¡Necesito entender las ... para poder utilizarlas!

otras **formas posibles de escribir una palabra**

favor: *to ask a favour of sb* pedir un favor a algn

pronunciación y **acento**

photograph /ˈfəʊtəgrɑːf; *USA* -græf/ ◆ *n* (*tb abrev* **photo**) fotografía ◆ **1** *vt* fotografiar **2** *vi* salir en una foto: *He photographs well.* Sale bien en fotos. **photographer** /fəˈtɒgrəfə(r)/ *n* fotógrafo, -a **photographic** /ˌfəʊtəˈgræfɪk/ *adj* fotográfico **photography** /fəˈtɒgrəfi/ *n* fotografía

ejemplos que te ayudarán a ver cómo se utiliza la palabra

fortunate /ˈfɔːtʃənət/ *adj* afortunado: *to be fortunate* tener suerte

notas de vocabulario para que aprendas palabras relacionadas con la que vas a utilizar

lata *nf* **1** (*envase*) can, tin

Can se utiliza para hablar de bebidas en lata: *una lata de Coca-Cola* a can of Coke. Para otros alimentos se puede usar **can** o **tin**: *una lata de sardinas* a can/tin of sardines. *Ver dibujo en* CONTAINER.

2 (*material*) tin **3** (*molestia*) pain: *¡Vaya una ~!* What a pain! LOC **dar la lata 1** (*molestar*) to be a pain: *¡Cuánta ~ das!* What a pain you are! **2** (*pedir con insistencia*) to pester: *Nos estuvo dando la ~ para que le compráramos la bici.* He kept pestering us to get him the bike. **de/en lata** tinned

notas culturales que te explicarán detalles interesantes y prácticos sobre las costumbres británicas

estanco *nm* tobacconist's [*pl* tobacconists]

En Gran Bretaña no hay estancos. Los sellos se venden en **post offices** (oficinas de correos), que realizan también algunas gestiones administrativas: pago del impuesto de circulación y 'TV licence', cobro de las pensiones, etc. Los **newsagents** también venden sellos, además de prensa, caramelos y cigarrillos. Ya quedan pocos **tobacconists**, establecimientos especializados en artículos para el fumador. Tampoco existen quioscos como tales sino puestos de periódicos o **news-stands**.

palabras que se utilizan sólo en situaciones concretas, por ejemplo al hablar con tus amigos, pero no con tu profesor

backside /ˈbæksaɪd/ *n* (*coloq*) trasero

Diccionario Oxford Pocket para estudiantes de inglés

Español–Inglés
Inglés–Español

Editores
Patrick Goldsmith · Mª Ángeles Pérez

Especialista en fonética
Michael Ashby

OXFORD UNIVERSITY PRESS

Oxford University Press
Great Clarendon Street, Oxford OX2 6PD

Oxford New York
Athens Auckland Bangkok Bogota Bombay
Buenos Aires Calcutta Cape Town Dar es Salaam
Delhi Florence Hong Kong Istanbul Karachi
Kuala Lumpur Madras Madrid Melbourne
Mexico City Nairobi Paris Singapore
Taipei Tokyo Toronto

and associated companies in
Berlin Ibadan

OXFORD and OXFORD ENGLISH
are trade marks of Oxford University Press

ISBN 0 19 431176 7

First published 1995
Seventh impression 1997

Diseño Holdsworth Associates, Isle of Wight

Cubierta Stonesfield Design, Stonesfield, Witney, Oxon

Illustraciones Martin Cox, Margaret Heath, Nigel Paige, Martin Shovel, Paul Thomas, Harry Venning, Michael Woods, Hardlines

Typeset in Great Britain by Tradespools Ltd, Frome, Somerset

Printed in Madrid, Spain, by Mateu Cromo Artes Gráficas S.A.

Índice

Introducción

El Oxford Pocket es el primer diccionario bilingüe de bolsillo concebido y escrito exclusivamente para estudiantes de inglés de nivel elemental a intermedio. Los miembros del grupo editorial que ha llevado a cabo el proyecto son lexicógrafos con una amplia experiencia en la enseñanza del inglés.

Nuestro objetivo fundamental ha sido el de elaborar un diccionario que guíe al estudiante en la primera etapa de su descubrimiento de la lengua inglesa y la cultura británica; de ahí los abundantes ejemplos de uso y las numerosas notas gramaticales, culturales y de vocabulario.

El Oxford Pocket pertenece a una nueva generación de diccionarios publicados por Oxford University Press, únicos por estar basados en el Corpus Nacional Británico (BNC). Dicho Corpus constituye una exhaustiva base de datos, con 100 millones de palabras cuidadosamente recopiladas a partir de fuentes variadas que reflejan con toda fidelidad el inglés que se habla en la actualidad en las Islas Británicas.

Queremos agradecer a los siguientes lexicógrafos su dedicación al proyecto: en el lado Español–Inglés, Marie Gorman, Mª José Rodríguez, Penny Fisher, Victoria Zaragoza, Mel Fraser, Raquel de Pedro y Mª Carmen Beaven; en el lado Inglés–Español, Enrique González Sardinero, Alayne Pullen, Margaret Jull Costa, Alison Sadler y Julie Watkins.

También queremos dar las gracias a Kate O'Neill, Ana Bremón y Judith Willis, cuya labor fue decisiva durante la fase final del proyecto, y a Idoia Noble por la creación y edición de las hojas de estudio y los apéndices.

Gracias también a Jeremy Munday, Olga Jimeno y Elisabeth Weeks por su colaboración, y a Margaret Hill, Joseph Díaz y Ane Ortega por su ayuda con la corrección de pruebas.

Patrick Goldsmith
Mª Ángeles Pérez

Test sobre el diccionario

Para que veas que el ***Diccionario Oxford Pocket*** te puede ayudar a aprender inglés, te proponemos un pequeño test que puedes responder consultando las entradas del diccionario.

1 ¿Cómo se llaman la hembra y la cría del ***cerdo*** en inglés?

2 ¿Cómo se dice ***fútbol*** en inglés americano?

3 ¿Cómo se llaman los palos de la ***baraja*** en inglés?

4 La palabra ***swimsuit*** está mal utilizada en la siguiente frase: *I like John's swimsuit.* ¿Sabrías sustituirla por la palabra correcta?

5 ¿Cómo puedes felicitar a un amigo por su ***cumpleaños***?

6 ¿Qué dicen los británicos cuando alguien ***estornuda***?

7 ¿Cuál es el menú típico de ***Navidad*** en el Reino Unido?

8 ¿Cuándo se celebra el equivalente al ***día*** de los ***inocentes*** en el Reino Unido?

9 ¿Hay alguna diferencia de pronunciación entre ***peace*** y ***piece***?

10 ¿De cuántas formas se puede pronunciar el sustantivo ***row*** y qué significa en cada caso?

HOW CAN THE OXFORD POCKET HELP ME?
OXFORD POCKET

Vocabulario

El ***Diccionario Oxford Pocket*** te ayudará a ampliar tu vocabulario de varias maneras: dándote detalles sobre palabras que ya conocías, introduciendo otras nuevas relacionadas con ellas, citando la versión americana cuando la hay, etc.

También podrás aprender expresiones típicas inglesas para utilizarlas en distintas situaciones.

Cada país tiene sus costumbres y celebraciones especiales. En este diccionario indicamos las más importantes del Reino Unido, para que así te resulte más fácil entender la cultura británica.

Pronunciación

En el lado inglés–español te mostramos la pronunciación de las palabras. Los símbolos fonéticos aparecen a pie de página. Consulta también la explicación que te ofrecemos en el interior de la contraportada.

11 ¿La palabra ***lung*** es un sustantivo, un adjetivo o un verbo?

12 ¿Hemos utilizado bien el sustantivo en la frase *I need some **information**s*? ¿Por qué?

13 ¿Sabrías corregir el verbo en la siguiente oración: *Jane **do** her homework in the library*?

14 ¿Cuál es el pasado simple del verbo *to **break***?

Gramática

Descubre si la palabra es un sustantivo, un verbo, un adverbio, etc consultando las partes de la oración que indicamos en cada entrada.

Comprueba si el sustantivo tiene un uso especial en inglés (a veces no se puede usar en plural porque es incontable).

En las entradas de los verbos te damos información sobre las formas más importantes (pasado y participio). Además, en el apéndice 2 encontrarás la lista de los verbos irregulares más importantes.

---

15 ¿Cómo se escribe ***party*** en plural?

16 ¿Cuál es la forma en *-ing* del verbo *to **hit***?

Escritura

También puedes utilizar el diccionario para asegurarte de cómo se escribe una palabra, ya que a menudo indicamos pequeños cambios dependiendo de la forma del verbo o de si la palabra está en plural.

---

17 ¿Cómo se dice ***cepillo*** de dientes? ¿Y ***cepillo*** para el pelo?

18 ¿Dónde te puedes hacer unos huevos fritos: en una ***frying-pan*** o en una ***saucepan***?

Explicaciones ilustradas

Para que puedas distinguir palabras de un mismo grupo, añadimos dibujos que te ayudarán a identificar exactamente la que necesitas.

---

19 ¿Cómo se expresa la siguiente ***fecha*** en inglés: *4 July 1996*?

20 ¿Cómo llamamos en inglés a una persona que ha nacido en ***Alemania***?

Información adicional

Consulta las hojas de estudio centrales y los apéndices finales para aprender a expresar la hora y las fechas, a utilizar las preposiciones, los verbos irregulares, nombres de lugar y persona, etc.

Respuestas

1 *Sow* y *piglet*. **2** *Soccer*. **3** *Hearts, diamonds, clubs* y *spades*. **4** *Swimming trunks*. **5** *Happy Birthday!* o *Many happy returns!* **6** *Bless you!* **7** Pavo y *Christmas pudding*. **8** El 1 de abril. **9** No. **10** De dos formas: /rəʊ/ (fila) y /raʊ/ (pelea). **11** Un sustantivo. **12** No, debería ser *I need some information* porque es incontable. **13** *Jane does her homework in the library*. **14** *Broke*. **15** *Parties*. **16** *Hitting*. **17** *Toothbrush* y *hairbrush*. **18** En una *frying-pan*. **19** *July the fourth, nineteen ninety-six* o *The fourth of July, nineteen ninety-six*. **20** *A German*.

Ejercicio 1

Al final de algunas entradas encontrarás la nota *Ver tb* seguida de una palabra. Si buscas la entrada correspondiente a dicha palabra descubrirás expresiones que dan traducciones interesantes ¡y a veces muy inesperadas!

Por ejemplo, al final de la entrada **asco** decimos *Ver tb* CARA. Si vas a la entrada **cara** encontrarás la expresión **poner cara de asco,** que en inglés se dice *to make a face.*

Adivina a qué expresiones hacemos referencia en las siguientes entradas y descubre cómo se traducen al inglés:

1 burro
2 longitud
3 detrás
4 ambiente
5 angelito

Busca el significado de las expresiones a las que nos referimos en las siguientes entradas:

6 *water*
7 *bird*
8 *bucket*
9 *basket*
10 *bright*

Ejercicio 2

Completa las siguientes oraciones utilizando la preposición adecuada:

1 Everybody **laughed** ...... the joke.
2 We were very **pleased** ...... the hotel.
3 It took her a long time to **recover** ...... the accident.
4 He's very **proud** ...... his new motorbike.
5 The house is quite **close** ...... the shops.

Ejercicio 3

Consulta el diccionario para escoger la estructura verbal correcta:

1 Have you **finished** .... (clean) your room?
2 He **keeps** .... (phone) me up.
3 I've **persuaded** Jan .... (come) to the party.
4 Try to **avoid** .... (make) mistakes.
5 She **asked** me .... (shut) the door.

Respuestas

Ejercicio 1

1 no ver tres en un burro *to be blind as a bat*
2 salto de longitud *long jump*
3 estar con la mosca detrás de la oreja *to smell a rat*
4 medio ambiente *environment*
5 soñar con los angelitos *to have sweet dreams*
6 like a fish out of water *como un pulpo en un garaje*
7 the early bird catches the worm *a quien madruga, Dios le ayuda*
8 to kick the bucket *estirar la pata*
9 to put all your eggs in one basket *jugárselo todo a una carta*
10 to look on the bright side *mirar el lado bueno de las cosas*

Ejercicio 2

1 *at* **2** *with* **3** *from* **4** *of* **5** *to*

Ejercicio 3

1 *cleaning* **2** *phoning* **3** *to come* **4** *making* **5** *to shut*

Aa

a *prep*

- **dirección** to: *Van a Sevilla.* They are going to Seville. ◊ *¿Te vas a casa?* Are you going home? ◊ *Se acercó a mí.* She came up to me.
- **posición** on: *a la izquierda* on the left ◊ *a este lado* on this side ◊ *Estaban sentados a la mesa.* They were sitting at the table.
- **distancia**: *a diez kilómetros de aquí* ten kilometres from here
- **tiempo 1** (*gen*) at: *a las doce* at twelve o'clock ◊ *a los sesenta años* at (the age of) sixty ◊ *Estamos a dos de enero.* It's the second of January. **2** (*después de*): *al año de su llegada* a year after his arrival ◊ *Volvieron a las cuatro horas.* They returned four hours later.
- **indicando finalidad** to: *Voy a repetirlo.* I'm going to do it again. ◊ *Me agaché a recogerlo.* I bent down to pick it up.
- **indicando modo o manera**: *ir a pie* to go on foot ◊ *Hazlo a tu manera.* Do it your way. ◊ *vestir a lo hippy* to dress like a hippy
- **complemento directo**: *No conozco a tu hermano.* I don't know your brother. ◊ *Llama al camarero.* Call the waiter over.
- **complemento indirecto 1** (*gen*) to: *Dáselo a tu hermano.* Give it to your brother. **2** (*para*) for: *Le compré una bicicleta a mi hija.* I bought a bicycle for my daughter. **3** (*de*) from: *No le copies el examen a Juan.* Don't copy from Juan.
- **otras construcciones 1** (*medida, reparto*) at: *Tocan a tres por persona.* It works out at three each. ◊ *Iban a 60 kilómetros por hora.* They were going at 60 kilometres an hour. **2** (*tarifa*) a, per (*más formal*): *cinco libras al mes* five pounds a month **3** (*precio*): *Están a 50 pesetas el kilo.* They are 50 pesetas a kilo. **4** (*Dep*): *Ganaron tres a cero.* They won three nil. ◊ *Empataron a dos.* They drew two all. **5** (*en órdenes*): *¡A trabajar!* Let's do some work! ◊ *Sal a buscarla.* Go out and look for her. LOC **¡a (por) él, ella, etc!** get him, her, etc! **¿a qué ...?** what ... for?: *¿A qué fuiste?* What did you go for? *Ver tb* AL

abadía *nf* abbey [*pl* abbeys]

abajo ◆ *adv* **1** (*posición*) below: *desde ~* from below **2** (*en un edificio*) downstairs: *el vecino de ~* the man who lives downstairs ◊ *Hay otro baño ~.* There is another toilet downstairs. **3** (*dirección*) down: *calle/escaleras ~* down the street/stairs ◆ **¡abajo!** *interj* down with ...! LOC **echar abajo 1** (*edificio*) to knock *sth* down **2** (*gobierno*) to bring *sth* down **el de abajo** the bottom one **hacia abajo** downwards **más abajo 1** (*más lejos*) further down: *en esta misma calle, más ~* further down this street **2** (*en sentido vertical*) lower down: *Pon el cuadro más ~.* Put the picture lower down. *Ver tb* AHÍ, ALLÁ, ALLÍ, ARRIBA, BOCA, CABEZA, CALLE, CUESTA, PARTE[1], RÍO, RODAR

abalanzarse *v pron* **1 ~ sobre** to pounce **on *sth/sb***: *Me abalancé sobre mi adversario.* I pounced on my opponent. **2 ~ hacia** to rush **towards *sth/sb***: *El público se abalanzó hacia la puerta.* The crowd rushed towards the door.

abandonado, -a *pp, adj* (*edificio*) derelict *Ver tb* ABANDONAR

abandonar ◆ *vt* **1** (*gen*) to abandon: *~ una criatura/un animal* to abandon a child/an animal ◊ *~ un proyecto* to abandon a project **2** (*lugar*) to leave: *~ la sala* to leave the room **3** (*fig*) to desert: *Mis amigos no me abandonarían.* My friends would never desert me. **4** (*Informát*) to quit ◆ *vi* **1** (*desistir*) to give up: *No abandones.* Don't give up. **2** (*Dep*) to withdraw

abanicar(se) *vt, v pron* to fan (yourself)

abanico *nm* **1** (*gen*) fan **2** (*gama*) range: *un amplio ~ de opciones* a wide range of options

abarrotado, -a *pp, adj ~* **(de)** crammed **(with *sth*)** LOC **abarrotado (de gente)** crowded *Ver tb* ABARROTAR

abarrotar *vt* to fill *sth* to overflowing: *El público abarrotaba la sala.* The audience filled the hall to overflowing.

abastecer ◆ *vt* to supply *sb* **(with *sth*)**: *La granja abastece de huevos a todo el pueblo.* The farm supplies the whole village with eggs. ◆ **abastecerse** *v pron* **abastecerse de** to stock up **on *sth***: *~se de harina* to stock up on flour

abastecimiento *nm* **1** (*acción*)

supplying: *¿Quién se encarga del ~ de las tropas?* Who is in charge of supplying the troops? **2** (*suministro*) supply: *controlar el ~ de agua* to regulate the water supply

abasto *nm* LOC **no dar abasto**: *Con tantas cosas que hacer no doy ~.* I've got far too many things to do.

abatible *adj* **1** (*asiento*) reclining: *asientos ~s* reclining seats **2** (*plegable*) folding

abdicar *vt, vi* ~ (**en**) to abdicate (**in favour of *sb***): *Eduardo VIII abdicó (la corona) en su hermano.* Edward the Eighth abdicated in favour of his brother.

abdomen *nm* abdomen

abdominal ◆ *adj* abdominal ◆ **abdominales** *nm* **1** (*músculos*) stomach muscles, abdominal muscles (*científ*) **2** (*ejercicios*) sit-ups: *hacer ~es* to do sit-ups

abecedario *nm* alphabet

abedul *nm* birch (tree)

abeja *nf* bee LOC **abeja obrera** worker (bee) **abeja reina** queen bee

abejorro *nm* bumble-bee

abertura *nf* **1** (*hueco*) gap **2** (*grieta*) crack

abeto *nm* fir (tree)

abierto, -a *pp, adj* **1** ~ (**a**) open (**to *sth*/*sb***): *Deja la puerta abierta.* Leave the door open. ◊ *~ al público* open to the public ◊ *El caso sigue ~.* The case is still open. **2** (*grifo*) running: *dejar un grifo ~* to leave a tap running **3** (*cremallera*) undone: *Llevas la bragueta abierta.* Your flies are undone. **4** (*persona*) sociable *Ver tb* ABRIR

abismo *nm* **1** (*gen*) abyss **2** ~ **entre...** gulf **between...**: *Hay un ~ entre tú y yo.* There is a gulf between us.

ablandar(se) *vt, v pron* to soften: *El calor ablanda la mantequilla.* Heat softens butter.

ablusado, -a *pp, adj* loose-fitting

abobado, -a *adj Ver* ATONTADO

abofetear *vt* to slap

abogacía *nf* legal profession LOC **ejercer/practicar la abogacía** to practise law

abogado, -a *nm-nf* lawyer

> **Lawyer** es un término general que comprende los distintos tipos de abogado en Gran Bretaña. **Solicitor** es el abogado que asesora legalmente y prepara los documentos relacionados con sus clientes. Puede también intervenir en juicios, pero sólo si se trata de tribunales inferiores. **Barrister** es el abogado con facultad para actuar en todos los tribunales. El **solicitor** le ayuda a preparar el caso pero normalmente es el **barrister** quien se dirige al juez.

LOC **abogado defensor** defence counsel **abogado del diablo** devil's advocate

abolición *nf* abolition

abolir *vt* to abolish

abolladura *nf* dent: *Mi coche tiene bastantes ~s.* There are quite a few dents in my car.

abollar *vt* to dent: *Me has abollado el coche.* You've dented my car.

abombado, -a *pp, adj* convex

abonar ◆ *vt* (*tierra*) to fertilize ◆ **abonar(se)** *vt, v pron* **abonar(se) a 1** (*publicación, servicio*) to subscribe **to *sth*** **2** (*espectáculo*) to buy a season ticket **for *sth***

abono *nm* **1** (*fertilizante*) fertilizer **2** (*pago*) payment: *mediante el ~ de 100 pesetas* on payment of 100 pesetas **3** (*espectáculo, transporte*) season ticket: *sacar/comprar un ~* to take out a season ticket

abordaje *nm* (*barco*) boarding

abordar *vt* **1** (*barco*) to board **2** (*asunto, problema*) to approach

aborigen *nmf* native

aborrecer *vt* **1** (*detestar*) to detest *sth*/*doing sth* **2** (*animal*) to abandon

abortar *vi* **1** (*espontáneamente*) to have a miscarriage **2** (*voluntariamente*) to have an abortion

aborto *nm* **1** (*espontáneo*) miscarriage: *sufrir un ~* to have a miscarriage **2** (*provocado*) abortion

abotonar *vt* to button *sth* (up): *Le abotoné la camisa.* I buttoned (up) his shirt.

abovedado, -a *pp, adj* vaulted

abrasador, ~a *adj* burning

abrasar ◆ *vt* to burn ◆ *vi* **1** (*gen*) to be boiling hot: *Ten cuidado con la sopa que abrasa.* Be careful, the soup is boiling hot. **2** (*sol*) to beat down ◆ **abrasarse** *v pron* **1** (*gen*) to burn yourself **2** (*al sol*) to get sunburnt: *Ponte una camiseta, te vas a ~.* Put on a T-shirt or you'll get sunburnt.

abrasivo, -a *adj, nm* abrasive

abrazar *vt* to hug, to embrace (*más*

formal): *Abrazó a sus hijos.* She hugged her children.

abrazo *nm* hug, embrace (*más formal*) LOC **un abrazo/un fuerte abrazo** love/lots of love: *Dales un ~ a tus padres.* Give my love to your parents. ◊ *Os mando un fuerte ~.* Lots of love.

abrebotellas *nm* bottle-opener

abrecartas *nm* paperknife [*pl* paperknives]

abrelatas *nm* tin-opener

abreviación *nf* shortening

abreviar ◆ *vt* (*palabra*) to abbreviate ◆ *vi* (*ahorrar tiempo*) to save time LOC **¡abrevia!** hurry up!

abreviatura *nf* abbreviation (***for/of sth***)

abridor *nm* opener

abrigado, -a *pp, adj* **1** (*lugar*) sheltered **2** (*persona*): *bien ~* well wrapped up ◊ *Vas demasiado ~.* You've got too much on. *Ver tb* ABRIGAR

abrigar ◆ *vt* **1** (*prenda*) to keep *sb* warm: *Esa bufanda te abrigará.* That scarf will keep you warm. **2** (*arropar*) to wrap *sb* up: *Abriga bien a la niña.* Wrap the child up well. ◆ *vi* to be warm: *Esta chaqueta abriga mucho.* This cardigan is very warm. ◆ **abrigarse** *v pron* to wrap up: *Abrígate, hace mucho frío.* Wrap up well, it's very cold outside.

abrigo *nm* coat: *Ponte el ~.* Put your coat on. LOC **al abrigo de** sheltered from *sth*: *al ~ de la lluvia* sheltered from the rain **de abrigo** warm: *prendas de ~* warm clothes

abril *nm* April (*abrev* Apr) ☛ *Ver ejemplos en* ENERO

abrir ◆ *vt* **1** (*gen*) to open: *No abras la ventana.* Don't open the window. ◊ *~ fuego* to open fire **2** (*grifo, gas*) to turn *sth* on **3** (*túnel*) to bore **4** (*agujero, camino*) to make ◆ *vi* (*abrir la puerta*) to open up: *¡Abre!* Open up! ◆ **abrirse** *v pron* **1** (*gen*) to open: *De repente se abrió la puerta.* Suddenly the door opened. **2** (*tierra*) to crack LOC **abrirse camino en la vida** to get on in life **abrirse la cabeza** to split your head open **abrir (un) expediente** to take proceedings (*against sb*) **en un abrir y cerrar de ojos** in the twinkling of an eye **no abrir el pico/la boca** not to say a word: *No abrió la boca en toda la tarde.* He didn't say a word all afternoon. *Ver tb* PASO

abrochar(se) *vt, v pron* **1** (*gen*) to do *sth* up (***for sb***): *Abróchate el abrigo.* Do your coat up. **2** (*broche, cinturón*) to fasten

abrupto, -a *adj* (*terreno*) rugged

ábside *nm* apse

absolución *nf* **1** (*Relig*) absolution: *dar la ~* to give absolution **2** (*Jur*) acquittal

absoluto, -a *adj* absolute: *conseguir la mayoría absoluta* to obtain an absolute majority LOC **en absoluto**: *nada en ~* nothing at all ◊ *—¿Te importa? —En ~.* 'Do you mind?' 'Not at all.'

absolver *vt* **1** (*Relig*) to absolve *sb* (***from sth***) **2** (*Jur*) to acquit *sb* (***of sth***): *El juez absolvió al acusado.* The defendant was acquitted.

absorbente *adj* absorbent

absorber *vt* to absorb: *~ un líquido/olor* to absorb a liquid/smell

abstención *nf* abstention (***from sth***)

abstenerse *v pron ~* (**de**) to abstain (***from sth***): *~ de beber/del tabaco* to abstain from drinking/smoking ◊ *El diputado se abstuvo.* The MP abstained.

abstinencia *nf* LOC *Ver* SÍNDROME

abstracto, -a *adj* abstract

abstraído, -a *pp, adj* (*preocupado*) preoccupied

absurdo, -a *adj* absurd

abuchear *vt* to boo

abuelo, -a *nm-nf* **1** (*gen*) grandad [*fem* granny] (*coloq*), grandfather [*fem* grandmother] **2 abuelos** grandparents: *en casa de mis ~s* at my grandparents'

abultar *vi* to be bulky: *Esta caja abulta demasiado.* This box is too bulky. ◊ *Abulta muy poco.* It hardly takes up any room at all. ◊ *¿Abulta mucho?* Does it take up much room?

aburrido, -a ◆ *pp, adj* (*que aburre*) boring: *un discurso ~* a boring speech ◊ *No seas tan ~.* Don't be so boring. ◆ *nm-nf* bore: *Eres un ~.* You're a bore. LOC **estar aburrido** to be bored *Ver tb* ABURRIR

aburrimiento *nm* boredom: *¡Qué ~ de película!* What a boring film! ◊ *Como de puro ~.* I eat from sheer boredom. LOC *Ver* MORIR(SE)

aburrir ◆ *vt* **1** (*gen*) to bore: *Espero no estar aburriéndote.* I hope I'm not boring you. ◊ *Me aburre este programa* This programme is boring. **2** (*hartar*): *Me aburrís con vuestras quejas.* I'm sick of your moaning. ◆ **aburrirse** *v pron* to get bored LOC **aburrirse como una ostra** to be bored stiff

abusar *vi ~* (**de**) to abuse *sth/sb* [*vt*]: *No*

abuses de su confianza. Don't abuse his trust. ◊ *Declaró que abusaron de ella.* She claims to have been sexually abused. LOC **abusar del alcohol, tabaco, etc** to drink, smoke, etc too much

abuso *nm* ~ (**de**) abuse: *¡Es un ~!* That's outrageous! LOC **abuso del tabaco, etc** excessive smoking, etc

acá *adv*: *Ven ~.* Come here. ◊ *Ponlo más (para) ~.* Bring it nearer. LOC **de acá para allá**: *Llevo todo el día de ~ para allá.* I've been running around all day. ◊ *He andado de ~ para allá buscándote.* I've been looking for you everywhere.

acabado, -a *pp, adj*: *una palabra acabada en "d"* a word ending in 'd' ◊ *~ en punta* coming to a point *Ver tb* ACABAR

acabar ◆ *vt, vi* ~ (**de**) to finish (*sth/doing sth*): *Aún no he acabado el artículo.* I haven't finished the article yet. ◊ *Tengo que ~ de lavar el coche.* I must finish washing the car. ◊ *La función acaba a las tres.* The show finishes at three. ◆ *vi* **1** ~ (**en/por**) to end up: *Ese vaso acabará por romperse.* That glass will end up broken. ◊ *~ en la ruina/arruinado* to end up penniless ◊ *Acabé cediendo.* I ended up giving in. **2** ~ **de hacer algo** to have just done sth: *Acabo de verle.* I've just seen him. **3** ~ **en (a)** (*forma*) to end **in *sth***: *Acaba en punta.* It ends in a point. **(b)** (*palabra*) to end **with *sth***: *¿En qué acaba, en "d" o en "z"?* What does it end with? A 'd' or a 'z'? **4** ~ **con (a)** (*persona*) to be the death **of *sb***: *Vas a ~ conmigo.* You'll be the death of me. **(b)** (*poner fin*) to put an end **to *sth***: *~ con la injusticia* to put an end to injustice ◆ **acabarse** *v pron* to run out (**of *sth***): *Se nos ha acabado el café.* We've run out of coffee. LOC **acabar mal**: *Esto tiene que ~ mal.* No good can come of this. ◊ *Ese chico acabará mal.* That boy will come to no good. **¡se acabó!** that's it!

acabóse *nm* LOC **ser el acabóse** to be the limit

academia *nf* **1** (*gen*) academy [*pl* academies]: *~ militar* military academy **2** (*escuela*) school: *~ de idiomas* language school

académico, -a *adj* academic: *curso/expediente ~* academic year/record

acampada *nf* LOC **ir de acampada** to go camping

acampar *vi* to camp

acantilado *nm* cliff

acariciar *vt* **1** (*persona*) to caress **2** (*animal*) to stroke

acaso *adv* **1** (*quizás*) perhaps **2** (*en preguntas*): *¿~ dije yo eso?* Did I say that? LOC **por si acaso** just in case

acatar *vt* (*leyes, órdenes*) to obey

acatarrarse *v pron* to catch a cold

acceder *vi* ~ (**a**) **1** (*estar de acuerdo*) to agree (**to *sth*/to do *sth***) **2** (*institución*) to be admitted **to *sth***: *Las mujeres podrán ~ al ejército.* Women will be admitted to the army.

accesible *adj* accessible (***to sb***)

acceso *nm* ~ (**a**) **1** (*gen, Informát*) access (**to *sth/sb***): *la puerta de ~ a la cocina* the door into the kitchen ◊ *~ a la cámara blindada* access to the strongroom **2** (*vía de entrada*) approach (**to *sth***): *Hay cuatro ~s al palacio.* There are four approaches to the palace. **3** ~ **de** fit: *Le dan ~s de tos.* He has coughing fits.

accesorio *nm* accessory [*pl* accessories]

accidentado, -a ◆ *pp, adj* **1** (*terreno*) rugged **2** (*difícil*) difficult: *un viaje ~* a difficult journey ◆ *nm-nf* casualty [*pl* casualties]

accidental *adj* accidental: *muerte ~* accidental death

accidente *nm* **1** (*gen*) accident: *~ de tráfico* traffic accident ◊ *sufrir un ~* to have an accident **2** (*Geog*) (geographical) feature LOC **accidente aéreo/de coche** plane/car crash

acción *nf* **1** (*gen*) action: *entrar en ~* to go into action ◊ *~ criminal/legal* criminal/legal action **2** (*obra*) act: *una mala ~* a wrongful act **3** (*Fin*) share LOC **una buena acción** a good deed

accionar *vt* to work

accionista *nmf* shareholder

acebo *nm* **1** (*hoja*) holly **2** (*árbol*) holly bush

acechar *vt, vi* to lie in wait (**for *sth/sb***): *El enemigo acechaba en la oscuridad.* The enemy lay in wait in the darkness.

acecho *nm* LOC **estar al acecho** to lie in wait (*for sth/sb*)

aceite *nm* oil: *~ de girasol/oliva* sunflower/olive oil LOC *Ver* BALSA[1], UNTAR

aceituna *nf* olive: *~s rellenas/sin hueso* stuffed/pitted olives

aceleración *nf* acceleration

acelerador *nm* accelerator

acelerar *vt, vi* to accelerate: *Acelera, que se cala.* Accelerate or you'll stall. LOC **acelerar el paso** to quicken your pace

acelerón *nm* LOC **dar un acelerón** (*vehículo*) to put your foot down

acelga *nf* chard [*incontable*]: *~s con besamel* chard in white sauce

acento *nm* accent: *con ~ en la última sílaba* with an accent on the last syllable ◊ *hablar con ~ extranjero* to speak with a foreign accent LOC *Ver* PEGAR

acentuar ◆ *vt* **1** (*poner tilde*) to accent: *Acentúa las siguientes palabras.* Put the accents on the following words. **2** (*resaltar, agravar*) to accentuate ◆ **acentuarse** *v pron* (*llevar tilde*) to have an accent: *Se acentúa en la segunda sílaba.* It's got an accent on the second syllable.

aceptable *adj* acceptable (**to sb**)

aceptar *vt* **1** (*gen*) to accept: *Por favor acepta este pequeño regalo.* Please accept this small gift. ◊ *¿Vas a ~ su oferta?* Are you going to accept their offer? **2** (*acceder a*) to agree **to do sth**: *Aceptó marcharse.* He agreed to leave.

acera *nf* pavement

acerca *adv* LOC **acerca de** about, concerning (*más formal*)

acercar ◆ *vt* **1** (*aproximar*) to bring *sth* closer (**to sth/sb**): *Acercó el micrófono a la boca.* He brought the microphone closer to his mouth. **2** (*dar*) to pass: *Acércame ese cuchillo.* Pass me that knife. **3** (*en vehículo*) to give *sb* a lift: *Me acercaron a casa/a la estación.* They gave me a lift home/to the station. ◆ **acercarse** *v pron* **acercarse (a)** to get closer (**to sth/sb**): *Se acerca mi cumpleaños.* My birthday is getting closer. ◊ *Acércate a mí.* Come closer.

acero *nm* steel: *~ inoxidable* stainless steel

acertado, -a *pp, adj* **1** (*correcto*) right: *la respuesta acertada* the right answer **2** (*inteligente*) clever: *una idea acertada* a clever idea *Ver tb* ACERTAR

acertante *nmf* winner

acertar ◆ *vt* to guess: *~ la respuesta* to guess the answer ◆ *vi* **1** *~* **(en/con)** (*al elegir*) to get *sth* right **2** (*al obrar*) to be right **to do sth**: *Hemos acertado al negarnos.* We were right to refuse. **3** *~* **(a/en)** (*al disparar*) to hit *sth* [*vt*]: *~ en el blanco* to hit the target

acertijo *nm* riddle

achaque *nm* ailment: *los ~s de la edad* old people's ailments ◊ *Siempre con tus ~s.* You're always complaining of aches and pains.

achatar ◆ *vt* to flatten ◆ **achatarse** *v pron* to get flattened

achicar *vt* **1** (*empequeñecer*) to make *sth* smaller **2** (*agua*) to bail *water* out

achicharrar ◆ *vt* **1** (*quemar*) to burn **2** (*calor*) to scorch **3** (*picar*): *Nos achicharraron los mosquitos.* We were bitten to death by the mosquitoes. ◆ **achicharrarse** *v pron* (*pasar calor*) to roast: *Nos achicharraremos en la playa.* We'll roast on the beach.

¡achís! *interj* atishoo!

> La persona que estornuda suele disculparse con **excuse me!** La gente a su alrededor puede decir **bless you!**, aunque muchas veces no dicen nada.

achuchar ◆ *vt* **1** (*abrazar*) to hug **2** (*estrujar*) to crush ◆ **achucharse** *v pron* to kiss and cuddle

achuchón *nm* **1** (*enfermedad*) turn: *Le ha dado otro ~.* He's had another turn. **2** (*abrazo*) hug

acidez *nf* acidity LOC **acidez de estómago** heartburn

ácido, -a ◆ *adj* (*sabor*) sharp ◆ *nm* acid LOC *Ver* LLUVIA

acierto *nm* **1** (*respuesta correcta*) correct answer **2** (*buena idea*) good idea: *Ha sido un ~ venir.* It was a good idea to come.

aclamar *vt* to acclaim

aclarar ◆ *vt* **1** (*explicar*) to clarify: *¿Puedes ~ este punto?* Can you clarify this point? **2** (*enjuagar*) to rinse **3** (*color*) to lighten ◆ *vi, v imp* (*cielo*) to clear up ◆ **aclararse** *v pron* (*entender*) to understand: *A ver si me aclaro.* Let's see if I can understand this. LOC **¡a ver si te aclaras!** make up your mind!

acné *nm* acne

acobardar ◆ *vt* to intimidate ◆ **acobardarse** *v pron* **acobardarse (ante/por)** to feel intimidated (**by sth/sb**)

acogedor, ~a *adj* (*lugar*) cosy

acoger *vt* **1** (*invitado, idea, noticia*) to welcome: *Me acogió con una sonrisa.* He welcomed me with a smile. ◊ *Acogieron la propuesta con entusiasmo.* They welcomed the proposal. **2** (*refugiado, huérfano*) to take *sb* in

acomodado, -a *pp, adj* (*con dinero*) well off *Ver tb* ACOMODARSE

acomodador, ~a *nm-nf* usher [*fem* usherette]

acomodarse *v pron* **1** (*instalarse*) to settle down: *Se acomodó en el sofá.* He settled down on the sofa. **2** ~ **a** (*adaptarse*) to adjust **to *sth***

acompañar *vt* **1** (*gen*) to go with *sth/sb*, to accompany (*más formal*): *la cinta que acompaña el libro* the tape which accompanies the book ◊ *Voy de paseo. ¿Me acompañas?* I'm going for a walk. Are you coming (with me)? **2** (*Mús*) to accompany *sb* (**on *sth***): *Su hermana le acompañaba al piano.* His sister accompanied him on the piano.

acomplejarse *v pron* to get a complex

acondicionado, -a *pp, adj* LOC *Ver* AIRE

aconsejable *adj* advisable

aconsejar *vt* to advise *sb* (**to do *sth***): *Te aconsejo que aceptes ese trabajo.* I advise you to accept that job. ◊ *—¿Lo compro? —No te lo aconsejo.* 'Shall I buy it?' 'I wouldn't advise you to.'

acontecimiento *nm* event: *Fue todo un ~.* It was quite an event.

acoplarse *v pron* ~ (**a**) to fit in (**with *sth/sb***): *Trataremos de acoplarnos a vuestro horario.* We'll try to fit in with your timetable.

acorazado, -a ◆ *pp, adj* armour-plated ◆ *nm* battleship

acordar ◆ *vt* to agree (**to do *sth***): *Acordamos volver al trabajo.* We agreed to return to work. ◆ **acordarse** *v pron* **acordarse** (**de**) to remember: *Acuérdate de echar la carta.* Remember to post the letter. ◊ *No me acuerdo de su nombre.* I can't remember his name. LOC **acordarse de haber hecho algo** to remember doing sth: *Me acuerdo de haberlo visto.* I remember seeing it. ☛ *Ver nota en* REMEMBER **¡te acordarás!** you'll regret it!

acorde *nm* (*Mús*) chord

acordeón *nm* accordion

acordonar *vt* (*lugar*) to cordon *sth* off

acorralar *vt* (*persona*) to corner

acortar ◆ *vt* to shorten ◆ **acortarse** *v pron* to get shorter

acostado, -a *pp, adj* LOC **estar acostado 1** (*tumbado*) to be lying down **2** (*en la cama*) to be in bed *Ver tb* ACOSTAR

acostar ◆ *vt* to put *sb* to bed: *Tuvimos que ~le.* We had to put him to bed. ◆ **acostarse** *v pron* **1** (*ir a la cama*) to go to bed: *Deberías ~te temprano hoy.* You should go to bed early today. ◊ *Es hora de ~se.* Time for bed. **2** (*tumbarse*) to lie down ☛ *Ver nota en* LIE[2]

acostumbrado, -a *pp, adj* LOC **estar acostumbrado a** to be used to *sth/sb/doing sth*: *Está ~ a levantarse pronto.* He's used to getting up early. *Ver tb* ACOSTUMBRARSE

acostumbrarse *v pron* ~ (**a**) to get used **to *sth/sb/doing sth***: *~ al calor* to get used to the heat ◊ *Tendrás que acostumbrarte a madrugar.* You'll have to get used to getting up early.

acreedor, ~a *nm-nf* creditor LOC **ser acreedor de** to be worthy of *sth*

acribillar *vt* **1** (*gen*) to riddle: *~ a algn a balazos* to riddle sb with bullets **2** (*mosquitos*) to bite *sb* to death

acrobacia *nf* acrobatics: *Sus ~s recibieron grandes aplausos.* Her acrobatics were greeted with loud applause. ◊ *realizar ~s* to perform acrobatics

acróbata *nmf* acrobat

acta *nf* **1** (*reunión*) minutes [*pl*] **2** (*exámenes*) list of examination results

actitud *nf* attitude (**to/towards *sth/sb***)

activar *vt* **1** (*poner en marcha*) to activate: *~ un mecanismo* to activate a mechanism **2** (*acelerar*) to accelerate

actividad *nf* activity [*pl* activities]

activo, -a *adj* active

acto *nm* **1** (*acción, Teat*) act: *un ~ violento* an act of violence ◊ *una obra en cuatro ~s* a four-act play **2** (*ceremonia*) ceremony [*pl* ceremonies]: *el ~ de clausura* the closing ceremony LOC **acto seguido** immediately afterwards **en el acto** straight away: *Me levanté en el ~.* I stood up straight away.

actor, -triz *nm-nf* actor [*fem* actress] ☛ *Ver nota en* ACTRESS LOC **actor/actriz principal** male/female lead

actuación *nf* performance

actual *adj* **1** (*del momento presente*) current: *el estado ~ de las obras* the current state of the building work **2** (*de hoy en día*) present-day: *La ciencia ~ se enfrenta a problemas éticos.* Present-day science faces ethical problems.

actualidad *nf* present situation: *la ~ de nuestro país* the present situation in our country LOC **de actualidad** topical: *estar de ~* to be topical ◊ *asuntos/temas de ~* topical issues

actualizar *vt* to update

actualmente *adv* (*ahora*) at the moment

actuar *vi* **1** (*artista*) to perform **2** ~ **de**

to act **as *sth***: ~ *de intermediario* to act as an intermediary

acuarela *nf* watercolour LOC *Ver* PINTAR

acuario[1] *nm* aquarium [*pl* aquariums/ aquaria]

acuario[2] (*tb* **Acuario**) *nm, nmf* (*Astrología*) Aquarius ☛ *Ver ejemplos en* AQUARIUS

acuático, -a *adj* **1** (*Biol*) aquatic **2** (*Dep*) water [*n atrib*]: *deportes ~s* water sports LOC *Ver* ESQUÍ

acudir *vi* **1** (*ir*) to go (***to sth/sb***): ~ *en ayuda de algn* to go to sb's aid **2** (*venir*) to come (***to sth/sb***): *Los recuerdos acudían a mi memoria.* Memories came flooding back. **3** (*recurrir*) to turn ***to sb***: *No sé a quién ~.* I don't know who to turn to.

acueducto *nm* aqueduct

acuerdo *nm* agreement: *llegar a un ~* to reach an agreement LOC **¡de acuerdo!** all right! **estar de acuerdo** to agree (*with sb*): *Estoy de ~ con él.* I agree with him. **ponerse de acuerdo** to agree (*to do sth*): *Se pusieron de ~ para ir juntos.* They agreed to go together.

acumular(se) *vt, v pron* to accumulate

acunar *vt* to rock

acupuntura *nf* acupuncture

acurrucarse *v pron* to curl up

acusación *nf* accusation: *hacer una ~ contra algn* to make an accusation against sb

acusado, -a *nm-nf* accused: *los ~s* the accused

acusar *vt* **1** (*gen*) to accuse *sb* (**of *sth*/ *doing sth***) **2** (*Jur*) to charge *sb* (**with *sth*/*doing sth***): ~ *a algn de asesinato* to charge sb with murder **3** (*mostrar*) to show signs of *sth*: ~ *el cansancio* to show signs of tiredness

acusica *nmf* (*tb* **acusón, -ona** *nm-nf*) tell-tale

acústica *nf* acoustics [*pl*]: *La ~ de este local no es muy buena.* The acoustics in this hall aren't very good.

adaptar ◆ *vt* to adapt: ~ *una novela para el teatro* to adapt a novel for the stage ◆ **adaptarse** *v pron* **1** (*aclimatarse*) to adapt (***to sth***): *~se a los cambios* to adapt to change **2** (*ajustarse*) to fit: *No se adapta bien.* It doesn't fit properly.

adecuado, -a *pp, adj*: *No es el momento ~.* This isn't the right time. ◊ *No encuentran a la persona adecuada para el puesto.* They can't find the right person for the job. ◊ *un traje ~ para la ocasión* a suitable dress for the occasion

adelantado, -a *pp, adj* **1** (*aventajado*) advanced: *Este niño está muy ~ para su edad.* This child is very advanced for his age. **2** (*que se ha hecho mucho*): *Llevo la tesis muy adelantada.* I'm getting on very well with my thesis. **3** (*en comparaciones*) ahead: *Vamos muy ~s con respecto a los de la otra clase.* We're way ahead of the other class. **4** (*reloj*) fast: *Llevas el reloj cinco minutos ~.* Your watch is five minutes fast. LOC **por adelantado** in advance *Ver tb* ADELANTAR

adelantar ◆ *vt* **1** (*objeto*) to move *sth* forward: *Adelanté un peón.* I moved a pawn forward. **2** (*acontecimiento, fecha*) to bring *sth* forward: *Queremos ~ el examen una semana.* We want to bring the exam forward a week. **3** (*reloj*) to put a *watch/clock* forward: *No te olvides de ~ el reloj una hora.* Don't forget to put your watch forward an hour. **4** (*sobrepasar*) to overtake: *El camión me adelantó en la curva.* The lorry overtook me on the bend. **5** (*conseguir*) to achieve: *¿Qué adelantamos con reñir?* What do we achieve by arguing? ◆ **adelantar(se)** *vi, v pron* (*reloj*) to gain: *Este reloj se adelanta.* This clock gains.

adelante ◆ *adv* forward: *un paso ~* a step forward ◆ **¡adelante!** *interj* **1** (*entre*) come in! **2** (*siga*) carry on! LOC **hacia/para adelante** forwards **más adelante 1** (*espacio*) further on **2** (*tiempo*) later *Ver tb* AHORA, HOY

adelanto *nm* advance: *los ~s de la medicina* advances in medicine ◊ *Pedí un ~.* I asked for an advance.

adelgazar *vi* to lose weight: ~ *tres kilos* to lose three kilos

además *adv* **1** (*también*) also: *Se le acusa ~ de estafa.* He's also accused of fraud. ☛ *Ver nota en* TAMBIÉN **2** (*lo que es más*) (and) what's more: *~, no creo que vengan.* What's more, I don't think they'll come. LOC **además de** as well as

adentro *adv* inside: *Está muy ~.* It's right inside. LOC **más adentro** further in **para mis adentros** to myself, yourself, etc: *Rió para sus ~s.* He laughed to himself. *Ver tb* MAR, TIERRA

adhesivo, -a ◆ *adj* adhesive ◆ *nm* (*pegatina*) sticker LOC *Ver* CINTA

adicto, -a ◆ *adj* ~ (**a**) addicted (**to *sth***) ◆ *nm-nf* addict

adiestrar *vt* to train *sth/sb* (**as/in sth**)
¡adiós! *interj* **1** (*despedida*) goodbye!, bye! (*más coloq*) **2** (*saludo al pasar*) hello! LOC **decir adiós con la mano** to wave goodbye (*to sth/sb*)
adivinanza *nf* riddle
adivinar *vt* to guess: *Adivina lo que traigo.* Guess what I've got. LOC **adivinar el pensamiento** to read *sb's* mind
adivino, -a *nm-nf* fortune-teller
adjetivo *nm* adjective
administración *nf* administration: *la ~ de la justicia* the administration of justice LOC **administración de lotería** lottery agency [*pl* lottery agencies]
administrador, ~a *nm-nf* administrator
administrar ◆ *vt* **1** (*gestionar*) to run, to manage (*más formal*): *~ un negocio* to run a business **2** (*dar*) to administer *sth* (**to sb**): *~ un medicamento/justicia* to administer a medicine/justice ◆ **administrarse** *v pron* to manage your money
administrativo, -a ◆ *adj* administrative ◆ *nm-nf* administrative assistant
admirable *adj* admirable
admiración *nf* (*signo de puntuación*) exclamation mark ☛ *Ver* págs 318–19.
admirador, ~a *nm-nf* admirer
admirar *vt* **1** (*apreciar*) to admire: *~ el paisaje* to admire the scenery **2** (*asombrar*) to amaze: *Me admira tu sabiduría.* Your knowledge amazes me.
admitir *vt* **1** (*aceptar*) to accept **2** (*culpa, error*) to admit: *Admito que ha sido culpa mía.* I admit (that) it was my fault. **3** (*dejar entrar en un sitio*) to admit *sth/sb* (**to sth**): *Me han admitido en el colegio.* I've been admitted to the school. LOC **no se admite(n)...**: *No se admiten perros.* No dogs. ◊ *No se admite a menores de 18 años.* No entrance to under-18s. ◊ *No se admiten tarjetas de crédito.* We do not accept credit cards.
adolescencia *nf* adolescence
adolescente *nmf* teenager, adolescent (*más formal*)
adonde *adv rel* where
adónde *adv interr* where: *¿~ vais?* Where are you going?
adoptar *vt* to adopt
adoptivo, -a *adj* **1** (*gen*) adopted: *hijo/país ~* adopted child/country **2** (*padres*) adoptive
adoquín *nm* paving stone
adorar *vt* to adore
adormecerse *v pron* to doze off
adormecido, -a *pp, adj* sleepy
adornar *vt* to decorate, to adorn (*más formal*)
adorno *nm* **1** (*gen*) decoration: *~s de Navidad* Christmas decorations **2** (*objeto*) ornament
adosado, -a *pp, adj* LOC *Ver* CHALÉ
adquirir *vt* **1** (*gen*) to acquire: *~ riqueza/fama* to acquire wealth/fame **2** (*comprar*) to buy LOC *Ver* IMPORTANCIA
adrede *adv* on purpose
aduana *nf* **1** (*oficina*) customs [*pl*]: *Pasamos la ~.* We went through customs. **2** (*derechos*) customs duty [*pl* customs duties]
adulterio *nm* adultery
adúltero, -a *adj* adulterous
adulto, -a *adj, nm-nf* adult: *las personas adultas* adults
adverbio *nm* adverb
adversario, -a *nm-nf* adversary [*pl* adversaries]
advertir *vt* **1** (*avisar*) to warn *sb* (**about/of sth**): *Les advertí del peligro.* I warned them about the danger. **2** (*decir*) to tell: *Ya te lo había advertido.* I told you so! ◊ *Te advierto que a mí me da lo mismo.* Mind you, it's all the same to me.
aéreo, -a *adj* **1** (*gen*) air [*n atrib*]: *tráfico ~* air traffic **2** (*vista, fotografía*) aerial LOC *Ver* ACCIDENTE, COMPAÑÍA, CORREO, FUERZA, PUENTE, VÍA
aerobic *nm* aerobics [*sing*]
aeronave *nf* aircraft [*pl* aircraft] LOC **aeronave espacial** spacecraft [*pl* spacecraft]
aeroplano *nm* aeroplane
aeropuerto *nm* airport: *Vamos a ir a buscarles al ~.* We're going to meet them at the airport.
aerosol *nm* aerosol
afectar *vt* to affect: *El golpe le afectó al oído.* The blow affected his hearing. ◊ *Su muerte me afectó mucho.* I was deeply affected by his death.
afecto *nm* affection LOC **tomar afecto** to become attached *to sth/sb*: *Le hemos tomado mucho ~ al perro.* We've become very attached to our dog.
afeitarse *v pron* **1** (*gen*) to shave: *~ la cabeza* to shave your head ◊ *¿Te has afeitado hoy?* Have you had a shave today? **2** (*barba, bigote*) to shave *sth* off: *Se afeitó el bigote.* He shaved his moustache off. LOC **cuchilla/hoja de afeitar**

razor blade *Ver tb* BROCHA, CREMA, MAQUINILLA

afeminado, -a *pp, adj* effeminate

aferrarse *v pron* ~ (**a**) to cling **to** ***sth/sb***: ~ *a una idea* to cling to an idea

afición *nf* **1** ~ (**a/por**) interest (**in** ***sth***): *Ahora hay menos ~ por la lectura.* Nowadays there's less interest in reading. **2** (*pasatiempo*) hobby [*pl* hobbies]: *Su ~ es la fotografía.* Her hobby is photography. LOC **por afición** as a hobby

aficionado, -a ◆ *pp, adj* **1** ~ **a** (*entusiasta*) keen **on** ***sth***: *Soy muy ~ al ciclismo.* I'm very keen on cycling. **2** (*amateur*) amateur: *una compañía de actores ~s* an amateur theatre company ◆ *nm-nf* **1** (*espectador*) **(a)** (*Dep, música pop*) fan: *un ~ al fútbol* a football fan **(b)** (*cine, música clásica, teatro*) lover: *un ~ a la ópera* an opera lover **2** (*amateur*) amateur: *No tocan mal para ser ~s.* They don't play badly for amateurs. *Ver tb* AFICIONARSE

aficionarse *v pron* ~ **a 1** (*pasatiempo*) to get keen **on** ***sth/doing sth***: *Se ha aficionado al ajedrez.* She's got very keen on chess. **2** (*placeres, vicios*) to acquire a taste **for** ***sth***: ~ *a la buena vida* to acquire a taste for the good life

afilado, -a *pp, adj* sharp *Ver tb* AFILAR

afilar *vt* to sharpen

afiliarse *v pron* ~ (**a**) to join: *Decidí afiliarme al partido.* I decided to join the party.

afinar *vt* (*instrumento musical*) to tune LOC **afinar la puntería** to take better aim

afirmar *vt* to state, to say (*más coloq*): *Afirmó sentirse preocupado.* He said that he was worried. LOC **afirmar con la cabeza** to nod (your head)

afirmativo, -a *adj* affirmative

aflojar ◆ *vt* to loosen: *Le aflojé la corbata.* I loosened his tie. ◆ **aflojarse** *v pron* **1** (*gen*) to loosen: *Me aflojé el cinturón.* I loosened my belt. **2** (*tornillo, nudo*) to come loose: *Se ha aflojado el nudo.* The knot has come loose.

afluente *nm* tributary [*pl* tributaries]

afónico, -a *adj* LOC **estar afónico** to have lost your voice **quedarse afónico** to lose your voice

afortunado, -a *adj* lucky, fortunate (*más formal*)

África *nf* Africa

africano, -a *adj, nm-nf* African

afrontar *vt* to face up to *sth*: ~ *la realidad* to face up to reality

afuera ◆ *adv* outside: *Vámonos ~.* Let's go outside. ◆ **afueras** *nf* outskirts: *Viven en las ~s de Roma.* They live on the outskirts of Rome.

agachar ◆ *vt* to lower: ~ *la cabeza* to lower your head ◆ **agacharse** *v pron* to bend down LOC **¡agáchate!/¡agachaos!** duck!

agarrado, -a *pp, adj* LOC *Ver* BAILAR; *Ver tb* AGARRAR

agarrar ◆ *vt* **1** (*asir*) to grab: *Me agarró del brazo.* He grabbed me by the arm. **2** (*sujetar*) to hold: *Agarra esto para que no se caiga.* Hold this and don't let it fall. **3** (*atrapar, contraer*) to catch: *Si agarro a ese mocoso lo mato.* If I catch the little brat I'll kill him. ◇ ~ *una pulmonía* to catch pneumonia ◆ **agarrarse** *v pron* **agarrarse** (**a**) to hold on (**to** ***sth/sb***): *Agárrate a mí.* Hold on to me. LOC *Ver* CABREO, TORO

agazaparse *v pron* to crouch (down)

agencia *nf* agency [*pl* agencies] LOC **agencia de viajes** travel agency [*pl* travel agencies]

agenda *nf* **1** (*calendario*) diary [*pl* diaries] **2** (*de direcciones y teléfonos*) address book

agente *nmf* **1** (*representante*) agent: *Eso trátelo con mi ~.* See my agent about that. **2** (*policía*) policeman/woman [*pl* policemen/women]

ágil *adj* (*persona*) agile

agilidad *nf* agility

agitado, -a *pp, adj* **1** (*vida, día*) hectic **2** (*mar*) rough *Ver tb* AGITAR

agitar *vt* **1** (*botella*) to shake: *Agítese antes de usarlo.* Shake (well) before using. **2** (*pañuelo, brazos*) to wave **3** (*alas*) to flap

agobiante *adj* **1** (*persona*) tiresome **2** (*calor*) stifling

agobiar ◆ *vt* **1** (*exigencias, problemas*) to overwhelm **2** (*meter prisa*) to rush: *No me agobies.* Don't rush me. ◆ **agobiarse** *v pron* to get worked up

agobio *nm* **1** (*calor*): *¡Qué ~! Abre un poco la ventana.* Phew! Open the window a bit. **2** (*preocupación*): *Para entonces estaré con el ~ de los exámenes.* I'll be in a sweat about the exams by then.

agonía ◆ *nf* agony [*pl* agonies] ◆ **agonías** *nmf* misery [*sing*]: *Eres una verdadera ~s.* You're a real misery.

agonizar *vi* to be dying

agosto *nm* August (*abrev* Aug) ☛ *Ver ejemplos en* ENERO LOC **hacer el/su agosto** to make a fortune

agotado, -a *pp, adj* **1** (*cansado*) worn out, exhausted (*más formal*) **2** (*existencias*) sold out **3** (*libros*) out of print *Ver tb* AGOTAR

agotador, ~a *adj* exhausting

agotamiento *nm* exhaustion

agotar ◆ *vt* **1** (*gen*) to exhaust: *~ un tema* to exhaust a subject **2** (*existencias, reservas*) to use *sth* up: *Hemos agotado las existencias.* We've used up all our supplies. **3** (*cansar*) to wear *sb* out: *Los niños me agotan.* The children wear me out. ◆ **agotarse** *v pron* **1** (*gen*) to run out: *Se me está agotando la paciencia.* My patience is running out. **2** (*libro, entradas*) to sell out

agraciado, -a *pp, adj* **1** (*físico*) attractive **2** (*número*) winning

agradable *adj* pleasant LOC **agradable a la vista/al oído** pleasing to the eye/ear

agradar *vi* to please *sb* [*vt*]: *Intenta ~ a todo el mundo.* He tries to please everyone.

agradecer *vt* to thank *sb* (**for *sth*/*doing sth***): *Agradezco mucho que hayáis venido.* Thank you very much for coming.

agradecido, -a *pp, adj* grateful: *Le quedo muy ~.* I am very grateful to you. *Ver tb* AGRADECER

agradecimiento *nm* gratitude: *Deberías mostrar tu ~.* You should show your gratitude. ◊ *unas palabras de ~* a few words of thanks

agrandar *vt* to enlarge

agrario, -a *adj* (*ley, reforma*) agrarian

agravar ◆ *vt* to make *sth* worse ◆ **agravarse** *v pron* to get worse

agredir *vt* to attack

agregar *vt* to add *sth* (***to sth***)

agresión *nf* aggression: *un pacto de no ~* a non-aggression pact

agresivo, -a *adj* aggressive

agrícola *adj* agricultural LOC *Ver* FAENA, PRODUCTO

agricultor, ~a *nm-nf* farmer

agricultura *nf* agriculture, farming (*más coloq*)

agridulce *adj* sweet and sour

agrietar(se) *vt, v pron* **1** (*gen*) to crack **2** (*piel*) to chap

agrio, -a *adj* **1** (*leche, vino, carácter*) sour **2** (*limón, experiencia*) bitter

agrónomo, -a *adj* agricultural LOC *Ver* INGENIERO, PERITO

agrupar ◆ *vt* to put *sth/sb* in a group ◆ **agruparse** *v pron* to get into groups: *~se de dos en dos* to get into groups of two

agua *nf* water LOC **agua corriente** running water **agua del grifo** tap water **agua dulce/salada** fresh/salt water: *peces de ~ salada* salt-water fish **agua mineral con/sin gas** fizzy/still mineral water **agua oxigenada** hydrogen peroxide **agua potable** drinking water **estar con el agua al cuello** to be in deep water *Ver tb* AHOGAR, BAILAR, BOLSA[1], CLARO, GOTA, MOLINO, TROMBA

aguacate *nm* avocado [*pl* avocados]

aguacero *nm* (heavy) shower

aguafiestas *nmf* spoilsport

aguanieve *nf* sleet

aguantar ◆ *vt* **1** (*gen*) to put up with *sth/sb*: *Tendrás que ~ el dolor.* You'll have to put up with the pain.

> Cuando la frase es negativa se utiliza mucho **to stand**: *No aguanto este calor.* I can't stand this heat. ◊ *No les aguanto.* I can't stand them. ◊ *¡No hay quien te aguante!* You're unbearable!

2 (*peso*) to take: *El puente no aguantó el peso del camión.* The bridge couldn't take the weight of the lorry. ◆ *vi* **1** (*durar*) to last: *La alfombra aguantará otro año.* The carpet will last another year. **2** (*esperar*) to hold on: *Aguanta, que ya casi hemos llegado.* Hold on, we're almost there. **3** (*resistir*) to hold: *Esta estantería no aguantará.* This shelf won't hold. ◆ **aguantarse** *v pron* to grin and bear it: *Yo también tengo hambre, pero me aguanto.* I'm hungry as well, but I grin and bear it. ◊ *Si no te gusta, te aguantas.* If you don't like it, tough! LOC **aguantar la respiración** to hold your breath

aguante *nm* **1** (*físico*) stamina: *Tienen muy poco ~.* They have very little stamina. **2** (*paciencia*) patience: *¡Tienes un ~!* You're so patient!

aguardiente *nm* eau-de-vie

aguarrás *nm* white spirit

agudo, -a ◆ *adj* **1** (*gen*) sharp: *una inteligencia aguda* a sharp mind **2** (*ángulo, dolor*) acute: *un dolor ~* an acute pain **3** (*sonido, voz*) high-pitched **4** (*gracioso*) witty: *un comentario ~* a witty remark **5** (*palabra*): *Es una palabra aguda.* The accent is on the last syllable. ◆ *nm* (*Mús*) treble [*incontable*]: *No se oyen bien los ~s.* You can't hear the treble very well.

aguijón *nm* (*insecto*) sting: *clavar el ~* to sting

águila *nf* eagle

aguja *nf* **1** (*gen*) needle: *enhebrar una ~* to thread a needle ◊ *~s de pino* pine needles **2** (*de reloj*) hand **3** (*de tocadiscos*) stylus [*pl* styluses/styli] LOC *Ver* BUSCAR

agujero *nm* hole: *hacer un ~* to make a hole

agujetas *nf* LOC **tener agujetas** to be stiff: *Tengo ~ en las piernas.* My legs are stiff.

ahí *adv* there: *~ van.* There they go ◊ *~ lo tienes.* There it is. ◊ *¡Ponte ~!* Stand over there! LOC **ahí abajo/arriba** down/up there: *¿Están mis libros ~ abajo?* Are my books down there? **ahí dentro/fuera** in/out there: *~ fuera hace un frío que pela.* It's freezing out there. **ahí mismo** right there **¡ahí va!** (*¡cógelo!*) catch! **por ahí 1** (*lugar determinado*) over there **2** (*lugar no determinado*): *He estado por ~.* I've been out. ◊ *ir por ~ a dar una vuelta* to go out for a walk

ahijado, -a *nm-nf* **1** (*sin distinción de sexo*) godchild [*pl* godchildren]: *Tengo dos ~s: un niño y una niña.* I've got two godchildren: one boy and one girl. **2** (*sólo masculino*) godson **3** (*sólo femenino*) god-daughter

ahogar ◆ *vt* **1** (*asfixiar*) to suffocate: *El humo me ahogaba.* The smoke was suffocating me. **2** (*en agua*) to drown ◆ **ahogarse** *v pron* **1** (*asfixiarse*) to suffocate: *Por poco se ahogan con el humo del incendio.* They nearly suffocated in the smoke from the fire. **2** (*en agua*) to drown **3** (*respirar mal*) to be unable to breathe: *Cuando me da el asma me ahogo.* When I have an asthma attack, I can't breathe. **4** (*al atragantarse*) to choke: *Casi me ahogo con esa espina.* I almost choked on that bone. LOC **ahogarse en un vaso de agua** to get worked up over nothing

ahora *adv* now: *¿Qué voy a hacer ~?* What am I going to do now? ◊ *~ voy.* I'm coming. LOC **ahora mismo 1** (*en este momento*) right now: *~ mismo no puedo.* I can't do it right now. **2** (*en seguida*) right away: *~ mismo te lo doy.* I'll give it to you right away. **de ahora en adelante** from now on **hasta ahora** up until now **¡hasta ahora!** see you soon!

ahorcado *nm* hangman: *jugar al ~* to play hangman

ahorcar(se) *vt, v pron* to hang (yourself)

En el sentido de *ahorcar* el verbo **to hang** es regular y por lo tanto forma el pasado añadiendo **-ed**.

ahorrador, ~a ◆ *adj* thrifty ◆ *nm-nf* saver LOC **ser poco ahorrador** to be bad with money

ahorrar *vt, vi* to save: *~ tiempo/dinero* to save time/money

ahorro *nm* saving: *mis ~s de toda la vida* my life savings LOC **cartilla/libreta de ahorro(s)** savings book *Ver tb* CAJA

ahumado, -a ◆ *pp, adj* smoked ◆ **ahumados** *nm* smoked fish [*incontable, v sing*] LOC *Ver* ARENQUE; *Ver tb* AHUMAR

ahumar ◆ *vt* **1** (*alimentos*) to smoke **2** (*habitación*) to fill *sth* with smoke ◆ **ahumarse** *v pron* **1** (*habitación*) to fill with smoke **2** (*ennegrecerse*) to blacken

ahuyentar *vt* to frighten *sth/sb* away

aire *nm* **1** (*gen*) air: *~ puro* fresh air **2** (*viento*) wind: *Hace mucho ~.* It's very windy. LOC **aire acondicionado** air-conditioning **al aire**: *con el pecho al ~* bare-chested ◊ *un vestido con la espalda al ~* a backless dress **al aire libre** in the open air: *un concierto al ~ libre* an open-air concert **a mi aire**: *Le gusta estar a su ~.* He likes to do his own thing. ◊ *Prefiero hacerlo a mi ~.* I'd prefer to do it my way. **darse aires de superioridad** to put on airs **saltar/volar por los aires** to blow up **tomar el aire** to get a breath of fresh air *Ver tb* BOMBA², EJÉRCITO, PISTOLA

airear ◆ *vt* to air ◆ **airearse** *v pron* to get some fresh air

aislado, -a *pp, adj* isolated: *casos ~s* isolated cases *Ver tb* AISLAR

aislante ◆ *adj* insulating ◆ *nm* insulator LOC *Ver* CINTA

aislar *vt* **1** (*separar*) to isolate *sth/sb* (**from** *sth/sb*) **2** (*incomunicar*) to cut *sth/sb* off (**from** *sth/sb*): *Las inundaciones aislaron la aldea.* The village was cut off by the floods. **3** (*con material aislante*) to insulate

ajedrez *nm* **1** (*juego*) chess **2** (*tablero y piezas*) chess set LOC *Ver* TABLERO

ajeno, -a *adj* **1** (*de otro*) somebody else's: *en casa ajena* in somebody else's house **2** (*de otros*) other people's: *meterse en los problemas ~s* to interfere in other people's lives

ajetreado, -a *pp, adj* **1** (*persona*) busy **2** (*día*) hectic

ajo *nm* garlic **LOC** *Ver* CABEZA, DIENTE

ajuar *nm* trousseau [*pl* trousseaus/ trousseaux]

ajustado, -a *pp, adj* tight: *un vestido muy ~* a tight-fitting dress *Ver tb* AJUSTAR

ajustar ◆ *vt* **1** (*gen*) to adjust: *~ la televisión* to adjust the television **2** (*apretar*) to tighten: *~ un tornillo* to tighten a screw ◆ *vi* to fit: *La puerta no ajusta.* The door doesn't fit. ◆ **ajustarse** *v pron* **ajustarse (a)** to fit in (**with** ***sth***): *Es lo que mejor se ajusta a nuestras necesidades.* It's what suits our needs best. **LOC ajustarle las cuentas a algn** to settle accounts with sb

al *prep* **+ inf 1** (*gen*) when: *Se echaron a reír al verme.* They burst out laughing when they saw me. **2** (*simultaneidad*) as: *Lo vi al salir.* I saw him as I was leaving. *Ver tb* A

ala *nf* **1** (*gen*) wing: *las ~s de un avión* the wings of a plane ◊ *el ~ conservadora del partido* the conservative wing of the party **2** (*sombrero*) brim: *un sombrero de ~ ancha* a wide-brimmed hat **LOC ala delta 1** (*aparato*) hang-glider **2** (*deporte*) hang-gliding

alabanza *nf* praise [*incontable*]: *Se deshicieron en ~s hacia ti.* They were full of praise for you.

alabar *vt* to praise *sth/sb* (**for** ***sth***): *Le alabaron por su valentía.* They praised him for his courage.

alacrán *nm* scorpion

alambrada *nf* wire fence

alambre *nm* wire

álamo *nm* poplar

alarde *nm* **LOC hacer alarde de** to show off about *sth*

alardear *vi* ~ (**de**) to boast (**about/of** ***sth***)

alargado, -a *pp, adj* long *Ver tb* ALARGAR

alargar ◆ *vt* **1** (*gen*) to extend: *~ una carretera* to extend a road **2** (*prenda*) to lengthen **3** (*duración*) to prolong: *~ la guerra* to prolong the war **4** (*estirar, brazo, mano*) to stretch *sth* out ◆ **alargarse** *v pron* **1** (*gen*) to get longer: *Los días se van alargando.* The days are getting longer. **2** (*prolongarse demasiado*) to drag on: *La reunión se alargó hasta las dos.* The meeting dragged on till two. **3** (*hablando, explicando*) to go on for too long

alarma *nf* alarm: *dar la (voz de) ~* to raise the alarm ◊ *Saltó la ~.* The alarm went off. **LOC alarma de incendios** fire alarm

alarmante *adj* alarming

alarmarse *v pron* ~ (**por**) to be alarmed (**at** ***sth***)

alba *nf* dawn: *al ~* at dawn

albañil *nm* **1** (*gen*) builder **2** (*que sólo pone ladrillos*) bricklayer

albaricoque *nm* apricot

albergar ◆ *vt* to house ◆ **albergarse** *v pron* to shelter

albergue *nm* **1** (*residencia*) hostel: *un ~ juvenil* a youth hostel **2** (*de montaña*) shelter

albóndiga *nf* meatball

albornoz *nm* bathrobe

alborotado, -a *pp, adj* **1** (*excitado*) in a state of excitement: *Los ánimos están ~s.* Feelings are running high. **2** (*con confusión*) in confusion: *La gente corría alborotada.* People were running around in confusion. *Ver tb* ALBOROTAR

alborotar ◆ *vt* **1** (*desordenar*) to mess *sth* up: *El viento nos alborotó el pelo.* The wind messed up our hair. **2** (*revolucionar*) to stir *sb* up: *~ al resto de la clase* to stir up the rest of the class ◆ *vi* (*armar jaleo*) to make a racket ◆ **alborotarse** *v pron* to get excited

alboroto *nm* **1** (*jaleo*) racket: *¿A qué viene tanto ~?* What's all the racket about? **2** (*disturbio*) disturbance: *El ~ hizo que viniera la policía.* The disturbance led the police to intervene.

álbum *nm* album

alcachofa *nf* artichoke

alcalde, -esa *nm-nf* mayor

alcance *nm* **1** (*gen*) reach: *fuera de tu ~* out of your reach **2** (*arma, emisora, telescopio*) range: *misiles de medio ~* medium-range missiles

alcanfor *nm* **LOC** *Ver* BOLA

alcantarilla *nf* sewer

alcantarillado *nm* sewage system

alcanzar ◆ *vt* **1** (*gen*) to reach: *~ un acuerdo* to reach an agreement **2** (*conseguir*) to achieve: *~ los objetivos* to achieve your objectives **3** (*pillar*) to catch *sb* up: *No pude ~los.* I couldn't catch them up. ◊ *Vete saliendo, ya te alcanzaré.* You go on—I'll catch you up. ◆ *vi* **1** (*ser suficiente*) to be enough: *La comida no alcanzará para todos.* There won't be enough food for everybody. **2** (*llegar*) to reach: *No alcanzo.* I can't reach.

alcaparra *nf* caper

alcohol *nm* alcohol LOC **sin alcohol** non-alcoholic *Ver tb* CERVEZA

alcohólico, -a *adj, nm-nf* alcoholic

alcoholismo *nm* alcoholism

aldea *nf* small village

aldeano, -a *nm-nf* villager

alegar *vt* **1** (*gen*) to claim: *Alegan que existió fraude.* They're claiming that there was a fraud. ◊ *Alegan no tener dinero.* They claim not to have money. **2** (*razones, motivos*) to cite: *Alegó motivos personales.* He cited personal reasons.

alegrar ◆ *vt* **1** (*hacer feliz*) to make *sb* happy: *La carta me alegró mucho.* The letter made me very happy. **2** (*animar*) **(a)** (*persona*) to cheer *sb* up: *Intentamos ~ a los ancianos.* We tried to cheer the old people up. **(b)** (*fiesta*) to liven *sth* up: *Los magos alegraron la fiesta.* The magicians livened up the party. **3** (*casa, lugar*) to brighten *sth* up ◆ **alegrarse** *v pron* **1** (*estar contento*) **(a) alegrarse (de/por)** to be pleased (**about *sth*/to do *sth***): *Me alegro de saberlo.* I am pleased to hear it. **(b) alegrarse por algn** to be delighted **for sb**: *Me alegro por vosotros.* I'm delighted for you. **2** (*cara, ojos*) to light up: *Se le alegró la cara.* His face lit up.

alegre *adj* **1** (*feliz*) happy **2** (*de buen humor*) cheerful: *Tiene un carácter ~.* He's a cheerful person. **3** (*música, espectáculo*) lively **4** (*color, habitación*) bright

alegría *nf* joy: *gritar/saltar de ~* to shout/jump for joy LOC **¡qué/vaya alegría!** great! *Ver tb* BOTAR, CABER

alejar ◆ *vt* **1** (*retirar*) to move *sth/sb* away (***from sth*/*sb***): *Debes ~lo de la ventana.* You should move it away from the window. **2** (*distanciar*) to distance *sth/sb* (***from sth*/*sb***): *El desacuerdo nos alejó de mis padres.* The disagreement distanced us from my parents. ◆ **alejarse** *v pron* **alejarse** (**de**) **1** (*apartarse*) to move away (***from sth*/*sb***): *~se de un objetivo* to move away from a goal ◊ *No os alejéis mucho.* Don't go too far away. **2** (*camino*) to leave

¡aleluya! *interj* alleluia!

alemán, -ana *adj, nm-nf, nm* German: *los alemanes* the Germans ◊ *hablar ~* to speak German LOC *Ver* PASTOR

Alemania *nf* Germany

alergia *nf* ~ (**a**) allergy [*pl* allergies] (**to *sth***): *tener ~ a algo* to be allergic to sth

alérgico, -a *adj* ~ (**a**) allergic (**to *sth***)

alero *nm* **1** (*tejado*) eaves [*pl*] **2** (*Dep*) winger

alerta ◆ *nf* alert: *en estado de ~* on alert ◊ *Dieron la (voz de) ~.* They gave the alert. ◆ *adj* alert (***to sth***)

alertar *vt* to alert *sb* (***to sth***): *Nos alertaron del riesgo.* They alerted us to the risk.

aleta *nf* **1** (*pez*) fin **2** (*buceador, foca*) flipper **3** (*vehículo*) wing

alfabético, -a *adj* alphabetical

alfabeto *nm* alphabet

alfalfa *nf* lucerne

alféizar *nm* (*ventana*) windowsill

alfil *nm* bishop

alfiler *nm* pin

alfombra *nf* **1** (*grande*) carpet **2** (*más pequeña*) rug

alfombrilla *nf* mat

alga *nf* **1** (*de agua dulce*) weed [*incontable*]: *El estanque está lleno de ~s.* The pond is full of weed. **2** (*de agua salada*) seaweed [*incontable*]

> También existe la palabra **algae**, pero es científica.

álgebra *nf* algebra

algo ◆ *pron* something, anything ☛La diferencia entre **something** y **anything** es la misma que hay entre **some** y **any**. *Ver nota en* SOME. ◆ *adv* **1 + adj** rather: *~ ingenuo* rather naive ☛ *Ver nota en* FAIRLY **2 + verbo** a bit: *Mi hija me ayuda ~.* My daughter helps me a bit. LOC **¿algo más?** (*tienda*) anything else? **en algo** in any way: *Si en ~ puedo ayudarles...* If I can help you in any way... **o algo así** or something like that **por algo será** there must be a reason

algodón *nm* **1** (*planta, fibra*) cotton **2** (*Med*) cotton wool [*incontable*]: *Me tapé los oídos con algodones.* I put cotton wool in my ears. LOC **algodón de azúcar/dulce** candyfloss

alguien *pron* somebody, anybody: *¿Crees que vendrá ~?* Do you think anybody will come? ☛La diferencia entre **somebody** y **anybody** es la misma que hay entre **some** y **any**. *Ver nota en* SOME.

Nótese que **somebody** y **anybody** llevan el verbo en singular, pero sin embargo suelen ir seguidos de un pronombre en plural (p.ej. 'their'): *Alguien se ha dejado el abrigo.* Somebody's left their coat behind.

algún *adj Ver* ALGUNO

alguno, -a ◆ *adj* **1** (*gen*) some, any: *Te he comprado ~s libros para que te entretengas.* I've bought you some books to pass the time. ◊ *¿Hay algún problema?* Are there any problems? ☛ *Ver nota en* SOME **2** (*con número*) several: *~s centenares de personas* several hundred people **3** (*uno que otro*) the occasional: *Habrá algún chubasco débil.* There will be the occasional light shower. ◆ *pron*: *~s de vosotros sois muy vagos.* Some of you are very lazy. ◊ *Seguro que ha sido ~ de vosotros.* It must have been one of you. ◊ *~s protestaron.* Some (people) protested. LOC **alguna cosa** something, anything ☛La diferencia entre **something** y **anything** es la misma que hay entre **some** y **any**. *Ver nota en* SOME. **algunas veces** sometimes **alguna vez** ever: *¿Has estado allí alguna vez?* Have you ever been there? **algún día** some day **en algún lugar/sitio/en alguna parte** somewhere, anywhere ☛La diferencia entre **somewhere** y **anywhere** es la misma que hay entre **some** y **any**. *Ver nota en* SOME.

aliado, -a ◆ *pp, adj* allied ◆ *nm-nf* ally [*pl* allies] *Ver tb* ALIARSE

alianza *nf* **1** (*unión*) alliance: *una ~ entre cinco partidos* an alliance between five parties **2** (*anillo*) wedding ring

aliarse *v pron* ~ (**con/contra**) to form an alliance (**with/against** ***sth/sb***)

alicates *nm* pliers: *Necesito unos ~.* I need a pair of pliers.

aliento *nm* breath: *tener mal ~* to have bad breath LOC **sin aliento** out of breath: *Vengo sin ~.* I'm out of breath.

alijo *nm* haul: *un ~ de 500kg de hachís* a haul of 500kg of hashish

alimaña *nf* pest

alimentación *nf* **1** (*acción*) feeding **2** (*dieta*) diet: *una ~ equilibrada* a balanced diet **3** (*comida*) food: *una tienda de ~* a food store

alimentar ◆ *vt* to feed *sth/sb* (**on/with** ***sth***): *~ a los caballos con heno* to feed the horses (on) hay ◆ *vi* to be nourishing: *Alimenta mucho.* It's very nourishing. ◆ **alimentarse** *v pron* **alimentarse de** to live **on** ***sth***

alimentario, -a *adj* food [*n atrib*]: *productos ~s* foodstuffs

alimenticio, -a *adj* nutritious: *Los plátanos son muy ~s.* Bananas are very nutritious.

alimento *nm* **1** (*comida*) food: *~s enlatados* tinned food(s) **2** (*valor nutritivo*): *Las lentejas tienen mucho ~.* Lentils are very nourishing.

alineación *nf* (*Dep*) line-up

alinear *vt* **1** (*poner en hilera*) to line *sth/sb* up **2** (*Dep*) to field

aliñar *vt* to dress *sth* (**with** ***sth***): *~ una ensalada* to dress a salad

alisar *vt* to smooth

alistarse *v pron* ~ (**en**) to enlist (**in** ***sth***)

aliviar *vt* to relieve: *~ el dolor* to relieve pain ◊ *El masaje me alivió un poco.* The massage made me feel a bit better.

alivio *nm* relief: *¡Qué ~!* What a relief! ◊ *Ha sido un ~ para todos.* It came as a relief to everybody.

allá *adv* **1** (*lugar*) (over) there: *Déjalo ~.* Leave it (over) there. ◊ *de Cuenca para ~* from Cuenca on **2** ~ **en/por...** (*tiempo*) back **in...**: *~ por los años 60* back in the 60s LOC **allá abajo/arriba** down/up there **allá dentro/fuera** in/out there **allá tú** it's your, his, etc problem **¡allá voy!** here I come! **el más allá** the afterlife **más allá 1** (*más lejos*) further on: *seis kilómetros más ~* six kilometres further on **2** (*hacia un lado*) further over: *correr la mesa más ~* to push the table further over **más allá de** beyond: *más ~ del río* beyond the river *Ver tb* ACÁ

allanar *vt* (*suelo*) to level

allí *adv* there: *Tengo un amigo ~.* I have a friend there. ◊ *¡~ están!* There they are! ◊ *a 30 kilómetros de ~* 30 kilometres from there ◊ *una chica que pasaba por ~* a girl who was passing by LOC **allí abajo/arriba** down/up there **allí dentro/fuera** in/out there **allí mismo** right there **es allí donde...** that's where...: *Es ~ donde me caí.* That's where I fell.

alma *nf* **1** (*gen*) soul: *No había ni un ~.* There wasn't a soul. **2** (*carácter, mente*) spirit: *un ~ noble* a noble spirit

almacén *nm* **1** (*edificio*) warehouse **2** (*habitación*) storeroom LOC *Ver* GRANDE

almacenar *vt* to store

almeja *nf* clam

almendra *nf* almond

almendro *nm* almond tree

almíbar *nm* syrup

almirante *nmf* admiral

almohada *nf* pillow LOC *Ver* CONSULTAR

almorzar ◆ *vi* to have a snack ◆ *vt* to have *sth* mid-morning

almuerzo *nm* mid-morning snack

alocado, -a *adj* **1** (*atolondrado*) scatty **2** (*precipitado, imprudente*) rash: *una decisión alocada* a rash decision

alojar ◆ *vt* **1** (*gen*) to accommodate: *El hotel puede ~ a 200 personas.* The hotel can accommodate 200 people. **2** (*sin cobrar*) to put *sb* up: *Tras el incendio nos alojaron en un colegio.* After the fire, they put us up in a school. ◆ **alojarse** *v pron* to stay: *Nos alojamos en un hotel.* We stayed in a hotel.

alpinismo *nm* mountaineering: *hacer ~* to go mountaineering

alpiste *nm* birdseed

alquilar *vt*

- **referido a la persona que coge algo en alquiler** to hire, to rent

> **To hire** se emplea para un plazo breve de tiempo, como en el caso de un coche o disfraz: *Alquiló un traje para la boda.* He hired a suit for the wedding. ◊ *Te compensa alquilar un coche.* You might as well hire a car.
> **To rent** implica periodos más largos, por ejemplo cuando alquilamos una casa o una habitación: *¿Cuánto me costaría alquilar un piso de dos habitaciones?* How much would it cost me to rent a two-bedroomed flat?

- **referido a la persona que deja algo en alquiler** to hire *sth* (out), to rent *sth* (out), to let *sth* (out)

> **To hire sth (out)** se emplea para un plazo breve de tiempo: *Viven de alquilar caballos a los turistas.* They make their living hiring (out) horses to tourists.
> **To rent sth (out)** se refiere a periodos largos de tiempo y se suele utilizar para referirnos a objetos, casas o habitaciones: *Alquilan habitaciones a estudiantes.* They rent (out) rooms to students. ◊ *una empresa que alquila electrodomésticos* a company that rents out household appliances
> **To let sth (out)** se refiere sólo a casas o habitaciones: *En nuestra casa se alquila un piso.* There's a flat to let in our block.

alquiler *nm* (*acción de alquilar*) **1** hire: *una compañía de ~ de coches* a car hire company **2** (*precio*) **(a)** (*gen*) hire charge **(b)** (*casa, habitación*) rent: *¿Has pagado el ~?* Have you paid the rent? LOC *Ver* COCHE

alquitrán *nm* tar

alrededor ◆ *adv* ~ (**de**) **1** (*en torno a*) around: *las personas a mi ~* the people around me **2** (*aproximadamente*) about: *Llegaremos ~ de las diez y media.* We'll get there at about half past ten. ◆ **alrededores** *nm* (*ciudad*) outskirts LOC *Ver* GIRAR, VUELTA

alta *nf* LOC **dar de/el alta a algn** to discharge sb (from hospital)

altar *nm* altar

altavoz *nm* loudspeaker: *Lo anunciaron por los altavoces.* They announced it over the loudspeakers.

alterar ◆ *vt* to alter ◆ **alterarse** *v pron* **1** (*enfadarse*) to get angry **2** (*ponerse nervioso*) to get nervous: *¡No te alteres!* Keep calm! LOC **alterar el orden público** to cause a breach of the peace

alternar ◆ *vt, vi* to alternate ◆ *vi* (*con gente*) to socialize

alternativa *nf* ~ (**a**) alternative (**to** *sth*): *Es nuestra única ~.* It is our only option.

alterno, -a *adj* alternate: *en días ~s* on alternate days

altitud *nf* height, altitude (*más formal*): *a 3.000 metros de ~* at an altitude of 3000 metres

alto, -a ◆ *adj* **1** (*gen*) tall, high

> **Tall** se usa para referirnos a personas, árboles y edificios que suelen ser estrechos además de altos: *el edificio más alto del mundo* the tallest building in the world ◊ *una niña muy alta* a tall girl. **High** se utiliza mucho con sustantivos abstractos: *altos niveles de contaminación* high levels of pollution ◊ *altos tipos de interés* high interest rates, y para referirnos a la altura sobre el nivel del mar: *La Paz es la capital más alta del mundo.* La Paz is the highest capital in the world.
> Los antónimos de **tall** son **short** y **small**, y el antónimo de **high** es **low**. Las dos palabras tienen en común el sustantivo **height**, *altura*.

2 (*mando, funcionario*) high-ranking **3** (*clase social, región*) upper: *el ~ Ebro* the upper Ebro **4** (*sonido, voz*) loud: *No pongas la música tan alta.* Don't play the music so loud. ◆ *adv* **1** (*poner, subir*) high: *Ese cuadro está muy ~.* That picture is too high up. **2** (*hablar, tocar*) loudly ◆ *nm* height: *Tiene tres metros de ~.* It is three metres high.

LOC alta fidelidad hi-fi **alta mar** the high sea(s): *El barco estaba en alta mar.* The ship was on the high sea. **¡alto!** stop! **alto el fuego** ceasefire **pasar por alto** to overlook *Ver tb* CLASE, CUELLO, HABLAR, POTENCIA

altura *nf* height: *caerse desde una ~ de tres metros* to fall from a height of three metres **LOC a estas alturas** at this stage **a la altura de...**: *una cicatriz a la ~ del codo* a scar near the elbow **altura máxima** maximum headroom **de gran/poca altura** high/low **tener dos, etc metros de altura** (*cosa*) to be two, etc metres high *Ver tb* SALTO

alubia *nf* bean

alucinación *nf* hallucination

alucinante *adj* amazing

alucinar *vi* **1** (*delirar*) to hallucinate **2** (*sorprenderse*): *Alucinábamos con sus comentarios.* We were amazed by his comments.

alud *nm* avalanche

aludido, -a *pp, adj* **LOC darse por aludido**: *No se dieron por ~s.* They didn't take the hint. ◊ *En seguida te das por ~.* You always take things personally.

alumbrado *nm* lighting

alumbrar ◆ *vt* to light *sth* (up): *Una gran lámpara alumbra la sala.* The room is lit by a huge lamp. ◆ *vi* to give off light: *Esa bombilla alumbra mucho.* That bulb gives off a lot of light. ◊ *Alumbra debajo de la cama.* Shine a light under the bed.

aluminio *nm* aluminium **LOC** *Ver* PAPEL

alumno, -a *nm-nf* **1** (*gen*) pupil: *uno de mis ~s* one of my pupils **2** (*universidad*) student

alzada *nf* height

alzar ◆ *vt* to raise: *~ el telón* to raise the curtain ◆ **alzarse** *v pron* **alzarse** (**contra**) to rebel (**against *sth/sb***): *Los militares se alzaron contra el gobierno.* The military rebelled against the government.

ama *nf* **LOC** *Ver* AMO

amable *adj* ~ (**con**) kind (**to *sb***): *Han sido muy ~s ayudándome.* It was very kind of them to help me. ◊ *Gracias, es usted muy ~.* Thank you, that's very kind of you. **LOC si es tan amable** (**de...**) if you would be so kind (as to...): *Si es tan ~ de cerrar la puerta.* If you would be so kind as to close the door.

amaestrar *vt* to train **LOC sin amaestrar** untrained

amamantar *vt* **1** (*persona*) to breast-feed **2** (*animal*) to suckle

amanecer[1] *nm* **1** (*alba*) dawn: *Nos levantamos al ~.* We got up at dawn. **2** (*salida del sol*) sunrise: *contemplar el ~* to watch the sunrise

amanecer[2] ◆ *v imp* to dawn: *Estaba amaneciendo.* Day was dawning. ◊ *Amaneció soleado.* It was sunny in the morning. ◆ *vi* (*despertarse*) to wake up: *Amanecí con dolor de cabeza.* I woke up with a headache.

amanerado, -a *pp, adj* **1** (*rebuscado*) affected **2** (*afeminado*) effeminate

amante ◆ *adj* loving: *~ padre y esposo* loving husband and father ◊ *~ de la música* music-loving ◆ *nmf* lover

amapola *nf* poppy [*pl* poppies]

amar *vt* to love

amargado, -a ◆ *pp, adj* bitter: *estar ~ por algo* to be bitter about sth ◆ *nm-nf* misery guts [*pl* misery guts]: *Son un par de ~s.* They're a couple of misery guts. *Ver tb* AMARGAR

amargar ◆ *vt* **1** (*persona*) to make *sb* bitter **2** (*ocasión*) to ruin: *Eso nos amargó las vacaciones.* That ruined our holiday. ◆ **amargarse** *v pron* to get upset: *No te amargues (la vida) por eso.* Don't get upset over something like that. **LOC amargarle la vida a algn** to make sb's life a misery

amargo, -a *adj* bitter

amarillento, -a *adj* yellowish

amarillo, -a ◆ *adj* **1** (*color*) yellow: *Es de color ~.* It is yellow. ◊ *Yo iba de ~.* I was wearing yellow. ◊ *pintar algo de ~* to paint sth yellow ◊ *el chico de la camisa amarilla* the boy in the yellow shirt **2** (*semáforo*) amber ◆ *nm* yellow: *No me gusta el ~.* I don't like yellow. **LOC** *Ver* PÁGINA, PRENSA

amarra *nf* (*Náut*) mooring rope **LOC** *Ver* SOLTAR

amarrar *vt* **1** (*gen*) to tie *sth/sb* up: *Le amarraron con cuerdas.* They tied him up with a rope. **2** (*Náut*) to moor

amasar *vt* **1** (*Cocina*) to knead **2** (*fortuna*) to amass

amateur *adj, nmf* amateur

amazona *nf* (*jinete*) horsewoman [*pl* horsewomen]

ámbar *nm* amber

ambición *nf* ambition

ambicionar *vt* (*desear*) to want: *Lo que más ambiciono es...* What I want more than anything else is...

ambicioso, -a *adj* ambitious
ambientación *nf (película, obra de teatro)* setting
ambientador *nm* air freshener
ambiental *adj* **1** *(gen)* background [*n atrib*]: *música ~* background music **2** *(del medio ambiente)* environmental **3** *(del aire)* atmospheric: *condiciones ~es* atmospheric conditions
ambientar *vt (novela, película)* to set *sth* **in...**
ambiente *nm* **1** *(gen)* atmosphere: *un ~ contaminado* a polluted atmosphere ◊ *El local tiene buen ~.* The place has a good atmosphere. ◊ *No hay ~ en la calle.* The streets are dead. **2** *(entorno)* environment: *El ~ familiar nos influye.* Our family environment has a big influence on us. LOC **estar en su ambiente** to be in your element **no estar en su ambiente** to be like a fish out of water *Ver tb* MEDIO
ambiguo, -a *adj* ambiguous
ambos, -as *pron* both (of us, you, them): *Me llevo bien con ~.* I get on well with both of them. ◊ *A ~ nos gusta viajar.* Both of us like travelling./We both like travelling.
ambulancia *nf* ambulance
ambulante *adj* travelling: *un circo ~* a travelling circus LOC *Ver* VENDEDOR
ambulatorio *nm* health centre
amén *nm* amen
amenaza *nf* threat
amenazador, ~a (*tb* **amenazante**) *adj* threatening
amenazar ♦ *vt* to threaten (***to do sth***): *Amenazaron con acudir a los tribunales.* They threatened to take them to court. ◊ *Le han amenazado de muerte* They've threatened to kill him. ◊ *Me amenazó con una navaja.* He threatened me with a knife. ♦ *v imp*: *Amenaza lluvia.* It looks like (it's going to) rain.
ameno, -a *adj* **1** *(entretenido)* entertaining: *una novela muy amena* a very entertaining novel **2** *(agradable)* pleasant: *una conversación muy amena* a very pleasant conversation
América *nf* America
americana *nf* jacket
americano, -a *adj, nm-nf* American
ametralladora *nf* machine-gun
amígdala *nf* tonsil: *Me operaron de las ~s.* I had my tonsils out.
amigo, -a ♦ *adj* **1** *(voz)* friendly **2** *(mano)* helping ♦ *nm-nf* friend: *mi mejor ~* my best friend ◊ *Es íntimo ~ mío.* He's a very close friend of mine. LOC **ser muy amigo(s)** to be good friends (*with sb*): *Soy muy ~ suyo.* We're good friends.
amiguismo *nm* favouritism
amistad *nf* **1** *(relación)* friendship: *romper una ~* to end a friendship **2** **amistades** friends: *Tiene ~es influyentes.* He's got friends in high places. LOC **entablar/hacer amistad** to become friends
amistoso, -a *adj* friendly
amnesia *nf* amnesia
amnistía *nf* amnesty [*pl* amnesties]
amo, -a *nm-nf* owner LOC **ama de casa** housewife [*pl* housewives] **ama de llaves** housekeeper
amodorrarse *v pron* **1** *(adormilarse)* to get drowsy **2** *(dormirse)* to doze off
amoniaco (*tb* **amoníaco**) *nm* ammonia
amontonar ♦ *vt* **1** *(apilar)* to pile *sth* up **2** *(acumular)* to amass: *~ trastos* to amass junk ♦ **amontonarse** *v pron* **1** *(gen)* to pile up: *Se me amontonó el trabajo.* My work piled up. **2** *(apiñarse)* to cram (***into...***): *Se amontonaron en el coche.* They crammed into the car.
amor *nm* love: *una canción/historia de ~* a love-song/love-story ◊ *el ~ de mi vida* the love of my life ◊ *con ~* lovingly LOC **amor propio** pride **hacer el amor a/con** to make love (to/with *sb*) **¡por (el) amor de Dios!** for God's sake!
amoratado, -a *pp, adj* **1** *(de frío)* blue **2** *(con cardenales)* black and blue: *Tenía todo el cuerpo ~.* My whole body was black and blue. **3** *(ojo)* black
amordazar *vt* to gag
amorío *nm* (love) affair
amoroso, -a *adj* **1** *(relativo al amor)* love [*n atrib*]: *vida/carta amorosa* love life/letter **2** *(cariñoso)* loving **3** *(suave)* fluffy: *un jersey ~* a fluffy jumper LOC *Ver* DESENGAÑO
amortiguador *nm* shock absorber
amotinarse *v pron* **1** *(preso, masas)* to riot **2** *(Náut, Mil)* to mutiny (***against sth/sb***)
amparar ♦ *vt* to protect *sth/sb* (***against/from sth/sb***): *La ley nos ampara contra los abusos.* The law protects us from abuse. ♦ **ampararse** *v pron* **1** **ampararse (de)** *(refugiarse)* to shelter (**from *sth/sb***): *~se de una tormenta* to shelter from a storm

2 ampararse en (*apoyarse*) to seek the protection **of *sth*/*sb***: *Se amparó en su familia.* He sought the protection of his family.

amparo *nm* **1** (*protección*) protection **2** (*lugar de abrigo*) shelter **3** (*apoyo*) support

amperio *nm* amp

ampliación *nf* **1** (*número, cantidad*) increase: *una ~ de plantilla* an increase in personnel **2** (*local, negocio, información*) expansion: *la ~ del aeropuerto* the expansion of the airport **3** (*plazo, acuerdo*) extension **4** (*Fot*) enlargement

ampliar *vt* **1** (*gen*) to extend: *~ el local/plazo de matrícula* to extend the premises/registration period **2** (*número, cantidad*) to increase: *La revista amplió su difusión.* The magazine increased its circulation. **3** (*negocio, imperio*) to expand **4** (*Fot*) to enlarge

amplificador *nm* amplifier

amplio, -a *adj* **1** (*gama, margen*) wide: *una amplia gama de productos* a wide range of goods **2** (*lugar*) spacious: *un piso ~* a spacious flat **3** (*ropa*) baggy

ampolla *nf* blister

amputar *vt* to amputate

amueblar *vt* to furnish LOC **sin amueblar** unfurnished

amuleto *nm* amulet LOC **amuleto de la suerte** good-luck charm

amurallado, -a *pp, adj* walled

analfabeto, -a *adj, nm-nf* illiterate [*adj*]: *ser un ~* to be illiterate ◊ *¡Pero mira que eres ~!* How stupid can you get!

analgésico *nm* painkiller

análisis *nm* analysis [*pl* analyses] LOC **análisis de sangre** blood test

analizar *vt* to analyse

anarquía *nf* anarchy

anarquismo *nm* anarchism

anarquista *adj, nmf* anarchist

anatomía *nf* anatomy [*pl* anatomies]

ancho, -a ◆ *adj* **1** (*de gran anchura*) wide: *el ~ mar* the wide sea **2** (*ropa*) baggy: *un jersey ~* a baggy jumper ◊ *La cintura me queda ancha.* The waist is too big. **3** (*sonrisa, hombros, espalda*) broad: *Es muy ~ de espaldas.* He's got broad shoulders. ☛ *Ver nota en* BROAD ◆ *nm* width: *¿Cuánto mide de ~?* How wide is it? ◊ *Tiene dos metros de ~.* It is two metres wide. LOC **a mis anchas 1** (*como en casa*) at home: *Ponte a tus anchas.* Make yourself at home. **2** (*con libertad*) quite happily: *Aquí los niños pueden jugar a sus anchas.* The children can play here quite happily. **quedarse tan ancho** not to be at all bothered

anchoa *nf* anchovy [*pl* anchovies]

anchura *nf* (*medida*) width: *No tiene suficiente ~.* It isn't wide enough.

anciano, -a ◆ *adj* elderly ◆ *nm-nf* elderly man/woman [*pl* elderly men/women]: *los ~s* the elderly LOC **asilo/residencia de ancianos** old people's home

ancla *nf* anchor LOC **echar el ancla/anclas** to drop anchor *Ver tb* LEVAR

andamio *nm* scaffolding [*incontable*]: *Hay ~s por todas partes.* There's scaffolding everywhere.

andar[1] ◆ *vi* **1** (*caminar*) to walk: *Vine andando.* I walked here. **2** (*funcionar*) to work: *Este reloj no anda.* This clock's not working. **3** (*estar*) to be: *¿Quién anda ahí?* Who's there? ◊ *~ ocupado/deprimido* to be busy/depressed ◊ *¿Qué andas buscando?* What are you looking for? **4** *~* **por** to be **about *sth***: *Debe ~ por los 50 años.* He must be about 50. ◆ **andarse** *v pron* **andarse con**: *No te andes con bromas.* Stop fooling around. ◊ *Habrá que ~se con cuidado.* We'll have to be careful. LOC **¡anda! 1** (*gen*) come on!: *¡Anda, no exageres!* Come on, don't exaggerate! ◊ *¡Anda, déjame en paz!* Come on, leave me alone! **2** (*sorpresa*) hey!: *¡Anda, si está lloviendo!* Hey, it's raining! ☛Para otras expresiones con **andar**, véanse las entradas del sustantivo, adjetivo, etc, p.ej. **andar a gatas** en GATO y **andarse con rodeos** en RODEO.

andar[2] *nm* **andares** walk [*sing*]: *Le reconocí por sus ~es.* I recognized him by his walk.

andén *nm* platform

andrajoso, -a *nm-nf* scruff

anécdota *nf* anecdote: *contar una ~* to tell an anecdote

anemia *nf* anaemia LOC **tener anemia** to be anaemic

anémico, -a *adj* anaemic

anestesia *nf* anaesthetic: *Me pusieron ~ general/local.* They gave me a general/local anaesthetic.

anestesiar *vt* to anaesthetize

anestesista *nmf* anaesthetist

anfetamina *nf* amphetamine

anfibio, -a ◆ *adj* amphibious ◆ *nm* amphibian

anfiteatro *nm* (*romano*) amphitheatre

anfitrión, -ona *nm-nf* host [*fem* hostess]

ángel *nm* angel: ~ *de la guarda* guardian angel LOC *Ver* SOÑAR

anginas *nf* tonsillitis [*incontable, v sing*]

anglicano, -a *adj, nm-nf* Anglican

anglosajón, -ona *adj, nm-nf* Anglo-Saxon

anguila *nf* eel

angula *nf* elver

ángulo *nm* angle: ~ *recto/agudo/obtuso* right/acute/obtuse angle ◊ *Yo veo las cosas desde otro* ~. I see things from a different angle.

angustia *nf* anguish: *Gritó con tremenda* ~. He cried out in anguish.

angustiado, -a *pp, adj* anxious: *Esperaba* ~. I waited anxiously. *Ver tb* ANGUSTIAR

angustiar ◆ *vt* to worry: *Me angustian los exámenes.* I am worried about my exams. ◆ **angustiarse** *v pron* **angustiarse (por) 1** (*inquietarse*) to worry (**about *sth*/*sb***): *No debes ~te cada vez que llegan tarde.* You mustn't worry every time they're late. **2** (*apenarse*) to get upset (**about *sth***)

anidar *vi* ~ (**en**) (*aves*) to nest (**in *sth***)

anilla *nf* ring

anillo *nm* ring LOC **venir como anillo al dedo** to be just right

animado, -a *pp, adj* **1** (*gen*) lively: *La fiesta estuvo muy animada.* It was a very lively party. **2** ~ (**a**) (*dispuesto*) keen (***to do sth***): *Yo estoy ~ a ir.* I am keen to go. LOC *Ver* DIBUJO; *Ver tb* ANIMAR

animal *adj, nm* animal [*n*]: ~ *doméstico/salvaje* domestic/wild animal ◊ *el reino* ~ the animal kingdom

animar ◆ *vt* **1** (*persona*) to cheer *sb* up: *Animé a mi hermana y dejó de llorar.* I cheered my sister up and she stopped crying. **2** (*conversación, partido*) to liven *sth* up **3** (*apoyar*) to cheer *sb* on: ~ *a un equipo* to cheer a team on ◆ **animarse** *v pron* **1** (*persona*) to cheer up: *¡Anímate hombre!* Cheer up! **2** (*decidirse*) to decide (***to do sth***): *A lo mejor me animo a ir.* I may decide to go. LOC **animar a algn a que haga algo** to encourage sb to do sth: *Yo les animo a que hagan deporte.* I'm encouraging them to take up sport.

ánimo *nm* spirits [*pl*]: *Estábamos bajos de* ~. Our spirits were low. LOC **¡ánimo!** cheer up!

aniquilar *vt* to annihilate: ~ *al adversario* to annihilate the enemy

anís *nm* **1** (*semilla*) aniseed **2** (*licor*) anisette

aniversario *nm* anniversary [*pl* anniversaries]: *nuestro* ~ *de boda* our wedding anniversary

ano *nm* anus [*pl* anuses]

anoche *adv* last night

anochecer ◆ *v imp* to get dark: *En invierno anochece temprano.* In winter it gets dark early. ◆ *nm* dusk: *al* ~ at dusk LOC **antes/después del anochecer** before/after dark

anónimo, -a ◆ *adj* anonymous ◆ *nm* (*carta*) anonymous letter LOC *Ver* SOCIEDAD

anorak *nm* anorak

anorexia *nf* anorexia (nervosa)

anormal *adj* abnormal: *un comportamiento* ~ abnormal behaviour

anotar ◆ *vt* to note *sth* down: *Anoté la dirección.* I noted down the address. ◆ **anotarse** *v pron* (*triunfo*) to score: *El equipo se anotó su primera victoria.* The team scored its first victory.

ansia *nf* **1** ~ (**de**) longing (**for *sth***): ~ *de cambio* a longing for change **2** ~ (**por**) desire (**for *sth*/*to do sth***): ~ *por mejorar* a desire to improve

ansiedad *nf* anxiety [*pl* anxieties]

antártico, -a ◆ *adj* Antarctic ◆ **Antártico** *nm* Antarctic Ocean LOC *Ver* CÍRCULO

ante[1] *prep* **1** (*gen*) before: *ante las cámaras* before the cameras ◊ *comparecer ante el juez* to appear before the judge **2** (*enfrentado con*) in the face of *sth*: *ante las dificultades* in the face of adversity LOC **ante todo** *Ver* TODO

ante[2] *nm* suede

anteanoche *adv* the night before last

anteayer *adv* the day before yesterday

antebrazo *nm* forearm

antelación *nf* LOC **con antelación** in advance: *con dos años de* ~ two years in advance

antemano *adv* LOC **de antemano** beforehand

antena *nf* **1** (*Radio, TV*) aerial **2** (*Zool*) antenna [*pl* antennae] LOC **antena parabólica** satellite dish **estar en antena** to be on the air

antepasado, -a *nm-nf* ancestor

anteponer *vt* (*poner delante*) to put *sth* in front of *sth*: *Anteponga el adjetivo al nombre.* Put the adjective before the noun.

anterior *adj* previous

antes *adv* **1** (*previamente*) before: *Ya lo habíamos discutido ~.* We had discussed it before. ☛ *Ver nota en* AGO **2** (*más temprano*) earlier: *Los lunes cerramos ~.* We close earlier on Mondays. LOC **antes de** before *sth/doing sth*: *~ de ir a la cama* before going to bed ◊ *~ de Navidad* before Christmas **antes que nada** above all **de antes** previous: *en el trabajo de ~* in my previous job **lo antes posible** as soon as possible *Ver tb* CONSUMIR, CUANTO

antiaéreo, -a *adj* anti-aircraft

antibala (*tb* **antibalas**) *adj* bulletproof LOC *Ver* CHALECO

antibiótico *nm* antibiotic

anticipación *nf* LOC **con anticipación** in advance: *reservar entradas con ~* to book tickets in advance

anticipado, -a *pp, adj* LOC **por anticipado** in advance *Ver tb* ANTICIPAR

anticipar *vt* **1** (*adelantar*) to bring *sth* forward: *Anticipamos la boda.* We brought the wedding forward. **2** (*dinero*) to advance *sth* (**to *sb***): *Me anticipó dos mil pesetas.* He advanced me two thousand pesetas. **3** (*sueldo, alquiler*) to pay *sth* in advance

anticipo *nm* (*dinero*) advance: *He pedido un ~ del sueldo.* I've asked for an advance on my salary.

anticonceptivo, -a *adj, nm* contraceptive: *los métodos ~s* contraceptive methods

anticuado, -a *adj, nm-nf* old-fashioned [*adj*]: *Esta camisa se ha quedado anticuada.* This shirt's old-fashioned. ◊ *¡Eres un ~, papá!* You're really old-fashioned, Dad!

anticuario *nm* antique shop

anticuerpo *nm* antibody [*pl* antibodies]

antidisturbios *adj* riot [*n atrib*]: *policía ~* riot police

antidoping LOC **control/prueba antidoping** drug test: *Dio positivo en la prueba ~* He tested positive.

antídoto *nm* ~ (**de/contra**) antidote (**to *sth***)

antidroga *adj* anti-drug: *organizar una campaña ~* to organize an anti-drug campaign

antifaz *nm* mask

antiguamente *adv* in the olden days

antigüedad *nf* **1** (*cualidad*) age: *la ~ de las viviendas* the age of the housing **2** (*en trabajo*) seniority **3** (*época*) ancient times **4** (*objeto*) antique: *tienda de ~es* antique shop

antiguo, -a *adj* **1** (*viejo*) old: *coches ~s* old cars **2** (*anterior*) former (*formal*), old: *la antigua Unión Soviética* the former Soviet Union ◊ *mi ~ jefe* my old boss **3** (*Hist*) ancient: *la Grecia antigua* ancient Greece LOC *Ver* CASCO, CHAPADO

antílope *nm* antelope

antipático, -a *adj* unpleasant

antipatriótico, -a *adj* unpatriotic

antirrobo *adj* anti-theft: *sistema ~* anti-theft device

antojarse *v pron*: *Iré cuando se me antoje.* I'll go when I feel like it. ◊ *Al niño se le antojó un robot.* The child took a fancy to a robot.

antojo *nm* **1** (*capricho*) whim **2** (*lunar*) birthmark LOC **tener antojo de** to have a craving for *sth* **tener antojos** to have cravings *Algunas embarazadas tienen ~s.* Some pregnant women have cravings.

antónimo, -a *adj, nm*: *¿Cuál es el ~ de alto?* What's the opposite of tall? ◊ *Alto y bajo son ~s.* Tall and short are opposites.

antorcha *nf* torch: *la ~ olímpica* the Olympic torch

antro *nm* (*local*) dive

anual *adj* annual

anualmente *adv* annually

anulación *nf* **1** (*gen*) cancellation: *la ~ del torneo* the cancellation of the tournament **2** (*matrimonio*) annulment

anular[1] *vt* **1** (*gen*) to cancel: *Tendremos que ~ la cena/el examen.* We'll have to cancel the dinner/exam. **2** (*matrimonio*) to annul **3** (*gol, tanto*) to disallow **4** (*votación*) to declare *sth* invalid

anular[2] *nm* (*dedo*) ring finger

anunciar ◆ *vt* **1** (*informar*) to announce: *Anunciaron el resultado por los altavoces.* They announced the result over the loudspeakers. **2** (*hacer publicidad*) to advertise ◆ **anunciarse** *v pron* **anunciarse (en ...)** (*hacer publicidad*) to advertise (**in ...**)

anuncio *nm* **1** (*prensa, televisión*) advertisement, advert (*más coloq*), ad (*coloq*) **2** (*cartel*) poster **3** (*declaración*) announcement LOC **anuncio**

luminoso neon sign **anuncio(s) por palabras** classified ad(s) *Ver tb* PROHIBIDO, TABLÓN

anzuelo *nm* hook **LOC** *Ver* MORDER(SE)

añadido, -a *pp, adj* **LOC** *Ver* IMPUESTO; *Ver tb* AÑADIR

añadir *vt* to add

añicos *nm* **LOC hacerse añicos** to shatter

año *nm* year: *todo el ~* all year (round) ◊ *todos los ~s* every year ◊ *~ académico/escolar* academic/school year **LOC año bisiesto** leap year **año(s) luz** light year(s) **de dos, etc años**: *una mujer de treinta años* a woman of thirty/a thirty-year-old woman ◊ *A Miguel, de 12 ~s, le gusta el cine.* Miguel, aged 12, likes films. **los años 50, 60, etc** the 50s, 60s, etc **quitarse años** to lie about your age **tener dos, etc años** to be two, etc (years old): *Tengo diez ~s.* I'm ten (years old). ◊ *¿Cuántos ~s tienes?* How old are you? ☛ *Ver nota en* OLD **un año sí y otro no** every other year *Ver tb* CURSO

añorar *vt* (*echar de menos*) to miss

apaciguar ◆ *vt* to appease ◆ **apaciguarse** *v pron* to calm down: *cuando se hayan apaciguado los ánimos* once everybody has calmed down

apagado, -a *pp, adj* **1** (*persona*) listless **2** (*color*) dull **3** (*volcán*) extinct **LOC estar apagado 1** (*luz, aparato*) to be off **2** (*fuego*) to be out *Ver tb* APAGAR

apagar ◆ *vt* **1** (*fuego*) to put *a fire* out **2** (*vela*) to blow *a candle* out **3** (*cigarro*) to stub *a cigarette* out **4** (*luz, aparato*) to switch *sth* off ◆ **apagarse** *v pron* to go out: *Se me apagó la vela/el cigarro.* My candle/cigarette went out.

apagón *nm* power cut

apañarse *v pron* (*darse maña*) to manage: *No me apaño a escribir con la izquierda.* I can't write with my left hand. **LOC apañárselas** (*arreglarse*) to get by: *Ya me las apañaré.* I'll get by.

aparador *nm* sideboard

aparato *nm* **1** (*máquina*) machine: *¿Cómo funciona este ~?* How does this machine work? **2** (*doméstico*) appliance **3** (*radio, televisión*) set **4** (*Anat*) system: *el ~ digestivo* the digestive system **5** (*para los dientes*) brace: *Me tienen que poner ~.* I've got to wear a brace. **6** (*Gimnasia*) apparatus [*incontable*]

aparatoso, -a *adj* spectacular

aparcamiento *nm* **1** (*parking*) car park **2** (*espacio*) parking space: *No encuentro ~.* I can't find a parking space.

aparcar *vt, vi* to park: *¿Dónde has aparcado?* Where have you parked? **LOC aparcar en doble fila** to double-park

aparecer ◆ *vi* **1** (*gen*) to appear: *Aparece mucho en la televisión.* He appears a lot on TV. **2** (*algn/algo que se había perdido*) to turn up: *Perdí las gafas pero aparecieron.* I lost my glasses but they turned up later. **3** (*figurar*) to be: *Mi número no aparece en la guía.* My number isn't in the directory. **4** (*llegar*) to show up: *A eso de las diez apareció Pedro.* Pedro showed up around ten. ◆ **aparecerse** *v pron* **aparecerse (a/ante)** to appear (**to *sb***)

aparejador, ~a *nm-nf* quantity surveyor

aparentar ◆ *vt* **1** (*fingir*) to pretend: *Tuve que ~ alegría.* I had to pretend I was happy. **2** (*edad*) to look: *Aparenta unos 50 años.* He looks about 50. ◆ *vi* to show off: *Les gusta ~.* They love showing off.

aparente *adj* apparent: *sin un motivo ~* for no apparent reason

aparición *nf* **1** (*gen*) appearance **2** (*Relig*) vision **3** (*fantasma*) apparition **LOC hacer (su) aparición** to appear

apariencia *nf* appearance **LOC** *Ver* GUARDAR

apartado, -a ◆ *pp, adj* remote ◆ *nm* **1** (*gen*) section **2** (*párrafo*) paragraph **LOC apartado de correos** post-office box (*abrev* PO box) *Ver tb* APARTAR

apartamento *nm* flat

apartar ◆ *vt* **1** (*obstáculo*) to move *sth* (out of the way) **2** (*alejar*) to separate *sth/sb* **from *sth/sb***: *Sus padres le apartaron de sus amigos.* His parents separated him from his friends. ◆ **apartarse** *v pron* to move (over): *Apártate, que estorbas.* Move (over), you're in the way. **LOC apartar la vista** to look away

aparte ◆ *adv* **1** (*a un lado*) aside: *Pondré estos papeles ~.* I'll set these documents aside. **2** (*separadamente*) separately: *Esto lo pago ~.* I'll pay for this separately. ◆ *adj* **1** (*diferente*) different: *un mundo* a different world **2** (*separado*) separate: *Dame una cuenta ~ para estas cosas.* Give me a separate bill for these items. **LOC aparte de 1** (*excepto*) apart from *sth/sb*: *~ de eso no pasó nada.* Apart from that nothing happened. ◊ *No lo dijo nadie ~ de mí.*

Nobody said it apart from me. **2** (*además de*) as well as: ~ *de bonito, parece práctico.* It's practical as well as pretty. *Ver tb* CASO, PUNTO

apasionado, -a ◆ *pp, adj* passionate: *un temperamento muy* ~ a very passionate temperament ◆ *nm-nf* ~ **de/por** lover **of** ***sth***: *los ~s de la ópera* opera lovers *Ver tb* APASIONAR

apasionante *adj* exciting

apasionar ◆ *vi* to love *sth/doing sth* [*vt*]: *Me apasiona el jazz.* I love jazz. ◆ **apasionarse** *v pron* **apasionarse con/por** to be mad **on** ***sth/sb***

apedrear *vt* to stone

apego *nm* ~ (**a/por**) affection **for** ***sth/sb*** LOC **tenerle apego** to be very attached *to sth*

apelación *nf* appeal

apelar *vi* to appeal: *Han apelado a nuestra generosidad.* They have appealed to our generosity. ◊ *Apelaron contra la sentencia.* They appealed against the sentence.

apellidarse *v pron*: *¿Cómo te apellidas?* What's your surname? ◊ *Se apellidan Morán.* Their surname's Morán.

apellido *nm* surname LOC *Ver* NOMBRE

apenado, -a *pp, adj* ~ (**por**) sad (**about** ***sth***) *Ver tb* APENAR

apenar ◆ *vt* to sadden: *Me apena pensar que no volveré a verte.* It saddens me to think that I won't see you again. ◆ **apenarse** *v pron* **apenarse** (**por**) to be upset (**about** ***sth***)

apenas *adv* **1** (*casi no*) hardly: ~ *había cola.* There was hardly any queue. ◊ ~ *dijeron nada.* They hardly said anything. ◊ *No vino* ~ *nadie.* Hardly anyone came. **2** (*casi nunca*) hardly ever: *Ahora* ~ *les vemos.* We hardly ever see them now. ☛ *Ver nota en* ALWAYS **3** (*escasamente*) scarcely: *Hace* ~ *un año.* Scarcely a year ago. **4** (*en cuanto*) as soon as: ~ *llegaron* as soon as they arrived

apéndice *nm* **1** (*Anat*) appendix [*pl* appendixes] **2** (*libro, documento*) appendix [*pl* appendices]

apendicitis *nf* appendicitis

aperitivo *nm* **1** (*bebida*) aperitif [*pl* aperitifs] **2** (*tapa*) appetizer

apertura *nf* **1** (*gen*) opening: *la ceremonia de* ~ the opening ceremony **2** (*comienzo*) beginning: *la* ~ *del curso* the beginning of the academic year

apestar *vi* ~ (**a**) to stink (**of** ***sth***) LOC *Ver* OLER

apetecer *vi* to fancy *sth/doing sth* [*vt*]: *¿Te apetece un café?* Do you fancy a coffee?

apetito *nm* appetite: *El paseo te abrirá el* ~. The walk will give you an appetite. ◊ *tener buen* ~ to have a good appetite

apiadarse *v pron* ~ **de** to take pity **on** ***sb***

apicultura *nf* bee-keeping

apilar *vt* to stack

apiñarse *v pron* to crowd (together)

apio *nm* celery

apisonadora *nf* steamroller

aplastante *adj* overwhelming: *ganar por mayoría* ~ to win by an overwhelming majority

aplastar *vt* **1** (*cosa hueca, persona*) to crush **2** (*cosa blanda, insecto*) to squash **3** (*derrotar*) to crush

aplaudir *vt, vi* to applaud

aplauso *nm* applause [*incontable*]: *grandes ~s* loud applause

aplazar *vt* **1** (*gen*) to put *sth* off, to postpone (*más formal*) **2** (*pago*) to defer

aplicable *adj* ~ (**a**) applicable (**to** ***sth/sb***)

aplicación *nf* application

aplicado, -a *pp, adj* **1** (*persona*) hardworking **2** ~ (**a**) applied (**to** ***sth***): *matemática aplicada* applied mathematics *Ver tb* APLICAR

aplicar ◆ *vt* **1** (*gen*) to apply *sth* (**to** ***sth***): ~ *una regla* to apply a rule ◊ *Aplique la crema sobre la zona afectada.* Apply the cream to the affected area. **2** (*poner en práctica*) to put *sth* to use: *Vamos a* ~ *los conocimientos aprendidos.* Let's put what we've learnt to use. ◆ **aplicarse** *v pron* **aplicarse** (**a/en**) to apply yourself (**to** ***sth***): *~se a una tarea* to apply yourself to a task

apoderarse *v pron* ~ **de** to take: *Se apoderaron de las joyas.* They took the jewels.

apodo *nm* nickname

apolítico, -a *adj* apolitical

apología *nf* ~ **de** defence **of** ***sth/sb***

aporrear *vt* **1** (*puerta*) to hammer **at** ***the door*** **2** (*piano*) to bang away **on** ***the piano***

aportación *nf* ~ **a/para** contribution **to** ***sth***

aportar *vt* to contribute: ~ *una idea*

interesante to contribute an interesting idea

aposta *adv* on purpose

apostar *vt, vi* ~ (**por**) to bet (**on** ***sth/sb***): ~ *por un caballo* to bet on a horse ◊ *Me apuesto lo que quieras a que no vienen.* I bet anything you like they won't come. ◊ *¿Qué te apuestas?* What do you bet?

apóstol *nm* apostle

apoyado, -a *pp, adj* ~ **en/sobre/contra** **1** (*descansando*) resting **on/against** ***sth***: *Tenía la cabeza apoyada en el respaldo.* I was resting my head on the back of the chair. **2** (*inclinado*) leaning **against** ***sth***: ~ *contra la pared* leaning against the wall ☛ *Ver dibujo en* LEAN[2]; *Ver tb* APOYAR

apoyar ◆ *vt* **1** (*gen*) to lean *sth* **against** ***sth***: *No lo apoyes contra la pared.* Don't lean it against the wall. ☛ *Ver dibujo en* LEAN[2] **2** (*descansar*) to rest *sth* **on/against** ***sth***: *Apoya la cabeza en mi hombro.* Rest your head on my shoulder. **3** (*defender*) to support: ~ *una huelga/a un compañero* to support a strike/colleague ◆ **apoyarse** *v pron* to lean **on/against** ***sth***: *~se en un bastón/contra una pared* to lean on a stick/against a wall

apoyo *nm* support: *una manifestación de ~ a la huelga* a demonstration in support of the strike

apreciar *vt* **1** (*cosa*) to value: *Aprecio el trabajo bien hecho.* I value a job well done. **2** (*persona*) to think highly **of** ***sb***: *Te aprecian mucho.* They think very highly of you. **3** (*percibir*) to see

aprecio *nm* regard (**for** ***sth/sb***) LOC **tenerle mucho aprecio a algn** to be very fond of sb

aprender ◆ *vt, vi* to learn: ~ *francés* to learn French ◊ *Deberías ~ a escuchar a los demás.* You should learn to listen to other people. ◊ *Quiero ~ a conducir.* I want to learn to drive. ◆ **aprenderse** *v pron* to learn: *~se tres capítulos* to learn three chapters ◊ *~se algo de memoria* to learn sth by heart

aprendiz, ~a *nm-nf* apprentice: ~ *de peluquero* apprentice hairdresser

aprendizaje *nm*: *el ~ de un idioma* learning a language

apresurarse *v pron* ~ **a** to hasten ***to do sth***: *Me apresuré a darles las gracias.* I hastened to thank them. LOC **¡apresúrate!** hurry up!

apretado, -a *pp, adj* **1** (*ajustado*) tight **2** (*gente*) squashed together *Ver tb* APRETAR

apretar ◆ *vt* **1** (*botón, pedal*) to press **2** (*tuerca, tapa, nudo*) to tighten **3** (*gatillo*) to pull **4** (*exigir*) to be strict **with** ***sb*** ◆ *vi* **1** (*ropa*) to be too tight (**for** ***sb***): *El pantalón me aprieta.* The trousers are too tight (for me). **2** (*zapatos*) to pinch ◆ **apretarse** *v pron* **apretarse** (**contra**) to squeeze up (**against** ***sth***) LOC **apretarse el cinturón** to tighten your belt

aprieto *nm* LOC **estar en aprietos/un aprieto** to be in a fix **poner en un aprieto** to put *sb* in a tight spot

aprisa *adv* fast LOC **¡aprisa!** hurry up!

aprobación *nf* approval LOC **dar su aprobación** to give your consent (*to sth*)

aprobado *nm* (*Educ*) pass ≃ D: *Saqué dos ~s.* I got two D's.

aprobar *vt* **1** (*examen, ley*) to pass: *Aprobé a la primera.* I passed first time. ◊ *No he aprobado ni una asignatura.* I haven't passed a single subject. **2** (*aceptar*) to approve **of** ***sth/sb***: *No apruebo su comportamiento.* I don't approve of their behaviour.

apropiado, -a *pp, adj* appropriate *Ver tb* APROPIARSE

apropiarse *v pron* ~ **de** to take: *Niegan haberse apropiado del dinero.* They say they didn't take the money.

aprovechado, -a *nm-nf* sponger

aprovechar ◆ *vt* **1** (*utilizar*) to use: ~ *bien el tiempo* to use your time well **2** (*recursos naturales*) to exploit: ~ *la energía solar* to exploit solar energy **3** (*oportunidad, abusar*) to take advantage of *sth/sb*: *Aproveché el viaje para visitar a mi hermano.* I took advantage of the journey to visit my brother. ◆ *vi*: *Aprovecha ahora que no está el jefe.* Seize the chance now that the boss isn't here. ◆ **aprovecharse** *v pron* **aprovecharse** (**de**) to take advantage (**of** ***sth/sb***) LOC **¡que aproveche!** enjoy your meal!

aproximado, -a *pp, adj* LOC *Ver* CÁLCULO; *Ver tb* APROXIMARSE

aproximarse *v pron* to approach, to draw near (*más coloq*): *Se aproximan los exámenes.* The exams are drawing near.

aptitud *nf* **1** (*gen*) aptitude (***for sth/doing sth***): *prueba de ~* aptitude test **2** **aptitudes** gift [*sing*]: *tener ~es musicales* to have a gift for music

apto, -a *adj* suitable (***for sth/to do sth***):

No son ~s para este trabajo. They're not suitable for this job.

apuesta *nf* bet: *hacer una ~* to make a bet

apuntar ◆ *vt* **1** (*anotar*) to note *sth* down: *Voy a ~ la dirección.* I'm going to note down the address. **2** (*inscribir*) to put *sb's* name down ◆ *vt, vi* to aim (*sth*) (**at sth/sb**): *Apunté demasiado alto.* I aimed too high. ◊ *Me apuntó con una pistola.* He aimed his gun at me. ◆ **apuntarse** *v pron* **1** (*inscribirse*) to put your name down (**for sth**), to enrol (*más formal*): *Me he apuntado a un curso de yudo.* I've enrolled for judo lessons. **2** (*Dep, triunfo*) to score: *El equipo se apuntó una gran victoria.* The team scored a great victory. LOC **apuntarse al paro** to sign on

apunte *nm* note: *coger/tomar ~s* to take notes

apuñalar *vt* to stab

apuro *nm* **1** (*aprieto*) fix: *Eso nos sacaría del ~.* That would get us out of this fix. **2 apuros** trouble [*sing*]: *un alpinista en ~s* a climber in trouble **3** (*vergüenza*) embarrassment: *¡Qué ~!* How embarrassing!

aquel, aquella *adj* that [*pl* those] LOC *Ver* ENTONCES

aquél, aquélla *pron* **1** (*cosa*) that one [*pl* those (ones)]: *Este coche es mío y ~ de Pedro.* This car's mine and that one is Pedro's. ◊ *Prefiero aquéllos.* I prefer those (ones). **2** (*persona*): *¿Conoces a aquéllos?* Do you know those people?

aquello *pron*: *¿Ves ~ de allí?* Can you see that thing over there? ◊ *No te imaginas lo que fue ~.* You can't imagine what it was like. ◊ *~ de tu jefe* that business involving your boss LOC **aquello que...** what...: *Recuerda ~ que tu madre siempre decía.* Remember what your mother always used to say.

aquí *adv* **1** (*lugar*) here: *Ya están ~.* They're here. ◊ *Es ~ mismo.* It's right here. **2** (*ahora*) now: *de ~ en adelante* from now on ◊ *Hasta ~ todo va bien.* Up till now everything's been fine. **3** (*presentaciones*) this is: *~ mi hermano, ~ un amigo.* This is my brother, this is a friend. LOC **(por) aquí cerca** near here **por aquí (por favor)** this way (please) *Ver tb* TIRO

árabe *nm* (*lengua*) Arabic

arábigo, -a *adj* LOC *Ver* NUMERACIÓN, NÚMERO

arado *nm* plough

arancel *nm* tariff

arandela *nf* **1** (*aro*) metal ring **2** (*para un tornillo*) washer

araña *nf* spider

arañar(se) *vt, v pron* to scratch: *Me he arañado los brazos cogiendo moras.* I scratched my arms picking blackberries.

arañazo *nm* scratch

arar *vt* to plough

arbitrar *vt* **1** (*Fútbol, Boxeo*) to referee **2** (*Tenis*) to umpire

arbitrario, -a *adj* arbitrary

árbitro, -a *nm-nf* **1** (*Fútbol, Boxeo*) referee **2** (*Tenis*) umpire **3** (*mediador*) arbitrator

árbol *nm* tree: *~ frutal* fruit tree LOC **árbol genealógico** family tree

arboleda *nf* grove

arbusto *nm* bush

arcada *nf* LOC **dar arcadas** to retch: *Me daban ~s.* I was retching.

arcén *nm* **1** (*autopista*) hard shoulder **2** (*carretera*) verge

archipiélago *nm* archipelago [*pl* archipelagos/archipelagoes]

archivador *nm* **1** (*mueble*) filing cabinet **2** (*carpeta*) file

archivar *vt* **1** (*clasificar*) to file **2** (*Informát*) to store: *~ datos* to store data **3** (*asunto*) to shelve

archivo *nm* **1** (*policía*) file **2** (*Hist*) archive(s) [*se usa mucho en plural*]: *un ~ histórico* historical archives

arcilla *nf* clay

arco *nm* **1** (*Arquit*) arch **2** (*Mat*) arc: *un ~ de 36°* a 36°arc **3** (*Dep, Mús*) bow: *el ~ y las flechas* a bow and arrows LOC **arco iris** rainbow: *¡Mira!, ha salido el ~ iris.* Look! There's a rainbow. *Ver tb* TIRO

arcón *nm* large chest

arder *vi* **1** (*quemarse*) to burn **2** (*estar muy caliente*) to be boiling hot: *La sopa está ardiendo.* The soup is boiling hot. LOC **estar que arde** (*persona*) to be fuming: *Tu padre está que arde.* Your father is fuming.

ardiente *adj* LOC *Ver* CAPILLA

ardilla *nf* squirrel

ardor *nm* (*entusiasmo*) enthusiasm LOC **ardor de estómago** heartburn

área *nf* area: *el ~ de un rectángulo* the area of a rectangle ◊ *un ~ de servicio* a service area

arena *nf* sand: *jugar en la ~* to play in

the sand LOC **arenas movedizas** quicksands *Ver tb* BANCO, CASTILLO

arenque *nm* herring LOC **arenque ahumado** kipper

Argentina *nf* Argentina

argentino, -a *adj, nm-nf* Argentine, Argentinian

argolla *nf* ring

argot *nm* **1** (*lenguaje coloquial*) slang **2** (*profesional*) jargon

argumento *nm* **1** (*razón*) argument: *los ~s a favor y en contra* the arguments for and against **2** (*Cine, Liter*) plot

árido, -a *adj* (*terreno, tema*) dry

aries (*tb* **Aries**) *nm, nmf* (*Astrología*) Aries ☛ *Ver ejemplos en* AQUARIUS

arisco, -a *adj* unfriendly

arista *nf* (*Geom*) edge

aristocracia *nf* aristocracy [*v sing o pl*]

aristócrata *nmf* aristocrat

aritmética *nf* arithmetic

arma *nf* **1** (*gen*) weapon: *~s nucleares* nuclear weapons **2 armas** arms: *un traficante de ~s* an arms dealer LOC **arma blanca** knife **arma de doble filo** double-edged sword **arma de fuego** firearm **arma homicida** murder weapon *Ver tb* CONTRABANDISTA, CONTRABANDO, ESCUDO

armada *nf* navy [*v sing o pl*] [*pl* navies]: *tres buques de la ~* three navy ships

armadura *nf* armour [*incontable*]: *una ~* a suit of armour

armamento *nm* arms [*pl*]: *el control de ~s* arms control LOC *Ver* CARRERA

armar *vt* **1** (*entregar armas*) to arm *sb* (**with *sth***): *Armaron a los soldados con fusiles.* They armed the soldiers with guns. **2** (*montar*) to assemble LOC **armar jaleo** to make a racket **armarse de paciencia** to be patient **armarse de valor** to pluck up courage **armar un lío** to kick up a fuss **armarse un lío** to get confused: *Con tantas puertas me armo un lío.* I get confused with all these doors. *Ver tb* BRONCA

armario *nm* **1** (*gen*) cupboard **2** (*para ropa*) wardrobe

armisticio *nm* armistice

armonía *nf* harmony [*pl* harmonies]

armónica *nf* mouth organ

arneses *nm* harness [*sing*]

aro *nm* **1** (*gen*) ring: *los ~s olímpicos* the Olympic rings **2** (*Gimnasia*) hoop

aroma *nm* aroma

aromático, -a *adj* aromatic

arpa *nf* harp

arpón *nm* harpoon

arqueología *nf* archaeology

arqueólogo, -a *nm-nf* archaeologist

arquitecto, -a *nm-nf* architect

arquitectura *nf* architecture

arrabal *nm* suburb

arraigado, -a *pp, adj* deep-rooted: *una costumbre muy arraigada* a deep-rooted custom *Ver tb* ARRAIGAR(SE)

arraigar(se) *vi, v pron* to take root

arrancar ♦ *vt* **1** (*sacar*) to pull *sth* out: *~ un clavo* to pull a nail out **2** (*planta*) to pull *sth* up: *~ los hierbajos* to pull the weeds up **3** (*página*) to tear *a page* out **4** (*quitar*) to pull *sth* off: *~ la etiqueta de una camisa* to pull the label off a shirt ♦ *vt, vi* (*motor*) to start

arranque *nm* **1** (*motor*) starting: *Tengo problemas con el ~.* I've got problems starting the car. **2** (*persona*) go: *una persona de poco ~* a person with very little go **3 ~ de** fit **of *sth***: *un ~ de celos* a fit of jealousy

arrasar ♦ *vt* to destroy: *El incendio arrasó varios edificios.* The fire destroyed several buildings. ♦ *vi* (*ganar*) to win hands down: *El equipo local arrasó.* The local team won hands down.

arrastrar ♦ *vt* **1** (*por el suelo*) to drag: *No arrastres los pies.* Don't drag your feet. **2** (*problema, deuda, asignatura*): *Todavía arrastro el catarro.* I haven't got over my cold yet. ◊ *Todavía arrastro la física de primero.* I still haven't passed my first year physics exam. ♦ **arrastrarse** *v pron* **1** (*gatear*) to crawl: *~se por el suelo* to crawl along the floor **2 arrastrarse** (**ante**) (*humillarse*) to grovel (**to *sb***)

¡arre! *interj* gee up!

arrear ♦ *vt* (*ganado*) to drive ♦ *vi*: *¡Arrea, que llegamos tarde!* Hurry up! We're late.

arrecife *nm* reef

arreglado, -a *pp, adj* **1** (*persona*) dressed up: *¿Dónde vas tan arreglada?* Where are you off to all dressed up? ◊ *una señora muy arreglada* a smartly dressed lady **2** (*ordenado*) tidy **3** (*asunto*) sorted out: *Ya está ~ el problema.* The problem's sorted out now. *Ver tb* ARREGLAR

arreglar ♦ *vt* **1** (*reparar*) to mend: *Van a venir a ~ la lavadora.* They're coming to mend the washing machine. **2** (*hacer obras*) to do *sth* up: *Estamos arreglando el cuarto de baño.* We're doing up the bathroom. **3** (*ordenar*) to tidy *sth* (up) **4** (*asunto, problema*) to sort *sth* out: *No te preocupes que yo lo arreglaré.* Don't worry, I'll sort it out. **5** (*ensalada*) to dress ◆ **arreglarse** *v pron* **1** (*acicalarse*) to get ready **2** (*mejorar*) to get better, to improve (*más formal*): *Si se arregla la situación económica…* If the economic situation improves… **3** (*salir bien*) to work out: *Al final todo se arregló.* It all worked out in the end. **4** (*apañarse*) to manage: *Hay poca comida pero ya nos arreglaremos.* There's not much food but we'll manage. LOC **arreglárselas** to get by

arreglo *nm* **1** (*reparación*) repair: *hacer ~s* to do repairs **2** (*acuerdo*) agreement LOC **no tiene arreglo 1** (*objeto*) it can't be mended **2** (*problema*) it can't be solved **3** (*persona*) he/she is a hopeless case

arrendar *vt* **1** (*ceder*) to rent *sth* out: *Arrendaron su casa de la playa el verano pasado.* They rented out their seaside home last summer. **2** (*tomar*) to rent: *Arrendé un apartamento en Santander.* I rented an apartment in Santander. ☛ *Ver nota en* ALQUILAR

arrepentido, -a *pp, adj* LOC **estar arrepentido (de)** to be sorry (for/about *sth*) *Ver tb* ARREPENTIRSE

arrepentimiento *nm* **1** (*pesar*) regret **2** (*Relig*) repentance

arrepentirse *v pron* ~ **(de) 1** (*lamentar*) to regret: *Me arrepiento de habérselo prestado.* I regret lending it to him. **2** (*pecado*) to repent (***of sth***)

arrestar *vt* **1** (*detener*) to arrest **2** (*encarcelar*) to imprison

arresto *nm* **1** (*detención*) arrest **2** (*prisión*) imprisonment: *10 meses de ~* 10 months' imprisonment

arriar *vt* to lower: *~ (la) bandera* to lower the flag

arriba ◆ *adv* **1** (*gen*) up: *aquel castillo allá ~* that castle up there ◊ *cuesta ~* up the hill ◊ *de cintura para ~* from the waist up **2** (*piso*) upstairs: *Viven ~.* They live upstairs. ◊ *los vecinos de ~* our upstairs neighbours ◆ **¡arriba!** *interj* come on!: *¡~ el Athletic!* Come on Athletic! LOC **arriba del todo** at the very top **¡arriba las manos!** hands up! **de arriba abajo 1** (*gen*) up and down: *Me miró de ~ abajo.* He looked me up and down. ◊ *mover algo de ~ abajo* to move something up and down **2** (*completamente*): *cambiar algo de ~ abajo* to change sth completely **hacia arriba** upwards *Ver tb* AHÍ, ALLÁ, ALLÍ, BOCA, CALLE, CUESTA, PARTE[1], RÍO

arriesgado, -a *pp, adj* **1** (*peligroso*) risky **2** (*audaz*) daring *Ver tb* ARRIESGAR

arriesgar ◆ *vt* to risk: *~ la salud/el dinero/la vida* to risk your health/money/life ◆ **arriesgarse** *v pron* to take a risk/risks: *Yo que tú no me arriesgaría.* If I were you I wouldn't take that risk. LOC *Ver* PELLEJO

arrimar ◆ *vt* to bring *sth* closer (***to sth***): *Arrima la silla a la estufa.* Bring your chair closer to the stove. ◆ **arrimarse** *v pron* **arrimarse (a)** to go/come near: *No te arrimes a la pared.* Don't go near that wall. ◊ *No te arrimes a esa puerta, está recién pintada.* Don't go near that door. It's just been painted.

arrinconar *vt* **1** (*cosa*) to discard **2** (*acorralar*) to corner **3** (*marginar*) to exclude

arrodillarse *v pron* to kneel (down)

arrogante *adj* arrogant

arrojar *vt* to throw: *~ piedras a la policía* to throw stones at the police

arrollar *vt* **1** (*peatón*) to run *sb* over: *Lo arrolló un coche.* A car ran him over. **2** (*viento, agua*) to carry *sth* away: *El viento arrolló el tejado.* The wind carried the roof away. **3** (*vencer*) to thrash

arropar(se) *vt, v pron* to wrap (*sb*) up: *Arrópate bien.* Wrap up well.

arroyo *nm* stream

arroz *nm* rice LOC **arroz con leche** rice pudding

arrozal *nm* ricefield

arruga *nf* **1** (*piel*) wrinkle **2** (*papel, ropa*) crease

arrugar(se) *vt, v pron* **1** (*piel*) to wrinkle **2** (*ropa*) to crease: *Esta falda se arruga en seguida.* This skirt creases very easily. **3** (*papel*) to crumple *sth* (up): *Dóblalo bien para que no se arrugue.* Fold it properly so that it doesn't get crumpled.

arruinar ◆ *vt* to ruin: *La tormenta ha arruinado las cosechas.* The storm has ruined the crops. ◆ **arruinarse** *v pron* to go bankrupt

arsenal *nm* (*armas*) arsenal

arsénico *nm* arsenic

arte *nm* **1** (*gen*) art: *una obra de ~* a work of art **2** (*habilidad*) skill (***at sth/ doing sth***): *Tienes ~ para pintar.* You show great skill at painting. LOC **como por arte de magia** as if by magic *Ver tb* BELLO

artefacto *nm* **1** (*dispositivo*) device: *un ~ explosivo* an explosive device **2** (*aparato extraño*) contraption

arteria *nf* artery [*pl* arteries]

artesanía *nf* **1** (*habilidad*) craftsmanship **2** (*productos*) handicrafts [*pl*] LOC **de artesanía** handmade

artesano, -a *nm-nf* craftsman/woman [*pl* craftsmen/women]

ártico, -a ◆ *adj* Arctic ◆ **Ártico** *nm* (*océano*) Arctic Ocean LOC *Ver* CÍRCULO

articulación *nf* **1** (*Anat, Mec*) joint **2** (*pronunciación*) articulation

artículo *nm* article: *Ojalá publiquen mi ~.* I hope my article gets published. ◊ *el ~ definido* the definite article

artificial *adj* artificial LOC *Ver* FUEGO, PULMÓN, RESPIRACIÓN

artillería *nf* artillery

artista *nmf* **1** (*gen*) artist **2** (*Cine, Teat*) actor [*fem* actress]

arzobispo *nm* archbishop

as *nm* ace: *el as de corazones* the ace of hearts ◊ *ases del ciclismo* ace cyclists ☛ *Ver nota en* BARAJA

asa *nf* handle

asado, -a *pp, adj, nm* roast: *cordero ~* roast lamb *Ver tb* ASAR

asalariado, -a *nm-nf* wage earner

asaltante *nmf* **1** (*agresor*) attacker **2** (*ladrón*) raider

asaltar *vt* **1** (*gen*) to raid: *Dos tipos asaltaron el banco.* Two men raided the bank. **2** (*persona*) to mug: *Nos asaltó un enmascarado.* We were mugged by a masked man.

asalto *nm* ~ (**a**) **1** (*gen*) raid (**on *sth***): *un ~ a una joyería* a raid on a jeweller's **2** (*a una persona*) attack (**on *sb***) **3** (*Boxeo*) round

asamblea *nf* **1** (*reunión*) meeting **2** (*parlamento*) assembly [*pl* assemblies]

asar ◆ *vt* **1** (*carne*) to roast **2** (*patata entera*) to bake ◆ **asarse** *v pron* to roast: *Me estoy asando vivo.* I'm roasting alive.

ascendente *nm* (*Astrología*) ascendant

ascender ◆ *vt* to promote *sb* (***to sth***): *Lo ascendieron a capitán.* He was promoted to captain. ◆ *vi* **1** (*elevarse*) to go up, to rise (*más formal*) **2** (*montañismo*) to climb (up) *sth* **3** (*trabajador*) to be promoted (***to sth***)

ascenso *nm* **1** (*temperatura, precios*) rise: *Habrá un ~ de las temperaturas.* There will be a rise in temperatures. **2** (*montaña*) ascent **3** (*de un empleado, de un equipo*) promotion

ascensor *nm* lift: *llamar al ~* to call the lift

asco *nm* LOC **dar asco**: *Los riñones me dan ~.* I can't stand kidney. ◊ *Este país da ~.* This country makes me sick. **estar hecho un asco 1** (*sitio*) to be filthy **2** (*persona*) to feel terrible **hacer ascos** to turn your nose up (*at sth*) **¡qué asco! 1** (*qué repugnante*) how revolting! **2** (*qué fastidio*) what a pain! **¡qué asco de...!**: *¡Qué ~ de tiempo!* What lousy weather! *Ver tb* CARA

ascua *nf* LOC **estar en ascuas** to be on tenterhooks

aseado, -a *pp, adj* **1** (*persona*) clean **2** (*lugar*) tidy *Ver tb* ASEARSE

asearse *v pron* **1** (*lavarse*) to have a wash **2** (*arreglarse*) to tidy yourself up

asegurar ◆ *vt* **1** (*garantizar*) to ensure: *~ que todo funcione* to ensure that everything works **2** (*afirmar*) to assure: *Asegura que no los vio.* She assures us she didn't see them. **3** (*con una compañía de seguros*) to insure *sth/sb* (***against sth***): *Quiero ~ el coche contra incendio y robo.* I want to insure my car against fire and theft. ◆ **asegurarse** *v pron* (*comprobar*) to make sure (***of sth/ that...***): *Asegúrate de cerrar las ventanas.* Please make sure you close the windows.

asentir *vi* LOC **asentir con la cabeza** to nod

aseo *nm* **1** (*limpieza*) cleanliness: *el ~ de la casa* cleaning the house **2** (*cuarto de baño*) bathroom LOC **aseo personal** personal hygiene

asesinar *vt* to murder: *Parece que le asesinaron.* He seems to have been murdered.

Existe también el verbo **to assassinate** y los sustantivos **assassination** (*asesinato*) y **assassin** (*asesino*), pero sólo se utilizan cuando nos referimos a un personaje importante: *¿Quién asesinó al ministro?* Who assassinated the minister? ◊ *Hubo un intento de asesinato contra el Presidente.* There was an assassination attempt on the President. ◊ *un asesino a sueldo* a hired assassin.

asesinato *nm* murder: *cometer un ~* to commit (a) murder ☛ *Ver nota en* ASESINAR

asesino, -a ◆ *nm-nf* murderer ☛ *Ver nota en* ASESINAR ◆ *adj* (*mirada*) murderous LOC *Ver* MANO

asfaltar *vt* to tarmac: *Han asfaltado la carretera.* They've tarmacked the road.

asfalto *nm* Tarmac®

asfixia *nf* suffocation, asphyxia (*más formal*)

asfixiar ◆ *vt* **1** (*con humo, gas*) to suffocate, to asphyxiate (*más formal*) **2** (*con una almohada*) to smother ◆ **asfixiarse** *v pron* to suffocate

así *adv, adj* **1** (*de este modo, como éste*) like this: *Sujétalo ~.* Hold it like this. **2** (*de ese modo, como ése*) like that: *Quiero un coche ~.* I want a car like that. ◊ *Con gente ~ da gusto trabajar.* It's nice working with people like that. ◊ *Yo soy ~.* That's the way I am. LOC **así, así** so so **así de grande, gordo, etc** this big, fat etc **así que** so: *No llegaban, ~ que me fui.* They didn't come so I left. ◊ *¡~ que os mudáis!* So you're moving, are you? **¡así se habla/hace!** well said/done! **o así** or so: *unos doce o ~* about twelve or so **y así sucesivamente** and so on (and so forth) *Ver tb* ALGO

Asia *nf* Asia

asiático, -a *adj, nm-nf* Asian

asiento *nm* seat

asignar *vt* to assign

asignatura *nf* subject: *He suspendido dos ~s.* I've failed two subjects.

asilo *nm* **1** (*residencia*) home **2** (*Pol*) asylum: *buscar ~ político* to seek political asylum LOC *Ver* ANCIANO

asimilar *vt* to assimilate

asistencia *nf* **1** (*presencia*) attendance **2** (*a enfermos*) care: *~ médica/sanitaria* medical/health care LOC *Ver* FALTA

asistenta *nf* cleaner

asistente *adj, nmf* ~ (**a**) present [*adj*] (**at** ***sth***): *entre los ~s a la reunión* among those present at the meeting LOC **asistente social** social worker

asistir ◆ *vi* ~ (**a**) (*acudir*) to attend: *~ a una clase/una reunión* to attend a lesson/meeting ◆ *vt* (*médico*) to treat: *¿Qué médico te asistió?* Which doctor treated you?

asma *nf* asthma

asmático, -a *adj, nm-nf* asthmatic

asno, -a *nm-nf* ass

asociación *nf* association

asociar ◆ *vt* to associate *sth/sb* (**with** ***sth/sb***): *~ el calor a las vacaciones* to associate good weather with the holidays ◆ **asociarse** *v pron* to form a partnership (**to do** ***sth***)

asomar ◆ *vt*: *~ la cabeza por la ventana* to put your head out of the window ◊ *~ la cabeza por la puerta* to put your head round the door ◆ **asomarse** *v pron*: *Me asomé a la ventana para verlo mejor.* I put my head out of the window to get a better look. ◊ *Asómate al balcón.* Come out onto the balcony.

asombrarse *v pron* to be amazed: *Se asombraron al vernos.* They were amazed to see us. ◊ *Me asombré del desorden.* I was amazed by the mess.

asombro *nm* amazement: *mirar con ~* to look in amazement ◊ *poner cara de ~* to look amazed

aspa *nf* (*molino*) sail

aspecto *nm* **1** (*apariencia*) look: *No puedo salir con este ~.* I can't go out looking like this. ◊ *Tu abuela no tiene muy buen ~.* Your granny doesn't look very well. **2** (*faceta*) aspect: *el ~ jurídico* the legal aspect

aspereza *nf* LOC *Ver* LIMAR

áspero, -a *adj* rough

aspirador *nm* (*tb* **aspiradora** *nf*) Hoover®: *pasar el ~* to hoover

aspirante *nmf* ~ (**a**) candidate (**for** ***sth***): *los ~s al puesto* the candidates for the job

aspirar ◆ *vt* **1** (*respirar*) to breathe *sth* in **2** (*máquina*) to suck *sth* up ◆ *vi* ~ **a** to aspire **to** ***sth***: *~ a ganar un sueldo decente* to aspire to a decent salary

aspirina *nf* aspirin: *tomarse una ~* to take an aspirin

asqueroso, -a *adj* **1** (*sucio*) filthy **2** (*repugnante*) disgusting

asta *nf* **1** (*bandera*) flagpole **2** (*toro*) horn LOC *Ver* MEDIO

asterisco *nm* asterisk

astilla *nf* splinter LOC *Ver* TAL

astillero *nm* shipyard

astro *nm* star

astrología *nf* astrology

astrólogo, -a *nm-nf* astrologer

astronauta *nmf* astronaut

astronomía *nf* astronomy

astrónomo, -a *nm-nf* astronomer

astucia *nf* **1** (*habilidad*) shrewdness: *tener mucha ~* to be very shrewd **2** (*malicia*) cunning **3** (*ardid*) trick:

Emplearon todo tipo de ~s para ganar. They used all kinds of tricks to win.

astuto, -a *adj* **1** (*hábil*) shrewd: *un hombre muy ~* a very shrewd man **2** (*malicioso*) cunning: *Elaboraron un ~ plan.* They devised a cunning plan.

asunto *nm* **1** (*tema*) matter: *un ~ de interés general* a matter of general interest **2** (*Pol*) affair LOC **no es asunto mío** it's none of my, your, etc business *Ver tb* DESCUBRIR, MINISTERIO, MINISTRO

asustar ◆ *vt* to scare, to frighten (*más formal*): *Me asustó el perro.* The dog frightened me. ◊ *¿Te asusta la oscuridad?* Are you scared of the dark? ◆ **asustarse** *v pron* to be scared (*más coloq*), to be frightened: *Te asustas por nada.* You're frightened of everything.

atacar *vt* to attack

atajar *vi* to take a short cut: *Podemos ~ por aquí.* We can take a short cut through here.

atajo *nm* short cut: *coger un ~* to take a short cut

ataque *nm* **1** ~ (**a/contra**) attack (**on *sth/sb***): *un ~ al corazón* a heart attack **2** (*risa, tos*) fit: *Le dio un ~ de tos.* He had a coughing fit. LOC **ataque de nervios** nervous breakdown *Ver tb* CARDIACO

atar ◆ *vt* to tie *sth/sb* (up): *Nos ataron las manos.* They tied our hands. ◊ *Ata bien el paquete.* Tie the parcel tightly. ◆ **atar(se)** *vt, v pron* to do *sth* up: *No puedo ~me los zapatos.* I can't do my shoes up.

atardecer *nm* dusk: *al ~* at dusk

atareado, -a *pp, adj* busy

atascar ◆ *vt* to block *sth* (up) ◆ **atascarse** *v pron* **1** (*gen*) to get stuck: *Siempre me atasco en esa palabra.* I always get stuck on that word. **2** (*mecanismo*) to jam

atasco *nm* (*coches*) traffic jam

ataúd *nm* coffin

atención ◆ *nf* attention ◆ **¡atención!** *interj* attention, please LOC **con atención** attentively **poner/prestar atención** to pay attention (*to sth/sb*) *Ver tb* LLAMAR

atender ◆ *vt* **1** (*recibir*) to see: *Tienen que ~ a muchas personas.* They have to see lots of people. **2** (*en una tienda*) to serve: *¿Le atienden?* Are you being served? **3** (*tarea, problema, solicitud*) to deal with *sth*: *Sólo atendemos casos urgentes.* We only deal with emergencies. **4** (*contestar*) to answer: *~ llamadas/al teléfono* to answer calls/the phone ◆ *vi* to pay attention (***to sth/sb***): *No atienden a lo que el profesor dice.* They don't pay any attention to what the teacher says.

atenerse *v pron* ~ **a 1** (*reglas, órdenes*) to abide by *sth*: *Nos atendremos a las normas.* We'll abide by the rules. **2** (*consecuencias*) to face: *Ateneos a las consecuencias.* You'll have to face the consequences. LOC **(no) saber a qué atenerse** (not) to know what to expect

atentado *nm* **1** (*ataque*) attack (**on *sth/sb***): *un ~ contra un cuartel del ejército* an attack on an army headquarters **2** (*intento de asesinato*) attempt on *sb's* life: *un ~ contra dos parlamentarios* an attempt on the lives of two MPs

atentamente *adv* (*fórmula de despedida*) Yours faithfully, Yours sincerely ☛ *Ver* págs 314–15. LOC *Ver* SALUDAR

atentar *vi* ~ **contra** to make an attempt on *sb's* life: *Atentaron contra el juez.* They made an attempt on the judge's life.

atento, -a *adj* **1** (*prestando atención*) attentive: *Escuchaban ~s.* They listened attentively. **2** (*amable*) kind LOC **estar atento a algo 1** (*mirar*) to watch out for sth: *estar ~ a la llegada del tren* to watch out for the train **2** (*prestar atención*) to pay attention to sth

ateo, -a *nm-nf* atheist: *ser ~* to be an atheist

aterrador, ~a *adj* terrifying

aterrizaje *nm* landing LOC **aterrizaje forzoso** emergency landing *Ver tb* TREN

aterrizar *vi* to land: *Aterrizaremos en Gatwick.* We shall be landing at Gatwick.

aterrorizar *vt* **1** (*dar miedo*) to terrify: *Me aterrorizaba que pudieran tirar la puerta.* I was terrified they might knock the door down. **2** (*con violencia*) to terrorize: *Esos matones aterrorizan a los vecinos.* Those thugs terrorize the neighbourhood.

atiborrarse *v pron* ~ (**de**) to stuff yourself (**with *sth***): *Nos atiborramos de langosta.* We stuffed ourselves with lobster.

ático *nm* **1** (*último piso*) top-floor flat **2** (*desván*) attic

atizar *vt* (*fuego*) to poke LOC **atizar un golpe** to hit *sth/sb*

atlántico, -a ◆ *adj* Atlantic ◆ **Atlántico** *nm* Atlantic (Ocean)

atlas *nm* atlas [*pl* atlases]

atleta *nmf* athlete

atlético, -a *adj* athletic

atletismo *nm* athletics [*sing*]

atmósfera *nf* atmosphere: ~ *cargada/de malestar* stuffy/uneasy atmosphere

atómico, -a *adj* atomic LOC *Ver* REACTOR

átomo *nm* atom

atontado, -a ◆ *pp, adj* **1** (*alelado*) groggy: *Esas pastillas me han dejado ~.* Those pills have made me groggy. **2** (*por un golpe*) stunned ◆ *nm-nf* dimwit *Ver tb* ATONTAR

atontar *vt* **1** (*marear*) to make *sb* dopey **2** (*volver tonto*) to dull your senses: *Esas revistas te atontan.* Magazines like these dull your senses.

atormentar *vt* to torment

atornillar *vt* to screw *sth* down/in/on: ~ *la última pieza* to screw on the last bit

atracador, ~a *nm-nf* **1** (*ladrón*) robber **2** (*en la calle*) mugger

atracar ◆ *vt* **1** (*asaltar*) to hold *sth/sb* up: ~ *una sucursal del Banco Central* to hold up a branch of the Central Bank **2** (*en la calle*) to mug: *Me han atracado en el metro.* I've been mugged on the underground. ◆ *vt, vi* (*barco*) to dock

atracción *nf* attraction: *una ~ turística* a tourist attraction ◊ *sentir ~ por algn* to be attracted to sb LOC *Ver* PARQUE

atraco *nm* **1** (*robo*) hold-up: *Cometieron un ~ en una joyería.* They held up a jeweller's shop. **2** (*en la calle*) mugging LOC *Ver* MANO

atracón *nm* LOC **darse un atracón** to stuff yourself full (*of sth*)

atractivo, -a ◆ *adj* attractive ◆ *nm* **1** (*cosa que atrae*) attraction: *uno de los ~s de la ciudad* one of the city's attractions **2** (*interés*) appeal [*incontable*] **3** (*persona*) charm

atraer *vt* **1** (*gen*) to attract: ~ *a los turistas* to attract tourists ◊ *Me atraen los hombres mediterráneos.* I'm attracted to Mediterranean men. **2** (*idea*) to appeal **to *sb***

atragantarse *v pron* **1** ~ (**con**) to choke (**on *sth***): *Me atraganté con una espina.* I choked on a bone. **2** (*objeto*) to get stuck in *sb's* throat: *Se le atragantó un hueso de aceituna.* An olive stone got stuck in his throat.

atrancarse *v pron* **1** (*tubería*) to get blocked **2** (*mecanismo, persona*) to get stuck

atrapado, -a *pp, adj* LOC **estar/quedarse atrapado** to be trapped *Ver tb* ATRAPAR

atrapar *vt* to catch

atrás *adv* back: *Vamos a ponernos más ~.* Let's sit further back. ◊ *Siempre se sientan ~.* They always sit at the back. LOC **dejar atrás** to leave *sth/sb* behind **echarse/volverse atrás** (*desdecirse*) to go back on your word **hacia/para atrás** backwards: *andar hacia ~* to walk backwards *Ver tb* CUENTA, MARCHA, PARTE[1]

atrasado, -a *pp, adj* **1** (*publicación, sueldo*) back: *los números ~s de una revista* the back numbers of a magazine **2** (*país, región*) backward **3** (*reloj*) slow: *Tu reloj va ~.* Your watch is slow. LOC **tener trabajo, etc atrasado** to be behind with your work, etc *Ver tb* ATRASAR

atrasar ◆ *vt* **1** (*aplazar*) to put *sth* off, to postpone (*más formal*): *Tuvieron que ~ la reunión una semana.* They had to postpone the meeting for a week. **2** (*reloj*) to put *sth* back: ~ *el reloj una hora* to put the clock back an hour ◆ **atrasar(se)** *vi, v pron* (*reloj*) to be slow: *(Se) atrasa cinco minutos.* It's five minutes slow.

atraso *nm* **1** (*demora*) delay [*pl* delays] **2** (*subdesarrollo*) backwardness

atravesar ◆ *vt* **1** (*cruzar*) to cross: ~ *la frontera* to cross the border **2** (*perforar, experimentar*) to go through *sth*: *Atraviesan una grave crisis.* They're going through a serious crisis. ◊ *La bala le atravesó el corazón.* The bullet went through his heart. ◆ **atravesarse** *v pron* **1** (*en el camino*) to block *sb's* path: *Se nos atravesó un elefante.* An elephant blocked our path. **2** (*en la garganta*) to get *sth* stuck in your throat: *Se me atravesó una espina.* I got a bone stuck in my throat.

atreverse *v pron* ~ (**a**) to dare (***do sth***): *No me atrevo a pedirle dinero.* I daren't ask him for money. ☛ *Ver nota en* DARE[1]

atrevido, -a *pp, adj* **1** (*gen*) daring: *una blusa/decisión atrevida* a daring blouse/decision **2** (*insolente*) cheeky *Ver tb* ATREVERSE

atributo *nm* attribute

atropellado *pp, adj* (*por un vehículo*): *Murió ~.* He died after being run over by a car. *Ver tb* ATROPELLAR

atropellar *vt* to run *sb* over: *Me atropelló un coche.* I was run over by a car.

atufar ◆ *vt* to make *sth* stink (**of sth**) ◆ *vi* ~ (**a**) to stink (**of sth**)

atún *nm* tuna [*pl* tuna]

audaz *adj* bold

audición *nf* **1** (*oído*) hearing: *perder* ~ to lose your hearing **2** (*prueba*) audition

audiencia *nf* audience: *el programa de mayor* ~ the programme with the largest audience

auditorio *nm* **1** (*audiencia*) audience **2** (*edificio*) concert hall

aula *nf* **1** (*de escuela*) classroom **2** (*de universidad*) lecture room

aullar *vi* to howl

aullido *nm* howl

aumentar ◆ *vt* **1** (*gen*) to increase: ~ *la competitividad* to increase competition **2** (*lupa, microscopio*) to magnify ◆ *vi* to increase: *Aumenta la población.* The population is increasing.

aumento *nm* rise, increase (*más formal*) (**in sth**): *un ~ de la población* an increase in population

aun *adv* even: ~ *así no lo aceptaría.* Even so, I wouldn't accept it.

aún *adv* **1** (*en oraciones afirmativas e interrogativas*) still: ~ *faltan dos horas.* There are still two hours to go. ◊ *¿~ estás aquí?* Are you still here? **2** (*en oraciones negativas e interrogativas-negativas*) yet: *—¿~ no te han contestado? —No, ~ no.* 'Haven't they written back yet?' 'No, not yet.' ☛ *Ver nota en* STILL[1] **3** (*en oraciones comparativas*) even: *Ésta me gusta ~ más.* I like this one even better.

aunque *conj* **1** (*a pesar de que*) although, though (*más coloq*)

> **Although** es más formal que **though**. Si se quiere dar más énfasis se puede usar **even though**: *No han querido venir, aunque sabían que estaríais.* They didn't want to come, although/though/even though they knew you'd be here.

2 (*incluso si*) even if: *Ven, ~ sea tarde.* Come along even if it's late.

auricular *nm* **1** (*teléfono*) receiver **2** **auriculares** headphones

aurora *nf* dawn

ausencia *nf* absence

ausentarse *v pron* ~ (**de**) **1** (*no ir*) to stay off: ~ *de la escuela* to stay off school **2** (*estar fuera*) to be away (**from ...**)

ausente ◆ *adj* absent (**from ...**): *Estaba ~ de la reunión.* He was absent from the meeting. ◆ *nmf* absentee

austeridad *nf* austerity

austero, -a *adj* austere

Australia *nf* Australia

australiano, -a *adj, nm-nf* Australian

Austria *nf* Austria

austriaco, -a (*tb* **austríaco, -a**) *adj, nm-nf* Austrian: *los ~s* the Austrians

auténtico, -a *adj* genuine, authentic (*más formal*): *un Renoir* ~ an authentic Renoir

auto *nm* (*coche*) car **LOC** *Ver* CHOQUE

autobiografía *nf* autobiography [*pl* autobiographies]

autobiográfico, -a *adj* autobiographical

autobús *nm* bus: *coger/perder el* ~ to catch/miss the bus **LOC** *Ver* PARADA

autocar *nm* coach

autodefensa *nf* self-defence

autodidacta *adj, nmf* self-taught [*adj*]: *Fue esencialmente un ~.* He was basically self-taught.

autoescuela *nf* driving school

autoestop *nm Ver* AUTOSTOP

autoestopista *nmf Ver* AUTOSTOPISTA

autógrafo *nm* autograph

automático, -a ◆ *adj* automatic ◆ *nm* (*Costura*) press-stud **LOC** *Ver* CAJERO, CONTESTADOR, PILOTO

automóvil *nm* car **LOC** *Ver* CEMENTERIO

automovilismo *nm* motor racing

automovilista *nmf* motorist

autonomía *nf* **1** (*autogobierno*) autonomy **2** (*independencia*) independence: *la ~ del poder judicial* the independence of the judiciary **3** (*territorio*) autonomous region

autonómico, -a *adj* regional: *las autoridades autonómicas* the regional authorities

autónomo, -a ◆ *adj* **1** (*gen*) autonomous **2** (*gobierno*) regional ◆ *adj, nm-nf* (*trabajador*) self-employed **LOC** *Ver* COMUNIDAD

autopista *nf* motorway [*pl* motorways]

autopsia *nf* post-mortem

autor, ~a *nm-nf* **1** (*escritor*) author **2** (*compositor musical*) composer **3** (*crimen*) perpetrator

autoridad *nf* authority [*pl* authorities]

autorización *nf* permission

autorizar *vt* **1** (*acción*) to authorize: *No han autorizado la huelga.* They haven't authorized the strike. **2** (*dar derecho*) to give *sb* the right (***to do sth***): *El cargo nos autoriza a utilizar un coche oficial.* The job gives us the right to use an official car.

autorretrato *nm* self-portrait

autoservicio *nm* **1** (*restaurante*) self-service restaurant **2** (*supermercado*) supermarket **3** (*gasolinera*) self-service petrol station

autostop *nm* hitch-hiking LOC **hacer autostop** to hitch-hike

autostopista *nmf* hitchhiker

autovía *nf* dual carriageway [*pl* dual carriageways]

auxilio *nm* help: *un grito de ~* a cry for help LOC *Ver* PRIMERO

avalancha *nf* avalanche

avanzar *vi* to advance

avaricia *nf* greed

avaricioso, -a *adj*, *nm-nf* greedy [*adj*]: *Es un ~.* He's greedy.

avaro, -a ◆ *adj* miserly ◆ *nm-nf* miser

ave *nf* bird

avellana ◆ *nf* hazelnut ◆ *nm* (*color*) hazel: *ojos de color ~* hazel eyes

avellano *nm* hazel

avemaría *nf* Hail Mary: *rezar tres ~s* to say three Hail Marys

avena *nf* oats [*pl*]

avenida *nf* avenue (*abrev* Ave)

aventura *nf* **1** (*peripecia*) adventure: *Vivimos una ~ fascinante.* We had a fascinating adventure. **2** (*amorío*) fling

aventurero, -a ◆ *adj* adventurous ◆ *nm-nf* adventurer

avergonzar ◆ *vt* **1** (*humillar*) to make *sb* feel ashamed: *~ a la familia* to make your family feel ashamed **2** (*abochornar*) to embarrass: *Tu manera de vestir me avergüenza.* The way you dress embarrasses me. ◆ **avergonzarse** *v pron* **1** (*arrepentirse*) to be ashamed (***of sth/doing sth***): *Me avergüenzo de haberles mentido.* I'm ashamed of having told them a lie. **2** (*sentirse incómodo*) to be embarrassed: *Se avergüenzan de su propia ignorancia.* They're embarrassed by their own ignorance.

avería *nf* **1** (*vehículo, mecanismo*) breakdown: *La ~ del coche me va a costar un ojo de la cara.* The breakdown's going to cost me an arm and a leg. **2** (*fallo*) fault: *una ~ en la instalación eléctrica* a fault in the electrical system

averiarse *v pron* (*Mec*) to break down

averiguar *vt* to find *sth* out, to discover (*más formal*)

avestruz *nm* ostrich

aviación *nf* **1** (*gen*) aviation: *~ civil* civil aviation **2** (*fuerzas aéreas*) air force

avinagrado, -a *pp*, *adj* (*vino*) vinegary

avión *nm* aeroplane, plane (*más coloq*) LOC **ir/viajar en avión** to fly **por avión** (*correo*) airmail

avioneta *nf* light aircraft [*pl* light aircraft]

avisar *vt* **1** (*informar*) to let *sb* know (***about sth***): *Avísame cuando lleguen.* Let me know when they arrive. **2** (*advertir*) to warn: *Te aviso que si no me pagas...* I'm warning you that if you don't pay... LOC **sin avisar**: *Vinieron sin ~.* They turned up unexpectedly. ◊ *Se fue de casa sin ~.* He left home without saying anything.

aviso *nm* **1** (*gen*) notice: *Cerrado hasta nuevo ~.* Closed until further notice. **2** (*advertencia*) warning: *sin previo ~* without prior warning

avispa *nf* wasp

avispero *nm* (*nido*) wasps' nest

axila *nf* armpit

¡ay! *interj* **1** (*de dolor*) ow! **2** (*de aflicción*) oh (dear)!

ayer *adv* yesterday LOC **antes de ayer** the day before yesterday **ayer por la noche** last night **de ayer**: *el periódico de ~* yesterday's paper ◊ *Este pan es de ~.* This bread isn't fresh.

ayuda *nf* help [*incontable*]: *Gracias por tu ~.* Thanks for your help. ◊ *Necesito ~.* I need some help.

ayudante *adj*, *nmf* assistant

ayudar *vt*, *vi* to help *sb* (***to do sth***): *¿Te ayudo?* Can I help you?

ayunar *vi* to fast

ayunas LOC **en ayunas**: *Estoy en ~.* I've had nothing to eat or drink.

ayuno *nm* fast: *40 días de ~* 40 days of fasting

ayuntamiento *nm* **1** (*concejo*) council [*v sing o pl*] **2** (*edificio*) town hall

azabache *nm* jet: *negro como el ~* jet black

azada *nf* hoe

azafata *nf* **1** (*de vuelo*) stewardess **2** (*de congresos*) hostess

azafrán *nm* saffron

azahar *nm* orange blossom

azar *nm* **1** (*casualidad*) chance: *juego de ~* game of chance **2** (*destino*) fate LOC **al**

azar at random: *Elige un número al ~.* Choose a number at random.
azote *nm* smack: *Como te pille te doy un ~.* I'll give you a smack if I catch you.
azotea *nf* (flat) roof [*pl* roofs]
azúcar *nm* sugar: *un terrón de ~* a lump of sugar LOC *Ver* ALGODÓN, FÁBRICA
azucarero *nm* sugar bowl LOC *Ver* REMOLACHA
azucarillo *nm* sugar lump
azucena *nf* lily [*pl* lilies]
azufre *nm* sulphur
azul *adj, nm* blue ☛ *Ver ejemplos en* AMARILLO LOC **azul celeste/marino** sky/ navy blue **azul turquesa** turquoise *Ver tb* PESCADO, PRÍNCIPE
azulejo *nm* tile

Bb

baba *nf* **1** (*de persona*) dribble **2** (*de animal*) foam LOC **caérsele la baba a algn** to dote *on sb*: *Se le cae la ~ por sus nietos.* She dotes on her grandchildren.
babear *vi* to dribble
babero *nm* bib
babi *nm* overall
Babia *nf* LOC **estar en Babia** to be daydreaming
babor *nm* port: *a ~* to port
babosa *nf* slug
baca *nf* roof-rack
bacalao *nm* cod [*pl* cod]
bache *nm* **1** (*hoyo*) pothole: *Estas carreteras tienen muchos ~s.* These roads are full of potholes. **2** (*dificultad*) bad patch: *atravesar un ~* to go through a bad patch
bachillerato *nm* secondary school
bacilo *nm* bacillus [*pl* bacilli]
bacon *nm* bacon
bacteria *nf* bacterium [*pl* bacteria]
bafle *nm* (loud)speaker
bahía *nf* bay [*pl* bays]
bailar ◆ *vt, vi* **1** (*danza*) to dance: *¿Bailas?* Would you like to dance? ◊ *~ un tango* to dance a tango **2** (*peonza*) to spin ◆ *vi* **1** (*estar suelto*) to be loose: *Me baila un diente.* I've got a loose tooth. **2** (*quedar grande*) to be too big (**for sb**): *Esta falda me baila.* This skirt's too big for me. LOC **bailar agarrado** to have a slow dance **bailar con la más fea** to draw the short straw **bailarle el agua a algn** to suck up to sb **sacar a bailar** to ask *sb* to dance
bailarín, -ina *nm-nf* dancer
baile *nm* **1** (*fiesta, danza*) dance: *El ~ empieza a las doce.* The dance begins at twelve. **2** (*acción*) dancing: *Me gusta mucho el ~.* I like dancing very much. LOC **baile de disfraces** fancy dress ball *Ver tb* PISTA
baja *nf* **1** (*precio*) fall (**in sth**): *una ~ en el precio del pan* a fall in the price of bread **2** (*ausencia autorizada*) sick leave: *pedir/solicitar la ~* to go on sick leave **3** (*Mil*) casualty [*pl* casualties]
bajada *nf* **1** (*descenso*) descent: *durante la ~* during the descent **2** (*pendiente*) slope: *La calle tiene mucha ~.* The street slopes steeply. **3** (*Econ*) fall (**in sth**): *Continúa la ~ de los tipos de interés.* Interest rates continue to fall. LOC **bajada de bandera** minimum fare
bajamar *nf* low tide
bajar ◆ *vt* **1** (*gen*) to get *sth* down: *¿Me ayuda a ~ la maleta?* Could you help me get my suitcase down? **2** (*traer, poner más abajo*) to bring *sth* down: *Bájalo un poco más.* Bring it down a bit. **3** (*llevar*) to take *sth* down: *¿Tenemos que ~ esta silla al segundo?* Do we have to take this chair down to the second floor? **4** (*ir/venir abajo*) to go/ come down: *~ la cuesta* to go down the hill **5** (*cabeza*) to bow **6** (*vista, voz*) to lower **7** (*volumen*) to turn *sth* down **8** (*precio*) to bring *a price* down, to lower (*más formal*) ◆ *vi* **1** (*ir/venir abajo*) to go/to come down: *¿Puede ~ a recepción, por favor?* Can you come down to reception, please? **2** (*temperatura, río*) to fall: *La temperatura ha bajado.* The temperature has fallen. **3** (*hinchazón*) to go down **4** (*marea*) to go out **5** (*precios*) to come down: *El pan ha vuelto a ~.* (The price of) bread has come down again. ◆ **bajar(se)** *vi,*

v pron **bajar(se)** **(de)** **1** (*automóvil*) to get out **(of *sth*)**: *Nunca (te) bajes de un coche en marcha.* Never get out of a moving car. **2** (*transporte público, caballo, bici*) to get off (*sth*): *~(se) de un autobús* to get off a bus **LOC** **bajarle los humos a algn** to take sb down a peg or two *Ver tb* ESCALERA

bajo[1] *nm* **1** (*vivienda*) ground-floor flat **2** (*ropa*) hem: *Tienes el ~ descosido.* Your hem has come undone. **3** (*voz*) bass **4** **bajos** (*coche*) underbody [*sing*]

bajo[2] *prep* under: *Nos resguardamos bajo un paraguas.* We sheltered under an umbrella. ◊ *bajo la lluvia* in the rain

bajo[3] *adv* **1** (*a poca altura*) low: *Los pájaros vuelan ~.* The birds are flying low. **2** (*suave*) quietly: *Toca más ~.* Play more quietly.

bajo, -a *adj* **1** (*persona*) short **2** **~** **(en)** low **(in *sth*)**: *una sopa baja en calorías* a low-calorie soup ◊ *La tele está demasiado baja.* The volume is too low. **3** (*zapato*) flat **4** (*voz*) quiet: *hablar en voz baja* to speak quietly/softly **5** (*metales nobles*) low quality: *oro ~* low quality gold **6** (*pobre*) poor: *los barrios ~s de la ciudad* the poor areas of the city **LOC** **estar bajo de moral** to be in low spirits *Ver tb* CLASE, CONTROL, GOLPE, HABLAR, PAÍS

bala *nf* (*arma*) bullet **LOC** **como una bala** like a shot *Ver tb* PRUEBA

balance *nm* **1** (*gen*) balance: *~ positivo/negativo* a positive/negative balance **2** (*número de víctimas*) toll

balancear(se) *vt, v pron* **1** (*gen*) to swing **2** (*cuna, mecedora*) to rock

balanza *nf* **1** (*instrumento*) scales [*pl*] **2** (*Com*) balance

balar *vi* to bleat

balazo *nm* **1** (*disparo*) shot **2** (*herida*) bullet wound

balbucear (*tb* **balbucir**) ◆ *vt, vi* (*adulto*) to stammer: *Balbuceó unas palabras.* He stammered a few words. ◆ *vi* (*bebé*) to babble

balcón *nm* balcony [*pl* balconies]: *salir al ~* to go out onto the balcony

balda *nf* shelf [*pl* shelves]

baldado, -a *pp, adj* (*cansado*) shattered: *Estoy ~ de tanto empapelar.* I'm shattered after all that wallpapering.

balde[1] *nm* bucket

balde[2] **LOC** **de balde** for nothing: *Entramos al cine de ~.* We got into the cinema for nothing. **en balde** in vain

baldosa *nf* **1** (*interior*) floor tile **2** (*exterior*) paving stone

baliza *nf* **1** (*Náut*) buoy [*pl* buoys] **2** (*Aviación*) beacon

ballena *nf* whale

ballet *nm* ballet

balneario *nm* spa

balón *nm* **1** (*gen*) ball **2** (*para cuerpos gaseosos*) bag **LOC** *Ver* CABEZAZO

baloncesto *nm* basketball: *jugar al ~* to play basketball

balonmano *nm* handball

balonvolea *nm* volleyball

balsa[1] *nf* (*charca*) pool **LOC** **como una balsa de aceite** (*mar*) as calm as a lake

balsa[2] *nf* (*embarcación*) raft

bambolearse *v pron* to sway

bambú *nm* bamboo: *una mesa de ~* a bamboo table

banca *nf* **1** (*bancos*) banks [*pl*]: *la ~ japonesa* Japanese banks **2** (*sector*) banking: *los sectores de ~ y comercio* the banking and business sectors

bancario, -a *adj* **LOC** *Ver* GIRO, TRANSFERENCIA

bancarrota *nf* bankruptcy **LOC** **estar en bancarrota** to be bankrupt

banco *nm* **1** (*gen, Fin*) bank: *~ de datos/sangre* data/blood bank **2** (*asiento*) bench **3** (*iglesia*) pew **4** (*peces*) shoal **LOC** **banco de arena** sandbank

banda[1] *nf* band: *una ~ del pelo* a hair band **LOC** **banda sonora** soundtrack **coger por banda** to get hold of *sb* *Ver tb* SAQUE

banda[2] *nf* **1** (*cuadrilla*) gang: *una ~ de gamberros* a gang of hooligans **2** (*grupo musical*) band **LOC** **banda terrorista** terrorist group

bandada *nf* **1** (*aves*) flock **2** (*peces*) shoal

bandeja *nf* tray [*pl* trays] **LOC** **poner/servir en bandeja** to hand *sb sth* on a plate

bandera *nf* **1** (*gen*) flag: *Las ~s están a media asta.* The flags are flying at half-mast. **2** (*Mil*) colours [*pl*] **LOC** **bandera blanca** white flag *Ver tb* BAJADA, JURAR

banderín *nm* pennant

bandido, -a *nm-nf* bandit

bando *nm* **1** (*Mil, Pol*) faction **2** (*en juegos*) side: *Jugaremos en ~s distintos.* We'll be playing on different sides.

banquero, -a *nm-nf* banker

banqueta *nf* stool: *subirse a una ~* to stand on a stool

banquete *nm* banquet (*formal*), dinner: *Dieron un ~ en su honor.* They organized a dinner in his honour.

banquillo *nm* **1** (*Dep*) bench: *Me dejaron en el ~.* I was left on the bench. **2** (*Jur*) dock: *estar en el ~* to be in the dock

bañado, -a *pp, adj* bathed: *~ en lágrimas/sudor/sangre* bathed in tears/sweat/blood LOC **bañado en oro/plata** gold-plated/silver-plated *Ver tb* BAÑAR

bañador *nm* **1** (*de hombre*) swimming trunks [*pl*]: *Ese ~ te queda pequeño.* Those swimming trunks are too small for you. ☛ Nótese que *un bañador* se dice **a pair of swimming trunks**. **2** (*de mujer*) swimming costume

bañar ◆ *vt* **1** (*gen*) to bath **2** (*en metal*) to plate *sth* (**with** *sth*) **3** (*Cocina*) to coat *sth* (**in/with** *sth*): *~ una tarta de chocolate* to coat a cake in chocolate ◆ **bañarse** *v pron* **1** (*bañera*) to have a bath **2** (*nadar*) to go for a swim

bañera *nf* bath

baño *nm* **1** (*en la bañera*) bath: *Me di un ~ de espuma.* I had a bubble bath. **2** (*mar, piscina*) swim: *¿Nos damos un ~?* Shall we go for a swim? **3** (*cuarto de baño*) bathroom **4** (*w.c.*) loo (*coloq*), toilet ☛ *Ver nota en* TOILET **5 baños** baths: *los ~s romanos* the Roman baths LOC **baño María** bain-marie: *cocer algo al ~ María* to cook sth in a bain-marie *Ver tb* CUARTO, GEL, GORRO, SAL, TRAJE

bar *nm* **1** (*bebidas alcohólicas*) pub **2** (*cafetería*) snack bar ☛ *Ver* pág 320. LOC **ir de bares** to go on a pub crawl

baraja *nf* pack of cards

Los palos de la baraja española (*oros, copas, espadas* y *bastos*) no tienen traducción porque en Gran Bretaña se utiliza la baraja francesa. La baraja francesa consta de 52 cartas divididas en cuatro *palos* o **suits**: **hearts** (*corazones*), **diamonds** (*diamantes*), **clubs** (*tréboles*) y **spades** (*picas*). Cada palo tiene un **ace** (*as*), **king** (*rey*), **queen** (*reina*), **jack** (*jota*), y nueve cartas numeradas del 2 al 10. Antes de empezar a jugar, se *baraja* (**shuffle**), se *corta* (**cut**) y se *reparten* las cartas (**deal**).

barajar *vt* to shuffle

barandilla (*tb* **baranda**) *nf* **1** (*de una escalera*) banister(s) [*se usa mucho en plural*]: *bajar por la ~* to slide down the banisters **2** (*de un balcón*) railing(s) [*se usa mucho en plural*]

barato, -a ◆ *adj* cheap: *Aquél es más ~.* That one's cheaper. ◆ *adv*: *comprar algo ~* to buy sth cheaply ◊ *Esa tienda vende ~.* Prices are low in that shop.

barba *nf* beard: *dejarse ~* to grow a beard ◊ *un hombre con ~* a bearded man LOC **por barba** each: *Tocamos a tres por ~.* There are three each. *Ver tb* SUBIR

barbacoa *nf* barbecue: *hacer una ~* to have a barbecue

barbaridad *nf* **1** (*gen*) barbarity **2** (*disparate*) nonsense [*incontable*]: *¡No digas ~es!* Don't talk nonsense! LOC **¡qué barbaridad!** good heavens!

bárbaro, -a ◆ *adj* **1** (*Hist*) barbarian **2** (*estupendo*) terrific: *¡Es un tío ~!* He's a terrific bloke! ◆ *nm-nf* barbarian ◆ *adv*: *pasarlo ~* to have a terrific time LOC **¡qué bárbaro!** good Lord!

barbecho *nm* fallow land LOC **dejar en barbecho** to leave *land* fallow

barbilla *nf* chin

barca *nf* (small) boat: *dar un paseo en ~* to go out in a boat ☛ *Ver nota en* BOAT LOC **barca de remos** rowing boat

barco *nm* **1** (*buque*) ship **2** (*más pequeño*) boat ☛ *Ver nota en* BOAT LOC **barco de vapor** steamship **barco de vela** sailing boat **ir en barco** to go by boat/ship

barítono *nm* baritone

barniz *nm* **1** (*madera*) varnish **2** (*cerámica*) glaze

barnizar *vt* **1** (*madera*) to varnish **2** (*cerámica*) to glaze

barómetro *nm* barometer

barón, -esa *nm-nf* baron [*fem* baroness]

barquillo *nm* wafer

barra *nf* bar: *Tomaban café sentados en la ~.* They were sitting at the bar having a coffee. LOC **barra de labios** lipstick **barra** (**de pan**) baguette ☛ *Ver dibujo en* PAN

barraca *nf* (*feria*) stall

barranco *nm* ravine

barrendero, -a *nm-nf* road sweeper

barrer ◆ *vt* **1** (*limpiar, arrasar*) to sweep: *Una ola de terror barrió el país.* A wave of terror swept the country. **2** (*derrotar*) to thrash: *Os vamos a ~.* We're going to thrash you. ◆ *vi* to sweep up: *Si tú barres, yo friego.* If you sweep up, I'll do the dishes.

barrera *nf* **1** (*gen*) barrier: *La ~ estaba subida.* The barrier was up. ◊ *la ~ de la* *comunicación* the language barrier **2** (*Fútbol*) wall

barricada *nf* barricade: *construir una ~* to build a barricade

barriga *nf* **1** (*estómago*) tummy [*pl* tummies]: *Me duele un poco la ~.* I've got tummy ache. **2** (*panza*) paunch: *Estás echando ~.* You're getting a paunch.

barril *nm* barrel LOC *Ver* CERVEZA

barrio *nm* **1** (*gen*) area: *Yo me crié en este ~.* I grew up in this area. **2** (*en las afueras*) suburb **3** (*zona típica*) quarter: *el ~ gótico* the Gothic quarter LOC **barrio de chabolas** shanty town **del barrio** local: *el carnicero del ~* the local butcher

barro *nm* **1** (*lodo*) mud: *¡No os metáis en el ~!* Stay away from that mud! **2** (*arcilla*) clay LOC **de barro** earthenware: *cacharros de ~* earthenware pots

barroco, -a *adj, nm* baroque

barrote *nm* iron bar

barullo *nm* **1** (*ruido*) racket: *armar mucho ~* to make a terrible racket **2** (*confusión*) muddle: *Se organizó un ~ tremendo.* There was a terrible muddle.

basar ◆ *vt* to base *sth* **on** *sth*: *Han basado la película en una novela.* They've based the film on a novel. ◆ **basarse** *v pron* **basarse en 1** (*persona*) to have grounds (**for** *sth*/**doing** *sth*): *¿En qué te basas para decir eso?* What grounds do you have for saying that? **2** (*teoría, película*) to be based **on** *sth*

báscula *nf* scales [*pl*]: *~ de baño* bathroom scales

base *nf* **1** (*gen*) base: *un jarrón con poca ~* a vase with a small base ◇ *~ militar* military base **2** (*fundamento*) basis [*pl* bases]: *La confianza es la ~ de la amistad.* Trust is the basis of friendship. LOC **base de datos** database **base espacial** space station *Ver tb* SALARIO

básico, -a *adj* basic

bastante ◆ *adj* **1** (*número considerable, mucho*): *Hace ~ tiempo que no he ido a verla.* It's quite a long time since I last visited her. ◇ *Tengo ~s cosas que hacer.* I've got quite a lot of things to do. **2** (*suficiente*) enough: *No tenemos ~ dinero.* We haven't got enough money. ◆ *pron* **1** (*mucho*) quite a lot **2** (*suficiente*) enough: *No, gracias; ya hemos comido ~s.* No thank you; we've had enough. ◆ *adv* **1 + adj/adv** quite: *Es ~ inteligente.* He's quite intelligent. ◇ *Leen ~ bien para su edad.* They read quite well for their age. ☛ *Ver nota en* FAIRLY **2** (*lo suficiente*) enough: *Hoy no has comido ~.* You haven't eaten enough today. **3** (*mucho*) quite a lot: *Aprendí ~ en tres meses.* I learnt quite a lot in three months.

bastar *vi* to be enough: *Bastará con 30.000 pesetas.* 30000 pesetas will be enough. LOC **¡basta (ya)!** that's enough!

basto (*tb* **bastos**) *nm* (*Naipes*) ☛ *Ver nota en* BARAJA

basto, -a *adj* **1** (*persona, tejido, lenguaje*) coarse **2** (*superficie*) rough

bastón *nm* walking stick LOC **bastón de esquí** ski pole

basura *nf* rubbish [*incontable*]: *En esta calle hay mucha ~.* There's a lot of rubbish in this street. ◇ *Esa película es una ~.* That film is rubbish. LOC **tirar algo a la basura** to throw sth away *Ver tb* CAMIÓN, CUBO

basurero, -a ◆ *nm-nf* dustman [*pl* dustmen] ◆ *nm* (*vertedero*) tip

bata *nf* **1** (*de casa*) dressing-gown **2** (*de colegio, de trabajo*) overall **3** (*de laboratorio*) lab coat **4** (*de hospital*) white coat

batalla *nf* battle LOC **de batalla** everyday: *Llevo las botas de ~.* I'm wearing my everyday boots. *Ver tb* CAMPO

batallón *nm* battalion

bate *nm* bat: *~ de béisbol* baseball bat

batería ◆ *nf* **1** (*Electrón, Mil*) battery [*pl* batteries]: *Se ha quedado sin ~.* The battery is flat. **2** (*Mús*) drums [*pl*]: *Jeff Porcaro en la ~.* Jeff Porcaro on drums. ◆ *nmf* drummer LOC **batería de cocina** set of saucepans ☛ *Ver dibujo en* SAUCEPAN

batido *nm* (*bebida*) milk shake: *un ~ de chocolate* a chocolate milk shake

batidora *nf* mixer

batín *nm* dressing-gown

batir *vt* **1** (*gen*) to beat: *~ huevos* to beat eggs ◇ *~ al contrincante* to beat your opponent **2** (*nata*) to whip **3** (*récord*) to break: *~ el récord mundial* to beat the world record

batuta *nf* baton

baúl *nm* trunk

bautismal *adj* baptismal: *pila ~* (baptismal) font

bautismo *nm* **1** (*iglesia católica*) baptism **2** (*iglesia protestante*) christening

bautizar *vt* **1** (*sacramento*) **(a)** (*iglesia católica*) to baptize **(b)** (*iglesia protestante*) to christen: *La bautizaremos con* *el nombre de Marta.* We're going to christen her Marta. **2** (*barco, invento*) to name

bautizo *nm* christening: *Mañana celebramos el ~ de mi hermano.* We're celebrating my brother's christening tomorrow.

baya *nf* (*Bot*) berry [*pl* berries]

bayeta *nf* cloth: *Pasa una ~ a la mesa por favor.* Can you give the table a wipe?

baza *nf* **1** (*Naipes*) trick: *Gané tres ~s.* I won three tricks. **2** (*recurso*) asset: *La experiencia es tu mejor ~.* Experience is your greatest asset.

bazo *nm* spleen

bebé *nm* baby [*pl* babies]

bebedor, ~a *nm-nf* heavy drinker

beber(se) *vt, vi, v pron* to drink: *Bébetelo todo.* Drink it up. ◊ *Se bebieron una botella entera de vino.* They drank a whole bottle of wine. LOC **beber a la salud de algn** to drink to sb's health **beber a morro (del grifo/de la botella)** to drink straight from the tap/bottle **beber a sorbos** to sip **beber como un cosaco** to drink like a fish **beber en vaso** to drink from a glass *Ver tb* TRAGO

bebida *nf* drink: *~ no alcohólica* non-alcoholic drink

bebido, -a *pp, adj* **1** (*ligeramente*) tipsy **2** (*borracho*) drunk *Ver tb* BEBER(SE)

beca *nf* **1** (*del Estado*) grant **2** (*de entidad privada*) scholarship

bedel *nmf* caretaker

beige *adj, nm* beige ☛ *Ver ejemplos en* AMARILLO

béisbol *nm* baseball

belén *nm* (*nacimiento*) crib: *Vamos a poner el ~.* Let's set up the crib.

belga *adj, nmf* Belgian: *los ~s* the Belgians

Bélgica *nf* Belgium

bélico, -a *adj* **1** (*actitud*) warlike **2** (*armas, juguetes*) war [*n atrib*]: *películas bélicas* war films

belleza *nf* beauty [*pl* beauties] LOC *Ver* CONCURSO, SALÓN

bello, -a *adj* beautiful LOC **bellas artes** fine art [*sing*] **la Bella Durmiente** Sleeping Beauty

bellota *nf* acorn

bendecir *vt* to bless LOC **bendecir la mesa** to say grace

bendición *nf* blessing LOC **dar/echar la bendición** to bless *sth/sb*

bendito, -a ◆ *adj* holy ◆ *nm-nf* **1** (*bonachón*) angel **2** (*tontorrón*) simple [*adj*]: *El pobre es un ~.* The poor man's a bit simple.

beneficiar ◆ *vt* ~ (**a**) to benefit *sth/sb* ◆ **beneficiarse** *v pron* **beneficiarse (con/de)** to benefit (**from** *sth*): *Se beneficiaron del descuento.* They benefited from the reduction.

beneficio *nm* **1** (*bien*) benefit **2** (*Com, Fin*) profit: *dar/obtener ~s* to produce/make a profit LOC **en beneficio de** to the advantage of *sth/sb*: *en ~ tuyo* to your advantage

beneficioso, -a *adj* beneficial

benéfico, -a *adj* charity [*n atrib*]: *obras benéficas* charity work ◊ *una institución benéfica* a charity

bengala *nf* **1** (*gen*) flare **2** (*de mano*) sparkler

benigno, -a *adj* **1** (*tumor*) benign **2** (*clima*) mild

benjamín, -ina *nm-nf* youngest child [*pl* youngest children]

berberecho *nm* cockle

berenjena *nf* aubergine

bermudas *nm o nf* Bermuda shorts

berrinche *nm* tantrum: *estar con/tener un ~* to have a tantrum

berro *nm* watercress [*incontable*]

berza *nf* cabbage

besamel *nf* white sauce

besar *vt* to kiss: *Le besó la mano.* He kissed her hand. ◊ *Me besó en la frente.* She kissed me on the forehead.

beso *nm* kiss: *Dale un ~ a tu prima.* Give your cousin a kiss. ◊ *Nos dimos un ~.* We kissed. LOC **tirar un beso** to blow (*sb*) a kiss *Ver tb* COMER

bestia ◆ *nf* beast ◆ *adj, nmf* brute [*n*]: *¡Qué ~ eres!* You're such a brute! LOC **a lo bestia** like crazy: *Conducen a lo ~.* They drive like crazy.

bestial *adj* **1** (*enorme*) huge: *Tengo un hambre ~.* I'm famished. **2** (*genial*) great

bestialidad *nf* **1** (*brutalidad*): *Hicieron muchas ~es.* They did a lot of disgusting things. **2** (*grosería*): *decir ~es* to be rude **3** (*estupidez*): *hacer/decir muchas ~es* to do/say a lot of stupid things LOC **una bestialidad** (*cantidad, número*) loads (*of sth*): *una ~ de gente* loads of people

besugo *nm* bream [*pl* bream]

betún *nm* (*calzado*) (shoe) polish: *Dales ~ a los zapatos.* Give your shoes a polish.

biberón *nm* bottle

Biblia *nf* Bible

bíblico, -a *adj* biblical

bibliografía *nf* bibliography [*pl* bibliographies]

biblioteca *nf* **1** (*edificio, conjunto de libros*) library [*pl* libraries] **2** (*mueble*) bookcase LOC *Ver* RATÓN

bibliotecario, -a *nm-nf* librarian

bicarbonato *nm* bicarbonate

bíceps *nm* biceps [*pl* biceps]

bicho *nm* **1** (*insecto*) insect, creepy-crawly (*coloq*) [*pl* creepy-crawlies] **2** (*cualquier animal*) animal LOC **¿qué bicho te ha picado?** what's up with you, him, her, etc? **ser un bicho raro** to be a bit of an oddball **ser un (mal) bicho** to be a nasty piece of work

bici *nf* bike

bicicleta *nf* bicycle, bike (*más coloq*): *¿Sabes montar en ~?* Can you ride a bike? ◊ *ir en ~ al trabajo* to cycle to work ◊ *dar un paseo en ~* to go for a ride on your bicycle LOC **bicicleta de carreras/montaña** racing/mountain bike

bidé *nm* bidet

bidón *nm* drum

bien[1] *adv* **1** (*gen*) well: *portarse ~* to behave well ◊ *Hoy no me encuentro ~.* I don't feel well today. ◊ *—¿Cómo está tu padre? —Muy ~, gracias.* 'How's your father?' 'Very well, thanks.' **2** (*de acuerdo, adecuado*) OK: *Les parecía ~.* They thought it was OK. ◊ *—¿Me lo dejas? —Está ~, pero ten cuidado.* 'Can I borrow it?' 'OK, but be careful.' **3** (*calidad, aspecto, olor, sabor*) good: *La escuela está ~.* The school is good. ◊ *¡Qué ~ huele!* That smells really good! **4** (*correctamente*): *Contesté ~ la pregunta.* I got the right answer. ◊ *Hablas ~ el español.* You speak good Spanish. LOC **andar/estar bien de** to have plenty of *sth* **¡(muy) bien!** (very) good! ☛ Para otras expresiones con **bien**, véanse las entradas del adjetivo, verbo, etc, p.ej. **bien considerado** en CONSIDERADO y **llevarse bien** en LLEVAR.

bien[2] *conj* LOC **bien ... bien ...** either ... or ...: *Iré ~ en tren,~ en autocar.* I'll go either by train or by coach.

bien[3] *nm* **1** (*lo bueno*) good: *el ~ y el mal* good and evil **2** (*Educ*) ≃ C: *sacar un ~* to get (a) C **3 bienes** possessions LOC **bienes de consumo** consumer goods **por el bien de** for the good of *sth/sb* **por tu bien** for your, his, her, etc own good *Ver tb* MAL

bien[4] *adj* well-to-do: *Son de familia ~.* They're from a well-to-do family. LOC *Ver* GENTE, NIÑO

bienestar *nm* well-being

bienvenida *nf* welcome: *dar la ~ a algn* to welcome sb

bienvenido, -a *adj* welcome

bigote *nm* **1** (*persona*) moustache: *un hombre con ~* a man with a moustache ◊ *Papá Noel llevaba unos grandes ~s.* Father Christmas had a large moustache. **2** (*gato*) whiskers [*pl*]

bikini *nm Ver* BIQUINI

biliar *adj* LOC *Ver* VESÍCULA

bilingüe *adj* bilingual

bilis *nf* bile

billar *nm* **1** (*juego*) billiards [*sing*]: *jugar al ~* to play billiards **2** (*mesa*) billiard table **3 billares** (*local*) billiard hall [*sing*]

billete *nm* **1** (*transporte, lotería*) ticket: *un ~ de avión* an airline ticket ◊ *sacar un ~* to get a ticket **2** (*dinero*) (bank) note: *~s de 1.000 (pesetas)* 1000-peseta notes LOC **billete de ida** single (ticket) **billete de ida y vuelta** return (ticket)

billetero *nm* (*tb* **billetera** *nf*) wallet

billón *nm* (*un millón de millones*) trillion ☛ *Ver nota en* BILLION

binario, -a *adj* binary

bingo *nm* **1** (*juego*) bingo: *jugar al ~* to play bingo **2** (*sala*) bingo hall

biodegradable *adj* biodegradable

biografía *nf* biography [*pl* biographies]

biología *nf* biology

biólogo, -a *nm-nf* biologist

biquini *nm* bikini [*pl* bikinis]

birlar *vt* to pinch: *Me han birlado la radio.* Somebody's pinched my radio.

birria *nf* rubbish [*incontable*]: *La película es una ~.* The film is rubbish. LOC **estar/ir hecho una birria** to be/look a right mess

bisabuelo, -a *nm-nf* **1** (*gen*) great-grandfather [*fem* great-grandmother] **2 bisabuelos** great-grandparents

bisagra *nf* hinge

bisiesto *adj* LOC *Ver* AÑO

bisnieto, -a *nm-nf* **1** (*gen*) great-grandson [*fem* great-granddaughter] **2 bisnietos** great-grandchildren

bisonte *nm* bison [*pl* bison]

bisté (*tb* **bistec**) *nm* steak

bisturí *nm* scalpel

bisutería *nf* costume jewellery
bit *nm* bit
bizco, -a *adj* cross-eyed
bizcocho *nm* sponge cake
biznieto, -a *nm-nf Ver* BISNIETO
blanca *nf* (*Mús*) minim LOC **estar sin blanca** to be stony broke
Blancanieves *n pr* Snow White
blanco, -a ◆ *adj* white: *pescado/vino ~* white fish/wine ☛ *Ver ejemplos en* AMARILLO ◆ *nm-nf* (*persona*) white man/woman [*pl* white men/women] ◆ *nm* **1** (*color*) white **2** (*diana*) target: *dar en el ~* to hit the target LOC **en blanco** blank: *un cheque/página en ~* a blank cheque/page **en blanco y negro** black and white: *ilustraciones en ~ y negro* black and white illustrations **más blanco que la nieve** as white as snow **quedarse en blanco** to go blank *Ver tb* ARMA, BANDERA, CHEQUE, PESCADO, PUNTA
blando, -a *adj* **1** (*gen*) soft: *queso ~* soft cheese ◊ *un profesor ~* a soft teacher **2** (*carne*) tender
blanquear *vt* **1** (*gen*) to whiten **2** (*encalar*) to whitewash **3** (*dinero*) to launder
blasfemar *vi* to blaspheme (***against sth/sb***)
blasfemia *nf* blasphemy [*incontable*]: *decir ~s* to blaspheme
blindado, -a *pp, adj* **1** (*vehículo*) armoured: *un coche ~* an armoured car **2** (*puerta*) reinforced
bloc *nm* writing pad
bloque *nm* **1** (*gen*) block: *un ~ de mármol* a marble block ◊ *un ~ de viviendas* a block of flats ☛ *Ver* pág 321. **2** (*Pol*) bloc
bloquear ◆ *vt* **1** (*obstruir*) to block: *~ el paso/una carretera* to block access/a road ◊ *~ a un jugador* to block a player **2** (*Mil*) to blockade ◆ **bloquearse** *v pron* (*persona*) to freeze
bloqueo *nm* **1** (*Dep*) block **2** (*Mil*) blockade
blusa *nf* blouse
bobada *nf* nonsense [*incontable*]: *decir ~s* to talk a lot of nonsense ◊ *Deja de hacer ~s.* Stop being silly.
bobina *nf* **1** (*hilo*) reel **2** (*Electrón, alambre*) coil
bobo, -a *adj, nm-nf* **1** (*tonto*) silly [*adj*] **2** (*ingenuo*) naive [*adj*]: *Eres un ~.* You're so naive.
boca *nf* **1** (*Anat*) mouth: *No hables con la ~ llena.* Don't talk with your mouth full. **2** (*entrada*) entrance: *la ~ del metro* the entrance to the underground LOC **boca abajo/arriba** (*tumbado*) face down/up **boca de incendio/riego** hydrant **el boca a boca** mouth-to-mouth resuscitation: *Le hicieron el ~ a ~.* They gave him mouth-to-mouth resuscitation. **quedarse con la boca abierta** (*por sorpresa*) to be dumbfounded *Ver tb* ABRIR, CALLAR, PALABRA
bocacalle *nf* side street: *Está en una ~ de la calle Santiago.* It's in a side street off Santiago Street.
bocadillo *nm* **1** (*emparedado*) roll: *un ~ de queso* a cheese roll **2** (*en un cómic*) speech bubble
bocado *nm* bite: *Se lo comieron de un ~.* They ate it all in one bite.
bocazas *nmf* big mouth: *¡Qué ~ eres!* You and your big mouth!
boceto *nm* **1** (*Arte*) sketch **2** (*idea general*) outline
bochorno *nm* **1** (*calor*): *Hace ~.* It's sultry. ◊ *un día de ~* a stiflingly hot day **2** (*corte*) embarrassment: *¡Qué ~!* How embarrassing!
bocina *nf* horn: *tocar la ~* to sound your horn
boda *nf* wedding: *aniversario de ~(s)* wedding anniversary ◊ *Mañana vamos de ~.* We're going to a wedding tomorrow.

Wedding se refiere a la ceremonia, **marriage** suele referirse al matrimonio como institución. En Gran Bretaña las bodas se pueden celebrar en una *iglesia* (a **church wedding**) o en un *juzgado* (a **registry office wedding**). La novia (**bride**) suele llevar *damas de honor* (**bridesmaids**). El *novio* (**groom**) no lleva *madrina*, sino que va acompañado del **best man** (normalmente su mejor amigo). Tampoco se habla del *padrino*, aunque la novia normalmente entra con su padre. Después de la ceremonia se da un *banquete* (a **reception**).

LOC **bodas de oro/plata** golden/silver wedding [*sing*]
bodega *nf* **1** (*para vino*) wine cellar **2** (*barco, avión*) hold: *en las ~s del barco* in the ship's hold
bodegón *nm* (*Arte*) still life [*pl* still lifes]
bofetada *nf* (*tb* **bofetón** *nm*) slap (in the face): *Me dio una ~.* She slapped me (in the face).
boicot *nm* boycott

boicotear *vt* to boycott

boina *nf* beret

bol *nm* bowl

bola *nf* **1** (*gen*) ball: *una ~ de cristal* a crystal ball **2** (*mentira*) lie: *Me metió una ~ tremenda.* He told me one heck of a lie. LOC **bola del mundo** globe **bola de nieve** snowball **bolas de alcanfor** mothballs **estar en bolas** to be starkers

bolera *nf* bowling alley [*pl* bowling alleys]

boletín *nm* bulletin: *~ informativo* news bulletin

boleto *nm* **1** (*lotería, rifa*) ticket **2** (*quiniela*) coupon

boli *nm* Biro® [*pl* Biros]

bolígrafo *nm* ballpoint pen

bollo *nm* **1** (*dulce*) bun **2** (*de pan*) roll ☛ *Ver dibujo en* PAN **3** (*abolladura*) dent: *Le he hecho un ~ al coche.* I dented the car. **4** (*chichón*) bump: *Me salió un ~.* I had a bump on my head.

bolo *nm* skittle: *jugar a los ~s* to play skittles

bolsa[1] *nf* **1** (*gen*) bag: *una ~ de deportes* a sports bag ◊ *una ~ de plástico* a plastic bag ◊ *una ~ de caramelos* a bag of sweets **2** (*patatas fritas*) packet ☛ *Ver dibujo en* CONTAINER **3** (*concentración*) pocket: *una ~ de aire* an air pocket LOC **bolsa de agua caliente** hot-water bottle **bolsa de trabajo** job vacancies **¡la bolsa o la vida!** your money or your life!

bolsa[2] *nf* stock exchange: *la ~ londinense* the London Stock Exchange

bolsillo *nm* pocket: *Está en el ~ de mi abrigo.* It's in my coat pocket. LOC **de bolsillo** pocket(-sized): *guía de ~* pocket guide *Ver tb* LIBRO

bolso *nm* handbag LOC **bolso de viaje** travel bag

bomba[1] *nf* **1** (*Mil*) bomb: *~ atómica* atomic bomb ◊ *colocar una ~* to plant a bomb **2** (*noticia*) bombshell LOC **bomba fétida** stink bomb **pasarlo bomba** to have a great time **carta/coche/paquete bomba** letter/car/parcel bomb

bomba[2] *nf* (*Tec*) pump LOC **bomba de aire** air pump

bombardear *vt* to bombard: *Me bombardearon a preguntas.* They bombarded me with questions.

bombero *nmf* fireman/woman [*pl* firemen/women] LOC **los bomberos** the fire brigade [*sing*] *Ver tb* COCHE, CUERPO, IDEA, PARQUE

bombilla *nf* light bulb

bombo *nm* **1** (*Mús*) bass drum **2** (*lotería*) lottery drum LOC **a bombo y platillo** with a great song and dance: *Lo anunciaron a ~ y platillo.* They made a great song and dance about it. **dar bombo** to make a fuss (*about sth/sb*)

bombón *nm* chocolate: *una caja de bombones* a box of chocolates

bombona *nf* cylinder: *~ de butano/oxígeno* gas/oxygen cylinder

bonachón, -ona *adj* good-natured

bondad *nf* goodness LOC **tener la bondad de** to be so good as *to do sth*: *¿Tiene la ~ de ayudarme?* Would you be so good as to help me?

bondadoso, -a *adj* ~ (**con**) kind (**to** ***sth/sb***)

bonito *nm* (*pez*) tuna [*pl* tuna]

bonito, -a *adj* nice: *una casa/voz bonita* a nice house/voice ◊ *¡Qué ~!* That's very nice!

bono *nm* **1** (*vale*) voucher **2** (*transporte*) season ticket

bono-bus (*tb* **bonobús**) *nm* ten journey bus ticket

boquerón *nm* anchovy [*pl* anchovies]

boquiabierto, -a *adj* (*sorprendido*) speechless

boquilla *nf* (*Mús*) mouthpiece LOC **decir algo de boquilla** to say sth without meaning it

borda *nf* side of the ship: *asomarse por la ~* to lean over the side of the ship LOC **echar/tirar por la borda** (*fig*) to throw *sth* away: *echar por la ~ una ocasión de oro* to throw away a golden opportunity

bordado, -a ◆ *pp, adj* **1** (*Costura*) embroidered: *~ a mano* hand-embroidered **2** (*perfecto*) brilliant: *He hecho un examen ~.* I did a brilliant exam. ◆ *nm* embroidery [*incontable*]: *un vestido con ~s en las mangas* a dress with embroidery on the sleeves *Ver tb* BORDAR

bordar *vt* **1** (*Costura*) to embroider **2** (*hacer perfectamente*) to do *sth* brilliantly

borde[1] *nm* **1** (*gen*) edge: *al ~ de la mesa* on the edge of the table **2** (*objeto circular*) rim: *el ~ del vaso* the rim of the glass LOC **al borde de** (*fig*) on the verge of *sth*: *al ~ de las lágrimas* on the verge of tears

borde[2] *adj* (*antipático*) stroppy

bordillo *nm* kerb

bordo *nm* LOC **a bordo** on board: *subir a ~ del avión* to get on board the plane

borrachera *nf*: *agarrar/coger una ~ (de whisky)* to get drunk (on whisky)

borracho, -a ◆ *adj* drunk ◆ *nm-nf* drunk, drunkard (*más formal*) LOC **(borracho) como una cuba** as drunk as a lord

borrador *nm* **1** (*texto provisional*) draft **2** (*pizarra*) board duster

borrar ◆ *vt* **1** (*con goma*) to rub *sth* out: *~ una palabra* to rub out a word **2** (*pizarra*) to clean **3** (*Informát*) to delete ◆ **borrarse** *v pron* **borrarse (de)** to withdraw **(from *sth*)**

borrasca *nf* storm

borrascoso, -a *adj* stormy

borrico, -a *nm-nf* ass: *¡No seas ~!* Don't be such an ass!

borrón *nm* ~ **(en)** smudge **(on *sth*)**: *hacer borrones* to make smudges

borroso, -a *adj* **1** (*impreciso*) blurred: *Sin gafas lo veo todo ~.* Everything is blurred without my glasses. **2** (*escritura*) illegible

bosque *nm* wood ☛ *Ver nota en* FOREST

bostezar *vi* to yawn

bostezo *nm* yawn

bota[1] *nf* boot: *~s de fútbol* football boots LOC **ponerse las botas** (*comer mucho*) to stuff yourself *Ver tb* COLGAR, GATO

bota[2] *nf* (*vino*) wineskin

botánica *nf* botany

botar ◆ *vt* **1** (*pelota*) to bounce **2** (*buque*) to launch **3** (*expulsar*) to throw *sb* out **(of *sth*)** ◆ *vi* to bounce: *Esta pelota bota mucho.* This ball is very bouncy. LOC **botar de alegría** to jump for joy **estar que bota** to be hopping mad

bote[1] *nm* boat LOC **bote salvavidas** lifeboat

bote[2] *nm* **1** (*gen*) tin **2** (*cerveza*) can ☛ *Ver dibujo en* CONTAINER LOC **estar de bote en bote** to be packed *Ver tb* CHUPAR

bote[3] *nm* (*pelota*) bounce LOC **dar/pegar botes** to bounce

botella *nf* bottle LOC **de/en botella** bottled: *Compramos la leche en ~.* We buy bottled milk. *Ver tb* BEBER, VERDE

botín[1] *nm* (*bota*) ankle boot

botín[2] *nm* (*dinero*) loot

botiquín *nm* **1** (*maletín*) first-aid kit **2** (*armario*) medicine chest **3** (*habitación*) sickroom

botón *nm* **1** (*ropa*) button: *Se te ha desabrochado un ~.* One of your buttons is undone. **2** (*control*) knob: *El ~ rojo es el del volumen.* The red knob is the volume control. **3 botones** (*en un hotel*) bellboy

bóveda *nf* vault

boxeador *nm* boxer

boxear *vi* to box

boxeo *nm* boxing LOC *Ver* COMBATE

bozal *nm* muzzle

braga *nf* **bragas** knickers

> Nótese que *unas bragas* se dice **a pair of knickers**: *Tienes unas bragas limpias en el cajón.* You've got a clean pair of knickers in the drawer.

bragueta *nf* flies [*pl*]: *Llevas la ~ bajada.* Your flies are undone.

brasa *nf* ember LOC **a la brasa** grilled: *chuletas a la ~* grilled chops

brasero *nm* electric heater

Brasil *nm* Brazil

brasileño, -a *adj, nm-nf* Brazilian

bravo, -a ◆ *adj* (*animal*) fierce ◆ **¡bravo!** *interj* bravo!

braza *nf* **1** (*Náut*) fathom **2** (*Natación*) breast-stroke LOC *Ver* NADAR

brazada *nf* (*Natación, remos*) stroke

brazalete *nm* armband

brazo *nm* **1** (*gen*) arm: *Me he roto el ~.* I've broken my arm. **2** (*lámpara*) bracket **3** (*río*) branch LOC **brazo de gitano** Swiss roll **del brazo** arm in arm **ponerse con los brazos en cruz** to stretch your arms out to the side **quedarse de brazos cruzados**: *No te quedes ahí de ~s cruzados y haz algo.* Don't just stand there! Do something. *Ver tb* COGIDO, CRUZAR

brea *nf* tar

brecha *nf* (*herida*) gash: *Me caí y me hice una ~ en la frente.* I fell and gashed my forehead.

breva *nf* LOC *Ver* HIGO

breve *adj* short: *una estancia ~* a short stay LOC **en breve** shortly **en breves palabras** in a few words **ser breve** (*hablando*) to be brief

bricolaje *nm* do-it-yourself (*abrev* DIY)

brigada ◆ *nf* **1** (*Mil*) brigade **2** (*policía*) squad: *la ~ antidisturbios/antidroga* the riot/drug squad ◆ *nmf* sergeant major

brillante ◆ *adj* **1** (*luz, color*) bright **2** (*superficie*) shiny **3** (*fenomenal*) brilliant ◆ *nm* diamond

brillar *vi* to shine: *Sus ojos brillaban de*

alegría. Their eyes shone with joy. ◊ *¡Cómo brilla!* Look how shiny it is!

brillo *nm* gleam LOC **sacar brillo** to make *sth* shine

brincar *vi* to jump

brinco *nm* jump LOC **dar/pegar un brinco/brincos** to jump: *dar ~s de alegría* to jump for joy

brindar ◆ *vi* ~ (**a/por**) to drink a toast (**to** ***sth/sb***): *Brindemos por su felicidad.* Let's drink (a toast) to their happiness. ◆ *vt* **1** (*dedicar*) to dedicate *sth* **to** ***sb*** **2** (*proporcionar*) to provide: ~ *ayuda* to provide help ◆ **brindarse** *v pron* **brindarse a** to offer ***to do sth***

brindis *nm* toast LOC **hacer un brindis** to drink a toast (*to sth/sb*)

brisa *nf* breeze

británico, -a ◆ *adj* British ◆ *nm-nf* Briton: *los ~s* the British LOC *Ver* ISLA

brocha *nf* brush ☛ *Ver dibujo en* BRUSH LOC **brocha de afeitar** shaving brush

broche *nm* **1** (*Costura*) fastener **2** (*joya*) brooch

broma *nf* joke: *Le gastaron muchas ~s.* They played a lot of jokes on him. LOC **broma pesada** practical joke **de/en broma** jokingly: *Lo digo en ~.* I'm only joking. **¡ni en broma(s)!** no way! *Ver tb* FUERA, GASTAR

bromear *vi* to joke

bromista *adj, nmf* joker [*n*]: *Es muy ~.* He's a real joker.

bronca *nf* **1** (*pelea*) row **2** (*reprimenda*) telling-off [*pl* tellings-off]: *Me han vuelto a echar la ~.* I've been told off again. LOC **armar/montar una bronca** to kick up a fuss

bronce *nm* bronze

bronceado *nm* (sun)tan

bronceador *nm* suntan lotion

broncearse *v pron* to get a suntan

bronquitis *nf* bronchitis [*incontable*]

brotar *vi* **1** (*plantas*) to sprout **2** (*flores*) to bud **3** (*líquido*) to gush (out) (***from sth***)

brote *nm* **1** (*gen*) shoot **2** (*flor*) bud **3** (*epidemia, violencia*) outbreak: *un ~ de cólera* an outbreak of cholera

bruces LOC **caerse de bruces** to fall flat on your face

bruja *nf* witch

brujería *nf* witchcraft

brujo *nm* **1** (*hechicero*) wizard **2** (*en tribus primitivas*) witch doctor

brújula *nf* compass

bruma *nf* mist

brusco, -a *adj* **1** (*repentino*) sudden **2** (*persona*) abrupt

brutal *adj* (*violento*) brutal

bruto, -a ◆ *adj* **1** (*necio*) thick: *¡No seas ~!* Don't be so thick! **2** (*grosero*) crude **3** (*peso, ingresos*) gross ◆ *nm-nf* **1** (*necio*) idiot **2** (*grosero*) slob

buceador, ~a *nm-nf* diver

bucear *vi* to dive

buceo *nm* diving: *practicar el ~* to go diving

budismo *nm* Buddhism

budista *adj, nmf* Buddhist

buen *adj Ver* BUENO

buenaventura *nf* LOC **decir/echar la buenaventura** to tell *sb's* fortune

bueno, -a ◆ *adj* **1** (*gen*) good: *Es una buena noticia.* That's good news. ◊ *Es ~ hacer ejercicio.* It is good to take exercise. **2** (*amable*) kind: *Fueron muy ~s conmigo.* They were very nice to me. **3** (*comida*) tasty **4** (*correcto*) right: *No andas por buen camino.* You're on the wrong road. **5** (*menudo*): *¡Buena la has hecho!* You've really messed it up this time! ◊ *¡Buena se va a poner tu madre!* Your mother'll get in a right old state! ◆ *nm-nf* goody [*pl* goodies]: *Ganó el ~.* The good guy won. ◊ *Lucharon los ~s contra los malos.* There was a fight between the goodies and the baddies. ◆ *adv*: *—¿Quieres ir al cine? —Bueno.* 'Would you like to go to the cinema?' 'OK.' ◊ *~, yo pienso que*... Well, I think that... LOC **el bueno de...** good old...: *el ~ de Enrique* good old Enrique **¡(muy) buenas!** good day! **por las buenas**: *Es mejor que lo hagas por las buenas.* It would be better if you did it willingly. ◊ *Te lo pido por las buenas.* I'm asking you nicely. **por las buenas o por las malas** whether you like it or not, whether he/she likes it or not, etc ☛ Para otras expresiones con **bueno**, véanse las entradas del sustantivo, p.ej. **¡buen provecho!** en PROVECHO y **hacer buenas migas** en MIGA.

buey *nm* ox [*pl* oxen] LOC *Ver* OJO

búfalo *nm* buffalo [*pl* buffalo/buffaloes]

bufanda *nf* scarf [*pl* scarves]

bufé (*tb* **bufet**) *nm* buffet

bufete *nm* (*abogado*) legal practice

buhardilla *nf* **1** (*ático*) loft **2** (*ventana*) dormer window

búho *nm* owl

buitre *nm* vulture

bujía *nf* (*Mec*) spark plug

buldog *nm* bulldog

bulla *nf* racket: *armar/meter* ~ to make a racket

bullicio *nm* **1** (*ruido*) racket **2** (*actividad*) hustle and bustle: *el ~ de la capital* the hustle and bustle of the capital

bulto *nm* **1** (*Med*) lump: *Me ha salido un ~ en la mano.* I've got a lump on my hand. **2** (*maleta*) luggage [*incontable*]: *sólo un ~ de mano* just one piece of hand luggage ◊ *Llevas demasiados ~s.* You've got too much luggage. **3** (*objeto indeterminado*) shape: *Me pareció ver un ~ que se movía.* I thought I saw a shape moving. LOC **a bulto** roughly: *A ~, calculo 500 personas.* I think there are roughly 500 people.

buque *nm* ship LOC **buque de guerra** warship

burbuja *nf* bubble: *un baño de ~s* a bubble bath LOC **con/sin burbujas** fizzy/still **hacer burbujas** to bubble **tener burbujas** (*bebida*) to be fizzy: *Tiene muchas ~s.* It's very fizzy.

burgués, -esa *adj* middle-class

burguesía *nf* middle class

burla *nf* **1** (*mofa*) mockery [*incontable*]: *un tono de ~* a mocking tone **2** (*broma*) joke: *Déjate de ~s.* Stop joking. LOC **hacer burla** to make fun *of sth/sb*: *No me hagas ~.* Don't make fun of me.

burlar ◆ *vt* (*eludir*) to evade: *~ la justicia* to evade justice ◆ **burlarse** *v pron* **burlarse (de)** to make fun **of *sth/sb***

burlón, -ona *adj* (*gesto, sonrisa*) mocking

burocracia *nf* (*excesivo papeleo*) red tape

burrada *nf* **1** (*tontería*): *Eso ha sido una verdadera ~.* That was a really stupid thing to do. ◊ *decir ~s* to talk nonsense **2** (*cantidad*) loads (**of *sth***): *Había una ~ de comida.* There was loads of food.

burro, -a ◆ *adj* **1** (*estúpido*) thick **2** (*cabezota*) pigheaded ◆ *nm-nf* **1** (*animal*) donkey [*pl* donkeys] **2** (*persona*) idiot: *el ~ de mi cuñado* my idiotic brother-in-law LOC **burro de carga** (*persona*) dogsbody [*pl* dogsbodies] *Ver tb* TRES

busca ◆ *nf* ~ (**de**) search (**for *sth/sb***): *Abandonaron la ~ del cadáver.* They abandoned the search for the body. ◆ *nm* bleeper LOC **en busca de** in search of *sth/sb*

buscador, ~a *nm-nf* LOC **buscador de oro** gold prospector **buscador de tesoros** treasure hunter

buscar ◆ *vt* **1** (*gen*) to look for *sth/sb*: *Busco trabajo.* I'm looking for work. **2** (*sistemáticamente*) to search **for *sth/sb***: *Usan perros para ~ droga.* They use dogs to search for drugs. **3** (*en un libro, en una lista*) to look *sth* up: *~ una palabra en el diccionario* to look a word up in the dictionary **4** (*recoger a algn*) **(a)** (*en coche*) to pick *sb* up: *Fuimos a ~le a la estación.* We picked him up at the station. **(b)** (*andando*) to meet **5** (*conseguir y traer*) to get: *Fui a ~ al médico.* I went to get the doctor. ◆ *vi* ~ (**en/por**) to look (**in/through *sth***): *Busqué en el archivo.* I looked in the file. LOC **buscar una aguja en un pajar** to look for a needle in a haystack **se busca** wanted: *Se busca apartamento.* Flat wanted. **te la estás buscando** you're asking for it

búsqueda *nf* ~ (**de**) search (**for *sth***): *la ~ de una solución pacífica* the search for a peaceful solution LOC **a la búsqueda de** in search of *sth*

busto *nm* bust

butaca *nf* **1** (*sillón*) armchair **2** (*Cine, Teat*) seat LOC *Ver* PATIO

butano *nm* gas, butane (*téc*): *Me he quedado sin ~.* I've run out of gas.

buzo *nm* diver

buzón *nm* **1** (*en la calle*) postbox **2** (*en una casa*) letter box LOC **echar al buzón** to post

byte *nm* (*Informát*) byte

Cc

cabal *adj* (*persona*) upright LOC **(no) estar en sus cabales** (not) to be in your right mind

cabalgar *vi* ~ **(en)** to ride **(on *sth*)**: *~ en mula es muy divertido.* Riding (on) a mule is great fun.

cabalgata *nf* procession: *la ~ de los Reyes Magos* the Twelfth Night procession

caballar *adj* LOC *Ver* GANADO

caballería *nf* **1** (*animal*) mount **2** (*Mil*) cavalry [*v sing o pl*] **3** (*caballeros andantes*) chivalry

caballeriza *nf* stable

caballero *nm* **1** (*gen*) gentleman [*pl* gentlemen]: *Mi abuelo era todo un ~.* My grandfather was a real gentleman. **2** (*Hist*) knight LOC **de caballero(s)**: *sección de ~s* menswear department

caballete *nm* **1** (*Arte*) easel **2** (*soporte*) trestle

caballitos *nm* merry-go-round [*sing*]

caballo *nm* **1** (*animal, Gimnasia*) horse **2** (*Ajedrez*) knight **3** (*Mec*) horsepower (*abrev* hp): *un motor de doce ~s* a twelve horsepower engine LOC **a caballo entre ...** halfway between ... **caballo de carrera(s)** racehorse **caballo de mar** sea horse *Ver tb* CARRERA, COLA[1], MONTAR, POTENCIA

cabaña *nf* (*choza*) hut

cabecear *vi* **1** (*afirmar, de sueño*) to nod **2** (*caballo*) to toss its head **3** (*Dep*): *~ a la red* to head the ball into the net

cabecera *nf* **1** (*gen*) head: *sentarse en la ~ de la mesa* to sit at the head of the table **2** (*periódico*) headline **3** (*página, documento*) heading LOC *Ver* MÉDICO

cabecero *nm* headboard

cabecilla *nmf* ringleader

cabello *nm* hair

caber *vi* **1** ~ **(en)** to fit **(in/into *sth*)**: *Mi ropa no cabe en la maleta.* My clothes won't fit in the suitcase. ◊ *¿Quepo?* Is there room for me? **2** ~ **por** to go **through *sth***: *El piano no cabía por la puerta.* The piano wouldn't go through the door. **3** (*ropa*) to fit: *Ya no me cabe este pantalón.* These trousers don't fit me any more. LOC **no cabe duda** there is no doubt **no caber en sí de contento/alegría** to be beside yourself with joy *Ver tb* DENTRO

cabestrillo *nm* sling: *con el brazo en ~* with your arm in a sling

cabeza *nf* **1** (*gen*) head: *tener buena/mala ~ para las matemáticas* to have a good head/to have no head for maths **2** (*lista, liga*) top: *en la ~ de la lista* at the top of the list **3** (*juicio*) sense: *¡Qué poca ~ tienes!* You've got no sense! LOC **cabeza abajo** upside down ☛ *Ver dibujo en* REVÉS **cabeza de ajo(s)** head of garlic **cabeza de familia** head of the household **de cabeza** headlong: *tirarse a la piscina de ~* to dive headlong into the swimming pool **estar mal/tocado de la cabeza** to be touched **ir en cabeza** to be in the lead **írsele la cabeza a algn** to feel dizzy **por cabeza** a/per head **ser un cabeza de chorlito** to be a scatterbrain **tener la cabeza a/llena de pájaros** to have your head in the clouds **tener la cabeza dura** to be stubborn *Ver tb* ABRIR, AFIRMAR, ASENTIR, DOLOR, ENTRAR, ESTRUJAR, LAVAR, METER, PERDER, PIE, SITUAR, SUBIR

cabezada *nf* LOC **dar cabezadas** (*dormirse*) to nod off **echar una cabezada** (*siesta*) to have/take forty winks

cabezazo *nm* **1** (*golpe*) butt **2** (*Dep*) header LOC **dar un cabezazo (al balón)** to head the ball

cabezota *adj, nmf* LOC **ser (un) cabezota** (*ser terco*) to be pig-headed

cabezudo *nm* LOC *Ver* GIGANTE

cabina *nf* **1** (*avión*) cockpit **2** (*barco*) cabin **3** (*camión*) cab LOC **cabina electoral** polling booth **cabina (telefónica/de teléfonos)** telephone box

cabizbajo, -a *adj* downcast

cable *nm* cable LOC **echar un cable** to lend *sb* a hand

cabo ◆ *nm* **1** (*extremo*) end **2** (*Náut*) rope **3** (*Geog*) cape: *el ~ de Buena Esperanza* the Cape of Good Hope ◆ *nmf* (*Mil*) corporal: *el ~ Ramos* Corporal Ramos LOC **al cabo de** after: *al ~ de un año* after a year **de cabo a rabo** from beginning to end **llevar a cabo** to carry *sth* out *Ver tb* FIN

cabra *nf* goat [*fem* nanny-goat] LOC **estar como una cabra** to be off your rocker

cabreado, -a *pp, adj* LOC **estar cabreado** to be in a bad mood *Ver tb* CABREAR

cabrear ◆ *vt* to annoy: *Lo que más mecabrea es que...* What annoys me most of all is that... ◆ **cabrearse** *v pron* **cabrearse (con) (por)** to get annoyed (**with** *sb*) (**about** *sth*)

cabreo *nm* LOC **agarrar(se)/coger(se) un cabreo** to go mad

cabrito *nm* (*animal*) kid

caca *nf* poo LOC **hacer caca** to do a poo (*coloq*)

cacahuete (*tb* **cacahué**) *nm* peanut

cacao[1] *nm* **1** (*planta*) cacao [*pl* cacaos] **2** (*en polvo*) cocoa **3** (*labios*) lipsalve

cacao[2] *nm* (*lío*) uproar LOC **tener un cacao mental** to be confused

cacarear *vi* **1** (*gallo*) to crow **2** (*gallina*) to cackle

cacería *nf* **1** (*gen*) hunt: *una ~ de elefantes* an elephant hunt **2** (*caza menor*) shoot LOC **ir de cacería 1** (*gen*) to go hunting **2** (*caza menor*) to go shooting

cacerola *nf* casserole ☛ *Ver dibujo en* SAUCEPAN

cacha *nf* thigh LOC **estar cachas 1** (*hombre*) to be a hunk **2** (*mujer*) to be muscly

cacharrazo *nm* **1** (*golpe*) bump **2** (*ruido*) racket LOC **darse un cacharrazo** (*conduciendo*) to have a prang

cacharro *nm* **1** (*vasija*) pot **2** (*vehículo*) old banger **3 cacharros** (*de cocina*) pots and pans: *No dejes los ~s sin fregar.* Don't forget to do the pots and pans.

cachear *vt* to frisk (*coloq*), to search: *Cachearon a todos los pasajeros.* All the passengers were searched.

cachete *nm* slap LOC **dar un cachete** to slap *sb*

cacho *nm* piece

cachondearse *v pron* to make fun of *sth/sb*

cachondeo *nm* joke: *No te lo tomes a ~.* Don't treat it as a joke. ◊ *Aquello era un ~, nadie se aclaraba.* It was a joke; no one knew what to do. LOC **estar de cachondeo** to be joking

cachondo, -a *adj* funny LOC **ser un cachondo mental** to be a real laugh

cachorro, -a *nm-nf* **1** (*perro*) puppy [*pl* puppies] **2** (*león, tigre*) cub

caco *nm* burglar ☛ *Ver nota en* THIEF

cactus (*tb* **cacto**) *nm* cactus [*pl* cacti/ cactuses]

cada *adj* **1** (*gen*) each: *Dieron un regalo a ~ niño.* They gave each child a present. ☛ *Ver nota en* EVERY **2** (*con expresiones de tiempo, con expresiones numéricas*) every: *~ semana/vez* every week/time ◊ *~ diez días* every ten days **3** (*con valor exclamativo*): *¡Dices ~ cosa!* The things you come out with! LOC **cada cosa a su tiempo** all in good time **cada cual** everyone **¿cada cuánto?** how often? **cada dos días, semanas, etc** every other day, week, etc **cada dos por tres** forever **cada loco con su tema** each to his own **cada uno** each (one): *~ uno valía 5.000 pesetas.* Each one cost 5000 pesetas. ◊ *Nos dieron una bolsa a ~ uno.* They gave each of us a bag./They gave us a bag each. **cada vez más** more and more: *~ vez hay más problemas.* There are more and more problems. ◊ *Estás ~ vez más guapa.* You're looking prettier and prettier. **cada vez mejor/peor** better and better/ worse and worse **cada vez menos**: *Tengo ~ vez menos dinero.* I've got less and less money. ◊ *~ vez hay menos alumnos.* There are fewer and fewer students. ◊ *Nos vemos ~ vez menos.* We see less and less of each other. **cada vez que...** whenever... **para cada...** between: *un libro para ~ dos/tres alumnos* one book between two/three students

cadáver *nm* corpse, body [*pl* bodies] (*más coloq*) LOC *Ver* DEPÓSITO

cadena *nf* **1** (*gen*) chain **2** (*Radio*) station **3** (*TV*) channel LOC **cadena perpetua** life imprisonment

cadera *nf* hip

cadete *nmf* cadet

caducar *vi* **1** (*documento, plazo*) to expire **2** (*alimento*) to go past its sell-by date **3** (*medicamento*) to be out of date: *¿Cuándo caduca?* When does it have to be used by?

caducidad *nf* LOC *Ver* FECHA

caduco, -a *adj* LOC *Ver* HOJA

caer ◆ *vi* **1** (*gen*) to fall: *La maceta cayó desde el balcón.* The plant pot fell off the balcony. ◊ *~ en la trampa* to fall into the trap ◊ *Mi cumpleaños cae en martes.* My birthday falls on a Tuesday. ◊ *Caía la noche.* Night was falling. **2** (*estar*) to be: *¿Por dónde cae su casa?* Where's their house? **3 ~ (en)** (*entender*) to get *sth* [*vt*]: *Ya caigo.* Now I get it. **4** (*persona*): *Le caíste muy bien a mi madre.* My mother really liked you. ◊ *Me cae fatal.* I can't stand him. ◊ *¿Qué tal te cayó su novia?* What did you think of his girlfriend? ◆ **caerse** *v pron* **1** (*gen*) to fall: *Cuidado, no te caigas.* Careful you don't fall. ◊ *Se me caen los pantalones.* My trousers are falling down. **2** (*diente, pelo*) to fall out: *Se le cae el pelo.* His hair is falling out. LOC **caérsele algo a algn** to drop sth: *Se me cayó el helado.* I dropped my ice cream. ☛Para otras expresiones con **caer**, véanse las entradas del sustantivo, adjetivo, etc, p. ej. **caer gordo** en GORDO y **caer como moscas** en MOSCA.

café *nm* **1** (*gen*) coffee: *¿Te apetece un ~?* Would you like some/a coffee? **2** (*establecimiento*) café ☛ *Ver* pág 320. LOC **café exprés** espresso [*pl* espressos] **café solo/con leche** black/white coffee **estar de mal café** to be in a bad mood **tener mal café** to be bad-tempered

cafeína *nf* caffeine: *sin ~* caffeine free

cafetal *nm* coffee plantation

cafetera *nf* coffee pot LOC **cafetera eléctrica** coffee-maker **cafetera exprés** espresso machine

cafetería *nf* snack bar ☛ *Ver* pág 320.

cafetero, -a *adj* **1** (*gen*) coffee [*n atrib*]: *la industria cafetera* the coffee industry **2** (*persona*): *ser muy ~* to be very fond of coffee

cafre *adj* (*bruto*) barbaric

cagalera *nf* the runs: *tener ~* to have the runs

cagarruta *nf* droppings [*pl*]: *~s de oveja* sheep droppings

cagueta *adj*, *nmf* chicken [*adj*]: *No seas ~.* Don't be chicken.

caída *nf* **1** (*gen*) fall: *una ~ de tres metros* a three-metre fall ◊ *la ~ del gobierno* the fall of the government **2** ~ **de** (*descenso*) fall **in** *sth*: *una ~ de los precios* a fall in prices **3** (*pelo*) loss: *prevenir la ~ del pelo* to prevent hair loss LOC **a la caída de la tarde/noche** at dusk/nightfall **caída libre** free fall

caído, -a ◆ *pp*, *adj* fallen: *un pino ~* a fallen pine ◆ *nm*: *los ~s en la guerra* those who died in the war LOC **caído del cielo 1** (*inesperado*) out of the blue **2** (*oportuno*): *Nos viene ~ del cielo.* It's a real godsend. *Ver tb* CAER

caimán *nm* alligator

caja *nf* **1** (*gen*) box: *una ~ de cartón* a cardboard box ◊ *una ~ de bombones* a box of chocolates ☛ *Ver dibujo en* CONTAINER **2** (*botellas*) **(a)** (*gen*) crate **(b)** (*vino*) case **3** (*ataúd*) coffin **4** (*supermercado*) checkout **5** (*otras tiendas*) cash desk **6** (*banco*) cashier's desk LOC **caja de ahorros** savings bank **caja de cambios/velocidades** gearbox **caja de herramientas** toolbox **caja fuerte** safe [*pl* safes] **caja negra** black box **caja registradora** till **hacer la caja** to cash up **la caja tonta** the box

cajero, -a *nm-nf* cashier LOC **cajero automático** cash machine

cajetilla *nf* packet: *una ~ de tabaco* a packet of cigarettes

cajón *nm* **1** (*mueble*) drawer **2** (*de madera*) crate

cal *nf* lime

cala *nf* cove

calabacín *nm* **1** (*grande*) marrow **2** (*pequeño*) courgette

calabaza *nf* pumpkin LOC **dar calabazas** to give *sb* the brush-off

calabozo *nm* **1** (*mazmorra*) dungeon **2** (*celda*) cell

calamar *nm* squid [*pl* squid]

calambre *nm* **1** (*muscular*) cramp [*incontable*]: *Me dan ~s en las piernas.* I get cramp in my legs. **2** (*electricidad*) (electric) shock: *¡Te va a dar ~!* You'll get a shock!

calamidad *nf* **1** (*desgracia*) misfortune: *pasar ~es* to suffer misfortune **2** (*persona*) useless [*adj*]: *Eres una ~.* You're useless.

calar ◆ *vt* (*mojar*) to soak: *La lluvia me caló hasta la camiseta.* The rain soaked through to my vest. ◊ *¡Me has calado la falda!* You've made my skirt soaking wet! ◆ **calarse** *v pron* **1** (*mojarse*) to get drenched **2** (*motor*) to stall: *Se me caló el coche.* I stalled the car. LOC **calarse hasta los huesos** to get soaked to the skin

calavera *nf* skull

calcar *vt* to trace

calcetín *nm* sock

calcinado, -a *pp*, *adj* charred *Ver tb* CALCINAR

calcinar *vt* to burn *sth* down: *El fuego calcinó la fábrica.* The fire burnt the factory down.

calcio *nm* calcium

calco *nm* **1** (*dibujo*) tracing: *papel de ~* tracing paper **2** (*imitación*) imitation

calculadora *nf* calculator

calcular *vt* **1** (*gen*) to work *sth* out, to calculate (*más formal*): *Calcula cuánto necesitamos.* Work out/calculate how much we need. **2** (*suponer*) to reckon: *Calculo que habrá 60 personas.* I reckon there must be around 60 people.

cálculo *nm* calculation: *Según mis ~s son 105.* It's 105 according to my calculations. ◊ *Tengo que hacer unos ~s antes de decidir.* I have to make some calculations before deciding. LOC **hacer un cálculo aproximado** to make a rough estimate

caldera *nf* boiler

calderilla *nf* small change

caldo *nm* **1** (*para cocinar*) stock: *~ de pollo* chicken stock **2** (*sopa*) broth [*incontable*]: *Para mí el ~ de verduras.* I'd like the vegetable broth.

calefacción *nf* heating: *~ central* central heating

calendario *nm* calendar

calentador *nm* heater: *~ de agua* water heater

calentamiento *nm* warm-up: *ejercicios de ~* warm-up exercises ◊ *Primero haremos un poco de ~.* We're going to warm up first.

calentar ◆ *vt* **1** (*gen*) to heat *sth* up: *Voy a ~te la cena.* I'll heat up your dinner. **2** (*templar*) to warm *sth/sb* up ◆ **calentarse** *v pron* **1** (*ponerse muy caliente*) to get very hot: *El motor se calentó demasiado.* The engine overheated. **2** (*templarse, Dep*) to warm up LOC *Ver* CASCO, SESO

calibre *nm* calibre: *una pistola del ~ 38* a 38 calibre gun ◊ *un imbécil de mucho ~* a complete idiot

calidad *nf* quality: *la ~ de vida en las ciudades* the quality of life in the cities ◊ *fruta de ~* quality fruit LOC **en calidad de** as: *en ~ de portavoz* as a spokesperson *Ver tb* RELACIÓN

cálido, -a *adj* warm

caliente *adj* **1** (*gen*) hot: *agua ~* hot water **2** (*templado*) warm: *La casa está ~.* The house is warm. ☛ *Ver nota en* FRÍO LOC *Ver* BOLSA[1], PERRITO

calificación *nf* **1** (*nota escolar*) mark: *buenas calificaciones* good marks ◊ *Obtuvo la ~ de notable.* He got a B. **2** (*descripción*) description: *Su comportamiento no merece otra ~.* His behaviour cannot be described in any other way.

calificar *vt* **1** (*corregir*) to mark **2** (*a un alumno*) to give *sb* a mark: *La calificaron con sobresaliente.* They gave her an A. **3** (*describir*) to label *sb* (**as sth**): *La calificaron de excéntrica.* They labelled her as eccentric.

caligrafía *nf* handwriting

callado, -a *pp, adj* **1** (*gen*) quiet: *Tu hermano está muy ~ hoy.* Your brother is very quiet today. **2** (*en completo silencio*) silent: *Permaneció ~.* He remained silent. LOC **más callado que un muerto** as quiet as a mouse *Ver tb* CALLAR

callar ◆ *vt* **1** (*persona*) to get *sb* to be quiet: *¡Calla a esos niños!* Get those children to be quiet! **2** (*información*) to keep quiet about *sth* ◆ **callar(se)** *vi, v pron* **1** (*no hablar*) to say nothing: *Prefiero ~(me).* I'd rather say nothing. **2** (*dejar de hablar o hacer ruido*) to go quiet, to shut up (*coloq*): *Dáselo, a ver si (se) calla.* Give it to him and see if he shuts up. LOC **¡calla!/¡cállate (la boca)!** be quiet!, shut up! (*coloq*)

calle *nf* **1** (*gen*) street (*abrev* St): *una ~ peatonal* a pedestrian street ◊ *Está en la ~ Goya.* It's in Goya Street.

> Cuando se menciona el número de la casa o portal se usa la preposición **at**: *Vivimos en la calle Goya 49.* We live at 49 Goya Street. ☛ *Ver nota en* STREET

2 (*Dep*) lane: *el corredor de la ~ dos* the athlete in lane two LOC **calle arriba/abajo** up/down the street **quedarse en la calle** (*sin trabajo*) to lose your job

callejero, -a *adj* LOC *Ver* PERRO

callejón *nm* alleyway [*pl* alleyways] LOC **callejón sin salida** cul-de-sac [*pl* cul-de-sacs]

callejuela (*tb* **calleja**) *nf* side street

callo *nm* **1** (*dedo del pie*) corn **2** (*mano, planta del pie*) callus [*pl* calluses] **3 callos** (*Cocina*) tripe [*incontable, v sing*]

calma *nf* calm: *mantener la ~* to keep calm LOC **¡(con) calma!** calm down! **tomarse algo con calma** to take sth easy: *Tómatelo con ~.* Take it easy. *Ver tb* PERDER

calmante *nm* **1** (*dolor*) painkiller **2** (*nervios*) tranquillizer

calmar ◆ *vt* **1** (*nervios*) to calm **2** (*dolor*) to relieve **3** (*hambre, sed*) to satisfy ◆ **calmarse** *v pron* to calm down

calor *nm* heat: *Hoy aprieta el ~.* It's stiflingly hot today. LOC **hacer calor** to be hot: *Hace mucho ~.* It's very hot. ◊ *¡Qué ~ hace!* It's so hot! **tener calor** to be/feel hot: *Tengo ~.* I'm hot. ☛ *Ver nota en* FRÍO; *Ver tb* ENTRAR

caloría *nf* calorie: *una dieta baja en ~s* a low-calorie diet ◊ *quemar ~s* to burn off calories

caluroso, -a *adj* **1** (*muy caliente*) hot: *Fue un día muy ~.* It was a very hot day. **2** (*tibio, fig*) warm: *una noche/ bienvenida calurosa* a warm night/ welcome

calva *nf* bald patch

calvo, -a *adj* bald: *quedarse ~* to go bald

calzada *nf* road

calzado *nm* footwear: *~ de piel* leather footwear

calzar ◆ *vt* **1** (*zapato*) to wear: *Calzo zapato plano.* I wear flat shoes. **2** (*número*) to take: *¿Qué número calzas?* What size do you take? **3** (*persona*) to put *sb's* shoes on: *¿Puedes ~ al niño?* Can you put the little boy's shoes on for him? ◆ **calzarse** *v pron* to put your shoes on LOC *Ver* VESTIR

calzoncillo *nm* **calzoncillos** underpants [*pl*] ☛Nótese que *unos calzoncillos* se dice **a pair of underpants**.

cama *nf* bed: *irse a la ~* to go to bed ◊ *¿Todavía estás en la ~?* Are you still in bed? ◊ *meterse en la ~* to get into bed ◊ *salir de la ~* to get out of bed LOC **cama individual/de matrimonio** single/ double bed *Ver tb* COCHE, SOFÁ

camada *nf* litter

camaleón *nm* chameleon

cámara ◆ *nf* **1** (*gen*) chamber: *la ~ legislativa* the legislative chamber ◊ *música de ~* chamber music **2** (*Cine, Fot*) camera ◆ *nmf* cameraman/woman [*pl* cameramen/women] LOC **a/en cámara lenta** in slow motion **cámara de fotos/fotográfica** camera

camarada *nmf* **1** (*Pol*) comrade **2** (*colega*) mate

camarero, -a *nm-nf* waiter [*fem* waitress]

camarote *nm* cabin

cambiante *adj* changing

cambiar ◆ *vt* **1** (*gen*) to change *sth* (**for** *sth*): *Voy a ~ mi coche por uno más grande.* I'm going to change my car for a bigger one. **2** (*dinero*) to change *sth* (**into** *sth*): *~ pesetas a/en libras* to change pesetas into pounds **3** (*intercambiar*) to exchange *sth* (**for** *sth*): *Si no te está bien lo puedes ~.* You can exchange it if it doesn't fit you. ◆ *vi* ~ (**de**) to change: *~ de trabajo/tren* to change jobs/trains ◊ *No van a ~.* They're not going to change. ◊ *~ de marcha* to change gear ◊ *~ de tema* to change the subject ◆ **cambiarse** *v pron* **1 cambiarse (de)** to change: *~se de zapatos* to change your shoes **2** (*persona*) to get changed: *Voy a ~me porque tengo que salir.* I'm going to get changed because I have to go out. LOC **cambiar de opinión** to change your mind **cambiar(se) de casa** to move house

cambio *nm* **1** ~ (**de**) (*gen*) change (**in/of** *sth*): *un ~ de temperatura* a change in temperature ◊ *Ha habido un ~ de planes.* There has been a change of plan. **2** (*intercambio*) exchange: *un ~ de impresiones* an exchange of views **3** (*dinero suelto*) change: *Me dieron mal el ~.* They gave me the wrong change. ◊ *¿Tiene ~ de 1.000 pesetas?* Have you got change for 1000 pesetas? **4** (*Fin*) exchange rate LOC **a cambio (de/de que)** in return (for *sth/doing sth*): *No recibieron nada a ~.* They got nothing in return. ◊ *a ~ de que me ayudes con las matemáticas* in return for you helping me with my maths **cambio de guardia** changing of the Guard **cambio de sentido** U-turn **en cambio** on the other hand *Ver tb* CAJA, PALANCA

camelar(se) *vt, v pron* **1** (*convencer*) to talk *sb* ***into doing sth***: *Me camelaré a tu padre para que te deje salir.* I'll talk your father into letting you go out. **2** (*halagar*) to butter *sb* up

camello, -a *nm-nf* **1** (*animal*) camel **2** (*traficante*) pusher

camelo *nm* **1** (*engaño*) con: *¡Vaya un ~!* What a con! **2** (*bulo*) cock and bull story: *Lo de su enfermedad es un ~.* His illness is a cock and bull story.

camerino *nm* dressing-room

camilla *nf* **1** (*Med*) stretcher **2** (*mesa*) (occasional) table

caminar ◆ *vi* to walk ◆ *vt* to cover: *Hemos caminado 150km.* We've covered 150km. LOC **ir caminando** to go on foot

caminata *nf* trek LOC **darse/pegarse una caminata** to do a lot of walking

camino *nm* **1** (*carretera no asfaltada*) track **2** (*ruta, medio*) way: *No me acuerdo del ~.* I can't remember the way. ◊ *Me la encontré en el ~.* I met her on the way. **3** ~ (**a/de**) (*senda*) path (**to** *sth*): *el ~ a la fama* the path to fame LOC **camino vecinal** minor road **coger/pillar de camino** to be on my, your, etc way **(estar/ir) camino de...** (to be) on the/your way to... **ir por buen/mal camino** to be on the right/wrong track **ponerse en camino** to set off *Ver tb* ABRIR, INGENIERO, MEDIO

camión *nm* lorry [*pl* lorries] LOC

camión cisterna tanker **camión de la basura** dustcart **camión de mudanzas** removal van

camionero, -a *nm-nf* lorry driver

camioneta *nf* van

camisa *nf* shirt LOC **camisa de fuerza** straitjacket

camiseta *nf* **1** (*gen*) T-shirt **2** (*Dep*) shirt: *la ~ número 11* the number 11 shirt **3** (*ropa interior*) vest

camisón *nm* nightdress, nightie (*coloq*)

camorra *nf* **1** (*jaleo*) shindy: *armar/ montar ~* to kick up a shindy **2** (*pelea*) fight: *buscar ~* to be looking for a fight

camorrista *nmf* troublemaker

campamento *nm* camp: *ir de ~* to go to a camp

campana *nf* **1** (*gen*) bell: *¿Oyes las ~s?* Can you hear the bells ringing? **2** (*extractor*) extractor hood LOC *Ver* VUELTA

campanada *nf* **1** (*campana*): *Sonaron las ~s.* The bells rang out. **2** (*reloj*) stroke: *las doce ~s de medianoche* the twelve strokes of midnight LOC **dar dos, etc campanadas** to strike two, etc: *El reloj dio seis ~s.* The clock struck six.

campanario *nm* belfry [*pl* belfries]

campaña *nf* (*Com, Pol, Mil*) campaign: *~ electoral* election campaign LOC *Ver* TIENDA

campeón, -ona *nm-nf* champion: *el ~ del mundo/de Europa* the world/ European champion

campeonato *nm* championship: *los Campeonatos Mundiales de Atletismo* the World Athletics Championships

campesino, -a *nm-nf* **1** (*agricultor*) farmworker

> También se puede decir **peasant**, pero tiene connotaciones de pobreza.

2 (*aldeano*) countryman/woman [*pl* countrymen/women]: *los ~s* country people

campestre *adj* LOC *Ver* COMIDA

camping *nm* campsite LOC **hacer camping** to camp **ir de camping** to go camping

campo *nm* **1** (*naturaleza*) country: *vivir en el ~* to live in the country **2** (*tierra de cultivo*) field: *~s de cebada* barley fields **3** (*paisaje*) countryside: *El ~ está precioso en abril.* The countryside looks lovely in April. **4** (*ámbito, Fís, Informát*) field: *~ magnético* magnetic field ◊ *el ~ de la ingeniería* the field of engineering **5** (*Dep*) **(a)** (*terreno*) pitch: *un ~ de rugby* a rugby pitch ◊ *salir al ~* to come out onto the pitch **(b)** (*estadio*) ground: *el ~ del Sevilla* Seville's ground **6** (*campamento*) camp: *~ de concentración/prisioneros* concentration/prison camp LOC **campo de batalla** battlefield **campo de golf** golf course **en campo contrario** (*Dep*) away: *jugar en ~ contrario* to play away *Ver tb* FAENA, MEDIO, PRODUCTO

camuflaje *nm* camouflage

camuflar *vt* to camouflage

cana *nf* grey hair: *tener ~s* to have grey hair

Canadá *nm* Canada

canadiense *adj, nmf* Canadian

canal *nm* **1** (*estrecho marítimo natural, TV, Informát*) channel: *un ~ de televisión* a TV channel ◊ *el ~ de la Mancha* the Channel **2** (*estrecho marítimo artificial, de riego*) canal: *el ~ de Suez* the Suez Canal LOC *Ver* INGENIERO ☛ *Ver nota en* TELEVISION

canario *nm* (*pájaro*) canary [*pl* canaries]

canasta *nf* basket: *meter una ~* to score a basket

cancelar *vt* **1** (*gen*) to cancel: *~ un vuelo/una reunión* to cancel a flight/ meeting **2** (*deuda*) to settle

cáncer ◆ *nm* cancer [*incontable*]: *~ de pulmón* lung cancer ◆ **cáncer** (*tb* **Cáncer**) *nm, nmf* (*Astrología*) Cancer ☛ *Ver ejemplos en* AQUARIUS

cancha *nf* **1** (*tenis, frontón, baloncesto*) court: *Los jugadores ya están en la ~.* The players are on court. **2** (*fútbol*) pitch

canción *nf* **1** (*Mús*) song **2** (*excusa*) story [*pl* stories]: *No me vengas con canciones.* Don't come to me with stories. LOC **canción de cuna** lullaby [*pl* lullabies]

candado *nm* padlock: *cerrado con ~* padlocked

candidato, -a *nm-nf* ~ (**a**) candidate (**for *sth***): *el ~ a la presidencia del club* the candidate for chair of the club

candidatura *nf* ~ (**a**) candidacy (**for *sth***): *renunciar a una ~* to withdraw your candidacy ◊ *Presentó su ~ al senado.* He is standing for the senate.

canela *nf* cinnamon

canelón *nm* **canelones** cannelloni [*incontable*]

cangrejo *nm* **1** (*de mar*) crab **2** (*de río*) crayfish [*pl* crayfish]

canguro ◆ *nm* kangaroo [*pl* kangaroos]

◆ *nmf* babysitter LOC **hacer de canguro** to babysit

caníbal *adj, nmf* cannibal [*n*]: *una tribu ~* a cannibal tribe

canibalismo *nm* cannibalism

canica *nf* marble: *jugar a las ~s* to play marbles

canino, -a *adj* canine LOC *Ver* HAMBRE

canjear *vt* to exchange *sth* (**for *sth***): *~ un vale* to exchange a voucher

canoa *nf* canoe

canoso, -a *adj* grey

cansado, -a *pp, adj* **1** ~ (**de**) (*fatigado*) tired (**from *sth*/*doing sth***): *Están ~s de tanto correr.* They're tired from all that running. **2** ~ **de** (*harto*) tired **of *sth*/*sb*/ *doing sth***: *¡Estoy ~ de ti!* I'm tired of you! **3** (*que fatiga*) tiring: *El viaje fue ~.* It was a tiring journey. LOC *Ver* VISTA; *Ver tb* CANSAR

cansancio *nm* tiredness LOC *Ver* MUERTO

cansar ◆ *vt* **1** (*fatigar*) to tire *sth/sb* (out) **2** (*aburrir, hartar*): *Me cansa tener que repetir las cosas.* I get tired of having to repeat things. ◆ *vi* to be tiring: *Este trabajo cansa mucho.* This work is very tiring. ◆ **cansarse** *v pron* **cansarse** (**de**) to get tired (**of *sth*/*sb*/ *doing sth***): *Se cansa en seguida.* He gets tired very easily.

cantante *nmf* singer LOC *Ver* VOZ

cantar ◆ *vt, vi* to sing ◆ *vi* **1** (*cigarra, pájaro pequeño*) to chirp **2** (*gallo*) to crow **3** (*oler mal*) to stink LOC **cantar las cuarenta/las verdades** to tell *sb* a few home truths **cantar victoria** to celebrate

cántaro *nm* pitcher LOC *Ver* LLOVER

cantautor, ~a *nm-nf* singer-songwriter

cante *nm* singing: *~ jondo* flamenco singing LOC **dar el cante** to stick out like a sore thumb

cantera *nf* **1** (*de piedra*) quarry [*pl* quarries] **2** (*Dep*) youth squad

cantidad ◆ *nf* **1** (*gen*) amount: *una ~ pequeña de pintura/agua* a small amount of paint/water ◊ *¿Cuánta ~ necesitas?* How much do you need? **2** (*personas, objetos*) number: *¡Qué ~ de coches!* What a lot of cars! ◊ *Había ~ de gente.* There were loads of people. **3** (*dinero*) amount, sum (*formal*) **4** (*magnitud*) quantity: *Prefiero la calidad a la ~.* I prefer quality to quantity. ◆ *adv* a lot: *Habla ~.* He talks a lot. LOC **en cantidades industriales** in huge amounts

cantimplora *nf* water bottle

canto[1] *nm* **1** (*arte*) singing: *estudiar ~* to study singing **2** (*canción, poema*) song: *un ~ a la belleza* a song to beauty

canto[2] *nm* **1** (*borde*) edge **2** (*cuchillo*) back LOC **de canto** on its/their side: *poner algo de ~* to put sth on its side

canto[3] *nm* (*piedra*) pebble LOC **darse con un canto en los dientes** to count yourself lucky

canturrear *vt, vi* to hum

caña *nf* **1** (*junco*) reed **2** (*bambú, azúcar*) cane: *~ de azúcar* sugar cane **3** (*cerveza*) glass of beer: *Me tomé cuatro ~s.* I had four glasses of beer. LOC **caña (de pescar)** fishing rod **dar/meter caña 1** (*azuzar*) to push *sb*: *Hay que meterle ~ para que estudie.* You have to push him to make him study. **2** (*coche*) to put your foot down

cañería *nf* pipe: *la ~ de desagüe* the drainpipe

cañón *nm* **1** (*de artillería*) cannon **2** (*fusil*) barrel: *una escopeta de dos cañones* a double-barrelled shotgun **3** (*Geog*) canyon: *el ~ del Colorado* the Grand Canyon

caoba *nf* mahogany

caos *nm* chaos [*incontable*]: *La noticia causó el ~.* The news caused chaos.

capa *nf* **1** (*gen*) layer: *la ~ de ozono* the ozone layer **2** (*pintura, barniz*) coat **3** (*prenda*) **(a)** (*larga*) cloak **(b)** (*corta*) cape

capacidad *nf* ~ (**de/para**) **1** (*gen*) capacity (**for *sth***): *una gran ~ de trabajo* a great capacity for work ◊ *un hotel con ~ para 300 personas* a hotel with capacity for 300 guests **2** (*aptitud*) ability (***to do sth***): *Tiene ~ para hacerlo.* She has the ability to do it.

capar *vt* to castrate

caparazón *nm* shell: *un ~ de tortuga* a tortoise shell

capataz *nmf* foreman/woman [*pl* foremen/women]

capaz *adj* ~ (**de**) capable (**of *sth*/*doing sth***): *Quiero gente ~ y trabajadora.* I want capable, hard-working people. LOC **ser capaz de** to be able *to do sth*: *No sé cómo fueron capaces de decírselo así.* I don't know how they could tell her like that. ◊ *No soy ~ de aprenderlo.* I just can't learn it.

capellán *nm* chaplain

Caperucita LOC **Caperucita Roja** Little Red Riding Hood

capicúa *nm* palindromic number

capilla *nf* chapel LOC **capilla ardiente** chapel of rest

capital ◆ *nf* capital ◆ *nm* (*Fin*) capital

capitalismo *nm* capitalism

capitalista *adj, nmf* capitalist

capitán, -ana ◆ *nm-nf* captain: *el ~ del equipo* the team captain ◆ *nmf* (*Mil*) captain

capítulo *nm* **1** (*libro*) chapter: *¿Por qué ~ te llegas?* What chapter are you on? **2** (*Radio, TV*) episode

capó *nm* (*coche*) bonnet

capote *nm* cape

capricho *nm* (*antojo*) whim: *los ~s de la moda* the whims of fashion LOC **dar un capricho a algn** to give sb a treat

caprichoso, -a *adj* **1** (*que quiere cosas*): *¡Qué niño más ~!* That child's never satisfied! **2** (*que cambia de idea*): *Tiene un carácter ~.* He's always changing his mind. ◊ *un cliente ~* a fussy customer

capricornio (*tb* **Capricornio**) *nm, nmf* Capricorn ☛ *Ver ejemplos en* AQUARIUS

captura *nf* **1** (*fugitivo*) capture **2** (*armas, drogas*) seizure

capturar *vt* **1** (*fugitivo*) to capture **2** (*armas, drogas*) to seize

capucha *nf* (*tb* **capuchón** *nm*) **1** (*prenda*) hood **2** (*bolígrafo*) top

capullo *nm* **1** (*flor*) bud **2** (*insecto*) cocoon

caqui *nm* khaki: *unos pantalones ~* a pair of khaki trousers ☛ *Ver ejemplos en* AMARILLO

cara *nf* **1** (*rostro*) face **2** (*descaro*) cheek: *¡Vaya ~!* What a cheek! **3** (*disco, papel, Geom*) side: *Escribí tres hojas por las dos ~s.* I wrote six sides. LOC **cara a cara** face to face **cara dura**: *Eres un ~ dura.* You've got a cheek! **cara o cruz** heads or tails **dar la cara** to face the music **partirle/romperle la cara a algn** to smash sb's face in **poner cara de asco** to make a face: *No pongas ~ de asco y cómetelo.* Don't make a face—just eat it. **tener buena/mala cara** (*persona*) to look well/ill **tener más cara que espalda** to be a cheeky so-and-so *Ver tb* COSTAR, VOLVER

carabina *nf* (*arma*) carbine LOC **hacer/ir de carabina** to play the chaperon

caracol *nm* **1** (*de tierra*) snail **2** (*de mar*) winkle LOC *Ver* ESCALERA

caracola *nf* conch

carácter *nm* **1** (*gen*) character: *un defecto de mi ~* a character defect **2** (*índole*) nature LOC **tener buen/mal carácter** to be good-natured/ill-tempered **tener mucho/poco carácter** to be strong-minded/weak-minded

característica *nf* characteristic

característico, -a *adj* characteristic

caracterizar ◆ *vt* **1** (*distinguir*) to characterize: *El orgullo caracteriza a este pueblo.* Pride characterizes this people. **2** (*disfrazar*) to dress *sb* up **as *sth*/*sb***: *Me caracterizaron de anciana.* They dressed me up as an old lady. ◆ **caracterizarse** *v pron* **caracterizarse de** to dress up **as *sth*/*sb***

¡caramba! *interj* **1** (*sorpresa*) goodness me! **2** (*enfado*) for heaven's sake!

caramelo *nm* **1** (*golosina*) sweet **2** (*azúcar quemado*) caramel

carantoña *nf* LOC **hacer carantoñas** to caress

caravana *nf* **1** (*expedición, roulotte*) caravan **2** (*tráfico*) tailback

carbón *nm* coal LOC **carbón vegetal** charcoal

carboncillo *nm* charcoal

carbonizar(se) *vt, v pron* to burn

carbono *nm* carbon LOC *Ver* DIÓXIDO, HIDRATO, MONÓXIDO

carburante *nm* fuel

carca *adj, nmf* old fogey [*n*] [*pl* old fogeys]: *¡Qué padres más ~s tienes!* Your parents are real old fogeys!

carcajada *nf* roar of laughter [*pl* roars of laughter] LOC *Ver* REÍR, SOLTAR

cárcel *nf* prison: *ir a la ~* to go to prison ◊ *Lo metieron en la ~.* They put him in prison.

carcelero, -a *nm-nf* jailer

cardenal *nm* **1** (*moratón*) bruise **2** (*Relig*) cardinal

cardiaco, -a (*tb* **cardíaco, -a**) *adj* LOC **ataque/paro cardiaco** cardiac arrest

cardinal *adj* cardinal

cardo *nm* thistle LOC **ser un cardo 1** (*feo*) to be as ugly as sin **2** (*antipático*) to be a prickly character

carecer *vi* ~ **de** to lack *sth* [*vt*]: *Carecemos de medicinas.* We lack medicines LOC **carece de sentido** it doesn't make sense

careta *nf* mask

carga *nf* **1** (*acción*) loading: *La ~ del buque llevó varios días.* Loading the ship took several days. ◊ *~ y descarga* loading and unloading **2** (*peso*) load: ~ *máxima* maximum load **3** (*mercancía*) **(a)** (*avión, barco*) cargo [*pl* cargoes] **(b)** (*camión*) load **4** (*explosivo, munición, Electrón*) charge: *una ~ eléctrica* an electric charge **5** (*obligación*) burden **6** (*bolígrafo*) refill LOC **¡a la carga!** charge! *Ver tb* BURRO

cargado, -a *pp, adj* **1** ~ **(de/con)** loaded **(with *sth*)**: *Venían ~s de maletas.* They were loaded down with suitcases. ◊ *un arma cargada* a loaded weapon **2** ~ **de** (*responsabilidades*) burdened down **with *sth*** **3** (*atmósfera*) stuffy **4** (*bebida*) strong: *un café muy ~* a very strong coffee *Ver tb* CARGAR

cargador *nm* (*Electrón*) charger: ~ *de pilas* battery charger

cargamento *nm* **1** (*avión, barco*) cargo [*pl* cargoes] **2** (*camión*) load

cargante *adj* pain in the neck [*n*]: *¡Qué tío más ~!* What a pain in the neck that bloke is!

cargar ◆ *vt* **1** (*gen*) to load: *Cargaron el camión de cajas.* They loaded the lorry with boxes. ◊ *~ un arma* to load a weapon **2** (*pluma, encendedor*) to fill **3** (*pila, batería*) to charge **4** (*suspender*) to fail *sb* **(*in sth*)**: *Me han cargado las matemáticas.* They've failed me in maths. ◆ *vi* **1** ~ **con (a)** (*llevar*) to carry *sth* [*vt*]: *Siempre me toca ~ con todo.* I always end up carrying everything. **(b)** (*responsabilidad*) to shoulder *sth* [*vt*] **2** ~ **(contra)** (*Mil*) to charge **(at *sb*)** ◆ **cargarse** *v pron* **1** (*romper*) to wreck: *¡Te vas a ~ la lavadora!* You're going to wreck the washing machine! **2** (*matar*) to kill **3** (*suspender*) to fail

cargo *nm* **1** (*gen*) post: *un ~ importante* an important post **2** (*Pol*) office: *el ~ de alcalde* the office of mayor **3 cargos** (*Jur*) charges LOC **dar/tener cargo de conciencia** to feel guilty: *Me da ~ de conciencia.* I feel guilty **hacerse cargo de 1** (*responsabilizarse*) to take charge of *sth* **2** (*cuidar de algn*) to look after *sb*

caricatura *nf* caricature: *hacer una ~* to draw a caricature

caricia *nf* caress LOC **hacer caricias** to caress

caridad *nf* charity: *vivir de la ~* to live on charity

caries *nf* **1** (*enfermedad*) tooth decay [*incontable*]: *para prevenir la ~* to prevent tooth decay **2** (*agujero*) hole: *Tengo ~ en la muela.* I've got a hole in my tooth.

cariño *nm* **1** (*afecto*) affection **2** (*delicadeza*) loving care: *Trata sus cosas con todo ~.* He treats his things with loving care. **3** (*apelativo*) sweetheart: *¡~ mío!* Sweetheart! LOC **cogerle cariño a algn** to become fond of sb **con cariño** (*en cartas*) with love **tenerle cariño a algo/algn** to be fond of sth/sb

cariñoso, -a *adj* ~ **(con)** **1** (*gen*) affectionate **(towards *sth/sb*)** **2** (*abrazo, saludos*) warm

caritativo, -a *adj* ~ **(con)** charitable **(to/towards *sb*)**

carmín *nm* lipstick

carnada (*tb* **carnaza**) *nf* bait

carnal *adj* (*sensual*) carnal LOC *Ver* PRIMO

carnaval *nm* carnival LOC *Ver* MARTES

carne *nf* **1** (*Anat, Relig, fruta*) flesh **2** (*alimento*) meat: *Me gusta la ~ bien hecha.* I like my meat well done.

> El inglés suele emplear distintas palabras para referirse al animal y a la carne que se obtiene de ellos: del *cerdo* (**pig**) se obtiene **pork**, de la *vaca* (**cow**), **beef**, del *ternero* (**calf**), **veal. Mutton** es la carne de la *oveja* (**sheep**), y del *cordero* (**lamb**) se obtiene la carne de cordero o **lamb**.

LOC **carne picada** mince **en carne viva** raw: *Tienes la rodilla en ~ viva.* Your knee is red and raw. **ser de carne y hueso** to be only human **tener carne de gallina** to have goose-pimples *Ver tb* PARRILLA, UÑA

carné (*tb* **carnet**) *nm* card LOC **carné de conducir** driving licence **carné de identidad** identity card **sacar(se) el carné de conducir** to pass your driving test *Ver tb* EXAMINAR, FOTO

carnero *nm* ram

carnicería *nf* **1** (*tienda*) butcher's [*pl* butchers] **2** (*matanza*) massacre

carnicero, -a *nm-nf* (*lit* y *fig*) butcher

carnívoro, -a *adj* carnivorous

caro, -a ◆ *adj* expensive, dear (*más coloq*) ◆ *adv*: *comprar/pagar algo muy ~* to pay a lot for sth LOC **costar/pagar caro** to cost *sb* dearly: *Pagarán ~ su error.* Their mistake will cost them dearly.

carpa[1] *nf* (*pez*) carp [*pl* carp]

carpa[2] *nf* (*entoldado*) marquee

carpeta *nf* folder

carpintería *nf* carpentry

carpintero, -a *nm-nf* carpenter

carraspear *vi* to clear your throat

carraspera *nf* hoarseness LOC **tener carraspera** to be hoarse

carrera *nf* **1** (*corrida*) run: *Ya no estoy para ~s.* I'm not up to running any more. **2** (*Dep*) race: *~ de relevos/sacos* relay/sack race **3 carreras** (*caballos*) races **4** (*licenciatura*) degree: *¿Qué ~ tienes?* What did you do your degree in? **5** (*profesión*) career: *Estoy en el mejor momento de mi ~.* I'm at the peak of my career. **6** (*medias*) ladder: *Tienes una ~ en las medias.* You've got a ladder in your tights. LOC **carrera de armamentos** arms race **carrera de caballos** horse race *Ver tb* BICICLETA, CABALLO, COCHE

carrerilla *nf* LOC **coger/tomar carrerilla** to take a run **decir algo de carrerilla** to reel sth off **saber(se) algo de carrerilla** to know sth by heart

carreta *nf* cart

carrete *nm* **1** (*bobina*) reel **2** (*Fot*) film: *Se me ha velado todo el ~.* The whole film is blurred. LOC **carrete de fotos** film

carretera *nf* road LOC **carretera comarcal/secundaria** B-road **carretera de circunvalación** ring road **carretera general/nacional** A-road **por carretera** by road *Ver tb* LUZ

carretilla *nf* wheelbarrow

carril *nm* **1** (*carretera*) lane: *~ de autobús/bicicletas* bus/cycle lane **2** (*raíl*) rail

carrillo *nm* cheek

carrito *nm* trolley [*pl* trolleys]: *~ de la compra* shopping trolley

carro *nm* **1** (*vehículo*) cart **2** (*supermercado, aeropuerto*) trolley [*pl* trolleys] **3** (*máquina de escribir*) carriage **4 el Carro** (*Osa Mayor*) the Plough LOC **carro de combate** tank

carrocería *nf* bodywork [*incontable*]

carromato *nm* caravan

carroña *nf* carrion

carroza ◆ *nf* **1** (*tirada por caballos*) carriage **2** (*en un desfile*) float ◆ *adj, nmf* old fogey [*n*] [*pl* old fogeys]: *¡No seas tan ~!* Don't be such an old fogey!

carruaje *nm* carriage

carrusel *nm* (*tiovivo*) merry-go-round

carta *nf* **1** (*misiva*) letter: *echar una ~* to post a letter ◊ *¿Tengo ~?* Are there any letters for me? ◊ *~ certificada/urgente* registered/express letter **2** (*naipe*) card: *jugar a las ~s* to play cards ☛ *Ver nota en* BARAJA **3** (*menú*) menu **4** (*documento*) charter LOC **carta de navegación** chart **echar las cartas** to tell *sb's* fortune *Ver tb* BOMBA[1]

cartabón *nm* set square

cartearse *v pron* ~ (**con**) to write **to** ***sb***

cartel *nm* poster: *poner un ~* to put up a poster LOC **cartel indicador** sign *Ver tb* PROHIBIDO

cartelera *nf* (*sección de periódico*) listings [*pl*]: *~ teatral* theatre listings LOC **en cartelera** on: *Lleva un mes en ~.* It has been on for a month.

cartera *nf* **1** (*billetero*) wallet **2** (*maletín*) briefcase **3** (*de colegio*) school bag

carterista *nmf* pickpocket

cartero, -a *nm-nf* postman/woman [*pl* postmen/women]

cartilla *nf* **1** (*Educ*) reader **2** (*libreta*) book: *~ de racionamiento/ahorros* ration/savings book LOC **cartilla de la seguridad social** medical card **cartilla del paro** unemployment card *Ver tb* LEER

cartón *nm* **1** (*material*) cardboard: *cajas de ~* cardboard boxes **2** (*huevos, cigarrillos, leche*) carton ☛ *Ver dibujo en* CONTAINER

cartucho *nm* (*proyectil, recambio*) cartridge

cartulina *nf* card

casa *nf* **1** (*vivienda*) **(a)** (*gen*) house **(b)** (*piso*) flat **(c)** (*edificio*) block of flats [*pl* blocks of flats] ☛ *Ver* pág 321. **2** (*hogar*) home: *No hay nada como estar en ~.* There's no place like home. **3** (*empresa*) company [*pl* companies]: *una ~ discográfica* a record company LOC **casa de empeño** pawnshop **casa de socorro** first-aid post **como una casa** huge: *una mentira como una ~* a huge lie **en casa** at home: *Me quedé en ~.* I stayed at home. ◊ *¿Está tu madre en ~?* Is your mother in? **en casa de** at *sb's* (house): *Estaré en ~ de mi hermana.* I'll be at my sister's house. ☛En lenguaje coloquial se omite la palabra 'house': *Estaré en ~ de Ana.* I'll be at Ana's. **ir a casa** to go home **ir a casa de** to go to *sb's* (house): *Iré a ~ de mis padres.* I'll go to my parents' (house). **pasar por casa de algn** to drop in (on sb): *Pasaré por tu casa mañana.* I'll drop in tomorrow. *Ver tb* AMO, CAMBIAR, LLEGAR

casaca *nf* (*blusón*) smock

casado, -a ◆ *pp, adj*: *estar ~ (con algn)* to be married (to sb) ◆ *nm-nf* married man/woman LOC *Ver* RECIÉN; *Ver tb* CASAR

casar ◆ *vi* ~ (**con**) to tally (**with *sth***): *Las cuentas no casaban.* The accounts didn't tally. ◆ **casarse** *v pron* **1** (*gen*) to get married: *¿Sabes quién se casa?* Guess who's getting married? **2 casarse con** to marry *sb*: *Jamás me casaré contigo.* I'll never marry you. LOC **casarse por la Iglesia/por lo civil** to get married in Church/a registry office ☛ *Ver nota en* BODA

cascabel *nm* bell LOC *Ver* SERPIENTE

cascada *nf* waterfall

cascado, -a *pp, adj* **1** (*roto*) clapped-out **2** (*voz*) cracked **3** (*persona*) worn out *Ver tb* CASCAR

cascajo *nm* nuts [*pl*]

cascanueces *nm* nutcrackers [*pl*]

cascar ◆ *vt* **1** (*gen*) to crack: ~ *un jarrón* to crack a vase **2** (*pegar*) to belt ◆ *vi* **1** (*charlar*) to chatter **2** (*morir*) to kick the bucket

cáscara *nf* **1** (*huevo, nuez*) shell: ~ *de huevo* eggshell **2** (*limón, naranja*) peel **3** (*plátano*) skin **4** (*cereal*) husk

cascarón *nm* eggshell

cascarrabias *nmf* grouch

casco *nm* **1** (*cabeza*) helmet: *llevar* ~ to wear a helmet **2** (*botella*) empty bottle [*pl* empties]: *Tengo que devolver estos ~s.* I've got to take these empties back. **3** (*animal*) hoof [*pl* hoofs/hooves] **4** (*barco*) hull **5 cascos** (*auriculares*) headphones LOC **calentarse/romperse los cascos** to rack your brains **casco antiguo/viejo** old town

cascote *nm* (*escombros*) rubble [*incontable*]: *La calle estaba llena de ~s.* The street was full of rubble.

caserío *nm* **1** (*casa*) farmhouse **2** (*aldea*) hamlet

casero, -a ◆ *adj* **1** (*gen*) home-made: *mermelada casera* home-made jam **2** (*persona*) home-loving ◆ *nm-nf* landlord/lady

caseta *nf* **1** (*feria*) sideshow **2** (*perro*) kennel **3** (*vestuario*) changing room

casete ◆ *nm* (*magnetófono*) cassette recorder ◆ *nm o nf* (*cinta*) cassette

> También se puede decir **tape**. **Rewind** es rebobinar y **fast forward** pasar hacia delante.

casi *adv* **1** (*en frases afirmativas*) almost, nearly: ~ *me caigo.* I almost/nearly fell. ◊ *Estaba ~ lleno.* It was almost/nearly full. ◊ *Yo ~ diría que...* I would almost say... ☛ *Ver nota en* NEARLY **2** (*en frases negativas*) hardly: *No la veo ~ nunca.* I hardly ever see her. ◊ *No vino ~ nadie.* Hardly anybody came. ◊ *No queda ~ nada.* There's hardly anything left. LOC **casi, casi** very nearly: *~, ~ llegaban a mil personas.* There were very nearly a thousand people.

casilla *nf* **1** (*Ajedrez, Damas*) square **2** (*formulario*) box: *marcar la ~ con una cruz* to put a tick in the box **3** (*cartas, llaves*) pigeon-hole LOC **sacar a algn de sus casillas** to drive sb up the wall

casillero *nm* **1** (*mueble*) pigeon-holes [*pl*] **2** (*marcador*) scoreboard

casino *nm* **1** (*juego*) casino [*pl* casinos] **2** (*de socios*) club

caso *nm* case: *en cualquier ~* in any case LOC **el caso es que... 1** (*el hecho es que...*) the fact is (that)...: *El ~ es que no puedo ir.* The fact is I can't go. **2** (*lo que importa*) the main thing is that...: *No importa cómo, el ~ es que vaya.* It doesn't matter how he goes, the main thing is that he goes. **en caso de** in the event of *sth*: *Rómpase en ~ de incendio.* Break the glass in the event of fire. **en caso de que...** if...: *En ~ de que te pregunte...* If he asks you... **en el mejor/peor de los casos** at best/worst **en todo caso** in any case **hacer caso a/de** to take notice of *sth/sb* **hacer/venir al caso** to be relevant **ser un caso** to be a right one **ser un caso aparte** to be something else **yo en tu caso** if I were you *Ver tb* TAL

caspa *nf* dandruff

casta *nf* **1** (*animal*) breed **2** (*grupo social*) caste LOC **de casta** thoroughbred

castaña *nf* **1** (*fruto*) chestnut **2 castañas**: *Tengo cincuenta ~s.* I'm fifty. LOC **sacarle a algn las castañas del fuego** to get sb out of a fix

castañetear *vi* (*dientes*) to chatter

castaño, -a ◆ *adj* brown: *ojos ~s* brown eyes ◊ *Tiene el pelo ~.* He's got brown hair. ◆ *nm* chestnut (tree)

castañuelas *nf* castanets

castellano *nm* (*lengua*) Castilian Spanish

castidad *nf* chastity

castigar *vt* **1** (*gen*) to punish *sb* (**for *sth***): *Me castigaron por mentir.* I was punished for telling lies. ◊ *Nos castigaron sin recreo.* We were kept in at break. **2** (*Dep*) to penalize

castigo *nm* punishment: *Habrá que ponerles un ~.* They'll have to be punished. ◊ *levantar un ~* to withdraw a punishment

castillo *nm* castle LOC **castillo de arena** sandcastle

casto, -a *adj* chaste

castor *nm* beaver

castrar *vt* to castrate

casual *adj* chance [*n atrib*]: *un encuentro ~* a chance meeting

casualidad *nf* chance: *Nos conocimos de/por pura ~.* We met by sheer chance. ◊ *¿No tendrás por ~ su teléfono?* You wouldn't have their number by any chance? LOC **da la casualidad (de) que...** it so happens that... **¡qué casualidad!** what a coincidence!

catalán *nm* (*lengua*) Catalan

catalizador *nm* (*de coche*) catalytic converter

catálogo *nm* catalogue

catar *vt* to taste

catarata *nf* **1** (*cascada*) waterfall **2** (*Med*) cataract

catarro *nm* cold: *Tengo ~.* I've got a cold. ◊ *coger un ~* to catch a cold

catástrofe *nf* catastrophe

cate *nm* (*suspenso*) fail: *¡Me han dado un ~!* I've failed!

catear *vt, vi* to fail

catecismo *nm* catechism

catedral *nf* cathedral

catedrático, -a *nm-nf* **1** (*de instituto*) head of department **2** (*de universidad*) professor

categoría *nf* **1** (*sección*) category [*pl* categories] **2** (*nivel*) level: *un torneo de ~ intermedia* an intermediate-level tournament **3** (*estatus*) status: *mi ~ profesional* my professional status LOC **de categoría 1** (*nivel, calidad*) first-rate **2** (*considerable*) serious: *una bronca de ~* a serious telling-off **de primera/segunda/tercera categoría** first-rate/second-rate/third-rate

categórico, -a *adj* categorical

catolicismo *nm* Catholicism

católico, -a *adj, nm-nf* Catholic [*n*]: *ser ~* to be a Catholic

catorce *nm, adj, pron* **1** (*gen*) fourteen **2** (*fecha*) fourteenth ☛ *Ver ejemplos en* ONCE *y* SEIS

cauce *nm* **1** (*río*) river bed **2** (*fig*) channel

caucho *nm* rubber

caudal *nm* (*agua*) flow: *el ~ del río* the flow of the river

caudaloso, -a *adj* large: *El Ebro es un río muy ~.* The Ebro is a very large river.

caudillo *nm* **1** (*líder*) leader **2** (*jefe militar*) commander

causa *nf* **1** (*origen, ideal*) cause: *la ~ principal del problema* the main cause of the problem ◊ *Lo abandonó todo por la ~.* He left everything for the cause. **2** (*motivo*) reason: *sin ~ aparente* for no apparent reason LOC **a/por causa de** because of *sth/sb*

causar *vt* **1** (*ser la causa de*) to cause: *~ la muerte/heridas/daños* to cause death/injury/damage **2** (*alegría, pena*): *Me causó una gran alegría/pena.* It made me very happy/sad. LOC *Ver* SENSACIÓN

cautela *nf* LOC **con cautela** cautiously

cauteloso, -a (*tb* **cauto, -a**) *adj* cautious

cautivador, ~a *adj* captivating

cautivar *vt* (*atraer*) to captivate

cautiverio *nm* captivity

cautivo, -a *adj, nm-nf* captive

cavar *vt, vi* to dig

caverna *nf* cavern

caviar *nm* caviar

cavilar *vi* to think deeply (**about sth**): *después de mucho ~* after much thought

caza[1] *nf* **1** (*cacería*) **(a)** (*gen*) hunting: *No me gusta la ~.* I don't like hunting. ◊ *ir de ~* to go hunting **(b)** (*caza menor*) shooting **2** (*animales*) game: *Nunca he comido ~.* I've never tried game. LOC **andar/ir a la caza de** to be after *sth/sb* **caza mayor** big game hunting **caza menor** shooting *Ver tb* FURTIVO, TEMPORADA

caza[2] *nm* (*avión*) fighter (plane)

cazador, ~a *nm-nf* hunter LOC *Ver* FURTIVO

cazadora *nf* (*chaqueta*) jacket: *una ~ de piel* a leather jacket

cazar ◆ *vt* **1** (*gen*) to hunt **2** (*capturar*) to catch: *~ mariposas* to catch butterflies **3** (*con escopeta*) to shoot **4** (*conseguir*) to land: *~ un buen empleo* to land a good job ◆ *vi* **1** (*gen*) to hunt **2** (*con escopeta*) to shoot

cazo *nm* **1** (*cacerola*) saucepan ☛ *Ver dibujo en* SAUCEPAN **2** (*cucharón*) ladle

cazuela *nf* casserole ☛ *Ver dibujo en* SAUCEPAN

cebada *nf* barley

cebar *vt* **1** (*engordar*) to fatten *sth/sb* up **2** (*atiborrar*) to fill *sth/sb* up: *Su* *madre los ceba.* Their mother fills them up.

cebo *nm* bait

cebolla *nf* onion

cebolleta *nf* **1** (*fresca*) spring onion **2** (*en vinagre*) pickled onion

cebra *nf* zebra LOC *Ver* PASO

ceder ◆ *vt* to hand *sth* over (**to sb**): ~ *el poder* to hand over power ◊ *Cedieron el edificio al ayuntamiento.* They handed over the building to the council. ◆ *vi* **1** (*transigir*) to give in (**to sth/sb**): *Es importante saber ~.* It's important to know how to give in gracefully. **2** (*intensidad, fuerza*) to ease off: *El viento cedió.* The wind eased off. **3** (*romperse*) to give way: *La estantería cedió por el peso.* The shelf gave way under the weight of the books. LOC **ceda el paso** give way: *No vi el ceda el paso.* I didn't see the Give Way sign. **ceder el paso** to give way **ceder la palabra** to hand over to *sb*

cedro *nm* cedar

cegar *vt* to blind: *Las luces me cegaron.* I was blinded by the lights.

ceguera *nf* blindness

ceja *nf* eyebrow

celda *nf* cell

celebración *nf* **1** (*fiesta, aniversario*) celebration **2** (*acontecimiento*): *La ~ de las elecciones será en junio.* The elections will be held in June.

celebrar ◆ *vt* **1** (*festejar*) to celebrate: ~ *un cumpleaños* to celebrate a birthday **2** (*llevar a cabo*) to hold: ~ *una reunión* to hold a meeting ◆ **celebrarse** *v pron* to take place

celeste *adj* heavenly LOC *Ver* AZUL

celo[1] *nm* **celos** jealousy [*incontable, v sing*]: *No son más que ~s.* That's just jealousy. ◊ *Sentía ~s.* He felt jealous. LOC **dar celos a algn** to make sb jealous **estar en celo 1** (*hembra*) to be on heat **2** (*macho*) to be in rut **tener celos (de algn)** to be jealous (of sb) *Ver tb* COMIDO

celo[2] *nm* Sellotape®

celofán *nm* Cellophane®: *papel de ~* Cellophane wrapping

celosía *nf* lattice

celoso, -a *adj, nm-nf* jealous [*adj*]: *Es un ~.* He's very jealous.

célula *nf* cell

celular *adj* cellular

celulitis *nf* cellulite

cementerio *nm* **1** (*gen*) cemetery [*pl* cemeteries] **2** (*de iglesia*) graveyard LOC **cementerio de automóviles** breaker's yard

cemento *nm* cement

cena *nf* dinner, supper: *¿Qué hay de ~?* What's for dinner? ☛ *Ver* pág 320. LOC *Ver* MERIENDA

cenar ◆ *vi* to have dinner, supper ◆ *vt* to have *sth* for dinner, supper: ~ *una tortilla* to have an omelette for supper ☛ *Ver* pág 320.

cencerro *nm* bell

cenicero *nm* ashtray [*pl* ashtrays]

Cenicienta *n pr* Cinderella

cenit *nm* zenith

ceniza *nf* ash: *esparcir las ~s* to scatter the ashes LOC *Ver* MIÉRCOLES

censo *nm* census [*pl* censuses] LOC **censo electoral** electoral register

censor, ~a *nm-nf* censor

censura *nf* censorship

censurar *vt* **1** (*libro, película*) to censor **2** (*reprobar*) to censure

centella *nf* spark

centellear *vi* **1** (*estrellas*) to twinkle **2** (*luz*) to flash

centena *nf* hundred: *unidades, decenas y ~s* hundreds, tens and units

centenar *nm* (*cien aproximadamente*) a hundred or so: *un ~ de espectadores* a hundred or so spectators LOC **centenares de...** hundreds of...: *~es de personas* hundreds of people

centenario *nm* centenary [*pl* centenaries]: *el ~ de su fundación* the centenary of its founding ◊ *el sexto ~ de su nacimiento* the 600th anniversary of his birth

centeno *nm* rye

centésimo, -a *adj, pron, nm-nf* hundredth: *una centésima de segundo* a hundredth of a second

centígrado, -a *adj* centigrade (*abrev* C): *cincuenta grados ~s* fifty degrees centigrade

centímetro *nm* centimetre (*abrev* cm): ~ *cuadrado/cúbico* square/cubic centimetre ☛ *Ver* Apéndice 1.

centinela *nmf* **1** (*Mil*) sentry [*pl* sentries] **2** (*vigía*) lookout

centollo *nm* crab

centrado, -a *pp, adj* **1** (*en el centro*): *El título no está bien ~.* The heading isn't in the centre. **2** (*persona*) settled *Ver tb* CENTRAR

central ◆ *adj* central: *calefacción ~* central heating ◆ *nf* **1** (*energía*) power station: *una ~ nuclear* a nuclear power station **2** (*oficina principal*) head office LOC **central lechera** dairy [*pl* dairies] **central telefónica** telephone exchange

centralita *nf* switchboard

centrar ◆ *vt* **1** (*colocar en el centro*) to centre: *~ la fotografía en una página* to centre the photo on a page **2** (*atención, mirada*) to focus *sth* ***on sth***: *Centraron sus críticas en el gobierno.* They focussed their criticism on the government. **3** (*esfuerzos*) to concentrate (*your efforts*) (***on sth/doing sth***) ◆ *vi* (*Dep*) to cross: *Rápidamente centró y su compañero marcó gol.* He crossed quickly and his team-mate scored. ◆ **centrarse** *v pron* **1 centrarse en** (*girar en torno*) to centre **on/around** ***sth/doing sth***: *La vida del estudiante se centra en el estudio.* Students' lives centre around studying. **2** (*adaptarse*) to settle down

céntrico, -a *adj*: *calles céntricas* city centre streets ◊ *un piso ~* a flat in the centre of town

centro *nm* centre: *el ~ de la ciudad* the city centre ◊ *el ~ de atención* the centre of attention LOC **centro comercial** shopping centre **centro cultural** arts centre **centro escolar** school **ir al centro** to go into town

ceño *nm* frown LOC *Ver* FRUNCIR

cepa *nf* **1** (*vid*) vine **2** (*árbol*) stump

cepillar ◆ *vt* **1** (*prenda de vestir, pelo*) to brush **2** (*madera*) to plane ◆ **cepillarse** *v pron* **1** (*prenda de vestir, pelo*) to brush: *~se la chaqueta/el pelo* to brush your jacket/hair **2** (*asesinar*) to bump *sb* off

cepillo *nm* **1** (*gen*) brush ☛ *Ver dibujo en* BRUSH **2** (*madera*) plane LOC **cepillo de dientes/pelo** toothbrush/hairbrush **cepillo de uñas** nail brush

cepo *nm* **1** (*trampa*) trap **2** (*para coche*) clamp

cera *nf* **1** (*gen*) wax **2** (*oídos*) earwax

cerámica *nf* pottery

cerca[1] *nf* (*valla*) fence

cerca[2] *adv* near (by): *Vivimos muy ~.* We live very near by. LOC **cerca de 1** (*a poca distancia*) near: *~ de aquí* near here **2** (*casi*) nearly: *El tren se retrasó ~ de una hora.* The train was nearly an hour late. **de cerca**: *Deja que lo vea de ~.* Let me see it close up. *Ver tb* AQUÍ, PILLAR

cercanías *nf* outskirts LOC *Ver* TREN

cercano, -a *adj* **1** ~ (**a**) (*gen*) close **to** ***sth***: *un amigo/pariente ~* a close friend/relative ◊ *fuentes cercanas a la familia* sources close to the family **2** ~ **a** (*referido a distancia*) near *sth/sb*; close **to** ***sth/sb***: *un pueblo ~ a Londres* a village close to/near London ☛ *Ver nota en* NEAR

cercar *vt* **1** (*poner una valla*) to fence *sth* in **2** (*rodear*) to surround

cerdo, -a ◆ *nm-nf* pig

> **Pig** es el sustantivo genérico, **boar** se refiere sólo al macho y su plural es 'boar' o 'boars'. Para referirnos sólo a la hembra utilizamos **sow**. **Piglet** es la cría del cerdo.

◆ *nm* (*carne*) pork: *lomo de ~* loin of pork LOC *Ver* MANTECA

cereal *nm* **1** (*planta, grano*) cereal **2 cereales** cereal [*gen incontable*]: *Desayuno ~es.* I have cereal for breakfast.

cerebral *adj* (*Med*) brain [*n atrib*]: *un tumor ~* a brain tumour LOC *Ver* CONMOCIÓN

cerebro *nm* **1** (*Anat*) brain **2** (*persona*) brains [*sing*]: *el ~ de la banda* the brains behind the gang

ceremonia *nf* ceremony [*pl* ceremonies]

cereza *nf* cherry [*pl* cherries]

cerezo *nm* cherry tree

cerilla *nf* match: *encender una ~* to strike a match ◊ *una caja de ~s* a box of matches

cero *nm* **1** (*gen*) nought: *un cinco y dos ~s* a five and two noughts ◊ *~ coma cinco* nought point five **2** (*temperaturas, grados*) zero: *temperaturas bajo ~* temperatures below zero ◊ *Estamos a diez grados bajo ~.* It's minus ten. **3** (*para teléfonos*) O ☛Se pronuncia 'ou': *Mi teléfono es el veintinueve, ~ dos, cuarenta.* My telephone number is two nine O two four O. **4** (*Dep*) **(a)** (*gen*) nil: *uno a ~* one nil ◊ *un empate a ~* a goalless draw **(b)** (*Tenis*) love: *quince a ~* fifteen love LOC **empezar/partir de cero** to start from scratch **ser un cero a la izquierda** to be a nobody ☛ *Ver* Apéndice 1.

cerrado, -a *pp, adj* **1** (*gen*) closed, shut (*más coloq*) ☛ *Ver nota en* SHUT **2** (*con llave*) locked **3** (*espacio*) enclosed **4** (*noche*) dark **5** (*curva*) sharp **6** (*acento*) broad: *En Glasgow hablan un inglés muy ~.* They speak English with a broad accent in Glasgow. LOC *Ver* HERMÉTICAMENTE; *Ver tb* CERRAR

cerradura *nf* lock

cerrajero, -a *nm-nf* locksmith

cerrar ◆ *vt* **1** (*gen*) to close, to shut (*más coloq*): *Cierra la puerta.* Shut the door. ◊ *Cerré los ojos.* I closed my eyes. **2** (*gas, llave de paso, grifo*) to turn *sth* off **3** (*sobre*) to seal **4** (*botella*) to put the top on *sth* ◆ *vi* to close, to shut (*más coloq*): *No cerramos para comer.* We don't close for lunch. ◆ **cerrarse** *v pron* to close, to shut (*más coloq*): *Se me cerró la puerta.* The door closed on me. ◊ *Se me cerraban los ojos.* My eyes were closing. LOC **cerrar con cerrojo** to bolt *sth* **cerrar con llave** to lock **¡cierra el pico!** shut up! **cerrar la puerta en las narices a algn** to shut the door in sb's face **cerrar(se) de un golpe/portazo** to slam *Ver tb* ABRIR

cerrojo *nm* bolt LOC **echar/correr el cerrojo** to bolt *sth Ver tb* CERRAR, DESCORRER

certeza (*tb* **certidumbre**) *nf* certainty [*pl* certainties] LOC **tener la certeza de que...** to be certain that...

certificado, -a ◆ *pp, adj* **1** (*documento*) certified **2** (*carta, correo*) registered: *por correo ~* by registered post ◆ *nm* certificate: *~ de defunción* death certificate LOC **certificado escolar** school leaving certificate *Ver tb* CERTIFICAR

certificar *vt* **1** (*dar por cierto*) to certify **2** (*carta, paquete*) to register

cervatillo *nm* fawn ☛ *Ver nota en* CIERVO

cerveza *nf* beer: *Me pone dos ~s, por favor.* Two beers, please. ◊ *Nos tomamos unas ~s con los de la oficina.* We had a few beers with the crowd from the office. LOC **cerveza de barril** draught beer **cerveza negra** stout **cerveza sin alcohol** alcohol-free beer *Ver tb* FÁBRICA, JARRA

cesar *vi* **1** ~ (**de**) to stop (***doing sth***) **2** ~ (**en**) (*dimitir*) to resign (**from *sth***) LOC **sin cesar** incessantly

césped *nm* **1** (*gen*) grass: *No pisar el ~.* Keep off the grass. **2** (*en un jardín privado*) lawn LOC *Ver* CORTAR

cesta *nf* basket: *una ~ con comida* a basket of food LOC **cesta de Navidad** Christmas hamper

cesto *nm* (big) basket LOC **cesto de la colada/ropa sucia** laundry basket

chabacano, -a *adj* vulgar

chabola *nf* shack LOC *Ver* BARRIO

chacal *nm* jackal

chacha *nf* **1** (*sirvienta*) maid **2** (*niñera*) nanny [*pl* nannies]

cháchara *nf* chatter: *¡Déjate de ~ !* Stop chattering! LOC **estar de cháchara** to chatter away

chachi *adj, adv* great: *¡Qué fiesta más ~!* What a great party! ◊ *pasárselo ~* to have a great time

chafar *vt* **1** (*aplastar*) to flatten: *~ el césped* to flatten the grass **2** (*arrugar*) to crumple **3** (*estropear*) to ruin: *Este cambio nos ha chafado el plan.* This change has ruined our plans.

chal *nm* shawl: *un ~ de seda* a silk shawl

chalado, -a ◆ *pp, adj* ~ (**por**) crazy (**about *sth*/*sb***): *Está ~ por ti.* He's crazy about you. ◆ *nm-nf* nutter *Ver tb* CHALARSE

chalarse *v pron* **1** (*enloquecer*) to go mad **2** ~ **por** to be crazy **about *sth*/*sb***: *Todas las chicas se chalaban por aquel actor.* All the girls were crazy about that actor.

chalé (*tb* **chalet**) *nm* **1** (*en la ciudad*) house: *un ~ en las afueras de Madrid* a house on the outskirts of Madrid **2** (*en la costa*) villa **3** (*en el campo*) cottage LOC **chalé adosado/individual** semi-detached/detached house ☛ *Ver pág 321.*

chaleco *nm* waistcoat LOC **chaleco antibalas** bulletproof vest **chaleco salvavidas** life jacket

champán (*tb* **champaña**) *nm* champagne

champiñón *nm* mushroom

champú *nm* shampoo [*pl* shampoos]: *~ anticaspa* anti-dandruff shampoo

chamuscar *vt* to singe

chamusquina *nf* LOC *Ver* OLER

chanchullo *nm* fiddle: *¡Qué ~!* What a fiddle! LOC **hacer chanchullos** to be on the fiddle

chancla (*tb* **chancleta**) *nf* flip-flop

chándal *nm* tracksuit

chantaje *nm* blackmail LOC **hacer chantaje** to blackmail

chantajear *vt* to blackmail *sb* (***into doing sth***)

chantajista *nmf* blackmailer

chapa *nf* **1** (*tapón*) bottle top **2** (*insignia*) badge **3** (*carrocería*) bodywork: *Saldrá caro porque hay que arreglar la ~.* It'll be expensive because they've got to repair the bodywork.

chapado, -a *pp, adj* (*metal*) plated: *un*

anillo ~ en oro a gold-plated ring **LOC chapado a la antigua** old-fashioned *Ver tb* CHAPAR

chapar *vi* (*estudiar*) to swot

chaparrón *nm* downpour: *¡Menudo ~!* What a downpour!

chapotear *vi* to splash about: *Los niños chapoteaban en los charcos.* The children were splashing about in the puddles.

chapucero, -a *adj, nm-nf* (*persona*) slapdash [*adj*]: *Ese fontanero es un ~.* That plumber is really slapdash.

chapurrear (*tb* **chapurrar**) *vt* to have a smattering of *sth*: *~ el italiano* to have a smattering of Italian

chapuza *nf* botch-up: *Ese dibujo es una ~.* You've made a real botch-up of that drawing. **LOC hacer chapuzas** (*arreglos*) to do odd jobs

chapuzón *nm* dip **LOC darse un chapuzón** to go for a dip

chaqué *nm* morning coat **LOC ir de chaqué** to wear morning dress

chaqueta *nf* jacket **LOC chaqueta de punto** cardigan

chaquetero, -a *nm-nf* turncoat

chaquetón *nm* jacket: *un ~ tres cuartos* a three-quarter length jacket

charanga *nf* brass band

charca *nf* pool

charco *nm* puddle

charcutería *nf* (*tienda*) delicatessen

charla *nf* **1** (*conversación*) chat **2** (*conferencia*) talk (**on *sth*/*sb***)

charlar *vi* to chat (***to sb***) (***about sth***)

charlatán, -ana ◆ *adj* talkative ◆ *nm-nf* **1** (*hablador*) chatterbox **2** (*indiscreto*) gossip

charol *nm* patent leather: *un bolso de ~* a patent leather bag

chárter *adj, nm*: *un (vuelo) ~* a charter flight

chascar ◆ *vt* **1** (*lengua*) to click **2** (*látigo*) to crack **3** (*dedos*) to snap ◆ *vi* **1** (*látigo*) to crack **2** (*madera*) to crackle

chasco *nm* (*decepción*) let-down, disappointment (*más formal*): *¡Vaya ~!* What a let-down! **LOC llevarse un chasco** to be disappointed

chasis *nm* chassis [*pl* chassis] **LOC estar/quedarse en el chasis** to be all skin and bone: *Se ha quedado en el ~.* He's all skin and bone.

chasquido *nm* **1** (*látigo*) crack **2** (*madera*) crackle **3** (*lengua*) click: *dar un ~ con la lengua* to click your tongue **4** (*dedos*) snap

chatarra *nf* **1** (*metal*) scrap [*incontable*]: *vender un coche como ~* to sell a car for scrap ◊ *Este frigorífico es una ~.* This fridge is only fit for scrap. **2** (*calderilla*) small change

chatarrero, -a *nm-nf* scrap merchant

chato *nm* glass of wine: *tomarse unos ~s* to have a few glasses of wine

chato, -a *adj* **1** (*persona*) snub-nosed **2** (*nariz*) snub **3** (*edificio, árbol*) squat

chaval, ~a *nm-nf* **1** (*gen*) boy [*fem* girl] **2 chavales** (*chicos y chicas*) youngsters, kids (*más coloq*) **LOC estar hecho un chaval** to look very young

chelín *nm* shilling

chepa *nf* hump

cheque *nm* cheque: *ingresar un ~* to pay a cheque in **LOC cheque de viaje** traveller's cheque **cheque en blanco/sin fondos** blank/bad cheque *Ver tb* PAGAR

chequeo *nm* check-up: *hacerse un ~* to have a check-up

chica *nf* (*criada*) maid *Ver tb* CHICO

chicha *nf* (*carne*) meat

chicharra *nf* (*insecto*) cicada

chicharrón *nm* crackling [*incontable*]

chichón *nm* lump: *tener un ~ en la frente* to have a lump on your forehead

chicle *nm* chewing gum [*incontable*]: *Cómprame un ~ de menta.* Buy me some spearmint chewing gum.

chico, -a *nm-nf* **1** (*gen*) boy [*fem* girl]: *el ~ de la oficina* the office boy **2 chicos** (*niños y niñas*) children, kids (*coloq*) **3** (*joven*) young man/woman [*pl* young men/women]: *un ~ de 25 años* a young man of twenty-five

chiflado, -a ◆ *pp, adj* (*loco*) touched ◆ *nm-nf* crackpot **LOC estar chiflado (por algo/algn)** to be mad (about sth/sb) *Ver tb* CHIFLAR

chifladura *nf* **1** (*locura*) madness **2** (*idea*) wild notion

chiflar ◆ *vi* **1** (*gen*) to whistle **2** (*encantar*) to love *sth/doing sth* [*vt*]: *Me chifla la paella.* I love paella. ◆ *vt* **1** (*con la boca*) to whistle: *~ una canción* to whistle a song **2** (*instrumento*) to blow ◆ **chiflarse** *v pron* **1** (*enloquecer*) to go mad **2 chiflarse con/por** (*entusiasmarse*) to be mad **about *sth*/*sb***: *Mi prima se chifla por los dibujos animados.* My cousin is mad about cartoons.

chile *nm* chilli [*pl* chillies]

chillar *vi* **1** (*gen*) to shout (***at sb***): *¡No me chilles!* Don't shout at me! ☛ *Ver nota en* SHOUT **2** (*berrear*) to scream **3** (*aves, frenos*) to screech **4** (*cerdo*) to squeal **5** (*ratón*) to squeak

chillido *nm* **1** (*persona*) shriek **2** (*ave, frenos*) screech **3** (*cerdo*) squeal **4** (*ratón*) squeak

chillón, -ona *adj* **1** (*persona*) noisy **2** (*sonido, color*) loud

chimenea *nf* **1** (*hogar*) fireplace: *Enciende la ~.* Light the fire. ◊ *sentados al lado de la ~* sitting by the fireplace **2** (*conducto de salida del humo*) chimney [*pl* chimneys]: *Desde aquí se ven las ~s de la fábrica.* You can see the factory chimneys from here. **3** (*de barco*) funnel

chimpancé *nm* chimpanzee

China *nf* China

chinchar ◆ *vt* to pester: *No me chinches más.* Stop pestering me. ◆ **chincharse** *v pron*: *¡Te chinchas!* Hard luck!

chinche *nf* bedbug

chincheta *nf* drawing-pin

chinchín *nm* (*brindis*) cheers!

chino, -a ◆ *adj, nm* Chinese: *hablar ~* to speak Chinese ◆ *nm-nf* Chinese man/woman [*pl* Chinese men/women]: *los ~s* the Chinese LOC *Ver* CUENTO, TINTA

chip *nm* chip

chipirón *nm* small squid [*pl* small squid]

chiquillo, -a *nm-nf* kid

chirimiri *nm* drizzle

chirimoya *nf* custard apple

chiringuito *nm* **1** (*quiosco*) refreshment stall **2** (*bar*) open-air café

chiripa *nf* stroke of luck: *¡Qué ~!* What a stroke of luck! LOC **de chiripa** by sheer luck

chirona *nf* nick: *estar en ~* to be in the nick

chirriar *vi* **1** (*bicicleta*) to squeak: *La cadena de mi bicicleta chirría.* My bicycle chain squeaks. **2** (*puerta*) to creak **3** (*frenos*) to screech **4** (*ave*) to squawk

chirrido *nm* **1** (*bicicleta*) squeak **2** (*puerta*) creak **3** (*frenos*) screech **4** (*ave*) squawk

¡chis! *interj* **1** (*¡silencio!*) sh! **2** (*¡oiga!*) hey!

chisme *nm* **1** (*cuento*) gossip [*incontable*]: *contar ~s* to gossip **2** (*trasto*) thing **3** (*aparato*) gadget, thingummy (*coloq*)

chismorrear *vi* to gossip

chismoso, -a ◆ *adj* gossipy ◆ *nm-nf* gossip: *¡Es un ~!* He's such a gossip!

chispa *nf* **1** (*gen*) spark **2** (*pizca*) bit: *Lleva una ~ de pimentón.* It's got a bit of paprika. LOC **estar algn que echa chispas** to be hopping mad **estar chispa** to be rather merry **tener chispa** to be witty

chispazo *nm* spark: *pegar un ~* to send out sparks

chispear *v imp* (*llover*) to spit: *Sólo chispeaba.* It was only spitting.

chistar *vi* LOC **sin chistar** without saying a word

chiste *nm* **1** (*hablado*) joke: *contar un ~* to tell a joke **2** (*dibujo*) cartoon LOC **coger el chiste** to get the joke

chistera *nf* top hat

chistoso, -a *adj* funny

chivar ◆ *vt, vi* to tell: *No le chives.* Don't tell him. ◊ *Me chivaron la última pregunta.* They told me the answer to the last question. ◆ **chivarse** *v pron* **1** (*entre niños*) to tell (on *sb*): *Me vio copiando y se chivó al profesor.* He saw me copying and told on me to the teacher. ◊ *Pienso ~me a mamá.* I'm going to tell mummy. **2** (*a la policía*) to grass

chivatazo *nm* tip-off LOC **dar el chivatazo** to tip *sb* off

chivato, -a *nm-nf* **1** (*gen*) tell-tale **2** (*de la policía*) grass

chivo, -a *nm-nf* kid

chocar ◆ *vi* **1** (*colisionar*) to crash: *El coche chocó contra una tapia.* The car crashed into a wall. ◊ *El balón chocó contra la puerta.* The ball crashed against the door. **2** (*sorprender*) to surprise: *Me chocó que se presentase sin avisar.* I was surprised he didn't tell us he was coming. ◆ *vt*: *¡Choca esos cinco!/ ¡Chócala!* Put it there!

chochear *vi* to go senile

chocolate *nm* **1** (*gen*) chocolate: *una tableta de ~* a bar of chocolate **2** (*líquido*) hot chocolate

chocolatina *nf* chocolate bar

chófer *nmf* **1** (*coche privado*) chauffeur **2** (*camión, autocar*) driver

chollo *nm* **1** (*trabajo*) cushy number **2** (*ganga*) bargain

chopo *nm* poplar

choque *nm* **1** (*colisión, ruido*) crash **2** (*enfrentamiento*) clash LOC **autos/ coches de choque** dodgems: *montarse en los coches de ~* to go on the dodgems

chorizo *nm* chorizo

chorlito *nm* LOC *Ver* CABEZA

chorrear *vi* **1** (*gotear*) to drip **2** (*estar empapado*) to be dripping wet: *Estas sábanas están chorreando.* These sheets are dripping wet.

chorro *nm* **1** (*gen*) jet **2** (*abundante*) gush **3** (*Cocina*) dash: *Añadir un ~ de limón.* Add a dash of lemon. LOC **a chorros**: *salir a ~s* to gush out

choza *nf* hut

chubasco *nm* shower: *inestable con claros y ~s* changeable with sunny spells and showers

chubasquero *nm* waterproof jacket

chuchería *nf* (*golosina*) sweet

chufa *nf* tiger nut: *horchata de ~s* tiger nut milk

chulear *vi* to show off

chuleta *nf* **1** (*alimento*) chop: *~s de cerdo* pork chops **2** (*para copiar*) crib

chuletilla *nf* cutlet

chulo, -a *adj* **1** (*persona*) cocky: *ponerse (en plan) ~* to get cocky **2** (*cosa*) lovely

chunga *nf* LOC **estar de chunga**: *No le hagas caso, está de ~.* Don't take any notice, he's only joking. **tomarse algo a chunga** to treat sth as a joke

chupa *nf* jacket

chupa-chups® *nm* lollipop

chupada *nf* **1** (*gen*) suck: *El niño le daba ~s al polo.* The boy was sucking his lolly. **2** (*cigarrillo*) puff: *dar una ~ a un cigarrillo* to have a puff of a cigarette

chupado, -a *pp, adj* **1** (*persona*) skinny ☛ *Ver nota en* DELGADO **2** (*cosa*) dead easy: *El examen estaba ~.* The exam was dead easy. *Ver tb* CHUPAR

chupar *vt* **1** (*gen*) to suck **2** (*absorber*) to soak *sth* up: *Esta planta chupa mucha agua.* This plant soaks up a lot of water. LOC **chupar del bote** to scrounge **chuparse el dedo 1** (*lit*) to suck your thumb **2** (*fig*): *¿Te crees que me chupo el dedo?* Do you think I'm stupid? **chuparse los dedos** to lick your fingers: *Estaba para ~se los dedos.* It was delicious.

chupatintas *nmf* pen-pusher

chupete *nm* dummy [*pl* dummies]

chupón, -ona *adj, nm-nf* (*aprovechado*) sponger [*n*]: *¡Mira que eres ~!* You're a real sponger!

churro *nm* **1** (*comida*) kind of doughnut **2** (*chapuza*) botch-up: *Me ha salido un ~.* I've made a botch of it. LOC **de churro**: *Me los encontré de ~.* I ran into them by pure chance. *Ver tb* VENDER

chutar ◆ *vi* to shoot ◆ **chutarse** *v pron* to shoot *sth* up LOC **ir que chuta 1** (*asunto*) to go really well **2** (*persona*): *20, y vas que chutas.* 20, and you can count yourself lucky.

cicatriz *nf* scar: *Me quedó una ~.* I was left with a scar.

cicatrizar *vi* to heal

ciclismo *nm* cycling: *hacer ~* to cycle

ciclista *nmf* cyclist LOC *Ver* VUELTA

ciclo *nm* cycle: *un ~ de cuatro años* a four-year cycle

ciclón *nm* cyclone

ciego, -a ◆ *adj* ~ (**de**) blind (**with** ***sth***): *quedarse ~* to go blind ◊ *~ de cólera* blind with rage ◆ *nm-nf* blind man/woman [*pl* blind men/women]: *una colecta para los ~s* a collection for the blind LOC **a ciegas**: *Lo han comprado a ciegas.* They bought it without seeing it. **ponerse ciego** (**a/de**) (*comida*) to stuff yourself (with *sth*) *Ver tb* GALLINA

cielo ◆ *nm* **1** (*firmamento*) sky [*pl* skies] **2** (*Relig*) heaven ◆ **¡cielos!** *interj* good heavens! LOC **ser un cielo** to be an angel *Ver tb* CAÍDO, SANTO, SÉPTIMO

ciempiés *nm* centipede

cien *nm, adj, pron* **1** (*gen*) a hundred: *Hoy cumple ~ años.* She's a hundred today. ◊ *Había ~ mil personas.* There were a hundred thousand people. **2** (*centésimo*) hundredth: *Soy el ~ de la lista.* I'm hundredth on the list. ☛ *Ver* Apéndice 1. LOC (**al**) **cien por cien** a hundred per cent **cien mil veces** hundreds of times **poner a algn a cien** to drive sb mad *Ver tb* OJO

ciencia *nf* **1** (*gen*) science **2 ciencias** (*Educ*) science [*sing*]: *mi profesor de ~s* my science teacher ◊ *Estudié ~s.* I studied science. LOC **ciencias empresariales** business studies [*sing*] **ciencias naturales** natural science [*sing*]

ciencia-ficción *nf* science fiction

científico, -a ◆ *adj* scientific ◆ *nm-nf* scientist

ciento *nm, adj* (a) hundred [*pl* hundred]: *~ sesenta y tres* a hundred and sixty-three ◊ *varios ~s* several hundred ☛ *Ver* Apéndice 1. LOC **cientos de…** hundreds of…: *~s de libras* hundreds of pounds **por ciento** per cent: *un/el 50 por ~ de la población* 50 per cent of the population *Ver tb* TANTO

cierre *nm* **1** (*acto de cerrar*) closure **2** (*collar, bolso*) clasp LOC *Ver* LIQUIDACIÓN

cierto, -a *adj* **1** (*gen*) certain: *con cierta inquietud* with a certain anxiety ◊ *Sólo están a ciertas horas del día.* They're only there at certain times of the day. **2** (*verdadero*) true: *Es ~.* It's true. LOC **hasta cierto punto** up to a point **por cierto** by the way

ciervo, -a *nm-nf* deer [*pl* deer]

> La palabra **deer** es el sustantivo genérico, **stag** (o **buck**) se refiere sólo al ciervo macho y **doe** sólo a la hembra. **Fawn** es el cervatillo.

cifra *nf* **1** (*gen*) figure: *un número de tres ~s* a three-figure number **2** (*teléfono*) digit: *un teléfono de seis ~s* a six-digit phone number **3** (*dinero*) figure: *una ~ de un millón de pesetas* a figure of one million pesetas

cigarrillo *nm* cigarette

cigüeña *nf* stork

cilíndrico, -a *adj* cylindrical

cilindro *nm* cylinder

cima *nf* top: *llegar a la ~* to reach the top

cimientos *nm* foundations

cinc *nm Ver* ZINC

cincel *nm* chisel

cinco *nm, adj, pron* **1** (*gen*) five **2** (*fecha*) fifth ☛ *Ver ejemplos en* SEIS

cincuenta *nm, adj, pron* **1** (*gen*) fifty **2** (*cincuentavo*) fiftieth ☛ *Ver ejemplos en* SESENTA

cine *nm* cinema: *ir al ~* to go to the cinema LOC **de cine** (*festival, director, crítico*) film: *un actor/director de ~* a film actor/director

cinematográfico, -a *adj* film [*n atrib*]: *la industria cinematográfica* the film industry

cínico, -a ◆ *adj* hypocritical ◆ *nm-nf* hypocrite

cinta *nf* **1** (*casete, vídeo*) tape: *una ~ virgen* a blank tape ☛ *Ver nota en* CASETE **2** (*lazo, máquina de escribir*) ribbon LOC **cinta adhesiva/aislante** sticky/insulating tape **cinta de vídeo** videotape **cinta para el pelo** hair band

cinto *nm* belt

cintura *nf* waist: *Tengo 60cm de ~.* I've got a 24 inch waist.

cinturón *nm* belt: *ser ~ negro* to be a black belt LOC **cinturón (de seguridad)** seat belt *Ver tb* APRETAR

ciprés *nm* cypress

circo *nm* **1** (*espectáculo*) circus [*pl* circuses] **2** (*anfiteatro*) amphitheatre

circuito *nm* **1** (*Dep*) track: *El piloto dio diez vueltas al ~.* The driver did ten laps of the track. **2** (*Electrón*) circuit

circulación *nf* **1** (*gen*) circulation: *mala ~ de la sangre* poor circulation **2** (*tráfico*) traffic LOC *Ver* CÓDIGO

circular[1] *adj, nf* circular: *una mesa ~* a round table ◊ *remitir una ~* to send out a circular

circular[2] ◆ *vt, vi* to circulate: *La sangre circula por las venas.* Blood circulates through your veins. ◊ *~ una carta* to circulate a letter ◆ *vi* **1** (*coche*) to drive: *Circulen con precaución.* Drive carefully. **2** (*tren, autobús*) to run **3** (*rumor*) to go round LOC **¡circulen!** move along!

círculo *nm* **1** (*gen*) circle: *formar un ~* to form a circle **2** (*asociación*) society [*pl* societies] LOC **círculo polar ártico/antártico** Arctic/Antarctic Circle **círculo vicioso** vicious circle

circunferencia *nf* **1** (*círculo*) circle: *El diámetro divide una ~ en dos partes iguales.* The diameter divides a circle into two equal halves. ◊ *dos ~s concéntricas* two concentric circles **2** (*perímetro*) circumference: *La Tierra tiene unos 40.000 kilómetros de ~.* The earth has a circumference of about 40 000 kilometres.

circunstancia *nf* circumstance

circunvalación *nf* LOC *Ver* CARRETERA

cirio *nm* candle LOC **armar/montar un cirio** to make a fuss

ciruela *nf* plum LOC **ciruela pasa** prune

ciruelo *nm* plum tree

cirugía *nf* surgery: *~ estética/plástica* cosmetic/plastic surgery

cirujano, -a *nm-nf* surgeon

cisco *nm* **1** (*jaleo*) racket: *armar un ~* to make a racket **2** (*discusión*) fuss: *Montó un ~ en la tienda.* He kicked up a fuss in the shop. LOC **hecho cisco** shattered

cisma *nm* schism

cisne *nm* swan

cisterna *nf* **1** (*depósito*) tank **2** (*baño*) cistern LOC *Ver* CAMIÓN

cita *nf* **1** (*amigos, pareja*) date **2** (*médico, abogado*) appointment: *Tengo una ~ con el dentista.* I've got a dental appointment. **3** (*frase*) quotation, quote (*coloq*)

citar ◆ *vt* **1** (*convocar*) to arrange to meet *sb* **2** (*Jur*) to summons **3** (*hacer referencia*) to quote (**from** ***sth/sb***)

◆ **citarse** *v pron* **citarse** (**con**) to arrange to meet (*sb*)

cítricos *nm* citrus fruits

ciudad *nf* **1** (*importante*) city [*pl* cities] **2** (*más pequeña*) town LOC **ciudad natal** home town

ciudadanía *nf* citizenship

ciudadano, -a ◆ *adj*: *por razones de seguridad ciudadana* for reasons of public safety ◊ *El alcalde pidió la colaboración ciudadana.* The mayor asked everyone to work together. ◆ *nm-nf* citizen: *ser ~ de la Comunidad Europea* to be a citizen of the European Community ◊ *Dio las gracias a todos los ~s de Simancas.* He thanked the people of Simancas. LOC *Ver* INSEGURIDAD

cívico, -a *adj* public-spirited: *sentido ~* public-spiritedness

civil ◆ *adj* civil: *un enfrentamiento ~* a civil disturbance ◆ *nmf* civilian LOC *Ver* CASAR, ESTADO, GUARDIA, REGISTRO

civilización *nf* civilization

civilizado, -a *pp, adj* civilized

civismo *nm* community spirit

clamar ◆ *vt* (*exigir*) to demand ◆ *vi* (*gritar*) to shout

clamor *nf* **1** (*gritos*) shouts [*pl*]: *el ~ de la muchedumbre* the shouts of the crowd **2** (*en espectáculos*) cheers [*pl*]: *el ~ del público* the cheers of the audience

clan *nm* clan

clandestino, -a *adj* clandestine

claqué *nm* tap-dancing

clara *nf* **1** (*huevo*) egg white **2** (*bebida*) shandy [*pl* shandies]

claraboya *nf* skylight

clarear *v imp* **1** (*despejarse*) to clear up **2** (*amanecer*) to get light

clarete *nm* rosé

claridad *nf* **1** (*luz*) light **2** (*fig*) clarity

clarificar *vt* to clarify

clarín *nm* bugle

clarinete *nm* clarinet

claro, -a ◆ *adj* **1** (*gen*) clear **2** (*color*) light: *verde ~* light green **3** (*luminoso*) bright **4** (*pelo*) fair **5** (*poco espeso*) thin ◆ *nm* **1** (*bosque*) clearing **2** (*Meteorología*) sunny spell ◆ *adv* clearly: *No oigo ~.* I can't hear clearly. ◆ **¡claro!** *interj* of course! LOC **claro que no** of course not **claro que sí** of course **dejar claro** to make *sth* clear **estar más claro que el agua** to be crystal clear **llevarlo claro** to have another think coming **poner en claro** to make *sth* clear

clase *nf* **1** (*gen, Ciencias, Sociol*) class: *Estudiamos en la misma ~.* We were in the same class. ◊ *viajar en primera ~* to travel first class **2** (*variedad*) kind: *distintas ~s de pan* different kinds of bread **3** (*aula*) classroom **4** (*lección*) lesson: *~s de conducir* driving lessons ◊ *~ particular* private lesson LOC **clase alta/baja/media** upper/lower/middle class(es) [*se usa mucho en plural*] **dar clase** to teach: *Doy ~ en un colegio privado.* I teach at an independent school. *Ver tb* COMPAÑERO

clásico, -a ◆ *adj* **1** (*Arte, Hist, Mús*) classical **2** (*típico*) classic: *el ~ comentario* the classic remark ◆ *nm* classic

clasificación *nf* **1** (*gen*) classification: *la ~ de las plantas* the classification of plants **2** (*Dep*): *partido de ~* qualifying match ◊ *El tenista alemán encabeza la ~ mundial.* The German player is number one in the world rankings. ◊ *la ~ general de la liga* the league table

clasificar ◆ *vt* to classify: *~ los libros por materias* to classify books according to subject ◆ **clasificarse** *v pron* **clasificarse** (**para**) to qualify (**for** *sth*): *~se para la final* to qualify for the final LOC **clasificarse en segundo, tercer, etc lugar** to come second, third, etc

clasificatorio, -a *adj* qualifying

clasista ◆ *adj* class-conscious ◆ *nmf* snob

claudicar *vi* to surrender

claustro *nm* **1** (*Arquit*) cloister **2** (*conjunto de profesores*) staff [*pl*] **3** (*reunión*) staff meeting

claustrofobia *nf* claustrophobia: *tener ~* to suffer from claustrophobia

claustrofóbico, -a *adj* claustrophobic

cláusula *nf* clause

clausura *nf* (*cierre*) closure LOC **de clausura** closing: *acto/discurso de ~* closing ceremony/speech

clausurar(se) *vt, v pron* to end

clavado, -a *pp, adj* **1** *~* **a** (*idéntico*) just like: *Esa sonrisa es clavada a la de su madre.* That smile is just like his mother's. **2** (*en punto*) on the dot: *las seis y media clavadas* half past six on the dot *Ver tb* CLAVAR

clavar ◆ *vt* **1** (*clavo, estaca*) to hammer *sth* **into** *sth*: *~ clavos en la pared* to hammer nails into the wall **2** (*cuchillo, puñal*) to stick *sth* **into** *sth*/*sb*: *Clavó el cuchillo en la mesa.* He stuck the knife into the table. **3** (*sujetar algo con clavos*) to nail: *Clavaron el cuadro en la pared.* They nailed the picture onto the wall. **4** (*estafar*) to rip *sb* off ◆ **clavarse** *v pron*: *Me he clavado una espina en el dedo.* I've got a thorn in my finger. ◊ *Ten cuidado, te vas a ~ el alfiler/las tijeras.* Be careful you don't hurt yourself with that pin/the scissors.

clave *nf* **1** (*código*) code **2** ~ (**de/para**) key (**to *sth***): *la ~ de su éxito* the key to their success **3** (*fundamental*) key [*n atrib*]: *factor/persona ~* key factor/person **4** (*Mús*) clef LOC **clave de sol/fa** treble/bass clef **ser clave** to be central *to sth*

clavel *nm* carnation

clavícula *nf* collarbone

clavo *nm* **1** (*gen*) nail **2** (*Cocina*) clove LOC **como un clavo** on the dot: *Salió a las dos como un ~.* It left at two on the dot. **dar en el clavo** to hit the nail on the head

claxon *nm* horn: *tocar el ~* to sound the horn

clero *nm* clergy [*pl*]

cliché *nm* **1** (*tópico*) cliché **2** (*Fot*) negative

cliente, -a *nm-nf* **1** (*tienda, restaurante*) customer: *uno de mis mejores ~s* one of my best customers **2** (*empresa*) client

clima *nm* **1** (*lit*) climate: *un ~ húmedo* a damp climate **2** (*fig*) atmosphere: *un ~ de cordialidad/tensión* a friendly/tense atmosphere

climatizado, -a *pp, adj* air-conditioned LOC *Ver* PISCINA

clímax *nm* climax

clínica *nf* clinic

clip *nm* **1** (*papel*) paper clip **2** (*pelo*) hair clip **3** (*vídeo*) video [*pl* videos]

cloaca *nf* sewer

cloro *nm* chlorine

clorofila *nf* chlorophyll

club *nm* club

coacción *nf* coercion

coaccionar *vt* to coerce *sb* (***into doing sth***)

coagular(se) *vt, v pron* to clot

coágulo *nm* clot

coala *nm Ver* KOALA

coalición *nf* coalition

coartada *nf* alibi [*pl* alibis]: *tener una buena ~* to have a good alibi

coba *nf* LOC **dar coba** to soft-soap *sb*

cobarde ◆ *adj* cowardly: *No seas ~.* Don't be so cowardly. ◆ *nmf* coward

cobardía *nf* cowardice [*incontable*]: *Es una ~.* It's an act of cowardice.

cobaya *nmf* guinea pig

cobertizo *nm* shed

cobijar ◆ *vt* to shelter *sb* (**from *sth***) ◆ **cobijarse** *v pron* **cobijarse** (**de**) to shelter (**from *sth***): *~se del frío* to shelter from the cold

cobra *nf* cobra

cobrador, ~a *nm-nf* **1** (*autobús*) conductor **2** (*deudas, recibos*) collector

cobrar ◆ *vt, vi* **1** (*gen*) to charge (*sb*) (***for sth***): *Me cobraron cien pesetas por un café.* They charged me a hundred pesetas for a coffee. ◊ *¿Me cobra, por favor?* Can I have the bill, please? **2** (*salario*): *Todavía no he cobrado las clases.* I still haven't been paid for those classes. ◊ *¡El jueves cobramos!* Thursday is pay day! ◆ *vt* **1** (*cheque*) to cash **2** (*adquirir*) to gain: *~ fuerza* to gain momentum ◆ *vi* to get a smack: *¡Vas a ~!* You'll get a smack! ◆ **cobrarse** *v pron* **1** (*gen*): *Cóbrese, por favor.* Here you are. ◊ *¿Te cobras las bebidas?* How much are the drinks? **2** (*costar*) to cost: *La guerra se ha cobrado muchas vidas.* The war has cost many lives. LOC **cobrar de más/menos** to overcharge/undercharge **cobrar el paro** to draw the dole *Ver tb* IMPORTANCIA

cobre *nm* copper

cobro *nm* **1** (*pago*) payment **2** (*recaudación*) charging LOC *Ver* LLAMADA, LLAMAR

Coca-Cola® *nf* Coke®

cocaína *nf* cocaine

cocción *nf* cooking: *tiempo de ~* cooking time

cocear *vi* to kick

cocer ◆ *vt* **1** (*hervir*) to boil **2** (*pan*) to bake **3** (*cerámica*) to fire ◆ *vi* **1** (*alimento*) to cook **2** (*líquido*) to boil: *El agua está cociendo.* The water is boiling. ◆ **cocerse** *v pron* **1** (*alimento*) to cook **2** (*tener calor*) to boil: *Me estoy cociendo con este jersey.* I'm boiling in this jumper. LOC **cocer a fuego lento** to simmer

coche *nm* **1** (*automóvil*) car: *ir en ~* to go by car **2** (*vagón, carruaje*) carriage **3** (*para bebé*) pram LOC **coche cama** sleeping car **coche de alquiler** hire car **coche de bomberos** fire engine **coche de carreras** racing car **coche fúnebre** hearse *Ver tb* ACCIDENTE, BOMBA[1], CHOQUE

cochera *nf* **1** (*coche*) garage **2** (*autobús*) depot

cochinillo *nm* sucking pig

cochino, -a *nm-nf* **1** (*animal*) pig ☛ *Ver nota en* CERDO **2** (*persona*) dirty beast

cocido *nm* stew LOC *Ver* JAMÓN

cocina *nf* **1** (*lugar*) kitchen **2** (*aparato*) cooker **3** (*arte de cocinar*) cookery: *un curso/libro de ~* a cookery course/book **4** (*gastronomía*) cooking: *la ~ china* Chinese cooking LOC *Ver* BATERÍA, MENAJE, PAÑO

cocinar *vt, vi* to cook: *No sé ~.* I can't cook.

cocinero, -a *nm-nf* cook: *ser buen ~* to be a good cook

coco *nm* **1** (*fruto*) coconut **2** (*cabeza*) nut **3** (*ser fantástico*) bogeyman **4** (*persona fea*) fright LOC **tener mucho coco** to be very brainy *Ver tb* COMER

cocodrilo *nm* crocodile LOC *Ver* LÁGRIMA

cocotero *nm* coconut palm

cóctel *nm* **1** (*bebida*) cocktail **2** (*reunión*) cocktail party

codazo *nm* **1** (*violento, para abrirse paso*): *Me abrí paso a ~s.* I elbowed my way through the crowd. **2** (*para llamar la atención*) nudge: *Me dio un ~.* He gave me a nudge.

codearse *v pron* ~ **con** to rub shoulders **with** ***sb***

codera *nf* (*parche*) elbow patch

codicia *nf* **1** (*avaricia*) greed **2** ~ **de** lust **for** ***sth***: *su ~ de poder/riquezas* their lust for power/riches

codiciar *vt* (*ambicionar*) to covet

codificar *vt* (*Informát*) to encode

código *nm* code LOC **código de (la) circulación** Highway Code **código postal** postcode

codo *nm* elbow LOC *Ver* HABLAR

codorniz *nf* quail [*pl* quail/quails]

coeficiente *nm* coefficient LOC **coeficiente de inteligencia** intelligence quotient (*abrev* IQ)

coexistencia *nf* coexistence

cofradía *nf* brotherhood

cofre *nm* case

cogedor *nm* dustpan

coger ◆ *vt* **1** (*tomar*) to take: *Coge los libros que quieras.* Take as many books as you like. ◊ *Prefiero ~ el autobús.* I'd rather take the bus. ◊ *Le cogí del brazo.* I took him by the arm. ◊ *He cogido dos entradas.* I've bought two tickets. **2** (*pillar*) to catch: *~ una pelota* to catch a ball ◊ *Los cogieron robando.* They were caught stealing. ◊ *~ un resfriado* to catch a cold **3** (*entender*) to get: *No lo cojo.* I don't get it. **4** (*fruta, flores*) to pick **5** (*tomar prestado*) to borrow: *¿Puedo ~ tu coche?* Can I borrow your car? ☛ *Ver dibujo en* BORROW **6** (*toro*) to gore ◆ **cogerse** *v pron* to hold: *Cógete de mi mano.* Hold my hand. ◊ *~se de la barandilla* to hold on to the railings LOC **coger y...** to up and *do sth*: *Cogí y me fui.* I upped and left. ☛Para otras expresiones con **coger**, véanse las entradas del sustantivo, adjetivo, etc, p.ej. **coger por banda** en BANDA y **coger la costumbre** en COSTUMBRE.

cogido, -a *pp, adj* (*reservado*) taken LOC **cogidos de la mano** holding hands **cogidos del brazo** arm in arm ☛ *Ver dibujo en* ARM; *Ver tb* COGER

cogorza *nf* LOC **coger una cogorza/mona** to get plastered

cogote *nm* back of the neck

coherencia *nf* coherence

cohete *nm* rocket

cohibir ◆ *vt* to inhibit ◆ **cohibirse** *v pron* to feel inhibited

coincidencia *nf* coincidence LOC **da la coincidencia de que...** it just so happens (that)...

coincidir *vi* **1** (*estar de acuerdo*) to agree (***with sb***) (***on/about sth***): *Coinciden conmigo en que es un chico estupendo.* They agree with me (that) he's a great lad. ◊ *Coincidimos en todo.* We agree on everything. **2** (*en un lugar*): *Coincidimos en el congreso.* We were both at the conference. **3** (*acontecimientos, resultados*) to coincide (***with sth***): *Espero que no me coincida con los exámenes.* I hope it doesn't coincide with my exams.

cojear *vi* ~ (**de**) **1** (*ser cojo*) to be lame (**in** ***sth***): *Cojeo del pie derecho.* I'm lame in my right foot. **2** (*por lesión*) to limp: *Todavía cojeo un poco, pero estoy mejor.* I'm still limping, but I feel better. **3** (*mueble*) to be wobbly LOC **cojear del mismo pie** to have the same faults (*as sb*)

cojera *nf* limp: *Casi no se le nota la ~.* He's got a very slight limp.

cojín *nm* cushion

cojo, -a ◆ *adj* **1** (*persona*): *estar ~ (de un pie)* to have a limp ◊ *Se quedó ~ después del accidente.* The accident left him with a limp. **2** (*animal*) lame **3** (*mueble*) wobbly ◆ *nm-nf* cripple LOC **andar/ir cojo** to limp *Ver tb* PATA

col *nf* cabbage LOC **coles de Bruselas** Brussels sprouts

cola[1] *nf* **1** (*animal*) tail **2** (*vestido*) train: *El vestido tiene un poco de ~.* The dress has a short train. **3** (*fila*) queue: *ponerse a la ~* to join the queue ◊ *Había mucha ~ para el cine.* There was a long queue for the cinema. LOC **¡a la cola!** get in the queue! **cola de caballo** ponytail **hacer cola** to queue *Ver tb* PIANO

cola[2] *nf* (*pegamento*) glue

colaboración *nf* collaboration: *hacer algo en ~ con algn* to do sth in collaboration with sb

colaborador, ~a *nm-nf* collaborator

colaborar *vi* ~ (**con**) (**en**) to collaborate (**with** *sb*) (**on** *sth*)

colada *nf* (*ropa*) wash: *hacer la ~* to do the washing LOC *Ver* CESTO

colado, -a *pp, adj* LOC **estar colado por algn** to be mad about sb *Ver tb* COLAR

colador *nm* **1** (*gen*) strainer **2** (*verduras*) colander

colar ◆ *vt* **1** (*infusión*) to strain **2** (*café*) to filter **3** (*verduras*) to drain ◆ *vi* to be believed: *Eso no va a ~.* Nobody is going to believe that. ◆ **colarse** *v pron* **1** (*líquido*) to seep ***through sth*** **2** (*persona*) **(a)** (*gen*) to sneak in: *Vi cómo se colaban.* I noticed them sneaking in. ◊ *Nos colamos en el autobús sin pagar.* We sneaked onto the bus without paying. **(b)** (*en una cola*) to push in: *¡Oiga, no se cuele!* Hey! No pushing in! **3** (*equivocarse*) to slip up **4 colarse por** (*enamorarse*) to fall **for** ***sb*** LOC **colarse en una fiesta** to gatecrash a party

colcha *nf* bedspread

colchón *nm* mattress

colchoneta *nf* **1** (*gimnasio*) mat **2** (*camping, playa*) air-bed

colección *nf* collection

coleccionar *vt* to collect

coleccionista *nmf* collector

colecta *nf* collection LOC **hacer una colecta** (*con fines caritativos*) to collect for charity

colectivo, -a *adj, nm* collective

colega *nmf* **1** (*compañero*) colleague: *un ~ mío* a colleague of mine **2** (*amigo*) friend

colegial, ~a *nm-nf* schoolboy/girl [*pl* schoolchildren]

colegio *nm* **1** (*Educ*) school: *Los niños están en el ~.* The children are at school. ◊ *ir al ~* to go to school ☛ *Ver nota en* SCHOOL **2** (*asociación*) association: *el ~ de médicos* the medical association LOC **colegio de curas/monjas** Catholic school **colegio de internos** boarding-school **colegio electoral** polling station **colegio mayor** hall of residence **colegio privado/público** independent/state school *Ver tb* MESA

cólera *nm* (*enfermedad*) cholera

colesterol *nm* cholesterol: *Me ha aumentado el ~.* My cholesterol (level) has gone up.

coleta *nf* pigtail LOC *Ver* CORTAR

colgado, -a *pp, adj* ~ **en/de** hanging **on/from** ***sth*** LOC **colgado al teléfono** on the phone **dejar a algn colgado** to leave sb in the lurch **estar colgado** (*drogado*) to be stoned **mal colgado**: *Creo que tienen el teléfono mal ~.* They must have left the phone off the hook. *Ver tb* COLGAR

colgante *nm* pendant

colgar ◆ *vt* **1** (*gen*) to hang *sth* ***from/on sth*** **2** (*prenda de vestir*) to hang *sth* up **3** (*ahorcar*) to hang: *Lo colgaron en 1215.* He was hanged in 1215. ☛ *Ver nota en* AHORCAR(SE) ◆ *vi* to hang (***from/on sth***) LOC **colgar (el teléfono)** to hang up: *Se enfadó y me colgó el teléfono.* He got angry and hung up. ◊ *No cuelgue, por favor.* Please hold the line. **colgar las botas** to retire **colgar los libros** to give up studying

cólico *nm* colic [*incontable*]

coliflor *nf* cauliflower

colilla *nf* cigarette end

colina *nf* hill

colirio *nm* eye drops [*pl*]

colisión *nf* collision (***with sth***): *una ~ de frente* a head-on collision

colitis *nf* diarrhoea [*incontable*]

collage *nm* collage: *hacer un ~* to make a collage

collar *nm* **1** (*adorno*) necklace: *un ~ de esmeraldas* an emerald necklace **2** (*perro, gato*) collar

collarín *nm* (surgical) collar

colmar *vt* LOC *Ver* GOTA

colmena *nf* beehive

colmillo *nm* **1** (*persona*) canine (tooth) **2** (*elefante, jabalí*) tusk

colmo *nm* LOC **ser el colmo** to be the limit **para colmo** to make matters worse

colocado, -a *pp, adj* LOC **estar colocado 1** (*bebido*) to be merry **2** (*drogado*) to be high **3** (*tener trabajo*) to be employed: *estar bien ~* to have a good job *Ver tb* COLOCAR

colocar ♦ *vt* **1** (*gen*) to place **2** (*bomba*) to plant **3** (*emplear*) to find *sb* a job (***with sb***) ♦ **colocarse** *v pron* **1** (*situarse*) to stand: *Colócate allí.* Stand over there. **2 colocarse** (**de/como**) to get a job (**as *sth***) **3 colocarse** (**con**) **(a)** (*alcohol*) to get drunk (**on *sth***) **(b)** (*drogas*) to get high (**on *sth***)

Colombia *nf* Colombia

colombiano, -a *adj, nm-nf* Colombian

colon *nm* colon

colonia[1] *nf* **1** (*gen*) colony [*pl* colonies] **2** (*grupo de viviendas*) housing estate

colonia[2] *nf* (*perfume*) cologne [*incontable*]: *echarse ~* to put (some) cologne on

colonial *adj* colonial

colonización *nf* colonization

colonizador, ~a ♦ *adj* colonizing ♦ *nm-nf* settler

colonizar *vt* to colonize

coloquial *adj* colloquial

coloquio *nm* discussion (***about sth***)

color *nm* colour LOC **de colores** coloured: *lápices de ~es* coloured pencils **en color**: *una televisión en ~* a colour TV *Ver tb* FAROLILLO, PEZ, TIZA, VIDRIERA

colorado, -a *adj* red LOC **estar colorado como un tomate/pimiento** to be as red as a beetroot **ponerse colorado** to blush *Ver tb* COLORÍN

colorante *adj, nm* colouring LOC **sin colorantes** no artificial colourings

colorear *vt* to colour *sth* (in)

colorete *nm* blusher: *darse un poco de ~* to put on some blusher

colorido *nm* colouring: *una ceremonia de gran ~* a very colourful ceremony

colorín *nm* **colorines** bright colours [*pl*]: *calcetines de colorines* brightly-coloured socks LOC **colorín colorado...** and they all lived happily ever after

columna *nf* **1** (*gen*) column **2** (*Anat*) spine LOC **columna vertebral 1** (*Anat*) spinal column **2** (*fig*) backbone

columpiar ♦ *vt* to give *sb* a swing ♦ **columpiarse** *v pron* to have a swing

columpio *nm* swing: *jugar en los ~s* to play on the swings

coma[1] *nm* (*Med*) coma: *estar en ~* to be in a coma LOC *Ver* ESTADO

coma[2] *nf* **1** (*puntuación*) comma ☛ *Ver* págs 318-9. **2** (*Mat*) point: *cuarenta ~ cinco (40,5)* forty point five (40·5) ☛ *Ver* Apéndice 1. LOC *Ver* PUNTO

comadreja *nf* weasel

comadrona *nf* midwife [*pl* midwives]

comandante *nmf* major

comando *nm* **1** (*Mil*) commando [*pl* commando/commandoes] **2** (*terrorista*) cell

comarca *nf* area

comarcal *adj* LOC *Ver* CARRETERA

comba *nf* **1** (*juego*) skipping **2** (*cuerda*) skipping rope LOC **jugar/saltar a la comba** to skip: *Están saltando a la ~.* They are skipping.

combate *nm* combat [*incontable*]: *soldados caídos en ~* soldiers killed in combat ◊ *Hubo feroces ~s.* There was fierce fighting. LOC **combate de boxeo** boxing match **de combate** fighter: *avión/piloto de ~* fighter plane/pilot *Ver tb* CARRO, FUERA

combatiente *nmf* combatant

combatir ♦ *vt* to combat: *~ a la guerrilla* to combat the guerrillas ♦ *vi ~* (**contra/por**) to fight (**against/for *sth/sb***): *~ contra los rebeldes* to fight (against) the rebels

combinación *nf* **1** (*gen*) combination: *la ~ de una caja fuerte* the combination of a safe **2** (*prenda*) slip

combinar ♦ *vt* **1** (*gen*) to combine **2** (*ropa*) to match *sth* (***with sth***) ♦ *vi* **1** (*colores*) to go ***with sth***: *El negro combina bien con todos los colores.* Black goes well with any colour. **2** (*ropa*) to match: *Esos zapatos no combinan con el bolso.* Those shoes don't match the handbag.

combustible ♦ *adj* combustible ♦ *nm* fuel

combustión *nf* combustion

comedia *nf* comedy [*pl* comedies] LOC **comedia musical** musical

comedor *nm* **1** (*casa, hotel*) dining-room **2** (*colegio, fábrica*) canteen ☛ *Ver* pág 320. **3** (*muebles*) dining-room suite

comentar *vt* **1** (*decir*) to say: *Se limitó a ~ que estaba enfermo.* He would only say he was sick. **2** (*tema*) to discuss

comentario *nm* comment, remark (*más coloq*): *hacer un ~* to make a comment/remark LOC **comentario de texto** textual criticism **hacer comentarios** to comment (*on sth/sb*) **sin comentarios** no comment

comentarista *nmf* commentator

comenzar *vt, vi ~* (**a**) to start (***sth/doing sth/to do sth***): *Comencé a sentirme mal.* I started to feel ill.

comer ♦ *vt* **1** (*ingerir*) to eat: *Deberías ~ algo antes de salir.* You should eat something before you go. **2** (*insectos*) to eat *sb* alive: *Me han comido los mosquitos.* I've been eaten alive by the mosquitoes. **3** (*Ajedrez, Damas*) to take ♦ *vi* **1** (*ingerir*) to eat: *Tu hijo no quiere ~.* Your son won't eat. **2** (*al mediodía*) to have lunch: *¿A qué hora comemos?* What time are we going to have lunch? ◊ *¿Qué hay para ~?* What's for lunch? ◊ *Mañana comemos fuera.* We're going out for lunch tomorrow. ♦ **comerse** *v pron* **1** (*ingerir*) to eat: *~se un bocadillo* to eat a sandwich **2** (*omitir*) to miss *sth* out: *~se una palabra* to miss a word out LOC **comer a besos** to smother *sb* with kisses **comer como una lima/fiera/vaca** to eat like a horse **comerle el coco a algn** to brainwash sb **comerse el coco** to worry yourself (*about sth/sb*) **dar/echar de comer** to feed

comercial *adj* commercial LOC *Ver* CENTRO, GALERÍA

comercializar *vt* to market

comerciante *nmf* (*dueño de una tienda*) shopkeeper

comerciar *vi* ~ **con 1** (*producto*) to trade (**in *sth***): *~ con armas* to trade in arms **2** (*persona*) to do business (**with *sb***)

comercio *nm* **1** (*negocio*) trade: *~ exterior* foreign trade **2** (*tienda*) shop: *Tienen un pequeño ~ .* They have a small shop. ◊ *¿A qué hora abre el ~?* What time do the shops open?

comestible ♦ *adj* edible ♦ **comestibles** *nm* LOC *Ver* TIENDA

cometa ♦ *nm* (*astro*) comet ♦ *nf* (*juguete*) kite

cometer *vt* **1** (*delito*) to commit **2** (*error*) to make

cometido *nm* **1** (*encargo*) assignment **2** (*obligación*) duty [*pl* duties]

cómic *nm* comic

comicios *nm* elections

cómico, -a ♦ *adj* **1** (*gracioso*) funny **2** (*de comedia*) comedy [*n atrib*]: *actor ~* comedy actor ♦ *nm-nf* comedian [*fem* comedienne] LOC *Ver* PELÍCULA

comida *nf* **1** (*alimento*) food: *Tenemos la nevera llena de ~.* The fridge is full of food. **2** (*desayuno, comida, cena*) meal: *una ~ ligera* a light meal **3** (*al mediodía*) lunch: *¿Qué hay de ~?* What's for lunch? ☛ *Ver* pág 320. LOC **comida campestre** picnic

comidilla *nf* LOC **ser la comidilla** to be the talk *of sth*

comido, -a *pp, adj*: *Ya vinieron ~s.* They had already eaten. LOC **comido por la envidia/la rabia/los celos** eaten up with envy/anger/jealousy *Ver tb* COMER

comienzo *nm* start, beginning (*más formal*) LOC **a comienzos de…** at the beginning of… **estar en sus comienzos** to be in its early stages **dar comienzo** to begin

comillas *nf* inverted commas ☛ *Ver* págs 318–19. LOC **entre comillas** in inverted commas

comilón, -ona ♦ *adj* greedy ♦ *nm-nf* big eater

comilona *nf* feast: *darse/pegarse una ~* to have a feast

comisaría *nf* police station

comisario *nm* superintendent

comisión *nf* commission: *una ~ del 10%* a 10% commission LOC **a comisión** on commission

comité *nm* committee [*v sing o pl*]

como ♦ *adv* **1** (*modo, en calidad de, según*) as: *Respondí ~ pude.* I answered as best I could. ◊ *Me lo llevé ~ recuerdo.* I took it home as a souvenir. ◊ *~ te iba diciendo…* As I was saying… **2** (*comparación, ejemplo*) like: *Tiene un coche ~ el nuestro.* He's got a car like ours. ◊ *infusiones ~ la manzanilla y la menta* herbal teas like camomile and peppermint ◊ *suave ~ la seda* smooth as silk **3** (*aproximadamente*) about: *Llamé ~ a diez personas.* I rang about ten people. ♦ *conj* **1** (*condición*) if: *~ vengas tarde, no podremos ir.* If you're late, we won't be able to go. **2** (*causa*) as: *~ llegué pronto, me preparé un café.* As I was early, I made myself a coffee. LOC **como que/si** as if: *Me trata ~ si fuera su hija.* He treats me as if I were his daughter.

En este tipo de expresiones lo más correcto es decir 'as if I/he/she/it **were**', pero hoy en día en el lenguaje hablado se usa mucho 'as if I/he/she/it **was**'.

como sea 1 (*a cualquier precio*) at all costs: *Tenemos que ganar ~ sea.* We must win at all costs. **2** (*no importa*): *—¿Cómo quieres el café? —~ sea.* 'How do you like your coffee?' 'As it comes.' **correr como un galgo** to run like the wind

cómo ♦ *adv* **1** (*interrogación*) how: *¿~ se traduce esta palabra?* How do you translate this word? ◊ *No sabemos ~*

pasó. We don't know how it happened. **2** (*¿por qué?*) why: *¿~ no me lo dijiste?* Why didn't you tell me? **3** (*cuando no se ha oído o entendido algo*) sorry: *¿Cómo? ¿Puedes repetir?* Sorry? Can you say that again? **4** (*exclamación*): *¡~ te pareces a tu padre!* You're just like your father! ◆ **¡cómo!** *interj* (*enfado, asombro*) what!: *¡Cómo! ¿No estás vestido aún?* What! Aren't you dressed yet? LOC **¿a cómo está/están?** how much is it/are they? **¿cómo es?** (*descripción*) what is he, she, it, etc like? **¿cómo es eso?** how come? **¿cómo es que...?** how come?: *¿~ es que no has salido?* How come you didn't go out? **¿cómo estás?** how are you? **¡cómo no!** of course! **¿cómo que...?** (*asombro, enfado*): *¿~ que no lo sabías?* What do you mean, you didn't know? **¡cómo voy a...!** how am I, are you, etc supposed to...!: *¡~ lo iba a saber!* How was I supposed to know!

cómoda *nf* chest of drawers [*pl* chests of drawers]

comodidad *nf* **1** (*confort*) comfort **2** (*conveniencia*) convenience: *la ~ de tener el metro cerca* the convenience of having the underground nearby

comodín *nm* joker

cómodo, -a *adj* **1** (*confortable*) comfortable: *sentirse ~* to feel comfortable **2** (*conveniente*) convenient: *Es muy ~ olvidarse del asunto.* It's very convenient to forget about it. LOC **ponerse cómodo** to make yourself comfortable

compact disc (*tb* **compacto**) *nm* **1** (*disco*) compact disc (*abrev* CD) **2** (*aparato*) CD player

compacto, -a *adj* compact LOC *Ver* DISCO

compadecer(se) *vt, v pron* **compadecer(se)** (**de**) to feel sorry **for** ***sb***

compaginar *vt* to combine *sth* (***with sth***): *~ el trabajo con la familia* to combine work with your family life

compañerismo *nm* comradeship

compañero, -a *nm-nf* **1** (*amigo*) companion **2** (*en pareja*) partner **3** (*en trabajo*) colleague LOC **compañero de clase** classmate **compañero de equipo** team-mate **compañero de habitación/piso** room-mate/flatmate

compañía *nf* company [*pl* companies]: *Trabaja en una ~ de seguros.* He works for an insurance company. LOC **compañía aérea** airline **hacer compañía a algn** to keep sb company

comparable *adj* ~ **a/con** comparable **to/with** ***sth/sb***

comparación *nf* comparison: *Esta casa no tiene ~ con la anterior.* There's no comparison between this house and the old one. LOC **en comparación con** compared to/with *sth/sb*

comparar *vt* to compare *sth/sb* (***to/with sth/sb***): *¡No compares esta ciudad con la mía!* Don't go comparing this town to mine!

compartimento (*tb* **compartimiento**) *nm* compartment

compartir *vt* to share: *~ un piso* to share a flat

compás *nm* **1** (*Mat, Náut*) compass **2** (*Mús*) **(a)** (*tiempo*) time: *el ~ de tres por cuatro* three four time **(b)** (*división de pentagrama*) bar: *los primeros compases de una sinfonía* the first bars of a symphony LOC *Ver* MARCAR

compasión *nf* pity, compassion (*más formal*) LOC **tener compasión de algn** to take pity on sb

compasivo, -a *adj* ~ (**con**) compassionate (**towards** ***sb***)

compatible *adj* compatible

compatriota *nmf* fellow countryman/woman [*pl* fellow countrymen/women]

compenetrarse *v pron* ~ (**con**) to get on well (**with** ***sb***)

compensación *nf* compensation

compensar ◆ *vt* **1** (*dos cosas*) to make up for *sth*: *para ~ la diferencia de precios* to make up for the difference in price **2** (*a una persona*) to repay *sb* (***for sth***): *No sé cómo ~les por todo lo que han hecho.* I don't know how to repay them for all they've done. ◆ *vi*: *No me compensa ir sólo media hora.* It's not worth going for half an hour. ◊ *A la larga compensa.* It's worth it in the long run.

competencia *nf* **1** (*rivalidad*) competition: *La ~ siempre es buena.* Competition is a good thing. **2** (*eficacia, habilidad*) competence: *falta de ~* incompetence LOC **hacer la competencia** to compete with *sth/sb*

competente *adj* competent: *un profesor ~* a competent teacher

competición *nf* competition

competir *vi* to compete: *~ por el título* to compete for the title ◊ *~ con empresas extranjeras* to compete with foreign companies

complacer *vt* to please: *Es bastante*

difícil ~les. They're rather hard to please.

complejo, -a *adj, nm* complex: *un ~ de oficinas* an office complex ◊ *tener ~ de gordo* to have a complex about being fat ◊ *tener ~ de superioridad* to have a superiority complex ◊ *Es un problema muy ~.* It's a very complex problem.

complemento *nm* **1** (*suplemento*) supplement: *como ~ a su dieta* as a dietary supplement **2** (*accesorio*) accessory [*pl* accessories]: *bisutería y ~s* costume jewellery and accessories **3** (*Gram*) object

completar *vt* to complete

completo, -a *adj* **1** (*entero*) complete: *la colección completa* the complete collection **2** (*lleno*) full: *El hotel está ~.* The hotel is full. **LOC** *Ver* JORNADA, PENSIÓN

complicado, -a *pp, adj* complicated *Ver tb* COMPLICAR

complicar ♦ *vt* **1** (*liar*) to complicate **2** (*implicar*) to implicate *sb* ***in sth*** ♦ **complicarse** *v pron* to become complicated **LOC complicarse la vida** to make life difficult for yourself

cómplice *nmf* accomplice (***in/to sth***)

complot (*tb* **compló**) *nm* plot

componer ♦ *vt* **1** (*formar*) to make *sth* up: *Cuatro relatos componen el libro.* The book is made up of four stories. **2** (*Mús*) to compose ♦ **componerse** *v pron* **componerse de** to consist **of *sth***: *El curso se compone de seis asignaturas.* The course consists of six subjects. **LOC componérselas** to manage (*to do sth*): *Me las compuse para salir.* I managed to go out.

comportamiento *nm* behaviour [*incontable*]: *Tuvieron un ~ ejemplar.* Their behaviour was exemplary.

comportarse *v pron* to behave

composición *nf* composition

compositor, ~a *nm-nf* composer

compota *nf* stewed fruit: *~ de manzana* stewed apple

compra *nf* purchase: *una buena ~* a good buy **LOC hacer/ir a la compra** to do the shopping **ir/salir de compras** to go shopping

comprar *vt* to buy: *Quiero ~les un regalo.* I want to buy them a present. ◊ *¿Me lo compras?* Will you buy it for me? ◊ *Le compré la bici a un amigo.* I bought the bike from a friend. **LOC comprar a plazos** to buy *sth* on hire purchase

comprender ♦ *vt, vi* (*entender*) to understand: *Mis padres no me comprenden.* My parents don't understand me. ◊ *Como usted comprenderá...* As you will understand... ♦ *vt* **1** (*darse cuenta*) to realize: *Han comprendido su importancia.* They've realized how important it is. **2** (*incluir*) to include

comprendido, -a *pp, adj*: *niños de edades comprendidas entre los 11 y 13 años* children aged between 11 and 13 *Ver tb* COMPRENDER

comprensión *nf* understanding **LOC tener/mostrar comprensión** to be understanding (*towards sb*)

comprensivo, -a *adj* understanding (***towards sb***)

compresa *nf* sanitary towel

comprimido, -a *pp, adj, nm* (*pastilla*) tablet **LOC** *Ver* PISTOLA

comprobar *vt* to check

comprometedor, ~a *adj* compromising

comprometer ♦ *vt* **1** (*obligar*) to commit *sb* ***to sth/doing sth*** **2** (*poner en un compromiso*) to put *sb* in an awkward position ♦ **comprometerse** *v pron* **1** (*dar tu palabra*) to promise (***to do sth***): *No me comprometo a ir.* I'm not promising I'll go. **2** (*en matrimonio*) to get engaged (***to sb***)

comprometido, -a *pp, adj* (*situación*) awkward *Ver tb* COMPROMETER

compromiso *nm* **1** (*obligación*) commitment: *El matrimonio es un gran ~.* Marriage is a great commitment. **2** (*acuerdo*) agreement **3** (*cita, matrimonial*) engagement **4** (*aprieto*) awkward situation: *Me pones en un ~.* You're putting me in an awkward position. **LOC por compromiso** out of a sense of duty **sin compromiso** without obligation

compuesto, -a ♦ *pp, adj* **1** (*gen*) compound: *palabras compuestas* compound words **2 ~ de/por** consisting **of *sth*** ♦ *nm* compound *Ver tb* COMPONER

comulgar *vi* (*Relig*) to take Communion

común *adj* **1** (*gen*) common: *un problema ~* a common problem ◊ *características comunes a un grupo* characteristics common to a group **2** (*compartido*) joint: *un esfuerzo ~* a joint effort **LOC poner algo en común** to discuss sth **tener algo en común 1** (*aficiones*) to share sth **2** (*parecerse*) to have sth in common *Ver tb* MERCADO, PUESTA, SENTIDO

comunicación *nf* **1** (*gen*) communication: *la falta de* ~ lack of communication **2** (*teléfono*): *Se cortó la* ~. We were cut off. LOC *Ver* MEDIO

comunicado, -a ◆ *pp, adj* (*transporte*): *Toda esa zona está mal comunicada.* All that area is poorly served by public transport. ◆ *nm* announcement *Ver tb* COMUNICAR

comunicar ◆ *vt* to communicate *sth* (***to sb***): *Han comunicado sus sospechas a la policía.* They've communicated their suspicions to the police. ◆ *vi* (*teléfono*) to be engaged: *Estaba comunicando.* It was engaged. ◆ **comunicar(se)** *vi, v pron* **comunicar(se)** (**con**) **1** (*gen*) to communicate (**with *sth/sb***): *Mi habitación (se) comunica con la tuya.* My room communicates with yours. ◊ *Me cuesta ~me con los demás.* I find it difficult to communicate with other people. **2** (*poner*se *en contacto*) to get in touch **with *sb***: *No puedo ~(me) con ellos.* I can't get in touch with them.

comunidad *nf* community [*v sing o pl*] [*pl* communities] LOC **comunidad autónoma** autonomous region **comunidad de vecinos** residents' association **Comunidad Europea (CE)** European Community (*abrev* EC)

comunión *nf* communion LOC **hacer la (primera) comunión** to take (your first) Communion

comunismo *nm* communism

comunista *adj, nmf* communist

con *prep* **1** (*gen*) with: *Vivo con mis padres.* I live with my parents. ◊ *Sujétalo con una chincheta.* Stick it up with a drawing pin. ◊ *¿Con qué lo limpias?* What do you clean it with? ☛ A veces se traduce por 'and': *pan con mantequilla* bread and butter ◊ *agua con azúcar* sugar and water. También se puede traducir por 'to': *¿Con quién hablabas?* Who were you talking to? ◊ *Es muy simpática con todo el mundo.* She is very nice to everybody. **2** (*contenido*) of: *una maleta con ropa* a suitcase (full) of clothes ◊ *un cubo con agua y jabón* a bucket of soapy water **3** (*a pesar de*): *Con lo duro que trabajan y no lo acabarán.* They're working so hard but they won't get it done. ◊ *¡Pero con lo que te gusta el chocolate!* But you're so fond of chocolate! **4 + inf**: *Con estudiar el fin de semana, aprobarás.* You'll pass if you study at the weekend. ◊ *Será suficiente con llamarles por teléfono.* All you'll need to do is phone them. LOC **con (tal de) que...** as long as...: *con tal de que me avises* as long as you tell me

cóncavo, -a *adj* concave

concebir ◆ *vt* **1** (*idea, plan, novela*) to conceive **2** (*entender*) to understand: *¡Es que no lo concibo!* I just don't understand! ◆ *vt, vi* (*quedar embarazada*) to conceive

conceder *vt* **1** (*gen*) to give: ~ *un préstamo a algn* to give sb a loan ◊ *¿Me concede unos minutos, por favor?* Could you spare me a couple of minutes, please? **2** (*premio, beca*) to award: *Me concedieron una beca.* I was awarded a scholarship. **3** (*reconocer*) to acknowledge: *Hay que ~les algún mérito.* We have to acknowledge that they have some merit.

concejal, ~a *nm-nf* (town) councillor

concejo *nm* (town) council

concentración *nf* concentration: *falta de* ~ lack of concentration

concentrado, -a ◆ *pp, adj* **1** (*persona*): *Estaba tan ~ en la lectura que no te oí entrar.* I was so immersed in the book that I didn't hear you come in. **2** (*sustancia*) concentrated ◆ *nm* concentrate: ~ *de uva* grape concentrate *Ver tb* CONCENTRAR

concentrar ◆ *vt* to concentrate ◆ **concentrarse** *v pron* **concentrarse** (**en**) to concentrate (**on *sth***): *Concéntrate en lo que haces.* Concentrate on what you are doing.

concepto *nm* **1** (*idea*) concept **2** (*opinión*) opinion: *No sé qué ~ tienes de mí.* I don't know what you think of me.

concha *nf* shell

conciencia *nf* **1** (*sentido moral*) conscience: *tener la ~ limpia* to have a clear conscience **2** (*conocimiento*) consciousness: ~ *de clase* class consciousness LOC **a conciencia** thoroughly **tener la conciencia tranquila** to have a clear conscience *Ver tb* CARGO, OBJETOR, REMORDER, REMORDIMIENTO

concienciar ◆ *vt* to make *sb* aware (***of sth***) ◆ **concienciarse** *v pron* to become aware (***of sth***)

concierto *nm* **1** (*recital*) concert **2** (*composición musical*) concerto [*pl* concertos]

concilio *nm* council

conciso, -a *adj* concise

conciudadano, -a *nm-nf* fellow citizen

concluir ◆ *vt, vi* (*terminar*) to

conclude, to finish (*más coloq*) ◆ *vt* (*deducir*) to conclude *sth* (***from sth***): *Concluyeron que era inocente.* They concluded that he was innocent.

conclusión *nf* conclusion: *llegar a/sacar una ~* to reach/draw a conclusion

concordar *vi ~* (**con**) (**en que...**) to agree (**with *sth/sb***) (**that...**): *Tu respuesta no concuerda con la suya.* Your answer doesn't agree with his. ◊ *Todos concuerdan en que fue un éxito.* Everyone agrees (that) it was a success.

concretar *vt* **1** (*precisar*) to specify **2** (*fecha*) to fix

concreto, -a *adj* **1** (*específico*) specific: *las tareas concretas que desempeñan* the specific tasks they perform **2** (*preciso*) definite: *una fecha concreta* a definite date

concurrido, -a *pp, adj* **1** (*lleno de gente*) crowded **2** (*popular*) popular

concursante *nmf* contestant

concursar *vi* **1** (*en un concurso*) to take part (***in sth***) **2** (*para un puesto*) to compete

concurso *nm* **1** (*juegos de habilidad, Dep*) competition **2** (*Radio, TV*) **(a)** (*de preguntas y respuestas*) quiz show **(b)** (*de juegos y pruebas*) game show LOC **concurso de belleza** beauty contest

condado *nm* county [*pl* counties]

conde, -esa *nm-nf* count [*fem* countess]

condecoración *nm* medal

condecorar *vt* to award *sb* a medal (***for sth***)

condena *nf* sentence LOC **poner una condena** to give *sb* a sentence

condenado, -a *pp, adj* **1** (*maldito*) wretched: *¡Ese ~ perro...!* That wretched dog...! **2** *~* **a** (*predestinado*) doomed (**to *sth***) *Ver tb* CONDENAR

condenar ◆ *vt* **1** (*desaprobar*) to condemn **2** (*Jur*) **(a)** (*a una pena*) to sentence *sb* (***to sth***): *~ a algn a muerte* to sentence sb to death **(b)** (*por un delito*) to convict *sb* (***of sth***) ◆ **condenarse** *v pron* to go to hell

condensado, -a *pp, adj* LOC *Ver* LECHE

condensar(se) *vt, v pron* to condense

condesa *nf Ver* CONDE

condescendiente *adj* **1** (*amable*) kind (***to sb***) **2** (*transigente*) tolerant (***of/towards sb***): *Sus padres son muy ~s con él.* His parents are very tolerant (towards him). **3** (*con aires de superioridad*) condescending: *una sonrisita ~* a condescending smile

condición *nf* **1** (*gen*) condition: *Ésa es mi única ~.* That is my one condition. ◊ *Lo hago con la ~ de que me ayudes.* I'll do it on condition that you help me. ◊ *Ellos pusieron las condiciones.* They laid down the conditions. ◊ *La mercancía llegó en perfectas condiciones.* The goods arrived in perfect condition. **2** (*social*) background LOC **estar en condiciones de 1** (*físicamente*) to be fit *to do sth* **2** (*tener la posibilidad*) to be in a position *to do sth* **sin condiciones** unconditional: *una rendición sin condiciones* an unconditional surrender ◊ *Aceptó sin condiciones.* He accepted unconditionally.

condicional *adj* conditional LOC *Ver* LIBERTAD

condicionar *vt* to condition: *La educación te condiciona.* You are conditioned by your upbringing.

condimentar *vt* to season *sth* (***with sth***)

condimento *nm* seasoning

condón *nm* condom

conducir ◆ *vt* **1** (*gen*) to drive **2** (*moto*) to ride **3** (*llevar*) to lead *sb* (***to sth***): *Las pistas nos condujeron al ladrón.* The clues led us to the thief. ◆ *vi* **1** (*vehículo*) to drive: *Estoy aprendiendo a ~.* I'm learning to drive. **2** *~* **a** (*llevar*) to lead **to *sth***: *Este camino conduce al palacio.* This path leads to the palace. LOC *Ver* CARNÉ, EXAMEN, EXAMINAR, PERMISO

conducta *nf* behaviour [*incontable*]

conducto *nm* **1** (*tubo*) pipe **2** (*Med*) duct

conductor, ~a *nm-nf* driver

> En inglés **conductor** significa *cobrador* o *revisor*.

conectar *vt* **1** (*unir*) to connect *sth* (up) (***with/to sth***): *~ la impresora al ordenador* to connect the printer to the computer **2** (*enchufar*) to plug *sth* in

conejillo *nm* LOC **conejillo de indias** guinea pig

conejo, -a *nm-nf* rabbit

> **Rabbit** es el sustantivo genérico, **buck** se refiere sólo al macho y su plural es 'buck' o 'bucks'. Para referirnos sólo a la hembra utilizamos **doe**.

conexión *nf* **1** *~* (**con**) connection (**to/**

with ***sth*****)** **2** ~ **(entre)** connection **(between...)**

confección *nf* LOC *Ver* CORTE

confeccionar *vt* to make

conferencia *nf* **1** (*charla*) lecture **2** (*por teléfono*) long-distance call: *poner una* ~ to make a long-distance call **3** (*congreso*) conference LOC *Ver* PRENSA

conferenciante *nmf* lecturer

confesar ◆ *vt, vi* **1** (*gen*) to confess (**to** ***sth/doing sth***): *Tengo que ~ que prefiero el tuyo.* I must confess I prefer yours. ◊ *~ un crimen/asesinato* to confess to a crime/murder ◊ *Confesaron haber robado el banco.* They confessed to robbing the bank. **2** (*cura*) to hear (*sb's*) confession: *Los domingos no confiesan.* They don't hear confessions on Sundays. ◊ *¿Quién te confiesa?* Who is your confessor? ◆ **confesarse** *v pron* **1** (*Relig*) **(a)** (*gen*) to go to confession **(b)** **confesarse de** to confess *sth*; to confess (**to** ***doing sth***) **2** (*declararse*): *Se confesaron autores/culpables del crimen.* They confessed they had committed the crime. LOC **confesar la verdad** to tell the truth

confesión *nf* confession

confesonario (*tb* **confesionario**) *nm* confessional

confesor *nm* confessor

confeti *nm* confetti

confianza *nf* **1** ~ **(en)** confidence (**in** ***sth/sb***): *No tienen mucha ~ en él.* They don't have much confidence in him. **2** (*naturalidad, amistad*): *tratar a algn con ~* to treat sb in a friendly way ◊ *Te lo puedo decir porque tenemos ~.* I can tell you because we're friends. LOC **confianza en uno mismo** self-confidence: *No tengo ~ en mí mismo.* I lack self-confidence. **de confianza** trustworthy: *un empleado de ~* a trustworthy employee **en confianza** in confidence *Ver tb* DIGNO

confiar ◆ *vi* ~ **en 1** (*fiarse*) to trust *sth/sb* [*vt*]: *Confía en mí.* Trust me. ◊ *No confío en los bancos.* I don't trust banks. **2** (*esperar*) to hope: *Confío en que no llueva.* I hope it doesn't rain. ◊ *Confío en que lleguen a tiempo.* I hope they arrive on time. ◆ *vt* to entrust *sth/sb* **with** ***sth***: *Sé que puedo ~le la organización de la fiesta.* I know I can entrust him with the arrangements for the party. ◆ **confiarse** *v pron* to be overconfident

confidencial *adj* confidential

confirmar *vt* to confirm

confitería *nf* **1** (*tienda*) confectioner's [*pl* confectioners] **2** (*ramo comercial*) confectionery

confitura *nf* preserve

conflicto *nm* conflict: *un ~ entre las dos potencias* a conflict between the two powers LOC **conflicto de intereses** clash of interests

conformarse *v pron* ~ **(con)** **1** (*gen*) to be happy (**with** ***sth/doing sth***): *Me conformo con un aprobado.* I'll be happy with a pass. ◊ *Se conforman con poco.* They're easily pleased. **2** (*resignarse*): *No me gusta, pero tendré que conformarme.* I don't like it, but I'll have to get used to the idea.

conforme ◆ *conj* as: *Se sentaban ~ iban entrando.* They sat down as they arrived. ◆ *adj* LOC **estar conforme (con)** **1** (*de acuerdo*) to agree with (*sth*): *Estoy ~ con las condiciones del contrato.* I agree with the terms of the contract. **2** (*contento*) to be satisfied (with *sth/sb*)

conformista *adj, nmf* conformist [*n*]

confundir ◆ *vt* **1** (*mezclar*) to mix *sth* up: *La bibliotecaria ha confundido todos los libros.* The librarian has mixed up all the books. ◊ *Sepáralos, no los confundas.* Separate them, don't mix them up. **2** (*dejar perplejo*) to confuse: *No me confundas.* Don't confuse me. **3** (*equivocar*) to mistake *sth/sb* **for** ***sth/sb***: *Creo que me ha confundido con otra persona.* I think you've mistaken me for somebody else. ◊ *~ la sal con el azúcar* to mistake the salt for the sugar ◆ **confundirse** *v pron* **confundirse (de)** (*equivocarse*): *~se de puerta* to knock/ring at the wrong door ◊ *Se ha confundido de número.* You've got the wrong number. ◊ *Todo el mundo se puede ~.* We all make mistakes.

confusión *nf* **1** (*falta de claridad*) confusion: *crear ~* to cause confusion **2** (*equivocación*) mistake: *Debe de haber sido una ~.* It must have been a mistake.

confuso, -a *adj* **1** (*poco claro*) confusing: *Sus indicaciones eran muy confusas.* His directions were very confusing. **2** (*desconcertado*) confused

congelador *nm* freezer

congelar ◆ *vt* to freeze ◆ **congelarse** *v pron* **1** (*helarse*) to freeze (over): *El lago se ha congelado.* The lake has frozen over. **2** (*tener frío*) to be freezing: *Me estoy congelando.* I'm freezing. **3** (*Med*) to get frostbite

congénito, -a *adj* congenital

congestionado, -a *pp, adj* **1** (*calles*) congested: *Las calles están congestionadas por el tráfico.* The streets are congested with traffic. **2** (*nariz*) blocked up: *Todavía tengo la nariz muy congestionada.* My nose is still blocked up. **3** (*cara*) flushed *Ver tb* CONGESTIONAR

congestionar ◆ *vt*: *El accidente congestionó el tráfico.* The accident caused traffic congestion. ◆ **congestionarse** *v pron* (*enrojecer*) to go red in the face

congreso *nm* congress LOC **Congreso de los Diputados** Congress ≃ Parliament (*GB*) ☛ *Ver* pág 322.

cónico, -a *adj* conical

conífera *nf* conifer

conjugar *vt* to conjugate

conjunción *nf* conjunction

conjuntivitis *nf* conjunctivitis [*incontable*]

conjunto *nm* **1** (*de objetos, obras*) collection **2** (*totalidad*) whole: *el ~ de la industria alemana* German industry as a whole **3** (*musical*) group **4** (*ropa*) outfit **5** (*Mat*) set

conjuro *nm* spell

conmigo *pron pers* with me: *Ven ~.* Come with me. ◊ *No quiere hablar ~.* He doesn't want to speak to me. LOC **conmigo mismo** with myself: *Estoy contenta ~ misma.* I'm very pleased with myself.

conmoción *nf* shock LOC **conmoción cerebral** concussion

conmovedor, ~a *adj* moving

conmover *vt* to move

cono *nm* cone

conocer *vt* **1** (*gen*) to know: *Les conozco de la universidad.* I know them from university. ◊ *Conozco muy bien París.* I know Paris very well. **2** (*a una persona por primera vez*) to meet: *Les conocí durante las vacaciones.* I met them during the holidays. **3** (*saber de la existencia*) to know **of *sth*/*sb***: *¿Conoces un buen hotel?* Do you know of a good hotel? LOC **conocer algo como la palma de la mano** to know sth like the back of your hand **conocer de vista** to know *sb* by sight **se conoce que...** it seems (that)... *Ver tb* ENCANTADO

conocido, -a ◆ *pp, adj* (*famoso*) well known ◆ *nm-nf* acquaintance *Ver tb* CONOCER

conocimiento *nm* knowledge [*incontable*]: *Pusieron a prueba sus ~s.* They put their knowledge to the test. LOC **perder/recobrar el conocimiento** to lose/regain conciousness **sin conocimiento** unconscious

conque *conj* so: *Es tarde, ~ acelera.* It's late, so hurry up.

conquista *nf* conquest

conquistador, ~a ◆ *adj* conquering ◆ *nm-nf* **1** (*gen*) conqueror: *Guillermo el Conquistador* William the Conqueror **2** (*América*) conquistador [*pl* conquistadores/conquistadors]

conquistar *vt* **1** (*Mil*) to conquer **2** (*enamorar*) to win *sb's* heart

consagrar *vt* **1** (*Relig*) to consecrate **2** (*dedicar*) to devote *sth* (**to *sth***): *Consagraron su vida al deporte.* They devoted their lives to sport. **3** (*lograr fama*) to establish *sth*/*sb* (**as *sth***): *La exposición lo consagró como pintor.* The exhibition established him as a painter.

consciente *adj* **1** ~ (**de**) conscious, aware (*más coloq*) (**of *sth***) **2** (*Med*) conscious

consecuencia *nf* **1** (*secuela*) consequence: *pagar las ~s* to suffer the consequences **2** (*resultado*) result: *como ~ de aquello* as a result of that

conseguir *vt* **1** (*obtener*) to obtain, to get (*más coloq*): *~ un visado* to obtain a visa ◊ *~ que algn haga algo* to get sb to do sth **2** (*lograr*) to achieve: *para ~ nuestros objetivos* to achieve our aims **3** (*ganar*) to win: *~ una medalla* to win a medal

consejo *nm* **1** (*recomendación*) advice [*incontable*]: *Te voy a dar un ~.* I'm going to give you some advice. ◊ *No sigas sus ~s.* Don't follow their advice. **2** (*organismo*) council LOC **consejo de administración** board of directors **el consejo de ministros** the Cabinet [*v sing o pl*] ☛ *Ver* pág 322.

consentimiento *nm* consent

consentir *vt* **1** (*tolerar*) to allow: *No consentiré que me trates así.* I won't allow you to treat me like this. ◊ *No se lo consientas.* Don't let him get away with it. **2** (*mimar*) to spoil: *Sus padres le consienten demasiado.* His parents really spoil him.

conserje *nmf* **1** (*gen*) porter **2** (*escuela, instituto*) caretaker **3** (*hotel*) receptionist

conserjería *nf* **1** (*gen*) porter's lodge

2 (*escuela, instituto*) caretaker's lodge 3 (*hotel*) reception

conserva *nf* **1** (*en lata*) tinned food: *tomates en ~* tinned tomatoes **2** (*en cristal*) bottled food

conservador, ~a *adj, nm-nf* conservative

conservante *nm* preservative

conservar *vt* **1** (*comida*) to preserve **2** (*cosas*) to keep: *Aún conservo sus cartas.* I've still got his letters. **3** (*calor*) to retain

conservatorio *nm* school of music

consideración *nf* **1** (*reflexión, cuidado*) consideration: *tomar algo en ~* to take sth into consideration **2** ~ **(por/hacia)** (*respeto*) respect (**for** ***sb***) LOC **con/sin consideración** considerately/inconsiderately

considerado, -a *pp, adj* (*respetuoso*) considerate LOC **bien/mal considerado**: *un médico bien ~* a highly regarded doctor ◊ *El apostar está mal ~ en este país.* Betting is frowned upon in this country. *Ver tb* CONSIDERAR

considerar *vt* **1** (*sopesar*) to weigh *sth* up, to consider (*más formal*): *~ los pros y los contras* to weigh up the pros and cons **2** (*ver, apreciar*) to regard *sth/sb* (**as** ***sth***): *La considero nuestra mejor jugadora.* I regard her as our best player.

consigna *nf* (*para equipaje*) left luggage office

consigo *pron pers* **1** (*él, ella*) with him/her **2** (*usted, ustedes*) with you **3** (*ellos, ellas*) with them LOC **consigo mismo** with himself, herself, etc

consistir *vi* ~ **en** to consist **of** ***sth/doing sth***: *Mi trabajo consiste en atender al público.* My work consists of dealing with the public.

consola *nf* control panel

consolación *nf* consolation: *premio de ~* consolation prize

consolar *vt* to console: *Traté de ~le por la pérdida de su madre.* I tried to console him for the loss of his mother.

consonante *nf* consonant

conspiración *nf* conspiracy [*pl* conspiracies]

constancia *nf* (*perseverancia*) perseverance

constante *adj* **1** (*continuo*) constant **2** (*perseverante*) hard-working: *Mi hijo es muy ~ en sus estudios.* My son works hard at his studies.

constar *vi* **1** (*ser cierto*) to be sure (**of** ***sth/that...***): *Me consta que ellos no lo hicieron.* I'm sure they didn't do it. **2** ~ **de** to consist **of** ***sth***: *La obra consta de tres actos.* The play consists of three acts.

constelación *nf* constellation

constipado, -a ◆ *pp, adj*: *Estoy ~.* I've got a bad cold. ◆ *nm* cold: *pillar un ~* to catch a cold

La palabra **constipated** no significa constipado, sino *estreñido*.

constitución *nf* constitution LOC *Ver* HIERRO

constitucional *adj* constitutional

constituir *vt* to be, to constitute (*formal*): *Puede ~ un riesgo para la salud.* It may be a health hazard.

construcción *nf* building, construction (*más formal*): *en ~* under construction ◊ *Trabajan en la ~.* They're builders.

constructor, ~a *nm-nf* builder

construir *vt, vi* to build: *~ un futuro mejor* to build a better future ◊ *No han empezado a ~ todavía.* They haven't started building yet.

consuelo *nm* consolation: *Es un ~ saber que no soy el único.* It is (of) some consolation to know that I am not the only one. ◊ *buscar ~ en algo* to seek consolation in sth

cónsul *nmf* consul

consulado *nm* consulate

consulta *nf* **1** (*pregunta*) question: *¿Le puedo hacer una ~?* Could I ask you something? **2** (*Med*) surgery [*pl* surgeries]: *La doctora tiene ~ hoy.* The doctor holds surgery today. LOC **de consulta** reference: *libros de ~* reference books

consultar *vt* **1** (*gen*) to consult *sth/sb* (**about** ***sth***): *Nos han consultado sobre ese tema.* They've consulted us about this matter. **2** (*palabra, dato*) to look *sth* up: *Consúltalo en el diccionario.* Look it up in the dictionary. LOC **consultar algo con la almohada** to sleep on sth

consultorio *nm* LOC **consultorio sentimental 1** (*Period*) problem page **2** (*Radio*) advice programme

consumición *nf* (*bebida*) drink: *una entrada con derecho a ~* a ticket entitling you to a drink

consumidor, ~a ◆ *adj* consuming: *países ~es de petróleo* oil-consuming countries ◆ *nm-nf* consumer

consumir *vt* **1** (*gen*) to consume: *un país que consume más de lo que produce* a country which consumes more than it produces **2** (*energía*) to use: *Este radiador consume mucha luz.* This radiator uses a lot of electricity. LOC **consumir preferentemente antes de...** best before...

consumo *nm* consumption LOC *Ver* BIEN[3]

contabilidad *nf* **1** (*cuentas*) accounts [*pl*]: *la ~ de una empresa* a firm's accounts **2** (*profesión*) accountancy LOC **llevar la contabilidad** to do the accounts

contable *nmf* accountant

contactar *vi, vt* ~ (**con**) to contact: *Intenté ~ con mi familia.* I tried to contact my family.

contacto *nm* contact LOC **mantenerse/ponerse en contacto con algn** to keep/get in touch with sb **poner a algn en contacto con algn** to put sb in touch with sb *Ver tb* LLAVE

contado LOC **al contado** cash: *pagar algo al ~* to pay cash for sth

contador *nm* meter: *el ~ del gas* the gas meter

contagiar ◆ *vt* to pass *sth* on ***to sb***: *Le contagió la varicela.* He passed the chickenpox on to her. ◆ **contagiarse** *v pron* to be contagious

contagioso, -a *adj* contagious

contaminación *nf* **1** (*gen*) pollution: *~ atmosférica* atmospheric pollution **2** (*radiactiva, alimenticia*) contamination

contaminar *vt, vi* **1** (*gen*) to pollute: *Los vertidos de la fábrica contaminan el río.* Waste from the factory is polluting the river. **2** (*radiactividad, alimentos*) to contaminate

contante *adj* LOC *Ver* DINERO

contar ◆ *vt* **1** (*enumerar, calcular*) to count: *Contó el número de viajeros.* He counted the number of passengers. **2** (*explicar*) to tell: *Nos contaron un cuento.* They told us a story. ◊ *Cuéntame lo de ayer.* Tell me about yesterday. ◆ *vi* **1** (*gen*) to count: *Cuenta hasta 50.* Count to 50. **2** ~ **con** (*confiar*) to count on *sth/sb*: *Cuento con ellos.* I'm counting on them. LOC **¿qué te cuentas?** how are things? *Ver tb* LARGO

contemplar *vt* to contemplate: *~ un cuadro/una posibilidad* to contemplate a painting/possibility

contemporáneo, -a *adj, nm-nf* contemporary [*pl* contemporaries]

contenedor *nm* **1** (*de basura*) bin **2** (*de mercancías*) container

contener *vt* **1** (*gen*) to contain: *Este texto contiene algunos errores.* This text contains a few mistakes. **2** (*aguantarse*) to hold *sth* back: *El niño no podía ~ el llanto.* The little boy couldn't hold back his tears.

contenido *nm* contents [*pl*]: *el ~ de un frasco* the contents of a bottle

contentarse *v pron* ~ **con** to be satisfied **with *sth***: *Se contenta con poco.* He's easily pleased.

contento, -a *adj* **1** (*feliz*) happy **2** ~ (**con/de**) (*satisfecho*) pleased (**with *sth/sb***): *Estamos ~s con el nuevo profesor.* We're pleased with the new teacher. LOC *Ver* CABER

contestación *nf* reply [*pl* replies]: *Espero ~.* I await your reply.

contestador *nm* LOC **contestador (automático)** answering machine

contestar ◆ *vt* ~ (**a**) to answer *sth*, to reply **to *sth*** (*más formal*): *Nunca contestan a mis cartas.* They never answer my letters. ◆ *vi* **1** (*dar una respuesta*) to answer, to reply (*más formal*) **2** (*replicar*) to answer back: *¡No me contestes!* Don't answer (me) back!

contigo *pron pers* with you: *Se fue ~.* He left with you. ◊ *Quiero hablar ~.* I want to talk to you. LOC **contigo mismo** with yourself

continente *nm* continent

continuación *nf* continuation LOC **a continuación** (*ahora*) next: *Y a ~ les ofrecemos una película de terror.* And next we have a horror film.

continuar *vi* **1** (*gen*) to go on (***with sth/doing sth***), to continue (***with sth/to do sth***) (*más formal*): *Continuaremos apoyándote.* We shall go on supporting you. **2** (*estar todavía*) to be still...: *Continúa haciendo mucho calor.* It's still very hot. LOC **continuará...** to be continued...

contorno *nm* **1** (*perfil*) outline **2** (*medida*) measurement: *~ de cintura* waist measurement

contra *prep* **1** (*gen*) against: *la lucha contra el crimen* the fight against crime ◊ *Ponte contra la pared.* Stand against the wall. **2** (*con verbos como lanzar, disparar, tirar*) at: *Lanzaron piedras contra las ventanas.* They threw stones at the windows. **3** (*con verbos como chocar, arremeter*) into: *Mi vehículo chocó contra el muro.* My car crashed into the wall. ◊ *Se estrelló contra un árbol.* He hit a tree. **4** (*golpe, ataque*) on: *Se dio un buen golpe contra el asfalto.* She fell down on the concrete. ◊ *un atentado contra su vida* an attempt on his life **5** (*resultado*) to: *Ganaron por once votos contra seis.* They won by eleven votes to six. **6** (*tratamiento, vacuna*) for: *una cura contra el cáncer* a cure for cancer **7** (*enfrentamiento*) versus (*abrev* v, vs): *el Madrid contra el Barcelona* Real Madrid v Barcelona LOC **en contra (de)** against (*sth/sb*): *¿Estás a favor o en contra?* Are you for or against? ◊ *en contra de su voluntad* against their will *Ver tb* PRO²

contraatacar *vi* to fight back

contraataque *nm* counter-attack

contrabajo *nm* (*instrumento*) double-bass

contrabandista *nmf* smuggler LOC **contrabandista de armas** gun-runner

contrabando *nm* **1** (*actividad*) smuggling **2** (*mercancía*) contraband LOC **contrabando de armas** gun-running **pasar algo de contrabando** to smuggle sth in

contradecir *vt* to contradict

contradicción *nf* contradiction

contradictorio, -a *adj* contradictory

contraer ◆ *vt* **1** (*gen*) to contract: ~ *un músculo* to contract a muscle ◊ ~ *deudas/la malaria* to contract debts/ malaria **2** (*compromisos, obligaciones*) to take *sth* on ◆ **contraerse** *v pron* (*materiales, músculos*) to contract LOC **contraer matrimonio** to get married (*to sb*)

contraluz *nm o nf* LOC **a contraluz** against the light

contrapeso *nm* counterweight

contrapié LOC **a contrapié** on the wrong foot

contraportada *nf* **1** (*libro*) back cover **2** (*revista, periódico*) back page

contrariedad *nf* setback

contrario, -a ◆ *adj* **1** (*equipo, opinión, teoría*) opposing **2** (*dirección, lado*) opposite **3** ~ **(a)** (*persona*) opposed (**to** ***sth***) ◆ *nm-nf* opponent LOC **al/por el contrario** on the contrary **de lo contrario** otherwise **llevar la contraria** to disagree: *Les gusta llevar siempre la contraria.* They always like to disagree. **(todo) lo contrario** (quite) the opposite: *Sus profesores opinan lo ~.* His teachers think the opposite. *Ver tb* CAMPO

contraseña *nf* password

contrastar *vt, vi* ~ **(con)** to contrast (*sth*) (**with** ***sth***): ~ *unos resultados con otros* to contrast one set of results with another

contraste *nm* contrast

contratar *vt* **1** (*gen*) to take *sb* on, to contract (*más formal*) **2** (*deportista, artista*) to sign *sb* on/up

contratiempo *nm* **1** (*problema*) setback **2** (*accidente*) mishap

contrato *nm* contract

contraventana *nf* shutter

contribuir *vi* **1** (*gen*) to contribute (*sth*) (**to/towards** ***sth***): *Contribuyeron con diez millones de pesetas a la construcción del hospital.* They contributed ten million pesetas to the construction of the hospital. **2** ~ **a hacer algo** to help **to do sth**: *Contribuirá a mejorar la imagen del colegio.* It will help (to) improve the school's image.

contribuyente *nmf* taxpayer

contrincante *nmf* rival

control *nm* **1** (*gen*) control: ~ *de natalidad* birth control ◊ *perder el* ~ to lose control **2** (*de policía, Dep*) checkpoint LOC **estar bajo/fuera de control** to be under/out of control *Ver tb* ANTIDOPING

controlar *vt* to control: ~ *a la gente/ una situación* to control people/a situation

convalidar *vt* to recognize: ~ *un título* to have a degree recognized

convencer ◆ *vt* **1** (*gen*) to convince *sb* (***of sth*/*to do sth*/*that…***): *Nos convencieron de que estaba bien.* They convinced us that it was right. **2** (*persuadir*) to persuade *sb* (***to do sth***): *A ver si le convences para que venga.* See if you can persuade him to come. ◆ *vi* to be convincing ◆ **convencerse** *v pron* **convencerse de** to get *sth* into your head: *Tienes que ~te de que se acabó.* You must get it into your head that it's over.

conveniente *adj* convenient: *una hora/un lugar* ~ a convenient time/ place LOC **ser conveniente**: *Creo que es ~ que salgamos de madrugada.* I think it's a good idea to leave early.

convenio *nm* agreement

convenir ◆ *vi* **1** (*ser conveniente*) to suit: *Haz lo que más te convenga.* Do whatever suits you best. **2** (*ser aconsejable*): *No te conviene trabajar tanto.* You shouldn't work so hard. ◊ *Convendría repasarlo.* We should go over it again. ◆ *vt, vi* ~ **(en)** to agree **on *sth*/to**

do sth: *Hay que ~ la fecha de la reunión.* We must agree on the date of the meeting.

convento *nm* **1** (*de monjas*) convent **2** (*de monjes*) monastery [*pl* monasteries]

conversación *nf* conversation: *un tema de ~* a topic of conversation

conversar *vi* to talk (***to/with sb***) (***about sth/sb***): *Conversamos sobre temas de actualidad.* We talked about current affairs.

convertir ◆ *vt* **1** (*gen*) to turn *sth/sb* ***into sth***: *Convirtieron su casa en museo.* His house was turned into a museum. **2** (*Relig*) to convert *sb* (***to sth***) ◆ **convertirse** *v pron* **1 convertirse en** (*llegar a ser*) to become **2 convertirse en** (*transformarse*) to turn into *sth*: *El príncipe se convirtió en rana.* The prince turned into a frog. **3 convertirse** (**a**) (*Relig*) to convert (***to sth***): *Se han convertido al islam.* They have converted to Islam. LOC **convertirse en realidad** to come true

convexo, -a *adj* convex

convivir *vi* to live together; to live with *sb*: *Convivieron antes de casarse.* They lived together before they got married. ◊ *Conviví con ella.* I lived with her.

convocar *vt* **1** (*huelga, elecciones, reunión*) to call: *~ una huelga general* to call a general strike **2** (*citar*) to summon: *~ a los líderes a una reunión* to summon the leaders to a meeting

convocatoria *nf* **1** (*huelga, elecciones*) call: *una ~ de huelga/elecciones* a strike call/a call for elections **2** (*Educ*): *Aprobé en la ~ de junio.* I passed in June. ◊ *Lo intentaré otra vez en la ~ de septiembre.* I'll try again in the September resits.

coñac *nm* brandy [*pl* brandies]

cooperar *vi* ~ (**con**) (**en**) to cooperate (**with *sb***) (**on *sth***): *Se negó a ~ con ellos en el proyecto.* He refused to cooperate with them on the project.

coordenada *nf* LOC *Ver* EJE

coordinar *vt* to coordinate

copa *nf* **1** (*vaso*) (wine) glass **2** (*bebida*) drink: *tomarse unas ~s* to have a few drinks **3** (*árbol*) top **4 Copa** (*Dep*) Cup: *la Copa de Europa* the European Cup **5 copas** (*Naipes*) ☛ *Ver nota en* BARAJA LOC **salir de copas** to go (out) drinking *Ver tb* SOMBRERO

copia *nf* copy [*pl* copies]: *hacer/sacar una ~* to make a copy

copiar ◆ *vt, vi* to copy *sth* (***from sth/sb***): *¿Has copiado este cuadro del original?* Did you copy this painting from the original? ◊ *Se lo copié a Luis.* I copied it from Luis. ◆ *vt* (*escribir*) to copy *sth* down: *Copiaban lo que el profesor iba diciendo.* They copied down what the teacher said.

copiloto *nmf* **1** (*avión*) copilot **2** (*automóvil*) co-driver

copión, -ona *nm-nf* copycat

copo *nm* flake: *~s de nieve* snowflakes

coquetear *vi* to flirt (***with sb***)

coqueto, -a ◆ *adj* (*que coquetea*) flirtatious ◆ *nm-nf* flirt: *Es un ~.* He's a flirt.

coral[1] *nm* (*Zool*) coral

coral[2] *nf* (*coro*) choir

corazón *nm* **1** (*gen*) heart: *en el fondo de su ~* at the bottom of his heart ◊ *en pleno ~ de la ciudad* in the very heart of the city **2** (*fruta*) core: *Pelar y quitar el ~.* Peel and remove the core. **3** (*dedo*) middle finger **4 corazones** (*Naipes*) hearts ☛ *Ver nota en* BARAJA LOC **de todo corazón** from the heart: *Lo digo de todo ~.* I'm speaking from the heart. **tener buen corazón** to be kind-hearted

corbata *nf* tie: *Todo el mundo iba con ~.* They were all wearing ties.

corchea *nf* (*Mús*) quaver

corcho *nm* **1** (*gen*) cork **2** (*pesca*) float

cordel *nm* string

cordero, -a *nm-nf* (*animal, carne*) lamb: *~ asado* roast lamb

cordillera *nf* mountain range: *la ~ Cantábrica* the Cantabrian mountains

cordón *nm* **1** (*cuerda*) cord **2** (*zapato*) (shoe)lace: *atarse los cordones de los zapatos* to do your shoelaces up **3** (*electricidad*) lead LOC **cordón policial** police cordon **cordón umbilical** umbilical cord

córnea *nf* cornea

córner *nm* corner

corneta *nf* bugle

coro *nm* (*Arquit, coral*) choir

corona *nf* **1** (*de un rey, la monarquía, diente, moneda*) crown **2** (*de flores*) wreath

coronación *nf* (*de un rey*) coronation

coronar *vt* to crown: *Le coronaron rey.* He was crowned king.

coronel *nmf* colonel

coronilla *nf* **1** (*gen*) crown **2** (*calva*) bald patch LOC **andar/ir de coronilla** to be rushed off your feet **estar hasta la coronilla** to be sick to death *of sth/sb/doing sth*

corporal *adj* **1** (*gen*) body [*n atrib*]: *lenguaje/temperatura ~* body language/ temperature **2** (*necesidades, funciones, contacto*) bodily: *las necesidades ~es* bodily needs

corpulento, -a *adj* hefty

corral *nm* farmyard

correa *nf* **1** (*gen*) strap: *~ del reloj* watch strap **2** (*para perro*) lead

corrección *nf* correction: *hacer correcciones en un texto* to make corrections to a text

correcto, -a *adj* correct: *el resultado ~* the correct result ◊ *Tu abuelo es muy ~.* Your grandfather is very correct.

corredizo, -a *adj* LOC *Ver* NUDO, PUERTA

corredor, ~a *nm-nf* **1** (*atleta*) runner **2** (*ciclista*) cyclist

corregir *vt* to correct: *~ exámenes* to correct exams ◊ *Corrígeme si lo digo mal.* Correct me if I get it wrong.

correo *nm* **1** (*gen*) post: *Me llegó en el ~ del jueves.* It came in Thursday's post. ◊ *votar por ~* to vote by post ☛ *Ver nota en* MAIL **2 correos** post office: *¿Dónde está ~s?* Where's the post office? ☛ *Ver nota en* ESTANCO LOC **correo aéreo** airmail **de correos** postal: *huelga/ servicio de ~s* postal strike/service **echar algo al correo** to post sth *Ver tb* APARTADO, TREN, VOTAR

correr ◆ *vi* **1** (*gen*) to run: *Corrían por el patio.* They were running round the playground. ◊ *Salí corriendo detrás de él.* I ran out after him. ◊ *Cuando me vio echó a ~.* He ran off when he saw me. **2** (*darse prisa*) to hurry: *No corras, aún tienes tiempo.* There's no need to hurry, you've still got time. ◊ *¡Corre!* Hurry up! **3** (*automóvil*) to go fast: *Su moto corre mucho.* His motor bike goes very fast. **4** (*conducir deprisa*) to drive fast **5** (*líquidos*) to flow: *El agua corría por la calle.* Water flowed down the street. ◆ *vt* **1** (*mover*) to move *sth* (along/down/ over/up): *Corre un poco la silla.* Move your chair over a bit. **2** (*cortina*) to draw **3** (*Dep*) to compete **in *sth***: *~ los 100 metros lisos* to compete in the 100 metres ◆ **correrse** *v pron* **1** (*moverse una persona*) to move up/over **2** (*tinta, maquillaje*) to run LOC *Ver* COMO, VOZ

correspondencia *nf* **1** (*correo*) correspondence **2** (*relación*) relation

corresponder *vi* **1** (*tener derecho*) to be entitled ***to sth***: *Te corresponde lo mismo que a los demás.* You're entitled to exactly the same as the others. **2** (*pertenecer, ser adecuado*): *Pon una cruz donde corresponda.* Tick as appropriate. ◊ *Ese texto corresponde a otra foto.* That text goes with another photo.

correspondiente *adj* **1** ~ (**a**) (*gen*) corresponding (**to *sth***): *¿Cuál es la expresión ~ en chino?* What's the corresponding expression in Chinese? ◊ *las palabras ~s a las definiciones* the words corresponding to the definitions **2** (*propio*) own: *Cada estudiante tendrá su título ~.* Each student will have their own diploma. **3** (*adecuado*) relevant: *presentar la documentación ~* to produce the relevant documents **4** ~ **a** for: *temas ~s al primer trimestre* subjects for the first term

corresponsal *nmf* correspondent

corrida *nf* LOC **corrida** (**de toros**) bullfight

corriente ◆ *adj* **1** (*normal*) ordinary: *gente ~* ordinary people **2** (*común*) common: *un árbol muy ~* a very common tree ◆ *nf* **1** (*agua, electricidad*) current: *Fueron arrastrados por la ~.* They were swept away by the current. **2** (*aire*) draught LOC **ponerse al corriente** to get up to date *Ver tb* AGUA, GENTE, NORMAL

corrimiento *nm* LOC **corrimiento de tierra**(**s**) landslide

corro *nm* **1** (*personas*) circle: *hacer (un) ~* to form a circle **2** (*juego*) ring-a-ring-a-roses

corroer(se) *vt, v pron* (*metales*) to corrode

corromper *vt* to corrupt

corrupción *nf* corruption

cortacésped *nm* lawnmower

cortado, -a *pp, adj* **1** (*cohibido*) embarrassed: *estar/quedarse ~* to be embarrassed **2** (*tímido*) shy *Ver tb* CORTAR

cortar ◆ *vt* **1** (*gen*) to cut: *Córtalo en cuatro trozos.* Cut it into four pieces. **2** (*agua, luz, parte del cuerpo, rama*) to cut *sth* off: *Han cortado el teléfono/gas.* The telephone/gas has been cut off. ◊ *La máquina le cortó un dedo.* The machine cut off one of his fingers. **3** (*con tijeras*) to cut *sth* out: *Corté los pantalones siguiendo el patrón.* I cut out the trousers following the pattern. **4** (*tráfico*) to stop **5** (*calle*) to close ◆ *vi* to cut: *Este cuchillo no corta.* This knife doesn't cut. ◊ *Ten cuidado que esas tije-*

ras cortan mucho. Be careful, those scissors are very sharp. ◆ **cortarse** *v pron* **1** (*herirse*) to cut: *Me corté la mano con los cristales.* I cut my hand on the glass. **2** (*leche, mahonesa*) to curdle **3** (*teléfono*): *Estábamos hablando y de repente se cortó.* We were talking and then suddenly we got cut off. **4** (*turbarse*) to get embarrassed LOC **cortar el césped** to mow the lawn **cortarse el pelo 1** (*uno mismo*) to cut your hair **2** (*en la peluquería*) to have your hair cut **cortarse la coleta** (*jubilarse*) to retire

cortaúñas *nm* nail clippers [*pl*]

corte[1] *nm* cut: *Sufrió varios ~s en el brazo.* He got several cuts on his arm. ◊ *un ~ de luz* a power cut LOC **corte de digestión** pains in your stomach [*pl*]: *sufrir un ~ de digestión* to get pains in your stomach **corte de pelo** haircut **corte (y confección)** dressmaking **dar/pegar un corte 1** (*de palabra*) to put *sb* down **2** (*con un gesto*) to snub **¡qué corte!** how embarrassing!

corte[2] *nf* **1** (*realeza*) court **2 las Cortes** the Spanish parliament [*sing*]

cortesía *nf* courtesy [*pl* courtesies]: *por ~* out of courtesy

corteza *nf* **1** (*árbol*) bark **2** (*pan*) crust **3** (*queso*) rind **4** (*fruta*) peel LOC **la corteza terrestre** the earth's crust

cortina *nf* curtain: *abrir/cerrar las ~s* to draw the curtains

corto, -a ◆ *adj* **1** (*gen*) short: *Ese pantalón te está ~.* Those trousers are too short for you. ◊ *una camisa de manga corta* a short-sleeved shirt **2** (*persona*) dim ◆ *nm* (*Cine*) short LOC **ni corto ni perezoso** without thinking twice **ser corto de vista** to be short-sighted *Ver tb* LUZ, PANTALÓN

cortocircuito *nm* short-circuit

cosa *nf* **1** (*gen*) thing: *Una ~ ha quedado clara…* One thing is clear… ◊ *Les van bien las ~s.* Things are going well for them. **2** (*algo*) something: *Te quería preguntar una ~.* I wanted to ask you something. **3** (*nada*) nothing, anything: *No hay ~ más impresionante que el mar.* There's nothing more impressive than the sea. **4 cosas** (*asuntos*) affairs: *Quiero solucionar primero mis ~s.* I want to sort out my own affairs first. ◊ *Nunca habla de sus ~s.* He never talks about his personal life. LOC **¡cosas de la vida!** that's life! **entre una cosa y otra** what with one thing and another **¡lo que son las cosas!** would you believe it! **¡qué cosa más rara!** how odd! **ser cosa de algn**: *Esta broma es ~ de mi hermana.* This joke must be my sister's doing. **ser poca cosa 1** (*herida*) not to be serious **2** (*persona*) to be a poor little thing **ver cosa igual/semejante**: *¿Habráse visto ~ igual?* Did you ever see anything like it? *Ver tb* ALGUNO, CADA, CUALQUIERA, OTRO

cosecha *nf* **1** (*gen*) harvest: *Este año habrá buena ~.* There's going to be a good harvest this year. **2** (*vino*) vintage: *la ~ del 85* the 1985 vintage

cosechar *vt, vi* to harvest

coser *vt, vi* to sew: *~ un botón* to sew a button on

cosmético, -a *adj, nm* cosmetic

cósmico, -a *adj* cosmic

cosmos *nm* cosmos

cosquillas *nf* LOC **hacer cosquillas** to tickle **tener cosquillas** to be ticklish: *Tengo muchas ~ en los pies.* My feet are very ticklish.

costa[1] *nf* coast: *Santander está en la ~ norte.* Santander is on the north coast.

costa[2] LOC **a costa de** at *sb's* expense: *a ~ nuestra* at our expense **a costa de lo que sea/a toda costa** at all costs *Ver tb* VIVIR

costado *nm* side: *Duermo de ~.* I sleep on my side.

costar *vi* **1** (*gen*) to cost: *El billete cuesta 30 libras.* The ticket costs £30. ◊ *El accidente costó la vida a cien personas.* The accident cost the lives of a hundred people. **2** (*tiempo*) to take: *Leerme el libro me costó un mes.* It took me a month to read the book. **3** (*resultar difícil*) to find it hard (***to do sth***): *Me cuesta levantarme temprano.* I find it hard to get up early. LOC **costar mucho/poco 1** (*dinero*) to be expensive/cheap **2** (*esfuerzo*) to be hard/easy **costar un riñón/un ojo de la cara** to cost an arm and a leg *Ver tb* CARO, CUÁNTO, TRABAJO

coste (*tb* **costo**) *nm* cost: *el ~ de la vida* the cost of living

costilla *nf* rib

costra *nf* scab

costumbre *nf* **1** (*de una persona*) habit: *Escuchamos la radio por ~.* We listen to the radio out of habit. **2** (*de un país*) custom: *Es una ~ española.* It's a Spanish custom. LOC **coger la costumbre** to get into the habit (*of doing sth*)

de costumbre usual: *más simpático que de ~* nicer than usual *Ver tb* QUITAR

costura *nf* **1** (*labor*) sewing: *una caja de ~* a sewing box **2** (*puntadas*) seam: *Se ha descosido el abrigo por la ~.* The seam of the coat has come undone.

cotidiano, -a *adj* daily

cotilla *nmf* gossip

cotillear *vi* to gossip

cotilleo *nm* gossip [*incontable*]: *No quiero ~s en la oficina.* I don't want any gossip in the office. ◊ *¿Sabes el último ~?* Have you heard the latest gossip?

coto *nm* **1** (*vedado*) preserve: *~ de caza* game preserve **2** (*parque natural*) reserve

cotorra *nf* parrot

coyote *nm* coyote

coz *nf* kick: *dar/pegar coces* to kick

cráneo *nm* skull, cranium [*pl* crania] (*científ*)

cráter *nm* crater

creación *nf* creation

creador, ~a *nm-nf* creator

crear ♦ *vt* **1** (*gen*) to create: *~ problemas* to create problems **2** (*empresa*) to set *sth* up ♦ **crearse** *v pron*: *~se enemigos* to make enemies

creatividad *nf* creativity

creativo, -a *adj* creative

crecer *vi* **1** (*gen*) to grow: *¡Cómo te ha crecido el pelo!* Hasn't your hair grown! **2** (*criarse*) to grow up: *Crecí en el campo.* I grew up in the country. **3** (*río*) to rise LOC **dejarse crecer el pelo, la barba, etc** to grow your hair, a beard, etc

creciente *adj* increasing LOC *Ver* CUARTO, LUNA

crecimiento *nm* growth

crédito *nm* **1** (*préstamo*) loan **2** (*forma de pago*) credit: *comprar algo a ~* to buy sth on credit

credo *nm* creed

crédulo, -a *adj* gullible

creencia *nf* belief [*pl* beliefs]

creer ♦ *vt, vi* **1** (*aceptar como verdad, tener fe*) to believe (***in sth/sb***): *~ en la justicia* to believe in justice ◊ *Nadie me creerá.* Nobody will believe me. **2** (*pensar*) to think: *Creen haber descubierto la verdad.* They think they've uncovered the truth. ◊ *¿Tú crees?* Do you think so? ◊ *—¿Lloverá mañana? —No creo.* 'Will it rain tomorrow?' 'I don't think so.' ♦ **creerse** *v pron* **1** (*gen*) to believe: *No me lo creo.* I don't believe it. **2** (*a uno mismo*) to think you are *sth/sb*: *Se cree muy listo.* He thinks he's very clever. ◊ *¿Qué se habrán creído?* Who do they think they are? LOC **creo que sí/no** I think so/I don't think so

creído, -a *pp, adj, nm-nf* (*engreído*) conceited [*adj*]: *ser un ~* to be conceited *Ver tb* CREER

crema *nf* **1** (*gen*) cream: *Date un poco de ~ en la espalda.* Put some cream on your back. ◊ *una bufanda color ~* a cream (coloured) scarf **2** (*pastelería*) confectioner's custard LOC **crema de afeitar** shaving cream *Ver tb* DESMAQUILLADOR, HIDRATANTE

cremallera *nf* zip: *No puedo subir la ~.* I can't do my zip up. ◊ *Bájame la ~ (del vestido).* Unzip my dress for me.

crematorio *nm* crematorium [*pl* crematoria]

crêpe *nf* pancake ☛ *Ver nota en* MARTES

crepúsculo *nm* twilight

cresta *nf* **1** (*gallo*) comb **2** (*otras aves, montaña, ola*) crest

creyente *nmf* believer LOC **no creyente** non-believer

cría *nf* **1** (*animal recién nacido*) baby [*pl* babies]: *una ~ de conejo* a baby rabbit **2** (*crianza*) breeding: *la ~ de perros* dog breeding

criadero *nm* farm LOC **criadero de perros** kennels [*pl*]

criado, -a *nm-nf* servant

criar ♦ *vt* **1** (*amamantar*) **(a)** (*persona*) to feed **(b)** (*animal*) to suckle **2** (*educar*) to bring *sb* up **3** (*ganado*) to rear ♦ **criarse** *v pron* to grow up: *Me crié en la ciudad.* I grew up in the city. LOC *Ver* MOHO

crimen *nm* **1** (*gen*) crime: *cometer un ~* to commit a crime **2** (*asesinato*) murder

criminal *adj, nmf* criminal

crin *nf* **crines** mane [*sing*]

crío, -a *nm-nf* **1** (*bebé*) baby [*pl* babies] **2** (*joven*) boy [*fem* girl], kid (*más coloq*): *Son unos ~s muy majos.* They're lovely kids.

crisis *nf* crisis [*pl* crises]

crisma[1] *nm* (*tarjeta de Navidad*) Christmas card

crisma[2] *nf* (*cabeza*) LOC *Ver* ROMPER

cristal *nm* **1** (*gen*) glass [*incontable*]: *Me corté con un ~ roto.* I cut myself on a piece of broken glass. **2** (*vidrio fino, mineral*) crystal: *una licorera de ~* a

crystal decanter **3** (*lámina*) pane: *el ~ de la ventana* the window pane
cristalero, -a *nm-nf* glazier
cristalino, -a *adj* (*agua*) crystal clear
cristianismo *nm* Christianity
cristiano, -a *adj*, *nm-nf* Christian
Cristo *n pr* Christ LOC **antes/después de Cristo** BC/AD **hecho un Cristo** a mess: *Tienes la cara hecha un ~*. Your face is a mess.
criterio *nm* **1** (*principio*) criterion [*pl* criteria] [*se usa mucho en plural*] **2** (*capacidad de juzgar, Jur*) judgement: *tener buen ~* to have sound judgement **3** (*opinión*) opinion: *según nuestro ~* in our opinion
crítica *nf* **1** (*gen*) criticism: *Estoy harta de tus ~s.* I'm fed up with your criticism. **2** (*en un periódico*) review, write-up (*más coloq*): *La obra ha tenido una ~ excelente.* The play got an excellent write-up. **3** (*conjunto de críticos*) critics [*pl*]: *bien acogida por la ~* well received by the critics
criticar *vt, vi* to criticize
crítico, -a *nm-nf* critic
crol *nm* crawl LOC *Ver tb* NADAR
cromo *nm* **1** (*de colección*) picture card **2** (*Quím*) chromium
crónico, -a *adj* chronic
cronológico, -a *adj* chronological
cronometrar *vt* to time
cronómetro *nm* (*Dep*) stopwatch
croqueta *nf* croquette
cross *nm* cross-country race: *participar en un ~* to take part in a cross-country race
cruasán *nm* croissant ☛ *Ver dibujo en* PAN
cruce *nm* **1** (*de carreteras*) junction: *Al llegar al ~, gira a la derecha.* Turn right when you reach the junction. **2** (*para peatones*) pedestrian crossing **3** (*híbrido*) cross: *un ~ de bóxer y doberman* a cross between a boxer and a Dobermann LOC *Ver* LUZ
crucero *nm* (*viaje*) cruise: *hacer un ~* to go on a cruise
crucificar *vt* to crucify
crucifijo *nm* crucifix
crucigrama *nm* crossword: *hacer un ~* to do a crossword
crudo, -a ◆ *adj* **1** (*sin cocinar*) raw **2** (*poco hecho*) underdone **3** (*clima, realidad*) harsh **4** (*ofensivo*) shocking: *unas escenas crudas* some shocking scenes ◆ *nm* crude oil
cruel *adj* cruel
crueldad *nf* cruelty [*pl* cruelties]
crujido *nm* **1** (*hojas secas, papel*) rustle **2** (*madera, huesos*) creak
crujiente *adj* (*alimentos*) crunchy
crujir *vi* **1** (*hojas secas*) to rustle **2** (*madera, huesos*) to creak **3** (*alimentos*) to crunch **4** (*dientes*) to grind
crustáceo *nm* crustacean
cruz *nf* cross: *Señale la respuesta con una ~*. Put a cross next to the answer. LOC **Cruz Roja** Red Cross *Ver tb* BRAZO, CARA
cruzado, -a *pp, adj* LOC *Ver* BRAZO, PIERNA; *Ver tb* CRUZAR
cruzar ◆ *vt* **1** (*gen*) to cross: *~ la calle/un río* to cross the street/a river ◊ *~ la calle corriendo* to run across the street ◊ *~ el río a nado* to swim across the river ◊ *~ las piernas* to cross your legs **2** (*palabras, miradas*) to exchange ◆ **cruzarse** *v pron* to meet (*sb*): *Nos cruzamos en el camino.* We met on the way. LOC **cruzar los brazos** to fold your arms
cuaderno *nm* **1** (*gen*) notebook **2** (*de ejercicios*) exercise book
cuadra *nf* stable
cuadrado, -a *adj, nm* square LOC **estar cuadrado** to be stockily-built *Ver tb* ELEVADO, RAÍZ; *Ver tb* CUADRAR
cuadrar ◆ *vi* ~ (**con**) to tally (**with** ***sth***): *La noticia no cuadra con lo ocurrido.* The news doesn't tally with what happened. ◆ *vt* (*Com*) to balance ◆ **cuadrarse** *v pron* to stand to attention
cuadrilla *nf* gang
cuadro *nm* **1** (*Arte*) painting **2 cuadros** (*tela*) check [*sing*]: *unos pantalones de ~s* check trousers ◊ *Los ~s te favorecen.* Check suits you. LOC **cuadro escocés** tartan *Ver tb* ÓLEO
cuádruple ◆ *adj* quadruple ◆ *nm* four times: *¿Cuál es el ~ de cuatro?* What is four times four?
cuajar(se) *vt, v pron* **1** (*leche*) to curdle **2** (*yogur*) to set
cual *pron rel* **1** (*persona*) whom: *Tengo diez alumnos, de los ~es dos son ingleses.* I've got ten students, two of whom are English. ◊ *la familia para la ~ trabaja* the family he works for ☛ *Ver nota en* WHOM **2** (*cosa*) which: *La pegó, lo ~ no está nada bien.* He hit her, which just isn't right. ◊ *un trabajo en el ~ me siento muy cómodo* a job I feel very comfortable in ☛ *Ver nota en* WHICH

LOC **con lo cual** so: *Lo he perdido, con lo ~ no podré prestárselo.* I've lost it, so I won't be able to lend it to him. *Ver tb* CADA

cuál *pron interr* **1** (*gen*) what: *¿~ es la capital de Perú?* What's the capital of Peru? **2** (*entre varios*) which (one): *¿~ prefieres?* Which one do you prefer? ☛ *Ver nota en* WHAT

cualidad *nf* quality [*pl* qualities]

cualquiera (*tb* **cualquier**) ◆ *adj* **1** (*gen*) any: *Coge cualquier autobús que vaya al centro.* Catch any bus that goes into town. ◊ *en cualquier caso* in any case ☛ *Ver nota en* SOME **2** (*uno cualquiera*) any old: *Trae un trapo ~.* Fetch any old cloth. ◆ **cualquiera** *pron* **1** (*cualquier persona*) anybody: *~ puede equivocarse.* Anybody can make a mistake. **2** (*entre dos*) either (one): *~ de los dos me sirve.* Either (of them) will do. ◊ *—¿Cuál de los dos libros cojo? —Cualquiera.* 'Which of the two books should I take?' 'Either one (of them).' **3** (*entre más de dos*) any (one): *en ~ de esas ciudades* in any one of those cities ◆ **cualquiera** *nmf* (*don nadie*) nobody: *No es más que un ~.* He is just a nobody. LOC **cualquier cosa** anything **cualquier cosa que...** whatever: *Cualquier cosa que pide, se la compran.* They buy her whatever she wants. **en cualquier lugar/parte/sitio** anywhere **por cualquier cosa** over the slightest thing: *Discuten por ~ cosa.* They argue over the slightest thing.

cuando ◆ *adv* when: *~ venga Juan iremos al zoo.* When Juan gets here, we'll go to the zoo. ◊ *Me atacaron ~ volvía del cine.* I was attacked as I was going home from the cinema. ◊ *Pásese por el banco ~ quiera.* Pop into the bank whenever you want. ◆ *conj* if: *~ lo dicen todos los periódicos, será verdad.* If all the papers say so, it must be true. LOC **de cuando en cuando** from time to time *Ver tb* VEZ

cuándo *adv interr* when: *¿~ te examinas?* When's your exam? ◊ *Pregúntale ~ llegará.* Ask him when he'll be arriving. LOC **¿desde cuándo?** how long...?: *¿Desde ~ juegas al tenis?* How long have you been playing tennis?

> También se puede decir **since when?** pero tiene un fuerte matiz irónico: *Pero tú ¿desde cuándo te interesas por el deporte?* And since when have you been interested in sport?

cuanto, -a ◆ *adj*: *Haz cuantas pruebas sean necesarias.* Do whatever tests are necessary. ◊ *Lo haré cuantas veces haga falta.* I will do it as many times as I have to. ◆ *pron*: *Le dimos ~ teníamos.* We gave him everything we had. ◊ *Llora ~ quieras.* Cry as much as you like. LOC **cuanto antes** as soon as possible **cuanto más/menos...** the more/less...: *~ más tiene, más quiere.* The more he has, the more he wants. ◊ *~ más lo pienso, menos lo entiendo.* The more I think about it, the less I understand. **en cuanto** as soon as: *En ~ me vieron, echaron a correr.* As soon as they saw me, they started running. **en cuanto a...** as for... **unos cuantos** a few: *unos ~s amigos* a few friends ◊ *Unos ~s llegaron tarde.* A few people were late.

cuánto, -a ◆ *adj*

- **uso interrogativo 1** (+ *sustantivo incontable*) how much: *¿~ dinero te has gastado?* How much money did you spend? **2** (+ *sustantivo contable*) how many: *¿Cuántas personas había?* How many people were there?
- **uso exclamativo**: *¡~ vino han bebido!* What a lot of wine they've drunk! ◊ *¡A cuántas personas ha ayudado!* He's helped so many people!

◆ *pron* how much [*pl* how many] ◆ *adv* **1** (*uso interrogativo*) how much **2** (*uso exclamativo*): *¡~ les quiero!* I'm so fond of them! LOC **¿a cuántos estamos?** what's the date today? **¿cuánto es/cuesta/vale?** how much is it? **¿cuánto (tiempo)/cuántos días, meses, etc?** how long...?: *¿~ has tardado en llegar?* How long did it take you to get here? ◊ *¿~s años llevas en Londres?* How long have you been living in London? *Ver tb* CADA

cuarenta *nm, adj, pron* **1** (*gen*) forty **2** (*cuadragésimo*) fortieth ☛ *Ver ejemplos en* SESENTA LOC **los cuarenta principales** the top forty *Ver tb* CANTAR

cuaresma *nf* Lent: *Estamos en ~.* It's Lent.

cuartel *nm* barracks [*v sing o pl*]: *El ~ está muy cerca de aquí.* The barracks is/are very near here. LOC **cuartel general** headquarters [*v sing o pl*]

cuartilla *nf* sheet of paper

cuarto *nm* room: *No entres en mi ~.* Don't go into my room. LOC **cuarto de baño** bathroom **cuarto de estar** living room **cuarto trastero** boxroom

cuarto, -a ◆ *adj, pron, nm-nf* fourth (*abrev* 4th) ☛ *Ver ejemplos en* SEXTO ◆ *nm* quarter: *un ~ de hora/kilo* a quarter of an hour/a kilo ◆ **cuarta** *nf* (*marcha*) fourth (gear) LOC **cuarto creciente/menguante** first/last quarter **cuartos de final** quarter finals **menos cuarto/y cuarto** a quarter to/a quarter past: *Llegaron a las diez menos ~.* They arrived at a quarter to ten. ◊ *Es la una y ~.* It's a quarter past one.

cuatro *nm, adj, pron* **1** (*gen*) four **2** (*fecha*) fourth ☛ *Ver ejemplos en* SEIS LOC **a cuatro patas** on all fours: *ponerse a ~ patas* to get down on all fours

cuatrocientos, -as *adj, pron, nm* four hundred ☛ *Ver ejemplos en* SEISCIENTOS

cuba *nf* barrel LOC *Ver* BORRACHO

cubertería *nf* cutlery set

cúbico, -a *adj* cubic: *metro ~* cubic metre LOC *Ver* RAÍZ

cubierta *nf* (*Náut*) deck: *subir a ~* to go up on deck

cubierto, -a ◆ *pp, adj* **1** ~ (**de/por**) covered (**in/with** ***sth***): *~ de manchas* covered in stains ◊ *El sillón estaba ~ por una sábana.* The chair was covered with a sheet. **2** (*cielo, día*) overcast **3** (*instalación*) indoor: *una piscina cubierta* an indoor swimming pool ◆ *nm* cutlery [*incontable*]: *Sólo me falta poner los ~s.* I've just got to put out the cutlery. ◊ *Todavía no ha aprendido a usar los ~s.* He hasn't learnt how to use a knife and fork yet. LOC **ponerse a cubierto** to take cover *from sth/sb* *Ver tb* PISCINA; *Ver tb* CUBRIR

cubilete *nm* (*para dados*) shaker

cubo *nm* **1** (*recipiente*) bucket **2** (*Geom*) cube LOC **cubo de la basura** dustbin

cubrir ◆ *vt* to cover *sth/sb* (**with** ***sth***): *Han cubierto las paredes de propaganda electoral.* They've covered the walls with election posters. ◊ *~ los gastos de desplazamiento* to cover travelling expenses ◆ *vi* (*en el agua*): *Os tengo prohibido nadar donde cubre.* You mustn't go out of your depth.

cucaracha *nf* cockroach

cuchara *nf* spoon LOC **cuchara de palo/madera** wooden spoon

cucharada *nf* spoonful: *dos ~s de azúcar* two spoonfuls of sugar

cucharadita *nf* teaspoonful

cucharilla *nf* teaspoon

cucharón *nm* ladle

cuchichear *vi* to whisper

cuchilla *nf* blade LOC *Ver* AFEITARSE

cuchillo *nm* knife [*pl* knives]

cuclillas LOC **en cuclillas** squatting **ponerse en cuclillas** to squat

cuco *nm* cuckoo [*pl* cuckoos] LOC *Ver* RELOJ

cucurucho *nm* **1** (*helado*) cornet **2** (*papel*) cone **3** (*gorro*) pointed hood

cuello *nm* **1** (*gen*) neck: *Me duele el ~.* My neck hurts. ◊ *el ~ de una botella* the neck of a bottle **2** (*prenda de vestir*) collar: *el ~ de la camisa* the shirt collar LOC **cuello alto/vuelto** polo-neck **cuello de pico** V-neck *Ver tb* AGUA, SOGA

cuenca *nf* (*Geog*) basin: *la ~ del Ebro* the Ebro basin LOC **cuenca minera** (*de carbón*) coalfield

cuenco *nm* (*recipiente*) bowl

cuenta *nf* **1** (*Com, Fin*) account: *una ~ corriente* a current account **2** (*factura*) bill: *¡Camarero, la ~ por favor!* Could I have the bill, please? ◊ *la ~ del teléfono* the phone bill **3** (*operación aritmética*) sum: *No me salen las ~s.* I can't work this out. **4** (*rosario*) bead LOC **cuenta atrás** countdown **darse cuenta de 1** (*gen*) to realize (*that...*): *Me di ~ de que no me estaban escuchando.* I realized (that) they weren't listening. **2** (*ver*) to notice *sth/that...* **echar/sacar la cuenta** to work *sth* out **hacer cuentas** to work *sth* out **hacer la cuenta de la vieja** to count on your fingers **por la cuenta que me trae** for my, your, etc own sake **salir de cuentas** to be due: *Sale de ~s a finales de julio.* She's due at the end of July. **tener/tomar en cuenta 1** (*hacer caso*) to bear *sth* in mind: *Tendré en ~ los consejos que me das.* I'll bear your advice in mind. **2** (*reprochar*) to take *sth* to heart: *No se lo tomes en ~.* Don't take it to heart. *Ver tb* AJUSTAR

cuentakilómetros *nm* ≃ milometer

cuentista *adj, nmf* **1** (*quejica*) whinger [*n*] **2** (*mentiroso*) fibber [*n*]: *¡Qué ~ eres!* You're such a fibber!

cuento *nm* **1** (*gen*) story [*pl* stories]: *~s de hadas* fairy stories ◊ *Cuéntame un ~.* Tell me a story. **2** (*mentira*) fib: *No me vengas con ~s.* Don't tell fibs. LOC **cuento chino** tall story **no venir a cuento** to be irrelevant: *Lo que dices no viene a ~.* What you say is irrelevant. **tener cuento** to put sth on: *Lo que tienes es ~.* You're just putting it on.

cuerda *nf* **1** (*gen*) rope: *una ~ de saltar* a skipping rope ◊ *átalo con una ~.* Tie it with some rope. **2** (*Mús*) string: *instrumentos de ~* stringed instruments LOC **cuerdas vocales** vocal chords **dar cuerda a algn** to encourage sb (to talk) **dar cuerda a un reloj** to wind up a clock/watch

cuerdo, -a *adj* sane

cuerno *nm* horn

cuero *nm* leather: *una cazadora de ~* a leather jacket LOC **en cueros** stark naked

cuerpo *nm* body [*pl* bodies] LOC **a cuerpo de rey** like a king **cuerpo de bomberos** fire brigade **de cuerpo entero** full-length: *una fotografía de ~ entero* a full-length photograph **ir a cuerpo** not to wear a coat/jacket

cuervo *nm* crow

cuesta *nf* slope LOC **a cuestas** on your back **cuesta abajo/arriba** downhill/ uphill

cuestión *nf* (*asunto, problema*) matter: *en ~ de horas* in a matter of hours ◊ *Es ~ de vida o muerte.* It's a matter of life or death. LOC **en cuestión** in question **la cuestión es…** the thing is…

cuestionario *nm* questionnaire: *rellenar un ~* to fill in a questionnaire

cueva *nf* cave

cuidado ◆ *nm* care ◆ **¡cuidado!** *interj* **1** (*gen*) look out!: *¡Cuidado! Viene un coche.* Look out! There's a car coming. **2 ~ con**: *¡~ con el perro!* Beware of the dog! ◊ *¡~ con el escalón!* Mind the step! LOC **al cuidado de** in charge of *sth/sb*: *Estoy al ~ de la oficina.* I'm in charge of the office. **con (mucho) cuidado** (very) carefully **tener cuidado (con)** to be careful (with *sth/sb*) *Ver tb* UNIDAD

cuidadoso, -a *adj* ~ (**con**) careful (**with** ***sth***): *Es muy ~ con sus juguetes.* He is very careful with his toys.

cuidar ◆ *vt, vi* ~ (**de**) to look after *sth/ sb*: *Siempre he cuidado mis plantas.* I've always looked after my plants. ◊ *¿Puedes ~ de los niños?* Can you look after the children? ◆ **cuidarse** *v pron* to look after yourself: *No se cuida nada.* She doesn't look after herself at all. ◊ *Cuídate.* Look after yourself. LOC *Ver* LÍNEA

culata *nf* (*arma*) butt LOC *Ver* TIRO

culebra *nf* snake

culebrón *nm* soap (opera)

culinario, -a *adj* culinary

culo *nm* (*trasero, botella, vaso*) bottom LOC *Ver* GAFAS

culpa *nf* fault: *No es ~ mía.* It isn't my fault. LOC **echar la culpa a algn (de algo)** to blame sb (for sth) **por culpa de** because of *sth/sb* **tener la culpa (de algo)** to be to blame (for sth): *Nadie tiene la ~ de lo que pasó.* Nobody is to blame for what happened.

culpabilidad *nf* guilt

culpable ◆ *adj* ~ (**de**) guilty (**of** ***sth***): *ser ~ de asesinato* to be guilty of murder ◆ *nmf* culprit LOC *Ver* DECLARAR

culpar *vt* to blame *sb* (***for sth***): *Me culpan de lo ocurrido.* They blame me for what happened.

cultivar *vt* to grow

cultivo *nm*: *el ~ de tomates* tomato growing

culto, -a ◆ *adj* **1** (*persona*) cultured **2** (*lengua, expresión*) formal ◆ *nm* **1** ~ (**a**) (*veneración*) worship (**of** ***sth/sb***): *el ~ al sol* sun worship ◊ *libertad de ~* freedom of worship **2** (*secta*) cult: *miembros de un nuevo ~ religioso* members of a new religious cult **3** (*misa*) service

cultura *nf* culture

cultural *adj* cultural LOC *Ver* CENTRO

cumbre *nf* summit

cumpleaños *nm* birthday [*pl* birthdays]: *El lunes es mi ~.* It's my birthday on Monday. ◊ *¡Feliz ~!* Happy Birthday! ☛También se puede decir 'Many happy returns!'.

cumplido, -a ◆ *pp, adj* LOC *Ver* RECIÉN; *Ver tb* CUMPLIR ◆ *nm* compliment LOC **sin cumplidos** without ceremony

cumplir ◆ *vt* **1** (*años*) to be: *En agosto cumplirá 30.* She'll be 30 in August. ◊ *¿Cuántos años cumples?* How old are you? **2** (*condena*) to serve ◆ *vt, vi* ~ (**con**) **1** (*orden*) to carry *sth* out **2** (*promesa, obligación*) to fulfil ◆ *vi* **1** (*hacer lo que corresponde*) to do your bit: *Yo he cumplido.* I've done my bit. **2** (*plazo*) to expire ◆ **cumplirse** *v pron* (*realizarse*) to come true: *Se cumplieron sus sueños.* His dreams came true. LOC **hacer algo por cumplir** to do sth to be polite: *No lo hagas por ~.* Don't do it just to be polite.

cuna *nf* (*bebé*) cot LOC *Ver* CANCIÓN

cundir *vi* **1** (*alimento*) to go a long way: *La pasta cunde mucho.* Pasta goes a long way. **2** (*extenderse*) to spread: *Cundió el pánico.* Panic spread. ◊ *Que no cunda el pánico.* Don't panic.

cuneta *nf* ditch

cuña *nf* wedge

cuñado, -a *nm-nf* brother-in-law [*fem* sister-in-law] [*pl* brothers-in-law/ sisters-in-law]

cuota *nf* fee: *la ~ de socio* the membership fee

cupón *nm* **1** (*vale*) coupon **2** (*para un sorteo*) ticket

cúpula *nf* dome

cura[1] *nf* **1** (*de una herida*) dressing: *Después de lavar la herida, aplique la ~.* After washing the wound apply the dressing. **2** (*curación, tratamiento*) cure: *~ de reposo* rest cure LOC **tener/ no tener cura** to be curable/incurable

cura[2] *nm* priest LOC *Ver* COLEGIO

curandero, -a *nm-nf* quack

curar ◆ *vt* **1** (*sanar*) to cure (*sb*) (**of *sth***): *Esas pastillas me han curado el catarro.* Those pills have cured my cold. **2** (*herida*) to dress **3** (*alimentos*) to cure ◆ **curarse** *v pron* **1 curarse (de)** (*ponerse bien*) to recover (**from *sth***): *El niño se curó del sarampión.* The little boy recovered from the measles. **2** (*herida*) to heal (over/up)

curiosidad *nf* curiosity LOC **por curiosidad** out of curiosity: *Entré por pura ~.* I went in out of pure curiosity. **tener curiosidad (por)** to be curious (about *sth*): *Tengo ~ por saber cómo son.* I'm curious to find out what they're like.

curioso, -a ◆ *adj* curious ◆ *nm-nf* **1** (*mirón*) onlooker **2** (*indiscreto*) busybody [*pl* busybodies]

currante *nmf* worker

currar *vi* to slave away

curre (*tb* **curro**) *nm* work: *ir al ~* to go to work

currículo *nm* **curriculum vitae** curriculum vitae (*abrev* cv)

cursi *adj* **1** (*persona*) affected: *¡Qué niña más ~!* What an affected little girl! **2** (*cosa*) flashy: *Viste muy ~.* He's a very flashy dresser.

cursillo *nm* short course

curso *nm* **1** (*gen*) course: *el ~ de un río* the course of a river ◊ *~s de idiomas* language courses **2** (*año académico*) school/academic year: *al final del ~* at the end of the school year **3** (*ciclo*) year: *Ese chico está en mi ~.* He's in the same year as me. ◊ *Estoy ya en tercer ~.* I'm now in the third year. LOC **el año/mes en curso** the current year/month *Ver tb* DELEGADO

cursor *nm* cursor

curtir *vt* to tan: *~ pieles* to tan leather hides

curva *nf* **1** (*línea, gráfico*) curve: *dibujar una ~* to draw a curve **2** (*carretera, río*) bend: *una ~ peligrosa/cerrada* a dangerous/sharp bend ◊ *Conduce con cuidado que hay muchas ~s.* There are a lot of bends so drive carefully.

curvo, -a *adj* **1** (*forma*) curved: *una línea curva* a curved line **2** (*doblado*) bent

custodia *nf* custody

custodiar *vt* to guard: *~ a los prisioneros/la caja fuerte* to guard the prisoners/safe

cutícula *nf* cuticle

cutis *nm* **1** (*piel*) skin **2** (*tez*) complexion: *Tu ~ es muy pálido.* You have a very pale complexion.

cutre *adj* (*lugar*) grotty

cuyo, -a *adj rel* whose: *Esa es la chica ~ padre me presentaron.* That's the girl whose father was introduced to me. ◊ *la casa cuyas puertas pintaste* the house whose doors you painted

Dd

dactilar *adj* LOC *Ver* HUELLA

dado *nm* dice [*pl* dice]: *echar/tirar los ~s* to roll the dice

dálmata *nmf* Dalmatian

daltónico, -a *adj* colour-blind

dama *nf* **1** (*señora*) lady [*pl* ladies] **2** (*empleada de la reina*) lady-in-waiting [*pl* ladies-in-waiting] **3** (*Ajedrez*) queen **4** (*en el juego de damas*) king **5 damas** draughts [*sing*]: *jugar a las ~s* to play draughts LOC **dama de honor** bridesmaid ☛ *Ver nota en* BODA

danés, -esa ◆ *adj, nm* Danish: *hablar ~* to speak Danish ◆ *nm-nf* Dane: *los daneses* the Danes LOC *Ver* GRANDE

danza *nf* dance

dañar *vt* **1** (*gen*) to damage: *La sequía*

dañó las cosechas. The drought damaged the crops. ◊ *El fumar puede ~ la salud.* Smoking can damage your health. **2** (*persona*) to hurt

dañino, -a *adj* harmful

daño *nm* damage (***to sth***) [*incontable*]: *La lluvia ha ocasionado muchos ~s.* The rain has caused a lot of damage. LOC **daños y perjuicios** damages **hacer daño** (*producir un dolor*) to hurt: *¡Ay, me haces ~!* Ouch, you're hurting me! **hacerse daño** to hurt yourself: *Me hice ~ en la mano.* I hurt my hand.

dar ◆ *vt* **1** (*gen*) to give: *Me dio la llave.* He gave me the key. ◊ *~le un susto a algn* to give sb a fright **2** (*Educ*) **(a)** (*profesor*) to teach: *~ ciencias* to teach science **(b)** (*alumno*) to have: *Doy clases de piano los lunes.* I have piano lessons on Mondays. **3** (*encender*) to turn *sth* on: *No des la luz todavía.* Don't turn the light on yet. **4** (*reloj*) to strike: *El reloj dio las doce.* The clock struck twelve. **5** (*fruto, flores*) to bear **6** (*olor*) to give *sth* off ◆ *vi* **1** ~ **a** to overlook *sth* [*vt*]: *El balcón da a una plaza.* The balcony overlooks a square. **2** ~ (**con/contra**) (*golpear*) to hit *sth/sb* [*vt*]: *El coche dio contra el árbol.* The car hit the tree. ◊ *La rama me dio en la cabeza.* The branch hit me on the head. **3** (*ataque*) to have: *Le dio un ataque al corazón/de tos.* He had a heart attack/a coughing fit. **4** (*hora*) to be: *¿Ya han dado las cinco?* Is it five o'clock yet? **5** (*luz*) to shine: *La luz me daba de lleno en los ojos.* The light was shining in my eyes. ◆ **darse** *v pron* **1** (*tomarse*) to have: *~se un baño/una ducha* to have a bath/ shower **2 darse** (**con/contra/en**) to hit: *Se dio con la rodilla en la mesa.* He hit his knee against the table. LOC **dárselas de** to make out you are *sth*: *dárselas de listo/inocente* to make out you're clever/innocent **no doy ni una** I, you, etc can't do anything right: *Hoy no das ni una.* You can't do anything right today. **se me da bien/mal** I am, you are, etc good/bad *at sth*: *Se le da muy mal el inglés.* He's very bad at English. ☛Para otras expresiones con **dar**, véanse las entradas del sustantivo, adjetivo, etc, p.ej. **dar calabazas** en CALABAZA y **dar la cara** en CARA.

dátil *nm* date

dato *nm* **1** (*información*) information [*incontable*]: *un ~ importante* an important piece of information **2 datos** (*Informát*) data [*incontable*]: *procesamiento de ~s* data processing LOC **datos personales** personal details *Ver tb* BASE

de *prep*

- **posesión 1** (*de algn*): *el libro de Pedro* Pedro's book ◊ *el perro de mis amigos* my friends' dog ◊ *Es de ella/mi abuela.* It's hers/my grandmother's. **2** (*de algo*): *una página del libro* a page of the book ◊ *las habitaciones de la casa* the rooms in the house ◊ *la catedral de León* León cathedral
- **origen, procedencia** from: *Son de Sevilla.* They are from Seville. ◊ *de Londres a Madrid* from London to Madrid
- **en descripciones de personas 1** (*cualidades físicas*) **(a)** (*gen*) with: *una niña de pelo rubio* a girl with fair hair **(b)** (*ropa, colores*) in: *la señora del vestido verde* the lady in the green dress **2** (*cualidades no físicas*) of: *una persona de gran carácter* a person of great character ◊ *una mujer de 30 años* a woman of 30
- **en descripciones de cosas 1** (*cualidades físicas*) **(a)** (*materia*): *un vestido de lino* a linen dress **(b)** (*contenido*) of: *un vaso de leche* a glass of milk **2** (*cualidades no físicas*) of: *un libro de gran interés* a book of great interest
- **tema, asignatura**: *un libro/profesor de física* a physics book/teacher ◊ *una clase de historia* a history class ◊ *No entiendo de política.* I don't understand anything about politics.
- **con números y expresiones de tiempo**: *más/menos de diez* more/less than ten ◊ *un sello de 45 pesetas* a 45 peseta stamp ◊ *un cuarto de kilo* a quarter of a kilo ◊ *de noche/día* at night/ during the day ◊ *a las diez de la mañana* at ten in the morning
- **agente** by: *un libro de Cela* a book by Cela ◊ *seguido de tres jóvenes* followed by three young people
- **causa**: *morirse de hambre* to die of hunger ◊ *Saltamos de alegría.* We jumped for joy.
- **otras construcciones**: *el mejor actor del mundo* the best actor in the world ◊ *Lo rompió de un golpe.* He broke it with one blow. ◊ *de un trago* in one gulp ◊ *¿Qué hay de postre?* What's for pudding?

debajo *adv* **1** (*gen*) underneath: *Llevo una camiseta ~.* I'm wearing a T-shirt underneath. ◊ *Coge el de ~.* Take the bottom one. **2** ~ **de** under: *Está ~ de la* *mesa.* It's under the table LOC **por debajo de** below *sth*: *por ~ de la rodilla* below the knee

debate *nm* debate: *hacer un ~* to have a debate

deber[1] ◆ *vt* **1 + sustantivo** to owe: *Te debo 3.000 pesetas/una explicación.* I owe you 3000 pesetas/an explanation. **2 + inf (a)** (*en presente o futuro*) must: *Debes estudiar/obedecer las reglas.* You must study/obey the rules. ◊ *La ley deberá ser anulada.* The law must be abolished. ☛ *Ver nota en* MUST **(b)** (*en pasado o condicional*) should: *Hace una hora que debías estar aquí.* You should have been here an hour ago. ◊ *No deberías salir así.* You shouldn't go out like that. ◆ *v aux* ~ **de 1** (*en frases afirmativas*) must: *Ya debe de estar en casa.* She must be home by now. **2** (*en frases negativas*): *No debe de ser fácil.* It can't be easy. ◆ **deberse** *v pron* to be due ***to sth***: *Esto se debe a la falta de fondos.* This is due to lack of funds.

deber[2] *nm* **1** (*obligación moral*) duty [*pl* duties]: *cumplir con un ~* to do your duty **2 deberes** (*Educ*) homework [*incontable, v sing*]: *hacer los ~es* to do your homework ◊ *El maestro nos pone muchos ~es.* Our teacher gives us lots of homework.

debido, -a *pp, adj* proper LOC **debido a** because of *sth/sb Ver tb* DEBER[1]

débil *adj* weak: *Está ~ del corazón.* He has a weak heart. LOC *Ver* PUNTO

debilidad *nf* weakness

debilitar(se) *vt, v pron* to weaken

década *nf* decade LOC **la década de los ochenta, noventa, etc** the eighties, nineties, etc [*pl*]

decadente *adj* decadent

decano, -a *nm-nf* dean

decapitar *vt* to behead

decena *nf* **1** (*Mat, numeral colectivo*) ten **2** (*aproximadamente*) about ten: *una ~ de personas/veces* about ten people/times

decente *adj* decent

decepción *nf* disappointment: *llevarse una ~* to be disappointed

decepcionante *adj* disappointing

decepcionar *vt* **1** (*desilusionar*) to disappoint: *Me decepcionó la película.* The film was disappointing. **2** (*fallar*) to let *sb* down: *Me has vuelto a ~.* You've let me down again.

decidir ◆ *vt, vi* to decide: *Han decidido vender la casa.* They've decided to sell the house. ◆ **decidirse** *v pron* **1 decidirse (a)** to decide (***to do sth***): *Al final me decidí a salir.* In the end I decided to go out. **2 decidirse por** to decide **on *sth/sb***: *Todos nos decidimos por el rojo.* We decided on the red one. LOC **¡decídete!** make up your mind!

decimal *adj, nm* decimal

décimo, -a *adj, pron, nm-nf* tenth ☛ *Ver ejemplos en* SEXTO LOC **tener unas décimas (de fiebre)** to have a slight temperature

decimotercero, -a *adj, pron* thirteenth ☛ Para *decimocuarto, decimoquinto*, etc, ver Apéndice 1.

decir[1] *vt* to say, to tell

> *Decir* se traduce generalmente por **to say**: *—Son las tres, dijo Rosa.* 'It's three o'clock,' said Rosa. ◊ *¿Qué ha dicho?* What did he say? Cuando especificamos la persona con la que hablamos, es más normal utilizar **to tell**: *Me dijo que llegaría tarde.* He told me he'd be late. ◊ *¿Quién te lo ha dicho?* Who told you? **To tell** se utiliza también para dar órdenes: *Me dijo que me lavara las manos.* She told me to wash my hands. *Ver tb nota en* SAY.

LOC **¡diga!** (*teléfono*) hello **digamos...** let's say...: *Digamos las seis.* Let's say six o'clock. **digo...** I mean...: *Cuesta cuatro, digo cinco mil pesetas.* It costs four, I mean five, thousand pesetas. **el qué dirán** what people will say **¡no me digas!** you don't say! **se dice que...** they say that... **sin decir nada** without a word ☛ Para otras expresiones con **decir**, véanse las entradas del sustantivo, adjetivo, etc, p.ej. **no decir ni jota** en JOTA y **decir tonterías** en TONTERÍA.

decir[2] *nm* saying LOC **es un decir** you know what I mean

decisión *nf* **1** (*gen*) decision: *la ~ del árbitro* the referee's decision **2** (*determinación*) determination: *Hace falta mucha ~.* You need a lot of determination. LOC **tomar una decisión** to make/take a decision

decisivo, -a *adj* decisive

declaración *nf* **1** (*gen*) declaration: *una ~ de amor* a declaration of love **2** (*manifestación pública, Jur*) statement: *No quiso hacer declaraciones.* He didn't want to make a statement. ◊ *La policía le tomó ~.* The police took his statement. **LOC declaración de la renta** tax return *Ver tb* PRESTAR

declarar ◆ *vt, vi* **1** (*gen*) to declare: *¿Algo que ~?* Anything to declare? **2** (*en público*) to state: *según declaró el ministro* according to the minister's statement **3** (*Jur*) to testify ◆ **declararse** *v pron* **1** (*gen*) to come out: *~se a favor/en contra de algo* to come out in favour of/against sth **2** (*incendio, epidemia*) to break out **3** (*confesar amor*): *Se me declaró.* He told me he loved me. **LOC declararse culpable/inocente** to plead guilty/not guilty

decoración *nf* **1** (*acción, adorno*) decoration **2** (*estilo*) décor

decorado *nm* set

decorar *vt* to decorate

dedal *nm* thimble

dedicación *nf* dedication: *Tu ~ a los pacientes es admirable.* Your dedication to your patients is admirable.

dedicar ◆ *vt* **1** (*gen*) to devote *sth* ***to sth/sb***: *Dedicaron su vida a los animales.* They devoted their lives to animals. ◊ *¿A qué dedicas el tiempo libre?* How do you spend your free time? **2** (*canción, poema*) to dedicate *sth* (***to sb***): *Dediqué el libro a mi padre.* I dedicated the book to my father. **3** (*ejemplar*) to autograph ◆ **dedicarse** *v pron* **dedicarse a**: *¿A qué te dedicas?* What do you do for a living? ◊ *Se dedica a las antigüedades.* He's in antiques.

dedicatoria *nf* dedication

dedillo LOC al dedillo by heart

dedo *nm* **1** (*de la mano*) finger **2** (*del pie*) toe **3** (*medida*) half an inch: *Ponga dos ~s de agua en la cazuela.* Put an inch of water in the pan. **LOC a dedo** (*en autostop*): *He venido a ~.* I hitch-hiked. **dedo anular/corazón/índice** ring/middle/index finger **dedo meñique 1** (*de la mano*) little finger **2** (*del pie*) little toe **dedo pulgar/gordo 1** (*de la mano*) thumb **2** (*del pie*) big toe **hacer dedo** to hitch-hike *Ver tb* ANILLO, CHUPAR, DOS

deducir *vt* **1** (*concluir*) to deduce *sth* (***from sth***): *Deduje que no estaba en casa.* I deduced that he wasn't at home. **2** (*restar*) to deduct *sth* (***from sth***)

defecto *nm* **1** (*gen*) defect: *un ~ en el habla* a speech defect **2** (*moral*) fault **3** (*ropa*) flaw ☛ *Ver nota en* MISTAKE **LOC encontrar/sacar defectos a todo** to find fault with everything

defectuoso, -a *adj* defective, faulty (*más coloq*)

defender ◆ *vt* to defend *sth/sb* (***against sth/sb***) ◆ **defenderse** *v pron* to get by: *No sé mucho inglés pero me defiendo.* I don't know much English but I get by.

defendido, -a *nm-nf* defendant

defensa ◆ *nf* defence: *las ~s del cuerpo* the body's defences ◊ *un equipo con muy buena ~* a team with a very good defence ◆ *nmf* (*Dep*) defender **LOC en defensa propia** in self-defence

defensivo, -a *adj* defensive **LOC estar/ponerse a la defensiva** to be/go on the defensive

defensor, ~a *adj* **LOC** *Ver* ABOGADO

deficiencia *nf* deficiency [*pl* deficiencies]

deficiente *adj, nmf* mentally deficient [*adj*]

definición *nf* definition

definir *vt* to define

definitivamente *adv* **1** (*para siempre*) for good: *Volvió ~ a su país.* He returned home for good. **2** (*de forma determinante*) definitely

definitivo, -a *adj* **1** (*gen*) final: *el resultado ~* the final result ◊ *el número ~ de víctimas* the final death toll **2** (*solución*) definitive **LOC en definitiva** in short

deformado, -a *pp, adj* (*prenda*) out of shape *Ver tb* DEFORMAR

deformar ◆ *vt* **1** (*cuerpo*) to deform **2** (*prenda*) to pull *sth* out of shape **3** (*imagen, realidad*) to distort ◆ **deformarse** *v pron* **1** (*cuerpo*) to become deformed **2** (*prenda*) to lose its shape

deforme *adj* deformed

defraudar *vt* **1** (*decepcionar*) to disappoint **2** (*estafar*) to defraud

degeneración *nf* degeneration

degenerado, -a *pp, adj, nm-nf* degenerate *Ver tb* DEGENERAR(SE)

degenerar(se) *vi, v pron* to degenerate

degradar ◆ *vt* to degrade ◆ **degradarse** *v pron* (*deteriorarse*) to deteriorate: *El suelo se ha degradado mucho.* The soil has deteriorated a lot.

dejar ◆ *vt* **1** (*gen*) to leave: *¿Dónde has dejado las llaves?* Where have you left the keys? ◊ *Déjalo para después.* Leave it till later. ◊ *¡Déjame en paz!* Leave me alone! **2** (*abandonar*) to give *sth* up: *~ el trabajo* to give up work **3** (*permitir*) to let *sb* (***do sth***): *Mis padres no me dejan salir por la noche.* My parents don't let me go out at night. **4** (*prestar*) to lend, to borrow: *¿Me dejas dinero?* Can you lend me some money? ◊ *¿Me dejas la moto?* Can I borrow your motor bike? ☛ *Ver dibujo en* BORROW ◆ *vi* ~ **de 1** (*parar*) to stop ***doing sth***: *Ha dejado de llover.* It's stopped raining. **2** (*abandonar una costumbre*) to give up ***doing sth***: ~ *de fumar* to give up smoking ◆ *v aux* + **participio**: *La noticia nos dejó preocupados.* We were worried by the news. ◆ **dejarse** *v pron* to leave: *Me dejé el paraguas en el autobús.* I left my umbrella on the bus. LOC ☛ Para expresiones con **dejar**, véanse las entradas del sustantivo, adjetivo, etc, p.ej. **dejar colgado** en COLGADO y **sin dejar rastro** en RASTRO.

del *Ver* DE

delantal *nm* apron

delante *adv* ~ (**de**) in front (**of** ***sth/sb***): *Si no ves la pizarra, ponte ~.* Sit at the front if you can't see the board. ◊ *Me lo contó estando otros ~.* She told me in front of other people. ◊ ~ *del televisor* in front of the television LOC **de delante**: *los asientos de ~* the front seats ◊ *el conductor de ~* the driver in front **hacia delante** forwards *Ver tb* PARTE[1]

delantero, -a ◆ *adj* front ◆ *nmf* (*Dep*) forward: *Juega de ~ centro.* He plays centre forward. LOC **llevar la delantera** to be in the lead

delatar *vt* to inform **on** ***sb***

delegación *nf* **1** (*comisión*) delegation: *una ~ de paz* a peace delegation **2** (*oficina*) office: *la ~ de Hacienda* the tax office

delegado, -a *nm-nf* (*Pol*) delegate LOC **delegado de curso** student representative

deletrear *vt* to spell

delfín *nm* dolphin

delgado, -a *adj* thin, slim

> **Thin** es la palabra más general para decir delgado y se puede utilizar para personas, animales o cosas. **Slim** se utiliza para referirnos a una persona delgada y con buen tipo. Existe también la palabra **skinny**, que significa *delgaducho*.

deliberado, -a *pp, adj* deliberate

delicadeza *nf* (*tacto*) tact: *Podías haberlo dicho con más ~.* You could have put it more tactfully. ◊ *Es una falta de ~.* It's very tactless. LOC **tener la delicadeza de** to have the courtesy *to do sth*

delicado, -a *adj* delicate

delicioso, -a *adj* delicious

delincuencia *nf* crime LOC **delincuencia juvenil** juvenile delinquency

delincuente *nmf* criminal

delineante *nmf* draughtsman/woman [*pl* draughtsmen/women]

delinquir *vi* to commit an offence

delirar *vi* **1** (*Med*) to be delirious **2** (*decir bobadas*) to talk nonsense

delito *nm* crime: *cometer un ~* to commit a crime

delta *nm* delta LOC *Ver* ALA

demanda *nf* **1** (*Com*) demand: *la oferta y la ~* supply and demand **2** (*Jur*) claim (**for** ***sth***): *presentar/poner una ~ por algo* to put in a claim for sth

demandar *vt* **1** (*exigir*) to demand **2** (*Jur*) to sue *sb* (**for** ***sth***)

demás ◆ *adj* other: *los ~ estudiantes* (the) other students ◆ *pron* (the) others: *Sólo vino Juan; los ~ se quedaron en casa.* Only Juan came; the others stayed at home. ◊ *ayudar a los ~* to help others LOC **lo demás** the rest: *Lo ~ no importa.* Nothing else matters. **y demás** and so on

demasiado, -a ◆ *adj* **1** (+ *sustantivo incontable*) too much: *Hay demasiada comida.* There is too much food. **2** (+ *sustantivo contable*) too many: *Llevas demasiadas cosas.* You're carrying too many things. ◆ *pron* too much [*pl* too many] ◆ *adv* **1** (*modificando a un verbo*) too much: *Fumas ~.* You smoke too much. **2** (*modificando a un adj o adv*) too: *Vas ~ deprisa.* You're going too fast. LOC **demasiadas veces** too often

democracia *nf* democracy [*pl* democracies]

demócrata *nmf* democrat

democrático, -a *adj* democratic

demonio *nm* **1** (*diablo*) devil **2** (*espíritu*) demon LOC **de mil/de todos los**

demonios: *Hace un frío de mil ~s.* It's freezing. **saber a demonios** to taste foul **ser un demonio** to be a (little) devil *Ver tb* DÓNDE

demostrar *vt* **1** (*probar*) to prove: *Le demostré que estaba equivocado.* I proved him wrong. **2** (*mostrar*) to show

denegar *vt* to refuse

densidad *nf* **1** (*gen*) density [*pl* densities] **2** (*niebla*) thickness

denso, -a *adj* dense

dentadura *nf* teeth [*pl*]: *~ postiza* false teeth

dentera *nf* LOC **dar dentera** to set *sb's* teeth on edge

dentífrico *nm* toothpaste

dentista *nmf* dentist

dentro *adv* **1** (*gen*) in/inside: *El gato está ~.* The cat is inside. ◊ *allí/aquí ~* in there/here **2** (*edificio*) indoors: *Prefiero que nos quedemos ~.* I'd rather stay indoors. **3 ~ de (a)** (*espacio*) in/inside: *~ del sobre* in/inside the envelope **(b)** (*tiempo*) in: *~ de una semana* in a week ◊ *~ de un rato* in a little while ◊ *~ de tres meses* in three months' time LOC **de/desde dentro** from (the) inside **dentro de lo que cabe** all things considered **dentro de nada** very soon **hacia dentro** in: *Mete la tripa hacia ~.* Pull your tummy in. **por dentro** (on the) inside: *pintado por ~* painted on the inside *Ver tb* AHÍ, ALLÁ, ALLÍ

denuncia *nf* **1** (*accidente, delito*) report: *presentar una ~* to report sth to the police **2** (*contra una persona*) complaint: *presentar una ~ contra algn* to make a formal complaint against sb

denunciar *vt* **1** (*gen*) to report *sth/sb* (**to sb**): *Denunció el robo de su bicicleta.* He reported the theft of his bicycle. ◊ *Me denunciaron a la policía.* They reported me to the police. **2** (*criticar*) to denounce

departamento *nm* **1** (*sección*) department **2** (*mueble, recipiente, tren*) compartment

depender *vi* **1 ~ de/de que/de si...** to depend **on sth/on whether...**: *Depende del tiempo que haga.* It depends on the weather. ◊ *Eso depende de que me traigas el dinero.* That depends on whether you bring me the money. ◊ *—¿Vendrás? —Depende.* 'Will you be coming?' 'That depends.' **2 ~ de algn (que...)** to be up **to sb (whether...)**: *Depende de mi jefe que pueda tener un día libre.* It's up to my boss whether I can have a day off. **3 ~ de** (*económicamente*) to be dependent **on *sth/sb***

dependiente, -a *nm-nf* shop assistant

depilar(se) *vt, v pron* **1** (*cejas*) to pluck **2** (*piernas, axilas*) **(a)** (*con cera*) to wax: *Me tengo que ~ para ir de vacaciones.* I must have my legs waxed before we go on holiday. **(b)** (*con maquinilla*) to shave

deporte *nm* sport: *¿Practicas algún ~?* Do you play any sports? LOC **hacer deporte** to get some exercise *Ver tb* PANTALÓN, ROPA

deportista ♦ *adj* keen on sport: *Siempre fue muy ~.* She's always been very keen on sport. ♦ *nmf* sportsman/woman [*pl* sportsmen/women]

deportivo, -a ♦ *adj* **1** (*gen*) sports [*n atrib*]: *competición deportiva* sports competition **2** (*conducta*) sporting: *una conducta poco deportiva* unsporting behaviour ♦ *nm* (*coche*) sports car

depósito *nm* tank: *el ~ de la gasolina* the petrol tank LOC **depósito de cadáveres** morgue

depresión *nf* depression

deprimente *adj* depressing

deprimir ♦ *vt* to depress ♦ **deprimirse** *v pron* to get depressed

deprisa *adv* quickly LOC **¡deprisa!** hurry up!

derecho, -a ♦ *adj* **1** (*diestro*) right: *romperse el pie ~* to break your right foot **2** (*recto*) straight: *Ese cuadro no está ~.* That picture isn't straight. ◊ *Ponte ~.* Sit up straight. **3** (*erguido*) upright ♦ **derecha** *nf* **1** (*gen*) right: *Es la segunda puerta a la derecha.* It's the second door on the right. ◊ *Cuando llegue al semáforo, tuerza a la derecha.* Turn right at the traffic lights. ◊ *Muévete un poco hacia la derecha.* Move a bit to the right. **2** (*mano*) right hand: *escribir con la derecha* to be right-handed **3** (*pie*) right foot ♦ **derecho** *nm* **1** (*anverso*) right side **2** (*facultad legal o moral*) right: *¿Con qué ~ entras aquí?* What right do you have to come in here? ◊ *los ~s humanos* human rights ◊ *el ~ de voto* the right to vote **3** (*estudios*) law ♦ **derecho** *adv* straight: *Vete ~ a casa.* Go straight home. LOC **de derecha(s)** right-wing **estar en su derecho** to be within my, your, etc rights: *Estoy en mi ~.* I'm within my rights. **la derecha** (*Pol*) the Right [*v sing o pl*] **¡no hay derecho!** it's not fair! **todo derecho** straight on: *Siga todo ~ hasta el final de* *la calle.* Go straight on to the end of the road. *Ver tb* HECHO, MANO, OJO

deriva *nf* LOC **a la deriva** adrift

derivar(se) *vi, v pron* **derivar(se) de 1** (*Ling*) to derive **from *sth* 2** (*proceder*) to stem **from *sth***

derramamiento *nm* LOC **derramamiento de sangre** bloodshed

derramar(se) *vt, v pron* to spill: *He derramado un poco de vino en la alfombra.* I've spilt some wine on the carpet. LOC **derramar sangre/lágrimas** to shed blood/tears

derrame *nm* haemorrhage

derrapar *vi* to skid

derretir(se) *vt, v pron* to melt

derribar *vt* **1** (*edificio*) to demolish **2** (*puerta*) to batter *a door* down **3** (*persona*) to knock *sb* down **4** (*avión, pájaro*) to bring *sth* down

derrochador, ~a ◆ *adj* wasteful ◆ *nm-nf* squanderer

derrochar *vt* **1** (*dinero*) to squander **2** (*rebosar*) to be bursting **with *sth***: *~ felicidad* to be bursting with happiness

derrota *nf* defeat

derrotar *vt* to defeat

derruir *vt* to demolish

derrumbamiento *nm* **1** (*hundimiento*) collapse **2** (*demolición*) demolition

derrumbar ◆ *vt* to demolish ◆ **derrumbarse** *v pron* to collapse

desabrigado, -a *pp, adj*: *Vas muy ~.* You're not very warmly dressed.

desabrochar ◆ *vt* to undo ◆ **desabrocharse** *v pron* to come undone: *Se me desabrochó la falda.* My skirt came undone.

desactivar *vt* to defuse

desafiar *vt* **1** (*retar*) to challenge *sb* (**to *sth***): *Te desafío a las damas.* I challenge you to a game of draughts. **2** (*peligro*) to brave

desafilado, -a *pp, adj* blunt

desafinado, -a *pp, adj* out of tune *Ver tb* DESAFINAR

desafinar *vi* **1** (*cantando*) to sing out of tune **2** (*instrumento*) to be out of tune **3** (*instrumentista*) to play out of tune

desafío *nm* challenge

desafortunado, -a *adj* unfortunate

desagradable *adj* unpleasant

desagradar *vi* to dislike *sth/doing sth* [*vt*]: *No me desagrada.* I don't dislike it.

desagradecido, -a *pp, adj* ungrateful

desagüe *nm* waste pipe

desahogarse *v pron* **1** (*gen*) to let off steam **2 ~ con algn** to confide **in sb**

desalentador, ~a *adj* discouraging

desaliñado, -a *pp, adj* scruffy

desalmado, -a *adj* heartless

desalojar *vt* to clear: *Desalojen la sala por favor.* Please clear the hall.

desamparado, -a *pp, adj* helpless

desangrarse *v pron* to bleed to death

desanimado, -a *pp, adj* (*deprimido*) depressed *Ver tb* DESANIMAR

desanimar ◆ *vt* to discourage ◆ **desanimarse** *v pron* to lose heart

desapacible *adj* unpleasant: *Hace un día muy ~.* The weather's very unpleasant today.

desaparecer *vi* to disappear LOC **desaparecer del mapa** to vanish off the face of the earth

desaparición *nf* disappearance

desapercibido, -a *adj* unnoticed: *pasar ~* to go unnoticed

desaprovechar *vt* to waste: *No desaproveches esta oportunidad.* Don't waste this opportunity.

desarmar *vt* **1** (*persona, ejército*) to disarm **2** (*desmontar*) to take *sth* to pieces

desarme *nm* disarmament: *el ~ nuclear* nuclear disarmament

desarrollado, -a *pp, adj* developed: *los países ~s* developed countries LOC **poco desarrollado** undeveloped *Ver tb* DESARROLLAR(SE)

desarrollar(se) *vt, v pron* to develop: *~ los músculos* to develop your muscles

desarrollo *nm* development LOC *Ver* VÍA

desastre *nm* disaster

desastroso, -a *adj* disastrous

desatar ◆ *vt* (*nudo, cuerda, animal*) to untie ◆ **desatarse** *v pron* **1** (*animal*) to get loose **2** (*paquete, cuerda*) to come undone: *Se me ha desatado un zapato.* One of my laces has come undone.

desatascar *vt* to unblock

desatender *vt* (*descuidar*) to neglect

desatornillar *vt* to unscrew

desatrancar *vt* **1** (*desatascar*) to unblock **2** (*puerta*) to unbolt

desautorizado, -a *pp, adj* unauthorized

desayunar ◆ *vi* to have breakfast: *Me gusta ~ en la cama.* I like having breakfast in bed. ◊ *antes de ~* before breakfast ◆ *vt* to have *sth* for breakfast: *¿Qué quieres ~?* What would you like for breakfast? ◊ *Sólo desayuno un café.* I just have a coffee for breakfast. ☛ *Ver* pág 320.

desayuno *nm* breakfast: *¿Te preparo el ~?* Shall I get you some breakfast? ☛ *Ver* pág 320.

desbandada *nf* LOC **salir en desbandada** to scatter in all directions

desbarajuste *nm* mess: *¡Qué ~!* What a mess!

desbaratar *vt* to foil: *~ un plan* to foil a plan

desbocado, -a *pp, adj* (*caballo*) runaway *Ver tb* DESBOCARSE

desbocarse *v pron* (*caballo*) to bolt

desbordar ◆ *vt*: *La basura desborda el cubo.* The bin is overflowing with rubbish. ◆ **desbordarse** *v pron* (*río*) to burst its banks

descafeinado, -a *adj* decaffeinated

descalificación *nf* (*Dep*) disqualification

descalificar *vt* (*Dep*) to disqualify: *Le descalificaron por hacer trampa.* He was disqualified for cheating.

descalzarse *v pron* to take your shoes off

descalzo, -a *adj* barefoot: *Me gusta andar descalza por la arena.* I love walking barefoot on the sand. ◊ *No andes ~.* Don't go round in your bare feet.

descampado *nm* area of open ground

descansado, -a *pp, adj* refreshed *Ver tb* DESCANSAR

descansar ◆ *vt, vi* to rest (*sth*) (**on** ***sth***): *Déjame ~ un rato.* Let me rest for a few minutes. ◊ *~ la vista* to rest your eyes ◆ *vi* to have a break: *Terminamos esto y descansamos cinco minutos.* We'll finish this and have a break for five minutes. LOC **¡que descanses!** sleep well!

descansillo *nm* landing

descanso *nm* **1** (*reposo*) rest: *El médico le mandó ~ y aire fresco.* The doctor prescribed rest and fresh air. **2** (*en el trabajo*) break: *trabajar sin ~* to work without a break **3** (*Dep*) half-time: *En el ~ iban tres a uno.* They were three one at half-time. **4** (*Teat*) interval: *Me encontré con ellos en el ~.* I met them during the interval.

descapotable *adj, nm* convertible

descarado, -a *adj* cheeky

descarga *nf* **1** (*mercancía*) unloading: *la carga y ~ de mercancías* the loading and unloading of goods **2** (*eléctrica*) shock

descargado, -a *pp, adj* (*pila, batería*) flat *Ver tb* DESCARGAR

descargar ◆ *vt* to unload: *~ un camión/una pistola* to unload a lorry/gun ◆ *vi* to break: *Por fin descargó la tormenta.* The storm finally broke. ◆ **descargarse** *v pron* (*pila, batería*) to go flat

descaro *nm* cheek: *¡Qué ~!* What (a) cheek!

descarriarse *v pron* to go off the straight and narrow

descarrilamiento *nm* derailment

descarrilar *vi* to be derailed: *El tren descarriló.* The train was derailed.

descartar *vt* to rule *sth/sb* out: *~ una posibilidad/a un candidato* to rule out a possibility/candidate

descendencia *nf* descendants [*pl*]

descender *vi* **1** (*ir/venir abajo*) to go/come down, to descend (*más formal*) **2** (*temperatura, precios, nivel*) to fall **3** ~ **de** (*familia*) to be descended **from** ***sb***: *Desciende de un príncipe ruso.* He's descended from a Russian prince. **4** (*Dep*) to be relegated: *Han descendido a tercera.* They've been relegated to the third division.

descendiente *nmf* descendant

descenso *nm* **1** (*bajada*) descent: *Es un ~ peligroso.* It's a dangerous descent. ◊ *El avión tuvo problemas en el ~.* The plane had problems during the descent. **2** (*temperatura*) drop ***in sth*** **3** (*precios*) fall ***in sth*** **4** (*Dep*) relegation

descifrar *vt* **1** (*mensaje*) to decode **2** (*escritura*) to decipher **3** (*enigma*) to solve

descodificador *nm* decoder

descodificar *vt* to decode

descolgado, -a *pp, adj* (*teléfono*) off the hook: *Lo han debido de dejar ~.* They must have left it off the hook. *Ver tb* DESCOLGAR

descolgar *vt* **1** (*algo colgado*) to take *sth* down: *Ayúdame a ~ el espejo.* Help me take the mirror down. **2** (*teléfono*) to pick *the phone* up

descolorido, -a *adj* faded

descomponer ◆ *vt* (*Quím*) to split *sth* (***into sth***) ◆ **descomponer(se)** *vt, v pron* (*pudrirse*) to rot

descompuesto, -a *pp, adj* LOC **estar**

descompuesto to have diarrhoea *Ver tb* DESCOMPONER

desconcertado, -a *pp, adj* LOC **estar/quedar desconcertado** to be taken aback: *Quedaron ~s ante mi negativa.* They were taken aback by my refusal. *Ver tb* DESCONCERTAR

desconcertar *vt* to disconcert: *Su reacción me desconcertó.* I was disconcerted by his reaction.

desconectar ◆ *vt* **1** (*luz, teléfono*) to disconnect: *Nos han desconectado el teléfono.* Our phone's been disconnected. **2** (*apagar*) to switch *sth* off **3** (*desenchufar*) to unplug ◆ **desconectarse** *v pron* **1** (*aparato*) to switch off **2** (*persona*) to cut yourself off (***from sth/sb***)

desconfiado, -a *pp, adj* wary *Ver tb* DESCONFIAR

desconfiar *vi* ~ **de** not to trust *sth/sb* [*vt*]: *Desconfía hasta de su sombra.* He doesn't trust anyone.

descongelar *vt* (*frigorífico, alimento*) to defrost

desconocer *vt* not to know: *Desconozco el porqué.* I don't know the reason.

desconocido, -a ◆ *pp, adj* **1** (*gen*) unknown: *un equipo ~* an unknown team **2** (*irreconocible*) unrecognizable: *Estaba ~ con ese disfraz.* He was unrecognizable in that disguise. ◊ *Últimamente está desconocida, siempre sonriendo.* She's been a changed woman recently; she's always smiling. ◆ *nm-nf* stranger *Ver tb* DESCONOCER

desconsiderado, -a *pp, adj* inconsiderate

descontado, -a *pp, adj* LOC **dar por descontado que...** to take it for granted that... **por descontado** of course *Ver tb* DESCONTAR

descontar *vt* **1** (*hacer un descuento*) to give a discount (***on sth***): *Descontaban el 10% en todos los juguetes.* They were giving a 10% discount on all toys. **2** (*restar*) to deduct: *Tienes que ~ los gastos del viaje.* You have to deduct your travelling expenses. **3** (*no contar*) not to count: *Si descontamos el mes de vacaciones...* If we don't count our month's holiday...

descontento, -a *adj* ~ (**con**) dissatisfied (**with *sth/sb***)

descorchar *vt* to uncork

descorrer *vt* to draw *sth* back: *~ las cortinas* to draw the curtains back LOC **descorrer el cerrojo** to unbolt the door

descortés *adj* rude

descoser ◆ *vt* to unpick ◆ **descoserse** *v pron* to come apart at the seams

descremado, -a *pp, adj* LOC *Ver* LECHE, YOGUR

describir *vt* to describe

descripción *nf* description

descuartizar *vt* **1** (*carnicero*) to carve *sth* up **2** (*asesino*) to chop *sth/sb* into pieces

descubierto, -a *pp, adj* uncovered LOC **al descubierto** (*al aire libre*) in the open air *Ver tb* DESCUBRIR

descubridor, ~a *nm-nf* discoverer

descubrimiento *nm* discovery [*pl* discoveries]

descubrir *vt* **1** (*encontrar, darse cuenta*) to discover: *~ una isla/vacuna* to discover an island/a vaccine ◊ *Descubrí que no tenía dinero.* I discovered I had no money. **2** (*averiguar*) to find *sth* (out): *Descubrí que me engañaban.* I found out that they were deceiving me. **3** (*estatua, placa*) to unveil LOC **se descubrió todo (el asunto/pastel)** it all came out

descuento *nm* discount: *Me hicieron un cinco por ciento de ~.* They gave me a five per cent discount. ◊ *Son 5.000 menos el ~.* It's 5000 before the discount.

descuidado, -a *pp, adj* **1** (*desatendido*) neglected **2** (*poco cuidadoso*) careless **3** (*desaliñado*) scruffy *Ver tb* DESCUIDAR

descuidar ◆ *vt* to neglect ◆ *vi* not to worry: *Descuida.* Don't worry. ◆ **descuidarse** *v pron*: *Si me descuido, pierdo el tren.* I nearly missed the train.

descuido *nm*: *El accidente ocurrió por un ~ del conductor.* The driver lost his concentration and caused an accident. ◊ *El perro se le escapó en un ~.* His attention wandered and he lost the dog.

desde *prep* **1** (*tiempo*) since: *Vivo en esta casa desde 1986.* I've been living in this house since 1986. ◊ *Desde que se fueron...* Since they left... ☛ *Ver nota en* FOR **2** (*lugar, cantidad*) from: *desde abajo* from below ◊ *Desde el apartamento se ve la playa.* You can see the beach from the flat. LOC **desde... hasta...** from... to...: *desde el 8 hasta el 15* from the 8th to the 15th

desear *vt* **1** (*suerte*) to wish ***sb sth***: *Te deseo suerte.* I wish you luck. **2**

(*anhelar*) to wish for *sth*: *¿Qué más podría ~?* What more could I wish for?

desembarcar ◆ *vt* **1** (*mercancía*) to unload **2** (*persona*) to set *sb* ashore ◆ *vi* to disembark

desembocadura *nf* **1** (*río*) mouth **2** (*calle*) end

desembocar *vi* ~ **en 1** (*río*) to flow **into *sth*** **2** (*calle, túnel*) to lead **to *sth***

desembolsar *vt* to pay *sth* (out)

desempatar *vi* **1** (*Dep*) to play off **2** (*Pol*) to break the deadlock

desempate *nm* play-off

desempeñar *vt* **1** (*cargo*) to hold: ~ *el puesto de decano* to hold the post of dean **2** (*papel*) to play

desempleado, -a *adj, nm-nf* unemployed [*adj*]: *los ~s* the unemployed

desempleo *nm* unemployment

desencajado, -a *pp, adj* **1** (*cara*) contorted **2** (*hueso*) dislocated

desenchufar *vt* to unplug

desenfadado, -a *pp, adj* **1** (*informal*) casual: *ropa desenfadada* casual clothes **2** (*sin inhibiciones*) uninhibited

desenfocado, -a *pp, adj* out of focus

desenfundar *vt* to pull *sth* out

desenganchar ◆ *vt* to unhook ◆ **desengancharse** *v pron* (*droga*) to come off drugs

desengañar ◆ *vt* **1** (*desilusionar*) to disillusion **2** (*revelar la verdad*) to open *sb's* eyes ◆ **desengañarse** *v pron* **1** (*desilusionarse*) to become disillusioned **2** (*enfrentarse a la verdad*) to face facts: *Desengáñate, no van a venir.* Face facts. They're not coming.

desengaño *nm* disappointment LOC **llevarse/sufrir un desengaño amoroso** to be disappointed in love

desenredarse *v pron* LOC **desenredarse el pelo** to get the tangles out of your hair

desenrollar(se) *vt, v pron* **1** (*papel*) to unroll **2** (*cable*) to unwind

desenroscar *vt* to unscrew

desenterrar *vt* to dig *sth* up: ~ *un hueso* to dig up a bone

desentonar *vi* ~ (**con**) to clash (**with *sth***): *¿Crees que estos colores desentonan?* Do you think these colours clash?

desenvolver ◆ *vt* to unwrap: ~ *un paquete* to unwrap a parcel ◆ **desenvolverse** *v pron* to get on: *Se desenvuelve bien en el trabajo/colegio.* He's getting on well at work/school.

deseo *nm* wish: *Piensa un ~.* Make a wish.

desértico, -a *adj* **1** (*zona*) desert [*n atrib*]: *una zona desértica* a desert area **2** (*clima*) arid

desertor, ~a *nm-nf* deserter

desesperación *nf* despair: *para ~ mía/de los médicos* to my despair/the despair of the doctors

desesperado, -a *pp, adj* **1** (*gen*) desperate: *Estoy ~ por verla.* I'm desperate to see her. **2** (*situación, caso*) hopeless LOC **a la desesperada** in desperation *Ver tb* DESESPERAR

desesperar ◆ *vt* to drive *sb* mad: *Le desesperaba no conseguir trabajo.* Not being able to get a job was driving him mad. ◆ *vi* ~ (**de**) to despair (**of *doing sth***): *No desesperes, aún puedes aprobar.* Don't despair. You can still pass.

desfasado, -a *pp, adj* out of date: *ideas desfasadas* out of date ideas

desfavorable *adj* unfavourable

desfigurar *vt* **1** (*estropear parte del cuerpo*) to disfigure **2** (*cambiar*) to distort: ~ *una imagen/los hechos* to distort an image/the facts

desfiladero *nm* gorge

desfilar *vi* **1** (*gen*) to march **2** (*modelos*) to parade

desfile *nm* parade LOC **desfile de modelos** fashion show

desgarrar(se) *vt, v pron* to tear: *~se el pantalón/un ligamento* to tear your trousers/a ligament

desgastar(se) *vt, v pron* **1** (*ropa, zapatos*) to wear (*sth*) out: ~ *unas botas* to wear out a pair of boots ◊ *Se me ha desgastado el jersey por los codos.* My sweater's worn at the elbows. **2** (*rocas*) to wear (*sth*) away, to erode (*más formal*)

desgaste *nm* **1** (*rocas*) erosion **2** (*por el uso*) wear: *Esta alfombra sufre mucho ~.* This rug gets very heavy wear.

desgracia *nf* misfortune: *Han tenido muchas ~s.* They've had many misfortunes. LOC **por desgracia** unfortunately **tener la desgracia de** to be unlucky enough *to do sth*

desgraciado, -a ◆ *pp, adj* **1** (*sin suerte*) unlucky **2** (*infeliz*) unhappy: *llevar una vida desgraciada* to lead an unhappy life ◆ *nm-nf* **1** (*pobre*) wretch **2** (*mala persona*) swine

deshabitado, -a *pp, adj* deserted

deshacer ◆ *vt* **1** (*nudo, paquete*) to

undo **2** (*cama*) to unmake **3** (*desmontar*) to take *sth* to pieces: ~ *un puzzle* to take a jigsaw to pieces **4** (*derretir*) to melt ◆ **deshacerse** *v pron* **1** (*nudo, costura*) to come undone **2** (*derretirse*) to melt **3 deshacerse de** to get rid of *sth/sb*: *~se de un coche viejo* to get rid of an old car **LOC** *Ver* MALETA

deshelar(se) *vt, v pron* to thaw

deshinchar ◆ *vt* (*desinflar*) to let *sth* down ◆ **deshincharse** *v pron* to go down

deshonesto, -a *adj* dishonest **LOC** *Ver* PROPOSICIÓN

desierto, -a ◆ *adj* deserted ◆ *nm* desert **LOC** *Ver* ISLA

designar *vt* **1** (*persona*) to appoint *sb* (***sth/to sth***): *Ha sido designado (como) presidente/para el puesto.* He has been appointed chairman/to the post. **2** (*sitio*) to designate *sth* (**as *sth***): ~ *Madrid como sede de los Juegos* to designate Madrid as the venue for the Games

desigual *adj* (*irregular*) uneven: *un terreno ~* uneven terrain

desigualdad *nf* inequality [*pl* inequalities]

desilusión *nf* disappointment **LOC llevarse una desilusión** to be disappointed

desilusionar *vt* to disappoint

desinfectante *nm* disinfectant

desinfectar *vt* to disinfect

desinflar ◆ *vt* to let *sth* down ◆ **desinflarse** *v pron* (*objeto inflado*) to go down

desintegración *nf* disintegration

desintegrarse *v pron* to disintegrate

desinterés *nm* lack of interest

desistir *vi* ~ (**de**) to give up (***sth/doing sth***): ~ *de buscar trabajo* to give up looking for work

desleal *adj* disloyal

deslizar ◆ *vt* **1** (*gen*) to slide: *Puedes ~ el asiento hacia adelante.* You can slide the seat forward. **2** (*con disimulo*) to slip: *Deslizó la carta en su bolsillo.* He slipped the letter into his pocket. ◆ **deslizarse** *v pron* to slide: *~se sobre el hielo* to slide on the ice

deslumbrante *adj* dazzling: *una luz/actuación ~* a dazzling light/performance

deslumbrar *vt* to dazzle

desmadrarse *v pron* to run wild

desmano LOC a desmano out of the way: *Nos pilla muy a ~.* It's well out of our way.

desmantelar *vt* to dismantle

desmaquillador, ~a *adj* **LOC crema/loción desmaquilladora** make-up remover

desmayarse *v pron* to faint

desmayo *nm* fainting fit **LOC darle a algn un desmayo** to faint

desmedido, -a *pp, adj* excessive

desmejorado, -a *pp, adj*: *La encontré un poco desmejorada.* She wasn't looking too well. ◊ *Está muy ~ desde la última vez que lo vi.* He's gone rapidly downhill since the last time I saw him.

desmelenarse *v pron* to let your hair down

desmentir *vt* to deny: *Desmintió las acusaciones.* He denied the accusations.

desmenuzar *vt* **1** (*gen*) to break *sth* into small pieces **2** (*pan, galletas*) to crumble *sth* (up)

desmontar ◆ *vt* **1** (*gen*) to take *sth* apart: ~ *una bici* to take a bike apart **2** (*andamio, estantería, tienda de campaña*) to take *sth* down ◆ *vi* (*bajar de un caballo*) to dismount

desmoralizarse *v pron* to lose heart: *Sigue adelante, no te desmoralices.* Keep going, don't lose heart.

desnatado, -a *pp, adj* **LOC** *Ver* LECHE, YOGUR

desnivel *nm*: *el ~ entre la casa y el jardín* the difference in level between the house and the garden

desnivelado, -a *pp, adj* not level: *El suelo está ~.* The ground isn't level.

desnudar ◆ *vt* to undress ◆ **desnudarse** *v pron* to get undressed: *Se desnudó y se metió en la cama.* He got undressed and went to bed.

desnudo, -a *adj* **1** (*persona*) naked: *El niño está medio ~.* The child is half-naked. **2** (*parte del cuerpo, vacío*) bare: *brazos ~s/paredes desnudas* bare arms/walls ☛ *Ver nota en* NAKED

desnutrido, -a *pp, adj* undernourished

desobedecer *vt* to disobey: ~ *órdenes/a tus padres* to disobey orders/your parents

desobediencia *nf* disobedience

desobediente *adj, nmf* disobedient [*adj*]: *¡Eres una ~!* You're a very disobedient girl!

desodorante *nm* deodorant

desolador, ~a *adj* devastating

desolar *vt* to devastate: *La noticia nos desoló.* We were devastated by the news.

desorden *nm* mess: *Perdona el ~.* Sorry for the mess. ◊ *Tenía la casa en ~.* The house was (in) a mess.

desordenado, -a *pp, adj, nm-nf* untidy [*adj*]: *¡Eres un ~!* You're so untidy! LOC **dejar algo desordenado** to mess sth up *Ver tb* DESORDENAR

desordenar *vt* to make *sth* untidy, to mess *sth* up (*más coloq*): *Me has desordenado el armario.* You've made a mess of my wardrobe.

desorganizado, -a *pp, adj, nm-nf* disorganized [*adj*]: *Ya sé que soy un ~.* I know I'm disorganized. *Ver tb* DESORGANIZAR

desorganizar *vt* to disrupt: *La huelga nos desorganizó las clases.* The classes were disrupted by the strike.

desorientar ◆ *vt* (*desconcertar*) to confuse: *Sus instrucciones me desorientaron.* I was confused by his directions. ◆ **desorientarse** *v pron* to get lost: *Me he desorientado.* I'm lost.

despachar *vt* **1** (*atender*) to serve **2** (*solucionar*) to settle: *Despachamos el tema en media hora.* We settled the matter in half an hour. **3** (*librarse de algn*) to get rid of *sb*: *Nos despachó rápido.* He soon got rid of us.

despacho *nm* **1** (*oficina*) office: *Nos recibió en su ~.* She saw us in her office. **2** (*en casa*) study [*pl* studies] LOC *Ver* MESA

despacio ◆ *adv* **1** (*lentamente*) slowly: *Conduce ~.* Drive slowly. **2** (*largo y tendido*) at length: *¿Por qué no lo hablamos más ~ durante la cena?* Why don't we talk about it at length over dinner? ◆ **¡despacio!** *interj* slow down! LOC *Ver* TORTUGA

despampanante *adj* stunning

despectivo, -a *adj* scornful: *en tono ~* in a scornful tone

despedida *nf* **1** (*gen*) goodbye, farewell (*más formal*): *cena de ~* farewell dinner **2** (*celebración*) leaving party LOC **despedida de soltero/soltera** stag/hen night

despedir ◆ *vt* **1** (*decir adiós*) to see *sb* off: *Fuimos a ~les a la estación.* We went to see them off at the station. **2** (*empleado*) to dismiss, to give *sb* the sack (*más coloq*) **3** (*calor, luz, olor*) to give *sth* off ◆ **despedirse** *v pron* **despedirse (de)** to say goodbye (**to *sth*/*sb***): *Ni siquiera se han despedido.* They didn't even say goodbye.

despegado, -a *pp, adj* **1** (*separado*) unstuck **2** (*persona*) cold: *Es muy despegada con su familia.* She's very cold towards her family. *Ver tb* DESPEGAR

despegar ◆ *vt* to pull *sth* off ◆ *vi* (*avión*) to take off: *El avión está despegando.* The plane is taking off. ◆ **despegarse** *v pron* to come off: *Se ha despegado el asa.* The handle's come off.

despegue *nm* take-off

despeinado, -a *pp, adj* untidy: *Estás ~.* Your hair's untidy. *Ver tb* DESPEINAR(SE)

despeinar(se) *vt, v pron* to mess your/sb's hair up: *No me despeines.* Don't mess my hair up.

despejado, -a *pp, adj* clear: *un cielo ~/una mente despejada* a clear sky/mind *Ver tb* DESPEJAR

despejar ◆ *vt* to clear: *¡Despejen la zona!* Clear the area! ◆ *v imp* (*cielo*) to clear up: *Despejó a eso de las cinco.* It cleared up at about five. ◆ **despejarse** *v pron* **1** (*nubes*) to clear (away) **2** (*despertarse*) to wake up

despensa *nf* larder

desperdiciar *vt* to waste

desperdicio *nm* **1** (*gen*) waste **2** **desperdicios** scraps

desperezarse *v pron* to stretch

desperfecto *nm* **1** (*deterioro*) damage [*incontable*]: *Sufrió algunos ~s.* It suffered some damage. **2** (*imperfección*) flaw

despertador *nm* alarm (clock): *He puesto el ~ para las siete.* I've set the alarm for seven. ☛ *Ver dibujo en* RELOJ

despertar ◆ *vt* **1** (*persona*) to wake *sb* up: *¿A qué hora quieres que te despierte?* What time do you want me to wake you up? **2** (*interés, sospecha*) to arouse ◆ **despertar(se)** *vi, v pron* to wake up LOC **tener (un) buen/mal despertar** to wake up in a good/bad mood

despido *nm* dismissal

despierto, -a *pp, adj* **1** (*no dormido*) awake: *¿Estás ~?* Are you awake? **2** (*espabilado*) bright LOC *Ver* SOÑAR; *Ver tb* DESPERTAR

despistado, -a *pp, adj* **1** (*por naturaleza*) absent-minded **2** (*distraído*) miles away: *Iba ~ y no les vi.* I was miles away and didn't see them. LOC **hacerse el despistado**: *Nos vio pero se hizo el ~.*

He saw us but pretended not to. *Ver tb* DESPISTAR

despistar *vt* **1** (*desorientar*) to confuse **2** (*dar esquinazo*) to shake *sb* off: *Despistó a la policía.* He shook off the police.

despiste *nm* absent-mindedness [*incontable*]: *¡Vaya ~ que llevas!* You're so absent-minded!

desplazado, -a *pp, adj* out of place: *sentirse ~* to feel out of place *Ver tb* DESPLAZAR

desplazar ◆ *vt* (*sustituir*) to take the place **of *sth*/*sb***: *El ordenador ha desplazado a la máquina de escribir.* Computers have taken the place of typewriters. ◆ **desplazarse** *v pron* to go: *Se desplazan a todos los sitios en taxi.* They go everywhere by taxi.

desplegar *vt* **1** (*mapa, papel*) to unfold **2** (*velas*) to unfurl **3** (*tropas, armamento*) to deploy

despliegue *nm* deployment

desplomarse *v pron* to collapse

despoblación *nf* depopulation

despoblado, -a *pp, adj* (*sin habitantes*) uninhabited

déspota *nmf* tyrant

despreciable *adj* despicable

despreciar *vt* **1** (*menospreciar*) to despise, to look down on *sb* (*más coloq*): *Despreciaban a los otros alumnos.* They looked down on the other pupils. **2** (*rechazar*) to reject: *Despreciaron nuestra ayuda.* They rejected our offer of help.

desprecio *nm* contempt (***for sth*/*sb***): *mostrar ~ por algn* to show contempt for sb

desprender ◆ *vt* **1** (*separar*) to take *sth* off, to remove (*más formal*): *Desprende la etiqueta.* Take the price tag off. **2** (*emanar*) to give *sth* off: *Esta estufa desprende gas.* This stove is giving off gas. ◆ **desprenderse** *v pron* **1** (*separarse*) to come off: *Se te ha desprendido un botón.* One of your buttons has come off. **2 desprenderse de** to get rid of *sth*: *Se desprendió de varios libros.* He got rid of some books.

desprendimiento *nm* LOC **desprendimiento de tierras** landslide

desprestigiar *vt* to discredit

desprevenido, -a *adj* LOC **coger/pillar a algn desprevenido** to catch sb unawares

desproporcionado, -a *adj* disproportionate (***to sth***)

desprovisto, -a *pp, adj* ~ **de** lacking **in *sth***

después *adv* **1** (*más tarde*) afterwards, later (*más coloq*): *~ dijo que no le había gustado.* He said afterwards he hadn't liked it. ◊ *Salieron poco ~.* They came out shortly afterwards. ◊ *Si estudias ahora, ~ puedes ver la tele.* If you do your homework now, you can watch TV later. ◊ *No me lo dijeron hasta mucho ~.* They didn't tell me until much later. **2** (*a continuación*) next: *¿Y qué pasó ~?* And what happened next? LOC **después de** after *sth/doing sth*: *~ de las dos* after two o'clock ◊ *~ de hablar con ellos* after talking to them ◊ *La farmacia está ~ del banco.* The chemist's is after the bank. **después de que** when: *~ de que acabes los deberes pon la mesa.* When you've finished your homework, you can lay the table. **después de todo** after all

despuntar *vi* **1** (*plantas*) to bud: *Ya despuntan los rosales.* The roses are starting to bud. **2** (*alba, día*) to break **3** (*persona*) to stand out

destacar ◆ *vt* to point *sth* out: *El profesor destacó varios aspectos de su obra.* The teacher pointed out various aspects of his work. ◆ **destacar(se)** *vi, v pron* to stand out: *El rojo destaca sobre el verde.* Red stands out against green.

destapar ◆ *vt* **1** (*quitar la tapa*) to take the lid **off *sth***: *~ una olla* to take the lid off a saucepan **2** (*en la cama*) to pull the bedclothes **off *sb***: *No me destapes.* Don't pull the bedclothes off me. ◆ **destaparse** *v pron* (*en la cama*) to throw the bedclothes off

destaponar(se) *vt, v pron* to unblock

desteñir(se) ◆ *vt, v pron* to fade: *Se te ha desteñido la falda.* Your skirt's faded. ◆ *vi*: *Esa camisa roja destiñe.* The colour runs in that red shirt.

destinar *vt* to post: *La han destinado a Vigo.* She's been posted to Vigo.

destinatario, -a *nm-nf* addressee

destino *nm* **1** (*sino*) fate **2** (*avión, barco, tren, pasajero*) destination **3** (*lugar de trabajo*): *Me van a cambiar de ~.* I'm going to be posted somewhere else. LOC **con destino a...** for...: *el ferry con ~ a Plymouth* the ferry for Plymouth

destornillador *nm* screwdriver

destrozado, -a *pp, adj* (*abatido*) devastated (**at/by sth**): *~ por la pérdida de su hijo* devastated by the loss of his son *Ver tb* DESTROZAR

destrozar *vt* **1** (*gen*) to destroy **2** (*hacer trozos*) to smash: *Destrozaron los cristales del escaparate.* They smashed the shop window. **3** (*arruinar*) to ruin: *~ la vida de algn* to ruin sb's life

destrucción *nf* destruction

destructivo, -a *adj* destructive

destructor *nm* (*Náut*) destroyer

destruir *vt* to destroy

desvalido, -a *adj* helpless

desvalijar *vt* **1** (*lugar*): *Me habían desvalijado el coche.* Everything had been stolen from my car. **2** (*persona*) to rob *sb* of all they have

desván *nm* loft

desvanecerse *v pron* **1** (*desmayarse*) to faint **2** (*desaparecer*) to disappear

desvariar *vi* **1** (*delirar*) to be delirious **2** (*decir disparates*) to talk nonsense

desvelar ◆ *vt* **1** (*espabilar*) to keep *sb* awake **2** (*revelar*) to reveal ◆ **desvelarse 1** (*espabilarse*) to wake up **2** (*desvivirse*) to do your utmost ***for sb***

desventaja *nf* disadvantage LOC **estar en desventaja** to be at a disadvantage

desvergonzado, -a *adj, nm-nf* **1** (*que no tiene vergüenza*) shameless [*adj*]: *ser un ~* to have no shame **2** (*insolente*) cheeky [*adj*]

desvestir ◆ *vt* to undress ◆ **desvestirse** *v pron* to get undressed

desviación *nf* **1** (*tráfico*) diversion **2** ~ (**de**) (*irregularidad*) deviation (**from *sth***)

desviar ◆ *vt* to divert: *~ el tráfico* to divert traffic ◊ *~ los fondos de una sociedad* to divert company funds ◆ **desviarse** *v pron* **1** (*carretera*) to branch off: *Verás que la carretera se desvía hacia la izquierda.* You'll see that the road branches off to the left. **2** (*coche*) to turn off LOC **desviar la mirada** to avert your eyes **desviarse del tema** to wander off the subject

desvío *nm* diversion

desvivirse *v pron* ~ **por** to live **for *sth/sb***: *Se desviven por sus hijos.* They live for their children.

detalladamente *adv* in detail

detallado, -a *pp, adj* detailed *Ver tb* DETALLAR

detallar *vt* **1** (*contar con detalle*) to give details **of *sth*** **2** (*especificar*) to specify

detalle *nm* **1** (*pormenor*) detail **2** (*atención*) gesture LOC **¡qué detalle!** how thoughtful! **tener muchos detalles (con algn)** to be very considerate (to sb)

detallista *adj* thoughtful: *Tú siempre tan ~.* You're always so thoughtful.

detectar *vt* to detect

detective *nmf* detective

detector *nm* detector: *un ~ de mentiras/metales* a lie/metal detector

detención *nf* **1** (*arresto*) arrest **2** (*paralización*) halt: *La falta de material motivó la ~ de las obras.* Lack of materials brought the building work to a halt.

detener ◆ *vt* **1** (*gen*) to stop **2** (*arrestar*) to arrest ◆ **detenerse** *v pron* to stop

detenidamente *adv* carefully

detenido, -a ◆ *pp, adj*: *estar/quedar ~* to be under arrest ◆ *nm-nf* person under arrest *Ver tb* DETENER

detergente *nm* detergent

deteriorar ◆ *vt* to damage ◆ **deteriorarse** *v pron* to deteriorate: *Su salud se deterioraba día a día.* Her health deteriorated by the day.

determinado, -a *pp, adj* **1** (*cierto*) certain: *en ~s casos* in certain cases **2** (*artículo*) definite *Ver tb* DETERMINAR

determinar *vt* to determine: *~ el precio de algo* to determine the price of sth

detestar *vt* to detest *sth/doing sth*, to hate *sth/doing sth* (*más coloq*)

detrás *adv* **1** (*gen*) behind: *Los otros vienen ~.* The others are coming behind. **2** (*atrás*) at/on the back: *El mercado está ~.* The market is at the back. ◊ *El precio está ~.* The price is on the back. LOC **detrás de 1** (*gen*) behind: *~ de nosotros/la casa* behind us/the house **2** (*después de*) after: *Fuma un cigarrillo ~ de otro.* He smokes one cigarette after another. **estar detrás de algn** (*gustar*) to be after sb **por detrás** from behind *Ver tb* MOSCA

deuda *nf* debt LOC **tener una deuda** to be in debt (*to sth/sb*): *tener una ~ con el banco* to be in debt to the bank

devaluar *vt* to devalue

devanarse *v pron* LOC *Ver* SESO

devastador, ~a *adj* devastating

devolución *nf* **1** (*artículo*) return: *la ~ de mercancías defectuosas* the return of defective goods **2** (*dinero*) refund

devolver ◆ *vt* **1** (*gen*) to return *sth* (**to *sth/sb***): *¿Devolviste los libros a la biblioteca?* Did you return the books to the library? **2** (*dinero*) to refund: *Se le devolverá el importe.* You will have your money refunded. **3** (*vomitar*) to bring *sth* up ◆ *vi* to be sick: *El niño ha devuelto.* The baby has been sick.

devorar *vt* to devour

devoto, -a *adj* (*piadoso*) devout

día *nm* **1** (*gen*) day [*pl* days]: *Pasamos el ~ en Madrid.* We spent the day in Madrid. ◊ *—¿Qué ~ es hoy? —Martes.* 'What day is it today?' 'Tuesday.' ◊ *al ~ siguiente* the following day **2** (*en fechas*): *Llegaron el ~ 10 de abril.* They arrived on 10 April. ☛ Se dice 'April the tenth' o 'the tenth of April': *Termina el ~ 15.* It ends on the 15th. LOC **al/por día** a day: *tres veces al ~* three times a day **¡buenos días!** good morning!, morning! (*más coloq*) **dar los buenos días** to say good morning **de día/durante el día** in the daytime/ during the daytime: *Duermen de ~.* They sleep in the daytime. **día festivo** holiday [*pl* holidays] **día de la madre/ del padre** Mother's/Father's Day **día de los enamorados** St Valentine's Day **día de los inocentes** ≃ April Fool's Day (*GB*) ☛ *Ver nota en* APRIL **día de Navidad** Christmas Day ☛ *Ver nota en* NAVIDAD **día de Reyes** 6 January **día de Todos los Santos** All Saints' Day ☛ *Ver nota en* HALLOWE'EN **día libre 1** (*no ocupado*) free day **2** (*sin ir a trabajar*) day off: *Mañana es mi ~ libre.* Tomorrow's my day off. **el día de mañana** in the future **estar al día** to be up to date **hacer buen día** to be a nice day: *Hace buen ~ hoy.* It's a nice day today. **hacerse de día** to get light **poner al día** to bring *sth/sb* up to date **ser de día** to be light **todos los días** every day ☛ *Ver nota en* EVERYDAY **un día sí y otro no** every other day *Ver tb* ALGUNO, HOY, MENÚ, PLENO, QUINCE, VIVIR

diabetes *nf* diabetes [*sing*]

diabético, -a *adj, nm-nf* diabetic

diablo *nm* devil LOC *Ver* ABOGADO

diadema *nf* (*cinta*) hair band

diagnóstico *nm* diagnosis [*pl* diagnoses]

diagonal *adj, nf* diagonal

diagrama *nm* diagram

dialecto *nm* dialect: *un ~ del inglés* a dialect of English

diálogo *nm* conversation: *Tuvimos un ~ interesante.* We had an interesting conversation.

diamante *nm* **1** (*piedra*) diamond **2** **diamantes** (*Naipes*) diamonds ☛ *Ver nota en* BARAJA

diámetro *nm* diameter

diapositiva *nf* slide: *una ~ en color* a colour slide

diariamente *adv* every day, daily (*más formal*)

diario, -a ◆ *adj* daily ◆ *nm* **1** (*periódico*) newspaper **2** (*personal*) diary [*pl* diaries] LOC **a diario** every day **de/para diario** everyday: *ropa de ~* everyday clothes ☛ *Ver nota en* EVERYDAY

diarrea *nf* diarrhoea [*incontable*]

dibujante *nmf* **1** (*Tec*) draughtsman/ woman [*pl* draughtsmen/women] **2** (*humor*) cartoonist

dibujar *vt* to draw

dibujo *nm* **1** (*Arte*) drawing: *estudiar ~* to study drawing ◊ *un ~* a drawing ◊ *Haz un ~ de tu familia.* Draw your family. **2** (*motivo*) pattern LOC **dibujo lineal** technical drawing **dibujos animados** cartoons

diccionario *nm* dictionary [*pl* dictionaries]: *Búscalo en el ~.* Look it up in the dictionary. ◊ *un ~ bilingüe* a bilingual dictionary

dicho, -a ◆ *pp, adj* that [*pl* those]: *~ año* that year ◆ *nm* (*refrán*) saying LOC **dicho de otra forma/manera** in other words **dicho y hecho** no sooner said than done *Ver tb* MEJOR; *Ver tb* DECIR[1]

diciembre *nm* December (*abrev* Dec) ☛ *Ver ejemplos en* ENERO

dictado *nm* dictation: *Vamos a hacer un ~.* We're going to do a dictation.

dictador, ~a *nm-nf* dictator

dictadura *nf* dictatorship: *durante la ~ militar* under the military dictatorship

dictar *vt, vi* to dictate LOC **dictar sentencia** to pass sentence

didáctico, -a *adj* LOC *Ver* MATERIAL

diecinueve *nm, adj, pron* **1** (*gen*) nineteen **2** (*fecha*) nineteenth ☛ *Ver ejemplos en* ONCE *y* SEIS

dieciocho *nm, adj, pron* **1** (*gen*) eighteen **2** (*fecha*) eighteenth ☛ *Ver ejemplos en* ONCE *y* SEIS

dieciséis *nm, adj, pron* **1** (*gen*) sixteen **2** (*fecha*) sixteenth ☛ *Ver ejemplos en* ONCE *y* SEIS

diecisiete *nm, adj, pron* **1** (*gen*) seventeen **2** (*fecha*) seventeenth ☛ *Ver ejemplos en* ONCE *y* SEIS

diente *nm* tooth [*pl* teeth] LOC **diente de ajo** clove of garlic **diente de leche**

milk tooth [*pl* milk teeth] *Ver tb* CANTO[3], CEPILLO, LAVAR, PASTA

diesel *nm* (*motor*) diesel engine

diestro, -a *adj* (*persona*) right-handed LOC **a diestro y siniestro** right, left and centre

dieta *nf* **1** (*gen*) diet: *estar a ~* to be on a diet **2 dietas** expenses

diez *nm, adj, pron* **1** (*gen*) ten **2** (*fechas*) tenth ☛ *Ver ejemplos en* SEIS LOC **sacar un diez** to get top marks

difamar *vt* **1** (*de palabra*) to slander **2** (*por escrito*) to libel

diferencia *nf* **1** ~ **con/entre** difference **between *sth and sth***: *Madrid tiene una hora de ~ con Londres.* There's an hour's difference between Madrid and London. ◊ *la ~ entre dos telas* the difference between two fabrics **2** ~ **(de)** difference **(in/of *sth*)**: *No hay mucha ~ de precio entre los dos.* There's not much difference in price between the two. ◊ *~ de opiniones* difference of opinion LOC **a diferencia de** unlike **con diferencia** by far: *Es el más importante con ~.* It's by far the most important.

diferenciar ◆ *vt* to differentiate *sth* **(*from sth*)**; to differentiate **between *sth and sth*** ◆ **diferenciarse** *v pron*: *No se diferencian en nada.* There's no difference between them. ◊ *¿En qué se diferencia?* What's the difference?

diferente ◆ *adj* ~ **(a/de)** different **(from/to *sth/sb*)** ◆ *adv* differently: *Pensamos ~.* We think differently.

difícil *adj* difficult

dificultad *nf* difficulty [*pl* difficulties]

difuminar *vt* to blur

difundir ◆ *vt* **1** (*Radio, TV*) to broadcast **2** (*publicar*) to publish **3** (*oralmente*) to spread ◆ **difundirse** *v pron* (*noticia, luz*) to spread

difunto, -a ◆ *adj* late: *el ~ presidente* the late president ◆ *nm-nf* deceased: *los familiares del ~* the family of the deceased

difusión *nf* **1** (*ideas*) dissemination **2** (*programas*) broadcasting **3** (*diario, revista*) circulation

digerir *vt* to digest

digestión *nf* digestion LOC **hacer la digestión**: *Todavía estoy haciendo la ~.* I've only just eaten. ◊ *Hay que hacer la ~ antes de bañarse.* You mustn't go swimming straight after meals. *Ver tb* CORTE[1]

digestivo, -a *adj* digestive: *el aparato ~* the digestive system

digital *adj* digital

dignarse *v pron* to deign ***to do sth***

dignidad *nf* dignity

digno, -a *adj* **1** (*gen*) decent: *el derecho a un trabajo ~* the right to a decent job **2** ~ **de** worthy **of *sth***: *~ de atención* worthy of attention LOC **digno de confianza** reliable

dilatar(se) *vt, v pron* **1** (*agrandar(se), ampliar(se)*) to expand **2** (*poros, pupilas*) to dilate

dilema *nm* dilemma

diluir ◆ *vt* **1** (*sólido*) to dissolve **2** (*líquido*) to dilute **3** (*salsa, pintura*) to thin ◆ **diluirse** *v pron* (*sólido*) to dissolve

diluvio *nm* flood LOC **el Diluvio Universal** the Flood

dimensión *nf* dimension: *la cuarta ~* the fourth dimension ◊ *las dimensiones de una sala* the dimensions of a room LOC **de grandes/enormes dimensiones** huge

diminutivo, -a *adj, nm* diminutive

diminuto, -a *adj* tiny

dimisión *nf* resignation: *Presentó su ~.* He handed in his resignation.

dimitir *vi* ~ **(de)** to resign **(from *sth*)**: *~ de un cargo* to resign from a post

Dinamarca *nf* Denmark

dinámico, -a ◆ *adj* dynamic ◆ **dinámica** *nf* dynamics [*sing*]

dinamita *nf* dynamite

dinamo (*tb* **dínamo**) *nf* dynamo [*pl* dynamos]

dinastía *nf* dynasty [*pl* dynasties]

dineral *nm* fortune: *Cuesta un ~.* It costs a fortune.

dinero *nm* money [*incontable*]: *¿Tienes ~?* Have you got any money? ◊ *Necesito ~.* I need some money. LOC **andar/estar mal de dinero** to be short of money **dinero contante y sonante** hard cash **dinero suelto** (loose) change

dinosaurio *nm* dinosaur

dioptría *nf*: *¿Cuántas ~s tienes?* How strong are your glasses?

dios *nm* god LOC **como Dios manda** proper(ly): *una oficina como Dios manda* a proper office ◊ *hacer algo como Dios manda* to do sth properly **¡Dios me libre!** God forbid! **¡Dios mío!** good God! **Dios sabe** God knows **ni Dios** not a soul **¡por Dios!** for God's sake! *Ver tb* AMOR, PEDIR

diosa *nf* goddess

dióxido *nm* dioxide LOC **dióxido de carbono** carbon dioxide

diploma *nm* diploma

diplomacia *nf* diplomacy

diplomado, -a *pp, adj* qualified: *una enfermera diplomada* a qualified nurse

diplomático, -a ◆ *adj* diplomatic ◆ *nm-nf* diplomat

diputación *nf* council: *la ~ provincial/regional* the provincial/regional council

diputado, -a *nm-nf* deputy [*pl* deputies] ≃ Member of Parliament (*abrev* MP) (*GB*) ☛ *Ver* pág 322. LOC *Ver* CONGRESO

dique *nm* dyke LOC **dique (seco)** dry dock

dirección *nf* **1** (*rumbo*) direction: *Iban en ~ contraria.* They were going in the opposite direction. ◊ *salir con ~ a Madrid* to set off for Madrid **2** (*señas*) address: *nombre y ~* name and address LOC **dirección prohibida** (*señal*) no entry **dirección única** one way: *Esa calle tiene ~ única.* That's a one-way street.

directamente *adv* (*derecho*) straight: *Volvimos ~ a Madrid.* We went straight back to Madrid.

directivo, -a ◆ *adj* management [*n atrib*]: *el equipo ~* the management team ◆ *nm-nf* director

directo, -a *adj* **1** (*gen*) direct: *un vuelo ~* a direct flight ◊ *¿Cuál es el camino más ~?* What's the most direct way? **2** (*tren*) through: *el tren ~ a Barcelona* the through train to Barcelona LOC **en directo** live: *una actuación en ~* a live performance *Ver tb* MÚSICA

director, ~a *nm-nf* **1** (*gen*) director: *~ artístico/financiero* artistic/financial director ◊ *un ~ de cine/teatro* a film/theatre director **2** (*colegio*) head **3** (*banco*) manager **4** (*periódico, editorial*) editor LOC **director (de orquesta)** conductor **director gerente** managing director

dirigente ◆ *adj* (*Pol*) ruling ◆ *nmf* **1** (*Pol*) leader **2** (*empresa*) manager LOC *Ver* MÁXIMO

dirigir ◆ *vt* **1** (*película, obra de teatro, tráfico*) to direct **2** (*carta, mensaje*) to address *sth* **to sth/sb** **3** (*arma, manguera, telescopio*) to point *sth* **at sth/sb** **4** (*debate, campaña, expedición, partido*) to lead **5** (*negocio*) to run ◆ **dirigirse** *v pron* **1 dirigirse a/hacia** (*ir*) to head for...: *~se hacia la frontera* to head for the border **2 dirigirse a** (*hablar*) to speak **to sb** **3 dirigirse a** (*por carta*) to write **to sb** LOC **dirigir la palabra** to speak *to sb*

disciplina *nf* **1** (*gen*) discipline: *mantener la ~* to maintain discipline **2** (*asignatura*) subject

discípulo, -a *nm-nf* **1** (*seguidor*) disciple **2** (*alumno*) pupil

disco *nm* **1** (*Mús*) record: *grabar/poner un ~* to make/play a record **2** (*Informát*) disk: *el ~ duro* the hard disk **3** (*Dep*) discus **4** (*semáforo*) light **5** (*objeto circular*) disc LOC **disco compacto** compact disc (*abrev* CD)

discográfico, -a *adj* record [*n atrib*]: *una empresa discográfica* a record company

discoteca *nf* disco [*pl* discos]

discotequero, -a *adj* (*música*) disco [*n atrib*]: *un ritmo ~* a disco beat

discreción *nf* discretion

discreto, -a *adj* **1** (*prudente*) discreet **2** (*mediocre*) unremarkable

discriminación *nf* discrimination (**against sb**): *la ~ racial* racial discrimination ◊ *la ~ de la mujer* discrimination against women

discriminar *vt* to discriminate **against sb**

disculpa *nf* **1** (*excusa*) excuse: *Esto no tiene ~.* There's no excuse for this. **2** (*pidiendo perdón*) apology [*pl* apologies] LOC *Ver* PEDIR

disculpar ◆ *vt* to forgive: *Disculpe la interrupción.* Forgive the interruption. ◊ *Disculpa que llegue tarde.* Sorry I'm late. ◆ **disculparse** *v pron* to apologize (**to sb**) (**for sth**): *Me disculpé con ella por no haber escrito.* I apologized to her for not writing.

discurso *nm* speech: *pronunciar un ~* to give a speech

discusión *nf* **1** (*debate*) discussion **2** (*disputa*) argument

discutido, -a *pp, adj* (*polémico*) controversial *Ver tb* DISCUTIR

discutir ◆ *vt* **1** (*debatir*) to discuss **2** (*cuestionar*) to question: *~ una decisión* to question a decision ◆ *vi* **1 ~ de/sobre** (*hablar*) to discuss *sth* [*vt*]: *~ de política* to discuss politics **2** (*reñir*) to argue (**with sb**) (**about sth**)

disecar *vt* **1** (*animal*) to stuff **2** (*flor*) to press **3** (*hacer la disección*) to dissect

diseñador, ~a *nm-nf* designer

diseñar *vt* **1** (*gen*) to design **2** (*plan*) to draw *sth* up

diseño *nm* design: ~ *gráfico* graphic design

disfraz *nm* fancy dress [*incontable*]: *un sitio donde alquilan disfraces* a shop where you can hire fancy dress **LOC** *Ver* BAILE

disfrazarse *v pron* ~ (**de**) (*para una fiesta*) to dress up (**as** ***sth/sb***): *Se disfrazó de Cenicienta.* She dressed up as Cinderella.

disfrutar ◆ *vi, vt* to enjoy *sth/doing sth*: *Disfrutamos bailando/con el fútbol.* We enjoy dancing/football. ◊ *Disfruto de buena salud.* I enjoy good health. ◆ *vi* (*pasarlo bien*) to enjoy yourself: *¡Que disfrutes mucho!* Enjoy yourself!

disgustado, -a *pp, adj* upset *Ver tb* DISGUSTAR

disgustar ◆ *vi* to upset *sb* [*vt*]: *Les disgustó mucho que suspendiera.* They were very upset he failed. ◆ **disgustarse** *v pron* to get upset: *Se disgusta siempre que llego tarde.* She gets upset whenever I'm late.

disgusto *nm* **1** (*tristeza*) sorrow: *Su decisión les causó un gran ~.* His decision caused them great sorrow. **2** (*desgracia*) accident: *Corres tanto que un día tendrás un ~.* You're going to have an accident if you carry on driving so fast. **LOC a disgusto** unwillingly: *hacer algo a ~* to do sth unwillingly **dar disgustos** to upset: *Da muchos ~s a sus padres.* He's always upsetting his parents. **llevarse un disgusto** to be upset: *Cuando me dieron las notas me llevé un ~.* I was upset when I got my results. *Ver tb* MATAR

disimular ◆ *vt* to hide: ~ *la verdad/una cicatriz* to hide the truth/a scar ◆ *vi* to pretend: *Disimula, haz como que no sabes nada.* Pretend you don't know anything. ◊ *¡Ahí vienen! ¡Disimula!* There they are! Pretend you haven't seen them.

disimulo *nm* **LOC con/sin disimulo** surreptitiously/openly

dislexia *nf* dyslexia

disléxico, -a *adj, nm-nf* dyslexic

dislocar(se) *vt, v pron* to dislocate

disminución *nf* drop (***in sth***): *una ~ en el número de accidentes* a drop in the number of accidents

disminuir ◆ *vt* to reduce: *Disminuye la velocidad.* Reduce your speed. ◆ *vi* to drop: *Han disminuido los precios.* Prices have dropped.

disolver(se) *vt, v pron* **1** (*en un líquido*) to dissolve: *Disuelva el azúcar en la leche.* Dissolve the sugar in the milk. **2** (*manifestación*) to break (*a demonstration*) up: *La manifestación se disolvió en seguida.* The demonstration broke up immediately.

disparado, -a *pp, adj* **LOC salir disparado** to shoot out (*of…*): *Salieron ~s del banco.* They shot out of the bank. *Ver tb* DISPARAR

disparar ◆ *vt, vi* to shoot: ~ *una flecha* to shoot an arrow ◊ *¡No disparen!* Don't shoot! ◊ *Disparaban contra todo lo que se movía.* They were shooting at everything that moved. ◊ ~ *a puerta* to shoot at goal ◆ **dispararse** *v pron* **1** (*arma, dispositivo*) to go off: *La pistola se disparó.* The pistol went off. **2** (*aumentar*) to shoot up: *Se han disparado los precios.* Prices have shot up.

disparate *nm* **1** (*dicho*) nonsense [*incontable*]: *¡No digas ~s!* Don't talk nonsense! **2** (*hecho*) stupid thing **LOC** *Ver* SARTA

disparo *nm* shot: *Murió a consecuencia de un ~.* He died from a gunshot wound. ◊ *Oí un ~.* I heard a shot.

dispersar(se) *vt, v pron* to disperse

disponer ◆ *vi* ~ **de 1** (*tener*) to have *sth* [*vt*] **2** (*utilizar*) to use *sth* [*vt*]: ~ *de tus ahorros* to use your savings ◆ **disponerse** *v pron* **disponerse a** to get ready **for** ***sth*****/to do** ***sth***: *Me disponía a salir cuando llegó mi suegra.* I was getting ready to leave when my mother-in-law arrived.

disponible *adj* available

dispuesto, -a *pp, adj* **1** (*ordenado*) arranged **2** (*preparado*) ready (***for sth***): *Todo está ~ para la fiesta.* Everything is ready for the party. **3** (*servicial*) willing **4** ~ **a** (*decidido*) prepared ***to do sth***: *No estoy ~ a dimitir.* I'm not prepared to resign. *Ver tb* DISPONER

disputado, -a *pp, adj* hard-fought *Ver tb* DISPUTAR

disputar ◆ *vt* (*Dep*) to play ◆ **disputarse** *v pron* to compete **for** ***sth***

disquete *nm* floppy disk ☛ *Ver dibujo en* ORDENADOR

distancia *nf* distance: *¿A qué ~ está la próxima gasolinera?* How far is it to the next petrol station? **LOC a mucha/poca distancia de…** a long way/not far from…: *a poca ~ de nuestra casa* not far from our house *Ver tb* MANDO

distante *adj* distant

distinción *nf* **1** (*gen*) distinction: *hacer distinciones* to make distinctions **2** (*premio*) award LOC **sin distinción de raza, sexo, etc** regardless of race, gender, etc

distinguido, -a *pp, adj* distinguished *Ver tb* DISTINGUIR

distinguir ◆ *vt* **1** (*gen*) to distinguish *sth/sb* (**from *sth/sb***): *¿Puedes ~ los machos de las hembras?* Can you distinguish the males from the females? ◇ *No puedo ~ a los dos hermanos.* I can't tell the difference between the two brothers. **2** (*divisar*) to make *sth* out: *~ una silueta* to make out an outline ◆ **distinguirse** *v pron* **distinguirse por** to be known **for *sth***: *Se distingue por su tenacidad.* He's known for his tenacity.

distinto, -a *adj* **1** ~ (**a/de**) different (**from/to *sth/sb***): *Es muy ~ de/a su hermana.* He's very different from/to his sister. **2 distintos** (*diversos*) various: *los ~s aspectos del problema* the various aspects of the problem

distracción *nf* (*pasatiempo*) pastime: *Su ~ favorita es leer.* Reading is her favourite pastime.

distraer ◆ *vt* **1** (*entretener*) to keep *sb* amused: *Les conté cuentos para ~los.* I told them stories to keep them amused. **2** (*apartar la atención*) to distract *sb* (**from *sth***): *No me distraigas (de mi labor).* Don't distract me (from what I'm doing). ◆ **distraerse** *v pron* **1 distraerse haciendo algo** (*pasar el tiempo*) to pass your time **doing sth 2** (*despistarse*) to be distracted: *Me distraje un momento.* I was distracted for a moment.

distraído, -a *pp, adj* absent-minded LOC **estar/ir distraído** to be miles away *Ver tb* DISTRAER

distribución *nf* **1** (*gen*) distribution **2** (*casa, piso*) layout

distribuir *vt* to distribute: *Distribuirán alimentos a/entre los refugiados.* They will distribute food to/among the refugees.

distrito *nm* district LOC **distrito electoral** (*parlamento*) constituency [*pl* constituencies]

disturbio *nm* riot

disuadir *vt* to dissuade *sb* (***from sth/doing sth***)

diversión *nf* **1** (*pasatiempo*) pastime **2** (*placer*) fun: *Pinto por ~.* I paint for fun. **3** (*espectáculo*) entertainment: *lugares de ~* places of entertainment

diverso, -a *adj* **1** (*variado, diferente*) different: *personas de ~ origen* people from different backgrounds **2 diversos** (*varios*) various: *El libro abarca ~s aspectos.* The book covers various aspects.

divertido, -a *pp, adj* **1** (*gracioso*) funny **2** (*agradable*) enjoyable: *unas vacaciones divertidas* an enjoyable holiday LOC **estar/ser** (**muy**) **divertido** to be (great) fun *Ver tb* DIVERTIR

divertir ◆ *vt* to amuse ◆ **divertirse** *v pron* to have fun LOC **¡que te diviertas!** have a good time!

dividir ◆ *vt* **1** (*gen*) to divide *sth* (up): *~ el trabajo/la tarta* to divide (up) the work/cake ◇ *~ algo en tres partes* to divide something into three parts ◇ *Lo dividieron entre sus hijos.* They divided it between their children. **2** (*Mat*) to divide *sth* (***by sth***): *~ ocho entre/por dos* to divide eight by two ◆ **dividir(se)** *vt, v pron* **dividir(se)** (**en**) to split (**into *sth***): *Ese asunto ha dividido a la familia.* That affair has split the family. ◇ *~se en dos facciones* to split into two factions

divino, -a *adj* divine

divisa *nf* (*dinero*) (foreign) currency [*gen incontable*]: *pagar en ~s* to pay in foreign currency

divisar *vt* to make *sth/sb* out

división *nf* division: *un equipo de primera ~* a first division team

divisorio, -a *adj* LOC *Ver* LÍNEA

divorciado, -a ◆ *pp, adj* divorced ◆ *nm-nf* divorcee *Ver tb* DIVORCIARSE

divorciarse *v pron* ~ (**de**) to get divorced (**from *sb***)

divorcio *nm* divorce

divulgar(se) *vt, v pron* to spread

do *nm* **1** (*nota de la escala*) doh **2** (*tonalidad*) C: *en do mayor* in C major

dobladillo *nm* hem

doblar ◆ *vt* **1** (*plegar*) to fold: *~ un papel en ocho* to fold a piece of paper into eight **2** (*torcer, flexionar*) to bend: *~ la rodilla/una barra de hierro* to bend your knee/an iron bar **3** (*duplicar*) to double: *Doblaron la oferta.* They doubled their offer. **4** (*esquina*) to turn **5** (*película*) to dub: *~ una película al portugués* to dub a film into Portuguese ◆ *vi* **1** (*girar*) to turn: *~ a la derecha* to turn right **2** (*campanas*) to toll

◆ **doblarse** *v pron* **1** (*cantidad*) to double **2** (*torcerse*) to bend

doble ◆ *adj* double ◆ *nm* **1** (*cantidad*) twice as much/many: *Cuesta el ~.* It costs twice as much. ◊ *Gana el ~ que yo.* She earns twice as much as me. ◊ *Había el ~ de gente.* There were twice as many people. **2 + adj** twice as...: *el ~ de ancho* twice as wide **3** (*persona parecida*) double **4** (*Cine*) stand-in LOC **de doble sentido** (*chiste, palabra*) with a double meaning *Ver tb* APARCAR, ARMA

doblez *nm* fold

doce *nm, adj, pron* **1** (*gen*) twelve **2** (*fecha*) twelfth ☛ *Ver ejemplos en* ONCE *y* SEIS

doceavo, -a *adj, nm* twelfth

docena *nf* dozen: *una ~ de personas* a dozen people LOC **a docenas** by the dozen

doctor, ~a *nm-nf* doctor (*abrev* Dr)

doctorado *nm* PhD: *estudiantes de ~* PhD students

doctrina *nf* doctrine

documentación *nf* **1** (*de una persona*) (identity) papers [*pl*]: *Me pidieron la ~.* They asked to see my (identity) papers. **2** (*de un coche*) documents [*pl*]

documental *nm* documentary [*pl* documentaries]

documento *nm* document LOC **Documento (Nacional) de Identidad (DNI)** identity card ☛En Gran Bretaña no hay DNIs.

dólar *nm* dollar

doler *vi* **1** (*gen*) to hurt: *Esto no te va a ~ nada.* This won't hurt (you) at all. ◊ *Me duele la pierna/el estómago.* My leg/stomach hurts. ◊ *Me dolió que no me apoyaran.* I was hurt by their lack of support. **2** (*cabeza, muela*) to ache: *Me duele la cabeza.* I've got a headache.

dolido, -a *pp, adj* **1** (*gen*) hurt: *Está ~ por lo que dijiste.* He's hurt at what you said. **2** ~ **con** upset **with** ***sb*** *Ver tb* DOLER

dolor *nm* **1** (*físico*) pain: *algo contra/para el ~* something for the pain **2** (*pena*) grief LOC **dolor de cabeza/muelas/oídos** headache/toothache/earache **dolor de estómago** stomach-ache *Ver tb* ESTREMECER(SE), GRITAR, RETORCER

dolorido, -a *adj* sore: *Tengo el hombro ~.* My shoulder is sore.

doloroso, -a *adj* painful

domador, ~a *nm-nf* tamer

domar *vt* **1** (*gen*) to tame **2** (*caballo*) to break *a horse* in

domesticar *vt* to domesticate

doméstico, -a *adj* **1** (*gen*) household [*n atrib*]: *tareas domésticas* household chores **2** (*animal*) domestic LOC *Ver* LABOR

domicilio *nm*: *cambio de ~* change of address ◊ *reparto/servicio a ~* delivery service

dominante *adj* dominant

dominar *vt* **1** (*gen*) to dominate: *~ a los demás* to dominate other people **2** (*idioma*) to be fluent **in** ***sth***: *Domina el ruso.* He's fluent in Russian. **3** (*materia, técnica*) to be good **at** ***sth***

domingo *nm* Sunday [*pl* Sundays] (*abrev* Sun) ☛ *Ver ejemplos en* LUNES LOC **Domingo de Ramos/Resurrección** Palm/Easter Sunday

dominguero, -a *nm-nf* Sunday driver

dominio *nm* **1** (*control*) control: *su ~ del balón* his ball control **2** (*lengua*) command **3** (*técnica*) mastery LOC **ser del dominio público** to be common knowledge

dominó *nm* (*juego*) dominoes [*sing*]: *jugar al ~* to play dominoes LOC *Ver* FICHA

don, doña *nm-nf* Mr [*fem* Mrs]: *don José Ruiz* Mr José Ruiz LOC **ser un don nadie** to be a nobody

donante *nmf* donor: *un ~ de sangre* a blood donor

donar *vt* to donate

donativo *nm* donation

donde *adv rel* **1** (*gen*) where: *la ciudad ~ nací* the city where I was born ◊ *Déjalo ~ puedas.* Leave it over there somewhere. ◊ *un lugar ~ vivir* a place to live **2** (*con preposición*): *la ciudad a/hacia ~ se dirigen* the city they're heading for ◊ *un alto de/desde ~ se ve el mar* a hill you can see the sea from ◊ *la calle por ~ pasa el autobús* the street the bus goes along

dónde *adv interr* where: *¿~ lo has puesto?* Where have you put it? ◊ *¿De ~ eres?* Where are you from? LOC **¿dónde demonios?** where on earth? **¿hacia dónde?** which way?: *¿Hacia ~ han ido?* Which way did they go? **¿por dónde se va a...?** how do you get to...?

donut *nm* doughnut ☛ *Ver dibujo en* PAN

doña *nf Ver* DON

dorado, -a *pp, adj* **1** (*gen*) gold [*n atrib*]: *un bolso ~* a gold bag ◊ *colores/*

tonos ~s gold colours/tones **2** (*época, pelo*) golden: *la época dorada* the golden age

dormir ◆ *vi* **1** (*gen*) to sleep: *No puedo ~.* I can't sleep. ◊ *No dormí nada.* I didn't sleep a wink. **2** (*estar dormido*) to be asleep: *mientras mi madre dormía* while my mother was asleep ◆ *vt* (*niño*) to get *sb* off to sleep ◆ **dormirse** *v pron* **1** (*conciliar el sueño*) to fall asleep, to get to sleep (*más coloq*) **2** (*despertarse tarde*) to oversleep: *Me dormí y llegué tarde a trabajar.* I overslept and was late for work. **3** (*parte del cuerpo*) to go to sleep: *Se me ha dormido la pierna.* My leg's gone to sleep. LOC **¡a dormir!** time for bed! **dormir como un lirón/tronco** to sleep like a log *Ver tb* SACO, SIESTA

dormitorio *nm* bedroom

dorsal *adj* LOC *Ver* ESPINA

dorso *nm* back: *al ~ de la tarjeta* on the back of the card

dos *nm, adj, pron* **1** (*gen*) two **2** (*fecha*) second ☛ *Ver ejemplos en* SEIS LOC **dos puntos** colon ☛ *Ver* págs 318–19. **estar/quedarse a dos velas 1** (*sin dinero*) to be broke **2** (*sin entender*) not to understand a thing **las/los dos** both: *las ~ manos* both hands ◊ *Fuimos los ~.* Both of us went./We both went. **no tener dos dedos de frente** to be (as) thick as two short planks *Ver tb* CADA, GOTA, VEZ

doscientos, -as *adj, pron, nm* two hundred ☛ *Ver ejemplos en* SEISCIENTOS

dosis *nf* dose

dotado, -a *pp, adj* ~ **de 1** (*de una cualidad*) endowed **with *sth***: *~ de inteligencia* endowed with intelligence **2** (*equipado*) equipped **with *sth***: *vehículos ~s de radio* vehicles equipped with a radio

dote *nf* **1** (*de una mujer*) dowry [*pl* dowries] **2 dotes** talent (***for sth/doing sth***) [*sing*]: *Tiene ~s de cómico.* He has a talent for comedy.

dragón *nm* dragon

drama *nm* drama

dramático, -a *adj* dramatic

droga *nf* **1** (*sustancia*) drug: *una ~ blanda/dura* a soft/hard drug **2 la droga** (*actividad*) drugs [*pl*]: *la lucha contra la ~* the fight against drugs LOC *Ver* TRÁFICO

drogadicto, -a *nm-nf* drug addict

drogar ◆ *vt* to drug ◆ **drogarse** *v pron* to take drugs

droguería *nf* shop selling household items and cleaning materials

dromedario *nm* dromedary [*pl* dromedaries]

ducha *nf* shower: *darse una ~* to have a shower LOC *Ver* GEL

ducharse *v pron* to have a shower

duda *nf* **1** (*incertidumbre*) doubt: *sin ~ (alguna)* without doubt ◊ *fuera de (toda) ~* beyond (all) doubt **2** (*problema*): *¿Tenéis alguna ~?* Are there any questions? LOC **sacar de dudas** to dispel *sb's* doubts *Ver tb* CABER, LUGAR

dudar ◆ *vt, vi* ~ (**de/que ...**) to doubt: *Lo dudo.* I doubt it. ◊ *¿Dudas de mi palabra?* Do you doubt my word? ◊ *Dudo que sea fácil.* I doubt that it'll be easy. ◆ *vi* **1** ~ **de** (*persona*) to mistrust *sb* [*vt*]: *Duda de todos.* She mistrusts everyone. **2** ~ **en** to hesitate ***to do sth***: *No dudes en preguntar.* Don't hesitate to ask. **3** ~ **entre**: *Dudamos entre los dos coches.* We couldn't make up our minds between the two cars.

dudoso, -a *adj* **1** (*incierto*) doubtful: *Estoy algo ~.* I'm rather doubtful. **2** (*sospechoso*) dubious: *un penalty ~* a dubious penalty

duelo *nm* (*enfrentamiento*) duel

duende *nm* elf [*pl* elves]

dueño, -a *nm-nf* **1** (*gen*) owner **2** (*bar, pensión*) landlord [*fem* landlady]

dulce ◆ *adj* **1** (*gen*) sweet: *un vino ~* a sweet wine **2** (*persona, voz*) gentle ◆ *nm* sweet LOC *Ver* AGUA, ALGODÓN

duna *nf* dune

dúo *nm* **1** (*composición*) duet **2** (*pareja*) duo [*pl* duos]

duodécimo, -a *adj, pron, nm-nf* twelfth

duque, -esa *nm-nf* duke [*fem* duchess]

> El plural de **duke** es 'dukes', pero cuando decimos *los duques* refiriéndonos al duque y la duquesa, se traduce por **the duke and duchess**.

duración *nf* **1** (*gen*) length: *la ~ de una película* the length of a film **2** (*bombilla, pila*) life: *pilas de larga ~* long-life batteries

durante *prep* during, for: *durante el concierto* during the concert ◊ *durante dos años* for two years

> **During** se utiliza para referirnos al tiempo o al momento en que se desarrolla una acción, y **for** cuando se especifica la duración de esta acción: *Me encontré mal durante la reunión.* I felt

ill during the meeting. ◇ *Anoche llovió durante tres horas.* Last night it rained for three hours.

durar *vi* to last: *La crisis duró dos años.* The crisis lasted two years. ◇ ~ *mucho* to last a long time ◇ *Duró poco.* It didn't last long.

durmiente *adj* LOC *Ver* BELLO

duro, -a ◆ *adj* **1** (*gen*) hard: *La mantequilla está dura.* The butter is hard. ◇ *una vida dura* a hard life ◇ *ser ~ con algn* to be hard on sb **2** (*castigo, clima, crítica, disciplina*) harsh **3** (*fuerte, resistente, carne*) tough: *Hay que ser ~ para sobrevivir.* You have to be tough to survive. ◆ *nm* five-peseta coin ◆ *adv* hard: *trabajar ~* to work hard LOC **duro de oído** hard of hearing *Ver tb* CABEZA, CARA, HUEVO, MANO, PAN

Ee

e *conj* and

ébano *nm* ebony

ebullición *nf* LOC *Ver* PUNTO

echado, -a *pp, adj* LOC **estar echado** to be lying down *Ver tb* ECHAR

echar ◆ *vt* **1** (*tirar*) to throw: *Echa el dado.* Throw the dice. **2** (*dar*) to give: *Échame un poco de agua.* Give me some water. **3** (*humo, olor*) to give *sth* off: *La chimenea echaba mucho humo.* The fire was giving off a lot of smoke. **4** (*correo*) to post: ~ *una carta (al correo)* to post a letter **5** (*película, programa*): *Echan una película muy buena esta noche.* There's a very good film on tonight. **6** (*expulsar*) **(a)** (*gen*) to throw *sb* out: *Nos echaron del bar.* We were thrown out of the bar. **(b)** (*escuela*) to expel: *Me han echado del colegio.* I've been expelled from school. **(c)** (*trabajo*) to sack **7** (*calcular*): *¿Cuántos años le echas?* How old do you think she is? ◆ *vi* ~ **a** to start ***doing sth/to do sth***: *Echaron a correr.* They started to run. ◆ **echarse** *v pron* **1** (*tumbarse*) to lie down **2** (*moverse*) to move: *~se a un lado* to move over **3 echarse a** (*comenzar*) to start ***doing sth/to do sth*** ☛ Para expresiones con **echar**, véanse las entradas del sustantivo, adjetivo, etc, p.ej. **echar a suertes** en SUERTE y **echarse la siesta** en SIESTA.

eclesiástico, -a *adj* ecclesiastical

eclipse *nm* eclipse

eco *nm* echo [*pl* echoes]: *Había ~ en la cueva.* The cave had an echo. LOC **ecos de sociedad** gossip column [*sing*]

ecología *nf* ecology

ecológico, -a *adj* ecological

ecologismo *nm* environmentalism

ecologista ◆ *adj* environmental: *grupos ~s* environmental groups ◆ *nmf* environmentalist

economía *nf* economy [*pl* economies]: *la ~ de nuestro país* our country's economy

económico, -a *adj* **1** (*que gasta poco*) economical: *un coche muy ~* a very economical car **2** (*Econ*) economic

economista *nmf* economist

ECU *nm* ECU/ecu

ecuación *nf* equation LOC **ecuación de segundo/tercer grado** quadratic/cubic equation

ecuador *nm* equator

ecuatorial *adj* equatorial

edad *nf* age: *¿Qué ~ tienen?* How old are they? ◇ *a tu ~* at your age ◇ *niños de todas las ~es* children of all ages LOC **de mi edad** my, your, etc age: *No había ningún chico de mi ~.* There wasn't anybody my age. **estar en la edad del pavo** to be at an awkward age **la Edad Media** the Middle Ages [*pl*]: *la Alta/Baja Edad Media* the Early/Late Middle Ages **no tener edad** to be too young/too old (*for sth/to do sth*) **tener edad** to be old enough (*for sth/to do sth*) *Ver tb* MAYOR, MEDIANO, TERCERO

edición *nf* **1** (*publicación*) publication **2** (*tirada, versión, Radio, TV*) edition: *la primera ~ del libro* the first edition of the book ◇ *~ pirata/semanal* pirate/weekly edition

edificar *vt, vi* (*construir*) to build

edificio *nm* building: *No queda nadie en el ~.* There is nobody left in the building.

editar *vt* **1** (*publicar*) to publish **2** (*preparar texto, Informát*) to edit

editor, ~a *nm-nf* **1** (*empresario*) publisher **2** (*textos, Period, Radio, TV*) editor

editorial ◆ *adj* (*sector*) publishing: *el mundo ~ de hoy* the publishing world of today ◆ *nm* (*periódico*) editorial ◆ *nf* publishing house: *¿De qué ~ es?* Who are the publishers?

edredón *nm* **1** (*gen*) quilt **2** (*nórdico*) duvet

educación *nf* **1** (*enseñanza*) education: *~ sanitaria/sexual* health/sex education **2** (*crianza*) upbringing: *Han tenido una buena ~.* They've been well brought up. LOC **educación física** physical education (*abrev* PE) **ser de buena/mala educación** to be good/bad manners (*to do sth*): *Bostezar es de mala ~.* It's bad manners to yawn. *Ver tb* FALTA

educado, -a *pp, adj* polite LOC **bien/mal educado** well-mannered/rude: *No seas tan mal ~.* Don't be so rude. *Ver tb* EDUCAR

educar *vt* **1** (*enseñar*) to educate **2** (*criar*) to bring *sb* up: *Es difícil ~ bien a los hijos.* It's difficult to bring your children up well. LOC **educar el oído** to train your ear

educativo, -a *adj* **1** (*gen*) educational: *juguetes ~s* educational toys **2** (*sistema*) education [*n atrib*]: *el sistema ~* the education system LOC *Ver* MATERIAL

efectivamente *adv* (*respuesta*) that's right: *—¿Dice que lo vendió ayer? —Efectivamente.* 'Did you say you sold it yesterday?' 'That's right.'

efectivo, -a ◆ *adj* effective ◆ *nm* cash LOC *Ver* PAGAR

efecto *nm* **1** (*gen, Ciencias*) effect: *hacer/no hacer ~* to have an effect/no effect **2** (*pelota*) spin: *La pelota iba con ~.* The ball had (a) spin on it. LOC **efecto invernadero** greenhouse effect **efectos (personales)** belongings **en efecto** indeed *Ver tb* SURTIR

efectuar *vt* to carry *sth* out: *~ un ataque/una prueba* to carry out an attack/a test

efervescente *adj* effervescent

eficaz *adj* **1** (*efectivo*) effective: *un remedio ~* an effective remedy **2** (*eficiente*) efficient

eficiente *adj* efficient: *un ayudante muy ~* a very efficient assistant

egoísta *adj, nmf* selfish [*adj*]: *No seas tan ~.* Don't be so selfish. ◊ *Son unos ~s.* They're really selfish.

¡eh! *interj* hey!: *¡Eh, cuidado!* Hey, watch out!

eje *nm* **1** (*ruedas*) axle **2** (*Geom, Geog, Pol*) axis [*pl* axes] LOC **eje de coordenadas** x and y axes [*pl*]

ejecutar *vt* **1** (*realizar*) to carry *sth* out: *~ una operación* to carry out an operation **2** (*pena de muerte, Jur, Informát*) to execute

ejecutivo, -a *adj, nm-nf* executive: *órgano ~* executive body ◊ *un ~ importante* an important executive LOC *Ver* PODER[2]

¡ejem! *interj* ahem!

ejemplar ◆ *adj* exemplary ◆ *nm* (*texto, disco*) copy [*pl* copies]

ejemplo *nm* example: *Espero que os sirva de ~.* Let this be an example to you. LOC **dar ejemplo** to set an example **por ejemplo** for example (*abrev* eg)

ejercer ◆ *vt* **1** (*profesión*) to practise: *~ la abogacía/medicina* to practise law/medicine **2** (*autoridad, poder, derechos*) to exercise ◆ *vi* to practise: *Ya no ejerzo.* I no longer practise.

ejercicio *nm* **1** (*gen*) exercise: *hacer un ~ de matemáticas* to do a maths exercise ◊ *Deberías hacer más ~.* You should take more exercise. **2** (*profesión*) practice

ejército *nm* army [*v sing o pl*] [*pl* armies]: *alistarse en el ~* to join the army LOC **ejército del aire** air force

el, la *art def* the: *El tren llegó tarde.* The train was late. ☛ *Ver nota en* THE LOC **el/la de... 1** (*posesión*): *La de Marisa es mejor.* Marisa's (one) is better. **2** (*característica*) the one (with...): *el de los ojos verdes/la barba* the one with green eyes/the beard ◊ *Prefiero la de lunares.* I'd prefer the spotted one. **3** (*ropa*) the one in...: *el del abrigo gris* the one in the grey coat ◊ *la de rojo* the one in red **4** (*procedencia*) the one from...: *el de Madrid* the one from Madrid

el/la que... 1 (*persona*) the one (who/that)...: *Ése no es el que vi.* He isn't the one I saw. **2** (*cosa*) the one (which/that)...: *La que compramos ayer era mejor.* The one (that) we bought yesterday was nicer. **3** (*quienquiera*) whoever: *El que llegue primero que haga café.* Whoever gets there first has to make the coffee.

él *pron pers* **1** (*persona*) **(a)** (*sujeto*) he: *José y él son primos.* José and he are cousins. **(b)** (*complemento, en comparaciones*) him: *Es para él.* It's for him. ◊

Eres más alta que él. You're taller than him. **2** (*cosa*) it: *He perdido el reloj y no puedo estar sin él.* I've lost my watch and I can't do without it. LOC **de él** (*posesivo*) his: *No son de ella, son de él.* They're not hers, they're his. **es él** it's him

elaborar *vt* **1** (*producto*) to produce **2** (*preparar*) to prepare: ~ *un informe* to prepare a report

elástico, -a *adj* **1** (*gen*) elastic **2** (*atleta*) supple

elección *nf* **1** (*gen*) choice: *no tener* ~ to have no choice **2 elecciones** election(s): *convocar elecciones* to call an election LOC **elecciones generales/legislativas** general election(s) **elecciones municipales** local election(s)

elector, ~a *nm-nf* voter

electorado *nm* electorate [*v sing o pl*]: *El ~ está desilusionado.* The electorate is/are disillusioned.

electoral *adj* electoral: *campaña ~* electoral campaign ◊ *lista ~* list of (election) candidates LOC *Ver* CABINA, COLEGIO, DISTRITO, LISTA

electricidad *nf* electricity

electricista *nmf* electrician

eléctrico, -a *adj* electric, electrical

> **Electric** se emplea para referirnos a electrodomésticos y aparatos eléctricos concretos, por ejemplo *electric razor/car/fence*, en frases hechas como *an electric shock*, y en sentido figurado en expresiones como *The atmosphere was electric.* **Electrical** se refiere a la electricidad en un sentido más general, como por ejemplo *electrical engineering, electrical goods* o *electrical appliances.*

LOC *Ver* CAFETERA, ENERGÍA, INSTALACIÓN, TENDIDO

electrocutarse *v pron* to be electrocuted

electrodo *nm* electrode

electrodoméstico *nm* electrical appliance

electrónico, -a ◆ *adj* electronic ◆ **electrónica** *nf* electronics [*sing*]

elefante, -a *nm-nf* elephant

elegante *adj* elegant

elegir *vt* **1** (*votar*) to elect: *Van a ~ un nuevo presidente.* They are going to elect a new president. **2** (*optar*) to choose: *No me dieron a ~.* They didn't let me choose. ◊ *~ entre matemáticas y latín* to choose between maths and Latin

elemental *adj* elementary

elemento *nm* **1** (*gen, Quím, Mat*) element: *los ~s de la tabla periódica* the elements of the periodic table **2** (*persona*): *¡Menudo ~ estás hecho!* You're a real handful!

elepé *nm* LP

elevado, -a *pp, adj* high: *temperaturas elevadas* high temperatures LOC **elevado al cuadrado/cubo** squared/cubed **elevado a cuatro, etc** (raised) to the power of four, etc *Ver tb* ELEVAR

elevar *vt* to raise: *~ el nivel de vida* to raise living standards

eliminación *nf* elimination

eliminar *vt* to eliminate

eliminatoria *nf* heat

elipse *nf* ellipse

ella *pron pers* **1** (*persona*) **(a)** (*sujeto*) she: *María y ~ son primas.* She and María are cousins. **(b)** (*complemento, en comparaciones*) her: *Es para ~.* It's for her. ◊ *Eres más alto que ~.* You're taller than her. **2** (*cosa*) it LOC **de ella** (*posesivo*) hers: *Ese collar era de ~.* This necklace was hers. **es ella** it's her

ello *pron* (*complemento*) it

ellos, -as *pron pers* **1** (*sujeto*) they **2** (*complemento, en comparaciones*) them: *Dígaselo a ~.* Tell them. LOC **de ellos** (*posesivo*) theirs **son ellos** it's them

elogiar *vt* to praise

emanciparse *v pron* to become independent

embajada *nf* embassy [*pl* embassies]

embajador, ~a *nm-nf* ambassador

embalarse *v pron*: *No te embales.* Slow down.

embalse *nm* (*pantano*) reservoir

embarazada *pp, adj, nf* pregnant (woman): *Está ~ de cinco meses.* She is five months pregnant.

embarazo *nm* pregnancy [*pl* pregnancies]

embarcación *nf* boat, craft [*pl* craft] (*más formal*) ☛ *Ver nota en* BOAT

embarcadero *nm* pier

embarcar ◆ *vt* **1** (*pasajeros*) to embark **2** (*mercancías*) to load ◆ *vi* to board: *El avión está listo para ~.* The plane is ready for boarding.

embargo *nm* LOC **sin embargo** however, nevertheless (*formal*) **y sin embargo...** and yet...

embarque *nm* LOC *Ver* PUERTA, TARJETA

embarrado, -a *pp, adj* muddy

embestida *nf (toro)* charge

embestir *vt, vi (toro)* to charge (**at *sth*/ *sb***)

emblema *nm* emblem

embolsar(se) *vt, v pron* to pocket: *Se embolsaron un dineral.* They pocketed a fortune.

emborracharse *v pron* ~ (**con**) to get drunk (**on *sth***)

emboscada *nf* ambush: *tender una ~ a algn* to lay an ambush for sb

embotellamiento *nm (tráfico)* traffic jam

embrague *nm* clutch: *pisar el ~* to put the clutch in

embrión *nm* embryo [*pl* embryos]

embrujado, -a *pp, adj* **1** *(persona)* bewitched **2** *(lugar)* haunted: *una casa embrujada* a haunted house

embrujo *nm* spell

embudo *nm* funnel

embutido *nm* cold meats [*pl*]

emergencia *nf* emergency [*pl* emergencies]

emigración *nf* **1** *(personas)* emigration **2** *(animales)* migration

emigrante *adj, nmf* emigrant [*n*]: *trabajadores ~s* emigrant labourers

emigrar *vi* **1** *(gen)* to emigrate **2** *(dentro de un mismo país, animales)* to migrate

eminencia *nf* **1** *(persona)* leading figure **2 Eminencia** Eminence

emisión *nf* **1** *(emanación)* emission **2** *(Radio, TV)* **(a)** *(programa)* broadcast **(b)** *(Tec)* transmission: *problemas con la ~* transmission problems

emisora *nf (Radio)* radio station

emitir *vt (Radio, TV)* to broadcast

emoción *nf* emotion

emocionante *adj* **1** *(conmovedor)* moving **2** *(apasionante)* exciting

emocionar ◆ *vt* **1** *(conmover)* to move **2** *(apasionar)* to thrill ◆ **emocionarse** *v pron* **1** *(conmoverse)* to be moved (**by *sth***) **2** *(apasionarse)* to get excited (**about *sth***)

empachado, -a *pp, adj* LOC **estar empachado** to have indigestion *Ver tb* EMPACHARSE

empacharse *v pron* to get indigestion

empacho *nm* indigestion [*incontable*]

empalagar *vt, vi* to be (too) sweet (**for *sb***): *Este licor empalaga.* This liqueur is too sweet.

empalagoso, -a *adj* **1** *(alimento)* oversweet **2** *(persona)* smarmy

empalmar ◆ *vt* to connect *sth* (**to/with *sth***) ◆ *vi (transportes)* to connect **with *sth***

empalme *nm* **1** *(gen)* connection **2** *(ferrocarril, carreteras)* junction

empanada *nf* pie ☛ *Ver nota en* PIE

empanadilla *nf* pasty [*pl* pasties]

empanado, -a *pp, adj* breaded

empañar ◆ *vt (vapor)* to cloud ◆ **empañarse** *v pron* to steam up

empapado, -a *pp, adj* soaked through *Ver tb* EMPAPAR

empapar ◆ *vt* **1** *(mojar)* to soak: *El último chaparrón nos empapó.* We got soaked in the last shower. ◊ *¡Me has empapado la falda!* You've made my skirt soaking wet! **2** *(absorber)* to soak *sth* up, to absorb *(más formal)* ◆ **empaparse** *v pron* to get soaked (through)

empapelar *vt* to (wall)paper

empaquetar *vt* to pack

emparejar ◆ *vt* **1** *(personas)* to pair *sb* off (***with sb***) **2** *(cosas)* to match *sth* (***with sth***): *~ las preguntas con las respuestas* to match the questions with the answers ◆ **emparejarse** *v pron* to pair off (***with sb***)

empastar *vt* to fill: *Me tienen que ~ tres muelas.* I've got to have three teeth filled.

empaste *nm* filling

empatado, -a *pp, adj* LOC **ir empatados**: *Cuando me fui iban ~s.* They were even when I left. ◊ *Van ~s a cuatro.* It's four all. *Ver tb* EMPATAR

empatar *vt, vi* **1** *(Dep)* **(a)** *(referido al resultado final)* to draw *(sth)* (***with sb***): *Empataron (el partido) con el Manchester United.* They drew (the match) with Manchester United. **(b)** *(en el marcador)* to equalize: *Tenemos que ~ antes del descanso.* We must equalize before half-time. **2** *(votación, concurso)* to tie (***with sb***) LOC **empatar a cero, uno, etc** to draw nil all, one all, etc

empate *nm* **1** ~ (a) *(Dep)* draw: *un ~ a dos* a two-all draw **2** *(votación, concurso)* tie LOC *Ver* GOL

empedrado *nm* cobbles [*pl*]

empeine *nm* instep

empeñado, -a *pp, adj* LOC **estar empeñado (en hacer algo)** to be determined (to do sth) *Ver tb* EMPEÑAR

empeñar ◆ *vt* to pawn ◆ **empeñarse** *v pron* **empeñarse (en)** to insist (**on *sth*/ *doing sth***): *No te empeñes, que no voy a ir.* I'm not going however much you insist.

empeño *nm* ~ (**en**/**por**) determination (***to do sth***) LOC **poner empeño** to take pains *with sth/to do sth Ver tb* CASA

empeorar ◆ *vt* to make *sth* worse ◆ *vi* to get worse: *La situación ha empeorado.* The situation has got worse.

emperador, -triz *nm-nf* emperor [*fem* empress]

empezar *vt, vi* ~ (**a**) to begin; to start (***sth*/*doing sth*/*to do sth***): *De repente empezó a llorar.* All of a sudden he started to cry. LOC **para empezar** to start with *Ver tb* CERO

empinado, -a *pp, adj* (*cuesta*) steep

empírico, -a *adj* empirical

empleado, -a[1] *pp, adj* LOC **¡te está bien empleado!** it serves you right! *Ver tb* EMPLEAR

empleado, -a[2] *nm-nf* **1** (*gen*) employee **2** (*oficina*) clerk

emplear *vt* **1** (*dar trabajo*) to employ **2** (*utilizar*) to use **3** (*tiempo, dinero*) to spend: *He empleado demasiado tiempo en esto.* I've spent too long on this. ◇ ~ *mal el tiempo* to waste your time

empleo *nm* **1** (*puesto de trabajo*) job: *conseguir un buen* ~ to get a good job ☛ *Ver nota en* WORK[1] **2** (*Pol*) employment LOC **estar sin empleo** to be unemployed *Ver tb* FOMENTO, OFERTA, OFICINA

empollar *vt, vi* **1** (*estudiar*) to swot (up) (**on**) ***sth***: *Esta noche tengo que ~ mucho.* I've got to do a lot of swotting tonight. ◇ *Acabo de ~ tres asignaturas.* I've just swotted up (on) three subjects. **2** (*ave*) to sit (**on *sth***): *Las gallinas empollan casi todo el día.* The hens sit for most of the day.

empollón, -ona *nm-nf* swot

empotrado, -a *pp, adj* built-in *Ver tb* EMPOTRARSE

empotrarse *v pron*: *El coche se empotró en el árbol.* The car embedded itself in the tree.

emprendedor, ~a *adj* enterprising

emprender *vt* **1** (*iniciar*) to begin **2** (*negocio*) to start *sth* (up) **3** (*viaje*) to set off **on *sth***: ~ *una gira* to set off on a tour LOC **emprender la marcha/viaje (hacia)** to set out (for ...)

empresa *nf* **1** (*Com*) company [*v sing o pl*] [*pl* companies] **2** (*proyecto*) enterprise LOC **empresa estatal/pública** state-owned company **empresa privada** private company

empresarial *adj* business [*n atrib*]: *sentido* ~ business sense

empresariales *nf* business studies [*sing*]

empresario, -a *nm-nf* **1** (*gen*) businessman/woman [*pl* businessmen/ women] **2** (*espectáculo*) impresario [*pl* impresarios]

empujar *vt* **1** (*gen*) to push: *¡No me empujes!* Don't push me! **2** (*carretilla, bicicleta*) to wheel **3** (*obligar*) to push *sb* ***into doing sth***: *Su familia la empujó a que hiciera periodismo.* Her family pushed her into studying journalism.

empujón *nm* shove: *dar un ~ a algn* to give sb a shove LOC **a empujones**: *Salieron a empujones.* They pushed (and shoved) their way out.

empuñar *vt* **1** (*de forma amenazadora*) to brandish **2** (*tener en la mano*) to hold

en *prep*

• **lugar 1** (*dentro*) in/inside: *Las llaves están en el cajón.* The keys are in the drawer. **2** (*dentro, con movimiento*) into: *Entró en la habitación.* He went into the room. **3** (*sobre*) on: *Está en la mesa.* It's on the table. **4** (*sobre, con movimiento*) onto: *Está goteando agua en el suelo.* Water is dripping onto the floor. **5** (*ciudad, país, campo*) in: *Trabajan en Vigo/el campo.* They work in Vigo/the country. **6** (*punto de referencia*) at

> Cuando nos referimos a un lugar sin considerarlo un área, sino como punto de referencia, utilizamos **at**: *Espérame en la esquina.* Wait for me at the corner. ◇ *Nos encontraremos en la estación.* We'll meet at the station. También se utiliza **at** para referirse a edificios donde la gente trabaja, estudia o se divierte: *Están en el colegio.* They're at school. ◇ *Mis padres están en el cine/ teatro.* My parents are at the cinema/ theatre. ◇ *Trabajo en el supermercado.* I work at the supermarket.

• **con expresiones de tiempo 1** (*meses, años, siglos, estaciones*) in: *en verano/el siglo XII* in the summer/the twelfth century **2** (*día*) on: *¿Qué hiciste en Nochevieja?* What did you do on New Year's Eve? ◇ *Cae en lunes.* It falls on a Monday. **3** (*Navidad, Semana Santa, momento*) at: *Siempre voy a casa en Navidades.* I always go home at Christmas. ◇ *en ese momento* at that moment

4 (*dentro de*) in: *Te veo en una hora.* I'll see you in an hour.

• **otras construcciones 1** (*medio de transporte*) by: *en tren/avión/coche* by train/plane/car **2 + inf** to do sth: *Fuimos los primeros en llegar.* We were the first to arrive.

enamorado, -a ◆ *pp, adj* in love: *estar ~ de algn* to be in love with sb ◆ *nm-nf* (*aficionado*) lover: *un ~ del arte* an art lover LOC *Ver* DÍA; *Ver tb* ENAMORAR

enamorar ◆ *vt* to win *sb's* heart ◆ **enamorarse** *v pron* **enamorarse (de)** to fall in love (**with *sth/sb***)

enano, -a ◆ *adj* **1** (*gen*) tiny **2** (*Bot, Zool*) dwarf [*n atrib*]: *una conífera enana* a dwarf conifer ◆ *nm-nf* dwarf [*pl* dwarfs/dwarves]

encabezamiento *nm* heading

encabezar *vt* to head

encadenar *vt* **1** (*atar*) to chain *sth/sb* (***to sth***) **2** (*ideas*) to link

encajar ◆ *vt* **1** (*colocar, meter*) to fit *sth* (***into sth***) **2** (*juntar*) to fit *sth* together: *Estoy tratando de ~ las piezas del puzzle.* I'm trying to fit the pieces of the jigsaw together. **3** (*noticia, suceso*) to take: *Encajaron resignadamente la noticia.* They took the news philosophically. ◆ *vi* to fit: *No encaja.* It doesn't fit. ◆ **encajarse** *v pron* **encajarse (en)** to get stuck (**in *sth***): *Esta puerta se ha encajado.* This door has stuck.

encaje *nm* lace

encalar *vt* to whitewash

encallar *vi* (*embarcación*) to run aground

encaminarse *v pron* ~ **a/hacia** to head (**for ...**): *Se encaminaron hacia su casa.* They headed for home.

encantado, -a *pp, adj* **1** ~ **(con)** (very) pleased (**with *sth/sb***) **2** ~ **de/de que** (very) pleased **to do sth/(that ...)**: *Estoy encantada de que hayáis venido.* I'm very pleased (that) you've come. **3** (*hechizado*) **(a)** (*gen*) enchanted: *un príncipe ~* an enchanted prince **(b)** (*edificio*) haunted: *una casa encantada* a haunted house LOC **encantado (de conocerle)** pleased to meet you *Ver tb* ENCANTAR

encantador, ~a *adj* lovely

encantamiento *nm* spell: *romper un ~* to break a spell

encantar ◆ *vt* to cast a spell **on *sth/sb*** ◆ *vi* to love *sth/doing sth* [*vt*]: *Me encanta ese vestido.* I love that dress. ◊ *Nos encanta ir al cine.* We love going to the cinema.

encanto *nm* charm: *Tiene mucho ~.* He's got a lot of charm. LOC **como por encanto** as if by magic **ser un encanto** to be lovely

encapricharse *v pron* ~ **(con/de)** to take a fancy **to *sth/sb***: *Se ha encaprichado con ese vestido.* She's taken a fancy to that dress.

encapuchado, -a *pp, adj* hooded: *dos hombres ~s* two hooded men

encarcelar *vt* to imprison

encargado, -a *pp, adj, nm-nf* in charge (***of sth/doing sth***): *¿Quién es el ~?* Who's in charge? ◊ *el juez ~ del caso* the judge in charge of the case ◊ *Eres la encargada de recoger el dinero.* You're in charge of collecting the money. *Ver tb* ENCARGAR

encargar ◆ *vt* **1** (*mandar*) to ask *sb* ***to do sth***: *Me encargaron que regara el jardín.* They asked me to water the garden. **2** (*producto*) to order: *Ya hemos encargado el sofá a la tienda.* We've already ordered the sofa from the shop. ◆ **encargarse** *v pron* **encargarse de 1** (*cuidar*) to look after *sth/sb*: *¿Quién se encarga del niño?* Who will look after the baby? **2** (*ser responsable*) to be in charge **of *sth/doing sth***

encargo *nm* **1** (*recado*) errand: *hacer un ~* to run an errand **2** (*Com*) order: *hacer/anular un ~* to place/cancel an order

encariñado, -a *pp, adj* LOC **estar encariñado con** to be fond of *sth/sb* *Ver tb* ENCARIÑARSE

encariñarse *v pron* ~ **con** to get attached **to *sth/sb***

encarrilar *vt* (*tren*) to put *sth* on the rails

encauzar *vt* **1** (*agua*) to channel **2** (*asunto*) to conduct

encendedor *nm* lighter

encender ◆ *vt* **1** (*con llama*) to light: *Encendimos una hoguera para calentarnos.* We lit a bonfire to warm ourselves. **2** (*aparato, luz*) to turn *sth* on: *Enciende la luz.* Turn the light on. ◆ **encenderse** *v pron* (*aparato, luz*) to come on: *Se ha encendido una luz roja.* A red light has come on.

encendido, -a *pp, adj* **1** (*con llama*) **(a)** (*con el verbo estar*) lit: *Vi que el fuego estaba ~.* I noticed that the fire was lit. **(b)** (*detrás de un sustantivo*) lighted: *un cigarrillo ~* a lighted cigarette **2** (*aparato, luz*) on: *Tenían la luz encendida.* The light was on. *Ver tb* ENCENDER

encerado *nm* (*pizarra*) blackboard

encerrar ◆ *vt* **1** (*gen*) to shut *sth/sb* up **2** (*con llave, encarcelar*) to lock *sth/sb* up ◆ **encerrarse** *v pron* **1** (*gen*) to shut yourself in **2** (*con llave*) to lock yourself in

encestar *vi* to score (a basket)

encharcado, -a *pp, adj* (*terreno*) covered with puddles

enchufado, -a *nm-nf* pet: *Es el ~ del profesor.* He is the teacher's pet. LOC **estar enchufado** (*persona*) to be well in

enchufar *vt* **1** (*aparato*) to plug *sth* in **2** (*recomendar, colocar*) to pull strings **for *sb***

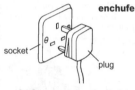

enchufe

socket

plug

enchufe *nm* **1** (*aparato*) **(a)** (*macho*) plug **(b)** (*hembra*) socket **2** (*contacto*) contacts [*pl*]: *Aprobaron gracias al ~.* It was thanks to their contacts that they passed. LOC **tener enchufe** to be well-connected

encía *nf* gum

enciclopedia *nf* encyclopedia [*pl* encyclopedias]

encima *adv* ~ **(de) 1** (*en*) on: *Déjalo ~ de la mesa.* Leave it on the table. **2** (*sobre*) on top (**of *sth/sb***): *Lo he dejado ~ de los otros discos.* I've put it on top of the other records. ◊ *Coge el de ~.* Take the top one. **3** (*cubriendo algo*) over: *poner una manta ~ del sofá* to put a blanket over the sofa **4** (*además*) on top of everything: *¡Y ~ te ríes!* And on top of everything, you stand there laughing! LOC **echarse encima** (*estar cerca*): *La Navidad se nos echa encima.* Christmas is just around the corner. **estar encima de algn** to be on sb's back **hacer algo por encima** to do sth superficially **llevar encima** to have *sth* on you: *No llevo un duro ~.* I haven't got a penny on me. **mirar por encima del hombro** to look down your nose at *sb* **por encima de** above: *El agua nos llegaba por ~ de las rodillas.* The water came above our knees. ◊ *Está por ~ de los demás.* He is above the rest. *Ver tb* QUITAR

encina *nf* holm-oak

encoger(se) *vi, v pron* to shrink: *En agua fría no encoge.* It doesn't shrink in cold water. LOC **encogerse de hombros** to shrug your shoulders

encolar *vt* to glue *sth* (together)

encontrar ◆ *vt* to find: *No encuentro mi reloj.* I can't find my watch. ◊ *Encontré a tu padre mucho mejor.* Your father is looking a lot better. ◆ **encontrarse** *v pron* **1 encontrarse (con)** (*persona*) **(a)** (*citarse*) to meet: *Decidimos ~nos en la librería.* We decided to meet in the bookshop. **(b)** (*por casualidad*) to run into *sb*: *Me la encontré en el súper.* I ran into her in the supermarket. **2** (*sentirse*) to feel: *Me encuentro mal.* I don't feel well. ◊ *¿Te encuentras bien?* Are you all right? LOC *Ver* DEFECTO

encorbatado, -a *pp, adj* wearing a tie

encorvarse *v pron* (*persona*) to become stooped

encuadernador, ~a *nm-nf* bookbinder

encuadernar *vt* to bind

encubrir *vt* **1** (*gen*) to conceal: *~ un delito* to conceal a crime **2** (*delincuente*) to harbour

encuentro *nm* **1** (*reunión*) meeting **2** (*Dep*) match

encuesta *nf* **1** (*gen*) survey [*pl* surveys]: *efectuar una ~* to carry out a survey **2** (*sondeo*) (opinion) poll: *según las últimas ~s* according to the latest polls

enderezar ◆ *vt* **1** (*poner derecho*) to straighten: *Endereza la espalda.* Straighten your back. **2** (*persona*) to correct ◆ **enderezarse** *v pron* to straighten (up): *¡Enderézate!* Stand up straight!

endeudarse *v pron* to get into debt

endibia *nf* chicory [*incontable*]

endulzar *vt* to sweeten

endurecer ◆ *vt* **1** (*gen*) to harden **2** (*músculos*) to firm *sth* up ◆ **endurecerse** *v pron* to harden

enemigo, -a *adj, nm-nf* enemy [*n*] [*pl* enemies]: *las tropas enemigas* the enemy troops

enemistarse *v pron* ~ **(con)** to fall out **(with *sb*)**

energía *nf* energy [*gen incontable*]: *~ nuclear* nuclear energy ◊ *No tengo ~s ni para levantarme de la cama.* I haven't even the energy to get out of bed. LOC **energía eléctrica** electric power

enero *nm* January (*abrev* Jan): *Los exámenes son en* ~. We've got exams in January. ◊ *Mi cumpleaños es el 12 de* ~. My birthday's (on) January 12. ☛Se dice 'January the twelfth' o 'the twelfth of January'.

enésimo, -a *adj* (*Mat*) nth LOC **por enésima vez** for the umpteenth time

enfadado, -a *pp, adj* ~ (**con**) (**por**) angry (**with** ***sb***) (**at/about** ***sth***): *Están ~s conmigo.* They're angry with me. ◊ *Pareces* ~. You look angry. *Ver tb* ENFADAR

enfadar ◆ *vt* to make *sb* angry ◆ **enfadarse** *v pron* **enfadarse** (**con**) (**por**) to get angry (**with** ***sb***) (**at/about** ***sth***): *No te enfades con ellos.* Don't get angry with them.

énfasis *nm* emphasis [*pl* emphases]

enfermar *vi* ~ (**de**) to fall ill (**with** ***sth***)

enfermedad *nf* **1** (*gen*) illness: *Acaba de salir de una ~ gravísima.* He has just recovered from a very serious illness. **2** (*Med, infecciosa, contagiosa*) disease: ~ *hereditaria/de Parkinson* hereditary/ Parkinson's disease ☛*Ver nota en* DISEASE

enfermería *nf* infirmary [*pl* infirmaries]

enfermero, -a *nm-nf* nurse

enfermo, -a ◆ *adj* ill, sick

> **Ill** y **sick** significan enfermo, pero no son intercambiables. **Ill** tiene que ir detrás de un verbo: *estar enfermo* to be ill ◊ *caer enfermo* to fall ill; **sick** suele ir delante de un sustantivo: *cuidar a un animal enfermo* to look after a sick animal, o cuando nos referimos a ausencias en la escuela o el lugar de trabajo: *Hay 15 niños enfermos.* There are 15 children off sick.
> Si utilizamos **sick** con un verbo como **be** o **feel**, no significa encontrarse enfermo, sino *tener ganas de vomitar*: *Tengo ganas de vomitar.* I feel sick.

◆ *nm-nf* **1** (*gen*) sick person ☛Cuando nos referimos al conjunto de los enfermos, decimos **the sick**: *cuidar de los enfermos* to look after the sick. **2** (*paciente*) patient LOC **ponerle enfermo a algn** to make sb sick

enfocar *vt* **1** (*ajustar*) to focus *sth* (**on** ***sth/sb***) **2** (*iluminar*) to shine a light **on** ***sth***: *Enfócame la caja de los fusibles.* Shine a light on the fuse box. **3** (*asunto, problema*) to approach

enfoque *nm* (*Fot*) focus [*pl* focuses/ foci]

enfrentamiento *nm* confrontation

enfrentar ◆ *vt* **1** (*encarar*) to bring *sb* face to face **with** ***sth/sb*** **2** (*enemistar*) to set *sb* at odds (**with** ***sb***): *Con sus habladurías enfrentaron a las dos hermanas.* With their gossip they set the two sisters at odds. ◆ **enfrentarse** *v pron* **1 enfrentarse a** (*gen*) to face: *El país se enfrenta a una profunda crisis.* The country is facing a serious crisis. **2 enfrentarse a** (*Dep*) to take *sb* on: *España se enfrenta a Austria en el Campeonato de Europa.* Spain is taking on Austria in the European Championship. **3 enfrentarse** (**con**) to argue (**with** ***sb***): *Si te enfrentas con ellos será peor.* You'll only make things worse if you argue with them.

enfrente *adv* ~ (**de**) opposite: *Mi casa está ~ del estadio.* My house is opposite the stadium. ◊ *el señor que estaba sentado* ~ the man sitting opposite ◊ *El hospital está* ~. The hospital is across the road.

enfriar ◆ *vt* to cool *sth* (down) ◆ **enfriarse** *v pron* **1** (*gen*) to get cold: *Se te está enfriando la sopa.* Your soup's getting cold. **2** (*acatarrarse*) to catch a cold

enfurecer ◆ *vt* to infuriate ◆ **enfurecerse** *v pron* **enfurecerse** (**con**) (**por**) to become furious (**with** ***sb***) (**at** ***sth***)

enganchar ◆ *vt* **1** (*acoplar*) to hitch: ~ *un remolque al tractor* to hitch a trailer to the tractor **2** (*garfio, anzuelo*) to hook ◆ **engancharse** *v pron* **1** (*atascarse*) to get caught: *Se me ha enganchado el zapato en la alcantarilla.* My shoe has got caught in the grating. **2** (*rasgarse*) to get snagged: *Se me han vuelto a ~ las medias.* My tights have got snagged again. **3** (*drogas*) to get hooked (***on sth***)

engañar ◆ *vt* **1** (*mentir*) to lie **to *sb***: *No me engañes.* Don't lie to me. ◊ *Me engañaron diciéndome que era de oro.* They told me it was gold but it wasn't. ☛ *Ver nota en* LIE[2] **2** (*ser infiel*) to cheat **on *sb*** ◆ **engañarse** *v pron* to fool yourself

engatusar *vt* to sweet-talk *sb* (***into doing sth***)

engendrar *vt* **1** (*concebir*) to conceive **2** (*causar*) to generate

engordar ◆ *vt* (*cebar*) to fatten *sth/sb* (up) ◆ *vi* **1** (*persona*) to put on weight: *He engordado mucho.* I've put on a lot of weight. **2** (*alimento*) to be fattening: *Los caramelos engordan.* Sweets are fattening.

engrasar *vt* **1** (*con grasa*) to grease **2** (*con aceite*) to oil

engreído, -a *pp, adj, nm-nf* conceited [*adj*]: *No eres más que un ~.* You're so conceited.

engullir *vt* to gobble *sth* (up/down)

enhebrar *vt* to thread

enhorabuena *nf* ~ (**por**) congratulations (**on *sth*/*doing sth***): *¡~ por los exámenes!* Congratulations on passing your exams! LOC **dar la enhorabuena** to congratulate *sb* (*on sth*)

enigma *nm* enigma

enjabonar(se) *vt, v pron* to soap: *Primero me gusta ~me la espalda.* I like to soap my back first.

enjambre *nm* swarm

enjaular *vt* to cage

enjuagar ◆ *vt* to rinse ◆ **enjuagarse** *v pron* to rinse (out) your mouth

enjugarse *v pron* (*sudor, lágrimas*) to wipe *sth* (away): *Se enjugó las lágrimas.* He wiped his tears away.

enlace *nm* **1** (*gen*) link **2** (*autobuses, trenes*) connection

enlatar *vt* to can

enlazar *vt, vi* to connect (*sth*) (***to/with sth***)

enloquecedor, ~a *adj* maddening

enloquecer ◆ *vi* **1** (*volverse loco*) to go mad: *El público enloqueció de entusiasmo.* The audience went mad with excitement. **2** (*gustar mucho*) to be mad about *sth*: *Los bombones me enloquecen.* I'm mad about chocolate. ◆ *vt* to drive *sb* mad

enmarcar *vt* to frame

enmascarar ◆ *vt* to mask ◆ **enmascararse** *v pron* to put on a mask

enmendar ◆ *vt* **1** (*errores, defectos*) to correct **2** (*daños*) to repair **3** (*ley*) to amend ◆ **enmendarse** *v pron* to mend your ways

enmienda *nf* (*ley*) amendment (***to sth***)

enmohecerse *v pron* to go mouldy

enmoquetar *vt* to carpet

enmudecer *vi* **1** (*perder el habla*) to go dumb **2** (*callar*) to go quiet

ennegrecer ◆ *vt* to blacken ◆ **ennegrecerse** *v pron* to go black

enojar ◆ *vt* to irritate ◆ **enojarse** *v pron* **enojarse** (**con**) (**por**) to get annoyed (**with *sb***) (**about *sth***)

enorgullecer ◆ *vt* to make *sb* proud: *Tu labor nos enorgullece.* We're proud of your achievements. ◆ **enorgullecerse** *v pron* to be proud ***of sth/sb***

enorme *adj* enormous LOC *Ver* DIMENSIÓN

enredadera *nf* creeper

enredar ◆ *vt* **1** (*pelo, cuerdas*) to get *sth* tangled (up) **2** (*involucrar*) to involve *sb* (***in sth***) ◆ *vi* ~ (**con/en**) to mess about (**with *sth***): *Siempre estás enredando en mis cosas.* You're always messing about with my things. ◆ **enredarse** *v pron* **1** (*pelo, cuerdas*) to get tangled (up) **2** **enredarse** (**en**) (*disputa, asunto*) to get involved (**in *sth***)

enrejado *nm* **1** (*jaula, ventana*) bars [*pl*] **2** (*para plantas*) trellis

enrevesado, -a *pp, adj* **1** (*gen*) complicated **2** (*persona*) awkward

enriquecer ◆ *vt* **1** (*lit*) to benefit **2** (*fig*) to enrich: *Enriqueció su vocabulario con la lectura.* He enriched his vocabulary by reading. ◆ **enriquecerse** *v pron* to get rich

enrojecer ◆ *vt* to redden ◆ **enrojecer(se)** *vi, v pron* **enrojecer(se)** (**de**) to go red (**with *sth***): *Enrojeció de ira.* He went red with anger.

enrolarse *v pron* ~ (**en**) to enlist (**in *sth***)

enrollado, -a *pp, adj* LOC **estar enrollado con algn** to be involved with sb **estar enrollado en algo** to be into sth *Ver tb* ENROLLAR

enrollar ◆ *vt* **1** (*enroscar*) to roll *sth* up **2** (*involucrar*) to talk *sb* ***into doing sth***: *Me han enrollado para ir al cine.* I've been talked into going to the cinema. ◆ *vi*: *Esta canción me enrolla cantidad.* This song is really great. ◆ **enrollarse** *v pron* **1** (*con explicaciones*) to go on **2** **enrollarse** (**con**) (*hablar*) to get talking (**to *sb***) **3 enrollarse con** (*amorío*) to get involved **with *sb***

enroscar *vt* **1** (*tapón*) to screw *sth* on: *Enrosca bien el tapón.* Screw the top on tightly. **2** (*piezas, tuercas*) to screw *sth* together

ensalada *nf* salad LOC **ensalada de lechuga/mixta** green/mixed salad

ensaladera *nf* salad bowl

ensamblar *vt* to assemble

ensanchar ◆ *vt* to widen ◆ **ensancharse** *v pron* **1** (*extenderse*) to widen **2** (*dar de sí*) to stretch: *Estos zapatos se han ensanchado.* These shoes have stretched.

ensangrentado, -a *pp, adj* bloodstained *Ver tb* ENSANGRENTAR

ensangrentar *vt* (*manchar*) to get blood on *sth*

ensayar *vt, vi* **1** (*gen*) to practise **2** (*Mús, Teat*) to rehearse

ensayo *nm* **1** (*experimento*) test: *un tubo de* ~ a test tube **2** (*Mús, Teat*) rehearsal **3** (*Liter*) essay [*pl* essays] LOC **ensayo general** dress rehearsal

enseguida *Ver* SEGUIDA

ensenada *nf* inlet

enseñado, -a *pp, adj* LOC **bien enseñado** well-trained **tener a algn mal enseñado**: *Los tienes muy mal ~s.* You spoil them. *Ver tb* ENSEÑAR

enseñanza *nf* **1** (*gen*) teaching **2** (*sistema nacional*) education: ~ *primaria/secundaria* primary/secondary education

enseñar *vt* **1** (*gen*) to teach *sth*; to teach *sb* **to do *sth***: *Enseña matemáticas.* He teaches maths. ◊ *¿Quién te enseñó a jugar?* Who taught you how to play? **2** (*mostrar*) to show: *Enséñame tu habitación.* Show me your room.

ensillar *vt* to saddle *sth* (up)

ensimismado, -a *pp, adj* **1** (*pensativo*) lost in thought **2** ~ (**en**) (*embebido*) engrossed **in *sth***: *Estaba muy ensimismada leyendo el libro.* She was deeply engrossed in her book.

ensordecedor, ~a *adj* deafening: *un ruido* ~ a deafening noise

ensordecer ◆ *vt* to deafen ◆ *vi* to go deaf: *Corres el peligro de ~.* You run the risk of going deaf.

ensuciar ◆ *vt* to get *sth* dirty: *No me ensucies la mesa.* Don't get the table dirty. ◊ *Te has ensuciado el vestido de aceite.* You've got oil on your dress. ◆ **ensuciarse** *v pron* to get dirty

ensueño *nm* LOC **de ensueño** dream: *una casa de* ~ a dream home

entablar *vt* (*comenzar*) to start *sth* (up): ~ *una conversación* to start up a conversation LOC *Ver* AMISTAD

entablillar *vt* to put *sth* in a splint

entender ◆ *vt* to understand: *No lo entiendo.* I don't understand. ◆ *vi* **1** (*gen*) to understand: *fácil/difícil de* ~ easy/difficult to understand **2** ~ **de** to be well up **in *sth***: *No entiendo mucho de eso.* I don't know much about that. ◆ **entenderse** *v pron* **entenderse** (**con**) to get on (**with *sb***): *Nos entendemos muy bien.* We get on very well. LOC **dar a entender** to imply **entender mal** to misunderstand **no entender ni jota**: *No entendí ni jota de lo que dijo.* I didn't understand a word he said.

entendido, -a ◆ *nm-nf* ~ (**en**) expert (**at/in/on *sth***) ◆ *interj*: *¡Entendido!* Right! ◊ *¿Entendido?* All right?

enterado, -a *pp, adj* LOC **estar enterado** (**de**) to know (about *sth*) **no darse por enterado** to turn a deaf ear (*to sth*) *Ver tb* ENTERAR

enterarse *v pron* ~ (**de**) **1** (*descubrir*) to find out (**about *sth***) **2** (*noticia*) to hear (**about *sth***): *Ya me he enterado de lo de tu abuelo.* I've heard about your grandfather. LOC **te vas a enterar** (*amenaza*) you, he, they, etc will get what for

entero, -a *adj* **1** (*completo*) whole, entire (*formal*) **2** (*intacto*) intact **3** (*leche*) full-cream LOC *Ver* CUERPO

enterrador, ~a *nm-nf* gravedigger

enterrar *vt* (*lit* y *fig*) to bury LOC **enterrarse en vida** to shut yourself away

entierro *nm* **1** (*gen*) funeral: *Había mucha gente en el ~.* There were a lot of people at the funeral. **2** (*sepelio*) burial LOC *Ver* VELA[1]

entonación *nf* intonation

entonar ◆ *vt* **1** (*cantar*) to sing **2** (*marcar el tono*) to pitch ◆ *vi* **1** (*Mús*) to sing in tune **2** ~ (**con**) to go (**with *sth***): *La colcha no entona con la moqueta.* The bedspread doesn't go with the carpet. ◆ **entonarse** *v pron* to perk up: *Date un baño, verás como te entonas.* Have a bath and you'll soon perk up.

entonces *adv* then LOC **en/por aquel entonces** at that time

entornado, -a *pp, adj* (*puerta*) ajar *Ver tb* ENTORNAR

entornar *vt* **1** (*gen*) to half-close **2** (*puerta*) to leave *the door* ajar

entorno *nm* **1** (*ambiente*) environment **2** (*círculo*) circle: ~ *familiar* family circle **3** (*alrededores*): *en el ~ de la ciudad* in and around the city

entrada *nf* **1** ~ **(en)** (*acción de entrar*) **(a)** (*gen*) entry **(into *sth*)**: *Prohibida la ~.* No entry. **(b)** (*club, asociación*) admission **(to *sth*)**: *No cobran ~ a los socios.* Admission is free for members. **2** (*billete*) ticket: *No hay ~s.* Sold out. **3** (*puerta*) entrance **(*to sth*)**: *Te espero a la ~.* I'll wait for you at the entrance. **4** (*primer pago*) deposit **(*on sth*)**: *dar una ~ del 20%* to pay a 20% deposit **5 entradas** (*pelo*) receding hairline: *Cada vez tienes más ~s.* Your hairline is receding fast. LOC **entrada gratuita/libre** free admission

entraña *nf* **entrañas** (*Anat*) entrails

entrañable *adj* (*querido*) much-loved

entrar *vi* **1 (a)** (*gen*) to go in/inside: *No me atreví a ~.* I didn't dare to go in. ◊ *El clavo no ha entrado bien.* The nail hasn't gone in properly. **(b)** (*pasar*) to come in/inside: *Hazle ~.* Ask him to come in. **2** ~ **en (a)** (*gen*) to go into..., to enter (*más formal*): *No entres en mi oficina cuando no estoy.* Don't go into my office when I'm not there. ◊ ~ *en detalles* to go into detail **(b)** (*pasar*) to come into..., to enter (*más formal*): *No entres en mi habitación sin llamar.* Knock before you come into my room. **3** ~ **en** (*ingresar*) **(a)** (*profesión, esfera social*) to enter *sth* [*vt*] **(b)** (*institución, club*) to join *sth* [*vt*] **4** (*caber*) **(a)** (*ropa*) to fit: *Esta falda no me entra.* This skirt doesn't fit (me). **(b)** ~ **(en)** to fit **(in/into *sth*)**: *No creo que entre en el maletero.* I don't think it'll fit in the boot. **5** (*marchas*) to engage: *La primera nunca entra bien.* First never seems to engage properly. LOC **entrar en calor** to warm up **entrar ganas de** to feel like *doing sth* **entrarle a algn el pánico** to be panic-stricken: *Me entró el pánico.* I was panic-stricken. **no me entra (en la cabeza)...** I, you, etc just don't understand... *Ver tb* PROHIBIDO

entre *prep* **1** (*dos cosas, personas*) between: *entre la tienda y el cine* between the shop and the cinema **2** (*más de dos cosas, personas*) among: *Nos sentamos entre los árboles.* We sat among the trees. **3** (*en medio*) somewhere between: *Tienes los ojos entre agrisados y azules.* Your eyes are somewhere between grey and blue. LOC **entre sí 1** (*dos personas*) each other: *Hablaban entre sí.* They were talking to each other. **2** (*varias personas*) among themselves: *Los muchachos lo discutían entre sí.* The boys were discussing it among themselves. **entre tanto** *Ver* ENTRETANTO **entre todos** together: *Lo haremos entre todos.* We'll do it together.

entreabierto, -a *adj* half-open

entreacto *nm* interval

entrecejo *nm* space between the eyebrows

entrecortado, -a *adj* **1** (*voz*) faltering **2** (*frases*) broken

entrecot *nm* fillet steak

entredicho *nm* LOC **poner en entredicho** to call *sth* into question

entrega *nf* **1** (*gen*) handing over: *la ~ del dinero* the handing over of the money **2** (*mercancía*) delivery **3** (*fascículo*) instalment: *Se publicará por ~s.* It will be published in instalments. LOC **entrega de medallas** medal ceremony **entrega de premios** prize-giving

entregado, -a *pp, adj* ~ **(a)** devoted **(to *sth/sb*)** *Ver tb* ENTREGAR

entregar ◆ *vt* **1** (*gen*) to hand *sth/sb* over **(*to sb*)**: ~ *los documentos/las llaves* to hand over the documents/keys ◊ ~ *a algn a las autoridades* to hand sb over to the authorities **2** (*premio, medallas*) to present *sth* **(*to sb*)** **3** (*mercancía*) to deliver ◆ **entregarse** *v pron* **entregarse (a) 1** (*rendirse*) to give yourself up, to surrender (*más formal*) **(to *sb*)**: *Se entregaron a la policía.* They gave themselves up to the police. **2** (*dedicarse*) to devote yourself **to *sth/sb***

entrenador, ~a *nm nf* **1** (*gen*) trainer **2** (*Dep*) coach

entrenamiento *nm* training

entrenar(se) *vt, v pron* to train

entrepierna *nf* crotch

entresuelo *nm* (*edificio*) first floor

entretanto *adv* in the meantime

entretener ◆ *vt* **1** (*demorar*) to keep: *No quiero ~te demasiado.* I won't keep you long. **2** (*divertir*) to keep *sb* amused **3** (*distraer*) to keep *sb* busy: *Entreténle mientras yo entro.* Keep him busy while I go in. ◆ **entretenerse** *v pron* **1 entretenerse (con)** (*disfrutar*): *Lo hago por ~me.* I just do it to pass the time. ◊ *Me entretengo con cualquier cosa.* I'm easily amused. **2** (*distraerse*) to hang about (**doing *sth***): *No os entretengáis y venid a casa en seguida.* Don't hang about; come home straight away.

entretenido, -a *pp, adj* entertaining LOC **estar entretenido** to be happy (*doing sth*) *Ver tb* ENTRETENER

entretenimiento *nm* **1** (*diversión*) entertainment **2** (*pasatiempo*) pastime

entrevista *nf* **1** (*reunión*) meeting **2** (*trabajo, Period*) interview

entrevistador, ~a *nm-nf* interviewer

entrevistar ◆ *vt* to interview ◆ **entrevistarse** *v pron* **entrevistarse (con)** to meet: *Se entrevistó con él en el hotel.* She met him in the hotel.

entristecer ◆ *vt* to sadden ◆ **entristecerse** *v pron* **entristecerse (por)** to be sad (**because of/about *sth***)

entrometerse *v pron* ~ **(en)** to interfere (**in *sth***)

entrometido, -a ◆ *pp, adj* meddlesome ◆ *nm-nf* meddler *Ver tb* ENTROMETERSE

enturbiar ◆ *vt* **1** (*líquido*) to make *sth* cloudy **2** (*relaciones, asunto*) to cloud ◆ **enturbiarse** *v pron* **1** (*líquido*) to become cloudy **2** (*relaciones, asunto*) to become muddled

entusiasmado, -a *pp, adj* LOC **estar entusiasmado (con)** to be delighted (at/about *sth*) *Ver tb* ENTUSIASMAR

entusiasmar ◆ *vt* to thrill ◆ **entusiasmarse** *v pron* **entusiasmarse (con/por)** to get excited (**about/over *sth***)

entusiasmo *nm* ~ **(por)** enthusiasm (**for *sth***) LOC **con entusiasmo** enthusiastically

enumerar *vt* to list, to enumerate (*formal*)

enunciado *nm* (*problema, teoría*) wording

enunciar *vt* to enunciate

envasado, -a *pp, adj* LOC **envasado al vacío** vacuum-packed *Ver tb* ENVASAR

envasar *vt* **1** (*embotellar*) to bottle **2** (*enlatar*) to can

envase *nm* **1** (*botella*) bottle **2** (*lata*) can **3** (*caja*) packet

envejecer ◆ *vi* (*persona*) to get old: *Ha envejecido mucho.* He's got very old. ◆ *vt* **1** (*persona, vino*) to age: *La enfermedad le ha envejecido.* Illness has aged him. **2** (*madera*) to season

envenenar ◆ *vt* to poison ◆ **envenenarse** *v pron*: *Se envenenaron comiendo setas.* They ate poisonous mushrooms.

enviado, -a *nm-nf* **1** (*emisario*) envoy [*pl* envoys] **2** (*Period*) correspondent: ~ *especial* special correspondent

enviar *vt* to send

enviciarse *v pron Ver* VICIARSE

envidia *nf* envy: *hacer algo por ~* to do sth out of envy ◊ *¡Qué ~!* I really envy you! LOC **dar envidia** to make *sb* jealous **tener envidia** to be jealous (*of sth/sb*) *Ver tb* COMIDO, MUERTO

envidiar *vt* to envy

envidioso, -a *adj, nm-nf* envious [*adj*]: *Eres un ~.* You're very envious.

envío *nm* **1** (*acción*) sending **2** (*paquete*) parcel **3** (*Com*) consignment LOC **envío contra reembolso** cash on delivery (*abrev* COD) *Ver tb* GASTO

enviudar *vi* to be widowed

envoltorio *nm* wrapper

envolver *vt* to wrap *sth/sb* (up) (***in sth***): *¿Se lo envolvemos?* Would you like it wrapped? LOC **envolver para regalo** to gift-wrap: *¿Me lo envuelve para regalo?* Can you gift-wrap it for me, please? *Ver tb* PAPEL

envuelto, -a *pp, adj* LOC **verse envuelto en** to find yourself involved in *sth Ver tb* ENVOLVER

enyesar *vt* to put *sth* in plaster: *Me enyesaron una pierna.* They put my leg in plaster.

epicentro *nm* epicentre

epidemia *nf* epidemic: *una ~ de cólera* a cholera epidemic

epilepsia *nf* epilepsy

episodio *nm* episode: *una serie de cinco ~s* a serial in five episodes

época *nf* **1** (*gen*) time: *en aquella ~* at that time ◊ *la ~ más fría del año* the coldest time of the year **2** (*era*) age: *la ~ de Felipe II* the age of Philip II LOC **de época** period: *mobiliario de ~* period furniture *Ver tb* GLACIAR

equilátero, -a *adj* LOC *Ver* TRIÁNGULO

equilibrio *nm* **1** (*gen*) balance: *mantener/perder el ~* to keep/lose your balance ◊ ~ *de fuerzas* balance of power **2** (*Fís*) equilibrium

equilibrista *nmf* **1** (*acróbata*) acrobat **2** (*en la cuerda floja*) tightrope walker

equino, -a *adj* LOC *Ver* GANADO

equipaje *nm* luggage [*incontable*]: *No llevo mucho ~.* I haven't got much luggage. ◊ ~ *de mano* hand luggage LOC **hacer el equipaje** to pack *Ver tb* EXCESO, RECOGIDA

equipar *vt* **1** (*gen*) to equip *sth/sb* (***with sth***): ~ *una oficina con muebles* to equip an office with furniture **2** (*ropa, Náut*) to fit *sth/sb* out (***with sth***): ~ *a los niños para el invierno* to fit the children out for the winter

equipo *nm* **1** (*grupo de personas*) team [*v sing o pl*]: *un ~ de fútbol* a football team ◊ *un ~ de expertos* a team of experts **2** (*equipamiento*) **(a)** (*gen*) equipment [*incontable*]: *un ~ de laboratorio* laboratory equipment **(b)** (*Dep*) gear: ~ *de caza/pesca* hunting/fishing gear LOC **equipo de música** hi-fi (system) *Ver tb* COMPAÑERO, TRABAJO

equitación *nf* horseriding

equivaler *vi* ~ **a** (*valer*) to be equivalent **to *sth***: *Esto equivale a mil pesetas.* That would be equivalent to one thousand pesetas.

equivocación *nf* **1** (*error*) mistake: *cometer una ~* to make a mistake **2** (*malentendido*) misunderstanding

equivocado, -a *pp, adj* wrong: *estar ~* to be wrong *Ver tb* EQUIVOCARSE

equivocarse *v pron* **1** ~ **(en)** (*confundirse*) to be wrong (**about *sth***): *En eso te equivocas.* You're wrong about that. **2** ~ **(de)**: *Se ha equivocado de número.* You have got the wrong number. ◊ ~ *de carretera* to take the wrong road

era[1] *nf* (*periodo*) era

era[2] *nf* (*Agricultura*) threshing floor

erección *nf* erection

erguir *vt* (*cabeza*) to hold *your head* up

erizo *nm* hedgehog LOC **erizo de mar** sea urchin

ermita *nf* hermitage

erosión *nf* erosion

erosionar *vt* to erode

erótico, -a *adj* erotic

errar ◆ *vt* to miss: *Erró el tiro.* He missed (with) his shot. ◆ *vi* (*vagar*) to wander

errata *nf* mistake

erróneo, -a *adj*: *La información era errónea.* The information was incorrect. ◊ *Tomaron la decisión errónea.* They made the wrong decision.

error *nm* mistake: *cometer un ~* to make a mistake ☛ *Ver nota en* MISTAKE

eructar *vi* to burp (*coloq*), to belch

eructo *nm* burp (*coloq*), belch

erupción *nf* **1** (*gen*) eruption **2** (*Med*) rash

esbelto, -a *adj* **1** (*delgado*) slender **2** (*elegante*) graceful

escabeche *nm* LOC **en escabeche** in brine

escabullirse *v pron* **1** (*irse*) to slip away **2** ~ **de/de entre** to slip **out of *sth***: ~ *de las manos* to slip out of your hands

escafandra *nf* diving-suit

escala *nf* **1** (*gen*) scale: *en una ~ de uno a diez* on a scale of one to ten **2** (*viajes*) stopover LOC **escala musical** scale **hacer escala** to stop (over) *in*...

escalada *nf* (*montaña*) climb

escalador, ~a *nm-nf* climber

escalar *vt, vi* to climb

escaleno *adj* LOC *Ver* TRIÁNGULO

escalera *nf* (*de un edificio*) stairs [*pl*], staircase (*más formal*): *La casa tiene una ~ antigua.* The house has an antique staircase. ◊ *Me caí por las ~s.* I fell down the stairs. LOC **bajar/subir las escaleras** to go downstairs/upstairs **escalera de caracol** spiral staircase **escalera de incendios** fire escape **escalera mecánica** escalator *Ver tb* RODAR

escalofrío *nm* shiver LOC **dar escalofríos** to send shivers down your spine **tener/sentir escalofríos** to shiver

escalón *nm* step

escalope *nm* escalope

escama *nf* scale

escandalizar *vt* to shock

escándalo *nm* **1** (*asunto*) scandal **2** (*ruido*) racket: *¡Qué ~!* What a racket! LOC **organizar/montar un escándalo** to make a scene

escandaloso, -a *adj* (*risa, color*) loud

escaño *nm* seat

escapada *nf* **1** (*fuga*) escape **2** (*viaje*) short break: *una ~ de fin de semana* a weekend break **3** (*Dep*) breakaway

escaparate *nm* shop window LOC **ir de escaparates** to go window-shopping

escapar(se) ◆ *vi, v pron* **escapar(se) (de) 1** (*lograr salir*) to escape (**from *sth/sb***): *El loro se escapó de la jaula.* The parrot escaped from its cage. **2** (*evitar*) to escape *sth* [*vt*]: ~ *de la justicia* to escape arrest ◆ **escaparse** *v pron* **1**

(*gas, líquido*) to leak **2** (*involuntariamente*): *Se le escapó un taco.* He accidentally swore. **3** (*secreto*) to let *sth* slip: *Se me escapó que estaba embarazada.* I let (it) slip that she was expecting. **4** (*detalles, oportunidad, medio de transporte*) to miss: *No se te escapa nada.* You don't miss a thing. LOC **dejar escapar 1** (*persona*) to let *sb* get away **2** (*oportunidad*) to let *sth* slip: *Has dejado ~ la mejor ocasión de tu vida.* You've let slip the chance of a lifetime.

escapatoria *nf* way out: *Es nuestra única ~.* It's the only way out.

escape *nm* (*gas, líquido*) leak LOC *Ver* TUBO

escaquearse *v pron* **1** (*gen*) to skive **2** ~ **de** to get out of *sth/doing sth*

escarabajo *nm* beetle

escarbar *vi, vt* (*tierra*) to dig

escarcha *nf* frost

escarchar *v imp*: *Anoche escarchó.* It was frosty last night.

escarmentado, -a *pp, adj* LOC **estar escarmentado** to have learnt your lesson *Ver tb* ESCARMENTAR

escarmentar ◆ *vt* to teach *sb* a lesson ◆ *vi* to learn your lesson: *No escarmientas, ¿eh?* Will you never learn?

escarola *nf* (*Bot*) endive

escarpia *nf* hook

escasear *vi* to be scarce

escasez *nf* shortage: *Hay ~ de profesorado.* There is a shortage of teachers.

escaso, -a *adj* **1** (+ *sustantivo contable en plural*) few: *a ~s metros de distancia* a few metres away **2** (+ *sustantivo incontable*) little: *La ayuda que recibieron fue escasa.* They received very little help. ◊ *debido al ~ interés* due to lack of interest ◊ *productos de escasa calidad* poor quality products **3** (*apenas*) only just (*coloq*), barely: *Tiene tres años ~s.* She is only just three. LOC **andar escaso de** to be short of *sth*

escayola *nf* plaster

escayolado, -a *pp, adj* in plaster: *Tengo el brazo ~.* My arm's in plaster. *Ver tb* ESCAYOLAR

escayolar *vt* (*Med*) to put *sth* in plaster

escena *nf* scene: *acto primero, ~ segunda* act one, scene two LOC **poner en escena** to stage

escenario *nm* **1** (*teatro, auditorio*) stage: *salir al ~* to come onto the stage **2** (*lugar*) scene: *el ~ del crimen* the scene of the crime

escenificar *vt* **1** (*representar*) to stage **2** (*adaptar*) to dramatize

esclarecer *vt* **1** (*explicar*) to clarify **2** (*delito*) to clear *sth* up: *~ un asesinato* to clear a murder up

esclavitud *nf* slavery

esclavizado, -a *pp, adj* LOC **tener esclavizado a algn** to treat sb like a slave *Ver tb* ESCLAVIZAR

esclavizar *vt* to enslave

esclavo, -a *adj, nm-nf* slave [*n*]: *Os tratan como a ~s.* You are treated like slaves. ◊ *ser ~ del dinero* to be a slave to money

esclusa *nf* lock

escoba *nf* **1** (*gen*) broom, brush ☛ *Ver dibujo en* BRUSH **2** (*de bruja*) broomstick

escobilla *nf* (*cuarto de baño*) toilet brush

escocer ◆ *vi* to sting ◆ **escocerse** *v pron* (*irritarse*) to get sore

escocés, -esa ◆ *adj* Scottish ◆ *nm-nf* Scotsman/woman [*pl* Scotsmen/women]: *los escoceses* the Scots LOC *Ver* CUADRO, FALDA

Escocia *nf* Scotland

escoger *vt, vi* to choose: *Escoge tú.* You choose. ◊ *~ entre dos cosas* to choose between two things ◊ *Hay que ~ del menú.* You have to choose from the menu.

escolar ◆ *adj* **1** (*gen*) school [*n atrib*]: *año/curso ~* school year ◊ *el comienzo de las vacaciones ~es* the start of the school holidays **2** (*sistema*) education [*n atrib*]: *el sistema ~* the education system ◆ *nmf* schoolboy [*fem* schoolgirl] [*pl* schoolchildren] LOC *Ver* CENTRO, CERTIFICADO

escolta *nf, nmf* escort

escoltar *vt* to escort

escombro *nm* **escombros** rubble [*incontable, v sing*]: *reducir algo a ~s* to reduce sth to rubble ◊ *un montón de ~s* a pile of rubble

esconder ◆ *vt* to hide: *Lo escondieron debajo de la cama.* They hid it under the bed. ◊ *Esconde el regalo para que no lo vea mi madre.* Hide the present from my mother. ◆ **esconderse** *v pron* **esconderse (de)** to hide **(from *sth/sb*)**: *¿De quién os escondéis?* Who are you hiding from?

escondido, -a *pp, adj* (*recóndito*) secluded LOC **a escondidas** in secret *Ver tb* ESCONDER

escondite *nm* **1** (*escondrijo*) hiding place **2** (*juego*) hide-and-seek: *jugar al ~* to play hide-and-seek

escopeta *nf* **1** (*gen*) rifle **2** (*de perdigones*) shotgun

escopetado, -a *adj* LOC **irse/salir escopetado** to rush out

escorpión[1] *nm* (*alacrán*) scorpion

escorpión[2] (*tb* **Escorpión, escorpio, Escorpio**) *nm, nmf* (*Astrología*) Scorpio [*pl* Scorpios] ☛ *Ver ejemplos en* AQUARIUS

escotado, -a *pp, adj* low-cut: *Es demasiado ~.* It's too low-cut. ◊ *un vestido ~ por detrás* a dress that comes down at the back *Ver tb* ESCOTAR[1]

escotar[1] *vt* (*prenda*) to lower the neckline of *sth*

escotar[2] *vi* to club together (***to do sth***): *Toda la clase escotó para comprar el regalo.* Everyone in the class clubbed together to buy the present.

escote[1] *nm* **1** (*prenda*) neckline: *¡Menudo ~!* That's some neckline! **2** (*pecho*) chest LOC **escote en pico** V-neck

escote[2] *nm* LOC **ir/pagar a escote 1** (*entre dos personas*) to go Dutch **2** (*entre más de dos personas*) to chip in: *Pagamos el regalo a ~.* We all chipped in to buy the present.

escotilla *nf* hatch

escozor *nm* sting

escribir ◆ *vt* **1** (*gen*) to write: *~ un libro* to write a book **2** (*ortografía*) to spell: *No sé ~lo.* I don't know how to spell it. ◊ *¿Cómo se escribe?* How do you spell it? ◆ *vi* to write: *Nunca me escribes.* You never write to me. ◊ *Todavía no sabe ~.* He can't write yet. ◆ **escribirse** *v pron* **escribirse con**: *Me gustaría ~me con un inglés.* I'd like to have an English pen pal. LOC **escribir a mano** to write *sth* in longhand *Ver tb* MÁQUINA

escrito, -a ◆ *pp, adj*: *poner algo por ~* to put sth in writing ◆ *nm* **1** (*carta*) letter **2** (*documento*) document *Ver tb* ESCRIBIR

escritor, ~a *nm-nf* writer

escritorio *nm* **1** (*mesa*) desk **2** (*buró*) bureau [*pl* bureaux/bureaus]

escritura *nf* **1** (*gen*) writing **2 Escritura(s)** Scripture: *la Sagrada Escritura/las Escrituras* the Holy Scripture(s)/the Scriptures

escrupuloso, -a *adj* **1** (*aprensivo*) fussy: *Déjame tu vaso, no soy ~.* Give me your glass. I'm not fussy. **2** (*honrado*) scrupulous

escrutinio *nm* (*recuento*) count

escuadra *nf* **1** (*regla*) set square **2** (*Mil*) squad

escuadrón *nm* squadron

escuchar *vt, vi* to listen (**to *sth/sb***): *Nunca me escuchas.* You never listen to me. ◊ *¡Escucha! ¿Lo oyes?* Listen! Can you hear it?

escudero *nm* squire

escudo *nm* **1** (*gen*) shield: *~ protector* protective shield **2** (*insignia*) emblem **3** (*moneda*) escudo [*pl* escudos] LOC **escudo de armas** coat of arms

escuela *nf* **1** (*gen*) school: *Iremos después de la ~.* We'll go after school. ◊ *El lunes no habrá ~.* There'll be no school on Monday. ◊ *Todos los días voy a la ~ en el autobús.* I go to school on the bus every day. ◊ *El martes iré a la ~ para hablar con tu profesor.* On Tuesday I'll go to the school to talk to your teacher. ☛ *Ver nota en* SCHOOL **2** (*academia*) college: *~ de policía* police college LOC **escuela primaria** primary school **escuela secundaria obligatoria** secondary school

> En Gran Bretaña hay escuelas estatales o públicas, **state schools**, y escuelas privadas, **independent schools**. Los **public schools** son un tipo de colegios privados más tradicionales y conocidos, como por ejemplo Eton y Harrow.

esculpir *vt, vi* to sculpt: *Me gustaría ~ en piedra.* I'd like to sculpt in stone.

escultor, ~a *nm-nf* sculptor [*fem* sculptress]

escultura *nf* sculpture

escupir ◆ *vt* **1** (*expectorar*) to spit *sth* (out) **2** (*a algn*) to spit **at *sb*** ◆ *vi* to spit

escupitajo *nm* spittle [*incontable*]: *Había un ~ en el suelo.* There was some spittle on the ground. ◊ *soltar un ~* to spit

escurreplatos *nm* plate rack

escurridor *nm* (*tb* **escurridora** *nf*) **1** (*verduras*) colander **2** (*escurreplatos*) plate rack

escurrir ◆ *vt* **1** (*ropa*) to wring *sth* (out) **2** (*platos, verduras, legumbres*) to drain ◆ *vi* **1** (*gen*) to drain: *Pon los platos a ~.* Leave the dishes to drain. **2** (*ropa*) to drip ◆ **escurrirse** *v pron* **escurrirse** (**de/entre/de entre**) to slip (**out of/from *sth***): *El jabón se le escurrió de entre las* *manos.* The soap slipped out of his hands.

ese *nf* LOC **hacer eses 1** (*gen*) to zigzag **2** (*persona*) to stagger

ese, -a *adj* that [*pl* those]: *a partir de ~ momento* from that moment on ◊ *esos libros* those books

ése, -a *pron* **1** (*cosa*) that one [*pl* those (ones)]: *Yo no quiero ~/ésos.* I don't want that one/those ones. **2** (*persona*): *¡Ha sido ésa!* It was her! ◊ *Yo no voy con ésos.* I'm not going with them.

esencia *nf* essence

esencial *adj* ~ **(para)** essential **(to/for *sth*)**

esfera *nf* **1** (*gen, Geom*) sphere **2** (*reloj*) face

esférico, -a *adj* spherical

esfinge *nf* sphinx

esforzarse *v pron* ~ **(en/para/por)** to try (hard) **(*to do sth*)**: *Se esforzaron mucho.* They tried very hard.

esfuerzo *nm* **1** (*gen*) effort: *Haz un ~ y come algo.* Make an effort to eat something. ◊ *No deberías hacer ~s, aún no estás recuperado.* You shouldn't overdo it, you're still recovering. **2** (*intento*) attempt **(*at doing sth/to do sth*)**: *en un último ~ por evitar el desastre* in a last attempt to avoid disaster LOC **sin esfuerzo** effortlessly

esfumarse *v pron* to vanish LOC **¡esfúmate!** get lost!

esgrima *nf* (*Dep*) fencing

esgrimir *vt* (*arma*) to wield

esguince *nm* (*Med*) sprain: *hacerse un ~ en el tobillo* to sprain your ankle

eslalon *nm* slalom

eslogan *nm* slogan

esmaltar *vt* to enamel

esmalte *nm* enamel LOC **esmalte de uñas** nail varnish

esmeralda *nf* emerald

esmerarse *v pron* ~ **(en/por)** to try very hard **(*to do sth*)**: *Esmérate un poco más.* Try a bit harder.

esmero *nm* LOC **con esmero** (very) carefully

esmoquin *nm* dinner jacket

esnifar *vt* **1** (*gen*) to sniff **2** (*cocaína*) to snort

esnob ◆ *adj* snobbish ◆ *nmf* snob

eso *pron* that: *¿Qué es ~?* What's that? ◊ *~ es, muy bien.* That's right, very good. LOC **a eso de** at about: *a ~ de la una* at about one o'clock ☛ *Ver nota en* AROUND[1] **¡de eso nada!** no way! **por eso** (*por esa razón*) so, therefore (*formal*)

esófago *nm* oesophagus [*pl* oesophagi/ oesophaguses]

esos, -as *adj Ver* ESE

ésos, -as *pron Ver* ÉSE

espabilado, -a *pp, adj* bright LOC **estar espabilado** to be wide awake *Ver tb* ESPABILAR

espabilar ◆ *vt* to wake *sb* up ◆ *vi* **1** (*gen*) to buck your ideas up: *¡A ver si espabilas de una vez!* It's about time you bucked your ideas up! **2** (*apresurarse*) to get a move on: *Espabila o perderás el tren.* Get a move on or you'll miss the train.

espacial *adj* space [*n atrib*]: *misión/ vuelo ~* space mission/flight LOC *Ver* AERONAVE, BASE, NAVE, TRAJE

espacio *nm* **1** (*gen, Mús*) space **2** (*sitio*) room: *En mi maleta hay ~ para tu jersey.* There is room for your jumper in my suitcase. **3** (*Radio, TV*) programme

espada *nf* **1** (*arma*) sword **2 espadas** (*Naipes*) ☛ *Ver nota en* BARAJA LOC **estar entre la espada y la pared** to be between the devil and the deep blue sea

espagueti *nm* **espaguetis** spaghetti [*incontable, v sing*]: *Me encantan los ~s.* I love spaghetti.

espalda *nf* **1** (*gen*) back: *Me duele la ~.* My back hurts. **2** (*natación*) backstroke: *100 metros ~* 100 metres backstroke LOC **dar la espalda** to turn your back on *sth/sb* **de espaldas**: *Ponte de ~s a la pared.* Stand with your back to the wall. ◊ *ver a algn de ~s* to see sb from behind **hacer algo a espaldas de algn** to do sth behind sb's back *Ver tb* CARA, NADAR

espantapájaros *nm* scarecrow

espantar ◆ *vt* **1** (*asustar*) to terrify **2** (*ahuyentar*) to drive *sth/sb* away ◆ *vi* **1** (*detestar*) to hate *sth/doing sth* [*vt*]: *Me espanta viajar sola.* I hate travelling alone. **2** (*horrorizar*) to appal: *Nos espantaron las condiciones del hospital.* We were appalled by conditions at the hospital.

espanto *nm* (*miedo*) fear LOC **de espanto** (*mucho*) terrible: *Hace un calor de ~.* It's terribly hot. **¡qué espanto!** how awful!

espantoso, -a *adj* dreadful

España *nf* Spain

español, ~a ◆ *adj, nm* Spanish:

hablar ~ to speak Spanish ◆ *nm-nf* Spaniard: *los ~es* the Spanish

esparadrapo *nm* plaster

esparcir *vt* to scatter

espárrago *nm* asparagus [*incontable*] LOC **espárragos trigueros** green asparagus [*incontable*]

esparto *nm* esparto

espatarrarse *v pron* to sprawl

espátula *nf* spatula

especia *nf* spice

especial *adj* special LOC **en especial 1** (*sobre todo*) especially: *Me gustan mucho los animales, en ~ los perros.* I'm very fond of animals, especially dogs. ☛ *Ver nota en* SPECIALLY **2** (*en concreto*) in particular: *Sospechan de uno de ellos en ~.* They suspect one of them in particular.

especialidad *nf* speciality [*pl* specialities]

especialista *nmf* ~ (**en**) specialist (**in** ***sth***): *un ~ en informática* a computer specialist

especializarse *v pron* ~ (**en**) to specialize (**in** ***sth***)

especialmente *adv* **1** (*sobre todo*) especially: *Me encantan los animales, ~ los gatos.* I love animals, especially cats. **2** (*en particular*) particularly: *Estoy ~ preocupada por el abuelo.* I'm particularly concerned about grandad. ◊ *No es un hombre ~ corpulento.* He's not a particularly fat man. **3** (*expresamente*) specially: *~ diseñado para minusválidos* specially designed for handicapped people ☛ *Ver nota en* SPECIALLY

especie *nf* **1** (*Biol*) species [*pl* species] **2** (*clase*) kind: *Era una ~ de barniz.* It was a kind of varnish.

especificar *vt* to specify

específico, -a *adj* specific

espécimen *nm* specimen

espectacular *adj* spectacular

espectáculo *nm* **1** (*gen*) spectacle: *un ~ impresionante* an impressive spectacle **2** (*función*) show LOC **dar un espectáculo** to make a scene *Ver tb* GUÍA, MUNDO

espectador, ~a *nm-nf* **1** (*Teat, Mús*) member of the audience **2** (*Dep*) spectator

espejismo *nm* mirage

espejo *nm* mirror LOC **espejo retrovisor** rear-view mirror **mirarse en el espejo** to look (at yourself) in the mirror

espera *nf* wait LOC *Ver* LISTA, SALA

esperanza *nf* hope LOC **esperanza de vida** life expectancy *Ver tb* ESTADO

esperar ◆ *vt* to wait for *sth/sb*, to expect, to hope

> Los tres verbos **to wait**, **to expect** y **to hope** significan esperar, pero no deben confundirse:
>
> **To wait** indica que una persona espera, sin hacer otra cosa, a que alguien llegue o a que algo suceda por fin: *Espérame, por favor.* Wait for me, please. ◊ *Estoy esperando al autobús.* I'm waiting for the bus. ◊ *Estamos esperando a que deje de llover.* We are waiting for it to stop raining.
>
> **To expect** se utiliza cuando lo esperado es lógico y muy probable: *Había más tráfico de lo que yo esperaba.* There was more traffic than I had expected. ◊ *Esperaba carta suya ayer, pero no recibí ninguna.* I was expecting a letter from him yesterday, but didn't receive one. Si una mujer está embarazada, también se dice **expect**: *Está esperando un bebé.* She's expecting a baby.
>
> Con **to hope** se expresa el deseo de que algo suceda o haya sucedido: *Espero volver a verte pronto.* I hope to see you again soon. ◊ *Espero que sí/no.* I hope so/not.

◆ *vi* to wait: *Estoy harta de ~.* I'm fed up of waiting.

esperma *nf* sperm

espesar(se) *vt, v pron* to thicken

espeso, -a *adj* thick: *La salsa está muy espesa.* This sauce is very thick.

espía *nmf* spy [*pl* spies]

espiar *vt, vi* to spy (**on sb**): *No me espíes.* Don't spy on me.

espiga *nf* (*cereal*) ear

espina *nf* **1** (*Bot*) thorn **2** (*pez*) bone LOC **darle a uno mala espina** to have a bad feeling *about sth*: *Ese asunto me da mala ~.* I've got a bad feeling about it. **espina dorsal** spine

espinaca *nf* spinach [*incontable*]: *Me encantan las ~s.* I love spinach.

espinilla *nf* **1** (*pierna*) shin **2** (*grano*) blackhead

espionaje *nm* spying: *Me acusan de ~.* I've been accused of spying. ◊ *Se dedica al ~.* He's a spy.

espiral *adj, nf* spiral

espiritismo *nm* spiritualism LOC **hacer espiritismo** to attend a séance

espíritu *nm* **1** (*gen*) spirit: ~ *de equipo* team spirit **2** (*alma*) soul LOC **Espíritu Santo** Holy Spirit

espiritual *adj* spiritual

espléndido, -a *adj* **1** (*magnífico*) splendid: *Fue una cena espléndida.* It was a splendid dinner. **2** (*generoso*) generous

espolvorear *vt* to sprinkle *sth* (**with** ***sth***)

esponja *nf* sponge

esponjoso, -a *adj* **1** (*pastel, pan*) light **2** (*lana*) soft

espontáneo, -a *adj* **1** (*impulsivo*) spontaneous **2** (*natural*) natural

esporádico, -a *adj* sporadic

esposar *vt* to handcuff

esposas *nf* handcuffs LOC **ponerle las esposas a algn** to handcuff sb

esposo, -a *nm-nf* husband [*fem* wife, *pl* wives]

espuela *nf* spur

espuma *nf* **1** (*gen*) foam **2** (*cerveza, huevo*) froth **3** (*jabón, champú*) lather **4** (*pelo*) mousse LOC **hacer espuma 1** (*olas*) to foam **2** (*jabón*) to lather

espumoso, -a *adj* (*vino*) sparkling

esqueje *nm* cutting

esquela *nf* LOC **esquela mortuoria** obituary [*pl* obituaries]

esquelético, -a *adj* (*flaco*) skinny ☛ *Ver nota en* DELGADO

esqueleto *nm* **1** (*Anat*) skeleton **2** (*estructura*) framework

esquema *nm* **1** (*diagrama*) diagram **2** (*resumen*) outline

esquí *nm* **1** (*tabla*) ski [*pl* skis] **2** (*Dep*) skiing LOC **esquí acuático** water-skiing: *hacer ~ acuático* to go water-skiing *Ver tb* BASTÓN, ESTACIÓN, PISTA

esquiador, ~a *nm-nf* skier

esquiar *vi* to ski: *Me gusta mucho ~.* I love skiing. ◊ *Esquían todos los fines de semana.* They go skiing every weekend.

esquilar *vt* to shear

esquimal *nmf* Eskimo [*pl* Eskimo/ Eskimos]

esquina *nf* corner: *Es la casa que hace ~ con Murillo.* It's the house that's on the corner of Murillo Street. LOC *Ver* VUELTA

esquinazo *nm* LOC **dar esquinazo** to give *sb* the slip

esquirol *nmf* blackleg

esquivar *vt* **1** (*gen*) to dodge **2** (*persona*) to avoid

esquizofrenia *nf* schizophrenia

esquizofrénico, -a *adj, nm-nf* schizophrenic

esta *adj Ver* ESTE

ésta *pron Ver* ÉSTE

estabilidad *nf* stability

estabilizar(se) *vt, v pron* to stabilize: *El enfermo se ha estabilizado.* The patient's condition has stabilized.

estable *adj* stable

establecer ◆ *vt* **1** (*crear*) to set *sth* up: ~ *una compañía* to set up a company **2** (*determinar, ordenar*) to establish: ~ *la identidad de una persona* to establish the identity of a person **3** (*récord*) to set ◆ **establecerse** *v pron* **1** (*afincarse*) to settle **2** (*en un negocio*) to set up: *~te por tu cuenta* to set up your own business

establo *nm* **1** (*vacas*) cowshed **2** (*caballos*) stable

estación *nf* **1** (*gen*) station: *¿Dónde está la ~ de autobuses?* Where's the bus station? **2** (*del año*) season LOC **estación de esquí** ski resort **estación de servicio** petrol station *Ver tb* JEFE

estadio *nm* (*Dep*) stadium [*pl* stadiums/stadia]

estadística *nf* **1** (*ciencia*) statistics [*sing*] **2** (*cifra*) statistic

estado *nm* **1** (*gen*) state: *la seguridad del ~* state security **2** (*condición médica*) condition: *Su ~ no reviste gravedad.* Her condition isn't serious. LOC **en estado de coma** in a coma **en mal estado 1** (*alimento*): *agua en mal ~* contaminated water ◊ *El pescado estaba en mal ~.* The fish was off. **2** (*carretera*) in a bad state of repair **estado civil** marital status **estar en estado (de buena esperanza)** to be expecting **los Estados Unidos** the United States (*abrev* US/USA) [*v sing o pl*] *Ver tb* GOLPE

estafa *nf* swindle

estafar *vt* to swindle *sb* (**out of** ***sth***): *Ha estafado millones de libras a los inversores.* He has swindled investors out of millions of pounds.

estalactita *nf* stalactite

estalagmita *nf* stalagmite

estallar *vi* **1** (*bomba*) to explode **2** (*globo*) to burst **3** (*guerra, epidemia*) to break out **4** (*escándalo, tormenta*) to break

estallido *nm* **1** (*bomba*) explosion **2** (*guerra*) outbreak

estampa *nf* (*dibujo*) picture

estampado, -a *pp, adj* (*tela*) patterned *Ver tb* ESTAMPAR

estampar ◆ *vt* **1** (*imprimir*) to print **2** (*arrojar*) to hurl *sth/sb* (**against *sth***) ◆ **estamparse** *v pron* **estamparse contra** to smash **into *sth***

estampida *nf* stampede

estancado, -a *pp, adj* (*agua*) stagnant *Ver tb* ESTANCARSE

estancarse *v pron* **1** (*agua*) to stagnate **2** (*negociación*) to come to a standstill

estancia *nf* **1** (*gen*) stay: *su ~ en el hospital* his stay in hospital **2** (*gastos*) living expenses [*pl*]: *pagar los viajes y la ~* to pay travel and living expenses

estanco *nm* tobacconist's [*pl* tobacconists]

En Gran Bretaña no hay estancos. Los sellos se venden en **post offices** (oficinas de correos), que realizan también algunas gestiones administrativas: pago del impuesto de circulación y 'TV licence', cobro de las pensiones, etc. Los **newsagents** también venden sellos, además de prensa, caramelos y cigarrillos. Ya quedan pocos **tobacconists**, establecimientos especializados en artículos para el fumador. Tampoco existen quioscos como tales sino puestos de periódicos o **news-stands**.

estándar *adj, nm* standard

estandarte *nm* banner

estanque *nm* (*jardín, parque*) pond

estante *nm* shelf [*pl* shelves]

estantería *nf* **1** (*gen*) shelves [*pl*]: *Esa ~ está torcida.* Those shelves are crooked. **2** (*libros*) bookcase

estaño *nm* tin

estar ◆ *v copul, vi* **1** (*gen*) to be: *¿Dónde está la biblioteca?* Where's the library? ◊ *¿Está Ana?* Is Ana in? ◊ *~ enfermo/cansado* to be ill/tired **2** (*aspecto*) to look: *Hoy estás muy guapo.* You look very nice today. ◆ *v aux* + **gerundio** to be **doing sth**: *Estaban jugando.* They were playing. ◆ **estarse** *v pron* to be: *~se callado/quieto* to be quiet/still LOC **está bien 1** (*de acuerdo*) OK: *—¿Me lo dejas? —Está bien.* 'Can I borrow it?' 'OK.' **2** (*¡basta!*) that's enough **¿estamos?** all right? **¡estamos buenos!** that's all we need! **estar a 1** (*fecha*): *Estamos a tres de mayo.* It's the third of May. **2** (*temperatura*): *En Canarias están a 30°C.* It's 30°C in the Canaries. **3** (*precio*): *¿A cuánto/cómo están los plátanos?* How much are the bananas? **estar al caer** to be due any time now **estar con** (*apoyar*) to be behind *sb*: *¡Ánimo, estamos contigo!* Go for it, we're behind you! **estar/ponerse bueno** to be/get well **estar que...**: *Estoy que me caigo de sueño.* I'm dead on my feet. **no estar para** not to be in the mood for *sth*: *No estoy para chistes.* I'm not in the mood for jokes. ☛Para otras expresiones con **estar**, véanse las entradas del sustantivo, adjetivo, etc, p.ej. **estar al día** en DÍA y **estar de acuerdo** en ACUERDO.

estárter *nm* choke

estatal *adj* state [*n atrib*]: *escuela ~* state school LOC *Ver* EMPRESA

estático, -a *adj* static

estatua *nf* statue

estatura *nf* height: *Es pequeño de ~.* He's short. ◊ *Es una mujer de mediana ~.* She's of average height.

estatuto *nm* statute

este *nm* east (*abrev* E): *en/por el ~* in the east ◊ *en la costa ~* on the east coast

este, -a *adj* this [*pl* these]

éste, -a *pron* **1** (*cosa*) this one [*pl* these (ones)]: *Prefiero aquel traje a ~.* I prefer that suit to this one. ◊ *¿Prefieres éstos?* Do you prefer these ones? **2** (*persona*): *¿Quién es ~?* Who's this? ◊ *La entrada se la he dado a ésta.* I've given the ticket to her.

estela *nf* **1** (*embarcación*) wake **2** (*avión*) vapour trail

estelar *adj* **1** (*Astron*) stellar **2** (*fig*) star [*n atrib*]: *un papel ~ en la nueva película* a star part in the new film

estera *nf* mat

estercolero *nm* dunghill

estéreo *adj, nm* stereo [*n*] [*pl* stereos]: *un casete ~* a stereo cassette player

estéril *adj* sterile

esterilizar *vt* to sterilize

esterlina *adj* sterling: *libras ~s* pounds sterling

esternón *nm* breastbone

estética *nf* aesthetics [*sing*]

esteticista *nmf* beautician

estético, -a *adj* aesthetic

estiércol *nm* dung

estilista *nmf* stylist

estilizar *vt* (*hacer delgado*): *Ese vestido*

te estiliza la figura. That dress makes you look very slim.

estilo *nm* **1** (*gen*) style: *tener mucho ~* to have a lot of style **2** (*Natación*) stroke: *~ espalda* backstroke ◊ *~ mariposa* butterfly (stroke) LOC **algo por el estilo** something like that: *pimienta o algo por el ~* pepper or something like that

estiloso, -a *adj* stylish

estima *nf* esteem LOC **tener estima a/por algn** to think highly of sb

estimado, -a *pp, adj* (*cartas*) dear ☛ *Ver* págs 314–15.

estimulante ◆ *adj* stimulating ◆ *nm* stimulant: *La cafeína es un ~.* Caffeine is a stimulant.

estimular *vt* to stimulate

estímulo *nm* stimulus [*pl* stimuli] (***to sth/to do sth***)

estirado, -a *pp, adj* (*altivo*) stiff *Ver tb* ESTIRAR

estirar ◆ *vt* **1** (*gen*) to stretch: *~ una cuerda* to stretch a rope tight **2** (*brazo, pierna*) to stretch *sth* out **3** (*dinero*) to spin *sth* out **4** (*alisar*) to smooth ◆ **estirarse** *v pron* **1** (*desperezarse*) to stretch **2** (*mostrarse generoso*) to be generous ◆ **estirar(se)** *vi, v pron* (*crecer*) to shoot up LOC **estirar la pata** to snuff it

estirón *nm* LOC **dar/pegar un estirón** (*crecer*) to shoot up

esto *pron* **1** (*gen*) this: *Hay que terminar con ~.* We've got to put a stop to this. ◊ *¿Qué es ~?* What's this? **2** (*vacilación*) er: *Quería decirte que, ~...* I wanted to tell you... er...

estofado *nm* stew

estómago *nm* stomach: *Me duele el ~.* I've got stomach-ache. LOC *Ver* ACIDEZ, ARDOR, DOLOR, PATADA

estorbar *vt, vi* to be in *sb's* way; to be in the way: *Si te estorban esas cajas dímelo.* Tell me if those boxes are in your way. ◊ *¿Estorbo?* Am I in the way?

estornudar *vi* to sneeze ☛ *Ver nota en* ¡ACHÍS!

estrago *nm* LOC **hacer estragos** to create havoc

estrangular *vt* to strangle

estraperlo *nm* black market LOC **de estraperlo** on the black market

estrategia *nf* strategy [*pl* strategies]

estratégico, -a *adj* strategic

estrato *nm* (*Geol, Sociol*) stratum [*pl* strata]

estrechar(se) ◆ *vt, v pron* **1** (*gen*) to narrow: *La carretera se estrecha a 50 metros.* The road narrows in 50 metres. **2** (*abrazar*) to embrace ◆ *vt* (*ropa*) to take *sth* in

estrecho, -a ◆ *adj* **1** (*gen*) narrow **2** (*ropa*) tight: *Esa falda te está estrecha.* That skirt's too tight (for you). ◆ *nm* strait(s) [*se usa mucho en plural*]: *el ~ de Bering* the Bering Strait(s)

estrella *nf* star: *~ polar* pole star ◊ *un hotel de tres ~s* a three-star hotel ◊ *una ~ de cine* a film star LOC **estrella fugaz** shooting star **estrella invitada** celebrity guest **ver las estrellas** to see stars

estrellado, -a *pp, adj* **1** (*noche, cielo*) starry **2** (*figura*) star-shaped *Ver tb* ESTRELLAR

estrellar ◆ *vt* to smash *sth* (***into/against sth***): *Estrellaron el coche contra un árbol.* They smashed the car into a tree. ◆ **estrellarse** *v pron* **1 estrellarse (contra)** (*chocarse*) to crash (**into *sth***): *~se contra otro vehículo* to crash into another vehicle **2** (*fracasar*) to founder

estremecer(se) *vt, v pron* to shake LOC **estremecerse de dolor** to wince with pain

estrenar *vt* **1** (*gen*): *Estreno zapatos.* I'm wearing new shoes. ◊ *¿Estrenas coche?* Is that a new car you're driving? **2** (*película*) to première **3** (*obra de teatro*) to stage *sth* for the first time

estreno *nm* **1** (*película*) première **2** (*obra de teatro*) first night

estreñido, -a *pp, adj* constipated *Ver tb* ESTREÑIR

estreñimiento *nm* constipation

estreñir ◆ *vt* to make *sb* constipated ◆ **estreñirse** *v pron* to become constipated

estrés *nm* stress LOC **tener estrés** to be suffering from stress

estresante *adj* stressful

estría *nf* **1** (*gen*) groove **2** (*piel*) stretch mark

estribillo *nm* **1** (*canción*) chorus **2** (*poema*) refrain

estribo *nm* stirrup

estribor *nm* starboard LOC **a estribor** to starboard

estricto, -a *adj* strict

estridente *adj* **1** (*sonido*) shrill **2** (*color*) gaudy

estrofa *nf* verse

estropajo *nm* scourer

estropear ◆ *vt* **1** (*gen*) to spoil: *Nos has estropeado los planes.* You've spoilt our plans. **2** (*aparato*) to break ◆ **estropearse** *v pron* **1** (*averiarse*) to break down **2** (*comida*) to go off

estructura *nf* structure

estruendo *nm* racket

estrujar *vt* **1** (*naranja, mano*) to squeeze **2** (*papel*) to crumple *sth* (up) LOC **estrujarse la cabeza/los sesos** to rack your brains

estuario *nm* estuary [*pl* estuaries]

estuche *nm* **1** (*pinturas, maquillaje, joyas*) box **2** (*lápices, instrumento musical*) case

estudiante *nmf* student: *un grupo de ~s de medicina* a group of medical students LOC *Ver* RESIDENCIA

estudiar *vt, vi* to study: *Me gustaría ~ francés.* I'd like to study French. ◊ *Estudia en un colegio privado.* She's at a private school. LOC **estudiar de memoria** to learn *sth* by heart *Ver tb* MATAR

estudio *nm* **1** (*gen*) study [*pl* studies]: *Han realizado ~s sobre la materia.* They've done studies on the subject. ◊ *Tiene todos los libros en el ~.* All her books are in the study. **2** (*apartamento*) studio flat **3** (*Cine, Fot, TV*) studio [*pl* studios] **4 estudios** education [*sing*]: *~s primarios* primary education LOC *Ver* JEFE, PLAN, PROGRAMA

estudioso, -a *adj* studious

estufa *nf* fire: *~ eléctrica/de gas* electric/gas fire

estupendo, -a *adj* fantastic

estúpido, -a ◆ *adj* stupid ◆ *nm-nf* idiot

etapa *nf* stage: *Hicimos el viaje en dos ~s.* We did the journey in two stages. LOC **por etapas** in stages

etcétera *nm* et cetera (*abrev* etc)

eternidad *nf* eternity LOC **una eternidad** ages: *Has tardado una ~.* You've been ages.

eternizarse *v pron* to spend ages (***doing sth***): *Se eterniza en el baño.* He spends ages in the bathroom.

eterno, -a *adj* eternal

ético, -a ◆ *adj* ethical ◆ **ética** *nf* ethics [*sing*]

etimología *nf* etymology [*pl* etymologies]

etiqueta *nf* **1** (*gen*) label: *la ~ de un paquete/una botella* the label on a parcel/bottle **2** (*precio*) price tag **3** (*Informát*) tag LOC **de etiqueta** formal: *traje de ~* formal dress

etiquetar *vt* to label

etnia *nf* ethnic group

étnico, -a *adj* ethnic

eucalipto *nm* eucalyptus [*pl* eucalyptuses/eucalypti]

Eucaristía *nf* Eucharist

euforia *nf* euphoria

eufórico, -a *adj* euphoric

eurodiputado, -a (*tb* **europarlamentario, -a**) *nm-nf* Euro MP

Europa *nf* Europe

europeo, -a *adj, nm-nf* European LOC *Ver* COMUNIDAD, UNIÓN

euskera *nm* Basque

eutanasia *nf* euthanasia

evacuación *nf* evacuation

evacuar *vt* **1** (*desalojar*) to vacate: *El público evacuó el cine.* The public vacated the cinema. **2** (*trasladar*) to evacuate: *~ a los refugiados* to evacuate the refugees

evadido, -a *nm-nf* escapee

evadir ◆ *vt* **1** (*eludir*) to evade: *~ impuestos* to evade taxes **2** (*dinero*) to smuggle *money* out of the country ◆ **evadirse** *v pron* **evadirse (de)** to escape (**from *sth***)

evaluación *nf* (*Educ*) assessment

evaluar *vt* to assess

evangelio *nm* gospel: *el ~ según San Juan* the gospel according to Saint John

evaporación *nf* evaporation

evaporar(se) *vt, v pron* to evaporate

evasión *nf* **1** (*fuga*) escape **2** (*distracción*) distraction LOC **evasión de impuestos** tax evasion

evasiva *nf* excuse: *Siempre estás con ~s.* You're always making excuses.

evidencia *nf* evidence LOC **poner a algn en evidencia** to make a fool of sb

evidente *adj* obvious

evitar *vt* **1** (*impedir*) to prevent: *~ una catástrofe* to prevent a disaster **2** (*rehuir*) to avoid *sth/sb/doing sth*: *Me evita a toda costa.* He does everything he can to avoid me. LOC **no lo puedo evitar** I, you, etc can't help it **si puedo evitarlo** if I, you, etc can help it

evocar *vt* to evoke

evolución *nf* **1** (*Biol*) evolution **2** (*desarrollo*) development

evolucionar *vi* **1** (*Biol*) to evolve **2** (*desarrollarse*) to develop

exactitud *nf* **1** (*gen*) exactness **2** (*descripción, reloj*) accuracy LOC **con**

exactitud exactly: *No se sabe con ~.* We don't know exactly.

exacto, -a ◆ *adj* **1** (*no aproximado*) exact: *Necesito las medidas exactas.* I need the exact measurements. ◊ *Dos kilos ~s.* Exactly two kilos. **2** (*descripción, reloj*) accurate: *No me dieron una descripción muy exacta.* They didn't give me a very accurate description. **3** (*idéntico*) identical: *Las dos copias son exactas.* The two copies are identical. ◆ **¡exacto!** *interj* exactly!

exageración *nf* exaggeration

exagerado, -a *pp, adj* **1** (*gen*) exaggerated: *No seas ~.* Don't exaggerate. **2** (*excesivo*) excessive: *El precio me parece ~.* I think the price is excessive. *Ver tb* EXAGERAR

exagerar *vt, vi* to exaggerate: *~ la importancia de algo* to exaggerate the importance of sth ◊ *No exageres.* Don't exaggerate.

exaltado, -a ◆ *pp, adj* angry (**about *sth***) ◆ *nm-nf* hothead: *un grupo de ~s* a group of hotheads *Ver tb* EXALTAR

exaltar ◆ *vt* (*alabar*) to praise ◆ **exaltarse** *v pron* to get heated

examen *nm* examination, exam (*más coloq*): *hacer un ~* to do an exam LOC **estar de exámenes** to be sitting exams **examen de conducir** driving test **examen de ingreso** entrance exam **examen de recuperación** resit **examen final** finals [*pl*] **examen tipo test** multiple-choice exam *Ver tb* PRESENTAR

examinador, ~a *nm-nf* examiner

examinar ◆ *vt* to examine ◆ **examinarse** *v pron* to have an exam: *Esta tarde me examino de francés.* I've got a French exam this afternoon. LOC **examinarse del carné de conducir** to take your driving test

excavación *nf* excavation

excavadora *nf* digger

excavar *vt* **1** (*gen*) to dig: *~ un túnel* to dig a tunnel ◊ *~ la tierra* to dig in the earth **2** (*Arqueología*) to excavate

excelencia *nf* LOC **Su Excelencia** His/Her Excellency **Su/Vuestra Excelencia** Your Excellency **por excelencia** par excellence

excelente *adj* excellent

excepción *nf* exception LOC **a/con excepción de** except (for) *sth/sb*

excepcional *adj* exceptional

excepto *prep* except (**for**) ***sth/sb***: *todos excepto yo* everybody except me ◊ *todos excepto el último* all of them except (for) the last one

exceptuar *vt*: *Exceptuando a uno, el resto son veteranos.* Except for one, the rest are all veterans.

excesivo, -a *adj* excessive: *Tienen una excesiva afición por el fútbol.* They're much too fond of football.

exceso *nm* ~ (**de**) excess (**of *sth***) LOC **con/en exceso** too much **exceso de equipaje** excess baggage

excitar ◆ *vt* **1** (*gen*) to excite **2** (*nervios*) to make *sb* nervous ◆ **excitarse** *v pron* to get excited (***about/over sth***)

exclamación *nf* (*signo de puntuación*) exclamation mark ☛ *Ver* págs 318–19.

exclamar *vi, vt* to exclaim

excluir *vt* to exclude *sth/sb* (**from *sth***)

exclusive *adv* exclusive: *hasta el 24 de enero ~* till 24 January exclusive

exclusivo, -a ◆ *adj* exclusive ◆ **exclusiva** *nf* (*reportaje*) exclusive

excomulgar *vt* to excommunicate

excomunión *nf* excommunication

excursión *nf* excursion LOC **ir/salir de excursión** to go on an excursion

excursionismo *nm* rambling: *hacer ~* to go rambling

excursionista *nmf* rambler

excusa *nf* excuse (**for *sth*/*doing sth***): *Siempre pone ~s para no venir.* He always finds an excuse not to come.

exento, -a *adj* ~ (**de**) **1** (*exonerado*) exempt (**from *sth***) **2** (*libre*) free (**from *sth***)

exhalar ◆ *vt* **1** (*gas, vapor, olor*) to give *sth* off **2** (*suspiro, queja*): *~ un suspiro de alivio* to heave a sigh of relief ◊ *~ un gemido de dolor* to groan with pain ◆ *vi* to breathe out, to exhale (*formal*)

exhaustivo, -a *adj* thorough, exhaustive (*formal*)

exhausto, -a *adj* exhausted

exhibición *nf* exhibition

exhibicionismo *nm* **1** (*gen*) exhibitionism **2** (*sexual*) indecent exposure

exhibicionista *nmf* **1** (*gen*) exhibitionist **2** (*sexual*) flasher (*coloq*)

exhibir ◆ *vt* **1** (*exponer*) to exhibit **2** (*película*) to show ◆ **exhibirse** *v pron* (*presumir*) to show off

exigencia *nf* **1** (*requerimiento*) requirement **2** (*pretensión*) demand (***for sth*/*that…***)

exigente *adj* **1** (*que pide mucho*) demanding **2** (*estricto*) strict

exigir *vt* **1** (*pedir*) to demand *sth* (**from *sb***): *Exijo una explicación.* I demand an explanation. **2** (*requerir*) to require: *Exige una preparación especial.* It requires special training. LOC *Ver* RESCATE

exiliado, -a ◆ *pp, adj* exiled ◆ *nm-nf* exile *Ver tb* EXILIAR

exiliar ◆ *vt* to exile *sb* (**from...**) ◆ **exiliarse** *v pron* **exiliarse (a/en)** to go into exile (**in...**)

exilio *nm* exile

existencia *nf* **1** (*hecho de existir*) existence **2 existencias (a)** (*gen*) stocks: *Se nos están acabando las ~s de carne.* Our stocks of meat are running low. **(b)** (*Com*) stock [*sing*]

existir *vi* **1** (*gen*) to exist: *Esa palabra no existe.* That word doesn't exist. **2** (*haber*): *No existe una voluntad de colaboración.* There is no spirit of cooperation.

éxito *nm* **1** (*gen*) success **2** (*disco, canción*) hit: *su último ~* their latest hit LOC **tener éxito** to be successful

exorcismo *nm* exorcism

exótico, -a *adj* exotic

expandir ◆ *vt* **1** (*gen*) to expand **2** (*incendio, rumor*) to spread ◆ **expandirse** *v pron* to spread

expansión *nf* **1** (*gen*) expansion **2** (*diversión*) relaxation

expansionar ◆ *vt* to expand ◆ **expansionarse** *v pron* **1** (*gen*) to expand **2 expansionarse (con)** (*divertirse*) to relax (**with *sth***)

expatriado, -a *pp, adj, nm-nf* expatriate [*n*]: *americanos ~s en España* expatriate Americans living in Spain *Ver tb* EXPATRIAR

expatriar ◆ *vt* to exile ◆ **expatriarse** *v pron* to emigrate

expectación *nf* **1** (*espera*) waiting: *Se acabó la ~.* The waiting came to an end. **2** (*interés*) expectancy: *La ~ está creciendo.* Expectancy is growing.

expectativa *nf* **1** (*esperanza*) expectation: *Superó mis ~s.* It exceeded my expectations. **2** (*perspectiva*) prospect: *~s electorales* electoral prospects LOC **estar a la expectativa** to be on the lookout (*for sth*)

expedición *nf* (*viaje*) expedition

expediente *nm* **1** (*documentación*) file: *los ~s municipales* council files **2** (*empleado, estudiante*) record: *tener un buen ~ académico* to have a good academic record **3** (*Jur*) proceedings [*pl*] LOC *Ver* ABRIR

expedir *vt* **1** (*carta, paquete*) to send **2** (*Administración*) to issue: *~ un pasaporte* to issue a passport

expensas *nf*: *a nuestras ~* at our expense

experiencia *nf* experience: *años de ~ laboral* years of work experience ◊ *Fue una gran ~.* It was a great experience. LOC **sin experiencia** inexperienced

experimentado, -a *pp, adj* (*persona*) experienced *Ver tb* EXPERIMENTAR

experimental *adj* experimental: *con carácter ~* on an experimental basis

experimentar ◆ *vi* ~ (**con**) to experiment (**with *sth***) ◆ *vt* **1** (*aumento, mejoría*) to show **2** (*cambio*) to undergo

experimento *nm* experiment: *hacer un ~* to carry out an experiment

experto, -a *nm-nf* ~ (**en**) expert (**at/in *sth*/*doing sth***)

expirar *vi* to expire

explanada *nf* open area

explicación *nf* explanation

explicar ◆ *vt* to explain *sth* (***to sb***): *Me explicó sus problemas.* He explained his problems to me. ◆ **explicarse** *v pron* (*entender*) to understand LOC **¿me explico?** do you see what I mean?

explorador, ~a *nm-nf* explorer

explorar *vt* **1** (*país, región*) to explore **2** (*Med*) to examine

explosión *nf* explosion: *una ~ nuclear* a nuclear explosion ◊ *la ~ demográfica* the population explosion LOC **hacer explosión** to explode

explosivo, -a *adj, nm* explosive

explotar *vi* (*hacer explosión*) to explode

exponer ◆ *vt* **1** (*cuadro*) to exhibit **2** (*ideas*) to present **3** (*vida*) to risk ◆ **exponerse** *v pron* **exponerse a** to expose yourself **to *sth***: *No te expongas demasiado al sol.* Don't stay out in the sun too long. LOC **exponerse a que...** to risk *sth*: *Te expones a que te multen.* You're risking a fine.

exportación *nf* export LOC *Ver* IMPORTACIÓN

exportador, ~a ◆ *adj* exporting: *los países ~es de petróleo* the oil exporting countries ◆ *nm-nf* exporter

exportar *vt* to export

exposición *nf* **1** (*de arte*) exhibition: *una ~ de fotografías* an exhibition of photographs ◊ *montar una ~* to put on an exhibition **2** (*de un tema*) presentation

exprés *adj* express: *una carta* ~ an express letter LOC *Ver* CAFÉ, CAFETERA, OLLA

expresar *vt* to express

expresión *nf* expression LOC *Ver* LIBERTAD

expresivo, -a *adj* **1** (*gen*) expressive: *una expresiva pieza musical* an expressive piece of music **2** (*mirada*) meaningful **3** (*afectuoso*) affectionate

expreso, -a *adj*, *nm* express

exprimidor *nm* **1** (*manual*) lemon-squeezer **2** (*eléctrico*) juice extractor

exprimir *vt* (*fruta*) to squeeze

expulsar *vt* **1** (*gen*) to expel *sb* (**from...**): *La van a ~ del colegio.* They're going to expel her (from school). **2** (*Dep*) to send *sb* off: *Fue expulsado del terreno de juego.* He was sent off (the pitch).

expulsión *nf* **1** (*gen*) expulsion: *Este año ha habido tres expulsiones en la escuela.* There have been three expulsions from the school this year. **2** (*Dep*) sending-off [*pl* sendings-off]

exquisito, -a *adj* **1** (*comida, bebida*) delicious **2** (*gusto, objeto*) exquisite

éxtasis *nm* ecstasy [*pl* ecstasies]

extender ◆ *vt* **1** (*desdoblar, desplegar*) to spread *sth* (out): *~ un mapa sobre la mesa* to spread a map out on the table **2** (*alargar*) to extend: *~ una mesa* to extend a table **3** (*brazo*) to stretch out *your arm* **4** (*alas, mantequilla, pintura*) to spread ◆ **extender(se)** *vi, v pron* to spread: *La epidemia se extendió por todo el país.* The epidemic spread through the whole country. ◆ **extenderse** *v pron* **1** (*en el espacio*) to stretch: *El jardín se extiende hasta el lago.* The garden stretches down to the lake. **2** (*en el tiempo*) to last: *El debate se extendió durante horas.* The debate lasted for hours.

extendido, -a *pp, adj* **1** (*general*) widespread **2** (*brazos*) outstretched *Ver tb* EXTENDER

extensión *nf* **1** (*superficie*) area: *una ~ de 30 metros cuadrados* an area of 30 square metres **2** (*duración*): *una gran ~ de tiempo* a long period of time ◊ *¿Cuál es la ~ del contrato?* How long is the contract for? **3** (*teléfono*) extension

extenso, -a *adj* **1** (*grande*) extensive **2** (*largo*) long

exterior ◆ *adj* **1** (*gen*) outer: *la capa ~ de la Tierra* the outer layer of the earth **2** (*comercio, política*) foreign: *política ~* foreign policy ◆ *nm* outside: *el ~ de la casa* the outside of the house ◊ *desde el ~ del teatro* from outside the theatre LOC *Ver* MINISTERIO, MINISTRO

exterminar *vt* to exterminate

externo, -a ◆ *adj* **1** (*gen*) external: *influencias externas* external influences **2** (*capa, superficie*) outer: *la capa externa de la piel* the outer layer of skin ◆ *nm-nf* day pupil LOC *Ver* USO

extinción *nf* (*especie*) extinction: *en peligro de ~* in danger of extinction

extinguir ◆ *vt* **1** (*fuego*) to put *sth* out **2** (*especie*) to wipe *sth* out ◆ **extinguirse** *v pron* **1** (*fuego*) to go out **2** (*especie*) to become extinct

extintor *nm* fire extinguisher

extirpar *vt* (*Med*) to remove

extra ◆ *adj* **1** (*superior*) top quality **2** (*adicional*) extra: *una capa ~ de barniz* an extra coat of varnish ◆ *nmf* (*Cine, Teat*) extra LOC *Ver* HORA

extraer *vt* **1** (*gen*) to extract *sth* **from** **sth/sb**: *~ oro de una mina* to extract gold from a mine ◊ *~ información de algn* to extract information from sb **2** (*sangre*) to take *a blood sample* **from sb**

extraescolar *adj*: *actividades ~es* extracurricular activities

extranjero, -a ◆ *adj* foreign ◆ *nm-nf* foreigner LOC **al/en el extranjero** abroad

extrañar ◆ *vt* **1** (*sorprender*) to surprise: *Me extrañó ver tanta gente.* I was surprised to see so many people. **2** (*echar de menos*) to miss: *Extraño mucho mi cama.* I really miss my bed. ◆ **extrañarse** *v pron* to be surprised (**at sth/sb**): *No me extraña que no quiera venir.* I'm not surprised he doesn't want to come. LOC **ya me extrañaba a mí** I thought it was strange

extraño, -a ◆ *adj* strange: *Oí un ruido ~.* I heard a strange noise. ◆ *nm-nf* stranger

extraordinario, -a *adj* **1** (*excelente*) excellent: *La comida estaba extraordinaria.* The food was excellent. **2** (*especial*) special: *edición extraordinaria* special edition **3** (*convocatoria, reunión*) extraordinary: *convocatoria extraordinaria* extraordinary meeting

extrarradio *nm* outskirts [*pl*]

extraterrestre ◆ *adj* extraterrestrial ◆ *nmf* alien

extraviado, -a *pp, adj* **1** (*persona, cosa*) lost **2** (*animal*) stray *Ver tb* EXTRAVIAR

extraviar ◆ *vt* to lose ◆ **extraviarse**

v pron **1** (*persona*) to get lost **2** (*animal*) to stray **3** (*objeto*) to be missing: *Se han extraviado mis gafas.* My glasses are missing.

extremar *vt*: ~ *las precauciones* to take strict precautions ◊ ~ *las medidas de control* to implement tight controls

extremidad *nf* **1** (*extremo*) end **2** **extremidades** (*cuerpo*) extremities

extremo, -a ◆ *adj* extreme: *un caso* ~ an extreme case ◊ *hacer algo con extrema precaución* to do sth with extreme care ◆ *nm* **1** (*punto más alto y más bajo*) extreme: *ir de un* ~ *a otro* to go from one extreme to another **2** (*punta*) end: *Coge el mantel por los ~s.* Take hold of the ends of the tablecloth. ◊ *Viven en el otro* ~ *de la ciudad.* They live at the other end of town. LOC *Ver* ORIENTE

extrovertido, -a *adj* extrovert [*n*]: *Es muy* ~. He's a real extrovert.

Ff

fa *nm* **1** (*nota de la escala*) fah **2** (*tonalidad*) F: *fa mayor* F major LOC *Ver* CLAVE

fábrica *nf* **1** (*gen*) factory [*pl* factories]: *una* ~ *de conservas* a canning factory **2** (*cemento, acero, ladrillos*) works [*v sing o pl*]: *Va a cerrar la* ~ *de acero.* The steelworks is/are closing down. LOC **fábrica de azúcar/papel** sugar mill/ paper mill **fábrica de cerveza** brewery [*pl* breweries]

fabricación *nf* manufacture, making (*más coloq*): ~ *de aviones* aircraft manufacture LOC **de fabricación española, holandesa, etc** made in Spain, Holland, etc

fabricado, -a *pp, adj* LOC **fabricado en ...** made in ... *Ver tb* FABRICAR

fabricante *nmf* manufacturer

fabricar *vt* to manufacture, to make (*más coloq*): ~ *coches* to manufacture cars LOC **fabricar en serie** to mass-produce

facha *nf* **1** (*aspecto*) look: *No me gusta mucho su* ~. I don't much like the look of him. **2** (*adefesio*) sight: *Con esa americana está hecho una* ~. He looks a real sight in that jacket.

fachada *nf* (*Arquit*) façade (*formal*), front: *la* ~ *del hospital* the front of the hospital

fácil *adj* **1** (*gen*) easy: *Es más* ~ *de lo que parece.* It's easier than it looks. ◊ *Eso es* ~ *de decir.* That's easy to say. **2** (*probable*): *No es* ~ *que me lo den.* They're unlikely to let me have it. ◊ *Es* ~ *que llegue tarde.* He will probably be late.

factor *nm* factor: *un* ~ *clave* a key factor

factura *nf* bill: *la* ~ *del gas/de la luz* the gas/electricity bill ◊ *Haz la* ~. Make out the bill.

facturar *vt* (*en aeropuerto*) to check *sth* in: *¿Ya has facturado las maletas?* Have you checked in the cases?

facultad *nf* **1** (*capacidad*) faculty [*pl* faculties]: *en plena posesión de sus ~es mentales* in full possession of his mental faculties ◊ *Ha perdido ~es.* He's lost his faculties. **2** (*Educ*) **(a)** (*universidad*) university: *un compañero de la* ~ a friend of mine from university **(b)** **Facultad** Faculty [*pl* Faculties]: ~ *de Filosofía y Letras* Faculty of Arts

faena *nf* **1** (*tarea*) job: *No le dediques mucho tiempo a esa* ~. Don't spend a lot of time on that job. **2** (*contratiempo*) nuisance: *Es una* ~, *pero qué se le va a hacer.* It's a nuisance but it can't be helped. **3** (*jugarreta*) dirty trick: *hacerle una (mala)* ~ *a algn* to play a dirty trick on sb LOC **faenas agrícolas/ del campo** farm work [*sing*]

faenar *vi* (*pescar*) to fish

faisán *nm* pheasant

faja *nf* **1** (*fajín*) sash **2** (*ropa interior*) girdle

fajo *nm* bundle: *un* ~ *de billetes nuevos* a bundle of crisp notes

falda *nf* **1** (*prenda*) skirt **2** (*montaña*) lower slope LOC **falda escocesa 1** (*gen*) tartan skirt **2** (*traje típico*) kilt **falda pantalón** culottes [*pl*]

faldero, -a *adj* LOC *Ver* PERRO

fallar ◆ *vi* **1** (*gen*) to fail: *Me falla la vista.* My eyesight's failing. **2** (*a un amigo*) to let *sb* down ◆ *vt* to miss: *El cazador falló el tiro.* The hunter missed. LOC **¡no falla!** it, he, etc is always the same: *Seguro que llega tarde, no falla nunca.* He's bound to be late; he's always the same.

fallecer *vi* to pass away

fallo *nm* **1** (*error*) mistake, error (*más formal*): *debido a un ~ humano* due to human error **2** (*defecto*) fault: *un ~ en los frenos* a fault in the brakes ☛ *Ver nota en* MISTAKE

falsificación *nf* forgery [*pl* forgeries]

falsificar *vt* to forge

falso, -a *adj* **1** (*gen*) false: *una falsa alarma* a false alarm **2** (*de imitación*) fake: *diamantes ~s* fake diamonds

falta *nf* **1 ~ de** (*carencia*) lack **of *sth***: *su ~ de ambición/respeto* his lack of ambition/respect **2** (*error*) mistake: *muchas ~s de ortografía* a lot of spelling mistakes **3** (*fútbol*) foul: *hacer (una) ~* to commit a foul LOC **falta (de asistencia)** absence: *Ya tienes tres ~s este mes.* That's three times you've been absent this month. ◊ *No quiero que me pongan ~.* I don't want to be marked absent. **falta de educación** rudeness: *¡Qué ~ de educación!* How rude! **hace(n) falta** to need *sth/to do sth* [*vt*]: *Me hace ~ un coche.* I need a car. ◊ *Hacen ~ cuatro sillas más.* We need four more chairs. ◊ *Llévatelo, no me hace ~.* Take it, I don't need it. ◊ *Te hace ~ estudiar más.* You need to study harder. ◊ *No hace ~ que vengas.* You don't have to come. **sin falta** without fail *Ver tb* PITAR

faltar *vi* **1** (*necesitar*) to need *sth/sb* [*vt*]: *Les falta cariño.* They need affection. ◊ *Aquí falta un director.* This place needs a manager. ◊ *Me faltan dos monedas para poder llamar.* I need two coins to make a phone call. ◊ *Faltan medicinas en muchos hospitales.* Many hospitals need medicines. **2** (*no estar*) to be missing: *¿Falta alguien?* Is there anybody missing? **3 ~ (a)** (*no acudir a un sitio*) to miss *sth* [*vt*]: *~ a una clase* to miss a lesson **4** (*quedar tiempo*): *Faltan diez minutos (para que se termine la clase).* There are ten minutes to go (till the end of the lesson). ◊ *¿Falta mucho para comer?* Is it long till lunch? ◊ *¿Te falta mucho?* Are you going to be long? LOC **faltar al respeto** to show no respect *to sb* **faltarle un tornillo a algn** to have a screw loose **¡lo que faltaba!** that's all I/we needed!

fama *nf* **1** (*celebridad*) fame: *alcanzar la ~* to achieve fame **2 ~ (de)** (*reputación*) reputation (**for *sth/doing sth***): *tener buena/mala ~* to have a good/bad reputation ◊ *Tiene ~ de ser un hueso.* He has a reputation for being very strict.

familia *nf* family [*v sing o pl*] [*pl* families]: *una ~ numerosa* a large family ◊ *¿Cómo está tu ~?* How's your family? ◊ *Mi ~ vive en Francia.* My family live in France. ◊ *Mi ~ es del norte.* My family is/are from the north.

> Hay dos formas posibles de expresar el apellido de la familia en inglés: con la palabra **family** ('the Robertson family') o poniendo el apellido en plural ('the Robertsons').

LOC **madre/padre de familia** mother/father **venir de familia** to run in the family *Ver tb* CABEZA

familiar ◆ *adj* **1** (*de la familia*) family [*n atrib*]: *lazos ~es* family ties **2** (*conocido*) familiar: *una cara ~* a familiar face. ◆ *nmf* (*pariente*) relative

famoso, -a *adj* ~ (**por**) **1** (*célebre*) famous (**for *sth***): *hacerse ~* to become famous **2** (*de mala fama*) notorious (**for *sth***): *Es ~ por su genio.* He's notorious for his bad temper.

fan *nmf* fan

fanático, -a *nm-nf* fanatic

fantasía *nf* fantasy [*pl* fantasies]: *Son ~s suyas.* That's just a fantasy of his.

fantasma *nm* ghost: *un relato de ~s* a ghost story LOC **ser (un) fantasma** (*chulo*) to be a show-off

fantástico, -a *adj* fantastic

farmacéutico, -a *nm-nf* chemist

farmacia *nf* **1** (*tienda*) chemist's [*pl* chemists]: *¿Dónde hay una ~ por aquí?* Is there a chemist's near here? ☛ *Ver nota en* PHARMACY **2** (*estudios*) pharmacy LOC **farmacia de guardia** duty chemist

faro *nm* **1** (*torre*) lighthouse **2** (*coche, moto*) headlight **3** (*bicicleta*) (bicycle) lamp

farol *nm* **1** (*lámpara*) lantern **2** (*fanfarronada*) bluff: *marcarse/tirarse un ~* to bluff

farola *nf* street light

farolillo *nm* paper lantern LOC **farolillos de colores** fairy lights

fascículo *nm* instalment: *publicar/vender algo en/por ~s* to publish/sell sth in instalments

fascinante *adj* fascinating

fascinar *vt* to fascinate: *Aquellos trucos fascinaron a los niños.* The children were fascinated by those tricks.

fascismo *nm* fascism

fascista *adj, nmf* fascist

fase *nf* stage, phase (*más formal*): *la ~ previa/clasificatoria* the preliminary/qualifying stage

fastidiar ◆ *vt* **1** (*molestar*) to annoy: *Deja de ~ a los niños.* Stop annoying the children. **2** (*estropear*) to ruin: *La lluvia nos fastidió los planes.* The rain ruined our plans. ◆ *vi*: *Me fastidia mucho tener que ir.* I'm really annoyed that I've got to go. ◊ *¿No te fastidia madrugar tanto?* Doesn't having to get up so early bother you? ◆ **fastidiarse** *v pron* to be ruined: *Se nos fastidiaron las vacaciones.* Our holidays were ruined. LOC **¡no fastidies!** you're kidding! **para que te fastidies** so there! **¡te fastidias!** tough!

fatal ◆ *adj* **1** (*muy malo*) terrible: *Tuvieron un año ~.* They had a terrible year. ◊ *Me encuentro ~.* I feel terrible. **2** (*irreparable*) fatal: *un accidente ~* a fatal accident ◆ *adv* really badly: *Se portaron ~.* They behaved really badly. LOC *Ver* OLER

fauna *nf* fauna

favor *nm* favour: *¿Me haces un ~?* Can you do me a favour? ◊ *pedirle un ~ a algn* to ask sb a favour LOC **a favor de** in favour of *sth/sb/doing sth*: *Estamos a ~ de actuar.* We're in favour of taking action. **por favor** please

favorable *adj* favourable

favorecer *vt* **1** (*gen*) to favour: *Estas medidas nos favorecen.* These measures favour us. **2** (*ropa, peinado*) to suit: *Te favorece el rojo.* Red suits you.

favoritismo *nm* favouritism

favorito, -a *adj, nm-nf* favourite

fax *nm* fax: *poner un ~* to send a fax ◊ *Lo mandaron por ~.* They faxed it.

fe *nf* faith (***in sth/sb***)

febrero *nm* February (*abrev* Feb) ☛ *Ver ejemplos en* ENERO

fecha *nf* **1** (*gen*) date: *¿A qué ~ estamos?* What's the date today? ◊ *Tiene ~ del 3 de mayo.* It is dated 3 May. **2 fechas** (*época*) time [*sing*]: *en/por estas ~s* at/around this time (of the year) LOC **fecha de caducidad** sell-by date **fecha límite/tope 1** (*solicitud*) closing date **2** (*proyecto*) deadline *Ver tb* PASADO

fecundar *vt* to fertilize

federación *nf* federation

felicidad *nf* **1** (*dicha*) happiness: *cara de ~* a happy face **2 felicidades (a)** (*gen*) best wishes (***on…***): *Te deseo muchas ~es por tu cumpleaños.* Best wishes on your birthday. **(b)** (*enhorabuena*) congratulations (***on sth/doing sth***): *~es por tu nuevo trabajo/por haber aprobado.* Congratulations on your new job/on passing your exams. LOC **¡felicidades!** Happy birthday!

felicitar *vt* **1** (*gen*) to congratulate *sb* (***on sth***): *Le felicité por el ascenso.* I congratulated him on his promotion. ◊ *¡Te felicito!* Congratulations! **2** (*fiestas*) to wish *sb* (a) happy…: *Me felicitaron las Navidades.* They wished me a happy Christmas.

feliz *adj* happy LOC **¡Feliz cumpleaños!** Happy birthday! **¡Feliz Navidad!** Happy/Merry Christmas! *Ver tb* VIAJE

felpudo *nm* doormat

femenino, -a *adj* **1** (*gen*) female: *el sexo ~* the female sex **2** (*Dep, moda*) women's: *el equipo ~* the women's team **3** (*característico de la mujer, Gram*) feminine: *Lleva ropa muy femenina.* She wears very feminine clothes. ☛ *Ver nota en* FEMALE

feminista *adj, nmf* feminist

fenomenal *adj* fantastic LOC **pasarlo fenomenal** to have a fantastic time

fenómeno *nm* **1** (*gen*) phenomenon [*pl* phenomena]: *~s climatológicos* meteorological phenomena **2** (*prodigio*) fantastic [*adj*]: *Este actor es un ~.* This actor is fantastic.

feo, -a *adj* **1** (*aspecto*) ugly: *una persona/casa fea* an ugly person/house **2** (*desagradable*) nasty: *Ésa es una costumbre muy fea.* That's a very nasty habit. LOC *Ver* BAILAR

féretro *nm* coffin

feria *nf* fair: *~ del libro* book fair ◊ *Ayer fuimos a la ~.* We went to the fair yesterday. LOC **feria de muestras** trade fair

fermentar *vt, vi* to ferment

feroz *adj* fierce LOC *Ver* HAMBRE

ferretería *nf* **1** (*tienda*) ironmonger's [*pl* ironmongers] **2** (*objetos*) hardware: *artículos de ~* hardware

ferrocarril *nm* railway, train (*más coloq*): *estación de ~* railway/train station ◊ *viajar por ~* to travel by train

ferry *nm* ferry [*pl* ferries]

fértil *adj* (*tierra, persona*) fertile

festín *nm* feast: *¡Vaya ~ que nos dimos!* What a feast we had!

festival *nm* festival

festividad *nf* **1** (*día festivo*) holiday [*pl*

holidays]: *la ~ del primero de mayo* the May Day holiday **2** (*Relig*) feast

festivo, -a *adj* LOC *Ver* DÍA

fétido, -a *adj* LOC *Ver* BOMBA[1]

feto *nm* foetus [*pl* foetuses]

fiable *adj* reliable

fiambre *nm* cold meat

fiambrera *nf* lunch box

fianza *nf* **1** (*Jur*) bail [*incontable*]: *una ~ de tres millones de pesetas* bail of three million pesetas **2** (*Com*) deposit LOC *Ver* LIBERTAD

fiar ◆ *vt* to let *sb* have *sth* on credit: *Me fiaron el pan.* They let me have the bread on credit. ◆ *vi* to give credit ◆ **fiarse** *v pron* **fiarse de** to trust: *No me fío de ella.* I don't trust her. LOC **ser de fiar** to be trustworthy

fibra *nf* fibre

ficción *nf* fiction

ficha *nf* **1** (*tarjeta*) (index) card **2** (*pieza de juego*) counter: *Se ha perdido una ~.* We've lost a counter. **3** (*equivalente al dinero*) token: *una ~ de teléfono* a telephone token LOC **fichas de dominó** dominoes **ficha médica/policial** medical/police record

fichaje *nm* (*Dep*) signing: *el nuevo ~ del Madrid* Madrid's new signing

fichar ◆ *vt* **1** (*policía*) to open a file **on** ***sb*** **2** (*Dep*) to sign *sb* (up) ◆ *vi* **1** ~ **(por)** (*Dep*) to sign **(for** ***sb*****)**: *~ por el Real Madrid* to sign for Real Madrid **2** (*en trabajo*) **(a)** (*al entrar*) to clock in **(b)** (*al salir*) to clock off

fichero *nm* **1** (*mueble*) filing cabinet **2** (*caja*) card index

fidelidad *nf* faithfulness LOC *Ver* ALTO

fideo *nm* noodle: *sopa de ~s* noodle soup LOC **estar hecho un fideo** to be as thin as a rake

fiebre *nf* **1** (*temperatura anormal*) temperature: *Te ha bajado/subido la ~.* Your temperature has gone down/up. ◊ *tener ~* to have a temperature ◊ *Tiene 38° de ~.* He's got a temperature of 38°. **2** (*enfermedad, fig*) fever: *~ amarilla* yellow fever LOC *Ver* DÉCIMO

fiel *adj* **1** ~ **(a)** (*leal*) faithful **(to** ***sth/sb*****)** **2** ~ **a** (*creencias, palabra*) true **to** ***sth***: *~ a sus ideas* true to his ideas

fieltro *nm* felt

fiera *nf* wild animal LOC **estar/ponerse hecho una fiera** to be furious/to blow your top *Ver tb* COMER

fiero, -a *adj* fierce

fiesta *nf* **1** (*celebración*) party [*pl* parties]: *dar una ~ de cumpleaños* to hold a birthday party **2** (*día festivo*) bank holiday [*pl* holidays]: *Mañana es ~.* Tomorrow is a bank holiday. **3 fiestas**: *las ~s navideñas* the Christmas festivities ◊ *las ~s del pueblo* the town festival LOC **fiesta nacional 1** (*fiesta oficial*) public holiday: *Mañana es ~ nacional.* It's a public holiday tomorrow. **2** (*toros*) bullfighting **hacer/tener fiesta** to have a day off *Ver tb* COLAR, SALA

figura *nf* figure: *una ~ de plastilina* a plasticine figure ◊ *una ~ política* a political figure

figurar ◆ *vi* **1** (*hallarse*) to be: *España figura entre los países de la UE.* Spain is one of the EU countries. **2** (*destacar*) to stand out from the crowd: *Les encanta ~.* They love standing out from the crowd. ◆ **figurarse** *v pron* to imagine: *Me figuro que ya habrán salido.* I imagine they must have left by now. ◊ *Ya me lo figuraba yo.* I thought as much.

fijamente *adv* LOC **mirar fijamente** to stare at *sth/sb*: *Me miró fijamente.* He stared at me.

fijar ◆ *vt* **1** (*gen*) to fix: *~ un precio/una fecha* to fix a price/date **2** (*atención*) to focus ◆ **fijarse** *v pron* **fijarse (en) 1** (*darse cuenta*) to see: *¿Te fijaste si estaban?* Did you see if they were there? **2** (*prestar atención*) to pay attention **(to** ***sth*****)**: *sin ~se en los detalles* without paying attention to detail **3** (*mirar*) to look **at** ***sth/sb***: *Se fijaba mucho en ti.* He was looking at you a lot. LOC *Ver* PROHIBIDO

fijo, -a ◆ *adj* **1** (*gen*) fixed: *Las patas están fijas al suelo.* The legs are fixed to the ground. **2** (*permanente*) permanent: *un puesto/contrato ~* a permanent post/contract ◆ *adv* definitely: *Aprobaré, ~.* I'll definitely pass.

fila *nf* **1** (*uno al lado de otro*) row: *Se sentaron en la primera/última ~.* They sat in the front/back row. **2** (*uno detrás de otro*) line: *Formad una ~.* Get in line. **3 filas** (*Mil, Pol*) ranks LOC **(en) fila india** (in) single file *Ver tb* APARCAR, ROMPER

filete *nm* **1** (*fino*) fillet: *~s de bacalao* cod fillets **2** (*grueso*) steak

filmar *vt* to film LOC *Ver* VÍDEO

filo *nm* cutting edge LOC *Ver* ARMA

filología *nf* philology LOC **filología hispánica, inglesa, etc** Spanish,

English, etc: *Soy licenciado en Filología Hispánica.* I've got a degree in Spanish.

filosofía *nf* philosophy [*pl* philosophies]

filósofo, -a *nm-nf* philosopher

filtrar ◆ *vt* to filter ◆ **filtrarse** *v pron* **1** (*gen*) to filter (in/out) (***through sth***): *La luz se filtraba por los resquicios.* Light was filtering in through the cracks. **2** (*líquido*) to leak (in/out) (***through sth***): *Se ha filtrado agua por la pared.* Water has leaked in through the wall.

filtro *nm* filter

fin *nm* **1** (*gen*) end: *a ~ de mes* at the end of the month ◊ *No es el ~ del mundo.* It's not the end of the world. **2** (*película, novela*) the end **3** (*finalidad*) purpose LOC **al/por fin** at last **al fin y al cabo** after all **en fin 1** (*bien*) well: *En ~, así es la vida.* Well, that's life. **2** (*en resumen*) in short **fin de semana** weekend: *Sólo nos vemos los ~es de semana.* We only see each other at weekends.

final ◆ *adj* final: *la decisión ~* the final decision ◆ *nm* **1** (*gen*) end: *a dos minutos del ~* two minutes from the end **2** (*novela, película*) ending: *un ~ feliz* a happy ending ◆ *nf* final: *la ~ de copa* the Cup Final LOC **a finales de...** at the end of...: *a ~es de año* at the end of the year *Ver tb* CUARTO, EXAMEN, OCTAVO, PUNTO, RECTA, RESULTADO

finalista *adj, nmf* finalist [*n*]: *Quedó ~ del torneo.* He reached the final. ◊ *los equipos ~s* the finalists

finca *nf* **1** (*casa en el campo*) country estate **2** (*terreno de cultivo*) (plot of) land

fingir *vt, vi* to pretend: *Seguro que está fingiendo.* He's probably just pretending. ◊ *Fingieron no vernos.* They pretended they hadn't seen us.

finlandés, -esa ◆ *adj, nm* Finnish: *hablar ~* to speak Finnish ◆ *nm-nf* Finn: *los finlandeses* the Finns

Finlandia *nf* Finland

fino, -a ◆ *adj* **1** (*delgado*) fine: *un lápiz ~* a fine pencil **2** (*dedos, talle*) slender **3** (*elegante*) posh (*coloq*): *¡Qué ~ te has vuelto!* You've become very posh! **4** (*educado*) polite **5** (*vista, oído*) keen ◆ *nm* (*vino*) dry 'fino' sherry LOC *Ver* SAL

firma *nf* **1** (*nombre*) signature: *Han recogido cien ~s.* They've collected a hundred signatures. **2** (*acto*) signing: *Hoy es la ~ del contrato.* The signing of the contract takes place today.

firmar *vt, vi* to sign: *Firme en la línea de puntos.* Sign on the dotted line.

firme *adj* firm: *un colchón ~* a firm mattress ◊ *Me mostré ~.* I stood firm. LOC **¡firmes!** attention! **ponerse firme** to stand to attention *Ver tb* TIERRA

fiscal ◆ *adj* tax [*n atrib*]: *los impuestos ~es* taxes ◆ *nmf* public prosecutor LOC *Ver* FRAUDE

fisgar *vt, vi ~* (**en**) to poke around **in *sth*** [*vi*]: *No me fisgues las cartas.* Don't poke around in my letters. ◊ *Alguien ha estado fisgando en mis cosas.* Somebody has been poking around in my things.

fisgón, -ona ◆ *adj* nosey ◆ *nm-nf* Nosey Parker

física *nf* physics [*sing*]

físico, -a ◆ *adj* physical ◆ *nm-nf* (*científico*) physicist ◆ *nm* (*aspecto*) appearance: *El ~ es muy importante.* Appearance is very important. LOC *Ver* EDUCACIÓN

flaco, -a *adj* **1** (*delgado*) thin, skinny (*coloq*) ☛ *Ver nota en* DELGADO **2** (*débil*) weak LOC *Ver* PUNTO

flamante *adj* **1** (*espléndido*) smart **2** (*nuevo*) brand-new

flamenco, -a ◆ *adj, nm* (*cante y baile*) flamenco ◆ *nm* (*ave*) flamingo [*pl* flamingos/flamingoes]

flan *nm* crème caramel LOC **estar como un flan** to be shaking like a leaf

flaquear *vi* to flag: *Me flaquean las fuerzas.* My strength is flagging.

flash *nm* flash

flato *nm* stitch: *No puedo correr más que me da el ~.* I can't run any further or I'll get a stitch.

flauta *nf* flute LOC *Ver* PITO

flautista *nmf* flautist

flecha *nf* arrow

flechazo *nm* love at first sight: *Fue un ~.* It was love at first sight.

fleco *nm* **flecos 1** (*adorno*) fringe: *una cazadora de cuero con ~s* a fringed leather jacket **2** (*borde deshilachado*) frayed edge

flemón *nm* abscess

flequillo *nm* fringe

flexible *adj* flexible

flojo, -a *adj* **1** (*poco apretado*) **(a)** (*gen*) loose: *un tornillo ~* a loose screw **(b)** (*goma, cuerda*) slack **2** (*sin fuerza*) weak: *un café ~* a weak coffee **3** (*sin calidad*) poor: *Tus deberes están bastante ~s.* Your homework is quite poor. LOC **estar flojo en algo** to be weak at/in sth: *Estoy muy ~ en historia.* I'm very weak at history.

flor *nf* **1** (*gen*) flower: *~es secas* dried flowers **2** (*árbol frutal, arbusto*) blossom [*gen incontable*]: *las ~es del almendro* almond blossom LOC **en flor** in bloom **la flor** (**y nata**) the crème de la crème **¡ni flores!** no idea!

flora *nf* flora

florecer *vi* **1** (*planta*) to flower **2** (*árbol frutal, arbusto*) to blossom **3** (*fig*) to flourish: *La industria está floreciendo.* Industry is flourishing.

florero *nm* vase

floristería *nf* florist's [*pl* florists]

flota *nf* fleet

flotador *nm* rubber ring

flotar *vi* to float: *El balón flotaba en el agua.* The ball was floating on the water.

flote LOC **a flote** afloat: *El barco/negocio sigue a ~.* The ship/business is still afloat. **sacar a flote 1** (*barco*) to refloat **2** (*negocio*) to put *a business* back on its feet **salir a flote** (*fig*) to pull through

fluido, -a ◆ *pp, adj* **1** (*circulación, diálogo*) free-flowing **2** (*lenguaje, estilo*) fluent ◆ *nm* fluid *Ver tb* FLUIR

fluir *vi* to flow

flúor *nm* **1** (*gas*) fluorine **2** (*dentífrico*) fluoride

fluorescente ◆ *adj* fluorescent ◆ *nm* fluorescent light

fluvial *adj* river [*n atrib*]: *el transporte ~* river transport

foca *nf* seal

foco *nm* **1** (*gen*) focus [*pl* focuses/foci]: *Eres el ~ de todas las miradas.* You're the focus of attention. **2** (*lámpara*) **(a)** (*gen*) spotlight: *Varios ~s iluminaban el monumento.* Several spotlights lit up the monument. **(b)** (*estadio*) floodlight

fogueo *nm* LOC **de fogueo** blank: *munición de ~* blank ammunition

folclore (*tb* **folklore**) *nm* folklore

folio *nm* sheet (of paper)

follaje *nm* foliage

folleto *nm* **1** (*librito*) **(a)** (*de publicidad*) brochure: *un ~ de viajes* a holiday brochure **(b)** (*de información, de instrucciones*) booklet **2** (*hoja*) leaflet: *Cogí un ~ con el horario.* I picked up a leaflet with the timetable in it.

follón *nm* **1** (*ruido*) racket: *¡Qué ~ arman los vecinos!* The neighbours are making a terrible racket! **2** (*desorden, confusión*) mess: *Me hice un ~ con los nombres.* I got into a real mess with their names. **3** (*problema*) trouble [*incontable*]: *No te metas en follones.* Don't get into trouble.

fomentar *vt* to promote

fomento *nm* promotion LOC **fomento de empleo** job creation

fondo *nm* **1** (*gen*) bottom: *llegar al ~ del asunto* to get to the bottom of things **2** (*mar, río*) bed **3** **(a)** (*calle, pasillo*) end: *Está al ~ del pasillo, a la derecha.* It's at the end of the corridor on the right. **(b)** (*habitación, escenario*) back: *al ~ del restaurante* at the back of the restaurant ◊ *la habitación del ~* the back room **4** (*bote*) kitty [*pl* kitties]: *poner/hacer un ~ (común)* to have a kitty **5 fondos** (*dinero*) funds: *recaudar ~s* to raise funds LOC **a fondo 1** (*con sustantivo*) thorough: *una revisión a ~* a thorough review **2** (*con verbo*) thoroughly: *Límpialo a ~.* Clean it thoroughly. **de fondo** (*Dep*) **1** (*Atletismo*) distance [*n atrib*]: *un corredor de ~* a distance runner **2** (*Esquí*) cross-country [*n atrib*]: *un esquiador de ~* a cross-country skier **en el fondo 1** (*a pesar de las apariencias*) deep down: *Dices que no, pero en el ~ sí que te importa.* You say you don't mind, but deep down you do. **2** (*en realidad*) basically: *En el ~ todos pensamos lo mismo.* We are basically in agreement. **sin fondo** bottomless *Ver tb* CHEQUE, MÚSICA

fontanero, -a *nm-nf* plumber

footing *nm* jogging: *hacer ~* to go jogging

forastero, -a *nm-nf* stranger

forcejear *vi* to struggle

forense *nmf* forensic scientist

forestal *adj* forest [*n atrib*]: *un guarda/incendio ~* a forest ranger/fire

forjar *vt* to forge LOC **forjarse ilusiones** to get your hopes up

forma *nf* **1** (*contorno*) shape: *en ~ de cruz* in the shape of a cross ◊ *La sala tiene ~ rectangular.* The room is rectangular. **2** (*modo*) way [*pl* ways]: *Si lo haces de esta ~ es más fácil.* It's easier if you do it this way. ◊ *Es su ~ de ser.* It's just the way he is. ◊ *¡Vaya ~ de conducir!* What a way to drive! LOC **de forma espontánea, indefinida, etc** spontaneously, indefinitely, etc **de todas formas** anyway **estar/ponerse en forma** to be/get fit *Ver tb* DICHO, MANTENER, PLENO

formación *nf* **1** (*gen*) formation: *la ~ de un gobierno* the formation of a government **2** (*educación*) education LOC **formación profesional** vocational training *Ver tb* INSTITUTO

formado, -a *pp, adj* LOC **estar formado por** to consist of *sth/sb Ver tb* FORMAR

formal *adj* **1** (*gen*) formal: *un noviazgo ~* a formal engagement **2** (*de fiar*) reliable **3** (*que se porta bien*) well behaved: *un niño muy ~* a very well behaved child

formar ◆ *vt* **1** (*crear*) to form: *~ un grupo* to form a group **2** (*educar*) to educate ◆ *vi* (*Mil*) to fall in: *¡A ~!* Fall in! ◆ **formarse** *v pron* **1** (*hacerse*) to form **2** (*educarse*) to train

fórmula *nf* formula [*pl* formulas/ formulae]

formulario *nm* form: *rellenar un ~* to fill in a form

forofo, -a *nm-nf* fan

forrado, -a *pp, adj* LOC **estar forrado** (*tener dinero*) to be rolling in it *Ver tb* FORRAR

forrar ◆ *vt* **1** (*el interior*) to line *sth* (***with sth***): *~ una caja de terciopelo* to line a box with velvet **2** (*el exterior*) to cover *sth* (***with sth***): *~ un libro con papel* to cover a book with paper ◆ **forrarse** *v pron* (*enriquecerse*) to make a packet: *Se han forrado vendiendo helados.* They've made a packet selling ice creams.

forro *nm* **1** (*interior*) lining: *poner un ~ a un abrigo* to put a lining in a coat **2** (*exterior*) cover

fortaleza *nf* **1** (*fuerza*) strength **2** (*fortificación*) fortress

fortuna *nf* **1** (*riqueza*) fortune **2** (*suerte*) fortune, luck (*más coloq*): *probar ~* to try your luck

forzado, -a *pp, adj* LOC *Ver* MARCHA, TRABAJO; *Ver tb* FORZAR

forzar *vt* to force

forzoso, -a *adj* LOC *Ver* ATERRIZAJE

fosa *nf* **1** (*hoyo*) ditch **2** (*sepultura*) grave

fosforescente *adj* phosphorescent LOC *Ver* ROTULADOR

fósforo *nm* **1** (*Quím*) phosphorus **2** (*cerilla*) match

fósil *nm* fossil

foso *nm* **1** (*hoyo*) ditch **2** (*de castillo*) moat

foto *nf* photo [*pl* photos]: *un álbum de ~s* a photograph album ◊ *Me hizo una ~.* He took my photo. LOC **foto de carné** passport photo **sacarse una foto** to have your photo taken *Ver tb* CÁMARA, CARRETE, MÁQUINA

fotocopia *nf* photocopy [*pl* photocopies]: *hacer/sacar una ~ de algo* to photocopy sth

fotocopiadora *nf* photocopier

fotocopiar *vt* to photocopy

fotogénico, -a *adj* photogenic

fotografía *nf* **1** (*actividad*) photography **2** (*foto*) photograph

fotografiar *vt* to photograph

fotográfico, -a *adj* LOC *Ver* CÁMARA

fotógrafo, -a *nm-nf* photographer

fotomatón *nm* photo booth

fracasado, -a *nm-nf* failure

fracasar *vi* **1** (*gen*) to fail **2** (*planes*) to fall through

fracaso *nm* failure

fracción *nf* **1** (*porción, Mat*) fraction **2** (*Pol*) faction

fractura *nf* fracture

fracturar(se) *vt, v pron* to fracture

frágil *adj* fragile

fragmento *nm* fragment

fraile *nm* monk

frambuesa *nf* raspberry [*pl* raspberries]

francamente *adv* (*muy*) really: *Es ~ difícil.* It's really hard.

francés, -esa ◆ *adj, nm* French: *hablar ~* to speak French ◆ *nm-nf* Frenchman/woman [*pl* Frenchmen/ women]: *los franceses* the French

Francia *nf* France

franco *nm* (*moneda*) franc

franco, -a *adj* **1** (*sincero*) frank **2** (*claro*) marked: *un ~ deterioro* a marked decline

franela *nf* flannel

franja *nf* strip

franquear *vt* (*carta, paquete*) to pay postage **on *sth***

franqueza *nf* frankness: *Hablemos con ~.* Let's be frank.

frasco *nm* **1** (*colonia, medicina*) bottle **2** (*conservas, mermelada*) jar

frase *nf* **1** (*oración*) sentence **2** (*locución*) phrase LOC **frase hecha** set phrase

fraternal (*tb* **fraterno, -a**) *adj* brotherly, fraternal (*más formal*): *el amor ~* brotherly love

fraude *nm* fraud LOC **fraude fiscal** tax evasion

fraudulento, -a *adj* fraudulent

frecuencia *nf* frequency [*pl* frequencies] LOC **con frecuencia** frequently, often (*más coloq*)

frecuentar *vt* **1** (*lugar*) to frequent **2** (*amigos*) to go around **with *sb***: *Ya no frecuento ese grupo de amigos.* I don't go around with that group of friends any more.

frecuente *adj* **1** (*reiterado*) frequent: *Tengo ~s ataques de asma.* I have frequent asthma attacks. **2** (*habitual*) common: *Es una práctica ~ en este país.* It is (a) common practice in this country.

fregadero *nm* sink

fregar ◆ *vt* to wash ◆ *vi* to do the washing-up LOC **fregar el suelo** to mop the floor **fregar los platos** to do the washing-up

fregona *nf* mop

freír(se) *vt, v pron* to fry

frenar *vi* to brake: *Frené de golpe.* I slammed on the brakes. LOC *Ver* SECO

frenazo *nm*: *Se oyó un ~.* There was a screech of brakes. LOC **dar un frenazo** to slam on the brakes

freno *nm* **1** (*vehículo*) brake: *Me fallaron los ~s.* My brakes failed. ◊ *poner/quitar el ~* to put on/release the brake(s) **2** (*reducción*) curb (**on *sth***): *un ~ a las exportaciones* a curb on exports LOC **freno de mano** handbrake

frente ◆ *nf* (*Anat*) forehead ◆ *nm* front: *un ~ frío* a cold front LOC **al frente** forward: *Di un paso al ~.* I took a step forward. **al frente de** in charge of *sth*: *Está al ~ de la empresa.* He's in charge of the company. **hacer frente a algo/algn** to stand up to sth/sb *Ver tb* DOS

fresa *nf* strawberry [*pl* strawberries]

fresca *nf* (*insolencia*) cheeky remark: *Me soltó una ~.* He made a cheeky remark to me.

fresco, -a ◆ *adj* **1** (*temperatura, ropa*) cool: *El día está algo ~.* It is rather cool today. ☛ *Ver nota en* FRÍO **2** (*comida*) fresh **3** (*noticia*) latest: *noticias frescas* the latest news ◆ *adj, nm-nf* (*persona*) cheeky so-and-so [*n*]: *El muy ~ me timó.* The cheeky so-and-so swindled me. LOC **hacer fresco** to be chilly: *Por la noche hace ~.* It's chilly at night. **tomar el fresco** to get some fresh air

fresno *nm* ash (tree)

fresón *nm* strawberry [*pl* strawberries]

frigorífico *nm* fridge, refrigerator (*más formal*)

frío, -a *adj, nm* cold: *Cierra la puerta, que entra ~.* Shut the door, you're letting the cold in.

> No se deben confundir las siguientes palabras: **cold** y **cool**, **hot** y **warm**. **Cold** indica una temperatura más baja que **cool** y muchas veces desagradable: *Ha sido un invierno muy frío.* It's been a terribly cold winter. **Cool** significa *fresco* más que frío: *Fuera hace calor, pero aquí se está fresquito.* It's hot outside but it's nice and cool in here. **Hot** describe una temperatura bastante más caliente que **warm**. **Warm** es más bien *cálido, templado* y muchas veces tiene connotaciones agradables. Compara los siguientes ejemplos: *No lo puedo beber, está muy caliente.* I can't drink it, it's too hot. ◊ *¡Qué calor hace aquí!* It's too hot here! ◊ *Siéntate al lado del fuego, pronto entrarás en calor.* Sit by the fire, you'll soon warm up.

LOC **coger frío** to catch cold **hacer frío** to be cold: *Hace mucho ~ en la calle.* It's very cold outside. ◊ *¡Hace un ~ que pela!* It's freezing! **pasar/tener frío** to be/feel cold: *Tengo ~ en las manos.* My hands are cold. *Ver tb* MORIR(SE), MUERTO, PELAR, SANGRE, TEMBLAR, TIESO

friolero, -a *adj, nm-nf*: *Soy muy ~.* I feel the cold a lot.

frito, -a *pp, adj* fried LOC **estar frito 1** (*dormido*) to be fast asleep **2** (*harto*) to be fed up **3** (*muerto*) to be a goner **quedarse frito** to doze off *Ver tb* HUEVO, PATATA; *Ver tb* FREÍR(SE)

frondoso, -a *adj* leafy

frontal *adj* **1** (*ataque*) frontal **2** (*choque, enfrentamiento*) head-on

frontera *nf* border, frontier (*más formal*): *pasar la ~* to cross the border ◊ *en la ~ francesa* on the French border ☛ *Ver nota en* BORDER

fronterizo, -a *adj* **1** (*gen*) border [*n atrib*]: *región fronteriza* border area **2** (*limítrofe*) neighbouring: *dos países ~s* two neighbouring countries

frontón *nm* **1** (*juego*) pelota **2** (*cancha*) pelota court

frotar(se) *vt, v pron* to rub LOC **frotarse las manos** to rub your hands together

fruncir *vt* (*Costura*) to gather LOC **fruncir el ceño** to frown

frustración *nf* frustration

fruta *nf* fruit [*gen incontable*]: *¿Quieres ~?* Do you want some fruit? ◊ *una pieza de ~* a piece of fruit LOC *Ver* MACEDONIA

frutal *adj* fruit [*n atrib*]: *un árbol ~* a fruit tree

frutería *nf* greengrocer's [*pl* greengrocers]

frutero, -a ◆ *nm-nf* greengrocer ◆ *nm* fruit bowl

fruto *nm* fruit LOC **frutos secos 1** (*de cáscara dura*) nuts **2** (*fruto desecado*) dried fruit [*incontable, v sing*]

fuego *nm* **1** (*gen*) fire: *encender el ~* to light the fire **2** (*para cigarro*) light: *¿Me das ~?* Have you got a light? LOC **a fuego lento/vivo** over a low/high heat **fuegos artificiales** fireworks *Ver tb* ALTO, ARMA, COCER, PRENDER

fuel (*tb* **fuel-oil**) *nm* oil

fuente *nf* **1** (*manantial*) spring **2** (*en una plaza, en un jardín*) fountain **3** (*bandeja*) dish: *una ~ de carne* a dish of meat **4** (*origen*) source: *~s cercanas al gobierno* sources close to the government

fuera ◆ *adv* **1** ~ (**de**) outside: *Se oían ruidos ~.* You could hear noises outside. ◊ *~ de España* outside Spain ◊ *Hay grietas por ~.* There are cracks on the outside. **2** (*no en casa*) out: *cenar ~* to eat out ◊ *Se pasan todo el día ~.* They're out all day. **3** (*de viaje*) away: *Está ~ en viaje de negocios.* He's away on business. **4** ~ **de** (*fig*) out **of *sth***: *~ de peligro/de lo normal* out of danger/the ordinary ◊ *Mantener ~ del alcance de los niños.* Keep out of reach of children. ◆ **¡fuera!** *interj* get out! LOC **dejar a algn fuera de combate** to knock sb out **estar fuera de combate 1** (*gen*) to be out of action **2** (*Boxeo*) to be knocked out **fuera (de) bromas** joking apart **fuera de juego** offside **fuera de sí** beside himself, herself, etc **fuera de tono** inappropriate *Ver tb* AHÍ, ALLÁ, ALLÍ, CONTROL

fuerte ◆ *adj* **1** (*gen*) strong: *un queso/olor muy ~* a very strong cheese/smell **2** (*lluvia, nevada, tráfico, pesado*) heavy: *un ~ ritmo de trabajo* a heavy work schedule **3** (*dolor, crisis, descenso*) severe **4** (*abrazo, comida*) big: *un desayuno ~* a big breakfast ◆ *adv* **1** (*con fuerza, intensamente*) hard: *tirar ~ de una cuerda* to pull a rope hard **2** (*firmemente*) tight: *¡Agárrate ~!* Hold on tight! **3** (*sonido*) loud: *No hables tan ~.* Don't talk so loud. ◊ *Ponlo más ~.* Turn it up. ◆ *nm* (*fortaleza*) fort LOC *Ver* ABRAZO, CAJA

fuerza *nf* **1** (*potencia, Fís, Mil, Pol*) force: *la ~ de la gravedad* the force of gravity ◊ *las ~s armadas* the armed forces **2** (*energía física*) strength [*incontable*]: *recobrar las ~s* to get your strength back ◊ *No tengo ~s para continuar.* I don't have the strength to carry on. LOC **a la fuerza 1** (*forzando*) by force: *Los sacaron a la ~.* They removed them by force. **2** (*por necesidad*): *Tengo que hacerlo a la ~.* I just have to do it. **fuerza de voluntad** will-power **fuerzas aéreas** air force [*sing*] *Ver tb* CAMISA

fuga *nf* **1** (*huida*) flight: *emprender la ~* to take flight **2** (*gas, agua*) leak

fugarse *v pron* **1** (*de un país*) to flee [*vt*]: *Se han fugado del país.* They have fled the country. **2** (*de la cárcel*) to escape (***from sth***) **3** (*de casa, del colegio*) to run away (***from sth***)

fugaz *adj* fleeting LOC *Ver* ESTRELLA

fugitivo, -a *nm-nf* fugitive

fulano, -a *nm-nf* so-and-so [*pl* so-and-so's]: *Imagínate que viene ~...* Just suppose so-and-so comes... LOC **(señor/don) Fulano de Tal** Mr So-and-so

fulminante *adj* **1** (*instantáneo*) immediate: *un éxito ~* an immediate success **2** (*mirada*) withering **3** (*muerte*) sudden

fumador, ~a *nm-nf* smoker LOC **¿fumador o no fumador?** (*en transportes, en restaurantes*) smoking or non-smoking?

fumar ◆ *vt, vi* to smoke: *~ en pipa* to smoke a pipe ◊ *Deberías dejar de ~.* You should give up smoking. ◆ **fumarse** *v pron* (*clase*) to skip LOC *Ver* PROHIBIDO, ROGAR

función *nf* **1** (*gen*) function: *Nuestra ~ es informar.* Our function is to inform. **2** (*Teat*) performance: *una ~ de gala* a gala performance

funcionamiento *nm* operation: *poner algo en ~* to put sth into operation

funcionar *vi* **1** (*gen*) to work: *La alarma no funciona.* The alarm doesn't work. ◊ *¿Cómo funciona?* How does it work? **2** ~ (**con**) to run (**on *sth***): *Este coche funciona con gasoil.* This car runs on diesel. LOC **no funciona** (*en un cartel*) out of order

funcionario, -a *nm-nf* civil servant

funda *nf* **1** (*estuche*) case: *una ~ de gafas* a glasses case **2** (*disco*) sleeve **3** (*almohada*) pillowcase **4** (*edredón, cojín*) cover

fundación *nf* (*institución*) foundation

fundador, ~a *adj, nm-nf* founder [*n*]: *los miembros ~es* the founder members

fundamental *adj* fundamental

fundar *vt* to found

fundir(se) *vt, v pron* **1** (*gen*) to melt: *~ queso* to melt cheese **2** (*fusible*) to blow: *Se fundieron los plomos.* The fuses blew.

fúnebre *adj* **1** (*para un funeral*) funeral [*n atrib*]: *la marcha ~* the funeral march **2** (*triste*) mournful LOC *Ver* COCHE, POMPA

funeral (*tb* **funerales**) *nm* funeral [*sing*]: *los ~es de un vecino* a neighbour's funeral

funeraria *nf* undertaker's [*pl* undertakers]

furgoneta *nf* van

furia *nf* fury LOC **con furia** furiously **estar hecho una furia** to be in a rage **ponerse hecho una furia** to fly into a rage

furioso, -a *adj* furious: *Estaba ~ con ella.* I was furious with her.

furtivo, -a *adj* furtive LOC **cazador/pescador furtivo** poacher **caza/pesca furtiva** poaching

fusible *nm* fuse: *Han saltado los ~s.* The fuses have blown.

fusil *nm* rifle

fusión *nf* **1** (*Fís*) fusion: *la ~ nuclear* nuclear fusion **2** (*hielo, metales*) melting **3** (*empresas, partidos políticos*) merger LOC *Ver* PUNTO

fusta *nf* riding crop

futbito *nm* five-a-side football

fútbol *nm* football, soccer (*más coloq*)

> En Estados Unidos sólo se dice **soccer**, para diferenciarlo del fútbol americano.

futbolín *nm* **1** (*juego*) table football **2** **futbolines** (*local*) amusement arcade [*sing*]

futbolista *nmf* footballer

futuro, -a *adj, nm* future

Gg

gabardina *nf* raincoat

gabinete *nm* **1** (*despacho*) office **2** (*Pol*) Cabinet [*v sing o pl*] LOC **gabinete de prensa** press office

gacela *nf* gazelle

gafar *vt* to put a jinx **on *sth/sb***

gafas *nf* **1** (*gen*) glasses, spectacles (*más formal*) (*abrev* specs): *un chico rubio, con ~* a fair boy with glasses ◊ *No le vi porque no llevaba ~.* I couldn't see him because I didn't have my glasses on. ◊ *Me tienen que poner ~.* I need glasses. **2** (*motociclista, esquiador, submarinista*) goggles LOC **gafas de culo de vaso** pebble glasses **gafas de sol** sunglasses

gafe *nmf* jinx LOC **ser/tener gafe** to be jinxed: *Es tan ~ que todo le sale mal.* He seems to be jinxed; nothing turns out right for him.

gaita *nf* **1** (*Mús*) bagpipe(s) [*se usa mucho en plural*]: *tocar la ~* to play the bagpipes **2** (*inconveniente*) pain: *¡Vaya ~!* What a pain! **3** (*rollo*): *¡Déjate de ~s!* Stop messing about!

gaitero, -a *nm-nf* piper

gajes *nm* LOC **ser gajes del oficio** to be part and parcel of the job

gajo *nm* segment

gala *nf* **1** (*recepción, ceremonia, actuación*) gala: *Asistiremos a la ~ inaugural.* We'll attend the gala opening. ◊ *una cena de ~* a gala dinner **2** **galas** best clothes: *Llevaré mis mejores ~s.* I'll wear my best clothes. LOC **ir/vestir de gala** to be dressed up

galáctico, -a *adj* galactic

galante *adj* gallant

galápago *nm* turtle

galardón *nm* award

galardonado, -a *pp, adj* prize-winning: *un autor/libro ~* a prize-winning author/book *Ver tb* GALARDONAR

galardonar *vt* to award *sb* a prize

galaxia *nf* galaxy [*pl* galaxies]

galería *nf* **1** (*Arte, Teat*) gallery [*pl* galleries]: *una ~ de arte* an art gallery ☛ *Ver nota en* MUSEUM **2** (*balcón*) balcony [*pl* balconies] LOC **galerías (comerciales)** shopping centre [*sing*]

Gales *nm* Wales

galés, -esa ◆ *adj, nm* Welsh: *hablar ~* to speak Welsh ◆ *nm-nf* Welshman/woman [*pl* Welshmen/women]: *los galeses* the Welsh

galgo *nm* greyhound LOC *Ver* COMO

gallego *nm* (*lengua*) Galician

galleta *nf* biscuit

gallina ◆ *nf* hen ◆ *adj, nmf* (*cobarde*) chicken [*n*]: *¡No seas tan ~!* Don't be such a chicken! LOC **la gallina/gallinita ciega** blind man's buff *Ver tb* CARNE, PIEL

gallinero *nm* **1** (*para gallinas*) hen house **2** (*griterío*) madhouse **3 el gallinero** (*Teat*) the gods [*pl*] (*coloq*), the gallery

gallo *nm* **1** (*ave*) cock **2** (*nota desafinada*) wrong note: *Le salió un ~.* He hit the wrong note. LOC *Ver* MISA, PATA

galón[1] *nm* (*uniforme*) stripe

galón[2] *nm* (*medida*) gallon

galopar *vi* to gallop: *salir a ~* to go for a gallop

galope *nm* gallop LOC **al galope**: *El caballo se puso al ~.* The horse started to gallop. ◊ *Se fueron al ~.* They galloped off.

gama *nf* range: *una amplia ~ de colores* a wide range of colours

gamba *nf* prawn

gamberrada *nf* LOC **hacer gamberradas** to make trouble

gamberrismo *nm* hooliganism

gamberro, -a *nm-nf* hooligan LOC **hacer el gamberro** to make trouble

gana *nf* LOC **como me da la gana** however I, you, etc want: *Lo haré como me dé la ~.* I'll do it however I want. **con/sin ganas** enthusiastically/half-heartedly **darle a algn la (real) gana** to want *to do sth*: *Lo hago por que me da la ~.* I'm doing it because I want to. **de buena/mala gana** willingly/reluctantly: *Lo hizo de mala ~.* She did it reluctantly. **hacer lo que me da la gana** to do as I, you, etc please: *Haz lo que te dé la ~.* Do what you like. **¡las ganas!** you wish! **tener/sentir ganas (de)** to feel like *sth/doing sth*: *Tengo ~s de comer algo.* I feel like having something to eat. *Ver tb* ENTRAR, QUITAR

ganadería *nf* **1** (*actividad*) livestock farming **2** (*conjunto de ganado*) livestock

ganadero, -a *nm-nf* livestock farmer

ganado *nm* livestock LOC **ganado caballar/equino** horses [*pl*] **ganado lanar/ovino** sheep [*pl*] **ganado porcino** pigs [*pl*] **ganado (vacuno)** cattle [*pl*]

ganador, ~a ◆ *adj* winning ◆ *nm-nf* winner

ganancia *nf* profit LOC *Ver* PÉRDIDA

ganar ◆ *vt* **1** (*sueldo, sustento*) to earn: *Este mes he ganado poco.* I didn't earn much this month. ◊ *~se la vida* to earn your living **2** (*premio, partido, guerra*) to win: *~ la lotería* to win the lottery ◊ *¿Quién ha ganado el partido?* Who won the match? **3** (*a un contrincante*) to beat: *Inglaterra ganó a Alemania.* England beat Germany. **4** (*conseguir*) to gain (***by/from sth/doing sth***): *¿Qué gano yo con decírtelo?* What do I gain by telling you? ◆ **ganarse** *v pron* **1** (*dinero, respeto*) to earn: *Se ha ganado el respeto de todos.* He has earned everybody's respect. **2** (*castigo, recompensa*) to deserve: *Te has ganado unas buenas vacaciones.* You deserve a holiday. LOC **ganarse el pan** to earn your living **ganar tiempo** to save time **salir ganando** to do well (*out of sth*): *He salido ganando con la reorganización.* I've done well out of the reorganization.

gancho *nm* **1** (*gen*) hook **2** (*cebo*) bait: *utilizar a algn como ~* to use sb as bait

gandul, ~a ◆ *adj* lazy ◆ *nm-nf* lazybones [*pl* lazybones]

gandulear *vi* to laze around

ganga *nf* bargain

gangrena *nf* gangrene

gángster *nm* gangster

ganso, -a *nm-nf* goose [*pl* geese]

> Si queremos especificar que se trata de un ganso macho, diremos **gander**.

garabatear *vt, vi* **1** (*dibujar*) to doodle **2** (*escribir*) to scribble

garabato *nm* **1** (*dibujo*) doodle **2** (*escritura*) scribble

garaje *nm* garage

garantía *nf* guarantee

garantizar *vt* **1** (*gen*) to guarantee: *Garantizamos la calidad del producto.* We guarantee the quality of the product. **2** (*asegurar*) to assure: *Vendrán, te lo garantizo.* They'll come, I assure you.

garbanzo *nm* chickpea

garbeo *nm* LOC **dar(se) un garbeo** to go for a stroll

garbo *nm* LOC **andar con garbo** to walk gracefully **tener garbo** to be graceful

garfio *nm* hook

garganta *nf* **1** (*Anat*) throat: *Me duele la ~.* I've got a sore throat. **2** (*Geog*) gorge LOC *Ver* NUDO

gargantilla *nf* necklace

gárgaras *nf* LOC **hacer gárgaras** to gargle

garita *nf* **1** (*centinela*) sentry box **2** (*portería*) porter's lodge

garra *nf* **1** (*animal*) claw **2** (*ave de rapiña*) talon **3** (*atractivo*): *Esta canción tiene mucha ~.* That song really has something. ◊ *Es una persona con ~.* He's a very attractive person.

garrafa *nf* carafe

garrafal *adj* monumental

garrapata *nf* tick

garrote *nm* **1** (*gen*) stick **2** (*tortura*) garrotte

gas *nm* **1** (*gen*) gas: *Huele a ~.* It smells of gas. **2 gases** (*Med*) wind [*incontable, v sing*]: *El bebé tiene ~es.* The baby's got wind. LOC **gases lacrimógenos** tear gas [*incontable, v sing*] *Ver tb* AGUA

gasa *nf* **1** (*tejido*) gauze **2** (*vendaje*) bandage

gaseosa *nf* (fizzy) lemonade

gaseoso, -a *adj* **1** (*Quím*) gaseous **2** (*bebida*) fizzy

gasóleo (*tb* **gas-oil**, **gasoil**) *nm* diesel

gasolina *nf* petrol LOC **gasolina normal** three-star petrol **gasolina súper** four-star petrol **gasolina sin plomo** unleaded petrol *Ver tb* INDICADOR

gasolinera *nf* petrol station

gastado, -a *pp, adj* (*desgastado*) worn out *Ver tb* GASTAR

gastar *vt* **1** (*dinero*) to spend *sth* (**on** ***sth/sb***) **2** (*consumir*) to use: *~ menos electricidad* to use less electricity **3** (*agotar*) to use *sth* up: *Me has gastado toda la colonia.* You've used up all my cologne. **4** (*talla*) to take: *~ la talla cuarenta de pantalones* to take size forty trousers LOC **gastar una broma** to play a joke *on sb*

gasto *nm* **1** (*dinero*) expense: *No gano ni para ~s.* I don't earn enough to cover my expenses. **2** (*agua, energía, gasolina*) consumption LOC **gastos de envío** postage and packing [*sing*]

gatear *vi* to crawl

gatillo *nm* trigger: *apretar el ~* to press the trigger

gato, -a ◆ *nm-nf* cat

Tom-cat o **tom** es un gato macho, **kittens** son los gatitos. Los gatos ronronean **(purr)** y hacen miau **(miaow)**.

◆ *nm* (*coche*) jack LOC **andar a gatas** to crawl **dar gato por liebre** to take *sb* in **el Gato con Botas** Puss in Boots **gato siamés** Siamese *Ver tb* PERRO

gaviota *nf* seagull

gay *adj, nm* gay

gel *nm* gel LOC **gel de baño/ducha** shower gel

gelatina *nf* **1** (*sustancia*) gelatine **2** (*Cocina*) jelly [*pl* jellies]

gemelo, -a ◆ *adj, nm-nf* twin [*n*]: *hermanas gemelas* twin sisters ◆ **gemelos** *nm* **1** (*anteojos*) binoculars **2** (*camisa*) cuff links

gemido *nm* **1** (*persona*) groan: *Se podían oír los ~s del enfermo.* You could hear the sick man groaning. **2** (*animal*) whine: *los ~s del perro* the whining of the dog

géminis (*tb* **Géminis**) *nm, nmf* (*Astrología*) Gemini ☛ *Ver ejemplos en* AQUARIUS

gemir *vi* **1** (*persona*) to groan **2** (*animal*) to whine

gene (*tb* **gen**) *nm* gene

genealógico, -a *adj* genealogical LOC *Ver* ÁRBOL

generación *nf* generation

general[1] *adj* general LOC **en general/por lo general** as a general rule *Ver tb* CARRETERA, CUARTEL, ELECCIÓN, ENSAYO

general[2] *nmf* (*Mil*) general

generalizar *vt, vi* to generalize: *No se puede ~.* You can't generalize.

generar *vt* to generate: *~ energía* to generate energy

género *nm* **1** (*tipo*) kind: *problemas de ese ~* problems of that kind **2** (*Arte, Liter*) genre **3** (*Gram*) gender **4** (*tela*) material ☛ *Ver nota en* TELA LOC **género policiaco** crime writing

generoso, -a *adj* generous: *Es muy ~ con sus amigos.* He is very generous to his friends.

genético, -a ◆ *adj* genetic ◆ **genética** *nf* genetics [*sing*]

genial *adj* brilliant: *una idea/un pianista ~* a brilliant idea/pianist

genio *nm* **1** ~ (**con/para**) (*lumbrera*) genius [*pl* geniuses] (**at** ***sth/doing sth***): *Eres un ~ haciendo arreglos.* You're a genius at doing repairs. **2** (*mal humor*) temper: *¡Qué ~ tienes!* What a temper you've got! LOC **estar de mal genio** to be in a bad mood **tener mal genio** to be bad-tempered

genital ◆ *adj* genital ◆ **genitales** *nm* genitals

gente *nf* people [*pl*]: *Había mucha ~.* There were a lot of people. ◊ *La ~ lloraba de alegría.* People were crying with joy. LOC **gente bien** well-off people **gente normal y corriente** ordinary people *Ver tb* ABARROTADO

geografía *nf* geography

geográfico, -a *adj* geographical

geología *nf* geology

geológico, -a *adj* geological

geometría *nf* geometry

geométrico, -a *adj* geometric(al)

geranio *nm* geranium

gerente *nmf* manager LOC *Ver* DIRECTOR

germen *nm* germ

germinar *vi* to germinate

gesticular *vi* **1** (*con las manos*) to gesticulate **2** (*con la cara*) to pull a face, to grimace (*formal*)

gesto *nm* **1** (*gen*) gesture: *un ~ simbólico* a symbolic gesture ◊ *comunicarse/hablar por ~s* to communicate by gesture **2** (*cara*) expression: *con ~ pensativo* with a thoughtful expression LOC **hacer un gesto/gestos 1** (*con la mano*) to signal (*to sb*): *Me hizo un ~ para que entrara.* He signalled to me to come in. **2** (*con la cara*) to pull a face/faces (*at sb*)

gigante ◆ *adj* **1** (*gen*) gigantic **2** (*Bot*) giant [*n atrib*]: *un olmo ~* a giant elm ◆ **gigante, -a** *nm-nf* giant [*fem* giantess] LOC **gigantes y cabezudos**: *¿Vienes a los ~s y cabezudos?* Are you coming to the carnival?

gigantesco, -a *adj* enormous

gimnasia *nf* **1** (*gen*) gymnastics [*sing*]: *el campeonato de ~ deportiva* the gymnastics championships **2** (*educación física*) physical education (*abrev* PE): *un profesor de ~* a PE teacher LOC **hacer gimnasia** to exercise, to work out (*más coloq*)

gimnasio *nm* gymnasium, gym (*más coloq*)

ginebra *nf* gin

gira *nf* tour LOC **estar/ir de gira** to be/go on tour

girar *vt, vi* to turn: *~ el volante hacia la derecha* to turn the steering wheel to the right LOC **girar alrededor de algo/algn** to revolve around sth/sb: *La Tierra gira alrededor del Sol.* The earth revolves around the sun.

girasol *nm* sunflower

giratorio, -a *adj* LOC *Ver* PUERTA

giro *nm* LOC **giro bancario** banker's draft **giro postal** postal order

gitano, -a *adj, nm-nf* gypsy [*n*] [*pl* gypsies] LOC *Ver* BRAZO

glacial *adj* **1** (*viento*) icy **2** (*temperatura*) freezing **3** (*periodo, zona*) glacial

glaciar *nm* glacier LOC **época/periodo glaciar** Ice Age

glándula *nf* gland

globo *nm* balloon: *una excursión en ~* a balloon trip LOC **el globo terráqueo** the globe

gloria *nf* **1** (*gen*) glory: *fama y ~* fame and glory **2** (*persona célebre*) great name: *las viejas ~s del deporte* the great sporting names of the past LOC **huele/sabe a gloria** it smells/tastes delicious

glotón, -ona ◆ *adj* greedy ◆ *nm-nf* glutton

glucosa *nf* glucose

gobernador, ~a *nm-nf* governor

gobernante ◆ *adj* governing ◆ *nmf* leader

gobernar *vt* **1** (*país*) to govern **2** (*barco*) to steer

gobierno *nm* government [*v sing o pl*]: *~ autónomo/central* regional/central government

gol *nm* goal: *marcar/meter un ~* to score a goal LOC **el gol del empate** the equalizer

golear *vt, vi*: *Alemania goleó a Holanda por cinco a cero.* Germany thrashed Holland five nil.

golf *nm* golf LOC *Ver* CAMPO

golfo[1] *nm* gulf: *el ~ Pérsico* the Persian Gulf

golfo[2] ◆ *nm* (*sinvergüenza*) scoundrel ◆ **golfa** *nf* tart

golondrina *nf* swallow

golosina *nf* sweet

goloso, -a *adj, nm-nf*: *ser muy/un ~* to have a sweet tooth ◊ *la gente golosa* people with a sweet tooth

golpe *nm* **1** (*gen*) blow: *un buen ~ en la cabeza* a severe blow to the head ◊ *Su muerte fue un duro ~ para nosotros.* Her death came as a heavy blow. ◊ *Lo mataron a ~s.* They beat him to death. **2** (*accidente*): *Me he dado un ~ en la cabeza.* I've banged my head. ◊ *No corras o nos daremos un ~.* Slow down or we'll have an accident. **3** (*moratón*) bruise **4** (*para llamar la atención*) knock: *Oí un ~ en la puerta.* I heard a knock on the door. ◊ *Di unos ~s en la puerta a ver si había alguien.* I knocked on the door to see if anybody was in. **5** (*Dep*) stroke LOC **de golpe (y porrazo)** out of the blue: *Hombre, si se lo dices de ~ y porrazo...* Well, if you tell him out of the blue... **de (un) golpe** in one go **golpe de estado** coup **no dar (ni) golpe** to be bone idle **tener buenos golpes** to be very funny **un golpe bajo**: *Eso fue un ~ bajo.* That was below the belt. *Ver tb* ATIZAR, CERRAR, LIAR

golpear *vt* **1** (*gen*) to bang: *Esa puerta golpea la pared.* That door is banging against the wall. **2** (*repetidamente*) to beat (**against/on** ***sth***): *El granizo golpeaba los cristales.* The hail was beating against the windows. ◊ *Golpeaban los tambores con fuerza.* They were beating the drums.

goma *nf* **1** (*de borrar, caucho*) rubber **2** (*banda elástica*) elastic band

gomina *nf* (hair) gel

gordo, -a ◆ *adj* **1** (*persona, animal*) fat **2** (*grueso*) thick **3** (*grave*) serious: *un error ~* a serious mistake ◆ *nm-nf* fat man/woman [*pl* fat men/women] ◆ *nm* (*lotería*) first prize LOC **caer gordo**: *Me cae muy ~.* I can't stand him. *Ver tb* DEDO, PEZ, SAL, SUDAR, VISTA

gorila *nm* **1** (*animal*) gorilla **2** (*guardaespaldas*) bodyguard

gorra *nf* cap LOC **de gorra** (*gratis*) free: *A ver si entramos de ~.* Let's see if we can get in free.

gorrión *nm* sparrow

gorro *nm* hat: *un ~ de lana/de cocinero* a woolly/chef's hat LOC **estar hasta el gorro** to be fed up to the back teeth *with sth/sb* **gorro de baño 1** (*para piscina*) swimming cap **2** (*para ducha*) shower cap

gorrón, -ona *nm-nf* scrounger

gota *nf* drop LOC **ser como dos gotas de agua** to be as like as two peas in a pod **ser la gota que colma el vaso** to be the last straw *Ver tb* SUDAR

gotear *vi* **1** (*gen*) to drip: *Ese grifo gotea.* That tap's dripping. **2** (*tubería*) to leak

gotera *nf* leak: *Cada vez que llueve tenemos ~s.* The roof leaks every time it rains.

gótico, -a *adj, nm* Gothic

gozar *vi* ~ (**con/de**) to enjoy ***sth/doing sth***: *Gozan fastidiando a la gente.* They enjoy annoying people. ◊ *~ de buena salud* to enjoy good health

grabación *nf* recording

grabado *nm* **1** (*gen*) engraving **2** (*en un libro*) illustration

grabadora *nf* tape recorder

grabar *vt* **1** (*sonido, imagen*) to record **2** (*metal, piedra*) to engrave LOC *Ver* VÍDEO

gracia *nf* **1** (*encanto, simpatía*) charm: *No es guapa pero tiene ~.* She's not pretty but there's something about her all the same. **2** (*elegancia, Relig*) grace **3 gracias** witty remarks: *Con sus ~s nos hizo reír.* She made us laugh with her witty remarks. LOC **dar las gracias** to thank *sb* (**for** ***sth/doing sth***): *sin darme las ~s* without thanking me **¡gracias!** thanks! (*coloq*) thank you!: *muchas ~s* thank you very much **gracias a...** thanks to *sth/sb*: *~s a ti, me han dado el puesto.* Thanks to you, I got the job. **hacer gracia** to amuse: *Me hace ~ su forma de hablar.* The way he talks amuses me. **¡qué gracia!** how funny! **tener gracia** to be funny: *Tus chistes no tienen ~.* Your jokes aren't funny. ◊ *No tiene ~ ¿sabes?* It's not funny, you know.

gracioso, -a *adj* funny, amusing (*formal*): *Ese chiste no me parece ~.* I don't find that joke very funny. LOC **hacerse el gracioso** to play the clown

grada *nf* stand: *Las ~s estaban llenas.* The stands were full.

grado *nm* **1** (*gen*) degree: *Estamos a dos ~s bajo cero.* It's two degrees below zero. ◊ *quemaduras de tercer ~* third-degree burns **2 grados** (*alcohol*): *Este vino tiene 12 ~s.* The alcoholic content of this wine is 12%. ◊ *Esta cerveza tiene muchos ~s.* This beer is very strong.

graduar ◆ *vt* (*regular*) to adjust: *Gradúa la temperatura, por favor.* Please adjust the temperature. ◆ **graduarse** *v pron* to graduate: *Se graduó en Derecho el año pasado.* She graduated in law last year. LOC **graduarse la vista** to have your eyes tested

gráfico, -a ◆ *adj* graphic ◆ **gráfico** *nm* (*tb* **gráfica** *nf*) graph LOC *Ver* REPORTERO

gramática *nf* grammar

gramo *nm* gram(me) (*abrev* g) ☛ *Ver* Apéndice 1.

gran *adj Ver* GRANDE

granate *adj, nm* maroon ☛ *Ver ejemplos en* AMARILLO

Gran Bretaña *nf* Great Britain (*abrev* GB)

grande *adj* **1** (*tamaño*) large, big (*más coloq*): *una casa/ciudad* ~ a big house/ city ◊ *¿~ o pequeño?* Large or small? ☛ *Ver nota en* BIG **2** (*fig*) big: *un gran problema* a big problem **3** (*número, cantidad*) large: *una gran cantidad de arena* a large amount of sand ◊ *una gran cantidad de gente* a large number of people **4** (*importante, notable*) great: *un gran músico* a great musician LOC **a grandes rasgos** in general terms **gran danés** Great Dane **grandes almacenes** department store [*sing*] **(la/una) gran parte de** most of: *Una gran parte de la audiencia eran niños.* Most of the audience were children. **pasarlo en grande** to have a great time *Ver tb* DIMENSIÓN, MANILLA, POTENCIA

granel LOC **a granel 1** (*vino*) from the cask **2** (*sin envasar*) loose: *bombones a* ~ loose chocolates

granero *nm* barn

granito *nm* granite

granizada *nf* hailstorm

granizado *nm* drink with crushed ice

granizar *v imp* to hail: *Anoche granizó.* It hailed last night.

granizo *nm* hail

granja *nf* farm

granjero, -a *nm-nf* farmer

grano *nm* **1** (*gen*) grain: *un ~ de arena* a grain of sand **2** (*semilla*) seed **3** (*café*) bean **4** (*en la piel*) spot: *Me han salido ~s.* I've come out in spots. LOC **ir al grano** to get to the point

grapa *nf* **1** (*para papel*) staple **2** (*Med*) stitch

grapadora *nf* stapler

grasa *nf* **1** (*gen*) fat: *Fríe las tortas con un poco de ~.* Fry the pancakes in a little fat. **2** (*suciedad*) grease LOC *Ver* UNTAR

grasiento, -a *adj* greasy

graso, -a *adj* (*cutis, pelo, comida*) greasy: *un champú para pelo ~* a shampoo for greasy hair

gratis *adj, adv* free: *La bebida era ~.* The drinks were free. ◊ *Los jubilados viajan ~.* Pensioners travel free. ◊ *trabajar ~* to work for nothing

grato, -a *adj* **1** (*agradable*) pleasant: *una grata sorpresa* a pleasant surprise **2** (*placentero*) pleasing: *~ al oído* pleasing to the ear

gratuito, -a *adj* free LOC *Ver* ENTRADA

grava *nf* gravel

grave *adj* **1** (*gen*) serious: *un problema/ una enfermedad ~* a serious problem/ illness **2** (*solemne*) solemn: *expresión ~* solemn expression **3** (*sonido, nota*) low: *El bajo produce sonidos ~s.* The bass guitar produces low notes. **4** (*voz*) deep

gravedad *nf* **1** (*Fís*) gravity **2** (*importancia*) seriousness LOC **de gravedad** seriously: *Está herido de ~.* He's seriously injured.

gravemente *adv* seriously

graznar *vi* **1** (*cuervo*) to caw **2** (*pato*) to quack

Grecia *nf* Greece

grelos *nm* turnip shoots

gremio *nm* **1** (*oficio*) trade **2** (*artesanos, artistas*) guild

griego, -a ◆ *adj, nm* Greek: *hablar ~* to speak Greek ◆ *nm-nf* Greek man/ woman [*pl* Greek men/women]: *los ~s* the Greeks

grieta *nf* crack

grifo *nm* tap: *abrir/cerrar el ~* to turn the tap on/off LOC *Ver* AGUA, BEBER

grillo *nm* cricket

grima *nf* LOC **dar grima** to set your teeth on edge

gripe *nf* flu [*incontable*]: *Tengo ~.* I've got (the) flu.

gris ◆ *adj* **1** (*color*) grey ☛ *Ver ejemplos en* AMARILLO **2** (*tiempo*) dull: *Hace un día ~.* It's a dull day. ◆ *nm* grey

gritar *vt, vi* to shout (**at sb**): *El profesor nos gritó para que nos calláramos.* The teacher shouted at us to be quiet. ◊ *Gritaron pidiendo ayuda.* They shouted for help. ☛ *Ver nota en* SHOUT LOC **gritar de dolor** to cry out in pain

grito *nm* **1** (*gen*) shout: *Oímos un ~.* We heard a shout. **2** (*auxilio, dolor, alegría*) cry [*pl* cries]: *~s de alegría* cries of joy LOC **a gritos/grito pelado** at the top of your voice **dar/pegar un grito** to shout *Ver tb* VOZ

grosella *nf* redcurrant LOC **grosella negra** blackcurrant

grosero, -a *adj, nm-nf* rude [*adj*]: *Eres un ~.* You're so rude.

grosor *nm* thickness: *Esta madera tiene dos centímetros de ~.* This piece of wood is two centimetres thick.

grúa *nf* **1** (*máquina*) crane **2** (*para vehículos*) **(a)** (*gen*) breakdown truck **(b)** (*de la policía*): *Avisamos ~.* Vehicles will be towed away. ◊ *Me ha llevado el coche la ~.* My car has been towed away.

grueso, -a *adj* thick
grumo *nm* lump: *una salsa con ~s* a lumpy sauce
gruñir *vi* **1** (*persona, cerdo*) to grunt **2** (*perro, león*) to growl **3** (*refunfuñar*) to grumble
gruñón, -ona *adj, nm-nf* grumpy [*adj*]: *Es una gruñona.* She's really grumpy.
grupo *nm* group: *Nos pusimos en ~s de seis.* We got into groups of six. ◊ *Me gusta el trabajo en ~.* I enjoy group work. LOC **grupo sanguíneo** blood group
gruta *nf* **1** (*natural*) cave **2** (*artificial*) grotto [*pl* grottoes/grottos]
guadaña *nf* scythe
guante *nm* glove LOC **echarle el guante a algn** to catch sb: *La policía les echó el ~.* The police caught them. *Ver tb* SENTAR
guantera *nf* glove compartment
guapo, -a *adj, nm-nf* **1** (*hombre*) good-looking (man) **2** (*mujer*) pretty (woman) LOC **estar guapo** to look nice: *Estás muy guapa con ese vestido.* You look really nice in that dress. **ir guapo** to look smart
guarda *nmf* **1** (*gen*) guard: *~ de seguridad* security guard **2** (*zoo*) keeper
guardabarros *nm* mudguard
guardaespaldas *nmf* bodyguard: *rodeado de ~* surrounded by bodyguards
guardar *vt* **1** (*gen*) to keep: *Guarda la entrada.* Keep your ticket. ◊ *~ un secreto* to keep a secret ◊ *¿Me puede ~ la vez?* Could you please keep my place in the queue? **2** (*recoger*) to put *sth* away: *Ya he guardado toda la ropa de invierno.* I've put away all my winter clothes. **3** (*custodiar*) to guard: *Dos soldados guardan la entrada al cuartel.* Two soldiers guard the entrance to the barracks. LOC **guardar la línea** to keep in shape **guardar las apariencias** to keep up appearances **guardarle rencor a algn** to bear sb a grudge: *No le guardo ningún rencor.* I don't bear him any grudge.
guardarropa *nm* (*en locales públicos*) cloakroom
guardería *nf* nursery [*pl* nurseries]
guardia ◆ *nmf* policeman/woman [*pl* policemen/women] ◆ *nf* guard LOC **de guardia** on duty: *el médico de ~* the doctor on duty ◊ *estar de ~* to be on duty **estar en guardia** to be on your guard **Guardia Civil** Civil Guard **guardia de tráfico** traffic warden **hacer guardia** to mount guard *Ver tb* CAMBIO, FARMACIA, MUNICIPAL, PAREJA, URBANO
guardián, -ana *nm-nf* guardian LOC *Ver* PERRO
guarecer ◆ *vt* to shelter *sb* (***from sth***) ◆ **guarecerse** *v pron* to take shelter (***from sth***)
guarida *nf* **1** (*gen*) den **2** (*ladrones*) hideout
guarnición *nf* **1** (*Cocina*) garnish: *una ~ de verduras* a garnish of vegetables **2** (*Mil*) garrison
guarrada *nf* **1** (*cochinada*) disgusting [*adj*]: *¡Qué ~ de cocina!* This kitchen is disgusting! **2** (*jugarreta*) dirty trick LOC **decir guarradas** to be filthy **hacer guarradas** to make a mess: *No hagas ~s con la comida.* Don't make a mess with your food.
guarro, -a *adj* filthy: *¡Qué ~ tienes el coche!* Your car's filthy!
guateque *nm* party [*pl* parties]
guau *nm* woof
guay *adj, adv* great [*adj*]: *Lo estamos pasando ~.* We're having a great time.
guerra *nf* war: *estar en ~* to be at war ◊ *en la Primera Guerra Mundial* during the First World War ◊ *declarar la ~ a algn* to declare war on sb LOC **dar guerra** to give *sb* trouble: *Estos niños dan mucha ~.* These kids are a real handful. *Ver tb* BUQUE
guerrero, -a ◆ *adj* **1** (*bélico*) warlike **2** (*niño*) boisterous ◆ *nm-nf* warrior ◆ **guerrera** *nf* tunic
guerrilla *nf* **1** (*grupo*) guerrillas [*pl*] **2** (*tipo de guerra*) guerrilla warfare
gueto *nm* ghetto [*pl* ghettoes]
guía ◆ *nmf* (*persona*) guide ◆ *nf* **1** (*gen*) guide: *~ turística/de hoteles* tourist/hotel guide **2** (*estudios*) prospectus [*pl* prospectuses]: *La universidad publica una ~ anual.* The university publishes a prospectus every year. LOC **guía (telefónica/de teléfonos)** telephone directory, phone book (*más coloq*): *Búscalo en la ~.* Look it up in the telephone directory. **guía del ocio/de espectáculos** What's On
guiar *vt* to guide LOC **guiarse por algo** to go by sth: *No deberías ~te por las apariencias.* You can't go by appearances.
guijarro *nm* pebble
guinda *nf* cherry [*pl* cherries]
guindilla *nf* chilli [*pl* chillies]

guiñar *vt, vi* to wink (***at sb***): *Me guiñó el ojo.* He winked at me.

guiño *nm* wink

guiñol *nm* puppet show LOC *Ver* TEATRO

guión *nm* **1** (*cine*) script **2** (*esquema*) plan **3** (*Ortografía*) **(a)** (*gen*) hyphen **(b)** (*diálogo*) dash ☛ *Ver* págs 318–19.

guisante *nm* pea

guisar *vt, vi* to cook

guiso *nm* stew

guitarra *nf* guitar

guitarrista *nmf* guitarist

gula *nf* greed

gusano *nm* **1** (*gen*) worm **2** (*en los alimentos*) maggot **3** (*de mariposa*) caterpillar LOC **gusano de seda** silkworm

gustar *vi* **1** (*gen*) to like *sth/doing sth* [*vt*]: *No me gusta.* I don't like it. ◊ *Les gusta pasear.* They like walking. ◊ *Me gusta cómo explica.* I like the way she explains things. **2** (*atraer sentimentalmente*) to fancy *sb* [*vt*]: *Creo que le gustas.* I think he fancies you. LOC **me gusta más** I, you, etc prefer *sth/doing sth*: *Me gusta más el vestido rojo.* I prefer the red dress.

gusto *nm* taste: *Tenemos ~s totalmente diferentes.* Our tastes are completely different. ◊ *Hizo un comentario de mal ~.* His remark was in bad taste. ◊ *para todos los ~s* to suit all tastes LOC **estar a gusto** to feel comfortable **¡mucho gusto!** pleased to meet you!

Hh

haba *nf* broad bean

haber ♦ *v aux* **1** (*tiempos compuestos*) to have: *He terminado.* I've finished. ◊ *Me habían dicho que vendrían.* They had told me they would come. **2** ~ **que** must: *Hay que ser valiente.* You must be brave. ♦ **haber** *v imp* there is, there are

> **There is** se utiliza con sustantivos en singular e incontables: *Hay una botella de vino en la mesa.* There's a bottle of wine on the table. ◊ *No hay pan.* There isn't any bread. ◊ *No había nadie.* There wasn't anybody.
> **There are** se utiliza con sustantivos en plural: *¿Cuántas botellas de vino hay?* How many bottles of wine are there?

LOC **de haber...** if...: *De ~lo sabido no le habría dicho nada.* If I'd known, I wouldn't have said anything. **¡haberlo dicho, hecho, etc!** you should have said so, done it, etc: *¡~lo dicho antes de salir!* You should have said so before we left! ☛Para otras expresiones con **haber**, véanse las entradas del sustantivo, adjetivo, etc, p.ej. **no hay derecho** en DERECHO y **no hay mal que por bien no venga** en MAL.

hábil *adj* **1** (*gen*) skilful: *un jugador muy ~* a very skilful player **2** (*astuto*) clever: *una maniobra muy ~* a clever move

habilidad *nf* skill

habilidoso, -a *adj* handy

habilitar *vt* (*edificio, local*) to convert

habitación *nf* **1** (*gen*) room: *un piso de cuatro habitaciones* a four-roomed flat **2** (*dormitorio*) bedroom LOC **habitación individual** single room *Ver tb* COMPAÑERO

habitante *nmf* inhabitant

habitar *vt, vi* ~ (**en**) to live **in...**: *la fauna que habita (en) los bosques* the animals that live in the woods

hábitat *nm* habitat

hábito *nm* habit LOC **coger el hábito** to get into the habit (*of doing sth*)

habitual *adj* **1** (*acostumbrado*) usual **2** (*cliente, lector, visitante*) regular

habituarse *v pron* ~ (**a**) to get used **to *sth/doing sth***: *Terminarás por habituarte.* You'll get used to it eventually.

habla *nf* **1** (*facultad*) speech **2** (*modo de hablar*) way of speaking: *el ~ andaluza* the Andalusian way of speaking LOC **de habla francesa, hispana, etc** French-speaking, Spanish-speaking, etc **sin habla** speechless: *Me dejó sin ~.* It left me speechless.

hablado, -a *pp, adj* spoken: *el inglés ~* spoken English *Ver tb* HABLAR

hablador, ~a ◆ *adj* talkative ◆ *nm-nf* chatterbox

hablante *nmf* speaker

hablar ◆ *vt* **1** (*idioma*) to speak: *¿Hablas ruso?* Do you speak Russian? **2** (*tratar*) to talk **about** ***sth***: *Ya lo hablaremos.* We'll talk about it. ◆ *vi* ~ (**con algn**) (**de/sobre algo/algn**) to speak, to talk (**to sb**) (**about sth/sb**)

To speak y **to talk** tienen prácticamente el mismo significado, aunque **to speak** es el término más general: *Habla más despacio.* Speak more slowly. ◊ *hablar en público* to speak in public ◊ *¿Puedo hablar con Juan?* Can I speak to Juan? **To talk** se utiliza más cuando nos referimos a una conversación o a un comentario, o cuando nos referimos a varios hablantes: *hablar de política* to talk about politics ◊ *Están hablando de nosotros.* They're talking about us. ◊ *Hablan de mudarse.* They're talking about moving. ◊ *Estuvimos hablando toda la noche.* We talked all night.

LOC **habla más alto/bajo** speak up/ lower your voice **hablar por los codos** to talk nineteen to the dozen **¡ni hablar!** no way! **no hablarse con algn** not to be on speaking terms with sb *Ver tb* ASÍ

hacer ◆ *vt*

- se traduce por **to make** en los siguientes casos: **1** (*fabricar*): ~ *bicicletas/una blusa* to make bicycles/a blouse **2** (*dinero, ruido, cama*): *Nunca haces la cama por la mañana.* You never make your bed in the morning. **3** (*comentario, promesa, esfuerzo*): *Tienes que ~ un esfuerzo.* You must make an effort. **4** (*amor*): *Haz el amor y no la guerra.* Make love, not war. **5** (*convertir en*): *Dicen que los sufrimientos te hacen más fuerte.* They say suffering makes you stronger. ☛ *Ver ejemplos en* MAKE[1]
- se traduce por **to do** en los siguientes casos: **1** cuando hablamos de una actividad sin decir de qué se trata: *¿Qué hacemos esta tarde?* What shall we do this afternoon? ◊ *Hago lo que puedo.* I do what I can. ◊ *Cuéntame lo que haces en el cole.* Tell me what you do at school. **2** cuando nos referimos a actividades como lavar, planchar, limpiar y comprar: *¿Cuándo haces la compra?* When do you do the shopping? ◊ *Si tú haces el baño, yo haré la cocina.* If you do the bathroom, I'll do the kitchen. **3** (*estudios*): ~ *los deberes/un examen/un curso* to do your homework/an exam/a course ◊ ~ *sumas y restas* to do sums **4** (*favor*): *¿Me haces un favor?* Will you do me a favour? ☛ *Ver ejemplos en* DO[2]
- **hacer** (**que...**) to get *sb* ***to do sth***: *Nos hacen venir todos los sábados.* They're getting us to come in every Saturday. ◊ *Hice que cambiaran el neumático.* I got them to change the tyre.
- **otros usos: 1** (*escribir*) to write: ~ *una redacción* to write an essay **2** (*pintar, dibujar*) to paint, to draw: ~ *un cuadro/una raya* to paint a picture/to draw a line **3** (*nudo*) to tie: ~ *un lazo* to tie a bow **4** (*distancia*): *Todos los días hago 50km.* I travel/drive 50km every day. ◊ *A veces hacemos cinco kilómetros corriendo.* We sometimes go for a five-kilometre run. **5** (*pregunta*) to ask: *¿Por qué haces tantas preguntas?* Why do you ask so many questions? **6** (*papel*) to play: *Hice el papel de Julieta.* I played the part of Juliet. **7** (*deportes*): ~ *judo/ aerobic* to do judo/aerobics ◊ ~ *ciclismo/alpinismo* to go cycling/ climbing

◆ *vi* ~ **de 1** (*oficio*) to work **as** ***sth***: *Hago de jardinero.* I'm working as a gardener. **2** (*ejercer*) to act **as** ***sth***: *No hagas de padre conmigo.* Don't act as if you were my father. **3** (*cosa*) to serve **as** ***sth***: *Una caja de cartón hacía de mesa.* A cardboard box served as a table. ◆ *v imp* **1** (*tiempo meteorológico*): *Hace frío/ calor/viento/sol.* It's cold/hot/windy/ sunny. ◊ *Hizo muy bueno el verano pasado.* We had very nice weather last summer. **2** (*tiempo cronológico*): *Me casé hace diez años.* I got married ten years ago. ◊ *Se habían conocido hacía pocos meses.* They had met a few months earlier. ◊ *¿Hace mucho que vives aquí?* Have you been living here long? ◊ *Hace años que nos conocemos.* We've known each other for ages. ☛ *Ver nota en* AGO ◆ **hacerse** *v pron* **1 + sustantivo** to become: *Se hizo taxista.* He became a taxi driver. **2 + adj**: *Me estoy haciendo viejo.* I'm getting old. ◊ *La última clase se me hace eterna.* The last lesson seems to go on for ever. **3 hacerse el/la + adj** to pretend to be *sth*: *No te hagas el sordo.* It's no good pretending to be deaf. ◊ *No te hagas la lista conmigo.* Don't try and be clever with me. **4** (*cuando otra persona realiza la acción*) to have *sth* done: *Se están haciendo una casa.* They're having a house built. ◊ *~se una foto* to have your photo taken LOC **desde hace/hacía... for...**: *Viven aquí desde hace dos años.* They've been living here for two years. **hacer bien/mal** to be right/wrong (*to do sth*): *¿Hice bien en ir?* Was I right to go? **hacer como que/si...** to pretend: *Hizo como que no me había visto.* He pretended he hadn't seen me. **hacerse pasar por...** to pass yourself off as *sth/sb*: *Se hizo pasar por el hijo del dueño.* He passed himself off as the owner's son. **hacer una de las suyas** to be up to his, her, etc old tricks again: *Nacho ha vuelto a ~ una de las suyas.* Nacho's been up to his old tricks again. **¿qué haces? 1** (*profesión*) what do you do?: *—¿Qué hace?—Es profesora.* 'What does she do?' 'She's a teacher.' **2** (*en este instante*) what are you doing?: *—Hola, ¿qué haces? —Ver una película.* 'Hi, what are you doing?' 'Watching a film.' ☛Para otras expresiones con **hacer**, véanse las entradas del sustantivo, adjetivo, etc, p.ej. **hacer el tonto** en TONTO y **hacer trampa(s)** en TRAMPA.

hacha *nf* axe LOC **ser un hacha** to be a genius (*at sth/doing sth*)

hacia *prep* **1** (*dirección*) towards: *ir hacia algo/algn* to go towards sth/sb **2** (*tiempo*) at about: *Llegaré hacia las tres.* I'll be there at about three. ◊ *hacia principios de verano* in early summer ☛ *Ver nota en* AROUND[1]

hacienda *nf* **1 Hacienda** the Treasury **2** (*finca*) estate LOC *Ver* MINISTERIO, MINISTRO

hada *nf* fairy [*pl* fairies]: *un cuento de ~s* a fairy story

¡hala! *interj* **1** (*¡qué barbaridad!*) good heavens! **2** (*enfático*) so there!: *Pues ahora no voy, ¡hala!* Well, now I'm not going, so there!

halagar *vt* to flatter

halcón *nm* falcon

hallar ◆ *vt* to find ◆ **hallarse** *v pron* to be

hallazgo *nm* **1** (*descubrimiento*) discovery [*pl* discoveries]: *Los científicos han hecho un gran ~.* Scientists have made an important discovery. **2** (*persona, cosa*) find: *La nueva bailarina ha sido un auténtico ~.* The new dancer is a real find.

halterofilia *nf* weightlifting

hamaca *nf* **1** (*gen*) hammock **2** (*playa*) deckchair

hambre *nf* hunger, starvation, famine

No deben confundirse las palabras **hunger**, **starvation** y **famine**:

Hunger es el término general y se usa en casos como: *hacer huelga de hambre* to go on (a) hunger strike, o para expresar un deseo: *hambre de conocimiento/poder* hunger for knowledge/power.

Starvation se refiere al hambre sufrida durante un periodo prolongado de tiempo: *Le dejaron morir de hambre.* They let him die of starvation. El verbo **to starve** significa *morir de hambre* y se utiliza mucho en la expresión: *Me muero de hambre.* I'm starving.

Famine es hambre que afecta normalmente a un gran número de personas y suele ser consecuencia de una catástrofe natural: *una población debilitada por el hambre* a population weakened by famine ◊ *A la larga sequía siguieron meses de hambre.* The long drought was followed by months of famine.

LOC **pasar hambre** to go hungry **tener hambre** to be hungry **tener un hambre canina/feroz** to be starving *Ver tb* MATAR, MUERTO

hambriento, -a *adj* **1** (*gen*) hungry: *La niña está hambrienta.* The baby is hungry. **2** (*muerto de hambre*) starving

hamburguesa *nf* hamburger, burger (*más coloq*)

hámster *nm* hamster

harapo *nm* rag

harina *nf* flour

hartarse *v pron* **1** ~ (**de**) (*cansarse*) to be fed up (**with *sth/sb/doing sth***): *Ya me he hartado de tus quejas.* I'm fed up with your complaints. **2** (*atiborrarse*) **(a)** (*gen*) to be full (up): *Comí hasta hartarme.* I ate till I was full (up). **(b)** ~ **de** to stuff yourself (**with *sth***): *Me harté de pasteles.* I stuffed myself with cakes.

harto, -a *adj* **1** (*lleno*) full **2** ~ (**de**) (*cansado*) fed up (**with *sth/sb/doing sth***): *Me tienes ~.* I'm fed up with you.

hasta ◆ *prep*

• **tiempo** until, till (*más coloq*)

Until se usa tanto en inglés formal como informal. **Till** se usa sobre todo en inglés hablado y no suele aparecer al principio de la frase: *No llegaré hasta las siete.* I won't be there until seven. ◊ *¿Hasta cuándo te quedas?* How long are you staying?

• **lugar 1** (*distancia*) as far as...: *Vinieron conmigo hasta Barcelona.* They came with me as far as Barcelona. **2** (*altura, longitud, cantidad*) up to...: *El agua llegó hasta aquí.* The water came up to here. **3** (*hacia abajo*) down to ...: *La falda me llega hasta los tobillos.* The skirt comes down to my ankles.

● **saludos** see you ...: *¡Hasta mañana/el lunes!* See you tomorrow/on Monday! ◊ *¡Hasta luego!* Bye!

◆ *adv* even: *Hasta yo lo hice.* Even I did it.

haya *nf* beech (tree)

hazaña *nf* exploit LOC **ser toda una hazaña** to be quite a feat

hebilla *nf* buckle

hebra *nf* (piece of) thread

hechicero, -a *nm-nf* wizard [*fem* witch]

hechizar *vt* to cast a spell (**on *sb***): *La bruja hechizó al príncipe.* The witch cast a spell on the Prince.

hechizo *nm* spell: *estar bajo un ~* to be under a spell

hecho, -a ◆ *pp, adj* **1** (*manufacturado*) made: *¿De qué está ~?* What's it made of? ◊ *~ a mano/máquina* handmade/ machine-made **2** (*cocinado*) done: *El pollo no está ~ todavía.* The chicken isn't done yet. ◊ *Me gusta la carne bien hecha.* I like my meat well done.

Un filete o carne poco hecha se dice **rare** y en su punto **medium rare**.

Ver tb HACER ◆ *nm* **1** (*gen*) fact **2** (*acontecimiento*) event: *su versión de los ~s* his version of the events LOC **¡bien hecho!** well done! **de hecho** in fact **hecho y derecho** grown: *un hombre ~ y derecho* a grown man **mal hecho**: *Si se lo dijiste, mal ~.* You shouldn't have told him. *Ver tb* CRISTO, DICHO, FRASE, TRATO

hectárea *nf* hectare (*abrev* ha)

helada *nf* frost

heladería *nf* ice cream parlour

helado, -a ◆ *pp, adj* **1** (*congelado*) frozen: *un estanque ~* a frozen pond **2** (*persona, habitación*) freezing: *Estoy ~.* I'm freezing! *Ver tb* HELAR(SE); ◆ *nm* ice cream: *~ de chocolate* chocolate ice cream LOC *Ver* TARTA

helar(se) ◆ *vt, vi, v pron* to freeze: *El frío ha helado las cañerías.* The pipes are frozen. ◊ *Nos vamos a ~ de frío.* We're going to freeze to death. ◆ *v imp*: *Anoche heló.* There was a frost last night.

helecho *nm* fern

hélice *nf* (*avión, barco*) propeller

helicóptero *nm* helicopter

helio *nm* helium

hembra *nf* **1** (*gen*) female: *un leopardo ~* a female leopard ☛ *Ver nota en* FEMALE **2** (*enchufe*) socket ☛ *Ver dibujo en* ENCHUFE

hemisferio *nm* hemisphere: *el ~ norte/ sur* the northern/southern hemisphere

hemorragia *nf* haemorrhage

heno *nm* hay

hepatitis *nf* hepatitis [*incontable*]

herbívoro, -a *adj* herbivorous

herboristería *nf* health food shop

heredar *vt* to inherit *sth* (**from *sb***): *A su muerte heredé sus propiedades.* On his death I inherited all his property.

heredero, -a *nm-nf* ~ (**de**) heir (**to *sth***): *el ~/la heredera del trono* the heir to the throne

También existe el femenino **heiress**, pero sólo se usa para referirnos a una *rica heredera*.

LOC *Ver* PRÍNCIPE

hereditario, -a *adj* hereditary

herencia *nf* inheritance

herida *nf* **1** (*gen*) injury [*pl* injuries] **2** (*bala, navaja*) wound

Es difícil saber cuándo usar **wound** y cuándo **injury**, o los verbos **to wound** y **to injure**.
Wound y **to wound** se utilizan para referirnos a heridas causadas por un arma (p.ej. una navaja, pistola, etc) de forma deliberada: *heridas de bala* gunshot wounds ◊ *La herida no tardará en cicatrizar.* The wound will soon heal. ◊ *Lo hirieron en la guerra.* He was wounded in the war.
Si la herida es resultado de un accidente utilizamos **injury** o **to injure**, que también se puede traducir a veces por *lesión* o *lesionarse*: *Sólo sufrió heridas leves.* He only suffered minor injuries. ◊ *Los trozos de cristal hirieron a varias personas.* Several people were injured by flying glass. ◊ *El casco protege a los jugadores de posibles lesiones cerebrales.* Helmets protect players from brain injuries.

herido, -a *nm-nf* casualty [*pl* casualties]

herir *vt* **1** (*gen*) to injure **2** (*bala, navaja*) to wound ☛ *Ver nota en* HERIDA

hermanastro, -a *nm-nf* stepbrother [*fem* stepsister]

Para referirnos a un hermano por parte de padre o de madre decimos

half-brother y **half-sister**: *Son hermanos por parte de padre.* They're half-brothers.

hermandad *nf* **1** (*entre hombres*) brotherhood **2** (*entre mujeres*) sisterhood **3** (*gremio*) association

hermano, -a *nm-nf* **1** (*pariente*) brother [*fem* sister]: *Tengo un ~ mayor.* I have an older brother. ◊ *mi hermana la pequeña* my youngest sister ◊ *Son dos ~s y tres hermanas.* There are two boys and three girls.

A veces decimos *hermanos* refiriéndonos a hermanos y hermanas, en cuyo caso debemos decir en inglés **brothers and sisters**: *¿Tienes hermanos?* Have you got any brothers and sisters? ◊ *Somos seis hermanos.* I've got five brothers and sisters.

2 (*comunidad religiosa*) brother [*fem* sister]: *el ~ Francisco* brother Francis LOC **hermano por parte de padre/madre** ☛ *Ver nota en* HERMANASTRO **hermanos siameses** Siamese twins

herméticamente *adv* LOC **herméticamente cerrado** airtight

hermético, -a *adj* airtight

hermoso, -a *adj* beautiful

hermosura *nf* beauty: *¡Qué ~!* How beautiful!

hernia *nf* hernia

héroe, heroína *nm-nf* hero [*pl* heroes] [*fem* heroine]

heroína *nf* (*droga*) heroin

herradura *nf* horseshoe

herramienta *nf* tool LOC *Ver* CAJA

herrar *vt* to shoe

herrería *nf* forge

herrero, -a *nm-nf* blacksmith

hervir *vt, vi* to boil: *La leche está hirviendo.* The milk is boiling. ◊ *Pon a ~ las patatas.* Put the potatoes on to boil. ◊ *Me hierve la sangre cuando me acuerdo.* Just thinking about it makes my blood boil.

heterosexual *adj, nmf* heterosexual

hexágono *nm* hexagon

hibernar *vi* to hibernate

hidratante *adj* moisturizing LOC **crema/leche hidratante** moisturizer

hidratar *vt* (*piel*) to moisturize

hidrato *nm* hydrate LOC **hidratos de carbono** carbohydrates

hidráulico, -a *adj* hydraulic: *energía/bomba hidráulica* hydraulic power/pump

hidroavión *nm* seaplane

hidroeléctrico, -a *adj* hydroelectric

hidrógeno *nm* hydrogen

hiedra *nf* ivy

hielo *nm* ice [*incontable*]: *Saca unos ~s.* Bring me some ice. ◊ *una bandeja para el ~* an ice cube tray LOC *Ver* HOCKEY, PISTA, ROMPER

hiena *nf* hyena

hierba *nf* **1** (*gen*) grass: *tumbarse en la ~* to lie down on the grass **2** (*Med, Cocina*) herb **3** (*marihuana*) pot LOC **mala hierba** weed

hierbabuena *nf* mint

hierro *nm* iron: *una barra de ~* an iron bar ◊ *~ forjado/fundido* wrought/cast iron LOC **tener una constitución/naturaleza de hierro** to have an iron constitution

hígado *nm* liver

higiene *nf* hygiene: *la ~ bucal/corporal* oral/personal hygiene

higiénico, -a *adj* hygienic LOC *Ver* PAPEL

higo *nm* fig LOC **de higos a brevas** once in a blue moon

higuera *nf* fig tree

hijastro, -a *nm-nf* stepson [*fem* stepdaughter] [*pl* stepchildren]

hijo, -a *nm-nf* son [*fem* daughter] [*pl* children]: *Tienen dos hijas y un ~.* They have two daughters and a son. ◊ *No tenemos ~s.* We don't have any children. LOC **hijo de papá** daddy's boy/girl **hijo único** only child: *Soy ~ único.* I'm an only child.

hilera *nf* **1** (*fila*) row: *una ~ de niños/árboles* a row of children/trees **2** (*Mil, hormigas*) column

hilo *nm* **1** (*gen*) thread: *un carrete de ~* a reel of thread ◊ *He perdido el ~ de la conversación.* I've lost the thread of the argument. **2** (*metal*) wire: *~ de acero/cobre* steel/copper wire **3** (*tela*) linen: *una falda de ~* a linen skirt

himno *nm* hymn LOC **himno nacional** national anthem

hincapié *nm* LOC **hacer hincapié en algo** to stress sth

hincar *vt* **1** (*diente*) to sink *your teeth* ***into sth***: *Hincó los dientes en la sandía.* He sank his teeth into the watermelon. **2** (*clavo, estaca*) to drive *sth* ***into sth***: *Hincó las estacas en la tierra.* He drove the stakes into the ground.

hincha *nmf* supporter

hinchado, -a *pp, adj* **1** (*gen*) swollen:

un brazo/pie ~ a swollen arm/foot **2** (*estómago*) bloated *Ver tb* HINCHAR

hinchar ♦ *vt* to blow *sth* up, to inflate (*más formal*): ~ *un balón* to blow up a ball ♦ **hincharse** *v pron* **1** (*gen*) to swell (up): *Se me ha hinchado el tobillo.* My ankle has swollen up. **2 hincharse (a/de)** to stuff yourself **(with *sth*)**: *Me hinché de pasteles.* I stuffed myself with cakes.

hinchazón *nf* (*Med*) swelling: *Parece que ha bajado la* ~. The swelling seems to have gone down.

hindú *adj, nmf* (*Relig*) Hindu

hinduismo *nm* Hinduism

hipermercado *nm* superstore

hipermétrope *adj* long-sighted

hipermetropía *nf* long-sightedness: *tener* ~ to be long-sighted

hípica *nf* riding

hípico, -a *adj* riding [*n atrib*]: *club/concurso* ~ riding club/competition

hipnotizar *vt* to hypnotize

hipo *nm* hiccups [*pl*]: *Tengo* ~. I've got the hiccups. ◊ *quitar el* ~ to cure the hiccups

hipócrita ♦ *adj* hypocritical ♦ *nmf* hypocrite

hipódromo *nm* racecourse

hipopótamo *nm* hippo [*pl* hippos]

Hippopotamus es la palabra científica.

hipótesis *nf* hypothesis [*pl* hypotheses]

hippy (*tb* **hippie**) *adj, nmf* hippie

hispanohablante ♦ *adj* Spanish-speaking ♦ *nmf* Spanish speaker

histeria *nf* hysteria: *Le dio un ataque de* ~. He became hysterical.

histérico, -a *adj, nm-nf* hysterical [*adj*] LOC **ponerse histérico** to have hysterics **ser un histérico** to get worked up about things

historia *nf* **1** (*gen*) history: ~ *antigua/natural* ancient/natural history ◊ *He aprobado* ~. I've passed history. **2** (*relato*) story [*pl* stories]: *Cuéntanos una* ~. Tell us a story. LOC **dejarse de historias** to get to the point

historiador, ~a *nm-nf* historian

historial *nm* record LOC **historial médico** medical history **historial profesional** curriculum vitae (*abrev* cv)

histórico, -a *adj* **1** (*gen*) historical: *documentos/personajes* ~*s* historical documents/figures **2** (*importante*) historic: *un triunfo/acuerdo* ~ a historic victory/agreement

historieta *nf* **1** (*tebeo, cómic*) cartoon: *Les encantan las ~s de Batman.* They love Batman cartoons. **2** (*anécdota*) story [*pl* stories]

hobby *nm* hobby [*pl* hobbies]

hocico *nm* **1** (*gen*) muzzle **2** (*cerdo*) snout

hockey *nm* hockey LOC **hockey sobre hielo** ice hockey

hogar *nm* **1** (*casa*) home: ~ *dulce* ~. Home sweet home. **2** (*familia*) family: *casarse y fundar un* ~ to get married and start a family **3** (*chimenea*) fireplace

hogareño, -a *adj* (*persona*) home-loving: *ser muy* ~ to love being at home

hoguera *nf* bonfire: *hacer una* ~ to make a bonfire ☛ *Ver nota en* BONFIRE NIGHT

hoja *nf* **1** (*gen*) leaf [*pl* leaves]: *las ~s de un árbol* the leaves of a tree ◊ *En otoño se caen las ~s.* Leaves fall off the trees in autumn. **2** (*libro, periódico*) page **3** (*folio*) sheet (of paper): *Dame una* ~ *de papel.* Can I have some paper, please? ◊ *una* ~ *en blanco* a clean sheet of paper **4** (*arma blanca, herramienta*) blade LOC **de hoja caduca/perenne** deciduous/evergreen **pasar la hoja/página** to turn over *Ver tb* AFEITARSE

hojalata *nf* tin plate

hojaldre *nm* puff pastry

hojear *vt* **1** (*pasar hojas*) to flick through *sth*: ~ *una revista* to flick through a magazine **2** (*mirar por encima*) to glance **at *sth***: ~ *el periódico* to glance at the paper

¡hola! *interj* hi! (*coloq*), hello!

Holanda *nf* Holland

holandés, -esa ♦ *adj, nm* Dutch: *hablar* ~ to speak Dutch ♦ *nm-nf* Dutchman/woman [*pl* Dutchmen/women]: *los holandeses* the Dutch

holgazán, -ana ♦ *adj* lazy ♦ *nm-nf* lazybones [*pl* lazybones]: *Es un* ~. He's a lazybones.

holgazanear *vi* to laze around

hollín *nm* soot

holocausto *nm* holocaust: *un* ~ *nuclear* a nuclear holocaust

holograma *nm* hologram

hombre ♦ *nm* **1** (*gen*) man [*pl* men]: *el* ~ *contemporáneo* modern man ◊ *tener una conversación de* ~ *a* ~ to have a man-to-man talk ◊ *el* ~ *de la calle* the man in the street **2** (*humanidad*) mankind: *la evolución del ~* the evolution of mankind ☛ *Ver nota en* MAN[1] ◆ **¡hombre!** *interj*: *¡Hombre! qué bien que hayas venido.* Great! You've come! ◊ *¡Hombre! ¿qué haces aquí?* Well I never! What are you doing here? LOC **hacerse hombre** to grow up **hombre del tiempo** weatherman [*pl* weathermen] **hombre lobo** werewolf [*pl* werewolves] **hombre rana** frogman [*pl* frogmen] *Ver tb* NEGOCIO

hombrera *nf* shoulder pad

hombro *nm* shoulder LOC **llevar/sacar a hombros** to carry *sth/sb* on your shoulders *Ver tb* ENCIMA, ENCOGER(SE), MANGA

homenaje *nm* homage [*incontable*]: *hacer un ~ a algn* to pay homage to sb LOC **en homenaje a** in honour of *sth/sb*

homicida *nmf* murderer [*fem* murderess] LOC *Ver* ARMA

homicidio *nm* homicide

homogéneo, -a *adj* homogeneous

homónimo *nm* homonym

homosexual *adj*, *nmf* homosexual

hondo, -a *adj* deep: *Es un pozo muy ~.* It's a very deep well. LOC *Ver* PLATO

honestidad *nf* honesty: *Nadie duda de su ~.* Nobody doubts his honesty.

honesto, -a *adj* honest: *una persona honesta* an honest person

hongo *nm* fungus [*pl* fungi/funguses] LOC **hongo venenoso** toadstool

honor *nm* **1** (*gen*) honour: *el invitado de ~* the guest of honour ◊ *Es un gran ~ para mí estar hoy aquí.* It's a great honour for me to be here today. **2** (*buen nombre*) good name: *El ~ del banco está en peligro.* The bank's good name is at risk. LOC **tener el honor de** to have the honour of *doing sth Ver tb* DAMA, PALABRA

honra *nf* honour LOC **¡(y) a mucha honra!** and proud of it!

honradez *nf* honesty

honrado, -a *pp*, *adj* honest *Ver tb* HONRAR

honrar *vt* **1** (*mostrar respeto*) to honour *sb* (**with sth**): *un acto para ~ a los soldados* a ceremony to honour the soldiers **2** (*ennoblecer*) to do *sb* credit: *Tu comportamiento te honra.* Your behaviour does you credit.

hora *nf* **1** (*gen*) hour: *La clase dura dos ~s.* The class lasts two hours. ◊ *120km por ~* 120km an hour **2** (*reloj*, *momento*, *horario*) time: *¿Qué ~ es?* What time is it? ◊ *¿A qué ~ vienen?* What time are they coming? ◊ *a cualquier ~ del día* at any time of the day ◊ *~s de consulta/oficina/visita* surgery/office/visiting hours ◊ *a la ~ de la comida/cena* at lunchtime/dinner time **3** (*cita*) appointment: *Tengo ~ en el dentista.* I've got a dental appointment. LOC **entre horas** between meals: *Nunca como entre ~.* I never eat between meals. **hora punta** rush hour **horas extras** overtime [*sing*] **pasarse las horas muertas haciendo algo** to do sth for hours on end **ser hora de**: *Es ~ de irse a la cama.* It's time to go to bed. ◊ *Creo que ya es ~ de que nos vayamos.* I think it's time we were going. ◊ *Ya era ~ de que nos escribieses.* It was about time you wrote to us. **¡ya era hora!** about time too! *Ver tb* PEDIR, ÚLTIMO

horario *nm* **1** (*clases*, *tren*) timetable **2** (*consulta*, *trabajo*) hours [*pl*]: *El ~ de oficina es de nueve a tres.* Office hours are nine to three. LOC **horario al público** opening hours [*pl*]

horca *nf* **1** (*cadalso*) gallows [*pl* gallows] **2** (*Agricultura*) pitchfork

horchata *nf* tiger nut milk

horizontal *adj* horizontal

horizonte *nm* horizon: *en el ~* on the horizon

hormiga *nf* ant

hormigón *nm* concrete

hormigueo *nm* pins and needles [*pl*]: *Siento un ~ en las yemas de los dedos.* I've got pins and needles in my fingers.

hormiguero *nm* **1** (*agujero*) ants' nest **2** (*montículo*) anthill LOC *Ver* OSO

hormona *nf* hormone

horno *nm* **1** (*gen*) oven: *encender el ~* to turn the oven on ◊ *Esta sala es un ~.* It's like an oven in here. **2** (*Tec*) furnace **3** (*cerámica*, *ladrillos*) kiln LOC **al horno** roast: *pollo al ~* roast chicken

horóscopo *nm* horoscope

horquilla *nf* **1** (*para cabello*) hairgrip **2** (*palo*, *rama*, *bicicleta*) fork LOC **horquilla de moño** hairpin

horrible *adj* awful

horror *nm* **1** (*miedo*) horror: *un grito de ~* a cry of horror ◊ *los ~es de la guerra* the horrors of war **2** (*mucho*): *Les han gustado ~es.* They loved them. ◊ *Había un ~ de coches.* There were loads of cars. LOC **¡qué horror!** how awful! **tenerle horror a** to hate *sth/doing sth*

horrorizar ◆ *vt* to frighten: *Le horroriza la oscuridad.* He's frightened of the dark. ◆ *vi* to hate *sth/doing sth* [*vt*]: *Me horroriza ese vestido.* I hate that dress.

horroroso, -a *adj* **1** (*aterrador*) horrific: *un incendio* ~ a horrific fire **2** (*muy feo*) hideous: *Tiene una nariz horrorosa.* He's got a hideous nose. **3** (*malo*) awful: *Hace un tiempo* ~. The weather is awful.

hortaliza *nf* vegetable

hortera *adj* naff

hospedarse *v pron* to stay

hospital *nm* hospital ☛ *Ver nota en* SCHOOL

hospitalidad *nf* hospitality

hospitalizar *vt* to hospitalize

hostal *nm* hotel

hostelería *nf* (*estudios*) catering and hotel management

hotel *nm* hotel

hoy *adv* today: *Hay que terminarlo* ~. We've got to get it finished today. LOC **de hoy**: *la música de* ~ present-day music ◊ *el periódico de* ~ today's paper ◊ *Este pan no es de* ~. This bread isn't fresh. **de hoy en adelante** from now on **hoy (en) día** nowadays

hoyo *nm* hole: *hacer/cavar un* ~ to dig a hole

hoyuelo *nm* dimple

hoz *nf* sickle

hucha *nf* money box

hueco, -a ◆ *adj* hollow: *Este muro está* ~. This wall is hollow. ◊ *sonar a* ~ to sound hollow ◆ *nm* **1** (*cavidad*) space: *Aprovecha este* ~. Use this space. **2** (*espacio en blanco*) gap: *Completa los ~s con preposiciones.* Fill in the gaps with prepositions. **3** (*rato libre*) free time [*incontable*]: *El lunes por la tarde tengo un* ~. I've got some free time on Monday afternoon.

huelga *nf* strike: *estar/ponerse en* ~ to be/go on strike ◊ *una* ~ *general/de hambre* a general/hunger strike

huelguista *nmf* striker

huella *nf* **1** (*pie, zapato*) footprint **2** (*animal, vehículo*) track: *~s de oso* bear tracks LOC **huella (dactilar)** fingerprint **sin dejar huella** without trace: *Desaparecieron sin dejar* ~. They disappeared without trace.

huérfano, -a *adj, nm-nf* orphan [*n*]: *~s de guerra* war orphans ◊ *ser* ~ to be an orphan LOC **huérfano de madre/padre** motherless/fatherless **quedarse huérfano de madre/padre** to lose your mother/father

huerta *nf* **1** (*huerto grande*) market garden **2** (*tierra de regadío*) irrigated region

huerto *nm* **1** (*gen*) vegetable garden **2** (*sólo de árboles frutales*) orchard

hueso *nm* **1** (*Anat*) bone **2** (*fruta*) stone **3** (*color*) ivory LOC **estar/quedarse en los huesos** to be nothing but skin and bone **ser un hueso 1** (*persona*) to be strict: *Mi profesor es un* ~. My teacher is strict. **2** (*asignatura, libro*) to be a hard grind *Ver tb* CALAR, CARNE

huésped, ~a *nm-nf* guest

hueva *nf* **huevas 1** (*Zool*) spawn [*incontable*]: *~s de rana* frog spawn **2** (*Cocina*) roe [*incontable*]

huevo *nm* egg: *poner un* ~ to lay an egg LOC **huevo duro/frito** hard-boiled/fried egg **huevos revueltos** scrambled eggs

huida *nf* escape, flight (*más formal*)

huir ◆ *vi* ~ **(de)** to escape **(from *sth/sb*)**: *Huyeron de la prisión.* They escaped from prison. ◆ *vt, vi* ~ **(de)** to avoid *sth/sb*: *No nos huyas.* Don't try to avoid us. ◊ *Conseguimos* ~ *de la prensa.* We managed to avoid the press. LOC **huir del país** to flee the country

hule *nm* oilcloth

humanidad *nf* humanity [*pl* humanities]

humanitario, -a *adj* humanitarian: *ayuda humanitaria* humanitarian aid

humano, -a ◆ *adj* **1** (*gen*) human: *el cuerpo* ~ the human body ◊ *los derechos ~s* human rights **2** (*comprensivo, justo*) humane: *un sistema judicial más* ~ a more humane judicial system ◆ *nm* human being

humareda *nf* cloud of smoke

humedad *nf* **1** (*gen*) damp: *Esta pared tiene* ~. This wall is damp. **2** (*atmósfera*) humidity

humedecer ◆ *vt* to dampen: ~ *la ropa para plancharla* to dampen clothes before ironing them ◆ **humedecerse** *v pron* to get wet

húmedo, -a *adj* **1** (*gen*) damp: *Estos calcetines están ~s.* These socks are damp. **2** (*aire, calor*) humid **3** (*lugar*) wet: *un país* ~ a wet country ☛ *Ver nota en* MOIST

humildad *nf* humility

humilde *adj* humble

humillante *adj* humiliating

humo *nm* **1** (*gen*) smoke: *Había demasiado* ~. There was too much smoke. ◊ *Salía* ~ *por la puerta.* There was smoke coming out of the door. **2** (*coche*) fumes [*pl*]: *el ~ del tubo de escape* exhaust fumes **3 humos** (*arrogancia*) airs: *darse muchos ~s* to put on airs LOC *Ver* BAJAR, SUBIR

humor *nm* **1** (*gen*) humour: *tener sentido del ~* to have a sense of humour ◊ *~ negro* black humour **2** (*comicidad*) comedy: *una serie de ~* a comedy series LOC **estar de buen/mal humor** to be in a good/bad mood **estar de humor** to be in the mood (*for sth/doing sth*) **poner a algn de mal humor** to make sb angry **tener buen/mal humor** to be good-tempered/bad-tempered

humorista *nmf* humorist

hundido, -a *pp, adj* **1** (*barco*) sunken: *un galeón ~* a sunken galleon **2** (*persona*) depressed *Ver tb* HUNDIR

hundir ♦ *vt* **1** (*gen*) to sink: *Una bomba hundió el barco.* A bomb sunk the boat. ◊ *~ los pies en la arena* to sink your feet into the sand **2** (*persona*) to destroy ♦ **hundirse** *v pron* **1** (*irse al fondo*) to sink **2** (*derrumbarse*) to collapse: *El puente se hundió.* The bridge collapsed. **3** (*negocio*) to go under: *Muchas empresas se han hundido.* Many firms have gone under.

huracán *nm* hurricane

hurgar ♦ *vi ~* **en** to rummage **in/through** ***sth***: *No hurgues en mis cosas.* Don't rummage through my things. ♦ **hurgarse** *v pron* to pick: *~se las narices* to pick your nose

¡hurra! *interj* hurrah!

husmear ♦ *vi* **1** (*olfatear*) to sniff around **2** (*curiosear*) to snoop around: *La policía ha estado husmeando por aquí.* The police have been snooping around here. ♦ *vt* (*olfatear*) to sniff

Ii

iceberg *nm* iceberg

ida *nf* outward journey: *durante la ~* on the way there LOC **ida y vuelta** there and back (*coloq*): *Son tres horas ~ y vuelta.* It's three hours there and back. *Ver tb* BILLETE, PARTIDO

idea *nf* **1** (*ocurrencia*) idea: *Tengo una ~.* I've got an idea. **2** (*concepto*) concept: *la ~ de la democracia* the concept of democracy **3 ideas** (*ideología*) convictions: *~s políticas/religiosas* political/religious convictions LOC **mala idea**: *No lo hice con mala ~.* I meant well. ◊ *¡Qué mala ~!* What a swine! **¡ni idea!** I haven't a clue! **tener ideas de bombero** to have strange ideas

ideal *adj, nm* ideal: *Eso sería lo ~.* That would be ideal/the ideal thing. ◊ *Es un hombre sin ~es.* He's a man without ideals.

idealista ♦ *adj* idealistic ♦ *nmf* idealist

idealizar *vt* to idealize

ídem *pron* (*en una lista*) ditto ☛ *Ver nota en* DITTO LOC **ídem de ídem**: *Es un fresco y el hijo ~ de ~.* He's got a real cheek and the same goes for his son.

idéntico, -a *adj* ~ (**a**) identical (**to** ***sth/sb***): *gemelos ~s* identical twins ◊ *Es ~ al mío.* It's identical to mine.

identidad *nf* identity [*pl* identities] LOC *Ver* CARNÉ, DOCUMENTO

identificar ♦ *vt* to identify ♦ **identificarse** *v pron* **identificarse con** to identify **with** ***sth/sb***: *No acababa de ~me con el personaje principal.* I couldn't quite identify with the main character. LOC **sin identificar** unidentified

ideología *nf* ideology [*pl* ideologies]

idioma *nm* language

idiota ♦ *adj* stupid ♦ *nmf* idiot: *¡Qué ~ (es)!* What an idiot (he is)! ◊ *¡Qué ~ eres!* You stupid thing!

idiotez *nf* stupidity: *el colmo de la ~* the height of stupidity LOC **decir idioteces** to talk nonsense

ido, -a *pp, adj* **1** (*distraído*) absent-minded **2** (*loco*) crazy *Ver tb* IR

ídolo *nm* idol

iglesia *nf* (*institución, edificio*) church: *la Iglesia católica* the Catholic Church ☛ *Ver nota en* SCHOOL LOC *Ver* CASAR

ignorante ♦ *adj* ignorant ♦ *nmf* ignoramus [*pl* ignoramuses]

ignorar *vt* **1** (*desconocer*) not to know: *Ignoro si han salido ya.* I don't know if they've already left. **2** (*hacer caso omiso*) to ignore

igual ♦ *adj* **1** (*gen*) equal: *Todos los*

ciudadanos son ~es. All citizens are equal. ◊ *A es ~ a B.* A is equal to B. **2 ~ (a/que)** (*idéntico*) the same (**as *sth/sb***): *Esa falda es ~ que la tuya.* That skirt is the same as yours. ◆ *nmf* equal ◆ *adv* **1 ~ de** equally: *Son ~ de culpables.* They are equally guilty. **2 ~ de ... que as ... as**: *Son ~ de responsables que nosotros.* They are as responsible as we are. **3** (*probablemente*) probably: *~ no vienen.* They probably won't come. **LOC me da igual** it's all the same to me, you, etc *Ver tb* COSA

igualar *vt* **1** (*Dep*) to equalize **2** (*terreno*) to level

igualmente *adv* equally **LOC ¡igualmente!** the same to you!

ilegal *adj* illegal

ileso, -a *adj* unharmed: *resultar ~* to escape unharmed

ilimitado, -a *adj* unlimited

iluminado, -a *pp, adj* **~ (con)** lit (up) (**with *sth***): *La cocina estaba iluminada con velas.* The kitchen was lit (up) with candles. *Ver tb* ILUMINAR

iluminar *vt* to light *sth* up: *~ un monumento* to light a monument up

ilusión *nf* **1** (*noción falsa*) illusion **2** (*sueño*) dream: *Era la ~ de su vida.* It was her dream. **LOC hacerse ilusiones** to build up your hopes **me hace mucha ilusión** I am, you are, etc really looking forward *to sth/doing sth*: *Le hace mucha ~ ir en avión.* She's really looking forward to going on a plane. **me hizo mucha ilusión** I was, you were, etc delighted (*with sth/to do sth*) **¡qué ilusión!** how lovely! *Ver tb* FORJAR

ilusionado, -a *pp, adj* **1** (*esperanzado*) enthusiastic: *Vine muy ~ al puesto.* I was very enthusiastic when I started. **2 ~ con** excited **about *sth/doing sth***: *Están muy ~s con el viaje.* They're really excited about the trip.

iluso, -a ◆ *adj* gullible ◆ *nm-nf* mug: *Es un auténtico ~.* He's a real mug.

ilustración *nf* (*dibujo*) illustration **LOC la Ilustración** the Enlightenment

ilustrar *vt* to illustrate

ilustre *adj* illustrious: *personalidades ~s* illustrious figures

imagen *nf* **1** (*gen*) image: *Los espejos distorsionaban su ~.* The mirrors distorted his image. ◊ *Me gustaría un cambio de ~.* I'd like to change my image. **2** (*Cine, TV*) picture

imaginación *nf* imagination

imaginario, -a *adj* imaginary

imaginar(se) *vt, v pron* to imagine: *Me imagino (que sí).* I imagine so. ◊ *¡Imagínate!* Just imagine!

imán *nm* magnet

imbécil ◆ *adj* stupid: *No seas ~.* Don't be stupid. ◆ *nmf* idiot: *¡Cállate, ~!* Be quiet, you idiot!

imitación *nf* imitation **LOC de imitación** fake

imitar *vt* **1** (*copiar*) to imitate **2** (*parodiar*) to mimic: *Imita fenomenal a los profesores.* He's really good at mimicking the teachers.

impacientar ◆ *vt* to exasperate ◆ **impacientarse** *v pron* **impacientarse (por)** to get worked up (**about *sth***)

impaciente *adj* impatient

impacto *nm* **1** (*colisión, impresión, repercusión*) impact: *el ~ ambiental* the impact on the environment **2** (*huella*) hole: *dos ~s de bala* two bullet holes

impar *adj* odd: *número ~* odd number

imparcial *adj* unbiased

impecable *adj* impeccable

impedido, -a *pp, adj, nm-nf* disabled [*adj*]: *ser un ~* to be disabled *Ver tb* IMPEDIR

impedimento *nm* **1** (*obstáculo*) obstacle **2** (*Jur*) impediment

impedir *vt* **1** (*paso*) to block *sth* (up): *~ la entrada* to block the entrance (up) **2** (*imposibilitar*) to prevent *sth/sb* (***from doing sth***): *La lluvia impidió que se celebrase la boda.* The rain prevented the wedding from taking place. ◊ *Nada te lo impide.* There's nothing stopping you.

impenetrable *adj* impenetrable

impepinable *adj* undeniable

imperativo, -a *adj, nm* imperative

imperdible *nm* safety pin

imperfección *nf* imperfection

imperialismo *nm* imperialism

imperio *nm* empire

impermeable ◆ *adj* waterproof ◆ *nm* mac

> **Mac** es la abreviatura de **mackintosh**, pero esta última forma se usa mucho menos.

impersonal *adj* impersonal

impertinente *adj* impertinent

implantar *vt* to introduce: *Quieren ~ un nuevo sistema.* They want to introduce a new system.

implicar *vt* **1** (*mezclar a algn en algo*) to implicate: *Le implicaron en el asesi-*

nato. He was implicated in the murder. **2** (*significar*) to imply

imponer ◆ *vt* to impose: ~ *condiciones/una multa* to impose conditions/a fine ◆ **imponerse** *v pron* to prevail (**over *sth*/*sb***): *La justicia se impuso.* Justice prevailed.

importación *nf* import: *la ~ de trigo* the import of wheat ◊ *reducir la ~* to reduce imports LOC **de importación** imported: *un coche de ~* an imported car **de importación y exportación** import-export: *un negocio de ~ y exportación* an import-export business

importador, ~a *nm-nf* importer

importancia *nf* importance LOC **adquirir/cobrar importancia** to become important **no tiene importancia** it doesn't matter **sin importancia** unimportant *Ver tb* QUITAR, RESTAR

importante *adj* **1** (*gen*) important: *Es ~ que asistas a clase.* It's important for you to attend lectures. **2** (*considerable*) considerable: *un número ~ de ofertas* a considerable number of offers

importar[1] *vt* to import: *España importa petróleo.* Spain imports oil.

importar[2] *vi* **1** (*tener importancia*) to matter: *Lo que importa es la salud.* Health is what matters most. ◊ *No importa.* It doesn't matter. **2** (*preocupar*) to care (**about *sth*/*sb***): *No me importa lo que piensen.* I don't care what they think. ◊ *No parecen ~le sus hijos.* He doesn't seem to care about his children. ◊ *¡Claro que me importa!* Of course I care! LOC **me importa un pepino, pimiento, pito, etc** I, you, etc couldn't care less **no me importa** I, you, etc don't mind (*sth/doing sth*): *No me importa levantarme temprano.* I don't mind getting up early. **¿te importa...?** do you mind...?: *¿Te importa cerrar la puerta?* Do you mind shutting the door? ◊ *¿Te importa que abra la ventana?* Do you mind if I open the window?

importe *nm* **1** (*cantidad*) amount: *el ~ de la deuda* the amount of the debt **2** (*coste*) cost: *el ~ de la reparación* the cost of the repair

imposible *adj, nm* impossible: *No pidas ~s.* Don't ask (for) the impossible.

impotente *adj* impotent

imprenta *nf* **1** (*taller*) printer's **2** (*máquina*) printing press

imprescindible *adj* essential

impresión *nf* **1** (*sensación*) impression **2** (*proceso*) printing: *listo para ~* ready for printing LOC **me da la impresión de que...** I get the feeling that...

impresionante *adj* **1** (*gen*) impressive: *un logro ~* an impressive achievement **2** (*espectacular*) striking: *una belleza ~* striking beauty

impresionar *vt* **1** (*gen*) to impress: *Me impresiona su eficacia.* I am impressed by her efficiency. **2** (*emocionar*) to move: *El final me impresionó mucho.* The ending was very moving. **3** (*desagradablemente*) to shock: *Nos impresionó el accidente.* We were shocked by the accident.

impreso, -a ◆ *adj* printed ◆ *nm* form: *rellenar un ~* to fill in a form

impresora *nf* printer ☛ *Ver dibujo en* ORDENADOR

imprevisto, -a ◆ *adj* unforeseen ◆ *nm*: *Ha surgido un ~.* Something unexpected has come up. ◊ *Tengo un dinero ahorrado para ~s.* I've got some money put aside for a rainy day.

imprimir *vt* **1** (*imprenta*) to print **2** (*huella*) to imprint

improvisar *vt* to improvise

imprudente *adj* **1** (*gen*) rash **2** (*conductor*) careless

impuesto *nm* tax: *libre de ~s* tax free LOC **Impuesto sobre el Valor Añadido** value added tax (*abrev* VAT) *Ver tb* EVASIÓN

impulsar *vt* **1** (*gen*) to drive: *La curiosidad me impulsó a entrar.* Curiosity drove me to enter. **2** (*estimular*) to stimulate: *~ la producción* to stimulate production

impulsivo, -a *adj* impulsive

impulso *nm* **1** (*gen*) impulse: *actuar por ~* to act on impulse **2** (*empujón*) boost: *El buen tiempo ha dado gran ~ al turismo.* The good weather has given tourism a boost.

impuro, -a *adj* impure

inaccesible *adj* inaccessible

inaceptable *adj* unacceptable

inadaptado, -a *adj* maladjusted

inadecuado, -a *adj* inappropriate

inadvertido, -a *adj* unnoticed: *pasar ~* to go unnoticed

inagotable *adj* **1** (*inacabable*) inexhaustible **2** (*incansable*) tireless

inaguantable *adj* unbearable

inalámbrico, -a *adj* cordless: *un teléfono ~* a cordless telephone

inapreciable *adj* (*valioso*) invaluable: *su ~ ayuda* their invaluable help

inauguración *nf* opening, inauguration (*formal*): *la ceremonia de ~* the opening ceremony ◊ *Había unas cien personas en la ~.* There were a hundred people at the inauguration.

inaugurar *vt* to open, to inaugurate (*formal*)

incapaz *adj* ~ **de** incapable **of *sth*/ *doing sth***: *Son incapaces de prestar atención.* They are incapable of paying attention.

incautarse *v pron* ~ **de** to seize: *La policía se incautó de 10kg de cocaína.* The police seized 10kg of cocaine.

incendiar ♦ *vt* to set fire **to *sth***: *Un loco ha incendiado la escuela.* A madman has set fire to the school. ♦ **incendiarse** *v pron* to catch fire: *El establo se incendió.* The stable caught fire.

incendio *nm* fire: *apagar un ~* to put out a fire LOC **incendio provocado** arson *Ver tb* ALARMA, BOCA, ESCALERA

incinerar *vt* **1** (*gen*) to incinerate **2** (*cadáver*) to cremate

incisivo *nm* incisor

inclinar ♦ *vt* **1** (*gen*) to tilt: *Inclina el paraguas un poco.* Tilt the umbrella a bit. **2** (*cabeza para asentir o saludar*) to nod ♦ **inclinarse** *v pron* **1** (*lit*) to lean: *El edificio se inclina hacia un lado.* The building leans over to one side. **2 inclinarse por** (*fig*): *Nos inclinamos por el partido verde.* Our sympathies lie with the Green Party.

incluido, -a *pp, adj* including: *con el IVA ~* including VAT LOC **todo incluido** all-in: *Son 10.000 pesetas todo ~.* It's 10000 pesetas all-in. *Ver tb* INCLUIR

incluir *vt* to include: *El precio incluye el servicio.* The price includes a service charge.

inclusive *adv* inclusive: *hasta el sábado ~* up to and including Saturday ◊ *del 3 al 7 ambos ~* from the 3rd to the 7th inclusive

incluso *adv* even: *~ me dieron dinero.* They even gave me money. ◊ *Eso sería ~ mejor.* That would be even better.

incógnito, -a *adj* LOC **de incógnito** incognito: *viajar de ~* to travel incognito

incoherente *adj* **1** (*confuso*) incoherent: *palabras ~s* incoherent words **2** (*ilógico*) inconsistent: *comportamiento ~* inconsistent behaviour

incoloro, -a *adj* colourless

incombustible *adj* fireproof

incomible *adj* inedible

incómodo, -a *adj* uncomfortable

incompatible *adj* incompatible

incompetente *adj, nmf* incompetent

incompleto, -a *adj* **1** (*gen*) incomplete: *información incompleta* incomplete information **2** (*sin acabar*) unfinished

incomprensible *adj* incomprehensible

incomunicado, -a *adj* **1** (*gen*) cut off: *Nos quedamos ~s por la nieve.* We were cut off by the snow. **2** (*preso*) in solitary confinement

inconfundible *adj* unmistakable

inconsciente ♦ *adj* unconscious: *El paciente está ~.* The patient is unconscious. ◊ *un gesto ~* an unconscious gesture ♦ *adj, nmf* (*irresponsable*) irresponsible [*adj*]: *Eres un ~.* You're so irresponsible.

incontable *adj* **1** (*gen*) countless **2** (*Ling*) uncountable

inconveniente ♦ *adj* **1** (*inoportuno, molesto*) inconvenient: *una hora ~* an inconvenient time **2** (*no apropiado*) inappropriate: *un comentario ~* an inappropriate comment ♦ *nm* **1** (*dificultad, obstáculo*) problem: *Han surgido algunos ~s.* Some problems have arisen. **2** (*desventaja*) disadvantage: *Tiene ventajas e ~s.* It has its advantages and disadvantages.

incorporación *nf* ~ (**a**) (*entrada*) entry (**into *sth***): *la ~ de España a la CE* Spain's entry into the EC

incorporado, -a *pp, adj* **1** ~ **a** (*gen*) incorporated **into *sth***: *nuevos vocablos ~s al idioma* new words incorporated into the language **2** (*Tec*) built-in: *con antena incorporada* with a built-in aerial *Ver tb* INCORPORAR

incorporar ♦ *vt* **1** (*persona*) to include *sb* (**in *sth***): *Me han incorporado al equipo.* I've been included in the team. **2** (*territorio*) to annex **3** (*persona tumbada*) to sit *sb* up: *Lo incorporé para que no se ahogara.* I sat him up so he wouldn't choke. ♦ **incorporarse** *v pron* **incorporarse** (**a**) **1** (*gen*) to join (*sth*) **2** (*trabajo*) to start (*sth*): *El lunes me incorporo a mi nuevo empleo.* I start my new job on Monday.

incorrecto, -a *adj* **1** (*erróneo*) incorrect **2** (*conducta*) impolite

increíble *adj* incredible

incrustarse *v pron* (*proyectil*): *La bala se incrustó en la pared.* The bullet embedded itself in the wall.

incubadora *nf* incubator
incubar(se) *vt, v pron* to incubate
inculto, -a *adj, nm-nf* ignorant [*adj*]: *Eres un ~.* You're so ignorant.
incultura *nf* lack of culture
incurable *adj* incurable
incursión *nf* (*Mil*) raid
indagación *nf* enquiry [*pl* enquiries]
indecente *adj* **1** (*sucio*) filthy: *Esta cocina está ~.* This kitchen is filthy. **2** (*espectáculo, gesto, lenguaje*) obscene **3** (*ropa*) indecent
indeciso, -a *adj, nm-nf* (*de carácter*) indecisive [*adj*]: *ser un ~* to be indecisive
indefenso, -a *adj* defenceless
indefinido, -a *adj* **1** (*periodo, Ling*) indefinite: *una huelga indefinida* an indefinite strike **2** (*color, edad, forma*) indeterminate
indemnizar *vt* to pay *sb* compensation (***for sth***)
independencia *nf* independence
independiente *adj* independent
independizarse *v pron* **1** (*individuo*) to leave home **2** (*país, colonia*) to gain independence
indestructible *adj* indestructible
India *nf* India
indicación *nf* **1** (*gen*) sign **2 indicaciones (a)** (*instrucciones*) instructions: *Siga las indicaciones del folleto.* Follow the instructions in the leaflet. **(b)** (*camino*) directions
indicado, -a *pp, adj* **1** (*conveniente*) suitable **2** (*convenido*) specified: *la fecha indicada en el documento* the date specified in the document **3** (*aconsejable*) advisable *Ver tb* INDICAR
indicador *nm* indicator LOC **indicador de gasolina/presión** petrol/pressure gauge *Ver tb* CARTEL
indicar *vt* **1** (*mostrar*) to show, to indicate (*más formal*): *~ el camino* to show the way **2** (*señalar*) to point *sth* out (***to sb***): *Indicó que se trataba de un error.* He pointed out that it was a mistake.
índice *nm* **1** (*gen*) index **2** (*dedo*) index finger LOC **índice (de materias)** table of contents **índice de natalidad** birth rate
índico, -a ◆ *adj* Indian ◆ **Índico** *nm* Indian Ocean
indiferencia *nf* indifference (***to sth/sb***)
indiferente *adj* indifferent (***to sth/sb***), not interested (***in sth/sb***) (*más coloq*): *Es ~ a la moda.* She isn't interested in fashion. LOC **ser indiferente**: *Es ~ que sea blanco o negro.* It doesn't matter whether it's black or white. **me es indiferente** I, you, etc don't care
indígena ◆ *adj* indigenous ◆ *nmf* native
indigestión *nf* indigestion
indignado, -a *pp, adj* indignant (***at/about/over sth***) *Ver tb* INDIGNAR
indignante *adj* outrageous
indignar ◆ *vt* to infuriate ◆ **indignarse** *v pron* **indignarse (con) (por)** to get angry (**with *sb***) (**about *sth***)
indigno, -a *adj* **1** (*despreciable*) contemptible **2 ~ de** unworthy **of *sth/sb***: *una conducta indigna de un director* behaviour unworthy of a director
indio, -a *adj, nm-nf* Indian: *los ~s* the Indians LOC *Ver* CONEJILLO, FILA
indirecta *nf* hint LOC **coger la indirecta** to take the hint **echar/lanzar/soltar una indirecta** to drop a hint
indirecto, -a *adj* indirect
indiscreción *nf*: *Fue una ~ por su parte preguntarlo.* She shouldn't have asked. ◊ *si no es ~* if you don't mind my asking
indiscutible *adj* indisputable
indispensable *adj* essential LOC **lo indispensable** the bare essentials [*v pl*]
indispuesto, -a *adj* (*enfermo*) not well: *No ha venido a clase porque está ~.* He hasn't come to school because he's not well.
individual *adj* individual LOC *Ver* CAMA, CHALÉ, HABITACIÓN
individuo, -a *nm-nf* individual
indudable *adj* undoubted LOC **es indudable que…** there is no doubt that…
indulto *nm* pardon: *El juez le concedió el ~.* The judge pardoned him.
industria *nf* industry [*pl* industries]: *~ alimentaria/siderúrgica* food/iron and steel industry
industrial ◆ *adj* industrial ◆ *nmf* industrialist LOC *Ver* CANTIDAD
industrialización *nf* industrialization
industrializar ◆ *vt* to industrialize ◆ **industrializarse** *v pron* to become industrialized
inédito, -a *adj* (*desconocido*) previously unknown
ineficaz *adj* **1** (*gen*) ineffective: *un tratamiento ~* ineffective treatment **2** (*persona*) inefficient
ineficiente *adj* (*persona*) inefficient

inercia *nf* inertia LOC **por inercia** through force of habit

inesperado, -a *adj* unexpected

inestable *adj* **1** (*gen*) unstable: *Tiene un carácter muy* ~. He's very unstable. **2** (*tiempo*) changeable

inevitable *adj* inevitable

inexperiencia *nf* inexperience

inexperto, -a *adj* inexperienced

infancia *nf* childhood LOC *Ver* JARDÍN

infantería *nf* infantry [*v sing o pl*] LOC **infantería de marina** marines [*pl*]

infantil *adj* **1** (*de niño*) children's: *literatura/programación* ~ children's books/programmes **2** (*inocente*) childlike: *una sonrisa* ~ a childlike smile **3** (*peyorativo*) childish, infantile (*más formal*): *No seas* ~. Don't be childish.

infarto *nm* heart attack

infección *nf* infection

infeccioso, -a *adj* infectious

infectar ◆ *vt* to infect *sth/sb* (**with sth**) ◆ **infectarse** *v pron* to become infected: *Se ha infectado la herida*. The wound has become infected.

infeliz ◆ *adj* unhappy ◆ *nmf* (*inocentón*) fool

inferior *adj* **1** ~ (**a**) (*gen*) inferior (**to** ***sth/sb***): *de una calidad* ~ *a la vuestra* inferior to yours **2** ~ (**a**) (*por debajo*) lower (**than** ***sth***): *una tasa de natalidad* ~ *a la del año pasado* a lower birth rate than last year

infidelidad *nf* infidelity [*pl* infidelities]

infiel *adj* unfaithful (***to sth/sb***): *Le ha sido* ~. He has been unfaithful to her.

infierno *nm* hell: *ir al* ~ to go to hell

infinidad *nf* (*multitud*) a great many: *una* ~ *de gente/cosas* a great many people/things

infinito, -a *adj* infinite: *Las posibilidades son infinitas*. The possibilities are infinite. ◊ *Se necesita una paciencia infinita*. You need infinite patience.

inflación *nf* inflation

inflamación *nf* (*Med*) swelling, inflammation (*formal*)

inflamarse *v pron* **1** (*encenderse*) to catch fire: *Se inflamó el depósito de la gasolina*. The petrol tank caught fire. **2** (*Med*) to swell: *Se me ha inflamado un poco el tobillo*. My ankle is a bit swollen.

inflar *vt* (*hinchar*) to blow *sth* up

influencia *nf* influence (**on/over** ***sth/sb***): *No tengo* ~ *sobre él*. I have no influence over him.

influir *vi* ~ **en** to influence *sth/sb* [*vt*]: *No quiero* ~ *en tu decisión*. I don't want to influence your decision.

información *nf* **1** (*gen*) information (**on/about** ***sth/sb***) [*incontable*]: *pedir* ~ to ask for information **2** (*noticias*) news [*sing*]: *La televisión ofrece mucha* ~ *deportiva*. There's a lot of sports news on television. **3** (*telefónica*) directory enquiries [*pl*] **4** (*recepción*) information desk LOC *Ver* OFICINA

informal ◆ *adj* (*ropa, acto*) informal: *una reunión* ~ an informal gathering ◆ *adj, nmf* unreliable [*adj*]: *Es un* ~, *siempre llega tarde*. He's very unreliable; he's always late.

informar ◆ *vt* **1** (*notificar*) to inform *sb* (**of/about** ***sth***): *Debemos* ~ *a la policía del accidente*. We must inform the police of the accident. **2** (*anunciar*) to announce: *La radio ha informado que…* It was announced on the radio that… ◆ *vi* ~ (**de/acerca de**) (*dar un informe*) to report (**on** ***sth***): ~ *de lo decidido en la reunión* to report on what was decided at the meeting ◆ **informarse** *v pron* **informarse** (**de/sobre/acerca de**) to find out (**about** ***sth/sb***): *Tengo que* ~*me de lo sucedido*. I've got to find out what happened.

informática *nf* **1** (*gen*) computing **2** (*carrera*) computer science

informe *nm* **1** (*documento, exposición oral*) report: *el* ~ *anual de una sociedad* the company's annual report ◊ *un* ~ *escolar* a school report **2 informes** information [*incontable, v sing*]: *de acuerdo con sus* ~*s* according to their information

infracción *nf* **1** (*gen*) offence: *una* ~ *de tráfico* a traffic offence **2** (*acuerdo, contrato, regla*) breach **of** ***sth***: *una* ~ *de la ley* a breach of the law

infrarrojo, -a *adj* infrared

infundado, -a *adj* unfounded

infundir *vt* **1** (*miedo*) to instil *sth* (**in/into** ***sb***) **2** (*sospechas*) to arouse *sb's suspicions* **3** (*respeto, confianza*) to inspire *sth* (**in** ***sb***)

infusión *nf* herbal tea

ingeniar *vt* to think *sth* up, to devise (*más formal*) LOC **ingeniárselas** to find a way (*to do sth/of doing sth*): *Nos las ingeniamos para entrar en la fiesta*. We found a way to get into the party. ◊ *Ingéniatelas como puedas*. You'll have to manage somehow.

ingeniería *nf* engineering

ingeniero, -a *nm-nf* engineer LOC **ingeniero agrónomo** agriculturalist **ingeniero de caminos, canales y puertos** civil engineer **ingeniero técnico** engineer

ingenio *nm* **1** (*inventiva*) ingenuity **2** (*humor*) wit **3** (*máquina, aparato*) device

ingenioso, -a *adj* **1** (*gen*) ingenious **2** (*perspicaz*) witty

ingenuo, -a *adj, nm-nf* **1** (*inocente*) innocent **2** (*crédulo*) naive [*adj*]: *¡Eres un ~!* You're so naive!

ingerir *vt* to consume

Inglaterra *nf* England

ingle *nf* groin

inglés, -esa ◆ *adj, nm* English: *hablar ~* to speak English ◆ *nm-nf* Englishman/woman [*pl* Englishmen/women]: *los ingleses* the English

ingrato, -a *adj* **1** (*persona*) ungrateful **2** (*trabajo, tarea*) thankless

ingrediente *nm* ingredient

ingresar ◆ *vi* ~ (**en**) **1** (*Mil, club*) to join *sth* [*vt*]: *~ en el ejército* to join the army **2** (*centro sanitario*): *Ingreso mañana.* I'm going into hospital tomorrow. ◊ *Ingresó en La Paz a las 4.30.* He was admitted to La Paz at 4.30. ◆ *vt* **1** (*hospital*): *Me tuvieron que ~.* I had to be taken into hospital. ◊ *Lo ingresan mañana.* They're admitting him tomorrow. **2** (*dinero*) to pay *sth* in: *~ dinero en una cuenta bancaria* to pay money into a bank account

ingreso *nm* **1** (*entrada*) **(a)** (*ejército*) enlistment (*in sth*) **(b)** (*organización*) entry (*into sth*): *el ~ de España en la CE* Spain's entry into the EC **(c)** (*hospital, institución*) admission (*to sth*) **2** (*dinero*) deposit **3 ingresos (a)** (*persona, institución*) income [*sing*] **(b)** (*Estado, municipio*) revenue [*sing*] LOC *Ver* EXAMEN

inhabitado, -a *adj* uninhabited

inhalador *nm* inhaler

inhalar *vt* to inhale

inherente *adj* ~ (**a**) inherent (**in** ***sth/sb***): *problemas ~s al cargo* problems inherent in the job

inhumano, -a *adj* **1** (*gen*) inhuman **2** (*injusto*) inhumane

iniciación *nf* ~ (**a**) **1** (*gen*) introduction (**to** ***sth***): *~ a la música* an introduction to music **2** (*rito*) initiation (**into** ***sth***)

inicial *adj, nf* initial

iniciar *vt* **1** (*comenzar*) to begin: *~ la reunión* to begin the meeting **2** (*reformas*) to initiate

iniciativa *nf* initiative: *tener ~* to show initiative ◊ *tomar la ~* to take the initiative LOC **por iniciativa propia** on your own initiative

inicio *nm* **1** (*principio*) beginning: *desde los ~s de su carrera* right from the beginning of his career **2** (*guerra, enfermedad*) outbreak

injusticia *nf* injustice: *Cometieron muchas ~s.* Many injustices were done. LOC **ser una injusticia**: *Es una ~.* It's not fair.

injusto, -a *adj* ~ (**con/para**) unfair (**on/to** ***sb***): *Es ~ para los demás.* It's unfair on the others.

inmaduro, -a *adj, nm-nf* (*persona*) immature [*adj*]

inmejorable *adj* **1** (*resultado, referencia, tiempo*) excellent **2** (*calidad, nivel*) top **3** (*precio, récord*) unbeatable

inmenso, -a *adj* **1** (*gen*) immense: *de una importancia inmensa* of immense importance **2** (*sentimientos*) great: *una alegría/pena inmensa* great happiness/sorrow LOC **la inmensa mayoría** the vast majority [*pl*]

inmigración *nf* immigration

inmigrado, -a *nm-nf* (*tb* **inmigrante** *nmf*) immigrant

inmigrar *vi* to immigrate

inmoral *adj* immoral

inmortal *adj, nmf* immortal

inmóvil *adj* still: *permanecer ~* to stand still

inmunidad *nf* immunity: *gozar de/tener ~ diplomática* to have diplomatic immunity

inmutarse *v pron*: *No se inmutaron.* They didn't turn a hair.

innato, -a *adj* innate

innovador, ~a *adj* innovative

innumerable *adj* innumerable

inocente ◆ *adj, nmf* innocent: *hacerse el ~* to play the innocent ◊ *Soy ~.* I'm innocent. ◆ *adj* **1** (*ingenuo*) naive **2** (*broma*) harmless LOC *Ver* DECLARAR, DÍA

inofensivo, -a *adj* harmless

inolvidable *adj* unforgettable

inoportuno, -a *adj* inopportune: *un momento ~* an inopportune moment LOC **¡qué inoportuno!** what a nuisance!

inoxidable *adj* (*acero*) stainless

inquieto, -a *adj* **1** (*agitado, activo*) restless: *un niño ~* a restless child **2** ~ (**por**) (*preocupado*) worried (**about** ***sth/***

sb): *Estoy ~ por los niños.* I'm worried about the children.

inquietud *nf* **1** (*preocupación*) anxiety **2 inquietudes** interest [*sing*]: *Es una persona sin ~es.* He's got no interest in anything.

inquilino, -a *nm-nf* tenant

insatisfecho, -a *adj* dissatisfied (***with sth/sb***)

inscribir ◆ *vt* **1** (*en un registro*) to register: *~ un nacimiento* to register a birth **2** (*matricular*) to enrol *sb*: *Voy a ~ a mi hijo en el colegio.* I'm going to enrol my son in school. **3** (*grabar*) to inscribe ◆ **inscribirse** *v pron* **1** (*curso*) to enrol (**for/on sth**) **2** (*organización, partido*) to join **3** (*competición, concurso*) to enter

inscripción *nf* **1** (*grabado*) inscription **2 (a)** (*registro*) registration **(b)** (*curso, ejército*) enrolment

insecticida *nm* insecticide

insecto *nm* insect

inseguridad *nf* **1** (*falta de confianza*) insecurity **2** (*tiempo, trabajo, proyecto*) uncertainty [*pl* uncertainties] LOC **inseguridad ciudadana** lack of safety on the streets

inseguro, -a *adj* **1** (*sin confianza en uno mismo*) insecure **2** (*peligroso*) unsafe **3** (*paso, voz*) unsteady

insensible *adj* **1** ~ **(a)** insensitive (**to sth**): *~ al frío/sufrimiento* insensitive to cold/suffering **2** (*miembro, nervio*) numb

inservible *adj* useless

insignia *nf* badge

insignificante *adj* insignificant

insinuación *nf* **1** (*sugerencia*) hint **2** (*ofensiva*) insinuation

insinuar *vt* **1** (*sugerir*) to hint: *Insinuó que había aprobado.* He hinted that I'd passed. **2** (*algo desagradable*) to insinuate: *¿Qué insinúas, que miento?* Are you insinuating that I'm lying?

insistente *adj* **1** (*con palabras*) insistent **2** (*actitud*) persistent

insistir *vi* ~ (**en/sobre**) to insist (**on *sth*/ *doing sth***): *Insistió en que fuéramos.* He insisted that we go.

insolación *nf* sunstroke [*incontable*]: *coger(se) una ~* to get sunstroke

insomnio *nm* insomnia

insonorizar *vt* to soundproof

insoportable *adj* unbearable

inspeccionar *vt* to inspect

inspector, ~a *nm-nf* inspector

inspiración *nf* inspiration

inspirar ◆ *vt* to inspire (*sb*) (**with *sth***): *Ese médico no me inspira ninguna confianza.* That doctor doesn't inspire me with confidence. ◆ **inspirarse** *v pron* **inspirarse (en)** to get inspiration (**from *sth***): *El autor se inspiró en un hecho real.* The author got his inspiration from a real-life event.

instalación *nf* **1** (*gen*) installation **2 instalaciones** facilities: *instalaciones deportivas* sports facilities LOC **instalación eléctrica** (electrical) wiring

instalar ◆ *vt* to install ◆ **instalarse** *v pron* **1** (*en una ciudad, país*) to settle (down) **2** (*en una casa*) to move ***into sth***: *Acabamos de ~nos en la nueva casa.* We've just moved into our new house.

instantáneo, -a *adj* instantaneous

instante *nm* moment: *en ese mismo ~* at that very moment

instinto *nm* instinct LOC **por instinto** instinctively

institución *nf* (*organismo*) institution

instituto *nm* **1** (*gen*) institute **2** (*Educ*) secondary school LOC **instituto de formación profesional** ≃ technical college (*GB*)

instrucción *nf* **1** (*Mil*) training **2 instrucciones** instructions: *instrucciones de uso* instructions for use

instructor, ~a *nm-nf* instructor

instrumental *nm* instruments [*pl*]: *el ~ médico* medical instruments

instrumento *nm* instrument

insubordinado, -a *adj* insubordinate (*formal*), rebellious

insuficiencia *nf* **1** (*deficiencia*) inadequacy [*pl* inadequacies] **2** (*Med*) failure: *~ cardiaca/renal* heart/kidney failure

insuficiente ◆ *adj* **1** (*escaso*) insufficient **2** (*deficiente*) inadequate ◆ *nm* fail ≃ F: *Le han puesto un ~.* He got an F.

insultar *vt* to insult

insulto *nm* insult

insuperable *adj* **1** (*hazaña, belleza*) matchless **2** (*dificultad*) insuperable **3** (*calidad, oferta*) unbeatable

insustituible *adj* irreplaceable

intachable *adj* irreproachable

intacto, -a *adj* **1** (*no tocado*) untouched **2** (*no dañado*) intact: *Su reputación permaneció intacta.* His reputation remained intact.

integración *nf* ~ (**en**) integration (**into *sth***)

integral *adj* comprehensive: *una*

reforma ~ a comprehensive reform ◊ *Es un idiota* ~. He's a complete idiot. LOC *Ver* PAN

integrarse *v pron* ~ **(en)** (*adaptarse*) to integrate **(into *sth*)**

integridad *nf* integrity

íntegro, -a *adj* whole: *mi sueldo* ~ my whole salary

intelectual *adj, nmf* intellectual

inteligencia *nf* intelligence LOC *Ver* COEFICIENTE

inteligente *adj* intelligent

intemperie *nf* LOC **a la intemperie** out in the open

intención *nf* intention: *tener malas intenciones* to have evil intentions LOC **con (mala) intención** maliciously **hacer algo con buena intención** to mean well: *Lo hizo con buena* ~. He meant well. **tener intención de** to intend *to do sth*: *Tenemos* ~ *de comprar un piso.* We intend to buy a flat.

intencionado, -a *adj* deliberate LOC **bien/mal intencionado** well-meaning/malicious

intensidad *nf* **1** (*gen*) intensity **2** (*corriente eléctrica, viento, voz*) strength

intensificar(se) *vt, v pron* to intensify

intensivo, -a *adj* intensive LOC *Ver* UNIDAD

intenso, -a *adj* **1** (*gen*) intense: *una ola de frío/calor* ~ intense cold/heat **2** (*vigilancia*) close **3** (*negociaciones*) intensive

intentar *vt* to try (*sth/to do sth*): *Inténtalo.* Just try.

intento *nm* attempt LOC **al primer, segundo, etc intento** at the first, second, etc attempt

intercambiar *vt* to exchange, to swap (*coloq*): ~ *prisioneros* to exchange prisoners ◊ ~ *cromos* to swap stickers

intercambio *nm* exchange LOC *Ver* VIAJE

interceder *vi* ~ **(a favor de/por)** to intervene **(on *sb's* behalf)**: *Intercedieron por mí.* They intervened on my behalf.

interés *nm* **1** ~ **(en/por)** interest **(in *sth*/*sb*)**: *La novela ha suscitado un gran* ~. The novel has aroused a lot of interest. ◊ *tener* ~ *en la política* to be interested in politics ◊ *a un 10% de* ~ at 10% interest **2** (*egoísmo*) self-interest: *Lo hicieron por puro* ~. They did it in their own self-interest. LOC **hacer algo sin ningún interés** to show no interest in sth: *Trabajan sin ningún* ~. They show no interest in their work. *Ver tb* CONFLICTO

interesante *adj* interesting

interesar ◆ *vi* to be interested **in *sth*/*doing sth***: *Nos interesa el arte.* We're interested in art. ◊ *¿Te interesa participar?* Are you interested in taking part? ◆ *vt* ~ **a algn (en algo)** to interest sb **(in sth)**: *No consiguió* ~ *al público en la reforma.* He didn't manage to interest the public in the reforms. ◆ **interesarse** *v pron* **interesarse por 1** (*mostrar interés*) to show (an) interest **in *sth***: *El director se interesó por mi obra.* The director showed (an) interest in my work. **2** (*preocuparse*) to ask **after *sth/sb***: *Se interesó por mi salud.* He asked after my health.

interferencia *nf* interference [*incontable*]: *Se han producido ~s en la emisión.* The programme has been affected by interference. ◊ *Hay muchas ~s.* We're getting a lot of interference.

interferir *vi* ~ **(en)** to meddle, to interfere (*más formal*) **(in *sth*)**: *Deja de* ~ *en mis asuntos.* Stop meddling in my affairs.

interior ◆ *adj* **1** (*gen*) inner: *una habitación* ~ an inner room **2** (*bolsillo*) inside **3** (*comercio, política*) domestic ◆ *nm* interior: *el* ~ *de un edificio/país* the interior of a building/country LOC *Ver* MINISTERIO, MINISTRO, ROPA

interjección *nf* interjection

intermediario, -a *nm-nf* **1** (*mediador*) mediator: *La ONU actuó de* ~ *en el conflicto.* The UN acted as a mediator in the conflict. **2** (*mensajero*) go-between [*pl* go-betweens] **3** (*Com*) middleman [*pl* middlemen]

intermedio, -a ◆ *adj* intermediate ◆ *nm* interval

interminable *adj* endless

intermitente *nm* (*coche*) indicator

internacional *adj* international

internado *nm* boarding school

internar *vt*: *Lo internaron en el hospital.* He was admitted to hospital. ◊ *Internaron a su padre en un asilo.* They got their father into a home.

interno, -a[1] *adj* **1** (*gen*) internal: *órganos ~s* internal organs **2** (*dentro de un país*) domestic: *comercio* ~ domestic trade **3** (*cara, parte*) inner: *la parte interna del muslo* the inner thigh

interno, -a[2] *nm-nf* **1** (*alumno*) boarder **2** (*cárcel*) inmate **3** (*residente*) resident LOC *Ver* COLEGIO

interpretación *nf* interpretation

interpretar *vt* **1** (*gen*) to interpret: ~ *la ley* to interpret the law **2** (*Cine, Teat, Mús*) to perform

intérprete *nmf* **1** (*gen*) interpreter **2** (*Teat, Cine, Mús*) performer

interrogación *nf* question mark ☛ *Ver* págs 318–19.

interrogar *vt* to question

interrogatorio *nm* interrogation

interrumpir *vt* **1** (*gen*) to interrupt: ~ *la emisión* to interrupt a programme ◊ *No me interrumpas.* Don't interrupt me. **2** (*tráfico, clase*) to disrupt: *Las obras interrumpirán el tráfico.* The roadworks will disrupt the traffic.

interruptor *nm* switch

interurbano, -a *adj* **1** (*gen*) inter-city: *servicios ~s* inter-city services **2** (*llamada*) long-distance

intervalo *nm* interval: *a ~s de media hora* at half-hourly intervals

intervenir ◆ *vi* **1** ~ (**en**) to intervene (**in** ***sth***): *Tuvo que ~ la policía.* The police had to intervene. **2** (*hablar*) to speak ◆ *vt* (*operar*) to operate (**on** ***sb***)

intestino *nm* intestine: ~ *delgado/grueso* small/large intestine

intimidad *nf* (*vida privada*) private life: *No le gusta que se metan en su ~.* He doesn't like people interfering in his private life. ◊ *el derecho a la ~* the right to privacy

íntimo, -a *adj* **1** (*gen*) intimate: *una conversación íntima* an intimate conversation **2** (*amistad, relación*) close: *Son ~s amigos.* They're very close friends.

intolerable *adj* intolerable

intriga *nf* **1** (*película, novela*) suspense: *una película con mucha ~* a film with lots of suspense **2** (*curiosidad*): *Chico, ¡qué ~! Cuéntamelo.* Come on, don't keep me in suspense. ◊ *¿No tienes ~ por saber dónde están?* Aren't you dying to know where they are?

intrigar *vt* to intrigue: *Ahora me intriga.* I'm intrigued now.

introducción *nf* introduction: *una ~ a la música* an introduction to music

introducir *vt* to put *sth* in; to put *sth* ***into sth***, to insert (*más formal*): *Introduzca la moneda en la ranura.* Insert the coin in the slot.

introvertido, -a ◆ *adj* introverted ◆ *nm-nf* introvert

intruso, -a *nm-nf* intruder

intuición *nf* intuition: *Contesté por ~.* I answered intuitively.

intuir *vt* to sense

inundación *nf* flood

inundar(se) *vt, v pron* to flood: *Se inundaron los campos.* The fields flooded.

inútil ◆ *adj* useless: *cacharros ~es* useless junk ◊ *Es un esfuerzo ~.* It's a waste of time. ◆ *nmf* good-for-nothing LOC **es inútil (que ...)**: *Es ~ que intentes convencerle.* It's pointless trying to convince him. ◊ *Es ~ que grites.* There's no point in shouting.

invadir *vt* to invade

inválido, -a ◆ *adj* (*Med*) disabled ◆ *nm-nf* disabled person

invasión *nf* invasion

invasor, ~a ◆ *adj* invading ◆ *nm-nf* invader

invencible *adj* invincible

inventar ◆ *vt* (*descubrir*) to invent: *Gutenberg inventó la imprenta.* Gutenberg invented the printing press. ◆ **inventar(se)** *vt, v pron* to make *sth* up: *~(se) una excusa* to make up an excuse ◊ *Te lo has inventado.* You've made that up.

invento *nm* invention: *Esto es un ~ mío.* This is an invention of mine.

inventor, ~a *nm-nf* inventor

invernadero *nm* greenhouse LOC *Ver* EFECTO

inversión *nf* (*Fin*) investment

inverso, -a *adj* **1** (*proporción*) inverse **2** (*orden*) reverse **3** (*dirección*) opposite: *en sentido ~ a la rotación* in the opposite direction to the rotation LOC **a la inversa** the other way round

invertebrado, -a *adj, nm* invertebrate

invertir *vt* (*tiempo, dinero*) to invest: *Han invertido diez millones en la compañía.* They've invested ten million pesetas in the company.

investigación *nf* ~ (**de/sobre**) **1** (*gen*) investigation (**into** ***sth***): *Habrá una ~ sobre el accidente.* There'll be an investigation into the accident. **2** (*científica, académica*) research [*incontable*] (**into/on** ***sth***): *Están haciendo un trabajo de ~ sobre la malaria.* They're doing research on malaria.

investigador, ~a *nm-nf* **1** (*gen*) investigator **2** (*científico, académico*) researcher LOC **investigador privado** private detective

investigar *vt, vi* **1** (*gen*) to investigate:

~ *un caso* to investigate a case **2** (*científico, académico*) to do research (**into/on sth**): *Están investigando sobre el virus del SIDA.* They're doing research on the Aids virus.

invierno *nm* winter: *ropa de ~* winter clothes ◊ *Nunca uso la bicicleta en ~.* I never ride my bike in the winter.

invisible *adj* invisible

invitación *nf* invitation (**to sth/to do sth**)

invitado, -a *pp, adj, nm-nf* guest [*n*]: *el artista ~* the guest artist ◊ *Los ~s llegarán a las siete.* The guests will arrive at seven. **LOC** *Ver* ESTRELLA; *Ver tb* INVITAR

invitar ◆ *vt* to invite *sb* (**to sth/to do sth**): *Me ha invitado a su fiesta de cumpleaños.* She's invited me to her birthday party. ◆ *vi* (*pagar*): *Invito yo.* I'll get this one. ◊ *Invita la casa.* It's on the house.

inyección *nf* injection: *poner una ~ a algn* to give sb an injection

ir ◆ *vi* **1** (*gen*) to go: *Van a Roma.* They're going to Rome. ◊ *ir en coche/tren/avión* to go by car/train/plane ◊ *ir a pie* to go on foot ◊ *¿Cómo te va (con tu novio)?* How are things going (with your boyfriend)? **2** (*estar, haber diferencia*) to be: *Íbamos sedientos.* We were thirsty. ◊ *ir bien/mal vestido* to be well/badly dressed ◊ *De nueve a doce van tres.* Nine from twelve is three. **3** (*sentar bien*) to suit *sb* [*vt*]: *Te va el pelo corto.* Short hair suits you. **4** (*funcionar*) to work: *El ascensor no va.* The lift's not working. **5** (*gustar*) to be into *sth*: *Le va la música pop.* She's really into pop. ◆ *v aux* **1** ~ **a hacer algo** **(a)** (*gen*) to be going **to do sth**: *Vamos a vender la casa.* We're going to sell the house. ◊ *Íbamos a comer cuando sonó el teléfono.* We were just going to eat when the phone rang. **(b)** (*en órdenes*) to go **and do sth**: *Ve a hablar con tu padre.* Go and talk to your father. **(c)** (*en sugerencias*): *¡Vamos a comer!* Let's go and eat! ◊ *¡Vamos a ver!* Let's see! **2** ~ **haciendo algo** to start **doing sth**: *Id preparando la mesa.* Start laying the table. ◆ **irse** *v pron* **1** (*marcharse*) to leave: *Mañana me voy a España.* I'm leaving for Spain tomorrow. ◊ *irse de casa* to leave home **2** (*mancha, luz, dolor*) to go: *Se ha ido la luz.* The electricity's gone (off). **3** (*líquido, gas*) to leak **LOC (a mí) ni me va ni me viene** that's nothing to do with me, you, etc **ir a dar a** (*calle*) to lead to *sth*: *Este camino va a dar al pueblo.* This track leads to the village. **ir a lo suyo** to think only of yourself: *Tú siempre vas a lo tuyo.* You always think only of yourself. **ir a por** to go and get *sth/sb*: *Tengo que ir a por pan.* I've got to go and get some bread. **ir con** (*combinar*) to go with *sth*: *Esos calcetines no van con estos zapatos.* Those socks don't go with these shoes. **ir de 1** (*vestido*) to be dressed as *sth/sb*/in *sth*: *Iba de payaso.* I was dressed as a clown. ◊ *ir de azul* to be dressed in blue **2** (*aparentar*): *Tu hermano va de liberal por la vida.* Your brother makes out he's a liberal. **3** (*película, libro*) to be about *sth*: *¿De qué va la película?* What's the film about? **ir por** (*llegarse*) to be up to *sth*: *Voy por la página 100.* I'm up to page 100. **¡qué va!** no way! **¡vamos!** come on!: *¡Vamos, que perdemos el tren!* Come on or we'll miss the train! **¡vaya! 1** (*sorpresa*) good heavens! **2** (*compasión*) oh dear!: *¡Vaya, cuánto lo siento!* Oh dear, I'm so sorry! **3** (*uso enfático*) what/what a(n)...: *¡Vaya película más mala!* What an awful film! **¡(ya) voy!** coming! ☛Para otras expresiones con **ir**, véanse las entradas del sustantivo, adjetivo, etc, p.ej. **ir empatados** en EMPATADO e **ir al grano** en GRANO.

iris *nm* iris **LOC** *Ver* ARCO

Irlanda *nf* Ireland **LOC Irlanda del Norte** Northern Ireland

irlandés, -esa ◆ *adj, nm* Irish: *hablar ~* to speak Irish ◆ *nm-nf* Irishman/woman [*pl* Irishmen/women]: *los irlandeses* the Irish

ironía *nf* irony [*pl* ironies]: *una de las ~s de la vida* one of life's little ironies

irónico, -a *adj, nm-nf* ironic [*adj*]: *ser un ~* to be ironic

irracional *adj* irrational: *un miedo ~* irrational fear

irreal *adj* unreal

irreconocible *adj* unrecognizable

irregular *adj* **1** (*gen*) irregular: *verbos ~es* irregular verbs ◊ *un latido ~* an irregular heartbeat **2** (*anormal*) abnormal: *una situación ~* an abnormal situation

irremediable *adj* irremediable: *una pérdida/un error ~* an irremediable loss/mistake ◊ *Eso ya es ~.* Nothing can be done about it now.

irreparable *adj* irreparable

irrepetible *adj* (*excelente*) unique: *una*

experiencia/obra de arte ~ a unique experience/work of art

irresistible *adj* irresistible: *un atractivo/una fuerza* ~ an irresistible attraction/force ◊ *Tenían unas ganas ~s de verse.* They were dying to see each other.

irrespetuoso, -a *adj* ~ **con/para con** disrespectful (**to/towards** ***sth/sb***)

irrespirable *adj* **1** (*aire*) unbreathable **2** (*ambiente*) unbearable

irresponsable *adj, nmf* irresponsible [*adj*]: *¡Eres un ~!* You're so irresponsible!

irreversible *adj* irreversible

irritar ◆ *vt* to irritate ◆ **irritarse** *v pron* **1 irritarse** (**con**) (**por**) to get annoyed (**with** ***sb***) (**about** ***sth***): *Se irrita por nada.* He gets annoyed very easily. **2** (*Med*) to get irritated

irrompible *adj* unbreakable

isla *nf* island: *las Islas Canarias* the Canary Islands LOC **isla desierta** desert island **las Islas Británicas** the British Isles

islámico, -a *adj* Islamic

isleño, -a *nm-nf* islander

isósceles *adj* LOC *Ver* TRIÁNGULO

istmo *nm* isthmus [*pl* isthmuses]: *el ~ de Panamá* the Isthmus of Panama

Italia *nf* Italy

italiano, -a *adj, nm-nf, nm* Italian: *los ~s* the Italians ◊ *hablar ~* to speak Italian

itinerario *nm* itinerary [*pl* itineraries], route (*más coloq*)

IVA *nm* VAT

izquierdo, -a ◆ *adj* left: *Me he roto el brazo ~.* I've broken my left arm. ◊ *la orilla izquierda del Sena* the left bank of the Seine ◆ **izquierda** *nf* left: *Siga por la izquierda.* Keep left. ◊ *conducir por la izquierda* to drive on the left ◊ *la casa de la izquierda* the house on the left ◊ La carretera se desvía hacia la izquierda. The road bears left. LOC **de izquierda(s)** left-wing: *grupos de izquierdas* left-wing groups **la izquierda** (*Pol*) the Left [*v sing o pl*]: *La izquierda ha ganado las elecciones.* The Left has/have won the election. *Ver tb* CERO, LEVANTAR, MANO

Jj

¡ja! *interj* ha! ha!

jabalí, -ina *nm-nf* wild boar [*pl* wild boar]

jabalina *nf* (*Dep*) javelin: *lanzamiento de ~* javelin throwing

jabón *nm* soap [*incontable*]: *una pastilla de ~* a bar of soap ◊ *~ de afeitar* shaving soap

jabonar(se) *vt, v pron Ver* ENJABONAR(SE)

jabonera *nf* soap dish

jacinto *nm* hyacinth

jadear *vi* to pant

jaguar *nm* jaguar

jalea *nf* LOC **jalea real** royal jelly

jaleo *nm* **1** (*ruido*) row: *Montaron un buen ~ en la discoteca.* They kicked up a terrible row at the disco. **2** (*desorden*) mess: *¡Vaya ~ que tienes en el despacho!* What a mess your office is! LOC *Ver* ARMAR

jamás *adv* never: *~ he conocido a alguien así.* I've never known anyone like him. ☛ *Ver nota en* ALWAYS LOC *Ver* NUNCA

jamón *nm* ham LOC **jamón cocido/de York** cooked ham **jamón serrano** cured ham

Japón *nm* Japan

japonés, -esa ◆ *adj, nm* Japanese: *hablar ~* to speak Japanese ◆ *nm-nf* Japanese man/woman [*pl* Japanese men/women]: *los japoneses* the Japanese

jaque *nm* check LOC **jaque mate** checkmate: *dar/hacer ~ mate* to checkmate

jaqueca *nf* migraine

jarabe *nm* mixture: *~ para la tos* cough mixture

jardín *nm* garden LOC **jardín de infancia** nursery school

jardinera *nf* (*macetero*) window box

jardinería *nf* gardening

jardinero, -a *nm-nf* gardener

jarra *nf* jug LOC **jarra de cerveza** beer mug

jarro *nm* (large) jug

jarrón *nm* vase

jauja *nf* LOC **¡esto es jauja!** this is heaven!

jaula *nf* cage

jefatura *nf* (*oficina central*) headquarters (*abrev* HQ) [*v sing o pl*]: *La ~ de policía está al final de la calle.* The police headquarters is/are at the end of the street.

jefe, -a *nm-nf* **1** (*superior*) boss: *ser el ~* to be the boss **2** (*de un colectivo*) head: *~ de departamento/estado* head of department/state **3** (*de una asociación*) leader: *el ~ de un partido* the party leader **4** (*de una tribu*) chief LOC **jefe de estación** station master **jefe de estudios 1** (*en el colegio*) deputy head **2** (*en una academia*) director of studies

jerarquía *nf* hierarchy [*pl* hierarchies]

jerez *nm* sherry

jeringuilla *nf* (*Med*) syringe

jeroglífico *nm* hieroglyph

jersey *nm* jumper

Jesucristo *n pr* Jesus Christ

jesuita *adj, nm* Jesuit

Jesús *n pr* LOC **¡Jesús!** (*al estornudar*) bless you! ☛ *Ver nota en* ¡ACHÍS!

jeta *nmf* scrounger LOC **tener jeta** to have a nerve: *¡Qué ~ tienes!* You've got a nerve!

jilguero *nm* goldfinch

jinete *nmf* **1** (*persona que va a caballo*) rider **2** (*yóquey*) jockey [*pl* jockeys]

jirafa *nf* giraffe

jolgorio *nm* celebrations [*pl*]: *El ~ continuó hasta bien entrada la noche.* The celebrations continued till well into the night.

jornada *nf* **1** (*gen*) day [*pl* days]: *una ~ de ocho horas* an eight-hour day ◊ *al final de la ~* at the end of the day **2 jornadas** (*congreso*) conference [*sing*] LOC **jornada completa/media jornada**: *Buscan a alguien que trabaje la ~ completa.* They're looking for someone to work full time. ◊ *trabajar media ~* to have a part-time job **jornada laboral** working day

jornalero, -a *nm-nf* casual labourer

joroba *nf* hump

jorobado, -a ◆ *pp, adj* hunched ◆ *nm-nf* hunchback *Ver tb* JOROBAR

jorobar *vt* **1** (*fastidiar*) to get on *sb's* nerves **2** (*estropear*) to muck *sth* up: *Alguien ha jorobado el vídeo.* Somebody's mucked up the video.

jota *nf* (*Naipes*) jack ☛ *Ver nota en* BARAJA LOC **no decir ni jota** not to say a word **no saber ni jota** not to know a thing (*about sth*): *No sé ni ~ de francés.* I don't know a word of French. *Ver* ENTENDER

joven ◆ *adj* young ◆ *nmf* **1** (*chico*) young man **2** (*chica*) girl, young woman (*más formal*) **3 jóvenes** young people

joya *nf* **1** (*gen*) jewellery [*incontable, v sing*]: *Las ~s estaban en la caja fuerte.* The jewellery was in the safe. ◊ *~s robadas* stolen jewellery **2** (*cosa, persona*) treasure: *Eres una ~.* You're a treasure.

joyería *nf* jeweller's [*pl* jewellers]

joyero, -a ◆ *nm-nf* jeweller ◆ *nm* jewellery box

juanete *nm* bunion

jubilación *nf* **1** (*retiro*) retirement **2** (*pensión*) pension

jubilado, -a ◆ *pp, adj* retired: *estar ~* to be retired ◆ *nm-nf* pensioner

jubilarse *v pron* to retire

judaísmo *nm* Judaism

judía *nf* bean LOC **judía verde** green bean

judicial *adj* LOC *Ver* PODER[2]

judío, -a ◆ *adj* Jewish ◆ *nm-nf* Jew

judo *nm* judo

juego *nm* **1** (*gen*) game: *~ de pelota* ball game ◊ *El tenista español gana tres ~s a uno.* The Spanish player is winning by three games to one. **2** (*azar*) gambling **3** (*conjunto*) set: *~ de llaves* set of keys LOC **a juego** matching: *Lleva falda y chaqueta a ~.* She's wearing a skirt and matching jacket. **estar (algo) en juego** to be at stake **hacer juego con** to match: *Los pendientes hacen ~ con el collar.* The earrings match the necklace. **juego de azar** game of chance **juego de mesa/salón** board game **juego de niños** child's play **juego de palabras** pun **juego limpio/sucio** fair/foul play **Juegos Olímpicos** Olympic Games **poner en juego** to put *sth* at stake *Ver tb* FUERA, TERRENO

juerga *nf*: *Montamos una gran ~ el día de la boda.* We had a big party on the day of the wedding. LOC **ir(se) de juerga** to go out

jueves *nm* Thursday [*pl* Thursdays] (*abrev* Thur(s)) ☛ *Ver ejemplos en* LUNES LOC **Jueves Santo** Maundy Thursday *Ver tb* OTRO

juez *nmf* judge

jugada *nf* move LOC **hacer una mala jugada** to play a dirty trick *on sb*

jugador, ~a *nm-nf* **1** (*competidor*) player **2** (*que apuesta*) gambler

jugar ◆ *vt* **1** (*gen*) to play: ~ *un partido de fútbol/una partida de cartas* to play a game of football/cards ◊ *El trabajo juega un papel importante en mi vida.* Work plays an important part in my life. **2** (*dinero*) to put *money* **on sth**: ~ *30.000 pesetas a un caballo* to put 30000 pesetas on a horse ◆ *vi* **1** ~ **(a)** (*gen*) to play: ~ *al fútbol* to play football **2** (*apostar*) to gamble ◆ **jugarse** *v pron* **1** (*apostar*) to gamble *sth* (away) **2** (*arriesgarse*) to risk: ~*se la vida* to risk your life LOC **jugar a la lotería** to buy a lottery ticket **jugar limpio/sucio** to play fair/dirty *Ver tb* COMBA, PASADA, PELLEJO

jugarreta *nf* LOC **hacer una jugarreta** to play a dirty trick *on sb*

jugo *nm* **1** (*gen*) juice **2** (*salsa*) gravy LOC **sacar jugo a algo** to get the most out of sth

jugoso, -a *adj* **1** (*gen*) juicy **2** (*carne*) succulent

juguete *nm* toy [*pl* toys] LOC **de juguete** toy: *camión de* ~ toy lorry

juguetería *nf* toyshop

juguetón, -ona *adj* playful

juicio *nm* **1** (*cualidad*) judgement: *Confío en el* ~ *de las personas.* I trust people's judgement. **2** (*sensatez*) (common) sense: *Careces totalmente de* ~. You're totally lacking in common sense. **3** (*opinión*) opinion: *emitir un* ~ to give an opinion **4** (*Jur*) trial LOC **a mi juicio** in my, your, etc opinion **llevar a juicio** to take *sth/sb* to court *Ver tb* MUELA, PERDER, SANO

juicioso, -a *adj* sensible

julio *nm* July (*abrev* Jul) ☛ *Ver ejemplos en* ENERO

jungla *nf* jungle

junio *nm* June (*abrev* Jun) ☛ *Ver ejemplos en* ENERO

juntar *vt* **1** (*poner juntos*) to put *sth/sb* together: *¿Juntamos las mesas?* Shall we put the tables together? **2** (*unir*) to join *sth* (together): *He juntado los dos trozos.* I've joined the two pieces (together). **3** (*reunir*) to get *people* together

junto, -a ◆ *adj* **1** (*gen*) together: *todos* ~*s* all together ◊ *Siempre estudiamos* ~*s.* We always study together. **2** (*cerca*) close together: *Los árboles están muy* ~*s.* The trees are very close together. ◆ *adv* **1** ~ **a** next to: *El cine está* ~ *al café.* The cinema is next to the café. **2** ~ **con** with

Júpiter *nm* Jupiter

jurado *nm* jury [*v sing o pl*] [*pl* juries]: *El* ~ *salió para deliberar.* The jury retired to consider its verdict.

juramento *nm* oath [*pl* oaths] LOC *Ver* PRESTAR

jurar *vt, vi* to swear LOC **jurar bandera** to swear allegiance to the flag **jurar lealtad a algo/algn** to swear allegiance to sth/sb

justicia *nf* **1** (*gen*) justice: *Espero que se haga* ~. I hope justice is done. **2** (*organización estatal*) law: *No te tomes la* ~ *por tu cuenta.* Don't take the law into your own hands.

justificar *vt* to justify

justo, -a ◆ *adj* **1** (*razonable*) fair: *una decisión justa* a fair decision **2** (*correcto, exacto*) right: *el precio* ~ the right price **3** (*apretado*) tight: *Esta falda me está muy justa.* This skirt is too tight for me. **4 justos** (*suficientes*) just enough: *Tenemos los platos* ~*s.* We have just enough plates. ◆ *adv* just, exactly (*formal*): *Lo encontré* ~ *donde dijiste.* I found it just where you told me. LOC **justo cuando…** just as…: *Llegaron* ~ *cuando nos marchábamos.* They arrived just as we were leaving.

juvenil *adj* **1** (*carácter*) youthful: *la moda* ~ young people's fashion **2** (*Dep*) junior LOC *Ver* DELINCUENCIA

juventud *nf* **1** (*edad*) youth **2** (*los jóvenes*) young people [*pl*]: *A la* ~ *de hoy en día le gusta tener libertad.* The young people of today like to have their freedom.

juzgado *nm* court

juzgar *vt* to judge LOC **juzgar mal** to misjudge

Kk

karaoke *nm* karaoke

karate (*tb* **kárate**) *nm* karate: *hacer ~* to do karate

kart *nm* go-kart

katiusca *nf* wellington (boot)

kilo *nm* kilo [*pl* kilos] (*abrev* kg) ☛ *Ver* Apéndice 1.

kilogramo *nm* kilogram(me) (*abrev* kg) ☛ *Ver* Apéndice 1.

kilómetro *nm* kilometre (*abrev* km) ☛ *Ver* Apéndice 1.

kilovatio *nm* kilowatt (*abrev* kw)

kimono *nm Ver* QUIMONO

kiosco *nm Ver* QUIOSCO

kiwi *nm* kiwi fruit [*pl* kiwi fruit]

kleenex® *nm* tissue

koala *nm* koala (bear)

Ll

la¹ ◆ *art def* the: *La casa es vieja.* The house is old. ☛ *Ver nota en* THE ◆ *pron pers* **1** (*ella*) her: *La sorprendió.* It surprised her. **2** (*cosa*) it: *Déjame que la vea.* Let me see it. **3** (*usted*) you LOC **la de/que...** *Ver* EL

la² *nm* **1** (*nota de la escala*) lah **2** (*tonalidad*) A: *la menor* A minor

laberinto *nm* **1** (*gen*) labyrinth **2** (*en un jardín*) maze

labio *nm* lip LOC *Ver* LEER, PINTAR

labor *nf* **1** (*trabajo*) work [*incontable*]: *Llevaron a cabo una gran ~.* They did some great work. **2** (*de coser*) needlework [*incontable*] **3** (*de punto*) knitting [*incontable*] LOC **labores domésticas** housework [*incontable, v sing*]

laborable *adj* working: *los días ~s* working days

laboratorio *nm* laboratory [*pl* laboratories], lab (*más coloq*)

labrador, ~a *nm-nf* **1** (*propietario*) small farmer **2** (*jornalero*) farm labourer

laca *nf* lacquer [*incontable*]

lacrimógeno, -a *adj Ver* GAS

lácteo, -a *adj* LOC *Ver* VÍA

ladera *nf* hillside

lado *nm* **1** (*gen*) side: *Un triángulo tiene tres ~s.* A triangle has three sides. ◊ *ver el ~ bueno de las cosas* to look on the bright side **2** (*lugar*) place: *de un ~ para otro* from one place to another ◊ *¿Nos vamos a otro ~?* Shall we go somewhere else? ◊ *en algún/ningún ~* somewhere/nowhere **3** (*dirección*) way: *Fueron por otro ~.* They went a different way. ◊ *mirar a todos ~s* to look in all directions ◊ *Se fueron cada uno por su ~.* They all went their separate ways. LOC **al lado 1** (*cerca*) really close by: *Está aquí al ~.* It's really close by. **2** (*contiguo*) next door: *el edificio de al ~* the building next door ◊ *los vecinos de al ~* the next-door neighbours **al lado de** next to *sth/sb*: *Se sentó al ~ de su amiga.* She sat down next to her friend. ◊ *Ponte a mi ~.* Stand next to me. **de lado** sideways: *ponerse de ~* to turn sideways **estar/ponerse del lado de algn** to be on/take sb's side: *¿De qué ~ estás?* Whose side are you on? **por un lado...por otro (lado)** on the one hand...on the other (hand) *Ver tb* OTRO

ladrar *vi* to bark (**at sb/sth**): *El perro no dejaba de ~nos.* The dog wouldn't stop barking at us.

ladrillo *nm* brick

ladrón, -ona ◆ *nm-nf* **1** (*gen*) thief [*pl* thieves]: *Los de esa frutería son unos ladrones.* They're a bunch of thieves at that greengrocer's. **2** (*en una casa*) burglar **3** (*en un banco*) robber ☛ *Ver nota en* THIEF ◆ *nm* (*Electrón*) adaptor

lagartija *nf* small lizard

lagarto, -a *nm-nf* lizard

lago *nm* lake

lágrima *nf* tear LOC **lágrimas de cocodrilo** crocodile tears *Ver tb* DERRAMAR(SE), LLORAR

laguna *nf* **1** (*lago*) (small) lake **2** (*omisión*) gap

lamentable *adj* **1** (*aspecto, condición*) pitiful **2** (*desafortunado*) regrettable

lamentar ◆ *vt* to regret *sth/doing sth/to do sth*: *Lamentamos haberos causado tanto trastorno.* We regret having caused you so much trouble. ◊ *Lamentamos comunicarle que...* We regret to inform you that... ◊ *Lo lamento mucho.* I am terribly sorry. ◆ **lamentarse** *v pron* to complain (**about sth**): *Ahora no sirve de nada ~se.* It's no use complaining now.

lamer *vt* to lick

lámina *nf* **1** (*hoja*) sheet **2** (*ilustración*) plate: *~s en color* colour plates

lámpara *nf* **1** (*de luz*) lamp: *una ~ de escritorio* a desk lamp **2** (*mancha*) stain LOC **lámpara de pie** standard lamp

lana *nf* wool LOC **de lana** woollen: *un jersey de ~* a woollen jumper **lana virgen** new wool *Ver tb* PERRO

lanar *adj* LOC *Ver* GANADO

lancha *nf* launch LOC **lancha motora** motor boat

langosta *nf* **1** (*de mar*) lobster **2** (*insecto*) locust

langostino *nm* king prawn

lánguido, -a *adj* languid

lanza *nf* spear

lanzamiento *nm* **1** (*misil, satélite, producto*) launch: *el ~ de su nuevo disco* the launch of their new album **2** (*bomba*) dropping **3** (*Dep*) throw: *Su último ~ fue el mejor.* His last throw was the best one.

lanzar ◆ *vt* **1** (*en un juego o deporte*) to throw *sth* **to sb**: *Lánzale la pelota a tu compañero.* Throw the ball to your team-mate. **2** (*con intención de hacer daño*) to throw *sth* **at sb** ☛ *Ver nota en* THROW[1] **3** (*misil, producto*) to launch **4** (*bomba*) to drop ◆ **lanzarse** *v pron* **1** (*arrojarse*) to throw yourself: *Me lancé al agua.* I threw myself into the water. **2 lanzarse sobre** to pounce **on** *sth/sb*: *Se lanzaron sobre mí/el dinero.* They pounced on me/the money. LOC *Ver* INDIRECTA, PARACAÍDAS

lapicero *nm* pencil

lápida *nf* gravestone

lápiz *nm* pencil: *lápices de colores* coloured pencils LOC **a lápiz** in pencil

largo, -a ◆ *adj* long: *El abrigo te está muy ~.* That coat is too long for you. ◆ *nm* length: *nadar seis ~s* to swim six lengths ◊ *¿Cuánto mide de ~?* How long is it? ◊ *Tiene cincuenta metros de ~.* It's fifty metres long. LOC **a lo largo** lengthways **a lo largo de 1** (*referido a espacio*) along... **2** (*referido a tiempo*) throughout...: *a lo ~ del día* throughout the day **es largo de contar** it's a long story **hacerse largo** to drag: *El día se me está haciendo muy ~.* Today is really dragging on. **¡largo (de aquí)!** clear off! **tener para largo**: *Yo aquí tengo para ~.* I'm going to be a long time. **pasar de largo** to go straight past *sth/sb Ver tb* LUZ

las *art def, pron pers Ver* LOS

lasaña *nf* lasagne

láser *nm* laser LOC *Ver* RAYO

lástima *nf* pity: *¡Qué ~!* What a pity! ◊ *Es una ~ tirarlo.* It's a pity to throw it away.

lastimar *vt* to hurt

lata *nf* **1** (*envase*) can, tin

> **Can** se utiliza para hablar de bebidas en lata: *una lata de Coca-Cola* a can of Coke. Para otros alimentos se puede usar **can** o **tin**: *una lata de sardinas* a can/tin of sardines. *Ver dibujo en* CONTAINER.

2 (*material*) tin **3** (*molestia*) pain: *¡Vaya una ~!* What a pain! LOC **dar la lata 1** (*molestar*) to be a pain: *¡Cuánta ~ das!* What a pain you are! **2** (*pedir con insistencia*) to pester: *Nos estuvo dando la ~ para que le compráramos la bici.* He kept pestering us to get him the bike. **de/en lata** tinned

lateral *adj, nm* side [*n*]: *una calle ~* a side street LOC *Ver* VOLTERETA

latido *nm* (*corazón*) (heart)beat

latifundio *nm* large estate

latigazo *nm* **1** (*golpe*) lash **2** (*chasquido*) crack

látigo *nm* whip

latín *nm* Latin

latino, -a *adj* Latin: *la gramática latina* Latin grammar ◊ *el temperamento ~* the Latin temperament

latir *vi* to beat

latitud *nf* latitude

latón *nm* brass

latoso, -a *adj, nm-nf* pain [*n*]: *¡Que niño más ~!* What a pain that child is!

laurel *nm* **1** (*Cocina*) bay leaf [*pl* bay leaves]: *una hoja de ~* a bay leaf ◊ *No tengo ~.* I haven't got any bay leaves. **2** (*árbol*) bay tree

lava *nf* lava

lavabo *nm* **1** (*pila*) washbasin **2** (*cuarto*

de baño) toilet: *¿Los ~s por favor?* Where are the toilets, please?

lavadora *nf* washing machine: *Pongo dos ~s al día.* I do two loads of washing a day.

lavanda *nf* lavender

lavandería *nf* **1** (*servicio*) laundry **2** (*establecimiento*) launderette

lavaplatos *nm* dishwasher

lavar ◆ *vt* to wash: *~ la ropa* to wash your clothes ◆ **lavarse** *v pron*: *Me gusta ~me con agua caliente.* I like to wash in hot water. ◊ *~se los pies* to wash your feet ◊ *Lávate bien.* Wash yourself thoroughly. ◊ *Me lavé antes de acostarme.* I had a wash before I went to bed. LOC **lavar a mano** to wash *sth* by hand **lavarse la cabeza** to wash your hair **lavarse los dientes** to brush your teeth

lavavajillas *nm* **1** (*lavaplatos*) dishwasher **2** (*detergente*) washing-up liquid

laxante *adj*, *nm* laxative

lazo *nm* **1** (*lazada*) bow: *una blusa con ~s rojos* a blouse with red bows **2** (*cinta*) ribbon: *Ponle un ~ en el pelo.* Put a ribbon in her hair.

le *pron pers* **1** (*él/ella/ello*) **(a)** (*complemento*) him/her/it: *Le vi el sábado por la tarde.* I saw him on Saturday afternoon. ◊ *Le compramos la casa.* We bought our house from him/her. ◊ *Vi a mi jefa pero no le hablé.* I saw my boss but I didn't speak to her. ◊ *Le vamos a comprar un vestido.* We're going to buy her a dress. ◊ *No le des importancia.* Ignore it. **(b)** (*partes del cuerpo, efectos personales*): *Le quitaron el carné.* They took away his identity card. ◊ *Le han arreglado la falda.* She's had her skirt mended. **2** (*usted*) **(a)** (*complemento*) you: *Le he hecho una pregunta.* I asked you a question. **(b)** (*partes del cuerpo, efectos personales*): *Tenga cuidado, o le robarán el bolso.* Be careful or they'll steal your bag.

leal *adj* **1** (*persona*) loyal (***to sth/sb***) **2** (*animal*) faithful (***to sb***)

lealtad *nf* loyalty (***to sth/sb***) LOC **con lealtad** loyally *Ver tb* JURAR

lección *nf* lesson LOC **preguntar/tomar la lección** to test *sb* (*on sth*): *Repasa los verbos, que luego te tomaré la ~.* Revise your verbs and then I'll test you (on them).

leche *nf* milk: *Se nos ha acabado la ~.* We've run out of milk. ◊ *¿Compro ~?* Shall I get some milk? LOC **leche descremada/desnatada** skimmed milk **leche en polvo** powdered milk **leche entera/condensada** full-cream/condensed milk *Ver tb* ARROZ, CAFÉ, DIENTE, HIDRATANTE

lechero, -a ◆ *adj* dairy [*n atrib*]: *una vaca lechera* a dairy cow ◆ *nm-nf* milkman [*pl* milkmen] LOC *Ver* CENTRAL

lechuga *nf* lettuce LOC *Ver* ENSALADA

lechuza *nf* barn owl

lector, ~a *nm-nf* reader

lectura *nf* reading: *Mi pasatiempo favorito es la ~.* My favourite hobby is reading.

leer *vt, vi* to read: *Léeme la lista.* Read me the list. ◊ *Me gusta ~.* I like reading. LOC **leer la cartilla** to tell *sb* off **leer los labios** to lip-read **leer para sí** to read to yourself

legal *adj* **1** (*Jur*) legal **2** (*persona*) trustworthy

legalizar *vt* to legalize

legaña *nf* sleep [*incontable*]: *Tienes los ojos llenos de ~s.* Your eyes are full of sleep.

legislación *nf* legislation

legislar *vi* to legislate

legislativo, -a *adj* LOC *Ver* ELECCIÓN, PODER[2]

legumbre *nf* pulse: *pasta y ~s* pasta and pulses

lejano, -a *adj* distant: *un lugar/pariente ~* a distant place/relative

lejía *nf* bleach

lejos *adv* ~ **(de)** far (away), a long way (away) (*más coloq*) (**from *sth/sb***): *No queda muy ~ de aquí.* It isn't very far (away) from here. LOC **a lo lejos** in the distance **de/desde lejos** from a distance *Ver tb* LLEGAR, PILLAR

lema *nm* **1** (*Com, Pol*) slogan **2** (*regla de conducta*) motto [*pl* mottoes]

lencería *nf* (*ropa interior*) lingerie

lengua *nf* **1** (*Anat*) tongue: *sacar la ~ a algn* to stick your tongue out at sb **2** (*idioma*) language LOC **irse de la lengua** to talk too much **las malas lenguas** gossip [*incontable*]: *Dicen las malas ~s que...* Gossip has it that... **lengua materna** mother tongue **no tener lengua** to have lost your tongue **tirarle a algn de la lengua** to make sb talk *Ver tb* PELO

lenguado *nm* sole [*pl* sole]

lenguaje *nm* **1** (*gen*) language **2** (*hablado*) speech

lengüeta *nf* tongue

lente *nf* lens [*pl* lenses]: *la ~ de la cámara* the camera lens ◊ *~s de contacto* contact lenses

lenteja *nf* lentil

lentilla *nf* contact lens [*pl* contact lenses]

lento, -a *adj* slow LOC **lento pero seguro** slowly but surely *Ver* CÁMARA, COCER, FUEGO, TORTUGA

leña *nf* firewood

leñador, ~a *nm-nf* woodcutter

leño *nm* log

leo (*tb* **Leo**) *nm, nmf* (*Astrología*) Leo [*pl* Leos] ☛ *Ver ejemplos en* AQUARIUS

león, -ona *nm-nf* lion [*fem* lioness]

leonera *nf* **1** (*habitación*) mess [*incontable*]: *No puedo vivir en esta ~.* I can't live in this mess. **2** (*madriguera*) lion's den

leopardo *nm* leopard

leotardos *nm* tights

lepra *nf* leprosy

leproso, -a ◆ *adj* leprous ◆ *nm-nf* leper

les *pron pers* **1** (*a ellos, a ellas*) **(a)** (*complemento*) them: *Les di todo lo que tenía.* I gave them everything I had. ◊ *Les compré un pastel.* I bought them a cake./I bought a cake for them. **(b)** (*partes del cuerpo, efectos personales*): *Les robaron el bolso.* Their bag was stolen. **2** (*a ustedes*) **(a)** (*complemento*) you: *¿Les apetece un café?* Would you like a coffee? **(b)** (*partes del cuerpo, efectos personales*): *¿Les quito los abrigos?* Shall I take your coats?

lesbiana *nf* lesbian

lesión *nf* **1** (*gen*) injury [*pl* injuries]: *lesiones graves* serious injuries **2** (*herida*) wound: *lesiones de bala* bullet wounds **3** (*hígado, riñón, cerebro*) damage [*incontable*] LOC ☛ *Ver nota en* HERIDA

lesionado, -a ◆ *pp, adj* injured: *Está ~.* He is injured. ◆ *nm-nf* injured person: *la lista de los ~s* the list of people injured *Ver tb* LESIONARSE

lesionarse *v pron* to hurt yourself: *Me lesioné la pierna.* I hurt my leg. ☛ *Ver nota en* HERIDA

letargo *nm* **1** (*sopor*) lethargy **2** (*hibernación*) hibernation

letra *nf* **1** (*abecedario, grafía*) letter **2** (*caracteres*) character: *las ~s chinas* Chinese characters **3** (*escritura*) writing **4** (*canción*) lyrics [*pl*]: *La ~ de esta canción es muy difícil.* The lyrics of this song are very difficult. LOC *Ver* PIE, PUÑO

letrero *nm* **1** (*nota*) notice: *Había un ~ en la puerta.* There was a notice on the door. **2** (*rótulo*) sign: *Pon el ~ de cerrado en la puerta.* Put the closed sign on the door.

leucemia *nf* leukaemia

levadizo, -a *adj* LOC *Ver* PUENTE

levadura *nf* yeast

levantar ◆ *vt* **1** (*gen*) to raise: *Levanta el brazo izquierdo.* Raise your left arm. ◊ *~ la moral/voz* to raise your spirits/voice **2** (*peso, tapa*) to lift *sth* up: *Levanta esa tapa.* Lift that lid up. **3** (*recoger*) to pick *sth/sb* up: *Le levantaron entre todos.* They picked him up between them. ◆ **levantarse** *v pron* **1** (*ponerse de pie*) to stand up **2** (*de la cama, viento*) to get up: *Suelo ~me temprano.* I usually get up early. LOC **levantarse con el pie izquierdo** to get out of bed on the wrong side

levar *vt* LOC **levar anclas** to weigh anchor

leve *adj* slight

ley *nf* **1** (*gen*) law: *la ~ de la gravedad* the law of gravity ◊ *ir contra la ~* to break the law **2** (*parlamento*) act LOC *Ver* PROYECTO

leyenda *nf* legend

liado, -a *pp, adj* LOC **estar liado con algo** to be busy with sth **estar liado con algn** to be having an affair with sb *Ver tb* LIAR

liar ◆ *vt* **1** (*atar*) to tie *sth* (up) **2** (*confundir*) to confuse: *No me líes.* Don't confuse me. **3** (*complicar*) to complicate: *Has liado aún más el asunto.* You've complicated things even more. ◆ **liarse** *v pron* **1 liarse (con/en)** to get confused **(about/over *sth*)**: *Se lía con las fechas.* He gets confused over dates. **2 liarse (en)** (*meterse*) to get involved **in *sth***: *Se va a ~ en política.* She's going to get involved in politics. LOC **liarse a golpes/palos** to come to blows (*with sb*)

libélula *nf* dragonfly [*pl* dragonflies]

liberación *nf* **1** (*país*) liberation **2** (*presos*) release

liberado, -a *pp, adj* **1** (*gen*) freed **2** (*mujer*) liberated *Ver tb* LIBERAR

liberal *adj, nmf* liberal

liberar *vt* **1** (*país*) to liberate **2** (*prisionero*) to free

libertad *nf* freedom LOC **libertad bajo fianza/provisional** bail: *salir en ~ bajo* *fianza* to be released on bail **libertad condicional** parole **libertad de expresión** freedom of speech **libertad de prensa** freedom of the press

libra[1] *nf* **1** (*dinero*) pound: *cincuenta ~s (£50)* fifty pounds ◊ *~s esterlinas* pounds sterling **2** (*peso*) pound (*abrev* lb) ☛ *Ver* Apéndice 1.

libra[2] (*tb* **Libra**) *nf, nmf* (*Astrología*) Libra ☛ *Ver ejemplos en* AQUARIUS

librar ◆ *vt* to save *sth/sb* ***from sth/doing sth***: *Le libraron de perecer en el incendio.* They saved him from the fire. ◆ **librarse** *v pron* **librarse (de)** **1** (*escaparse*) to get out of *sth/doing sth*: *Me libré de la mili.* I got out of doing military service. **2** (*desembarazarse*) to get rid of *sth/sb*: *Quiero ~me de esta estufa.* I want to get rid of this heater. **LOC librarse por los pelos** to escape by the skin of your teeth *Ver tb* DIOS

libre *adj* **1** (*gen*) free: *Soy ~ de hacer lo que quiera.* I'm free to do what I want. ◊ *¿Está ~ esta silla?* Is this seat free? **2** (*disponible*) vacant: *No quedan plazas ~s.* There are no vacant seats. **LOC** *Ver* AIRE, CAÍDA, DÍA, ENTRADA, LUCHA

librería *nf* **1** (*tienda*) bookshop **2** (*estantería*) bookcase

librero, -a *nm-nf* bookseller

libreta *nf* notebook **LOC** *Ver* AHORRO

libro *nm* book **LOC libro de bolsillo** paperback **libro de texto** textbook *Ver tb* COLGAR, SUSPENSE

licencia *nf* licence: *~ de pesca/armas* fishing/gun licence

licenciado, -a *pp, adj, nm-nf* ~ **(en)** graduate [*n*] **(in** ***sth*****)**: *~ en Ciencias Biológicas* a biology graduate ◊ *un ~ por la Universidad de Londres* a graduate from London University *Ver tb* LICENCIARSE

licenciarse *v pron* ~ **(en)** to graduate **(in** ***sth*****)**: *~ por la Universidad de Salamanca* to graduate from Salamanca University

licenciatura *nf* **1** (*título*) degree **2** (*estudios*) degree course

licor *nm* liqueur: *un ~ de manzana* an apple liqueur

licuadora *nf* liquidizer

líder *nmf* leader

liebre *nf* hare **LOC** *Ver* GATO

liendre *nf* nit

lienzo *nm* canvas

liga *nf* **1** (*gen*) league: *la ~ de baloncesto* the basketball league **2** (*cinta*) garter

ligamento *nm* ligament: *sufrir una fractura/rotura de ~s* to tear a ligament

ligar *vi* ~ **(con)**: *Me gusta ~ con las chicas.* I like chatting girls up. ◊ *~ mucho* to have a lot of success with boys/girls ◊ *Se ligó al más guapo de la clase.* She got off with the best looking boy in the class.

ligeramente *adv* slightly: *~ inestable* slightly unsettled

ligero, -a *adj* **1** (*gen*) light: *comida/ropa ligera* light food/clothing ◊ *tener el sueño ~* to sleep lightly **2** (*que casi no se nota*) slight: *un ~ acento andaluz* a slight Andalusian accent **3** (*ágil*) agile **LOC hacer algo a la ligera** to do sth hastily **tomarse algo a la ligera** to take sth lightly

light *adj* (*refresco*) diet [*n atrib*]: *Coca-Cola ~* Diet Coke ☛ *Ver nota en* LOW-CALORIE

lija *nf* sandpaper

lijar *vt* to sand

lila *nf, nm* lilac: *El ~ te sienta muy bien.* Lilac suits you.

lima *nf* **1** (*herramienta*) file: *~ de uñas* nail file **2** (*fruta*) lime **LOC** *Ver* COMER

limar *vt* to file **LOC limar asperezas** to smooth things over

limbo *nm* limbo **LOC estar en el limbo** to have your head in the clouds

limitación *nf* limitation: *Conoce sus limitaciones.* He knows his limitations.

limitado, -a *pp, adj* limited: *un número ~ de plazas* a limited number of places **LOC** *Ver* SOCIEDAD; *Ver tb* LIMITAR

limitar ◆ *vt* to limit ◆ *vi* ~ **con** to border **on ...**: *España limita con Portugal.* Spain borders on Portugal. ◆ **limitarse** *v pron* **limitarse a**: *Limítese a responder a la pregunta.* Just answer the question.

límite *nm* **1** (*gen*) limit: *el ~ de velocidad* the speed limit **2** (*Geog, Pol*) boundary [*pl* boundaries] ☛ *Ver nota en* BORDER **LOC sin límite** unlimited: *kilometraje sin ~* unlimited mileage ◊ *Tiene una paciencia sin ~.* She has unlimited patience. *Ver tb* FECHA

limón *nm* lemon: *un vestido amarillo ~* a lemon yellow dress **LOC** *Ver* RALLADURA

limonada *nf* (traditional) lemonade

limonero *nm* lemon tree

limosna *nf*: *Le dimos una ~.* We gave him some money. ◊ *Una ~ por favor.* Could you spare some change, please? **LOC** *Ver* PEDIR

limpiabotas *nmf* shoeshine

limpiaparabrisas *nm* windscreen wiper

limpiar ◆ *vt* **1** (*gen*) to clean: *Tengo que ~ los cristales.* I've got to clean the windows. **2** (*pasar un trapo*) to wipe **3** (*sacar brillo*) to polish ◆ **limpiarse** *v pron* to clean yourself up LOC **limpiar en seco** to dry-clean **limpiarse la nariz** to wipe your nose

limpieza *nf* **1** (*acción de limpiar*) cleaning: *productos de ~* cleaning products **2** (*pulcritud*) cleanliness LOC **limpieza en seco** dry-cleaning

limpio, -a ◆ *adj* **1** (*gen*) clean: *El hotel estaba bastante ~.* The hotel was quite clean. ◊ *Mantén limpia tu ciudad.* Keep your city tidy. **2** (*pelado*) skint ◆ *adv* fair: *jugar ~* to play fair LOC **pasar a limpio/poner en limpio** to make a fair copy *of sth* **sacar en limpio 1** (*entender*) to get *sth* out of *sth*: *No he sacado nada en ~.* I haven't got anything out of it. **2** (*dinero*) to clear: *Sacó en ~ cinco millones de pesetas.* He cleared five million pesetas. *Ver tb* JUEGO, JUGAR

lince *nm* lynx LOC **ser un lince** not to miss a trick: *Es un ~.* She never misses a trick.

lindo, -a *adj* LOC **de lo lindo**: *divertirse de lo ~* to have a great time

línea *nf*: *una ~ recta* a straight line LOC **cuidar/mantener la línea** to watch your weight **línea de meta** finishing line **línea divisoria** dividing line **por línea materna/paterna** on my, your, etc mother's/father's side *Ver tb* GUARDAR

lineal *adj* LOC *Ver* DIBUJO

lingote *nm* ingot

lingüística *nf* linguistics [*sing*]

lino *nm* **1** (*Bot*) flax **2** (*tela*) linen

linterna *nf* torch

lío *nm*: *¡Qué ~!* What a mess! ◊ *Le metieron en un ~.* They got him into trouble. LOC **estar hecho un lío** to be really confused **hacerse un lío** (*confundirse*) to get into a muddle *Ver tb* ARMAR

liquidación *nf* (*rebaja*) sale LOC **liquidación por cierre de negocio** clearance sale

liquidar *vt* **1** (*deuda*) to settle **2** (*negocio*) to liquidate **3** (*matar*) to bump *sb* off

líquido, -a *adj, nm* liquid: *Sólo puedo comer ~s.* I can only have liquids.

lira *nf* (*moneda*) lira

lírica *nf* lyric poetry

lirio *nm* iris

lirón *nm* dormouse [*pl* dormice] LOC *Ver* DORMIR

liso, -a *adj* **1** (*llano*) flat **2** (*suave*) smooth **3** (*sin adornos, de un solo color*) plain **4** (*pelo*) straight

lista *nf* list: *~ de la compra* shopping list LOC **lista de espera** waiting list **lista electoral** electoral roll **pasar lista** to take the register

listo, -a *adj* **1** (*inteligente*) clever **2** (*preparado*) ready: *Estamos ~s para salir.* We're ready to leave. LOC **pasarse de listo** to be too clever by half: *No te pases de ~ conmigo.* Don't try and be clever with me. *Ver tb* PREPARADO

litera *nf* **1** (*en casa*) bunk-bed: *Los niños duermen en ~s.* The children sleep in bunk-beds. **2** (*en barco*) bunk **3** (*en tren*) couchette

literatura *nf* literature

litro *nm* litre (*abrev* l): *medio ~* half a litre ☛ *Ver* Apéndice 1.

llaga *nf* ulcer

llama[1] *nf* (*de fuego*) flame LOC **estar en llamas** to be ablaze

llama[2] *nf* (*animal*) llama

llamada *nf* call: *hacer una ~ (telefónica)* to make a (phone) call ◊ *la ~ del deber* the call of duty LOC **llamada a cobro revertido** reverse charge call

llamado, -a *pp, adj* so-called: *el ~ Tercer Mundo* the so-called Third World *Ver tb* LLAMAR

llamar ◆ *vt* to call: *Se llama Ignacio pero le llaman Nacho.* His name's Ignacio but they call him Nacho. ◊ *~ a la policía* to call the police ◊ *Llámame cuando llegues.* Give me a ring when you get there. ◆ *vi* **1** (*telefonear*) to call: *¿Quién llama?* Who's calling? **2** (*puerta*) to knock: *Están llamando a la puerta* Someone's knocking at the door. **3** (*timbre*) to ring *sth* [*vt*]: *~ al timbre* to ring the bell ◆ **llamarse** *v pron* to be called: *¿Cómo te llamas?* What's your name? ◊ *Me llamo Ana.* I'm called Ana./My name's Ana. LOC **llamar a cobro revertido** to reverse the charges **llamar la atención 1** (*sobresalir*) to attract attention: *Se viste así para ~ la atención.* He dresses like that to attract attention. **2** (*sorprender*) to surprise: *Nos llamó la atención que volvieras sola.* We were surprised that you came back alone. **3** (*reprender*) to tell *sb* off **llamar por teléfono** to telephone *sb*, to give *sb* a ring (*más coloq*) *Ver tb* PAN

llamativo, -a *adj* **1** (*noticia*) striking **2** (*ostentoso*) flashy: *un coche muy ~* a flashy car

llano, -a ◆ *adj* **1** (*gen*) flat **2** (*sencillo*) simple ◆ *nm* plain LOC *Ver* PLATO

llanto *nm* crying

llanura *nf* plain

llave *nf* **1** ~ (**de**) (*gen*) key [*pl* keys] (**to** ***sth***): *la ~ del armario* the key to the wardrobe ◊ *la ~ de la puerta* the door key **2** (*Mec*) spanner LOC **bajo llave** under lock and key **echar la llave** to lock up **llave de contacto** ignition key **llave de paso** (*del agua*) stopcock *Ver tb* AMO, CERRAR

llavero *nm* keyring

llegada *nf* arrival

llegar *vi* **1** (*gen*) to arrive (**at/in...**): *Llegamos al aeropuerto/hospital a las cinco.* We arrived at the airport/hospital at five o'clock. ◊ *Llegué a Inglaterra hace un mes.* I arrived in England a month ago. ☛ *Ver nota en* ARRIVE **2** (*alcanzar*) to reach: *¿Llegas?* Can you reach? ◊ *~ a una conclusión* to reach a conclusion **3** (*bastar*) to be enough: *La comida no llegó para todos.* There wasn't enough food for everybody. **4** (*altura*) to come up *to sth*: *Mi hija ya me llega al hombro.* My daughter comes up to my shoulder. **5** ~ **hasta** (*extenderse*) to go **as far as...**: *La finca llega hasta el río.* The estate goes as far as the river. **6** (*tiempo*) to come: *cuando llegue el verano* when summer comes ◊ *Ha llegado el momento de...* The time has come to... LOC **estar al llegar** to be due any time: *Tu padre debe estar al ~.* Your father must be due any time now. **llegar a casa** to arrive home, to get home (*más coloq*) **llegar a hacer algo** (*lograr*) to manage to do sth **llegar a las manos** to come to blows **llegar a ser** to become **llegar a tiempo** to be on time **llegar lejos** to go far **llegar tarde/temprano** to be late/early **si no llega a ser por él** if it hadn't been for him, her, etc: *Si no llega a ser por él me mato.* If it hadn't been for him, I would have been killed.

llenar ◆ *vt* **1** (*gen*) to fill *sth/sb* (**with** ***sth***): *Llena la jarra de agua.* Fill the jug with water. ◊ *No lo llenes tanto que se sale.* Don't fill it too much or it'll run over. **2** (*satisfacer*) to satisfy: *Aquel estilo de vida no me llenaba.* That lifestyle didn't satisfy me. ◆ **llenarse** *v pron* **1** (*gen*) to fill (up) (**with** ***sth***): *La casa se llenó de invitados.* The house filled (up) with guests. **2** (*comiendo*) to stuff yourself (**with** ***sth***)

lleno, -a *adj* **1** (*gen*) full (**of** ***sth***): *Esta habitación está llena de humo.* This room is full of smoke. ◊ *No quiero más, estoy ~.* I don't want any more, I'm full. ◊ *El autobús estaba ~ hasta los topes.* The bus was full to bursting. **2** (*cubierto*) covered ***in/with sth***: *El techo estaba ~ de telarañas.* The ceiling was covered in cobwebs. LOC *Ver* CABEZA, LUNA

llevadero, -a *adj* bearable

llevar ◆ *vt* **1** (*gen*) to take: *Lleva las sillas a la cocina.* Take the chairs to the kitchen. ◊ *Me llevará un par de días arreglarlo.* It'll take me a couple of days to fix it. ◊ *Llevé el perro al veterinario.* I took the dog to the vet.

Cuando el hablante se ofrece a llevarle algo al oyente, se utiliza **to bring**: *No hace falta que vengas, te lo llevo el viernes.* You don't need to come, I'll bring it on Friday.

☛ *Ver dibujo en* TAKE **2** (*carga*) to carry: *Se ofreció a ~le la maleta.* He offered to carry her suitcase. **3** (*gafas, ropa, peinado*) to wear: *Lleva gafas.* She wears glasses. **4** (*conducir*) to drive: *¿Quién llevaba el coche?* Who was driving? **5** (*tener*) to have: *No llevaba dinero encima.* I didn't have any cash on me. ◊ *¿Llevas suelto?* Have you got any change? **6** (*tiempo*) to have been (***doing sth***): *Llevan dos horas esperando.* They've been waiting for two hours. ◊ *¿Cuánto tiempo llevas en Madrid?* How long have you been in Madrid? ◆ *vi* to lead to *sth*: *Esta carretera lleva a la desembocadura del río.* This road leads to the mouth of the river. ◆ *v aux* **+ participio** to have: *Llevo vistas tres películas esta semana.* I've seen three films this week. ◆ **llevarse** *v pron* **1** (*robar*) to take: *El ladrón se llevó el vídeo.* The thief took the video. **2** (*estar de moda*) to be in: *Este invierno se lleva el verde.* Green is in this winter. **3** (*Mat*) to carry: *22 y me llevo dos* 22 and carry two. LOC **llevarle a algn dos años, etc** to be two years, etc older than sb: *Me lleva seis meses.* She's six months older than me. **llevarse bien/mal** to get on well/badly (*with sb*) **para llevar** to take away: *una pizza para ~* a pizza to take away

☛Para otras expresiones con **llevar**, véanse las entradas del sustantivo, adjetivo, etc, p.ej. **llevar la voz cantante** en VOZ y **llevarse un disgusto** en DISGUSTO.

llorar *vi* **1** (*gen*) to cry: *No llores.* Don't cry. ◊ *ponerse a ~* to burst out crying ◊ *~ de alegría/rabia* to cry with joy/rage **2** (*ojos*) to water: *Me lloran los ojos.* My eyes are watering. LOC **llorar a lágrima viva/a moco tendido** to cry your eyes out

llorón, -ona *adj, nm-nf* cry-baby [*n*] [*pl* cry-babies]: *No seas tan ~.* Don't be such a cry-baby. LOC *Ver* SAUCE

llover *v imp* to rain: *Estuvo lloviendo toda la tarde.* It was raining all afternoon. ◊ *¿Llueve?* Is it raining? LOC **llover a cántaros** to pour: *Está lloviendo a cántaros.* It's pouring. *Ver tb* PARECER

llovizna *nf* drizzle

lloviznar *v imp* to drizzle

lluvia *nf* **1** (*gen*) rain: *La ~ no me dejó dormir.* The rain kept me awake. ◊ *un día de ~* a rainy day ◊ *Éstas son unas buenas botas para la ~.* These boots are good for wet weather. **2 ~ de** (*billetes, regalos, polvo*) shower **of *sth*** **3 ~ de** (*balas, piedras, golpes, insultos*) hail **of *sth*** LOC **bajo la lluvia** in the rain **lluvia ácida** acid rain **lluvia radiactiva** radioactive fallout

lluvioso, -a *adj* **1** (*zona, país, temporada*) wet **2** (*día, tarde, tiempo*) rainy

lo ◆ *art def* (*para sustantivar*) the...thing: *lo interesante/difícil es...* the interesting/difficult thing is... ◆ *pron pers* **1** (*él*) him: *Lo eché de casa.* I threw him out of the house. **2** (*cosa*) it: *¿Dónde lo tienes?* Where is it? ◊ *No me lo creo.* I don't believe it. ☛Cuando se usa como complemento directo de algunos verbos como *decir*, *saber* y *ser* no se traduce: *Te lo diré mañana.* I'll tell you tomorrow. ◊ *Todavía no eres médico pero lo serás.* You are not a doctor yet, but you will be. **3** (*usted*) you LOC **lo cual** which: *lo cual no es cierto* which isn't true **lo de... 1** (*posesión*): *Todo ese equipaje es lo de Juan.* All that luggage is Juan's. **2** (*asunto*): *Lo del viaje fue muy inesperado.* The journey came as a real surprise. ◊ *Lo de la fiesta era una broma ¿no?* What you said about the party was a joke, wasn't it? **lo mío 1** (*posesión*) my, your, etc things: *Todo lo mío es tuyo.* Everything I've got is yours. **2** (*afición*) my, your etc thing: *Lo suyo es la música.* Music's his thing. **lo que...** what: *No te imaginas lo que fue aquello.* You can't imagine what it was like. ◊ *Haré lo que digas.* I'll do whatever you say. ◊ *Haría lo que fuera por aprobar.* I'd do anything to pass.

lobo, -a *nm-nf* wolf [*pl* wolves]

> Si queremos especificar que se trata de una hembra, diremos **she-wolf**.

LOC *Ver* HOMBRE, PERRO

local ◆ *adj* local ◆ *nm* premises [*pl*]: *El ~ es bastante grande.* The premises are quite big.

localidad *nf* **1** (*pueblo*) village **2** (*ciudad pequeña*) town **3** (*Cine, Teat*) seat LOC **no hay localidades** sold out

localizar *vt* **1** (*encontrar*) to locate: *Han localizado su paradero.* They've located his whereabouts. **2** (*contactar*) to get hold of *sb*: *Llevo toda la mañana tratando de ~te.* I've been trying to get hold of you all morning.

loción *nf* lotion LOC *Ver* DESMAQUILLADOR

loco, -a ◆ *adj* mad: *volverse ~* to go mad ◊ *El chocolate me vuelve ~.* I'm mad about chocolate. ◆ *nm-nf* madman/woman [*pl* madmen/women] LOC **estar como loco (con)** (*encantado*) to be crazy about *sth/sb* **estar loco de** to be beside yourself with *sth*: *Está loca de alegría.* She's beside herself with joy. **estar loco de remate** to be round the bend **hacerse el loco** to pretend not to notice *Ver tb* CADA

locura *nf* (*disparate*) crazy thing: *He hecho muchas ~s.* I've done a lot of crazy things. ◊ *Es una ~ ir solo.* It's crazy to go alone.

locutor, ~a *nm-nf* (*de noticias*) newsreader

lodo *nm* mud

lógico, -a *adj* **1** (*normal*) natural: *Es ~ que te preocupes.* It's only natural that you're worried. **2** (*Fil*) logical

lograr *vt* **1** (*gen*) to get, to achieve (*más formal*): *Logré buenos resultados.* I got good results. **2 + inf** to manage ***to do sth***: *Logré convencerles.* I managed to persuade them. **3 ~ que...** to get *sb* ***to do sth***: *No lograrás que vengan.* You'll never get them to come.

logro *nm* achievement

lombriz *nf* worm

lomo *nm* **1** (*Anat*) back **2** (*Cocina*) loin: *~ de cerdo* (loin of) pork **3** (*libro*) spine

loncha *nf* slice LOC **en lonchas** sliced

longitud *nf* **1** (*gen*) length: *Tiene dos*

metros de ~. It is two metres long. **2** (*Geog*) longitude LOC *Ver* SALTO

lonja *nf* LOC **lonja** (**de pescado**) fish market

loro *nm* **1** (*ave*) parrot **2** (*persona*) windbag

los, las ◆ *art def* the: *los libros que compré ayer* the books I bought yesterday ☛ *Ver nota en* THE ◆ *pron pers* them: *Los/las vi en el cine.* I saw them at the cinema. LOC **de los/las de...**: *un terremoto de los de verdad* a really violent earthquake ◊ *El diseño del coche es de los de antes.* The design of the car is old-fashioned. **los/las de... 1** (*posesión*): *los de mi abuela* my grandmother's **2** (*característica*) the ones (with...): *Prefiero los de punta fina.* I prefer the ones with a fine point. ◊ *Me gustan las de cuadros.* I like the checked ones. **3** (*ropa*) the ones in...: *las de rojo* the ones in red **4** (*procedencia*) the ones from...: *los de Pamplona* the ones from Pamplona **los/las hay**: *Los hay con muy poco dinero.* There are some with very little money. ◊ *Dime si los hay o no.* Tell me if there are any or not. **los/las que... 1** (*personas*): *los que se encontraban en la casa* the ones who were in the house ◊ *los que tenemos que madrugar* those of us who have to get up early ◊ *Entrevistamos a todos los que se presentaron.* We interviewed everyone who applied. **2** (*cosas*) the ones (which/that)...: *las que compramos ayer* the ones we bought yesterday

losa *nf* flagstone

lote *nm* **1** (*gen*) set: *un ~ de libros* a set of books **2** (*Com*) batch LOC **darse un lote** to pet

lotería *nf* lottery [*pl* lotteries] LOC *Ver* ADMINISTRACIÓN, JUGAR

loto *nm* lotus [*pl* lotuses]

loza *nf* china: *un plato de ~* a china plate

lubina *nf* sea bass [*pl* sea bass]

lucha *nf* ~ (**contra/por**) fight (**against/for** ***sth/sb***): *la ~ contra la contaminación/por la igualdad* the fight against pollution/for equality LOC **lucha libre** wrestling

luchador, ~a ◆ *adj*, *nm-nf* fighter [*n*]: *Es un hombre muy ~.* He's a real fighter. ◆ *nm-nf* (*deportista*) wrestler

luchar *vi* **1** (*gen*) to fight (**for/against** ***sth/sb***); to fight *sth/sb*: *~ por la libertad* to fight for freedom ◊ *~ contra los prejuicios raciales* to fight racial prejudice **2** (*Dep*) to wrestle

lúcido, -a *adj* lucid

lucir ◆ *vt* (*ropa*) to wear ◆ *vi* **1** (*bombilla*) to give off light: *Esa farola no luce mucho.* That street lamp doesn't give off much light. **2** (*astro*) to shine **3** (*resaltar*) to look nice: *Esa figura luce mucho ahí.* That figure looks very nice there. **4** (*cundir*) to show: *Estudio mucho pero no me luce.* I work hard but it doesn't show. ◆ **lucirse** *v pron* to show off: *Lo hace para ~se.* He just does it to show off.

luego ◆ *adv* **1** (*más tarde*) later: *Te lo cuento ~.* I'll tell you later. **2** (*a continuación*) then: *Se baten los huevos y ~ se añade el azúcar.* Beat the eggs and then stir in the sugar. ◊ *Primero está el ambulatorio y ~ la farmacia.* First there's the hospital and then the chemist's. ◆ *conj* therefore: *Pienso, ~ existo.* I think therefore I am. LOC **desde luego** of course: *¡Desde ~ que no!* Of course not! **¡hasta luego!** bye!

lugar *nm* **1** (*gen*) place: *Me gusta este ~.* I like this place. ◊ *En esta fiesta estoy fuera de ~.* I feel out of place at this party. **2** (*posición, puesto*) position: *ocupar un ~ importante en la empresa* to have an important position in the firm **3** (*pueblo*) village: *los del ~* the people from the village LOC **dar lugar a algo** to cause sth **en lugar de** instead of *sth/sb/doing sth*: *En ~ de salir tanto, más te valdría estudiar.* Instead of going out so much, you'd be better off studying. **en primer, segundo, etc lugar 1** (*posición*) first, second, etc: *El equipo francés quedó clasificado en último ~.* The French team came last. **2** (*en un discurso*) first of all, secondly, etc: *En último ~...* Last of all... **lugar de nacimiento 1** (*gen*) birthplace **2** (*en impresos*) place of birth **sin lugar a dudas** undoubtedly **tener lugar** to take place: *El accidente tuvo ~ a las dos de la madrugada.* The accident took place at two in the morning. **yo en tu lugar** if I were you: *Yo, en tu ~, aceptaría la invitación.* If I were you, I'd accept the invitation. *Ver tb* ALGUNO, CLASIFICAR, CUALQUIERA, NINGUNO, OTRO

lúgubre *adj* gloomy

lujo *nm* luxury [*pl* luxuries]: *No puedo permitirme esos ~s.* I can't afford such luxuries. LOC **a todo lujo** in style: *Viven a todo ~.* They live in style. **de**

lujo luxury: *un apartamento de* ~ a luxury apartment

lujoso, -a *adj* luxurious

lujuria *nf* lust

lumbre *nf* **1** (*gen*) fire: *Nos sentamos al calor de la* ~. We sat down by the fire. **2** (*cocina*) stove: *Tengo la comida en la* ~. The food's on the stove.

luminoso, -a *adj* **1** (*gen*) bright: *una habitación/idea luminosa* a bright room/idea **2** (*que despide luz*) luminous: *un reloj* ~ a luminous watch LOC *Ver* ANUNCIO

luna *nf* **1** (*gen*) moon: *un viaje a la Luna* a trip to the moon **2** (*cristal*) glass **3** (*espejo*) mirror **4** (*parabrisas*) windscreen LOC **estar en la luna** to be miles away **luna creciente/menguante** waxing/waning moon **luna de miel** honeymoon **luna llena/nueva** full/new moon

lunar ◆ *adj* lunar ◆ *nm* **1** (*piel*) mole **2** (*dibujo*) polka dot: *una falda de ~es* a polka-dot skirt

lunático, -a *adj, nm-nf* lunatic

lunes *nm* Monday [*pl* Mondays] (*abrev* Mon): *el ~ por la mañana/tarde* on Monday morning/afternoon ◊ *Los ~ no trabajo.* I don't work on Mondays. ◊ *un ~ sí y otro no* every other Monday ◊ *Ocurrió el ~ pasado.* It happened last Monday. ◊ *Nos veremos el ~ que viene.* We'll meet next Monday. ◊ *Mi cumpleaños cae en ~ este año.* My birthday falls on a Monday this year. ◊ *Se casarán el ~ 25 de julio.* They're getting married on Monday July 25. ☛Se lee: 'Monday the twenty-fifth of July'

lupa *nf* magnifying glass

luto *nm* mourning: *una jornada de ~* a day of mourning LOC **estar de/llevar luto** to be in mourning (*for sb*) **ir de luto** to be dressed in mourning

luz *nf* **1** (*gen*) light: *encender/apagar la ~* to turn the light on/off ◊ *Hay mucha ~ en este piso.* This flat gets a lot of light. **2** (*electricidad*) electricity: *Con la tormenta se fue la ~.* The electricity went off during the storm. **3** (*día*) daylight **4 luces** (*inteligencia*): *tener muchas/pocas luces* to be bright/dim LOC **dar a luz** to give birth (to *sb*): *Dio a ~ una niña.* She gave birth to a baby girl. **luces cortas/de cruce** dipped headlights: *Puse las luces cortas.* I dipped my headlights. **luces de posición** sidelights **luces largas/de carretera** headlights **sacar a la luz** to bring *sth* (out) into the open **salir a la luz** (*secreto*) to come to light *Ver tb* AÑO, PLENO

Mm

macabro, -a *adj* macabre

macarra *nmf* flashy person

macarrón *nm* **macarrones** macaroni [*incontable, v sing*]: *Los macarrones son fáciles de hacer.* Macaroni is easy to cook.

macedonia *nf* LOC **macedonia (de frutas)** fruit salad

maceta *nf* flowerpot

machacar ◆ *vt* **1** (*aplastar*) **(a)** (*gen*) to crush: *~ ajo/nueces* to crush garlic/nuts **(b)** (*fruta, patata, zanahoria*) to mash **2** (*romper*) to smash: *El niño machacó los juguetes.* The child smashed his toys to bits. ◆ *vt, vi* to go over (and over) *sth*: *Les machaqué la canción hasta que se la aprendieron.* I went over and over the song until they learnt it.

machete *nm* machete

machismo *nm* machismo

machista *adj, nmf* sexist: *publicidad/sociedad ~* sexist advertising/society ◊ *Mi jefe es un ~ de tomo y lomo.* My boss is really sexist.

macho ◆ *adj, nm* **1** (*gen*) male: *una camada de dos ~s y tres hembras* a litter of two males and three females ◊ *¿Es ~ o hembra?* Is it male or female? ☛*Ver nota en* FEMALE **2** (*machote*) macho [*adj*]: *Ese tío va de ~.* He's a bit of a macho man. ◆ *nm* (*enchufe*) plug ☛*Ver dibujo en* ENCHUFE

macizo, -a *adj* (*objeto*) solid

madeja *nf* skein

madera *nf* **1** (*material*) wood [*gen incontable*]: *El roble es una ~ de gran calidad.* Oak is a high quality wood. ◊ ~

procedente de Noruega wood from Norway ◊ *hecho de ~* made of wood **2** (*tabla*) piece of wood: *Esa ~ puede servir para tapar el agujero.* We could use that piece of wood to block up the hole. **3** (*de construcción*) timber: *las ~s del tejado* the roof timbers LOC **de madera** wooden: *una silla/viga de ~* a wooden chair/beam **madera de pino, roble, etc** pine, oak, etc: *una mesa de ~ de pino* a pine table **tener madera de artista, líder, etc** to be a born artist, leader, etc **¡toca madera!** touch wood! *Ver tb* CUCHARA

madero *nm* **1** (*tronco*) log **2** (*tablón*) piece of timber

madrastra *nf* stepmother

madre *nf* mother: *ser ~ de dos hijos* to be the mother of two children LOC **¡madre mía!** good heavens! **madre soltera** single parent **madre superiora** Mother Superior *Ver tb* DÍA, FAMILIA, HUÉRFANO

madriguera *nf* **1** (*gen*) den: *una ~ de león/lobo* a lion's/wolf's den **2** (*conejo*) burrow

madrina *nf* **1** (*bautizo*) godmother **2** (*confirmación*) sponsor **3** (*boda*) woman who accompanies the groom, usually his mother ☛ *Ver nota en* BODA

madrugada *nf*: *a las dos de la ~* at two in the morning ◊ *en la ~ del viernes al sábado* in the early hours of Saturday morning

madrugar *vi* to get up early

madurar *vi* **1** (*fruta*) to ripen **2** (*persona*) to mature

maduro, -a *adj* **1** (*fruta*) ripe **2** (*de mediana edad*) middle-aged: *un hombre ya ~* a middle-aged man **3** (*sensato*) mature: *Javier es muy ~ para su edad.* Javier is very mature for his age.

maestro, -a *nm-nf* **1** (*educador*) teacher **2** ~ **(de/en)** (*figura destacada*) master: *un ~ del ajedrez* a chess master LOC *Ver* OBRA

mafia *nf* mafia: *la ~ de la droga* the drugs mafia ◊ *la Mafia* the Mafia

magdalena *nf* fairy cake

magia *nf* magic: *~ blanca/negra* white/black magic LOC *Ver* ARTE

mágico, -a *adj* (*ilusionismo*) magic: *poderes ~s* magic powers LOC *Ver* VARITA

magisterio *nm* (*estudios*) teacher training: *Elena estudió Magisterio en Valencia.* Elena trained as a teacher in Valencia.

magma *nm* magma

magnate *nmf* tycoon, magnate (*más formal*)

magnético, -a *adj* magnetic

magnetismo *nm* magnetism

magnetofón (*tb* **magnetófono**) *nm* tape recorder

magnífico, -a *adj, interj* wonderful: *Hizo un tiempo ~.* The weather was wonderful. ◊ *una magnífica nadadora* a wonderful swimmer

mago, -a *nm-nf* (*ilusionista*) magician LOC *Ver* REY

mahonesa *nf Ver* MAYONESA

maicena® *nf* cornflour

maillot *nm* (*Ciclismo*) jersey [*pl* jerseys]: *el ~ amarillo* the yellow jersey

maíz *nm* **1** (*planta*) maize **2** (*grano*) sweetcorn LOC *Ver* PALOMITA

Majestad *nf* Majesty [*pl* Majesties]: *Su ~* His/Her/Your Majesty

mal ◆ *adj Ver* MALO ◆ *adv* **1** (*gen*) badly: *portarse/hablar ~* to behave/speak badly ◊ *un trabajo ~ pagado* a poorly/badly paid job ◊ *Mi abuela oye muy ~.* My grandmother's hearing is very bad. ◊ *¡Qué ~ lo pasamos!* What a terrible time we had! **2** (*calidad, aspecto*) bad: *Esa chaqueta no está ~.* That jacket's not bad. **3** (*equivocadamente, moralmente*): *Has escogido ~.* You've made the wrong choice. ◊ *contestar ~ a una pregunta* to give the wrong answer ◊ *Está ~ que contestes a tu madre.* It's wrong to answer your mother back. ◆ *nm* **1** (*daño*) harm: *No te deseo ningún ~.* I don't wish you any harm. **2** (*problema*) problem: *La venta de la casa nos salvó de ~es mayores.* The sale of the house saved us any further problems. **3** (*Fil*) evil: *el bien y el ~* good and evil LOC **andar/estar mal de** to be short of *sth* **estar/encontrarse mal** to be/feel ill **no hay mal que por bien no venga** every cloud has a silver lining ☛Para otras expresiones con **mal**, véanse las entradas del sustantivo, adjetivo, etc, p.ej. **estar mal de la cabeza** en CABEZA y **¡menos mal!** en MENOS.

malcriar *vt* to spoil

maldad *nf* wickedness [*incontable*]: *Siempre se han caracterizado por su ~.* Their wickedness is notorious. ◊ *Ha sido una ~ por su parte.* It was a wicked thing to do.

maldecir *vt* to curse

maldición *nf* curse: *Nos ha caído una ~.* There's a curse on us. ◊ *echarle una*

~ *a algn* to put a curse on sb ◊ *No paraba de soltar maldiciones.* He kept cursing and swearing.

maldito, -a *pp, adj* **1** (*lit*) damned **2** (*fig*) wretched: *¡Estos ~s zapatos me aprietan!* These wretched shoes are too tight for me! *Ver tb* MALDECIR

maleducado, -a *pp, adj, nm-nf* rude [*adj*]: *¡Que niños tan ~s!* What rude children! ◊ *Eres un ~.* You're so rude!

malentendido *nm* misunderstanding: *Ha habido un ~.* There has been a misunderstanding.

malestar *nm* **1** (*indisposición*): *Siento un ~ general.* I don't feel very well. **2** (*inquietud*) unease: *Sus palabras causaron ~ en medios políticos.* His words caused unease in political circles.

maleta *nf* (suit)case LOC **hacer/deshacer la(s) maleta(s)** to pack/unpack

maletero *nm* boot

maletín *nm* **1** (*documentos*) briefcase **2** (*médico*) (doctor's) bag

malgastar *vt* to waste

malhablado, -a *adj, nm-nf* foul-mouthed [*adj*]: *ser un ~* to be foul-mouthed

malherido, -a *pp, adj* badly injured

maligno, -a *adj* (*Med*) malignant

malla *nf* **1** (*ballet, Gimnasia*) leotard **2** (*red*) mesh

malo, -a ◆ *adj* **1** (*gen*) bad: *una mala persona* a bad person ◊ *~s modales/mala conducta* bad manners/behaviour ◊ *Tuvimos muy mal tiempo.* We had very bad weather. **2** (*inadecuado*) poor: *mala alimentación/visibilidad* poor food/visibility ◊ *debido al mal estado del terreno* due to the poor condition of the ground **3** (*travieso*) naughty: *No seas ~ y bébete la leche.* Don't be naughty—drink up your milk. **4** ~ **en/para** (*torpe*) bad **at *sth*/*doing sth***: *Soy malísimo en matemáticas.* I'm hopeless at maths. ◆ *nm-nf* villain, baddy [*pl* baddies] (*coloq*): *El ~ muere en el último acto.* The villain dies in the last act. ◊ *Al final luchan los buenos contra los ~s.* At the end there is a fight between the goodies and the baddies. LOC **estar malo** to be ill **lo malo es que...** the trouble is (that)... ☛Para otras expresiones con **malo**, véanse las entradas del sustantivo, p.ej. **mala hierba** en HIERBA y **hacer una mala jugada** en JUGADA.

malpensado, -a *adj, nm-nf* **1** (*que siempre sospecha*) suspicious [*adj*]: *Eres un ~.* You've got a really suspicious mind. **2** (*obsceno*) dirty-minded: *¡Qué ~ eres!* What a dirty mind you've got!

maltratar *vt* to mistreat: *Dijeron que les habían maltratado.* They said they had been mistreated. ◊ *Nos maltrataron física y verbalmente.* We were subjected to physical and verbal abuse.

malucho, -a *adj* under the weather

malva ◆ *nf* (*flor*) mallow ◆ *nm* (*color*) mauve ☛ *Ver ejemplos en* AMARILLO

malvado, -a *adj* wicked

mama *nf* breast: *cáncer de ~* breast cancer

mamá *nf* mum ☛Los niños pequeños suelen decir **mummy**.

mamar *vi* to feed: *En cuanto termina de ~ se duerme.* He falls asleep as soon as he's finished feeding. LOC **dar de mamar** to breastfeed

mamífero *nm* mammal

mampara *nf* **1** (*en un mostrador de banco*) screen **2** (*pared*) partition

manada *nf* **1 (a)** (*gen*) herd: *una ~ de elefantes* a herd of elephants **(b)** (*lobos, perros*) pack **(c)** (*leones*) pride **2** (*gente*) crowd

manantial *nm* spring: *agua de ~* spring water

manar *vi* to flow (***from sth/sb***)

mancha *nf* **1** (*suciedad*) stain: *una ~ de grasa* a grease stain **2** (*leopardo*) spot

manchado, -a *pp, adj* **1** ~ **(de)** (*embadurnado*) stained (**with *sth***): *Llevas la camisa manchada de vino.* You've got a wine stain on your shirt. ◊ *una carta manchada de sangre/tinta* a bloodstained/ink-stained letter **2** (*animal*) spotted *Ver tb* MANCHAR

manchar ◆ *vt* to get *sth* dirty: *No manches el mantel.* Don't get the tablecloth dirty. ◊ *Has manchado el suelo de barro.* You've got mud on the floor. ◆ **mancharse** *v pron* to get dirty

manco, -a *adj* **1** (*sin un brazo*) one-armed **2** (*sin una mano*) one-handed

mandamiento *nm* (*Relig*) commandment

mandar ◆ *vt* **1** (*ordenar*) to tell *sb* **to do *sth***: *Mandó a los niños que se callaran.* He told the children to be quiet. **2** (*enviar*) to send: *Te he mandado una carta.* I've sent you a letter. ◊ *El ministerio ha mandado a un inspector.* The ministry has sent an inspector. **3** (*llevar*) to have *sth* done: *Lo voy a ~ a limpiar.* I'm going to have it cleaned.

◆ *vi* **1** (*gobierno*) to be in power **2** (*ser el jefe*) to be the boss (*coloq*), to be in charge LOC **mandar a algn a paseo/la porra** to tell sb to get lost *Ver tb* DIOS

mandarina *nf* tangerine

mandíbula *nf* jaw

mando *nm* **1 (a)** (*liderazgo*) leadership: *tener don de ~* to be a born leader **(b)** (*Mil*) command: *entregar/tomar el ~* to hand over/take command **2** (*Informát*) joystick ☛ *Ver dibujo en* ORDENADOR **3 mandos** controls: *cuadro de ~s* control panel LOC **mando a distancia** remote control

mandón, -ona *adj, nm-nf* bossy [*adj*]: *Eres un ~.* You're very bossy.

manecilla *nf* hand: *la ~ grande del reloj* the big hand of the clock

manejar *vt* **1** (*gen*) to handle: *~ un arma* to handle a weapon **2** (*máquina*) to operate **3** (*manipular*) to manipulate: *No te dejes ~.* Don't let yourself be manipulated.

manera *nf* ~ **(de) 1** (*modo*) way [*pl* ways] **(of *doing sth*)**: *su ~ de hablar/vestir* her way of speaking/dressing **2 maneras** manners: *buenas ~s* good manners ◊ *pedir algo de buenas ~s* to ask nicely for sth LOC **a mi manera** my, your, etc way **de todas (las) maneras** anyway **manera de ser**: *Es mi ~ de ser.* It's just the way I am. **no haber manera de** to be impossible *to do sth*: *No ha habido ~ de arrancar el coche.* It was impossible to start the car. **¡qué manera de ... !** what a way to ...!: *¡Qué ~ de hablar!* What a way to speak! *Ver tb* DICHO, NINGUNO

manga *nf* sleeve: *una camisa de ~ larga/corta* a long-sleeved/short-sleeved shirt LOC **estar manga por hombro** to be in a mess **sacarse algo de la manga** to make sth up **sin mangas** sleeveless

mangar *vt* to nick: *Me han mangado la cartera.* My wallet's been nicked.

mango[1] *nm* (*asa*) handle

mango[2] *nm* (*fruta*) mango [*pl* mangoes]

mangonear *vi* to boss people around

manguera *nf* hose

manía *nf* quirk: *Todo el mundo tiene sus pequeñas ~s.* Everybody's got their own little quirks. ◊ *¡Qué ~!* You're getting obsessed about it! LOC **cogerle/tenerle manía a algn** to have got it in for sb: *El profesor me ha cogido ~.* The teacher's got it in for me. **cogerle/tenerle manía a algo** to hate sth **tener la manía de hacer algo** to have the strange habit of doing sth *Ver tb* QUITAR

maniático, -a *adj* (*quisquilloso*) fussy

manicomio *nm* psychiatric hospital

manifestación *nf* **1** (*protesta*) demonstration **2** (*expresión*) expression: *una ~ de apoyo* an expression of support **3** (*declaración*) statement

manifestante *nmf* demonstrator

manifestar ◆ *vt* **1** (*opinión*) to express **2** (*mostrar*) to show ◆ **manifestarse** *v pron* to demonstrate: *~se en contra/a favor de algo* to demonstrate against/in favour of sth

manifiesto *nm* manifesto [*pl* manifestos/manifestoes]: *el ~ comunista* the Communist Manifesto

manilla *nf* **1** (*puerta*) handle **2** (*reloj*) hand LOC **la manilla grande/pequeña** the minute/hour hand

manillar *nm* handlebars [*pl*]

maniobra *nf* manoeuvre

maniobrar *vi* **1** (*gen*) to manoeuvre **2** (*ejército*) to be on manoeuvres

manipular *vt* **1** (*deshonestamente*) to manipulate: *~ los resultados de las elecciones* to manipulate the election results **2** (*lícitamente*) to handle: *~ alimentos* to handle food

maniquí *nm* dummy [*pl* dummies]

manirroto, -a *nm-nf* big spender

manitas ◆ *adj* handy ◆ *nmf*: *Mi hermana es la ~ de la casa.* My sister's the handy one around the house.

> El sustantivo **handyman** también significa *manitas*, pero se refiere sólo a un hombre: *Mi marido es un/muy manitas.* My husband's a handyman.

LOC **hacer manitas** to hold hands

manivela *nf* handle, crank (*téc*)

manjar *nm* delicacy [*pl* delicacies]

mano *nf* **1** (*gen*) hand: *Levanta la ~.* Put your hand up. ◊ *estar en buenas ~s* to be in good hands **2** (*animal*) forefoot [*pl* forefeet] **3** (*pintura*) coat LOC **a mano 1** (*cerca*) at hand: *¿Tienes un diccionario a ~?* Have you got a dictionary at hand? **2** (*manualmente*) by hand: *Hay que lavarlo a ~.* It needs washing by hand. ◊ *hecho a ~* handmade **a mano derecha/izquierda** on the right/left **atraco/robo a mano armada 1** (*lit*) armed robbery **2** (*fig*) daylight robbery **coger/pillar a algn con las manos en la masa** to catch sb red-handed **dar la mano** to hold *sb's* hand: *Dame la ~.* Hold my hand. **dar(se) la mano** to shake hands (*with sb*): *Se dieron la ~*. They shook hands. **de la mano** hand in hand (*with sb*): *Paseaban (cogidos) de la ~*. They were walking along hand in hand. **echar una mano** to give *sb* a hand **en mano** in person: *Entrégueselo en ~*. Give it to him in person. **la mano asesina** the murderer **mano de obra** labour **mano dura** firm hand **¡manos arriba!** hands up! **tener mano izquierda** to be tactful *Ver tb* ¡ADIÓS!, COGIDO, CONOCER, ESCRIBIR, FRENO, FROTAR(SE), LAVAR, LLEGAR, PÁJARO, SALUDAR, SEGUNDO

manojo *nm* bunch

manopla *nf* mitten

manosear *vt* to touch

manotazo *nm* slap

mansión *nf* mansion

manso, -a *adj* **1** (*animal*) tame **2** (*persona*) meek: *más ~ que un cordero* as meek as a lamb

manta *nf* blanket: *Ponle una ~*. Put a blanket over him.

manteca *nf* fat LOC **manteca (de cerdo)** lard

mantel *nm* tablecloth

mantener ◆ *vt* **1** (*conservar*) to keep: *~ la comida caliente* to keep food hot ◇ *~ una promesa* to keep a promise **2** (*económicamente*) to support: *~ a una familia de ocho* to support a family of eight **3** (*afirmar*) to maintain **4** (*sujetar*) to hold: *Mantén bien sujeta la botella*. Hold the bottle tight. ◆ **mantenerse** *v pron* to live ***on sth***: *~se a base de comida de lata* to live on tinned food LOC **mantenerse en forma** to keep fit **mantenerse en pie** to stand (up): *No puede ~se en pie*. He can't stand (up) any more. **mantener vivo** to keep *sth/sb* alive: *~ viva la ilusión* to keep your hopes alive *Ver tb* CONTACTO, LÍNEA, TRECE

mantenimiento *nm* maintenance

mantequilla *nf* butter

manual *adj*, *nm* manual: *~ de instrucciones* instruction manual LOC *Ver* TRABAJO

manufacturar *vt* to manufacture

manuscrito *nm* manuscript

manzana *nf* **1** (*fruta*) apple **2** (*de casas*) block LOC *Ver* VUELTA

manzanilla *nf* **1** (*planta*) camomile **2** (*infusión*) camomile tea

manzano *nm* apple tree

maña *nf* **1** (*habilidad*) skill **2 mañas** cunning [*incontable*]: *Empleó todas sus ~s para que lo ascendieran*. He used all his cunning to get promotion. LOC **tener/darse maña** to be good *at sth/doing sth*: *tener ~ para la carpintería* to be good at woodwork

mañana ◆ *nf* morning: *Se marcha esta ~*. He's leaving this morning. ◇ *a la ~ siguiente* the following morning ◇ *a las dos de la ~* at two o'clock in the morning ◇ *El examen es el lunes por la ~*. The exam is on Monday morning. ◇ *Salimos ~ por la ~*. We're leaving tomorrow morning. ☛ *Ver nota en* MORNING ◆ *nm* future: *No pienses en el ~*. Don't think about the future. ◆ *adv* tomorrow: *~ es sábado ¿no?* Tomorrow is Saturday, isn't it? ◇ *el periódico de ~* tomorrow's paper LOC **¡hasta mañana!** see you tomorrow! *Ver tb* DÍA, MEDIO, NOCHE, PASADO

mapa *nm* map: *Está en el ~*. It's on the map. LOC *Ver* DESAPARECER

mapamundi *nm* world map

maqueta *nf* model

maquillaje *nm* make-up [*incontable*]: *Ana se compra unos ~s carísimos*. Ana buys very expensive make-up.

maquillar ◆ *vt* to make *sb* up ◆ **maquillarse** *v pron* to put on your make-up: *No he tenido tiempo de ~me*. I haven't had time to put on my make-up.

máquina *nf* **1** (*gen*) machine: *~ de coser* sewing machine **2** (*tren*) engine LOC **escribir/pasar a máquina** to type **máquina de escribir** typewriter **máquina (de fotos)** camera **máquina tragaperras** fruit machine

maquinaria *nf* machinery

maquinilla *nf* LOC **maquinilla (de afeitar)** electric razor

maquinista *nmf* train driver

mar *nm o nf* sea: *Este verano quiero ir al ~*. I want to go to the seaside this summer.

> En inglés **sea** se escribe con mayúscula cuando aparece con el nombre de un mar: *el mar Negro* the Black Sea.

LOC **hacerse a la mar** to put out to sea **mar adentro** out to sea **por mar** by sea *Ver tb* ALTO, CABALLO, ERIZO, ORILLA

maratón *nm o nf* marathon

maravilla *nf* wonder LOC **hacer maravillas** to work wonders: *Este jarabe hace ~s*. This cough mixture works wonders. **¡qué maravilla!** how wonderful!

maravilloso, -a *adj* wonderful

marca *nf* **1** (*señal*) mark **2** (*productos de limpieza, alimentos, ropa*) brand: *una ~ de vaqueros* a brand of jeans **3** (*coches, motos, electrodomésticos, ordenadores, tabaco*) make: *¿Qué ~ de coche tienes?* What make of car have you got? **4** (*récord*) record: *batir/establecer una ~* to beat/set a record LOC **de marca**: *productos de ~* brand name goods ◊ *ropa de ~* designer clothes **marca (registrada)** (registered) trade mark

marcado, -a *pp, adj* (*fuerte*) strong: *hablar con ~ acento andaluz* to speak with a strong Andalusian accent *Ver tb* MARCAR

marcador *nm* (*Dep*) scoreboard

marcar ◆ *vt* **1** (*gen*) to mark: *~ el suelo con tiza* to mark the ground with chalk **2** (*ganado*) to brand **3** (*indicar*) to say: *El reloj marcaba las cinco.* The clock said five o'clock. ◆ *vt, vi* **1** (*Dep*) to score: *Marcaron (tres goles) en el primer tiempo.* They scored (three goals) in the first half. **2** (*teléfono*) to dial: *Has marcado mal.* You've dialled the wrong number. **3** (*pelo*) to set LOC **marcar el compás/ritmo** to beat time/ the rhythm

marcha *nf* **1** (*Mil, Mús, manifestación*) march **2** (*bicicleta, coche*) gear: *cambiar de ~* to change gear **3** (*velocidad*) speed: *reducir la ~* to reduce speed **4** (*animación*): *¡Qué ~ tenía el tío!* That guy was all go! ◊ *una fiesta con mucha ~* a very lively party ◊ *la ~ nocturna de Torremolinos* the night life in Torremolinos LOC **a marchas forzadas** against the clock **a toda marcha** at top speed **dar marcha atrás** to reverse **sobre la marcha** as I, you, etc go (along): *Lo decidiremos sobre la ~.* We'll decide as we go along. *Ver tb* EMPRENDER

marchar ◆ *vi* to go: *¿Cómo marchan las cosas?* How are things going? ◆ **marchar(se)** *vi, v pron* **marchar(se) (de)** to leave: *~se de casa* to leave home ◊ *¿Os marcháis ya?* Are you leaving already?

marchito, -a *adj* (*flor*) withered

marchoso, -a *adj* lively

marcial *adj* martial

marcianitos *nm* Space Invaders

marciano, -a *adj, nm-nf* Martian

marco *nm* **1** (*cuadro, puerta*) frame **2** (*moneda*) mark

marea *nf* tide: *~ alta/baja* high/low tide ◊ *Ha subido/bajado la ~.* The tide has come in/gone out. LOC **marea negra** oil slick *Ver tb* VIENTO

mareado, -a *pp, adj* **1** (*gen*) sick: *Estoy un poco ~.* I'm feeling rather sick. **2** (*harto*) sick and tired: *Me tiene ~ con la idea de la moto.* I'm sick and tired of him going on about that motor bike. *Ver tb* MAREAR

marear ◆ *vt* **1** (*gen*) to make *sb* feel sick: *Ese olor me marea.* That smell makes me feel sick. **2** (*hartar*) to get on *sb's* nerves: *La están mareando con esa música.* Their music is getting on her nerves. ◊ *¡No me marees!* Don't go on at me! ◆ **marearse** *v pron* **1** (*gen*) to get sick: *Me mareo en el asiento de atrás.* I get sick if I sit in the back seat. **2** (*perder el equilibrio*) to feel dizzy **3** (*en el mar*) to get seasick

maremoto *nm* tidal wave

mareo *nm* dizziness: *sufrir/tener ~s* to feel dizzy LOC *Ver* PASTILLA

marfil *nm* ivory

margarina *nf* margarine

margarita *nf* daisy [*pl* daisies]

margen ◆ *nf* bank ◆ *nm* **1** (*en una página*) margin **2** (*libertad*) room (***for sth***): *~ de duda* room for doubt LOC **al margen**: *Le dejan al ~ de todo.* They leave him out of everything.

marginado, -a ◆ *pp, adj* **1** (*persona*) left out: *sentirse ~* to feel left out **2** (*zona*) deprived ◆ *nm-nf* outcast *Ver tb* MARGINAR

marginar *vt* to shun

maría *nf* (*asignatura fácil*) easy subject

marica *nm* poof

marido *nm* husband

marihuana *nf* marijuana

marimandón, -ona *nm-nf* bossy [*adj*]

marina *nf* navy [*v sing o pl*]: *la Marina Mercante* the Merchant Navy LOC *Ver* INFANTERÍA

marinero, -a *adj, nm* sailor [*n*]: *una gorra marinera* a sailor hat

marino, -a ◆ *adj* **1** (*gen*) marine: *vida/contaminación marina* marine life/ pollution **2** (*aves, sal*) sea [*n atrib*] ◆ *nm* sailor LOC *Ver* AZUL

marioneta *nf* **1** (*gen*) puppet **2 marionetas** puppet show [*sing*]

mariposa *nf* butterfly [*pl* butterflies]: *los 200 metros ~* the 200 metres butterfly LOC *Ver* NADAR

mariquita *nf* ladybird

marisco *nm* shellfish

marisma *nf* marsh

marítimo, -a *adj* **1** (*pueblo, zona*) coastal **2** (*puerto, ruta*) sea [*n atrib*]: *puerto ~* sea port LOC *Ver* PASEO

marketing *nm* marketing

mármol *nm* marble

marqués, -esa *nm-nf* marquis [*fem* marchioness]

marranada *nf* **1** (*suciedad*) filthy [*adj*]: *La calle quedó hecha una ~.* The street was filthy. **2** (*asquerosidad*) disgusting [*adj*]: *Lo que estás haciendo con la comida es una ~.* What you're doing with your food is disgusting.

marrano, -a ◆ *adj* filthy ◆ *nm-nf* pig ☛ *Ver nota en* CERDO

marrón *adj, nm* brown ☛ *Ver ejemplos en* AMARILLO

Marte *nm* Mars

martes *nm* Tuesday [*pl* Tuesdays] (*abrev* Tue(s)) ☛ *Ver ejemplos en* LUNES LOC **Martes de Carnaval** Shrove Tuesday

> El Martes de Carnaval también se llama **Pancake Day** porque es típico comer crêpes con zumo de limón y azúcar.

martes y trece ≃ Friday the thirteenth (*GB*)

martillo *nm* hammer

mártir *nmf* martyr

marxismo *nm* marxism

marzo *nm* March (*abrev* Mar) ☛ *Ver ejemplos en* ENERO

más ◆ *adv*

- **uso comparativo** more (***than sth/sb***): *Es ~ alta/inteligente que yo.* She's taller/more intelligent than me. ◊ *Tú has viajado ~ que yo.* You have travelled more than me/than I have. ◊ *~ de cuatro semanas* more than four weeks ◊ *Me gusta ~ que el tuyo.* I like it better than yours. ◊ *durar/trabajar ~* to last longer/work harder ◊ *Son ~ de las dos.* It's gone two.

> En comparaciones como *más blanco que la nieve, más sordo que una tapia,* etc el inglés utiliza la construcción **as ... as**: 'as white as snow', 'as deaf as a post'.

- **uso superlativo** most (***in/of...***): *el edificio ~ antiguo de la ciudad* the oldest building in the town ◊ *el ~ simpático de todos* the nicest one of all ◊ *la tienda que ~ libros ha vendido* the shop that has sold most books

> Cuando el superlativo se refiere sólo a dos cosas o personas, se utiliza la forma **more** o **-er**. Compárense las frases siguientes: *¿Cuál es la cama más cómoda (de las dos)?* Which bed is more comfortable? ◊ *¿Cuál es la cama más cómoda de la casa?* Which is the most comfortable bed in the house?

- **con pronombres negativos, interrogativos e indefinidos** else: *Si tienes algo ~ que decirme...* If you've got anything else to tell me... ◊ *¿Alguien ~?* Anyone else? ◊ *nada/nadie ~* nothing/nobody else ◊ *¿Qué ~ puedo hacer por vosotros?* What else can I do for you?
- **otras construcciones 1** (*exclamaciones*): *¡Qué paisaje ~ hermoso!* What lovely scenery! ◊ *¡Es ~ aburrido!* He's so boring! **2** (*negaciones*) only: *No sabemos ~ que lo que ha dicho la radio.* We only know what it said on the radio. ◊ *Esto no lo sabe nadie ~ que tú.* Only you know this.

◆ *nm, prep* plus: *Dos ~ dos, cuatro.* Two plus two is four. LOC **a más no poder**: *Gritamos a ~ no poder.* We shouted as loud as we could. **de lo más...** really: *una cara de lo ~ antipática* a really nasty face **de más 1** (*que sobra*) too much, too many: *Hay dos sillas de ~.* There are two chairs too many. ◊ *Pagaste tres libras de ~.* You paid three pounds too much. **2** (*de sobra*) spare: *No te preocupes, yo llevo un bolígrafo de ~.* Don't worry. I've got a spare pen. **más bien** rather: *Es ~ bien feo, pero muy simpático.* He's rather ugly, but very nice. **más o menos** *Ver* MENOS **más que nada** particularly **por más que** however much: *Por ~ que grites...* However much you shout... **¿qué más da?** what difference does it make? **sin más ni más** just like that ☛ Para otras expresiones con **más**, véanse las entradas del adjetivo, adverbio, etc, p.ej. **más callado que un muerto** en CALLADO y **más que nunca** en NUNCA.

masa *nf* **1** (*gen*) mass: *~ atómica* atomic mass ◊ *una ~ de gente* a mass of people **2** (*pan*) dough LOC **de masas** mass: *cultura/movimientos de ~s* mass culture/movements *Ver tb* MANO

masaje *nm* massage: *¿Me das un poco de ~ en la espalda?* Can you massage my back for me?

mascar *vt, vi* to chew

máscara *nf* mask

mascota *nf* mascot

masculino, -a *adj* **1** (*gen*) male: *la población masculina* the male population **2** (*Dep, moda*) men's: *la prueba masculina de los 100 metros* the men's 100 metres **3** (*característico del hombre, Gram*) masculine ☛ *Ver nota en* MALE

masivo, -a *adj* huge, massive (*más formal*): *una afluencia masiva de turistas* a huge influx of tourists

masticar *vt, vi* to chew: *Hay que ~ bien la comida.* You should chew your food thoroughly.

mástil *nm* **1** (*barco*) mast **2** (*bandera*) flagpole

masturbarse *v pron* to masturbate

mata *nf* bush

matadero *nm* slaughterhouse

matanza *nf* slaughter

matar *vt, vi* to kill: *~ el tiempo* to kill time ◊ *¡Te voy a ~!* I'm going to kill you! LOC **matar a disgustos** to make *sb's* life a misery **matar a tiros/de un tiro** to shoot *sb* dead **matar dos pájaros de un tiro** to kill two birds with one stone **matar el hambre**: *Compramos fruta para ~ el hambre.* We bought some fruit to keep us going. **matarse a estudiar/trabajar** to work like mad

matasellos *nm* postmark

mate[1] *nm* (*Ajedrez*) mate LOC *Ver* JAQUE

mate[2] *adj* (*sin brillo*) matt

matemáticas *nf* mathematics (*abrev* maths) [*v sing o pl*]: *Se le dan bien las ~.* He's good at maths.

matemático, -a ◆ *adj* mathematical ◆ *nm-nf* mathematician

materia *nf* **1** (*gen*) matter: *~ orgánica* organic matter **2** (*asignatura, tema*) subject: *ser un experto en la ~* to be an expert on the subject LOC **materia prima** raw material *Ver tb* ÍNDICE

material ◆ *adj* material ◆ *nm* **1** (*materia, datos*) material: *un ~ resistente al fuego* fire-resistant material ◊ *Tengo todo el ~ que necesito para el artículo.* I've got all the material I need for the article. **2** (*equipo*) equipment [*incontable*]: *~ deportivo/de laboratorio* sports/laboratory equipment LOC **material didáctico/educativo** teaching materials [*pl*]

materialista ◆ *adj* materialistic ◆ *nmf* materialist

maternal *adj* motherly, maternal (*más formal*)

maternidad *nf* **1** (*condición*) motherhood, maternity (*formal*) **2** (*clínica*) maternity ward

materno, -a *adj* **1** (*maternal*) motherly: *amor ~* motherly love **2** (*parentesco*) maternal: *abuelo ~* maternal grandfather LOC *Ver* LENGUA, LÍNEA

matinal *adj* morning [*n atrib*]: *un vuelo ~* a morning flight

matiz *nm* **1** (*color*) shade **2** (*rasgo*) nuance: *matices de significado* nuances of meaning ◊ *un ~ irónico* a touch of irony

matizar *vt* **1** (*puntualizar*) to clarify: *Me gustaría que matizara sus palabras.* I'd like you to clarify what you said. **2** (*armonizar*) to blend

matón *nm* bully [*pl* bullies]

matorral *nm* scrub [*incontable*]: *Estábamos escondidos en unos ~es.* We were hidden in the scrub.

matrícula *nf* **1** (*inscripción*) registration: *Se ha abierto la ~.* Registration has begun. **2** (*vehículo*) **(a)** (*número*) registration number: *Apunté la ~.* I wrote down the registration number. **(b)** (*placa*) number plate

matricular(se) *vt, v pron* to enrol (*sb*) (***in sth***): *Todavía no me he matriculado.* I still haven't enrolled.

matrimonio *nm* **1** (*gen*) marriage ☛ *Ver nota en* BODA **2** (*pareja*) (married) couple LOC *Ver* CAMA, CONTRAER, PROPOSICIÓN

matriz *nf* **1** (*Anat*) womb **2** (*Mat*) matrix [*pl* matrices/matrixes]

matutino, -a *adj* morning [*n atrib*]: *al final de la sesión matutina* at the end of the morning session

maullar *vi* to miaow

máximo, -a ◆ *adj* maximum: *temperatura máxima* maximum temperature ◊ *Tenemos un plazo ~ de diez días para pagar.* We've got a maximum of ten days in which to pay. ◊ *el ~ anotador de la liga* the top scorer in the league ◆ *nm* maximum: *un ~ de diez personas* a maximum of ten people ◆ **máxima** *nf* maximum temperature: *Sevilla dio la máxima con 35°C.* Seville had the maximum temperature with 35°C. LOC **al máximo**: *Debemos aprovechar los recursos al ~.* We must make maximum use of our resources. ◊ *Me esforcé al ~.* I tried my best. **como máximo** at most **máximo dirigente** leader *Ver tb* ALTURA

mayo *nm* May ☛ *Ver ejemplos en* ENERO

mayonesa *nf* mayonnaise [*incontable*]

mayor ◆ *adj*
• **uso comparativo 1** (*tamaño*) bigger (***than sth***): *Londres es ~ que Madrid.* London is bigger than Madrid. ◊ *~ de lo que parece* bigger than it looks **2** (*edad*) older (***than sb***): *Soy ~ que mi hermano.* I'm older than my brother. ☛ *Ver nota en* ELDER
• **uso superlativo** ~ (**de**) (*edad*) oldest (**in ...**): *Es el alumno ~ de la clase.* He's the oldest student in the class. ☛ *Ver nota en* ELDER
• **otros usos 1** (*adulto*) grown-up: *Sus hijos son ya ~es.* Their children are grown-up now. **2** (*anciano*) old **3** (*principal*) **(a)** (*gen*) main: *la plaza ~* the main square **(b)** (*calle*) high: *calle ~* high street **4** (*Mús*) major: *en do ~* in C major
◆ *nmf* **1** ~ (**de**) oldest (one) (**in/of ...**): *El ~ tiene quince años.* The oldest (one) is fifteen. ◊ *la ~ de las tres hermanas* the oldest of the three sisters ☛ *Ver nota en* ELDER **2 mayores** (*adultos*) grown-ups: *Los ~es no llegarán hasta las ocho.* The grown-ups won't get here till eight. **LOC al por mayor** wholesale **de mayor** when I, you, etc grow up: *De ~ quiero ser médico.* I want to be a doctor when I grow up. **hacerse mayor** to grow up **la mayor parte** (**de**) most (of *sth/sb*): *La ~ parte son católicos.* Most of them are Catholics. **ser mayor de edad**: *Cuando sea ~ de edad podré votar.* I'll be able to vote when I'm eighteen. ◊ *Puede sacarse el carné de conducir porque es ~ de edad.* He can get his driving licence because he is over eighteen. *Ver tb* CAZA[1], COLEGIO, PERSONA

mayordomo *nm* butler

mayoría *nf* majority [*pl* majorities]: *obtener la ~ absoluta* to get an absolute majority **LOC la mayoría de ...** most (of ...): *A la ~ de nosotros nos gusta.* Most of us like it. ◊ *La ~ de los ingleses prefiere vivir en el campo.* Most English people prefer to live in the country. ☛ *Ver nota en* MOST; *Ver tb* INMENSO

mayúscula *nf* capital letter **LOC con mayúscula** with a capital letter **en mayúsculas** in capitals

mazapán *nm* marzipan

mazo *nm* (*martillo*) mallet

me *pron pers* **1** (*complemento*) me: *¿No me viste?* Didn't you see me? ◊ *Dámelo.* Give it to me. ◊ *¡Cómpramelo!* Buy it for me. **2** (*partes del cuerpo, efectos personales*): *Me voy a lavar las manos.* I'm going to wash my hands. **3** (*reflexivo*) (myself): *Me vi en el espejo.* I saw myself in the mirror. ◊ *Me vestí en seguida.* I got dressed straight away.

mear *vi* to pee

mecánica *nf* mechanics [*sing*]

mecánico, -a ◆ *adj* mechanical ◆ *nmf* mechanic **LOC** *Ver* ESCALERA

mecanismo *nm* mechanism: *el ~ de un reloj* a watch mechanism

mecanografía *nf* typing

mecanografiar *vt* to type

mecanógrafo, -a *nm-nf* typist

mecedora *nf* rocking chair

mecer(se) *vt, v pron* **1** (*columpio*) to swing **2** (*cuna, bebé, barca*) to rock

mecha *nf* **1** (*vela*) wick **2** (*bomba*) fuse **3 mechas** (*pelo*) highlights **LOC a toda mecha** at full speed

mechero *nm* lighter

mechón *nm* lock

medalla *nf* medal: *~ de oro* gold medal **LOC** *Ver* ENTREGA

media[1] *nf* **1** (*promedio*) average **2** (*Mat*) mean **3** (*reloj*): *Son las tres y ~.* It's half past three.

media[2] *nf* **medias** tights

mediados LOC a mediados de... in the middle of... **hacia mediados de...** around the middle of...

mediano, -a *adj* **1** (*gen*) medium: *de tamaño ~* of medium size ◊ *Uso la talla mediana.* I take a medium size. **2** (*regular*): *de mediana estatura/inteligencia* of average height/intelligence **LOC de mediana edad** middle-aged

medianoche *nf* midnight: *Llegaron a ~.* They arrived at midnight.

medicamento *nm* medicine

medicina *nf* medicine: *recetar una ~* to prescribe a medicine

médico, -a ◆ *adj* medical: *un reconocimiento ~* a medical examination ◆ *nm-nf* doctor: *ir al ~* to go to the doctor's **LOC médico de cabecera** GP *Ver tb* FICHA, HISTORIAL, RECONOCIMIENTO

medida *nf* **1** (*extensión*) measurement: *¿Qué ~s tiene esta habitación?* What are the measurements of this room? ◊ *El sastre me tomó las ~s.* The tailor took my measurements. **2** (*unidad, norma*) measure: *pesos y ~s* weights and measures ◊ *Habrá que tomar ~s al respecto.* Something must be done about it. **LOC** (**hecho**) **a medida** (made) to measure

medieval *adj* medieval

medio, -a ◆ *adj* **1** (*la mitad de*) half a, half an: *media botella de vino* half a bottle of wine ◊ *media hora* half an hour **2** (*promedio, normal*) average: *temperatura/velocidad media* average temperature/speed ◊ *un chico de inteligencia media* a boy of average intelligence ◆ *adv* half: *Cuando llegó estábamos ~ dormidos.* We were half asleep when he arrived. ◆ *nm* **1** (*centro*) middle: *una plaza con un quiosco en el ~* a square with a newsstand in the middle **2** (*entorno*) environment **3** (*Mat*) half [*pl* halves]: *Dos ~s suman un entero.* Two halves make a whole. **4** (*procedimiento, recurso*) means [*pl* means]: *~ de transporte* means of transport ◊ *No tienen ~s para comprar una casa.* They lack the means to buy a house. LOC **a media asta** at half-mast **a media mañana/tarde** in the middle of the morning/afternoon **a medio camino** halfway: *A ~ camino paramos a descansar.* We stopped to rest halfway. **en medio de** in the middle of *sth* **estar/ponerse en medio** to be/get in the way: *No puedo pasar, siempre estás en ~.* I can't get by—you're always (getting) in the way. **medias tintas** half measures: *No me gustan las medias tintas.* I don't like half measures. **medio ambiente** environment **medio campo** midfield: *un jugador de ~ campo* a midfield player **medio (de comunicación)** medium [*pl* media]: *un ~ tan poderoso como la televisión* a powerful medium like TV **medio mundo** lots of people [*pl*] **y medio** and a half: *kilo y ~ de tomates* one and a half kilos of tomatoes ◊ *Tardamos dos horas y media.* It took us two and a half hours. *Ver tb* CLASE, EDAD, JORNADA, PENSIÓN, TÉRMINO, VUELTA

mediodía *nm* midday: *Llegaron al ~.* They arrived at lunchtime. ◊ *la comida del ~* the midday meal

medir ◆ *vt* to measure: *~ la cocina* to measure the kitchen ◆ *vi*: *—¿Cuánto mides?* 'How tall are you?' ◊ *La mesa mide 1,50m de largo por 1m de ancho.* The table is 1·50m long by 1m wide.

meditar *vt, vi* ~ (**sobre**) to think (**about** ***sth***): *Meditó sobre su respuesta.* He thought about his answer.

mediterráneo, -a *adj, nm* Mediterranean

médula (*tb* **medula**) *nf* marrow: *~ ósea* bone marrow

medusa *nf* jellyfish [*pl* jellyfish]

mejicano, -a *adj, nm-nf Ver* MEXICANO

Méjico *nm Ver* MÉXICO

mejilla *nf* cheek

mejillón *nm* mussel

mejor ◆ *adj, adv* (*uso comparativo*) better (**than** ***sth/sb***): *Tienen un piso ~ que el nuestro.* Their flat is better than ours. ◊ *Me siento mucho ~.* I feel much better. ◊ *cuanto antes ~* the sooner the better ◊ *Cantas ~ que yo.* You're a better singer than me. ◆ *adj, adv, nmf* (*uso superlativo*) ~ (**de**) best (**in/of/that…**): *mi ~ amigo* my best friend ◊ *el ~ equipo de la liga* the best team in the league ◊ *Es la ~ de la clase.* She's the best in the class. ◊ *el que ~ canta* the one who sings best LOC **a lo mejor** maybe **hacer algo lo mejor posible** to do your best: *Preséntate al examen y hazlo lo ~ posible.* Go to the exam and do your best. **mejor dicho** I mean: *cinco, ~ dicho, seis* five, I mean six *Ver tb* CADA, CASO

mejorar ◆ *vt* **1** (*gen*) to improve: *~ las carreteras* to improve the roads **2** (*enfermo*) to make *sb* feel better ◆ *vi* to improve: *Si las cosas no mejoran…* If things don't improve… ◆ **mejorarse** *v pron* to get better: *¡Que te mejores!* Get well soon!

mejoría *nf* improvement (**in** ***sth/sb***): *la ~ de su estado de salud* the improvement in his health

melancólico, -a *adj* sad

melena *nf* hair: *llevar ~ suelta* to wear your hair loose

mellizo, -a *adj, nm-nf* twin [*n*]

melocotón *nm* peach

melocotonero *nm* peach tree

melodía *nf* tune

melón *nm* melon

membrillo *nm* quince

memorable *adj* memorable

memoria *nf* **1** (*gen*) memory: *Tienes buena ~.* You've got a good memory. ◊ *perder la ~* to lose your memory **2** **memorias** (*autobiografía*) memoirs LOC **de memoria** by heart: *saberse algo de ~* to know something by heart **hacer memoria** to try to remember *Ver tb* ESTUDIAR

memorizar *vt* to memorize

menaje *nm* LOC **menaje de cocina** kitchenware

mención *nf* mention

mencionar *vt* to mention LOC **sin mencionar** not to mention

mendigar *vt, vi* to beg (**for** ***sth***): *~ comida* to beg for food

mendigo, -a *nm-nf* beggar

mendrugo *nm* crust

menear *vt* **1** (*sacudir*) to shake **2** (*cabeza*) **(a)** (*para decir que sí*) to nod **(b)** (*para decir que no*) to shake **3** (*cola*) to wag

menestra *nf* vegetable stew

menguante *adj* (*luna*) waning LOC *Ver* CUARTO

menopausia *nf* menopause

menor ◆ *adj*

• **uso comparativo 1** (*tamaño*) smaller (***than sth***): *Mi jardín es ~ que el tuyo.* My garden is smaller than yours. **2** (*edad*) younger (***than sb***): *Eres ~ que ella.* You're younger than her.

• **uso superlativo** ~ **(de)** (*edad*) youngest (**in ...**): *el alumno ~ de la clase* the youngest student in the class ◊ *el hermano ~ de María* María's youngest brother

• **música** minor: *una sinfonía en mi ~* a symphony in E minor

◆ *nmf* **1** ~ **(de)** youngest (one) (**in/of ...**): *La ~ tiene cinco años.* The youngest (one) is five. ◊ *el ~ de la clase* the youngest in the class **2** (*menor de edad*) minor: *No se sirve alcohol a ~es.* Alcohol will not be served to minors. LOC **al por menor** retail **menor de 18, etc años**: *Prohibida la entrada a los ~es de 18 años.* No entry for under-18s. *Ver tb* CAZA[1], PAÑO

menos ◆ *adv* menos **uso comparativo** less (***than sth/sb***): *A mí sírveme ~.* Give me less. ◊ *Tardé ~ de lo que yo pensaba.* It took me less time than I thought it would.

> Con sustantivos contables es más correcta la forma **fewer**, aunque cada vez más gente utiliza **less**: *Había menos gente/coches que ayer.* There were fewer people/cars than yesterday. *Ver tb nota en* LESS.

• **uso superlativo** least (***in/of...***): *la ~ habladora de la familia* the least talkative member of the family ◊ *el alumno que ~ trabaja* the student who works least

> Con sustantivos contables es más correcta la forma **fewest**, aunque cada vez más gente utiliza **least**: *la clase con menos alumnos* the class with fewest pupils *Ver tb nota en* LESS.

◆ *prep* **1** (*excepto*) except: *Fueron todos ~ yo.* Everybody went except me. **2** (*hora*) to: *Son las doce ~ cinco.* It's five to twelve. **3** (*Mat, temperatura*) minus: *Estamos a ~ diez grados.* It's minus ten. ◊ *Cinco ~ tres, dos.* Five minus three is two. ◆ *nm* (*signo matemático*) minus (sign) LOC **al menos** at least **a menos que** unless: *a ~ que deje de llover* unless it stops raining **de menos** too little, too few: *Me dieron mil pesetas de ~.* They gave me a thousand pesetas too little. ◊ *tres tenedores de ~* three forks too few **echar de menos** to miss *sth/sb/doing sth*: *Echaremos de ~ el ir al cine.* We'll miss going to the cinema. **lo menos** the least: *¡Es lo ~ que puedo hacer!* It's the least I can do! ◊ *lo ~ posible* as little as possible **más o menos** more or less **¡menos mal!** thank goodness! **por lo menos** at least

mensaje *nm* message

mensajero, -a *nm-nf* messenger

menstruación *nf* menstruation

mensual *adj* monthly: *un salario ~* a monthly salary

menta *nf* mint

mental *adj* mental LOC *Ver* CACAO[2]

mentalidad *nf* mentality [*pl* mentalities] LOC **tener una mentalidad abierta/estrecha** to be open-minded/narrow-minded

mentalizar *vt* (*concienciar*) to make *sb* aware (***of sth***): *~ a la población de la necesidad de cuidar del medio ambiente* to make people aware of the need to look after the environment

mente *nf* mind LOC **tener algo en mente** to have sth in mind: *¿Tienes algo en ~?* Do you have anything in mind?

mentir *vi* to lie: *¡No me mientas!* Don't lie to me! ☛ *Ver nota en* LIE[2]

mentira *nf* lie: *contar/decir ~s* to tell lies ◊ *¡Eso es ~!* That isn't true! LOC **una mentira piadosa** a white lie *Ver tb* PARECER

mentiroso, -a ◆ *adj* deceitful: *una persona mentirosa* a deceitful person ◆ *nm-nf* liar

menú *nm* menu: *No estaba en el ~.* It wasn't on the menu. LOC **menú del día** set menu

menudo, -a *adj* **1** (*pequeño*) small **2** (*en exclamaciones*): *¡Menuda suerte tienes!* You're so lucky! ◊ *¡Menuda gracia me hace tener que cocinar!* It's not much fun having to cook! LOC **a menudo** often

meñique *nm* **1** (*de la mano*) little finger **2** (*del pie*) little toe

mercadillo *nm* street market

mercado *nm* market: *Lo compré en el ~.* I bought it at the market. LOC **el Mercado Común** the Common Market

mercancía *nf* goods [*pl*]: *La ~ estaba defectuosa.* The goods were damaged. LOC *Ver* TREN, VAGÓN

mercería *nf* (*sección*) haberdashery

mercurio *nm* **1** (*Quím*) mercury **2** **Mercurio** (*planeta*) Mercury

merecer(se) *vt, v pron* to deserve: *(Te) mereces un castigo.* You deserve to be punished. ◊ *El equipo mereció perder.* The team deserved to lose. LOC *Ver* PENA

merecido, -a *pp, adj* well deserved: *una victoria bien merecida* a well deserved victory LOC **lo tienes bien merecido** it serves you right *Ver tb* MERECER(SE)

merendar ♦ *vt* to have *sth* for tea: *¿Qué queréis ~?* What do you want for tea? ♦ *vi* **1** (*gen*) to have tea: *Merendamos a las seis.* We have tea at six o'clock. ☛ *Ver* pág 320. **2** (*al aire libre*) to have a picnic

merengue *nm* (*Cocina*) meringue

meridiano *nm* meridian

merienda *nf* **1** (*gen*) tea: *Termínate la ~.* Eat up your tea. **2** (*al aire libre*) picnic: *Fueron de ~ al campo.* They went for a picnic in the country. LOC **merienda-cena** early dinner ☛ *Ver* pág 320.

mérito *nm* merit LOC **tener mérito** to be praiseworthy

merluza *nf* hake [*pl* hake]

mermelada *nf* **1** (*gen*) jam: *~ de melocotón* peach jam **2** (*de cítricos*) marmalade

mero, -a *adj* mere: *Fue una mera casualidad.* It was mere coincidence.

mes *nm* month: *Dentro de un ~ empiezan las vacaciones.* The holidays start in a month. ◊ *el ~ pasado/que viene* last/next month ◊ *a primeros de ~* at the beginning of the month LOC **al mes 1** (*cada mes*) a month: *¿Cuánto gastas al ~?* How much do you spend a month? **2** (*transcurrido un mes*) within a month: *Al ~ de empezar enfermó.* Within a month of starting he fell ill. **estar de dos, etc meses** to be two, etc months pregnant **por meses** monthly: *Nos pagan por ~es.* We're paid monthly. **un mes sí y otro no** every other month *Ver tb* CURSO, ÚLTIMO

mesa *nf* table: *No pongas los pies en la ~.* Don't put your feet on the table. ◊ *¿Nos sentamos a la ~?* Shall we sit at the table? LOC **mesa (de despacho/colegio)** desk **mesa redonda** (*lit* y *fig*) round table **poner la mesa** to lay/set the table **quitar/recoger la mesa** to clear the table *Ver tb* BENDECIR, JUEGO, TENIS

meseta *nf* plateau [*pl* plateaus/plateaux]

mesilla (*tb* **mesita**) *nf* LOC **mesilla (de noche)** bedside table

mesón *nm* inn

mestizo, -a *adj, nm-nf* (person) of mixed race

meta *nf* **1** (*Atletismo*) finishing line: *el primero en cruzar la ~* the first across the finishing line **2** (*objetivo*) goal: *alcanzar una ~* to achieve a goal LOC *Ver* PROPIO

metáfora *nf* metaphor

metal *nm* metal

metálico, -a *adj* **1** (*gen*) metal [*n atrib*]: *una barra metálica* a metal bar **2** (*color, sonido*) metallic LOC **en metálico** cash: *un premio en ~* a cash prize *Ver tb* PAGAR, TELA

metedura *nf* LOC **metedura de pata** blunder

meteorito *nm* meteor

meteorológico, -a *adj* weather [*n atrib*], meteorological (*formal*): *un parte ~* a weather bulletin

meter ♦ *vt* **1** (*gen*) to put: *Mete el coche en el garaje.* Put the car in the garage. ◊ *¿Dónde has metido mis llaves?* Where have you put my keys? ◊ *Metí 2.000 pesetas en mi cuenta.* I put 2000 pesetas into my account. **2** (*gol, canasta*) to score ♦ **meterse** *v pron* **1** (*introducirse*) to get into *sth*: *~se en la cama/ducha* to get into bed/the shower ◊ *Se me ha metido una piedra en el zapato.* I've got a stone in my shoe. **2** (*involucrarse, interesarse*) to get involved ***in sth***: *~se en política* to get involved in politics **3** (*en los asuntos de otro*) to interfere (***in sth***): *Se meten en todo.* They interfere in everything. **4 meterse con** (*criticar*) to pick on *sb* LOC **meter la pata** to put your foot in it **meter las narices** to poke/stick your nose *into sth* **meterle miedo a algn** to frighten sb **meter prisa** to rush: *No me metas prisa.* Don't rush me. **meter ruido**: *No metas ruido.* Don't make any noise. ◊ *El coche mete mucho ruido.* The car is really noisy. **metérsele a algn en la cabeza hacer algo** to take it into your head to do sth *Ver tb* CAÑA

método *nm* method

metomentodo *nmf* busybody [*pl* busybodies]

metralleta *nf* sub-machine gun

métrico, -a *adj* metric: *el sistema ~* the metric system

metro[1] *nm* **1** (*medida*) metre (*abrev* m): *los 200 ~s braza* the 200 metres breaststroke ◊ *Se vende por ~s.* It's sold by the metre. ☛ *Ver* Apéndice 1. **2** (*cinta para medir*) tape-measure

metro[2] *nm* underground: *Podemos ir en ~.* We can go there on the underground.

El metro de Londres se llama **tube**: *Cogimos el último metro.* We caught the last tube.

mexicano, -a *adj, nm-nf* Mexican

México *nm* (*país*) Mexico

mezcla *nf* **1** (*gen*) mixture: *una ~ de aceite y vinagre* a mixture of oil and vinegar **2** (*tabaco, alcohol, café, té*) blend **3** (*racial, social, musical*) mix

mezclar ◆ *vt* **1** (*gen*) to mix: *Hay que ~ bien los ingredientes.* Mix the ingredients well. **2** (*desordenar*) to get *sth* mixed up: *No mezcles las fotos.* Don't get the photos mixed up. ◆ **mezclarse** *v pron* **1** (*alternar*) to mix ***with sb***: *No quiere ~se con la gente del pueblo.* He doesn't want to mix with people from the village. **2** (*meterse*) to get mixed up ***in sth***: *No quiero ~me en asuntos de familia.* I don't want to get mixed up in family affairs.

mezquita *nf* mosque

mi[1] *adj pos* my: *mis amigos* my friends

mi[2] *nm* **1** (*nota de la escala*) mi **2** (*tonalidad*) E: *mi mayor* E major

mí *pron pers* me: *¿Es para mí?* Is it for me? ◊ *No me gusta hablar de mí misma.* I don't like talking about myself.

miau *nm* miaow ☛ *Ver nota en* GATO

microbio *nm* microbe, germ (*más coloq*)

micrófono *nm* microphone, mike (*más coloq*)

microondas *nm* microwave (oven)

microscopio *nm* microscope

miedo *nm* fear (**of sth/sb/doing sth**): *el ~ a volar/al fracaso* fear of flying/failure LOC **coger miedo** to be scared *of sth/sb/doing sth* **dar miedo** to frighten, to scare (*más coloq*): *Sus amenazas no me dan ningún ~.* His threats don't frighten me. **pasar miedo** to be frightened: *Pasé un ~ espantoso.* I was terribly frightened. **por miedo a/de** for fear of *sth/sb/doing sth*: *No lo hice por ~ a que me riñieran.* I didn't do it for fear of being scolded. **¡qué miedo!** how scary! **tener miedo** to be afraid (*of sth/sb/doing sth*), to be scared (*más coloq*): *Tiene mucho ~ a los perros.* He's very scared of dogs. ◊ *¿Tenías ~ de suspender?* Were you afraid you'd fail? *Ver tb* METER, MORIR(SE), MUERTO, PELÍCULA

miel *nf* honey LOC *Ver* LUNA

miembro *nm* **1** (*gen*) member: *hacerse ~* to become a member **2** (*Anat*) limb

mientras ◆ *adv* in the meantime ◆ *conj* **1** (*simultaneidad*) while: *Canta ~ pinta.* He sings while he paints. **2** (*tanto tiempo como, siempre que*) as long as: *Aguanta ~ te sea posible.* Put up with it as long as you can. LOC **mientras que** while **mientras tanto** in the meantime

miércoles *nm* Wednesday [*pl* Wednesdays] (*abrev* Wed) ☛ *Ver ejemplos en* LUNES LOC **Miércoles de Ceniza** Ash Wednesday

miga *nf* crumb: *~s de galleta* biscuit crumbs LOC **hacer buenas migas** to get on well (*with sb*)

migración *nf* migration

mil *nm, adj, pron* **1** (*gen*) (a) thousand: *~ personas* a thousand people ◊ *un billete de cinco ~* a five-thousand peseta note

Mil puede traducirse también por **one thousand** cuando va seguido de otro número: *mil trescientos sesenta* one thousand three hundred and sixty, o para dar énfasis: *Te dije mil, no dos mil.* I said one thousand, not two.
De 1.100 a 1.900 es muy frecuente usar las formas **eleven hundred, twelve hundred, etc**: *una carrera de mil quinientos metros* a fifteen hundred metre race.

2 (*años*): *en 1600* in sixteen hundred ◊ *1713* seventeen thirteen ◊ *el año 2000* the year two thousand ☛ *Ver* Apéndice 1. LOC **a/por miles** in their thousands **miles de...** thousands of...: *~es de moscas* thousands of flies **mil millones** (a) billion: *Ha costado tres ~ millones de pesetas.* It cost three billion pesetas. *Ver tb* CIEN, DEMONIO

milagro *nm* miracle

milésimo, -a *adj, pron, nm-nf* thousandth: *una milésima de segundo* a thousandth of a second

mili *nf* military service: *Está en la ~.* He's doing his military service.

milímetro *nm* millimetre (*abrev* mm) ☛ *Ver* Apéndice 1.

militar ◆ *adj* military: *uniforme ~* military uniform ◆ *nmf* soldier: *Mi padre era ~.* My father was in the army. **LOC** *Ver* SERVICIO

milla *nf* mile

millar *nm* thousand [*pl* thousand]: *dos ~es de libros* two thousand books **LOC millares de...** thousands of...: *~es de personas* thousands of people

millón *nm* million [*pl* million]: *dos millones trescientas quince* two million three hundred and fifteen ◇ *Tengo un ~ de cosas que hacer.* I've got a million things to do. ☛ *Ver* Apéndice 1. **LOC millones de...** millions of...: *millones de partículas* millions of particles *Ver tb* MIL

millonario, -a *nm-nf* millionaire [*fem* millionairess] ☛ *Ver nota en* MILLIONAIRE

mimar *vt* to spoil

mimbre *nm* wicker: *un cesto de ~* a wicker basket

mímica *nf* (*lenguaje*) sign language **LOC hacer mímica** to mime

mimo ◆ *nm* **mimos 1** (*cariño*) fuss [*incontable*]: *Los niños necesitan ~s.* Children need to be made a fuss of. **2** (*excesiva tolerancia*): *No le des tantos ~s.* Don't spoil him. ◆ *nmf* mime artist

mina *nf* **1** (*gen*) mine: *una ~ de carbón* a coal mine **2** (*lápiz*) lead

mineral *nm* mineral **LOC** *Ver* AGUA

minero, -a ◆ *adj* mining [*n atrib*]: *varias empresas mineras* several mining companies ◆ *nm-nf* miner **LOC** *Ver* CUENCA

miniatura *nf* miniature

minifalda *nf* miniskirt

mínimo, -a ◆ *adj* **1** (*menor*) minimum: *la tarifa mínima* the minimum charge **2** (*insignificante*) minimal: *La diferencia entre ellos era mínima.* The difference between them was minimal. ◆ *nm* minimum: *reducir al ~ la contaminación* to cut pollution to a minimum **LOC como mínimo** at least *Ver tb* SALARIO

ministerio *nm* (*Pol, Relig*) ministry [*pl* ministries] **LOC Ministerio de Asuntos Exteriores** Ministry of Foreign Affairs ≃ Foreign Office (*GB*) **Ministerio de Hacienda** Ministry of Finance ≃ Treasury (*GB*) **Ministerio del Interior** Ministry of the Interior ≃ Home Office (*GB*)

ministro, -a *nm-nf* minister: *el Ministro español de Educación y Ciencia* the Spanish Minister for Education

Nótese que en Gran Bretaña el jefe de un ministerio no se llama 'minister' sino **Secretary of State** o simplemente **Secretary**: *el Ministro de Educación* the Secretary of State for Education/ Education Secretary.

LOC Ministro de Asuntos Exteriores ≃ Foreign Secretary (*GB*) **Ministro de Hacienda** ≃ Chancellor of the Exchequer (*GB*) **Ministro del Interior** ≃ Home Secretary (*GB*) *Ver tb* CONSEJO, PRIMERO

minoría *nf* minority [*v sing o pl*] [*pl* minorities] **LOC ser minoría** to be in the minority

minúsculo, -a ◆ *adj* **1** (*diminuto*) tiny **2** (*letra*) small, lower case (*más formal*): *una "m" minúscula* a small 'm' ◆ **minúscula** *nf* small letter, lower case letter (*más formal*)

minusválido, -a *adj, nm-nf* disabled [*adj*]: *asientos reservados para los ~s* seats for the disabled

minutero *nm* minute hand

minuto *nm* minute: *Espere un ~.* Just a minute. **LOC** *Ver* PULSACIÓN

mío, -a *adj pos, pron pos* mine: *Estos libros son ~s.* These books are mine.

Nótese que *un amigo mío* se traduce por **a friend of mine** porque significa *uno de mis amigos.*

miope *adj* short-sighted

miopía *nf* short-sightedness

mirada *nf* **1** (*gen*) look: *tener una ~ inexpresiva* to have a blank look (on your face) **2** (*vistazo*) glance: *Sólo me dio tiempo a echar una ~ rápida al periódico.* I only had time for a glance at the newspaper. **LOC** *Ver* DESVIAR

mirador *nm* viewpoint

mirar ◆ *vt* **1** (*gen*) to look **at sth/sb**: *~ el reloj* to look at the clock **2** (*observar*) to watch: *Estaban mirando cómo jugaban los niños.* They were watching the children play. ◆ *vi* to look: *~ hacia arriba/abajo* to look up/down ◇ *~ por una ventana/un agujero* to look out of a window/through a hole **LOC ¡mira que...!**: *¡Mira que casarse con ese sinvergüenza!* Fancy marrying that good-for-nothing! ◇ *¡Mira que eres despistado!* You're so absent-minded! **se mire como/por donde se mire** whichever way you look at it ☛ Para otras expresiones con **mirar**, véanse las entradas del sustantivo, adjetivo, etc, p.ej. **mirar de reojo** en REOJO y **mirar fijamente** en FIJAMENTE.

mirilla *nf* spyhole

mirlo *nm* blackbird

misa *nf* mass LOC **misa del gallo** midnight mass

miserable ◆ *adj* **1** (*sórdido, escaso*) miserable: *un cuarto/sueldo ~* a miserable room/wage **2** (*persona, vida*) wretched ◆ *nmf* **1** (*malvado*) wretch **2** (*tacaño*) miser

miseria *nf* **1** (*pobreza*) poverty **2** (*cantidad pequeña*) pittance: *Gana una ~.* He earns a pittance.

misil *nm* missile

misión *nf* mission

misionero, -a *nm-nf* missionary [*pl* missionaries]

mismo, -a ◆ *adj* **1** (*idéntico*) same: *al ~ tiempo* at the same time ◊ *Vivo en la misma casa que él.* I live in the same house as him. **2** (*uso enfático*): *Yo ~ lo vi.* I saw it myself. ◊ *estar en paz contigo ~* to be at peace with yourself ◊ *la princesa misma* the princess herself ◆ *pron* same one: *Es la misma que vino ayer.* She's the same one who came yesterday. ◆ *adv*: *delante ~ de mi casa* right in front of my house ◊ *Te prometo hacerlo hoy ~.* I promise you I'll get it done today. LOC **lo mismo** the same: *Póngame lo ~ de siempre.* I'll have the same as usual. **me da lo mismo** I, you, etc don't mind: *—¿Café o té? —Me da lo ~.* 'Coffee or tea?' 'I don't mind.' *Ver tb* AHÍ, AHORA, ALLÍ, COJEAR, CONFIANZA, VESTIR

misterio *nm* mystery [*pl* mysteries]

misterioso, -a *adj* mysterious

mitad *nf* half [*pl* halves]: *La ~ de los diputados votó en contra.* Half the MPs voted against. ◊ *en la primera ~ del partido* in the first half of the match ◊ *partir algo por la ~* to cut sth in half LOC **a/por (la) mitad (de)**: *Haremos una parada a ~ de camino.* We'll stop halfway. ◊ *La botella estaba a la ~.* The bottle was half empty. **a mitad de precio** half-price: *Lo compré a ~ de precio.* I bought it half-price.

mitin *nm* meeting: *dar un ~* to hold a meeting

mito *nm* **1** (*leyenda*) myth **2** (*persona famosa*) legend: *Es un ~ del fútbol español.* He's a Spanish football legend.

mitología *nf* mythology

mixto, -a *adj* (*colegio, instituto*) coeducational LOC *Ver* ENSALADA

mobiliario *nm* furniture

mochila *nf* rucksack

moco *nm* **mocos** LOC **tener mocos** to have a runny nose *Ver tb* LLORAR

moda *nf* fashion: *seguir la ~* to follow fashion LOC **(estar/ponerse) de moda** (to be/become) fashionable: *un bar de ~* a fashionable bar **pasarse de moda** to go out of fashion *Ver tb* PASADO

modales *nm* manners: *tener buenos ~* to have good manners

modelo ◆ *nm* **1** (*gen*) model: *un ~ a escala* a scale model **2** (*ropa*) style: *Tenemos varios ~s de chaqueta.* We've got several styles of jacket. ◆ *nmf* (*persona*) model LOC *Ver* DESFILE

moderado, -a *pp, adj* moderate *Ver tb* MODERAR

moderador, ~a *nm-nf* moderator

moderar *vt* **1** (*velocidad*) to reduce **2** (*lenguaje*) to mind: *Modera tus palabras.* Mind your language.

modernizar(se) *vt, v pron* to modernize

moderno, -a *adj* modern

modestia *nf* modesty

modesto, -a *adj* modest

modificar *vt* **1** (*cambiar*) to change **2** (*Gram*) to modify

modisto, -a ◆ *nm-nf* (*diseñador*) designer ◆ **modista** *nf* (*costurera*) dressmaker

modo *nm* **1** (*manera*) way [*pl* ways] (***of doing sth***): *un ~ especial de reír* a special way of laughing ◊ *Lo hace del mismo ~ que yo.* He does it the same way as me. **2 modos** (*modales*) manners: *malos ~s* bad manners LOC **a mi modo** my, your, etc way: *Dejadles que lo hagan a su ~.* Let them do it their way. **de modo que** (*por tanto*) so: *Has estudiado poco, de ~ que no puedes aprobar.* You haven't studied much, so you won't pass. **de todos modos** anyway *Ver tb* NINGUNO

moflete *nm* chubby cheek

mogollón *nm* an awful lot (***of sth***): *un ~ de dinero* an awful lot of money ◊ *Se aprende (un) ~.* You learn an awful lot.

moho *nm* mould LOC **criar/tener moho** to go/be mouldy

mojado, -a *pp, adj* wet *Ver tb* MOJAR

mojar ◆ *vt* **1** (*gen*) to get *sth/sb* wet: *No mojes el suelo.* Don't get the floor wet. **2** (*pringar*) to dip: *~ el pan en la sopa* to dip your bread in the soup ◆ **mojarse** *v pron* to get wet: *~se los pies* to get your feet wet ◊ *¿Te has mojado?* Did you get wet?

molde *nm* **1** (*Cocina*) tin **2** (*de yeso*) cast: *un ~ de yeso* a plaster cast LOC *Ver* PAN

molécula *nf* molecule

moler *vt* **1** (*café, trigo*) to grind **2** (*cansar*) to wear *sb* out LOC **moler a palos** to give *sb* a beating

molestar ♦ *vt* **1** (*importunar*) to bother: *Siento ~te a estas horas.* I'm sorry to bother you so late. **2** (*interrumpir*) to disturb: *No quiere que la molesten mientras trabaja.* She doesn't want to be disturbed while she's working. **3** (*ofender*) to upset ♦ *vi* to be a nuisance: *No quiero ~.* I don't want to be a nuisance. ♦ **molestarse** *v pron* (*tomarse trabajo*) **molestarse (en)** to bother (***to do sth***): *Ni se molestó en contestar mi carta.* He didn't even bother to reply to my letter. LOC **no molestar** do not disturb **¿te molesta que...?** do you mind if...?: *¿Te molesta que fume?* Do you mind if I smoke?

molestia *nf* **1** (*dolor*) discomfort [*incontable*] **2 molestias** inconvenience [*sing*]: *causar ~s a algn* to cause inconvenience to sb ◊ *Disculpen las ~s.* We apologize for any inconvenience. LOC **si no es molestia** if it's no bother **tomarse la molestia de** to take the trouble *to do sth*

molesto, -a *adj* **1** (*que fastidia*) annoying **2** (*disgustado*) annoyed (***with sb***): *Está ~ conmigo por lo del coche.* He's annoyed with me about the car.

molino *nm* mill LOC **molino de agua/viento** watermill/windmill

momento *nm* **1** (*gen*) moment: *Espera un ~.* Hold on a moment. **2** (*periodo*) time [*incontable*]: *en estos ~s de crisis* at this time of crisis LOC **al momento** immediately **del momento** contemporary: *el mejor cantante del ~* the best contemporary singer **de momento** for the moment: *De ~ tengo bastante trabajo.* I've got enough work for the moment. **por el momento** for the time being *Ver tb* NINGUNO

momia *nf* mummy [*pl* mummies]

monaguillo *nm* altar boy

monarca *nmf* monarch

monarquía *nf* monarchy [*pl* monarchies]

monasterio *nm* monastery [*pl* monasteries]

monda (*tb* **mondadura**) *nf* **1** (*frutas*) peel [*incontable*] **2** (*hortalizas*) peeling: *~s de patata* potato peelings LOC **ser la monda** (*ser divertido*) to be a scream

mondar *vt* to peel LOC *Ver* RISA

moneda *nf* **1** (*pieza*) coin: *¿Tienes una ~ de 50?* Have you got a 50 peseta coin? **2** (*unidad monetaria*) currency [*pl* currencies]: *la ~ francesa* the French currency

monedero *nm* purse

monitor, ~a ♦ *nm-nf* instructor: *un ~ de gimnasia* a gym instructor ♦ *nm* (*pantalla*) monitor

monja *nf* nun LOC *Ver* COLEGIO

monje *nm* monk

mono, -a ♦ *adj* pretty: *Va siempre muy mona.* She always looks very pretty. ◊ *¡Qué niño más ~!* What a pretty baby! ♦ *nm-nf* (*animal*) monkey [*pl* monkeys] ♦ *nm* (*traje*) overalls [*pl*]: *Llevaba un ~ azul.* He was wearing blue overalls.

monolito *nm* monolith

monólogo *nm* monologue

monopatín *nm* skateboard

monopolio *nm* monopoly [*pl* monopolies]

monótono, -a *adj* monotonous

monóxido *nm* monoxide LOC **monóxido de carbono** carbon monoxide

monstruo *nm* **1** (*gen*) monster: *un ~ de tres ojos* a three-eyed monster **2** (*genio*) genius [*pl* geniuses]: *un ~ de las matemáticas* a mathematical genius

montado, -a *pp, adj*: *~ en un caballo/una motocicleta* riding a horse/a motor bike *Ver tb* MONTAR

montaje *nm* **1** (*máquina*) assembly: *una cadena de ~* an assembly line **2** (*truco*) set-up: *Seguro que todo es un ~.* I bet it's all a set-up.

montaña *nf* **1** (*gen*) mountain: *en lo alto de una ~* at the top of a mountain **2** (*tipo de paisaje*) mountains [*pl*]: *Prefiero la ~ a la playa.* I prefer the mountains to the seaside. LOC **montaña rusa** roller-coaster *Ver tb* BICICLETA

montañismo *nm* mountaineering

montañoso, -a *adj* mountainous LOC *Ver* SISTEMA

montar ♦ *vt* **1** (*establecer*) to set *sth* up: *~ un negocio* to set up a business **2** (*máquina*) to assemble **3** (*tienda de campaña*) to put *a tent* up **4** (*nata*) to whip ♦ *vi* to ride: *~ en bici* to ride a bike ◊ *botas/traje de ~* riding boots/clothes ♦ **montar(se)** *vi, v pron* to get on (*sth*): *Montaron dos pasajeros.* Two passengers got on. LOC **montar a caballo** to ride: *Me gusta ~ a caballo.* I like riding. **montárselo bien**: *¡Qué bien se lo montan!* They've really got it made! *Ver tb* BRONCA, ESCÁNDALO, SILLA

monte *nm* **1** (*gen*) mountain **2** (*con nombre propio*) Mount: *el ~ Everest* Mount Everest

montón *nm* **1** (*pila*) pile: *un ~ de arena/libros* a pile of sand/books **2** (*muchos*) lot (**of sth**): *un ~ de problemas* a lot of problems ◊ *Tienes montones de amigos.* You've got lots of friends. LOC **del montón** ordinary: *una chica del ~* an ordinary girl

montura *nf* (*gafas*) frame

monumento *nm* monument

moño *nm* bun: *Siempre va peinada con ~.* She always wears her hair in a bun. LOC *Ver* HORQUILLA

moqueta *nf* carpet

mora *nf* mulberry [*pl* mulberries]

morado, -a *adj, nm* purple ☛ *Ver ejemplos en* AMARILLO LOC **ponerse morado (de)** to stuff yourself (with *sth*)

moral ◆ *adj* moral ◆ *nf* **1** (*principios*) morality **2** (*ánimo*) morale: *La ~ está baja.* Morale is low. LOC *Ver* BAJO

moraleja *nf* moral

morcilla *nf* black pudding

mordaza *nf* gag LOC **ponerle una mordaza a algn** to gag sb: *Los asaltantes le pusieron una ~.* The robbers gagged him.

mordedura *nf* bite

morder(se) *vt, vi, v pron* to bite: *El perro me mordió en la pierna.* The dog bit my leg. ◊ *Mordí la manzana.* I bit into the apple. ◊ *~se las uñas* to bite your nails LOC **estar que muerde**: *No le preguntes; está que muerde.* Don't ask him; he'll bite your head off. **morder el anzuelo** to swallow the bait

mordisco *nm* bite LOC **dar/pegar un mordisco** to bite

mordisquear *vt* to nibble

moreno, -a *adj* **1** (*pelo, piel*) dark: *Mi hermana es mucho más morena que yo.* My sister's much darker than me. **2** (*bronceado, azúcar, pan*) brown: *ponerse ~* to go brown

morfina *nf* morphine

moribundo, -a *adj* dying

morir(se) *vi, v pron* to die: *~ de un infarto/en un accidente* to die of a heart attack/in an accident LOC **morirse de aburrimiento** to be bored stiff **morirse de frío** to be freezing **morirse de miedo** to be scared stiff **morirse por hacer algo** to be dying to do sth *Ver tb* MOSCA, RISA

moro, -a ◆ *adj* Moorish ◆ *nm-nf* Moor

morro *nm* **1** (*animal*) snout **2** (*avión, coche*) nose LOC **¡vaya morro!/¡qué morro!** what a cheek! *Ver tb* BEBER

morrón *adj* LOC *Ver* PIMIENTO

morsa *nf* walrus [*pl* walruses]

morse *nm* Morse Code

mortadela *nf* mortadella

mortal ◆ *adj* **1** (*gen*) mortal: *Los seres humanos son ~es.* Human beings are mortal. ◊ *pecado ~* mortal sin **2** (*enfermedad, accidente*) fatal **3** (*veneno, enemigo*) deadly **4** (*aburrimiento, ruido, trabajo*) dreadful: *La película es de una pesadez ~.* The film is dreadfully boring. ◆ *nmf* mortal LOC *Ver* RESTO

mortalidad *nf* mortality

mortero *nm* mortar

mortuorio, -a *adj* LOC *Ver* ESQUELA

moruno, -a *adj* LOC *Ver* PINCHO

mosaico *nm* mosaic

mosca *nf* fly [*pl* flies] LOC **caer/morir como moscas** to drop like flies **estar con la mosca detrás de la oreja** to smell a rat **¿qué mosca te ha picado?** what's eating you?

mosquito *nm* mosquito [*pl* mosquitoes]

mostaza *nf* mustard

mosto *nm* grape juice: *Dos ~s, por favor.* Two glasses of grape juice, please.

mostrador *nm* **1** (*tienda, aeropuerto*) counter **2** (*bar*) bar

mostrar ◆ *vt* to show: *Mostraron mucho interés por ella.* They showed great interest in her. ◆ **mostrarse** *v pron* (*parecer*) to seem: *Se mostraba algo pesimista.* He seemed rather pessimistic.

mota *nf* speck

mote *nm* nickname: *Me pusieron de ~ "la flaca".* They nicknamed me 'Skinny'.

motín *nm* mutiny [*pl* mutinies]

motivar *vt* **1** (*causar*) to cause **2** (*incentivar*) to motivate

motivo *nm* reason (**for sth**): *el ~ de nuestro viaje* the reason for our trip ◊ *por ~s de salud* for health reasons ◊ *Se enfadó conmigo sin ~ alguno.* He got angry with me for no reason.

moto (*tb* **motocicleta**) *nf* motor bike: *ir en ~* to ride a motor bike

motociclismo *nm* motorcycling

motociclista *nmf* motorcyclist

motocross *nm* motocross

motor, ~a ♦ *adj* motive: *potencia motora* motive power ♦ *nm* engine, motor ☛ *Ver nota en* ENGINE ♦ **motora** *nf* motor boat LOC *Ver* VUELO

movedizo, -a *adj* LOC *Ver* ARENA

mover(se) *vt, vi, v pron* to move: *~ una pieza del ajedrez* to move a chess piece ◊ *Te toca ~*. It's your move. ◊ *Muévete un poco para que me siente.* Move up a bit so I can sit down.

movido, -a *pp, adj* **1** (*ajetreado*) busy: *Hemos tenido un mes muy ~*. We've had a very busy month. **2** (*foto*) blurred *Ver tb* MOVER(SE)

móvil *adj* mobile

movimiento *nm* **1** (*gen*) movement: *un leve ~ de la mano* a slight movement of the hand ◊ *el ~ obrero/romántico* the labour/Romantic movement **2** (*marcha*) motion: *El coche estaba en ~*. The car was in motion. ◊ *poner algo en ~* to set sth in motion **3** (*actividad*) activity

mu *nm* moo LOC **no decir ni mu** not to open your mouth

muchacho, -a *nm-nf* **1** (*gen*) boy, lad (*más coloq*) [*fem* girl] **2 muchachos** (*chicos y chicas*) youngsters

muchedumbre *nf* crowd

mucho, -a ♦ *adj*

• **en oraciones afirmativas** a lot of *sth*: *Tengo ~ trabajo.* I've got a lot of work. ◊ *Había ~s coches.* There were a lot of cars.

• **en oraciones negativas e interrogativas** **1** (+ *sustantivo incontable*) much, a lot of *sth* (*más coloq*): *No tiene mucha suerte.* He doesn't have much luck. ◊ *¿Tomas ~ café?* Do you drink a lot of coffee? **2** (+ *sustantivo contable*) many, a lot of *sth* (*más coloq*): *No había ~s ingleses.* There weren't many English people.

• **otras construcciones**: *¿Tienes mucha hambre?* Are you very hungry? ◊ *hace ~ tiempo* a long time ago ♦ *pron* **1** (*en oraciones afirmativas*) a lot: *~s de mis amigos* a lot of my friends **2** (*en oraciones negativas e interrogativas*) much [*pl* many] ☛ *Ver nota en* MANY ♦ *adv* **1** (*gen*) a lot: *Se parece ~ a su padre.* He's a lot like his father. ◊ *Tu amigo viene ~ por aquí.* Your friend comes round here a lot. ◊ *trabajar ~* to work hard **2** (*con formas comparativas*) much: *Eres ~ mayor que ella.* You're much older than her. ◊ *~ más interesante* much more interesting **3** (*mucho tiempo*) a long time: *Llegaron ~ antes que nosotros.* They got here a long time before us. ◊ *hace ~* a long time ago **4** (*en respuestas*) very: *—¿Estás cansado? —No ~*. 'Are you tired?' 'Not very.' ◊ *—¿Te gustó? —Mucho.* 'Did you like it?' 'Very much.' LOC **como mucho** at most **ni mucho menos** far from it **por mucho que...** however much...: *Por ~ que insistas...* However much you insist...

mudanza *nf* move LOC **estar de mudanza** to be moving (house) *Ver tb* CAMIÓN

mudar(se) ♦ *vt, vi, v pron* (*cambiar*) **mudar(se) (de)** to change: *Hay que ~ al bebé.* The baby needs changing. ◊ *~se de camisa* to change your shirt ♦ **mudar(se)** *vt, v pron* **mudar(se) (de)** to move: *~se de casa* to move house

mudo, -a *adj* dumb: *Es ~ de nacimiento.* He was born dumb. LOC *Ver* PELÍCULA

mueble *nm* **1** (*gen*) piece of furniture: *un ~ muy elegante* a lovely piece of furniture **2 muebles** (*conjunto*) furniture [*incontable, v sing*]: *Los ~s estaban cubiertos de polvo.* The furniture was covered in dust.

mueca *nf* LOC **hacer muecas** to make/pull faces (*at sb*)

muela *nf* (back) tooth [*pl* (back) teeth] LOC **muela del juicio** wisdom tooth *Ver tb* DOLOR

muelle *nm* **1** (*resorte*) spring **2** (*de un puerto*) wharf [*pl* wharves]

muerte *nf* death LOC **dar muerte a algo/algn** to kill sth/sb **de mala muerte** horrible: *un barrio de mala ~* a horrible neighbourhood *Ver tb* PENA, REO, SUSTO

muerto, -a *pp, adj, nm-nf* dead [*adj*]: *La habían dado por muerta.* They had given her up for dead. ◊ *El pueblo se queda ~ durante el invierno.* The town is dead in winter. ◊ *los ~s en la guerra* the war dead ◊ *Hubo tres ~s en el accidente.* Three people were killed in the accident. LOC **muerto de cansancio** dead tired **muerto de envidia** green with envy **muerto de frío/hambre** freezing/starving **muerto de miedo** scared to death **muerto de sed** dying of thirst *Ver tb* CALLADO, HORA, NATURALEZA, PESAR[1], PUNTO, VIVO; *Ver tb* MORIR(SE)

muestra *nf* **1** (*Med, Estadística, mercancía*) sample: *una ~ de sangre* a blood sample **2** (*prueba*) token: *una ~*

de amor a token of love **3** (*señal*) sign: *dar ~s de cansancio* to show signs of fatigue LOC *Ver* FERIA

mugir *vi* **1** (*vaca*) to moo **2** (*toro*) to bellow

mugre *nf* filth

mujer *nf* **1** (*gen*) woman [*pl* women] **2** (*esposa*) wife [*pl* wives] LOC *Ver* NEGOCIO

muleta *nf* (*para andar*) crutch: *andar con ~s* to walk on crutches

mullido, -a *pp*, *adj* soft

mulo, -a *nm-nf* mule

multa *nf* fine LOC **poner una multa** to fine: *Le han puesto una ~.* He's been fined.

multinacional ♦ *adj* multinational ♦ *nf* multinational company [*pl* multinational companies]

múltiple *adj* **1** (*no simple*) multiple: *una fractura ~* a multiple fracture **2** (*numerosos*) numerous: *en ~s casos* on numerous occasions

multiplicación *nf* multiplication

multiplicar *vt*, *vi* (*Mat*) to multiply: *~ dos por cuatro* to multiply two by four ◊ *¿Ya sabes ~?* Do you know how to do multiplication yet?

multirracial *adj* multiracial

multitud *nf* **1** (*muchedumbre*) crowd [*v sing o pl*] **2** *~* **de** (*muchos*) a lot **of** ***sth***: *(una) ~ de problemas* a lot of problems

mundial ♦ *adj* world [*n atrib*]: *el récord ~* the world record ♦ *nm* world championship: *los Mundiales de Atletismo* the World Athletics Championships ◊ *el Mundial de fútbol* the World Cup

mundo *nm* world: *dar la vuelta al ~* to go round the world LOC **el mundo del espectáculo** show business **todo el mundo** everybody *Ver tb* BOLA, MEDIO, VUELTA

munición *nf* ammunition [*incontable*]: *quedarse sin municiones* to run out of ammunition

municipal *adj* municipal LOC **guardia/policía municipal 1** (*individuo*) policeman/woman [*pl* policemen/women] **2** (*cuerpo*) local police force *Ver tb* ELECCIÓN

municipio *nm* **1** (*unidad territorial*) town **2** (*ayuntamiento*) town council

muñeca *nf* **1** (*juguete*) doll: *¿Te gusta jugar con ~s?* Do you like playing with dolls? **2** (*parte del cuerpo*) wrist: *fracturarse la ~* to fracture your wrist

muñeco *nm* **1** (*juguete*) doll: *un ~ de trapo* a rag doll **2** (*de un ventrílocuo, maniquí*) dummy [*pl* dummies] LOC **muñeco de nieve** snowman [*pl* snowmen] **muñeco de peluche** soft toy

muñequera *nf* wristband

mural *nm* mural

muralla *nf* wall(s) [*se usa mucho en plural*]: *la ~ medieval* the medieval walls

murciélago *nm* bat

murmullo *nm* murmur: *el ~ de su voz/del viento* the murmur of his voice/the wind

murmurar ♦ *vt*, *vi* (*hablar en voz baja*) to mutter ♦ *vi* (*cotillear*) to gossip (***about sth/sb***)

muro *nm* wall

musa *nf* muse

musaraña *nf* LOC *Ver* PENSAR

muscular *adj* muscle [*n atrib*]: *una lesión ~* a muscle injury

músculo *nm* muscle

musculoso, -a *adj* muscular

museo *nm* museum: *Está en el Museo del Prado.* It's in the Prado Museum. ☛ *Ver nota en* MUSEUM

musgo *nm* moss

música *nf* music: *No me gusta la ~ clásica.* I don't like classical music. LOC **música de fondo** background music **música en directo** live music *Ver tb* EQUIPO

musical *adj*, *nm* musical LOC *Ver* COMEDIA, ESCALA

músico *nmf* musician

muslo *nm* **1** (*gen*) thigh **2** (*ave*) leg

musulmán, -ana *adj*, *nm-nf* Muslim

mutante *adj*, *nmf* mutant

mutilar *vt* to mutilate

mutuamente *adv* each other, one another: *Se odian ~.* They hate each other. ☛ *Ver nota en* EACH OTHER

mutuo, -a *adj* mutual

muy *adv* **1** (*gen*) very: *Están ~ bien/cansados.* They're very well/tired. ◊ *~ despacio/temprano* very slowly/early **2** (*+ sustantivo*): *El ~ sinvergüenza se ha marchado sin pagar.* The swine's gone off without paying. ◊ *Es ~ hombre.* He's a real man. LOC **muy bien** (*de acuerdo*) OK **Muy Sr mío/Sra mía** Dear Sir/Madam ☛ *Ver* págs 314–15. **por muy... que...** however...: *Por ~ simpático que sea...* However nice he is...

Nn

nabo *nm* turnip
nácar *nm* mother-of-pearl
nacer *vi* **1** (*persona, animal*) to be born: *¿Dónde naciste?* Where were you born? ◇ *Nací en 1971.* I was born in 1971. **2** (*río*) to rise **3** (*planta, pelo, plumas*) to grow LOC **nacer para actor, cantante, etc** to be a born actor, singer, etc
nacido, -a *pp, adj* LOC *Ver* RECIÉN; *Ver tb* NACER
naciente *adj* (*sol*) rising
nacimiento *nm* **1** (*gen*) birth: *fecha de ~* date of birth **2** (*río*) source **3** (*pelo, uña*) root **4** (*belén*) crib LOC **de nacimiento**: *Es ciega de ~.* She was born blind. ◇ *ser español de ~* to be Spanish by birth *Ver tb* LUGAR
nación *nf* nation LOC *Ver* ORGANIZACIÓN
nacional *adj* **1** (*de la nación*) national: *la bandera ~* the national flag **2** (*no internacional*) domestic: *el mercado ~* the domestic market ◇ *vuelos/salidas ~es* domestic flights/departures LOC *Ver* CARRETERA, DOCUMENTO, FIESTA, HIMNO
nacionalidad *nf* **1** (*gen*) nationality [*pl* nationalities] **2** (*ciudadanía*) citizenship
nacionalizar ◆ *vt* to nationalize ◆ **nacionalizarse** *v pron* to become a British, Spanish, etc citizen
nada ◆ *pron* **1** (*gen*) nothing, anything

> **Nothing** se utiliza cuando el verbo va en forma afirmativa en inglés y **anything** cuando va en negativa: *No queda nada.* There's nothing left. ◇ *No tengo nada que perder.* I've nothing to lose. ◇ *No quiero nada.* I don't want anything. ◇ *No tienen nada en común.* They haven't anything in common. ◇ *¿No quieres nada?* Don't you want anything?

2 (*Tenis*) love: *treinta, ~* thirty love ◆ *adv* at all: *No está ~ claro.* It's not at all clear. LOC **de nada 1** (*sin importancia*) little: *Es un arañazo de ~.* It's only a little scratch. **2** (*exclamación*) you're welcome: *—Gracias por la cena. —¡De ~!* 'Thank you for the meal.' 'You're welcome!'

> También se puede decir **don't mention it.**

nada más 1 (*eso es todo*) that's all **2** (*sólo*) only: *Tengo un hijo ~ más.* I only have one son. **nada más hacer algo**: *Lo reconocí ~ más verle.* I recognized him as soon as I saw him. **nada más y nada menos que... 1** (*persona*) none other than...: *~ más y ~ menos que el Presidente* none other than the President **2** (*cantidad*) no less than...: *~ más y ~ menos que 100 personas* no less than 100 people *Ver tb* DENTRO
nadador, ~a *nm-nf* swimmer
nadar *vi* to swim: *No sé ~.* I can't swim. LOC **nadar a braza/mariposa** to do (the) breast stroke/butterfly **nadar a crol** to do the crawl **nadar a espalda** to do backstroke
nadie *pron* nobody: *Eso no lo sabe ~.* Nobody knows that. ◇ *No había ~ más.* There was nobody else there.

> Nótese que cuando el verbo en inglés va en forma negativa, usamos **anybody**: *Está enfadado y no habla con nadie.* He is angry and won't talk to anybody.

LOC *Ver* DON
nado LOC **a nado**: *Cruzaron el río a ~.* They swam across the river.
naipe *nm* (playing) card ☛ *Ver nota en* BARAJA
nana *nf* lullaby [*pl* lullabies]
naranja ◆ *nf* (*fruta*) orange ◆ *adj, nm* (*color*) orange ☛ *Ver ejemplos en* AMARILLO LOC *Ver* RALLADURA
naranjada *nf* orangeade
naranjo *nm* orange tree
narcótico *nm* **narcóticos** drugs
narcotraficante *nmf* drug dealer
narcotráfico *nm* drug trafficking
nariz *nf* nose: *Suénate la ~.* Blow your nose. LOC **estar hasta las narices (de)** to be fed up (with *sth/sb/doing sth*) **¡narices!** rubbish! **no me sale de las narices** I, you, etc don't feel like doing it *Ver tb* CERRAR, LIMPIAR, METER
narrador, ~a *nm-nf* narrator
narrar *vt* to tell
nasal *adj* LOC *Ver* TABIQUE
nata *nf* **1** (*gen*) cream: *~ montada* whipped cream **2** (*de leche hervida*) skin LOC *Ver* FLOR
natación *nf* swimming
natal *adj* native: *país ~* native country LOC *Ver* CIUDAD
natalidad *nf* birth rate LOC *Ver* ÍNDICE

natillas *nf* custard [*incontable, v sing*]

nativo, -a *adj, nm-nf* native

nato, -a *adj* born: *un músico* ~ a born musician

natural *adj* **1** (*gen*) natural: *causas ~es* natural causes ◊ *¡Es ~!* It's only natural! **2** (*fruta, flor*) fresh **3** (*espontáneo*) unaffected: *un gesto* ~ an unaffected gesture LOC **ser natural de...** to come from... *Ver tb* CIENCIA

naturaleza *nf* nature LOC **naturaleza muerta** still life **por naturaleza** by nature *Ver tb* HIERRO

naturalidad *nf*: *con la mayor ~ del mundo* as if it were the most natural thing in the world LOC **con naturalidad** naturally

naturalmente *adv* of course: *Sí, ~ que sí.* Yes, of course.

naufragar *vi* to be wrecked

naufragio *nm* shipwreck

náufrago, -a *nm-nf* castaway [*pl* castaways]

náusea *nf* LOC **dar náuseas** to make *sb* feel sick **sentir/tener náuseas** to feel sick

náutico, -a *adj* sailing: *club* ~ sailing club

navaja *nf* **1** (*poco afilada*) penknife [*pl* penknives] **2** (*arma*) knife [*pl* knives]: *Me sacaron la ~ en la calle.* They pulled a knife on me in the street. LOC *Ver* PUNTA

navajazo *nm* knife wound: *Tenía un ~ en la cara.* He had a knife wound on his face. LOC **dar un navajazo** to stab

nave *nf* **1** (*Náut*) ship **2** (*iglesia*) nave LOC **nave espacial** spaceship

navegación *nf* navigation LOC *Ver* CARTA

navegar *vi* **1** (*barcos*) to sail **2** (*aviones*) to fly

navidad (*tb* **Navidad**) *nf* Christmas: *¡Feliz Navidad!* Happy Christmas! ◊ *Siempre nos reunimos en Navidad.* We always get together at Christmas.

> En Gran Bretaña apenas se celebra el día de Nochebuena o **Christmas Eve**. El día más importante es el 25 de diciembre, llamado **Christmas Day**. La familia se levanta por la mañana y todos abren los regalos que ha traído **Father Christmas**. Hacia las 3 de la tarde habla la Reina por la televisión, y después se toma el **Christmas dinner**: pavo y **Christmas pudding** (una especie de pastel de frutos secos). **Boxing Day** es el día después de Navidad y es fiesta nacional.

LOC *Ver* CESTA

navideño, -a *adj* Christmas [*n atrib*]

necesario, -a *adj* necessary: *Haré lo que sea ~.* I'll do whatever's necessary. ◊ *No lleves más de lo ~.* Only take what you need. ◊ *No es ~ que vengas.* You don't have to come. LOC **si es necesario** if necessary

neceser *nm* sponge bag

necesidad *nf* **1** (*cosas imprescindibles*) necessity [*pl* necessities]: *La calefacción es una ~.* Heating is a necessity. **2** ~ **(de)** need (**for *sth*/to do *sth***): *No veo la ~ de ir en coche.* I don't see the need to go by car. LOC **no hay necesidad** there's no need (*for sth/to do sth*) **pasar necesidades** to suffer hardship *Ver tb* PRIMERO

necesitado, -a ◆ *pp, adj* (*pobre*) needy ◆ *nm-nf*: *ayudar a los ~s* to help the poor *Ver tb* NECESITAR

necesitar *vt* to need

negado, -a *pp, adj, nm-nf* useless LOC **ser (un) negado** to be useless (*at sth/doing sth*): *Soy un ~ para las matemáticas.* I'm useless at maths. *Ver tb* NEGAR

negar ◆ *vt* **1** (*hecho*) to deny ***sth*/*doing sth*/*that*...**: *Negó haber robado el cuadro.* He denied stealing the picture. **2** (*permiso, ayuda*) to refuse: *Nos negaron la entrada en el país.* We were refused admittance into the country. ◆ **negarse** *v pron* **negarse a** to refuse ***to do sth***: *Se negaron a pagar.* They refused to pay.

negativa *nf* refusal

negativo, -a *adj, nm* negative

negociación *nf* negotiation

negociante *nmf* businessman/woman [*pl* businessmen/women]

negociar *vt, vi* to negotiate

negocio *nm* **1** (*comercio, asunto*) business: *hacer ~s* to do business ◊ *Muchos ~s han fracasado.* A lot of businesses have gone broke. ◊ *Los ~s son los ~s.* Business is business. ◊ *Estoy aquí por/de ~s.* I'm here on business. **2** (*irónicamente*) bargain: *¡Vaya ~ hemos hecho!* Some bargain we got there! LOC **hombre/mujer de negocios** businessman/woman [*pl* businessmen/women] *Ver tb* LIQUIDACIÓN

negro, -a ◆ *adj, nm* black ☛ *Ver ejemplos en* AMARILLO ◆ *nm-nf* black man/woman [*pl* black men/women] LOC *Ver*

BLANCO, CAJA, CERVEZA, GROSELLA, MAREA, OVEJA

Neptuno *nm* Neptune

nervio *nm* **1** (*gen*) nerve: *Eso son los ~s.* That's nerves. **2** (*carne*) gristle: *Esta carne tiene mucho ~.* This meat is very gristly. **LOC poner los nervios de punta** to set *sb's* nerves on edge *Ver tb* ATAQUE

nerviosismo *nm* nervousness

nervioso, -a *adj* **1** (*gen*) nervous: *el sistema ~* the nervous system ◊ *estar ~* to be nervous **2** (*Anat, célula, fibra, impulso*) nerve [*n atrib*]: *tejido ~* nerve tissue **LOC poner nervioso a algn** to get on sb's nerves **ponerse nervioso** to get worked up

neto, -a *adj* net: *ingresos ~s* net income ◊ *peso ~* net weight

neumático *nm* tyre

neumonía *nf* pneumonia [*incontable*]: *coger una ~* to catch pneumonia

neutral *adj* neutral

neutro, -a *adj* **1** (*gen*) neutral **2** (*Biol, Gram*) neuter

neutrón *nm* neutron

nevada *nf* snowfall

nevado, -a *pp, adj* (*cubierto de nieve*) snow-covered *Ver tb* NEVAR

nevar *v imp* to snow: *Creo que va a ~.* I think it's going to snow. **LOC** *Ver* PARECER

nevera *nf* fridge

ni *conj* **1** (*doble negación*) neither... nor...: *Ni tú ni yo hablamos inglés.* Neither you nor I speak English. ◊ *Ni lo sabe ni le importa.* He neither knows nor cares. ◊ *No ha dicho ni que sí ni que no.* He hasn't said either yes or no. **2** (*ni siquiera*) not even: *Ni él mismo sabe lo que gana.* Not even he knows how much he earns. **LOC ni aunque** even if: *ni aunque me diesen dinero* not even if they paid me **¡ni que fuera...!** anyone would think...: *¡Ni que yo fuera millonario!* Anyone would think I was a millionaire! **ni una palabra, un día, etc más** not another word, day, etc more **ni uno** not a single (one): *No me queda ni una peseta.* I haven't got a single peseta left. **ni yo (tampoco)** neither am I, do I, have I, etc: *—Yo no voy a la fiesta. —Ni yo tampoco.* 'I'm not going to the party.' 'Neither am I.'

nicotina *nf* nicotine

nido *nm* nest: *hacer un ~* to build a nest

niebla *nf* fog: *Hay mucha ~.* It's very foggy.

nieto, -a *nm-nf* **1** (*gen*) grandson [*fem* granddaughter] **2 nietos** grandchildren

nieve *nf* snow **LOC** *Ver* BLANCO, BOLA, MUÑECO, PUNTO

ningún *adj Ver* NINGUNO

ninguno, -a ◆ *adj* no, any: *No es ningún imbécil.* He's no fool.

> Se utiliza **no** cuando el verbo va en forma afirmativa en inglés: *Aún no ha llegado ningún alumno.* No pupils have arrived yet. ◊ *No mostró ningún entusiasmo.* He showed no enthusiasm. **Any** se utiliza cuando el verbo va en negativa: *No le dio ninguna importancia.* He didn't pay any attention to it.

◆ *pron* **1** (*entre dos personas o cosas*) neither, either

> **Neither** se utiliza cuando el verbo va en forma afirmativa en inglés: —¿Cuál de los dos prefieres? —Ninguno. 'Which one do you prefer?' 'Neither (of them).' **Either** se utiliza cuando va en negativa: *No reñí con ninguno de los dos.* I didn't argue with either of them.

2 (*entre más de dos personas o cosas*) none: *Había tres, pero no queda ~.* There were three, but there are none left. ◊ *~ de los concursantes acertó.* None of the participants got the right answer. **LOC de ninguna manera/de ningún modo** no way! (*coloq*), certainly not!: *No quiso quedarse de ninguna manera.* He absolutely refused to stay. **en ningún lugar/sitio/en ninguna parte** nowhere, anywhere

> **Nowhere** se utiliza cuando el verbo va en afirmativa en inglés: *Al final no iremos a ningún sitio.* We'll go nowhere in the end. **Anywhere** se utiliza cuando va en negativa: *No lo encuentro en ninguna parte.* I can't find it anywhere.

en ningún momento never: *En ningún momento pensé que lo harían.* I never thought they would do it.

niñez *nf* childhood

niño, -a *nm-nf* **1** (*sin distinción de sexo*) **(a)** (*gen*) child [*pl* children] **(b)** (*recién nacido*) baby [*pl* babies]: *tener un ~* to have a baby **2** (*masculino*) boy **3** (*femenino*) girl **LOC niño bien/pera/pijo** rich kid **niño prodigio** child prodigy [*pl* child prodigies] *Ver tb* JUEGO

nitrógeno *nm* nitrogen

nivel *nm* **1** (*gen*) level: *~ del agua/mar*

water/sea level ◊ *a todos los ~es* in every respect **2** (*calidad, preparación*) standard: *un excelente ~ de juego* an excellent standard of play LOC **nivel de vida** standard of living *Ver tb* PASO

nivelar *vt* **1** (*superficie, terreno*) to level **2** (*desigualdades*) to even *sth* out

no ◆ *adv* **1** (*respuesta*) no: *No, gracias.* No, thank you. ◊ *He dicho que no.* I said no. **2** (*referido a verbos, adverbios, frases*) not: *No lo sé.* I don't know. ◊ *No es un buen ejemplo.* It's not a good example. ◊ *¿Empezamos ya o no?* Are we starting now or not? ◊ *Por supuesto que no.* Of course not. ◊ *Que yo sepa, no.* Not as far as I know. **3** (*doble negación*): *No sale nunca.* He never goes out. ◊ *No sé nada de fútbol.* I know nothing about football. **4** (*palabras compuestas*) non-: *no fumador* non-smoker ◊ *fuentes no oficiales* unofficial sources ◆ *nm* no [*pl* noes]: *un no categórico* a categorical no LOC **¿a que no...? 1** (*confirmando*): *¿A que no han venido?* They haven't come, have they? **2** (*desafío*) I bet...: *¿A que no ganas?* I bet you don't win. **¿no?**: *Hoy es jueves ¿no?* Today is Thursday, isn't it? ◊ *Lo compraste, ¿no?* You did buy it, didn't you? ◊ *¡Para quieta! ¿no?* Keep still, will you! ☛ Para otras expresiones con **no**, véanse las entradas del verbo, sustantivo, etc, p.ej. **no pegar ojo** en PEGAR y **no obstante** en OBSTANTE.

noble ◆ *adj* **1** (*gen*) noble **2** (*madera, material*) fine ◆ *nmf* nobleman/woman [*pl* noblemen/women]

nobleza *nf* nobility

noche *nf* night: *el lunes por la ~* on Monday night ◊ *las diez de la ~* ten o'clock at night LOC **¡buenas noches!** good night!

> **Good night** se utiliza sólo como fórmula de despedida. Si se quiere saludar con *buenas noches*, decimos **good evening**: *Buenas noches, damas y caballeros.* Good evening ladies and gentlemen.

dar las buenas noches to say good night **de la noche a la mañana** overnight **de noche 1** (*trabajar, estudiar*) at night **2** (*función, vestido*) evening: *sesión de ~* evening performance **esta noche** tonight **hacerse de noche** to get dark *Ver tb* AYER, CAÍDA, MESILLA, TRAJE

Nochebuena *nf* Christmas Eve: *El día de ~ nos reunimos todos.* We all get together on Christmas Eve. ☛ *Ver nota en* NAVIDAD

Nochevieja *nf* New Year's Eve: *¿Qué hiciste en ~?* What did you do on New Year's Eve?

noción *nf* notion LOC **tener nociones de algo** to have a basic grasp of sth

nocivo, -a *adj* ~ **(para)** harmful **(to *sth/sb*)**

nocturno, -a *adj* **1** (*gen*) night [*n atrib*]: *servicio ~ de autobuses* night bus service **2** (*clases*) evening [*n atrib*]

nogal *nm* walnut (tree)

nómada ◆ *adj* nomadic ◆ *nmf* nomad

nombrar *vt* **1** (*citar*) to mention *sb's name*: *sin ~lo* without mentioning his name **2** (*designar a algn para un cargo*) to appoint

nombre *nm* **1 (a)** (*gen*) name **(b)** (*en formularios*) first name ☛ *Ver nota en* MIDDLE NAME **2** (*Gram*) noun: *~ común* common noun LOC **en nombre de** on behalf of *sb*: *Le dio las gracias en ~ del presidente.* He thanked her on behalf of the president. **nombre de pila** Christian name **nombre propio** proper noun **nombre y apellidos** full name

nómina *nf* (*sueldo*) pay

nominar *vt* to nominate *sth/sb* (**for *sth***): *Fue nominada al Óscar.* She was nominated for an Oscar.

nones *nm* odd numbers LOC *Ver* PAR

nordeste (*tb* **noreste**) *nm* **1** (*punto cardinal, región*) north-east (*abrev* NE) **2** (*viento, dirección*) north-easterly

noria *nf* (*feria*) big wheel

norma *nf* rule LOC **tener por norma hacer/no hacer algo** to always/never do sth: *Tengo por ~ no comer entre horas.* I never eat between meals.

normal *adj* **1** (*común*) normal: *el curso ~ de los acontecimientos* the normal course of events ◊ *Es lo ~.* That's the normal thing. **2** (*corriente*) ordinary: *un empleo ~* an ordinary job **3** (*estándar*) standard: *el procedimiento ~* the standard procedure LOC **normal y corriente** ordinary *Ver tb* GASOLINA, GENTE

normalizar ◆ *vt* (*relaciones, situación*) to restore *sth* to normal ◆ **normalizarse** *v pron* to return to normal

noroeste *nm* **1** (*punto cardinal, región*) north-west (*abrev* NW) **2** (*dirección, viento*) north-westerly

norte *nm* north (*abrev* N): *en el ~ de España* in the north of Spain ◊ *en la* *costa* ~ on the north coast LOC *Ver* IRLANDA

Noruega *nf* Norway

noruego, -a *adj, nm-nf, nm* Norwegian: *los ~s* the Norwegians ◊ *hablar ~* to speak Norwegian

nos *pron pers* **1** (*complemento*) us: *Nos han visto.* They've seen us. ◊ *Nunca nos dicen la verdad.* They never tell us the truth. ◊ *Nos han mentido.* They've lied to us. ◊ *Nos han preparado la cena.* They've made supper for us. **2** (*partes del cuerpo, efectos personales*): *Nos quitamos el abrigo.* We took our coats off. **3** (*reflexivo*) (ourselves): *Nos divertimos mucho.* We enjoyed ourselves very much. ◊ *Nos acabamos de bañar.* We've just had a bath. ◊ *¡Vámonos!* Let's go! **4** (*recíproco*) each other, one another: *Nos queremos mucho.* We love each other very much. ☛ *Ver nota en* EACH OTHER

nosotros, -as *pron pers* **1** (*sujeto*) we: *Tú no lo sabes. ~ sí.* You don't know. We do. ◊ *Lo haremos ~.* We'll do it. **2** (*complemento, en comparaciones*) us: *¿Vienes con ~?* Are you coming with us? ◊ *Hace menos deporte que ~.* He does less sport than us. LOC **entre nosotros** (*confidencialmente*) between ourselves **somos nosotros** it's us

nota *nf* **1** (*gen*) note: *Te dejé una ~ en la cocina.* I left you a note in the kitchen. **2** (*Educ*) mark: *sacar buenas/malas ~s* to get good/bad marks LOC **las notas** report [*sing*]: *El jueves me dan las ~s.* I'm getting my report on Thursday. **tomar nota** to take note (*of sth*)

notable *nm* (*Educ*) ≃ B

notar ◆ *vt* **1** (*advertir*) to notice: *No he notado ningún cambio.* I haven't noticed any change. **2** (*encontrar*): *Lo noto muy triste.* He seems very sad. ◆ **notarse** *v pron* **1** (*sentirse*) to feel: *Se nota la tensión.* You can feel the tension. **2** (*verse*) to show: *No se le notan los años.* He doesn't look his age. LOC **se nota que...** you can tell (that)...: *Se notaba que estaba nerviosa.* You could tell she was nervous.

notario, -a *nm-nf* ≃ solicitor ☛ *Ver nota en* ABOGADO

noticia *nf* **1** (*gen*) news [*incontable, v sing*]: *Te tengo que dar una buena/mala ~.* I've got some good/bad news for you. ◊ *Las ~s son alarmantes.* The news is alarming. **2** (*Period, TV*) news item LOC **las noticias** the news [*sing*]: *Lo han dicho en las ~s de las tres.* It was on the three o'clock news. **tener noticias de algn** to hear from sb: *¿Tenéis ~s de tu hermana?* Have you heard from your sister?

notificar *vt* to notify *sb* **of** *sth*: *Notificamos el robo a la policía.* We notified the police of the theft.

novato, -a ◆ *adj* inexperienced ◆ *nm-nf* **1** (*gen*) beginner **2** (*colegio*) new pupil **3** (*cuartel*) new recruit

novecientos, -as *adj, pron, nm* nine hundred ☛ *Ver ejemplos en* SEISCIENTOS

novedad *nf* **1** (*gen*) novelty [*pl* novelties]: *la ~ de la situación* the novelty of the situation ◊ *El ordenador es para mí una ~.* Computers are a novelty to me. ◊ *la gran ~ de la temporada* the latest thing **2** (*cambio*) change: *No hay ~ en el estado del enfermo.* There's no change in the patient's condition. **3** (*noticia*) news [*incontable, v sing*]: *¿Alguna ~?* Any news?

novela *nf* novel: *~ de aventuras/espionaje* adventure/spy novel LOC **novela rosa/policiaca** romantic/detective novel

novelista *nmf* novelist

noveno, -a *adj, pron, nm-nf* ninth ☛ *Ver ejemplos en* SEXTO

noventa *nm, adj, pron* **1** (*gen*) ninety **2** (*nonagésimo*) ninetieth ☛ *Ver ejemplos en* SESENTA

noviembre *nm* November (*abrev* Nov) ☛ *Ver ejemplos en* ENERO

novillo *nm* young bull LOC **hacer novillos** to play truant

novio, -a *nm-nf* **1** (*gen*) boyfriend [*fem* girlfriend]: *¿Tienes novia?* Have you got a girlfriend? **2** (*prometido*) fiancé [*fem* fiancée] **3** (*en la boda, recién casados*) (bride)groom [*fem* bride] ☛ *Ver nota en* BODA LOC **los novios 1** (*en una boda*) the bride and groom **2** (*recién casados*) the newly-weds **ser novios**: *Hace dos años que somos ~s.* We've been going out together for two years. *Ver tb* VESTIDO

nube *nf* cloud LOC **estar en las nubes** to have your head in the clouds

nublado, -a *pp, adj* cloudy *Ver tb* NUBLARSE

nublarse *v pron* **1** (*cielo*) to cloud over **2** (*vista*) to be blurred

nubosidad *nf* LOC **nubosidad variable** patchy cloud

nuca *nf* nape (of the neck)

nuclear *adj* nuclear LOC *Ver* REACTOR

núcleo *nm* nucleus [*pl* nuclei]

nudillo *nm* knuckle

nudo *nm* knot: *hacer/deshacer un ~* to tie/undo a knot LOC **nudo corredizo** slip-knot **tener un nudo en la garganta** to have a lump in your throat

nuera *nf* daughter-in-law [*pl* daughters-in-law]

nuestro, -a ◆ *adj pos* our: *nuestra familia* our family ◆ *pron pos* ours: *Vuestro coche es mejor que el ~.* Your car is better than ours.

Nótese que *una amiga nuestra* se traduce por **a friend of ours** porque significa *una de nuestras amigas.*

nueve *nm, adj, pron* **1** (*gen*) nine **2** (*fecha*) ninth ☛ *Ver ejemplos en* SEIS

nuevo, -a *adj* **1** (*gen*) new: *¿Son ~s esos zapatos?* Are those new shoes? **2** (*adicional*) further: *Se han presentado ~s problemas.* Further problems have arisen. LOC **de nuevo** again *Ver tb* LUNA

nuez *nf* **1** (*fruto*) walnut **2** (*Anat*) Adam's apple LOC **nuez moscada** nutmeg

nulo, -a *adj* **1** (*inválido*) invalid: *un acuerdo ~* an invalid agreement **2** (*inexistente*) non-existent: *Las posibilidades son prácticamente nulas.* The chances are almost non-existent. **3** ~ **en/para** hopeless **at *sth*/*doing sth***: *Soy ~ para el deporte.* I'm hopeless at sport. LOC *Ver* VOTO

numeración *nf* numbers [*pl*] LOC **numeración arábiga/romana** Arabic/ Roman numerals [*pl*]

numeral *nm* numeral

numerar ◆ *vt* to number ◆ **numerarse** *v pron* to number off

número *nm* **1** (*gen*) number: *un ~ de teléfono* a telephone number ◊ *~ par/impar* even/odd number **2** (*talla*) size: *¿Qué ~ de zapatos usas?* What size shoe do you take? **3** (*publicación*) issue (*formal*), number: *un ~ atrasado* a back issue **4** (*Teat*) act: *un ~ circense* a circus act LOC **estar en números rojos** to be in the red **número de matrícula** registration number **número primo** prime number **números arábigos/romanos** Arabic/Roman numerals

numeroso, -a *adj* **1** (*grande*) large: *una familia numerosa* a large family **2** (*muchos*) numerous: *en numerosas ocasiones* on numerous occasions

nunca *adv* never, ever

Never se utiliza cuando el verbo va en afirmativa en inglés: *Nunca he estado en París.* I've never been to Paris. **Ever** se utiliza cuando el verbo va en negativa: *Nunca pasa nada.* Nothing ever happens. ◊ *sin ver nunca el sol* without ever seeing the sun ☛ *Ver nota en* ALWAYS

LOC **casi nunca** hardly ever: *No nos vemos casi ~.* We hardly ever see each other. **como nunca** better than ever **más que nunca** more than ever: *Hoy hace más calor que ~.* It's hotter than ever today. **nunca jamás** never ever: *~ jamás volveré a dejarle nada.* I'll never ever lend him anything again. **nunca más** never again

nupcial *adj* wedding [*n atrib*]

nutria *nf* otter

nutrición *nf* nutrition

nutritivo, -a *adj* nutritious

Ñ ñ

¡ñam! *interj* LOC **¡ñam, ñam!** yum-yum!

ñoño, -a *adj, nm-nf* **1** (*remilgado*) affected [*adj*] **2** (*puritano*) prim [*adj*]

ñu *nm* wildebeest [*pl* wildebeest]

Oo

o *conj* or: *¿Té o café?* Tea or coffee? ◊ *O te comes todo, o no sales a jugar.* If you don't eat it all up, you're not going out to play.

oasis *nm* oasis [*pl* oases]

obedecer ◆ *vt* to obey: *~ a tus padres* to obey your parents ◆ *vi* to do as you are told: *¡Obedece!* Do as you're told!

obediente *adj* obedient

obispo *nm* bishop

objetar *vt* to object

objetivo, -a ◆ *adj* objective ◆ *nm* **1** (*finalidad*) objective, aim (*más coloq*): *~s a largo plazo* long-term objectives **2** (*Mil*) target **3** (*Fot*) lens

objeto *nm* **1** (*cosa, Gram*) object **2** (*propósito*) purpose LOC **objetos perdidos** lost property [*sing*]: *oficina de ~s perdidos* lost property office

objetor, ~a *nm-nf* LOC **objetor (de conciencia)** conscientious objector

oblicuo, -a *adj* oblique

obligación *nf* obligation LOC **tener (la) obligación de** to be obliged *to do sth*

obligado, -a *pp, adj* LOC **estar obligado a** to have *to do sth*: *Estamos ~s a cambiarlo.* We have to change it. **sentirse/verse obligado** to feel obliged *to do sth Ver tb* OBLIGAR

obligar *vt* to force *sb* ***to do sth***: *Me obligaron a entregar el maletín.* They forced me to hand over the case.

obligatorio, -a *adj* compulsory: *la enseñanza obligatoria* compulsory education LOC *Ver* ESCUELA

oboe *nm* oboe

obra *nf* **1** (*gen*) work: *una ~ de arte* a work of art ◊ *la ~ completa de Machado* the complete works of Machado **2** (*acción*) deed: *realizar buenas ~s* to do good deeds **3** (*lugar en construcción*) site: *Hubo un accidente en la ~.* There was an accident at the site. **4 obras** (*de carretera*) roadworks LOC **obra maestra** masterpiece **obra (teatral/de teatro)** play [*pl* plays] *Ver tb* MANO

obrero, -a ◆ *adj* **1** (*familia, barrio*) working-class **2** (*sindicato*) labour [*n atrib*]: *el movimiento ~* the labour movement ◆ *nm-nf* worker LOC *Ver* ABEJA

obsceno, -a *adj* obscene

observación *nf* observation: *capacidad de ~* powers of observation LOC **estar en observación** to be under observation

observador, ~a ◆ *adj* observant ◆ *nm-nf* observer

observar *vt* **1** (*mirar*) to observe, to watch (*más coloq*): *Observaba a la gente desde mi ventana.* I was watching people from my window. **2** (*notar*) to notice: *¿Has observado algo extraño en él?* Have you noticed anything odd about him?

observatorio *nm* observatory [*pl* observatories]

obsesión *nf* obsession (***with sth/sb/doing sth***): *una ~ por las motos/ganar* an obsession with motor bikes/winning LOC **tener obsesión por** to be obsessed with *sth/sb/doing sth*

obsesionar ◆ *vt* to obsess: *Le obsesionan los libros.* He's obsessed with books. ◆ **obsesionarse** *v pron* to become obsessed (***with sth/sb/doing sth***)

obstaculizar *vt* to block

obstáculo *nm* obstacle

obstante LOC **no obstante** nevertheless, however (*más coloq*)

obstruir *vt* **1** (*cañería, lavabo*) to block **2** (*dificultar*) to obstruct: *~ la justicia* to obstruct justice

obtener *vt* to obtain, to get (*más coloq*): *~ un préstamo/el apoyo de algn* to get a loan/sb's support

obvio, -a *adj* obvious

oca *nf* **1** (*animal*) goose [*pl* geese] **2** (*juego*) ≃ snakes and ladders (*GB*) [*sing*]

ocasión *nf* **1** (*vez*) occasion: *en numerosas ocasiones* on numerous occasions **2** (*oportunidad*) opportunity [*pl* opportunities], chance (*más coloq*) (***to do sth***): *una ~ única* a unique opportunity LOC **de ocasión**: *precios de ~* bargain prices ◊ *coches de ~* second-hand cars

occidental ◆ *adj* western: *el mundo ~* the western world ◆ *nmf* westerner

occidente *nm* west: *las diferencias entre Oriente y Occidente* the differences between East and West

océano *nm* ocean

En inglés **ocean** se escribe con mayúscula cuando aparece con el nombre de un océano: *el océano Índico* the Indian Ocean.

ochenta *nm, adj, pron* **1** (*gen*) eighty **2** (*octogésimo*) eightieth ☛ *Ver ejemplos en* SESENTA

ocho *nm, adj, pron* **1** (*gen*) eight **2** (*fecha*) eighth ☛ *Ver ejemplos en* SEIS

ochocientos, -as *adj, pron, nm* eight hundred ☛ *Ver ejemplos en* SEISCIENTOS

ocio *nm* leisure: *tiempo/ratos de ~* leisure time LOC *Ver* GUÍA

octavo, -a *adj, pron, nm-nf* eighth ☛ *Ver ejemplos en* SEXTO LOC **octavos de final** round prior to quarter-finals

octubre *nm* October (*abrev* Oct) ☛ *Ver ejemplos en* ENERO

oculista *nmf* eye specialist

ocultar ◆ *vt* to hide *sth/sb* (***from sth/sb***): *Me ocultaron de la policía.* They hid me from the police. ◊ *No tengo nada que ~.* I have nothing to hide. ◆ **ocultarse** *v pron* to hide (***from sth/sb***): *el sitio donde se ocultaban* the place where they were hiding

ocupado, -a *pp, adj* **1** ~ (**en/con**) (*persona*) busy (**with** ***sth/sb***); busy (***doing sth***): *Si llaman, di que estoy ~.* If anyone calls, say I'm busy. **2** (*teléfono, wáter*) engaged **3** (*asiento, taxi*) taken: *¿Está ~ este sitio?* Is this seat taken? **4** (*país*) occupied *Ver tb* OCUPAR

ocupar *vt* **1** (*espacio, tiempo*) to take up *sth*: *Ocupa media página.* It takes up half a page. ◊ *Ocupa todo mi tiempo libre.* It takes up all my spare time. **2** (*cargo oficial*) to hold **3** (*país*) to occupy

ocurrencia *nf* idea LOC **¡qué ocurrencia(s)!** what will you, he, etc think of next?

ocurrir ◆ *vi* to happen, to occur (*más formal*): *Lo que ocurrió fue...* What happened was that... ◊ *No quiero que vuelva a ~.* I don't want it to happen again. ◆ **ocurrirse** *v pron* to occur ***to sb***; to think ***of sth/doing sth***: *Se me acaba de ~ que...* It has just occurred to me that... ◊ *¿Se te ocurre algo?* Can you think of anything?

odiar *vt* to hate *sth/sb/doing sth*: *Odio cocinar.* I hate cooking.

odio *nm* hatred (***for/of sth/sb***)

odioso, -a *adj* horrible

oeste *nm* west (*abrev* W): *en/por el ~* in the west ◊ *en la costa ~* on the west coast ◊ *más al ~* further west LOC *Ver* PELÍCULA

ofender ◆ *vt* to offend ◆ **ofenderse** *v pron* to take offence (***at sth***): *Te ofendes por cualquier tontería.* You take offence at the slightest thing.

ofensa *nf* offence

ofensiva *nf* offensive

ofensivo, -a *adj* offensive

oferta *nf* **1** (*gen*) offer: *una ~ especial* a special offer **2** (*Econ, Fin*) supply: *La demanda supera a la ~.* Demand outstrips supply. LOC **de/en oferta** on special offer **ofertas de empleo** job vacancies

oficial ◆ *adj* official ◆ *nmf* (*policía, Mil*) officer LOC **no oficial** unofficial

oficina *nf* office: *~ de correos* post office ◊ *Estaré en la ~.* I'll be at the office. LOC **oficina de empleo** job centre **oficina de información y turismo** tourist information centre

oficinista *nmf* office worker

oficio *nm* trade: *Es fontanero de ~.* He is a plumber by trade. ◊ *aprender un ~* to learn a trade LOC *Ver* GAJES

ofrecer ◆ *vt* to offer: *Nos ofrecieron un café.* They offered us a cup of coffee. ◆ **ofrecerse** *v pron* **ofrecerse (a/para)** to volunteer (***to do sth***): *Me ofrecí para llevarles a casa.* I volunteered to take them home.

oída LOC **de oídas**: *Le conozco de ~s pero no nos han presentado.* I've heard a lot about him but we've yet to be introduced.

oído *nm* **1** (*Anat*) ear **2** (*sentido*) hearing LOC **al oído**: *Dímelo al ~.* Whisper it in my ear. **de oído** by ear: *Toco el piano de ~.* I play the piano by ear. **tener buen oído** to have a good ear *Ver tb* DOLOR, DURO, EDUCAR, ZUMBAR

oír *vt* **1** (*percibir sonidos*) to hear: *No oyeron el despertador.* They didn't hear the alarm. ◊ *No te oí entrar.* I didn't hear you come in. **2** (*escuchar*) to listen (**to** ***sth/sb***): *~ la radio* to listen to the radio LOC **¡oiga! 1** (*gen*) excuse me! **2** (*por teléfono*) hello! *Ver tb* PARED

ojal *nm* buttonhole

¡ojalá! *interj* **1** (*espero que*) I hope...: *¡~ ganen!* I hope they win! ◊ *—Verás como apruebas. —¡Ojalá!* 'I'm sure you'll pass.' 'I hope so!' **2** (*ya quisiera yo*) if only: *¡~ pudiera ir!* If only I could go!

ojeada *nf* glance: *con una sola ~* at a glance LOC **echar una ojeada** to have a (quick) look (*at sth*)

ojeras *nf* bags under the eyes: *¡Qué ~ tienes!* You've got huge bags under your eyes.

ojo *nm* **1** (*gen*) eye: *Es morena con los ~s verdes.* She has dark hair and green eyes. ◊ *tener los ~s saltones* to have bulging eyes **2** (*cerradura*) keyhole **3** (*cuidado*) (be) careful: *¡~ con esa jarra!* (Be) careful with that jug! ◊ *Debes tener ~ con lo que haces.* You must be careful what you do. LOC **andar con cien ojos** to be very careful **a ojo** roughly: *Lo calculé a ~.* I worked it out roughly. **con los ojos vendados** blindfold **echarle un ojo a algo/algn** (*cuidar*) to keep an eye on sth/sb **mirar a los ojos** to look into *sb's* eyes **mirarse a los ojos** to look into each other's eyes **ojo de buey** (*ventana*) porthole **ojos que no ven...** what the eye doesn't see, the heart doesn't grieve over **ser el ojo derecho de algn** to be the apple of sb's eye *Ver tb* ABRIR, COSTAR, PEGAR, PINTAR, QUITAR, RABILLO, SOMBRA, VENDAR

ola *nf* wave

¡olé! (*tb* **¡ole!**) *interj* bravo!

oleaje *nm* swell: *un fuerte ~* a heavy swell

óleo *nm* oil LOC **cuadro/pintura al óleo** oil painting *Ver tb* PINTAR

oler *vt, vi* ~ (**a**) to smell (**of** *sth*): *~ a pintura* to smell of paint ◊ *¿A qué huele?* What's that smell? ◊ *Ese perfume huele bien.* That perfume smells nice. ☛ *Ver nota en* SMELL LOC **oler a chamusquina** (*fig*) to smell fishy **oler a quemado** to smell of burning **oler fatal/que apesta** to stink **olerse algo** to suspect sth **olerse la tostada** to smell a rat *Ver tb* GLORIA

olfatear *vt* **1** (*oler*) to sniff **2** (*seguir el rastro*) to scent

olfato *nm* (*sentido*) smell LOC **tener olfato** to have a nose *for sth*: *Tienen ~ para las antigüedades.* They have a nose for antiques.

olimpiada (*tb* **olimpíada**) *nf* Olympics [*pl*] LOC **las Olimpiadas** the Olympic Games

olímpico, -a *adj* Olympic: *el récord ~* the Olympic record LOC *Ver* JUEGO, VILLA

oliva *nf* olive

olivar *nm* olive grove

olivo *nm* olive tree

olla *nf* LOC **olla (exprés/a presión)** pressure cooker ☛ *Ver dibujo en* SAUCEPAN

olmo *nm* elm (tree)

olor *nm* smell (**of** *sth*): *Había un ~ a rosas/quemado.* There was a smell of roses/burning.

oloroso, -a *adj* sweet-smelling

olvidadizo, -a *adj* forgetful

olvidado, -a *pp, adj* LOC **dejar(se) algo olvidado** to leave sth (behind): *No te lo dejes ~.* Don't leave it behind. *Ver tb* OLVIDAR(SE)

olvidar(se) *vt, v pron* **1** (*gen*) to forget: *Olvidé (comprar) el detergente.* I forgot (to buy) the washing-powder. **2** (*dejar*) to leave *sth* (behind): *Olvidé el paraguas en el autobús.* I left my umbrella on the bus.

ombligo *nm* navel, tummy-button (*coloq*)

omitir *vt* to omit, to leave *sth* out (*más coloq*)

once *nm, adj, pron* **1** (*gen*) eleven **2** (*fecha*) eleventh **3** (*títulos*) the Eleventh: *Alfonso XI* Alfonso XI ☛ Se lee: 'Alfonso the Eleventh'. *Ver ejemplos en* SEIS

onceavo, -a *adj, nm* eleventh

onda *nf* wave: *~ sonora/expansiva* sound/shock wave ◊ *~ corta/media/larga* short/medium/long wave

ondear ◆ *vt* to wave: *~ una pancarta* to wave a banner ◆ *vi* (*bandera*) to fly

ondulado, -a *pp, adj* **1** (*pelo*) wavy **2** (*superficie*) undulating **3** (*cartón, papel*) corrugated

ONU *nf* UN

opaco, -a *adj* opaque

opción *nf* option: *No tiene otra ~.* He has no option.

opcional *adj* optional

ópera *nf* opera

operación *nf* **1** (*gen*) operation: *sufrir una ~ cardiaca* to have a heart operation ◊ *una ~ policial* a police operation **2** (*Fin*) transaction

operar ◆ *vt* to operate **on** *sb*: *Me operaron de apendicitis.* I had my appendix out. ◆ *vi* to operate ◆ **operarse** *v pron* to have an operation: *Tengo que ~me del pie.* I've got to have an operation on my foot.

opinar *vt* to think: *¿Qué opinas?* What do you think?

opinión *nf* opinion: *en mi ~* in my opinion LOC **tener buena/mala opinión de** to have a high/low opinion of *sth/sb* *Ver tb* CAMBIAR

oponente *nmf* opponent

oponer ◆ *vt* to offer: *~ resistencia a algo/algn* to offer resistance to sth/sb ◆ **oponerse** *v pron* **1 oponerse a** to oppose: *~se a una idea* to oppose an idea **2** (*poner reparos*) to object: *Iré a la* *fiesta si mis padres no se oponen.* I'll go to the party if my parents don't object.

oportunidad *nf* **1** (*gen*) chance, opportunity [*pl* opportunities] (*más formal*): *Tuve la ~ de ir al teatro.* I had the chance to go to the theatre. **2** (*ganga*) bargain

oportuno, -a *adj* **1** (*en buen momento*) timely: *una visita oportuna* a timely visit **2** (*adecuado*) appropriate: *Tu respuesta no fue muy oportuna.* Your reply wasn't very appropriate.

oposición *nf* **1** (*gen*) opposition (***to sth/sb***): *el líder de la ~* the leader of the opposition **2** (*examen*) examination LOC **hacer oposiciones** (**a**) to sit an examination (for *sth*)

opresivo, -a *adj* oppressive

oprimir *vt* **1** (*tiranizar*) to oppress **2** (*apretar*) to be too tight: *La cinturilla de la falda me oprimía.* The waistband on my skirt was too tight.

optar *vi* **1** ~ **por** to opt **for *sth*/*to do sth***: *Optaron por seguir estudiando.* They opted to carry on studying. **2** ~ **a** (*solicitar*) to apply **for *sth***: *~ a una plaza en el ayuntamiento* to apply for a job with the council

optativo, -a *adj* optional

óptico, -a ◆ *adj* optical ◆ *nm-nf* optician ◆ **óptica** *nf* (*establecimiento*) optician's [*pl* opticians]

optimismo *nm* optimism

optimista ◆ *adj* optimistic ◆ *nmf* optimist

opuesto, -a *pp, adj* **1** (*extremo, lado, dirección*) opposite: *El frío es lo ~ al calor.* Cold is the opposite of heat. **2** (*dispar*) different: *Mis dos hermanos son totalmente ~s.* My two brothers are totally different. LOC *Ver* POLO; *Ver tb* OPONER

oración *nf* **1** (*Relig*) prayer: *rezar una ~* to say a prayer **2** (*Gram*) **(a)** (*gen*) sentence: *una ~ compuesta* a complex sentence **(b)** (*proposición*) clause: *una ~ subordinada* a subordinate clause

oral *adj* oral

orar *vi* to pray

órbita *nf* (*Astron*) orbit

orden ◆ *nm* order: *en/por ~ alfabético* in alphabetical order ◊ *por ~ de importancia* in order of importance ◆ *nf* **1** (*gen*) order: *por ~ del juez* by order of the court ◊ *la ~ franciscana* the Franciscan Order **2** (*Jur*) warrant: *una ~ de registro* a search warrant LOC *Ver* ALTERAR

ordenado, -a *pp, adj* tidy: *una niña/habitación muy ordenada* a very tidy girl/room *Ver tb* ORDENAR

ordenador

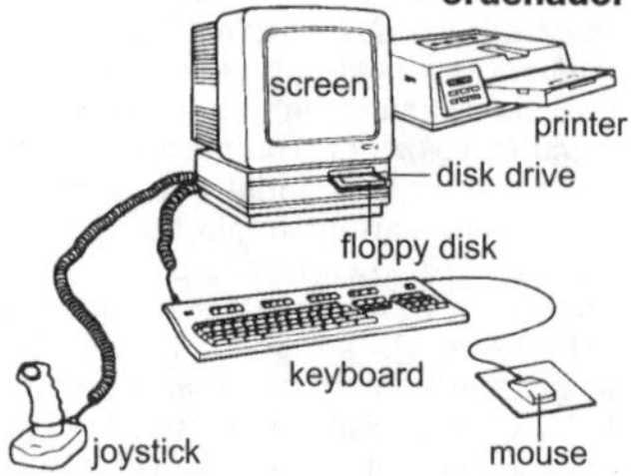

ordenador *nm* computer LOC **ordenador personal** personal computer (*abrev* PC)

ordenar *vt* **1** (*habitación*) to tidy *a room* up: *¿Podrías ~ tu habitación?* Could you tidy your bedroom up? **2** (*apuntes, carpetas*) to put *sth* in order: *~ las tarjetas alfabéticamente* to put the cards in alphabetical order **3** (*mandar*) to order *sb* ***to do sth***: *Me ordenó que me sentara.* He ordered me to sit down.

ordeñar *vt* to milk

ordinario, -a ◆ *adj* (*habitual*) ordinary: *acontecimientos ~s* ordinary events ◆ *adj, nm-nf* (*vulgar*) common [*adj*]: *Son unos ~s.* They're common.

orégano *nm* oregano

oreja *nf* ear LOC *Ver* MOSCA

orfanato (*tb* **orfelinato**) *nm* orphanage

organismo *nm* **1** (*Biol*) organism **2** (*organización*) organization

organización *nf* organization: *organizaciones internacionales* international organizations ◊ *una ~ juvenil* a youth group LOC **Organización de las Naciones Unidas (ONU)** the United Nations (*abrev* UN)

organizador, ~a ◆ *adj* organizing ◆ *nm-nf* organizer

organizar ◆ *vt* to organize ◆ **organizarse** *v pron* (*persona*) to get yourself organized: *Debería ~me mejor.* I should get myself better organized. LOC *Ver* ESCÁNDALO

órgano *nm* (*Anat, Mús*) organ

orgullo *nm* pride: *herir el ~ de algn* to hurt sb's pride

orgulloso, -a *adj, nm-nf* proud [*adj*]: *Está ~ de sí mismo.* He is proud of himself. ◊ *Son unos ~s.* They're very proud.

orientado, -a *pp, adj* LOC **estar orientado a/hacia** (*edificio, habitación*) to face: *El balcón está ~ hacia el sureste.* The balcony faces southeast. *Ver tb* ORIENTAR

oriental ◆ *adj* eastern: *Europa Oriental* Eastern Europe ◆ *nmf* oriental [*adj*]: *En mi clase hay dos ~es.* There are two Eastern people in my class.

Existe la palabra **Oriental** como sustantivo en inglés, pero es preferible no usarla porque puede ofender.

orientar ◆ *vt* **1** (*colocar*) to position: *~ una antena* to position an aerial **2** (*dirigir*) to direct: *El policía les orientó.* The policeman directed them. ◆ **orientarse** *v pron* (*encontrar el camino*) to find your way around

oriente *nm* east LOC **el Oriente Próximo/Extremo Oriente** the Near/Far East

origen *nm* origin LOC **dar origen a** to give rise to *sth*

original *adj, nm* original LOC *Ver* VERSIÓN

originar ◆ *vt* to lead to *sth* ◆ **originarse** *v pron* to start: *Se originó un incendio en el bosque.* A fire started in the woods.

orilla *nf* **1** (*borde*) edge: *a la ~ del camino* at the edge of the path **2** (*río*) bank: *a ~s del Sena* on the banks of the Seine **3** (*lago, mar*) shore LOC **a la orilla del mar/río** on the seashore/riverside

orina *nf* urine

orinar ◆ *vi* to urinate, to pass water (*más coloq*) ◆ **orinarse** *v pron* to wet yourself

oro *nm* **1** (*gen*) gold: *tener un corazón de ~* to have a heart of gold ◊ *una medalla de ~* a gold medal **2 oros** (*Naipes*) ☛ *Ver nota en* BARAJA LOC **no es oro todo lo que reluce** all that glitters is not gold *Ver tb* BAÑADO, BODA, BUSCADOR, SIGLO

orquesta *nf* **1** (*de música clásica*) orchestra **2** (*de música ligera*) band: *una ~ de baile/jazz* a dance/jazz band LOC *Ver* DIRECTOR

ortografía *nf* spelling: *faltas de ~* spelling mistakes

orzuelo *nm* sty(e) [*pl* sties/styes]: *Me ha salido un ~.* I've got a stye.

os *pron pers* **1** (*complemento*) you: *Os invito a cenar.* I'll take you out for a meal. ◊ *Os lo di ayer.* I gave it to you yesterday. **2** (*partes del cuerpo, efectos personales*): *Quitaos el abrigo.* Take your coats off. **3** (*reflexivo*) (yourselves): *¿Os divertisteis?* Did you enjoy yourselves? **4** (*recíproco*) each other, one another: *¿Os veis con mucha frecuencia?* Do you see each other very often? ☛ *Ver nota en* EACH OTHER

oscilar *vi* **1** (*lámpara, péndulo*) to swing **2 ~ entre** (*precios, temperaturas*) to vary **from *sth* to *sth***: *El precio oscila entre las cinco y las siete libras.* The price varies from five to seven pounds.

oscurecer ◆ *vt* to darken ◆ **oscurecer(se)** *v imp, v pron* to get dark

oscuridad *nf* **1** (*lit*) darkness: *la ~ de la noche* the darkness of the night ◊ *Me da miedo la ~.* I'm afraid of the dark. **2** (*fig*) obscurity: *vivir en la ~* to live in obscurity

oscuro, -a *adj* **1** (*lit*) dark: *azul ~* dark blue **2** (*fig*) obscure: *un ~ poeta* an obscure poet LOC **a oscuras** in the dark: *Nos quedamos a oscuras.* We were left in the dark.

oso, -a *nm-nf* bear: *~ polar* polar bear LOC **oso de peluche** teddy bear **oso hormiguero** anteater

ostra *nf* oyster LOC **¡ostras!** (*sorpresa*) good heavens! *Ver tb* ABURRIR

otoño *nm* autumn: *en ~* in (the) autumn

otorgar *vt* to award *sth* (***to sb***)

otro, -a ◆ *adj* another, other

Another se usa con sustantivos en singular y **other** con sustantivos en plural: *No hay otro tren hasta las cinco.* There isn't another train until five. ◊ *en otra ocasión* on another occasion ◊ *¿Tienes otros colores?* Have you got any other colours? **Other** también se utiliza en expresiones como: *la otra noche* the other night ◊ *mi otro hermano* my other brother.

A veces **another** va seguido de un número y un sustantivo plural cuando tiene el sentido de "más": *Me quedan otros tres exámenes.* I've got another three exams to do. También se puede decir en estos casos 'I've got three more exams.'

◆ *pron* another (one) [*pl* others]: *un día u ~* one day or another ◊ *¿Tienes ~?* Have you got another (one)? ◊ *No me gustan. ¿Tienes ~s?* I don't like these ones. Have you got any others? ☛ **El otro, la otra** se traducen por 'the other one': *¿Dónde está el otro?* Where's the other one? LOC **en otro lugar/sitio/en otra parte** somewhere else **lo otro 1** (*la otra cosa*) the other thing: *¿Cuál era lo ~ que querías?* What was the other thing you wanted? **2** (*lo demás*) the rest:

Lo ~ no importa. The rest doesn't matter. **nada del otro jueves** nothing to write home about **otra cosa** something else: *Había otra cosa que quería decirte.* There was something else I wanted to tell you.

Si la oración es negativa podemos decir **nothing else** o **anything else**, dependiendo de si hay o no otra partícula negativa en la frase: *No hay otra cosa.* There's nothing else./There isn't anything else. ◊ *No pudieron hacer otra cosa.* They couldn't do anything else.

otra vez again: *He suspendido otra vez.* I've failed again. **otro(s) tanto(s)** as much/as many again: *Me ha pagado 5.000 pesetas y aún me debe ~ tanto.* He's paid me 5000 pesetas and still owes me as much again. **por otra parte/otro lado** on the other hand *Ver tb* COSA, MES, SEMANA, SITIO

oval (*tb* **ovalado, -a**) *adj* oval

ovario *nm* ovary [*pl* ovaries]

oveja *nf* sheep [*pl* sheep]: *un rebaño de ~s* a flock of sheep LOC **oveja negra** black sheep

ovillo *nm* ball: *un ~ de lana* a ball of wool LOC **hacerse un ovillo** to curl up

ovino, -a *adj* LOC *Ver* GANADO

ovni *nm* UFO [*pl* UFOs]

oxidado, -a *pp, adj* rusty *Ver tb* OXIDAR(SE)

oxidar(se) *vt, v pron* to rust: *Se han oxidado las tijeras.* The scissors have rusted.

oxígeno *nm* oxygen

oyente *nmf* **1** (*Radio*) listener **2** (*Educ*) unregistered student

ozono *nm* ozone: *la capa de ~* the ozone layer

Pp

pabellón *nm* **1** (*exposición*) pavilion: *el ~ de Francia* the French pavilion **2** (*Dep*) sports hall **3** (*hospital*) block

pacer *vi* to graze

pachucho, -a *adj* **1** (*persona*) poorly **2** (*planta*) limp

paciencia *nf* patience: *Se me está acabando la ~.* My patience is wearing thin. LOC **¡paciencia!** be patient! **tener paciencia** to be patient: *Hay que tener ~.* You must be patient. *Ver tb* ARMAR

paciente *adj, nmf* patient

pacificar ◆ *vt* to pacify ◆ **pacificarse** *v pron* to calm down

pacífico, -a ◆ *adj* peaceful ◆ **Pacífico** *adj, nm* Pacific: *el (océano) Pacífico* the Pacific (Ocean)

pacifista *nmf* pacifist

pactar ◆ *vt* to agree **on *sth***: *Pactaron un alto el fuego.* They agreed on a ceasefire. ◆ *vi* to make an agreement (***with sb***) (***to do sth***)

pacto *nm* agreement: *romper un ~* to break an agreement

padecer *vt, vi* ~ **(de)** to suffer (**from *sth***): *Padece dolores de cabeza.* He suffers from headaches. LOC **padecer de la espalda, del corazón, etc** to have back, heart, etc trouble

padrastro *nm* **1** (*gen*) stepfather **2** (*pellejo*) hangnail

padre *nm* **1** (*gen*) father: *Es ~ de dos hijos.* He is the father of two children. ◊ *el ~ García* Father García **2 padres** (*padre y madre*) parents LOC *Ver* DÍA, FAMILIA, HUÉRFANO, VIDA

padrenuestro *nm* Our Father: *rezar dos ~s* to say two Our Fathers

padrino *nm* **1** (*bautizo*) godfather **2** (*boda*) man who accompanies the bride, usually her father ☛ *Ver nota en* BODA **3 padrinos** godparents

paella *nf* paella

paga *nf* **1** (*sueldo*) pay **2** (*propina*) pocket money

pagano, -a *adj* pagan

pagar ◆ *vt* to pay **(for) *sth***: *~ las deudas/los impuestos* to pay your debts/taxes ◊ *Mi abuelo me paga los estudios.* My grandfather is paying for my education. ◆ *vi* to pay: *Pagan bien.* They pay well. LOC **¡me las pagarás!** you'll pay for this! **pagar con cheque/tarjeta** to pay (*for sth*) by cheque/credit card **pagar el pato** to carry the can **pagar en efectivo/metálico** to pay (*for sth*) in cash *Ver tb* CARO

página *nf* page (*abrev* p): *en la ~ tres* on

page three LOC **páginas amarillas** yellow pages *Ver tb* HOJA

pago *nm* (*dinero*) payment: *efectuar/hacer un ~* to make a payment

país *nm* country [*pl* countries] LOC **los Países Bajos** the Netherlands *Ver tb* HUIR

paisaje *nm* landscape ☛ *Ver nota en* SCENERY

paisano, -a *nm-nf* **1** (*compatriota*) fellow countryman/woman [*pl* fellow countrymen/women] **2** (*pueblerino*) countryman/woman [*pl* countrymen/women] LOC **de paisano 1** (*militar*) in civilian dress **2** (*policía*) in plain clothes

paja *nf* **1** (*gen*) straw **2** (*en un texto/discurso*) waffle

pajar *nm* hay loft LOC *Ver* BUSCAR

pajarita *nf* **1** (*corbata*) bow-tie **2** (*de papel*) ≃ paper aeroplane (*GB*)

pájaro *nm* bird LOC **más vale pájaro en mano...** a bird in the hand is worth two in the bush *Ver tb* CABEZA, MATAR

paje *nm* page

pala *nf* **1** (*gen*) shovel **2** (*playa*) spade: *jugar con el cubo y la ~* to play with your bucket and spade

palabra *nf* word: *una ~ de tres letras* a three-letter word ◊ *Te doy mi ~.* I give you my word. ◊ *No dijo ni ~.* He didn't say a word. ◊ *en otras ~s* in other words LOC **coger la palabra** to take *sb* at their word **dejar a algn con la palabra en la boca** to cut sb short: *Me dejó con la ~ en la boca y se fue.* He cut me short and walked off. **¡palabra (de honor)!** honestly! **tener la última palabra** to have the last word (*on sth*) *Ver tb* ANUNCIO, BREVE, CEDER, DIRIGIR, JUEGO, SOLTAR

palabrota *nf* swear word: *decir ~s* to swear

palacio *nm* palace

paladar *nm* palate LOC *Ver* VELO

palanca *nf* lever: *En caso de emergencia, tirar de la ~.* In an emergency, pull the lever. LOC **palanca de cambio** gear lever

palangana *nf* bowl

palco *nm* box

paleta *nf* **1** (*albañil*) trowel **2** (*pintor*) palette

paleto, -a *adj, nm-nf* country bumpkin [*n*]: *No seas tan ~.* Don't be such a country bumpkin.

palidecer *vi* to go pale

pálido, -a *adj* pale: *rosa ~* pale pink LOC **ponerse/quedarse pálido** to go pale

palillo *nm* **1** (*de dientes*) toothpick **2 palillos (a)** (*para tambor*) drumsticks **(b)** (*para comida*) chopsticks LOC **estar hecho un palillo** to be as thin as a rake

paliza ♦ *nf* beating: *El Atlético les metió una buena ~.* Atlético gave them a sound beating. ♦ *adj, nmf* (*pelmazo*) bore [*n*]: *Ese tío es un ~.* What a bore that man is! LOC **darse una paliza** to wear yourself out (*doing sth*): *Nos dimos una buena ~ a estudiar.* We wore ourselves out studying. **dar una paliza a algn** (*pegar*) to beat sb up

palma *nf* **1** (*mano*) palm **2** (*árbol*) palm (tree) LOC **dar palmas 1** (*aplaudir*) to clap **2** (*acompañamiento*) to clap in time (*to sth*): *Le acompañaban dando ~s.* They clapped in time to the music. *Ver tb* CONOCER

palmada *nf* pat: *Me dio una ~ en la espalda.* He gave me a pat on the back. LOC **dar palmadas** to clap: *Dio tres ~.* He clapped three times.

palmera *nf* palm (tree)

palmo *nm*: *Es un ~ más alto que yo.* He's several inches taller than me. LOC **palmo a palmo** inch by inch

palo *nm* **1** (*gen*) stick **2** (*disgusto*) blow: *Su muerte fue un gran ~ para mí.* Her death was a great blow to me. **3** (*barco*) mast **4** (*Naipes*) suit ☛ *Ver nota en* BARAJA **5** (*golf*) (golf) club LOC **a palo seco** on its own **de palo** wooden: *cuchara/pata de ~* wooden spoon/leg *Ver tb* CUCHARA, LIAR, MOLER, TAL

paloma *nf* **1** (*gen*) pigeon: *una ~ mensajera* a carrier pigeon **2** (*blanca*) dove: *la ~ de la paz* the dove of peace

palomar *nm* dovecote

palomita *nf* LOC **palomitas (de maíz)** popcorn [*incontable, v sing*]: *¿Quieres unas ~s?* Would you like some popcorn?

palpar(se) *vt, vi, v pron* to feel: *El médico me palpó el vientre.* The doctor felt my stomach. ◊ *Se palpó los bolsillos.* He felt his pockets.

palpitar *vi* to beat

pan *nm* **1** (*gen*) bread [*incontable*]: *Me gusta el ~ recién hecho.* I like freshly-baked bread. ◊ *¿Quieres ~?* Do you want some bread? ☛ *Ver nota en* BREAD **2** (*pieza*) **(a)** (*barra*) baguette; French loaf [*pl* French loaves]: *¿Me da tres ~es?* Could I have three baguettes, please? **(b)** (*hogaza*) (round) loaf [*pl* (round) loaves] LOC **(llamar) al pan pan y al**

vino vino to call a spade a spade **pan duro** stale bread **pan integral/de molde** wholemeal/sliced bread **pan rallado** breadcrumbs [*pl*] *Ver tb* BARRA, GANAR

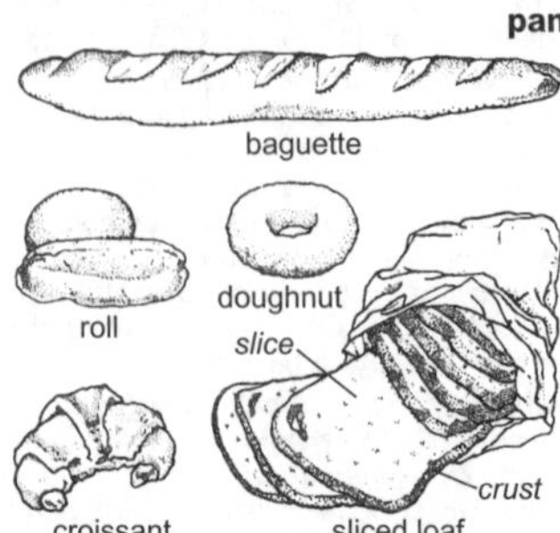

pana *nf* corduroy: *Ponte los pantalones de ~.* Wear your corduroy trousers.

panadería *nf* baker's [*pl* bakers]

panadero, -a *nm-nf* baker

panal *nm* honeycomb

pancarta *nf* **1** (*de cartón*) placard **2** (*de tela*) banner

páncreas *nm* pancreas

panda¹ *nm* (*animal*) panda

panda² (*tb* **pandilla**) *nf* friends [*pl*]: *Vendrá toda la ~.* All my friends are coming.

pandereta *nf* tambourine

panfleto *nm* pamphlet

pánico *nm* panic LOC **tenerle pánico a algo/algn** to be scared stiff of sth/sb: *Le tienen ~ al mar.* They're scared stiff of the sea. *Ver tb* ENTRAR, PRESA

panorama *nm* **1** (*vista*) view: *contemplar un hermoso ~* to look at a lovely view **2** (*perspectiva*) prospect: *¡Menudo ~!* What a prospect!

pantalla *nf* **1** (*gen*) screen: *una ~ de ordenador* a computer screen ☛ *Ver dibujo en* ORDENADOR **2** (*lámpara*) lampshade

pantalón (*tb* **pantalones**) *nm* trousers [*pl*]: *No encuentro el ~ del pijama.* I can't find my pyjama trousers.

> **Trousers** es una palabra plural en inglés, por lo tanto para referirnos a *un pantalón* o *unos pantalones* utilizamos **some/a pair of trousers**: *Llevaba un pantalón viejo.* He was wearing some old trousers/an old pair of trousers. ◊ *Necesito unos pantalones negros.* I need a pair of black trousers.

LOC **pantalón corto/de deporte** shorts [*pl*] **pantalones vaqueros** jeans *Ver tb* FALDA

pantano *nm* **1** (*embalse*) reservoir **2** (*terreno*) marsh

pantera *nf* panther

pantis *nm* tights

pañal *nm* nappy [*pl* nappies]: *cambiar el ~ a un niño* to change a baby's nappy

paño *nm* (*bayeta*) cloth LOC **en paños menores** in your underwear **paño de cocina** tea towel

pañuelo *nm* **1** (*moquero*) handkerchief [*pl* handkerchiefs/handkerchieves] **2** (*cabeza, cuello*) scarf [*pl* scarves] LOC **pañuelo de papel** tissue

papa *nm* pope: *el ~ Juan Pablo II* Pope John Paul II

papá *nm* **1** (*padre*) dad: *Pregúntaselo a ~.* Ask your dad. ☛Los niños pequeños suelen decir **daddy**. **2 papás** mum and dad LOC **Papá Noel** Father Christmas ☛ *Ver nota en* NAVIDAD; *Ver tb* HIJO

papagayo *nm* parrot

papel *nm* **1** (*material*) paper [*incontable*]: *una hoja de ~* a sheet of paper ◊ *La acera está llena de ~es.* The pavement is covered in bits of paper. ◊ *servilletas de ~* paper napkins ◊ *~ cuadriculado/reciclado* squared/recycled paper **2** (*recorte, cuartilla*) piece of paper: *anotar algo en un ~* to note sth down on a piece of paper **3** (*personaje, función*) part: *hacer el ~ de Otelo* to play the part of Othello ◊ *Jugará un ~ importante en la reforma.* It will play an important part in the reform. LOC **papel de aluminio** foil **papel de envolver/regalo** wrapping paper **papel higiénico** toilet paper **papel principal/secundario** (*Cine, Teat*) leading/supporting role *Ver tb* FÁBRICA, PAÑUELO, VASO

papeleo *nm* paperwork

papelera *nf* **1** (*gen*) waste-paper basket: *Tíralo a la ~.* Throw it in the waste-paper basket. **2** (*en la calle*) litter bin

papelería *nf* stationer's [*pl* stationers]

papeleta *nf* **1** (*electoral*) ballot paper **2** (*sorteo, rifa*) raffle ticket

paperas *nf* mumps [*sing*]: *tener ~* to have (the) mumps

papilla *nf* (*de bebé*) baby food

paquete *nm* **1** (*comida, tabaco*) packet: *un ~ de cigarrillos* a packet of cigarettes ☛ *Ver dibujo en* CONTAINER **2** (*bulto*) parcel: *mandar un ~ por correo* to post a parcel ☛ *Ver nota en* PARCEL **LOC ir de paquete** to ride pillion *Ver tb* BOMBA[1]

par ◆ *adj* even: *números ~es* even numbers ◆ *nm* **1** (*pareja*) pair: *un ~ de calcetines* a pair of socks **2** (*número indefinido*) couple: *hace un ~ de meses* a couple of months ago **LOC a la par** (*a la vez*) at the same time **de par en par** wide open: *dejar la puerta de ~ en ~* to leave the door wide open **pares y nones** (*juego*) odds and evens

para *prep* **1** (*gen*) for: *muy útil para la lluvia* very useful for the rain ◊ *demasiado complicado para mí* too complicated for me ◊ *¿Para qué lo quieres?* What do you want it for? **2 + inf** to do sth: *Han venido para quedarse.* They've come to stay. ◊ *Lo hice para no molestarte.* I did it so as not to bother you. **3** (*futuro*): *Lo necesito para el lunes.* I need it for Monday. ◊ *Estará acabado para el otoño.* It will be finished by autumn. **4** (*dirección*): *Ahora mismo voy para casa.* I'm going home now. ◊ *Van para allá.* They're on their way. **LOC para eso**: *Para eso, me compro uno nuevo.* I might as well buy a new one. ◊ *¿Para eso me has hecho venir?* You got me here just for that? **para que...** so (that)...: *Les reprendió para que no lo volvieran a hacer.* He told them off so that they wouldn't do it again. **para sí** to yourself: *hablar para sí* to talk to yourself

parábola *nf* **1** (*Biblia*) parable **2** (*Geom*) parabola

parabólico, -a *adj* **LOC** *Ver* ANTENA

parabrisas *nm* windscreen

paracaídas *nm* parachute **LOC lanzarse/tirarse en paracaídas** to parachute

paracaidista *nmf* parachutist

parachoques *nm* bumper

parada *nf* **1** (*gen*) stop: *Bájate en la próxima ~.* Get off at the next stop. **2** (*Dep*) save: *El guardameta hizo una ~ fantástica.* The goalkeeper made a spectacular save. **LOC parada de autobús** bus stop **parada de taxis** taxi rank **tener parada** to stop: *Este tren tiene ~ en todas las estaciones.* This train stops at every station.

parado, -a ◆ *pp, adj* **1** (*desempleado*) unemployed **2** (*paralizado*) at a standstill: *Las obras están paradas desde hace dos meses.* The roadworks have been at a standstill for two months. **3** (*cohibido*) shy ◆ *nm-nf* unemployed person: *los ~s* the unemployed **LOC salir bien/mal parado** to come off well/badly *Ver tb* PARAR

paraguas *nm* umbrella: *abrir/cerrar un ~* to put up/take down an umbrella

paragüero *nm* umbrella stand

paraíso *nm* paradise **LOC paraíso terrenal** heaven on earth

paraje *nm* spot

paralelas *nf* parallel bars

paralelo, -a *adj* ~ (**a**) parallel (**to** ***sth***): *líneas paralelas* parallel lines

parálisis *nf* paralysis [*incontable*]

paralítico, -a *adj* paralysed: *quedarse ~ de cintura para abajo* to be paralysed from the waist down

paralizar *vt* to paralyse

páramo *nm* moor

parapente *nm* paragliding

parar ◆ *vt* **1** (*gen*) to stop: *Para el coche.* Stop the car. **2** (*gol*) to save ◆ **parar(se)** *vi, v pron* to stop: *El tren no paró.* The train didn't stop. ◊ *Me paré a hablar con una amiga.* I stopped to talk to a friend. **LOC ir a parar** to end up: *Fueron a ~ a la cárcel.* They ended up in prison. ◊ *¿Dónde habrá ido a ~?* Where can it have got to? **no parar** to be always on the go **para parar un tren** to feed an army: *Tenemos comida para ~ un tren.* We've got enough food here to feed an army. **sin parar** non-stop: *trabajar sin ~* to work non-stop *Ver tb* SECO

pararrayos *nm* lightning conductor

parásito *nm* parasite

parcela *nf* (*terreno*) plot

parche *nm* patch

parchís *nm* ludo

parcial ◆ *adj* **1** (*incompleto*) partial: *una solución ~* a partial solution **2** (*partidista*) biased ◆ *nm* mid-year assessment exam

parecer ◆ *vi* **1** (*dar la impresión*) to seem: *Parecen (estar) seguros.* They seem certain. ◊ *Parece que fue ayer.* It seems like only yesterday. **2** (*tener aspecto*) **(a) + adj** to look: *Parece más joven de lo que es.* She looks younger than she really is. **(b) + sustantivo** to look like *sth/sb*: *Parece una actriz.* She looks like an actress. **3** (*opinar*) to think: *Me pareció que no tenía razón.* I thought he was wrong. ◊ *¿Qué te parecieron mis primos?* What did you think of my cousins? ◊ *No me parece bien que* *no les llames.* I think you ought to phone them. ◊ *¿Te parece bien mañana?* Is tomorrow all right? ◆ **parecerse** *v pron* **parecerse (a) 1** (*personas*) **(a)** (*físicamente*) to look alike; to look like *sb*: *Se parecen mucho.* They look very much alike. ◊ *Te pareces mucho a tu hermana.* You look very much like your sister. **(b)** (*en carácter*) to be alike; to be like *sb*: *Nos llevamos mal porque nos parecemos mucho.* We don't get on because we are so alike. ◊ *En eso te pareces a tu padre.* You're like your father in that. **2** (*cosas*) to be similar **(to *sth*)**: *Se parece mucho al mío.* It's very similar to mine. LOC **al parecer/según parece** apparently **parece mentira (que...)**: *¡Parece mentira!* I can hardly believe it! ◊ *Parece mentira que seas tan despistado.* How can you be so absent-minded? **parece que va a llover/nevar** it looks like rain/snow

parecido, -a ◆ *pp, adj* ~ **(a) 1** (*personas*) alike; like *sb*: *¡Sois tan ~s!* You're so alike! ◊ *Eres muy parecida a tu madre.* You're like your mother. **2** (*cosas*) similar **(to *sth*)**: *Tienen estilos ~s.* They have similar styles. ◊ *Ese vestido es muy ~ al de Ana.* That dress is very similar to Ana's. ◆ *nm* similarity LOC **algo parecido** something like that *Ver tb* PARECER

pared *nf* wall: *Hay varios carteles en la ~.* There are several posters on the wall. LOC **las paredes oyen** walls have ears *Ver tb* ESPADA, SUBIR

pareja *nf* **1** (*relación amorosa*) couple: *Hacen muy buena ~.* They make a really nice couple. **2** (*animales, equipo*) pair: *la ~ vencedora del torneo* the winning pair **3** (*cónyuge, compañero, de juegos, de baile*) partner: *No puedo jugar porque no tengo ~.* I can't play because I haven't got a partner. ◊ *Ana vino con su ~.* Ana came with her partner. LOC **en parejas** two by two: *Entraron en ~s.* They went in two by two. **una pareja de la policía/guardia civil** two policemen/two civil guards

parentela *nf* relations [*pl*]

parentesco *nm* relationship LOC **tener parentesco con algn** to be related to sb

paréntesis *nm* (*signo*) brackets [*pl*]: *abrir/cerrar el ~* to open/close (the) brackets ☛ *Ver* págs 318–19. LOC **entre paréntesis** in brackets

pariente, -a *nm-nf* relation: *~ cercano/lejano* close/distant relation

parir *vt, vi* to give birth **(to *sth*/*sb*)** LOC **poner a algn a parir** to call sb all the names under the sun

parking *nm* car park: *un ~ subterráneo* an underground car park

parlamentario, -a ◆ *adj* parliamentary ◆ *nm-nf* Member of Parliament (*abrev* MP) ☛ *Ver* pág 322 .

parlamento *nm* parliament [*v sing o pl*] ☛ *Ver* pág 322.

parlanchín, -ina ◆ *adj* talkative ◆ *nm-nf* chatterbox

paro *nm* **1** (*desempleo*) unemployment **2** (*huelga*) strike LOC **(estar) en paro** (to be) unemployed *Ver tb* APUNTAR, CARDIACO, CARTILLA, COBRAR

parpadear *vi* **1** (*ojos*) to blink **2** (*luz*) to flicker

párpado *nm* eyelid

parque *nm* **1** (*jardín*) park **2** (*bebé*) playpen LOC **parque de atracciones** amusement park **parque de bomberos** fire station

parrafada *nf* LOC *Ver* SOLTAR

párrafo *nm* paragraph

parrilla *nf* grill LOC **carne/pescado a la parrilla** grilled meat/fish

párroco *nm* parish priest

parroquia *nf* **1** (*iglesia*) parish church **2** (*comunidad*) parish

parte[1] *nf* **1** (*gen*) part: *tres ~s iguales* three equal parts ◊ *¿En qué ~ de la ciudad vives?* What part of the town do you live in? ◊ *las dos terceras ~s* two thirds ◊ *Vete a hacer ruido a otra ~.* Go and make a noise somewhere else. ◊ *Esto te lo arreglan en cualquier ~.* This can be repaired anywhere. **2** (*persona*) party [*pl* parties]: *la ~ contraria* the opposing party LOC **de parte de algn** on behalf of sb: *de ~ de todos nosotros* on behalf of us all **¿de parte de quién?** (*por teléfono*) who's calling? **en/por todas partes** everywhere **la parte de abajo/arriba** the bottom/top **la parte de atrás/delante** the back/front **por mi parte** as far as I am, you are, etc concerned: *Por nuestra ~ no hay ningún problema.* As far as we're concerned there's no problem. **por partes** bit by bit: *Estamos arreglando el tejado por ~s.* We're repairing the roof bit by bit. **por una parte... por la otra...** on the one hand... on the other...: *Por una ~ me alegro, pero por la otra me da pena.* On the one hand I'm pleased, but on the other I think it's sad. **tomar parte en algo** to take part in sth *Ver tb* ALGUNO, CUALQUIERA, GRANDE, MAYOR, NINGUNO, OTRO, SALUDAR, SEXTO

parte² *nm* report: ~ *médico/ meteorológico* medical/weather report LOC **dar parte** to inform *sb* (*of/about sth*)

participación *nf* **1** (*intervención*) participation: *la ~ del público* audience participation **2** (*Fin, lotería*) share

participante ◆ *adj* participating: *los países ~s* the participating countries ◆ *nmf* participant

participar *vi* ~ (**en**) to participate, to take part (*más coloq*) (**in *sth***): ~ *en un proyecto* to participate in a project

partícula *nf* particle

particular *adj* **1** (*gen*) characteristic: *Cada vino tiene su sabor ~.* Each wine has its own characteristic taste. **2** (*privado*) private: *clases ~es* private tuition

partida *nf* **1** (*juego*) game: *echar una ~ de ajedrez* to have a game of chess **2** (*nacimiento, matrimonio, defunción*) certificate **3** (*mercancía*) consignment

partidario, -a ◆ *adj* ~ **de** in favour **of *sth/doing sth***: *No soy ~ de hacer eso.* I'm not in favour of doing that. ◆ *nm-nf* supporter

partido *nm* **1** (*Pol*) party [*pl* parties] **2** (*Dep*) match: *ver un ~ de fútbol* to watch a football match LOC **partido de ida/ vuelta** first/second leg **sacar partido a/ de algo** to make the most of sth

partir ◆ *vt* **1** (*con cuchillo*) to cut *sth* (up): ~ *la tarta* to cut up the cake **2** (*con las manos*) to break *sth* (off): *¿Me partes un pedazo de pan?* Could you break me off a piece of bread? **3** (*frutos secos*) to crack ◆ *vi* (*marcharse*) to leave (**for...**): *Parten mañana hacia Madrid.* They're leaving for Madrid tomorrow. ◆ **partirse** *v pron* **1** (*gen*) to split: *Si te caes te partirás la cabeza.* You'll split your head open if you fall. **2** (*diente, alma*) to break LOC **a partir de** from...(on): *a ~ de las nueve de la noche* from 9pm onwards ◊ *a ~ de entonces* from then on ◊ *a ~ de mañana* starting from tomorrow *Ver tb* CARA, CERO, RISA

partitura *nf* score

parto *nm* birth LOC **estar de parto** to be in labour

parvulario *nm* nursery school

pasa *nf* raisin LOC *Ver* CIRUELA

pasada *nf* LOC **de pasada** in passing **hacer/jugar una mala pasada** to play a dirty trick *on sb* **¡qué pasada de...!**: *¡Qué ~ de moto!* What a fantastic bike!

pasadizo *nm* passage

pasado, -a ◆ *pp, adj* **1** (*día, semana, mes, verano, etc*) last: *el martes ~* last Tuesday **2** (*Gram, época*) past: *siglos ~s* past centuries **3** (*comida*) **(a)** (*demasiado hecha*) overdone **(b)** (*estropeada*) off ◆ *nm* past LOC **estar pasado de fecha** (*producto*) to be past its sell-by date **pasado de moda** (*ropa*) unfashionable **pasado mañana** the day after tomorrow *Ver tb* PASAR

pasajero, -a *nm-nf* passenger: *un barco de ~s* a passenger boat

pasamontañas *nm* balaclava

pasaporte *nm* passport

pasar ◆ *vi* **1** (*gen*) to pass: *La moto pasó a toda velocidad.* The motor bike passed at top speed. ◊ *Pasaron tres horas.* Three hours passed. ◊ *Ya han pasado dos días desde que llamó.* It's two days since he phoned. ◊ *¡Cómo pasa el tiempo!* Doesn't time fly! ◊ *Ese autobús pasa por el museo.* That bus goes past the museum. **2** (*entrar*) to come in: *¿Puedo ~?* May I come in? **3** (*ir*) to go: *Mañana pasaré por el banco.* I'll go to the bank tomorrow. **4** (*ocurrir*) to happen: *A mí me pasó lo mismo.* The same thing happened to me. ◆ *vt* **1** (*gen*) to pass: *¿Me pasas ese libro?* Can you pass me that book, please? ◊ *Hace punto para ~ el tiempo.* She knits to pass the time. **2** (*periodo de tiempo*) to spend: *Pasamos la tarde/dos horas charlando.* We spent the afternoon/two hours chatting. ◆ **pasarse** *v pron* **1** (*ir demasiado lejos*): *No te pases comiendo.* Don't eat too much. ◊ *¡Esta vez te has pasado!* You've gone too far this time! ◊ *~se de parada* to go past your stop **2** (*comida*) **(a)** (*ponerse mala*) to go off **(b)** (*demasiado cocinada*) to be overcooked: *Se te ha pasado el arroz.* The rice is overcooked. **3** (*olvidarse*) to forget: *Se me pasó completamente lo del entrenamiento.* I completely forgot about the training session. LOC **¿pasa algo?** anything the matter? **pasar de algo/algn**: *Paso de ella.* I couldn't care less about her. ◊ *Pasa de todo.* He couldn't care less. **pasarlo bien** to have a good time **pasarlo mal** to have a hard time: *Lo está pasando muy mal.* She's having a very hard time. **pasar por algo/algn** to pass for sth/sb: *Esa chica pasa por italiana.* That girl could easily pass for an Italian. **pasar sin** to manage without *sth/sb*: *No puedo ~ sin coche.* I can't manage without a car. **¿qué pasa?** (*¿hay problemas?*) what's the matter? ☛Para otras expresiones con **pasar**, véanse las entradas del sustantivo, adjetivo, etc, p.ej. **pasarlo bomba** en BOMBA[1] y **pasarse de listo** en LISTO.

pasatiempo *nm* **1** (*afición*) hobby [*pl* hobbies] **2 pasatiempos** (*en un periódico*) puzzles: *la página de ~s* the puzzle page

pascua *nf* **1** (*Semana Santa*) Easter **2 pascuas** (*navidades*) Christmas: *¡Felices Pascuas!* Happy Christmas! LOC *Ver* SANTO

pase *nm* pass: *No puedes entrar sin ~.* You can't get in without a pass.

pasear *vt, vi* to walk: *~ al perro* to walk the dog ◊ *Todos los días salgo a ~.* I go for a walk every day.

paseo *nm* **1** (*a pie*) walk **2** (*en bicicleta, en caballo*) ride **3** (*avenida*) avenue LOC **dar un paseo** to go for a walk **paseo marítimo** prom (*coloq*), promenade *Ver tb* MANDAR

pasillo *nm* **1** (*gen*) corridor: *No corras por los ~s.* Don't run along the corridors. **2** (*iglesia, avión, teatro*) aisle

pasión *nf* passion LOC **tener pasión por algo/algn** to be mad about sth/sb

pasivo, -a ◆ *adj* passive ◆ **pasiva** *nf* (*Gram*) passive (voice)

pasmado, -a ◆ *pp, adj* amazed (**at/by sth**): *Me quedé ~ ante su insolencia.* I was amazed at their insolence. ◆ *nm-nf* halfwit

paso *nm* **1** (*gen*) step: *dar un ~ adelante/atrás* to step forward/back ◊ *un ~ hacia la paz* a step towards peace **2** (*acción de pasar*) passage: *el ~ del tiempo* the passage of time **3** (*camino*) way (through): *Por aquí no hay ~.* There's no way through. **4** (*teléfono, contador*) unit **5 pasos** footsteps: *Me ha parecido oír ~s.* I thought I heard footsteps. LOC **abrir/dejar paso** to make way (*for sth/sb*): *¡Dejen ~ a la ambulancia!* Make way for the ambulance! ◊ *Nos abrimos ~ a codazos entre la gente.* We elbowed our way through the crowd. **a paso de tortuga** at snail's pace **de paso 1** (*en el camino*) on the way: *Me pilla de ~.* It's on my way. **2** (*al mismo tiempo*): *Lleva esto a la oficina y de ~ habla con la secretaria.* Take this to the office, and while you're there have a word with the secretary. **paso a nivel/de cebra/de peatones** level/zebra/ pedestrian crossing **paso a paso** step by step **paso subterráneo 1** (*para peatones*) subway [*pl* subways] **2** (*para coches*) underpass **salir del paso** to get by: *Estudian lo justo para salir del ~.* They do just enough work to get by. *Ver tb* ACELERAR, CEDER, LLAVE, PROHIBIDO

pasta *nf* **1** (*plasta*) paste: *Mézclese hasta que la ~ quede espesa.* Mix to a thick paste. **2** (*masa*) **(a)** (*de pan*) dough **(b)** (*de tarta*) pastry **3** (*fideos, macarrones*) pasta **4** (*galleta*) biscuit **5** (*dinero*) dough **6** (*libro*) cover LOC **pasta de dientes** toothpaste

pastar *vt, vi* to graze

pastel *nm* **1** (*gen*) cake: *un ~ de cumpleaños* a birthday cake **2** (*Arte*) pastel LOC *Ver* DESCUBRIR

pastelería *nf* cake shop

pastilla *nf* **1** (*píldora*) tablet **2** (*chocolate*) square **3** (*jabón*) bar LOC **pastillas contra el mareo** travel-sickness pills

pasto *nm* pasture

pastor, ~a *nm-nf* shepherd [*fem* shepherdess] LOC **pastor alemán** Alsatian *Ver tb* PERRO

pata *nf* **1** (*gen*) leg: *la ~ de la mesa* the table leg **2** (*pie*) **(a)** (*cuadrúpedo con uñas*) paw: *El perro se ha hecho daño en la ~.* The dog has hurt its paw. **(b)** (*pezuña*) hoof [*pl* hoofs/hooves]: *las ~s de un caballo* a horse's hooves **3** (*animal*) duck ☛ *Ver nota en* PATO LOC **andar a la pata coja** to hop **mala pata** bad luck: *¡Qué mala ~ tienen!* They're so unlucky! **patas arriba**: *La casa está ~s arriba.* The house is a tip. **patas de gallo** crow's feet *Ver tb* CUATRO, ESTIRAR, METEDURA, METER

patada *nf* **1** (*puntapié*) kick: *Le dio una ~ a la mesa.* He kicked the table. **2** (*en el suelo*) stamp LOC **caer/sentar como una patada (en el estómago)** to be like a kick in the teeth **echar a algn a patadas** to kick sb out

patalear *vi* **1** (*en el suelo*) to stamp (your feet) **2** (*en el aire*) to kick (your feet)

pataleta *nf* tantrum: *agarrarse una ~* to throw a tantrum

patata

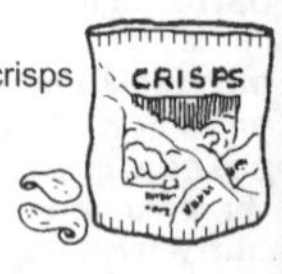

patata *nf* potato [*pl* potatoes] LOC **patatas fritas 1** (*de bolsa*) crisps **2** (*Cocina*) chips *Ver tb* PURÉ

patatús *nm* LOC **darle a algn un patatús 1** (*desmayarse*) to faint **2** (*disgustarse*) to have a fit

paté *nm* pâté

patear(se) *vi, vt, v pron* (*andar mucho*) to tramp round: *Nos pateamos la ciudad entera.* We tramped round the whole city.

patente *nf* patent

paternal *adj* fatherly, paternal (*más formal*)

paternidad *nf* fatherhood, paternity (*formal*)

paterno, -a *adj* **1** (*paternal*) fatherly **2** (*parentesco*) paternal: *abuelo ~* paternal grandfather LOC *Ver* LÍNEA

patilla *nf* **1** (*pelo*) sideboard **2** (*gafas*) arm

patín *nm* **1** (*con ruedas*) roller skate **2** (*con cuchilla*) ice-skate **3** (*embarcación*) pedal boat

patinador, ~a *nm-nf* skater

patinaje *nm* skating: *~ sobre hielo/artístico* ice-skating/figure-skating LOC *Ver* PISTA

patinar *vi* **1** (*persona*) to skate **2** (*vehículo*) to skid

patinete *nm* scooter

patio *nm* **1** (*gen*) courtyard **2** (*colegio*) playground LOC **patio de butacas** stalls [*pl*]

patito, -a *nm-nf* duckling

pato, -a *nm-nf* duck

> **Duck** es el sustantivo genérico. Para referirnos sólo al macho decimos **drake**. **Ducklings** son los patitos.

LOC **ser (un) pato** to be clumsy *Ver tb* PAGAR

patoso, -a *adj, nm-nf* clumsy [*adj*]: *Eres un ~.* You're so clumsy!

patria *nf* (native) country

patriota *nmf* patriot

patriotismo *nm* patriotism

patrocinador, ~a *nm-nf* sponsor

patrocinar *vt* to sponsor

patrón, -ona ◆ *nm-nf* (*Relig*) patron saint: *San Isidro es el ~ de Madrid.* Saint Isidore is the patron saint of Madrid. ◆ *nm* (*Costura*) pattern

patrulla *nf* patrol: *un coche ~* a patrol car

patrullar *vt, vi* to patrol

pausa *nf* pause LOC **hacer una pausa** to have a short break

pavimento *nm* surface

pavo, -a *nm-nf* turkey [*pl* turkeys] LOC **pavo real** peacock [*fem* peahen] *Ver tb* EDAD

payasada *nf* LOC **hacer payasadas** to play the fool: *Siempre estás haciendo ~s.* You're always playing the fool.

payaso, -a *nm-nf* clown LOC **hacer el payaso** to clown around

paz *nf* peace: *plan de ~* peace plan ◊ *en tiempo(s) de ~* in peacetime LOC **dejar en paz** to leave *sth/sb* alone: *No me dejan en ~.* They won't leave me alone. **hacer las paces** to make it up (*with sb*): *Han hecho las paces.* They've made it up.

pe *nf* LOC **de pe a pa** from beginning to end

peaje *nm* toll

peatón *nm* pedestrian LOC *Ver* PASO

peatonal *adj* pedestrian [*n atrib*]: *calle ~* pedestrian street

peca *nf* freckle: *Me han salido muchas ~s.* I've come out in freckles.

pecado *nm* sin

pecador, ~a *nm-nf* sinner

pecar *vi* to sin LOC **pecar de** to be too...: *Pecas de confiado.* You're too trusting.

pecera *nf* goldfish bowl

pecho *nm* **1** (*gen*) chest: *Tengo catarro de ~.* I've got a cold on my chest. **2** (*sólo mujer*) **(a)** (*busto*) bust **(b)** (*mama*) breast LOC **tomarse algo a pecho 1** (*en serio*) to take sth seriously: *Se toma el trabajo demasiado a ~.* He takes his work too seriously. **2** (*ofenderse*) to take sth to heart: *Era una broma, no te lo tomes a ~.* It was a joke; don't take it to heart.

pechuga *nf* (*ave*) breast: *~ de pollo* chicken breast

pedagogía *nf* education

pedagógico, -a *adj* educational

pedal *nm* pedal

pedalear *vi* to pedal

pedante ◆ *adj* pedantic ◆ *nmf* pedant

pedazo *nm* piece, bit (*más coloq*): *un ~ de tarta* a piece of cake LOC **caerse algo a pedazos** to fall to pieces **hacerse pedazos** to smash (to pieces)

pediatra *nmf* paediatrician

pedido *nm* order: *hacer un ~* to place an order

pedir *vt* **1** (*gen*) to ask (*sb*) **for *sth***: *~ pan/la cuenta* to ask for bread/the bill ◊ *~ ayuda a los vecinos* to ask the neighbours for help **2** (*permiso, favor, cantidad*) to ask (*sb*) (*sth*): *Te quiero ~*

un favor. I want to ask you a favour. ◊ *Piden dos mil libras.* They're asking two thousand pounds. **3** ~ **a algn que haga algo** to ask sb **to do sth**: *Me pidió que esperara.* He asked me to wait. **4** (*encargar*) to order: *De primero pedimos sopa.* We ordered soup as a starter. LOC **pedir disculpas/perdón** to apologize (*to sb*) (*for sth*) **pedir hora** to make an appointment **pedir** (**limosna**) to beg **pedir prestado** to borrow: *Me pidió prestado el coche.* He borrowed my car. ☛ *Ver dibujo en* BORROW **te pido por Dios/por lo que más quieras que...** I beg you to... *Ver tb* RESCATE

pedo *nm* (*gases*) fart LOC **tirarse un pedo** to fart

pedrada *nf*: *Lo recibieron a ~s.* They threw stones at him.

pega *nf* **1** (*inconveniente*) drawback: *La mayor ~ de vivir aquí es el ruido.* The main drawback to living here is the noise. **2** (*problema*) snag: *Surgieron algunas ~s.* There were a few snags. LOC **poner pegas**: *¿Crees que me pondrán ~s para matricularme?* Do you think I'll have trouble registering?

pegadizo, -a *adj* (*música*) catchy

pegajoso, -a *adj* **1** (*pringoso*) sticky **2** (*cargante*) clingy

pegamento *nm* glue

pegar ◆ *vt* **1** (*golpear*) to hit **2** (*adherir*) to stick: ~ *una etiqueta en un paquete* to stick a label on a parcel ◊ ~ *una taza rota* to stick a broken cup together **3** (*acercar*) to put *sth* **against sth**: *Pegó la cama a la ventana.* He put his bed against the window. **4** (*contagiar*) to give: *Me has pegado la gripe.* You've given me your flu. ◆ *vi* **1** (*ropa, colores*) to go (**with sth**): *La chaqueta no pega con la falda.* The jacket doesn't go with the skirt. **2** (*sol, bebida*) to be strong ◆ **pegarse** *v pron* **1** (*pelearse*) to fight **2** (*adherirse, comida*) to stick **3** (*enfermedad*) to be catching LOC **dale que te pego** like mad: *Está dale que te pego al piano.* She's playing the piano like mad. **estar pegando a** (*muy cerca*) to be right next to... **no pegar ojo** not to sleep a wink **pegársela a algn** (*ser infiel*) to cheat on sb **pegársele a algn un acento** to pick up an accent **pegar un tiro** to shoot: *Se pegó un tiro.* He shot himself. *Ver tb* BOTE[3], BRINCO, CAMINATA, CORTE[1], ESTIRÓN, GRITO, MORDISCO, PELLIZCO, TOQUE, TORTA, VIDA

pegatina *nf* sticker

pegote *nm* patch

peinado, -a ◆ *pp, adj*: *¿Todavía no estás peinada?* Haven't you done your hair yet? ◆ *nm* hairstyle LOC **ir bien/mal peinado**: *Iba muy bien peinada.* Her hair looked really nice. ◊ *Siempre va muy mal ~.* His hair always looks a mess. *Ver tb* PEINAR

peinar ◆ *vt* **1** (*gen*) to comb *sb's* hair: *Déjame que te peine.* Let me comb your hair. **2** (*peluquero*) to do *sb's* hair: *Voy a que me peinen.* I'm going to have my hair done. **3** (*zona*) to comb ◆ **peinarse** *v pron* to comb your hair: *Péinate antes de salir.* Comb your hair before you go out.

peine *nm* comb

pelado, -a *pp, adj* LOC **estar pelado** (*sin dinero*) to be broke *Ver tb* GRITO; *Ver tb* PELAR

pelar ◆ *vt* **1** (*gen*) to peel: ~ *una naranja* to peel an orange **2** (*guisantes, mariscos*) to shell **3** (*caramelo*) to unwrap ◆ **pelarse** *v pron* to peel: *Se te va a ~ la nariz.* Your nose will peel. LOC **pelarse de frío** to freeze to death

peldaño *nm* step

pelea *nf* fight: *meterse en una ~* to get into a fight ◊ *Siempre están de ~.* They're always fighting.

pelear(se) *vi, v pron* **1** (*luchar*) to fight (**for/against/over sth/sb**): *Los niños se peleaban por los juguetes.* The children were fighting over the toys. **2** (*reñir*) to quarrel

peletería *nf* furrier's [*pl* furriers]

pelícano (*tb* **pelicano**) *nm* pelican

película *nf* film LOC **echar una película** to show a film **película cómica/de risa** comedy [*pl* comedies] **película del oeste** western **película de miedo** horror film **película muda** silent film **película policiaca** thriller *Ver tb* SUSPENSE

peligrar *vi* to be in danger

peligro *nm* danger: *Está en ~.* He's in danger. ◊ *fuera de ~* out of danger

peligroso, -a *adj* dangerous

pelirrojo, -a ◆ *adj* red-haired, ginger (*más coloq*) ◆ *nm-nf* redhead

pellejo *nm* **1** (*gen*) skin **2** (*en una uña*) hangnail LOC **arriesgar/jugarse el pellejo** to risk your neck

pellizcar *vt* to pinch

pellizco *nm* **1** (*sal*) pinch **2** (*pedacito*) little bit: *un ~ de pan* a little bit of bread LOC **dar/pegar un pellizco** to pinch

pelo *nm* **1** (*gen*) hair: *tener el ~ rizado/liso* to have curly/straight hair **2** (*piel de animal*) coat: *Ese perro tiene un ~ muy suave.* That dog has a silky coat. LOC **no tener pelos en la lengua** not to mince your words **ponérsele los pelos de punta a algn**: *Se me pusieron los ~s de punta.* My hair stood on end. **por los pelos** by the skin of your teeth: *Se libraron del accidente por los ~s.* They missed having an accident by the skin of their teeth. **tomarle el pelo a algn** to pull sb's leg *Ver tb* CEPILLO, CINTA, CORTAR, CORTE[1], DESENREDARSE, LIBRAR, RECOGER, SOLTAR, TOMADURA

pelota ◆ *nf* **1** (*balón*) ball: *una ~ de tenis* a tennis ball **2** (*cabeza*) head ◆ *adj, nmf* creep [*n*]: *No seas ~.* Don't be such a creep. LOC **estar en pelotas** to be stark naked **hacer la pelota/rosca** to suck up to *sb*

pelotón *nm* (*ciclismo*) bunch

peluca *nf* wig

peluche *nm* plush LOC *Ver* MUÑECO, OSO

peludo, -a *adj* **1** (*gen*) hairy: *unos brazos ~s* hairy arms **2** (*animal*) long-haired

peluquería *nf* **1** (*gen*) hairdresser's [*pl* hairdressers] **2** (*para hombres*) barber's [*pl* barbers]

peluquero, -a *nm-nf* **1** (*gen*) hairdresser **2** (*para hombres*) barber

peluquín *nm* toupee

pelusa (*tb* **pelusilla**) *nf* **1** (*cara, fruta*) down **2** (*tela, suciedad*) ball of fluff LOC **tener pelusa a/de algn** to be jealous of sb

pena *nf* **1** (*tristeza*) sorrow: *ahogar las ~s* to drown your sorrows **2** (*lástima*) pity: *¡Qué ~ que no puedas venir!* What a pity you can't come! **3** (*condena*) sentence **4 penas** (*problemas*) troubles: *No me cuentes tus ~s.* Don't tell me your troubles. LOC **dar pena 1** (*persona*) to feel sorry *for sb*: *Esos niños me dan mucha ~.* I feel very sorry for those children. **2** (*cosa, situación*): *Me da ~ que os tengáis que marchar.* I'm sorry you have to go. **merecer/valer la pena** to be worth *doing sth*: *Vale la ~ leerlo.* It's worth reading. ◊ *No merece la pena.* It's not worth it. **pena de muerte** death penalty

penal *adj* penal

penalty *nm* penalty [*pl* penalties]: *meter un gol de ~* to score from a penalty ◊ *meter un ~* to score a penalty LOC *Ver* PITAR

pendiente ◆ *adj* **1** (*asunto, factura, problema*) outstanding **2** (*decisión, veredicto*) pending ◆ *nm* earring ◆ *nf* slope: *una ~ suave/pronunciada* a gentle/steep slope LOC **estar pendiente (de algo/algn) 1** (*vigilar*) to keep an eye on sth/sb: *Estate ~ de los niños.* Keep an eye on the children. **2** (*estar atento*) to be attentive (to sth/sb): *Estaba muy ~ de sus invitados.* He was very attentive to his guests. **3** (*estar esperando*) to be waiting (for sth): *Estamos ~s de su decisión.* We're waiting for his decision.

pene *nm* penis

penetrante *adj* **1** (*gen*) penetrating: *una mirada ~* a penetrating look **2** (*frío, viento*) bitter

penetrar *vt, vi* ~ **(en) 1** (*entrar*) to enter, to get into *sth* (*más coloq*): *El agua penetró en la bodega.* The water got into the cellar. **2** (*bala, flecha, sonido*) to pierce: *La bala le penetró el corazón.* The bullet pierced his heart.

penicilina *nf* penicillin

península *nf* peninsula

penique *nm* penny [*pl* pence]: *Cuesta 50 ~s.* It's 50 pence. ◊ *una moneda de cinco ~s* a five-pence piece ☛ *Ver* Apéndice 1.

penitencia *nf* penance: *hacer ~* to do penance

pensamiento *nm* thought LOC *Ver* ADIVINAR

pensar *vt, vi* **1** ~ **(en)** to think **(about/of** ***sth/sb*****)**; to think **(about/of** ***doing sth*****)**: *Piensa un número.* Think of a number. ◊ *¿En qué piensas?* What are you thinking about? ◊ *Estamos pensando en casarnos.* We're thinking about getting married. ◊ *¿Piensas que vendrán?* Do you think they'll come? ◊ *¿En quién piensas?* Who are you thinking about? **2** (*opinar*) to think *sth* ***of sth/sb***: *¿Qué piensas de Juan?* What do you think of Juan? ◊ *No pienses mal de ellos.* Don't think badly of them. **3** (*tener decidido*): *Pensábamos irnos mañana.* We were going to go tomorrow. ◊ *No pienso ir.* I'm not going. ◊ *¿Piensas venir?* Are you going to come? LOC **pensándolo bien...** on second thoughts... **pensar en las musarañas** to daydream **piénsalo/piénsatelo** think it over **¡ni pensarlo!** no way!

pensativo, -a *adj* thoughtful

pensión *nf* **1** (*jubilación, subsidio*) pension: *una ~ de viudedad* a widow's pension **2** (*hostal*) guest house LOC **pensión completa/media pensión** full/ half board

pensionista *nmf* pensioner

pentagrama *nm* staff

penúltimo, -a ◆ *adj* penultimate, last *sth/sb* but one (*más coloq*): *el ~ capítulo* the penultimate chapter ◊ *la penúltima parada* the last stop but one ◆ *nm-nf* last but one

peñón *nm* rock: *el Peñón (de Gibraltar)* the Rock (of Gibraltar)

peón *nm* **1** (*obrero*) labourer **2** (*Ajedrez*) pawn

peonza *nf* spinning top: *bailar una ~* to spin a top

peor ◆ *adj, adv* (*uso comparativo*) worse (**than sth/sb**): *Este coche es ~ que aquél.* This car is worse than that one. ◊ *Hoy me encuentro mucho ~.* I feel much worse today. ◊ *Fue ~ de lo que me esperaba.* It was worse than I had expected. ◊ *Cocina aún ~ que su madre.* She's an even worse cook than her mother. ◆ *adj, adv, nmf* (*uso superlativo*) ~ (**de**) worst (**in/of/...**): *Soy el ~ corredor del mundo.* I'm the worst runner in the world. ◊ *la ~ de todas* the worst of all ◊ *el que ~ canta* the one who sings worst LOC *Ver* CADA, CASO

pepinillo *nm* gherkin: *~s en vinagre* pickled gherkins

pepino *nm* cucumber LOC *Ver* IMPORTAR[2]

pepita *nf* **1** (*semilla*) seed **2** (*oro*) nugget: *~s de oro* gold nuggets

pequeño, -a ◆ *adj* **1** (*gen*) small: *un ~ problema/detalle* a small problem/ detail ◊ *El cuarto es demasiado ~.* The room is too small. ◊ *Todas las faldas se me han quedado pequeñas.* All my skirts are too small for me now. ☛ *Ver nota en* SMALL **2** (*joven*) little: *cuando yo era ~* when I was little ◊ *los niños ~s* little children **3** (*el más joven*) youngest: *mi hijo ~* my youngest son **4** (*poco importante*) minor: *unos ~s cambios* a few minor changes ◆ *nm-nf* youngest (one): *El ~ está estudiando derecho.* The youngest one is studying law. LOC *Ver* MANILLA

pera *nf* pear LOC *Ver* NIÑO

peral *nm* pear tree

percha *nf* **1** (*de armario*) hanger: *Cuelga el traje en una ~.* Put your suit on a hanger. **2** (*de pie*) coat stand **3** (*de pared*) coat hook

perdedor, ~a ◆ *adj* losing: *el equipo ~* the losing team ◆ *nm-nf* loser: *ser un buen/mal ~* to be a good/bad loser

perder ◆ *vt* **1** (*gen*) to lose: *~ altura/peso* to lose height/weight ◊ *He perdido el reloj.* I've lost my watch. **2** (*medio de transporte, oportunidad*) to miss: *~ el autobús/avión* to miss the bus/plane ◊ *¡No pierda esta oportunidad!* Don't miss this opportunity! **3** (*desperdiciar*) to waste: *~ el tiempo* to waste time ◊ *sin ~ un minuto* without wasting a minute ◆ *vi* **1** ~ (**a**) to lose (**at sth**): *Hemos perdido.* We've lost. ◊ *~ al ajedrez* to lose at chess **2** (*salir perjudicado*) to lose out: *Tú eres el único que pierde.* You're the only one to lose out. ◆ *vt, vi* **1** (*líquido, gas*) to leak: *El depósito pierde (gasolina).* The tank is leaking (petrol). ◊ *~ aceite/gas* to have an oil/ gas leak **2** (*aire*) to lose air ◆ **perderse** *v pron* **1** (*gen*) to get lost: *Si no llevas mapa te perderás.* If you don't take a map you'll get lost. **2** (*película, espectáculo*) to miss: *No te pierdas esa película.* Don't miss that film. LOC **echar algo a perder** to ruin sth **perder algo/a algn de vista** to lose sight of sth/sb **perder el rastro** to lose track *of sth/sb* **perder la cabeza/el juicio** to go mad **perder la calma** to lose your temper **salir perdiendo** to lose out *Ver tb* CONOCIMIENTO

pérdida *nf* **1** (*gen*) loss: *Su marcha fue una gran ~.* His leaving was a great loss. ◊ *sufrir ~s económicas* to lose money **2** (*de tiempo*) waste: *Esto es una ~ de tiempo.* This is a waste of time. **3 pérdidas** (*daños*) damage [*incontable, v sing*]: *Las ~s a causa de la tormenta son cuantiosas.* The storm damage is extensive. LOC **no tiene pérdida** you can't miss it **pérdidas y ganancias** profit and loss

perdido, -a *pp, adj* **1** (*gen*) lost: *Estoy completamente perdida.* I'm completely lost. **2** (*perro*) stray **3** (*sucio*): *Te has puesto ~.* You're filthy. ◊ *Has puesto la alfombra perdida de barro.* You've covered the carpet in mud. LOC *Ver* OBJETO; *Ver tb* PERDER

perdigón *nm* pellet

perdiz *nf* partridge

perdón ◆ *nm* forgiveness ◆ **¡perdón!** *interj* sorry! ☛ *Ver nota en* EXCUSE LOC *Ver* PEDIR

perdonar *vt* **1** (*gen*) to forgive *sb* (**for sth/doing sth**): *¿Me perdonas?* Will you forgive me? ◊ *Jamás le perdonaré lo que me hizo.* I'll never forgive him for what he did. **2** (*deuda, obligación, condena* to let *sb* off *sth*: *Me perdonó las mil pesetas que le debía.* He let me off the thousand pesetas I owed him. LOC **perdona, perdone, etc 1** (*para pedir disculpas*) sorry: *¡Ay! Perdone, ¿le he pisado?* Sorry, did I stand on your foot? **2** (*para llamar la atención*) excuse me: *¡Perdone! ¿Tiene hora?* Excuse me! Have you got the time, please? **3** (*cuando no se ha oído bien*) sorry, I beg your pardon (*más formal*): *—Soy la señora de Rodríguez. —¿Perdone? ¿Señora de qué?* 'I am Mrs Rodríguez.' 'Sorry? Mrs who?' ☛ *Ver nota en* EXCUSE

peregrinación *nf* (*tb* **peregrinaje** *nm*) pilgrimage: *ir en ~* to go on a pilgrimage

peregrino, -a *nm-nf* pilgrim

perejil *nm* parsley

perenne *adj* LOC *Ver* HOJA

pereza *nf*: *Después de comer me entra mucha ~.* I always feel very sleepy after lunch. ◊ *¡Qué ~ tener que levantarme ahora!* I really don't feel like getting up now.

perezoso, -a *adj, nm-nf* lazy [*adj*]: *Mi hermano es un ~.* My brother is really lazy. LOC *Ver* CORTO

perfeccionar *vt* (*mejorar*) to improve: *Quiero ~ mi alemán.* I want to improve my German.

perfecto, -a *adj* perfect

perfil *nm* **1** (*persona*) profile: *Está más guapo de ~.* He's better looking in profile. ◊ *un retrato de ~* a profile portrait ◊ *Ponte de ~.* Stand sideways. **2** (*edificio, montaña*) outline

perfilar *vt* (*dibujo*) to draw the outline **of *sth***

perfumado, -a *pp, adj* scented *Ver tb* PERFUMAR

perfumar ◆ *vt* to perfume ◆ **perfumarse** *v pron* to put perfume on

perfume *nm* perfume

perfumería *nf* perfumery [*pl* perfumeries]

perímetro *nm* perimeter

periódico, -a ◆ *adj* periodic ◆ *nm* newspaper, paper (*más coloq*) LOC *Ver* PUESTO, QUIOSCO, REPARTIDOR

periodismo *nm* journalism

periodista *nmf* journalist

periodo (*tb* **período**) *nm* period LOC **tener el periodo** to have your period *Ver tb* GLACIAR

periquito *nm* budgerigar, budgie (*coloq*)

perito *nmf* expert (***in sth***) LOC **perito agrónomo** agronomist

perjudicar *vt* **1** (*salud*) to damage **2** (*intereses*) to prejudice

perjudicial *adj* ~ (**para**) (*salud*) bad (**for *sth*/*sb***): *El tabaco es ~ para la salud.* Cigarettes are bad for your health.

perjuicio *nm* harm: *ocasionar un ~ a algn* to cause/do sb harm LOC **ir en perjuicio de algn** to go against sb *Ver tb* DAÑO

perla *nf* pearl LOC **ir/venir de perlas** to come in (very) handy: *Me viene de ~s.* It will come in very handy.

permanecer *vi* to remain, to be (*más coloq*): *~ pensativo/sentado* to remain thoughtful/seated ◊ *Permanecí despierta toda la noche.* I was awake all night.

permanente ◆ *adj* permanent ◆ *nf* perm LOC **hacerse la permanente** to have your hair permed *Ver tb* VADO

permiso *nm* **1** (*autorización*) permission (***to do sth***): *pedir/dar ~* to ask for/give permission **2** (*documento*) permit: *~ de residencia/trabajo* residence/work permit **3** (*vacación*) leave: *Estoy de ~.* I'm on leave. ◊ *He pedido una semana de ~.* I've asked for a week off. LOC **con (su) permiso**: *Con ~, ¿puedo pasar?* May I come in? ◊ *Me siento aquí, con su ~.* I'll sit here, if you don't mind. **permiso de conducir** driving licence

permitir ◆ *vt* **1** (*dejar*) to let *sb* (***do sth***): *Permítame ayudarle.* Let me help you. ◊ *No me lo permitirían.* They wouldn't let me. **2** (*autorizar*) to allow *sb* ***to do sth***: *No permiten entrar sin corbata.* You are not allowed in without a tie. ☛ *Ver nota en* ALLOW ◆ **permitirse** *v pron* **1** (*atreverse, tomarse*) to take: *Se permite demasiadas confianzas con ellos.* He takes too many liberties with them. **2** (*económicamente*) to afford: *No nos lo podemos ~.* We can't afford it. LOC **¿me permite...?** may I...?: *¿Me permite su mechero?* May I use your lighter?

permutación *nf* (*Mat*) permutation

pero ◆ *conj* but: *lento ~ seguro* slowly but surely ◆ *nm* (*defecto*) fault: *Le encuentras ~s a todo.* You find fault with everything.

perpendicular ◆ *adj* perpendicular (***to sth***) ◆ *nf* perpendicular

perpetuo, -a *adj* perpetual LOC *Ver* CADENA

perplejo, -a *adj* puzzled: *Me quedé ~.* I was puzzled.

perra *nf* **1** (*animal*) bitch ☞ *Ver nota en* PERRO **2** (*rabieta*) tantrum: *cogerse una ~* to throw a tantrum **3 perras** cash [*incontable*]: *ganar unas ~s* to earn some cash LOC **no tener una perra** to be broke

perrera *nf* kennel

perrito, -a *nm-nf* puppy [*pl* puppies] ☞ *Ver nota en* PERRO LOC **perrito caliente** hot dog

perro, -a *nm-nf* dog

Para referirnos sólo a la hembra, decimos **bitch**. A los perros recién nacidos se les llama **puppies**.

LOC **de perros** lousy: *un día de ~s* a lousy day **llevarse como el perro y el gato** to fight like cat and dog **perro callejero** stray (dog) **perro de lanas** spaniel **perro de San Bernardo** St Bernard **perro faldero** (*lit* y *fig*) lapdog **perro guardián** guard dog **perro ladrador...** his/her bark is worse than his/her bite **perro lobo** Alsatian **perro pastor** sheepdog *Ver tb* CRIADERO, VIDA

persecución *nf* **1** (*gen*) pursuit: *La policía iba en ~ de los atracadores.* The police went in pursuit of the robbers. **2** (*Pol, Relig*) persecution

perseguir *vt* **1** (*gen*) to pursue: *~ un coche/objetivo* to pursue a car/an objective **2** (*Pol, Relig*) to persecute

persiana *nf* shutters [*pl*]: *subir/bajar las ~s* to raise/lower the shutters

persistente *adj* persistent

persistir *vi* to persist (***in sth***)

persona *nf* person [*pl* people]: *miles de ~s* thousands of people LOC **persona mayor** grown-up **por persona** a head: *5.000 pesetas por ~* 5000 pesetas a head **ser (una) buena persona** to be nice: *Son muy buenas ~s.* They're very nice.

personaje *nm* **1** (*de un libro, una película*) character: *el ~ principal* the main character **2** (*persona importante*) personality [*pl* personalities]

personal ◆ *adj* personal ◆ *nm* staff [*v sing o pl*] LOC *Ver* ASEO, DATO, EFECTO, ORDENADOR

personalidad *nf* personality [*pl* personalities]

perspectiva *nf* **1** (*gen*) perspective: *A ese cuadro le falta ~.* The perspective's not quite right in that painting. **2** (*vista*) view **3** (*en el futuro*) prospect: *buenas ~s* good prospects

perspicacia *nf* insight

perspicaz *adj* perceptive

persuadir ◆ *vt* to persuade ◆ **persuadirse** *v pron* to become convinced (***of sth/that...***)

persuasivo, -a *adj* persuasive

pertenecer *vi* to belong ***to sth/sb***: *Este collar perteneció a mi abuela.* This necklace belonged to my grandmother.

perteneciente *adj ~* **a** belonging **to *sth/sb***: *los países ~s a la UE* the countries belonging to the EU

pertenencia *nf* **1** (*a un partido, club, etc*) membership **2 pertenencias** belongings

pértiga *nf* pole LOC *Ver* SALTO

pertinente *adj* relevant

pervertir *vt* to pervert

pesa *nf* weight LOC **hacer pesas** to do weight training

pesadez *nf* **1** (*aburrimiento*): *¡Qué ~ de película!* What a boring film! **2** (*molestia*) nuisance: *Estas moscas son una ~.* These flies are a nuisance.

pesadilla *nf* nightmare: *Anoche tuve una ~.* I had a nightmare last night.

pesado, -a ◆ *pp, adj* **1** (*gen*) heavy: *una maleta/comida pesada* a heavy suitcase/meal **2** (*aburrido*) boring ◆ *adj, nm-nf* (*pelmazo*) pain [*n*]: *Son unos ~s.* They're a pain. ◊ *No seas ~.* Don't be such a pain. LOC *Ver* BROMA, TÍO; *Ver tb* PESAR[1]

pésame *nm* condolences [*pl*]: *Mi más sentido ~.* My deepest condolences. LOC **dar el pésame** to offer *sb* your condolences

pesar[1] ◆ *vt* to weigh: *~ una maleta* to weigh a suitcase ◆ *vi* **1** (*gen*) to weigh: *¿Cuánto pesas?* How much do you weigh? ◊ *¡Cómo pesa!* It weighs a ton! **2** (*tener mucho peso*) to be heavy: *¡Este paquete sí que pesa!* This parcel is very heavy. ◊ *¿Te pesa?* Is it very heavy? ◊ *¡No pesa nada!* It hardly weighs a thing! LOC **pesar como un muerto** to weigh a ton

pesar[2] *nm* (*tristeza*) sorrow LOC **a pesar de algo** in spite of sth: *Fuimos a ~ de la lluvia.* We went in spite of the rain. **a pesar de que...** although...: *A ~ de que implicaba riesgos...* Although it was risky...

pesca *nf* fishing: *ir de ~* to go fishing LOC *Ver* FURTIVO

pescadería *nf* fishmonger's [*pl* fishmongers]

pescadero, -a *nm-nf* fishmonger

pescadilla *nf* small hake [*pl* small hake]

pescado *nm* fish [*incontable*]: *Voy a comprar ~.* I'm going to buy some fish. ◊ *Es un tipo de ~.* It's a kind of fish. ☛ *Ver nota en* FISH LOC **pescado azul/blanco** blue/white fish *Ver tb* LONJA, PARRILLA

pescador, ~a *nm-nf* fisherman/woman [*pl* fishermen/women] LOC *Ver* FURTIVO

pescar ◆ *vi* to fish: *Habían salido a ~.* They'd gone out fishing. ◆ *vt* (*coger*) to catch: *Pesqué dos truchas.* I caught two trout. ◊ *~ una pulmonía* to catch pneumonia LOC *Ver* CAÑA

peseta *nf* peseta

pesimista ◆ *adj* pessimistic ◆ *nmf* pessimist

pésimo, -a *adj* dreadful

peso *nm* **1** (*gen*) weight: *ganar/perder ~* to put on/lose weight ◊ *vender algo a ~* to sell sth by weight ◊ *~ bruto/neto* gross/net weight **2** (*balanza*) scales [*pl*]: *Este ~ no es muy exacto.* These scales aren't very accurate. LOC **de peso** (*fig*) **1** (*persona*) influential **2** (*asunto*) weighty *Ver tb* QUITAR

pesquero, -a ◆ *adj* fishing [*n atrib*]: *un puerto ~* a fishing port ◆ *nm* fishing boat

pestaña *nf* (*ojo*) eyelash

pestañear *vi* to blink LOC **sin pestañear** without batting an eyelid: *Escuchó la noticia sin ~.* He heard the news without batting an eyelid.

peste *nf* **1** (*enfermedad*) plague **2** (*mal olor*) stink: *¡Qué ~ hay!* What a stink! LOC **decir/echar pestes (de)** to slag *sth/sb* off

pestillo *nm* catch: *echar el ~* to put the catch on

petaca *nf* **1** (*para tabaco*) tobacco pouch **2** (*para licores*) hip flask LOC **hacer la petaca** to make an apple-pie bed *for sb*

pétalo *nm* petal

petardo *nm* **1** (*explosivo*) banger **2** (*tostón*) bore: *Es un ~ de película.* The film is a real bore.

petición *nf* **1** (*gen*) request: *hacer una ~ de ayuda* to make a request for help **2** (*instancia*) petition: *redactar una ~* to draw up a petition

petirrojo *nm* robin

peto *nm* dungarees [*pl*]

petróleo *nm* oil: *un pozo de ~* an oil well

petrolero *nm* oil tanker

pez *nm* fish [*pl* fish]: *peces de agua dulce* freshwater fish ◊ *Hay dos peces en la pecera.* There are two fish in the goldfish bowl. ☛ *Ver nota en* FISH LOC **pez de colores** goldfish [*pl* goldfish] **pez gordo** big shot

pezón *nm* **1** (*persona*) nipple **2** (*animal*) teat

pezuña *nf* hoof [*pl* hoofs/hooves]

piadoso, -a *adj* devout LOC *Ver* MENTIRA

pianista *nmf* pianist

piano *nm* piano [*pl* pianos]: *tocar una pieza al ~* to play a piece of music on the piano LOC **piano de cola** grand piano

piar *vi* to chirp

pica *nf* **picas** (*Naipes*) spades ☛ *Ver nota en* BARAJA

picadero *nm* riding school

picado, -a *pp, adj* **1** (*diente*) bad **2** (*mar*) choppy **3** (*enfadado*) cross: *Creo que están ~s conmigo.* I think they're cross with me. LOC **caer en picado** to nosedive *Ver tb* CARNE; *Ver tb* PICAR

picadura *nf* **1** (*mosquito, serpiente*) bite: *una ~ de serpiente* a snake bite **2** (*abeja, avispa*) sting

picajoso, -a *adj* touchy

picante *adj* (*Cocina*) hot: *una salsa ~* a hot sauce

picapica *nm* (*chuche*) sherbet LOC *Ver* POLVO

picaporte *nm* door-handle

picar ◆ *vt, vi* **1** (*pájaro*) to peck **2** (*mosquito, serpiente*) to bite **3** (*abeja, avispa*) to sting **4** (*comer*): *¿Te apetece ~ algo?* Do you fancy something to eat? ◊ *Acabo de ~ un poco de queso.* I've just had some cheese. ◊ *Nos pusieron unas cosas para ~.* They gave us some nibbles. ◆ *vt* **1** (*carne*) to mince **2** (*cebolla, verdura*) to chop *sth* (up) ◆ *vi* **1** (*producir picor*) to itch: *Este jersey pica.* This jumper makes me itch. **2** (*ojos*) to sting: *Me pican los ojos.* My eyes are stinging. **3** (*pez*) to bite: *¡Ha picado uno!* I've got a bite! **4** (*ser picante*) to be hot: *¡Esta salsa pica muchísimo!* This sauce is terribly hot! **5** (*caer en la trampa*) to fall for it: *Le conté una mentira y picó.* I told him a lie and he fell for it. ◆ **picarse** *v pron* **1** (*diente, fruta*) to go bad **2** (*vino, nata*) to go off **3 picarse (con) (por)** (*enfadarse*) to get annoyed **(with** *sb*) **(about** *sth*): *Se pica* *por todo.* He's always getting annoyed about something. LOC *Ver* BICHO, MOSCA

picardía *nf* craftiness: *tener mucha* ~ to be very crafty ◊ *Tienes que hacerlo con* ~. You have to be crafty.

pichón *nm* young pigeon

picnic *nm* picnic: *ir de* ~ to go for a picnic

pico *nm* **1** (*pájaro*) beak **2** (*montaña*) peak: *los* ~*s cubiertos de nieve* the snow-covered peaks **3** (*herramienta*) pick LOC **y pico 1** (*gen*) odd: *dos mil y* ~ *pesetas/personas* two thousand odd pesetas/people ◊ *Tiene treinta y* ~ *años.* He's thirty something. **2** (*hora*) just after: *Eran las dos y* ~. It was just after two. *Ver tb* CERRAR, CUELLO, ESCOTE[1]

picor *nm* **1** (*picazón*) itch: *Tengo* ~ *en la espalda.* I've got an itchy back. **2** (*escozor*) stinging **3** (*garganta*) tickle

picotazo *nm* **1** (*mosquito*) bite **2** (*abeja, avispa*) sting: *No te muevas o te pegará un* ~. Don't move or it'll sting you. **3** (*pájaro*) peck

pie *nm* **1** (*gen*) foot [*pl* feet]: *el* ~ *derecho/izquierdo* your right/left foot ◊ *tener los* ~*s planos* to have flat feet **2** (*estatua, columna*) pedestal **3** (*copa*) stem **4** (*lámpara*) stand LOC **al pie de la letra** word for word **andar(se) con pies de plomo** to tread carefully **a pie** on foot **de pies a cabeza** from top to toe **estar de pie** to be standing (up) **hacer pie**: *No hago* ~. My feet don't touch the bottom. **no tener ni pies ni cabeza** to be absurd **ponerse de pie** to stand up *Ver tb* COJEAR, LÁMPARA, LEVANTAR, MANTENER, PLANTA

piedad *nf* **1** (*compasión*) mercy (*on sb*): *Señor ten* ~. Lord have mercy. **2** (*devoción*) piety **3** (*imagen, escultura*) pietà

piedra *nf* stone: *una pared de* ~ a stone wall ◊ *una* ~ *preciosa* a precious stone LOC **quedarse de piedra** to be speechless *Ver tb* TIRO

piel *nf* **1** (*Anat*) skin: *tener la* ~ *blanca/morena* to have fair/dark skin **2** (*con pelo*) fur: *un abrigo de* ~*es* a fur coat **3** (*cuero*) leather: *una cartera de* ~ a leather wallet **4** (*fruta*) **(a)** (*gen*) skin: *Quítale la* ~ *a las uvas.* Peel the grapes. **(b)** (*patata, cítricos*) peel LOC **piel de gallina** goose-pimples: *Se me puso la* ~ *de gallina.* I got goose-pimples.

pienso *nm* **1** (*para ganado*) fodder **2** (*para perros*) dried dog food

pierna *nf* leg: *romperse una* ~ to break your leg ◊ *cruzar/estirar las* ~*s* to cross/stretch your legs LOC **con las piernas cruzadas** cross-legged

pieza *nf* **1** (*gen, Ajedrez, Mús*) piece **2** (*Mec*) part: *una* ~ *de recambio* a spare part LOC **quedarse de una pieza** to be speechless

pigmento *nm* pigment

pijama *nm* pyjamas [*pl*]: *Ese* ~ *te queda pequeño.* Those pyjamas are too small for you. ☛Nótese que *un pijama* se dice **a pair of pyjamas**: *Mete dos* ~*s en la maleta.* Pack two pairs of pyjamas.

pijo, -a ◆ *adj* posh: *la zona pija de la ciudad* the posh part of the city ◆ *adj, nm-nf* snob [*n*]: *No puede ser más* ~. He is a real snob. LOC *Ver* NIÑO

pila *nf* **1** (*montón*) pile: *una* ~ *de periódicos* a pile of newspapers **2** (*gran cantidad*): *Tienen la* ~ *de dinero.* They've got loads of money. ◊ *Ese tío tiene ya una* ~ *de años.* That bloke's getting on. **3** (*Electrón*) battery [*pl* batteries]: *Se han acabado las* ~*s.* The batteries have run out. **4** (*fregadero*) sink LOC *Ver* NOMBRE

pilar *nm* pillar

píldora *nf* pill: *¿Estás tomando la* ~*?* Are you on the pill?

pillaje *nm* plunder

pillar ◆ *vt* **1** (*gen*) to catch: *¡A que no me pillas!* I bet you can't catch me! ◊ ~ *una pulmonía* to catch pneumonia ◊ *Pillé a un chaval robando manzanas.* I caught a boy stealing apples. **2** (*atropellar*) to run *sb* over: *Le pilló un coche.* He was run over by a car. ◆ **pillarse** *v pron* **pillarse (con/en)** to get *sth* caught (**in** *sth*): *Me pillé el dedo en la puerta.* I got my finger caught in the door. LOC **pillar cerca/lejos de algo** to be near sth/a long way from sth: *El colegio me pilla muy cerca de casa.* My school is very near my house. *Ver tb* CAMINO, DESPREVENIDO, MANO

pilotar *vt* **1** (*avión*) to fly **2** (*coche*) to drive

piloto *nmf* **1** (*avión*) pilot **2** (*coche*) racing driver LOC **piloto automático** automatic pilot: *El avión iba con el* ~ *automático.* The plane was on automatic pilot.

pimentón *nm* paprika

pimienta *nf* pepper

pimiento *nm* pepper LOC **pimiento morrón** red pepper *Ver tb* COLORADO, IMPORTAR[2]

pimpón *nm* ping-pong

pinar *nm* pine wood

pincel *nm* paintbrush

pinchadiscos *nmf* disc jockey [*pl* disc jockeys] (*abrev* DJ)

pinchar ◆ *vt* **1** (*gen*) to prick: ~ *a algn con un alfiler* to prick sb with a pin **2** (*balón, neumático*) to puncture **3** (*Med*) to give *sb* an injection ◆ *vi* **1** (*planta espinosa*) to be prickly: *Ten cuidado que pinchan.* Be careful, they're very prickly. **2** (*tener un pinchazo*) to have a puncture: *He pinchado dos veces en una semana.* I've had two punctures in a week. ◆ **pincharse** *v pron* **1** (*neumático*) to puncture: *Se me ha pinchado una rueda.* I've got a puncture. **2** **pincharse (con)** to prick yourself **(on/ with *sth*)**: *~se con una aguja* to prick yourself on/with a needle

pinchazo *nm* puncture: *arreglar un ~* to mend a puncture

pincho *nm* **1** (*punta aguda*) spike: *Ese cardo tiene ~s.* That thistle's got spikes. **2** (*aperitivo*): *tomar un ~* to have a snack ◊ *un ~ de tortilla* a portion of Spanish omelette LOC **pincho moruno** kebab

ping-pong *nm Ver* PIMPÓN

pingüino *nm* penguin

pino *nm* pine (tree) LOC **hacer el pino** to do a handstand *Ver tb* QUINTO

pinta *nf* **1** (*aspecto*) look: *No me gusta la ~ de ese pescado.* I don't like the look of that fish. **2** (*medida*) pint ☛ *Ver* Apéndice 1. LOC **tener pinta (de)** to look (like *sth*): *Con ese traje tienes ~ de payaso.* You look like a clown in that suit. ◊ *Estos pasteles tienen muy buena ~.* Those cakes look very nice.

pintada *nf* graffiti [*incontable*]: *Había ~s por toda la pared.* There was graffiti all over the wall. ◊ *Había una ~ que decía…* There was graffiti saying…

pintado, -a *pp, adj* LOC **ir/sentar/venir que ni pintado** to be perfect: *Ese trabajo me va que ni ~.* A job like that is just perfect for me. **pintado de** painted: *Las paredes están pintadas de azul.* The walls are painted blue. *Ver tb* RECIÉN; *Ver tb* PINTAR

pintar ◆ *vt, vi* to paint: ~ *una pared de rojo* to paint a wall red ◊ *Me gusta ~.* I like painting. ◆ *vt* (*colorear*) to colour *sth* (in): *El niño había pintado la casa de azul.* The little boy had coloured the house blue. ◊ *Dibujó una pelota y luego la pintó.* He drew a ball and then coloured it in. ◆ *vi* to write: *Este boli no pinta.* This pen doesn't write. ◆ **pintarse** *v pron* **1** (*gen*) to paint: *~se las uñas* to paint your nails **2** (*maquillarse*) to put on your make-up: *No he tenido tiempo de ~me.* I haven't had time to put on my make-up. LOC **pintar al óleo/a la acuarela** to paint in oils/ watercolours **pintarse los labios/ojos** to put on your lipstick/eye make-up

pintor, ~a *nm-nf* painter

pintoresco, -a *adj* picturesque: *un paisaje ~* a picturesque landscape

pintura *nf* **1** (*gen*) painting: *La ~ es una de mis aficiones.* Painting is one of my hobbies. **2** (*producto*) paint: *una mano de ~* a coat of paint **3** **pinturas** (*lápices de colores*) coloured pencils LOC *Ver* ÓLEO

pinza *nf* **1** (*para tender*) clothes-peg **2** (*de pelo*) clip **3** (*cangrejo, langosta*) pincer **4** **pinzas** **(a)** (*gen*) tweezers: *unas ~s para las cejas* tweezers **(b)** (*azúcar, hielo, carbón*) tongs

piña *nf* **1** (*pino*) pine cone **2** (*fruta tropical*) pineapple

piñón *nm* (*Bot*) pine nut

pío *nm* (*sonido*) tweet LOC **no decir ni pío** not to open your mouth

piojo *nm* louse [*pl* lice]

pionero, -a ◆ *adj* pioneering ◆ *nm-nf* pioneer (***in sth***): *un ~ de la cirugía estética* a pioneer in cosmetic surgery

pipa *nf* **1** (*para fumar*) pipe: *fumar en ~* to smoke a pipe ◊ *la ~ de la paz* the pipe of peace **2** (*semilla de girasol*) sunflower seed

pipeta *nf* pipette

pique *nm* (*enfado*) quarrel: *Siempre están de ~.* They're always quarrelling. LOC **irse a pique** (*negocio*) to go bust

piquete *nmf* picket

pirado, -a *pp, adj* nuts: *estar ~* to be nuts *Ver tb* PIRARSE

piragua *nf* canoe

piragüismo *nm* canoeing: *hacer ~* to go canoeing

pirámide *nf* pyramid

pirarse *v pron* to clear off LOC **pirárselas** to leg it

pirata *adj, nmf* pirate [*n*]: *un barco/una emisora ~* a pirate boat/radio station

piratear *vt* **1** (*disco, vídeo*) to pirate **2** (*entrar en un sistema informático*) to hack **into *sth***

pirómano, -a *nm-nf* arsonist

piropo *nm* **1** (*cumplido*) compliment **2** (*en la calle*): *echar un ~* to whistle at sb

pirueta *nf* pirouette

pirulí *nm* lollipop

pis *nm* pee LOC **hacer pis** to have a pee

pisada *nf* **1** (*sonido*) footstep **2** (*huella*) footprint

pisar ◆ *vt* **1** (*gen*) to step **on/in** ***sth***: *~le el pie a algn* to step on sb's foot ◊ *~ un charco* to step in a puddle **2** (*tierra*) to tread *sth* down **3** (*acelerador, freno*) to put your foot **on** ***sth*** **4** (*dominar*) to walk all over *sb*: *No te dejes ~.* Don't let people walk all over you. **5** (*idea*) to pinch: *~le a algn una idea* to pinch an idea from sb ◆ *vi* to tread LOC *Ver* PROHIBIDO

piscina *nf* swimming pool LOC **piscina climatizada/cubierta** heated/indoor pool

piscis (*tb* **Piscis**) *nm, nmf* Pisces ☛ *Ver ejemplos en* AQUARIUS

piso *nm* **1** (*suelo, planta*) floor: *Vivo en el tercer ~.* I live on the third floor. **2** (*apartamento*) flat LOC **de dos, etc pisos** (*edificio*) two-storey, etc: *un bloque de cinco ~s* a five-storey block *Ver tb* COMPAÑERO

pisotear *vt* **1** (*pisar*) to stamp **on** ***sth*** **2** (*fig*) to trample **on** ***sth***: *~ los derechos de algn* to trample on sb's rights

pisotón *nm* LOC **dar un pisotón a algn** to tread on sb's foot

pista *nf* **1** (*huella*) track(s) [*se usa mucho en plural*]: *seguir la ~ de un animal* to follow an animal's tracks ◊ *Le he perdido la ~ a Manolo.* I've lost track of Manolo. **2** (*dato*) clue: *Dame más ~s.* Give me more clues. **3** (*carreras*) track: *una ~ al aire libre/cubierta* an outdoor/indoor track **4** (*Aeronáut*) runway [*pl* runways] LOC **estar sobre la pista de algn** to be on sb's trail **pista de baile** dance floor **pista de esquí** ski slope **pista de hielo/patinaje** ice rink/ skating-rink **pista de squash/tenis** squash/tennis court

pistacho *nm* pistachio [*pl* pistachios]

pistola *nf* gun, pistol (*téc*) LOC **pistola de aire comprimido** airgun *Ver tb* PUNTA

pitar ◆ *vt* (*abuchear*) to boo ◆ *vi* **1** (*policía, árbitro*) to blow your whistle (**at** ***sth/sb***): *El guardia nos pitó.* The policeman blew his whistle at us. **2** (*claxon*) to hoot (**at** ***sth/sb***): *El conductor me pitó.* The driver hooted at me. LOC **irse/salir pitando** to dash off **pitar un penalty/una falta** to award a penalty/free kick

pitido *nm* **1** (*tren, árbitro, policía*) whistle: *los ~s del tren* the whistle of the train **2** (*claxon*) hoot **3** (*despertador*) ring

pito *nm* whistle LOC **entre pitos y flautas** what with one thing and another

pitón *nm* python

pizarra *nf* **1** (*en una clase*) blackboard: *salir a la ~* to go out to the blackboard **2** (*roca*) slate: *un tejado de ~* a slate roof

pizca *nf*: *una ~ de sal* a pinch of salt ◊ *una ~ de humor* a touch of humour LOC **ni pizca**: *Hoy no hace ni ~ de frío.* It's not at all cold today. ◊ *No tiene ni ~ de gracia.* It's not the least bit funny.

pizza *nf* pizza

placa *nf* **1** (*lámina, Fot, Geol*) plate: *~s de acero* steel plates ◊ *La ~ de la puerta dice "dentista".* The plate on the door says 'dentist'. **2** (*conmemorativa*) plaque: *una ~ conmemorativa* a commemorative plaque **3** (*policía*) badge

placer *nm* pleasure: *un viaje de ~* a pleasure trip ◊ *Tengo el ~ de presentarles al Dr García.* It is my pleasure to introduce Dr García.

plaga *nf* plague: *una ~ de mosquitos* a plague of mosquitoes

plan *nm* **1** (*gen*) plan: *He cambiado de ~es.* I've changed my plans. ◊ *¿Tienes ~ para el sábado?* Have you got anything planned for Saturday? **2** (*humor*): *Si sigues en ese ~, me voy.* If you're going to carry on like this, I'm going. LOC **plan de estudios** curriculum [*pl* curriculums/curricula]

plancha *nf* (*electrodoméstico*) iron LOC **a la plancha** grilled

planchar ◆ *vt* to iron: *~ una camisa* to iron a shirt ◆ *vi* to do the ironing: *Hoy me toca ~.* I've got to do the ironing today.

planear¹ *vt* (*organizar*) to plan: *~ la fuga* to plan your escape

planear² *vi* (*avión, pájaro*) to glide

planeta *nm* planet

planificación *nf* planning

plano, -a ◆ *adj* flat: *una superficie plana* a flat surface ◆ *nm* **1** (*nivel*) level: *Las casas están construidas en distintos ~s.* The houses are built on different levels. ◊ *en el ~ personal* on a personal level **2** (*diagrama*) **(a)** (*ciudad, metro*) map **(b)** (*Arquit*) plan **3** (*Cine*) shot LOC *Ver* PRIMERO

planta *nf* **1** (*Bot*) plant **2** (*piso*) floor: *Vivo en la ~ baja.* I live on the ground floor. LOC **planta del pie** sole

plantación *nf* plantation

plantado, -a *pp, adj* LOC **dejar plantado** to stand *sb* up *Ver tb* PLANTAR

plantar *vt* **1** (*gen*) to plant **2** (*dar plantón*) to stand *sb* up

planteamiento *nm* formulation

plantear ◆ *vt* to raise: ~ *dudas/preguntas* to raise doubts/questions ◊ *El libro plantea temas muy importantes.* The book raises very important issues. ◆ **plantearse** *v pron* to think **(about sth/doing sth)**: *¡Eso ni me lo planteo!* I don't even think about that!

plantilla *nf* **1** (*zapato*) insole **2** (*para dibujar*) template **3** (*personal*) staff [*v sing o pl*]

plástico, -a ◆ *adj* plastic: *la cirujía plástica* plastic surgery ◆ *nm* plastic [*gen incontable*]: *un envase de* ~ a plastic container ◊ *Tápalo con un* ~. Cover it with a plastic sheet. LOC *Ver* VASO

plastificar *vt* to laminate

plastilina *nf* plasticine®

plata *nf* silver: *un anillo de* ~ a silver ring LOC *Ver* BAÑADO, BODA

plataforma *nf* platform

plátano *nm* **1** (*fruta*) banana **2** (*árbol*) plane tree

plateado, -a *pp, adj* **1** (*color*) silver: *pintura plateada* silver paint **2** (*revestido de plata*) silver-plated

platillo *nm* **1** (*taza*) saucer **2 platillos** cymbals LOC **platillo volante** flying saucer *Ver tb* BOMBO

platino *nm* platinum

plato *nm* **1** (*utensilio*) **(a)** (*gen*) plate: *¡Ya se ha roto otro* ~*!* There goes another plate! **(b)** (*para debajo de la taza*) saucer **2** (*guiso*) dish: *un* ~ *típico del país* a national dish **3** (*parte de la comida*) course: *De primer* ~ *comí sopa.* I had soup for my first course. ◊ *el* ~ *fuerte* the main course LOC **plato hondo/sopero** soup plate **plato llano/de postre** dinner/dessert plate *Ver tb* FREGAR, SECAR

plató *nm* set LOC **salir al plató** to go/come onto the stage

playa *nf* beach: *Pasamos el verano en la* ~. We spent the summer on the beach.

playeras *nf* **1** (*gen*) canvas shoes **2** (*para deporte*) trainers

plaza *nf* **1** (*espacio abierto*) square: *la* ~ *mayor* the main square **2** (*mercado*) market (place) **3** (*asiento*) seat: *¿Queda alguna* ~ *en el autobús?* Are there any seats left on the bus? **4** (*puesto de trabajo*) post **5** (*en un curso*) place: *Ya no quedan* ~*s.* There are no places left. LOC **plaza de toros** bullring

plazo *nm* **1** (*periodo*): *el* ~ *de matrícula* the enrolment period ◊ *Tenemos un mes de* ~ *para pagar.* We've got a month to pay. ◊ *El* ~ *vence mañana.* The deadline is tomorrow. **2** (*pago*) instalment: *pagar algo a* ~*s* to pay for sth in instalments LOC *Ver* COMPRAR

plegable *adj* folding: *una cama* ~ a folding bed

plegar *vt* to fold

pleito *nm* lawsuit

pleno, -a *adj* full: *Soy miembro de* ~ *derecho.* I'm a full member. ◊ ~*s poderes* full powers LOC **a plena luz del día** in broad daylight **en pleno...** (right) in the middle of...: *en* ~ *invierno* in the middle of winter ◊ *en* ~ *centro de la ciudad* right in the centre of the city **estar en plena forma** to be in peak condition

pliegue *nm* **1** (*gen*) fold: *La tela caía formando* ~*s.* The material hung in folds. **2** (*falda*) pleat

plomo *nm* **1** (*metal*) lead **2 plomos** fuses: *Se han fundido los* ~*s.* The fuses have blown. LOC *Ver* GASOLINA, PIE

pluma *nf* **1** (*gen*) feather: *un colchón de* ~*s* a feather mattress **2** (*estilográfica*) fountain pen **3 plumas** (*prenda de abrigo*) ski jacket

plumero *nm* feather duster

plumífero *nm* (*prenda*) ski jacket

plural *adj, nm* plural

Plutón *nm* Pluto

plutonio *nm* plutonium

población *nf* **1** (*conjunto de personas*) population: *la* ~ *activa* the working population **2** (*localidad*) **(a)** (*ciudad grande*) city [*pl* cities] **(b)** (*ciudad pequeña*) town **(c)** (*pueblo*) village

poblado *nm* village

pobre ◆ *adj* poor ◆ *nmf* **1** (*gen*) poor man/woman [*pl* poor men/women]: *los ricos y los* ~*s* the rich and the poor **2** (*desgraciado*) poor thing: *¡Pobre! Tiene hambre.* He's hungry, poor thing!

pobreza *nf* poverty

pocilga *nf* pigsty [*pl* pigsties]

poco, -a ◆ *adj* **1** (+ *sustantivo incontable*) little, not much (*más coloq*): *Tienen muy* ~ *interés.* They have very little interest. ◊ *Tengo* ~ *dinero.* I don't have much money. **2** (+ *sustantivo contable*) few, not many (*más coloq*): *en muy* *pocas ocasiones* on very few occasions ◊ *Tiene ~s amigos.* He hasn't got many friends. ☛ *Ver nota en* LESS ◆ *pron* little [*pl* few]: *Vinieron muy ~s.* Very few came. ◆ *adv* **1** (*gen*) not much: *Come ~ para lo alto que está.* He doesn't eat much for his height. **2** (*poco tiempo*) not long: *La vi hace ~.* I saw her not long ago/recently. **3** (+ *adj*) not very: *Es ~ inteligente.* He's not very intelligent. LOC **a poco de** shortly after: *a ~ de irte* shortly after you left **poco a poco** gradually **poco más/menos (de)** just over/under: *~ menos de 5.000 personas* just under 5000 people **por poco** nearly: *Por ~ me atropellan.* I was nearly run over. **un poco** a little, a bit (*más coloq*): *un ~ más/mejor* a little more/better ◊ *un ~ de azúcar* a bit of sugar ◊ *Espera un ~.* Wait a bit. **unos pocos** a few: *unos ~s claveles* a few carnations ◊ *—¿Cuántos quieres? —Dame unos ~s.* 'How many would you like?' 'Just a few.' ☛Para otras expresiones con **poco**, véanse las entradas del sustantivo, adjetivo, etc, p.ej. **ser poca cosa** en COSA y **al poco tiempo** en TIEMPO. ☛ *Ver nota en* FEW

podar *vt* to prune

poder[1] *vt, vi* **1** (*gen*) can ***do sth***, to be able ***to do sth***: *Puedo escoger Londres o Madrid.* I can choose London or Madrid. ◊ *No podía creérmelo.* I couldn't believe it. ◊ *Desde entonces no ha podido andar.* He hasn't been able to walk since then. ☛ *Ver nota en* CAN[2] **2** (*tener permiso*) can, may (*más formal*): *¿Puedo hablar con Andrés?* Can I talk to Andrés? ☛ *Ver nota en* MAY **3** (*probabilidad*) may, could, might

> El uso de **may**, **could**, **might** depende del grado de probabilidad de realizarse la acción: **could** y **might** expresan menor probabilidad que **may**: *Pueden llegar en cualquier momento.* They may arrive at any minute. ◊ *Podría ser peligroso.* It could/might be dangerous.

LOC **no poder más** (*estar cansado*) to be exhausted **poder con** to cope with *sth*: *No puedo con tantos deberes.* I can't cope with so much homework. **puede (que ...)** maybe: *Puede que sí, puede que no.* Maybe, maybe not. **se puede/no se puede**: *¿Se puede?* May I come in? ◊ *No se puede fumar aquí.* You can't smoke in here. ☛Para otras expresiones con **poder**, véanse las entradas del sustantivo, adjetivo, etc, p.ej. **a más no poder** en MÁS y **sálvese quien pueda** en SALVAR.

poder[2] *nm* power: *tomar el ~* to seize power LOC **el poder ejecutivo/judicial/legislativo** the executive/judiciary/legislature

poderoso, -a *adj* powerful

podrido, -a *pp, adj* rotten: *una manzana/sociedad podrida* a rotten apple/society

poema *nm* poem

poesía *nf* **1** (*gen*) poetry: *la ~ épica* epic poetry **2** (*poema*) poem

poeta *nmf* poet

poético, -a *adj* poetic

poetisa *nf* poet

polaco, -a ◆ *adj, nm* Polish: *hablar ~* to speak Polish ◆ *nm-nf* Pole: *los ~s* the Poles

polar *adj* polar LOC *Ver* CÍRCULO

polea *nf* pulley [*pl* pulleys]

polémico, -a ◆ *adj* controversial ◆ **polémica** *nf* controversy [*pl* controversies]

polen *nm* pollen

poli ◆ *nmf* cop ◆ *nf* cops [*pl*]: *Viene la ~.* The cops are coming.

policía ◆ *nmf* policeman/woman [*pl* policemen/women] ◆ *nf* police [*pl*]: *La ~ está investigando el caso.* The police are investigating the case. LOC *Ver* MUNICIPAL, PAREJA, URBANO

policiaco, -a (*tb* **policíaco, -a**) *adj* LOC *Ver* GÉNERO, NOVELA, PELÍCULA

policial *adj* LOC *Ver* CORDÓN, FICHA

polideportivo *nm* sports centre

polígono *nm* **1** (*Geom*) polygon **2** (*zona*) estate: *un ~ industrial* an industrial estate

polilla *nf* moth

politécnico, -a *adj* polytechnic

política *nf* **1** (*Pol*) politics [*sing*]: *meterse en ~* to get involved in politics **2** (*postura, programa*) policy [*pl* policies]: *la ~ exterior* foreign policy

político, -a ◆ *adj* **1** (*Pol*) political: *un partido ~* a political party **2** (*diplomático*) diplomatic **3** (*familia*) in-law: *padre ~* father-in-law ◊ *mi familia política* my in-laws ◆ *nm-nf* politician: *un ~ de izquierdas* a left-wing politician

póliza *nf* **1** (*seguros*) policy [*pl* policies]: *hacerse una ~* to take out a policy **2** (*sello*) stamp

polizón *nmf* stowaway [*pl* stowaways]: *colarse de ~* to stow away

pollito (*tb* **polluelo**) *nm* chick

pollo *nm* chicken: ~ *asado* roast chicken

polo *nm* **1** (*Geog, Fís*) pole: *el ~ Norte/Sur* the North/South Pole **2** (*helado*) ice lolly [*pl* ice lollies] **3** (*camisa*) polo shirt LOC **ser polos opuestos** (*carácter*) to be like chalk and cheese

Polonia *nf* Poland

polución *nf* pollution

polvareda *nf* cloud of dust: *levantar una ~* to raise a cloud of dust

polvo *nm* **1** (*suciedad*) dust: *Hay mucho ~ en la librería.* There's a lot of dust on the bookshelf. ◊ *Estás levantando ~.* You're kicking up the dust. **2** (*Cocina, Quím*) powder **3 polvos** (*tocador*) powder [*incontable, v sing*] LOC **estar hecho polvo** (*cansado*) to be shattered **limpiar/quitar el polvo (a/de)** to dust (*sth*) **polvos de picapica** itching powder [*incontable, v sing*] **polvos de talco** talcum powder [*incontable, v sing*] *Ver tb* LECHE, TRAPO

pólvora *nf* gunpowder

polvoriento, -a *adj* dusty

polvorín *nm* (*almacén*) magazine

pomada *nf* ointment

pomelo *nm* grapefruit [*pl* grapefruit/grapefruits]

pomo *nm* **1** (*puerta*) doorknob **2** (*cajón*) knob

pompa *nf* **1** (*burbuja*) bubble: *hacer ~s de jabón* to blow bubbles **2** (*solemnidad*) pomp LOC **pompas fúnebres 1** (*entierro*) funeral [*sing*] **2** (*funeraria*) undertaker's

pompis *nm* bottom

pomposo, -a *adj* pompous: *un lenguaje retórico y ~* rhetorical, pompous language

pómulo *nm* cheekbone

poner ◆ *vt* **1** (*colocar*) to put: *Pon los libros sobre la mesa/en una caja.* Put the books on the table/in a box. **2** (*aparato*) to put *sth* on: *~ la radio* to put on the radio **3** (*disco*) to play **4** (*reloj*) to set: *Pon el despertador a las seis.* Set the alarm for six. **5** (*vestir*) to put *sth* on (**for sb**): *Ponle la bufanda a tu hermano.* Put your brother's scarf on for him. **6** (*servir*) to give: *Ponme un poco más de sopa.* Give me some more soup please. **7** (*huevos*) to lay **8** (*deberes*) to set **9** (*película, programa*) to show: *¿Qué ponen esta noche?* What's on tonight? **10** (*obra de teatro*) to put *a play* on **11** (*sábana, mantel*) to put *sth* on: *Pon el mantel/la sábana.* Put the tablecloth on the table./Put the sheet on the bed. ◆ **ponerse** *v pron* **1** (*de pie*) to stand: *Ponte a mi lado.* Stand next to me. **2** (*sentado*) to sit **3** (*vestirse*) to put *sth* on: *¿Qué me pongo?* What shall I put on? **4** (*sol*) to set **5 + adj** to get: *Se puso enfermo.* He got ill. ◊ *¡No te pongas chulo conmigo!* Don't get cheeky with me! **6 ponerse a** to start ***doing sth/to do sth***: *Se ha puesto a nevar.* It's started snowing. ◊ *Ponte a estudiar.* Get on with some work. **7 ponerse de** to get covered **in *sth***: *¡Cómo te has puesto de pintura!* You're covered in paint! ☛Para expresiones con **poner**, véanse las entradas del sustantivo, adjetivo, etc, p.ej. **poner pegas** en PEGA y **ponerse rojo** en ROJO.

poni (*tb* **poney**) *nm* pony [*pl* ponies]

pontífice *nm* pontiff: *el Sumo Pontífice* the Supreme Pontiff

popa *nf* stern

popular *adj* popular

por *prep*

- **lugar 1** (*con verbos de movimiento*): *circular por la derecha/izquierda* to drive on the right/left ◊ *¿Pasas por una farmacia?* Are you going past a chemist's? ◊ *pasar por el centro de París* to go through the centre of Paris ◊ *Pasaré por tu casa mañana.* I'll drop in tomorrow. ◊ *viajar por Europa* to travel round Europe **2** (*con verbos como coger, agarrar*) by: *Lo cogí por el brazo.* I grabbed him by the arm.
- **tiempo 1** (*tiempo determinado*): *por la mañana/tarde* in the morning/afternoon ◊ *por la noche* at night ◊ *mañana por la mañana/noche* tomorrow morning/night **2** (*duración*) for: *sólo por unos días* only for a few days ☛*Ver nota en* FOR
- **causa**: *Se suspende por el mal tiempo.* It's been cancelled because of bad weather. ◊ *hacer algo por dinero* to do sth for money ◊ *Lo despidieron por robar/vago.* He was sacked for stealing/being lazy.
- **finalidad**: *Por ti haría cualquier cosa.* I'd do anything for you. ◊ *por ver las noticias* to watch the news ◊ *por no perderlo* so as not to miss it
- **agente** by: *firmado por…* signed by… ◊ *pintado por El Greco* painted by El Greco
- **hacia/en favor de** for: *sentir cariño*

por algn to feel affection for sb ◊ *¡Vote por nosotros!* Vote for us!

• **con expresiones numéricas**: *4 por 3 son 12.* 4 times 3 is 12. ◊ *Mide 7 por 2.* It measures 7 by 2. ◊ *50 libras por hora* 50 pounds an/per hour

• **otras construcciones 1** (*medio, instrumento*): *por correo/mar/avión* by post/sea/air **2** (*sustitución*): *Ella irá por mí.* She'll go instead of me. ◊ *Lo compré por dos millones.* I bought it for two million pesetas. **3** (*sucesión*) by: *uno por uno* one by one ◊ *paso por paso* step by step **4 + adj/adv** however: *Por simple que...* However simple... ◊ *Por mucho que trabajes...* However much you work... LOC **por mí** as far as I am, you are, etc concerned **por qué** why: *No dijo por qué no venía.* He didn't say why he wasn't coming. ◊ *¿Por qué no?* Why not? **por que** (*finalidad*) *ver* PORQUE

porcelana *nf* porcelain

porcentaje *nm* percentage

porcino, -a *adj* LOC *Ver* GANADO

pornografía *nf* pornography

pornográfico, -a *adj* pornographic

poro *nm* pore

poroso, -a *adj* porous

porque *conj* **1** (*razón*) because: *No viene ~ no quiere.* He's not coming because he doesn't want to. **2** (*finalidad*) so (that): *Vine ~ tuvieses compañía.* I came so (that) you'd have company.

porqué *nm* ~ **(de)** reason **(for *sth*)**: *el ~ de la huelga* the reason for the strike LOC **¿por qué?** *ver* POR

porquería *nf* **1** (*suciedad*): *En esta cocina hay mucha ~.* This kitchen is filthy. **2** (*golosina*) junk (food) [*incontable, v sing*]: *Deja de comer ~s.* Stop eating junk food.

porra *nf* (*de policía*) truncheon LOC *Ver* MANDAR

porrazo *nm* LOC *Ver* GOLPE

porro *nm* joint

portaaviones *nm* aircraft carrier

portada *nf* **1** (*libro, revista*) cover **2** (*disco*) sleeve

portafolios *nm* folder

portal *nm* (entrance) hall

portarse *v pron* to behave: *~ bien/mal* to behave well/badly ◊ *Pórtate bien.* Be good.

portátil *adj* portable: *una televisión ~* a portable television

portavoz *nmf* spokesperson [*pl* spokespersons/spokespeople]

> Existen las formas **spokesman** y **spokeswoman**, pero se prefiere usar **spokesperson** porque se refiere tanto a un hombre como a una mujer: *los portavoces de la oposición* spokespersons for the opposition.

portazo *nm* bang LOC **dar un portazo** to slam the door *Ver tb* CERRAR

portería *nf* **1** (*garita*) porter's lodge **2** (*Dep*) goal

portero, -a *nm-nf* **1** (*de un edificio público*) caretaker **2** (*de un edificio privado*) porter **3** (*Dep*) goalkeeper

Portugal *nm* Portugal

portugués, -esa ◆ *adj, nm* Portuguese: *hablar ~* to speak Portuguese. ◆ *nm-nf* Portuguese man/woman [*pl* Portuguese men/women]: *los portugueses* the Portuguese

porvenir *nm* future: *tener un buen ~* to have a good future ahead of you

posar ◆ *vi* (*para una foto*) to pose ◆ **posarse** *v pron* **1 posarse (en/sobre)** (*aves, insectos*) to land **(on *sth*) 2** (*polvo, sedimento*) to settle **(on *sth*)**

posavasos *nm* coaster

posdata *nf* postscript (*abrev* PS)

poseer *vt* (*ser dueño*) to own

posesivo, -a *adj* possessive

posibilidad *nf* possibility [*pl* possibilities] LOC **tener (muchas) posibilidades de...** to have a (good) chance of *doing sth*

posible *adj* **1** (*gen*) possible: *Es ~ que ya hayan llegado.* It's possible that they've already arrived. **2** (*potencial*) potential: *un ~ accidente* a potential accident LOC **hacer (todo) lo posible por/para** to do your best *to do sth Ver tb* ANTES, MEJOR

posición *nf* position: *Terminaron en última ~.* They finished last.

positivo, -a *adj* positive: *La prueba dio positiva.* The test was positive.

poso *nm* (*sedimento*) dregs [*pl*]

postal ◆ *adj* postal ◆ *nf* postcard LOC *Ver* CÓDIGO, GIRO

poste *nm* **1** (*gen*) pole: *~ telegráfico* telegraph pole **2** (*Dep*) (goal)post: *El balón dio en el ~.* The ball hit the post.

póster *nm* poster

posterior *adj* ~ **(a) 1** (*tiempo*): *un suceso ~* a subsequent event ◊ *los años ~es a la guerra* the years after the war **2** (*lugar*): *en la parte ~ del autocar* at the back of the bus ◊ *la fila ~ a la vuestra* the row behind yours

postizo, -a *adj* false: *dentadura postiza* false teeth

postre *nm* dessert, pudding (*más coloq*): *¿Qué hay de ~?* What's for pudding? ◊ *De ~ me tomé una tarta.* I had cake for dessert. LOC *Ver* PLATO

postura *nf* **1** (*del cuerpo*) position: *dormir en mala ~* to sleep in an awkward position **2** (*actitud*) stance

potable *adj* drinkable LOC *Ver* AGUA

potaje *nm* (*de garbanzos*) chickpea stew

potencia *nf* power: *~ atómica/económica* atomic/economic power ◊ *una ~ de 80 vatios* 80 watts of power LOC **de alta/gran potencia** powerful **potencia (en caballos)** horsepower [*pl* horsepower] (*abrev* hp)

potente *adj* powerful

potra *nf* LOC **tener potra** to be jammy: *¡Qué ~ tienes!* You're so jammy! *Ver tb* POTRO

potro, -a ◆ *nm-nf* foal

Foal es el sustantivo genérico. Para referirnos sólo al macho decimos **colt**. **Filly** se refiere sólo a la hembra y su plural es 'fillies'.

◆ *nm* (*Gimnasia*) vaulting horse

pozo *nm* well: *un ~ de petróleo* an oil well

práctica *nf* **1** (*gen*) practice: *En teoría funciona, pero en la ~...* It's all right in theory, but in practice... ◊ *poner algo en ~* to put sth into practice **2** (*Educ*) practical

prácticamente *adv* practically

practicante ◆ *adj* practising: *Soy católico ~.* I'm a practising Catholic. ◆ *nmf* nurse

practicar *vt* **1** (*gen*) to practise: *~ la medicina* to practise medicine **2** (*deporte*) to play: *¿Practicas algún deporte?* Do you play any sports?

práctico, -a *adj* practical

pradera *nf* meadow

prado *nm* meadow

preámbulo *nm* **1** (*prólogo*) introduction **2** (*rodeos*): *Déjate de ~s.* Stop beating about the bush.

precaución *nf* precaution: *tomar precauciones contra incendios* to take precautions against fire LOC **con precaución** carefully: *Circulen con ~.* Drive carefully. **por precaución** as a precaution

preceder *vt* ~ **a** to precede, to go/come before *sth/sb* (*más coloq*): *El adjetivo precede al nombre.* The adjective goes before the noun. ◊ *Al incendio precedió una gran explosión.* A huge explosion preceded the fire.

precepto *nm* rule

precinto *nm* seal

precio *nm* price: *~s de fábrica* factory prices ◊ *¿Qué ~ tiene la habitación doble?* How much is a double room? LOC *Ver* MITAD, RELACIÓN

preciosidad *nf* lovely [*adj*]: *Ese vestido es una ~.* That dress is lovely.

precioso, -a *adj* **1** (*valioso*) precious: *el ~ don de la libertad* the precious gift of freedom ◊ *una piedra preciosa* a precious stone **2** (*persona, cosa*) lovely: *¡Qué gemelos tan ~s!* What lovely twins!

precipicio *nm* precipice

precipitaciones *nf* (*lluvia*) rainfall [*incontable, v sing*]: *~ abundantes* heavy rainfall

precipitado, -a *pp, adj* hasty *Ver tb* PRECIPITARSE

precipitarse *v pron* **1** (*sin pensar*) to be hasty: *No te precipites, piénsatelo bien.* Don't be hasty. Think it over. **2** (*arrojarse*) to throw yourself **out of *sth***: *El paracaidista se precipitó al vacío desde el avión.* The parachutist jumped out of the plane.

precisar *vt* **1** (*necesitar*) to need, to require (*más formal*) **2** (*especificar*) to specify: *~ hasta el mínimo detalle* to specify every detail

precisión *nf* accuracy LOC **con precisión** accurately

preciso, -a *adj*: *decir algo en el momento ~* to say sth at the right moment LOC **ser preciso** (*necesario*): *No fue ~ recurrir a los bomberos.* They didn't have to call the fire brigade. ◊ *Es ~ que vengas.* You must come.

precoz *adj* (*niño*) precocious

predecir *vt* to foretell

predicar *vt, vi* to preach

predominante *adj* predominant

preescolar *adj* pre-school: *niños en edad ~* pre-school children

prefabricado, -a *pp, adj* prefabricated

prefacio *nm* preface

preferencia *nf* preference

preferible *adj* preferable LOC **ser preferible**: *Es ~ que no entres ahora.* It would be better not to go in now.

preferido, -a *pp, adj, nm-nf* favourite *Ver tb* PREFERIR

preferir *vt* to prefer *sth/sb* (**to** ***sth/sb***): *Prefiero el té al café.* I prefer tea to coffee. ◊ *Prefiero estudiar por las mañanas.* I prefer to study in the morning.

> Cuando se pregunta qué prefiere una persona, se suele utilizar **would prefer** si se trata de dos cosas o **would rather** si se trata de dos acciones, por ejemplo: *¿Prefieres té o café?* Would you prefer tea or coffee? ◊ *¿Prefieres ir al cine o ver un vídeo?* Would you rather go to the cinema or watch a video? Para contestar a este tipo de preguntas se suele utilizar **I would rather, he/she would rather**, etc o **I'd rather, he'd/she'd rather**, etc: *—¿Prefieres té o café? —Prefiero té.* 'Would you prefer tea or coffee?' 'I'd rather have tea, please.' ◊ *—¿Quieres salir? —No, prefiero quedarme en casa esta noche.* 'Would you like to go out?' 'No, I'd rather stay at home tonight.'
> Nótese que **would rather** siempre va seguido de infinitivo sin TO.

prefijo *nm* **1** (*Ling*) prefix **2** (*teléfono*) code: *¿Cuál es el ~ de Madrid?* What's the code for Madrid?

pregonar *vt* (*divulgar*): *Lo ha ido pregonando por todo el colegio.* He's told the whole school.

pregunta *nf* question: *contestar a una ~* to answer a question LOC **hacer una pregunta** to ask a question

preguntar ◆ *vt, vi* to ask ◆ *vi* ~ **por 1** (*buscando algo/a algn*) to ask **for** ***sth/sb***: *Vino un señor preguntando por ti.* A man was asking for you. **2** (*interesándose por algn*) to ask **after** ***sb***: *Pregúntale por el pequeño.* Ask after her little boy. **3** (*interesándose por algo*) to ask **about** ***sth***: *Le pregunté por el examen.* I asked her about the exam. ◆ **preguntarse** *v pron* to wonder: *Me pregunto quién será a estas horas.* I wonder who it can be at this time of night. LOC *Ver* LECCIÓN

preguntón, -ona *adj* nosey

prehistórico, -a *adj* prehistoric

prejuicio *nm* prejudice

prematuro, -a *adj* premature

premiar *vt* to award *sb* a prize: *Premiaron al novelista.* The novelist was awarded a prize. ◊ *Fue premiado con un Óscar.* He was awarded an Oscar.

premio *nm* **1** (*gen*) prize: *Gané el primer ~.* I won first prize. ◊ *~ de consolación* consolation prize **2** (*recompensa*) reward: *como ~ a tu esfuerzo* as a reward for your efforts LOC *Ver* ENTREGA

prenatal *adj* antenatal

prenda *nf* **1** (*ropa*) garment **2 prendas** (*juego*) forfeits LOC *Ver* SOLTAR

prender ◆ *vt* (*con alfileres*) to pin *sth* (**to/on** ***sth***): *Prendí la manga con alfileres.* I pinned on the sleeve. ◆ *vi* to light: *Si está mojado no prende.* It won't light if it's wet. ◆ **prenderse** *v pron* to catch fire LOC **prender fuego** to set light *to sth*: *Prendieron fuego al carbón.* They set light to the coal.

prensa *nf* **1** (*Tec, imprenta*) press: *~ hidraúlica* hydraulic press **2** (*periódicos*) papers [*pl*]: *No te olvides de comprar la ~.* Don't forget to buy the papers. **3 la prensa** (*periodistas*) the press [*v sing o pl*]: *Acudió toda la ~ internacional.* All the international press was/were there. LOC **conferencia/rueda de prensa** press conference **prensa amarilla** gutter press *Ver tb* GABINETE, LIBERTAD

prensar *vt* to press

preñado, -a *pp, adj* pregnant

preocupación *nf* worry [*pl* worries]

preocupar ◆ *vt* to worry: *Me preocupa la salud de mi padre.* My father's health worries me. ◆ **preocuparse** *v pron* **preocuparse** (**por**) to worry (**about** ***sth/sb***): *No te preocupes por mí.* Don't worry about me.

preparación *nf* **1** (*gen*) preparation: *tiempo de ~: 10 minutos* preparation time: 10 minutes **2** (*entrenamiento*) training: *~ profesional/física* professional/physical training

preparado, -a *pp, adj* **1** (*listo*) ready: *La cena está preparada.* Dinner is ready. **2** (*persona*) qualified LOC **preparados, listos, ¡ya!** ready, steady, go! *Ver tb* PREPARAR

preparador, ~a *nm-nf* trainer

preparar ◆ *vt* to prepare, to get *sth/sb* ready (*más coloq*) (**for** ***sth***): *~ la cena* to get supper ready ◆ **prepararse** *v pron* **prepararse para** to prepare **for** ***sth***: *Se prepara para examinarse de conducir.* He's preparing for his driving test.

preparativos *nm* preparations

preposición *nf* preposition

presa *nf* **1** (*gen*) prey [*incontable*]: *aves de ~* birds of prey **2** (*embalse*) dam LOC **ser presa del pánico** to be seized by panic

presagio *nm* omen

prescindir *vi* ~ **de 1** (*privarse*) to do without (*sth*): *No puedo ~ del coche.* I can't do without the car. **2** (*deshacerse*) to dispense with *sb*: *Prescindieron del entrenador.* They dispensed with the trainer.

presencia *nf* **1** (*gen*) presence: *Su ~ me pone nerviosa.* I get nervous when he's around. **2** (*apariencia*) appearance: *buena/mala ~* pleasant/unattractive appearance

presencial *adj* **LOC** *Ver* TESTIGO

presenciar *vt* **1** (*ser testigo*) to witness: *Mucha gente presenció el accidente.* Many people witnessed the accident. **2** (*estar presente*) to attend: *Presenciaron el partido más de 10.000 espectadores.* More than 10000 spectators attended the match.

presentación *nf* **1** (*gen*) presentation: *La ~ es muy importante.* Presentation is very important. **2 presentaciones** introductions: *No has hecho las presentaciones.* You haven't introduced us.

presentador, ~a *nm-nf* presenter

presentar ◆ *vt* **1** (*gen*) to present (*sb*) (**with** ***sth***); to present (*sth*) (***to sb***): *~ un programa* to present a programme ◊ *Presentó las pruebas ante el juez.* He presented the judge with the evidence. **2** (*dimisión*) to tender: *Presentó su dimisión.* She tendered her resignation. **3** (*denuncia, demanda, queja*) to make: *~ una denuncia* to make an official complaint **4** (*persona*) to introduce *sb* (***to sb***): *¿Cuándo nos la presentarás?* When are you going to introduce her to us? ◊ *Os presento a mi marido.* This is my husband.

> Hay varias formas de presentar a la gente en inglés según el grado de formalidad de la situación, por ejemplo: 'John, meet Mary.' (*informal*); 'Mrs Smith, this is my daughter Jane' (*informal*); 'May I introduce you. Sir Godfrey, this is Mr Jones. Mr Jones, Sir Godfrey.' (*formal*). Cuando te presentan a alguien, se puede responder 'Hello' o 'Nice to meet you' si la situación es informal, o 'How do you do?' si es formal. A 'How do you do?' la otra persona responde 'How do you do?'

◆ **presentarse** *v pron* **1** (*a elecciones*) to stand (***for sth***): *~se a diputado* to stand for parliament **2** (*aparecer*) to turn up: *Se presenta cuando le da la gana.* He turns up whenever he feels like it. **LOC presentarse (a un examen)** to take an exam: *No me presenté.* I didn't take the exam. *Ver tb* VOLUNTARIO

presente ◆ *adj, nmf* present [*adj*]: *los ~s* those present ◆ *nm* (*Gram*) present

presentimiento *nm* feeling: *Tengo el ~ de que...* I have a feeling that...

presentir *vt* to have a feeling (***that...***): *Presiento que vas a aprobar.* I've got a feeling that you're going to pass.

preservativo *nm* condom

presidencia *nf* **1** (*gen*) presidency [*pl* presidencies]: *la ~ de un país* the presidency of a country **2** (*club, comité, empresa, partido*) chairmanship

presidencial *adj* presidential

presidente, -a *nm-nf* **1** (*gen*) president **2** (*club, comité, empresa, partido*) chairman/woman [*pl* chairmen/women]

> Cada vez se utiliza más la palabra **chairperson** [*pl* chairpersons] para evitar el sexismo.

presidiario, -a *nm-nf* convict

presidio *nm* prison

presidir *vt* to preside **at/over** ***sth***: *El secretario presidirá la asamblea.* The secretary will preside at/over the meeting.

presión *nf* pressure: *la ~ atmosférica* atmospheric pressure **LOC** *Ver* INDICADOR, OLLA

presionar *vt* **1** (*apretar*) to press **2** (*forzar*) to put pressure on *sb* (***to do sth***): *No le presiones.* Don't put pressure on him.

preso, -a ◆ *adj*: *estar ~* to be in prison ◊ *Se lo llevaron ~.* They took him prisoner. ◆ *nm-nf* prisoner

prestado, -a *pp, adj*: *No es mío, es ~.* It's not mine. I borrowed it. ◊ *¿Por qué no se lo pides ~?* Why don't you ask him if you can borrow it? **LOC dejar prestado** to lend: *Te lo dejo ~ si tienes cuidado.* I'll lend it to you if you're careful. ☛ *Ver dibujo en* BORROW; *Ver tb* PEDIR; *Ver tb* PRESTAR

préstamo *nm* loan

prestar *vt* to lend: *Le presté mis libros.* I lent her my books. ◊ *¿Me lo prestas?* Can I borrow it? ◊ *¿Me prestas 100 pesetas?* Can you lend me 100 pesetas, please? ☛ *Ver dibujo en* BORROW **LOC prestar declaración** to give evidence **prestar juramento** to take an oath *Ver tb* ATENCIÓN

prestigio *nm* prestige LOC **de mucho prestigio** very prestigious

presumido, -a *pp, adj* vain *Ver tb* PRESUMIR

presumir *vi* **1** (*gen*) to show off: *Les encanta ~.* They love showing off. **2 ~ de**: *Presume de listo.* He thinks he's clever. ◊ *Siempre están presumiendo de su coche.* They're forever bragging about their car.

presunto, -a *adj* alleged: *el ~ criminal* the alleged criminal

presupuesto *nm* **1** (*cálculo anticipado*) estimate: *He pedido que me den un ~ para el cuarto de baño.* I've asked for an estimate for the bathroom. **2** (*de gastos*) budget: *No quiero pasarme del ~.* I don't want to exceed my budget.

pretender *vt* **1** (*querer*): *¿Qué pretendes de mí?* What do you want from me? ◊ *Si pretendes ir sola, ni lo sueñes.* Don't even think about going alone. ◊ *¿No pretenderá quedarse en nuestra casa?* He's not expecting to stay at our house, is he? ◊ *No pretenderás que me lo crea, ¿no?* You don't expect me to believe that, do you? **2** (*intentar*) to try ***to do sth***: *¿Qué pretende decirnos?* What's he trying to tell us?

pretexto *nm* excuse: *Siempre encuentras algún ~ para no fregar.* You always find some excuse not to wash up.

prevención *nf* prevention

prevenido, -a *pp, adj* **1** (*preparado*) prepared: *estar ~ para algo* to be prepared for sth **2** (*prudente*) prudent: *ser ~* to be prudent *Ver tb* PREVENIR

prevenir *vt* **1** (*evitar*) to prevent: *~ un accidente* to prevent an accident **2** (*avisar*) to warn *sb* ***about sth***: *Te previne de lo que planeaban.* I warned you about what they were planning.

prever *vt* to foresee

previo, -a *adj*: *experiencia previa* previous experience ◊ *sin ~ aviso* without prior warning

previsor, ~a *adj* far-sighted

prieto, -a *adj* tight: *Estos zapatos me están muy ~s.* These shoes are too tight.

prima *nf* bonus [*pl* bonuses]

primario, -a ◆ *adj* primary: *color ~* primary colour ◊ *enseñanza primaria* primary education ◆ **primaria** *nf* (*escuela*) primary school: *maestra de primaria* primary school teacher LOC *Ver* ESCUELA

primavera *nf* spring: *en ~* in (the) spring

primer *adj Ver* PRIMERO

primera *nf* **1** (*automóvil*) first (gear): *Puse la ~ y salí zumbando.* I put it into first and sped off. **2** (*clase*) first class: *viajar en ~* to travel first class LOC **a la primera** first time: *Me salió bien a la ~.* I got it right first time.

primero, -a ◆ *adj* **1** (*gen*) first (*abrev* 1st): *primera clase* first class ◊ *Me gustó desde el primer momento.* I liked it from the first moment. **2** (*principal*) main, principal (*más formal*): *el primer país azucarero del mundo* the principal sugar-producing country in the world ◆ *pron, nm-nf* **1** (*gen*) first (one): *Fuimos los ~s en salir.* We were the first (ones) to leave. ◊ *llegar el ~* to come first **2** (*mejor*) top: *Eres el ~ de la clase.* You're top of the class. ◆ *nm* (*plato*) starter: *Tomamos sopa de ~.* We had soup as a starter. ◆ *adv* first: *Prefiero hacer los deberes ~.* I'd rather do my homework first. LOC **de primera necesidad** absolutely essential **primer ministro** prime minister ☛ *Ver* pág 322. **primeros auxilios** first aid [*incontable, v sing*] **primer plano** close-up

primitivo, -a *adj* primitive

primo, -a *nm-nf* (*pariente*) cousin LOC **primo carnal/segundo** first/second cousin *Ver tb* MATERIA, NÚMERO

princesa *nf* princess

principal *adj* main, principal (*más formal*): *comida/oración ~* main meal/clause ◊ *Eso es lo ~.* That's the main thing. LOC *Ver* ACTOR, CUARENTA, PAPEL

príncipe *nm* prince

> El plural de **prince** es 'princes', pero si nos referimos a la pareja de príncipes, diremos **prince and princess**: *Los príncipes nos recibieron en palacio.* The prince and princess received us at the palace.

LOC **príncipe azul** Prince Charming **príncipe heredero** Crown prince

principiante, -a *nm-nf* beginner

principio *nm* **1** (*comienzo*) beginning: *al ~ de la novela* at the beginning of the novel ◊ *desde el ~* from the beginning **2** (*concepto, moral*) principle LOC **al principio** at first **a principio(s) de...** at the beginning of...: *a ~s del año* at the beginning of the year ◊ *a ~s de enero* in early January

pringarse *v pron* **~ con/de** to get covered **in *sth***: *Se pringaron de pintura.* They got covered in paint.

pringoso, -a *adj* sticky

prioridad *nf* priority [*pl* priorities]

prisa *nf* hurry [*incontable*]: *No hay ~.* There's no hurry. ◊ *Con las ~s se me olvidó desenchufarlo.* I was in such a hurry that I forgot to unplug it. LOC **darse prisa** to hurry up **tener prisa** to be in a hurry *Ver tb* METER

prisión *nf* prison

prisionero, -a *nm-nf* prisoner LOC **hacer prisionero** to take *sb* prisoner

prismáticos *nm* binoculars

privado, -a *pp, adj* private: *en ~* in private LOC *Ver* COLEGIO, EMPRESA, INVESTIGADOR

privilegiado, -a ◆ *pp, adj* **1** (*excepcional*) exceptional: *una memoria privilegiada* an exceptional memory **2** (*favorecido*) privileged: *las clases privilegiadas* the privileged classes ◆ *nm-nf* privileged [*adj*]: *Somos unos ~s.* We're privileged people.

privilegio *nm* privilege

pro[1] *prep* for: *la organización pro ciegos* the society for the blind LOC **en pro de** in favour of *sth/sb*

pro[2] *nm* LOC **los pros y los contras** the pros and cons

proa *nf* bow(s) [*se usa mucho en plural*]

probabilidad *nf* ~ (**de**) chance (**of *sth*/ *doing sth***): *Creo que tengo muchas ~es de aprobar.* I think I've got a good chance of passing. ◊ *Tiene pocas ~es.* He hasn't got much chance.

probable *adj* likely, probable (*más formal*): *Es ~ que no esté en casa.* He probably won't be in. ◊ *Es muy ~ que llueva.* It's likely to rain. LOC **poco probable** unlikely

probador *nm* fitting room ☛También se dice **changing room**.

probar ◆ *vt* **1** (*demostrar*) to prove: *Esto prueba que yo tenía razón.* This proves I was right. **2** (*comprobar que funciona*) to try *sth* out: *~ la lavadora* to try out the washing machine **3** (*comida, bebida*) **(a)** (*por primera vez*) to try: *Nunca he probado el caviar.* I've never tried caviar. **(b)** (*catar, degustar*) to taste: *Prueba esto. ¿Está soso?* Taste this. Does it need salt? ◆ *vi* ~ (**a**) to try (***doing sth***): *¿Has probado a abrir la ventana?* Have you tried opening the window? ◊ *He probado con todo y no hay manera.* I've tried everything but with no success. ◆ **probar(se)** *vt, v pron* (*ropa*) to try *sth* on

probeta *nf* test tube

problema *nm* problem

procedencia *nf* origin

procedente *adj* ~ **de** from...: *el tren ~ de Bilbao* the train from Bilbao

proceder *vi* ~ **de** to come **from...**: *La sidra procede de la manzana.* Cider comes from apples.

procedimiento *nm* procedure [*gen incontable*]: *según los ~s establecidos* according to established procedure

procesador *nm* processor: *~ de datos/ textos* data/word processor

procesamiento *nm* processing LOC *Ver* TEXTO

procesar *vt* **1** (*juzgar*) to prosecute *sb* (**for *sth*/*doing sth***): *La procesaron por fraude.* She was prosecuted for fraud. **2** (*producto, Informát*) to process

procesión *nf* procession

proceso *nm* **1** (*gen*) process: *un ~ químico* a chemical process **2** (*Jur*) proceedings [*pl*]

procurar *vt* **1** ~ **hacer algo** to try **to do sth**: *Procuremos descansar.* Let's try to rest. **2** ~ **que** to make sure (**that...**): *Procuraré que vengan.* I'll make sure they come. ◊ *Procura que todo esté en orden.* Make sure everything's OK.

prodigio *nm* (*persona*) prodigy [*pl* prodigies] LOC *Ver* NIÑO

producción *nf* **1** (*gen*) production: *la ~ del acero* steel production **2** (*agrícola*) harvest **3** (*industrial, artística*) output

producir *vt* to produce: *~ aceite/papel* to produce oil/paper LOC *Ver* VÉRTIGO

producto *nm* product: *~s de belleza/ limpieza* beauty/cleaning products LOC **productos agrícolas/del campo** agricultural/farm produce ☛ *Ver nota en* PRODUCT

productor, ~a ◆ *adj* producing: *un país ~ de petróleo* an oil-producing country ◆ *nm-nf* producer ◆ **productora** *nf* production company [*pl* production companies]

profesión *nf* profession, occupation ☛ *Ver nota en* WORK[1]

profesional *adj, nmf* professional: *un ~ del ajedrez* a professional chess player LOC *Ver* FORMACIÓN, HISTORIAL, INSTITUTO

profesor, ~a *nm-nf* **1** (*gen*) teacher: *un ~ de geografía* a geography teacher **2** (*de universidad*) lecturer

profesorado *nm* teachers [*pl*]: *El ~ está muy descontento.* The teachers are very unhappy. ◊ *la formación del ~* teacher training

profeta, -isa *nm-nf* prophet [*fem* prophetess]

profundidad *nf* depth: *a 400 metros de ~* at a depth of 400 metres LOC **poca profundidad** shallowness

profundo, -a *adj* deep: *una voz profunda* a deep voice ◊ *sumirse en un sueño ~* to fall into a deep sleep LOC **poco profundo** shallow

programa *nm* **1** (*gen*) programme: *un ~ de televisión* a TV programme **2** (*Informát*) program **3** (*temario de una asignatura*) syllabus [*pl* syllabuses] LOC **programa de estudios** curriculum **programa de risa** comedy programme

programación *nf* programmes [*pl*]: *la ~ infantil* children's programmes

programador, ~a *nm-nf* (*Informát*) programmer

programar ◆ *vt* **1** (*elaborar*) to plan **2** (*aparato*) to set: *~ el vídeo* to set the video ◆ *vt, vi* (*Informát*) to program

progresar *vi* to make progress: *Ha progresado mucho.* He's made good progress.

progreso *nm* progress [*incontable*]: *hacer ~s* to make progress

prohibido, -a *pp, adj*: *circular por dirección prohibida* to drive the wrong way LOC **prohibido el paso/entrar** no entry **prohibido fijar anuncios/carteles** no fly-posting **prohibido fumar** no smoking **prohibido pisar el césped** keep off the grass *Ver tb* DIRECCIÓN; *Ver tb* PROHIBIR

prohibir ◆ *vt* **1** (*gen*) to forbid *sb* ***to do sth***: *Mi padre me ha prohibido salir de noche.* My father has forbidden me to go out at night. ◊ *Le han prohibido los dulces.* She's been forbidden to eat sweets. **2** (*oficialmente*) to ban *sth/sb* (***from doing sth***): *Han prohibido la circulación por el centro.* Traffic has been banned in the town centre. ◆ **prohibirse** *v pron*: *Se prohibe fumar.* No smoking.

prójimo *nm* neighbour: *amar al ~* to love your neighbour

prólogo *nm* prologue

prolongar ◆ *vt* to prolong (*formal*), to make *sth* longer: *~ la vida de un enfermo* to prolong a patient's life ◆ **prolongarse** *v pron* to go on: *La reunión se prolongó demasiado.* The meeting went on too long.

promedio *nm* average LOC **como promedio** on average

promesa *nf* promise: *cumplir/hacer una ~* to keep/make a promise ◊ *una joven ~* a young woman with great promise

prometer *vt* to promise: *Te prometo que volveré.* I promise I'll come back. ◊ *Te lo prometo.* I promise.

prometido, -a *nm-nf* fiancé [*fem* fiancée]

promoción *nf* **1** (*gen*) promotion: *la ~ de una película* the promotion of a film **2** (*curso*) year: *un compañero de mi ~* one of the people in my year

promover *vt* (*fomentar*) to promote: *~ el diálogo* to promote dialogue

pronombre *nm* pronoun

pronosticar *vt* to forecast

pronóstico *nm* **1** (*predicción*) forecast: *el ~ del tiempo* the weather forecast **2** (*Med*) prognosis [*pl* prognoses]: *Sufrió heridas de ~ grave.* He was seriously injured. ◊ *¿Cuál es el ~ de los especialistas?* What do the specialists think?

pronto *adv* **1** (*en seguida*) soon: *Vuelve ~.* Come back soon. ◊ *lo más ~ posible* as soon as possible **2** (*rápidamente*) quickly: *Por favor, doctor, venga ~.* Please, doctor, come quickly. **3** (*temprano*) early LOC **de pronto** suddenly **¡hasta pronto!** see you soon!

pronunciación *nf* pronunciation

pronunciar ◆ *vt* **1** (*sonidos*) to pronounce **2** (*discurso*) to give: *~ un discurso* to give a speech ◆ *vi*: *Pronuncias muy bien.* Your pronunciation is very good. ◆ **pronunciarse** *v pron* **pronunciarse en contra/a favor de** to speak out **against/in favour of *sth***: *~se en contra de la violencia* to speak out against violence

propaganda *nf* **1** (*publicidad*) advertising: *hacer ~ de un producto* to advertise a product **2** (*material publicitario*): *Estaban repartiendo ~ de la nueva discoteca.* They were handing out flyers for the new disco. ◊ *En el buzón no había más que ~.* The letter box was full of adverts. **3** (*Pol*) propaganda: *~ electoral* election propaganda

propagar(se) *vt, v pron* to spread: *El viento propagó las llamas.* The wind spread the flames.

propenso, -a *adj* ~ **a** prone **to *sth*/to *do sth***

propiedad *nf* property [*pl* properties]: *~ particular/privada* private property ◊ *las ~es medicinales de las plantas* the medicinal properties of plants

propietario, -a *nm-nf* owner

propina *nf* tip: *¿Dejamos ~?* Shall we leave a tip? ◊ *Le di tres libras de ~.* I gave him a three-pound tip.

propio, -a *adj* **1** (*de uno*) my, your, etc own: *Todo lo que haces es en beneficio ~.* Everything you do is for your own benefit. **2** (*mismo*) himself [*fem* herself] [*pl* themselves]: *El ~ pintor inauguró la exposición.* The painter himself opened the exhibition. **3** (*característico*) typical ***of sb***: *Llegar tarde es ~ de ella.* It's typical of her to be late. LOC **en propia meta/puerta**: *un gol en propia puerta* an own goal ◊ *marcar en propia meta* to score an own goal *Ver tb* AMOR, DEFENSA, INICIATIVA, NOMBRE

proponer ♦ *vt* **1** (*medida, plan*) to propose: *Te propongo un trato.* I've got a deal for you. **2** (*acción*) to suggest ***doing sth***/(***that...***): *Propongo ir al cine esta tarde.* I suggest going to the cinema this evening. ◊ *Propuso que nos marchásemos.* He suggested (that) we should leave. ♦ **proponerse** *v pron* to set out ***to do sth***: *Me propuse acabarlo.* I set out to finish it.

proporción *nf* **1** (*relación, tamaño*) proportion: *El largo debe estar en ~ con el ancho.* The length must be in proportion to the width. **2** (*Mat*) ratio: *La ~ de niños y niñas es de uno a tres.* The ratio of boys to girls is one to three.

proposición *nf* proposal LOC **hacer proposiciones deshonestas** to make improper suggestions **proposición de matrimonio** proposal (of marriage): *hacerle una ~ de matrimonio a algn* to propose to sb

propósito *nm* **1** (*intención*) intention: *buenos ~s* good intentions **2** (*objetivo*) purpose: *El ~ de esta reunión es...* The purpose of this meeting is... LOC **a propósito 1** (*adrede*) on purpose **2** (*por cierto*) by the way

propuesta *nf* proposal: *Desestimaron la ~.* The proposal was turned down.

prórroga *nf* **1** (*de un plazo*) extension **2** (*Dep*) extra time

prosa *nf* prose

prospecto *nm* **1** (*de instrucciones*) instructions [*pl*]: *¿Te has leído el ~?* Have you read the instructions? **2** (*de propaganda*) leaflet

prosperar *vi* to prosper

prosperidad *nf* prosperity

próspero, -a *adj* prosperous

prostituta *nf* prostitute

protagonista *nmf* main character

protagonizar *vt* to star **in *sth***: *Protagonizan la película dos actores desconocidos.* Two unknown actors star in this film.

protección *nf* protection

protector, ~a *adj* protective (***towards sb***)

proteger *vt* to protect *sb* (***against/from sth/sb***): *El sombrero te protege del sol.* Your hat protects you from the sun.

proteína *nf* protein

protesta *nf* protest: *Ignoraron las ~s de los alumnos.* They ignored the pupils' protests. ◊ *una carta de ~* a letter of protest

protestante *adj, nmf* Protestant

protestantismo *nm* Protestantism

protestar *vi* **1** ~ (**por**) (*quejarse*) to complain (**about *sth***): *Deja ya de ~.* Stop complaining. **2** ~ (**contra/por**) (*reivindicar*) to protest (**against/about *sth***): *~ contra una ley* to protest against a law

prototipo *nm* **1** (*primer ejemplar*) prototype: *el ~ de las nuevas locomotoras* the prototype for the new engines **2** (*modelo*) epitome: *el ~ del hombre moderno* the epitome of modern man

provecho *nm* benefit LOC **¡buen provecho!** enjoy your meal! **sacar provecho** to benefit *from sth*

proverbio *nm* proverb

providencia *nf* providence

provincia *nf* province: *un pueblo de la ~ de Valladolid* a town in the province of Valladolid

provisional *adj* provisional LOC *Ver* LIBERTAD

provocado, -a *pp, adj* LOC *Ver* INCENDIO; *Ver tb* PROVOCAR

provocar *vt* **1** (*hacer enfadar*) to provoke **2** (*causar*) to cause: *~ un accidente* to cause an accident **3** (*incendio*) to start

proximidad *nf* nearness, proximity (*más formal*): *la ~ del mar* the nearness/proximity of the sea

próximo, -a *adj* **1** (*siguiente*) next: *la próxima parada* the next stop ◊ *el mes/martes ~* next month/Tuesday **2** (*en el tiempo*): *La Navidad/primavera está próxima.* It will soon be Christmas/spring. LOC *Ver* ORIENTE

proyectar *vt* **1** (*reflejar*) to project: *~ una imagen sobre una pantalla* to project an image onto a screen **2** (*Cine*) to show: ~ *diapositivas/una película* to show slides/a film

proyectil *nm* projectile

proyecto *nm* **1** (*gen*) project: *Estamos casi al final del ~.* We're almost at the end of the project. **2** (*plan*) plan: *¿Tienes algún ~ para el futuro?* Have you got any plans for the future? LOC **proyecto de ley** bill

proyector *nm* projector

prudencia *nf* good sense LOC **con prudencia** carefully: *conducir con ~* to drive carefully

prudente *adj* **1** (*sensato*) sensible: *un hombre/una decisión ~* a sensible man/decision **2** (*cauto*) careful

prueba *nf* **1** (*gen*) test: *una ~ de aptitud* an aptitude test ◊ *hacerse la ~ del embarazo* to have a pregnancy test **2** (*Mat*) proof **3** (*Dep*): *Hoy comienzan las ~s de salto de altura.* The high jump competition begins today. **4** (*Jur*) evidence [*incontable*]: *No hay ~s contra mí.* There's no evidence against me. LOC **a prueba** on trial: *Me admitieron a ~ en la fábrica.* I was taken on at the factory for a trial period. **a prueba de balas** bulletproof **poner a prueba a algn** to test sb *Ver tb* ANTIDOPING

psicología *nf* psychology

psicólogo, -a *nm-nf* psychologist

psiquiatra *nmf* psychiatrist

psiquiatría *nf* psychiatry

psiquiátrico *nm* psychiatric hospital

púa *nf* **1** (*animal*) spine **2** (*peine*) tooth [*pl* teeth] **3** (*Mús*) plectrum [*pl* plectra]

pub *nm* bar ☛ *Ver* pág 320.

pubertad *nf* puberty

pubis *nm* pubis

publicación *nf* publication LOC **de publicación semanal** weekly: *una revista de ~ semanal* a weekly magazine

publicar *vt* **1** (*gen*) to publish: *~ una novela* to publish a novel **2** (*divulgar*) to publicize

publicidad *nf* **1** (*gen*) publicity: *Han dado demasiada ~ al caso.* The case has had too much publicity. **2** (*propaganda*) advertising: *hacer ~ en la tele* to advertise on TV

publicitario, -a *adj* advertising: *una campaña publicitaria* an advertising campaign LOC *Ver* VALLA

público, -a ◆ *adj* **1** (*gen*) public: *la opinión pública* public opinion ◊ *transporte ~* public transport **2** (*del Estado*) state [*n atrib*]: *una escuela pública* a state school ◊ *el sector ~* the state sector ◆ *nm* **1** (*gen*) public [*v sing o pl*]: *abierto/cerrado al ~* open/closed to the public ◊ *El ~ está a favor de la nueva ley.* The public is/are in favour of the new law. ◊ *hablar en ~* to speak in public **2** (*clientela*) clientele: *un ~ selecto* a select clientele **3** (*espectadores*) audience [*v sing o pl*] LOC *Ver* ALTERAR, COLEGIO, DOMINIO, EMPRESA, HORARIO, RELACIÓN

puchero *nm* **1** (*recipiente*) cooking pot **2** (*cocido*) stew LOC **hacer pucheros** to pout

pudiente *adj* wealthy

pudor *nm* shame

pudrirse *v pron* to rot

pueblo *nm* **1** (*gente*) people [*pl*]: *el ~ español* the Spanish people **2** (*con población pequeña*) village **3** (*con población grande*) town

puente *nm* bridge: *un ~ colgante* a suspension bridge LOC **hacer puente** to have a long weekend **puente aéreo** shuttle service **puente levadizo** drawbridge

puerco, -a *nm-nf* pig ☛ *Ver nota en* CERDO

puericultor, ~a *nm-nf* paediatrician

puerro *nm* leek

puerta *nf* **1** (*gen*) door: *la ~ principal/trasera* the front/back door ◊ *Llaman a la ~.* There's somebody at the door. **2** (*de una ciudad, palacio*) gate **3** (*Dep*) goal: *Tiró a ~ pero falló.* He shot at goal but missed. LOC **coger la puerta** to clear off **puerta corrediza/giratoria** sliding/revolving door **puerta de embarque** gate *Ver tb* CERRAR, PROPIO

puerto *nm* **1** (*gen*) port: *un ~ comercial/pesquero* a commercial/fishing port **2** (*de montaña*) pass LOC *Ver* INGENIERO

pues *conj* well: *~ como íbamos diciendo…* Well, as we were saying… ◊ *¡~ a mí no me dijo nada!* Well, he didn't mention it to me! ◊ *¿Que no te apetece salir?, ~ no salgas.* You don't feel like going out? Well, don't.

puesta *nf* LOC **puesta a punto** (*motor*) tuning **puesta de sol** sunset **puesta en común** round table

puesto, -a ◆ *pp, adj* **1** (*gen*): *Dejaré la mesa puesta.* I'll leave the table laid. ◊ *No lo envuelva, me lo llevo ~.* There's no need to put it in a bag. I'll wear it. **2** (*bien arreglado*) smart ◆ *nm* **1** (*lugar*) place: *El ciclista español ocupa el primer ~.* The Spanish cyclist is in first place. ◊ *llegar en tercer ~* to be third ◊ *¡Todo el mundo a sus ~s!* Places, everyone! **2** (*empleo*) job: *solicitar un ~ de trabajo* to apply for a job ◊ *Su mujer tiene un buen ~.* His wife's got a good job. ☛ *Ver nota en* WORK[1] **3** (*caseta*) **(a)** (*en un mercado*) stall **(b)** (*en una feria*) stand LOC **estar (muy) puesto en algo** to know a lot about sth **puesto de periódicos** news-stand *Ver tb* PONER

puf *nm* pouffe

púgil *nm* boxer

pulcritud *nf* neatness

pulcro, -a *adj* neat

pulga *nf* flea LOC **tener malas pulgas** to have a bad temper

pulgada *nf* inch (*abrev* in) ☛ *Ver* Apéndice 1.

pulgar *nm* **1** (*de la mano*) thumb **2** (*del pie*) big toe

Pulgarcito *n pr* Tom Thumb

pulir ◆ *vt* to polish ◆ **pulirse** *v pron* (*dinero*) to squander

pulmón *nm* lung LOC **pulmón artificial** iron lung

pulmonar *adj* lung [*n atrib*]: *una infección ~* a lung infection

pulmonía *nf* pneumonia [*incontable*]: *coger una ~* to catch pneumonia

pulpa *nf* pulp

púlpito *nm* pulpit

pulpo *nm* octopus [*pl* octopuses]

pulsación *nf* (*corazón*) pulse rate: *Con el ejercicio aumenta el número de pulsaciones.* Your pulse rate increases after exercise. LOC **pulsaciones por minuto** (*mecanografía*): *160 pulsaciones por minuto* forty words per minute

pulsar *vt* **1** (*gen*) to press: *Pulse la tecla dos veces.* Press the key twice. **2** (*timbre*) to ring

pulsera *nf* **1** (*brazalete*) bracelet **2** (*de reloj*) strap

pulso *nm* **1** (*Mec*) pulse: *Tienes el ~ muy débil.* You have a very weak pulse. ◊ *El médico me tomó el ~.* The doctor took my pulse. **2** (*mano firme*) (steady) hand: *tener buen ~* to have a steady hand ◊ *Me tiembla el ~.* My hand is trembling. LOC **a pulso** with my, your, etc bare hands: *Me levantó a ~.* He lifted me up with his bare hands. **echar un pulso** to arm-wrestle

pulverizador *nm* spray [*pl* sprays]

pulverizar *vt* **1** (*rociar*) to spray **2** (*destrozar*) to pulverize

puma *nm* puma

punki (*tb* **punk**) *adj, nmf* punk [*n*]

punta *nf* **1** (*cuchillo, arma, pluma, lápiz*) point **2** (*lengua, dedo, isla, iceberg*) tip: *Lo tengo en la ~ de la lengua.* It's on the tip of my tongue. **3** (*extremo, pelo*) end: *~s estropeadas* split ends ◊ *en la otra ~ de la mesa* at the other end of the table **4** (*clavo*) tack LOC **a punta de navaja/pistola** at knifepoint/gunpoint **de punta a punta**: *de ~ a ~ de Madrid* from one side of Madrid to the other **de punta en blanco** dressed up to the nines **sacar punta** (*afilar*) to sharpen *Ver tb* HORA, NERVIO, PELO

puntada *nf* stitch: *Dale una ~ a ese dobladillo.* Put a stitch in the hem.

puntapié *nm* kick: *Le di un ~.* I kicked him.

puntería *nf* aim: *¡Qué ~ la mía!* What a good aim I've got! LOC **tener buena/mala puntería** to be a good/bad shot *Ver tb* AFINAR

puntiagudo, -a *adj* pointed

puntilla *nf* LOC **de puntillas** on tiptoe: *andar de ~s* to walk on tiptoe ◊ *Entré/salí de ~s.* I tiptoed in/out.

punto *nm* **1** (*gen*) point: *en todos los ~s del país* all over the country ◊ *Pasemos al siguiente ~.* Let's go on to the next point. ◊ *Perdimos por dos ~s.* We lost by two points. **2** (*signo de puntuación*) full stop ☛ *Ver* págs 318–19. **3** (*grado*) extent: *¿Hasta qué ~ es cierto?* To what extent is this true? **4** (*Costura, Med*) stitch: *Me dieron tres ~s.* I had three stitches. LOC **al/en su punto** (*carne*) medium rare **a punto de nieve** stiffly beaten: *batir/montar las claras a ~ de nieve* to beat egg whites until they are stiff **con puntos y comas** down to the last detail **de punto** knitted: *un vestido de ~* a knitted dress **en punto** precisely: *Son las dos en ~.* It's two o'clock precisely. **estar a punto de hacer algo 1** (*gen*) to be about to do sth: *Está a ~ de terminar.* It's about to finish. **2** (*por poco*) to nearly do sth: *Estuvo a ~ de perder la vida.* He nearly lost his life. **hacer punto** to knit **punto débil/flaco** weak point **punto de ebullición/fusión** boiling point/melting point **punto de vista** point of view **punto final** full stop **punto muerto 1** (*coche*) neutral

2 (*negociaciones*) deadlock **puntos suspensivos** dot dot dot **punto y aparte** new paragraph **punto y coma** semicolon ☛ *Ver* págs 318–19. *Ver tb* CHAQUETA, CIERTO, DOS, PUESTA, TECNOLOGÍA

puntuación *nf* **1** (*escritura*) punctuation: *signos de ~* punctuation marks **2** (*competición, examen*) mark(s) [*se usa mucho en plural*]: *Todo depende de la ~ que le den los jueces.* It all depends on what marks the judges award him. ◊ *Obtuvo la ~ más alta de todos.* He got the highest mark of all.

puntual *adj* punctual

> **Punctual** se suele utilizar para referirnos a la cualidad o virtud de una persona: *Es importante ser puntual.* It's important to be punctual. Cuando nos referimos a la idea de *llegar a tiempo* se utiliza la expresión **on time**: *Procura ser/llegar puntual.* Try to get there on time. ◊ *Este chico nunca es puntual.* He's always late./He's never on time.

puntualidad *nf* punctuality

puntuar *vt* **1** (*escritura*) to punctuate **2** (*calificar*) to mark

punzada *nf* sharp pain: *Siento ~s en la barriga.* I've got sharp pains in my stomach.

punzante *adj* sharp: *un objeto ~* a sharp object

puñado *nm* handful: *un ~ de arroz* a handful of rice

puñal *nm* dagger

puñalada *nf* stab

puñetazo *nm* punch: *Me dio un ~ en todo el estómago.* He punched me in the stomach.

puño *nm* **1** (*mano cerrada*) fist **2** (*manga*) cuff **3** (*bastón, paraguas*) handle **4** (*espada*) hilt LOC **como puños** great big ...: *mentiras como ~s* great big lies **de su puño y letra** in his/her own handwriting *Ver tb* VERDAD

pupila *nf* pupil

pupitre *nm* desk

purasangre *nm* thoroughbred

puré *nm* **1** (*muy espeso*) purée: *~ de tomate/manzana* tomato/apple purée **2** (*sopa cremosa*) soup [*incontable*]: *~ de lentejas* lentil soup ◆ *Voy a hacer un ~.* I'm going to make some soup. LOC **estar hecho puré** to be shattered **puré de patatas** mashed potato [*incontable*]

pureza *nf* purity

purgatorio *nm* purgatory

purificar *vt* to purify

puritanismo *nm* puritanism

puritano, -a ◆ *adj* **1** (*ñoño*) puritanical **2** (*Relig*) Puritan ◆ *nm-nf* Puritan

puro *nm* **1** (*cigarro*) cigar **2** (*castigo*): *Me cayó un buen ~ por no hacer los deberes.* I got into real trouble for not doing my homework.

puro, -a *adj* **1** (*gen*) pure: *oro ~* pure gold ◊ *por pura casualidad* purely by chance **2** (*enfático*) simple: *la pura verdad* the simple truth LOC *Ver* SUGESTIÓN

púrpura *nf* purple

purpurina *nf* glitter

pus *nm* pus

puzzle *nm* jigsaw: *hacer un ~* to do a jigsaw

Qq

que[1] *pron rel*

- **sujeto 1** (*personas*) who: *el hombre ~ vino ayer* the man who came yesterday ◊ *Mi hermana, ~ vive allí, dice que es precioso.* My sister, who lives there, says it's lovely. **2** (*cosas*) that: *el coche ~ está aparcado en la plaza* the car that's parked in the square ☛Cuando **que** equivale a *el cual, la cual,* etc, se traduce por **which**: *Este edificio, ~ antes fue sede del Gobierno, hoy es una biblioteca.* This building, which previously housed the Government, is now a library.
- **complemento** ☛El inglés prefiere no traducir **que** cuando funciona como complemento, aunque también es correcto usar **that/who** para personas y **that/which** para cosas: *el chico ~ conociste en Roma* the boy (that/who) you met in Rome ◊ *la revista ~ me prestaste ayer* the magazine (that/

which) you lent me yesterday LOC **el que/la que/los que/las que** *Ver* EL

que² *conj* **1** (*con oraciones subordinadas*) (that): *Dijo ~ vendría esta semana.* He said (that) he would come this week. ◊ *Quiero ~ viajes en primera.* I want you to travel first class. **2** (*en comparaciones*): *Mi hermano es más alto ~ tú.* My brother's taller than you. **3** (*en mandatos*): *¡~ te calles!* Shut up! ◊ *¡~ lo paséis bien!* Have a good time! **4** (*resultado*) (that): *Estaba tan cansada ~ me quedé dormida.* I was so tired (that) I fell asleep. **5** (*otras construcciones*): *Sube la radio ~ no la oigo.* Turn the radio up—I can't hear it. ◊ *Cuando lavo el coche se queda ~ parece nuevo.* When I wash the car, it looks like new. ◊ *No hay día ~ no llueva.* There isn't a single day when it doesn't rain. ◊ *¡Cómo dices! ¿~ se ha pasado el plazo?* What! It's too late to apply? LOC **¡que sí/no!** yes/no!

qué ◆ *adj*

- **interrogación** what: *¿~ hora es?* What time is it? ◊ *¿En ~ piso vives?* What floor do you live on? ☛Cuando existen sólo pocas posibilidades solemos usar **which**: *¿Qué coche cogemos hoy? ¿El tuyo o el mío?* Which car shall we take today? Yours or mine?
- **exclamación** **1** (+ *sustantivos contables en plural e incontables*) what: *¡~ casas más bonitas!* What lovely houses! ◊ *¡~ valor!* What courage! **2** (+ *sustantivos contables en singular*) what a: *¡~ vida!* What a life! **3** (*cuando traduce por adjetivo*) how: *¡~ rabia/horror!* How annoying/awful!

◆ *pron* what: *¿Qué? Habla más alto.* What? Speak up. ◊ *No sé ~ quieres.* I don't know what you want. ◆ *adv* how: *¡~ interesante!* How interesting! LOC **¡qué bien!** great! **¡qué de...!** what a lot of...!: *¡~ de turistas!* What a lot of tourists! **¡qué mal!** oh no! **¿qué tal? 1** (*saludo*) how are things? **2** (*¿cómo está/están?*) how is/are...?: *¿~ tal tus padres?* How are your parents? **3** (*¿cómo es/son?*) what is/are *sth/sb* like?: *¿~ tal la película?* What was the film like? **¡qué va!** no way! **¿y a mí qué?** what's it to me, you, etc?

quebrado *nm* fraction

quebrar *vi* to go bankrupt

queda *nf* LOC *Ver* TOQUE

quedar ◆ *vi* **1** (*haber*) to be left: *¿Queda café?* Is there any coffee left? ◊ *Quedan tres días para las vacaciones.* There are three days left before we go on holiday. ◊ *Quedan cinco kilómetros para Granada.* It's still five kilometres to Granada. **2** (*tener*) to have *sth* left: *Todavía nos quedan dos botellas.* We've still got two bottles left. ◊ *No me queda dinero.* I haven't got any money left. **3** (*citarse*) to meet: *¿Dónde quedamos?* Where shall we meet? ◊ *He quedado con ella a las tres.* I've arranged to meet her at three o'clock. **4** (*estar situado, llegar*) to be: *¿Dónde queda tu hotel?* Where is your hotel? ◊ *Quedamos terceros en el concurso.* We were third in the competition. **5** (*ropa*): *¿Qué tal le queda la chaqueta?* How does the jacket look on her? ◊ *La falda me quedaba grande.* The skirt was too big for me. ◊ *Ese jersey te queda muy bien.* That jumper really suits you. **6 ~ en** to agree ***to do sth***: *Quedamos en vernos el martes.* We agreed to meet on Tuesday. ◆ **quedarse** *v pron* **1** (*en un sitio*) to stay: *~se en la cama/en casa* to stay in bed/at home **2 + adj** to go: *~se calvo/ciego* to go bald/blind **3 quedarse** (**con**) to keep: *Quédese con el cambio.* Keep the change. LOC **quedar bien/mal** to make a good/bad impression (*on sb*): *He quedado muy mal con Raúl.* I made a bad impression on Raúl. **quedarse con algn** (*tomar el pelo*) to pull sb's leg **quedarse sin algo** to run out of sth: *Me he quedado sin cambio.* I've run out of change. ☛Para otras expresiones con **quedar**, véanse las entradas del sustantivo, adjetivo, etc, p.ej. **quedarse de piedra** en PIEDRA y **quedarse tan ancho** en ANCHO.

queja *nf* complaint

quejarse *v pron* ~ (**de/por**) to complain, to moan (*más coloq*) (**about *sth*/*sb***)

quejica *nmf* whinger

quejido *nm* **1** (*de dolor*) moan **2** (*lamento, suspiro*) sigh **3** (*animal*) whine

quemado, -a *pp, adj* (*harto, enfadado*) fed up: *Estoy muy ~ con ellos.* I'm fed up with them. LOC **saber a quemado** to taste burnt *Ver tb* OLER; *Ver tb* QUEMAR

quemadura *nf* **1** (*gen*) burn: *~s de segundo grado* second-degree burns **2** (*con líquido hirviendo*) scald LOC **quemadura de sol** sunburn [*incontable*]: *Esta crema es para las ~s de sol.* This cream is for sunburn.

quemar ◆ *vt* **1** (*gen*) to burn: *Vas a ~ la tortilla.* You're going to burn the omelette. **2** (*edificio, bosque*) to burn *sth* down: *Ha quemado ya tres edificios.* He's already burnt down three buildings. ◆ *vi* to be hot: *¡Cómo quema!* It's very hot! ◆ **quemarse** *v pron* **1 quemarse (con)** (*persona*) to burn *sth/yourself* (**on** ***sth***): *~se la lengua* to burn your tongue ◊ *Me quemé con la sartén.* I burnt myself on the frying-pan. **2** (*comida*) to be burnt **3** (*agotarse*) to burn yourself out **4** (*con el sol*) to get sunburnt: *En seguida me quemo.* I get sunburnt very easily.

querer ◆ *vt* **1** (*amar*) to love **2** (*algo, hacer algo*) to want: *¿Cuál quieres?* Which one do you want? ◊ *Quiero salir.* I want to go out. ◊ *Quiere que vayamos a su casa.* He wants us to go to his house. ◊ *De primero, quiero sopa de pescado.* I'd like fish soup to start with. ☛ *Ver nota en* WANT ◆ *vi* to want to: *No quiero.* I don't want to. ◊ *Pues claro que quiere.* Of course he wants to. LOC **querer decir** to mean: *¿Qué quiere decir esta palabra?* What does this word mean? **queriendo** (*a propósito*) on purpose **quisiera...** I, he, etc would like *to do sth*: *Quisiera saber por qué siempre llegas tarde.* I'd like to know why you're always late. **sin querer**: *Perdona, ha sido sin ~.* Sorry, it was an accident.

querido, -a *pp, adj* dear *Ver tb* QUERER

queso *nm* cheese: *~ rallado* grated cheese ◊ *No me gusta el ~.* I don't like cheese. ◊ *un sandwich de ~* a cheese sandwich

quicio *nm* LOC **sacar de quicio** to drive *sb* mad

quiebra *nf* bankruptcy [*pl* bankruptcies]

quien *pron rel* **1** (*sujeto*) who: *Fue mi hermano ~ me lo dijo.* It was my brother who told me. ◊ *Aquí no hay ~ trabaje.* No one can work here. **2** (*complemento*) ☛El inglés prefiere no traducir **quien** cuando funciona como complemento, aunque también es correcto usar **who** o **whom**: *Es a mi madre a ~ quiero ver.* It's my mother I want to see. ◊ *Fue a él a ~ se lo dije.* He was the one I told. ◊ *El chico con ~ la vi ayer es su primo.* The boy (who) I saw her with yesterday is her cousin. ◊ *la actriz de ~ se ha escrito tanto* the actress about whom so much has been written **3** (*cualquiera*) whoever: *Invita a ~ quieras.* Invite whoever you want. ◊ *~ esté a favor, que levante la mano.* Those in favour, raise your hands. ◊ *Paco, Julián o ~ sea* Paco, Julián or whoever

quién *pron interr* who: *¿~ es?* Who is it? ◊ *¿A ~ viste?* Who did you see? ◊ *¿~es vienen?* Who's coming? ◊ *¿Para ~ es este regalo?* Who is this present for? ◊ *¿De ~ hablas?* Who are you talking about? LOC **¿de quién...?** (*posesión*) whose...?: *¿De ~ es este abrigo?* Whose is this coat?

quienquiera *pron* whoever: *~ que sea el culpable recibirá su castigo.* Whoever is responsible will be punished.

quieto, -a *adj* still: *estarse/quedarse ~* to keep still

química *nf* chemistry

químico, -a ◆ *adj* chemical ◆ *nm-nf* chemist

quimono *nm* kimono [*pl* kimonos]

quince *nm, adj, pron* **1** (*gen*) fifteen **2** (*fecha*) fifteenth ☛ *Ver ejemplos en* ONCE *y* SEIS LOC **quince días** fortnight: *Sólo vamos ~ días.* We're only going for a fortnight.

quinceañero, -a *nm-nf* (*adolescente*) teenager

quincena *nf* (*quince días*) two weeks [*pl*]: *la segunda ~ de enero* the last two weeks of January

quiniela *nf* **quinielas** football pools [*pl*] LOC **hacer la(s) quiniela(s)** to do the pools

quinientos, -as *adj, pron, nm* five hundred ☛ *Ver ejemplos en* SEISCIENTOS

quinto, -a ◆ *adj, pron, nm-nf* fifth ☛ *Ver ejemplos en* SEXTO ◆ **quinta** *nf* (*marcha*) fifth (gear) LOC **en el quinto pino** in the middle of nowhere

quiosco *nm* stand LOC **quiosco de periódicos** news-stand

quiquiriquí *nm* cock-a-doodle-doo

quirófano *nm* (operating) theatre

quirúrgico, -a *adj* surgical: *una intervención quirúrgica* an operation

quisquilloso, -a *adj* **1** (*exigente*) fussy **2** (*susceptible*) touchy

quitamanchas *nm* stain remover

quitar ◆ *vt* **1** (*gen*) to take *sth* off/down/out: *Quita tus cosas de mi escritorio.* Take your things off my desk. ◊ *Quítale el jersey.* Take his jumper off. ◊ *Quitó el cartel.* He took the poster down. **2** (*Mat, sustraer*) to take *sth* away (**from** ***sth/sb***): *Si a tres le quitas uno...* If you take one (away) from three... ◊*Me quitaron el carnet de conducir.* I had my driving licence taken away. **3** (*mancha*) to remove, to get *a stain* out (*más coloq*) **4** (*dolor*) to relieve **5** (*tiempo*) to take up *sb's time*: *Los niños me quitan mucho tiempo.* The children take up a lot of my time. ◆ **quitarse** *v pron* **1** (*ropa, gafas, maquillaje*) to take *sth* off: *Quítate los zapatos.* Take your shoes off. **2** (*mancha*) to come out: *Esta mancha no se quita.* This stain won't come out. LOC **no quitar la vista/los ojos (de encima)** not to take your eyes off *sth/sb* **¡quita (de ahí)!/¡quítate de en medio!** get out of the way! **quitar importancia** to play *sth* down: *Siempre quita importancia a sus triunfos.* She always plays down her achievements. **quitarse de encima a algn** to get rid of sb **quitarse la costumbre/manía** to kick the habit (*of doing sth*): *~se la costumbre de morderse las uñas* to kick the habit of biting your nails **quitarse las ganas** to go off the idea (*of doing sth*): *Se me han quitado las ganas de ir al cine.* I've gone off the idea of going to the cinema. **quitarse un peso de encima**: *Me he quitado un gran peso de encima.* That's a great weight off my mind. *Ver tb* MESA, POLVO

quizá (*tb* **quizás**) *adv* perhaps: *—¿Crees que vendrá? —Quizás sí.* 'Do you think she'll come?' 'Perhaps.'

Rr

rábano (*tb* **rabanito**) *nm* radish

rabia *nf* **1** (*ira*) anger **2** (*Med*) rabies [*sing*]: *El perro tenía la ~.* The dog had rabies. LOC **dar rabia** to drive *sb* mad: *Me da muchísima ~.* It really drives me mad. *Ver tb* COMIDO

rabieta *nf* tantrum: *Le dan muchas ~s.* He's always throwing tantrums.

rabillo *nm* LOC **con/por el rabillo del ojo** out of the corner of your eye

rabioso, -a *adj* **1** (*furioso*) furious: *Me contestó ~.* He replied furiously. **2** (*Med*) rabid: *un perro ~* a rabid dog

rabo *nm* **1** (*animal*) tail **2** (*planta, fruta*) stalk LOC *Ver* CABO

rácano, -a ◆ *adj* **1** (*tacaño*) stingy **2** (*vago*) lazy ◆ *nm-nf* **1** (*tacaño*) skinflint **2** (*vago*) lazybones [*pl* lazybones]

racha *nf* **1** (*serie*) run: *una ~ de suerte* a run of good luck ◊ *una ~ de desgracias* a series of misfortunes **2** (*viento*) gust LOC **pasar una mala racha** to be going through a bad patch

racial *adj* racial: *la discriminación ~* racial discrimination ◊ *relaciones ~es* race relations

racimo *nm* bunch

ración *nf* (*comida*) portion, helping (*más coloq*): *Media ~ de calamares, por favor.* A small portion of squid, please. ◊ *Tomaron unas buenas raciones.* They took big helpings.

racional *adj* rational

racionamiento *nm* rationing: *el ~ del agua* water rationing

racismo *nm* racism

racista *adj, nmf* racist

radar *nm* radar [*incontable*]: *los ~es enemigos* enemy radar

radiactivo, -a *adj* radioactive LOC *Ver* LLUVIA

radiador *nm* radiator

radiante *adj* **1** (*brillante*) bright: *Lucía un sol ~.* The sun was shining brightly. **2** (*persona*) radiant: *~ de alegría* radiant with happiness

radical *adj, nmf* radical

radicar *vi* ~ **en** to lie **in** ***sth***: *El éxito del grupo radica en su originalidad.* The group's success lies in their originality.

radio[1] *nm* **1** (*Geom*) radius [*pl* radii] **2** (*rueda*) spoke

radio[2] *nm* (*Quím*) radium

radio[3] *nf* radio [*pl* radios]: *oír/escuchar la ~* to listen to the radio LOC **en/por la radio** on the radio: *Lo he oído en la ~.* I heard it on the radio. ◊ *hablar por la ~* to speak on the radio

radioaficionado, -a *nm-nf* radio ham

radiocasete *nm* radio cassette player

radiografía *nf* X-ray [*pl* X-rays]: *hacer una ~* to take an X-ray

radioyente *nmf* listener

ráfaga *nf* **1** (*viento*) gust **2** (*luz*) flash: *dar la ~* to flash your lights **3** (*dispa-*

ros) burst: *una ~ de disparos* a burst of gunfire

raído, -a *pp, adj* threadbare

raíl *nm* rail

raíz *nf* root LOC **echar raíces 1** (*planta*) to take root **2** (*persona*) to put down roots **raíz cuadrada/cúbica** square/cube root: *La ~ cuadrada de 49 es 7.* The square root of 49 is 7.

raja *nf* **1** (*fisura*) crack **2** (*herida*) cut **3** (*de alimentos*) slice: *una ~ de sandía* a slice of watermelon

rajar ◆ *vt* **1** (*cortar*) to slit: *Me rajaron los neumáticos.* They slit my tyres. **2** (*apuñalar*) to stab ◆ **rajarse** *v pron* **1** (*romperse*) to crack: *El espejo se ha rajado.* The mirror has cracked. **2** (*echarse atrás*) to back out

rajatabla LOC **a rajatabla** to the letter

rallado *pp, adj* LOC *Ver* PAN; *Ver tb* RALLAR

ralladura *nf* LOC **ralladura de limón/naranja** grated lemon/orange rind

rallar *vt* to grate

rama *nf* branch: *la ~ de un árbol* the branch of a tree ◊ *una ~ de la filosofía* a branch of philosophy LOC **andarse/irse por las ramas** to beat about the bush

ramo *nm* **1** (*de flores*) bunch **2** (*sector*) sector LOC *Ver* DOMINGO

rampa *nf* ramp

rana *nf* frog LOC **salir rana** to be a disappointment *Ver tb* HOMBRE

rancio, -a *adj* **1** (*mantequilla*) rancid: *Sabe a ~.* It tastes rancid. **2** (*pan*) stale **3** (*olor*) musty: *El sótano olía a ~.* The basement smelt musty. **4** (*persona*) unfriendly

rango *nm* rank

ranura *nf* slot: *Hay que introducir la moneda por la ~.* You have to put the coin in the slot.

rapapolvo *nm* LOC **echar un rapapolvo** to give *sb* a telling-off

rapar *vt* (*pelo*) to crop

rapaz *nf* (*ave*) bird of prey

rape *nm* monkfish

rapidez *nf* speed LOC **con rapidez** quickly

rápido, -a ◆ *adj* **1** (*breve*) quick: *¿Puedo hacer una llamada rápida?* Can I make a quick phone call? **2** (*veloz*) fast: *un corredor ~* a fast runner ☛ *Ver nota en* FAST[1] ◆ *adv* quickly ◆ *nm* (*río*) rapids [*pl*]

raptar *vt* to kidnap

rapto *nm* kidnapping

raptor, ~a *nm-nf* kidnapper

raqueta *nf* racket: *una ~ de tenis* a tennis racket

raro, -a *adj* **1** (*extraño*) strange: *una manera muy rara de hablar* a very strange way of speaking ◊ *¡Qué ~!* How strange! **2** (*poco común*) rare: *una planta rara* a rare plant LOC *Ver* BICHO, COSA

ras *nm* LOC **a ras de** level with *sth*: *a ~ del suelo* along the floor

rascacielos *nm* skyscraper

rascar ◆ *vt* **1** (*con las uñas*) to scratch: *Oí al perro rascando la puerta.* I heard the dog scratching at the door. **2** (*superficie*) to scrape *sth* (**off** *sth*): *Rascamos la pintura del suelo.* We scraped the paint off the floor. ◆ *vi* to be rough: *Estas toallas rascan.* These towels are rough. ◆ **rascarse** *v pron* to scratch: *~se la cabeza* to scratch your head

rasgado *pp, adj* (*ojos*) almond-shaped *Ver tb* RASGAR

rasgar ◆ *vt* to tear *sth* (up) ◆ **rasgarse** *v pron* to tear

rasgo *nm* **1** (*gen*) feature: *los ~s distintivos de su obra* the distinctive features of her work **2** (*personalidad*) characteristic **3** (*de la pluma*) stroke LOC *Ver* GRANDE

rasguño *nm* scratch

raso, -a ◆ *adj* **1** (*llano*) flat **2** (*cucharada, medida*) level **3** (*balón*) low ◆ *nm* satin

raspar ◆ *vt* **1** (*arañar*) to scratch **2** (*quitar*) to scrape *sth* (**off** *sth*): *Raspa el papel de la pared.* Scrape the paper off the wall. ◆ *vi* to be rough: *Esta toalla raspa.* This towel is rough. ◆ **rasparse** *v pron* to graze: *~se la mano* to graze your hand

rastra *nf* LOC **a rastras**: *Se acercó a ~s.* He crawled over. ◊ *Trajo la bolsa a ~s.* He dragged the bag in. ◊ *No querían irse, los tuve que sacar a ~s.* They didn't want to go so I had to drag them away.

rastrear *vt* **1** (*seguir la pista*) to follow: *Los perros rastreaban el olor.* The dogs followed the scent. **2** (*zona*) to comb

rastreo *nm* search: *Realizaron un ~ de los bosques.* They searched the woods.

rastrillo *nm* rake

rastro *nm* **1** (*huella, pista*) trail: *Los perros siguieron el ~.* The dogs followed the trail. ◊ *No había ni ~ de ella.* There was no trace of her. **2** (*mercadillo*) flea market LOC **sin dejar rastro** without trace *Ver tb* PERDER

rata ◆ *nf* rat ◆ *adj, nmf* (*persona*) mean [*adj*]

ratificar *vt* **1** (*tratado, acuerdo*) to ratify **2** (*noticia*) to confirm

rato *nm* while: *Un ~ más tarde sonó el teléfono.* The telephone rang a while later. LOC **al (poco) rato** shortly after: *Llegaron al poco ~ de irte tú.* They arrived shortly after you left. **a ratos** sometimes **para rato**: *Todavía tengo para ~, no me esperes.* I've still got a lot to do, so don't wait for me. **pasar el rato** to pass the time

ratón *nm* (*animal, Informát*) mouse [*pl* mice] ☛ *Ver dibujo en* ORDENADOR LOC **el ratón/ratoncito Pérez** the tooth fairy **ratón de biblioteca** bookworm

ratonera *nf* **1** (*trampa*) mousetrap **2** (*madriguera*) mousehole

raya *nf* **1** (*gen*) line: *marcar una ~* to draw a line **2** (*listas*) stripe: *una camisa de ~s* a striped shirt **3** (*pelo*) parting: *un peinado con ~ en medio* a hairstyle with a centre parting **4** (*pantalón*) crease LOC **pasarse de la raya** to go too far: *Esta vez te has pasado de la ~.* This time you've gone too far. **tener a algn a raya** to keep a tight rein on sb *Ver tb* TRES

rayar ◆ *vt* to scratch ◆ *vi* ~ **(en/con)** to border **on** ***sth***: *Mi admiración por él rayaba en la devoción.* My admiration for him bordered on devotion.

rayo *nm* **1** (*gen*) ray [*pl* rays]: *un ~ de sol* a ray of sunshine ◊ *los ~s del sol* the sun's rays **2** (*Meteorología*) lightning [*incontable*]: *Los ~s y los truenos me asustan.* Thunder and lightning frighten me. LOC **rayo láser** laser beam **rayos X** X-rays

raza *nf* **1** (*humana*) race **2** (*animal*) breed: *¿De qué ~ es?* What breed is it? LOC **de raza** (*perro*) pedigree

razón *nf* reason (***for sth/doing sth***): *La ~ de su dimisión es obvia.* The reason for his resignation is obvious. LOC **llevar/tener razón** to be right **no tener razón** to be wrong

razonable *adj* reasonable

razonamiento *nm* reasoning

razonar ◆ *vi* (*pensar*) to think: *No razonaba con claridad.* He wasn't thinking clearly. ◆ *vt* (*explicar*) to give reasons **for** ***sth***: *Razona tu respuesta.* Give reasons for your answer.

re *nm* **1** (*nota de la escala*) ray **2** (*tonalidad*) D: *re mayor* D major

reacción *nf* reaction

reaccionar *vi* to react

reactor *nm* **1** (*motor*) jet engine **2** (*avión*) jet LOC **reactor atómico/nuclear** nuclear reactor

readmitir *vt* to readmit *sb* (***to...***): *Le readmitieron en el colegio.* He was readmitted to school.

real[1] *adj* (*caso, historia*) true LOC *Ver* GANA

real[2] *adj* (*de reyes*) royal LOC *Ver* JALEA, PAVO

realidad *nf* reality [*pl* realities] LOC **en realidad** actually **hacerse realidad** to come true *Ver tb* CONVERTIR

realismo *nm* realism

realista ◆ *adj* realistic ◆ *nmf* realist

realización *nf* **1** (*proyecto, trabajo*) carrying out: *Yo me encargaré de la ~ del plan.* I'll take charge of carrying out the plan. **2** (*objetivo, sueño*) fulfilment

realizar ◆ *vt* **1** (*llevar a cabo*) to carry *sth* out: *~ un proyecto* to carry out a project **2** (*sueño, objetivo*) to fulfil ◆ **realizarse** *v pron* **1** (*hacerse realidad*) to come true: *Mis sueños se realizaron.* My dreams came true. **2** (*persona*) to fulfil yourself

realmente *adv* really

realzar *vt* to enhance

reanimar ◆ *vt* to revive ◆ **reanimarse** *v pron* **1** (*fortalecerse*) to get your strength back **2** (*volver en sí*) to regain consciousness

reanudar *vt* **1** (*gen*) to resume: *~ el trabajo* to resume work **2** (*amistad, relación*) to renew

rearme *nm* rearmament

rebaja *nf* **1** (*descuento*) discount: *Nos hicieron una ~.* They gave us a discount. **2 rebajas** sales: *las ~s de verano/enero* the summer/January sales

rebajar ◆ *vt* **1** (*gen*) to reduce: *~ una condena* to reduce a sentence ◊ *Nos rebajó un 15 por ciento.* He gave us a 15 per cent reduction. **2** (*color*) to soften **3** (*humillar*) to humiliate: *Me rebajó delante de todos.* He humiliated me in front of everyone. ◆ **rebajarse** *v pron* **1 rebajarse (a hacer algo)** to lower yourself (**by doing sth**): *No me rebajaría a aceptar tu dinero.* I wouldn't lower myself by accepting your money. **2 rebajarse ante algn** to bow down **to sb**

rebanada *nf* slice: *dos ~s de pan* two slices of bread ☛ *Ver dibujo en* PAN

rebaño *nm* **1** (*ovejas*) flock **2** (*ganado*) herd

rebelarse *v pron* ~ (**contra**) to rebel (**against *sth*/*sb***)

rebelde ◆ *adj* **1** (*gen*) rebel [*n atrib*]: *el general* ~ the rebel general **2** (*espíritu*) rebellious **3** (*niño*) difficult ◆ *nmf* rebel

rebelión *nf* rebellion

rebobinar *vt* to rewind

rebosante *adj* ~ (**de**) overflowing (**with *sth***): ~ *de alegría* overflowing with joy

rebosar *vi, vt* to be overflowing ***with sth***

rebotar *vi* **1** (*gen*) to bounce (***off sth***): *El balón rebotó en el aro.* The ball bounced off the hoop. **2** (*bala*) to ricochet (***off sth***)

rebote *nm* rebound LOC **de rebote** on the rebound

rebozar *vt* **1** (*con pan rallado*) to cover *sth* in breadcrumbs **2** (*con harina*) to dip *sth* in batter

rebuznar *vi* to bray

recado *nm* **1** (*mensaje*) message: *dejar (un)* ~ to leave a message **2** (*encargo*) errand: *Tengo que hacer unos ~s.* I have to run a few errands.

recaer *vi* **1** (*Med*) to have a relapse **2** (*vicio*) to go back to your old ways **3** ~ **en (a)** (*responsabilidad, sospecha*) to fall **on *sb***: *Todas las sospechas recayeron sobre mí.* Suspicion fell on me. **(b)** (*premio*) to go **to *sth*/*sb***: *El premio recayó en mi grupo.* The prize went to my group.

recalcar *vt* to stress

recalentar ◆ *vt* to warm *sth* up ◆ **recalentarse** *v pron* to overheat

recambio *nm* **1** (*gen*) spare (part) **2** (*bolígrafo*) refill

recapacitar ◆ *vt* to think *sth* over ◆ *vi* to think things over

recargado, -a *pp, adj* **1** (*de peso*) overloaded **2** (*estética*): *Iba un poco recargada para mi gusto.* She was a bit overdressed for my taste. *Ver tb* RECARGAR

recargar *vt* **1** (*cargar de nuevo*) **(a)** (*pila, batería*) to recharge **(b)** (*arma*) to reload **(c)** (*pluma*) to refill **2** (*de peso*) to overload

recargo *nm* surcharge

recaudar *vt* to collect

recepción *nf* reception

recepcionista *nmf* receptionist

receta *nf* **1** (*Cocina*) recipe (***for sth***): *Tienes que darme la ~ de este plato.* You must give me the recipe for this dish. **2** (*Med*) prescription: *Sólo se vende con ~.* Only available on prescription.

recetar *vt* to prescribe

rechazar *vt* to turn *sth*/*sb* down: *Rechazaron nuestra propuesta.* Our proposal was turned down.

rechistar *vi*: *¡A mí ni me rechistes!* Don't answer back! ◇ *¡Hazlo sin ~!* Shut up and get on with it!

rechupete LOC **de rechupete** delicious

recibir *vt* **1** (*gen*) to receive, to get (*más coloq*): *Recibí tu carta.* I received/got your letter. **2** (*persona*) to welcome: *Salió a ~nos.* He came out to welcome us.

recibo *nm* **1** (*comprobante*) receipt: *Para cambiarlo necesita el ~.* You'll need the receipt if you want to exchange it. **2** (*factura*) bill: *el ~ de la luz* the electricity bill

reciclar *vt* (*materiales*) to recycle

recién *adv* recently: ~ *creado* recently formed LOC **los recién casados** the newly-weds **recién cumplidos**: *Tengo 15 años ~ cumplidos.* I've just turned 15. **recién pintado** (*cartel*) wet paint **un recién nacido** a newborn baby

reciente *adj* **1** (*pan, huella*) fresh **2** (*acontecimiento*) recent

recipiente *nm* container

recitar *vt* to recite

reclamación *nf* complaint: *hacer/presentar una* ~ to make/lodge a complaint

reclamar ◆ *vt* to demand: *Reclaman justicia.* They are demanding justice. ◆ *vi* to complain: *Deberías ~, no funciona.* This doesn't work so you ought to complain.

reclinar ◆ *vt* to lean *sth* (**on *sth*/*sb***): *Reclinó la cabeza en mi hombro.* He leant his head on my shoulder. ◆ **reclinarse** *v pron* (*persona*) to lean back (***against sth*/*sb***)

recluso, -a *nm-nf* prisoner

recluta *nmf* recruit

recobrar ◆ *vt* **1** (*gen*) to regain, to get *sth* back (*más coloq*): ~ *el dinero* to get your money back **2** (*salud, memoria*) to recover, to get *sth* back (*más coloq*): ~ *la memoria* to get your memory back ◆ **recobrarse** *v pron* to recover (***from sth***): *~se de una enfermedad* to recover from an illness LOC *Ver* CONOCIMIENTO

recogedor *nm* dustpan

recogepelotas *nmf* ballboy [*fem* ballgirl]

recoger ◆ *vt* **1** (*objeto caído*) to pick *sth* up: *Recoge el pañuelo.* Pick up the handkerchief. **2** (*reunir*) to collect: ~ *firmas* to collect signatures **3** (*ordenar*) to tidy: ~ *la casa* to tidy the house **4** (*ir a buscar*) to pick *sth/sb* up: ~ *a los niños del colegio* to pick the children up from school ◆ *vi* to tidy up: *¿Me ayudas a ~?* Will you help me tidy up? ◆ **recogerse** *v pron* **1** (*irse a casa*) to go home **2** (*acostarse*) to go to bed LOC **recogerse el pelo** (*en una coleta*) to tie your hair back *Ver tb* MESA

recogida *nf* LOC **recogida de equipaje(s)** baggage reclaim

recogido, -a *pp, adj* **1** (*tranquilo*) quiet **2** (*pelo*) up: *Estás mejor con el pelo ~.* You look better with your hair up. *Ver tb* RECOGER

recomendación *nf* recommendation: *Fuimos por ~ de mi hermano.* We went on my brother's recommendation.

recomendado, -a *pp, adj* recommended: *muy* ~ highly recommended

recomendar *vt* to recommend

recompensa *nf* reward LOC **en/como recompensa (por)** as a reward (for *sth*)

recompensar *vt* to reward *sb* (**for sth**)

reconciliarse *v pron* to make (it) up (**with sb**): *Riñeron pero se han reconciliado.* They quarrelled but they've made (it) up now.

reconocer *vt* **1** (*gen*) to recognize: *No la reconocí.* I didn't recognize her. **2** (*admitir*) to admit: ~ *un error* to admit a mistake **3** (*examinar*) to examine: ~ *a un paciente* to examine a patient

reconocido, -a *pp, adj* (*apreciado*) well known: *un ~ sociólogo* a well known sociologist *Ver tb* RECONOCER

reconocimiento *nm* recognition LOC **reconocimiento (médico)** medical: *Tienes que hacerte un ~ médico.* You have to have a medical.

reconquista *nf* reconquest LOC **la Reconquista** the Reconquest (of Spain)

reconstruir *vt* **1** (*gen*) to rebuild **2** (*hechos, suceso*) to reconstruct

recopilar *vt* to collect

récord *nm* record: *batir/tener un ~* to break/hold a record

recordar *vt* **1 ~le algo a algn** to remind *sb* (**about sth/to do sth**): *Recuérdame que compre pan.* Remind me to buy some bread. ◊ *Recuérdamelo mañana o se me olvidará.* Remind me tomorrow or I'll forget. **2** (*por asociación*) to remind *sb* **of sth/sb**: *Me recuerda a mi hermano.* He reminds me of my brother. ◊ *¿Sabes a qué/quién me recuerda esta canción?* Do you know what/who this song reminds me of? ☛ *Ver nota en* REMIND **3** (*acordarse*) to remember *sth/doing sth*: *No recuerdo su nombre.* I can't remember his name. ◊ *No recuerdo habértelo dicho.* I don't remember telling you. ◊ *Recuerdo que los vi.* I remember seeing them. ☛ *Ver nota en* REMEMBER LOC **que yo recuerde** as far as I remember **te recuerdo que...** remember...: *Te recuerdo que mañana tienes un examen.* Remember you've got an exam tomorrow.

recorrer *vt* **1** (*gen*) to go **round...**: *Recorrimos Francia en tren.* We went round France by train. **2** (*distancia*) to cover, to do (*más coloq*): *Tardamos tres horas en ~ un kilómetro.* It took us three hours to do one kilometre.

recorrido *nm* route: *el ~ del autobús* the bus route

recortar *vt* **1** (*artículo, figura*) to cut *sth* out: *Recorté la foto de una revista vieja.* I cut the photograph out of an old magazine. **2** (*lo que sobra*) to trim **3** (*gastos*) to cut

recrearse *v pron* ~ **con/en** to take pleasure **in *sth/doing sth***: ~ *con las desgracias ajenas* to take pleasure in other people's misfortunes

recreo *nm* break: *A las once salimos al ~.* Break is at eleven. LOC **de recreo** recreational

recta *nf* straight line LOC **recta final 1** (*Dep*) home straight **2** (*fig*) closing stages [*pl*]: *en la ~ final de la campaña* in the closing stages of the campaign

rectangular *adj* rectangular

rectángulo *nm* rectangle LOC *Ver* TRIÁNGULO

rectificar *vt* **1** (*gen*) to rectify: *La empresa tendrá que ~ los daños.* The company will have to rectify the damage. **2** (*actitud, conducta*) to improve

recto, -a ◆ *adj* straight ◆ *nm* rectum [*pl* rectums/recta] LOC **todo recto** straight on

recuadro *nm* (*casilla*) box

recuerdo *nm* **1** (*memoria*) memory [*pl* memories]: *Guardo un buen ~ de su amistad.* I have happy memories of our friendship. **2** (*turismo*) souvenir **3 recuerdos** regards: *Dale ~s de mi parte.* Give him my regards. ◊ *Mi madre te* *manda ~s.* My mother sends her regards.

recuperación *nf Ver* EXAMEN

recuperar ♦ *vt* **1** (*gen*) to recover: *Confío en que recupere la vista.* I'm sure he'll recover his sight. **2** (*tiempo, clases*) to make *sth* up: *Tienes que ~ tus horas de trabajo.* You'll have to make up the time. **3** (*Educ*) to pass a resit: *He recuperado historia.* I've passed the history resit. ♦ **recuperarse** *v pron* **recuperarse de** to recover **from** ***sth***

recurrir *vi* ~ **a 1** (*utilizar*) to resort **to** ***sth*** **2** (*pedir ayuda*) to turn **to** ***sb***: *No tenía a quién ~.* I had no one to turn to.

recurso *nm* **1** (*medio*) resort: *como último ~* as a last resort **2 recursos** resources: *~s humanos/económicos* human/economic resources

red *nf* **1** (*Dep, Caza, Pesca*) net **2** (*Informát, Comunicaciones*) network: *la ~ de ferrocarriles/carreteras* the railway/road network **3** (*organizaciones, sucursales*) chain LOC **caer en la red** to fall into the trap

redacción *nf* essay [*pl* essays]: *hacer una ~ sobre tu ciudad* to write an essay on your town

redactar *vt, vi* to write: *~ una carta* to write a letter ◊ *Para ser tan pequeño redacta bien.* He writes well for his age.

redactor, ~a *nm-nf* (*Period*) editor

redada *nf* raid: *efectuar una ~* to carry out a raid

redicho, -a *nm-nf* know-all

redoblar *vi* (*tambor*) to roll

redomado, -a *adj* out-and-out: *un mentiroso ~* an out-and-out liar

redonda *nf* (*Mús*) semibreve

redondear *vt* **1** (*gen*) to round *sth* off: *~ un negocio* to round off a business deal **2** (*precio, cifra*) to round *sth* up/down

redondo, -a *adj* round: *en números ~s* in round figures LOC **a la redonda**: *No había ninguna casa en diez kilómetros a la redonda.* There were no houses within ten kilometres. **salir redondo** to turn out perfectly: *Nos salió todo ~.* It all turned out perfectly for us. *Ver tb* MESA

reducción *nf* reduction

reducido, -a *pp, adj* (*pequeño*) small *Ver tb* REDUCIR

reducir *vt* to reduce: *~ la velocidad* to reduce speed ◊ *El fuego redujo la casa a cenizas.* The fire reduced the house to ashes. LOC **todo se reduce a...** it all boils down to...

redundancia *nf* redundancy

reelegir *vt* to re-elect: *Le han reelegido como su representante.* They've re-elected him as their representative.

reembolsar *vt* **1** (*cantidad pagada*) to refund **2** (*gastos*) to reimburse

reembolso *nm* LOC **contra reembolso** cash on delivery (*abrev* COD) *Ver tb* ENVÍO

reemplazar *vt* to replace *sth/sb* (**with** ***sth/sb***)

reencarnación *nf* reincarnation

reencarnarse *v pron* ~ (**en**) to be reincarnated (**in/as** ***sth/sb***)

referencia *nf* reference (**to** ***sth/sb***): *servir de/como ~* to serve as a (point of) reference ◊ *Con ~ a su carta...* With reference to your letter... ◊ *tener buenas ~s* to have good references LOC **hacer referencia a** to refer to *sth/sb*

referéndum (*tb* **referendo**) *nm* referendum [*pl* referendums/referenda]

referente *adj* ~ **a** regarding *sth/sb* LOC **(en lo) referente a** with regard to *sth/sb*

referirse *v pron* ~ **a** to refer **to** ***sth/sb***: *¿A qué te refieres?* What are you referring to?

refilón LOC **de refilón**: *Me miraba de ~.* He was looking at me out of the corner of his eye. ◊ *La vi sólo de ~.* I only caught a glimpse of her.

refinería *nf* refinery [*pl* refineries]

reflejar *vt* to reflect

reflejo, -a ♦ *adj* reflex [*n atrib*]: *un acto ~* a reflex action ♦ *nm* **1** (*gen*) reflection: *Veía mi ~ en el espejo.* I could see my reflection in the mirror. **2** (*reacción*) reflex: *tener buenos ~s* to have good reflexes **3 reflejos** (*pelo*) streaks

reflexionar *vi* ~ (**sobre**) to reflect (**on** ***sth***)

reforestación *nf* reafforestation

reforma *nf* **1** (*gen*) reform **2** (*en un edificio*) alteration: *cerrado por ~s* closed for alterations

reformar ♦ *vt* **1** (*gen*) to reform: *~ una ley/a un delincuente* to reform a law/delinquent **2** (*edificio*) to make alterations **to** ***sth*** ♦ **reformarse** *v pron* to mend your ways

reformatorio *nm* young offenders' institution

reforzar *vt* to reinforce *sth* (**with** ***sth***)

refrán *nm* saying: *Como dice el ~...* As the saying goes...

refrescante *adj* refreshing

refrescar ◆ *vt* **1** (*enfriar*) to cool **2** (*memoria*) to refresh **3** (*conocimientos*) to brush up ***on sth***: *Necesito ~ mi inglés.* I have to brush up on my English. ◆ *v imp* to get cooler: *Por las noches refresca.* It gets cooler at night. ◆ **refrescarse** *v pron* to freshen up

refresco *nm* soft drink

refrigerar *vt* to refrigerate

refuerzo *nm* reinforcement

refugiado, -a *nm-nf* refugee: *un campo de ~s* a refugee camp

refugiar ◆ *vt* to shelter *sth/sb* (***from sth/sb***) ◆ **refugiarse** *v pron* **refugiarse** (**de**) to take refuge (**from *sth***): *~se de la lluvia* to take refuge from the rain

refugio *nm* refuge: *un ~ de montaña* a mountain refuge

refunfuñar *vi* to grumble (***about sth***)

regadera *nf* watering can LOC **estar como una regadera** to be as mad as a hatter

regadío *nm* irrigation: *tierra de ~* irrigated land

regalar *vt* **1** (*hacer un regalo*) to give: *Me regaló un ramo de flores.* She gave me a bunch of flowers. **2** (*cuando no se quiere algo*) to give *sth* away: *Voy a ~ tus muñecas.* I'm going to give your dolls away.

regaliz *nm* liquorice

regalo *nm* **1** (*obsequio*) present **2** (*fig*) gift: *La última pregunta fue un ~.* That last question was an absolute gift. LOC *Ver* ENVOLVER, PAPEL

regañadientes LOC **a regañadientes** reluctantly

regañar *vt* to tell *sb* off (***for sth/doing sth***)

regar *vt* **1** (*planta, jardín*) to water **2** (*esparcir*) to scatter

regate *nm* (*Fútbol*) dribble

regatear *vt, vi* **1** (*precio*) to haggle (***over/about sth***) **2** (*Fútbol*) to dribble

regazo *nm* lap

regenerar ◆ *vt* to regenerate ◆ **regenerarse** *v pron* **1** (*gen*) to regenerate **2** (*persona*) to mend your ways

regente *adj, nmf* regent: *el príncipe ~* the Prince Regent

régimen *nm* **1** (*Pol, normas*) regime: *un ~ muy liberal* a very liberal regime **2** (*dieta*) diet: *estar a ~* to be on a diet

regimiento *nm* regiment

región *nf* region

regional *adj* regional

regir ◆ *vt* **1** (*país, sociedad*) to rule **2** (*empresa, proyecto*) to run ◆ *vi* **1** (*ley*) to be in force: *El convenio rige desde el pasado día 15.* The agreement has been in force since the 15th. **2** (*persona*) to be all there: *No le hagas caso, no rige muy bien.* Don't take any notice of him; he's not all there.

registrado, -a *pp, adj* LOC *Ver* MARCA; *Ver tb* REGISTRAR

registrador, ~a *adj* LOC *Ver* CAJA

registrar ◆ *vt* **1** (*inspeccionar*) to search **2** (*grabar, hacer constar*) to record: *~ información* to record information ◆ **registrarse** *v pron* to register

registro *nm* **1** (*inscripción*) registration **2** (*inspección*) search **3** (*lugar, oficina*) registry [*pl* registries] LOC **registro civil** registry office

regla *nf* **1** (*gen*) rule: *Va contra las ~s del colegio.* It's against the school rules. ◊ *por ~ general* as a general rule **2** (*instrumento*) ruler **3** (*menstruación*) period LOC **en regla** in order

reglamentario, -a *adj* regulation [*n atrib*]: *uniforme ~* regulation uniform

reglamento *nm* regulations [*pl*]

regocijarse *v pron* to be delighted (***at/with sth***): *Se regocijaron con la noticia.* They were delighted at the news.

regocijo *nm* delight

regresar *vi* to go/come back (***to...***): *No quieren ~ a su país.* They don't want to go back to their own country. ◊ *Creo que regresan mañana.* I think they're coming back tomorrow.

regreso *nm* return (***to...***): *a mi ~ a la ciudad* on my return to the city

reguero *nm* trickle: *un ~ de agua/aceite* a trickle of water/oil

regular[1] *vt* to regulate

regular[2] ◆ *adj* **1** (*gen*) regular: *verbos ~es* regular verbs **2** (*mediocre*) poor: *Sus notas han sido muy ~es.* His marks have been very poor. **3** (*mediano*) medium: *de altura ~* of medium height ◆ *adv*: *—¿Qué tal te va? —Regular.* 'How are things?' 'So so.' ◊ *El negocio va ~.* Business isn't going too well. ◊ *La abuela está ~ (de salud).* Granny is poorly. LOC *Ver* VUELO

regularidad *nf* regularity LOC **con regularidad** regularly

rehabilitación *nf* rehabilitation: *programas para la ~ de delincuentes* rehabilitation programmes for young offenders

rehabilitar *vt* to rehabilitate

rehacer *vt* to redo LOC **rehacer la vida** to rebuild your life

rehén *nmf* hostage

rehogar *vt* to fry *sth* lightly

rehuir *vt* to avoid *sth/sb/doing sth*: *Rehuyó mi mirada.* She avoided my gaze.

rehusar *vt* to refuse *sth/to do sth*: *Rehusaron venir.* They refused to come. ◊ *Rehusé su invitación.* I turned their invitation down.

reina *nf* queen LOC *Ver* ABEJA

reinado *nm* reign

reinar *vi* **1** (*gobernar*) to reign **2** (*prevalecer*) to prevail

reincidir *vi* ~ (**en**) to relapse (**into *sth*/ *doing sth***)

reiniciar *vt* to resume: ~ *el trabajo* to resume work

reino *nm* **1** (*gen*) kingdom: *el ~ animal* the animal kingdom **2** (*ámbito*) realm LOC **el Reino Unido** the United Kingdom (*abrev* UK)

reintegro *nm* **1** (*gen*) refund **2** (*en un sorteo*) return of stake

reír ◆ *vi* to laugh: *echarse a ~* to burst out laughing ◆ *vt* to laugh **at *sth***: *Le ríen todas las gracias.* They laugh at all his jokes. ◆ **reírse** *v pron* **1 reírse con algn** to have a laugh **with sb**: *Siempre nos reímos con él.* We always have a laugh with him. **2 reírse con algo** to laugh **at sth 3 reírse de** to laugh **at *sth*/ *sb***: *¿De qué te ríes?* What are you laughing at? ◊ *Siempre se ríen de mí.* They always laugh at me. LOC **reír(se) a carcajadas** to split your sides (laughing)

reivindicación *nf* **1** (*derecho*) claim (***for sth***) **2** ~ (**de**) (*atentado*): *No se ha producido una ~ de la bomba.* Nobody has claimed responsibility for the bomb.

reivindicar *vt* **1** (*reclamar*) to claim **2** (*atentado*) to claim responsibility **for *sth***

reja *nf* **1** (*ventana*) grille **2 rejas** bars: *entre ~s* behind bars

rejilla *nf* **1** (*gen*) grille **2** (*alcantarilla*) grating

rejuvenecer *vt* to make *sb* look younger

relación *nf* **1** ~ (**con**) (*gen*) relationship (**with *sth*/*sb***): *mantener relaciones con algn* to have a relationship with sb ◊ *Nuestra ~ es puramente laboral.* Our relationship is strictly professional. **2** ~ (**entre**) (*conexión*) connection (**between …**) LOC **con/en relación a** in/ with relation to *sth/sb* **relación calidad precio** value for money **relaciones públicas** public relations (*abrev* PR)

relacionado, -a *pp, adj* ~ (**con**) related (**to *sth***) *Ver tb* RELACIONAR

relacionar ◆ *vt* to relate *sth* (***to/with sth***): *Los médicos relacionan los problemas del corazón con el estrés.* Doctors relate heart disease with stress. ◆ **relacionarse** *v pron* **relacionarse** (**con**) to mix (**with *sb***)

relajación *nf* **1** (*gen*) relaxation: *técnicas de ~* relaxation techniques **2** (*tensión*) easing: *la ~ de las tensiones internacionales* the easing of international tension

relajar ◆ *vt* to relax: *Relaja la mano.* Relax your hand. ◆ **relajarse** *v pron* **1** (*gen*) to relax: *Tienes que ~te.* You must relax. **2** (*reglas, disciplina*) to become lax

relamer ◆ *vt* to lick *sth* clean ◆ **relamerse** *v pron* to lick your lips

relámpago *nm* **1** (*tormenta*) lightning [*incontable*]: *Un ~ y un trueno anunciaron la tormenta.* A flash of lightning and a clap of thunder heralded the storm. ◊ *Me asustan los ~s.* Lightning frightens me. **2** (*rápido*) lightning [*n atrib*]: *un viaje/una visita ~* a lightning trip/visit

relatar *vt* to relate

relatividad *nf* relativity

relativo, -a *adj* **1** (*no absoluto*) relative: *Hombre, eso es ~.* Well, that depends. **2** ~ **a** relating (**to *sth***)

relato *nm* **1** (*cuento*) story [*pl* stories]: *un ~ histórico* a historical story **2** (*descripción*) account: *hacer un ~ de los hechos* to give an account of events

relax *nm*: *Pintar me sirve de ~.* Painting relaxes me. ◊ *No tengo ni un momento de ~.* I don't get a moment's rest.

relevar ◆ *vt* **1** (*sustituir*) to take over (**from *sb***): *Estuve de guardia hasta que me relevó un compañero.* I was on duty until a colleague took over from me. **2** (*de un cargo*) to relieve *sb* **of *sth***: *Ha sido relevado del cargo.* He has been relieved of his duties. ◆ **relevarse** *v pron* to take turns (***at sth/doing sth***)

relevo *nm* **1** (*gen*) relief: *El ~ no tardará en llegar.* The relief will be here soon. **2** (*turno*) shift: *¿Quién va a organizar los ~s?* Who is going to organize the shifts? **3 relevos** (*Dep*): *una carrera de ~s* a relay race

relieve *nm* **1** (*Geog*): *una región de ~ accidentado* an area with a rugged landscape ◊ *un mapa en ~* a relief map **2** (*importancia*) significance: *un acontecimiento de ~ internacional* an event of international significance

religión *nf* religion

religioso, -a ◆ *adj* religious ◆ *nm-nf* monk [*fem* nun]

relinchar *vi* to neigh

reliquia *nf* relic

rellenar *vt* **1** (*gen*) to fill *sth* (***with sth***): *Rellené las tartaletas de/con fruta.* I filled the cases with fruit. **2** (*volver a llenar*) to refill: *No hacía más que ~ los vasos.* He just kept on refilling everybody's glasses. **3** (*formulario, impreso*) to fill *sth* in: *~ un formulario* to fill in a form

relleno *nm* **1** (*gen*) filling: *pasteles con ~ de nata* cream cakes **2** (*cojín*) stuffing

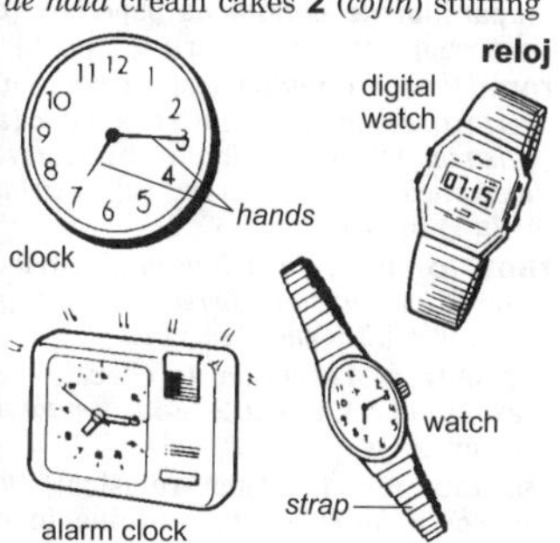

reloj *nm* **1** (*gen*) clock: *¿Qué hora tiene el ~ de la cocina?* What time does the kitchen clock say? **2** (*de pulsera, de bolsillo*) watch: *Tengo el ~ atrasado.* My watch is slow. **LOC contra reloj** against the clock **reloj de cuco** cuckoo clock **reloj de sol** sundial *Ver tb* CUERDA

relojería *nf* watchmaker's [*pl* watchmakers]

relojero, -a *nm-nf* watchmaker

relucir *vi* to shine **LOC** *Ver* ORO, TRAPO

remangar(se) *vt, v pron* **1** (*manga, pantalón*) to roll *sth* up: *Se remangó los pantalones.* He rolled up his trousers. **2** (*falda*) to lift

remar *vi* to row

rematar *vt* **1** (*gen*) to finish *sth/sb* off: *Remataré el informe este fin de semana.* I'll finish off the report this weekend. **2** (*Dep*) to shoot: *La pelota pasó al capitán, que remató la jugada.* The ball went to the captain, who shot at goal.

remate *nm* **1** (*término*) end **2** (*extremo*) top: *el ~ de una torre* the top of a tower **3** (*borde*) edging: *un ~ de encaje* a lace edging **4** (*Dep*) shot: *El portero evitó el ~.* The goalkeeper saved the shot. **LOC de remate**: *ser un imbécil de ~* to be a total idiot *Ver tb* LOCO

remediar *vt* **1** (*solucionar*) to remedy: *~ la situación* to remedy the situation **2** (*daño*) to repair: *Quisiera ~ el daño que he causado.* I'd like to repair the damage I've caused. **LOC no lo puedo remediar** I, you, etc can't help it

remedio *nm* ~ (**para/contra**) remedy [*pl* remedies] (**for *sth***) **LOC no tener más remedio (que…)** to have no choice (but to…)

remendar *vt* **1** (*gen*) to mend **2** (*calcetines*) to darn

remiendo *nm* (*Costura*) patch

remite *nm* return address

remitente *nmf* sender

remo *nm* **1** (*instrumento*) oar **2** (*Dep*) rowing: *practicar el ~* to row ◊ *un club de ~* a rowing club **LOC a remo**: *Cruzaron el estrecho a ~.* They rowed across the straits. *Ver tb* BARCA

remojar *vt* to soak

remojo *nm*: *Pon los garbanzos a ~.* Soak the chickpeas.

remolacha *nf* beetroot **LOC remolacha azucarera** sugar beet

remolcar *vt* to tow

remolino *nm* **1** (*gen*) eddy [*pl* eddies] **2** (*en río*) whirlpool **3** (*pelo*) cow-lick

remolón, -ona ◆ *adj* lazy ◆ *nm-nf* lazybones [*pl* lazybones]

remolque *nm* trailer

remontar ◆ *vt* **1** (*cuesta, río*) to go up *sth* **2** (*dificultad*) to overcome **3** (*partido, marcador*) to turn *sth* round: *El equipo no consiguió ~ el partido.* The team didn't manage to turn the match round. ◆ **remontarse** *v pron* **remontarse a** (*hecho, tradición*) to date back **to *sth*** **LOC remontar el vuelo** to soar

remorder *vi* LOC **remorderle a algn la conciencia** to have a guilty conscience

remordimiento *nm* remorse [*incontable*] LOC **tener remordimientos (de conciencia)** to feel guilty

remoto, -a *adj* remote: *una posibilidad remota* a remote possibility

remover *vt* **1** (*líquido*) to stir **2** (*ensalada*) to toss **3** (*tierra*) to turn *sth* over **4** (*asunto*) to bring *sth* up

renacimiento *nm* **1** (*resurgimiento*) revival **2 Renacimiento** Renaissance

renacuajo *nm* tadpole

rencor *nm* resentment LOC *Ver* GUARDAR

rencoroso, -a *adj* resentful

rendición *nf* surrender

rendido, -a *pp, adj* (*agotado*) worn out, exhausted (*más formal*) *Ver tb* RENDIR

rendija *nf* crack

rendimiento *nm* **1** (*gen*) performance: *su ~ en los estudios* his academic performance ◊ *un motor de alto ~* a high-performance engine **2** (*producción*) output

rendir *vt* (*cansar*) to tire *sb* out ◆ *vi*: *Rindo mucho mejor por la mañana.* I work much better in the mornings. ◆ **rendirse** *v pron* **1** (*gen*) to give up: *No te rindas.* Don't give up. **2** (*Mil*) to surrender (***to sth/sb***) LOC **rendir culto** to worship

renegar *vi* **1** ~ **de** to renounce *sth* [*vt*]: *~ de la religión/política* to renounce your religion/politics **2** (*quejarse*) to grumble (***about sth***): *Deja ya de ~.* Stop grumbling.

renglón *nm* line

reno *nm* reindeer [*pl* reindeer]

renovación *nf* **1** (*gen*) renewal: *la fecha de ~* the renewal date **2** (*estructural*) renovation: *Están haciendo renovaciones en el edificio.* They're doing renovation work in the building.

renovar *vt* **1** (*gen*) to renew: *~ un contrato/el pasaporte* to renew a contract/your passport **2** (*edificio*) to renovate **3** (*modernizar*) to modernize

renta *nf* **1** (*alquiler*) rent **2** (*Fin, ingresos*) income: *el impuesto sobre la ~* income tax LOC *Ver* DECLARACIÓN

rentable *adj* profitable: *un negocio ~* a profitable deal

renunciar *vt* ~ **a 1** (*gen*) to renounce: *~ a una herencia/un derecho* to renounce an inheritance/a right **2** (*puesto*) to resign (**from *sth***): *Renunció a su cargo.* She resigned from her post.

reñido, -a *pp, adj* hard-fought: *El partido estuvo muy ~.* It was a hard-fought match. *Ver tb* REÑIR

reñir ◆ *vt* to tell *sb* off (***for sth/doing sth***): *Me riñó por no haber regado las plantas.* He told me off for not watering the plants. ◆ *vi* ~ **(con) (por) 1** (*discutir*) to argue (**with *sb***) (**about/over *sth***): *No riñáis por eso.* Don't argue over something like that. **2** (*enemistarse*) to fall out (**with *sb***) (**about/over *sth***): *Creo que ha reñido con su novia.* I think he's fallen out with his girlfriend.

reo *nmf* accused LOC **reo de muerte** condemned person

reojo LOC **mirar de reojo** to look *at sb* out of the corner of your eye

reparación *nf* repair: *reparaciones en el acto* repairs while you wait ◊ *Esta casa necesita reparaciones.* This house is in need of repair.

reparar ◆ *vt* to repair ◆ *vi* ~ **en** to notice *sth*/(*that...*): *Reparé en que sus zapatos estaban mojados.* I noticed (that) his shoes were wet.

reparo *nm* reservation LOC **poner reparos** to find fault *with sth*

repartidor, ~a *nm-nf* delivery man/woman [*pl* delivery men/women] LOC **repartidor de periódicos** paperboy [*pl* paperboys] [*fem* papergirl]

repartir *vt* **1** (*dividir*) to share *sth* (out): *~ el trabajo* to share the work out **2 (a)** (*distribuir*) to distribute **(b)** (*correo, mercancías*) to deliver **(c)** (*cartas, golpes*) to deal

reparto *nm* **1** (*distribución*) distribution **2** (*mercancías, correo*) delivery [*pl* deliveries] **3** (*Cine, Teat*) cast

repasar *vt* **1** (*revisar*) to check: *~ un texto* to check a text **2** (*Educ, estudiar*) to revise

repaso *nm* **1** (*Educ*) revision: *Hoy vamos a hacer ~.* We're going to do some revision today. ◊ *dar un ~ a algo* to revise sth **2** (*revisión, inspección*) check

repatriar *vt* to repatriate

repelente *adj, nmf* (*persona*) know-all [*n*]: *un niño ~* a know-all

repente *nm* LOC **de repente** suddenly

repentino, -a *adj* sudden

repercusión *nf* repercussion

repercutir *vi* to have repercussions: *Podría ~ en la economía.* It could have repercussions on the economy.

repertorio *nm* (*musical*) repertoire

repetición *nf* repetition

repetir ◆ *vt* to repeat: *¿Puede repetírmelo?* Could you repeat that please? ◊ *No te lo pienso ~.* I'm not going to tell you again. ◆ *vi* **1** (*servirse otro poco*) to have another helping: *¿Puedo ~?* Can I have another helping? **2** (*ajo, cebolla, pimiento*) to repeat (**on** ***sb***): *Me está repitiendo el pimiento.* The peppers are repeating (on me). **3** (*volver a hacer*) to do *sth* again: *Lo voy a tener que ~.* I'm going to have to do it again. ◆ **repetirse** *v pron* **1** (*acontecimiento*) to happen again: *¡Y que no se repita!* And don't let it happen again! **2** (*persona*) to repeat yourself

repicar *vt, vi* to ring

repisa *nf* **1** (*gen*) ledge **2** (*chimenea*) mantelpiece **3** (*ventana*) windowsill

repleto, -a *adj* ~ (**de**) full (**of** ***sth/sb***)

replicar ◆ *vt* to retort: *—¿Quién ha pedido tu opinión? —replicó.* 'Who asked you?' he retorted ◆ *vi* to answer back: *No me repliques ¿eh?* Don't answer me back!

repollo *nm* cabbage

reponer ◆ *vt* **1** (*combustible, provisiones*) to replenish **2** (*película*) to rerun ◆ **reponerse** *v pron* **reponerse** (**de**) to recover (**from** ***sth***)

reportaje *nm* documentary [*pl* documentaries]: *Esta noche ponen un ~ sobre la India.* There's a documentary about India tonight.

reportero, -a *nm-nf* reporter LOC **reportero gráfico** press photographer

reposacabezas *nm* headrest

reposar *vi* **1** (*gen*) to rest: *Necesitas ~.* You need to rest. **2** (*yacer*) to lie: *Sus restos reposan en este cementerio.* His remains lie in this cemetery. ☛ *Ver nota en* LIE[2]

reposo *nm* **1** (*descanso*) rest: *Los médicos le han mandado ~.* The doctors have told him to rest. **2** (*paz*) peace: *No tengo ni un momento de ~.* I don't get a moment's peace.

repostar *vi* to refuel

repostería *nf* confectionery: *La ~ se me da muy mal.* I'm not very good at baking.

represalia *nf* reprisal: *Esperemos que no haya ~s contra los vecinos.* Let's hope there are no reprisals against the local people.

representación *nf* **1** (*gen*) representation **2** (*Teat*) performance

representante *nmf* **1** (*gen*) representative: *el ~ del partido* the party representative **2** (*Cine, Teat*) agent: *el ~ de la actriz* the actress's agent

representar *vt* **1** (*organización, país*) to represent: *Representaron a España en las Olimpíadas.* They represented Spain in the Olympics. **2** (*cuadro, estatua*) to depict: *El cuadro representa una batalla.* The painting depicts a battle. **3** (*simbolizar*) to symbolize: *El verde representa la esperanza.* Green symbolizes hope. **4** (*Teat*) **(a)** (*obra*) to perform **(b)** (*papel*) to play: *Representó el papel de Otelo.* He played the part of Othello. **5** (*edad*) to look: *Representa unos 30 años.* She looks about 30.

representativo, -a *adj* representative

represión *nf* repression

represivo, -a *adj* repressive

reprimido, -a *pp, adj, nm-nf* repressed [*adj*]: *Es un ~.* He's repressed.

reprochar *vt* to reproach *sb* ***for sth/doing sth***: *Me reprochó el no haberle llamado.* He reproached me for not telephoning him.

reproducción *nf* reproduction

reproducir(se) *vt, v pron* to reproduce

reptar *vi* **1** (*serpiente*) to slither **2** (*persona*) to crawl

reptil *nm* reptile

república *nf* republic

republicano, -a *adj, nm-nf* republican

repuesto *nm* spare part LOC **de repuesto** spare: *un carrete de ~* a spare film

repugnante *adj* revolting

reputación *nf* reputation: *tener buena/mala ~* to have a good/bad reputation

requemado *pp, adj* burnt

requisar *vt* to seize: *La policía les requisó los documentos.* The police seized their documents.

requisito *nm* requirement (***for sth/to do sth***)

res *nf* (farm) animal

resaca *nf* **1** (*mar*) undertow **2** (*borrachera*) hangover: *tener ~* to have a hangover

resaltar ◆ *vt* **1** (*color, belleza*) to bring *sth* out **2** (*poner énfasis*) to highlight ◆ *vi* to stand out (***from sth***) LOC **hacer resaltar** to bring *sth* out

resbaladizo, -a *adj* slippery

resbalar ◆ *vi* **1** (*vehículo*) to skid **2** (*superficie*) to be slippery **3** ~ (**por**) to slide (**along/down** ***sth***): *La lluvia resbalaba por los cristales.* The rain slid down the windows. ◆ **resbalar(se)** *vi, v pron* to slip (***on sth***): *Resbalé con una mancha de aceite.* I slipped on a patch of oil. LOC **resbalarle algo a algn** not to care about sth: *Los estudios le resbalan.* He doesn't care about school.

resbalón *nm* slip: *dar/pegarse un ~* to slip

rescatar *vt* **1** (*salvar*) to rescue *sb* (***from sth***) **2** (*recuperar*) to recover *sth* (***from sth/sb***): *Pudieron ~ el dinero.* They were able to recover the money.

rescate *nm* **1** (*salvación*) rescue: *las labores de ~* rescue work **2** (*pago*) ransom: *pedir un elevado ~* to demand a high ransom LOC **exigir/pedir rescate por algn** to hold sb to ransom

rescoldo *nm* embers [*pl*]

reseco, -a *adj* very dry

resentirse *v pron* **1** (*deteriorarse*) to deteriorate: *Su salud empieza a ~.* His health is starting to deteriorate. **2** (*enfadarse*) to be annoyed (***with sb***) (***about sth***): *Se resintió con ella porque le mintió.* He was annoyed with her because she'd lied to him. **3** (*dolerse*) to hurt: *La pierna aún se resiente de la caída.* My leg still hurts from the fall.

reserva ◆ *nf* **1** (*hotel, viaje, restaurante*) reservation: *hacer una ~* to make a reservation **2** ~ **(de)** reserve(s) [*se usa mucho en plural*]: *una buena ~ de carbón* good coal reserves ◊ *~s de petróleo* oil reserves **3** (*gasolina*) reserve tank **4** (*animales, plantas*) reserve ◆ *nmf* (*Dep*) reserve

reservado, -a *pp, adj* (*persona*) reserved *Ver tb* RESERVAR

reservar *vt* **1** (*guardar*) to save: *Resérvame un sitio.* Save me a place. **2** (*pedir con antelación*) to book: *Quiero ~ una mesa para tres.* I'd like to book a table for three.

resfriado *nm* cold

resfriarse *v pron* to catch a cold

resguardar ◆ *vt* to protect *sth/sb* ***against/from sth*** ◆ **resguardarse** *v pron* **resguardarse (de)** to shelter (**from** ***sth***): *~se de la lluvia* to shelter from the rain

resguardo *nm* ticket

residencia *nf* residence LOC **residencia de estudiantes** hall (of residence) *Ver tb* ANCIANO

residuo *nm* **residuos** waste [*incontable, v sing*]: *~s tóxicos* toxic waste

resina *nf* resin

resistencia *nf* (*física*) strength: *No tengo mucha ~.* I'm not very strong.

resistir ◆ *vt* **1** (*soportar*) to withstand: *Las chabolas no resistieron el vendaval.* The shanty town didn't withstand the hurricane. **2** (*peso*) to take: *El puente no resistirá el peso de ese camión.* The bridge won't take the weight of that lorry. **3** (*tentación*) to resist *sth/doing sth*: *No lo pude ~ y me comí todos los pasteles.* I couldn't resist eating all the cakes. ◆ *vi* to hold up ◆ **resistirse** *v pron* to refuse ***to do sth***: *Me resistía a creerlo.* I refused to believe it.

resolver *vt* **1** (*problema, misterio, caso*) to solve **2** ~ **hacer algo** to resolve **to do sth**: *Hemos resuelto no decírselo.* We've resolved not to tell her.

resonar *vi* **1** (*metal, voz*) to ring **2** (*retumbar*) to resound

resoplar *vi* to puff and pant: *Deja de ~.* Stop puffing and panting.

respaldar *vt* to back *sth/sb* up: *Mis padres siempre me respaldaron.* My parents always backed me up.

respaldo *nm* **1** (*silla*) back **2** (*apoyo*) support

respectivo, -a *adj* respective

respecto *nm* LOC **con respecto a** with regard to *sth/sb*

respetable *adj* respectable: *una persona/cantidad ~* a respectable person/amount

respetar *vt* **1** (*estimar*) to respect *sth/sb* (***for sth***): *~ las opiniones de los demás* to respect other people's opinions **2** (*código, signo*) to obey: *~ las señales de tráfico* to obey road signs

respeto *nm* **1** ~ **(a/hacia)** (*consideración, veneración*) respect (**for** ***sth/sb***): *el ~ a los demás/la naturaleza* respect for others/nature **2** ~ **a** (*miedo*) fear **of** ***sth***: *tenerle ~ al agua* to be afraid of water LOC *Ver* FALTAR

respetuoso, -a *adj* respectful

respiración *nf*: *ejercicios de ~* breathing exercises ◊ *quedarse sin ~* to be out of breath ◊ *contener la ~* to hold your breath LOC **respiración artificial** artificial respiration **respiración boca a boca** mouth-to-mouth resuscitation *Ver tb* AGUANTAR

respirar *vt, vi* to breathe: *~ aire puro* to breathe fresh air ◊ *Respira hondo.* Take a deep breath. LOC **no dejar a algn respirar** not to give sb a minute's peace

respiratorio, -a *adj* respiratory

resplandecer *vi* to shine

resplandeciente *adj* shining

resplandor *nm* **1** (*gen*) brightness: *el ~ de la lámpara* the brightness of the lamp **2** (*fuego*) blaze

responder ◆ *vt, vi* ~ (**a**) to answer, to reply (*más formal*): *Tengo que ~ a estas cartas.* I have to reply to these letters. ◊ *~ a una pregunta* to answer a question ◆ *vi* **1** (*reaccionar*) to respond (**to *sth***): *~ a un tratamiento* to respond to treatment ◊ *Los frenos no respondían.* The brakes didn't respond. **2** ~ **de/por** to answer **for *sth/sb***: *¡No respondo de mí!* I won't answer for my actions! ◊ *Yo respondo por él.* I'll answer for him.

responsabilidad *nf* responsibility [*pl* responsibilities]

responsabilizarse *v pron* **responsabilizarse (de)** to assume responsibility (**for *sth***): *Me responsabilizo de mis decisiones.* I assume responsibility for my decisions.

responsable ◆ *adj* responsible (***for sth***): *¿Quién es el ~ de este barullo?* Who is responsible for this row? ◆ *nmf* (*encargado*) person in charge: *el ~ de las obras* the person in charge of the building work ◊ *Los ~s se entregaron.* Those responsible gave themselves up.

respuesta *nf* **1** (*contestación*) answer, reply [*pl* replies] (*más formal*): *No hemos obtenido ~.* We haven't had a reply. ◊ *una ~ clara* a clear answer ◊ *Quiero una ~ a mi pregunta.* I want an answer to my question. **2** (*reacción*) response (***to sth***): *una ~ favorable* a favourable response

resquebrajar(se) *vt, v pron* to crack

resta *nf* (*Mat*) subtraction

restablecer ◆ *vt* **1** (*gen*) to restore: *~ el orden* to restore order **2** (*diálogo, negociaciones*) to resume ◆ **restablecerse** *v pron* to recover (***from sth***): *Tardó varias semanas en ~se.* He took several weeks to recover.

restar *vt* to subtract (*formal*), to take *sth* away: *~ 3 de 7* to take 3 away from 7 LOC **restar(le) importancia a algo** to play sth down

restauración *nf* restoration

restaurador, ~a *nm-nf* restorer

restaurante *nm* restaurant ☛ *Ver pág* 320. LOC *Ver* VAGÓN

restaurar *vt* to restore

resto *nm* **1** (*gen*) rest: *El ~ te lo contaré mañana.* I'll tell you the rest tomorrow. **2** (*Mat*) remainder: *¿Qué ~ te da?* What's the remainder? **3 restos (a)** (*comida*) leftovers **(b)** (*Arqueología*) remains LOC **restos mortales** mortal remains

restregar ◆ *vt* to scrub ◆ **restregarse** *v pron* to rub: *El pequeño se restregaba los ojos.* The little boy was rubbing his eyes.

resucitar ◆ *vi* (*Relig*) to rise from the dead ◆ *vt* (*Med*) to resuscitate

resultado *nm* result: *como ~ de la pelea* as a result of the fight LOC **dar/no dar resultado** to be successful/unsuccessful **resultado final** (*Dep*) final score

resultar *vi* **1** (*ser, quedar*) to be: *Resulta difícil de creer.* It's hard to believe. ◊ *Su cara me resulta familiar.* His face is familiar to me. **2** ~ **que...** to turn out (**that...**): *Resultó que se conocían.* It turned out (that) they knew each other.

resumen *nm* summary [*pl* summaries]: *~ informativo* news summary LOC **en resumen** in short

resumir *vt* **1** (*gen*) to summarize: *~ un libro* to summarize a book **2** (*concluir*) to sum *sth* up: *Resumiendo,...* To sum up,...

resurrección *nf* resurrection LOC *Ver* DOMINGO

retablo *nm* (*altar*) altarpiece

retal *nm* remnant

retardado, -a *pp, adj* delayed: *de acción retardada* delayed-action

retención *nf* (*tráfico*) hold-up

retener *vt* **1** (*guardar*) to keep **2** (*memorizar*) to remember **3** (*detener*) to hold: *~ a algn en contra de su voluntad* to hold sb against their will

retina *nf* retina

retirada *nf* **1** (*de una profesión*) retirement: *Anunció su ~ del fútbol.* He announced his retirement from football. **2** (*de soldados vencidos*) retreat: *El general ordenó la ~.* The general ordered a retreat.

retirado, -a *pp, adj* **1** (*remoto*) remote **2** (*jubilado*) retired *Ver tb* RETIRAR

retirar ◆ *vt* to withdraw (*sth/sb*) (***from sth***): *~le el carné a algn* to withdraw sb's licence ◊ *~ una revista de la circulación* to withdraw a magazine from circulation ◆ **retirarse** *v pron* **1** (*irse*) to withdraw (***from sth***): *~se de una lucha* to withdraw from a fight **2** (*jubilarse*) to retire (***from sth***): *Se retiró de la política.* He retired from politics. **3** (*Mil*) to retreat

retiro *nm* **1** (*jubilación*) retirement **2** (*pensión*) retirement pension **3** (*lugar*) retreat

reto *nm* challenge

retocar *vt* (*pintura, fotos*) to retouch

retoque *nm* finishing touch: *dar los últimos ~s a un dibujo* to put the finishing touches to a drawing

retorcer *vt* to twist: *Me retorció el brazo.* He twisted my arm. LOC **retorcerse de dolor** to writhe in pain **retorcerse de risa** to double up with laughter

retornable *adj* returnable LOC **no retornable** non-returnable

retorno *nm* return

retortijón *nm* cramp: *retortijones de barriga* stomach cramps

retransmisión *nf* broadcast: *una ~ en directo/diferido* a live/recorded broadcast

retransmitir *vt* to broadcast

retrasado, -a ◆ *pp, adj* **1** (*atrasado*) behind (**with sth**): *Voy muy ~ en mi trabajo.* I'm very behind with my work. **2** (*país, región*) backward ◆ *adj, nm-nf* retarded [*adj*]: *~s mentales* mentally retarded people *Ver tb* RETRASAR

retrasar ◆ *vt* **1** (*retardar*) to hold *sth/sb* up, to delay (*más formal*): *Retrasaron todos los vuelos.* All the flights were delayed. **2** (*reloj*) to put *sth* back: *~ el reloj una hora* to put your watch back an hour ◆ **retrasarse** *v pron* **1** (*llegar tarde*) to be late: *Siento haberme retrasado.* Sorry I'm late. **2** (*en trabajo*) to fall behind (***in*/*with* sth**): *Empezó a ~se en sus estudios.* He began to fall behind in his studies. **3** (*reloj*) to be slow: *Este reloj se retrasa diez minutos.* This watch is ten minutes slow.

retraso *nm* **1** (*demora*) delay [*pl* delays]: *Algunos vuelos sufrieron ~s.* Some flights were subject to delays. ◊ *Empezó con cinco minutos de ~.* It began five minutes late. **2** (*subdesarrollo*) backwardness LOC **llevar/tener retraso** to be late: *El tren lleva cinco horas de ~.* The train is five hours late.

retratar *vt* **1** (*pintar*) to paint *sb's* portrait: *El artista la retrató en 1897.* The artist painted her portrait in 1897. **2** (*Fot*) to take a photograph (**of *sth/sb***) **3** (*describir*) to portray: *La obra retrata la vida aristocrática.* The play portrays aristocratic life.

retrato *nm* **1** (*cuadro*) portrait **2** (*foto*) photograph **3** (*descripción*) portrayal LOC **retrato robot** identikit picture

retroceder *vi* **1** (*gen*) to go back: *Éste no es el camino, retrocedamos.* We're going the wrong way, let's go back. **2** (*echarse atrás*) to back down: *No retrocederé ante las dificultades.* I won't back down in the face of adversity.

retroceso *nm* **1** (*movimiento*) backward movement **2** (*de arma*) recoil **3** (*Econ*) recession: *~ económico* economic recession

retrovisor *nm* rear-view mirror LOC *Ver* ESPEJO

retumbar *vt* to resound

reúma *nm* rheumatism

reunificar *vt* to reunify

reunión *nf* **1** (*gen*) meeting: *Mañana tenemos una ~ importante.* We've got an important meeting tomorrow. **2** (*encuentro*) reunion: *una ~ de antiguos alumnos* a school reunion

reunir ◆ *vt* **1** (*gen*) to gather *sth/sb* together: *Reuní a mis amigas/la familia.* I gathered my friends/family together. **2** (*información*) to collect **3** (*dinero*) to raise **4** (*cualidades*) to have: *~ cualidades para ser líder* to have leadership qualities ◆ **reunirse** *v pron* to meet: *Nos reuniremos esta tarde.* We'll meet this evening.

revancha *nf* revenge LOC **tomarse la revancha** to get/take your revenge (*for sth*)

revelado *nm* developing

revelar *vt* **1** (*gen*) to reveal: *Nunca nos reveló su secreto.* He never revealed his secret to us. **2** (*Fot*) to develop

reventado, -a *pp, adj* (*cansado*) shattered *Ver tb* REVENTAR(SE)

reventar(se) *vt, vi, v pron* to burst: *Si comes más vas a ~.* If you eat any more you'll burst. ◊ *~ de alegría* to be bursting with happiness LOC **me revienta** I, you, etc hate *doing sth*: *Me revienta tener que levantarme temprano.* I hate having to get up early.

reverencia *nf* LOC **hacer una reverencia** **1** (*hombres*) to bow **2** (*mujeres*) to curtsey

reversible *adj* reversible

reverso *nm* **1** (*papel*) back **2** (*moneda*) reverse

revertido, -a *pp, adj* LOC *Ver* LLAMADA

revés *nm* **1** (*tela*) wrong side **2** (*Dep*) backhand **3** (*bofetada*) slap **4** (*contratiempo*) setback: *sufrir un ~* to suffer a setback LOC **al revés 1** (*mal*) wrong: *¡Todo me está saliendo al ~!* Everything's going wrong for me! **2** (*al contrario*) the other way round: *Yo lo hice al ~ que tú.* I did it the other way round from you. **al/del revés 1** (*con lo de arriba abajo*) upside down **2** (*con lo de dentro afuera*) inside out: *Llevas puesto el jersey al ~.* Your jumper's on inside out. **3** (*con lo de delante atrás*) back to front

revestir *vt* (*cubrir*) to cover

revisar *vt* to check: *Vinieron a ~ el gas.* They came to check the gas.

revisión *nf* **1** (*gen*) revision **2** (*vehículo*) service **3** (*Med*) check-up

revisor, ~a *nm-nf* ticket inspector

revista *nf* **1** (*publicación*) magazine **2** (*Teat*) revue **3** (*Mil*) review: *pasar ~ a las tropas* to review the troops

revivir *vt, vi* to revive: *~ el pasado/una vieja amistad* to revive the past/an old friendship

revolcar ◆ *vt* to knock *sb* over ◆ **revolcarse** *v pron* **1** (*gen*) to roll about: *Nos revolcamos en el césped.* We rolled about on the lawn. **2** (*en agua, barro*) to wallow

revolotear *vi* to fly about

revoltoso, -a *adj, nm-nf* naughty [*adj*]: *Eres un ~.* You're very naughty.

revolución *nf* revolution

revolucionar *vt* **1** (*transformar*) to revolutionize **2** (*alborotar*) to stir *sb* up: *No revoluciones a todo el mundo.* Don't stir everybody up.

revolucionario, -a *adj, nm-nf* revolutionary [*pl* revolutionaries]

revolver ◆ *vt* **1** (*remover*) **(a)** (*gen*) to stir: *Revuélvelo bien.* Stir it well. **(b)** (*ensalada*) to toss **2** (*desordenar*) **(a)** (*gen*) to mess *sth* up: *No revuelvas los cajones.* Don't mess the drawers up. **(b)** (*ladrones*) to turn *sth* upside down: *Los ladrones revolvieron el piso.* The burglars turned the flat upside down. **3** (*estómago*) to turn ◆ *vi* (*fisgar*) to rummage: *Estuvo revolviendo en el bolso un rato.* She spent some time rummaging through her bag.

revólver *nm* revolver

revuelta *nf* revolt

revuelto, -a *pp, adj* **1** (*desordenado*) untidy **2** (*agitado*) worked up: *El pueblo anda ~ con las elecciones.* People are worked-up about the elections. **3** (*estómago*) upset: *Tengo el estómago ~.* I've got an upset stomach. LOC *Ver* HUEVO; *Ver tb* REVOLVER

rey *nm* **1** (*monarca*) king

> El plural de **king** es regular ('kings'), pero cuando decimos *los reyes* refiriéndonos al rey y la reina, se dice **the king and queen**.

2 Reyes Epiphany LOC **los Reyes Magos** the Three Wise Men *Ver tb* CUERPO, DÍA

rezagado, -a ◆ *pp, adj*: *Venga, no te quedes ~.* Come on, don't get left behind. ◆ *nm-nf* straggler

rezar ◆ *vt* to say: *~ una oración* to say a prayer ◆ *vi* ~ **(por)** to pray **(for *sth/sb*)**

ría *nf* estuary [*pl* estuaries]

riachuelo *nm* stream

riada *nf* flood

ribera *nf* **1** (*orilla*) bank **2** (*vega*) riverside

rico, -a ◆ *adj* **1** ~ **(en)** rich **(in *sth*)**: *una familia rica* a rich family ◇ *~ en minerales* rich in minerals **2** (*comida*) delicious **3** (*mono*) sweet: *¡Qué bebé más ~!* What a sweet little baby! ◆ *nm-nf* rich man/woman [*pl* rich men/women]: *los ~s* the rich

ridiculez *nf*: *¡Qué ~!* How ridiculous! ◇ *Lo que dice es una ~.* He's talking rubbish.

ridiculizar *vt* to ridicule

ridículo, -a *adj* ridiculous LOC **dejar/poner a algn en ridículo** to make a fool of sb **hacer el ridículo** to make a fool of yourself

riego *nm* (*Agricultura*) irrigation **LOC riego sanguíneo** circulation *Ver tb* BOCA

riel *nm* rail

rienda *nf* rein **LOC dar rienda suelta** to give free rein *to sth/sb* **llevar las riendas** to be in charge (*of sth*)

riesgo *nm* risk: *Corren el ~ de perder su dinero.* They run the risk of losing their money. **LOC a todo riesgo** (*seguro*) comprehensive

rifa *nf* raffle

rifar *vt* to raffle

rifle *nm* rifle

rígido, -a *adj* **1** (*tieso*) rigid **2** (*severo*) strict: *Tiene unos padres muy ~s.* She has very strict parents.

riguroso, -a *adj* **1** (*estricto*) strict **2** (*minucioso*) thorough **3** (*castigo*) harsh

rima *nf* rhyme

rimar *vi* to rhyme

rimbombante *adj* (*lenguaje*) pompous

rímel *nm* mascara: *darse/ponerse ~* to apply mascara

rincón *nm* corner: *en un tranquilo ~ de Asturias* in a quiet corner of Asturias

rinoceronte *nm* rhino [*pl* rhinos]

> **Rhinoceros** es la palabra científica.

riña *nf* **1** (*pelea*) fight **2** (*discusión*) row

riñón *nm* **1** (*órgano*) kidney [*pl* kidneys] **2 riñones** (*zona lumbar*) lower back [*sing*] **LOC** *Ver* COSTAR

río *nm* river

> En inglés **river** se escribe con mayúscula cuando aparece con el nombre de un río: *el río Amazonas* the River Amazon.

LOC río abajo/arriba downstream/upstream

riqueza *nf* **1** (*dinero*) wealth [*incontable*]: *amontonar ~s* to amass wealth **2** (*cualidad*) richness: *la ~ del terreno* the richness of the land

risa *nf* **1** (*gen*) laugh: *una ~ nerviosa/contagiosa* a nervous/contagious laugh ◊ *¡Qué ~!* What a laugh! **2 risas** laughter [*incontable*]: *Se oían las ~s de los pequeños.* You could hear the children's laughter. **LOC dar risa** to make *sb* laugh **me dio la risa** I, you, etc got the giggles **mondarse/morirse/partirse de risa** to fall about laughing *Ver tb* PELÍCULA, PROGRAMA, RETORCER

risueño, -a *adj* **1** (*cara*) smiling **2** (*persona*) cheerful

ritmo *nm* **1** (*Mús*) rhythm, beat (*más coloq*): *seguir el ~* to keep time **2** (*velocidad*) rate: *el ~ de crecimiento* the growth rate **LOC ritmo de vida** pace of life **tener ritmo 1** (*persona*) to have a good sense of rhythm **2** (*melodía*) to have a good beat *Ver tb* MARCAR

rito *nm* rite

ritual *nm* ritual

rival *adj, nmf* rival

rizado, -a *pp, adj* curly: *Tengo el pelo ~.* I've got curly hair. *Ver tb* RIZAR

rizar ◆ *vt* to curl ◆ **rizarse** *v pron* to go curly: *Con la lluvia se me ha rizado el pelo.* My hair's gone curly because of the rain. **LOC rizar el rizo** to complicate things

rizo *nm* **1** (*pelo*) curl **2** (*Aeronáut*) loop **LOC** *Ver* RIZAR

robar ◆ *vt* **1** (*banco, tienda, persona*) to rob: *~ un banco* to rob a bank **2** (*dinero, objetos*) to steal: *Me han robado el reloj.* My watch has been stolen. **3** (*casa, caja fuerte*) to break into *sth*: *Le enseñaron a ~ cajas fuertes.* They taught him how to break into a safe. ◆ *vi* **1** (*gen*) to steal: *Le echaron del colegio por ~.* He was expelled for stealing. **2** (*a una persona*) to rob: *¡Me han robado!* I've been robbed! **3** (*en una casa*): *Han robado en casa de los vecinos.* Our neighbours house has been broken into. ☛ *Ver nota en* ROB **4** (*Naipes*) to draw: *Te toca ~.* It's your turn to draw.

roble *nm* oak (tree)

robo *nm* **1** (*de un banco, una tienda, o una persona*) robbery [*pl* robberies]: *el ~ al supermercado* the supermarket robbery ◊ *He sido víctima de un ~.* I've been robbed. **2** (*de objetos*) theft: *acusado de ~* accused of theft ◊ *~ de coches/bicicletas* car/bicycle theft **3** (*de una casa, oficina*) burglary [*pl* burglaries]: *El domingo hubo tres ~s en esta calle.* There were three burglaries in this street on Sunday. **4** (*estafa*) rip-off: *¡Vaya ~!* That's a rip-off! ☛ *Ver nota en* THEFT **LOC** *Ver* MANO

robot *nm* robot **LOC** *Ver* RETRATO

robusto, -a *adj* robust

roca *nf* rock

roce *nm* **1** (*rozamiento*) rubbing **2** (*discusión*) clash: *Ya he tenido varios ~*

con él. I've already clashed with him several times.

rociar *vt* to spray *sth* (***with sth***): *Hay que ~ las plantas dos veces al día.* The plants should be sprayed twice a day.

rocío *nm* dew

rocoso, -a *adj* rocky

rodaballo *nm* turbot [*pl* turbot]

rodaja *nf* slice: *una ~ de melón* a slice of melon **LOC en rodajas**: *Córtalo en ~s.* Slice it. ◊ *piña en ~s* pineapple rings

rodaje *nm* **1** (*Cine*) filming, shooting (*más coloq*): *el ~ de una serie de televisión* the filming of a TV series **2** (*coche*): *El coche está todavía en ~.* I'm still running my car in.

rodar ◆ *vi* **1** (*dar vueltas*) to roll: *Las canicas ruedan.* Marbles roll. ◊ *Las rocas rodaron por el precipicio.* The rocks rolled down the cliff. **2** (*ir de un lado a otro*) to lie around: *Esta carta lleva un mes rodando por la oficina.* This letter has been lying around the office for a month now. ◆ *vt* **1** (*película*) to film, to shoot (*más coloq*) **2** (*vehículo, motor*) to run *sth* in: *Todavía estoy rodando el coche.* I'm still running the car in. **LOC rodar escaleras abajo** to fall down the stairs

rodear ◆ *vt* **1** (*gen*) to surround *sth/sb* (***with sth/sb***): *Hemos rodeado al enemigo.* We've surrounded the enemy. ◊ *Sus amigas la rodearon para felicitarla.* She was surrounded by friends wanting to congratulate her. **2** (*con los brazos*): *Sus brazos me rodearon.* He put his arms around me. ◆ *vt, vi* ~ (**por**) to make a detour: *Podemos ~ (por) el bosque.* We can make a detour through the woods. ◆ **rodearse** *v pron* **rodearse de** to surround yourself **with** ***sth/sb***: *Les encanta ~se de gente joven.* They love to surround themselves with young people.

rodeo *nm* **1** (*desvío*) detour: *Tuvimos que dar un ~ de cinco kilómetros.* We had to make a five-kilometre detour. **2** (*espectáculo*) rodeo [*pl* rodeos] **LOC andarse con rodeos** to beat about the bush

rodilla *nf* knee **LOC de rodillas**: *Todo el mundo estaba de ~s.* Everyone was kneeling down. ◊ *Tendrás que pedírmelo de ~s.* You'll have to get down on your knees and beg. **ponerse de rodillas** to kneel (down)

rodillera *nf* **1** (*Dep*) kneepad **2** (*Med*) knee support **3** (*parche*) knee patch

rodillo *nm* **1** (*Cocina*) rolling pin **2** (*pintura, máquina de escribir*) roller

roedor *nm* rodent

roer *vt* to gnaw (**at**) ***sth***: *El perro roía su hueso.* The dog was gnawing (at) its bone.

rogar *vt* **1** (*suplicar*) to beg (*sb*) **for *sth***; to beg (*sth*) **of *sb***: *Le rogaron misericordia.* They begged him for mercy. ◊ *Les rogué que me soltasen.* I begged them to let me go. **2** (*pedir*): *Tranquilízate, te lo ruego.* Calm down, please. ◊ *Me rogaron que me fuera.* They asked me to go. **3** (*rezar*) to pray: *Roguemos al Señor.* Let us pray. **LOC hacerse de rogar** to play hard to get **se ruega no fumar** please do not smoke **se ruega silencio** silence please

rojizo, -a *adj* reddish

rojo, -a *adj, nm* red ☛ *Ver ejemplos en* AMARILLO **LOC al rojo vivo** (*metal*) red-hot **ponerse rojo** to go red *Ver tb* CAPERUCITA, CRUZ, NÚMERO

rollo *nm* **1** (*gen*) roll: *~s de papel higiénico* toilet rolls ◊ *un ~ de película* a roll of film **2** (*pesadez, aburrimiento*): *¡Qué ~ de libro!* What a boring book! ◊ *Esa clase es un ~.* That class is really boring. ◊ *Ese tío me parece un ~.* I find that bloke so boring. **3** (*asunto*): *¿Qué ~s te traes?* What are you up to? ◊ *Está metido en un ~ muy raro.* He's involved in something very odd. ◊ *¿Te va el ~ de los coches?* Are you into cars? **4** (*amorío*) fling

románico, -a *adj* (*Arquit*) Romanesque

romano, -a *adj* Roman **LOC** *Ver* NUMERACIÓN, NÚMERO

romántico, -a *adj, nm-nf* romantic

rombo *nm* rhombus [*pl* rhombuses]

romero *nm* rosemary

rompecabezas *nm* **1** (*puzzle*) jigsaw: *hacer un ~* to do a jigsaw **2** (*acertijo*) puzzle

rompeolas *nm* breakwater

romper ◆ *vt* **1** (*gen*) to break: *Rompí el cristal de un pelotazo.* I broke the window with my ball. ◊ *~ una promesa* to break a promise **2** (*papel, tela*) to tear: *He roto la falda con un clavo.* I've torn my skirt on a nail. ◊ *Rompió la carta.* He tore up the letter. **3** (*ropa, zapatos*) to wear *sth* out: *Rompe todos los jerséis por los codos.* He wears out all his jumpers at the elbows. ◆ *vi* **1** ~ **con** to fall out **with *sb***: *~ con la familia política* to fall out with your in-laws

2 (*novios*) to split up **(with *sb*)** ◆ **romperse** *v pron* **1** (*gen*) to break: *Me rompí el brazo jugando al fútbol.* I broke my arm playing football. ◊ *Se ha roto sola.* It broke of its own accord. **2** (*tela, papel*) to tear: *Esta tela se rompe fácilmente.* This material tears easily. **3** (*cuerda*) to snap **4** (*ropa, zapatos*) to wear out: *Seguro que se rompen a los dos días.* They're bound to wear out in no time. LOC **romper el hielo** to break the ice **romper filas** to fall out **romperse la crisma** to crack your head open *Ver tb* CARA, CASCO

ron *nm* rum

roncar *vi* to snore

ronco, -a *adj* (*afónico*) hoarse: *Me quedé ~ de gritar.* I shouted myself hoarse.

ronda *nf* round: *Esta ~ la pides tú.* It's your round. ◊ *Tu casa no está incluida en mi ~.* Your house isn't on my round. LOC **hacer la ronda 1** (*policía*) to pound the beat **2** (*soldado, vigilante*) to be on patrol **3** (*repartidor*) to do your round

ronronear *vi* to purr

ronroneo *nm* purr: *Se oía el ~ del gato.* You could hear the cat purring.

roña *nf* (*mugre*) dirt: *Tienes ~ en el cuello.* You've got dirt on your collar.

roñoso, -a *adj* **1** (*mugriento*) grimy **2** (*tacaño*) stingy

ropa *nf* **1** (*de persona*) clothes [*pl*]: *~ infantil* children's clothes ◊ *~ usada/sucia* second-hand/dirty clothes ◊ *¿Qué ~ me pongo hoy?* What shall I wear today? **2** (*de uso doméstico*) linen: *~ blanca/de cama* household/bed linen LOC **ropa de deportes** sportswear **ropa interior** underwear *Ver tb* CESTO

ropero *nm* wardrobe

rosa ◆ *nf* rose ◆ *adj, nm* pink ☛ *Ver ejemplos en* AMARILLO LOC *Ver* NOVELA

rosado, -a *adj* pink

rosal *nm* rose bush

rosario *nm* (*Relig*) rosary [*pl* rosaries]: *rezar el ~* to say the rosary

rosca *nf* **1** (*pan*) (ring-shaped) roll **2** (*tornillo*) thread LOC **pasarse de rosca 1** (*persona*) to go over the top **2** (*tornillo*) to have a worn thread: *Esta tuerca está pasada de ~.* The thread is worn on this screw. *Ver tb* PELOTA, TAPÓN

rostro *nm* **1** (*cara*) face: *La expresión de su ~ lo decía todo.* The look on his face said it all. **2** (*cara dura*) cheek: *¡Vaya ~ que tienes!* You've got a cheek!

rotación *nf* rotation: *~ de cultivos* crop rotation

roto ◆ *pp, adj* (*cansado*) worn-out ◆ *nm* hole *Ver tb* ROMPER

rótula *nf* kneecap

rotulador *nm* felt-tip pen LOC **rotulador fosforescente** highlighter

rotular *vt* (*poner rótulos*) to put the lettering **on *sth***

rótulo *nm* **1** (*en un cartel, mapa*) lettering [*incontable*]: *Los ~s son demasiado pequeños.* The lettering's too small. **2** (*letrero*) sign

rotundo, -a *adj* **1** (*contundente*) resounding: *un sí/fracaso ~* a resounding 'yes'/flop **2** (*negativa*) emphatic

roulotte *nf* caravan

rozar ◆ *vt, vi* **1** (*gen*) to brush **(*against sth/sb*)**: *Le rocé el vestido.* I brushed against her dress. ◊ *La pelota me rozó la pierna.* The ball grazed my leg. **2** (*raspar*) to rub: *Estas botas me rozan atrás.* These boots rub at the back. ◊ *El guardabarros roza con la rueda.* The mudguard rubs against the wheel. ◆ *vt* (*hacer un rozón*) to scratch: *No me roces el coche.* Don't scratch my car.

rubeola (*tb* **rubéola**) *nf* German measles [*sing*]

rubí *nm* ruby [*pl* rubies]

rubio, -a *adj* fair, blond(e)

> **Fair** se usa sólo si el rubio es natural y **blond** tanto si es natural como si es teñido: *Es rubio.* He's got fair/blond hair. ☛ *Ver tb nota en* BLOND

LOC *Ver tb* TABACO, TEÑIR

rueda *nf* **1** (*gen*) wheel: *~ delantera/trasera* front/back wheel ◊ *cambiar la ~* to change the wheel **2** (*neumático*) tyre: *Se me ha pinchado una ~.* I've got a puncture. LOC *Ver* PRENSA, SILLA

ruedo *nm* ring: *El torero dio la vuelta al ~.* The bullfighter paraded round the ring.

ruego *nm* plea

rugby *nm* rugby: *un partido de ~* rugby match

rugido *nm* roar

rugir *vi* to roar

ruido *nm* noise: *No hagas ~.* Don't make any noise. ◊ *Oí ~s raros y me dio miedo.* I heard some strange noises and got frightened. ◊ *¿Tú has oído un ~?* Did you hear something? LOC *Ver* METER

ruidoso, -a *adj* noisy

ruina *nf* **1** (*gen*) ruin: *La ciudad estaba en ~s.* The city was in ruins. ◊ *las ~s d* *una ciudad romana* the ruins of a Roman city ◊ ~ *económica* financial ruin **2** (*hundimiento*) collapse: *Ese edificio amenaza ~.* That building is in danger of collapsing. LOC **estar en la ruina** to be broke **ser la/una ruina**: *Las bodas son una ~.* Weddings cost a fortune.

ruiseñor *nm* nightingale

ruleta *nf* roulette

rulo *nm* roller

rumba *nf* rumba

rumbo *nm* **1** (*camino, dirección*) direction **2** (*avión, barco*) course: *El barco puso ~ sur.* The ship set course southwards. LOC **(con) rumbo a** bound for: *El barco iba con ~ a Santander.* The ship was bound for Santander.

rumiante *adj, nm* ruminant

rumiar *vi* (*vaca*) to ruminate (*téc*), to chew the cud

rumor *nm* **1** (*noticia*) rumour: *Corre el ~ de que se van a casar.* There's a rumour going round that they're getting married. **2** (*murmullo*) murmur

rumorear *vt* LOC **se rumorea que...** there are rumours (that...): *Se rumorea que han hecho un fraude.* There are rumours about a fraud.

rural *adj* rural

Rusia *nf* Russia

ruso, -a *adj, nm-nf, nm* Russian: *los ~s* the Russians ◊ *hablar ~* to speak Russian LOC *Ver* MONTAÑA

rústico, -a *adj* rustic

ruta *nf* route: *la ~ de la seda* the silk route ◊ *¿Qué ~ seguiremos?* What route will we take?

rutina *nf* routine: *inspecciones de ~* routine inspections ◊ *No quiere cambiar la ~ diaria.* She doesn't want to change her daily routine. ◊ *Se ha convertido en ~.* It's become a routine.

Ss

sábado *nm* Saturday [*pl* Saturdays] (*abrev* Sat) ☛ *Ver ejemplos en* LUNES

sábana *nf* sheet

saber ◆ *vt* **1** (*gen*) to know: *No supe qué contestar.* I didn't know what to say. ◊ *No sé nada de mecánica.* I don't know anything about mechanics. ◊ *Sabía que volvería.* I knew he would be back. ◊ *¡Ya lo sé!* I know! **2** ~ **hacer algo** can: *¿Sabes nadar?* Can you swim? ◊ *No sé escribir a máquina.* I can't type. **3** (*enterarse*) to find out: *Lo supe ayer.* I found out yesterday. **4** (*idioma*) to speak: *Sabe mucho inglés.* He speaks good English. ◆ *vi* **1** (*gen*) to know: *Le tengo mucho aprecio, ¿sabes?* I'm very fond of her, you know. ◊ *¿Sabes? Manolo se casa.* Know what? Manolo's getting married. ◊ *Nunca se sabe.* You never know. **2** ~ **de** (*tener noticias*) to hear **of** ***sth/sb***: *Nunca más supimos de él.* That was the last we heard of him. **3** ~ **(a)** to taste **(of** ***sth*)**: *Sabe a menta.* It tastes of mint. ◊ *¡Qué bien sabe!* It tastes really good! LOC **no sé qué/cuántos** something or other: *Me habló de no sé qué.* He talked to me about something or other. **¡qué sé yo!/¡yo qué sé!** how should I know? **que yo sepa** as far as I know **saber mal 1** (*lit*) to have a nasty taste **2** (*fig*) not to like...: *Me sabe mal que me mientas.* I don't like you telling me lies. ☛Para otras expresiones con **saber**, véanse las entradas del sustantivo, adjetivo, etc, p.ej. **no saber ni jota** en JOTA y **saber(se) algo de carrerilla** en CARRERILLA.

sabiduría *nf* wisdom

sabio, -a *adj* wise

sabor *nm* ~ **(a) 1** (*gusto*) taste **(of** ***sth*)**: *El agua no tiene ~.* Water is tasteless. ◊ *Tiene un ~ muy raro.* It tastes very strange. **2** (*gusto que se añade a un producto*) flavour: *Lo hay de siete ~es distintos.* It comes in seven different flavours. ◊ *¿De qué ~ lo quieres?* Which flavour would you like? LOC **con sabor a** flavoured: *un yogur con ~ a plátano* a banana-flavoured yogurt

saborear *vt* to savour: *Le gusta ~ su café.* He likes to savour his coffee.

sabotaje *nm* sabotage

sabotear *vt* to sabotage

sabroso, -a *adj* delicious

sacacorchos *nm* corkscrew

sacapuntas *nm* pencil sharpener

sacar ◆ *vt* **1** (*fuera*) to take *sth/sb* out

(**of sth**): *Sacó una carpeta del cajón.* He took a folder out of the drawer. ◊ *El dentista le sacó una muela.* The dentist took his tooth out. ◊ ~ *la basura* to take the rubbish out **2** (*conseguir*) to get: *¿Qué has sacado en matemáticas?* What did you get in maths? ◊ *No sé de dónde ha sacado el dinero.* I don't know where she got the money from. **3** (*parte del cuerpo*) to stick *sth* out: *No me saques la lengua.* Don't stick your tongue out at me. ◊ ~ *la cabeza por la ventanilla* to stick your head out of the window ◊ *¡Casi me sacas un ojo!* You nearly poked my eye out! **4** (*producir*) to make *sth* (**from sth**): *Sacan la mantequilla de la leche.* They make butter from milk. ◆ *vt, vi* (*Tenis*) to serve ◆ **sacarse** *v pron*: *¡Sácate las manos de los bolsillos!* Take your hands out of your pockets. ☛Para expresiones con **sacar**, véanse las entradas del sustantivo, adjetivo, etc, p.ej. **sacar de quicio** en QUICIO y **sacar punta** en PUNTA.

sacarina *nf* saccharin

sacerdote *nm* priest

saciar *vt* **1** (*hambre, ambición, deseo*) to satisfy **2** (*sed*) to quench

saco *nm* **1** (*grande*) sack **2** (*pequeño*) bag LOC **saco de dormir** sleeping bag

sacramento *nm* sacrament

sacrificar ◆ *vt* to sacrifice: *Sacrificó su carrera para tener hijos.* She sacrificed her career to have children. ◊ *Lo sacrifiqué todo para sacar adelante a mi familia.* I sacrificed everything for my family. ◆ **sacrificarse** *v pron* **sacrificarse** (**por/para**) to make sacrifices: *Mis padres se han sacrificado mucho.* My parents have made a lot of sacrifices.

sacrificio *nm* sacrifice: *Tendrás que hacer algunos ~s.* You'll have to make some sacrifices.

sacudida *nf* (*eléctrica*) shock: *Me pegó una buena ~.* I got an electric shock.

sacudir ◆ *vt* **1** (*gen*) to shake: *Sacude el mantel.* Shake the tablecloth. ◊ ~ *la arena (de la toalla)* to shake the sand off (the towel) **2** (*pegar*) to give *sb* a smack ◆ **sacudirse** *v pron* to brush *sth* (off): *~se la caspa del abrigo* to brush the dandruff off your coat

sádico, -a *nm-nf* sadist

sagitario (*tb* **Sagitario**) *nm, nmf* (*Astrología*) Sagittarius ☛*Ver ejemplos en* AQUARIUS

sagrado, -a *adj* **1** (*Relig*) holy: *un lugar ~* a holy place ◊ *la Sagrada Familia* the Holy Family **2** (*intocable*) sacred: *Los domingos para mí son ~s.* My Sundays are sacred.

sal *nf* salt LOC **sales de baño** bath salts **sal fina/gorda** table/sea salt

sala *nf* **1** (*gen*) room: ~ *de juntas* meeting room **2** (*casa*) sitting room **3** (*Cine*) screen: *La ~ 1 es la más grande.* Screen 1 is the largest. **4** (*hospital*) ward LOC **sala de espera** waiting-room **sala de estar** sitting room **sala de fiestas** disco [*pl* discos]

salado, -a *pp, adj* **1** (*gusto*) salty **2** (*gracioso*) amusing LOC *Ver* AGUA

salario *nm* salary [*pl* salaries] LOC **salario base/mínimo** basic/minimum wage

salchicha *nf* sausage

salchichón *nm* salami [*incontable*]

saldar *vt* (*cuenta, deuda*) to settle

saldo *nm* **1** (*en una cuenta*) balance **2** (*rebaja*) sale

salero *nm* (*para la sal*) salt cellar

salida *nf* **1** (*acción de salir*) way out (**of sth**): *a la ~ del cine* on the way out of the cinema **2** (*puerta*) exit: *la ~ de emergencia* the emergency exit **3** (*avión, tren*) departure: *~s nacionales/internacionales* domestic/international departures ◊ *el tablero de ~s* the departures board LOC **salida del sol** sunrise *Ver tb* CALLEJÓN

salir ◆ *vi* **1** (*ir/venir fuera*) to go/come out: *¿Salimos al jardín?* Shall we go out into the garden? ◊ *No quería ~ del baño.* He wouldn't come out of the bathroom. ◊ *Salí a ver qué pasaba.* I went out to see what was going on. **2** (*partir*) to leave: *¿A qué hora sale el avión?* What time does the plane leave? ◊ *Hemos salido de casa a las dos.* We left home at two. ◊ *El tren sale del andén número cinco.* The train leaves from platform five. ◊ ~ *para Irún* to leave for Irún **3** (*alternar*) to go out: *Anoche salimos a cenar.* We went out for a meal last night. ◊ *Sale con un estudiante.* She's going out with a student. **4** (*producto, flor*) to come out: *El disco/libro sale en abril.* The record/book is coming out in April. **5** (*sol*) **(a)** (*amanecer*) to rise **(b)** (*de entre las nubes*) to come out: *Por la tarde salió el sol.* The sun came out in the afternoon. **6** ~ **de** (*superar*): ~ *de una operación* to pull through an operation ◊ ~ *de la droga* to come off drugs **7** ~ **a algn** (*parecerse*) to take after sb **8** ~ **a/por** (*costar*) to work out **at *sth***: *Sale a*

6.000 pesetas el metro. It works out at 6000 pesetas a metre. **9** (*al hacer cuentas*): *A mí me sale 18.* I make it 18. **10** (*resultar*) to turn out: *¿Qué tal te salió la receta?* How did the recipe turn out? ◊ *El viaje salió fenomenal.* The trip turned out really well. **11** (*saber hacer algo*): *Todavía no me sale bien el pino.* I still can't do handstands properly. ◆ **salirse** *v pron* **1** (*gen*) to come off: *Se ha salido una pieza.* A piece has come off. ◊ *El coche se salió de la carretera.* The car came off the road. **2** (*líquido*) to leak LOC **salirse con la suya** to get your own way ☛Para otras expresiones con **salir**, véanse las entradas del sustantivo, adjetivo, etc, p.ej. **salir de copas** en COPA y **salir rana** en RANA.

saliva *nf* saliva

salmo *nm* psalm

salmón ◆ *nm* salmon [*pl* salmon] ◆ *adj, nm* (*color*) salmon ☛ *Ver ejemplos en* AMARILLO

salmonete *nm* red mullet [*pl* red mullet]

salón *nm* **1** (*de una casa*) sitting room **2** (*de un hotel*) lounge LOC **salón de belleza** beauty salon **salón de actos** main hall *Ver tb* JUEGO

salpicadero *nm* dashboard

salpicar *vt* to splash *sth/sb* (***with sth***): *Un coche me salpicó los pantalones.* A car splashed my trousers.

salsa *nf* **1** (*gen*) sauce: *~ de tomate* tomato sauce **2** (*de jugo de carne*) gravy

saltamontes *nm* grasshopper

saltar ◆ *vt* to jump: *El caballo saltó la valla.* The horse jumped the fence. ◆ *vi* **1** (*gen*) to jump: *Saltaron al agua/por la ventana.* They jumped into the water/out of the window. ◊ *Salté de la silla cuando oí el timbre.* I jumped up from my chair when I heard the bell. ◊ *~ sobre algn* to jump on sb **2** (*alarma*) to go off ◆ **saltarse** *v pron* **1** (*omitir*) to skip: *~se una comida* to skip a meal **2** (*cola, semáforo*) to jump *~se un semáforo* to jump the lights LOC **saltar a la vista** to be obvious *Ver tb* AIRE, COMBA

salto *nm* **1** (*gen*) jump: *Los niños daban ~s de alegría.* The children were jumping for joy. ◊ *Atrevesé el arroyo de un ~.* I jumped over the stream. **2** (*pájaro, conejo, canguro*) hop: *El conejo se escapó dando ~s.* The rabbit hopped away to safety. **3** (*de trampolín*) dive **4** (*salto vigoroso, progreso*) leap LOC **salto de altura/longitud** high jump/long jump **salto de/con pértiga** pole-vault

saltón, -ona *adj* (*ojos*) bulging

salud *nf* health: *estar bien/mal de ~* to be in good/poor health LOC **¡salud!** cheers! *Ver tb* BEBER

saludable *adj* healthy

saludar *vt* to say hello (***to sb***), to greet (*más formal*): *Me vio pero no me saludó.* He saw me but didn't say hello. LOC **le saluda atentamente** Yours faithfully, Yours sincerely ☛ *Ver* págs 314–15. **salúdale de mi parte** give him my regards **saludar con la mano** to wave (*to sb*)

saludo *nm* **1** (*gen*) greeting **2 saludos** best wishes, regards (*más formal*): *Te mandan ~s.* They send their regards.

salvación *nf* salvation: *Has sido mi ~.* You've saved my life.

salvador, ~a *nm-nf* saviour

salvajada *nf* atrocity [*pl* atrocities] LOC **ser una salvajada** to be outrageous

salvaje *adj* **1** (*gen*) wild: *animales ~s* wild animals **2** (*pueblo, tribu*) uncivilized

salvamento *nm* rescue: *equipo de ~* rescue team

salvar ◆ *vt* **1** (*gen*) to save: *El cinturón de seguridad le salvó la vida.* The seat belt saved his life. **2** (*obstáculo*) to cross: *~ un río* to cross a river ◆ **salvarse** *v pron* to survive LOC **¡sálvese quien pueda!** every man for himself!

salvavidas *nm* lifebelt LOC *Ver* BOTE[1], CHALECO

salvo *prep* except: *Todos vinieron salvo él.* Everybody came except him. LOC **estar a salvo** to be safe **salvo que...** unless...: *Lo haré, salvo que me digas lo contrario.* I'll do it, unless you say otherwise.

San *adj* Saint (*abrev* St)

sanar *vi* **1** (*herida*) to heal **2** (*enfermo*) to recover

sanción *nf* **1** (*castigo*) sanction: *sanciones económicas* economic sanctions **2** (*multa*) fine

sancionar *vt* **1** (*penalizar*) to penalize **2** (*económicamente*) to sanction

sandalia *nf* sandal

sandía *nf* watermelon

sandwich *nm* sandwich

sangrar *vt, vi* to bleed: *Estoy sangrando por la nariz.* I've got a nosebleed.

sangre *nf* blood: *donar ~* to give blood LOC **a sangre fría** in cold blood **hacerse sangre**: *Me caí y me hice ~ en la rodilla.* I fell and cut my knee. **tener sangre fría** (*serenidad*) to keep your cool *Ver tb* ANÁLISIS, DERRAMAMIENTO, DERRAMAR(SE), SUDAR

sangría *nf* sangria

sangriento, -a *adj* **1** (*lucha*) bloody **2** (*herida*) bleeding

sanguíneo, -a *adj* blood [*n atrib*]: *grupo ~* blood group LOC *Ver* RIEGO

sanidad *nf* **1** (*pública*) public health **2** (*higiene*) sanitation

sanitario, -a *adj* **1** (*de salud*) health [*n atrib*]: *medidas sanitarias* health measures **2** (*de higiene*) sanitary

sano, -a *adj* **1** (*clima, vida, ambiente, cuerpo, comida*) healthy **2** (*en forma*) fit **3** (*madera*) sound LOC **no estar en su sano juicio** not to be in your right mind **sano y salvo** safe and sound

santiamén LOC **en un santiamén** in no time at all

santo, -a ◆ *adj* **1** (*Relig*) holy: *la santa Biblia* the Holy Bible **2** (*enfático*): *No salimos de casa en todo el ~ día.* We didn't go out of the house all day. ◆ *nm-nf* **1** (*gen*) saint: *Esa mujer es una santa.* That woman is a saint. **2** (*título*) Saint (*abrev* St) ◆ *nm* saint's day: *¿Cuándo es tu ~?* When is your saint's day? ☛En Gran Bretaña no se celebran los santos. LOC **se me ha ido el santo al cielo** it's gone right out of my head **ser un santo varón** to be a saint **¡y santas pascuas!** and that's that! *Ver tb* DÍA, ESPÍRITU, JUEVES, SEMANA, VIERNES

santuario *nm* shrine

sapo *nm* toad

saque *nm* **1** (*Fútbol*) kick-off **2** (*Tenis*) service LOC **saque de banda** throw-in **tener buen saque** (*comiendo*) to be a big eater

saquear *vt* **1** (*ciudad*) to sack **2** (*despensa*) to raid **3** (*robar*) to loot

sarampión *nm* measles [*sing*]

sarcástico, -a *adj* sarcastic

sardina *nf* sardine

sargento *nmf* sergeant

sarta *nf* string LOC **decir una sarta de disparates/tonterías** to talk a load of rubbish **una sarta de mentiras** a pack of lies

sartén *nf* frying-pan ☛ *Ver dibujo en* SAUCEPAN

sastre, -a *nm-nf* tailor

satélite *nm* satellite LOC *Ver* VÍA

satén *nm* satin

satisfacción *nf* satisfaction

satisfacer ◆ *vt* **1** (*gen*) to satisfy: *~ el hambre/la curiosidad* to satisfy your hunger/curiosity **2** (*sed*) to quench **3** (*ambición, sueño*) to fulfil ◆ *vi* **1** (*gen*) to satisfy *sb* [*vt*]: *Nada le satisface.* He's never satisfied. **2** (*complacer*) to please *sb* [*vt*]: *Me satisface poder hacerlo.* I'm pleased to be able to do it.

satisfactorio, -a *adj* satisfactory

satisfecho, -a *pp, adj* **1** (*gen*) satisfied (***with sth***): *un cliente ~* a satisfied customer **2** (*complacido*) pleased (***with sth/sb***): *Estoy muy satisfecha del rendimiento de mis alumnos.* I'm very pleased with the way my pupils are working. LOC **darse por satisfecho** to be happy *with sth*: *Me daría por ~ con un aprobado.* I'd be happy with a pass. **satisfecho de sí mismo** self-satisfied *Ver tb* SATISFACER

Saturno *nm* Saturn

sauce *nm* willow LOC **sauce llorón** weeping willow

sauna *nf* sauna

savia *nf* (*Bot*) sap

saxofón *nm* saxophone (*abrev* sax)

sazonar *vt* to season

se *pron pers*

- **reflexivo 1** (*él, ella, ello*) himself, herself, itself: *Se compró un compact disc.* He bought himself a CD. ◊ *Se hizo daño.* She hurt herself. **2** (*usted, ustedes*) yourself [*pl* yourselves] **3** (*ellos, ellas*) themselves **4** (*partes del cuerpo, efectos personales*): *Se lavó las manos.* He washed his hands. ◊ *Se secó el pelo.* She dried her hair.
- **recíproco** each other, one another: *Se quieren.* They love each other. ☛ *Ver nota en* EACH OTHER
- **pasivo**: *Se construyó hace años.* It was built a long time ago. ◊ *Se registraron tres muertos.* Three deaths were recorded. ◊ *Se dice que están arruinados.* They are said to be broke. ◊ *No se admiten tarjetas de crédito.* No credit cards. ◊ *Se prohíbe fumar.* No smoking.
- **impersonal**: *Se vive bien aquí.* Life here is terrific. ◊ *Se les recompensará.* They'll get their reward.
- **en lugar de le, les** him, her, you, them: *Se lo di.* I gave it to him/her. ◊ *Se lo robamos.* We stole it from them.

secador *nm* hairdryer

secadora *nf* tumble-dryer

secar ◆ *vt, vi* to dry ◆ **secarse** *v pron* **1** (*gen*) to dry: *Se secó las lágrimas.* He dried his tears. **2** (*planta, río, estanque, tierra, herida*) to dry up: *El estanque se había secado.* The pond had dried up. LOC **secar los platos** to dry up

sección *nf* **1** (*gen, Arquit, Mat*) section **2** (*tienda*) department: ~ *de caballeros* menswear department **3** (*periódico, revista*) pages [*pl*]: *la* ~ *deportiva* the sports pages LOC **sección transversal** cross-section

seco, -a *adj* **1** (*gen*) dry: *¿Está ~?* Is it dry? ◊ *un clima muy* ~ a very dry climate **2** (*persona*) unfriendly **3** (*sin vida*) dead: *hojas secas* dead leaves **4** (*frutos, flores*) dried: *higos ~s* dried figs **5** (*sonido, golpe*) sharp LOC **a secas** just: *Me dijo que no, a secas.* He just said 'no'. **frenar/parar en seco** to stop dead *Ver tb* DIQUE, FRUTO, LIMPIAR, LIMPIEZA, PALO

secretaría *nf* **1** (*oficina para matricularse*) admissions office **2** (*cargo*) secretariat: *la* ~ *de la ONU* the UN secretariat **3** (*oficina del secretario*) secretary's office

secretariado *nm* (*estudios*) secretarial course

secretario, -a *nm-nf* secretary [*pl* secretaries]

secreto, -a *adj, nm* secret LOC **en secreto** secretly

secta *nf* sect

sector *nm* **1** (*zona, industria*) sector **2** (*grupo de personas*) section: *un pequeño* ~ *de la población* a small section of the population

secuencia *nf* sequence

secuestrador, ~a *nm-nf* **1** (*de una persona*) kidnapper **2** (*de un avión*) hijacker

secuestrar *vt* **1** (*persona*) to kidnap **2** (*avión*) to hijack

secuestro *nm* **1** (*de una persona*) kidnapping **2** (*de un avión*) hijacking

secundario, -a *adj* secondary LOC *Ver* CARRETERA, ESCUELA, PAPEL

sed *nf* thirst LOC **tener/pasar sed** to be thirsty: *Tengo mucha* ~. I'm very thirsty. *Ver tb* MUERTO

seda *nf* silk: *una camisa de* ~ a silk shirt LOC *Ver* GUSANO

sedante *nm* sedative

sede *nf* headquarters (*abrev* HQ) [*v sing o pl*]

sediento, -a *adj* thirsty

sedimento *nm* sediment

seducción *nf* seduction

seducir *vt* to seduce

seductor, ~a ◆ *adj* seductive ◆ *nm-nf* seducer

segadora *nf* combine harvester

segar *vt* to cut

segmento *nm* segment

segregar *vt* to segregate *sth/sb* (***from sth/sb***)

seguida LOC **en seguida** straight away

seguido, -a *pp, adj* in a row: *cuatro veces seguidas* four times in a row ◊ *Lo hizo tres días ~s.* He did it three days running. LOC **todo seguido** straight on *Ver tb* ACTO; *Ver tb* SEGUIR

seguir ◆ *vt* **1** (*gen*) to follow: *Sígueme.* Follow me. **2** (*estudios*) to do: *Estoy siguiendo un curso de francés.* I'm doing a French course. ◆ *vi* **1** (*gen*) to go on (***doing sth***): *Sigue hasta la plaza.* Go on till you reach the square. ◊ *Siguieron trabajando hasta las nueve.* They went on working till nine. **2** (*en una situación*) to be still…: *¿Sigue enferma?* Is she still poorly? ◊ *Sigo en el mismo trabajo.* I'm still in the same job. LOC *Ver* TRECE

según ◆ *prep* according to *sth/sb*: ~ *ella/los planes* according to her/the plans ◆ *adv* **1** (*dependiendo de*) depending on *sth*: ~ *sea el tamaño* depending on what size it is ◊ *Tal vez lo haga, ~.* I might do it; it depends. **2** (*de acuerdo con, a medida que*) as: ~ *van entrando* as they come in

segundero *nm* second hand

segundo, -a ◆ *adj, pron, nm-nf* second (*abrev* 2nd) ☛ *Ver ejemplos en* SEXTO ◆ *nm* **1** (*tiempo*) second **2** (*plato*) main course: *¿Qué quieres de ~?* What would you like as a main course? ◆ **segunda** *nf* (*marcha*) second (gear) LOC **de segunda mano** second-hand *Ver tb* ECUACIÓN, PRIMO

seguramente *adv* probably

seguridad *nf* **1** (*contra accidente*) safety: *la* ~ *ciudadana/vial* public/road safety **2** (*contra un ataque/robo, garantía*) security: *controles de* ~ security checks **3** (*certeza*) certainty **4** (*en sí mismo*) self-confidence LOC **Seguridad Social** ≃ National Health Service (*GB*) *Ver tb* CARTILLA, CINTURÓN

seguro, -a ◆ *adj* **1** (*sin riesgo*) safe: *un lugar ~* a safe place **2** (*convencido*) sure: *Estoy segura de que vendrán.* I'm sure they'll come. **3** (*firme, bien sujeto*) secure ◆ *nm* **1** (*póliza*) insurance [*incontable*]: *sacarse un ~ de vida* to take out life insurance **2** (*mecanismo*) safety catch ◆ *adv* for certain: *No lo saben ~.* They don't know for certain. LOC **seguro que...**: *~ que llegan tarde.* They're bound to be late. *Ver tb* LENTO

seis *nm, adj, pron* **1** (*gen*) six: *el número ~* number six ◊ *sacar un ~ en un examen* to get six in an exam ◊ *El ~ sigue al cinco.* Six comes after five. ◊ *~ y tres son nueve.* Six and three are/make nine. ◊ *~ por tres (son) dieciocho.* Three sixes (are) eighteen. **2** (*fecha, sexto*) sixth: *en el minuto ~* in the sixth minute ◊ *Fuimos el 6 de mayo.* We went on 6 May ☛Se lee: 'the sixth of May'. LOC **a las seis** at six o'clock **dar las seis** to strike six: *Dieron las ~ en el reloj.* The clock struck six. **las seis menos cinco, etc** five, etc to six **las seis menos cuarto** a quarter to six **las seis y cinco, etc** five, etc past six **las seis y cuarto** a quarter past six **las seis y media** half past six **seis de cada diez** six out of ten **son las seis** it's six o'clock ☛Para más información sobre el uso de los números, fechas, etc, ver Apéndice 1.

seiscientos, -as ◆ *adj, pron* six hundred: *~ cuarenta y dos* six hundred and forty-two ◊ *Éramos ~ en la boda.* There were six hundred of us at the wedding. ◊ *hace ~ años* six hundred years ago ◆ *nm* six hundred LOC **seiscientos un(o), seiscientos dos, etc** six hundred and one, six hundred and two, etc ☛ *Ver* Apéndice 1.

selección *nf* **1** (*gen*) selection **2** (*equipo*) (national) team: *la ~ española de baloncesto* the Spanish basketball team

seleccionar *vt* to select

selectividad *nf* university entrance exam

selecto, -a *adj* select: *un grupo/restaurante ~* a select group/restaurant

sellar *vt* **1** (*cerrar*) to seal: *~ un sobre/una amistad* to seal an envelope/a friendship **2** (*marcar con un sello*) to stamp: *~ una carta/un pasaporte* to stamp a letter/passport

sello *nm* (*correos*) stamp: *Dos ~s para España, por favor.* Two stamps for Spain, please. ◊ *Ponle un ~ a la postal.* Put a stamp on the postcard. ☛ *Ver nota en* STAMP

selva *nf* jungle

semáforo *nm* traffic lights [*pl*]: *un ~ en rojo* a red light

semana *nf* week: *la ~ pasada/que viene* last/next week ◊ *dos veces por ~* twice a week LOC **Semana Santa** Easter: *¿Qué vais a hacer en Semana Santa?* What are you doing at Easter?

> También existe la expresión **Holy Week**, pero se usa solamente para referirse a las festividades religiosas.

una semana sí y otra no every other week *Ver tb* FIN

semanal *adj* **1** (*de cada semana*) weekly: *una revista ~* a weekly magazine **2** (*a la semana*): *Tenemos una hora ~ de gimnasia.* We have one hour of PE a week.

sembrar *vt* **1** (*gen*) to sow: *~ trigo/un campo* to sow wheat/a field **2** (*hortalizas*) to plant: *Han sembrado ese campo de patatas.* They've planted that field with potatoes.

semejante *adj* **1** (*parecido*) similar: *un modelo ~ a éste* a model similar to this one **2** (*tal*): *¿Cómo pudiste hacer ~ cosa?* How could you do a thing like that? LOC *Ver* COSA

semejanza *nf* similarity [*pl* similarities]

semen *nm* semen

semicírculo *nm* semicircle

semicorchea *nf* (*Mús*) semiquaver

semifinal *nf* semifinal

semifinalista *nmf* semifinalist

semilla *nf* seed

seminario *nm* **1** (*clase*) seminar **2** (*Relig*) seminary [*pl* seminaries]

senado *nm* senate

senador, ~a *nm-nf* senator

sencillez *nf* simplicity

sencillo, -a ◆ *adj* **1** (*gen*) simple: *una comida sencilla* a simple meal **2** (*persona*) straightforward ◆ *nm* (*disco*) single: *el último ~ del grupo* the group's latest single

senda *nf* path

seno *nm* breast

sensación *nf* feeling LOC **causar/hacer sensación 1** (*hacer furor*) to cause a sensation **2** (*emocionar*) to make an impression *on sb*: *Volver a verle me causó una gran ~.* Seeing him again made a deep impression on me.

sensacional *adj* sensational

sensatez *nf* good sense

sensato, -a *adj* sensible

sensibilidad *nf* sensitivity

sensible *adj* **1** (*gen*) sensitive (**to** ***sth***): *Mi piel es muy ~ al sol.* My skin is very sensitive to the sun. ◊ *Es una niña muy ~.* She's a very sensitive child. **2** (*grande*) noticeable: *una mejora ~* a noticeable improvement

sensual *adj* sensual

sentada *nf* (*protesta*) sit-in **LOC de/en una sentada** in one go

sentado, -a *pp, adj* sitting, seated (*más formal*): *Estaban ~s a la mesa.* They were sitting at the table. ◊ *Se quedaron ~s.* They remained seated. **LOC dar algo por sentado** to assume sth *Ver tb* SENTAR

sentar ◆ *vt* to sit: *Sentó al niño en su cochecito.* He sat the baby in its pram. ◆ *vi* to suit: *Te sienta mejor el rojo.* The red one suits you better. ◊ *¿Qué tal me sienta?* How does it look? ◆ **sentarse** *v pron* to sit (down): *Siéntese.* Sit down, please. ◊ *Nos sentamos en el suelo.* We sat (down) on the floor. **LOC sentar bien/mal 1** (*ropa*) to suit/not to suit *sb*: *Este vestido me sienta muy mal.* This dress doesn't suit me at all. **2** (*alimentos*) to agree/not to agree *with sb*: *El café no me sienta bien.* Coffee doesn't agree with me. **3** (*hacer buen efecto*) to do *sb* good/no good: *Me sentó bien el descanso.* The rest did me good. **4** (*tomar bien/mal*): *Me sentó mal que no me invitaran.* I was upset that I wasn't invited. **sentar como un guante** to fit like a glove **sentar (la) cabeza** to settle down *Ver tb* PATADA, PINTADO, TIRO

sentencia *nf* **1** (*Jur*) sentence **2** (*dicho*) maxim **LOC** *Ver* DICTAR

sentenciar *vt* to sentence *sb* ***to sth***

sentido *nm* **1** (*gen*) sense: *los cinco ~s* the five senses ◊ *~ del humor* sense of humour ◊ *No tiene ~.* It doesn't make sense. **2** (*significado*) meaning **3** (*dirección*) direction **LOC sentido común** common sense **sentido único** one way: *una calle de ~ único* a one-way street *Ver tb* CARECER, DOBLE, SEXTO

sentimental *adj* **1** (*gen*) sentimental: *valor ~* sentimental value **2** (*vida*) love [*n atrib*]: *vida ~* love life **LOC** *Ver* CONSULTORIO

sentimiento *nm* feeling

sentir ◆ *vt* **1** (*gen*) to feel: *~ frío/hambre* to feel cold/hungry **2** (*oír*) to hear **3** (*lamentar*) to be sorry **about** ***sth***/(***that…***): *Siento no poder ayudarte.* I'm sorry (that) I can't help you. ◊ *Sentimos mucho tu desgracia.* We're very sorry about your bad luck. ◆ **sentirse** *v pron* to feel: *Me siento muy bien.* I feel very well. **LOC lo siento (mucho)** I'm (very) sorry *Ver tb* ESCALOFRÍO, GANA, NÁUSEA, OBLIGADO, SIMPATÍA, SOLO

seña *nf* **1** (*gesto*) sign **2 señas** (*dirección*) address [*sing*] **LOC hacer señas** to signal: *Me hacían ~s para que parase.* They were signalling to me to stop.

señal *nf* **1** (*gen*) sign: *~es de tráfico* road signs ◊ *Es una buena/mala ~.* It's a good/bad sign. ◊ *en ~ de protesta* as a sign of protest **2** (*marca*) mark **3** (*teléfono*) tone: *la ~ para marcar/de ocupado* the dialling/engaged tone **LOC dar señales** to show signs *of sth/doing sth* **hacer una señal/señales** to signal: *El conductor me hacía ~es.* The driver was signalling to me.

señalar *vt* **1** (*marcar*) to mark: *Señala las faltas con un lápiz rojo.* Mark the mistakes in red pencil. **2** (*mostrar, afirmar*) to point *sth* out: *~ algo en un mapa* to point sth out on a map ◊ *Señaló que…* He pointed out that…

señalizar *vt* to signpost

señor, ~a ◆ *nm-nf* **1** (*adulto*) man [*fem* lady] [*pl* men/ladies]: *Hay un ~ que quiere hablar contigo.* There's a man who wants to talk to you. ◊ *una peluquería de señoras* a ladies' hairdresser **2** (*delante del apellido*) Mr [*fem* Mrs] [*pl* Mr and Mrs]: *¿Está el ~ López?* Is Mr López in? ◊ *los ~es de Soler* Mr and Mrs Soler **3** (*delante del nombre o de cargos*): *La señora Luisa es la costurera.* Luisa is the dressmaker. ◊ *el ~ alcalde* the mayor **4** (*para llamar la atención*) excuse me!: *¡Señor! Se le ha caído el billete.* Excuse me! You've dropped your ticket. **5** (*de cortesía*) sir [*fem* madam] [*pl* gentlemen/ladies]: *Buenos días ~.* Good morning, sir. ◊ *Señoras y señores…* Ladies and gentlemen… ◆ *nm* **Señor** Lord ◆ **señora** *nf* (*esposa*) wife [*pl* wives] **LOC ¡no señor!** no way! **¡señor!** good Lord! **¡sí señor!** too right! *Ver tb* MUY

señorita *nf* **1** (*fórmula de cortesía*) Miss, Ms

Miss se utiliza con el apellido o con el nombre y el apellido: 'Miss Jones' o 'Miss Mary Jones'. Nunca se utiliza sólo con el nombre propio: *Llame a la*

señorita Elena/a la señorita Pelayo. Phone Elena/Miss Pelayo.
Ms se usa para mujeres casadas o solteras cuando no se conoce su estado civil.

2 (*maestra*) teacher: *La ~ nos pone muchos deberes.* Our teacher gives us a lot of homework. **3** (*para llamar la atención*) excuse me: *¡Señorita! ¿Me puede atender, por favor?* Excuse me! Can you serve me please?

separación *nf* **1** (*gen*) separation **2** (*distancia*) gap: *Hay siete metros de ~.* There's a seven-metre gap.

separado, -a *pp, adj* **1** (*matrimonio*) separated: *—¿Soltera o casada? —Separada.* 'Married or single?' 'Separated.' **2** (*distinto*) separate: *llevar vidas separadas* to lead separate lives LOC **por separado** separately *Ver tb* SEPARAR

separar ♦ *vt* **1** (*gen*) to separate *sth/sb* (***from sth/sb***): *Separa las bolas rojas de las verdes.* Separate the red balls from the green ones. **2** (*alejar*) to move *sth/sb* away (***from sth/sb***): *~ la mesa de la ventana* to move the table away from the window **3** (*guardar*) to put *sth* aside: *Sepárame un pan.* Put a loaf aside for me. ♦ **separarse** *v pron* **1** (*gen*) to separate, to split up (*más coloq*): *Se separó de su marido.* She separated from her husband. ◊ *Nos separamos a mitad de camino.* We split up halfway. **2** (*apartarse*) to move away (***from sth/sb***): *~se de la familia* to move away from your family

separatista *adj, nmf* separatist

sepia *nf* cuttlefish [*pl* cuttlefish]

septiembre (*tb* **setiembre**) *nm* September (*abrev* Sept) ☛ *Ver ejemplos en* ENERO

séptimo, -a *adj, pron, nm-nf* seventh ☛ *Ver ejemplos en* SEXTO LOC **estar en el séptimo cielo** to be in seventh heaven

sepultura *nf* grave

sequía *nf* drought

ser¹ ♦ *v copul, vi* **1** (*gen*) to be: *Es alta.* She's tall. ◊ *Soy de Jaén.* I'm from Jaén. ◊ *Dos y dos son cuatro.* Two and two are four. ◊ *Son las siete.* It's seven o'clock. ◊ *—¿Cuánto es? —Son 320 pesetas.* 'How much is it?' '(It's) 320 pesetas.' ◊ *—¿Quién es? —Soy Ana.* 'Who's that?' 'It's Ana.' ◊ *En mi familia somos seis.* There are six of us in my family.

En inglés se utiliza el artículo indefinido **a/an** delante de profesiones en oraciones con el verbo 'to be': *Es médico/ingeniero.* He's a doctor/an engineer.

2 ~ de (*material*) to be made **of *sth***: *Es de aluminio.* It's made of aluminium. ♦ *v aux* to be: *Será juzgado el lunes.* He will be tried on Monday. LOC **a no ser que...** unless... **es más** what's more **¡eso es!** that's right! **es que...**: *Es que no me apetece.* I just don't feel like it. ◊ *¡Es que es muy caro!* It's very expensive! ◊ *¿Es que no os conocíais?* Didn't you know each other, then? **lo que sea** whatever **no sea que/no vaya a ser que** (just) in case **o sea**: *¿O sea que os vais mañana?* So you're leaving tomorrow, are you? ◊ *El día 17, o sea el martes pasado.* The 17th, that is to say last Tuesday. **por si fuera poco** to top it all **¿qué es de...?**: *¿Qué es de tu hermana?* What's your sister been up to? ◊ *¿Qué es de vuestra vida?* What have you been up to? **sea como sea/sea lo que sea/sea quien sea** no matter how/what/who **si no es/fuera por** if it weren't for *sth/sb* **si yo fuera** if I were **soy yo** it's me, you, etc ☛ Para otras expresiones con **ser**, véanse las entradas del sustantivo, adjetivo, etc, p.ej. **ser el colmo** en COLMO y **ser tartamudo** en TARTAMUDO.

ser² *nm* being: *un ~ humano/vivo* a human/living being

sereno, -a ♦ *adj* calm ♦ *nm* nightwatchman [*pl* nightwatchmen]

serial *nm* serial ☛ *Ver nota en* SERIES

serie *nf* series [*pl* series]: *una ~ de desgracias* a series of disasters ◊ *una nueva ~ televisiva* a new TV series ☛ *Ver nota en* SERIES LOC *Ver* FABRICAR

serio, -a *adj* **1** (*gen*) serious: *un libro/asunto ~* a serious book/matter **2** (*cumplidor*) reliable: *Es un hombre de negocios ~.* He's a reliable businessman. LOC **en serio** seriously: *tomar algo en ~* to take sth seriously ◊ *¿Lo dices en ~?* Are you serious? **ponerse serio con algn** to get cross with sb

sermón *nm* (*Relig*) sermon LOC **echar un sermón** to give *sb* a lecture *Ver tb* SOLTAR

serpentina *nf* streamer

serpiente *nf* snake LOC **serpiente de cascabel** rattlesnake

serrano, -a *adj* LOC *Ver* JAMÓN

serrar *vt* to saw *sth* (up): *Serré la madera.* I sawed up the wood.

serrín *nm* sawdust

servicio *nm* **1** (*gen, Tenis*) service: ~ *de autobuses* bus service **2** (*doméstico*) domestic help **3** (*cuarto de baño*) toilet: *¿Los ~s por favor?* Where are the toilets, please? ☛ *Ver nota en* TOILET LOC **hacer el servicio (militar)** to do (your) military service *Ver tb* ESTACIÓN

servilleta *nf* napkin: *~s de papel* paper napkins

servilletero *nm* napkin-ring

servir ◆ *vt* to serve: *Tardaron mucho en ~nos.* They took a long time to serve us. ◊ *¿Te sirvo un poco más?* Would you like some more? ◆ *vi* **1** (*gen, Tenis*) to serve: ~ *en la marina* to serve in the navy **2** ~ **de/como/para** to serve **as *sth*/ to do *sth***: *Sirvió para aclarar las cosas.* It served to clarify things. ◊ *La caja me sirvió de mesa.* I used the box as a table. **3** ~ **para** (*usarse*) to be (used) **for *doing sth***: *Sirve para cortar.* It is used for cutting. ◊ *¿Para qué sirve?* What do you use it for? ◆ **servirse** *v pron* (*comida*) to help yourself (**to *sth***): *Me serví ensalada.* I helped myself to salad. ◊ *Sírvase usted mismo.* Help yourself. LOC **no servir 1** (*utensilio*) to be no good (*for doing sth*): *Este cuchillo no sirve para cortar carne.* This knife is no good for cutting meat. **2** (*persona*) to be no good *at sth/doing sth*: *No sirvo para enseñar.* I'm no good at teaching. *Ver tb* BANDEJA

sesenta *nm, adj, pron* **1** (*gen*) sixty **2** (*sexagésimo*) sixtieth: *Estás el ~ en la lista.* You're sixtieth on the list. ◊ *el ~ aniversario* the sixtieth anniversary LOC **los sesenta** (*los años 60*) the sixties **sesenta y un(o), sesenta y dos, etc** sixty-one, sixty-two, etc ☛ *Ver* Apéndice 1.

sesión *nf* **1** (*gen*) session: ~ *de entrenamiento/clausura* training/closing session **2** (*Cine*) showing **3** (*Teat*) performance

seso *nm* brain LOC **calentarse/ devanarse los sesos** to rack your brains *Ver tb* ESTRUJAR

seta *nf* mushroom LOC **seta venenosa** toadstool

setecientos, -as *adj, pron, nm* seven hundred ☛ *Ver ejemplos en* SEISCIENTOS

setenta *nm, adj, pron* **1** (*gen*) seventy **2** (*septuagésimo*) seventieth ☛ *Ver ejemplos en* SESENTA

seudónimo *nm* pseudonym

severo, -a *adj* **1** (*intenso*) severe: *un golpe* ~ a severe blow **2** ~ **(con)** (*estricto*) strict (**with *sb***): *Mi padre era muy ~ con nosotros.* My father was very strict with us. **3** (*castigo, crítica*) harsh

sexista *adj, nmf* sexist

sexo *nm* sex

sexto, -a ◆ *adj* **1** (*gen*) sixth: *la sexta hija* the sixth daughter **2** (*en títulos*): *Felipe VI* Philip VI ☛ Se lee: 'Philip the Sixth'. ☛ *Ver* Apéndice 1. ◆ *pron, nm-nf* sixth: *Es el ~ de la familia.* He's sixth in the family. ◊ *Fui ~ en cruzar la meta.* I was the sixth to finish. ◆ *nm* **1** sixth: *cinco ~s* five sixths **2** (*piso*) sixth floor: *Vivo en el ~.* I live on the sixth floor. **3** (*vivienda*) sixth-floor flat: *Viven en un ~.* They live in a sixth-floor flat. LOC **la/ una sexta parte** a sixth **sexto sentido** sixth sense

sexual *adj* **1** (*gen*) sexual: *acoso ~* sexual harassment **2** (*educación, órganos, vida*) sex [*n atrib*]

sexualidad *nf* sexuality

si[1] *nm* (*Mús*) **1** (*nota de la escala*) ti **2** (*tonalidad*) B: *si mayor* B major

si[2] *conj* **1** (*gen*) if: *Si llueve no iremos.* If it rains, we won't go. ◊ *Si fuera rico me compraría una moto.* If I were rich, I'd buy a motorbike. ☛ Es más correcto decir 'if I/he/she/it **were**', pero hoy en día en el lenguaje hablado se suele usar 'if I/he/she/it **was**'. **2** (*duda*) whether: *No sé si quedarme o marcharme.* I don't know whether to stay or go. **3** (*deseo*) if only: *¡Si me lo hubieras dicho antes!* If only you had told me before! **4** (*protesta*) but: *¡Si no me lo habías dicho!* But you didn't tell me! **5** (*enfático*) really: *Si será despistada.* She's really scatterbrained. LOC **si no** otherwise

sí[1] ◆ *adv* **1** (*gen*) yes: *—¿Quieres un poco más? —Sí.* 'Would you like a bit more?' 'Yes, please.' **2** (*énfasis*): *Sí que estoy contenta.* I am really happy. ◊ *Ella no irá, pero yo sí.* She's not going but I am. ◆ *nm*: *Contestó con un tímido sí.* He shyly said yes. ◊ *Aún no me ha dado el sí.* He still hasn't said yes. LOC **¡eso sí que no!** definitely not!

sí[2] *pron pers* **1** (*él*) himself: *Hablaba para sí (mismo).* He was talking to himself. **2** (*ella*) herself: *Sólo sabe hablar de sí misma.* She can only talk about herself. **3** (*ello*) itself: *El problema se solucionó por sí mismo.* The problem solved itself. **4** (*ellos, ellas*) themselves **5** (*impersonal, usted*) yourself: *querer algo para sí* to want sth for yourself ☛ *Ver nota en* YOU **6** (*ustedes*) yourselves LOC **darse de sí** (*prendas, zapatos*) to stretch **de por sí/en sí** (**mismo**) in itself

siamés, -esa *adj* LOC *Ver* GATO, HERMANO

sida (*tb* **SIDA**) *nm* AIDS/Aids

siderurgia *nf* iron and steel industry

siderúrgico, -a *adj* iron and steel [*n atrib*]: *el sector ~ español* the Spanish iron and steel sector

sidra *nf* cider

siembra *nf* sowing

siempre *adv* always: *~ dices lo mismo.* You always say the same thing. ◊ *~ he vivido con mis primos.* I've always lived with my cousins. ☛ *Ver nota en* ALWAYS LOC **como siempre** as usual **de siempre** (*acostumbrado*) usual: *Nos veremos en el sitio de ~.* We'll meet in the usual place. **lo de siempre** the usual thing **para siempre 1** (*permanentemente*) for good: *Me marcho de España para ~.* I'm leaving Spain for good. **2** (*eternamente*) for ever: *Nuestro amor es para ~.* Our love will last for ever. **siempre que...** whenever...: *~ que vamos de vacaciones te pones enfermo.* Whenever we go on holiday you get ill.

sien *nf* temple

sierra *nf* **1** (*herramienta*) saw **2** (*región*) mountains [*pl*]: *una casita en la ~* a cottage in the mountains **3** (*Geog*) mountain range

siesta *nf* siesta LOC **dormir/echarse la siesta** to have a siesta

siete *nm, adj, pron* **1** (*gen*) seven **2** (*fecha*) seventh ☛ *Ver ejemplos en* SEIS LOC **tener siete vidas** to have nine lives

sigilosamente *adv* very quietly

sigla *nf* **siglas**: *¿Cuáles son las ~s de...?* What's the abbreviation for...? ◊ *CE son las ~s de la Comunidad Europea.* CE stands for 'Comunidad Europea'.

siglo *nm* **1** (*centuria*) century [*pl* centuries]: *en el ~ XX* in the 20th century ☛Se lee: 'in the twentieth century'. **2** (*era*) age: *Vivimos en el ~ de los ordenadores.* We live in the age of computers. LOC **Siglo de Oro** Golden Age

significado *nm* meaning

significar *vt, vi* to mean (*sth*) (**to sb**): *¿Qué significa esta palabra?* What does this word mean? ◊ *Él significa mucho para mí.* He means a lot to me.

signo *nm* **1** (*gen*) sign: *los ~s del zodíaco* the signs of the zodiac **2** (*imprenta, fonética*) symbol LOC **signo de admiración/interrogación** exclamation/question mark ☛ *Ver* págs 318–19.

siguiente ◆ *adj* next: *al día ~* the next day ◆ *nmf* next one: *Que pase la ~.* Tell the next one to come in. LOC **lo siguiente** the following

sílaba *nf* syllable

silbar *vt, vi* **1** (*gen*) to whistle: *~ una canción* to whistle a tune **2** (*abuchear*) to boo

silbato *nm* whistle: *El árbitro tocó el ~.* The referee blew the whistle.

silbido *nm* **1** (*gen*) whistle: *el ~ del viento* the whistling of the wind **2** (*protesta, serpiente*) hiss **3** (*oídos*) buzzing

silenciar *vt* **1** (*persona*) to silence **2** (*suceso*) to hush *sth* up

silencio *nm* silence: *En la clase había ~ absoluto.* There was total silence in the classroom. LOC **¡silencio!** be quiet! *Ver tb* ROGAR

silencioso, -a *adj* **1** (*en silencio, callado*) silent: *La casa estaba completamente silenciosa.* The house was totally silent. ◊ *un motor ~* a silent engine **2** (*tranquilo*) quiet: *una calle muy silenciosa* a very quiet street

silla *nf* **1** (*mueble*) chair: *sentado en una ~* sitting on a chair **2** (*de niño*) pushchair LOC **silla de montar** saddle **silla de ruedas** wheelchair

sillón *nm* armchair: *sentado en un ~* sitting in an armchair

silueta *nf* silhouette

silvestre *adj* wild

simbólico, -a *adj* symbolic

simbolizar *vt* to symbolize

símbolo *nm* symbol

simétrico, -a *adj* symmetrical

similar *adj* ~ (**a**) similar (**to** ***sth/sb***)

simio, -a *nm-nf* ape

simpatía *nf* charm LOC **sentir/tener simpatía hacia/por algn** to like sb

simpático, -a *adj* nice: *Es una chica muy simpática.* She's a very nice girl. ◊ *Me pareció/cayó muy ~.* I thought he was very nice.

> Nótese que **sympathetic** no significa simpático sino *comprensivo, compasivo*: *Todos fueron muy comprensivos.* Everyone was very sympathetic.

LOC **hacerse el simpático**: *Se estaba haciendo el ~.* He was trying to be nice.

simpatizante *nmf* sympathizer: *ser ~ del partido liberal* to be a liberal party sympathizer

simpatizar *vi* (*llevarse bien*) to get on (well) (***with sb***)

simple *adj* **1** (*sencillo, fácil*) simple: *No es tan ~ como parece.* It's not as simple as it looks. **2** (*mero*): *Es un ~ apodo.* It's just a nickname. LOC **a simple vista** at first glance

simplificar *vt* to simplify

simultáneo, -a *adj* simultaneous

sin *prep* **1** (*gen*) without: *sin azúcar* without sugar ◊ *sin pensar* without thinking ◊ *Salió sin decir nada.* She went out without saying anything. ◊ *Salieron sin que nadie les viera.* They left without anybody seeing them. **2** (*por hacer*): *Los platos estaban todavía sin fregar.* The dishes still hadn't been done. ◊ *Tuve que dejar el trabajo sin terminar.* I had to leave the work unfinished. LOC **sin embargo** *Ver* EMBARGO

sinagoga *nf* synagogue

sinceridad *nf* sincerity

sincero, -a *adj* sincere

sincronizar *vt* to synchronize: *Sincronicemos los relojes.* Let's synchronize our watches.

sindicato *nm* (trade) union: *el ~ de mineros* the miners' union

síndrome *nm* syndrome LOC **síndrome de abstinencia** withdrawal symptoms [*pl*] **síndrome de inmunodeficiencia adquirida (SIDA)** Acquired Immune Deficiency Syndrome (*abrev* AIDS)

sinfonía *nf* symphony [*pl* symphonies]

sinfónico, -a *adj* **1** (*música*) symphonic **2** (*orquesta*) symphony [*n atrib*]: *orquesta sinfónica* symphony orchestra

singular *adj* (*Gram*) singular

siniestro, -a *adj* sinister: *aspecto ~* sinister appearance LOC *Ver* DIESTRO

sino *conj* but: *no sólo en Madrid, ~ también en otros sitios* not only in Madrid but in other places as well ◊ *No haces ~ criticar.* You do nothing but criticize.

sinónimo, -a ◆ *adj* ~ (**de**) synonymous (**with *sth***) ◆ *nm* synonym

síntoma *nm* symptom

sintonizar *vt, vi* to tune in (***to sth***): *~ (con) la BBC* to tune in to the BBC

sinvergüenza *nmf* scoundrel

siquiera *adv* **1** (*en frase negativa*) even: *Ni ~ me llamaste.* You didn't even phone me. ◊ *sin vestirme ~* without even getting dressed **2** (*al menos*) at least: *Dame ~ una idea.* At least give me an idea.

sirena *nf* **1** (*señal acústica*) siren: *~ de policía* police siren **2** (*mujer-pez*) mermaid

sirviente, -a *nm-nf* servant

sísmico, -a *adj* seismic

sistema *nm* **1** (*gen*) system: *~ político/educativo* political/education system ◊ *el ~ solar* the solar system **2** (*método*) method: *los ~s pedagógicos modernos* modern teaching methods LOC **sistema montañoso** mountain range

sitio *nm* **1** (*gen*) place: *un ~ para dormir* a place to sleep **2** (*espacio*) room: *¿Hay ~?* Is there any room? ◊ *Creo que no habrá ~ para todos.* I don't think there'll be enough room for everybody. **3** (*asiento*) seat: *La gente buscaba ~.* People were looking for seats. LOC **hacer sitio** to make room (*for sth/sb*) **ir de un sitio a/para otro** to rush around *Ver tb* ALGUNO, CUALQUIERA, NINGUNO, OTRO

situación *nf* situation: *una ~ difícil* a difficult situation

situado, -a *pp, adj* situated *Ver tb* SITUAR

situar ◆ *vt* **1** (*colocar*) to put, to place (*más formal*): *Me sitúa en una posición muy comprometida.* This puts me in a very awkward position. **2** (*en un mapa*) to find: *Sitúame Suiza en el mapa.* Find Switzerland on the map. ◆ **situarse** *v pron* (*clasificación*) to be: *~se entre las cinco primeras* to be among the top five LOC **situarse a la cabeza** to lead the field

slogan *nm Ver* ESLOGAN

smoking *nm Ver* ESMOQUIN

snob *adj, nmf Ver* ESNOB

¡so! *interj* whoa!

sobaco *nm* armpit

sobar *vt* **1** (*cosa*) to finger: *Deja de ~ la tela.* Stop fingering the material. **2** (*persona*) to paw

soberano, -a *adj, nm-nf* sovereign

sobornar *vt* to bribe

soborno *nm*: *intento de ~* attempted bribery ◊ *aceptar ~s* to accept/take bribes

sobra *nf* **1** (*exceso*) surplus: *Hay ~ de mano de obra barata.* There is a surplus of cheap labour. **2 sobras** (*restos*) leftovers LOC **de sobra 1** (*suficiente*) plenty (of *sth*): *Hay comida de*

~. There's plenty of food. ◊ *Tenemos tiempo de ~*. We have plenty of time. **2** (*muy bien*) very well: *Sabes de ~ que no me gusta*. You know very well that I don't like it.

sobrar *vi* **1** (*quedar*): *Sobra queso de anoche*. There's some cheese left (over) from last night. **2** (*haber más de lo necesario*): *Sobra tela para la falda*. There's plenty of material for the skirt. ◊ *Sobran dos sillas*. There are two chairs too many. **3** (*estar de más*) **(a)** (*cosa*) to be unnecessary: *Sobran las palabras*. Words are unnecessary. **(b)** (*persona*) to be in the way: *Aquí sobramos*. We're in the way here. LOC **sobrarle algo a algn 1** (*quedar*) to have sth left: *Me sobran dos caramelos*. I've got two sweets left. **2** (*tener demasiado*) to have too much/many...: *Me sobra trabajo*. I've got too much work.

sobre[1] *nm* **1** (*carta*) envelope **2** (*envoltorio*) packet: *un ~ de sopa* a packet of soup

sobre[2] *prep* **1** (*encima de*) on: *sobre la mesa* on the table **2** (*por encima, sin tocar*) over: *Volamos sobre Madrid*. We flew over Madrid. **3** (*temperatura*) above: *un grado sobre cero* one degree above zero **4** (*acerca de, expresando aproximación*) about: *una película sobre Escocia* a film about Scotland ◊ *Llegaré sobre las ocho*. I'll arrive about eight. LOC **sobre todo** *ver* TODO

sobrecargado, -a *pp, adj* overloaded: *una línea sobrecargada* an overloaded line

sobredosis *nf* overdose

sobremesa *nf* **1** (*conversación*) after-dinner chat: *estar de ~* to have an after-dinner chat ◊ *La ~ estuvo muy agradable*. We had a very nice chat after dinner. **2** (*programa de TV*) afternoon [*n atrib*]: *la programación de ~* afternoon television

sobrenatural *adj* supernatural

sobrentenderse (*tb* **sobreentenderse**) *v pron* to be understood

sobrepasar *vt* **1** (*cantidad, límite, medida, esperanzas*) to exceed: *Sobrepasó los 170km por hora*. It exceeded 170km an hour. **2** (*rival, récord*) to beat

sobresaliente ◆ *adj* outstanding: *una actuación ~* an outstanding performance ◆ *nm* (*Educ*) ≃ A: *Saqué tres ~s*. I got three A's.

sobresalir *vi* **1** (*objeto, parte del cuerpo*) to stick out, to protrude (*formal*) **2** (*destacar, resaltar*) to stand out (**from sth/sb**): *Sobresale entre sus compañeras*. She stands out from her friends.

sobresaltar *vt* to startle

sobrevivir *vi* to survive

sobrino, -a *nm-nf* nephew [*fem* niece]

> A veces decimos *sobrinos* refiriéndonos a sobrinos y sobrinas, en cuyo caso debemos decir en inglés **nephews and nieces**: *¿Cuántos sobrinos tienes?* How many nephews and nieces have you got?

sobrio, -a *adj* sober

sociable *adj* sociable

social *adj* social LOC *Ver* ASISTENTE, CARTILLA, SEGURIDAD

socialismo *nm* socialism

socialista *adj, nmf* socialist

sociedad *nf* **1** (*gen*) society [*pl* societies]: *una ~ de consumo* a consumer society **2** (*Com*) company [*pl* companies] LOC **sociedad anónima** public limited company (*abrev* plc) **sociedad limitada** limited company (*abrev* Ltd) *Ver tb* ECO

socio, -a *nm-nf* **1** (*club*) member: *hacerse ~ de un club* to become a member of a club/to join a club **2** (*Com*) partner

sociología *nf* sociology

sociólogo, -a *nm-nf* sociologist

socorrer *vt* to help

socorrido, -a *pp, adj* handy: *una excusa socorrida* a handy excuse *Ver tb* SOCORRER

socorrismo *nm* life-saving

socorrista *nmf* lifeguard

socorro ◆ *nm* help ◆ **¡socorro!** *interj* help! LOC *Ver* CASA

sofá *nm* sofa LOC **sofá cama** sofa bed

sofisticado, -a *adj* sophisticated

sofocante *adj* stifling: *Hacía un calor ~*. It was stiflingly hot.

sofocar ◆ *vt* **1** (*fuego*) to smother **2** (*rebelión*) to put *sth* down ◆ **sofocarse** *v pron* **1** (*de calor*) to suffocate: *Me estaba sofocando en el metro*. I was suffocating on the underground. **2** (*quedarse sin aliento*) to get out of breath **3** (*irritarse*) to get worked up

sofoco *nm* **1** (*vergüenza*) embarrassment: *¡Qué ~!* How embarrassing! **2** (*sudores*) hot flush

soga *nf* rope LOC **estar con la soga al cuello** to be in a fix

soja *nf* soya

sol[1] *nm* sun: *Me daba el ~ en la cara.* The sun was shining on my face. ◊ *sentarse al ~* to sit in the sun ◊ *una tarde de ~* a sunny afternoon LOC **de sol a sol** from morning to night **hacer sol** to be sunny **no dejar a algn ni a sol ni a sombra** not to leave sb in peace **tomar el sol** to sunbathe *Ver tb* GAFAS, PUESTA, QUEMADURA, RELOJ, SALIDA

sol[2] *nm* **1** (*nota de la escala*) soh **2** (*tonalidad*) G: *~ bemol* G flat LOC *Ver* CLAVE

solamente *adv Ver* SÓLO

solapa *nf* **1** (*chaqueta*) lapel **2** (*libro, sobre*) flap

solar[1] *adj* (*del sol*) solar

solar[2] *nm* (*terreno*) plot

soldado *nmf* soldier

soldar *vt* to solder

soleado, -a *adj* sunny

solemne *adj* solemn

soler *vi* **1** (*en presente*) to usually do sth: *No suelo desayunar.* I don't usually have breakfast. ☛ *Ver nota en* ALWAYS **2** (*en pasado*) used to do sth: *Solíamos visitarlo en el verano.* We used to visit him in the summer. ◊ *No solíamos salir.* We didn't use to go out. ☛ *Ver nota en* USED TO

solfeo *nm* music theory

solicitante *nmf* applicant (***for sth***)

solicitar *vt* **1** (*gen*) to request: *~ una entrevista* to request an interview **2** (*empleo, beca*) to apply **for *sth***

solicitud *nf* **1** (*petición*) request (***for sth***): *una ~ de información* a request for information **2** (*instancia*) application (***for sth***): *una ~ de trabajo* a job application ◊ *rellenar una ~* to fill in an application (form)

solidez *nf* solidity

solidificar(se) *vt, v pron* **1** (*gen*) to solidify **2** (*agua*) to freeze

sólido, -a *adj, nm* solid

solista *nmf* soloist

solitario, -a ◆ *adj* **1** (*sin compañía*) solitary: *Lleva una vida solitaria.* She leads a solitary life. **2** (*lugar*) lonely: *las calles solitarias* the lonely streets ◆ *nm* (*Naipes*) patience [*incontable*]: *hacer un ~* to play a game of patience

sollozo *nm* sob

solo, -a ◆ *adj* **1** (*sin compañía*) alone: *Estaba sola en casa.* She was alone in the house. **2** (*sin ayuda*) by myself, yourself, etc: *El niño ya come ~.* He can eat by himself now. ☛ *Ver nota en* ALONE ◆ *nm* solo [*pl* solos]: *hacer un ~* to play/sing a solo LOC **estar a solas** to be alone **estar/sentirse solo** to be/feel lonely **quedarse solo** to be (left) on your own *Ver tb* CAFÉ

sólo (*tb* **solamente**) *adv* only: *Trabajo ~ los sábados.* I only work on Saturdays. ◊ *Es ~ un chiquillo.* He's only a child. ◊ *Tan ~ te pido una cosa.* I'm just asking you one thing. LOC **no sólo ... sino también ...** not only ... but also ...

solomillo *nm* fillet (steak)

soltar ◆ *vt* **1** (*desasir*) to let go **of *sth/sb***: *¡Suéltame!* Let go of me! **2** (*dejar caer*) to drop **3** (*dejar libre*) to set *sth/sb* free, to release (*más formal*) **4** (*perro*) to set *a dog* loose **5** (*cable, cuerda*) to let *sth* out: *Suelta un poco de cuerda.* Let the rope out a bit. **6** (*olor, humo*) to give *sth* off: *Suelta mucho humo.* It gives off a lot of smoke. **7** (*dinero*) to cough *sth* up **8** (*grito, suspiro*) to let *sth* out ◆ **soltarse** *v pron* **1** (*separarse*) to let go (***of sth/sb***): *No te sueltes de mi mano.* Don't let go of my hand. **2 soltarse (en)** to get the hang **of *sth***: *Ya se está soltando en inglés.* She's getting the hang of English now. LOC **no soltar palabra/prenda** not to say a word **soltar amarras** to cast off **soltarse el pelo** to let your hair down **soltar una carcajada** to burst out laughing **soltar una parrafada/un sermón** to give *sb* a lecture (*on sth*) *Ver tb* INDIRECTA, TACO

soltero, -a ◆ *adj* single: *ser/estar ~* to be single ◆ *nm-nf* single man/woman [*pl* single men/women] LOC *Ver* DESPEDIDA, MADRE

solterón, -ona *nm-nf* bachelor [*fem* old maid]: *Es un ~ empedernido.* He is a confirmed bachelor.

soltura *nf* **1** (*desparpajo*) self-confidence: *Se desenvuelve con ~.* He's very confident. **2** (*facilidad*): *Habla francés con ~.* She speaks fluent French. ◊ *conducir con ~* to drive well ◊ *coger ~ con el ordenador* to get the hang of the computer

soluble *adj* soluble: *aspirina ~* soluble aspirin

solución *nf* solution (***to sth***): *encontrar la ~ del problema* to find a solution to the problem

solucionar *vt* to solve: *Lo solucionaron*

con una llamada. They solved the problem with a phone call.

solvente *adj* solvent

sombra
CAFE
a shadow
They're sitting
in the shade.

sombra *nf* **1** (*ausencia de sol*) shade: *Nos sentamos en la ~.* We sat in the shade. ◊ *El árbol daba ~ al coche.* The car was shaded by the tree. ◊ *Me estás haciendo ~.* You're keeping the sun off me. **2** (*silueta*) shadow: *proyectar una ~* to cast a shadow ◊ *No es ni la ~ de lo que era.* She is a shadow of her former self. **LOC sombra (de ojos)** eyeshadow *Ver tb* SOL[1]

sombreado, -a *adj* shady

sombrero *nm* hat **LOC sombrero de copa** top hat

sombrilla *nf* (*playa*) sunshade

someter ◆ *vt* **1** (*dominar*) to subdue **2** (*exponer*) to subject *sth/sb* ***to sth***: *~ a los presos a torturas* to subject prisoners to torture ◊ *Sometieron el metal al calor.* The metal was subjected to heat. **3** (*buscar aprobación*) to submit *sth* (***to sth/sb***): *Tienen que ~ el proyecto al consejo.* The project must be submitted to the council. ◆ **someterse** *v pron* (*rendirse*) to surrender (***to sb***) **LOC someter a votación** to put *sth* to the vote

somnífero *nm* sleeping pill

sonado, -a *pp, adj* **1** (*comentado*) much talked-about: *la sonada dimisión del ministro* the much talked-about resignation of the minister **2** (*impresionante*) incredible **LOC estar sonado** to be bonkers *Ver tb* SONAR

sonajero *nm* rattle

sonámbulo, -a *nm-nf* sleepwalker

sonante *adj* **LOC** *Ver* DINERO

sonar ◆ *vi* **1** (*alarma, sirena*) to go off **2** (*timbre, campanilla, teléfono*) to ring **3** ~ **(a)** to sound: *Esta pared suena a hueco.* This wall sounds hollow. ◊ *El piano suena de maravilla.* The piano sounds great. ◊ *¿Cómo te suena este párrafo?* How does this paragraph sound to you? **4** (*ser familiar*) to ring a bell: *Ese nombre me suena.* That name rings a bell. **5** (*tripas*) to rumble: *Me sonaban las tripas.* My tummy was rumbling. ◆ **sonarse** *v pron* (*nariz*) to blow your nose

sonda *nf* (*Med*) probe

sondear *vt* **1** (*persona*) to sound *sb* out (***about/on sth***) **2** (*opinión, mercado*) to test

sondeo *nm* (*opinión, mercado*) poll: *un ~ de opinión* an opinion poll

sonido *nm* sound

sonoro, -a *adj* **1** (*Tec*) sound [*n atrib*]: *efectos ~s* sound effects **2** (*voz*) loud **LOC** *Ver* BANDA

sonreír *vi* to smile (***at sb***): *Me sonrió.* He smiled at me.

sonriente *adj* smiling

sonrisa *nf* smile

sonrojarse *v pron* to blush

sonrosado, -a *adj* rosy

soñador, ~a *nm-nf* dreamer

soñar ◆ *vi* ~ **con 1** (*durmiendo*) to dream **about** ***sth/sb***: *Anoche soñé contigo.* I dreamt about you last night. **2** (*desear*) to dream **of *doing sth***: *Sueño con una moto.* I dream of having a motor bike. ◊ *Sueñan con ser famosos.* They dream of becoming famous. ◆ *vt* to dream: *No sé si lo he soñado.* I don't know if I dreamt it. **LOC ni lo sueñes** no chance **soñar con los angelitos** to have sweet dreams **soñar despierto** to daydream

sopa *nf* soup: *~ de sobre/fideos* packet/noodle soup **LOC hasta en la sopa** all over the place

sopero, -a ◆ *adj* soup [*n atrib*]: *cuchara sopera* soup spoon ◆ **sopera** *nf* soup tureen **LOC** *Ver* PLATO

soplar ◆ *vt* **1** (*para apagar algo*) to blow *sth* out: *~ una vela* to blow out a candle **2** (*para enfriar algo*) to blow **on** ***sth***: *~ la sopa* to blow on your soup **3** (*decir en voz baja*) to whisper: *Me soplaba las respuestas.* He whispered the answers to me. **4** (*chivarse*) **(a)** (*entre niños*) to tell (on *sb*): *Si no me lo devuelves se lo soplo a la maestra.* If you don't give it back to me, I'll tell the teacher on you. **(b)** (*a la policía*) to grass ◆ *vi* **1** (*persona, viento*) to blow **2** (*beber*) to drink

soplo *nm* **1** (*gen*) blow: *Apagó todas las*

velas de un ~. He blew out the candles in one go. **2** (*viento*) gust

soplón, -ona *nm-nf* **1** (*gen*) tell-tale **2** (*de la policía*) grass

soportales *nm* arcade [*sing*]: *los* ~ *de la plaza* the arcade round the square

soportar *vt* to put up with *sth/sb*: ~ *el calor* to put up with the heat ☛Cuando la frase es negativa se utiliza mucho **to stand**: *No la soporto.* I can't stand her. ◊ *No soporto tener que esperar.* I can't stand waiting.

soporte *nm* **1** (*gen*) support **2** (*estantería*) bracket

soprano *nf* soprano [*pl* sopranos]

sorber *vt, vi* **1** (*líquido*) **(a)** (*gen*) to sip **(b)** (*con una pajita*) to suck **2** (*por las narices*) to sniff

sorbete *nm* sorbet

sorbo *nm* sip: *tomar un* ~ *de café* to have a sip of coffee **LOC** *Ver* BEBER(SE)

sordera *nf* deafness

sórdido, -a *adj* sordid

sordo, -a *adj, nm-nf* deaf [*adj*]: *un colegio especial para ~s* a special school for the deaf ◊ *quedarse* ~ to go deaf **LOC hacerse el sordo** to turn a deaf ear (*to sth/sb*) **sordo como una tapia** as deaf as a post

sordomudo, -a ◆ *adj* deaf and dumb ◆ *nm-nf* deaf mute

sorprendente *adj* surprising

sorprender ◆ *vt* **1** (*gen*) to surprise: *Me sorprende que no haya llegado todavía.* I'm surprised he hasn't arrived yet. **2** (*coger desprevenido*) to catch *sb* (unawares): *Los sorprendió robando.* He caught them stealing. ◊ *Sorprendieron a los atracadores.* They caught the robbers unawares. ◆ **sorprenderse** *v pron* to be surprised: *Se sorprendieron al vernos.* They were surprised to see us.

sorprendido, -a *pp, adj* surprised *Ver tb* SORPRENDER

sorpresa *nf* surprise **LOC coger por sorpresa** to take *sb* by surprise

sortear *vt* **1** (*echar a suertes*) to draw lots **for *sth*** **2** (*rifar*) to raffle **3** (*golpe, obstáculo*) to dodge **4** (*dificultad, trabas*) to overcome

sorteo *nm* **1** (*lotería, adjudicación*) draw **2** (*rifa*) raffle

sortija *nf* ring

SOS *nm* SOS: *enviar un* ~ to send out an SOS

sosegado, -a *pp, adj* calm *Ver tb* SOSEGARSE

sosegarse *v pron* to calm down

sosiego *nm* calm

soso, -a *adj* **1** (*comida*) tasteless: *La sopa está algo sosa.* This soup needs a little salt. **2** (*persona*) dull **3** (*chiste*): *Los chistes que cuentan son ~s.* Their jokes aren't funny.

sospecha *nf* suspicion

sospechar *vt, vi* ~ **(de)** to suspect: *Sospechan del joven como terrorista.* They suspect the young man of being a terrorist. **LOC ¡ya (me) lo sospechaba!** just as I thought!

sospechoso, -a ◆ *adj* suspicious ◆ *nm-nf* suspect

sostén *nm* (*sujetador*) bra

sostener ◆ *vt* **1** (*sujetar*) to hold **2** (*peso, carga*) to support **3** (*afirmar*) to maintain ◆ **sostenerse** *v pron* to stand up

sostenido, -a *pp, adj* (*Mús*) sharp: *fa* ~ F sharp *Ver tb* SOSTENER

sotana *nf* cassock

sótano *nm* basement

sport *nm* **LOC de sport** casual: *zapatos/ropa de* ~ casual shoes/clothes

squash *nm* squash **LOC** *Ver* PISTA

stop *nm* (*tráfico*) stop sign

stress *nm Ver* ESTRÉS

su *adj pos* **1** (*de él*) his **2** (*de ella*) her **3** (*de objeto, animal, concepto*) its **4** (*de ellos/ellas*) their **5** (*impersonal*) their: *Cada cual tiene su opinión.* Everyone has their own opinion. **6** (*de usted, de ustedes*) your

suave *adj* **1** (*color, luz, música, piel, ropa, voz*) soft **2** (*superficie*) smooth **3** (*brisa, persona, curva, pendiente, sonido*) gentle **4** (*castigo, clima, sabor*) mild **5** (*ejercicios, lluvia, viento*) light

suavizante *nm* **1** (*pelo*) conditioner **2** (*ropa*) (fabric) softener

suavizar *vt* **1** (*piel*) to moisturize **2** (*pelo*) to condition

subasta *nf* auction

subcampeón, -ona *nm-nf* runner-up [*pl* runners-up]

subconsciente *adj, nm* subconscious

subdesarrollado, -a *adj* underdeveloped

subdesarrollo *nm* underdevelopment

súbdito, -a *nm-nf* subject: *una súbdita británica* a British subject

subida *nf* **1** (*acción*) ascent **2**

(*pendiente*) hill: *al final de esta ~* at the top of this hill **3** (*aumento*) rise (***in sth***): *una ~ de precios* a rise in prices

subido, -a *pp, adj* (*color*) bright *Ver tb* SUBIR

subir ◆ *vt* **1** (*llevar*) to take/bring *sth* up: *Subió las maletas a la habitación.* He took the suitcases up to the room. **2** (*poner más arriba*) to put *sth* up: *Súbelo un poco más.* Put it a bit higher. **3** (*levantar*) to lift *sth* up: *Subí el equipaje al tren.* I lifted the luggage onto the train. **4** (*ir/venir arriba*) to go/come up: *~ una calle* to go up a street **5** (*volumen*) to turn *sth* up **6** (*precios*) to put *sth* up, to raise (*más formal*) ◆ *vi* **1** (*ir/venir arriba*) to go/come up: *Subimos al segundo piso.* We went up to the second floor. ◊ *~ al tejado* to go up onto the roof **2** (*temperatura, río*) to rise **3** (*marea*) to come in **4** (*precios*) to go up (in price): *Ha subido la gasolina.* Petrol has gone up in price. **5** (*volumen, voz*) to get louder ◆ **subir(se)** *vi, v pron* **subir(se)** (**a**) **1** (*automóvil*) to get in; to get into *sth*: *Subí al taxi.* I got into the taxi. **2** (*transporte público, caballo, bici*) to get on (*sth*) LOC **subirse a la cabeza** to go to your head **subirse a las barbas** to walk all over *sb* **subírsele los humos a algn** to become high and mighty **subirse por las paredes** to hit the roof *Ver tb* ESCALERA

subjetivo, -a *adj* subjective

subjuntivo, -a *adj, nm* subjunctive

sublevación *nf* uprising

sublime *adj* sublime

submarinismo *nm* scuba-diving

submarinista *nmf* scuba-diver

submarino, -a ◆ *adj* underwater ◆ *nm* submarine

subnormal ◆ *adj* subnormal ◆ *nmf* (*como insulto*) cretin

subordinado, -a *pp, adj, nm-nf* subordinate

subrayar *vt* to underline

subsidio *nm* benefit: *~ de enfermedad/paro* sickness/unemployment benefit

subsistir *vi* to subsist (***on sth***)

subterráneo, -a *adj* underground LOC *Ver* PASO

subtítulo *nm* subtitle

suburbio *nm* **1** (*alrededores*) suburb **2** (*barrio bajo*) slum quarter

subvencionar *vt* to subsidize

sucedáneo *nm* substitute (***for sth***)

suceder *vi* **1** (*ocurrir*) to happen (***to sth/sb***): *¡Que no vuelva a ~!* Don't let it happen again! **2** (*cargo, trono*) to succeed: *Su hijo le sucederá en el trono.* His son will succeed to the throne.

sucesión *nf* succession

sucesivamente *adv* successively LOC *Ver* ASÍ

suceso *nm* **1** (*acontecimiento*) event: *los ~s de los últimos días* the events of the past few days **2** (*incidente*) incident

sucesor, -a *nm-nf* ~ (**a**) successor (***to sth/sb***): *Todavía no han nombrado a su sucesora.* They've yet to name her successor.

suciedad *nf* dirt

sucio, -a *adj* dirty LOC **en sucio** in rough: *Escribe la redacción en ~ primero.* Write the essay in rough first. *Ver tb* CESTO, JUEGO, JUGAR, TRAPO

suculento, -a *adj* succulent

sucursal *nf* branch

sudadera *nf* sweatshirt

sudar *vi* to sweat LOC **sudar la gota gorda/sangre/tinta** to sweat blood

sudeste *nm* **1** (*punto cardinal, región*) south-east (*abrev* SE): *la fachada ~ del edificio* the south-east face of the building **2** (*viento, dirección*) south-easterly: *en dirección ~* in a south-easterly direction

sudoeste *nm* **1** (*punto cardinal, región*) south-west (*abrev* SW) **2** (*viento, dirección*) south-westerly

sudor *nm* sweat

sudoroso, -a *adj* sweaty

Suecia *nf* Sweden

sueco, -a ◆ *adj, nm* Swedish: *hablar ~* to speak Swedish ◆ *nm-nf* Swede: *los ~s* the Swedes

suegro, -a *nm-nf* **1** (*gen*) father-in-law [*fem* mother-in-law] **2 suegros** parents-in-law, in-laws (*más coloq*)

suela *nf* sole: *zapatos con ~ de goma* rubber-soled shoes

sueldo *nm* **1** (*gen*) pay [*incontable*]: *pedir un aumento de ~* to ask for a pay increase **2** (*mensual*) salary [*pl* salaries]

suelo *nm* **1** (*superficie de la tierra*) ground: *caer al ~* to fall (to the ground) **2** (*dentro de un edificio*) floor **3** (*terreno*) land LOC *Ver* FREGAR

suelto, -a ◆ *adj* loose: *una página suelta* a loose page ◊ *Siempre llevo el pelo ~.* I always wear my hair loose. ◊ *Creo que hay un tornillo ~.* I think there's a screw loose. ◆ *nm* small change LOC *Ver* DINERO, RIENDA

sueño *nm* **1** (*descanso*) sleep: *debido a la falta de ~* due to lack of sleep ◊ *No dejes que te quite el ~.* Don't lose any sleep over it. **2** (*somnolencia*) drowsiness: *Estas pastillas producen ~.* These pills make you drowsy. **3** (*lo soñado, ilusión*) dream: *Fue un ~ hecho realidad.* It was a dream come true. LOC **caerse de sueño** to be dead on your feet **dar sueño** to make *sb* drowsy **tener sueño** to be sleepy

suerte *nf* **1** (*fortuna*) luck: *¡Buena ~ con el examen!* Good luck with your exam! ◊ *dar/traer buena/mala ~* to bring good/bad luck **2** (*destino*) fate LOC **de la suerte** lucky: *mi número de la ~* my lucky number **echar a suertes** to toss for *sth*: *Lo echamos a ~s.* We tossed for it. **por suerte** fortunately **tener mala suerte** to be unlucky **tener suerte** to be lucky *Ver tb* AMULETO

suéter *nm* sweater

suficiente ◆ *adj* enough: *No tengo arroz ~ para tantas personas.* I haven't got enough rice for all these people. ◊ *¿Serán ~s?* Will there be enough? ◊ *Gano lo ~ para vivir.* I earn enough to live on. ◆ *nm* (*exámenes*) pass ≃ D

sufrido, -a *pp, adj* (*persona*) long-suffering *Ver tb* SUFRIR

sufrimiento *nm* suffering

sufrir ◆ *vt* **1** (*gen*) to suffer: *~ una derrota/lesión* to suffer a defeat/an injury **2** (*tener*) to have: *~ un accidente/ataque al corazón* to have an accident/a heart attack ◊ *La ciudad sufre problemas de tráfico.* The city has traffic problems. **3** (*cambio*) to undergo ◆ *vi* ~ (**de**) to suffer (**from *sth***): *Sufre del corazón.* He suffers from heart trouble. LOC *Ver* DESENGAÑO

sugerencia *nf* suggestion

sugerir *vt* to suggest

sugestión *nf* LOC **es (pura) sugestión** it's all in the mind

sugestionar ◆ *vt* to influence ◆ **sugestionarse** *v pron* to convince yourself ***that…***

suicidarse *v pron* to commit suicide

suicidio *nm* suicide

Suiza *nf* Switzerland

suizo, -a ◆ *adj* Swiss ◆ *nm-nf* Swiss man/woman [*pl* Swiss men/women]: *los ~s* the Swiss

sujetador *nm* (*prenda*) bra

sujetar ◆ *vt* **1** (*agarrar*) to hold: *Sujeta bien el paraguas.* Hold the umbrella tight. **2** (*asegurar*) to fasten: *~ unos papeles con un clip* to fasten papers together with a paper clip ◆ **sujetarse** *v pron* **sujetarse (a)** (*agarrarse*) to hold on (**to *sth***): *Sujétate a mi brazo.* Hold on to my arm

sujeto, -a ◆ *pp, adj* **1** (*atado*) fastened: *El equipaje iba bien ~.* The luggage was tightly fastened. **2** (*cogido*): *Dos policías lo tenían ~.* Two policemen were holding him down. **3** (*fijo*) secure: *El gancho no estaba bien ~.* The hook wasn't secure. **4** ~ **a** (*sometido*) subject **to *sth***: *Estamos ~s a las reglas del club.* We are subject to the rules of the club. ◆ *nm* **1** (*tipo*) character **2** (*Gram*) subject *Ver tb* SUJETAR

suma *nf* sum: *hacer una ~* to do a sum

sumar *vt, vi* to add (*sth*) up: *Suma dos y cinco.* Add up two and five. ◊ *¿Sabéis ~?* Can you add up?

sumergible *adj* water-resistant

sumergir(se) *vt, v pron* to submerge

suministrar *vt* to supply (*sb*) (**with *sth***): *Me suministró los datos.* He supplied me with the information.

sumiso, -a *adj* submissive

súper *nm* supermarket LOC *Ver* GASOLINA

superar ◆ *vt* **1** (*dificultad, problema*) to overcome, to get over *sth* (*más coloq*): *He superado el miedo a volar.* I've got over my fear of flying. **2** (*récord*) to beat **3** (*prueba*) to pass **4** (*ser mejor*) to surpass: *~ las expectativas* to surpass expectations ◊ *El equipo español superó a los italianos en juego.* The Spanish team outplayed the Italians. ◆ **superarse** *v pron* to better yourself

superficial *adj* superficial

superficie *nf* **1** (*gen*) surface: *la ~ del agua* the surface of the water **2** (*Mat, extensión*) area

superfluo, -a *adj* **1** (*gen*) superfluous: *detalles ~s* superfluous detail **2** (*gastos*) unnecessary

superior ◆ *adj* **1** ~ (**a**) (*gen*) higher (**than *sth/sb***): *una cifra 20 veces ~ a la normal* a figure 20 times higher than normal ◊ *estudios ~es* higher education **2** ~ (**a**) (*calidad*) superior (**to *sth/sb***): *Fue ~ a su rival.* He was superior to his rival. **3** (*posición*) top: *el ángulo ~ izquierdo* the top left-hand corner ◊ *el labio ~* the upper/top lip ◆ *nm* superior

superiora *nf* (*Relig*) Mother Superior
superioridad *nf* superiority LOC *Ver* AIRE
supermercado *nm* supermarket
superpoblado, -a *pp, adj* overpopulated
superstición *nf* superstition
supersticioso, -a *adj* superstitious
supervisar *vt* to supervise
superviviente ◆ *adj* surviving ◆ *nmf* survivor
suplemento *nm* supplement: *el ~ dominical* the Sunday supplement
suplente *adj, nmf* **1** (*gen*) relief [*n atrib*]: *un conductor ~* a relief driver **2** (*maestro*) supply teacher **3** (*Fútbol*) substitute [*n*]: *estar de ~* to be a substitute
supletorio, -a *adj* (*cama, mesa*) spare
súplica *nf* plea
suplicar *vt* to beg (*sb*) (**for *sth***): *Le supliqué que no lo hiciera.* I begged him not to do it. ◊ *~ piedad* to beg for mercy
suplicio *nm* **1** (*tortura*) torture: *Estos tacones son un ~.* These high heels are torture. **2** (*experiencia*) ordeal: *Aquellas horas de incertidumbre fueron un ~.* Those hours of uncertainty were an ordeal.
suponer *vt* **1** (*creer*) to suppose: *Supongo que vendrán.* I suppose they'll come. ◊ *Supongo que sí/no.* I suppose so/not. **2** (*significar*) to mean: *Esos ahorros suponen mucho para nosotros.* Those savings mean a lot to us. LOC **supón/supongamos que...** supposing...
suposición *nf* supposition
supositorio *nm* suppository [*pl* suppositories]
supremacía *nf* supremacy (**over *sth*/*sb***)
supremo, -a *adj* supreme LOC *Ver* TRIBUNAL
suprimir *vt* **1** (*omitir, excluir*) to leave *sth* out: *Yo suprimiría este párrafo.* I'd leave this paragraph out. **2** (*abolir*) to abolish: *~ una ley* to abolish a law
supuesto, -a *pp, adj* (*presunto*) alleged: *el ~ culpable* the alleged culprit LOC **dar por supuesto** to take *sth* for granted **por supuesto (que...)** of course *Ver tb* SUPONER
sur *nm* south (*abrev* S): *en el ~ de Francia* in the south of France ◊ *Queda al ~ de Barcelona.* It's south of Barcelona. ◊ *en la costa ~* on the south coast
surco *nm* **1** (*agricultura, arruga*) furrow **2** (*en el agua*) wake **3** (*disco, metal*) groove
sureste *nm Ver* SUDESTE
surf *nm* surfing: *hacer/practicar el ~* to go surfing
surgir *vi* to arise: *Espero que no surja ningún problema.* I hope that no problems arise.
suroeste *nm Ver* SUDOESTE
surtido, -a ◆ *pp, adj* (*variado*) assorted: *bombones ~s* assorted chocolates ◆ *nm* selection: *Tienen muy poco ~.* They've got a very poor selection. *Ver tb* SURTIR
surtidor *nm* **1** (*fuente*) fountain **2** (*gasolina*) pump
surtir *vt* LOC **surtir efecto** to have an effect
susceptible *adj* (*irritable*) touchy
suscribirse *v pron* ~ (**a**) **1** (*publicación*) to take out a subscription (**to *sth***) **2** (*asociación*) to become a member (**of *sth***)
suscripción *nf* subscription
susodicho, -a *adj, nm-nf* abovementioned [*adj*]: *los ~s* the abovementioned
suspender ◆ *vt, vi* to fail: *He suspendido el inglés.* I've failed English. ◊ *~ en dos asignaturas* to fail two subjects ◆ *vt* **1** (*interrumpir*) to suspend: *El árbitro suspendió el partido media hora.* The referee suspended the game for half an hour. **2** (*aplazar*) to postpone
suspense *nm* suspense LOC **libro/película de suspense** thriller
suspensivo, -a *adj* LOC *Ver* PUNTO
suspenso *nm* fail ≃ F: *Tengo dos ~s.* I got F in two subjects. ◊ *Hubo muchos ~s en historia.* A lot of people failed history.
suspirar *vi* to sigh
suspiro *nm* sigh
sustancia *nf* substance
sustancial *adj* substantial
sustancioso, -a *adj* (*comida*) nourishing
sustantivo *nm* noun
sustento *nm* **1** (*alimento*) sustenance **2** (*soporte, apoyo*) support
sustitución *nf* **1** (*permanente*) replacement **2** (*temporal, Dep*) substitution
sustituir *vt* (*suplir*) to stand in **for *sb***:

Me sustituirá mi ayudante. My assistant will stand in for me.

sustituto, -a *nm-nf* **1** (*permanente*) replacement: *Están buscando un ~ para el jefe de personal.* They're looking for a replacement for the personnel manager. **2** (*suplente*) stand-in

susto *nm* **1** (*miedo, sobresalto*) fright: *¡Qué ~ me has dado/pegado!* What a fright you gave me! **2** (*falsa alarma*) scare LOC **llevarse un susto de muerte** to get the fright of your life

sustraer *vt* (*Mat*) to subtract

susurrar *vt, vi* to whisper

susurro *nm* whisper

sutil *adj* subtle

suyo, -a *adj pos, pron pos* **1** (*de él*) his: *Es culpa suya.* It's his fault. ◊ *un despacho junto al ~* an office next to his **2** (*de ella*) hers

Nótese que *un amigo suyo* se traduce por 'a friend of his, hers, etc' porque significa *uno de sus amigos.*

3 (*de animal*) its **4** (*de usted/ustedes*) yours **5** (*de ellas/ellos*) theirs LOC **ser muy suyo** to be a bit strange

Tt

tabaco *nm* **1** (*gen*) tobacco: *~ de pipa* pipe tobacco **2** (*cigarrillos*) cigarettes [*pl*]: *Me he quedado sin ~.* I've run out of cigarettes. LOC **tabaco rubio/negro** Virginia/black tobacco

tábano *nm* horsefly [*pl* horseflies]

tabarra *nf* pain in the neck LOC **dar la tabarra** to be a nuisance

taberna *nf* pub ☛ *Ver* pág 320.

tabique *nm* partition: *tirar un ~* to knock down a partition LOC **tabique nasal** nasal septum (*científ*)

tabla *nf* **1** (*de madera sin alisar*) plank: *un puente construido con ~s* a bridge made from planks **2** (*de madera pulida, plancha*) board: *~ de planchar* ironing board **3** (*lista, índice, Mat*) table: *~ de equivalencias* conversion table ◊ *saberse las ~s (de multiplicar)* to know your (multiplication) tables LOC **a raja tabla** *Ver* RAJATABLA **la tabla del dos, etc** the two, etc times table **tabla de windsurf** windsurfer

tablero *nm* **1** (*gen*) board: *Lo escribió en el ~.* He wrote it up on the board. **2** (*panel*) panel: *~ de control/mandos* control/instrument panel LOC **tablero de ajedrez** chessboard

tableta *nf* **1** (*Med*) tablet **2** (*chocolate*) bar

tablón *nm* plank LOC **tablón (de anuncios)** noticeboard

tabú *nm* taboo [*pl* taboos]: *un tema/una palabra ~* a taboo subject/word

taburete *nm* stool

tacaño, -a ◆ *adj* mean, stingy (*más coloq*) ◆ *nm-nf* skinflint

tachadura *nf* (*tb* **tachón** *nm*) crossing out [*pl* crossings out]: *lleno de ~s* full of crossings out

tachar *vt* to cross *sth* out: *Tacha todos los adjetivos.* Cross out all the adjectives.

taco *nm* **1** (*Tec, gen*) plug: *Tapó el agujero con un ~.* He plugged the hole. **2** (*para clavos/tornillos*) wall plug **3** (*jamón, queso*) piece: *Sólo he comido unos ~s de jamón.* I've only had a few pieces of ham. ◊ *Voy a traer unos ~s de queso.* I'm going to bring some cheese. LOC **decir/soltar tacos** to swear

tacón *nm* heel: *Se me ha roto el ~.* I've broken my heel. ◊ *Nunca lleva tacones.* She never wears high heels. LOC **de tacón** high-heeled

táctica *nf* **1** (*estrategia*) tactics [*pl*]: *la ~ de guerra de los romanos* Roman military tactics ◊ *un cambio de ~* a change of tactics **2** (*maniobra*) tactic: *una brillante ~ electoral* a brilliant electoral tactic

tacto *nm* sense of touch: *tener un ~ muy desarrollado* to have a highly developed sense of touch ◊ *reconocer algo por el ~* to recognize sth by touch

tajada *nf* **1** (*trozo*) slice **2** (*corte*) cut: *una ~ en el dedo* a cut on your finger

tajante *adj* adamant: *una negativa ~* an adamant refusal

tal *adj* **1** (+ *sustantivos contables en plural e incontables*) such: *en ~es situaciones* in such situations ◊ *un hecho de ~ gravedad* a matter of such importance **2** (+ *sustantivos contables en* *singular*) such a: *¿Cómo puedes decir ~ cosa?* How can you say such a thing? LOC **con tal de** to: *Haría cualquier cosa con ~ de ganar.* I'd do anything to win. **de tal palo tal astilla** like father like son **el/la tal** the so-called: *La ~ esposa no era más que su cómplice.* His so-called wife was only his accomplice. **en tal caso** in that case **(ser) tal para cual** to be two of a kind **un/una tal** a: *Le ha llamado un ~ Luis Moreno.* A Luis Moreno rang for you. **tal como** the way: *Se escribe ~ como suena.* It's spelt the way it sounds. **tales como...** such as... **tal vez** maybe *Ver tb* FULANO, QUÉ

taladradora *nf* **1** (*taladro*) drill **2** (*de papel*) hole punch

taladrar *vt* **1** (*pared, madera*) to drill a hole **in *sth***: *Los albañiles taladraron el cemento.* The workmen drilled a hole in the cement. **2** (*billete*) to punch

talar *vt* (*árboles*) to fell

talco *nm* talc LOC *Ver* POLVO

talento *nm* **1** (*habilidad*) talent (**for *sth*/*doing sth***): *Tiene ~ para la música/pintar.* He has a talent for music/painting. **2** (*inteligencia*) ability: *Tiene ~ pero no le gusta estudiar.* He's got ability but doesn't like studying.

talla *nf* **1** (*prenda*) size: *¿Qué ~ de camisa usas?* What size shirt do you take? ◊ *No tienen la ~.* They haven't got the right size. **2** (*escultura*) carving

tallar *vt* **1** (*madera, piedra*) to carve: *~ algo en coral* to carve sth in coral **2** (*joya, cristal*) to cut

taller *nm* **1** (*gen*) workshop: *un ~ de teatro/carpintería* a theatre/joiner's workshop **2** (*Mec*) garage **3** (*Arte*) studio [*pl* studios]

tallo *nm* stem

talón[1] *nm* (*pie, zapato*) heel

talón[2] *nm* cheque: *un ~ por valor de...* a cheque for... ◊ *ingresar/cobrar un ~* to pay in/cash a cheque

talonario *nm* **1** (*cheques*) cheque book **2** (*billetes, recibos*) book

tamaño *nm* size: *¿Qué ~ tiene la caja?* What size is the box? ◊ *ser del/tener el mismo ~* to be the same size

también *adv* also, too, as well

> **Too** y **as well** suelen ir al final de la frase: *Yo también quiero ir.* I want to go too/as well. ◊ *Yo también llegué tarde.* I was late too/as well. **Also** es la variante más formal y se coloca delante del verbo principal, o detrás si es un verbo auxiliar: *También venden zapatos.* They also sell shoes. ◊ *He conocido a Jane y también a sus padres.* I've met Jane and I've also met her parents.

LOC **yo también** me too: *—Quiero un bocadillo. —Yo ~.* 'I want a roll.' 'Me too.' *Ver tb* SÓLO

tambor *nm* drum: *tocar el ~* to play the drum ◊ *el ~ de una lavadora* the drum of a washing machine

tampoco *adv* neither, nor, either: *—No he visto esa película. —Yo ~.* 'I haven't seen that film.' 'Neither have I./Me neither./Nor have I.' ◊ *—No me gusta. —A mí ~.* 'I don't like it.' 'Nor do I./Neither do I./I don't either.' ◊ *Yo ~ fui.* I didn't go either. ☛ *Ver nota en* NEITHER

tampón *nm* tampon

tan *adv* **1** (*delante de adjetivo/adverbio*) so: *No creo que sea ~ ingenuo.* I don't think he's so naive. ◊ *No creí que llegarías ~ tarde.* I didn't think you'd be this late. ◊ *Es ~ difícil que...* It's so hard that... **2** (*detrás de sustantivo*) such: *No me esperaba un regalo ~ caro.* I wasn't expecting such an expensive present. ◊ *Son unos niños ~ buenos que...* They're such good children that... ◊ *¡Qué casa ~ bonita tienes!* What a lovely house you've got! LOC **tan...como...** as...as...: *Es ~ apuesto como su padre.* He's as smart as his father. ◊ *~ pronto como llegues* as soon as you arrive

tangente *adj, nf* tangent [*n*]

tanque *nm* tank

tantear *vt* **1** (*persona*) to sound *sb* out **2** (*situación*) to weigh *sth* up

tanto *nm* **1** (*cantidad*) so much: *Me dan un ~ al mes.* They give me so much a month. **2** (*gol*) goal: *marcar un ~* to score a goal LOC **poner al tanto** to fill *sb* in (*on sth*): *Me puso al ~ de la situación.* He filled me in on what was happening. **un tanto** (*bastante*) rather **un tanto por ciento** a percentage *Ver tb* MIENTRAS, OTRO

tanto, -a ◆ *adj* **1** (+ *sustantivo incontable*) so much: *No me pongas ~ arroz.* Don't give me so much rice. ◊ *Nunca había pasado tanta hambre.* I'd never been so hungry. **2** (+ *sustantivo contable*) so many: *¡Había tanta gente!* There were so many people! ◊ *¡Tenía ~s problemas!* He had so many problems! ◆ *pron* so much [*pl* so many]: *¿Por qué has comprado ~s?* Why did you buy so many? ◆ *adv* **1** (*gen*) so much: *He* *comido ~ que no me puedo mover.* I've eaten so much (that) I can't move. **2** (*tanto tiempo*) so long: *¡Hace ~ que no te veo!* I haven't seen you for so long! **3** (*tan rápido*) so fast: *No corras ~ con el coche.* Don't drive so fast. **4** (*tan a menudo*) so often LOC **a/hasta las tantas** in/until the small hours **entre tanto** *Ver* ENTRETANTO **no ser para tanto**: *¡Sé que te duele, pero no es para ~!* I know it hurts but it's not as bad as all that! **por (lo) tanto** therefore **tanto ... como ... 1** (*en comparaciones*) **(a)** (+ *sustantivo incontable*) as much ... as ...: *Bebí tanta cerveza como tú.* I drank as much beer as you. **(b)** (+ *sustantivo contable*) as many ... as ...: *No tenemos ~s amigos como antes.* We haven't got as many friends as we had before. **2** (*los dos*) both ... and ...: *Lo sabían ~ él como su hermana.* He and his sister both knew. **tanto si ... como si ...** whether ... or ...: *~ si llueve como si no* whether it rains or not **y tantos 1** (*con cantidad, con edad*) odd: *cuarenta y tantas personas* forty-odd people **2** (*con año*): *mil novecientos sesenta y ~s* nineteen sixty something *Ver tb* MIENTRAS

tapa *nf* **1** (*tapadera*) lid: *Pon la ~.* Put the lid on. **2** (*libro*) cover **3** (*zapatos*) heel: *Estas botas necesitan ~s.* These boots need new heels. **4** (*aperitivo*) **(a)** (*ración*) portion: *una ~ de ensaladilla rusa* a portion of Russian salad **(b) tapas** tapas: *tomar unas ~s* to have some tapas

tapadera *nf* **1** (*tapa*) lid **2** (*fig*) cover: *La empresa es sólo una ~.* The firm is just a cover.

tapar ♦ *vt* **1** (*cubrir*) to cover *sth/sb* (***with sth***): *~ una herida con una venda* to cover a wound with a bandage **2** (*abrigar*) to wrap *sth/sb* up (***in sth***): *La tapé con una manta.* I wrapped her up in a blanket. **3** (*con una tapa*) to put the lid **on *sth***: *Tapa la cazuela.* Put the lid on the saucepan. **4** (*con un tapón*) to put the top **on *sth***: *~ la pasta de dientes* to put the top on the toothpaste **5** (*agujero, gotera*) to stop *sth* (up) (***with sth***): *Tapé los agujeros con yeso.* I stopped (up) the holes with plaster. **6** (*obstruir*) to block: *La porquería tapó el desagüe.* The rubbish blocked the drainpipe. **7** (*la vista*) to block *sb's* view **of *sth***: *No me tapes la tele.* Don't block my view of the TV. ♦ **taparse** *v pron* **taparse (con)** to wrap up (**in *sth***): *Tápate bien.* Wrap up well.

tapia *nf* wall LOC *Ver* SORDO

tapicería *nf* (*coche, mueble*) upholstery [*incontable*]

tapiz *nm* tapestry [*pl* tapestries]

tapizar *vt* (*mueble, coche*) to upholster

tapón *nm* **1** (*gen*) top **2** (*de corcho*) cork **3** (*Tec, bañera, para los oídos*) plug: *ponerse tapones en los oídos* to put plugs in your ears **4** (*cerumen*) earwax [*incontable*]: *Creo que tengo tapones porque no oigo bien.* I must have wax in my ears because I can't hear properly. LOC **tapón de rosca** screw top

taponarse *v pron* to get blocked: *Se me ha taponado la nariz.* My nose is blocked.

taquigrafía *nf* shorthand

taquilla *nf* **1** (*estación, Dep*) ticket office **2** (*Cine, Teat*) box office **3** (*armario*) locker

tarántula *nf* tarantula

tararear *vt, vi* to hum

tardar *vi* to take (time) ***to do sth***: *¡Cómo tarda tu hermana!* Your sister's taking a long time! ◊ *Tardaron bastante en contestar.* It took them a long time to reply. ◊ *Tardé dos meses en recuperarme.* It took me two months to get better. LOC **no tardar nada** not to be long: *No tardes.* Don't be long. **se tarda ...** it takes ...: *En coche se tarda dos horas.* It takes two hours by car.

tarde ♦ *nf* afternoon, evening: *El concierto es por la ~.* The concert is in the afternoon/evening. ◊ *Llegaron el domingo por la ~.* They arrived on Sunday afternoon/evening. ◊ *Te veré mañana por la ~.* I'll see you tomorrow afternoon/evening. ◊ *¿Qué haces esta ~?* What are you doing this afternoon/evening? ◊ *a las cuatro de la ~* at four o'clock in the afternoon

> **Afternoon** se utiliza desde el mediodía hasta aproximadamente las seis de la tarde, y **evening** desde las seis de la tarde hasta la hora de acostarse. *Ver tb nota en* MORNING.

♦ *adv* **1** (*gen*) late: *Nos levantamos ~.* We got up late. ◊ *Me voy, que se hace ~.* I'm off; it's getting late. **2** (*demasiado tarde*) too late: *Es ~ para llamarles por teléfono.* It's too late to ring them. LOC **¡buenas tardes!** good afternoon/evening! **tarde o temprano** sooner or later *Ver tb* CAÍDA, LLEGAR

tarea *nf* **1** (*actividad*) task: *una ~ imposible* an impossible task **2** (*deberes*) homework [*incontable*]: *No nos han puesto ~ para el lunes.* We haven't got any homework to do for Monday.

tarima *nf* platform

tarjeta *nf* card: ~ *de crédito* credit card ◊ ~ *de Navidad* Christmas card ◊ *Le sacaron ~ amarilla.* He was given a yellow card. LOC **tarjeta de embarque** boarding card *Ver tb* PAGAR

tarro *nm* jar ☛ *Ver dibujo en* CONTAINER

tarta *nf* **1** (*pastel*) cake **2** (*de hojaldre*) tart, pie: *una ~ de manzana* an apple tart/pie ☛ *Ver nota en* PIE LOC **tarta helada** ice cream cake

tartamudear *vt* to stutter

tartamudo, -a *adj, nm-nf*: *los ~s* people who stutter LOC **ser tartamudo** to have a stutter

tasa *nf* **1** (*índice*) rate: *la ~ de natalidad* the birth rate **2** (*impuesto*) tax **3** (*cuota*) fee: *~s académicas* tuition fees

tasca *nf* bar

tatarabuelo, -a *nm-nf* **1** (*gen*) great-great-grandfather [*fem* great-great-grandmother] **2 tatarabuelos** great-great-grandparents

tatuaje *nm* tattoo [*pl* tattoos]

tauro (*tb* **Tauro**) *nm, nmf* (*Astrología*) Taurus ☛ *Ver ejemplos en* AQUARIUS

taxi *nm* taxi LOC *Ver* PARADA

taxista *nmf* taxi driver

taza *nf* **1** (*gen*) cup: *una ~ de café* a cup of coffee **2** (*sin platillo*) mug ☛ *Ver dibujo en* MUG **3** (*retrete*) bowl

tazón *nm* bowl

te *pron pers* **1** (*complemento*) you: *¿Te ha visto?* Did he see you? ◊ *Te he traído un libro.* I've brought you a book. ◊ *Te escribiré pronto.* I'll write to you soon. ◊ *Te lo he comprado.* I've bought it for you. **2** (*partes del cuerpo, efectos personales*): *Quítate el abrigo.* Take your coat off. ◊ *¿Te duele la espalda?* Is your back hurting? **3** (*reflexivo*) (yourself): *Te vas a hacer daño.* You'll hurt yourself. ◊ *Vístete.* Get dressed.

té *nm* tea: *¿Te apetece un té?* Would you like a cup of tea?

teatral *adj* LOC *Ver* OBRA

teatro *nm* theatre: *el ~ clásico/moderno* classical/modern theatre LOC **echarle teatro a algo** to put on an act: *Le duele el pie, pero también le echa un poco de ~.* His foot does hurt, but he's putting on a bit of an act. **teatro de guiñol** puppet theatre *Ver tb* OBRA

tebeo *nm* comic

techo *nm* **1** (*gen*) ceiling: *Hay una mancha de humedad en el ~.* There's a damp patch on the ceiling. **2** (*coche*) roof [*pl* roofs]

tecla *nf* key [*pl* keys]: *tocar una ~* to press a key

teclado *nm* keyboard ☛ *Ver dibujo en* ORDENADOR

teclear *vt* (*ordenador*) to key *sth* in: *Teclee su número personal.* Key in your personal identification number (PIN).

técnica *nf* **1** (*método*) technique **2** (*tecnología*) technology: *los avances de la ~* technological advances

técnico, -a ◆ *adj* technical: *Estudié en una escuela técnica.* I went to a technical college. ◆ *nm-nf* technician LOC *Ver* INGENIERO

tecnología *nf* technology [*pl* technologies] LOC **tecnología punta** state-of-the-art technology

teja *nf* tile

tejado *nm* roof [*pl* roofs]

tejer *vt* **1** (*gen*) to weave: ~ *una cesta* to weave a basket **2** (*araña, gusano*) to spin **3** (*hacer punto*) to knit

tejido *nm* **1** (*tela*) fabric ☛ *Ver nota en* TELA **2** (*Anat*) tissue

tela *nf* cloth, material, fabric

> **Cloth** es la palabra más general para decir tela y se puede utilizar tanto para referirnos a la tela con la que se hacen los trajes, cortinas, etc, como para describir de qué está hecha una cosa *Está hecho de tela.* It's made of cloth. ◊ *una bolsa de tela* a cloth bag. **Material** y **fabric** se utilizan sólo para referirnos a tela que se usa en sastrería y tapicería, aunque **fabric** suele indicar que tiene distintos colores. **Material** y **fabric** son sustantivos contables e incontables, mientras que **cloth** suele ser incontable cuando significa *tela*: *Algunas telas encogen al lavar.* Some materials/fabrics shrink when you wash them. ◊ *Necesito más tela para las cortinas.* I need to buy some more cloth/material/fabric for the curtains.

LOC **tela metálica** wire netting

telaraña *nf* cobweb

tele *nm Ver* TELEVISIÓN

telecomunicaciones *nf* telecommunications [*pl*]

telediario *nm* news [*sing*]: *¿A qué hora es el ~?* What time is the news on? ◊ *Lo dijeron en el ~ de las tres.* It was on the three o'clock news. ◊ *Ni siquiera he podido ver el ~ hoy.* I haven't even had time to watch the news today.

teleférico *nm* cable car

telefonazo *nm* ring: *Dame un ~ mañana.* Give me a ring tomorrow.

telefonear *vt, vi* to telephone, to phone (*coloq*)

telefónico, -a *adj* telephone, phone (*coloq*) [*n atrib*]: *hacer una llamada telefónica* to make a phone call LOC *Ver* CABINA, CENTRAL, GUÍA

telefonista *nmf* telephonist

teléfono *nm* **1** (*aparato*) telephone, phone (*coloq*): *¡Ana, al ~!* Phone for you, Ana! ◊ *Está hablando por ~ con su madre.* She's on the phone to her mother. ◊ *¿Puedes coger el ~?* Can you answer the phone? **2** (*número*) phone number: *¿Tienes mi ~?* Have you got my phone number? LOC *Ver* CABINA, COLGADO, COLGAR, GUÍA, LLAMAR

telegrama *nm* telegram: *poner un ~* to send a telegram

telenovela *nf* soap (opera)

teleobjetivo *nm* telephoto lens

telepatía *nf* telepathy

telescopio *nm* telescope

telesilla *nm* chairlift

telespectador, ~a *nm-nf* viewer

telesquí *nm* ski lift

teletexto *nm* teletext

televisar *vt* to televise

televisión *nf* television (*abrev* TV), telly (*coloq*): *salir en la ~* to be on television ◊ *Enciende/apaga la ~.* Turn the TV on/off. ◊ *¿Qué ponen en la ~ esta noche?* What's on the telly tonight? ◊ *Estábamos viendo la ~.* We were watching television. ☛ *Ver nota en* TELEVISION

televisor *nm* television (set) (*abrev* TV)

télex *nm* telex [*pl* telexes]

telón *nm* curtain: *Subieron el ~.* The curtain went up.

tema *nm* **1** (*gen*) subject: *el ~ de una charla/poema* the subject of a talk/poem ◊ *No cambies de ~.* Don't change the subject. **2** (*Mús*) theme **3** (*cuestión importante*) question: *~s ecológicos/económicos* ecological/economic questions LOC *Ver* CADA, DESVIAR

temario *nm* syllabus [*pl* syllabuses]

temblar *vi* **1** ~ **(de)** (*gen*) to tremble **(with *sth*)**: *La mujer temblaba de miedo.* The woman was trembling with fear. ◊ *Le temblaba la voz.* His voice trembled. **2** (*edificio, muebles*) to shake: *El terremoto hizo ~ el pueblo entero.* The earthquake made the whole village shake. LOC **temblar de frío** to shiver

temblor *nm* tremor: *un ligero ~ en la voz* a slight tremor in his voice ◊ *un ~ de tierra* an earth tremor

temer ◆ *vt* to be afraid **of *sth/sb/doing sth***: *Le teme a la oscuridad.* He's afraid of the dark. ◊ *Temo equivocarme.* I'm afraid of making mistakes. ◆ **temerse** *v pron* to be afraid: *Me temo que no vendrán.* I'm afraid they won't come.

temible *adj* fearful

temor *nm* fear: *No lo dije por ~ a que se enfadase.* I didn't say it for fear of offending him.

temperamento *nm* temperament: *Tiene mucho ~.* He is very temperamental.

temperatura *nf* temperature: *Mañana bajarán las ~s.* Temperatures will fall tomorrow.

tempestad *nf* storm

templado, -a *pp, adj* **1** (*clima*) mild **2** (*comida, líquidos*) lukewarm

templo *nm* temple LOC *Ver* VERDAD

temporada *nf* **1** (*periodo de tiempo*) time: *Llevaba enfermo una larga ~.* He had been ill for a long time. **2** (*época*) season: *la ~ futbolística* the football season ◊ *la ~ alta/baja* the high/low season LOC **de temporada** seasonal **temporada de caza** open season

temporal ◆ *adj* temporary ◆ *nm* storm

temprano, -a *adj, adv* early: *Llegó por la mañana ~.* He arrived early in the morning. LOC *Ver* TARDE

tenaz *adj* tenacious

tenazas *nf* pliers

tendedero *nm* **1** (*cuerda*) clothes line **2** (*plegable*) clothes horse **3** (*lugar*) drying-room

tendencia *nf* **1** (*gen*) tendency [*pl* tendencies]: *Tiene ~ a engordar.* He has a tendency to put on weight. **2** (*moda*) trend: *las últimas ~s de la moda* the latest trends in fashion

tender ◆ *vt* (*ropa*) **1** (*fuera*) to hang *sth* out: *Todavía tengo que ~ la ropa.* I've still got to hang the washing out.

2 (*dentro*) to hang *sth* up ◆ *vi* ~ **a**: *Tiende a complicar las cosas.* He tends to complicate things. ◊ *La economía tiende a recuperarse.* The economy is recovering. ◆ **tenderse** *v pron* to lie down ☞ *Ver nota en* LIE[2]

tendero, -a *nm-nf* shopkeeper

tendido, -a *pp, adj* **1** (*persona*) lying: *Estaba ~ en el sofá.* He was lying on the sofa. **2** (*ropa*): *La colada está tendida.* The washing is on the line. LOC **tendido eléctrico** cables [*pl*] *Ver tb* LLORAR; *Ver tb* TENDER

tendón *nm* tendon

tenebroso, -a *adj* sinister

tenedor *nm* fork

tener ◆ *vt*

• **posesión** to have

> Existen dos formas para expresar *tener* en presente: *to have got* y *to have.* **To have got** es más frecuente y no necesita un auxiliar en oraciones negativas e interrogativas: *¿Tienes hermanos?* Have you got any brothers or sisters? ◊ *No tiene dinero.* He hasn't got any money. **To have** siempre va acompañado de un auxiliar en interrogativa y negativa: Do you have any brothers or sisters? ◊ He doesn't have any money. En los demás tiempos verbales se utiliza *to have*: *Cuando era pequeña tenía una bicicleta.* I had a bicycle when I was little.

• **estados, actitudes 1** (*edad, tamaño*) to be: *Mi hija tiene diez años.* My daughter is ten (years old). ◊ *Tiene tres metros de largo.* It's three metres long. **2** (*sentir, tener una actitud*) to be

> Cuando "tener" significa "sentir", el inglés utiliza el verbo *to be* con un adjetivo mientras que en español usamos un sustantivo: *Tengo mucha hambre.* I'm very hungry. *tener calor/frío/sed/miedo* to be hot/cold/thirsty/frightened ◊ *Le tengo un gran cariño a tu madre.* I'm very fond of your mother. *tener cuidado/paciencia* to be careful/patient.

• **en construcciones con adjetivos**: *Me tiene harta de tanto esperar.* I'm sick of waiting for him. ◊ *Tienes las manos sucias.* Your hands are dirty. ◊ *Tengo a mi madre enferma.* My mother is ill.

◆ *v aux* **1** ~ **que hacer algo** to have **to do sth**: *Tuvieron que irse en seguida.* They had to leave straight away. ◊ *Tienes que decírselo.* You must tell him. ☞ *Ver nota en* MUST **2 + participio**: *Lo tienen todo planeado.* It's all arranged. ◊ *Su comportamiento nos tiene preocupados.* We're worried about the way he's been behaving. LOC **tener a algn por algo** to think sb is sth: *Parece que me tienes por idiota.* You seem to think I'm an idiot. **tener que ver** (*asunto*) to have to do with *sth/sb*: *Pero ¿eso qué tiene que ver?* What's that got to do with it? ◊ *Eso no tiene nada que ver.* That's got nothing to do with it. ☞Para otras expresiones con **tener**, véanse las entradas del sustantivo, adjetivo, etc, p.ej. **tener agujetas** en AGUJETAS y **tener chispa** en CHISPA.

teniente *nmf* lieutenant

tenis *nm* tennis LOC **tenis de mesa** table tennis *Ver tb* PISTA

tenista *nmf* tennis player

tenor *nm* tenor

tensar *vt* to tighten: ~ *las cuerdas de una raqueta* to tighten the strings of a racket

tensión *nf* **1** (*gen*) tension: *la ~ de una cuerda* the tension of a rope ◊ *Hubo mucha ~ durante la cena.* There was a lot of tension during dinner. **2** (*eléctrica*) voltage: *cables de alta ~* high voltage cables **3** (*Med*) blood pressure

tenso, -a *adj* tense

tentación *nf* temptation: *No pude resistir la ~ de comérmelo.* I couldn't resist the temptation to eat it up. ◊ *caer en la ~* to fall into temptation

tentáculo *nm* tentacle

tentador, ~a *adj* tempting

tentar *vt* **1** (*inducir*) to tempt: *Me tienta la idea de irme de vacaciones.* I'm tempted to go on holiday. **2** (*palpar*) to feel

tentativa *nf* attempt

tenue *adj* (*luz, sonido, línea*) faint

teñir ◆ *vt* to dye: ~ *una camisa de rojo* to dye a shirt red ◆ **teñirse** *v pron* to dye your hair: *~se de moreno* to dye your hair dark brown ◊ *Me toca ~me esta semana.* I've got to dye my hair this week. LOC **teñirse de rubio** to bleach your hair

teología *nf* theology

teoría *nf* theory [*pl* theories]

teórico, -a *adj* theoretical

terapia *nf* therapy [*pl* therapies]: ~ *de grupo* group therapy

tercer *adj Ver* TERCERO

tercero, -a ◆ *adj, pron, nm-nf* third

(*abrev* 3rd) ☛ *Ver ejemplos en* SEXTO ◆ *nm* third party: *seguro a/contra ~s* third-party insurance ◆ **tercera** *nf* (*marcha*) third (gear) LOC **a la tercera va la vencida** third time lucky **tercera edad**: *actividades para la tercera edad* activities for senior citizens *Ver tb* ECUACIÓN

tercio *nm* third: *dos ~s de la población* two thirds of the population

terciopelo *nm* velvet

térmico, -a *adj* thermal

terminación *nf* ending

terminal *adj, nf, nm* terminal: *enfermos ~es* terminally ill patients ◊ *~ de pasajeros* passenger terminal

terminar ◆ *vt* to finish ◆ *vi* **1** ~ (**en algo**) to end (**in sth**): *Las fiestas terminan el próximo lunes.* The festivities end next Monday. ◊ *La manifestación terminó en tragedia.* The demonstration ended in tragedy. **2** ~ (**de hacer algo**) to finish (**doing sth**): *He terminado de hacer los deberes.* I've finished doing my homework. **3** ~ **haciendo/por hacer algo** to end up **doing sth**: *Terminamos riéndonos.* We ended up laughing. **4** ~ **como/igual que...** to end up **like** ***sth/sb***: *Vas a ~ igual que tu padre.* You'll end up like your father. ◆ **terminarse** *v pron* **1** (*acabarse*) to run out: *Se ha terminado el azúcar.* The sugar's run out. ◊ *Se nos ha terminado el pan.* We've run out of bread. **2** (*llegar a su fin*) to be over: *Se terminó la fiesta.* The party's over.

término *nm* **1** (*gen*) term: *en ~s generales* in general terms **2** (*fin*) end LOC **por término medio** on average

termo *nm* Thermos flask®

termómetro *nm* thermometer LOC **poner el termómetro** to take *sb's* temperature

termostato *nm* thermostat

ternero, -a ◆ *nm-nf* calf [*pl* calves] ◆ **ternera** *nf* (*Cocina*) veal

ternura *nf* tenderness: *tratar a algn con ~* to treat sb tenderly

terráqueo, -a *adj* LOC *Ver* GLOBO

terrateniente *nmf* landowner

terraza *nf* **1** (*balcón*) balcony [*pl* balconies] **2** (*bar*): *Sentémonos en la ~.* Let's sit outside. ◊ *¿Ya han puesto la ~?* Have they put the tables out yet? **3** (*Agricultura*) terrace

terremoto *nm* earthquake

terrenal *adj* LOC *Ver* PARAÍSO

terreno *nm* **1** (*tierra*) land [*incontable*]: *un ~ muy fértil* very fertile land ◊ *Compraron un ~.* They bought some land. **2** (*fig*) field: *el ~ de la biología* the field of biology LOC **sobre el terreno 1** (*en el lugar*) on the spot **2** (*sobre la marcha*) as I, you, etc go along **terreno de juego** pitch

terrestre *adj* land [*n atrib*]: *un animal/ataque ~* a land animal/attack LOC *Ver* CORTEZA

terrible *adj* terrible

territorio *nm* territory [*pl* territories]

terrón *nm* lump: *un ~ de azúcar* a sugar lump

terror *nm* terror LOC **de terror** (*película, novela*) horror [*n atrib*]: *una película de ~* a horror film

terrorífico, -a *adj* terrifying

terrorismo *nm* terrorism

terrorista *adj, nmf* terrorist LOC *Ver* BANDA[2]

tertulia *nf* get-together: *hacer/tener una ~* to have a get-together

tesis *nf* thesis [*pl* theses]

tesón *nm* determination: *trabajar con ~* to work with determination

tesorero, -a *nm-nf* treasurer

tesoro *nm* treasure: *encontrar un ~ escondido* to find hidden treasure ◊ *¡Eres un ~!* You're a treasure! LOC *Ver* BUSCADOR

test *nm* LOC *Ver* EXAMEN

testamento *nm* **1** (*Jur*) will: *hacer ~* to make a will **2 Testamento** Testament: *el Antiguo/Nuevo Testamento* the Old/New Testament

testarudo, -a *adj* stubborn

testículo *nm* testicle

testigo ◆ *nmf* witness ◆ *nm* (*Dep*) baton: *entregar el ~* to pass the baton LOC **ser testigo de algo** to witness sth **testigo presencial** eyewitness

tetera *nf* teapot

tetilla *nf* (*biberón*) teat

Tetra Brik® (*tb* **tetrabik**) *nm* carton ☛ *Ver dibujo en* CONTAINER

tétrico, -a *adj* gloomy

textil *adj* textile [*n atrib*]: *una fábrica ~* a textile factory

texto *nm* text LOC **procesamiento/tratamiento de textos** word processing *Ver tb* COMENTARIO, LIBRO

textualmente *adv* word for word

textura *nf* texture

tez *nf* complexion

ti *pron pers* you: *Lo hago por ti.* I'm

doing it for you. ◇ *Siempre estás pensando en ti misma.* You're always thinking of yourself.

tibio, -a *adj* lukewarm

tiburón *nm* shark

ticket *nm Ver* TIQUE

tiempo *nm* **1** (*gen*) time: *en ~s de los romanos* in Roman times ◇ *Hace mucho ~ que vivo aquí.* I've been living here for a long time. ◇ *en mi ~ libre* in my spare time ◇ *¿Cuánto ~ hace que estudias inglés?* How long have you been studying English? **2** (*meteorológico*) weather: *Ayer hizo buen/mal ~.* The weather was good/bad yesterday. **3** (*bebé*): *¿Qué ~ tiene?* How old is she? **4** (*Dep*) half [*pl* halves]: *el primer ~* the first half **5** (*verbal*) tense LOC **al poco tiempo** soon afterwards **a tiempo**: *Todavía estás a ~ de mandarlo.* You've still got time to send it. **con el tiempo** in time: *Lo entenderás con el ~.* You'll understand in time. **con tiempo (de sobra)** in good time: *Avísame con ~.* Let me know in good time. **del tiempo 1** (*fruta*) seasonal **2** (*bebida*) at room temperature **hacer tiempo** to while away your time *Ver tb* CADA, CUÁNTO, GANAR, HOMBRE, LLEGAR

tienda *nf* shop LOC **ir de tiendas** to go shopping **tienda (de campaña)** tent: *montar/quitar una ~* to put up/take down a tent **tienda de comestibles** grocer's [*pl* grocers]

tierno, -a *adj* **1** (*gen*) tender: *un filete ~* a tender steak ◇ *una mirada tierna* a tender look **2** (*pan*) fresh

tierra *nf* **1** (*por oposición al mar, campo, fincas*) land [*incontable*]: *viajar por ~* to travel by land ◇ *cultivar la ~* to work the land ◇ *Vendió las ~s de su familia.* He sold his family's land. **2** (*para plantas, terreno*) soil: *~ para las macetas* soil for the plants ◇ *una ~ fértil* fertile soil **3** (*suelo*) ground: *Cayó a ~.* He fell to the ground. **4** (*patria*) home: *costumbres de mi ~* customs from back home **5 Tierra** (*planeta*) earth: *La Tierra es un planeta.* The earth is a planet. LOC **echar por tierra** to ruin **tierra adentro** inland **¡tierra a la vista!** land ahoy! **tierra firme** dry land **Tierra Santa** the Holy Land **tomar tierra** to land *Ver tb* CORRIMIENTO, DESPRENDIMIENTO, TOMA

tieso, -a *adj* **1** (*gen*) stiff: *Me molesta llevar los cuellos ~s.* I can't stand wearing stiff collars. **2** (*recto*) straight: *¡Ponte ~!* Stand up straight! LOC **dejar a algn tieso** (*asombrar*) to leave sb speechless: *La noticia nos dejó ~s.* The news left us speechless. **quedarse tieso (de frío)** to be frozen stiff

tiesto *nm* flowerpot

tifón *nm* typhoon

tigre, -esa *nm-nf* tiger [*fem* tigress]

tijera *nf* **tijeras** scissors [*pl*]

> **Scissors** es una palabra plural en inglés, por lo tanto para referirnos a *unas tijeras* utilizamos **some/a pair of scissors**: *Necesito unas tijeras nuevas.* I need some new scissors/a new pair of scissors.

tila *nf* (*infusión*) lime tea

timar *vt* to swindle *sth/sb* (**out of** ***sth***): *Le timaron 40.000 pesetas.* They swindled him out of 40000 pesetas.

timbre *nm* **1** (*campanilla*) bell: *tocar el ~* to ring the bell **2** (*voz*) pitch: *Tiene un ~ de voz muy alto.* He has a very high-pitched voice.

tímido, -a *adj, nm-nf* shy [*adj*]: *Es un ~.* He's shy.

timo *nm* swindle, rip-off (*más coloq*): *¡Vaya ~!* What a rip-off!

timón *nm* rudder

tímpano *nm* (*oído*) eardrum

tinaja *nf* large earthenware jar

tinieblas *nf* darkness [*sing*]

tinta *nf* ink: *un dibujo a ~* an ink drawing LOC **saber algo de buena tinta** to have sth on good authority **tinta china** Indian ink *Ver tb* MEDIO, SUDAR

tinte *nm* **1** (*producto*) dye **2** (*tintorería*) dry-cleaner's [*pl* dry-cleaners]

tinto ◆ *adj* (*vino*) red ◆ *nm* red wine

tintorería *nf* dry-cleaner's [*pl* dry-cleaners]

tío, -a *nm-nf* **1** (*familiar*) uncle [*fem* aunt, auntie (*más coloq*)]: *el ~ Daniel* Uncle Daniel **2 tíos** uncle and aunt: *Voy a casa de mis ~s.* I'm going to my uncle and aunt's. **3** (*individuo*) guy [*pl* guys] [*fem* girl]: *ese ~ de ahí* that guy over there

> Cuando se usan como apelativos, *tío* y *tía* no siempre se traducen en inglés: *¿Qué haces, tía?* What are you doing?

LOC **¡qué tío (más pesado)!** what a pain!

tiovivo *nm* merry-go-round

típico, -a *adj* **1** (*característico*) typical (**of** ***sth/sb***): *Eso es ~ de Pepe.* That's just typical of Pepe. **2** (*tradicional*) traditional: *un baile/traje ~* a traditional dance/costume

ipo *nm* **1** (*gen*) kind (***of sth***): *el ~ de persona nerviosa* the nervous kind ◊ *todo ~ de gente/animales* all kinds of people/animals ◊ *No es mi ~.* He's not my type. **2** (*cuerpo*) **(a)** (*de mujer*) figure: *Tiene un ~ bonito.* She has a nice figure. **(b)** (*de hombre*) body **3** (*individuo*) guy [*pl* guys]: *¡Qué ~ más feo!* What an ugly guy! LOC *Ver* EXAMEN

ique *nm* **1** (*recibo*) receipt **2** (*entrada*) ticket

ira *nf* **1** (*papel, tela*) strip: *Corta el papel en ~s.* Cut the paper into strips. **2** (*zapato*) strap LOC **la tira (de)** loads (of sth): *Tienes la ~ de amigos.* You've got loads of friends. ◊ *Hace la ~ de tiempo que no voy al teatro.* It's been ages since I last went to the theatre. ◊ *Gastas la ~.* You spend loads of money.

irachinas *nm* catapult

irada *nf* **1** (*turno*) throw **2** (*distancia*) way: *Hasta mi casa hay una buena ~.* It's quite a way to my house. LOC **de/en una tirada** in one go

rado, -a *pp, adj* **1** (*en el suelo*) lying around): *~ en el suelo* lying on the ground ◊ *Lo dejaron todo ~.* They left everything lying around. **2** (*muy barato*) dirt cheap **3** (*muy fácil*) dead easy: *Esta asignatura está tirada.* This subject is dead easy. LOC **dejar a algn irado** to let sb down *Ver tb* TIRAR

rador, ~a ◆ *nm-nf* shot: *Es un buen ~.* He's a good shot. ◆ *nm* (*cajón, puerta*) knob

ralíneas *nm* drawing pen

ranizar *vt* to tyrannize

rante ◆ *adj* **1** (*gen*) tight: *Pon la uerda bien ~.* Make sure the rope is ight. **2** (*ambiente, situación*) tense ◆ *nm* **1** (*vestido*) shoulder strap **2 tirantes** braces

rar ◆ *vt* **1** (*gen*) to throw *sth* (***to sb***): *Los niños tiraban piedras.* The children were throwing stones. ◊ *Tírale la pelota a tu compañero.* Throw the ball to your team-mate.

Cuando se tira algo a alguien con intención de hacerle daño, se usa **to throw sth at sb**: *Le tiraban piedras al pobre gato.* They were throwing stones at the poor cat.

(*desechar*) to throw *sth* away: *Tíralo, está muy viejo.* Throw it away, it's really old now. **3** (*derramar*) to spill: *Ten cuidado, vas a ~ el café.* Be careful r you'll spill the coffee. **4** (*tumbar*) to knock *sth/sb* over: *Cuidado con ese jarrón, no lo tires.* Careful you don't knock that vase over. **5** (*malgastar*) to waste: *~ el dinero* to waste money ◆ *vi* **1** ~ **(de)** (*gen*) to pull *sth* [*vt*]: *Tira de la cadena.* Pull the chain. **2** ~ **a**: *Tiene el pelo tirando a rubio.* He's got blondish hair. ◊ *rosa tirando a rojo* pinky red ◊ *Tira un poco a la familia de su madre.* He looks a bit like his mother's side of the family. **3** (*disparar, Dep*) to shoot (***at sth/sb***): *~ a puerta* to shoot at goal **4** (*atraer*) to fancy *sth/sb/doing sth* [*vt*]: *Me tira ese chico.* I fancy that boy. ◊ *No me tira nada estudiar.* I really don't like studying. ◆ **tirarse** *v pron* **1** (*lanzarse*) to jump: *~se por la ventana/al agua* to jump out of the window/into the water **2** (*pasar el tiempo*) to spend: *Me tiré toda la semana estudiando.* I spent the whole week studying. LOC **tirando**: *—¿Cómo anda tu madre? —Tirando.* 'How's your mother?' 'Not so bad.' ◊ *Vamos tirando.* We're doing OK. ☛Para otras expresiones con **tirar**, véanse las entradas del sustantivo, adjetivo, etc, p.ej. **tirar algo a la basura** en BASURA y **tirar la toalla** en TOALLA.

tirita *nf* plaster

tiritar *vi* ~ **(de)** to shiver (**with *sth***): *~ de frío* to shiver with cold

tiro *nm* **1** (*lanzamiento*) throw **2** (*disparo, Dep*) shot: *un ~ a puerta* a shot at goal **3** (*herida de disparo*) bullet wound: *un ~ en la cabeza* a bullet wound in the head **4** (*chimenea*) draught LOC **a tiro de piedra (de aquí)** a stone's throw away (from here) **caer/sentar como un tiro**: *Me sentó como un ~ que me dijese eso.* I was really upset when he said that. ◊ *La cena me sentó como un ~.* Dinner didn't agree with me. **ni a tiros** for love nor money: *Este niño no come ni a ~s.* This child won't eat for love nor money. **salir el tiro por la culata** to backfire **tiro con arco** archery *Ver tb* MATAR, PEGAR

tirón *nm* **1** (*gen*) tug: *dar un ~ de pelo* to give sb's hair a tug ◊ *Sentí un ~ en la manga.* I felt a tug on my sleeve. **2** (*robo*): *ser víctima de un ~* to have your bag snatched

tiroteo *nm* **1** (*entre policía y delincuentes*) shoot-out: *Murió en el ~.* He died in the shoot-out. **2** (*ruido de disparos*) shooting [*incontable*]: *Escuchamos un ~ desde la calle.* We heard shooting out in the street. **3** (*durante una guerra*) fighting

títere *nm* **1** (*muñeco*) puppet **2 títeres** (*guiñol*) puppet show [*sing*]

titulado, -a *pp, adj* (*libro, película*) called, entitled (*más formal*) *Ver tb* TITULAR[1]

titular[1] ♦ *vt* to call: *No sé cómo ~ el poema.* I don't know what to call the poem. ♦ **titularse** *v pron* **titularse (en)** (*graduarse*) to graduate (**in** ***sth***): *~se en historia* to graduate in history

titular[2] ♦ *adj*: *el equipo ~* the first team ◊ *un jugador ~* a first team player ♦ *nmf* (*pasaporte, cuenta bancaria*) holder ♦ *nm* headline: *Estaba en los ~es de esta mañana.* It was in the headlines this morning.

título *nm* **1** (*gen*) title: *¿Qué ~ le has puesto a tu novela?* What title have you given your novel? ◊ *Mañana boxearán por el ~.* They're fighting for the title tomorrow. **2** (*estudios*) degree: *obtener el ~ de abogado* to get a degree in law ◊ *~ universitario* university degree **3** (*diploma*) degree certificate: *Quiero enmarcar el ~.* I want to frame my degree certificate.

tiza *nf* chalk [*gen incontable*]: *Dame una ~.* Give me a piece of chalk. ◊ *Tráeme unas ~s.* Bring me some chalk. LOC **tizas de colores** coloured chalks

toalla *nf* towel: *~ de baño/de las manos* bath/hand towel LOC **tirar la toalla** to throw in the towel

tobillera *nf* ankle support

tobillo *nm* ankle: *Me he torcido el ~.* I've sprained my ankle.

tobogán *nm* (*parque*) slide

tocadiscos *nm* record player

tocar ♦ *vt* **1** (*gen*) to touch: *¡No lo toques!* Don't touch it! **2** (*palpar*) to feel: *¿Me dejas ~ la tela?* Can I feel the fabric? **3** (*Mús*) to play: *~ la guitarra/un villancico* to play the guitar/a carol **4** (*hacer sonar*) **(a)** (*campana, timbre*) to ring **(b)** (*bocina, sirena*) to sound ♦ *vi* **1** (*Mús*) to play **2** (*turno*) to be *sb's* turn (***to do sth***): *Te toca tirar.* It's your turn to throw. ◊ *¿Ya me toca?* Is it my turn yet? **3** (*en un sorteo*) to win: *Me tocó una muñeca.* I won a doll. LOC *Ver* MADERA

tocateja LOC **a tocateja**: *Pagamos el coche a ~.* We paid for the car in cash.

tocayo, -a *nm-nf* namesake: *¡Somos ~s!* We've got the same name!

tocino *nm* pork fat

todavía *adv* **1** (*en oraciones afirmativas e interrogativas*) still: *¿~ vives en Londres?* Do you still live in London? **2** (*en oraciones negativas e interrogativas negativas*) yet: *~ no están maduras* They're not ripe yet. ◊ *—¿~ no te han contestado? —No, ~ no.* 'Haven't they written back yet?' 'No, not yet.' ☛ *Ver nota en* STILL[1] **3** (*en oraciones comparativas*) even: *Ella pinta ~ mejor.* She paints even better.

todo *nm* whole: *considerado como un ~* taken as a whole

todo, -a ♦ *adj* **1** (*gen*) all: *He hecho ~ el trabajo.* I've done all the work. ◊ *Lleva ~ el mes enfermo.* You've been ill all month. ◊ *Van a limpiar ~s los edificios del pueblo.* They're going to clean up all the buildings in the village.

> Con un sustantivo contable en singular, el inglés prefiere utilizar **the whole**: *Van a limpiar todo el edificio.* They're going to clean the whole building.

2 (*cada*) every: *~s los días me levanto a las siete.* I get up at seven every day. ☛ *Ver nota en* EVERY ♦ *pron* **1** (*gen*) all: *Eso es ~ por hoy.* That's all for today. ◊ *ante/después de ~* above/after all ◊ *A ~s nos gustó la obra.* We all/All of us liked the play. **2** (*todas las cosas*) everything: *~ lo que te dije era verdad.* Everything I told you was true. **3** (*cualquier cosa*) anything: *Mi loro come de ~.* My parrot eats anything. **4 todos** everyone, everybody [*sing*]: *~s dicen lo mismo.* Everyone says the same thing.

> Nótese que **everyone** y **everybody** llevan el verbo en singular, pero sin embargo suelen ir seguidos de un pronombre en plural (p.ej. 'their'): *¿Todos tenéis vuestros lápices?* Has everyone got their pencils?

LOC **ante todo** above all **a todo esto** by the way **por toda España, todo el mundo, etc** throughout Spain, the world, etc **sobre todo** especially ☛Para otras expresiones con **todo**, véanse las entradas del sustantivo, adjetivo, etc, p.ej. **todo el mundo** en MUNDO y **todo recto** en RECTO.

toldo *nm* awning

tolerar *vt* **1** (*soportar*) to bear, to tolerate (*más formal*): *No tolera a las personas como yo.* He can't bear people like me. **2** (*consentir*) to let *sb* get away with *sth*: *Te toleran demasiadas cosas.* They let you get away with too much.

toma *nf* **1** (*gen*) taking: *la ~ de la ciudad* the taking of the city **2** (*medicina*) do

3 (*Cine, TV*) take LOC **toma de tierra** earth: *El cable está conectado a la ~ de tierra.* The cable is earthed.

omadura *nf* LOC **tomadura de pelo 1** (*burla*) joke **2** (*estafa*) rip-off

omar ◆ *vt* **1** (*gen*) to take: ~ *una decisión* to take a decision ◊ ~ *apuntes/precauciones* to take notes/precautions ◊ *¿Por quién me has tomado?* Who do you take me for? **2** (*comer, beber*) to have: *¿Qué vas a ~?* What are you going to have? ◆ *vi*: *Toma, es para ti.* Here, it's for you. ◆ **tomarse** *v pron* to take: *He decidido ~me unos días de descanso.* I've decided to take a few days off. ◊ *No deberías habértelo tomado así.* You shouldn't have taken it like that. LOC **¡toma!** goodness me! ☛Para otras expresiones con **tomar**, véanse las entradas del sustantivo, adjetivo, etc, p.ej. **tomar el sol** en SOL y **tomarle el pelo a algn** en PELO.

omate *nm* tomato [*pl* tomatoes] LOC **ponerse como un tomate** to go as red as a beetroot *Ver tb* COLORADO

omillo *nm* thyme

omo *nm* volume

on *nm* LOC **sin ton ni son** for no particular reason

onalidad *nf* **1** (*Mús*) key [*pl* keys] **2** (*color*) tone

onel *nm* barrel

onelada *nf* ton

ónica *nf* (*bebida*) tonic: *Dos ~s, por favor.* Two tonics, please.

ónico, -a ◆ *adj* (*Ling*) stressed ◆ *nm* tonic

ono *nm* **1** (*gen*) tone: *¡No me hables en ese ~!* Don't speak to me in that tone of voice! **2** (*color*) shade **3** (*Mús*) key [*pl* keys] LOC *Ver* FUERA

ntear *vi* to fool around (***with sb***)

ntería ◆ *nf* **1** (*acción, dicho*) silly thing: *Siempre discutimos por ~s.* We're always arguing over silly little things. **2** (*cosa de poco valor*) (little) thing: *He comprado unas ~s para la cena.* I've bought a couple of things for dinner. ◆ **tonterías!** *interj* nonsense! [*incontable*]: *¡Eso son ~s!* That's nonsense! LOC **decir tonterías** to talk nonsense **dejarse de tonterías** to stop messing about *Ver tb* SARTA

nto, -a ◆ *adj* silly, stupid

> **Silly** y **stupid** son prácticamente sinónimos, aunque **stupid** es un poco más fuerte: *una excusa tonta* a silly excuse ◊ *No seas tan tonto, y deja de llorar.* Don't be so stupid; stop crying.

◆ *nm-nf* fool LOC **hacer el tonto** to play the fool *Ver tb* CAJA

toparse *v pron* ~ **con** to bump **into *sth*/*sb***

tope *nm* **1** (*puerta*) doorstop **2** (*límite*) limit: *¿Hay una edad ~?* Is there an age limit? LOC **a tope/hasta los topes**: *El supermercado estaba a ~.* The supermarket was packed. ◊ *Estoy a ~ de trabajo.* I'm up to my eyes in work. *Ver tb* FECHA

tópico, -a ◆ *adj* (*común*) hackneyed ◆ *nm* cliché LOC *Ver* USO

topo *nm* mole

toque *nm* **1** (*golpecito*) tap **2** (*matiz*) touch: *dar el ~ final a algo* to put the finishing touch to sth LOC **darle/pegarle un toque a algn** (*llamar*) to give sb a ring **toque de queda** curfew

toquilla *nf* shawl

tórax *nm* thorax [*pl* thoraxes/thoraces]

torbellino *nm* whirlwind

torcedura *nf* sprain

torcer ◆ *vt* **1** (*gen*) to twist: *Le torció el brazo.* She twisted his arm. **2** (*cabeza*) to turn ◆ *vi* to turn: ~ *a la derecha/izquierda* to turn right/left ◆ **torcerse** *v pron* (*tobillo, muñeca*) to sprain: *Se torció el tobillo.* He sprained his ankle.

torcido, -a *pp, adj* **1** (*dientes, nariz*) crooked **2** (*cuadro, ropa*) not straight: *¿No ves que el cuadro está ~?* Can't you see the picture isn't straight? **3** (*muñeca, tobillo*) sprained *Ver tb* TORCER

torear *vt, vi* to fight (a bull) LOC **torear a algn** to tease sb

torero, -a ◆ *nm-nf* bullfighter ◆ **torera** *nf* bolero jacket

tormenta *nf* storm: *Se avecina una ~.* There's a storm brewing. ◊ *Parece que va a haber ~.* It looks like there's going to be a storm.

tormento *nm* **1** (*tortura*) torture **2** (*persona, animal*) pest: *Este niño es un ~.* This child's a pest.

tornado *nm* tornado [*pl* tornadoes]

torneo *nm* **1** (*gen*) tournament **2** (*atletismo*) meeting

tornillo *nm* **1** (*gen*) screw: *apretar un ~* to put a screw in **2** (*para tuerca*) bolt LOC *Ver* FALTAR

torniquete *nm* **1** (*Med*) tourniquet **2** (*puerta de entrada*) turnstile

torno *nm* **1** (*mecanismo elevador*) winch

2 (*alfarero*) (potter's) wheel **3** (*dentista*) drill

toro *nm* **1** (*animal*) bull **2 toros**: *ir a los ~s* to go to a bullfight ◇ *A mi hermano le encantan los ~s.* My brother loves bullfighting. LOC **agarrar/coger al toro por los cuernos** to take the bull by the horns *Ver tb* CORRIDA, PLAZA

torpe *adj* **1** (*manazas*) clumsy **2** (*zoquete*) slow

torpedo *nm* torpedo [*pl* torpedoes]

torpeza *nf* **1** (*gen*) clumsiness **2** (*lentitud*) slowness

torrar(se) *vt, v pron* to roast

torre *nf* **1** (*gen*) tower **2** (*electricidad*) pylon **3** (*telecomunicaciones*) mast **4** (*Ajedrez*) rook, castle (*más coloq*) LOC **torre de vigilancia** watch tower

torrencial *adj* torrential: *lluvias ~es* torrential rain

torrente *nm* (*río*) torrent

torrija *nf* French toast [*incontable*]

torso *nm* torso [*pl* torsos]

torta *nf* **1** (*Panadería*) cake **2** (*crêpe*) pancake **3** (*bofetada*) smack LOC **dar/pegar una torta/un tortazo** to smack **ni torta** not a thing: *No oigo ni ~.* I can't hear a thing.

tortazo *nm* smack LOC *Ver* TORTA

tortícolis *nm o nf* crick in your neck: *Me ha producido ~.* It's given me a crick in my neck.

tortilla *nf* omelette

tortuga *nf* **1** (*de tierra*) tortoise **2** (*de mar*) turtle LOC **ir más despacio/lento que una tortuga** to go at a snail's pace *Ver tb* PASO

tortura *nf* torture: *métodos de ~* methods of torture

torturar *vt* to torture

tos *nf* cough: *El humo del tabaco me produce ~.* Cigarette smoke makes me cough.

toser *vi* to cough

tostada *nf* toast [*incontable*]: *Se me han quemado las ~s.* I've burnt the toast. ◇ *una ~ con mermelada* a slice of toast with jam LOC *Ver* OLER

tostador *nm* (*tb* **tostadora** *nf*) toaster

tostar *vt* **1** (*pan, frutos secos*) to toast **2** (*café*) to roast **3** (*piel*) to tan

total ◆ *adj, nm* total ◆ *adv* so: *~, que has suspendido.* So you failed. ◇ *~, que les pillaron desprevenidos.* To cut a long story short, they caught them unawares. LOC **en total** altogether: *Somos diez en ~.* There are ten of us altogether.

tóxico, -a *adj* toxic

toxicómano, -a *nm-nf* drug addict

trabajador, ~a ◆ *adj* hard-working ◆ *nm-nf* worker: *~es cualificados/nc cualificados* skilled/unskilled workers

trabajar *vi, vt* to work: *Trabaja parc una compañía inglesa.* She works fo an English company. ◇ *Nunca he traba jado de profesora.* I've never worked a a teacher. ◇ *¿En qué trabaja tı hermana?* What does your sister do? ◇ *~ la tierra* to work the land LOC *Ve* MATAR

trabajo *nm* **1** (*gen*) work [*incontable*] *Tengo mucho ~.* I've got a lot of work t do. ◇ *Debes ponerte al día con el ~ atra sado.* You must get up to date wit your work. ◇ *Me dieron la noticia en e ~.* I heard the news at work. **2** (*emplec* job: *dar (un) ~ a algn* to give sb a job *un ~ bien pagado* a well-paid job *quedarse sin ~* to lose your job ☛ *Ve nota en* WORK[1] **3** (*en el colegio*) projec *hacer un ~ sobre el medio ambiente* t do a project on the environment LO **costar/llevar trabajo**: *Me cuesta madrugar.* I find it hard to get up earl ◇ *Este vestido me ha llevado mucho ~* This dress was a lot of work. **estar si trabajo** to be out of work **trabajo de/e equipo** teamwork **trabajos forzado** hard labour [*sing*] **trabajos manuale** arts and crafts *Ver tb* BOLSA[1]

trabalenguas *nm* tongue-twister

tractor *nm* tractor

tradición *nf* tradition: *seguir una familiar* to follow a family tradition

tradicional *adj* traditional

traducción *nf* translation (***from st*** (***into sth***): *hacer una ~ del español ruso* to do a translation from Spanis into Russian

traducir *vt, vi* to translate (***from st*** (***into sth***): *~ un libro del francés inglés* to translate a book from Fren into English ☛ *Ver nota en* INTERPRE

traductor, ~a *nm-nf* translator

traer ◆ *vt* **1** (*gen*) to bring: *¿Qué quier que te traiga?* What shall I bring yo ☛ *Ver dibujo en* TAKE **2** (*causar*) cause: *El nuevo sistema nos va a problemas.* The new system is going cause problems. ◆ **traerse** *v pron* bring *sth/sb* (with you): *Tráete u almohada.* Bring a pillow with yc LOC **traerse algo (entre manos)** to up to sth: *¿Qué te traes entre man* What are you up to?

traficante *nmf* dealer: *un ~ de armas* an arms dealer

traficar *vi* ~ **con/en** to deal **in *sth*:** *Traficaban con drogas.* They dealt in drugs.

tráfico *nm* traffic: *Hay mucho ~ en el centro.* There's a lot of traffic in the town centre. LOC **tráfico de drogas** (*delito*) drug trafficking *Ver tb* GUARDIA

tragaperras *nf* fruit machine

tragar ◆ *vt, vi* **1** (*ingerir*) to swallow: *Me duele la garganta al ~.* My throat hurts when I swallow. **2** (*soportar*) to put up with *sth*: *No sé cómo puedes ~ tanto.* I don't know how you put up with it. ◆ **tragarse** *v pron* to swallow: *Me tragué un hueso de aceituna.* I swallowed an olive stone. ◊ *~se el orgullo* to swallow your pride ◊ *Se ha tragado lo del ascenso de Miguel.* He's swallowed the story about Miguel's promotion. ◊ *~se un libro/una película* to get through a book/to sit through a film

tragedia *nf* tragedy [*pl* tragedies]

trágico, -a *adj* tragic

trago *nm* **1** (*gen*) drink: *un ~ de agua* a drink of water **2** (*disgusto*) shock LOC **beberse/tomar algo de (un) trago** to drink sth in one go

traición *nf* **1** (*gen*) betrayal: *cometer ~ contra tus amigos* to betray your friends **2** (*contra el Estado*) treason: *Le juzgarán por alta ~.* He will be tried for high treason. LOC **a traición**: *Le dispararon a ~.* They shot him in the back. ◊ *Lo hicieron a ~.* They went behind his back.

traicionar *vt* **1** (*gen*) to betray: *~ a un compañero/una causa* to betray a friend/cause **2** (*nervios*) to let *sb* down: *Los nervios me traicionaron.* My nerves let me down.

traidor, ~a *nm-nf* traitor

traje *nm* **1** (*dos piezas*) suit: *Juan lleva un ~ muy elegante.* Juan is wearing a very smart suit. **2** (*de un país, de una región*) dress [*incontable*]: *Me encanta el ~ típico aragonés.* I love Aragonese regional dress. LOC **traje de baño 1** (*de hombre*) swimming trunks [*pl*] **2** (*de mujer*) swimming costume **traje de noche** evening dress **traje espacial** spacesuit

trama *nf* plot

tramar *vt* to plot: *Sé que están tramando algo.* I know they're up to something.

tramitar *vt* to process

trámite *nm* procedure [*incontable*]: *Cumplió con los ~s habituales.* He followed the usual procedure. LOC **en trámite(s) de** in the process of *doing sth*: *Estamos en ~s de divorcio.* We are in the process of getting a divorce.

tramo *nm* **1** (*carretera*) stretch **2** (*escalera*) flight

trampa *nf* **1** (*gen*) trap: *caer en una ~* to fall into a trap ◊ *tenderle una ~ a algn* to set a trap for sb **2** (*en un juego*) cheating [*incontable*]: *Una ~ más y estás eliminado.* Any more cheating and you're out of the game. ◊ *Eso es ~.* That's cheating. LOC **hacer trampa(s)** to cheat: *Siempre haces ~s.* You always cheat.

trampilla *nf* trapdoor

trampolín *nm* **1** (*gen*) springboard: *La gimnasta tomó impulso desde el ~.* The gymnast jumped off the springboard. **2** (*Natación*) diving board: *tirarse del ~* to dive from the board

tramposo, -a *adj, nm-nf* cheat [*n*]: *No seas tan ~.* Don't be such a cheat.

tranquilidad *nf* **1** (*gen*) calm: *un ambiente de ~* an atmosphere of calm ◊ *¡Qué ~, no tener que trabajar!* What a relief, no work! ◊ *la ~ del campo* the peace of the countryside **2** (*espíritu*) peace of mind: *Para tu ~, te diré que es cierto.* For your peace of mind, I can tell you it is true.

tranquilizante *nm* (*medicamento*) tranquillizer

tranquilizar ◆ *vt* **1** (*gen*) to calm *sb* down: *No consiguió tranquilizarla.* He couldn't calm her down. **2** (*aliviar*) to reassure: *Las noticias le tranquilizaron.* The news reassured him. ◆ **tranquilizarse** *v pron* to calm down: *Tranquilízate, que pronto llegarán.* Calm down, they'll soon be here.

tranquilo, -a *adj* **1** (*gen*) calm: *Es una mujer muy tranquila.* She's a very calm person. ◊ *La mar está tranquila.* The sea is calm. **2** (*lento*) laid-back: *Es tan ~ que me pone nerviosa.* He is so laid-back he makes me nervous. **3** (*apacible*) quiet: *Vivo en una zona tranquila.* I live in a quiet area. LOC **tan tranquilo** not bothered: *Suspendió y se quedó tan tranquila.* She failed, but she didn't seem bothered. *Ver tb* CONCIENCIA

transatlántico *nm* liner

transbordo *nm* LOC **hacer transbordo**

to change: *Tuvimos que hacer dos ~s.* We had to change twice.

transcripción *nf* transcription: *una ~ fonética* a phonetic transcription

transcurrir *vi* **1** (*tiempo*) to pass: *Han transcurrido dos días desde su partida.* Two days have passed since he left. **2** (*ocurrir*) to take place

transeúnte *nmf* passer-by [*pl* passers-by]

transferencia *nf* transfer LOC **transferencia bancaria** credit transfer

transferir *vt* to transfer

transformador *nm* transformer

transformar ◆ *vt* to transform *sth/sb* (*into sth*): *~ un lugar/a una persona* to transform a place/person ◆ **transformarse** *v pron* **transformarse en** to turn into *sth/sb*: *La rana se transformó en príncipe.* The frog turned into a prince.

transfusión *nf* transfusion: *Le hicieron dos transfusiones (de sangre).* He was given two (blood) transfusions.

transición *nf* transition

transistor *nm* (transistor) radio

transitivo, -a *adj* transitive

transmitir ◆ *vt* to transmit: *~ una enfermedad* to transmit a disease ◊ *Les transmitimos la noticia.* We passed the news on to them. ◆ *vt, vi* (*programa*) to broadcast: *~ un partido* to broadcast a match

transparentar(se) *vi, v pron*: *Esa tela (se) transparenta demasiado.* That material is really see-through. ◊ *Con esa falda se te transparentan las piernas.* You can see your legs through that skirt.

transparente *adj* **1** (*gen*) transparent: *El cristal es ~.* Glass is transparent. **2** (*ropa*): *una blusa ~* a see-through blouse ◊ *Es demasiado ~.* You can see right through it.

transportar *vt* to carry

transporte *nm* transport: *~ público/escolar* public/school transport ◊ *El ~ marítimo es más barato que el aéreo.* Sending goods by sea is cheaper than by air.

transportista *nmf* carrier

transversal *adj* transverse: *eje ~* transverse axis ◊ *La Gran Vía es ~ a la calle Mayor.* The Gran Vía crosses the Calle Mayor. LOC *Ver* SECCIÓN

tranvía *nm* tram

trapecio *nm* **1** (*circo*) trapeze **2** (*Geom*) trapezium [*pl* trapeziums]

trapecista *nmf* trapeze artist

trapo *nm* **1** (*limpieza*) cloth **2 trapos** (*ropa*) clothes LOC **sacar (a relucir) los trapos sucios** to wash your dirty linen in public **trapo de cocina** tea towel **trapo del polvo** duster **trapo viejo** old rag

tráquea *nf* windpipe, trachea [*pl* tracheas/tracheae] (*científ*)

tras *prep* **1** (*después de*) after: *día tras día* day after day **2** (*detrás de*) behind: *La puerta se cerró tras ella.* The door closed behind her. **3** (*más allá de*) beyond: *Tras las montañas está el mar.* Beyond the mountains is the sea. LOC **andar/estar/ir tras algo/algn** to be after sth/sb

trasero, -a ◆ *adj* back: *la puerta trasera* the back door ◆ *nm* bottom, backside (*coloq*)

trasladar ◆ *vt* **1** (*gen*) to move: *Trasladaron todas mis cosas al otro despacho.* They moved all my things to the other office. **2** (*destinar*) to transfer: *Lo han trasladado al servicio de inteligencia.* He's been transferred to the intelligence service. ◆ **trasladarse** *v pron* to move: *Nos trasladamos al número tres.* We moved to number three.

traslado *nm* **1** (*mudanza, desplazamiento*) move **2** (*cambio de destino*) transfer

traslucir *vt* to reveal

trasluz *nm* LOC **al trasluz** against the light: *mirar los negativos al ~* to look at the negatives against the light

trasnochar *vi* to stay up late

traspapelarse *v pron* to be mislaid

traspasar *vt* **1** (*atravesar*) to go through *sth*: *~ la barrera del sonido* to go through the sound barrier **2** (*líquido*) to soak **3** (*Dep*) to transfer *sb* (*to sth*): *Han traspasado a tres jugadores del Celta.* Three Celta players have been transferred. **4** (*negocio*) to sell

traspié *nm* LOC **dar un traspié** to trip

trasplantar *vt* to transplant

trasplante *nm* transplant

trastada *nf* LOC **hacer trastadas/una trastada**: *Ese niño no deja de hacer ~s.* That boy is always up to mischief. ◊ *Deja de hacer ~s de una vez.* Don't be so naughty!

trastero *nm* boxroom LOC *Ver* CUARTO

trasto *nm* **1** (*cosa*) junk [*incontable*]

Tienes la habitación llena de ~s. Your room is full of junk. **2** (*niño*) little devil: *Esos niños son unos ~s.* Those children are little devils.

trastornar ◆ *vt* **1** (*gen*) to upset: *La huelga ha trastornado todos mis planes.* The strike has upset all my plans. **2** (*volver loco*) to drive *sb* out of their mind ◆ **trastornarse** *v pron* **1** (*persona*) to go crazy **2** (*planes*) to be upset

tratado *nm* (*Pol*) treaty [*pl* treaties]

tratamiento *nm* **1** (*gen*) treatment: *un ~ contra la celulitis* treatment for cellulite **2** (*Informát*) processing LOC *Ver* TEXTO

tratar ◆ *vt* **1** (*gen*) to treat: *Nos gusta que nos traten bien.* We like people to treat us well. **2** (*discutir*) to deal with *sth*: *Trataremos estas cuestiones mañana.* We will deal with these matters tomorrow. ◆ *vi* **1** ~ **de/sobre** (*gen*) to be **about** ***sth***: *La película trata sobre el mundo del espectáculo.* The film is about show business. **2** ~ **con** to deal **with** ***sth/sb***: *No trato con ese tipo de gente.* I don't have any dealings with people like that. **3** (*intentar*) to try ***to do sth***: *Trata de llegar a tiempo.* Try to/and get there on time. ☛ *Ver nota en* TRY. ◆ **tratarse** *v pron* **tratarse de** to be **about** ***sth/sb/doing sth***: *Se trata de tu hermano.* It's about your brother. ◊ *Se trata de aprender, no de aprobar.* It's about learning, not just passing. LOC **tratar a algn de tú/usted** to be on familiar/formal terms with sb

trato *nm* **1** (*gen*) treatment: *el mismo ~ para todos* the same treatment for everyone **2** (*relación*): *Debemos mejorar nuestro ~ con los vecinos.* We must try to get on with our neighbours a bit better. ◊ *Nuestro ~ no es muy bueno.* We don't get on very well. **3** (*acuerdo*) deal: *hacer/cerrar un ~* to make/close a deal LOC **malos tratos** ill-treatment [*incontable*]: *Sufrieron malos ~s en la cárcel.* They were subjected to ill-treatment in prison. **tener/no tener trato con algn** to see/not to see sb: *No tengo demasiado ~ con ellos.* I don't see much of them. **trato hecho** it's a deal!

trauma *nm* trauma

través LOC **a través de** through: *Corría a ~ del bosque.* He was running through the wood. ◊ *Huyeron a ~ del parque/de los campos.* They ran across the park/fields.

travesti (*tb* **travestí**) *nmf* transvestite

travesura *nf* prank LOC **hacer travesuras** to play pranks

travieso, -a *adj* naughty

trayecto *nm* route: *Este tren hace el ~ Madrid-Barcelona.* This train runs on the Madrid-Barcelona route.

trayectoria *nf* trajectory [*pl* trajectories]

trazar *vt* **1** (*línea, plano*) to draw **2** (*plan, proyecto*) to devise (*formal*), to draw *sth* up: *~ un plan* to draw up a plan

trébol *nm* **1** (*Bot*) clover **2 tréboles** (*Naipes*) clubs ☛ *Ver nota en* BARAJA

trece *nm, adj, pron* **1** (*gen*) thirteen **2** (*fecha*) thirteenth ☛ *Ver ejemplos en* ONCE *y* SEIS LOC **mantenerse/seguir en sus trece** to stand your ground *Ver tb* MARTES

treceavo, -a *adj, nm* thirteenth ☛ Para *catorceavo*, *quinceavo*, etc, ver Apéndice 1.

trecho *nm* stretch: *un ~ peligroso* a dangerous stretch of road

tregua *nf* truce: *romper una ~* to break a truce

treinta *nm, adj, pron* **1** (*gen*) thirty **2** (*trigésimo*) thirtieth ☛ *Ver ejemplos en* SESENTA

tremendo, -a *adj* **1** (*gen*) terrible: *un disgusto/dolor ~* a terrible blow/pain **2** (*positivo*) tremendous: *El niño tiene una fuerza tremenda.* That child is tremendously strong. ◊ *Tuvo un éxito ~.* It was a tremendous success.

tren *nm* train: *coger/perder el ~* to catch/miss the train ◊ *Fui a Londres en ~.* I went to London by train. LOC **a todo tren 1** (*con lujo*) in style **2** (*muy rápido*) flat out **estar como un tren** to be a stunner **tren correo/de mercancías** mail/goods train **tren de aterrizaje** undercarriage: *bajar el ~ de aterrizaje* to lower the undercarriage **tren de cercanías** local train **tren de vida** lifestyle *Ver tb* PARAR

trenca *nf* duffel coat

trenza *nf* plait: *Hazte una ~.* Do your hair in a plait.

trepar *vi* to climb; to climb (up) *sth*: *~ a un árbol* to climb (up) a tree

tres *nm, adj, pron* **1** (*gen*) three **2** (*fecha*) third ☛ *Ver ejemplos en* SEIS LOC **no ver tres en un burro** to be blind as a bat **tres en raya** noughts and crosses [*sing*] *Ver tb* CADA

trescientos, -as *adj, pron, nm* three hundred ☛ *Ver ejemplos en* SEISCIENTOS

tresillo *nm* three-piece suite

triangular *adj* triangular

triángulo *nm* triangle LOC **triángulo equilátero/escaleno/isósceles** equilateral/scalene/isosceles triangle **triángulo rectángulo** right-angled triangle

tribu *nf* tribe

tribuna *nf* stand: *Tenemos entradas de ~.* We've got stand tickets. ◊ *Han montado una ~.* They've put up a stand.

tribunal *nm* **1** (*gen*) court: *comparecer ante el ~* to appear before the court **2** (*en un examen*) examining board: *Me ha tocado un ~ muy estricto.* The examiners were very strict. LOC **llevar a los tribunales** to take *sth/sb* to court **Tribunal Supremo** ≃ High Court (*GB*)

triciclo *nm* tricycle, trike (*coloq*)

trigo *nm* wheat

trigonometría *nf* trigonometry

trillar *vt* to thresh

trillizos, -as *nm-nf* triplets

trimestral *adj* quarterly: *revistas/facturas ~es* quarterly magazines/bills

trimestre *nm* **1** (*gen*) quarter **2** (*Educ*) term

trinar *vi* (*pájaro*) to sing

trinchera *nf* trench

trineo *nm* **1** (*gen*) sledge **2** (*de caballos*) sleigh: *Papá Noel viaja siempre en ~.* Father Christmas always travels by sleigh.

trinidad *nf* trinity

trino *nm* trill

trío *nm* trio [*pl* trios]

tripa *nf* **1** (*intestino*) gut **2** (*vientre*) stomach, tummy [*pl* tummies] (*más coloq*): *tener dolor de ~* to have a tummy ache **3** (*barriga*) belly [*pl* bellies]

triple ◆ *adj* triple: *~ salto* triple jump ◆ *nm* three times: *Nueve es el ~ de tres.* Nine is three times three. ◊ *Éste es el ~ de grande que el otro.* This one's three times bigger than the other one. ◊ *Gana el ~ que yo.* He earns three times as much as me.

triplicado, -a *pp, adj* LOC **por triplicado** in triplicate *Ver tb* TRIPLICAR(SE)

triplicar(se) *vt, v pron* to treble

tripulación *nf* crew [*v sing o pl*]

tripular *vt* **1** (*barco*) to sail **2** (*avión*) to fly

triste *adj* **1** (*gen*) sad: *estar/sentirse ~* to be/feel sad **2** (*deprimente, deprimido habitación*) gloomy: *un paisaje/una habitación ~* a gloomy landscape/room

tristeza *nf* **1** (*gen*) sadness **2** (*melancolía*) gloominess

triturar *vt* **1** (*carne*) to mince **2** (*cosas duras*) to crush **3** (*papel*) to shred

triunfal *adj* **1** (*arco, entrada*) triumphal **2** (*gesto, regreso*) triumphant

triunfar *vi* **1** (*tener éxito*) to succeed: *~ en la vida* to succeed in life ◊ *Esta canción va a ~ en el extranjero.* This song will do well abroad. **2** ~ (**en**) (*ganar*) to win: *~ a cualquier precio* to win at any price **3** ~ (**sobre**) to triumph (**over** *sth/sb*): *Triunfaron sobre sus enemigos.* They triumphed over their enemies.

triunfo *nm* **1** (*Pol, Mil*) victory [*pl* victories] **2** (*logro personal, proeza*) triumph: *un ~ de la ingeniería* a triumph of engineering **3** (*Mús, éxito*) hit: *sus últimos ~s cinematográficos* his latest box-office hits **4** (*Naipes*) trump

trivial *adj* trivial

trivialidad *nf* **1** (*cosa trivial*) triviality [*pl* trivialities] **2** (*comentario*) trite remark: *decir ~es* to make trite remarks

triza *nf* LOC **hacer trizas 1** (*gen*) to shatter: *Terminé hecho ~s.* I was shattered by the end. **2** (*papel, tela*) to tear *sth* to shreds

trocear *vt* to cut *sth* into pieces

trofeo *nm* trophy [*pl* trophies]

trola *nf* fib: *contar/meter ~s* to tell fibs

tromba *nf* LOC **tromba** (**de agua**) downpour: *Ayer cayó una buena ~ de agua.* It really poured down yesterday.

trombón *nm* (*instrumento*) trombone

trompa *nf* (*Zool*) **1** (*elefante*) trunk **2** (*insecto*) proboscis LOC **coger(se) una trompa** to get plastered

trompeta *nf* (*instrumento*) trumpet

tronar *v imp* to thunder: *¡Está tronando!* It's thundering!

troncharse *v pron*: *~ de risa* to split your sides (laughing)

tronco *nm* **1** (*árbol, Anat*) trunk **2** (*leño*) log LOC *Ver* DORMIR

trono *nm* throne: *subir al ~* to come to the throne ◊ *el heredero del ~* the heir to the throne

tropa *nf* troop

tropezar(se) *vi, v pron* **tropezar(se) (con) 1** (*caerse*) to trip (**over *sth***): ~ *con una raíz* to trip over a root **2** (*problemas*) to come up against *sth*: *Hemos tropezado con serias dificultades.* We've come up against serious difficulties.

tropezón *nm* (*traspié*) stumble

tropical *adj* tropical

trópico *nm* tropic: *el ~ de Cáncer/Capricornio* the tropic of Cancer/Capricorn

trote *nm* **1** (*gen*) trot: *ir al ~* to go at a trot **2** (*actividad intensa*): *Tanto ~ acabará conmigo.* All this rushing around will finish me off. LOC **no estar para muchos/esos trotes**: *Ya no estoy para esos ~s.* I'm not up to it any more.

trozo *nm* piece: *un ~ de pan* a piece of bread ◊ *Corta la carne a ~s.* Cut the meat into pieces.

trucha *nf* trout [*pl* trout]

truco *nm* trick LOC **coger el truco** to get the hang (*of sth*) **tener truco** to have a catch: *Esa oferta tiene ~.* There's a catch to that offer.

trueno *nm* thunder [*incontable*]: *¿No has oído un ~?* Wasn't that a clap of thunder? ◊ *Los ~s han cesado.* The thunder's stopped. ◊ *rayos y ~s* thunder and lightning

trufa *nf* truffle

tu *adj pos* your: *tus libros* your books

tú *pron pers* you: *¿Eres tú?* Is that you? LOC *Ver* YO

tuberculosis *nf* tuberculosis (*abrev* TB)

tubería *nf* pipe: *Se ha roto una ~.* A pipe has burst.

tubo *nm* **1** (*de conducción*) pipe **2** (*recipiente*) tube: *un ~ de pasta de dientes* a tube of toothpaste ☛ *Ver dibujo en* CONTAINER LOC **tubo de escape** exhaust

tuerca *nf* nut

tuerto, -a *adj* one-eyed LOC **ser tuerto** to be blind in one eye

tugurio *nm* **1** (*chabola*) hovel **2** (*bar*) dive

tulipán *nm* tulip

tumba *nf* **1** (*gen*) grave **2** (*mausoleo*) tomb: *la ~ de Marx* Marx's tomb

tumbar ♦ *vt* to knock *sth/sb* down: *Me tumbó de un guantazo.* He knocked me over. ♦ **tumbarse** *v pron* to lie down: *Se tumbó unos minutos.* He lay down for a few minutes. ☛ *Ver nota en* LIE[2]

tumbo *nm* LOC **dar tumbos 1** (*tambalearse*) to stagger **2** (*tener dificultades*) to lurch from one crisis to another

tumbona *nf* **1** (*gen*) lounger **2** (*hamaca*) deckchair

tumor *nm* tumour: ~ *benigno/cerebral* benign/brain tumour

tumulto *nm* (*multitud*) crowd

túnel *nm* tunnel: *pasar por un ~* to go through a tunnel

tupido, -a *pp, adj* **1** (*gen*) dense **2** (*tela*) densely woven

turbante *nm* turban

turbio, -a *adj* **1** (*líquido*) cloudy **2** (*asunto*) shady

turismo *nm* **1** (*industria*) tourism **2** (*turistas*) tourists [*pl*]: *un 40% del ~ que visita nuestra zona* 40% of the tourists visiting our area LOC **hacer turismo 1** (*por un país*) to tour: *hacer ~ por África* to tour round Africa **2** (*por una ciudad*) to go sightseeing *Ver tb* OFICINA

turista *nmf* tourist

turnarse *v pron* ~ **(con) (para)** to take it in turns (**with *sb***) (***to do sth***): *Nos turnamos para hacer la limpieza de la casa.* We take it in turns to do the housework.

turno *nm* **1** (*orden*) turn: *Espera tu ~ en la cola.* Wait your turn in the queue. **2** (*trabajo*) shift: ~ *de día/noche* day/night shift LOC **estar de turno** to be on duty

turquesa *nf* LOC *Ver* AZUL

turrón *nm* Spanish nougat [*incontable*]

tutear(se) *vt, v pron* to be on familiar terms (**with *sb***)

tutor, ~a *nm-nf* **1** (*Jur*) guardian **2** (*profesor*) tutor

tuyo, -a *adj pos, pron pos* yours: *Esos zapatos no son ~s.* Those shoes aren't yours. ◊ *No es asunto ~.* That's none of your business.

Nótese que *un amigo tuyo* se traduce por 'a friend of yours' porque significa *uno de tus amigos*.

Uu

u *conj* or

¡uf! *interj* **1** (*alivio, cansancio, sofoco*) phew!: *¡Uf, qué calor!* Phew, it's hot! **2** (*asco*) ugh!: *¡Uf, qué mal huele!* Ugh, what an awful smell!

úlcera *nf* ulcer

últimamente *adv* lately

ultimátum *nm* ultimatum [*pl* ultimatums]

último, -a ◆ *adj* **1** (*gen*) last: *el ~ episodio* the last episode ◊ *estos ~s días* the last few days ◊ *Te lo digo por última vez.* I'm telling you for the last time. **2** (*más reciente*) latest: *la última moda* the latest fashion **3** (*más alto*) top: *en el ~ piso* on the top floor **4** (*más bajo*) bottom: *Están en última posición de la liga.* They are bottom of the league. ◆ *nm-nf* **1** (*gen*) last (one): *Fuimos los ~s en llegar.* We were the last (ones) to arrive. **2** (*mencionado en último lugar*) latter LOC **ir/vestir a la última** to be fashionably dressed **a última hora 1** (*en último momento*) at the last moment **2** (*al final de un día*) late: *a última hora de la tarde de ayer* late yesterday evening ◊ *a última hora del martes* late last Tuesday **a últimos de mes** at the end of the month

ultraderecha *nf* extreme right

ultramarinos *nm* grocer's [*pl* grocers]

umbilical *adj* LOC *Ver* CORDÓN

umbral *nm* threshold: *en el ~ del nuevo siglo* on the threshold of the new century

un, una ◆ *art indef* **1** a, an ☛ La forma **an** se emplea delante de sonido vocálico: *un árbol* a tree ◊ *un brazo* an arm ◊ *una hora* an hour **2 unos** some: *Necesito unos zapatos nuevos.* I need some new shoes. ◊ *Ya que vas, compra unos plátanos.* Get some bananas while you're there. ◊ *Tienes unos ojos preciosos.* You've got beautiful eyes. ◆ *adj Ver* UNO

unanimidad *nf* unanimity LOC **por unanimidad** unanimously

undécimo, -a *adj, pron, nm-nf* eleventh

único, -a ◆ *adj* **1** (*solo*) only: *la única excepción* the only exception **2** (*excepcional*) extraordinary: *una mujer única* an extraordinary woman **3** (*sin igual*) unique: *una obra de arte única* a unique work of art ◆ *nm-nf* only one: *Es la única que sabe nadar.* She's the only one who can swim. LOC *Ver* DIRECCIÓN, HIJO, SENTIDO

unidad *nf* **1** (*gen*) unit: *~ de medida* unit of measurement **2** (*unión*) unity: *falta de ~* lack of unity LOC **Unidad de Vigilancia Intensiva/Cuidados Intensivos (UVI/UCI)** intensive care unit

unido, -a *pp, adj* close: *una familia muy unida* a very close family ◊ *Están muy ~s.* They're very close. LOC *Ver* ESTADO, ORGANIZACIÓN, REINO; *Ver tb* UNIR

unificar *vt* to unify

uniforme ◆ *adj* **1** (*gen*) uniform: *de tamaño ~* of uniform size **2** (*superficie*) even ◆ *nm* uniform LOC **con/de uniforme**: *soldados de ~* uniformed soldiers ◊ *colegiales con ~* children in school uniform

unión *nf* **1** (*gen*) union: *la ~ monetaria* monetary union **2** (*unidad*) unity: *La ~ es nuestra mejor arma.* Unity is our best weapon. **3** (*acción*) joining (together): *la ~ de las dos partes* the joining together of the two parts LOC **Unión Europea (UE)** European Union (*abrev* EU)

unir ◆ *vt* **1** (*intereses, personas*) to unite: *los objetivos que nos unen* the aims that unite us **2** (*piezas, objetos*) to join **3** (*carretera, ferrocarril*) to link ◆ **unirse** *v pron* **unirse a** to join: *Se unieron al grupo.* They joined the group.

universal *adj* **1** (*gen*) universal: *Provocan condena ~.* They arouse universal condemnation. **2** (*historia, literatura*) world [*n atrib*]: *historia ~* world history LOC *Ver* DILUVIO

universidad *nf* university [*pl* universities]: *ir a la ~* to go to university

universo *nm* universe

uno, -a ◆ *adj* **1** (*cantidad*) one: *He dicho un kilo, no dos.* I said one kilo, not two. **2** (*primero*) first: *el día ~ de mayo* the first of May **3 unos** (*aproximadamente*): *~s quince días* about a fortnight ◊ *Sólo estaré ~s días.* I'll only be there a few days. ◊ *Tendrá ~s 50 años.* He must be about 50. ◆ *pron* **1** (*gen*) one: *No tenía corbata y le dejé una.* He didn't have a tie, so I lent him one. **2** (*uso impersonal*) you, one (*más formal*): *~ no sabe a qué atenerse.* You don't know what to think, do you? **3 unos**: *A ~s les gusta y a otros no.* Some (people) like it; some don't. ◆ *nm* one: *~, dos, tres* one, two, three LOC **¡a la una, a las dos, a las tres!** ready, steady, go! **de uno en uno** one by one: *Mételos de ~ en ~.* Put them in one by one. **es la una** it's one o'clock **(los) unos a (los) otros** each other, one another: *Se ayudaban (los) ~s a (los) otros.* They helped each other. ☛ *Ver nota en* EACH OTHER ☛ *Para más información sobre el uso del numeral uno, ver ejemplos en* SEIS.

untar *vt* **1** (*extender*) to spread *sth* ***on sth***: *~ las tostadas con/de mermelada* to spread jam on toast **2** (*en salsa*) to dip: *~ patatas fritas en tomate* to dip chips in tomato sauce LOC **untar con aceite/grasa** to grease: *~ un molde con aceite* to grease a tin

uña *nf* **1** (*mano*) (finger)nail: *morderse las ~s* to bite your nails **2** (*pie*) toenail LOC **ser uña y carne** to be inseparable *Ver tb* CEPILLO, ESMALTE

uranio *nm* uranium

Urano *nm* Uranus

urbanización *nf* (housing) estate

urbano, -a *adj* urban LOC **guardia/policía urbano** municipal policeman

urgencia *nf* **1** (*emergencia, caso urgente*) emergency [*pl* emergencies]: *en caso de ~* in case of emergency **2 urgencias** (*en un hospital*) casualty (department) [*sing*]

urgente *adj* **1** (*gen*) urgent: *un pedido/trabajo ~* an urgent order/job **2** (*correo*) express

urna *nf* **1** (*cenizas*) urn **2** (*Pol*) ballot box

urraca *nf* magpie

usado, -a *pp, adj* **1** (*de segunda mano*) second-hand: *ropa usada* second-hand clothes **2** (*desgastado*) worn out: *unos zapatos ~s* worn out shoes *Ver tb* USAR

usar *vt* **1** (*utilizar*) to use: *Uso mucho el ordenador.* I use the computer a lot. **2** (*ponerse*) to wear: *¿Qué colonia usas?* What cologne do you wear?

uso *nm* use: *instrucciones de ~* instructions for use LOC **de uso externo/tópico** (*pomada*) for external application

usted *pron pers* you: *Todo se lo debo a ~es.* I owe it all to you.

usuario, -a *nm-nf* user

utensilio *nm* **1** (*herramienta*) tool **2** (*cocina*) utensil

útero *nm* womb

útil ◆ *adj* useful ◆ **útiles** *nm* equipment [*incontable, v sing*]

utilidad *nf* usefulness LOC **tener mucha utilidad** to be very useful

utilizar *vt* to use

utopía *nf* Utopia

uva *nf* grape LOC **estar de mala uva** to be in a foul mood **tener mala uva** to be bad-tempered

UVI (*tb* **UCI**) *nf Ver* UNIDAD

Vv

vaca *nf* **1** (*animal*) cow **2** (*carne*) beef LOC **estar como una vaca** to be very fat *Ver tb* COMER

vacación *nf* holiday [*pl* holidays] LOC **estar/ir(se) de vacaciones** to be/go on holiday

vaciar *vt* **1** (*gen*) to empty *sth* (out) (***into sth***): *Vaciemos esta caja.* Let's empty (out) that box. **2** (*un lugar*) to clear *sth* (***of sth***): *Quiero que vacíes tu cuarto de trastos.* I want you to clear your room of junk.

vacío, -a ◆ *adj* empty: *una caja/casa vacía* an empty box/house ◆ *nm* vacuum LOC *Ver* ENVASADO

vacuna *nf* vaccine: *la ~ contra la polio* the polio vaccine

vacunar *vt* to vaccinate *sth/sb* (***against sth***): *Tenemos que ~ al perro contra la rabia.* We've got to have the dog vaccinated against rabies.

vacuno, -a *adj* LOC *Ver* GANADO

vado *nm* (*de un río*) ford LOC **vado permanente** keep clear (at all times)

vagabundo, -a ◆ *adj* **1** (*persona*) wandering **2** (*animal*) stray ◆ *nm-nf* tramp

vagar *vi* to wander: *Pasaron toda la noche vagando por las calles de la* *ciudad.* They spent all night wandering the city streets.

vagina *nf* vagina

vago, -a[1] ◆ *adj* lazy ◆ *nm-nf* slacker LOC **hacer el vago** to laze about/ around

vago, -a[2] *adj* vague: *una respuesta vaga* a vague answer ◊ *un ~ parecido* a vague resemblance

vagón *nm* carriage: *~ de pasajeros* passenger carriage LOC **vagón de mercancías** freight wagon **vagón restaurante** dining car

vaho *nm* **1** (*vapor*) steam **2** (*aliento*) breath

vainilla *nf* vanilla

vaivén *nm* swinging: *el ~ del péndulo* the swinging of the pendulum

vajilla *nf* **1** (*gen*) crockery [*incontable*] **2** (*juego completo*) dinner service

vale *nm* **1** (*cupón*) voucher **2** (*recibo*) receipt **3** (*entrada*) (free) ticket

valentía *nf* courage

valer ◆ *vt* **1** (*costar*) to cost: *El libro valía 1.500 pesetas.* The book cost 1500 pesetas. **2** (*tener un valor*) to be worth: *Una libra vale unas 200 pesetas.* One pound is worth about 200 pesetas. ◆ *vi* **1** (*servir*) to do: *Este vaso vale como florero.* This glass will do as a vase. ◊ *¿Para qué vale esto?* What's that for? ☛Para decir *no valer* se emplea **to be no good**: *Tiré todos los bolígrafos que no valían.* I threw away all the pens that were no good. **2** (*ser suficiente*) to be enough: *¿Vale con esto?* Is this enough? **3** *~* **por** to entitle *sb* **to** ***sth***: *Este cupón vale por un descuento.* This coupon entitles you to a discount. **4** *~* (**para**) (*persona*) to be good: *Yo no valdría para maestra.* I'd be no good as a teacher. **5** (*estar permitido*) to be allowed: *No vale hacer trampas.* No cheating. **6** (*documento*) to be valid: *Este pasaporte ya no vale.* This passport is no longer valid. **7** (*ropa*) to fit: *Esa falda ya no me vale.* That skirt doesn't fit me any more. ◆ **valerse** *v pron* **valerse de** to use: *Se valió de todos los medios para triunfar.* He used every means possible to get on. LOC **más vale ...**: *Más vale que cojas el paraguas.* You'd better take your umbrella. ◊ *Más te vale decir la verdad.* You're better off telling the truth. **¡no vale!** (*no es justo*) that's not fair! **no valer para nada** to be useless **vale** (*de acuerdo*) OK **valerse (por sí mismo)** to get around (on your own) *Ver tb* CUÁNTO, PENA

válido, -a *adj* valid

valiente *adj, nmf* brave [*adj*]: *¡Eres un ~!* You're very brave!

valioso, -a *adj* valuable

valla *nf* **1** (*cerca*) fence **2** (*Dep*) hurdle: *los 500 metros ~s* the 500 metres hurdles LOC **valla publicitaria** hoarding

vallar *vt* to fence

valle *nm* valley [*pl* valleys]

valor *nm* **1** (*gen*) value: *Tiene un gran ~ sentimental para mí.* It has great sentimental value for me. **2** (*precio*) price: *Las joyas alcanzaron un ~ muy alto.* The jewels fetched a very high price. **3** (*valentía*) courage: *Me falta ~.* I haven't got the courage. LOC **sin valor** worthless *Ver tb* ARMAR, IMPUESTO

valorar *vt* **1** (*gen*) to value *sth* (***at sth***): *Valoraron el anillo en un millón de pesetas.* The ring was valued at a million pesetas. **2** (*considerar*) to assess: *Llegó el momento de ~ los resultados.* It was time to assess the results.

vals *nm* waltz

válvula *nf* valve: *la ~ de escape/ seguridad* the exhaust/safety valve

vampiro *nm* **1** (*murciélago*) vampire bat **2** (*Cine*) vampire

vandalismo *nm* vandalism

vanguardia *nf* **1** (*Mil*) vanguard **2** (*Arte*) avant-garde: *teatro de ~* avant-garde theatre

vanguardismo *nm* (*Arte, Liter*) avant-gardism

vanidad *nf* vanity

vanidoso, -a *adj, nm-nf* vain [*adj*]: *Eres un ~.* You're so vain.

vano, -a *adj* vain: *un intento ~* a vain attempt LOC **en vano** in vain

vapor *nm* **1** (*gen*) steam: *una locomotora de ~* a steam engine ◊ *una plancha de ~* a steam iron **2** (*Quím*) vapour: *~es tóxicos* toxic vapours LOC **al vapor** steamed *Ver tb* BARCO

vaquero, -a ◆ *adj* (*tela*) denim [*n atrib*]: *cazadora vaquera* denim jacket ◆ *nm-nf* (*pastor*) cowherd ◆ *nm* **1** (*cowboy*) cowboy [*pl* cowboys] **2 vaqueros** jeans

vara *nf* **1** (*palo*) stick **2** (*rama*) branch

variable ◆ *adj* (*carácter*) changeable ◆ *nf* variable LOC *Ver* NUBOSIDAD

variación *nf* variation: *ligeras variaciones de presión* slight variations in pressure

variar *vt, vi* **1** (*dar variedad, ser variado*) to vary: *Los precios varían según el restaurante.* Prices vary depending on the restaurant. ◊ *Hay que ~ la alimentación.* You should vary your diet. **2** (*cambiar*) to change: *No varía en plural.* It doesn't change in the plural. LOC **para variar** for a change

varicela *nf* chickenpox

variedad *nf* variety [*pl* varieties]

varilla *nf* rod

varios, -as *adj, pron* several: *en varias ocasiones* on several occasions ◊ *Hay varias posibilidades.* There are several possibilities. ◊ *~ de vosotros tendréis que estudiar más.* Several of you will have to work harder.

varita *nf* stick LOC **varita mágica** magic wand

variz *nf* varicose vein

varón *nm* (*hijo*) boy: *Nos gustaría un ~.* We would like a boy. LOC *Ver* SANTO

varonil *adj* manly, virile (*formal*): *una voz ~* a manly voice

vasco, -a *adj, nm-nf* Basque: *el País Vasco* the Basque Country

vasija *nf* vessel

vaso *nm* **1** (*gen*) glass: *un ~ de agua* a glass of water **2** (*Anat, Bot*) vessel: *~s capilares/sanguíneos* capillary/blood vessels LOC **vaso de plástico/papel** plastic/paper cup *Ver tb* AHOGAR, BEBER, GAFAS, GOTA

vatio *nm* watt: *una bombilla de 60 ~s* a 60-watt light bulb

vecinal *adj* LOC *Ver* CAMINO

vecindario *nm* **1** (*barrio*) neighbourhood: *una de las escuelas del ~* one of the schools in the neighbourhood **2** (*vecinos*) residents [*pl*]: *Todo el ~ salió a la calle.* All the residents took to the streets.

vecino, -a ◆ *adj* neighbouring: *países ~s* neighbouring countries ◆ *nm-nf* neighbour: *¿Qué tal son tus ~s?* What are your neighbours like? LOC *Ver* COMUNIDAD

veda *nf* close season: *El salmón está en ~.* It's the close season for salmon.

vegetación *nf* **1** (*gen*) vegetation **2** **vegetaciones** (*Med*) adenoids

vegetal ◆ *adj* vegetable [*n atrib*]: *aceites ~es* vegetable oils ◊ *el reino ~* the vegetable kingdom ◆ *nm* vegetable LOC *Ver* CARBÓN

vegetar *vi* **1** (*Bot*) to grow **2** (*persona*) to be a vegetable

vegetariano, -a *adj, nm-nf* vegetarian: *ser ~* to be a vegetarian

vehículo *nm* vehicle

veinte *nm, adj, pron* **1** (*gen*) twenty **2** (*vigésimo*) twentieth: *el siglo ~* the twentieth century ☛ *Ver ejemplos en* SESENTA

vejestorio *nm* old man

vejez *nf* old age

vejiga *nf* bladder

vela[1] *nf* **1** (*cirio*) candle: *encender/apagar una ~* to light/put out a candle **2** (*mocos*): *Se te cae la ~.* Your nose is running. LOC **estar/pasarse la noche en vela 1** (*gen*) to stay up all night **2** (*con un enfermo*) to keep watch (*over sb*) **¿quién te ha dado vela en este entierro?** who asked you to butt in? *Ver tb* DOS

vela[2] *nf* **1** (*de un barco*) sail **2** (*Dep*) sailing: *practicar la ~* to go sailing LOC *Ver* BARCO

velada *nf* evening

velar ◆ *vt* **1** (*cadáver*) to keep vigil **over sb** **2** (*enfermo*) to sit up **with sb** ◆ *vi ~* **por** to look after *sth/sb*: *Tu padrino velará por ti.* Your godfather will look after you.

velarse *v pron* (*carrete*) to be exposed: *No abras la máquina que se vela el carrete.* Don't open the camera or you'll expose the film.

velatorio *nm* wake

velero *nm* sailing boat

veleta *nf* weathervane

vello *nm* (*Anat*) hair: *tener ~ en las piernas* to have hair on your legs

velo *nm* veil LOC **velo del paladar** soft palate

velocidad *nf* **1** (*rapidez*) speed: *la ~ del sonido* the speed of sound ◊ *trenes de gran ~* high-speed trains **2** (*Mec*) gear: *cambiar de ~* to change gear ◊ *un coche con cinco ~es* a car with a five-speed gearbox LOC *Ver* CAJA

velocímetro *nm* speedometer

velocista *nmf* sprinter

velódromo *nm* velodrome, cycle track (*más coloq*)

veloz *adj* fast: *No es tan ~ como yo.* He isn't as fast as me. ☛ *Ver nota en* FAST[1]

vena *nf* vein LOC **darle la vena a algn** to take it into your head *to do sth*: *Me dio la ~ y me fui de compras.* I took it into my head to go shopping. **estar en vena** to be on form

vencedor, ~a ◆ *adj* **1** (*gen*) winning: *el equipo* ~ the winning team **2** (*país, ejército*) victorious ◆ *nm-nf* **1** (*gen*) winner: *el ~ de la prueba* the winner of the competition **2** (*Mil*) victor

vencer ◆ *vt* **1** (*Dep*) to beat: *Nos vencieron en la semifinal.* We were beaten in the semifinal. **2** (*Mil*) to defeat **3** (*rendir*) to overcome: *Me venció el sueño.* I was overcome with sleep. ◆ *vi* **1** (*gen*) to win: *Venció el equipo visitante.* The visiting team won. **2** (*plazo*) to expire: *El plazo venció ayer.* The deadline expired yesterday. **3** (*pago*) to be due: *El pago del préstamo vence hoy.* Repayment of the loan is due today.

vencido, -a ◆ *pp, adj*: *darse por* ~ to give in ◆ *nm-nf* loser: *vencedores y ~s* winners and losers LOC *Ver* TERCERO; *Ver tb* VENCER

venda *nf* bandage: *Me puse una ~ en el dedo.* I bandaged (up) my finger.

vendado, -a *pp, adj* LOC *Ver* OJO; *Ver tb* VENDAR

vendar *vt* to bandage *sth/sb* (up): *Me vendaron el tobillo.* They bandaged (up) my ankle. ◊ *La vendaron de pies a cabeza.* She was bandaged from head to foot. LOC **vendarle los ojos a algn** to blindfold sb

vendaval *nm* hurricane

vendedor, ~a *nm-nf* **1** (*viajante*) salesman/woman [*pl* salesmen/women] **2** (*dependiente*) shop assistant LOC **vendedor ambulante** hawker

vender ◆ *vt* to sell: *Venden el piso de arriba.* The upstairs flat is for sale. ◆ **venderse** *v pron* **1** (*estar a la venta*) to be on sale: *Se venden en el mercado.* They are on sale in the market. **2** (*dejarse sobornar*) to sell yourself LOC **se vende** for sale **venderse como churros** to sell like hot cakes

vendimia *nf* grape harvest

vendimiar *vi* to harvest grapes

veneno *nm* poison

venenoso, -a *adj* poisonous LOC *Ver* HONGO, SETA

venganza *nf* revenge

vengarse *v pron* to take revenge (**on sb**) (**for sth**): *Se vengó de lo que le hicieron.* He took revenge for what they'd done to him. ◊ *Me vengaré de él.* I'll get my revenge on him.

venir ◆ *vi* **1** (*gen*) to come: *¡Ven aquí!* Come here! ◊ *Nunca vienes a verme.* You never come to see me. ◊ *No me vengas con excusas.* Don't come to me with excuses. **2** (*volver*) to be back: *Vengo en seguida.* I'll be back in a minute. **3** (*estar*) to be: *Viene en todos los periódicos.* It's in all the papers. ◊ *Hoy vengo un poco cansado.* I'm a bit tired today. ◆ *v aux* ~ **haciendo algo** to have been **doing sth**: *Hace años que te vengo diciendo lo mismo.* I've been telling you the same thing for years. LOC **que viene** next: *el martes que viene* next Tuesday **venir bien/mal** (*convenir*) to suit/not to suit: *Mañana me viene muy mal.* Tomorrow doesn't suit me. ☞Para otras expresiones con **venir**, véanse las entradas del sustantivo, adjetivo, etc, p.ej. **no venir a cuento** en CUENTO y **venir de familia** en FAMILIA.

venta *nf* sale: *en* ~ for sale

ventaja *nf* advantage: *Vivir en el campo tiene muchas ~s.* Living in the country has a lot of advantages. LOC **llevarle ventaja a algn** to have an advantage over sb

ventana *nf* window

ventanilla *nf* (*coche*) window: *Baja/sube la ~.* Open/shut the window.

ventilación *nf* ventilation

ventilador *nm* fan

ventilar *vt* (*habitación, ropa*) to air

ventrílocuo, -a *nm-nf* ventriloquist

Venus *nm* Venus

ver ◆ *vt* **1** (*gen*) to see: *Hace mucho que no la veo.* I haven't seen her for a long time. ◊ *¿Lo ves?, ya te has vuelto a caer.* You see? You've fallen down again. ◊ *No veo por qué.* I don't see why. ◊ *¿Ves aquel edificio de allí?* Can you see that building over there? **2** (*televisión*) to watch: ~ *la tele* to watch TV **3** (*examinar*) to look at *sth*: *Necesito ~lo con más calma.* I need more time to look at it. ◆ *vi* to see: *Espera, voy a ~.* Wait, I'll go and see. ◆ **verse** *v pron* **1 verse** (**con**) to meet (*sb*): *Me vi con tu hermana en el parque.* I met your sister in the park. **2** (*estar*) to be: *Nunca me había visto en una situación igual.* I'd never been in a situation like that. LOC **a ver si... 1** (*deseo*) I hope...: *A ~ si apruebo esta vez.* I hope I pass this time. **2** (*temor*) what if...: *¡A ~ si les ha pasado algo!* What if something has happened to them? **3** (*ruego, mandato*) how about...?: *A ~ si me escribes de una vez.* How about writing to me sometime? **ver venir algo** to see it coming:

Lo estaba viendo venir. I could see it coming ☛Para otras expresiones con **ver**, véanse las entradas del sustantivo, adjetivo, etc, p.ej. **tener que ver** en TENER y **ver visiones** en VISIÓN.

veraneante *nmf* holiday-maker

veranear *vi* to spend the summer: ~ *en la playa* to spend the summer by the sea

veraneo *nm* holiday: *estar/ir de* ~ to be/go on holiday

verano *nm* summer: *En* ~ *hace mucho calor.* It's very hot in (the) summer. ◊ *las vacaciones de* ~ the summer holidays

verbena *nf* dance: *la* ~ *de San Juan* the Midsummer Night dance

verbo *nm* verb

verdad *nf* truth: *Di la* ~. Tell the truth. LOC **ser verdad** to be true: *No puede ser* ~. It can't be true. **ser una verdad como un puño/templo** to be as plain as the nose on your face **¿verdad?**: *Este coche es más rápido, ¿verdad?* This car's faster, isn't it? ◊ *No te gusta la leche, ¿verdad?* You don't like milk, do you? *Ver tb* CANTAR, CONFESAR

verdadero, -a *adj* true: *la verdadera historia* the true story

verde ◆ *adj* **1** (*gen*) green ☛*Ver ejemplos en* AMARILLO **2** (*fruta*) unripe: *Todavía están ~s.* They're not ripe yet. **3** (*obsceno*) dirty: *chistes ~s* dirty jokes ◆ *nm* **1** (*color*) green **2** (*hierba*) grass **3 los verdes** (*Pol*) the Greens LOC **ponerle verde a algn** (*hablando de algn*) to slag sb off **verde botella** bottle-green *Ver tb* JUDÍA, VIEJO, ZONA

verdugo *nm* **1** (*persona*) executioner **2** (*pasamontañas*) balaclava

verdura *nf* vegetable(s) [*se usa mucho en plural*]: *frutas y ~s* fruit and vegetables ◊ *La* ~ *es muy sana.* Vegetables are good for you. ◊ *sopa de ~s* vegetable soup

vergonzoso, -a *adj* **1** (*tímido*) shy **2** (*indignante*) disgraceful

vergüenza *nf* **1** (*timidez, sentido del ridículo*) embarrassment: *¡Qué ~!* How embarrassing! **2** (*sentido de culpabilidad, modestia*) shame: *No tienes ~.* You've got no shame. ◊ *Le daba ~ confesarlo.* He was ashamed to admit it. LOC **dar/pasar vergüenza** to be embarrassed: *Me da ~ preguntarles.* I'm too embarrassed to ask them.

verídico, -a *adj* true

verificar *vt* to check

verja *nf* **1** (*cerca*) railing(s) [*se usa mucho en plural*]: *saltar una ~ de hierro* to jump over some iron railings **2** (*puerta*) gate: *Cierra la ~, por favor.* Shut the gate, please.

verruga *nf* wart

versión *nf* version LOC **en versión original** (*película*) with subtitles

verso *nm* **1** (*línea de un poema*) line **2** (*género literario*) poetry **3** (*poema*) verse

vértebra *nf* vertebra [*pl* vertebrae]

vertebrado, -a *adj, nm* vertebrate

vertebral *adj* LOC *Ver* COLUMNA

vertedero *nm* tip

verter *vt* **1** (*en un recipiente*) to pour: *Vierte la leche en otra taza.* Pour the milk into another cup. **2** (*residuos*) to dump

vertical *adj* **1** (*gen*) vertical: *una línea ~* a vertical line **2** (*posición*) upright: *en posición ~* in an upright position

vértice *nm* vertex [*pl* vertexes/vertices]

vértigo *nm* vertigo: *tener ~* to get vertigo LOC **dar/producir vértigo** to make *sb* dizzy

vesícula *nf* LOC **vesícula** (**biliar**) gall bladder

vestíbulo *nm* **1** (*entrada, recibidor*) hall **2** (*teatro, cine, hotel*) foyer

vestido *nm* dress: *Llevas un ~ precioso.* You're wearing a beautiful dress. LOC **vestido de novia** wedding dress

vestir ◆ *vt* **1** (*gen*) to dress: *Vestí a los niños.* I got the children dressed. **2** (*llevar*) to wear: *Él vestía un traje gris.* He was wearing a grey suit. ◆ **vestir(se)** *vi, v pron* **vestir(se)** (**de**) to dress (**in** *sth*): ~ *bien/de blanco* to dress well/in white ◆ **vestirse** *v pron* to get dressed: *Vístete o llegarás tarde.* Get dressed or you'll be late. LOC **el mismo que viste y calza** the very same *Ver tb* GALA, ÚLTIMO

vestuario *nm* **1** (*ropa, Cine, Teat*) wardrobe **2** (*Dep*) changing room

veterano, -a ◆ *adj* experienced: *el jugador más ~ del equipo* the most experienced player in the team ◆ *nm-nf* veteran: *ser ~* to be a veteran

veterinaria *nf* veterinary science

veterinario, -a *nm-nf* vet

veto *nm* veto [*pl* vetoes]

vez *nf* time: *tres veces al año* three times a year ◊ *Te lo he dicho cien veces.* I've told you hundreds of times. ◊ *Gano* *cuatro veces más que él.* I earn four times as much as he does. LOC **a la vez (que)** at the same time (as): *Lo dijimos a la ~.* We said it at the same time. ◊ *Terminó a la ~ que yo.* He finished at the same time as I did. **a veces** sometimes **de una vez**: *¡Contéstalo de una ~!* Hurry up and answer! **de una vez por todas** once and for all **de vez en cuando** from time to time **dos veces** twice **en vez de** instead of *sth/sb/doing sth* **érase una vez...** once upon a time there was... **una vez** once *Ver tb* ALGUNO, CADA, CIEN, DEMASIADO, OTRO

vía *nf* **1** (*Ferrocarril*) **(a)** (*raíles*) track: *la ~ del tren* the train track **(b)** (*andén*) platform **2 vías** (*Med*) tract [*sing*]: *~s respiratorias* respiratory tract LOC **en vías de desarrollo** developing: *países en ~s de desarrollo* developing countries **(por) vía aérea** (*correos*) (by) airmail **Vía Láctea** Milky Way **vía satélite** satellite: *una conexión ~ satélite* a satellite link

viajante *nmf* sales rep

viajar *vi* to travel: *~ en avión/coche* to travel by plane/car

viaje *nm* journey [*pl* journeys], trip, travel

> Las palabras **travel**, **journey** y **trip** no deben confundirse.
> El sustantivo **travel** es incontable y se refiere a la actividad de viajar en general: *Sus principales aficiones son los libros y los viajes.* Her main interests are reading and travel. **Journey** y **trip** se refieren a un viaje concreto. **Journey** indica sólo el desplazamiento de un lugar a otro: *El viaje fue agotador.* The journey was exhausting. **Trip** incluye también la estancia: *¿Qué tal tu viaje a París?* How did your trip to Paris go? ◊ *un viaje de negocios* a business trip
> Otras palabras que se utilizan para referirnos a viajes son **voyage** y **tour**. **Voyage** es un viaje largo por mar: *Colón es famoso por sus viajes al Nuevo Mundo.* Columbus is famous for his voyages to the New World. **Tour** es un viaje organizado donde se va parando en distintos sitios: *Jane va a hacer un viaje por Tierra Santa.* Jane is going on a tour around the Holy Land.

LOC **¡buen/feliz viaje!** have a good trip! **estar/irse de viaje** to be/go away **viaje de intercambio** exchange visit *Ver tb* AGENCIA, BOLSO, CHEQUE, EMPRENDER

viajero, -a *nm-nf* **1** (*pasajero*) passenger **2** (*turista*) traveller: *un ~ incansable* a tireless traveller

vial *adj* road [*n atrib*]: *educación ~* road safety awareness

víbora *nf* viper

vibrar *vi* to vibrate

vicepresidente, -a *nm-nf* vice-president

vicesecretario, -a *nm-nf* deputy secretary [*pl* deputy secretaries]

viceversa *adv* vice versa

viciarse *v pron* ~ **(con)** to get hooked **(on** ***sth*****)**

vicio *nm* **1** (*gen*) vice: *No tengo ~s.* I don't have any vices. **2** (*adicción*) addiction: *El juego se convirtió en ~.* Gambling became an addiction. LOC **coger/tener el vicio de algo** to get/be addicted to sth **darse al vicio** to turn to drink, drugs, etc

vicioso, -a *adj* depraved LOC *Ver* CÍRCULO

víctima *nf* victim: *ser ~ de un robo* to be the victim of a burglary

victoria *nf* **1** (*gen*) victory [*pl* victories] **2** (*Dep*) win: *una ~ en campo contrario* an away win LOC *Ver* CANTAR

victorioso, -a *adj* LOC **salir victorioso** to triumph

vid *nf* vine

vida *nf* **1** (*gen*) life [*pl* lives]: *¿Qué es de tu ~?* How's life? **2** (*sustento*) living: *ganarse la ~* to make a living LOC **con vida** alive: *Siguen con ~.* They're still alive. **darse/pegarse la vida padre** to live the life of Riley **de toda la vida**: *La conozco de toda la ~.* I've known her all my life. ◊ *amigos de toda la ~* lifelong friends **en la vida** never: *En la ~ he visto una cosa igual.* I've never seen anything like it. **¡esto es vida!** this is the life! **llevar una vida de perros** to lead a dog's life **para toda la vida** for life *Ver tb* ABRIR, AMARGAR, BOLSA[1], COMPLICAR, COSA, ENTERRAR, ESPERANZA, NIVEL, RITMO, SIETE, TREN

vídeo *nm* **1** (*gen*) video [*pl* videos] **2** (*aparato*) video recorder LOC **filmar, grabar en vídeo** to film/to tape *Ver tb* CINTA

videocámara *nf* video camera

videoclip *nm* video [*pl* videos]

videoclub *nm* video shop

videojuego *nm* video game

videoteca *nf* video library [*pl* video libraries]

vidriera *nf* LOC **vidriera (de colores)** stained-glass window

vidrio *nm* glass [*incontable*]: *una botella de* ~ a glass bottle

vieira *nf* scallop

viejo, -a ◆ *adj* old: *estar/hacerse* ~ to look/get old ◆ *nm-nf* old man/woman [*pl* old men/women] LOC **viejo verde** dirty old man *Ver tb* CASCO, TRAPO

viento *nm* wind LOC **contra viento y marea** come hell or high water **hacer viento** to be windy: *Hacía demasiado* ~. It was too windy. *Ver tb* MOLINO

vientre *nm* **1** (*abdomen*) belly [*pl* bellies] **2** (*matriz*) womb

viernes *nm* Friday [*pl* Fridays] (*abrev* Fri) ☛ *Ver ejemplos en* LUNES LOC **Viernes Santo** Good Friday

viga *nf* **1** (*madera*) beam **2** (*metal*) girder

vigente *adj* current LOC **estar vigente** to be in force

vigía *nmf* lookout

vigilancia *nf* (*control*) surveillance: *Van a aumentar la* ~. They're going to step up surveillance. LOC *Ver* TORRE, UNIDAD

vigilante *nmf* guard

vigilar *vt* **1** (*prestar atención, atender*) to keep an eye on *sth/sb* **2** (*enfermo*) to look after *sb* **3** (*custodiar*) to guard: ~ *la frontera/a los presos* to guard the border/prisoners **4** (*examen*) to invigilate

vigor *nm* **1** (*Jur*) force: *entrar en* ~ to come into force **2** (*energía*) vigour

villa *nf* (*chalé*) villa LOC **villa olímpica** Olympic village

villancico *nm* (Christmas) carol

vilo LOC **en vilo** (*intranquilo*) on tenterhooks: *Nos has tenido en ~ toda la noche.* You've kept us on tenterhooks all night.

vinagre *nm* vinegar

vinagreras *nf* cruets

vinagreta *nf* vinaigrette

vínculo *nm* link

vinícola *adj* wine [*n atrib*]: *industria* ~ wine industry ◊ *región* ~ wine-growing region

vinicultor, ~a *nm-nf* wine-grower

vino *nm* wine: *¿Te apetece un* ~*?* Would you like a glass of wine? ◊ ~ *blanco/tinto/de mesa* white/red/table wine LOC *Ver* PAN

viña *nf* (*tb* **viñedo** *nm*) vineyard

viñeta *nf* (*tira cómica*) comic strip

violación *nf* **1** (*delito*) rape **2** (*transgresión, profanación*) violation

violador, ~a *nm-nf* rapist

violar *vt* **1** (*forzar*) to rape **2** (*incumplir*) to break **3** (*profanar*) to violate

violencia *nf* violence

violentar *vt* **1** (*forzar*) to force: ~ *una cerradura* to force a lock **2** (*incomodar*) to make *sb* uncomfortable

violento, -a *adj* **1** (*gen*) violent: *una película violenta* a violent film **2** (*incómodo*) embarrassing: *una situación violenta* an embarrassing situation

violeta *adj, nf, nm* violet ☛ *Ver ejemplos en* AMARILLO

violín *nm* violin

violinista *nmf* violinist

violoncelo *nm* cello [*pl* cellos]

virar *vi* to swerve: *Tuvo que ~ rápidamente hacia la derecha.* He had to swerve to the right.

virgen ◆ *adj* **1** (*gen*) virgin: *bosques vírgenes* virgin forests ◊ *aceite de oliva* ~ extra virgin olive oil **2** (*cinta*) blank ◆ *nmf* virgin: *la Virgen de Fátima* the Virgin of Fatima ◊ *ser* ~ to be a virgin LOC *Ver tb* LANA

virginidad *nf* virginity

virgo (*tb* **Virgo**) *nm, nmf* (*Astrología*) Virgo [*pl* Virgos] ☛ *Ver ejemplos en* AQUARIUS

viril *adj* manly, virile (*formal*)

virilidad *nf* manliness

virtualmente *adv* virtually

virtud *nf* virtue: *tu mayor* ~ your greatest virtue

virtuoso, -a *adj* (*honesto*) virtuous

viruela *nf* **1** (*Med*) smallpox **2** (*ampolla*) pockmark

virus *nm* virus [*pl* viruses]

visado *nm* visa: ~ *de entrada/salida* entry/exit visa

visar *vt* (*pasaporte*) to stamp a visa in *a passport*

viscoso, -a *adj* viscous

visera *nf* **1** (*gorra*) peaked cap **2** (*de deportista*) eye-shade

visibilidad *nf* visibility: *poca* ~ poor visibility

visible *adj* visible

visillo *nm* net curtain

visión *nf* **1** (*vista*) (eye)sight: *perder la ~ en un ojo* to lose the sight of one eye **2** (*punto de vista*) view: *una ~ personal/de conjunto* a personal/an overall view **3** (*alucinación*) vision: *tener una* ~

to have a vision. LOC **ver visiones** to hallucinate

visita *nf* **1** (*gen*) visit: *horario de ~(s)* visiting hours **2** (*visitante*) visitor: *Me parece que tienes ~.* I think you've got visitors/a visitor. LOC **hacer una visita** to pay *sb* a visit

visitante ◆ *adj* visiting: *el equipo ~* the visiting team ◆ *nmf* visitor: *los ~s del palacio* visitors to the palace

visitar *vt* to visit: *Fui a ~le al hospital.* I went to visit him in hospital.

visón *nm* mink

víspera *nf* day before (*sth*): *Dejé todo preparado la ~.* I got everything ready the day before. ◊ *la ~ del examen* the day before the exam

También existe la palabra **eve**, que se usa cuando es la víspera de una fiesta religiosa o de un acontecimiento importante: *la víspera de San Juan* Midsummer Eve ◊ *Llegaron la víspera de las elecciones.* They arrived on the eve of the elections.

LOC **en vísperas de** just before *sth*: *en ~s de exámenes* just before the exams

vista *nf* **1** (*gen*): *Lo operaron de la ~.* He had an eye operation. ◊ *La zanahoria es muy buena para la ~.* Carrots are very good for your eyes. **2** (*panorama*) view: *la ~ desde mi habitación* the view from my room ◊ *con ~s al mar* overlooking the sea **3** (*instinto*): *un político con mucha ~* a very far-sighted politician ◊ *Tienes mucha ~ para los negocios.* You've got a good eye for business. LOC **dejar algo a la vista**: *Déjalo a la ~ para que no se me olvide.* Leave it where I can see it or I'll forget it. **en vista de** in view of *sth*: *en ~ de lo ocurrido* in view of what has happened **hacer la vista gorda** to turn a blind eye (*to sth*) **¡hasta la vista!** see you! **tener (la) vista cansada** to be long-sighted *Ver tb* APARTAR, CONOCER, CORTO, GRADUAR, PERDER, PUNTO, QUITAR, SALTAR, SIMPLE, TIERRA

vistazo *nm* look: *Con un ~ tengo suficiente.* Just a quick look will do. LOC **dar/echar un vistazo** to have a look (*at sth/sb*)

visto, -a *pp, adj* LOC **estar bien/mal visto** to be well thought of/frowned upon **estar muy visto** to be unoriginal: *Eso ya está muy ~.* That's not very original. ◊ *La minifalda está muy vista.* Miniskirts have been around for ages. **por lo visto** apparently **visto bueno** approval *Ver tb* VER

vistoso, -a *adj* colourful

visual *adj* visual

vital *adj* **1** (*Biol*) life [*n atrib*]: *el ciclo ~* the life cycle **2** (*persona*) full of life **3** (*decisivo*) vital

vitalidad *nf* vitality

vitamina *nf* vitamin: *la ~ C* vitamin C

viticultura *nf* wine-growing

vitrina *nf* glass cabinet

viudo, -a ◆ *adj* widowed: *Se quedó viuda muy joven.* She was widowed at an early age. ◆ *nm-nf* widower [*fem* widow]

viva ◆ *nm* cheer: *¡Tres ~s al campeón!* Three cheers for the champion! ◆ **¡viva!** *interj* hooray!: *¡~, he aprobado!* Hooray! I've passed! ◊ *¡~ el rey!* Long live the king!

víveres *nm* provisions

vivero *nm* **1** (*plantas*) nursery [*pl* nurseries]: *un ~ de árboles* a tree nursery **2** (*peces*) fish farm

vivienda *nf* **1** (*gen*) housing [*incontable*]: *el problema de la ~* the housing problem **2** (*casa*) house: *buscar ~* to look for a house **3** (*piso*) flat: *bloques de ~s* blocks of flats

vivir ◆ *vi* **1** (*gen*) to live: *Vivió casi setenta años.* He lived for almost seventy years. ◊ *¿Dónde vives?* Where do you live? ◊ *Viven en León/el segundo.* They live in León/on the second floor. ◊ *¡Qué bien vives!* What a nice life you have! **2** (*subsistir*) to live on *sth*: *No sé de qué viven.* I don't know what they live on. ◊ *Vivimos con 40.000 pesetas al mes.* We live on 40000 pesetas a month. **3** (*existir*) to be alive: *Mi bisabuelo aún vive.* My great-grandfather is still alive. ◆ *vt* to live (***through sth***): *Vive tu vida.* Live your own life. ◊ *~ una mala experiencia* to live through a bad experience LOC **no dejar vivir** not to leave *sb* in peace: *El jefe no nos deja ~.* Our boss won't leave us in peace. **vivir a costa de algn** to live off sb **vivir al día** to live from hand to mouth

vivo, -a *adj* **1** (*gen*) living: *seres ~s* living beings ◊ *lenguas vivas* living languages **2** (*persona*) clever **3** (*luz, color, ojos*) bright **4** (*activo*) lively: *una ciudad viva* a lively city LOC **en vivo** (*en directo*) live **estar vivo** to be alive: *¿Está ~?* Is he alive? **vivo o muerto** dead or alive *Ver tb* CARNE, FUEGO, LLORAR, MANTENER, ROJO

vocabulario *nm* vocabulary [*pl* vocabularies]

vocación *nf* vocation

vocal ◆ *adj* vocal ◆ *nf* (*letra*) vowel ◆ *nmf* member LOC *Ver* CUERDA

vocalizar *vi* to speak clearly

vocear *vt, vi* to shout

vodka *nm* vodka

volador, ~a *adj* flying

volante ◆ *adj* flying ◆ *nm* **1** (*automóvil*) steering wheel **2** (*de tela*) frill **3** (*médico*) referral note: *un ~ para el otorrino* a referral note for the ENT specialist LOC *Ver* PLATILLO

volar ◆ *vi* **1** (*gen*) to fly: *Volamos a Roma desde Madrid.* We flew to Rome from Madrid. ◊ *El tiempo vuela.* Time flies. **2** (*con el viento*) to blow away: *El sombrero voló por los aires.* His hat blew away. ◆ *vt* (*hacer explotar*) to blow *sth* up: *~ un edificio* to blow up a building LOC **volando** (*de prisa*) in a rush: *Fuimos volando a la estación.* We rushed off to the station. *Ver tb* AIRE

volcán *nm* volcano [*pl* volcanoes]

volcar ◆ *vt* **1** (*derribar*) to knock *sth* over: *Los chicos volcaron el contenedor.* The children knocked the wheely bin over. **2** (*vaciar*) to empty *sth* out ◆ **volcar(se)** *vi, v pron* to overturn: *El coche volcó al patinar.* The car skidded and overturned. ◆ **volcarse** *v pron* **volcarse con** to do anything **for *sb***: *Se vuelca con sus nietos.* She will do anything for her grandchildren.

voleibol *nm* volleyball

voleo *nm* LOC **a voleo** at random

voltaje *nm* voltage

voltereta *nf* somersault: *dar una ~* to do a somersault LOC **voltereta lateral** cartwheel

voltio *nm* volt

voluble *adj* changeable

volumen *nm* volume: *Compré el primer ~.* I bought the first volume. ◊ *bajar/subir el ~* to turn the volume down/up

voluntad *nf* **1** (*gen*) will: *No tiene ~ propia.* He has no will of his own. ◊ *contra mi ~* against my will **2** (*deseo*) wishes [*pl*]: *Debemos respetar su ~.* We must respect his wishes. LOC **buena voluntad** goodwill: *mostrar buena ~* to show goodwill *Ver tb* FUERZA

voluntario, -a ◆ *adj* voluntary ◆ *nm-nf* volunteer: *Trabajo de ~.* I work as a volunteer. LOC **presentarse/salir voluntario** to volunteer

volver ◆ *vi* **1** (*regresar*) to go/come back: *Volví a casa.* I went back home. ◊ *Vuelve aquí.* Come back here. ◊ *¿A qué hora volverás?* What time will you be back? **2 ~ a hacer algo** to do sth again: *No vuelvas a decirlo.* Don't say that again. ◆ *vt* to turn: *Volví la cabeza.* I turned my head. ◊ *Me volvió la espalda.* He turned his back on me. ◆ **volverse** *v pron* **1 volverse (a/hacia)** to turn **(to/towards *sth/sb*)**: *Se volvió y me miró.* She turned round and looked at me. ◊ *Se volvió hacia Elena.* He turned towards Elena. **2** (*convertirse*) to become: *Se ha vuelto muy tranquilo.* He's become very calm. ◊ *~se loco* to go mad LOC **volver en sí** to come round **volver la cara** to look the other way

vomitar ◆ *vt* to bring *sth* up: *Vomité toda la cena.* I brought up all my dinner. ◆ *vi* to be sick, to vomit (*más formal*): *Tengo ganas de ~.* I think I'm going to be sick.

vómito *nm* vomit, sick (*más coloq*)

vosotros, -as *pron pers* you: *¿ ~ vais a la fiesta?* Are you going to the party?

votación *nf* vote LOC **hacer una votación** to vote *Ver tb* SOMETER

votar *vt, vi* to vote (**for *sth/sb***): *Voté a los verdes.* I voted Green/for the Greens. ◊ *~ a favor/en contra de algo* to vote for/against sth LOC **votar por correo** to have a postal vote

voto *nm* **1** (*Pol*) vote: *100 ~s a favor y dos en contra* 100 votes in favour, two against **2** (*Relig*) vow LOC **voto nulo** spoilt ballot paper

voz *nf* **1** (*gen*) voice: *decir algo en ~ alta/baja* to say sth in a loud/quiet voice **2** (*grito*) shout: *Dale una ~ a tu hermano para que venga.* Give your brother a shout. ◊ *dar/pegar voces* to shout LOC **a voz en grito** at the top of your voice **correr la voz** to spread the word (*that…*) **llevar la voz cantante** to be the boss

vuelo *nm* **1** (*gen*) flight: *el ~ Santiago-Madrid* the Santiago-Madrid flight ◊ *~s nacionales/internacionales* domestic/international flights **2** (*prenda*): *Esa falda tiene mucho ~.* That skirt's very full. LOC **cogerlas (todas) al vuelo** to catch on fast **vuelo regular** scheduled flight **vuelo sin motor** gliding *Ver tb* REMONTAR

vuelta *nf* **1** (*regreso*) return: *la ~ a la normalidad* the return to normality ◊ *Te veré a la ~.* I'll see you when I get back. **2** (*Dep*) lap: *Dieron tres ~s a la pista.* They did three laps of the track.

3 (*cambio*) change: *Quédese con la ~.* Keep the change. LOC **a la vuelta de la esquina** (just) round the corner: *El verano está a la ~ de la esquina.* Summer's just round the corner. **dar (dos, etc) vueltas a/alrededor de algo** to go round sth (twice, etc): *La Luna da ~s alrededor de la Tierra.* The moon goes round the earth. **dar la vuelta a la manzana/al mundo** to go round the block/world **darle la vuelta a algo** to turn sth over: *Dale la ~ al filete.* Turn the steak over. **darle vueltas a algo 1** (*gen*) to turn sth: *Siempre le doy dos ~s a la llave.* I always turn the key twice. **2** (*comida*) to stir sth: *No dejes de dar ~s al caldo.* Keep stirring the broth. **3** (*pensar*) to worry about sth: *Deja de darle ~s al asunto.* Stop worrying about it. **dar media vuelta** to turn round **dar vueltas** to spin: *La Tierra da ~s sobre su eje.* The earth spins on its axis. **(ir/salir a) dar una vuelta** to go out (for a walk) **vuelta ciclista** cycle race **vuelta de campana** somersault: *El coche dio tres ~s de campana.* The car somersaulted three times. *Ver tb* BILLETE, IDA, PARTIDO

vuestro, -a ◆ *adj pos* your: *vuestra casa* your house ◆ *pron pers* yours: *¿Son éstos los ~s?* Are these yours?

Nótese que *un primo vuestro* se traduce por 'a cousin of yours' porque significa *uno de vuestros primos.*

vulgar *adj* vulgar

Ww

walkie-talkie *nm* walkie-talkie

walkman® *nm* Walkman® [*pl* Walkmans]

wáter *nm* toilet

waterpolo *nm* water polo

whisky *nm* whisky [*pl* whiskies]

windsurf *nm* windsurfing: *practicar el ~* to go windsurfing LOC *Ver* TABLA

xilófono *nm* xylophone

Yy

y *conj* **1** (*copulativa*) and: *chicos y chicas* boys and girls **2** (*en interrogaciones*) and what about...?: *¿Y tú?* And what about you? **3** (*para expresar las horas*) past: *Son las dos y diez.* It's ten past two. LOC **¿y qué?** so what?

ya ◆ *adv* **1** (*referido al presente o al pasado*) already: *Ya son las tres.* It's already three o'clock. ◊ *¿Ya lo has terminado?* Have you finished it already? ◊ *Estaba muy enfermo pero ya está bien.* He was very ill but he's fine now. ☛ *Ver nota en* YET **2** (*referido al futuro*): *Ya veremos.* We'll see. ◊ *Ya te escribirán.* They'll write to you (eventually). **3** (*uso enfático*): *Ya lo sé.* I know. ◊ *Sí, ya entiendo.* Yes, I understand. ◊ *Ya verás, ya.* Just you wait and see. ◆ **¡ya!** *interj* of course! LOC **ya no...**: *Ya no vivo allí.* I don't live there any more. **¡ya voy!** coming! *Ver tb* BASTAR

yacimiento *nm* **1** (*Geol*) deposit **2** (*Arqueología*) site

yanqui *adj*, *nmf* Yankee [*n*]: *la hospitalidad* ~ Yankee hospitality

yate *nm* yacht

yegua *nf* mare

yema *nf* **1** (*huevo*) (egg) yolk **2** (*dedo*) (finger)tip: *No siento las ~s de los dedos.* I can't feel my fingertips. ◊ *la ~ del pulgar* the tip of the thumb **3** (*Bot*) bud

yerba *nf Ver* HIERBA

yerno *nm* son-in-law [*pl* sons-in-law]

yeso *nm* plaster

yo *pron pers* **1** (*sujeto*) I: *Iremos mi hermana y yo.* My sister and I will go. ◊ *Lo haré yo mismo.* I'll do it myself. **2** (*en comparaciones, con preposición*) me: *excepto yo* except (for) me ◊ *Llegaste antes que yo.* You got here before me. LOC **soy yo** it's me **¿yo?** me?: *¿Quién dices? ¿Yo?* Who do you mean? Me? **yo que tú** if I were you: *Yo que tú no iría.* I wouldn't go if I were you.

yodo *nm* iodine

yoga *nm* yoga: *hacer ~* to practise yoga

yogur *nm* yoghurt LOC **yogur descremado/desnatado** low-fat yoghurt

yóquey (*tb* **yoqui**) *nmf* jockey [*pl* jockeys]

yudo *nm* judo

yugular *adj*, *nf* jugular

Zz

zafiro *nm* sapphire

zaguán *nm* hallway

zamarra *nf* **1** (*chaqueta de piel*) sheepskin jacket **2** (*chaqueta gruesa*) heavy jacket

zambomba *nf* traditional percussion instrument

zambullirse *v pron* (*bañarse*) to take a dip

zampar ◆ *vi* to stuff yourself ◆ **zampar(se)** *vt*, *v pron* to wolf *sth* down

zanahoria *nf* carrot

zancada *nf* stride

zancadilla *nf* LOC **echar/poner la zancadilla** to trip *sb* up: *Le pusiste la ~.* You tripped him up.

zángano, -a *nm-nf* lazybones [*pl* lazybones]

zanja *nf* trench

zanjar *vt* to put an end to *sth*

zapatería *nf* shoe shop

zapatero, -a *nm-nf* shoemaker

zapatilla *nf* **1** (*pantufla*) slipper **2** (*Dep*) trainer **3** (*ballet, tenis*) shoe

zapato *nm* shoe: *~s planos* flat shoes ◊ *~s de tacón* high-heeled shoes

zarandear *vt* to shake: *La zarandeó para que dejara de gritar.* He shook her to stop her shouting.

zarpa *nf* paw LOC **echar la(s) zarpa(s)** to get your hands on *sth/sb*

zarpar *vi* ~ (**hacia/con rumbo a**) to set sail (**for...**): *El buque zarpó hacia Malta.* The boat set sail for Malta.

zarza *nf* bramble

zarzamora *nf* blackberry [*pl* blackberries]

¡zas! *interj* bang!

zigzag *nm* zigzag: *un camino en ~* a zigzag path

zinc *nm* zinc

zodiaco (*tb* **zodíaco**) *nm* zodiac: *los signos del ~* the signs of the zodiac

zombi *adj*, *nmf* zombie [*n*]: *ir ~* to go round like a zombie

zona *nf* **1** (*área*) area: *~ industrial/residencial* industrial/residential area **2** (*Anat, Geog, Mil*) zone: *~ fronteriza/neutral* border/neutral zone LOC **zona norte, etc** north, etc: *la ~ sur de la ciudad* the south of the city **zonas verdes** parks

zoo (*tb* **zoológico**) *nm* zoo [*pl* zoos]

zopenco, -a ◆ *adj* stupid ◆ *nm-nf* twit

zoquete ◆ *adj* thick ◆ *nmf* dimwit

zorro, -a ◆ *nm-nf* (*animal*) fox [*fem* vixen] ◆ *nm* (*piel*) fox fur: *un abrigo de ~* a fox fur coat LOC **estar/quedarse hecho unos zorros** to be shattered

zueco *nm* clog

zulo *nm* cache

zumbado, -a *pp*, *adj* (*loco*) crazy *Ver tb* ZUMBAR

zumbar *vt*, *vi* LOC **salir zumbando** to

rush off: *Miró su reloj y salió zumbando.* He looked at his watch and rushed off. **zumbarle los oídos a algn** to have a buzzing in your ears

zumbido *nm* **1** (*insecto*) buzzing [*incontable*]: *Se oían los ~s de las moscas.* You could hear the flies buzzing. **2** (*máquina*) humming [*incontable*]

zumo *nm* (fruit) juice: ~ *de piña* pineapple juice ◊ ~ *de naranja natural* fresh orange juice

zurcir *vt* to darn LOC **¡que te zurzan!** get lost!

zurdo, -a *adj* left-handed: *ser* ~ to be left-handed

zurrar *vt* to wallop

zurrón *nm* bag

Hojas de estudio

He aquí la lista de apartados que hemos elaborado para ayudarte con el inglés:

Preposiciones de lugar

The lamp is **above** the table.

The meat is **on** the table.

The cat is **under** the table.

The lorry is **in front of** the car.

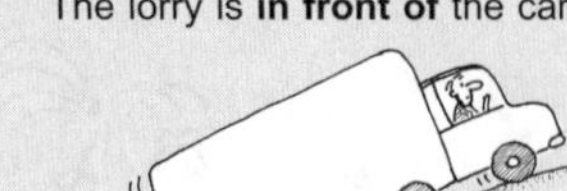

The car is **behind** the lorry.

Sam is **between** Tom and Kim.

Kim is **next to/beside** Sam.

The bird is **in/ inside** the cage.

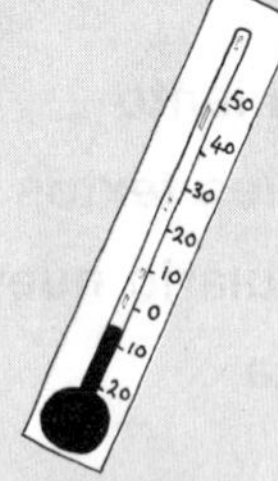

The temperature is **below** zero.

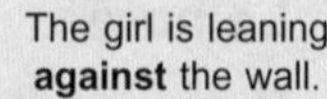

The girl is leaning **against** the wall.

Tom is **opposite** Kim.

The house is **among** the trees.

Preposiciones de movimiento

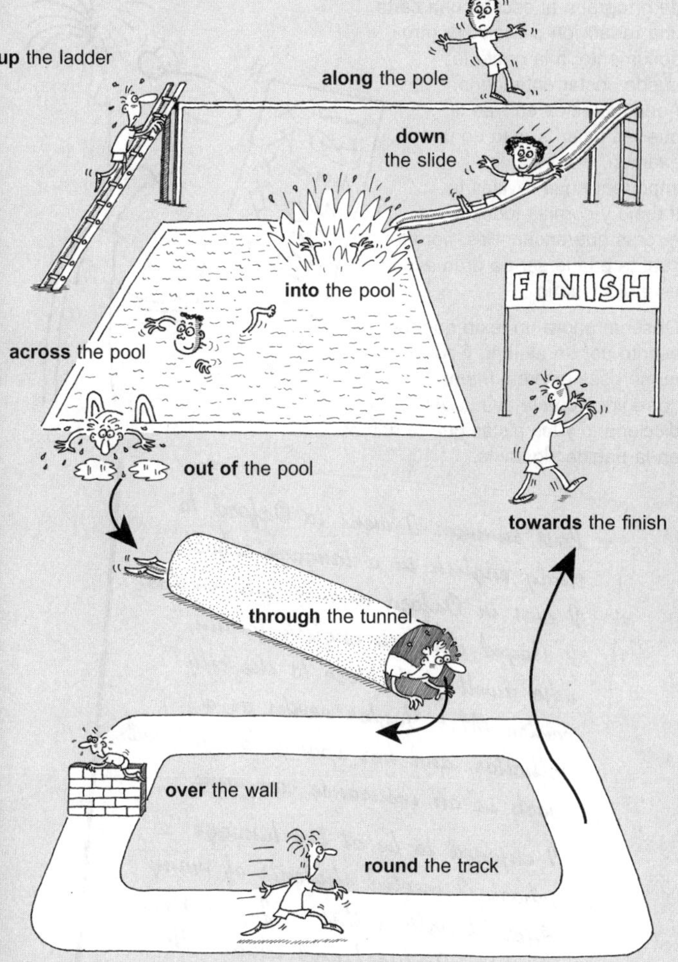

Cómo corregir tus propios textos

Si cometes muchos errores y faltas de ortografía al escribir una carta, una redacción o cualquier otro documento, a la gente le puede costar entenderlo. Además, estos errores te pueden bajar la nota en un examen. Por eso, es importante que revises tu trabajo y corrijas todos los errores que encuentres, para lo cual te puede ser de gran ayuda este diccionario.

Observa ahora un texto que fue escrito por un alumno y contiene numerosos errores. Intenta corregirlos con la ayuda del diccionario y las pistas que te damos en la página siguiente.

Last summer I went to Oxford to study english in a langage school. I was in Oxford during two months. I stayed with an english family, who dwell quite close to the city centre. Mrs Taylor works as a sollicitor, and her spouse has a good work in an insuranse company.

I enjoyed to be at the langage school. I meeted students of many diferent nationalitys – Japanesse, Italien, Portugal and spain. The professors were very sympathetic and teached me a lot, but I didn't like making so many homeworks!

Pistas para la corrección de textos

1 ¿He utilizado la palabra correcta?

En este diccionario incluimos notas sobre palabras que la gente tiende a confundir. Busca entradas como ***sympathetic, work*** o cualquier otra que te haga dudar.

2 ¿He escogido el estilo más adecuado?

Puede que algunas de las palabras que has utilizado sean demasiado formales o informales para el texto que has escrito. Compruébalo en las entradas correspondientes de nuestro diccionario.

3 ¿He combinado correctamente las palabras?

¿Se dice *to* ***make*** *your* ***homework*** o *to* ***do*** *your* ***homework***? Si no estás seguro, consulta las entradas de los verbos correspondientes, donde encontrarás un ejemplo que lo aclare.

4 ¿Qué preposición debo utilizar?

¿Se dirá ***close to*** o ***close from***? Las preposiciones en inglés pueden llegar a ser una pesadilla... ¡¡parece que cada sustantivo, adjetivo y verbo lleva una preposición diferente!! Este diccionario te ayudará a la hora de hacer la elección.

5 ¿He acertado con la estructura sintáctica?

¿***Enjoy to do sth*** o ***enjoy doing sth***? La entrada ***enjoy*** te ayudará a solucionar esta duda. Asegúrate de comprobar este tipo de estructuras en el texto.

6 ¿He cometido faltas de ortografía?

Ten cuidado con aquellas palabras que se parecen a las de tu propia lengua, ya que a menudo se escriben de distinta manera. Fíjate también en los nombres de países y nacionalidades (encontrarás una lista en el apéndice 4). Comprueba las terminaciones del plural, las formas en *-ing*, las dobles consonantes, etc.

7 ¿Es el texto gramaticalmente correcto?

¿Te has fijado en si los sustantivos son contables o incontables? ¿Has utilizado el pasado y el participio correctos en los verbos? Consulta la lista de verbos irregulares del apéndice 2 para asegurarte.

Ahora ya puedes darle la vuelta a la página para comprobar las respuestas.

Respuestas

Last summer I went to Oxford to study **E**nglish in a lang**u**age school. I was in Oxford **for** two months. I stayed with an **E**nglish family, who **live** quite close to the city centre. Mrs Taylor work**s** as a solicitor, and her **husband** has a good **job** in an insuran**c**e company.

I enjoyed **being** at the lang**u**age school. I **met** students of many di**ff**erent nationalit**ies** – Japan**ese**, Itali**a**n, Portug**uese** and **Spanish**. The **teachers** were very **nice** and **taught** me a lot, but I didn't like **doing** so **much** homework!

Cómo archivar el vocabulario nuevo

A la hora de aprender vocabulario, es importante ordenar y archivar todas aquellas palabras nuevas que quieras recordar. He aquí algunas sugerencias sobre cómo hacerlo.

Cuadernos de vocabulario

A

B

A muchos estudiantes les gusta tener un cuaderno especial para anotar el vocabulario. Hay dos maneras de organizar dicho cuaderno: por *temas* (como en el dibujo A) o por *orden alfabético* (dibujo B). Escribe unas cuantas palabras al principio, y añade después otras a medida que las vayas aprendiendo.

Fichas de vocabulario

parte delantera de la ficha

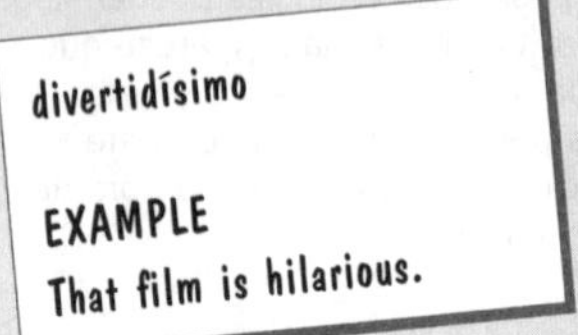

parte trasera de la ficha

Otra manera de organizar el vocabulario es escribir cada palabra nueva en una ficha y guardar todas las fichas en un fichero. Escribe la palabra en una cara de la ficha y la traducción, acompañada de algún ejemplo, en la otra cara. Esto te vendrá bien cuando quieras repasar lo que has aprendido: miras la palabra e intentas recordar cómo se traduce al español; o, si lo prefieres, miras la traducción y tratas de adivinar de qué palabra se trata.

Cómo anotar información adicional sobre una palabra

Puede que te interese recordar ciertos detalles sobre una palabra. Búscalos en el diccionario y decide cuáles quieres anotar en tu cuaderno o en tus fichas de vocabulario. Trata de dar siempre un ejemplo, te ayudará a recordar cómo se usa la palabra en inglés.

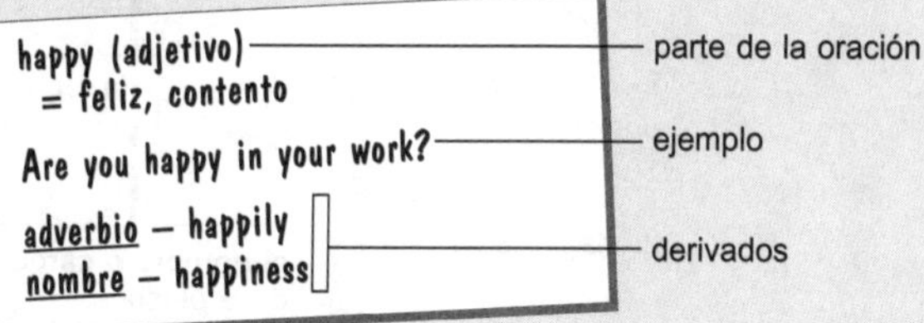

happy (adjetivo)
= feliz, contento
Are you happy in your work?
adverbio – happily
nombre – happiness
parte de la oración
ejemplo
derivados

Ejercicio 1

Decide, con la ayuda del diccionario, cuáles son los detalles más importantes de las siguientes palabras, y a continuación anótalos.

bleed **deaf** **on the ball** **fluent** **swap**

Cuadros sinópticos y diagramas

A veces puede ser interesante agrupar las palabras por familias. Observa los dos métodos que mostramos a continuación:

a) Cuadros sinópticos

Deporte	Persona	Lugar
football	footballer	pitch
athletics	athlete	track
golf	golfer	course
tennis	tennis player	court

b) Diagramas

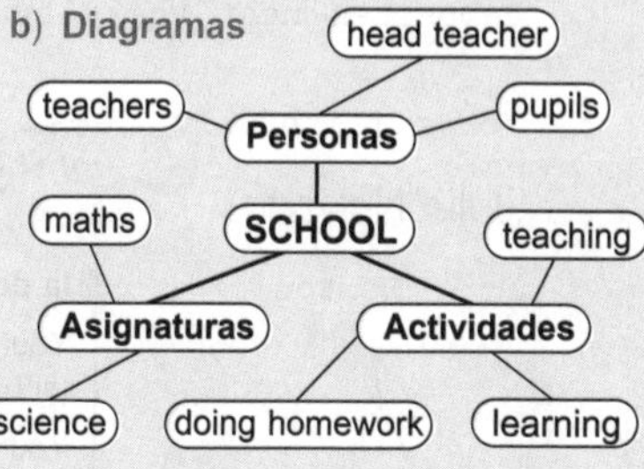

Ejercicio 2

a) *Haz un cuadro sinóptico utilizando palabras que se refieran a trabajos, lugares de trabajo y cosas que la gente utiliza en el trabajo.*

b) *Haz un diagrama que muestre vocabulario relacionado con las vacaciones. Puedes agrupar las palabras según se refieran a lugares donde alojarse, métodos de transporte o actividades.*

Cómo redactar una carta

Cartas formales

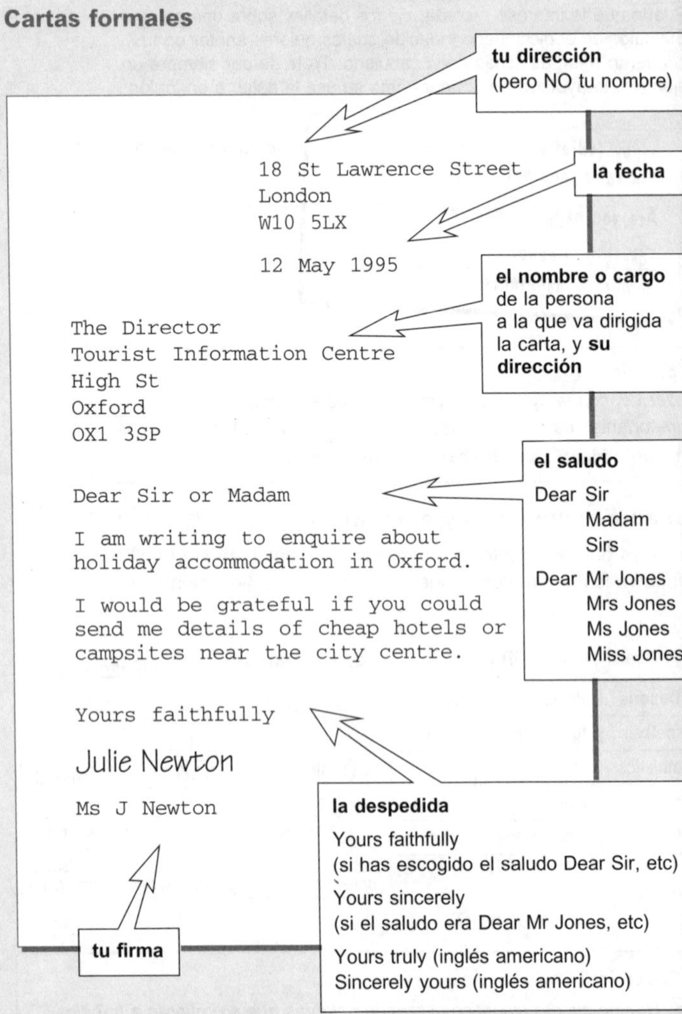
18 St Lawrence Street
London
W10 5LX

12 May 1995

The Director
Tourist Information Centre
High St
Oxford
OX1 3SP

Dear Sir or Madam

I am writing to enquire about holiday accommodation in Oxford.

I would be grateful if you could send me details of cheap hotels or campsites near the city centre.

Yours faithfully

Julie Newton

Ms J Newton

Recuerda que este tipo de cartas deben redactarse en estilo formal y por lo tanto debes evitar utilizar contracciones como *I'm*, *I'd*, etc.

Cartas informales

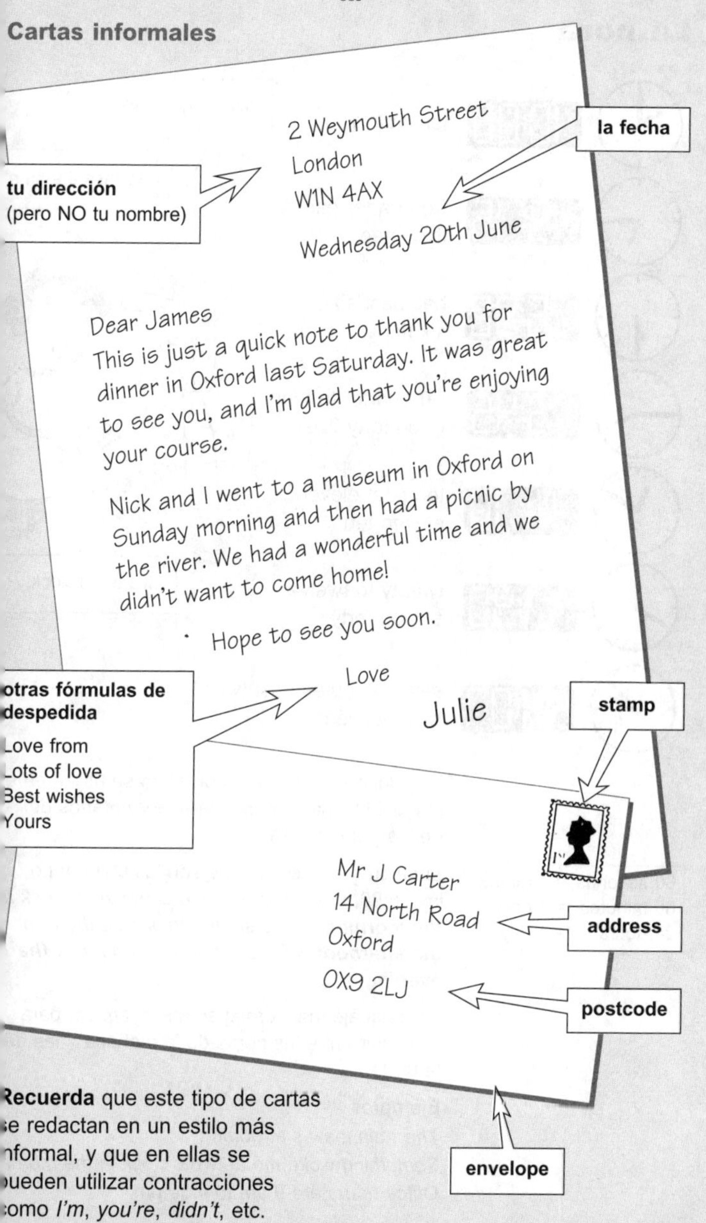

2 Weymouth Street
London
W1N 4AX
Wednesday 20th June
Dear James
This is just a quick note to thank you for dinner in Oxford last Saturday. It was great to see you, and I'm glad that you're enjoying your course.
Nick and I went to a museum in Oxford on Sunday morning and then had a picnic by the river. We had a wonderful time and we didn't want to come home!
Hope to see you soon.
Love
Julie
la fecha
tu dirección
(pero NO tu nombre)
otras fórmulas de despedida
Love from
Lots of love
Best wishes
Yours
stamp
Mr J Carter
14 North Road
Oxford
OX9 2LJ
address
postcode
envelope

Recuerda que este tipo de cartas se redactan en un estilo más informal, y que en ellas se pueden utilizar contracciones como *I'm*, *you're*, *didn't*, etc.

La hora

14:07 seven minutes past two
two o seven*

* El "reloj de veinticuatro horas" no se utiliza en e lenguaje hablado, salvo para leer horarios de trenes y autobuses.

60 seconds	=	1 minute
60 minutes	=	1 hour
24 hours	=	1 day

Si quieres especificar que son las 06:00 y no las 18:00, puedes expresarlo como *six o'clock* ***i*** ***the morning***. 15:30 se diría *half past three* ***in the afternoon*** y 22:00 sería *ten o'clock* ***in the evening***.

En lenguaje más formal se utiliza *am/pm* para distinguir entre las horas de la mañana y las de la tarde.

Ejemplos

The train leaves at 06:56.
Something woke me at two o'clock in the morni
Office hours are 9 am to 4:30 pm.

Vamos a llamar por teléfono

¿Cómo se expresan los números de teléfono?

36920 three six nine two o (Se pronuncia /əʊ/.)
25844 two five eight double four

Para hacer una *llamada telefónica* (a **telephone call**), *levantamos el auricular* (**pick up** the **receiver**) y *marcamos un número de teléfono* (**dial** a telephone number). Cuando *el teléfono suena* (the telephone **rings**), la persona a la que llamamos *lo contesta* (**answers** it). Si esa persona está hablando por teléfono en ese momento, el teléfono estará *comunicando* (**engaged**).

La puntuación inglesa

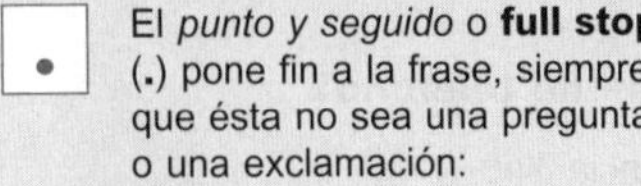

El *punto y seguido* o **full stop** (**.**) pone fin a la frase, siempre que ésta no sea una pregunta o una exclamación:

We're leaving now.
That's all.
Thank you.

También se utiliza en abreviaturas:

Acacia Ave.
Walton St.

? El *signo de interrogación* o **question mark** (**?**) se pone al final de una frase interrogativa directa:

'Who's that man?' Jenny asked.

pero nunca al final de una interrogativa indirecta:

Jenny asked who the man was.

! El *signo de admiración* o **exclamation mark** (**!**) se pone al final de una frase que expresa sorpresa, entusiasmo, miedo, etc:

What an amazing story!
How well you look!
Oh no! The cat's been run over!

También se utiliza con interjecciones y palabras onomatopéyicas:

Bye!
Ow!
Crash!

, La coma o **comma** (**,**) indica una breve pausa dentro de una frase:

I ran all the way to the station, but I still missed the train.
However, he may be wrong.

También utilizamos la coma para citar a una persona o para introducir una frase en estilo directo:

Fiona said, 'I'll help you.'
'I'll help you', said Fiona, 'but you'll have to wait till Monday.'

La coma puede separar los elementos de una enumeración o de una lista (no es obligatoria delante de *'and'*).

It was a cold, rainy day.
This shop sells records, tapes, and compact discs.

: Los *dos puntos* o **colon** (**:**) se utilizan para introducir citas largas o listas de objetos:

There is a choice of main course: roast beef, turkey or omelette.

; El *punto y coma* o **semicolon** (**;**) se utiliza para separar dos partes bien diferenciadas dentro de una oración:

John wanted to go; I did not.

También puede separar elementos de una lista cuando ya hemos utilizado la coma:

The school uniform consists of navy skirt or trousers; grey, white or pale blue shirt; navy jumper or cardigan.

' El *apóstrofo* o **apostrophe** (') puede indicar dos cosas:

a) que se ha omitido una letra, como en el caso de las contracciones

hasn't, don't, I'm y *he's*

b) el genitivo sajón:

Peter's scarf
Jane's mother
my friend's car

Cuando un sustantivo acaba en *s*, no siempre es necesario añadir una segunda *s*, p. ej. en

Jesus' family

Observa que la posición del apóstrofo es distinta cuando acompaña a sustantivos que están en singular y en plural:

the girl's keys
(= las llaves de una niña)
the girls' keys
(= las llaves de varias niñas)

" " Las *comillas simples y dobles*, **quotation marks** (' ') e **inverted commas** (" "), se utilizan para introducir las palabras o los pensamientos de una persona:

'Come and see,' said Martin.
Angela shouted, 'Over here!'
'Will they get here on time?' she wondered.

Las comillas también pueden introducir el título de un libro, de una película, etc:

'Pinocchio' is the first film I ever saw.
'Have you read "Emma"?' he asked.

- El *guión* o **hyphen** (-) se usa para unir dos palabras que forman una unidad:

dining room
a ten-ton truck

También se usa para unir un prefijo a una palabra:

non-violent
anti-British

y en números compuestos:

thirty-four
seventy-nine

Cuando tenemos que partir una palabra al final de una línea, lo hacemos por medio de un guión.

— La *raya* o **dash** (–) se utiliza para separar una frase o explicación dentro de una oración más amplia. También la podemos encontrar al final de la oración, para resumir su contenido:

A few people – not more than ten – had already arrived.
The burglars had taken the furniture, the TV and stereo, the paintings – absolutely everything.

( ) El *paréntesis* o **brackets ( )** sirve para resaltar información adicional dentro de una oración:

Two of the runners (Johns and Smith) finished the race in under an hour.

Los números y letras que indican distintos apartados se marcan también mediante paréntesis:

The camera has three main advantages:
1) *its compact size*
2) *its low price and*
3) *the quality of the photographs.*

What would you do if you won a lot of money?
a) *save it*
b) *travel round the world*
c) *buy a new house*

¿Dónde comemos hoy?

¿En un café? ¿En un pub?

En Gran Bretaña, los **cafés** abren sólo hasta media tarde y no sirven bebidas alcohólicas. Éstas se toman en el **pub**, donde a veces se dan también comidas y cenas rápidas. **Cafeteria** o **canteen** es el local donde comen los estudiantes cuando están en el colegio y los empleados en el trabajo. En un **tea-shop** (o **coffee-shop** en los grandes almacenes) te puedes tomar un café o un té con pasteles.

¿En un restaurante?

Un **restaurant** es un lugar más refinado y más caro que un **café**, donde se toman comidas completas. En el **café** se sirven solamente aperitivos y comidas ligeras. En un **take-away** se vende la comida ya lista para llevar y consumir fuera del local.

¿A qué hora se come?

El desayuno

El desayuno tradicional inglés o **cooked breakfast** (huevos, bacon, salchichas, etc) se toma normalmente los sábados y los domingos. Entre semana es más normal tomar café con tostadas o bollería, cereales, etc.

La comida, la merienda y la cena

Dinner, **lunch**, **tea** y **supper** significan cosas distintas según las personas y las regiones.

Dinner es la comida principal y se prepara normalmente al final de la tarde.

Al mediodía se suele tomar el **lunch**, que es casi siempre una comida ligera, como una ensalada o un sandwich.

Tea puede ser la merienda-cena que se les da a los niños o el té con pastas que meriendan los mayores.

Hay gente que llama **supper** a la cena ligera que se toma antes de acostarse.

Gran Bretaña	España
breakfast	desayuno
lunch	comida
tea	merienda (merienda-cena para los niños)
dinner/supper	cena

La comida de los domingos

Los domingos es frecuente tomar el **Sunday lunch**, generalmente **roast meat** (*asado de carne*) con verduras.

Las casas en Gran Bretaña

Una **detached house** es una vivienda unifamiliar que no tiene ningún edificio adosado.

Una **semi-detached house** está adosada a otra casa por uno de sus lados.

Una **terraced house** forma parte de una hilera de casas adosadas entre sí.

Un **block of flats** es un edificio moderno, dividido en pisos y más alto que las casas tradicionales.

Un **cottage** es una casa pequeña, a menudo antigua y de aspecto coqueto, construida en el campo o en un pueblo pequeño.

Un **bungalow** es una casa de una sola planta. La mayoría de los **bungalows** son de construcción moderna.

En Gran Bretaña, la mayoría de la gente vive en una casa, excepto en las grandes ciudades, donde muchas personas viven en pisos. Cuando alguien quiere comprar o vender una casa, se pone en contacto con un **estate agent** (agencia inmobiliaria) y por lo general pide un **mortgage** (hipoteca) a una **building society** (una especie de caja de ahorros). La gente que vive en una casa alquilada tiene que pagar el dinero del alquiler (the **rent**) al dueño o dueña de la casa (the **landlord** o **landlady**).

Las instituciones británicas

El parlamento

El parlamento británico (the **British Parliament**) está dividido en dos cámaras, la Cámara de los Comunes (the **House of Commons**) y la Cámara de los Lores (the **House of Lords**). La Cámara de los Comunes está compuesta por 650 parlamentarios (**Members of Parliament** o **MPs**) elegidos directamente por los ciudadanos británicos. La Cámara de los Lores tiene más de 1.000 miembros. Se les llama **Lords** y pueden ser aristócratas, obispos, etc, o bien ciudadanos escogidos para el cargo por su contribución a la sociedad británica.

El gobierno

El primer ministro (the **Prime Minister**) escoge a unos 20 ministros (**ministers**) para formar su gabinete (**Cabinet**). La mayoría de los miembros del gabinete están a cargo de un ministerio, p. ej., el **Chancellor of the Exchequer** está al frente del Ministerio de Hacienda (the **Treasury**), y el **Foreign Secretary** dirige el Ministerio de Asuntos Exteriores (the **Foreign Office**).

Las elecciones

Cada cinco años se celebran las elecciones generales (a **general election**), y los habitantes de cada distrito electoral (**constituency**) votan a un político para que les represente en el parlamento. También se celebran elecciones locales (**local elections**), en las que la gente vota a un concejal para el ayuntamiento de su ciudad, barrio o distrito. Todas las personas mayores de 18 años tienen derecho a votar.

Aa

A, a /eɪ/ *n* (*pl* **A's**, **a's** /eɪz/) **1** A, a: *A for Andrew* A de Andrés ◊ *'bean' (spelt) with an 'a'* bean con "a" ◊ *'Awful' begins/starts with an 'A'.* "Awful" empieza por "A". ◊ *'Data' ends in an 'a'.* "Data" termina en "a". **2** (*Educ*) sobresaliente: *to get (an) A in English* sacar un sobresaliente en lengua y literatura inglesa **3** (*Mús*) la

a /ə, eɪ/ (*tb* **an** /ən, æn/) *art indef* ☛ **A, an** corresponde al español *un, una* excepto en los siguientes casos: **1** (*números*): *a hundred and twenty people* ciento veinte personas **2** (*profesiones*): *My mother is a solicitor.* Mi madre es abogada. **3** por: *200 words a minute* 200 palabras por minuto ◊ *50p a dozen* 50 peniques la docena **4** (*con desconocidos*) un(a) tal: *Do we know a Tim Smith?* ¿Conocemos a un tal Tim Smith?

aback /əˈbæk/ *adv Ver* TAKE

abandon /əˈbændən/ *vt* abandonar: *We abandoned the attempt.* Abandonamos el intento. ◊ *an abandoned baby/car/village* un bebé/coche/pueblo abandonado

abbess /ˈæbes/ *n* abadesa

abbey /ˈæbi/ *n* (*pl* **-eys**) abadía

abbot /ˈæbət/ *n* abad

abbreviate /əˈbriːvieɪt/ *vt* abreviar **abbreviation** *n* **1** abreviación **2** abreviatura

ABC /ˌeɪ biː ˈsiː/ *n* **1** abecedario **2** abecé

abdicate /ˈæbdɪkeɪt/ *vt, vi* abdicar: *to abdicate (all) responsibility* declinar toda responsabilidad

abdomen /ˈæbdəmən/ *n* abdomen **abdominal** /æbˈdɒmɪnl/ *adj* abdominal

abduct /əbˈdʌkt, æb-/ *vt* secuestrar **abduction** *n* secuestro

abide /əˈbaɪd/ *vt* soportar: *I can't abide them.* No los puedo soportar. PHR V **to abide by sth 1** (*veredicto, decisión*) acatar algo **2** (*promesa*) cumplir con algo

ability /əˈbɪləti/ *n* (*pl* **-ies**) **1** (*talento*) capacidad, aptitud: *her ability to accept change* su capacidad para asumir los cambios ◊ *Despite his ability as a dancer...* A pesar de sus aptitudes como bailarín... **2** habilidad

ablaze /əˈbleɪz/ *adj* **1** en llamas: *to set sth ablaze* prender fuego a algo **2 to be ~ with sth** resplandecer de algo: *The garden was ablaze with flowers.* El jardín estaba inundado de flores.

able[1] /ˈeɪbl/ *adj* **to be ~ to do sth** poder hacer algo: *Will he be able to help you?* ¿Podrá ayudarte? ◊ *They are not yet able to swim.* No saben nadar todavía. ☛ *Ver nota en* CAN[2] LOC *Ver* BRING

able[2] /ˈeɪbl/ *adj* (**abler**, **ablest**) capaz

abnormal /æbˈnɔːml/ *adj* anormal **abnormality** /ˌæbnɔːˈmæləti/ *n* (*pl* **-ies**) anormalidad

aboard /əˈbɔːd/ *adv, prep* a bordo: *aboard the ship* a bordo del barco ◊ *Welcome aboard.* Bienvenidos a bordo.

abode /əˈbəʊd/ *n* (*fml*) morada LOC *Ver* FIXED

abolish /əˈbɒlɪʃ/ *vt* abolir **abolition** *n* abolición

abominable /əˈbɒmɪnəbl; *USA* -mən-/ *adj* abominable

abort /əˈbɔːt/ **1** *vt, vi* (*Med*) abortar **2** *vt* abortar: *They aborted the launch.* Detuvieron el lanzamiento.

abortion /əˈbɔːʃn/ *n* aborto (*intencionado*): *to have an abortion* abortar ☛ *Comparar con* MISCARRIAGE

abortive /əˈbɔːtɪv/ *adj* fracasado: *an abortive coup/attempt* un golpe de estado/intento fracasado

abound /əˈbaʊnd/ *vi* ~ (**with sth**) abundar (en algo)

about[1] /əˈbaʊt/ *adv* **1** (*tb* **around**) más o menos: *about the same height as you* más o menos de tu misma altura **2** (*tb* **around**) hacia: *I got home at about half past seven.* Llegué a casa hacia las siete y media. ☛ *Ver nota en* AROUND[1] **3** (*tb* **around**) por aquí: *She's somewhere about.* Está por aquí. ◊ *There are no jobs about at the moment.* De momento no sale ningún trabajo. **4** casi: *Dinner's about ready.* La cena está casi lista. LOC **to be about to do sth** estar a punto de hacer algo

about[2] /əˈbaʊt/ (*tb* **around**, **round**) *part*

adv **1** de un lado a otro: *I could hear people moving about.* Oía gente yendo de un lado para otro. **2** aquí y allá: *People were standing about in the street.* Había gente parada por la calle. ☛ Para los usos de **about** en PHRASAL VERBS ver las entradas de los verbos correspondientes, p.ej. **to lie about** en LIE².

about³ /əˈbaʊt/ *prep* **1** por: *papers strewn about the room* papeles esparcidos por la habitación ◊ *She's somewhere about the place.* Anda por aquí. **2** sobre: *a book about flowers* un libro sobre flores ◊ *What's the book about?* ¿De qué trata el libro? **3** [*con adjetivos*]: *angry/happy about sth* enfadado por/contento con algo **4** (*característica*): *There's something about her I like.* Tiene algo que me atrae. LOC **how/what about?**: *What about his car?* ¿Y su coche? ◊ *How about going swimming?* ¿Qué os parece ir a nadar?

above¹ /əˈbʌv/ *adv* arriba: *the people in the flat above* la gente del piso de arriba ◊ *children aged eleven and above* niños de once años y mayores

above² /əˈbʌv/ *prep* **1** por encima de, más arriba de: *1000 metres above sea level* 1.000 metros por encima del nivel del mar ◊ *I live in a house above the village.* Vivo en una casa más arriba del pueblo. **2** más de: *above 50%* más del 50% LOC **above all** sobre todo

abrasive /əˈbreɪsɪv/ *adj* **1** (*persona*) brusco y desagradable **2** (*superficie*) áspero: *abrasive paper* papel de lija

abreast /əˈbrest/ *adv* ~ (**of sth/sb**): *to cycle two abreast* andar en bicicleta parejo con algn ◊ *A car came abreast of us.* Un coche se puso a nuestra altura. LOC **to be/keep abreast of sth** estar/mantenerse al corriente de algo

abroad /əˈbrɔːd/ *adv* en el extranjero: *to go abroad* ir al extranjero ◊ *Have you ever been abroad?* ¿Has estado en el extranjero?

abrupt /əˈbrʌpt/ *adj* **1** (*cambio*) repentino, brusco **2** (*persona*) brusco, cortante: *He was very abrupt with me.* Fue muy brusco conmigo.

absence /ˈæbsəns/ *n* **1** ausencia: *absences due to illness* ausencias por enfermedad **2** [*sing*] ausencia, falta: *the complete absence of noise* la total ausencia de ruido ◊ *in the absence of new evidence* a falta de nuevas pruebas LOC *Ver* CONSPICUOUS

absent /ˈæbsənt/ *adj* **1** ausente **2** distraído

absentee /ˌæbsənˈtiː/ *n* ausente

absent-minded /ˌæbsənt ˈmaɪndɪd/ *adj* distraído

absolute /ˈæbsəluːt/ *adj* absoluto

absolutely /ˈæbsəluːtli/ *adv* **1** absolutamente: *You are absolutely right.* Tienes toda la razón. ◊ *Are you absolutely sure/certain that…?* ¿Estás completamente seguro de que…? ◊ *It's absolutely essential/necessary that…* Es imprescindible que… **2** [*en negativa*]: *absolutely nothing* nada en absoluto **3** (*mostrando acuerdo con algn*): *Oh absolutely!* ¡Sin duda!

absolve /əbˈzɒlv/ *vt* ~ **sb** (**from/of sth**) absolver a algn (de algo)

absorb /əbˈsɔːb/ *vt* **1** absorber, asimilar: *The root hairs absorb the water.* Los pelos de la raíz absorben el agua. ◊ *easily absorbed into the bloodstream* fácilmente asimilado por la sangre ◊ *to absorb information* asimilar información **2** amortiguar: *to absorb the shock* amortiguar el golpe

absorbed /əbˈsɔːbd/ *adj* absorto

absorbing /əbˈsɔːbɪŋ/ *adj* absorbente (*libro, película, etc*)

absorption /əbˈsɔːpʃn/ *n* **1** (*líquidos*) absorción **2** (*minerales, ideas*) asimilación

abstain /əbˈsteɪn/ *vi* ~ (**from sth**) abstenerse (de algo)

abstract /ˈæbstrækt/ ◆ *adj* abstracto ◆ *n* (*Arte*) obra de arte abstracto LOC **in the abstract** en abstracto

absurd /əbˈsɜːd/ *adj* absurdo: *How absurd!* ¡Qué disparate! ◊ *You look absurd in that hat.* Estás ridículo con ese sombrero. **absurdity** *n* (*pl* **-ies**) absurdo: *our absurdities and inconsistencies* nuestros absurdos e incoherencias ◊ *the absurdity of…* lo absurdo de…

abundance /əˈbʌndəns/ *n* abundancia

abundant /əˈbʌndənt/ *adj* abundante

abuse /əˈbjuːz/ ◆ *vt* **1** abusar de: *to abuse your power* abusar de su poder **2** insultar **3** maltratar ◆ /əˈbjuːs/ *n* **1** abuso: *human rights abuses* abusos contra los derechos humanos **2** [*incontable*] insultos: *They shouted abuse at* *him.* Le gritaron insultos. **3** malos tratos **abusive** *adj* insultante, grosero

academic /ˌækəˈdemɪk/ *adj* **1** académico **2** especulativo

academy /əˈkædəmi/ *n* (*pl* **-ies**) academia

accelerate /əkˈseləreɪt/ *vt, vi* acelerar **acceleration** *n* **1** aceleración **2** (*vehículo*) reprise **accelerator** *n* acelerador

accent /ˈæksent, ˈæksənt/ *n* **1** acento **2** énfasis **3** tilde

accentuate /əkˈsentʃueɪt/ *vt* **1** acentuar **2** resaltar **3** agravar

accept /əkˈsept/ **1** *vt, vi* aceptar **2** *vt, vi* admitir: *I've been accepted by the University.* Me han admitido en la universidad. **3** *vt* (*máquina*): *The machine only accepts 10p coins.* La máquina sólo funciona con monedas de diez peniques. LOC *Ver* FACE VALUE

acceptable /əkˈseptəbl/ *adj* ~ (**to sb**) aceptable (para algn)

acceptance /əkˈseptəns/ *n* **1** aceptación **2** aprobación

access /ˈækses/ *n* ~ (**to sth/sb**) acceso (a algo/algn)

accessible /əkˈsesəbl/ *adj* accesible

accessory /əkˈsesəri/ *n* (*pl* **-ies**) **1** accesorio **2** [*gen pl*] (*ropa*) complemento LOC **accessory** (**to sth**) cómplice (de algo)

accident /ˈæksɪdənt/ *n* **1** accidente **2** casualidad LOC **by accident 1** accidentalmente **2** por casualidad **3** por descuido **accidental** /ˌæksɪˈdentl/ *adj* **1** accidental **2** casual

acclaim /əˈkleɪm/ ◆ *vt* aclamar ◆ *n* [*incontable*] elogios

accommodate /əˈkɒmədeɪt/ *vt* **1** alojar **2** (*vehículo*): *The car can accommodate four people.* El coche es de cuatro plazas.

accommodation /əˌkɒməˈdeɪʃn/ *n* **1** (*GB*) alojamiento **2** vivienda

accompaniment /əˈkʌmpənimənt/ *n* acompañamiento

accompany /əˈkʌmpəni/ *vt* (*pret, pp* **-ied**) acompañar

accomplice /əˈkʌmplɪs; *USA* əˈkɒm-/ *n* cómplice

accomplish /əˈkʌmplɪʃ; *USA* əˈkɒm-/ *vt* llevar a cabo

accomplished /əˈkʌmplɪʃt/ *adj* consumado

accomplishment /əˈkʌmplɪʃmənt/ *n* **1** logro **2** talento

accord /əˈkɔːd/ ◆ *n* acuerdo LOC **in accord** (**with sth/sb**) en concordancia (con algo/algn) **of your own accord** por decisión propia ◆ **1** *vi* ~ **with sth** (*fml*) concordar con algo **2** *vt* (*fml*) otorgar, conceder

accordance /əˈkɔːdns/ *n* LOC **in accordance with sth** de acuerdo con algo

accordingly /əˈkɔːdɪŋli/ *adv* **1** por lo tanto, por consiguiente **2** en consecuencia: *to act accordingly* obrar en consecuencia

according to *prep* según

accordion /əˈkɔːdiən/ *n* acordeón

account /əˈkaʊnt/ ◆ *n* **1** (*Fin, Com*) cuenta: *current account* cuenta corriente **2** factura **3 accounts** [*pl*] contabilidad **4** relato, relación LOC **by/from all accounts** por lo que dicen **of no account** sin ninguna importancia **on account of sth** a causa de algo **on no account; not on any account** bajo ningún concepto, de ninguna manera **on this/that account** según esto/eso **to take account of sth; to take sth into account** tener algo en cuenta **to take sth/sb into account** considerar algo/a algn ◆ *vi* ~ (**to sb**) **for sth** rendir cuentas (a algn) de algo

accountable /əˈkaʊntəbl/ *adj* ~ (**to sb**) (**for sth**) responsable (ante algn) (de algo) **accountability** /əkaʊntəˈbɪləti/ *n* responsabilidad de la que hay que dar cuenta

accountancy /əˈkaʊntənsi/ *n* contabilidad

accountant /əˈkaʊntənt/ *n* contable

accumulate /əˈkjuːmjəleɪt/ *vt, vi* acumular(se) **accumulation** *n* acumulación

accuracy /ˈækjərəsi/ *n* precisión

accurate /ˈækjərət/ *adj* exacto: *an accurate shot* un disparo certero

accusation /ˌækjuˈzeɪʃn/ *n* acusación

accuse /əˈkjuːz/ *vt* ~ **sb** (**of sth**) acusar a algn (de algo): *He was accused of murder.* Fue acusado de asesinato. **the accused** *n* (*pl* **the accused**) el acusado, la acusada **accusingly** *adv*: *to look accusingly at sb* lanzar una mirada acusadora a algn

accustomed /ə'kʌstəmd/ *adj* ~ **to sth** acostumbrado a algo: *to be accustomed to sth* estar acostumbrado a algo ◊ *to become/get/grow accustomed to sth* acostumbrarse a algo

ace /eɪs/ *n* as

ache /eɪk/ ◆ *n* dolor *Ver tb* BACKACHE, HEADACHE, TOOTHACHE ◆ *vi* doler

achieve /ə'tʃiːv/ *vt* **1** (*objetivo, éxito*) alcanzar **2** (*resultados*) conseguir **achievement** *n* logro

aching /'eɪkɪŋ/ *adj* dolorido

acid /'æsɪd/ ◆ *n* ácido ◆ *adj* **1** (*sabor*) ácido, agrio **2** (*tb* **acidic**) ácido **acidity** /ə'sɪdəti/ *n* acidez

acid rain *n* lluvia ácida

acknowledge /ək'nɒlɪdʒ/ *vt* **1** reconocer **2** (*carta*) acusar recibo de **3** darse por enterado **acknowledg(e)ment** *n* **1** reconocimiento **2** acuse de recibo **3** agradecimiento (*en un libro, etc*)

acne /'ækni/ *n* acné

acorn /'eɪkɔːn/ *n* bellota

acoustic /ə'kuːstɪk/ *adj* acústico **acoustics** *n* [*pl*] acústica

acquaintance /ə'kweɪntəns/ *n* **1** amistad **2** conocido LOC **to make sb's acquaintance/to make the acquaintance of sb** (*fml*) conocer a algn (*por primera vez*) **acquainted** *adj* familiarizado: *to become/get acquainted with sb* (llegar a) conocer a algn

acquiesce /ˌækwi'es/ *vi* (*fml*) ~ **(in sth)** consentir (algo/en algo); aceptar (algo) **acquiescence** *n* consentimiento

acquire /ə'kwaɪə(r)/ *vt* **1** (*conocimientos, posesiones*) adquirir **2** (*información*) obtener **3** (*reputación*) adquirir, ganarse **4** hacerse con, apoderarse de

acquisition /ˌækwɪ'zɪʃn/ *n* adquisición

acquit /ə'kwɪt/ *vt* (**-tt-**) ~ **sb (of sth)** absolver a algn (de algo) **acquittal** *n* absolución

acre /'eɪkə(r)/ *n* acre

acrobat /'ækrəbæt/ *n* acróbata

across /ə'krɒs; *USA* ə'krɔːs/ *part adv, prep* **1** [*suele traducirse por un verbo*] de un lado a otro: *to swim across* cruzar nadando ◊ *to walk across the border* cruzar la frontera a pie ◊ *to take the path across the fields* tomar el camino que atraviesa los campos **2** al otro lado: *We were across in no time.* Llegamos al otro lado en un periquete. ◊ *from across the room* desde el otro lado de la habitación **3** sobre, a lo largo de: *a bridge across the river* un puente sobre el río ◊ *A branch lay across the path.* Había una rama atravesada en el camino. **4** de ancho: *The river is half a mile across.* El río tiene media milla de ancho. ☛ Para los usos de **across** en PHRASAL VERBS ver las entradas de los verbos correspondientes, p.ej. **to come across** en COME.

acrylic /ə'krɪlɪk/ *adj, n* acrílico

act /ækt/ ◆ *n* **1** acto: *an act of violence/kindness* un acto de violencia/amabilidad **2** (*Teat*) acto **3** número: *a circus act* un número de circo **4** (*Jur*) decreto LOC **in the act of doing sth** en el momento de hacer algo **to get your act together** (*coloq*) organizarse **to put on an act** (*coloq*) fingir ◆ **1** *vi* actuar **2** *vi* comportarse **3** *vt* (*Teat*) hacer el papel de LOC *Ver* FOOL

acting¹ /'æktɪŋ/ *n* teatro: *his acting career* su carrera como actor ◊ *Her acting was awful.* Actuó muy mal.

acting² /'æktɪŋ/ *adj* en funciones: *He was acting chairman at the meeting.* Actuó como presidente en la reunión. ☛ Sólo se usa antes de sustantivo.

action /'ækʃn/ *n* **1** acción **2** medidas: *Drastic action is needed.* Hay que tomar medidas drásticas. **3** acto **4** (*Mil*) acción: *to go into action* entrar en acción LOC **in action** en acción **out of action**: *This machine is out of action.* Esta máquina no funciona. **to put sth into action** poner algo en práctica **to take action** tomar medidas *Ver tb* COURSE

activate /'æktɪveɪt/ *vt* activar

active /'æktɪv/ *adj* **1** activo: *to take an active part in sth* participar activamente en algo ◊ *to take an active interest in sth* interesarse vivamente por algo **2** (*volcán*) en actividad

activity /æk'tɪvəti/ *n* (*pl* **-ies**) **1** actividad **2** bullicio

actor /'æktə(r)/ *n* actor, actriz ☛ *Ver nota en* ACTRESS

actress /'æktrəs/ *n* actriz

Hay mucha gente que prefiere el término **actor** tanto para el femenino como para el masculino, aunque a veces para diferenciar se usa **female actor**.

actual /ˈæktʃuəl/ *adj* **1** exacto: *What were his actual words?* ¿Qué es lo que dijo exactamente? **2** verdadero: *based on actual events* basado en hechos reales **3** propiamente dicho: *the actual city centre* el centro propiamente dicho ☛ *Comparar con* CURRENT 1, PRESENT-DAY LOC **in actual fact** en realidad

actually /ˈæktʃuəli/ *adv* **1** en realidad, de hecho: *He's actually very bright.* La verdad es que es muy inteligente. **2** exactamente: *What did she actually say?* ¿Qué dijo exactamente? **3** *Actually, my name's Sue, not Ann.* A propósito, me llamo Sue, no Ann. **4** (*para dar énfasis*): *You actually met her?* ¿De verdad la conociste? **5** hasta: *He actually expected me to leave.* Hasta esperaba que me fuera. ☛ *Comparar con* AT PRESENT *en* PRESENT, CURRENTLY *en* CURRENT

acupuncture /ˈækjʊpʌŋktʃə(r)/ *n* acupuntura

acute /əˈkjuːt/ *adj* **1** extremo: *to become more acute* agudizarse **2** agudo: *acute angle* ángulo agudo ◊ *acute appendicitis* apendicitis aguda **3** (*remordimiento*) profundo

AD /ˌeɪˈdiː/ *abrev* **anno domini** después de Cristo

ad /æd/ *n* (*coloq*) **advertisement** anuncio (*publicidad*)

adamant /ˈædəmənt/ *adj* ~ (**about/in sth**) firme, categórico en cuanto a algo: *He was adamant about staying behind.* Se empeñó en quedarse.

adapt /əˈdæpt/ *vt, vi* adaptar(se) **adaptable** *adj* **1** (*persona*): *to learn to be adaptable* aprender a adaptarse **2** (*aparatos, etc*) adaptable **adaptation** *n* adaptación

adaptor /əˈdæptə(r)/ *n* ladrón (*Elec*), adaptador

add /æd/ *vt* añadir LOC **to add A and B together** sumar A y B PHR V **to add sth on (to sth)** añadir algo (a algo) **to add to sth 1** aumentar algo **2** ampliar algo **to add up** (*coloq*) encajar: *His story doesn't add up.* Hay cosas en su relato que no encajan. **to add (sth) up** sumar (algo) **to add up to sth** ascender a algo: *The bill adds up to £40.* La cuenta asciende a 40 libras.

adder /ˈædə(r)/ *n* víbora

addict /ˈædɪkt/ *n* adicto, -a: *drug addict* toxicómano **addicted** /əˈdɪktɪd/ *adj* adicto **addiction** /əˈdɪkʃn/ *n* adicción **addictive** /əˈdɪktɪv/ *adj* adictivo

addition /əˈdɪʃn/ *n* **1** incorporación **2** adquisición **3** (*Mat*): *Children are taught addition and subtraction.* Los niños aprenden a sumar y a restar. LOC **in addition** por añadidura **in addition (to sth)** además (de algo) **additional** *adj* adicional

additive /ˈædətɪv/ *n* aditivo

address /əˈdres; *USA* ˈædres/ ◆ *n* **1** dirección, señas: *address book* libreta de direcciones **2** discurso LOC *Ver* FIXED ◆ *vt* **1** (*carta, etc*) dirigir **2** ~ **sb** dirigirse a algn **3** ~ (**yourself to**) **sth** hacer frente a algo

adept /əˈdept/ *adj* hábil

adequate /ˈædɪkwət/ *adj* **1** adecuado **2** aceptable

adhere /ədˈhɪə(r)/ *vi* (*fml*) **1** adherirse **2** ~ **to sth** (*creencia, etc*) observar algo **adherence** *n* ~ (**to sth**) **1** adherencia (a algo) **2** observación (de algo) **adherent** *n* adepto, -a

adhesive /ədˈhiːsɪv/ *adj, n* adhesivo

adjacent /əˈdʒeɪsnt/ *adj* adyacente

adjective /ˈædʒɪktɪv/ *n* adjetivo

adjoining /əˈdʒɔɪnɪŋ/ *adj* contiguo, colindante

adjourn /əˈdʒɜːn/ **1** *vt* aplazar **2** *vt, vi* (*reunión, sesión*) suspender(se)

adjust /əˈdʒʌst/ **1** *vt* ajustar, arreglar **2** *vt, vi* ~ (**sth**) (**to sth**) adaptar algo (a algo); adaptarse (a algo) **adjustment** *n* **1** ajuste, modificación **2** adaptación

administer /ədˈmɪnɪstə(r)/ *vt* **1** administrar **2** (*organización*) dirigir **3** (*castigo*) aplicar

administration /ədˌmɪnɪˈstreɪʃn/ *n* administración, dirección

administrative /ədˈmɪnɪstrətɪv/ *adj* administrativo

administrator /ədˈmɪnɪstreɪtə(r)/ *n* administrador, -ora

admirable /ˈædmərəbl/ *adj* admirable

admiral /ˈædmərəl/ *n* almirante

admiration /ˌædməˈreɪʃn/ *n* admiración

admire /ədˈmaɪə(r)/ *vt* admirar, elogiar **admirer** *n* admirador, -ora **admiring** *adj* lleno de admiración

admission /ədˈmɪʃn/ *n* **1** entrada,

admisión **2** reconocimiento **3** (*hospital*) ingreso

admit /əd'mɪt/ (-tt-) **1** *vt* ~ **sb** dejar entrar, admitir, ingresar a algn **2** *vt, vi* ~ (**to**) **sth** confesar algo (*crimen*), reconocer algo (*error*) **admittedly** *adv*: *Admittedly*... Hay que admitir que...

adolescent /ˌædə'lesnt/ *adj, n* adolescente **adolescence** *n* adolescencia

adopt /ə'dɒpt/ *vt* adoptar **adopted** *adj* adoptivo **adoption** *n* adopción

adore /ə'dɔː(r)/ *vt* adorar: *I adore cats.* Me encantan los gatos.

adorn /ə'dɔːn/ *vt* adornar

adrenalin /ə'drenəlɪn/ *n* adrenalina

adrift /ə'drɪft/ *adj* a la deriva

adult /'ædʌlt, ə'dʌlt/ ◆ *adj* adulto, mayor de edad ◆ *n* adulto, -a

adultery /ə'dʌltəri/ *n* adulterio

adulthood /'ædʌlthʊd/ *n* madurez

advance /əd'vɑːns; *USA* -'væns/ ◆ *n* **1** avance **2** (*sueldo*) adelanto LOC **in advance 1** de antemano **2** con antelación **3** por adelantado ◆ *adj* anticipado: *advance warning* previo aviso ◆ **1** *vi* avanzar **2** *vt* hacer avanzar **advanced** *adj* avanzado **advancement** *n* **1** desarrollo **2** (*trabajo*) ascenso

advantage /əd'vɑːntɪdʒ; *USA* -'væn-/ *n* **1** ventaja **2** provecho LOC **to take advantage of sth 1** aprovecharse de algo **2** sacar provecho de algo **to take advantage of sth/sb** abusar de algo/algn **advantageous** /ˌædvən'teɪdʒəs/ *adj* ventajoso

advent /'ædvent/ *n* **1** advenimiento **2** **Advent** (*Relig*) adviento

adventure /əd'ventʃə(r)/ *n* aventura **adventurer** *n* aventurero, -a **adventurous** *adj* **1** aventurero **2** aventurado **3** audaz

adverb /'ædvɜːb/ *n* adverbio

adversary /'ædvəsəri; *USA* -seri/ *n* (*pl* **-ies**) adversario, -a

adverse /'ædvɜːs/ *adj* **1** adverso **2** (*crítica*) negativo **adversely** *adv* negativamente

adversity /əd'vɜːsəti/ *n* (*pl* **-ies**) adversidad

advert /'ædvɜːt/ *n* (*GB, coloq*) anuncio (*publicidad*)

advertise /'ædvətaɪz/ **1** *vt* anunciar **2** *vi* hacer publicidad **3** *vi* ~ **for sth/sb** buscar algo/a algn **advertisement** /əd'vɜːtɪsmənt; *USA* ˌædvər'taɪzmənt/ (*tb* **advert, ad**) *n* ~ (**for sth/sb**) anuncio (de algo/algn) **advertising** *n* **1** publicidad: *advertising campaign* campaña publicitaria **2** anuncios

advice /əd'vaɪs/ *n* [*incontable*] consejo(s): *a piece of advice* un consejo ◇ *I asked for her advice.* Le pedí consejo. ◇ *to seek/take legal advice* consultar a un abogado

advisable /əd'vaɪzəbl/ *adj* aconsejable

advise /əd'vaɪz/ *vt, vi* **1** aconsejar, recomendar: *to advise sb to do sth* aconsejar a algn que haga algo ◇ *You would be well advised to*... Sería prudente... **2** asesorar **adviser** (*USA* **advisor**) *n* consejero, -a, asesor, -ora **advisory** *adj* consultivo

advocacy /'ædvəkəsi/ *n* ~ **of sth** apoyo a algo

advocate /'ædvəkeɪt/ *vt* abogar por

aerial /'eəriəl/ ◆ *n* (*USA* **antenna**) antena ◆ *adj* aéreo

aerobics /eə'rəʊbɪks/ *n* [*sing*] aerobic

aerodynamic /ˌeərəʊdaɪ'næmɪk/ *adj* aerodinámico

aeroplane /'eərəpleɪn/ (*USA* **airplane**) *n* avión

aesthetic /iːs'θetɪk/ (*USA* **esthetic** /es'θetɪk/) *adj* estético

affair /ə'feə(r)/ *n* **1** asunto: *the Watergate affair* el caso Watergate **2** acontecimiento **3** aventura (amorosa), lío: *to have an affair with sb* estar liado con algn LOC *Ver* STATE[1]

affect /ə'fekt/ *vt* **1** afectar, influir en **2** conmover, emocionar ☛ *Comparar con* EFFECT

affection /ə'fekʃn/ *n* cariño **affectionate** *adj* ~ (**towards sth/sb**) cariñoso (con algo/algn)

affinity /ə'fɪnəti/ *n* (*pl* **-ies**) **1** afinidad **2** simpatía

affirm /ə'fɜːm/ *vt* afirmar, sostener

afflict /ə'flɪkt/ *vt* afligir: *to be afflicted with* sufrir de

affluent /'æfluənt/ *adj* rico, opulento **affluence** *n* riqueza, opulencia

afford /ə'fɔːd/ *vt* **1** permitirse (el lujo): *Can you afford it?* ¿Te lo puedes permitir? **2** proporcionar **affordable** *adj* asequible

afield /ə'fiːld/ *adv* LOC **far/further afield** muy lejos/más allá: *from as far* *afield as...* desde lugares tan lejanos como...

afloat /ə'fləʊt/ *adj* a flote

afraid /ə'freɪd/ *adj* **1 to be ~ (of sth/sb)** tener miedo (de algo/algn) **2 to be ~ to do sth** no atreverse a hacer algo **3 to be ~ for sb** temer por algn LOC **I'm afraid (that...)** me temo que..., lo siento, pero...: *I'm afraid so/not.* Me temo que sí/no.

afresh /ə'freʃ/ *adv* de nuevo

after /'ɑːftə(r); *USA* 'æf-/ ◆ *adv* **1** después: *soon after* poco después ◊ *the day after* al día siguiente **2** detrás: *She came running after.* Llegó corriendo detrás. ◆ *prep* **1** después de: *after doing your homework* después de hacer los deberes ◊ *after lunch* después de comer ◊ *the day after tomorrow* pasado mañana **2** detrás de, tras: *time after time* una y otra vez **3** (*búsqueda*): *They're after me.* Me están buscando. ◊ *What are you after?* ¿Qué estás buscando? ◊ *She's after a job in advertising.* Está buscando un trabajo en publicidad. **4** *We named him after you.* Le pusimos tu nombre. LOC **after all** después de todo, al fin y al cabo ◆ *conj* después de que

aftermath /'ɑːftəmɑːθ; *USA* 'æf-/ *n* [*sing*] secuelas LOC **in the aftermath of** en el periodo subsiguiente a

afternoon /ˌɑːftə'nuːn; *USA* ˌæf-/ *n* tarde: *tomorrow afternoon* mañana por la tarde LOC **good afternoon** buenas tardes ☛ *Ver nota en* MORNING, TARDE

afterthought /'ɑːftəθɔːt; *USA* 'æf-/ *n* ocurrencia tardía

afterwards /'ɑːftəwədz; *USA* 'æf-/ (*USA tb* **afterward**) *adv* después: *shortly/soon afterwards* poco después

again /ə'gen, ə'geɪn/ *adv* otra vez, de nuevo: *once again* una vez más ◊ *never again* nunca más ◊ *Don't do it again.* No vuelvas a hacerlo. LOC **again and again** una y otra vez **then/there again** por otra parte *Ver tb* NOW, OVER, TIME, YET

against /ə'genst, ə'geɪnst/ *prep* **1** (*contacto*) contra: *Put the piano against the wall.* Pon el piano contra la pared. **2** (*oposición*) en contra de, contra: *We were rowing against the current.* Remábamos contra la corriente. **3** (*contraste*) sobre: *The mountains stood out against the blue sky.* Las montañas se recortaban sobre el azul del cielo. ☛ Para los usos de **against** en PHRASAL VERBS ver las entradas de los verbos correspondientes, p.ej. **to come up against** en COME.

age /eɪdʒ/ ◆ *n* **1** edad: *to be six years of age* tener seis años **2** vejez: *It improves with age.* Mejora con el tiempo. **3** época, era **4** eternidad: *It's ages since I saw her.* Hace años que no la veo. LOC **age of consent** edad legal para mantener relaciones sexuales **to come of age** alcanzar la mayoría de edad **under age** demasiado joven, menor de edad *Ver tb* LOOK[1] ◆ *vt, vi* (*pt pres* **ageing** *o* **aging** *pret, pp* **aged** /eɪdʒd/) (hacer) envejecer

aged /'eɪdʒd/ ◆ *adj* **1** de ...años de edad: *He died aged 81.* Murió a la edad de 81 años. **2** /'eɪdʒɪd/ anciano ◆ /'eɪdʒɪd/ *n* [*pl*] **the aged** los ancianos

ageing (*tb* **aging**) /'eɪdʒɪŋ/ ◆ *adj* **1** avejentado **2** (*irón*) no tan joven ◆ *n* envejecimiento

agency /'eɪdʒənsi/ *n* (*pl* **-ies**) agencia, organismo

agenda /ə'dʒendə/ *n* orden del día

agent /'eɪdʒənt/ *n* agente, representante

aggravate /'ægrəveɪt/ *vt* **1** agravar **2** fastidiar **aggravating** *adj* irritante **aggravation** *n* **1** fastidio **2** agravamiento

aggression /ə'greʃn/ *n* [*incontable*] agresión, agresividad: *an act of aggression* un asalto

aggressive /ə'gresɪv/ *adj* agresivo

agile /'ædʒaɪl; *USA* 'ædʒl/ *adj* ágil **agility** /ə'dʒɪləti/ *n* agilidad

aging *Ver* AGEING

agitated /'ædʒɪteɪtɪd/ *adj* agitado: *to get agitated* desazonarse **agitation** *n* **1** inquietud, perturbación **2** (*Pol*) agitación

ago /ə'gəʊ/ *adv* hace: *ten years ago* hace diez años ◊ *How long ago did she die?* ¿Cuánto hace que murió? ◊ *as long ago as 1950* ya en 1950

Ago se usa con el pasado simple y el pasado continuo, pero nunca con el pretérito perfecto: *She arrived a few minutes ago.* Ha llegado/Llegó hace unos minutos. Con el pretérito pluscuamperfecto se usa **before** o **earlier**:

She had arrived two days before. Había llegado hacía dos días/dos días antes. ☛ *Ver ejemplos en* FOR 3

agonize, -ise /ˈæɡənaɪz/ *vi* ~ (**about/over sth**) atormentarse (por/con motivo de algo): *to agonize over a decision* pasar muchos apuros tratando de decidir algo **agonized, -ised** *adj* angustiado **agonizing, -ising** *adj* **1** angustioso, acongojante **2** (*dolor*) horroroso

agony /ˈæɡəni/ *n* (*pl* **-ies**) **1** *to be in agony* tener unos dolores horrorosos **2** (*coloq*): *It was agony!* ¡Fue una pesadilla!

agree /əˈɡriː/ **1** *vi* ~ (**with sb**) (**on/about sth**) estar de acuerdo (con algn) (en/sobre algo): *They agreed with me on all the major points.* Estuvieron de acuerdo conmigo en todos los puntos fundamentales. **2** *vi* ~ (**to sth**) consentir (en algo); acceder (a algo): *He agreed to let me go.* Consintió en que me fuera. **3** *vt* acordar: *It was agreed that...* Se acordó que... **4** *vi* llegar a un acuerdo **5** *vi* concordar **6** *vt* (*informe, etc*) aprobar PHR V **to agree with sb** sentarle bien a algn (*comida, clima*): *The climate didn't agree with him.* El clima no le sentaba bien. **agreeable** *adj* **1** agradable **2** ~ (**to sth**) conforme (con algo)

agreement /əˈɡriːmənt/ *n* **1** conformidad, acuerdo **2** convenio, acuerdo **3** (*Com*) contrato LOC **in agreement with** de acuerdo con

agriculture /ˈæɡrɪkʌltʃə(r)/ *n* agricultura **agricultural** /ˌæɡrɪˈkʌltʃərəl/ *adj* agrícola

ah! /ɑː/ *interj* ¡ah!

ahead /əˈhed/ ◆ *part adv* **1** hacia adelante: *She looked (straight) ahead.* Miró hacia adelante. **2** próximo: *during the months ahead* durante los próximos meses **3** por delante: *the road ahead* la carretera que se abre por delante de nosotros LOC **to be ahead** llevar ventaja ☛ Para los usos de **ahead** en PHRASAL VERBS ver las entradas de los verbos correspondientes, p.ej. **to press ahead** en PRESS. ◆ *prep* ~ **of sth/sb 1** (por) delante de algo/algn: *directly ahead of us* justo delante de nosotros **2** antes que algo/algn LOC **to be/get ahead of sth/sb** llevar ventaja a/adelantarse a algo/algn

aid /eɪd/ ◆ *n* **1** ayuda **2** auxilio: *to come/go to sb's aid* acudir en auxilio de algn **3** apoyo LOC **in aid of sth/sb** a beneficio de algo/algn ◆ *vt* ayudar, facilitar

Aids (*tb* **AIDS**) /eɪdz/ *abrev* **acquired immune deficiency syndrome** SIDA (=síndrome de inmunodeficiencia adquirida)

ailment /ˈeɪlmənt/ *n* achaque, dolencia

aim /eɪm/ ◆ **1** *vt, vi* **to aim** (**sth**) (**at sth/sb**) (*arma*) apuntar (a algo/algn) (con algo) **2** *vt* **to aim sth at sth/sb** dirigir algo contra algo/algn: *to be aimed at sth/doing sth* tener como objetivo algo/hacer algo ◊ *She aimed a blow at his head.* Le dirigió un golpe a la cabeza. **3** *vi* **to aim at/for sth** aspirar a algo **4** *vi* **to aim to do sth** tener la intención de hacer algo ◆ *n* **1** objetivo, propósito **2** puntería LOC **to take aim** apuntar

aimless /ˈeɪmləs/ *adj* sin objeto **aimlessly** *adv* sin rumbo

ain't /eɪnt/ (*coloq*) **1** = AM/IS/ARE NOT *Ver* BE **2** = HAS/HAVE NOT *Ver* HAVE

air /eə(r)/ ◆ *n* aire: *air fares* tarifas aéreas ◊ *air pollution* contaminación atmosférica LOC **by air** en avión, por vía aérea **in the air**: *There's something in the air.* Se está tramando algo. **to be on the air** estar en antena **to give yourself/put on airs** darse aires **(up) in the air**: *The plan is still up in the air.* El proyecto sigue en el aire. *Ver tb* BREATH, CLEAR, OPEN, THIN ◆ *vt* **1** airear **2** (*ropa*) orear **3** (*queja*) ventilar

air-conditioned /ˈeə kəndɪʃənd/ *adj* climatizado **air-conditioning** *n* aire acondicionado

aircraft /ˈeəkrɑːft/ *n* (*pl* **aircraft**) avión, aeronave

airfield /ˈeəfiːld/ *n* aeródromo

air force *n* [*v sing o pl*] fuerza(s) aérea(s)

air hostess *n* azafata

airline /ˈeəlaɪn/ *n* línea aérea **airliner** *n* avión (de pasajeros)

airmail /ˈeəmeɪl/ *n* correo aéreo: *by airmail* por vía aérea

airplane /ˈeəpleɪn/ *n* (*USA*) avión

airport /ˈeəpɔːt/ *n* aeropuerto

air raid *n* ataque aéreo

airtight /ˈeətaɪt/ *adj* hermético

aisle /aɪl/ *n* pasillo

akin /ə'kɪn/ *adj* ~ **to sth** semejante a algo

alarm /ə'lɑːm/ ◆ *n* **1** alarma: *to raise/ sound the alarm* dar la alarma **2** (*tb* **alarm clock**) (reloj) despertador ☛ *Ver dibujo en* RELOJ **3** (*tb* **alarm bell**) timbre de alarma LOC *Ver* FALSE ◆ *vt* alarmar: *to be/become/get alarmed* alarmarse **alarming** *adj* alarmante

alas! /ə'læs/ *interj* ¡por desgracia!

albeit /ˌɔːl'biːɪt/ *conj* (*fml*) aunque

album /'ælbəm/ *n* álbum

alcohol /'ælkəhɒl; *USA* -hɔːl/ *n* alcohol: *alcohol-free* sin alcohol **alcoholic** /ˌælkə'hɒlɪk/ *adj, n* alcohólico, -a

ale /eɪl/ *n* cerveza

alert /ə'lɜːt/ ◆ *adj* despierto ◆ *n* **1** alerta: *to be on the alert* estar alerta **2** aviso: *bomb alert* aviso de bomba ◆ *vt* ~ **sb (to sth)** alertar a algn (de algo)

algae /'ældʒiː, 'ælgi/ *n* [*v sing o pl*] algas

algebra /'ældʒɪbrə/ *n* álgebra

alibi /'æləbaɪ/ *n* coartada

alien /'eɪliən/ ◆ *adj* **1** extraño **2** extranjero **3** ~ **to sth/sb** ajeno a algo/algn ◆ *n* **1** (*fml*) extranjero, -a **2** extraterrestre **alienate** *vt* enajenar

alight /ə'laɪt/ *adj*: *to be alight* estar ardiendo LOC *Ver* SET[2]

align /ə'laɪn/ **1** *vt* ~ **sth (with sth)** alinear algo (con algo) **2** *v refl* ~ **yourself with sb** (*Pol*) aliarse con algn

alike /ə'laɪk/ ◆ *adj* **1** parecido: *to be/ look alike* parecerse **2** igual: *No two are alike.* No hay dos iguales. ◆ *adv* igual, del mismo modo: *It appeals to young and old alike.* Atrae a viejos y jóvenes por igual. LOC *Ver* GREAT

alive /ə'laɪv/ *adj* [*nunca delante de sustantivo*] **1** vivo, con vida: *to stay alive* sobrevivir **2** en el mundo: *He's the best player alive.* Es el mejor jugador del mundo. ☛ *Comparar con* LIVING LOC **alive and kicking** vivito y coleando **to keep sth alive 1** (*tradición*) conservar algo **2** (*recuerdo*) mantener fresco algo **to keep yourself alive** sobrevivir

all /ɔːl/ ◆ *adj* **1** todo: *all four of us* los cuatro **2** *He denied all knowledge of the crime.* Negó todo conocimiento del crimen. LOC **all but** casi: *It was all but impossible.* Era casi imposible. **not all that...** no muy... **not as...as all that**: *They're not as rich as all that.* No son tan ricos. **on all fours** a gatas *Ver tb* FOR ◆ *pron* **1** todo: *I ate all of it.* Me lo comí todo. ◊ *All of us liked it.* Nos gustó a todos. ◊ *Are you all going?* ¿Os vais todos? **2** *All I want is...* Lo único que quiero es... LOC **all in all** en conjunto **all the more** tanto más, aún más **at all**: *if it's at all possible* si existe la más mínima posibilidad **in all** en total **not at all 1** no, en absoluto **2** (*respuesta*) de nada ◆ *adv* **1** todo: *all in white* todo de blanco ◊ *all alone* completamente solo **2** *all excited* muy emocionado **3** (*Dep*): *The score is two all.* Están empatados a dos. LOC **all along** (*coloq*) todo el tiempo **all but** casi **all over 1** por todas partes **2** *That's her all over.* Eso es muy propio de ella. **all the better** tanto mejor **all too** demasiado **to be all for sth** estar totalmente a favor de algo

allegation /ˌælə'geɪʃn/ *n* acusación

allege /ə'ledʒ/ *vt* alegar **alleged** *adj* presunto **allegedly** *adv* supuestamente

allegiance /ə'liːdʒəns/ *n* lealtad

allergic /ə'lɜːdʒɪk/ *adj* ~ **(to sth)** alérgico (a algo)

allergy /'ælədʒi/ *n* (*pl* **-ies**) alergia

alleviate /ə'liːvieɪt/ *vt* aliviar **alleviation** *n* alivio

alley /'æli/ *n* (*pl* **-eys**) (*tb* **alleyway**) callejón

alliance /ə'laɪəns/ *n* alianza

allied /ə'laɪd, 'ælaɪd/ *adj* ~ **(to sth) 1** relacionado (con algo) **2** (*Pol*) aliado (a algo)

alligator /'ælɪgeɪtə(r)/ *n* caimán

allocate /'æləkeɪt/ *vt* asignar **allocation** *n* asignación

allot /ə'lɒt/ *vt* (**-tt-**) ~ **sth (to sth/sb)** asignar algo (a algo/algn) **allotment** *n* **1** asignación **2** (*GB*) parcela

all-out /ˌɔːl 'aʊt/ ◆ *adj* total ◆ *adv* LOC **to go all out** no reparar en nada

allow /ə'laʊ/ *vt* **1** ~ **sth/sb to do sth** permitir a algo/algn que haga algo: *Dogs are not allowed.* No se admiten perros.

Allow se usa igualmente en inglés formal y coloquial. La forma pasiva **be allowed to** es muy corriente. **Permit** es una palabra muy formal y se usa fundamentalmente en lenguaje escrito.

Let es informal y se usa mucho en inglés hablado.

2 conceder **3** calcular **4** admitir PHR V **to allow for sth** tener algo en cuenta **allowable** *adj* admisible, permisible

allowance /əˈlaʊəns/ *n* **1** límite permitido **2** subvención LOC **to make allowances for sth/sb** tener algo en cuenta/ ser indulgente con algn

alloy /ˈælɔɪ/ *n* aleación

all right (*tb* **alright**) *adj, adv* **1** bien: *Did you get here all right?* ¿Te ha sido fácil llegar? **2** (*adecuado*): *The food was all right.* La comida no estaba mal. **3** (*consentimiento*) de acuerdo **4** *That's him all right.* Seguro que es él.

all-round /ˌɔːl ˈraʊnd/ *adj* **1** general **2** (*persona*) completo

all-time /ˈɔːl taɪm/ *adj* de todos los tiempos

ally /əˈlaɪ/ ◆ *vt, vi* (*pret, pp* **allied**) ~ (**yourself**) **with/to sth/sb** aliarse con algo/algn ◆ /ˈælaɪ/ *n* (*pl* **-ies**) aliado, -a

almond /ˈɑːmənd/ *n* **1** almendra **2** (*tb* **almond tree**) almendro

almost /ˈɔːlməʊst/ *adv* casi ☛ *Ver nota en* NEARLY

alone /əˈləʊn/ *adj, adv* **1** solo: *Are you alone?* ¿Estás sola?

Nótese que **alone** no se usa delante de sustantivo y es una palabra neutra, mientras que **lonely** sí puede ir delante del sustantivo y siempre tiene connotaciones negativas: *I want to be alone.* Quiero estar solo. ◊ *She was feeling very lonely.* Se sentía muy sola. ◊ *a lonely house* una casa solitaria.

2 sólo: *You alone can help me.* Sólo tú puedes ayudarme. LOC **to leave/let sth/ sb alone** dejar algo/a algn en paz *Ver tb* LET[1]

along /əˈlɒŋ; *USA* əˈlɔːŋ/ ◆ *prep* por, a lo largo de: *a walk along the beach* un paseo por la playa ◆ *part adv*: *I was driving along.* Iba conduciendo. ◊ *Bring some friends along (with you).* Tráete a algunos amigos.

Along se emplea a menudo con verbos de movimiento en tiempos continuos cuando no se menciona ningún destino y generalmente no se traduce en español.

LOC **along with** junto con **come along!** ¡vamos! ☛ Para los usos de **along** en PHRASAL VERBS ver las entradas de los verbos correspondientes, p.ej. **to get along** en GET.

alongside /əˌlɒŋˈsaɪd; *USA* əlɔːŋˈsaɪd/ *prep, adv* junto (a): *A car drew up alongside.* Un coche se paró junto al nuestro.

aloud /əˈlaʊd/ *adv* **1** en voz alta **2** a voces

alphabet /ˈælfəbet/ *n* alfabeto

already /ɔːlˈredi/ *adv* ya: *We got there at 6.30 but Martin had already left.* Llegamos a las 6.30, pero Martin ya se había marchado. ◊ *Have you already eaten?* ¿Has comido ya? ◊ *Surely you are not going already!* ¡No te irás a marchar ya! ☛ *Ver nota en* YET

alright /ɔːlˈraɪt/ *Ver* ALL RIGHT

also /ˈɔːlsəʊ/ *adv* también, además: *I've also met her parents.* También he conocido a sus padres. ◊ *She was also very rich.* Además era muy rica. ☛ *Ver nota en* TAMBIÉN

altar /ˈɔːltə(r)/ *n* altar

alter /ˈɔːltə(r)/ **1** *vt, vi* cambiar **2** *vt* (*ropa*) arreglar: *The skirt needs altering.* La falda necesita arreglos. **alteration** *n* **1** cambio **2** (*ropa*) arreglo

alternate /ɔːlˈtɜːnət; *USA* ˈɔːltərneɪt/ ◆ *adj* alterno ◆ /ˈɔːltɜːneɪt/ *vt, vi* alternar(se)

alternative /ɔːlˈtɜːnətɪv/ ◆ *n* alternativa: *She had no alternative but to…* No tuvo más remedio que… ◆ *adj* alternativo

although (*USA tb* **altho**) /ɔːlˈðəʊ/ *conj* aunque

altitude /ˈæltɪtjuːd; *USA* -tuːd/ *n* altitud

altogether /ˌɔːltəˈgeðə(r)/ *adv* **1** completamente: *I don't altogether agree.* No estoy completamente de acuerdo. **2** en total **3** *Altogether, it was disappointing.* En general, fue decepcionante.

aluminium /ˌæljəˈmɪniəm/ (*USA* **aluminum** /əˈluːmɪnəm/) *n* aluminio

always /ˈɔːlweɪz/ *adv* siempre LOC **as always** como siempre

La posición de los *adverbios de frecuencia* (**always**, **never**, **ever**, **usually**, etc) depende del verbo al que acompañan, es decir, van detrás de los verbos auxiliares y modales (**be**, **have**, **can**, etc) y delante de los demás verbos: *I have* *never visited her.* Nunca he ido a visitarla. ◊ *I am always tired.* Siempre estoy cansado. ◊ *I usually go shopping on Mondays.* Normalmente voy a la compra los lunes.

am[1] /əm, m, æm/ *Ver* BE

am[2] (*USA* **AM**) /ˌeɪ ˈem/ *abrev* de la mañana: *at 11am* a las once de la mañana ☛ *Ver nota en* PM

amalgam /əˈmælgəm/ *n* amalgama

amalgamate /əˈmælgəmeɪt/ *vt, vi* fusionar(se)

amateur /ˈæmətə(r)/ *adj, n* **1** aficionado, -a **2** (*pey*) chapucero, -a

amaze /əˈmeɪz/ *vt* asombrar: *to be amazed at/by sth* quedar asombrado por algo **amazement** *n* asombro **amazing** *adj* asombroso

ambassador /æmˈbæsədə(r)/ *n* embajador, -ora

amber /ˈæmbə(r)/ *adj, n* ámbar

ambiguity /ˌæmbɪˈgjuːəti/ *n* (*pl* **-ies**) ambigüedad

ambiguous /æmˈbɪgjuəs/ *adj* ambiguo

ambition /æmˈbɪʃn/ *n* ambición

ambitious /æmˈbɪʃəs/ *adj* ambicioso

ambulance /ˈæmbjələns/ *n* ambulancia

ambush /ˈæmbʊʃ/ *n* emboscada

amen /ɑːˈmen, eɪˈmen/ *interj, n* amén

amend /əˈmend/ *vt* enmendar **amendment** enmienda

amends /əˈmendz/ *n* [*pl*] LOC **to make amends (to sb) (for sth)** compensar (a algn) (por algo)

amenities /əˈmiːnətiz; *USA* əˈmenətiz/ *n* [*pl*] **1** comodidades **2** instalaciones (*públicas*)

amiable /ˈeɪmiəbl/ *adj* amable

amicable /ˈæmɪkəbl/ *adj* amistoso

amid /əˈmɪd/ (*tb* **amidst** /əˈmɪdst/) *prep* (*fml*) entre, en medio de: *Amid all the confusion, the thieves got away.* Entre tanta confusión, los ladrones se escaparon.

ammunition /ˌæmjuˈnɪʃn/ *n* [*incontable*] **1** municiones: *live ammunition* fuego real **2** (*fig*) argumentos (*para discutir*)

amnesty /ˈæmnəsti/ *n* (*pl* **-ies**) amnistía

among /əˈmʌŋ/ (*tb* **amongst** /əˈmʌŋst/) *prep* entre (*más de dos cosas/personas*): *I was among the last to leave.* Fui de los últimos en marcharse. ☛ *Ver dibujo en* ENTRE

amount /əˈmaʊnt/ ◆ *vi* ~ **to sth 1** ascender a algo: *Our information doesn't amount to much.* No tenemos muchos datos. ◊ *John will never amount to much.* John nunca llegará a nada. **2** equivaler a algo ◆ *n* **1** cantidad **2** (*factura*) importe **3** (*dinero*) suma LOC **any amount of**: *any amount of money* todo el dinero que quiera

amphibian /æmˈfɪbiən/ *adj, n* anfibio

amphitheatre (*USA* **-ter**) /ˈæmfɪθɪətə(r)/ *n* anfiteatro

ample /ˈæmpl/ *adj* **1** abundante **2** (*suficiente*) bastante **3** (*extenso*) amplio **amply** *adv* ampliamente

amplify /ˈæmplɪfaɪ/ *vt* (*pret, pp* **-fied**) **1** amplificar **2** (*relato, etc*) ampliar **amplifier** *n* amplificador

amuse /əˈmjuːz/ *vt* **1** hacer gracia **2** distraer, divertir **amusement** *n* **1** diversión **2** atracción: *amusement arcade* salón recreativo ◊ *amusement park* parque de atracciones **amusing** *adj* divertido, gracioso

an *Ver* A

anaemia (*USA* **anemia**) /əˈniːmiə/ *n* anemia **anaemic** (*USA* **anemic**) *adj* anémico

anaesthetic (*USA* **anesthetic**) /ˌænəsˈθetɪk/ *n* anestesia: *to give sb an anaesthetic* anestesiar a algn

analogy /əˈnælədʒi/ *n* (*pl* **-ies**) analogía: *by analogy with* por analogía con

analyse (*USA* **analyze**) /ˈænəlaɪz/ *vt* analizar

analysis /əˈnæləsɪs/ *n* (*pl* **-yses** /-əsiːz/) análisis LOC **in the last/final analysis** a fin de cuentas

analyst /ˈænəlɪst/ *n* analista, psicólogo, -a

analytic(al) /ˌænəˈlɪtɪk(l)/ *adj* analítico

anarchist /ˈænəkɪst/ *adj, n* anarquista

anarchy /ˈænəki/ *n* anarquía **anarchic** /əˈnɑːkɪk/ *adj* anárquico

anatomy /əˈnætəmi/ *n* (*pl* **-ies**) anatomía

ancestor /ˈænsestə(r)/ *n* antepasado, -a **ancestral** /ænˈsestrəl/ *adj* ancestral: *ancestral home* casa de los antepasados **ancestry** /ˈænsestri/ *n* (*pl* **-ies**) ascendencia

anchor /ˈæŋkə(r)/ ◆ *n* **1** ancla **2** (*fig*)

soporte LOC **at anchor** anclado *Ver tb* WEIGH ◆ *vt, vi* anclar

ancient /ˈeɪnʃənt/ *adj* **1** antiguo **2** (*coloq*) viejísimo

and /ænd, ənd/ *conj* **1** y **2** con: *bacon and eggs* huevos con bacon **3** (*números*): *one hundred and three* ciento tres **4** a: *Come and help me.* Ven a ayudarme. **5** [*con comparativos*]: *bigger and bigger* cada vez más grande **6** (*repetición*): *They shouted and shouted.* Gritaron sin parar. ◊ *I've tried and tried.* Lo he intentado repetidas veces. LOC *Ver* TRY

anecdote /ˈænɪkdəʊt/ *n* anécdota

anemia, anemic (*USA*) *Ver* ANAEMIA

anesthetic (*USA*) *Ver* ANAESTHETIC

angel /ˈeɪndʒl/ *n* ángel: *guardian angel* ángel de la guarda

anger /ˈæŋgə(r)/ ◆ *n* ira ◆ *vt* enfadar

angle /ˈæŋgl/ *n* **1** ángulo **2** punto de vista LOC **at an angle** inclinado

angling /ˈæŋglɪŋ/ *n* pesca (con caña)

angry /ˈæŋgri/ *adj* (**-ier**, **-iest**) **1** ~ (**at/about sth**); ~ (**with sb**) enfadado (por algo); enfadado (con algn) **2** (*cielo*) tormentoso LOC **to get angry** enfadarse **to make sb angry** enfadar a algn **angrily** *adv* con ira

anguish /ˈæŋgwɪʃ/ *n* angustia **anguished** *adj* angustiado

angular /ˈæŋgjələ(r)/ *adj* **1** angular **2** (*facciones*) anguloso **3** (*complexión*) huesudo

animal /ˈænɪml/ *n* animal: *animal experiments* experimentos con animales

animate /ˈænɪmət/ ◆ *adj* animado (*vivo*) ◆ /ˈænɪmeɪt/ *vt* animar

ankle /ˈæŋkl/ *n* tobillo

anniversary /ˌænɪˈvɜːsəri/ *n* (*pl* **-ies**) aniversario

announce /əˈnaʊns/ *vt* anunciar (*hacer público*) **announcement** *n* anuncio (*en público*) LOC **to make an announcement** comunicar algo **announcer** *n* locutor, -ora (*radio, etc*)

annoy /əˈnɔɪ/ *vt* fastidiar **annoyance** *n* fastidio: *much to our annoyance* para fastidio nuestro **annoyed** *adj* enfadado LOC **to get annoyed** enfadarse **annoying** *adj* molesto

annual /ˈænjuəl/ *adj* anual **annually** *adv* anualmente

anonymity /ˌænəˈnɪməti/ *n* anonimato

anonymous /əˈnɒnɪməs/ *adj* anónimo

another /əˈnʌðə(r)/ ◆ *adj* otro: *another one* otro (más) ◊ *another five* cinco más ◊ *I'll do it another time.* Lo haré en otro momento. ☛ *Ver nota en* OTRO ◆ *pron* otro, -a: *one way or another* de una manera u otra ☛ El plural del *pron* **another** es **others**. *Ver tb* ONE ANOTHER

answer /ˈɑːnsə(r); *USA* ˈænsər/ ◆ *n* **1** respuesta: *I phoned, but there was no answer.* Llamé, pero no contestaban. **2** solución **3** (*Mat*) resultado LOC **in answer** (**to sth**) en respuesta (a algo) **to have/know all the answers** saberlo todo ◆ **1** *vt, vi* ~ (**sth/sb**) contestar (a algo/algn): *to answer the door* abrir la puerta **2** *vt* (*acusación, propósito*) responder a **3** *vt* (*ruegos*) oír PHR V **to answer back** replicar (*con insolencia*) **to answer for sth/sb** responder de algo/por algn **to answer to sb** (**for sth**) responder ante algn (de algo) **to answer to sth** responder a algo (*descripción*)

ant /ænt/ *n* hormiga

antagonism /ænˈtægənɪzəm/ *n* antagonismo **antagonistic** *adj* hostil

antenna /ænˈtenə/ *n* **1** (*pl* **-nae** /-niː/) (*insecto*) antena **2** (*pl* **-s**) (*USA*) (*Radio, TV*) antena

anthem /ˈænθəm/ *n* himno

anthology /ænˈθɒlədʒi/ *n* (*pl* **-ies**) antología

anthropology /ˌænθrəˈpɒlədʒi/ *n* antropología **anthropological** /ˌænθrəpəˈlɒdʒɪkl/ *adj* antropológico **anthropologist** /ˌænθrəˈpɒlədʒɪst/ *n* antropólogo, -a

antibiotic /ˌæntibaɪˈɒtɪk/ *adj, n* antibiótico

antibody /ˈæntibɒdi/ *n* (*pl* **-ies**) anticuerpo

anticipate /ænˈtɪsɪpeɪt/ *vt* **1** ~ **sth** prever algo: *as anticipated* de acuerdo con lo previsto ◊ *We anticipate some difficulties.* Contamos con tener algunas dificultades. **2** ~ **sth/sb** anticiparse a algo/algn

anticipation /ænˌtɪsɪˈpeɪʃn/ *n* **1** previsión **2** expectación

antics /ˈæntɪks/ *n* [*pl*] payasadas

antidote /ˈæntidəʊt/ *n* ~ (**for/to sth**) antídoto (contra algo)

antiquated /ˈæntɪkweɪtɪd/ *adj* anticuado

antique /ænˈtiːk/ ◆ *n* (*objeto*) antigüedad: *an antique shop* una tienda de antigüedades ◆ *adj* antiguo (*generalmente de objetos valiosos*) **antiquity** /æn'tɪkwəti/ *n* (*pl* **-ies**) antigüedad

antithesis /æn'tɪθəsɪs/ *n* (*pl* **-ses** /æn'tɪθəsiːz/) antítesis

antler /'æntlə(r)/ *n* **1** [*incontable*] asta de ciervo, reno, alce **2 antlers** [*pl*] cornamenta

anus /'eɪnəs/ *n* (*pl* ~**es**) ano

anxiety /æŋ'zaɪəti/ *n* (*pl* **-ies**) **1** inquietud, preocupación **2** (*Med*) ansiedad **3** ~ **for sth/to do sth** ansia de algo/de hacer algo

anxious /'æŋkʃəs/ *adj* **1** ~ (**about sth**) preocupado (por algo): *an anxious moment* un momento de inquietud **2** ~ **to do sth** ansioso por hacer algo **anxiously** *adv* con ansia

any /'eni/ ◆ *adj, pron* ☛ *Ver nota en* SOME

- **frases interrogativas 1** *Have you got any cash?* ¿Tienes dinero? **2** algo (de): *Do you know any French?* ¿Sabes algo de francés? **3** algún: *Are there any problems?* ¿Hay algún problema? ☛ En este sentido el sustantivo suele ir en plural en inglés.
- **frases negativas 1** *He hasn't got any friends.* No tiene amigos. ◊ *There isn't any left.* No queda nada. ☛ *Ver nota en* NINGUNO **2** [*uso enfático*]: *We won't do you any harm.* No te haremos ningún daño.
- **frases condicionales 1** *If I had any relatives...* Si tuviera parientes... **2** algo (de): *If he's got any sense, he won't go.* Si tiene un mínimo de sentido común, no irá. **3** algún: *If you see any mistakes, tell me.* Si ves algún error, dímelo. ☛ En este sentido el sustantivo suele ir en plural en inglés.

En las frases condicionales se puede emplear la palabra **some** en vez de **any** en muchos casos: *If you need some help, tell me.* Si necesitas ayuda, dímelo.

- **frases afirmativas 1** cualquier(a): *just like any other boy* igual que cualquier otro niño **2** *Take any one you like.* Coge el que quieras. **3** todo: *Give her any help she needs.* Préstale toda la ayuda que necesite.

◆ *adv* [*antes de comparativo*] más: *She doesn't work here any longer.* Ya no trabaja aquí. ◊ *I can't walk any faster.* No puedo andar más deprisa. ◊ *She doesn't live here any more.* Ya no vive aquí.

anybody /'enibɒdi/ (*tb* **anyone**) *pron* **1** alguien: *Is anybody there?* ¿Hay alguien? **2** [*en frases negativas*] nadie: *I can't see anybody.* No veo a nadie. ☛ *Ver nota en* NOBODY **3** [*en frases afirmativas*]: *Invite anybody you like.* Invita a quien quieras. ◊ *Ask anybody.* Pregúntale a cualquiera. **4** [*en frases comparativas*] nadie: *He spoke more than anybody.* Habló más que nadie. ☛ *Ver nota en* EVERYBODY, SOMEBODY LOC **anybody else** alguien más: *Anybody else would have refused.* Cualquier otro se habría negado. *Ver tb* GUESS

anyhow /'enihaʊ/ *adv* **1** (*coloq* **any old how**) de cualquier manera **2** (*tb* **anyway**) de todas formas

anyone /'eniwʌn/ *Ver* ANYBODY

anyplace /'enipleɪs/ (*USA*) *Ver* ANYWHERE

anything /'eniθɪŋ/ *pron* **1** algo: *Is anything wrong?* ¿Pasa algo? ◊ *Is there anything in these rumours?* ¿Hay algo de verdad en estos rumores? **2** [*en frases afirmativas*] cualquier cosa, todo: *We'll do anything you say.* Haremos lo que nos digas. **3** [*frases negativas y comparativas*] nada: *He never says anything.* Nunca dice nada. ◊ *It was better than anything he'd seen before.* Era mejor que nada que hubiera visto antes. ☛ *Ver nota en* NOBODY, SOMETHING LOC **anything but**: *It was anything but pleasant.* Fue todo menos agradable. ◊ *'Are you tired?' 'Anything but.'* —¿Estás cansado? —¡En absoluto! **if anything**: *I'm a pacifist, if anything.* En todo caso, soy pacifista.

anyway /'eniweɪ/ *Ver* ANYHOW 2

anywhere /'enɪweə(r)/ (*USA* **anyplace**) *adv, pron* **1** [*en frases interrogativas*] en/a alguna parte **2** [*en frases afirmativas*]: *I'd live anywhere.* Viviría en cualquier sitio. ◊ *anywhere you like* donde quieras **3** [*en frases negativas*] en/a/por ninguna parte: *I didn't go anywhere special.* No fui a ningún sitio especial. ◊ *I haven't got anywhere to stay.* No tengo donde alojarme. ☛ *Ver nota en* NOBODY **4** [*en frases comparativas*]: *more beautiful than anywhere* más bonito que ningún otro sitio ☛ *Ver nota en* SOMEWHERE LOC *Ver* NEAR

apart /ə'pɑːt/ *adv* **1** *The two men were five metres apart.* Los dos hombres estaban a cinco metros uno del otro. ◊ *They are a long way apart.* Están muy lejos el uno del otro. **2** aislado **3** separado: *They live apart.* Viven separados. ◊ *I can't pull them apart.* No puedo separarlos. LOC **to take sth apart 1** desmontar algo **2** (*fig*) hacer pedazos algo *Ver tb* JOKE, POLE

apart from (*USA tb* **aside from**) *prep* aparte de

apartment /ə'pɑːtmənt/ *n* apartamento

apathy /'æpəθi/ *n* apatía **apathetic** /ˌæpə'θetɪk/ *adj* apático

ape /eɪp/ ◆ *n* simio ◆ *vt* remedar

apologetic /əˌpɒlə'dʒetɪk/ *adj* de disculpa: *an apologetic look* una mirada de disculpa ◊ *to be apologetic (about sth)* disculparse (por algo)

apologize, -ise /ə'pɒlədʒaɪz/ *vi* ~ (**for sth**) disculparse (por algo)

apology /ə'pɒlədʒi/ *n* (*pl* **-ies**) disculpa LOC **to make no apologies/apology (for sth)** no disculparse (por algo)

apostle /ə'pɒsl/ *n* apóstol

appal (*USA tb* **appall**) /ə'pɔːl/ *vt* (**-ll-**) horrorizar: *He was appalled at/by her behaviour.* Le horrorizó su comportamiento. **appalling** *adj* espantoso, horrible

apparatus /ˌæpə'reɪtəs; *USA* -'rætəs/ *n* [*incontable*] aparato (*en un gimnasio, laboratorio*)

apparent /ə'pærənt/ *adj* **1** evidente: *to become apparent* hacerse evidente **2** aparente: *for no apparent reason* sin motivo aparente **apparently** *adv* al parecer: *Apparently not.* Parece que no.

appeal /ə'piːl/ ◆ *vi* **1** ~ (**to sb**) **for sth** pedir algo (a algn) **2** ~ **to sb to do sth** hacer un llamamiento a algn para que haga algo **3** apelar **4** ~ (**to sb**) atraer (a algn) **5** ~ (**against sth**) (*sentencia, etc*) recurrir (algo) ◆ *n* **1** llamamiento: *an appeal for help* un llamamiento pidiendo ayuda **2** súplica **3** atractivo **4** recurso: *appeal(s) court* tribunal de apelación **appealing** *adj* **1** atractivo: *to look appealing* tener un aspecto atractivo **2** suplicante

appear /ə'pɪə(r)/ *vi* **1** aparecer: *to appear on TV* salir en televisión **2** parecer: *You appear to have made a mistake.* Parece que has cometido un error. = SEEM **3** (*fantasma*) aparecerse **4** (*acusado*) comparecer **appearance** *n* **1** apariencia **2** aparición LOC **to keep up appearances** mantener las apariencias

appendicitis /əˌpendə'saɪtɪs/ *n* apendicitis

appendix /ə'pendɪks/ *n* **1** (*pl* **-dices** /-dɪsiːz/) (*escrito*) apéndice **2** (*pl* **-dixes**) (*Anat*) apéndice

appetite /'æpɪtaɪt/ *n* **1** apetito: *to give sb an appetite* abrir el apetito a algn **2** apetencia LOC *Ver* WHET

applaud /ə'plɔːd/ *vt, vi* aplaudir **applause** *n* [*incontable*] aplausos: *a big round of applause* un fuerte aplauso

apple /'æpl/ *n* **1** manzana **2** (*tb* **apple tree**) manzano

appliance /ə'plaɪəns/ *n* aparato: *electrical/kitchen appliances* electrodomésticos

applicable /'æplɪkəbl, ə'plɪkəbl/ *adj* aplicable

applicant /'æplɪkənt/ *n* solicitante, aspirante

application /ˌæplɪ'keɪʃn/ *n* **1** solicitud: *application form* impreso de solicitud **2** aplicación

applied /ə'plaɪd/ *adj* aplicado

apply /ə'plaɪ/ (*pret, pp* **applied**) **1** *vt* aplicar **2** *vt* (*fuerza, etc*) ejercer: *to apply the brakes* frenar **3** *vi* hacer una solicitud **4** *vi* ser aplicable: *In this case, the condition does not apply.* En este caso, no es aplicable esta condición. PHR V **to apply for sth** solicitar algo **to apply to sth/sb** aplicarse a algo/algn: *This applies to men and women.* Esto se aplica tanto a los hombres como a las mujeres. **to apply yourself (to sth)** aplicarse (a algo)

appoint /ə'pɔɪnt/ *vt* **1** nombrar **2** (*fml*) (*hora, lugar*) señalar **appointment** *n* **1** (*acto*) nombramiento **2** puesto **3** cita (*profesional*)

appraisal /ə'preɪzl/ *n* evaluación, estimación

appreciate /ə'priːʃieɪt/ **1** *vt* apreciar **2** *vt* (*ayuda, etc*) agradecer **3** *vt* (*problema, etc*) comprender **4** *vi* revalorizarse **appreciation** *n* **1** (*gen, Fin*) apreciación **2** agradecimiento **3** valoración **appreciative** *adj* **1** ~ (**of sth**) agradecido (por algo) **2** (*mirada, comentario*) de admiración **3** (*público*) agradecido

apprehend /ˌæprɪˈhend/ *vt* detener, capturar **apprehension** *n* aprensión: *filled with apprehension* lleno de aprensión **apprehensive** *adj* aprensivo

apprentice /əˈprentɪs/ *n* **1** aprendiz, -iza: *apprentice plumber* aprendiz de fontanero **2** principiante **apprenticeship** *n* aprendizaje

approach /əˈprəʊtʃ/ ◆ **1** *vt, vi* acercarse (a) **2** *vt* ~ **sb** (*para ayuda*) acudir a algn **3** *vt* (*tema, persona*) abordar ◆ *n* **1** llegada **2** aproximación **3** acceso **4** enfoque

appropriate[1] /əˈprəʊprieɪt/ *vt* apropiarse de

appropriate[2] /əˈprəʊpriət/ *adj* **1** apropiado, adecuado **2** (*momento, etc*) oportuno **appropriately** *adv* apropiadamente, adecuadamente

approval /əˈpruːvl/ *n* aprobación, visto bueno LOC **on approval** a prueba

approve /əˈpruːv/ **1** *vt* aprobar **2** *vi* ~ (**of sth**) estar de acuerdo (con algo) **3** *vi* ~ (**of sb**): *I don't approve of him.* No tengo un buen concepto de él. **approving** *adj* de aprobación

approximate /əˈprɒksɪmət/ ◆ *adj* aproximado ◆ /əˈprɒksɪmeɪt/ *vi* ~ **to sth** aproximarse a algo **approximately** *adv* aproximadamente

apricot /ˈeɪprɪkɒt/ *n* **1** albaricoque **2** (*tb* **apricot tree**) albaricoquero **3** color albaricoque

April /ˈeɪprəl/ *n* (*abrev* **Apr**) abril: *April Fool's Day* día de los inocentes ☛ *Ver nota y ejemplos en* JANUARY

April Fool's Day es el 1 de abril.

apron /ˈeɪprən/ *n* delantal

apt /æpt/ *adj* (**apter**, **aptest**) acertado LOC **to be apt to do sth** tener tendencia a hacer algo **aptly** *adv* acertadamente

aptitude /ˈæptɪtjuːd; *USA* -tuːd/ *n* aptitud

aquarium /əˈkweəriəm/ *n* (*pl* **-riums** *o* **-ria**) acuario

Aquarius /əˈkweəriəs/ *n* Acuario: *My sister is (an) Aquarius.* Mi hermana es acuario. ◊ *born under Aquarius* nacido acuario.

aquatic /əˈkwætɪk/ *adj* acuático

arable /ˈærəbl/ *adj* cultivable: *arable farming* agricultura ◊ *arable land* tierra de cultivo

arbitrary /ˈɑːbɪtrəri; *USA* ˈɑːbɪtreri/ *adj* **1** arbitrario **2** indiscriminado

arbitrate /ˈɑːbɪtreɪt/ *vt, vi* arbitrar **arbitration** *n* arbitrio

arc /ɑːk/ *n* arco

arcade /ɑːˈkeɪd/ *n* **1** galería: *amusement arcade* salón recreativo **2** [*sing*] soportales

arch /ɑːtʃ/ ◆ *n* arco ◆ *vt, vi* **1** (*espalda*) arquear(se) **2** (*cejas*) enarcar(se)

archaeology (*USA* **archeology**) /ˌɑːkiˈɒlədʒi/ *n* arqueología **archaeological** (*USA* **archeological**) /ˌɑːkiəˈlɒdʒɪkl/ *adj* arqueológico **archaeologist** (*USA* **archeologist**) /ˌɑːkiˈɒlədʒɪst/ *n* arqueólogo, -a

archaic /ɑːˈkeɪɪk/ *adj* arcaico

archbishop /ˌɑːtʃˈbɪʃəp/ *n* arzobispo

archer /ˈɑːtʃə(r)/ *n* arquero, -a **archery** *n* tiro con arco

architect /ˈɑːkɪtekt/ *n* arquitecto, -a

architecture /ˈɑːkɪtektʃə(r)/ *n* arquitectura **architectural** /ˌɑːkɪˈtektʃərəl/ *adj* arquitectónico

archive /ˈɑːkaɪv/ *n* archivo

archway /ˈɑːtʃweɪ/ *n* arco (*arquitectónico*)

ardent /ˈɑːdnt/ *adj* ferviente, entusiasta

ardour (*USA* **ardor**) /ˈɑːdə(r)/ *n* fervor

arduous /ˈɑːdjuəs; *USA* -dʒʊ-/ *adj* arduo

are /ə(r), ɑː(r)/ *Ver* BE

area /ˈeəriə/ *n* **1** superficie **2** (*Mat*) área **3** (*Geog*) zona, región: *area manager* director regional **4** (*de uso específico*) zona, recinto **5** (*de actividad, etc*) área

arena /əˈriːnə/ *n* **1** (*Dep*) estadio **2** (*circo*) pista **3** (*plaza de toros*) ruedo **4** (*fig*) ámbito

aren't /ɑːnt/ = ARE NOT *Ver* BE

arguable /ˈɑːgjuəbl/ *adj* **1** *It is arguable that...* Podemos afirmar que... **2** discutible **arguably** *adv* probablemente

argue /ˈɑːgjuː/ **1** *vi* discutir **2** *vt, vi* argumentar: *to argue for/against* dar argumentos a favor de/en contra de

argument /ˈɑːgjumənt/ *n* **1** discusión: *to have an argument* discutir ☛ *Comparar con* ROW[3] **2** ~ (**for/against**

sth) argumento a favor de/en contra de algo

arid /ˈærɪd/ *adj* árido

Aries /ˈeəriːz/ *n* aries ☛ *Ver ejemplos en* AQUARIUS

arise /əˈraɪz/ *vi* (*pret* **arose** /əˈrəʊz/ *pp* **arisen** /əˈrɪzn/) **1** (*problema*) surgir **2** (*oportunidad*) presentarse **3** (*tormenta*) levantarse **4** (*situación, etc*) producirse: *should the need arise* si fuera preciso **5** (*cuestión, etc*) plantearse **6** (*antic*) alzarse

aristocracy /ˌærɪˈstɒkrəsi/ *n* [*v sing o pl*] (*pl* **-ies**) aristocracia

aristocrat /ˈærɪstəkræt; *USA* əˈrɪst-/ *n* aristócrata **aristocratic** /ˌærɪstəˈkrætɪk/ *adj* aristocrático

arithmetic /əˈrɪθmətɪk/ *n* aritmética: *mental arithmetic* cálculo mental

ark /ɑːk/ *n* arca

arm

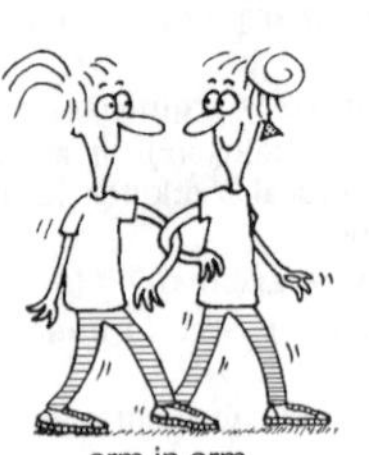

arm in arm

arms crossed/ folded

arm /ɑːm/ ◆ *n* **1** brazo: *I've broken my arm.* Me he roto el brazo.

Nótese que en inglés las partes del cuerpo van normalmente precedidas por un adjetivo posesivo (*my, your, her, etc*).

2 (*camisa, etc*) manga LOC **arm in arm** (**with sb**) del brazo (de algn) *Ver tb* CHANCE, FOLD ◆ *vt, vi* armar(se): *to arm yourself with sth* armarse con/de algo

armament /ˈɑːməmənt/ *n* armamento: *armaments factory* fábrica de armamento

armchair /ɑːmˈtʃeə(r)/ *n* sillón

armed /ɑːmd/ *adj* armado

armed forces (*tb* **armed services**) *n* fuerzas armadas

armed robbery *n* atraco a mano armada

armistice /ˈɑːmɪstɪs/ *n* armisticio

armour (*USA* **armor**) /ˈɑːmə(r)/ *n* [*incontable*] **1** armadura: *a suit of armour* una armadura **2** blindaje LOC *Ver* CHINK **armoured** (*USA* **armored**) *adj* **1** (*vehículo*) blindado **2** (*barco*) acorazado

armpit /ˈɑːmpɪt/ *n* axila

arms /ɑːmz/ *n* [*pl*] **1** armas: *arms race* carrera armamentista **2** escudo (de armas) LOC **to be up in arms (about/over sth)** estar en pie de guerra (por algo)

army /ˈɑːmi/ *n* [*v sing o pl*] (*pl* **armies**) ejército

arose *pret de* ARISE

around[1] /əˈraʊnd/ (*tb* **about**) *adv* **1** más o menos: *around 200 people* más o menos 200 personas **2** hacia: *around 1850* hacia 1850

En expresiones temporales, la palabra **about** suele ir precedida por las preposiciones **at**, **on**, **in**, etc, mientras que la palabra **around** no requiere preposición: *around/at about five o'clock* a eso de las cinco ◇ *around/on about 15 June* hacia el 15 de junio.

3 por aquí: *There are few good teachers around.* No hay muchos profesores buenos por aquí.

around[2] /əˈraʊnd/ (*tb* **round**, **about**) *part adv* **1** de aquí para allá: *I've been dashing (a)round all morning.* Llevo toda la mañana de aquí para allá. **2** a su alrededor: *to look (a)round* mirar (algn) a su alrededor ☛ Para los usos de **around** en PHRASAL VERBS ver las entradas de los verbos correspondientes, p.ej. **to lie around** en LIE[2].

around[3] /əˈraʊnd/ (*tb* **round**) *prep* **1** por: *to travel (a)round the world* viajar por todo el mundo **2** alrededor de: *sitting (a)round the table* sentados alrededor de la mesa

arouse /əˈraʊz/ *vt* **1** suscitar **2** excitar (sexualmente) **3** ~ **sb** (**from sth**) despertar a algn (de algo)

arrange /əˈreɪndʒ/ *vt* **1** disponer **2** ordenar **3** (*evento*) organizar **4** ~ **for sb to do sth** asegurarse de que algn haga algo **5** ~ **to do sth/that...** quedar en hacer algo/en que... **6** (*Mús*) arreglar **arrangement** *n* **1** disposición **2** arreglo **3** acuerdo **4** **arrangements** [*pl*] preparativos

arrest /əˈrest/ ◆ *vt* **1** (*delincuente*) detener **2** (*fml*) (*inflación, etc*) contener **3** (*atención*) atraer ◆ *n* **1** detención **2** *cardiac arrest* paro cardiaco LOC **to be under arrest** estar/quedar detenido

arrival /əˈraɪvl/ *n* **1** llegada **2** (*persona*): *new/recent arrivals* recién llegados

arrive /əˈraɪv/ *vi* **1** llegar

> **¿Arrive in** o **arrive at? Arrive in** se utiliza cuando se llega a un país o a una población: *When did you arrive in England?* ¿Cuándo llegaste a Inglaterra? **Arrive at** se usa seguido de lugares específicos como un edificio, una estación, etc: *We'll phone you as soon as we arrive at the airport.* Os llamaremos en cuanto lleguemos al aeropuerto. El uso de **at** seguido del nombre de una población implica que se está considerando esa población como un punto en un itinerario. Nótese que "llegar a casa" se dice *to arrive home.*

2 (*coloq*) (*éxito*) llegar a la cima

arrogant /ˈærəgənt/ *adj* arrogante **arrogance** *n* arrogancia

arrow /ˈærəʊ/ *n* flecha

arson /ˈɑːsn/ *n* incendio criminal

art /ɑːt/ *n* **1** arte: *a work of art* una obra de arte **2 the arts** [*pl*] las Bellas Artes: *the Arts Minister* el ministro de Cultura **3 arts** [*pl*] (*asignatura*) letras: *Bachelor of Arts* Licenciado (en una carrera de Humanidades) **4** maña

artery /ˈɑːtəri/ *n* (*pl* **-ies**) arteria

arthritis /ɑːˈθraɪtɪs/ *n* artritis **arthritic** *adj, n* artrítico, -a

artichoke /ˈɑːtɪtʃəʊk/ *n* alcachofa

article /ˈɑːtɪkl/ *n* **1** artículo: *definite/indefinite article* artículo definido/indefinido **2** *articles of clothing* prendas de vestir

articulate[1] /ɑːˈtɪkjələt/ *adj* capaz de expresarse con claridad

articulate[2] /ɑːˈtɪkjuleɪt/ *vt, vi* articular: *articulated lorry* camión articulado

artificial /ˌɑːtɪˈfɪʃl/ *adj* artificial

artillery /ɑːˈtɪləri/ *n* artillería

artisan /ˌɑːtɪˈzæn; *USA* ˈɑːrtɪzn/ *n* artesano, -a

artist /ˈɑːtɪst/ *n* artista

artistic /ɑːˈtɪstɪk/ *adj* artístico

artwork /ˈɑːtwɜːk/ *n* material gráfico (*en una publicación*)

as /əz, æz/ ◆ *prep* **1** (*en calidad de*) como: *Treat me as a friend.* Trátame como a un amigo. ◊ *Use this plate as an ashtray.* Usa este plato como cenicero. **2** (*con profesiones*) de: *to work as a waiter* trabajar de camarero **3** (*cuando algn es/era*) de: *as a child* de pequeño

> Nótese que para comparaciones y ejemplos usamos **like**: *a car like yours* un coche como el tuyo ◊ *Romantic poets, like Byron, Shelley, etc* poetas románticos (tales) como Byron, Shelley, etc.

◆ *adv* **1 as ... as** tan ... como: *She is as tall as me/as I am.* Es tan alta como yo. ◊ *as soon as possible* lo antes posible ◊ *I earn as much as her/as she does.* Gano tanto como ella. **2** (*según*) como: *as you can see* como puedes ver ◆ *conj* **1** mientras: *I watched her as she combed her hair.* La miré mientras se peinaba. **2** como: *as you weren't there...* como no estabas... **3** tal como: *Leave it as you find it.* Déjalo tal como lo encuentres. LOC **as for sth/sb** en cuanto a algo/algn **as from** (*esp USA* **as of**): *as from/of 12 May* a partir del 12 de mayo **as if/as though** como si: *as if nothing had happened* como si no hubiera sucedido nada **as it is** vista la situación **as many 1** tantos: *We no longer have as many members.* Ya no tenemos tantos socios. **2** otros tantos: *four jobs in as many months* cuatro trabajos en otros tantos meses **as many again/more** otros tantos **as many as 1** *I didn't win as many as him.* No gané tantos como él. **2** hasta: *as many as ten people* hasta diez personas **3** *You ate three times as many as I did.* Comiste tres veces más que yo. **as many ... as** tantos ... como **as much**: *I don't have as much as you.* No tengo tanto como tú. ◊ *I thought as much.* Eso es lo que a mí me parecía. **as much again** otro tanto **as to sth/as regards sth** en cuanto a algo **as yet** hasta ahora

asbestos /æsˈbestəs, əzˈbestəs/ *n* amianto

ascend /əˈsend/ (*fml*) **1** *vi* ascender **2** *vt* (*escaleras, trono*) subir (a)

ascendancy /əˈsendənsi/ *n* ~ (**over sth/sb**) ascendiente (sobre algo/algn)

ascent /əˈsent/ *n* ascenso

ascertain /ˌæsəˈteɪn/ *vt* (*fml*) averiguar

ascribe /ə'skraɪb/ *vt* ~ **sth to sth/sb** atribuir algo a algo/algn
ash /æʃ/ *n* **1** (*tb* **ash tree**) fresno **2** ceniza
ashamed /ə'ʃeɪmd/ *adj* ~ (**of sth/sb**) avergonzado (de algo/algn) LOC **to be ashamed to do sth** darle vergüenza a uno hacer algo
ashore /ə'ʃɔː(r)/ *adv, prep* en/a tierra: *to go ashore* desembarcar
ashtray /'æʃtreɪ/ *n* cenicero
Ash Wednesday *n* miércoles de Ceniza
aside /ə'saɪd/ ◆ *adv* **1** a un lado **2** en reserva ◆ *n* aparte (*Teatro*)
aside from *prep* (*esp USA*) aparte de
ask /ɑːsk; *USA* æsk/ **1** *vt, vi* **to ask** (**sb**) (**sth**) preguntar (algo) (a algn): *to ask a question* hacer una pregunta ◊ *to ask about sth* preguntar acerca de algo **2** *vt, vi* **to ask** (**sb**) **for sth** pedir algo (a algn) **3** *vt* **to ask sb to do sth** pedir a algn que haga algo **4** *vt* **to ask sb** (**to sth**) invitar a algn (a algo) LOC **don't ask me!** (*coloq*) ¡yo qué sé! **for the asking** con sólo pedirlo **to ask for trouble/it** (*coloq*) buscársela **to ask sb out** pedirle a algn que salga con uno (como pareja) **to ask sb round** invitar a algn (a tu casa) PHR V **to ask after sb** preguntar cómo está algn **to ask for sb** preguntar por algn (*para verle*)
asleep /ə'sliːp/ *adj* dormido: *to fall asleep* dormirse ◊ *fast/sound asleep* profundamente dormido

Nótese que **asleep** no se usa antes de un sustantivo, por lo tanto, para traducir "un niño dormido" tendríamos que decir *a sleeping baby*.

asparagus /ə'spærəgəs/ *n* [*incontable*] espárrago(s)
aspect /'æspekt/ *n* **1** (*de una situación, etc*) aspecto **2** (*Arquit*) orientación
asphalt /'æsfælt; *USA* -fɔːlt/ *n* asfalto
asphyxiate /əs'fɪksieɪt/ *vt* asfixiar
aspiration /ˌæspə'reɪʃn/ *n* aspiración
aspire /ə'spaɪə(r)/ *vi* ~ **to sth** aspirar a algo: *aspiring musicians* aspirantes a músicos
aspirin /'æsprɪn, 'æspərɪn/ *n* aspirina
ass /æs/ *n* **1** asno **2** (*coloq*) (*idiota*) burro
assailant /ə'seɪlənt/ *n* (*fml*) agresor, -ora
assassin /ə'sæsɪn; *USA* -sn/ *n* asesino, -a **assassinate** *vt* asesinar **assassination** *n* asesinato ☛ *Ver nota en* ASESINAR
assault /ə'sɔːlt/ ◆ *vt* agredir ◆ *n* **1** agresión **2** ~ (**on sth/sb**) ataque (contra algo/algn)
assemble /ə'sembl/ **1** *vt, vi* reunir(se) **2** *vt* (*Mec*) montar
assembly /ə'sembli/ *n* (*pl* **-ies**) **1** asamblea **2** (*escuela*) reunión matinal **3** montaje: *assembly line* cadena de montaje
assert /ə'sɜːt/ *vt* **1** afirmar **2** (*derechos, etc*) hacer valer LOC **to assert yourself** imponerse **assertion** *n* afirmación
assertive /ə'sɜːtɪv/ *adj* firme, que se hace valer
assess /ə'ses/ *vt* **1** (*propiedad, etc*) valorar **2** (*impuestos, etc*) calcular **assessment** *n* **1** valoración **2** análisis **assessor** *n* tasador, -ora
asset /'æset/ *n* **1** ventaja, baza: *to be an asset to sth/sb* ser muy valioso para algo/algn **2 assets** [*pl*] (*Com*) bienes
assign /ə'saɪn/ *vt* **1** ~ **sth to sb** asignar algo a algn **2** ~ **sb to sth** asignar a algn a algo
assignment /ə'saɪnmənt/ *n* **1** (*en colegio*) trabajo **2** misión **3** (*en el extranjero*) destino
assimilate /ə'sɪməleɪt/ **1** *vt* asimilar **2** *vi* ~ **into sth** asimilarse a algo
assist /ə'sɪst/ *vt* (*fml*) *vi* ayudar, asistir **assistance** *n* (*fml*) **1** ayuda **2** auxilio
assistant /ə'sɪstənt/ *n* **1** ayudante **2** (*tb* **sales/shop assistant**) dependiente, -a **3** *the assistant manager* la subdirectora
associate[1] /ə'səʊʃiət/ *n* socio, -a
associate[2] /ə'səʊʃieɪt/ **1** *vt* ~ **sth/sb with sth/sb** relacionar algo/a algn con algo/algn **2** *vi* ~ **with sb** tratar con algn
association /əˌsəʊsi'eɪʃn/ *n* **1** asociación **2** implicación
assorted /ə'sɔːtɪd/ *adj* **1** variados **2** (*galletas, etc*) surtidos
assortment /ə'sɔːtmənt/ *n* variedad, surtido
assume /ə'sjuːm; *USA* ə'suːm/ *vt* **1** suponer **2** dar por sentado **3** (*expresión, nombre falso*) adoptar **4** (*significado*) adquirir **5** (*control*) asumir
assumption /ə'sʌmpʃn/ *n* **1** supuesto **2** (*de poder, etc*) toma

assurance /ə'ʃɔːrəns; *USA* ə'ʃʊərəns/ *n* **1** garantía **2** confianza

assure /ə'ʃʊə(r)/ **1** *vt* asegurar **2** *vt* ~ **sb of sth** prometer algo a algn **3** *vt* ~ **sb of sth** convencer a algn de algo **4** *v refl* ~ **yourself that...** cerciorarse de que... **assured** *adj* seguro LOC **to be assured of sth** tener algo asegurado

asterisk /'æstərɪsk/ *n* asterisco

asthma /'æsmə; *USA* 'æzmə/ *n* asma **asthmatic** *adj, n* asmático, -a

astonish /ə'stɒnɪʃ/ *vt* asombrar **astonishing** *adj* asombroso **astonishingly** *adv* increíblemente **astonishment** *n* asombro

astound /ə'staʊnd/ *vt* dejar atónito: *We were astounded to find him playing chess with his dog.* Nos quedamos atónitos al encontrarlo jugando al ajedrez con el perro. **astounding** *adj* increíble

astray /ə'streɪ/ *adv* LOC **to go astray** extraviarse

astride /ə'straɪd/ *adv, prep* ~ **(sth)** a horcajadas (en algo)

astrology /ə'strɒlədʒi/ *n* astrología

astronaut /'æstrənɔːt/ *n* astronauta

astronomy /ə'strɒnəmi/ *n* astronomía **astronomer** *n* astrónomo, -a **astronomical** /ˌæstrə'nɒmɪkl/ *adj* astronómico

astute /ə'stjuːt; *USA* ə'stuːt/ *adj* astuto

asylum /ə'saɪləm/ *n* **1** asilo **2** (*tb* **lunatic asylum**) (*antic*) manicomio

at /æt, ət/ *prep* **1** (*posición*) en: *at home* en casa ◊ *at the door* en la puerta ◊ *at the top* en lo alto ☛ *Ver nota en* EN **2** (*tiempo*): *at 3.35* a las 3.35 ◊ *at dawn* al amanecer ◊ *at times* a veces ◊ *at night* por la noche ◊ *at Christmas* en Navidades ◊ *at the moment* de momento **3** (*precio, frecuencia, velocidad*) a: *at 70kph* a 70km/h ◊ *at full volume* a todo volumen ◊ *two at a time* de dos en dos **4** (*hacia*): *to stare at sb* mirar fijamente a algn **5** (*reacción*): *surprised at sth* sorprendido por algo ◊ *At this, she fainted.* Y entonces, se desmayó. **6** (*actividad*) en: *She's at work.* Está en el trabajo. ◊ *to be at war* estar en guerra ◊ *children at play* niños jugando

ate *pret de* EAT

atheism /'eɪθiɪzəm/ *n* ateísmo **atheist** *n* ateo, -a

athlete /'æθliːt/ *n* atleta

athletic /æθ'letɪk/ *adj* atlético **athletics** *n* [*sing*] atletismo

atlas /'ætləs/ *n* **1** atlas **2** (*de carreteras*) mapa

atmosphere /'ætməsfɪə(r)/ *n* **1** atmósfera **2** ambiente

atom /'ætəm/ *n* **1** átomo **2** (*fig*) ápice

atomic /ə'tɒmɪk/ *adj* atómico: *atomic weapons* armas nucleares

atrocious /ə'trəʊʃəs/ *adj* **1** atroz **2** pésimo **atrocity** /ə'trɒsəti/ *n* (*pl* **-ies**) atrocidad

attach /ə'tætʃ/ *vt* **1** atar **2** unir **3** (*documentos*) adjuntar **4** (*fig*): *to attach importance to sth* dar importancia a algo **attached** *adj*: *to be attached to sth/sb* tenerle cariño a algo/algn LOC *Ver* STRING **attachment** *n* **1** accesorio **2** ~ **to sth** apego a algo

attack /ə'tæk/ ◆ *n* ~ **(on sth/sb)** ataque (contra algo/algn) ◆ *vt, vi* atacar **attacker** *n* agresor, -ora

attain /ə'teɪn/ *vt* alcanzar **attainment** *n* éxito

attempt /ə'tempt/ ◆ *vt* intentar: *to attempt to do sth* intentar hacer algo ◆ *n* **1** ~ **(at doing/to do sth)** intento (de hacer algo) **2** atentado **attempted** *adj*: *attempted robbery* intento de robo ◊ *attempted murder* asesinato frustrado

attend /ə'tend/ **1** *vt, vi* ~ **(sth)** asistir (a algo) **2** *vi* ~ **to sth/sb** ocuparse de algo/algn **attendance** *n* asistencia LOC **in attendance** presente

attendant /ə'tendənt/ *n* encargado, -a

attention /ə'tenʃn/ ◆ *n* atención: *for the attention of...* a la atención de... LOC *Ver* CATCH, FOCUS, PAY ◆ **attention!** *interj* (*Mil*) ¡firmes!

attentive /ə'tentɪv/ *adj* atento

attic /'ætɪk/ *n* desván

attitude /'ætɪtjuːd; *USA* -tuːd/ *n* actitud

attorney /ə'tɜːni/ *n* (*pl* **-eys**) **1** (*USA*) abogado, -a **2** apoderado, -a

Attorney-General /əˌtɜːni 'dʒenrəl/ *n* **1** (*GB*) asesor, -ora legal del gobierno **2** (*USA*) procurador, -ora general

attract /ə'trækt/ *vt* **1** atraer **2** (*atención*) llamar **attraction** *n* **1** atracción **2** atractivo **attractive** *adj* **1** (*persona*) atractivo **2** (*salario, etc*) interesante

attribute /'ætrɪbjuːt/ ◆ *n* atributo ◆ /ə'trɪbjuːt/ *vt* ~ **sth to sth** atribuir algo a algo

aubergine /ˈəʊbəʒiːn/ ◆ *n* berenjena ◆ *adj* (*color*) morado

auction /ˈɔːkʃn, ˈɒkʃn/ ◆ *n* subasta ◆ *vt* subastar **auctioneer** /ˌɔːkʃəˈnɪə(r)/ *n* subastador, -ora

audible /ˈɔːdəbl/ *adj* audible

audience /ˈɔːdiəns/ *n* **1** [*v sing o pl*] (*teatro, etc*) público **2** ~ **with sb** audiencia con algn

audit /ˈɔːdɪt/ ◆ *n* auditoría ◆ *vt* auditar

audition /ɔːˈdɪʃn/ ◆ *n* audición ◆ *vi* ~ **for sth** presentarse a una audición para algo

auditor /ˈɔːdɪtə(r)/ *n* auditor, -ora

auditorium /ˌɔːdɪˈtɔːriəm/ *n* (*pl* **-ria** *o* **-riums**) auditorio

August /ˈɔːgəst/ *n* (*abrev* **Aug**) agosto ☛ *Ver nota y ejemplos en* JANUARY

aunt /ɑːnt; *USA* ænt/ *n* tía: *Aunt Louise* la tía Luisa ◊ *my aunt and uncle* mis tíos **auntie** (*tb* **aunty**) (*coloq*) *n* tía

au pair /ˌəʊ ˈpeə(r)/ *n* au pair

austere /ɒˈstɪə(r), ɔːˈstɪə(r)/ *adj* austero **austerity** *n* austeridad

authentic /ɔːˈθentɪk/ *adj* auténtico

authenticity /ˌɔːθenˈtɪsəti/ *n* autenticidad

author /ˈɔːθə(r)/ *n* autor, -ora

authoritarian /ɔːˌθɒrɪˈteəriən/ *adj, n* autoritario, -a

authoritative /ɔːˈθɒrətətɪv; *USA* -teɪtɪv/ *adj* **1** (*libro, etc*) de gran autoridad **2** (*voz, etc*) autoritario

authority /ɔːˈθɒrəti/ *n* (*pl* **-ies**) autoridad LOC **to have it on good authority that...** saber de buena fuente que...

authorization, -isation /ˌɔːθəraɪˈzeɪʃn; *USA* -rɪˈz-/ *n* autorización

authorize, -ise /ˈɔːθəraɪz/ *vt* autorizar

autobiographical /ˌɔːtəˌbaɪəˈgræfɪkl/ *adj* autobiográfico

autobiography /ˌɔːtəbaɪˈɒgrəfi/ *n* (*pl* **-ies**) autobiografía

autograph /ˈɔːtəgrɑːf; *USA* -græf/ ◆ *n* autógrafo ◆ *vt* firmar

automate /ˈɔːtəmeɪt/ *vt* automatizar

automatic /ˌɔːtəˈmætɪk/ ◆ *adj* automático ◆ *n* **1** arma automática **2** coche automático **automatically** *adv* automáticamente

automation /ˌɔːtəˈmeɪʃn/ *n* automatización

automobile /ˈɔːtəməbiːl, -məʊ-/ *n* (*esp USA*) automóvil

autonomous /ɔːˈtɒnəməs/ *adj* autónomo **autonomy** *n* autonomía

autopsy /ˈɔːtɒpsi/ *n* (*pl* **-ies**) autopsia

autumn /ˈɔːtəm/ (*USA* **fall**) *n* otoño

auxiliary /ɔːgˈzɪliəri/ *adj, n* auxiliar

avail /əˈveɪl/ *n* LOC **to no avail** en vano

available /əˈveɪləbl/ *adj* disponible

avalanche /ˈævəlɑːnʃ; *USA* -læntʃ/ *n* avalancha

avant-garde /ˌævɒŋ ˈgɑːd/ *adj* vanguardista

avenue /ˈævənjuː; *USA* -nuː/ *n* **1** (*abrev* **Ave**) avenida **2** (*fig*) camino

average /ˈævərɪdʒ/ ◆ *n* promedio: *on average* como media ◆ *adj* **1** medio: *average earnings* el sueldo medio **2** (*coloq, pey*) mediocre PHR V **to average out (at sth)**: *It averages out at 10%.* Sale a un promedio del 10%.

aversion /əˈvɜːʃn/ *n* aversión

avert /əˈvɜːt/ *vt* **1** (*mirada*) apartar **2** (*crisis, etc*) evitar

aviation /ˌeɪviˈeɪʃn/ *n* aviación

avid /ˈævɪd/ *adj* ávido

avocado /ˌævəˈkɑːdəʊ/ *n* (*pl* ~**s**) aguacate

avoid /əˈvɔɪd/ *vt* **1** ~ **(doing) sth** evitar (hacer) algo: *She avoided going.* Evitó ir. **2** (*responsabilidad, etc*) eludir

await /əˈweɪt/ *vt* (*fml*) ~ **sth 1** estar en espera de algo **2** aguardar algo: *A surprise awaited us.* Nos aguardaba una sorpresa. ☛ *Comparar con* WAIT

awake /əˈweɪk/ ◆ *adj* **1** despierto **2** ~ **to sth** (*peligro, etc*) consciente de algo ◆ *vt, vi* (*pret* **awoke** /əˈwəʊk/ *pp* **awoken** /əˈwəʊkən/) despertar(se)

Los verbos **awake** y **awaken** sólo se emplean en lenguaje formal o literario. La expresión normal es **to wake (sb) up**.

awaken /əˈweɪkən/ **1** *vt, vi* despertar(se) ☛ *Ver nota en* AWAKE **2** *vt* ~ **sb to sth** (*peligro, etc*) advertir a algn de algo

award /əˈwɔːd/ ◆ *vt* (*premio, etc*) conceder ◆ *n* premio, galardón

aware /əˈweə(r)/ *adj* ~ **of sth** consciente de algo LOC **as far as I am aware** que yo sepa **to make sb aware of**

sth informar a algn de algo *Ver tb* BECOME **awareness** *n* conciencia

away /əˈweɪ/ *part adv* **1** (*indicando distancia*): *The hotel is two kilometres away.* El hotel está a dos kilómetros. ◊ *It's a long way away.* Queda muy lejos. **2** [*con verbos de movimiento*] irse de una determinada manera: *He limped away.* Se fue cojeando. **3** [*uso enfático con tiempos continuos*]: *I was working away all night.* Pasé toda la noche trabajando. **4** por completo: *The snow had melted away.* La nieve se había derretido del todo. **5** (*Dep*) fuera (de casa): *an away win* una victoria fuera de casa LOC *Ver* RIGHT ☛ Para los usos de **away** en PHRASAL VERBS ver las entradas de los verbos correspondientes, p.ej. **to get away** en GET.

awe /ɔː/ *n* admiración LOC **to be in awe of sb** sentirse intimidado por algn **awesome** *adj* impresionante

awful /ˈɔːfl/ *adj* **1** (*accidente, etc*) horroroso **2** *an awful lot of money* un montón de dinero **awfully** *adv* terriblemente: *I'm awfully sorry.* Lo siento muchísimo.

awkward /ˈɔːkwəd/ *adj* **1** (*momento, etc*) inoportuno **2** (*sensación, etc*) incómodo **3** (*persona*) difícil **4** (*movimiento*) desgarbado

awoke *pret de* AWAKE

awoken *pp de* AWAKE

axe (*USA* **ax**) /æks/ ◆ *n* hacha LOC **to have an axe to grind** tener un interés particular en algo ◆ *vt* **1** (*servicio, etc*) cortar **2** despedir

axis /ˈæksɪs/ *n* (*pl* **axes** /ˈæksiːz/) eje

axle /ˈæksl/ *n* eje (*de ruedas*)

aye (*tb* **ay**) /aɪ/ *interj, n* (*antic*) sí: *The ayes have it.* Han ganado los síes. ☛ **Aye** *es corriente en Escocia y en el norte de Inglaterra.*

Bb

B, b /biː/ *n* (*pl* **B's, b's** /biːz/) **1** B, b: *B for Benjamin* B de Barcelona ☛ *Ver ejemplos en* A, a **2** (*Educ*) notable: *to get (a) B in Science* sacar un notable en Ciencias **3** (*Mús*) si

babble /ˈbæbl/ ◆ *n* **1** (*voces*) murmullo **2** (*bebé*) balbuceo ◆ *vt, vi* farfullar, balbucear

babe /beɪb/ *n* (*USA, coloq*) muñeca (*chica*)

baby /ˈbeɪbi/ *n* (*pl* **babies**) **1** bebé: *a newborn baby* un recién nacido ◊ *a baby girl* una niña **2** (*animal*) cría **3** (*USA, coloq*) cariño

babysit /ˈbeɪbisɪt/ *vi* (**-tt-**) (*pret* **-sat**) ~ (**for sb**) cuidar a un niño (de algn) **babysitter** *n* canguro

bachelor /ˈbætʃələ(r)/ *n* soltero: *a bachelor flat* un piso de soltero

back[1] /bæk/ ◆ *n* **1** parte de atrás, parte de detrás **2** dorso **3** revés **4** espalda: *to lie on your back* estar tumbado boca arriba **5** (*silla*) respaldo LOC **at the back of your/sb's mind** en lo (más) recóndito de la mente **back to back** espalda con espalda **back to front** al revés ☛ *Ver dibujo en* REVÉS **behind sb's back** a espaldas de algn **to be glad, pleased, etc to see the back of sth/sb** alegrarse de librarse de algo/algn **to be on sb's back** estar encima de algn **to get/put sb's back up** sacar de quicio a algn **to have your back to the wall** estar entre la espada y la pared *Ver tb* BREAK[1], PAT, TURN ◆ *adj* **1** trasero: *the back door* la puerta trasera **2** (*número de revista*) atrasado LOC **by/through the back door** por la puerta de atrás ◆ *adv, part adv* **1** (*movimiento, posición*) hacia atrás: *Stand well back.* Manténganse alejados. ◊ *a mile back* una milla más atrás **2** (*regreso, repetición*) de vuelta: *They are back in power.* Están en el poder otra vez. ◊ *on the way back* a la vuelta ◊ *to go there and back* ir y volver **3** (*tiempo*) allá: *back in the seventies* allá por los años setenta ◊ *a few years back* hace algunos años **4** (*reciprocidad*): *He smiled back (at her).* Le devolvió la sonrisa. LOC **to get/have your own back (on sb)** (*coloq*) vengarse (de algn) **to go, travel, etc back and forth** ir y venir ☛ Para los usos de **back** en PHRASAL VERBS ver las entradas de los verbos correspondientes, p.ej. **to go back** en GO[1].

back[2] /bæk/ **1** *vt* ~ **sth/sb** (**up**) respaldar algo/a algn **2** *vt* financiar **3** *vt* apostar por **4** *vi* ~ (**up**) dar marcha atrás PHR V **to back away** (**from sth/sb**) retroceder (ante algo/algn) **to back down**; (*USA*) **to back off** retractarse **to back on to sth**: *Our house backs on to the river.* La parte de atrás de nuestra casa da al río. **to back out** (**of an agreement, etc**) echarse atrás (de un acuerdo, etc)

backache /ˈbækeɪk/ *n* dolor de espalda

backbone /ˈbækbəʊn/ *n* **1** columna vertebral **2** fortaleza, empuje

backcloth /ˈbækklɒθ/ (*tb* **backdrop** /ˈbækdrɒp/) *n* telón de fondo

backfire /ˌbækˈfaɪə(r)/ *vi* **1** (*coche*) petardear **2** ~ (**on sb**) (*fig*) salirle (a algn) el tiro por la culata

background /ˈbækgraʊnd/ *n* **1** fondo **2** contexto **3** clase social, educación, formación

backing /ˈbækɪŋ/ *n* **1** respaldo, apoyo **2** (*Mús*) acompañamiento

backlash /ˈbæklæʃ/ *n* reacción violenta

backlog /ˈbæklɒg/ *n* atraso: *a huge backlog of work* un montón de trabajo atrasado

backpack /ˈbækpæk/ *n* mochila

back seat *n* (*coche*) asiento trasero LOC **to take a back seat** pasar a segundo plano

backside /ˈbæksaɪd/ *n* (*coloq*) trasero

backstage /ˌbækˈsteɪdʒ/ *adv* entre bastidores

backup /ˈbækʌp/ *n* **1** refuerzos, asistencia **2** (*Informát*) copia

backward /ˈbækwəd/ *adj* **1** hacia atrás: *a backward glance* una mirada hacia atrás **2** atrasado

backward(s) /ˈbækwədz/ *adv* **1** hacia atrás **2** de espaldas: *He fell backwards.* Se cayó de espaldas. **3** al revés LOC **backward(s) and forward(s)** de un lado a otro

backyard /ˌbækˈjɑːd/ (*tb* **yard**) *n* (*GB*) patio trasero

bacon /ˈbeɪkən/ *n* bacon ☛ *Comparar con* HAM, GAMMON

bacteria /bækˈtɪəriə/ *n* [*pl*] bacterias

bad /bæd/ *adj* (*comp* **worse** /wɜːs/ *superl* **worst** /wɜːst/) **1** malo: *It's bad for your health.* Es malo para la salud. ◇ *This film's not bad.* Esta película no está mal. **2** grave **3** (*dolor de cabeza, etc*) fuerte LOC **to be bad at sth**: *I'm bad at Maths.* Se me dan mal las matemáticas. **to be in sb's bad books**: *I'm in his bad books.* Me ha puesto en su lista negra. **to go through/hit a bad patch** (*coloq*) pasar/tener una mala racha **too bad 1** una pena: *It's too bad you can't come.* Es una pena que no puedas venir. **2** (*irón*) ¡peor para ti! *Ver tb* FAITH, FEELING

bade *pret de* BID *en* LOC **to bid/say farewell to sb** *en* FAREWELL

badge /bædʒ/ *n* **1** insignia, chapa **2** (*fig*) símbolo

badger /ˈbædʒə(r)/ *n* tejón

bad language *n* palabrotas

badly /ˈbædli/ *adv* (*comp* **worse** /wɜːs/ *superl* **worst** /wɜːst/) **1** mal: *It's badly made.* Está mal hecho. **2** (*dañar, etc*): *The house was badly damaged.* La casa sufrió muchos daños. **3** (*necesitar, etc*) con urgencia LOC (**not**) **to be badly off** (no) andar mal de fondos

badminton /ˈbædmɪntən/ *n* bádminton

bad-tempered /ˌbæd ˈtempəd/ *adj* de mal genio

baffle /ˈbæfl/ *vt* **1** desconcertar **2** frustrar **baffling** *adj* desconcertante

bag /bæg/ *n* bolsa, bolso ☛ *Ver dibujo en* CONTAINER LOC **bags of sth** (*coloq*) un montón de algo **to be in the bag** (*coloq*) estar en el bote *Ver tb* LET[1], PACK

baggage /ˈbægɪdʒ/ *n* equipaje

bagpipe /ˈbægpaɪp/ (*tb* **bagpipes, pipes**) *n* gaita: *bagpipe music* música de gaita

baguette /bæˈget/ *n* barra de pan ☛ *Ver dibujo en* PAN

bail /beɪl/ *n* [*incontable*] fianza, libertad bajo fianza LOC **to go/stand bail** (**for sb**) pagar la fianza (de algn)

bailiff /ˈbeɪlɪf/ *n* alguacil

bait /beɪt/ *n* cebo

bake /beɪk/ **1** *vt, vi* (*pan, pastel*) hacer(se): *a baking tin* un molde **2** *vt, vi* (*patatas*) asar(se) **baker** *n* **1** panadero, -a **2 baker's** panadería **bakery** *n* (*pl* **-ies**) panadería

baked beans *n* [*pl*] judías en salsa de tomate: *a can of baked beans* una lata de judías en salsa de tomate

balance /ˈbæləns/ ◆ *n* **1** equilibrio: *to lose your balance* perder el equilibrio **2** (*Fin*) saldo, balance **3** (*instrumento*) balanza LOC **on balance** bien mirado *Ver tb* CATCH ◆ **1** *vi* ~ (**on sth**) mantener el equilibrio (sobre algo) **2** *vt* ~ **sth** (**on sth**) mantener algo en equilibrio (sobre algo) **3** *vt* equilibrar **4** *vt* compensar, contrarrestar **5** *vt, vi* (*cuentas*) (hacer) cuadrar

balcony /ˈbælkəni/ *n* (*pl* **-ies**) balcón

bald /bɔːld/ *adj* calvo

ball /bɔːl/ *n* **1** (*Dep*) balón, pelota, bola **2** esfera, ovillo **3** baile (de etiqueta) LOC (**to be**) **on the ball** (*coloq*) (estar) al tanto **to have a ball** (*coloq*) pasárselo bomba **to start/set the ball rolling** empezar

ballad /ˈbæləd/ *n* balada, romance

ballet /ˈbæleɪ/ *n* ballet

ballet dancer *n* bailarín, -ina

balloon /bəˈluːn/ *n* globo

ballot /ˈbælət/ *n* votación

ballot box *n* urna (*electoral*)

ballroom /ˈbɔːlruːm/ *n* salón de baile: *ballroom dancing* baile de salón

bamboo /ˌbæmˈbuː/ *n* bambú

ban /bæn/ ◆ *vt* (**-nn-**) prohibir ◆ *n* **ban** (**on sth**) prohibición (de algo)

banana /bəˈnɑːnə; *USA* bəˈnænə/ *n* plátano: *banana skin* piel de plátano

band /bænd/ *n* **1** cinta, franja **2** (*en baremos*) escalón (de tributación), escala **3** (*Mús, Radio*) banda: *a jazz band* un grupo de jazz **4** (*de ladrones, etc*) banda

andage /ˈbændɪdʒ/ ◆ *n* vendaje ◆ *vt* vendar

andwagon /ˈbændwægən/ *n* LOC **to climb/jump on the bandwagon** (*coloq*) subirse al mismo carro/tren

ang /bæŋ/ ◆ **1** *vt* dar un golpe en: *He banged his fist on the table.* Dio un golpe en la mesa con el puño. ◊ *I banged the box down on the floor.* Tiré la caja al suelo de un golpe. **2** *vt* ~ **your head, etc** (**against/on sth**) darse en la cabeza, etc (con algo) **3** *vi* ~ **into sth/sb** darse contra algo/algn **4** *vi* (*petardo, etc*) estallar **5** *vi* (*puerta, etc*) dar golpes ◆ *n* **1** golpe **2** estallido ◆ (*coloq*) *adv* justo, completamente: *bang on time* justo a tiempo ◊ *bang up to date* completamente al día LOC **bang goes sth** se acabó algo **to go bang** (*coloq*) estallar ◆ **bang!** *interj* ¡pum!

banger /ˈbæŋə(r)/ *n* (*GB, coloq*) **1** salchicha **2** petardo **3** (*coche*) cacharro: *an old banger* un viejo cacharro

banish /ˈbænɪʃ/ *vt* desterrar

banister /ˈbænɪstə(r)/ *n* barandilla, pasamanos

bank[1] /bæŋk/ *n* orilla (*de río, lago*) ☛ *Comparar con* SHORE

bank[2] /bæŋk/ ◆ *n* banco: *bank manager* director de banco ◊ *bank statement* estado de cuenta ◊ *bank account* cuenta bancaria ◊ *bank balance* saldo bancario LOC *Ver* BREAK[1] ◆ **1** *vt* (*dinero*) ingresar **2** *vi* tener cuenta: *Who do you bank with?* ¿En qué banco tienes cuenta? PHR V **to bank on sth/sb** contar con algo/algn **banker** *n* banquero, -a

bank holiday *n* (*GB*) día festivo

bankrupt /ˈbæŋkrʌpt/ *adj* en bancarrota LOC **to go bankrupt** ir a la bancarrota **bankruptcy** *n* bancarrota, quiebra

banner /ˈbænə(r)/ *n* pancarta, estandarte

banning /ˈbænɪŋ/ *n* prohibición

banquet /ˈbæŋkwɪt/ *n* banquete

baptism /ˈbæptɪzəm/ *n* bautismo, bautizo **baptize, -ise** *vt* bautizar

bar /bɑː(r)/ ◆ *n* **1** barra **2** bar ☛ *Ver* pág 320. **3** (*de chocolate*) tableta **4** (*de jabón*) pastilla **5** (*Mús*) compás **6** prohibición LOC **behind bars** (*coloq*) entre rejas ◆ *vt* (**-rr-**) **to bar sb from doing sth** prohibir a algn hacer algo LOC **to bar the way** cerrar el paso ◆ *prep* excepto

barbarian /bɑːˈbeəriən/ *n* bárbaro, -a **barbaric** /bɑːˈbærɪk/ *adj* bárbaro

barbecue /ˈbɑːbɪkjuː/ *n* barbacoa

barbed wire /ˌbɑːbd ˈwaɪə(r)/ *n* alambre de espino

barber /ˈbɑːbə(r)/ *n* peluquero: *the barber's* la peluquería

bar chart *n* gráfico de barras

bare /beə(r)/ *adj* (**barer**, **barest**) **1** desnudo ☛ *Ver nota en* NAKED **2**

descubierto **3** ~ (**of sth**): *a room bare of furniture* una habitación sin muebles **4** mínimo: *the bare essentials* lo mínimo **barely** *adv* apenas

barefoot /ˈbeəfʊt/ *adv* descalzo

bargain /ˈbɑːɡən/ ◆ *n* **1** trato **2** ganga LOC **into the bargain** además *Ver tb* DRIVE ◆ *vi* **1** negociar **2** regatear PHR V **to bargain for sth** (*coloq*) esperar algo **bargaining 1** negociación: *pay bargaining* negociaciones salariales **2** regateo

barge /bɑːdʒ/ *n* barcaza

baritone /ˈbærɪtəʊn/ *n* barítono

bark[1] /bɑːk/ *n* corteza (*árbol*)

bark[2] /bɑːk/ ◆ *n* ladrido ◆ **1** *vi* ladrar **2** *vt, vi* (*persona*) gritar **barking** *n* ladridos

barley /ˈbɑːli/ *n* cebada

barmaid /ˈbɑːmeɪd/ *n* camarera

barman /ˈbɑːmən/ *n* (*pl* **-men** /-mən/) (*USA* **bartender**) camarero

barn /bɑːn/ *n* granero

barometer /bəˈrɒmɪtə(r)/ *n* barómetro

baron /ˈbærən/ *n* barón

baroness /ˈbærənɪs/ *n* baronesa

barracks /ˈbærəks/ *n* [*v sing o pl*] cuartel

barrage /ˈbærɑːʒ; *USA* bəˈrɑːʒ/ *n* **1** (*Mil*) descarga de fuego **2** (*quejas, preguntas, etc*) bombardeo

barrel /ˈbærəl/ *n* **1** barril, tonel **2** cañón

barren /ˈbærən/ *adj* árido, improductivo (*tierra, etc*)

barricade /ˌbærɪˈkeɪd/ ◆ *n* barricada ◆ *vt* bloquear (con una barricada) PHR V **to barricade yourself in** encerrarse (poniendo barricadas)

barrier /ˈbæriə(r)/ *n* barrera

barrister /ˈbærɪstə(r)/ *n* abogado, -a ☛ *Ver nota en* ABOGADO

barrow /ˈbærəʊ/ *n Ver* WHEELBARROW

bartender /ˈbɑːtendə(r)/ *n* (*USA*) camarero

base /beɪs/ ◆ *n* base ◆ *vt* **1** basar **2 to be based in/at** tener su base en

baseball /ˈbeɪsbɔːl/ *n* béisbol

basement /ˈbeɪsmənt/ *n* sótano

bash /bæʃ/ ◆ *vt, vi* (*coloq*) **1** golpear fuertemente **2** ~ **your head, elbow, etc** (**against/on/into sth**) darse un golpe en la cabeza, el codo, etc (con algo) ◆ *n* golpe fuerte LOC **to have a bash** (**at sth**) (*coloq*) intentar (algo)

basic /ˈbeɪsɪk/ ◆ *adj* **1** fundamental **2** básico **3** elemental ◆ **basics** *n* [*pl*] lo esencial, la base **basically** *adv* básicamente

basin /ˈbeɪsn/ *n* **1** (*tb* **washbasin**) lavabo ☛ *Comparar con* SINK **2** cuenco **3** (*Geog*) cuenca

basis /ˈbeɪsɪs/ *n* (*pl* **bases** /ˈbeɪsiːz/) base: *on the basis of sth* basándose en algo LOC *Ver* REGULAR

basket /ˈbɑːskɪt; *USA* ˈbæskɪt/ *n* cesta, cesto: *a waste-paper basket* papelera LOC *Ver* EGG

basketball /ˈbɑːskɪtbɔːl; *USA* ˈbæs-/ *n* baloncesto

bass /beɪs/ ◆ *n* **1** (*cantante*) bajo **2** graves: *to turn up the bass* subir los graves **3** (*tb* **bass guitar**) bajo **4** (*tb* **double bass**) contrabajo ◆ *adj* bajo ☛ *Comparar con* TREBLE[2]

bat[1] /bæt/ *n* murciélago

bat[2] /bæt/ ◆ *n* bate ◆ *vt, vi* (-tt-) batear LOC **not to bat an eyelid** (*coloq*) no pestañear

batch /bætʃ/ *n* lote

bath /bɑːθ; *USA* bæθ/ ◆ *n* (*pl* ~**s** /bɑːðz; *USA* bæðz/) **1** baño: *to have/take a bath* darse un baño **2** bañera ◆ *vt* (*GB*) bañar

bathe /beɪð/ **1** *vt* (*ojos, herida*) lavar **2** *vi* (*GB*) bañarse

bathroom /ˈbɑːθruːm; *USA* ˈbæθ-/ *n* **1** (*GB*) (cuarto de) baño **2** (*USA, euf* mismo) aseo ☛ *Ver nota en* TOILET

baton /ˈbætn, ˈbætɒn; *USA* bəˈtɒn/ *n* **1** (*policía*) porra **2** (*Mús*) batuta **3** (*Dep*) testigo

battalion /bəˈtæliən/ *n* batallón

batter /ˈbætə(r)/ **1** *vt* ~ **sb** apalear a algn: *to batter sb to death* matar a algn a palos **2** *vt, vi* ~ (**at/on**) **sth** aporrear algo PHR V **to batter sth down** derribar algo a golpes **battered** *adj* deformado

battery /ˈbætəri/ *n* (*pl* **-ies**) **1** batería, pila (*Elec*) **2** de cría intensiva: *a battery hen* gallina de cría industrial ☛ *Comparar con* FREE-RANGE

battle /ˈbætl/ ◆ *n* batalla, lucha LOC *Ver* FIGHT, WAGE ◆ *vi* **1** ~ (**with/against sth/sb**) (**for sth**) luchar (con/contra algo/algn) (por algo) **2** ~ (**on**) seguir luchando

be

presente	*contracciones*	*negativa contracciones*	*pasado*
I **am**	I**'m**	I**'m not**	I **was**
you **are**	you**'re**	you **aren't**	you **were**
he/she/it **is**	he**'s**/she**'s**/it**'s**	he/she/it **isn't**	he/she/it **was**
we **are**	we**'re**	we **aren't**	we **were**
you **are**	you**'re**	you **aren't**	you **were**
they **are**	they**'re**	they **aren't**	they **were**

forma en -ing **being** *participio pasado* **been**

battlefield /ˈbætlfiːld/ (*tb* **battleground**) *n* campo de batalla

battlements /ˈbætlmənts/ *n* [*pl*] almenas

battleship /ˈbætlʃɪp/ *n* acorazado

bauble /ˈbɔːbl/ *n* adorno, chuchería

bawl /bɔːl/ **1** *vi* berrear **2** *vt* gritar

bay /beɪ/ ◆ *n* **1** bahía **2** *loading bay* zona de carga **3** (*tb* **bay tree**) laurel **4** caballo pardo LOC **to hold/keep sth/sb at bay** mantener algo/a algn a raya ◆ *vi* aullar

bayonet /ˈbeɪənət/ *n* bayoneta

bay window *n* ventana (*en forma de mirador redondo*)

bazaar /bəˈzɑː(r)/ *n* **1** bazar **2** mercadillo benéfico *Ver tb* FÊTE

BC /ˌbiːˈsiː/ *abrev* **before Christ** antes de Cristo

be /bi, biː/ ☛ Para los usos de **be** con **there** ver THERE.

• **v intransitivo 1** ser: *Life is unfair.* La vida es injusta. ◊ *'Who is it?' 'It's me.'* —¿Quién es? —Soy yo. ◊ *It's John's.* Es de John. ◊ *Be quick!* ¡Date prisa! ◊ *I was late.* Llegué tarde. **2** (*estado*) estar: *How are you?* ¿Cómo estás? ◊ *Is he alive?* ¿Está vivo?

Compara las dos oraciones: *He's bored.* Está aburrido. ◊ *He's boring.* Es aburrido. Con adjetivos terminados en **-ed**, como *interested, tired,* etc, el verbo **to be** expresa un estado y se traduce por "estar", mientras que con adjetivos terminados en *-ing*, como *interesting, tiring,* etc, expresa una cualidad y se traduce por "ser".

3 (*localización*) estar: *Mary's upstairs.* Mary está arriba. **4** (*origen*) ser: *She's from Italy.* Es italiana. **5** [*sólo en tiempo perfecto*] visitar: *I've never been to Spain.* Nunca he estado en España. ◊ *Has the plumber been yet?* ¿Ha venido ya el fontanero? ◊ *I've been into town.* He ido al centro. ☛ A veces **been** se utiliza como participio de **go**. *Ver nota en* GO[1] **6** tener: *I'm right, aren't I?* ¿A que tengo razón? ◊ *I'm hot/afraid.* Tengo calor/miedo. ◊ *Are you in a hurry?* ¿Tienes prisa?

Nótese que en español se usa **tener** con sustantivos como *calor, frío, hambre, sed,* etc, mientras que en inglés se usa **be** con el adjetivo correspondiente.

7 (*edad*) tener: *He is ten (years old).* Tiene diez años. ☛ *Ver nota en* OLD, YEAR **8** (*tiempo*): *It's cold/hot.* Hace frío/calor. ◊ *It's foggy.* Hay niebla. **9** (*medida*) medir: *He is six feet tall.* Mide 1,80m. **10** (*hora*) ser: *It's two o'clock.* Son las dos. **11** (*precio*) costar: *How much is that dress?* ¿Cuánto cuesta ese vestido? **12** (*Mat*) ser: *Two and two is/are four.* Dos y dos son cuatro.

• **v auxiliar 1** [*con participios para formar la pasiva*]: *He was killed in the war.* Lo mataron en la guerra. ◊ *It is said that he is/He is said to be rich.* Dicen que es rico. **2** [*con -ing para formar tiempos continuos*]: *What are you doing?* ¿Qué haces/Qué estás haciendo? ◊ *I'm just coming!* ¡Ya voy! **3** [*con infinitivo*]: *I am to inform you that…* Debo informarle que… ◊ *They were to be married.* Se iban a casar. ☛ Para expresiones con **be**, véanse las entradas del sustantivo, adjetivo, etc, p.ej. **to be a drain on sth** en DRAIN. PHR V **to be through (to sth/sb)** (*GB*) tener línea (con algo/algn) **to be through (with sth/sb)** haber terminado (con algo/algn)

beach /biːtʃ/ ◆ *n* playa ◆ *vt* varar

beacon /ˈbiːkən/ *n* **1** faro **2** (*hoguera*) almenara **3** (*tb* **radio beacon**) radiobaliza

bead /biːd/ *n* **1** cuenta **2 beads** [*pl*] collar de cuentas **3** (*de sudor, etc*) gota

beak /biːk/ *n* pico

beaker /ˈbiːkə(r)/ *n* vaso alto (*de plástico*)

beam /biːm/ ◆ *n* **1** viga, travesaño **2** (*de luz*) rayo **3** (*de linterna, etc*) haz de luz **4** sonrisa radiante ◆ *vi*: *to beam at sb* echar una sonrisa radiante a algn ◆ *vt* transmitir (*programa, mensaje*)

bean /biːn/ *n* **1** (*semilla*): *kidney beans* alubias rojas ◇ *broad beans* habas *Ver tb* BAKED BEANS **2** (*vaina*) judía **3** (*café, cacao*) grano

bear[1] /beə(r)/ *n* oso

bear[2] /beə(r)/ (*pret* **bore** /bɔː(r)/ *pp* **borne** /bɔːn/) **1** *vt* aguantar **2** *vt* (*firma, etc*) llevar **3** *vt* (*carga*) soportar **4** *vt* (*gastos*) hacerse cargo de **5** *vt* (*responsabilidad*) asumir **6** *vt* resistir: *It won't bear close examination.* No resistirá un examen a fondo. **7** *vt* (*fml*) (*hijo*) dar a luz **8** *vt* (*cosecha, resultado*) producir **9** *vi* (*carretera, etc*) torcer LOC **to bear a grudge** guardar rencor **to bear a resemblance to sth/sb** tener un parecido a algo/algn **to bear little relation to sth** tener poca relación con algo **to bear sth/sb in mind** tener a algo/algn en cuenta *Ver tb* GRIN PHR V **to bear sth/sb out** confirmar algo/lo que algn ha dicho **to bear with sb** tener paciencia con algn **bearable** *adj* tolerable

beard /bɪəd/ *n* barba **bearded** *adj* barbudo, con barba

bearer /ˈbeərə(r)/ *n* **1** (*noticias, cheque*) portador, -ora **2** (*documento*) titular

bearing /ˈbeərɪŋ/ *n* (*Náut*) marcación LOC **to get/take your bearings** orientarse **to have a bearing on sth** tener que ver con algo

beast /biːst/ *n* animal, bestia: *wild beasts* fieras

beat /biːt/ ◆ (*pret* **beat** *pp* **beaten** /ˈbiːtn/) **1** *vt* golpear **2** *vt* (*metal, huevos, alas*) batir **3** *vt* (*tambor*) tocar **4** *vt, vi* dar golpes (en) **5** *vi* (*corazón*) latir **6** *vi* ~ **against/on sth** batir (contra) algo **7** *vt* ~ **sb (at sth)** vencer a algn (a algo) **8** *vt* (*récord*) batir **9** *vt* (*fig*): *Nothing beats home cooking.* No hay nada como la cocina casera. LOC **off the beaten track** (en un lugar) apartado **to beat about the bush** andarse con rodeos PHR V **to beat sb up** dar una paliza a algn ◆ *n* **1** ritmo **2** (*tambor*) redoble **3** (*policía*) ronda **beating** *n* **1** (*castigo, derrota*) paliza **2** batir **3** (*corazón*) latido LOC **to take a lot of/some beating** ser difícil de superar

beautiful /ˈbjuːtɪfl/ *adj* **1** hermoso **2** magnífico **beautifully** *adv* estupendamente

beauty /ˈbjuːti/ *n* (*pl* **-ies**) **1** belleza **2** (*persona o cosa*) preciosidad

beaver /ˈbiːvə(r)/ *n* castor

became *pret de* BECOME

because /bɪˈkɒz; *USA* -kɔːz/ *conj* porque **because of** *prep* a causa de, debido a: *because of you* por ti

beckon /ˈbekən/ **1** *vi* ~ **to sb** hacer señas a algn **2** *vt* llamar con señas

become /bɪˈkʌm/ *vi* (*pret* **became** /bɪˈkeɪm/ *pp* **become**) **1** [+ *sustantivo*] llegar a ser, convertirse en, hacerse: *She became a doctor.* Se hizo médico. **2** [+ *adj*] ponerse, volverse: *to become fashionable* ponerse de moda ◇ *She became aware that…* Se dio cuenta de que… *Ver tb* GET LOC **to become aware of sth** darse cuenta de algo **to become of sth/sb** pasar con algo/algn: *What will become of me?* ¿Que será de mí?

bed /bed/ *n* **1** cama: *a single/double bed* una cama individual/de matrimonio ◇ *to make the bed* hacer la cama

> Nótese que en las siguientes expresiones no se usa el artículo determinado en inglés: *to go to bed* irse a la cama ◇ *It's time for bed.* Es hora de irse a la cama.

2 (*tb* **river bed**) lecho (*de un río*) **3** (*tb* **sea bed**) fondo (*del océano*) **4** (*flores*) macizo *Ver tb* FLOWER BED

bed and breakfast (*tb abrev* **B & B, b & b**) *n* pensión y desayuno

bedclothes /ˈbedkləʊðz/ (*tb* **bedding**) *n* [*pl*] ropa de cama

bedroom /ˈbedruːm/ *n* dormitorio

bedside /ˈbedsaɪd/ *n* cabecera: *bedside table* mesilla de noche

bedsit /ˈbedsɪt/ *n* (*GB*) habitación con cama y cocina

bedspread /ˈbedspred/ *n* colcha

bedtime /ˈbedtaɪm/ *n* hora de acostarse

bee /biː/ *n* abeja

beech /biːtʃ/ (*tb* **beech tree**) *n* haya

beef /biːf/ *n* carne de vaca: *roast beef* rosbif ☛ *Ver nota en* CARNE

beefburger /ˈbiːfbɜːɡə(r)/ *n* hamburguesa ☛ *Comparar con* BURGER, HAMBURGER

beehive /ˈbiːhaɪv/ *n* colmena

been /biːn, bɪn; *USA* bɪn/ *pp de* BE

beer /bɪə(r)/ *n* cerveza ☛ *Comparar con* BITTER, ALE, LAGER

beetle /ˈbiːtl/ *n* escarabajo

beetroot /ˈbiːtruːt/ (*USA* **beet**) *n* remolacha (*cocida*)

before /bɪˈfɔː(r)/ ◆ *adv* antes: *the day/week before* el día/la semana anterior ◊ *I've never seen her before.* No la había visto nunca. ◆ *prep* **1** antes de (que), antes que: *before lunch* antes de comer ◊ *the day before yesterday* anteayer ◊ *He arrived before me.* Llegó antes que yo. **2** ante: *right before my eyes* ante mis propios ojos **3** delante de: *He puts his work before everything else.* Antepone su trabajo a todo lo demás. ◆ *conj* antes de que: *before he goes on holiday* antes de que se vaya de vacaciones

beforehand /bɪˈfɔːhænd/ *adv* de antemano

beg /beɡ/ (**-gg-**) **1** *vt, vi* **to beg (sth/for sth) (from sb)** mendigar: *They had to beg (for) scraps from shopkeepers.* Tenían que mendigar sobras a los tenderos. **2** *vt* **to beg sb to do sth** suplicar a algn que haga algo ☛ *Comparar con* ASK LOC **to beg sb's pardon 1** pedir perdón a algn **2** pedir a algn que repita lo que ha dicho **beggar** *n* mendigo, -a

begin /bɪˈɡɪn/ *vt, vi* (**-nn-**) (*pret* **began** /bɪˈɡæn/ *pp* **begun** /bɪˈɡʌn/) ~ **(doing/to do sth)** empezar (a hacer algo): *Shall I begin?* ¿Empiezo yo? LOC **to begin with 1** para empezar **2** al principio **beginner** *n* principiante **beginning** *n* **1** comienzo, principio: *at/in the beginning* al principio ◊ *from beginning to end* de principio a fin **2** origen

behalf /bɪˈhɑːf; *USA* -ˈhæf/ *n* LOC **on behalf of sb/on sb's behalf**; *USA* **in behalf of sb/in sb's behalf** en nombre de algn/en su nombre

behave /bɪˈheɪv/ *vi* ~ **well, badly, etc (towards sb)** comportarse bien, mal, etc (con algn): *Behave yourself!* ¡Pórtate bien! ◊ *well-behaved* bien educado

behaviour (*USA* **behavior**) /bɪˈheɪvjə(r)/ *n* comportamiento

behind /bɪˈhaɪnd/ ◆ *prep* **1** detrás de, tras: *I put it behind the cupboard.* Lo puse detrás del armario. ◊ *What's behind this sudden change?* ¿Qué hay detrás de este cambio repentino? **2** retrasado con respecto a: *to be behind schedule* ir retrasado (con respecto a los planes) **3** a favor de ◆ *adv* **1** atrás: *to leave sth behind* dejar algo atrás ◊ *to look behind* mirar hacia atrás ◊ *He was shot from behind.* Le dispararon por la espalda. ◊ *to stay behind* quedarse ☛ *Comparar con* FRONT **2** ~ **(in/with sth)** atrasado (en/con algo) ◆ *n* (*eufemismo*) trasero

being /ˈbiːɪŋ/ *n* **1** ser: *human beings* seres humanos **2** existencia LOC **to come into being** crearse

belated /bɪˈleɪtɪd/ *adj* tardío

belch /beltʃ/ ◆ *vi* eructar ◆ *n* eructo

belief /bɪˈliːf/ *n* **1** creencia **2** ~ **in sth** confianza, fe en algo LOC **beyond belief** increíble **in the belief that...** confiando en que... *Ver tb* BEST

believe /bɪˈliːv/ *vt, vi* creer: *I believe so.* Creo que sí. LOC **believe it or not** aunque no te lo creas *Ver tb* LEAD[2] PHR V **to believe in sth/sb** creer en algo, confiar en algo/algn **believable** *adj* creíble **believer** *n* creyente LOC **to be a (great/firm) believer in sth** ser (gran) partidario de algo

bell /bel/ *n* **1** campana, campanilla **2** timbre: *to ring the bell* tocar el timbre

bellow /ˈbeləʊ/ ◆ **1** *vi* bramar **2** *vt, vi* gritar ◆ *n* **1** bramido **2** grito

belly /ˈbeli/ *n* (*pl* **-ies**) **1** (*coloq*) (*persona*) barriga **2** (*animal*) panza

belong /bɪˈlɒŋ; *USA* -ˈlɔːŋ/ *vi* **1** ~ **to sth/sb** pertenecer a algo/algn: *Who does this belong to?* ¿A quién pertenece esto? **2** deber estar: *Where does this belong?* ¿Dónde se pone esto? **belongings** *n* [*pl*] pertenencias

below /bɪˈləʊ/ ◆ *prep* (por) debajo de, bajo: *five degrees below freezing* cinco grados bajo cero ◆ *adv* (más) abajo: *above and below* arriba y abajo

belt /belt/ *n* **1** cinturón **2** (*Mec*) cinta, correa: *conveyor belt* cinta transportadora **3** (*Geog*) zona LOC **below the belt** golpe bajo: *That remark was rather below the belt.* Ese comentario fue un golpe bajo.

bemused /bɪˈmjuːzd/ *adj* perplejo

bench /bentʃ/ *n* **1** (*asiento*) banco **2**

(*GB, Pol*) escaño **3 the bench** la magistratura

benchmark /ˈbentʃmɑːk/ *n* punto de referencia

bend /bend/ ◆ (*pret, pp* **bent** /bent/) **1** *vt, vi* doblar(se) **2** *vi* (*tb* **to bend down**) agacharse, inclinarse PHR V **to be bent on (doing) sth** estar empeñado en (hacer) algo ◆ *n* **1** curva **2** (*tubería*) codo

beneath /bɪˈniːθ/ ◆ *prep* (*fml*) **1** bajo, debajo de **2** indigno de ◆ *adv* abajo

benefactor /ˈbenɪfæktə(r)/ *n* benefactor, -ora

beneficial /ˌbenɪˈfɪʃl/ *adj* beneficioso, provechoso

benefit /ˈbenɪfɪt/ ◆ *n* **1** beneficio: *to be of benefit to* ser beneficioso para **2** subsidio: *unemployment benefit* subsidio de desempleo **3** función benéfica LOC **to give sb the benefit of the doubt** conceder a algn el beneficio de la duda ◆ (*pret, pp* **-fited**, *USA tb* **-fitted**) **1** *vt* beneficiar **2** *vi* ~ (**from/by sth**) beneficiarse, sacar provecho (de algo)

benevolent /bəˈnevələnt/ *adj* **1** benévolo **2** benéfico **benevolence** *n* benevolencia

benign /bɪˈnaɪn/ *adj* benigno

bent /bent/ ◆ *pret, pp de* BEND ◆ *n* ~ (**for sth**) facilidad (para algo); inclinación (por algo)

bequeath /bɪˈkwiːð/ *vt* (*fml*) ~ **sth (to sb)** legar algo (a algn)

bequest /bɪˈkwest/ *n* (*fml*) legado

bereaved /bɪˈriːvd/ *adj* (*fml*) afligido por la muerte de un ser querido **bereavement** *n* pérdida (de un ser querido)

beret /ˈbereɪ; *USA* bəˈreɪ/ *n* boina

berry /ˈberi/ *n* (*pl* **-ies**) baya

berserk /bəˈsɜːk/ *adj* loco: *to go berserk* volverse loco

berth /bɜːθ/ ◆ *n* **1** (*barco*) camarote **2** (*tren*) litera **3** (*Náut*) atracadero ◆ *vt, vi* atracar (*un barco*)

beset /bɪˈset/ *vt* (**-tt-**) (*pret, pp* **beset**) (*fml*) acosar: *beset by doubts* acosado por las dudas

beside /bɪˈsaɪd/ *prep* junto a, al lado de LOC **beside yourself (with sth)** fuera de sí (por algo)

besides /bɪˈsaɪdz/ ◆ *prep* **1** además de **2** aparte de: *No one writes to me besides you.* Nadie me escribe más que tú. ◆ *adv* además

besiege /bɪˈsiːdʒ/ *vt* **1** (*lit y fig*) asediar **2** acosar

best /best/ ◆ *adj* (*superl de* **good**) mejor: *the best dinner I've ever had* la mejor cena que he comido en mi vida ◊ *the best footballer in the world* el mejor futbolista del mundo ◊ *my best friend* mi mejor amigo *Ver tb* GOOD, BETTER LOC **best before**: *best before January 1999* consumir antes de enero 1999 **best wishes**: *Best wishes, Ann.* Un fuerte abrazo, Ann. ◊ *Give her my best wishes.* Dale muchos recuerdos. ◆ *adv* (*superl de* **well**) **1** mejor: *best dressed* mejor vestido ◊ *Do as you think best.* Haz lo que te parezca más oportuno. **2** más: *best-known* más conocido LOC **as best you can** lo mejor que puedas ◆ *n* **1 the best** el/la mejor: *She's the best by far.* Ella es con mucho la mejor. **2 the best** lo mejor: *to want the best for sb* querer lo mejor para algn **3 (the) ~ of sth**: *We're (the) best of friends.* Somos excelentes amigos. LOC **at best** en el mejor de los casos **to be at its/your best** estar algo/algn en su mejor momento **to do/try your (level/very) best** hacer todo lo posible **to make the best of sth** sacar el máximo partido de algo **to the best of your belief/knowledge** que tú sepas

best man *n* padrino (de boda) ☞ *Ver nota en* BODA

best-seller /ˌbest ˈselə(r)/ *n* éxito editorial/de ventas

bet /bet/ ◆ *vt* (**-tt-**) (*pret, pp* **bet** o **betted**) **to bet on sth** apostar en algo LOC **I bet (that)...** (*coloq*) *I bet you he doesn't come.* ¡A que no viene! ◆ *n* apuesta: *to place/put a bet (on sth)* apostar (por algo)

betide /bɪˈtaɪd/ LOC *Ver* WOE

betray /bɪˈtreɪ/ *vt* **1** (*país, principios*) traicionar **2** (*secreto*) revelar **betrayal** *n* traición

better /ˈbetə(r)/ ◆ *adj* (*comp de* **good**) mejor: *It was better than I expected.* Fue mejor de lo que esperaba. ◊ *He is much better today.* Hoy está mucho mejor *Ver tb* BEST, GOOD LOC **(to be) little/no better than...** no valer más que... **to get better** mejorar **to have seen/known better days** no ser lo que era *Ver tb* ALL ◆ *adv* **1** (*comp de* **well**) mejor: *She sings better than me/than* *(do).* Canta mejor que yo. **2** más: *I like him better than before.* Me gusta más que antes. LOC **better late than never** (*refrán*) más vale tarde que nunca **better safe than sorry** (*refrán*) más vale prevenir que curar **I'd, you'd, etc better/best (do sth)** ser mejor (que haga, hagas, etc algo): *I'd better be going now.* Será mejor que me vaya ahora. **to be better off (doing sth)**: *He'd be better off leaving now.* Más le valdría irse ahora. **to be better off (without sth/sb)** estar mejor (sin algo/ algn) *Ver tb* KNOW, SOON ◆ *n* (algo) mejor: *I expected better of him.* Esperaba más de él. LOC **to get the better of sb** vencer a algn: *His shyness got the better of him.* Le venció la timidez.

betting shop *n* despacho de apuestas

between /bɪˈtwiːn/ ◆ *prep* entre (*dos cosas/personas*) ☛ *Ver dibujo en* ENTRE ◆ *adv* (*tb* **in between**) en medio

beware /bɪˈweə(r)/ *vi* ~ **(of sth/sb)** tener cuidado (con algo/algn)

bewilder /bɪˈwɪldə(r)/ *vt* dejar perplejo **bewildered** *adj* perplejo **bewildering** *adj* desconcertante **bewilderment** *n* perplejidad

bewitch /bɪˈwɪtʃ/ *vt* hechizar

beyond /bɪˈjɒnd/ *prep, adv* más allá LOC **to be beyond sb** (*coloq*): *It's beyond me.* No lo puedo entender.

bias /ˈbaɪəs/ *n* **1** ~ **towards sth/sb** predisposición a favor de algo/algn **2** ~ **against sth/sb** prejuicios contra algo/ algn **3** parcialidad **biassed** (*tb* **biased**) *adj* parcial

bib /bɪb/ *n* **1** babero **2** peto (*de delantal*)

bible /ˈbaɪbl/ *n* biblia **biblical** *adj* bíblico

bibliography /ˌbɪbliˈɒgrəfi/ *n* (*pl* **-ies**) bibliografía

biceps /ˈbaɪseps/ *n* (*pl* **biceps**) bíceps

bicker /ˈbɪkə(r)/ *vi* discutir (*por asuntos triviales*)

bicycle /ˈbaɪsɪk(ə)l/ *n* bicicleta: *to ride a bicycle* andar en bicicleta

bid /bɪd/ ◆ *vt, vi* (**-dd-**) (*pret, pp* **bid**) **1** (*subasta*) pujar **2** (*Com*) hacer ofertas LOC *Ver* FAREWELL ◆ *n* **1** (*subasta*) puja **2** (*Com*) oferta **3** intento: *to make a bid for sth* intentar conseguir algo **bidder** *n* postor, -ora

bide /baɪd/ *vt* LOC **to bide your time** esperar el momento oportuno

biennial /baɪˈeniəl/ *adj* bienal

big /bɪg/ ◆ *adj* (**bigger**, **biggest**) **1** grande: *the biggest desert in the world* el desierto más grande del mundo

> **Big** y **large** describen el tamaño, la capacidad o la cantidad de algo, pero **big** es menos formal.

2 mayor: *my big sister* mi hermana mayor **3** (*decisión*) importante **4** (*error*) grave LOC **a big cheese/fish/noise/shot** (*coloq*) un pez gordo **big business**: *This is big business.* Esto es una mina. **the big time** (*coloq*) el estrellato ◆ *adv* (**bigger**, **biggest**) (*coloq*) a lo grande: *Let's think big.* Vamos a planearlo a lo grande.

bigamy /ˈbɪgəmi/ *n* bigamia

bigoted /ˈbɪgətɪd/ *adj* intolerante

bike /baɪk/ *n* (*coloq*) **1** bici **2** (*tb* **motor bike**) moto

bikini /bɪˈkiːni/ *n* bikini

bilingual /ˌbaɪˈlɪŋgwəl/ *adj, n* bilingüe

bill[1] /bɪl/ ◆ *n* **1** (*USA* **check**) factura: *phone/gas bills* recibos del teléfono/del gas ◊ *a bill for 5000 pesetas* una factura de 5.000 pesetas **2** (*restaurante, hotel*) cuenta: *The bill, please.* La cuenta, por favor. **3** programa **4** proyecto de ley **5** (*USA*): *a ten-dollar bill* un billete de diez dólares LOC **to fill/fit the bill** satisfacer los requisitos *Ver tb* FOOT ◆ *vt* **1** *to bill sb for sth* pasar la factura (de algo) a algn **2** anunciar (*en un programa*)

bill[2] /bɪl/ *n* pico

billboard /ˈbɪlbɔːd/ *n* (*USA*) valla publicitaria

billiards /ˈbɪliədz/ *n* [*sing*] billar **billiard** *adj billiard ball/room/table* bola/sala/mesa de billar

billing /ˈbɪlɪŋ/ *n*: *to get top/star billing* encabezar el cartel

billion /ˈbɪljən/ *adj, n* mil millones

> Antiguamente **a billion** equivalía a un billón, pero hoy en día equivale a mil millones. **A trillion** equivale a un millón de millones, es decir, a un billón.

☛ *Ver* Apéndice 1.

bin /bɪn/ *n* **1** cubo: *waste-paper bin* papelera **2** (*GB*) *Ver* DUSTBIN

binary /ˈbaɪnəri/ *adj* binario

bind[1] /baɪnd/ *vt* (*pret, pp* **bound** /baʊnd/) **1** ~ **sth/sb (together)** atar algo/a algn **2** ~ **sth/sb (together)** (*fig*) unir, ligar algo/a algn **3** ~ **sb/yourself (to sth)** obligar a algn/obligarse (a algo)

bind[2] /baɪnd/ *n* (*coloq*) **1** lata: *It's a terrible bind.* Es un latazo. **2** apuro: *I'm in a bit of a bind.* Estoy en un apuro.

binder /ˈbaɪndə(r)/ *n* archivador

binding /ˈbaɪndɪŋ/ ◆ *n* **1** encuadernación **2** ribete ◆ *adj* ~ **(on/upon sb)** vinculante (para algn)

binge /bɪndʒ/ ◆ *n* (*coloq*) juerga ◆ *vi* atracarse de comida, emborracharse

bingo /ˈbɪŋgəʊ/ *n* bingo

binoculars /bɪˈnɒkjələz/ *n* [*pl*] gemelos, prismáticos

biochemical /ˌbaɪəʊˈkemɪkl/ *adj* bioquímico

biochemist /ˌbaɪəʊˈkemɪst/ *n* bioquímico, -a **biochemistry** *n* bioquímica

biographical /ˌbaɪəˈgræfɪkl/ *adj* biográfico

biography /baɪˈɒgrəfi/ *n* (*pl* **-ies**) biografía **biographer** *n* biógrafo, -a

biology /baɪˈɒlədʒi/ *n* biología **biological** /baɪəˈlɒdʒɪkl/ *adj* biológico **biologist** /baɪˈɒlədʒɪst/ *n* biólogo, -a

bird /bɜːd/ *n* ave, pájaro: *bird of prey* ave de rapiña **LOC** *Ver* EARLY

biro® /ˈbaɪrəʊ/ (*tb* **Biro**) *n* (*pl* **~s**) bolígrafo

birth /bɜːθ/ *n* **1** nacimiento **2** natalidad **3** parto **4** cuna, origen **LOC to give birth (to sth/sb)** dar a luz (a algo/algn)

birthday /ˈbɜːθdeɪ/ *n* **1** cumpleaños: *Happy birthday!* ¡Feliz cumpleaños! ◊ *birthday card* tarjeta de cumpleaños **2** aniversario

birthplace /ˈbɜːθpleɪs/ *n* lugar de nacimiento

biscuit /ˈbɪskɪt/ *n* galleta

bishop /ˈbɪʃəp/ *n* **1** obispo **2** alfil

bit[1] /bɪt/ *n* trocito, pedacito: *I've got a bit of shopping to do.* Tengo que hacer algunas compras. **LOC a bit 1** un poco: *a bit tired* un poco cansado **2** mucho: *It rained quite a bit.* Llovió mucho. **a bit much** (*coloq*) demasiado **bit by bit** poco a poco **bits and pieces** (*coloq*) cosillas **not a bit; not one (little) bit** en absoluto: *I don't like it one little bit.* No me gusta nada. **to bits**: *to pull/tear sth to bits* hacer algo pedazos ◊ *to fall to bits* hacerse pedazos ◊ *to smash (sth) to bits* hacer algo/hacerse añicos ◊ *to take sth to bits* desarmar algo **to do your bit** (*coloq*) hacer tu parte

bit[2] /bɪt/ *n* bocado (*para un caballo*)

bit[3] /bɪt/ *n* (*Informát*) bit

bit[4] *pret de* BITE

bitch /bɪtʃ/ *n* perra ☛ *Ver nota en* PERRO

bite /baɪt/ ◆ (*pret* **bit** /bɪt/ *pp* **bitten** /ˈbɪtn/) **1** *vt, vi* ~ **(into sth)** morder (algo): *to bite your nails* morderse las uñas **2** *vt* (*insecto*) picar ◆ *n* **1** mordisco **2** bocado **3** picadura

bitter /ˈbɪtə(r)/ ◆ *adj* **(-est) 1** amargo **2** resentido **3** glacial ◆ *n* (*GB*) cerveza amarga **bitterly** *adv* amargamente: *It's bitterly cold.* Hace un frío que pela. **bitterness** *n* amargura

bizarre /bɪˈzɑː(r)/ *adj* **1** (*suceso*) insólito **2** (*aspecto*) estrafalario

black /blæk/ ◆ *adj* **(-er, -est) 1** (*lit y fig*) negro: *black eye* ojo morado ◊ *black market* mercado negro **2** (*cielo, noche*) oscuro **3** (*café, té*) solo ◆ *n* **1** negro **2** (*persona*) negro, -a ◆ **PHR V to black out** perder el conocimiento

blackberry /ˈblækbəri, -beri/ *n* (*p*[l] **-ies**) **1** mora **2** zarza

blackbird /ˈblækbɜːd/ *n* mirlo

blackboard /ˈblækbɔːd/ *n* pizarra

blackcurrant /ˌblækˈkʌrənt/ *n* grosella negra

blacken /ˈblækən/ *vt* **1** (*reputación, etc*) manchar **2** ennegrecer

blacklist /ˈblæklɪst/ ◆ *n* lista negra ◆ *vt* poner en la lista negra

blackmail /ˈblækmeɪl/ ◆ *n* chantaje ◆ *vt* chantajear **blackmailer** *n* chantajista

blacksmith /ˈblæksmɪθ/ (*tb* **smith**) [*n*] herrero, -a

bladder /ˈblædə(r)/ *n* vejiga

blade /bleɪd/ *n* **1** (*cuchillo, etc*) hoja [**2**] (*patín*) cuchilla **3** (*ventilador*) aspa [**4**] (*remo*) pala **5** (*hierba*) brizna

blame /bleɪm/ ◆ *vt* **1** culpar: *He blame[s] it on her/He blames her for it.* Le ech[a] la culpa a ella. ☛ Nótese que **to blam[e] sb for sth** es igual que **to blame st[h] on sb. 2** [*en oraciones negativas*]: *Yo[u] couldn't blame him for being annoye[d].* No me extraña que se enfadara. **LOC t[o] be to blame (for sth)** tener la culpa (d[e] algo) ◆ *n* ~ **(for sth)** culpa (de algo) **LO**[C]

to lay/to put the blame (for sth) on sb echar la culpa (de algo) a algn

bland /blænd/ *adj* (**-er**, **-est**) soso

blank /blæŋk/ ◆ *adj* **1** (*papel, cheque, etc*) en blanco **2** (*pared, espacio, etc*) desnudo **3** (*casete*) virgen **4** (*municiones*) de fogueo **5** (*expresión*) vacío ◆ *n* **1** espacio en blanco **2** (*tb* **blank cartridge**) bala de fogueo

blanket /ˈblæŋkɪt/ ◆ *n* manta ◆ *adj* general ◆ *vt* cubrir (*por completo*)

blare /bleə(r)/ *vi* ~ (**out**) sonar a todo volumen

blasphemy /ˈblæsfəmi/ *n* [*gen incontable*] blasfemia **blasphemous** *adj* blasfemo

blast /blɑːst; *USA* blæst/ ◆ *n* **1** explosión **2** onda expansiva **3** ráfaga: *a blast of air* una ráfaga de viento LOC *Ver* FULL ◆ *vt* volar (*con explosivos*) PHR V **to blast off** (*Aeronáut*) despegar ◆ **blast!** *interj* maldición **blasted** *adj* (*coloq*) condenado

blatant /ˈbleɪtnt/ *adj* descarado

blaze /bleɪz/ ◆ *n* **1** incendio **2** hoguera **3** [*sing*] **a ~ of sth**: *a blaze of colour* una explosión de color ◊ *in a blaze of publicity* con mucha publicidad ◆ *vi* **1** arder **2** brillar **3** (*fig*): *eyes blazing* echando chispas por los ojos

blazer /ˈbleɪzə(r)/ *n* chaqueta: *a school blazer* una americana de uniforme

bleach /bliːtʃ/ ◆ *vt* blanquear ◆ *n* lejía

bleak /bliːk/ *adj* (**-er**, **-est**) **1** (*paisaje*) inhóspito **2** (*tiempo*) crudo **3** (*día*) gris y deprimente **4** (*fig*) poco prometedor **bleakly** *adv* desoladamente **bleakness** *n* **1** desolación **2** crudeza

bleed /bliːd/ *vi* (*pret, pp* **bled** /bled/) sangrar **bleeding** *n* hemorragia

blemish /ˈblemɪʃ/ ◆ *n* mancha ◆ *vt* manchar

blend /blend/ ◆ **1** *vt, vi* mezclar(se) **2** *vi* difuminarse PHR V **to blend in (with sth)** armonizar (con algo) ◆ *n* (*aprob*) mezcla **blender** *n Ver* LIQUIDIZER *en* LIQUID

bless /bles/ *vt* (*pret, pp* **blessed** /blest/) bendecir LOC **bless you! 1** ¡que Dios te bendiga! **2** ¡Jesús! (*al estornudar*) ☛ *Ver nota en* ¡ACHÍS! **to be blessed with sth** gozar de algo

blessed /ˈblesɪd/ *adj* **1** santo **2** bendito **3** (*coloq*): *the whole blessed day* todo el santo día

blessing /ˈblesɪŋ/ *n* **1** bendición **2** [*gen sing*] visto bueno LOC **it's a blessing in disguise** (*refrán*) no hay mal que por bien no venga

blew *pret de* BLOW

blind /blaɪnd/ ◆ *adj* ciego LOC *Ver* TURN ◆ *vt* **1** (*momentáneamente*) deslumbrar **2** cegar ◆ *n* **1** persiana **2 the blind** los ciegos **blindly** *adv* ciegamente **blindness** *n* ceguera

blindfold /ˈblaɪndfəʊld/ ◆ *n* venda (*en los ojos*) ◆ *vt* vendar los ojos a ◆ *adv* con los ojos vendados

blink /blɪŋk/ ◆ *vi* parpadear ◆ *n* parpadeo

bliss /blɪs/ *n* [*incontable*] (una) dicha **blissful** *adj* dichoso

blister /ˈblɪstə(r)/ *n* **1** ampolla **2** (*pintura*) burbuja

blistering /ˈblɪstərɪŋ/ *adj* abrasador (*calor*)

blitz /blɪts/ *n* **1** (*Mil*) ataque relámpago **2** (*coloq*) ~ (**on sth**) campaña (contra/sobre algo)

blizzard /ˈblɪzəd/ *n* ventisca (de nieve)

bloated /ˈbləʊtɪd/ *adj* hinchado

blob /blɒb/ *n* gota (*líquido espeso*)

bloc /blɒk/ *n* [*v sing o pl*] bloque

block /blɒk/ ◆ *n* **1** (*piedra, hielo, etc*) bloque **2** (*edificios*) manzana, bloque **3** (*entradas, acciones, etc*) paquete: *a block booking* una reserva en grupo **4** obstáculo, impedimento: *a mental block* un bloqueo mental LOC *Ver* CHIP ◆ *vt* **1** atascar, bloquear **2** tapiar **3** impedir

blockade /blɒˈkeɪd/ ◆ *n* bloqueo (*Mil*) ◆ *vt* bloquear (*puerto, ciudad, etc*)

blockage /ˈblɒkɪdʒ/ *n* **1** obstrucción **2** bloqueo **3** atasco

blockbuster /ˈblɒkbʌstə(r)/ *n* libro o película que rompe récords

block capitals (*tb* **block letters**) *n* [*pl*] mayúsculas

bloke /bləʊk/ *n* (*GB, coloq*) tío, tipo

blond (*tb* **blonde**) /blɒnd/ ◆ *adj* (**-er**, **-est**) rubio ◆ *n* rubio, -a ☛ La variante **blonde** se suele escribir cuando nos referimos a una mujer. *Ver nota en* RUBIO

blood /blʌd/ *n* sangre: *blood group* grupo sanguíneo ◊ *blood pressure* presión arterial ◊ *blood test* análisis de sangre LOC *Ver* FLESH *Ver tb* COLD-BLOODED

bloodshed /ˈblʌdʃed/ *n* derramamiento de sangre

bloodshot /ˈblʌdʃɒt/ *adj* inyectado en sangre

blood sports *n* [*pl*] caza

bloodstream /ˈblʌdstriːm/ *n* flujo sanguíneo

bloody /ˈblʌdi/ ◆ *adj* (**-ier**, **-iest**) **1** ensangrentado **2** sanguinolento **3** (*batalla, etc*) sangriento ◆ *adj, adv* (*GB, coloq*): *That bloody car!* ¡Ese maldito coche!

bloom /bluːm/ ◆ *n* flor ◆ *vi* florecer

blossom /ˈblɒsəm/ ◆ *n* flor (*de árbol frutal*) ◆ *vi* florecer ☛ *Comparar con* FLOWER

blot /blɒt/ ◆ *n* **1** borrón **2** ~ **on sth** (*fig*) mancha en algo ◆ *vt* (**-tt-**) **1** (*carta, etc*) emborronar **2** (*con secante*) secar: *blotting-paper* (papel) secante PHR V **to blot sth out 1** (*memoria, etc*) borrar algo **2** (*panorama, luz, etc*) tapar algo

blotch /blɒtʃ/ *n* mancha (*esp en la piel*)

blouse /blaʊz; *USA* blaʊs/ *n* blusa

blow /bləʊ/ ◆ (*pret* **blew** /bluː/ *pp* **blown** /bləʊn/ *o* **blowed**) **1** *vi* soplar **2** *vi* (*movido por el viento*): *to blow shut/open* cerrarse/abrirse de golpe **3** *vi* (*silbato*) sonar **4** *vt* (*silbato*) tocar **5** *vt* (*viento, etc*) llevar: *The wind blew us towards the island.* El viento nos llevó hacia la isla. LOC **blow it!** ¡maldita sea! **to blow your nose** sonarse (la nariz)

PHR V **to blow away** irse volando (llevado por el viento)

to blow down/over ser derribado por el viento **to blow sth/sb down/over** derribar algo/a algn (*el viento*)

to blow sth out apagar algo

to blow over pasar sin más (*tormenta, escándalo*)

to blow up 1 (*bomba, etc*) explotar **2** (*tormenta, escándalo*) estallar **3** (*coloq*) cabrearse **to blow sth up 1** (*reventar*) volar algo **2** (*globo, etc*) inflar algo **3** (*Fot*) ampliar algo **4** (*coloq*) (*asunto*) exagerar algo

◆ *n* ~ (**to sth/sb**) golpe (para algo/algn) LOC **a blow-by-blow account, description, etc (of sth)** un relato, descripción, etc (de algo) con pelos y señales **at one blow/at a single blow** de un (solo) golpe **to come to blows (over sth)** llegar a las manos (por algo)

blue /bluː/ ◆ *adj* **1** azul **2** (*coloq*) triste **3** (*película, etc*) verde ◆ *n* **1** azul **2 the blues** [*v sing o pl*] (*Mús*) el blues **3 the blues** [*pl*] la depre LOC **out of the blue** de repente

blueprint /ˈbluːprɪnt/ *n* ~ (**for sth**) anteproyecto (de algo)

bluff /blʌf/ ◆ *vi* marcarse/tirarse un farol ◆ *n* fanfarronada

blunder /ˈblʌndə(r)/ ◆ *n* metedura de pata ◆ *vi* cometer una equivocación

blunt /blʌnt/ ◆ *vt* embotar ◆ *adj* (**-er**, **-est**) **1** despuntado **2** romo: *blunt instrument* instrumento contundente **3** (*negativa*) liso y llano: *to be blunt with sb* hablar a algn sin rodeos **4** (*comentario*) brusco

blur /blɜː(r)/ ◆ *n* imagen borrosa ◆ *vt* (**-rr-**) **1** hacer borroso **2** (*diferencia*) atenuar **blurred** *adj* borroso

blurt /blɜːt/ PHR V **to blurt sth out** soltar algo

blush /blʌʃ/ ◆ *vi* sonrojarse ◆ *n* sonrojo **blusher** *n* colorete

boar /bɔː(r)/ *n* (*pl* **boar** *o* ~**s**) **1** jabalí **2** verraco ☛ *Ver nota en* CERDO

board /bɔːd/ ◆ *n* **1** tabla: *ironing board* tabla de planchar **2** (*tb* **blackboard**) pizarra **3** (*tb* **noticeboard**) tablón de anuncios **4** (*ajedrez, etc*) tablero **5** cartoné **6 the board** (*tb* **the board of directors**) [*v sing o pl*] junta directiva **7** (*comida*) pensión: *full/half board* pensión completa/media pensión LOC **above board** limpio **across the board** en todos los niveles: *a 10% pay increase across the board* un aumento general de sueldo del 10% **on board** a bordo ◆ *vt* ~ **sth** (**up/over**) cubrir algo con tablas **2** *vi* embarcar **3** *vt* subir a

boarder /ˈbɔːdə(r)/ *n* **1** (*colegio*) interno, -a **2** (*casa de huéspedes*) huésped, -eda

boarding card (*tb* **boarding pass**) *n* tarjeta de embarque

boarding house *n* casa de huéspedes

boarding school *n* internado

boast /bəʊst/ ◆ **1** *vi* ~ (**about/of sth**) alardear (de algo) **2** *vt* (*fml*) gozar de: *The town boasts a famous museum.* La ciudad presume de tener un museo famoso. ◆ *n* alarde **boastful** *adj* presuntuoso **2** pretencioso

boat /bəʊt/ *n* **1** barco: *to go by boat*

en barco **2** barca: *rowing boat* barca de remos ◊ *boat race* regata **3** buque LOC *Ver* SAME

Boat y ship tienen significados muy similares, pero **boat** se suele utilizar para embarcaciones más pequeñas.

bob /bɒb/ *vi* (**-bb-**) **to bob** (**up and down**) (*en el agua*) balancearse PHR V **to bob up** surgir

bobby /ˈbɒbi/ *n* (*pl* **-ies**) (*GB, coloq*) poli

bode /bəʊd/ *vt* (*fml*) presagiar, augurar LOC **to bode ill/well** (**for sth/sb**) ser de mal agüero/buena señal (para algo/ algn)

bodice /ˈbɒdɪs/ *n* corpiño

bodily /ˈbɒdɪli/ ◆ *adj* del cuerpo, corporal ◆ *adv* **1** a la fuerza **2** en conjunto

body /ˈbɒdi/ *n* (*pl* **bodies**) **1** cuerpo **2** cadáver **3** [*v sing o pl*] grupo: *a government body* un organismo gubernamental **4** conjunto LOC **body and soul** en cuerpo y alma

bodyguard /ˈbɒdigɑːd/ *n* **1** guardaespaldas **2** (*grupo*) guardia personal

bodywork /ˈbɒdiwɜːk/ *n* [*incontable*] carrocería

bog /bɒg/ ◆ *n* **1** ciénaga **2** (*GB, coloq*) retrete ◆ *v* (**-gg-**) PHR V **to get bogged down 1** (*fig*) estancarse **2** (*lit*) atascarse **boggy** *adj* cenagoso

bogey (*tb* **bogy**) /ˈbəʊgi/ *n* (*pl* **bogeys**) (*tb* **bogeyman**) coco (*espíritu maligno*)

bogus /ˈbəʊgəs/ *adj* falso, fraudulento

boil[1] /bɔɪl/ *n* forúnculo

boil[2] /bɔɪl/ ◆ **1** *vt, vi* hervir **2** *vt* (*huevo*) cocer PHR V **to boil down to sth** reducirse a algo **to boil over** rebosarse ◆ *n* LOC **to be on the boil** estar hirviendo **boiling** *adj* hirviendo: *boiling point* punto de ebullición ◊ *boiling hot* al rojo vivo

boiler /ˈbɔɪlə(r)/ *n* caldera: *boiler suit* mono

boisterous /ˈbɔɪstərəs/ *adj* bullicioso, alborotado

bold /bəʊld/ *adj* (**-er**, **-est**) **1** valiente **2** osado, atrevido **3** bien definido, marcado **4** llamativo LOC **to be/make so bold** (**as to do sth**) (*fml*) atreverse (a hacer algo) *Ver tb* FACE[1] **boldly** *adv* **1** resueltamente **2** audazmente, atrevidamente **3** marcadamente **boldness** *n* **1** valentía **2** audacia, atrevimiento

bolster /ˈbəʊlstə(r)/ *vt* **1** ~ **sth** (**up**) reforzar algo **2** ~ **sb** (**up**) alentar a algn

bolt[1] /bəʊlt/ ◆ *n* **1** cerrojo **2** perno **3** *a bolt of lightning* un rayo ◆ *vt* **1** cerrar con cerrojo **2** ~ **A to B**; ~ **A and B together** atornillar A a B

bolt[2] /bəʊlt/ ◆ **1** *vi* (*caballo*) desbocarse **2** *vi* salir disparado **3** *vt* ~ **sth** (**down**) engullir algo ◆ *n* LOC **to make a bolt/ dash/run for it** intentar escapar

bomb /bɒm/ ◆ *n* **1** bomba: *bomb disposal* desarticulación de bombas ◊ *bomb scare* amenaza de bomba ◊ *to plant a bomb* poner una bomba **2 the bomb** la bomba atómica LOC **to go like a bomb** (*coloq*) ir como un rayo *Ver tb* COST ◆ **1** *vt, vi* bombardear **2** *vt, vi* poner una bomba (*en un edificio, etc*) **3** *vi* ~ **along, down, up, etc** (*GB, coloq*) ir zumbando

bombard /bɒmˈbɑːd/ *vt* **1** bombardear **2** (*a preguntas, etc*) acosar **bombardment** *n* bombardeo

bomber /ˈbɒmə(r)/ *n* **1** (*avión*) bombardero **2** persona que pone bombas

bombing /ˈbɒmɪŋ/ *n* **1** bombardeo **2** atentado con explosivos

bombshell /ˈbɒmʃel/ *n* bomba: *The news came as a bombshell.* La noticia cayó como una bomba.

bond /bɒnd/ ◆ *vt* unir ◆ *n* **1** pacto **2** lazos **3** bono: *Government bonds* bonos del Tesoro **4 bonds** [*pl*] cadenas

bone /bəʊn/ ◆ *n* **1** hueso **2** (*pez*) espina LOC **bone dry** completamente seco **to be a bone of contention** ser la manzana de la discordia **to have a bone to pick with sb** tener una queja sobre algn **to make no bones about sth** no andarse con rodeos en cuanto a algo *Ver tb* CHILL, WORK[2] ◆ *vt* deshuesar

bone marrow *n* médula

bonfire /ˈbɒnfaɪə(r)/ *n* hoguera

Bonfire Night *n* (*GB*)

El 5 de noviembre se celebra en Gran Bretaña lo que llaman **Bonfire Night**. La gente hace hogueras por la noche y hay fuegos artificiales para recordar aquel 5 de noviembre de 1605 cuando Guy Fawkes intentó quemar el Parlamento.

bonnet /ˈbɒnɪt/ *n* **1** (*bebé*) gorrito **2** (*señora*) sombrero **3** (*USA* **hood**) capó

bonus /ˈbəʊnəs/ *n* **1** plus: *a productivity*

bonus un plus de productividad **2** (*fig*) ventaja añadida

bony /ˈbəʊni/ *adj* **1** óseo **2** lleno de espinas/huesos **3** huesudo

boo /buː/ ◆ *vt, vi* abuchear ◆ *n* (*pl* **boos**) abucheo ◆ **boo!** *interj* ¡bu!

booby-trap /ˈbuːbi træp/ *n* trampa (explosiva)

book[1] /bʊk/ *n* **1** libro: *book club* club del libro **2** libreta **3** cuaderno **4** (*cheques*) talonario **5 the books** [*pl*] las cuentas: *to do the books* llevar las cuentas LOC **to be in sb's good books** gozar del favor de algn **to do sth by the book** hacer algo según las normas *Ver tb* BAD, COOK, LEAF, TRICK

book[2] /bʊk/ **1** *vt, vi* reservar, hacer una reserva **2** *vt* contratar **3** *vt* (*coloq*) (*policía*) fichar **4** *vt* (*Dep*) sancionar LOC **to be booked up 1** agotarse las localidades **2** (*coloq*): *I'm booked up.* No tengo ni un hueco en la agenda. PHR V **to book in** registrarse

bookcase /ˈbʊkkeɪs/ *n* librería (*mueble*)

booking /ˈbʊkɪŋ/ *n* (*esp GB*) reserva

booking office *n* (*esp GB*) taquilla

booklet /ˈbʊklət/ *n* folleto

bookmaker /ˈbʊkmeɪkə(r)/ (*tb* **bookie**) *n* corredor, -ora de apuestas

bookseller /ˈbʊkˌselə(r)/ *n* librero, -a

bookshelf /ˈbʊkʃelf/ *n* (*pl* **-shelves** /-ʃelvz/) estante para libros

bookshop /ˈbʊkʃɒp/ (*USA tb* **bookstore**) *n* librería

boom /buːm/ ◆ *vi* resonar, retumbar ◆ *n* estruendo

boost /buːst/ ◆ *vt* **1** (*ventas, confianza*) aumentar **2** (*moral*) levantar ◆ *n* **1** aumento **2** estímulo grato

boot /buːt/ *n* **1** bota **2** (*USA* **trunk**) (*coche*) maletero LOC *Ver* TOUGH

booth /buːð; *USA* buːθ/ *n* **1** caseta **2** cabina: *polling/telephone booth* cabina electoral/telefónica

booty /ˈbuːti/ *n* botín

booze /buːz/ ◆ *n* (*coloq*) bebida (alcohólica) ◆ *vi* (*coloq*): *to go out boozing* ir de cogorza

border /ˈbɔːdə(r)/ ◆ *n* **1** frontera

> **Border** y **frontier** se usan para referirse a la división entre países o estados, pero sólo **border** suele usarse para hablar de fronteras naturales: *The river forms the border between the two countries.* El río constituye la frontera entre los dos países. Por otro lado, **boundary** se utiliza para las divisiones entre áreas más pequeñas, como por ejemplo los condados.

2 (*jardín*) arriate **3** borde, ribete ◆ *vt* limitar con, lindar con PHR V **to border on sth** rayar en algo

borderline /ˈbɔːdəlaɪn/ *n* límites LOC **a borderline case** un caso dudoso

bore[1] *pret de* BEAR[2]

bore[2] /bɔː(r)/ ◆ *vt* **1** aburrir **2** (*agujero*) hacer (*con taladro*) ◆ *n* **1** (*persona*) aburrido, -a **2** rollo, lata **3** (*escopeta*) calibre **bored** *adj* aburrido: *I am bored.* Estoy aburrido. **boredom** *n* aburrimiento **boring** *adj* aburrido: *He is boring.* Es aburrido.

born /bɔːn/ ◆ *pp* nacido LOC **to be born** nacer: *She was born in Bath.* Nació en Bath. ◊ *He was born blind.* Es ciego de nacimiento. ◆ *adj* [*sólo antes de sustantivo*] nato: *He's a born actor.* Es un actor nato.

borne *pp de* BEAR[2]

borough /ˈbʌrə; *USA* -rəʊ/ *n* municipio

borrow

She's **lending** her son some money.

He's **borrowing** some money from his mother.

borrow /ˈbɒrəʊ/ *vt* ~ **sth** (**from sth/sb**) pedir (prestado) algo (a algo/algn) ☛ Lo más normal en español es cambiar la estructura, y emplear un verbo como "prestar" o "dejar": *Could I borrow a pen?* ¿Me dejas un bolígrafo? **borrower** *n* prestatario, -a **borrowing** *n* crédito: *public sector borrowing* crédito al sector público

bosom /ˈbʊzəm/ *n* **1** (*ret*) pecho, busto **2** (*fig*) seno

boss /bɒs/ ◆ *n* (*coloq*) jefe, -a ◆ *vt* ~ **sb about/around** (*pey*) dar órdenes a algn; mangonear a algn **bossy** *adj* (**-ier**, **-iest**) (*pey*) mandón

botany /ˈbɒtəni/ *n* botánica **botanical** /bəˈtænɪkl/ (*tb* **botanic**) *adj* botánico **botanist** /ˈbɒtənɪst/ *n* botánico, -a

both /bəʊθ/ ◆ *pron, adj* ambos, -as, los/las dos: *both of us* nosotros dos ◊ *Both of us went./We both went.* Los dos fuimos. ◆ *adv* **both ... and ...** a la vez ... y ...: *The report is both reliable and readable.* El informe es a la vez fiable e interesante. ◊ *both you and me* tanto tú como yo ◊ *He both plays and sings.* Canta y toca. LOC *Ver* NOT ONLY ... BUT ALSO *en* ONLY

bother /ˈbɒðə(r)/ ◆ **1** *vt* molestar **2** *vt* preocupar: *What's bothering you?* ¿Qué es lo que te preocupa? **3** *vi* ~ (**to do sth**) molestarse (en hacer algo): *He didn't even bother to say thank you.* No se molestó ni siquiera en dar las gracias. **4** *vi* ~ **about sth/sb** preocuparse por algo/algn LOC **I can't be bothered (to do sth)** no me apetece (hacer algo) **I'm not bothered** me da igual ◆ *n* molestia ◆ **bother!** *interj* ¡puñetas!

bottle /ˈbɒtl/ ◆ *n* **1** botella **2** frasco **3** biberón ◆ *vt* **1** embotellar **2** envasar

bottle bank *n* contenedor de vidrio

bottom /ˈbɒtəm/ *n* **1** (*colina, página, escaleras*) pie **2** (*mar, barco, taza*) fondo **3** (*Anat*) trasero **4** (*calle*) final **5** último: *He's bottom of the class.* Es el último de la clase. **6** *bikini bottom* la braga del bikini ◊ *pyjama bottoms* pantalones de pijama LOC **to be at the bottom of sth** estar detrás de algo **to get to the bottom of sth** llegar al fondo de algo *Ver tb* ROCK[1]

bough /baʊ/ *n* rama

bought *pret, pp de* BUY

boulder /ˈbəʊldə(r)/ *n* roca (*grande*)

bounce /baʊns/ ◆ **1** *vt, vi* botar **2** *vi* (*coloq*) (*cheque*) ser devuelto PHR V **to bounce back** (*coloq*) recuperarse ◆ *n* bote

bound[1] /baʊnd/ ◆ *vi* saltar ◆ *n* salto

bound[2] /baʊnd/ *adj* ~ **for ...** con destino a ...

bound[3] *pret, pp de* BIND[1]

bound[4] /baʊnd/ *adj* **1 to be ~ to do sth**: *You're bound to pass the exam.* Seguro que apruebas el examen. **2** obligado (*por la ley o el deber*) LOC **bound up with sth** ligado a algo

boundary /ˈbaʊndri/ *n* (*pl* **-ies**) límite, frontera ☛ *Ver nota en* BORDER

boundless /ˈbaʊndləs/ *adj* ilimitado

bounds /baʊndz/ *n* [*pl*] límites LOC **out of bounds** prohibido

bouquet /buˈkeɪ/ *n* **1** (*flores*) ramo **2** buqué

bourgeois /ˌbʊəˈʒwɑː/ *adj, n* burgués, -esa

bout /baʊt/ *n* **1** (*actividad*) racha **2** (*enfermedad*) ataque **3** (*boxeo*) combate

bow[1] /bəʊ/ *n* **1** lazo **2** (*Dep, violín*) arco

bow[2] /baʊ/ ◆ **1** *vi* inclinarse, hacer una reverencia **2** *vt* (*cabeza*) inclinar, bajar ◆ *n* **1** reverencia **2** (*tb* **bows** [*pl*]) (*Náut*) proa

bowel /ˈbaʊəl/ *n* **1** (*Med*) [*a menudo pl*] intestino(s) **2 bowels** [*pl*] (*fig*) entrañas

bowl[1] /bəʊl/ *n* **1** cuenco ☛ **Bowl** se usa en muchas formas compuestas, cuya traducción es generalmente una sola palabra: *a fruit bowl* un frutero ◊ *a sugar bowl* un azucarero ◊ *a salad bowl* una ensaladera. **2** plato hondo **3** tazón **4** (*retrete*) taza

bowl[2] /bəʊl/ ◆ *n* **1** (*bolos*) bola **2 bowls** [*sing*] bochas ◆ *vt, vi* lanzar (la pelota)

bowler /ˈbəʊlə(r)/ *n* **1** (*Dep, críquet*) lanzador, -ora **2** (*tb* **bowler hat**) bombín

bowling /ˈbəʊlɪŋ/ *n* [*incontable*] bolos: *bowling alley* bolera

bow tie *n* pajarita

box[1] /bɒks/ ◆ *n* **1** caja: *cardboard box* caja de cartón ☛ *Ver dibujo en* CONTAINER **2** estuche **3** (*correo*) buzón **4** (*Teat*) palco **5** (*teléfono*) cabina **6 the box** (*coloq, GB*) la tele ◆ *vt* (*tb* **to box up**) embalar

box[2] /bɒks/ *vt, vi* boxear (contra)

boxer /ˈbɒksə(r)/ *n* **1** boxeador **2** bóxer

boxing /ˈbɒksɪŋ/ *n* boxeo

Boxing Day *n* 26 de diciembre ☛ *Ver nota en* NAVIDAD

box number *n* apartado de correos

box-office /ˈbɒks ɒfɪs/ *n* taquilla

boy /bɔɪ/ *n* **1** niño: *It's a boy!* ¡Es un niño! **2** hijo: *his eldest boy* su hijo mayor ◊ *I've got three children, two boys and one girl.* Tengo tres hijos: dos chicos y una chica. **3** chico, muchacho: *boys and girls* chicos y chicas

boycott /ˈbɔɪkɒt/ ◆ *vt* boicotear ◆ *n* boicot

boyfriend /ˈbɔɪfrend/ *n* novio: *Is he your boyfriend, or just a friend?* ¿Es tu novio o sólo un amigo?

boyhood /ˈbɔɪhʊd/ *n* niñez

boyish /ˈbɔɪɪʃ/ *adj* **1** (*hombre*) aniñado, juvenil **2** (*mujer*): *She has a boyish figure.* Tiene tipo de muchacho.

bra /brɑː/ *n* sujetador

brace /breɪs/ ◆ *n* **1** (*para los dientes*) aparato **2 braces** (*USA* **suspenders**) [*pl*] tirantes ◆ *v refl* ~ **yourself (for sth)** prepararse (para algo) PHR V **to brace up** (*USA*) animarse **bracing** *adj* estimulante

bracelet /ˈbreɪslət/ *n* pulsera

bracket /ˈbrækɪt/ ◆ *n* **1** paréntesis: *in brackets* entre paréntesis ☛ *Ver* pág 318–9. **2** (*Tec*) soporte **3** categoría: *the 20-30 age bracket* el grupo de edad de 20 a 30 años ◆ *vt* **1** poner entre paréntesis **2** agrupar

brag /bræg/ *vi* (**-gg-**) ~ **(about sth)** fanfarronear (de algo)

braid /breɪd/ *n* (*USA*) *Ver* PLAIT

brain /breɪn/ *n* **1** cerebro: *He's the brains of the family.* Es el cerebro de la familia. **2 brains** [*pl*] sesos **3** mente LOC **to have sth on the brain** (*coloq*) tener algo metido en la cabeza *Ver tb* PICK, RACK **brainless** *adj* insensato, estúpido **brainy** *adj* (**-ier**, **-iest**) (*coloq*) inteligente

brainwash /ˈbreɪnwɒʃ/ *vt* ~ **sb (into doing sth)** lavar el cerebro a algn (para que haga algo) **brainwashing** *n* lavado de cerebro

brake /breɪk/ ◆ *n* freno: *to put on/apply the brake(s)* frenar/echar el freno ◆ *vt, vi* frenar: *to brake hard* frenar de golpe

bramble /ˈbræmbl/ *n* zarzamora

bran /bræn/ *n* salvado

branch /brɑːntʃ; *USA* bræntʃ/ ◆ *n* **1** rama **2** sucursal: *your nearest/local branch* la sucursal más cercana/del barrio ◆ PHR V **to branch off** desviarse, ramificarse **to branch out (into sth)** extenderse (a algo), comenzar (con algo): *They are branching out into Eastern Europe.* Están comenzando a operar en Europa del Este.

brand /brænd/ ◆ *n* **1** (*Com*) marca (*productos de limpieza, tabaco, ropa, alimentos*) ☛ *Comparar con* MAKE[2] **2** forma: *a strange brand of humour* un sentido del humor muy peculiar ◆ *vt* **1** (*ganado*) marcar **2** ~ **sb (as sth)** etiquetar a algn (de algo)

brandish /ˈbrændɪʃ/ *vt* blandir

brand new *adj* completamente nuevo

brandy /ˈbrændi/ *n* coñac

brash /bræʃ/ *adj* (*pey*) descarado **brashness** *n* desparpajo

brass /brɑːs; *USA* bræs/ *n* **1** latón **2** [*v sing o pl*] (*Mús*) instrumentos de metal

bravado /brəˈvɑːdəʊ/ *n* bravuconería

brave /breɪv/ ◆ *vt* **1** (*peligro, intemperie, etc*) desafiar **2** (*dificultades*) soportar ◆ *adj* (**-er**, **-est**) valiente LOC *Ver* FACE[1]

brawl /brɔːl/ *n* reyerta

breach /briːtʃ/ ◆ *n* **1** (*contrato, etc*) incumplimiento **2** (*ley*) violación **3** (*relaciones*) ruptura **4** (*seguridad*) fallo LOC **breach of confidence/faith/trust** abuso de confianza ◆ *vt* **1** (*contrato, etc*) incumplir **2** (*ley*) violar **3** (*muro, defensas*) abrir una brecha en

bread /bred/ *n* **1** [*incontable*] pan: *I bought a loaf/two loaves of bread.* Compré una barra/dos barras de pan. ◊ *a slice of bread* una rebanada de pan **2** [*contable*] (tipo de) pan ☛ Nótese que el plural **breads** sólo se usa para referirse a distintos tipos de pan, no a varias piezas de pan. *Ver dibujo en* PAN

breadcrumbs /ˈbredkrʌmz/ *n* [*pl*] pan rallado: *fish in breadcrumbs* pescado empanado

breadth /bredθ/ *n* **1** amplitud **2** anchura

break[1] /breɪk/ (*pret* **broke** /brəʊk/ *pp* **broken** /ˈbrəʊkən/) **1** *vt* romper: *to break sth in two/in half* romper algo en dos/por la mitad ◊ *She's broken her leg.* Se ha roto la pierna. ☛ **Break** no se usa con materiales flexibles, como la tela o el papel. *Ver tb* ROMPER **2** *vi* romperse, hacerse pedazos **3** *vt* (*ley*) violar **4** *vt* (*promesa, palabra*) no cumplir **5** *vt* (*récord*) batir **6** *vt* (*caída*) amortiguar **7** *vt* (*viaje*) interrumpir **8** *vi* hacer un descanso: *Let's break for coffee.* Vamos a parar para tomar un café. **9** *vt* (*voluntad*) quebrantar **10** *vt* (*mala costumbre*) dejar **11** *vt* (*código*) descifrar **12** *vt* (*caja fuerte*) forzar **13** *v* (*tiempo*) cambiar **14** *vi* (*tormenta, escándalo*) estallar **15** *vi* (*noticia, historia*) hacerse público **16** *vi* (*voz*) quebrarse, cambiar **17** *vi* (*olas, aguas*) romper: *Her waters broke.* Rompió aguas. LOC **break it up!** ¡basta ya! **to break the bank** (*coloq*) arruinar: *A meal out won't break the bank.* Cenar fuera no nos va a arruinar. **to break the news** (**to sb**) dar la (mala) noticia (a algn) **to break your back** (**to do sth**) sudar tinta (para hacer algo) *Ver tb* WORD

PHR V **to break away** (**from sth**) separarse (de algo), romper (con algo)

to break down 1 (*coche*) averiarse: *We broke down.* Se nos averió el coche. **2** (*máquina*) estropearse **3** (*persona*) venirse abajo: *He broke down and cried.* Rompió a llorar. **4** (*negociaciones*) romperse **to break sth down 1** echar abajo algo **2** vencer algo **3** descomponer algo

to break in forzar la entrada **to break into sth 1** (*ladrones*) entrar en algo **2** (*mercado*) introducirse en algo **3** (*empezar a hacer algo*): *to break into a run* echar a correr ◊ *He broke into a cold sweat.* Le dio un sudor frío.

to break off dejar de hablar **to break sth off 1** partir algo (*trozo*) **2** romper algo (*compromiso*)

to break out 1 (*epidemia*) declararse **2** (*guerra, violencia*) estallar **3** (*incendio*) producirse **4** llenarse: *I've broken out in spots.* Me he llenado de granos.

to break through sth abrirse camino a través de algo

to break up 1 (*reunión*) disolverse **2** (*relación*) terminarse **3** *The school breaks up on 20 July.* Las clases terminan el 20 de julio. **to break** (**up**) **with sb** romper con algn **to break sth up** disolver, hacer fracasar algo

break[2] /breɪk/ *n* **1** rotura, abertura **2** descanso, vacaciones cortas, recreo: *a coffee break* un descanso para tomar café **3** ruptura, cambio: *a break in the routine* un cambio de rutina **4** (*coloq*) golpe de suerte LOC **to give sb a break** dar un respiro a algn **to make a break** (**for it**) intentar escapar *Ver tb* CLEAN

breakdown /ˈbreɪkdaʊn/ *n* **1** avería **2** (*salud*) crisis: *a nervous breakdown* una crisis nerviosa **3** (*estadística*) análisis

breakfast /ˈbrekfəst/ *n* desayuno: *to have breakfast* desayunar ☛ *Ver pág 320. Ver tb* BED AND BREAKFAST

break-in /ˈbreɪk ɪn/ *n* robo

breakthrough /ˈbreɪkθruː/ *n* avance (importante)

breast /brest/ *n* seno, pecho (*de mujer*): *breast cancer* cáncer de mama

breath /breθ/ *n* aliento: *to take a deep breath* respirar a fondo LOC **a breath of fresh air** un soplo de aire fresco (**to be**) **out of/short of breath** (estar) sin aliento **to get your breath** (**again/back**) recuperar el aliento **to say sth, speak, etc under your breath** decir algo, hablar, etc entre susurros **to take sb's breath away** dejar a algn boquiabierto *Ver tb* CATCH, HOLD, WASTE

breathe /briːð/ **1** *vi* respirar **2** *vt, vi* ~ (**sth**) (**in/out**) aspirar, expirar (algo) LOC **not to breathe a word** (**of/about sth**) (**to sb**) no soltar ni una palabra (de algo) (a algn) **to breathe down sb's neck** (*coloq*) estar encima de algn **to breathe life into sth/sb** infundir vida a algo/algn **breathing** *n* respiración: *heavy breathing* resuello

breathless /ˈbreθləs/ *adj* jadeante, sin aliento

breathtaking /ˈbreθteɪkɪŋ/ *adj* impresionante, vertiginoso

breed /briːd/ ◆ (*pret, pp* **bred** /bred/) **1** *vi* (*animal*) reproducirse **2** *vt* (*ganado*) criar **3** *vt* producir, engendrar: *Dirt breeds disease.* La suciedad produce enfermedad. ◆ *n* raza, casta

breeze /briːz/ *n* brisa

brew /bruː/ **1** *vt* (*cerveza*) elaborar **2** *vt, vi* (*té*) hacer(se) **3** *vi* (*fig*) prepararse: *Trouble is brewing.* Se está preparando jaleo.

bribe /braɪb/ ◆ *n* soborno ◆ *vt* ~ **sb** (**into doing sth**) sobornar a algn (para que haga algo) **bribery** *n* cohecho, soborno

brick /brɪk/ ◆ *n* ladrillo LOC *Ver* DROP ◆ PHR V **to brick sth in/up** enladrillar algo

bride /braɪd/ *n* novia LOC **the bride and groom** los novios

bridegroom /ˈbraɪdgruːm/ (*tb* **groom**) *n* novio (*en una boda*): *the bride and groom* los novios

bridesmaid /ˈbraɪdzmeɪd/ *n* dama de honor ☛ *Ver nota en* BODA

bridge /brɪdʒ/ ◆ *n* **1** puente **2** vínculo

◆ *vt* LOC **to bridge a/the gap between...** acortar la distancia entre...

bridle /ˈbraɪdl/ *n* brida

brief /briːf/ *adj* (**-er**, **-est**) breve LOC **in brief** en pocas palabras **briefly** *adv* **1** brevemente **2** en pocas palabras

briefcase /ˈbriːfkeɪs/ *n* maletín

briefs /briːfs/ *n* [*pl*] **1** calzoncillos **2** bragas ☛ *Ver nota en* PAIR

bright /braɪt/ ◆ *adj* (**-er**, **-est**) **1** brillante, luminoso: *bright eyes* ojos vivos **2** (*color*) vivo **3** (*sonrisa, expresión, carácter*) radiante, alegre **4** (*inteligente*) listo LOC *Ver* LOOK[1] ◆ *adv* (**-er**, **-est**) brillantemente

brighten /ˈbraɪtn/ **1** *vi* ~ (**up**) animarse, despejar (*tiempo*) **2** *vt* ~ **sth** (**up**) animar algo

brightly /ˈbraɪtli/ *adv* **1** brillantemente **2** *brightly lit* con mucha iluminación ◊ *brightly painted* pintado con colores vivos **3** radiantemente, alegremente

brightness /ˈbraɪtnəs/ *n* **1** brillo, claridad **2** alegría **3** inteligencia

brilliant /ˈbrɪliənt/ *adj* **1** brillante **2** genial **brilliance** *n* **1** brillo, resplandor **2** brillantez

brim /brɪm/ *n* **1** borde: *full to the brim* lleno hasta el borde **2** ala (*de sombrero*)

bring /brɪŋ/ *vt* (*pret, pp* **brought** /brɔːt/) ☛ *Ver nota en* LLEVAR **1** ~ (**with you**) traer (consigo) **2** llevar: *Can I bring a friend to your party?* ¿Puedo llevar a un amigo a tu fiesta? ☛ *Ver dibujo en* TAKE **3** (*acciones judiciales*) entablar LOC **to be able to bring yourself to do sth**: *I couldn't bring myself to tell her.* No tuve fuerzas para decírselo. **to bring sb to justice** llevar a algn ante los tribunales **to bring sb up to date** poner a algn al día **to bring sth home to sb** hacer que algn comprenda algo **to bring sth (out) into the open** sacar algo a la luz **to bring sth to a close** concluir algo **to bring sth/sb to life** animar algo/a algn **to bring sth up to date** actualizar algo **to bring tears to sb's eyes/a smile to sb's face** hacerle llorar/sonreír a algn **to bring up the rear** ir a la cola *Ver tb* CHARGE, PEG, QUESTION
PHR V **to bring sth about/on** provocar algo
to bring sth back 1 restaurar algo **2** hacer pensar en algo
to bring sth down 1 derribar algo, derrocar algo **2** (*inflación, etc*) reducir algo, bajar algo
to bring sth forward adelantar algo
to bring sth in introducir algo (*ley*)
to bring sth off (*coloq*) lograr algo
to bring sth on yourself buscarse algo
to bring sth out 1 producir algo **2** publicar algo **3** realzar algo
to bring sb round/over (to sth) convencer a algn (de algo) **to bring sb round/to** hacer que algn vuelva en sí
to bring together reconciliar, unir
to bring sb up criar a algn: *She was brought up by her granny.* La crió su abuela. ☛ *Comparar con* EDUCATE, RAISE 8 **to bring sth up 1** vomitar algo **2** sacar algo a colación

brink /brɪŋk/ *n* borde: *on the brink of war* al borde de la guerra

brisk /brɪsk/ *adj* (**-er**, **-est**) **1** (*paso*) enérgico **2** (*negocio*) activo

brittle /ˈbrɪtl/ *adj* **1** quebradizo **2** (*fig*) frágil

broach /brəʊtʃ/ *vt* abordar

broad /brɔːd/ *adj* (**-er**, **-est**) **1** ancho **2** (*sonrisa*) amplio **3** (*esquema, acuerdo*) general, amplio: *in the broadest sense of the word* en el sentido más amplio de la palabra

> Para referirnos a la distancia entre los dos extremos de algo es más corriente utilizar **wide**: *The gate is four metres wide.* La verja tiene cuatro metros de ancho. **Broad** se utiliza para referirnos a características geográficas: *a broad expanse of desert* una amplia extensión de desierto, y también en frases como: *broad shoulders* espalda ancha.

LOC **in broad daylight** en pleno día

broad bean *n* haba

broadcast /ˈbrɔːdkɑːst; *USA* ˈbrɔːdkæst/ ◆ (*pret, pp* **broadcast**) **1** *vt* (*Radio, TV*) transmitir **2** *vt* (*opinión, etc*) propagar **3** *vi* emitir ◆ *n* transmisión: *party political broadcast* espacio electoral

broaden /ˈbrɔːdn/ *vt, vi* ~ (**out**) ensanchar(se)

broadly /ˈbrɔːdli/ *adv* **1** ampliamente: *smiling broadly* con una amplia sonrisa **2** en general: *broadly speaking* hablando en términos generales

broccoli /ˈbrɒkəli/ *n* brécol

brochure /ˈbrəʊʃə(r); *USA* brəʊˈʃʊər/ *n* folleto (*esp de viajes o publicidad*)

broke /brəʊk/ ◆ *adj* (*coloq*) sin blanca LOC **to go broke** quebrar (*negocio*) ◆ *pret de* BREAK[1]

broken /ˈbrəʊkən/ ◆ *adj* **1** roto **2** (*corazón, hogar*) destrozado ◆ *pp de* BREAK[1]

bronchitis /brɒŋˈkaɪtɪs/ *n* [*incontable*] bronquitis: *to catch bronchitis* coger una bronquitis

bronze /brɒnz/ ◆ *n* bronce ◆ *adj* de (color) bronce

brooch /brəʊtʃ/ *n* broche

brood /bruːd/ *vi* ~ (**on/over sth**) dar vueltas a algo

brook /brʊk/ *n* arroyo

broom /bruːm, brʊm/ *n* **1** escoba ☛ *Ver dibujo en* BRUSH **2** (*Bot*) retama **broomstick** *n* (palo de) escoba

broth /brɒθ; *USA* brɔːt/ *n* [*incontable*] caldo

brother /ˈbrʌðə(r)/ *n* **1** hermano: *Does she have any brothers or sisters?* ¿Tiene hermanos? ◊ *Brother Luke* el Hermano Luke **2** (*fig*) cofrade **brotherhood** *n* [*v sing o pl*] **1** hermandad **2** cofradía **brotherly** *adj* fraternal

brother-in-law /ˈbrʌðər ɪn lɔː/ *n* (*pl* **-ers-in-law**) cuñado

brought *pret, pp de* BRING

brow /braʊ/ *n* **1** (*Anat*) frente ☛ La palabra más normal es **forehead**. **2** [*gen pl*] (*tb* **eyebrow**) ceja **3** (*colina*) cima

brown /braʊn/ ◆ *adj, n* (**-er**, **-est**) **1** marrón **2** (*pelo*) castaño **3** (*piel, azúcar*) moreno **4** (*oso*) pardo **5** *brown bread/rice* pan/arroz integral ◊ *brown paper* papel de embalar ◆ *vt, vi* dorar(se) **brownish** *adj* pardusco

brownie /ˈbraʊni/ *n* **1** (*GB tb* **Brownie**) niña exploradora **2** (*USA*) bizcocho de chocolate y nueces

browse /braʊz/ *vi* **1** ~ (**through sth**) (*tienda*) echar un vistazo (a algo) **2** ~ (**through sth**) (*revista*) hojear (algo) **3** pacer

bruise /bruːz/ ◆ *n* **1** cardenal **2** (*fruta*) golpe ◆ **1** *vt, vi* ~ (**yourself**) (*persona*) magullar(se) **2** *vt* (*fruta*) golpear **bruising** *n* [*incontable*]: *He had a lot of bruising.* Tenía muchas magulladuras.

brush /brʌʃ/ ◆ *n* **1** cepillo **2** escobón **3** pincel **4** brocha **5** (*Electrón*) escobilla **6** cepillado **7** ~ **with sth** (*fig*) roce con algo ◆ *vt* **1** cepillar: *to brush your hair/teeth* cepillarse el pelo/los dientes **2** barrer **3** ~ **past/against sth/sb** rozarse contra algo/con algn PHR V **to brush sth aside** hacer caso omiso de algo **to brush sth up/to brush up on sth** pulir algo (*idioma, etc*)

brusque /bruːsk; *USA* brʌsk/ *adj* brusco (*comportamiento, voz*)

Brussels sprout (*tb* **sprout**) *n* col de Bruselas

brutal /ˈbruːtl/ *adj* brutal **brutality** /bruːˈtæləti/ *n* (*pl* **-ies**) brutalidad

brute /bruːt/ ◆ *n* **1** bestia **2** bruto ◆ *adj* bruto **brutish** *adj* brutal

bubble /ˈbʌbl/ ◆ *n* **1** burbuja **2** pompa: *to blow bubbles* hacer pompas ◆ *vi* **1** borbotear **2** burbujear **bubbly** *adj* (**-ier**, **-iest**) **1** burbujeante, efervescente **2** (*persona*) saleroso

bubble bath *n* espuma para baño

bubblegum /ˈbʌblgʌm/ *n* chicle (*que hace globos*)

buck[1] /bʌk/ *n* macho (*de ciervo, conejo*) ☛ *Ver nota en* CIERVO, CONEJO

buck[2] /bʌk/ *vi* dar brincos LOC **to buck the trend** ir contra la corriente PHR V **to buck sb up** (*coloq*) animar a algn

buck[3] /bʌk/ *n* **1** (*USA, coloq*) (*dólar*) pavo **2** [*gen pl*] (*coloq*) pasta LOC **the buck stops here** yo soy el último responsable **to make a fast/quick buck** hacer uno su agosto

bucket /ˈbʌkɪt/ *n* **1** cubo **2** (*máquina excavadora*) pala LOC *Ver* KICK

buckle /ˈbʌkl/ ◆ *n* hebilla ◆ **1** *vt* ~ **sth**

(**up**) abrochar algo **2** *vi* (*piernas*) doblarse **3** *vt, vi* (*metal*) deformar(se)

bud /bʌd/ *n* **1** (*flor*) capullo **2** (*Bot*) yema

Buddhism /ˈbʊdɪzəm/ *n* budismo **Buddhist** *adj, n* budista

budding /ˈbʌdɪŋ/ *adj* en ciernes

buddy /ˈbʌdi/ *n* (*pl* **-ies**) (*coloq*) colega (*amiguete*) ☛ Se emplea sobre todo entre chicos y se usa mucho en Estados Unidos.

budge /bʌdʒ/ *vt, vi* **1** mover(se) **2** (*opinión*) ceder

budgerigar /ˈbʌdʒərɪˌgɑː(r)/ *n* periquito

budget /ˈbʌdʒɪt/ ◆ *n* **1** presupuesto: *a budget deficit* un déficit presupuestario **2** (*Pol*) presupuestos generales ◆ **1** *vt* hacer los presupuestos para **2** *vi* (*gastos*) planificarse **3** *vi* ~ **for sth** contar con algo **budgetary** *adj* presupuestario

buff /bʌf/ ◆ *n* entusiasta: *a film buff* un entusiasta del cine ◆ *adj, n* beige

buffalo /ˈbʌfələʊ/ *n* (*pl* **buffalo** *o* ~**es**) **1** búfalo **2** (*USA*) bisonte

buffer /ˈbʌfə(r)/ *n* **1** (*lit y fig*) amortiguador **2** (*vía*) tope **3** (*Informát*) memoria intermedia **4** (*GB, coloq*) (*tb* **old buffer**) vejestorio

buffet[1] /ˈbʊfeɪ; *USA* bəˈfeɪ/ *n* **1** cafetería: *buffet car* coche bar/restaurante **2** bufé

buffet[2] /ˈbʌfɪt/ *vt* zarandear **buffeting** *n* zarandeo

bug /bʌg/ ◆ *n* **1** chinche, bicho **2** (*coloq*) virus, infección **3** (*coloq*) (*Informát*) error de programación **4** (*coloq*) micrófono oculto ◆ *vt* (**-gg-**) **1** poner un micrófono escondido en **2** escuchar mediante un micrófono oculto **3** (*coloq, esp USA*) sacar de quicio

buggy /ˈbʌgi/ *n* (*pl* **-ies**) **1** todoterreno **2** (*esp USA*) cochecito de niño

build /bɪld/ *vt* (*pret, pp* **built** /bɪlt/) **1** construir **2** crear, producir PHR V **to build sth in 1** empotrar algo **2** (*fig*) incorporar algo **to build on sth** partir de la base de algo **to build up 1** intensificarse **2** acumularse **to build sth/sb up** poner algo/a algn muy bien **to build sth up 1** (*colección*) acumular algo **2** (*negocio*) crear algo

builder /ˈbɪldə(r)/ *n* constructor, -ora

building /ˈbɪldɪŋ/ *n* **1** edificio **2** construcción

building site *n* **1** solar **2** (*construcción*) obra

building society *n* (*GB*) banco hipotecario

build-up /ˈbɪld ʌp/ *n* **1** aumento gradual **2** acumulación **3** ~ (**to sth**) preparación (para algo) **4** propaganda

built *pret, pp de* BUILD

built-in /ˌbɪlt ˈɪn/ *adj* **1** empotrado **2** incorporado

built-up /ˌbɪlt ˈʌp/ *adj* edificado: *built-up areas* zonas edificadas

bulb /bʌlb/ *n* **1** (*Bot*) bulbo **2** (*tb* **light bulb**) bombilla

bulge /bʌldʒ/ ◆ *n* **1** bulto **2** (*coloq*) aumento (transitorio) ◆ *vi* **1** ~ (**with sth**) rebosar (de algo) **2** abombarse

bulk /bʌlk/ *n* **1** volumen: *bulk buying* compra al por mayor **2** mole **3 the bulk (of sth)** la mayor parte (de algo) LOC **in bulk 1** al por mayor **2** a granel **bulky** *adj* (**-ier**, **-iest**) voluminoso

bull /bʊl/ *n* **1** toro **2** (*dardos*) centro de la diana

bulldoze /ˈbʊldəʊz/ *vt* **1** (*con excavadora*) aplanar **2** derribar

bullet /ˈbʊlɪt/ *n* bala

bulletin /ˈbʊlətɪn/ *n* **1** (*declaración*) parte **2** boletín: *news bulletin* boletín de noticias ◊ *bulletin-board* tablón (de avisos)

bulletproof /ˈbʊlɪtpruːf/ *adj* antibalas

bullfight /ˈbʊlfaɪt/ *n* corrida de toros **bullfighter** *n* torero, -a **bullfighting** *n* toreo

bullion /ˈbʊliən/ *n* oro/plata (*en lingotes*)

bullring /ˈbʊlrɪŋ/ *n* plaza de toros

bull's-eye /ˈbʊlz aɪ/ *n* (centro del) blanco

bully /ˈbʊli/ ◆ *n* (*pl* **-ies**) matón, -ona ◆ *vt* (*pret, pp* **bullied**) meterse con algn, intimidar a algn

bum /bʌm/ ◆ *n* (*coloq*) **1** (*GB*) culo **2** (*USA*) vagabundo, -a ◆ *v* (*coloq*) PHR V **to bum around** vaguear

bumble-bee /ˈbʌmbl biː/ *n* abejorro

bump /bʌmp/ ◆ **1** *vt* ~ **sth** (**against/on sth**) dar(se) con algo (contra/en algo) **2** *vi* ~ **into sth/sb** darse con algo/algn PHR V **to bump into sb** toparse con algn **to bump sb off** (*coloq*) cargarse a algn

◆ *n* **1** golpe **2** sacudida **3** (*Anat*) chichón **4** bache **5** abolladura

bumper /ˈbʌmpə(r)/ ◆ *n* parachoques: *bumper car* auto de choque ◆ *adj* abundante

bumpy /ˈbʌmpi/ *adj* (**-ier**, **-iest**) **1** (*superficie*) desigual **2** (*carretera*) accidentado **3** (*viaje*) agitado

bun /bʌn/ *n* **1** bollo (dulce) **2** moño

bunch /bʌntʃ/ ◆ *n* **1** (*uvas, plátanos*) racimo **2** (*flores*) ramo **3** (*hierbas, llaves*) manojo **4** [*v sing o pl*] (*coloq*) grupo ◆ *vt, vi* agrupar(se), apiñar(se)

bundle /ˈbʌndl/ ◆ *n* **1** (*ropa, papeles*) fardo **2** haz **3** (*billetes*) fajo ◆ *vt* ~ **sth** (**together/up**) empaquetar algo

bung /bʌŋ/ ◆ *n* tapón ◆ *vt* **1** taponar **2** (*GB, coloq*) poner

bungalow /ˈbʌŋgələʊ/ *n* bungalow ☛ *Ver* pág 321.

bungle /ˈbʌŋgl/ **1** *vt* echar a perder **2** *vi* fracasar, meter la pata

bunk /bʌŋk/ *n* litera LOC **to do a bunk** (*GB, coloq*) pirárselas

bunny /ˈbʌni/ (*tb* **bunny-rabbit**) *n* conejito

bunting /ˈbʌntɪŋ/ *n* [*incontable*] banderolas

buoy /bɔɪ; *USA* ˈbuːi/ ◆ *n* boya ◆ PHR V **to buoy sb up** animar a algn **to buoy sth up** mantener algo a flote

buoyant /ˈbɔɪənt; *USA* ˈbuːjənt/ *adj* (*Econ*) boyante

burble /ˈbɜːbl/ *vi* **1** (*arroyo*) susurrar **2** ~ (**on**) (**about sth**) farfullar (algo)

burden /ˈbɜːdn/ ◆ *n* **1** carga **2** peso ◆ *vt* **1** cargar **2** (*fig*) agobiar **burdensome** *adj* agobiante

bureau /ˈbjʊərəʊ/ *n* (*pl* **-reaux** *o* **-reaus** /-rəʊz/) **1** (*GB*) escritorio **2** (*USA*) cómoda **3** (*esp USA, Pol*) departamento (de gobierno) **4** agencia: *travel bureau* agencia de viajes

bureaucracy /bjʊəˈrɒkrəsi/ *n* (*pl* **-ies**) burocracia **bureaucrat** /ˈbjʊərəkræt/ *n* burócrata **bureaucratic** /ˌbjʊərəˈkrætɪk/ *adj* burocrático

burger /ˈbɜːgə(r)/ *n* (*coloq*) hamburguesa

> La palabra **burger** se usa mucho en compuestos como *cheeseburger* hamburguesa con queso.

burglar /ˈbɜːglə(r)/ *n* ladrón, -ona: *burglar alarm* alarma antirrobo ☛ *Ver nota en* THIEF **burglary** *n* (*pl* **-ies**) robo (*en una casa*) ☛ *Ver nota en* THEFT **burgle** *vt* robar en ☛ *Ver nota en* ROB

burgundy /ˈbɜːgəndi/ *n* **1** (*tb* **Burgundy**) (*vino*) borgoña **2** color burdeos

burial /ˈberiəl/ *n* entierro

burly /ˈbɜːli/ *adj* (**-ier**, **-iest**) fornido

burn /bɜːn/ ◆ (*pret, pp* **burnt** /bɜːnt/ *o* **burned**) ☛ *Ver nota en* DREAM **1** *vt, vi* quemar: *to be badly burnt* sufrir graves quemaduras **2** *vi* (*lit y fig*) arder: *a burning building* un edificio en llamas ◊ *to burn to do sth/for sth* arder en deseos de (hacer) algo **3** *vi* escocer **4** *vi* (*luz, etc*): *He left the lamp burning.* Dejó la lámpara encendida. **5** *vt*: *The boiler burns oil.* La caldera funciona con petróleo. ◆ *n* quemadura

burner /ˈbɜːnə(r)/ *n* quemador (*cocina*)

burning /ˈbɜːnɪŋ/ *adj* **1** ardiente **2** (*vergüenza*) intenso **3** (*tema*) candente

burnt /bɜːnt/ ◆ *pret, pp de* BURN ◆ *adj* quemado

burp /bɜːp/ ◆ **1** *vi* eructar **2** *vt* (*bebé*) hacer eructar ◆ *n* eructo

burrow /ˈbʌrəʊ/ ◆ *n* madriguera ◆ *vt* excavar

burst /bɜːst/ ◆ *vt, vi* (*pret, pp* **burst**) **1** reventar(se) **2** explotar: *The river burst its banks.* El río se desbordó. LOC **to be bursting to do sth** reventar por hacer algo **to burst open** abrirse de golpe **to burst out laughing** echar(se) a reír PHR V **to burst into sth 1** *to burst into a room* irrumpir en un cuarto **2** *to burst into tears* romper a llorar **to burst out** salir de golpe (*de un cuarto*) ◆ *n* **1** (*ira, etc*) arranque **2** (*disparos*) ráfaga **3** (*aplausos*) salva

bury /ˈberi/ *vt* (*pp* **buried**) **1** enterrar **2** sepultar **3** (*cuchillo, etc*) clavar **4** *She buried her face in her hands.* Ocultó la cara en las manos.

bus /bʌs/ *n* (*pl* **buses**) autobús: *bus conductor/conductress* cobrador, -ora de autobús ◊ *bus driver* conductor, -ora de autobús ◊ *bus stop* parada (de autobús)

bush /bʊʃ/ *n* **1** arbusto: *a rose bush* un rosal ☛ *Comparar con* SHRUB **2 the bush** el monte LOC *Ver* BEAT **bushy** *adj* **1** (*barba*) poblado **2** (*rabo*) peludo **3** (*planta*) frondoso

busily /ˈbɪzɪli/ *adv* afanosamente

business /ˈbɪznəs/ *n* **1** [*incontable*] negocios **2** [*antes de sustantivo*]: *business card* tarjeta comercial ◊ *business studies* ciencias empresariales ◊ *a business trip* un viaje de negocios **3** negocio, empresa **4** asunto: *It's none of your business!* ¡No es asunto tuyo! **5** (*en una reunión*): *any other business* ruegos y preguntas LOC **business before pleasure** (*refrán*) primero es la obligación que la devoción **on business** en viaje de negocios **to do business with sb** hacer negocios con algn **to get down to business** ir al grano **to go out of business** quebrar **to have no business doing sth** no tener derecho a hacer algo *Ver tb* BIG, MEAN[1], MIND

businesslike /ˈbɪznəslaɪk/ *adj* **1** formal **2** sistemático

businessman /ˈbɪznəsmən/ *n* (*pl* **-men** /-mən/) hombre de negocios

businesswoman /ˈbɪznɪswʊmən/ *n* (*pl* **-women**) mujer de negocios

busk /bʌsk/ *vi* tocar música en un lugar público **busker** *n* músico callejero

bust[1] /bʌst/ *n* **1** (*escultura*) busto **2** (*Anat*) pecho

bust[2] /bʌst/ ◆ *vt, vi* (*pret, pp* **bust** *o* **busted**) (*coloq*) romper(se) ☛ *Ver nota en* DREAM ◆ *adj* (*coloq*) roto LOC **to go bust** ir a la quiebra

bustle /ˈbʌsl/ ◆ *vi* ~ (**about**) trajinar ◆ *n* (*tb* **hustle and bustle**) bullicio, ajetreo **bustling** *adj* bullicioso

busy /ˈbɪzi/ ◆ *adj* (**busier**, **busiest**) **1** ~ (**at/with sth**) ocupado (con algo) **2** (*sitio*) concurrido **3** (*temporada*) de mucha actividad **4** (*programa*) apretado **5** (*USA*): *The line is busy.* Está comunicando. ◆ *v refl* ~ **yourself with (doing) sth** ocuparse con algo/haciendo algo

busybody /ˈbɪzibɒdi/ *n* (*pl* **-ies**) entrometido, -a

but /bʌt, bət/ ◆ *conj* **1** pero **2** sino: *Not only him but me too.* No sólo él, sino yo también. ◊ *What could I do but cry?* ¿Qué podía hacer sino llorar? ◆ *prep* excepto: *nobody but you* sólo tú LOC **but for sth/sb** de no haber sido por algo/algn **we can but hope, try, etc** sólo nos queda esperar, intentar, etc

butcher /ˈbʊtʃə(r)/ ◆ *n* carnicero, -a ◆ *vt* **1** (*animal*) matar **2** (*persona*) matar brutalmente

butcher's /ˈbʊtʃəz/ (*tb* **butcher's shop**) *n* carnicería

butler /ˈbʌtlə(r)/ *n* mayordomo

butt /bʌt/ ◆ *n* **1** tonel **2** aljibe **3** culata **4** (*cigarrillo*) colilla **5** (*coloq, USA*) culo **6** blanco ◆ *vt* dar un cabezazo a PHR V **to butt in** (*coloq*) interrumpir

butter /ˈbʌtə(r)/ ◆ *n* mantequilla ◆ *vt* untar con mantequilla

buttercup /ˈbʌtəkʌp/ *n* botón de oro

butterfly /ˈbʌtəflaɪ/ *n* (*pl* **-ies**) mariposa LOC **to have butterflies (in your stomach)** tener los nervios en el estómago

buttock /ˈbʌtək/ *n* nalga

button /ˈbʌtn/ ◆ *n* botón ◆ *vt, vi* ~ **(sth) (up)** abrochar(se)

buttonhole /ˈbʌtnhəʊl/ *n* ojal

buttress /ˈbʌtrəs/ *n* contrafuerte

buy /baɪ/ ◆ *vt* (*pret, pp* **bought** /bɔːt/) **1 to buy sth for sb; to buy sb sth** comprar algo a algn/para algn: *He bought his girlfriend a present.* Compró un regalo para su novia. ◊ *I bought one for myself for £10.* Yo me compré uno por diez libras. **2 to buy sth from sb** comprar algo a algn ◆ *n* compra: *a good buy* una buena compra **buyer** *n* comprador, -ora

buzz /bʌz/ ◆ *n* **1** zumbido **2** (*voces*) murmullo **3** *I get a real buzz out of flying.* Ir en avión me entusiasma. **4** (*coloq*) telefonazo ◆ *vi* zumbar PHR V **buzz off!** (*coloq*) ¡lárgate!

buzzard /ˈbʌzəd/ *n* águila ratonera

buzzer /ˈbʌzə(r)/ *n* timbre eléctrico

by /baɪ/ ◆ *prep* **1** por: *by post* por correo ◊ *ten (multiplied) by six* diez (multiplicado) por seis ◊ *designed by Wren* diseñado por Wren **2** al lado de, junto a: *Sit by me.* Siéntate a mi lado. **3** antes de, para: *to be home by ten o'clock* estar en casa para las diez **4** de: *by day/night* de día/noche ◊ *by birth/profession* de nacimiento/profesión ◊ *a novel by Steinbeck* una novela de Steinbeck **5** en: *to go by boat, car, bicycle* ir en barco, coche, bicicleta ◊ *two by two* de dos en dos **6** según: *by my watch* según mi reloj **7** con: *to pay by cheque* pagar con un cheque **8** a: *little by little* poco a poco **9** a base de: *by working hard* a base de trabajar duro **10 by doing sth** haciendo algo: *Let me begin by saying…* Permítanme que empiece diciendo... LOC **to have/keep sth by you** tener algo a mano ◆ *adv* LOC **by and by** dentro de poco **by the by** a propósito **to go, drive, run, etc by** pasar por delante (en coche, corriendo, etc) **to keep/put sth by** guardar algo para más tarde *Ver tb* LARGE

bye! /baɪ/ (*tb* **bye-bye!** /ˌbaɪˈbaɪ, bəˈbaɪ/) *interj* (*coloq*) ¡adiós!

by-election /ˈbaɪ ɪlekʃn/ *n*: *She won the by-election.* Ganó las elecciones parciales.

bygone /ˈbaɪɡɒn/ *adj* pasado

by-law /ˈbaɪ lɔː/ (*tb* **bye-law**) *n* ordenanza municipal

bypass /ˈbaɪpɑːs; *USA* -pæs/ ◆ *n* (carretera de) circunvalación ◆ *vt* **1** circunvalar **2** evitar

by-product /ˈbaɪ prɒdʌkt/ *n* **1** (*lit*) subproducto **2** (*fig*) consecuencia

bystander /ˈbaɪstændə(r)/ *n* presente: *seen by bystanders* visto por los presentes

Cc

C, c /siː/ *n* (*pl* **C's, c's** /siːz/) **1** C, c: *C for Charlie* C de Cáceres ☛ *Ver ejemplos en* A, a **2** (*Educ*) bien: *to get (a) C in Physics* sacar un bien en Física **3** (*Mús*) do

cab /kæb/ *n* **1** taxi **2** cabina (*de un camión*)

cabbage /ˈkæbɪdʒ/ *n* col

cabin /ˈkæbɪn/ *n* **1** (*Náut*) camarote **2** (*Aeronáut*) cabina (de pasajeros): *pilot's cabin* cabina de mando **3** cabaña

cabinet /ˈkæbɪnət/ *n* **1** armario: *bathroom cabinet* armario de baño ◊ *drinks cabinet* mueble bar **2 the Cabinet** [*v sing o pl*] gabinete ☛ Ver pág 322.

cable /ˈkeɪbl/ *n* **1** cable **2** amarra

cable car *n* teleférico

cackle /ˈkækl/ ◆ *n* **1** cacareo **2** carcajada desagradable ◆ *vt* **1** (*gallina*) cacarear **2** (*persona*) reírse a carcajadas

cactus /ˈkæktəs/ *n* (*pl* ~**es** *o* **cacti** /ˈkæktaɪ/) cacto, cactus

cadet /kəˈdet/ *n* cadete

Caesarean (*USA* **Cesarian**) /siˈzeəriən/ (*tb* **Caesarean section**) *n* cesárea

café /ˈkæfeɪ; *USA* kæˈfeɪ/ *n* café ☛ Ver pág 320

cafeteria /ˌkæfəˈtɪəriə/ *n* restaurante de autoservicio ☛ Ver pág 320.

caffeine /ˈkæfiːn/ *n* cafeína

cage /keɪdʒ/ ◆ *n* jaula ◆ *vt* enjaular

cagey /ˈkeɪdʒi/ *adj* (**cagier**, **cagiest**) ~ (**about sth**) (*coloq*) reservado: *He's very cagey about his family.* No suelta prenda sobre su familia.

cake /keɪk/ *n* pastel: *birthday cake* tarta de cumpleaños LOC **to have your cake and eat it** (*coloq*) nadar y guardar la ropa *Ver tb* PIECE

caked /keɪkt/ *adj* ~ **with sth** cubierto de algo: *caked with mud* cubierto de barro

calamity /kəlˈæməti/ *n* (*pl* **-ies**) calamidad

calculate /ˈkælkjuleɪt/ *vt* calcular LOC **to be calculated to do sth** estar pensado para hacer algo **calculating** *adj* calculador **calculation** *n* cálculo

calculator /ˈkælkjʊleɪtə(r)/ *n* calculadora

calendar /ˈkælɪndə(r)/ *n* calendario: *calendar month* mes (de calendario)

calf[1] /kɑːf; *USA* kæf/ *n* (*pl* **calves** /kɑːvz; *USA* kævz/) **1** becerro, ternero ☛ *Ver nota en* CARNE **2** cría (*de foca, etc*)

calf[2] /kɑːf; *USA* kæf/ *n* (*pl* **calves** /kɑːvz; *USA* kævz/) pantorrilla

calibre (*USA* **caliber**) /ˈkælɪbə(r)/ *n* calibre, valía

call /kɔːl/ ◆ *n* **1** grito, llamada **2** (*Ornitología*) canto **3** visita **4** (*tb* **phone call**, **ring**) llamada (telefónica) **5** ~ **for sth**: *There isn't much call for such things.* Hay poca demanda para esas cosas. LOC **(to be) on call** (estar) de guardia *Ver tb* CLOSE[1], PORT ◆ **1** *vi* ~ **(out) (to sb) (for sth)** llamar a voces (a algn) (pidiendo algo): *I thought I heard some-*

body calling. Creí que había oído llamar a alguien. ◊ *She called to her father for help.* Pidió ayuda a su padre a voces. **2** *vt* ~ **sth** (**out**) gritar algo (a voces), llamar (a voces): *Why didn't you come when I called (out) your name?* ¿Por qué no viniste cuando te llamé? **3** *vt, vi* llamar (por teléfono) **4** *vt* (*taxi, ambulancia*) llamar **5** *vt* llamar: *Please call me at seven o'clock.* Por favor llámame a las siete. **6** *vt* llamarse: *What's your dog called?* ¿Cómo se llama el perro? **7** *vi* ~ (**in/round**) (**on sb**); ~ (**in/round**) (**at...**) visitar (a algn), pasarse (por...): *Let's call (in) on John/ at John's house.* Vamos a pasar por casa de John. ◊ *He was out when I called (round) (to see him).* No estaba cuando fui a su casa. ◊ *Will you call in at the supermarket for some eggs?* ¿Puedes pasarte por el supermercado a comprar huevos? **8** *vi* ~ **at** (*tren*) tener parada en **9** *vt* (*reunión, elección*) convocar LOC **to call it a day** (*coloq*) dejarlo por hoy: *Let's call it a day.* Dejémoslo por hoy. *Ver tb* QUESTION

PHR V **to call by** (*coloq*) pasar: *Could you call by on your way home?* ¿Puedes pasar al volver a casa?

to call for sb ir a buscar a algn: *I'll call for you at seven o'clock.* Iré a buscarte a las siete. **to call for sth** requerir algo: *The situation calls for prompt action.* La situación requiere acción rápida.

to call sth off cancelar algo, abandonar algo

to call sb out llamar a algn: *to call out the troops/the fire brigade* llamar al ejército/ a los bomberos

to call sb up 1 (*esp USA*) (*por teléfono*) llamar a algn **2** llamar a algn a filas

caller /ˈkɔːlə(r)/ *n* **1** el/la que llama (por teléfono) **2** visita

callous /ˈkæləs/ *adj* insensible, cruel

calm /kɑːm; *USA* kɑːlm/ ◆ *adj* (**-er, -est**) tranquilo ◆ *n* calma ◆ *vt, vi* ~ (**sb**) (**down**) calmar(se), tranquilizar(se): *Just calm down a bit!* ¡Tranquilízate un poco!

calorie /ˈkæləri/ *n* caloría

calves *plural de* CALF[1,2]

came *pret de* COME

camel /ˈkæml/ *n* **1** camello **2** beige (*color*)

camera /ˈkæmərə/ *n* cámara (fotográfica): *a television/video camera* una cámara de televisión/vídeo

camouflage /ˈkæməflɑːʒ/ ◆ *n* camuflaje ◆ *vt* camuflar

camp /kæmp/ ◆ *n* campamento: *concentration camp* campo de concentración ◆ *vi* acampar: *to go camping* ir de camping

campaign /kæmˈpeɪn/ ◆ *n* campaña ◆ *vi* ~ (**for/against sth/sb**) hacer campaña (a favor de/en contra de algo/algn) **campaigner** *n* militante

campsite /ˈkæmpsaɪt/ (*tb* **camping site**) *n* camping

campus /ˈkæmpəs/ *n* (*pl* ~**es**) ciudad universitaria

can[1] /kæn/ ◆ *n* lata: *a can of sardines* una lata de sardinas ◊ *a petrol can* un bidón (de gasolina) LOC *Ver* CARRY ☛ *Ver nota en* LATA *y dibujo en* CONTAINER. ◆ *vt* (**-nn-**) enlatar, hacer conservas en lata de

can[2] /kən, kæn/ *v modal* (*neg* **cannot** /ˈkænɒt/ *o* **can't** /kɑːnt; *USA* kænt/ *pret* **could** /kəd, kʊd/ *neg* **could not** *o* **couldn't** /ˈkʊdnt/)

> **Can** es un verbo modal al que sigue un infinitivo sin TO, y las oraciones interrogativas y negativas se construyen sin el auxiliar *do*. Sólo tiene presente: *I can't swim.* No sé nadar; y pasado, que también tiene un valor condicional: *He couldn't do it.* No pudo hacerlo. ◊ *Could you come?* ¿Podrías venir? Cuando queremos utilizar otras formas, tenemos que usar **to be able to**: *Will you be able to come?* ¿Podrás venir? ◊ *I'd like to be able to go.* Me gustaría poder ir.

- **posibilidad** poder: *We can catch a bus from here.* Podemos coger un autobús aquí. ◊ *She can be very forgetful.* A veces es muy olvidadiza.
- **conocimentos, habilidades** saber: *They can't read or write.* No saben leer ni escribir. ◊ *Can you swim?* ¿Sabes nadar? ◊ *He couldn't answer the question.* No supo contestar a la pregunta.
- **permiso** poder: *Can I open the window?* ¿Puedo abrir la ventana? ◊ *You can't go swimming today.* No puedes ir a nadar hoy. ☛ *Ver nota en* MAY
- **ofrecimientos, sugerencias, peticiones** poder: *Can I help?* ¿Puedo ayudarle? ◊ *We can eat in a restaurant,*

if you want. Podemos comer en un restaurante si quieres. ◊ *Could you help me with this box?* ¿Me puede ayudar con esta caja? ☛ *Ver nota en* MUST

• **con verbos de percepción**: *You can see it everywhere.* Se puede ver por todas partes. ◊ *She could hear them clearly.* Los oía claramente. ◊ *I can smell something burning.* Huele a quemado. ◊ *She could still taste the garlic.* Le quedaba en la boca el sabor a ajo.

• **incredulidad, perplejidad**: *I can't believe it.* No lo puedo creer. ◊ *Whatever can they be doing?* ¿Qué estarán haciendo? ◊ *Where can she have put it?* ¿Dónde lo habrá puesto?

canal /kəˈnæl/ *n* **1** canal **2** tubo, conducto: *the birth canal* el canal del parto

canary /kəˈneəri/ *n* (*pl* **-ies**) canario

cancel /ˈkænsl/ *vt, vi* (**-ll-**, *USA* **-l-**) **1** (*vuelo, pedido, vacaciones*) cancelar ☛ *Comparar con* POSTPONE **2** (*contrato*) anular PHR V **to cancel (sth) out** eliminarse, eliminar algo **cancellation** *n* cancelación

Cancer /ˈkænsə(r)/ *n* cáncer ☛ *Ver ejemplos en* AQUARIUS

cancer /ˈkænsə(r)/ *n* [*incontable*] cáncer

candid /ˈkændɪd/ *adj* franco

candidate /ˈkændɪdət, -deɪt; *USA* -deɪt/ *n* **1** candidato, -a **2** persona que se presenta a un examen **candidacy** *n* candidatura

candle /ˈkændl/ *n* **1** vela **2** (*Relig*) cirio

candlelight /ˈkændl laɪt/ *n* luz de una vela

candlestick /ˈkændlstɪk/ *n* **1** candelero **2** candelabro

candy /ˈkændi/ *n* **1** [*incontable*] golosinas **2** (*pl* **-ies**) (*USA*) golosina (*caramelo, bombón, etc*)

cane /keɪn/ *n* **1** (*Bot*) caña **2** mimbre **3** bastón **4 the cane** palmeta

canister /ˈkænɪstə(r)/ *n* **1** lata (*de café, té, galletas*) **2** bote (de humo)

cannibal /ˈkænɪbl/ *n* caníbal

cannon /ˈkænən/ *n* (*pl* **cannon** *o* **~s**) cañón

canoe /kəˈnuː/ *n* canoa, piragua **canoeing** *n* piragüismo

canopy /ˈkænəpi/ *n* (*pl* **-ies**) **1** toldo, marquesina **2** dosel **3** (*fig*) techo

canteen /kænˈtiːn/ *n* cantina ☛ *Ver* pág 320.

canter /ˈkæntə(r)/ *n* medio galope

canvas /ˈkænvəs/ *n* **1** lona **2** (*Arte*) lienzo

canvass /ˈkænvəs/ **1** *vt, vi* ~ **(sb) (for sth)** pedir apoyo (a algn) (para algo) **2** *vt, vi* (*Pol*): *to canvass for/on behalf of sb* hacer campaña por algn ◊ *to go out canvassing (for votes)* salir a captar votos **3** *vt* (*opinión*) sondear

canyon /ˈkænjən/ *n* cañón (*Geol*)

cap /kæp/ ◆ *n* **1** gorra **2** cofia **3** gorro **4** tapa, tapón ◆ *vt* (**-pp-**) superar LOC **to cap it all** para colmo

capability /ˌkeɪpəˈbɪləti/ *n* (*pl* **-ies**) **1** capacidad, aptitud **2 capabilities** [*pl*] potencial

capable /ˈkeɪpəbl/ *adj* capaz

capacity /kəˈpæsəti/ *n* (*pl* **-ies**) **1** capacidad: *filled to capacity* lleno a rebosar/completo **2** nivel máximo de producción: *at full capacity* a pleno rendimiento LOC **in your capacity as sth** en su calidad de algo

cape /keɪp/ *n* **1** capotillo **2** (*Geog*) cabo

caper /ˈkeɪpə(r)/ ◆ *vi* ~ **(about)** brincar ◆ *n* (*coloq*) broma, travesura

capillary /kəˈpɪləri; *USA* ˈkæpɪləri/ *n* (*pl* **-ies**) capilar

capital[1] /ˈkæpɪtl/ ◆ *n* **1** (*tb* **capital city**) capital **2** (*tb* **capital letter**) mayúscula **3** (*Arquit*) capitel ◆ *adj* **1** capital: *capital punishment* pena de muerte **2** mayúsculo

capital[2] /ˈkæpɪtl/ *n* capital: *capital gains* plusvalía ◊ *capital goods* bienes de capital LOC **to make capital (out) of sth** sacar partido de algo **capitalism** *n* capitalismo **capitalist** *adj, n* capitalista **capitalize, -ise** *vt* (*Fin*) capitalizar PHR V **to capitalize on sth** aprovecharse de algo, sacar partido de algo

capitulate /kəˈpɪtʃuleɪt/ *vi* ~ **(to sth/sb)** capitular (ante algo/algn)

capricious /kəˈprɪʃəs/ *adj* caprichoso

Capricorn /ˈkæprɪkɔːn/ *n* capricornio ☛ *Ver ejemplos en* AQUARIUS

capsize /kæpˈsaɪz; *USA* ˈkæpsaɪz/ *vt, vi* volcar(se)

capsule /ˈkæpsjuːl; *USA* ˈkæpsl/ *n* cápsula

captain /ˈkæptɪn/ ◆ *n* **1** (*Dep, Náut*) capitán, -ana **2** (*avión*) comandante ◆ *vt* capitanear, ser el capitán de **captaincy** *n* capitanía

caption /ˈkæpʃn/ *n* **1** encabezamiento, título **2** pie (de foto) **3** (*Cine, TV*) rótulo

captivate /ˈkæptɪveɪt/ *vt* cautivar **captivating** *adj* cautivador, encantador

captive /ˈkæptɪv/ ◆ *adj* cautivo LOC **to hold/take sb captive/prisoner** tener preso/apresar a algn ◆ *n* preso, -a, cautivo, -a **captivity** /kæpˈtɪvəti/ *n* cautividad

captor /ˈkæptə(r)/ *n* captor, -ora

capture /ˈkæptʃə(r)/ ◆ *vt* **1** capturar **2** (*interés, etc*) atraer **3** (*Mil*) tomar **4** (*fig*): *She captured his heart.* Le conquistó el corazón. **5** (*Arte*) captar ◆ *n* **1** captura **2** (*ciudad*) toma

car /kɑː(r)/ *n* **1** (*tb* **motor car**, *USA* **automobile**) coche, automóvil: *by car* en coche ◊ *car accident* accidente de coche ◊ *car bomb* coche-bomba **2** (*Ferrocarril*): *dining car* coche restaurante **3** (*USA, Ferrocarril*) vagón

caramel /ˈkærəmel/ *n* **1** caramelo (*azúcar quemado*) **2** color caramelo

carat (*USA* **karat**) /ˈkærət/ *n* quilate

caravan /ˈkærəvæn/ *n* **1** (*USA* **trailer**) caravana: *caravan site* cámping para caravanas **2** carromato **3** caravana (*de camellos*)

carbohydrate /ˌkɑːbəʊˈhaɪdreɪt/ *n* hidrato de carbono

carbon /ˈkɑːbən/ *n* **1** carbono: *carbon dating* datar por medio de la técnica del carbono 14 ◊ *carbon dioxide/monoxide* dióxido/monóxido de carbono **2** *carbon paper* papel carbón ☛ *Comparar con* COAL

carbon copy *n* (*pl* **-ies**) **1** copia al carbón **2** (*fig*) réplica: *She's a carbon copy of her sister.* Es idéntica a su hermana.

carburettor /ˌkɑːbəˈretə(r)/ (*USA* **carburetor** /ˌkɑːrbəˈreɪtər/) *n* carburador

carcass (*tb* **carcase**) /ˈkɑːkəs/ *n* **1** restos (*de pollo, etc*) **2** res muerta lista para trocear

card /kɑːd/ *n* **1** tarjeta **2** ficha: *card index* fichero **3** (*de socio, de identidad, etc*) carnet **4** carta, naipe **5** [*incontable*] cartulina LOC **on the cards** (*coloq*) probable **to get your cards/give sb their cards** (*coloq*) ser despedido/despedir a algn *Ver tb* LAY[1], PLAY

cardboard /ˈkɑːdbɔːd/ *n* cartón

cardholder /ˈkɑːdˌhəʊldə(r)/ *n* poseedor, -ora de tarjeta (de crédito)

cardiac /ˈkɑːdiæk/ *adj* cardiaco

cardigan /ˈkɑːdɪgən/ *n* chaqueta (*de punto*)

cardinal /ˈkɑːdɪnl/ ◆ *adj* **1** (*pecado, etc*) cardinal **2** (*regla, etc*) fundamental ◆ *n* (*Relig*) cardenal

care /keə(r)/ ◆ *n* **1** ~ (**over sth/in doing sth**) cuidado (con algo/al hacer algo): *to take care* tener cuidado **2** atención: *child care provision* servicio de cuidado de los niños **3** preocupación LOC **care of sb** (*correos*) a la atención de algn **that takes care of that** eso zanja la cuestión **to take care of sth/sb** encargarse de algo/algn **to take care of yourself/sth/sb** cuidarse/cuidar algo/a algn **to take sb into/put sb in care** poner a algn (esp a un niño) al cuidado de una institución ◆ *vi* **1** ~ (**about sth**) importarle a algn (algo): *See if I care.* ¿Y a mí qué me importa? **2** ~ **to do sth** querer hacer algo LOC **for all I, you, etc care** para lo que a mí me, a ti te, etc importa **I, you, etc couldn't care less** me, te, etc importa un comino PHR V **to care for sb 1** querer a algn **2** cuidar a algn **to care for sth 1** gustarle algo a algn **2** apetecerle algo a algn

career /kəˈrɪə(r)/ ◆ *n* (*actividad profesional*) carrera: *career prospects* perspectivas profesionales ☛ *Comparar con* DEGREE 2 ◆ *vi* correr a toda velocidad

carefree /ˈkeəfriː/ *adj* libre de preocupaciones

careful /ˈkeəfl/ *adj* **1** *to be careful (about/of/with sth)* tener cuidado (con algo) **2** (*trabajo, etc*) cuidadoso **carefully** *adv* con cuidado, cuidadosamente: *to listen/think carefully* escuchar con atención/pensar bien LOC *Ver* TREAD

careless /ˈkeələs/ *adj* **1** ~ (**about sth**) descuidado, despreocupado (con algo): *to be careless of sth* no preocuparse por algo **2** imprudente

carer /ˈkeərə(r)/ *n* cuidador, -ora (*de persona anciana o enferma*)

caress /kəˈres/ ◆ *n* caricia ◆ *vt* acariciar

caretaker /ˈkeəteɪkə(r)/ ◆ *n* (*GB*)

conserje, portero, -a, vigilante ◆ *adj* interino

cargo /ˈkɑːgəʊ/ *n* (*pl* ~**es**, *USA* ~**s**) **1** carga **2** cargamento

caricature /ˈkærɪkətjʊə(r)/ ◆ *n* caricatura ◆ *vt* caricaturizar

caring /ˈkeərɪŋ/ *adj* caritativo: *a caring image* una imagen caritativa

carnation /kɑːˈneɪʃn/ *n* clavel

carnival /ˈkɑːnɪvl/ *n* carnaval

carnivore /ˈkɑːnɪvɔː(r)/ *n* carnívoro **carnivorous** *adj* carnívoro

carol /ˈkærəl/ *n* villancico

car park *n* aparcamiento

carpenter /ˈkɑːpəntə(r)/ *n* carpintero, -a **carpentry** *n* carpintería

carpet /ˈkɑːpɪt/ ◆ *n* moqueta, alfombra ◆ *vt* enmoquetar, alfombrar **carpeting** *n* [*incontable*] moqueta

carriage /ˈkærɪdʒ/ *n* **1** carruaje **2** (*USA* **car**) (*Ferrocarril*) vagón **3** (*correos*) porte **carriageway** *n* carril

carrier /ˈkæriə(r)/ *n* **1** portador **2** empresa de transportes

carrier bag *n* (*GB*) bolsa (*de plástico/papel*)

carrot /ˈkærət/ *n* **1** zanahoria **2** (*fig*) caramelo

carry /ˈkæri/ (*pret, pp* **carried**) **1** *vt* llevar: *to carry a gun* estar armado ☛ *Ver nota en* WEAR **2** *vt* soportar **3** *vt* (*votación*) aprobar **4** *v refl* ~ **yourself**: *She carries herself well.* Anda con mucha elegancia. **5** *vi* oírse: *Her voice carries well.* Tiene una voz muy fuerte. LOC **to carry the can** (**for sth**) (*coloq*) cargar con la culpa (de algo) **to carry the day** triunfar **to carry weight** tener gran peso
PHR V **to carry sth/sb away 1** (*lit*) llevar(se) algo/a algn **2** (*fig*): *Don't get carried away.* No te entusiasmes.
to carry sth off 1 salir airoso de algo **2** realizar algo **to carry sth/sb off** llevar(se) algo/a algn
to carry on (**with sb**) (*coloq*) tener una aventura (con algn) **to carry on** (**with sth/doing sth**); **to carry sth on** continuar (con algo/haciendo algo): *to carry on a conversation* mantener una conversación
to carry sth out 1 (*promesa, orden, etc*) cumplir **2** (*plan, investigación, etc*) llevar a cabo
to carry sth through llevar a término algo

carry-on /ˈkæri ɒn/ *n* (*coloq, esp GB*) lío

cart /kɑːt/ ◆ *n* carro ◆ *vt* acarrear PHR V **to cart sth about/around** (*coloq*) cargar con algo **to cart sth/sb off** (*coloq*) llevarse (algo/a algn)

carton /ˈkɑːtn/ *n* caja, cartón ☛ *Ver dibujo en* CONTAINER

cartoon /kɑːˈtuːn/ *n* **1** caricatura **2** tira cómica **3** dibujos animados **4** (*Arte*) cartón **cartoonist** *n* caricaturista

cartridge /ˈkɑːtrɪdʒ/ *n* **1** cartucho **2** (*de cámara, etc*) carrete

carve /kɑːv/ **1** *vt, vi* esculpir: *carved out of/from/in marble* esculpido en mármol **2** *vt, vi* (*madera*) tallar **3** *vt* (*iniciales, etc*) grabar **4** *vt, vi* (*carne*) trinchar PHR V **to carve sth out** (**for yourself**) ganarse algo **to carve sth up** (*coloq*) repartir algo **carving** *n* escultura, talla

cascade /kæˈskeɪd/ *n* cascada

case[1] /keɪs/ *n* **1** (*gen, Med, Gram*) caso: *It's a case of...* Se trata de... **2** argumento(s): *There is a case for...* Hay razones para... **3** (*Jur*) causa: *the case for the defence/prosecution* la defensa/la acusación LOC **in any case** en cualquier caso (**just**) **in case** por si acaso **to make** (**out**) **a case** (**for sth**) presentar argumentos convincentes (para algo) *Ver tb* BORDERLINE, JUST

case[2] /keɪs/ *n* **1** estuche **2** cajón (*de embalaje*) **3** caja (*de vino*) **4** maleta

cash /kæʃ/ ◆ *n* [*incontable*] dinero (en metálico): *to pay (in) cash* pagar en metálico ◊ *cash card* tarjeta de cajero automático ◊ *cash price* precio al contado ◊ *cash dispenser/cashpoint* cajero automático ◊ *cash flow* movimiento de fondos ◊ *cash desk* caja ◊ *to be short of cash* andar justo de dinero LOC **cash down** pago al contado **cash on delivery** (*abrev* **COD**) pago a la entrega *Ver tb* HARD ◆ *vt* hacer efectivo PHR V **to cash in** (**on sth**) aprovecharse (de algo) **to cash sth in** canjear algo

cashier /kæˈʃɪə(r)/ *n* cajero, -a

cashmere /ˌkæʃˈmɪə(r)/ *n* cachemir

casino /kəˈsiːnəʊ/ *n* (*pl* ~**s**) casino

cask /kɑːsk; *USA* kæsk/ *n* barril

casket /ˈkɑːskɪt; *USA* ˈkæskɪt/ *n* **1** cofre (*para joyas, etc*) **2** (*USA*) ataúd

casserole /ˈkæsərəʊl/ *n* **1** (*tb* **casser-**

ole dish) cazuela ☛ *Ver dibujo en* SAUCEPAN **2** guisado

cassette /kəˈset/ *n* cinta: *cassette deck/player/recorder* pletina/casete/grabadora

cast /kɑːst; *USA* kæst/ ◆ *n* **1** [*v sing o pl*] (*Teat*) reparto **2** (*Arte*) vaciado ◆ *vt* (*pret, pp* **cast**) **1** (*Teat*): *to cast sb as Othello* dar a algn el papel de Otelo **2** arrojar, lanzar **3** (*mirada*) echar **4** (*sombra*) proyectar **5** (*voto*) emitir: *to cast your vote* votar LOC **to cast an eye/your eye(s) over sth** echar un vistazo a algo **to cast a spell on sth/sb** hechizar algo/a algn **to cast doubt (on sth)** hacer dudar (de algo) PHR V **to cast about/around for sth** buscar algo **to cast sth/sb aside** dejar de lado algo/a algn **to cast sth off** deshacerse de algo

castaway /ˈkɑːstəweɪ; *USA* ˈkæst-/ *n* náufrago, -a

caste /kɑːst; *USA* kæst/ *n* casta: *caste system* sistema de castas

cast iron ◆ *n* hierro colado ◆ *adj* **1** de hierro colado **2** (*constitución*) de hierro **3** (*coartada*) sin mella

castle /ˈkɑːsl; *USA* ˈkæsl/ *n* **1** castillo **2** (*ajedrez*) (*tb* **rook**) torre

castrate /kæˈstreɪt; *USA* ˈkæstreɪt/ *vt* castrar **castration** *n* castración

casual /ˈkæʒuəl/ *adj* **1** (*ropa*) informal **2** (*trabajo*) ocasional: *casual worker* trabajador por horas **3** superficial: *a casual acquaintance* un conocido ◊ *a casual glance* un vistazo **4** (*encuentro*) fortuito **5** (*comentario*) sin importancia **6** (*comportamiento*) despreocupado, informal: *casual sex* promiscuidad sexual **casually** *adv* **1** como por casualidad **2** informalmente **3** temporalmente **4** despreocupadamente

casualty /ˈkæʒuəlti/ *n* (*pl* **-ies**) víctima, baja

cat /kæt/ *n* **1** gato: *cat food* comida para gatos ☛ *Ver nota en* GATO **2** felino: *big cat* felino salvaje LOC *Ver* LET[1]

catalogue (*USA tb* **catalog**) /ˈkætəlɒg; *USA* -lɔːg/ ◆ *n* **1** catálogo **2** (*fig*): *a catalogue of disasters* una serie de desastres ◆ *vt* catalogar **cataloguing** *n* catalogación

catalyst /ˈkætəlɪst/ *n* catalizador

catapult /ˈkætəpʌlt/ ◆ *n* tirachinas, catapulta ◆ *vt* catapultar

cataract /ˈkætərækt/ *n* catarata (*Geog, Med*)

catarrh /kəˈtɑː(r)/ *n* catarro, flujo catarral

catastrophe /kəˈtæstrəfi/ *n* catástrofe **catastrophic** /ˌkætəˈstrɒfɪk/ *adj* catastrófico

catch /kætʃ/ ◆ (*pret, pp* **caught** /kɔːt/) **1** *vt, vi* coger: *Here, catch!* ¡Toma! **2** *vt* atrapar, agarrar **3** *vt* sorprender **4** *vt* (*coloq*) pillar **5** *vt* (*USA, coloq*) ir a ver: *I'll catch you later.* Te veré luego. **6** *vt* ~ **sth (in/on sth)** enganchar algo (en/con algo): *He caught his thumb in the door.* Se pilló el dedo con la puerta. **7** *vt* (*Med*) contagiarse de, coger **8** *vt* oír, entender **9** *vi* (*fuego*) prenderse LOC **to catch fire** incendiarse **to catch it** (*coloq*): *You'll catch it!* ¡Te la vas a ganar! **to catch sb off balance** coger desprevenido a algn **to catch sb's attention/eye** captar la atención de algn **to catch sight/a glimpse of sth/sb** vislumbrar algo/a algn **to catch your breath 1** recuperar el aliento **2** contener la respiración **to catch your death (of cold)** (*coloq*) pillarse una pulmonía *Ver tb* BALANCE, CROSSFIRE, EARLY, FANCY

PHR V **to catch at sth** *Ver* TO CLUTCH AT STH *en* CLUTCH

to catch on (*coloq*) hacerse popular **to catch on (to sth)** (*coloq*) entender (algo)

to catch sb out 1 coger en falta a algn **2** (*béisbol, etc*) eliminar a algn al coger la pelota

to be caught up in sth estar metido en algo **to catch up (on sth)** ponerse al día (con algo) **to catch up (with sb)/to catch sb up** alcanzar a algn

◆ *n* **1** acción de coger (especialmente una pelota) **2** captura **3** (*peces*) pesca **4** (*coloq, fig*): *He's a good catch.* Es un buen partido. **5** cierre, cerradura **6** (*fig*) trampa: *It's a catch-22 (situation).* Es una situación sin salida. **catching** *adj* contagioso **catchy** *adj* (**-ier**, **-iest**) pegadizo (*fig*), fácil de recordar

catchment area *n* distrito

catchphrase /ˈkætʃfreɪz/ *n* dicho (*de persona famosa*)

catechism /ˈkætəkɪzəm/ *n* catecismo

categorical /ˌkætəˈgɒrɪkl; *USA* -ˈgɔːr-/ (*tb* **categoric**) *adj* **1** (*respuesta*) categórico **2** (*rechazo*) rotundo **3** (*regla*) terminante **categorically** *adv* categóricamente

categorize, -ise /ˈkætəgəraɪz/ *vt* clasificar

category /ˈkætəgəri; *USA* -gɔːri/ *n* (*pl* **-ies**) categoría

cater /ˈkeɪtə(r)/ *vi* abastecer: *to cater for a party* proveer la comida para una fiesta ◊ *to cater for all tastes* atender a todos los gustos **catering** *n* comida: *the catering industry* la hostelería

caterpillar /ˈkætəpɪlə(r)/ *n* **1** oruga **2** (*tb* **Caterpillar track**®) cadena (*de tanque, etc*)

cathedral /kəˈθiːdrəl/ *n* catedral

Catholic /ˈkæθlɪk/ *adj*, *n* católico, -a **Catholicism** /kəˈθɒləsɪzəm/ *n* catolicismo

cattle /ˈkætl/ *n* [*pl*] ganado

caught *pret*, *pp de* CATCH LOC *Ver* CROSSFIRE

cauldron /ˈkɔːldrən/ (*tb* **caldron**) *n* caldera

cauliflower /ˈkɒlɪflaʊə(r); *USA* ˈkɔːli-/ *n* coliflor

cause /kɔːz/ ◆ *vt* causar LOC *Ver* HAVOC ◆ *n* **1** ~ (**of sth**) causa (de algo) **2** ~ (**for sth**) motivo, razón (de/para algo): *cause for complaint/to complain* motivo de queja LOC *Ver* ROOT[1]

causeway /ˈkɔːzweɪ/ *n* carretera o camino más elevado que el terreno a los lados

caustic /ˈkɔːstɪk/ *adj* **1** cáustico **2** (*fig*) mordaz

caution /ˈkɔːʃn/ ◆ *vt* **1** ~ **against sth** advertir contra algo **2** amonestar ◆ *n* **1** precaución, cautela: *to exercise extreme caution* extremar las precauciones **2** amonestación LOC **to throw/fling caution to the winds** liarse la manta a la cabeza **cautionary** *adj* **1** de advertencia **2** ejemplar: *a cautionary tale* un relato ejemplar

cautious /ˈkɔːʃəs/ *adj* ~ (**about/of sth**) cauteloso (con algo): *a cautious driver* un conductor precavido **cautiously** *adv* con cautela

cavalry /ˈkævlri/ *n* [*v sing o pl*] caballería

cave /keɪv/ ◆ *n* cueva: *cave painting* pintura rupestre ◆ PHR V **to cave in 1** derrumbarse **2** (*fig*) ceder

cavern /ˈkævən/ *n* caverna **cavernous** *adj* cavernoso

cavity /ˈkævəti/ *n* (*pl* **-ies**) **1** cavidad **2** caries

cease /siːs/ *vt*, *vi* (*fml*) cesar, terminar: *to cease to do sth* dejar de hacer algo

ceasefire /ˈsiːsfaɪə(r)/ *n* alto el fuego

ceaseless /ˈsiːsləs/ *adj* incesante

cede /siːd/ *vt* ~ **sth** (**to**) ceder algo (a)

ceiling /ˈsiːlɪŋ/ *n* **1** techo **2** altura máxima **3** (*fig*) tope, límite

celebrate /ˈselɪbreɪt/ **1** *vt* celebrar **2** *vi* festejar **3** *vt* (*fml*) alabar **celebrated** *adj* ~ (**for sth**) célebre (por algo) **celebration** *n* celebración: *in celebration of* en conmemoración de **celebratory** /ˌseləˈbreɪtəri/ *adj* conmemorativo, festivo

celebrity /səˈlebrəti/ *n* (*pl* **-ies**) celebridad

celery /ˈseləri/ *n* apio

cell /sel/ *n* **1** celda **2** (*Anat*, *Pol*) célula **3** (*Electrón*) pila

cellar /ˈselə(r)/ *n* sótano

cellist /ˈtʃelɪst/ *n* violonchelista

cello /ˈtʃeləʊ/ *n* (*pl* ~**s**) violonchelo

cellular /ˈseljulə(r)/ *adj* celular

cement /sɪˈment/ ◆ *n* cemento ◆ *vt* **1** revestir de cemento, pegar con cemento **2** (*fig*) cimentar

cemetery /ˈsemətri; *USA* -teri/ *n* (*pl* **-ies**) cementerio municipal ☛ *Comparar con* CHURCHYARD

censor /ˈsensə(r)/ ◆ *n* censor, -ora ◆ *vt* censurar **censorship** *n* [*incontable*] censura

censure /ˈsenʃə(r)/ ◆ *vt* ~ **sb** (**for**) censurar a algn (por) ◆ *n* censura

census /ˈsensəs/ *n* (*pl* ~**es**) censo

cent /sent/ *n* (*USA*) centavo

centenary /senˈtiːnəri; *USA* ˈsentəneri/ *n* (*pl* **-ies**) centenario

center (*USA*) *Ver* CENTRE

centimetre /ˈsentɪmiːtə(r)/ *n* (*abrev* **cm**) centímetro

centipede /ˈsentɪpiːd/ *n* ciempiés

central /ˈsentrəl/ *adj* **1** (*en una población*) céntrico: *central London* el centro de Londres **2** central: *central heating* calefacción central **3** principal **centralize, -ise** *vt* centralizar **centralization, -isation** *n* centralización **centrally** *adv* centralmente

centre (*USA* **center**) /ˈsentə(r)/ ◆ *n* **1**

centro: *the town centre* el centro de la ciudad **2** núcleo: *a centre of commerce* un núcleo comercial **3 the centre** [*v sing o pl*] (*Pol*) el centro: *a centre party* un partido de centro **4** (*fútbol*) delantero centro **5** (*rugby*) centrocampista ◆ *vt, vi* centrar(se) PHR V **to centre (sth) on/upon/(a)round sth/sb** centrar algo/ centrarse en/alrededor de algo/algn

centre forward (*tb* **centre**) *n* delantero centro

centre half *n* medio centro

century /ˈsentʃəri/ *n* (*pl* **-ies**) **1** siglo **2** (*críquet*) cien carreras

cereal /ˈsɪəriəl/ *n* cereal(es)

cerebral /ˈserəbrəl; *USA* səˈriːbrəl/ *adj* cerebral

ceremonial /ˌserɪˈməʊniəl/ *adj, n* ceremonial

ceremony /ˈserəməni; *USA* -məʊni/ *n* (*pl* **-ies**) ceremonia

certain /ˈsɜːtn/ ◆ *adj* **1** seguro: *That's far from certain.* Eso dista mucho de ser seguro. ◊ *It is certain that he'll be elected.* Es seguro que será elegido. **2** cierto: *to a certain extent* hasta cierto punto **3** tal: *a certain Mr Brown* un tal Sr Brown LOC **for certain** con seguridad **to make certain (that...)** asegurarse (de que...) **to make certain of (doing) sth** asegurarse de (que se haga) algo ◆ *pron* ~ **of...**: *certain of those present* algunos de los presentes **certainly** *adv* **1** con toda certeza ☛ *Comparar con* SURELY **2** (*como respuesta*) desde luego: *Certainly not!* ¡Desde luego que no! **certainty** *n* (*pl* **-ies**) certeza

certificate /səˈtɪfɪkət/ *n* **1** certificado: *doctor's certificate* baja médica **2** (*nacimiento, etc*) partida

certify /ˈsɜːtɪfaɪ/ *vt* (*pret, pp* **-fied**) **1** certificar **2** (*tb* **to certify insane**): *He was certified (insane).* Declararon que no estaba en posesión de sus facultades mentales. **certification** *n* certificación

Cesarian (*USA*) *Ver* CAESAREAN

chain /tʃeɪn/ ◆ *n* **1** cadena: *chain mail* cota de malla ◊ *chain reaction* reacción en cadena **2** (*Geog*) cordillera LOC **in chains** encadenado ◆ *vt* ~ **sth/sb (up)** encadenar algo/a algn

chainsaw /ˈtʃeɪnsɔː/ *n* sierra mecánica

chain-smoke /ˈtʃeɪn sməʊk/ *vi* fumar uno tras otro

chair /tʃeə(r)/ ◆ *n* **1** silla: *Pull up a chair.* Toma asiento. ◊ *easy chair* sillón **2 the chair** (*reunión*) la presidencia, el presidente, la presidenta **3** (*USA*) (*tb* **the electric chair**) la silla eléctrica **4** cátedra ◆ *vt* presidir (*reunión*)

chairman /ˈtʃeəmən/ *n* (*pl* **-men** /-mən/) presidente ☛ Se prefiere utilizar la forma **chairperson**, que se refiere tanto a un hombre como a una mujer.

chairperson /ˈtʃeəpɜːsn/ *n* presidente, -a

chairwoman /ˈtʃeəwʊmən/ *n* (*pl* **-women**) presidenta ☛ Se prefiere utilizar la forma **chairperson**, que se refiere tanto a un hombre como a una mujer.

chalet /ˈʃæleɪ/ *n* chalé (*esp de estilo suizo*)

chalk /tʃɔːk/ ◆ *n* [*gen incontable*] **1** (*Geol*) creta **2** tiza: *a piece/stick of chalk* una tiza ◆ PHR V **to chalk sth up** apuntarse algo

challenge /ˈtʃælɪndʒ/ ◆ *n* **1** desafío: *to issue a challenge to sb* desafiar a algn **2** reto ◆ *vt* **1** desafiar **2** dar el alto a **3** (*derecho, etc*) poner en duda **4** (*trabajo, etc*) estimular **challenger** *n* **1** (*Dep*) aspirante **2** desafiador, -ora **challenging** *adj* estimulante, exigente

chamber /ˈtʃeɪmbə(r)/ *n* cámara: *chamber music* música de cámara ◊ *chamber of commerce* cámara de comercio

champagne /ʃæmˈpeɪn/ *n* champán

champion /ˈtʃæmpiən/ ◆ *n* **1** (*Dep, etc*) campeón, -ona: *the defending/reigning champion* el actual campeón **2** (*causa*) defensor, -ora ◆ *vt* defender **championship** *n* campeonato: *world championship* campeonato mundial

chance /tʃɑːns; *USA* tʃæns/ ◆ *n* **1** azar **2** casualidad: *a chance meeting* un encuentro casual **3** posibilidad **4** oportunidad **5** riesgo LOC **by (any) chance** por casualidad **on the (off) chance** por si acaso **the chances are (that)...** (*coloq*) lo más probable es que... **to take a chance (on sth)** correr el riesgo (de algo) **to take chances** arriesgarse *Ver tb* STAND ◆ *vt* ~ **doing sth** correr el riesgo de hacer algo LOC **to chance**

your arm/luck (*coloq*) arriesgarse PHR V **to chance on/upon sth/sb** encontrarse con algo/algn por casualidad

chancellor /ˈtʃɑːnsələ(r); *USA* ˈtʃæns-/ *n* **1** canciller: *Chancellor of the Exchequer* Ministro de Economía y Hacienda **2** (*GB*) (*universidad*) rector honorario, rectora honoraria

chandelier /ˌʃændəˈlɪə(r)/ *n* (lámpara de) araña

change /tʃeɪndʒ/ ◆ **1** *vt, vi* cambiar(se): *to change your mind* cambiar de opinión **2** *vt* ~ **sth/sb (into sth)** convertir algo/a algn (en algo) **3** *vi* ~ **from sth (in)to sth** pasar de algo a algo LOC **to change hands** cambiar de manos **to change places (with sb) 1** cambiarse el sitio (con algn) **2** (*fig*) cambiarse (por algn) **to change your mind** cambiar de opinión **to change your tune** (*coloq*) cambiar de actitud PHR V **to change back into sth 1** (*ropa*) ponerse algo otra vez **2** volver a convertirse en algo **to change into sth 1** ponerse algo **2** transformarse en algo **to change over (from sth to sth)** cambiar (de algo a algo) ◆ *n* **1** cambio: *a change of socks* otro par de calcetines **2** transbordo **3** [*incontable*] monedas: *loose change* suelto **4** (*dinero*) vuelta LOC **a change for the better/worse** un cambio a mejor/peor **a change of heart** un cambio de actitud **for a change** por variar **the change of life** la menopausia **to make a change** cambiar las cosas *Ver tb* CHOP **changeable** *adj* variable

changeover /ˈtʃeɪndʒəʊvə(r)/ *n* cambio (*p.ej. de un sistema político a otro*)

changing room *n* probador, vestuario

channel /ˈtʃænl/ ◆ *n* **1** (*TV*) cadena, canal **2** (*Radio*) banda **3** cauce **4** canal (de navegación) **5** (*fig*) vía ◆ *vt* (**-ll-**, *USA tb* **-l-**) **1** encauzar **2** acanalar

chant /tʃɑːnt; *USA* tʃænt/ ◆ *n* **1** (*Relig*) canto (litúrgico) **2** (*multitud*) consigna, canción ◆ *vt, vi* **1** (*Relig*) cantar **2** (*multitud*) gritar, corear

chaos /ˈkeɪɒs/ *n* [*incontable*] caos: *to cause chaos* provocar un caos **chaotic** /keɪˈɒtɪk/ *adj* caótico

chap /tʃæp/ *n* (*coloq, GB*) tío: *He's a good chap.* Es un buen tío.

chapel /ˈtʃæpl/ *n* capilla

chaplain /ˈtʃæplɪn/ *n* capellán

chapped /tʃæpt/ *adj* agrietado

chapter /ˈtʃæptə(r)/ *n* **1** capítulo **2** época LOC **chapter and verse** con pelos y señales

char /tʃɑː(r)/ *vt, vi* (**-rr-**) carbonizar(se), chamuscar(se)

character /ˈkærəktə(r)/ *n* **1** carácter: *character references* referencias personales ◊ *character assassination* difamación **2** (*coloq*) tipo **3** (*Liter*) personaje: *the main character* el protagonista **4** reputación LOC **in/out of character** típico/poco típico (de algn)

characteristic /ˌkærəktəˈrɪstɪk/ ◆ *adj* característico ◆ *n* rasgo, característica **characteristically** *adv*: *His answer was characteristically frank.* Respondió con la franqueza que lo caracteriza.

characterize, -ise /ˈkærəktəraɪz/ *vt* **1** ~ **sth/sb as sth** calificar algo/a algn de algo **2** caracterizar: *It is characterized by...* Se caracteriza por... **characterization, -isation** *n* descripción, caracterización

charade /ʃəˈrɑːd; *USA* ʃəˈreɪd/ *n* (*fig*) farsa

charcoal /ˈtʃɑːkəʊl/ *n* **1** carbón vegetal **2** (*Arte*) carboncillo **3** (*tb* **charcoal grey**) color gris marengo

charge /tʃɑːdʒ/ ◆ *n* **1** acusación **2** (*Mil*) carga **3** (*Dep*) ataque **4** (*animales*) embestida **5** cargo: *free of charge* gratis/sin cargo adicional **6** cargo: *to leave a child in a friend's charge* dejar a un amigo a cargo de un niño **7** carga (*eléctrica o de un arma*) LOC **in charge (of sth/sb)** a cargo (de algo/algn): *Who's in charge here?* ¿Quién es el encargado aquí? **in/under sb's charge** a cargo/bajo el cuidado de algn **to bring/press charges against sb** presentar cargos contra algn **to have charge of sth** estar a cargo de algo **to take charge (of sth)** hacerse cargo (de algo) *Ver tb* EARTH, REVERSE ◆ **1** *vt* ~ **sb (with sth)** acusar a algn (de algo) **2** *vt, vi* ~ **(at sth/sb)** (*Mil, Dep*) lanzarse (contra algo/algn): *The children charged down/up the stairs.* Los niños se lanzaron escaleras abajo/arriba. **3** *vt, vi* ~ **(at sth/sb)** (*animal*) embestir (algo/a algn) **4** *vt, vi* cobrar **5** *vt* (*pistola, pila*) cargar **6** *vt* (*fml*) encomendar PHR V **to charge sth (up) (to sb)** cargar algo a la cuenta (de algn)

chargeable *adj* **1** imponible, sujeto a pago **2** ~ **to sb** (*pago*) a cargo de algn

chariot /ˈtʃæriət/ *n* carro

charisma /kəˈrɪzmə/ *n* carisma **charismatic** /ˌkærɪzˈmætɪk/ *adj* carismático

charitable /ˈtʃærətəbl/ *adj* **1** caritativo **2** bondadoso **3** (*organización*) benéfico

charity /ˈtʃærəti/ *n* (*pl* **-ies**) **1** caridad **2** comprensión **3** (*organismo*) organización benéfica: *for charity* con fines benéficos

charm /tʃɑːm/ ◆ *n* **1** encanto **2** amuleto: *a charm bracelet* una pulsera de colgantes **3** hechizo LOC *Ver* WORK[2] ◆ *vt* encantar: *a charmed life* una vida afortunada PHR V **to charm sth from/out of sth/sb** conseguir algo de algo/algn por medio del encanto **charming** *adj* encantador

chart /tʃɑːt/ ◆ *n* **1** carta de navegación **2** gráfico: *flow chart* organigrama **3 the charts** [*pl*] (*discos*) los cuarenta principales ◆ *vt: to chart the course/the progress of sth* hacer un gráfico de la trayectoria/del progreso de algo

charter /ˈtʃɑːtə(r)/ ◆ *n* **1** estatutos: *royal charter* autorización real **2** flete: *a charter flight* un vuelo chárter ◊ *a charter plane/boat* un avión/barco fletado ◆ *vt* **1** otorgar autorización a **2** (*avión*) fletar **chartered** *adj* diplomado: *chartered accountant* auditor

chase /tʃeɪs/ ◆ **1** *vt*, *vi* (*lit y fig*) perseguir: *He's always chasing (after) women.* Siempre anda persiguiendo mujeres. **2** *vt* (*coloq*) andar detrás de PHR V **to chase about, around, etc** correr de un lado para otro **to chase sth/sb away, off, out, etc** echar/ahuyentar algo/a algn **to chase sth up** (*GB, coloq*) agilizar algo ◆ *n* **1** persecución **2** (*animales*) caza

chasm /ˈkæzəm/ *n* abismo

chassis /ˈʃæsi/ *n* (*pl* **chassis** /ˈʃæsiz/) chasis

chaste /tʃeɪst/ *adj* **1** casto **2** (*estilo*) sobrio

chastened /ˈtʃeɪsnd/ *adj* **1** escarmentado **2** (*tono*) sumiso **chastening** *adj* que sirve de escarmiento

chastity /ˈtʃæstəti/ *n* castidad

chat /tʃæt/ ◆ *n* charla: *chat show* programa de entrevistas ◆ *vi* (**-tt-**) ~ (**to/with sb**) (**about sth**) charlar (con algn) (de algo) PHR V **to chat sb up** (*GB, coloq*) enrollarse con algn **chatty** *adj* (**-ier**, **-iest**) **1** (*persona*) parlanchín **2** (*carta*) informal

chatter /ˈtʃætə(r)/ ◆ *vi* **1** ~ (**away/on**) parlotear **2** (*mono*) chillar **3** (*pájaro*) trinar **4** (*dientes*) castañetear ◆ *n* parloteo

chauffeur /ˈʃəʊfə(r); *USA* ʃəʊˈfɜːr/ ◆ *n* chófer ◆ *vt* ~ **sb around** hacer de chófer para algn; llevar en coche a algn

chauvinism /ˈʃəʊvɪnɪzəm/ *n* chovinismo, patriotería

chauvinist /ˈʃəʊvɪnɪst/ ◆ *n* chovinista, patriotero, -a ◆ *adj* (*tb* **chauvinistic** /ˌʃəʊvɪˈnɪstɪk/) chovinista

cheap /tʃiːp/ ◆ *adj* (**-er**, **-est**) **1** barato **2** económico **3** de mala calidad **4** (*coloq*) (*comentario, chiste, etc*) ordinario **5** (*coloq, USA*) tacaño LOC **cheap at the price** regalado ◆ *adv* (*coloq*) (**-er**, **-est**) barato LOC **not to come cheap** (*coloq*): *Success doesn't come cheap.* El éxito no lo regalan. **to be going cheap** (*coloq*) estar de oferta ◆ *n* LOC **on the cheap** (*coloq*) por/con cuatro cuartos **cheapen** *vt* abaratar: *to cheapen yourself* rebajarse **cheaply** *adv* barato, a bajo precio

cheat /tʃiːt/ ◆ **1** *vi* hacer trampas **2** *vi* (*colegio*) copiar(se) **3** *vt* engañar PHR V **to cheat sb (out) of sth** quitar algo a algn (por medio de engaños) **to cheat on sb** engañar a algn (*siendo infiel*) ◆ *n* **1** tramposo, -a **2** engaño, trampa

check /tʃek/ ◆ **1** *vt* comprobar, revisar *Ver tb* DOUBLE-CHECK **2** *vt*, *vi* asegurar(se) **3** *vt* contener **4** *vi* detenerse LOC **to check (sth) for sth** comprobar que no haya algo (en algo) PHR V **to check in (at...)**; **to check into...** registrarse (*en un hotel*) **to check sth in** facturar algo (*equipaje*) **to check sth off** tachar algo de una lista **to check out (of...)** saldar la cuenta y marcharse (*de un hotel*) **to check sth/sb out** (*USA*) hacer averiguaciones sobre algo/algn **to check (up) on sth/sb** hacer averiguaciones sobre algo/algn ◆ *n* **1** comprobación, revisión **2** investigación **3** jaque *Ver tb* CHECKMATE **4** (*USA*) *Ver* CHEQUE **5** (*USA*) *Ver* BILL[1] 1 LOC **to hold/keep sth in check** contener/controlar algo **checked** (*tb* **check**) *adj* a cuadros

check-in /ˈtʃek ɪn/ *n* facturación (*en un aeropuerto*)

checklist /ˈtʃeklɪst/ *n* lista

checkmate /ˈtʃekmeɪt/ (*tb* **mate**) *n* jaque mate

checkout /ˈtʃekaʊt/ *n* **1** caja (*en una tienda*) **2** acto de pagar y marcharse de un hotel

checkpoint /ˈtʃekpɔɪnt/ *n* puesto de control

check-up /ˈtʃek ʌp/ *n* **1** chequeo (*médico*) **2** comprobación

cheek /tʃiːk/ *n* **1** mejilla **2** (*fig*) cara: *What (a) cheek!* ¡Qué descaro! LOC *Ver* TONGUE **cheeky** *adj* (**-ier**, **-iest**) descarado

cheer /tʃɪə(r)/ ◆ **1** *vt, vi* aclamar, vitorear **2** *vt* animar, alegrar: *to be cheered by sth* animarse con algo PHR V **to cheer sb on** alentar a algn **to cheer (sth/sb) up** alegrar (algo), animar (a algn): *Cheer up!* ¡Anímate! ◆ *n* ovación, vítor: *Three cheers for…* ¡Tres hurras por…! **cheerful** *adj* **1** alegre **2** agradable **cheery** *adj* (**-ier**, **-iest**) alegre

cheering /ˈtʃɪərɪŋ/ ◆ *n* [*incontable*] vítores ◆ *adj* alentador, reconfortante

cheerio! /ˌtʃɪəriˈəʊ/ *interj* (*GB*) ¡adiós!

cheers! /tʃɪəz/ *interj* (*GB*) **1** ¡salud! **2** ¡adiós! **3** ¡gracias!

cheese /tʃiːz/ *n* queso: *Would you like some cheese?* ¿Quieres queso? ◊ *a wide variety of cheeses* una amplia selección de quesos LOC *Ver* BIG

cheesecake /ˈtʃiːzkeɪk/ *n* tarta de queso

cheetah /ˈtʃiːtə/ *n* guepardo

chef /ʃef/ *n* cocinero, -a jefe

chemical /ˈkemɪkl/ ◆ *adj* químico ◆ *n* sustancia química

chemist /ˈkemɪst/ *n* **1** farmacéutico, -a ☛ *Comparar con* PHARMACIST **2** químico, -a **chemist's (shop)** farmacia ☛ *Ver nota en* PHARMACY

chemistry /ˈkemɪstri/ *n* química

cheque (*USA* **check**) /tʃek/ *n* cheque: *by cheque* con cheque ◊ *cheque card* tarjeta bancaria que garantiza el pago de cheques

cheque book (*USA* **checkbook**) *n* talonario (de cheques)

cherish /ˈtʃerɪʃ/ *vt* **1** (*libertad, tradiciones*) valorar **2** (*persona*) querer, cuidar **3** (*esperanza*) abrigar **4** (*recuerdo*) guardar con cariño

cherry /ˈtʃeri/ *n* (*pl* **-ies**) **1** cereza **2** (*tb* **cherry tree**) (*árbol*) cerezo: *cherry blossom* flor del cerezo **3** (*tb* **cherry red**) (*color*) rojo cereza

cherub /ˈtʃerəb/ *n* (*pl* **~s** *o* **~im**) querubín

chess /tʃes/ *n* ajedrez: *chessboard* tablero de ajedrez

chest /tʃest/ *n* **1** arcón: *chest of drawers* cómoda **2** pecho (*tórax*) ☛ *Comparar con* BREAST LOC **to get it/something off your chest** (*coloq*) quitarse un peso de encima, desahogarse

chestnut /ˈtʃesnʌt/ ◆ *n* **1** castaña **2** (*árbol, madera*) castaño **3** (*coloq*) batallita ◆ *adj, n* (color) caoba

chew /tʃuː/ *vt* ~ **sth (up)** masticar algo: *chewing gum* chicle PHR V **to chew sth over** (*coloq*) rumiar algo

chewing gum *n* [*incontable*] chicle

chick /tʃɪk/ *n* polluelo

chicken /ˈtʃɪkɪn/ ◆ *n* **1** (*carne*) pollo **2** (*ave*) gallina *Ver tb* COCK, HEN **3** (*coloq*) miedica ◆ PHR V **to chicken out** (*coloq*) rajarse ◆ *adj* (*coloq*) cobarde

chickenpox /ˈtʃɪkɪnpɒks/ *n* [*incontable*] varicela

chickpea /ˈtʃɪkpiː/ *n* garbanzo

chicory /ˈtʃɪkəri/ *n* [*incontable*] **1** endibia **2** achicoria

chief /tʃiːf/ ◆ *n* jefe, -a ◆ *adj* principal **chiefly** *adv* **1** sobre todo **2** principalmente

chieftain /ˈtʃiːftən/ *n* cacique (*de tribu o clan*)

child /tʃaɪld/ *n* (*pl* **~ren** /ˈtʃɪldrən/) **1** niño, -a: *child benefit* subvención familiar ◊ *child care* puericultura ◊ *child care provisions* servicios de cuidado de los niños ◊ *child minder* persona que cuida niños en casa ◊ *children's clothes/television* ropa para niños/programación infantil **2** hijo, -a: *an only child* un hijo único **3** (*fig*) producto LOC **child's play** (*coloq*) juego de niños **childbirth** *n* parto **childhood** *n* infancia, niñez **childish** *adj* **1** infantil **2** (*pey*) inmaduro: *to be childish* portarse como un niño **childless** *adj* sin hijos **childlike** *adj* (*aprob*) de (un) niño

chili (*USA*) *Ver* CHILLI

chill /tʃɪl/ ◆ *n* **1** frío **2** resfriado: *to catch/get a chill* resfriarse **3** escalofrío ◆ **1** *vt* helar **2** *vt, vi* (*comestibles*) enfriar(se), refrigerar(se): *frozen and* *chilled foods* alimentos congelados y refrigerados LOC **to chill sb to the bone/marrow** helar a algn hasta los huesos **chilling** *adj* escalofriante **chilly** *adj* (**-ier**, **-iest**) frío

chilli (*USA* **chili**) /ˈtʃɪli/ *n* (*pl* ~**es**) **1** (*tb* **chilli pepper**) guindilla **2** pimentón

chime /tʃaɪm/ ◆ *n* **1** repique **2** campanada ◆ *vi* repicar PHR V **to chime in (with sth)** (*coloq*) interrumpir (diciendo algo)

chimney /ˈtʃɪmni/ *n* (*pl* **-eys**) chimenea: *chimney sweep* deshollinador, -ora

chimp /tʃɪmp/ *n* (*coloq*) *Ver* CHIMPANZEE

chimpanzee /ˌtʃɪmpænˈziː/ *n* chimpancé

chin /tʃɪn/ *n* barbilla LOC **to keep your chin up** (*coloq*) poner al mal tiempo buena cara *Ver tb* CUP

china /ˈtʃaɪnə/ *n* **1** porcelana **2** vajilla (de porcelana)

chink /tʃɪŋk/ *n* grieta, abertura LOC **a chink in sb's armour** el punto débil de algn

chip /tʃɪp/ ◆ *n* **1** trocito **2** (*madera*) astilla **3** mella, desportilladura **4** patata frita (*larga*) ☛ *Ver dibujo en* PATATA **5** (*USA*) *Ver* CRISP **6** (*casino*) ficha **7** (*Electrón*) chip LOC **a chip off the old block** (*coloq*) de tal palo tal astilla **to have a chip on your shoulder** (*coloq*) estar resentido ◆ *vt, vi* mellar(se), desconchar(se) PHR V **to chip away at sth** minar algo (*destruir poco a poco*) **to chip in (with sth)** (*coloq*) **1** (*comentario*) interrumpir (diciendo algo) **2** (*dinero*) contribuir (con algo) **chippings** *n* [*pl*] **1** grava **2** (*tb* **wood chippings**) virutas de madera

chirp /tʃɜːp/ ◆ *n* **1** gorjeo **2** (*grillo*) canto ◆ *vi* **1** gorjear **2** (*grillo*) cantar **chirpy** *adj* alegre

chisel /ˈtʃɪzl/ ◆ *n* cincel, escoplo ◆ *vt* **1** cincelar: *finely chiselled features* rasgos elegantes **2** (*con cincel*) tallar

chivalry /ˈʃɪvəlri/ *n* **1** caballería **2** caballerosidad

chive /tʃaɪv/ *n* [*gen pl*] cebollino

chloride /ˈklɔːraɪd/ *n* cloruro

chlorine /ˈklɔːriːn/ *n* cloro

chock-a-block /ˌtʃɒk ə ˈblɒk/ *adj* ~ **(with sth)** atestado (de algo)

chock-full /ˌtʃɒk ˈfʊl/ *adj* ~ **(of sth)** lleno a rebosar (de algo)

chocolate /ˈtʃɒklət/ ◆ *n* **1** chocolate: *milk/plain chocolate* chocolate con/sin leche **2** bombón ◆ *adj* **1** (*salsa, pastel, etc*) de chocolate **2** color chocolate

choice /tʃɔɪs/ ◆ *n* **1** ~ **(between...)** elección (entre...): *to make a choice* escoger **2** selección **3** posibilidad: *If I had the choice...* Si de mí dependiera... LOC **out of/from choice** por decisión propia **to have no choice** no tener más remedio ◆ *adj* (**-er**, **-est**) **1** de calidad **2** escogido

choir /ˈkwaɪə(r)/ *n* [*v sing o pl*] coro: *choir boy* niño de coro

choke /tʃəʊk/ ◆ **1** *vi* ~ **(on sth)** atragantarse con algo: *to choke to death* asfixiarse **2** *vt* ahogar, estrangular **3** *vt* ~ **sth (up) (with sth)** atascar algo (con algo) PHR V **to choke sth back** contener algo ◆ *n* estárter

cholera /ˈkɒlərə/ *n* cólera

cholesterol /kəˈlestərɒl/ *n* colesterol

choose /tʃuːz/ (*pret* **chose** /tʃəʊz/ *pp* **chosen** /tʃəʊzn/) **1** *vt, vi* ~ **(between A and/or B)**; ~ **(A from B)** elegir, escoger (entre A y B); (A de entre B) **2** *vt* ~ **sth/sb as sth**: *She was chosen as chair*: La eligieron presidente. **3** *vt* (*Dep*) seleccionar **4** *vt, vi* ~ **(to do sth)** decidir (hacer algo) **5** *vi* preferir: *whenever I choose* cuando me apetece LOC *Ver* PICK **choosy** (*tb* **choosey**) *adj* (**-ier**, **-iest**) (*coloq*) melindroso, quisquilloso

chop /tʃɒp/ ◆ *vt, vi* (**-pp-**) **1** ~ **sth (up) (into sth)** cortar algo (en algo): *to chop sth in two* partir algo por la mitad ◊ *chopping board* tabla de cortar **2** picar, trocear **3** (*GB, coloq*) reducir LOC **to chop and change** cambiar de opinión varias veces PHR V **to chop sth down** talar algo **to chop sth off (sth)** cortar algo ◆ *n* **1** hachazo **2** golpe **3** chuleta (*carne*) **chopper** *n* **1** hacha **2** (*carne*) tajadera **3** (*coloq*) helicóptero **choppy** *adj* (**-ier**, **-iest**) picado (*mar*)

chopsticks /ˈtʃɒpstɪks/ *n* [*pl*] palillos chinos

choral /ˈkɔːrəl/ *adj* coral (*de coro*)

chord /kɔːd/ *n* acorde

chore /tʃɔː(r)/ *n* trabajo (*rutinario*): *household chores* quehaceres domésticos

choreography /ˌkɒriˈɒgrəfi; *USA*

ˌkɔːri-/ *n* coreografía **choreographer** *n* coreógrafo, -a

chorus /ˈkɔːrəs/ ◆ *n* [*v sing o pl*] **1** (*Mús, Teat*) coro: *chorus girl* corista **2** estribillo **LOC in chorus** a coro ◆ *vt* corear

chose *pret de* CHOOSE

chosen *pp de* CHOOSE

Christ /kraɪst/ (*tb* **Jesus**, **Jesus Christ**) *n* Cristo

christen /ˈkrɪsn/ *vt* bautizar (con el nombre de) **christening** *n* bautismo

Christian /ˈkrɪstʃən/ *adj, n* cristiano, -a **Christianity** /ˌkrɪstiˈænəti/ *n* cristianismo

Christian name (*tb* **first name**) *n* nombre de pila

Christmas /ˈkrɪsməs/ *n* Navidad: *Christmas Day* Día de Navidad ◊ *Christmas Eve* Nochebuena ◊ *Merry/Happy Christmas!* ¡Feliz Navidad! ☛ *Ver nota en* NAVIDAD

chrome /krəʊm/ *n* cromo

chromium /ˈkrəʊmiəm/ *n* cromo: *chromium-plating/plated* cromado

chromosome /ˈkrəʊməsəʊm/ *n* cromosoma

chronic /ˈkrɒnɪk/ *adj* **1** crónico **2** (*mentiroso, alcohólico, etc*) empedernido

chronicle /ˈkrɒnɪkl/ ◆ *n* crónica ◆ *vt* registrar

chrysalis /ˈkrɪsəlɪs/ *n* (*pl* ~**es**) crisálida

chubby /ˈtʃʌbi/ *adj* (**-ier**, **-iest**) regordete *Ver tb* FAT

chuck /tʃʌk/ *vt* (*coloq*) **1** tirar **2** ~ **sth (in/up)** dejar algo **PHR V to chuck sth away/out** tirar algo (a la basura) **to chuck sb out** echar a algn

chuckle /ˈtʃʌkl/ ◆ *vi* reírse para uno mismo ◆ *n* risita

chum /tʃʌm/ *n* (*coloq*) colega

chunk /tʃʌŋk/ *n* trozo **chunky** *adj* (**-ier**, **-iest**) macizo

church /tʃɜːtʃ/ *n* iglesia: *church hall* salón parroquial **LOC to go to church** ir a misa/ir al oficio ☛ *Ver nota en* SCHOOL

churchyard /ˈtʃɜːtʃjɑːd/ (*tb* **graveyard**) *n* cementerio (*alrededor de una iglesia*) ☛ *Comparar con* CEMETERY

churn /tʃɜːn/ **1** *vt* ~ **sth (up)** (*agua, barro*) remover algo **2** *vi* (*aguas*) agitarse **3** *vi* (*estómago*) revolverse **PHR V to churn sth out** (*coloq*) fabricar como churros (*libros, etc*)

chute /ʃuːt/ *n* **1** tobogán (*para mercancías o desechos*) **2** (*piscina*) tobogán

cider /ˈsaɪdə(r)/ *n* sidra

cigar /sɪˈgɑː(r)/ *n* puro

cigarette /ˌsɪgəˈret; *USA* ˈsɪgərət/ *n* cigarrillo: *cigarette butt/end* colilla

cinder /ˈsɪndə(r)/ *n* ceniza

cinema /ˈsɪnəmə/ *n* cine

cinnamon /ˈsɪnəmən/ *n* canela

circle /ˈsɜːkl/ ◆ *n* **1** círculo, circunferencia: *the circumference of a circle* el perímetro de una circunferencia **2** corro: *to stand in a circle* hacer un corro **3** (*Teat*) anfiteatro (*primer piso*) **LOC to go round in circles** no hacer progresos *Ver tb* FULL, VICIOUS ◆ *vt* **1** dar una vuelta/vueltas a **2** rodear **3** marcar con un círculo

circuit /ˈsɜːkɪt/ *n* **1** gira **2** vuelta **3** pista **4** (*Electrón*) circuito

circular /ˈsɜːkjələ(r)/ ◆ *adj* redondo, circular ◆ *n* circular

circulate /ˈsɜːkjəleɪt/ *vt, vi* (hacer) circular

circulation /ˌsɜːkjəˈleɪʃn/ *n* **1** circulación **2** (*periódico*) tirada

circumcise /ˈsɜːkəmsaɪz/ *vt* circuncidar **circumcision** /ˌsɜːkəmˈsɪʒn/ *n* circuncisión

circumference /səˈkʌmfərəns/ *n* circunferencia: *the circumference of a circle* el perímetro de una circunferencia ◊ *the circumference of the earth* la circunferencia de la Tierra

circumstance /ˈsɜːkəmstəns/ *n* **1** circunstancia **2 circumstances** [*pl*] situación económica **LOC in/under no circumstances** en ningún caso **in/under the circumstances** dadas las circunstancias

circus /ˈsɜːkəs/ *n* circo

cistern /ˈsɪstən/ *n* **1** cisterna **2** depósito

cite /saɪt/ *vt* **1** citar **2** (*USA, Mil*) mencionar

citizen /ˈsɪtɪzn/ *n* ciudadano, -a **citizenship** *n* ciudadanía

citrus /ˈsɪtrəs/ *adj* cítrico: *citrus fruit(s)* cítricos

city /ˈsɪti/ *n* (*pl* **cities**) **1** ciudad: *city centre* centro de la ciudad **2 the City** la City (*centro financiero de Londres*)

civic /ˈsɪvɪk/ *adj* **1** municipal: *civic centre* centro municipal **2** cívico

civil /ˈsɪvl/ *adj* **1** civil: *civil strife* disensión social ◊ *civil law* código/derecho civil ◊ *civil rights/liberties* derechos del ciudadano ◊ *the Civil Service* la Administración Pública ◊ *civil servant* funcionario (del Estado) **2** educado, atento

civilian /səˈvɪliən/ *n* civil

civilization, -isation /ˌsɪvəlaɪˈzeɪʃn; *USA* -əlɪˈz-/ *n* civilización

civilized, -ised /ˈsɪvəlaɪzd/ *adj* civilizado

clad /klæd/ *adj* (*fml*) ~ (**in sth**) vestido (de algo)

claim /kleɪm/ ◆ **1** *vt, vi* ~ (**for sth**) reclamar (algo) **2** *vt* afirmar, sostener **3** *vt* (*atención*) merecer **4** *vt* (*vidas*) cobrarse ◆ *n* **1** ~ (**for sth**) reclamación (de algo) **2** ~ (**against sth/sb**) reclamación, demanda (contra algo/algn) **3** ~ (**on sth/sb**) derecho (sobre algo/algn) **4** ~ (**to sth**) derecho (a algo) **5** afirmación, pretensión LOC *Ver* LAY[1], STAKE **claimant** *n* demandante

clam /klæm/ ◆ *n* almeja ◆ *v* (**-mm-**) PHR V **to clam up** (*coloq*) cerrar el pico

clamber /ˈklæmbə(r)/ *vi* trepar (*esp con dificultad*)

clammy /ˈklæmi/ *adj* (**-ier**, **-iest**) sudoroso, pegajoso

clamour (*USA* **clamor**) /ˈklæmə(r)/ ◆ *n* clamor, griterío ◆ *vi* **1** clamar **2** ~ **for sth** pedir algo a voces **3** ~ **against sth** protestar a gritos contra algo

clamp /klæmp/ ◆ *n* **1** (*tb* **cramp**) grapa **2** abrazadera **3** cepo ◆ *vt* **1** sujetar **2** poner el cepo a PHR V **to clamp down on sth/sb** (*coloq*) apretar los tornillos a algo/algn

clampdown /ˈklæmpdaʊn/ *n* ~ (**on sth**) restricción (de algo); medidas drásticas (contra algo)

clan /klæn/ *n* [*v sing o pl*] clan

clandestine /klænˈdestɪn/ *adj* (*fml*) clandestino

clang /klæŋ/ ◆ *n* tañido (*metálico*) ◆ *vt, vi* (hacer) sonar

clank /klæŋk/ *vi* hacer un ruido metálico (*cadenas, maquinaria*)

clap /klæp/ ◆ (**-pp-**) **1** *vt, vi* aplaudir **2** *vt*: *to clap your hands (together)* batir palmas ◊ *to clap sb on the back* dar una palmada en la espalda a algn ◆ *n* **1** aplauso **2** *a clap of thunder* un trueno **clapping** *n* aplausos

clarify /ˈklærəfaɪ/ *vt* (*pret, pp* **-fied**) aclarar **clarification** *n* aclaración

clarinet /ˌklærəˈnet/ *n* clarinete

clarity /ˈklærəti/ *n* lucidez, claridad

clash /klæʃ/ ◆ **1** *vt, vi* (hacer) chocar (*con ruido*) **2** *vi* ~ (**with sb**) tener un enfrentamiento (con algn) **3** *vi* ~ (**with sb**) (**on/over sth**) discrepar (con algn) (en algo) **4** *vi* (*fechas*) coincidir **5** *vi* (*colores*) desentonar ◆ *n* **1** estruendo **2** enfrentamiento **3** ~ (**on/over sth**) discrepancia (por algo): *a clash of interests* un conflicto de intereses

clasp /klɑːsp; *USA* klæsp/ ◆ *n* cierre ◆ *vt* apretar

class /klɑːs; *USA* klæs/ ◆ *n* **1** clase: *They're in class.* Están en clase. ◊ *class struggle/system* lucha/sistema de clases **2** categoría: *They are not in the same class.* No tienen comparación. LOC **in a class of your/its own** sin par ◆ *vt* ~ **sth/sb** (**as sth**) clasificar algo/a algn (como algo)

classic /ˈklæsɪk/ *adj, n* clásico (*típico*): *It was a classic case.* Fue un caso típico

classical /ˈklæsɪkl/ *adj* clásico

classification /ˌklæsɪfɪˈkeɪʃn/ *n* **1** clasificación **2** categoría

classify /ˈklæsɪfaɪ/ *vt* (*pret, pp* **-fied**) clasificar **classified** *adj* **1** clasificado: *classified advertisements/ads* anuncios por palabras **2** confidencial

classmate /ˈklɑːsmeɪt; *USA* ˈklæs-/ *n* compañero, -a de clase

classroom /ˈklɑːsruːm, -rʊm; *USA* ˈklæs-/ *n* aula, clase

classy /ˈklɑːsi; *USA* ˈklæsi/ *adj* (**-ier**, **-iest**) con mucho estilo

clatter /ˈklætə(r)/ ◆ *n* (*tb* **clattering** /-ərɪŋ/) **1** estrépito **2** (*tren*) triquitraque ◆ **1** *vt, vi* hacer ruido (*con platos, etc*) **2** *vi* (*tren*) traquetear

clause /klɔːz/ *n* **1** (*Gram*) proposición **2** (*Jur*) cláusula

claw /klɔː/ ◆ *n* **1** garra **2** (*gato*) uña **3** (*cangrejo*) pinza **4** (*máquina*) garfio ◆ *vt* arañar

clay /kleɪ/ *n* arcilla, barro

clean /kliːn/ ◆ *adj* (**-er**, **-est**) **1** limpio: *to wipe clean* limpiar **2** (*Dep*) que juega limpio **3** (*papel, etc*) en blanco LOC

make a clean break (with sth) cortar por completo (con algo) ◆ *vt, vi* limpiar(se) PHR V **to clean sth from/off sth** limpiar algo de algo **to clean sb out** (*coloq*) dejar a algn sin un duro **to clean sth out** limpiar algo a fondo **to clean (sth) up** limpiar (algo): *to clean up your image* mejorar algn su imagen **cleaning** *n* limpieza (*trabajo*) **cleanliness** /ˈklenlinəs/ *n* limpieza (*cualidad*) **cleanly** *adv* limpiamente

clean-cut /ˌkliːn ˈkʌt/ *adj* **1** pulcro **2** (*rasgos*) muy bien perfilado

cleaner /ˈkliːnə(r)/ *n* **1** limpiador, -ora **2 cleaners** [*pl*] tintorería

cleanse /klenz/ *vt* ~ **sth/sb (of sth) 1** limpiar en profundidad algo/a algn (de algo) **2** (*fig*) purificar algo/a algn (de algo) **cleanser** *n* **1** producto de limpieza **2** (*para cara*) crema limpiadora

clean-shaven /ˌkliːn ˈʃeɪvn/ *adj* afeitado

clean-up /ˈkliːn ʌp/ *n* limpieza

clear /klɪə(r)/ ◆ *adj* (**-er**, **-est**) **1** claro: *Are you quite clear about what the job involves?* ¿Tienes claro lo que implica el trabajo? **2** (*tiempo, cielo, carretera*) despejado **3** (*cristal*) transparente **4** (*recepción*) nítido **5** (*conciencia*) tranquilo **6** libre: *clear of debt* libre de deudas ◊ *to keep next weekend clear* dejar libre el fin de semana que viene LOC **(as) clear as day** más claro que el agua **(as) clear as mud** nada claro **in the clear** (*coloq*) **1** fuera de sospecha **2** fuera de peligro **to make sth clear/plain (to sb)** dejar algo claro (a algn) *Ver tb* CRYSTAL ◆ **1** *vi* (*tiempo*) despejar(se) **2** *vt* (*duda*) despejar **3** *vi* (*agua*) aclararse **4** *vt* (*tubería*) desatascar **5** *vt* (*de gente*) desalojar **6** *vt* ~ **sb (of sth)** absolver a algn (de algo): *to clear your name* limpiar tu nombre **7** *vt* (*obstáculo*) salvar LOC **to clear the air** aclarar las cosas **to clear the table** quitar la mesa PHR V **to clear (sth) away/up** recoger (algo) **to clear off** (*coloq*) largarse **to clear sth out** ordenar algo **to clear up** despejarse **to clear sth up** dejar algo claro ◆ *adv* (**-er**, **-est**) **1** claramente **2** completamente LOC **to keep/stay/steer clear (of sth/sb)** mantenerse alejado (de algo/algn)

clearance /ˈklɪərəns/ *n* **1** despeje: *a clearance sale* una liquidación **2** espacio libre **3** autorización

clear-cut /ˌklɪə ˈkʌt/ *adj* definido

clear-headed /ˌklɪə ˈhedɪd/ *adj* de mente despejada

clearing /ˈklɪərɪŋ/ *n* claro (*de bosque*)

clearly /klɪəli/ *adv* claramente

clear-sighted /ˌklɪə ˈsaɪtɪd/ *adj* lúcido

cleavage /ˈkliːvɪdʒ/ *n* escote

clef /klef/ *n* clave (*Mús*)

clench /klentʃ/ *vt* apretar (*puños, dientes*)

clergy /ˈklɜːdʒi/ *n* [*pl*] clero

clergyman /ˈklɜːdʒimən/ *n* (*pl* **-men** /-mən/) **1** clérigo **2** sacerdote anglicano ☛ *Ver nota en* PRIEST

clerical /ˈklerɪkl/ *adj* **1** de oficina: *clerical staff* personal administrativo **2** (*Relig*) eclesiástico

clerk /klɑːk; *USA* klɜːrk/ *n* **1** oficinista, empleado, -a **2** (*ayuntamiento, juzgado*) secretario, -a **3** (*USA*) (*tb* **desk clerk**) recepcionista **4** (*USA*) (*en tienda*) dependiente, -a

clever /ˈklevə(r)/ *adj* (**-er**, **-est**) **1** listo **2** hábil: *to be clever at sth* tener aptitud para algo **3** ingenioso **4** astuto LOC **to be too clever** pasarse de listo **cleverness** *n* inteligencia, habilidad, astucia

cliché /ˈkliːʃeɪ/ *n* cliché

click /klɪk/ ◆ *n* **1** clic **2** chasquido **3** taconazo ◆ **1** *vt*: *to click your heels* dar un taconazo ◊ *to click your fingers* chasquear los dedos **2** *vi* (*cámara, etc*) hacer clic **3** *vi* (*hacerse amigos*) conectar **4** *vi* caer en la cuenta LOC **to click open/shut** abrir(se)/cerrar(se) con un clic

client /ˈklaɪənt/ *n* **1** cliente, -a **2** (*de abogado*) defendido, -a

clientele /ˌkliːənˈtel; *USA* ˌklaɪənˈtel/ *n* clientela

cliff /klɪf/ *n* acantilado, precipicio

climate /ˈklaɪmət/ *n* clima: *the economic climate* las condiciones económicas

climax /ˈklaɪmæks/ *n* clímax

climb /klaɪm/ ◆ *vt, vi* **1** escalar **2** subir: *The road climbs steeply.* La carretera es muy empinada. **3** trepar **4** (*sociedad*) ascender LOC **to go climbing** hacer alpinismo *Ver tb* BANDWAGON PHR V **to climb down 1** (*fig*) dar marcha atrás **2** bajar **to climb out of sth 1** *to climb out of bed* levantarse de la cama **2** (*coche, etc*) bajarse de algo **to climb (up) on to**

sth subirse a algo **to climb up sth** subirse a algo, trepar por algo ◆ *n* **1** escalada, subida **2** pendiente

climber /ˈklaɪmə(r)/ *n* alpinista

clinch /klɪntʃ/ *vt* **1** (*trato, etc*) cerrar **2** (*partido, etc*) ganar **3** (*victoria, etc*) conseguir: *That clinched it.* Eso fue decisivo.

cling /klɪŋ/ *vi* (*pret, pp* **clung** /klʌŋ/) ~ **(on) to sth/sb** (*lit y fig*) agarrarse/aferrarse a algo/algn: *to cling to each other* abrazarse estrechamente **clinging** *adj* **1** (*tb* **clingy**) (*ropa*) ceñido **2** (*pey*) (*persona*) pegajoso

clinic /ˈklɪnɪk/ *n* clínica

clinical /ˈklɪnɪkl/ *adj* **1** clínico **2** (*fig*) imparcial

clink /klɪŋk/ **1** *vi* tintinear **2** *vt*: *They clinked glasses.* Brindaron.

clip /klɪp/ ◆ *n* **1** clip **2** (*joya*) alfiler ◆ *vt* (**-pp-**) **1** cortar, recortar **2** ~ **sth (on) to sth** prender algo a algo (con un clip) PHR V **to clip sth together** unir algo (con un clip)

clique /kliːk/ *n* camarilla

cloak /kləʊk/ ◆ *n* capa ◆ *vt* envolver: *cloaked in secrecy* rodeado de un gran secreto

cloakroom /ˈkləʊkruːm/ *n* **1** guardarropa **2** (*GB, eufemismo*) aseo ☛ *Ver nota en* TOILET

clock /klɒk/ ◆ *n* **1** reloj (*de pared o de mesa*) ☛ *Ver dibujo en* RELOJ **2** (*coloq*) cuentakilómetros **3** (*coloq*) taxímetro LOC **(a)round the clock** las veinticuatro horas ◆ *vt* cronometrar PHR V **to clock in/on** fichar (*en el trabajo*) **to clock off/out** fichar (*al salir*) **to clock sth up** registrar algo, acumular algo **clockwise** *adv, adj* en el sentido de las agujas del reloj

clockwork /ˈklɒkwɜːk/ ◆ *adj* con mecanismo de relojería ◆ *n* mecanismo LOC **like clockwork** como un reloj, a pedir de boca

clog /klɒg/ ◆ *n* zueco ◆ *vt, vi* ~ **(sth) (up)** obstruir(se), atascar(se)

cloister /ˈklɔɪstə(r)/ *n* claustro

close[1] /kləʊs/ ◆ *adj* (**-er, -est**) **1** (*pariente*) cercano **2** (*amigo*) íntimo **3** (*vínculos, etc*) estrecho **4** (*vigilancia*) estricto **5** (*examen*) minucioso **6** (*Dep, partido*) muy reñido **7** (*tiempo*) bochornoso, pesado **8** ~ **to sth** cerca de algo, al lado de algo: *close to tears* casi llorando **9** ~ **to sb** (*emocionalmente*) unido a alguien LOC **it/that was a close call/shave** (*coloq*) me, te, etc ha faltado el pelo de un calvo **to keep a close eye/watch on sth/sb** mantener algo/a algn bajo estricta vigilancia ◆ *adv* (**-er, -est**) (*tb* **close by**) cerca LOC **close on** casi **close together** juntos **closely** *adv* **1** estrechamente **2** atentamente **3** (*examinar*) minuciosamente **closeness** *n* **1** proximidad **2** intimidad

close[2] /kləʊz/ ◆ **1** *vt, vi* cerrar(se) **2** *vt, vi* (*reunión, etc*) concluir(se) LOC **to close your mind to sth** no querer saber nada de algo PHR V **to close down 1** (*empresa*) cerrar (definitivamente) **2** (*emisora*) cerrar la emisión **to close sth down** cerrar algo (*empresa, etc*) **to close in** (*día*) acortarse **to close in (on sth/sb)** (*niebla, noche, enemigo*) venirse encima (de algo/algn) ◆ *n* final: *towards the close of* a finales de LOC **to come/draw to a close** llegar a su fin *Ver tb* BRING **closed** *adj* cerrado: *a closed door* una puerta cerrada

close-knit /ˌkləʊs ˈnɪt/ *adj* unido como una piña (*comunidad, etc*)

closet /ˈklɒzɪt/ *n* (*USA*) armario

close-up /ˈkləʊs ʌp/ *n* primer plano

closing /ˈkləʊzɪŋ/ *adj* **1** último **2** (*fecha*) límite **3** *closing time* hora de cierre

closure /ˈkləʊʒə(r)/ *n* cierre

clot /klɒt/ *n* **1** coágulo **2** (*GB, coloq, joc*) bobo, -a

cloth /klɒθ; *USA* klɔːθ/ *n* (*pl* **~s** /klɒθs; *USA* klɔːðz/) **1** tela, paño ☛ *Ver nota en* TELA **2** trapo

clothe /kləʊð/ *vt* ~ **sb/yourself (in sth)** vestir(se) (de algo)

clothes /kləʊðz; *USA* kləʊz/ *n* [*pl*] ropa: *clothes line* cuerda para tender la ropa ◇ *clothes-peg* pinza (para tender la ropa) ☛ *Comparar con* ROPA

clothing /ˈkləʊðɪŋ/ *n* ropa: *the clothing industry* la industria textil ☛ *Comparar con* ROPA

cloud /klaʊd/ ◆ *n* nube ◆ **1** *vt* (*juicio*) ofuscar **2** *vt* (*asunto*) complicar **3** *vi* (*expresión*) ensombrecerse PHR V **to cloud over** nublarse **cloudless** *adj* despejado **cloudy** *adj* (**-ier, -iest**) **1** nublado **2** (*recuerdo*) vago

clout /klaʊt/ ◆ *n* (*coloq*) **1** tortazo **2** (*fig*) influencia ◆ *vt* (*coloq*) dar un tortazo a

clove /kləʊv/ *n* **1** clavo (*especia*) **2** **clove of garlic** diente de ajo

clover /ˈkləʊvə(r)/ *n* trébol

clown /klaʊn/ *n* payaso, -a

club /klʌb/ ◆ *n* **1** club **2** *Ver* NIGHTCLUB **3** porra **4** palo (*de golf*) **5** **clubs** [*pl*] (*cartas*) trébol ☛ *Ver nota en* BARAJA ◆ *vt, vi* (**-bb-**) aporrear: *to club sb to death* matar a algn a porrazos PHR V **to club together** (**to do sth**) hacer un fondo (para hacer algo)

clue /kluː/ *n* **1** ~ (**to sth**) pista (de algo) **2** indicio **3** (*crucigrama*) definición LOC **not to have a clue** (*coloq*) **1** no tener ni idea **2** ser un inútil

clump /klʌmp/ *n* grupo (*plantas, etc*)

clumsy /ˈklʌmzi/ *adj* (**-ier**, **-iest**) **1** torpe, desgarbado **2** tosco

clung *pret, pp de* CLING

cluster /ˈklʌstə(r)/ ◆ *n* grupo ◆ PHR V **to cluster/be clustered** (**together**) **round sth/sb** apiñarse alrededor de algo/algn

clutch /klʌtʃ/ ◆ *vt* **1** (*tener*) apretar, estrechar **2** (*coger*) agarrar PHR V **to clutch at sth** agarrarse a/de algo ◆ *n* **1** embrague **2** **clutches** [*pl*] (*pey*) garras

clutter /ˈklʌtə(r)/ ◆ *n* (*pey*) desorden, confusión ◆ *vt* (*pey*) ~ **sth** (**up**) atestar algo

coach /kəʊtʃ/ ◆ *n* **1** autocar **2** (*Ferrocarril*) vagón, coche *Ver tb* CARRIAGE 2 **3** carroza **4** entrenador, -ora **5** profesor, -ora particular ◆ **1** *vt* (*Dep*) entrenar: *to coach a swimmer for the Olympics* entrenar a una nadadora para las Olimpiadas **2** *vt, vi* ~ (**sb**) (**for/in sth**) dar clases particulares (de algo) (a algn) **coaching** *n* entrenamiento, preparación

coal /kəʊl/ *n* **1** carbón **2** trozo de carbón: *hot/live coals* brasas

coalfield /ˈkəʊlfiːld/ *n* **1** yacimiento de carbón **2** [*gen pl*] mina de carbón

coalition /ˌkəʊəˈlɪʃn/ *n* [*v sing o pl*] coalición

coal mine (*tb* **pit**) *n* mina de carbón

coarse /kɔːs/ *adj* (**-er**, **-est**) **1** (*arena, etc*) grueso **2** (*tela, manos*) áspero **3** vulgar **4** (*lenguaje, persona*) grosero **5** (*chiste*) verde

coast /kəʊst/ ◆ *n* costa ◆ *vi* **1** (*coche*) ir en punto muerto **2** (*bicicleta*) ir sin pedalear **coastal** *adj* costero

coastguard /ˈkəʊstgɑːd/ *n* (servicio de) guardacostas

coastline /ˈkəʊstlaɪn/ *n* litoral

coat /kəʊt/ ◆ *n* **1** abrigo, chaquetón: *coat-hanger* perchero **2** **white coat** bata (*blanca*) **3** (*animal*) pelo, lana **4** (*pintura*) capa, mano ◆ *vt* ~ **sth** (**in/with sth**) cubrir, bañar, rebozar algo (de algo) **coating** *n* capa, baño

coax /kəʊks/ *vt* ~ **sb into/out of** (**doing**) **sth**; ~ **sb to do sth** engatusar, persuadir a algn (para que haga/deje de hacer algo) PHR V **to coax sth out of/from sb** sonsacar algo a algn

cobble /ˈkɒbl/ (*tb* **cobblestone**) *n* adoquín

cobweb /ˈkɒbweb/ *n* telaraña

cocaine /kəʊˈkeɪn/ *n* cocaína

cock /kɒk/ ◆ *n* **1** gallo **2** macho ◆ *vt* **1** (*esp animales*) levantar (*pata, orejas*) **2** (*fusil*) amartillar

cockney /ˈkɒkni/ ◆ *adj* del este de Londres ◆ *n* **1** (*pl* **-eys**) nativo, -a del este de Londres **2** dialecto de éstos

cockpit /ˈkɒkpɪt/ *n* cabina (del piloto)

cocktail /ˈkɒkteɪl/ *n* **1** cóctel **2** (*de fruta*) macedonia **3** (*coloq, fig*) mezcla

cocoa /ˈkəʊkəʊ/ *n* **1** cacao **2** (*bebida*) chocolate

coconut /ˈkəʊkənʌt/ *n* coco

cocoon /kəˈkuːn/ *n* **1** (*gusano*) capullo **2** (*fig*) caparazón

cod /kɒd/ *n* bacalao

code /kəʊd/ *n* **1** código **2** (*mensaje*) clave: *code name* nombre de guerra

coercion /kəʊˈɜːʃn/ *n* coacción

coffee /ˈkɒfi; *USA* ˈkɔːfi/ *n* **1** café: *coffee bar/shop* cafetería **2** color café

coffin /ˈkɒfɪn/ *n* ataúd

cog /kɒg/ *n* **1** rueda dentada **2** (*de rueda dentada*) diente

cogent /ˈkəʊdʒənt/ *adj* contundente

coherent /kəʊˈhɪərənt/ *adj* **1** coherente **2** (*habla*) inteligible

coil /kɔɪl/ ◆ *n* **1** rollo **2** (*serpiente*) anillo **3** (*anticonceptivo*) diu ◆ **1** *vt* ~ **sth** (**up**) enrollar algo **2** *vt, vi* ~ (**yourself**) **up** (**around sth**) enroscarse (en algo)

coin /kɔɪn/ ◆ *n* moneda ◆ *vt* acuñar

coincide /ˌkəʊɪnˈsaɪd/ *vi* ~ (**with sth**) coincidir (con algo)

coincidence /kəʊˈɪnsɪdəns/ *n* **1** casualidad **2** (*fml*) coincidencia

coke /kəʊk/ *n* **1** **Coke®** Coca-Cola® **2** (*coloq*) coca **3** coque

cold /kəʊld/ ◆ *adj* (**-er**, **-est**) frío ☛ *Ver nota en* FRÍO **LOC** **to be cold** **1** (*persona*) tener frío **2** (*tiempo*) hacer frío **3** (*objeto*) estar frío **4** (*lugares, periodos de tiempo*) ser (muy) frío **to get cold** **1** enfriarse **2** coger frío **3** (*tiempo*) ponerse frío **to get/have cold feet** (*coloq*) sentir mieditis ◆ *n* **1** frío **2** resfriado: *to catch (a) cold* resfriarse ◆ *adv* de improviso

cold-blooded /ˌkəʊld ˈblʌdɪd/ *adj* **1** (*Biol*) de sangre fría **2** desalmado

collaboration /kəˌlæbəˈreɪʃn/ *n* **1** colaboración **2** colaboracionismo

collapse /kəˈlæps/ ◆ *vi* **1** derrumbarse, desplomarse **2** caer desmayado **3** (*negocio, etc*) hundirse **4** (*valor*) caer en picado **5** (*mueble, etc*) plegarse ◆ *n* **1** derrumbamiento **2** caída en picado **3** (*Med*) colapso

collar /ˈkɒlə(r)/ *n* **1** (*camisa, etc*) cuello **2** (*perro*) collar

collateral /kəˈlætərəl/ *n* garantía

colleague /ˈkɒliːg/ *n* colega, compañero, -a (*de profesión*)

collect /kəˈlekt/ ◆ **1** *vt* recoger: *collected works* obras completas **2** *vt* ~ **sth (up/together)** juntar, reunir algo **3** *vt* (*datos*) recopilar **4** *vt* (*fondos, impuestos*) recaudar **5** *vt* (*sellos, monedas*) coleccionar **6** *vi* (*muchedumbre*) reunirse **7** *vi* (*polvo, agua*) acumularse ◆ *adj, adv* (*USA*) a cobro revertido **LOC** *Ver* REVERSE **collection** *n* **1** colección **2** recogida **3** (*en iglesia*) colecta **4** conjunto, grupo **collector** *n* coleccionista

collective /kəˈlektɪv/ *adj, n* colectivo

college /ˈkɒlɪdʒ/ *n* **1** centro de educación superior *Ver tb* TECHNICAL COLLEGE **2** (*GB*) colegio universitario (*Oxford, Cambridge, etc*) **3** (*USA*) universidad

collide /kəˈlaɪd/ *vi* ~ **(with sth/sb)** chocar (con algo/algn)

colliery /ˈkɒliəri/ *n* (*pl* **-ies**) (*GB*) mina de carbón *Ver tb* COAL MINE

collision /kəˈlɪʒn/ *n* choque

collusion /kəˈluːʒn/ *n* confabulación

colon /ˈkəʊlən/ *n* **1** colon **2** dos puntos ☛ *Ver* págs 318–19.

colonel /ˈkɜːnl/ *n* coronel

colonial /kəˈləʊniəl/ *adj* colonial

colony /ˈkɒləni/ *n* [*v sing o pl*] (*pl* **-ies**) colonia

colossal /kəˈlɒsl/ *adj* colosal

colour (*USA* **color**) /ˈkʌlə(r)/ ◆ *n* **1** color: *colour-blind* daltónico **2** **colours** [*pl*] (*equipo, partido, etc*) colores **3** **colours** [*pl*] (*Mil*) bandera **LOC** **to be/feel off colour** (*coloq*) no estar muy católico ◆ *vt* **1** colorear, pintar **2** (*afectar*) marcar **3** (*juicio*) ofuscar **PHR V** **to colour sth in** colorear algo **to colour (up) (at sth)** ruborizarse (ante algo) **coloured** (*USA* **colored**) *adj* **1** de colores: *cream-coloured* (de) color crema **2** (*pey*) (*persona*) de color **3** (*exagerado*) adornado **colourful** (*USA* **colorful**) *adj* **1** lleno de color, llamativo **2** (*personaje, vida*) interesante **colouring** (*USA* **coloring**) *n* **1** colorido **2** tez **3** colorante **colourless** (*USA* **colorless**) *adj* **1** incoloro, sin color **2** (*personaje, estilo*) gris

colt /kəʊlt/ *n* potro ☛ *Ver nota en* POTRO

column /ˈkɒləm/ *n* columna

coma /ˈkəʊmə/ *n* coma

comb /kəʊm/ ◆ *n* **1** peine **2** (*adorno*) peineta ◆ **1** *vt* peinar **2** *vt, vi* ~ **(through) sth (for sth/sb)** rastrear, peinar algo (en busca de algo/algn)

combat /ˈkɒmbæt/ ◆ *n* [*incontable*] combate ◆ *vt* combatir, luchar contra

combination /ˌkɒmbɪˈneɪʃn/ *n* combinación

combine /kəmˈbaɪn/ **1** *vt, vi* combinar(se) **2** *vi* ~ **with sth/sb** (*Com*) fusionarse con algo/algn **3** *vt* (*cualidades*) reunir

come /kʌm/ *vi* (*pret* **came** /keɪm/ *pp* **come**) **1** venir: *to come running* venir corriendo **2** llegar **3** recorrer **4** (*posición*) ser: *to come first* ser el/lo primero ◊ *It came as a surprise.* Fue una sorpresa. **5** (*resultar*): *to come undone* desatarse **6** ~ **to/into + sustantivo**: *to come to a halt* pararse ◊ *to come into a fortune* heredar una fortuna **LOC** **come what may** pase lo que pase **to come to nothing; not to come to anything** quedarse en nada **when it comes to (doing) sth** cuando se trata de (hacer) algo ☛ Para otras expresiones con

come, véanse las entradas del sustantivo, adjetivo, etc, p.ej. **to come of age** en AGE.

PHR V **to come about (that...)** ocurrir, suceder (que...)

to come across sth/sb encontrar algo/encontrarse con algn

to come along 1 aparecer, presentarse **2** venir también **3** *Ver* TO COME ON

to come apart deshacerse

to come away (from sth) desprenderse (de algo) **to come away (with sth)** marcharse, irse (con algo)

to come back volver

to come by sth 1 (*obtener*) conseguir algo **2** (*recibir*) adquirir algo

to come down 1 (*precios, temperatura*) bajar **2** desplomarse, venirse abajo

to come forward ofrecerse

to come from... ser de...: *Where do you come from?* ¿De dónde eres?

to come in 1 entrar: *Come in!* ¡Adelante! **2** llegar **to come in for sth** (*crítica, etc*) recibir algo

to come off 1 (*mancha*) quitarse **2** (*pieza*): *Does it come off?* ¿Se puede quitar? **3** (*coloq*) tener éxito, resultar (*plan*) **to come off (sth)** caerse, desprenderse (de algo)

to come on 1 (*actor*) salir a la escena **2** (*tb* **to come along**) hacer progresos

to come out 1 salir **2** ponerse de manifiesto **3** declararse homosexual **to come out with sth** soltar algo, salir con algo

to come over (to...) (*tb* **to come round (to...)**) venir (a...) **to come over sb** invadir a algn: *I can't think what came over me.* No sé qué me pasó.

to come round (*tb* **to come to**) volver en sí **to come round (to...)** (*tb* **to come over (to...)**) venir (a...)

to come through (sth) sobrevivir (algo)

to come to sth 1 ascender a algo **2** llegar a algo

to come up 1 (*planta, sol*) salir **2** (*tema*) surgir **to come up against sth** tropezar con algo **to come up to sb** acercarse a algn

comeback /ˈkʌmbæk/ *n*: *to make/stage a comeback* reaparecer en escena

comedian /kəˈmiːdiən/ *n* (*fem* **comedienne** /kəˌmiːdiˈen/) humorista, cómico, -a

comedy /ˈkɒmədi/ *n* (*pl* **-ies**) **1** comedia **2** comicidad

comet /ˈkɒmɪt/ *n* cometa

comfort /ˈkʌmfət/ ◆ *n* **1** bienestar, comodidad **2** consuelo **3 comforts** [*pl*] comodidades ◆ *vt* consolar

comfortable /ˈkʌmftəbl; *USA* -fərt-/ *adj* **1** cómodo **2** (*victoria*) fácil **3** (*mayoría*) amplia **comfortably** *adv* (*ganar*) cómodamente LOC **to be comfortably off** vivir con holgura

comic /ˈkɒmɪk/ ◆ *adj* cómico ◆ *n* **1** (*USA* **comic book**) cómic, tebeo **2** humorista, cómico, -a

coming /ˈkʌmɪŋ/ ◆ *n* **1** llegada **2** (*Relig*) advenimiento ◆ *adj* próximo

comma /ˈkɒmə/ *n* coma (*Ortografía*) ☛ *Ver* págs 318–19.

command /kəˈmɑːnd; *USA* -ˈmænd/ ◆ **1** *vt* ordenar **2** *vt, vi* tener el mando (de) **3** *vt* (*recursos*) disponer de **4** *vt* (*vista*) tener **5** *vt* (*respeto*) infundir **6** *vt* (*atención*) llamar ◆ *n* **1** orden **2** (*Informát*) orden, comando **3** (*Mil*) mando **4** (*idioma*) dominio **commander** *n* **1** (*Mil*) comandante **2** jefe, -a

commemorate /kəˈmeməreɪt/ *vt* conmemorar

commence /kəˈmens/ *vt, vi* (*fml*) dar comienzo (a)

commend /kəˈmend/ *vt* **1** elogiar **2** (*fml*) ~ **sb to sb** recomendar a algn a algn **commendable** *adj* meritorio, digno de mención

comment /ˈkɒment/ ◆ *n* **1** comentario **2** [*incontable*] comentarios: *'No comment.'* "Sin comentarios." ◆ *vi* **1** ~ **(that...)** comentar (que...) **2** ~ **(on sth)** hacer comentarios (sobre algo)

commentary /ˈkɒməntri; *USA* -teri/ *n* (*pl* **-ies**) **1** (*Dep*) comentarios **2** (*texto*) comentario

commentator /ˈkɒmenˌteɪtə(r)/ *n* comentarista

commerce /ˈkɒmɜːs/ *n* comercio ☛ Se usa más la palabra **trade**.

commercial /kəˈmɜːʃl/ ◆ *adj* **1** comercial **2** (*derecho*) mercantil **3** (*TV, Radio*) financiado por medio de la publicidad ☛ *Ver nota en* TELEVISION ◆ *n* anuncio

commission /kəˈmɪʃn/ ◆ *n* **1** (*porcentaje, organismo*) comisión **2** encargo ◆ *vt* encargar

commissioner /kəˈmɪʃənə(r)/ *n* comisario (*a cargo de un departamento*)

commit /kəˈmɪt/ **(-tt-) 1** *vt* cometer **2** *vt*

~ **sth/sb to sth** entregar algo/a algn a algo: *to commit sth to memory* aprenderse algo de memoria **3** *v refl* ~ **yourself (to sth/to doing sth)** comprometerse (a algo/a hacer algo) ☛ *Comparar con* ENGAGED *en* ENGAGE **4** *v refl* ~ **yourself (on sth)** definirse (en algo) **commitment** *n* **1** ~ **(to sth/to do sth)** compromiso (con algo/de hacer algo) ☛ *Comparar con* ENGAGEMENT 1 **2** entrega

committee /kəˈmɪti/ *n* [*v sing o pl*] comité

commodity /kəˈmɒdəti/ *n* (*pl* **-ies**) **1** producto **2** (*Fin*) mercancía

common /ˈkɒmən/ ◆ *adj* **1** corriente **2** ~ **(to sth/sb)** común (a algo/algn): *common sense* sentido común **3** (*pey*) ordinario, vulgar ☛ *Comparar con* ORDINARY **LOC in common** en común ◆ *n* **1** (*tb* **common land**) tierra comunal **2 the Commons** *Ver* THE HOUSE OF COMMONS **commonly** *adv* generalmente

commonplace /ˈkɒmənpleɪs/ *adj* normal

commotion /kəˈməʊʃn/ *n* revuelo

communal /ˈkɒmjənl, kəˈmjuːnl/ *adj* comunal

commune /ˈkɒmjuːn/ *n* [*v sing o pl*] comuna

communicate /kəˈmjuːnɪkeɪt/ **1** *vt* ~ **sth (to sth/sb)** comunicar algo (a algo/ algn) **2** *vi* ~ **(with sth/sb)** comunicarse (con algo/algn) **communication** *n* **1** comunicación **2** mensaje

communion /kəˈmjuːniən/ (*tb* **Holy Communion**) *n* comunión

communiqué /kəˈmjuːnɪkeɪ; *USA* kəˌmjuːnəˈkeɪ/ *n* comunicado

communism /ˈkɒmjunɪzəm/ *n* comunismo **communist** *adj*, *n* comunista

community /kəˈmjuːnəti/ *n* [*v sing o pl*] (*pl* **-ies**) **1** comunidad: *community centre* centro social **2** (*de expatriados*) colonia

commute /kəˈmjuːt/ *vi* viajar para ir al trabajo **commuter** *n* persona que tiene que viajar para ir al trabajo

compact /kəmˈpækt/ ◆ *adj* compacto ◆ /ˈkɒmpækt/ *n* (*tb* **powder compact**) polvera

compact disc *n* (*abrev* **CD**) disco compacto, compact disc

companion /kəmˈpæniən/ *n* compañero, -a **companionship** *n* compañerismo

company /ˈkʌmpəni/ *n* (*pl* **-ies**) **1** compañía **2** [*v sing o pl*] (*Com*) compañía, empresa **LOC to keep sb company** hacer compañía a algn *Ver tb* PART

comparable /ˈkɒmpərəbl/ *adj* ~ **(to/ with sth/sb)** comparable (a algo/algn)

comparative /kəmˈpærətɪv/ *adj* **1** comparativo **2** relativo

compare /kəmˈpeə(r)/ **1** *vt* ~ **sth with/ to sth** comparar algo con algo **2** *vi* ~ **(with sth/sb)** compararse (con algo/ algn)

comparison /kəmˈpærɪsn/ *n* ~ **(of sth and/to/with sth)** comparación (de algo con algo) **LOC there's no comparison** no hay punto de comparación

compartment /kəmˈpɑːtmənt/ *n* compartimento

compass /ˈkʌmpəs/ *n* **1** brújula **2** (*tb* **compasses** [*pl*]) compás

compassion /kəmˈpæʃn/ *n* compasión **compassionate** *adj* compasivo

compatible /kəmˈpætəbl/ *adj* compatible

compel /kəmˈpel/ *vt* (**-ll-**) (*fml*) **1** obligar **2** forzar **compelling** *adj* **1** irresistible **2** (*motivo*) apremiante **3** (*argumento*) convincente *Ver tb* COMPULSION

compensate /ˈkɒmpenseɪt/ **1** *vt, vi* ~ **(sb) (for sth)** compensar (a algn) (por algo) **2** *vt* ~ **sb (for sth)** indemnizar a algn (por algo) **3** *vi* ~ **(for sth)** contrarrestar (algo) **compensation** *n* **1** compensación **2** indemnización

compete /kəmˈpiːt/ *vi* **1** ~ **(against/ with sb) (in sth) (for sth)** competir (con algn) (en algo) (por algo) **2** ~ **(in sth)** (*Dep*) tomar parte (en algo)

competent /ˈkɒmpɪtənt/ *adj* **1** ~ **(as/ at/in sth)** competente (como/para/en algo) **2** ~ **(to do sth)** competente (para hacer algo) **competence** *n* aptitud, eficiencia

competition /ˌkɒmpəˈtɪʃn/ *n* **1** competición, concurso **2** ~ **(with sb/ between...) (for sth)** enfrentamiento (con algn/entre...) (por algo) **3 the competition** [*v sing o pl*] la competencia

competitive /kəmˈpetətɪv/ *adj* competitivo

competitor /kəmˈpetɪtə(r)/ *n* competi

dor, -ora, concursante *Ver tb* CONTESTANT *en* CONTEST

compile /kəmˈpaɪl/ *vt* compilar

complacency /kəmˈpleɪsnsi/ *n* ~ (**about sth/sb**) autosatisfacción (con algo/algn) **complacent** *adj* satisfecho de sí mismo

complain /kəmˈpleɪn/ *vi* **1** ~ (**to sb**) (**about/at/of sth**) quejarse (a algn) (de algo) **2** ~ (**that...**) quejarse (de que...) **complaint** *n* **1** queja, reclamación **2** (*Med*) afección

complement /ˈkɒmplɪmənt/ ◆ *n* **1** ~ (**to sth**) complemento (para algo) **2** dotación ◆ *vt* complementar ☛ *Comparar con* COMPLIMENT **complementary** /ˌkɒmplɪˈmentri/ *adj* ~ (**to sth**) complementario (a algo)

complete /kəmˈpliːt/ ◆ *vt* **1** completar **2** terminar **3** (*impreso*) rellenar ◆ *adj* **1** completo **2** total **3** (*éxito*) rotundo **4** terminado **completely** *adv* completamente, totalmente **completion** *n* **1** conclusión **2** formalización del contrato de venta (*de una casa*)

complex /ˈkɒmpleks/ ◆ *adj* complejo, complicado ◆ *n* complejo

complexion /kəmˈplekʃn/ *n* **1** tez, cutis **2** (*fig*) cariz

compliance /kəmˈplaɪəns/ *n* obediencia: *in compliance with* conforme a

complicate /ˈkɒmplɪkeɪt/ *vt* complicar **complicated** *adj* complicado **complication** *n* complicación

compliment /ˈkɒmplɪmənt/ ◆ *n* **1** cumplido: *to pay sb a compliment* hacer un cumplido a algn **2 compliments** [*pl*] (*fml*) saludos: *with the compliments of* con un atento saludo de ◆ *vt* ~ **sb** (**on sth**) felicitar a algn (por algo) ☛ *Comparar con* COMPLEMENT **complimentary** /ˌkɒmplɪˈmentri/ *adj* **1** elogioso, favorable **2** (*entrada, etc*) de regalo

comply /kəmˈplaɪ/ *vi* (*pret, pp* **complied**) ~ (**with sth**) obedecer (algo)

component /kəmˈpəʊnənt/ ◆ *n* **1** componente **2** (*Mec*) pieza ◆ *adj*: *component parts* piezas integrantes

compose /kəmˈpəʊz/ **1** *vt* (*Mús*) componer **2** *vt* (*escrito*) redactar **3** *vt* (*pensamientos*) poner en orden **4** *v refl* ~ **yourself** serenarse **composed** *adj* sereno **composer** *n* compositor, -ora

composition /ˌkɒmpəˈzɪʃn/ *n* **1** composición **2** (*colegio*) redacción *Ver tb* ESSAY

compost /ˈkɒmpɒst/ *n* abono

composure /kəmˈpəʊʒə(r)/ *n* calma

compound /ˈkɒmpaʊnd/ ◆ *adj, n* compuesto ◆ *n* recinto ◆ /kəmˈpaʊnd/ *vt* agravar

comprehend /ˌkɒmprɪˈhend/ *vt* comprender (*en su totalidad*) *Ver tb* UNDERSTAND **comprehensible** *adj* ~ (**to sb**) comprensible (para algn) **comprehension** *n* comprensión

comprehensive /ˌkɒmprɪˈhensɪv/ *adj* global, completo

comprehensive school *n* (*GB*) instituto de enseñanza secundaria

compress /kəmˈpres/ *vt* **1** comprimir **2** (*argumento, tiempo*) condensar **compression** *n* compresión

comprise /kəmˈpraɪz/ *vt* **1** constar de **2** formar

compromise /ˈkɒmprəmaɪz/ ◆ *n* acuerdo ◆ **1** *vi* ~ (**on sth**) llegar a un acuerdo (en algo) **2** *vt* comprometer **compromising** *adj* comprometedor

compulsion /kəmˈpʌlʃn/ *n* ~ (**to do sth**) **1** obligación (de hacer algo) **2** deseo irresistible (de hacer algo)

compulsive /kəmˈpʌlsɪv/ *adj* **1** irresistible **2** compulsivo **3** (*jugador*) empedernido

compulsory /kəmˈpʌlsəri/ *adj* **1** obligatorio **2** (*despido*) forzoso LOC **compulsory purchase** expropiación

computer /kəmˈpjuːtə(r)/ *n* ordenador: *computer programmer* programador de ordenadores ☛ *Ver dibujo en* ORDENADOR **computerize, -ise** *vt* informatizar **computing** *n* informática

comrade /ˈkɒmreɪd; *USA* -ræd/ *n* **1** (*Pol*) camarada **2** compañero, -a

con /kɒn/ ◆ *n* (*coloq*) estafa: *con artist/man* estafador LOC *Ver* PRO ◆ *vt* (*coloq*) (**-nn-**) **to con sb** (**out of sth**) estafar (algo) a algn

conceal /kənˈsiːl/ *vt* **1** ocultar **2** (*alegría*) disimular

concede /kənˈsiːd/ *vt* **1** conceder **2** ~ **that...** admitir que...

conceit /kənˈsiːt/ *n* vanidad **conceited** *adj* vanidoso

conceivable /kənˈsiːvəbl/ *adj* concebible **conceivably** *adv* posiblemente

conceive /kən'siːv/ *vt, vi* **1** concebir **2** ~ **(of) sth** imaginar algo

concentrate /'kɒnsntreɪt/ *vt, vi* concentrar(se) **concentration** *n* concentración

concept /'kɒnsept/ *n* concepto

conception /kən'sepʃn/ *n* **1** concepción **2** idea

concern /kən'sɜːn/ ◆ **1** *vt* tener que ver con: *as far as I am concerned* por lo que a mí se refiere/en cuanto a mí **2** *vt* referirse a **3** *v refl* ~ **yourself with sth** interesarse por algo **4** *vt* preocupar ◆ *n* **1** preocupación **2** interés **3** negocio **concerned** *adj* preocupado LOC **to be concerned with sth** tratar de algo **concerning** *prep* **1** acerca de **2** en lo que se refiere a

concert /'kɒnsət/ *n* concierto: *concert hall* sala de conciertos

concerted /kən'sɜːtɪd/ *adj* **1** (*ataque*) coordinado **2** (*intento, esfuerzo*) conjunto

concerto /kən'tʃɜːtəʊ/ *n* (*pl* ~**s**) concierto

concession /kən'seʃn/ *n* **1** concesión **2** (*Fin*) desgravación

conciliation /kənˌsɪli'eɪʃn/ *n* conciliación **conciliatory** /kən'sɪliətəri/ *adj* conciliador

concise /kən'saɪs/ *adj* conciso

conclude /kən'kluːd/ **1** *vt, vi* concluir **2** *vt* ~ **that...** llegar a la conclusión de que... **3** *vt* (*acuerdo*) concertar **conclusion** *n* conclusión LOC *Ver* JUMP

conclusive /kən'kluːsɪv/ *adj* definitivo, decisivo

concoct /kən'kɒkt/ *vt* **1** (*frec pey*) elaborar **2** (*pretexto*) inventar **3** (*plan, intriga*) tramar **concoction** *n* **1** mezcolanza **2** (*líquido*) mejunje

concord /'kɒŋkɔːd/ *n* concordia, armonía

concourse /'kɒŋkɔːs/ *n* vestíbulo (*de edificio*)

concrete /'kɒŋkriːt/ ◆ *adj* concreto, tangible ◆ *n* hormigón

concur /kən'kɜː(r)/ *vi* (**-rr-**) (*fml*) ~ **(with sth/sb) (in sth)** estar de acuerdo, coincidir (con algo/algn) (en algo) **concurrence** *n* acuerdo **concurrent** *adj* simultáneo (con algo) **concurrently** *adv* al mismo tiempo

concussion /kən'kʌʃn/ *n* conmoción cerebral

condemn /kən'dem/ *vt* **1** ~ **sth/sb (for/as)** condenar algo/a algn (por) **2** ~ **sb (to sth/to do sth)** condenar a algn (a algo/a hacer algo) **3** (*edificio*) declarar ruinoso **condemnation** *n* condena

condensation /ˌkɒnden'seɪʃn/ *n* **1** condensación **2** vaho **3** (*texto*) versión resumida

condense /kən'dens/ *vt, vi* ~ **(sth) (into/to sth) 1** condensar algo (en algo); condensarse (en algo) **2** resumir algo (en algo); resumirse (en algo)

condescend /ˌkɒndɪ'send/ *vi* ~ **to do sth** dignarse hacer algo

condition /kən'dɪʃn/ ◆ *n* **1** estado, condición **2** *to be out of condition* no estar en forma **3** (*contrato*) requisito **4** **conditions** [*pl*] circunstancias, condiciones LOC **on condition (that...)** a condición de que... **on no condition** (*fml*) bajo ningún concepto **on one condition** (*fml*) con una condición *Ver tb* MINT ◆ *vt* **1** condicionar, determinar **2** acondicionar **conditional** *adj* condicional: *to be conditional on/upon sth* depender de algo **conditioner** *n* suavizante

condolence /kən'dəʊləns/ *n* [*gen pl*] condolencia: *to give/send your condolences* dar el pésame

condom /'kɒndɒm/ *n* preservativo, condón

condone /kən'dəʊn/ *vt* **1** condonar **2** (*abuso*) sancionar

conducive /kən'djuːsɪv; *USA* -'duːs-/ *adj* ~ **to sth** propicio para algo

conduct /'kɒndʌkt/ ◆ *n* **1** conducta **2** ~ **of sth** gestión de algo ◆ /kən'dʌkt/ **1** *vt* guiar **2** *vt* dirigir **3** *vt* (*investigación*) llevar a cabo **4** *vt* (*orquesta*) dirigir **5** *v refl* ~ **yourself** (*fml*) comportarse **6** *vt* (*Electrón*) conducir **conductor** *n* **1** (*Mús*) director, -ora **2** (*GB*) (*autobús*) cobrador, -ora

Para referirnos al conductor de un autobús, decimos **driver**.

3 (*USA*) (*GB* **guard**) (*Ferrocarril*) jefe, -a de tren **4** (*Electrón*) conductor

cone /kəʊn/ *n* **1** cono **2** (*helado*) barquillo **3** (*Bot*) piña (*de pino, etc*)

confectionery /kən'fekʃənəri/ *n* [*incontable*] dulces

confederation /kənˌfedəˈreɪʃn/ *n* confederación

confer /kənˈfɜː(r)/ *vi* (**-rr-**) **1** deliberar **2** ~ **with sb** consultar a algn **3** ~ **sth (on)** (*título, etc*) conceder algo (a)

conference /ˈkɒnfərəns/ *n* **1** congreso: *conference hall* sala de conferencias ☛ *Comparar con* LECTURE **2** (*discusión*) reunión

confess /kənˈfes/ **1** *vt* confesar **2** *vi* confesarse: *to confess to sth* confesar algo **confession** *n* **1** confesión **2** (*crimen*) declaración de culpabilidad

confide /kənˈfaɪd/ *vt* ~ **sth to sb** confiar secretos, etc a algn PHR V **to confide in sb** hacer confidencias a algn

confidence /ˈkɒnfɪdəns/ *n* **1** ~ **(in sth/sb)** confianza (en algn/algo): *confidence trick* timo **2** confidencia LOC **to take sb into your confidence** hacer confidencias a algn *Ver tb* BREACH, STRICT, VOTE **confident** *adj* **1** seguro (de sí mismo) **2** *to be confident of sth* confiar en algo ◊ *to be confident that...* confiar en que... **confidential** /ˌkɒnfɪˈdenʃl/ *adj* **1** confidencial **2** (*tono, etc*) de confianza **confidently** *adv* con toda confianza

confine /kənˈfaɪn/ *vt* **1** confinar: *to be confined to bed* tener que guardar cama **2** limitar **confined** *adj* limitado (*espacio*) **confinement** *n* confinamiento LOC *Ver* SOLITARY

confines /ˈkɒnfaɪnz/ *n* [*pl*] (*fml*) límites

confirm /kənˈfɜːm/ *vt* confirmar **confirmed** *adj* empedernido

confirmation /ˌkɒnfəˈmeɪʃn/ *n* confirmación

confiscate /ˈkɒnfɪskeɪt/ *vt* confiscar

conflict /ˈkɒnflɪkt/ ◆ *n* conflicto ◆ /kənˈflɪkt/ *vi* ~ **(with sth)** discrepar (de algo) **conflicting** *adj* discrepante: *conflicting evidence* pruebas contradictorias

conform /kənˈfɔːm/ *vi* **1** ~ **to sth** atenerse a algo **2** seguir las reglas **3** ~ **with/to sth** ajustarse a algo **conformist** *n* conformista **conformity** (*fml*) *n* conformidad: *in conformity with* de conformidad con

confront /kənˈfrʌnt/ *vt* hacer frente a, enfrentarse con: *They confronted him with the facts.* Le hicieron afrontar los hechos. **confrontation** *n* enfrentamiento

confuse /kənˈfjuːz/ *vt* **1** ~ **sth/sb with sth/sb** confundir algo/a algn con algo/algn **2** (*persona*) desorientar **3** (*asunto*) complicar **confused** *adj* **1** confuso **2** (*persona*) desorientado: *to get confused* desorientarse/ofuscarse **confusing** *adj* confuso ☛ *Comparar con* CONFUSO **confusion** *n* confusión

congeal /kənˈdʒiːl/ *vi* coagularse

congenial /kənˈdʒiːniəl/ *adj* agradable LOC **congenial to sb** atractivo para algn **congenial to sth** propicio para algo

congenital /kənˈdʒenɪtl/ *adj* congénito

congested /kənˈdʒestɪd/ *adj* ~ **(with sth)** congestionado (de algo) **congestion** *n* colapso, congestión

conglomerate /kənˈglɒmərət/ *n* grupo (*de empresas*)

congratulate /kənˈgrætʃuleɪt/ *vt* ~ **sb (on)** felicitar a algn (por) **congratulation** *n* felicitación LOC **congratulations!** ¡enhorabuena!

congregate /ˈkɒŋgrɪgeɪt/ *vi* congregarse **congregation** *n* [*v sing o pl*] feligreses

congress /ˈkɒŋgres; *USA* -grəs/ *n* [*v sing o pl*] congreso **congressional** /kənˈgreʃənl/ *adj* del congreso

conical /ˈkɒnɪkl/ *adj* cónico

conifer /ˈkɒnɪfə(r)/ *n* conífera

conjecture /kənˈdʒektʃə(r)/ *n* **1** conjetura **2** [*incontable*] conjeturas

conjunction /kənˈdʒʌŋkʃn/ *n* (*Gram*) conjunción LOC **in conjunction with** conjuntamente con

conjure /ˈkʌndʒə(r)/ *vi* hacer juegos de manos PHR V **to conjure sth up 1** (*imagen, etc*) evocar algo **2** hacer aparecer algo como por arte de magia **3** (*espíritu*) invocar **conjurer** *n* prestidigitador, -ora

connect /kəˈnekt/ **1** *vt, vi* (*gen, Electrón*) conectar(se) **2** *vt* (*habitaciones*) comunicar **3** *vt* emparentar: *connected by marriage* emparentados políticamente **4** *vt* ~ **sth/sb (with sth/sb)** relacionar algo/a algn (con algo/algn) **5** *vt* ~ **sb (with sb)** (*teléf*) poner a algn (con algn) **connection** *n* **1** conexión **2** relación **3** (*transporte*) enlace LOC **in connection with** en relación con **to have connections** tener enchufe

connoisseur /ˌkɒnəˈsɜː(r)/ *n* conocedor, -ora, experto, -a

conquer /ˈkɒŋkə(r)/ *vt* **1** conquistar **2**

vencer, derrotar **conqueror** *n* **1** conquistador, -ora **2** vencedor, -ora

conquest /ˈkɒŋkwest/ *n* conquista

conscience /ˈkɒnʃəns/ *n* (*moral*) conciencia LOC **to have sth on your conscience** pesar algo sobre la conciencia de algn *Ver tb* EASE

conscientious /ˌkɒnʃiˈenʃəs/ *adj* concienzudo: *conscientious objector* objetor de conciencia

conscious /ˈkɒnʃəs/ *adj* **1** consciente **2** (*esfuerzo, decisión*) deliberado **consciously** *adv* deliberadamente **consciousness** *n* **1** conocimiento **2** **consciousness** (**of sth**) conciencia (sobre algo)

conscript /ˈkɒnskrɪpt/ *n* recluta **conscription** *n* reclutamiento (*obligatorio*)

consecrate /ˈkɒnsɪkreɪt/ *vt* consagrar

consecutive /kənˈsekjətɪv/ *adj* consecutivo

consent /kənˈsent/ ◆ *vi* ~ (**to sth**) acceder (a algo) ◆ *n* consentimiento LOC *Ver* AGE

consequence /ˈkɒnsɪkwəns; *USA* -kwens/ *n* **1** [*gen pl*] consecuencia: *as a/in consequence of sth* a consecuencia de algo **2** (*fml*) importancia

consequent /ˈkɒnsɪkwənt/ *adj* (*fml*) **1** consiguiente **2** ~ **on/upon sth** que resulta de algo **consequently** *adv* por consiguiente

conservation /ˌkɒnsəˈveɪʃn/ *n* conservación, ahorro: *conservation area* zona protegida

conservative /kənˈsɜːvətɪv/ ◆ *adj* **1** conservador **2** **Conservative** (*Pol*) conservador *Ver tb* TORY ◆ *n* conservador, -ora

conservatory /kənˈsɜːvətri; *USA* -tɔːri/ *n* (*pl* **-ies**) **1** galería acristalada contigua a una casa **2** (*Mús*) conservatorio

conserve /kənˈsɜːv/ *vt* **1** conservar **2** (*energía*) ahorrar **3** (*fuerzas*) reservar **4** (*naturaleza*) proteger

consider /kənˈsɪdə(r)/ *vt* **1** considerar: *to consider doing sth* pensar hacer algo **2** tener en cuenta

considerable /kənˈsɪdərəbl/ *adj* considerable **considerably** *adv* bastante

considerate /kənˈsɪdərət/ *adj* ~ (**towards sth/sb**) considerado (con algo/algn)

consideration /kənˌsɪdəˈreɪʃn/ *n* **1** consideración: *It is under consideration.* Lo están considerando. **2** factor LOC **to take sth into consideration** tener algo en cuenta

considering /kənˈsɪdərɪŋ/ *conj* teniendo en cuenta

consign /kənˈsaɪn/ *vt* ~ **sth/sb** (**to sth**) abandonar algo/a algn (a/en algo): *consigned to oblivion* relegado al olvido **consignment** *n* **1** envío **2** pedido

consist /kənˈsɪst/ *v* PHR V **to consist of sth** consistir en algo, estar formado de algo

consistency /kənˈsɪstənsi/ *n* (*pl* **-ies**) **1** consistencia **2** (*actitud*) coherencia

consistent /kənˈsɪstənt/ *adj* **1** (*persona*) consecuente **2** ~ (**with sth**) en concordancia (con algo) **consistently** *adv* **1** constantemente **2** (*actuar*) consecuentemente

consolation /ˌkɒnsəˈleɪʃn/ *n* consuelo

console /kənˈsəʊl/ *vt* consolar

consolidate /kənˈsɒlɪdeɪt/ *vt, vi* consolidar(se)

consonant /ˈkɒnsənənt/ *n* consonante

consortium /kənˈsɔːtiəm; *USA* -ˈsɔːrʃɪəm/ *n* (*pl* **-tia** /-tɪə; *USA* -ʃɪə/) consorcio

conspicuous /kənˈspɪkjuəs/ *adj* **1** llamativo: *to make yourself conspicuous* llamar la atención **2** (*irón*) **to be ~ for sth** distinguirse por algo **3** visible LOC **to be conspicuous by your/its absence** brillar algn/algo por su ausencia **conspicuously** *adv* notablemente

conspiracy /kənˈspɪrəsi/ *n* (*pl* **-ies**) **1** conspiración **2** conjura **conspiratorial** /kənˌspɪrəˈtɔːriəl/ *adj* conspirador

conspire /kənˈspaɪə(r)/ *vi* conspirar

constable /ˈkʌnstəbl; *USA* ˈkɒn-/ *n* (agente de) policía

constant /ˈkɒnstənt/ ◆ *adj* **1** constante, continuo **2** (*amigo, seguidor, etc*) fiel ◆ *n* constante **constantly** *adv* constantemente

constipated /ˈkɒnstɪpeɪtɪd/ *adj* estreñido

constipation /ˌkɒnstɪˈpeɪʃn/ *n* estreñimiento

constituency /kənˈstɪtjuənsi/ *n* (*pl* **-ies**) **1** distrito electoral **2** votantes

constituent /kənˈstɪtjuənt/ *n* **1** (*Pol*) elector, -ora **2** componente

container

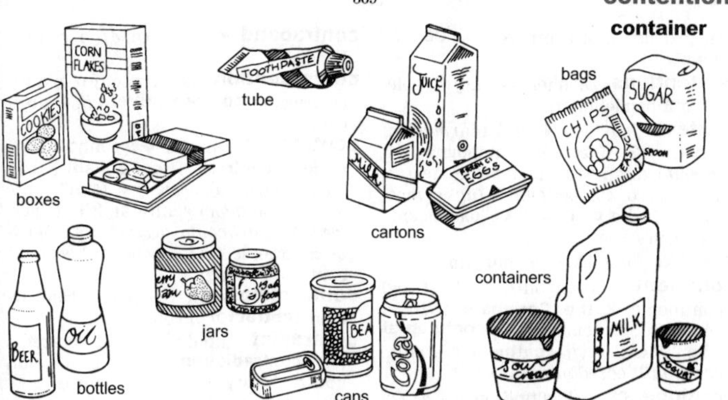

constitute /ˈkɒnstɪtjuːt/ *vt* constituir

constitution /ˌkɒnstɪˈtjuːʃn; *USA* -ˈtuːʃn/ *n* constitución **constitutional** *adj* constitucional

constraint /kənˈstreɪnt/ *n* **1** coacción **2** limitación

constrict /kənˈstrɪkt/ *vt* **1** apretar **2** limitar

construct /kənˈstrʌkt/ *vt* construir ☛ La palabra más normal es **build**. **construction** *n* construcción

construe /kənˈstruː/ *vt* interpretar

consul /ˈkɒnsl/ *n* cónsul

consulate /ˈkɒnsjələt; *USA* -səl-/ *n* consulado

consult /kənˈsʌlt/ *vt, vi* consultar: *consulting room* consultorio **consultant** *n* **1** asesor, -ora **2** (*Med*) especialista **consultancy** *n* asesoría **consultation** *n* consulta

consume /kənˈsjuːm; *USA* -ˈsuːm/ *vt* consumir: *He was consumed with envy.* Lo consumía la envidia. **consumer** *n* consumidor, -ora

consummate /kənˈsʌmət/ ◆ *adj* (*fml*) **1** consumado **2** (*habilidad, etc*) extraordinario ◆ /ˈkɒnsəmeɪt/ *vt* (*fml*) **1** culminar **2** (*matrimonio*) consumar

consumption /kənˈsʌmpʃn/ *n* **1** consumo **2** (*antic, Med*) tisis

contact /ˈkɒntækt/ ◆ *n* (*gen, Electrón*) contacto: *contact lens* lentilla LOC **to make contact** (**with sth**/**sb**) ponerse en contacto (con algo/algn) ◆ *vt* ponerse en contacto con

contagious /kənˈteɪdʒəs/ *adj* contagioso

contain /kənˈteɪn/ *vt* contener: *to contain yourself* contenerse **container** *n* **1** recipiente **2** contenedor: *container lorry/ship* camión/buque contenedor

contaminate /kənˈtæmɪneɪt/ *vt* contaminar

contemplate /ˈkɒntəmpleɪt/ **1** *vt, vi* contemplar, meditar (sobre) **2** *vt* considerar: *to contemplate doing sth* considerar la idea de hacer algo

contemporary /kənˈtemprəri; *USA* -pəreri/ ◆ *adj* **1** contemporáneo **2** de la época ◆ *n* (*pl* **-ies**) coetáneo, -a

contempt /kənˈtempt/ *n* **1** desprecio **2** (*tb* **contempt of court**) desacato (al tribunal) LOC **beneath contempt** despreciable *Ver tb* HOLD **contemptible** *adj* despreciable **contemptuous** *adj* desdeñoso, despectivo

contend /kənˈtend/ **1** *vi* ~ **with sth** luchar contra algo: *She's had a lot of problems to contend with.* Ha tenido que enfrentarse con muchos problemas. **2** *vi* ~ (**for sth**) competir, luchar (por algo) **3** *vt* afirmar **contender** *n* contendiente

content[1] /ˈkɒntent/ (*tb* **contents** [*pl*]) *n* contenido: *table of contents* índice de materias

content[2] /kənˈtent/ ◆ *adj* ~ (**with sth**/**to do sth**) contento (con algo/con hacer algo); satisfecho con algo ◆ *v refl* ~ **yourself with sth** contentarse con algo **contented** *adj* satisfecho **contentment** *n* contento, satisfacción

contention /kənˈtenʃn/ *n* **1** liza: *the teams in contention for…* los equipos en liza por... **2** controversia **LOC** *Ver* BONE

contentious /kənˈtenʃəs/ *adj* **1** polémico **2** pendenciero

contest /kənˈtest/ ◆ *vt* **1** (*afirmación*) rebatir **2** (*decisión*) impugnar **3** (*premio, escaño*) disputar ◆ /ˈkɒntest/ *n* **1** concurso, competición **2** (*fig*) competición, lucha **contestant** /kənˈtestənt/ *n* concursante

context /ˈkɒntekst/ *n* contexto

continent /ˈkɒntɪnənt/ *n* **1** (*Geog*) continente **2 the Continent** (*GB*) el continente europeo **continental** /ˌkɒntɪˈnentl/ *adj* continental: *continental quilt* edredón nórdico

contingency /kənˈtɪndʒənsi/ *n* (*pl* **-ies**) **1** eventualidad **2** contingencia: *contingency plan* plan de emergencia

contingent /kənˈtɪndʒənt/ *n* [*v sing o pl*] **1** (*Mil*) contingente **2** representación

continual /kənˈtɪnjuəl/ *adj* continuo **continually** *adv* continuamente

¿**Continual** o **continuous**? **Continual** y **continually** suelen emplearse para describir acciones que se repiten sucesivamente y a menudo tienen un matiz negativo: *His continual phone calls started to annoy her.* Sus continuas llamadas empezaban a fastidiarla. **Continuous** y **continuously** se utilizan para describir acciones ininterrumpidas: *There has been a continuous improvement in his work.* Su trabajo ha mostrado una mejora constante. ◊ *It has rained continuously here for three days.* Ha llovido sin parar durante tres días.

continuation /kənˌtɪnjuˈeɪʃn/ *n* continuación

continue /kənˈtɪnjuː/ *vt, vi* continuar, seguir: *to continue doing sth/to do sth* continuar haciendo algo **continued** *adj* continuo **continuing** *adj* continuado

continuity /ˌkɒntɪˈnjuːəti; *USA* -ˈnuː-/ *n* continuidad

continuous /kənˈtɪnjuəs/ *adj* constante, continuo **continuously** *adv* continuamente, sin parar ☛ *Ver nota en* CONTINUAL

contort /kənˈtɔːt/ **1** *vt* (re)torcer **2** *vi* contorsionarse, retorcerse

contour /ˈkɒntʊə(r)/ *n* contorno

contraband /ˈkɒntrəbænd/ *n* contrabando

contraception /ˌkɒntrəˈsepʃn/ *n* anticoncepción **contraceptive** *adj, n* anticonceptivo

contract /ˈkɒntrækt/ ◆ *n* contrato **LOC under contract (to sth/sb)** bajo contrato (con algo/algn) ◆ /kənˈtrækt/ **1** *vt* (*trabajador*) contratar **2** *vt* (*enfermedad, matrimonio, deudas*) contraer **3** *vi* contraerse **4** *vi* ~ **with sb** hacer un contrato con algn

contraction /kənˈtrækʃən/ *n* contracción **contractor** *n* contratista

contradict /ˌkɒntrəˈdɪkt/ *vt* contradecir **contradiction** *n* contradicción **contradictory** *adj* contradictorio

contrary /ˈkɒntrəri; *USA* -treri/ ◆ *adj* contrario ◆ *adv* ~ **to sth** en contra de algo; contrario a algo ◆ **the contrary** *n* lo contrario **LOC on the contrary** por el contrario

contrast /kənˈtrɑːst; *USA* -ˈtræst/ ◆ *vt, vi* ~ **(A and/with B)** contrastar (A con B) ◆ /ˈkɒntrɑːst; *USA* -træst/ *n* contraste

contribute /kənˈtrɪbjuːt/ **1** *vt, vi* contribuir **2** *vt, vi* ~ **(sth) to sth** (*artículo*) escribir (algo) para algo **3** *vi* ~ **to sth** (*debate*) participar en algo **contributor** *n* **1** contribuyente **2** (*publicación*) colaborador, -ora **contributory** *adj* **1** que contribuye **2** (*plan de jubilación*) contributivo

contribution /ˌkɒntrɪˈbjuːʃn/ *n* **1** contribución, aportación **2** (*publicación*) artículo

control /kənˈtrəʊl/ ◆ *n* **1** control, mando, dominio: *to be in control of sth* tener el control de algo/tener algo bajo control **2 controls** [*pl*] mandos **LOC to be out of control 1** estar fuera de control: *Her car went out of control.* Perdió el control del coche. **2** (*persona*) desmandarse ◆ **1** *vt* controlar, tener el mando de **2** *vt* (*coche*) manejar **3** *v refl* ~ **yourself** dominarse **4** *vt* (*ley*) regular **5** *vt* (*gastos, inflación*) contener

controversial /ˌkɒntrəˈvɜːʃl/ *adj* controvertido, polémico

controversy /ˈkɒntrəvɜːsi, kənˈtrɒvəsi/ *n* (*pl* **-ies**) ~ **(about/over sth)** controversia (acerca de algo)

convene /kənˈviːn/ **1** *vt* convocar **2** *vi* reunirse

convenience /kənˈviːniəns/ *n* **1** comodidad: *public conveniences* lavabos **2** conveniencia

convenient /kənˈviːniənt/ *adj* **1** *if it's convenient (for you)* si te viene bien **2** (*momento*) oportuno **3** práctico **4** (*accesible*) a mano **5** ~ **for sth** bien situado en relación con algo **conveniently** *adv* oportunamente (*tb irón*)

convent /ˈkɒnvənt; *USA* -vent/ *n* convento

convention /kənˈvenʃn/ *n* **1** congreso **2** convencionalismo **3** (*acuerdo*) convención **conventional** *adj* convencional LOC **conventional wisdom** sabiduría popular

converge /kənˈvɜːdʒ/ *vi* **1** converger **2** ~ **(on sth)** (*personas*) juntarse (en algo) **convergence** *n* convergencia

conversant /kənˈvɜːsnt/ *adj* (*fml*) ~ **with sth** versado en algo: *to become conversant with* familiarizarse con

conversation /ˌkɒnvəˈseɪʃn/ *n* conversación: *to make conversation* dar conversación

converse[1] /kənˈvɜːs/ *vi* (*fml*) conversar

converse[2] /ˈkɒnvɜːs/ **the converse** *n* lo contrario **conversely** *adv* a la inversa

conversion /kənˈvɜːʃn; *USA* kənˈvɜːrʒn/ *n* ~ **(from sth) (into/to sth)** conversión (de algo) (en/a algo)

convert /kənˈvɜːt/ ◆ *vt, vi* **1** ~ **(sth) (from sth) (into/to sth)** convertir algo (de algo) (en algo); convertirse (de algo) (en algo): *The sofa converts (in)to a bed.* El sofá se hace cama. **2** ~ **(sb) (from sth) (to sth)** (*Relig*) convertir a algn (de algo) (a algo); convertirse (de algo) (a algo) ◆ /ˈkɒnvɜːt/ *n* ~ **(to sth)** converso, -a (a algo)

convertible /kənˈvɜːtəbl/ ◆ *adj* ~ **(into/to sth)** convertible (en algo) ◆ *n* descapotable

convey /kənˈveɪ/ *vt* **1** (*fml*) llevar, transportar **2** (*idea, agradecimiento*) expresar **3** (*saludos*) enviar **4** (*propiedad*) traspasar **conveyor** (*tb* **conveyor belt**) *n* cinta transportadora

convict /kənˈvɪkt/ ◆ *vt* ~ **sb (of sth)** declarar culpable a algn (de algo) ◆ /ˈkɒnvɪkt/ *n* presidiario, -a: *an escaped convict* un preso fugado **conviction** *n* **1** ~ **(for sth)** condena (por algo) **2** ~ **(that...)** convicción (de que...): *to lack conviction* no ser convincente

convince /kənˈvɪns/ *vt* **1** ~ **sb (that.../of sth)** convencer a algn (de que.../de algo) **2** (*esp USA*) determinar **convinced** *adj* convencido **convincing** *adj* convincente

convulse /kənˈvʌls/ *vt* convulsionar: *convulsed with laughter* muerto de risa **convulsion** *n* [*gen pl*] convulsión

cook /kʊk/ ◆ **1** *vi* (*persona*) cocinar, hacer la comida **2** *vi* (*comida*) cocer **3** *vt* preparar: *The potatoes aren't cooked.* Las patatas no están hechas. LOC **to cook the books** (*coloq, pey*) falsificar los libros de contabilidad PHR V **to cook sth up** (*coloq*): *to cook up an excuse* montarse una excusa ◆ *n* cocinero, -a

cooker /ˈkʊkə(r)/ *n* cocina (*electrodoméstico*) *Ver tb* STOVE

cookery /ˈkʊkəri/ *n* [*incontable*] cocina: *Oriental cookery* la cocina oriental

cooking /ˈkʊkɪŋ/ *n* [*incontable*] cocina: *French cooking* cocina francesa ◊ *to do the cooking* hacer la comida ◊ *cooking apple* manzana de guisar

cool /kuːl/ ◆ *adj* **(-er, -est) 1** fresco ☛ *Ver nota en* FRÍO **2** (*coloq*) impasible **3** ~ **(about sth/towards sb)** indiferente (a algo/algn) **4** (*acogida*) frío LOC **to keep/stay cool** no perder la calma: *Keep cool!* ¡Tranquilo! ◆ *vt, vi* ~ **(sth) (down/off)** enfriarse, enfriar algo PHR V **to cool (sb) down/off** calmarse, calmar a algn ◆ **the cool** *n* [*incontable*] el fresco LOC **to keep/lose your cool** (*coloq*) mantener/perder la calma

cooperate /kəʊˈɒpəreɪt/ *vi* **1** ~ **(with sb) (in doing/to do sth)** cooperar (con algn) (para hacer algo) **2** ~ **(with sb) (on sth)** cooperar (con algn) (en algo) **3** colaborar **cooperation** *n* **1** cooperación **2** colaboración

cooperative /kəʊˈɒpərətɪv/ ◆ *adj* **1** cooperativo **2** dispuesto a colaborar ◆ *n* cooperativa

coordinate /kəʊˈɔːdɪneɪt/ *vt* coordinar

cop /kɒp/ *n* (*coloq*) poli

cope /kəʊp/ *vi* ~ **(with sth)** arreglárselas (con algo); hacer frente a algo: *I can't cope.* No puedo más.

copious /ˈkəʊpiəs/ *adj* (*fml*) copioso, abundante

copper /ˈkɒpə(r)/ *n* **1** cobre **2** (*coloq, GB*) policía

copy /ˈkɒpi/ ◆ *n* (*pl* **copies**) **1** copia **2** (*libro, disco, etc*) ejemplar **3** (*revista, etc*) número **4** texto (*para imprimir*) ◆ *vt* (*pret, pp* **copied**) **1** ~ **sth (down/out) (in/into sth)** copiar algo (en algo) **2** fotocopiar **3** ~ **sth/sb** copiar, imitar algo/a algn

copyright /ˈkɒpiraɪt/ ◆ *n* derechos de autor, copyright ◆ *adj* registrado, protegido por los derechos de autor

coral /ˈkɒrəl; *USA* ˈkɔːrəl/ ◆ *n* coral ◆ *adj* de coral, coralino

cord /kɔːd/ *n* **1** cordón **2** (*USA*) *Ver* FLEX **3** (*coloq*) pana **4 cords** [*pl*] pantalón de pana

cordon /ˈkɔːdn/ ◆ *n* cordón ◆ PHR V **to cordon sth off** acordonar algo

corduroy /ˈkɔːdərɔɪ/ *n* pana

core /kɔː(r)/ *n* **1** (*fruta*) corazón **2** centro, núcleo: *a hard core* un núcleo arraigado LOC **to the core** hasta la médula

cork /kɔːk/ *n* corcho

corkscrew /ˈkɔːkskruː/ *n* sacacorchos

corn /kɔːn/ *n* **1** (*GB*) cereal **2** (*USA*) maíz **3** callo

corner /ˈkɔːnə(r)/ ◆ *n* **1** (*desde dentro*) rincón **2** (*desde fuera*) esquina **3** (*tb* **corner kick**) córner, saque de esquina LOC **(just) round the corner** a la vuelta de la esquina ◆ **1** *vt* acorralar **2** *vi* coger una curva **3** *vt* monopolizar: *to corner the market in sth* hacerse con el mercado de algo

cornerstone /ˈkɔːnəstəʊn/ *n* piedra angular

cornflour /ˈkɔːnflaʊə(r)/ *n* maicena

corollary /kəˈrɒləri; *USA* ˈkɒrəleri/ *n* ~ **(of/to sth)** (*fml*) consecuencia lógica (de algo)

coronation /ˌkɒrəˈneɪʃn; *USA* ˌkɔːr-/ *n* coronación

coroner /ˈkɒrənə(r); *USA* ˈkɔːr-/ *n* juez de instrucción (*en casos de muerte violenta o accidentes*)

corporal /ˈkɔːpərəl/ ◆ *n* (*Mil*) cabo ◆ *adj*: *corporal punishment* castigo corporal

corporate /ˈkɔːpərət/ *adj* **1** colectivo **2** corporativo

corporation /ˌkɔːpəˈreɪʃn/ *n* [*v sing o pl*] **1** corporación municipal, Ayuntamiento **2** corporación

corps /kɔː(r)/ *n* [*v sing o pl*] (*pl* **corps** /kɔːz/) cuerpo

corpse /kɔːps/ *n* cadáver

correct /kəˈrekt/ ◆ *adj* correcto: *Would I be correct in saying...?* ¿Me equivoco si digo...? ◆ *vt* corregir

correlation /ˌkɒrəˈleɪʃn; *USA* ˌkɔːr-/ *n* ~ **(with sth)/(between...)** correlación (con algo)/(entre...)

correspond /ˌkɒrəˈspɒnd; *USA* ˌkɔːr-/ *vi* **1** ~ **(with sth)** coincidir (con algo) **2** ~ **(to sth)** equivaler (a algo) **3** ~ **(with sb)** cartearse (con algn) **correspondence** *n* correspondencia **correspondent** *n* corresponsal **corresponding** *adj* correspondiente

corridor /ˈkɒrɪdɔː(r); *USA* ˈkɔːr-/ *n* pasillo

corrosion /kəˈrəʊʒn/ *n* corrosión

corrugated /ˈkɒrəgeɪtɪd/ *adj* ondulado

corrupt /kəˈrʌpt/ ◆ *adj* **1** corrupto, deshonesto **2** depravado ◆ *vt* corromper, sobornar **corruption** *n* corrupción

cosmetic /kɒzˈmetɪk/ *adj* cósmetico: *cosmetic surgery* cirugía estética **cosmetics** *n* [*pl*] cosméticos

cosmopolitan /ˌkɒzməˈpɒlɪtən/ *adj, n* cosmopolita

cost /kɒst; *USA* kɔːst/ ◆ *vt* **1** (*pret, pp* **cost**) costar, valer **2** (*pret, pp* **costed**) (*Com*) presupuestar LOC **to cost a bomb** costar un dineral *Ver tb* EARTH ◆ *n* **1** coste: *whatever the cost* cueste lo que cueste ◊ *cost-effective* rentable *Ver tb* PRICE **2 costs** [*pl*] costas, gastos LOC **at all costs** a toda costa *Ver tb* COUNT **costly** *adj* (**-ier**, **-iest**) costoso

costume /ˈkɒstjuːm; *USA* -tuːm/ *n* **1** traje **2 costumes** [*pl*] (*Teat*) vestuario

cosy (*USA* **cozy**) /ˈkəʊzi/ *adj* (**-ier**, **-iest**) acogedor

cot /kɒt/ *n* **1** (*USA* **crib**) cuna **2** (*USA*) camastro

cottage /ˈkɒtɪdʒ/ *n* casita (*de campo*) ☛ *Ver* pág 321.

cotton /ˈkɒtn/ *n* **1** algodón **2** hilo (*de algodón*)

cotton wool *n* [*incontable*] algodón

couch /kaʊtʃ/ ◆ *n* diván ◆ *vt* (*fml*) ~ **sth (in sth)** expresar algo (en algo)

cough /kɒf; *USA* kɔːf/ ◆ **1** *vi* toser **2** *vt*

~ **sth up** escupir algo **PHR V to cough (sth) up** (*GB, coloq*) soltar (algo) ◆ *n* tos

could *pret de* CAN[2]

council /ˈkaʊnsl/ *n* [*v sing o pl*] **1** consejo municipal, ayuntamiento: *council flat/house* vivienda protegida perteneciente al ayuntamiento **2** consejo **councillor** (*USA tb* **councilor**) *n* concejal, -ala

counsel /ˈkaʊnsl/ ◆ *n* **1** (*fml*) consejo *Ver tb* ADVICE **2** (*pl* **counsel**) abogado ☛ *Ver nota en* ABOGADO ◆ *vt* (**-ll-**, *USA* **-l-**) (*fml*) aconsejar **counselling** (*USA tb* **counseling**) *n* asesoramiento, orientación **counsellor** (*USA tb* **counselor**) *n* **1** asesor, -ora, consejero, -a **2** (*USA o Irl*) abogado, -a

count[1] /kaʊnt/ **1** *vt, vi* ~ (**sth**) (**up**) contar (algo) **2** *vi* ~ (**as sth**) contar (como algo) **3** *vi* ~ (**for sth**) importar, contar (para algo) **4** *vi* valer **5** *v refl*: *to count yourself lucky* considerarse afortunado **LOC to count the cost** (**of sth**) pagar las consecuencias (de algo) **PHR V to count down** hacer la cuenta atrás **to count sth/sb in** contar algo/a algn **to count on sth/sb** contar con algo/algn **to count sth/sb out** (*coloq*) no contar con algo/algn **to count towards sth** contribuir a algo

count[2] /kaʊnt/ *n* **1** conde **2** recuento, cuenta

countdown /ˈkaʊntdaʊn/ *n* ~ (**to sth**) cuenta atrás (de algo)

countenance /ˈkaʊntənəns/ ◆ *vt* (*fml*) aprobar, tolerar ◆ *n* rostro, semblante

counter /ˈkaʊntə(r)/ ◆ **1** *vi* rebatir, contraatacar **2** *vt* (*ataque*) contestar, responder a ◆ *n* **1** (*juego*) ficha **2** contador **3** mostrador ◆ *adv* ~ **to sth** en contra de algo

counteract /ˌkaʊntərˈækt/ *vt* contrarrestar

counter-attack /ˈkaʊntər ətæk/ *n* contraataque

counterfeit /ˈkaʊntəfɪt/ *adj* falso

counterpart /ˈkaʊntəpɑːt/ *n* **1** homólogo, -a **2** equivalente

counter-productive /ˌkaʊntə prəˈdʌktɪv/ *adj* contraproducente

countess /ˈkaʊntəs/ *n* condesa

countless /ˈkaʊntləs/ *adj* innumerable

country /ˈkʌntri/ *n* (*pl* **-ies**) **1** país **2** [*sing*] patria **3** [*incontable*] (*tb* **the country**) campo, campiña: *country life* la vida rural **4** zona, tierra

countryman /ˈkʌntrimən/ *n* (*pl* **-men** /-mən/) **1** compatriota **2** campesino, -a ☛ *Ver nota en* CAMPESINO

countryside /ˈkʌntrisaɪd/ *n* [*incontable*] **1** campo, campiña **2** paisaje

countrywoman /ˈkʌntriwʊmən/ *n* (*pl* **-women**) **1** compatriota **2** campesina

county /ˈkaʊnti/ *n* (*pl* **-ies**) condado

coup /kuː/ *n* (*pl* ~**s** /kuːz/) (*Fr*) **1** (*tb* **coup d'état** /kuːdeɪˈtɑː/) (*pl* ~**s d'état**) golpe (de estado) **2** éxito

couple /ˈkʌpl/ ◆ *n* **1** pareja (*relación amorosa*): *a married couple* un matrimonio **2** par **LOC a couple of** un par de, unos, -as cuantos, -as ◆ *vt* **1** asociar, acompañar: *coupled with sth* junto con algo **2** acoplar, enganchar

coupon /ˈkuːpɒn/ *n* cupón, vale

courage /ˈkʌrɪdʒ/ *n* valor **LOC** *Ver* DUTCH, PLUCK **courageous** /kəˈreɪdʒəs/ *adj* **1** (*persona*) valiente **2** (*intento*) valeroso

courgette /kʊəˈʒet/ *n* calabacín

courier /ˈkʊriə(r)/ *n* **1** guía turístico, -a (*persona*) **2** mensajero, -a

course /kɔːs/ *n* **1** curso, transcurso **2** (*barco, avión, río*) rumbo, curso: *to be on/off course* seguir el rumbo/un rumbo equivocado **3** ~ (**in/on sth**) (*Educ*) curso (de algo) **4** ~ **of sth** (*Med*) tratamiento de algo **5** (*golf*) campo **6** (*carreras*) pista **7** (*comida*) plato **LOC a course of action** una línea de actuación **in the course of sth** en el transcurso de algo **of course** por supuesto *Ver tb* DUE, MATTER

court /kɔːt/ ◆ *n* **1** ~ (**of law**) juzgado, tribunal: *a court case* un pleito ◊ *court order* orden judicial *Ver tb* HIGH COURT **2** (*Dep*) pista **3 Court** corte **LOC to go to court** (**over sth**) ir a juicio (por algo) **to take sb to court** demandar a algn ◆ *vt* **1** cortejar **2** (*peligro, etc*) exponerse a

courteous /ˈkɜːtiəs/ *adj* cortés

courtesy /ˈkɜːtəsi/ *n* (*pl* **-ies**) cortesía **LOC** (**by**) **courtesy of sb** (por) gentileza de algn

court martial *n* (*pl* ~**s martial**) consejo de guerra

courtship /ˈkɔːtʃɪp/ *n* noviazgo

courtyard /ˈkɔːtjɑːd/ *n* patio

cousin /ˈkʌzn/ (*tb* **first cousin**) *n* primo (hermano), prima (hermana)

cove /kəʊv/ *n* cala

covenant /ˈkʌvənənt/ *n* convenio, pacto

cover /ˈkʌvə(r)/ ◆ **1** *vt* ~ **sth (up/over) (with sth)** cubrir algo (con algo) **2** *vt* ~ **sth/sb in/with sth** cubrir algo/a algn de algo **3** *vt* (*cazuela, cara*) tapar **4** *vt* (*timidez, etc*) disimular **5** *vt* abarcar **6** *vt* tratar, encargarse de **7** *vi* ~ **for sb** sustituir a algn PHR V **to cover (sth) up** (*pey*) ocultar (algo) **to cover up for sb** cubrir las espaldas a algn ◆ *n* **1** cubierta **2** funda **3** (*libro*) tapa **4** (*revista*) portada **5 the covers** [*pl*] las mantas **6** ~ (**for sth**) (*fig*) tapadera (para algo) **7** identidad falsa **8** (*Mil*) protección **9** ~ (**for sb**) sustitución (de algn) **10** ~ (**against sth**) seguro (contra algo) LOC **from cover to cover** de principio a fin **to take cover (from sth)** resguardarse (de algo) **under cover of sth** al amparo de algo *Ver tb* DIVE **coverage** *n* cobertura **covering** *n* **1** envoltura **2** capa

covert /ˈkʌvət; *USA* ˈkəʊvɜːrt/ *adj* **1** secreto, encubierto **2** (*mirada*) furtivo

cover-up /ˈkʌvər ʌp/ *n* (*pey*) encubrimiento

covet /ˈkʌvət/ *vt* codiciar

cow /kaʊ/ *n* vaca ☛ *Ver nota en* CARNE

coward /ˈkaʊəd/ *n* cobarde **cowardice** *n* [*incontable*] cobardía **cowardly** *adj* cobarde

cowboy /ˈkaʊbɔɪ/ *n* **1** vaquero **2** (*GB, coloq*) pirata (*albañil, fontanero, etc*)

coy /kɔɪ/ *adj* (**coyer**, **coyest**) **1** tímido (*por coquetería*) **2** reservado

cozy /ˈkəʊzi/ *adj* (*USA*) *Ver* COSY

crab /kræb/ *n* cangrejo

crack /kræk/ ◆ *n* **1** ~ (**in sth**) grieta (en algo) **2** ~ (**in sth**) (*fig*) defecto (de algo) **3** rendija, abertura **4** chasquido, (r)estallido LOC **the crack of dawn** (*coloq*) el amanecer ◆ **1** *vt, vi* resquebrajar(se): *a cracked cup* una taza agrietada **2** *vt* ~ **sth (open)** abrir algo **3** *vi* ~ **(open)** abrirse (*rompiéndose*) **4** *vt* (*nuez*) cascar **5** *vt* ~ **sth (on/against sth)** golpear algo (contra algo) **6** *vt, vi* chascar **7** *vt* (*látigo*) restallar **8** *vi* desmoronarse **9** *vt* (*resistencia*) quebrantar **10** *vt* (*coloq*) resolver **11** *vi* (*voz*) quebrarse **12** *vt* (*coloq*) (*chiste*) contar LOC **to get cracking** (*coloq*) poner manos a la obra PHR V **to crack down (on sth/sb)** tomar medidas enérgicas (contra algo/algn) **to crack up** (*coloq*) agotarse (*física o mentalmente*)

crackdown /ˈkrækdaʊn/ *n* ~ **(on sth)** medidas enérgicas (contra algo)

cracker /ˈkrækə(r)/ *n* **1** galleta salada **2** petardo **3** (*tb* **Christmas cracker**) petardo sorpresa

crackle /ˈkrækl/ ◆ *vi* crepitar ◆ *n* (*tb* **crackling**) crujido, chisporroteo

cradle /ˈkreɪdl/ ◆ *n* (*lit y fig*) cuna ◆ *vt* acunar

craft /krɑːft; *USA* kræft/ ◆ *n* **1** artesanía: *a craft fair* una feria de artesanía **2** (*destreza*) oficio **3** embarcación ◆ *vt* fabricar artesanalmente

craftsman /ˈkrɑːftsmən; *USA* ˈkræfts-/ *n* (*pl* **-men** /-mən/) **1** artesano **2** (*fig*) artista **craftsmanship** *n* **1** artesanía **2** arte

crafty /ˈkrɑːfti; *USA* ˈkræfti/ *adj* (**-ier**, **-iest**) astuto, ladino

crag /kræg/ *n* despeñadero **craggy** *adj* escarpado

cram /kræm/ **1** *vt* ~ **A into B** atiborrar, llenar B de A; meter A en B (*a presión*) **2** *vi* ~ **into sth** meterse con dificultad en algo; abarrotar algo **3** *vi* (*coloq*) empollar

cramp /kræmp/ ◆ *n* [*incontable*] (*muscular*) **1** calambre, tirón **2 cramps** (*tb* **stomach cramps**) [*pl*] retortijones ◆ *vt* (*movimiento, desarrollo, etc*) obstaculizar **cramped** *adj* **1** (*letra*) apretado **2** (*espacio*) exiguo

crane /kreɪn/ *n* **1** (*Ornitología*) grulla **2** (*Mec*) grúa

crank /kræŋk/ *n* **1** (*Mec*) manivela **2** (*coloq*) bicho raro

crash /kræʃ/ ◆ *n* **1** estrépito **2** accidente, choque: *crash helmet* casco protector **3** (*Com*) quiebra **4** (*bolsa*) caída ◆ **1** *vt* (*coche*) tener un accidente con: *He crashed his car last Monday.* Tuvo un accidente con el coche el lunes pasado. **2** *vt, vi* ~ **(sth) (into sth)** (*vehículo*) estrellar algo/estrellarse (contra algo): *He crashed into a lamppost.* Se estrelló contra una farola. ◆ *adj* (*curso, dieta*) intensivo

crash landing *n* aterrizaje forzoso

crass /kræs/ *adj* (*pey*) **1** sumo **2** majadero

crate /kreɪt/ *n* **1** cajón **2** caja (*para botellas*)

crater /ˈkreɪtə(r)/ *n* cráter

crave /kreɪv/ **1** *vt, vi* ~ **(for) sth** anhelar algo **2** *vt* (*antic*) (*perdón*) suplicar **craving** *n* ~ **(for sth)** ansia, antojo (de algo)

crawl /krɔːl/ ◆ *vi* **1** andar a gatas, arrastrarse **2** (*tb* **to crawl along**) (*tráfico*) avanzar a paso de tortuga **3** (*coloq*) ~ **(to sb)** hacer la pelota (a algn) LOC **crawling with sth** lleno/cubierto de algo ◆ *n* **1** paso de tortuga **2** (*natación*) crol

crayon /ˈkreɪən/ *n* **1** lápiz de colores, cera (de colores) **2** (*Arte*) pastel

craze /kreɪz/ *n* moda, fiebre

crazy /ˈkreɪzi/ *adj* (**-ier**, **-iest**) (*coloq*) **1** loco **2** (*idea*) disparatado **3** *crazy paving* pavimento de piezas irregulares

creak /kriːk/ *vi* crujir, chirriar

cream[1] /kriːm/ ◆ *n* **1** nata: *cream cheese* queso para untar **2** crema, pomada **3 the cream** la flor y nata ◆ *adj, n* color crema **creamy** *adj* (**-ier**, **-iest**) cremoso

cream[2] /kriːm/ *vt* batir PHR V **to cream sth off** quedarse con lo mejor de algo

crease /kriːs/ ◆ *n* **1** arruga, pliegue **2** (*pantalón*) raya ◆ *vt, vi* arrugar(se)

create /kriˈeɪt/ *vt* crear, producir: *to create a fuss* montar un número **creation** *n* creación **creative** *adj* creativo

creator /kriːˈeɪtə(r)/ *n* creador, -ora

creature /ˈkriːtʃə(r)/ *n* criatura: *living creatures* seres vivos ◇ *a creature of habit* un animal de costumbres ◇ *creature comforts* necesidades básicas

crèche /kreʃ/ *n* (*GB*) guardería infantil

credentials /krəˈdenʃlz/ *n* [*pl*] **1** credenciales **2** (*para un trabajo*) currículo

credibility /ˌkredəˈbɪləti/ *n* credibilidad

credible /ˈkredəbl/ *adj* verosímil, creíble

credit /ˈkredɪt/ ◆ *n* **1** crédito: *on credit* a crédito ◇ *creditworthy* solvente **2** saldo positivo: *to be in credit* tener saldo positivo **3** (*contabilidad*) haber **4** mérito **5 credits** [*pl*] títulos de crédito LOC **to be a credit to sth/sb** hacer honor a algo/algn **to do sb credit** honrar a algn ◆ *vt* **1** ~ **sth/sb with sth** atribuir el mérito de algo a algo/algn **2** (*Fin*) abonar **3** creer **creditable** *adj* encomiable **creditor** *n* acreedor, -ora

creed /kriːd/ *n* credo

creek /kriːk; *USA* krɪk/ *n* **1** (*GB*) cala **2** (*USA*) riachuelo LOC **to be up the creek (without a paddle)** (*coloq*) estar apañado

creep /kriːp/ ◆ *vi* (*pret, pp* **crept**) **1** deslizarse (sigilosamente): *to creep up on sb* aproximarse sigilosamente a algn/coger desprevenido a algn **2** (*fig*): *A feeling of drowsiness crept over him.* Le invadió una sensación de sopor. **3** (*planta*) trepar ◆ *n* (*coloq*) pelota LOC **to give sb the creeps** (*coloq*) dar a algn repelús **creepy** *adj* (**-ier**, **-iest**) (*coloq*) *adj* espeluznante

cremation /krəˈmeɪʃn/ *n* incineración (*del cadáver*)

crematorium /ˌkreməˈtɔːriəm/ *n* (*pl* **-riums** *o* **-ria** /-ɔːriə/) (*USA* **crematory** /ˈkremətɔːri/) crematorio

crept *pret, pp de* CREEP

crescendo /krəˈʃendəʊ/ *n* (*pl* **~s**) **1** (*Mús*) crescendo **2** (*fig*) cúspide

crescent /ˈkresnt/ *n* **1** media luna: *a crescent moon* la media luna **2** calle en forma de media luna

cress /kres/ *n* berro

crest /krest/ *n* **1** cresta **2** (*colina*) cima **3** (*Heráldica*) blasón

crestfallen /ˈkrestfɔːlən/ *adj* cabizbajo

crevice /ˈkrevɪs/ *n* grieta (*en roca*)

crew /kruː/ *n* [*v sing o pl*] **1** tripulación: *cabin crew* tripulación (de un avión) **2** (*remo, cine*) equipo

crew-cut /ˈkruː kʌt/ *n* corte de pelo a cepillo

crib /krɪb/ ◆ *n* **1** pesebre **2** (*USA*) cuna **3** (*plagio*) copia ◆ *vt, vi* copiar, plagiar

cricket /ˈkrɪkɪt/ *n* **1** (*Zool*) grillo **2** (*Dep*) críquet **cricketer** *n* jugador, -ora (*de críquet*)

crime /kraɪm/ *n* **1** delito, crimen **2** delincuencia

criminal /ˈkrɪmɪnl/ ◆ *adj* **1** delictivo, criminal: *criminal damage* daños y perjuicios ◇ *a criminal record* antecedentes penales **2** (*derecho*) penal **3** inmoral ◆ *n* delincuente, criminal

crimson /ˈkrɪmzn/ *adj* carmesí

cringe /krɪndʒ/ *vi* **1** (*por miedo*) encogerse **2** (*fig*) morirse de vergüenza

cripple /ˈkrɪpl/ ◆ *n* inválido, -a ◆ *vt* **1**

dejar inválido **2** (*fig*) perjudicar seriamente **crippling** *adj* **1** (*enfermedad*) que deja inválido **2** (*deuda*) agobiante

crisis /ˈkraɪsɪs/ *n* (*pl* **crises** /-siːz/) crisis

crisp /krɪsp/ ◆ *adj* (**-er**, **-est**) **1** crujiente **2** (*verduras*) fresco **3** (*papel*) tieso **4** (*tiempo*) seco y frío **5** (*manera*) tajante ◆ *n* (*tb* **potato crisp**) (*USA* **potato chip**, **chip**) patata frita (*de bolsa*) ☛ *Ver dibujo en* PATATA **crisply** *adv* tajantemente **crispy** *adj* (**-ier**, **-iest**) crujiente

criterion /kraɪˈtɪəriən/ *n* (*pl* **-ria** /-rɪə/) criterio

critic /ˈkrɪtɪk/ *n* **1** detractor, -ora **2** (*cine*) crítico, -a **critical** *adj* **1** crítico: *to be critical of sth/sb* criticar algo/a algn ◊ *critical acclaim* el aplauso de la crítica **2** (*persona*) criticón **3** (*momento*) crítico, crucial **4** (*estado*) crítico **critically** *adv* **1** críticamente **2** *critically ill* gravemente enfermo

criticism /ˈkrɪtɪsɪzəm/ *n* **1** crítica **2** [*incontable*] críticas: *He can't take criticism.* No soporta que lo critiquen. **3** [*incontable*] crítica: *literary criticism* crítica literaria

criticize, -ise /ˈkrɪtɪsaɪz/ *vt* criticar

critique /krɪˈtiːk/ *n* análisis crítico

croak /krəʊk/ ◆ *vi* **1** croar **2** (*fig*) gruñir ◆ *n* (*tb* **croaking**) croar

crochet /ˈkrəʊʃeɪ; *USA* krəʊˈʃeɪ/ *n* (labor de) ganchillo

crockery /ˈkrɒkəri/ *n* [*incontable*] loza, vajilla

crocodile /ˈkrɒkədaɪl/ *n* cocodrilo

crocus /ˈkrəʊkəs/ *n* (*pl* **~es** /-siz/) azafrán

crony /ˈkrəʊni/ *n* (*pl* **-ies**) (*pey*) compinche

crook /krʊk/ *n* (*coloq*) ladrón **crooked** /ˈkrʊkɪd/ *adj* (**-er**, **-est**) **1** torcido **2** (*camino*) tortuoso **3** (*coloq*) (*persona*) deshonesto **4** (*acción*) poco limpio

crop /krɒp/ ◆ *n* **1** cosecha **2** cultivo **3** (*fig*) montón ◆ *vt* (**-pp-**) **1** (*pelo*) cortar muy corto **2** (*animales*) pacer PHR V **to crop up** surgir, aparecer

croquet /ˈkrəʊkeɪ; *USA* krəʊˈkeɪ/ *n* croquet

cross /krɒs; *USA* krɔːs/ ◆ *n* **1** cruz **2** ~ (**between ...**) cruce, mezcla (de ...) ◆ **1** *vt, vi* cruzar, atravesar: *Shall we cross over?* ¿Pasamos al otro lado? **2** *vt, vi* ~ (**each other/one another**) cruzarse **3** *v refl* ~ **yourself** santiguarse **4** *vt* llevar la contraria a **5** *vt* ~ **sth with sth** (*Zool, Bot*) cruzar algo con algo LOC **cross your fingers (for me)** deséame suerte **to cross your mind** pasar por la mente, ocurrírsele a uno *Ver tb* DOT PHR V **to cross sth off/out/through** tachar algo: *to cross sb off the list* borrar a algn de la lista ◆ *adj* (**-er**, **-est**) **1** enfadado: *to get cross* enfadarse **2** (*viento*) de costado

crossbar /ˈkrɒsbɑː(r); *USA* ˈkrɔːs-/ *n* **1** barra **2** (*Dep*) larguero

crossbow /ˈkrɒsbəʊ; *USA* ˈkrɔːs-/ *n* ballesta

cross-country /ˌkrɒs ˈkʌntri; *USA* ˌkrɔːs/ *adj, adv* campo a través

cross-examine /ˌkrɒs ɪgˈzæmɪn; *USA* ˌkrɔːs/ *vt* interrogar

cross-eyed /ˈkrɒs aɪd; *USA* ˈkrɔːs/ *adj* bizco

crossfire /ˈkrɒsfaɪə(r); *USA* ˈkrɔːs-/ *n* fuego cruzado, tiroteo (cruzado) LOC **to get caught in the crossfire** encontrarse entre dos fuegos

crossing /ˈkrɒsɪŋ; *USA* ˈkrɔːs-/ *n* **1** (*viaje*) travesía **2** (*carretera*) cruce **3** paso a nivel **4** paso para peatones *Ver* ZEBRA CROSSING **5** *border crossing* frontera

cross-legged

cross-legged

with her legs crossed

cross-legged /ˌkrɒs ˈlegd; *USA* ˌkrɔːs/ *adj, adv* con las piernas cruzadas

crossly /ˈkrɒsli/ *adv* con enfado

crossover /ˈkrɒsəʊvə(r)/ *n* paso

cross purposes *n* LOC **at cross purposes**: *We're (talking) at cross purposes.* Aquí hay un malentendido.

cross-reference /ˌkrɒs ˈrefrəns; *USA* ˌkrɔːs/ *n* referencia

crossroads /ˈkrɒsrəʊdz; *USA* ˈkrɔːs-/ *n* **1** cruce, encrucijada **2** (*fig*) encrucijada

cross-section /ˌkrɒs ˈsekʃn; *USA* ˌkrɔːs/ *n* **1** sección **2** muestra representativa

crossword /ˈkrɒswɜːd; *USA* ˈkrɔːs-/ (*tb* **crossword puzzle**) *n* crucigrama

crotch /krɒtʃ/ *n Ver* CRUTCH

crouch /kraʊtʃ/ *vi* agacharse, agazaparse, ponerse en cuclillas

crow /krəʊ/ ◆ *n* cuervo LOC **as the crow flies** en línea recta ◆ *vi* **1** cantar **2** ~ **(over sth)** jactarse (de algo)

crowbar /ˈkrəʊbɑː(r)/ *n* palanca

crowd /kraʊd/ ◆ *n* [*v sing o pl*] **1** multitud **2** (*espectadores*) concurrencia **3 the crowd** (*pey*) las masas **4** (*coloq*) gente, grupo (de amigos) LOC **crowds of/a crowd of** un montón de *Ver tb* FOLLOW ◆ *vt* (*espacio*) llenar PHR V **to crowd (a)round (sth/sb)** apiñarse (alrededor de algo/algn) **to crowd in** entrar en tropel **to crowd sth/sb in** apiñar algo/a algn **crowded** *adj* **1** lleno (de gente) **2** (*fig*) repleto

crown /kraʊn/ ◆ *n* **1** corona: *crown prince* príncipe heredero **2 the Crown** (*GB, Jur*) el estado **3** (*cabeza*) coronilla **4** (*sombrero*) copa **5** (*colina*) cumbre **6** (*diente*) corona ◆ *vt* coronar

crucial /ˈkruːʃl/ *adj* ~ **(to/for sth/sb)** crucial (para algo/algn)

crucifix /ˈkruːsəfɪks/ *n* crucifijo

crucify /ˈkruːsɪfaɪ/ *vt* (*pret, pp* **-fied**) (*lit y fig*) crucificar

crude /kruːd/ *adj* (**-er**, **-est**) **1** burdo ☛ *Comparar con* RAW **2** grosero

crude oil *n* crudo (*petróleo*)

cruel /kruːəl/ *adj* (**-ller**, **-llest**) ~ **(to sth/sb)** cruel (con algo/algn) **cruelty** *n* (*pl* **-ies**) crueldad

cruise /kruːz/ ◆ *vi* **1** hacer un crucero **2** (*avión*) volar (a velocidad de crucero) **3** (*coche*) ir a velocidad constante ◆ *n* crucero (*viaje*) **cruiser** *n* **1** (*barco*) crucero **2** (*tb* **cabin-cruiser**) lancha motora con camarotes

crumb /krʌm/ *n* **1** miga **2** (*fig*) migaja **3 crumbs!** ¡caramba!

crumble /ˈkrʌmbl/ **1** *vi* ~ **(away)** desmoronarse, deshacerse **2** *vt* deshacer **3** *vt, vi* (*Cocina*) desmenuzar(se)

crumbly *adj* (**-ier**, **-iest**) que se desmorona, que se deshace en migas

crumple /ˈkrʌmpl/ *vt, vi* ~ **(sth) (up)** arrugarse, arrugar algo

crunch /krʌntʃ/ ◆ **1** *vt* ~ **sth (up)** morder algo (*haciendo ruido*) **2** *vt, vi* (hacer) crujir ◆ *n* crujido **crunchy** *adj* (**-ier**, **-iest**) crujiente

crusade /kruːˈseɪd/ *n* cruzada **crusader** *n* **1** (*Hist*) cruzado **2** luchador, -ora

crush /krʌʃ/ ◆ *vt* **1** aplastar: *to be crushed to death* morir aplastado **2** ~ **sth (up)** (*roca, etc*) triturar algo: *crushed ice* hielo picado **3** (*ajo, etc*) majar **4** (*fruta*) exprimir **5** moler **6** (*ropa*) arrugar **7** (*ánimo*) abatir ◆ *n* **1** (*gentío*) aglomeración **2** ~ **(on sb)** (*coloq*) enamoramiento (breve) (de algn): *I had a crush on my teacher.* Me colgué de mi profesora. **3** (*fruta*) jugo **crushing** *adj* aplastante (*derrota, golpe*)

crust /krʌst/ *n* corteza ☛ *Ver dibujo en* PAN **crusty** *adj* (**-ier**, **-iest**) (de corteza) crujiente

crutch /krʌtʃ/ *n* **1** muleta **2** (*fig*) apoyo **3** (*tb* **crotch**) entrepierna

crux /krʌks/ *n* quid

cry /kraɪ/ ◆ (*pret, pp* **cried**) **1** *vi* **to cry (over sth/sb)** llorar (por algo/algn): *to cry for joy* llorar de alegría ◊ *cry-baby* llorón **2** *vt, vi* **to cry (sth) (out)** gritar (algo) LOC **it's no use crying over spilt milk** a lo hecho, pecho **to cry your eyes/heart out** llorar a lágrima viva PHR V **to cry off** echarse atrás **to cry out for sth** (*fig*) pedir algo a gritos ◆ *n* (*pl* **cries**) **1** grito **2** llorera: *to have a (good) cry* desahogarse llorando LOC *Ver* HUE **crying** *adj* LOC **a crying shame** una verdadera lástima

crypt /krɪpt/ *n* cripta

cryptic /ˈkrɪptɪk/ *adj* críptico

crystal /ˈkrɪstl/ *n* (*gen, Quím*) cristal LOC **crystal clear 1** cristalino **2** (*significado*) claro como el agua

cub /kʌb/ *n* **1** (*león, tigre, zorro*) cachorro **2** osezno **3** lobezno **4 the Cubs** [*pl*] los lobatos

cube /kjuːb/ *n* **1** cubo **2** (*esp alimento*) cubito: *sugar cube* terrón de azúcar **cubic** *adj* cúbico

cubicle /ˈkjuːbɪkl/ *n* **1** cubículo **2** probador **3** (*piscina*) vestuario **4** (*aseos*) retrete

cuckoo /ˈkʊkuː/ *n* (*pl* ~**s**) cuco

cucumber /ˈkjuːkʌmbə(r)/ *n* pepino

cuddle /ˈkʌdl/ ◆ **1** *vt* tener en brazos **2** *vt, vi* abrazar(se) PHR V **to cuddle up (to sb)** acurrucarse junto a algn ◆ *n* abrazo **cuddly** *adj* (**-ier**, **-iest**) (*aprob, coloq*) mimoso: *cuddly toy* muñeco de peluche

cue /kjuː/ ◆ *n* **1** señal **2** (*Teat*) entrada: *He missed his cue.* Perdió su entrada. **3** ejemplo: *to take your cue from sb* seguir el ejemplo de algn **4** (*tb* **billiard cue**) taco (*de billar*) LOC **(right) on cue** en el momento preciso ◆ *vt* **1 to cue sb (in)** dar la señal a algn **2 to cue sb (in)** (*Teat*) dar la entrada a algn

cuff /kʌf/ ◆ *n* **1** (*ropa*) puño **2** manotazo LOC **off the cuff** de improviso ◆ *vt* dar un manotazo a

cuff link *n* gemelo (*de camisa*)

cuisine /kwɪˈziːn/ *n* (*Fr*) cocina (*arte de cocinar*)

cul-de-sac /ˈkʌl də sæk/ *n* (*pl* ~**s**) (*Fr*) callejón sin salida

cull /kʌl/ *vt* **1** (*información*) entresacar **2** (*animales*) matar (*para controlar el número*)

culminate /ˈkʌlmɪneɪt/ *vi* (*fml*) ~ **in sth** culminar en algo **culmination** *n* culminación

culottes /kjuːˈlɒts/ *n* [*pl*] falda pantalón

culprit /ˈkʌlprɪt/ *n* culpable

cult /kʌlt/ *n* **1** ~ **(of sth/sb)** culto (a algo/algn) **2** moda

cultivate /ˈkʌltɪveɪt/ *vt* **1** cultivar **2** (*fig*) fomentar **cultivated** *adj* **1** (*persona*) culto **2** cultivado **cultivation** *n* cultivo

cultural /ˈkʌltʃərəl/ *adj* cultural

culture /ˈkʌltʃə(r)/ *n* **1** cultura: *culture shock* choque cultural **2** (*Biol, Bot*) cultivo **cultured** *adj* **1** (*persona*) culto **2** *cultured pearl* perla cultivada

cum /kʌm/ *prep*: *a kitchen-cum-dining room* una cocina-comedor

cumbersome /ˈkʌmbəsəm/ *adj* **1** engorroso **2** voluminoso

cumulative /ˈkjuːmjələtɪv; *USA* -leɪtɪv/ *adj* **1** acumulado **2** acumulativo

cunning /ˈkʌnɪŋ/ ◆ *adj* **1** (*persona, acción*) astuto **2** (*aparato*) ingenioso **3** (*USA*) (*guapo*) mono ◆ *n* [*incontable*] astucia, maña **cunningly** *adv* astutamente

cup /kʌp/ ◆ *n* **1** taza: *paper cup* vaso de papel ☛ *Ver dibujo en* MUG **2** (*premio*) copa LOC **(not) to be sb's cup of tea** (*coloq*) (no) ser plato del gusto de algn ◆ *vt* (*manos*) hacer un cuenco con, hacer bocina con: *She cupped a hand over the receiver.* Tapó el teléfono con la mano. LOC **to cup your chin/face in your hands** apoyar la barbilla/la cara en las manos

cupboard /ˈkʌbəd/ *n* armario, alacena: *cupboard love* amor interesado

Wardrobe es un armario para colgar ropa.

cupful /ˈkʌpfʊl/ *n* taza (*cantidad*)

curate /ˈkjʊərət/ *n* (*iglesia anglicana*) coadjutor, -ora (del párroco)

curative /ˈkjʊərətɪv/ *adj* curativo

curator /kjʊəˈreɪtə(r); *USA* ˈkjʊərətər/ *n* conservador, -ora (*de museo*)

curb /kɜːb/ ◆ *n* **1** (*fig*) freno **2** (*USA*) (*tb* **kerb**) bordillo (de la acera) ◆ *vt* frenar

curd /kɜːd/ *n* cuajada: *curd cheese* requesón

curdle /ˈkɜːdl/ *vt, vi* cortar(se) (*leche, etc*)

cure /kjʊə(r)/ ◆ *vt* **1** curar **2** (*fig*) sanear **3** (*alimentos*) curar ◆ *n* **1** cura, curación **2** (*fig*) remedio

curfew /ˈkɜːfjuː/ *n* toque de queda

curious /ˈkjʊəriəs/ *adj* **1** (*interesado*) curioso: *I'm curious to…* Tengo curiosidad por… **2** (*extraño*) curioso **curiosity** /ˌkjʊəriˈɒsəti/ *n* (*pl* **-ies**) **1** curiosidad **2** cosa rara

curl /kɜːl/ ◆ *n* **1** rizo **2** (*humo*) voluta ◆ **1** *vt, vi* rizar(se) **2** *vi*: *The smoke curled upwards.* El humo subía en espiral PHR V **to curl up 1** rizarse **2** acurrucarse **curly** *adj* (**-ier**, **-iest**) rizado

currant /ˈkʌrənt/ *n* **1** pasa **2** grosella (negra)

currency /ˈkʌrənsi/ *n* (*pl* **-ies**) **1** moneda: *foreign/hard currency* divisa extranjera/fuerte **2** aceptación: *to gain currency* generalizarse

current /ˈkʌrənt/ ◆ *n* corriente ◆ *adj* **1** actual: *current affairs* temas de actualidad *Ver tb* ACCOUNT **2** generalizado **currently** *adv* actualmente

curriculum /kəˈrɪkjələm/ *n* (*pl* ~**s** *o* **-la** /-lə/) plan de estudios

curry /ˈkʌri/ ◆ *n* (*pl* **-ies**) (plato al) curry ◆ *vt* (*pp* **curried**) LOC **to curry favour (with sb)** dar coba (a algn)

curse /kɜːs/ ◆ *n* **1** maldición **2** maleficio **3** desgracia **4 the curse** (*coloq*) la regla ◆ *vt, vi* maldecir LOC **to be cursed with sth** estar atribulado por algo

cursory /ˈkɜːsəri/ *adj* rápido, superficial

curt /kɜːt/ *adj* (*manera de hablar*) brusco

curtail /kɜːˈteɪl/ *vt* acortar **curtailment** *n* **1** (*poder*) limitación **2** interrupción

curtain /ˈkɜːtn/ *n* **1** cortina: *to draw the curtains* abrir/correr las cortinas ◊ *lace/net curtains* visillos **2** (*Teat*) telón **3** (*coloq*) **curtains** [*pl*] ~ **(for sth/sb)** el fin (para algo/algn)

curtsy (*tb* **curtsey**) /ˈkɜːtsi/ ◆ *vi* (*pret, pp* **curtsied** *o* **curtseyed**) (*sólo mujeres*) hacer una reverencia ◆ *n* (*pl* **-ies** *o* **-eys**) reverencia

curve /kɜːv/ ◆ *n* curva ◆ *vi* describir/hacer una curva **curved** *adj* **1** curvo **2** (*tb* **curving**) en curva, arqueado

cushion /ˈkʊʃn/ ◆ *n* **1** cojín **2** (*fig*) colchón ◆ *vt* **1** amortiguar **2** ~ **sth/sb (against sth)** (*fig*) proteger algo/a algn (de algo)

custard /ˈkʌstəd/ *n* [*incontable*] natillas

custodian /kʌˈstəʊdiən/ *n* **1** guardián, -ana **2** (*museo, etc*) conservador, -ora

custody /ˈkʌstədi/ *n* **1** custodia: *in custody* bajo custodia **2** *to remand sb in custody* ordenar la detención de algn

custom /ˈkʌstəm/ *n* **1** costumbre **2** clientela **customary** *adj* acostumbrado, habitual: *It is customary to...* Es costumbre... **customer** *n* cliente

customs /ˈkʌstəmz/ *n* [*pl*] **1** (*tb* **customs duty**) derechos de aduana **2** (*tb* **the customs**) aduana

cut /kʌt/ ◆ (**-tt-**) (*pret, pp* **cut**) **1** *vt, vi* cortar(se): *to cut sth in half* partir algo por la mitad *Ver tb* CHOP **2** *vt* (*gema*) tallar: *cut glass* cristal tallado **3** *vt* (*fig*) herir **4** *vt* reducir, recortar **5** *vt* (*precio*) rebajar *Ver tb* SLASH **6** *vt* (*suprimir*) cortar **7** *vt* (*motor*) apagar LOC **cut it/that out!** (*coloq*) ¡basta ya! **to cut it/things fine** dejar algo hasta el último momento **to cut sth short** truncar algo **to cut sth/sb short** interrumpir algo/a algn

PHR V **to cut across sth 1** rebasar algo **2** atajar por algo

to cut back (on sth) recortar algo **to cut sth back** podar algo

to cut down (on sth): *to cut down on smoking* fumar menos **to cut sth down 1** talar algo **2** reducir algo

to cut in (on sth/sb) 1 (*coche*) meterse (delante de algo/algn) **2** interrumpir (algo/a algn)

to cut sb off 1 desheredar a algn **2** (*teléf*): *I've been cut off.* Se ha cortado la línea. **to cut sth off 1** cortar algo: *to cut 20 seconds off the record* mejorar el récord en 20 segundos **2** (*pueblo*) aislar algo: *to be cut off* quedar incomunicado

to be cut out to be sth; to be cut out for sth (*coloq*) estar hecho para algo, tener madera de algo **to cut sth out 1** recortar algo **2** (*información*) suprimir algo **3** *to cut out sweets* dejar de comer dulces

to cut sth up cortar algo (en pedazos), picar algo

◆ *n* **1** corte, incisión **2** reducción, recorte, rebaja **3** (*carne*) pieza **4** (*ropa*) corte **5** (*coloq*) (*ganancias*) parte LOC **a cut above sth/sb** (*coloq*) (algo) superior a algo/algn *Ver tb* SHORT CUT

cutback /ˈkʌtbæk/ *n* recorte, reducción

cute /kjuːt/ *adj* (**cuter, cutest**) (*coloq, a veces ofen*) mono, lindo

cutlery /ˈkʌtləri/ *n* [*incontable*] cubiertos

cutlet /ˈkʌtlət/ *n* chuleta

cut-off /ˈkʌt ɒf/ (*tb* **cut-off point**) *n* límite

cut-price /ˌkʌt ˈpraɪs/ *adj, adv* a precio reducido

cut-throat /ˈkʌt θrəʊt/ *adj* despiadado

cutting /ˈkʌtɪŋ/ ◆ *n* **1** (*periódico, etc*) recorte **2** (*Bot*) esqueje ◆ *adj* **1** (*viento*) cortante **2** (*comentario*) mordaz

cyanide /ˈsaɪənaɪd/ *n* cianuro

cycle /ˈsaɪkl/ ◆ *n* **1** ciclo **2** (*obras*) serie **3** bicicleta ◆ *vi* ir en bicicleta: *to go cycling* ir de paseo en bici **cyclic** (*tb* **cyclical**) *adj* cíclico **cycling** *n* ciclismo **cyclist** *n* ciclista

cyclone /ˈsaɪkləʊn/ *n* ciclón

cylinder /ˈsɪlɪndə(r)/ *n* **1** cilindro **2** (*gas*) bombona **cylindrical** /səˈlɪndrɪkl/ *adj* cilíndrico

cymbal /ˈsɪmbl/ *n* platillo (*música*)

cynic /ˈsɪnɪk/ *n* mal pensado, -a, desconfiado, -a **cynical** *adj* **1** que desconfía de todo **2** sin escrúpulos **cynicism** *n* **1** desconfianza **2** falta de escrúpulos

cypress /ˈsaɪprəs/ *n* ciprés

cyst /sɪst/ *n* quiste

cystic fibrosis /ˌsɪstɪk faɪˈbrəʊsɪs/ *n* [*incontable*] fibrosis pulmonar

czar (*tb* **tsar**) /zɑː(r)/ *n* zar

czarina (*tb* **tsarina**) /zɑːˈriːnə/ *n* zarina

Dd

D, d /diː/ *n* (*pl* **D's, d's** /diːz/) **1** D, d: *D for David* D de dedo ☛ *Ver ejemplos en* A, a **2** (*Educ*) aprobado: *to get (a) D in Maths* sacar un aprobado en Matemáticas **3** (*Mús*) re

dab /dæb/ ◆ *vt, vi* (**-bb-**) **to dab (at) sth** tocar algo ligeramente **PHR V to dab sth on (sth)** poner un poco de algo (en algo) ◆ *n* poquito

dad /dæd/ (*tb* **daddy** /ˈdædi/) *n* (*coloq*) papá

daffodil /ˈdæfədɪl/ *n* narciso

daft /dɑːft; *USA* dæft/ *adj* (**-er**, **-est**) (*coloq*) bobo, ridículo

dagger /ˈdægə(r)/ *n* puñal, daga

daily /ˈdeɪli/ ◆ *adj* diario, cotidiano ◆ *adv* a diario, diariamente ◆ *n* (*pl* **-ies**) diario (*periódico*)

dairy /ˈdeəri/ *n* (*pl* **-ies**) lechería

dairy farm *n* vaquería **dairy farming** *n* industria lechera

dairy produce (*tb* **dairy products**) *n* productos lácteos

daisy /ˈdeɪzi/ *n* (*pl* **-ies**) margarita

dale /deɪl/ *n* valle

dam /dæm/ ◆ *n* presa (*de un río*) ◆ *vt* embalsar

damage /ˈdæmɪdʒ/ ◆ *vt* **1** dañar **2** perjudicar **3** estropear ◆ *n* **1** [*incontable*] daño **2 damages** [*pl*] daños y perjuicios **damaging** *adj* perjudicial

Dame /deɪm/ *n* (*GB*) título aristocrático concedido a mujeres

damn /dæm/ ◆ *vt* condenar ◆ (*tb* **damned**) (*coloq*) *adj* maldito ◆ **damn!** *interj* ¡mecachis! **damnation** *n* condenación **damning** *adj* contundente (*críticas, pruebas*)

damp /dæmp/ ◆ *adj* (**-er**, **-est**) húmedo ☛ *Ver nota en* MOIST ◆ *n* humedad ◆ *vt* **1** (*tb* **dampen**) mojar **2** ~ **sth (down)** amortiguar algo; sofocar algo

dance /dɑːns; *USA* dæns/ ◆ *vt, v*[...] bailar ◆ *n* baile **dancer** *n* bailarín, -in[...] **dancing** *n* baile

dandelion /ˈdændɪlaɪən/ *n* diente d[...] león

dandruff /ˈdændrʌf/ *n* caspa

danger /ˈdeɪndʒə(r)/ *n* peligro **LOC t**[...] **be in danger of sth** estar en peligro d[...] algo: *They're in danger of losing thei*[...] *jobs.* Corren el peligro de quedarse si[...] empleo. **dangerous** *adj* **1** peligroso [...] nocivo

dangle /ˈdæŋgl/ *vi* colgar

dank /dæŋk/ *adj* (**-er**, **-est**) (*pe*[...]) húmedo y frío

dare[1] /deə(r)/ *v modal, vi* (*neg* **dare no**[...] *o* **daren't** /deənt/ *o* **don't/doesn't dar**[...] *pret* **dared not** *o* **didn't dare**) (*en frase*[...] *negativas y en preguntas*) atreverse **LOC don't you dare** ni se te ocurr[...] *Don't (you) dare tell her!* ¡No se t[...] ocurra decírselo! **how dare you** ¡cómo te atreves! **I dare say** diría yo[...]

Cuando **dare** es un verbo modal [...] sigue un infinitivo sin TO, y construy[...] las oraciones negativas e interrogat[...] vas y el pasado sin el auxiliar *d*[...] *Nobody dared speak.* Nadie se atrevió [...] hablar. ◊ *I daren't ask my boss for a d*[...] *off.* No me atrevo a pedirle a mi jefe u[...] día libre.

dare[2] /deə(r)/ *vt* ~ **sb (to do sth)** des[...] fiar a algn (a hacer algo)

daring /ˈdeərɪŋ/ ◆ *n* atrevimient[...] osadía ◆ *adj* atrevido, audaz

dark /dɑːk/ ◆ **the dark** *n* la oscurida[...] **LOC before/after dark** antes/despu[...] del anochecer ◆ *adj* (**-er**, **-est**) **1** oscur[...]

to get/grow dark anochecer ◊ *dark green* verde oscuro **2** (*persona, tez*) moreno **3** secreto **4** triste, agorero: *These are dark days.* Estamos en tiempos difíciles. LOC **a dark horse** una persona de talentos ocultos

darken /ˈdɑːkən/ *vt, vi* oscurecer(se)

dark glasses *n* [*pl*] gafas oscuras

darkly /ˈdɑːkli/ *adv* **1** misteriosamente **2** con pesimismo

darkness /ˈdɑːknəs/ *n* oscuridad, tinieblas: *in darkness* a oscuras

darkroom /ˈdɑːkruːm/ *n* cuarto de revelado

darling /ˈdɑːlɪŋ/ *n* encanto: *Hello, darling!* ¡Hola, cariño!

dart[1] /dɑːt/ *n* dardo: *to play darts* jugar a los dardos

dart[2] /dɑːt/ *vi* precipitarse PHR V **to dart away/off** salir disparado

dash /dæʃ/ ◆ *n* **1** ~ (**of sth**) pizca (de algo) **2** guión ☛ *Ver* págs 318–19. **3** raya LOC **to make a dash for sth** precipitarse hacia algo *Ver tb* BOLT[2] ◆ **1** *vi* apresurarse: *I must dash.* Tengo que darme prisa. **2** *vi* ir a toda prisa: *He dashed across the room.* Cruzó la sala a toda prisa. ◊ *I dashed upstairs.* Subí las escaleras a todo correr. **3** *vt* (*esperanzas, etc*) desbaratar PHR V **to dash sth off** hacer algo a toda prisa

dashboard /ˈdæʃbɔːd/ *n* salpicadero

data /ˈdeɪtə, ˈdɑːtə; *USA* ˈdætə/ *n* **1** [*sing*] (*Informát*) datos **2** [*v sing o pl*] información

database /ˈdeɪtəbeɪs/ *n* base de datos

date[1] /deɪt/ ◆ *n* **1** fecha **2** (*coloq*) cita LOC **out of date 1** pasado de moda **2** desfasado **3** caducado **up to date 1** al día **2** actualizado **to date** hasta la fecha *Ver tb* BRING ◆ *vt* **1** fechar **2** (*fósiles, cuadros*) datar **dated** *adj* **1** pasado de moda **2** desfasado

date[2] /deɪt/ *n* dátil

daughter /ˈdɔːtə(r)/ *n* hija

daughter-in-law /ˈdɔːtər ɪn lɔː/ *n* (*pl* **-ers-in-law**) nuera

daunting /ˈdɔːntɪŋ/ *adj* sobrecogedor: *the daunting task of…* la impresionante tarea de…

dawn /dɔːn/ ◆ *n* amanecer: *from dawn till dusk* de sol a sol LOC *Ver* CRACK ◆ *vi* amanecer

day /deɪ/ *n* **1** día: *all day* todo el día **2** jornada **3 days** [*pl*] época LOC **by day/night** de día/noche **day after day** día tras día **day by day** día a día **day in, day out** todos los días sin excepción **from one day to the next** de un día para otro **one/some day**; **one of these days** algún día, un día de éstos **the day after tomorrow** pasado mañana **the day before yesterday** anteayer **these days** hoy en día **to this day** aun ahora *Ver tb* BETTER, CALL, CARRY, CLEAR, EARLY, FINE

daydream /ˈdeɪdriːm/ ◆ *n* ensueño ◆ *vi* soñar despierto

daylight /ˈdeɪlaɪt/ *n* luz del día: *in daylight* de día LOC *Ver* BROAD

day off *n* día libre

day return *n* billete de ida y vuelta para un mismo día

daytime /ˈdeɪtaɪm/ *n* día: *in the daytime* de día

day-to-day /ˌdeɪ tə ˈdeɪ/ *adj* día a día

day trip *n* excursión de un día

daze /deɪz/ *n* LOC **in a daze** aturdido **dazed** *adj* aturdido

dazzle /ˈdæzl/ *vt* deslumbrar

dead /ded/ ◆ *adj* **1** muerto **2** (*hojas*) seco **3** (*brazos, etc*) dormido **4** (*pilas*) gastado **5** (*teléfono*): *The line's gone dead.* Se ha cortado la línea. ◆ *adv* completamente: *You are dead right.* Tienes toda la razón. LOC *Ver* FLOG, DROP, STOP ◆ *n* LOC **in the/at dead of night** en plena noche **deaden** *vt* **1** (*sonido*) amortiguar **2** (*dolor*) aliviar

dead end *n* callejón sin salida

dead heat *n* empate

deadline /ˈdedlaɪn/ *n* fecha/hora límite

deadlock /ˈdedlɒk/ *n* punto muerto

deadly /ˈdedli/ *adj* (**-ier**, **-iest**) mortal LOC *Ver* EARNEST

deaf /def/ *adj* (**-er**, **-est**) sordo: *deaf and dumb* sordomudo **deafen** *vt* ensordecer **deafening** *adj* ensordecedor **deafness** *n* sordera

deal[1] /diːl/ *n* LOC **a good/great deal** mucho: *It's a good/great deal warmer today.* Hace mucho más calor hoy.

deal[2] /diːl/ *n* **1** trato **2** contrato

deal[3] /diːl/ *vt, vi* (*pret, pp* **dealt** /delt/) (*golpe, naipes*) dar PHR V **to deal in sth** comerciar en algo: *to deal in drugs/arms* traficar en drogas/armas **to deal**

with sb 1 tratar a/con algn **2** castigar a algn **3** ocuparse de algn **to deal with sth 1** (*un problema*) resolver algo **2** (*una situación*) manejar algo **3** (*un tema*) tratar de algo

dealer /ˈdiːlə(r)/ *n* **1** vendedor, -ora, comerciante **2** (*de drogas, armas*) traficante **3** (*naipes*) mano

dealing /ˈdiːlɪŋ/ *n* (*drogas, armas*) tráfico LOC **to have dealings with sth/sb** tratar con algo/algn

dealt *pret, pp de* DEAL[3]

dean /diːn/ *n* **1** deán **2** (*universidad*) decano, -a

dear /dɪə(r)/ ♦ *adj* (**-er**, **-est**) **1** querido **2** (*carta*): *Dear Sir* Muy señor mío ◊ *Dear Jason,...* Querido Jason:... ☛ *Ver* págs 314–15. **3** (*GB*) caro LOC **oh dear!** ¡vaya! ♦ *n* cariño **dearly** *adv* mucho

death /deθ/ *n* muerte: *death certificate* certificado de defunción ◊ *death penalty/sentence* pena/condena de muerte ◊ *to beat sb to death* matar a algn a palos LOC **to put sb to death** dar muerte a algn *Ver tb* CATCH, MATTER, SICK **deathly** *adj* (**-lier**, **-liest**) sepulcral: *deathly cold/pale* frío/pálido como un muerto

debase /dɪˈbeɪs/ *vt* ~ **sth/sb/yourself** degradarse/degradar algo/a algn

debatable /dɪˈbeɪtəbl/ *adj* discutible

debate /dɪˈbeɪt/ ♦ *n* debate ♦ *vt, vi* debatir

debit /ˈdebɪt/ ♦ *n* débito ♦ *vt* cobrar

debris /ˈdeɪbriː; *USA* dəˈbriː/ *n* escombros

debt /det/ *n* deuda LOC **to be in debt** tener deudas **debtor** *n* deudor, -ora

decade /ˈdekeɪd; *USA* diˈkeɪd/ *n* década

decadent /ˈdekədənt/ *adj* decadente **decadence** *n* decadencia

decaffeinated /ˌdiːˈkæfɪneɪtɪd/ *adj* descafeinado

decay /dɪˈkeɪ/ ♦ *vi* **1** (*dientes*) picarse **2** descomponerse **3** decaer ♦ *n* [*incontable*] **1** (*tb* **tooth decay**) caries **2** descomposición

deceased /dɪˈsiːst/ ♦ *adj* (*fml*) difunto ♦ **the deceased** *n* el difunto, la difunta

deceit /dɪˈsiːt/ *n* **1** (*doblez*) falsedad **2** engaño **deceitful** *adj* **1** mentiroso **2** engañoso

deceive /dɪˈsiːv/ *vt* engañar

December /dɪˈsembə(r)/ *n* (*abrev* **Dec**) diciembre ☛ *Ver nota y ejemplos en* JANUARY

decency /ˈdiːsnsi/ *n* decencia, decoro

decent /ˈdiːsnt/ *adj* **1** decente, correcto **2** adecuado, aceptable **3** amable

deception /dɪˈsepʃn/ *n* engaño

deceptive /dɪˈseptɪv/ *adj* engañoso

decide /dɪˈsaɪd/ **1** *vi* ~ (**against sth/sb**) decidirse (en contra de algo/algn) **2** *vi* ~ **on sth/sb** optar por algo/algn **3** *vt* decidir, determinar **decided** *adj* **1** (*claro*) marcado **2** ~ (**about sth**) decidido, resuelto (en algo)

decimal /ˈdesɪml/ *adj, n* decimal: *decimal point* coma decimal

decipher /dɪˈsaɪfə(r)/ *vt* descifrar

decision /dɪˈsɪʒn/ *n* ~ (**on/against sth**) decisión (sobre/en contra de algo): *decision-making* toma de decisiones

decisive /dɪˈsaɪsɪv/ *adj* **1** decisivo **2** decidido, resuelto

deck /dek/ *n* **1** (*Náut*) cubierta **2** (*autobús*) piso **3** (*USA*) baraja **4** (*tb* **cassette deck**, **tape deck**) pletina

deckchair /ˈdektʃeə(r)/ *n* tumbona

declaration /ˌdekləˈreɪʃn/ *n* declaración

declare /dɪˈkleə(r)/ **1** *vt* declarar **2** *vi* ~ **for/against sth/sb** pronunciarse a favor/en contra de algo/algn

decline /dɪˈklaɪn/ ♦ **1** *vt* declinar **2** *vi* ~ **to do sth** negarse a hacer algo **3** *vi* disminuir ♦ *n* **1** disminución **2** decadencia, deterioro

decompose /ˌdiːkəmˈpəʊz/ *vt, vi* descomponer(se), pudrir(se)

décor /ˈdeɪkɔː(r); *USA* deɪˈkɔːr/ *n* [*incontable*] decoración

decorate /ˈdekəreɪt/ *vt* **1** ~ **sth** (**with sth**) adornar algo (con/de algo) **2** empapelar, pintar **3** ~ **sb** (**for sth**) condecorar a algn (por algo) **decoration** *n* **1** decoración **2** adorno **3** condecoración

decorative /ˈdekərətɪv; *USA* ˈdekəreɪtɪv/ *adj* decorativo

decoy /ˈdiːkɔɪ/ *n* señuelo

decrease /dɪˈkriːs/ ♦ **1** *vi* disminuir **2** *vt* reducir ♦ /ˈdiːkriːs/ *n* ~ (**in sth**) disminución, reducción (en/de algo)

decree /dɪˈkriː/ ♦ *n* decreto ♦ *vt* (*pret, pp* **decreed**) decretar

decrepit /dɪˈkrepɪt/ *adj* decrépito

dedicate /ˈdedɪkeɪt/ *vt* dedicar, consagrar **dedication** *n* **1** dedicación **2** dedicatoria

deduce /dɪˈdjuːs; *USA* dɪˈduːs/ *vt* deducir (*teoría, conclusión, etc*)

deduct /dɪˈdʌkt/ *vt* deducir (*impuestos, gastos, etc*) **deduction** *n* deducción

deed /diːd/ *n* **1** (*fml*) acción, obra **2** hazaña **3** (*Jur*) escritura

deem /diːm/ *vt* (*fml*) considerar

deep /diːp/ ◆ *adj* (**-er**, **-est**) **1** profundo **2** de profundidad: *This pool is only one metre deep.* Esta piscina sólo tiene un metro de profundidad. **3** (*respiración*) hondo **4** (*voz, sonido, etc*) grave **5** (*color*) intenso **6** ~ **in sth** sumido, absorto en algo ◆ *adv* (**-er**, **-est**) muy profundo, con profundidad: *Don't go in too deep!* ¡No te metas muy adentro! LOC **deep down** (*coloq*) en el fondo **to go/run deep** estar muy arraigado **deeply** *adv* profundamente, a fondo, muchísimo

deepen /ˈdiːpən/ *vt, vi* hacer(se) más profundo, aumentar

deep-freeze /ˌdiːp ˈfriːz/ *n* *Ver* FREEZER

deer /dɪə(r)/ *n* (*pl* **deer**) ciervo ☛ *Ver nota en* CIERVO

default /dɪˈfɔːlt/ ◆ *n* **1** incumplimiento **2** incomparecencia LOC **by default** por incomparecencia ◆ *vi* **1** no comparecer **2** ~ (**on sth**) dejar incumplido (algo) ◆ *adj* (*Informát*) por defecto

defeat /dɪˈfiːt/ ◆ *vt* **1** derrotar **2** (*fig*) frustar ◆ *n* derrota: *to admit/accept defeat* darse por vencido

defect[1] /dɪˈfekt/ *vi* **1** ~ (**from sth**) desertar (de algo) **2** ~ **to sth** pasarse a algo **defection** *n* **1** deserción **2** exilio **defector** *n* desertor, -ora

defect[2] /ˈdiːfekt, dɪˈfekt/ *n* defecto ☛ *Ver nota en* MISTAKE **defective** /dɪˈfektɪv/ *adj* defectuoso

defence (*USA* **defense**) /dɪˈfens/ *n* **1** ~ (**of sth**) (**against sth**) defensa (de algo) (contra algo) **2 the defence** [*v sing o pl*] (*juicio*) la defensa **defenceless** *adj* indefenso **defend** /dɪˈfend/ *vt* ~ **sth/sb** (**against/from sth/sb**) defender, proteger algo/a algn (de algo/algn) **defendant** *n* acusado, -a, inculpado, -a ☛ *Comparar con* PLAINTIFF **defensive** /dɪˈfensɪv/ *adj* ~ (**about sth**) a la defensiva (sobre algo) LOC **to put sb/to be on the defensive** poner a algn/estar a la defensiva

defer /dɪˈfɜː(r)/ *vt* (**-rr-**) ~ **sth to sth** posponer algo para algo **deference** /ˈdefərəns/ *n* deferencia, respeto LOC **in deference to sth/sb** por deferencia a algo/algn

defiance /dɪˈfaɪəns/ *n* desafío, desobediencia **defiant** *adj* desafiante

deficiency /dɪˈfɪʃnsi/ *n* (*pl* **-ies**) deficiencia **deficient** *adj* ~ (**in sth**) deficiente (en algo)

define /dɪˈfaɪn/ *vt* ~ **sth** (**as sth**) definir algo (como algo)

definite /ˈdefɪnət/ *adj* **1** definitivo, concreto **2** ~ (**about sth/that…**) seguro (sobre algo/de que…) **3** definido: *definite article* artículo definido **definitely** *adv* **1** definitivamente **2** sin duda alguna

definition /ˌdefɪˈnɪʃn/ *n* definición

definitive /dɪˈfɪnətɪv/ *adj* definitivo, determinante

deflate /diːˈfleɪt/ *vt, vi* deshinchar(se), desinflar(se)

deflect /dɪˈflekt/ *vt* ~ **sth** (**from sth**) desviar algo (de algo)

deform /dɪˈfɔːm/ *vt* deformar **deformed** *adj* deforme **deformity** *n* (*pl* **-ies**) deformidad

defrost /ˌdiːˈfrɒst; *USA* ˌdiːˈfrɔːst/ *vt* descongelar

deft /deft/ *adj* hábil

defunct /dɪˈfʌŋkt/ *adj* (*fml*) muerto, fenecido

defuse /ˌdiːˈfjuːz/ *vt* **1** (*bomba*) desactivar **2** (*tensión, crisis*) atenuar

defy /dɪˈfaɪ/ *vt* (*pret, pp* **defied**) **1** desafiar **2** ~ **sb to do sth** retar, desafiar a algn a que haga algo

degenerate /dɪˈdʒenəreɪt/ *vi* ~ (**from sth**) (**into sth**) degenerar (de algo) (a algo) **degeneration** *n* degeneración

degrade /dɪˈgreɪd/ *vt* degradar **degradation** *n* degradación

degree /dɪˈgriː/ *n* **1** grado **2** título: *a university degree* un título universitario ◇ *to choose a degree course* escoger una carrera LOC **by degrees** poco a poco

deity /ˈdeɪəti/ *n* (*pl* **-ies**) deidad

dejected /dɪˈdʒektɪd/ *adj* desanimado

delay /dɪˈleɪ/ ◆ **1** *vt* retrasar: *The train was delayed.* El tren se retrasó.

☛ *Comparar con* LATE **2** *vi* esperar, tardar: *Don't delay!* ¡No esperes! **3** *vt* aplazar: *delayed action* de acción retardada ◆ *n* retraso **delaying** *adj* dilatorio: *delaying tactics* tácticas de distracción

delegate /ˈdelɪgət/ ◆ *n* delegado ◆ /ˈdelɪgeɪt/ *vt* ~ **sth** (**to sb**) encomendar algo (a algn) **delegation** *n* [*v sing o pl*] delegación

delete /dɪˈliːt/ *vt* borrar, tachar **deletion** *n* borrado, eliminación

deliberate¹ /dɪˈlɪbərət/ *adj* deliberado

deliberate² /dɪˈlɪbəreɪt/ *vi* ~ (**about/on sth**) (*fml*) deliberar (sobre algo) **deliberation** *n* [*gen pl*] deliberación

delicacy /ˈdelɪkəsi/ *n* (*pl* **-ies**) **1** delicadeza **2** manjar

delicate /ˈdelɪkət/ *adj* delicado: *delicate china* porcelana fina ◊ *a delicate colour* un color suave ◊ *a delicate flavour* un exquisito sabor

delicatessen /ˌdelɪkəˈtesn/ *n* charcutería (*especializada en productos importados*)

delicious /dɪˈlɪʃəs/ *adj* delicioso

delight¹ /dɪˈlaɪt/ *n* deleite: *the delights of travelling* el placer de viajar LOC **to take delight in** (**doing**) **sth 1** deleitarse en (hacer) algo **2** (*pey*) regodearse en (hacer) algo

delight² /dɪˈlaɪt/ **1** *vt* encantar **2** *vi* ~ **in** (**doing**) **sth** regodearse en algo/haciendo algo **delighted** *adj* **1** ~ (**at/with sth**) encantado (con algo) **2** ~ (**to do sth/that...**) encantado (de hacer algo/de que...)

delightful /dɪˈlaɪtfl/ *adj* encantador

delinquent /dɪˈlɪŋkwənt/ *adj*, *n* delincuente **delinquency** *n* delincuencia

delirious /dɪˈlɪriəs/ *adj* delirante: *delirious with joy* loco de contento **delirium** *n* delirio

deliver /dɪˈlɪvə(r)/ *vt* **1** (*correo, géneros*) repartir **2** (*recado*) comunicar **3** (*discurso*) pronunciar **4** (*Med*) asistir a un parto **5** (*golpe*) dar **delivery** *n* (*pl* **-ies**) **1** reparto **2** entrega **3** parto LOC *Ver* CASH

delta /ˈdeltə/ *n* delta

delude /dɪˈluːd/ *vt* engañar

deluge /ˈdeljuːdʒ/ ◆ *n* (*fml*) **1** tromba de agua **2** (*fig*) lluvia ◆ *vt* ~ **sth/sb** (**with sth**) inundar algo/a algn (de algo)

delusion /dɪˈluːʒn/ *n* engaño, espejismo

de luxe /də ˈlʌks, -ˈlʊks/ *adj* de lujo

demand /dɪˈmɑːnd; *USA* dɪˈmænd/ ◆ *n* **1** ~ (**for sb to do sth**) exigencia (de que algn haga algo) **2** ~ (**that...**) exigencia (de que...) **3** ~ (**for sth/sb**) demanda (de algo/algn) LOC **in demand** solicitado **on demand** a petición *Ver tb* SUPPLY ◆ *vt* **1** exigir **2** requerir **demanding** *adj* exigente

demise /dɪˈmaɪz/ *n* (*fml*) fallecimiento: *the demise of the business* el fracaso del negocio

demo /ˈdeməʊ/ *n* (*pl* ~**s**) (*coloq*) manifestación

democracy /dɪˈmɒkrəsi/ *n* (*pl* **-ies**) democracia **democrat** /ˈdeməkræt/ *n* demócrata **democratic** /ˌdeməˈkrætɪk/ *adj* democrático

demographic /ˌdeməˈgræfɪk/ *adj* demográfico

demolish /dɪˈmɒlɪʃ/ *vt* derribar **demolition** *n* demolición

demon /ˈdiːmən/ *n* demonio **demonic** *adj* diabólico

demonstrate /ˈdemənstreɪt/ **1** *vt* demostrar **2** *vi* ~ (**against/in favour of sth/sb**) manifestarse (en contra/a favor de algo/algn) **demonstration** *n* **1** demostración **2** ~ (**against/in favour of sth/sb**) manifestación (en contra/a favor de algo/algn)

demonstrative /dɪˈmɒnstrətɪv/ *adj* **1** cariñoso **2** (*Gram*) demostrativo

demonstrator /ˈdemənstreɪtə(r)/ *n* manifestante

demoralize, -ise /dɪˈmɒrəlaɪz; *USA* -ˈmɔːr-/ *vt* desmoralizar

demure /dɪˈmjʊə(r)/ *adj* recatado

den /den/ *n* guarida

denial /dɪˈnaɪəl/ *n* **1** ~ (**that.../of sth**) negación (de que.../de algo) **2** ~ **of sth** denegación, rechazo

denim /ˈdenɪm/ *n* tela vaquera

denomination /dɪˌnɒmɪˈneɪʃn/ *n* secta

denounce /dɪˈnaʊns/ *vt* ~ **sth/sb** (**to sb**) (**as sth**) denunciar algo/a algn (a algn) (como algo): *An informer denounced him to the police (as a terrorist).* Un delator lo denunció a la policía (como terrorista).

dense /dens/ *adj* (**-er**, **-est**) denso **density** *n* (*pl* **-ies**) densidad

dent /dent/ ◆ *n* abolladura ◆ *vt, vi* abollar(se)

dental /ˈdentl/ *adj* dental

dentist /ˈdentɪst/ *n* dentista

denunciation /dɪˌnʌnsiˈeɪʃn/ *n* denuncia

deny /dɪˈnaɪ/ *vt* (*pret, pp* **denied**) **1** negar **2** (*verdad*) desmentir

deodorant /diˈəʊdərənt/ *n* desodorante

depart /dɪˈpɑːt/ *vi* (*fml*) ~ (**for...**) (**from...**) salir (hacia...) (de...)

department /dɪˈpɑːtmənt/ *n* (*abrev* **Dept**) **1** departamento, sección **2** ministerio **departmental** /ˌdiːpɑːtˈmentl/ *adj* de departamento

department store *n* grandes almacenes

departure /dɪˈpɑːtʃə(r)/ *n* **1** ~ (**from...**) partida (de...) **2** (*de avión, tren*) salida

depend /dɪˈpend/ *vi* LOC **that depends; it (all) depends** depende PHR V **to depend on/upon sth/sb 1** contar con algo/algn **2** confiar en algo/algn **to depend on sth/sb** (**for sth**) depender de algo/algn (para algo) **dependable** *adj* fiable

dependant (*esp USA* **-ent**) /dɪˈpendənt/ *n* persona bajo el cargo de otra **dependence** *n* ~ (**on/upon sth/sb**) dependencia (de algo/algn) **dependent** *adj* **1 to be ~ on/upon sth/sb** depender de algo/algn **2** (*persona*) poco independiente

depict /dɪˈpɪkt/ *vt* representar

depleted /dɪˈpliːtɪd/ *adj* reducido

deplore /dɪˈplɔː(r)/ *vt* **1** condenar **2** lamentar

deploy /dɪˈplɔɪ/ *vt, vi* desplegar(se)

deport /dɪˈpɔːt/ *vt* deportar **deportation** *n* deportación

depose /dɪˈpəʊz/ *vt* destituir, deponer

deposit /dɪˈpɒzɪt/ ◆ *vt* **1** (*dinero*) ingresar, imponer **2 ~ sth** (**with sb**) (*bienes*) dejar algo (a cargo de algn) ◆ *n* **1** (*Fin*) depósito: *deposit account* cuenta a plazo fijo **2** ingreso, imposición: *safety deposit box* caja de seguridad **3** (*alquiler*) fianza **4** ~ (**on sth**) señal, desembolso inicial (para algo) **5** depósito, sedimento

depot /ˈdepəʊ; *USA* ˈdiːpəʊ/ *n* **1** depósito, almacén **2** (*para vehículos*) parque **3** (*USA*) estación (*de tren o de autobuses*)

depress /dɪˈpres/ *vt* deprimir **depression** *n* depresión

deprive /dɪˈpraɪv/ *vt* ~ **sth/sb of sth** privar algo/a algn de algo **deprived** *adj* necesitado

deprivation /deprɪˈveɪʃn/ *n* pobreza, privación

depth /depθ/ *n* profundidad LOC **in depth** a fondo, en profundidad

deputation /ˌdepjuˈteɪʃn/ *n* [*v sing o pl*] delegación

deputize, -ise /ˈdepjətaiz/ *vi* ~ (**for sb**) sustituir a algn

deputy /ˈdepjəti/ *n* (*pl* **-ies**) **1** sustituto, -a, suplente: *deputy chairman* vicepresidente **2** (*Pol*) diputado, -a

deranged /dɪˈreɪndʒd/ *adj* trastornado, loco

deregulation /ˌdiːregjʊˈleɪʃn/ *vt* liberalización (*ventas, servicios, etc*)

derelict /ˈderəlɪkt/ *adj* abandonado (*edificio*)

deride /dɪˈraɪd/ *vt* ridiculizar, mofarse de

derision /dɪˈrɪʒn/ *n* mofa(s) **derisive** /dɪˈraɪsɪv/ *adj* burlón **derisory** /dɪˈraɪsəri/ *adj* irrisorio

derivation /ˌderɪˈveɪʃn/ *n* derivación **derivative** *n* derivado

derive /dɪˈraɪv/ **1** *vt* ~ **sth from sth** obtener, sacar algo de algo: *to derive comfort from sth* hallar consuelo en algo **2** *vt, vi* ~ **from sth** derivar de algo

derogatory /dɪˈrɒgətri; *USA* -tɔːri/ *adj* despectivo

descend /dɪˈsend/ *vt, vi* (*fml*) descender **descendant** *n* descendiente

descent /dɪˈsent/ *n* **1** descenso **2** ascendencia

describe /dɪˈskraɪb/ *vt* ~ **sth/sb** (**as sth**) describir algo/a algn (como algo) **description** *n* descripción

desert[1] /ˈdezət/ *n* desierto

desert[2] /dɪˈzɜːt/ **1** *vt* ~ **sth/sb** abandonar algo/a algn **2** *vi* (*Mil*) desertar **deserted** *adj* desierto **deserter** *n* desertor, -ora

deserve /dɪˈzɜːv/ *vt* merecer LOC *Ver* RICHLY *en* RICH **deserving** *adj* digno

design /dɪˈzaɪn/ ◆ *n* **1** ~ (**for/of sth**) diseño (de algo) **2** plan **3** dibujo ◆ *vt* diseñar

designate /ˈdezɪgneɪt/ *vt* **1** ~ **sth/sb** (**as**) **sth** (*fml*) designar algo/a algn algo **2** nombrar

designer /dɪˈzamə(r)/ *n* diseñador, -ora

desirable /dɪˈzaɪərəbl/ *adj* deseable

desire /dɪˈzaɪə(r)/ ◆ *n* **1** ~ (**for sth/sb**) deseo (de/por algo/algn) **2** ~ (**to do sth**) deseo (de hacer algo) **3** ~ (**for sth/to do sth**) ansias (de algo/de hacer algo): *He had no desire to see her.* No sentía ninguna gana de verla. ◆ *vt* desear

desk /desk/ *n* mesa (*de trabajo*)

desktop /ˈdesktɒp/ *adj*: *a desktop computer* un ordenador personal ◊ *desktop publishing* tratamiento de textos avanzado

desolate /ˈdesələt/ *adj* **1** (*paisaje*) desolado, desierto **2** (*futuro*) desolador **desolation** *n* **1** desolación **2** desconsuelo

despair /dɪˈspeə(r)/ ◆ *vi* (*fml*) ~ (**of sth/doing sth**) perder las esperanzas (de algo/de hacer algo) ◆ *n* desesperación **despairing** *adj* desesperado

despatch /dɪˈspætʃ/ *n, vt Ver* DISPATCH

desperate /ˈdespərət/ *adj* desesperado

despicable /dɪˈspɪkəbl/ *adj* despreciable

despise /dɪˈspaɪz/ *vt* despreciar

despite /dɪˈspaɪt/ *prep* a pesar de

despondent /dɪˈspɒndənt/ *adj* abatido, desalentado

despot /ˈdespɒt/ *n* déspota

dessert /dɪˈzɜːt/ (*tb* **sweet**) *n* postre ☛ La palabra más normal es **pudding**.

dessertspoon /dɪˈzɜːtspuːn/ *n* **1** cuchara de postre **2** (*tb* **dessertspoonful**) cucharada (*de postre*)

destination /ˌdestɪˈneɪʃn/ *n* destino (*de avión, barco, etc*)

destined /ˈdestɪnd/ *adj* (*fml*) destinado: *It was destined to fail.* Estaba condenado a fracasar.

destiny /ˈdestəni/ *n* (*pl* **-ies**) destino (*hado*)

destitute /ˈdestɪtjuːt; *USA* -tuːt/ *adj* indigente

destroy /dɪˈstrɔɪ/ *vt* destruir **destroyer** *n* destructor

destruction /dɪˈstrʌkʃn/ *n* destrucción **destructive** *adj* destructivo

detach /dɪˈtætʃ/ *vt* ~ **sth** (**from sth**) separar algo (de algo) **detachable** *adj* que se puede separar

detached /dɪˈtætʃd/ *adj* **1** imparcial **2** (*vivienda*) no unido a otra casa: *detached house* chalé ☛ *Comparar con* SEMI-DETACHED *y ver* pág 321.

detachment /dɪˈtætʃmənt/ *n* **1** imparcialidad **2** (*Mil*) destacamento

detail /ˈdiːteɪl; *USA* dɪˈteɪl/ ◆ *n* detalle, pormenor LOC **in detail** en detalle, detalladamente **to go into detail(s)** entrar en detalles ◆ *vt* detallar **detailed** *adj* detallado

detain /dɪˈteɪn/ *vt* retener **detainee** *n* detenido, -a

detect /dɪˈtekt/ *vt* **1** detectar **2** (*fraude*) descubrir **detectable** *adj* detectable **detection** *n* descubrimiento: *to escape detection* pasar inadvertido/desapercibido

detective /dɪˈtektɪv/ *n* detective, policía de paisano: *detective story* novela policiaca

detention /dɪˈtenʃn/ *n* retención: *detention centre* centro de detención preventiva

deter /dɪˈtɜː(r)/ *vt* (**-rr-**) ~ **sb** (**from doing sth**) disuadir a algn (de hacer algo)

detergent /dɪˈtɜːdʒənt/ *adj, n* detergente

deteriorate /dɪˈtiərɪəreɪt/ *vi* deteriorarse, empeorar **deterioration** *n* deterioro

determination /dɪˌtɜːmɪˈneɪʃn/ *n* determinación

determine /dɪˈtɜːmɪn/ *vt* determinar, decidir: *determining factor* factor determinante ◊ *to determine the cause of an accident* determinar la causa de un accidente **determined** *adj* ~ (**to do sth**) resuelto (a hacer algo)

determiner /dɪˈtɜːmɪnə(r)/ *n* (*Gram*) determinante

deterrent /dɪˈterənt; *USA* -ˈtɜː-/ *n* **1** escarmiento **2** argumento disuasorio **3** (*Mil*) fuerza disuasoria: *nuclear deterrent* fuerza disuasoria nuclear

detest /dɪˈtest/ *vt* detestar *Ver tb* HATE

detonate /ˈdetəneɪt/ *vt, vi* detonar

detour /ˈdiːtʊə(r); *USA* dɪˈtʊər/ *n* desvío ☛ *Comparar con* DIVERSION

detract /dɪˈtrækt/ *vi* ~ **from sth** restar mérito a algo: *The incident detracted from our enjoyment of the evening.* El incidente le restó placer a nuestra velada.

detriment /ˈdetrɪmənt/ *n* LOC **to the**

detriment of sth/sb en detrimento de algo/algn **detrimental** /ˌdetrɪˈmentl/ *adj* ~ (**to sth/sb**) perjudicial (para/a algo/algn)

devalue /ˌdiːˈvæljuː/ *vt, vi* devaluar(se) **devaluation** *n* devaluación

devastate /ˈdevəsteɪt/ *vt* **1** devastar, asolar **2** (*persona*) desolar, destrozar **devastating** *adj* **1** devastador **2** desastroso **devastation** *n* devastación

develop /dɪˈveləp/ **1** *vt, vi* desarrollar(se) **2** *vt* (*plan, estrategia*) elaborar **3** *vt, vi* (*Fot*) revelar(se) **4** *vt* (*terreno*) urbanizar, construir en **developed** *adj* desarrollado **developer** *n* promotor, -ora **developing** *adj* en (vías de) desarrollo

development /dɪˈveləpmənt/ *n* **1** desarrollo, evolución: *development area* polo de desarrollo ◊ *There has been a new development.* Ha cambiado la situación. **2** (*de terrenos*) urbanización **3** (*tb* **developing**) (*Fot*) revelado

deviant /ˈdiːviənt/ *adj, n* **1** desviado, -a **2** (*sexual*) pervertido, -a

deviate /ˈdiːvieɪt/ *vi* ~ (**from sth**) desviarse (de algo) **deviation** *n* ~ (**from sth**) desviación (de algo)

device /dɪˈvaɪs/ *n* **1** aparato, dispositivo, mecanismo: *explosive device* artefacto explosivo ◊ *nuclear device* ingenio nuclear **2** (*plan*) ardid, estratagema LOC *Ver* LEAVE

devil /ˈdevl/ *n* demonio, diablo: *You lucky devil!* ¡Tienes una suerte del diablo!

devious /ˈdiːviəs/ *adj* **1** enrevesado, intrincado **2** (*método, persona*) poco escrupuloso

devise /dɪˈvaɪz/ *vt* idear, elaborar

devoid /dɪˈvɔɪd/ *adj* ~ **of sth** desprovisto, exento de algo

devolution /ˌdiːvəˈluːʃn; *USA* ˌdev-/ *n* **1** descentralización **2** (*de poderes*) delegación

devote /dɪˈvəʊt/ **1** *v refl* ~ **yourself to sth/sb** dedicarse a algo/algn **2** *vt* ~ **sth to sth/sb** dedicar algo a algo/algn **3** *vt* ~ **sth to sth** (*recursos*) destinar algo a algo **devoted** *adj* ~ (**to sth/sb**) fiel, leal (a algo/algn): *They're devoted to each other.* Están entregados el uno al otro.

devotee /ˌdevəˈtiː/ *n* devoto, -a

devotion /dɪˈvəʊʃn/ *n* ~ (**to sth/sb**) devoción (por/a algo/algn)

devour /dɪˈvaʊə(r)/ *vt* devorar

devout /dɪˈvaʊt/ *adj* **1** devoto, piadoso **2** (*esperanza, deseo*) sincero **devoutly** *adv* **1** piadosamente, con devoción **2** sinceramente

dew /djuː; *USA* duː/ *n* rocío

dexterity /dekˈsterəti/ *n* destreza

diabetes /ˌdaɪəˈbiːtiːz/ *n* [*incontable*] diabetes **diabetic** *adj, n* diabético, -a

diabolic /ˌdaɪəˈbɒlɪk/ (*tb* **diabolical**) *adj* diabólico

diagnose /ˈdaɪəgnəʊz; *USA* ˌdaɪəgˈnəʊs/ *vt* ~ **sth** (**as sth**) diagnosticar: *I've been diagnosed as having hepatitis.* Me han diagnosticado una hepatitis. **diagnosis** /ˌdaɪəgˈnəʊsɪs/ *n* (*pl* **-oses** /-ˈnəʊsiːz/) diagnóstico **diagnostic** *adj* diagnóstico

diagonal /daɪˈægənl/ *adj, n* diagonal **diagonally** *adv* diagonalmente

diagram /ˈdaɪəgræm/ *n* diagrama

dial /ˈdaɪəl/ ◆ *n* **1** (*instrumento*) indicador **2** (*teléfono*) disco **3** (*reloj*) esfera ◆ *vt* (**-ll-**, *USA* **-l-**) marcar: *to dial a wrong number* marcar un número equivocado

dialect /ˈdaɪəlekt/ *n* dialecto

dialling code *n* prefijo

dialling tone *n* tono de marcar

dialogue (*USA tb* **dialog**) /ˈdaɪəlɒg; *USA* -lɔːg/ *n* diálogo

diameter /daɪˈæmɪtə(r)/ *n* diámetro: *It is 15cm in diameter.* Tiene 15cm de diámetro.

diamond /ˈdaɪəmənd/ *n* **1** diamante **2** rombo **3** *diamond jubilee* sexagésimo aniversario **4 diamonds** [*pl*] (*en cartas*) diamantes ☛ *Ver nota en* BARAJA

diaphragm /ˈdaɪəfræm/ *n* diafragma

diarrhoea (*USA* **diarrhea**) /ˌdaɪəˈrɪə/ *n* [*incontable*] diarrea

diary /ˈdaɪəri/ *n* (*pl* **-ies**) **1** diario **2** agenda

dice[1] /daɪs/ *n* (*pl* **dice**) dado: *to roll/throw the dice* tirar/lanzar los dados ◊ *to play dice* jugar a los dados

dice[2] /daɪs/ *vt* cortar en trozos

dictate /dɪkˈteɪt; *USA* ˈdɪkteɪt/ *vt, vi* ~ (**sth**) (**to sb**) dictar (algo) (a algn) PHR V **to dictate to sb**: *You can't dictate to your children how to run their lives.* No puedes decirles a tus hijos cómo vivir su vida. **dictation** *n* dictado

dictator /dɪkˈteɪtə(r); *USA* ˈdɪkteɪtər/ *n* dictador **dictatorship** *n* dictadura

dictionary /ˈdɪkʃənri; *USA* -neri/ *n* (*pl* **-ies**) diccionario

did *pret de* DO

didactic /daɪˈdæktɪk/ *adj* (*fml, a veces pey*) didáctico

didn't /ˈdɪd(ə)nt/ = DID NOT *Ver* DO

die /daɪ/ *vi* (*pret, pp* **died** *pt pres* **dying**) (*lit y fig*) morir: *to die of/from sth* morir de algo **LOC to be dying for sth/to do sth** morirse por algo/por hacer algo **PHR V to die away 1** disminuir poco a poco hasta desaparecer **2** (*ruido*) alejarse hasta perderse **to die down 1** apagarse gradualmente, disminuir **2** (*viento*) amainar **to die off** morir uno tras otro **to die out 1** (*Zool*) extinguirse **2** (*tradiciones*) desaparecer

diesel /ˈdiːzl/ *n* diesel: *diesel fuel/oil* gasóleo

diet /ˈdaɪət/ ◆ *n* dieta, régimen ☛ *Comparar con* REGIME **LOC to be/go on a diet** estar/ponerse a régimen ☛ *Ver nota en* LOW-CALORIE ◆ *vi* estar/ponerse a régimen **dietary** *adj* dietético

differ /ˈdɪfə(r)/ *vi* **1** ~ (**from sth/sb**) ser diferente de algo/algn **2** ~ (**with sb**) (**about/on sth**) no estar de acuerdo (con algn) (sobre/en algo)

difference /ˈdɪfrəns/ *n* diferencia: *to make up the difference (in price)* poner la diferencia (en el precio) ◊ *a difference of opinion* una desavenencia **LOC it makes all the difference** lo cambia todo **it makes no difference** da lo mismo **what difference does it make?** ¿qué más da?

different /ˈdɪfrənt/ *adj* **1** ~ (**from sth/sb**) diferente, distinto (a/de algo/algn) **2** ~ (**than sth/sb**) (*USA*) diferente, distinto (a/de algo/algn) **differently** *adv* de otra manera, de distinta manera

differentiate /ˌdɪfəˈrenʃieɪt/ *vt, vi* ~ **between A and B**; ~ **A from B** distinguir, diferenciar entre A y B; A de B **differentiation** *n* diferenciación

difficult /ˈdɪfɪkəlt/ *adj* difícil **difficulty** *n* (*pl* **-ies**) **1** dificultad: *with great difficulty* a duras penas **2** (*situación difícil*) apuro, aprieto: *to get/run into difficulties* verse en un apuro/encontrarse en apuros ◊ *to make difficulties for sb* poner obstáculos a algn

diffident /ˈdɪfɪdənt/ *adj* que tiene poca confianza en sí mismo **diffidence** *n* falta de confianza en sí mismo

dig /dɪg/ ◆ *vt, vi* (**-gg-**) (*pret, pp* **dug** /dʌg/) **1** cavar: *to dig for sth* cavar en busca de algo **2 to dig (sth) into sth** clavar algo/clavarse en algo: *The chair-back was digging into his back.* El respaldo de la silla se le clavaba en la espalda. **LOC to dig your heels in** mantenerse en sus trece **PHR V to dig in** (*coloq*) (*comida*) atacar **to dig sth/sb out** sacar algo/a algn (cavando) **to dig sth up 1** (*planta*) sacar de la tierra **2** (*un objeto oculto*) desenterrar **3** (*calle*) levantar ◆ *n* excavación **digger** *n* excavadora

digest¹ /ˈdaɪdʒest/ *n* **1** resumen **2** compendio

digest² /daɪˈdʒest/ *vt, vi* digerir(se) **digestion** *n* digestión

digit /ˈdɪdʒɪt/ *n* dígito **digital** *adj* digital

dignified /ˈdɪgnɪfaɪd/ *adj* digno

dignitary /ˈdɪgnɪtəri; *USA* -teri/ *n* dignatario, -a

dignity /ˈdɪgnəti/ *n* dignidad

digression /daɪˈgreʃn/ *n* digresión

dike *Ver* DYKE

dilapidated /dɪˈlæpɪdeɪtɪd/ *adj* **1** ruinoso **2** (*vehículo*) destartalado

dilemma /dɪˈlemə, daɪ-/ *n* dilema

dilute /daɪˈljuːt; *USA* -ˈluːt/ *vt* **1** diluir **2** (*fig*) suavizar, debilitar

dim /dɪm/ ◆ *adj* (**dimmer**, **dimmest**) **1** (*luz*) débil, tenue **2** (*recuerdo, noción*) vago **3** (*perspectiva*) poco prometedor, sombrío **4** (*coloq*) (*persona*) lerdo **5** (*vista*) turbio ◆ (**-mm-**) **1** *vt* (*luz*) bajar **2** *vi* (*luz*) apagarse poco a poco **3** *vt, vi* (*fig*) empañar(se), apagar(se)

dime /daɪm/ *n* (*Can, USA*) moneda de 10 centavos

dimension /dɪˈmenʃn, daɪ-/ *n* dimensión

diminish /dɪˈmɪnɪʃ/ *vt, vi* disminuir

diminutive /dɪˈmɪnjətɪv/ ◆ *adj* diminuto ◆ *adj, n* diminutivo

dimly /ˈdɪmli/ *adv* **1** (*iluminar*) débilmente **2** (*recordar*) vagamente **3** (*ver*) apenas

dimple /ˈdɪmpl/ *n* hoyuelo

din /dɪn/ *n* [*sing*] **1** (*de gente*) alboroto **2** (*de máquinas*) estruendo

dine /daɪn/ *vi* (*fml*) ~ (**on sth**) cenar, comer (algo) *Ver tb* DINNER **PHR V to dine out** cenar/comer fuera **diner** *n* **1**

comensal **2** (*USA*) restaurante (*de carretera*)

dinghy /ˈdɪŋgi/ *n* (*pl* **dinghies**) **1** bote, barca **2** (*de goma*) lancha neumática

dingy /ˈdɪndʒi/ *adj* (**-ier**, **-iest**) **1** (*deprimente*) sombrío **2** sucio

dining room comedor

dinner /ˈdɪnə(r)/ *n* **1** [*incontable*] cena, almuerzo: *to have dinner* cenar/almorzar/comer **2** cena (de gala) ☛ *Ver nota en* NAVIDAD **3** (*tb* **dinner party**) (*entre amigos*) cena ☛ *Ver* pág 320.

dinner jacket *n* esmoquin

dinosaur /ˈdaɪnəsɔː(r)/ *n* dinosaurio

diocese /ˈdaɪəsɪs/ *n* diócesis

dioxide /daɪˈɒksaɪd/ *n* dióxido

dip /dɪp/ ◆ (**-pp-**) **1** *vt* **to dip sth (in/into sth)** meter, mojar, bañar algo (en algo) **2** *vi* descender **3** *vt, vi* bajar: *to dip the headlights (of a car)* bajar las luces (de un coche) ◆ *n* **1** (*coloq*) chapuzón **2** (*Geog*) depresión **3** declive **4** (*precios, etc*) baja

diploma /dɪˈpləʊmə/ *n* diploma

diplomacy /dɪˈpləʊməsi/ *n* diplomacia **diplomat** /ˈdɪpləmæt/ *n* diplomático, -a **diplomatic** /ˌdɪpləˈmætɪk/ *adj* (*lit y fig*) diplomático **diplomatically** *adv* diplomáticamente, con diplomacia

dire /ˈdaɪə(r)/ *adj* (**direr**, **direst**) **1** (*fml*) horrible, extremo **2** (*coloq*) fatal

direct /dɪˈrekt, daɪ-/ ◆ *vt* dirigir: *Could you direct me to...?* ¿Podría indicarme el camino a...? ◆ *adj* **1** directo **2** franco **3** total ◆ *adv* **1** directamente: *You don't have to change, the train goes direct to London.* No tienes que hacer trasbordo, el tren va directamente a Londres. **2** en persona

direct debit *n* cargo bancario

direction /dɪˈrekʃn, daɪ-/ *n* **1** dirección, sentido **2 directions** [*pl*] instrucciones: *to ask (sb) for directions* preguntar (a algn) el camino a algún sitio

directive /dɪˈrektɪv, daɪ-/ *n* directriz

directly /dɪˈrektli, daɪ-/ *adv* **1** directamente: *directly opposite (sth)* justo enfrente (de algo) **2** en seguida

directness /dɪˈrektnəs, daɪ-/ *n* franqueza

director /dɪˈrektə(r), daɪ-/ *n* director, -ora

directorate /dɪˈrektərət, daɪ-/ *n* **1** junta directiva **2** Dirección General (de...)

directory /dəˈrektəri, daɪ-/ *n* (*pl* **-ies**) guía (*telefónica, etc*), directorio

dirt /dɜːt/ *n* **1** suciedad, mugre **2** tierra **3** (*coloq*) grosería, porquería LOC *Ver* TREAT

dirty /ˈdɜːti/ ◆ *vt, vi* (*pret, pp* **dirtied**) ensuciar(se) ◆ *adj* (**-ier**, **-iest**) **1** (*lit y fig*) sucio **2** (*chiste, libro, etc*) verde: *dirty word* palabrota **3** (*coloq*) sucio: *dirty trick* mala pasada

disability /ˌdɪsəˈbɪləti/ *n* (*pl* **-ies**) **1** incapacidad **2** (*Med*) minusvalía

disabled /dɪsˈeɪbld/ ◆ *adj* incapacitado ◆ **the disabled** *n* [*pl*] los minusválidos

disadvantage /ˌdɪsədˈvɑːntɪdʒ; *USA* -ˈvæn-/ *n* desventaja LOC **to put sb/be at a disadvantage** poner a algn/estar en desventaja **disadvantaged** *adj* perjudicado **disadvantageous** *adj* desventajoso

disagree /ˌdɪsəˈgriː/ *vi* (*pret, pp* **-reed**) ~ (**with sth/sb**) (**about/on sth**) no estar de acuerdo (con algo/algn) (sobre algo): *He disagreed with her on how to spend the money.* No estuvo de acuerdo con ella sobre cómo gastar el dinero. PHR V **to disagree with sb** sentarle mal a algn (*comida, clima*) **disagreeable** *adj* desagradable **disagreement** *n* **1** desacuerdo **2** discrepancia

disappear /ˌdɪsəˈpɪə(r)/ *vi* desaparecer: *It disappeared into the bushes.* Desapareció entre los matorrales. **disappearance** *n* desaparición

disappoint /ˌdɪsəˈpɔɪnt/ *vt* decepcionar, defraudar **disappointed** *adj* **1** ~ (**about/at/by sth**) decepcionado, defraudado (por algo) **2** ~ (**in/with sth/sb**) decepcionado (con algo/algn): *I'm disappointed in you.* Me has decepcionado. **disappointing** *adj* decepcionante **disappointment** *n* decepción

disapproval /ˌdɪsəˈpruːvl/ *n* desaprobación

disapprove /ˌdɪsəˈpruːv/ *vi* **1** ~ (**of sth**) desaprobar (algo) **2** ~ (**of sb**) tener mala opinión (de algn) **disapproving** *adj* de desaprobación

disarm /dɪsˈɑːm/ *vt, vi* desarmar(se) **disarmament** *n* desarme

disassociate /ˌdɪsəˈsəʊʃieɪt/ *Ver* DISSOCIATE

disaster /dɪˈzɑːstə(r); *USA* -ˈzæs-/ *n* desastre **disastrous** *adj* desastroso, catastrófico

disband /dɪsˈbænd/ *vt, vi* disolver(se)

disbelief /ˌdɪsbɪˈliːf/ *n* incredulidad

disc (*tb USA* **disk**) /dɪsk/ *n* disco *Ver tb* DISK

discard /dɪˈskɑːd/ *vt* desechar, deshacerse de

discern /dɪˈsɜːn/ *vt* **1** percibir **2** discernir

discernible /dɪˈsɜːnəbl/ *adj* perceptible

discharge /dɪsˈtʃɑːdʒ/ ◆ *vt* **1** (*residuos*) verter **2** (*Mil*) licenciar **3** (*Med, paciente*) dar de alta **4** (*deber*) desempeñar ◆ /ˈdɪstʃɑːdʒ/ *n* **1** (*eléctrica, de cargamento, de artillería*) descarga **2** (*residuo*) vertido **3** (*Mil*) licenciamiento **4** (*Jur*): *conditional discharge* libertad condicional **5** (*Med*) supuración

disciple /dɪˈsaɪpl/ *n* discípulo, -a

discipline /ˈdɪsəplɪn/ ◆ *n* disciplina ◆ *vt* disciplinar **disciplinary** *adj* disciplinario

disc jockey *n* (*pl* **-eys**) (*abrev* **DJ**) pinchadiscos

disclose /dɪsˈkləʊz/ *vt* (*fml*) revelar **disclosure** /dɪsˈkləʊʒə(r)/ *n* revelación

disco /ˈdɪskəʊ/ (*tb* **discotheque** /ˈdɪskətek/) *n* (*pl* ~**s**) discoteca

discolour (*USA* **discolor**) /dɪsˈkʌlə(r)/ *vt, vi* decolorar

discomfort /dɪsˈkʌmfət/ *n* [*incontable*] incomodidad

disconcerted /ˌdɪskənˈsɜːtɪd/ *adj* desconcertado **disconcerting** *adj* desconcertante

disconnect /ˌdɪskəˈnekt/ *vt* **1** desconectar **2** (*luz*) cortar **disconnected** *adj* inconexo, incoherente

discontent /ˌdɪskənˈtent/ (*tb* **discontentment**) *n* ~ (**with/over sth**) descontento (con algo) **discontented** *adj* descontento

discontinue /ˌdɪskənˈtɪnjuː/ *vt* suspender, interrumpir

discord /ˈdɪskɔːd/ *n* (*fml*) **1** discordia **2** (*Mús*) disonancia **discordant** /dɪsˈkɔːdənt/ *adj* **1** (*opiniones*) discorde **2** (*sonido*) disonante

discount[1] /dɪsˈkaʊnt; *USA* ˈdɪskaʊnt/ *vt* **1** descartar, ignorar **2** (*Com*) descontar, rebajar

discount[2] /ˈdɪskaʊnt/ *n* descuento LOC **at a discount** a precio rebajado

discourage /dɪsˈkʌrɪdʒ/ *vt* **1** desanimar **2** ~ **sth** oponerse a algo; aconsejar que no se haga algo **3** ~ **sb from doing sth** disuadir a algn de hacer algo **discouraging** *adj* desalentador

discover /dɪsˈkʌvə(r)/ *vt* descubrir **discovery** *n* (*pl* **-ies**) descubrimiento

discredit /dɪsˈkredɪt/ *vt* desacreditar

discreet /dɪˈskriːt/ *adj* discreto

discrepancy /dɪsˈkrepənsi/ *n* (*pl* **-ies**) discrepancia

discretion /dɪˈskreʃn/ *n* **1** discreción **2** albedrío LOC **at sb's discretion** a juicio de algn

discriminate /dɪˈskrɪmɪneɪt/ *vi* **1** ~ (**between...**) distinguir (entre...) **2** ~ **against/in favour of sb** discriminar a algn; dar trato de favor a algn **discriminating** *adj* perspicaz **discrimination** *n* **1** discernimiento, buen gusto **2** discriminación

discuss /dɪˈskʌs/ *vt* ~ **sth** (**with sb**) hablar, tratar de algo (con algn) **discussion** *n* debate, deliberación ☛ *Comparar con* ARGUMENT

disdain /dɪsˈdeɪn/ *n* desdén, desprecio

disease /dɪˈziːz/ *n* enfermedad, afección

En general, **disease** se usa para enfermedades específicas como *heart disease, Parkinson's disease*, mientras que **illness** se suele referir a la enfermedad como estado o al periodo en que uno está enfermo. *Ver ejemplos en* ILLNESS

diseased *adj* enfermo

disembark /ˌdɪsɪmˈbɑːk/ *vi* ~ (**from sth**) desembarcar (de algo) (*barcos y aviones*)

disenchanted /ˌdɪsɪnˈtʃɑːntɪd/ *adj* ~ (**with sth/sb**) desengañado, desilusionado (con algo/algn)

disentangle /ˌdɪsɪnˈtæŋgl/ *vt* **1** desenredar **2** ~ **sth/sb** (**from sth**) liberar algo/a algn (de algo)

disfigure /dɪsˈfɪgə(r); *USA* -gjər/ *vt* desfigurar

disgrace /dɪsˈgreɪs/ ◆ *vt* deshonrar: *to disgrace yourself* deshonrar su nombre ◆ *n* **1** desgracia, deshonra **2** ~ (**to sth/sb**) vergüenza (para algo/algn) LOC **in disgrace** (**with sb**) desacreditado (ante algn) **disgraceful** *adj* vergonzoso

disgruntled /dɪsˈgrʌntld/ *adj* **1** ~ **(at/ about sth)** disgustado (por algo) **2** ~ **(with sb)** disgustado (con algn)

disguise /dɪsˈgaɪz/ ◆ *vt* **1** ~ **sth/sb (as sth/sb)** disfrazar, disimular algo/a algn (de algo/algn) **2** (*voz*) cambiar **3** (*emoción*) disimular ◆ *n* disfraz LOC **in disguise** disfrazado *Ver tb* BLESSING

disgust /dɪsˈgʌst/ *n* asco, repugnancia

dish /dɪʃ/ ◆ *n* **1** (*guiso*) plato: *the national dish* el plato típico nacional **2** (*para servir*) fuente: *to wash/do the dishes* fregar los platos ◆ PHR V **to dish sth out 1** (*comida*) servir algo **2** (*dinero*) repartir algo a manos llenas **to dish sth up** servir algo

disheartened /dɪsˈhɑːtnd/ *adj* desalentado, desanimado **disheartening** *adj* desalentador

dishevelled (*USA* **disheveled**) /dɪˈʃevld/ *adj* **1** (*pelo*) despeinado **2** (*ropa, apariencia*) desaliñado

dishonest /dɪsˈɒnɪst/ *adj* **1** (*persona*) deshonesto **2** fraudulento **dishonesty** *n* falta de honradez

dishonour (*USA* **dishonor**) /dɪsˈɒnə(r)/ ◆ *n* deshonor, deshonra ◆ *vt* deshonrar **dishonourable** (*USA* **dishonorable**) *adj* deshonroso

dishwasher /ˈdɪʃwɒʃə(r)/ *n* lavavajillas, lavaplatos

disillusion /ˌdɪsɪˈluːʒn/ ◆ *n* (*tb* **disillusionment**) ~ **(with sth)** desengaño, desencanto (con algo) ◆ *vt* desengañar, desencantar

disinfect /ˌdɪsɪnˈfekt/ *vt* desinfectar **disinfectant** *n* desinfectante

disintegrate /dɪsˈɪntɪgreɪt/ *vt, vi* desintegrar(se), desmoronar(se) **disintegration** *n* desintegración, desmoronamiento

disinterested /dɪsˈɪntrəstɪd/ *adj* desinteresado

disjointed /dɪsˈdʒɔɪntɪd/ *adj* inconexo

disk /dɪsk/ *n* **1** (*esp USA*) *Ver* DISC **2** (*Informát*) disco

disk drive *n* unidad de disco ☛ *Ver dibujo en* ORDENADOR

diskette /dɪsˈket/ *n* disquete

dislike /dɪsˈlaɪk/ ◆ *vt* no gustar, tener aversión a ◆ *n* ~ **(of sth/sb)** aversión (por/a algo/algn); antipatía (a/hacia algn) LOC **to take a dislike to sth/sb** cogerle aversión a algo/algn, cogerle antipatía a algn

dislocate /ˈdɪsləkeɪt; *USA* -ləʊk-/ *vt* dislocarse **dislocation** *n* dislocación

dislodge /dɪsˈlɒdʒ/ *vt* ~ **sth/sb (from sth)** desalojar, sacar algo/a algn (de algo)

disloyal /dɪsˈlɔɪəl/ *adj* ~ **(to sth/sb)** desleal (a algo/con algn) **disloyalty** *n* deslealtad

dismal /ˈdɪzməl/ *adj* **1** triste **2** (*coloq*) pésimo

dismantle /dɪsˈmæntl/ *vt* **1** desarmar, desmontar **2** (*fig, buque, edificio*) desmantelar

dismay /dɪsˈmeɪ/ ◆ *n* ~ **(at sth)** consternación (ante algo) ◆ *vt* llenar de consternación

dismember /dɪsˈmembə(r)/ *vt* desmembrar

dismiss /dɪsˈmɪs/ *vt* **1** ~ **sb (from sth)** despedir, destituir a algn (de algo) **2** ~ **sth/sb (as sth)** descartar, desechar algo/a algn (por ser algo) **dismissal** *n* **1** despido **2** rechazo **dismissive** *adj* desdeñoso

dismount /dɪsˈmaʊnt/ *vi* ~ **(from sth)** desmontar, apearse (de algo)

disobedient /ˌdɪsəˈbiːdiənt/ *adj* ~ **(to sth/sb)** desobediente (de algo/a algn) **disobedience** *n* desobediencia

disobey /ˌdɪsəˈbeɪ/ *vt, vi* desobedecer

disorder /dɪsˈɔːdə(r)/ *n* desorden: *in disorder* desordenado **disorderly** *adj* **1** desordenado **2** indisciplinado, descontrolado LOC *Ver* DRUNK[1]

disorganized, -ised /dɪsˈɔːgənaɪzd/ *adj* desorganizado

disorientate /dɪsˈɔːriənteɪt/ *vt* desorientar

disown /dɪsˈəʊn/ *vt* renegar de

dispatch (*tb* **despatch**) /dɪˈspætʃ/ ◆ *vt* (*fml*) **1** enviar **2** (*reunión, comida*) despachar ◆ *n* **1** envío **2** (*Period*) despacho

dispel /dɪˈspel/ *vt* (-ll-) disipar

dispense /dɪˈspens/ *vt* repartir PHR V **to dispense with sth/sb** prescindir de algo/algn

disperse /dɪˈspɜːs/ *vt, vi* dispersar(se) **dispersal** (*tb* **dispersion**) *n* dispersión

displace /dɪsˈpleɪs/ *vt* **1** desplazar (a) **2** reemplazar

display /dɪˈspleɪ/ ◆ *vt* **1** exponer,

exhibir **2** (*emoción, etc*) mostrar, manifestar **3** (*Informát*) mostrar en pantalla ◆ *n* **1** exposición, exhibición **2** demostración **3** (*Informát*) pantalla (*de información*) LOC **on display** expuesto

disposable /dɪˈspəʊzəbl/ *adj* **1** desechable **2** (*Fin*) disponible

disposal /dɪˈspəʊzl/ *n* desecho, vertido LOC **at your/sb's disposal** a su disposición/a la disposición de algn

disposed /dɪˈspəʊzd/ *adj* dispuesto LOC **to be ill/well disposed towards sth/sb** estar mal/bien dispuesto hacia algo/algn

disposition /ˌdɪspəˈzɪʃn/ *n* modo de ser, manera

disproportionate /ˌdɪsprəˈpɔːʃənət/ *adj* desproporcionado

disprove /ˌdɪsˈpruːv/ *vt* refutar (*teoría*)

dispute /dɪˈspjuːt/ ◆ *n* **1** discusión **2** conflicto, disputa LOC **in dispute 1** en discusión **2** (*Jur*) en litigio ◆ *vt, vi* discutir, poner en duda

disqualify /dɪsˈkwɒlɪfaɪ/ *vt* (*pret, pp* **-fied**) descalificar: *to disqualify sb from doing sth* inhabilitar a algn para hacer algo

disregard /ˌdɪsrɪˈɡɑːd/ ◆ *vt* hacer caso omiso de (*consejo, error*) ◆ *n* ~ **(for/of sth/sb)** indiferencia (hacia algo/algn)

disreputable /dɪsˈrepjətəbl/ *adj* **1** de mala reputación **2** (*método, aspecto*) vergonzoso

disrepute /ˌdɪsrɪˈpjuːt/ *n* desprestigio

disrespect /ˌdɪsrɪˈspekt/ *n* falta de respeto

disrupt /dɪsˈrʌpt/ *vt* desbaratar, interrumpir **disruption** *n* trastorno, molestia(s)

disruptive /dɪsˈrʌptɪv/ *adj* molesto, que causa molestias

dissatisfaction /ˌdɪsˌsætɪsˈfækʃn/ *n* descontento

dissatisfied /dɪˈsætɪsfaɪd/ *adj* ~ **(with sth/sb)** descontento (con algo/algn)

dissent /dɪˈsent/ *n* desacuerdo **dissenting** *adj* en desacuerdo, contrario

dissertation /ˌdɪsəˈteɪʃn/ *n* ~ **(on sth)** tesina (sobre algo)

dissident /ˈdɪsɪdənt/ *adj, n* disidente

dissimilar /dɪˈsɪmɪlə(r)/ *adj* ~ **(from/to sth/sb)** distinto (de algo/algn)

dissociate /dɪˈsəʊʃieɪt/ (*tb* **disassociate** /ˌdɪsəˈsəʊʃieɪt/) **1** *v refl* ~ **yourself from sth/sb** desligarse de algo/algn **2** *vt* disociar

dissolve /dɪˈzɒlv/ **1** *vt, vi* disolver(se) **2** *vi* desvanecerse

dissuade /dɪˈsweɪd/ *vt* ~ **sb (from sth/doing sth)** disuadir a algn (de algo/hacer algo)

distance /ˈdɪstəns/ ◆ *n* distancia: *from/at a distance* a distancia LOC **in the distance** a lo lejos ◆ *vt* ~ **sb (from sth/sb)** distanciar a algn (de algo/algn) **distant** *adj* **1** distante, lejano **2** (*pariente*) lejano

distaste /dɪsˈteɪst/ *n* ~ **(for sth/sb)** aversión (a algo/algn) **distasteful** *adj* desagradable

distil (*USA* **distill**) /dɪˈstɪl/ *vt* (**-ll-**) ~ **sth (off/out) (from sth)** destilar algo (de algo) **distillery** *n* destilería

distinct /dɪˈstɪŋkt/ *adj* **1** claro **2** ~ **(from sth)** distinto (de algo): *as distinct from sth* en contraposición a algo **distinction** *n* **1** distinción **2** honor **distinctive** *adj* particular

distinguish /dɪˈstɪŋɡwɪʃ/ **1** *vt* ~ **A (from B)** distinguir A (de B) **2** *vi* ~ **between A and B** distinguir entre A y B **3** *v refl* ~ **yourself** distinguirse

distort /dɪˈstɔːt/ *vt* **1** deformar, distorsionar **2** (*fig*) tergiversar **distortion** *n* **1** distorsión **2** tergiversación

distract /dɪˈstrækt/ *vt* ~ **sb (from sth)** distraer a algn (de algo) **distracted** *adj* distraído **distraction** *n* distracción: *to drive sb to distraction* volver loco a algn

distraught /dɪˈstrɔːt/ *adj* consternado

distress /dɪˈstres/ *n* **1** angustia **2** dolor **3** peligro: *a distress signal* una señal de peligro **distressed** *adj* afligido **distressing** *adj* penoso

distribute /dɪˈstrɪbjuːt/ *vt* ~ **sth (to/among sth/sb)** repartir, distribuir algo (a/entre algo/algn) **distribution** *n* distribución **distributor** *n* distribuidor, -ora

district /ˈdɪstrɪkt/ *n* **1** distrito, región **2** zona

distrust /dɪsˈtrʌst/ ◆ *n* [*sing*] desconfianza ◆ *vt* desconfiar de **distrustful** *adj* desconfiado

disturb /dɪˈstɜːb/ *vt* **1** molestar, interrumpir: *I'm sorry to disturb you.* Siento molestarte. **2** (*silencio, sueño*) perturbar LOC **do not disturb** no molestar **to disturb the peace** perturbar la paz y el orden **disturbance** *n* **1** molestia: *to cause a disturbance* causar alteraciones **2** disturbios **disturbed** *adj* trastornado **disturbing** *adj* inquietante

disuse /dɪsˈjuːs/ *n* desuso: *to fall into disuse* caer en desuso **disused** *adj* abandonado

ditch /dɪtʃ/ ◆ *n* zanja ◆ *vt* (*coloq*) abandonar

dither /ˈdɪðə(r)/ *vi* (*coloq*) ~ (**about sth**) vacilar (sobre algo)

ditto /ˈdɪtəʊ/ *n* ídem

Ditto se suele referir al símbolo (") que se utiliza para evitar las repeticiones en una lista.

dive /daɪv/ ◆ *vi* (*pret* **dived** *o USA* **dove** /dəʊv/ *pp* **dived**) **1** ~ (**from/off sth**) (**into sth**) tirarse de cabeza (desde algo) (en algo) **2** (*submarino*) sumergirse **3** ~ (**down**) (**for sth**) (*persona*) bucear (en busca de algo) **4** (*avión*) bajar en picado **5** ~ **into/under sth** meterse en/debajo de algo LOC **to dive for cover** buscar cobijo precipitadamente ◆ *n* salto **diver** *n* buzo, -a

diverge /daɪˈvɜːdʒ/ *vi* **1** ~ (**from sth**) (*líneas, carreteras*) divergir (de algo) **2** (*fml*) (*opiniones*) diferir **divergence** *n* divergencia **divergent** *adj* divergente

diverse /daɪˈvɜːs/ *adj* diverso **diversification** *n* diversificación **diversify** *vt, vi* (*pret, pp* **-fied**) diversificar(se)

diversion /daɪˈvɜːʃn; *USA* -ˈvɜːrʒn/ *n* desvío (*ocasionado por obras, etc*)

diversity /daɪˈvɜːsəti/ *n* diversidad

divert /daɪˈvɜːt/ *vt* ~ **sth/sb** (**from sth**) (**to sth**) desviar algo/a algn (de algo) (a algo)

divide /dɪˈvaɪd/ **1** *vt* ~ **sth** (**up**) (**into sth**) dividir algo (en algo) **2** *vi* ~ (**up**) **into sth** dividirse en algo **3** *vt* ~ **sth** (**out/up**) (**between/among sb**) dividir, repartir algo (entre algn) **4** *vt* ~ **sth** (**between A and B**) dividir, repartir algo (entre A y B) **5** *vt* separar **6** *vt* ~ **sth by sth** (*Mat*) dividir algo por algo **divided** *adj* dividido

dividend /ˈdɪvɪdend/ *n* dividendo

divine /dɪˈvaɪn/ *adj* divino

diving /daɪvɪŋ/ *n* buceo

diving board *n* trampolín

division /dɪˈvɪʒn/ *n* **1** división **2** sección, departamento (*en una empresa*) **divisional** *adj* divisionario

divorce /dɪˈvɔːs/ ◆ *n* divorcio ◆ *vt* divorciarse de: *to get divorced* divorciarse **divorcee** /dɪˌvɔːˈsiː/ *n* divorciado, -a

divulge /daɪˈvʌldʒ/ *vt* ~ **sth** (**to sb**) revelar algo (a algn)

DIY /ˌdiː aɪ ˈwaɪ/ *abrev* **do-it-yourself**

dizzy /ˈdɪzi/ *adj* (**-ier**, **-iest**) mareado **dizziness** *n* mareo, vértigo

DJ /ˌdiː ˈdʒeɪ/ *abrev* **disc jockey**

do

presente	*negativa contracciones*
I **do**	I **don't**
you **do**	you **don't**
he/she/it **does**	he/she/it **doesn't**
we **do**	we **don't**
you **do**	you **don't**
they **do**	they **don't**
pasado	**did**
forma en -ing	**doing**
participio pasado	**done**

do¹ /duː/ *v aux* ☛ En español, **do** no se traduce. Lleva el tiempo y la persona del verbo principal de la oración.

- **frases interrogativas y negativas**: *Does she speak French?* ¿Habla francés? ◊ *Did you go home?* ¿Os fuisteis a casa? ◊ *She didn't go to Paris.* No fue a París. ◊ *He doesn't want to come with us.* No quiere venir con nosotros.
- **question tags 1** [*oración afirmativa*]: **do** + n't + sujeto (pron pers)?: *John lives here, doesn't he?* John vive aquí, ¿verdad? **2** [*oración negativa*]: **do** + sujeto (pron pers)?: *Mary doesn't know, does she?* Mary no lo sabe, ¿verdad? **3** [*oración afirmativa*]: **do** + sujeto (pron pers)?: *So you told them, did you?* O sea que se lo dijiste, ¿no?
- **en afirmativas con un uso enfático**: *He does look tired.* De verdad que se le ve cansado. ◊ *Well, I did warn you.* Bueno, ya te advertí. ◊ *Oh, do be quiet!* ¡Cállate ya!
- **para evitar repeticiones**: *He drives better than he did a year ago.* Conduce mejor de lo que lo hacía hace un año. ◊ *She knows more than he does.* Ella sabe más que él. ◊ *'Who won?' 'I did.'* —¿Quién ganó? —Yo. ◊ *'He smokes.' 'So do I.'* —Él fuma. —Yo también. ◊ *Peter didn't go and neither did I.* Peter no fue

y yo tampoco. ◊ *You didn't know her but I did.* Tú no la conocías pero yo sí.

do² /duː/ (*3ª pers sing pres* **does** /dʌz/ *pret* **did** /dɪd/ *pp* **done** /dʌn/)

• *vt, vi* hacer ☛ Usamos **to do** cuando hablamos de una actividad sin decir exactamente de qué se trata, como por ejemplo, cuando va acompañado de palabras como *something, nothing, anything, everything*, etc: *What are you doing this evening?* ¿Qué vas a hacer esta tarde? ◊ *Are you doing anything tomorrow?* ¿Vas a hacer algo mañana? ◊ *We'll do what we can to help you.* Haremos lo que podamos para ayudarte. ◊ *What does she want to do?* ¿Qué quiere hacer? ◊ *I've got nothing to do.* No tengo nada que hacer. ◊ *What can I do for you?* ¿En qué puedo servirle? ◊ *I have a number of things to do today.* Hoy tengo varias cosas que hacer. ◊ *Do as you please.* Haz lo que quieras. ◊ *Do as you're told!* ¡Haz lo que se te dice!

• **to do + the, my, etc + -ing** *vt* (*obligaciones y hobbies*) hacer: *to do the washing up* hacer/fregar los platos ◊ *to do the ironing* planchar ◊ *to do the/your shopping* hacer la compra

• **to do + (the, my, etc) + sustantivo** *vt*: *to do your homework* hacer los deberes ◊ *to do a test/an exam* hacer un examen ◊ *to do an English course* hacer un curso de inglés ◊ *to do business* hacer negocios ◊ *to do your duty* cumplir con tu deber ◊ *to do your job* hacer tu trabajo ◊ *to do the housework* hacer la casa ◊ *to do your hair/to have your hair done* arreglarse el pelo/ir a la peluquería

• **otros usos 1** *vt*: *to do your best* hacer lo que se pueda ◊ *to do good* hacer el bien ◊ *to do sb a favour* hacerle un favor a algn **2** *vi* ser suficiente, servir: *Will £10 do?* ¿Será suficiente con diez libras? ◊ *All right, a pencil will do.* Da igual, un lápiz servirá. **3** *vi* venir bien: *Will next Friday do?* ¿Te viene bien el viernes? **4** *vi* ir: *She's doing well at school.* Va bien en la escuela. ◊ *How's the business doing?* ¿Qué tal va el negocio? ◊ *He did badly in the exam.* Le fue mal en el examen.

LOC **it/that will never/won't do**: *It (simply) won't do.* No puede ser. ◊ *It would never do to…* No estaría bien que… **that does it!** (*coloq*) ¡se acabó! **that's done it** (*coloq*) ¡la hemos hecho buena! **that will do!** ¡ya está bien! **to be/have to do with sth/sb** tener que ver con algo/algn: *What's it got to do with you?* ¡Y a ti que te importa! ☛ Para otras expresiones con **do**, véanse las entradas del sustantivo adjetivo, etc, p.ej. **to do your bit** en BIT¹.

PHR V **to do away with sth** deshacerse de algo, abolir algo

to do sth up 1 abrochar(se) algo **2** atar(se) algo **3** envolver algo **4** renovar algo

to do with 1 *I could do with a good night's sleep.* Me haría bien dormir toda la noche. ◊ *We could do with a holiday.* Nos sentarían bien unas vacaciones. **2** *She won't have anything to do with him.* No quiere tener nada que ver con él.

to do without (sth/sb) pasarse sin (algo/algn) ☛ *Ver tb ejemplos en* MAKE

do³ /duː/ *n* (*pl* **dos** *o* **do's** /duːz/) LOC **do's and don'ts** reglas

docile /ˈdəʊsaɪl; *USA* ˈdɒsl/ *adj* dócil

dock¹ /dɒk/ ◆ *n* **1** dársena **2 docks** [*pl*] puerto ◆ **1** *vt, vi* (*Náut*) (hacer) entrar en dique, atracar (en un muelle) **2** *vi* llegar en barco **3** *vt, vi* (*Aeronáut*) acoplar(se)

dock² /dɒk/ *n* banquillo (de los acusados)

dock³ /dɒk/ *vt* reducir (*sueldo*)

doctor /ˈdɒktə(r)/ ◆ *n* (*abrev* **Dr**) (*Med*) médico, -a **2** ~ **(of sth)** (*título*) doctor, -ora (en algo) ◆ *vt* (*coloq*) amañar **2** (*comestibles*) adulterar

doctorate /ˈdɒktərət/ *n* doctorado

doctrine /ˈdɒktrɪn/ *n* doctrina

document /ˈdɒkjumənt/ ◆ *n* documento ◆ *vt* documentar

documentary /ˌdɒkjuˈmentri/ *adj*, *n* (*pl* **-ies**) documental

dodge /dɒdʒ/ **1** *vi* hacer un quiebro: *She dodged round the corner.* Hizo un quiebro y dobló la esquina. ◊ *to dodge awkward questions* eludir preguntas embarazosas **2** *vt* (*golpe*) esquivar **3** (*perseguidor*) dar esquinazo a

dodgy /ˈdɒdʒi/ *adj* (**-ier**, **-iest**) (*coloq esp GB*) problemático: *Sounds a bit dodgy to me.* Me huele a chamusquina. ◊ *a dodgy situation* una situación delicada ◊ *a dodgy wheel* una rueda defectuosa

doe /dəʊ/ *n* cierva, coneja, liebre hembra ☛ *Ver nota en* CIERVO, CONEJO

does /dəz, dʌz/ *Ver* DO

doesn't /ˈdʌz(ə)nt/ = DOES NOT *Ver* DO

dog /dɒg; *USA* dɔːg/ ◆ *n* perro LOC *Ver* TREAT ◆ *vt* (**-gg-**) seguir: *He was dogged by misfortune.* Le persiguió la mala suerte.

dogged /ˈdɒgɪd; *USA* ˈdɔːgɪd/ *adj* (*aprob*) tenaz **doggedly** *adv* tenazmente

doggie (*tb* **doggy**) /ˈdɒgi; *USA* ˈdɔːgi/ *n* (*coloq*) perrito

dogsbody /ˈdɒgzbɒdi; *USA* ˈdɔːg-/ *n* (*pl* **-ies**) (*GB*) chico, -a para todo

do-it-yourself /ˌduː ɪt jəˈself/ *n* (*abrev* **DIY**) bricolaje

the dole /dəʊl/ *n* (*GB, coloq*) subsidio de desempleo: *to be/go on the dole* estar/quedarse en paro

doll /dɒl; *USA* dɔːl/ *n* muñeca

dollar /ˈdɒlə(r)/ *n* dólar: *a dollar bill* un billete de dólar

dolly /ˈdɒli; *USA* ˈdɔːli/ *n* muñequita

dolphin /ˈdɒlfɪn/ *n* delfín

domain /dəˈmeɪn/ *n* **1** (*lit*) propiedad **2** campo: *outside my domain* fuera de mi competencia

dome /dəʊm/ *n* cúpula **domed** *adj* abovedado

domestic /dəˈmestɪk/ *adj* **1** doméstico **2** nacional **domesticated** *adj* **1** doméstico **2** casero

dominant /ˈdɒmɪnənt/ *adj* dominante **dominance** *n* dominación

dominate /ˈdɒmɪneɪt/ *vt, vi* dominar **domination** *n* dominio

domineering /ˌdɒmɪˈnɪərɪŋ/ *adj* dominante

dominion /dəˈmɪniən/ *n* dominio

domino /ˈdɒmɪnəʊ/ *n* **1** (*pl* **~es**) ficha de dominó **2 dominoes** [*sing*]: *to play dominoes* jugar al dominó

donate /dəʊˈneɪt; *USA* ˈdəʊneɪt/ *vt* donar **donation** *n* **1** donativo **2** [*incontable*] donación

done /dʌn/ ◆ *pp de* DO² ◆ *adj* hecho

donkey /ˈdɒŋki/ *n* (*pl* **-eys**) burro

donor /ˈdəʊnə(r)/ *n* donante

don't /dəʊnt/ = DO NOT *Ver* DO¹,²

doom /duːm/ *n* [*sing*] **1** (*fml*) perdición: *to send a man to his doom* mandar a un hombre a la muerte **2** pesimismo **doomed** *adj* condenado: *doomed to failure* destinado al fracaso

door /dɔː(r)/ *n* **1** puerta **2** *Ver* DOORWAY LOC (**from**) **door to door** de puerta en puerta: *a door-to-door salesman* un vendedor a domicilio **out of doors** al aire libre

doorbell /ˈdɔːbel/ *n* timbre (*de puerta*)

doormat /ˈdɔːmæt/ *n* felpudo

doorstep /ˈdɔːstep/ *n* peldaño de la puerta LOC **on your doorstep** a un paso

doorway /ˈdɔːweɪ/ *n* vano (*de puerta*)

dope¹ /dəʊp/ *n* (*coloq*) imbécil

dope² /dəʊp/ *vt* narcotizar

dope test *n* prueba antidoping

dormant /ˈdɔːmənt/ *adj* inactivo

dormitory /ˈdɔːmətri; *USA* -tɔːri/ *n* (*pl* **-ies**) dormitorio

dosage /ˈdəʊsɪdʒ/ *n* dosificación

dose /dəʊs/ *n* dosis

dot /dɒt/ ◆ *n* punto LOC **on the dot** (*coloq*) a la hora en punto ◆ *vt* (**-tt-**) poner un punto sobre LOC **to dot your/the i's and cross your/the t's** dar los últimos retoques

dote /dəʊt/ *vi* ~ **on sth/sb** adorar algo/a algn **doting** *adj* devoto

double¹ /ˈdʌbl/ ◆ *adj* doble: *double figures* número de dos cifras ◊ *She earns double what he does.* Gana el doble que él. ◆ *adv*: *to see double* ver doble ◊ *bent double* encorvado ◊ *to fold a blanket double* doblar una manta en dos

double² /ˈdʌbl/ *n* **1** doble **2 doubles** [*pl*] dobles: *mixed doubles* dobles mixtos

double³ /ˈdʌbl/ **1** *vt, vi* duplicar(se) **2** *vt* ~ **sth** (**up/over/across/back**) doblar algo (en dos) **3** *vi* ~ **as sth** hacer de algo PHR V **to double back** volver sobre sus pasos **to double** (**sb**) **up**: *to be doubled up with laughter* partirse de risa ◊ *to double up with pain* doblarse de dolor

double-barrelled /ˌdʌbl ˈbærəld/ *adj* **1** (*escopeta*) de dos cañones **2** (*GB*) (*apellido*) compuesto

double bass *n* contrabajo

double bed *n* cama de matrimonio

double-breasted /ˌdʌbl ˈbrestɪd/ *adj* cruzado

double-check /ˌdʌbl ˈtʃek/ *vt* volver a comprobar

double-cross /ˌdʌbl ˈkrɒs/ *vt* engañar

double-decker /ˌdʌbl ˈdekə(r)/ (*tb* **double-decker bus**) *n* autobús de dos pisos

double-edged /ˌdʌbl ˈedʒd/ *adj* de doble filo

double glazed *adj* con cristal doble

double glazing *n* doble acristalamiento

doubly /ˈdʌbli/ *adv* doblemente: *to make doubly sure of sth* volver a asegurarse de algo

doubt /daʊt/ ◆ *n* **1** ~ (**about sth**) duda (sobre algo) **2** ~ **as to (whether)...** duda sobre (si)... LOC **beyond a/all/any doubt** fuera de toda duda **in doubt** dudoso **no doubt**; **without (a) doubt** sin duda *Ver tb* BENEFIT, CAST ◆ *vt, vi* dudar **doubter** *n* escéptico, -a **doubtless** *adv* sin duda

doubtful /ˈdaʊtfl/ *adj* dudoso: *to be doubtful about (doing) sth* tener dudas sobre (si hacer) algo **doubtfully** *adv* sin convicción

dough /dəʊ/ *n* masa

doughnut /ˈdəʊnʌt/ *n* donut ☛ *Ver dibujo en* PAN

dour /dʊə(r)/ *adj* (*fml*) austero

douse (*tb* **dowse**) /daʊs/ *vt* ~ **sth/sb (in/with sth)** empapar algo/a algn (de algo)

dove¹ /dʌv/ *n* paloma

dove² (*USA*) *pret de* DIVE

dowdy /ˈdaʊdi/ *adj* (**-ier, -iest**) (*pey*) **1** (*ropa*) sin gracia **2** (*persona*) vestido con un estilo muy gris

down¹ /daʊn/ *part adv* **1** abajo: *face down* boca abajo **2** bajo: *Inflation is down this month.* La inflación ha bajado este mes. ◊ *to be £50 down* faltarle a algn 50 libras **3** *Ten down, five to go.* Van diez, quedan cinco. **4** (*Informát*): *The computer's down.* El ordenador está estropeado. LOC **down with sth/sb!** ¡abajo algo/algn! **to be/feel down** (*coloq*) estar con la depre ☛ Para los usos de **down** en PHRASAL VERBS ver las entradas de los verbos correspondientes, p.ej. **to go down** en GO¹.

down² /daʊn/ *prep* abajo: *down the hill* colina abajo ◊ *down the corridor on the right* bajando el pasillo a la derecha ◊ *He ran his eyes down the list.* Recorrió la lista de arriba abajo.

down³ /daʊn/ *n* **1** plumones **2** pelusa

down-and-out /ˈdaʊn ən ˌaʊt/ *n* vagabundo, -a

downcast /ˈdaʊnkɑːst; *USA* -kæst/ *adj* abatido

downfall /ˈdaʊnfɔːl/ *n* [*sing*] caída: *Drink will be your downfall.* La bebida será tu ruina.

downgrade /ˈdaʊngreɪd/ *vt* ~ **sth/sb (from ... to ...)** degradar algo/a algn (de ... a ...)

downhearted /ˌdaʊnˈhɑːtɪd/ *adj* desanimado

downhill /ˌdaʊnˈhɪl/ *adv, adj* cuesta abajo LOC **to be (all) downhill (from here/there)** ser (todo) coser y cantar (a partir de ahora/entonces) **to go downhill** ir cuesta abajo

downmarket /ˌdaʊnˈmɑːkɪt/ *adj* de, para la gran masa, vulgar

downpour /ˈdaʊnpɔː(r)/ *n* chaparrón

downright /ˈdaʊnraɪt/ ◆ *adj* total: *downright stupidity* estupidez declarada ◆ *adv* completamente

the downs /daʊnz/ *n* [*pl*] las lomas

downside /ˈdaʊnsaɪd/ *n* inconvenient

Down's syndrome *n* síndrome de Down

downstairs /ˌdaʊnˈsteəz/ ◆ *adv* (escaleras) abajo ◆ *adj* (en el/del piso de abajo ◆ *n* [*sing*] planta baja

downstream /ˌdaʊnˈstriːm/ *adv* rí abajo

down-to-earth /ˌdaʊn tuː ˈɜːθ/ *ad* práctico, con los pies en la tierra

downtown /ˌdaʊnˈtaʊn/ *adv* (*USA* a/en el centro (*de ciudad*)

downtrodden /ˈdaʊntrɒdn/ *adj* opr mido

downturn /ˈdaʊntɜːn/ *n* bajada: *downturn in sales* un descenso en la ventas

down under *adv, n* (en) las antípoda

downward /ˈdaʊnwəd/ ◆ *adj* haci abajo: *a downward trend* una tendenc a la baja ◆ *adv* (*tb* **downwards**) hac abajo

downy /daʊni/ *adj* con pelusa

dowry /ˈdaʊri/ *n* (*pl* **-ies**) dote

dowse *Ver* DOUSE

doze /dəʊz/ ◆ *vi* dormitar PHR V

doze off dar una cabezada ◆ *n* cabezada

dozen /ˈdʌzn/ *n* (*abrev* **doz**) docena: *There were dozens of people.* Había muchísima gente. ◊ *two dozen eggs* dos docenas de huevos

dozy /ˈdəʊzi/ *adj* (**-ier**, **-iest**) amodorrado

drab /dræb/ *adj* monótono, gris

draft /drɑːft; *USA* dræft/ ◆ *n* **1** borrador: *a draft bill* un anteproyecto de ley **2** (*Fin*) orden de pago, letra de cambio **3** (*USA*) **the draft** la llamada a filas **4** (*USA*) *Ver* DRAUGHT ◆ *vt* **1** hacer un borrador de **2** (*USA*, *Mil*) llamar al servicio militar **3** ~ **sth/sb** (**in**) destacar algo/a algn

lrafty (*USA*) *Ver* DRAUGHTY

lrag¹ /dræg/ *n* **1 a drag** (*coloq*) (*persona, cosa*) un rollo **2** (*coloq*): *a man dressed in drag* un hombre vestido de mujer

lrag² /dræg/ (**-gg-**) **1** *vt, vi* arrastrar(se) **2** *vi* (*tiempo*) pasar lentamente **3** *vt* (*Náut*) dragar **4** *vi* ~ (**on**) hacerse eterno

lragon /ˈdrægən/ *n* dragón

lragonfly /ˈdrægənflaɪ/ *n* libélula

lrain /dreɪn/ ◆ *n* **1** desagüe **2** alcantarilla **LOC to be a drain on sth** ser un agujero continuo de algo ◆ *vt* **1** (*platos, verduras, etc*) escurrir **2** (*terreno, lago, etc*) drenar **LOC to be/feel drained** estar/sentirse agotado: *She felt drained of all energy.* Se sentía completamente agotada. **PHR V to drain away 1** (*lit*) perderse **2** (*fig*) consumirse (*lentamente*) **drainage** *n* drenaje

raining board *n* escurreplatos

rainpipe /ˈdreɪnpaɪp/ *n* tubería de desagüe

rama /ˈdrɑːmə/ *n* **1** obra de teatro **2** drama: *drama school* escuela dramática ◊ *drama student* estudiante de arte dramático **dramatic** *adj* dramático **dramatically** *adv* dramáticamente, de modo impresionante

ramatist /ˈdræmətɪst/ *n* dramaturgo, -a **dramatization, -isation** *n* dramatización **dramatize, -ise** *vt, vi* (*lit y fig*) dramatizar

rank *pret de* DRINK

rape /dreɪp/ *vt* **1** ~ **sth across/round/over sth** (*tejido*) colgar algo sobre algo **2** ~ **sth/sb** (**in/with sth**) cubrir, envolver algo/a algn (en/con algo)

drastic /ˈdræstɪk/ *adj* **1** drástico **2** grave **drastically** *adv* drásticamente

draught /drɑːft/ (*USA* **draft** /dræft/) *n* **1** corriente (*de aire*) **2 draughts** [*sing*] damas (*juego*) **LOC on draught** de barril

draughtsman /ˈdrɑːftsmən; *USA* ˈdræfts-/ *n* (*pl* **-men** /-mən/) delineante

draughty /ˈdrɑːfti/ (*USA* **drafty** /ˈdræfti/) *adj* (**-ier**, **-iest**) con muchas corrientes (*de aire*)

draw¹ /drɔː/ *n* **1** [*gen sing*] sorteo ☛ *Comparar con* RAFFLE **2** empate

draw² /drɔː/ (*pret* **drew** /druː/ *pp* **drawn** /drɔːn/) **1** *vt, vi* dibujar, trazar **2** *vi*: *to draw level with sb* alcanzar a algn ◊ *to draw near* acercarse **3** *vt* (*cortinas*) correr, descorrer **4** *vt* (*conclusión*) sacar: *to draw comfort from sth/sb* hallar consuelo en algo/algn ◊ *to draw inspiration from sth* inspirarse en algo ◊ *to draw a distinction* hacer una distinción ◊ *to draw an analogy/a parallel* establecer una analogía/un paralelo **5** *vt* (*sueldo*) cobrar **6** *vt* provocar, causar **7** *vt* ~ **sb** (**to sth/sb**) atraer a algn (hacia algo/algn) **8** *vi* (*Dep*) empatar **LOC** *Ver* CLOSE²

PHR V to draw back retroceder, retirarse **to draw sth back** retirar algo, descorrer algo

to draw in (*tren*) entrar en la estación

to draw on/upon sth hacer uso de algo

to draw out 1 (*día*) alargarse **2** (*tren*) salir de la estación

to draw up 1 pararse **2** (*silla*) acercar

to draw sth up redactar algo

drawback /ˈdrɔːbæk/ *n* ~ (**of/to sth/to doing sth**) inconveniente, desventaja (de algo/de hacer algo)

drawer /drɔː(r)/ *n* cajón

drawing /ˈdrɔːɪŋ/ *n* dibujo

drawing pin *n* chincheta

drawing-room /ˈdrɔːɪŋ ruːm/ *n* salón

drawl /drɔːl/ *n* voz cansina

drawn¹ *pp de* DRAW²

drawn² /drɔːn/ *adj* demacrado

dread /dred/ ◆ *n* terror ◆ *vt* tener terror a: *I dread to think what will happen.* Sólo pensar qué pasará me horroriza. **dreadful** *adj* **1** terrible, espantoso **2** horrible, pésimo: *I feel dreadful.* Me siento fatal. ◊ *I feel* *dreadful about what happened.* Me da vergüenza lo que pasó. ◊ *How dreadful!* ¡Qué horror! **dreadfully** *adv* **1** terriblemente **2** muy mal **3** muy: *I'm dreadfully sorry.* Lo siento muchísimo.

dream /driːm/ ◆ *n* (*lit y fig*) sueño: *to have a dream about sth/sb* soñar con algo/algn ◊ *to go around in a dream/live in a dream world* vivir de ensueños ◆ (*pret, pp* **dreamt** /dremt/ *o* **dreamed**) **1** *vt, vi* ~ (**about/of sth/doing sth**) soñar (con algo/con hacer algo): *I dreamt (that) I could fly.* Soñé que podía volar. **2** *vt* imaginar: *I never dreamt (that) I'd see you again.* Nunca imaginé que te volvería a ver.

Algunos verbos poseen tanto formas regulares como irregulares para el pasado y el participio pasado: **dream**: **dreamed/dreamt**, **spoil**: **spoiled/spoilt**, etc. En inglés británico se prefieren las formas irregulares (**dreamt**, **spoilt**, etc), mientras que en inglés americano se utilizan las formas regulares (**dreamed**, **spoiled**, etc). Sin embargo, cuando el participio funciona como adjetivo siempre se usa la forma irregular: *a spoilt child* un niño mimado.

dreamer *n* soñador, -ora **dreamy** *adj* (**-ier**, **-iest**) **1** soñador, distraído **2** vago **dreamily** *adv* distraídamente

dreary /ˈdrɪəri/ (*tb antic* **drear** /drɪə(r)/) *adj* (**-ier**, **-iest**) **1** deprimente **2** aburrido

dredge /dredʒ/ *vt, vi* dragar **dredger** (*tb* **dredge**) *n* draga

drench /drentʃ/ *vt* empapar: *to get drenched to the skin/drenched through* calarse hasta los huesos ◊ *(absolutely) drenched* hecho una sopa

dress /dres/ ◆ *n* **1** vestido **2** [*incontable*] ropa: *to have no dress sense* no saber vestirse *Ver tb* FANCY DRESS ◆ **1** *vt, vi* vestir(se): *to dress as sth* vestirse de algo ◊ *to dress smartly* vestir bien ☛ Cuando nos referimos simplemente a la acción de vestirse decimos **get dressed**. **2** *vt* (*herida*) curar **3** *vt* (*ensalada*) aliñar **LOC** (**to be**) **dressed in sth** (ir) vestido de algo **PHR V to dress (sb) up (as sth/sb)** disfrazarse/disfrazar a algn (de algo/algn) **to dress (sb) up (in sth)** disfrazarse/disfrazar a algn (con algo) **to dress sth up** disfrazar algo **to dress up** ponerse de punta en blanco

dress circle *n* (*GB, Teat*) principal

dresser /ˈdresə(r)/ *n* **1** aparador **2** (*USA*) tocador

dressing /ˈdresɪŋ/ *n* **1** vendaje **2** aliño

dressing gown *n* bata

dressing room *n* vestuario, camerino

dressing table *n* tocador

dressmaker /ˈdresmeɪkə(r)/ (*tb* **dress designer**) *n* modisto, -a **dressmaking** *n* corte y confección

drew *pret de* DRAW[2]

dribble /ˈdrɪbl/ **1** *vi* babear **2** *vt, vi* regatear

dried *pret, pp de* DRY

drier (*tb* **dryer**) /ˈdraɪə(r)/ *n* secador*a* *Ver tb* TUMBLE-DRIER

drift /drɪft/ ◆ *vi* **1** flotar **2** (*arena, nieve*) amontonarse **3** ir a la deriva: *to drift into (doing) sth* hacer algo a la deriva ◆ *n* **1** [*sing*] idea general **2** montón: *snow drifts* montones de nieve **drifter** *n* vagabundo

drill /drɪl/ ◆ *n* **1** taladro: *a dentist's drill* un torno de dentista **2** instrucción **3** ejercicio **4** rutina ◆ *vt* **1** taladrar, perforar **2** instruir

drily *Ver* DRYLY

drink /drɪŋk/ ◆ *n* bebida: *a drink of water* un trago de agua ◊ *to go for a drink* ir a tomar algo ◊ *a soft drink* un refresco ◆ *vt, vi* (*pret* **drank** /dræŋk/ *pp* **drunk** /drʌŋk/) beber: *Don't drink and drive.* Si bebes, no conduzcas. **LOC to drink sb's health** beber a la salud de algn **PHR V to drink (a toast) to sth/sb** brindar por algo/algn **to drink sth down/up** beber algo de un trago **to drink sth in** embeberse en algo **drinker** *n* bebedor **drinking** *n* el beber

drinking water *n* agua potable

drip /drɪp/ ◆ *vi* (**-pp-**) gotear **LOC to be dripping with sth** estar chorreando algo ◆ *n* **1** gota **2** (*Med*) gotero: *to be on a drip* tener puesto un gotero

drive /draɪv/ ◆ (*pret* **drove** /drəʊv/ *pp* **driven** /ˈdrɪvn/) **1** *vt, vi* conducir: *Can you drive?* ¿Sabes conducir? **2** *vi* viajar en coche: *Did you drive?* ¿Has venido en coche? **3** *vt* llevar (en coche) **4** *vt*: *to drive cattle* arrear ganado ◊ *to drive sb crazy* volver loco a algn ◊ *to drive sb to drink* llevar a algn a la bebida **5**

impulsar LOC **to be driving at sth**: *What are you driving at?* ¿Qué insinúas? **to drive a hard bargain** ser un negociador duro PHR V **to drive away**; **to drive off** alejarse en coche **to drive sth/sb back/off** ahuyentar algo/a algn **to drive (sb) on** empujar (a algn) ◆ *n* **1** vuelta, viaje (*en coche, etc*): *to go for a drive* dar una vuelta en coche **2** (*USA* **driveway**) (*en una casa*) camino de la entrada **3** (*Dep*) golpe directo, drive **4** empuje **5** campaña **6** (*Mec*) mecanismo de transmisión: *four-wheel drive* tracción en las cuatro ruedas ◊ *a left-hand drive car* un coche con el volante a la izquierda **7** (*Informát*): *disk drive* unidad de disco

drive-in /ˈdraɪv ɪn/ *n* (*USA*) lugar al aire libre, sobre todo cines, restaurantes, etc donde se sirve a los clientes sin que tengan que salir del coche

driven *pp de* DRIVE

driver /ˈdraɪvə(r)/ *n* chófer: *train driver* maquinista LOC **to be in the driver's seat** tener la sartén por el mango

driving licence (*USA* **driver's license**) *n* carnet de conducir

driving school *n* autoescuela

driving test *n* examen de conducir

drizzle /ˈdrɪzl/ ◆ *n* llovizna ◆ *vi* lloviznar

drone /drəʊn/ ◆ *vi* zumbar: *to drone on about sth* hablar sobre algo en un tono monótono ◆ *n* zumbido

drool /druːl/ *vi* babear: *to drool over sth/sb* caérsele la baba a uno por algo/algn

droop /druːp/ *vi* **1** caer **2** (*flor*) marchitarse **3** (*ánimo*) decaer **drooping** (*tb* **droopy**) *adj* **1** caído **2** (*flor*) marchito

drop /drɒp/ ◆ *n* **1** gota: *Would you like a drop of wine?* ¿Te apetece un vaso de vino? **2** [*sing*] caída: *a sheer drop* un precipicio ◊ *a drop in prices* una caída de los precios ◊ *a drop in temperature* un descenso de la temperatura LOC **at the drop of a hat** sin pensarlo dos veces **to be (only) a drop in the ocean** no ser más que una gota de agua en el océano ◆ **(-pp-) 1** *vi* caer: *He dropped to his knees.* Se arrodilló. **2** *vt* dejar caer: *to drop a bomb* lanzar una bomba ◊ *to drop anchor* echar el ancla **3** *vi* desplomarse: *I feel ready to drop.* Estoy que me caigo. ◊ *to work till you drop* matarse a trabajar **4** *vt, vi* disminuir, caer: *to drop prices* reducir precios **5** *vt* ~ **sth/sb (off)** (*pasajero, paquete*) dejar algo/a algn **6** *vt* omitir: *He's been dropped from the team.* Lo han excluido del equipo. **7** *vt* ~ **sb** romper con algn **8** *vt* ~ **sth** (*hábito, actitud*) dejar: *Drop everything!* ¡Déjalo todo! ◊ *Can we drop the subject?* ¿Podemos olvidar el tema? LOC **to drop a brick** (*coloq*) meter la pata **to drop a hint (to sb)/drop (sb) a hint** soltar una indirecta (a algn) **to drop dead** (*coloq*) quedarse en el sitio: *Drop dead!* ¡Vete al cuerno! **to drop sb a line** (*coloq*) mandarle unas líneas a algn *Ver tb* LET[1] PHR V **to drop back**; **to drop behind** quedarse atrás, rezagarse **to drop by/in/over/round**: *Why don't you drop by?* ¿Por qué no te pasas por casa? ◊ *They dropped in for breakfast.* Se pasaron a desayunar. ◊ *Drop round some time.* Ven a vernos alguna vez. **to drop in on sb** hacer una visita informal a algn **to drop off** (*coloq*) quedarse dormido **to drop out (of sth)** retirarse (de algo): *to drop out (of university)* dejar los estudios ◊ *to drop out (of society)* automarginarse

drop-out /ˈdrɒp aʊt/ *n* marginado, -a

droppings /ˈdrɒpɪŋz/ *n* [*pl*] excrementos (*de animales o pájaros*)

drought /draʊt/ *n* sequía

drove *pret de* DRIVE

drown /draʊn/ *vt, vi* ahogar(se) PHR V **to drown sth/sb out** ahogar (a algo/algn): *His words were drowned out by the music.* La música ahogó sus palabras.

drowsy /ˈdraʊzi/ *adj* (**-ier**, **-iest**) adormilado: *This drug can make you drowsy.* Este fármaco puede producir somnolencia.

drudgery /ˈdrʌdʒəri/ *n* trabajo pesado

drug /drʌg/ ◆ *n* **1** (*Med*) fármaco, medicamento: *drug company* empresa farmacéutica **2** droga: *to be on drugs* consumir drogas habitualmente ◆ *vt* (**-gg-**) drogar

drug abuse *n* abuso de drogas

drug addict *n* drogadicto, -a **drug addiction** *n* drogadicción

drugstore /ˈdrʌgstɔː(r)/ *n* (*USA*) farmacia que también vende comestibles, periódicos, etc *Ver tb* PHARMACY

drum /drʌm/ ◆ *n* **1** (*Mús*) tambor, batería: *to play the drums* tocar la batería **2** tambor, bidón ◆ (**-mm-**) **1** *vi* tocar el tambor **2** *vt, vi* ~ **(sth) on sth** tamborilear (con algo) en algo PHR V **to drum sth into sb/into sb's head** machacarle algo a algn **to drum sb out (of sth)** echar a algn (de algo) **to drum sth up** esforzarse por conseguir algo (*apoyo, clientes, etc*): *to drum up interest in sth* fomentar el interés en algo **drummer** *n* batería

drumstick /ˈdrʌmstɪk/ *n* **1** (*Mús*) baqueta **2** (*Cocina*) pata (*de pollo, etc*)

drunk[1] /drʌŋk/ ◆ *adj* borracho: *to be drunk with joy* estar ebrio de alegría LOC **drunk and disorderly**: *to be charged with being drunk and disorderly* ser acusado de borrachera y alboroto **to get drunk** emborracharse ◆ *n* *Ver* DRUNKARD

drunk[2] *pp de* DRINK

drunkard /ˈdrʌŋkəd/ *n* borracho, -a

drunken /ˈdrʌŋkən/ *adj* borracho: *to be charged with drunken driving* ser acusado de conducir en estado de embriaguez **drunkenness** *n* embriaguez

dry /draɪ/ ◆ *adj* (**drier**, **driest**) **1** seco: *dry white wine* vino blanco seco ◊ *Tonight will be dry.* Esta noche no va a llover. **2** árido **3** (*humor*) irónico LOC *Ver* BONE, HIGH[1], HOME, RUN ◆ *vt, vi* (*pret, pp* **dried**) secar(se): *He dried his eyes.* Se secó las lágrimas. PHR V **to dry out** secarse **to dry up** (*río*), secarse **to dry sth up** secar (*platos, etc*) ◆ *n* LOC **in the dry** a cubierto

dry-clean /draɪ ˈkliːn/ *vt* limpiar en seco **dry-cleaner's** *n* tintorería **dry-cleaning** *n* limpieza en seco

dryer *Ver* DRIER

dry land *n* tierra firme

dryly (*tb* **drily**) /ˈdraɪli/ *adv* en tono seco

dryness /ˈdraməs/ *n* **1** sequedad **2** aridez **3** (*humor*) ironía

dual /ˈdjuːəl; *USA* ˈduːəl/ *adj* doble

dual carriageway *n* (*GB*) autovía

dub /dʌb/ *vt* (**-bb-**) doblar: *dubbed into English* doblado al inglés **dubbing** *n* doblaje

dubious /ˈdjuːbiəs; *USA* ˈduː-/ *adj* **1** *to be dubious about sth* tener dudas acerca de algo **2** (*pey*) (*conducta*) sospechoso **3** (*honor*) discutible **dubiously** *adv* **1** de un modo sospechoso **2** en tono dudoso

duchess (*tb* **Duchess** *en títulos*) /ˈdʌtʃəs/ *n* duquesa

duck /dʌk/ ◆ *n* pato, -a ☛ *Ver nota en* PATO ◆ **1** *vi* agachar la cabeza: *He ducked behind a rock.* Se escondió detrás de una roca. **2** *vt* (*responsabilidad*) eludir PHR V **to duck out of sth** (*coloq*) escaquearse de algo

duct /dʌkt/ *n* conducto

dud /dʌd/ ◆ *adj* (*coloq*) **1** defectuoso **2** inútil **3** (*cheque*) sin fondos ◆ *n* (*coloq*): *This battery is a dud.* Esta pila es defectuosa.

due /djuː; *USA* duː/ ◆ *adj* **1** *the money due to them* el dinero que se les debe ◊ *Our thanks are due to…* Quedamos agradecidos a… ◊ *Payment is due on the fifth.* El próximo pago vence el cinco. **2** *The bus is due (in) at five o'clock.* El autobús tiene la llegada a las cinco. ◊ *She's due to arrive soon.* Debe llegar pronto. ◊ *She's due back on Thursday.* Se la espera el jueves. **3 due (for) sth**: *I reckon I'm due (for) a holiday.* Creo que me merezco unas vacaciones. **4** debido: *with all due respect* con el debido respeto ◊ *It's all due to her efforts.* Se lo debemos todo a su esfuerzo. LOC **in due course** a su debido tiempo ◆ **dues** *n* [*pl*] cuota LOC **to give sb their due** para ser justo ◆ *adv*: *due south* directamente al sur

duel /ˈdjuːəl; *USA* ˈduːəl/ *n* duelo

duet /djuˈet; *USA* duːˈet/ *n* dúo (*pieza musical*)

duffle coat /ˈdʌfl kəʊt/ *n* trenca

dug *pret, pp de* DIG

duke (*tb* **Duke** *en títulos*) /djuːk; *USA* duːk/ *n* duque

dull /dʌl/ *adj* (**-er**, **-est**) **1** (*tiempo*) gris **2** (*color*) apagado **3** (*superficie*) deslustrado **4** (*luz*) sombrío: *a dull glow* una luz mortecina **5** (*dolor, ruido*) sordo **6** aburrido, soso **7** (*filo*) embotado **dully** *adv* con desgana

duly /ˈdjuːli; *USA* ˈduːli/ *adv* **1** debidamente **2** a su debido tiempo

dumb /dʌm/ *adj* (**-er**, **-est**) **1** mudo: *to be deaf and dumb* ser sordomudo **2** (*coloq*) tonto **dumbly** *adv* sin hablar

dumbfounded (*tb* **dumfounded**

/dʌmˈfaʊndɪd/ (*tb* **dumbstruck**) *adj* mudo de asombro

dummy /ˈdʌmi/ ◆ *n* (*pl* **-ies**) **1** maniquí **2** imitación **3** chupete **4** (*coloq*) imbécil ◆ *adj* postizo: *dummy run* ensayo

dump /dʌmp/ ◆ *vt, vi* **1** verter, tirar: *No dumping.* Prohibido tirar basuras. ◊ *dumping ground* vertedero **2** (*coloq, pey*) abandonar **3** deshacerse de ◆ *n* **1** vertedero **2** (*Mil*) depósito **3** (*coloq, pey*) antro

dumpling /ˈdʌmplɪŋ/ *n* bola de una masa especial que se come en Gran Bretaña con los estofados

dumps /dʌmps/ *n* [*pl*] LOC **to be (down) in the dumps** (*coloq*) estar mustio

dune /djuːn; *USA* duːn/ (*tb* **sand-dune**) *n* duna

dung /dʌŋ/ *n* boñigas, estiércol

dungarees /ˌdʌŋgəˈriːz/ *n* [*pl*] pantalones de peto

dungeon /ˈdʌndʒən/ *n* mazmorra

duo /ˈdjuːəʊ; *USA* ˈduːəʊ/ *n* (*pl* **duos**) dúo

dupe /djuːp; *USA* duːp/ *vt* engañar

duplicate /ˈdjuːplɪkeɪt; *USA* ˈduː-/ ◆ *vt* duplicar ◆ /ˈdjuːplɪkət; *USA* ˈduː-/ *adj, n* duplicado: *a duplicate (letter)* una copia

durable /ˈdjʊərəbl; *USA* ˈdʊə-/ ◆ *adj* duradero ◆ *n* [*pl*] (*tb* **consumer durables**) electrodomésticos **durability** /ˌdjʊərəˈbɪləti; *USA* ˌdʊə-/ *n* durabilidad

duration /djuˈreɪʃn; *USA* du-/ *n* duración LOC **for the duration** (*coloq*) durante el tiempo que dure

duress /djuˈres; *USA* du-/ *n* LOC **to do sth under duress** hacer algo bajo coacción

during /ˈdjʊərɪŋ; *USA* ˈdʊər-/ *prep* durante: *during the meal* mientras comíamos ☛ *Ver ejemplos en* FOR 3 *y nota en* DURANTE

dusk /dʌsk/ *n* crepúsculo: *at dusk* al atardecer

dusky /ˈdʌski/ *adj* (**-ier**, **-iest**) moreno

dust /dʌst/ ◆ *n* polvo: *gold dust* oro en polvo ◆ *vt, vi* limpiar el polvo PHR V **to dust sth/sb down/off** quitarle el polvo a algo/algn **to dust sth with sth** espolvorear algo de algo

dustbin /ˈdʌstbɪn/ *n* cubo de basura

duster /ˈdʌstə(r)/ *n* trapo (del polvo): *feather duster* plumero

dustman /ˈdʌstmən/ *n* (*pl* **-men** /-mən/) barrendero, basurero

dustpan /ˈdʌstpæn/ *n* recogedor

dusty /ˈdʌsti/ *adj* (**-ier**, **-iest**) polvoriento

Dutch /dʌtʃ/ *adj* LOC **Dutch courage** (*coloq, joc*) valor infundido por el alcohol **to go Dutch (with sb)** pagar a escote

dutiful /ˈdjuːtɪfl; *USA* ˈduː-/ *adj* (*fml*) obediente, concienzudo **dutifully** *adv* obedientemente, cumplidamente

duty /ˈdjuːti; *USA* ˈduːti/ *n* (*pl* **duties**) **1** deber, obligación: *to do your duty (by sb)* cumplir uno con su deber (para con algn) **2** obligación, función: *duty officer* oficial de guardia ◊ *the duties of the president* las obligaciones de la presidenta **3** ~ (**on sth**) aranceles (sobre algo) *Ver tb* TARIFF 2 LOC **to be on/off duty** estar/no estar de servicio

duty-free /ˈdjuːti friː; *USA* ˈduːti-/ *adj* libre de impuestos

duvet /ˈduːveɪ/ *n* edredón nórdico

dwarf /dwɔːf/ ◆ *n* (*pl* **dwarfs** *o* **dwarves** /dwɔːvz/) enano, -a ◆ *vt* empequeñecer: *a house dwarfed by skyscrapers* una casa empequeñecida por los rascacielos

dwell /dwel/ *vi* (*pret, pp* **dwelt** /dwelt/ *o* **dwelled**) ~ **in/at sth** (*antic, ret*) morar en algo PHR V **to dwell on/upon sth 1** insistir en algo, extenderse en algo **2** dejarse obsesionar por algo **dwelling** (*tb* **dwelling place**) *n* morada, vivienda

dwindle /ˈdwɪndl/ *vi* disminuir, reducirse: *to dwindle (away) (to nothing)* quedar reducido (a la nada)

dye /daɪ/ ◆ *vt, vi* (*3ª pers sing pres* **dyes** *pret, pp* **dyed** *pt pres* **dyeing**) teñir(se): *to dye sth blue* teñir algo de azul ◆ *n* tinte (*para el pelo, la ropa, etc*)

dying /ˈdaɪɪŋ/ *adj* **1** (*persona*) moribundo, agonizante **2** (*palabras, momentos, etc*) último: *her dying wish* su último deseo ◊ *a dying breed* una raza en vías de extinción

dyke /daɪk/ (*tb* **dike**) *n* **1** dique **2** acequia

dynamic /daɪˈnæmɪk/ *adj* dinámico

dynamics /daɪˈnæmɪks/ *n* [*pl*] dinámica

dynamism /ˈdaɪnəmɪzəm/ *n* dinamismo

dynamite /ˈdaɪnəmaɪt/ ◆ *n* (*lit y fig*) dinamita ◆ *vt* dinamitar

dynamo /ˈdaɪnəməʊ/ *n* (*pl* ~**s**) dinamo, dínamo

dynasty /ˈdɪnəsti; *USA* ˈdaɪ-/ *n* (*pl* **-ies**) dinastía

dysentery /ˈdɪsəntri; *USA* -teri/ *n* disentería

dyslexia /dɪsˈleksiə/ (*tb* **word-blindness**) *n* dislexia **dyslexic** *adj*, *n* disléxico, -a

dystrophy /ˈdɪstrəfi/ *n* distrofia

Ee

E, e /iː/ *n* (*pl* **E's**, **e's** /iːz/) **1** E, e: *E for Edward* E de Enrique ☛ *Ver ejemplos en* A, a **2** (*Educ*) aprobado bajo: *to get (an) E in French* sacar (un) aprobado bajo en Francés **3** (*Mús*) mi

each /iːtʃ/ ◆ *adj* cada: *each for himself* cada cual por su cuenta

> **Each** casi siempre se traduce por "cada (uno)" y **every** por "todo(s)". Una excepción importante es cuando se expresa la repetición de algo a intervalos fijos de tiempo: *The Olympics are held every four years.* Los Juegos Olímpicos se celebran cada cuatro años. *Ver tb nota en* EVERY.

◆ *pron* cada uno (*de dos o más*) ◆ *adv* cada uno: *We have two each.* Tenemos dos cada uno.

each other *pron* uno a otro (*mutuamente*) ☛ **Each other** se suele utilizar para referirse a dos personas y **one another** a más de dos: *We love each other.* Nos queremos. ◊ *They all looked at one another.* Todos se miraron (entre sí).

eager /ˈiːgə(r)/ *adj* ~ (**for sth/to do sth**) ávido (de algo); ansioso (por hacer algo): *eager to please* ansioso por complacer **eagerly** *adv* con impaciencia/ilusión **eagerness** *n* ansia

eagle /ˈiːgl/ *n* águila

ear[1] /ɪə(r)/ *n* **1** oreja **2** oído: *to have an ear/a good ear for sth* tener buen oído para algo LOC **to be all ears** (*coloq*) ser todo oídos **to be up to your ears/eyes in sth** estar hasta el cuello de algo *Ver tb* PLAY, PRICK

ear[2] /ɪə(r)/ *n* espiga

earache /ˈɪəreɪk/ *n* [*gen sing*] dolor de oídos

eardrum /ˈɪədrʌm/ *n* tímpano

earl /ɜːl/ *n* conde

early /ˈɜːli/ ◆ *adj* (**-ier**, **-iest**) **1** temprano **2** (*muerte*) prematuro **3** (*jubilación*) anticipado **4** (*primero*): *my earliest memories* mis primeros recuerdos ◊ *at an early age* a una edad temprana ◆ *adv* (**-ier**, **-iest**) **1** temprano **2** con anticipación **3** prematuramente **4** a principios de: *early last week* a principios de la semana pasada LOC **as early as...**: *as early as 1988* ya en 1988 **at the earliest** como muy pronto **early bird** (*joc*) madrugador **early on** al poco de empezar: *earlier on* anteriormente **it's early days (yet)** (*esp GB*) es demasiado pronto **the early bird catches the worm** (*refrán*) al que madruga, Dios le ayuda **the early hours** la madrugada

earmark /ˈɪəmɑːk/ *vt* (*fig*) destinar

earn /ɜːn/ *vt* **1** (*dinero*) ganar: *to earn a living* ganarse la vida **2** merecer(se)

earnest /ˈɜːnɪst/ *adj* **1** (*carácter*) serio **2** (*deseo, etc*) ferviente LOC **in (deadly) earnest 1** de veras **2** en serio: *She was in deadly earnest.* Hablaba con la mayor seriedad. **earnestly** *adv* con empeño **earnestness** *n* fervor

earnings /ˈɜːnɪŋz/ *n* [*pl*] ingresos

earphones /ˈɪəfəʊnz/ *n* [*pl*] auriculares

earring /ˈɪərɪŋ/ *n* pendiente

earshot /ˈɪəʃɒt/ *n* LOC **(to be) out of/within earshot** (estar) fuera del/al alcance del oído

earth /ɜːθ/ ◆ *n* **1 the Earth** (*planeta*) la Tierra **2** (*Geol*) tierra **3** (*Electrón*) tierra LOC **how/what/why, etc on earth/in the world** (*coloq*) ¿cómo/qué/por qué demonios?: *What on earth are you doing?* ¿Qué demonios estás haciendo? **to charge/cost/pay the earth** (*coloq*) cobrar/costar/pagar un dineral **to come back/down to earth (with a bang/bump)** (*coloq*) bajar de las nubes ◆ *vt* (*Electrón, esp GB*) conectar a tierra

earthly /ˈɜːθli/ *adj* **1** (*lit*) terrenal **2** (*coloq, fig*) concebible: *You haven't an earthly (chance) of winning.* No tienes la más remota posibilidad de ganar. ☛ En este sentido suele usarse en frases negativas o interrogativas.

earthquake /ˈɜːθkweɪk/ (*tb* **quake**) *n* terremoto

ease /iːz/ ◆ *n* **1** facilidad **2** desahogo **3** alivio LOC **(to be/feel) at (your) ease** (estar/sentirse) relajado *Ver tb* ILL, MIND ◆ *vt* **1** (*dolor*) aliviar **2** (*tensión*) reducir **3** (*tráfico*) disminuir **4** (*situación*) suavizar **5** (*restricción*) aflojar LOC **to ease sb's conscience/mind** tranquilizar la conciencia/mente de algn PHR V **to ease (sth/sb) across, along, etc sth** mover (algo/a algn) cuidadosamente a través de, a lo largo de, etc algo **to ease off/up** aligerarse **to ease up on sth/sb** moderarse con algo/algn

easel /ˈiːzl/ *n* caballete (*de artista*)

easily /ˈiːzəli/ *adv* **1** fácilmente *Ver tb* EASY **2** seguramente: *It's easily the best.* Es seguramente el mejor. **3** muy probablemente

east /iːst/ ◆ *n* **1** (*tb* **the east, the East**) (*abrev* **E**) (el) este: *Newcastle is in the East of England.* Newcastle está al este de Inglaterra. ◊ *eastbound* en/con dirección este **2 the East** (el) Oriente ◆ *adj* (del) este, oriental: *east winds* vientos del este ◆ *adv* al este: *They headed east.* Fueron hacia el este. *Ver tb* EASTWARD(S)

Easter /ˈiːstə(r)/ *n* Pascua: *Easter egg* huevo de Pascua

eastern /ˈiːstən/ (*tb* **Eastern**) *adj* (del) este, oriental

eastward(s) /ˈiːstwəd(z)/ *adv* hacia el este *Ver tb* EAST *adv*

easy /ˈiːzi/ ◆ *adj* (**-ier**, **-iest**) **1** fácil **2** tranquilo: *My mind is easier now.* Estoy más tranquilo ahora. LOC **I'm easy** (*coloq, esp GB*) me da igual ◆ *adv* (**-ier**, **-iest**) LOC **easier said than done** más fácil decirlo que hacerlo **take it easy!** ¡cálmate! **to go easy on/with sth/sb** (*coloq*) tomárselo con tranquilidad con algo/algn **to take it/things easy** tomarse las cosas con calma *Ver tb* FREE

easygoing /ˌiːziˈɡəʊɪŋ/ *adj* tolerante: *She's very easygoing.* Es de trato muy fácil.

eat /iːt/ *vt, vi* (*pret* **ate** /et; *USA* eɪt/ *pp* **eaten** /ˈiːtn/) comer LOC **to be eaten up with sth** estar consumido por algo **to be eating sb** estar inquietando a algn: *What's eating you?* ¿Qué te atormenta? **to eat out of sb's hand** estar sometido a algn: *She had him eating out of her hand.* Lo tenía totalmente dominado. **to eat your words** tragarse las palabras *Ver tb* CAKE PHR V **to eat away at sth/eat sth away 1** (*lit*) erosionar algo **2** (*fig*) consumir algo **to eat into sth 1** corroer algo, desgastar algo **2** (*fig*) mermar algo (*reservas*) **to eat out** comer fuera **to eat (sth) up** comérselo todo **to eat sth up** (*fig*) devorar algo: *This car eats up petrol!* Este coche chupa un montón de gasolina. **eater** *n*: *He's a big eater.* Es un comilón.

eavesdrop /ˈiːvzdrɒp/ *vi* (**-pp-**) ~ **(on sth/sb)** espiar (algo/a algn) (*escuchar*)

ebb /eb/ ◆ *vi* **to ebb (away) 1** (*marea*) bajar **2** (*fig*) disminuir ◆ **the ebb** *n* [*sing*] (*lit y fig*) (el) reflujo LOC **on the ebb** en decadencia **the ebb and flow (of sth)** los altibajos (de algo)

ebony /ˈebəni/ *n* ébano

echo /ˈekəʊ/ ◆ *n* (*pl* **echoes**) **1** eco, resonancia **2** (*fig*) imitación ◆ **1** *vt* ~ **sth (back)**: *The tunnel echoed back their words.* El eco del túnel repitió sus palabras. **2** *vt* (*fig*) repetir, reflejar algo **3** *vi* resonar

ecological /ˌiːkəˈlɒdʒɪkl/ *adj* ecológico **ecologically** *adv* ecológicamente

ecology /iˈkɒlədʒi/ *n* ecología **ecologist** *n* ecologista

economic /ˌiːkəˈnɒmɪk, ˌekəˈnɒmɪk/ *adj* **1** (*desarrollo, crecimiento, política*) económico ☛ *Comparar con* ECONOMICAL **2** rentable

economical /ˌiːkəˈnɒmɪkl, ˌekəˈnɒmɪkl/ *adj* (*combustible, aparato,* *estilo*) económico ☛ A diferencia de **economic**, **economical** puede ser calificado por palabras como *more, less, very*, etc: *a more economical car* un coche más económico LOC **to be economical with the truth** decir las verdades a medias **economically** *adv* económicamente

economics /ˌiːkəˈnɒmɪks, ˌekəˈnɒmɪks/ *n* [*sing*] **1** economía **2** (*Educ*) económicas **economist** *n* economista

economize, -ise /ɪˈkɒnəmaɪz/ *vi* economizar: *to economize on petrol* ahorrar gasolina

economy /ɪˈkɒnəmi/ *n* (*pl* **-ies**) economía: *to make economies* economizar ◊ *economy size* envase de ahorro

ecstasy /ˈekstəsi/ *n* (*pl* **-ies**) éxtasis: *to be in/go into ecstasy/ecstasies (over sth)* extasiarse (con algo) **ecstatic** /ɪkˈstætɪk/ *adj* extasiado

edge /edʒ/ ◆ *n* **1** filo (*de cuchillo, etc*) **2** borde LOC **to be on edge** estar con los nervios de punta **to have an/the edge on/over sth/sb** (*coloq*) tener ventaja sobre algo/algn **to take the edge off sth** suavizar algo ◆ *vt, vi* ~ (**sth**) (**with sth**) bordear (algo) (de algo) PHR V **to edge** (**your way**) **along, away, etc** avanzar, alejarse, etc poco a poco: *I edged slowly towards the door.* Me fui acercando poco a poco hacia la puerta.

edgy /ˈedʒi/ *adj* (*coloq*) nervioso

edible /ˈedəbl/ *adj* comestible

edit /ˈedɪt/ *vt* **1** (*libro*) preparar una edición de **2** (*texto*) editar **edition** *n* edición

editor /ˈedɪtə(r)/ *n* director, -ora (*de periódico, etc*): *the arts editor* el director/la directora de la sección de cultura

educate /ˈedʒukeɪt/ *vt* educar (*académicamente*): *He was educated abroad.* Se educó en el extranjero. ☛ *Comparar con* RAISE, TO BRING SB UP *en* BRING **educated** *adj* culto LOC **an educated guess** una predicción con fundamento

education /ˌedʒuˈkeɪʃn/ *n* **1** educación, enseñanza **2** pedagogía **educational** *adj* educativo, educacional, docente

eel /iːl/ *n* anguila

eerie (*tb* **eery**) /ˈɪəri/ *adj* (**-ier**, **-iest**) misterioso, horripilante

effect /ɪˈfekt/ ◆ *n* efecto: *It had no effect on her.* No le hizo ningún efecto. LOC **for effect** para impresionar **in effect** en realidad **to come into effect** entrar en vigor **to take effect 1** surtir efecto **2** entrar en vigor **to no effect** inútilmente **to this effect** con este propósito *Ver tb* WORD ◆ (*fml*) *vt* efectuar (*una cura, un cambio*) ☛ *Comparar con* AFFECT

effective /ɪˈfektɪv/ *adj* **1** (*sistema, medicina*) ~ (**in doing sth**) eficaz (para hacer algo) **2** de mucho efecto **effectively** *adv* **1** eficazmente **2** en efecto **effectiveness** *n* eficacia

effeminate /ɪˈfemɪnət/ *adj* afeminado

efficient /ɪˈfɪʃnt/ *adj* **1** (*persona*) eficiente **2** (*máquina, etc*) eficaz **efficiency** *n* eficiencia **efficiently** *adv* eficientemente

effort /ˈefət/ *n* **1** esfuerzo: *to make an effort* esforzarse/hacer un esfuerzo **2** intento

eg /ˌiːˈdʒiː/ *abrev* por ejemplo (=p.ej.)

egg /eg/ ◆ *n* huevo LOC **to put all your eggs in one basket** jugárselo todo a una carta ◆ PHR V **to egg sb on** (**to do sth**) animar mucho a algn (a que haga algo)

eggplant /ˈegplɑːnt/ *n* (*esp USA*) *Ver* AUBERGINE

eggshell /ˈegʃel/ *n* cáscara de huevo

ego /ˈegəʊ; *USA* ˈiːgəʊ/ *n* ego: *to boost sb's ego* levantar la moral a algn

eight /eɪt/ *adj, pron, n* ocho ☛ *Ver ejemplos en* FIVE **eighth 1** *adj* octavo **2** *pron, adv* el octavo, la octava, los octavos, las octavas **3** *n* octava parte, octavo ☛ *Ver ejemplos en* FIFTH

eighteen /ˌeɪˈtiːn/ *adj, pron, n* dieciocho ☛ *Ver ejemplos en* FIVE **eighteenth 1** *adj* decimoctavo **2** *pron, adv* el decimoctavo, la decimoctava, los decimoctavos, las decimoctavas **3** *n* dieciochava parte, dieciochavo ☛ *Ver ejemplos en* FIFTH

eighty /ˈeɪti/ *adj, pron, n* ochenta ☛ *Ver ejemplos en* FIFTY, FIVE **eightieth 1** *adj, pron* octogésimo **2** *n* ochentava parte, ochentavo ☛ *Ver ejemplos en* FIFTH

either /ˈaɪðə(r); ˈiːðər/ ◆ *adj* **1** cualquiera de los dos: *Either kind of flour will do.* Cualquiera de los dos tipos de harina sirve. ◊ *either way...* de cualquiera de las dos maneras... **2**

ambos: *on either side of the road* en ambos lados de la calle **3** [*en frases negativas*] ninguno de los dos ◆ *pron* **1** cualquiera, uno u otro **2** ninguno: *I don't want either of them.* No quiero ninguno de los dos. ☛ *Ver nota en* NINGUNO ◆ *adv* **1** tampoco: *'I'm not going.' 'I'm not either.'* —No pienso ir. —Yo tampoco. **2 either ... or ...** o ... o ..., ni ... ni ... ☛ *Comparar con* ALSO, TOO *y ver nota en* NEITHER

eject /iˈdʒekt/ **1** *vt* (*fml*) expulsar **2** *vt* arrojar **3** *vi* eyectar

elaborate[1] /ɪˈlæbərət/ *adj* complicado, intrincado

elaborate[2] /ɪˈlæbəreɪt/ *vi* ~ (**on sth**) dar detalles (sobre algo)

elapse /ɪˈlæps/ *vi* (*fml*) pasar (*tiempo*)

elastic /ɪˈlæstɪk/ ◆ *adj* **1** elástico **2** flexible ◆ *n* goma (elástica)

elastic band *n* goma elástica

elated /iˈleɪtɪd/ *adj* jubiloso

elbow /ˈelbəʊ/ *n* codo

elder /ˈeldə(r)/ *adj, pron* mayor: *Pitt the Elder* Pitt el Viejo

> Los comparativos más normales de **old** son **older** y **oldest**: *He is older than me.* Es mayor que yo. ◊ *the oldest building in the city* el edificio más antiguo de la ciudad. Cuando se comparan las edades de las personas, sobre todo de los miembros de una familia, **elder** y **eldest** se usan muy a menudo como adjetivos y como pronombres: *my eldest brother* mi hermano el mayor ◊ *the elder of the two brothers* el mayor de los dos hermanos. Nótese que **elder** y **eldest** no se pueden usar con *than* y como adjetivos sólo pueden ir delante del sustantivo.

elderly *adj* anciano: *the elderly* los ancianos

eldest /ˈeldɪst/ *adj, pron* mayor ☛ *Ver nota en* ELDER

elect /ɪˈlekt/ *vt* elegir **election** *n* elección ☛ *Ver* pág 322. **electoral** *adj* electoral **electorate** *n* [*v sing o pl*] electorado

electric /ɪˈlektrɪk/ *adj* eléctrico **electrical** *adj* eléctrico ☛ *Ver nota en* ELÉCTRICO **electrician** /ɪˌlekˈtrɪʃn/ *n* electricista **electricity** /ɪˌlekˈtrɪsəti/ *n* electricidad: *to switch off the electricity* cortar la corriente **electrification** *n* electrificación **electrify** *vt* (*pret, pp* **-fied**) **1** electrificar **2** (*fig*) electrizar

electrocute /ɪˈlektrəkjuːt/ *vt* **to be electrocuted** electrocutarse

electrode /ɪˈlektrəʊd/ *n* electrodo

electron /ɪˈlektrɒn/ *n* electrón

electronic /ɪˌlekˈtrɒnɪk/ *adj* electrónico **electronics** *n* [*sing*] electrónica

elegant /ˈelɪgənt/ *adj* elegante **elegance** *n* elegancia

element /ˈelɪmənt/ *n* elemento

elementary /ˌelɪˈmentri/ *adj* elemental: *elementary school* escuela primaria

elephant /ˈelɪfənt/ *n* elefante

elevator /ˈelɪveɪtə(r)/ *n* (*USA*) ascensor

eleven /ɪˈlevn/ *adj, pron, n* once ☛ *Ver ejemplos en* FIVE **eleventh** **1** *adj* undécimo **2** *pron, adv* el undécimo, la undécima, los undécimos, las undécimas **3** *n* onceava parte, onceavo ☛ *Ver ejemplos en* FIFTH

elicit /iˈlɪsɪt/ *vt* (*fml*) obtener

eligible /ˈelɪdʒəbl/ *adj*: *to be eligible for sth* tener derecho a algo ◊ *to be eligible to do sth* cubrir los requisitos para hacer algo ◊ *an eligible bachelor* un soltero deseable

eliminate /ɪˈlɪmɪneɪt/ *vt* **1** eliminar **2** (*enfermedad, pobreza*) erradicar

elk /elk/ *n* alce

elm /elm/ (*tb* **elm tree**) *n* olmo

elope /ɪˈləʊp/ *vi* fugarse con su amante

eloquent /ˈeləkwənt/ *adj* elocuente

else /els/ *adv* [*con pronombres indefinidos, interrogativos o negativos, y con adverbios*]: *Did you see anybody else?* ¿Viste a alguien más? ◊ *anyone else* cualquier otra persona ◊ *everyone/everything else* todos los/todo lo demás ◊ *It must have been somebody else.* Ha debido ser otro. ◊ *nobody else* nadie más ◊ *Anything else?* ¿Algo más? ◊ *somewhere else* a/en otra parte ◊ *What else?* ¿Qué más? **elsewhere** *adv* en, a o de otra parte

elude /iˈluːd/ *vt* escaparse de **elusive** *adj* escurridizo: *an elusive word* una palabra difícil de recordar

emaciated /ɪˈmeɪʃieɪtɪd/ *adj* demacrado

emanate /ˈeməneɪt/ *vi* ~ **from sth/sb** emanar, provenir de algo/algn

emancipation /ɪˌmænsɪˈpeɪʃn/ *n* emancipación

embankment /ɪmˈbæŋkmənt/ *n* terraplén, ribazo
embargo /ɪmˈbɑːɡəʊ/ *n* (*pl* **~es** /-ɡəʊz/) prohibición, embargo
embark /ɪmˈbɑːk/ *vt, vi* **1** ~ (**for...**) embarcar (con rumbo a...) **2** ~ **on sth** emprender algo
embarrass /ɪmˈbærəs/ *vt* avergonzar, turbar **embarrassing** *adj* embarazoso **embarrassment** *n* **1** vergüenza **2** (*persona o cosa que incomoda*) estorbo
embassy /ˈembəsi/ *n* (*pl* **-ies**) embajada
embedded /ɪmˈbedɪd/ *adj* **1** empotrado **2** (*dientes, espada*) clavado, hincado
ember /ˈembə(r)/ *n* ascua
embezzlement /ɪmˈbezlmənt/ *n* desfalco
embittered /ɪmˈbɪtəd/ *adj* amargado
embody /ɪmˈbɒdi/ *vt* (*pret, pp* **-died**) (*fml*) encarnar **embodiment** *n* personificación
embrace /ɪmˈbreɪs/ ◆ *vt, vi* abrazar(se) ◆ *n* abrazo
embroider /ɪmˈbrɔɪdə(r)/ *vt, vi* bordar **embroidery** *n* [*incontable*] bordado
embryo /ˈembriəʊ/ *n* (*pl* **~s** /-əʊz/) embrión
emerald /ˈemərəld/ *n* esmeralda
emerge /iˈmɜːdʒ/ *vi* ~ (**from sth**) emerger, surgir (de algo): *It emerged that...* Salió a relucir que... **emergence** *n* aparición, surgimiento
emergency /iˈmɜːdʒənsi/ *n* (*pl* **-ies**) emergencia: *emergency exit* salida de emergencia
emigrate /ˈemɪɡreɪt/ *vi* emigrar **emigrant** *n* emigrante **emigration** *n* emigración
eminent /ˈemɪnənt/ *adj* eminente
emission /iˈmɪʃn/ *n* (*fml*) emanación
emit /iˈmɪt/ *vt* (**-tt-**) **1** (*rayos, sonidos*) emitir **2** (*olores, vapores*) despedir
emotion /ɪˈməʊʃn/ *n* emoción **emotional** *adj* emocional, excitable **emotive** *adj* emotivo
empathy /ˈempəθi/ *n* empatía
emperor /ˈempərə(r)/ *n* emperador
emphasis /ˈemfəsɪs/ *n* (*pl* **-ases** /-əsiːz/) ~ (**on sth**) énfasis (en algo) **emphatic** *adj* categórico, enfático
emphasize, -ise /ˈemfəsaɪz/ *vt* enfatizar, recalcar
empire /ˈempaɪə(r)/ *n* imperio
employ /ɪmˈplɔɪ/ *vt* emplear **employee** *n* empleado **employer** *n* patrón, -ona **employment** *n* empleo, trabajo ☛ *Ver nota en* WORK[1]
empress /ˈemprəs/ *n* emperatriz
empty /ˈempti/ ◆ *adj* **1** vacío **2** vano, inútil ◆ (*pret, pp* **emptied**) **1** *vt* ~ **sth** (**out**) (**onto/into sth**) vaciar, verter algo (en algo) **2** *vt* (*habitación, edificio*) desalojar **3** *vi* ~ vaciarse, quedar vacío **emptiness** *n* **1** vacío **2** (*fig*) futilidad
empty-handed /ˌempti ˈhændɪd/ *adj* con las manos vacías
enable /ɪˈneɪbl/ *vt* ~ **sb to do sth** permitir a algn hacer algo
enact /ɪˈnækt/ *vt* (*fml*) **1** (*Teat*) representar **2** llevar a cabo
enamel /ɪˈnæml/ *n* esmalte
enchanting /ɪnˈtʃɑːntɪŋ; *USA* -ˈtʃænt-/ *adj* encantador
encircle /ɪnˈsɜːkl/ *vt* rodear, cercar
enclose /ɪnˈkləʊz/ *vt* **1** ~ **sth** (**with sth**) cercar algo (de algo) **2** adjuntar: *I enclose.../Please find enclosed...* Le remito adjunto... **enclosure** *n* documento adjunto, anexo
encore /ˈɒŋkɔː(r)/ ◆ *interj* ¡otra! ◆ *n* repetición, bis
encounter /ɪnˈkaʊntə(r)/ ◆ *vt* (*fml*) encontrarse con ◆ *n* encuentro
encourage /ɪnˈkʌrɪdʒ/ *vt* **1** ~ **sb** (**in sth/to do sth**) animar, alentar a algn (en algo/a hacer algo) **2** fomentar, estimular **encouragement** *n* ~ (**to sb**) (**to do sth**) aliento, estímulo (a algn) (para hacer algo) **encouraging** *adj* alentador
encyclopedia (*tb* **-paedia**) /ɪnˌsaɪkləˈpiːdiə/ *n* enciclopedia
end /end/ ◆ *n* **1** final, extremo: *from end to end* de punta a punta **2** (*palo, etc*) punta **3** (*hilo, etc*) cabo **4** *the east end of town* la parte/zona del este de la ciudad **5** (*tiempo*) fin, final: *at the end of* a final/a finales de ◇ *from beginning to end* de principio a fin **6** propósito, fin **7** (*Dep*) campo, lado LOC (**to be**) **at an end** tocar a su fin, haber terminado (ya) **in the end** al final **on end 1** de punta **2** *for days on end* durante varios días **to be at the end of your tether** no poder uno más *Ver tb* LOOSE, MEANS[1], ODDS, WIT ◆ *vt, vi* terminar, acabar PHR V **to end in sth 1** (*forma*) terminar en algo **2** (*resultado*) acabar en algo: *Thei*

argument ended in tears. Su discusión acabó en lágrimas. **to end up (as sth/ doing sth)** terminar (siendo algo/ haciendo algo) **to end up (in...)** ir a parar (a...) (*lugar*)

endanger /ɪnˈdeɪndʒə(r)/ *vt* poner en peligro

endear /ɪnˈdɪə(r)/ *vt* (*fml*) ~ **sb/ yourself to sb** hacerse querer por algn; granjearse las simpatías de algn **endearing** *adj* atractivo

endeavour (*USA* **-vor**) /ɪnˈdevə(r)/ ◆ *n* (*fml*) esfuerzo ◆ *vi* (*fml*) ~ **to do sth** esforzarse por hacer algo

ending /ˈendɪŋ/ *n* final

endless /ˈendləs/ *adj* **1** interminable, sin fin: *endless possibilities* infinitas posibilidades **2** (*paciencia*) incansable

endorse /ɪnˈdɔːs/ *vt* **1** aprobar **2** (*cheque*) endosar **endorsement** *n* **1** aprobación **2** endoso **3** (*en carné de conductor*) nota de sanción

endow /ɪnˈdaʊ/ *vt* ~ **sth/sb with sth** dotar algo/a algn de algo **endowment** *n* dotación (*dinero*)

endurance /ɪnˈdjʊərəns; *USA* -ˈdʊə-/ *n* resistencia

endure /ɪnˈdjʊə(r); *USA* -ˈdʊər/ **1** *vt* soportar, aguantar ☛ En negativa es más corriente decir **can't bear** o **can't stand**. **2** *vi* perdurar **enduring** *adj* duradero

enemy /ˈenəmi/ *n* (*pl* **-ies**) enemigo, -a

energy /ˈenədʒi/ *n* [*gen incontable*] (*pl* **-ies**) energía **energetic** /ˌenəˈdʒetɪk/ *adj* enérgico

enforce /ɪnˈfɔːs/ *vt* hacer cumplir (*ley*) **enforcement** *n* aplicación

engage /ɪnˈgeɪdʒ/ **1** *vt* ~ **sb (as sth)** (*fml*) contratar a algn (como algo) **2** *vt* (*fml*) (*tiempo, pensamientos*) ocupar **3** *vt* (*fml*) (*atención*) llamar **4** *vi* ~ **(with sth)** (*Mec*) encajar (con algo) PHR V **to engage in sth** dedicarse a algo **to engage sb in sth** ocupar a algn en algo **engaged** *adj* **1** ocupado, comprometido **2** (*GB*) (*USA* **busy**) (*Telec*) comunicando **3** ~ **(to sb)** prometido (a algn): *to get engaged* prometerse **engaging** *adj* atractivo

engagement /ɪnˈgeɪdʒmənt/ *n* **1** compromiso matrimonial **2** (*periodo*) noviazgo **3** cita, compromiso

engine /ˈendʒɪn/ *n* **1** motor: *The engine is overheating.* El motor del coche está demasiado caliente.

> La palabra **engine** se utiliza para referirnos al motor de un vehículo y **motor** para el de los electrodomésticos. **Engine** normalmente es de gasolina y **motor** eléctrico.

2 (*tb* **locomotive**) locomotora: *engine driver* maquinista

engineer /ˌendʒɪˈnɪə(r)/ ◆ *n* **1** ingeniero, -a **2** (*teléfono, mantenimiento, etc*) técnico, -a **3** (*en barco o avión*) maquinista **4** (*USA*) maquinista ◆ *vt* **1** (*coloq, frec pey*) maquinar **2** construir

engineering /ˌendʒɪˈnɪərɪŋ/ *n* ingeniería

engrave /ɪnˈgreɪv/ *vt* ~ **B on A/A with B** grabar B en A **engraving** *n* grabado

engrossed /ɪnˈgrəʊst/ *adj* absorto

enhance /ɪnˈhɑːns; *USA* -ˈhæns/ *vt* **1** aumentar, mejorar **2** (*aspecto*) realzar

enjoy /ɪnˈdʒɔɪ/ *vt* **1** disfrutar de: *Enjoy your meal!* ¡Que aproveche! **2** ~ **doing sth** gustarle a algn hacer algo LOC **to enjoy yourself** pasarlo bien: *Enjoy yourself!* ¡Que lo pases bien! **enjoyable** *adj* agradable, divertido **enjoyment** *n* satisfacción, disfrute: *He spoiled my enjoyment of the film.* Me arruinó la película.

enlarge /ɪnˈlɑːdʒ/ *vt* ampliar **enlargement** *n* ampliación

enlighten /ɪnˈlaɪtn/ *vt* ~ **sb (about/as to/on sth)** aclarar (algo) a algn **enlightened** *adj* **1** (*persona*) culto **2** (*política*) inteligente **enlightenment** *n* (*fml*) **1** aclaración **2 the Enlightenment** el Siglo de las Luces

enlist /ɪnˈlɪst/ **1** *vi* ~ **(in/for sth)** (*Mil*) alistarse (en algo) **2** *vt* ~ **sth/sb (in/for sth)** reclutar algo/a algn (en/para algo)

enmity /ˈenməti/ *n* enemistad

enormous /ɪˈnɔːməs/ *adj* enorme **enormously** *adv* enormemente: *I enjoyed it enormously.* Me gustó muchísimo.

enough /ɪˈnʌf/ ◆ *adj, pron* suficiente, bastante: *Is that enough food for ten?* ¿Será suficiente comida para diez? ◊ *That's enough!* ¡Ya basta! ◊ *I've saved up enough to go on holiday.* He ahorrado lo suficiente para ir de vacaciones. LOC **to have had enough (of sth/sb)** estar harto (de algo/algn) ◆ *adv*

1 ~ (**for sth/sb**) (lo) bastante (para algo/algn) **2** ~ (**to do sth**) (lo) bastante (como para hacer algo): *Is it near enough to go on foot?* ¿Está lo bastante cerca como para ir andando? ☛ Nótese que **enough** siempre aparece después del adjetivo y **too** delante: *You're not old enough./You're too young.* Eres demasiado joven. *Comparar con* TOO LOC **curiously, oddly, strangely, etc enough** lo curioso, extraño, etc es que...

enquire (*tb* **inquire**) /ɪnˈkwaɪə(r)/ (*fml*) **1** *vt* preguntar **2** *vi* ~ (**about sth/sb**) pedir información (sobre algo/algn) **enquiring** (*tb* **inquiring**) *adj* **1** (*mente*) curioso **2** (*mirada*) inquisitiva **enquiry** *n Ver* INQUIRY

enrage /ɪnˈreɪdʒ/ *vt* enfurecer

enrich /ɪnˈrɪtʃ/ *vt* ~ **sth/sb** (**with sth**) enriquecer algo/algn (con algo)

enrol (*esp USA* **enroll**) /ɪnˈrəʊl/ *vt, vi* (**-ll-**) ~ (**sb**) (**in/as sth**) inscribirse/ inscribir a algn, matricularse/ matricular a algn (en/como algo) **enrolment** (*esp USA* **enrollment**) *n* inscripción, matrícula

ensure (*USA* **insure**) /ɪnˈʃʊə(r)/ *vt* asegurar (*garantizar*)

entangle /ɪnˈtæŋgl/ *vt* ~ **sth/sb** (**in/ with sth**) enredar algo/a algn (en algo) **entanglement** *n* enredo

enter /ˈentə(r)/ **1** *vt* entrar en: *The thought never entered my head.* La idea ni se me pasó por la cabeza. **2** *vt, vi* ~ (**for**) **sth** inscribirse en algo **3** *vt* (*colegio, universidad*) matricularse en **4** *vt* (*hospital, sociedad*) ingresar en **5** *vt* ~ **sth** (**up**) (**in sth**) anotar algo (en algo) PHR V **to enter into sth** **1** (*negociaciones*) iniciar **2** (*un acuerdo*) llegar a **3** tener que ver: *What he wants doesn't enter into it.* Lo que él quiera no tiene nada que ver.

enterprise /ˈentəpraɪz/ *n* **1** (*actividad*) empresa **2** espíritu emprendedor **enterprising** *adj* emprendedor

entertain /ˌentəˈteɪn/ *vt, vi* **1** recibir (*en casa*) **2** ~ **sb** (**with sth**) (*divertir*) entretener a algn (con algo) **3** (*idea*) albergar **entertainer** *n* artista de variedades **entertaining** *adj* entretenido, divertido **entertainment** *n* entretenimiento, diversión

enthralling /ɪnˈθrɔːlɪŋ/ *adj* cautivador

enthusiasm /ɪnˈθjuːziæzəm; *USA* -ˈθuː-/ *n* ~ (**for/about sth**) entusiasmo (por algo) **enthusiast** *n* entusiasta **enthusiastic** /ɪnˌθjuːziˈæstɪk/ *adj* entusiasta

entice /ɪnˈtaɪs/ *vt* tentar

entire /ɪnˈtaɪə(r)/ *adj* entero, todo **entirely** *adv* totalmente, enteramente **entirety** *n* totalidad

entitle /ɪnˈtaɪtl/ *vt* **1** ~ **sb to** (**do**) **sth** dar derecho a algn a (hacer) algo **2** (*libro*) titular **entitlement** *n* derecho

entity /ˈentəti/ *n* (*pl* **-ies**) entidad, ente

entrance /ˈentrəns/ *n* ~ (**to sth**) entrada (de algo)

entrant /ˈentrənt/ *n* ~ (**for sth**) participante (en algo)

entrepreneur /ˌɒntrəprəˈnɜː(r)/ *n* empresario

entrust /ɪnˈtrʌst/ *vt* ~ **sb with sth/sth to sb** confiar algo a algn

entry /ˈentri/ *n* (*pl* **-ies**) **1** ~ (**into sth**) entrada, ingreso (en algo): *No entry.* Prohibido el paso. **2** (*diario*) apunte, anotación **3** (*diccionario*) entrada

enunciate /ɪˈnʌnsieɪt/ *vt, vi* pronunciar, articular

envelop /ɪnˈveləp/ *vt* ~ **sth/sb** (**in sth**) envolver algo/a algn (en algo)

envelope /ˈenvələʊp, ˈɒn-/ *n* sobre (*para carta*)

enviable /ˈenviəbl/ *adj* envidiable **envious** *adj* envidioso: *to be envious of* tener envidia de/envidiar

environment /ɪnˈvaɪrənmənt/ **the environment** *n* el medio ambiente **environmental** /ɪnˌvaɪrənˈmentl/ *adj* del medio ambiente **environmentalist** *n* ecologista

envisage /ɪnˈvɪzɪdʒ/ *vt* imaginar(se)

envoy /ˈenvɔɪ/ *n* enviado, -a

envy /ˈenvi/ ◆ *n* envidia ◆ *vt* (*pret, pp* **envied**) envidiar

enzyme /ˈenzaɪm/ *n* enzima

ephemeral /ɪˈfemərəl/ *adj* efímero

epic /ˈepɪk/ ◆ *n* épica, epopeya ◆ *adj* épico

epidemic /ˌepɪˈdemɪk/ *n* epidemia

epilepsy /ˈepɪlepsi/ *n* epilepsia **epileptic** /ˌepɪˈleptɪk/ *adj, n* epiléptico, -a

episode /ˈepɪsəʊd/ *n* episodio

epitaph /ˈepɪtɑːf; *USA* -tæf/ *n* epitafio

epitome /ɪˈpɪtəmi/ *n* LOC **to be the**

epitome of sth ser la más pura expresión de algo

epoch /ˈiːpɒk; *USA* ˈepək/ *n* (*fml*) época

equal /ˈiːkwəl/ ◆ *adj, n* igual: *equal opportunities* igualdad de oportunidades LOC **to be on equal terms (with sb)** tener una relación de igual a igual (con algn) ◆ *vt* (**-ll-**) (*USA* **-l-**) **1** igualar **2** (*Mat*): *13 plus 29 equals 42.* 13 más 29 son 42. **equality** /ɪˈkwɒləti/ *n* igualdad **equally** *adv* **1** igualmente **2** equitativamente

equate /iˈkweɪt/ *vt* ~ **sth (to/with sth)** equiparar, comparar algo (con algo)

equation /ɪˈkweɪʒn/ *n* ecuación

equator /ɪˈkweɪtə(r)/ *n* ecuador

equilibrium /ˌiːkwɪˈlɪbriəm, ˌek-/ *n* equilibrio

equinox /ˈiːkwɪnɒks, ˈek-/ *n* equinoccio

equip /ɪˈkwɪp/ *vt* (**-pp-**) ~ **sth/sb (with sth) (for sth)** equipar, proveer algo/a algn (con/de algo) (para algo) **equipment** *n* [*incontable*] equipo, equipamiento

equitable /ˈekwɪtəbl/ *adj* (*fml*) equitativo, justo

equivalent /ɪˈkwɪvələnt/ *adj, n* ~ **(to sth)** equivalente (a algo)

era /ˈɪərə/ *n* era

eradicate /ɪˈrædɪkeɪt/ *vt* erradicar

erase /ɪˈreɪz; *USA* ɪˈreɪs/ *vt* ~ **sth (from sth)** borrar algo (de algo) ☛ Para las marcas de lápiz utilizamos **rub out**. **eraser** (*USA*) (*GB* **rubber**) *n* goma (de borrar)

erect /ɪˈrekt/ ◆ *vt* erigir ◆ *adj* **1** erguido **2** (*pene*) erecto **erection** *n* erección

erode /ɪˈrəʊd/ *vt* erosionar

erotic /ɪˈrɒtɪk/ *adj* erótico

errand /ˈerənd/ *n* recado: *to run errands for sb* hacer recados para algn

erratic /ɪˈrætɪk/ *adj* (*frec pey*) irregular

error /ˈerə(r)/ *n* (*fml*) error: *to make an error* cometer un error ◇ *The letter was sent to you in error.* Se le envió la carta por error. ☛ **Mistake** es un término más corriente que **error**. Sin embargo, en algunas construcciones sólo se puede utilizar **error**: *human error* error humano ◇ *an error of judgement* una equivocación. *Ver nota en* MISTAKE LOC *Ver* TRIAL

erupt /ɪˈrʌpt/ *vi* **1** (*volcán*) entrar en erupción **2** (*violencia*) estallar

escalate /ˈeskəleɪt/ *vt, vi* **1** aumentar **2** intensificar(se) **escalation** *n* escalada

escalator /ˈeskəleɪtə(r)/ *n* escalera mecánica

escapade /ˌeskəˈpeɪd, ˈeskəpeɪd/ *n* aventura

escape /ɪˈskeɪp/ ◆ **1** *vi* ~ **(from sth/sb)** escapar (de algo/algn) **2** *vt, vi* salvarse (de): *They escaped unharmed.* Salieron ilesos. **3** *vi* (*gas, líquido*) fugarse LOC **to escape (sb's) notice** pasar inadvertido (a algn) *Ver tb* LIGHTLY ◆ *n* **1** ~ **(from sth)** fuga (de algo): *to make your escape* darse a la fuga **2** (*de gas, fluido*) escape LOC *Ver* NARROW

escort /ˈeskɔːt/ ◆ *n* **1** [*v sing o pl*] escolta **2** (*fml*) acompañante ◆ /ɪˈskɔːt/ *vt* ~ **sb (to sth)** acompañar a algn (a algo)

especially /ɪˈspeʃəli/ *adv* sobre todo, especialmente ☛ *Ver nota en* SPECIAL

espionage /ˈespiənɑːʒ/ *n* espionaje

essay /ˈeseɪ/ *n* **1** (*Liter*) ensayo **2** (*colegio*) redacción

essence /ˈesns/ *n* esencia **essential** *adj* **1** ~ **(to/for sth)** imprescindible (para algo) **2** fundamental **essentially** *adv* básicamente

establish /ɪˈstæblɪʃ/ *vt* ~ **sth/sb/yourself** establecer(se) **established** *adj* **1** (*negocio*) sólido **2** (*religión*) oficial **establishment** *n* **1** establecimiento **2** institución **3 the Establishment** (*GB*) el "establishment", el sistema

estate /ɪˈsteɪt/ *n* **1** finca **2** (*bienes*) herencia **3** *Ver* HOUSING ESTATE

estate agent *n* agente inmobiliario

estate (car) *n* ranchera, coche familiar

esteem /ɪˈstiːm/ *n* LOC **to hold sth/sb in high/low esteem** tener una buena/mala opinión de algo/algn

esthetic (*USA*) *Ver* AESTHETIC

estimate /ˈestɪmət/ ◆ *n* **1** cálculo **2** valoración **3** (*cálculo previo*) presupuesto ◆ /ˈestɪmeɪt/ *vt* calcular

estimation /ˌestɪˈmeɪʃn/ *n* juicio

estranged /ɪˈstreɪndʒd/ *adj* LOC **to be estranged from sb 1** estar enemistado con algn **2** vivir separado de algn

estuary /ˈestʃuəri; *USA* -ueri/ *n* (*pl* **-ies**) estuario

etching /etʃɪŋ/ *n* grabado (al aguafuerte)

eternal /ɪˈtɜːnl/ *adj* eterno **eternity** *n* eternidad

ether /ˈiːθə(r)/ *n* éter **ethereal** *adj* etéreo

ethics /ˈeθɪks/ *n* [*sing*] ética **ethical** *adj* ético

ethnic /ˈeθnɪk/ *adj* étnico

ethos /ˈiːθɒs/ *n* (*fml*) carácter

etiquette /ˈetɪket, -kət/ *n* etiqueta (*modales*)

Euro-MP /ˈjʊərəʊ empiː/ *n* eurodiputado, -a

evacuate /ɪˈvækjueɪt/ *vt* evacuar (*a personas*) **evacuee** /ɪˌvækjuˈiː/ *n* evacuado, -a

evade /ɪˈveɪd/ *vt* evadir, eludir

evaluate /ɪˈvæljueɪt/ *vt* evaluar

evaporate /ɪˈvæpəreɪt/ *vt, vi* evaporar(se) **evaporation** *n* evaporación

evasion /ɪˈveɪʒn/ *n* evasión **evasive** *adj* evasivo

eve /iːv/ *n* LOC **on the eve of sth 1** (*lit*) la víspera de algo **2** (*fig*) en vísperas de algo

even[1] /ˈiːvn/ ◆ *adj* **1** (*superficie*) llano, liso **2** (*color*) uniforme **3** (*temperatura*) constante **4** (*competición, puntuación*) igualado **5** (*número*) par ☛ *Comparar con* ODD ◆ PHR V **to even out** allanar(se), nivelar(se) **to even sth out** repartir algo equitativamente **to even sth up** nivelar algo

even[2] /ˈiːvn/ *adv* **1** [*uso enfático*] aun, hasta: *He didn't even open the letter.* Ni siquiera abrió la carta. **2** [*con adj o adv comparativo*] aun LOC **even if/though** aunque, aun cuando **even so** aun así, no obstante

evening /ˈiːvnɪŋ/ *n* **1** tarde, noche: *tomorrow evening* mañana por la tarde/noche ◊ *an evening class* una clase nocturna ◊ *evening dress* traje de noche/de etiqueta ◊ *the evening meal* la cena ◊ *an evening paper* un periódico de la tarde ☛ *Ver nota en* MORNING, TARDE **2** atardecer LOC **good evening** buenas tardes, buenas noches ☛ *Ver nota en* NOCHE

evenly /ˈiːvənli/ *adv* **1** de modo uniforme **2** (*repartir, etc*) equitativamente

event /ɪˈvent/ *n* suceso, acontecimiento LOC **at all events/in any event** en todo caso **in the event** al final **in the event of sth** en caso de (que) **eventful** *adj* memorable

eventual /ɪˈventʃuəl/ *adj* final **eventually** *adv* finalmente

ever /ˈevə(r)/ *adv* nunca, jamás: *more than ever* más que nunca ◊ *for ever (and ever)* para siempre (jamás) ◊ *Has it ever happened before?* ¿Ha pasado alguna vez antes? LOC **ever since** desde entonces ☛ *Ver nota en* ALWAYS, NUNCA

every /ˈevri/ *adj* cada, todos (los): *every (single) time* cada vez ◊ *every 10 minutes* cada 10 minutos

> Utilizamos **every** para referirnos a todos los elementos de un grupo en conjunto: *Every player was on top form.* Todos los jugadores estaban en plena forma. **Each** se utiliza para referirnos individualmente a cada uno de ellos: *The Queen shook hands with each player after the game.* La Reina le dio la mano a cada jugador después del partido. *Ver tb nota en* EACH.

LOC **every last...** hasta el último... **every now and again/then** de vez en cuando **every other** uno sí y otro no: *every other week* cada dos semanas **every so often** alguna que otra vez

everybody /ˈevribɒdi/ (*tb* **everyone** /ˈevriwʌn/) *pron* todos, todo el mundo

> **Everybody**, **anybody** y **somebody** llevan el verbo en singular, pero suelen ir seguidos por un pronombre en plural, salvo en lenguaje formal: *Somebody has left their coat behind.* Alguien se ha dejado el abrigo.

everyday /ˈevrideɪ/ *adj* cotidiano, de todos los días: *for everyday use* para uso diario ◊ *in everyday use* de uso corriente

> **Everyday** sólo se usa antes de un sustantivo. No se debe confundir con la expresión **every day**, que significa "todos los días".

everything /ˈevriθɪŋ/ *pron* todo

everywhere /ˈevriweə(r)/ *adv* (en/a/por) todas partes

evict /ɪˈvɪkt/ *vt* ~ **sth/sb (from sth)** desahuciar algo/a algn (de algo)

evidence /ˈevɪdəns/ *n* [*incontable*] **1** (*derecho*) pruebas: *insufficient evidence* falta de pruebas **2** (*derecho*) testimonio

evident *adj* ~ **(to sb) (that…)** evidente (para algn) (que…) **evidently** *adv* obviamente

evil /ˈiːvl/ ◆ *adj* malvado, muy malo ◆ *n (fml)* mal

evocative /ɪˈvɒkətɪv/ *adj* ~ **(of sth)** evocador (de algo)

evoke /ɪˈvəʊk/ *vt* evocar

evolution /ˌiːvəˈluːʃn; *USA* ˌev-/ *n* evolución

evolve /iˈvɒlv/ *vi* evolucionar

ewe /juː/ *n* oveja hembra

exact /ɪgˈzækt/ *adj* exacto

exacting /ɪgˈzæktɪŋ/ *adj* exigente

exactly /ɪgˈzæktli/ *adv* exactamente LOC **exactly!** ¡exacto!

exaggerate /ɪgˈzædʒəreɪt/ *vt* exagerar **exaggerated** *adj* exagerado

exam /ɪgˈzæm/ *n (Educ)* examen: *to sit an exam* presentarse a un examen

examination /ɪgˌzæmɪˈneɪʃn/ *n (fml)* **1** examen **2** reconocimiento, revisión **examine** *vt* revisar, examinar

example /ɪgˈzɑːmpl; *USA* -ˈzæmpl/ *n* ejemplo LOC **for example** (*abrev* **eg**) por ejemplo *Ver tb* SET[2]

exasperate /ɪgˈzɑːspəreɪt/ *vt* exasperar **exasperation** *n* exasperación

excavate /ˈekskəveɪt/ *vt, vi* excavar

exceed /ɪkˈsiːd/ *vt* exceder(se en), superar **exceedingly** *adv* sumamente

excel /ɪkˈsel/ *vi* (**-ll-**) ~ **in/at sth** sobresalir, destacar en algo

excellent /ˈeksələnt/ *adj* excelente **excellence** *n* excelencia

except /ɪkˈsept/ *prep* **1** ~ **(for) sth/sb** excepto algo/algn **2** ~ **that…** excepto que… **exception** *n* excepción **exceptional** *adj* excepcional

excerpt /ˈeksɜːpt/ *n* ~ **(from sth)** extracto (de algo)

excess /ɪkˈses/ *n* exceso **excessive** *adj* excesivo

exchange /ɪksˈtʃeɪndʒ/ ◆ *n* cambio, intercambio ◆ *vt* **1** ~ **A for B** cambiar A por B **2** ~ **sth (with sb)** cambiar algo (con algn)

the Exchequer /ɪksˈtʃekə(r)/ *n (GB)* Ministerio de Economía y Hacienda

excite /ɪkˈsaɪt/ *vt* excitar **excitable** *adj* excitable **excited** *adj* excitado, emocionado **excitement** *n* emoción **exciting** *adj* emocionante

exclaim /ɪkˈskleɪm/ *vi* exclamar **exclamation** *n* exclamación

exclamation mark *n* signo de admiración ☛ *Ver págs 318–19.*

exclude /ɪkˈskluːd/ *vt* ~ **sth/sb (from sth)** excluir algo/a algn (de algo) **exclusion** *n* ~ **(of sth/sb) (from sth)** exclusión (de algo/algn) (de algo)

exclusive /ɪkˈskluːsɪv/ *adj* **1** exclusivo **2** ~ **of sth/sb** sin incluir algo/a algn

excursion /ɪkˈskɜːʃn; *USA* -ɜːrʒn/ *n* excursión

excuse /ɪkˈskjuːs/ ◆ *n* ~ **(for sth/doing sth)** excusa (por/para algo/hacer algo) ◆ /ɪkˈskjuːz/ *vt* **1** ~ **sth/sb (for sth/doing sth)** disculpar algo/a algn (por algo/por hacer algo) **2** ~ **sb (from sth)** dispensar a algn (de algo)

> Se dice **excuse me** cuando se quiere interrumpir o abordar a algn: *Excuse me, sir!* ¡Oiga, señor!
> Decimos **sorry** cuando tenemos que pedir perdón por algo que hemos hecho: *I'm sorry I'm late.* Siento llegar tarde. ◊ *Did I hit you? I'm sorry!* ¿Te he dado? ¡Perdona! En inglés americano se usa **excuse me** en vez de **sorry**.

execute /ˈeksɪkjuːt/ *vt* ejecutar **execution** *n* ejecución **executioner** *n* verdugo

executive /ɪgˈzekjətɪv/ *n* ejecutivo, -a

exempt /ɪgˈzempt/ ◆ *adj* ~ **(from sth)** exento (de algo) ◆ *vt* ~ **sth/sb (from sth)** eximir algo/a algn (de algo); dispensar a algn (de algo) **exemption** *n* exención

exercise /ˈeksəsaɪz/ ◆ *n* ejercicio ◆ **1** *vi* hacer ejercicio **2** *vt (derecho, poder)* ejercer

exert /ɪgˈzɜːt/ **1** *vt* ~ **sth (on sth/sb)** ejercer algo (sobre algo/algn) **2** *v refl* ~ **yourself** esforzarse **exertion** *n* esfuerzo

exhaust[1] /ɪgˈzɔːst/ *n* **1** (*tb* **exhaust fumes**) gases del tubo de escape **2** (*tb* **exhaust pipe**) tubo de escape

exhaust[2] /ɪgˈzɔːst/ *vt* agotar **exhausted** *adj* exhausto **exhausting** *adj* agotador **exhaustion** *n* agotamiento **exhaustive** *adj* exhaustivo

exhibit /ɪgˈzɪbɪt/ ◆ *n* objeto expuesto ◆ **1** *vt, vi* exponer **2** *vt* manifestar

exhibition /ˌeksɪˈbɪʃn/ *n* exposición

exhilarating /ɪgˈzɪləreɪtɪŋ/ *adj*

estimulante, emocionante **exhilaration** *n* euforia

exile /ˈeksaɪl/ ◆ *n* **1** exilio **2** (*persona*) exiliado, -a ◆ *vt* exiliar

exist /ɪgˈzɪst/ *vi* **1** ~ (**in sth**) existir (en algo) **2** ~ (**on sth**) subsistir (a base de algo) **existence** *n* existencia **existing** *adj* existente

exit /ˈeksɪt/ *n* salida

exotic /ɪgˈzɒtɪk/ *adj* exótico

expand /ɪkˈspænd/ *vt, vi* **1** (*metal, etc*) dilatar(se) **2** (*negocio*) ampliar(se) PHR V **to expand on sth** ampliar algo

expanse /ɪkˈspæns/ *n* ~ (**of sth**) extensión (de algo)

expansion /ɪkˈspænʃn/ *n* **1** expansión **2** desarrollo

expansive /ɪkˈspænsɪv/ *adj* comunicativo

expatriate /ˌeksˈpætriət; *USA* -ˈpeɪt-/ *n* expatriado, -a

expect /ɪkˈspekt/ *vt* **1** ~ **sth** (**from sth/sb**) esperar algo (de algo/algn) ☛ *Ver nota en* ESPERAR **2** (*esp GB, coloq*) suponer **expectant** *adj* expectante: *expectant mother* mujer embarazada **expectancy** *n* expectación *Ver tb* LIFE EXPECTANCY **expectation** *n* ~ (**of sth**) expectativa (de algo) LOC **against/contrary to** (**all**) **expectation(s)** contra todas las previsiones

expedition /ˌekspəˈdɪʃn/ *n* expedición

expel /ɪkˈspel/ *vt* (**-ll-**) ~ **sth/sb** (**from sth**) expulsar algo/a algn (de algo)

expend /ɪkˈspend/ *vt* ~ **sth** (**on/upon sth/doing sth**) (*fml*) emplear algo (en algo/hacer algo)

expendable /ɪkˈspendəbl/ *adj* (*fml*) **1** (*cosas*) desechable **2** (*personas*) prescindible

expenditure /ɪkˈspendɪtʃə(r)/ *n* gasto(s)

expense /ɪkˈspens/ *n* gasto(s), coste **expensive** *adj* caro, costoso

experience /ɪkˈspɪəriəns/ ◆ *n* experiencia ◆ *vt* experimentar **experienced** *adj* experimentado

experiment /ɪkˈsperɪmənt/ ◆ *n* experimento ◆ *vi* ~ (**on/with sth**) hacer experimentos, experimentar (con algo)

expert /ˈekspɜːt/ *adj, n* ~ (**at/in/on sth/at doing sth**) experto, -a, perito, -a (en algo/en hacer algo) **expertise** /ˌekspɜːˈtiːz/ *n* conocimientos (técnicos), pericia

expire /ɪkˈspaɪə(r)/ *vi* vencer, caducar: *My passport's expired.* Mi pasaporte ha caducado. **expiry** *n* vencimiento

explain /ɪkˈspleɪn/ *vt* ~ **sth** (**to sb**) explicar, aclarar algo (a algn): *Explain this to me.* Explícame esto. **explanation** *n* ~ (**of/for sth**) explicación, aclaración (de algo) **explanatory** /ɪkˈsplænətri; *USA* -tɔːri/ *adj* explicativo, aclaratorio

explicit /ɪkˈsplɪsɪt/ *adj* explícito

explode /ɪkˈspləʊd/ *vt, vi* estallar, explotar

exploit[1] /ˈeksplɔɪt/ *n* proeza, hazaña

exploit[2] /ɪkˈsplɔɪt/ *vt* explotar (*personas, recursos*) **exploitation** *n* explotación

explore /ɪkˈsplɔː(r)/ *vt, vi* explorar **exploration** *n* exploración, investigación **explorer** *n* explorador, -ora

explosion /ɪkˈspləʊʒn/ *n* explosión **explosive** *adj, n* explosivo

export /ˈekspɔːt/ ◆ *n* (artículo de) exportación ◆ /ɪkˈspɔːt/ *vt, vi* exportar

expose /ɪkˈspəʊz/ **1** *vt* ~ **sth/sb** (**to sth**) exponer algo/a algn (a algo) **2** *v refl* ~ **yourself** (**to sth**) exponerse (a algo) **3** *vt* (*persona culpable*) desenmascarar **exposed** *adj* descubierto **exposure** *n* **1** ~ (**to sth**) exposición (a algo): *to die of exposure* morir de frío (a la intemperie) **2** (*de falta*) descubrimiento, revelación

express /ɪkˈspres/ ◆ *adj* **1** (*Ferrocarril*) rápido **2** (*entrega*) urgente **3** (*deseo, etc*) expreso ◆ *adv* **1** por envío urgente **2** en tren rápido ◆ *vt* ~ **sth** (**to sb**) expresar algo (a algn): *to express yourself* expresarse ◆ *n* **1** (*tb* **express train**) rápido **2** servicio/envío urgente

expression /ɪkˈspreʃn/ *n* **1** expresión **2** muestra, expresión: *as an expression of his gratitude* como muestra de su gratitud **3** expresividad

expressive /ɪkˈspresɪv/ *adj* expresivo

expressly /ɪkˈspresli/ *adv* expresamente

expulsion /ɪkˈspʌlʃn/ *n* expulsión

exquisite /ˈekskwɪzɪt, ɪkˈskwɪzɪt/ *adj* exquisito

extend /ɪkˈstend/ **1** *vt* extender, ampliar **2** *vi* extenderse: *to extend as far as sth* llegar hasta algo **3** *vt* (*estancia, vida*) prolongar **4** *vt* (*plazo, crédito*) prorrogar **5** *vt* (*mano*) tender **6** *vt* (*bienvenida*) dar

extension /ɪkˈstenʃn/ *n* **1** extensión **2** ~ **(to sth)** ampliación, anexo (de algo): *to build an extension to sth* hacer ampliaciones a algo **3** (*periodo*) prolongación **4** (*plazo*) prórroga **5** (*Telec*) supletorio **6** (*Telec*) extensión (*número*)

extensive /ɪkˈstensɪv/ *adj* **1** extenso **2** (*daños*) cuantioso **3** (*conocimiento*) amplio **4** (*uso*) frecuente **extensively** *adv* **1** extensamente **2** (*usar*) comúnmente

extent /ɪkˈstent/ *n* alcance, grado: *the full extent of the losses* el valor real de las pérdidas LOC **to a large/great extent** en gran parte **to a lesser extent** en menor grado **to some/a certain extent** hasta cierto punto **to what extent** hasta qué punto

exterior /ɪkˈstɪəriə(r)/ ◆ *adj* exterior ◆ *n* **1** exterior **2** (*persona*) aspecto

exterminate /ɪkˈstɜːmɪneɪt/ *vt* exterminar

external /ɪkˈstɜːnl/ *adj* externo, exterior

extinct /ɪkˈstɪŋkt/ *adj* **1** (*animal*) extinto, desaparecido: *to become extinct* extinguirse **2** (*volcán*) inactivo

extinguish /ɪkˈstɪŋgwɪʃ/ *vt* extinguir, apagar ☛ La palabra más normal es **put out**. **extinguisher** *n* extintor

extort /ɪkˈstɔːt/ *vt* ~ **sth (from sb) 1** (*dinero*) obtener algo (de algn) mediante extorsión **2** (*confesión*) sacar algo (a algn) por la fuerza **extortion** *n* extorsión

extortionate /ɪkˈstɔːʃənət/ *adj* **1** (*precio*) exorbitante **2** (*exigencia*) excesivo

extra /ˈekstrə/ ◆ *adj* **1** adicional, de más, extra: *extra charge* recargo ◊ *Wine is extra.* El vino no está incluido. **2** de sobra **3** (*Dep*): *extra time* prórroga ◆ *adv* súper, extra: *to pay extra* pagar un suplemento ◆ *n* **1** extra **2** (*precio*) suplemento **3** (*Cine*) extra

extract /ɪkˈstrækt/ ◆ *vt* **1** ~ **sth (from sth)** extraer algo (de algo) **2** ~ **sth (from sth/sb)** conseguir algo (de algo/algn) ◆ /ˈekstrækt/ *n* **1** extracto **2** pasaje

extraordinary /ɪkˈstrɔːdnri; *USA* -dəneri/ *adj* extraordinario

extravagant /ɪkˈstrævəgənt/ *adj* **1** extravagante **2** exagerado **extravagance** *n* extravagancia

extreme /ɪkˈstriːm/ *adj, n* extremo: *with extreme care* con sumo cuidado **extremely** *adv* extremadamente **extremist** *n* extremista **extremity** /ɪkˈstreməti/ *n* (*pl* **-ies**) extremidad

extricate /ˈekstrɪkeɪt/ *vt* (*fml*) ~ **sth/sb (from sth)** sacar algo/a algn (de algo)

extrovert /ˈekstrəvɜːt/ *n* extrovertido, -a

exuberant /ɪgˈzjuːbərənt; *USA* -ˈzuː-/ *adj* desbordante de vida y entusiasmo

exude /ɪgˈzjuːd; *USA* -ˈzuːd/ *vt, vi* **1** (*fml*) exudar **2** (*fig*) rebosar

eye /aɪ/ ◆ *n* ojo: *to have sharp eyes* tener muy buena vista LOC **before your very eyes** delante de tus mismas narices **in the eyes of sb/in sb's eyes** en opinión de algn **in the eyes of the law** a los ojos de la ley **(not) to see eye to eye with sb** (no) estar plenamente de acuerdo con algn **to keep an eye on sth/sb** echarle un ojo a algo/algn *Ver tb* BRING, CAST, CATCH, CLOSE[1], CRY, EAR[1], MEET[1], MIND, NAKED, TURN ◆ *vt* (*pt pres* **eyeing**) mirar

eyeball /ˈaɪbɔːl/ *n* globo ocular

eyebrow /ˈaɪbraʊ/ *n* ceja LOC *Ver* RAISE

eye-catching /ˈaɪ kætʃɪŋ/ *adj* vistoso

eyelash /ˈaɪlæʃ/ (*tb* **lash**) *n* pestaña

eye-level /ˈaɪ levl/ *adj* a la altura de los ojos

eyelid /ˈaɪlɪd/ (*tb* **lid**) *n* párpado LOC *Ver* BAT[2]

eyesight /ˈaɪsaɪt/ *n* vista

eyewitness /ˈaɪwɪtnəs/ *n* testigo ocular

Ff

F, f /ef/ *n* (*pl* **F's**, **f's** /efs/) **1** F, f: *F for Frederick* F de Francia ☛ *Ver ejemplos en* A, a **2** (*Educ*) suspenso: *to get (an) F in History* sacar un suspenso en Historia **3** (*Mús*) fa

fable /ˈfeɪbl/ *n* fábula

fabric /ˈfæbrɪk/ *n* **1** tejido, tela ☛ *Ver nota en* TELA **2 the ~ (of sth)** [*sing*] (*lit y fig*) la estructura (de algo)

fabulous /ˈfæbjələs/ *adj* **1** fabuloso **2** de leyenda

façade /fəˈsɑːd/ *n* (*lit y fig*) fachada

face[1] /feɪs/ *n* **1** cara, rostro: *to wash your face* lavarse la cara ◊ *face down(wards)/up(wards)* boca abajo/arriba **2** cara: *the South face of...* la cara sur de... ◊ *a rock face* una pared de roca **3** esfera (*de reloj*) **4** superficie LOC **face to face** cara a cara: *to come face to face with sth* enfrentarse con algo **in the face of sth 1** a pesar de algo **2** frente a algo **on the face of it** (*coloq*) a primera vista **to make/pull faces/a face** hacer muecas **to put a bold, brave, good, etc face on it/on sth** poner al mal tiempo buena cara **to sb's face** a la cara ☛ *Comparar con* BEHIND SB'S BACK *en* BACK[1] *Ver tb* BRING, CUP, SAVE, STRAIGHT

face[2] /feɪs/ *vt* **1** estar de cara a: *They sat down facing each other.* Se sentaron uno frente al otro. **2** dar a: *a house facing the park* una casa que da al parque **3** enfrentarse con **4** (*fig*) afrontar: *to face facts* afrontar los hechos **5** (*sentencia, multa*) correr el riesgo de recibir **6** revestir LOC *Ver* LET[1] PHR V **to face up to sth/sb** enfrentarse a algo/algn

faceless /ˈfeɪsləs/ *adj* anónimo

facelift /ˈfeɪslɪft/ *n* **1** estiramiento (*facial*) **2** (*fig*) lavado de cara

facet /ˈfæsɪt/ *n* faceta

facetious /fəˈsiːʃəs/ *adj* (*pey*) gracioso

face value *n* valor nominal LOC **to accept/take sth at its face value** tomar algo literalmente

facial /ˈfeɪʃl/ ◆ *adj* facial ◆ *n* tratamiento facial

facile /ˈfæsaɪl; *USA* ˈfæsl/ *adj* (*pey*) simplista

facilitate /fəˈsɪlɪteɪt/ *vt* (*fml*) facilitar

facility /fəˈsɪləti/ *n* **1** [*sing*] facilidad **2 facilities** [*pl*]: *sports/banking facilities* instalaciones deportivas/servicios bancarios

fact /fækt/ *n* hecho: *in fact* de hecho ◊ *the fact that...* el hecho de que... LOC **facts and figures** (*coloq*) pelos y señales **the facts of life** (*eufemismo*) de dónde vienen los niños, la sexualidad *Ver tb* ACTUAL, MATTER, POINT

factor /ˈfæktə(r)/ *n* factor

factory /ˈfæktəri/ *n* (*pl* **-ies**) fábrica: *a shoe factory* una fábrica de zapatos ◊ *factory workers* obreros de fábrica

factual /ˈfæktʃuəl/ *adj* basado en los hechos

faculty /ˈfæklti/ *n* (*pl* **-ies**) **1** facultad: *Arts Faculty* Facultad de Filosofía y Letras **2** (*USA*) profesorado

fad /fæd/ *n* **1** manía **2** moda

fade /feɪd/ *vt, vi* **1** decolorar(se) **2** (*tela*) desteñir(se) PHR V **to fade away** ir desapareciendo poco a poco

fag /fæg/ *n* **1** [*sing*] (*coloq*) faena **2** (*GB, coloq*) cigarrillo **3** (*USA, ofen*) maricón

fail /feɪl/ ◆ **1** *vt* (*examen, candidato*) suspender **2** *vi* ~ **(in sth)** fracasar (en algo): *to fail in your duty* faltar al deber **3** *vi* ~ **to do sth**: *They failed to notice anything unusual.* No notaron nada extraño. **4** *vi* (*fuerzas, motor, etc*) fallar **5** *vi* (*salud*) deteriorarse **6** *vi* (*cosecha*) arruinarse **7** *vi* (*negocio*) quebrar ◆ *n* suspenso LOC **without fail** sin falta

failing /ˈfeɪlɪŋ/ ◆ *n* **1** debilidad **2** defecto ◆ *prep* a falta de: *failing this* si esto no es posible

failure /ˈfeɪljə(r)/ *n* **1** fracaso **2** fallo: *heart failure* paro cardiaco ◊ *engine failure* avería del motor **3** ~ **to do sth**: *His failure to answer puzzled her.* Le extrañó que no contestara.

faint /feɪnt/ ◆ *adj* (**-er**, **-est**) **1** (*sonido*) débil **2** (*rastro*) leve **3** (*parecido*) ligero **4** (*esperanza*) pequeño **5** ~ **(from/with sth)** mareado (de/por algo): *to feel faint* estar mareado ◆ *vi* desmayarse ◆ *n* [*sing*] desmayo **faintly** *adv* **1** débilmente **2** vagamente

fair /feə(r)/ ◆ *n* feria: *a trade fair* una feria de muestras ◊ *a fun fair* un parque de atracciones ◆ *adj* (**-er**, **-est**) **1** ~ (**to/on sb**) justo, imparcial (con algn) **2** (*tiempo*) despejado **3** (*pelo*) rubio ☛ *Ver nota en* RUBIO **4** (*idea*) bastante bueno: *a fair size* bastante grande LOC **fair and square 1** merecidamente **2** claramente **fair game** objeto legítimo de persecución o burla **fair play** juego limpio **to have, etc (more than) your fair share of sth**: *We had more than our fair share of rain.* Nos llovió más de lo que cabía esperar.

fair-haired /ˌfeə ˈheəd/ *adj* rubio

fairly /ˈfeəli/ *adv* **1** justamente, equitativamente **2** [*antes de adj o adv*] bastante: *It's fairly easy.* Es bastante fácil. ◊ *It's fairly good.* No está mal. ◊ *fairly quickly* bastante rápido

Los adverbios **fairly**, **quite**, **rather** y **pretty** modifican la intensidad de los adjetivos o adverbios a los que acompañan, y pueden significar "bastante", "hasta cierto punto" o "no muy". **Fairly** es el de grado más bajo.

fairy /ˈfeəri/ *n* (*pl* **-ies**) hada: *fairy tale* cuento de hadas ◊ *fairy godmother* hada madrina

faith /feɪθ/ *n* ~ (**in sth/sb**) fe (en algo/algn) LOC **in bad/good faith** de mala/buena fe **to put your faith in sth/sb** confiar en algo/algn *Ver tb* BREACH

faithful /ˈfeɪθfl/ *adj* fiel, leal **faithfully** *adv* fielmente LOC *Ver* YOURS

fake /feɪk/ ◆ *n* imitación ◆ *adj* falso ◆ **1** *vt* (*firma, documento*) falsificar **2** *vt, vi* fingir

falcon /ˈfɔːlkən; *USA* ˈfælkən/ *n* halcón

fall /fɔːl/ ◆ *n* **1** (*lit y fig*) caída **2** baja, descenso **3** *a fall of snow* una nevada **4** (*USA*) otoño **5** [*gen pl*] (*Geog*) catarata ◆ *vi* (*pret* **fell** /fel/ *pp* **fallen** /ˈfɔːlən/) **1** (*lit y fig*) caer(se) **2** (*precio, temperatura*) bajar

A veces el verbo **fall** tiene el sentido de "volverse", "quedarse", "ponerse", p. ej. *He fell asleep.* Se quedó dormido. ◊ *He fell ill.* Cayó enfermo

LOC **to fall in love** (**with sb**) enamorarse (de algn) **to fall short of sth** no alcanzar algo **to fall victim to sth** sucumbir a algo, enfermar con algo *Ver tb* FOOT

PHR V **to fall apart** deshacerse

to fall back retroceder **to fall back on sth/sb** recurrir a algo/algn

to fall behind (**sb/sth**) quedar(se) atrás, quedarse detrás de algo/algn **to fall behind with sth** retrasarse con algo/en hacer algo

to fall down 1 (*persona, objeto*) caerse **2** (*plan*) fracasar

to fall for sb (*coloq*) colarse por algn **to fall for sth** (*coloq*) tragarse algo (trampa)

to fall in 1 (*techo*) desplomarse **2** (*Mil*) formar

to fall off descender, flojear

to fall on/upon sb recaer en algn

to fall out (**with sb**) reñir (con algn)

to fall over caerse **to fall over sth/sb** tropezar con algo/algn

to fall through fracasar, irse a pique

fallen /ˈfɔːlən/ ◆ *adj* caído ◆ *pp de* FALL

false /fɔːls/ *adj* **1** falso **2** (*dentadura, etc*) postizo **3** (*reclamación*) fraudulento LOC **a false alarm** una falsa alarma **a false move** un paso en falso **a false start 1** (*Dep*) salida nula **2** intento fallido

falsify /ˈfɔːlsɪfaɪ/ *vt* (*pret, pp* **-fied**) falsificar

falter /ˈfɔːltə(r)/ *vi* **1** (*persona*) vacilar **2** (*voz*) titubear

fame /feɪm/ *n* fama

familiar /fəˈmɪliə(r)/ *adj* **1** familiar (*conocido*) **2** ~ **with sth/sb** familiarizado con algo/algn **familiarity** /fəˌmɪliˈærəti/ *n* **1** ~ **with sth** conocimientos de algo **2** familiaridad

family /ˈfæməli/ *n* [*v sing o pl*] (*pl* **-ies**) familia: *family name* apellido ◊ *family man* hombre casero ◊ *family tree* árbol genealógico ☛ *Ver nota en* FAMILIA LOC *Ver* RUN

famine /ˈfæmɪn/ *n* hambre ☛ *Ver nota en* HAMBRE

famous /ˈfeɪməs/ *adj* famoso

fan /fæn/ ◆ *n* **1** abanico **2** ventilador **3** fan, hincha ◆ *vt* (**-nn-**) **1 to fan (yourself)** abanicar(se) **2** (*disputa, fuego*) atizar PHR V **to fan out** desplegarse en abanico

fanatic /fəˈnætɪk/ *n* fanático, -a **fanatic(al)** *adj* fanático

fanciful /ˈfænsɪfl/ *adj* **1** (*idea*) extravagante **2** (*persona*) fantasioso

fancy /ˈfænsi/ ◆ *n* **1** capricho **2** fantasía ◆ *adj* fuera de lo corriente: *nothing fancy* nada extravagante ◆ *vt* (*pret, pp* **fancied**) **1** imaginarse **2** (*coloq*) apetecer **3** (*GB, coloq*) gustar: *I don't fancy him.* No lo encuentro atractivo. LOC **fancy (that)!** ¡quién lo iba a decir! **to catch/take sb's fancy** cautivar a algn: *whatever takes your fancy* lo que más te apetezca **to fancy yourself as sth** (*coloq*) presumir de algo **to take a fancy to sth/sb** encapricharse con algo/algn

fancy dress *n* [*incontable*] disfraz

fantastic /fænˈtæstɪk/ *adj* fantástico

fantasy /ˈfæntəsi/ *n* (*pl* **-ies**) fantasía

far /fɑː(r)/ ◆ *adj* (*comp* **farther** /ˈfɑːðə(r)/ *o* **further** /ˈfɜːðə(r)/ *superl* **farthest** /ˈfɑːðɪst/ *o* **furthest** /ˈfɜːðɪst/) *Ver tb* FURTHER, FURTHEST **1** extremo: *the far end* el otro extremo **2** opuesto: *on the far bank* en la margen opuesta **3** (*antic*) lejano ◆ *adv* (*comp* **farther** /ˈfɑːðə(r)/ o **further** /ˈfɜːðə(r)/ *superl* **furthest** /ˈfɜːðɪst/) *ver tb* FURTHER, FURTHEST **1** lejos: *Is it far?* ¿Está lejos? ◊ *How far is it?* ¿A qué distancia está? ☛ En este sentido se usa en frases negativas o interrogativas. En frases afirmativas es mucho más frecuente decir **a long way**. **2** [*con preposiciones*] muy: *far above/far beyond* sth muy por encima/mucho más allá de algo **3** [*con comparativos*] mucho: *It's far easier for him.* Es mucho más fácil para él. LOC **as far as** hasta **as/so far as** por lo que: *as far as I know* que yo sepa **as/so far as sth/sb is concerned** por lo que se refiere a algn/algo **by far** con mucho **far and wide** por todas partes **far away** muy lejos **far from it** (*coloq*) ni mucho menos **to be far from (doing) sth** distar mucho de (hacer) algo **to go too far** pasarse **in so far as** en la medida en que **so far 1** hasta ahora **2** hasta cierto punto *Ver tb* AFIELD, FEW

faraway /ˈfɑːrəweɪ/ *adj* **1** remoto **2** (*expresión*) distraído

fare /feə(r)/ ◆ *n* tarifa, precio del billete ◆ *vi* (*fml*) *to fare well/badly* irle bien/mal a uno

farewell /ˌfeəˈwel/ ◆ *interj* (*antic, fml*) adiós ◆ *n* despedida: *farewell party* fiesta de despedida LOC **to bid/say farewell to sth/sb** despedirse de algo/algn ☛ *Comparar con* BADE

farm /fɑːm/ ◆ *n* granja ◆ **1** *vt, vi* labrar **2** *vt* criar

farmer /ˈfɑːmə(r)/ *n* granjero, -a, agricultor, -ora

farmhouse /ˈfɑːmhaʊs/ *n* granja (*casa*)

farming /ˈfɑːmɪŋ/ *n* agricultura, ganadería

farmyard /ˈfɑːmjɑːd/ *n* corral

fart /fɑːt/ ◆ *n* (*coloq*) pedo ◆ *vi* (*coloq*) tirarse un pedo

farther /ˈfɑːðə(r)/ *adv* (*comp de* **far**) más lejos: *I can swim farther than you.* Puedo nadar más lejos que tú. ☛ *Ver nota en* FURTHER

farthest /ˈfɑːðɪst/ *adj, adv* (*superl de* **far**) *Ver* FURTHEST

fascinate /ˈfæsɪneɪt/ *vt* fascinar **fascinating** *adj* fascinante

fascism /ˈfæʃɪzəm/ *n* fascismo **fascist** *adj, n* fascista

fashion /ˈfæʃn/ ◆ *n* **1** moda **2** [*sing*] manera LOC **to be/go out of fashion** estar pasado/pasar de moda **to be in/come into fashion** estar/ponerse de moda *Ver tb* HEIGHT ◆ *vt* moldear, hacer

fashionable /ˈfæʃnəbl/ *adj* de moda

fast[1] /fɑːst; *USA* fæst/ ◆ *adj* (**-er**, **-est**) **1** rápido

> Tanto **fast** como **quick** significan rápido, pero **fast** suele utilizarse para describir a una persona o cosa que se mueve a mucha velocidad: *a fast horse/car/runner* un caballo/coche/corredor rápido, mientras que **quick** se refiere a algo que se realiza en un breve espacio de tiempo: *a quick decision/visit* una decisión/visita rápida.

2 (*reloj*) adelantado LOC *Ver* BUCK[3] ◆ *adv* (**-er**, **-est**) rápido, rápidamente

fast[2] /fɑːst; *USA* fæst/ ◆ *adj* **1** fijo **2** (*color*) que no destiñe ◆ *adv*: *fast asleep* dormido profundamente LOC *Ver* HOLD, STAND

fast[3] /fɑːst; *USA* fæst/ ◆ *vi* ayunar ◆ *n* ayuno

fasten /ˈfɑːsn; *USA* ˈfæsn/ **1** *vt* ~ **sth (down)** asegurar algo **2** *vt* ~ **sth (up)** abrochar algo **3** *vt* sujetar, fijar: *to fasten sth (together)* unir algo **4** *vi* cerrarse, abrocharse

fastidious /fəˈstɪdiəs, fæ-/ *adj* puntilloso, exigente

fat /fæt/ ◆ *adj* (**fatter**, **fattest**) gordo: *You're getting fat.* Estás engordando.

☛ Otras palabras menos directas que **fat** son **chubby**, **stout**, **plump** y **overweight**. ◆ *n* **1** grasa **2** manteca

fatal /ˈfeɪtl/ *adj* **1** ~ (**to sth/sb**) mortal (para algo/algn) **2** (*fml*) fatídico **fatality** /fəˈtæləti/ *n* (*pl* **-ies**) víctima mortal

fate /feɪt/ *n* destino, suerte **fated** *adj* predestinado **fateful** *adj* fatídico

father /ˈfɑːðə(r)/ ◆ *n* padre: *Father Christmas* Papá Noel ☛ *Ver nota en* NAVIDAD ◆ *vt* engendrar LOC **like father, like son** de tal palo, tal astilla

father-in-law /ˈfɑːðər ɪn lɔː/ *n* (*pl* **-ers-in-law**) suegro

fatigue /fəˈtiːg/ ◆ *n* fatiga, cansancio ◆ *vt* fatigar

fatten /ˈfætn/ *vt* **1** (*un animal*) cebar **2** (*alimento*) engordar: *Butter is very fattening.* La mantequilla engorda mucho. *Ver tb* TO LOSE/PUT ON WEIGHT *en* WEIGHT

fatty /ˈfæti/ *adj* **1** (**-ier**, **-iest**) (*Med*) adiposo **2** (*alimento*) graso

fault /fɔːlt/ ◆ *vt* criticar: *He can't be faulted.* Es irreprochable. ◆ *n* **1** defecto, fallo ☛ *Ver nota en* MISTAKE **2** culpa: *Whose fault is it?* ¿Quién tiene la culpa? **3** (*Dep*) falta **4** (*Geol*) falla LOC **to be at fault** tener la culpa *Ver tb* FIND

faultless /ˈfɔːltləs/ *adj* sin tacha, impecable

faulty /ˈfɔːlti/ *adj* (**-ier**, **-iest**) defectuoso

fauna /ˈfɔːnə/ *n* fauna

favour (*USA* **favor**) /ˈfeɪvə(r)/ ◆ *n* favor: *to ask a favour of sb* pedir un favor a algn LOC **in favour of (doing) sth** a favor de (hacer) algo *Ver tb* CURRY ◆ *vt* **1** favorecer **2** preferir, ser partidario, -a de (*idea*)

favourable (*USA* **favor-**) /ˈfeɪvərəbl/ *adj* **1** ~ (**for sth**) favorable (para algo) **2** ~ (**to/toward sth/sb**) a favor (de algo/algn)

favourite (*USA* **favor-**) /ˈfeɪvərɪt/ ◆ *n* favorito, -a ◆ *adj* preferido

fawn /fɔːn/ ◆ *n* ciervo menor de un año ☛ *Ver nota en* CIERVO ◆ *adj*, *n* beige

fax /fæks/ ◆ *n* fax ◆ *vt* **1 to fax sb** mandar un fax a algn **2 to fax sth (to sb)** mandar algo por fax (a algn)

fear /fɪə(r)/ ◆ *vt* temer a: *I fear so.* Me temo que sí. ◆ *n* miedo, temor: *to shake with fear* temblar de miedo LOC **for fear of (doing) sth** por temor a (hacer) algo **for fear (that/lest)...** por temor a... **in fear of sth/sb** con miedo de algo/algn

fearful /ˈfɪəfl/ *adj* horrendo, terrible

fearless /ˈfɪələs/ *adj* intrépido

fearsome /ˈfɪəsəm/ *adj* temible

feasible /ˈfiːzəbl/ *adj* factible **feasibility** /ˌfiːzəˈbɪləti/ *n* viabilidad

feast /fiːst/ ◆ *n* **1** festín **2** (*Relig*) fiesta ◆ *vi* banquetear

feat /fiːt/ *n* proeza, hazaña

feather /ˈfeðə(r)/ *n* pluma

feature /ˈfiːtʃə(r)/ ◆ *n* **1** característica **2 features** [*pl*] facciones ◆ *vt*: *featuring Jack Lemmon* protagonizada por Jack Lemmon **featureless** *adj* sin rasgos característicos

February /ˈfebruəri; *USA* -ueri/ *n* (*abrev* **Feb**) febrero ☛ *Ver nota y ejemplos en* JANUARY

fed *pret*, *pp de* FEED

federal /ˈfedərəl/ *adj* federal

federation /ˌfedəˈreɪʃn/ *n* federación

fed up *adj* ~ (**about/with sth/sb**) (*coloq*) harto (de algo/algn)

fee /fiː/ *n* **1** [*gen pl*] honorarios **2** cuota (*de club*) **3** *school fees* matrícula del colegio

feeble /ˈfiːbl/ *adj* (**-er**, **-est**) **1** débil **2** (*pey*) (*excusa*) endeble

feed /fiːd/ ◆ (*pret*, *pp* **fed** /fed/) **1** *vi* ~ (**on sth**) alimentarse, nutrirse (de algo) **2** *vt* dar de comer a, alimentar **3** *vt* (*datos, etc*) suministrar ◆ *n* **1** comida **2** pienso

feedback /ˈfiːdbæk/ *n* reacción

feel /fiːl/ ◆ (*pret*, *pp* **felt** /felt/) **1** *vt* sentir, tocar: *He feels the cold a lot.* Es muy sensible al frío. ◊ *She felt the water.* Comprobó la temperatura del agua. **2** *vi* sentirse: *I felt like a fool.* Me sentí como un idiota. ◊ *to feel sick/sad* sentirse enfermo/triste ◊ *to feel cold/hungry* tener frío/hambre **3** *vt*, *vi* (*pensar*) opinar: *How do you feel about him?* ¿Qué opinas de él? **4** *vi* (*cosa*) parecer: *It feels like leather.* Parece de piel. LOC **to feel as if/as though...**: *I feel as if I'm going to be sick.* Me parece que voy a vomitar. **to feel good** sentirse bien **to feel like (doing) sth**: *I felt like hitting him.* Me dieron ganas de darle de patadas. **to feel sorry for sb**

compadecer a algn: *I felt sorry for the children.* Los niños me dieron lástima. **to feel sorry for yourself** sentir lástima de uno mismo **to feel yourself** sentirse bien **to feel your way** ir a tientas *Ver tb* COLOUR, DOWN[1], DRAIN, EASE **PHR V to feel about** (**for sth**) buscar (algo) a tientas **to feel for sb** sentir pena por algn **to feel up to** (**doing**) **sth** sentirse capaz de (hacer) algo ◆ *n*: *Let me have a feel.* Déjame tocarlo. **LOC to get the feel of sth/of doing sth** (*coloq*) familiarizarse con algo

feeling /ˈfiːlɪŋ/ *n* **1** ~ (**of...**) sensación (de...): *I've got a feeling that...* Tengo la sensación de que... **2** [*sing*] (*opinión*) sentir **3** [*gen pl*] sentimiento **4** sensibilidad: *to lose all feeling* perder toda la sensibilidad **LOC bad/ill feeling** resentimiento *Ver tb* MIXED *en* MIX

feet *plural de* FOOT

fell /fel/ **1** *pret de* FALL **2** *vt* (*árbol*) talar **3** *vt* derribar

fellow /ˈfeləʊ/ *n* **1** compañero: *fellow countryman, -men* compatriota, -as ◇ *fellow passenger* compañero, -a de viaje ◇ *fellow Spaniards* compatriotas españoles **2** (*coloq*) tío: *He's a nice fellow.* Es un buen tío.

fellowship /ˈfeləʊʃɪp/ *n* **1** compañerismo **2** beca

felt[1] *pret, pp de* FEEL

felt[2] /felt/ *n* fieltro

female /ˈfiːmeɪl/ ◆ *adj* **1** femenino ☛ Se aplica a las características físicas de las mujeres: *the female figure* la figura femenina. *Comparar con* FEMININE **2** hembra

Female y **male** especifican el sexo de personas o animales: *a female friend, a male colleague; a female rabbit, a male eagle, etc.*

3 de la mujer: *female equality* la igualdad de la mujer ◆ *n* hembra

feminine /ˈfemənɪn/ *adj, n* femenino (*propio de la mujer*)

Feminine se aplica a las cualidades que consideramos típicas de una mujer. Compárese con EFFEMINATE.

feminism /ˈfemənɪzəm/ *n* feminismo **feminist** *n* feminista

fence[1] /fens/ ◆ *n* **1** valla, cerca **2** alambrada ◆ *vt* cercar

fence[2] /fens/ *vi* practicar la esgrima **fencing** *n* esgrima

fend /fend/ **PHR V to fend for yoursel[f]** cuidar de sí mismo **to fend sth/sb of[f]** rechazar algo/a algn

ferment /fəˈment/ ◆ *vt, vi* fermentar ◆ /ˈfɜːment/ *n* ebullición (*fig*)

fern /fɜːn/ *n* helecho

ferocious /fəˈrəʊʃəs/ *adj* feroz

ferocity /fəˈrɒsəti/ *n* ferocidad

ferry /ˈferi/ ◆ *n* (*pl* **-ies**) **1** ferry: *ca[r] ferry* transbordador de coches **2** bals[a] (*para cruzar ríos*) ◆ *vt* (*pret, pp* **ferried**) transportar

fertile /ˈfɜːtaɪl; *USA* ˈfəːrtl/ *adj* **1** férti[l] fecundo **2** (*fig*) abonado

fertility /fəˈtɪləti/ *n* fertilidad

fertilization, -isation /ˌfɜːtəlaɪˈzeɪʃn/ *n* fertilización

fertilize, -ise /ˈfɜːtəlaɪz/ *vt* **1** fertiliza[r] **2** abonar **fertilizer, -iser** *n* **1** fertil[i]zante **2** abono

fervent /ˈfɜːvənt/ (*tb* **fervid**) *a[dj]* ferviente

fester /ˈfestə(r)/ *vi* infectarse

festival /ˈfestɪvl/ *n* **1** (*de arte, cin[e]*) festival **2** (*Relig*) fiesta

fetch /fetʃ/ *vt* **1** traer **2** buscar, ir [a] recoger ☛ *Ver dibujo en* TAKE **3** alca[n]zar (*precio*)

fête /feɪt/ *n* fiesta: *the village fête* fiesta del pueblo *Ver tb* BAZAAR

feud /fjuːd/ ◆ *n* rencilla ◆ *vi* ~ (**wi[th] sth/sb**) tener una reyerta (con alg[o]/ algn)

feudal /ˈfjuːdl/ *adj* feudal **feudalism** feudalismo

fever /ˈfiːvə(r)/ *n* (*lit y fig*) fiebre **feve[r]ish** *adj* febril

few /fjuː/ *adj, pron* **1** (**fewer**, **fewes[t]**) pocos: *every few minutes* cada poc[os] minutos ◇ *fewer than six* menos de se[is] ☛ *Ver nota en* LESS **2 a few** unos cua[n]tos, algunos

¿Few o **a few**? *Few* tiene un senti[do] negativo y equivale a "poco". *A f[ew]* tiene un sentido mucho más positiv[o y] equivale a "unos cuantos", "alguno[s]". Compara las siguientes oraciones: *F[ew] people turned up.* Vino poca gente. *I've got a few friends coming for dinn[er].* Vienen unos cuantos amigos a cena[r].

LOC a good few; **quite a few**; **not a f[ew]**

un buen número (de), bastantes **few and far between** escasos, contadísimos

iancé (*fem* **fiancée**) /fɪˈɒnseɪ; *USA* ˌfiːɑːnˈseɪ/ *n* prometido, -a

ib /fɪb/ ◆ *n* (*coloq*) cuento (*mentira*) ◆ *vi* (*coloq*) (**-bb-**) contar cuentos

ibre (*USA* **fiber**) /ˈfaɪbə(r)/ *n* (*lit y fig*) fibra **fibrous** *adj* fibroso

ickle /ˈfɪkl/ *adj* voluble

iction /ˈfɪkʃn/ *n* ficción

iddle /ˈfɪdl/ ◆ *n* (*coloq*) **1** violín **2** estafa ◆ **1** *vt* (*coloq*) (*gastos, etc*) falsear **2** *vi* tocar el violín **3** *vi* ~ (**about/around**) **with sth** juguetear con algo LOC *Ver* FIT[1] PHR V **to fiddle around** perder el tiempo **fiddler** *n* violinista

iddly /ˈfɪdli/ *adj* (*coloq*) complicado

idelity /fɪˈdeləti; *USA* faɪ-/ *n* ~ (**to sth/sb**) fidelidad (a algo/algn) ☛ La palabra más normal es **faithfulness**.

ield /fiːld/ *n* (*lit y fig*) campo

iend /fiːnd/ *n* **1** desalmado, -a **2** (*coloq*) entusiasta **fiendish** *adj* (*coloq*) endiablado

ierce /fɪəs/ *adj* (**-er**, **-est**) **1** (*animal*) feroz **2** (*oposición*) fuerte

fteen /ˌfɪfˈtiːn/ *adj, pron, n* quince ☛ *Ver ejemplos en* FIVE **fifteenth 1** *adj* decimoquinto **2** *pron, adv* el decimoquinto, la decimoquinta, los decimoquintos, las decimoquintas **3** *n* quinceava parte, quinceavo ☛ *Ver ejemplos en* FIFTH

fth (*abrev* **5th**) /fɪfθ/ ◆ *adj* quinto: *We live on the fifth floor.* Vivimos en el quinto piso. ◊ *It's his fifth birthday today.* Hoy cumple cinco años. ◆ *pron, adv* el quinto, la quinta, los quintos, las quintas: *She came fifth in the world championships.* Llegó la quinta en los campeonatos del mundo. ◊ *the fifth to arrive* el quinto en llegar ◊ *I was fifth on the list.* Yo era la quinta de la lista. ◊ *I've had four cups of coffee already, so this is my fifth.* Ya me he tomado cuatro tazas de café, así que ésta es la quinta. ◆ *n* **1** quinto, quinta parte: *three fifths* tres quintos **2 the fifth** el (día) cinco: *They'll be arriving on the fifth of March.* Llegarán el (día) cinco de marzo. **3** (*tb* **fifth gear**) quinta: *to change into fifth* meter la quinta

La abreviatura de los números ordinales se hace poniendo el número en cifra seguido por las dos últimas letras de la palabra: *1st, 2nd, 3rd, 20th, etc.*

☛ *Ver* Apéndice 1.

fifty /ˈfɪfti/ *adj, pron, n* cincuenta: *the fifties* los años cincuenta ◊ *to be in your fifties* tener cincuenta y pico años ☛ *Ver ejemplos en* FIVE LOC **to go fifty-fifty** pagar a medias **fiftieth 1** *adj, pron* quincuagésimo **2** *n* cincuentava parte, cincuentavo ☛ *Ver ejemplos en* FIFTH *y* Apéndice 4.

fig /fɪg/ *n* **1** higo **2** (*tb* **fig tree**) higuera

fight /faɪt/ ◆ *n* **1** ~ (**for/against sth/sb**) lucha, pelea (por/contra algo/algn): *A fight broke out in the pub.* Se armó una pelea en el bar. **2** combate

Cuando se trata de un conflicto continuado (normalmente en situaciones de guerra), se suele usar **fighting**: *There has been heavy/fierce fighting in the capital.* ◊ Ha habido combates intensos/encarnizados en la capital.

3 ~ (**to do sth**) lucha (por hacer algo) ◆ (*pret, pp* **fought** /fɔːt/) **1** *vi, vt* ~ (**against/with sth/sb**) (**about/over sth**) luchar (contra algo/algn) (por algo): *They fought (against/with) the Germans.* Lucharon contra los alemanes. **2** *vi, vt* ~ (**sb/with sb**) (**about/over sth**) pelearse (con algn) (por algo): *They fought (with) each other about/over the money.* Se pelearon por el dinero. **3** *vt* (*corrupción, droga*) combatir LOC **to fight a battle** (**against sth**) librar una batalla (contra algo) **to fight it out**: *They must fight it out between them.* Deben arreglarlo entre ellos. **to fight tooth and nail** defenderse como gato panza arriba **to fight your way across, into, through, etc sth** abrirse camino hacia, en, por, etc algo **to give up without a fight** rendirse sin luchar **to put up a good/poor fight** ponerle mucho/poco empeño a algo *Ver tb* PICK PHR V **to fight back** contraatacar **to fight for sth** luchar por algo **to fight sth/sb off** repeler algo/a algn

fighter /ˈfaɪtə(r)/ *n* **1** luchador, -ora, combatiente **2** caza (*avión*)

figure /ˈfɪgə(r); *USA* ˈfɪgjər/ ◆ *n* **1** cifra, número **2** [*gen sing*] cantidad, suma **3** figura: *a key figure* un personaje clave **4** tipo: *to have a good figure* tener buen tipo **5** silueta LOC **to put a figure on sth** dar una cifra sobre algo, poner precio a algo *Ver tb* FACT ◆ **1** *vi* ~ (**in sth**) figurar (en algo) **2** (*coloq*) *vi*: *It/That figures.* Se comprende. **3** *vt* (*esp USA*) figurarse: *It's what I figured.* Es lo que me figuraba. PHR V **to figure sth out** entender algo

file /faɪl/ ◆ *n* **1** carpeta **2** expediente: *to be on file* estar archivado **3** (*Informát*) fichero **4** lima **5** fila: *in single file* en fila india LOC *Ver* RANK ◆ **1** *vt* ~ **sth** (**away**) archivar algo **2** *vt* (*demanda*) presentar **3** *vt* limar **4** *vi* ~ (**past sth**) desfilar (ante algo) **5** *vi* ~ **in/out, etc** entrar/salir, etc en fila

fill /fɪl/ **1** *vi* ~ (**with sth**) llenarse (de algo) **2** *vt* ~ **sth** (**with sth**) llenar algo (de algo) **3** *vt* (*grieta*) rellenar **4** *vt* (*diente*) empastar **5** *vt* (*cargo*) ocupar LOC *Ver* BILL[1] PHR V **to fill in** (**for sb**) sustituir (a algn) **to fill sth in/out** rellenar algo (*formulario, etc*) **to fill sb in** (**on sth**) poner a algn al tanto (de algo)

fillet /ˈfɪlɪt/ *n* filete

filling /ˈfɪlɪŋ/ *n* **1** empaste **2** relleno

film /fɪlm/ ◆ *n* **1** película (*capa fina*) **2** película: *film-maker* cineasta ◊ *film-making* cinematografía ◊ *film star* estrella de cine ◆ *vt* filmar **filming** *n* rodaje

filter /ˈfɪltə(r)/ ◆ *n* filtro ◆ *vt, vi* filtrar(se)

filth /fɪlθ/ *n* **1** porquería **2** groserías **3** guarradas (*revistas, etc*)

filthy /ˈfɪlθi/ *adj* (**-ier**, **-iest**) **1** (*costumbre, etc*) asqueroso **2** (*manos, mente*) sucio **3** obsceno **4** (*coloq*) desagradable: *a filthy temper* un carácter insoportable

fin /fɪn/ *n* aleta

final /ˈfaɪnl/ ◆ *n* **1** *the men's final(s)* la final masculina **2** **finals** [*pl*] (exámenes) finales ◆ *adj* último, final LOC *Ver* ANALYSIS, STRAW

finally /ˈfaɪnəli/ *adv* **1** por último **2** finalmente **3** por fin, al final

finance /ˈfaɪnæns, fəˈnæns/ ◆ *n* finanzas: *finance company* (compañía) financiera ◊ *the finance minister* el secretario de Hacienda ◆ *vt* financiar **financial** /faɪˈnænʃl, fəˈnæ-/ *adj* financiero, económico: *financial year* ejercicio fiscal

find /faɪnd/ *vt* (*pret, pp* **found** /faʊnd/) **1** encontrar, hallar **2** buscar: *They came here to find work.* Vinieron para buscar trabajo. **3** *to find sb guilty* declarar a algn culpable LOC **to find fault** (**with sth/sb**) sacar faltas (a algo/algn) **to find your feet** acostumbrarse **to find your way** encontrar el camino *Ver tb* MATCH[2], NOWHERE PHR V **to find** (**sth**) **out** enterarse (de algo) **to find sb out** descubrirle el juego a algn **finding** *n* **1** descubrimiento **2** fallo

fine /faɪn/ ◆ *adj* (**finer**, **finest**) **1** excelente: *I'm fine.* Estoy bien. ◊ *You're a fine one to talk!* ¡Mira quién habla! **2** (*seda, polvo, etc*) fino **3** (*rasgos*) delicado **4** (*tiempo*) bueno: *a fine day* una día estupendo **5** (*distinción*) sutil LOC *Ver* CUT ◆ *adv* (*coloq*) bien: *That suits me fine.* Eso me va muy bien. LOC **one fine day** un buen día ◆ *n* multa ◆ *vt* ~ **sb** (**for doing sth**) multar a algn (por hacer algo)

fine art (*tb* **the fine arts**) *n* bellas artes

finger /ˈfɪŋɡə(r)/ *n* dedo (*de la mano*): *little finger* dedo meñique ◊ *forefinger/first finger* dedo índice ◊ *middle finger* dedo corazón ◊ *ring finger* dedo anular *Ver tb* THUMB ☛ *Comparar con* TOE LOC **to be all fingers and thumbs** ser un manazas **to put your finger on sth** señalar/identificar algo (con precisión) *Ver tb* CROSS, WORK[2]

fingernail /ˈfɪŋɡəneɪl/ *n* uña (*de la mano*)

fingerprint /ˈfɪŋɡəprɪnt/ *n* huella dactilar

fingertip /ˈfɪŋɡətɪp/ *n* yema del dedo LOC **to have sth at your fingertips** saberse algo al dedillo

finish /ˈfɪnɪʃ/ ◆ **1** *vt, vi* ~ (**sth/doing sth**) terminar (algo/de hacer algo) **2** *vt* ~ **sth** (**off/up**) (*comida*) acabar (algo) PHR V **to finish up**: *He could finish up dead.* Podría acabar muerto. ◆ *n* **1** acabado **2** meta

finishing line *n* línea de meta

fir /fɜː(r)/ (*tb* **fir tree**) *n* abeto

fire /ˈfaɪə(r)/ ◆ **1** *vt, vi* disparar: *to fire at sth/sb* hacer fuego sobre algo/algn **2** *vt* (*insultos*) soltar **3** *vt* (*coloq*) ~ **sb** despedir a algn **4** *vt* (*imaginación*) estimular ◆ *n* **1** fuego **2** estufa **3** incendio **4** disparos LOC **on fire** en llamas: *to be on fire* estar ardiendo **to be/come under fire** **1** encontrarse bajo fuego enemigo **2** (*fig*) ser objeto de severas críticas *Ver tb* CATCH, FRYING-PAN, SET[2]

firearm /ˈfaɪərɑːm/ *n* [*gen pl*] arma de fuego

fire engine *n* coche de bomberos

fire escape *n* escalera de incendios

fire extinguisher (*tb* **extinguisher**) *n* extintor

firefighter /ˈfaɪəˌfaɪtə(r)/ *n* bombero

fireman /ˈfaɪəmən/ *n* (*pl* **-men** /-mən/) bombero

fireplace /ˈfaɪəpleɪs/ *n* hogar (*chimenea*)

fire station *n* parque de bomberos

firewood /ˈfaɪəwʊd/ *n* leña

firework /ˈfaɪəwɜːk/ *n* **1** cohete **2 fireworks** [*pl*] fuegos artificiales

firing /ˈfaɪərɪŋ/ *n* tiroteo: *firing line* línea de fuego ◊ *firing squad* pelotón de fusilamiento

firm /fɜːm/ ◆ *n* [*v sing o pl*] firma, empresa ◆ *adj* (**-er**, **-est**) firme LOC **a firm hand** mano dura **to be on firm ground** pisar terreno firme *Ver tb* BELIEVER en BELIEVE ◆ *adv* LOC *Ver* HOLD

first (*abrev* **1st**) /fɜːst/ ◆ *adj* primero: *a first night* un estreno ◊ *first name* nombre de pila ◆ *adv* **1** primero: *to come first in the race* ganar la carrera **2** por primera vez: *I first came to Oxford in 1989.* Vine a Oxford por primera vez en 1989. **3** en primer lugar **4** antes: *Finish your dinner first.* Antes termina de cenar. ◆ *pron* el primero, la primera, los primeros, las primeras ◆ *n* **1 the first** el (día) uno **2** (*tb* **first gear**) primera ☛ *Ver ejemplos en* FIFTH LOC **at first** al principio **at first hand** de buena tinta **first come, first served** por orden de llegada **first of all 1** al principio **2** en primer lugar **first thing** a primera hora **first things first** lo primero es lo primero **from first to last** de principio a fin **from the (very) first** desde el primer momento **to put sth/sb first** poner algo/a algn por encima de todo *Ver tb* HEAD[1]

first aid *n* primeros auxilios: *first aid kit* botiquín

first class ◆ *n* primera (clase): *first class ticket* billete de primera ◊ *first class stamp* sello urgente ◆ *adv* en primera: *to travel first class* viajar en primera ◊ *to send sth first class* mandar algo urgente

first-hand /ˌfɜːst ˈhænd/ *adj, adv* de primera mano

firstly /ˈfɜːstli/ *adv* en primer lugar

first-rate /ˌfɜːst ˈreɪt/ *adj* excelente, de primera categoría

fish /fɪʃ/ *n* **1** [*contable*] pez **2** [*incontable*] pescado: *fish and chips* pescado con patatas fritas

> **Fish** como sustantivo contable tiene dos formas para el plural: **fish** y **fishes**. **Fish** es la forma más normal. **Fishes** es una forma anticuada, técnica o literaria.

LOC **an odd/a queer fish** (*coloq*) un tipo raro **like a fish out of water** como un pulpo en un garaje *Ver tb* BIG

fisherman /ˈfɪʃəmən/ *n* (*pl* **-men** /-mən/) pescador

fishing /ˈfɪʃɪŋ/ *n* la pesca

fishmonger /ˈfɪʃmʌŋgə(r)/ *n* (*GB*) pescadero, -a: *fishmonger's* pescadería

fishy /ˈfɪʃi/ *adj* (**-ier**, **-iest**) **1** a pescado (*oler, saber*) **2** (*coloq*) sospechoso, raro: *There's something fishy going on.* Aquí hay gato encerrado.

fist /fɪst/ *n* puño **fistful** puñado

fit[1] /fɪt/ *adj* (**fitter**, **fittest**) **1 fit (for sth/sb/to do sth)** apto, en condiciones, adecuado (para algo/algn/para hacer algo): *a meal fit for a king* una comida digna de un rey **2 fit to do sth** (*coloq*) listo (para hacer algo) **3** en forma LOC **(as) fit as a fiddle** hecho una rosa **to keep fit** mantenerse en forma

fit[2] /fɪt/ ◆ (**-tt-**) (*pret, pp* **fitted**, *USA* **fit**) **1** *vi* **to fit (in/into sth)** caber: *It doesn't fit in/into the box.* No cabe en la caja. **2** *vt* entrar en: *These shoes don't fit (me).* Estos zapatos me van muy justos. **3** *vt* **to fit sth with sth** equipar algo de algo **4** *vt* **to fit sth on(to) sth** poner algo a/en algo **5** *vt* cuadrar con: *to fit a description* cuadrar con una descripción LOC **to fit (sb) like a glove** venir (a algn) como un guante *Ver tb* BILL[1] PHR V **to fit in (with sth/sb)** encajar (con algo/algn) ◆ *n* LOC **to be a good, tight, etc fit** quedar a algn bien, ajustado, etc

fit[3] /fɪt/ *n* ataque (*de risa, tos, etc*) LOC **to have/throw a fit**: *She'll have/throw a fit!* ¡Le va a dar un ataque!

fitness /ˈfɪtnəs/ *n* forma (física)

fitted /ˈfɪtɪd/ *adj* **1** (*moqueta*) instalado **2** (*habitación*) amueblado

fitting /ˈfɪtɪŋ/ ◆ *adj* apropiado ◆ *n* **1** repuesto, pieza **2** (*vestido*) prueba: *fitting room* probador

five /faɪv/ *adj, pron, n* cinco: *page/chapter five* la página/el capítulo (número) cinco ◊ *five past nine* las nueve y cinco ◊ *on 5 May* el 5 de mayo ◊ *all five of them* los cinco ◊ *There were five of us.* Éramos cinco. ☛ *Ver* Apéndice 1. **fiver** *n* (*GB, coloq*) (billete de) cinco libras

fix /fɪks/ ◆ *n* (*coloq*) lío: *to be in/get yourself into a fix* estar/meterse en un lío ◆ *vt* **1 to fix sth (on sth)** fijar algo (en algo) **2** arreglar **3** establecer **4 to fix sth (for sb)** (*comida*) preparar algo (para algn) **5** (*coloq*) amañar **6** (*coloq*) ajustar las cuentas a PHR V **to fix on sth/sb** decidirse por algo/algn **to fix sb up (with sth)** (*coloq*) procurar algo a algn **to fix sth up 1** arreglar algo **2** reparar/retocar algo

fixed /fɪkst/ *adj* fijo LOC **(of) no fixed abode/address** sin paradero fijo

fixture /ˈfɪkstʃə(r)/ *n* **1** accesorio fijo de una casa **2** cita deportiva **3** (*coloq*) inamovible

fizz /fɪz/ *vi* **1** estar en efervescencia **2** silbar

fizzy /ˈfɪzi/ *adj* (**-ier**, **-iest**) con gas, gaseoso

flabby /ˈflæbi/ *adj* (*coloq, pey*) (**-ier**, **-iest**) fofo

flag /flæg/ ◆ *n* **1** bandera **2** banderín ◆ *vi* (**-gg-**) flaquear

flagrant /ˈfleɪgrənt/ *adj* flagrante

flair /fleə(r)/ *n* **1** [*sing*] ~ **for sth** aptitud para algo **2** elegancia

flake /fleɪk/ ◆ *n* copo ◆ *vi* ~ **(off/away)** desconcharse

flamboyant /flæmˈbɔɪənt/ *adj* **1** (*persona*) extravagante **2** (*vestido*) llamativo

flame /fleɪm/ *n* (*lit y fig*) llama

flammable /ˈflæməbl/ (*tb* **inflammable**) *adj* inflamable

flan /flæn/ *n* tarta, tartaleta ☛ *Ver nota en* PIE

La palabra española **flan** se traduce por **crème caramel** en inglés.

flank /flæŋk/ ◆ *n* **1** (*persona*) costado **2** (*animal*) ijada **3** (*Mil*) flanco ◆ *vt* flanquear

flannel /ˈflænl/ *n* **1** franela **2** toalla de cara

flap /flæp/ ◆ *n* **1** (*sobre*) solapa **2** (*bolso*) tapa **3** (*mesa*) hoja plegable **4** (*Aeronáut*) alerón ◆ (**-pp-**) **1** *vt, vi* agitar(se) **2** *vt* (*alas*) batir

flare /fleə(r)/ ◆ *n* **1** bengala **2** destello **3** acampanamiento ◆ *vi* **1** llamear **2** (*fig*) estallar: *Tempers flared.* Se encendieron los ánimos. PHR V **to flare up 1** (*fuego*) avivarse **2** (*conflicto*) estallar **3** (*problema*) reavivarse

flash /flæʃ/ ◆ *n* **1** destello: *a flash of lightning* un relámpago **2** (*fig*) golpe: *a flash of genius* un golpe de genio **3** (*Fot, noticias*) flash LOC **a flash in the pan**: *It was no flash in the pan.* No ocurrió de chiripa. **in a/like a flash** en un santiamén ◆ **1** *vi* centellear, brillar: *It flashed on and off.* Se encendía y apagaba. **2** *vt* dirigir (*luz*): *to flash your headlights* lanzar ráfagas con los faros **3** *vt* mostrar rápidamente (*imagen*) PHR V **to flash by, past, through, etc** pasar, cruzar, etc como un rayo

flashy /ˈflæʃi/ *adj* (**-ier**, **-iest**) ostentoso, llamativo

flask /flɑːsk; *USA* flæsk/ *n* **1** termo **2** (*licores*) petaca

flat /flæt/ ◆ *n* **1** piso **2 the ~ of sth** la parte plana de algo: *the flat of your hand* la palma de la mano **3** [*gen pl*] (*Geog*): *mud flats* marismas **4** (*Mús*) bemol ☛ *Comparar con* SHARP **5** (*USA coloq*) pinchazo ◆ *adj* (**flatter**, **flattest**) **1** plano, liso, llano **2** (*rueda*) desinflado **3** (*batería*) descargado **4** (*bebida*) sin gas **5** (*Mús*) desafinado **6** (*precio, etc*) único ◆ *adv* (**flatter**, **flattest**): *to lie down flat* tumbarse completamente LOC **flat out** a tope (*trabajar, correr etc*) **in 10 seconds, etc flat** en sólo 10 segundos, etc

flatly /ˈflætli/ *adv* rotundamente, de lleno (*decir, rechazar, negar*)

flatten /ˈflætn/ **1** *vt* ~ **sth (out)** aplanar algo, alisar algo **2** *vt* ~ **sth/sb** aplastar, arrasar algo/a algn **3** *vi* ~ **(out)** (*paisaje*) allanarse

flatter /ˈflætə(r)/ **1** *vt* adular, halagar: *was flattered by your invitation.* Me halagó tu invitación. **2** *vt* (*ropa, etc*) favorecer **3** *v refl* ~ **yourself (that)** hacerse ilusiones (de que) **flattering** *adj* favorecedor, halagador

flaunt /flɔːnt/ *vt* (*pey*) ~ **sth** alardear de algo

flavour (*USA* **flavor**) /ˈfleɪvə(r)/ ◆ *n* sabor, gusto ◆ *vt* dar sabor a, condimentar

flaw /flɔː/ *n* **1** (*objetos*) desperfecto **2** (*plan, carácter*) fallo, defecto **flawed** *adj* defectuoso **flawless** *adj* impecable

flea /fliː/ *n* pulga: *flea market* rastro (mercado)

fleck /ˈflek/ *n* ~ (**of sth**) mota de algo (*polvo, color*)

flee /fliː/ (*pret, pp* **fled** /fled/) **1** *vi* huir, escapar **2** *vt* abandonar

fleet /fliːt/ *n* [*v sing o pl*] flota (*de coches, pesquera*)

flesh /fleʃ/ *n* **1** carne **2** (*de fruta*) pulpa LOC **flesh and blood** carne y hueso **in the flesh** en persona **your own flesh and blood** (pariente) de tu propia sangre

flew *pret de* FLY

flex /fleks/ ◆ *n* (*USA* **cord**) flexible ◆ *vt* flexionar

flexible /ˈfleksəbl/ *adj* flexible

flick /flɪk/ ◆ *n* **1** capirotazo **2** movimiento rápido: *a flick of the wrist* un giro de muñeca ◆ *vt* **1** pegar **2** ~ **sth** (**off, on, etc**) mover algo rápidamente PHR V **to flick through** (**sth**) hojear algo rápidamente

flicker /ˈflɪkə(r)/ ◆ *vi* parpadear: *a flickering light* una luz vacilante ◆ *n* **1** (*luz*) parpadeo **2** (*fig*) atisbo

flight /flaɪt/ *n* **1** vuelo **2** huida **3** (*aves*) bandada **4** (*escalera*) tramo LOC **to take** (**to**) **flight** darse a la fuga

flimsy /ˈflɪmzi/ *adj* (**-ier**, **-iest**) **1** (*tela*) fino **2** (*objetos, excusa*) endeble, débil

flinch /flɪntʃ/ *vi* **1** retroceder **2** ~ **from sth/from doing sth** echarse atrás ante algo/a la hora de hacer algo

fling /flɪŋ/ ◆ *vt* (*pret, pp* **flung** /flʌŋ/) **1** ~ **sth** (**at sth**) arrojar, lanzar algo (contra algo): *She flung her arms around him.* Le echó los brazos al cuello. **2** dar un empujón a: *He flung open the door.* Abrió la puerta de un golpe. LOC *Ver* CAUTION ◆ *n* **1** juerga **2** aventurilla

flint /flɪnt/ *n* **1** pedernal **2** piedra (*de mechero*)

flip /flɪp/ (**-pp-**) **1** *vt* echar: *to flip a coin* echar una moneda a cara o cruz **2** *vt, vi* ~ (**sth**) (**over**) dar a algo/darse la vuelta **3** *vi* (*coloq*) ponerse como una fiera

flippant /ˈflɪpənt/ *adj* ligero, frívolo

flirt /flɜːt/ ◆ *vi* flirtear ◆ *n* ligón, -ona: *He's a terrible flirt.* Siempre está flirteando.

flit /flɪt/ *vi* (**-tt-**) revolotear

float /fləʊt/ ◆ **1** *vi* flotar **2** *vi* (*nadador*) hacer la plancha **3** *vt* (*barco*) poner a flote **4** *vt* (*proyecto,idea*) proponer ◆ *n* **1** corcho **2** boya **3** flotador **4** (*carnaval*) carroza

flock /flɒk/ ◆ *n* **1** rebaño (*de ovejas*) **2** bandada **3** tropel ◆ *vi* **1** agruparse **2** ~ **into/to sth** acudir en tropel a algo

flog /flɒg/ *vt* (**-gg-**) **1** azotar **2** ~ **sth** (**off**) (**to sb**) (*GB, coloq*) vender algo (a algn) LOC **to flog a dead horse** malgastar saliva

flood /flʌd/ ◆ *n* **1** inundación **2 the Flood** (*Relig*) el Diluvio **3** (*fig*) torrente, avalancha ◆ *vt, vi* inundar(se) PHR V **to flood in** llegar en avalancha

flooding /ˈflʌdɪŋ/ *n* [*incontable*] inundación, inundaciones

floodlight /ˈflʌdlaɪt/ ◆ *n* foco ◆ *vt* (*pret, pp* **floodlighted** *o* **floodlit** /-lɪt/) iluminar con focos

floor /flɔː(r)/ ◆ *n* **1** suelo: *on the floor* en el suelo **2** planta, piso **3** (*mar, valle*) fondo ◆ *vt* **1** (*contrincante*) tumbar **2** (*coloq, fig*) dejar fuera de combate

floorboard /ˈflɔːbɔːd/ *n* tabla (*del suelo*)

flop /flɒp/ ◆ *n* (*coloq*) fracaso ◆ *vi* (**-pp-**) **1** desplomarse **2** (*coloq*) (*obra, negocio*) fracasar

floppy /flɒpi/ *adj* (**-ier**, **-iest**) **1** flojo, flexible **2** (*orejas*) colgante

floppy disk (*tb* **floppy**, **diskette**) *n* disquete ☛ *Ver dibujo en* ORDENADOR

flora /ˈflɔːrə/ *n* [*pl*] flora

floral /ˈflɔːrəl/ *adj* de flores: *floral tribute* corona de flores

florist /ˈflɒrɪst; *USA* ˈflɔːr-/ *n* florista **florist's** *n* floristería

flounder /ˈflaʊndə(r)/ *vi* **1** vacilar **2** balbucear **3** caminar con dificultad

flour /ˈflaʊə(r)/ *n* harina

flourish /ˈflʌrɪʃ/ ◆ **1** *vi* prosperar, florecer **2** *vt* (*arma*) blandir ◆ *n* **1** floreo **2** *a flourish of the pen* una rúbrica

flow /fləʊ/ ◆ *n* **1** flujo **2** caudal **3**

circulación **4** suministro ◆ *vi* (*pret, pp* **-ed**) **1** (*lit y fig*) fluir: *to flow into the sea* desembocar en el mar **2** circular **3** flotar **4** (*marea*) subir LOC *Ver* EBB PHR V **to flow in/out**: *Is the tide flowing in or out?* ¿La marea está subiendo o bajando? **to flow in/into sth** llegar sin parar a algo

flower /ˈflaʊə(r)/ ◆ *n* flor ☛ *Comparar con* BLOSSOM ◆ *vi* florecer

flower bed *n* macizo de flores

flowering /ˈflaʊərɪŋ/ ◆ *n* florecimiento ◆ *adj* que da flores (*planta*)

flowerpot /ˈflaʊəpɒt/ *n* tiesto

flown *pp de* FLY

flu /fluː/ *n* [*incontable*] (*coloq*) gripe

fluctuate /ˈflʌktʃueɪt/ *vi* ~ (**between...**) fluctuar, variar (entre...)

fluent /ˈfluːənt/ *adj* **1** (*Ling*): *She's fluent in Russian.* Habla ruso con soltura. ◊ *She speaks fluent French.* Domina el francés. **2** (*orador*) elocuente **3** (*estilo*) fluido

fluff /flʌf/ *n* **1** pelusa: *a piece of fluff* una pelusa **2** (*aves*) plumón **3** (*en el cuerpo humano*) vello **fluffy** *adj* (**-ier, -iest**) **1** lanudo, velludo, cubierto de pelusa **2** mullido, esponjoso

fluid /ˈfluːɪd/ ◆ *adj* **1** fluido, líquido **2** (*plan*) flexible **3** (*situación*) variable, inestable **4** (*estilo, movimiento*) fluido, suelto ◆ *n* **1** líquido **2** (*Quím, Biol*) fluido

fluke /fluːk/ *n* (*coloq*) chiripa

flung *pret, pp de* FLING

flurry /ˈflʌri/ *n* (*pl* **-ies**) **1** ráfaga: *a flurry of snow* una nevisca **2** ~ (**of sth**) (*de actividad, emoción*) frenesí (de algo)

flush /flʌʃ/ ◆ *n* rubor: *hot flushes* sofocos ◆ **1** *vi* ruborizarse **2** *vt* (*wáter*) tirar de la cadena

fluster /ˈflʌstə(r)/ *vt* aturdir: *to get flustered* ponerse nervioso

flute /fluːt/ *n* flauta

flutter /ˈflʌtə(r)/ ◆ **1** *vi* (*pájaro*) revolotear, aletear **2** *vt, vi* (*alas*) agitar(se), batir(se) **3** *vi* (*cortina, bandera, etc*) ondear **4** *vt* (*objeto*) menear ◆ *n* **1** (*alas*) aleteo **2** (*pestañas*) pestañeo **3** *all of a/in a flutter* alterado/nervioso

fly /flaɪ/ ◆ *n* (*pl* **flies**) **1** mosca **2** (*tb* **flies** [*pl*]) bragueta ◆ (*pret* **flew** /fluː/ *pp* **flown** /fləʊn/) **1** *vi* volar: *to fly away/off* irse volando **2** *vi* (*persona*) ir/viajar en avión: *to fly in/out/back* llegar/partir/regresar (en avión) **3** *vt* (*avión*) pilotar **4** *vt* (*pasajeros o mercancías*) transportar (en avión) **5** *vi* ir de prisa: *I must fly.* Me voy corriendo. **6** *vi* (*repentinamente*): *The wheel flew off.* La rueda salió disparada. ◊ *The door flew open.* La puerta se abrió de golpe. **7** *vi* (*flotar al aire*) ondear **8** *vt* (*bandera*) enarbolar **9** *vt* (*cometa*) volar LOC **to fly high** ser ambicioso *Ver tb* CROW, LET[1], TANGENT PHR V **to fly at sb** lanzarse sobre algn

flying /ˈflaɪɪŋ/ ◆ *n* volar: *flying lessons* clases de vuelo ◆ *adj* volador

flying saucer *n* platillo volante

flying start *n* LOC **to get off to a flying start** empezar con buen pie

flyover /ˈflaɪəʊvə(r)/ *n* paso elevado

foam /fəʊm/ ◆ *n* **1** espuma **2** (*tb* **foam rubber**) gomaespuma ◆ *vi* echar espuma

focus /ˈfəʊkəs/ ◆ *n* (*pl* ~**es** *o* **foci** /ˈfəʊsaɪ/) foco LOC **to be in focus/out of focus** estar enfocado/desenfocado ◆ (**-s-** *o* **-ss-**) **1** *vt, vi* enfocar **2** *vt* ~ **sth on sth** concentrar algo (*esfuerzo, etc*) en algo LOC **to focus your attention/mind on sth** centrarse en algo

fodder /ˈfɒdə(r)/ *n* forraje

foetus (*USA* **fetus**) /ˈfiːtəs/ *n* feto

fog /fɒg; *USA* fɔːg/ ◆ *n* niebla ☛ *Comparar con* HAZE, MIST ◆ *vi* (**-gg-**) (*tb* **to fog up**) empañarse

foggy /ˈfɒgi; *USA* ˈfɔːgi/ *adj* (**-ier, -iest**): *a foggy day* un día de niebla

foil /fɔɪl/ ◆ *n* lámina: *aluminium foil* papel de aluminio ◆ *vt* frustrar

fold /fəʊld/ ◆ **1** *vt, vi* doblar(se) plegar(se) **2** *vi* (*coloq*) (*empresa, negocio*) irse abajo **3** *vi* (*coloq*) (*obra de teatro*) cerrar LOC **to fold your arms** cruzar los brazos PHR V **to fold (sth) back/down/up** doblar algo/doblarse ◆ *n* **1** pliegue **2** redil

folder /ˈfəʊldə(r)/ *n* carpeta

folding /ˈfəʊldɪŋ/ *adj* plegable ☛ Se usa sólo antes de sustantivo: *a folding table/bed* una mesa/cama plegable

folk /fəʊk/ ◆ *n* **1** gente: *country folk* gente de pueblo **2** **folks** [*pl*] (*coloq*) gente **3** **folks** [*pl*] (*coloq*) parientes ◆ *adj* folklórico, popular

follow /ˈfɒləʊ/ *vt, vi* **1** seguir **2** (*explicación*) entender **3** ~ (**from sth**) resultar, ser la consecuencia (de algo) LOC **a**

follows como sigue **to follow the crowd** hacer lo que hacen los demás PHR V **to follow on** seguir: *to follow on from sth* ser una consecuencia de algo **to follow sth through** seguir con algo hasta el final **to follow sth up** redondear algo, completar algo

follower /ˈfɒləʊə(r)/ *n* seguidor, -ora

following /ˈfɒləʊɪŋ/ ◆ *adj* siguiente ◆ *n* **1 the following** [*v sing o pl*] lo siguiente/lo que sigue **2** seguidores ◆ *prep* tras: *following the burglary* tras el robo

follow-up /ˈfɒləʊ ʌp/ *n* continuación

fond /fɒnd/ *adj* (**-er**, **-est**) **1** [*antes de sustantivo*] cariñoso: *fond memories* gratos recuerdos ◊ *a fond smile* una sonrisa cariñosa **2 to be ~ of sb** tenerle cariño a algn **3 to be ~ of (doing) sth** ser aficionado a (hacer) algo **4** (*esperanza*) vano

fondle /ˈfɒndl/ *vt* acariciar

food /fuːd/ *n* alimento, comida LOC **(to give sb) food for thought** (dar a algn) algo en que pensar

food processor *n* robot de cocina

foodstuffs /ˈfuːdstʌfs/ *n* [*pl*] alimentos

fool /fuːl/ ◆ *n* (*pey*) tonto, loco LOC **to act/play the fool** hacer(se) el tonto **to be no fool** no tener un pelo de tonto **to be nobody's fool** no dejarse engañar por nadie **to make a fool of yourself/sb** ponerse/poner a algn en ridículo ◆ **1** *vi* bromear **2** *vt* engañar PHR V **to fool about/around** perder el tiempo: *Stop fooling about with that knife!* ¡Para de jugar con ese cuchillo!

foolish /ˈfuːlɪʃ/ *adj* **1** tonto **2** ridículo

foolproof /ˈfuːlpruːf/ *adj* infalible

foot /fʊt/ ◆ *n* **1** (*pl* **feet** /fiːt/) pie: *at the foot of the stairs* al pie de las escaleras **2** (*pl* **feet** *o* **foot**) (*abrev* **ft**) (*unidad de longitud*) pie (*30,48 centímetros*) ☛ *Ver* Apéndice 1. LOC **on foot** a pie **to fall/land on your feet** salirle a algn las cosas redondas **to put your feet up** descansar **to put your foot down** cerrarse en banda **to put your foot in it** meter la pata *Ver tb* COLD, FIND, SWEEP ◆ *vt* LOC **to foot the bill (for sth)** pagar los gastos (de algo)

football /ˈfʊtbɔːl/ *n* **1** fútbol **2** balón (de fútbol) **footballer** *n* futbolista

footing /ˈfʊtɪŋ/ *n* [*incontable*] **1** equilibrio: *to lose your footing* perder el equilibrio **2** (*fig*) situación: *on an equal footing* en igualdad de condiciones

footnote /ˈfʊtnəʊt/ *n* nota (a pie de página)

footpath /ˈfʊtpɑːθ; *USA* -pæθ/ *n* sendero, acera: *public footpath* camino público

footprint /ˈfʊtprɪnt/ *n* [*gen pl*] huella

footstep /ˈfʊtstep/ *n* pisada, paso

footwear /ˈfʊtweə(r)/ *n* [*incontable*] calzado

for /fə(r), fɔː(r)/ ◆ *prep* **1** para: *a letter for you* una carta para ti ◊ *What's it for?* ¿Para qué sirve? ◊ *the train for Glasgow* el tren que va a Glasgow ◊ *It's time for supper.* Es hora de cenar. **2** por: *for her own good* por su propio bien ◊ *What can I do for you?* ¿Qué puedo hacer por ti? ◊ *to fight for your country* luchar por su país **3** (*en expresiones de tiempo*) durante, desde hace: *They are going for a month.* Se van por un mes. ◊ *How long are you here for?* ¿Cuánto tiempo estarás aquí? ◊ *I haven't seen him for two days.* No lo veo desde hace dos días.

> ¿**For** o **since**? Cuando **for** se traduce por "desde hace" se puede confundir con **since**, "desde". Las dos palabras se usan para expresar el tiempo que ha durado la acción del verbo, pero **for** especifica la duración de la acción y **since** el comienzo de dicha acción: *I've been living here for three months.* Vivo aquí desde hace tres meses. ◊ *I've been living here since August.* Vivo aquí desde agosto. Nótese que en ambos casos se usa el pretérito perfecto o el pluscuamperfecto, nunca el presente. *Ver tb nota en* AGO

4 [*con infinitivo*]: *There's no need for you to go.* No hace falta que vayas. ◊ *It's impossible for me to do it.* Me es imposible hacerlo. **5** (*otros usos de for*): *I for Irene* I de Irene ◊ *for miles and miles* milla tras milla ◊ *What does he do for a job?* ¿Qué trabajo tiene? LOC **for all**: *for all his wealth* a pesar de toda su riqueza **to be for/against sth** estar a favor/en contra de algo **to be for it** (*coloq*): *He's for it now!* ¡Se la va a cargar! ☛ Para los usos de **for** en PHRASAL VERBS ver las entradas de los verbos correspondientes, p.ej. **to look for** en LOOK. ◆ *conj* (*fml, antic*) ya que

forbade (*tb* **forbad**) *pret de* FORBID

forbid /fəˈbɪd/ *vt* (*pret* **forbade** /fəˈbæd; *USA* fəˈbeɪd/ *o* **forbad** *pp* **forbidden** /fəˈbɪdn/) ~ **sb to do sth** prohibir a algn hacer algo: *It is forbidden to smoke.* Se prohibe fumar. ◊ *They forbade them from entering.* Les prohibieron entrar. **forbidding** *adj* imponente, amenazante

force /fɔːs/ ◆ *n* (*lit y fig*) fuerza: *the armed forces* las fuerzas armadas LOC **by force** a la fuerza **in force** en vigor: *to be in/come into force* estar/entrar en vigor ◆ *vt* ~ **sth/sb (to do sth)** forzar, obligar a algo/algn (a hacer algo) PHR V **to force sth on sb** imponer algo a algn

forcible /ˈfɔːsəbl/ *adj* **1** a/por la fuerza **2** convincente **forcibly** *adv* **1** por la fuerza **2** enérgicamente

ford /fɔːd/ ◆ *n* vado ◆ *vt* vadear

fore /fɔː(r)/ ◆ *adj* delantero, anterior ◆ *n* proa LOC **to be/come to the fore** destacarse/hacerse importante

forearm /ˈfɔːrɑːm/ *n* antebrazo

forecast /ˈfɔːkɑːst; *USA* -kæst/ ◆ *vt* (*pret, pp* **forecast** *o* **forecasted**) pronosticar ◆ *n* pronóstico

forefinger /ˈfɔːfɪŋgə(r)/ *n* dedo índice

forefront /ˈfɔːfrʌnt/ *n* LOC **at/in the forefront of sth** en la vanguardia de algo

foreground /ˈfɔːgraʊnd/ *n* primer plano

forehead /ˈfɒrɪd, ˈfɔːhed; *USA* ˈfɔːrɪd/ *n* (*Anat*) frente

foreign /ˈfɒrən; *USA* ˈfɔːr-/ *adj* **1** extranjero **2** exterior: *foreign exchange* divisas ◊ *Foreign Office/Secretary* Ministerio/Ministro, -a de Asuntos Exteriores **3** (*fml*) ~ **to sth/sb** ajeno a algo/algn

foreigner /ˈfɒrənə(r)/ *n* extranjero, -a

foremost /ˈfɔːməʊst/ ◆ *adj* más destacado ◆ *adv* principalmente

forerunner /ˈfɔːrʌnə(r)/ *n* precursor, -ora

foresee /fɔːˈsiː/ *vt* (*pret* **foresaw** /fɔːˈsɔː/ *pp* **foreseen** /fɔːˈsiːn/) prever **forseeable** *adj* previsible LOC **for/in the foreseeable future** en un futuro previsible

foresight /ˈfɔːsaɪt/ *n* previsión

foresook *pret de* FORSAKE

forest /ˈfɒrɪst; *USA* ˈfɔːr-/ *n* bosque: *rainforest* selva tropical

Tanto **forest** como **wood** significan "bosque", pero **wood** es más pequeño.

foretell /fɔːˈtel/ *vt* (*pret, pp* **foretold** /fɔːˈtəʊld/) (*fml*) predecir

forever /fəˈrevə(r)/ *adv* **1** (*tb* **for ever**) para siempre **2** siempre

foreword /ˈfɔːwɜːd/ *n* prefacio

forgave *pret de* FORGIVE

forge /fɔːdʒ/ ◆ *n* fragua ◆ *vt* **1** (*lazos, metal*) forjar **2** (*dinero, etc*) falsificar PHR V **to forge ahead** progresar con rapidez

forgery /ˈfɔːdʒəri/ *n* (*pl* **-ies**) falsificación

forget /fəˈget/ (*pret* **forgot** /fəˈgɒt/ *pp* **forgotten** /fəˈgɒtn/) **1** *vt, vi* ~ **(sth/to do sth)** olvidarse (de algo/hacer algo): *He forgot to pay me.* Se le olvidó pagarme. **2** *vt* (*dejar de pensar en*) olvidar LOC **not forgetting...** sin olvidarse de... PHR V **to forget about sth/sb** olvidársele a uno algo/algn **2** olvidar algo/a algn **forgetful** *adj* **1** olvidadizo **2** descuidado

forgive /fəˈgɪv/ *vt* (*pret* **forgave** /fəˈgeɪv/ *pp* **forgiven** /fəˈgɪvn/) perdonar: *Forgive me for interrupting.* Perdóname por interrumpir. **forgiveness** *n* perdón: *to ask (for) forgiveness (for sth)* pedir perdón (por algo) **forgiving** *adj* indulgente

forgot *pret de* FORGET

forgotten *pp de* FORGET

fork /fɔːk/ ◆ *n* **1** tenedor **2** (*Agric*) horca **3** bifurcación ◆ *vi* **1** (*camino*) bifurcarse **2** (*persona*): *to fork left* torcer a la izquierda PHR V **to fork out (for/on sth)** (*coloq*) aflojar la pasta (para algo)

form /fɔːm/ ◆ *n* **1** forma: *in the form of sth* en forma de algo **2** formulario: *tax form* impreso de la renta ◊ *application form* hoja de solicitud **3** formas: *as a matter of form* para guardar las formas **4** curso: *in the first form* en primero LOC **in/off form** en forma/en baja forma *Ver tb* SHAPE ◆ **1** *vt* formar, constituir: *to form an idea (of sth/sb)* formarse una idea (de algo/algn) **2** *vi* formarse

formal /ˈfɔːml/ *adj* **1** (*ademán, etc*) ceremonioso **2** (*comida/ropa*) de etiqueta **3** (*declaración, etc*) oficial **4** (*formación*) convencional

formality /fɔːˈmæləti/ *n* (*pl* **-ies**) **1** formalidad, ceremonia **2** trámite: *legal formalities* requisitos legales

formally /ˈfɔːməli/ *adv* **1** oficialmente **2** de etiqueta

format /ˈfɔːmæt/ *n* formato

formation /fɔːˈmeɪʃn/ *n* formación

former /ˈfɔːmə(r)/ ◆ *adj* **1** antiguo: *the former champion* el antiguo campeón **2** anterior: *in former times* en tiempos pasados **3** primero: *the former option* la primera opción ◆ **the former** *pron* aquello, aquél, -la, -los, -las: *The former was much better than the latter.* Aquélla fue mucho mejor que ésta. ☛ *Comparar con* LATTER

formerly /ˈfɔːməli/ *adv* **1** anteriormente **2** antiguamente

formidable /ˈfɔːmɪdəbl/ *adj* **1** extraordinario, formidable **2** (*tarea*) tremendo

formula /ˈfɔːmjələ/ *n* (*pl* **~s** *o en uso científico* **-lae** /ˈfɔːmjʊliː/) fórmula

forsake /fəˈseɪk/ *vt* (*pret* **forsook** /fəˈsʊk/ *pp* **forsaken** /fəˈseɪkən/) **1** (*fml*) ~ **sth** renunciar a algo **2** abandonar

fort /fɔːt/ *n* fortificación, fuerte

forth /fɔːθ/ *adv* (*fml*) en adelante: *from that day forth* desde aquel día LOC **and (so on and) so forth** y demás *Ver tb* BACK[1]

forthcoming /ˌfɔːθˈkʌmɪŋ/ *adj* **1** venidero, próximo: *the forthcoming election* las próximas elecciones **2** de próxima aparición **3** disponible ☛ No se usa antes de sustantivo: *No offer was forthcoming.* No hubo ninguna oferta. **4** (*persona*) comunicativo ☛ No se usa antes de sustantivo.

forthright /ˈfɔːθraɪt/ *adj* **1** (*persona*) directo **2** (*oposición*) enérgico

fortieth *Ver* FORTY

fortification /ˌfɔːtɪfɪˈkeɪʃn/ *n* fortalecimiento

fortify /ˈfɔːtɪfaɪ/ *vt* (*pret, pp* **fortified**) **1** fortificar **2** ~ **sb/yourself** fortalecer(se)

fortnight /ˈfɔːtnaɪt/ *n* quincena (*dos semanas*): *a fortnight today* de hoy en quince días

fortnightly /ˈfɔːtnaɪtli/ ◆ *adj* quincenal ◆ *adv* cada quince días, quincenalmente

fortress /ˈfɔːtrəs/ *n* fortaleza

fortunate /ˈfɔːtʃənət/ *adj* afortunado: *to be fortunate* tener suerte

fortune /ˈfɔːtʃuːn/ *n* **1** fortuna: *to be worth a fortune* valer una fortuna **2** suerte LOC *Ver* SMALL

forty /ˈfɔːti/ *adj, pron, n* cuarenta ☛ *Ver ejemplos en* FIFTY, FIVE **fortieth 1** *adj, pron* cuadragésimo **2** *n* cuarentava parte, cuarentavo ☛ *Ver ejemplos en* FIFTH

forward /ˈfɔːwəd/ ◆ *adj* **1** hacia adelante **2** delantero: *a forward position* una posición avanzada **3** para el futuro: *forward planning* planificación para el futuro **4** atrevido, descarado ◆ *adv* **1** (*tb* **forwards**) adelante, hacia adelante **2** en adelante: *from that day forward* a partir de entonces LOC *Ver* BACKWARD(S) ◆ *vt* ~ **sth (to sb)** remitir algo (a algn): *please forward* se ruega enviar ◊ *forwarding address* dirección (a la que han de remitirse las cartas) ◆ *n* delantero, -a

fossil /ˈfɒsl/ *n* (*lit y fig*) fósil

foster /ˈfɒstə(r)/ *vt* **1** fomentar **2** acoger en una familia

fought *pret, pp de* FIGHT

foul /faʊl/ ◆ *adj* **1** (*agua, lenguaje*) sucio **2** (*comida, olor, sabor*) asqueroso **3** (*carácter, humor, tiempo*) horrible ◆ *n* falta (*Dep*) ◆ *vt* cometer una falta contra (*Dep*) PHR V **to foul sth up** estropear algo

foul play *n* crimen

found[1] *pret, pp de* FIND

found[2] /faʊnd/ *vt* **1** fundar **2** fundamentar: *founded on fact* basado en la realidad

foundation /faʊnˈdeɪʃn/ *n* **1** fundación **2 the foundations** [*pl*] los cimientos **3** fundamento **4** (*tb* **foundation cream**) maquillaje de fondo

founder /ˈfaʊndə(r)/ *n* fundador, -ora

fountain /ˈfaʊntən; *USA* -tn/ *n* fuente, surtidor

fountain pen *n* estilográfica

four /fɔː(r)/ *adj, pron, n* cuatro ☛ *Ver ejemplos en* FIVE

fourteen /ˌfɔːˈtiːn/ *adj, pron, n* catorce ☛ *Ver ejemplos en* FIVE **fourteenth 1** *adj* decimocuarto **2** *pron, adv* el decimocuarto, la decimocuarta, los decimocuartos, las decimocuartas **3** *n* catorceava parte, catorceavo ☛ *Ver ejemplos en* FIFTH

fourth (*abrev* **4th**) /fɔːθ/ ◆ *adj* cuarto ◆ *pron, adv* el cuarto, la cuarta, los cuartos, las cuartas ◆ *n* **1 the fourth** el (día) cuatro **2** (*tb* **fourth gear**) cuarta ☛ *Ver ejemplos en* FIFTH

Para hablar de proporciones, "un cuarto" se dice **a quarter**: *We ate a quarter of the cake each.* Nos comimos un cuarto del pastel cada uno.

fowl /faʊl/ *n* (*pl* **fowl** *o* **~s**) ave (*de corral*)

fox /fɒks/ *n* (*fem* **vixen** /ˈvɪksn/) zorro

foyer /ˈfɔɪeɪ; *USA* ˈfɔɪər/ *n* vestíbulo

fraction /ˈfrækʃn/ *n* fracción

fracture /ˈfræktʃə(r)/ ◆ *n* fractura ◆ *vt, vi* fracturar(se)

fragile /ˈfrædʒaɪl; *USA* -dʒl/ *adj* (*lit y fig*) frágil, delicado

fragment /ˈfrægmənt/ ◆ *n* fragmento, parte ◆ /frægˈment/ *vt, vi* fragmentar(se)

fragrance /ˈfreɪgrəns/ *n* fragancia, aroma, perfume

fragrant /ˈfreɪgrənt/ *adj* aromático, fragante

frail /freɪl/ *adj* frágil, delicado ☛ Se aplica sobre todo a personas ancianas o enfermas.

frame /freɪm/ ◆ *n* **1** marco **2** armazón, estructura **3** (*gafas*) montura LOC **frame of mind** estado de ánimo ◆ *vt* **1** enmarcar **2** (*pregunta, etc*) formular **3** (*coloq*) ~ **sb** declarar en falso para incriminar a algn

framework /ˈfreɪmwɜːk/ *n* **1** armazón, estructura **2** marco, coyuntura

franc /fræŋk/ *n* franco (*moneda*)

frank /fræŋk/ *adj* franco, sincero

frantic /ˈfræntɪk/ *adj* frenético, desesperado

fraternal /frəˈtɜːnl/ *adj* fraternal

fraternity /frəˈtɜːnəti/ *n* (*pl* **-ies**) **1** fraternidad **2** hermandad, cofradía, sociedad

fraud /frɔːd/ *n* **1** (*delito*) fraude **2** (*persona*) impostor, -ora

fraught /frɔːt/ *adj* **1** ~ **with sth** lleno, cargado de algo **2** preocupante, tenso

fray /freɪ/ *vt, vi* desgastar(se), raer(se), deshilachar(se)

freak /friːk/ *n* (*coloq, pey*) bicho raro

freckle /ˈfrekl/ *n* peca **freckled** *adj* pecoso

free /friː/ ◆ *adj* (**freer** /friːə(r)/ **freest** /ˈfriːɪst/) **1** libre: *free speech* libertad de expresión ◊ *free will* libre albedrío ◊ *to set sb free* poner a algn en libertad ◊ *to be free of/from sth/sb* estar libre de algo/algn **2** (*sin atar*) suelto, libre **3** gratis, gratuito: *admission free* entrada libre ◊ *free of charge* gratis **4** ~ **with sth** generoso con algo **5** (*pey*) desvergonzado: *to be too free (with sb)* tomarse demasiadas libertades (con algn) LOC **free and easy** relajado, informal **of your own free will** por voluntad propia **to get, have, etc a free hand** tener las manos libres ◆ *vt* (*pret, pp* **freed**) **1** ~ **sth/sb (from sth)** liberar algo/a algn (de algo) **2** ~ **sth/sb of/from sth** librar, eximir algo/a algn de algo **3** ~ **sth/sb (from sth)** soltar algo/a algn (de algo) ◆ *adv* gratis **freely** *adv* **1** libremente, copiosamente **2** generosamente

freedom /ˈfriːdəm/ *n* **1** ~ **(of sth)** libertad (de algo): *freedom of speech* libertad de expresión **2** ~ **(to do sth)** libertad (para hacer algo) **3** ~ **from sth** inmunidad contra algo

free-range /ˌfriː ˈreɪndʒ/ *adj* de corral: *free-range eggs* huevos de corral ☛ *Comparar con* BATTERY 2

freeway /ˈfriːweɪ/ *n* (*USA*) autopista

freeze /friːz/ ◆ (*pret* **froze** /frəʊz/ *pp* **frozen** /ˈfrəʊzn/) **1** *vt, vi* helar(se), congelar(se): *I'm freezing!* ¡Estoy muerto de frío! ◊ *freezing point* punto de congelación **2** *vt, vi* (*comida, precios, salarios, fondos*) congelar(se) **3** quedarse rígido: *Freeze!* ¡No te muevas! ◆ *n* **1** (*tb* **freeze-up**) helada **2** (*de salarios, precios*) congelación

freezer /ˈfriːzə(r)/ (*tb* **deep-freeze**) congelador

freight /freɪt/ *n* carga

French window (*USA tb* **French door**) *n* puerta (*que da a un jardín, porche, etc*)

frenzied /ˈfrenzid/ *adj* frenético, enloquecido

frenzy /ˈfrenzi/ *n* [*gen sing*] frenesí

frequency /ˈfriːkwənsi/ *n* (*pl* **-ies**) frecuencia

frequent /ˈfriːkwənt/ ◆ *adj* frecuente ◆ /friˈkwent/ *vt* frecuentar

frequently /ˈfriːkwəntli/ *adv* c

frecuencia, frecuentemente ☛ *Ver nota en* ALWAYS

fresh /freʃ/ *adj* (**-er**, **-est**) **1** nuevo, otro **2** reciente **3** (*alimentos, aire, tiempo, tez*) fresco **4** (*agua*) dulce LOC *Ver* BREATH **freshly** *adv* recién: *freshly baked* recién sacado del horno **freshness** *n* **1** frescura **2** novedad

freshen /ˈfreʃn/ **1** *vt* ~ **freshen sth** (**up**) dar nueva vida a algo **2** *vi* (*viento*) refrescar PHR V **to freshen** (**yourself**) **up** arreglarse

freshwater /ˈfreʃˌwɔːtə(r)/ *adj* de agua dulce

fret /fret/ *vi* (**-tt-**) ~ (**about/at/over sth**) apurarse, preocuparse (por algo)

friar /ˈfraɪə(r)/ *n* fraile

friction /ˈfrɪkʃn/ *n* **1** fricción, rozamiento **2** fricción, desavenencia

Friday /ˈfraɪdeɪ, ˈfraɪdi/ *n* (*abrev* **Fri**) viernes ☛ *Ver ejemplos en* MONDAY LOC **Good Friday** Viernes Santo

fridge /frɪdʒ/ *n* (*coloq*) nevera: *fridge-freezer* frigorífico de dos puertas

fried /fraɪd/ ◆ *pret, pp de* FRY ◆ *adj* frito

friend /frend/ *n* **1** amigo, -a **2** ~ **of/to sth** partidario, -a de algo LOC **to be friends** (**with sb**) ser amigo (de algn) **to have friends in high places** tener enchufes **to make friends** hacer amigos **to make friends with sb** hacerse amigo (de algn)

friendly /ˈfrendli/ *adj* (**-ier**, **-iest**) **1** (*persona*) simpático, amable ☛ Nótese que **sympathetic** se traduce por "compasivo". **2** (*relación, consejo*) amistoso **3** (*gesto, palabras*) amable **4** (*ambiente, lugar*) acogedor **5** (*partido*) amistoso **friendliness** *n* simpatía, cordialidad

friendship /ˈfrendʃɪp/ *n* amistad

fright /fraɪt/ *n* susto: *to give sb/get a fright* dar un susto a algn/darse un susto

frighten /ˈfraɪtn/ *vt* asustar, dar miedo a **frightened** *adj* asustado: *to be frightened (of sth/sb)* tener miedo (a/de algo/algn) LOC *Ver* WIT **frightening** *adj* alarmante, aterrador

frightful /ˈfraɪtfl/ *adj* **1** horrible, espantoso **2** (*coloq*) (*para enfatizar*): *a frightful mess* un desorden terrible **frightfully** *adv* (*coloq*): *I'm frightfully sorry.* Lo siento muchísimo.

frigid /ˈfrɪdʒɪd/ *adj* frígido

frill /frɪl/ *n* **1** (*costura*) volante **2** [*gen pl*] (*fig*) adorno: *no frills* sin adornos

fringe /frɪndʒ/ ◆ *n* **1** flequillo **2** flecos **3** (*fig*) margen ◆ *vt* LOC **to be fringed by/with sth** estar bordeado por/con algo

frisk /frɪsk/ **1** *vt* (*coloq*) cachear **2** *vi* retozar **frisky** *adj* retozón, juguetón

frivolity /frɪˈvɒləti/ *n* frivolidad

frivolous /ˈfrɪvələs/ *adj* frívolo

fro /frəʊ/ *adv Ver* TO

frock /frɒk/ *n* vestido

frog /frɒg; *USA* frɔːg/ *n* **1** rana **2** (*coloq, ofen*) gabacho, -a

from /frəm, frɒm/ *prep* **1** de (*procedencia*): *from Madrid to London* de Madrid a Londres ◊ *I'm from New Zealand.* Soy de Nueva Zelanda. ◊ *from bad to worse* de mal en peor ◊ *the train from Soria* el tren (procedente) de Soria ◊ *a present from a friend* un regalo de un amigo ◊ *to take sth away from sb* quitarle algo a algn **2** (*tiempo, situación*) desde: *from above/below* desde arriba/abajo ◊ *from time to time* de vez en cuando ◊ *from yesterday* desde ayer ☛ *Ver nota en* SINCE **3** por: *from choice* por elección ◊ *from what I can gather* por lo que yo entiendo **4** entre: *to choose from...* elegir entre... **5** con: *Wine is made from grapes.* El vino se hace con uvas. **6** (*Mat*): *13 from 34 leaves 21.* 34 menos 13 son 21. LOC **from...on**: *from now on* de ahora en adelante ◊ *from then on* desde entonces ☛ Para los usos de **from** en PHRASAL VERBS ver las entradas de los verbos correspondientes, p.ej. **to hear from** en HEAR.

front /frʌnt/ ◆ *n* **1 the** ~ (**of sth**) el frente, la (parte) delantera (de algo): *If you can't see the board, sit at the front.* Si no ves la pizarra, siéntate delante. ◊ *The number is shown on the front of the bus.* El número está puesto en la parte delantera del autobús. **2 the front** (*Mil*) el frente **3** fachada: *a front for sth* una fachada para algo **4** terreno: *on the financial front* en el terreno económico ◆ *adj* delantero, de delante (*rueda, habitación, etc*) ◆ *adv* LOC **in front** delante: *the row in front* la fila de delante ☛ *Ver dibujo en* DELANTE **up front** (*coloq*) por adelantado *Ver tb* BACK[1] ◆ *prep* LOC **in front of 1** delante de **2** ante ☛ Nótese que **enfrente de** se traduce por **opposite**. *Ver dibujo en* ENFRENTE

front cover *n* portada

front door *n* puerta de entrada

frontier /ˈfrʌntɪə(r); *USA* frʌnˈtɪər/ *n* ~ (**with sth/between…**) frontera (con algo/entre…) ☛ *Ver nota en* BORDER

front page *n* primera plana

front row *n* primera fila

frost /frɒst; *USA* frɔːst/ ◆ *n* **1** helada **2** escarcha ◆ *vt, vi* cubrir de escarcha **frosty** *adj* (**-ier**, **-iest**) **1** helado **2** cubierto de escarcha

froth /frɒθ; *USA* frɔːθ/ ◆ *n* espuma ◆ *vi* hacer espuma

frown /fraʊn/ ◆ *n* ceño ◆ *vi* fruncir el ceño PHR V **to frown on/upon sth** desaprobar algo

froze *pret de* FREEZE

frozen *pp de* FREEZE

fruit /fruːt/ *n* **1** [*gen incontable*] fruta: *fruit and vegetables* frutas y verduras ◊ *tropical fruits* frutas tropicales **2** fruto: *the fruit(s) of your labours* el fruto de su trabajo

fruitful /ˈfruːtfl/ *adj* fructífero, provechoso

fruition /fruˈɪʃn/ *n* realización: *to come to fruition* verse realizado

fruitless /ˈfruːtləs/ *adj* infructuoso

frustrate /frʌˈstreɪt; *USA* ˈfrʌstreɪt/ *vt* frustrar, desbaratar

fry /fraɪ/ *vt, vi* (*pret, pp* **fried** /fraɪd/) freír(se)

frying-pan /ˈfraɪɪŋ pæn/ (*USA* **frypan**) *n* sartén ☛ *Ver dibujo en* SAUCEPAN LOC **out of the frying-pan into the fire** de Guatemala a guatepeor

fuel /ˈfjuːəl/ *n* **1** combustible **2** carburante

fugitive /ˈfjuːdʒətɪv/ *adj, n* ~ (**from sth/sb**) fugitivo, -a, prófugo, -a (de algo/algn)

fulfil (*USA* **fulfill**) /fʊlˈfɪl/ *vt* (**-ll-**) **1** (*promesa*) cumplir **2** (*tarea*) llevar a cabo **3** (*deseo*) satisfacer **4** (*función*) realizar

full /fʊl/ ◆ *adj* (**-er**, **-est**) **1** ~ (**of sth**) lleno (de algo) **2** ~ **of sth** obsesionado por algo **3** ~ (**up**) hasta arriba: *I'm full up.* Ya no puedo más. **4** (*hotel, instrucciones*) completo **5** (*discusiones*) extenso **6** (*sentido*) amplio **7** (*investigación*) detallado **8** (*ropa*) holgado LOC (**at**) **full blast** a tope (**at**) **full speed** a toda mecha **full of yourself** (*pey*): *You're very full of yourself.* Estás hecho un creído. **in full** detalladamente, íntegramente **in full swing** en plena marcha **to come full circle** volver al principio **to the full** al máximo ◆ *adv* **1** *full in the face* en plena cara **2** muy: *You know full well that…* Sabes muy bien que…

full board *n* pensión completa

full-length /ˌfʊl ˈleŋθ/ *adj* **1** (*espejo*) de cuerpo entero **2** (*ropa*) largo

full stop (*tb* **full point**, *USA* **period**) *n* punto (y seguido) ☛ *Ver* págs 318–9.

full-time /ˌfʊl ˈtaɪm/ *adj, adv* jornada completa

fully /ˈfʊli/ *adv* **1** completamente **2** del todo **3** por lo menos: *fully two hours* por lo menos dos horas

fumble /ˈfʌmbl/ *vi* ~ (**with sth**) manipular torpemente algo

fume /fjuːm/ ◆ *n* [*gen pl*] humo: *poisonous fumes* gases tóxicos ◆ *vi* echar humo (*de rabia*)

fun /fʌn/ ◆ *n* diversión: *to have fun* pasarlo bien ◊ *to take the fun out of sth* quitar toda la gracia a algo LOC **to make fun of sth/sb** reírse de algo/algn *Ver tb* POKE ◆ *adj* (*coloq*) divertido, entretenido

function /ˈfʌŋkʃn/ ◆ *n* **1** función **2** ceremonia ◆ *vi* **1** funcionar **2** ~ **as sth** servir, hacer de algo

fund /fʌnd/ ◆ *n* **1** fondo (*de dinero*) **2** **funds** [*pl*] fondos ◆ *vt* financiar, subvencionar

fundamental /ˌfʌndəˈmentl/ ◆ *adj* ~ (**to sth**) fundamental (para algo) ◆ *n* [*gen pl*] fundamento

funeral /ˈfjuːnərəl/ *n* **1** funeral, entierro: *funeral parlour* funeraria **2** cortejo fúnebre

fungus /ˈfʌŋgəs/ *n* (*pl* **-gi** /-gaɪ, -dʒaɪ/ *o* **-guses** /-gəsɪz/) hongo

funnel /ˈfʌnl/ ◆ *n* **1** embudo **2** (*de un barco*) chimenea ◆ *vt* (**-ll-**, *USA* **-l-**) canalizar

funny /ˈfʌni/ *adj* (**-ier**, **-iest**) **1** gracioso, divertido **2** extraño, raro

fur /fɜː(r)/ *n* **1** pelo (*de animal*) **2** piel: *a fur coat* un abrigo de pieles

furious /ˈfjʊəriəs/ *adj* **1** ~ (**at sth/with sb**) furioso (con algo/algn) **2** (*esfuerzo, lucha, tormenta*) violento **3** (*debate*) acalorado **furiously** *adv* violentamente, furiosamente

furnace /ˈfɜːnɪs/ *n* caldera

furnish /ˈfɜːnɪʃ/ *vt* **1** ~ **sth** (**with sth**) amueblar algo (con algo): *a furnished flat* un piso amueblado **2** ~ **sth/sb with sth** suministrar algo a algo/algn **furnishings** *n* [*pl*] mobiliario

furniture /ˈfɜːnɪtʃə(r)/ *n* [*incontable*] mobiliario, muebles: *a piece of furniture* un mueble

furrow /ˈfʌrəʊ/ ◆ *n* surco ◆ *vt* hacer surcos en: *a furrowed brow* una frente arrugada

furry /ˈfɜːri/ *adj* (**-ier**, **-iest**) **1** peludo **2** de peluche

further /ˈfəːðə(r)/ ◆ *adj* **1** (*tb* **farther**) más lejos: *¿Which is further?* ¿Cuál está más lejos? **2** más: *until further notice* hasta nuevo aviso ◊ *for further details/ information...* para más información... ◆ *adv* **1** (*tb* **farther**) más lejos: *How much further is it to Oxford?* ¿Cuánto falta para Oxford? **2** además: *Further to my letter...* En relación a mi carta... **3** más: *to hear nothing further* no tener más noticias LOC *Ver* AFIELD

¿Farther o **further?** Los dos son comparativos de **far**, pero sólo son sinónimos cuando nos referimos a distancias: *Which is further/farther?* ¿Cuál está más lejos?

furthermore /ˌfɜːðəˈmɔː(r)/ *adv* además

furthest /ˈfɜːðɪst/ *adj, adv* (*superl de* **far**) más lejano/alejado: *the furthest corner of Europe* el punto más lejano de Europa

fury /ˈfjʊəri/ *n* furia, rabia

fuse /fjuːz/ ◆ *n* **1** fusible **2** mecha **3** (*USA tb* **fuze**) espoleta ◆ **1** *vi* fundirse **2** *vt* ~ **sth** (**together**) soldar algo

fusion /ˈfjuːʒn/ *n* fusión

fuss /fʌs/ ◆ *n* [*incontable*] alboroto, jaleo, lío LOC **to make a fuss of/over sb** mimar a algn **to make a fuss of/over sth** dar mucho bombo a algo **to make, kick up, etc a fuss** (**about/over sth**) armar un escándalo (por algo) ◆ *vi* **1** ~ (**about**) preocuparse (*por una menudencia*) **2** ~ **over sb** mimar a algn

fussy /ˈfʌsi/ *adj* (**-ier**, **-iest**) **1** quisquilloso, -a **2** ~ (**about sth**) exigente (con algo)

futile /ˈfjuːtaɪl; *USA* -tl/ *adj* inútil

future /ˈfjuːtʃə(r)/ ◆ *n* **1** futuro: *in the near future* en un futuro cercano **2** porvenir LOC **in future** en el futuro, de ahora en adelante *Ver tb* FORESEE ◆ *adj* futuro

fuzzy /ˈfʌzi/ *adj* (**-ier**, **-iest**) **1** velludo, peludo **2** borroso **3** (*mente*) embotado

Gg

G, g /dʒiː/ *n* (*pl* **G's**, **g's** /dʒiːz/) **1** G, g: *G for George* G de Gerona ☛ *Ver ejemplos en* A, a **2** (*Mús*) sol

gab /gæb/ *n* LOC *Ver* GIFT

gable /ˈgeɪbl/ *n* hastial (*triángulo de fachada que soporta el tejado*)

gadget /ˈgædʒɪt/ *n* aparato

gag /gæg/ ◆ *n* **1** (*lit y fig*) mordaza **2** gag ◆ *vt* (**-gg-**) (*lit y fig*) amordazar

gage (*USA*) *Ver* GAUGE

gaiety /ˈgeɪəti/ *n* alegría

gain /geɪn/ ◆ *n* **1** ganancia **2** aumento, subida ◆ **1** *vt* adquirir, ganar: *to gain control* adquirir control **2** *vt* aumentar, subir, ganar: *to gain two kilos* engordar dos kilos ◊ *to gain speed* ganar velocidad **3** *vi* ~ **by/from** (**doing**) **sth** beneficiarse de (hacer) algo **4** *vi* (*reloj*) adelantarse PHR V **to gain on sth/sb** ir alcanzando algo/a algn

gait /geɪt/ *n* [*sing*] paso, andar

galaxy /ˈgæləksi/ *n* (*pl* **-ies**) galaxia

gale /geɪl/ *n* temporal

gallant /ˈgælənt/ *adj* **1** (*fml*) valiente **2** *tb* /ˌgəˈlænt/ galante **gallantry** *n* valentía

gallery /ˈɡæləri/ *n* (*pl* **-ies**) **1** (*tb* **art gallery**) museo ☛ *Ver nota en* MUSEUM **2** (*tienda*) galería **3** (*Teat*) galería

galley /ˈɡæli/ *n* (*pl* **-eys**) **1** cocina (*en un avión o un barco*) **2** (*Náut*) galera

gallon /ˈɡælən/ *n* (*abrev* **gall**) galón

gallop /ˈɡæləp/ ◆ *vt, vi* (hacer) galopar ◆ *n* (*lit y fig*) galope

the gallows /ˈɡæləʊz/ *n* (la) horca

gamble /ˈɡæmbl/ ◆ *vt, vi* (*dinero*) jugar PHR V **to gamble on (doing) sth** confiar en (hacer) algo, arriesgarse a (hacer) algo ◆ *n* **1** jugada **2** (*fig*): *to be a gamble* ser arriesgado **gambler** *n* jugador, -ora **gambling** *n* juego

game /ɡeɪm/ ◆ *n* **1** juego **2** partido ☛ *Comparar con* MATCH² **3** (*naipes, ajedrez*) partida **4 games** [*pl*] educación física **5** [*incontable*] caza LOC *Ver* FAIR, MUG ◆ *adj*: *Are you game?* ¿Te animas?

gammon /ˈɡæmən/ *n* [*incontable*] jamón (fresco salado) ☛ *Comparar con* BACON, HAM

gang /ɡæŋ/ ◆ *n* [*v sing o pl*] **1** banda, pandilla **2** cuadrilla ◆ PHR V **to gang up on sb** juntarse contra algn

gangster /ˈɡæŋstə(r)/ *n* gángster

gangway /ˈɡæŋweɪ/ *n* **1** pasarela **2** (*GB*) pasillo (*entre sillas, etc*)

gaol /dʒeɪl/ *Ver* JAIL

gap /ɡæp/ *n* **1** hueco, abertura **2** espacio **3** (*tiempo*) intervalo **4** (*fig*) separación **5** (*deficiencia*) laguna, vacío LOC *Ver* BRIDGE

gape /ɡeɪp/ *vi* **1** ~ (**at sth/sb**) mirar boquiabierto (algo/a algn) **2** abrirse, quedar abierto **gaping** *adj* enorme: *a gaping hole* un agujero enorme

garage /ˈɡærɑːʒ, ˈɡærɪdʒ; *USA* ɡəˈrɑːʒ/ *n* **1** garaje **2** taller **3** estación de servicio

garbage /ˈɡɑːbɪdʒ/ *n* (*USA*) [*incontable*] (*lit y fig*) basura

garbled /ˈɡɑːbld/ *adj* confuso

garden /ˈɡɑːdn/ ◆ *n* jardín ◆ *vi* trabajar en el jardín **gardener** *n* jardinero, -a **gardening** *n* jardinería

gargle /ˈɡɑːɡl/ *vi* hacer gárgaras

garish /ˈɡeərɪʃ/ *adj* chillón (*color, ropa*)

garland /ˈɡɑːlənd/ *n* guirnalda

garlic /ˈɡɑːlɪk/ *n* [*incontable*] ajo: *clove of garlic* diente de ajo

garment /ˈɡɑːmənt/ *n* (*fml*) prenda (*de vestir*)

garnish /ˈɡɑːnɪʃ/ ◆ *vt* adornar, aderezar ◆ *n* adorno

garrison /ˈɡærɪsn/ *n* [*v sing o pl*] guarnición (*militar*)

gas /ɡæs/ ◆ *n* (*pl* ~**es**, *tb USA* **gasses**) **1** gas: *gas mask* máscara antigás **2** (*USA, coloq*) gasolina ◆ *vt* (**-ss-**) asfixiar con gas

gash /ɡæʃ/ *n* herida profunda

gasoline /ˈɡæsəliːn/ *n* (*USA*) gasolina

gasp /ɡɑːsp/ ◆ **1** *vi* dar un grito ahogado **2** *vi* jadear: *to gasp for air* hacer esfuerzos para respirar **3** *vt* ~ **sth** (**out**) decir algo con voz entrecortada ◆ *n* jadeo, grito ahogado

gas station *n* (*USA*) gasolinera

gate /ɡeɪt/ *n* puerta, portón, cancela

gatecrash /ˈɡeɪtkræʃ/ *vt, vi* colarse (en)

gateway /ˈɡeɪtweɪ/ *n* **1** entrada, puerta **2** ~ **to sth** (*fig*) pasaporte hacia algo

gather /ˈɡæðə(r)/ **1** *vi* juntarse, reunirse **2** *vi* (*muchedumbre*) formarse **3** *vt* ~ **sth/sb** (**together**) reunir/juntar algo; reunir a algn **4** *vt* (*flores, fruta*) recoger **5** *vt* deducir, tener entendido **6** *vt* ~ **sth** (**in**) (*costura*) fruncir algo **7** *vt* (*velocidad*) cobrar PHR V **to gather round** acercarse **to gather round sth/sb** agruparse en torno a algo/algn **to gather sth up** recoger algo **gathering** *n* reunión

gaudy /ˈɡɔːdi/ *adj* (**-ier**, **-iest**) (*pey*) chillón, llamativo

gauge /ɡeɪdʒ/ ◆ *n* **1** medida **2** (*Ferrocarril*) ancho de vía **3** indicador ◆ *vt* **1** calibrar, calcular **2** juzgar

gaunt /ɡɔːnt/ *adj* demacrado

gauze /ɡɔːz/ *n* gasa

gave *pret de* GIVE

gay /ɡeɪ/ ◆ *adj* **1** gay, homosexual **2** (*antic*) alegre ◆ *n* gay

gaze /ɡeɪz/ ◆ *vi* ~ (**at sth/sb**) mirar fijamente (algo/a algn): *They gazed into each other's eyes.* Se miraron fijamente a los ojos. ◆ *n* [*sing*] mirada fija y larga

GCSE /ˌdʒiːsiːesˈiː/ *abrev* (*GB*) **General Certificate of Secondary Education** bachillerato elemental

gear /ɡɪə(r)/ ◆ *n* **1** equipo: *camping gear* equipo de acampada **2** (*automóvil*) marcha, velocidad: *out of gear* en punt

iː	i	ɪ	e	æ	ɑː	ʌ	ʊ	uː
see	happy	sit	ten	hat	arm	cup	put	too

muerto ◊ *to change gear* cambiar de velocidad *Ver tb* REVERSE **3** (*Mec*) engranaje ◆ **PHR V to gear sth to/towards sth** adaptar algo a algo, enfocar algo a algo **to gear (sth/sb) up (for/to do sth)** prepararse (para algo/para hacer algo), preparar algo/a algn (para algo/para hacer algo)

gearbox /ˈgɪəbɒks/ *n* caja de cambios

geese *plural de* GOOSE

gem /dʒem/ *n* **1** piedra preciosa **2** (*fig*) joya

Gemini /ˈdʒemɪnaɪ/ *n* géminis ☛ *Ver ejemplos en* AQUARIUS

gender /ˈdʒendə(r)/ *n* **1** (*Gram*) género **2** sexo

gene /dʒiːn/ *n* gen

general /ˈdʒenrəl/ ◆ *adj* general: *as a general rule* por regla general ◊ *the general public* el público/la gente (en general) **LOC in general** en general ◆ *n* general

general election *n* elecciones generales

generalize, -ise /ˈdʒenrəlaɪz/ *vi* ~ (**about sth**) generalizar (sobre algo) **generalization, -isation** *n* generalización

generally /ˈdʒenrəli/ *adv* generalmente, por lo general: *generally speaking...* en términos generales...

general practice *n* (*GB*) medicina general

general practitioner *n* (*abrev* **GP**) (*GB*) médico de cabecera

general-purpose /ˌdʒenrəl ˈpɜːpəs/ *adj* de uso general

generate /ˈdʒenəreɪt/ *vt* generar **generation** *n* generación: *the older/younger generation* los mayores/jóvenes ◊ *the generation gap* el conflicto generacional

generator /ˈdʒenəreɪtə(r)/ *n* generador

generosity /ˌdʒenəˈrɒsəti/ *n* generosidad

generous /ˈdʒenərəs/ *adj* **1** (*persona, regalo*) generoso **2** (*ración*) abundante: *a generous helping* una buena porción

genetic /dʒəˈnetɪk/ *adj* genético **genetics** *n* [*sing*] genética

genial /ˈdʒiːniəl/ *adj* afable

genital /ˈdʒenɪtl/ *adj* genital **genitals** (*tb* **genitalia** /ˌdʒenɪˈteɪliə/) *n* [*pl*] (*fml*) genitales

genius /ˈdʒiːniəs/ *n* (*pl* **geniuses**) genio

genocide /ˈdʒenəsaɪd/ *n* genocidio

gent /dʒent/ *n* **1 the Gents** [*sing*] (*GB, coloq*) servicios (de caballeros) **2** (*coloq, joc*) caballero

genteel /dʒenˈtiːl/ *adj* (*pey*) remilgado **gentility** /dʒenˈtɪləti/ *n* (*aprob, irón*) finura

gentle /ˈdʒentl/ *adj* (**-er**, **-est**) **1** (*persona, carácter*) amable, benévolo **2** (*brisa, caricia, ejercicio*) suave **3** (*animal*) manso **4** (*declive, toque*) ligero **gentleness** *n* **1** amabilidad **2** suavidad **3** mansedumbre **gently** *adv* **1** suavemente **2** (*freír*) a fuego lento **3** (*persuadir*) poco a poco

gentleman /ˈdʒentlmən/ *n* (*pl* **-men** /-mən/) caballero *Ver tb* LADY

genuine /ˈdʒenjuɪn/ *adj* **1** (*cuadro*) auténtico **2** (*persona*) sincero

geography /dʒiˈɒgrəfi/ *n* geografía **geographer** /dʒiˈɒgrəfə(r)/ *n* geógrafo, -a **geographical** /ˌdʒiːəˈgræfɪkl/ *adj* geográfico

geology /dʒiˈɒlədʒi/ *n* geología **geological** /ˌdʒiːəˈlɒdʒɪkl/ *adj* geológico **geologist** /dʒiˈɒlədʒɪst/ *n* geólogo, -a

geometry /dʒiˈɒmətri/ *n* geometría **geometric** /dʒɪəˈmetrɪk/ (*tb* **geometrical** /-ɪkl/) *adj* geométrico

geriatric /ˌdʒeriˈætrɪk/ *adj, n* geriátrico, -a

germ /dʒɜːm/ *n* germen, microbio

get /get/ (**-tt-**) (*pret* **got** /gɒt/ *pp* **got**, *USA* **gotten** /ˈgɒtn/)

- **to get + n/pron** *vt* recibir, conseguir, coger: *to get a shock* llevarse un susto ◊ *to get a letter* recibir una carta ◊ *How much did you get for your car?* ¿Cuánto te han dado por el coche? ◊ *She gets bad headaches.* Sufre de fuertes dolores de cabeza. ◊ *I didn't get the joke.* No cogí el chiste.
- **to get + objeto + infinitivo o -ing** *vt* **to get sth/sb doing sth/to do sth** hacer, conseguir que algo/algn haga algo: *to get the car to start* hacer que el coche arranque ◊ *to get him talking* hacerle hablar
- **to get + objeto + participio** *vt* (*con actividades que queremos que sean realizadas por otra persona para nosotros*): *to get your hair cut* cortarse el pelo ◊ *You should get your watch repaired.*

Deberías llevar tu reloj a arreglar. ☛ *Comparar con* HAVE 6

• **to get + objeto + adj** *vt* (*conseguir que algo se vuelva/haga...*): *to get sth right* acertar algo ◊ *to get the children ready for school* dejar a los niños listos para ir a la escuela ◊ *to get (yourself) ready* arreglarse

• **to get + adj** *vi* volverse, hacerse: *to get wet* mojarse ◊ *It's getting late.* Se está haciendo tarde. ◊ *to get better* mejorar/recuperarse

• **to get + participio** *vt*: *to get fed up with sth* hartarse de algo ◊ *to get used to sth* acostumbrarse a algo ◊ *to get lost* perderse

Algunas combinaciones frecuentes de **to get + participio** se traducen por verbos pronominales: *to get bored* aburrirse ◊ *to get divorced* divorciarse ◊ *to get dressed* vestirse ◊ *to get drunk* emborracharse ◊ *to get married* casarse. Para conjugarlos, añadimos la forma correspondiente de **get**: *She soon got used to it.* Se acostumbró enseguida. ◊ *I'm getting dressed.* Me estoy vistiendo. ◊ *We'll get married in the summer.* Nos casaremos este verano. **Get + participio** se utiliza también para expresar acciones que ocurren o se realizan de forma accidental, inesperada o repentina: *I got caught in a heavy rainstorm.* Me pilló una tormenta muy fuerte. ◊ *Simon got hit by a ball.* A Simon le dieron un pelotazo.

• **otros usos 1** *vi* **to get to do sth** llegar a hacer algo: *to get to know sb* (llegar a) conocer a algn **2** *vt, vi* **to have got (to do) sth** tener (que hacer) algo *Ver tb* HAVE **3** *vi* **to get to...** (*movimiento*) llegar a...: *Where have they got to?* ¿Dónde se han metido?

LOC to get away from it all (*coloq*) huir de todo y de todos **to get (sb) nowhere**; **not to get (sb) anywhere** (*coloq*) no llevar (a algn) a ninguna parte **to get there** lograrlo ☛ Para otras expresiones con **get**, véanse las entradas del sustantivo, adjetivo, etc, p.ej. **to get the hang of sth** en HANG.

• **PHR V**

to get about/(a)round 1 (*persona, animal*) salir, moverse **2** (*rumor, noticia*) circular, correr

to get sth across (to sb) comunicar algo (a algn)

to get ahead (of sb) adelantarse (a algn)

to get along with sb; **to get along (together)** llevarse bien (con algn)

to get (a)round to (doing) sth encontrar tiempo para (hacer) algo

to get at sb (*coloq*) tomarla con algn **to get at sth** (*coloq*) insinuar algo: *What are you getting at?* ¿Qué quieres decir?

to get away (from...) irse, salir (de...)

to get away with (doing) sth quedarse sin castigo por (hacer) algo

to get back regresar **to get back at sb** (*coloq*) vengarse de algn **to get sth back** recuperar, recobrar algo

to get behind (with sth) retrasarse (con/en algo)

to get by (lograr) pasar

to get down 1 bajar **2** (*niños*) levantarse (de la mesa) **to get down to (doing) sth** ponerse a hacer algo **to get sb down** (*coloq*) deprimir a algn

to get in; **to get into sth 1** (*tren*) llegar (a algún sitio) **2** (*persona*) volver (a casa) **3** subirse (a algo) (*vehículo*) **to get sth in** recoger algo

to get off (sth) 1 salir (del trabajo) **2** (*vehículo*) bajar (de algo) **to get off with sb** (*GB, coloq*) ligar, enrollarse con algn

to get sth off (sth) quitar algo (de algo)

to get on 1 (*tb* **to get along**) irle a algn: *How did you get on?* ¿Cómo te fue? **2** tener éxito **3** (*tb* **to get along**) arreglárselas **to get on**; **to get onto sth** subirse (a algo) **to get on to sth** ponerse a hablar de algo, pasar a considerar algo **to get on with sb**; **to get on (together)** (*tb* **to get along**) llevarse bien (con algn) **to get on with sth** seguir con algo: *Get on with your work!* ¡Sigan trabajando! **to get sth on** poner(se) algo

to get out (of sth) 1 salir (de algo): *Get out (of here)!* ¡Fuera de aquí! **2** (*vehículo*) bajar (de algo) **to get out of (doing) sth** librarse de (hacer) algo **to get sth out of sth/sb** sacar algo de algo/algn

to get over sth 1 (*problema, timidez*) superar algo **2** olvidar algo **3** recuperarse de algo

to get round sb (*coloq*) convencer a algn **to get (a)round to (doing) sth** encontrar tiempo para (hacer) algo

to get through sth 1 (*dinero, comida*) consumir algo **2** (*tarea*) terminar algo

to get through (**to sb**) (*por teléfono*) ponerse en contacto (con algn) **to get through to sb** entenderse con algn
to get together (**with sb**) reunirse (con algn) **to get sth/sb together** reunir, juntar algo/a algn
to get up levantarse **to get up to sth 1** llegar a algo **2** meterse en algo **to get sb up** levantar a algn

getaway /ˈgetəweɪ/ *n* fuga: *getaway car* coche de fuga

ghastly /ˈgɑːstli; *USA* ˈgæstli/ *adj* (**-ier, -iest**) espantoso: *the whole ghastly business* todo el asqueroso asunto

ghetto /ˈgetəʊ/ *n* (*pl* **~s**) gueto

ghost /gəʊst/ *n* fantasma LOC **to give up the ghost** entregar el alma **ghostly** *adj* (**-ier**, **-iest**) fantasmal

ghost story *n* historia de terror

giant /ˈdʒaɪənt/ *n* gigante

gibberish /ˈdʒɪbərɪʃ/ *n* tonterías

giddy /ˈgɪdi/ *adj* (**-ier**, **-iest**) mareado: *The dancing made her giddy.* El baile la mareó.

gift /gɪft/ *n* **1** regalo *Ver tb* PRESENT **2** ~ (**for sth/doing sth**) don (para algo/hacer algo) **3** (*coloq*) ganga LOC **to have the gift of the gab** tener mucha labia *Ver tb* LOOK[1] **gifted** *adj* dotado

gift token (*tb* **gift voucher**) *n* vale de regalo

gift-wrap /ˈgɪft ræp/ *vt* envolver en papel de regalo

gig /gɪg/ *n* (*coloq*) actuación (*musical*)

gigantic /dʒaɪˈgæntɪk/ *adj* gigantesco

giggle /ˈgɪgl/ ◆ *vi* ~ (**at sth/sb**) reírse tontamente (de algo/algn) ◆ *n* **1** risita **2** broma: *I only did it for a giggle.* Sólo lo hice por hacer una gracia. **3 the giggles** [*pl*]: *a fit of the giggles* un ataque de risa

gilded /ˈgɪldɪd/ (*tb* **gilt** /gɪlt/) *adj* dorado

gimmick /ˈgɪmɪk/ *n* truco publicitario o de promoción

gin /dʒɪn/ *n* ginebra: *a gin and tonic* un gin-tonic

ginger /ˈdʒɪndʒə(r)/ ◆ *n* jengibre ◆ *adj* pelirrojo: *ginger hair* pelo pelirrojo ◇ *a ginger cat* un gato romano

gingerly /ˈdʒɪndʒəli/ *adv* cautelosamente, sigilosamente

gipsy *Ver* GYPSY

giraffe /dʒəˈrɑːf; *USA* -ˈræf/ *n* jirafa

girl /gɜːl/ *n* niña, chica

girlfriend /ˈgɜːlfrend/ *n* **1** novia **2** (*esp USA*) amiga

gist /dʒɪst/ *n* LOC **to get the gist of sth** captar lo esencial de algo

give /gɪv/ ◆ (*pret* **gave** /geɪv/ *pp* **given** /ˈgɪvn/) **1** *vt* ~ **sth** (**to sb**); ~ (**sb**) **sth** dar algo (a algn): *I gave each of the boys an apple.* Le di una manzana a cada uno de los chicos. ◇ *It gave us rather a shock.* Nos dio un buen susto. **2** *vi* ~ (**to sth**) dar dinero (para algo) **3** *vi* ceder **4** *vt* (*tiempo, pensamiento*) dedicar **5** *vt* contagiar: *You've given me your cold.* Me has contagiado tu resfriado. **6** *vt* conceder: *I'll give you that.* Te reconozco eso. **7** *vt* dar: *to give a lecture* dar una conferencia LOC **don't give me that!** ¿te crees que soy tonto? **give or take sth**: *an hour and a half, give or take a few minutes* una hora y media, más o menos **not to give a damn, a hoot, etc** (**about sth/sb**) (*coloq*) importar a algn un bledo (algo/algn): *She doesn't give a damn about it.* Le importa un bledo. ☛ Para otras expresiones con **give**, véanse las entradas del sustantivo, adjetivo, etc, p.ej. **to give rise to sth** en RISE.
PHR V **to give sth away** regalar algo **to give sth/sb away** delatar algo/a algn
to give (**sb**) **back sth**; **to give sth back** (**to sb**) devolver algo (a algn)
to give in (**to sth/sb**) ceder (a algo/algn) **to give sth in** entregar algo
to give sth out repartir algo
to give up abandonar, rendirse **to give sth up**; **to give up doing sth** dejar algo, dejar de hacer algo: *to give up hope* perder las esperanzas ◇ *to give up smoking* dejar de fumar
◆ *n* LOC **give and take** toma y daca

given /ˈgɪvn/ ◆ *adj, prep* dado ◆ *pp de* GIVE

glad /glæd/ *adj* (**gladder**, **gladdest**) **1 to be ~ (about sth/to do sth/that…)** alegrarse (de algo/de hacer algo/de que…): *I'm glad (that) you could come.* Me alegro de que pudieras venir. **2 to be ~ to do sth** tener mucho gusto en hacer algo: *'Can you help?' 'I'd be glad to.'* —¿Puedes ayudar? —Con mucho gusto. **3 to be ~ of sth** agradecer algo

Glad y **pleased** se utilizan para referirse a una circunstancia o un hecho concretos: *Are you glad/pleased about*

getting the job? ¿Estás contento de haber conseguido el trabajo? **Happy** describe un estado mental y puede preceder al sustantivo al que acompaña: *Are you happy in your new job?* ¿Estás contento en tu nuevo trabajo? ◊ *a happy occasion* una ocasión feliz ◊ *happy memories* recuerdos felices.

gladly *adv* con gusto

glamour (*USA* **glamor**) /ˈglæmə(r)/ *n* glamour **glamorous** *adj* **1** (*persona*) seductor **2** (*trabajo*) atractivo

glance /glɑːns; *USA* glæns/ ◆ *vi* ~ **at/down/over/through sth** echar un vistazo/una mirada a algo ◆ *n* mirada (rápida), vistazo: *to take a glance at sth* echar un vistazo a algo LOC **at a glance** a simple vista

gland /glænd/ *n* glándula

glare /gleə(r)/ ◆ *n* **1** luz deslumbrante **2** mirada airada ◆ *vi* ~ **at sth/sb** mirar airadamente a algo/algn **glaring** *adj* **1** (*error*) evidente **2** (*expresión*) airado **3** (*luz*) deslumbrante **glaringly** *adv*: *glaringly obvious* muy evidente

glass /glɑːs; *USA* glæs/ *n* **1** [*incontable*] vidrio, cristal: *a pane of glass* una lámina de cristal ◊ *broken glass* cristales rotos **2** copa, vaso: *a glass of water* un vaso de agua **3 glasses** (*tb* **spectacles**) [*pl*] gafas: *I need a new pair of glasses.* Necesito unas gafas nuevas. LOC *Ver* RAISE ☛ *Ver nota en* PAIR

glaze /gleɪz/ ◆ *n* **1** (*cerámica*) barniz **2** (*Cocina*) glaseado ◆ *vt* **1** (*cerámica*) vidriar **2** (*cocina*) glasear *Ver tb* DOUBLE GLAZING PHR V **to glaze over** ponerse vidrioso **glazed** *adj* **1** (*ojos*) inexpresivo **2** (*cerámica*) vidriado

gleam /gliːm/ ◆ *n* **1** destello **2** brillo ◆ *vi* **1** destellar **2** brillar, relucir **gleaming** *adj* reluciente

glean /gliːn/ *vt* sacar (*información*)

glee /gliː/ *n* regocijo **gleeful** *adj* eufórico **gleefully** *adv* con euforia

glen /glen/ *n* valle estrecho

glide /glaɪd/ ◆ *n* deslizamiento ◆ *vi* **1** deslizarse **2** (*en el aire*) planear **glider** *n* planeador

glimmer /ˈglɪmə(r)/ *n* **1** luz tenue **2** ~ **(of sth)** (*fig*) chispa (de algo): *a glimmer of hope* un rayo de esperanza

glimpse /glɪmps/ ◆ *n* visión momentánea LOC *Ver* CATCH ◆ *vt* vislumbrar

glint /glɪnt/ ◆ *vi* **1** destellar **2** (*ojos*) brillar ◆ *n* **1** destello **2** (*ojos*) chispa

glisten /ˈglɪsn/ *vi* relucir (*esp superficie mojada*)

glitter /ˈglɪtə(r)/ ◆ *vi* relucir ◆ *n* **1** brillo **2** (*fig*) esplendor

gloat /gləʊt/ *vi* ~ **(about/over sth)** relamerse, regocijarse (de algo)

global /ˈgləʊbl/ *adj* **1** mundial **2** global

globe /gləʊb/ *n* **1** globo **2** globo terráqueo

gloom /gluːm/ *n* **1** penumbra **2** tristeza **3** pesimismo **gloomy** *adj* (**-ier**, **-iest**) **1** (*lugar*) oscuro **2** (*día*) triste **3** (*pronóstico*) poco prometedor **4** (*aspecto, voz, etc*) triste **5** (*carácter*) melancólico

glorious /ˈglɔːriəs/ *adj* **1** glorioso **2** espléndido

glory /ˈglɔːri/ ◆ *n* **1** gloria **2** esplendor ◆ *vi* ~ **in sth 1** vanagloriarse de algo **2** enorgullecerse de algo

gloss /glɒs/ ◆ *n* **1** brillo **2** (*tb* **gloss paint**) pintura de esmalte ☛ *Comparar con* MATT **3** (*fig*) lustre **4** ~ **(on sth)** glosa (de algo) ◆ PHR V **to gloss over sth** pasar algo por alto **glossy** *adj* (**-ier**, **-iest**) reluciente, lustroso

glossary /ˈglɒsəri/ *n* (*pl* **-ies**) glosario

glove /glʌv/ *n* guante LOC *Ver* FIT[2]

glow /gləʊ/ ◆ *vi* **1** estar candente **2** brillar (suavemente) **3** (*cara*) enrojecerse **4** ~ **(with sth)** (*esp salud*) rebosar (de algo) ◆ *n* **1** luz suave **2** arrebol **3** (sentimiento de) satisfacción

glucose /ˈgluːkəʊs/ *n* glucosa

glue /gluː/ ◆ *n* cola (*de pegar*), pegamento ◆ *vt* (*pt pres* **gluing**) pegar

glutton /ˈglʌtn/ *n* **1** glotón, -ona **2** ~ **for sth** (*coloq, fig*) amante de algo: *to be a glutton for punishment* hacerse el mártir

gnarled /nɑːld/ *adj* **1** (*árbol, mano*) retorcido **2** (*tronco*) nudoso

gnaw /nɔː/ *vt, vi* **1** ~ **(at) sth** roer algo **2** ~ **(at) sb** atormentar a algn

gnome /nəʊm/ *n* gnomo

go[1] /gəʊ/ *vi* (*3ª pers sing pres* **goes** /gəʊz/ *pret* **went** /went/ *pp* **gone** /gɒn; *USA* gɔːn/) **1** ir: *I went to bed at ten o'clock.* Me fui a la cama a las diez. ◊ *to go home* irse a casa

Been se usa como participio pasado de **go** para expresar que alguien ha ido a un lugar y ha vuelto: *Have you ever*

been to London? ¿Has ido alguna vez a Londres? **Gone** implica que esa persona no ha regresado todavía: *John's gone to Peru. He'll be back in May.* John se ha ido a Perú. Volverá en mayo.

2 irse, marcharse **3** (*tren, etc*) salir **4 to go + -ing** ir: *to go fishing/swimming/camping* ir a pescar/a nadar/de camping **5 to go for a + sustantivo** ir: *to go for a walk* ir a dar un paseo **6** (*progreso*) ir, salir: *How's it going?* ¿Cómo te va? ◊ *All went well.* Todo salió bien. **7** (*máquina*) funcionar **8** volverse, quedarse: *to go mad/blind/pale* volverse loco/quedarse ciego/palidecer *Ver tb* BECOME **9** hacer (*emitir un sonido*): *Cats go 'miaow'.* Los gatos hacen "miau". **10** desaparecer, terminarse: *My headache's gone.* Se me ha pasado el dolor de cabeza. ◊ *Is it all gone?* ¿Se ha acabado? **11** gastarse, romperse **12** (*tiempo*) pasar **LOC to be going to do sth**: *We're going to buy a house.* Vamos a comprar una casa. ◊ *He's going to fall!* ¡Se va a caer! ☛ Para otras expresiones con **go**, véanse las entradas del sustantivo, adjetivo, etc, p.ej. **to go astray** en ASTRAY.

PHR V to go about (*tb* **to go (a)round**) **1** [*con adj o -ing*] andar: *to go about naked* andar desnudo **2** (*rumor*) circular **to go about (doing) sth**: *How should I go about telling him?* ¿Cómo debería decírselo?

to go ahead (with sth) seguir adelante (con algo)

to go along with sth/sb estar conforme con algo/con lo que dice algn

to go (a)round (*tb* **to go about**) **1** [*con adj o -ing*] andar (por ahí) **2** (*rumor*) circular

to go away 1 irse (de viaje) **2** (*mancha*) desaparecer

to go back volver **to go back on sth** faltar a algo (*promesa, etc*)

to go by pasar: *as time goes by* con el tiempo

to go down 1 bajar **2** (*barco*) hundirse **3** (*sol*) ponerse **to go down (with sb)** (*película, obra*) ser recibido (por algn)

to go for sb atacar a algn **to go for sth/sb** ir por algo/algn: *That goes for you too.* Eso vale para ti también.

to go in entrar **to go in (sth)** caber (en algo) **to go in for (doing) sth** interesarse por (hacer) algo (*hobby, etc*)

to go into sth 1 decidir dedicarse a algo (*profesión*) **2** examinar algo: *to go into (the) details* entrar en detalles

to go off 1 irse, marcharse **2** (*arma*) dispararse **3** (*bomba*) explotar **4** (*alarma*) sonar **5** (*luz*) apagarse **6** (*alimentos*) pasarse **7** (*acontecimiento*) salir: *It went off well.* Salió muy bien. **to go off sth/sb** perder interés en algo/algn **to go off with sth** llevarse algo

to go on 1 seguir adelante **2** (*luz*) encenderse **3** suceder: *What's going on here?* ¿Qué pasa aquí? **4** (*situación*) continuar, durar **to go on (about sth/sb)** no parar de hablar (de algo/algn) **to go on (with sth/doing sth)** seguir (con algo/haciendo algo)

to go out 1 salir **2** (*luz*) apagarse

to go over sth 1 examinar algo **2** (*de nuevo*) repasar algo **to go over to sth** pasarse a algo (*opinión, partido*)

to go round 1 girar, dar vueltas **2** (*cantidad*) alcanzar **to go (a)round** (*tb* **to go about**) **1** [*con adj o -ing*] andar (por ahí) **2** (*rumor*) circular

to go through ser aprobado (*ley, etc*) **to go through sth 1** revisar, registrar algo **2** (*de nuevo*) repasar algo **3** sufrir, pasar por algo **to go through with sth** llevar algo a cabo, seguir adelante con algo

to go together hacer juego, armonizar

to go up 1 subir **2** (*edificio*) levantarse **3** estallar, explotar

to go with sth ir bien, hacer juego con algo

to go without pasar privaciones **to go without sth** pasarse sin algo

go[2] /gəʊ/ *n* (*pl* **goes** /gəʊz/) **1** turno: *Whose go is it?* ¿A quién le toca? *Ver* TURN **2** (*coloq*) empuje **LOC to be on the go** (*coloq*) no parar **to have a go (at sth/doing sth)** (*coloq*) probar suerte (con algo), intentar (hacer algo)

goad /gəʊd/ *vt* ~ **sb (into doing sth)** incitar a algn (a hacer algo)

go-ahead /ˈgəʊ əhed/ ◆ **the go-ahead** *n* luz verde ◆ *adj* emprendedor

goal /gəʊl/ *n* **1** portería **2** gol **3** (*fig*) meta **goalkeeper** (*tb coloq* **goalie**) *n* portero, -a **goalpost** *n* poste de la portería

goat /gəʊt/ *n* cabra

gobble /ˈgɒbl/ *vt* ~ **sth (up/down)** engullir algo

go-between /ˈgəʊ bɪtwiːn/ *n* intermediario, -a

god /gɒd/ *n* **1** dios **2 God** [*sing*] Dios LOC *Ver* SAKE, KNOW

godchild /ˈgɒdtʃaɪld/ *n* ahijado, -a

god-daughter /ˈgɒd dɔːtə(r)/ *n* ahijada

goddess /ˈgɒdes/ *n* diosa

godfather /ˈgɒdfɑːðə(r)/ *n* padrino

godmother /ˈgɒdmʌðə(r)/ *n* madrina

godparent /ˈgɒdpeərənt/ *n* **1** padrino, madrina **2 godparents** [*pl*] padrinos

godsend /ˈgɒdsend/ *n* regalo del cielo

godson /ˈgɒdsʌn/ *n* ahijado

goggles /ˈgɒglz/ *n* [*pl*] gafas (*protectoras*)

going /ˈgəʊɪŋ/ *n* **1** [*sing*] (*marcha*) partida **2** *Good going!* ¡Bien hecho! ◊ *That was good going.* Ha sido muy rápido. ◊ *The path was rough going.* El camino estaba en muy mal estado. LOC **to get out, etc while the going is good** irse, etc mientras se puede

gold /gəʊld/ *n* oro: *a gold bracelet* una pulsera de oro LOC **(as) good as gold** más bueno que el pan

gold dust *n* oro en polvo

golden /ˈgəʊldən/ *adj* **1** de oro **2** (*color y fig*) dorado LOC *Ver* WEDDING

goldfish /ˈgəʊldfɪʃ/ *n* pez de colores

golf /gɒlf/ *n* golf: *golf course* campo de golf **golf club** *n* **1** club de golf **2** palo de golf **golfer** *n* golfista

gone /gɒn; *USA* gɔːn/ ◆ *pp de* GO[1] ◆ *prep*: *It was gone midnight.* Eran las doce pasadas.

gonna /ˈgɒnə/ (*coloq*) = GOING TO *en* GO[1]

good /gʊd/ ◆ *adj* (*comp* **better** /ˈbetə(r)/ *superl* **best** /best/) **1** bueno: *good nature* bondad **2** *to be good at sth* tener aptitud para algo **3** ~ **to sb** bueno, amable con algn **4** *Vegetables are good for you.* Las verduras son buenas para la salud. LOC **as good as** prácticamente **good for you, her, etc!** (*coloq*) ¡bien hecho! ☛ Para otras expresiones con **good**, véanse las entradas del sustantivo, adjetivo, etc, p.ej. **a good many** en MANY. ◆ *n* **1** bien **2 the good** los buenos LOC **for good** para siempre **to be no good (doing sth)** no servir de nada (hacer algo) **to do sb good** hacer bien a algn

goodbye /ˌgʊdˈbaɪ/ *interj*, *n* adiós: *to say goodbye* despedirse ☛ Otras palabras más informales son: **bye**, **cheerio** y **cheers**.

good-humoured /ˌgʊd ˈhjuːməd/ *adj* **1** afable **2** de buen humor

good-looking /ˌgʊd ˈlʊkɪŋ/ *adj* guapo

good-natured /ˌgʊd ˈneɪtʃəd/ *adj* **1** amable **2** de buen corazón

goodness /ˈgʊdnəs/ ◆ *n* **1** bondad **2** valor nutritivo ◆ *interj* ¡cielos! LOC *Ver* KNOW

goods /gʊdz/ *n* [*pl*] **1** bienes **2** artículos, mercancías, productos

goodwill /ˌgʊdˈwɪl/ *n* buena voluntad

goose /guːs/ *n* (*pl* **geese** /giːs/) (*masc* **gander** /ˈgændə(r)/) ganso, -a, oca

gooseberry /ˈgʊzbəri; *USA* ˈguːsberi/ *n* (*pl* **-ies**) grosella silvestre

goose-pimples /ˈguːs pɪmplz/ *n* [*pl*] (*tb* **goose-flesh**) carne de gallina

gorge /gɔːdʒ/ *n* cañón (*Geog*)

gorgeous /ˈgɔːdʒəs/ *adj* **1** magnífico **2** (*coloq*) guapísimo

gorilla /gəˈrɪlə/ *n* gorila

gory /ˈgɔːri/ *adj* (**gorier**, **goriest**) **1** sangriento **2** morboso

go-slow /ˌgəʊ ˈsləʊ/ *n* huelga de celo

gospel /ˈgɒspl/ *n* evangelio

gossip /ˈgɒsɪp/ ◆ *n* **1** [*incontable*] (*pey*) chismes **2** (*pey*) chismoso, -a ◆ *vi* ~ **(with sb) (about sth)** cotillear (con algn) (de algo)

got *pret, pp de* GET

Gothic /ˈgɒθɪk/ *adj* gótico

gotten (*USA*) *pp de* GET

gouge /gaʊdʒ/ *vt* hacer (*agujero*) PHR V **to gouge sth out** excavar algo

gout /gaʊt/ *n* gota

govern /ˈgʌvn/ **1** *vt, vi* gobernar **2** *vt* (*acto, negocio*) regir **governing** *adj* rector

governess /ˈgʌvənəs/ *n* institutriz

government /ˈgʌvənmənt/ *n* [*v sing o pl*] gobierno LOC **in government** en el gobierno **governmental** /ˌgʌvnˈmentl/ *adj* gubernamental

governor /ˈgʌvənə(r)/ *n* **1** gobernador, -ora **2** director, -ora

gown /gaʊn/ *n* **1** vestido largo **2** (*Educ, Jur*) toga **3** (*Med*) bata

GP /ˌdʒiːˈpiː/ *abrev* **general practitioner**

grab /græb/ ◆ (**-bb-**) **1** *vt* agarrar **2** *vt*

(*atención*) captar **3** *vi* ~ **at sth/sb** tratar de agarrar algo/a algn **4** *vt* ~ **sth (from sth/sb)** quitar algo (a algn) PHR V **to grab hold of sth/sb** agarrar algo/a algn, hacerse con algo/algn ◆ *n* LOC **to make a grab for/at sth** intentar hacerse con algo

grace /greɪs/ ◆ *n* **1** gracia, elegancia **2** plazo: *five days' grace* cinco días de gracia **3** *to say grace* bendecir la mesa ◆ *vt* **1** adornar **2** ~ **sth/sb (with sth)** honrar algo/a algn (con algo) **graceful** *adj* **1** grácil, elegante **2** delicado (*cortés*)

gracious /ˈgreɪʃəs/ *adj* **1** afable **2** elegante, lujoso

grade /greɪd/ ◆ *n* **1** clase, categoría **2** (*Educ*) nota **3** (*USA, Educ*) curso **4** (*USA, Geog*) pendiente LOC **to make the grade** (*coloq*) tener éxito ◆ *vt* **1** clasificar **2** (*USA, Educ*) calificar (*examen*) **grading** *n* clasificación

gradient /ˈgreɪdiənt/ *n* (*GB*) pendiente

gradual /ˈgrædʒuəl/ *adj* **1** gradual, paulatino **2** (*pendiente*) suave **gradually** *adv* paulatinamente, poco a poco

graduate /ˈgrædʒʊət/ ◆ *n* **1** ~ **(in sth)** licenciado, -a (en algo) **2** (*USA*) diplomado, -a, graduado, -a ◆ /ˈgrædʒʊeɪt/ **1** *vi* ~ **(in sth)** licenciarse (en algo) **2** *vi* ~ **(in sth)** (*USA*) graduarse (en algo) **3** *vt* graduar **graduation** *n* graduación

graffiti /grəˈfiːti/ *n* [*incontable*] pintadas

graft /grɑːft; *USA* græft/ ◆ *n* (*Bot, Med*) injerto ◆ *vt* ~ **sth (onto sth)** injertar algo (en algo)

grain /greɪn/ *n* **1** [*incontable*] cereales **2** grano **3** veta (*madera*)

gram (*tb* **gramme**) /græm/ *n* (*abrev* **g**) gramo ☛ *Ver* Apéndice 1.

grammar /ˈgræmə(r)/ *n* gramática (*libro, reglas*)

grammar school *n* **1** (*GB*) instituto (para alumnos de 12 a 18 años) **2** (*USA*) escuela primaria

grammatical /grəˈmætɪkl/ *adj* **1** gramatical **2** (gramaticalmente) correcto

gramme /græm/ *n Ver* GRAM

gramophone /ˈgræməfəʊn/ *n* (*antic*) gramófono

grand /grænd/ ◆ *adj* (**-er**, **-est**) **1** espléndido, magnífico, grandioso **2** (*antic, coloq, Irl*) estupendo **3 Grand** (*títulos*) gran **4** *grand piano* piano de cola ◆ *n* (*pl* **grand**) (*coloq*) mil dólares o libras

grandad /ˈgrændæd/ *n* (*coloq*) abuelo, yayo

grandchild /ˈgræntʃaɪld/ *n* (*pl* **-children**) nieto, -a

granddaughter /ˈgrændɔːtə(r)/ *n* nieta

grandeur /ˈgrændʒə(r)/ *n* grandiosidad, grandeza

grandfather /ˈgrænfɑːðə(r)/ *n* abuelo

grandma /ˈgrænmɑː/ *n* (*coloq*) abuela, yaya

grandmother /ˈgrænmʌðə(r)/ *n* abuela

grandpa /ˈgrænpɑː/ *n* (*coloq*) abuelo, yayo

grandparent /ˈgrænpeərənt/ *n* abuelo, -a

grandson /ˈgrænsʌn/ *n* nieto

grandstand /ˈgrændstænd/ *n* (*Dep*) tribuna

granite /ˈgrænɪt/ *n* granito

granny /ˈgræni/ *n* (*pl* **-ies**) (*coloq*) abuela, yaya

grant /grɑːnt/ ◆ *vt* ~ **sth (to sb)** conceder algo (a algn) LOC **to take sth/sb for granted** dar algo por descontado, no darse cuenta de lo que vale algn ◆ *n* **1** subvención **2** (*Educ*) beca

grape /greɪp/ *n* uva

grapefruit /ˈgreɪpfruːt/ *n* (*pl* **grapefruit** *o* **~s**) pomelo

grapevine /ˈgreɪpvaɪn/ *n* **1** viña **2 the grapevine** (*fig*) radio macuto: *to hear sth on the grapevine* oír algo por ahí

graph /grɑːf; *USA* græf/ *n* gráfico

graphic /ˈgræfɪk/ *adj* gráfico **graphics** *n* [*pl*]: *computer graphics* gráficos por ordenador

grapple /ˈgræpl/ *vi* ~ **(with sth/sb)** (*lit y fig*) luchar (con algo/algn)

grasp /grɑːsp; *USA* græsp/ ◆ *vt* **1** agarrar **2** (*oportunidad*) aprovechar **3** comprender ◆ *n* **1** (*fig*) alcance: *within/beyond the grasp of* al alcance/fuera del alcance de **2** conocimiento **grasping** *adj* codicioso

grass /grɑːs; *USA* græs/ *n* hierba, césped

grasshopper /ˈgrɑːshɒpə(r)/ *n* saltamontes

grassland /ˈgrɑːslænd, -lənd/ (*tb* **grasslands** [*pl*]) *n* pastos

grass roots *n* bases

grassy /grɑːsi; *USA* græsi/ *adj* (**-ier**, **-iest**) herboso

grate /greɪt/ ◆ **1** *vt* rallar **2** *vi* chirriar **3** *vi* ~ (**on sth/sb**) (*fig*) irritar (algo/a algn) ◆ *n* parrilla (*de chimenea*)

grateful /ˈgreɪtfl/ *adj* ~ (**to sb**) (**for sth**); ~ (**that…**) agradecido (a algn) (por algo); agradecido (de que…)

grater /greɪtə(r)/ *n* rallador

gratitude /ˈgrætɪtjuːd; *USA* -tuːd/ *n* ~ (**to sb**) (**for sth**) gratitud (a algn) (por algo)

grave /greɪv/ ◆ *adj* (**-er**, **-est**) (*fml*) grave, serio ☛ La palabra más normal es **serious**. ◆ *n* tumba

gravel /ˈgrævl/ *n* gravilla

graveyard /ˈgreɪvjɑːd/ (*tb* **churchyard**) *n* cementerio (*alrededor de una iglesia*) ☛ *Comparar con* CEMETERY

gravity /ˈgrævəti/ *n* **1** (*Fís*) gravedad **2** (*fml*) seriedad ☛ Una palabra más normal es **seriousness**.

gravy /ˈgreɪvi/ *n* salsa (*hecha con el jugo de la carne*)

gray /greɪ/ (*USA*) *Ver* GREY

graze /greɪz/ ◆ **1** *vi* pacer **2** *vt* ~ **sth** (**against/on sth**) (*pierna, etc*) raspar algo (con algo) **3** *vt* rozar ◆ *n* raspadura (*Med*)

grease /griːs/ ◆ *n* **1** grasa **2** (*Mec*) lubricante **3** brillantina ◆ *vt* engrasar **greasy** *adj* (**-ier**, **-iest**) grasiento

great /greɪt/ ◆ *adj* (**-er**, **-est**) **1** gran, grande: *in great detail* con gran detalle ◊ *the world's greatest tennis player* la mejor tenista del mundo ◊ *We're great friends.* Somos muy amigos. ◊ *I'm not a great reader.* No tengo mucha afición a la lectura. **2** (*distancia*) largo **3** (*edad*) avanzado **4** (*cuidado*) mucho **5** (*coloq*) estupendo: *We had a great time.* Lo pasamos genial. ◊ *It's great to see you!* ¡Qué alegría verte! **6** ~ **at sth** muy bueno en algo **7** (*coloq*) muy: *a great big dog* un perro enorme LOC **great minds think alike** los grandes cerebros siempre coinciden *Ver tb* BELIEVER *en* BELIEVE, DEAL[1], EXTENT ◆ *n* [*gen pl*] (*coloq*): *one of the jazz greats* una de las grandes figuras del jazz **greatly** *adv* muy, mucho: *greatly exaggerated* muy exagerado ◊ *It varies greatly.* Varía mucho. **greatness** *n* grandeza

great-grandfather /ˌgreɪt ˈgrænfɑːðə(r)/ *n* bisabuelo

great-grandmother /ˌgreɪt ˈgrænmʌðə(r)/ *n* bisabuela

greed /griːd/ *n* **1** ~ (**for sth**) codicia (de algo) **2** gula **greedily** *adv* **1** codiciosamente **2** vorazmente **greedy** *adj* (**-ier**, **-iest**) **1** ~ (**for sth**) codicioso (de algo) **2** glotón

green /griːn/ ◆ *adj* (**-er**, **-est**) verde ◆ *n* **1** verde **2 greens** [*pl*] verduras **3** prado **greenery** *n* verde, follaje

greengrocer /ˈgriːnˌgrəʊsə(r)/ *n* (*GB*) verdulero, -a: *greengrocer's (shop)* verdulería

greenhouse /ˈgriːnhaʊs/ *n* invernadero: *greenhouse effect* efecto invernadero

greet /griːt/ *vt* **1** ~ **sb** saludar a algn: *He greeted me with a smile.* Me recibió con una sonrisa. ☛ *Comparar con* SALUTE **2** ~ **sth with sth** recibir, acoger algo con algo **greeting** *n* **1** saludo **2** recibimiento

grenade /grəˈneɪd/ *n* granada (de *mano*)

grew *pret de* GROW

grey (*USA tb* **gray**) /greɪ/ ◆ *adj* (**-er**, **-est**) **1** (*lit y fig*) gris **2** (*pelo*) blanco: *to go/turn grey* encanecer ◊ *grey-haired* canoso ◆ *n* (*pl* **greys**) gris

greyhound /ˈgreɪhaʊnd/ *n* galgo

grid /grɪd/ *n* **1** rejilla **2** (*eléc, gas*) red **3** (*mapa*) cuadrícula

grief /griːf/ *n* ~ (**over/at sth**) dolor, pesar (por algo) LOC **to come to grief** (*coloq*) **1** fracasar **2** sufrir un accidente

grievance /ˈgriːvns/ *n* ~ (**against sb**) **1** (motivo de) queja (contra algn) **2** (de *trabajadores*) reivindicación (contra algn)

grieve /griːv/ (*fml*) **1** *vt* afligir, dar pena a **2** *vi* ~ (**for/over/about sth/sb**) llorar la pérdida (de algo /algn) **3** *vi* ~ **at/about/over sth** lamentarse de algo, afligirse por algo

grill /grɪl/ ◆ *n* **1** parrilla **2** (*plato*) parrillada **3** *Ver* GRILLE ◆ **1** *vt, vi* asar(se) a la parrilla **2** *vt* (*coloq, fig*) freír a preguntas

grille (*tb* **grill**) /grɪl/ *n* rejilla, reja

grim /grɪm/ *adj* (**grimmer**, **grimmest**) (*persona*) severo, ceñudo **2** (*lugar*) triste, lúgubre **3** deprimente, triste macabro, siniestro

grimace /grɪˈmeɪs; *USA* ˈgrɪməs/ ◆

mueca ◆ *vi* ~ (**at sth/sb**) hacer muecas (a algo/algn)

grime /graɪm/ *n* mugre **grimy** *adj* (**-ier**, **-iest**) mugriento

grin /grɪn/ ◆ *vi* (**-nn-**) ~ (**at sth/sb**) sonreír de oreja a oreja (a algo/algn) LOC **to grin and bear it** poner al mal tiempo buena cara ◆ *n* sonrisa

grind /graɪnd/ ◆ (*pret*, *pp* **ground** /graʊnd/) **1** *vt*, *vi* moler(se) **2** *vt* afilar **3** *vt* (*dientes*) rechinar **4** *vt* (*esp USA*) (*carne*) picar LOC **to grind to a halt/standstill 1** pararse chirriando **2** (*proceso*) detenerse gradualmente *Ver tb* AXE ◆ *n* (*coloq*): *the daily grind* la rutina cotidiana

grip /grɪp/ ◆ (**-pp-**) **1** *vt*, *vi* agarrar(se), asir(se) **2** *vt* (*mano*) coger **3** *vt* (*atención*) absorber ◆ *n* **1** ~ (**on sth/sb**) agarre, adherencia (a algo/algn) **2** ~ (**on sth/sb**) (*fig*) dominio, control, presión (sobre algo/algn) **3** agarradero, asidero LOC **to come/get to grips with sth/sb** (*lit y fig*) enfrentarse a algo/algn **gripping** *adj* fascinante, que se agarra

grit /grɪt/ ◆ *n* **1** arena, arenilla **2** valor, determinación ◆ *vt* (**-tt-**) cubrir con arena LOC **to grit your teeth 1** apretar los dientes **2** (*fig*) armarse de valor

groan /grəʊn/ ◆ *vi* **1** ~ (**with sth**) gemir (de algo) **2** (*muebles, etc*) crujir **3** ~ (**on**) (**about/over sth**) quejarse (de algo) **4** ~ (**at sth/sb**) quejarse (a algo/algn) ◆ *n* **1** gemido **2** quejido **3** crujido

grocer /ˈgrəʊsə(r)/ *n* **1** tendero, -a **2** **grocer's** (*tb* **grocery shop**, **grocery store**) tienda de comestibles, ultramarinos **groceries** *n* [*pl*] comestibles

groggy /ˈgrɒgi/ *adj* (**-ier**, **-iest**) mareado, grogui

groin /grɔɪn/ *n* bajo vientre: *a groin injury* una herida en la ingle

groom /gruːm/ ◆ *n* **1** mozo, -a de cuadra **2** = BRIDEGROOM LOC *Ver* BRIDE ◆ *vt* **1** (*caballo*) cepillar **2** (*pelo*) arreglar **3** ~ **sb** (**for sth/to do sth**) preparar a algn (para algo/para hacer algo)

groove /gruːv/ *n* ranura, estría, surco

grope /grəʊp/ *vi* **1** andar a tientas **2** ~ (**about**) **for sth** buscar algo a tientas; titubear buscando algo

gross /grəʊs/ ◆ *n* (*pl* **gross** *o* **grosses**) gruesa (*doce docenas*) ◆ *adj* (**-er**, **-est**) **1** repulsivamente gordo **2** grosero **3** (*exageración*) flagrante **4** (*error, negligencia*) craso **5** (*injusticia, indecencia*) grave **6** (*total*) bruto ◆ *vt* recaudar, ganar (*en bruto*) **grossly** *adv* extremadamente

grotesque /grəʊˈtesk/ *adj* grotesco

ground /graʊnd/ ◆ *n* **1** (*lit*) suelo, tierra, terreno **2** (*fig*) terreno **3** zona, campo (*de juego*) **4** **grounds** [*pl*] jardines **5** [*gen pl*] motivo, razón **6** **grounds** [*pl*] poso, sedimento LOC **on the ground** en el suelo, sobre el terreno **to get off the ground 1** ponerse en marcha, resultar factible **2** (*avión*) despegar **to give/lose ground** (**to sth/sb**) ceder/perder terreno (frente a algo/algn) **to the ground** (*destruir*) completamente *Ver tb* FIRM, MIDDLE, THIN ◆ *vt* **1** (*avión*) impedir que despegue **2** (*coloq*) castigar sin salir ◆ *pret*, *pp de* GRIND ◆ *adj* **1** molido **2** (*esp USA*) (*carne*) picado **grounding** *n* [*sing*] ~ (**in sth**) base, conceptos fundamentales de algo **groundless** *adj* infundado

ground floor *n* **1** planta baja **2** **ground-floor** [*antes de sustantivo*] de/en la planta baja *Ver tb* FLOOR

group /gruːp/ ◆ *n* [*v sing o pl*] (*gen*, *Mús*) grupo ◆ *vt*, *vi* ~ (**together**) agrupar(se) **grouping** *n* agrupación

grouse /graʊs/ *n* (*pl* **grouse**) urogallo

grove /grəʊv/ *n* arboleda

grovel /ˈgrɒvl/ *vi* (**-ll-**, *USA* **-l-**) (*pey*) ~ (**to sb**) humillarse (ante algn) **grovelling** *adj* servil

grow /grəʊ/ (*pret* **grew** /gruː/ *pp* **grown** /grəʊn/) **1** *vi* crecer **2** *vt* (*pelo, barba*) dejar crecer **3** *vt* cultivar **4** *vt* hacerse (*algo*): *to grow old/rich* envejecer/enriquecerse **5** *vi*: *He grew to rely on her.* Llegó a depender de ella. PHR V **to grow into sth** convertirse en algo **to grow on sb** empezar a gustarle a uno cada vez más **to grow up 1** desarrollarse **2** crecer: *when I grow up* cuando sea mayor ◊ *Oh, grow up!* ¡Déjate ya de niñerías! *Ver tb* GROWN-UP **growing** *adj* creciente

growl /graʊl/ ◆ *vi* gruñir ◆ *n* gruñido

grown /grəʊn/ ◆ *adj* adulto: *a grown man* un adulto ◆ *pp de* GROW

grown-up /ˌgrəʊn ˈʌp/ ◆ *adj* mayor ◆ /ˈgrəʊn ʌp/ *n* adulto

growth /grəʊθ/ *n* **1** crecimiento **2** ~ (**in/of sth**) aumento (de algo) **3** [*sing*] brotes **4** tumor

grub /grʌb/ *n* **1** larva **2** (*coloq*) papeo
grubby /ˈgrʌbi/ *adj* (**-ier**, **-iest**) (*coloq*) sucio
grudge /grʌdʒ/ ◆ *vt* ~ **sb sth 1** envidiar algo a algn **2** escatimar algo a algn ◆ *n* rencor: *to bear sb a grudge/have a grudge against sb* guardar rencor a algn LOC *Ver* BEAR[2] **grudgingly** *adv* de mala gana, a regañadientes
gruelling (*USA* **grueling**) /ˈgruːəlɪŋ/ *adj* muy duro, penoso
gruesome /ˈgruːsəm/ *adj* espantoso, horrible
gruff /grʌf/ *adj* (*voz*) tosco, áspero
grumble /ˈgrʌmbl/ ◆ *vi* refunfuñar: *to grumble about/at/over sth* quejarse de algo ◆ *n* queja
grumpy /ˈgrʌmpi/ *adj* (**-ier**, **-iest**) (*coloq*) gruñón
grunt /grʌnt/ ◆ *vi* gruñir ◆ *n* gruñido
guarantee /ˌgærənˈtiː/ ◆ *n* ~ (**of sth/that...**) garantía (de algo/de que...) ◆ *vt* **1** garantizar **2** (*préstamo*) avalar
guard /gɑːd/ ◆ *vt* **1** proteger, guardar **2** ~ **sb** vigilar a algn PHR V **to guard against sth** protegerse contra algo ◆ *n* **1** guardia, vigilancia: *to be on guard* estar de guardia ◊ *guard dog* perro guardián **2** guardia, centinela **3** [*v sing o pl*] guardia (*grupo de soldados*) **4** (*maquinaria*) dispositivo de seguridad **5** (*GB*, *Ferrocarril*) jefe de tren LOC **to be off/on your guard** estar desprevenido/alerta **guarded** *adj* cauteloso, precavido
guardian /ˈgɑːdiən/ *n* **1** guardián, -ana: *guardian angel* ángel de la guarda **2** tutor, -ora
guerrilla (*tb* **guerilla**) /gəˈrɪlə/ *n* guerrillero, -a: *guerrilla war(fare)* guerra de guerrillas
guess /ges/ ◆ *vt, vi* **1** adivinar **2** ~ **at sth** imaginar algo **3** (*coloq*, *esp USA*) creer, pensar: *I guess so/not.* Supongo que sí/no. ◆ *n* suposición, conjetura, cálculo: *to have/make a guess (at sth)* intentar adivinar algo ◊ *guesswork* conjeturas LOC **it's anybody's guess** nadie lo sabe *Ver tb* HAZARD
guest /gest/ *n* **1** invitado, -a **2** huésped, -eda: *guest house* casa de huéspedes/pensión
guidance /ˈgaɪdns/ *n* orientación, supervisión
guide /gaɪd/ ◆ *n* **1** (*persona*) guía **2** (*tb* **guidebook**) guía (*turística*) **3** (*tb* **Guide, Girl Guide**) guía (*de los scouts*) ◆ *vt* **1** guiar, orientar: *to guide sb to sth* llevar a algn hasta algo **2** influenciar **guided** *adj* con guía
guideline /ˈgaɪdlaɪn/ *n* directriz, pauta
guilt /gɪlt/ *n* culpa, culpabilidad **guilty** *adj* (**-ier**, **-iest**) culpable LOC *Ver* PLEAD
guinea pig /ˈgɪni pɪg/ *n* (*lit y fig*) cobaya, conejillo de Indias
guise /gaɪz/ *n* apariencia
guitar /gɪˈtɑː(r)/ *n* guitarra
gulf /gʌlf/ *n* **1** (*Geog*) golfo **2** abismo, sima
gull /gʌl/ (*tb* **seagull**) *n* gaviota
gullible /ˈgʌləbl/ *adj* crédulo
gulp /gʌlp/ ◆ *vt* **1** ~ **sth (down)** tragarse algo **2** *vi* tragar saliva ◆ *n* trago
gum /gʌm/ *n* **1** (*Anat*) encía **2** goma, pegamento **3** chicle *Ver* BUBBLEGUM, CHEWING GUM
gun /gʌn/ ◆ *n* **1** arma (*de fuego*) **2** escopeta *Ver tb* MACHINE-GUN, PISTOL, RIFLE, SHOTGUN ◆ *v* (**-nn-**) PHR V **to gun sb down** (*coloq*) matar/herir gravemente a algn a tiros
gunfire /ˈgʌnfaɪə(r)/ *n* fuego (*disparos*)
gunman /ˈgʌnmən/ *n* (*pl* **-men** /-mən/) pistolero
gunpoint /ˈgʌnpɔɪnt/ *n* LOC **at gunpoint** a punta de pistola
gunpowder /ˈgʌnpaʊdə(r)/ *n* pólvora
gunshot /ˈgʌnʃɒt/ *n* disparo
gurgle /ˈgɜːgl/ *vi* gorjear, gorgotear
gush /gʌʃ/ *vi* **1** ~ **(out) (from sth)** salir a borbotones, manar (de algo) **2** ~ **(over sth/sb)** (*pey*, *fig*) hablar con demasiado entusiasmo (de algo/algn)
gust /gʌst/ *n* ráfaga
gusto /ˈgʌstəʊ/ *n* (*coloq*) entusiasmo
gut /gʌt/ ◆ *n* **1 guts** [*pl*] (*coloq*) tripas **2 guts** [*pl*] (*fig*) agallas **3** intestino: *a gut reaction/feeling* una reacción visceral/un instinto ◆ *vt* (**-tt-**) **1** destripar **2** destruir por dentro
gutter /ˈgʌtə(r)/ *n* **1** cuneta: *the gutter press* la prensa amarilla **2** canalón
guy /gaɪ/ *n* (*coloq*) tío
guzzle /ˈgʌzl/ ~ **sth (down/up)** (*coloq*) *vt* zamparse, tragarse algo

gymnasium /dʒɪmˈneɪziəm/ (*pl* **-siums** *o* **-sia** /-zɪə/) (*coloq* **gym**) *n* gimnasio

gymnastics /dʒɪmˈnæstɪks/ (*coloq* **gym**) *n* [*sing*] gimnasia **gymnast** /ˈdʒɪmnæst/ *n* gimnasta

gynaecologist (*USA* **gyne-**) /ˌgaməˈkɒlədʒɪst/ *n* ginecólogo, -a

gypsy (*tb* **gipsy, Gypsy**) /ˈdʒɪpsi/ *n* (*pl* **-ies**) gitano, -a

Hh

H, h /eɪtʃ/ *n* (*pl* **H's, h's** /ˈeɪtʃɪz/) H, h: *H for Harry* H de huevo ☛ *Ver ejemplos en* A, a

habit /ˈhæbɪt/ *n* **1** costumbre, hábito **2** (*Relig*) hábito

habitation /ˌhæbɪˈteɪʃn/ *n* habitación: *not fit for human habitation* no apto para ser habitado

habitual /həˈbɪtʃuəl/ *adj* habitual

hack[1] /hæk/ *vt, vi* ~ **(at) sth** golpear algo (*con algo cortante*)

hack[2] /hæk/ *vt, vi* ~ **(into) (sth)** (*Informát, coloq*) lograr acceso (a algo) ilegalmente **hacking** *n* acceso ilegal

had /həd, hæd/ *pret, pp de* HAVE

hadn't /ˈhæd(ə)nt/ = HAD NOT *Ver* HAVE

haemoglobin (*USA* **hem-**) /ˌhiːməˈgləʊbɪn/ *n* hemoglobina

haemorrhage (*USA* **hem-**) /ˈhemərɪdʒ/ *n* hemorragia

haggard /ˈhægəd/ *adj* demacrado

haggle /ˈhægl/ *vi* ~ **(over/about sth)** regatear (por algo)

hail[1] /heɪl/ ◆ *n* [*incontable*] granizo ◆ *vi* granizar

hail[2] /heɪl/ *vt* **1** llamar a (*para atraer la atención*) **2** ~ **sth/sb as sth** aclamar algo/a algn como algo

hailstone /ˈheɪlstəʊn/ *n* piedra (*de granizo*)

hailstorm /ˈheɪlstɔːm/ *n* granizada

hair /heə(r)/ *n* **1** pelo, cabello **2** vello LOC *Ver* PART

hairbrush /ˈheəbrʌʃ/ *n* cepillo (*para el pelo*) ☛ *Ver dibujo en* BRUSH

haircut /ˈheəkʌt/ *n* corte de pelo: *to have/get a haircut* cortarse el pelo

hairdo /ˈheəduː/ *n* (*pl* **~s**) (*coloq*) peinado

hairdresser /ˈheədresə(r)/ *n* peluquero, -a **hairdresser's** *n* peluquería (*tienda*) **hairdressing** *n* peluquería (*arte*)

hairdryer /ˈheədraɪə(r)/ *n* secador (*de pelo*)

hairpin /ˈheəpɪn/ *n* horquilla de moño: *hairpin bend* curva muy cerrada

hairstyle /ˈheəstaɪl/ *n* peinado

hairy /ˈheəri/ *adj* (**-ier, -iest**) peludo

half /hɑːf; *USA* hæf/ ◆ *n* (*pl* **halves** /hɑːvz; *USA* hævz/) mitad, medio: *The second half of the book is more interesting.* La segunda mitad del libro es más interesante. ◊ *two and a half hours* dos horas y media ◊ *Two halves make a whole.* Dos medios hacen un entero. LOC **to break, etc sth in half** partir, etc algo por la mitad **to go halves (with sb)** ir a medias (con algn) ◆ *adj, pron* mitad, medio: *half the team* la mitad del equipo ◊ *half an hour* media hora ◊ *to cut sth by half* reducir algo a la mitad LOC **half (past) one, two, etc** la una, las dos, etc y media ◆ *adv* a medio, a medias: *The job will have been only half done.* Habrán hecho el trabajo sólo a medias. ◊ *half built* a medio construir

half board *n* media pensión

half-brother /ˈhɑːf brʌðə(r); *USA* ˈhæf-/ *n* hermano por parte de padre/madre ☛ *Ver nota en* HERMANASTRO

half-hearted /ˌhɑːf ˈhɑːtɪd; *USA* ˈhæf-/ *adj* poco entusiasta **half-heartedly** *adv* sin entusiasmo

half-sister /ˈhɑːf sɪstə(r); *USA* ˈhæf-/ *n* hermana por parte de padre/madre ☛ *Ver nota en* HERMANASTRO

half-term /ˌhɑːf ˈtɜːm; *USA* ˌhæf-/ *n* (*GB*) vacaciones escolares de una semana a mediados de cada trimestre

half-time /ˌhɑːf ˈtaɪm; *USA* ˌhæf-/ *n* (*Dep*) descanso

halfway /ˌhɑːf ˈweɪ; *USA* ˌhæf-/ *adj, adv* a medio camino, a mitad: *halfway between London and Glasgow* a medio camino entre Londres y Glasgow

halfwit /ˈhɑːfwɪt; *USA* ˈhæf-/ *n* lelo, -a

hall /hɔːl/ *n* **1** (*tb* **hallway**) vestíbulo, entrada **2** (*de conciertos o reuniones*) sala **3** (*tb* **hall of residence**) colegio mayor, residencia universitaria

hallmark /ˈhɔːlmɑːk/ *n* **1** (*de metales preciosos*) contraste **2** (*fig*) sello

Hallowe'en /ˌhæləʊˈiːn/ *n*

> **Hallowe'en** (31 de octubre) significa la víspera de Todos los Santos y es la noche de los fantasmas y las brujas. Mucha gente vacía una calabaza, le da forma de cara y pone una vela dentro. Los niños se disfrazan y van por las casas pidiendo caramelos o dinero. Cuando les abres la puerta dicen **trick or treat** ("o nos das algo o te gastamos una broma").

hallucination /həˌluːsɪˈneɪʃn/ *n* alucinación

hallway *Ver* HALL

halo /ˈheɪləʊ/ *n* (*pl* **haloes** *o* **~s**) halo, aureola

halt /hɔːlt/ ◆ *n* parada, alto, interrupción LOC *Ver* GRIND ◆ *vt, vi* parar(se), detener(se): *Halt!* ¡Alto!

halting /ˈhɔːltɪŋ/ *adj* vacilante, titubeante

halve /hɑːv; *USA* hæv/ *vt* **1** partir por la mitad **2** reducir a la mitad

halves *plural de* HALF

ham /hæm/ *n* jamón cocido

hamburger /ˈhæmbɜːgə(r)/ (*tb* **burger**) *n* hamburguesa

hamlet /ˈhæmlət/ *n* aldea, caserío

hammer /ˈhæmə(r)/ ◆ *n* martillo ◆ **1** *vt* martillear **2** *vi* (*coloq, fig*) dar una paliza a PHR V **to hammer sth in** clavar algo (a martillazos)

hammock /ˈhæmək/ *n* hamaca

hamper[1] /ˈhæmpə(r)/ *n* (*GB*) cesta (*para alimentos*)

hamper[2] /ˈhæmpə(r)/ *vt* obstaculizar

hamster /ˈhæmstə(r)/ *n* hámster

hand /hænd/ ◆ *n* **1** mano **2** [*sing*] (*tb* **handwriting**) letra **3** (*reloj, etc*) manecilla, aguja ☛ *Ver dibujo en* RELOJ **4** peón, jornalero **5** (*Náut*) tripulante **6** (*naipes*) mano **7** (*medida*) palmo LOC **by hand** a mano: *made by hand* hecho a mano ◊ *delivered by hand* entregado en mano **(close/near) at hand** a mano: *He lives close at hand.* Vive muy cerca. **hand in hand 1** cogidos de la mano **2** (*fig*) muy unido, a la par **hands up!** ¡manos arriba! **in hand 1** disponible, en reserva **2** entre manos **on hand** disponible **on the one hand ... on the other (hand) ...** por un lado ... por otro ... **out of hand 1** descontrolado **2** sin pensarlo **to give/lend sb a hand** echar una mano a algn **to hand** a mano *Ver tb* CHANGE, CUP, EAT, FIRM, FIRST, FREE, HEAVY, HELP, HOLD, MATTER, PALM, SHAKE, UPPER ◆ *vt* pasar PHR V **to hand sth back (to sb)** devolver algo (a algn) **to hand sth in (to sb)** entregar algo (a algn) **to hand sth out (to sb)** repartir algo (a algn)

handbag /ˈhændbæg/ (*USA* **purse**) *n* bolso

handbook /ˈhændbʊk/ *n* manual, guía

handbrake /ˈhændbreɪk/ *n* freno de mano

handcuff /ˈhændkʌf/ ◆ *vt* esposar ◆ **handcuffs** *n* [*pl*] esposas

handful /ˈhændfʊl/ *n* (*pl* **~s**) (*lit y fig*) puñado: *a handful of students* un puñado de estudiantes LOC **to be a (real) handful** (*coloq*) ser una pesadilla

handicap /ˈhændikæp/ ◆ *n* **1** (*Med*) minusvalía **2** (*Dep*) desventaja ◆ *vt* (**-pp-**) **1** perjudicar **2** (*Dep*) compensar

handicapped *adj* minusválido

handicrafts /ˈhændikrɑːfts; *USA* -kræfts/ *n* [*pl*] artesanía

handkerchief /ˈhæŋkətʃɪf, -tʃiːf/ *n* (*pl* **-chiefs** *o* **-chieves** /-tʃiːvz/) pañuelo (*de bolsillo*)

handle /ˈhændl/ ◆ *n* **1** mango ☛ *Ver dibujo en* SAUCEPAN **2** manilla **3** asa ☛ *Ver dibujo en* MUG ◆ *vt* **1** manejar **2** (*maquinaria*) operar **3** (*gente*) tratar **4** soportar

handlebars /ˈhændlbɑːz/ *n* [*pl*] manillar

handmade /ˌhændˈmeɪd/ *adj* hecho a mano, de artesanía

> En inglés se pueden formar adjetivos compuestos para todas las destrezas manuales: p.ej. **hand-built** (construido a mano), **hand-knitted** (tricotado a

mano), **hand-painted** (pintado a mano), etc.

handout /ˈhændaʊt/ *n* **1** donativo **2** folleto **3** declaración (*por escrito para la prensa*)

handshake /ˈhændʃeɪk/ *n* apretón de manos

handsome /ˈhænsəm/ *adj* **1** guapo ☛ Se aplica sobre todo a los hombres. **2** (*regalo*) generoso

handwriting /ˈhændraɪtɪŋ/ *n* **1** escritura **2** letra

handwritten /ˌhændˈrɪtn/ *adj* escrito a mano

handy /ˈhændi/ *adj* (**-ier**, **-iest**) **1** práctico **2** a mano

hang /hæŋ/ ◆ (*pret, pp* **hung** /hʌŋ/) **1** *vt* colgar **2** *vi* estar colgado **3** *vi* (*ropa, pelo*) caer **4** (*pret, pp* **hanged**) *vt, vi* ahorcar(se) **5** *vi* ~ (**above/over sth/sb**) pender (sobre algo/algn) PHR V **to hang about/around** (*coloq*) **1** holgazanear **2** esperar (*sin hacer nada*) **to hang (sth) out** tender algo **to hang up (on sb)** (*coloq*) colgar (a algn) (*el teléfono*) ◆ *n* LOC **to get the hang of sth** (*coloq*) coger el tranquillo a algo

hangar /ˈhæŋə(r)/ *n* hangar

hanger /ˈhæŋə(r)/ (*tb* **clothes hanger**, **coat-hanger**) *n* percha

hang-glider /ˈhæŋ glaɪdə(r)/ *n* ala delta **hang-gliding** *n* vuelo en ala delta

hangman /ˈhæŋmən/ *n* (*pl* **-men** /-mən/) **1** verdugo (*de horca*) **2** (*juego*) el ahorcado

hangover /ˈhæŋəʊvə(r)/ *n* resaca

hang-up /ˈhæŋ ʌp/ *n* (*argot*) trauma, complejo

haphazard /hæpˈhæzəd/ *adj* al azar, de cualquier manera

happen /ˈhæpən/ *vi* ocurrir, suceder, pasar: *whatever happens* pase lo que pase ◊ *if you happen to go into town* si por casualidad vas al centro **happening** *n* suceso, acontecimiento

happy /ˈhæpi/ *adj* (**-ier**, **-iest**) **1** feliz: *a happy marriage/memory/child* un matrimonio/recuerdo/niño feliz **2** contento: *Are you happy in your work?* ¿Estás contento con tu trabajo? ☛ *Ver nota en* GLAD **happily** *adv* **1** felizmente **2** afortunadamente **happiness** *n* felicidad

harass /ˈhærəs, həˈræs/ *vt* hostigar, acosar **harassment** *n* hostigamiento, acoso

harbour (*USA* **harbor**) /ˈhɑːbə(r)/ ◆ *n* puerto ◆ *vt* **1** proteger, dar cobijo a **2** (*sospechas*) albergar

hard /hɑːd/ ◆ *adj* (**-er**, **-est**) **1** duro **2** difícil: *It's hard to tell.* Es difícil saber con seguridad. ◊ *It's hard for me to say no.* Me cuesta decir que no. ◊ *hard to please* exigente **3** duro, agotador: *a hard worker* una persona trabajadora **4** (*persona, trato*) duro, severo, cruel **5** (*bebida*) alcohólico LOC **hard cash** dinero contante **hard luck** (*coloq*) mala pata **the hard way** por la vía difícil **to have/give sb a hard time** (hacer) pasar a algn un mal rato **to take a hard line (on/over sth)** adoptar una postura tajante (en algo) *Ver tb* DRIVE ◆ *adv* (**-er**, **-est**) **1** (*trabajar, llover*) mucho, duro: *She hit her head hard.* Se dio un fuerte golpe en la cabeza. ◊ *to try hard* esforzarse **2** (*tirar*) fuerte **3** (*pensar*) detenidamente **4** (*mirar*) fijamente LOC **to be hard put to do sth** tener dificultad en hacer algo **to be hard up** andar mal de dinero

hardback /ˈhɑːdbæk/ *n* libro de tapas duras: *hardback edition* edición de tapas duras ☛ *Comparar con* PAPERBACK

hard disk *n* disco duro

harden /ˈhɑːdn/ **1** *vt, vi* endurecer(se) **2** *vt* (*fig*) curtir: *hardened criminal* criminal habitual **hardening** *n* endurecimiento

hardly /ˈhɑːdli/ *adv* **1** apenas: *I hardly know her.* Apenas la conozco. **2** difícilmente: *It's hardly surprising.* No es ninguna sorpresa. ◊ *He's hardly the world's best cook.* No es el mejor cocinero del mundo. **3** *hardly anybody* casi nadie ◊ *hardly ever* casi nunca

hardship /ˈhɑːdʃɪp/ *n* apuro, privación

hardware /ˈhɑːdweə(r)/ *n* **1** ferretería: *hardware store* ferretería **2** (*Mil*) armamentos **3** (*Informát*) hardware

hard-working /ˌhɑːd ˈwɜːkɪŋ/ *adj* trabajador

hardy /ˈhɑːdi/ *adj* (**-ier**, **-iest**) **1** robusto **2** (*Bot*) resistente

hare /heə(r)/ *n* liebre

harm /hɑːm/ ◆ *n* daño, mal: *He meant no harm.* No tenía malas intenciones. ◊

have

presente	contracciones	negativa contracciones	pasado contracciones
I **have**	I**'ve**	I **haven't**	I**'d**
you **have**	you**'ve**	you **haven't**	you**'d**
he/she/it **has**	he**'s**/she**'s**/it**'s**	he/she/it **hasn't**	he**'d**/she**'d**/it**'d**
we **have**	we**'ve**	we **haven't**	we**'d**
you **have**	you**'ve**	you **haven't**	you**'d**
they **have**	they**'ve**	they **haven't**	they**'d**

pasado **had** *forma en -ing* **having** *participio pasado* **had**

There's no harm in asking. No se pierde nada con preguntar. ◊ *(There's) no harm done.* No pasó nada. LOC **out of harm's way** a buen recaudo **to come to harm**: *You'll come to no harm.* No te pasará nada. **to do more harm than good** ser peor el remedio que la enfermedad ◆ *vt* **1** (*persona*) hacer daño a **2** (*cosa*) dañar **harmful** *adj* dañino, nocivo, perjudicial **harmless** *adj* **1** inocuo **2** inocente, inofensivo

harmony /ˈhɑːməni/ *n* (*pl* **-ies**) armonía

harness /ˈhɑːnɪs/ ◆ *n* [*sing*] arreos ◆ *vt* **1** (*caballo*) enjaezar **2** (*rayos solares*) aprovechar

harp /hɑːp/ ◆ *n* arpa ◆ PHR V **to harp on (about) sth** hablar repetidamente de algo

harsh /hɑːʃ/ *adj* (**-er**, **-est**) **1** (*textura, voz*) áspero **2** (*color, luz*) chillón **3** (*ruido, etc*) estridente **4** (*clima, etc*) riguroso **5** (*castigo, etc*) severo **6** (*palabra, profesor*) duro **harshly** *adv* duramente, severamente

harvest /ˈhɑːvɪst/ ◆ *n* cosecha ◆ *vt* cosechar

has /həz, hæz/ *Ver* HAVE

hasn't /ˈhæz(ə)nt/ = HAS NOT *Ver* HAVE

hassle /ˈhæsl/ ◆ *n* (*coloq*) **1** (*complicación*) lío, rollo: *It's a lot of hassle.* Es mucho lío. **2** molestias: *Don't give me any hassle!* ¡Déjame en paz! ◆ *vt* (*coloq*) molestar

haste /heɪst/ *n* prisa LOC **in haste** de prisa **hasten** /ˈheɪsn/ **1** *vi* darse prisa **2** *vt* acelerar **hastily** *adv* precipitadamente **hasty** *adj* (**-ier**, **-iest**) precipitado

hat /hæt/ *n* sombrero LOC *Ver* DROP

hatch¹ /hætʃ/ *n* **1** trampilla **2** ventanilla (*para pasar comida*)

hatch² /hætʃ/ **1** *vi* ~ (**out**) salir del huevo **2** *vi* (*huevo*) abrirse **3** *vt* incubar **4** *vt* ~ **sth** (**up**) tramar algo

hate /heɪt/ ◆ *vt* **1** odiar **2** lamentar: *I hate to bother you, but...* Siento molestarte, pero... ◆ *n* **1** odio **2** (*coloq*): *pet hate* bestia negra **hateful** *adj* odioso **hatred** *n* odio

haul /hɔːl/ ◆ *vt* tirar, arrastrar ◆ *n* **1** (*distancia*) camino **2** redada (*de peces*) **3** botín

haunt /hɔːnt/ ◆ *vt* **1** (*fantasma*) aparecerse en **2** (*lugar*) frecuentar **3** (*pensamiento*) atormentar ◆ *n* lugar predilecto **haunted** *adj* embrujado (*casa*)

have /həv, hæv/ ◆ *v aux* haber: *'I've finished my work.' 'So have I.'* —He terminado mi trabajo. —Yo también. ◊ *He's gone home, hasn't he?* Se ha ido a casa, ¿no? ◊ *'Have you seen it?' 'Yes, I have./No, I haven't.'* —¿Lo has visto? —Sí./No. ◆ *vt* **1** (*tb* **to have got**) tener: *She's got a new car.* Tiene un coche nuevo. ◊ *to have flu/a headache* tener la gripe/dolor de cabeza ☛ *Ver nota en* TENER **2** ~ (**got**) **sth to do** tener algo que hacer: *I've got a bus to catch.* Tengo que coger el autobús. **3** ~ (**got**) **to do sth** tener que hacer algo: *I've got to go to the bank.* Tengo que ir al banco. ◊ *Did you have to pay a fine?* ¿Tuviste que pagar una multa? ◊ *It has to be done.* Hay que hacerlo. **4** (*tb* **to have got**) llevar: *Have you got any money on you?* ¿Llevas encima dinero? **5** tomar: *to have a bath/wash* tomar un baño/lavarse ◊ *to have a cup of coffee* tomar un café ◊ *to have breakfast/lunch/dinner* desayunar/comer/cenar ☛ Nótese que la estructura **to have + sustantivo** a menudo se expresa en español con un verbo. **6** ~ **sth done** hacer/mandar hacer algo: *to have your hair cut* cortarse el pelo ◊ *to have a dress made* encargar que te hagan un vestido ◊ *She had her bag stolen.* Le robaron el bolso. **7** consentir: *I won't have it!* ¡No lo consentiré! LOC **to have had it** (*coloq*): *The TV has had it.* La tele ha cascado. **to have it (that)**: *Rumour has it that...* Se dice que... ◊ *As luck would have it...* Como quiso la suerte... **to have to do with sth/sb** tener que ver con algo/algn: *It has nothing to do with me.* No tiene nada que ver conmigo. ☛ Para otras expresiones con **have**, véanse las entradas del sustantivo, adjetivo, etc, p.ej. **to have a sweet tooth** en SWEET. PHR V **to have sth back**: *Let me have it back soon.* Devuélvemelo pronto. **to have sb on** (*coloq*) tomar el pelo a algn: *You're having me on!* ¡Me estás tomando el pelo! **to have sth on 1** (*ropa*) llevar algo puesto: *He's got a tie on today.* Hoy lleva corbata. **2** estar ocupado con algo: *I've got a lot on.* Estoy muy ocupado. ◊ *Have you got anything on tonight?* ¿Tienes algún plan para esta noche?

haven /ˈheɪvn/ *n* refugio

haven't /ˈhæv(ə)nt/ = HAVE NOT *Ver* HAVE

havoc /ˈhævək/ *n* estragos LOC **to wreak/cause/play havoc with sth** hacer estragos en algo

hawk /hɔːk/ *n* halcón

hay /heɪ/ *n* heno: *hay fever* alergia al polen

hazard /ˈhæzəd/ ◆ *n* peligro, riesgo: *a health hazard* un peligro para la salud ◆ *vt* LOC **to hazard a guess** aventurar una opinión **hazardous** *adj* peligroso, arriesgado

haze /heɪz/ *n* bruma ☛ *Comparar con* FOG, MIST

hazel /ˈheɪzl/ ◆ *n* avellano ◆ *adj* color avellana

hazelnut /ˈheɪzlnʌt/ *n* avellana

hazy /ˈheɪzi/ *adj* (**hazier**, **haziest**) **1** brumoso **2** (*idea, etc*) vago **3** (*persona*) confuso

he /hiː/ ◆ *pron pers* él: *He's in Paris.* Está en París. ☛ El *pron pers* no se puede omitir en inglés. *Comparar con* HIM ◆ *n* [*sing*]: *Is it a he or a she?* ¿Es macho o hembra?

head[1] /hed/ *n* **1** cabeza: *It never entered my head.* Jamás se me ocurrió. ◊ *to have a good head for business* tener talento para los negocios **2 a/per head** por cabeza: *ten pounds a head* diez libras por cabeza **3** cabecera: *the head of the table* la cabecera de la mesa **4** jefe, -a: *the heads of government* los jefes de gobierno **5** director, -ora (*de un colegio*) LOC **head first** de cabeza **heads or tails?** ¿cara o cruz? **not to make head or tail of sth** no conseguir entender algo: *I can't make head (n)or tail of it.* No consigo entenderlo. **to be/go above/over your head** pasarle por encima **to go to your head** subírsele a la cabeza a algn *Ver tb* HIT, SHAKE, TOP[1]

head[2] /hed/ *vt* **1** encabezar **2** (*Dep*) dar de cabeza PHR V **to head for sth** dirigirse a algo, ir camino de algo

headache /ˈhedeɪk/ *n* **1** dolor de cabeza **2** quebradero de cabeza

heading /ˈhedɪŋ/ *n* encabezamiento, apartado

headlight /ˈhedlaɪt/ (*tb* **headlamp**) *n* faro

headline /ˈhedlaɪn/ *n* **1** titular **2 the headlines** [*pl*] resumen de noticias

headmaster /hedˈmɑːstə(r)/ *n* director (*de un colegio*)

headmistress /ˌhedˈmɪstrəs/ *n* directora (*de un colegio*)

head office *n* sede central

head-on /hed ˈɒn/ *adj, adv* de frente: *a head-on collision* una colisión de frente

headphones /ˈhedfəʊnz/ *n* [*pl*] auriculares

headquarters /ˌhedˈkwɔːtəz/ *n* (*abrev* **HQ**) [*v sing o pl*] oficina principal

head start *n*: *You had a head start over me.* Me llevabas ventaja.

headway /ˈhedweɪ/ *n* LOC **to make headway** avanzar

heal /hiːl/ **1** *vi* cicatrizar, sanar **2** *vt* ~ **sth/sb** sanar, curar algo/a algn

health /helθ/ *n* salud: *health centre* ambulatorio LOC *Ver* DRINK

healthy /ˈhelθi/ *adj* (**-ier**, **-iest**) **1** (*lit*) sano **2** saludable (*estilo de vida, etc*)

heap /hiːp/ ◆ *n* montón ◆ *vt* ~ **sth (up)** amontonar algo

hear /hɪə(r)/ (*pret, pp* **heard** /hɜːd/) **1** *vt, vi* oír: *I couldn't hear a thing.* No oía nada. ◊ *I heard someone laughing.* Oí a alguien que se reía. **2** *vt* escuchar **3** *vt* (*Jur*) ver PHR V **to hear about sth** enterarse de algo **to hear from sb** tener noticias de algn **to hear of sth/sb** oír hablar de algo/algn

hearing /ˈhɪərɪŋ/ *n* **1** (*tb* **sense of hearing**) oído **2** (*Jur*) vista, audiencia

heart /hɑːt/ *n* **1** corazón: *heart attack/ failure* ataque/paro cardiaco **2** (*centro*): *the heart of the matter* el quid del asunto **3** (*de lechuga, etc*) cogollo **4** **hearts** [*pl*] (*en cartas*) corazones ☛ *Ver nota en* BARAJA LOC **at heart** en el fondo **by heart** de memoria **to take heart** alentarse **to take sth to heart** tomar algo a pecho **your/sb's heart sinks**: *When I saw the queue my heart sank.* Cuando vi la cola se me cayó el alma a los pies. *Ver tb* CHANGE, CRY, SET[2]

heartbeat /ˈhɑːtbiːt/ *n* latido (*del corazón*)

heartbreak /ˈhɑːtbreɪk/ *n* congoja, angustia **heartbreaking** *adj* que parte el corazón, angustioso **heartbroken** *adj* acongojado, angustiado

hearten /ˈhɑːtn/ *vt* animar **heartening** *adj* alentador

heartfelt /ˈhɑːtfelt/ *adj* sincero

hearth /hɑːθ/ *n* **1** chimenea **2** (*lit y fig*) hogar

heartless /ˈhɑːtləs/ *adj* inhumano, cruel

hearty /ˈhɑːti/ *adj* (**-ier**, **-iest**) **1** (*enhorabuena*) cordial **2** (*persona*) jovial (*a veces en exceso*) **3** (*comida*) abundante

heat /hiːt/ ◆ *n* **1** calor **2** (*Dep*) prueba clasificatoria LOC **to be on heat**; *USA* **to be in heat** estar en celo ◆ *vt, vi* ~ (**up**) calentar(se) **heated** *adj* **1** *a heated pool* una piscina climatizada ◊ *centrally heated* con calefacción central **2** (*discusión, persona*) acalorado **heater** *n* calefactor (*aparato*)

heath /hiːθ/ *n* brezal

heathen /ˈhiːðn/ *n* no creyente

heather /ˈheðə(r)/ *n* brezo

heating /ˈhiːtɪŋ/ *n* calefacción

heatwave /ˈhiːtweɪv/ *n* ola de calor

heave /hiːv/ ◆ **1** *vt, vi* arrastrar(se) (*con esfuerzo*) **2** *vi* ~ (**at/on sth**) tirar con esfuerzo (de algo) **3** (*coloq*) *vt* arrojar (*algo pesado*) ◆ *n* tirón, empujón

heaven /ˈhevn/ (*tb* **Heaven**) *n* (*Relig*) cielo LOC *Ver* KNOW, SAKE

heavenly /ˈhevnli/ *adj* **1** (*Relig*) celestial **2** (*Astron*) celeste **3** (*coloq*) divino

heavily /ˈhevɪli/ *adv* **1** muy, mucho: *heavily loaded* muy cargado ◊ *to rain heavily* llover muchísimo **2** pesadamente

heavy /ˈhevi/ *adj* (**-ier**, **-iest**) **1** pesado: *How heavy is it?* ¿Cuánto pesa? **2** más de lo normal: *heavy traffic* un tráfico denso **3** (*facciones, movimiento*) torpe LOC **with a heavy hand** con mano dura

heavyweight /ˈheviweɪt/ *n* **1** peso pesado **2** (*fig*) figura (importante)

heckle /ˈhekl/ *vt, vi* interrumpir

hectare /ˈhekteə(r)/ *n* hectárea

hectic /ˈhektɪk/ *adj* frenético

he'd /hiːd/ **1** = HE HAD *Ver* HAVE **2** = HE WOULD *Ver* WOULD

hedge /hedʒ/ ◆ *n* **1** seto **2** ~ (**against sth**) protección (contra algo) ◆ *vt, vi* esquivar

hedgehog /ˈhedʒhɒg; *USA* -hɔːg/ *n* erizo

heed /hiːd/ ◆ *vt* (*fml*) prestar atención a ◆ *n* LOC **to take heed** (**of sth**) hacer caso (de algo)

heel /hiːl/ *n* **1** talón **2** tacón LOC *Ver* DIG

hefty /ˈhefti/ *adj* (**-ier**, **-iest**) (*coloq*) **1** fornido **2** (*objeto*) pesado **3** (*golpe*) fuerte

height /haɪt/ *n* **1** estatura **2** altura **3** (*Geog*) altitud **4** (*fig*) cumbre, colmo: *at/ in the height of summer* en pleno verano LOC **the height of fashion** la última moda ☛ *Ver nota en* ALTO

heighten /ˈhaɪtn/ *vt, vi* intensificar, aumentar

heir /eə(r)/ *n* ~ (**to sth**) heredero, -a (de algo)

heiress /ˈeərəs/ *n* heredera

held *pret, pp de* HOLD

helicopter /ˈhelɪkɒptə(r)/ *n* helicóptero

hell /hel/ *n* infierno: *to go to hell* ir al infierno ☛ Nótese que **hell** no lleva artículo. LOC **a/one hell of a ...** (*coloq*): *I got a hell of a shock.* Me llevé un susto terrible. **hellish** *adj* infernal

he'll /hiːl/ = HE WILL *Ver* WILL

hello /həˈləʊ/ *interj, n* hola: *Say hello for me.* Saluda de mi parte.

helm /helm/ *n* timón

helmet /ˈhelmɪt/ *n* casco

help /help/ ◆ **1** *vt, vi* ayudar: *Help!* ¡Socorro! ◊ *How can I help you?* ¿En qué puedo servirle? **2** *v refl* ~ **yourself (to sth)** servirse algo **LOC a helping hand**: *to give/lend (sb) a helping hand* echar una mano (a algn) **can/could not help sth**: *I couldn't help laughing.* No pude contener la risa. ◊ *He can't help it.* No lo puede evitar. **it can't/couldn't be helped** no hay/había remedio **PHR V to help (sb) out** echar un cable (a algn) ◆ *n* [*incontable*] **1** ayuda: *It wasn't much help.* No sirvió de mucho. **2** asistencia

helper /ˈhelpə(r)/ *n* ayudante

helpful /ˈhelpfl/ *adj* **1** servicial **2** amable **3** (*consejo, etc*) útil

helping /ˈhelpɪŋ/ *n* porción

helpless /ˈhelpləs/ *adj* **1** indefenso **2** desamparado **3** imposibilitado

helter-skelter /ˌheltə ˈskeltə(r)/ ◆ *n* tobogán (*en espiral*) ◆ *adj* precipitado

hem /hem/ ◆ *n* dobladillo ◆ *vt* (**-mm-**) coser el dobladillo de **PHR V to hem sth/sb in 1** cercar algo/a algn **2** cohibir a algn

hemisphere /ˈhemɪsfɪə(r)/ *n* hemisferio

hemo- (*USA*) *Ver* HAEMO-

hen /hen/ *n* gallina

hence /hens/ *adv* **1** (*tiempo*) desde ahora: *3 years hence* de aquí a 3 años **2** (*por esta razón*) de ahí, por eso

henceforth /ˌhensˈfɔːθ/ *adv* (*fml*) de ahora en adelante

hepatitis /ˌhepəˈtaɪtɪs/ *n* [*incontable*] hepatitis

her /hə, ɜː(r), ə(r), hɜː(r)/ ◆ *pron pers* **1** [*como objeto directo*] la: *I saw her.* La vi. **2** [*como objeto indirecto*] le, a ella: *I asked her to come.* Le pedí que viniera. ◊ *I said it to her.* Se lo dije a ella. **3** [*después de preposición y del verbo* **to be**] ella: *I think of her often.* Pienso en ella a menudo. ◊ *She took it with her.* Se lo llevó consigo. ◊ *It wasn't her.* No fue ella. ☛ *Comparar con* SHE ◆ *adj pos* su(s) (*de ella*): *her book(s)* su(s) libro(s) ☛ **Her** se usa también para referirse a coches, barcos o naciones. *Comparar con* HERS *y ver nota en* MY

herald /ˈherəld/ ◆ *n* heraldo ◆ *vt* anunciar (*llegada, comienzo*) **heraldry** *n* heráldica

herb /hɜːb; *USA* ɜːrb/ *n* hierba (fina) **herbal** *adj* (a base) de hierbas: *herbal tea* infusión

herd /hɜːd/ ◆ *n* manada, piara (*de vacas, cabras y cerdos*) ☛ *Comparar con* FLOCK ◆ *vt* llevar en manada

here /hɪə(r)/ ◆ *adv* aquí: *I live a mile from here.* Vivo a una milla de aquí. ◊ *Please sign here.* Firme aquí, por favor.

En las oraciones que empiezan con **here** el verbo se coloca detrás del sujeto si éste es un pronombre: *Here they are, at last!* Ya llegan ¡por fin! ◊ *Here it is, on the table!* Aquí está, encima de la mesa. Y antes si es un sustantivo: *Here comes the bus.* Ya llega el autobús.

LOC here and there aquí y allá **here you are** aquí tiene **to be here** llegar: *They'll be here any minute.* Están a punto de llegar. ◆ *interj* **1** ¡oye! **2** (*ofreciendo algo*) ¡toma! **3** (*respuesta*) ¡presente!

hereditary /həˈredɪtri; *USA* -teri/ *adj* hereditario

heresy /ˈherəsi/ *n* (*pl* **-ies**) herejía

heritage /ˈherɪtɪdʒ/ *n* [*gen sing*] patrimonio

hermit /ˈhɜːmɪt/ *n* ermitaño, -a

hero /ˈhɪərəʊ/ *n* (*pl* ~**es**) **1** protagonista (*de novela, película, etc*) **2** (*persona*) héroe, heroína: *sporting heroes* los héroes del deporte **heroic** /həˈrəʊɪk/ *adj* heroico **heroism** /ˈherəʊɪzəm/ *n* heroísmo

heroin /ˈherəʊɪn/ *n* heroína (*droga*)

heroine /ˈherəʊɪn/ *n* heroína (*persona*)

herring /ˈherɪŋ/ *n* (*pl* **herring** *o* ~**s**) arenque **LOC** *Ver* RED

hers /hɜːz/ *pron pos* suyo, -a, -os, -as (*de ella*): *a friend of hers* un amigo suyo ◊ *Where are hers?* ¿Dónde están los suyos?

herself /hɜːˈself/ *pron* **1** [*uso reflexivo*] se, a ella misma: *She bought herself a book.* Se compró un libro. **2** [*después de preposición*] sí (misma): *'I am free', she said to herself.* "Soy libre" – se dijo a sí misma. **3** [*uso enfático*] ella misma: *She told me the news herself.* Me contó la noticia ella misma.

he's /hiːz/ **1** = HE IS *Ver* BE **2** = HE HAS *Ver* HAVE

hesitant /ˈhezɪtənt/ *adj* vacilante, indeciso

hesitate /ˈhezɪteɪt/ *vi* **1** dudar: *Don't hesitate to call.* No dudes en llamar. **2** vacilar **hesitation** *n* vacilación, duda

heterogeneous /ˌhetərəˈdʒiːniəs/ *adj* heterogéneo

heterosexual /ˌhetərəˈsekʃuəl/ *adj, n* heterosexual

hexagon /ˈheksəgən; *USA* -gɒn/ *n* hexágono

heyday /ˈheɪdeɪ/ *n* (días de) apogeo

hi! /haɪ/ *interj* (*coloq*) ¡hola!

hibernate /ˈhaɪbəneɪt/ *vi* hibernar **hibernation** *n* hibernación

hiccup (*tb* **hiccough**) /ˈhɪkʌp/ *n* **1** hipo: *I got (the) hiccups.* Me dio el hipo. **2** (*coloq*) problema

hid *pret de* HIDE[1]

hidden /ˈhɪdn/ **1** *pp de* HIDE[1] **2** *adj* oculto, escondido

hide[1] /haɪd/ *vi* (*pret* **hid** /hɪd/ *pp* **hidden** /ˈhɪdn/) **1** ~ (**from sb**) esconderse, ocultarse (de algn): *The child was hiding under the bed.* El niño estaba escondido debajo de la cama. **2** ~ **sth** (**from sb**) ocultar algo (a algn): *The trees hid the house from view.* Los árboles ocultaban la casa.

hide[2] /haɪd/ *n* piel (*de animal*)

hide-and-seek /ˌhaɪd n ˈsiːk/ *n* escondite: *to play hide-and-seek* jugar al escondite

hideous /ˈhɪdiəs/ *adj* espantoso

hiding[1] /ˈhaɪdɪŋ/ *n* LOC **to be in/go into hiding** estar escondido/ocultarse

hiding[2] /ˈhaɪdɪŋ/ *n* (*coloq*) tunda

hierarchy /ˈhaɪərɑːki/ *n* (*pl* **-ies**) jerarquía

hieroglyphics /ˌhaɪərəˈglɪfɪks/ *n* jeroglíficos

hi-fi /ˈhaɪ faɪ/ *adj, n* (*coloq*) (equipo de) alta fidelidad

high[1] /haɪ/ *adj* (**-er**, **-est**) **1** (*precio, techo, velocidad*) alto ☛ *Ver nota en* ALTO **2** *to have a high opinion of sb* tener buena opinión de algn ◊ *high hopes* grandes esperanzas **3** (*viento*) fuerte **4** (*ideales, ganancias*) elevado: *to set high standards* poner el listón muy alto ◊ *I have it on the highest authority* lo sé de muy buena fuente ◊ *she has friends in high places* tiene amigos muy influyentes **5** *the high life* la vida de lujo ◊ *the high point of the evening* el mejor momento de la tarde **6** (*sonido*) agudo **7** *in high summer* en pleno verano ◊ *high season* temporada alta **8** (*coloq*) ~ (**on sth**) ciego (de algo) (*drogas, alcohol*) LOC **high and dry** plantado: *to leave sb high and dry* dejar plantado a algn **to be X metres, feet, etc high** medir X metros, pies, etc de altura: *The wall is six feet high.* La pared mide seis pies de altura. ◊ *How high is it?* ¿Cuánto mide de altura? *Ver tb* ESTEEM, FLY

high[2] /haɪ/ ◆ *n* punto alto ◆ *adv* (**-er**, **-est**) alto, a gran altura

highbrow /ˈhaɪbraʊ/ *adj* (*frec pey*) culto, intelectual

high-class /ˌhaɪ ˈklɑːs/ *adj* de categoría

High Court *n* Tribunal Supremo

higher education *n* educación superior

high jump *n* salto de altura

highland /ˈhaɪlənd/ *n* [*gen pl*] región montañosa

high-level /ˌhaɪ ˈlevl/ *adj* de alto nivel

highlight /ˈhaɪlaɪt/ ◆ *n* **1** punto culminante, aspecto notable **2** [*gen pl*] (*en el pelo*) reflejo ◆ *vt* poner de relieve, (hacer) resaltar

highly /ˈhaɪli/ *adv* **1** muy, altamente, sumamente: *highly unlikely* altamente improbable **2** *to think/speak highly of sb* tener muy buena opinión/hablar muy bien de algn

highly strung *adj* nervioso

Highness /ˈhaɪnəs/ *n* alteza

high-powered /ˌhaɪ ˈpaʊəd/ *adj* **1** (*coche*) de gran potencia **2** (*persona*) enérgico, dinámico

high pressure /ˌhaɪ ˈpreʃə/ ◆ *n* (*Meteor*) altas presiones ◆ *adj* estresante

high-rise /ˈhaɪ raɪz/ ◆ *n* torre (*de muchos pisos*) ◆ *adj* **1** (*edificio*) de muchos pisos **2** (*piso*) de un edificio alto

high school *n* (*esp USA*) escuela de enseñanza secundaria

high street *n* calle mayor: *high-street shops* tiendas de la calle principal

high-tech (*tb* **hi-tech**) /ˌhaɪ ˈtek/ *adj* (*coloq*) de alta tecnología

high tide (*tb* **high water**) *n* pleamar

highway /ˈhaɪweɪ/ *n* **1** (*esp USA*) carretera, autopista **2** vía pública: *Highway Code* código de circulación

hijack /ˈhaɪdʒæk/ ◆ *vt* **1** secuestrar

(*fig*) acaparar ◆ *n* secuestro **hijacker** *n* secuestrador, -ora

hike /haɪk/ ◆ *n* caminata ◆ *vi* ir de excursión a pie **hiker** *n* caminante, excursionista

hilarious /hɪˈleəriəs/ *adj* divertidísimo, muy cómico

hill /hɪl/ *n* **1** colina, cerro **2** cuesta, pendiente **hilly** *adj* montañoso

hillside /ˈhɪlsaɪd/ *n* ladera

hilt /hɪlt/ *n* empuñadura LOC (**up**) **to the hilt 1** hasta el cuello **2** (*apoyar*) incondicionalmente

him /hɪm/ *pron pers* **1** [*como objeto directo*] lo, le: *I hit him.* Le pegué. **2** [*como objeto indirecto*] le: *Give it to him.* Dáselo. **3** [*después de preposición y del verbo* **to be**] él: *He always has it with him.* Siempre lo tiene consigo. ◊ *It must be him.* Debe de ser él. ☛ *Comparar con* HE

himself /hɪmˈself/ *pron* **1** [*uso reflexivo*] se **2** [*después de preposición*] sí (mismo): *'I tried', he said to himself.* "Lo intenté" – se dijo a sí mismo. **3** [*uso enfático*] él mismo: *He said so himself.* Él mismo lo dijo.

hinder /ˈhɪndə(r)/ *vt* entorpecer, dificultar: *It seriously hindered him in his work.* Le entorpeció seriamente en su trabajo. ◊ *Our progress was hindered by bad weather.* El mal tiempo dificultó nuestro trabajo.

hindrance /ˈhɪndrəns/ *n* ~ (**to sth/sb**) estorbo, obstáculo (para algo/algn)

hindsight /ˈhaɪndsaɪt/ *n*: *with (the benefit of)/in hindsight* viéndolo a posteriori

Hindu /ˌhɪnˈduː; *USA* ˈhɪnduː/ *adj, n* hindú **Hinduism** *n* hinduismo

hinge /hɪndʒ/ ◆ *n* bisagra, gozne ◆ PHR V **to hinge on sth** depender de algo

hint /hɪnt/ ◆ *n* **1** insinuación, indirecta **2** indicio **3** consejo ◆ **1** *vi* ~ **at sth** referirse indirectamente a algo **2** *vt, vi* ~ (**to sb**) **that...** insinuar (a algn) que...

hip /hɪp/ *n* cadera

hippopotamus /ˌhɪpəˈpɒtəməs/ *n* (*pl* **-muses** /-məsɪz/ *o* **-mi** /-maɪ/) (*tb* **hippo**) hipopótamo

hire /ˈhaɪə(r)/ ◆ *vt* **1** alquilar **2** (*persona*) contratar ☛ *Ver nota en* ALQUILAR ◆ *n* alquiler: *Bicycles for hire.* Se alquilan bicicletas. ◊ *hire purchase* compra a plazos

his /hɪz/ **1** *adj pos* su(s) (*de él*): *his bag(s)* su(s) bolsa(s) **2** *pron pos* suyo, -a, -os, -as (*de él*): *a friend of his* un amigo suyo ◊ *He lent me his.* Me dejó el suyo. ☛ *Ver nota en* MY

hiss /hɪs/ ◆ **1** *vi* sisear, silbar **2** *vt, vi* (*desaprobación*) silbar ◆ *n* silbido, siseo

historian /hɪˈstɔːriən/ *n* historiador, -ora

historic /hɪˈstɒrɪk; *USA* -ˈstɔːr-/ *adj* histórico **historical** *adj* histórico ☛ *Comparar con* HISTÓRICO

history /ˈhɪstri/ *n* (*pl* **-ies**) **1** historia **2** (*Med*) historial

hit /hɪt/ ◆ *vt* (**-tt-**) (*pret, pp* **hit**) **1** golpear: *to hit a nail* darle a un clavo **2** alcanzar: *He's been hit in the leg by a bullet.* Fue alcanzado en la pierna por una bala. **3** chocar contra **4 to hit sth** (**on/against sth**) golpearse algo (con/contra algo): *I hit my knee against the table.* Me golpeé la rodilla contra la mesa. **5** (*pelota*) dar a **6** afectar: *Rural areas have been worst hit by the strike.* Las zonas rurales han sido las más afectadas por la huelga. LOC **to hit it off** (**with sb**) (*coloq*): *Pete and Sue hit it off immediately.* Pete y Sue se cayeron bien desde el principio. **to hit the nail on the head** dar en el clavo *Ver tb* HOME PHR V **to hit back** (**at sth/sb**) contestar (a algo/algn), devolver el golpe (a algo/algn) **to hit out** (**at sth/sb**) lanzarse (contra algo/algn) ◆ *n* **1** golpe **2** éxito

hit-and-run /ˌhɪt ən ˈrʌn/ *adj*: *a hit-and-run driver* conductor que atropella a alguien y se da a la fuga

hitch¹ /hɪtʃ/ *vt, vi*: *to hitch (a ride)* hacer autostop ◊ *Can I hitch a lift with you as far as the station?* ¿Me puedes llevar hasta la estación? PHR V **to hitch sth up 1** (*pantalones*) subirse algo un poco **2** (*falda*) remangarse

hitch² /hɪtʃ/ *n* pega: *without a hitch* sin dificultades

hitch-hike /ˈhɪtʃ haɪk/ *vi* hacer autostop **hitch-hiker** *n* autostopista

hi-tech *Ver* HIGH-TECH

hive /haɪv/ (*tb* **beehive**) *n* colmena

hoard /hɔːd/ ◆ *n* **1** tesoro **2** provisión ◆ *vt* acaparar

hoarding /ˈhɔːdɪŋ/ (*USA* **billboard**) *n* valla publicitaria

hoarse /hɔːs/ *adj* ronco

hoax /həʊks/ *n* broma de mal gusto: *a hoax bomb warning* un aviso de bomba falso

hob /hɒb/ *n* plancha

hockey /ˈhɒki/ *n* hockey

hoe /həʊ/ *n* azada

hog /hɒg; *USA* hɔːg/ ◆ *n* cerdo ◆ *vt* (*coloq*) acaparar

hoist /hɔɪst/ *vt* izar, levantar

hold /həʊld/ ◆ (*pret, pp* **held** /held/) **1** *vt* sostener, tener en la mano: *to hold hands* ir cogidos de la mano **2** *vt* agarrarse a **3** *vt, vi* (*peso*) aguantar **4** *vt* (*criminal, rehén, etc*) retener, tener detenido **5** *vt* (*opinión*) sostener **6** *vt* tener espacio para: *It won't hold you all.* No vais a caber todos. **7** *vt* (*puesto, cargo*) ocupar **8** *vt* (*conversación*) mantener **9** *vt* (*reunión, elecciones*) celebrar **10** *vt* (*poseer*) tener **11** *vt* (*fml*) considerar **12** *vi* (*oferta, acuerdo*) ser válido **13** *vt* (*título*) ostentar **14** *vi* (*al teléfono*) esperar LOC **don't hold your breath!** ¡espérate sentado! **hold it!** (*coloq*) ¡espera! **to hold fast to sth** aferrarse a algo **to hold firm to sth** mantenerse firme en algo **to hold hands (with sb)** ir de la mano (con algn) **to hold sb to ransom** (*fig*) chantajear a algn **to hold sth/sb in contempt** despreciar algo/a algn **to hold the line** no colgar el teléfono **to hold your breath** contener el aliento *Ver tb* BAY, CAPTIVE, CHECK, ESTEEM
PHR V **to hold sth against sb** (*coloq*) tener algo en contra de algn
to hold sth/sb back refrenar algo/a algn **to hold sth back** ocultar algo
to hold forth echar un discurso
to hold on (to sth/sb) agarrarse (a algo/algn) **to hold sth on/down** sujetar algo
to hold out 1 (*provisiones*) durar **2** (*persona*) aguantar
to hold up (a bank, etc) atracar (un banco, etc) **to hold sth/sb up** retrasar algo/a algn
to hold with sth estar de acuerdo con algo
◆ *n* **1** *to keep a firm hold of sth* tener algo bien agarrado **2** (*judo*) llave **3** ~ **(on/over sth/sb)** influencia, control (sobre algo/algn) **4** (*barco, avión*) bodega LOC **to take hold of sth/sb** coger algo/a algn **to get hold of sb** ponerse en contacto con algn

holdall /ˈhəʊldɔːl/ *n* bolsa de viaje

holder /ˈhəʊldə(r)/ *n* **1** titular **2** poseedor, -ora **3** recipiente

hold-up /ˈhəʊld ʌp/ *n* **1** (*tráfico*) atasco **2** retraso **3** atraco

hole /həʊl/ *n* **1** agujero **2** perforación **3** (*carretera*) bache **4** boquete **5** madriguera **6** (*coloq*) aprieto **7** (*Dep*) hoyo LOC *Ver* PICK

holiday /ˈhɒlədeɪ/ ◆ *n* **1** fiesta **2** (*USA* **vacation**) vacaciones: *to be/go on holiday* estar/ir de vacaciones ◆ *vi* estar de vacaciones

holiday-maker /ˈhɒlədeɪ meɪkə(r)/ *n* veraneante

holiness /ˈhəʊlinəs/ *n* santidad

hollow /ˈhɒləʊ/ ◆ *adj* **1** hueco **2** (*cara, ojos*) hundido **3** (*sonido*) sordo **4** (*fig*) poco sincero, falso ◆ *n* **1** hoyo **2** hondonada **3** hueco ◆ *vt* (*tb* **to hollow sth out**) ahuecar algo

holly /ˈhɒli/ *n* acebo

holocaust /ˈhɒləkɔːst/ *n* holocausto

holy /ˈhəʊli/ *adj* (**holier**, **holiest**) **1** santo **2** sagrado **3** bendito

homage /ˈhɒmɪdʒ/ *n* [*incontable*] (*fml*) homenaje: *to pay homage to sth/sb* rendir homenaje a algo/algn

home /həʊm/ ◆ *n* **1** (*hogar*) casa, hogar **2** (*de ancianos, etc*) residencia **3** (*fig*) cuna **4** (*Zool*) hábitat **5** (*carrera*) meta LOC **at home 1** en casa **2** a sus anchas **3** en mi, su, nuestro, etc país ◆ *adj* **1** (*vida*) familiar: *home comforts* las comodidades del hogar **2** (*cocina, películas, etc*) casero **3** (*no extranjero*) nacional: *the Home Office* el Ministerio del Interior **4** (*Dep*) de/en casa **5** (*pueblo, país*) natal ◆ *adv* **1** a casa: *to go home* irse a casa **2** (*fijar, clavar, etc*) a fondo LOC **home and dry** a salvo **to hit/strike home** dar en el blanco *Ver tb* BRING

homeland /ˈhəʊmlænd/ *n* tierra natal, patria

homeless /ˈhəʊmləs/ ◆ *adj* sin hogar ◆ **the homeless** *n* [*pl*] las personas sin hogar

homely /ˈhəʊmli/ *adj* (**-ier**, **-iest**) **1** (*GB*) (*persona*) sencillo **2** (*ambiente, lugar*) familiar **3** (*USA, pey*) chabacano

home-made /ˌhəʊm ˈmeɪd/ *adj* casero, hecho en casa

homesick /ˈhəʊmsɪk/ *adj* nostálgico: *to be/feel homesick* tener morriña

homework /ˈhəʊmwɜːk/ *n* [*incontable*] (*colegio*) deberes

homicide /ˈhɒmɪsaɪd/ *n* homicidio ☛ *Comparar con* MANSLAUGHTER, MURDER **homicidal** /ˌhɒmɪˈsaɪdl/ *adj* homicida

homogeneous /ˌhɒməˈdʒiːniəs/ *adj* homogéneo

homosexual /ˌhɒməˈsekʃuəl/ *adj, n* homosexual **homosexuality** /ˌhɒməsekʃuˈæləti/ *n* homosexualidad

honest /ˈɒnɪst/ *adj* **1** (*persona*) honrado **2** (*afirmación*) franco, sincero **3** (*sueldo*) justo **honestly** *adv* **1** honradamente **2** [*uso enfático*] de verdad, francamente

honesty /ˈɒnəsti/ *n* **1** honradez, honestidad **2** franqueza

honey /ˈhʌni/ *n* **1** miel **2** (*coloq, USA*) (*tratamiento*) cariño

honeymoon /ˈhʌnimuːn/ *n* (*lit y fig*) luna de miel

honk /hɒŋk/ *vt, vi* tocar la bocina

honorary /ˈɒnərəri; *USA* ˈɒnəreri/ *adj* **1** honorífico **2** (*doctor*) honoris causa **3** (*no remunerado*) honorario

honour (*USA* **honor**) /ˈɒnə(r)/ ◆ *n* **1** honor **2** (*título*) condecoración **3** **honours** [*pl*] distinción: *(first class) honours degree* licenciatura (con la nota más alta) **4 your Honour**, **his/her Honour** su Señoría LOC **in honour of sth/sb; in sth's/sb's honour** en honor de/a algo/algn ◆ *vt* **1** ~ **sth/sb (with sth)** honrar algo/a algn (con algo) **2** ~ **sth/sb (with sth)** condecorar a algn (con algo) **3** (*opinión, etc*) respetar **4** (*compromiso/deuda*) cumplir (con)

honourable (*USA* **honorable**) /ˈɒnərəbl/ *adj* **1** honorable **2** honroso

hood /hʊd/ *n* **1** capucha **2** (*coche*) capota **3** (*USA*) *Ver* BONNET

hoof /huːf/ *n* (*pl* ~**s** *o* **hooves** /huːvz/) casco, pezuña

hook /hʊk/ ◆ *n* **1** gancho, garfio **2** (*pesca*) anzuelo LOC **off the hook** descolgado (*teléfono*) **to let sb/get sb off the hook** (*coloq*) dejar que algn se salve/sacar a algn del apuro ◆ *vt, vi* enganchar LOC **to be hooked (on sb)** (*coloq*) estar chiflado (por algn) **to be/get hooked (on sth)** (*coloq*) estar enganchado/engancharse (a algo)

hooligan /ˈhuːlɪgən/ *n* gamberro, -a **hooliganism** *n* gamberrismo

hoop /huːp/ *n* aro

hooray! /hʊˈreɪ/ *interj Ver* HURRAH

hoot /huːt/ ◆ *n* **1** (*búho*) ululato **2** (*bocina*) bocinazo ◆ **1** *vi* (*búho*) ulular **2** *vi* ~ **(at sth/sb)** (*coche*) pitar (a algo/algn) **3** *vt* (*bocina*) tocar

Hoover® /ˈhuːvə(r)/ ◆ *n* aspiradora ◆ *vt, vi* pasar la aspiradora (a)

hooves /huːvz/ *n plural de* HOOF

hop /hɒp/ ◆ *vi* (**-pp-**) **1** (*persona*) saltar a la pata coja **2** (*animal*) dar saltitos ◆ *n* **1** salto **2** (*Bot*) lúpulo

hope /həʊp/ ◆ *n* **1** ~ **(of/for sth)** esperanza (de/para algo) **2** ~ **(of doing sth/that…)** esperanza (de hacer algo/de que…) ◆ **1** *vi* ~ **(for sth)** esperar (algo) **2** *vt* ~ **to do sth/that…** esperar hacer algo/que…: *I hope not/so.* Espero que no/sí. LOC **I should hope not!** ¡faltaría más! ☛ *Ver nota en* ESPERAR

hopeful /ˈhəʊpfl/ *adj* **1** (*persona*) esperanzado, confiado: *to be hopeful that…* tener la esperanza de que… **2** (*situación*) prometedor, esperanzador **hopefully** *adv* **1** con optimismo, con esperanzas **2** con un poco de suerte

hopeless /ˈhəʊpləs/ *adj* **1** inútil, desastroso **2** (*tarea*) imposible **hopelessly** *adv* (*enfático*) totalmente

horde /hɔːd/ *n* (*a veces pey*) multitud: *hordes of people* mareas de gente

horizon /həˈraɪzn/ *n* **1 the horizon** el horizonte **2 horizons** [*gen pl*] (*fig*) perspectiva

horizontal /ˌhɒrɪˈzɒntl; *USA* ˌhɔːr-/ *adj, n* horizontal

hormone /ˈhɔːməʊn/ *n* hormona

horn /hɔːn/ *n* **1** cuerno, asta **2** (*Mús*) instrumento de viento con pabellón como el de la trompeta **3** (*coche, etc*) bocina

horoscope /ˈhɒrəskəʊp; *USA* ˈhɔːr-/ *n* horóscopo

horrendous /hɒˈrendəs/ *adj* **1** horrendo **2** (*coloq*) (*excesivo*) tremendo

horrible /ˈhɒrəbl; *USA* ˈhɔːr-/ *adj* horrible

horrid /ˈhɒrɪd; *USA* ˈhɔːrɪd/ *adj* horrible, horroroso

horrific /həˈrɪfɪk/ *adj* horripilante, espantoso

horrify /ˈhɒrɪfaɪ; *USA* ˈhɔːr-/ *vt* (*pret, pp* **-fied**) horrorizar **horrifying** *adj* horroroso, horripilante

horror /ˈhɒrə(r); *USA* ˈhɔːr-/ *n* horror: *horror film* película de terror

horse /hɔːs/ *n* caballo LOC *Ver* DARK, FLOG, LOOK[1]

horseman /ˈhɔːsmən/ *n* (*pl* **-men** /-mən/) jinete

horsepower /ˈhɔːspaʊə(r)/ *n* (*pl* **horsepower**) (*abrev* **hp**) caballo de vapor

horseshoe /ˈhɔːsʃuː/ *n* herradura

horsewoman /ˈhɔːswʊmən/ *n* (*pl* **-women**) amazona

horticulture /ˈhɔːtɪkʌltʃə(r)/ *n* horticultura **horticultural** /ˌhɔːtɪˈkʌltʃərəl/ *adj* hortícola

hose /həʊz/ (*tb* **hosepipe**) *n* manguera, manga

hospice /ˈhɒspɪs/ *n* hospital (*para incurables*)

hospitable /hɒˈspɪtəbl, ˈhɒspɪtəbl/ *adj* hospitalario

hospital /ˈhɒspɪtl/ *n* hospital ☛ *Ver nota en* SCHOOL

hospitality /ˌhɒspɪˈtæləti/ *n* hospitalidad

host /həʊst/ ◆ *n* **1** multitud, montón: *a host of admirers* una multitud de admiradores **2** (*fem tb* **hostess**) anfitrión, -ona **3** (*TV*) presentador, -ora **4 the Host** (*Relig*) la hostia ◆ *vt*: *Barcelona hosted the 1992 Olympic Games.* Barcelona fue la sede de los Juegos Olímpicos de 1992.

hostage /ˈhɒstɪdʒ/ *n* rehén

hostel /ˈhɒstl/ *n* hostal: *youth hostel* albergue juvenil

hostess /ˈhəʊstəs, -tes/ *n* **1** anfitriona **2** (*TV*) presentadora **3** azafata

hostile /ˈhɒstaɪl; *USA* -tl/ *adj* **1** hostil **2** (*territorio*) enemigo

hostility /hɒˈstɪləti/ *n* hostilidad

hot /hɒt/ *adj* (**hotter**, **hottest**) **1** (*agua, comida, objeto*) caliente ☛ *Ver nota en* FRÍO **2** (*día*) caluroso: *in hot weather* cuando hace calor **3** (*sabor*) picante LOC **to be hot 1** (*persona*) tener calor **2** (*tiempo*): *It's very hot.* Hace mucho calor. *Ver tb* PIPING *en* PIPE

hotel /həʊˈtel/ *n* hotel

hotly /ˈhɒtli/ *adv* ardientemente, enérgicamente

hound /haʊnd/ ◆ *n* perro de caza ◆ *vt* acosar

hour /ˈaʊə(r)/ *n* **1** hora: *half an hour* media hora **2 hours** [*pl*] horario: *office/opening hours* el horario de oficina/apertura **3** [*gen sing*] momento LOC **after hours** después del horario de trabajo/de apertura **on the hour** a la hora en punto *Ver tb* EARLY **hourly** *adv, adj* cada hora

house /haʊs/ ◆ *n* (*pl* ~**s** /ˈhaʊzɪz/) **1** casa **2** (*Teat*) sala de espectáculos: *There was a full house.* Se llenó al completo. LOC **on the house** cortesía de la casa *Ver tb* MOVE ◆ /haʊz/ *vt* alojar, albergar

household /ˈhaʊshəʊld/ *n*: *a large household* una casa de mucha gente ◇ *household chores* faenas domésticas **householder** *n* dueño, -a de la casa

housekeeper /ˈhaʊskiːpə(r)/ *n* ama de llaves **housekeeping** *n* **1** gobierno de la casa **2** gastos de la casa

the House of Commons (*tb* **the Commons**) *n* [*v sing o pl*] la Cámara de los Comunes ☛ *Ver* pág 322.

the House of Lords (*tb* **the Lords**) *n* [*v sing o pl*] la Cámara de los Lores ☛ *Ver* pág 322.

the Houses of Parliament *n* el Parlamento (británico)

housewife /ˈhaʊswaɪf/ *n* (*pl* **-wives**) ama de casa

housework /ˈhaʊswɜːk/ *n* [*incontable*] tareas domésticas

housing /ˈhaʊzɪŋ/ *n* [*incontable*] vivienda, alojamiento

housing estate *n* urbanización

hover /ˈhɒvə(r); *USA* ˈhʌvər/ *vi* **1** (*ave*) planear **2** (*objeto*) quedarse suspendido (en el aire) **3** (*persona*) rondar

hovercraft /ˈhɒvəkrɑːft/ *n* (*pl* **hovercraft**) aerodeslizador

how /haʊ/ ◆ *adv interr* **1** cómo: *How can that be?* ¿Cómo puede ser? ◇ *Tell me how to spell it.* Dime cómo se escribe. *How is your job?* ¿Cómo va el trabajo? *How are you?* ¿Qué tal estás? **3** *How old are you?* ¿Cuántos años tienes? ◇ *How fast were you going?* ¿A qué velocidad ibas? **4 how many** cuántos **how much** cuánto: *How much is it?* ¿Cuánto es? *How many letters did you write*

¿Cuántas cartas escribiste? LOC **how about?**: *How about it?* ¿Qué te parece? **how are you?** ¿cómo estás? **how come ...?** ¿cómo es que ...? **how do you do?** es un placer

How do you do? se usa en presentaciones formales, y se contesta con *how do you do?* En cambio **how are you?** se usa en situaciones informales, y se responde según se encuentre uno: *fine, very well, not too well, etc.*

◆ *adv* (*fml*) ¡qué ...!: *How cold it is!* ¡Qué frío hace! ◊ *How you've grown!* ¡Cómo has crecido! ◆ *conj* como: *I dress how I like.* Me visto como quiero.

however /haʊˈevə(r)/ ◆ *adv* **1** sin embargo **2** por muy/mucho que: *however strong you are* por muy fuerte que seas ◊ *however hard he tries* por mucho que lo intente ◆ *conj* (*tb* **how**) como: *how(ever) you like* como quieras ◆ *adv interr* cómo: *However did she do it?* ¿Cómo consiguió hacerlo?

howl /haʊl/ ◆ *n* **1** aullido **2** grito ◆ *vi* **1** aullar **2** dar alaridos

hub /hʌb/ *n* **1** (*rueda*) cubo **2** (*fig*) eje

hubbub /ˈhʌbʌb/ *n* jaleo, algarabía

huddle /ˈhʌdl/ ◆ *vi* **1** acurrucarse **2** apiñarse ◆ *n* corrillo

hue /hjuː/ *n* (*fml*) **1** (*color, significado*) matiz **2** color LOC **hue and cry** griterío

huff /hʌf/ *n* enfurruñamiento: *to be in a huff* estar enfurruñado

hug /hʌg/ ◆ *n* abrazo: *to give sb a hug* darle un abrazo a algn ◆ *vt* (**-gg-**) abrazar

huge /hjuːdʒ/ *adj* enorme

hull /hʌl/ *n* casco (*de un barco*)

hullo *Ver* HELLO

hum /hʌm/ ◆ *n* **1** zumbido **2** (*voces*) murmullo ◆ (**-mm-**) **1** *vi* zumbar **2** *vt, vi* tararear **3** *vi* (*coloq*) bullir: *to hum with activity* bullir de actividad

human /ˈhjuːmən/ *adj, n* humano: *human being* ser humano ◊ *human rights* derechos humanos ◊ *human nature* la naturaleza humana ◊ *the human race* el género humano

humane /hjuːˈmeɪn/ *adj* humanitario, humano

humanitarian /hjuːˌmænɪˈteəriən/ *adj* humanitario

humanity /hjuːˈmænəti/ *n* **1** humanidad **2** **humanities** [*pl*] humanidades

humble /ˈhʌmbl/ ◆ *adj* (**-er**, **-est**) humilde ◆ *vt*: *to humble yourself* adoptar una actitud humilde

humid /ˈhjuːmɪd/ *adj* húmedo **humidity** /hjuːˈmɪdəti/ *n* humedad

Humid y **humidity** sólo se refieren a la humedad atmosférica. ☛ *Ver nota en* MOIST

humiliate /hjuːˈmɪlieɪt/ *vt* humillar **humiliating** *adj* humillante, vergonzoso **humiliation** *n* humillación

humility /hjuːˈmɪləti/ *n* humildad

hummingbird /ˈhʌmɪŋbɜːd/ *n* colibrí

humorous /ˈhjuːmərəs/ *adj* humorístico, divertido

humour (*USA* **humor**) /ˈhjuːmə(r)/ ◆ *n* **1** humor **2** (*comicidad*) gracia ◆ *vt* seguir la corriente a, complacer

hump /hʌmp/ *n* joroba, giba

hunch[1] /hʌntʃ/ *n* corazonada, presentimiento

hunch[2] /hʌntʃ/ *vt, vi* ~ (**sth**) (**up**) encorvar algo/encorvarse

hundred /ˈhʌndrəd/ ◆ *adj, pron* cien, ciento ☛ *Ver ejemplos en* FIVE ◆ *n* ciento, centenar **hundredth** **1** *adj, pron* centésimo **2** *n* centésima parte ☛ *Ver ejemplos en* FIFTH

hung *pret, pp de* HANG

hunger /ˈhʌŋgə(r)/ ◆ *n* hambre ☛ *Ver nota en* HAMBRE ◆ PHR V **to hunger for/after sth** anhelar algo, tener sed de algo

hungry /ˈhʌŋgri/ *adj* (**-ier**, **-iest**) hambriento: *I'm hungry.* Tengo hambre.

hunk /hʌŋk/ *n* (buen) trozo

hunt /hʌnt/ ◆ *vt, vi* **1** cazar, ir de cacería **2** ~ (**for sth/sb**) buscar (algo/a algn) ◆ *n* **1** caza, cacería **2** búsqueda, busca **hunter** *n* cazador, -ora

hunting /ˈhʌntɪŋ/ *n* caza, cacería

hurdle /ˈhɜːdl/ *n* **1** valla **2** (*fig*) obstáculo

hurl /hɜːl/ *vt* **1** lanzar, arrojar **2** (*insultos, etc*) soltar

hurrah! /həˈrɑː/ (*tb* **hooray!**) *interj* ~ (**for sth/sb**) ¡viva! (algo/algn)

hurricane /ˈhʌrɪkən; *USA* -keɪn/ *n* huracán

hurried /ˈhʌrid/ *adj* apresurado, rápido

hurry /ˈhʌri/ ◆ *n* [*sing*] prisa LOC **to be**

in a hurry tener prisa ◆ *vt, vi* (*pret, pp* **hurried**) dar(se) prisa, apresurar(se) PHR V **to hurry up** (*coloq*) darse prisa

hurt /hɜːt/ (*pret, pp* **hurt**) **1** *vt* lastimar, hacer daño a: *to get hurt* hacerse daño **2** *vi* doler: *My leg hurts.* Me duele la pierna. **3** *vt* (*apenar*) herir, ofender **4** *vt* (*intereses, reputación, etc*) perjudicar, dañar **hurtful** *adj* hiriente, cruel, perjudicial

hurtle /ˈhɜːtl/ *vi* precipitarse

husband /ˈhʌzbənd/ *n* marido

hush /hʌʃ/ ◆ *n* [*sing*] silencio ◆ PHR V **to hush sth/sb up** acallar algo/a algn

husky /ˈhʌski/ ◆ *adj* (**-ier**, **-iest**) ronco ◆ *n* (*pl* **-ies**) perro esquimal

hustle /ˈhʌsl/ ◆ *vt* **1** empujar a **2** (*coloq*) meter prisa a ◆ *n* LOC **hustle and bustle** ajetreo

hut /hʌt/ *n* choza, cabaña

hybrid /ˈhaɪbrɪd/ *adj n*, híbrido

hydrant /ˈhaɪdrənt/ *n* boca de riego: *fire hydrant* boca de incendio

hydraulic /haɪˈdrɔːlɪk/ *adj* hidráulico

hydroelectric /ˌhaɪdrəʊɪˈlektrɪk/ *adj* hidroeléctrico

hydrogen /ˈhaɪdrədʒən/ *n* hidrógeno

hyena (*tb* **hyaena**) /haɪˈiːnə/ *n* hiena

hygiene /ˈhaɪdʒiːn/ *n* higiene **hygienic** *adj* higiénico

hymn /hɪm/ *n* himno

hype /haɪp/ ◆ *n* (*coloq*) propaganda (exagerada) ◆ PHR V **to hype sth (up)** (*coloq*) anunciar algo exageradamente

hypermarket /ˈhaɪpəmɑːkɪt/ *n* (*GB*) hipermercado

hyphen /ˈhaɪfn/ *n* guión ☛ *Ver* págs 318–19.

hypnosis /hɪpˈnəʊsɪs/ *n* hipnosis

hypnotic /hɪpˈnɒtɪk/ *adj* hipnótico

hypnotism /ˈhɪpnətɪzəm/ *n* hipnotismo **hypnotist** *n* hipnotizador, -ora

hypnotize, -ise /ˈhɪpnətaɪz/ *vt* (*lit y fig*) hipnotizar

hypochondriac /ˌhaɪpəˈkɒndriæk/ *n* hipocondríaco, -a

hypocrisy /hɪˈpɒkrəsi/ *n* hipocresía

hypocrite /ˈhɪpəkrɪt/ *n* hipócrita **hypocritical** /ˌhɪpəˈkrɪtɪkl/ *adj* hipócrita

hypothesis /haɪˈpɒθəsɪs/ *n* (*pl* **-ses** /-siːz/) hipótesis

hypothetical /ˌhaɪpəˈθetɪkl/ *adj* hipotético

hysteria /hɪˈstɪəriə/ *n* histeria

hysterical /hɪˈsterɪkl/ *adj* **1** (*risa, etc*) histérico **2** (*coloq*) para partirse de risa

hysterics /hɪˈsterɪks/ *n* [*pl*] **1** crisis de histeria **2** (*coloq*) ataque de risa

Ii

I, i /aɪ/ *n* (*pl* **I's, i's** /aɪz/) I, i: *I for Isaac* I de Italia ☛ *Ver ejemplos en* A, a

I /aɪ/ *pron pers* yo: *I am 15 (years old).* Tengo quince años. ☛ El *pron pers* no se puede omitir en inglés. *Comparar con* ME 3

ice /aɪs/ ◆ *n* [*incontable*] hielo: *ice cube* cubito de hielo ◆ *vt* glasear

iceberg /ˈaɪsbɜːg/ *n* iceberg

icebox /ˈaɪsbɒks/ *n* **1** (*USA*) nevera **2** congelador

ice cream *n* helado

ice lolly /ˌaɪs ˈlɒli/ *n* (*pl* **-ies**) polo

ice rink *n* pista de hielo

ice-skate /ˈaɪs skeɪt/ ◆ *n* patín de cuchilla ◆ *vi* patinar sobre hielo **ice skating** *n* patinaje sobre hielo

icicle /ˈaɪsɪkl/ *n* carámbano

icing /ˈaɪsɪŋ/ *n* glaseado: *icing sugar* azúcar glas

icon (*tb* **ikon**) /ˈaɪkɒn/ *n* **1** (*Relig*) icono **2** (*Informát*) símbolo gráfico

icy /ˈaɪsi/ *adj* (**icier**, **iciest**) **1** helado **2** (*fig*) gélido

I'd /aɪd/ **1** = I HAD *Ver* HAVE **2** = I WOULD *Ver* WOULD

idea /aɪˈdɪə/ *n* **1** idea **2** ocurrencia: *What an idea!* ¡Qué ocurrencia! LOC **to get/have the idea that...** tener la impresión de que... **to get the idea** sacar la idea **to give sb ideas** meter algn ideas en la cabeza **to have no idea** no tener ni idea

ideal /aɪˈdiːəl/ ◆ *adj* ~ (**for sth/sb**) ideal (para algo/algn) ◆ *n* ideal

idealism /aɪˈdiːəlɪzəm/ *n* idealismo **idealist** *n* idealista **idealistic** /ˌaɪdiəˈlɪstɪk/ *adj* idealista

idealize, -ise /aɪˈdiːəlaɪz/ *vt* idealizar

ideally /aɪˈdiːəli/ *adv* en el mejor de los casos: *to be ideally suited* complementarse de una forma ideal ◊ *Ideally, they should all help.* Lo ideal sería que todos ayudaran.

identical /aɪˈdentɪkl/ *adj* ~ (**to/with sth/sb**) idéntico a algo/algn

identification /aɪˌdentɪfɪˈkeɪʃn/ *n* identificación: *identification papers* documento de identidad ◊ *identification parade* rueda de reconocimiento

identify /aɪˈdentɪfaɪ/ *vt* (*pret, pp* **-fied**) **1** ~ **sth/sb as sth/sb** identificar algo/a algn como algo/algn **2** ~ **sth with sth** identificar algo con algo

identity /aɪˈdentəti/ *n* (*pl* **-ies**) **1** identidad **2** *a case of mistaken identity* un error de identificación

ideology /ˌaɪdiˈɒlədʒi/ *n* (*pl* **-ies**) ideología

idiom /ˈɪdiəm/ *n* **1** modismo, locución **2** (*individuo, época*) lenguaje

idiosyncrasy /ˌɪdiəˈsɪŋkrəsi/ *n* idiosincrasia

idiot /ˈɪdiət/ *n* (*coloq, pey*) idiota **idiotic** /ˌɪdiˈɒtɪk/ *adj* estúpido

idle /ˈaɪdl/ ◆ *adj* (**idler**, **idlest**) **1** holgazán **2** desocupado **3** (*maquinaria*) parado **4** vano, inútil ◆ PHR V **to idle sth away** desperdiciar algo **idleness** *n* ociosidad, holgazanería

idol /ˈaɪdl/ *n* ídolo **idolize, -ise** *vt* idolatrar

idyllic /ɪˈdɪlɪk; *USA* aɪˈd-/ *adj* idílico

ie /ˌaɪ ˈiː/ *abrev* es decir

if /ɪf/ *conj* **1** si: *If he were here…* Si estuviera él aquí… **2** cuando, siempre que: *if in doubt* en caso de duda **3** (*tb* **even if**) aunque, incluso si LOC **if I were you** yo que tú, yo en tu lugar **if only** ojalá: *If only I had known!* ¡De haberlo sabido! **if so** de ser así

igloo /ˈɪgluː/ *n* (*pl* ~**s**) iglú

ignite /ɪgˈnaɪt/ *vt, vi* prender (fuego a), encender(se) **ignition** *n* **1** ignición **2** (*Mec*) encendido

ignominious /ˌɪgnəˈmɪniəs/ *adj* vergonzoso

ignorance /ˈɪgnərəns/ *n* ignorancia

ignorant /ˈɪgnərənt/ *adj* ignorante: *to be ignorant of sth* desconocer algo

ignore /ɪgˈnɔː(r)/ *vt* **1** ~ **sth/sb** no hacer caso de algo/a algn **2** ~ **sb** ignorar a algn **3** ~ **sth** pasar algo por alto

I'll /aɪl/ **1** = I SHALL *Ver* SHALL **2** = I WILL *Ver* WILL

ill /ɪl/ ◆ *adj* **1** (*USA* **sick**) enfermo: *to fall/be taken ill* caer enfermo ◊ *to feel ill* sentirse mal **2** malo ☛ *Ver nota en* ENFERMO ◆ *adv* mal: *to speak ill of sb* hablar mal de algn ☛ Se emplea mucho en compuestos, p.ej. **ill-fated** infortunado, **ill-equipped** mal equipado, **ill-advised** imprudente, poco aconsejable. LOC **ill at ease** incómodo, molesto *Ver tb* BODE, DISPOSED, FEELING ◆ *n* (*fml*) mal, daño

illegal /ɪˈliːgl/ *adj* ilegal

illegible /ɪˈledʒəbl/ *adj* ilegible

illegitimate /ˌɪləˈdʒətɪmət/ *adj* ilegítimo

ill feeling *n* rencor

ill health *n* mala salud

illicit /ɪˈlɪsɪt/ *adj* ilícito

illiterate /ɪˈlɪtərət/ *adj* **1** analfabeto **2** ignorante

illness /ˈɪlnəs/ *n* enfermedad: *mental illness* enfermedad mental ◊ *absences due to illness* absentismo por enfermedad ☛ *Ver nota en* DISEASE

illogical /ɪˈlɒdʒɪkl/ *adj* ilógico

ill-treatment /ˌɪl ˈtriːtmənt/ *n* maltrato

illuminate /ɪˈluːmɪneɪt/ *vt* iluminar **illuminating** *adj* revelador **illumination** *n* **1** iluminación **2** **illuminations** [*pl*] (*GB*) luminarias

illusion /ɪˈluːʒn/ *n* ilusión (*idea equivocada*) LOC **to be under an illusion** engañarse a uno mismo

illusory /ɪˈluːsəri/ *adj* ilusorio

illustrate /ˈɪləstreɪt/ *vt* ilustrar **illustration** *n* **1** ilustración **2** ejemplo

illustrious /ɪˈlʌstriəs/ *adj* ilustre

I'm /aɪm/ = I AM *Ver* BE

image /ˈɪmɪdʒ/ *n* imagen **imagery** *n* imágenes

imaginary /ɪˈmædʒɪnərɪ; *USA* -ənerɪ/ *adj* imaginario

imagination /ɪˌmædʒɪˈneɪʃn/ *n*

imaginación **imaginative** /ɪˈmædʒɪnətɪv/ *adj* imaginativo

imagine /ɪˈmædʒɪn/ *vt* imaginar(se)

imbalance /ɪmˈbæləns/ *n* desequilibrio

imbecile /ˈɪmbəsiːl; *USA* -sl/ *n* imbécil

imitate /ˈɪmɪteɪt/ *vt* imitar

imitation /ˌɪmɪˈteɪʃn/ *n* **1** (*acción y efecto*) imitación **2** copia, reproducción

immaculate /ɪˈmækjələt/ *adj* **1** inmaculado **2** (*ropa*) impecable

immaterial /ˌɪməˈtɪəriəl/ *adj* irrelevante

immature /ˌɪməˈtjʊə(r); *USA* -ˈtʊər/ *adj* inmaduro

immeasurable /ɪˈmeʒərəbl/ *adj* inconmensurable

immediate /ɪˈmiːdiət/ *adj* **1** inmediato: *to take immediate action* actuar de inmediato **2** (*familia, parientes*) más cercano **3** (*necesidad, etc*) urgente

immediately /ɪˈmiːdiətli/ ◆ *adv* **1** inmediatamente **2** directamente ◆ *conj* (*GB*) en cuanto: *immediately I saw her* en cuanto la vi/nada más verla

immense /ɪˈmens/ *adj* inmenso

immerse /ɪˈmɜːs/ *vt* (*lit y fig*) sumergir(se) **immersion** *n* inmersión

immigrant /ˈɪmɪgrənt/ *adj, n* inmigrante

immigration /ˌɪmɪˈgreɪʃn/ *n* inmigración

imminent /ˈɪmɪnənt/ *adj* inminente

immobile /ɪˈməʊbaɪl; *USA* -bl/ *adj* inmóvil

immobilize, -ise /ɪˈməʊbəlaɪz/ *vt* inmovilizar

immoral /ɪˈmɒrəl; *USA* ɪˈmɔːrəl/ *adj* inmoral

immortal /ɪˈmɔːtl/ *adj* **1** (*alma, vida*) inmortal **2** (*fama*) imperecedero **immortality** /ˌɪmɔːˈtæləti/ *n* inmortalidad

immovable /ɪˈmuːvəbl/ *adj* **1** (*objeto*) inmóvil **2** (*persona, actitud*) inflexible

immune /ɪˈmjuːn/ *adj* ~ (**to/against sth**) inmune (a algo) **immunity** *n* inmunidad

immunize, -ise /ˈɪmjʊnaɪz/ *vt* ~ **sb** (**against sth**) inmunizar a algn (contra algo) **immunization, -isation** *n* inmunización

imp /ɪmp/ *n* **1** diablillo **2** (*niño*) pillo

impact /ˈɪmpækt/ *n* **1** (*lit y fig*) impacto **2** (*coche*) choque

impair /ɪmˈpeə(r)/ *vt* deteriorar, debilitar: *impaired vision* vista debilitada **impairment** *n* deficiencia

impart /ɪmˈpɑːt/ *vt* **1** conferir **2** ~ **sth** (**to sb**) impartir algo (a algn)

impartial /ɪmˈpɑːʃl/ *adj* imparcial

impasse /ˈæmpɑːs; *USA* ˈɪmpæs/ *n* (*fig*) callejón sin salida

impassioned /ɪmˈpæʃnd/ *adj* apasionado

impassive /ɪmˈpæsɪv/ *adj* impasible

impatience /ɪmˈpeɪʃns/ *n* impaciencia

impatient /ɪmˈpeɪʃnt/ *adj* impaciente

impeccable /ɪmˈpekəbl/ *adj* impecable

impede /ɪmˈpiːd/ *vt* obstaculizar

impediment /ɪmˈpedɪmənt/ *n* **1** ~ (**to sth/sb**) obstáculo (para algo/algn) **2** (*habla*) defecto

impel /ɪmˈpel/ *vt* (**-ll-**) impulsar

impending /ɪmˈpendɪŋ/ *adj* inminente

impenetrable /ɪmˈpenɪtrəbl/ *adj* impenetrable

imperative /ɪmˈperətɪv/ ◆ *adj* **1** (*esencial*) urgente, imprescindible **2** (*tono de voz*) imperativo ◆ *n* imperativo

imperceptible /ˌɪmpəˈseptəbl/ *adj* imperceptible

imperfect /ɪmˈpɜːfɪkt/ *adj, n* imperfecto

imperial /ɪmˈpɪəriəl/ *adj* imperial **imperialism** *n* imperialismo

impersonal /ɪmˈpɜːsənl/ *adj* impersonal

impersonate /ɪmˈpɜːsəneɪt/ *vt* **1** imitar **2** hacerse pasar por

impertinent /ɪmˈpɜːtɪnənt/ *adj* impertinente

impetus /ˈɪmpɪtəs/ *n* **1** impulso, ímpetu **2** (*Fís*) impulso

implausible /ɪmˈplɔːzəbl/ *adj* inverosímil

implement /ˈɪmplɪmənt/ ◆ *n* utensilio ◆ *vt* **1** llevar a cabo, realizar **2** (*decisión*) poner en práctica **3** (*ley*) aplicar **implementation** *n* **1** realización, puesta en práctica **2** (*ley*) aplicación

implicate /ˈɪmplɪkeɪt/ *vt* ~ **sb** (**in sth**) involucrar a algn (en algo)

implication /ˌɪmplɪˈkeɪʃn/ *n* **1** ~ (**for**

sth/sb) consecuencia (para algo/algn) **2** implicación (*delito*)

implicit /ɪmˈplɪsɪt/ *adj* **1** ~ (**in sth**) implícito (en algo) **2** absoluto

implore /ɪmˈplɔː(r)/ *vt* implorar, suplicar

imply /ɪmˈplaɪ/ *vt* (*pret, pp* **implied**) **1** dar a entender **2** implicar, suponer

import /ɪmˈpɔːt/ ◆ *vt* **1** importar **2** (*fig*) traer ◆ *n* /ˈɪmpɔːt/ importación

important /ɪmˈpɔːtnt/ *adj* importante: *vitally important* de suma importancia **importance** *n* importancia

impose /ɪmˈpəʊz/ *vt* ~ **sth** (**on sth/sb**) imponer algo (a/sobre algo/algn) PHR V **to impose on/upon sth/sb** abusar (de la hospitalidad) de algo/algn **imposing** *adj* imponente **imposition** *n* ~ (**on sth/sb**) **1** imposición (sobre algo/algn) (*restricción, etc*) **2** molestia

impossible /ɪmˈpɒsəbl/ ◆ *adj* **1** imposible **2** intolerable ◆ **the impossible** *n* lo imposible **impossibility** /ɪmˌpɒsəˈbɪləti/ *n* imposibilidad

impotence /ˈɪmpətəns/ *n* impotencia **impotent** *adj* impotente

impoverished /ɪmˈpɒvərɪʃt/ *adj* empobrecido

impractical /ɪmˈpræktɪkl/ *adj* poco práctico

impress /ɪmˈpres/ **1** *vt* impresionar a **2** *vt* ~ **sth on/upon sb** recalcar algo a algn **3** *vi* causar buena impresión

impression /ɪmˈpreʃn/ *n* **1** impresión: *to be under the impression that…* tener la impresión de que… **2** imitación

impressive /ɪmˈpresɪv/ *adj* impresionante

imprison /ɪmˈprɪzn/ *vt* encarcelar a **imprisonment** *n* encarcelamiento *Ver tb* LIFE

improbable /ɪmˈprɒbəbl/ *adj* improbable, poco probable

impromptu /ɪmˈprɒmptjuː; *USA* -tuː/ *adj* improvisado

improper /ɪmˈprɒpə(r)/ *adj* **1** incorrecto, indebido **2** impropio **3** (*transacción*) irregular

improve /ɪmˈpruːv/ *vt, vi* mejorar PHR V **to improve on/upon sth** superar algo **improvement** *n* **1** ~ (**on/in sth**) mejora (de algo): *to be an improvement on sth* suponer una mejora sobre **2** reforma

improvise /ˈɪmprəvaɪz/ *vt, vi* improvisar

impulse /ˈɪmpʌls/ *n* impulso LOC **on impulse** sin pensar

impulsive /ɪmˈpʌlsɪv/ *adj* impulsivo

in /ɪn/ ◆ *prep* **1** en: *in here/there* aquí/ahí dentro **2** [*después de superlativo*] de: *the best shops in town* las mejores tiendas de la ciudad **3** (*tiempo*): *in the morning* por la mañana ◊ *in the daytime* de día ◊ *ten in the morning* las diez de la mañana **4** *I'll see you in two days (time).* Te veré dentro de dos días. ◊ *He did it in two days.* Lo hizo en dos días. **5** por: *5p in the pound* cinco peniques por libra ◊ *one in ten people* una de cada diez personas **6** (*descripción, método*): *the girl in glasses* la chica de gafas ◊ *covered in mud* cubierto de barro ◊ *Speak in English.* Habla en inglés. **7 + ing**: *In saying that, you're contradicting yourself.* Al decir eso te contradices a ti mismo. LOC **in that** en tanto que ◆ *part adv* **1 to be in** estar (*en casa*): *Is anyone in?* ¿Hay alguien? **2** (*tren, etc*): *to be/get in* haber llegado/llegar ◊ *Applications must be in by…* Las solicitudes deberán llegar antes del… **3** de moda LOC **to be in for sth** (*coloq*) esperarle a uno algo: *He's in for a surprise!* ¡Vaya sorpresa que se va a llevar! **to be/get in on sth** (*coloq*) participar en algo, enterarse de algo **to have (got) it in for sb** (*coloq*): *He's got it in for me.* Me tiene manía. ☛ Para los usos de **in** en PHRASAL VERBS ver las entradas de los verbos correspondientes, p.ej. **to go in** en GO[1]. ◆ *n* LOC **the ins and outs (of sth)** los pormenores (de algo)

inability /ˌɪnəˈbɪləti/ *n* ~ (**of sb**) (**to do sth**) incapacidad (de algn) (para hacer algo)

inaccessible /ˌɪnækˈsesəbl/ *adj* **1** ~ (**to sb**) inaccesible (para algn) **2** (*fig*) incomprensible (para algn)

inaccurate /ɪnˈækjərət/ *adj* inexacto, impreciso

inaction /ɪnˈækʃn/ *n* pasividad

inadequate /ɪnˈædɪkwət/ *adj* **1** insuficiente **2** incapaz

inadvertently /ˌɪnədˈvɜːtəntli/ *adv* por descuido, sin darse cuenta

inappropriate /ˌɪnəˈprəʊpriət/ *adj* ~ (**to/for sth/sb**) poco apropiado, impropio (para algo/algn)

inaugural /ɪˈnɔːgjərəl/ *adj* **1** inaugural **2** (*discurso*) de apertura

inaugurate /ɪˈnɔːgjəreɪt/ *vt* **1** ~ **sb (as sth)** investir a algn (como algo) **2** inaugurar

incapable /ɪnˈkeɪpəbl/ *adj* **1** ~ **of (doing) sth** incapaz de (hacer) algo **2** incompetente

incapacity /ˌɪnkəˈpæsəti/ *n* ~ **(for sth/ to do sth)** incapacidad (para algo/ hacer algo)

incense /ˈɪnsens/ *n* incienso

incensed /ɪnˈsenst/ *adj* ~ **(by/at sth)** furioso (por algo)

incentive /ɪnˈsentɪv/ *n* ~ **(to do sth)** incentivo, aliciente (para hacer algo)

incessant /ɪnˈsesnt/ *adj* incesante **incessantly** *adv* sin parar

incest /ˈɪnsest/ *n* incesto

inch /ɪntʃ/ *n* (*abrev* **in**) pulgada (*25,4 milímetros*) ☛ *Ver* Apéndice 1. LOC **not to give an inch** no ceder ni un palmo

incidence /ˈɪnsɪdəns/ *n* ~ **of sth** frecuencia, tasa, caso de algo

incident /ˈɪnsɪdənt/ *n* incidente, episodio: *without incident* sin novedad

incidental /ˌɪnsɪˈdentl/ *adj* **1** ocasional, fortuito **2** sin importancia, secundario, marginal **3** ~ **to sth** propio de algo **incidentally** *adv* **1** a propósito **2** de paso

incisive /ɪnˈsaɪsɪv/ *adj* **1** (*comentario*) incisivo **2** (*tono*) mordaz **3** (*cerebro*) penetrante

incite /ɪnˈsaɪt/ *vt* ~ **sb (to sth)** incitar a algn (a algo)

inclination /ˌɪnklɪˈneɪʃn/ *n* **1** inclinación, tendencia **2** ~ **to/for/towards sth** disposición para algo/a hacer algo **3** ~ **to do sth** deseo de hacer algo

incline /ɪnˈklaɪn/ ◆ *vt, vi* inclinar(se) ◆ /ˈɪŋklaɪn/ *n* pendiente **inclined** *adj* **to be ~ to do sth 1** (*voluntad*) inclinarse a hacer algo; estar dispuesto a hacer algo **2** (*tendencia*) ser propenso a algo/hacer algo

include /ɪnˈkluːd/ *vt* ~ **sth/sb (in/ among sth)** incluir algo/a algn (en algo) **including** *prep* incluido, inclusive

inclusion /ɪnˈkluːʒn/ *n* inclusión

inclusive /ɪnˈkluːsɪv/ *adj* **1** incluido: *to be inclusive of sth* incluir algo **2** inclusive

incoherent /ˌɪnkəʊˈhɪərənt/ *adj* incoherente

income /ˈɪŋkʌm/ *n* ingresos: *income tax* impuesto sobre la renta

incoming /ˈɪnkʌmɪŋ/ *adj* entrante

incompetent /ɪnˈkɒmpɪtənt/ *adj, n* incompetente

incomplete /ˌɪnkəmˈpliːt/ *adj* incompleto

incomprehensible /ɪnˌkɒmprɪˈhensəbl/ *adj* incomprensible

inconceivable /ˌɪnkənˈsiːvəbl/ *adj* inconcebible

inconclusive /ˌɪnkənˈkluːsɪv/ *adj* no concluyente: *The meeting was inconclusive.* La reunión no alcanzó ninguna conclusión.

incongruous /ɪnˈkɒŋgruəs/ *adj* incongruente

inconsiderate /ˌɪnkənˈsɪdərət/ *adj* desconsiderado

inconsistent /ˌɪnkənˈsɪstənt/ *adj* inconsecuente

inconspicuous /ˌɪnkənˈspɪkjuəs/ *adj* **1** apenas visible **2** poco llamativo: *to make yourself inconspicuous* procurar pasar inadvertido

inconvenience /ˌɪnkənˈviːniəns/ ◆ *n* **1** [*incontable*] inconveniente **2** molestia ◆ *vt* incomodar

inconvenient /ˌɪnkənˈviːniənt/ *adj* **1** molesto, incómodo **2** (*momento*) inoportuno

incorporate /ɪnˈkɔːpəreɪt/ *vt* **1** ~ **sth (in/into sth)** incorporar algo (a algo) **2** ~ **sth (in/into sth)** incluir algo (en algo) **3** (*USA, Com*) constituir en sociedad anónima: *incorporated company* sociedad anónima

incorrect /ˌɪnkəˈrekt/ *adj* incorrecto

increase /ˈɪŋkriːs/ ◆ *n* ~ **(in sth)** aumento (de algo) LOC **on the increase** (*coloq*) en aumento ◆ **1** *vt, vi* aumentar **2** *vt, vi* incrementar(se) **increasing** *adj* creciente **increasingly** *adv* cada vez más

incredible /ɪnˈkredəbl/ *adj* increíble

indecisive /ˌɪndɪˈsaɪsɪv/ *adj* **1** indeciso **2** no concluyente

indeed /ɪnˈdiːd/ *adv* **1** [*uso enfático*] de verdad: *Thank you very much indeed!* ¡Muchísimas gracias! **2** (*comentario, respuesta o reconocimiento*) de veras:

Did you indeed? ¿De veras? **3** (*fml*) en efecto, de hecho

indefensible /ˌɪndɪˈfensəbl/ *adj* intolerable (*comportamiento*)

indefinite /ɪnˈdefɪnət/ *adj* **1** vago **2** indefinido: *indefinite article* artículo indefinido **indefinitely** *adv* **1** indefinidamente **2** por tiempo indefinido

indelible /ɪnˈdeləbl/ *adj* imborrable

indemnity /ɪnˈdemnəti/ *n* **1** indemnización **2** indemnidad

independence /ˌɪndɪˈpendəns/ *n* independencia

independent /ˌɪndɪˈpendənt/ *adj* **1** independiente **2** (*colegio*) privado

in-depth /ˌɪn ˈdepθ/ *adj* exhaustivo

indescribable /ˌɪndɪˈskraɪbəbl/ *adj* indescriptible

index /ˈɪndeks/ *n* **1** (*pl* **indexes**) (*libro*) índice: *index finger* dedo índice ◊ *index-linked* actualizado según el coste de la vida ◊ *the retail price index* el índice de precios al consumo **2** (*pl* **indexes**) (*tb* **card index**) (*archivo*) ficha **3** (*pl* **indices** /ˈɪndɪsiːz/) (*Mat*) exponente

indicate /ˈɪndɪkeɪt/ **1** *vt* indicar **2** *vi* poner el intermitente

indication /ˌɪndɪˈkeɪʃn/ *n* **1** indicación **2** indicio, señal

indicative /ɪnˈdɪkətɪv/ *adj* indicativo

indicator /ˈɪndɪkeɪtə(r)/ *n* **1** indicador **2** (*coche*) intermitente

indices *plural de* INDEX 3

indictment /ɪnˈdaɪtmənt/ *n* **1** acusación **2** procesamiento **3** (*fig*) crítica

indifference /ɪnˈdɪfrəns/ *n* indiferencia

indifferent /ɪnˈdɪfrənt/ *adj* **1** indiferente **2** (*pey*) mediocre

indigenous /ɪnˈdɪdʒənəs/ *adj* (*fml*) indígena

indigestion /ˌɪndɪˈdʒestʃən/ *n* [*incontable*] indigestión

indignant /ɪnˈdɪgnənt/ *adj* indignado

indignation /ˌɪndɪgˈneɪʃn/ *n* indignación

indignity /ɪnˈdɪgnəti/ *n* humillación

indirect /ˌɪndəˈrekt, -daɪˈr-/ *adj* indirecto **indirectly** *adv* indirectamente

indiscreet /ˌɪndɪˈskriːt/ *adj* indiscreto

indiscretion /ˌɪndɪˈskreʃn/ *n* indiscreción

indiscriminate /ˌɪndɪˈskrɪmɪnət/ *adj* indiscriminado

indispensable /ˌɪndɪˈspensəbl/ *adj* imprescindible

indisputable /ˌɪndɪˈspjuːtəbl/ *adj* irrefutable

indistinct /ˌɪndɪˈstɪŋkt/ *adj* confuso (*poco claro*)

individual /ˌɪndɪˈvɪdʒuəl/ ◆ *adj* **1** suelto **2** individual **3** personal **4** particular, original ◆ *n* individuo **individually** *adv* **1** por separado **2** individualmente

individualism /ˌɪndɪˈvɪdʒuəlɪzəm/ *n* individualismo

indoctrination /ɪnˌdɒktrɪˈneɪʃn/ *n* adoctrinamiento

indoor /ˈɪndɔː(r)/ *adj* interior: *indoor (swimming) pool* piscina cubierta ◊ *indoor activities* actividades de sala

indoors /ˌɪnˈdɔːz/ *adv* en casa

induce /ɪnˈdjuːs; *USA* -ˈduːs/ *vt* **1** ~ **sb to do sth** inducir a algn que haga algo **2** causar **3** (*Med*) provocar el parto de

induction /ɪnˈdʌkʃn/ *n* iniciación: *an induction course* un curso de introducción

indulge /ɪnˈdʌldʒ/ **1** *vt*: *to indulge yourself* darse el placer/capricho **2** *vt* (*capricho*) complacer, satisfacer **3** *vi* ~ (**in sth**) darse el gusto de algo

indulgence /ɪnˈdʌlgəns/ *n* **1** tolerancia **2** vicio, placer **indulgent** *adj* indulgente

industrial /ɪnˈdʌstriəl/ *adj* **1** industrial: *industrial estate* polígono industrial **2** laboral **industrialist** *n* empresario

industrialization, -isation /ɪnˌdʌstrɪəlaɪˈzeɪʃn; *USA* -lɪˈz-/ *n* industrialización

industrialize, -ise /ɪnˈdʌstrɪəlaɪz/ *vt* industrializar

industrious /ɪnˈdʌstriəs/ *adj* trabajador

industry /ˈɪndəstri/ *n* (*pl* **-ies**) **1** industria **2** (*fml*) aplicación

inedible /ɪnˈedəbl/ *adj* (*fml*) no comestible

ineffective /ˌɪnɪˈfektɪv/ *adj* **1** ineficaz **2** (*persona*) incapaz

inefficiency /ˌɪnɪˈfɪʃnsi/ *n* incompetencia **inefficient** *adj* **1** ineficaz **2** incompetente

ineligible /ɪnˈelɪdʒəbl/ *adj* **to be ~ (for sth/to do sth)** no tener derecho a/para algo/hacer algo

inept /ɪˈnept/ *adj* inepto

inequality /ˌɪnɪˈkwɒləti/ *n* (*pl* **-ies**) desigualdad

inert /ɪˈnɜːt/ *adj* inerte

inertia /ɪˈnɜːʃə/ *n* inercia

inescapable /ˌɪnɪˈskeɪpəbl/ *adj* ineludible

inevitable /ɪnˈevɪtəbl/ *adj* inevitable **inevitably** *adv* inevitablemente

inexcusable /ˌɪnɪkˈskjuːzəbl/ *adj* imperdonable

inexhaustible /ˌɪnɪgˈzɔːstəbl/ *adj* inagotable

inexpensive /ˌɪnɪkˈspensɪv/ *adj* económico

inexperience /ˌɪnɪkˈspɪəriəns/ *n* inexperiencia **inexperienced** *adj* sin experiencia: *inexperienced in business* inexperto en los negocios

inexplicable /ˌɪnɪkˈsplɪkəbl/ *adj* inexplicable

infallible /ɪnˈfæləbl/ *adj* infalible **infallibility** /ɪnˌfæləˈbɪləti/ *n* infalibilidad

infamous /ˈɪnfəməs/ *adj* infame

infancy /ˈɪnfənsi/ *n* **1** infancia: *in infancy* de niño **2** (*fig*): *It was still in its infancy.* Todavía estaba en mantillas.

infant /ˈɪnfənt/ ◆ *n* niño pequeño: *infant school* escuela primaria (hasta los 7 años) ◊ *infant mortality rate* tasa de mortalidad infantil ☛ **Baby, toddler** y **child** son palabras más normales. ◆ *adj* naciente

infantile /ˈɪnfəntaɪl/ *adj* (*ofen*) infantil

infantry /ˈɪnfəntri/ *n* [*v sing o pl*] infantería

infatuated /ɪnˈfætʃueɪtɪd/ *adj* **~ (with/by sth/sb)** encaprichado (con algo/algn) **infatuation** *n* **~ (with/for sth/sb)** encaprichamiento (con algo/algn)

infect /ɪnˈfekt/ *vt* **1** infectar **2** (*fig*) contagiar **infection** *n* infección **infectious** *adj* infeccioso

infer /ɪnˈfɜː(r)/ *vt* (**-rr-**) **1** deducir **2** insinuar **inference** *n* conclusión: *by inference* por deducción

inferior /ɪnˈfɪəriə(r)/ *adj, n* inferior **inferiority** /ɪnˌfɪəriˈɒrəti/ *n* inferioridad: *inferiority complex* complejo de inferioridad

infertile /ɪnˈfɜːtaɪl; *USA* -tl/ *adj* estéril **infertility** /ˌɪnfɜːˈtɪləti/ *n* esterilidad

infest /ɪnˈfest/ *vt* infestar **infestation** *n* plaga

infidelity /ˌɪnfɪˈdeləti/ *n* (*fml*) infidelidad

infiltrate /ˈɪnfɪltreɪt/ *vt, vi* infiltrar(se)

infinite /ˈɪnfɪnət/ *adj* infinito **infinitely** *adv* muchísimo

infinitive /ɪnˈfɪnətɪv/ *n* infinitivo

infinity /ɪnˈfɪnəti/ *n* **1** infinidad **2** infinito

infirm /ɪnˈfɜːm/ *adj* débil, achacoso **infirmity** *n* (*pl* **-ies**) **1** debilidad **2** achaque

infirmary /ɪnˈfɜːməri/ *n* (*pl* **-ies**) hospital

inflamed /ɪnˈfleɪmd/ *adj* **1** (*Med*) inflamado **2 ~ (by/with sth)** (*fig*) acalorado (por algo)

inflammable /ɪnˈflæməbl/ *adj* inflamable

Nótese que **inflammable** y **flammable** son sinónimos.

inflammation /ˌɪnfləˈmeɪʃn/ *n* inflamación

inflate /ɪnˈfleɪt/ *vt, vi* inflar(se), hinchar(se)

inflation /ɪnˈfleɪʃn/ *n* inflación

inflexible /ɪnˈfleksəbl/ *adj* inflexible

inflict /ɪnˈflɪkt/ *vt* **~ sth (on sb) 1** (*sufrimiento, derrota*) infligir algo (a algn) **2** (*daño*) causar algo (a algn) **3** (*coloq, gen joc*) imponer algo a algn

influence /ˈɪnfluəns/ ◆ *n* **1** influencia **2** enchufe ◆ *vt* **1 ~ sth** influir en/sobre algo **2 ~ sb** influenciar a algn

influential /ˌɪnfluˈenʃl/ *adj* influyente

influenza /ˌɪnfluˈenzə/ (*fml*) (*coloq* **flu** /fluː/) *n* gripe

influx /ˈɪnflʌks/ *n* afluencia

inform /ɪnˈfɔːm/ **1** *vt* **~ sb (of/about sth)** informar a algn (de algo) **2** *vi* **~ against/on sb** delatar a algn **informant** *n* informante

informal /ɪnˈfɔːml/ *adj* **1** (*charla, reunión, etc*) informal, no oficial **2** (*persona, tono*) campechano **3** (*vestir*) sin etiqueta

information /ˌɪnfəˈmeɪʃn/ *n* [*incontable*] información: *a piece of information* un dato ◊ *I need some information on…* Necesito información sobre…

information technology *n* informática

informative /ɪnˈfɔːmətɪv/ *adj* informativo

informer /ɪnˈfɔːmə(r)/ *n* soplón, -ona

infrastructure /ˈɪnfrəˌstrʌktʃə(r)/ *n* infraestructura

infrequent /ɪnˈfriːkwənt/ *adj* poco frecuente

infringe /ɪnˈfrɪndʒ/ *vt* infringir, violar

infuriate /ɪnˈfjʊərieɪt/ *vt* enfurecer **infuriating** *adj* exasperante

ingenious /ɪnˈdʒiːniəs/ *adj* ingenioso

ingenuity /ˌɪndʒəˈnjuːəti; *USA* -ˈnuː-/ *n* ingenio

ingrained /ɪnˈgreɪnd/ *adj* arraigado

ingredient /ɪnˈgriːdiənt/ *n* ingrediente

inhabit /ɪnˈhæbɪt/ *vt* habitar

inhabitant /ɪnˈhæbɪtənt/ *n* habitante

inhale /ɪnˈheɪl/ **1** *vi* respirar **2** *vi* (*fumador*) tragarse el humo **3** *vt* inhalar

inherent /ɪnˈhɪərənt, -ˈher-/ *adj* ~ (**in sth/sb**) inherente (a algo/algn) **inherently** *adv* intrínsecamente

inherit /ɪnˈherɪt/ *vt* heredar **inheritance** *n* herencia

inhibit /ɪnˈhɪbɪt/ *vt* **1** ~ **sb** (**from doing sth**) impedir a algn (hacer algo) **2** (*un proceso, etc*) dificultar **inhibited** *adj* cohibido **inhibition** *n* inhibición

inhospitable /ˌɪnhɒˈspɪtəbl/ *adj* **1** inhospitalario **2** (*fig*) inhóspito

inhuman /ɪnˈhjuːmən/ *adj* inhumano, despiadado

initial /ɪˈnɪʃl/ ◆ *adj*, *n* inicial ◆ *vt* (**-ll-**, *USA* **-l-**) poner las iniciales en **initially** *adv* en un principio, inicialmente

initiate /ɪˈnɪʃɪeɪt/ *vt* **1** (*fml*) iniciar **2** (*proceso*) entablar **initiation** *n* iniciación

initiative /ɪˈnɪʃətɪv/ *n* iniciativa

inject /ɪnˈdʒekt/ *vt* inyectar **injection** *n* inyección

injure /ˈɪndʒə(r)/ *vt* herir, lesionar: *Five people were injured in the crash.* Cinco personas resultaron heridas en el accidente. ☛ *Ver nota en* HERIDA **injured** *adj* **1** herido, lesionado **2** (*tono*) ofendido

injury /ˈɪndʒəri/ *n* (*pl* **-ies**) **1** herida, lesión: *injury time* tiempo de descuento ☛ *Ver nota en* HERIDA **2** (*fig*) perjuicio

injustice /ɪnˈdʒʌstɪs/ *n* injusticia

ink /ɪŋk/ *n* tinta

inkling /ˈɪŋklɪŋ/ *n* ~ (**of sth/that…**) indicio, idea (de algo/de que…)

inland /ˈɪnlənd/ ◆ *adj* (del) interior ◆ /ˌɪnˈlænd/ *adv* hacia el interior

Inland Revenue *n* (*GB*) Hacienda

in-laws /ˈɪn lɔːz/ *n* [*pl*] (*coloq*) familia política

inlet /ˈɪnlet/ *n* **1** ensenada **2** entrada

inmate /ˈɪnmeɪt/ *n* interno, -a (*en un recinto vigilado*)

inn /ɪn/ *n* (*GB*) **1** taberna **2** (*antic*) posada

innate /ɪˈneɪt/ *adj* innato

inner /ˈɪnə(r)/ *adj* **1** interior **2** íntimo

innermost /ˈɪnəməʊst/ *adj* **1** (*fig*) más secreto/íntimo **2** más recóndito

innocent /ˈɪnəsnt/ *adj* inocente **innocence** *n* inocencia

innocuous /ɪˈnɒkjuəs/ *adj* **1** (*comentario*) inofensivo **2** (*sustancia*) inocuo

innovate /ˈɪnəveɪt/ *vi* introducir novedades **innovation** *n* innovación **innovative** (*tb* **innovatory**) *adj* innovador

innuendo /ˌɪnjuˈendəʊ/ *n* (*pey*) insinuación

innumerable /ɪˈnjuːmərəbl; *USA* ɪˈnuː-/ *adj* innumerable

inoculate /ɪˈnɒkjuleɪt/ (*tb* **innoculate**) *vt* vacunar **inoculation** *n* vacuna

input /ˈɪnpʊt/ *n* **1** contribución **2** (*Informát*) entrada

inquest /ˈɪŋkwest/ *n* ~ (**on sb/into sth**) investigación (judicial) (acerca de algn/algo)

inquire *Ver* ENQUIRE

inquiry (*tb* **enquiry**) /ɪnˈkwaɪəri; *USA* ˈɪnkwəri/ *n* (*pl* **-ies**) **1** (*fml*) pregunta **2** **inquiries** [*pl*] oficina de información **3** investigación

inquisition /ˌɪnkwɪˈzɪʃn/ *n* (*fml*) interrogatorio

inquisitive /ɪnˈkwɪzətɪv/ *adj* inquisitivo

insane /ɪnˈseɪn/ *adj* loco

insanity /ɪnˈsænəti/ *n* demencia, locura

insatiable /ɪnˈseɪʃəbl/ *adj* insaciable

inscribe /ɪnˈskraɪb/ *vt* ~ **sth** (**in/on sth**) grabar algo (en algo) **inscribed** *adj* grabado: *a plaque inscribed with a quotation from Dante* una placa con una cita de Dante grabada

inscription /ɪnˈskrɪpʃn/ *n* inscripción (*en piedra, etc*), dedicatoria (*de un libro*)

insect /ˈɪnsekt/ *n* insecto **insecticide** /ɪnˈsektɪsaɪd/ *n* insecticida

insecure /ˌɪnsɪˈkjʊə(r)/ *adj* inseguro **insecurity** *n* inseguridad

insensitive /ɪnˈsensətɪv/ *adj* **1** ~ (**to sth**) (*persona*) insensible (a algo) **2** (*acto*) falto de sensibilidad **insensitivity** /ɪnˌsensəˈtɪvəti/ *n* insensibilidad

inseparable /ɪnˈseprəbl/ *adj* inseparable

insert /ɪnˈsɜːt/ *vt* introducir, insertar

inside /ɪnˈsaɪd/ ◆ *n* **1** interior: *The door was locked from the inside.* La puerta estaba cerrada por dentro. **2 insides** [*pl*] (*coloq*) tripas LOC **inside out 1** del revés: *You've got your jumper on inside out.* Llevas el jersey del revés. ☛ *Ver dibujo en* REVÉS **2** de arriba abajo: *She knows these streets inside out.* Se conoce estas calles como la palma de la mano. ◆ *adj* [*antes de sustantivo*] **1** interior, interno: *the inside pocket* el bolsillo interior **2** interno: *inside information* información interna ◆ *prep* (*USA* **inside of**) dentro de: *Is there anything inside the box?* ¿Hay algo dentro de la caja? ◆ *adv* (a)dentro: *Let's go inside.* Vamos adentro. ◊ *Pete's inside.* Pete está dentro. **insider** *n* alguien de dentro (*empresa, grupo*)

insight /ˈɪnsaɪt/ *n* **1** perspicacia, entendimiento **2** ~ (**into sth**) idea, percepción (de algo)

insignificant /ˌɪnsɪgˈnɪfɪkənt/ *adj* insignificante **insignificance** *n* insignificancia

insincere /ˌɪnsɪnˈsɪə(r)/ *adj* falso, hipócrita **insincerity** *n* insinceridad

insinuate /ɪnˈsɪnjueɪt/ *vt* insinuar **insinuation** *n* insinuación

insist /ɪnˈsɪst/ *vi* **1** ~ (**on sth**) insistir (en algo) **2** ~ **on** (**doing**) **sth** empeñarse en (hacer) algo: *She always insists on a room to herself.* Siempre se empeña en tener una habitación para ella sola.

insistence /ɪnˈsɪstəns/ *n* insistencia **insistent** *adj* insistente

insolent /ˈɪnsələnt/ *adj* insolente **insolence** *n* insolencia

insomnia /ɪnˈsɒmniə/ *n* insomnio

inspect /ɪnˈspekt/ *vt* **1** inspeccionar **2** (*equipaje*) registrar **inspection** *n* inspección **inspector** *n* **1** inspector, -ora **2** (*de billetes*) revisor, -ora

inspiration /ˌɪnspəˈreɪʃn/ *n* inspiración

inspire /ɪnˈspaɪə(r)/ *vt* **1** inspirar **2** ~ **sb** (**with sth**) (*entusiasmo, etc*) infundir algo (en algn)

instability /ˌɪnstəˈbɪləti/ *n* inestabilidad

install (*USA tb* **instal**) /ɪnˈstɔːl/ *vt* instalar

installation /ˌɪnstəˈleɪʃn/ *n* instalación

instalment (*USA tb* **installment**) /ɪnˈstɔːlmənt/ *n* **1** (*publicaciones*) entrega, fascículo **2** (*televisión*) episodio **3** ~ (**on sth**) (*pago*) plazo (de algo): *to pay in instalments* pagar a plazos

instance /ˈɪnstəns/ *n* caso LOC **for instance** por ejemplo

instant /ˈɪnstənt/ ◆ *n* instante ◆ *adj* **1** inmediato **2** *instant coffee* café instantáneo **instantly** *adv* inmediatamente, de inmediato

instantaneous /ˌɪnstənˈteɪniəs/ *adj* instantáneo

instead /ɪnˈsted/ ◆ *adv* en vez de eso ◆ *prep* ~ **of sth/sb** en vez de algo/algn

instigate /ˈɪnstɪgeɪt/ *vt* instigar **instigation** *n* instigación

instil (*USA* **instill**) /ɪnˈstɪl/ *vt* (**-ll-**) ~ **sth** (**in/into sb**) infundir algo (a algn)

instinct /ˈɪnstɪŋkt/ *n* instinto **instinctive** /ɪnˈstɪŋktɪv/ *adj* instintivo

institute /ˈɪnstɪtjuːt; *USA* -tuːt/ ◆ *n* instituto, centro ◆ *vt* (*fml*) iniciar (*investigación*)

institution /ˌɪnstɪˈtjuːʃn; *USA* -ˈtuːʃn/ *n* institución **institutional** *adj* institucional

instruct /ɪnˈstrʌkt/ *vt* **1** ~ **sb** (**in sth**) enseñar (algo) a algn **2** dar instrucciones

instruction /ɪnˈstrʌkʃn/ *n* **1 instruction(s)** (**to do sth**) instrucción, -iones (para hacer algo) **2** ~ (**in sth**) formación (en algo)

instructive /ɪnˈstrʌktɪv/ *adj* instructivo

instructor /ɪnˈstrʌktə(r)/ *n* profesor, -ora, instructor, -ora

instrument /ˈɪnstrəmənt/ *n* instrumento

instrumental /ˌɪnstrəˈmentl/ *adj* **1 to be ~ in doing sth** contribuir materialmente a hacer algo **2** (*Mús*) instrumental

insufferable /ɪnˈsʌfrəbl/ *adj* insufrible

insufficient /ˌɪnsəˈfɪʃnt/ *adj* insuficiente

insular /ˈɪnsjələ(r); *USA* -sələr/ *adj* estrecho de miras

insulate /ˈɪnsjuleɪt; *USA* -səl-/ *vt* aislar **insulation** *n* aislamiento

insult /ˈɪnsʌlt/ ◆ *n* insulto ◆ /ɪnˈsʌlt/ *vt* insultar **insulting** *adj* insultante

insurance /ɪnˈʃɔːrəns; *USA* -ˈʃʊər-/ *n* [*incontable*] seguro (*Fin*)

insure /ɪnˈʃʊə(r)/ *vt* **1** ~ **sth/sb (against sth)** asegurar algo/a algn (contra algo): *to insure sth for £5000* asegurar algo en 5.000 libras **2** (*USA*) *Ver* ENSURE

intake /ˈɪnteɪk/ *n* **1** (*personas*) número admitido: *We have an annual intake of 20.* Admitimos a 20 cada año. **2** (*de comida, etc*) consumo

integral /ˈɪntɪgrəl/ *adj* esencial: *an integral part of sth* una parte fundamental de algo

integrate /ˈɪntɪgreɪt/ *vt, vi* integrar(se) **integration** *n* integración

integrity /ɪnˈtegrəti/ *n* integridad

intellectual /ˌɪntəˈlektʃuəl/ *adj, n* intelectual **intellectually** *adv* intelectualmente

intelligence /ɪnˈtelɪdʒəns/ *n* inteligencia **intelligent** *adj* inteligente **intelligently** *adv* inteligentemente

intend /ɪnˈtend/ *vt* **1** ~ **to do sth** pensar hacer algo; tener la intención de hacer algo **2 intended for sth/sb** destinado a algo/algn: *It is intended for Sally.* Está destinado a Sally. ◇ *They're not intended for eating/to be eaten.* No son para comer. **3** ~ **sb to do sth**: *I intend you to take over.* Es mi intención que te hagas cargo. ◇ *You weren't intended to hear that remark.* Tú no tenías que haber oído ese comentario. **4** ~ **sth as sth**: *It was intended as a joke.* Se suponía que era una broma.

intense /ɪnˈtens/ *adj* (**-er**, **-est**) **1** intenso **2** (*emociones*) ardiente, fuerte **3** (*persona*) nervioso, serio **intensely** *adv* intensamente, sumamente **intensify** *vt, vi* (*pret, pp* **-fied**) intensificar(se), aumentar(se) **intensity** *n* intensidad, fuerza

intensive /ɪnˈtensɪv/ *adj* intensivo: *intensive care* cuidados intensivos

intent /ɪnˈtent/ ◆ *adj* **1** (*concentrado*) atento **2 to be** ~ **on/upon doing sth** estar resuelto a hacer algo **3 to be** ~ **on/upon (doing) sth** estar absorto en algo/haciendo algo ◆ *n* LOC **to all intents (and purposes)** a efectos prácticos

intention /ɪnˈtenʃn/ *n* intención: *to have the intention of doing sth* tener la intención de hacer algo ◇ *I have no intention of doing it.* No tengo intención de hacerlo. **intentional** *adj* intencionado *Ver tb* DELIBERATE[1] **intentionally** *adv* intencionadamente

intently /ɪnˈtentli/ *adv* atentamente

interact /ˌɪntərˈækt/ *vi* **1** (*personas*) relacionarse entre sí **2** (*cosas*) influirse mutuamente **interaction** *n* **1** relación (*entre personas*) **2** interacción

intercept /ˌɪntəˈsept/ *vt* interceptar

interchange /ˌɪntəˈtʃeɪndʒ/ ◆ *vt* intercambiar ◆ /ˈɪntətʃeɪndʒ/ *n* intercambio **interchangeable** /ˌɪntəˈtʃeɪndʒəbl/ *adj* intercambiable

interconnect /ˌɪntəkəˈnekt/ *vi* **1** interconectarse, conectarse entre sí **2** (*tb* **intercommunicate**) comunicarse entre sí **interconnected** *adj*: *to be interconnected* tener conexión entre sí **interconnection** *n* conexión

intercourse /ˈɪntəkɔːs/ *n* (*fml*) relaciones sexuales, coito

interest /ˈɪntrəst/ ◆ *n* **1** ~ **(in sth)** interés (por algo): *It is of no interest to me.* No me interesa. **2** afición: *her main interest in life* lo que más le interesa en la vida **3** (*Fin*) interés LOC **in sb's interest(s)** en interés de algn **in the interest(s) of sth** en aras de/con el fin de: *in the interest(s) of safety* por razones de seguridad *Ver tb* VEST[2] ◆ *vt* **1** interesar **2** ~ **sb in sth** hacer que algn se interese por algo

interested /ˈɪntrəstɪd/ *adj* interesado: *to be interested in sth* interesarse por algo

interesting /ˈɪntrəstɪŋ/ *adj* interesante **interestingly** *adv* curiosamente

interfere /ˌɪntəˈfɪə(r)/ *vi* **1** ~ **(in sth)** entrometerse (en algo) **2** ~ **with sth** toquetear algo **3** ~ **with sth** interponerse en algo, dificultar algo **interference** *n* [*incontable*] **1** ~ **(in sth)**

intromisión (en algo) **2** (*Radio*) interferencias **3** (*USA, Dep*) *Ver* OBSTRUCTION **interfering** *adj* entrometido

interim /ˈɪntərɪm/ ◆ *adj* provisional ◆ *n* LOC **in the interim** en el ínterin

interior /ɪnˈtɪəriə(r)/ *adj, n* interior

interlude /ˈɪntəluːd/ *n* intermedio

intermediate /ˌɪntəˈmiːdiət/ *adj* intermedio

intermission /ˌɪntəˈmɪʃn/ *n* descanso (*Teat*)

intern /ɪnˈtɜːn/ *vt* internar

internal /ɪnˈtɜːnl/ *adj* interno, interior: *internal affairs* asuntos internos ◇ *internal injuries* heridas internas ◇ *internal market* mercado interior **internally** *adv* internamente, interiormente

international /ˌɪntəˈnæʃnəl/ ◆ *adj* internacional ◆ *n* (*Dep*) **1** campeonato internacional **2** jugador, -ora internacional **internationally** *adv* internacionalmente

interpret /ɪnˈtɜːprɪt/ *vt* **1** interpretar, entender **2** traducir

> **Interpret** se utiliza para referirse a la traducción oral, y **translate** a la traducción escrita.

interpretation interpretación **interpreter** *n* intérprete ☛ *Comparar con* TRANSLATOR *en* TRANSLATE

interrelated /ˌɪntərɪˈleɪtɪd/ *adj* interrelacionado

interrogate /ɪnˈterəgeɪt/ *vt* interrogar **interrogation** *n* interrogación **interrogator** *n* interrogador, -ora

interrogative /ˌɪntəˈrɒgətɪv/ *adj* interrogativo

interrupt /ˌɪntəˈrʌpt/ *vt, vi* interrumpir: *I'm sorry to interrupt but there's a phone call for you.* Perdonad que os interrumpa, pero te llaman por teléfono. **interruption** *n* interrupción

intersect /ˌɪntəˈsekt/ *vi* cruzarse, cortar(se) **intersection** *n* intersección, cruce

interspersed /ˌɪntəˈspɜːst/ *adj* ~ **with sth** salteado de algo

intertwine /ˌɪntəˈtwaɪn/ *vt, vi* entrelazar(se)

interval /ˈɪntəvl/ *n* **1** intervalo **2** (*GB, Teat*) entreacto **3** (*Dep*) descanso

intervene /ˌɪntəˈviːn/ *vi* (*fml*) **1** ~ (**in sth**) intervenir (en algo) **2** (*tiempo*) transcurrir **3** interponerse **intervening** *adj* intermedio

intervention /ˌɪntəˈvenʃn/ *n* intervención

interview /ˈɪntəvjuː/ ◆ *n* entrevista ◆ *vt* entrevistar **interviewee** *n* entrevistado, -a **interviewer** *n* entrevistador, -ora

interweave /ˌɪntəˈwiːv/ *vt, vi* (*pret* **-wove** /-ˈwəʊv/ *pp* **-woven** /-ˈwəʊvn/) entretejer(se)

intestine /ɪnˈtestɪn/ *n* intestino: *small/large intestine* intestino delgado/grueso

intimacy /ˈɪntɪməsi/ *n* intimidad

intimate[1] /ˈɪntɪmət/ *adj* **1** (*amigo, restaurante, etc*) íntimo **2** (*amistad*) estrecho **3** (*fml*) (*conocimiento*) profundo

intimate[2] /ˈɪntɪmeɪt/ *vt* ~ **sth** (**to sb**) (*fml*) dar a entender, insinuar algo (a algn) **intimation** *n* (*fml*) indicación, indicio

intimidate /ɪnˈtɪmɪdeɪt/ *vt* intimidar **intimidation** *n* intimidación

into /ˈɪntə/ ☛ Antes de vocal y al final de la frase se pronuncia /ˈɪntuː/. *prep* **1** (*dirección*) en, dentro de: *to come into a room* entrar en una habitación ◇ *He put it into the box.* Lo metió dentro de la caja. **2** a: *to get into a bus* subir al autobús ◇ *She went into town.* Fue al centro. ◇ *to translate into Spanish* traducir al español **3** (*tiempo, distancia*): *long into the night* bien entrada la noche ◇ *far into the distance* a lo lejos **4** (*Mat*): *12 into 144 goes 12 times.* 144 dividido por 12 son 12. LOC **to be into sth** (*coloq*): *She's into motor bikes.* Es muy aficionada a las motos. ☛ Para los usos de **into** en PHRASAL VERBS ver las entradas de los verbos correspondientes, p.ej. **to look into** en LOOK[1].

intolerable /ɪnˈtɒlərəbl/ *adj* intolerable, insufrible

intolerance /ɪnˈtɒlərəns/ *n* intolerancia, intransigencia

intolerant /ɪnˈtɒlərənt/ *adj* (*pey*) intolerante

intonation /ˌɪntəˈneɪʃn/ *n* entonación

intoxicated /ɪnˈtɒksɪkeɪtɪd/ *adj* (*fml, lit y fig*) ebrio

intoxication /ɪnˌtɒksɪˈkeɪʃn/ *n* embriaguez

intrepid /ɪnˈtrepɪd/ *adj* intrépido

intricate /ˈɪntrɪkət/ *adj* intrincado, complejo

intrigue /ˈɪntriːg, ɪnˈtriːg/ ◆ *n* intriga ◆ /ɪnˈtriːg/ **1** *vi* intrigar **2** *vt* fascinar **intriguing** *adj* intrigante, fascinante

intrinsic /ɪnˈtrɪnsɪk, -zɪk/ *adj* intrínseco

introduce /ˌɪntrəˈdjuːs; *USA* -ˈduːs/ *vt* **1** ~ **sth/sb (to sb)** presentar algo/algn (a algn) ☛ *Ver nota en* PRESENTAR **2** ~ **sb to sth** iniciar a algn en algo **3** (*producto, reforma, etc*) introducir

introduction /ˌɪntrəˈdʌkʃn/ *n* **1** presentación **2** ~ **(to sth)** prólogo (de algo) **3** [*sing*] ~ **to sth** iniciación a/en algo **4** [*incontable*] introducción (*producto, reforma, etc*)

introductory /ˌɪntrəˈdʌktəri/ *adj* **1** (*capítulo, curso*) preliminar **2** (*oferta*) introductorio

introvert /ˈɪntrəvɜːt/ *n* introvertido, -a

intrude /ɪnˈtruːd/ *vi* (*fml*) **1** importunar, molestar **2** ~ **(on/upon sth)** entrometerse, inmiscuirse (en algo) **intruder** *n* intruso, -a **intrusion** *n* **1** [*incontable*] invasión **2** [*contable*] intromisión **intrusive** *adj* intruso

intuition /ˌɪntjuˈɪʃn; *USA* -tu-/ *n* intuición

intuitive /ɪnˈtjuːɪtɪv; *USA* -ˈtuː-/ *adj* intuitivo

inundate /ˈɪnʌndeɪt/ *vt* ~ **sth/sb (with sth)** inundar algo/a algn (de algo): *We were inundated with applications.* Nos vimos inundados de solicitudes.

invade /ɪnˈveɪd/ *vt, vi* invadir **invader** *n* invasor, -ora

invalid /ˈɪnvəlɪd, ˈɪnvəliːd/ ◆ *n* inválido, -a ◆ /ɪnˈvælɪd/ *adj* no válido

invalidate /ɪnˈvælɪdeɪt/ *vt* invalidar, anular

invaluable /ɪnˈvæljuəbl/ *adj* inestimable

invariably /ɪnˈveəriəbli/ *adv* invariablemente

invasion /ɪnˈveɪʒn/ *n* invasión

invent /ɪnˈvent/ *vt* inventar **invention** *n* **1** invención **2** invento **inventive** *adj* **1** (*poderes*) de invención **2** que tiene mucha imaginación **inventiveness** *n* inventiva **inventor** *n* inventor, -ora

inventory /ˈɪnvəntri; *USA* -tɔːri/ *n* (*pl* **-ies**) inventario

invert /ɪnˈvɜːt/ *vt* invertir: *in inverted commas* entre comillas

invertebrate /ɪnˈvɜːtɪbrət/ *adj, n* invertebrado

invest /ɪnˈvest/ **1** *vt* invertir **2** *vi* ~ **(in sth)** invertir (en algo)

investigate /ɪnˈvestɪgeɪt/ *vt, vi* investigar

investigation /ɪnˌvestɪˈgeɪʃn/ *n* ~ **into sth** investigación de algo

investigative /ɪnˈvestɪgətɪv; *USA* -geɪtɪv/ *adj*: *investigative journalism* periodismo de investigación

investigator /ɪnˈvestɪgeɪtə(r)/ *n* investigador, -ora

investment /ɪnˈvestmənt/ *n* ~ **(in sth)** inversión (en algo)

investor /ɪnˈvestə(r)/ *n* inversor, -ora

invigorating /ɪnˈvɪgəreɪtɪŋ/ *adj* vigorizante, estimulante

invincible /ɪnˈvɪnsəbl/ *adj* invencible

invisible /ɪnˈvɪzəbl/ *adj* invisible

invitation /ˌɪnvɪˈteɪʃn/ *n* invitación

invite /ɪnˈvaɪt/ ◆ *vt* **1** ~ **sb (to/for sth)/(to do sth)** invitar a algn (a algo)/(a hacer algo): *to invite trouble* buscarse problemas **2** (*sugerencias, aportes*) pedir, solicitar PHR V **to invite sb back 1** invitar a algn a casa (*para corresponder a su invitación previa*) **2** invitar a algn a volver con uno a su casa **to invite sb in** invitar a algn a entrar **to invite sb out** invitar a algn a salir **to invite sb over/round** invitar a algn a casa ◆ /ˈɪnvaɪt/ *n* (*coloq*) invitación **inviting** /ɪnˈvaɪtɪŋ/ *adj* **1** atractivo, tentador **2** (*comida*) apetitoso

invoice /ˈɪnvɔɪs/ ◆ *n* ~ **(for sth)** factura (de algo) ◆ *vt* ~ **sth/sb** pasar factura a algo/algn

involuntary /ɪnˈvɒləntri/ *adj* involuntario

involve /ɪnˈvɒlv/ *vt* **1** suponer, implicar: *The job involves me/my living in London.* El trabajo requiere que viva en Londres. **2** ~ **sb in sth** hacer participar a algn en algo: *to be involved in sth* participar en algo **3** ~ **sb in sth** meter, enredar a algn en algo: *Don't involve me in your problems.* No me mezcles en tus problemas. **4** ~ **sb in sth** (*esp crimen*) involucrar a algn en algo: *to be/get involved in sth* estar involucrado/involucrarse en algo **5 to be/become/get involved with sb** (*pey*) estar enredado, enredarse con algn **6 to be/ become/get involved with sb** (*emocionalmente*) estar liado, liarse con algn **involved** *adj* complicado, enrevesado **involvement** *n* **1** ~ (**in sth**) implicación, compromiso, participación (en algo) **2** ~ (**with sb**) compromiso, relación (con algn)

inward /ˈɪnwəd/ ◆ *adj* **1** (*pensamientos, etc*) interior, íntimo: *to give an inward sigh* suspirar uno para sí **2** (*dirección*) hacia dentro ◆ *adv* (*tb* **inwards**) hacia dentro **inwardly** *adv* **1** por dentro **2** (*suspirar, sonreír, etc*) para sí

IQ /ˌaɪˈkjuː/ *abrev* **intelligence quotient** coeficiente de inteligencia: *She's got an IQ of 120.* Tiene un coeficiente de inteligencia de 120.

iris /ˈaɪrɪs/ *n* **1** (*Anat*) iris **2** (*Bot*) lirio

iron /ˈaɪən; *USA* ˈaɪərn/ ◆ *n* **1** (*Quím*) hierro: *the Iron Curtain* el Telón de Acero **2** (*para ropa*) plancha ◆ *vt* planchar PHR V **to iron sth out 1** (*arrugas*) planchar algo **2** (*problemas, etc*) resolver, allanar **ironing** *n* **1** planchado: *to do the ironing* planchar ◊ *ironing board* tabla de planchar **2** ropa por planchar, ropa planchada

ironic /aɪˈrɒnɪk/ *adj* irónico: *It is ironic that we only won the last match.* Resulta irónico que sólo hayamos ganado el último partido. ◊ *He gave an ironic smile.* Sonrió con sorna. ☛ *Comparar con* SARCASTIC *en* SARCASM **ironically** *adv* irónicamente, con ironía: *He smiled ironically.* Sonrió con sorna.

irony /ˈaɪrəni/ *n* (*pl* **-ies**) ironía

irrational /ɪˈræʃənl/ *adj* irracional **irrationality** /ɪræʃəˈnæləti/ *n* irracionalidad **irrationally** *adv* de forma irracional

irrelevant /ɪˈreləvənt/ *adj* que no viene al caso: *irrelevant remarks* observaciones que no vienen al caso **irrelevance** *n* algo que no viene al caso: *the irrelevance of the curriculum to their own life* lo poco que el programa tiene que ver con sus vidas

irresistible /ˌɪrɪˈzɪstəbl/ *adj* irresistible **irresistibly** *adv* irresistiblemente

irrespective of /ˌɪrɪˈspektɪv əv/ *prep* sin consideración a

irresponsible /ˌɪrɪˈspɒnsəbl/ *adj* irresponsable: *It was irresponsible of you.* Fue una irresponsabilidad de tu parte.

irresponsibility /ˌɪrɪˌspɒnsəˈbɪləti/ *n* irresponsabilidad **irresponsibly** *adv* de forma irresponsable

irrigation /ˌɪrɪˈgeɪʃn/ *n* regadío

irritable /ˈɪrɪtəbl/ *adj* irritable **irritability** /ˌɪrɪtəˈbɪləti/ *n* irritabilidad **irritably** *adv* con irritación

irritate /ˈɪrɪteɪt/ *vt* irritar: *He's easily irritated.* Se irrita con facilidad. **irritating** *adj* irritante: *How irritating!* ¡Qué fastidio! **irritation** *n* irritación

is /s, z, ɪz/ *Ver* BE

Islam /ɪzˈlɑːm, ˈɪzlɑːm/ *n* Islam

island /ˈaɪlənd/ *n* (*abrev* **I**, **Is**) isla: *a desert island* una isla desierta **islander** *n* isleño, -a

isle /aɪl/ *n* (*abrev* **I**, **Is**) isla ☛ Se usa sobre todo en nombres de lugares, p.ej. *the Isle of Man. Comparar con* ISLAND

isn't /ˈɪznt/ = IS NOT *Ver* BE

isolate /ˈaɪsəleɪt/ *vt* ~ **sth/sb** (**from sth/ sb**) aislar algo/a algn (de algo/algn) **isolated** *adj* aislado **isolation** *n* aislamiento LOC **in isolation** (**from sth/sb**) aislado (de algo/algn): *Looked at in isolation...* Considerado fuera del contexto...

issue /ˈɪʃuː, ˈɪsjuː/ ◆ *n* **1** asunto, cuestión **2** emisión, provisión **3** (*de una revista, etc*) número LOC **to make an issue** (**out**) **of sth** hacer de algo un problema: *Let's not make an issue of it.* No lo convirtamos en un problema. ◆ **1** *vt* ~ **sth** (**to sb**) distribuir algo (a algn) **2** *vt* ~ **sb with sth** proveer a algn de algo **3** *vt* (*visado, etc*) expedir **4** *vt* publicar **5** *vt* (*sellos, etc*) poner en circulación **6** *vt* (*llamada*) emitir **7** *vi* ~ **from sth** (*fml*) salir de algo

it /ɪt/ *pron pers*

- **como sujeto y objeto** ☛ **It** sustituye a un animal o una cosa. También se puede utilizar para referirse a un bebé. **1** [*como sujeto*] él, ella, ello: *Where is it?* ¿Dónde está? ◊ *The baby is crying, I think it's hungry.* El bebé está llorando, creo que tiene hambre. ◊ *Who is it?* ¿Quién es? ◊ *It's me.* Soy yo. ☛ El *pron pers* no se puede omitir en inglés. **2** [*como objeto directo*] lo, la: *Did you buy it?* ¿Lo compraste? ◊ *Give it to me.* Dámelo. **3** [*como objeto indirecto*] le: *Give it some milk.* Dale un poco de leche. **4** [*después de preposición*]: *That* *box is heavy. What's inside it?* Esa caja pesa mucho, ¿qué hay dentro?

• **frases impersonales** ☛ En muchos casos **it** carece de significado, y se utiliza como sujeto gramatical para construir oraciones que en español suelen ser impersonales. Normalmente no se traduce. **1** (*de tiempo, distancia y tiempo atmosférico*): *It's ten past twelve.* Son las doce y diez. ◊ *It's May 12.* Es el 12 de mayo. ◊ *It's two miles to the beach.* Hay dos millas hasta la playa. ◊ *It's a long time since they left.* Hace mucho tiempo que se marcharon. ◊ *It's raining.* Está lloviendo. ◊ *It's hot.* Hace calor. **2** (*en otras construcciones*): *Does it matter what colour the hat is?* ¿Importa de qué color sea el sombrero? ◊ *I'll come at seven if it's convenient.* Vendré a las siete, si te va bien. ◊ *It's Jim who's the clever one, not his brother.* Es Jim el que es listo, no su hermano.

LOC **that's it 1** ya está **2** eso es todo **3** ya está bien **4** eso es **that's just it** ahí está el problema **this is it** llegó la hora

italics /ɪˈtælɪks/ *n* [*pl*] cursiva

itch /ɪtʃ/ ◆ *n* picor ◆ *vi* picar: *My leg itches.* Me pica la pierna. ◊ *to be itching to do sth* tener muchas ganas de hacer algo **itchy** *adj* que pica: *My skin is itchy.* Me pica la piel.

it'd /ˈɪtəd/ **1** = IT HAD *Ver* HAVE **2** = IT WOULD *Ver* WOULD

item /ˈaɪtəm/ *n* **1** artículo **2** (*tb* **news item**) noticia

itinerary /aɪˈtɪnərəri; *USA* -reri/ *n* (*pl* **-ies**) itinerario

it'll /ˈɪtl/ = IT WILL *Ver* WILL

its /ɪts/ *adj pos* su(s) (*que pertenece a una cosa, un animal o un bebé.*): *The table isn't in its place.* La mesa no está en su sitio. ☛ *Ver nota en* MY

it's /ɪts/ **1** = IT IS *Ver* BE **2** = IT HAS *Ver* HAVE ☛ *Comparar con* ITS

itself /ɪtˈself/ *pron* **1** [*uso reflexivo*] se: *The cat was washing itself.* El gato se estaba lavando. **2** [*uso enfático*] él mismo, ella misma, ello mismo **3** *She is kindness itself.* Es la bondad personificada. LOC **by itself 1** por sí mismo **2** solo **in itself** de por sí

I've /aɪv/ = I HAVE *Ver* HAVE

ivory /ˈaɪvəri/ *n* marfil

ivy /ˈaɪvi/ *n* hiedra

Jj

J, j /dʒeɪ/ *n* (*pl* **J's, j's** /dʒeɪz/) J, j: *J for Jack* J de Juan ☛ *Ver ejemplos en* A, a

jab /dʒæb/ ◆ *vt, vi* (**-bb-**) pinchar: *He jabbed his finger at the door.* Apuntó a la puerta con el dedo. ◊ *She jabbed at a potato with her fork.* Intentó ensartar una patata con su tenedor. PHR V **to jab sth into sth/sb** hincar algo en algo/a algn ◆ *n* **1** inyección **2** pinchazo **3** golpe

jack /dʒæk/ *n* **1** (*Mec*) gato **2** (*tb* **knave**) jota (*baraja francesa*)

jackal /ˈdʒækl/ *n* chacal

jackdaw /ˈdʒækdɔː/ *n* grajilla

jacket /ˈdʒækɪt/ *n* **1** americana, chaqueta ☛ *Comparar con* CARDIGAN **2** cazadora **3** (*de un libro*) sobrecubierta

jackpot /ˈdʒækpɒt/ *n* premio gordo

jade /dʒeɪd/ *adj, n* jade

jaded /ˈdʒeɪdɪd/ *adj* (*pey*) agotado, con falta de entusiasmo

jagged /ˈdʒægɪd/ *adj* dentado

jaguar /ˈdʒægjʊə(r)/ *n* jaguar

jail /dʒeɪl/ *n* cárcel

jam /dʒæm/ ◆ *n* **1** mermelada ☛ *Comparar con* MARMALADE **2** atasco: *traffic jam* embotellamiento **3** (*coloq*) aprieto: *to be in/get into a jam* estar/meterse en un aprieto ◆ (**-mm-**) **1** *vt* **to jam sth into, under, etc sth** meter algo a la fuerza en, debajo, etc de algo: *He jammed the flowers into a vase.* Metió las flores en un jarrón, todas apretujadas. **2** *vt, vi* apretujar(se): *The three of them were jammed into a phone booth.* Los tres estaban apretujados en una cabina de teléfonos. **3** *vt, vi* atascar(se), obstruir(se) **4** *vt* (*Radio*) interferir

jangle /ˈdʒæŋgl/ *vt, vi* (hacer) sonar de manera discordante

January /ˈdʒænjuəri; *USA* -jʊeri/ *n* (*abrev* **Jan**) enero: *They are getting married this January/in January.* Se van a casar en enero. ◊ *on January 1st* el 1 de enero ◊ *every January* todos los meses de enero ◊ *next January* en enero del año que viene ☛ Los nombres de los meses en inglés se escriben con mayúscula.

jar[1] /dʒɑː(r)/ *n* **1** tarro, bote ☛ *Ver dibujo en* CONTAINER **2** jarra

jar[2] /dʒɑː(r)/ (**-rr-**) **1** *vi* **to jar (on sth/sb)** irritar (algo/a algn) **2** *vi* **to jar (with sth)** (*fig*) desentonar (con algo) **3** *vt* golpear

jargon /ˈdʒɑːgən/ *n* jerga

jasmine /ˈdʒæzmɪn; *USA* ˈdʒæzmən/ *n* jazmín

jaundice /ˈdʒɔːndɪs/ *n* ictericia **jaundiced** *adj* amargado

javelin /ˈdʒævlɪn/ *n* jabalina

jaw /dʒɔː/ *n* **1** [*gen pl*] (*persona*) mandíbula **2** (*animal*) quijada **3 jaws** [*pl*] fauces

jazz /dʒæz/ ◆ *n* jazz ◆ PHR V **to jazz sth up** animar algo **jazzy** (*coloq*) *adj* vistoso

jealous /ˈdʒeləs/ *adj* **1** celoso: *He's very jealous of her male friends.* Tiene muchos celos de sus amigos. **2** envidioso: *I'm very jealous of your new car.* Tu coche nuevo me da mucha envidia. **jealousy** *n* [*gen incontable*] (*pl* **-ies**) celos, envidia

jeans /dʒiːnz/ *n* [*pl*] (pantalones) vaqueros ☛ *Ver nota en* PAIR

Jeep® /dʒiːp/ *n* jeep, vehículo todo terreno

jeer /dʒɪə(r)/ ◆ *vt, vi* ~ **(at) (sth/sb) 1** mofarse (de algo/algn) **2** abuchear (a algo/algn) ◆ *n* burla, abucheo

jelly /ˈdʒeli/ *n* (*pl* **-ies**) **1** gelatina (*de sabores*) **2** jalea

jellyfish /ˈdʒelifɪʃ/ *n* (*pl* **jellyfish** *o* **~es**) medusa (*Zool*)

jeopardize, -ise /ˈdʒepədaɪz/ *vt* poner en peligro

jeopardy /ˈdʒepədi/ *n* LOC **(to be, put, etc) in jeopardy** (estar, poner, etc) en peligro

jerk /dʒɜːk/ ◆ *n* **1** sacudida, tirón **2** (*coloq, pey*) idiota ◆ *vt, vi* sacudir(se), mover(se) a sacudidas

jet[1] /dʒet/ *n* **1** (*tb* **jet aircraft**) jet, reactor **2** (*de agua, gas*) chorro

jet[2] /dʒet/ *n* azabache: *jet-black* negro azabache

jetty /ˈdʒeti/ *n* (*pl* **-ies**) embarcadero, malecón

Jew /dʒuː/ *n* judío, -a *Ver tb* JUDAISM

jewel /ˈdʒuːəl/ *n* **1** joya **2** piedra preciosa **jeweller** (*USA* **jeweler**) *n* joyero, -a **jeweller's** (*tb* **jeweller's shop**) *n* joyería **jewellery** (*tb* **jewelry**) *n* [*incontable*] joyas: *jewellery box/case* joyero

Jewish /ˈdʒuːɪʃ/ *adj* judío

jigsaw /ˈdʒɪgsɔː/ (*tb* **jigsaw puzzle**) *n* rompecabezas

jingle /ˈdʒɪŋgl/ ◆ *n* **1** [*sing*] tintineo **2** anuncio cantado ◆ *vt, vi* (hacer) tintinear

jinx /dʒɪŋks/ ◆ *n* (*coloq*) gafe ◆ *vt* (*coloq*) gafar

job /dʒɒb/ *n* **1** (puesto de) trabajo, empleo ☛ *Ver nota en* WORK[1] **2** tarea **3** deber, responsabilidad LOC **a good job** (*coloq*): *It's a good job you've come.* Menos mal que has venido. **out of a job** en el paro

jobcentre /ˈdʒɒbˌsentə(r)/ *n* (*GB*) oficina de empleo

jobless /ˈdʒɒbləs/ *adj* parado

jockey /ˈdʒɒki/ *n* (*pl* **-eys**) jockey

jog /dʒɒg/ ◆ *n* [*sing*] **1** empujoncito **2** *to go for a jog* ir a hacer footing ◆ (**-gg-**) **1** *vt* empujar (ligeramente) **2** *vi* hacer footing LOC **to jog sb's memory** refrescar la memoria a algn

jogger /ˈdʒɒgə(r)/ *n* persona que hace footing

jogging /ˈdʒɒgɪŋ/ *n* footing

join /dʒɔɪn/ ◆ *n* **1** juntura **2** costura ◆ **1** *vt* ~ **sth (on)to sth** unir, juntar algo con algo **2** *vi* ~ **up (with sth/sb)** juntarse (con algo/algn); unirse a algo/algn **3** *vt* ~ **sb** reunirse con algn **4** *vt, vi* (*club etc*) hacerse socio (de), afiliarse (a) **5** *vt vi* (*empresa*) unirse (a) **6** *vt* (*UE, etc*) ingresar en PHR V **to join in (sth)** participar en (algo)

joiner /ˈdʒɔɪnə(r)/ *n* (*GB*) carpintero, -a

joint[1] /dʒɔɪnt/ *adj* conjunto, mutuo colectivo

joint[2] /dʒɔɪnt/ *n* **1** (*Anat*) articulación **2** junta, ensambladura **3** cuarto de carne

4 (*argot, pey*) antro **5** (*argot*) porro **jointed** *adj* articulado, plegable

joke /dʒəʊk/ ◆ *n* **1** chiste: *to tell a joke* contar un chiste **2** broma: *to play a joke on sb* gastar una broma a algn **3** [*sing*] cachondeo: *The new dog laws are a joke.* La nueva ley sobre perros es un cachondeo. ◆ *vi* ~ (**with sb**) bromear (con algn) LOC **joking apart** bromas aparte

joker /ˈdʒəʊkə(r)/ *n* **1** (*coloq*) bromista **2** (*coloq*) hazmerreír **3** (*cartas*) comodín

jolly /ˈdʒɒli/ ◆ *adj* (**-ier**, **-iest**) alegre, jovial ◆ *adv* (*GB, coloq*) muy

jolt /dʒəʊlt/ ◆ **1** *vi* traquetear **2** *vt* sacudir ◆ *n* **1** sacudida **2** susto

jostle /ˈdʒɒsl/ *vt, vi* empujar(se), codear(se)

jot /dʒɒt/ *v* (**-tt-**) PHR V **to jot sth down** apuntar algo

journal /ˈdʒɜːnl/ *n* **1** revista, periódico (*especializado*) **2** diario **journalism** *n* periodismo **journalist** *n* periodista

journey /ˈdʒɜːni/ *n* (*pl* **-eys**) viaje, recorrido ☛ *Ver nota en* VIAJE

joy /dʒɔɪ/ *n* **1** alegría: *to jump for joy* saltar de alegría **2** encanto LOC *Ver* PRIDE **joyful** *adj* alegre **joyfully** *adv* alegremente

joystick /ˈdʒɔɪstɪk/ *n* (*Aeronáut, Informát*) mando ☛ *Ver dibujo en* ORDENADOR

jubilant /ˈdʒuːbɪlənt/ *adj* jubiloso **jubilation** *n* júbilo

jubilee /ˈdʒuːbɪliː/ *n* aniversario

Judaism /ˈdʒuːdeɪɪzəm; *USA* -dəɪzəm/ *n* judaísmo

judge /dʒʌdʒ/ ◆ *n* **1** juez, -eza **2** (*de competición*) juez, -eza, árbitro, -a **3** ~ (**of sth**) conocedor, -ora (de algo) ◆ *vt, vi* juzgar, considerar, calcular: *judging by/from…* a juzgar por…

judgement (*tb* **judgment** *esp Jur*) /ˈdʒʌdʒmənt/ *n* juicio: *to use your own judgement* actuar según su propio entender

judicious /dʒuˈdɪʃəs/ *adj* juicioso **judiciously** *adv* juiciosamente

judo /ˈdʒuːdəʊ/ *n* judo

jug /dʒʌg/ (*USA* **pitcher**) *n* jarra

juggle /ˈdʒʌgl/ *vt, vi* **1** ~ (**sth/with sth**) hacer juegos malabares (con algo) **2** ~ (**with**) **sth** (*fig*) dar vueltas a algo: *She juggles home, career and children.* Se las arregla para llevar casa, trabajo e hijos al mismo tiempo.

juice /dʒuːs/ *n* zumo, jugo **juicy** *adj* (**-ier**, **-iest**) **1** jugoso **2** (*coloq*) (*cuento, etc*) sabroso

July /dʒuˈlaɪ/ *n* (*abrev* **Jul**) julio ☛ *Ver nota y ejemplos en* JANUARY

jumble /ˈdʒʌmbl/ ◆ *vt* ~ **sth** (**up**) revolver algo ◆ *n* **1** revoltijo **2** (*GB*) objetos o ropa usados para un rastrillo benéfico

jumbo /ˈdʒʌmbəʊ/ *adj* (*coloq*) (de tamaño) súper

jump /dʒʌmp/ ◆ *n* **1** salto *Ver tb* HIGH JUMP, LONG JUMP **2** aumento ◆ **1** *vt, vi* saltar: *to jump up and down* dar saltos ◊ *to jump up* levantarse de un salto **2** *vi* sobresaltarse: *It made me jump.* Me sobresaltó. **3** *vi* aumentar LOC **to jump the queue** (*GB*) colarse **to jump to conclusions** sacar conclusiones precipitadas **jump to it** (*coloq*) ¡volando! *Ver tb* BANDWAGON PHR V **to jump at sth** aprovechar una oportunidad con entusiasmo

jumper /ˈdʒʌmpə(r)/ *n* **1** (*GB*) jersey ☛ *Ver nota en* SWEATER **2** saltador, -ora

jumpy /ˈdʒʌmpi/ *adj* (**-ier**, **-iest**) (*coloq*) nervioso

junction /ˈdʒʌŋkʃn/ *n* cruce (*Aut*)

June /dʒuːn/ *n* (*abrev* **Jun**) junio ☛ *Ver nota y ejemplos en* JANUARY

jungle /ˈdʒʌŋgl/ *n* jungla

junior /ˈdʒuːnɪə(r)/ ◆ *adj* **1** subalterno **2** (*abrev* **Jr**) júnior **3** (*GB*) *junior school* escuela primaria ◆ *n* **1** subalterno, -a **2** [*precedido de adjetivos posesivos*]: *He is three years her junior.* Es tres años más joven que ella. **3** (*GB*) alumno, -a de escuela primaria

junk /dʒʌŋk/ *n* [*incontable*] **1** (*coloq*) trastos **2** baratijas

junk food *n* (*coloq, pey*) [*incontable*] tentempiés o comidas preparadas (gen poco nutritivos)

junk mail *n* propaganda

Jupiter /ˈdʒuːpɪtə(r)/ *n* Júpiter

juror /ˈdʒʊərə(r)/ *n* miembro del jurado

jury /ˈdʒʊəri/ *n* [*v sing o pl*] (*pl* **-ies**) jurado

just /dʒʌst/ ◆ *adv* **1** justo, exactamente: *It's just what I need.* Es justo lo que necesito. ◊ *That's just it!* ¡Exacto! ◊ *just here* aquí mismo **2** ~ **as** justo cuando; justo como: *She arrived just as we were* *leaving*. Llegó justo cuando nos íbamos. ◊ *It's just as I thought.* Es justo como/lo que yo pensaba. **3 ~ as ... as ...** igual de ... que ...: *She's just as clever as her mother.* Es igual de lista que su madre. **4 to have ~ done sth** acabar de hacer algo: *She has just left.* Acaba de marcharse. ◊ *We had just arrived when ...* Acabábamos de llegar cuando ... ◊ *'Just married'* "Recién casados" **5 (only) ~** por muy poco: *I can (only) just reach the shelf.* Llego al estante a duras penas. **6 ~ over/under**: *It's just over a kilo.* Pasa un poco del kilo. **7** ahora: *I'm just going.* Ahora mismo me voy. **8 to be ~ about/going to do sth** estar a punto de hacer algo: *I was just about/going to phone you.* Estaba a punto de llamarte. **9** sencillamente: *It's just one of those things.* Es una de esas cosas que pasan, nada más. **10** *Just let me say something!* ¡Déjame hablar un momento! **11** sólo: *I waited an hour just to see you.* Esperé una hora sólo para poder verte. ◊ *just for fun* para reírnos un poco LOC **it is just as well (that ...)** menos mal (que)... **just about** (*coloq*) casi: *I know just about everyone.* Conozco más o menos a todo el mundo. **just in case** por si acaso **just like 1** igual que: *It was just like old times.* Fue como en los viejos tiempos. **2** típico de: *It's just like her to be late.* Es muy propio de ella llegar tarde. **just like that** sin más **just now 1** en estos momentos **2** hace un momento ◆ *adj* **1** justo **2** merecido

justice /ˈdʒʌstɪs/ *n* **1** justicia **2** juez, -eza: *justice of the peace* juez de paz LOC **to do justice to sth/sb 1** hacerle justicia a algo/algn **2** *We couldn't do justice to her cooking.* No pudimos hacer los honores a su comida. **to do yourself justice**: *He didn't do himself justice in the exam.* Podía haber hecho el examen mucho mejor. *Ver tb* BRING, MISCARRIAGE

justifiable /ˌdʒʌstɪˈfaɪəbl, ˈdʒʌstɪfaɪəbl/ *adj* justificable **justifiably** *adv* justificadamente: *She was justifiably angry.* Estaba enfadada, y con razón.

justify /ˈdʒʌstɪfaɪ/ *vt* (*pret, pp* **-fied**) justificar

justly /ˈdʒʌstli/ *adv* justamente, con razón

jut /dʒʌt/ *v* (**-tt-**) PHR V **to jut out** sobresalir

juvenile /ˈdʒuːvənaɪl/ ◆ *n* menor ◆ *adj* **1** juvenil **2** (*pey*) pueril

juxtapose /ˌdʒʌkstəˈpəʊz/ *vt* (*fml*) contraponer **juxtaposition** *n* contraposición

Kk

K, k /keɪ/ *n* (*pl* **K's, k's** /keɪz/) K, k: *K for king* k de kilo ☛ *Ver ejemplos en* A, a

kaleidoscope /kəˈlaɪdəskəʊp/ *n* calidoscopio

kangaroo /ˌkæŋgəˈruː/ *n* (*pl* **~s**) canguro

karate /kəˈrɑːti/ *n* karate

kebab /kɪˈbæb/ *n* pincho moruno

keel /kiːl/ ◆ *n* quilla ◆ PHR V **to keel over** (*coloq*) desplomarse

keen /kiːn/ *adj* (**-er, -est**) **1** entusiasta **2 to be ~ (that .../to do sth)** estar ansioso (de que .../de hacer algo); tener ganas (de hacer algo) **3** (*interés*) grande **4** (*olfato*) fino **5** (*oído, inteligencia*) agudo LOC **to be keen on sth/sb** gustarle a uno algo/algn **keenly** *adv* **1** con entusiasmo **2** (*sentir*) profundamente

keep /kiːp/ ◆ (*pret, pp* **kept** /kept/) **1** *vi* quedarse, permanecer: *Keep still!* ¡Estáte quieto! ◊ *Keep quiet!* ¡Cállate! ◊ *to keep warm* no enfriarse **2** *vi* **~ (on) doing sth** seguir haciendo algo; no parar de hacer algo: *He keeps interrupting me.* No para de interrumpirme. **3** *vt* [*con adj, adv o -ing*] mantener, tener: *to keep sb waiting* hacer esperar a algn ◊ *to keep sb amused/happy* tener a algn entretenido/contento ◊ *Don't keep us in suspense.* No nos tengas en suspenso. **4** *vt* entretener, retener: *What kept you?* ¿Por qué has tardado tanto? **5** *vt* guardar, tener: *Will you keep my place in th* *queue?* ¿Me guardas el sitio en la cola? **6** *vt* (*no devolver*) quedarse con: *Keep the change.* Quédese con la vuelta. **7** *vt* (*negocio*) tener, ser propietario de **8** *vt* (*animales*) criar, tener **9** *vt* (*secreto*) guardar **10** *vi* (*alimentos*) conservarse (fresco), durar **11** *vt* (*diario*) escribir, llevar **12** *vt* (*cuentas, registro*) llevar **13** *vt* (*familia, persona*) mantener **14** *vt* (*cita*) acudir a **15** *vt* (*promesa*) cumplir ☛ Para expresiones con **keep**, véanse las entradas del sustantivo, adjetivo, etc, p.ej. **to keep your word** en WORD.

PHR V **to keep away** (**from sth/sb**) mantenerse alejado (de algo/algn) **to keep sth/sb away** (**from sth/sb**) mantener alejado algo/a algn (de algo/algn)

to keep sth (**back**) **from sb** ocultar algo a algn

to keep sth down mantener algo bajo

to keep sb from (**doing**) **sth** impedir, no dejar a algn hacer algo **to keep** (**yourself**) **from doing sth** evitar hacer algo

to keep off (**sth**) no acercarse (a algo), no tocar (algo): *Keep off the grass.* Prohibido pisar el césped. **to keep sth/sb off** (**sth/sb**) no dejar a algo/algn acercarse (a algo/algn): *Keep your hands off me!* ¡No me toques!

to keep on (**at sb**) (**about sth/sb**) no parar de dar la tabarra (a algn) (sobre algo/algn)

to keep (**sth/sb**) **out** (**of sth**) no dejar (a algo/algn) entrar (en algo): *Keep Out!* ¡Prohibida la entrada!

to keep (**yourself**) **to yourself** guardar las distancias **to keep sth to yourself** guardarse algo (para sí)

to keep up (**with sth/sb**) seguir el ritmo (de algo/algn) **to keep sth up** mantener algo, seguir haciendo algo: *Keep it up!* ¡Dale!

◆ *n* manutención

keeper /ˈkiːpə(r)/ *n* **1** (*zoo*) guarda **2** (*en museo*) conservador, -ora **3** portero, -a

keeping /ˈkiːpɪŋ/ *n* LOC **in/out of keeping** (**with sth**) de acuerdo/en desacuerdo (con algo) **in sb's keeping** al cuidado de algn

kennel /ˈkenl/ *n* perrera

kept *pret, pp de* KEEP

kerb (*esp USA* **curb**) /kɜːb/ *n* bordillo

ketchup /ˈketʃəp/ *n* catchup

kettle

kettle /ˈketl/ *n* hervidora eléctrica

key /kiː/ ◆ *n* (*pl* **keys**) **1** llave: *the car keys* las llaves del coche **2** (*Mús*) tono **3** tecla **4 key** (**to sth**) clave (de algo): *Exercise is the key (to good health).* El ejercicio es la clave (de la buena salud). ◆ *adj* clave ◆ *vt* **to key sth** (**in**) teclear algo

keyboard /ˈkiːbɔːd/ *n* teclado ☛ *Ver dibujo en* ORDENADOR

keyhole /ˈkiːhəʊl/ *n* ojo de la cerradura

khaki /ˈkɑːki/ *adj, n* caqui

kick /kɪk/ ◆ **1** *vt* dar una patada a **2** *vt* (*pelota*) golpear (*con el pie*): *to kick the ball into the river* tirar la pelota al río de una patada **3** *vi* (*persona*) patalear **4** *vi* (*animal*) cocear LOC **to kick the bucket** (*coloq*) estirar la pata *Ver tb* ALIVE PHR V **to kick off** hacer el saque inicial **to kick sb out** (**of sth**) (*coloq*) echar a algn (de algo) ◆ *n* **1** puntapié, patada **2** (*coloq*): *for kicks* para divertirse

kick-off /ˈkɪk ɒf/ *n* saque inicial

kid /kɪd/ ◆ *n* **1** (*coloq*) crío, -a: *How are your wife and the kids?* ¿Qué tal tu mujer y los críos? **2** (*coloq, esp USA*): *his kid sister* su hermana menor **3** (*Zool*) cabrito **4** (*piel*) cabritilla ◆ (**-dd-**) **1** *vt, vi* (*coloq*) estar de broma: *Are you kidding?* ¿Estás de broma? **2** *v refl* **to kid yourself** engañarse a sí mismo

kidnap /ˈkɪdnæp/ *vt* (**-pp-**, *USA* **-p-**) secuestrar **kidnapper** *n* secuestrador, -ora **kidnapping** *n* secuestro

kidney /ˈkɪdni/ *n* (*pl* **-eys**) riñón

kill /kɪl/ ◆ *vt, vi* matar: *Smoking kills.* Fumar mata. ◊ *She was killed in a car crash.* Se mató en un accidente de coche. LOC **to kill time** matar el tiempo PHR V **to kill sth/sb off** exterminar algo, rematar a algn ◆ *n* (*animal matado*) pieza LOC **to go/move in for the kill** entrar a matar **killer** *n* asesino, -a

killing /ˈkɪlɪŋ/ *n* matanza LOC **to make a killing** hacer el agosto

kiln /kɪln/ *n* horno para cerámica

kilo /ˈkiːləʊ/ (*tb* **kilogramme**, **kilogram**) /ˈkɪləgræm/ *n* (*pl* ~**s**) (*abrev* **kg**) kilo(gramo) ☛ *Ver* Apéndice 1.

kilometre (*USA* **-meter**) /kɪlˈɒmɪtə(r)/ *n* (*abrev* **km**) kilómetro

kilt /kɪlt/ *n* falda escocesa

kin /kɪn/ (*tb* **kinsfolk**) *n* [*pl*] (*antic, fml*) familia *Ver tb* NEXT OF KIN

kind[1] /kaɪnd/ *adj* (**-er**, **-est**) amable

kind[2] /kaɪnd/ *n* tipo, clase: *the best of its kind* el mejor de su categoría LOC **in kind 1** en especie **2** (*fig*) con la misma moneda **kind of** (*coloq*) en cierto modo: *kind of scared* como asustado *Ver tb* NOTHING

kindly /ˈkaɪndli/ ◆ *adv* **1** amablemente **2** *Kindly leave me alone!* ¡Haz el favor de dejarme en paz! LOC **not to take kindly to sth/sb** no gustarle algo/algn a uno ◆ *adj* (**-ier**, **-iest**) amable

kindness /ˈkaɪndnəs/ *n* **1** amabilidad, bondad **2** favor

king /kɪŋ/ *n* rey

kingdom /ˈkɪŋdəm/ *n* reino

kingfisher /ˈkɪŋfɪʃə(r)/ *n* martín pescador

kinship /ˈkɪnʃɪp/ *n* parentesco

kiosk /ˈkiːɒsk/ *n* **1** quiosco **2** (*antic, GB*) (*teléf*) cabina

kipper /ˈkɪpə(r)/ *n* arenque ahumado

kiss /kɪs/ ◆ *vt, vi* besar(se) ◆ *n* beso LOC **the kiss of life** el boca a boca

kit /kɪt/ *n* **1** equipo **2** conjunto para ensamblaje

kitchen /ˈkɪtʃɪn/ *n* cocina

kite /kaɪt/ *n* cometa

kitten /ˈkɪtn/ *n* gatito ☛ *Ver nota en* GATO

kitty /ˈkɪti/ *n* (*pl* **-ies**) (*coloq*) fondo (*de dinero*)

knack /næk/ *n* tranquillo: *to get the knack of sth* cogerle el tranquillo a algo

knead /niːd/ *vt* amasar

knee /niː/ *n* rodilla LOC **to be/go (down) on your knees** estar/ponerse de rodillas

kneecap /ˈniːkæp/ *n* rótula

kneel /niːl/ *vi* (*pret, pp* **knelt** /nelt/, *esp USA* **kneeled**) ☛ *Ver nota en* DREAM ~ **(down)** arrodillarse

knew *pret de* KNOW

knickers /ˈnɪkəz/ *n* [*pl*] (*GB*) bragas: *a pair of knickers* unas bragas ☛ *Ver nota en* PAIR

knife /naɪf/ ◆ *n* (*pl* **knives** /naɪvz/) cuchillo ◆ *vt* acuchillar

knight /naɪt/ ◆ *n* **1** caballero **2** (*ajedrez*) caballo ◆ *vt* nombrar caballero/Sir **knighthood** *n* título de caballero

knit /nɪt/ (**-tt-**) (*pret, pp* **knitted**) **1** *vt* ~ **sth (for sb)** tejer algo (a algn) **2** *vi* hacer punto **3** *Ver* CLOSE-KNIT **knitting** *n* [*incontable*] labor de punto: *knitting needle* aguja (de hacer punto)

knitwear /ˈnɪtweə(r)/ *n* [*incontable*] (prendas de) punto

knob /nɒb/ *n* **1** (*de puerta, cajón*) tirador **2** (*de radio, televisor*) mando (*que gira*) **3** (*árbol*) nudo

knock /nɒk/ ◆ **1** *vt, vi* golpear: *to knock your head on the ceiling* pegarse con la cabeza en el techo **2** *vi*: *to knock at/on the door* llamar a la puerta **3** *vt* (*coloq*) criticar PHR V **to knock sb down** atropellar a algn **to knock sth down** derribar algo **to knock off (sth)** (*coloq*): *to knock off (work)* terminar de trabajar **to knock sth off** hacer un descuento de algo (*una cantidad*) **to knock sth/sb off (sth)** tirar algo/a algn (de algo) **to knock sb out 1** (*boxeo*) dejar K.O. a algn **2** dejar inconsciente a algn **3** (*coloq*) dejar boquiabierto a algn **to knock sth/sb over** tirar algo/a algn ◆ *n* **1** *There was a knock at the door* Llamaron a la puerta. **2** (*lit y fig*) golpe

knockout /ˈnɒkaʊt/ *n* **1** K.O. **2** *knockout (tournament)* eliminatoria

knot /nɒt/ ◆ *n* **1** nudo **2** corrillo (*de gente*) ◆ *vt* (*pret, pp* **-tt-**) hacer un nudo a, anudar

know /nəʊ/ ◆ (*pret* **knew** /njuː; *USA* nuː/ *pp* **known** /nəʊn/) **1** *vt, vi* ~ **(how to do sth)** saber (hacer algo): *to know how to swim* saber nadar ◊ *Let me know if…* Avísame si… **2** *vt*: *I've never known anyone to…* Nunca se ha visto que… **3** *vt* conocer: *to get to know sb* llegar a conocer a algn LOC **for all you know** por lo (poco) que uno sabe **God/goodness/Heaven knows** (bien) sabe Dios **to know best** saber uno lo que hace **to know better (than that/than to do sth)**: *You ought to know better* ¡Parece mentira que tú hayas hecho eso! ◊ *I should have known better*

Debería haber espabilado. **you never know** nunca se sabe *Ver tb* ANSWER, ROPE PHR V **to know of sth/sb** saber de algo/algn: *Not that I know of.* Que yo sepa, no. ◆ *n* LOC **to be in the know** (*coloq*) estar en el ajo

knowing /ˈnəʊɪŋ/ *adj* (*mirada*) de complicidad **knowingly** *adv* intencionadamente

knowledge /ˈnɒlɪdʒ/ *n* [*incontable*] **1** conocimiento(s): *not to my knowledge* que yo sepa, no **2** saber LOC **in the knowledge that...** a sabiendas de que... **knowledgeable** *adj* que posee muchos conocimientos sobre algo

known *pp de* KNOW

knuckle /ˈnʌkl/ ◆ *n* nudillo ◆ PHR V **to knuckle down (to sth)** (*coloq*) poner manos a la obra **to knuckle under** (*coloq*) doblegarse

Koran /kəˈrɑːn; *USA* -ˈræn/ *n* Corán

Ll

L, l /el/ *n* (*pl* **L's, l's** /elz/) L, l: *L for Lucy* L de Lugo ☛ *Ver ejemplos en* A, a

label /ˈleɪbl/ ◆ *n* etiqueta ◆ *vt* (**-ll-**, *USA* **-l-**) **1** etiquetar, poner etiquetas a **2** ~ **sth/sb as sth** (*fig*) calificar algo/a algn de algo

laboratory /ləˈbɒrətri; *USA* ˈlæbrətɔːri/ *n* (*pl* **-ies**) laboratorio

laborious /ləˈbɔːriəs/ *adj* **1** laborioso **2** penoso

labour (*USA* **labor**) /ˈleɪbə(r)/ ◆ *n* **1** [*incontable*] trabajo **2** [*incontable*] mano de obra: *parts and labour* los repuestos y la mano de obra ◊ *labour relations* relaciones laborales **3** [*incontable*] parto: *to go into labour* ponerse de parto **4 Labour** (*tb* **the Labour Party**) [*v sing o pl*] (*GB*) el Partido Laborista ☛ *Comparar con* LIBERAL 3, TORY ◆ *vi* esforzarse **laboured** (*USA* **labored**) *adj* **1** dificultoso **2** pesado **labourer** (*USA* **laborer**) *n* trabajador, -ora

labyrinth /ˈlæbərɪnθ/ *n* laberinto

lace /leɪs/ ◆ *n* **1** encaje **2** (*tb* **shoelace**) cordón ◆ *vt, vi* atar(se) (*con un lazo*)

lack /læk/ ◆ *vt* ~ **sth** carecer de algo LOC **to be lacking** faltar **to be lacking in sth** carecer de algo ◆ *n* [*incontable*] falta, carencia

lacquer /ˈlækə(r)/ *n* laca

lacy /ˈleɪsi/ *adj* de encaje

lad /læd/ *n* (*coloq*) muchacho

ladder /ˈlædə(r)/ *n* **1** escalera de mano **2** carrera (*en las medias, etc*) **3** (*fig*) escala (*social, profesional, etc*)

laden /ˈleɪdn/ *adj* ~ (**with sth**) cargado (de algo)

ladies /ˈleɪdiz/ *n* **1** *plural de* LADY **2** *Ver* LADY 4

lady /ˈleɪdi/ *n* (*pl* **ladies**) **1** señora: *Ladies and gentlemen...* Señoras y señores... *Ver tb* GENTLEMAN **2** dama **3 Lady** Lady (*como título nobiliario*) *Ver tb* LORD **4 Ladies** [*sing*] (*GB*) lavabo de señoras

ladybird /ˈleɪdibɜːd/ *n* mariquita

lag /læg/ ◆ *vi* (**-gg-**) LOC **to lag behind (sth/sb)** quedarse atrás (con respecto a algo/algn) ◆ *n* (*tb* **time lag**) retraso

lager /ˈlɑːgə(r)/ *n* cerveza rubia ☛ *Comparar con* BEER

lagoon /ləˈguːn/ *n* **1** albufera **2** laguna

laid *pret, pp de* LAY[1]

laid-back /ˌleɪd ˈbæk/ *adj* (*coloq*) tranquilo

lain *pp de* LIE[2]

lake /leɪk/ *n* lago

lamb /læm/ *n* cordero ☛ *Ver nota en* CARNE

lame /leɪm/ *adj* **1** cojo **2** (*excusa, etc*) poco convincente

lament /ləˈment/ *vt, vi* ~ (**for/over sth/sb**) lamentar(se) (de algo/algn)

lamp /læmp/ *n* lámpara

lamp-post /ˈlæmp pəʊst/ *n* farola

lampshade /ˈlæmpʃeɪd/ *n* pantalla (de lámpara)

land /lænd/ ◆ *n* **1** tierra: *by land* por

tierra ◊ *on dry land* en tierra firme **2** tierra(s): *arable land* tierra de cultivo ◊ *a plot of land* una parcela **3 the land** campo: *to work on the land* dedicarse a la agricultura **4** país: *the finest in the land* el mejor del país ◆ **1** *vt, vi* ~ (**sth/sb**) (**at…**) desembarcar (algo/a algn) (en…) **2** *vt* (*avión*) poner en tierra **3** *vi* aterrizar **4** *vi* caer: *The ball landed in the water.* La pelota cayó al agua. **5** *vi* (*pájaro*) posarse **6** *vt* (*coloq*) (*lograr*) conseguir, obtener LOC *Ver* FOOT PHR V **to land sb with sth/sb** (*coloq*) cargarle a algn con algo/algn: *I got landed with the washing up.* A mí me tocó fregar.

landing /ˈlændɪŋ/ *n* **1** aterrizaje **2** desembarco **3** (*escalera*) rellano

landlady /ˈlændleɪdi/ *n* (*pl* **-ies**) **1** casera **2** patrona (*de un pub o una pensión*)

landlord /ˈlændlɔːd/ *n* **1** casero **2** patrón (*de un pub o una pensión*)

landmark /ˈlændmɑːk/ *n* **1** (*lit*) punto destacado **2** (*fig*) hito

landowner /ˈlændəʊnə(r)/ *n* terrateniente

landscape /ˈlændskeɪp/ *n* paisaje ☛ *Ver nota en* SCENERY

landslide /ˈlændslaɪd/ *n* **1** (*lit*) desprendimiento (*de tierras*) **2** (*tb* **landslide victory**) (*fig*) victoria aplastante

lane /leɪn/ *n* **1** camino **2** callejón **3** carril: *slow/fast lane* carril de la derecha/de aceleración **4** (*Dep*) calle

language /ˈlæŋgwɪdʒ/ *n* **1** lenguaje: *to use bad language* decir palabrotas **2** idioma, lengua

lantern /ˈlæntən/ *n* farol

lap¹ /læp/ *n* regazo

lap² /læp/ *n* vuelta (*Dep*)

lap³ /læp/ (**-pp-**) **1** *vi* (*agua*) chapotear **2** *vt* **to lap sth** (**up**) lamer algo PHR V **to lap sth up** (*coloq*) tragarse algo

lapel /ləˈpel/ *n* solapa

lapse /læps/ ◆ *n* **1** error, lapso **2** ~ (**into sth**) caída (en algo) **3** (*de tiempo*) lapso, periodo: *after a lapse of six years* al cabo de seis años ◆ *vi* **1** ~ (**from sth**) (**into sth**) caer (de algo) (en algo): *to lapse into silence* quedarse callado **2** (*Jur*) caducar

larder /ˈlɑːdə(r)/ *n* despensa

large /lɑːdʒ/ ◆ *adj* (**-er**, **-est**) **1** grande: *small, medium or large* pequeña, mediana o grande ◊ *to a large extent* en gran parte **2** extenso, amplio ☛ *Ver nota en* BIG LOC **by and large** en términos generales *Ver tb* EXTENT ◆ *n* LOC **at large 1** en libertad **2** en general: *the world at large* todo el mundo

largely /ˈlɑːdʒli/ *adv* en gran parte

large-scale /ˈlɑːdʒ skeɪl/ *adj* **1** a gran escala, extenso **2** (*mapa*) a gran escala

lark /lɑːk/ *n* alondra

laser /ˈleɪzə(r)/ *n* láser: *laser printer* impresora láser

lash /læʃ/ ◆ *n* **1** azote **2** *Ver* EYELASH ◆ *vt* **1** azotar **2** (*rabo*) sacudir PHR V **to lash out at/against sth/sb 1** emprenderla a golpes contra algo/algn **2** arremeter contra algo/algn

lass /læs/ (*tb* **lassie** /ˈlæsi/) *n* muchacha (*esp en Escocia y el N de Inglaterra*)

last /lɑːst; *USA* læst/ ◆ *adj* **1** último: *last thing at night* lo último por la noche ☛ *Ver nota en* LATE **2** pasado: *last month* el mes pasado ◊ *last night* anoche ◊ *the night before last* anteanoche LOC **as a/in the last resort** en último recurso **to have the last laugh** reírse el último **to have the last word** tener la última palabra *Ver tb* ANALYSIS, EVERY, FIRST, STRAW, THING ◆ *n* **1 the last** (**of sth**) el último/la última (de algo): *the last but one* el penúltimo/la penúltima **2 the last** el/la anterior LOC **at** (**long**) **last** por fin ◆ *adv* **1** último: *He came last.* Llegó el último. **2** por última vez LOC (**and**) **last but not least** y por último, aunque no por ello de menos importancia ◆ **1** *vt, vi* ~ (**for**) **hours, days, etc** durar horas, días, etc **2** *vi* perdurar **lasting** *adj* duradero, permanente **lastly** *adv* por último

latch /lætʃ/ ◆ *n* **1** aldaba **2** picaporte ◆ PHR V **to latch on** (**to sth**) (*coloq*) enterarse (de algo) (*explicación, etc*)

late /leɪt/ ◆ *adj* (**later**, **latest**) **1** tarde, tardío: *to be late* llegar tarde ◊ *My flight was an hour late.* Mi vuelo se retrasó una hora. **2** *in the late 19th century* a finales del siglo XIX ◊ *in her late twenties* rondando la treintena **3 latest** lo último, el más reciente

El superlativo **latest** significa el más reciente, el más nuevo: *the latest technology* la tecnología más reciente. El adjetivo **last** significa el último de una serie: *The last bus is at twelve.* El último autobús sale a las doce.

4 [*antes de sustantivo*] difunto LOC **at the latest** a más tardar ◆ *adv* (**later**) tarde: *He arrived half an hour late.* Llegó con media hora de retraso. LOC **later on** más tarde *Ver tb* BETTER, SOON

ately /ˈleɪtli/ *adv* últimamente

ather /ˈlɑːðə(r); *USA* ˈlæð-/ *n* espuma

atitude /ˈlætɪtjuːd; *USA* -tuːd/ *n* latitud

he latter /ˈlætə(r)/ *pron* el segundo ☛ *Comparar con* FORMER

augh /lɑːf; *USA* læf/ ◆ *vi* reír(se) LOC algo/algn *Ver* BURST PHR V **to laugh at sth/sb 1** reírse de algo/algn **2** burlarse de algo/algn ◆ *n* **1** risa, carcajada **2** (*coloq*) (*suceso o persona*): *What a laugh!* ¡Es para partirse de risa! LOC **to be good for a laugh** ser una juerga *Ver tb* LAST **laughable** *adj* risible **laughter** *n* [*incontable*] risa(s): *to roar with laughter* reírse a carcajadas

aunch[1] /lɔːntʃ/ ◆ *vt* **1** (*proyectil, ataque, campaña*) lanzar **2** (*buque nuevo*) botar PHR V **to launch into sth** (*discurso, etc*) comenzar algo ◆ *n* lanzamiento

aunch[2] /lɔːntʃ/ *n* lancha

aunderette /lɔːnˈdret/ *n* lavandería (*establecimiento donde uno va a lavar la ropa*) ☛ *Comparar con* LAUNDRY

aundry /ˈlɔːndri/ *n* (*pl* **-ies**) **1** colada: *to do the laundry* hacer la colada ☛ La palabra más corriente para "colada" es **washing**. **2** lavandería industrial: *laundry service* servicio de lavandería ☛ *Comparar con* LAUNDERETTE

ava /ˈlɑːvə/ *n* lava

avatory /ˈlævətri/ *n* (*pl* **-ies**) (*fml*) **1** retrete **2** (*público*) aseos **3** (*en casa particular*) lavabo ☛ *Ver nota en* TOILET

avender /ˈlævəndə(r)/ *n* espliego, lavanda

avish /ˈlævɪʃ/ *adj* **1** pródigo, generoso **2** abundante

aw /lɔː/ *n* **1** (*tb* **the law**) ley: *against the law* en contra de la ley **2** (*carrera*) derecho LOC **law and order** orden público *Ver tb* EYE **lawful** *adj* legal, legítimo *Ver tb* LEGAL

awn /lɔːn/ *n* césped

awsuit /ˈlɔːsuːt/ *n* pleito

lawyer /ˈlɔːjə(r)/ *n* abogado, -a ☛ *Ver nota en* ABOGADO

lay[1] /leɪ/ *vt, vi* (*pret, pp* **laid** /leɪd/) **1** colocar, poner **2** (*cimientos*) echar **3** (*cable, etc*) tender **4** extender ☛ *Ver nota en* LIE[2] **5** (*huevos*) poner LOC **to lay claim to sth** reclamar algo **to lay your cards on the table** poner las cartas sobre la mesa *Ver tb* BLAME, TABLE PHR V **to lay sth aside** poner algo a un lado **to lay sth down 1** (*armas*) deponer **2** (*regla, principio, etc*) estipular, establecer **to lay sb off** (*coloq*) despedir a algn **to lay sth on 1** (*gas, luz, etc*) instalar algo **2** (*coloq*) (*facilitar*) proveer algo **to lay sth out 1** (*sacar a la vista*) disponer algo **2** (*argumento*) exponer algo **3** (*jardín, ciudad*) hacer el trazado de algo: *well laid out* bien distribuido/planificado

lay[2] *pret de* LIE[2]

lay[3] /leɪ/ *adj* **1** laico **2** (*no experto*) lego

lay-by /ˈleɪ baɪ/ *n* (*pl* **-bys**) (*GB*) área de descanso (*carretera*)

layer /ˈleɪə(r)/ *n* **1** capa **2** (*Geol*) estrato **layered** *adj* en capas

lazy /ˈleɪzi/ *adj* (**lazier**, **laziest**) **1** vago **2** perezoso

lead[1] /led/ *n* plomo **leaded** *adj* con plomo

lead[2] /liːd/ ◆ *n* **1** iniciativa **2** (*competición*) ventaja: *to be in the lead* llevar la delantera **3** (*Teat*) papel principal **4** (*naipes*) mano: *It's your lead.* Tú eres mano. **5** (*indicio*) pista **6** (*de perro, etc*) correa **7** (*Electrón*) cable ◆ (*pret, pp* **led** /led/) **1** *vt* llevar, conducir **2** *vt* ~ **sb (to do sth)** llevar a algn (a hacer algo) **3** *vi* ~ **to/into sth** (*puerta, etc*) dar, llevar (a algo): *This door leads into the garden.* Esta puerta da al jardín. ◊ *This road leads back to town.* Por este camino se vuelve a la ciudad. **4** *vi* ~ **to sth** dar lugar a algo **5** *vt* (*vida*) llevar **6** *vi* llevar la delantera **7** *vt* encabezar **8** *vt, vi* (*naipes*) salir LOC **to lead sb to believe (that)...** hacer creer a algn (que)... **to lead the way (to sth)** mostrar el camino (a algo) PHR V **to lead up to sth** preparar el terreno para algo **leader** *n* líder, dirigente **leadership** *n* **1** liderazgo **2** [*v sing o pl*] (*cargo*) jefatura **leading** *adj* principal, más importante

leaf /liːf/ *n* (*pl* **leaves** /liːvz/) hoja LOC **to take a leaf out of sb's book** seguir el ejemplo de algn *Ver tb* TURN **leafy** *adj* (**-ier**, **-iest**) frondoso: *leafy vegetables* verduras de hoja

leaflet /ˈliːflət/ *n* folleto

league /liːg/ *n* **1** (*alianza*) liga **2** (*coloq*) (*categoría*) clase LOC **in league (with sb)** confabulado (con algn)

leak /liːk/ ◆ *n* **1** agujero, gotera **2** fuga, escape **3** (*fig*) filtración ◆ **1** *vi* (*recipiente*) estar agujereado, tener fuga **2** *vi* (*gas o líquido*) salirse, escaparse **3** *vt* dejar escapar

lean¹ /liːn/ *adj* (**-er**, **-est**) **1** (*persona, animal*) delgado, flaco **2** magro

lean

She is **leaning against** a tree. He is **leaning out of** a window.

lean² /liːn/ (*pret, pp* **leant** /lent/ *o* **leaned**) *Ver nota en* DREAM **1** *vi* inclinar(se), ladear(se): *to lean out of the window* asomarse a la ventana ◊ *to lean back/forward* inclinarse hacia atrás/adelante **2** *vt, vi* ~ **against/on sth** apoyar(se) contra/en algo **leaning** *n* inclinación

leap /liːp/ ◆ *vi* (*pret, pp* **leapt** /lept/ *o* **leaped**) **1** saltar, brincar **2** (*corazón*) dar un salto ◆ *n* salto

leap year *n* año bisiesto

learn /lɜːn/ *vt, vi* (*pret, pp* **learnt** /lɜːnt/ *o* **learned**) *Ver nota en* DREAM **1** aprender **2** ~ **(of/about) sth** enterarse de algo LOC **to learn your lesson** escarmentar *Ver tb* ROPE **learner** *n* aprendiz, -iza, principiante **learning** *n* **1** (*acción*) aprendizaje **2** (*conocimientos*) erudición

lease /liːs/ ◆ *n* contrato de arrendamiento LOC *Ver* NEW ◆ *vt* ~ **sth (to/from sb)** arrendar algo (a algn) (*propietario o inquilino*)

least /liːst/ ◆ *pron* (*superl de* **little**) menos: *It's the least I can do.* Es lo menos que puedo hacer. LOC **at least** al menos, por lo menos **not in the least** en absoluto **not least** especialmente *Ver tb* LAST ◆ *adj* menor ◆ *adv* menos: *when I least expected it* cuando menos lo esperaba

leather /ˈleðə(r)/ *n* cuero

leave /liːv/ ◆ (*pret, pp* **left** /left/) **1** *vt, vi* dejar: *Leave it to me.* Yo me encargo. **2** *vt, vi* irse (de), salir (de) **3** *vi* **to be left** quedar: *You've only got two days left.* Sólo te quedan dos días. ◊ *to be left over* sobrar LOC **to leave sb to their own devices/to themselves** dejar a algn a su libre albedrío *Ver tb* ALONE PHR V **to leave behind** dejar (atrás), olvidar ◆ *n* permiso (*vacaciones*) LOC **on leave** de permiso

leaves *plural de* LEAF

lecture /ˈlektʃə(r)/ ◆ *n* **1** conferencia: *to give a lecture* dar una conferencia ☛ *Comparar con* CONFERENCE **2** (*reprimenda*) sermón LOC **lecture theatre** aula magna ◆ **1** *vi* ~ **(on sth)** dar una conferencia/conferencias (sobre algo) **2** *vt* ~ **sb (for/about sth)** sermonear a algn (por/sobre algo) **lecturer** *n* **1** ~ **(in sth)** (*de universidad*) profesor, -ora (de algo) **2** conferenciante

led *pret, pp de* LEAD²

ledge /ledʒ/ *n* **1** repisa: *the window ledge* el alféizar **2** (*Geog*) plataforma

leek /liːk/ *n* puerro

left¹ *pret, pp de* LEAVE

left² /left/ ◆ *n* **1** izquierda: *on the left* a la izquierda **2 the Left** [*v sing o pl*] (*Pol*) la izquierda ◆ *adj* izquierdo ◆ *adv* a la izquierda: *Turn/Go left.* Gira a la izquierda.

left-hand /ˈleft hænd/ *adj* a/de (la) izquierda: *on the left-hand side* a mano izquierda **left-handed** *adj* zurdo

left luggage office *n* consigna

leftover /ˈleftəʊvə(r)/ *adj* sobrante **leftovers** *n* [*pl*] sobras

left wing *adj* izquierdista

leg /leg/ *n* **1** pierna **2** (*de animal, mueble*) pata **3** (*carne*) pierna, muslo **4** (*pantalón*) pernera LOC **to give sb a leg up** (*coloq*) ayudar a algn a subirse a algo **not to have a leg to stand on** (*coloq*) no tener uno nada que lo respalde *Ver tb* PULL, STRETCH

legacy /ˈlegəsi/ *n* (*pl* **-ies**) **1** legado **2** (*fig*) patrimonio

legal /ˈliːgl/ *adj* jurídico, legal: *to ta*

legal action against sb entablar un proceso legal contra algn *Ver tb* LAWFUL *en* LAW **legality** /lɪˈgæləti/ *n* legalidad **legalization, -isation** *n* legalización **legalize, -ise** *vt* legalizar

legend /ˈledʒənd/ *n* leyenda **legendary** *adj* legendario

leggings /ˈlegɪŋz/ *n* [*pl*] mallas (*pantalón*)

legible /ˈledʒəbl/ *adj* legible

legion /ˈliːdʒən/ *n* legión

legislate /ˈledʒɪsleɪt/ *vi* ~ (**for/against sth**) legislar (para/contra algo) **legislation** *n* legislación **legislative** *adj* legislativo **legislature** *n* (*fml*) asamblea legislativa

legitimacy /lɪˈdʒɪtɪməsi/ *n* (*fml*) legitimidad

legitimate /lɪˈdʒɪtɪmət/ *adj* **1** legítimo, lícito **2** justo, válido

leisure /ˈleʒə(r); *USA* ˈliːʒər/ *n* ocio: *leisure time* tiempo libre LOC **at your leisure** cuando te venga bien

leisure centre *n* centro recreativo

leisurely /ˈleʒəli; *USA* ˈliːʒərli/ ◆ *adj* pausado, relajado ◆ *adv* tranquilamente

lemon /ˈlemən/ *n* limón

lemonade /ˌleməˈneɪd/ *n* **1** gaseosa **2** limonada

lend /lend/ *vt* (*pret, pp* **lent** /lent/) prestar LOC *Ver* HAND ☛ *Ver dibujo en* BORROW

length /leŋθ/ *n* **1** largo, longitud: *20 metres in length* 20 metros de largo **2** duración: *for some length of time* durante un buen rato/una temporada LOC **to go to any, great, etc lengths** (**to do sth**) hacer todo lo posible (por hacer algo) **lengthen** *vt, vi* alargar(se), prolongar(se) **lengthy** *adj* (**-ier**, **-iest**) largo

lenient /ˈliːniənt/ *adj* **1** indulgente **2** (*tratamiento*) clemente

lens /lenz/ *n* (*pl* **lenses**) **1** (*cámara*) objetivo **2** lente: *contact lenses* lentillas

lent *pret, pp de* LEND

lentil /ˈlentl/ *n* lenteja

Leo /ˈliːəʊ/ *n* (*pl* **Leos**) leo ☛ *Ver ejemplos en* AQUARIUS

leopard /ˈlepəd/ *n* leopardo

lesbian /ˈlezbiən/ *n* lesbiana

less /les/ ◆ *adv* ~ (**than…**) menos (que/de…): *less often* con menos frecuencia LOC **less and less** cada vez menos *Ver tb* EXTENT, MORE ◆ *adj, pron* ~ (**than…**) menos (que/de…): *I have less than you.* Tengo menos que tú.

> **Less** se usa como comparativo de **little** y normalmente va con sustantivos incontables: *'I've got very little money.' 'I have even less money (than you).'* —Tengo poco dinero. —Yo tengo aún menos (que tú). **Fewer** es el comparativo de **few** y normalmente va con sustantivos en plural: *fewer accidents, people, etc* menos accidentes, gente, etc. Sin embargo, en el inglés hablado se utiliza más **less** que **fewer**, aunque sea con sustantivos en plural.

lessen **1** *vi* disminuir **2** *vt* reducir **lesser** *adj* menor: *to a lesser extent* en menor grado

lesson /ˈlesn/ *n* **1** clase: *four English lessons a week* cuatro clases de inglés a la semana ☛ *Comparar con* CLASE **2** lección LOC *Ver* LEARN, TEACH

let[1] /let/ *vt* (**-tt-**) (*pret, pp* **let**) dejar, permitir: *to let sb do sth* dejar a algn hacer algo ◊ *My dad won't let me smoke in my bedroom.* Mi padre no me deja fumar en mi habitación. *Ver nota en* ALLOW.

> **Let us** + infinitivo sin TO se utiliza para hacer sugerencias. Excepto en el habla formal, normalmente se usa la contracción **let's**: *Let's go!* ¡Vamos! En negativa, se usa **let's not** o **don't let's**: *Let's not argue.* No discutamos.

LOC **let alone** mucho menos: *I can't afford new clothes, let alone a holiday.* No me puedo permitir ropa nueva, y mucho menos unas vacaciones. **let's face it** (*coloq*) reconozcámoslo **let us say** digamos **to let fly at sth/sb** atacar algo/a algn **to let fly with sth** disparar con algo **to let off steam** (*coloq*) desahogarse **to let sb know sth** informar a algn de algo **to let sth/sb go**; **to let go of sth/sb** soltar algo/a algn **to let sth/sb loose** soltar algo/a algn **to let sth slip**: *I let it slip that I was married.* Se me escapó que estaba casado. **to let the cat out of the bag** irse de la lengua **to let the matter drop/rest** dejar el asunto tranquilo **to let yourself go** dejarse llevar por el instinto *Ver tb* HOOK PHR V **to let sb down** fallar a algn **to let sb in/out** dejar entrar/salir a algn **to let sb off (sth)** perdonar (algo) a algn **to let sth off 1** (*arma*) disparar algo **2** (*fuegos artificiales*) hacer estallar algo

let² /let/ *vt* (**-tt-**) (*pret, pp* **let**) (*GB*) **to let sth (to sb)** alquilar algo (a algn) LOC **to let** se alquila

lethal /ˈliːθl/ *adj* letal

lethargy /ˈleθədʒi/ *n* aletargamiento **lethargic** /ləˈθɑːdʒɪk/ *adj* aletargado

let's /lets/ = LET US *Ver* LET¹ 2

letter /ˈletə(r)/ *n* **1** letra **2** carta: *to post a letter* echar una carta al correo LOC **to the letter** al pie de la letra

letter box *n* **1** (*tb* **postbox**) buzón (*en la calle*) **2** ranura en la puerta de una casa por la que se echan las cartas

lettuce /ˈletɪs/ *n* lechuga

leukaemia (*USA* **leukemia**) /luːˈkiːmiə/ *n* leucemia

level /ˈlevl/ ◆ *adj* **1** raso **2** ~ **(with sth/sb)** al nivel (de algo/algn) LOC *Ver* BEST ◆ *n* nivel: *1000 metres above sea-level* a 1.000 metros sobre el nivel del mar ◊ *noise levels* el nivel de ruido ◊ *high-/low-level negotiations* negociaciones de alto/bajo nivel ◆ *vt* (**-ll-**, *USA* **-l-**) nivelar PHR V **to level sth at sth/sb** dirigir algo a algo/algn (*críticas, etc*) **to level off/out** estabilizarse

level crossing *n* paso a nivel

lever /ˈliːvə(r); *USA* ˈlevər/ *n* palanca **leverage** *n* **1** (*fig*) influencia **2** (*lit*) fuerza de la palanca, apalancamiento

levy /ˈlevi/ ◆ *vt* (*pret, pp* **levied**) imponer (*impuestos, etc*) ◆ *n* **1** exacción **2** impuesto

liability /ˌlaɪəˈbɪləti/ *n* (*pl* **-ies**) **1** ~ **(for sth)** responsabilidad (por algo) **2** (*coloq*) problema **liable** *adj* **1** responsable: *to be liable for sth* ser responsable de algo **2** ~ **to sth** sujeto a algo **3** ~ **to sth** propenso a algo **4** ~ **to do sth** tendente a hacer algo

liaison /liˈeɪzn; *USA* ˈlɪəzɒn/ *n* **1** vinculación **2** relación sexual

liar /ˈlaɪə(r)/ *n* mentiroso, -a

libel /ˈlaɪbl/ *n* libelo, difamación

liberal /ˈlɪbərəl/ *adj* **1** liberal **2** libre **3 Liberal** (*Pol*) liberal: *the Liberal Democrats* el Partido Demócrata Liberal ☛ *Comparar con* LABOUR 4, TORY

liberate /ˈlɪbəreɪt/ *vt* ~ **sth/sb (from sth)** liberar algo/a algn (de algo) **liberated** *adj* liberado **liberation** *n* liberación

liberty /ˈlɪbəti/ *n* (*pl* **-ies**) libertad *Ver tb* FREEDOM LOC **to take liberties** tomarse libertades

Libra /ˈliːbrə/ *n* libra ☛ *Ver ejemplos en* AQUARIUS

library /ˈlaɪbrəri; *USA* -breri/ *n* (*pl* **-ies**) biblioteca **librarian** /laɪˈbreəriən/ *n* bibliotecario, -a

lice *plural de* LOUSE

licence (*USA* **license**) /ˈlaɪsns/ *n* licencia: *a driving licence* un carnet de conducir *Ver* OFF-LICENCE **2** (*fml*) permiso

lick /lɪk/ ◆ *vt* lamer ◆ *n* lametón

licorice (*USA*) *Ver* LIQUORICE

lid /lɪd/ *n* tapa ☛ *Ver dibujo en* SAUCEPAN

lie¹ /laɪ/ ◆ *vi* (*pret, pp* **lied** *pt pres* **lying**) **to lie (to sb) (about sth)** mentir (a algn) (sobre algo) ◆ *n* mentira: *to tell lies* decir mentiras

lie² /laɪ/ *vi* (*pret* **lay** /leɪ/ *pp* **lain** /leɪn/ *pt pres* **lying**) **1** echarse, yacer **2** estar: *the life that lay ahead of him* la vida que le esperaba ◊ *The problem lies in...* El problema está en... **3** extenderse PHR V **to lie about/around 1** pasar el tiempo sin hacer nada **2** estar esparcido: *Don't leave all your clothes lying around.* No dejes toda la ropa por ahí tirada. **to lie back** recostarse **to lie down** echarse **to lie in** (*GB*) (*USA* **to sleep in**) (*coloq*) quedarse en la cama

Compárense los verbos **lie** y **lay**. El verbo **lie** (**lay, lain, lying**) es intransitivo y significa "estar echado": *I was feeling ill, so I lay down on the bed for a while.* Me sentía mal, así que me eché un rato. Es importante no confundirlo con **lie** (**lied, lied, lying**), que significa "mentir". Por otro lado, **lay** (**laid, laid, laying**) es transitivo y tiene el significado de "poner sobre": *She laid her dress on the bed to keep it neat.* Puso el vestido sobre la cama para que no se arrugara.

lieutenant /lefˈtenənt; *USA* luːˈt-/ *n* teniente

life /laɪf/ (*pl* **lives** /laɪvz/) *n* **1** vida: *late in life* a una avanzada edad ◊ *a friend for life* un amigo de por vida ◊ *home life* la vida casera *Ver* LONG-LIFE **2** (*tb* **l**

sentence, **life imprisonment**) cadena perpetua LOC **to come to life** animarse **to take your (own) life** suicidarse *Ver tb* BREATHE, BRING, FACT, KISS, MATTER, NEW, PRIME, TIME, TRUE, WALK, WAY

lifebelt /ˈlaɪfbelt/ (*tb* **lifebuoy**) *n* salvavidas

lifeboat /ˈlaɪfbəʊt/ *n* bote salvavidas

life expectancy *n* (*pl* **-ies**) esperanza de vida

lifeguard /ˈlaɪfgɑːd/ *n* socorrista

life jacket *n* chaleco salvavidas

lifelong /ˈlaɪflɒŋ/ *adj* de toda la vida

lifestyle /ˈlaɪfstaɪl/ *n* estilo de vida

lifetime /ˈlaɪftaɪm/ *n* toda una vida LOC **the chance, etc of a lifetime** la oportunidad, etc de tu vida

lift /lɪft/ ◆ **1** *vt* ~ **sth/sb (up)** levantar algo/a algn **2** *vt* (*embargo, toque de queda*) levantar **3** *vi* (*neblina, nubes*) disiparse PHR V **to lift off** despegar ◆ *n* **1** impulso **2** (*USA* **elevator**) ascensor **3** *to give sb a lift* llevar a algn en coche LOC *Ver* THUMB

light /laɪt/ ◆ *n* **1** luz: *to turn on/off the light* encender/apagar la luz **2 (traffic) lights** [*pl*] semáforo **3 a light**: *Have you got a light?* ¿Tienes fuego? LOC **in the light of sth** considerando algo **to come to light** salir a la luz *Ver tb* SET[2] ◆ *adj* (**-er**, **-est**) **1** (*habitación*) luminoso, claro **2** (*color, tono*) claro **3** ligero: *two kilos lighter* dos kilos menos **4** (*golpe, viento*) suave ◆ (*pret, pp* **lit** /lɪt/ *o* **lighted**) **1** *vt, vi* encender(se) **2** *vt* iluminar, alumbrar ☛ Generalmente se usa **lighted** como *adj* antes del sustantivo: *a lighted candle* una vela encendida, y **lit** como verbo: *He lit the candle.* Encendió la vela. PHR V **to light up (with sth)** iluminarse (de algo) (*cara, ojos*) ◆ *adv*: *to travel light* viajar ligero (de equipaje)

light bulb *Ver* BULB

lighten /ˈlaɪtn/ *vt, vi* **1** iluminar(se) **2** aligerar(se) **3** alegrar(se)

lighter /ˈlaɪtə(r)/ *n* encendedor

light-headed /ˌlaɪt ˈhedɪd/ *adj* mareado

light-hearted /ˌlaɪt ˈhɑːtɪd/ *adj* **1** despreocupado **2** (*comentario*) desenfadado

lighthouse /ˈlaɪthaʊs/ *n* faro

lighting /ˈlaɪtɪŋ/ *n* **1** iluminación **2** *street lighting* alumbrado público

lightly /ˈlaɪtli/ *adv* **1** ligeramente, levemente, suavemente **2** ágilmente **3** a la ligera LOC **to get off/escape lightly** (*coloq*) salir bien parado

lightness /ˈlaɪtnəs/ *n* **1** claridad **2** ligereza **3** suavidad **4** agilidad

lightning /ˈlaɪtnɪŋ/ *n* [*incontable*] relámpago, rayo

lightweight /ˈlaɪtweɪt/ ◆ *n* peso ligero (*boxeo*) ◆ *adj* **1** ligero **2** (*boxeador*) de peso ligero

like[1] /laɪk/ *vt* gustar: *Do you like fish?* ¿Te gusta el pescado? ◊ *I like swimming.* Me gusta nadar. LOC **if you like** si quieres **likeable** *adj* agradable

like[2] /laɪk/ ◆ *prep* **1** como: *to look/be like sb* parecerse a algn **2** (*comparación*) como, igual que: *He cried like a child.* Lloró como un niño. ◊ *He acted like our leader.* Se comportó como si fuera nuestro líder. **3** (*ejemplo*) como, tal como: *European countries like Spain, France, etc* países europeos (tales) como España, Francia, etc ☛ *Comparar con* AS **4 like + -ing** como + infinitivo: *It's like baking a cake.* Es como hacer un pastel. LOC *Ver* JUST ◆ *conj* (*coloq*) **1** como: *It didn't end quite like I expected it to.* No terminó como esperaba. **2** como si *Ver tb* AS IF/THOUGH *en* AS

likely /ˈlaɪkli/ ◆ *adj* (**-ier**, **-iest**) **1** probable: *It isn't likely to rain.* No es probable que llueva. ◊ *She's very likely to ring me/It's very likely that she'll ring me.* Es muy probable que me llame. **2** apropiado ◆ *adv* LOC **not likely!** (*coloq*) ¡ni hablar! **likelihood** *n* [*sing*] probabilidad

liken /ˈlaɪkən/ ~ **to sth** (*fml*) *vt* comparar con algo

likeness /ˈlaɪknəs/ *n* parecido: *a family likeness* un aire de familia

likewise /ˈlaɪkwaɪz/ *adv* (*fml*) **1** de la misma forma: *to do likewise* hacer lo mismo **2** asimismo

liking /ˈlaɪkɪŋ/ *n* LOC **to sb's liking** (*fml*) del agrado de algn **to take a liking to sb** coger simpatía a algn

lilac /ˈlaɪlək/ *n* (color) lila

lily /ˈlɪli/ *n* (*pl* **lilies**) **1** lirio **2** azucena

limb /lɪm/ *n* (*Anat*) brazo, pierna (*de persona*)

lime[1] /laɪm/ *n* cal

lime[2] /laɪm/ ◆ *n* lima, limero ◆ *adj*, *n* (*tb* **lime green**) (color) verde lima

limelight /ˈlaɪmlaɪt/ *n*: *in the limelight* en candelero

limestone /ˈlaɪmstəʊn/ *n* piedra caliza

limit[1] /ˈlɪmɪt/ *n* límite: *the speed limit* el límite de velocidad LOC **within limits** dentro de ciertos límites **limitation** *n* limitación **limitless** *adj* ilimitado

limit[2] /ˈlɪmɪt/ *vt* ~ **sth/sb** (**to sth**) limitar algo/a algn (a algo) **limited** *adj* limitado **limiting** *adj* restrictivo

limousine /ˈlɪməziːn, ˌlɪməˈziːn/ *n* limusina

limp[1] /lɪmp/ *adj* **1** flácido **2** débil

limp[2] /lɪmp/ ◆ *vi* cojear ◆ *n* cojera: *to have a limp* ser/estar cojo

line[1] /laɪn/ *n* **1** línea, raya **2** fila **3 lines** [*pl*] (*Teat*): *to learn your lines* aprender tu papel **4 lines** [*pl*] copias (*castigo*) **5** cuerda: *a fishing line* un sedal (de pesca) ◊ *a clothes line* un tendedero **6** línea telefónica: *The line is engaged.* Está comunicando. **7** vía **8** [*sing*]: *the official line* la postura oficial LOC **along/on the same, etc lines** del mismo, etc estilo **in line with sth** conforme a algo *Ver tb* DROP, HARD, HOLD, TOE

line[2] /laɪn/ *vt* alinear(se) PHR V **to line up** (**for sth**) ponerse en fila (para algo) **lined** *adj* **1** (*papel*) rayado **2** (*rostro*) arrugado

line[3] /laɪn/ *vt* ~ **sth** (**with sth**) forrar, revestir algo (de algo) **lined** *adj* forrado, revestido **lining** *n* **1** forro **2** revestimiento

line drawing *n* dibujo a lápiz o pluma

linen /ˈlɪnɪn/ *n* **1** lino **2** ropa blanca

liner /ˈlaɪnə(r)/ *n* transatlántico

linger /ˈlɪŋgə(r)/ *vi* **1** (*persona*) quedarse mucho tiempo **2** (*duda, olor, memoria*) perdurar, persistir

linguist /ˈlɪŋgwɪst/ *n* **1** políglota, **2** lingüista **linguistic** /lɪŋˈgwɪstɪk/ *adj* lingüístico **linguistics** *n* [*sing*] lingüística

link /lɪŋk/ ◆ *n* **1** eslabón **2** lazo **3** vínculo **4** conexión: *satellite link* vía satélite ◆ *vt* **1** unir: *to link arms* cogerse del brazo **2** vincular, relacionar PHR V **to link up** (**with sth/sb**) unirse (con algo/algn)

lion /ˈlaɪən/ *n* león: *a lion-tamer* un domador de leones ◊ *a lion-cub* un cachorro de león

lip /lɪp/ *n* labio

lip-read /ˈlɪp riːd/ *vi* (*pret, pp* **lip-read** /-red/) leer los labios

lipstick /ˈlɪpstɪk/ *n* lápiz de labios

liqueur /lɪˈkjʊə(r); *USA* -ˈkɜːr/ *n* licor

liquid /ˈlɪkwɪd/ ◆ *n* líquido ◆ *adj* líquido **liquidize, -ise** *vt* licuar **liquidizer, -iser** (*tb* **blender**) *n* licuadora

liquor /ˈlɪkə(r)/ *n* **1** (*GB*) alcohol **2** (*USA*) bebida fuerte

liquorice (*USA* **licorice**) /ˈlɪkərɪs/ *n* regaliz

lisp /lɪsp/ ◆ *n* ceceo ◆ *vt, vi* cecear

list /lɪst/ ◆ *n* lista: *to make a list* hacer una lista ◊ *waiting list* lista de espera ◆ *vt* **1** enumerar, hacer una lista de **2** catalogar

listen /ˈlɪsn/ *vi* **1** ~ (**to sth/sb**) escuchar (a algo/algn) **2** ~ **to sth/sb** hacer caso a algo/algn PHR V **to listen** (**out**) **for** estar atento a **listener** *n* **1** (*Radio*) oyente **2** *a good listener* uno que sabe escuchar

lit *pret, pp de* LIGHT

literacy /ˈlɪtərəsi/ *n* capacidad de leer y escribir

literal /ˈlɪtərəl/ *adj* literal **literally** *adv* literalmente

literary /ˈlɪtərəri; *USA* -reri/ *adj* literario

literate /ˈlɪtərət/ *adj* que sabe leer y escribir

literature /ˈlɪtrətʃə(r); *USA* -tʃʊər/ *n* **1** literatura **2** (*coloq*) información

litre (*USA* **liter**) /ˈliːtə(r)/ *n* (*abrev* **l**) litro ☛ *Ver* Apéndice 1.

litter /ˈlɪtə(r)/ ◆ *n* **1** (*papel, etc en la calle*) basura **2** (*Zool*) camada ◆ *vt* estar esparcido por: *Newspapers littered the floor.* Había periódicos tirados por el suelo.

litter bin *n* papelera

little /ˈlɪtl/ ◆ *adj* ☛ El comparativo **littler** y el superlativo **littlest** son poco frecuentes y normalmente se usan **smaller** y **smallest**. **1** pequeño: *When I was little…* Cuando era pequeño… ◊ *my little brother* mi hermano pequeño ◊ *little finger* meñique ◊ *Poor little thing!* ¡Pobrecillo! **2** poco: *to wait a little while* esperar un poco ☛ *Ver nota en* LESS

¿**Little** o **a little**? *Little* tiene un sentido negativo y equivale a "poco". *A little* tiene un sentido mucho más positivo, equivale a "algo de". Compara las siguientes oraciones: *I've got little hope.* Tengo pocas esperanzas. ◊ *You should always carry a little money with you.* Siempre deberías llevar algo de dinero encima.

◆ *n, pron* poco: *There was little anyone could do.* No se pudo hacer nada. *I only want a little.* Sólo quiero un poco. ◆ *adv* poco: *little more than an hour ago* hace poco más de una hora LOC **little by little** poco a poco **little or nothing** casi nada

live¹ /laɪv/ ◆ *adj* **1** vivo **2** (*bomba, etc*) activado **3** (*Electrón*) conectado **4** (*TV*) en directo **5** (*grabación*) en vivo ◆ *adv* en directo

live² /lɪv/ *vi* **1** vivir: *Where do you live?* ¿Dónde vives? **2** (*fig*) permanecer vivo PHR V **to live for sth** vivir para algo **to live on** seguir viviendo **to live on sth** vivir de algo **to live through sth** sobrevivir algo **to live up to sth** estar a la altura de su fama **to live with sth** aceptar algo

livelihood /ˈlaɪvlihʊd/ *n* medio de subsistencia

lively /ˈlaɪvli/ *adj* (**-ier**, **-iest**) **1** (*persona, imaginación*) vivo **2** (*conversación, fiesta*) animado

liver /ˈlɪvə(r)/ *n* hígado

lives *plural de* LIFE

livestock /ˈlaɪvstɒk/ *n* ganado

living /ˈlɪvɪŋ/ ◆ *n* vida: *to earn/make a living* ganarse la vida ◊ *What do you do for a living?* ¿Cómo te ganas la vida? ◊ *cost/standard of living* coste de la vida/nivel de vida ◆ *adj* [*sólo antes de sustantivo*] vivo: *living creatures* seres vivos ☛ *Comparar con* ALIVE LOC **in/within living memory** que se recuerda

living room (*GB* **sitting room**) *n* cuarto de estar

lizard /ˈlɪzəd/ *n* lagarto, lagartija

load /ləʊd/ ◆ *n* **1** carga **2 loads (of sth)** [*pl*] (*coloq*) montones (de algo) LOC **a load of (old) rubbish, etc** (*coloq*): *What a load of rubbish!* ¡Vaya montón de chorradas! ◆ **1** *vt* ~ **sth (into/onto sth/sb)** cargar algo (en algo/algn) **2** *vt* ~ **sth (up) (with sth)** cargar algo (con/de algo) **3** *vt* ~ **sth/sb (down)** cargar (con mucho peso) algo/a algn **4** *vi* ~ **(up)/(up with sth)** cargar algo (con algo) **loaded** *adj* cargado LOC **a loaded question** una pregunta con segundas

loaf /ləʊf/ *n* (*pl* **loaves** /ləʊvz/) pan (*de molde, redondo, etc*): *a loaf of bread* una hogaza de pan ☛ *Ver dibujo en* PAN

loan /ləʊn/ *n* préstamo

loathe /ləʊð/ *vt* abominar **loathing** *n* aborrecimiento

loaves *plural de* LOAF

lobby /ˈlɒbi/ ◆ *n* (*pl* **-ies**) **1** vestíbulo **2** [*v sing o pl*] (*Pol*) grupo (*de presión*) ◆ *vt* (*pret, pp* **lobbied**) ~ (**sb**) (**for sth**) presionar (a algn) (para algo)

lobster /ˈlɒbstə(r)/ *n* langosta

local /ˈləʊkl/ *adj* **1** local, de la zona: *local authority* gobierno provincial/regional **2** (*Med*) localizado: *local anaesthetic* anestesia local **locally** *adv* localmente

locate /ləʊˈkeɪt; *USA* ˈləʊkeɪt/ *vt* **1** localizar **2** situar

location /ləʊˈkeɪʃn/ *n* **1** lugar **2** localización **3** (*persona*) paradero LOC **to be on location** rodar en exteriores

loch /lɒk, lɒx/ *n* (*Escocia*) lago

lock /lɒk/ ◆ *n* **1** cerradura **2** (*canal*) esclusa ◆ *vt, vi* **1** cerrar con llave **2** (*volante, etc*) bloquear(se) PHR V **to lock sth away/up** guardar algo bajo llave **to lock sb up** encerrar a algn

locker /ˈlɒkə(r)/ *n* taquilla (*armario*)

lodge /lɒdʒ/ ◆ *n* **1** casa del guarda **2** (*de caza, pesca, etc*) pabellón **3** portería ◆ *vi* **1** ~ (**with sb/at**...) hospedarse (con algn/en casa de...) **2** ~ **in sth** alojarse en algo **lodger** *n* huésped **lodging** *n* **1** alojamiento: *board and lodging* alojamiento y comida **2 lodgings** [*pl*] habitaciones

loft /lɒft; *USA* lɔːft/ *n* desván

log¹ /lɒg; *USA* lɔːg/ *n* **1** tronco **2** leño

log² /lɒg; *USA* lɔːg/ ◆ *n* diario de vuelo/navegación ◆ *vt* (**-gg-**) anotar PHR V **to log in/on** (*Informát*) entrar en sesión **to log off/out** (*Informát*) salir de sesión

logic /ˈlɒdʒɪk/ *n* lógica **logical** *adj* lógico

logo /ˈləʊgəʊ/ *n* (*pl* ~**s**) logotipo

lollipop /ˈlɒlipɒp/ *n* piruleta

lonely /ˈləʊnli/ *adj* **1** solo: *to feel lonely* sentirse solo ☛ *Ver nota en* ALONE **2** solitario **loneliness** *n* soledad **loner** *n* solitario, -a

long[1] /lɒŋ; *USA* lɔːŋ/ ◆ *adj* (**longer** /lɒŋgə(r)/**longest** /lɒŋgɪst/) **1** (*longitud*) largo: *It's two metres long.* Mide dos metros de largo. **2** (*tiempo*): *a long time ago* hace mucho tiempo ◊ *How long are the holidays?* ¿Cuánto duran las vacaciones? LOC **at the longest** como máximo **in the long run** a la larga *Ver tb* TERM ◆ *adv* (**longer** /lɒŋgə(r)/**longest** /lɒŋgɪst/) **1** mucho (tiempo): *Stay as long as you like.* Quédate cuanto quieras. ◊ *long ago* hace mucho tiempo ◊ *long before/after* mucho antes/después **2** todo: *the whole night long* toda la noche ◊ *all day long* todo el día LOC **as/so long as** con tal de que **for long** mucho tiempo **no longer/not any longer**: *I can't stay any longer.* No me puedo quedar más.

long[2] /lɒŋ; *USA* lɔːŋ/ *vi* **1** ~ **for sth/to do sth** ansiar algo/hacer algo **2** ~ **for sb to do sth** estar deseando que algn haga algo **longing** *n* anhelo

long-distance /ˌlɒŋ ˈdɪstəns/ *adj, adv* de larga distancia: *to phone long-distance* poner una conferencia

longitude /ˈlɒndʒɪtjuːd; *USA* -tuːd/ *n* longitud (*Geog*) ☛ *Comparar con* LATITUDE

long jump *n* salto de longitud

long-life /ˌlɒŋ ˈlaɪf/ *adj* de larga duración

long-range /ˌlɒŋ ˈreɪndʒ/ *adj* **1** a largo plazo **2** de largo alcance

long-sighted /ˈlɒŋ saɪtɪd/ *adj* hipermétrope

long-standing /ˌlɒŋ ˈstændɪŋ/ *adj* de hace mucho tiempo

long-suffering /ˌlɒŋ ˈsʌfərɪŋ/ *adj* resignado

long-term /ˌlɒŋ ˈtɜːm/ *adj* a largo plazo

loo /luː/ *n* (*pl* **loos**) (*GB, coloq*) cuarto de baño ☛ *Ver nota en* TOILET

look[1] /lʊk/ *vi* **1** mirar: *She looked out of the window.* Miró por la ventana. **2** parecer: *You look tired.* Pareces cansada. **3** ~ **onto sth** dar a algo LOC **don't look a gift horse in the mouth** (*refrán*) a caballo regalado no le mires el dentado (**not**) **to look yourself** (no) parecer uno mismo **to look on the bright side** mirar el lado bueno de las cosas **to look sb up and down** mirar a algn de arriba abajo **to look your age** aparentar uno la edad que tiene

PHR V **to look after yourself/sb** cuidarse/cuidar a algn

to look at sth 1 examinar algo **2** considerar algo **to look at sth/sb** mirar algo/a algn

to look back (**on sth**) pensar (en algo) pasado

to look down on sth/sb (*coloq*) despreciar algo/a algn

to look for sth/sb buscar algo/a algn

to look forward to sth/doing sth tener ganas de algo/hacer algo

to look into sth investigar algo

to look on mirar (sin tomar parte)

look out: *Look out!* ¡Cuidado! **to look out** (**for sth/sb**) fijarse (por si se ve algo/algn)

to look sth over examinar algo

to look round 1 volver la cabeza para mirar **2** mirar por ahí **to look round sth** visitar algo

to look up 1 alzar la vista **2** (*coloq*) mejorar **to look up to sb** admirar a algn **to look sth up** buscar algo (*en un diccionario o en un libro*)

look[2] /lʊk/ *n* **1** mirada, vistazo: *to have/take a look at sth* echar un vistazo a algo **2** *to have a look for sth* buscar algo **3** aspecto, aire **4** moda **5 looks** [*pl*] físico: *good looks* belleza

lookout /ˈlʊkaʊt/ *n* vigía LOC **to be on the lookout for sth/sb**; **to keep a lookout for sth/sb** *Ver* TO LOOK OUT (FOR STH/SB) *en* LOOK[1]

loom /luːm/ ◆ *n* telar ◆ *vi* **1** ~ (**up**) surgir, asomar(se) **2** (*fig*) amenazar, vislumbrarse

loony /ˈluːni/ *n* (*pl* **-ies** *adj*) (*coloq, pey*) loco, -a

loop /luːp/ ◆ *n* **1** curva, vuelta **2** (*con nudo*) lazo ◆ **1** *vi* dar vueltas **2** *vt*: *to loop sth round/over sth* pasar algo alrededor de/por algo

loophole /ˈluːphəʊl/ *n* escapatoria

loose /luːs/ ◆ *adj* (**-er**, **-est**) **1** suelto: *loose change* (dinero) suelto **2** (*que se puede quitar*) flojo **3** (*vestido*) holgado, ancho **4** (*moral*) relajado LOC **to be at a loose end** no tener nada que hacer *Ver tb* LET[1] ◆ *n* LOC **to be on the loose** andar suelto **loosely** *adv* **1** sin apretar **2** libremente, aproximadamente

loosen /ˈluːsn/ **1** *vt, vi* aflojar(se), soltar(se), desatar(se) **2** *vt* (*control*) relajar PHR V **to loosen up 1** relajarse, soltarse **2** entrar en calor

loot /luːt/ ◆ *n* botín ◆ *vt, vi* saquear **looting** *n* saqueo

lop /lɒp/ *vt* (**-pp-**) podar PHR V **to lop sth off/away** cortar algo

lopsided /ˌlɒp ˈsaɪdɪd/ *adj* **1** torcido **2** (*fig*) desequilibrado

lord /lɔːd/ *n* **1** señor **2 the Lord** el Señor: *the Lord's Prayer* el padrenuestro **3 the Lords** *Ver* THE HOUSE OF LORDS **4 Lord** (*GB*) (*título*) Lord *Ver tb* LADY **lordship** *n* LOC **your/his Lordship** su Señoría

lorry /ˈlɒri; *USA* ˈlɔːri/ *n* (*pl* **-ies**) (*tb esp USA* **truck**) camión

lose /luːz/ (*pret, pp* **lost** /lɒst; *USA* lɔːst/) **1** *vt, vi* perder: *He lost his title to the Russian.* El ruso le quitó el título. **2** *vt* ~ **sb sth** hacer perder algo a algn: *It lost us the game.* Nos costó el partido. **3** *vi* (*reloj*) atrasarse LOC **to lose your mind** volverse loco **to lose your nerve** acobardarse **to lose sight of sth/sb** perder algo/a algn de vista: *We must not lose sight of the fact that...* Debemos tener presente el hecho de que... **to lose your touch** perder facultades **to lose your way** perderse *Ver tb* COOL, GROUND, TEMPER[1], TOSS, TRACK, WEIGHT PHR V **to lose out (on sth)/(to sth/sb)** (*coloq*) salir perdiendo (en algo)/(con respecto a algo/algn) **loser** *n* perdedor, -ora, fracasado, -a

loss /lɒs; *USA* lɔːs/ *n* pérdida LOC **to be at a loss** estar desorientado

lost /lɒst/ ◆ *adj* perdido: *to get lost* perderse LOC **get lost!** (*argot*) ¡piérdete! ◆ *pret, pp de* LOSE

lost property *n* objetos perdidos

lot[1] /lɒt/ ◆ **the (whole) lot** *n* todo(s): *That's the lot!* ¡Eso es todo! ◆ **a lot, lots** *pron* (*coloq*) mucho(s): *He spends a lot on clothes.* Gasta mucho en ropa. ◆ **a lot of, lots of** *adj (coloq)* mucho(s): *lots of people* un montón de gente ◇ *What a lot of presents!* ¡Qué cantidad de regalos! ☛ *Ver nota en* MANY *Ver tb* MUCHO LOC **to see a lot of sb** ver bastante a algn ◆ *adv* mucho: *It's a lot colder today.* Hoy hace mucho más frío. ◇ *Thanks a lot.* Muchas gracias.

lot[2] /lɒt/ *n* **1** lote **2** grupo: *What do you lot want?* ¿Qué queréis vosotros? ◇ *I don't go out with that lot.* No salgo con ésos. **3** suerte (*destino*)

lotion /ˈləʊʃn/ *n* loción

lottery /ˈlɒtəri/ *n* (*pl* **-ies**) lotería

loud /laʊd/ ◆ *adj* (**-er**, **-est**) **1** (*volumen*) alto **2** (*grito*) fuerte **3** (*color*) chillón ◆ *adv* (**-er**, **-est**) alto: *Speak louder.* Habla más alto. LOC **out loud** en voz alta

loudspeaker /laʊdˈspiːkə(r)/ (*tb* **speaker**) *n* altavoz

lounge /laʊndʒ/ ◆ *vi* ~ (**about/around**) gandulear ◆ *n* **1** cuarto de estar **2** sala: *departure lounge* sala de embarque **3** salón

louse /laʊs/ *n* (*pl* **lice** /laɪs/) piojo

lousy /ˈlaʊzi/ *adj* (**-ier**, **-iest**) terrible

lout /laʊt/ *n* gamberro

lovable /ˈlʌvəbl/ *adj* encantador

love /lʌv/ ◆ *n* **1** amor: *love story/song* historia/canción de amor ☛ Nótese que con personas se dice **love** *for* **somebody** y con cosas **love** *of* **something**. **2** (*Dep*) cero LOC **to be in love (with sb)** estar enamorado (de algn) **to give/send sb your love** dar/mandar recuerdos a algn **to make love (to sb)** hacer el amor (con algn) *Ver tb* FALL ◆ *vt* **1** amar, querer: *Do you love me?* ¿Me quieres? **2** *She loves horses.* Le encantan los caballos. ◇ *I'd love to come.* Me encantaría ir.

love affair *n* aventura amorosa

lovely /ˈlʌvli/ *adj* (**-ier**, **-iest**) **1** precioso **2** encantador **3** muy agradable: *We had a lovely time.* Lo pasamos muy bien.

lovemaking /ˈlʌvmeɪkɪŋ/ *n* relaciones sexuales

lover /ˈlʌvə(r)/ *n* amante

loving /ˈlʌvɪŋ/ *adj* cariñoso **lovingly** *adv* amorosamente

low /ləʊ/ ◆ *adj* (**lower**, **lowest**) **1** bajo: *low pressure* baja presión ◇ *high and low temperatures* temperaturas altas y bajas ◇ *lower lip* labio inferior ◇ *lower case* minúsculas ◇ *the lower middle classes* la clase media baja ☛ *Comparar con* HIGH[1], UPPER **2** (*voz, sonido*) grave **3** abatido LOC **to keep a low profile** procurar pasar desapercibido *Ver tb* ESTEEM ◆ *adv* (**lower**, **lowest**) bajo: *to shoot low* disparar bajo LOC *Ver* STOOP ◆ *n* mínimo

low-alcohol /ˌləʊ ˈælkəhɒl/ *adj* bajo en alcohol

low-calorie /ˌləʊ ˈkæləri/ *adj* bajo en calorías

Low-calorie es el término general para referirnos a los productos bajos en calorías o "light". Para bebidas se usa **diet**: *diet drinks* bebidas bajas en calorías.

low-cost /ˌləʊ ˈkɒst/ *adj* barato
lower /ˈləʊə(r)/ *vt, vi* bajar(se)
low-fat /ˌləʊ ˈfæt/ *adj* de bajo contenido graso: *low-fat yogurt* yogur descremado
low-key /ˌləʊ ˈkiː/ *adj* discreto
lowlands /ˈləʊləndz/ *n* [*pl*] tierras bajas **lowland** *adj* de las tierras bajas
low tide *n* marea baja
loyal /ˈlɔɪəl/ *adj* ~ (**to sth/sb**) fiel a algo/algn **loyalist** *n* partidario del régimen **loyalty** *n* (*pl* **-ies**) lealtad
luck /lʌk/ *n* suerte: *a stroke of luck* un golpe de suerte LOC **no such luck** ¡ojalá! **to be in/out of luck** estar de suerte/tener la negra *Ver tb* CHANCE, HARD
lucky /ˈlʌki/ *adj* (**-ier**, **-iest**) **1** (*persona*) afortunado **2** *It's lucky she's still here.* Suerte que todavía está aquí. ◊ *a lucky number* un número de la suerte **luckily** *adv* por suerte
ludicrous /ˈluːdɪkrəs/ *adj* ridículo
luggage /ˈlʌgɪdʒ/ (*USA* **baggage**) *n* [*incontable*] equipaje
luggage rack *n* parrilla del equipaje
lukewarm /ˌluːkˈwɔːm/ *adj* tibio
lull /lʌl/ ◆ *vt* **1** calmar **2** arrullar ◆ *n* periodo de calma
lumber /ˈlʌmbə(r)/ **1** *vt* ~ **sb with sth/sb** hacer a algn cargar con algo/algn **2** *vi* moverse pesadamente **lumbering** *adj* torpe, pesado
lump /lʌmp/ ◆ *n* **1** trozo: *sugar lump* terrón de azúcar **2** grumo **3** (*Med*) bulto ◆ *vt* ~ **sth/sb together** juntar algo/a algn **lumpy** *adj* (**-ier**, **-iest**) **1** (*salsa, etc*) lleno de grumos **2** (*colchón, etc*) lleno de bollos
lump sum *n* pago único
lunacy /ˈluːnəsi/ *n* [*incontable*] locura
lunatic /ˈluːnətɪk/ *n* loco, -a
lunch /lʌntʃ/ ◆ *n* almuerzo, comida: *to have lunch* comer ◊ *the lunch hour* la hora de la comida LOC *Ver* PACKED *en* PACK ◆ *vi* comer ☛ *Ver* pág 320.
lunchtime /ˈlʌntʃtaɪm/ *n* la hora de comer
lung /lʌŋ/ *n* pulmón
lurch /lɜːtʃ/ ◆ *n* sacudida ◆ *vi* **1** tambalearse **2** dar un bandazo
lure /lʊə(r)/ ◆ *n* atractivo ◆ *vt* atraer
lurid /ˈlʊərɪd/ *adj* **1** (*color*) chillón **2** (*descripción, historia*) horripilante
lurk /lɜːk/ *vi* acechar
luscious /ˈlʌʃəs/ *adj* (*comida*) exquisito
lush /lʌʃ/ *adj* (*vegetación*) exuberante
lust /lʌst/ ◆ *n* **1** lujuria **2** ~ **for sth** sed de algo ◆ *vi* ~ **after/for sth/sb** codiciar algo; desear a algn
luxurious /lʌgˈʒʊəriəs/ *adj* lujoso
luxury /ˈlʌkʃəri/ *n* (*pl* **-ies**) lujo: *a luxury hotel* un hotel de lujo
lying *Ver* LIE[1,2]
lyric /ˈlɪrɪk/ ◆ **lyrics** *n* [*pl*] letra (*de una canción*) ◆ *adj Ver* LYRICAL
lyrical /ˈlɪrɪkl/ *adj* lírico

Mm

M, m /em/ *n* (*pl* **M's**, **m's** /emz/) M, m: *M for Mary* M de María ☛ *Ver ejemplos en* A, a
mac (*tb* **mack**) /mæk/ *n* (*GB, coloq*) *Ver* MACKINTOSH
macabre /məˈkɑːbrə/ *adj* macabro
macaroni /ˌmækəˈrəʊni/ *n* [*incontable*] macarrones
machine /məˈʃiːn/ (*lit y fig*) *n* máquina
machine-gun /məˈʃiːn gʌn/ *n* ametralladora
machinery /məˈʃiːnəri/ *n* maquinaria
mackintosh /ˈmækɪntɒʃ/ (*tb* **mac**, **mack** /mæk/) *n* (*GB*) gabardina
mad /mæd/ *adj* (**madder**, **maddest**) loco: *to be/go mad* estar/volverse loco *to be mad about sth/sb* estar loco por algo/algn **2** (*coloq, esp USA*) **mad** (**at/with sb**) furioso (con algn) LOC **like**

mad (*coloq*) como loco **madly** locamente: *to be madly in love with sb* estar perdidamente enamorado de algn **madness** *n* locura

madam /ˈmædəm/ *n* [*sing*] (*fml*) señora

maddening /ˈmædnɪŋ/ *adj* exasperante

made *pret, pp de* MAKE[1]

magazine /ˌmægəˈziːn; *USA* ˈmægəziːn/ *n* (*abrev* **mag**) (*coloq*) revista

maggot /ˈmægət/ *n* gusano

magic /ˈmædʒɪk/ ◆ *n* (*lit y fig*) magia LOC **like magic** como por arte de magia ◆ *adj* mágico **magical** *adj* mágico **magician** *n* mago, -a *Ver tb* CONJURER *en* CONJURE

magistrate /ˈmædʒɪstreɪt/ *n* magistrado, juez municipal: *the magistrates' court* el Juzgado de Paz

magnet /ˈmægnət/ *n* imán **magnetic** /mægˈnetɪk/ *adj* magnético **magnetism** /ˈmægnətɪzəm/ *n* magnetismo **magnetize, -ise** *vt* imantar

magnetic field *n* campo magnético

magnificent /mægˈnɪfɪsnt/ *adj* magnífico **magnificence** *n* magnificencia

magnify /ˈmægnɪfaɪ/ *vt, vi* (*pret, pp* **-fied**) aumentar **magnification** *n* (capacidad de) aumento

magnifying glass *n* lupa

magnitude /ˈmægnɪtjuːd; *USA* -tuːd/ *n* magnitud

mahogany /məˈhɒgəni/ *adj, n* caoba

maid /meɪd/ *n* **1** criada **2** (*Hist*) doncella

maiden /ˈmeɪdn/ *n* (*Hist*) doncella

maiden name *n* apellido de soltera

> En los países de habla inglesa, muchas mujeres toman el apellido del marido cuando se casan.

mail /meɪl/ ◆ *n* [*incontable*] (*esp USA*) correo

> La palabra **post** sigue siendo más normal que **mail** en el inglés británico, aunque **mail** se ha ido introduciendo, especialmente en compuestos como **electronic mail**, **junk mail** y **airmail**.

◆ *vt* ~ **sth (to sb)** enviar por correo algo (a algn)

mailbox /ˈmeɪlbɒks/ (*USA*) (*GB* **letter box**) *n* buzón

mailman /ˈmeɪlmæn/ *n* (*USA*) (*pl* **-men** /-mən/) *Ver* POSTMAN

mail order *n* venta por correo

maim /meɪm/ *vt* mutilar

main[1] /meɪn/ *adj* principal: *main course* segundo plato LOC **in the main** en general **the main thing** lo principal **mainly** *adv* principalmente

main[2] /meɪn/ *n* **1** cañería: *a gas main* una tubería del gas **2 the mains** [*pl*] la red de suministros

mainland /ˈmeɪnlænd/ *n* tierra firme, continente

main line *n* (*Ferrocarril*) línea principal

mainstream /ˈmeɪnstriːm/ *n* corriente principal

maintain /meɪnˈteɪn/ *vt* **1** ~ **sth (with sth/sb)** mantener algo (con algo/algn) **2** conservar: *well-maintained* bien cuidado **3** sostener

maintenance /ˈmeɪntənəns/ *n* **1** mantenimiento **2** pensión de manutención

maize /meɪz/ *n* maíz ☛ Cuando nos referimos al maíz cocinado decimos **sweetcorn**. *Comparar con* CORN

majestic /məˈdʒestɪk/ *adj* majestuoso

majesty /ˈmædʒəsti/ *n* (*pl* **-ies**) **1** majestuosidad **2 Majesty** majestad

major /ˈmeɪdʒə(r)/ ◆ *adj* **1** de (gran) importancia: *to make major changes* realizar cambios de importancia ◊ *a major road/problem* una carretera principal/un problema importante **2** (*Mús*) mayor ◆ *n* comandante

majority /məˈdʒɒrəti; *USA* -ˈdʒɔːr-/ *n* (*pl* **-ies**) **1** [*v sing o pl*] mayoría: *The majority was/were in favour.* La mayoría estaba a favor. **2** [*antes de sustantivo*] mayoritario: *majority rule* gobierno mayoritario

make[1] /meɪk/ *vt* (*pret, pp* **made** /meɪd/) **1** (*causar o crear*): *to make an impression* impresionar ◊ *to make a note of sth* anotar algo **2** (*llevar a cabo*): *to make an improvement/change* hacer una mejora/un cambio ◊ *to make an effort* hacer un esfuerzo ◊ *to make a phone call* hacer una llamada de teléfono ◊ *to make a visit/trip* hacer una visita/un viaje **3** (*proponer*): *to make an offer/a promise* hacer una oferta/una promesa ◊ *to make plans* hacer planes **4** (*otros usos*): *to make a mistake* cometer un error ◊ *to make an excuse* poner una excusa ◊ *to make a comment* hacer un comentario ◊ *to make a noise/hole/list* hacer un ruido/un agujero/una lista **5** ~ **sth** (**from/out of sth**) hacer algo (con/de algo): *He made a meringue from egg white.* Hizo un merengue con clara de huevo. ◊ *What's it made (out) of?* ¿De qué está hecho? ◊ *made in Japan* fabricado en Japón **6** ~ **sth** (**for sb**) hacer algo (para/a algn): *She makes films for children.* Hace películas para niños. ◊ *I'll make you a meal/cup of coffee.* Te voy a preparar una comida/taza de café. **7** ~ **sth into sth** convertir algo en algo; hacer algo con algo: *We can make this room into a bedroom.* Podemos convertir esta habitación en dormitorio. **8** ~ **sth/sb + adj/sust**: *He made me angry.* Hizo que me enfadara. ◊ *That will only make things worse.* Eso sólo empeorará las cosas. ◊ *He made my life hell.* Me hizo la vida imposible. **9** ~ **sth/sb do sth** hacer que algo/algn haga algo ☛ El verbo en infinitivo que viene después de **make** se pone sin TO, salvo en pasiva: *I can't make him do it.* No puedo obligarle a hacerlo. ◊ *You've made her feel guilty.* Has hecho que se sienta culpable. ◊ *He was made to wait at the police station.* Le hicieron esperar en la comisaría. **10** ~ **sb sth** hacer a algn algo: *to make sb king* hacer a algn rey **11** llegar a ser: *He'll make a good teacher.* Tiene madera de profesor. **12** (*dinero*) hacer: *She makes lots of money.* Gana una fortuna. **13** (*coloq*) conseguir llegar a: *Can you make it (to the party)?* ¿Podrás venir (a la fiesta)? LOC **to make do with sth** arreglárselas (con algo) **to make it** (*coloq*) triunfar **to make the most of sth** sacar el mayor provecho de algo ☛ Para otras expresiones con **make**, véanse las entradas del sustantivo, adjetivo, etc, p.ej. **to make love** en LOVE.

PHR V **to be made for sb/each other** estar hecho para algn/estar hechos el uno para el otro **to make for sth** contribuir a (mejorar) algo **to make for sth/sb** dirigirse hacia algo/algn: *to make for home* dirigirse hacia casa

to make sth of sth/sb opinar algo de algo/algn: *What do you make of it all?* ¿Qué opinas de todo esto?

to make off (**with sth**) largarse (con algo)

to make sth out escribir algo: *to make out a cheque for £10* escribir un cheque por valor de diez libras **to make sth/sb out 1** entender algo/a algn **2** distinguir algo/a algn: *to make out sb's handwriting* descifrar la escritura de algn

to make up for sth compensar algo **to make up** (**with sb**) hacer las paces (con algn) **to make sb up** maquillar a algn **to make sth up 1** formar algo: *the groups that make up our society* los grupos que constituyen nuestra sociedad **2** inventar algo: *to make up an excuse* inventarse una excusa **to make** (**yourself**) **up** maquillarse

make[2] /meɪk/ *n* marca (*electrodomésticos, coches, etc*) ☛ *Comparar con* BRAND

maker /ˈmeɪkə(r)/ *n* fabricante

makeshift /ˈmeɪkʃɪft/ *adj* provisional, improvisado

make-up /ˈmeɪk ʌp/ *n* [*incontable*] **1** maquillaje **2** constitución **3** carácter

making /ˈmeɪkɪŋ/ *n* fabricación LOC **to be the making of sb** ser la clave del éxito de algn **to have the makings of sth 1** (*persona*) tener madera de algo **2** (*cosa*) tener los ingredientes para ser algo

male /meɪl/ ◆ *adj* **1** masculino ☛ Se aplica a las características físicas de los hombres: *The male voice is deeper than the female.* La voz de los hombres es más profunda que la de las mujeres. *Comparar con* MASCULINE **2** macho ☛ *Ver nota en* FEMALE ◆ *n* macho varón

malice /ˈmælɪs/ *n* malevolencia, mala intención **malicious** /məˈlɪʃəs/ *adj* mal intencionado

malignant /məˈlɪgnənt/ *adj* maligno

mall /mæl, mɔːl/ (*tb* **shopping mall**) *n* centro comercial

malnutrition /ˌmælnjuːˈtrɪʃn; *USA* -nuː-/ *n* desnutrición

malt /mɔːlt/ *n* malta

mammal /ˈmæml/ *n* mamífero

mammoth /ˈmæməθ/ ◆ *n* mamut ◆ *adj* colosal

man[1] /mæn/ *n* (*pl* **men** /men/) hombre *a young man* un (hombre) joven ◊ *man's shirt* una camisa de caballero LOC **the man in the street** (*GB*) el ciudadano de a pie

Man y **mankind** se utilizan con el significado genérico de "todos los hombres y mujeres". Sin embargo, mucha gente considera este uso discriminatorio, y prefiere utilizar palabras como **humanity, the human race** (singular) o **humans, human beings, people** (plural).

man² /mæn/ *vt* (**-nn-**) **1** (*oficina*) dotar de personal **2** (*nave*) tripular

manage /ˈmænɪdʒ/ **1** *vt* (*empresa*) dirigir **2** *vt* (*propiedades*) administrar **3** *vi* ~ (**without sth/sb**) arreglárselas (sin algo/algn): *I can't manage on £50 a week.* No me llega con 50 libras a la semana. **4** *vt, vi*: *to manage to do sth* conseguir hacer algo ◊ *Can you manage all of it?* ¿Puedes con todo eso? ◊ *Can you manage six o'clock?* ¿Puedes venir a las seis? ◊ *I couldn't manage another mouthful.* Ya no puedo comer ni un bocado más. **manageable** *adj* **1** manejable **2** (*persona o animal*) tratable, dócil

management /ˈmænɪdʒmənt/ *n* dirección, gestión: *a management committee* comité directivo/consejo de administración ◊ *a management consultant* asesor de dirección de empresas

manager /ˈmænɪdʒə(r)/ *n* **1** director, -ora, gerente **2** (*de una propiedad*) administrador, -ora **3** (*Teat*) mánager, empresario, -a **4** (*Dep*) mánager **manageress** *n* administradora, gerente **managerial** /ˌmænəˈdʒɪəriəl/ *adj* directivo, administrativo, de gerencia

managing director *n* director, -ora general

mandate /ˈmændeɪt/ *n* ~ (**to do sth**) mandato (para hacer algo) **mandatory** /ˈmændətəri; *USA* -tɔːri/ *adj* preceptivo

mane /meɪn/ *n* **1** (*caballo*) crin **2** (*león o persona*) melena

maneuver (*USA*) *Ver* MANOEUVRE

manfully /ˈmænfəli/ *adv* valientemente

mangle /ˈmæŋgl/ *vt* mutilar, destrozar

manhood /ˈmænhʊd/ *n* edad viril

mania /ˈmeɪniə/ *n* manía **maniac** *adj, n* maniaco, -a: *to drive like a maniac* conducir como un loco

manic /ˈmænɪk/ *adj* **1** maniaco **2** frenético

manicure /ˈmænɪkjʊə(r)/ *n* manicura

manifest /ˈmænɪfest/ *vt* manifestar, mostrar: *to manifest itself* manifestarse/hacerse patente **manifestation** *n* manifestación **manifestly** *adv* manifiestamente

manifesto /ˌmænɪˈfestəʊ/ *n* (*pl* **~s** *o* **~es**) manifiesto

manifold /ˈmænɪfəʊld/ *adj* (*fml*) múltiple

manipulate /məˈnɪpjuleɪt/ *vt* manipular, manejar **manipulation** *n* manipulación **manipulative** *adj* manipulador

mankind /mænˈkaɪnd/ *n* género humano ☛ *Ver nota en* MAN¹

manly /ˈmænli/ *adj* (**-ier**, **-iest**) varonil, viril

man-made /ˌmæn ˈmeɪd/ *adj* artificial

manned /mænd/ *adj* tripulado

manner /ˈmænə(r)/ *n* **1** manera, forma **2** actitud, modo de comportarse **3** **manners** [*pl*] modales: *good/bad manners* buena educación/mala educación ◊ *It's bad manners to stare.* Es de mala educación mirar fijamente. ◊ *He has no manners.* Es un mal educado.

mannerism /ˈmænərɪzəm/ *n* peculiaridad

manoeuvre (*USA* **maneuver**) /məˈnuːvə(r)/ ◆ *n* maniobra ◆ *vt, vi* maniobrar

manor /ˈmænə(r)/ *n* **1** (*territorio*) señorío **2** (*tb* **manor house**) casa señorial

manpower /ˈmænpaʊə(r)/ *n* mano de obra

mansion /ˈmænʃn/ *n* **1** mansión **2** casa solariega

manslaughter /ˈmænslɔːtə(r)/ *n* homicidio involuntario ☛ *Comparar con* HOMICIDE, MURDER

mantelpiece /ˈmæntlˌpiːs/ (*tb* **chimney-piece**) *n* repisa de la chimenea

manual /ˈmænjuəl/ ◆ *adj* manual ◆ *n* manual: *a training manual* un manual de instrucciones **manually** *adv* manualmente

manufacture /ˌmænjʊˈfæktʃə(r)/ *vt* **1** fabricar ☛ *Comparar con* PRODUCE **2** (*pruebas*) inventar **manufacturer** *n* fabricante

manure /məˈnjʊə(r)/ *n* estiércol

manuscript /ˈmænjuskrɪpt/ *adj, n* manuscrito

many /ˈmeni/ *adj, pron* **1** mucho, -a, -os, -as: *Many people would disagree.*

Mucha gente no estaría de acuerdo. ◊ *I haven't got many left.* No me quedan muchos. ◊ *In many ways, I regret it.* En cierta manera, lo lamento.

Mucho se traduce según el sustantivo al que acompaña o sustituye. En oraciones afirmativas usamos **a lot (of)**: *She's got a lot of money.* Tiene mucho dinero. ◊ *Lots of people are poor.* Mucha gente es pobre. En oraciones negativas e interrogativas usamos **many** o **a lot of** cuando el sustantivo es contable: *I haven't seen many women as bosses.* No he visto muchas mujeres de jefe. Y usamos **much** o **a lot of** cuando el sustantivo es incontable: *I haven't eaten much (food).* No he comido mucho. *Ver tb* MUCHO

2 ~ **a sth**: *Many a politician has been ruined by scandal.* Muchos políticos han sido arruinados por escándalos. ◊ *many a time* muchas veces LOC **a good/great many** muchísimos *Ver tb* so

map /mæp/ ◆ *n* **1** mapa **2** (*ciudad*) plano **3** carta LOC **to put sth/sb on the map** dar a conocer algo/a algn ◆ *vt* (**-pp-**) levantar mapas de PHR V **to map sth out 1** planear algo **2** (*idea*) exponer algo

maple /ˈmeɪpl/ *n* arce

marathon /ˈmærəθən; *USA* -θɒn/ *n* maratón: *to run a marathon* tomar parte en un maratón ◊ *The interview was a real marathon.* Fue una entrevista maratoniana.

marble /ˈmɑːbl/ *n* **1** mármol: *a marble statue* una estatua de mármol **2** canica

March /mɑːtʃ/ *n* (*abrev* **Mar**) marzo ☛ *Ver nota y ejemplos en* JANUARY

march /mɑːtʃ/ ◆ *vi* marchar: *The students marched on Parliament.* Los estudiantes se manifestaron ante el Parlamento. LOC **to get your marching orders** ser despedido *Ver tb* QUICK PHR V **to march sb away/off** llevarse a algn **to march in** entrar resueltamente **to march past (sb)** desfilar (ante algn) **to march up to sb** abordar a algn con resolución ◆ *n* marcha LOC **on the march** en marcha **marcher** *n* manifestante

mare /ˈmeə(r)/ *n* yegua

margarine /ˌmɑːdʒəˈriːn; *USA* ˈmɑːrdʒərɪn/ (*GB, coloq* **marge** /mɑːdʒ/) *n* margarina

margin /ˈmɑːdʒɪn/ *n* margen **marginal** *adj* **1** marginal **2** (*notas*) al margen **marginally** *adv* ligeramente

marina /məˈriːnə/ *n* puerto de recreo

marine /məˈriːn/ ◆ *adj* **1** marino **2** marítimo ◆ *n* infante de marina: *the Marines* la Infantería de Marina

marital /ˈmærɪtl/ *adj* conyugal: *marital status* estado civil

maritime /ˈmærɪtaɪm/ *adj* marítimo

mark /mɑːk/ ◆ *n* **1** marca **2** señal: *punctuation marks* signos de puntuación **3** nota: *a good/poor mark* una nota buena/mediocre LOC **on your marks, (get) set, go!** preparados, listos, ¡ya! **to be up to the mark** dar la talla **to make your mark** alcanzar el éxito *Ver tb* OVERSTEP ◆ *vt* **1** marcar **2** señalar **3** (*exámenes*) corregir LOC **to mark time 1** (*Mil*) marcar el paso **2** (*fig*) hacer tiempo **mark my words** acuérdate de lo que te estoy diciendo PHR V **to mark sth up/down** aumentar/rebajar el precio de algo **marked** /mɑːkt/ *adj* notable **markedly** /ˈmɑːkɪdli/ *adv* (*fml*) de forma notable

marker /ˈmɑːkə(r)/ *n* marca: *a marker buoy* una boya de señalización

market /ˈmɑːkɪt/ ◆ *n* mercado LOC **in the market for sth** (*coloq*) interesado en comprar algo **on the market** en el mercado: *to put sth on the market* poner algo en venta ◆ *vt* **1** vender **2** ~ **sth (to sb)** ofertar algo (a algn) **marketable** *adj* vendible

marketing /ˈmɑːkətɪŋ/ *n* marketing

market place (*tb* **market square**) *n* plaza del mercado

market research *n* estudio de mercado

marmalade /ˈmɑːməleɪd/ *n* mermelada (*de cítricos*)

maroon /məˈruːn/ *adj, n* granate (*color*)

marooned /məˈruːnd/ *adj* abandonado (p. ej. en una isla desierta)

marquee /mɑːˈkiː/ *n* carpa (*entoldado*)

marriage /ˈmærɪdʒ/ *n* **1** (*institución*) matrimonio **2** (*ceremonia*) boda ☛ *Ver nota en* BODA

married /ˈmærid/ *adj* ~ **(to sb)** casado (con algn): *to get married* casarse ◊ *married couple* un matrimonio

marrow[1] /ˈmærəʊ/ *n* médula, tuétano LOC *Ver* CHILL

marrow[2] /ˈmærəʊ/ *n* calabacín

marry /ˈmæri/ *vt, vi* (*pret, pp* **married**) casar(se) *Ver tb* MARRIED

Mars /mɑːz/ *n* Marte

marsh /mɑːʃ/ *n* ciénaga

marshal /ˈmɑːʃl/ ◆ *n* **1** mariscal **2** (*USA*) alguacil ◆ *vt* (**-ll-**, *USA* **-l-**) **1** (*tropas*) formar **2** (*ideas, datos*) ordenar

marshy /ˈmɑːʃi/ *adj* (**-ier**, **-iest**) pantanoso

martial /ˈmɑːʃl/ *adj* marcial

Martian /ˈmɑːʃn/ *adj, n* marciano, -a

martyr /ˈmɑːtə(r)/ *n* mártir **martyrdom** *n* martirio

marvel /ˈmɑːvl/ ◆ *n* maravilla, prodigio ◆ *vi* (**-ll-**, *USA* **-l-**) ~ **at sth** maravillarse ante algo **marvellous** (*USA* **marvelous**) *adj* maravilloso, excelente: *We had a marvellous time.* Lo pasamos de maravilla. ◊ *(That's) marvellous!* ¡Estupendo!

Marxism /ˈmɑːksɪzəm/ *n* marxismo **Marxist** *adj, n* marxista

marzipan /ˈmɑːzɪpæn, ˌmɑːzɪˈpæn/ *n* mazapán

mascara /mæˈskɑːrə; *USA* -ˈskærə/ *n* rímel

mascot /ˈmæskət, -skɒt/ *n* mascota

masculine /ˈmæskjəlɪn/ *adj, n* masculino (*propio del hombre*)

Masculine se aplica a las cualidades que consideramos típicas de un hombre.

masculinity /ˌmæskjuˈlɪnəti/ *n* masculinidad

mash /mæʃ/ ◆ *n* (*GB, coloq*) puré (de patatas) ◆ *vt* **1** ~ **sth** (**up**) machacar, triturar algo **2** hacer puré de: *mashed potatoes* puré de patata

mask /mɑːsk; *USA* mæsk/ ◆ *n* **1** (*lit y fig*) máscara, careta **2** antifaz **3** (*cirujano*) mascarilla ◆ *vt* **1** (*rostro*) enmascarar **2** tapar **3** (*fig*) encubrir, enmascarar **masked** *adj* **1** enmascarado **2** (*atracador*) encapuchado

mason[1] /ˈmeɪsn/ *n* cantero, albañil

mason[2] (*tb* **Mason**) /ˈmeɪsn/ *n* masón **masonic** (*tb* **Masonic**) /məˈsɒnɪk/ *adj* masónico

masonry /ˈmeɪsənri/ *n* albañilería, mampostería

masquerade /ˌmɑːskəˈreɪd; *USA* ˌmæsk-/ ◆ *n* mascarada, farsa ◆ *vi* ~ **as sth** hacerse pasar por algo; disfrazarse de algo

mass[1] (*tb* **Mass**) /mæs/ *n* (*Relig, Mús*) misa

mass[2] /mæs/ ◆ *n* **1** ~ (**of sth**) masa (de algo) **2** montón, gran cantidad: *masses of letters* un montón de cartas **3** [*usado como adj*] masivo, de masas: *a mass grave* una fosa común ◊ *mass hysteria* histeria colectiva ◊ *mass media* medios de comunicación de masas **4 the masses** [*pl*] las masas LOC **the (great) mass of...** la (inmensa) mayoría de... **to be a mass of sth** estar cubierto/lleno de algo ◆ *vt, vi* **1** juntar(se) (en masa), reunir(se) **2** (*Mil*) formar(se), concentrar(se)

massacre /ˈmæsəkə(r)/ ◆ *n* masacre ◆ *vt* masacrar

massage /ˈmæsɑːʒ; *USA* məˈsɑːʒ/ ◆ *vt* dar masaje a ◆ *n* masaje

massive /ˈmæsɪv/ *adj* **1** enorme, monumental **2** macizo, sólido **massively** *adv* enormemente

mass-produce /ˌmæs prəˈdjuːs/ *vt* fabricar en serie

mass production *n* fabricación en serie

mast /mɑːst; *USA* mæst/ *n* **1** (*barco*) mástil **2** (*televisión*) torre

master /ˈmɑːstə(r); *USA* ˈmæs-/ ◆ *n* **1** amo, dueño, señor **2** maestro **3** (*Náut*) capitán **4** (*cinta*) original **5** *master bedroom* dormitorio principal LOC **a master plan** un plan infalible ◆ *vt* **1** dominar **2** controlar **masterful** *adj* **1** con autoridad **2** dominante

masterly /ˈmɑːstəli; *USA* ˈmæs-/ *adj* magistral

mastermind /ˈmɑːstəmaɪnd; *USA* ˈmæs-/ ◆ *n* cerebro ◆ *vt* planear, dirigir

masterpiece /ˈmɑːstəpiːs; *USA* ˈmæs-/ *n* obra maestra

Master's degree (*tb* **Master's**) *n* máster

mastery /ˈmɑːstəri; *USA* ˈmæs-/ *n* **1** ~ (**of sth**) dominio (de algo) **2** ~ (**over sth/sb**) supremacía (sobre algo/algn)

masturbate /ˈmæstəbeɪt/ *vi* masturbarse **masturbation** *n* masturbación

mat /mæt/ *n* **1** estera, felpudo **2**

colchoneta **3** salvamanteles **4** maraña *Ver tb* MATTED

match¹ /mætʃ/ *n* cerilla

match² /mætʃ/ *n* **1** (*Dep*) partido, encuentro **2** igual **3** ~ **(for sth/sb)** complemento (para algo/algn) LOC **a good match** un buen partido **to find/to meet your match** encontrar la horma de tu zapato

match³ /mætʃ/ **1** *vt, vi* combinar con **2** *vt* hacer juego (con): *matching shoes and handbag* zapatos y bolso a juego **3** *vt* igualar PHR V **to match up** coincidir **to match up to sth/sb** igualar algo/a algn **to match sth up (with sth)** acoplar algo (a algo)

matchbox /ˈmætʃbɒks/ *n* caja de cerillas

mate¹ /meɪt/ ◆ *n* **1** (*GB, coloq*) amigo, compañero **2** ayudante **3** (*Náut*) segundo de a bordo **4** (*Zool*) pareja ◆ *vt, vi* aparear(se)

mate² /meɪt/ (*tb* **checkmate**) *n* jaque mate

material /məˈtɪəriəl/ ◆ *n* **1** material: *raw materials* materias primas **2** tela ☛ *Ver nota en* TELA ◆ *adj* material **materially** *adv* sensiblemente

materialism /məˈtɪəriəlɪzəm/ *n* materialismo **materialist** *n* materialista **materialistic** /məˌtɪəriəˈlɪstɪk/ *adj* materialista

materialize, -ise /məˈtɪəriəlaɪz/ *vi* convertirse en realidad

maternal /məˈtɜːnl/ *adj* **1** maternal **2** (*familiares*) materno

maternity /məˈtɜːnəti/ *n* maternidad

mathematical /ˌmæθəˈmætɪkl/ *adj* matemático **mathematician** /ˌmæθəməˈtɪʃn/ *n* matemático, -a **mathematics** /ˌmæθəˈmætɪks/ *n* [*sing*] matemáticas

maths /mæθs/ *n* [*sing*] (*coloq*) matemáticas

matinée /ˈmætɪneɪ; *USA* ˌmætnˈeɪ/ *n* matiné (*cine, teatro*)

mating /ˈmeɪtɪŋ/ *n* apareamiento LOC **mating season** época de celo

matrimony /ˈmætrɪməni; *USA* -məʊni/ *n* (*fml*) matrimonio **matrimonial** /ˌmætrɪˈməʊniəl/ *adj* matrimonial

matron /ˈmeɪtrən/ *n* enfermera jefe

matt (*USA* **matte**) /mæt/ *adj* **1** mate (*color*) **2** (*tb* **matt paint**) pintura mate ☛ *Comparar con* GLOSS

matted /ˈmætɪd/ *adj* enmarañado

matter /ˈmætə(r)/ ◆ *n* **1** asunto: *I have nothing further to say on the matter.* No tengo nada más que decir al respecto. **2** (*Fís*) materia **3** material: *printed matter* impresos LOC **a matter of hours, minutes, days, etc** cosa de horas, minutos, días, etc **a matter of life and death** cuestión de vida o muerte **a matter of opinion** cuestión de opinión **as a matter of course** por costumbre **as a matter of fact** en realidad **for that matter** si vamos a eso **no matter who, what, where, when, etc**: *no matter what he says* diga lo que diga ◊ *no matter how rich he is* por muy rico que sea ◊ *no matter what* pase lo que pase **(to be) a matter of...** (ser) cuestión de... **to be the matter (with sth/sb)** (*coloq*) pasarle a algo/algn: *What's the matter with him?* ¿Qué le pasa? ◊ *Is anything the matter?* ¿Pasa algo? ◊ *What's the matter with my dress?* ¿Qué pasa con mi vestido? **to take matters into your own hands** decidir obrar por cuenta propia *Ver tb* LET¹, MINCE, WORSE ◆ *vi* ~ **(to sb)** importar (a algn)

matter-of-fact /ˌmætər əv ˈfækt/ *adj* **1** (*estilo*) prosaico **2** (*persona*) impasible **3** realista

mattress /ˈmætrəs/ *n* colchón

mature /məˈtjʊə(r); *USA* -ˈtʊər/ ◆ *adj* **1** maduro **2** (*Com*) vencido ◆ **1** *vi* madurar **2** *vi* (*Com*) vencer **3** *vt* hacer madurar **maturity** *n* madurez

maul /mɔːl/ *vt* **1** maltratar **2** (*fiera*) herir seriamente

mausoleum /ˌmɔːsəˈliːəm/ *n* mausoleo

mauve /məʊv/ *adj, n* malva

maverick /ˈmævərɪk/ *n* LOC **to be a maverick** ir por libre

maxim /ˈmæksɪm/ *n* máxima

maximize, -ise /ˈmæksɪmaɪz/ *vt* potenciar/llevar al máximo

maximum /ˈmæksɪməm/ *adj, n* (*pl* **maxima** /ˈmæksɪmə/) (*abrev* **max**) máximo

May /meɪ/ *n* mayo ☛ *Ver nota y ejemplos en* JANUARY

may /meɪ/ *v modal* (*pret* **might** /maɪt/ *neg* **might not** *o* **mightn't** /ˈmaɪtnt/)

May es un verbo modal al que sigue un infinitivo sin TO, y las oraciones interrogativas y negativas se construyen sin el auxiliar *do*. Sólo tiene do

iː	i	ɪ	e	æ	ɑː	ʌ	ʊ	uː
see	happy	sit	ten	hat	arm	cup	put	too

formas: presente, **may**, y pasado, **might**.

1 (*permiso*) poder: *You may come if you wish.* Puedes venir si quieres. ◇ *May I go to the toilet?* ¿Puedo ir al servicio? ◇ *You may as well go home.* Más vale que vuelvas a casa.

Para pedir permiso, **may** se considera más cortés que **can**, aunque **can** es mucho más normal: *Can I come in?* ¿Puedo pasar? ◇ *May I get down from the table?* ¿Puedo levantarme de la mesa? ◇ *I'll take a seat, if I may.* Tomaré asiento, si no le importa. Sin embargo, en el pasado se usa **could** mucho más que **might**: *She asked if she could come in.* Preguntó si podía pasar.

2 (*tb* **might**) (*posibilidad*) poder (que): *They may/might not come.* Puede que no vengan. ☛ *Ver nota en* PODER[1] LOC **be that as it may** sea como fuere

maybe /ˈmeɪbi/ *adv* quizá(s)

mayhem /ˈmeɪhem/ *n* [*incontable*] alboroto

mayonnaise /ˌmeɪəˈneɪz; *USA* ˈmeɪəneɪz/ *n* mayonesa

mayor /meə(r); *USA* ˈmeɪər/ *n* alcalde **mayoress** /meəˈres/ *n* **1** (*tb* **lady mayor**) alcaldesa **2** esposa del alcalde

maze /meɪz/ *n* laberinto

me /miː/ *pron pers* **1** [*como objeto*] me: *Don't hit me.* No me pegues. ◇ *Tell me all about it.* Cuéntame todo. **2** [*después de preposición*] mí: *as for me* en cuanto a mí ◇ *Come with me.* Ven conmigo. **3** [*cuando va sólo o después del verbo* **to be**] yo: *Hello, it's me.* Hola, soy yo. ☛ *Comparar con* I

meadow /ˈmedəʊ/ *n* prado

meagre (*USA* **meager**) /ˈmiːgə(r)/ *adj* escaso, pobre

meal /miːl/ *n* comida LOC **to make a meal of sth** (*coloq*) hacer algo con una atención o un esfuerzo exagerado *Ver tb* SQUARE

mean[1] /miːn/ *vt* (*pret, pp* **meant** /ment/) **1** querer decir, significar: *Do you know what I mean?* ¿Sabes lo que quiero decir? ◇ *What does 'cuero' mean?* ¿Qué quiere decir "cuero"? **2** ~ **sth (to sb)** significar algo (para algn): *You know how much Jane means to me.* Sabes lo mucho que Jane significa para mí. ◇ *That name doesn't mean anything to me.* Ese nombre no me dice nada. **3** suponer: *His new job means him travelling more.* Su nuevo trabajo significa que tiene que viajar más. **4** pretender: *I didn't mean to.* Ha sido sin querer. ◇ *I meant to have washed the car today.* Pensaba haber lavado el coche hoy. **5** decir en serio: *She meant it as a joke.* No lo dijo en serio. ◇ *I'm never coming back—I mean it!* ¡No volveré nunca, lo digo en serio! LOC **I mean** (*coloq*) quiero decir: *It's very warm, isn't it? I mean, for this time of year.* Hace mucho calor ¿no? Quiero decir, para esta época del año. ◇ *We went there on Tuesday, I mean Thursday.* Fuimos el martes, quiero decir, el jueves. **to be meant for each other** estar hechos el uno para el otro **to mean business** (*coloq*) ir en serio **to mean well** tener buenas intenciones

mean[2] /miːn/ *adj* (**-er**, **-est**) **1** ~ **(with sth)** tacaño (con algo) **2** ~ **(to sb)** mezquino (con algn)

mean[3] /miːn/ *n* **1** término medio **2** (*Mat*) media **mean** *adj* medio

meander /mɪˈændə(r)/ *vi* **1** (*río*) serpentear **2** (*persona*) deambular **3** (*conversación*) divagar

meaning /ˈmiːnɪŋ/ *n* significado **meaningful** *adj* trascendente **meaningless** *adj* sin sentido

means[1] /miːnz/ *n* [*v sing o pl*] manera LOC **a means to an end** un medio para conseguir un fin **by all means** (*fml*) desde luego *Ver tb* WAY

means[2] /miːnz/ *n* [*pl*] medios

meant *pret, pp de* MEAN[1]

meantime /ˈmiːntaɪm/ *adv* mientras tanto LOC **in the meantime** mientras tanto

meanwhile /ˈmiːnwaɪl/ *adv* mientras tanto

measles /ˈmiːzlz/ *n* [*incontable*] sarampión

measurable /ˈmeʒərəbl/ *adj* **1** medible **2** sensible

measure /ˈmeʒə(r)/ ◆ *vt, vi* medir PHR V **to measure sth/sb up (for sth)** medir algo/a algn: *The tailor measured me up for a suit.* El sastre me ha tomado medidas para un traje. **to measure up (to sth)** estar a la altura (de algo) ◆ *n* medida: *weights and measures* pesos y medidas ◇ *to take measures to do sth* tomar medidas para *hacer algo* LOC **a measure of sth** signo de algo **for good measure** para no quedarse cortos **half measures** medias tintas **to make sth to measure** hacer algo a medida

measured /ˈmeʒəd/ *adj* **1** (*lenguaje*) comedido **2** (*pasos*) pausado

measurement /ˈmeʒəmənt/ *n* **1** medición **2** medida

meat /miːt/ *n* carne

meatball /ˈmiːtbɔːl/ *n* albóndiga

meaty /ˈmiːti/ *adj* (**-ier**, **-iest**) **1** carnoso **2** (*fig*) jugoso

mechanic /məˈkænɪk/ *n* mecánico, -a **mechanical** *adj* mecánico **mechanically** *adv* mecánicamente: *I'm not mechanically minded.* No sirvo para las máquinas.

mechanics /məˈkænɪks/ *n* **1** [*sing*] mecánica (*ciencia*) **2 the mechanics** [*pl*] (*fig*) mecánica, funcionamiento

mechanism /ˈmekənɪzəm/ *n* mecanismo

medal /ˈmedl/ *n* medalla **medallist** (*USA* **medalist**) *n* medallista

medallion /məˈdæliən/ *n* medallón

meddle /ˈmedl/ *vi* (*pey*) **1** ~ **(in sth)** entrometerse (en algo) **2** ~ **with sth** jugar con algo

media /ˈmiːdiə/ *n* **1 the media** [*pl*] medios de comunicación: *media studies* estudios de periodismo **2** *plural de* MEDIUM[1]

mediaeval *Ver* MEDIEVAL

mediate /ˈmiːdieɪt/ *vi* mediar **mediation** *n* mediación **mediator** *n* mediador, -ora

medic /ˈmedɪk/ *n* (*coloq*) **1** médico, -a **2** estudiante de medicina

medical /ˈmedɪkl/ ◆ *adj* **1** médico: *medical student* estudiante de medicina **2** clínico ◆ *n* (*coloq*) reconocimiento médico

medication /ˌmedɪˈkeɪʃn/ *n* medicación

medicinal /məˈdɪsɪnl/ *adj* medicinal

medicine /ˈmedsn; *USA* ˈmedɪsn/ *n* medicina

medieval (*tb* **mediaeval**) /ˌmediˈiːvl; *USA* ˌmiːd-/ *adj* medieval

mediocre /ˌmiːdɪˈəʊkə(r)/ *adj* mediocre **mediocrity** /ˌmiːdɪˈɒkrəti/ *n* **1** mediocridad **2** (*persona*) mediocre

meditate /ˈmedɪteɪt/ *vi* ~ **(on sth)** meditar (sobre algo) **meditation** *n* meditación

medium[1] /ˈmiːdɪəm/ ◆ *n* **1** (*pl* **media**) medio **2** (*pl* ~**s**) punto medio *Ver tb* MEDIA ◆ *adj* medio: *I'm medium.* Uso la talla mediana.

medium[2] /ˈmiːdɪəm/ *n* médium

medley /ˈmedli/ *n* (*pl* **-eys**) popurrí

meek /miːk/ *adj* (**-er**, **-est**) manso **meekly** *adv* mansamente

meet[1] /miːt/ (*pret, pp* **met** /met/) **1** *vt, vi* encontrar(se): *What time shall we meet?* ¿A qué hora quedamos? ◇ *Our eyes met across the table.* Nuestras miradas se cruzaron en la mesa. ◇ *Will you meet me at the station?* ¿Irás a esperarme a la estación? **2** *vi* reunirse **3** *vt, vi* conocer(se): *Pleased to meet you.* Encantado de conocerle. ◇ *I'd like you to meet...* Quiero presentarte a... **4** *vt, vi* enfrentar(se) **5** *vt* (*demanda*) satisfacer: *They failed to meet payments on their loan.* No pudieron pagar las letras del préstamo. LOC **to meet sb's eye** mirar a algn a los ojos *Ver tb* MATCH[2] PHR V **to meet up (with sb)** coincidir (con algn) **to meet with sb** (*USA*) reunirse con algn

meet[2] /miːt/ *n* **1** (*GB*) partida de caza **2** (*USA, Dep*) encuentro *Ver tb* MEETING 3

meeting /ˈmiːtɪŋ/ *n* **1** encuentro: *meeting place* lugar de encuentro **2** (*discusión*) reunión: *Annual General Meeting* junta general anual **3** (*Dep*) encuentro *Ver tb* MEET[2] **4** (*Pol*) reunión

megaphone /ˈmegəfəʊn/ *n* megáfono

melancholy /ˈmelənkɒli/ ◆ *n* melancolía ◆ *adj* **1** (*persona*) melancólico **2** (*cosa*) triste

mêlée /ˈmeleɪ; *USA* ˈmeɪleɪ/ *n* (*Fr*) mel[é]

mellow /ˈmeləʊ/ ◆ *adj* (**-er**, **-est**) **1** (*fruta*) maduro **2** (*vino*) añejo **3** (*color*) suave **4** (*sonido*) dulce **5** (*actitud*) comprensivo **6** (*coloq*) alegre (*de beber*) ◆ **1** *vt, vi* (*persona*) ablandarse **2** *vi* (*vino*) envejecer

melodious /məˈləʊdiəs/ *adj* melodioso

melodrama /ˈmelədrɑːmə/ *n* melodrama **melodramatic** /ˌmelədrəˈmætɪk/ *adj* melodramático

melody /ˈmelədi/ *n* (*pl* **-ies**) melodía **melodic** /məˈlɒdɪk/ *adj* melódico

melon /ˈmelən/ *n* melón

melt /melt/ **1** *vt, vi* derretir(se): *meltin*

point punto de fusión **2** *vi* (*fig*) deshacerse: *to melt in the mouth* deshacerse en la boca **3** *vt, vi* disolver(se) **4** *vt, vi* (*fig*) ablandar(se) PHR V **to melt away** disolverse, fundirse **to melt sth down** fundir algo **melting** *n* **1** derretimiento **2** fundición

melting pot *n* amalgama (*de razas, culturas, etc*) LOC **to be in/go into the melting pot** estar en proceso de cambio

member /ˈmembə(r)/ *n* **1** miembro: *Member of Parliament (MP)* diputado, -a ◊ *a member of the audience* uno de los asistentes **2** (*club*) socio **3** (*Anat*) miembro **membership** *n* **1** afiliación: *to apply for membership* solicitar la entrada ◊ *membership card* tarjeta de socio **2** (número de) miembros/socios

membrane /ˈmembreɪn/ *n* membrana

memento /məˈmentəʊ/ *n* (*pl* **-os** *o* **-oes**) recuerdo

memo /ˈmeməʊ/ *n* (*pl* **~s**) (*coloq*) circular: *an inter-office memo* una circular

memoir /ˈmemwɑː(r)/ *n* memoria

memorabilia /ˌmemərəˈbɪliə/ *n* [*pl*] recuerdos

memorable /ˈmemərəbl/ *adj* memorable

memorandum /ˌmeməˈrændəm/ *n* (*pl* **-anda** /-də/ *o* **~s**) **1** memorándum, memorando **2** ~ **(to sb)** nota (a algn) **3** (*Jur*) minuta

memorial /məˈmɔːriəl/ *n* ~ **(to sth/sb)** monumento conmemorativo (de algo/algn)

memorize, -ise /ˈmeməraɪz/ *vt* memorizar

memory /ˈmeməri/ *n* (*pl* **-ies**) **1** memoria: *from memory* de memoria *Ver tb* BY HEART *en* HEART **2** recuerdo LOC **in memory of sb/to the memory of sb** en memoria de algn *Ver tb* JOG, LIVING, REFRESH

men *plural de* MAN[1]

menace /ˈmenəs/ ◆ *n* **1** ~ **(to sth/sb)** amenaza (para algo/algn) **2 a menace** (*coloq, joc*) un peligro ◆ *vt* ~ **sth/sb (with sth)** amenazar algo/a algn (con algo) **menacing** *adj* amenazador

menagerie /məˈnædʒəri/ *n* casa de fieras

mend /mend/ ◆ **1** *vt* arreglar *Ver tb* FIX **2** *vi* curarse LOC **to mend your ways** reformarse ◆ *n* remiendo LOC **on the mend** (*coloq*) mejorando **mending** *n* **1** arreglo (*de la ropa*) **2** ropa para arreglar

menfolk /ˈmenfəʊk/ *n* [*pl*] hombres

meningitis /ˌmenɪnˈdʒaɪtɪs/ *n* meningitis

menopause /ˈmenəpɔːz/ *n* menopausia

menstrual /ˈmenstruəl/ *adj* menstrual

menstruation /ˌmenstruˈeɪʃn/ *n* menstruación

menswear /ˈmenzweə(r)/ *n* ropa de caballero

mental /ˈmentl/ *adj* **1** mental: *mental hospital* hospital para enfermos mentales **2** (*coloq, pey*) mal de la cabeza **mentally** *adv* mentalmente: *mentally ill/disturbed* enfermo/trastornado mental

mentality /menˈtæləti/ *n* (*pl* **-ies**) **1** mentalidad **2** (*fml*) intelecto

mention /ˈmenʃn/ ◆ *vt* mencionar, decir, hablar de: *worth mentioning* digno de mención LOC **don't mention it** no hay de qué **not to mention...** por no hablar de..., sin contar... ◆ *n* mención, alusión

mentor /ˈmentɔː(r)/ *n* mentor

menu /ˈmenjuː/ *n* **1** menú, carta **2** (*Informát*) menú

mercantile /ˈmɜːkəntaɪl; *USA* -tiːl, -tɪl/ *adj* mercantil

mercenary /ˈmɜːsənəri; *USA* -neri/ ◆ *adj* **1** mercenario **2** (*fig*) interesado ◆ *n* (*pl* **-ies**) mercenario, -a

merchandise /ˈmɜːtʃəndaɪz/ *n* [*incontable*] mercancía(s), mercadería(s) **merchandising** *n* comercialización

merchant /ˈmɜːtʃənt/ *n* **1** comerciante, mayorista (que comercia con el extranjero) *Ver tb* DEAL[3], DEALER **2** (*Hist*) mercader **3** *merchant bank* banco comercial ◊ *merchant navy* marina mercante

merciful *Ver* MERCY

Mercury /ˈmɜːkjəri/ *n* Mercurio

mercury /ˈmɜːkjəri/ (*tb* **quicksilver**) *n* mercurio

mercy /ˈmɜːsi/ *n* **1** compasión, clemencia: *to have mercy on sb* tener compasión de algn ◊ *mercy killing* eutanasia **2** *It's a mercy that...* Es una suerte que... LOC **at the mercy of sth/sb** a merced de algo/algn **merciful** *adj* **1** ~ **(to/towards sb)** compasivo, clemente (con algn) **2**

(*suceso*) feliz **mercifully** *adv* **1** compasivamente, con piedad **2** felizmente **merciless** *adj* ~ **(to/towards sb)** despiadado (con algn)

mere /mɪə(r)/ *adj* mero, simple: *He's a mere child.* No es más que un niño. ◊ *mere coincidence* pura casualidad ◊ *the mere thought of him* con sólo pensar en él LOC **the merest...** el menor...: *The merest glimpse was enough.* Un simple vistazo fue suficiente. **merely** *adv* sólo, meramente

merge /mɜːdʒ/ *vt, vi* ~ **(sth) (with/into sth) 1** (*Com*) fusionar algo/fusionarse (con/en algo): *Three small companies merged into one large one.* Tres empresas pequeñas se fusionaron para formar una grande. **2** (*fig*) entremezclar algo/entremezclarse, unir algo/unirse (con/en algo): *Past and present merge in Oxford.* En Oxford se entremezclan el pasado y el presente. **merger** *n* fusión

meringue /məˈræŋ/ *n* merengue

merit /ˈmerɪt/ ◆ *n* mérito: *to judge sth on its merits* juzgar algo según sus méritos ◆ *vt* (*fml*) merecer, ser digno de

mermaid /ˈmɜːmeɪd/ *n* sirena

merry /ˈmeri/ *adj* (**-ier**, **-iest**) **1** alegre: *Merry Christmas!* ¡Feliz Navidad! **2** (*coloq*) alegre, chispado (*de beber*) LOC **to make merry** (*antic*) divertirse **merriment** *n* (*fml*) alegría, regocijo: *amid merriment* entre risas

merry-go-round /ˈmeri gəʊ raʊnd/ *n* tiovivo

mesh /meʃ/ ◆ *n* **1** malla: *wire mesh* tela metálica **2** (*Mec*) engranaje **3** (*fig*) red ◆ *vi* ~ **(with sth) 1** engranar (con algo) **2** (*fig*) encajar (con algo)

mesmerize, -ise /ˈmezməraɪz/ *vt* hipnotizar

mess /mes/ ◆ *n* **1** desastre: *This kitchen's a mess!* ¡Esta cocina está hecha una porquería! **2** (*coloq, eufemismo*) (*excremento*) inmundicia **3** enredo, lío **4** guarro, -a **5** (*Mil*) (*USA tb* **mess hall**) comedor ◆ *vt* (*USA, coloq*) desordenar PHR V **to mess about/around 1** hacer el tonto **2** pasar el rato **to mess sb about/around**; **to mess about/around with sb** tratar con desconsideración a algn **to mess sth about/around**; **to mess about/around with sth** enredar con algo

to mess sb up (*coloq*) traumatizar a algn **to mess sth up 1** ensuciar algo, enredar algo: *Don't mess up my hair!* ¡No me despeines! **2** hacer algo de forma chapucera

to mess with sth/sb (*coloq*) entrometerse en algo/en los asuntos de algn

message /ˈmesɪdʒ/ *n* **1** recado **2** mensaje **3** encargo LOC **to get the message** (*coloq*) enterarse

messenger /ˈmesɪndʒə(r)/ *n* mensajero, -a

Messiah /məˈsaɪə/ (*tb* **messiah**) *n* Mesías

messy /ˈmesi/ *adj* (**-ier**, **-iest**) **1** sucio **2** revuelto, desordenado **3** (*fig*) embrollado

met *pret, pp de* MEET[1]

metabolism /məˈtæbəlɪzəm/ *n* metabolismo

metal /ˈmetl/ *n* metal: *metalwork* trabajo del metal **metallic** /məˈtælɪk/ *adj* metálico

metamorphose /ˌmetəˈmɔːfəʊz/ *vt, vi* (*fml*) convertir(se) **metamorphosis** /ˌmetəˈmɔːfəsɪs/ *n* (*pl* **-oses** /-əsiːz/) (*fml*) metamorfosis

metaphor /ˈmetəfə(r)/ *n* metáfora **metaphorical** /ˌmetəˈfɒrɪkl; *USA* -ˈfɔːr-/ *adj* metafórico ☛ *Comparar con* LITERAL

metaphysics /ˌmetəˈfɪzɪks/ *n* [*incontable*] metafísica **metaphysical** *adj* metafísico

meteor /ˈmiːtɪɔː(r)/ *n* meteorito **meteoric** /ˌmiːtiˈɒrɪk; *USA* -ˈɔːr-/ *adj* meteórico

meteorite /ˈmiːtiəraɪt/ *n* meteorito

meter /ˈmiːtə(r)/ ◆ *n* **1** contador **2** (*USA*) *Ver* METRE ◆ *vt* medir

methane /ˈmiːθeɪn/ (*tb* **marsh gas**) *n* metano

method /ˈmeθəd/ *n* método: *a method of payment* un sistema de pago **methodical** /məˈθɒdɪkl/ *adj* metódico **methodology** *n* metodología

Methodist /ˈmeθədɪst/ *adj, n* metodista

methylated spirits /ˌmeθəleɪtɪd ˈspɪrɪts/ (*coloq, GB* **meths**) *n* alcohol desnaturalizado

meticulous /məˈtɪkjələs/ *adj* meticuloso

metre (*USA* **meter**) /ˈmiːtə(r)/ *n* (*abrev*

m) metro ☛ *Ver* Apéndice 1. **metric** /ˈmetrɪk/ *adj* métrico: *the metric system* el sistema métrico decimal

metropolis /məˈtrɒpəlɪs/ *n* (*pl* **-lises**) metrópoli **metropolitan** /ˌmetrəˈpɒlɪtən/ *adj* metropolitano

miaow /miˈaʊ/ ◆ *interj* miau ◆ *n* maullido ◆ *vi* maullar

mice *plural de* MOUSE

mickey /ˈmɪki/ *n* LOC **to take the mickey (out of sb)** (*coloq*) burlarse (de algn)

micro /ˈmaɪkrəʊ/ (*tb* **microcomputer**) *n* ordenador personal

microbe /ˈmaɪkrəʊb/ *n* microbio

microchip /ˈmaɪkrəʊtʃɪp/ (*tb* **chip**) *n* microchip

microcosm /ˈmaɪkrəkɒzəm/ *n* microcosmos

micro-organism /ˌmaɪkrəʊˈɔːgənɪzəm/ *n* microorganismo

microphone /ˈmaɪkrəfəʊn/ *n* micrófono

microprocessor /ˈmaɪkrəʊˈprəʊsesə(r)/ *n* microprocesador

microscope /ˈmaɪkrəskəʊp/ *n* microscopio **microscopic** /ˌmaɪkrəˈskɒpɪk/ *adj* microscópico

microwave /ˈmaɪkrəweɪv/ *n* **1** microonda **2** (*tb* **microwave oven**) microondas

mid /mɪd/ *adj*: *in mid-July* a mediados de julio ◊ *mid-morning* media mañana ◊ *in mid sentence* a mitad de frase ◊ *midlife crisis* crisis de los cuarenta

mid-air /ˌmɪd ˈeə(r)/ *n* en el aire: *in mid-air* en el aire ◊ *to leave sth in mid-air* dejar algo sin resolver

midday /ˌmɪdˈdeɪ/ *n* mediodía

middle /ˈmɪdl/ ◆ *n* **1 the middle** [*sing*] medio, centro: *in the middle of the night* en mitad de la noche **2** (*coloq*) cintura LOC **in the middle of nowhere** (*coloq*) en el quinto pino ◆ *adj* central, medio: *middle finger* dedo corazón ◊ *middle management* ejecutivos de nivel intermedio LOC **the middle ground** terreno neutral **(to take/follow) a middle course** (tomar/seguir) una línea media

middle age *n* madurez **middle-aged** *adj* de mediana edad

middle class *n* clase media: *the middle classes* la clase media **middle-class** *adj* de clase media

middleman /ˈmɪdlmæn/ *n* (*pl* **-men** /-men/) intermediario

middle name *n* segundo nombre

> En los países de habla inglesa, utilizan dos nombres y un apellido.

middle-of-the-road /ˌmɪdl əv ðə ˈrəʊd/ *adj* (*frec pey*) moderado

middleweight /ˈmɪdlweɪt/ *n* peso medio

midfield /ˌmɪdˈfiːld/ *n* centro del campo: *midfield player* centrocampista **midfielder** *n* centrocampista

midge /mɪdʒ/ *n* mosquito

midget /ˈmɪdʒɪt/ *n* enano

midnight /ˈmɪdnaɪt/ *n* medianoche

midriff /ˈmɪdrɪf/ *n* abdomen

midst /mɪdst/ *n* medio: *in the midst of* en medio de LOC **in our midst** entre nosotros

midsummer /ˌmɪdˈsʌmə(r)/ *n* periodo alrededor del solsticio de verano (*21 de junio*): *Midsummer('s) Day* día de San Juan (24 de junio)

midway /ˌmɪdˈweɪ/ *adv* ~ **(between ...)** a medio camino (entre ...)

midweek /ˌmɪdˈwiːk/ *n* entre semana LOC **in midweek** a mediados de semana

midwife /ˈmɪdwaɪf/ *n* (*pl* **-wives** /-waɪvz/) comadrón, -ona **midwifery** /ˈmɪdwɪfəri/ *n* obstetricia

midwinter /ˌmɪdˈwɪntə(r)/ *n* periodo alrededor del solsticio de invierno (*21 de diciembre*)

miffed /mɪft/ *adj* (*coloq*) cabreado

might[1] /maɪt/ *v modal* (*neg* **might not** *o* **mightn't** /ˈmaɪtnt/) **1** *pret de* MAY **2** (*tb* **may**) (*posibilidad*) poder (que): *They may/might not come.* Puede que no vengan. ◊ *I might be able to.* Es posible que pueda. **3** (*fml*): *Might I make a suggestion?* ¿Podría hacer una sugerencia? ◊ *And who might she be?* Y ¿ésa quién será? ◊ *You might at least offer to help!* Lo menos que podrías hacer es echar una mano. ◊ *You might have told me!* ¡Me lo podías haber dicho! ☛ *Ver nota en* MAY, PODER[1]

might[2] /maɪt/ *n* [*incontable*] fuerza: *with all their might* con todas sus fuerzas ◊ *military might* poderío militar **mightily** *adv* (*coloq*) enormemente

mighty *adj* (**-ier**, **-iest**) **1** poderoso, potente **2** enorme

migraine /ˈmiːgreɪn; *USA* ˈmaɪgreɪn/ *n* migraña

migrant /ˈmaɪgrənt/ ◆ *adj* **1** (*persona*) emigrante **2** (*animal, ave*) migratorio ◆ *n* emigrante

migrate /maɪˈgreɪt; *USA* ˈmaɪgreɪt/ *vi* migrar **migratory** /ˈmaɪgrətri, maɪˈgreɪtəri; *USA* ˈmaɪgrətɔːri/ *adj* migratorio

mike /maɪk/ *n* micrófono

mild /maɪld/ *adj* (**-er**, **-est**) **1** (*carácter*) apacible **2** (*clima*) templado: *a mild winter* un invierno suave **3** (*sabor, etc*) suave **4** (*enfermedad, castigo*) leve **5** ligero **mildly** *adv* ligeramente, un tanto: *mildly surprised* un tanto sorprendido LOC **to put it mildly** por no decir otra cosa, cuando menos

mildew /ˈmɪldjuː; *USA* ˈmɪlduː/ *n* moho

mild-mannered /ˌmaɪld ˈmænəd/ *adj* apacible, manso

mile /maɪl/ *n* **1** milla **2 miles** (*coloq*): *He's miles better.* Él es mucho mejor. **3** *esp* **the mile** carrera de una milla LOC **miles from anywhere/nowhere** en el quinto pino **to be miles away** (*coloq*) estar en la inopia **to see/tell, etc sth a mile off** (*coloq*) notar algo a la legua **mileage** *n* **1** recorrido en millas, kilometraje **2** (*coloq*, *fig*) ventaja

milestone /ˈmaɪlstəʊn/ *n* **1** mojón (*en carretera*) **2** (*fig*) hito

milieu /ˈmiːljɜː; *USA* ˌmiːˈljɜː/ *n* (*pl* **-eus** *o* **-eux**) entorno social

militant /ˈmɪlɪtənt/ ◆ *adj* militante ◆ *n* militante

military /ˈmɪlətri; *USA* -teri/ ◆ *adj* militar ◆ *n* [*v sing o pl*] los militares, el ejército

militia /məˈlɪʃə/ *n* [*v sing o pl*] milicia **militiaman** *n* (*pl* **-men** /-mən/) miliciano

milk /mɪlk/ ◆ *n* leche: *milk products* productos lácteos ◊ *milk shake* batido LOC *Ver* CRY ◆ *vt* **1** ordeñar **2** (*fig*) chupar **milky** *adj* (**-ier**, **-iest**) **1** (*té, café, etc*) con leche **2** lechoso

milkman /ˈmɪlkmən/ *n* (*pl* **-men** /-mən/) lechero

mill /mɪl/ ◆ *n* **1** molino **2** molinillo **3** fábrica: *steel mill* acerería ◆ *vt* moler PHR V **to mill about/around** arremolinarse **miller** *n* molinero, -a

millennium /mɪˈleniəm/ *n* (*pl* **-ia** /-nɪə/ *o* **-iums**) **1** milenio **2 the millennium** (*fig*) la edad de oro

millet /ˈmɪlɪt/ *n* mijo

million /ˈmɪljən/ *adj*, *n* **1** millón ☛ *Ver ejemplos en* FIVE **2** (*fig*) sinfín LOC **one, etc in a million** excepcional **millionth 1** *adj* millonésimo **2** *n* millonésima parte ☛ *Ver ejemplos en* FIFTH

millionaire /ˌmɪljəˈneə(r)/ *n* (*fem* **millionairess**) millonario, -a

> En un contexto comercial **millionaire** también se emplea para el femenino, porque **millionairess** suele usarse para describir a una mujer de la alta sociedad con una gran fortuna familiar.

millstone /ˈmɪlstəʊn/ *n* piedra de molino LOC **a millstone round your/sb's neck** una carga enorme (para algn)

mime /maɪm/ ◆ *n* mimo: *a mime artist* un, -a mimo ◆ *vt*, *vi* hacer mimo, imitar

mimic /ˈmɪmɪk/ ◆ *vt* (*pret*, *pp* **mimicked** *pt pres* **mimicking**) imitar ◆ *n* imitador, -ora **mimicry** *n* imitación

mince /mɪns/ ◆ *vt* picar (*carne*) LOC **not to mince matters**; **not to mince (your) words** no andarse con rodeos ◆ *n* (*USA* **ground beef**) carne picada

mincemeat /ˈmɪnsmiːt/ *n* relleno de frutas LOC **to make mincemeat of sth/sb** (*coloq*) hacer picadillo algo/a algn

mince pie *n* pastelillo navideño relleno de frutas

mind /maɪnd/ ◆ *n* **1** ánimo **2** (*intelecto*) mente, cerebro: *mind-boggling* increíble **3** pensamiento(s): *My mind was on other things.* Estaba pensando en otra cosa. **4** juicio: *to be sound in mind and body* estar sano en cuerpo y alma LOC **in your mind's eye** en la imaginación **to be in two minds about (doing) sth** estar indeciso sobre (si hacer) algo **to be on your mind**: *What's on your mind?* ¿Qué te preocupa? **to be out of your mind** (*coloq*) estar como una cabra **to come/spring to mind** ocurrírsele a algn **to have a (good) mind to do sth** (*coloq*) tener ganas de hacer algo **to have a mind of your own** ser una persona de mente independiente **to have sth/sb in mind (for sth)** tener algo/a algn pensado (para algo) **to keep your mind on sth** concentrarse en algo **to make up your**

mind decidir(se) **to my mind** a mi parecer **to put/set your/sb's mind at ease/rest** tranquilizarse/tranquilizar a algn **to put/set/turn your mind to sth** centrarse en algo, proponerse algo **to take your/sb's mind off sth** distraerse/distraer a algn de algo *Ver tb* BACK[1], BEAR[2], CHANGE, CLOSE[2], CROSS, FOCUS, FRAME, GREAT, PREY, SIGHT, SLIP, SOUND[2], SPEAK, STATE[1], UPPERMOST ◆ **1** *vt* cuidar de **2** *vt, vi* (*importar*): *I wouldn't mind a drink.* No vendría mal tomar algo. ◊ *Do you mind if I smoke?* ¿Te molesta si fumo? ◊ *I don't mind.* Me da igual. ◊ *Would you mind going tomorrow?* ¿Te importa ir mañana? **3** *vt* preocuparse de: *Don't mind him.* No le hagas caso. **4** *vt, vi* tener cuidado (con): *Mind your head!* ¡Cuidado con la cabeza! LOC **do you mind?** (*irón, pey*) ¿Te importa? **mind you; mind** (*coloq*) a decir verdad **never mind** no importa **never you mind** (*coloq*) no preguntes **to mind your own business** no meterse en lo que no le importa a algn PHR V **to mind out (for sth/sb)** tener cuidado (con algo/algn) **minder** *n* cuidador, -ora **mindful** *adj* (*fml*) consciente **mindless** *adj* tonto

mine[1] /maɪn/ *pron pos* mío, -a, -os, -as: *a friend of mine* un amigo mío ◊ *Where's mine?* ¿Dónde está la mía? ☛ *Comparar con* MY

mine[2] /maɪn/ ◆ *n* mina: *mine worker* minero, -a ◆ *vt* **1** extraer (*minerales*) **2** (*lit y fig*) minar **3** sembrar minas en **miner** *n* minero, -a

minefield /ˈmaɪnfiːld/ *n* **1** campo de minas **2** (*fig*) terreno peligroso/delicado

mineral /ˈmɪnərəl/ *n* mineral: *mineral water* agua mineral

mingle /ˈmɪŋgl/ **1** *vi* charlar con gente (*en una fiesta, reunión, etc*): *The president mingled with his guests.* El presidente charló con los invitados. **2** *vi* ~ (**with sth**) mezclarse (con algo) **3** *vt* mezclar

miniature /ˈmɪnətʃə(r); *USA* ˈmɪnɪətʃʊər/ *n* miniatura

minibus /ˈmɪnibʌs/ *n* (*GB*) microbús

minicab /ˈmɪnikæb/ *n* (*GB*) radiotaxi

minimal /ˈmɪnɪməl/ *adj* mínimo

minimize, -ise /ˈmɪnɪmaɪz/ *vt* minimizar

minimum /ˈmɪnɪməm/ ◆ *n* (*pl* **minima** /-mə/) (*abrev* **min**) [*gen sing*] mínimo: *with a minimum of effort* con un esfuerzo mínimo ◆ *adj* mínimo: *There is a minimum charge of…* Se cobra un mínimo de…

mining /ˈmaɪnɪŋ/ *n* minería: *the mining industry* la industria minera

minister /ˈmɪnɪstə(r)/ ◆ *n* **1** (*USA* **secretary**) ~ (**for/of sth**) secretario, -a (de algo) ☛ *Ver nota en* MINISTRO **2** ministro, -a (*protestante*) ☛ *Ver nota en* PRIEST ◆ *vi* ~ **to sth/sb** (*fml*) atender a algo/algn **ministerial** /ˌmɪnɪˈstɪəriəl/ *adj* ministerial

ministry /ˈmɪnɪstri/ *n* (*pl* **-ies**) **1** (*USA* **department**) (*Pol*) ministerio **2** **the ministry** clero (*protestante*): *to enter/go into/take up the ministry* hacerse pastor/sacerdote

mink /mɪŋk/ *n* visón

minor /ˈmaɪnə(r)/ ◆ *adj* **1** secundario: *minor repairs* pequeñas reparaciones ◊ *minor injuries* heridas leves **2** (*Mús*) menor ◆ *n* menor de edad

minority /maɪˈnɒrəti; *USA* -ˈnɔːr-/ *n* [*v sing o pl*] (*pl* **-ies**) minoría: *a minority vote* un voto minoritario LOC **to be in a/the minority** estar en (una/la) minoría

mint /mɪnt/ ◆ *n* **1** menta **2** pastilla de menta **3** (*tb* **the Royal Mint**) la Real Casa de la Moneda **4** [*sing*] (*coloq*) dineral LOC **in mint condition** en perfectas condiciones ◆ *vt* acuñar

minus /ˈmaɪnəs/ ◆ *prep* **1** menos **2** (*coloq*) sin: *I'm minus my car today.* Estoy sin coche hoy. **3** (*temperatura*) bajo cero: *minus five* cinco grados bajo cero ◆ *adj* (*Educ*) bajo: *B minus (B-)* notable bajo ◆ *n* **1** (*tb* **minus sign**) (signo) menos **2** (*coloq*) desventaja: *the pluses and minuses of sth* los más y los menos de algo

minute[1] /ˈmɪnɪt/ *n* **1** minuto **2** minuto, momento: *Wait a minute!/Just a minute!* ¡Un momento! **3** instante: *at that very minute* en ese preciso instante **4** nota (*oficial*) **5** **minutes** [*pl*] actas (*de una reunión*) LOC **not for a/one minute/moment** (*coloq*) ni por un segundo **the minute/moment (that)…** en cuanto…

minute[2] /maɪˈnjuːt; *USA* -ˈnuːt/ *adj* (**-er**, **-est**) **1** diminuto **2** minucioso **minutely** *adv* minuciosamente

miracle /ˈmɪrəkl/ *n* milagro: *a miracle cure* una cura milagrosa LOC **to do/**

work miracles/wonders (*coloq*) hacer milagros **miraculous** /mɪˈrækjələs/ *adj* **1** milagroso: *He had a miraculous escape.* Salió ileso de milagro. **2** (*coloq*) asombroso

mirage /ˈmɪrɑːʒ, mɪˈrɑːʒ/ *n* espejismo

mirror /ˈmɪrə(r)/ ◆ *n* **1** espejo: *mirror image* réplica exacta/imagen invertida **2** (*en coche*) retrovisor **3** (*fig*) reflejo ◆ *vt* reflejar

mirth /mɜːθ/ *n* (*fml*) **1** risa **2** alegría

misadventure /ˌmɪsədˈventʃə(r)/ *n* **1** (*fml*) desgracia **2** (*Jur*): *death by misadventure* muerte accidental

misbehave /ˌmɪsbɪˈheɪv/ *vi* portarse mal **misbehaviour** (*USA* **misbehavior**) *n* mal comportamiento

miscalculation /ˌmɪskælkjuˈleɪʃn/ *n* error de cálculo

miscarriage /ˌmɪsˈkærɪdʒ, ˈmɪs-/ *n* (*Med*) aborto (*espontáneo*) LOC **miscarriage of justice** error judicial

miscellaneous /ˌmɪsəˈleɪniəs/ *adj* variado: *miscellaneous expenditure* gastos varios

mischief /ˈmɪstʃɪf/ *n* **1** travesura, diablura: *to keep out of mischief* no hacer travesuras **2** daño **mischievous** *adj* **1** (*niño*) travieso **2** (*sonrisa*) pícaro

misconceive /ˌmɪskənˈsiːv/ *vt* (*fml*) interpretar mal: *a misconceived project* un proyecto mal planteado **misconception** *n* idea equivocada: *It is a popular misconception that...* Es un error corriente el creer que...

misconduct /ˌmɪsˈkɒndʌkt/ *n* (*fml*) **1** (*Jur*) mala conducta: *professional misconduct* error profesional **2** (*Com*) mala administración

miser /ˈmaɪzə(r)/ *n* avaro, -a **miserly** *adj* (*pey*) **1** avaro **2** mísero

miserable /ˈmɪzrəbl/ *adj* **1** triste, infeliz **2** despreciable **3** miserable: *miserable weather* tiempo de perros ◊ *I had a miserable time.* Lo pasé muy mal. **miserably** *adv* **1** tristemente **2** miserablemente: *Their efforts failed miserably.* Sus esfuerzos fueron un fracaso total.

misery /ˈmɪzəri/ *n* (*pl* **-ies**) **1** tristeza, sufrimiento: *a life of misery* una vida de perros **2** [*gen pl*] miseria **3** (*GB, coloq*) aguafiestas LOC **to put sb out of their misery** (*lit y fig*) acabar con la agonía/el sufrimiento de algn

misfortune /ˌmɪsˈfɔːtʃuːn/ *n* desgracia

misgiving /ˌmɪsˈɡɪvɪŋ/ *n* [*gen pl*] duda (*aprensión*)

misguided /ˌmɪsˈɡaɪdɪd/ *adj* (*fml*) equivocado: *misguided generosity* generosidad mal entendida

mishap /ˈmɪshæp/ *n* **1** contratiempo **2** percance

misinform /ˌmɪsɪnˈfɔːm/ *vt* ~ **sb (about sth)** (*fml*) informar mal a algn (sobre algo)

misinterpret /ˌmɪsɪnˈtɜːprɪt/ *vt* interpretar mal **misinterpretation** *n* interpretación errónea

misjudge /ˌmɪsˈdʒʌdʒ/ *vt* **1** juzgar mal **2** calcular mal

mislay /ˌmɪsˈleɪ/ *vt* (*pret, pp* **mislaid**) extraviar

mislead /ˌmɪsˈliːd/ *vt* (*pret, pp* **misled** /-ˈled/) ~ **sb (about/as to sth)** llevar a conclusiones erróneas a algn (respecto a algo): *Don't be misled by...* No te dejes engañar por... **misleading** *adj* engañoso

mismanagement /ˌmɪsˈmænɪdʒmənt/ *n* mala administración

misogynist /mɪˈsɒdʒɪnɪst/ *n* misógino

misplaced /ˌmɪsˈpleɪst/ *adj* **1** mal colocado **2** (*afecto, confianza*) inmerecido **3** fuera de lugar

misprint /ˈmɪsprɪnt/ *n* errata

misread /ˌmɪsˈriːd/ *vt* (*pret, pp* **misread** /-ˈred/) **1** leer mal **2** interpretar mal

misrepresent /ˌmɪsˌreprɪˈzent/ *vt* ~ **sb** tergiversar las palabras de algn

Miss /mɪs/ *n* señorita (=Srta.) ☛ *Ver nota en* SEÑORITA

miss /mɪs/ ◆ **1** *vt, vi* no acertar, fallar: *to miss your footing* dar un traspié **2** *vt* no ver: *You can't miss it.* No tiene pérdida. ◊ *I missed what you said.* Se me escapó lo que dijiste. ◊ *to miss the point* no ver la intención **3** *vt* (*no llegar a tiempo para*) perder **4** *vt* sentir/advertir la falta de **5** *vt* echar de menos **6** *vt* evitar: *to narrowly miss (hitting) sth* esquivar algo por un pelo LOC **not to miss much**; **not to miss a trick** (*coloq*) ser muy espabilado PHR V **to miss sth/sb out** olvidarse de algo/a algn **to miss out (on sth)** (*coloq*) perder la oportunidad (de algo) ◆ *n* tiro errado LOC **to give sth a miss** (*coloq*) pasar de algo

missile /ˈmɪsaɪl; *USA* ˈmɪsl/ *n* **1** proyectil **2** (*Mil*) misil

missing /ˈmɪsɪŋ/ *adj* **1** extraviado **2** que falta: *He has a tooth missing.* Le falta un diente. **3** desaparecido: *missing persons* desaparecidos

mission /ˈmɪʃn/ *n* misión

missionary /ˈmɪʃənri; *USA* -neri/ *n* (*pl* **-ies**) misionero, -a

mist /mɪst/ ◆ *n* **1** neblina ☛ *Comparar con* FOG, HAZE **2** (*fig*) bruma: *lost in the mists of time* perdido en la noche de los tiempos ◆ PHR V **to mist over/up** empañar(se) **misty** *adj* (**-ier**, **-iest**) **1** (*tiempo*) con neblina **2** (*fig*) borroso

mistake /mɪˈsteɪk/ ◆ *n* error, equivocación: *to make a mistake* equivocarse

> Las palabras **mistake**, **error**, **fault** y **defect** están relacionadas. **Mistake** y **error** significan lo mismo, pero **error** es más formal. **Fault** indica la culpabilidad de una persona: *It's all your fault.* Es todo culpa tuya. También puede indicar una imperfección: *an electrical fault* un fallo eléctrico ◊ *He has many faults.* Tiene muchos defectos. **Defect** es una imperfección más grave.

LOC **and no mistake** (*coloq*) sin duda alguna **by mistake** por equivocación ◆ *vt* (*pret* **mistook** /mɪˈstʊk/ *pp* **mistaken** /mɪˈsteɪkən/) **1** equivocarse de: *I mistook your meaning/what you meant.* Entendí mal lo que dijiste. **2** ~ **sth/sb for sth/sb** confundir algo/a algn con algo/algn LOC **there's no mistaking sth/sb** es imposible confundir a algo/algn **mistaken** *adj* ~ (**about sth/sb**) equivocado (sobre algo/algn): *if I'm not mistaken* si no me equivoco **mistakenly** *adv* erróneamente, por equivocación

mister /ˈmɪstə(r)/ *n* (*abrev* **Mr**) Señor

mistletoe /ˈmɪsltəʊ/ *n* muérdago

mistook *pret de* MISTAKE

mistreat /ˌmɪsˈtriːt/ *vt* maltratar

mistress /ˈmɪstrəs/ *n* **1** señora *Ver tb* MASTER **2** (*de situación, animal*) dueña **3** (*esp GB*) profesora **4** querida

mistrust /ˌmɪsˈtrʌst/ ◆ *vt* desconfiar de ◆ *n* ~ (**of sth/sb**) desconfianza (hacia algo/algn)

misty *Ver* MIST

misunderstand /ˌmɪsʌndəˈstænd/ *vt, vi* (*pret, pp* **misunderstood** /ˌmɪsˌʌndəˈstʊd/) entender mal **misunderstanding** *n* **1** malentendido **2** desavenencia

misuse /ˌmɪsˈjuːs/ *n* **1** (*palabra*) mal empleo **2** (*fondos*) malversación **3** abuso

mitigate /ˈmɪtɪgeɪt/ *vt* (*fml*) mitigar, atenuar

mix /mɪks/ ◆ **1** *vt, vi* mezclar(se) **2** *vi* **to mix (with sth/sb)** tratar con algo/algn: *She mixes well with other children.* Se relaciona bien con otros niños. LOC **to be/get mixed up in sth** (*coloq*) estar metido/meterse en algo PHR V **to mix sth in(to sth)** añadir algo (a algo) **to mix sth/sb up (with sth/sb)** confundir algo/a algn (con algo/algn) ◆ *n* **1** mezcla **2** (*Cocina*) preparado **mixed** *adj* **1** mixto **2** surtido **3** (*tiempo*) variable LOC **to have mixed feelings (about sth/sb)** tener sentimientos encontrados (sobre algo/algn) **mixer** *n* **1** mezclador **2** (*coloq*): *to be a good/bad mixer* ser sociable/insociable **mixture** *n* **1** mezcla **2** combinación **mix-up** *n* (*coloq*) confusión

moan /məʊn/ ◆ **1** *vt, vi* gemir, decir gimiendo **2** *vi* ~ (**about sth**) (*coloq*) quejarse (de algo) ◆ *n* **1** gemido **2** (*coloq*) queja

moat /məʊt/ *n* foso (*de castillo*)

mob /mɒb/ ◆ *n* [*v sing o pl*] **1** chusma **2** (*coloq*) banda (*de delincuentes*), mafia ◆ *vt* (**-bb-**) acosar

mobile /ˈməʊbaɪl; *USA* -bl *tb* -biːl/ *adj* **1** móvil: *mobile library* biblioteca ambulante ◊ *mobile home* caravana **2** (*cara*) cambiante **mobility** /məʊˈbɪləti/ *n* movilidad

mobilize, -ise /ˈməʊbəlaɪz/ **1** *vt, vi* (*Mil*) movilizar(se) **2** *vt* organizar

mock /mɒk/ ◆ **1** *vt* burlarse de **2** *vi* ~ (**at sth/sb**) burlarse (de algo/algn): *a mocking smile* una sonrisa burlona ◆ *n* LOC **to make (a) mock of sth/sb** poner algo/a algn en ridículo ◆ *adj* **1** ficticio: *mock battle* simulacro de combate **2** falso, de imitación **mockery** *n* [*incontable*] **1** burla **2** ~ (**of sth**) parodia (de algo) LOC **to make a mockery of sth** poner algo en ridículo

mode /məʊd/ *n* (*fml*) **1** (*de transporte*) medio **2** (*de producción*) modo **3** (*de pensar*) forma

model /ˈmɒdl/ ◆ *n* **1** modelo **2** maqueta: *scale model* maqueta a escala

◊ *model car* coche en miniatura ◆ *vt, vi* (**-ll-**, *USA* **-l-**) pasar modelos, ser modelo PHR V **to model yourself/sth on sth/sb** basarse/basar algo en algo/algn **modelling** (*USA* **modeling**) *n* **1** modelado **2** trabajo de modelo

moderate /ˈmɒdərət/ ◆ *adj* **1** moderado: *Cook over a moderate heat.* Cocinar a fuego lento. **2** regular ◆ *n* moderado, -a ◆ /ˈmɒdəreɪt/ *vt, vi* moderar(se): *a moderating influence* una influencia moderadora **moderation** *n* moderación LOC **in moderation** con moderación

modern /ˈmɒdn/ *adj* moderno: *to study modern languages* estudiar idiomas **modernity** /məˈdɜːnəti/ *n* modernidad **modernize, -ise** *vt, vi* modernizar(se)

modest /ˈmɒdɪst/ *adj* **1** modesto **2** pequeño, moderado **3** (*suma, precio*) módico **4** ~ (**about sth**) (*aprob*) modesto (con algo) **5** recatado **modesty** *n* modestia

modify /ˈmɒdɪfaɪ/ *vt* (*pret, pp* **-fied**) modificar ☛ La palabra más normal es **change**.

module /ˈmɒdjuːl; *USA* -dʒuːl/ *n* módulo **modular** *adj* modular

mogul /ˈməʊgl/ *n* magnate

moist /mɔɪst/ *adj* húmedo: *a rich, moist fruit cake* un bizcocho de frutas sabroso y esponjoso ◊ *in order to keep your skin soft and moist* para mantener tu piel suave e hidratada

Tanto **moist** como **damp** se traducen por "húmedo"; **damp** es el término más frecuente y puede tener un matiz negativo: *damp walls* paredes con humedad ◊ *Use a damp cloth.* Use un trapo húmedo. ◊ *cold damp rainy weather* tiempo lluvioso, frío y húmedo.

moisten /ˈmɔɪsn/ *vt, vi* humedecer(se) **moisture** /ˈmɔɪstʃə(r)/ *n* humedad **moisturize, -ise** *vt* hidratar **moisturizer, -iser** *n* crema hidratante

molar /ˈməʊlə(r)/ *n* molar, muela

mold (*USA*) *Ver* MOULD[1,2]

moldy (*USA*) *Ver* MOULDY *en* MOULD[2]

mole /məʊl/ *n* **1** lunar **2** (*lit y fig*) topo

molecule /ˈmɒlɪkjuːl/ *n* molécula **molecular** *adj* molecular

molest /məˈlest/ *vt* **1** agredir sexualmente **2** fastidiar

mollify /ˈmɒlɪfaɪ/ *vt* (*pret, pp* **-fied**) calmar, apaciguar

molten /ˈməʊltən/ *adj* fundido

mom (*USA, coloq*) *Ver* MUM

moment /ˈməʊmənt/ *n* momento, instante: *One moment/Just a moment/Wait a moment.* Un momento. ◊ *I shall only be/I won't be a moment.* En seguida termino. LOC **at a moment's notice** inmediatamente, casi sin aviso **at the moment** de momento, por ahora **for the moment/present** de momento, por ahora **the moment of truth** la hora de la verdad *Ver tb* MINUTE[1], SPUR

momentary /ˈməʊməntri; *USA* -teri/ *adj* momentáneo **momentarily** *adv* momentáneamente

momentous /məˈmentəs, məʊˈm-/ *adj* trascendental

momentum /məˈmentəm, məʊˈm-/ *n* **1** impulso, ímpetu **2** (*Fís*) momento: *to gain/gather momentum* cobrar velocidad

monarch /ˈmɒnək/ *n* monarca **monarchy** *n* (*pl* **-ies**) monarquía

monastery /ˈmɒnəstri; *USA* -teri/ *n* (*pl* **-ies**) monasterio

monastic /məˈnæstɪk/ *adj* monástico

Monday /ˈmʌndeɪ, ˈmʌndi/ *n* (*abrev* **Mon**) lunes ☛ Los nombres de los días de la semana en inglés llevan mayúscula: *every Monday* todos los lunes ◊ *last/next Monday* el lunes pasado/que viene ◊ *the Monday before last/after next* hace dos lunes/dentro de dos lunes ◊ *Monday morning/evening* el lunes por la mañana/tarde ◊ *Monday week/a week on Monday* el lunes que viene no, el siguiente ◊ *I'll see you (on) Monday.* Nos veremos el lunes. ◊ *We usually play badminton on Mondays/on a Monday.* Solemos jugar al bádminton los lunes. ◊ *The museum is open Monday to Friday.* El museo abre de lunes a viernes. ◊ *Did you read the article about Italy in Monday's paper?* ¿Leíste el artículo sobre Italia en el periódico del lunes?

monetary /ˈmʌnɪtri; *USA* -teri/ *adj* monetario

money /ˈmʌni/ *n* [*incontable*] dinero: *to spend/save money* gastar/ahorrar dinero ◊ *to earn/make money* ganar/hacer dinero ◊ *money worries* preocupaciones económicas LOC **to get you**

money's worth recibir buena calidad (*en una compra o servicio*)

monitor /ˈmɒnɪtə(r)/ ◆ *n* **1** (*TV, Informát*) monitor **2** (*elecciones*) observador, -ora ◆ *vt* **1** controlar, observar **2** (*Radio*) escuchar **monitoring** *n* control, supervisión

monk /mʌŋk/ *n* monje

monkey /ˈmʌŋki/ *n* (*pl* **-eys**) **1** mono **2** (*coloq*) (*niño*) diablillo

monogamy /məˈnɒgəmi/ *n* monogamia **monogamous** *adj* monógamo

monolithic /ˌmɒnəˈlɪθɪk/ *adj* (*lit y fig*) monolítico

monologue (*USA tb* **monolog**) /ˈmɒnəlɒg; *USA* -lɔːg/ *n* monólogo

monopolize, -ise /məˈnɒpəlaɪz/ *vt* monopolizar

monopoly /məˈnɒpəli/ *n* (*pl* **-ies**) monopolio

monoxide /mɒˈnɒksaɪd/ *n* monóxido

monsoon /ˌmɒnˈsuːn/ *n* **1** monzón **2** época de los monzones

monster /ˈmɒnstə(r)/ *n* monstruo **monstrous** /ˈmɒnstrəs/ *adj* monstruoso

monstrosity /mɒnˈstrɒsəti/ *n* (*pl* **-ies**) monstruosidad

month /mʌnθ/ *n* mes: *£14 a month* 14 libras al mes ◊ *I haven't seen her for months.* Hace meses que no la veo.

monthly /ˈmʌnθli/ ◆ *adj* mensual ◆ *adv* mensualmente ◆ *n* (*pl* **-ies**) publicación mensual

monument /ˈmɒnjumənt/ *n* ~ (**to sth**) monumento (a algo) **monumental** /ˌmɒnjuˈmentl/ *adj* **1** monumental **2** (*fig*) excepcional **3** (*negativo*) garrafal

moo /muː/ *vi* mugir

mood /muːd/ *n* **1** humor: *to be in a good/bad mood* estar de buen/mal humor **2** mal humor: *He's in a mood.* Está de mal humor. **3** ambiente **4** (*Gram*) modo LOC **to be in the/in no mood to do sth/for** (**doing**) **sth** (no) estar de humor para (hacer) algo **moody** *adj* (**-ier**, **-iest**) **1** de humor antojadizo **2** malhumorado

moon /muːn/ ◆ *n* luna: *moonbeam* rayo de luna ◊ *moonless* sin luna LOC **over the moon** (*coloq*) loco de contento ◆ *vi* ~ (**about/around**) (*coloq*) ir de aquí para allá distraídamente

moonlight /ˈmuːnlaɪt/ ◆ *n* luz de la luna ◆ *vi* (*pret, pp* **-lighted**) (*coloq*) estar pluriempleado **moonlit** *adj* iluminado por la luna

Moor /mʊə(r)/ *n* moro, -a **Moorish** *adj* moro

moor¹ /mʊə(r)/ *n* **1** páramo **2** (*de caza*) coto

moor² /mʊə(r)/ *vt, vi* ~ **sth** (**to sth**) amarrar algo (a algo) **mooring** *n* **1** **moorings** [*pl*] amarras **2** amarradero

moorland /ˈmʊələnd/ *n* páramo

mop /mɒp/ ◆ *n* **1** fregona **2** (*pelo*) pelambrera ◆ *vt* (**-pp-**) **1** limpiar, fregar **2** (*cara*) enjugarse PHR V **to mop sth up** limpiar algo

mope /məʊp/ *vi* abatirse PHR V **to mope about/around** andar deprimido

moped /ˈməʊped/ *n* moto (*ciclomotor*)

moral /ˈmɒrəl; *USA* ˈmɔːrəl/ ◆ *n* **1** moraleja **2** **morals** [*pl*] moralidad ◆ *adj* **1** moral **2** *a moral tale* un cuento con moraleja **moralistic** /mɒrəˈlɪstɪk/ *adj* (*gen pey*) moralista **morality** /məˈræləti/ *n* moral, moralidad: *standards of morality* valores morales **moralize, -ise** *vt, vi* ~ (**about/on sth**) (*gen pey*) moralizar (sobre algo) **morally** *adv* moralmente: *to behave morally* comportarse honradamente

morale /məˈrɑːl; *USA* -ˈræl/ *n* moral (*ánimo*)

morbid /ˈmɔːbɪd/ *adj* **1** morboso **2** (*Med*) patológico **morbidity** /mɔːˈbɪdəti/ *n* **1** morbosidad **2** (*Med*) patología

more /mɔː(r)/ ◆ *adj* más: *more money than sense* más dinero que buen sentido ◊ *more food than could be eaten* más comida de la que se podía comer ◆ *pron* más: *You've had more to drink than me/than I have.* Has bebido más que yo. ◊ *more than £50* más de 50 libras ◊ *I hope we'll see more of you.* Espero que te veremos más a menudo. ◆ *adv* **1** más ☛ Se usa para formar comparativos de *adjs* y *advs* de dos o más sílabas: *more quickly* más de prisa ◊ *more expensive* más caro **2** más: *once more* una vez más ◊ *It's more of a hindrance than a help.* Estorba más que ayuda. ◊ *That's more like it!* ¡Eso es! ◊ *even more so* aún más LOC **to be more than happy, glad, willing, etc to do sth** hacer algo con mucho gusto **more and more** cada vez más, más y más **more or less** más o menos: *more or less finished* casi terminado **what is more** es más, además *Ver tb* ALL

tʃ	dʒ	v	θ	ð	s	z	ʃ
chin	June	van	thin	then	so	zoo	she

moreover /mɔːˈrəʊvə(r)/ *adv* además, por otra parte

morgue /mɔːg/ *n* morgue

morning /ˈmɔːnɪŋ/ *n* **1** mañana: *on Sunday morning* el domingo por la mañana ◊ *tomorrow morning* mañana por la mañana ◊ *on the morning of the wedding* la mañana de la boda **2** madrugada: *in the early hours of Sunday morning* en la madrugada del domingo ◊ *at three in the morning* a las tres de la madrugada **3** [*antes de sustantivo*] de la mañana, matinal: *the morning papers* los periódicos de la mañana LOC **good morning!** ¡buenos días! ☛ En el uso familiar, muchas veces se dice simplemente **morning!** en vez de **good morning!** **in the morning 1** por la mañana: *eleven o'clock in the morning* las once de la mañana **2** (*del día siguiente*): *I'll ring her up in the morning.* La llamaré mañana por la mañana.

Utilizamos la preposición **in** con **morning**, **afternoon** y **evening** para referirnos a un periodo determinado del día: *at three o'clock in the afternoon* a las tres de la tarde, y **on** para hacer referencia a un punto en el calendario: *on a cool May morning* en una fría mañana de mayo ◊ *on Monday afternoon* el lunes por la tarde ◊ *on the morning of the 4th of September* el cuatro de septiembre por la mañana. Sin embargo, en combinación con **tomorrow**, **this**, **that** y **yesterday** no se usa preposición: *They'll leave this evening.* Se marchan esta tarde. ◊ *I saw her yesterday morning.* La vi ayer por la mañana.

moron /ˈmɔːrɒn/ *n* (*coloq, ofen*) imbécil

morose /məˈrəʊs/ *adj* huraño **morosely** *adv* malhumoradamente

morphine /ˈmɔːfiːn/ *n* morfina

morsel /ˈmɔːsl/ *n* bocado

mortal /ˈmɔːtl/ ◆ *n* mortal ◆ *adj* mortal **mortality** /mɔːˈtæləti/ *n* **1** mortalidad **2** mortandad

mortar /ˈmɔːtə(r)/ *n* **1** argamasa, mortero **2** (*cañón*) mortero **3** mortero, almirez

mortgage /ˈmɔːgɪdʒ/ ◆ *n* hipoteca: *mortgage (re)payment* pago hipotecario ◆ *vt* hipotecar

mortify /ˈmɔːtɪfaɪ/ *vt* (*pret, pp* **-fied**) humillar

mortuary /ˈmɔːtʃəri; *USA* ˈmɔːtʃʊeri/ *n* (*pl* **-ies**) depósito de cadáveres

mosaic /məʊˈzeɪɪk/ *n* mosaico

Moslem *Ver* MUSLIM

mosque /mɒsk/ *n* mezquita

mosquito /məsˈkiːtəʊ, mɒs-/ *n* (*pl* **-oes**) mosquito: *mosquito net* mosquitero

moss /mɒs; *USA* mɔːs/ *n* musgo

most /məʊst/ ◆ *adj* **1** más, la mayor parte de: *Who got (the) most votes?* ¿Quién consiguió más votos? ◊ *We spent most time in Rome.* Pasamos la mayor parte del tiempo en Roma. **2** la mayoría de, casi todo: *most days* casi todos los días ◆ *pron* **1** el, la, lo, los, las más: *I ate (the) most.* Yo fui el que más comió. ◊ *the most I could offer you* lo máximo que le podría ofrecer **2** la mayoría de: *most of the day* casi todo el día ◊ *Most of you know.* La mayoría de vosotros sabe

Most es el superlativo de **much** y de **many** y se usa con sustantivos incontables o en plural: *Who's got most time?* ¿Quién es el que tiene más tiempo? ◊ *most children* la mayoría de los niños. Sin embargo, delante de pronombres o cuando el sustantivo al que precede lleva *the* o un adjetivo posesivo o demostrativo, se usa **most of**: *most of my friends* la mayoría de mis amigos ◊ *most of us* la mayoría de nosotros ◊ *most of these records* la mayoría de estos discos.

◆ *adv* **1** más ☛ Se usa para formar el superlativo de locuciones adverbiales, adjetivos y adverbios de dos o más sílabas: *This is the most interesting book I've read for a long time.* Éste es el libro más interesante que he leído en mucho tiempo. ◊ *What upset me (the) most was that…* Lo que más me dolió es que… *most of all* sobre todo **2** muy: *most likely* muy probablemente LOC **at (the) most** como mucho/máximo **mostly** *adv* principalmente, por lo general

moth /mɒθ; *USA* mɔːθ/ *n* **1** mariposa nocturna **2** (*tb* **clothes-moth**) polilla

mother /ˈmʌðə(r)/ ◆ *n* madre ◆ *vt* **1** criar **2** mimar **motherhood** *n* maternidad **mother-in-law** *n* (*pl* **-ers-in-law**) suegra **motherly** *adj* maternal **mother**…

to-be *n* (*pl* **-ers-to-be**) futura madre **mother tongue** *n* lengua materna

motif /məʊˈtiːf/ *n* **1** motivo, adorno **2** tema

motion /ˈməʊʃn/ ◆ *n* **1** movimiento: *motion picture* película de cine **2** (*en reunión*) moción LOC **to go through the motions (of doing sth)** (*coloq*) fingir (hacer algo) **to put/set sth in motion** poner algo en marcha *Ver tb* SLOW ◆ **1** *vi* ~ **to/for sb to do sth** hacer señas a algn para que haga algo **2** *vt* indicar con señas: *to motion sb in* indicar a algn que entre **motionless** *adj* inmóvil

motivate /ˈməʊtɪveɪt/ *vt* motivar

motive /ˈməʊtɪv/ *n* ~ **(for sth)** motivo, móvil (de algo): *He had an ulterior motive.* Iba detrás de algo. ☛ La traducción más normal de "motivo" es **reason**.

motor /ˈməʊtə(r)/ *n* **1** motor ☛ *Ver nota en* ENGINE **2** (*GB, antic, joc*) coche **motoring** *n* automovilismo **motorist** *n* conductor, -ora de coche **motorize, -ise** *vt* motorizar

motor bike *n* (*coloq*) moto

motor boat *n* lancha motora

motor car *n* (*fml, antic*) coche

motorcycle /ˈməʊtəsaɪkl/ *n* motocicleta

motor racing *n* carreras de coches

motorway /ˈməʊtəweɪ/ *n* autopista

mottled /ˈmɒtld/ *adj* moteado

motto /ˈmɒtəʊ/ *n* (*pl* **-oes**) lema

mould[1] (*USA* **mold**) /məʊld/ ◆ *n* molde ◆ *vt* moldear

mould[2] (*USA* **mold**) /məʊld/ *n* moho **mouldy** (*USA* **moldy**) *adj* mohoso

mound /maʊnd/ *n* **1** montículo **2** montón

mount /maʊnt/ ◆ *n* **1** monte **2** soporte, montura **3** (*animal*) montura, caballería **4** (*de cuadro*) marco ◆ **1** *vt* (*caballo, etc*) subirse a **2** *vt* (*cuadro*) enmarcar **3** *vt* organizar, montar **4** *vt* instalar **5** *vi* ~ **(up) (to sth)** crecer (hasta alcanzar algo) **mounting** *adj* creciente

mountain /ˈmaʊntən; *USA* -ntn/ *n* **1** montaña: *mountain range* cordillera **2** **the mountains** [*pl*] (*por contraste con la costa*) la montaña **mountaineer** /ˌmaʊntɪˈnɪə(r)/ *n* alpinista **mountaineering** /ˌmaʊntɪˈnɪərɪŋ/ *n* alpinismo

mountainous /ˈmaʊntənəs/ *adj* montañoso

mountainside /ˈmaʊntənsaɪd/ *n* falda de montaña

mourn /mɔːn/ **1** *vi* lamentarse **2** *vi* estar de luto **3** *vt*: *to mourn sth/sb* lamentar algo/llorar la muerte de algn **mourner** *n* doliente **mournful** *adj* triste, lúgubre **mourning** *n* luto, duelo: *in mourning* de luto

mouse /maʊs/ *n* (*pl* **mice** /maɪs/) ratón ☛ *Ver dibujo en* ORDENADOR

mousse /muːs/ *n* **1** mousse **2** espuma (*para el pelo*)

moustache /məˈstɑːʃ/ (*USA* **mustache** /ˈmʌstæʃ/) *n* bigote(s)

mouth /maʊθ/ *n* (*pl* ~**s** /maʊðz/) **1** boca **2** (*de río*) desembocadura LOC *Ver* LOOK[1] **mouthful** *n* **1** bocado **2** (*líquido*) trago

mouthpiece /ˈmaʊθpiːs/ *n* **1** (*Mús*) boquilla **2** (*de teléfono*) micrófono **3** (*fig*) portavoz

movable /ˈmuːvəbl/ *adj* movible

move /muːv/ ◆ *n* **1** movimiento **2** (*de casa*) mudanza **3** (*de trabajo*) cambio **4** (*ajedrez, etc*) jugada, turno **5** paso LOC **to get a move on** (*coloq*) darse prisa **to make a move 1** actuar **2** ponerse en marcha *Ver tb* FALSE ◆ **1** *vi* mover(se): *Don't move!* ¡No te muevas! ◇ *It's your turn to move.* Te toca mover. **2** *vt, vi* trasladar(se), cambiar(se) (de sitio): *He has been moved to London.* Lo han trasladado a Londres. ◇ *I'm going to move the car before they give me a ticket.* Voy a cambiar el coche de sitio antes de que me pongan una multa. ◇ *They sold the house and moved to Scotland.* Vendieron la casa y se trasladaron a Escocia. **3** *vi* ~ **(in)/(out)** mudarse: *They had to move out.* Tuvieron que dejar la casa. **4** *vt* ~ **sb** conmover a algn **5** *vt* ~ **sb (to do sth)** inducir a algn (a hacer algo) LOC **to move house** cambiar de casa, mudarse (de casa) *Ver tb* KILL

PHR V **to move about/around** moverse (de acá para allá)

to move (sth) away alejarse, alejar algo

to move forward avanzar

to move in instalarse

to move on seguir (viajando)

to move out mudarse

movement /ˈmuːvmənt/ *n* **1** movimiento **2** [*incontable*] ~ **(towards/away from sth)** tendencia (hacia/a distanciarse de algo) **3** (*Mec*) mecanismo

movie /ˈmuːvi/ (*esp USA*) *n* película (*de cine*): *to go to the movies* ir al cine

moving /muːvɪŋ/ *adj* **1** móvil **2** conmovedor

mow /məʊ/ *vt* (*pret* **mowed** *pp* **mown** /məʊn/ *o* **mowed**) segar, cortar PHR V **to mow sb down** aniquilar a algn **mower** *n* cortacésped

MP /ˌem ˈpiː/ *abrev* (*GB*) **Member of Parliament** diputado, -a ☛ *Ver* pág 322.

Mr /ˈmɪstə(r)/ *abrev* señor (=Sr.)

Mrs /ˈmɪsɪz/ *abrev* señora (=Sra.)

Ms /mɪz, məz/ *abrev* señora (=Sra.) ☛ *ver nota en* SEÑORITA

much /mʌtʃ/ ◆ *adj* mucho: *so much traffic* tanto tráfico ◆ *pron* mucho: *How much is it?* ¿Cuánto es? ◊ *too much* demasiado ◊ *as much as you can* todo lo que puedas ◊ *for much of the day* la mayor parte del día ☛ *Ver nota en* MANY *Ver tb* MUCHO ◆ *adv* mucho: *Much to her surprise...* Para gran sorpresa suya... ◊ *much-needed* muy necesario ◊ *much too cold* demasiado frío LOC **much as** por más que **much the same** prácticamente igual **not much of a...**: *He's not much of an actor.* No es gran cosa como actor. *Ver tb* AS, SO

muck /mʌk/ ◆ *n* **1** estiércol **2** (*coloq, esp GB*) porquería ◆ *v* (*coloq, esp GB*) PHR V **to muck about/around** hacer el indio **to muck sth up** echar algo a perder **mucky** *adj* (**-ier**, **-iest**) sucio

mucus /ˈmjuːkəs/ *n* [*incontable*] mucosidad

mud /mʌd/ *n* barro, lodo: *mudguard* guardabarros LOC *Ver* CLEAR **muddy** *adj* (**-ier**, **-iest**) **1** embarrado: *muddy footprints* pisadas de barro **2** (*fig*) turbio, poco claro

muddle /ˈmʌdl/ ◆ *vt* **1** ~ **sth (up)** revolver algo **2** ~ **sth/sb (up)** armar un lío con algo/a algn **3** ~ **A (up) with B**; ~ **A and B (up)** confundir A con B ◆ *n* **1** desorden **2** ~ **(about/over sth)** confusión, lío (con algo): *to get (yourself) into a muddle* armarse un lío **muddled** *adj* enrevesado

muffled /ˈmʌfld/ *vt* **1** (*grito*) ahogado **2** (*voz*) apagado **3** ~ **(up) (in sth)** (*ropa*) arrebujado (en algo)

cup and saucer

mug

mug /mʌg/ ◆ *n* **1** taza (alta) **2** (*coloq, pey, joc*) jeta **3** (*coloq*) bobo, -a LOC **a mug's game** (*pey, GB*) una pérdida de tiempo ◆ *vt* (**-gg-**) atracar **mugger** *n* atracador, -ora **mugging** *n* atraco

muggy /ˈmʌgi/ *adj* (**-ier**, **-iest**) bochornoso (*tiempo*)

mulberry /ˈmʌlbəri; *USA* ˈmʌlberi/ *n* **1** (*tb* **mulberry tree**, **mulberry bush**) morera **2** mora **3** morado

mule /mjuːl/ *n* **1** mulo, -a **2** babucha, chinela

mull /mʌl/ PHR V **to mull sth over** meditar algo

multicoloured (*USA* **multicolored**) /ˌmʌltiˈkʌləd/ *adj* multicolor

multilingual /ˌmʌltiˈlɪŋgwəl/ *adj* políglota

multinational /ˌmʌltiˈnæʃnəl/ *adj, n* multinacional

multiple /ˈmʌltɪpl/ ◆ *adj* múltiple ◆ *n* múltiplo

multiple sclerosis /ˌmʌltɪpl skləˈrəʊsɪs/ *n* esclerosis múltiple

multiplication /ˌmʌltɪplɪˈkeɪʃn/ *n* multiplicación: *multiplication table/sign* tabla/signo de multiplicar

multiplicity /ˌmʌltɪˈplɪsəti/ *n* ~ **of sth** multiplicidad de algo

multiply /ˈmʌltɪplaɪ/ *vt, vi* (*pret, pp* **-lied**) multiplicar(se)

multi-purpose /ˌmʌlti ˈpɜːpəs/ *adj* multiuso

multi-storey /ˌmʌlti ˈstɔːri/ *adj* de varios pisos: *multi-storey car park* aparcamiento de varios pisos

multitude /ˈmʌltɪtjuːd; *USA* -tuːd/ *n* (*fml*) multitud

mum /mʌm/ (*USA* **mom** /mɒm/) *n* (*coloq*) mamá

mumble /ˈmʌmbl/ *vt, vi* musitar, farfullar: *Don't mumble.* Habla alto y claro

mummy /ˈmʌmi/ *n* (*pl* **-ies**) **1** (*USA* **mommy** /ˈmɒmi/) (*coloq*) mamá **2** momia

mumps /mʌmps/ *n* [*sing*] paperas

munch /mʌntʃ/ *vt, vi* ~ **(on) sth** ronzar, mascar algo

mundane /mʌnˈdeɪn/ *adj* corriente, mundano

municipal /mjuːˈnɪsɪpl/ *adj* municipal

munitions /mjuːˈnɪʃnz/ *n* municiones

mural /ˈmjʊərəl/ *n* mural

murder /ˈmɜːdə(r)/ ◆ *n* **1** asesinato, homicidio ☛ *Comparar con* MANSLAUGHTER, HOMICIDE **2** (*coloq*, *fig*) una pesadilla LOC **to get away with murder** (*frec joc, coloq*) hacer lo que le dé la gana a uno ◆ *vt* asesinar, matar ☛ *Ver nota en* ASESINAR **murderer** *n* asesino, -a **murderous** *adj* **1** homicida: *a murderous look* una mirada asesina **2** (*muy desagradable*) matador

murky /mɜːki/ *adj* (**-ier**, **-iest**) **1** lóbrego, sombrío **2** (*lit y fig*) turbio

murmur /mɜːmə(r)/ ◆ *n* murmullo LOC **without a murmur** sin rechistar ◆ *vt, vi* susurrar

muscle /ˈmʌsl/ ◆ *n* **1** músculo: *Don't move a muscle!* ¡No muevas ni las pestañas! **2** (*fig*) poder ◆ PHR V **to muscle in (on sth/sb)** (*coloq, pey*) participar sin derecho (en algo) **muscular** *adj* **1** muscular **2** musculoso

muse /mjuːz/ ◆ *n* musa ◆ **1** *vi* ~ **(about/over/on/upon sth)** meditar (algo); reflexionar (sobre algo) **2** *vt*: *'How interesting,' he mused.* "Qué interesante," - dijo pensativo.

museum /mjuˈziəm/ *n* museo

> **Museum** se utiliza para referirse a los museos en los que se exponen esculturas, piezas históricas, científicas, etc. **Gallery** o **art gallery** se utilizan para referirse a museos en los que se exponen principalmente cuadros y esculturas.

mushroom /ˈmʌʃrʊm, -ruːm/ ◆ *n* seta, champiñón ◆ *vi* (*a veces pey*) crecer como hongos

mushy /mʌʃi/ *adj* **1** blando **2** (*coloq, pey*) sensiblero

music /ˈmjuːzɪk/ *n* **1** música: *a piece of music* una pieza musical ◇ *music-hall* teatro de variedades **2** (*texto*) partitura **musical** *adj* musical, de música: *to be musical* tener talento para la música **musical** (*tb* **musical comedy**) *n* comedia musical **musician** *n* músico **musicianship** *n* maestría musical

musk /mʌsk/ *n* (perfume de) almizcle

musket /ˈmʌskɪt/ *n* mosquete

Muslim /ˈmʊzlɪm; *USA* ˈmʌzləm/ (*tb* **Moslem** /ˈmɒzləm/) *adj, n* musulmán, -ana *Ver tb* ISLAM

muslin /ˈmʌzlɪn/ *n* muselina

mussel /ˈmʌsl/ *n* mejillón

must /məst, mʌst/ ◆ *v modal* (*neg* **must not** *o* **mustn't** /ˈmʌsnt/)

> **Must** es un verbo modal al que sigue un infinitivo sin TO, y las oraciones interrogativas y negativas se construyen sin el auxiliar *do*: *Must you go?* ¿Tienes que irte? ◇ *We mustn't tell her.* No debemos decírselo. **Must** sólo tiene la forma del presente: *I must leave early.* Tengo que salir temprano. Cuando necesitamos otras formas utilizamos **to have to**: *He'll have to come tomorrow.* Tendrá que venir mañana. ◇ *We had to eat quickly.* Tuvimos que comer rápido.

• **obligación y prohibición** deber, tener que: *'Must you go so soon?' 'Yes, I must.'* —¿Tienes que irte tan pronto? —Sí.

> **Must** se emplea para dar órdenes o para hacer que alguien o uno mismo siga un determinado comportamiento: *The children must be back by four.* Los niños tienen que volver a las cuatro. ◇ *I must stop smoking.* Tengo que dejar de fumar. Cuando las órdenes son impuestas por un agente externo, p.ej. por una ley, una regla, etc, usamos **to have to**: *The doctor says I have to stop smoking.* El médico dice que tengo que dejar de fumar. ◇ *You have to send it before Tuesday.* Tiene que mandarlo antes del martes. En negativa, **must not** o **mustn't** expresan una prohibición: *You mustn't open other people's post.* No debes abrir el correo de otras personas. Sin embargo, **haven't got to** o **don't have to** expresan que algo no es necesario, es decir, que hay una ausencia de obligación: *You don't have to go if you don't want to.* No tienes que ir si no quieres.

• **sugerencia** tener que: *You must come to lunch one day.* Tienes que venir a comer un día de estos. ☛ En la mayoría de los casos, para hacer sugerencias y dar consejos se usa **ought to** o **should.**

• **probabilidad** deber: *You must be hungry.* Debes de tener hambre. ◊ *You must be Mr Smith.* Vd. debe ser el señor Smith.

LOC **if I, you, etc must** si no hay más remedio

◆ *n* (*coloq*): *It's a must.* Es imprescindible. ◊ *His new book is a must.* Su último libro no te lo puedes perder.

mustache (*USA*) *Ver* MOUSTACHE

mustard /ˈmʌstəd/ *n* **1** (*planta, semilla y salsa*) mostaza **2** color mostaza

muster /ˈmʌstə(r)/ **1** *vt, vi* reunir(se) **2** *vt* reunir, juntar: *to muster (up) enthusiasm* cobrar entusiasmo ◊ *to muster a smile* conseguir sonreír

musty /ˈmʌsti/ *adj* (**-ier**, **-iest**) **1** rancio: *to smell musty* oler a rancio **2** (*pey, fig*) pasado, rancio, viejo

mutant /ˈmjuːtənt/ *adj, n* mutante

mutate /mjuːˈteɪt; *USA* ˈmjuːteɪt/ **1** *vi* ~ (**into sth**) transformarse (en algo) **2** *vi* ~ (**into sth**) (*Biol*) mutar (a algo) **3** *vt* mutar **mutation** *n* mutación

mute /mjuːt/ ◆ *adj* mudo ◆ *n* **1** (*Mús*) sordina **2** (*antic*) (*persona*) mudo, -a ◆ *vt* **1** amortiguar **2** (*Mús*) poner sordina a **muted** *adj* **1** (*sonidos, colores*) apagado **2** (*crítica, etc*) velado **3** (*Mús*) sordo

mutilate /ˈmjuːtɪleɪt/ *vt* mutilar

mutiny /ˈmjuːtəni/ *n* (*pl* **-ies**) motín **mutinous** *adj* (*fig*) rebelde

mutter /ˈmʌtə(r)/ **1** *vt, vi* ~ (**sth**) (**to sb**) (**about sth**) hablar entre dientes, murmurar (algo) (a algn) (sobre algo) **2** *vi* ~ (**about/against/at sth/sb**) refunfuñar (de algo/algn)

mutton /ˈmʌtn/ *n* (carne de) carnero ☛ *Ver nota en* CARNE

mutual /ˈmjuːtʃuəl/ *adj* **1** mutuo **2** común: *a mutual friend* un amigo común **mutually** *adv* mutuamente: *mutually beneficial* beneficioso para ambas partes

muzzle /ˈmʌzl/ ◆ *n* **1** hocico **2** bozal **3** (*de arma de fuego*) boca ◆ *vt* **1** poner bozal **2** (*fig*) amordazar

my /maɪ/ *adj pos* mi, mío: *It was my fault.* Ha sido culpa mía/mi culpa. ◊ *My God!* ¡Dios mío! ◊ *My feet are cold.* Tengo los pies fríos.

En inglés se usa el posesivo delante de partes del cuerpo y prendas de vestir. *Comparar con* MINE 1

myopia /maɪˈəʊpiə/ *n* miopía **myopic** /maɪˈɒpɪk/ *adj* miope

myriad /ˈmɪriəd/ ◆ *n* miríada ◆ *adj*: *their myriad activities* sus muchas actividades

myself /maɪˈself/ *pron* **1** [*uso reflexivo*] me: *I cut myself.* Me corté. ◊ *I said to myself…* Dije para mí… **2** [*uso enfático*] yo mismo, -a: *I myself will do it.* Yo misma lo haré. LOC (**all**) **by myself** solo

mysterious /mɪˈstɪəriəs/ *adj* misterioso

mystery /ˈmɪstri/ *n* (*pl* **-ies**) **1** misterio: *It's a mystery to me.* No logro entenderlo. **2** *mystery tour* viaje sorpresa ◊ *the mystery assailant* el agresor misterioso **3** obra de teatro, novela, etc de misterio

mystic /ˈmɪstɪk/ ◆ *n* místico, -a ◆ *adj* (*tb* **mystical**) místico **mysticism** *n* misticismo, mística

mystification /ˌmɪstɪfɪˈkeɪʃn/ *n* **1** misterio, perplejidad **2** (*pey*) confusión (*deliberada*)

mystify /ˈmɪstɪfaɪ/ *vt* (*pret, pp* **-fied**) dejar perplejo **mystifying** *adj* desconcertante

mystique /mɪˈstiːk/ *n* (*aprob*) [*sing*] misterio

myth /mɪθ/ *n* mito **mythical** *adj* mítico

mythology /mɪˈθɒlədʒi/ *n* mitología

mythological /ˌmɪθəˈlɒdʒɪkl/ *adj* mitológico

Nn

N, n /en/ *n* (*pl* **N's**, **n's** /enz/) N, n: *N for Nellie* N de nata ☛ *Ver ejemplos en* A, a

nag /næg/ *vt, vi* (**-gg-**) **to nag (at) sb 1** dar la lata a algn **2** regañar a algn **3** (*dolor, sospecha*) corroer a algn **nagging** *adj* **1** (*dolor, sospecha*) persistente **2** (*persona*) criticón, pesado

nail /neɪl/ ◆ *n* **1** uña: *nail file* lima de uñas ◊ *nail varnish/polish* esmalte de uñas *Ver tb* FINGERNAIL, TOENAIL **2** clavo **LOC** *Ver* FIGHT, HIT ◆ **PHR V to nail sb down (to sth)** conseguir que algn se comprometa (a algo), conseguir que algn dé una respuesta concreta (sobre algo) **to nail sth to sth** clavar algo a/en algo

naive (*tb* **naïve**) /naɪˈiːv/ *adj* ingenuo

naked /ˈneɪkɪd/ *adj* **1** desnudo: *stark naked* en cueros

"Desnudo" se traduce de tres formas en inglés: **bare**, **naked** y **nude**. **Bare** se usa para referirse a partes del cuerpo: *bare arms*, **naked** generalmente se refiere a todo el cuerpo: *a naked body* y **nude** se usa para hablar de desnudos artísticos y eróticos: *a nude figure*.

2 (*llama*) descubierto **LOC with the naked eye** a simple vista

name /neɪm/ ◆ *n* **1** nombre: *What's your name?* ¿Cómo te llamas? ◊ *first/Christian name* nombre (de pila) **2** apellido ☛ *Comparar con* SURNAME **3** fama **4** personaje **LOC by name** de nombre **by/of the name of** (*fml*) llamado **in the name of sth/sb** en nombre de algo/algn ◆ *vt* **1** ~ **sth/sb sth** llamar algo/a algn algo **2** ~ **sth/sb (after sb)** (*USA*) ~ **sth/sb (for sb)** poner nombre a algn; poner a algo/algn el nombre de algn **3** (*identificar*) nombrar **4** (*fecha, precio*) fijar

nameless /ˈneɪmləs/ *adj* anónimo, sin nombre

namely /ˈneɪmli/ *adv* a saber

namesake /ˈneɪmseɪk/ *n* tocayo, -a

nanny /ˈnæni/ *n* (*pl* **-ies**) (*GB*) niñera

nap /næp/ *n* sueñecito, siesta: *to have/take a nap* echarse una siesta

nape /neɪp/ (*tb* **nape of the neck**) *n* nuca

napkin /ˈnæpkɪn/ (*tb* **table napkin**) *n* servilleta

nappy /ˈnæpi/ *n* (*pl* **-ies**) pañal

narcotic /nɑːˈkɒtɪk/ *adj, n* narcótico

narrate /nəˈreɪt; *USA* ˈnæreɪt/ *vt* narrar, contar **narrator** *n* narrador, -ora

narrative /ˈnærətɪv/ ◆ *n* **1** relato **2** narrativa ◆ *adj* narrativo

narrow /ˈnærəʊ/ ◆ *adj* (**-er**, **-est**) **1** estrecho **2** limitado **3** (*ventaja, mayoría*) escaso **LOC to have a narrow escape** escaparse por los pelos ◆ *vt, vi* hacer(se) más estrecho, estrechar(se), disminuir **PHR V to narrow (sth) down to sth** reducir algo/reducirse a algo **narrowly** *adv He narrowly escaped drowning.* Por poco se ahogó.

narrow-minded /ˌnærəʊ ˈmaɪndɪd/ *adj* estrecho de miras

nasal /ˈneɪzl/ *adj* **1** nasal **2** (*voz*) gangoso

nasty /ˈnɑːsti; *USA* ˈnæs-/ *adj* (**-ier**, **-iest**) **1** desagradable **2** (*olor*) repugnante **3** (*persona*) antipático: *to be nasty to sb* tratar muy mal a algn **4** (*situación, crimen*) feo **5** grave, peligroso: *That's a nasty cut.* ¡Qué corte tan malo!

nation /ˈneɪʃn/ *n* nación

national /ˈnæʃnəl/ ◆ *adj* nacional: *national service* servicio militar ◆ *n* ciudadano, -a, súbdito, -a

National Health Service *n* (*abrev* **NHS**) servicio de asistencia sanitaria de la Seguridad Social

National Insurance *n* (*GB*) Seguridad Social: *National Insurance contributions* contribuciones a la Seguridad Social

nationalism /ˈnæʃnəlɪzəm/ *n* nacionalismo **nationalist** *adj, n* nacionalista

nationality /ˌnæʃəˈnæləti/ *n* (*pl* **-ies**) nacionalidad

nationalize, -ise /ˈnæʃnəlaɪz/ *vt* nacionalizar

nationally /ˈnæʃnəli/ *adv* nacionalmente, a escala nacional

nationwide /ˌneɪʃnˈwaɪd/ *adj, adv* en

todo el territorio nacional, a escala nacional

native /ˈneɪtɪv/ ◆ *n* **1** nativo, -a, natural **2** (*frec pey*) indígena **3** (*se traduce por adj*) originario: *The koala is a native of Australia.* El koala es originario de Australia. ◆ *adj* **1** natal: *native land* patria ◇ *native language/tongue* lengua materna **2** indígena, nativo **3** innato **4 ~ to...** originario de...

natural /ˈnætʃrəl/ *adj* **1** natural **2** nato, innato

naturalist /ˈnætʃrəlɪst/ *n* naturalista

naturally /ˈnætʃrəli/ *adv* **1** naturalmente, con naturalidad **2** por supuesto

nature /ˈneɪtʃə(r)/ *n* **1** (*tb* **Nature**) naturaleza **2** carácter: *good nature* buen carácter ◇ *It's not in my nature to...* No soy capaz de... **3** [*incontable*] tipo, índole LOC **in the nature of sth** como algo

naughty /ˈnɔːti/ *adj* (**-ier**, **-iest**) **1** (*coloq*) travieso: *to be naughty* portarse mal **2** atrevido

nausea /ˈnɔːsiə; *USA* ˈnɔːʒə/ *n* náusea

nauseating /ˈnɔːzieɪtɪŋ/ *adj* asqueroso, nauseabundo

nautical /ˈnɔːtɪkl/ *adj* náutico

naval /ˈneɪvl/ *adj* naval, marítimo

nave /neɪv/ *n* nave

navel /ˈneɪvl/ *n* ombligo

navigate /ˈnævɪgeɪt/ **1** *vi* navegar **2** *vi* (*en coche*) guiar **3** *vt* (*barco*) gobernar **4** *vt* (*río, mar*) navegar por **navigation** *n* **1** navegación **2** náutica **navigator** *n* navegante

navy /ˈneɪvi/ *n* (**1** *pl* **-ies**) flota **2 the navy, the Navy** [*sing*] la armada **3** (*tb* **navy-blue**) azul marino

Nazi /ˈnɑːtsi/ *n* nazi

near /nɪə(r)/ ◆ *adj* (**-er**, **-est**) **1** (*lit*) cercano: *Which town is nearer?* ¿Qué ciudad está más cerca? ◇ *to get nearer* acercarse

> Nótese que antes de sustantivo se usa el adjetivo **nearby** en vez de **near**: *a nearby village* un pueblo cercano ◇ *The village is very near.* El pueblo está muy cerca. Sin embargo, cuando queremos utilizar otras formas del adjetivo, como el superlativo, tenemos que utilizar **near**: *the nearest shop* la tienda más cercana.

2 (*fig*) próximo: *in the near future* en un futuro próximo ◆ *prep* cerca de: *I live near the station.* Vivo cerca de la estación. ◇ *Is there a bank near here?* ¿Hay algún banco cerca de aquí? ◇ *near the beginning* hacia el principio ◆ *adv* (**-er**, **-est**) cerca: *I live quite near.* Vivo bastante cerca. ◇ *We are getting near to Christmas.* Ya falta poco para la Navidad.

> Nótese que *I live nearby* es más corriente que *I live near*, pero **nearby** no suele ir modificado por **quite**, **very**, etc: *I live quite near.*

LOC **not to be anywhere near**; **to be nowhere near** no acercarse ni con mucho, no parecerse en nada *Ver tb* HAND ◆ *vt, vi* acercarse (a)

nearby /ˌnɪəˈbaɪ/ ◆ *adj* cercano ◆ *adv* cerca: *She lives nearby.* Vive cerca (de aquí/allí). ☞ *Ver nota en* NEAR

nearly /ˈnɪəli/ *adv* casi: *He nearly won.* Por poco ganó.

> A menudo **almost** y **nearly** son intercambiables. Sin embargo, sólo **almost** se puede usar para calificar otro adverbio en **-ly**: *almost completely* casi completamente, y sólo **nearly** puede ser calificado por otros adverbios: *I very nearly left.* Me faltó muy poco para irme.

LOC **not nearly** ni con mucho, para nada

neat /niːt/ *adj* (**-er**, **-est**) **1** ordenado, bien cuidado **2** (*persona*) pulcro y ordenado **3** (*letra*) claro **4** (*coloq, esp USA*) estupendo **5** (*bebida*) solo **neatly** *adv* **1** ordenadamente, pulcramente **2** hábilmente

necessarily /ˌnesəˈserəli, ˈnesəsərəli/ *adv* forzosamente, necesariamente

necessary /ˈnesəsəri; *USA* -seri/ *adj* **1** necesario: *Is it necessary for us to meet/necessary that we meet?* ¿Es necesario que nos reunamos? ◇ *if necessary* si resulta necesario **2** inevitable

necessitate /nəˈsesɪteɪt/ *vt* (*fml*) requerir

necessity /nəˈsesəti/ *n* (*pl* **-ies**) **1** necesidad **2** artículo de primera necesidad

neck /nek/ *n* cuello: *to break your neck* desnucarse *Ver tb* PAIN LOC **neck and neck (with sth/sb)** a la par (con algo/algn) **(to be) up to your neck in sth** (estar) metido hasta el cuello en algo

Ver tb BREATHE, MILLSTONE, RISK, SCRUFF, WRING

necklace /ˈnekləs/ *n* collar

neckline /ˈneklaɪn/ *n* escote

need /niːd/ ◆ *v modal* (*neg* **need not** *o* **needn't** /ˈniːdnt/) (*obligación*) tener que: *You needn't have come.* No hacía falta que vinieras. ◊ *Need I explain it again?* ¿Es necesario que lo explique otra vez?

Cuando **need** es un verbo modal le sigue un infinitivo sin TO, y las oraciones interrogativas y negativas se construyen sin el auxiliar *do*.

◆ *vt* **1** necesitar: *Do you need any help?* ¿Necesitas ayuda? ◊ *It needs painting.* Hace falta pintarlo. **2** ~ **to do sth** (*obligación*) tener que hacer algo: *Do we really need to leave so early?* ¿Es realmente necesario que salgamos tan temprano? ☛ En este sentido se puede usar el verbo modal, pero es más formal: *Need we really leave so early?* ◆ *n* ~ (**for sth**) necesidad (de algo) LOC **if need be** si fuera necesario **to be in need of sth** necesitar algo

needle /ˈniːdl/ *n* aguja LOC *Ver* PIN

needless /ˈniːdləs/ *adj* innecesario LOC **needless to say** ni que decir tiene

needlework /ˈniːdlwɜːk/ *n* [*incontable*] costura, bordado

needy /ˈniːdi/ *adj* necesitado

negative /ˈnegətɪv/ ◆ *adj* negativo ◆ *n* negativo (*de foto*)

neglect /nɪˈglekt/ ◆ *vt* **1** ~ **sth/sb** descuidar algo/a algn **2** ~ **to do sth** olvidar hacer algo ◆ *n* abandono

negligent /ˈneglɪdʒənt/ *adj* negligente **negligence** *n* negligencia

negligible /ˈneglɪdʒəbl/ *adj* insignificante

negotiate /nɪˈgəʊʃieɪt/ **1** *vt, vi* ~ (**sth**) (**with sb**) negociar (algo) (con algn) **2** *vt* (*obstáculo*) salvar **negotiation** *n* [*a menudo pl*] negociación

neigh /neɪ/ ◆ *vi* relinchar ◆ *n* relincho

neighbour (*USA* **neighbor**) /ˈneɪbə(r)/ *n* **1** vecino, -a **2** prójimo, -a **neighbourhood** (*USA* **-borhood**) *n* **1** (*distrito*) barrio **2** (*personas*) vecindario **neighbouring** (*USA* **-boring**) *adj* vecino, contiguo

neither /ˈnaɪðə(r), ˈniːðə(r)/ ◆ *adj, pron* ninguno ☛ *Ver nota en* NINGUNO ◆ *adv* **1** tampoco

Cuando **neither** significa "tampoco" se puede sustituir por **nor**. Con ambos se utiliza la estructura: **neither/nor + v aux/v modal + sujeto**: *'I didn't go.' 'Neither/nor did I.'* — Yo no fui. — Yo tampoco. ◊ *I can't swim and neither/nor can my brother.* Yo no sé nadar y mi hermano tampoco.

Either puede significar "tampoco", pero requiere un verbo en negativa y su posición en la frase es distinta: *I don't like it, and I can't afford it either.* No me gusta, y tampoco puedo comprarlo. ◊ *My sister didn't go either.* Mi hermana tampoco fue. ◊ *'I haven't seen that film.' 'I haven't either.'* – No he visto esa película. – Yo tampoco.

2 neither ... nor ni ... ni

neon /ˈniːɒn/ *n* neón

nephew /ˈnevjuː, ˈnefjuː/ *n* sobrino: *I've got two nephews and one niece.* Tengo dos sobrinos y una sobrina.

Neptune /ˈneptjuːn; *USA* -tuːn/ *n* Neptuno

nerve /nɜːv/ *n* **1** nervio: *nerve-racking* desesperante **2** valor **3** (*pey, coloq*) cara: *You've got a nerve!* ¡Qué cara tienes! LOC **to get on your/sb's nerves** (*coloq*) ponerle a uno/algn los nervios de punta *Ver tb* LOSE

nervous /ˈnɜːvəs/ *adj* **1** (*Anat*) nervioso: *nervous breakdown* depresión nerviosa **2** ~ (**about/of sth/doing sth**) nervioso (ante algo/la idea de hacer algo) **nervousness** *n* nerviosismo

nest /nest/ *n* (*lit y fig*) nido

nestle /ˈnesl/ **1** *vi* arrellanarse **2** *vi* (*pueblo*) estar situado al abrigo de **3** *vt, vi* ~ (**sth**) **against/on, etc sth/sb** recostar algo/recostarse (sobre algo/algn)

net /net/ ◆ *n* **1** (*lit y fig*) red **2** [*incontable*] malla, tul: *net curtains* visillos ◆ *adj* (*tb* **nett**) **1** (*peso, sueldo*) neto **2** (*resultado*) final **netting** *n* red: *wire netting* tela metálica

netball /ˈnetbɔːl/ *n* juego parecido al baloncesto muy popular en los colegios de niñas en GB

nettle /ˈnetl/ *n* ortiga

network /ˈnetwɜːk/ ◆ *n* **1** red **2** (*TV*) red de cadenas (de radio y televisión) ◆ *vt* retransmitir

neurotic /njʊəˈrɒtɪk; *USA* nʊ-/ *adj, n* neurótico, -a

neutral /ˈnjuːtrəl; *USA* ˈnuː-/ *adj* **1** neutral **2** (*color*) neutro

never /ˈnevə(r)/ *adv* **1** nunca **2** *That will never do.* Eso es totalmente inaceptable. LOC **well, I never (did)!** ¡no me digas! ☛ *Ver nota en* ALWAYS, NUNCA

nevertheless /ˌnevəðəˈles/ *adv* (*fml*) sin embargo

new /njuː; *USA* nuː/ *adj* (**newer**, **newest**) **1** nuevo: *What's new?* ¿Qué hay de nuevo? **2 new (to sth)** nuevo (en algo) **3** otro: *a new job* otro trabajo LOC **a new lease of life**; *USA* **a new lease on life** una nueva vida **(as) good as new** como nuevo *Ver tb* TURN **newly** *adv* recién **newness** *n* novedad

newcomer /ˈnjuːkʌmə(r)/ *n* recién llegado, -a

news /njuːz; *USA* nuːz/ *n* [*incontable*] **1** noticia(s): *The news is not good.* Las noticias no son buenas. ◊ *a piece of news* una noticia ◊ *Have you got any news?* ¿Tienes noticias? ◊ *It's news to me.* Ahora me entero. **2 the news** las noticias, el informativo LOC *Ver* BREAK[1]

newsagent /ˈnjuːʒeɪdʒənt/ (*USA* **newsdealer**) *n* vendedor, -ora de periódicos: *newsagent's* quiosco (de periódicos) ☛ *Ver nota en* ESTANCO

newspaper /ˈnjuːsˌpeɪpə(r); *USA* ˈnuːz-/ *n* periódico

news-stand /ˈnjuːs stænd; *USA* ˈnuːz/ *n* quiosco de periódicos

new year *n* año nuevo: *New Year's Day/Eve* Día de Año Nuevo/Nochevieja

next /nekst/ ◆ *adj* **1** próximo, siguiente: *(the) next time you see her* la próxima vez que la veas ◊ *(the) next day* al día siguiente ◊ *next month* el mes que viene ◊ *It's not ideal, but it's the next best thing.* No es ideal, pero es lo mejor que hay. **2** (*contiguo*) de al lado LOC **the next few days, months, etc** los próximos/siguientes días, meses, etc *Ver tb* DAY ◆ **next to** *prep* **1** (*situación*) al lado de, junto a **2** (*orden*) después de **3** casi: *next to nothing* casi nada ◊ *next to last* el penúltimo ◆ *adv* **1** después, ahora: *What shall we do next?* ¿Qué hacemos ahora? ◊ *What did they do next?* ¿Qué hicieron después? **2** *when we next meet* la próxima vez que nos veamos **3** (*comparación*): *the next oldest* el siguiente en antigüedad ◆ **the next** [*sing*] el/la siguiente, el próximo, l próxima: *Who's next?* ¿Quién es (siguiente?

next door *adj, adv*: *next-door neigh bour* vecino de al lado ◊ *the room nex door* la habitación de al lado ◊ *They liu next door.* Viven en la puerta de al lad(

next of kin *n* pariente(s) má cercano(s) *Ver tb* KIN

nibble /ˈnɪbl/ *vt, vi* ~ **(at sth)** mordi quear, picar (algo)

nice /naɪs/ *adj* (**nicer**, **nicest**) **1** ~ **(t sb)** simpático, amable (con algı ☛ Nótese que **sympathetic** se traduc por "compasivo". **2** bonito: *You loo nice.* Estás muy guapo. **3** agradable: *t have a nice time* pasarlo bien ◊ *It smel nice.* Huele bien. **4** (*tiempo*) buen(o) LO **nice and...** (*coloq*) bastante: *nice an warm* calentito **nicely** *adv* **1** bien amablemente

niche /nɪtʃ, niːʃ/ *n* **1** hornacina **2** (*fi* rincón, lugar

nick /nɪk/ ◆ *n* **1** muesca, cor pequeño, mella **2 the nick** (*GB, colo* la chirona, la comisaría LOC **in the nic of time** justo a tiempo ◆ *vt* **1** hacer(s un corte en, mellar **2** ~ **sth (from st sb)** birlar algo (de algo/a algn)

nickel /ˈnɪkl/ *n* **1** níquel **2** (*Can, US* moneda de 5 centavos

nickname /ˈnɪkneɪm/ ◆ *n* apodo, mo ◆ *vt* apodar

nicotine /ˈnɪkətiːn/ *n* nicotina

niece /niːs/ *n* sobrina

night /naɪt/ *n* **1** noche: *the night befo last* anteanoche ◊ *night school* escue nocturna ◊ *night shift* turno de noche (*Teat*) representación: *first/openir night* estreno LOC **at night** de noch por la noche: *ten o'clock at night* a l diez de la noche **good night** buen noches, hasta mañana (*como fórmu de despedida*) *Ver tb* DAY, DEAD ☛ *V nota en* NOCHE

nightclub /ˈnaɪtklʌb/ *n* discoteca, sa de fiestas

nightdress /ˈnaɪtdres/ *n* (*tb col* **nightie, nighty**) *n* camisón

nightfall /ˈnaɪtfɔːl/ *n* anochecer

nightingale /ˈnaɪtɪŋgeɪl; *USA* -tng-/ ruiseñor

nightlife /ˈnaɪtlaɪf/ *n* vida nocturna

nightly /ˈnaɪtli/ ◆ *adv* todas las noches, cada noche ◆ *adj* **1** nocturno **2** (*regular*) de todas las noches

nightmare /ˈnaɪtmeə(r)/ *n* (*lit y fig*) pesadilla **nightmarish** *adj* de pesadilla, espeluznante

night-time /ˈnaɪt taɪm/ *n* noche

nil /nɪl/ *n* **1** (*Dep*) cero **2** nulo

nimble /ˈnɪmbl/ *adj* (**-er**, **-est**) **1** ágil **2** (*mente*) despierto

nine /naɪn/ *adj, pron, n* nueve ☛ *Ver ejemplos en* FIVE **ninth 1** *adj* noveno **2** *pron, adv* el noveno, la novena, los novenos, las novenas **3** *n* novena parte, noveno ☛ *Ver ejemplos en* FIFTH

nineteen /ˌnaɪnˈtiːn/ *adj, pron, n* diecinueve ☛ *Ver ejemplos en* FIVE **nineteenth 1** *adj* decimonoveno **2** *pron, adv* el decimonoveno, la decimonovena, los decimonovenos, las decimonovenas **3** *n* diecinueveava parte, diecinueveavo ☛ *Ver ejemplos en* FIFTH

ninety /ˈnaɪnti/ *adj, pron, n* noventa ☛ *Ver ejemplos en* FIFTY, FIVE **ninetieth 1** *adj, pron* nonagésimo **2** *n* noventava parte, noventavo ☛ *Ver ejemplos en* FIFTH

nip /nɪp/ (**-pp-**) **1** *vt* pellizcar **2** *vi* (*coloq*) correr: *to nip out* salir un momento

nipple /ˈnɪpl/ *n* pezón, tetilla

nitrogen /ˈnaɪtrədʒən/ *n* nitrógeno

no /nəʊ/ ◆ *adj neg* [*antes de sustantivo*] **1** ninguno: *No two people think alike.* No hay dos personas que piensen igual. ☛ *Ver nota en* NINGUNO **2** (*prohibición*): *No smoking.* Prohibido fumar. **3** (*para enfatizar una negación*): *She's no fool.* No es ninguna tonta. ◊ *It's no joke.* No es broma. ◆ *adv neg* [*antes de adj comparativo y adv*] no: *His car is no bigger/more expensive than mine.* Su coche no es más grande/caro que el mío. ◆ *interj* ¡no!

nobility /nəʊˈbɪləti/ *n* nobleza

noble /ˈnəʊbl/ *adj, n* (**-er** /ˈnəʊblə(r)/ **-est** /ˈnəʊblɪst/) noble

nobody /ˈnəʊbədi/ ◆ *pron* (*tb* **no one** /ˈnəʊwʌn/) nadie

En inglés no se pueden usar dos negativas en la misma frase. Como las palabras **nobody**, **nothing** y **nowhere** son negativas, el verbo siempre tiene que ir en afirmativa: *Nobody saw him.* No le vio nadie. ◊ *She said nothing.* No dijo nada. ◊ *Nothing happened.* No pasó nada. Cuando el verbo va en negativa tenemos que usar **anybody**, **anything** y **anywhere**: *I didn't see anybody.* No vi a nadie. ◊ *She didn't say anything.* No dijo nada.

◆ *n* (*pl* **-ies**) don nadie

nocturnal /nɒkˈtɜːnl/ *adj* nocturno

nod /nɒd/ ◆ (**-dd-**) **1** *vt, vi* asentir con la cabeza: *He nodded (his head) in agreement.* Asintió (con la cabeza). **2** *vi* **to nod (to/at sb)** saludar con la cabeza (a algn) **3** *vt, vi* indicar/hacer una señal con la cabeza **4** *vi* dar cabezadas PHR V **to nod off** (*coloq*) dormirse ◆ *n* inclinación de la cabeza LOC **to give (sb) the nod** dar permiso (a algn) para hacer algo

noise /nɔɪz/ *n* ruido LOC **to make a noise (about sth)** armar un escándalo (por algo) *Ver tb* BIG **noisily** *adv* ruidosamente, escandalosamente **noisy** *adj* (**-ier**, **-iest**) **1** ruidoso **2** bullicioso

nomad /ˈnəʊmæd/ *n* nómada **nomadic** /nəʊˈmædɪk/ *adj* nómada

nominal /ˈnɒmɪnl/ *adj* nominal **nominally** *adv* en apariencia, de nombre

nominate /ˈnɒmɪneɪt/ *vt* **1** ~ **sb (as sth) (for sth)** nombrar a algn (como algo) (para algo) **2** ~ **sth (as sth)** establecer, designar algo (como algo) **nomination** *n* nombramiento

nominee /ˌnɒmɪˈniː/ *n* candidato, -a

none /nʌn/ ◆ *pron* **1** ninguno, -a, -os, -as: *None (of them) is/are alive now.* Ya no queda ninguno vivo. **2** [*con sustantivos o pronombres incontables*] nada: *'Is there any bread left?' 'No, none.'* —¿Queda algo de pan? —No, no queda nada. **3** (*fml*) nadie: *and none more so than…* y nadie más que… LOC **none but** sólo **none other than** ni más ni menos que ◆ *adv* **1** *I'm none the wiser.* Sigo sin entender nada. ◊ *He's none the worse for it.* No le ha pasado nada. **2** *none too clean* nada limpio

nonetheless *adv* /ˌnʌnðəˈles/ sin embargo

non-existent /ˌnɒn ɪɡˈzɪstənt/ *adj* inexistente

non-fiction /ˌnɒn ˈfɪkʃn/ *n* obras que no pertenecen al género de ficción

nonsense /ˈnɒnsns; *USA* -sens/ *n* [*incontable*] **1** disparates **2** chorradas, tonterías **nonsensical** /nɒnˈsensɪkl/ *adj* absurdo

non-stop /ˌnɒn ˈstɒp/ ◆ *adj* **1** (*vuelo, etc*) directo **2** ininterrumpido ◆ *adv* **1** directamente, sin hacer escala **2** sin parar, ininterrumpidamente (*hablar, trabajar, etc*)

noodle /ˈnuːdl/ *n* fideo

noon /nuːn/ *n* (*fml*) mediodía: *at noon* al mediodía ◊ *twelve noon* las doce en punto

no one *Ver* NOBODY

noose /nuːs/ *n* nudo corredizo, lazo

nor /nɔː(r)/ *conj, adv* **1** ni **2** (ni…) tampoco: *Nor do I.* Yo tampoco. ☛ *Ver nota en* NEITHER

norm /nɔːm/ *n* norma

normal /ˈnɔːml/ ◆ *adj* normal ◆ *n* lo normal: *Things are back to normal.* Las cosas han vuelto a la normalidad. **normally** *adv* normalmente ☛ *Ver nota en* ALWAYS

north /nɔːθ/ ◆ *n* (*tb* **the north**, **the North**) (*abrev* **N**) (el) norte: *Leeds is in the North of England.* Leeds está en el norte de Inglaterra. ◊ *northbound* en/ con dirección norte ◆ *adj* (del) norte: *north winds* vientos del norte ◆ *adv* al norte: *We are going north on Tuesday.* Nos vamos al norte el martes. *Ver tb* NORTHWARD(S)

north-east /ˌnɔːθ ˈiːst/ ◆ *n* (*abrev* **NE**) noreste ◆ *adj* (del) noreste ◆ *adv* hacia el noreste **north-eastern** *adj* (del) noreste

northern /ˈnɔːðən/ (*tb* **Northern**) *adj* (del) norte: *She has a northern accent.* Tiene acento del norte. ◊ *the northern hemisphere* el hemisferio norte **northerner** *n* norteño, -a

northward(s) /ˈnɔːθwəd(z)/ *adv* hacia el norte *Ver tb* NORTH *adv*

north-west /ˌnɔːθ ˈwest/ ◆ *n* (*abrev* **NW**) noroeste ◆ *adj* (del) noroeste ◆ *adv* hacia el noroeste **north-western** *adj* (del) noroeste

nose /nəʊz/ ◆ *n* **1** nariz **2** (*avión*) morro **3** (*lit y fig*) olfato LOC *Ver* BLOW ◆ PHR V **to nose about/around** (*coloq*) husmear

nosey (*tb* **nosy**) /ˈnəʊzi/ *adj* (**-ier**, **-iest**) (*coloq, pey*) curioso, fisgón

nostalgia /nɒˈstældʒə/ *n* nostalgia

nostril /ˈnɒstrəl/ *n* fosa nasal: *nostrils* nariz

not /nɒt/ *adv* no: *I hope not.* Espero que no. ◊ *I'm afraid not.* Me temo que no. ◊ *Certainly not!* ¡Ni hablar! ◊ *Not any more.* Ya no. ◊ *Not even…* Ni siquiera…

> **Not** se usa para formar la negativa con verbos auxiliares y modales (**be**, **do**, **have**, **can**, **must**, etc) y muchas veces se usa en su forma contracta **-n't**: *She is not/isn't going.* ◊ *We did not/didn't go.* ◊ *I must not/mustn't go.* La forma no contracta (**not**) tiene un uso más formal o enfático y se usa para formar la negativa de los verbos subordinados: *He warned me not to be late.* Me advirtió que no llegara tarde. ◊ *I expect not.* Supongo que no. ☛ *Comparar con* NO

LOC **not at all 1** (*respuesta*) de nada *Ver tb* WELCOME **2** nada, en lo más mínimo **not that…** no es que…: *It's not that I mind…* No es que me importe…

notably /ˈnəʊtəbli/ *adv* notablemente

notch /nɒtʃ/ ◆ *n* **1** mella **2** grado ◆ PHR V **to notch sth up** (*coloq*) apuntarse algo

note /nəʊt/ ◆ *n* **1** (*tb Mús*) nota: *to make a note (of sth)* tomar nota (de algo) ◊ *to take notes* tomar apuntes ◊ *notepaper* papel de cartas **2** (*tb* **bank note**, *USA* **bill**) billete **3** (*piano, etc*) tecla ◆ *vt* advertir, fijarse en PHR V **to note sth down** anotar algo **noted** *adj* (**for/as sth**) célebre (por/por ser algo)

notebook /ˈnəʊtbʊk/ *n* cuaderno, libreta

noteworthy /ˈnəʊtwɜːði/ *adj* digno de mención

nothing /ˈnʌθɪŋ/ *pron* **1** nada ☛ *Ver nota en* NOBODY **2** cero LOC **for nothing 1** gratis **2** en vano **nothing much** no gran cosa **nothing of the kind/sort** nada por el estilo **to have nothing to do with sth/sb** no tener nada que ver con algo/algn

notice /ˈnəʊtɪs/ ◆ *n* **1** anuncio, cartel: *noticeboard* tablón de anuncios **2** aviso: *until further notice* hasta nuevo aviso ◊ *to give one month's notice* avisar con un mes de antelación **3** dimisión, carta de despido **4** reseña LOC **to take no notice/not to take any notice (of sth/sb)** no hacer caso (de algo/algn) *Ver tb* ESCAPE, MOMENT ◆ *vt* **1** darse cuenta **2** prestar atención a, fijarse en **noticeable** *adj* perceptible

notify /ˈnəʊtɪfaɪ/ *vt* (*pret, pp* **-fied**) (*fml*) ~ **sb (of sth)**; ~ **sth to sb** notificar (algo) a algn

notion /ˈnəʊʃn/ *n* **1** ~ **(that...)** noción, idea (de que...) **2** [*incontable*] ~ **(of sth)** idea (de algo): *without any notion of what he would do* sin tener idea de lo que haría

notorious /nəʊˈtɔːriəs/ *adj* (*pey*) ~ **(for/as sth)** conocido, famoso (por/por ser algo)

notwithstanding /ˌnɒtwɪθˈstændɪŋ/ *prep, adv* (*fml*) a pesar de, no obstante

nought /nɔːt/ *n* cero

noun /naʊn/ *n* nombre, sustantivo

nourish /ˈnʌrɪʃ/ *vt* **1** nutrir **2** (*fml, fig*) alimentar **nourishing** *adj* nutritivo

novel /ˈnɒvl/ ◆ *adj* original ◆ *n* novela **novelist** *n* novelista

novelty /ˈnɒvlti/ *n* (*pl* **-ies**) novedad

November /nəʊˈvembə(r)/ *n* (*abrev* **Nov**) noviembre ☛ *Ver nota y ejemplos en* JANUARY

novice /ˈnɒvɪs/ *n* novato, -a, principiante

now /naʊ/ ◆ *adv* **1** ahora: *by now* ya ◊ *right now* ahora mismo **2** ahora bien LOC **(every) now and again/then** de vez en cuando ◆ *conj* **now (that...)** ahora que..., ya que...

nowadays /ˈnaʊədeɪz/ *adv* hoy (en) día

nowhere /ˈnəʊweə(r)/ *adv* a/en/por ninguna parte: *There's nowhere to park.* No hay donde aparcar. ☛ *Ver nota en* NOBODY LOC **to be nowhere to be found/seen** no aparecer por ninguna parte *Ver tb* MIDDLE, NEAR

nozzle /ˈnɒzl/ *n* boquilla

nuance /ˈnjuːɑːns; *USA* ˈnuː-/ *n* matiz

nuclear /ˈnjuːkliə(r); *USA* ˈnuː-/ *adj* nuclear

nucleus /ˈnjuːkliəs; *USA* ˈnuː-/ *n* (*pl* **nuclei** /-kliaɪ/) núcleo

nude /njuːd; *USA* nuːd/ ◆ *adj* desnudo (integral) (*artístico y erótico*) ☛ *Ver nota en* NAKED ◆ *n* desnudo LOC **in the nude** desnudo **nudity** *n* desnudez

nudge /nʌdʒ/ *vt* **1** dar un codazo a *Ver tb* ELBOW **2** empujar suavemente

nuisance /ˈnjuːsns; *USA* ˈnuː-/ *n* **1** molestia **2** (*persona*) pesado, -a

null /nʌl/ *adj* LOC **null and void** nulo

numb /nʌm/ ◆ *adj* entumecido: *numb with shock* paralizado del susto ◆ *vt* **1** entumecer **2** (*fig*) paralizar

number /ˈnʌmbə(r)/ ◆ *n* (*abrev* **No**) número *Ver* REGISTRATION NUMBER LOC **a number of...** varios/ciertos... ◆ *vt* **1** numerar **2** ascender a

number plate *n* placa de la matrícula

numerical /njuːˈmerɪkl; *USA* nuː-/ *adj* numérico

numerous /ˈnjuːmərəs; *USA* ˈnuː-/ *adj* (*fml*) numeroso

nun /nʌn/ *n* monja

nurse /nɜːs/ ◆ *n* **1** enfermero, -a **2** (*tb* **nursemaid**) niñera *Ver tb* NANNY ◆ **1** *vt* (*lit y fig*) cuidar **2** *vt, vi* amamantar(se) **3** *vt* acunar **4** *vt* (*sentimientos*) alimentar *Ver tb* NURTURE 2 **nursing** *n* **1** enfermería: *nursing home* residencia privada de la tercera edad **2** cuidado (*de enfermos*)

nursery /ˈnɜːsəri/ *n* (*pl* **-ies**) **1** guardería infantil: *nursery education* educación preescolar ◊ *nursery rhyme* canción infantil *Ver tb* CRÈCHE, PLAYGROUP **2** habitación de los niños **3** vivero

nurture /ˈnɜːtʃə(r)/ *vt* **1** (*niño*) criar **2** alimentar **3** (*fig*) fomentar

nut /nʌt/ *n* **1** fruto seco **2** tuerca **3** (*coloq, pey*) (*GB* **nutter**) chiflado, -a **4** fanático, -a **nutty** *adj* (**-ier**, **-iest**) **1** *a nutty flavour* un sabor a fruto seco **2** (*coloq*) chiflado

nutcase /ˈnʌtkeɪs/ *n* (*coloq*) chiflado, -a

nutcrackers /ˈnʌtkrækəz/ *n* [*pl*] cascanueces

nutmeg /ˈnʌtmeg/ *n* nuez moscada

nutrient /ˈnjuːtriənt; *USA* ˈnuː-/ *n* (*fml*) nutriente, sustancia nutritiva

nutrition /njuˈtrɪʃn; *USA* nu-/ *n* nutrición **nutritional** *adj* nutritivo **nutritious** *adj* nutritivo

nuts /nʌts/ *adj* (*coloq*) **1** loco **2** ~ **about/on sth/sb** loco por algo/algn

nutshell /ˈnʌtʃel/ *n* cáscara (*de fruto seco*) LOC **(to put sth) in a nutshell** (decir algo) en pocas palabras

nutty *Ver* NUT

nylon /ˈnaɪlɒn/ *n* nilón, nailon

nymph /nɪmf/ *n* ninfa

Oo

O, o /əʊ/ *n* (*pl* **O's, o's** /əʊz/) **1** O, o: *O for Oliver* O de Óscar ☛ *Ver ejemplos en* A, a **2** cero

Cuando se nombra el cero en una serie de números, p.ej. 01865, se pronuncia como la letra **O**: /ˌəʊ wʌn eɪt sɪks ˈfaɪv/.

oak /əʊk/ (*tb* **oak tree**) *n* roble

oar /ɔː(r)/ *n* remo

oasis /əʊˈeɪsɪs/ *n* (*pl* **oases** /-siːz/) (*lit y fig*) oasis

oath /əʊθ/ *n* **1** juramento **2** palabrota LOC **on/under oath** bajo juramento

oats /əʊts/ *n* [*pl*] (copos de) avena

obedient /əˈbiːdiənt/ *adj* obediente **obedience** *n* obediencia

obese /əʊˈbiːs/ *adj* (*fml*) obeso

obey /əˈbeɪ/ *vt, vi* obedecer

obituary /əˈbɪtʃuəri; *USA* -tʃʊeri/ *n* (*pl* **-ies**) necrología

object /ˈɒbdʒɪkt/ ◆ *n* **1** objeto **2** objetivo, propósito **3** (*Gram*) complemento ◆ /əbˈdʒekt/ *vi* ~ (**to sth/sb**) oponerse (a algo/algn); estar en contra (de algo/algn): *If he doesn't object.* Si no tiene inconveniente.

objection /əbˈdʒekʃn/ *n* ~ (**to/against sth/doing sth**) oposición (a algo/a hacer algo); protesta contra algo; inconveniente en hacer algo

objective /əbˈdʒektɪv/ *adj, n* objetivo: *to remain objective* mantener la objetividad

obligation /ˌɒblɪˈgeɪʃn/ *n* **1** obligación **2** (*Com*) compromiso LOC **to be under an/no obligation** (**to do sth**) (no) tener obligación (de hacer algo)

obligatory /əˈblɪgətri; *USA* -tɔːri/ *adj* (*fml*) obligatorio, de rigor

oblige /əˈblaɪdʒ/ *vt* **1** obligar **2** ~ **sb** (**with sth/by doing sth**) (*fml*) complacer a algn; hacer el favor a algn (de hacer algo) **obliged** *adj* ~ (**to sb**) (**for sth/doing sth**) agradecido (a algn) (por algo/hacer algo) LOC **much obliged** se agradece **obliging** *adj* atento

obliterate /əˈblɪtəreɪt/ *vt* (*fml*) eliminar

oblivion /əˈblɪviən/ *n* olvido

oblivious /əˈblɪviəs/ *adj* ~ **of/to sth** no consciente de algo

oblong /ˈɒblɒŋ; *USA* -lɔːŋ/ ◆ *n* rectángulo ◆ *adj* rectangular

oboe /ˈəʊbəʊ/ *n* oboe

obscene /əbˈsiːn/ *adj* obsceno

obscure /əbˈskjʊə(r)/ ◆ *adj* **1** poco claro **2** desconocido ◆ *vt* oscurecer, esconder

observant /əbˈzɜːvənt/ *adj* observador

observation /ˌɒbzəˈveɪʃn/ *n* observación

observatory /əbˈzɜːvətri; *USA* -tɔːri/ *n* (*pl* **-ies**) observatorio

observe /əbˈzɜːv/ *vt* **1** observar **2** (*fml*) (*fiesta*) guardar **observer** *n* observador, -ora

obsess /əbˈses/ *vt* obsesionar **obsession** *n* ~ (**with/about sth/sb**) obsesión (con algo/algn) **obsessive** *adj* (*pey*) obsesivo

obsolete /ˈɒbsəliːt/ *adj* obsoleto

obstacle /ˈɒbstəkl/ *n* obstáculo

obstetrician /ˌɒbstəˈtrɪʃn/ *n* tocólogo, -a

obstinate /ˈɒbstɪnət/ *adj* obstinado

obstruct /əbˈstrʌkt/ *vt* obstruir

obstruction /əbˈstrʌkʃn/ *n* obstrucción

obtain /əbˈteɪn/ *vt* obtener **obtainable** *adj* que se puede conseguir

obvious /ˈɒbviəs/ *adj* obvio **obviously** *adv* obviamente

occasion /əˈkeɪʒn/ *n* **1** ocasión **2** acontecimiento LOC **on the occasion of sth** (*fml*) con motivo de algo

occasional /əˈkeɪʒənl/ *adj* esporádico: *She reads the occasional book.* Lee algún que otro libro. **occasionally** *adv* de vez en cuando ☛ *Ver nota en* ALWAYS

occupant /ˈɒkjəpənt/ *n* ocupante

occupation /ˌɒkjuˈpeɪʃn/ *n* **1** ocupación **2** profesión ☛ *Ver nota en* WORK

occupational /ˌɒkjuˈpeɪʃənl/ *adj* laboral: *occupational hazards* gajes del oficio **2** (*terapia*) ocupacional

occupier /ˈɒkjʊpaɪə(r)/ *n* ocupante

occupy /ˈɒkjupaɪ/ (*pret, pp* **occupied**

1 *vt* ocupar **2** *v refl* ~ **yourself (in doing sth/with sth)** entretenerse (haciendo algo con algo)

occur /əˈkɜː(r)/ *vi* (*pret, pp* **occurred**) **1** ocurrir, producirse **2** (*fml*) aparecer **3** ~ **to sb** ocurrirse a algn

occurrence /əˈkʌrəns/ *n* **1** hecho, caso **2** (*fml*) existencia, aparición **3** frecuencia ☛ *Comparar con* OCURRENCIA

ocean /ˈəʊʃn/ *n* océano **LOC** *Ver* DROP ☛ *Ver nota en* OCÉANO

o'clock /əˈklɒk/ *adv*: *six o'clock* las seis (en punto)

October /ɒkˈtəʊbə(r)/ *n* (*abrev* **Oct**) octubre ☛ *Ver nota y ejemplos en* JANUARY

octopus /ˈɒktəpəs/ *n* (*pl* ~**es**) pulpo

odd /ɒd/ *adj* **1** (**odder**, **oddest**) raro **2** (*número*) impar **3** (*fascículo*) suelto **4** (*zapato*) desparejado **5** sobrante **6** *thirty-odd* treinta y pico ◊ *twelve pounds odd* doce libras y pico **7** *He has the odd beer.* Toma una cerveza de vez en cuando. **LOC to be the odd man/one out** ser el único desparejado, sobrar *Ver tb* FISH

oddity /ˈɒdəti/ *n* (*pl* **-ies**) **1** (*tb* **oddness**) rareza **2** cosa rara **3** (*persona*) bicho raro

oddly /ˈɒdli/ *adv* extrañamente: *Oddly enough...* Lo extraño es que...

odds /ɒdz/ *n* [*pl*] **1** probabilidades: *The odds are that...* Lo más probable es que... **2** apuestas **LOC it makes no odds** da lo mismo **odds and ends** (*GB, coloq*) cosas sin valor, chismes **to be at odds (with sb) (over/on sth)** estar reñido (con algn) (por algo), discrepar (sobre algo)

odour (*USA* **odor**) /ˈəʊdə(r)/ *n* (*fml*) olor: *body odour* olor corporal ☛ **Odour** se usa en contextos más formales que **smell** y a veces implica que es un olor desagradable.

of /əv, ɒv/ *prep* **1** de: *a girl of six* una niña de seis años ◊ *It's made of wood.* Es de madera. ◊ *two kilos of rice* dos kilos de arroz ◊ *It was very kind of him.* Fue muy amable de su parte. **2** (*con posesivos*) de: *a friend of John's* un amigo de John ◊ *a cousin of mine* un primo mío **3** (*con cantidades*): *There were five of us.* Éramos cinco. ◊ *most of all* más que nada ◊ *The six of us went.* Fuimos los seis. **4** (*fechas y tiempo*) de: *the first of March* el uno de marzo **5** (*causa*) de: *What did she die of?* ¿De qué murió?

off /ɒf; *USA* ɔːf/ ◆ *adj* **1** (*comida*) pasado **2** (*leche*) cortado ◆ *part adv* **1** (*a distancia*): *five miles off* a cinco millas de distancia ◊ *some way off* a cierta distancia ◊ *not far off* no (muy) lejos **2** (*quitado*): *You left the lid off.* Lo dejaste destapado. ◊ *with her shoes off* descalza **3** *I must be off.* Tengo que irme. **4** (*coloq*): *The meeting is off.* Se ha cancelado la reunión. **5** (*gas, electricidad*) desconectado **6** (*máquinas, etc*) apagado **7** (*grifo*) cerrado **8** *a day off* un día libre **9** *five per cent off* un cinco por ciento de descuento *Ver* WELL OFF **LOC off and on; on and off** de cuando en cuando **to be off (for sth)** (*coloq*): *How are you off for cash?* ¿Cómo estás de dinero? ☛ *Comparar con* BADLY, BETTER ◆ *prep* **1** de: *to fall off sth* caerse de algo **2** *a street off the main road* una calle que sale de la carretera principal **3** *off the coast* a cierta distancia de la costa **4** (*coloq*) sin ganas de: *to be off your food* estar desganado **LOC come off it!** ¡anda ya! ☛ Para los usos de **off** en PHRASAL VERBS ver las entradas de los verbos correspondientes, p.ej. **to go off** en GO[1].

off-duty /ˈɒf djuːti/ *adj* fuera de servicio

offence (*USA* **offense**) /əˈfens/ *n* **1** delito **2** ofensa **LOC to take offence (at sth)** ofenderse (por algo)

offend /əˈfend/ *vt* ofender: *to be offended* ofenderse **offender** *n* **1** infractor, -ora **2** delincuente

offensive /əˈfensɪv/ ◆ *adj* **1** ofensivo, insultante **2** (*olor, etc*) repugnante ◆ *n* ofensiva

offer /ˈɒfə(r); *USA* ˈɔːf-/ ◆ *vt, vi* ofrecer: *to offer to do sth* ofrecerse a/para hacer algo ◆ *n* oferta **offering** *n* **1** ofrecimiento **2** ofrenda

offhand /ˌɒfˈhænd; *USA* ˌɔːf-/ ◆ *adv* improvisadamente, así, de pronto ◆ *adj* hosco

office /ˈɒfɪs; *USA* ˈɔːf-/ *n* **1** oficina: *office hours* horas de oficina **2** despacho **3** cargo: *to take office* entrar en funciones **LOC in office** en el poder

officer /ˈɒfɪsə(r); *USA* ˈɔːf-/ *n* **1** (*ejército*)

oficial **2** (*gobierno*) funcionario, -a **3** (*tb* **police officer**) agente

official /əˈfɪʃl/ ◆ *adj* oficial ◆ *n* funcionario, -a **officially** *adv* oficialmente

off-licence /ˈɒf laɪsns/ *n* (*GB*) tienda de vinos y licores

off-peak /ˌɒf ˈpiːk; *USA* ˌɔːf/ *adj* **1** (*precio, tarifa*) de temporada baja **2** (*periodo*) de menor consumo

off-putting /ˈɒf pʊtɪŋ; *USA* ˌɔːf/ *adj* (*coloq*) **1** desconcertante **2** (*persona*) desagradable

offset /ˈɒfset; *USA* ˈɔːf-/ *vt* (**-tt-**) (*pret, pp* **offset**) contrarrestar

offshore /ˌɒfˈʃɔː(r); *USA* ˌɔːf-/ *adj* **1** (*isla*) cercano a la costa **2** (*brisa*) terral **3** (*pesca*) de bajura

offside /ˌɒfˈsaɪd; *USA* ˌɔːf-/ *adj, adv* fuera de juego

offspring /ˈɒfsprɪŋ; *USA* ˈɔːf-/ *n* (*pl* **offspring**) (*fml*) **1** hijo(s), descendencia **2** cría(s)

often /ˈɒfn, ˈɒftən; *USA* ˈɔːfn/ *adv* **1** a menudo, muchas veces: *How often do you see her?* ¿Cada cuánto la ves? **2** con frecuencia ☛ *Ver nota en* ALWAYS *Ver tb* EVERY

oh! /əʊ/ *interj* **1** ¡oh!, ¡ah! **2** *Oh yes I will.* ¡Y tanto que lo haré! ◊ *Oh no you won't!* ¡De eso nada!

oil /ɔɪl/ ◆ *n* **1** petróleo: *oilfield* yacimiento petrolífero ◊ *oil rig* plataforma/torre de perforación ◊ *oil tanker* petrolero ◊ *oil well* pozo petrolífero **2** aceite **3** (*Arte*) óleo ◆ *vt* lubricar **oily** *adj* (**oilier**, **oiliest**) **1** oleoso **2** aceitoso

oil slick *n* mancha de petróleo

okay (*tb* **OK**) /ˌəʊˈkeɪ/ ◆ *adj, adv* (*coloq*) bien ◆ *interj* ¡vale! ◆ *vt* dar el visto bueno a ◆ *n* consentimiento, visto bueno

old /əʊld/ ◆ *adj* (**older**, **oldest**) ☛ *Ver nota en* ELDER **1** viejo: *old age* vejez ◊ *old people* (los) ancianos ◊ *the Old Testament* el Antiguo Testamento **2** *How old are you?* ¿Cuántos años tienes? ◊ *She is two (years old).* Tiene dos años.

> Para decir "tengo diez años", decimos *I am ten* o *I am ten years old.* Sin embargo, para decir "un chico de diez años", decimos *a boy of ten* o *a ten-year-old boy.* ☛ *Ver nota en* YEAR

3 (*anterior*) antiguo LOC *Ver* CHIP ◆ **the old** *n* [*pl*] los ancianos

old-fashioned /ˌəʊld ˈfæʃnd/ *adj* **1** pasado de moda **2** tradicional

olive /ˈɒlɪv/ ◆ *n* **1** aceituna **2** (*tb* **olive tree**) olivo: *olive oil* aceite de oliva ◆ *adj* **1** (*tb* **olive green**) verde oliva **2** (*piel*) cetrino

the Olympic Games *n* [*pl*] **1** (*Hist*) los Juegos Olímpicos **2** (*tb* **the Olympics**) la Olimpiada

omelette (*tb* **omelet**) /ˈɒmlət/ *n* tortilla

omen /ˈəʊmen/ *n* presagio

ominous /ˈɒmɪnəs/ *adj* ominoso

omission /əˈmɪʃn/ *n* omisión, olvido

omit /əˈmɪt/ *vt* (**-tt-**) **1** ~ **doing/to do** dejar de hacer algo **2** omitir

omnipotent /ɒmˈnɪpətənt/ *adj* omnipotente

on /ɒn/ ◆ *part adv* **1** (*con un sentido de continuidad*): *to play on* seguir tocando ◊ *further on* más lejos/más allá ◊ *from that day on* a partir de aquel día **2** (*ropa, etc*) puesto **3** (*máquinas, etc*) conectado, encendido **4** (*grifo*) abierto **5** programado: *When is the film on?* ¿A qué hora empieza la película? LOC **on and on** sin parar *Ver tb* OFF ◆ *prep* **1** (*tb* **upon**) en, sobre: *on the table* en/sobre la mesa ◊ *on the wall* en la pared **2** (*transporte*): *to go on the train/bus* ir en tren/autobús ◊ *to go on foot* ir a pie **3** (*fechas*): *on Sunday(s)* el/los domingo(s) ◊ *on 3 May* el tres de mayo **4** (*tb* **upon**) [+ *ing*]: *on arriving home* al llegar a casa **5** (*acerca de*) sobre **6** (*consumo*): *to be on drugs* estar tomando drogas ◊ *to live on fruit/on £20 a week* vivir de fruta/mantenerse con 20 libras a la semana **7** *to speak on the telephone* hablar por teléfono **8** (*actividad, estado, etc*) de: *on holiday* de vacaciones ◊ *to be on duty* estar de servicio ☛ Para los usos de **on** en PHRASAL VERBS ver las entradas de los verbos correspondientes, p.ej. **to get on** en GET.

once /wʌns/ ◆ *conj* una vez que: *Once he'd gone…* Una vez que se hubo ido… ◆ *adv* una vez: *once a week* una vez a la semana LOC **at once 1** en seguida **2** a la vez **once again/more** una vez más **once and for all** de una vez por todas **once in a while** de vez en cuando **once or twice** un par de veces **once upon a time** érase una vez

oncoming /ˈɒnkʌmɪŋ/ *adj* en dirección contraria

one¹ /wʌn/ *adj, pron, n* uno, una ☛ *Ver ejemplos en* FIVE

one² /wʌn/ ◆ *adj* **1** un(o), una: *one morning* una mañana **2** único: *the one way to succeed* la única forma de triunfar **3** mismo: *of one mind* de la misma opinión ◆ *pron* **1** [*después de adjetivo*]: *the little ones* los pequeños ◇ *I prefer this/that one.* Prefiero éste/ése. ◇ *Which one?* ¿Cuál? ◇ *another one* otro ◇ *It's better than the old one.* Es mejor que el viejo. **2** el, los, la, las que: *the one at the end* el que está al final **3** uno, una: *I need a pen. Have you got one?* Necesito un bolígrafo. ¿Tienes uno? ◇ *one of her friends* uno de sus amigos ◇ *to tell one from the other* distinguir el uno del otro **4** [*como sujeto*] (*fml*) uno, -a: *One must be sure.* Uno debe estar seguro. ☛ *Ver nota en* YOU LOC **(all) in one** a la vez **one by one** uno a uno **one or two** unos cuantos

one another *pron* los unos a los otros, el uno al otro ☛ *Ver nota en* EACH OTHER

one-off /ˌwʌn ˈɒf/ *adj, n* (algo) excepcional/único

oneself /wʌnˈself/ *pron* **1** [*uso reflexivo*]: *to cut oneself* cortarse **2** [*uso enfático*] uno mismo: *to do it oneself* hacerlo uno mismo

one-way /ˌwʌn ˈweɪ/ *adj* **1** de sentido único **2** (*billete*) de ida

ongoing /ˈɒngəʊɪŋ/ *adj* **1** en curso **2** actual

onion /ˈʌnjən/ *n* cebolla

on-line /ˌɒn ˈlaɪn/ *adj, adv* en línea (*Informát*)

onlooker /ˈɒnlʊkə(r)/ *n* espectador, -ora

only /ˈəʊnli/ ◆ *adv* solamente, sólo LOC **not only... but also** no sólo... sino (también) **only just 1** *I've only just arrived.* Acabo de llegar. **2** *I can only just see.* Apenas si puedo ver. *Ver tb* IF ◆ *adj* único: *He is an only child.* Es hijo único. ◆ *conj* (*coloq*) sólo que, pero

onset /ˈɒnset/ *n* llegada, inicio

onslaught /ˈɒnslɔːt/ *n* ~ **(on sth/sb)** ataque (contra algo/algn)

onto (*tb* **on to**) /ˈɒntə, ˈɒntuː/ *prep* en, sobre, a: *to climb (up) onto sth* subirse a algo PHR V **to be onto sb** (*coloq*) seguir la pista de algn **to be onto sth** haber dado con algo

onward /ˈɒnwəd/ ◆ *adj* (*fml*) hacia delante: *your onward journey* la continuación de tu viaje ◆ *adv* (*tb* **onwards**) **1** hacia adelante **2** en adelante: *from then onwards* a partir de entonces

ooze /uːz/ **1** *vt, vi* ~ **(with) sth** rezumar (algo) **2** *vt, vi* ~ **from/out of sth** rezumar (de algo)

opaque /əʊˈpeɪk/ *adj* opaco

open /ˈəʊpən/ ◆ *adj* **1** abierto: *Don't leave the door open.* No dejes la puerta abierta. **2** (*vista*) despejado **3** público **4** (*fig*): *to leave sth open* dejar algo pendiente LOC **in the open air** al aire libre *Ver tb* BURST, CLICK, WIDE ◆ **1** *vt, vi* abrir(se) **2** *vt* (*proceso*) empezar **3** *vt, vi* (*edificio, exposición, etc*) inaugurar(se) PHR V **to open into/onto sth** dar a algo **to open sth out** desplegar algo **to open up** (*coloq*) abrirse **to open (sth) up** abrir algo, abrirse: *Open up!* ¡Abra(n)! ◆ **the open** *n* el aire libre LOC **to come (out) into the open** salir a la luz *Ver tb* BRING **opener** *n* abridor **openly** *adv* abiertamente **openness** *n* franqueza

open-air /ˌəʊpən ˈeə(r)/ *adj* al aire libre

opening /ˈəʊpnɪŋ/ ◆ *n* **1** (*hueco*) abertura **2** (*acto*) apertura **3** comienzo **4** (*tb* **opening-night**) (*Teat*) estreno **5** inauguración **6** (*trabajo*) vacante **7** oportunidad ◆ *adj* primero

open-minded /ˌəʊpən ˈmaɪndɪd/ *adj* abierto

opera /ˈɒprə/ *n* ópera: *opera house* teatro de la ópera

operate /ˈɒpəreɪt/ **1** *vt, vi* (*máquina*) funcionar, manejar **2** *vi* (*empresa*) operar **3** *vt* (*servicio*) ofrecer **4** *vt* (*negocio*) dirigir **5** *vt, vi* (*Mec*) accionar(se) **6** *vi* ~ **(on sb) (for sth)** (*Med*) operar (a algn) (de algo): *operating theatre* quirófano

operation /ˌɒpəˈreɪʃn/ *n* **1** operación **2** funcionamiento LOC **to be in/come into operation 1** estar/entrar en funcionamiento **2** (*Jur*) estar/entrar en vigor **operational** *adj* **1** de funcionamiento **2** operativo, en funcionamiento

operative /ˈɒpərətɪv, *USA* -reɪt-/ ◆ *adj* **1** en funcionamiento **2** (*Jur*) en vigor **3** (*Med*) operatorio ◆ *n* operario, -a

operator /ˈɒpəreɪtə(r)/ *n* operario, -a:

radio operator radiotelegrafista ◊ *switchboard operator* telefonista/ operador, -ora

opinion /əˈpɪniən/ *n* ~ (**of/about sth/ sb**) opinión (de/sobre/acerca de algo/ algn) LOC **in my opinion** en mi opinión *Ver tb* MATTER

opinion poll *Ver* POLL 4

opponent /əˈpəʊnənt/ *n* **1** ~ (**at/in sth**) adversario, -a, contrincante (en algo) **2** *to be an opponent of sth* ser contrario, -a a algo

opportunity /ˌɒpəˈtjuːnəti; *USA* -ˈtuːn-/ *n* (*pl* **-ies**) ~ (**for/of doing sth**); ~ (**to do sth**) oportunidad (de hacer algo) LOC **to take the opportunity to do sth/of doing sth** aprovechar la ocasión para hacer algo

oppose /əˈpəʊz/ *vt* **1** ~ **sth** oponerse a algo **2** ~ **sb** enfrentarse a algn **opposed** *adj* contrario: *to be opposed to sth* ser contrario a algo LOC **as opposed to**: *quality as opposed to quantity* calidad más que cantidad **opposing** *adj* contrario

opposite /ˈɒpəzɪt/ ◆ *adj* **1** de enfrente: *the house opposite* la casa de enfrente **2** contrario: *the opposite sex* el otro sexo ◆ *adv* enfrente: *She was sitting opposite.* Estaba sentada enfrente. ◆ *prep* ~ **to sth/sb** en frente de algo/algn; frente a algo/algn: *opposite each other* frente a frente ◆ *n* ~ (**of sth**) lo contrario (de algo) ☛ *Ver dibujo en* ENFRENTE

opposition /ˌɒpəˈzɪʃn/ *n* ~ (**to sth/sb**) oposición (a algo/algn)

oppress /əˈpres/ *vt* **1** oprimir **2** agobiar **oppressed** *adj* oprimido **oppression** *n* opresión **oppressive** *adj* **1** opresivo **2** agobiante, sofocante

opt /ɒpt/ *vi* **to opt to do sth** optar por hacer algo PHR V **to opt for sth** optar por algo **to opt out (of sth)** optar por no hacer algo, no participar (en algo)

optical /ˈɒptɪkl/ *adj* óptico

optician /ɒpˈtɪʃn/ *n* **1** óptico, -a **2 optician's** (*tienda*) óptica

optimism /ˈɒptɪmɪzəm/ *n* optimismo **optimist** *n* optimista **optimistic** /ˌɒptɪˈmɪstɪk/ *adj* ~ (**about sth**) optimista (sobre/en cuanto a algo)

optimum /ˈɒptɪməm/ (*tb* **optimal**) *adj* óptimo

option /ˈɒpʃn/ *n* opción **optional** *adj* opcional, optativo

or /ɔː(r)/ *conj* **1** o, u *Ver tb* EITHER **2** (*de otro modo*) o, si no **3** [*después de negativa*] ni *Ver tb* NEITHER LOC **or so**: *an hour or so* una hora más o menos **sth/ sb/somewhere or other** (*coloq*) algo/ algn/en alguna parte *Ver tb* RATHER, WHETHER

oral /ˈɔːrəl/ ◆ *adj* **1** (*hablado*) oral **2** (*Anat*) bucal, oral ◆ *n* (examen) oral

orange /ˈɒrɪndʒ; *USA* ˈɔːr-/ ◆ *n* **1** naranja **2** (*tb* **orange tree**) naranjo **3** (*color*) el naranja ◆ *adj* (color) naranja, anaranjado

orbit /ˈɔːbɪt/ ◆ *n* (*lit y fig*) órbita ◆ *vt, vi* ~ (**sth/around sth**) describir una órbita (alrededor de algo)

orchard /ˈɔːtʃəd/ *n* huerto

orchestra /ˈɔːkɪstrə/ *n* [*v sing o pl*] orquesta

orchid /ˈɔːkɪd/ *n* orquídea

ordeal /ɔːˈdiːl, ˈɔːdiːl/ *n* experiencia terrible, suplicio

order /ˈɔːdə(r)/ ◆ *n* **1** (*disposición, calma*) orden: *in alphabetical order* por/en orden alfabético **2** (*mandato*) orden **3** (*Com*) pedido **4** [*v sing o pl*] (*Mil, Relig*) orden LOC **in order 1** en orden, en regla **2** (*aceptable*) permitido **in order that...** para que... **in order to...** para... **in running/ working order** en perfecto estado de funcionamiento **out of order** estropeado: *It's out of order.* No funciona. *Ver tb* LAW, MARCHING *en* MARCH, PECKING *en* PECK ◆ **1** *vt* ~ **sb to do sth** ordenar, mandar a algn hacer algo/que haga algo **2** *vt* ~ **sth (for sb)** pedir, encargar algo (para algn) **3** *vt, vi* ~ **(sth) (for sb)** (*comida, etc*) pedir (algo) (para algn) **4** *vt* (*fml*) poner en orden, ordenar, organizar PHR V **to order sb about/around** mandar a algn de acá para allá, ser mandón con algn

orderly /ˈɔːdəli/ *adj* **1** ordenado, metódico **2** disciplinado, pacífico

ordinary /ˈɔːdnri; *USA* ˈɔː rdəneri/ *adj* corriente, normal, medio: *ordinary people* gente corriente ☛ *Comparar con* COMMON 3 LOC **out of the ordinary** fuera de lo común, extraordinario

ore /ɔː(r)/ *n* mineral metalífero: *gold/ iron ore* mineral de oro/hierro

oregano /ˌɒrɪˈɡɑːnəʊ/ *n* orégano

organ /ˈɔːɡən/ *n* (*Mús, Anat*), órgano

organic /ɔːˈɡænɪk/ *adj* orgánico

organism /ˈɔːgənɪzəm/ *n* organismo
organization, -isation /ˌɔːgənaɪˈzeɪʃn; *USA* -nɪˈz-/ *n* organización **organizational, -isational** *adj* organizativo
organize, -ise /ˈɔːgənaɪz/ **1** *vt, vi* organizar(se) **2** *vt* (*pensamientos*) poner en orden **organizer, -iser** *n* organizador, -ora
orgy /ˈɔːdʒi/ *n* (*pl* **-ies**) (*lit y fig*) orgía
orient /ˈɔːrɪənt/ ◆ *vt* (*esp USA*) *Ver* ORIENTATE ◆ **the Orient** *n* Oriente **oriental** /ˌɔːriˈentl/ *adj* oriental
orientate /ˈɔːriənteɪt/ (*USA* **orient**) *vt* ~ **sth/sb** (**towards sth/sb**) orientar algo/a algn (hacia algo/algn): *to orientate yourself* orientarse **orientation** *n* orientación
origin /ˈɒrɪdʒɪn/ *n* **1** origen **2** [*a menudo pl*] origen, ascendencia
original /əˈrɪdʒənl/ ◆ *adj* **1** original **2** primero, primitivo ◆ *n* original LOC **in the original** en su idioma/versión original **originality** /əˌrɪdʒəˈnæləti/ *n* originalidad **originally** *adv* **1** con originalidad **2** en un/al principio, antiguamente
originate /əˈrɪdʒɪneɪt/ **1** *vi* ~ **in/from sth** originarse, tener su origen en algo; provenir de algo **2** *vi* (*comenzar*) nacer, empezar **3** *vt* originar, crear
ornament /ˈɔːnəmənt/ *n* (objeto de) adorno, ornamento **ornamental** /ˌɔːnəˈmentl/ *adj* decorativo, de adorno
ornate /ɔːˈneɪt/ *adj* (*frec pey*) **1** ornamentado, recargado **2** (*lenguaje, estilo*) florido
orphan /ˈɔːfn/ ◆ *n* huérfano, -a ◆ *vt*: *to be orphaned* quedarse huérfano **orphanage** *n* orfanato
orthodox /ˈɔːθədɒks/ *adj* ortodoxo
ostrich /ˈɒstrɪtʃ/ *n* avestruz
other /ˈʌðə(r)/ ◆ *adj* **1** [*con sustantivos en plural*] otro: *other books* otros libros ◇ *Have you got other plans?* ¿Tienes otros planes? **2** [*con sustantivos en singular o en plural cuando va precedido de* the, some *o* any, *adjetivos posesivos o demostrativos*] otro: *All their other children have left home.* Sus otros hijos ya se han marchado de casa. ◇ *That other car was better.* Aquel otro coche era mejor. ◇ *some other time* otro día ☛ *Ver nota en* OTRO LOC **the other day, morning, week, etc** el otro día, la otra mañana, semana, etc *Ver tb* EVERY, OR, WORD ◆ *pron* **1 others** [*pl*] otros, -as: *Others have said this before.* Otros han dicho esto antes. ◇ *Have you got any others?* ¿Tienes más? **2 the other** el otro, la otra: *I'll keep one and she can have the other.* Me quedo con uno y dejo el otro para ella. **3 the others** [*pl*] los, las demás: *This shirt is too small and the others are too big.* Esta camisa es demasiado pequeña y las demás, demasiado grandes. ◆ **other than** *prep* **1** excepto, a parte de **2** de otra manera que
otherwise /ˈʌðəwaɪz/ ◆ *adv* **1** (*fml*) de otra manera **2** por lo demás ◆ *conj* si no, de no ser así ◆ *adj* distinto
otter /ˈɒtə(r)/ *n* nutria
ouch! /aʊtʃ/ *interj* ¡ay!
ought to /ˈɔːt tə, ˈɔːt tuː/ *v modal* (*neg* **ought not** *o* **oughtn't** /ˈɔːtnt/)

Ought to es un verbo modal, y las oraciones interrogativas y negativas se construyen sin el auxiliar *do*.

1 (*sugerencias y consejos*): *You ought to do it.* Deberías hacerlo. ◇ *I ought to have gone.* Debería haber ido. ☛ *Comparar con* MUST **2** (*probabilidad*): *Five ought to be enough.* Con cinco habrá suficiente.
ounce /aʊns/ *n* (*abrev* **oz**) onza (*28,35 gramos*) ☛ *Ver* Apéndice 1.
our /ɑː(r), ˈaʊə(r)/ *adj pos* nuestro, -a, -os, -as: *Our house is in the centre.* Nuestra casa está en el centro. ☛ *Ver nota en* MY
ours /ɑːz, ˈaʊəz/ *pron pos* nuestro, -a, -os, -as: *a friend of ours* una amiga nuestra ◇ *Where's ours?* ¿Dónde está el nuestro?
ourselves /ɑːˈselvz, aʊəˈselvz/ *pron* **1** [*uso reflexivo*] nos **2** [*uso enfático*] nosotros mismos LOC **by ourselves 1** a solas **2** sin ayuda, solos
out /aʊt/ ◆ *part adv* **1** fuera: *to be out* no estar (en casa)/haber salido **2** *The sun is out.* Ha salido el sol. **3** pasado de moda **4** (*coloq*) (*posibidad, etc*) descartado **5** (*luz, etc*) apagado **6** *to call out (loud)* llamar en voz alta **7** (*cálculo*) equivocado: *The bill is out by five pounds.* Se han equivocado en cinco libras en la cuenta. **8** (*jugador*) eliminado **9** (*pelota*) fuera (*de la línea*) *Ver tb* OUT OF LOC **to be out to do sth** estar

decidido a hacer algo ☛ Para los usos de **out** en PHRASAL VERBS ver las entradas de los verbos correspondientes, p.ej. **to pick out** en PICK. ◆ *n* LOC *Ver* IN

outbreak /ˈaʊtbreɪk/ *n* **1** brote **2** (*guerra*) estallido

outburst /ˈaʊtbɜːst/ *n* **1** explosión **2** (*emoción*) estallido

outcast /ˈaʊtkɑːst; *USA* -kæst/ *n* marginado, -a, paria

outcome /ˈaʊtkʌm/ *n* resultado

outcry /ˈaʊtkraɪ/ *n* (*pl* **-ies**) protestas

outdo /ˌaʊtˈduː/ *vt* (*3ª pers sing pres* **-does** /-ˈdʌz/ *pret* **-did** /-ˈdɪd/ *pp* **-done** /-ˈdʌn/) superar

outdoor /ˈaʊtdɔː(r)/ *adj* al aire libre: *outdoor swimming pool* piscina descubierta

outdoors /ˌaʊtˈdɔːz/ *adv* al aire libre, fuera

outer /ˈaʊtə(r)/ *adj* externo, exterior

outfit /ˈaʊtfɪt/ *n* (*ropa*) conjunto

outgoing /ˈaʊtgəʊɪŋ/ *adj* **1** que sale, de salida **2** (*Pol*) cesante, saliente **3** extrovertido

outgrow /ˌaʊtˈgrəʊ/ *vt* (*pret* **outgrew** /-ˈgruː/ *pp* **outgrown** /-ˈgrəʊn/) **1** *He's outgrown his shoes.* Sus zapatos se le han quedado pequeños. **2** (*hábito, etc*) cansarse de, abandonar

outing /ˈaʊtɪŋ/ *n* excursión

outlandish /aʊtˈlændɪʃ/ *adj* estrafalario

outlaw /ˈaʊtlɔː/ ◆ *vt* declarar ilegal ◆ *n* forajido

outlet /ˈaʊtlet/ *n* **1** ~ (**for sth**) desagüe, salida (para algo) **2** ~ (**for sth**) (*fig*) desahogo (para algo) **3** (*Com*) punto de venta

outline /ˈaʊtlaɪn/ ◆ *n* **1** contorno, perfil **2** líneas generales, esbozo ◆ *vt* **1** perfilar, esbozar **2** exponer en líneas generales

outlive /ˌaʊtˈlɪv/ *vt* ~ **sth/sb** sobrevivir a algo/algn

outlook /ˈaʊtlʊk/ *n* **1** ~ (**onto/over sth**) perspectiva (sobre algo) **2** ~ (**on sth**) (*fig*) punto de vista (sobre algo) **3** ~ (**for sth**) perspectiva, pronóstico (para algo)

outnumber /ˌaʊtˈnʌmbə(r)/ *vt* ~ **sb** superar en número a algn

out of /ˈaʊt əv/ *prep* **1** fuera de: *I want that dog out of the house.* Quiero ese perro fuera de la casa. ◊ *to jump out of bed* saltar de la cama **2** (*causa*) por: *out of interest* por interés **3** de: *eight out of every ten* ocho de cada diez ◊ *to copy sth out of a book* copiar algo de un libro **4** (*material*) de, con: *made out of plastic* (hecho) de plástico **5** sin: *to be out of work* estar sin trabajo

outpost /ˈaʊtpəʊst/ *n* (puesto de) avanzada

output /ˈaʊtpʊt/ *n* **1** producción **2** (*Fís*) potencia

outrage /ˈaʊtreɪdʒ/ ◆ *n* **1** atrocidad **2** escándalo **3** ira ◆ /aʊtˈreɪdʒ/ *vt* ~ **sth/sb** ultrajar a algo/algn **outrageous** *adj* **1** escandaloso, monstruoso **2** extravagante

outright /ˈaʊtraɪt/ ◆ *adv* **1** (*sin reservas*) abiertamente, de plano **2** instantáneamente, de golpe **3** en su totalidad **4** (*ganar*) rotundamente ◆ *adj* **1** abierto **2** (*ganador*) indiscutible **3** (*negativa*) rotundo

outset /ˈaʊtset/ *n* LOC **at/from the outset (of sth)** al/desde el principio (de algo)

outside /ˌaʊtˈsaɪd/ ◆ *n* exterior: *on/from the outside* por/desde fuera ◆ *prep* (*esp USA* **outside of**) fuera de: *Wait outside the door.* Espera en la puerta. ◆ *adv* fuera, afuera ◆ /ˈaʊtsaɪd/ *adj* exterior, de fuera

outsider /ˌaʊtˈsaɪdə(r)/ *n* **1** forastero, -a **2** (*pey*) intruso, -a **3** (*competidor*) desconocido, -a

outskirts /ˈaʊtskɜːts/ *n* [*pl*] afueras

outspoken /aʊtˈspəʊkən/ *adj* sincero, franco

outstanding /aʊtˈstændɪŋ/ *adj* **1** destacado, excepcional **2** (*visible*) sobresaliente **3** (*pago, trabajo*) pendiente

outstretched /ˌaʊtˈstretʃt/ *adj* extendido, abierto

outward /ˈaʊtwəd/ *adj* **1** externo, exterior **2** (*viaje*) de ida **outwardly** *adv* por fuera, aparentemente **outwards** *adv* hacia fuera

outweigh /ˌaʊtˈweɪ/ *vt* pesar más que, importar más que

oval /ˈəʊvl/ *adj* oval, ovalado

ovary /ˈəʊvəri/ *n* (*pl* **-ies**) ovario

oven /ˈʌvn/ *n* horno *Ver tb* STOVE

over /ˈəʊvə(r)/ ◆ *part adv* **1** *to knock sth over* tirar/volcar algo ◊ *to fall over* caer(se) **2** *to turn sth over* dar la vuelta a algo **3** (*lugar*): *over here/there* por aquí/allí ◇ *They came over to see us.* Vinieron a vernos. **4 left over** de sobra: *Is there any food left over?* ¿Queda algo de comida? **5** (*más*): *children of five and over* niños de cinco años en adelante **6** terminado LOC **(all) over again** otra vez, de nuevo **over and done with** terminado para siempre **over and over (again)** una y otra vez *Ver tb* ALL ◆ *prep* **1** sobre, por encima de: *clouds over the mountains* nubes por encima de las montañas **2** al otro lado de: *He lives over the road.* Vive al otro lado de la calle. **3** más de: *(for) over a month* (durante) más de un mes **4** (*tiempo*) durante, mientras: *We'll discuss it over lunch.* Lo discutiremos durante la comida. **5** (*a causa de*): *an argument over money* una discusión por cuestiones de dinero LOC **over and above** además de ☛ Para los usos de **over** en PHRASAL VERBS ver las entradas de los verbos correspondientes, p.ej. **to think over** en THINK.

over- /ˈəʊvə(r)/ *pref* **1** excesivamente: *over-ambitious* excesivamente ambicioso **2** (*edad*) mayor de: *the over-60s* los mayores de sesenta años

overall /ˌəʊvərˈɔːl/ ◆ *adj* **1** total **2** (*general*) global **3** (*ganador*) absoluto ◆ *adv* **1** en total **2** en general ◆ /ˈəʊvərɔːl/ *n* **1** (*GB*) guardapolvo, bata **2 overalls** [*pl*] mono

overbearing /ˌəʊvəˈbeərɪŋ/ *adj* dominante

overboard /ˈəʊvəbɔːd/ *adv* por la borda

overcame *pret de* OVERCOME

overcast /ˌəʊvəˈkɑːst; *USA* -ˈkæst/ *adj* nublado, cubierto

overcharge /ˌəʊvəˈtʃɑːdʒ/ *vt, vi* ~ **(sb) (for sth)** cobrar de más (a algn) (por algo)

overcoat /ˈəʊvəkəʊt/ *n* abrigo

overcome /ˌəʊvəˈkʌm/ *vt* (*pret* **overcame** /-ˈkeɪm/ *pp* **overcome**) **1** (*dificultad, etc*) superar, dominar **2** abrumar, invadir: *overcome by fumes/smoke* vencido por los gases/el humo ◇ *overcome with/by emotion* embargado por la emoción

overcrowded /ˌəʊvəˈkraʊdɪd/ *adj* atestado (de gente) **overcrowding** *n* congestión, hacinamiento

overdo /ˌəʊvəˈduː/ *vt* (*pret* **overdid** /-ˈdɪd/ *pp* **overdone** /-ˈdʌn/) **1** exagerar, pasarse con **2** cocer demasiado LOC **to overdo it/things** pasarse (de la raya)

overdose /ˈəʊvədəʊs/ *n* sobredosis

overdraft /ˈəʊvədrɑːft; *USA* -dræft/ *n* descubierto (*en una cuenta bancaria*)

overdue /ˌəʊvəˈdjuː; *USA* -ˈduː/ *adj* **1** retrasado **2** (*Fin*) vencido y no pagado

overestimate /ˌəʊvərˈestɪmeɪt/ *vt* sobreestimar

overflow /ˌəʊvəˈfləʊ/ ◆ **1** *vt, vi* desbordarse **2** *vi* rebosar ◆ /ˈəʊvəfləʊ/ *n* **1** desbordamiento **2** derrame **3** (*tb* **overflow pipe**) cañería de desagüe

overgrown /ˌəʊvəˈgrəʊn/ *adj* **1** crecido, grande **2** ~ **(with sth)** (*jardín*) cubierto (de algo)

overhang /ˌəʊvəˈhæŋ/ *vt, vi* (*pret, pp* **overhung** /-ˈhʌŋ/) sobresalir/colgar (por encima): *overhanging* sobresaliente

overhaul /ˌəʊvəˈhɔːl/ ◆ *vt* revisar, poner a punto ◆ /ˈəʊvəhɔːl/ *n* revisión, puesta a punto

overhead /ˈəʊvəhed/ ◆ *adj* **1** elevado **2** (*cable*) aéreo **3** (*luz*) de techo ◆ /ˌəʊvəˈhed/ *adv* por encima de la cabeza, en alto, por lo alto

overhear /ˌəʊvəˈhɪə(r)/ *vt* (*pret, pp* **overheard** /-ˈhɜːd/) oír (*por casualidad*)

overhung *pret, pp de* OVERHANG

overjoyed /ˌəʊvəˈdʒɔɪd/ *adj* **1** ~ **(at sth)** eufórico (por/con algo **2** ~ **(to do sth)** contentísimo (de hacer algo)

overland /ˈəʊvəlænd/ ◆ *adj* terrestre ◆ *adv* por tierra

overlap /ˌəʊvəˈlæp/ ◆ *vt, vi* **(-pp-)** **1** superponer(se) **2** (*fig*) coincidir en parte (con) ◆ /ˈəʊvəlæp/ *n* **1** superposición **2** (*fig*) coincidencia

overleaf /ˌəʊvəˈliːf/ *adv* en la página siguiente

overload /ˌəʊvəˈləʊd/ ◆ *vt* ~ **sth/sb (with sth)** sobrecargar algo/a algn (de algo) ◆ /ˌəʊvələʊd/ *n* sobrecarga

overlook /ˌəʊvəˈlʊk/ *vt* **1** dar a, tener vista a **2** pasar por alto **3** no notar **4** (*perdonar*) dejar pasar

overnight /ˌəʊvəˈnaɪt/ ◆ *adv* **1** por la

noche **2** (*coloq*) de la noche a la mañana ◆ *adj* **1** de la noche, para una noche **2** (*coloq*) (*éxito*) repentino

overpower /ˌəʊvəˈpaʊə(r)/ *vt* dominar, vencer, reducir **overpowering** *adj* agobiante, arrollador

overran *pret de* OVERRUN

overrate /ˌəʊvəˈreɪt/ *vt* sobreestimar, sobrevalorar

override /ˌəʊvəˈraɪd/ *vt* (*pret* **overrode** /-ˈrəʊd/ *pp* **overridden** /-ˈrɪdn/) **1** ~ **sth/sb** hacer caso omiso de algo/algn **2** tener preferencia **overriding** /ˌəʊvəˈraɪdɪŋ/ *adj* capital, primordial

overrule /ˌəʊvəˈruːl/ *vt* denegar, anular

overrun /ˌəʊvəˈrʌn/ (*pret* **overran** /-ˈræn/ *pp* **overrun**) **1** *vt* invadir **2** *vi* rebasar (su tiempo)

oversaw *pret de* OVERSEE

overseas /ˌəʊvəˈsiːz/ ◆ *adj* exterior, extranjero ◆ *adv* en el/al extranjero

oversee /ˌəʊvəˈsiː/ *vt* (*pret* **oversaw** /-ˈsɔː/ *pp* **overseen** /-ˈsiːn/) supervisar, inspeccionar

overshadow /ˌəʊvəˈʃædəʊ/ *vt* **1** (*entristecer*) ensombrecer **2** (*persona, logro*) eclipsar

oversight /ˈəʊvəsaɪt/ *n* omisión, olvido

oversleep /ˌəʊvəˈsliːp/ *vi* (*pret, pp* **overslept** /-ˈslept/) quedarse dormido (*no despertarse a tiempo*)

overspend /ˌəʊvəˈspend/ (*pret, pp* **overspent** /-ˈspent/) **1** *vi* gastar en exceso **2** *vt* (*presupuesto*) pasarse de

overstate /ˌəʊvəˈsteɪt/ *vt* exagerar

overstep /ˌəʊvəˈstep/ *vt* (**-pp-**) pasarse LOC **to overstep the mark** pasarse de la raya

overt /ˈəʊvɜːt; *USA* əʊˈvɜːrt/ *adj* (*fml*) abierto

overtake /ˌəʊvəˈteɪk/ (*pret* **overtook** /-ˈtʊk/ *pp* **overtaken** /-ˈteɪkən/) **1** *vt, vi* (*coche*) adelantar (a) **2** *vt* (*fig*) sobrecoger, sobrepasar

overthrow /ˌəʊvəˈθrəʊ/ ◆ *vt* (*pret* **overthrew** /-ˈθruː/ *pp* **overthrown** /-ˈθrəʊn/) derrocar ◆ *n* derrocamiento

overtime /ˈəʊvətaɪm/ *n, adv* horas extras

overtone /ˈəʊvətəʊn/ *n* [*gen pl*] connotación

overtook *pret de* OVERTAKE

overture /ˈəʊvətjʊə(r)/ *n* (*Mús*) obertura LOC **to make overtures (to sb)** hacer propuestas (a algn)

overturn /ˌəʊvəˈtɜːn/ **1** *vt, vi* volcar, dar la vuelta (a) **2** *vt* (*decisión*) anular

overview /ˈəʊvəvjuː/ *n* (*fml*) perspectiva (general)

overweight /ˌəʊvəˈweɪt/ *adj*: *to be overweight* tener exceso de peso *Ver nota en* FAT

overwhelm /ˌəʊvəˈwelm/ *vt* **1** abatir, derribar **2** (*fig*) abrumar **overwhelming** *adj* abrumador

overwork /ˌəʊvəˈwɜːk/ *vt, vi* (hacer) trabajar en exceso

owe /əʊ/ *vt, vi* deber, estar en deuda

owing to /ˈəʊɪŋ tu/ *prep* debido a, a causa de

owl /aʊl/ *n* búho, lechuza

own /əʊn/ ◆ *adj, pron* propio, mío, tuyo, suyo, nuestro, vuestro: *It was my own idea.* Fue idea mía. LOC **of your own** propio: *a house of your own* una casa propia **(all) on your own 1** (completamente) solo **2** por sí solo, sin ayuda *Ver tb* BACK[1] ◆ *vt* poseer, tener, ser dueño de PHR V **to own up (to sth)** (*coloq*) confesarse culpable (de algo)

owner /ˈəʊnə(r)/ *n* dueño, -a **ownership** *n* [*incontable*] propiedad

ox /ɒks/ *n* (*pl* **oxen** /ˈɒksn/) buey

oxygen /ˈɒksɪdʒən/ *n* oxígeno

oyster /ˈɔɪstə(r)/ *n* ostra

ozone /ˈəʊzəʊn/ *n* ozono: *ozone layer* capa de ozono

Pp

P, p /piː/ *n* (*pl* **P's**, **p's** /piːz/) P, p: *P for Peter* P de Paco ☛ *Ver ejemplos en* A, a

pace /peɪs/ ◆ *n* **1** paso **2** ritmo LOC **to keep pace (with sth/sb) 1** ir al mismo paso (que algo/algn) **2** mantenerse al corriente (de algo/algn) ◆ *vt* (*con inquietud*) pasearse por LOC **to pace up and down (a room, etc)** pasearse con inquietud (por una habitación, etc)

pacemaker /ˈpeɪsmeɪkə(r)/ *n* (*Med*) marcapasos

pacify /ˈpæsɪfaɪ/ *vt* (*pret, pp* **-fied**) **1** (*temores, ira*) apaciguar **2** (*región*) pacificar

pack /pæk/ ◆ *n* **1** mochila **2** envase: *The pack contains a pen, ten envelopes and twenty sheets of writing paper.* El envase contiene un bolígrafo, diez sobres y veinte hojas de papel de carta. ☛ *Ver nota en* PARCEL **3** (*cigarrillos*) paquete **4** (*animal*) carga **5** [*v sing o pl*] (*perros*) jauría **6** [*v sing o pl*] (*lobos*) manada **7** (*USA* **deck**) (*cartas*) baraja ◆ **1** *vt* (*maleta*) hacer **2** *vi* hacer las maletas **3** *vt* llevar **4** *vt* embalar **5** *vt* ~ **sth into sth** poner algo en algo **6** *vt* ~ **sth in sth** envolver algo con algo **7** *vt* (*caja*) llenar **8** *vt* (*comida*) empaquetar, envasar **9** *vt* (*habitación*) atestar LOC **to pack your bags** irse PHR V **to pack sth in** (*coloq*) dejar algo: *I've packed in my job.* He dejado mi trabajo. **to pack (sth/sb) into sth** apiñarse en algo, apiñar algo/a algn en algo **to pack up** (*coloq*) cascar (*averiarse*) **packed** *adj* **1** a tope **2** ~ **with sth** abarrotado, lleno de algo LOC **packed lunch** almuerzo para llevar

package /ˈpækɪdʒ/ ◆ *n* **1** paquete ☛ *Ver nota en* PARCEL **2** (*equipaje*) bulto ◆ *vt* envasar **packaging** *n* embalaje

package holiday (*tb* **package tour**) *n* viaje organizado

packet /ˈpækɪt/ *n* paquete ☛ *Ver dibujo en* CONTAINER *y nota en* PARCEL

packing /ˈpækɪŋ/ *n* **1** embalaje **2** rollono

pact /pækt/ *n* pacto

pad /pæd/ ◆ *n* **1** almohadilla **2** (*papel*) bloc ◆ *vt* (**-dd-**) acolchar PHR V **to pad about, along, around, etc** andar (con pasos suaves) **to pad sth out** (*fig*) alargar algo con paja (*libro, etc*) **padding** *n* **1** acolchado **2** (*fig*) paja

paddle /ˈpædl/ ◆ *n* pala (*remo*) LOC **to have a paddle** mojarse los pies *Ver tb* CREEK ◆ **1** *vt* (*barca*) dirigir (remando) **2** *vi* remar **3** *vi* mojarse los pies

paddock /ˈpædək/ *n* prado (*donde pastan los caballos*)

padlock /ˈpædlɒk/ *n* candado

paediatrician (*USA* **pedi-**) /ˌpiːdiəˈtrɪʃn/ *n* pediatra

pagan /ˈpeɪgən/ *adj, n* pagano, -a

page /peɪdʒ/ ◆ *n* (*abrev* **p**) página ◆ *vt* llamar por el altavoz/busca

paid /peɪd/ ◆ *pret, pp de* PAY ◆ *adj* **1** (*empleado*) a sueldo **2** (*trabajo*) remunerado LOC **to put paid to sth** acabar con algo

pain /peɪn/ *n* **1** dolor: *Is she in pain?* ¿Sufre? ◇ *painkiller* calmante ◇ *I've got a pain in my neck.* Me duele el cuello. **2** ~ **(in the neck)** (*coloq*) (*esp persona*) peñazo LOC **to be at pains to do sth** esforzarse por hacer algo **to take great pains with/over sth** esmerarse mucho en algo **pained** *adj* **1** afligido **2** ofendido **painful** *adj* **1** dolorido: *to be painful* doler **2** doloroso **3** (*deber*) penoso **4** (*decisión*) desagradable **painfully** *adv* terriblemente **painless** *adj* **1** que no duele **2** (*procedimiento*) sin dificultades

painstaking /ˈpeɪnzteɪkɪŋ/ *adj* **1** (*trabajo*) laborioso **2** (*persona*) concienzudo

paint /peɪnt/ ◆ *n* pintura ◆ *vt, vi* pintar **painter** *n* pintor, -ora **painting** *n* **1** pintura **2** cuadro

paintbrush /ˈpeɪntbrʌʃ/ *n* pincel, brocha ☛ *Ver dibujo en* BRUSH

paintwork /ˈpeɪntwɜːk/ *n* pintura (*superficie*)

pair /peə(r)/ ◆ *n* **1** par: *a pair of trousers* unos pantalones/un pantalón

> Las palabras que designan objetos compuestos por dos elementos (como tenazas, tijeras, pantalones, etc), llevan el verbo en plural: *My trousers are very*

tight. Los pantalones me están muy justos. Cuando nos referimos a más de uno, utilizamos la palabra **pair**: *I've got two pairs of trousers.* Tengo dos pantalones.

2 [*v sing o pl*] pareja (*animales, equipo*): *the winning pair* la pareja ganadora ☛ *Comparar con* COUPLE ◆ PHR V **to pair off/up (with sb)** emparejarse (con algn) **to pair sb off (with sb)** emparejar a algn (con algn)

pajamas (*USA*) *Ver* PYJAMAS

pal /pæl/ *n* (*coloq*) **1** compañero, -a **2** colega

palace /ˈpæləs/ *n* palacio

palate /ˈpælət/ *n* paladar

pale /peɪl/ ◆ *adj* (**paler**, **palest**) **1** pálido **2** (*color*) claro **3** (*luz*) tenue LOC **to go/turn pale** palidecer ◆ *n* LOC **beyond the pale** (*conducta*) inaceptable

pall /pɔːl/ ◆ *vi* ~ **(on sb)** cansar (a algn) (*de aburrimiento*) ◆ *n* **1** paño mortuorio **2** (*fig*) manto

pallid /ˈpælɪd/ *adj* pálido

pallor /ˈpælə(r)/ *n* palidez

palm /pɑːm/ ◆ *n* **1** (*mano*) palma **2** (*tb* **palm tree**) palmera, palma LOC **to have sb in the palm of your hand** tener a algn en un puño ◆ PHR V **to palm sth/sb off (on sb)** (*coloq*) endosarle algo/algn (a algn)

paltry /ˈpɔːltri/ *adj* (**-ier**, **-iest**) insignificante

pamper /ˈpæmpə(r)/ *vt* (*frec pey*) mimar

pamphlet /ˈpæmflət/ *n* **1** folleto **2** (*político*) octavilla, panfleto

pan /pæn/ *n* término genérico que abarca cazuelas, cacerolas, cazos, ollas y sartenes ☛ *Ver dibujo en* SAUCEPAN *Ver tb* FLASH

pancake /ˈpænkeɪk/ *n* crêpe ☛ *Ver nota en* MARTES

panda /ˈpændə/ *n* panda

pander /ˈpændə(r)/ PHR V **to pander to sth/sb** (*pey*) complacer a algo/algn, condescender con algo/algn

pane /peɪn/ *n* cristal: *pane of glass* hoja de vidrio ◊ *window-pane* cristal (de ventana)

panel /ˈpænl/ *n* **1** (*pared, puerta*) panel **2** (*mandos*) panel **3** [*v sing o pl*] (*TV, Radio*) panel **4** [*v sing o pl*] comisión, jurado **panelled** (*USA* **paneled**) *adj* (revestido) con paneles **panelling** (*USA* **paneling**) *n* revestimiento (*p.ej. de las paredes*): *oak panelling* paneles de roble

pang /pæŋ/ *n* (*lit y fig*) punzada

panic /ˈpænɪk/ ◆ *n* pánico: *panic-stricken* preso del pánico ◆ *vt, vi* (**-ck-**) aterrar(se), dejarse llevar por el pánico

pant /pænt/ *vi* jadear

panther /ˈpænθə(r)/ *n* **1** pantera **2** (*USA*) puma

panties /ˈpæntiz/ *n* (*coloq*) [*pl*] bragas

pantomime /ˈpæntəmaɪm/ *n* **1** (*GB*) representación teatral con música para la Navidad, basada en cuentos de hadas **2** (*fig*) farsa

pantry /ˈpæntri/ *n* (*pl* **-ies**) despensa

pants /pænts/ *n* [*pl*] **1** (*GB*) calzoncillos, bragas **2** (*USA*) pantalones ☛ *Ver nota en* PAIR

paper /ˈpeɪpə(r)/ ◆ *n* **1** [*incontable*] papel: *a piece of paper* una hoja/un pedazo de papel **2** periódico **3** (*tb* **wallpaper**) papel pintado **4 papers** [*pl*] documentación **5 papers** [*pl*] papeles, papeleo **6** examen **7** (*científico, académico*) artículo, ponencia LOC **on paper 1** por escrito **2** (*fig*) en teoría ◆ *vt* empapelar

paperback /ˈpeɪpəbæk/ *n* libro en rústica

paperwork /ˈpeɪpəwɜːk/ *n* [*incontable*] **1** papeleo **2** tareas administrativas

par /pɑː(r)/ *n* LOC **below par** (*coloq*) en baja forma **to be on a par with sth/sb** estar en pie de igualdad con algo/algn

parable /ˈpærəbl/ *n* parábola (*cuento*)

parachute /ˈpærəʃuːt/ *n* paracaídas

parade /pəˈreɪd/ ◆ *n* **1** desfile **2** (*tb* **parade ground**) plaza de armas ◆ **1** *vi* desfilar **2** *vi* (*Mil*) pasar revista **3** *vt* (*pey*) (*conocimientos*) hacer alarde de **4** *vt* (*esp por las calles*) exhibir

paradise /ˈpærədaɪs/ *n* paraíso

paradox /ˈpærədɒks/ *n* paradoja

paraffin /ˈpærəfɪn/ *n* queroseno

paragraph /ˈpærəgrɑːf; *USA* -græf/ *n* párrafo

parallel /ˈpærəlel/ ◆ *adj* (en) paralelo ◆ *n* **1** (*gen, Geog*) paralelo **2** paralela

paralyse (*USA* **paralyze**) /ˈpærəlaɪz/ *vt* paralizar

paralysis /pəˈræləsɪs/ *n* [*incontable*] **1** parálisis **2** (*fig*) paralización

paramount /ˈpærəmaʊnt/ *adj* primordial: *of paramount importance* de suma importancia

paranoid /ˈpærənɔɪd/ *n, adj* **1** paranoico, -a **2** (*fig*) maniático, -a

paraphrase /ˈpærəfreɪz/ *vt* parafrasear

parasite /ˈpærəsaɪt/ *n* parásito

parcel /ˈpɑːsl/ (*USA* **package**) *n* paquete

> **Parcel** (USA **package**) se usa para referirse a los paquetes que se envían por correo. Para hablar de los paquetes que se entregan en mano utilizamos **package**. **Packet** (USA **pack**) es el término que utilizamos para referirnos a un paquete o una bolsa que contiene algún producto que se vende en una tienda: *a packet of cigarettes/crisps*. **Pack** se utiliza para hablar de un conjunto de cosas diferentes que se venden juntas: *The pack contains needles and thread*. El envase contiene agujas e hilo. *Ver tb* PACKAGING *en* PACKAGE *y dibujo en* CONTAINER

parched /pɑːtʃt/ *adj* **1** reseco **2** (*persona*) muerto de sed

parchment /ˈpɑːtʃmənt/ *n* pergamino

pardon /ˈpɑːdn/ ◆ *n* **1** perdón **2** (*Jur*) indulto LOC *Ver* BEG ◆ *vt* (*fml*) perdonar LOC **pardon?** (*USA* **pardon me?**) ¿cómo dice?, ¿qué has dicho? **pardon me!** ¡perdón!

parent /ˈpeərənt/ *n* madre, padre: *parent company* empresa matriz **parentage** *n* **1** ascendencia **2** padres **parental** /pəˈrentl/ *adj* de los padres **parenthood** /ˈpeərənthʊd/ *n* maternidad, paternidad

parish /ˈpærɪʃ/ *n* [*v sing o pl*] parroquia: *parish priest* párroco

park /pɑːk/ ◆ *n* **1** parque: *parkland* zona verde/parque **2** (*USA*) campo (de deportes) ◆ *vt, vi* aparcar

parking /ˈpɑːkɪŋ/ *n* aparcamiento: *parking ticket/fine* multa por aparcamiento indebido ◊ *parking meter* parquímetro

parliament /ˈpɑːləmənt/ *n* [*v sing o pl*] parlamento: *Member of Parliament* diputado, -a ☛ *Ver* pág 322. **parliamentary** /ˌpɑːləˈmentri/ *adj* parlamentario

parlour (*USA* **parlor**) /ˈpɑːlə(r)/ *n* sala (de recibir)

parody /ˈpærədi/ *n* (*pl* **-ies**) parodia

parole /pəˈrəʊl/ *n* libertad condicional

parrot /ˈpærət/ *n* loro

parsley /ˈpɑːsli/ *n* perejil

parsnip /ˈpɑːsnɪp/ *n* chirivía

part /pɑːt/ ◆ *n* **1** parte: *in part exchange* como parte del pago **2** pieza **3** (*TV*) episodio **4** (*cine, teatro*) papel **5 parts** [*pl*] región: *She's not from these parts*. No es de aquí. LOC **for my part** por mi parte **for the most part** por lo general **on the part of sb/on sb's part**: *It was an error on my part*. Fue un error por mi parte. **the best/better part of sth** la mayor parte de algo: *for the best part of a year* casi un año **to take part (in sth)** tomar parte (en algo) **to take sb's part** ponerse de parte de algn ◆ **1** *vt, vi* separar(se) **2** *vt, vi* apartar(se) **3** *vt* partir LOC **to part company (with sb)** separarse (de algn), despedirse (de algn) **to part your hair** hacerse la raya PHR V **to part with sth 1** renunciar a algo **2** (*dinero*) gastar algo

partial /ˈpɑːʃl/ *adj* **1** parcial **2** ~ (**towards sth/sb**) predispuesto (a favor de algo/algn) LOC **to be partial to sth/sb** ser aficionado a algo/algn **partially** *adv* **1** parcialmente **2** de manera parcial

participant /pɑːˈtɪsɪpənt/ *n* participante

participate /pɑːˈtɪsɪpeɪt/ *vi* ~ (**in sth**) participar (en algo) **participation** *n* participación

particle /ˈpɑːtɪkl/ *n* partícula

particular /pəˈtɪkjələ(r)/ ◆ *adj* **1** (*concreto*) en particular: *in this particular case* en este caso en particular **2** (*excepcional*) especial **3** ~ (**about sth**) exigente (con algo) ◆ **particulars** *n* [*pl*] datos **particularly** *adv* **1** particularmente, especialmente **2** en particular

parting /ˈpɑːtɪŋ/ *n* **1** despedida **2** (*pelo*) raya

partisan /ˌpɑːtɪˈzæn, ˈpɑːtɪzæn; *USA* ˈpɑːrtɪzn/ ◆ *adj* parcial ◆ *n* **1** partidario, -a **2** (*Mil*) partisano, -a

partition /pɑːˈtɪʃn/ *n* **1** (*Pol*) división **2** tabique

partly /ˈpɑːtli/ *adv* en parte

partner /ˈpɑːtnə(r)/ *n* **1** (*Com*) socio **2** (*baile, deportes, relación*) pareja **partnership** *n* **1** asociación **2** (*Com*) sociedad (comanditaria)

partridge /ˈpɑːtrɪdʒ/ *n* perdiz

part-time /ˌpɑːt ˈtaɪm/ *adj, adv* **1** por horas **2** (*curso*) a tiempo parcial

party /ˈpɑːti/ *n* (*pl* **-ies**) **1** (*reunión*) fiesta **2** (*Pol*) partido **3** grupo **4** (*Jur*) parte LOC **to be (a) party to sth** participar en algo

pass /pɑːs; *USA* pæs/ ◆ *n* **1** (*examen*) aprobado **2** (*permiso*) pase **3** (*autobús, etc*) bono **4** (*Dep*) pase **5** (*montaña*) puerto LOC **to make a pass at sb** (*coloq*) insinuarse a algn ◆ **1** *vt, vi* pasar **2** *vt* (*barrera*) cruzar **3** *vt* (*límite*) superar **4** *vt* (*examen, ley*) aprobar **5** *vi* suceder

PHR V **to pass as sth/sb** *Ver* TO PASS FOR STH/SB

to pass away (*eufemismo*) morir

to pass by (sth/sb) pasar al lado (de algo/algn) **to pass sth/sb by 1** dejar algo/a algn de lado **2** ignorar algo/a algn

to pass for sth/sb pasar por algo/algn (*ser tomado por*)

to pass sth/sb off as sth/sb hacer pasar algo/a algn por algo/algn

to pass out desmayarse

to pass sth round circular algo

to pass sth up (*coloq*) rechazar algo (*oportunidad*)

passable /ˈpɑːsəbl; *USA* ˈpæs-/ *adj* **1** aceptable **2** transitable

passage /ˈpæsɪdʒ/ *n* **1** (*tb* **passageway**) pasadizo, pasillo **2** (*extracto*) pasaje **3** paso

passenger /ˈpæsɪndʒə(r)/ *n* pasajero, -a

passer-by /ˌpɑːsə ˈbaɪ; *USA* ˌpæsər/ *n* (*pl* **-s-by** /ˌpɑːsəz ˈbaɪ/) transeúnte

passing /ˈpɑːsɪŋ; *USA* ˈpæs-/ ◆ *adj* **1** pasajero **2** (*referencia*) de pasada **3** (*tráfico*) que pasa ◆ *n* **1** paso **2** (*fml*) desaparición LOC **in passing** de pasada

passion /ˈpæʃn/ *n* pasión **passionate** *adj* apasionado, ardiente

passive /ˈpæsɪv/ ◆ *adj* pasivo ◆ *n* (*tb* **passive voice**) (voz) pasiva

passport /ˈpɑːspɔːt; *USA* ˈpæs-/ *n* pasaporte

password /ˈpɑːswɜːd/ (*tb* **watchword**) *n* contraseña

past /pɑːst; *USA* pæst/ ◆ *adj* **1** pasado **2** antiguo: *past students* antiguos alumnos **3** último: *the past few days* los últimos días **4** (*tiempo*) acabado: *The time is past.* Se ha acabado el tiempo. ◆ *n* **1** pasado **2** (*tb* **past tense**) pretérito, pasado ◆ *prep* **1** *half past two* las dos y media ◊ *past midnight* más de medianoche ◊ *It's past five o'clock.* Son las cinco pasadas. **2** (*con verbos de movimiento*): *to walk past sth/sb* pasar por delante de algo/al lado de algn **3** más allá de, después de: *It's past your bedtime.* Ya debías estar en cama. LOC **not to put it past sb (to do sth)** creer a algn capaz (de hacer algo) ◆ *adv* al lado, por delante: *to walk past* pasar por delante

paste /peɪst/ *n* **1** pasta, masa **2** cola **3** paté

pastime /ˈpɑːstaɪm; *USA* ˈpæs-/ *n* pasatiempo

pastor /ˈpɑːstə(r); *USA* ˈpæs-/ *n* pastor (*sacerdote*)

pastoral /ˈpɑːstərəl; *USA* ˈpæs-/ *adj* **1** pastoril, bucólico **2** *pastoral care* atención personal

pastry /ˈpeɪstri/ *n* (*pl* **-ies**) **1** masa (*de una tarta, etc*) **2** pastel (*de bollería*)

pasture /ˈpɑːstʃə(r); *USA* ˈpæs-/ *n* pasto

pat /pæt/ ◆ *vt* (**-tt-**) **1** dar golpecitos a, dar una palmadita a **2** acariciar ◆ *n* **1** palmadita **2** caricia **3** (*mantequilla*) trozo LOC **to give sb a pat on the back** felicitar a algn

patch /pætʃ/ ◆ *n* **1** (*tela*) parche **2** (*color*) mancha **3** (*niebla, etc*) zona **4** trozo (*donde se cultivan verduras, etc*) **5** (*GB, coloq*) (*área de trabajo*) zona LOC **not to be a patch on sth/sb** no tener ni comparación con algo/algn *Ver tb* BAD ◆ *vt* echar un parche a PHR V **to patch sth up 1** ponerle parches a algo **2** (*disputa*) resolver **patchy** *adj* (**-ier, -iest**) **1** irregular: *patchy rain/fog* chubascos/bancos de niebla **2** desigual **3** (*conocimientos*) con lagunas

patchwork /ˈpætʃwɜːk/ *n* **1** labor de aguja a base de parches geométricos **2** (*fig*) tapiz

patent /ˈpeɪtnt; *USA* ˈpætnt/ ◆ *adj* **1** patente **2** (*Com*) patentado ◆ *n* patente ◆ *vt* patentar **patently** *adv* claramente

paternal /pəˈtɜːnl/ *adj* **1** paternal **2** paterno

path /pɑːθ; *USA* pæθ/ *n* **1** (*tb* **pathway**, **footpath**) sendero **2** paso **3** trayectoria **4** (*fig*) camino

pathetic /pəˈθetɪk/ *adj* **1** patético **2** (*coloq*) (*insuficiente*) lamentable

pathological /ˌpæθəˈlɒdʒɪkl/ *adj* pato

lógico **pathology** /pəˈθɒlədʒi/ *n* patología

pathos /ˈpeɪθɒs/ *n* patetismo

patience /ˈpeɪʃns/ *n* **1** [*incontable*] paciencia **2** (*GB*) (*juego de cartas*) solitario LOC *Ver* TRY

patient /ˈpeɪʃnt/ ◆ *n* paciente ◆ *adj* paciente

patio /ˈpætiəʊ/ *n* (*pl* ~**s** /-əʊz/) **1** terraza **2** patio

patriarch /ˈpeɪtriɑːk; *USA* ˈpæt-/ *n* patriarca

patriot /ˈpætriət; *USA* ˈpeɪt-/ *n* patriota **patriotic** /ˌpætrɪˈɒtɪk; *USA* ˌpeɪt-/ *adj* patriótico

patrol /pəˈtrəʊl/ ◆ *vt* (**-ll-**) **1** patrullar **2** (*guardia*) hacer la ronda ◆ *n* patrulla

patron /ˈpeɪtrən/ *n* **1** patrocinador, -ora **2** (*antic*) mecenas **3** cliente **patronage** *n* **1** patrocinio **2** (*cliente regular*) apoyo **3** patronazgo

patronize, -ise /ˈpætrənaɪz; *USA* ˈpeɪt-/ *vt* **1** tratar condescendientemente a **2** apadrinar, patrocinar **patronizing, -ising** *adj* condescendiente

pattern /ˈpætn/ *n* **1** dibujo (*en tela, etc*) **2** (*costura, etc*) patrón **3** pauta, tendencia **patterned** *adj* estampado

pause /pɔːz/ ◆ *n* pausa *Ver tb* BREAK[2] ◆ *vi* hacer una pausa, pararse

pave /peɪv/ *vt* pavimentar LOC **to pave the way (for sth/sb)** preparar el camino (para algo/algn)

pavement /ˈpeɪvmənt/ *n* **1** (*USA* **sidewalk**) acera **2** (*USA*) pavimento

pavilion /pəˈvɪliən/ *n* **1** (*GB*) pabellón **2** quiosco

paving /ˈpeɪvɪŋ/ *n* pavimento: *paving stone* losa

paw /pɔː/ ◆ *n* **1** pata **2** (*coloq, joc*) mano ◆ *vt* manosear

pawn[1] /pɔːn/ *n* (*lit y fig*) peón (*ajedrez*)

pawn[2] /pɔːn/ *vt* empeñar

pawnbroker /ˈpɔːnˌbrəʊkə(r)/ *n* prestamista

pay /peɪ/ ◆ *n* [*incontable*] sueldo: *a pay rise/increase* un aumento de sueldo ◊ *pay claim* reclamación salarial ◊ *pay day* día de paga ◊ *pay packet* sobre de la paga *Ver tb* INCOME ◆ (*pret, pp* **paid**) **1** *vt* **to pay sth (to sb) (for sth)** pagar algo (a algn) (por algo) **2** *vt, vi* **to pay (sb) (for sth)** pagar (algo) (a algn) **3** *vi* ser rentable **4** *vi* valer la pena **5** *vt, vi* compensar LOC **to pay attention (to sth/sb)** prestar atención (a algo/algn) **to pay sb a compliment/pay a compliment to sb** hacer un cumplido a algn **to pay sth/sb a visit** visitar algo/a algn *Ver tb* EARTH

PHR V **to pay sb back** devolver el dinero a algn **to pay sb back sth; to pay sth back** devolver algo (a algn)

to pay sth in ingresar algo

to pay off (*coloq*) dar fruto, valer la pena **to pay sb off** pagar y despedir a algn **to pay sth off** terminar de pagar algo

to pay up pagar del todo

payable *adj* pagadero

payment /ˈpeɪmənt/ *n* **1** pago **2** [*incontable*]: *in/as payment for* como recompensa a/en pago a

pay-off /ˈpeɪ ɒf/ *n* (*coloq*) **1** pago, soborno **2** recompensa

payroll /ˈpeɪrəʊl/ *n* nómina

PC /ˌpiː ˈsiː/ *abrev* (*pl* **PCs**) **1 personal computer** ordenador personal **2 police constable** (agente de) policía

PE /ˌpiː ˈiː/ *abrev* **physical education** educación física

pea /piː/ *n* guisante

peace /piːs/ *n* **1** paz **2** tranquilidad: *peace of mind* tranquilidad de conciencia LOC **peace and quiet** paz y tranquilidad **to be at peace (with sth/sb)** estar en armonía (con algo/algn) **to make (your) peace (with sb)** hacer las paces (con algn) *Ver tb* DISTURB **peaceful** *adj* **1** pacífico **2** tranquilo

peach /piːtʃ/ *n* **1** melocotón **2** (*tb* **peach tree**) melocotonero **3** color melocotón

peacock /ˈpiːkɒk/ *n* pavo real

peak /piːk/ ◆ *n* **1** (*montaña*) pico, cumbre **2** punta **3** visera **4** punto máximo ◆ *adj* máximo: *peak hours* horas punta ◊ *in peak condition* en condiciones óptimas ◆ *vi* alcanzar el punto máximo **peaked** *adj* **1** en punta **2** (*gorra*) con visera

peal /piːl/ *n* **1** (*campanas*) repique **2** *peals of laughter* carcajadas

peanut /ˈpiːnʌt/ *n* **1** cacahuete **2** **peanuts** [*pl*] (*coloq*) migajas

pear /peə(r)/ *n* **1** pera **2** (*tb* **pear tree**) peral

pearl /pɜːl/ *n* **1** perla **2** (*fig*) joya

peasant /ˈpeznt/ *n* **1** campesino, -a

☛ *Ver nota en* CAMPESINO **2** (*coloq, pey*) palurdo, -a

peat /piːt/ *n* turba (*carbón*)

pebble /ˈpebl/ *n* guijarro

peck /pek/ ◆ **1** *vt, vi* picotear **2** (*coloq*) *vt* dar un besito a LOC **pecking order** (*coloq*) orden jerárquico ◆ *n* **1** picotazo **2** (*coloq*) besito

peckish /ˈpekɪʃ/ *adj* (*coloq*) hambriento: *to feel peckish* tener ganas de picar algo

peculiar /prˈkjuːliə(r)/ *adj* **1** extraño **2** especial **3** ~ (**to sth/sb**) peculiar (de algo/algn) **peculiarity** /pɪˌkjuːliˈærəti/ *n* (*pl* **-ies**) **1** peculiaridad **2** [*incontable*] rarezas **peculiarly** *adv* **1** especialmente **2** característicamente **3** de una manera extraña

pedal /ˈpedl/ ◆ *n* pedal ◆ *vi* (*pret* **-ll-**, *USA* **-l-**) pedalear

pedantic /prˈdæntɪk/ *adj* (*pey*) **1** maniático **2** pedante **3** redicho

pedestrian /pəˈdestriən/ ◆ *n* peatón: *pedestrian precinct/crossing* zona peatonal/paso de peatones ◆ *adj* (*pey*) pedestre

pediatrician (*USA*) *Ver* PAEDIATRICIAN

pedigree /ˈpedɪgriː/ ◆ *n* **1** (*animal*) pedigrí **2** (*persona*) genealogía **3** casta ◆ *adj* **1** con pedigrí **2** (*caballo*) de raza

pee /piː/ ◆ *vi* (*coloq*) hacer pis ◆ *n* (*coloq*) pis

peek /piːk/ *vi* ~ **at sth/sb** echar una mirada a algo/algn ☛ Implica una mirada rápida y muchas veces furtiva.

peel /piːl/ ◆ *vt, vi* pelar(se) PHR V **to peel (away/off) 1** (*papel pintado*) despegarse **2** (*pintura*) desconcharse **to peel sth away/back/off 1** despegar algo **2** quitar algo ◆ *n* [*incontable*] **1** piel **2** corteza **3** cáscara

> Para cáscaras duras, como de nuez o de huevo, se usa **shell** en vez de **peel**. Para la corteza del limón se utiliza **rind** o **peel**, mientras que para la naranja se usa sólo **peel**. **Skin** se utiliza para la piel del plátano y para otras frutas con piel más fina, como el melocotón.

peep /piːp/ ◆ *vi* **1** ~ **at sth/sb** echar una ojeada a algo/algn ☛ Implica una mirada rápida y muchas veces cautelosa. **2** ~ **over, through, etc sth** atisbar por encima de, por, etc algo PHR V **to peep out/through** asomarse ◆ *n* **1** vistazo **2** pío LOC **to have/take a peep at sth/sb** echar una ojeada a algo/algn

peer /pɪə(r)/ ◆ *vi* ~ **at sth/sb** mirar algo/a algn ☛ Implica una mirada prolongada que a veces supone esfuerzo. PHR V **to peer out (of sth)** sacar la cabeza (por algo) ◆ *n* **1** igual **2** contemporáneo, -a **3** (*GB*) noble **the peerage** *n* [*v sing o pl*] los pares, la nobleza

peeved /piːvd/ *adj* (*coloq*) molesto (*enfadado*)

peg /peg/ ◆ *n* **1** (*tb* **clothes-peg**) pinza **2** (*en la pared*) colgador LOC **to bring/take sb down a peg (or two)** bajarle a alguien los humos ◆ *vt* (*pp, pret* **-gg-**) **1** (*precios, sueldos*) fijar (el nivel de) **2 to peg sth to sth** ligar algo a algo

pejorative /prˈdʒɒrətɪv; *USA* -ˈdʒɔːr-/ *adj* (*fml*) peyorativo

pelican /ˈpelɪkən/ *n* pelícano

pellet /ˈpelɪt/ *n* **1** (*papel, etc*) bola **2** perdigón **3** (*fertilizantes, etc*) gránulo

pelt /pelt/ ◆ *n* **1** pellejo **2** piel ◆ *vt* (*coloq*) ~ **sb with sth** tirar cosas a algn LOC **to pelt down (with rain)** llover a cántaros PHR V **to pelt along, down, up, etc (sth)** ir a todo meter (por algún sitio): *They pelted down the hill.* Bajaron la colina a todo meter.

pelvis /ˈpelvɪs/ *n* pelvis **pelvic** *adj* pelviano

pen /pen/ *n* **1** bolígrafo, pluma **2** corral **3** (*para ovejas*) redil **4** (*bebé*) parque

penalize, -ise /ˈpiːnəlaɪz/ *vt* **1** penalizar, sancionar **2** perjudicar

penalty /ˈpenlti/ *n* (*pl* **-ies**) **1** (*castigo*) pena **2** multa **3** desventaja **4** (*Dep*) penalización **5** (*fútbol*) penalti

pence /pens/ *n* (*abrev* **p**) peniques

pencil /ˈpensl/ *n* lápiz: *pencil-sharpener* sacapuntas

pendant /ˈpendənt/ *n* colgante

pending /ˈpendɪŋ/ ◆ *adj* (*fml*) pendiente ◆ *prep* en espera de

pendulum /ˈpendjələm; *USA* -dʒʊləm/ *n* péndulo

penetrate /ˈpenɪtreɪt/ *vt* penetrar (*organización*) infiltrar PHR V **to penetrate into sth** introducirse en algo **to penetrate through sth** atravesar algo **penetrating** *adj* **1** perspicaz **2** (*mirada, sonido*) penetrante

penfriend /ˈpenfrend/ *n* amigo, -a por correspondencia

penguin /ˈpeŋgwɪn/ *n* pingüino

penicillin /ˌpenɪˈsɪlɪn/ *n* penicilina

peninsula /pəˈnɪnsjələ; *USA* -nsələ/ *n* península

penis /ˈpiːnɪs/ *n* pene

penknife /ˈpennaɪf/ *n* (*pl* **-knives** /naɪvz/) **1** navaja **2** cortaplumas

penniless /ˈpeniləs/ *adj* sin dinero

penny /ˈpeni/ *n* **1** (*pl* **pence**) (*dinero*) penique **2** (*pl* **pennies**) (*fig*) *It was worth every penny.* Valía lo que costaba. **3** (*pl* **pennies**) (*USA, coloq*) centavo

pension /ˈpenʃn/ ◆ *n* pensión ◆ PHR V **to pension sb off** jubilar a algn **to pension sth off** desechar algo **pensioner** *n* jubilado, -a

penthouse /ˈpenthaʊs/ *n* ático (*generalmente de lujo*)

pent-up /ˈpent ʌp/ *adj* **1** (*ira, etc*) contenido **2** (*deseo*) reprimido

penultimate /penˈʌltɪmət/ *adj* penúltimo

people /ˈpiːpl/ ◆ *n* **1** [*pl*] gente: *People are saying that…* Dice la gente que… **2** personas: *ten people* diez personas ☛ *Comparar con* PERSON **3 the people** [*pl*] (*público*) el pueblo **4** (*nación*) pueblo (*sólo en este sentido es contable*) ◆ *vt* poblar

pepper /ˈpepə(r)/ *n* **1** pimienta: *peppercorn* grano de pimienta **2** (*legumbre*) pimiento

peppermint /ˈpepəmɪnt/ *n* **1** menta **2** (*tb* **mint**) caramelo de menta

per /pə(r)/ *prep* por: *per person* por persona ◊ *£60 per day* 60 libras al día ◊ *per annum* al año

perceive /pəˈsiːv/ *vt* (*fml*) **1** (*observar*) percibir, divisar **2** (*considerar*) interpretar

per cent /pə ˈsent/ *adj, adv* por ciento **percentage** *n* porcentaje: *percentage increase* aumento porcentual

perceptible /pəˈseptəbl/ *adj* **1** perceptible **2** (*mejora, etc*) sensible

perception /pəˈsepʃn/ *n* (*fml*) **1** percepción **2** sensibilidad, perspicacia **3** punto de vista

perceptive /pəˈseptɪv/ *adj* (*fml*) perspicaz

perch /pɜːtʃ/ ◆ *n* **1** (*para pájaros*) percha **2** posición (elevada) **3** (*pez*) perca ◆ *vi* **1** (*pájaro*) posarse **2** (*persona, edificio*) encaramarse ☛ Casi siempre se utiliza en pasiva o como participio pasado.

percussion /pəˈkʌʃn/ *n* percusión

perennial /pəˈreniəl/ *adj* perenne

perfect[1] /ˈpɜːfɪkt/ *adj* **1** perfecto **2** ~ **for sth/sb** ideal para algo/algn **3** completo: *a perfect stranger* un perfecto extraño

perfect[2] /pəˈfekt/ *vt* perfeccionar

perfection /pəˈfekʃn/ *n* perfección LOC **to perfection** a la perfección **perfectionist** *n* perfeccionista

perfectly /ˈpɜːfɪktli/ *adv* **1** perfectamente **2** completamente

perforate /ˈpɜːfəreɪt/ *vt* perforar **perforated** *adj* perforado **perforation** *n* **1** perforación **2** perforado

perform /pəˈfɔːm/ **1** *vt* (*función*) desempeñar **2** *vt* (*operación, ritual, trabajo*) realizar **3** *vt* (*compromiso*) cumplir **4** *vt* (*danza, obra de teatro*) representar **5** *vt, vi* (*música*) interpretar **6** *vt, vi* (*teatro*) actuar, representar

performance /pəˈfɔːməns/ *n* **1** (*deberes*) cumplimiento **2** (*estudiante, empleado*) rendimiento **3** (*empresa*) resultados **4** (*Cine*) sesión **5** (*Mús*) actuación, interpretación **6** (*Teat*) representación: *the evening performance* la función de la tarde

performer /pəˈfɔːmə(r)/ *n* **1** (*Mús*) intérprete **2** (*Teat*) actor, actriz **3** (*variedades*) artista

perfume /ˈpɜːfjuːm; *USA* pərˈfjuːm/ *n* perfume

perhaps /pəˈhæps, præps/ *adv* quizá(s), tal vez, a lo mejor: *perhaps not* puede que no *Ver tb* MAYBE

peril /ˈperəl/ *n* peligro, riesgo

perimeter /pəˈrɪmɪtə(r)/ *n* perímetro

period /ˈpɪəriəd/ *n* **1** periodo: *over a period of three years* a lo largo de tres años **2** época: *period dress/furniture* prendas/muebles de época **3** (*Educ*) clase **4** (*Med*) periodo, regla **5** (*esp USA*) *Ver* FULL STOP

periodic /ˌpɪəriˈɒdɪk/ (*tb* **periodical** /ˌpɪəriˈɒdɪkl/) *adj* periódico

periodical /ˌpɪəriˈɒdɪkl/ *n* revista

perish /ˈperɪʃ/ *vi* (*fml*) perecer, fallecer **perishable** *adj* perecedero

perjury /ˈpɜːdʒəri/ *n* perjurio

perk /pɜːk/ ◆ *v (coloq)* PHR V **to perk up** **1** animarse, sentirse mejor **2** (*negocios, tiempo*) mejorar ◆ *n (coloq)* beneficio (adicional) (*de un trabajo, etc*)

perm /pɜːm/ ◆ *n* permanente ◆ *vt*: *to have your hair permed* hacerse la permanente

permanent /ˈpɜːmənənt/ *adj* **1** permanente, fijo **2** (*daño*) irreparable, para siempre **permanently** *adv* permanentemente, para siempre

permissible /pəˈmɪsəbl/ *adj* permisible, admisible

permission /pəˈmɪʃn/ *n* ~ (**for sth/to do sth**) permiso, autorización (para algo/para hacer algo)

permissive /pəˈmɪsɪv/ *adj* (*frec pey*) permisivo

permit /pəˈmɪt/ ◆ *vt, vi* (**-tt-**) (*fml*) permitir: *If time permits...* Si da tiempo... ☛ *Ver nota en* ALLOW ◆ /ˈpɜːmɪt/ *n* **1** permiso, autorización **2** (*de entrada*) pase

perpendicular /ˌpɜːpənˈdɪkjələ(r)/ *adj* **1** ~ (**to sth**) perpendicular (a algo) **2** (*pared de roca*) vertical

perpetrate /ˈpɜːpətreɪt/ *vt* (*fml*) perpetrar

perpetual /pəˈpetʃuəl/ *adj* **1** perpetuo, continuo **2** constante, interminable

perpetuate /pəˈpetʃueɪt/ *vt* perpetuar

perplexed /pəˈplekst/ *adj* perplejo

persecute /ˈpɜːsɪkjuːt/ *vt* ~ **sb** (**for sth**) perseguir a algn (por algo) (*p.ej. raza, religión, etc*) **persecution** *n* persecución

persevere /ˌpɜːsɪˈvɪə(r)/ *vi* **1** ~ (**in/with sth**) perseverar (en algo) **2** ~ (**with sb**) seguir insistiendo (con algn) **perseverance** *n* perseverancia

persist /pəˈsɪst/ *vi* **1** ~ (**in sth/in doing sth**) insistir, empeñarse (en algo/en hacer algo) **2** ~ **with sth** continuar con algo **3** persistir **persistence** *n* **1** perseverancia **2** persistencia **persistent** *adj* **1** porfiado, pertinaz **2** continuo, persistente

person /ˈpɜːsn/ *n* persona ☛ El plural *persons* sólo se usa en lenguaje formal. *Comparar con* PEOPLE LOC **in person** en persona **personal** *adj* personal: *personal assistant* secretario de dirección ◊ *personal column(s)* anuncios por palabras LOC **to become/get personal** empezar a hacer críticas personales

personality /ˌpɜːsəˈnæləti/ *n* (*pl* **-ies**) personalidad **personalized, -ised** *adj* **1** marcado con las iniciales de uno **2** con membrete **personally** *adv* personalmente: *to know sb personally* conocer a algn personalmente LOC **to take it personally** darse por aludido **to take sth personally** ofenderse por algo

personify /pəˈsɒnɪfaɪ/ *vt* (*pret, pp* **-fied**) personificar

personnel /ˌpɜːsəˈnel/ *n* [*v sing o pl*] (departamento de) personal: *personnel officer* jefe de personal

perspective /pəˈspektɪv/ *n* perspectiva LOC **to put sth in** (**its right/true**) **perspective** poner algo en su sitio

perspire /pəˈspaɪə(r)/ *vi* (*fml*) transpirar **perspiration** *n* **1** sudor **2** transpiración ☛ La palabra más normal es **sweat**.

persuade /pəˈsweɪd/ *vt* **1** ~ **sb to do sth** persuadir a algn de que haga algo **2** ~ **sb** (**of sth**) convencer a algn (de algo) **persuasion** *n* **1** persuasión **2** creencia, opinión **persuasive** *adj* **1** convincente **2** persuasivo

pertinent /ˈpɜːtɪnənt; *USA* -tənənt/ *adj* (*fml*) pertinente

perturb /pəˈtɜːb/ *vt* (*fml*) perturbar

pervade /pəˈveɪd/ *vt* ~ **sth** **1** (*olor*) extenderse por algo **2** (*luz*) difundirse por algo **3** (*obra, libro*) impregnar algo **pervasive** (*tb* **pervading**) *adj* generalizado

perverse /pəˈvɜːs/ *adj* **1** (*persona*) terco, retorcido **2** (*decisión, comportamiento*) a mala idea **3** (*placer, deseo*) perverso **perversion** *n* **1** corrupción **2** perversión **3** tergiversación

pervert /pəˈvɜːt/ ◆ *vt* **1** tergiversar **2** corromper ◆ /ˈpɜːvɜːt/ *n* pervertido, -a

pessimist /ˈpesɪmɪst/ *n* pesimista **pessimistic** /ˌpesɪˈmɪstɪk/ *adj* pesimista

pest /pest/ *n* **1** insecto o animal dañino: *pest control* control de plagas **2** (*coloq, fig*) plasta

pester /ˈpestə(r)/ *vt* molestar

pet /pet/ ◆ *n* **1** animal doméstico **2** (*pey*) enchufado, -a ◆ *adj* **1** predilecto **2** (*animal*) domesticado

petal /ˈpetl/ *n* pétalo

peter /ˈpiːtə(r)/ PHR V **to peter out** **1** agotarse poco a poco **2** (*conversación*) apagarse

petition /pəˈtɪʃn/ *n* petición

petrol /ˈpetrəl/ (*USA* **gasoline**, **gas**) *n* gasolina: *petrol station* gasolinera

petroleum /pəˈtrəʊliəm/ *n* petróleo

petrol station *n* gasolinera

petticoat /ˈpetɪkəʊt/ *n* combinación, enaguas

petty /ˈpeti/ (**-ier**, **-iest**) *adj* (*pey*) **1** insignificante **2** (*delito, gasto*) menor: *petty cash* dinero para gastos menores **3** (*persona, conducta*) mezquino

pew /pjuː/ *n* banco de iglesia

phantom /ˈfæntəm/ ◆ *n* fantasma ◆ *adj* ilusorio

pharmaceutical /ˌfɑːməˈsjuːtɪkl; *USA* -ˈsuː-/ *adj* farmacéutico

pharmacist /ˈfɑːməsɪst/ *n* farmacéutico, -a ☛ *Comparar con* CHEMIST

pharmacy /ˈfɑːməsi/ *n* (*pl* **-ies**) farmacia

> "Farmacia" se dice **pharmacy** o **chemist's (shop)** en inglés británico y **drugstore** en inglés americano.

phase /feɪz/ ◆ *n* fase, etapa ◆ *vt* escalonar PHR V **to phase sth in/out** introducir/retirar algo de una manera escalonada

pheasant /ˈfeznt/ *n* (*pl* **pheasant** *o* ~**s**) faisán

phenomena *n plural de* PHENOMENON

phenomenal /fəˈnɒmɪnl/ *adj* fenomenal

phenomenon /fəˈnɒmɪnən; *USA* -nɒn/ *n* (*pl* **-ena** /-ɪnə/) fenómeno

phew! /fjuː/ *interj* ¡uf!

philanthropist /fɪˈlænθrəpɪst/ *n* filántropo, -a

philosopher /fɪˈlɒsəfə(r)/ *n* filósofo, -a

philosophical /ˌfɪləˈsɒfɪkl/ (*tb* **philosophic**) *adj* filosófico

philosophy /fəˈlɒsəfi/ *n* (*pl* **-ies**) filosofía

phlegm /flem/ *n* flema **phlegmatic** *adj* flemático

phobia /ˈfəʊbiə/ *n* fobia

phone /fəʊn/ *Ver* TELEPHONE

phonecard® /ˈfəʊnkɑːd/ *n* tarjeta para llamar por teléfono

phone-in /ˈfəʊn ɪn/ *n* programa de radio o televisión abierto al público

phon(e)y /ˈfəʊni/ *adj* (*coloq*) (**-ier**, **-iest**) falso

photo /ˈfəʊtəʊ/ *n* (*pl* ~**s** /-təʊz/) *Ver* PHOTOGRAPH

photocopier /ˈfəʊtəʊˌkɒpiə(r)/ *n* fotocopiadora

photocopy /ˈfəʊtəʊkɒpi/ ◆ *vt* (*pret, pp* **-pied**) fotocopiar ◆ *n* (*pl* **-ies**) fotocopia

photograph /ˈfəʊtəgrɑːf; *USA* -græf/ ◆ *n* (*tb abrev* **photo**) fotografía ◆ **1** *vt* fotografiar **2** *vi* salir en una foto: *He photographs well.* Sale bien en fotos. **photographer** /fəˈtɒgrəfə(r)/ *n* fotógrafo, -a **photographic** /ˌfəʊtəˈgræfɪk/ *adj* fotográfico **photography** /fəˈtɒgrəfi/ *n* fotografía

phrase /freɪz/ ◆ *n* **1** Conjunto de palabras que no contiene verbo conjugado, por ejemplo: *a bar of chocolate* ◇ *running fast* **2** expresión, frase: *phrase book* libro de frases *Ver tb* CATCHPHRASE LOC *Ver* TURN ◆ *vt* **1** expresar **2** (*Mús*) frasear

physical /ˈfɪzɪkl/ ◆ *adj* físico: *physical fitness* buena forma física ◆ *n* reconocimiento médico **physically** *adv* físicamente: *physically fit* en buena forma física ◇ *physically handicapped* minusválido

physician /fɪˈzɪʃn/ *n* médico, -a

physicist /ˈfɪzɪsɪst/ *n* físico, -a

physics /ˈfɪzɪks/ *n* [*sing*] física

physiology /ˌfɪziˈɒlədʒi/ *n* fisiología

physiotherapy /ˌfɪziəʊˈθerəpi/ *n* fisioterapia **physiotherapist** *n* fisioterapeuta

physique /fɪˈziːk/ *n* físico (*aspecto*)

pianist /ˈpɪənɪst/ *n* pianista

piano /pɪˈænəʊ/ *n* (*pl* ~**s** /-nəʊz/) piano: *piano stool* taburete de piano

pick /pɪk/ ◆ **1** *vt* elegir, seleccionar ☛ *Ver nota en* CHOOSE **2** *vt* (*flor, fruta, etc*) coger **3** *vt* escarbar: *to pick your teeth* escarbarse los dientes ◇ *to pick your nose* hurgarse la nariz ◇ *to pick a hole (in sth)* hacer un agujero (en algo) **4** *vt* ~ **sth from/off sth** quitar, recoger algo de algo **5** *vt* (*cerradura*) forzar **6** *vi* ~ **at sth** comer algo con poca gana LOC **to pick a fight/quarrel (with sb)** buscar pelea (con algn) **to pick and choose** ser muy exigente **to pick holes in sth** encontrar defectos en algo **to pick sb's brains** explotar los conocimientos de algn **to pick sb's pocket** robarle la cartera a algn **to pick up speed** cobrar velocidad *Ver tb* BONE

PHR V **to pick on sb 1** meterse con algn **2** elegir a algn (*para un trabajo desagradable*)
to pick sth out 1 identificar algo **2** destacar algo **to pick sth/sb out 1** escoger algo/a algn **2** (*en una multitud, etc*) distinguir algo/a algn
to pick up 1 mejorar **2** (*viento*) soplar más fuerte **3** seguir **to pick sb up 1** (*esp en coche*) (ir a) recoger a algn **2** (*coloq*) ligar con algn **3** detener a algn **to pick sth up 1** aprender algo **2** (*enfermedad, acento, costumbre*) coger algo **to pick sth/sb up** (re)coger algo/a algn **to pick yourself up** levantarse
◆ *n* **1** (derecho de) elección, selección: *Take your pick.* Coge el/la que quieras. **2 the pick** (**of sth**) lo mejor (de algo) **3** pico

pickle /ˈpɪkl/ *n* **1** encurtidos **2** vinagre, salmuera LOC **to be in a pickle** estar en un lío

pickpocket /ˈpɪkpɒkɪt/ *n* carterista

picnic /ˈpɪknɪk/ *n* picnic

pictorial /pɪkˈtɔːriəl/ *adj* **1** gráfico **2** (*Arte*) pictórico

picture /ˈpɪktʃə(r)/ ◆ *n* **1** cuadro **2** ilustración **3** foto **4** retrato **5** (*fig*) preciosidad **6** imagen, idea **7** (*TV*) imagen **8** (*GB*) película **9 the pictures** [*pl*] el cine LOC **to put sb in the picture** poner a algn al corriente ◆ **1** *v refl* ~ **yourself** imaginarse **2** *vt* retratar, fotografiar

picturesque /ˌpɪktʃəˈresk/ *adj* pintoresco

pie /paɪ/ *n* **1** (*dulce*) tarta, pastel: *apple pie* tarta de manzana **2** (*salado*) empanada

Pie es una tarta o empanada de hojaldre o masa que tiene tapa y relleno dulce o salado. **Tart** y **flan** se usan para las tartas dulces que tienen una base de hojaldre o masa pero que no tienen tapa.

piece /piːs/ ◆ *n* **1** pedazo **2** pieza: *to take sth to pieces* desmontar algo **3** trozo **4** (*papel*) hoja **5** *a piece of advice/news* un consejo/una noticia ☛ A **piece of...** o **pieces of...** se usa con sustantivos incontables. **6** (*Mús*) obra **7** (*Period*) artículo **8** moneda LOC **in one piece** sano y salvo **to be a piece of cake** (*coloq*) estar chupado *Ver tb* BIT[1] ◆ PHR V **to piece sth together 1** (*pruebas, datos, etc*) juntar algo **2** (*pasado*) reconstruir algo, atar cabos

piecemeal /ˈpiːsmiːl/ ◆ *adv* poco a poco ◆ *adj* gradual

pier /pɪə(r)/ *n* paseo marítimo, embarcadero

pierce /pɪəs/ *vt* **1** (*bala, cuchillo*) atravesar **2** perforar: *to have your ears pierced* hacerse los agujeros en las orejas **3** (*sonido, etc*) penetrar en **piercing** *adj* **1** (*grito*) agudo **2** (*mirada, ojos*) penetrante

piety /ˈpaɪəti/ *n* piedad (*religiosa*)

pig /pɪg/ *n* **1** (*coloq, pey*) cerdo ☛ *Ver nota en* CARNE, CERDO **2** (*tb* **greedy pig**) glotón, -ona

pigeon /ˈpɪdʒɪn/ *n* **1** paloma **2** pichón

pigeon-hole /ˈpɪdʒɪn həʊl/ *n* casilla

piglet /ˈpɪglət/ *n* cerdito ☛ *Ver nota en* CERDO

pigment /ˈpɪgmənt/ *n* pigmento

pigsty /ˈpɪgstaɪ/ *n* (*pl* **-ies**) (*lit y fig*) pocilga

pigtail /ˈpɪgteɪl/ *n* **1** trenza **2** (*torero*) coleta

pile /paɪl/ ◆ *n* **1** montón **2** ~ (**of sth**) (*coloq*) un montón de algo ◆ *vt* amontonar, apilar: *to be piled with sth* estar colmado de algo PHR V **to pile in/out** entrar/salir en tropel **to pile up** amontonarse **2** (*vehículos*) chocarse unos contra otros **to pile sth up** amontonar algo

pile-up /ˈpaɪl ʌp/ *n* accidente múltipl[e]

pilgrim /ˈpɪlgrɪm/ *n* peregrino, [-a] **pilgrimage** *n* peregrinación

pill /pɪl/ *n* **1** píldora **2 the pill** (*colo[q]*) (*anticonceptivo*) la píldora

pillar /ˈpɪlə(r)/ *n* pilar

pillar box *n* (*GB*) buzón

pillow /ˈpɪləʊ/ *n* almohada **pillowcas[e]** *n* funda de almohada

pilot /ˈpaɪlət/ ◆ *n* **1** piloto **2** (*T[V]*) programa piloto ◆ *adj* piloto (*exper[i]mental*)

pimple /ˈpɪmpl/ *n* grano (*en la piel*)

PIN /pɪn/ (*tb* **PIN number**) *n* **person[al] identification number** número secre[to] (*de la tarjeta de crédito*)

pin /pɪn/ ◆ *n* **1** alfiler **2** broche **3** clav[ija] LOC **pins and needles** hormigueo ◆ (**-nn-**) **1** (*con alfileres*) prender, sujet[ar] **2** (*persona, brazos*) sujetar PHR V **to p[in]**

sb down 1 hacer que algn concrete 2 (*en el suelo*) inmovilizar a algn

incer /ˈpɪnsə(r)/ *n* **1** (*Zool*) pinza **2** **pincers** [*pl*] tenazas *Ver nota en* PAIR

inch /pɪntʃ/ ◆ **1** *vt* pellizcar **2** *vt, vi* (*zapatos, etc*) apretar **3** *vt* ~ **sth (from sth/sb)** (*coloq*) birlar algo (de algo/a algn) ◆ *n* **1** pellizco **2** (*sal, etc*) pizca LOC **at a pinch** en caso de necesidad

ine /paɪn/ ◆ *n* (*tb* **pine tree**) pino ◆ *vi* **1** ~ **(away)** languidecer, consumirse **2** ~ **for sth/sb** echar de menos, añorar algo/a algn

ineapple /ˈpaɪnæpl/ *n* piña

ing /pɪŋ/ *n* **1** sonido (metálico) **2** (*de bala*) silbido

ing-pong /ˈpɪŋ pɒŋ/ (*tb* **table tennis**) *n* (*coloq*) pimpón

ink /pɪŋk/ ◆ *adj* **1** rosa, rosado **2** (*de vergüenza, etc*) colorado ◆ *n* **1** rosa **2** (*Bot*) clavelina

innacle /ˈpɪnəkl/ *n* **1** (*fig*) cúspide **2** (*Arquit*) pináculo **3** (*de montaña*) pico

inpoint /ˈpɪnpɔɪnt/ *vt* **1** localizar exactamente **2** poner el dedo en, precisar

nt /paɪnt/ *n* **1** (*abrev* **pt**) pinta (*0,568 litros*) ☛ *Ver* Apéndice 1. **2** *to have a pint* tomar una caña

n-up /ˈpɪn ʌp/ *n* foto (*de persona atractiva, clavada en la pared*)

oneer /ˌpaɪəˈnɪə(r)/ ◆ *n* (*lit y fig*) pionero, -a ◆ *vt* ser pionero en **pioneering** *adj* pionero

ous /ˈpaɪəs/ *adj* **1** piadoso, devoto **2** (*pey*) beato

p /pɪp/ *n* pepita

pe /paɪp/ ◆ *n* **1** tubería, conducto **2** **pipes** [*pl*] cañería(s) **3** pipa **4** (*Mús*) flauta **5** **pipes** [*pl*] *Ver* BAGPIPE ◆ *vt* transportar (*por tubería, gaseoducto, oleoducto*) PHR V **to pipe down** (*coloq*) callarse **piping** *adj* LOC **piping hot** hirviendo

peline /ˈpaɪplaɪn/ *n* tubería, gaseoducto, oleoducto LOC **to be in the pipeline** **1** (*pedido*) estar tramitándose **2** (*cambio, propuesta, etc*) estar preparándose

acy /ˈpaɪrəsi/ *n* piratería

ate /ˈpaɪrət/ ◆ *n* pirata ◆ *vt* piratear

sces /ˈpaɪsiːz/ *n* piscis ☛ *Ver ejemplos en* AQUARIUS

stol /ˈpɪstl/ *n* pistola

ston /ˈpɪstən/ *n* pistón

pit /pɪt/ ◆ *n* **1** foso **2** (*de carbón*) pozo **3** hoyo (*en una superficie*) **4 the pit** (*GB, Teat*) platea **5** (*garaje*) foso **6 the pits** [*pl*] (*carreras de coches*) box **7** (*esp USA*) hueso (*de una fruta*) LOC **to be the pits** (*coloq*) ser pésimo ◆ *v* (**-tt-**) PHR V **to pit sth/sb against sth/sb** oponer algo/a algn con algo/algn

pitch /pɪtʃ/ ◆ *n* **1** (*Dep*) campo **2** (*intensidad, Mús*) tono **3** (*tejado*) inclinación **4** (*GB*) puesto (*en mercado, calle*) **5** brea: *pitch-black* negro como la boca del lobo ◆ **1** *vt* montar (*tienda de campaña*) **2** *vt* (*ideas*) expresar **3** *vt* lanzar, arrojar **4** *vi* tirarse **5** *vi* (*barco*) cabecear PHR V **to pitch in** (*coloq*) **1** poner manos a la obra **2** comer con buen apetito **to pitch in (with sth)** ayudar (con algo), colaborar **pitched** *adj* (*batalla*) campal

pitcher /ˈpɪtʃə(r)/ *n* **1** (*GB*) cántaro **2** (*USA*) jarra

pitfall /ˈpɪtfɔːl/ *n* escollo

pith /pɪθ/ *n* médula

pitiful /ˈpɪtɪfl/ *adj* **1** lastimoso, conmovedor **2** penoso

pitiless /ˈpɪtiləs/ *adj* **1** despiadado **2** (*fig*) implacable

pity /ˈpɪti/ ◆ *n* **1** pena, compasión **2** lástima, pena LOC **to take pity on sb** apiadarse de algn ◆ *vt* (*pret, pp* **pitied**) compadecerse de: *I pity you.* Me das pena.

pivot /ˈpɪvət/ *n* **1** pivote **2** (*fig*) eje

placard /ˈplækɑːd/ *n* pancarta

placate /pləˈkeɪt; *USA* ˈpleɪkeɪt/ *vt* apaciguar a

place /pleɪs/ ◆ *n* **1** sitio, lugar **2** (*en superficie*) parte **3** (*asiento, posición*) puesto, plaza, sitio **4** *It's not my place to...* No me compete... **5** (*coloq*) casa LOC **all over the place** (*coloq*) **1** en todas partes **2** en desorden **in place** en su sitio **in the first, second, etc place** en primer, segundo, etc lugar **out of place 1** desplazado, fuera de lugar **2** fuera de lugar **to take place** tener lugar, ocurrir *Ver tb* CHANGE, HAPPEN ◆ *vt* **1** poner, colocar **2** ~ **sb** identificar a algn **3** ~ **sth (with sth/sb)** (*pedido, apuesta*) hacer algo (en algo/a algn): *We placed an order for... with...* Hicimos un pedido de... a... **4** situar

plague /pleɪg/ ◆ *n* **1** peste **2** ~ **of sth**

plaga de algo ◆ *vt* **1** importunar, atormentar **2** acosar

plaice /pleɪs/ *n* (*pl* **plaice**) platija

plain /pleɪn/ ◆ *adj* (**-er**, **-est**) **1** claro **2** franco, directo **3** sencillo: *plain flour* harina (sin levadura) ◊ *plain chocolate* chocolate puro **4** liso, neutro, sin dibujo: *plain paper* papel liso **5** (*físico*) sin atractivo LOC **to make sth plain** dejar algo claro *Ver tb* CLEAR ◆ *adv* simplemente: *It's just plain stupid.* Es simplemente estúpido. **plainly** *adv* **1** claramente, con claridad **2** evidentemente

plain clothes *adj* de paisano

plaintiff /ˈpleɪntɪf/ *n* demandante

plait /plæt/ (*USA* **braid**) *n* trenza

plan /plæn/ ◆ *n* **1** plan, programa **2** plano **3** esquema LOC *Ver* MASTER ◆ (**-nn-**) **1** *vt* planear, proyectar: *What do you plan to do?* ¿Qué piensas hacer? **2** *vi* hacer planes PHR V **to plan sth out** planificar algo

plane /pleɪn/ *n* **1** (*tb* **aeroplane**, *USA* **airplane**) avión: *plane crash* accidente de aviación **2** plano **3** cepillo (de carpintero)

planet /ˈplænɪt/ *n* planeta

plank /plæŋk/ *n* **1** tabla, tablón **2** (*fig*) elemento fundamental (*de política, etc*)

planner /ˈplænə(r)/ *n* planificador, -ora

planning /ˈplænɪŋ/ *n* planificación: *planning permission* permiso de obras

plant /plɑːnt; *USA* plænt/ ◆ *n* **1** planta: *plant pot* tiesto **2** (*Mec*) maquinaria, equipo **3** fábrica ◆ *vt* **1** plantar **2** (*jardín, campo*) sembrar **3** (*coloq*) (*objetos robados, etc*) colocar **4** (*dudas, etc*) sembrar

plantation /plænˈteɪʃn, plɑːn-/ *n* **1** (*finca*) plantación **2** arboleda

plaque /plɑːk; *USA* plæk/ *n* placa (*tb dental*)

plaster /ˈplɑːstə(r); *USA* ˈplæs-/ ◆ *n* **1** yeso, enlucido **2** (*tb* **plaster of Paris**) escayola: *to put sth in plaster* escayolar algo **3** (*tb* **sticking plaster**) esparadrapo, tirita ◆ *vt* **1** enyesar **2** embadurnar **3** (*fig*) llenar, cubrir

plastic /ˈplæstɪk/ ◆ *n* plástico ◆ *adj* **1** de plástico **2** (*flexible*) plástico

plasticine® /ˈplæstəsiːn/ *n* plastilina

plate /pleɪt/ *n* **1** plato **2** (*metal*) placa, plancha: *plate glass* vidrio cilindrado **3** vajilla (de oro/plata) **4** (*imprenta*) lámina

plateau /ˈplætəʊ; *USA* plæˈtəʊ/ *n* (*pl* ~s o **-eaux** /-təʊz/) meseta

platform /ˈplætfɔːm/ *n* **1** tribuna **2** andén **3** (*Pol*) programa

platinum /ˈplætɪnəm/ *n* platino

platoon /pləˈtuːn/ *n* (*Mil*) sección

plausible /ˈplɔːzəbl/ *adj* **1** creíble **2** (*persona*) convincente

play /pleɪ/ ◆ *n* **1** (*Teat*) obra **2** (*movimiento*) holgura **3** (*de fuerzas, personalidades, etc*) interacción LOC **a play on words** un juego de palabras **at pla**[y] jugando **in play** en broma *Ver* [tb] CHILD, FAIR, FOOL ◆ **1** *vt, vi* jugar **2** *vt* [...] **sb** (*Dep*) jugar con algn **3** *vt* (*naipe*[s]) jugar **4** *vt, vi* (*instrumento*) tocar: [*to*] *play the guitar* tocar la guitarra **5** (*disco, cinta*) poner **6** *vi* (*música*) son[ar] **7** *vt* (*golpe*) dar **8** *vt* (*broma pesad*[a]) gastar **9** *vt* (*papel dramático*) interpr[e]tar, hacer de **10** *vt, vi* (*escena, obr*[a]) representar(se) **11** *vt* hacer(se): *to pl*[ay] *the fool* hacer el tonto **12** *vt* (*manguer*[a]) dirigir LOC **to play it by ear** (*colo*[q]) improvisar **to play (sth) by ear** toc[ar] (algo) de oído **to play truant** hac[er] novillos **to play your cards well/rig**[ht] jugar bien tus cartas *Ver tb* HAV[E] PHR V **to play along (with sb)** segui[r] la corriente (a algn) **to play sth do**[wn] restar importancia a algo **to play A** [off] **against B** enfrentar a A y B **to play (s**[b]**) up** (*coloq*) dar guerra (a algn) **playe**[r] **1** jugador, -ora **2** (*Mús*) músico **play**[ful] *adj* **1** juguetón **2** (*humor*) alegre [**3**] (*comentario*) en broma

playground /ˈpleɪgraʊnd/ *n* patio [de] recreo), parque infantil

playgroup /ˈpleɪgruːp/ *n* guardería

playing card (*tb* **card**) *n* carta, nai[pe]

playing field *n* campo de deportes

play-off /ˈpleɪ ɒf/ *n* partido de dese[m]pate

playtime /ˈpleɪtaɪm/ *n* recreo

playwright /ˈpleɪraɪt/ *n* dramaturgo[, -a]

plea /pliː/ *n* **1** ~ (**for sth**) petición [(de] algo) **2** súplica **3** pretexto: *on a plea* [*of*] *ill health* bajo pretexto de padecer m[ala] salud **4** (*Jur*) declaración, alegaci[ón:] *plea of guilty/not guilty* declaración [de] culpabilidad/inocencia LOC **to mak**[e a] **plea for sth** pedir algo

plead /pliːd/ (*pret, pp* **pleaded**, *U*[SA] ...

pled /pled/) **1** *vi* ~ (**with sb**) suplicar (a algn) **2** *vi* ~ **for sth** pedir algo **3** *vi* ~ **for sb** hablar en favor de algn **4** *vt* (*defensa*) alegar LOC **to plead guilty/not guilty** declararse culpable/inocente

pleasant /ˈpleznt/ *adj* (**-er**, **-est**) agradable **pleasantly** *adv* **1** agradablemente, gratamente **2** con amabilidad

please /pli:z/ ◆ **1** *vt, vi* complacer **2** *vt* ser un placer para **3** *vi*: *for as long as you please* todo el tiempo que te parezca ◇ *I'll do whatever I please.* Haré lo que me dé la gana. LOC **as you please** como quieras **please yourself!** ¡Haz lo que te dé la gana! ◆ *interj* **1** ¡por favor! **2** (*fml*) *Please come in.* Haga el favor de entrar. ◇ *Please do not smoke.* Se ruega no fumar. LOC **please do!** ¡por supuesto! **pleased** *adj* **1** contento ☛ *Ver nota en* GLAD **2** ~ (**with sth/sb**) satisfecho (de algo/con algn) LOC **to be pleased to do sth** alegrarse de hacer algo, tener el placer de hacer algo: *I'd be pleased to come.* Me encantaría ir. **pleased to meet you** encantado de conocerle **pleasing** *adj* **1** grato, agradable **2** (*futuro*) halagüeño

pleasure /ˈpleʒə(r)/ *n* placer: *It gives me pleasure to…* Tengo el placer de… LOC **my pleasure** no hay de qué **to take pleasure in sth** disfrutar con algo **with pleasure** con mucho gusto *Ver tb* BUSINESS **pleasurable** *adj* placentero

pled (*USA*) *pret, pp de* PLEAD

pledge /pledʒ/ ◆ *n* **1** promesa, compromiso **2** (*fianza*) prenda ◆ **1** *vt, vi* (*fml*) prometer, comprometerse **2** *vt* (*joyas, etc*) empeñar

plentiful /ˈplentɪfl/ *adj* abundante: *a plentiful supply* un suministro abundante LOC **to be in plentiful supply** abundar

plenty /ˈplenti/ ◆ *pron* **1** mucho, de sobra: *plenty to do* mucho que hacer **2** bastante: *That's plenty, thank you.* Ya basta, gracias. ◆ *adv* **1** (*coloq*) lo bastante: *plenty high enough* lo bastante alto **2** (*USA*) mucho LOC **plenty more 1** de sobra **2** (*personas*) otros muchos

pliable /ˈplaɪəbl/ (*tb* **pliant** /ˈplaɪənt/) *adj* **1** flexible **2** influenciable

pliers /ˈplaɪəz/ *n* [*pl*] alicates: *a pair of pliers* unos alicates ☛ *Ver nota en* PAIR

plight /plaɪt/ *n* **1** (mala) situación **2** crisis

plod /plɒd/ *vi* (**-dd-**) caminar con dificultad PHR V **to plod away** (**at sth**) trabajar con empeño (en algo)

plonk /plɒŋk/ PHR V **to plonk sth down** dejar caer algo pesadamente

plot /plɒt/ ◆ *n* **1** parcela **2** solar **3** (*libro, película*) argumento **4** complot, intriga ◆ **1** *vt* (**-tt-**) (*rumbo, etc*) trazar **2** *vt* (*intriga*) urdir **3** *vi* conjurarse, intrigar

plough (*USA* **plow**) /plaʊ/ ◆ *n* arado ◆ *vt, vi* arar LOC **to plough** (**your way**) **through sth** abrirse camino por/entre algo PHR V **to plough sth back** (*ganancias*) reinvertir algo **to plough into sth/sb** chocar contra algo/algn

ploy /plɔɪ/ *n* ardid, táctica

pluck /plʌk/ ◆ *vt* **1** coger, arrancar **2** desplumar **3** (*cejas*) depilarse **4** (*cuerda*) pulsar **5** (*guitarra*) puntear LOC **to pluck up courage** (**to do sth**) armarse de valor (y hacer algo) ◆ *n* (*coloq*) valor, agallas

plug /plʌg/ ◆ *n* **1** tapón **2** (*Electrón*) enchufe (*macho*) ☛ *Ver dibujo en* ENCHUFE **3** bujía **4** (*coloq*) propaganda ◆ *vt* (**-gg-**) **1** (*agujero*) tapar **2** (*escape*) sellar **3** (*oídos*) taponar **4** (*hueco*) rellenar **5** (*coloq*) hacer propaganda de PHR V **to plug sth in**(**to sth**) enchufar algo (en algo)

plum /plʌm/ *n* **1** ciruela **2** (*tb* **plum tree**) ciruelo

plumage /ˈplu:mɪdʒ/ *n* plumaje

plumber /ˈplʌmə(r)/ *n* fontanero, -a **plumbing** *n* fontanería

plummet /ˈplʌmɪt/ *vi* **1** caer en picado **2** (*fig*) bajar drásticamente

plump /plʌmp/ ◆ *adj* **1** rollizo *Ver tb* FAT **2** mullido ◆ PHR V **to plump for sth/sb** decidirse por algo/algn, elegir algo/a algn

plunder /ˈplʌndə(r)/ *vt* saquear

plunge /plʌndʒ/ ◆ **1** *vi* caer (en picado), precipitarse **2** *vt* (*fig*) sumir **3** *vi* zambullirse **4** *vt* sumergir **5** *vt* (*en bolsillo, bolsa, etc*) meter **6** *vt* (*cuchillo, etc*) hundir ◆ *n* **1** caída **2** zambullida **3** (*precios*) bajón LOC **to take the plunge** dar el gran paso

plural /ˈplʊərəl/ *adj, n* plural

plus /plʌs/ ◆ *prep* **1** (*Mat*) más: *Five plus six equals eleven.* Cinco más seis son once. **2** además de: *plus the fact that…* además de que… ◆ *conj* además ◆ *adj* **1** como mínimo: *£500 plus* 500 libras como mínimo ◊ *He must be forty plus.* Debe de tener cuarenta y pico años. **2** (*Electrón, Mat*) positivo ◆ *n* **1** (*tb* **plus sign**) signo (de) más **2 a ~ (for sb)** (*coloq*) un punto a favor (de algn): *the pluses and minuses of sth* los más y los menos de algo

plush /plʌʃ/ *adj* (*coloq*) lujoso, de lujo

Pluto /ˈpluːtəʊ/ *n* Plutón

plutonium /pluːˈtəʊniəm/ *n* plutonio

ply /plaɪ/ ◆ *n* **1** *Ver* PLYWOOD **2** (*papel*) capa **3** (*lana*) cabo ◆ *vt* (*pret, pp* **plied** /plaɪd/) **1** (*fml*) (*oficio*) ejercer: *to ply your trade* desempeñar uno su trabajo **2** (*ruta*) hacer: *This ship plied between the Indies and Spain.* Este barco hacía la ruta entre las Indias y España. PHR V **to ply sb with drink/food** dar de beber/comer a algn (constantemente) **to ply sb with questions** acosar a algn de preguntas

plywood /ˈplaɪwʊd/ *n* madera contrachapada

pm (*USA* **PM**) /ˌpiː ˈem/ *abrev* de la tarde: *at 4.30pm* a las cuatro y media de la tarde

> Nótese que cuando decimos **am** o **pm** con las horas, no se puede usar **o'clock**: *Shall we meet at three o'clock/3pm?* ¿Quedamos a las tres (de la tarde)?

pneumatic /njuːˈmætɪk; *USA* nuː-/ *adj* neumático: *pneumatic drill* martillo neumático

pneumonia /njuːˈməʊniə; *USA* nuː-/ *n* [*incontable*] **1** pulmonía **2** (*Med*) neumonía

PO /ˌpiːˈəʊ/ *abrev* **Post Office**

poach /pəʊtʃ/ **1** *vt* cocer **2** *vt* (*huevo*) escalfar **3** *vt, vi* cazar/pescar furtivamente **4** *vt* (*idea*) robar **poacher** *n* cazador, -ora, pescador, -ora (*furtivo*)

pocket /ˈpɒkɪt/ ◆ *n* **1** bolsillo: *pocket money* propina (para niños) ◊ *pocket knife* navaja ◊ *pocket-sized* tamaño bolsillo **2** núcleo LOC **to be out of pocket** terminar perdiendo dinero *Ver tb* PICK ◆ *vt* **1** meterse en el bolsillo **2** embolsarse

pod /pɒd/ *n* vaina (*judías, etc*)

podium /ˈpəʊdiəm/ *n* podio

poem /ˈpəʊɪm/ *n* poema

poet /ˈpəʊɪt/ *n* poeta

poetic /pəʊˈetɪk/ *adj* poético: *poetic justice* justicia divina

poetry /ˈpəʊətri/ *n* poesía

poignant /ˈpɔɪnjənt/ *adj* conmovedor

point /pɔɪnt/ ◆ *n* **1** (*gen, Geom*) punto **2** (*gen, Geog*) punta **3** (*Mat*) coma **4** cuestión: *the point is…* la cuestión es… **5** sentido: *What's the point?* ¿Para qué? **6** (*tb* **power point**) enchufe **7 points** [*pl*] (*GB, Ferrocarril*) agujas LOC **in point of fact** de hecho **point of view** punto de vista **to be beside the point** no tener nada que ver **to make a point of doing sth** asegurarse de hacer algo **to make your point** dejar clara una idea, propuesta, etc **to take sb's point** entender lo que algn dice **to the point** al caso, al grano *Ver tb* PROVE, SORE, STRONG ◆ **1** *vi* ~ **(at/to sth/sb)** señalar (con el dedo) (algo/a algn); apuntar (hacia algo/algn) **2** *vi* ~ **to sth** (*fig*) indicar, señalar algo **3** *vt* ~ **sth at sb** apuntar a algn con algo: *to point your finger (at sth/sb)* indicar (algo/a algn) con el dedo PHR V **to point sth out (to sb)** señalar algo a (a algn)

point-blank /ˌpɔɪnt ˈblæŋk/ ◆ *adj* **1** *at point-blank range* a bocajarro **2** (*negativa*) tajante ◆ *adv* **1** a bocajarro **2** (*fig*) de forma tajante

pointed /ˈpɔɪntɪd/ *adj* **1** afilado, puntiagudo **2** (*fig*) intencionado

pointer /ˈpɔɪntə(r)/ *n* **1** indicador **2** puntero **3** (*coloq*) sugerencia **4** pista

pointless /ˈpɔɪntləs/ *adj* **1** sin sentido **2** inútil

poise /pɔɪz/ *n* **1** elegancia **2** aplomo **poised** *adj* **1** suspendido **2** con aplomo

poison /ˈpɔɪzn/ ◆ *n* veneno ◆ *vt* **1** envenenar **2** (*mente*) emponzoñar **poisoning** *n* envenenamiento **poisonous** *adj* venenoso

poke /pəʊk/ *vt* dar (*con el dedo, etc*): *to poke your finger into sth* meter el dedo en algo LOC **to poke fun at sth/sb** burlarse de algo/algn PHR V **to poke about/around** (*coloq*) **1** fisgonear **2** curiosear **to poke out (of sth)/through (sth)** asomar (por algo)

poker /ˈpəʊkə(r)/ *n* **1** atizador **2** póquer

poker-faced /ˌpəʊkə ˈfeɪst/ *adj* de rostro impasible

poky /ˈpəʊki/ *adj* (*coloq*) (**pokier**, **pokiest**) diminuto

polar /ˈpəʊlə(r)/ *adj* polar: *polar bear* oso polar

pole /pəʊl/ *n* **1** (*Geog, Fís*) polo **2** palo: *pole-vault* salto con pértiga **3** (*telegráfico*) poste LOC **to be poles apart** estar en extremos opuestos ☛ *Comparar con* SER POLOS OPUESTOS *en* POLO

police /pəˈliːs/ ◆ *n* [*pl*] policía: *police constable/officer* (agente de) policía ◊ *police force* cuerpo de policía ◊ *police state* estado policial ◊ *police station* comisaría (de policía) ◆ *vt* vigilar

policeman /pəˈliːsmən/ *n* (*pl* **-men** /-mən/) policía

policewoman /pəˈliːswʊmən/ *n* (*pl* **-women**) policía

policy /ˈpɒləsi/ *n* (*pl* **-ies**) **1** política **2** (*seguros*) póliza

polio /ˈpəʊliəʊ/ (*fml* **poliomyelitis**) *n* polio(mielitis)

polish /ˈpɒlɪʃ/ ◆ *vt* **1** sacar brillo a, encerar, pulimentar **2** (*gafas, zapatos*) limpiar **3** (*fig*) pulir PHR V **to polish sb off** cepillarse a algn (*matar*) **to polish sth off** (*coloq*) **1** zampar algo **2** (*trabajo*) cepillarse algo ◆ *n* **1** lustre **2** brillo **3** (*muebles*) cera **4** (*zapatos*) betún **5** (*uñas*) esmalte **6** (*fig*) finura, refinamiento **polished** *adj* **1** brillante, pulido **2** (*manera, estilo*) refinado, pulido **3** (*actuación*) impecable

polite /pəˈlaɪt/ *adj* **1** cortés **2** (*persona*) educado **3** (*comportamiento*) correcto

political /pəˈlɪtɪkl/ *adj* político

politician /ˌpɒləˈtɪʃn/ *n* político, -a

politics /ˈpɒlətɪks/ *n* **1** [*v sing o pl*] política **2** [*pl*] opiniones políticas **3** [*sing*] (*asignatura*) ciencias políticas

poll /pəʊl/ *n* **1** elección **2** votación: *to take a poll on something* someter algo a votación **3 the polls** [*pl*] las urnas **4** encuesta, sondeo

pollen /ˈpɒlən/ *n* polen

pollute /pəˈluːt/ *vt* ~ **sth** (**with sth**) **1** contaminar algo (de algo) **2** (*fig*) corromper **pollution** *n* **1** contaminación **2** (*fig*) corrupción

polo /ˈpəʊləʊ/ *n* polo (*deporte*)

polo neck *n* cuello alto/vuelto (*jersey*)

polyester /ˌpɒlɪˈestə(r); *USA* ˈpɒliːestər/ *n* poliéster

polystyrene /ˌpɒliˈstaɪriːn/ *n* poliestireno

polythene /ˈpɒlɪθiːn/ *n* polietileno

pomp /pɒmp/ *n* **1** pompa **2** (*pey*) ostentación

pompous /ˈpɒmpəs/ *adj* (*pey*) **1** pomposo **2** (*persona*) presumido

pond /pɒnd/ *n* estanque, charca

ponder /ˈpɒndə(r)/ *vt, vi* ~ (**on/over sth**) reflexionar (sobre algo)

pony /ˈpəʊni/ *n* (*pl* **ponies**) poni: *pony-trekking* excursión en poni ◊ *ponytail* cola de caballo

poodle /ˈpuːdl/ *n* perro de lanas, caniche

pool /puːl/ ◆ *n* **1** charca **2** charco **3** (*tb* **swimming pool**) piscina **4** (*luz*) haz **5** (*río*) pozo **6** estanque **7** (*dinero*) fondo (común) **8** billar americano **9 the (football) pools** [*pl*] las quinielas ◆ *vt* (*recursos, ideas*) aunar, juntar

poor /pʊə(r)/ ◆ *adj* (**-er**, **-est**) **1** pobre **2** malo: *in poor taste* de mal gusto **3** (*nivel*) bajo LOC *Ver* FIGHT ◆ **the poor** *n* [*pl*] los pobres

poorly /pɔːli; *USA* pʊərli/ ◆ *adv* **1** mal **2** pobremente ◆ *adj* mal, enfermo

pop /pɒp/ ◆ *n* **1** pequeño estallido **2** taponazo **3** (*coloq*) (*bebida*) gaseosa **4** (*USA*) papá **5** (música) pop ◆ *adv*: *to go pop* hacer ¡pum!, reventar ◆ (**-pp-**) **1** *vi* dar un taponazo **2** *vi* hacer ¡pum! **3** *vt, vi* (*globo*) estallar **4** *vt* (*corcho*) hacer saltar PHR V **to pop across, back, down, out, etc** (*coloq*) cruzar, volver, bajar, salir, etc (*rápida o repentinamente*) **to pop sth back, in, etc** (*coloq*) devolver, meter, etc algo (*rápida o repentinamente*) **to pop in** visitar (*brevemente*) **to pop out** (**of sth**) salir (de algo) (*repentinamente*) **to pop up** aparecer (*de repente*)

popcorn /ˈpɒpkɔːn/ *n* palomitas de maíz

pope /pəʊp/ *n* papa

poplar /ˈpɒplə(r)/ *n* álamo, chopo

poppy /ˈpɒpi/ *n* (*pl* **-ies**) amapola

popular /ˈpɒpjələ(r)/ *adj* **1** popular: *(not) to be popular with sb* (no) caer bien a algn **2** de moda: *Polo-necks are very popular this season.* Los jerseys de cuello alto se llevan mucho esta temporada. **3** corriente: *the popular press* la prensa sensacionalista **4** (*creencia*) generalizado **popularize, -ise** *vt* **1** popularizar **2** vulgarizar

population /ˌpɒpjuˈleɪʃn/ *n* población: *population explosion* explosión demográfica

porcelain /ˈpɔːsəlɪn/ *n* [*incontable*] porcelana

porch /pɔːtʃ/ *n* **1** porche **2** (*USA*) portal, terraza

pore /pɔː(r)/ ◆ *n* poro ◆ PHR V **to pore over sth** estudiar algo detenidamente

pork /pɔːk/ *n* (carne de) cerdo ☛ *Ver nota en* CARNE

porn /pɔːn/ *n* (*coloq*) porno

pornography /pɔːˈnɒɡrəfi/ *n* pornografía

porous /ˈpɔːrəs/ *adj* poroso

porpoise /ˈpɔːpəs/ *n* marsopa

porridge /ˈpɒrɪdʒ; *USA* ˈpɔːr-/ *n* [*incontable*] gachas de avena

port /pɔːt/ *n* **1** puerto **2** (*barco*) babor **3** (*vino*) oporto LOC **port of call** puerto de escala

portable /ˈpɔːtəbl/ *adj* portátil

porter /ˈpɔːtə(r)/ *n* **1** (*estación, hotel*) mozo, maletero **2** portero

porthole /ˈpɔːthəʊl/ *n* portilla

portion /ˈpɔːʃn/ *n* **1** porción **2** (*comida*) ración

portrait /ˈpɔːtreɪt, -trət/ *n* **1** retrato **2** (*fig*) cuadro

portray /pɔːˈtreɪ/ *vt* **1** retratar **2** ~ **sth/sb (as sth)** (*Teat*) representar algo/a algn (como algo) **portrayal** *n* representación

pose /pəʊz/ ◆ **1** *vi* (*para retratarse*) posar **2** *vi* (*pey*) comportarse de forma afectada **3** *vi* ~ **as sth/sb** hacerse pasar por algo/algn **4** *vt* (*dificultad, pregunta*) presentar ◆ *n* **1** postura **2** (*pey*) pose

posh /pɒʃ/ *adj* (**-er**, **-est**) **1** (*hotel, coche, etc*) de lujo **2** (*zona*) elegante **3** (*esp pey*) (*acento*) afectado **4** (*pey*) pijo

position /pəˈzɪʃn/ ◆ *n* **1** posición **2** situación **3** ~ **(on sth)** (*opinión*) posición respecto a algo **4** (*trabajo*) puesto LOC **to be in a/no position to do sth** estar/no estar en condiciones de hacer algo ◆ *vt* colocar, situar

positive /ˈpɒzətɪv/ *adj* **1** positivo **2** definitivo, categórico **3** ~ **(about sth/that...)** seguro (de algo/de que...) **4** total, auténtico: *a positive disgrace* un escándalo total **positively** *adv* **1** positivamente **2** con optimismo **3** categóricamente **4** verdaderamente

possess /pəˈzes/ *vt* **1** poseer, tener **2** dominar: *What possessed you to do that?* ¿Cómo se te ocurrió hacer eso? **possession** *n* **1** posesión **2 possessions** [*pl*] pertenencias LOC **to be in possession of sth** tener algo

possibility /ˌpɒsəˈbɪləti/ *n* (*pl* **-ies**) **1** posibilidad: *within/beyond the bounds of possibility* dentro/más allá de lo posible **2 possibilities** [*pl*] potencial *Ver tb* CHANCE

possible /ˈpɒsəbl/ *adj* posible: *if possible* si es posible ◊ *as quickly as possible* lo más rápido posible LOC **to make sth possible** posibilitar algo **possibly** *adv* posiblemente: *You can't possibly go.* No puedes ir de ninguna manera.

post /pəʊst/ ◆ *n* **1** poste, estaca, palo **2** (*trabajo*) puesto **3** (*esp USA* **mail**) correo: *postcode* código postal ◊ *first/second post* primer/segundo correo ☛ *Ver nota en* MAIL ◆ *vt* **1** (*esp USA* **to mail**) echar (al correo), mandar **2** (*Mil*) destinar, enviar **3** (*soldado*) apostar LOC **to keep sb posted (about sth)** tener/mantener a algn al corriente (de algo)

postage /ˈpəʊstɪdʒ/ *n* franqueo: *postage stamp* sello (de correo)

postal /ˈpəʊstl/ *adj* postal, de correos: *postal vote* voto por correo

postbox /ˈpəʊstbɒks/ *n* buzón (*en la calle*) ☛ *Comparar con* LETTER BOX

postcard /ˈpəʊstkɑːd/ *n* (tarjeta) postal

poster /ˈpəʊstə(r)/ *n* **1** (*anuncio*) cartel **2** póster

posterity /pɒˈsterəti/ *n* posteridad

postgraduate /ˌpəʊstˈɡrædʒuət/ *adj, n* posgraduado, -a

posthumous /ˈpɒstjʊməs; *USA* ˈpɒstʃəməs/ *adj* póstumo

postman /ˈpəʊstmən/ (*USA* **mailman**) *n* (*pl* **-men** /-mən/) cartero

post-mortem /ˌpəʊst ˈmɔːtəm/ *n* autopsia

post office *n* (oficina de) correos ☛ *Ver nota en* ESTANCO

postpone /pəˈspəʊn/ *vt* aplazar

postscript /ˈpəʊstskrɪpt/ *n* **1** posdata **2** (*fig*) nota final

posture /ˈpɒstʃə(r)/ *n* **1** postura **2** actitud

post-war /ˌpəʊst ˈwɔː(r)/ *adj* de la posguerra

postwoman /ˈpəʊst wʊmən/ *n* (*pl* **-women**) cartero

pot /pɒt/ *n* **1** olla: *pots and pans* batería de cocina **2** tarro **3** (*decorativo*) cacharro **4** (*planta*) tiesto **5** (*coloq*) marihuana LOC **to go to pot** (*coloq*) echarse a perder

potassium /pəˈtæsiəm/ *n* potasio

potato /pəˈteɪtəʊ/ *n* (*pl* **-oes**) patata

potent /ˈpəʊtnt/ *adj* potente, poderoso **potency** *n* fuerza

potential /pəˈtenʃl/ ◆ *adj* potencial ◆ *n* ~ **for sth** potencial de/para algo **potentially** *adv* potencialmente

pothole /ˈpɒthəʊl/ *n* **1** (*Geol*) cueva **2** (*carretera*) bache

potted /ˈpɒtɪd/ *adj* **1** en conserva **2** (*relato*) resumido

potter /ˈpɒtə(r)/ ◆ PHR V **to potter about/around (sth)** hacer trabajillos (en algo) ◆ *n* alfarero, -a **pottery** *n* **1** (*lugar, arte*) alfarería **2** (*objetos*) cerámica

potty /ˈpɒti/ ◆ *adj* (**-ier, -iest**) (*GB, coloq*) **1** (*loco*) ido **2** ~ **about sth/sb** loco por algo/algn ◆ *n* (*pl* **-ies**) (*coloq*) orinal

pouch /paʊtʃ/ *n* **1** bolsa pequeña **2** (*tabaco*) petaca **3** (*Zool*) bolsa

poultry /ˈpəʊltri/ *n* [*incontable*] aves (de corral)

pounce /paʊns/ *vi* **1** ~ **(on sth/sb)** abalanzarse (sobre algo/algn) **2** (*fig*) saltar (sobre algo/algn)

pound /paʊnd/ ◆ *n* **1** (*dinero*) libra (£) **2** (*abrev* **lb**) libra (*0,454 kilogramos*) ☛ *Ver* Apéndice 1. ◆ **1** *vi* ~ **(at sth)** golpear (en algo) **2** *vi* correr pesadamente **3** *vi* ~ **(with sth)** latir fuertemente (de algo) (*miedo, emoción, etc*) **4** *vt* machacar **5** *vt* aporrear **pounding** *n* **1** (*lit y fig*) paliza **2** (*olas*) embate

pour /pɔː(r)/ **1** *vi* fluir, correr **2** *vi* (*tb* **to pour with rain**) llover a cántaros **3** *vt* (*bebida*) servir PHR V **to pour in 1** entrar a raudales **2** inundar **to pour sth in** echar algo (*añadir*) **to pour out (of sth) 1** fluir (de algo) **2** (*personas*) salir en tropel (de algo) **to pour sth out 1** (*bebida*) servir algo **2** (*expresar*) sacar algo

pout /paʊt/ *vi* **1** hacer un mohín **2** (*provocativamente*) poner morritos

poverty /ˈpɒvəti/ *n* **1** pobreza **2** miseria **3** (*de idea*) falta **poverty-stricken** *adj* necesitado

powder /ˈpaʊdə(r)/ ◆ *n* [*gen incontable*] polvo ◆ *vt* empolvar: *to powder your face* empolvarse la cara **powdered** *adj* en polvo

power /ˈpaʊə(r)/ ◆ *n* **1** poder: *power-sharing* poder compartido **2 powers** [*pl*] capacidad, facultades **3** fuerza **4** potencia **5** energía **6** (*electricidad*) luz: *power cut* corte eléctrico ◊ *power station* central eléctrica ◊ *power point* enchufe LOC **the powers that be** (*esp irón*) los que mandan **to do sb a power of good** (*coloq*) ser muy beneficioso para algn ◆ *vt* impulsar, potenciar **powerful** *adj* **1** poderoso **2** (*máquina*) potente **3** (*brazos, golpe, bebida*) fuerte **4** (*imagen, obra*) intenso **powerless** *adj* **1** sin poder, impotente **2** ~ **to do sth** impotente para hacer algo

practicable /ˈpræktɪkəbl/ *adj* factible

practical /ˈpræktɪkl/ *adj* **1** práctico: *practical joke* broma **2** (*persona*) pragmático **practically** *adv* prácticamente, de forma práctica

practice /ˈpræktɪs/ *n* **1** práctica **2** (*Dep*) entrenamiento **3** (*Mús*) ejercicios **4** (*Med*) consultorio *Ver tb* GENERAL PRACTICE **5** (*profesión*) ejercicio LOC **to be out of practice** haber perdido práctica

practise (*USA* **practice**) /ˈpræktɪs/ **1** *vt, vi* practicar **2** *vi* (*Dep*) entrenarse **3** *vt* (*Dep*) practicar **4** *vt, vi* ~ **(as sth)** (*profesión*) ejercer (de algo) **5** *vt* (*cualidad*) ejercitar **practised** (*USA* **practiced**) *adj* ~ **(in sth)** experto (en algo)

practitioner /prækˈtɪʃənə(r)/ *n* **1** experto, -a **2** médico, -a *Ver tb* GENERAL PRACTITIONER

pragmatic /prægˈmætɪk/ *adj* pragmático

praise /preɪz/ ◆ *vt* **1** elogiar **2** (*a Dios*) alabar ◆ *n* [*incontable*] **1** elogio(s) **2** halago **3** (*Relig*) alabanza **praiseworthy** *adj* loable

pram /præm/ (*USA* **buggy**) *n* cochecito (de niño)

prawn /prɔːn/ *n* gamba

pray /preɪ/ *vi* rezar, orar

prayer /preə(r)/ *n* oración

preach /priːtʃ/ **1** *vt, vi* (*Relig*) predicar **2** *vi* ~ **(at/to sb)** (*pey*) sermonear (a algn) **3** *vt* aconsejar **preacher** *n* predicador, -ora

precarious /prɪˈkeəriəs/ *adj* precario

precaution /prɪˈkɔːʃn/ *n* precaución **precautionary** *adj* cautelar

precede /prɪˈsiːd/ *vt* **1** preceder a **2** (*discurso*) introducir

precedence /ˈpresɪdəns/ *n* precedencia

precedent /ˈpresɪdənt/ *n* precedente

preceding /prɪˈsiːdɪŋ/ *adj* **1** precedente **2** (*tiempo*) anterior

precinct /ˈpriːsɪŋkt/ *n* **1** (*tb* **precincts**) recinto **2** (*GB*) zona: *pedestrian precinct* zona peatonal

precious /ˈpreʃəs/ ◆ *adj* **1** precioso (*valioso*) ☛ *Comparar con* PRECIOSO **2** ~ **to sb** de gran valor para algn ◆ *adv* LOC **precious few/little** muy poco, -a, -os, -as

precipice /ˈpresəpɪs/ *n* precipicio

precise /prɪˈsaɪs/ *adj* **1** exacto, preciso **2** (*explicación*) claro **3** (*persona*) meticuloso **precisely** *adv* **1** exactamente, precisamente **2** (*hora*) en punto **3** con precisión **precision** *n* exactitud, precisión

preclude /prɪˈkluːd/ *vt* (*fml*) excluir

precocious /prɪˈkəʊʃəs/ *adj* precoz

preconceived /ˌpriːkənˈsiːvd/ *adj* preconcebido **preconception** *n* idea preconcebida

precondition /ˌpriːkənˈdɪʃn/ *n* condición previa

predator /ˈpredətə(r)/ *n* depredador **predatory** *adj* **1** (*animal*) depredador **2** (*persona*) buitre

predecessor /ˈpriːdɪsesə(r); *USA* ˈpredə-/ *n* predecesor, -ora

predicament /prɪˈdɪkəmənt/ *n* situación difícil, apuro

predict /prɪˈdɪkt/ *vt* **1** predecir, prever **2** pronosticar **predictable** *adj* previsible **prediction** *n* predicción, pronóstico

predominant /prɪˈdɒmɪnənt/ *adj* predominante **predominantly** *adv* predominantemente

pre-empt /pri ˈempt/ *vt* adelantarse a

preface /ˈprefəs/ *n* **1** prefacio, prólogo **2** (*discurso*) introducción

prefer /prɪˈfɜː(r)/ *vt* (-rr-) preferir: *Would you prefer cake or biscuits?* ¿Qué prefieres, bizcocho o galletas? ☛ *Ver nota en* PREFERIR **preferable** /ˈprefrəbl/ *adj* preferible **preferably** /ˈprefrəbli/ preferiblemente **preference** /ˈprefrəns/ *n* preferencia LOC **in preference to sb/sth** en lugar de algn/algo **preferential** /ˌprefəˈrenʃl/ *adj* preferente

prefix /ˈpriːfɪks/ *n* prefijo

pregnant /ˈpregnənt/ *adj* **1** embarazada **2** (*animal*) preñada **pregnancy** *n* (*pl* **-ies**) embarazo

prejudice /ˈpredʒudɪs/ ◆ *n* **1** [*incontable*] prejuicios **2** prejuicio **3** parcialidad LOC **without prejudice to sth/sb** sin detrimento de algo/algn ◆ *vt* **1** (*persona*) predisponer **2** (*decisión, resultado*) influir en **3** perjudicar **prejudiced** *adj* **1** parcial **2** intolerante LOC **to be prejudiced against sth/sb** estar predispuesto contra algo/algn

preliminary /prɪˈlɪmɪnəri; *USA* -neri/ ◆ *adj* **1** preliminar **2** (*Dep*) eliminatorio ◆ **preliminaries** *n* [*pl*] preliminares

prelude /ˈpreljuːd/ *n* **1** (*Mús*) preludio **2** (*fig*) prólogo

premature /ˈprematjʊə(r); *USA* ˌpriːməˈtʊər/ *adj* prematuro

premier /ˈpremiə(r); *USA* ˈpriːmiər/ ◆ *n* primer ministro, primera ministra ☛ *Ver* pág 322. ◆ *adj* principal

première /ˈpremɪeə(r); *USA* prɪˈmɪər/ *n* estreno

premises /ˈpremɪsɪz/ *n* [*pl*] **1** (*tienda, bar, etc*) local **2** (*empresa*) oficinas **3** (*gen*) edificio

premium /ˈpriːmiəm/ *n* (*pago*) prima LOC **to be at a premium** escasear

preoccupation /priɒkjuˈpeɪʃn/ *n* ~ (**with sth**) preocupación (por algo) **preoccupied** *adj* **1** preocupado **2** abstraído

preparation /ˌprepəˈreɪʃn/ *n* **1** preparación **2** **preparations** [*pl*] (**for sth**) preparativos (para algo)

preparatory /prɪˈpærətri; *USA* -tɔːri/ *adj* preparatorio

prepare /prɪˈpeə(r)/ **1** *vi* ~ **for sth/to do sth** prepararse para algo/para hacer algo; hacer preparativos para algo **2** *v* preparar LOC **to be prepared to do sth** estar dispuesto a hacer algo

preposterous /prɪˈpɒstərəs/ *ad* absurdo

prerequisite /ˌpriːˈrekwəzɪt/ (*tb* **pre-condition**) *n* (*fml*) ~ (**for/of sth**) requisito, condición previa (para algo)

prerogative /prɪˈrɒgətɪv/ *n* prerrogativa

prescribe /prɪˈskraɪb/ *vt* **1** (*medicina*) recetar **2** recomendar

prescription /prɪˈskrɪpʃn/ *n* **1** (*lit y fig*) receta **2** (*acción*) prescripción

presence /ˈprezns/ *n* **1** presencia **2** asistencia **3** existencia

present /ˈpreznt/ ◆ *adj* **1** ~ **(at/in sth)** presente (en algo) (*lugar, sustancia*) **2** (*tiempo*) actual **3** (*mes, año*) corriente LOC **to the present day** hasta hoy ◆ *n* **1 the present** (*tiempo*) el presente **2** regalo: *to give sb a present* regalar algo a algn LOC **at present** actualmente *Ver tb* MOMENT ◆ /prɪˈzent/ *vt* **1** presentar: *to present yourself* presentarse **2** ~ **sb with sth**; ~ **sth (to sb)** hacer entrega de algo (a algn): ~ *sb with a problem* plantearle a algn un problema **3** (*argumento*) exponer **4** ~ **itself (to sb)** (*oportunidad*) presentarse a algn **5** (*Teat*) representar **presentable** /prɪˈzentəbl/ *adj* **1** presentable **2** (*decente*) visible

presentation /ˌpreznˈteɪʃn; *USA* ˌpriːzen-/ *n* **1** presentación **2** (*argumento*) exposición **3** (*Teat*) representación **4** (*premio*) entrega

present-day /ˌpreznt ˈdeɪ/ *adj* actual

presenter /prɪˈzentə(r)/ *n* presentador, -ora

presently /ˈprezntli/ *adv* **1** (*GB*) [*futuro: generalmente al final de la frase*] en un momento, dentro de poco: *I will follow on presently.* Voy dentro de un momento. **2** (*GB*) [*pasado: generalmente al principio de la frase*] al poco tiempo: *Presently he got up to go.* Al poco tiempo se levantó para marcharse. **3** (*GB*) luego **4** (*esp USA*) actualmente

preservation /ˌprezəˈveɪʃn/ *n* conservación, preservación

preservative /prɪˈzɜːvətɪv/ *adj, n* conservante

preserve /prɪˈzɜːv/ ◆ *vt* **1** conservar (*comida, etc*) **2** ~ **sth (for sth)** preservar algo (para algo) **3** ~ **sb (from sth/sb)** preservar, proteger a algn (de algn/algo) ◆ *n* **1** [*gen pl*] conserva, confitura **2** (*caza, lit y fig*) coto: *the exclusive preserve of party members* el coto privado de los miembros del partido

preside /prɪˈzaɪd/ *vi* ~ **(over/at sth)** presidir (algo)

presidency /ˈprezɪdənsi/ *n* (*pl* **-ies**) presidencia

president /ˈprezɪdənt/ *n* presidente, -a **presidential** /ˌprezɪˈdenʃl/ *adj* presidencial

press /pres/ ◆ *n* **1** (*tb* **the Press**) [*v sing o pl*] la prensa: *press conference* rueda de prensa ◊ *press cutting* recorte de prensa ◊ *press release* comunicado de prensa **2** planchado **3** lagar **4** (*tb* **printing-press**) imprenta ◆ **1** *vt, vi* apretar **2** *vt* pulsar, presionar **3** *vi* ~ **(up) against sb** arrimarse a algn **4** *vt* (*uvas*) pisar **5** *vt* (*aceitunas, flores*) prensar **6** *vt* planchar **7** *vt* ~ **sb (for sth/to do sth)** presionar a algn (para que haga algo) LOC **to be pressed for time** andar muy escaso de tiempo *Ver tb* CHARGE PHR V **to press ahead/on (with sth)** seguir adelante (con algo) **to press for sth** presionar para que se haga algo

pressing /ˈpresɪŋ/ *adj* acuciante, urgente

press-up /ˈpres ʌp/ (*esp USA* **push-up**) *n* flexión

pressure /ˈpreʃə(r)/ ◆ *n* ~ **(of sth)**; ~ **(to do sth)** presión (de algo); presión (para hacer algo): *pressure cooker* olla a presión ◊ *pressure gauge* manómetro ◊ *pressure group* grupo de presión LOC **to put pressure on sb (to do sth)** presionar a algn (para que haga algo) ◆ *vt Ver* PRESSURIZE

pressure cooker *n* olla a presión ☛ *Ver dibujo en* SAUCEPAN

pressurize, -ise /ˈpreʃəraɪz/ (*tb* **pressure**) *vt* **1** ~ **sb into (doing) sth** presionar a algn para que haga algo **2** (*Fís*) presurizar

prestige /preˈstiːʒ/ *n* prestigio **prestigious** *adj* prestigioso

presumably /prɪˈzjuːməbli/ *adv* es de suponer que

presume /prɪˈzjuːm; *USA* -ˈzuːm/ *vt* asumir: *I presume so.* Eso creo.

presumption /prɪˈzʌmpʃn/ *n* **1** presunción **2** atrevimiento

presumptuous /prɪˈzʌmptʃuəs/ *adj* impertinente

presuppose /ˌpriːsəˈpəʊz/ *vt* presuponer

pretence (*USA* **pretense**) /prɪˈtens/ *n* **1** [*incontable*] engaño(s): *They abandoned all pretence of objectivity.* Dejaron de fingir que eran objetivos. **2** (*fml*) ostentación

pretend /prɪˈtend/ ◆ *vt, vi* **1** fingir **2** pretender **3** ~ **to be sth** jugar a algo: *They're pretending to be explorers.* Están jugando a los exploradores. ◆ (*coloq*) *adj* **1** de juguete **2** fingido

pretentious /prɪˈtenʃəs/ *adj* pretencioso

pretext /ˈpriːtekst/ *n* pretexto

pretty /ˈprɪti/ ◆ *adj* (**-ier**, **-iest**) **1** bonito **2** (*mujer*) guapa LOC **not to be a pretty sight** no ser nada agradable ◆ *adv* bastante *Ver tb* QUITE 1 ☛ *Ver nota en* FAIRLY, RATHER LOC **pretty much/well** más o menos

prevail /prɪˈveɪl/ *vi* **1** (*ley, condiciones*) imperar **2** predominar **3** (*fig*) prevalecer PHR V **to prevail (up)on sb to do sth** (*fml*) convencer a algn para que haga algo **prevailing** (*fml*) *adj* **1** reinante **2** (*viento*) predominante

prevalent /ˈprevələnt/ *adj* (*fml*) **1** difundido **2** predominante **prevalence** *n* **1** difusión **2** predominancia

prevent /prɪˈvent/ *vt* **1** ~ **sb from doing sth** impedir que algn haga algo **2** ~ **sth** evitar, prevenir algo

prevention /prɪˈvenʃn/ *n* prevención

preventive /prɪˈventɪv/ *adj* preventivo

preview /ˈpriːvjuː/ *n* preestreno

previous /ˈpriːviəs/ *adj* anterior LOC **previous to doing sth** antes de hacer algo **previously** *adv* anteriormente

pre-war /ˌpriː ˈwɔː(r)/ *adj* de (la) preguerra

prey /preɪ/ ◆ *n* [*incontable*] (*lit y fig*) presa ◆ *vi* LOC **to prey on sb's mind** preocupar a algn PHR V **to prey on sth/sb 1** cazar algo/a algn **2** vivir a costa de algo/algn

price /praɪs/ ◆ *n* precio: *to go up/down in price* subir/bajar de precio LOC **at any price** a toda costa **not at any price** por nada del mundo *Ver tb* CHEAP ◆ *vt* **1** fijar el precio de **2** valorar **3** poner el precio a **priceless** *adj* que no tiene precio

prick /prɪk/ ◆ *n* **1** punzada **2** pinchazo ◆ *vt* pinchar (*fig*) remorder (*la conciencia*) LOC **to prick up your ears 1** levantar las orejas **2** aguzar el oído

prickly /ˈprɪkli/ *adj* (**-ier**, **-iest**) **1** espinoso **2** que pica **3** (*coloq*) malhumorado

pride /praɪd/ ◆ *n* **1** ~ **(in sth)** orgullo (por algo) **2** (*pey*) orgullo, soberbia LOC **(to be) sb's pride and joy** (ser) la niña de los ojos de algn **to take pride in sth** hacer algo con orgullo ◆ *vt* LOC **to pride yourself on sth** preciarse de algo

priest /priːst/ *n* sacerdote, cura **priesthood** *n* **1** sacerdocio **2** clero

> En inglés se usa la palabra **priest** para referirse normalmente a los sacerdotes católicos. Los párrocos anglicanos se llaman **clergyman** o **vicar**, y los de las demás religiones protestantes, **minister**.

prig /prɪg/ *n* (*pey*) mojigato, -a **priggish** *adj* mojigato

prim /prɪm/ *adj* (*pey*) (**primmer**, **primmest**) **1** remilgado **2** (*aspecto*) recatado

primarily /ˈpraɪmərəli; *USA* praɪˈmerəli/ *adv* principalmente, sobre todo

primary /ˈpraɪməri; *USA* -meri/ ◆ *adj* **1** primario: *primary school* escuela primaria **2** primordial **3** principal ◆ *n* (*pl* **-ies**) (*USA*) (*tb* **primary election**) eleccion primaria

prime /praɪm/ ◆ *adj* **1** principal **2** de primera: *a prime example* un ejemplo excelente ◆ *n* LOC **in your prime/in the prime of life** en la flor de la vida ◆ *vt* **1** ~ **sb (for sth)** preparar a algn (para algo) **2** ~ **sb (with sth)** poner al tanto a algn (de algo)

Prime Minister *n* primer ministro, primera ministra ☛ *Ver* pág 322.

primeval (*tb* **primaeval**) /praɪˈmiːvl/ *adj* primigenio

primitive /ˈprɪmətɪv/ *adj* primitivo

primrose /ˈprɪmrəʊz/ ◆ *n* prímula ◆ *adj, n* amarillo pálido

prince /prɪns/ *n* príncipe

princess /ˌprɪnˈses/ *n* princesa

principal /ˈprɪnsəpl/ ◆ *adj* principal ◆ *n* director, -ora, rector, -ora (*colegio, universidad*)

principle /ˈprɪnsəpl/ *n* (*gen*) principio *a woman of principle* una mujer de principios LOC **in principle** en principio **on principle** por principio

print /prɪnt/ ◆ *vt* **1** imprimir **2** (*Period*) publicar **3** escribir con letras de imprenta **4** (*tela*) estampar PHR V **to print (sth) out** imprimir (algo) (*Informát*) ◆ *n* **1** (*tipografía*) letra **2** huella **3**

(*Arte*) grabado **4** (*Fot*) copia **5** tela estampada LOC **in print 1** (*libro*) en venta **2** publicado **out of print** agotado *Ver tb* SMALL **printer** *n* **1** (*persona*) impresor, -ora **2** (*máquina*) impresora ☛ *Ver dibujo en* ORDENADOR **3 the printers** [*pl*] (*taller*) imprenta **printing** *n* **1** imprenta (*técnica*): *a printing error* una errata **2** (*libros, etc*) impresión **printout** *n* copia impresa (*esp Informát*)

prior /ˈpraɪə(r)/ ◆ *adj* previo ◆ **prior to** *adv* **1 prior to doing sth** antes de hacer algo **2 prior to sth** anterior a algo **priority** *n* (*pl* **-ies**) ~ (**over sth/sb**) prioridad (sobre algo/algn) LOC **to get your priorities right** saber cuáles son tus prioridades

prise (*USA tb* **prize**) /praɪz/ PHR V **to prise sth apart, off, open, etc (with sth)** separar, quitar, abrir, etc algo (haciendo palanca con algo)

prison /ˈprɪzn/ *n* cárcel: *prison camp* campo de concentración **prisoner** *n* **1** preso, -a **2** (*cautivo*) prisionero, -a **3** detenido, -a **4** (*en juzgado*) acusado, -a LOC *Ver* CAPTIVE

privacy /ˈprɪvəsi; *USA* ˈpraɪv-/ *n* intimidad

private /ˈpraɪvət/ ◆ *adj* **1** privado: *private enterprise* empresa privada ◇ *private eye* detective privado **2** (*de individuo*) particular **3** (*persona*) reservado **4** (*lugar*) íntimo ◆ *n* **1** (*Mil*) soldado raso **2 privates** [*pl*] (*coloq*) partes (pudendas) LOC **in private** en privado **privately** *adv* en privado **privatize, -ise** *vt* privatizar

privilege /ˈprɪvəlɪdʒ/ *n* **1** privilegio **2** (*Jur*) inmunidad **privileged** *adj* **1** privilegiado **2** (*información*) confidencial

privy /ˈprɪvi/ *adj* LOC **to be privy to sth** (*fml*) tener conocimiento de algo

prize[1] /praɪz/ ◆ *n* premio ◆ *adj* **1** premiado **2** de primera **3** (*irón*) de remate **prize** *vt* estimar

prize[2] (*USA*) *Ver* PRISE

pro /prəʊ/ ◆ *n* LOC **the pros and (the) cons** los pros y los contras ◆ *adj, n* (*coloq*) profesional

probable /ˈprɒbəbl/ *adj* probable: *It seems probable that he'll arrive tomorrow.* Parece probable que llegue mañana. **probability** /ˌprɒbəˈbɪləti/ *n* (*pl* **-ies**) probabilidad LOC **in all probability** con toda probabilidad **probably** *adv* probablemente

En inglés se suele usar el adverbio en los casos en que se usaría *es probable que* en español: *They will probably go.* Es probable que vayan.

probation /prəˈbeɪʃn; *USA* prəʊ-/ *n* **1** libertad condicional **2** (*empleado*) prueba: *a three-month probation period* un periodo de prueba de tres meses

probe /prəʊb/ ◆ *n* sonda ◆ **1** *vt, vi* (*Med*) sondar **2** *vt, vi* explorar **3** *vt* ~ **sb about/on sth** examinar a algn de algo **4** *vi* ~ (**into sth**) investigar (algo) **probing** *adj* (*pregunta*) penetrante

problem /ˈprɒbləm/ *n* problema LOC *Ver* TEETHE **problematic(al)** *adj* **1** problemático **2** (*discutible*) dudoso

procedure /prəˈsiːdʒə(r)/ *n* **1** procedimiento **2** (*gestión*) trámite(s)

proceed /prəˈsiːd, prəʊ-/ *vi* **1** proceder **2** ~ (**to sth/to do sth**) pasar (a algo/a hacer algo) **3** (*fml*) avanzar, ir **4** ~ (**with sth**) (*continue*) continuar, ir adelante (con algo) **proceedings** *n* [*pl*] **1** acto **2** (*Jur*) proceso **3** (*reunión*) actas

proceeds /ˈprəʊsiːdz/ *n* [*pl*] ~ (**of/from sth**) ganancias (de algo)

process /ˈprəʊses; *USA* ˈprɒses/ ◆ *n* **1** (*método*) procedimiento **2** (*Jur*) proceso LOC **in the process** al hacerlo **to be in the process of (doing) sth** estar haciendo algo ◆ *vt* **1** (*alimento, materia prima*) tratar **2** (*solicitud*) tramitar **3** (*Fot*) revelar *Ver tb* DEVELOP **4** (*Informát*) procesar **processing** *n* **1** tratamiento **2** (*Fot*) revelado **3** (*Informát*) proceso: *word processing* tratamiento de textos

procession /prəˈseʃn/ *n* desfile, procesión

processor /ˈprəʊsesə(r)/ *n* procesador *Ver* MICROPROCESSOR, FOOD PROCESSOR

proclaim /prəˈkleɪm/ *vt* proclamar **proclamation** *n* **1** proclama **2** (*acto*) proclamación

prod /prɒd/ ◆ *vt, vi* (**-dd-**) ~ (**at**) **sth/sb** pinchar algo/a algn ◆ *n* **1** (*lit y fig*) pinchazo **2** pincho

prodigious /prəˈdɪdʒəs/ *adj* prodigioso

prodigy /ˈprɒdədʒi/ *n* (*pl* **-ies**) prodigio

produce /prəˈdjuːs; *USA* -ˈduːs/ ◆ *vt* **1** producir ☛ *Comparar con* MANUFACTURE **2** (*cultivo*) dar **3** (*cría*) tener **4** ~

sth (from/out of sth) sacar algo (de algo) **5** (*Teat*) poner en escena **6** (*Cine, TV*) producir ◆ /ˈprɒdjuːs; *USA* -duːs/ *n* [*incontable*] productos: *produce of France* producto de Francia ☛ *Ver nota en* PRODUCT **producer** *n* **1** (*gen, Cine, TV*) productor, -ora ☛ *Comparar con* DIRECTOR, CONSUMER *en* CONSUME **2** (*Teat*) director, -ora, de escena

product /ˈprɒdʌkt/ *n* producto: *Coal was once a major industrial product.* El carbón fue en un tiempo uno de los productos industriales más importantes.

> **Product** se utiliza para referirse a productos industriales, mientras que **produce** se usa para los productos del campo.

production /prəˈdʌkʃn/ *n* producción: *production line* cadena de montaje

productive /prəˈdʌktɪv/ *adj* productivo **productivity** /ˌprɒdʌkˈtɪvəti/ *n* productividad

profess /prəˈfes/ *vt* (*fml*) **1** ~ **to be sth** pretender ser algo; declararse algo **2** ~ **(yourself) sth** declarar(se) algo **3** (*Relig*) profesar **professed** *adj* **1** supuesto **2** declarado, -a

profession /prəˈfeʃn/ *n* profesión ☛ *Ver nota en* WORK[1] **professional** *adj* profesional

professor /prəˈfesə(r)/ *n* (*abrev* **Prof**) **1** (*GB*) catedrático, -a de universidad **2** (*USA*) profesor, -ora de universidad

proficiency /prəˈfɪʃnsi/ *n* ~ **(in sth/doing sth)** competencia, capacidad en algo/para hacer algo **proficient** *adj* ~ **(in/at sth/doing sth)** competente en algo: *She's very proficient in/at swimming.* Es una nadadora muy compentente.

profile /ˈprəʊfaɪl/ *n* perfil

profit /ˈprɒfɪt/ ◆ *n* **1** ganancia(s), beneficio(s): *to do sth for profit* hacer algo con fines lucrativos ◊ *to make a profit of £20* sacar un beneficio de 20 libras ◊ *to sell at a profit* vender con ganancia ◊ *profit-making* lucrativo **2** (*fig*) beneficio, provecho ◆ PHR V **to profit from sth** beneficiarse de algo **profitable** *adj* **1** rentable **2** provechoso

profound /prəˈfaʊnd/ *adj* profundo **profoundly** *adv* profundamente, extremadamente

profusely /prəˈfjuːsli/ *adv* profusa mente

profusion /prəˈfjuːʒn/ *n* profusión abundancia LOC **in profusion** en abun dancia

programme (*USA* **program**) /ˈprəʊ græm; *USA* -grəm/ ◆ *n* program ☛ En lenguaje infórmatico se escrib **program**. ◆ *vt, vi* (**-mm-**, *USA* **-m-**) programar **programmer** (*tb* **compute programmer**) (*USA* **-m-**) *n* programa dor, -ora **programming** (*USA* **-m-**) programación

progress /ˈprəʊgres; *USA* ˈprɒg-/ ◆ [*incontable*] **1** progreso(s) **2** (*mov miento*) avance: *to make progress* avan zar LOC **in progress** en marcha /prəˈgres/ *vi* avanzar

progressive /prəˈgresɪv/ *adj* **1** progre sivo **2** (*Pol*) progresista

prohibit /prəˈhɪbɪt; *USA* prəʊ-/ *vt* (*fm* **1** ~ **sth/sb (from doing sth)** prohibi algo/a algn (hacer algo) **2** ~ **sth**; ~ **s (from doing sth)** impedir algo; a alg (hacer algo) **prohibition** *n* prohibición

project /ˈprɒdʒekt/ ◆ *n* proyecto /prəˈdʒekt/ **1** *vt* proyectar **2** *vi* sobresa lir **projection** *n* proyección **projector** proyector (*de cine*): *overhead projecto* retroproyector

prolific /prəˈlɪfɪk/ *adj* prolífico

prologue (*USA tb* **prolog**) /ˈprəʊlɒ *USA* -lɔːg/ *n* ~ **(to sth)** (*lit y fig*) prólog (de algo)

prolong /prəˈlɒŋ; *USA* -ˈlɔːŋ/ *vt* prolon gar, alargar

promenade /ˌprɒməˈnɑːd; *USA* -ˈneɪd (*GB, coloq* **prom**) *n* paseo marítimo

prominent /ˈprɒmɪnənt/ *adj* **1** promi nente **2** importante

promiscuous /prəˈmɪskjuəs/ *a* promiscuo

promise /ˈprɒmɪs/ ◆ *n* **1** promesa **2** *show promise* ser prometedor ◆ *vt,* prometer **promising** *adj* prometedor

promote /prəˈməʊt/ *vt* **1** promove fomentar **2** (*en el trabajo*) ascender (*Com*) promocionar **promoter** *n* prom tor, -ora **promotion** *n* **1** ascenso promoción, fomento

prompt /prɒmpt/ ◆ *adj* **1** sin dilació **2** (*servicio*) rápido **3** (*persona*) puntu ◆ *adv* en punto ◆ **1** *vt* ~ **sb to do s** incitar a algn a hacer algo **2** *vt* (*rea ción*) provocar **3** *vt, vi* (*Teat*) apunt

promptly *adv* **1** con prontitud **2** puntualmente **3** al punto

prone /prəʊn/ *adj* ~ **to sth** propenso a algo

pronoun /ˈprəʊnaʊn/ *n* pronombre

pronounce /prəˈnaʊns/ *vt* **1** pronunciar **2** declarar **pronounced** *adj* **1** (*acento*) fuerte **2** (*mejora*) marcado **3** (*movimiento*) pronunciado

pronunciation /prəˌnʌnsiˈeɪʃn/ *n* pronunciación

proof /pru:f/ *n* **1** [*incontable*] prueba(s) **2** comprobación

prop /prɒp/ ◆ *n* **1** (*lit y fig*) apoyo **2** puntal ◆ *vt* (**-pp-**) ~ **sth (up) against sth** apoyar algo contra algo PHR V **to prop sth up 1** sujetar algo **2** (*pey, fig*) respaldar algo

propaganda /ˌprɒpəˈgændə/ *n* propaganda

propel /prəˈpel/ *vt* (**-ll-**) **1** impulsar **2** (*Mec*) propulsar **propellant** *adj, n* propulsor

propeller /prəˈpelə(r)/ *n* hélice

propensity /prəˈpensəti/ *n* (*fml*) ~ (**for/to sth**) propensión (a algo)

proper /ˈprɒpə(r)/ *adj* **1** debido **2** adecuado **3** de verdad **4** correcto **5** decente **6** *the house proper* la casa propiamente dicha **properly** *adv* **1** bien **2** (*comportarse*) con propiedad **3** adecuadamente

property /ˈprɒpəti/ *n* (*pl* **-ies**) **1** propiedad **2** [*incontable*] bienes: *personal property* bienes muebles

prophecy /ˈprɒfəsi/ *n* (*pl* **-ies**) profecía

prophesy /ˈprɒfəsaɪ/ (*pret, pp* **-sied**) **1** *vt* predecir **2** *vi* profetizar

prophet /ˈprɒfɪt/ *n* profeta

proportion /prəˈpɔ:ʃn/ *n* proporción: *sense of proportion* sentido de la proporción LOC **out of (all) proportion 1** desmesuradamente **2** desproporcionado *Ver tb* THING **proportional** *adj* ~ (**to sth**) proporcional a algo; en proporción con algo

proposal /prəˈpəʊzl/ *n* **1** propuesta **2** (*tb* **proposal of marriage**) propuesta de matrimonio

propose /prəˈpəʊz/ **1** *vt* (*sugerencia*) proponer **2** *vt* ~ **to do sth/doing sth** proponerse hacer algo **3** *vi* ~ (**to sb**) pedir la mano (a algn)

proposition /ˌprɒpəˈzɪʃn/ *n* **1** proposición **2** propuesta

proprietor /prəˈpraɪətə(r)/ *n* propietario, -a

prose /prəʊz/ *n* prosa

prosecute /ˈprɒsɪkju:t/ *vt* procesar: *prosecuting lawyer* fiscal **prosecution** *n* **1** enjuiciamiento, procesamiento **2** [*v sing o pl*] (*abogado*) acusación **prosecutor** *n* fiscal

prospect /ˈprɒspekt/ *n* **1** perspectiva **2** ~ (**of sth/doing sth**) expectativa(s), posibilidad(es) (de algo/hacer algo) **3** (*antic*) panorama, vista **prospective** /prəˈspektɪv/ *adj* **1** futuro **2** probable

prospectus /prəˈspektəs/ *n* prospecto (*folleto promocional*)

prosper /ˈprɒspə(r)/ *vi* prosperar **prosperity** /prɒˈsperəti/ *n* prosperidad **prosperous** *adj* próspero

prostitute /ˈprɒstɪtju:t; *USA* -tu:t/ *n* **1** prostituta **2 male prostitute** prostituto **prostitution** *n* prostitución

prostrate /ˈprɒstreɪt/ *adj* **1** postrado **2** ~ (**with sth**) abatido (por algo)

protagonist /prəˈtægənɪst/ *n* **1** protagonista **2** ~ (**of sth**) defensor, -ora (de algo)

protect /prəˈtekt/ *vt* ~ **sth/sb (against/from sth)** proteger algo/a algn (contra/de algo) **protection** *n* **1** ~ (**for sth**) protección (de/para algo) **2** ~ (**against sth**) protección (contra algo)

protective /prəˈtektɪv/ *adj* protector

protein /ˈprəʊti:n/ *n* proteína

protest /ˈprəʊtest/ ◆ *n* protesta ◆ /prəˈtest/ **1** *vi* ~ (**about/at/against sth**) protestar (por/de/contra algo) **2** *vt* declarar **protester** *n* manifestante *Ver tb* DEMONSTRATOR

Protestant /ˈprɒtɪstənt/ *adj, n* protestante

prototype /ˈprəʊtətaɪp/ *n* prototipo

protrude /prəˈtru:d; *USA* prəʊ-/ *vi* ~ (**from sth**) sobresalir (de algo): *protruding teeth* dientes salientes

proud /praʊd/ *adj* (**-er, -est**) **1** (*aprob*) ~ (**of sth/sb**) orgulloso (de algo/algn) **2** (*aprob*) ~ (**to do sth/that ...**) orgulloso (de hacer algo/de que ...) **3** (*pey*) soberbio **proudly** *adv* con orgullo

prove /pru:v/ *vt* (*pp* **proved**, *USA* **proven** /ˈpru:vn/) **1** ~ **sth (to sb)** probar, demostrar algo (a algn) **2** *vt, vi*

~ (**yourself**) (**to be**) **sth** resultar (ser) algo: *The task proved (to be) very difficult.* La tarea resultó (ser) muy difícil. LOC **to prove your point** demostrar que se está en lo cierto

proven /ˈpruːvn/ ♦ *adj* comprobado ♦ (*USA*) *pp de* PROVE

proverb /ˈprɒvɜːb/ *n* proverbio **proverbial** *adj* **1** proverbial **2** por todos conocido

provide /prəˈvaɪd/ *vt* ~ **sb** (**with sth**); ~ **sth** (**for sb**) proporcionar, suministrar algo a algn PHR V **to provide for sb** mantener a algn **to provide for sth 1** prevenir algo **2** estipular algo

provided /prəˈvaɪdɪd/ (*tb* **providing**) *conj* ~ (**that...**) a condición de que, con tal (de) que

province /ˈprɒvɪns/ *n* **1** provincia **2 the provinces** [*pl*] provincias **3** competencia: *It's not my province.* Está fuera de mi competencia. **provincial** /prəˈvɪnʃl/ *adj* **1** provincial **2** (*pey*) de provincias, provinciano

provision /prəˈvɪʒn/ *n* **1** ~ **of sth** suministro, abastecimiento de algo **2** *to make provision for sb* asegurar el porvenir de algn ◊ *to make provision against/for sth* prever algo **3 provisions** [*pl*] víveres, provisiones **4** (*Jur*) disposición, estipulación

provisional /prəˈvɪʒənl/ *adj* provisional

proviso /prəˈvaɪzəʊ/ *n* (*pl* **~s**) condición

provocation /ˌprɒvəˈkeɪʃn/ *n* provocación **provocative** /prəˈvɒkətɪv/ *adj* provocador, provocativo

provoke /prəˈvəʊk/ *vt* **1** (*persona*) provocar **2** ~ **sb into doing sth/to do sth** inducir, incitar a algn a hacer algo **3** ~ **sth** provocar, causar algo

prow /praʊ/ *n* proa

prowess /ˈpraʊəs/ *n* **1** proeza **2** habilidad

prowl /praʊl/ *vt, vi* ~ (**about/around**) rondar, merodear

proximity /prɒkˈsɪməti/ *n* proximidad

proxy /ˈprɒksi/ *n* **1** apoderado, -a, representante **2** poder: *by proxy* por poderes

prude /pruːd/ *n* (*pey*) mojigato, -a

prudent /ˈpruːdnt/ *adj* prudente

prune[1] /pruːn/ *n* ciruela pasa

prune[2] /pruːn/ *vt* **1** podar **2** (*fig*) recortar **pruning** *n* poda

pry /praɪ/ (*pret, pp* **pried** /praɪd/) **1** *v*. **to pry** (**into sth**) entrometerse (en algo) fisgonear **2** *vt* (*esp USA*) *Ver* PRISE

PS /ˌpiːˈes/ *abrev* **postscript** posdata (=P.D.)

psalm /sɑːm/ *n* salmo

pseudonym /ˈsjuːdənɪm; *USA* ˈsuːdənɪm/ *n* seudónimo

psyche /ˈsaɪki/ *n* psique, psiquis

psychiatry /saɪˈkaɪətri; *USA* sɪ-/ *n* psiquiatría **psychiatric** /ˌsaɪkiˈætrɪk/ *adj* psiquiátrico **psychiatrist** /saɪˈkaɪətrɪst/ *n* psiquiatra

psychic /ˈsaɪkɪk/ *adj* **1** (*tb* **psychical**) psíquico **2** (*persona*): *to be psychic* tener poderes parapsicológicos

psychoanalysis /ˌsaɪkəʊəˈnæləsɪs/ (*tb* **analysis**) *n* psicoanálisis

psychology /saɪˈkɒlədʒi/ *n* psicología **psychological** /ˌsaɪkəˈlɒdʒɪkl/ *adj* psicológico **psychologist** /saɪˈkɒlədʒɪst/ *n* psicólogo, -a

pub /pʌb/ *n* (*GB*) bar ☛ *Ver* pág 320.

puberty /ˈpjuːbəti/ *n* pubertad

pubic /ˈpjuːbɪk/ *adj* púbico: *pubic hair* vello púbico

public /ˈpʌblɪk/ ♦ *adj* público: *public convenience* aseos públicos ◊ *public house* bar ♦ *n* **1** público **2 the public** [*v sing o pl*] el público LOC **in public** en público

publication /ˌpʌblɪˈkeɪʃn/ *n* publicación

publicity /pʌbˈlɪsəti/ *n* publicidad: *publicity campaign* campaña publicitaria

publicize, -ise /ˈpʌblɪsaɪz/ *vt* **1** hacer público **2** promover, promocionar

publicly /ˈpʌblɪkli/ *adv* públicamente

public school *n* **1** (*GB*) colegio privado **2** (*USA*) colegio público ☛ *Ver nota en* ESCUELA

publish /ˈpʌblɪʃ/ *vt* **1** publicar **2** hacer público **publisher** *n* **1** editor, -ora (casa) editorial **publishing** *n* mundo editorial: *publishing house* casa editorial

pudding /ˈpʊdɪŋ/ *n* **1** (*GB*) postre *Ver nota en* NAVIDAD **2** pudin, budín **3** *black pudding* morcilla

puddle /ˈpʌdl/ *n* charco

puff /pʌf/ ♦ *n* **1** soplo, resoplido

(*humo, vapor*) bocanada **3** (*coloq*) (*cigarrillo*) chupada **4** (*coloq*) aliento ◆ **1** *vi* jadear **2** *vi* ~ **(away) at/on sth** (*pipa, etc*) chupar algo **3** *vt* (*humo*) salir a bocanadas **4** *vt* (*cigarro, etc*) chupar PHR V **to puff sb out** (*coloq*) dejar a algn sin aliento **to puff sth out** hinchar algo **to puff up** hincharse **puffed** (*tb* **puffed out**) (*coloq*) *adj* sin aliento **puffy** *adj* (**-ier**, **-iest**) hinchado (*esp cara*)

pull /pʊl/ ◆ *n* **1** ~ **(at/on sth)** tirón (en algo) **2 the** ~ **of sth** la atracción, la llamada de algo **3** *It was a hard pull.* Resultó un duro esfuerzo. ◆ **1** *vt* dar un tirón a, tirar de **2** *vi* ~ **(at/on sth)** tirar de algo **3** *vt* (*carro, etc*) tirar de **4** *vt*: *to pull a muscle* darle a algn un tirón en un músculo **5** *vt* (*gatillo*) apretar **6** *vt* (*corcho, muela, pistola*) sacar LOC **to pull sb's leg** (*coloq*) tomarle el pelo a algn **to pull strings (for sb)** (*coloq*) tocar teclas, enchufar a algn **to pull your socks up** (*GB, coloq*) esforzarse por mejorar **to pull your weight** poner todo su esfuerzo *Ver tb* FACE[1]
PHR V **to pull sth apart** partir algo en dos
to pull sth down 1 bajar algo **2** (*edificio*) derribar algo
to pull into sth; **pull in (to sth) 1** (*tren*) llegar a algo **2** (*coche*) detenerse en algo
to pull sth off (*coloq*) conseguir algo
to pull out (of sth) 1 retirarse (de algo) **2** salir (de algo) **to pull sth out** sacar algo **to pull sth/sb out (of sth)** retirar algo/a algn (de algo)
to pull over hacerse a un lado (*coche, etc*)
to pull yourself together dominarse
to pull up detenerse **to pull sth up 1** alzar algo **2** (*planta*) arrancar algo

ulley /ˈpʊli/ *n* (*pl* **-eys**) polea

ullover /ˈpʊləʊvə(r)/ *n* jersey ☛ *Ver nota en* SWEATER

ulp /pʌlp/ *n* **1** pulpa **2** (*de madera*) pasta

ulpit /ˈpʊlpɪt/ *n* púlpito

ulsate /pʌlˈseɪt; *USA* ˈpʌlseɪt/ (*tb* **pulse**) *vi* palpitar, latir

ulse /pʌls/ *n* **1** (*Med*) pulso **2** ritmo **3** pulsación **4** [*gen pl*] legumbre seca

umice /ˈpʌmɪs/ (*tb* **pumice stone**) *n* piedra pómez

ummel /ˈpʌml/ (*tb* **pommel**) *vt* (**-ll-**, *USA tb* **-l-**) aporrear

pump /pʌmp/ ◆ *n* **1** bomba: *petrol pump* surtidor de gasolina **2** zapatilla ◆ **1** *vt* bombear **2** *vi* dar a la bomba **3** *vi* (*corazón*) latir **4** ~ **sb (for sth)** (*coloq*) sonsacar a algn; sonsacarle algo a algn PHR V **to pump sth up** inflar algo

pumpkin /ˈpʌmpkɪn/ *n* calabaza

pun /pʌn/ *n* **pun (on sth)** juego de palabras (con algo)

punch /pʌntʃ/ ◆ *n* **1** punzón **2** (*para billetes*) taladradora **3** (*bebida*) ponche **4** puñetazo ◆ *vt* **1** perforar, picar: *to punch a hole in sth* hacer un agujero en algo **2** dar un puñetazo a

punch-up /ˈpʌntʃ ʌp/ *n* (*GB, coloq*) pelea a puñetazos

punctual /ˈpʌŋktʃuəl/ *adj* puntual ☛ *Ver nota en* PUNTUAL **punctuality** /ˌpʌŋktʃuˈæləti/ *n* puntualidad

punctuate /ˈpʌŋktʃueɪt/ *vt* **1** (*Gram*) puntuar **2** ~ **sth (with sth)** interrumpir algo (con algo)

puncture /ˈpʌŋktʃə(r)/ ◆ *n* pinchazo ◆ **1** *vt, vi* pinchar(se) **2** *vt* (*Med*) perforar

pundit /ˈpʌndɪt/ *n* entendido, -a

pungent /ˈpʌndʒənt/ *adj* **1** acre **2** punzante **3** (*fig*) mordaz

punish /ˈpʌnɪʃ/ *vt* castigar **punishment** *n* **1** castigo **2** (*fig*) paliza

punitive /ˈpjuːnətɪv/ *adj* (*fml*) **1** punitivo **2** desorbitado

punk /pʌŋk/ ◆ *n* **1** (*tb* **punk rock**) (*tb* **punk rocker**) punk **2** (*pey, coloq, esp USA*) gamberro ◆ *adj* punki

punt /pʌnt/ *n* (*GB*) bote largo y plano que se impulsa con una pértiga

punter /ˈpʌntə(r)/ *n* (*GB*) **1** apostante **2** (*coloq*) cliente, miembro del público

pup /pʌp/ *n* **1** *Ver* PUPPY **2** cría

pupil /ˈpjuːpl/ *n* **1** alumno, -a **2** discípulo, -a **3** pupila (*del ojo*)

puppet /ˈpʌpɪt/ *n* **1** (*lit*) marioneta **2** (*fig*) títere

puppy /ˈpʌpi/ (*pl* **-ies**) (*tb* **pup** /pʌp/) *n* cachorro, -a

purchase /ˈpɜːtʃəs/ ◆ *n* (*fml*) compra, adquisición LOC *Ver* COMPULSORY ◆ *vt* (*fml*) comprar **purchaser** *n* (*fml*) comprador, -ora

pure /pjʊə(r)/ *adj* (**purer**, **purest**) puro **purely** *adv* puramente, simplemente

purée /ˈpjʊəreɪ; *USA* pjʊəˈreɪ/ *n* puré

purge /pɜːdʒ/ ◆ *vt* ~ **sth/sb (of/from**

sth) purgar algo/algn (de algo) ◆ *n* **1** purga **2** purgante

purify /ˈpjʊərɪfaɪ/ *vt* (*pret, pp* **-fied**) purificar

puritan /ˈpjʊərɪtən/ *adj, n* puritano, -a **puritanical** /ˌpjʊərɪˈtænɪkl/ *adj* (*pey*) puritano

purity /ˈpjʊərəti/ *n* pureza

purple /ˈpɜːpl/ *adj, n* morado

purport /pəˈpɔːt/ *vt* (*fml*) *It purports to be...* Pretende ser...

purpose /ˈpɜːpəs/ *n* **1** propósito, motivo: *purpose-built* construido con un fin específico **2** determinación: *to have a/no sense of purpose* (no) tener una meta en la vida LOC **for the purpose of** al efecto de **for this purpose** para este fin **on purpose** a propósito *Ver tb* INTENT **purposeful** *adj* decidido **purposely** *adv* intencionadamente

purr /pɜː(r)/ *vi* ronronear

purse /pɜːs/ ◆ *n* **1** monedero ☛ *Comparar con* WALLET **2** (*USA*) bolso ◆ *vt*: *to purse your lips* fruncir los labios

pursue /pəˈsjuː; *USA* -ˈsuː/ *vt* (*fml*) **1** perseguir ☛ La palabra más normal es **chase**. **2** (*actividad*) dedicarse a **3** (*conversación*) continuar (con)

pursuit /pəˈsjuːt; *USA* -ˈsuːt/ *n* (*fml*) **1** ~ **of sth** búsqueda de algo **2** [*gen pl*] actividad LOC **in pursuit of sth** en busca de algo **in pursuit (of sth/sb)** persiguiendo (algo/a algn)

push /pʊʃ/ ◆ *n* empujón LOC **to get/to give sb the push** (*GB, coloq*) ser despedido/dar la patada a algn ◆ **1** *vt, vi* empujar: *to push past sb* pasar a algn empujando **2** *vt, vi* ~ **(on/against) sth** (*botón*) apretar **3** *vt* (*coloq*) (*idea*) promover LOC **to be pushed for sth** (*coloq*) andar justo de algo PHR V **to push ahead/forward/on (with sth)** seguir adelante (con algo) **to push sb around** (*coloq*) mangonear a algn **to push in** colarse **to push off** (*coloq*) largarse

pushchair /ˈpʊʃtʃeə(r)/ *n* silla de niño

push-up /ˈpʊʃ ʌp/ *n* (*esp USA*) *Ver* PRESS-UP

pushy /ˈpʊʃi/ *adj* (**-ier**, **-iest**) (*coloq, pey*) avasallador

puss /pʊs/ *n* minino **pussy** (*pl* **-ies**) (*tb* **pussy-cat**) *n* gatito

put /pʊt/ *vt* (**-tt-**) (*pret, pp* **put**) **1** poner, colocar, meter: *Did you put sugar in my tea?* ¿Me has echado azúcar en el té? ◊ *to put sb out of work* dejar a algn sin trabajo ◊ *Put them together.* Júntalos. **2** decir, expresar **3** (*pregunta, sugerencia*) hacer **4** (*tiempo, esfuerzo*) dedicar ☛ Para expresiones con **put**, véanse las entradas del sustantivo, adjetivo, etc, p.ej. **to put sth right** en RIGHT.

PHR V **to put sth across/over** comunicar algo **to put yourself across/over** expresarse

to put sth aside 1 dejar algo a un lado **2** (*dinero*) ahorrar, separar algo

to put sth away guardar algo

to put sth back 1 devolver algo a su lugar, guardar algo **2** (*reloj*) retrasar algo **3** (*posponer*) aplazar algo

to put sth by 1 (*dinero*) ahorrar algo **2** (*reservar*) guardar algo

to put sb down (*coloq*) humillar, despreciar a algn **to put sth down 1** poner algo (en el suelo, etc) **2** dejar, soltar algo **3** (*escribir*) apuntar algo **4** (*rebelión*) sofocar algo, reprimir algo **5** (*animal*) sacrificar algo **to put sth down to sth** atribuir algo a algo

to put sth forward 1 (*propuesta*) presentar algo **2** (*sugerencia*) hacer algo **3** (*reloj*) adelantar algo

to put sth into (doing) sth dedicar algo a (hacer) algo, invertir algo en (hacer) algo

to put sb off 1 decir a algn que no venga **2** distraer a algn **to put sb off (sth/doing sth)** quitarle a algn las ganas (de algo/de hacer algo)

to put sth on 1 (*ropa*) ponerse algo **2** (*luz, etc*) poner, encender algo **3** engordar algo: *to put on weight* engordar ◊ *to put on two kilos* engordar dos kilos **4** (*obra de teatro*) hacer, montar algo **5** fingir algo

to put sb out [*gen pasiva*] enfadar a algn **to put sth out 1** sacar algo **2** (*luz, fuego*) apagar algo **3** (*mano*) tender algo **to put yourself out (to do sth)** (*coloq*) molestarse (en hacer algo)

to put sth through llevar a cabo algo (*plan, reforma, etc*) **to put sb through sth** someter a algn a algo **to put sb through (to sb)** poner a algn (con algn) (*por teléfono*)

to put sth to sb sugerir, proponer algo a algn

to put sth together armar, montar algo (*aparato*)

to put sb up alojar a algn **to put sth up 1** (*mano*) levantar algo **2** (*edificio*) construir, levantar algo **3** (*letrero, etc*) poner algo **4** (*precio*) subir algo **to put up with sth/sb** aguantar algo/a algn

putrid /ˈpjuːtrɪd/ *adj* **1** podrido, putrefacto **2** (*color, etc*) asqueroso

putty /ˈpʌti/ *n* masilla (*para ventanas*)

puzzle /ˈpʌzl/ ◆ *n* **1** acertijo **2** misterio ◆ *vt* desconcertar PHR V **to puzzle sth out** resolver algo **to puzzle over sth** devanarse los sesos sobre algo

pygmy /ˈpɪgmi/ ◆ *n* pigmeo, -a ◆ *adj* enano: *pygmy horse* caballo enano

pyjamas /pəˈdʒɑːməz/ (*USA* **pajamas** /-ˈdʒæm-/) *n* [*pl*] pijama: *a pair of pyjamas* un pijama ☛ **Pyjama** se usa en singular cuando va delante de otro sustantivo: *pyjama trousers* el pantalón de pijama. *Ver tb nota en* PAIR

pylon /ˈpaɪlən; *USA* ˈpaɪlɒn/ *n* torre de conducción eléctrica

pyramid /ˈpɪrəmɪd/ *n* pirámide

python /ˈpaɪθn; *USA* ˈpaɪθɒn/ *n* pitón

Qq

Q, q /kjuː/ *n* (*pl* **Q's, q's** /kjuːz/) Q, q: *Q for Queenie* Q de Quito ☛ *Ver ejemplos en* A, a

quack /kwæk/ ◆ *n* **1** graznido **2** (*coloq, pey*) curandero, -a ◆ *vi* graznar

quadruple /ˈkwɒdrʊpl; *USA* kwɒˈdruːpl/ ◆ *adj* cuádruple ◆ *vt, vi* cuadruplicar(se)

quagmire /ˈkwægmaɪə(r), kwɒg-/ *n* (*lit y fig*) atolladero

quail /kweɪl/ ◆ *n* (*pl* **quail** *o* ~**s**) codorniz ◆ *vi* ~ (**at sth/sb**) acobardarse ante algo/algn

quaint /kweɪnt/ *adj* **1** (*idea, costumbre, etc*) curioso **2** (*lugar, edificio*) pintoresco

quake /kweɪk/ ◆ *vi* temblar ◆ (*coloq*) *n* terremoto

qualification /ˌkwɒlɪfɪˈkeɪʃn/ *n* **1** (*diploma, etc*) título **2** requisito **3** modificación: *without qualification* sin reserva **4** calificación

qualified /ˈkwɒlɪfaɪd/ *adj* **1** titulado **2** cualificado, capacitado **3** (*éxito, etc*) limitado

qualify /ˈkwɒlɪfaɪ/ (*pret, pp* **-fied**) **1** *vt* ~ **sb** (**for sth/to do sth**) capacitar a algn (para algo/para hacer algo); dar derecho a algn a algo/a hacer algo **2** *vi* ~ **for sth/to do sth** tener derecho a algo/a hacer algo **3** *vt* (*declaración*) modificar **4** *vi* ~ (**as sth**) obtener el título (de algo) **5** *vi* ~ (**as sth**) contar (como algo) **6** *vi* ~ (**for sth**) cumplir los requisitos (para algo) **7** *vi* ~ (**for sth**) (*Dep*) clasificarse (para algo) **qualifying** *adj* eliminatorio

qualitative /ˈkwɒlɪtətɪv; *USA* -teɪt-/ *adj* cualitativo

quality /ˈkwɒləti/ *n* (*pl* **-ies**) **1** calidad **2** clase **3** cualidad **4** característica

qualm /kwɑːm/ *n* escrúpulo

quandary /ˈkwɒndəri/ *n* LOC **to be in a quandary 1** tener un dilema **2** estar en un aprieto

quantify /ˈkwɒntɪfaɪ/ *vt* (*pret, pp* **-fied**) cuantificar

quantitative /ˈkwɒntɪtətɪv; *USA* -teɪt-/ *adj* cuantitativo

quantity /ˈkwɒntəti/ *n* (*pl* **-ies**) cantidad

quarantine /ˈkwɒrəntiːn; *USA* ˈkwɔːr-/ *n* cuarentena

quarrel /ˈkwɒrəl; *USA* ˈkwɔːrəl/ ◆ *n* **1** riña **2** queja LOC *Ver* PICK ◆ *vi* (**-ll-**, *USA* **-l-**) ~ (**with sb**) (**about/over sth**) reñir (con algn) (por algo) **quarrelsome** *adj* pendenciero

quarry /ˈkwɒri; *USA* ˈkwɔːri/ *n* (*pl* **-ies**) **1** presa **2** cantera

quart /kwɔːt/ *n* (*abrev* **qt**) cuarto de galón (= 1,14 litros)

quarter /ˈkwɔːtə(r)/ *n* **1** cuarto: *It's (a) quarter to/past one.* Es la una menos/y cuarto. **2** una cuarta parte: *a quarter full* lleno en una cuarta parte **3** (*recibos, etc*) trimestre **4** barrio **5** (*USA*) veinticinco centavos **6 quarters** [*pl*] (*esp Mil*) alojamiento LOC **in/from all quarters** en/de todas partes

quarter-final /ˌkwɔːtə ˈfaɪnəl/ *n* cuartos de final

quarterly /ˈkwɔːtəli/ ◆ *adj* trimestral ◆ *adv* trimestralmente ◆ *n* revista trimestral

quartet /kwɔːˈtet/ *n* cuarteto

quartz /kwɔːts/ *n* cuarzo

quash /kwɒʃ/ *vt* **1** (*sentencia*) anular **2** (*rebelión*) sofocar **3** (*rumor, sospecha, etc*) poner fin a

quay /kiː/ (*tb* **quayside**) /ˈkiːsaɪd/ *n* muelle

queen /kwiːn/ *n* **1** reina **2** (*baraja*) dama

queer /kwɪə(r)/ ◆ *adj* raro LOC *Ver* FISH ◆ *n* (*argot, ofen*) maricón ☛ *Comparar con* GAY

quell /kwel/ *vt* **1** (*revuelta, etc*) aplastar **2** (*miedo, dudas, etc*) disipar

quench /kwentʃ/ *vt* apagar (*sed, fuego, pasión*)

query /ˈkwɪəri/ ◆ *n* (*pl* **-ies**) (*pregunta*) duda: *Have you got any queries?* ¿Tienes alguna duda? ◆ *vt* (*pret, pp* **queried**) cuestionar

quest /kwest/ *n* (*fml*) búsqueda

question /ˈkwestʃən/ ◆ *n* **1** pregunta: *to ask/answer a question* hacer/responder a una pregunta **2** ~ (**of sth**) cuestión (de algo) LOC **to be out of the question** ser impensable **to bring/call sth into question** poner algo en duda *Ver tb* LOADED *en* LOAD ◆ *vt* **1** hacer preguntas a, interrogar a **2** ~ **sth** dudar de algo **questionable** *adj* dudoso

questioning /ˈkwesʃənɪŋ/ ◆ *n* interrogatorio ◆ *adj* inquisitivo, expectante

question mark *n* signo de interrogación ☛ *Ver* págs 318–19.

questionnaire /ˌkwestʃəˈneə(r)/ *n* cuestionario

queue /kjuː/ ◆ *n* cola (*de personas, etc*) LOC *Ver* JUMP ◆ *vi* ~ (**up**) hacer cola

quick /kwɪk/ ◆ *adj* (**-er**, **-est**) **1** rápido: *Be quick!* ¡Date prisa! ☛ *Ver nota en* FAST[1] **2** (*persona, mente, etc*) agudo, listo LOC **a quick temper** un genio vivo **quick march!** ¡paso ligero! **to be quick to do sth** no tardar en hacer algo *Ver tb* BUCK[3] ◆ *adv* (**-er**, **-est**) rápido, rápidamente

quicken /ˈkwɪkən/ *vt, vi* **1** acelerar(se) **2** (*ritmo, interés*) avivar(se)

quickly /ˈkwɪkli/ *adv* de prisa, rápidamente

quid /kwɪd/ *n* (*pl* **quid**) (*coloq, GB*) libra: *It's five quid each.* Son cinco libras cada uno.

quiet /ˈkwaɪət/ ◆ *adj* (**-er**, **-est**) **1** (*lugar, vida*) tranquilo **2** callado: *Be quiet!* ¡Cállate! **3** silencioso ◆ *n* **1** silencio **2** tranquilidad LOC **on the quiet** a la chita callando *Ver tb* PEACE **quieten** (*esp USA* **quiet**) *vt* ~ (**sth/sb**) (**down**) (*esp GB*) calmar (algo/a algn) PHR V **to quieten down** tranquilizarse, calmarse

quietly /ˈkwaɪətli/ *adv* **1** en silencio **2** tranquilamente **3** en voz baja

quietness /ˈkwaɪətnəs/ *n* tranquilidad

quilt /kwɪlt/ (*tb* **continental quilt**) *n* edredón

quintet /kwɪnˈtet/ *n* quinteto

quirk /kwɜːk/ *n* **1** rareza **2** capricho **quirky** *adj* extraño

quit /kwɪt/ (**-tt-**) (*pret, pp* **quit** *o* **quitted**) (*coloq*) **1** *vt, vi* (*trabajo, etc*) dejar **2** *vt* (*coloq*) ~ (**doing**) **sth** dejar (de hacer) algo **3** *vi* marcharse

quite /kwaɪt/ *adv* **1** bastante: *He played quite well.* Jugó bastante bien. **2** totalmente, absolutamente: *quite empty/sure* absolutamente vacío/seguro ◇ *She played quite brilliantly.* Tocó de maravilla. ☛ *Ver nota en* FAIRLY LOC **quite a**; **quite some** (*aprob, esp USA*) todo un: *It gave me quite a shock.* Me dio un buen susto. **quite a few** un número considerable

quiver /ˈkwɪvə(r)/ ◆ *vi* temblar, estremecerse ◆ *n* temblor, estremecimiento

quiz /kwɪz/ ◆ *n* (*pl* **quizzes**) concurso, prueba (*de conocimientos*) ◆ *vt* (**-zz-**) ~ **sb** (**about sth/sb**) interrogar a algn (sobre algo/algn) **quizzical** *adj* inquisitivo

quorum /ˈkwɔːrəm/ *n* [*gen sing*] quórum

quota /ˈkwəʊtə/ *n* **1** cupo **2** cuota, parte

quotation /kwəʊˈteɪʃn/ *n* **1** (*tb* **quote**) (*de un libro, etc*) cita **2** (*Fin*) cotización **3** presupuesto

quotation marks (*tb* **quotes**) *n* [*pl*] comillas ☛ *Ver* págs 318–19.

quote /kwəʊt/ ◆ **1** *vt, vi* citar **2** *vt* dar un presupuesto **3** *vt* cotizar ◆ *n* **1** *Ver* QUOTATION 1 **2** *Ver* QUOTATION 3 **quotes** [*pl*] *Ver* QUOTATION MARKS

iː	i	ɪ	e	æ	ɑː	ʌ	ʊ	uː
see	happy	sit	ten	hat	arm	cup	put	too

Rr

R, r /ɑː(r)/ *n* (*pl* **R's, r's** /ɑːz/) R, r: *R for Robert* R de Ramón ☛ *Ver ejemplos en* A, a

rabbit /ˈræbɪt/ *n* conejo ☛ *Ver nota en* CONEJO

rabid /ˈræbɪd/ *adj* rabioso

rabies /ˈreɪbiːz/ *n* [*incontable*] rabia (*enfermedad*)

race[1] /reɪs/ *n* raza: *race relations* relaciones raciales

race[2] /reɪs/ ◆ *n* carrera LOC *Ver* RAT ◆ **1** *vi* (*en carrera*) correr **2** *vi* correr a toda velocidad **3** *vi* competir **4** *vi* (*pulso, corazón*) latir muy rápido **5** *vt* ~ **sb** echar una carrera con algn **6** *vt* (*caballo*) hacer correr, presentar

racecourse /ˈreɪskɔːs/ (*USA* **racetrack**) *n* hipódromo

racehorse /ˈreɪshɔːs/ *n* caballo de carreras

racetrack /ˈreɪstræk/ *n* **1** circuito (de automovilismo, etc) **2** (*USA*) *Ver* RACECOURSE

racial /ˈreɪʃl/ *adj* racial

racing /ˈreɪsɪŋ/ *n* carreras: *horse racing* carreras de caballos ◊ *racing car/bike* coche/moto de carreras

racism /ˈreɪsɪzəm/ *n* racismo **racist** *adj, n* racista

rack /ræk/ ◆ *n* **1** soporte **2** (*para equipaje*) rejilla *Ver* ROOF-RACK **3 the rack** el potro ◆ *vt* LOC **to rack your brain(s)** devanarse los sesos

racket /ˈrækɪt/ *n* **1** (*tb* **racquet**) raqueta **2** alboroto **3** timo

racquet *Ver* RACKET 1

racy /ˈreɪsi/ *adj* (**racier**, **raciest**) **1** (*estilo*) vivo **2** (*chiste*) picante

radar /ˈreɪdɑː(r)/ *n* [*incontable*] radar

radiant /ˈreɪdiənt/ *adj* ~ (**with sth**) radiante (de algo): *radiant with joy* radiante de alegría **radiance** *n* resplandor

radiate /ˈreɪdieɪt/ **1** *vt, vi* (*luz, alegría*) irradiar **2** *vi* (*de un punto central*) salir

radiation /ˌreɪdiˈeɪʃn/ *n* radiación: *radiation sickness* enfermedad por radiación

radiator /ˈreɪdɪeɪtə(r)/ *n* radiador

radical /ˈrædɪkl/ *adj, n* radical

radio /ˈreɪdiəʊ/ *n* (*pl* ~**s**) radio: *radio station* emisora (de radio)

radioactive /ˌreɪdiəʊˈæktɪv/ *adj* radiactivo **radioactivity** /ˌreɪdiəʊækˈtɪvəti/ *n* radiactividad

radish /ˈrædɪʃ/ *n* rábano

radius /ˈreɪdiəs/ *n* (*pl* **radii** /-diaɪ/) radio

raffle /ˈræfl/ *n* rifa

raft /rɑːft; *USA* ræft/ *n* balsa: *life raft* balsa salvavidas

rafter /ˈrɑːftə(r); *USA* ˈræf-/ *n* viga (*del techo*)

rag /ræg/ *n* **1** trapo **2 rags** [*pl*] andrajos **3** (*coloq, pey*) periodicucho

rage /reɪdʒ/ ◆ *n* (*ira*) cólera: *to fly into a rage* montar en cólera LOC **to be all the rage** hacer furor ◆ *vi* **1** ponerse furioso **2** (*tormenta*) rugir **3** (*batalla*) continuar con furia

ragged /ˈrægɪd/ *adj* **1** (*ropa*) roto **2** (*persona*) andrajoso

raging /ˈreɪdʒɪŋ/ *adj* **1** (*dolor, sed*) atroz **2** (*mar*) enfurecido **3** (*tormenta*) violento

raid /reɪd/ ◆ *n* **1** ~ (**on sth**) ataque (contra algo) **2** ~ (**on sth**) (*robo*) asalto (a algo) **3** (*policial*) redada ◆ *vt* **1** (*policía*) registrar **2** (*fig*) saquear **raider** *n* asaltante

rail /reɪl/ *n* **1** barandilla **2** (*cortinas*) riel **3** (*Ferrocarril*) raíl **4** (*Ferrocarril*): *rail strike* huelga de ferroviarios ◊ *by rail* por ferrocarril

railing /ˈreɪlɪŋ/ (*tb* **railings**) *n* verja

railroad /ˈreɪlrəʊd/ *n* (*USA*) ferrocarril

railway /ˈreɪlweɪ/ *n* **1** ferrocarril: *railway station* estación de ferrocarril **2** (*tb* **railway line/track**) vía férrea

rain /reɪn/ ◆ *n* (*lit y fig*) lluvia: *It's pouring with rain.* Está lloviendo a cántaros. ◆ *vi* (*lit y fig*) llover: *It's raining hard.* Está lloviendo mucho.

rainbow /ˈreɪnbəʊ/ *n* arco iris

raincoat /ˈreɪnkəʊt/ *n* gabardina

rainfall /ˈreɪnfɔːl/ *n* [*incontable*] precipitaciones

rainforest /ˈreɪnfɒrɪst/ *n* selva tropical

rainy /ˈremi/ *adj* (**-ier**, **-iest**) lluvioso
raise /reɪz/ ◆ *vt* **1** levantar **2** (*salarios, precios*) subir **3** (*esperanzas*) aumentar **4** (*nivel*) mejorar **5** (*alarma*) dar **6** (*tema*) plantear **7** (*préstamo, fondos*) conseguir **8** (*niños, animales*) criar ☛ *Comparar con* EDUCATE, TO BRING SB UP *en* BRING **9** (*ejército*) reclutar LOC **to raise your eyebrows** (**at sth**) arquear las cejas (por algo) **to raise your glass** (**to sb**) alzar las copas (por algn) ◆ *n* (*USA*) aumento (*salarial*)
raisin /ˈreɪzn/ *n* pasa *Ver tb* SULTANA
rake /reɪk/ ◆ *n* **1** rastrillo **2** (*Agricultura*) rastro ◆ *vt, vi* rastrillar LOC **to rake it in** forrarse PHR V **to rake sth up** (*coloq*) sacar a relucir algo (*pasado, etc*)
rally /ˈræli/ ◆ (*pret, pp* **rallied**) **1** *vi* ~ (**round**) cerrar filas **2** *vt* ~ **sb** (**round sb**) reunir (a algn) (en torno a algn) **3** *vi* recuperarse ◆ *n* (*pl* **-ies**) **1** mitin **2** (*tenis, etc*) peloteo **3** (*coches*) rally
ram /ræm/ ◆ *n* carnero ◆ (**-mm-**) **1** *vi* **to ram into sth** chocar (con algo) **2** *vt* (*puerta, etc*) empujar con fuerza **3** *vt* **to ram sth in, into, on, etc sth** meter algo en algo a la fuerza
ramble /ˈræmbl/ ◆ *vi* ~ (**on**) (**about sth/sb**) (*fig*) divagar (acerca de algo/ algn) ◆ *n* excursión a pie **rambler** *n* excursionista **rambling** *adj* **1** laberíntico **2** (*Bot*) trepador **3** (*discurso*) que se va por las ramas
ramp /ræmp/ *n* **1** rampa **2** (*en carretera*) desnivel
rampage /ræmˈpeɪdʒ/ ◆ *vi* desmandarse ◆ /ˈræmpeɪdʒ/ *n* desmán LOC **to be/go on the rampage** desmandarse
rampant /ˈræmpənt/ *adj* **1** desenfrenado **2** (*plantas*) exuberante
ramshackle /ˈræmʃækl/ *adj* destartalado
ran *pret de* RUN
ranch /rɑːntʃ; *USA* ræntʃ/ *n* rancho, granja
rancid /ˈrænsɪd/ *adj* rancio
random /ˈrændəm/ ◆ *adj* al azar ◆ *n* LOC **at random** al azar
rang *pret de* RING²
range /reɪndʒ/ ◆ *n* **1** (*montañas*) cadena **2** gama **3** (*productos*) línea **4** escala **5** (*visión, sonido*) campo (de alcance) **6** (*armas*) alcance ◆ **1** *vi* ~ **from sth to sth** extenderse, ir desde algo hasta algo **2** *vi* ~ **from sth to sth**; ~ **between sth and sth** (*cifra*) oscilar entre algo y algo **3** *vt* alinear **4** *vi* ~ (**over/through sth**) recorrer (algo)
rank /ræŋk/ ◆ *n* **1** categoría **2** (*Mil*) grado, rango LOC **the rank and file** la base ◆ **1** *vt* ~ **sth/sb** (**as sth**) clasificar algo/a algn (como algo); considerar algo/a algn (algo) **2** *vi* situarse: *high-ranking* de alto rango
ransack /ˈrænsæk/ *vt* **1** ~ **sth** (**for sth**) volver algo patas arriba en busca de algo **2** desvalijar
ransom /ˈrænsəm/ *n* rescate LOC *Ver* HOLD
rap /ræp/ ◆ *n* **1** golpe seco **2** (*Mús*) rap ◆ *vt, vi* (**-pp-**) golpear
rape /reɪp/ ◆ *vt* violar ☛ *Ver nota en* VIOLATE ◆ *n* **1** violación **2** (*Bot*) colza **rapist** *n* violador
rapid /ˈræpɪd/ *adj* rápido **rapidity** /rəˈpɪdəti/ *n* (*fml*) rapidez **rapidly** *adv* (muy) deprisa
rapport /ræˈpɔː(r); *USA* -ˈpɔːrt/ *n* compenetración
rapt /ræpt/ *adj* ~ (**in sth**) absorto (en algo)
rapture /ˈræptʃə(r)/ *n* éxtasis **rapturous** *adj* entusiasta
rare¹ /reə(r)/ *adj* (**rarer**, **rarest**) poco común: *a rare opportunity* una ocasión poco frecuente **rarely** *adv* pocas veces ☛ *Ver nota en* ALWAYS **rarity** *n* (*pl* **-ies**) rareza
rare² /reə(r)/ *adj* poco hecho (*carne*)
rash¹ /ræʃ/ *n* sarpullido
rash² /ræʃ/ *adj* (**rasher**, **rashest**) imprudente, precipitado: *In a rash moment I promised her…* En un arrebato le prometí…
raspberry /ˈrɑːzbəri; *USA* ˈræzberi/ *n* (*pl* **-ies**) frambuesa
rat /ræt/ *n* rata LOC **the rat race** (*coloq, pey*) la carrera de la vida moderna
rate¹ /reɪt/ *n* **1** razón (*proporción*): *at a rate of 50 a/per week* a razón de cincuenta por semana ◊ *the exchange rate/the rate of exchange* el tipo de cambio **2** tarifa: *an hourly rate of pay* una tarifa por hora ◊ *interest rate* el tipo de interés LOC **at any rate** de todos modos **at this/that rate** (*coloq*) a este/ ese paso
rate² /reɪt/ **1** *vt, vi* estimar, valorar

highly rated tenido en gran estima **2** *vt* considerar como

rather /ˈrɑːðə(r); *USA* ˈræð-/ *adv* algo, bastante: *I rather suspect...* Me inclino a sospechar...

Rather con una palabra de sentido positivo implica sorpresa por parte del hablante: *It was a rather nice present.* Fue un regalo realmente estupendo. También se utiliza cuando queremos criticar algo: *This room looks rather untidy.* Esta habitación está bastante desordenada. ☛ *Ver nota en* FAIRLY

LOC **I'd, you'd, etc rather...(than)**: *I'd rather walk than wait for the bus.* Prefiero ir andando a esperar el autobús. **or rather** o mejor dicho **rather than** *prep* mejor que

rating /ˈreɪtɪŋ/ *n* **1** clasificación: *a high/low popularity rating* un nivel alto/bajo de popularidad **2 the ratings** [*pl*] (*TV*) los niveles de popularidad

ratio /ˈreɪʃiəʊ/ *n* (*pl* ~**s**) ratio: *The ratio of boys to girls in this class is three to one.* La ratio de niños y niñas en esta clase es de tres a una.

ration /ˈræʃn/ ◆ *n* ración ◆ *vt* ~ **sth/sb (to sth)** racionar algo/a algn (a algo) **rationing** *n* racionamiento

rational /ˈræʃnəl/ *adj* racional, razonable **rationality** /ræʃəˈnæləti/ *n* racionalidad **rationalization, -isation** *n* racionalización **rationalize, -ise** *vt* racionalizar

rattle /ˈrætl/ ◆ **1** *vt* hacer sonar **2** *vi* hacer ruido, tintinear PHR V **rattle along, off, past, etc** traquetear **to rattle sth off** farfullar algo ◆ *n* **1** traqueteo **2** carraca, sonajero

ravage /ˈrævɪdʒ/ *vt* devastar

rave /reɪv/ *vi* **1** ~ **(at/against/about sth/sb)** despotricar (contra algo/algn) **2** ~ **(on) about sth/sb** (*coloq*) poner por las nubes algo/a algn

raven /ˈreɪvn/ *n* cuervo

raw /rɔː/ *adj* **1** crudo **2** sin refinar: *raw silk* seda bruta ◊ *raw material* materia prima **3** (*herida*) en carne viva

ray /reɪ/ *n* rayo: *X-rays* rayos X

razor /ˈreɪzə(r)/ *n* maquinilla/navaja de afeitar

razor blade *n* cuchilla de afeitar

reach /riːtʃ/ ◆ **1** *vi* ~ **for sth** alargar la mano para coger algo **2** *vi* ~ **out (to sth/sb)** alargar la mano (a algo/algn) **3** *vt* alcanzar **4** *vt* localizar **5** *vt* llegar a: *to reach an agreement* llegar a un acuerdo ◆ *n* LOC **beyond/out of/within (your) reach** fuera del alcance/al alcance (de algn) **within (easy) reach (of sth/sb)** a corta distancia (de algo/algn)

react /riˈækt/ *vi* **1** ~ **(to sth/sb)** reaccionar (a/ante algo/algn) **2** ~ **(against sth/sb)** oponerse (a algo/algn) **reaction** *n* ~ **(to sth/sb)** reacción (a/ante algo/algn) **reactionary** *adj* reaccionario

reactor /riˈæktə(r)/ *n* **1** (*tb* **nuclear reactor**) reactor nuclear **2** reactor

read /riːd/ (*pret, pp* **read** /red/) **1** *vt, vi* ~ **(about/of sth/sb)** leer (sobre algo/algn) **2** *vt* ~ **sth (as sth)** interpretar algo (como algo) **3** *vi* (*telegrama, etc*) decir, rezar **4** *vi* (*contador, etc*) marcar PHR V **to read on** seguir leyendo **to read sth into sth** atribuir algo a algo **to read sth out** leer algo en voz alta **readable** *adj* leíble **reading** *n* lectura: *reading glasses* gafas para leer

reader /ˈriːdə(r)/ *n* lector, -ora **readership** *n* [*incontable*] número de lectores

ready /ˈredi/ *adj* (**-ier**, **-iest**) **1** ~ **(for sth/to do sth)** listo, preparado (para algo/para hacer algo): *to get ready* prepararse **2** ~ **(to do sth)** dispuesto (a hacer algo): *He's always ready to help his friends.* Siempre está dispuesto a ayudar a sus amigos. **3** ~ **to do sth** a punto de hacer algo **4** a mano **readily** *adv* **1** de buena gana **2** fácilmente **readiness** *n* disposición: *(to do sth) in readiness for sth* (hacer algo) en preparación de algo ◊ *her readiness to help* su disposición para ayudar

ready-made /ˈredi meɪd/ *adj* **1** (*ropa, etc*) de confección **2** ya hecho: *You can buy ready-made curtains.* Puedes comprar cortinas ya hechas.

real /ˈriːəl/ *adj* **1** real, verdadero: *real life* la vida real **2** verdadero, auténtico: *That's not his real name.* Ese no es su nombre verdadero. ◊ *The meal was a real disaster.* La comida fue un verdadero desastre.

realism /ˈriːəlɪzəm/ *n* realismo **realist** *n* realista **realistic** /ˌriːəˈlɪstɪk/ *adj* realista

reality /riˈæləti/ *n* (*pl* **-ies**) realidad LOC **in reality** en realidad

realize, -ise /ˈriːəlaɪz/ *vt* **1** ~ **sth** darse

cuenta de algo: *Not realizing that…* Sin darse cuenta de que… **2** (*plan, ambición*) cumplir **realization, -isation** *n* comprensión

really /ˈriːəli/ *adv* **1** [+ *verbo*] de verdad: *I really mean that.* Te lo digo de verdad. **2** [+ *adj*] muy, realmente: *Is it really true?* ¿Es realmente cierto? **3** (*expresa sorpresa, interés, duda, etc*): *Really?* ¿En serio?

realm /relm/ *n* (*fig*), terreno: *the realms of possibility* el ámbito de lo posible

reap /riːp/ *vt* segar

reappear /ˌriːəˈpɪə(r)/ *vi* reaparecer **reappearance** *n* reaparición

rear[1] /rɪə(r)/ **the rear** *n* [*sing*] (*fml*) la parte trasera: *a rear window* una ventana trasera LOC *Ver* BRING

rear[2] /rɪə(r)/ **1** *vt* criar **2** *vi* ~ (**up**) (*caballo*) encabritarse **3** *vt* erguir

rearrange /ˌriːəˈreɪndʒ/ *vt* **1** arreglar, cambiar **2** (*planes*) volver a organizar

reason /ˈriːzn/ ◆ *n* **1** ~ (**for sth/doing sth**) razón, motivo (de/para algo/para hacer algo) **2** ~ (**why…/that…**) razón, motivo (por la/el que…/de que…) **3** razón, sentido común LOC **by reason of sth** (*fml*) en virtud de algo **in/within reason** dentro de lo razonable **to make sb see reason** hacer entrar en razón a algn *Ver tb* STAND ◆ *vi* razonar **reasonable** *adj* **1** razonable, sensato **2** tolerable, regular **reasonably** *adv* **1** bastante **2** con sensatez **reasoning** *n* razonamiento

reassure /ˌriːəˈʃʊə(r)/ *vt* tranquilizar **reassurance** *n* **1** consuelo, tranquilidad **2** palabras tranquilizadoras **reassuring** *adj* tranquilizador

rebate /ˈriːbeɪt/ *n* bonificación

rebel /ˈrebl/ ◆ *n* rebelde ◆ /rɪˈbel/ *vi* (**-ll-**) rebelarse **rebellion** /rɪˈbeljən/ *n* rebelión **rebellious** /rɪˈbeljəs/ *adj* rebelde

rebirth /ˌriːˈbɜːθ/ *n* **1** renacimiento **2** resurgimiento

rebound /rɪˈbaʊnd/ ◆ *vi* **1** ~ (**from/off sth**) rebotar (en algo) **2** ~ (**on sb**) repercutir (en algn) ◆ /ˈriːbaʊnd/ *n* rebote LOC **on the rebound** de rebote

rebuff /rɪˈbʌf/ ◆ *n* **1** desaire **2** rechazo ◆ *vt* **1** desairar **2** rechazar

rebuild /ˌriːˈbɪld/ *vt* (*pret, pp* **rebuilt** /ˌriːˈbɪlt/) reconstruir

rebuke /rɪˈbjuːk/ ◆ *vt* reprender ◆ *n* reprimenda

recall /rɪˈkɔːl/ *vt* **1** llamar **2** (*embajador, etc*) retirar **3** (*libro*) reclamar **4** (*parlamento*) convocar **5** recordar *Ver tb* REMEMBER

recapture /ˌriːˈkæptʃə(r)/ *vt* **1** recobrar, reconquistar **2** (*fig*) revivir, reproducir

recede /rɪˈsiːd/ *vi* **1** retroceder: *receding chin* barbilla retraída ◇ *receding hair(line)* entradas **2** (*marea*) bajar

receipt /rɪˈsiːt/ *n* **1** ~ (**for sth**) (*fml*) recibo (de algo): *to acknowledge receipt of sth* acusar recibo de algo ◇ *a receipt for your expenses* un recibo de tus gastos **2 receipts** [*pl*] ingresos

receive /rɪˈsiːv/ *vt* **1** recibir, acoger **2** (*herida*) sufrir

receiver /rɪˈsiːvə(r)/ *n* **1** (*radio, TV*) receptor **2** (*teléfono*) auricular: *to lift/pick up the receiver* descolgar (el receptor) **3** destinatario, -a

recent /ˈriːsnt/ *adj* reciente: *in recent years* en los últimos años **recently** *adv* **1** recientemente: *until recently* hasta hace poco **2** (*tb* **recently-**) recién: *a recently-appointed director* una directora recién nombrada

reception /rɪˈsepʃn/ *n* **1** recepción: *reception desk* (mesa de) recepción **2** acogida **receptionist** *n* recepcionista

receptive /rɪˈseptɪv/ *adj* ~ (**to sth**) receptivo (a algo)

recess /rɪˈses; *USA* ˈriːses/ *n* **1** (*parlamento*) periodo de vacaciones **2** descanso **3** (*USA*) (*en escuela*) recreo **4** (*nicho*) hueco **5** [*gen pl*] escondrijo, lugar recóndito

recession /rɪˈseʃn/ *n* recesión

recharge /ˌriːˈtʃɑːdʒ/ *vt* recargar

recipe /ˈresəpi/ *n* **1** ~ (**for sth**) (*cocina*) receta (de algo) **2** ~ **for sth** (*fig*) receta para/de algo

recipient /rɪˈsɪpiənt/ *n* **1** destinatario, -a **2** (*dinero, etc*) beneficiario, -a

reciprocal /rɪˈsɪprəkl/ *adj* recíproco

reciprocate /rɪˈsɪprəkeɪt/ *vt* (*fml*) *vi* corresponder

recital /rɪˈsaɪtl/ *n* recital

recite /rɪˈsaɪt/ *vt* **1** recitar **2** enumerar

reckless /ˈrekləs/ *adj* **1** temerario **2** imprudente

reckon /ˈrekən/ *vt* **1** considerar **2** creer

3 calcular PHR V **to reckon on sth/sb** contar con algo/algn **to reckon with sth/sb** contar con algn, tomar algo en consideración: *There is still your father to reckon with.* Todavía hay que vérselas con tu padre. **reckoning** *n* [*sing*] **1** cálculos: *by my reckoning* según mis cálculos **2** cuentas

reclaim /rɪˈkleɪm/ *vt* **1** recuperar **2** (*materiales, etc*) reciclar **reclamation** *n* recuperación

recline /rɪˈklaɪn/ *vt, vi* reclinar(se), recostar(se) **reclining** *adj* reclinable (*silla*)

recognition /ˌrekəgˈnɪʃn/ *n* reconocimiento: *in recognition of sth* en reconocimiento a algo ◊ *to have changed beyond recognition* estar irreconocible

recognize, -ise /ˈrekəgnaɪz/ *vt* reconocer **recognizable, -isable** *adj* reconocible

recoil /rɪˈkɔɪl/ *vi* **1** ~ **(at/from sth/sb)** sentir repugnancia (ante algo/algn) **2** retroceder

recollect /ˌrekəˈlekt/ *vt* recordar **recollection** *n* recuerdo

recommend /ˌrekəˈmend/ *vt* recomendar

recompense /ˈrekəmpens/ ◆ *vt* (*fml*) ~ **sb (for sth)** recompensar a algn (por algo) ◆ *n* (*fml*) [*sing*] recompensa

reconcile /ˈrekənsaɪl/ *vt* **1** reconciliar **2** ~ **sth (with sth)** conciliar algo (con algo) **3** *to reconcile yourself to sth* resignarse a algo **reconciliation** *n* [*sing*] **1** conciliación **2** reconciliación

reconnaissance /rɪˈkɒnɪsns/ *n* reconocimiento (*Mil, etc*)

reconsider /ˌriːkənˈsɪdə(r)/ **1** *vt* reconsiderar **2** *vi* recapacitar

reconstruct /ˌriːkənˈstrʌkt/ *vt* ~ **sth (from sth)** reconstruir algo (a partir de algo)

record /ˈrekɔːd; *USA* ˈrekərd/ ◆ *n* **1** registro: *to make/keep a record of sth* hacer/llevar un registro de algo **2** historial: *a criminal record* antecedentes penales **3** disco: *a record company* una casa discográfica **4** récord: *to beat/break a record* batir/superar un récord LOC **to put/set the record straight** dejar/poner las cosas claras ◆ /rɪˈkɔːd/ *vt* **1** registrar, anotar **2** ~ **(sth) (from sth) (on sth)** grabar (algo) (de algo) (en algo) **3** (*termómetro, etc*) marcar

record-breaking /ˈrekɔːd breɪkɪŋ/ *adj* sin precedentes

recorder /rɪˈkɔːdə(r)/ *n* **1** flauta dulce **2** *Ver* TAPE RECORDER, VIDEO

recording /rɪˈkɔːdɪŋ/ *n* grabación

record player *n* tocadiscos

recount /rɪˈkaʊnt/ *vt* ~ **sth (to sb)** referir algo (a algn)

recourse /rɪˈkɔːs/ *n* recurso LOC **to have recourse to sth/sb** (*fml*) recurrir a algo/algn

recover /rɪˈkʌvə(r)/ **1** *vt* recuperar, recobrar: *to recover consciousness* recobrar el conocimiento **2** *vi* ~ **(from sth)** recuperarse, reponerse (de algo)

recovery /rɪˈkʌvəri/ *n* **1** (*pl* **-ies**) recuperación, rescate **2** [*sing*] ~ **(from sth)** restablecimiento (de algo)

recreation /ˌrekriˈeɪʃn/ *n* **1** pasatiempo, esparcimiento **2** (hora del) recreo: *recreation ground* campo de deportes

recruit /rɪˈkruːt/ ◆ *n* recluta ◆ *vt* ~ **sb (as/to sth)** reclutar a algn (como/para algo) **recruitment** *n* reclutamiento

rectangle /ˈrektæŋgl/ *n* rectángulo

rector /ˈrektə(r)/ *n* párroco *Ver tb* VICAR **rectory** *n* casa del párroco

recuperate /rɪˈkuːpəreɪt/ **1** (*fml*) *vi* ~ **(from sth)** recuperarse, reponerse (de algo) **2** *vt* recuperar

recur /rɪˈkɜː(r)/ *vi* (**-rr-**) repetirse, volver a aparecer

recycle /ˌriːˈsaɪkl/ *vt* reciclar **recyclable** *adj* reciclable **recycling** *n* reciclaje

red /red/ ◆ *adj* (**redder**, **reddest**) **1** rojo: *a red dress* un vestido rojo **2** (*rostro*) colorado **3** (*vino*) tinto LOC **a red herring** una pista falsa ◆ *n* rojo: *The traffic lights are on red.* El semáforo está en rojo. **reddish** *adj* rojizo

redeem /rɪˈdiːm/ *vt* **1** redimir: *to redeem yourself* salvarse **2** recompensar **3** ~ **sth (from sth/sb)** desempeñar algo (de algo/algn)

redemption /rɪˈdempʃn/ *n* (*fml*) redención

redevelopment /ˌriːdɪˈveləpmənt/ *n* nueva edificación, reurbanización

redo /ˌriːˈduː/ *vt* (*pret* **redid** /-ˈdɪd/ *pp* **redone** /-ˈdʌn/) rehacer

red tape *n* papeleo

reduce /rɪˈdjuːs; *USA* -ˈduːs/ **1** *vt* ~ **sth**

(**from sth to sth**) reducir, disminuir algo (de algo a algo) **2** *vt* ~ **sth** (**by sth**) disminuir, rebajar algo (en algo) **3** *vi* reducirse **4** *vt* ~ **sth/sb** (**from sth**) **to sth**: *The house was reduced to ashes.* La casa se redujo a cenizas. ◊ *to reduce sb to tears* hacer llorar a algn **reduced** *adj* rebajado

reduction /rɪˈdʌkʃn/ *n* **1** ~ (**in sth**) reducción (de algo) **2** ~ (**of sth**) rebaja, descuento ~ (de algo): *a reduction of 5%* un descuento del 5%

redundancy /rɪˈdʌndənsi/ *n* (*pl* **-ies**) despido (*por cierre de empresa o reducción de plantilla*): *redundancy pay* indemnización por despido

redundant /rɪˈdʌndənt/ *adj* **1** *to be made redundant* ser despedido por cierre de empresa o reducción de plantilla **2** superfluo

reed /riːd/ *n* junco

reef /riːf/ *n* arrecife

reek /riːk/ *vi* (*pey*) ~ (**of sth**) (*lit y fig*) apestar (a algo)

reel /riːl/ ◆ *n* **1** bobina, carrete **2** (*película*) rollo ◆ *vi* **1** tambalearse **2** (*cabeza*) dar vueltas PHR V **to reel sth off** recitar algo (de una tirada)

re-enter /ˌriː ˈentə(r)/ *vt* ~ **sth** volver a entrar, reingresar en algo **re-entry** *n* reentrada

refer /rɪˈfɜː(r)/ (**-rr-**) **1** *vi* ~ **to sth/sb** referirse a algo/algn **2** *vt, vi* remitir(se)

referee /ˌrefəˈriː/ ◆ *n* **1** (*Dep*) árbitro, -a **2** juez árbitro **3** (*GB*) (*para empleo*) persona que da referencias ◆ *vt, vi* arbitrar

reference /ˈrefərəns/ *n* referencia LOC **in/with reference to sth/sb** (*esp Com*) en/con referencia a algo/algn

referendum /ˌrefəˈrendəm/ *n* (*pl* ~**s**) referéndum

refill /ˌriːˈfɪl/ ◆ *vt* rellenar ◆ /ˈriːfɪl/ *n* relleno, recambio

refine /rɪˈfaɪn/ *vt* **1** refinar **2** (*modelo, técnica, etc*) pulir **refinement** *n* **1** refinamiento **refinery** *n* (*pl* **-ies**) **1** refinería **2** (*Mec*) refinación **3** sutileza

reflect /rɪˈflekt/ **1** *vt* reflejar **2** *vt* (*luz*) reflectar **3** *vi* ~ (**on/upon sth**) reflexionar (en algo) LOC **to reflect on sth/sb**: *to reflect well/badly on sth/sb* decir mucho/poco en favor de algo/algn **reflection** (*GB tb* **reflexion**) *n* **1** reflejo **2** (*acto, pensamiento*) reflexión LOC **on reflection** pensándolo bien **to be a reflection on sth/sb** dar mala impresión de algo/algn

reflex /ˈriːfleks/ (*tb* **reflex action**) *n* reflejo

reform /rɪˈfɔːm/ ◆ *vt, vi* reformar(se) ◆ *n* reforma **reformation** *n* **1** reforma **2** **the Reformation** la Reforma

refrain[1] /rɪˈfreɪn/ *n* (*fml*) estribillo

refrain[2] /rɪˈfreɪn/ *vi* (*fml*) ~ (**from sth**) abstenerse (de algo): *Please refrain from smoking in the hospital.* Por favor absténganse de fumar en el hospital.

refresh /rɪˈfreʃ/ *vt* refrescar LOC **to refresh sb's memory** (**about sth/sb**) refrescar la memoria a algn (sobre algo/algn) **refreshing** *adj* **1** refrescante **2** (*fig*) alentador

refreshments /rɪˈfreʃməntz/ *n* [*pl*] refrigerios: *The restaurant offers delicious meals and refreshments.* El restaurante ofrece deliciosas comidas y refrigerios.

> **Refreshment** se usa en singular cuando va delante de otro sustantivo: *There will be a refreshment stop.* Habrá una parada para tomar algo.

refrigerate /rɪˈfrɪdʒəreɪt/ *vt* refrigerar **refrigeration** *n* refrigeración

refrigerator /rɪˈfrɪdʒəreɪtə(r)/ (*coloq* **fridge** /frɪdʒ/) *n* frigorífico *Ver tb* FREEZER

refuge /ˈrefjuːdʒ/ *n* **1** ~ (**from sth/sb**) refugio (de algo/algn): *to take refuge* refugiarse **2** (*Pol*) asilo ☛ *Comparar con* ASYLUM

refugee /ˌrefjuˈdʒiː; *USA* ˈrefjʊdʒɪː/ *n* refugiado, -a

refund /riˈfʌnd/ ◆ *vt* reembolsar ◆ /ˈriːfʌnd/ *n* reembolso

refusal /rɪˈfjuːzl/ *n* **1** denegación, rechazo **2** ~ (**to do sth**) negativa (a hacer algo)

refuse[1] /rɪˈfjuːz/ **1** *vt* rechazar, rehusar: *to refuse an offer* rechazar una oferta ◊ *to refuse (sb) entry/entry (to sb)* negar la entrada (a algn) **2** *vi* ~ (**to do sth**) negarse (a hacer algo)

refuse[2] /ˈrefjuːs/ *n* [*incontable*] desperdicios

regain /rɪˈgeɪn/ *vt* recuperar: *to regain consciousness* recobrar el conocimiento

regal /ˈriːgl/ *adj* regio

regard /rɪˈgɑːd/ ◆ *vt* **1** ~ **sth/sb as sth**

considerar algo/a algn algo **2** (*fml*) ~ **sth/sb (with sth)** mirar algo/a algn (con algo) LOC **as regards sth/sb** en/por lo que se refiere a algo/algn ◆ *n* **1** ~ **to/for sth/sb** respeto a/por algo/algn: *with no regard for/to speed limits* sin respetar los límites de velocidad **2 regards** [*pl*] (*en cartas*) saludos LOC **in this/that/one regard** en este/ese/un aspecto **in/with regard to sth/sb** con respecto a algo/algn **regarding** *prep* referente a **regardless** *adv* (*coloq*) pase lo que pase **regardless of** *prep* sea cual sea, sin tener en cuenta

regime /reɪˈʒiːm, ˈreʒiːm/ *n* régimen (*gobierno, reglas, etc*) ☛ *Comparar con* DIET

regiment /ˈredʒɪmənt/ *n* [*v sing o pl*] regimiento **regimented** *adj* reglamentado

region /ˈriːdʒən/ *n* región LOC **in the region of sth** alrededor de algo

register /ˈredʒɪstə(r)/ ◆ *n* **1** registro **2** (*en el colegio*) lista: *to call the register* pasar lista ◆ **1** *vt* ~ **sth (in sth)** registrar algo (en algo) **2** *vi* ~ **(at/for/with sth)** matricularse, inscribirse (en/para/con algo) **3** *vt* (*cifras, etc*) registrar **4** *vt* (*sorpresa, etc*) acusar, mostrar **5** *vt* (*correo*) mandar certificado

registered post *n* correo certificado: *to send sth by registered post* mandar algo por correo certificado

registrar /ˌredʒɪˈstrɑː(r), ˈredʒɪstrɑː(r)/ *n* **1** funcionario, -a (*del registro civil, etc*) **2** (*Educ*) vicerrector, -ora (*al cargo de matriculación, exámenes, etc*)

registration /ˌredʒɪˈstreɪʃn/ *n* **1** matriculación **2** inscripción

registration number *n* número de la matrícula

registry office /ˈredʒɪstri ɒfɪs/ (*tb* **register office**) *n* registro civil

regret /rɪˈgret/ ◆ *n* **1** ~ **(at/about sth)** pesar (por algo) **2** ~ **(for sth)** remordimiento (por algo) ◆ *vt* (**-tt-**) **1** lamentar **2** arrepentirse de **regretfully** *adv* con pesar, con pena **regrettable** *adj* lamentable

regular /ˈregjələ(r)/ ◆ *adj* **1** regular: *to take regular exercise* hacer ejercicio con regularidad **2** habitual LOC **on a regular basis** con regularidad ◆ *n* cliente habitual **regularity** /ˌregjuˈlærəti/ *n* regularidad **regularly** *adv* **1** regularmente **2** con regularidad

regulate /ˈregjuleɪt/ *vt* regular, reglamentar **regulation** *n* **1** regulación **2** [*gen pl*] norma: *safety regulations* normas de seguridad

rehabilitate /ˌriːəˈbɪlɪteɪt/ *vt* rehabilitar **rehabilitation** *n* rehabilitación

rehearse /rɪˈhɜːs/ *vt, vi* ~ **(sb) (for sth)** ensayar (con algn) (algo) **rehearsal** *n* ensayo: *a dress rehearsal* un ensayo general

reign /reɪn/ ◆ *n* reinado ◆ *vi* ~ **(over sth/sb)** reinar (sobre algo/algn)

reimburse /ˌriːɪmˈbɜːs/ *vt* **1** ~ **sth (to sb)** reembolsar algo (a algn) **2** ~ **sb (for sth)** reembolsar a algn (los gastos de algo)

rein /reɪn/ *n* rienda

reindeer /ˈreɪndɪə(r)/ *n* (*pl* **reindeer**) reno

reinforce /ˌriːɪnˈfɔːs/ *vt* reforzar **reinforcement** *n* **1** consolidación, refuerzo **2 reinforcements** [*pl*] (*Mil*) refuerzos

reinstate /ˌriːɪnˈsteɪt/ *vt* (*fml*) ~ **sth/sb (in/as sth)** restituir algo/a algn (en algo)

reject /rɪˈdʒekt/ ◆ *vt* rechazar ◆ /ˈriːdʒekt/ *n* **1** marginado, -a **2** cosa defectuosa **rejection** *n* rechazo

rejoice /rɪˈdʒɔɪs/ *vi* (*fml*) ~ **(at/in/over sth)** alegrarse, regocijarse (por/de algo)

rejoin /ˌriːˈdʒɔɪn/ *vt* **1** reincorporarse a **2** volver a juntarse con

relapse /rɪˈlæps/ ◆ *vi* recaer ◆ *n* recaída

relate /rɪˈleɪt/ **1** *vt* ~ **sth (to sb)** (*fml*) relatar algo (a algn) **2** *vt* ~ **sth to/with sth** relacionar algo con algo **3** *vi* ~ **to sth/sb** estar relacionado con algo/algn **4** *vi* ~ **(to sth/sb)** (*entender*) identificarse (con algo/algn) **related** *adj* **1** relacionado **2** ~ **(to sb)** emparentado (con algn): *to be related by marriage* ser pariente(s) político(s)

relation /rɪˈleɪʃn/ *n* **1** ~ **(to sth/between ...)** relación (con algo/entre ...) **2** pariente, -a **3** parentesco: *What relation are you?* ¿Que parentesco tenéis? ◇ *Is he any relation (to you)?* ¿Es familiar tuyo? LOC **in/with relation to** (*fml*) con relación a *Ver tb* BEAR[2] **relationship** *n* **1** ~ **(between A and B)**; ~ **(of A to/with B)** relación entre A y B **2** (relación de) parentesco **3** relación (*sentimental o sexual*)

relative /ˈrelətɪv/ ◆ *n* pariente, -a ◆ *adj* relativo

relax /rɪˈlæks/ **1** *vt, vi* relajar(se) **2** *vt* aflojar **relaxation** *n* **1** relajación **2** descanso **3** pasatiempo **relaxing** *adj* relajante

relay /ˈriːleɪ/ ◆ *n* **1** relevo, tanda **2** (*tb* **relay race**) carrera de relevos ◆ /ˈriːleɪ, rɪˈleɪ/ *vt* (*pret, pp* **relayed**) **1** transmitir **2** (*GB, TV, Radio*) retransmitir

release /rɪˈliːs/ ◆ *vt* **1** liberar **2** poner en libertad **3** soltar: *to release your grip on sth/sb* soltar algo/a algn **4** (*noticia*) dar a conocer **5** (*disco*) poner a la venta **6** (*película*) estrenar ◆ *n* **1** liberación **2** puesta en libertad **3** (*acto*) aparición (*de un disco, etc*), publicación, estreno: *The film is on general release.* Pasan la película en todos los cines.

relegate /ˈrelɪgeɪt/ *vt* **1** relegar **2** (*esp GB, Dep*) bajar **relegation** *n* **1** relegación **2** (*Dep*) descenso

relent /rɪˈlent/ *vi* ceder **relentless** *adj* **1** implacable **2** (*ambición*) tenaz

relevant /ˈreləvənt/ *adj* pertinente, que viene al caso **relevance** (*tb* **relevancy**) *n* pertinencia

reliable /rɪˈlaɪəbl/ *adj* **1** (*persona*) de confianza **2** (*datos*) fiable **3** (*fuente*) fidedigno **4** (*método, aparato*) seguro **reliability** /rɪˌlaɪəˈbɪləti/ *n* fiabilidad

reliance /rɪˈlaɪəns/ *n* ~ **on sth/sb** dependencia de algo/algn; confianza en algo/algn

relic /ˈrelɪk/ *n* reliquia

relief /rɪˈliːf/ *n* **1** alivio: *much to my relief* para mi consuelo **2** ayuda, auxilio **3** (*persona*) relevo **4** (*Arte, Geog*) relieve

relieve /rɪˈliːv/ **1** *vt* aliviar **2** *v refl* ~ **yourself** (*eufemismo*) hacer uno sus necesidades **3** *vt* relevar PHR V **to relieve sb of sth** quitar algo a algn

religion /rɪˈlɪdʒən/ *n* religión **religious** *adj* religioso

relinquish /rɪˈlɪŋkwɪʃ/ *vt* (*fml*) **1** ~ **sth** (**to sb**) renunciar a algo (en favor de algn) **2** abandonar ☛ La palabra más normal es **give sth up**.

relish /ˈrelɪʃ/ ◆ *n* ~ (**for sth**) gusto (por algo) ◆ *vt* ~ **sth** disfrutar algo

reluctant /rɪˈlʌktənt/ *adj* ~ (**to do sth**) reacio (a hacer algo) **reluctance** *n* desgana **reluctantly** *adv* de mala gana

rely /rɪˈlaɪ/ *v* (*pret, pp* **relied**) PHR V **to rely on/upon sth/sb** (**to do sth**) depender de, confiar en, contar con algo/algn (para hacer algo)

remain /rɪˈmeɪn/ (*fml*) *vi* **1** quedar(se) ☛ La palabra más normal es **stay**. **2** (*continuar*) permanecer, seguir siendo **remainder** *n* [*sing*] resto (*tb Mat*) **remains** *n* [*pl*] **1** restos **2** ruinas

remand /rɪˈmɑːnd; *USA* -ˈmænd/ ◆ *vt*: *to remand sb in custody/on bail* poner a algn en prisión preventiva/en libertad bajo fianza ◆ *n* custodia LOC **on remand** detenido, -a

remark /rɪˈmɑːk/ ◆ *vt* comentar, mencionar PHR V **to remark on/upon sth/sb** hacer un comentario sobre algo/algn ◆ *n* comentario **remarkable** *adj* **1** extraordinario **2** ~ (**for sth**) notable (por algo)

remedial /rɪˈmiːdiəl/ *adj* **1** (*acción, medidas*) reparador, rectificador **2** (*clases*) para niños con dificultades de aprendizaje

remedy /ˈremədi/ ◆ *n* (*pl* **-ies**) remedio ◆ *vt* (*pret, pp* **-died**) remediar

remember /rɪˈmembə(r)/ *vt, vi* acordarse (de): *as far as I remember* que yo recuerde ◊ *Remember that we have visitors tonight.* Recuerda que tenemos visita esta noche. ◊ *Remember to phone your mother.* Acuérdate de llamar a tu madre.

> **Remember** varía de significado según se use con infinitivo o con una forma en **-ing**. Cuando va seguido de infinitivo, éste hace referencia a una acción que todavía no se ha realizado: *Remember to post that letter.* Acuérdate de echar esa carta. Cuando se usa seguido por una forma en **-ing**, éste se refiere a una acción que ya ha tenido lugar: *I remember posting that letter.* Recuerdo haber echado esa carta al correo.

PHR V **to remember sb to sb** dar recuerdos de algn a algn: *Remember me to Anna.* Dale recuerdos de mi parte a Anna. *Comparar con* REMIND **remembrance** *n* conmemoración, recuerdo

remind /rɪˈmaɪnd/ *vt* ~ **sb** (**to do sth**) recordar a algn (que haga algo): *Remind me to phone my mother.* Recuérdame que llame a mi madre. ☛ *Com* *parar con 'Remember to phone your mother' en* REMEMBER PHR V **to remind sb of sth/sb**

La construcción **to remind sb of sth/sb** se utiliza cuando una cosa o una persona te recuerdan a algo o a alguien: *Your brother reminds me of John.* Tu hermano me recuerda a John. ◊ *That song reminds me of my first girlfriend.* Esa canción me recuerda a mi primera novia.

reminder *n* **1** recuerdo, recordatorio **2** aviso

reminisce /ˌremɪˈnɪs/ *vi* ~ (**about sth**) rememorar (algo)

reminiscent /ˌremɪˈnɪsnt/ *adj* ~ **of sth/sb** con reminiscencias de algo/algn **reminiscence** *n* recuerdo, evocación

remnant /ˈremnənt/ *n* **1** resto **2** (*fig*) vestigio **3** retal (*tela*)

remorse /rɪˈmɔːs/ *n* [*incontable*] ~ (**for sth**) remordimiento (por algo) **remorseless** *adj* **1** despiadado **2** implacable

remote /rɪˈməʊt/ *adj* (**-er**, **-est**) **1** (*lit y fig*) remoto, lejano, alejado **2** (*persona*) distante **3** (*posibilidad*) remoto **remotely** *adv* remotamente

remove /rɪˈmuːv/ *vt* **1** ~ **sth** (**from sth**) quitar(se) algo (de algo): *to remove your coat* quitarse el abrigo ☛ Es más normal decir **take off**, **take out**, etc. **2** (*fig*) eliminar **3** ~ **sb** (**from sth**) sacar, destituir a algn (de algo) **removable** *adj* que se puede quitar **removal** *n* **1** eliminación **2** mudanza

the Renaissance /rɪˈneɪsns; *USA* ˈrenəsɑːns/ *n* el Renacimiento

render /ˈrendə(r)/ *vt* (*fml*) **1** (*servicio, etc*) prestar **2** hacer: *She was rendered speechless.* Quedó estupefacta. **3** (*Mús, Arte*) interpretar

rendezvous /ˈrɒndɪvuː/ *n* (*pl* **rendezvous** /-z/) **1** cita *Ver tb* APPOINTMENT *en* APPOINT **2** lugar de reunión

renegade /ˈrenɪgeɪd/ *n* (*fml, pey*) renegado, -a, rebelde

renew /rɪˈnjuː; *USA* -ˈnuː/ *vt* **1** renovar **2** (*reestablecer*) reanudar **3** reafirmar **renewable** *adj* renovable **renewal** *n* renovación

renounce /rɪˈnaʊns/ *vt* (*fml*) renunciar a: *He renounced his right to be king.* Renunció a su derecho al trono.

renovate /ˈrenəveɪt/ *vt* restaurar

renowned /rɪˈnaʊnd/ *adj* ~ (**as/for sth**) famoso (como/por algo)

rent /rent/ ◆ *n* alquiler LOC **for rent** (*esp USA*) se alquila(n) ☛ *Ver nota en* ALQUILAR ◆ *vt* **1** ~ **sth** (**from sb**) alquilar algo (de algn): *I rent a garage from a neighbour.* Un vecino me alquila su garaje. **2** ~ **sth** (**out**) (**to sb**) alquilar algo (a algn): *We rented out the house to some students.* Les alquilamos nuestra casa a unos estudiantes. **rental** *n* alquiler (*coches, electrodomésticos, etc*)

reorganize, -ise /ˌriˈɔːgənaɪz/ *vt, vi* reorganizar(se)

rep /rep/ *n* (*coloq*) *Ver* REPRESENTATIVE

repaid *pret, pp de* REPAY

repair /rɪˈpeə(r)/ ◆ *vt* **1** reparar *Ver tb* FIX, MEND **2** remediar ◆ *n* reparación: *It's beyond repair.* No tiene arreglo. LOC **in a good state of/in good repair** en buen estado

repay /rɪˈpeɪ/ *vt* (*pret, pp* **repaid**) **1** (*dinero, favor*) devolver **2** (*persona*) reembolsar **3** (*préstamo, deuda*) pagar **4** (*amabilidad*) corresponder a **repayment** *n* **1** reembolso, devolución **2** (*cantidad*) pago

repeat /rɪˈpiːt/ ◆ **1** *vt, vi* repetir(se) **2** *vt* (*confidencia*) contar ◆ *n* repetición **repeated** *adj* **1** repetido **2** reiterado **repeatedly** *adv* repetidamente, en repetidas ocasiones

repel /rɪˈpel/ *vt* (**-ll-**) **1** repeler **2** (*oferta, etc*) rechazar **3** repugnar

repellent /rɪˈpelənt/ ◆ *adj* ~ (**to sb**) repelente (para algn) ◆ *n*: *insect repellent* loción antimosquitos

repent /rɪˈpent/ *vt, vi* ~ (**of**) **sth** arrepentirse de algo **repentance** *n* arrepentimiento

repercussion /ˌriːpəˈkʌʃn/ *n* [*gen pl*] repercusión

repertoire /ˈrepətwɑː(r)/ *n* repertorio (*de un músico, actor, etc*)

repertory /ˈrepətri; *USA* -tɔːri/ (*tb* **repertory company/theatre** *o coloq* **rep**) *n* compañía de repertorio

repetition /ˌrepəˈtɪʃn/ *n* repetición **repetitive** /rɪˈpetətɪv/ *adj* repetitivo

replace /rɪˈpleɪs/ *vt* **1** colocar de nuevo en su sitio **2** reponer **3** reemplazar **4** (*algo roto*) cambiar: *to replace a broken window* cambiar el cristal roto de una ventana **5** destituir **replacement** *n* **1**

sustitución, reemplazo **2** (*persona*) suplente **3** (*pieza*) repuesto

replay /ˈriːpleɪ/ *n* **1** partido de desempate **2** (*TV*) repetición

reply /rɪˈplaɪ/ ◆ *vi* (*pret*, *pp* **replied**) responder, contestar *Ver tb* ANSWER ◆ *n* (*pl* **-ies**) contestación, respuesta

report /rɪˈpɔːt/ ◆ **1** *vt* ~ **sth** informar de/sobre algo; comunicar, dar parte de algo **2** *vt* (*crimen, culpable*) denunciar **3** *vi* ~ (**on sth**) informar (acerca de/sobre algo) **4** *vi* ~ **to/for sth** (*trabajo, etc*) presentarse en/a algo: *to report sick* darse de baja por enfermedad **5** ~ **to sb** rendir cuentas a algn ◆ *n* **1** informe **2** noticia **3** (*Period*) reportaje **4** informe escolar **5** (*pistola*) detonación **reportedly** *adv* según nuestras fuentes **reporter** *n* reportero, -a

represent /ˌreprɪˈzent/ *vt* **1** representar **2** describir **representation** *n* representación

representative /ˌreprɪˈzentətɪv/ ◆ *adj* representativo ◆ *n* **1** representante **2** (*USA*, *Pol*) diputado, -a

repress /rɪˈpres/ *vt* **1** reprimir **2** contener **repression** *n* represión

reprieve /rɪˈpriːv/ *n* **1** indulto **2** (*fig*) respiro

reprimand /ˈreprɪmɑːnd; *USA* -mænd/ ◆ *vt* reprender ◆ *n* reprimenda

reprisal /rɪˈpraɪzl/ *n* represalia

reproach /rɪˈprəʊtʃ/ ◆ *vt* ~ **sb** (**for/with sth**) reprochar (algo) a algn ◆ *n* reproche LOC **above/beyond reproach** por encima de toda crítica

reproduce /ˌriːprəˈdjuːs; *USA* -ˈduːs/ *vt*, *vi* reproducir(se) **reproduction** *n* reproducción **reproductive** *adj* reproductor

reptile /ˈreptaɪl; *USA* -tl/ *n* reptil

republic /rɪˈpʌblɪk/ *n* república **republican** *adj* republicano

repugnant /rɪˈpʌgnənt/ *adj* repugnante

repulsive /rɪˈpʌlsɪv/ *adj* repulsivo

reputable /ˈrepjətəbl/ *adj* **1** (*persona*) de buena reputación, de confianza **2** (*empresa*) acreditado

reputation /ˌrepjuˈteɪʃn/ *n* reputación, fama

repute /rɪˈpjuːt/ *n* (*fml*) reputación, fama **reputed** *adj* **1** supuesto **2** *He is reputed to be*... Tiene fama de ser.../Se dice que es... **reputedly** *adv* según se dice

request /rɪˈkwest/ ◆ *n* ~ (**for sth**) petición, solicitud (de algo): *to make a request for sth* pedir algo ◆ *vt* ~ **sth** (**from/of sb**) pedir algo (a algn) ☛ La palabra más normal es **ask**.

require /rɪˈkwaɪə(r)/ *vt* **1** requerir **2** (*fml*) necesitar ☛ La palabra más normal es **need**. **3** (*fml*) ~ **sb to do sth** exigir a algn que haga algo **requirement** *n* **1** necesidad **2** requisito

rescue /ˈreskjuː/ ◆ *vt* rescatar, salvar ◆ *n* rescate, salvamento: *rescue operation/team* operación/equipo de rescate LOC **to come/go to sb's rescue** acudir en ayuda de algn **rescuer** *n* salvador, -ora

research /rɪˈsɜːtʃ, ˈriːsɜːtʃ/ ◆ *n* [*incontable*] ~ (**into/on sth**) investigación (sobre algo) (*no policial*) ◆ *vi* ~ (**into/on**) **sth** investigar (algo) **researcher** *n* investigador, -ora

resemble /rɪˈzembl/ *vt* parecerse a **resemblance** *n* parecido LOC *Ver* BEAR[2]

resent /rɪˈzent/ *vt* resentirse de/por **resentful** *adj* **1** (*mirada, etc*) de resentimiento **2** resentido **resentment** *n* resentimiento

reservation /ˌrezəˈveɪʃn/ *n* **1** reserva **2** (*duda*) reserva: *I have reservations on that subject.* Tengo ciertas reservas sobre ese tema.

reserve /rɪˈzɜːv/ ◆ *vt* **1** reservar **2** (*derecho*) reservarse ◆ *n* **1** reserva(s) **2** **reserves** [*pl*] (*Mil*) reservistas LOC **in reserve** de reserva **reserved** *adj* reservado

reservoir /ˈrezəvwɑː(r)/ *n* **1** (*lit*) embalse **2** (*fig*) cúmulo, pozo

reshuffle /ˌriːˈʃʌfl/ *n* reorganización

reside /rɪˈzaɪd/ *vi* (*fml*) residir

residence /ˈrezɪdəns/ *n* (*fml*) **1** residencia: *hall of residence* colegio mayor **2** (*ret*) casa

resident /ˈrezɪdənt/ ◆ *n* **1** residente **2** (*hotel*) huésped, -eda ◆ *adj* residente: *to be resident* residir **residential** /ˌrezɪˈdenʃl/ *adj* **1** de viviendas **2** (*curso*) con alojamiento incluido

residue /ˈrezɪdjuː; *USA* -duː/ *n* residuo

resign /rɪˈzaɪn/ *vt*, *vi* dimitir PHR V **to resign yourself to sth** resignarse a algo **resignation** *n* **1** dimisión **2** resignación

resilient /rɪˈzɪliənt/ *adj* **1** (*material*)

elástico **2** (*persona*) resistente **resilience** *n* **1** elasticidad **2** capacidad de recuperación

resist /rɪˈzɪst/ **1** *vi* resistir **2** *vt* resistirse (a): *I had to buy it, I couldn't resist it.* Tuve que comprarlo, no lo pude resistir. **3** *vt* (*presión, reforma*) oponerse a, oponer resistencia a

resistance /rɪˈzɪstəns/ *n* ~ (**to sth/sb**) resistencia (a algo/algn): *He didn't put up/offer much resistance.* No presentó gran oposición. ◊ *the body's resistance to diseases* la resistencia del organismo a las enfermedades

resolute /ˈrezəluːt/ *adj* resuelto, decidido ☛ La palabra más normal es **determined**. **resolutely** *adv* **1** con firmeza **2** resueltamente

resolution /ˌrezəˈluːʃn/ *n* **1** resolución **2** propósito: *New Year resolutions* propósitos para el año nuevo

resolve /rɪˈzɒlv/ (*fml*) **1** *vi* ~ **to do sth** resolverse a hacer algo **2** *vi* acordar: *The senate resolved that...* El Senado acordó que... **3** *vt* (*disputa, crisis*) resolver

resort[1] /rɪˈzɔːt/ ◆ *vt* ~ **to sth** recurrir a algo: *to resort to violence* recurrir a la violencia ◆ *n* LOC *Ver* LAST

resort[2] /rɪˈzɔːt/ *n*: *a seaside resort* un centro turístico costero ◊ *a ski resort* una estación de esquí

resounding /rɪˈzaʊndɪŋ/ *adj* rotundo: *a resounding success* un éxito rotundo

resource /rɪˈsɔːs/ *n* recurso **resourceful** *adj* de recursos: *She is very resourceful.* Tiene mucho ingenio para salir de apuros.

respect /rɪˈspekt/ ◆ *n* **1** ~ (**for sth/sb**) respeto, consideración (por algo/algn) **2** concepto: *in this respect* en este sentido LOC **with respect to sth** (*fml*) por lo que respecta a algo ◆ *vt* ~ **sb** (**as/for sth**) respetar a algn (como/por algo): *I respect them for their honesty.* Los respeto por su honradez. ◊ *He respected her as a detective.* La respetaba como detective. **respectful** *adj* respetuoso

respectable /rɪˈspektəbl/ *adj* **1** respetable, decente **2** considerable

respective /rɪˈspektɪv/ *adj* respectivo: *They all got on with their respective jobs.* Todos volvieron a sus respectivos trabajos.

respite /ˈrespaɪt/ *n* **1** respiro **2** alivio

respond /rɪˈspɒnd/ *vi* **1** ~ (**to sth**) responder (a algo): *The patient is responding to treatment.* El paciente está respondiendo al tratamiento. **2** contestar: *I wrote to them last week but they haven't responded.* Les escribí la semana pasada, pero no han contestado. ☛ Para decir "contestar", **answer** y **reply** son palabras más normales.

response /rɪˈspɒns/ *n* ~ (**to sth/sb**) **1** respuesta, contestación (a algo/algn): *In response to your inquiry...* En contestación a su pregunta... **2** reacción (a algo/algn)

responsibility /rɪˌspɒnsəˈbɪləti/ *n* (*pl* **-ies**) ~ (**for sth**); ~ (**for/to sb**) responsabilidad (por algo); responsabilidad (sobre/ante algn): *to take full responsibility for sth/sb* asumir toda la responsabilidad por algo/algn

responsible /rɪˈspɒnsəbl/ *adj* ~ (**for sth/doing sth**); ~ **to sth/sb** responsable (de algo/hacer algo); ante algo/algn: *She's responsible for five patients.* Tiene cinco pacientes a su cargo. ◊ *to act in a responsible way* comportarse de una forma responsable.

responsive /rɪˈspɒnsɪv/ *adj* **1** receptivo: *a responsive audience* un público receptivo **2** sensible: *to be responsive (to sth)* ser sensible (a algo)

rest[1] /rest/ ◆ **1** *vt, vi* descansar **2** *vt, vi* ~ (**sth**) **on/against sth** apoyar algo/apoyarse en/contra algo **3** (*fml*) *vi* quedar: *to let the matter rest* dejar el asunto ◆ *n* descanso: *to have a rest* tomarse un descanso ◊ *to get some rest* descansar LOC **at rest** en reposo, en paz **to come to rest** pararse *Ver tb* MIND **restful** *adj* descansado, sosegado

rest[2] /rest/ *n* **the** ~ (**of sth**) **1** [*incontable*] el resto (de algo) **2** [*pl*] los/las demás, los otros, las otras (de algo): *the rest of the players* los demás jugadores

restaurant /ˈrestrɒnt; *USA* -tərənt/ *n* restaurante ☛ *Ver* pág 320.

restless /ˈrestləs/ *adj* **1** agitado **2** inquieto: *to become/grow restless* impacientarse **3** *to have a restless night* pasar una mala noche

restoration /ˌrestəˈreɪʃn/ *n* **1** devolución **2** restauración **3** restablecimiento

restore /rɪˈstɔː(r)/ *vt* **1** ~ **sth** (**to sth/sb**) (*fml*) (*confianza, salud*) devolver algo (a algo/algn) **2** (*orden, paz*) restablecer **3** (*bienes*) restituir **4** (*monarquía*) restaurar

restrain /rɪˈstreɪn/ **1** *vt* ~ **sb** contener a algn **2** *v refl* ~ **yourself** contenerse **3** *vt* (*entusiasmo*) dominar, contener **4** *vt* (*lágrimas*) contener **restrained** *adj* moderado, comedido

restraint /rɪˈstreɪnt/ *n* (*fml*) **1** compostura **2** limitación, restricción **3** comedimiento

restrict /rɪˈstrɪkt/ *vt* limitar **restricted** limitado: *to be restricted to sth* estar restringido a algo **restriction** *n* restricción **restrictive** *adj* restrictivo

result /rɪˈzʌlt/ ◆ *n* resultado: *As a result of...* A consecuencia de... ◆ *vi* ~ (**from sth**) ser el resultado (de algo); originarse (por algo) PHR V **to result in sth** terminar en algo

resume /rɪˈzjuːm; *USA* -ˈzuːm/ (*fml*) **1** *vt, vi* reanudar(se) **2** *vt* recobrar, volver a tomar **resumption** *n* [*sing*] (*fml*) reanudación

resurgence /rɪˈsɜːdʒəns/ *n* (*fml*) resurgimiento

resurrect /ˌrezəˈrekt/ *vt* resucitar: *to resurrect old traditions* hacer revivir viejas tradiciones **resurrection** *n* resurrección

resuscitate /rɪˈsʌsɪteɪt/ *vt* reanimar **resuscitation** *n* reanimación

retail /ˈriːteɪl/ ◆ *n* venta al por menor: *retail price* precio de venta al público ◆ *vt, vi* vender(se) al público **retailer** *n* (comerciante) minorista

retain /rɪˈteɪn/ *vt* (*fml*) **1** quedarse con **2** conservar **3** retener **4** quedarse con (*en la memoria*)

retaliate /rɪˈtælieɪt/ *vi* ~ (**against sth/sb**) vengarse (de algo/algn); tomar represalias (contra algo/algn) **retaliation** *n* ~ (**against sth/sb/for sth**) represalia (contra algo/algn/por algo)

retarded /rɪˈtɑːdɪd/ *adj* retrasado

retch /retʃ/ *vi* dar arcadas

retention /rɪˈtenʃn/ *n* (*fml*) retención, conservación

rethink /ˌriːˈθɪŋk/ *vt* (*pret, pp* **rethought** /-ˈθɔːt/) reconsiderar

reticent /ˈretɪsnt/ *adj* reservado **reticence** *n* reserva

retire /rɪˈtaɪə(r)/ **1** *vt, vi* jubilar(se) **2** *vi* (*fml, joc*) retirarse a sus aposentos **3** *vi* (*fml, Mil*) retirarse **retired** *adj* jubilado **retiring** *adj* **1** retraído **2** que se jubila

retirement /rɪˈtaɪəmənt/ *n* jubilación, retiro

retort /rɪˈtɔːt/ ◆ *n* réplica, contestación ◆ *vt* replicar

retrace /rɪˈtreɪs/ *vt* desandar (*camino*): *to retrace your steps* volver sobre tus pasos

retract /rɪˈtrækt/ *vt, vi* (*fml*) **1** (*declaración*) retractarse (de) **2** (*garra, uña, etc*) retraer(se) **3** replegar(se)

retreat /rɪˈtriːt/ ◆ *vi* batirse en retirada ◆ *n* **1** retirada **2 the retreat** (*Mil*) retreta **3** retiro **4** refugio

retrial /ˌriːˈtraɪəl/ *n* nuevo juicio

retribution /ˌretrɪˈbjuːʃn/ *n* (*fml*) **1** justo castigo **2** venganza

retrieval /rɪˈtriːvl/ *n* (*fml*) recuperación

retrieve /rɪˈtriːv/ *vt* **1** (*fml*) recobrar **2** (*Informát*) recuperar **3** (*perro de caza*) cobrar (*la pieza matada*) **retriever** *n* perro de caza

retrograde /ˈretrəgreɪd/ *adj* (*fml*) retrógrado

retrospect /ˈretrəspekt/ *n* LOC **in retrospect** mirando hacia atrás

retrospective /ˌretrəˈspektɪv/ ◆ *adj* **1** retrospectivo **2** retroactivo ◆ *n* exposición retrospectiva

return /rɪˈtɜːn/ ◆ **1** *vi* regresar, volver **2** *vt* devolver **3** *vt* (*Pol*) elegir **4** *vt* (*fml*) declarar **5** (*síntoma*) reaparecer ◆ *n* **1** vuelta, regreso: *on my return* a mi vuelta **2** ~ (**to sth**) retorno (a algo) **3** reaparición **4** devolución **5** declaración: *(income-)tax return* declaración de la renta **6** ~ (**on sth**) rendimiento (de algo) **7** (*tb* **return ticket**) billete de ida y vuelta ☛ *Comparar con* SINGLE **8** [*antes de sustantivo*] de vuelta: *return journey* viaje de vuelta LOC **in return** (**for sth**) en recompensa/a cambio (de algo)

returnable /rɪˈtɜːnəbl/ *adj* **1** (*dinero*) reembolsable **2** (*envase*) retornable

reunion /riːˈjuːniən/ *n* reunión, reencuentro

reunite /ˌriːjuːˈnaɪt/ *vt, vi* **1** reunir(se), reencontrar(se) **2** reconciliar(se)

rev /rev/ ◆ *n* [*gen pl*] (*coloq*) revolución

(*de motor*) ◆ *v* (-**vv**-) PHR V **to rev (sth) up** acelerar (algo)

revalue /ˌriːˈvæljuː/ *vt* **1** (*propiedad, etc*) revalorar **2** (*moneda*) revalorizar **revaluation** *n* revalorización

revamp /ˌriːˈvæmp/ *vt* (*coloq*) modernizar

reveal /rɪˈviːl/ *vt* **1** (*secretos, datos, etc*) revelar **2** mostrar, descubrir **revealing** *adj* **1** revelador **2** (*vestido*) atrevido

revel /ˈrevl/ *vi* (-**ll**-, *USA* -**l**-) PHR V **to revel in sth/doing sth** deleitarse en algo/en hacer algo

revelation /ˌrevəˈleɪʃn/ *n* revelación

revenge /rɪˈvendʒ/ ◆ *n* venganza LOC **to take (your) revenge (on sb)** vengarse (de algn) ◆ *vt* vengar LOC **to revenge yourself/be revenged (on sb)** vengarse (de algn)

revenue /ˈrevənjuː; *USA* -ənuː/ *n* ingresos: *a source of government revenue* una fuente de ingresos del gobierno

reverberate /rɪˈvɜːbəreɪt/ *vi* **1** resonar **2** (*fig*) tener repercusiones **reverberation** *n* **1** (*coloq*) retumbo **2 reverberations** [*pl*] (*fig*) repercusiones

revere /rɪˈvɪə(r)/ *vt* (*fml*) venerar

reverence /ˈrevərəns/ *n* reverencia (*veneración*)

reverend /ˈrevərənd/ (*tb* **the Reverend**) *adj* (*abrev* **Rev**, **Revd**) reverendo

reverent /ˈrevərənt/ *adj* reverente

reversal /rɪˈvɜːsl/ *n* **1** (*opinión*) cambio **2** (*suerte, fortuna*) revés **3** (*Jur*) revocación **4** (*de papeles*) inversión

reverse /rɪˈvɜːs/ ◆ *n* **1 the ~ (of sth)** lo contrario (de algo): *quite the reverse* todo lo contrario **2** reverso **3** (*papel*) dorso **4** (*tb* **reverse gear**) marcha atrás ◆ **1** *vt* invertir **2** *vt, vi* poner en/ir marcha atrás **3** *vt* (*decisión*) revocar LOC **to reverse (the) charges** (*USA* **to call collect**) llamar a cobro revertido

revert /rɪˈvɜːt/ *vi* **1** ~ **to sth** volver a algo (*estado, tema, etc anterior*) **2** ~ **(to sth/sb)** (*propiedad, etc*) revertir (a algo/algn)

review /rɪˈvjuː/ ◆ *n* **1** examen, revisión **2** informe **3** (*crítica*) reseña **4** (*gen, Mil*) revista ◆ *vt* **1** reconsiderar **2** examinar **3** hacer una reseña de **4** (*Mil*) pasar revista a **reviewer** *n* crítico, -a

revise /rɪˈvaɪz/ **1** *vt* revisar **2** *vt* modificar **3** *vt, vi* (*GB*) repasar (*para examen*)

revision /rɪˈvɪʒn/ *n* **1** revisión **2** modificación **3** (*GB*) repaso: *to do some revision* repasar

revival /rɪˈvaɪvl/ *n* **1** restablecimiento **2** (*moda*) resurgimiento **3** (*Teat*) reposición

revive /rɪˈvaɪv/ **1** *vt, vi* (*enfermo*) reanimar(se) **2** *vt* (*recuerdos*) refrescar **3** *vt, vi* (*economía*) reactivar(se) **4** *vt* (*Teat*) reponer

revoke /rɪˈvəʊk/ *vt* (*fml*) revocar

revolt /rɪˈvəʊlt/ ◆ **1** *vi* ~ **(against sth/sb)** sublevarse, rebelarse contra algo/algn **2** *vt* repugnar a, dar asco a: *The smell revolted him.* El olor le repugnaba. ◆ *n* ~ **(over sth)** sublevación, rebelión (por algo)

revolting /rɪˈvəʊltɪŋ/ *adj* (*coloq*) repugnante

revolution /ˌrevəˈluːʃn/ *n* revolución **revolutionary** *n* (*pl* -**ies**) *adj* revolucionario, -a

revolve /rɪˈvɒlv/ *vt, vi* (hacer) girar PHR V **to revolve around sth/sb** centrarse en/girar alrededor de algo/algn

revolver /rɪˈvɒlvə(r)/ *n* revólver

revulsion /rɪˈvʌlʃn/ *n* repugnancia

reward /rɪˈwɔːd/ ◆ *n* recompensa ◆ *vt* recompensar **rewarding** *adj* gratificante

rewrite /ˌriːˈraɪt/ *vt* (*pret* **rewrote** /-rəʊt/ *pp* **rewritten** /-ˈrɪtn/) volver a escribir

rhetoric /ˈretərɪk/ *n* retórica

rhinoceros /raɪˈnɒsərəs/ *n* (*pl* **rhinoceros** *o* ~**es**) rinoceronte

rhubarb /ˈruːbɑːb/ *n* ruibarbo

rhyme /raɪm/ ◆ *n* **1** rima **2** (*poema*) verso *Ver* NURSERY ◆ *vt, vi* rimar

rhythm /ˈrɪðəm/ *n* ritmo

rib /rɪb/ *n* costilla (*Anat*): *ribcage* caja torácica

ribbon /ˈrɪbən/ *n* cinta LOC **to tear, cut, etc sth to ribbons** hacer algo trizas

rice /raɪs/ *n* arroz: *rice field* arrozal ◊ *brown rice* arroz integral ◊ *rice pudding* arroz con leche

rich /rɪtʃ/ *adj* (-**er**, -**est**) **1** rico: *to become/get rich* enriquecerse ◊ *to be rich in sth* ser rico/abundar en algo **2** (*lujoso*) suntuoso **3** (*tierra*) fértil **4** (*pey*) (*comida*) pesado, empalagoso **the rich** *n* [*pl*] los ricos **riches** *n* riqueza(s) **richly** *adv* LOC **to richly deserve sth** tener algo bien merecido

rickety /ˈrɪkəti/ *adj* (*coloq*) **1** (*estructura*) desvencijado **2** (*mueble*) cojo

rid /rɪd/ *vt* (**-dd-**) (*pret, pp* **rid**) **to rid sth/sb of sth/sb** librar algo/a algn de algo/algn; eliminar algo de algo LOC **to be/get rid of sth/sb** deshacerse/librarse de algo/algn

ridden /ˈrɪdn/ ◆ *pp de* RIDE ◆ *adj* ~ **with/by sth** agobiado, acosado por algo

riddle[1] /ˈrɪdl/ *n* **1** acertijo, adivinanza **2** misterio, enigma

riddle[2] /ˈrɪdl/ *vt* **1** (*a balazos*) acribillar **2** (*pey, fig*): *to be riddled with sth* estar plagado/lleno de algo

ride /raɪd/ ◆ (*pret* **rode** /rəʊd/ *pp* **ridden** /ˈrɪdn/) **1** *vt* (*caballo*) montar a **2** *vt* (*bicicleta, etc*) montar en **3** *vi* montar a caballo **4** *vi* (*en vehículo*) viajar, ir ◆ *n* **1** (*a caballo*) paseo **2** (*en vehículo*) viaje: *to go for a ride* ir a dar una vuelta LOC **to take sb for a ride** (*coloq*) dar gato por liebre a algn **rider** *n* **1** jinete **2** ciclista **3** motociclista

ridge /rɪdʒ/ *n* **1** (*montaña*) cresta **2** (*tejado*) caballete

ridicule /ˈrɪdɪkjuːl/ ◆ *n* ridículo ◆ *vt* ridiculizar **ridiculous** /rɪˈdɪkjələs/ *adj* ridículo, absurdo

riding /ˈraɪdɪŋ/ *n* equitación: *I like riding.* Me gusta montar a caballo.

rife /raɪf/ *adj* (*fml*): *to be rife (with sth)* abundar (en algo)

rifle /ˈraɪfl/ *n* fusil, rifle

rift /rɪft/ *n* **1** (*Geog*) grieta **2** (*fig*) división

rig /rɪg/ ◆ *vt* (**-gg-**) amañar PHR V **to rig sth up** armar algo, improvisar algo ◆ *n* **1** (*tb* **rigging**) aparejo, jarcia **2** aparato

right /raɪt/ ◆ *adj* **1** correcto, cierto: *You are quite right.* Tienes toda la razón. ◊ *Are these figures right?* ¿Son estas cifras correctas? **2** adecuado, correcto: *Is this the right colour for the curtains?* ¿Es éste el color adecuado para las cortinas? ◊ *to be on the right road* ir por buen camino **3** (*momento*) oportuno: *It wasn't the right time to say that.* No era el momento oportuno para decir aquello. **4** (*pie, mano*) derecho **5** justo: *It's not right to pay people so badly.* No es justo pagar tan mal a la gente. ◊ *He was right to do that.* Hizo lo correcto al obrar así. **6** (*GB, coloq*) de remate: *a right fool* un tonto de remate *Ver tb* ALL RIGHT LOC **to get sth right** acertar, hacer algo bien **to get sth right/straight** dejar algo claro **to put/set sth/sb right** corregir algo/a algn, arreglar algo *Ver tb* CUE, SIDE ◆ *adv* **1** bien, correctamente: *Have I spelt your name right?* ¿He escrito bien tu nombre? **2** exactamente: *right beside you* justo a tu lado **3** completamente: *right to the end* hasta el final **4** a la derecha: *to turn right* torcer a la derecha **5** inmediatamente: *I'll be right back.* Vuelvo ahora mismo. LOC **right now** ahora mismo **right/straight away/off** en seguida *Ver tb* SERVE ◆ *n* **1** bien: *right and wrong* el bien y el mal **2** ~ (**to sth/to do sth**) derecho a algo/a hacer algo: *human rights* los derechos humanos **3** (*tb Pol*) derecha: *on the right* a la derecha LOC **by rights 1** en buena ley **2** en teoría **in your own right** por derecho propio **to be in the right** tener razón ◆ *vt* **1** enderezar **2** corregir

right angle *n* ángulo recto

righteous /ˈraɪtʃəs/ *adj* **1** (*fml*) (*persona*) recto, honrado **2** (*indignación*) justificado **3** (*pey*) virtuoso

rightful /ˈraɪtfl/ *adj* [*sólo antes de sustantivo*] legítimo: *the rightful heir* el heredero legítimo

right-hand /ˈraɪt hænd/ *adj*: *on the right-hand side* a mano derecha LOC **right-hand man** brazo derecho **right-handed** *adj* diestro

rightly /ˈraɪtli/ *adv* correctamente, justificadamente: *rightly or wrongly* mal que bien

right wing ◆ *n* derecha ◆ *adj* de derecha(s), derechista

rigid /ˈrɪdʒɪd/ *adj* **1** rígido **2** (*actitud*) inflexible

rigour (*USA* **rigor**) /ˈrɪgə(r)/ *n* (*fml*) rigor **rigorous** *adj* riguroso

rim /rɪm/ *n* **1** borde ☛ *Ver dibujo en* MUG **2** [*gen pl*] (*gafas*) montura **3** llanta

rind /raɪnd/ *n* corteza (*de bacon, queso, limón*) ☛ *Ver nota en* PEEL

ring[1] /rɪŋ/ ◆ *n* **1** anillo: *ring road* carretera de circunvalación **2** aro **3** círculo **4** (*tb* **circus ring**) pista (*de circo*) **5** (*tb* **boxing ring**) ring **6** (*tb* **bullring**) ruedo ◆ *vt* (*pret, pp* **-ed**) **1** ~ **sth/sb (with sth)**

rodear algo/a algn (de algo) **2** (*esp pájaro*) anillar

ring² /rɪŋ/ ◆ (*pret* **rang** /ræŋ/ *pp* **rung** /rʌŋ/) **1** *vi* sonar **2** *vt* (*timbre*) tocar **3** *vi* ~ (**for sth/sb**) llamar (a algo/algn) **4** *vi* (*oídos*) zumbar **5** *vt, vi* (*GB*) ~ (**sth/sb**) (**up**) llamar a algo/algn (*por teléfono*) PHR V **to ring (sb) back** volver a llamar (a algn), devolver la llamada (a algn) **to ring off** (*GB*) colgar ◆ *n* **1** (*timbre*) timbrazo **2** (*campanas*) toque **3** [*sing*] sonido **4** (*GB, coloq*): *to give sb a ring* dar un telefonazo a algn

ringleader /ˈrɪŋˌliːdə(r)/ *n* (*pey*) cabecilla

rink /rɪŋk/ *n* pista *Ver* ICE RINK

rinse /rɪns/ ◆ *vt* **1** ~ **sth** (**out**) enjuagar algo **2** (*quitar el jabón*) aclarar ◆ *n* **1** aclarado **2** tinte

riot /ˈraɪət/ ◆ *n* disturbio, motín LOC *Ver* RUN ◆ *vi* causar disturbios, amotinarse **rioting** *n* disturbios **riotous** *adj* **1** desenfrenado, bullicioso (*fiesta*) **2** (*fml, Jur*) alborotador

rip /rɪp/ ◆ *vt, vi* (**-pp-**) rasgar(se): *to rip sth open* abrir algo desgarrándolo PHR V **rip sb off** (*coloq*) timar a algn **rip sth off/out** arrancar algo **to rip sth up** desgarrar algo ◆ *n* desgarrón

ripe /raɪp/ *adj* **1** (*fruta, queso*) maduro **2** ~ (**for sth**) listo (para algo): *The time is ripe for his return.* Ha llegado la hora de que regrese. **ripen** *vt, vi* madurar

rip-off /ˈrɪp ɒf/ *n* (*coloq*) timo, robo

ripple /ˈrɪpl/ ◆ *n* **1** onda, rizo **2** murmullo (*de risas, interés, etc*) ◆ *vt, vi* ondular(se)

rise /raɪz/ ◆ *vi* (*pret* **rose** /rəʊz/ *pp* **risen** /ˈrɪzn/) **1** subir **2** (*voz*) alzarse **3** (*fml*) (*persona, viento*) levantarse **4** ~ (**up**) (**against sth/sb**) (*fml*) sublevarse (contra algo/algn) **5** (*sol, luna*) salir **6** ascender (*en rango*) **7** (*río*) nacer **8** (*nivel de un río*) crecer ◆ *n* **1** subida, ascenso **2** (*cantidad*) subida, aumento **3** cuesta **4** (*USA* **raise**) aumento (*de sueldo*) LOC **to give rise to sth** (*fml*) dar lugar a algo

rising /ˈraɪzɪŋ/ ◆ *n* **1** (*Pol*) levantamiento **2** (*sol, luna*) salida ◆ *adj* **1** creciente **2** (*sol*) naciente

risk /rɪsk/ ◆ *n* ~ (**of sth/that...**) riesgo (de algo/de que...) LOC **at risk** en peligro **to take a risk/risks** arriesgarse *Ver tb* RUN ◆ *vt* **1** arriesgar(se a) **2** ~ **doing sth** exponerse, arriesgarse a hacer algo LOC **to risk your neck** jugarse el pellejo **risky** *adj* (**-ier**, **-iest**) arriesgado

rite /raɪt/ *n* rito

ritual /ˈrɪtʃuəl/ ◆ *n* ritual, rito ◆ *adj* ritual

rival /ˈraɪvl/ ◆ *n* ~ (**for/in sth**) rival (para/en algo) ◆ *adj* rival ◆ *vt* (**-ll-**, *USA tb* **-l-**) ~ **sth/sb** (**for/in sth**) rivalizar con algo/algn (en algo) **rivalry** *n* (*pl* **-ies**) rivalidad

river /ˈrɪvə(r)/ *n* río: *river bank* orilla (del río) ☛ *Ver nota en* RÍO **riverside** *n* orilla (del río)

rivet /ˈrɪvɪt/ *vt* **1** (*lit*) remachar **2** (*ojos*) clavar **3** (*atraer*) fascinar **riveting** *adj* fascinante

road /rəʊd/ *n* **1** (*entre ciudades*) carretera: *roadblock* control (policial) ◊ *road sign* señal de tráfico ◊ *road safety* seguridad vial ◊ *across/over the road* al otro lado de la carretera ◊ *road accident* accidente de tráfico **2 Road** (*abrev* **Rd**) (*en nombres de calles*): *Banbury Road* la calle Banbury LOC **by road** por carretera **on the road to sth** en camino de algo **roadside** *n* borde de la carretera: *roadside café* bar de carretera **roadway** *n* calzada

roadworks /ˈrəʊdwɜːks/ *n* [*pl*] obras: *There were roadworks on the motorway.* Había obras en la autopista.

roam /rəʊm/ **1** *vt* vagar por, recorrer **2** *vi* vagar

roar /rɔː(r)/ ◆ *n* **1** (*león, etc*) rugido **2** estruendo: *roars of laughter* carcajadas ◆ **1** *vi* gritar: *to roar with laughter* reírse a carcajadas **2** *vi* (*león, etc*) rugir **3** *vt* decir a gritos **roaring** *adj* LOC **to do a roaring trade** (**in sth**) hacer un negocio redondo (en algo)

roast /rəʊst/ ◆ **1** *vt, vi* (*carne*) asar(se) **2** *vt, vi* (*café, etc*) tostar(se) **3** *vi* (*persona*) asarse ◆ *adj, n* asado: *roast beef* rosbif

rob /rɒb/ *vt* (**-bb-**) **to rob sth/sb** (**of sth**) robar (algo) a algo/algn

Los verbos **rob**, **steal** y **burgle** significan "robar". **Rob** se utiliza con complementos de persona o lugar: *He robbed me (of all my money).* Me robó (todo mi dinero). **Steal** se usa cuando mencionamos el objeto robado (de un lugar o a una persona): *He stole all my money (from me).* Me robó todo mi dinero.

Burgle se refiere a robos en casas particulares o tiendas, normalmente cuando los dueños están fuera: *The house has been burgled.* Han robado en la casa.

robber *n* **1** ladrón, -ona **2** (*tb* **bank robber**) atracador, -ora ☛ *Ver nota en* THIEF **robbery** *n* (*pl* **-ies**) **1** robo **2** (*violento*) atraco ☛ *Ver nota en* THEFT

robe /rəʊb/ *n* **1** bata **2** (*ceremonial*) manto

robin /ˈrɒbɪn/ *n* petirrojo

robot /ˈrəʊbɒt/ *n* robot

robust /rəʊˈbʌst/ *adj* robusto, enérgico

rock[1] /rɒk/ *n* **1** roca: *rock climbing* escalada (montañismo) **2** (*USA*) piedra LOC **at rock bottom** en su punto más bajo, por los suelos **on the rocks 1** (*coloq*) en crisis **2** (*coloq*) (*bebida*) con hielo

rock[2] /rɒk/ **1** *vt, vi* mecer(se): *rocking chair* mecedora **2** *vt* (*niño*) arrullar **3** *vt, vi* (*lit y fig*) estremecer(se), sacudir(se)

rock[3] /rɒk/ (*tb* **rock music**) *n* (música) rock

rocket /ˈrɒkɪt/ ◆ *n* cohete ◆ *vi* aumentar muy rápidamente

rocky /ˈrɒki/ *adj* (**-ier**, **-iest**) **1** rocoso **2** (*fig*) inestable

rod /rɒd/ *n* **1** barra **2** vara

rode *pret de* RIDE

rodent /ˈrəʊdnt/ *n* roedor

rogue /rəʊg/ *n* **1** (*antic*) sinvergüenza **2** (*joc*) pícaro, -a

role (*tb* **rôle**) /rəʊl/ *n* papel: *role model* modelo a imitar

roll /rəʊl/ ◆ *n* **1** rollo **2** (*de fotos*) carrete **3** panecillo ☛ *Ver dibujo en* PAN **4** (*con relleno*) bocadillo **5** balanceo **6** registro, lista: *roll-call* (acto de pasar) lista **7** (*USA, coloq*) (*GB* **bankroll**) fajo ◆ **1** *vt, vi* (hacer) rodar **2** *vt, vi* dar vueltas (a algo) **3** *vt, vi* ~ (**up**) enrollar(se) **4** *vt, vi* ~ (**up**) envolver(se) **5** *vt* (*cigarrillo*) liar **6** *vt* allanar con un rodillo **7** *vt, vi* balancear(se) LOC **to be rolling in it** (*coloq*) estar forrado *Ver tb* BALL PHR V **to roll in** (*coloq*) llegar en grandes cantidades **to roll on** (*tiempo*) pasar **to roll sth out** extender algo **to roll over** darse la vuelta **to roll up** (*coloq*) presentarse **rolling** *adj* ondulante

roller /ˈrəʊlə(r)/ *n* **1** rodillo **2** rulo

roller-coaster /ˈrəʊlə kəʊstə(r)/ *n* montaña rusa

roller skate *n* patín

rolling pin *n* rodillo (*de cocina*)

romance /rəʊˈmæns/ *n* **1** romanticismo: *the romance of foreign lands* el romanticismo de las tierras lejanas **2** amor, amorío: *a holiday romance* una aventura de verano **3** novela de amor

romantic /rəʊˈmæntɪk/ *adj* romántico

romp /rɒmp/ ◆ *vi* ~ (**about/around**) retozar, corretear ◆ *n* **1** retozo **2** (*coloq*) (*cine, teatro, literatura*) obra divertida y sin pretensiones

roof /ru:f/ *n* (*pl* ~**s**) **1** tejado **2** (*coche*) techo **roofing** *n* techumbre

roof-rack /ˈru:f ræk/ *n* baca

rooftop /ˈru:ftɒp/ *n* **1** azotea **2** tejado

room /ru:m, rʊm/ *n* **1** habitación, cuarto, sala *Ver* DINING-ROOM, LIVING ROOM **2** sitio: *Is there room for me?* ¿Hay sitio para mí? ◊ *room to breathe* espacio para respirar **3** *There's no room for doubt.* No cabe duda. ◊ *There's room for improvement.* Podría mejorarse. **roomy** *adj* (**-ier**, **-iest**) espacioso

room service *n* servicio de habitaciones

room temperature *n* temperatura ambiente

roost /ru:st/ ◆ *n* percha (*para aves*) ◆ *vi* posarse para dormir

root /ru:t/ ◆ *n* raíz: *square root* raíz cuadrada LOC **the root cause** (**of sth**) la causa fundamental (de algo) **to put down** (**new**) **roots** echar raices ◆ PHR V **to root sth out 1** erradicar algo, arrancar algo de raíz **2** (*coloq*) encontrar algo **to root about/around for sth** revolver (*en busca de algo*) **to root for sth/sb** (*coloq*) apoyar/animar algo/a algn

rope /rəʊp/ ◆ *n* cuerda LOC **to show sb/know/learn the ropes** enseñarle a algn/conocer/aprender el oficio ◆ PHR V **to rope sb in** (**to do sth**) (*coloq*) enganchar a algn (para hacer algo) **to rope sth off** acordonar un lugar

rope ladder *n* escala de cuerda

rosary /ˈrəʊzəri/ *n* (*pl* **-ies**) rosario (*oración y cuentas*)

rose[1] *pret de* RISE

rose[2] /rəʊz/ *n* rosa

rosé /ˈrəʊzeɪ; *USA* rəʊˈzeɪ/ *n* (vino) rosado

rosette /rəʊˈzet/ *n* escarapela

rosy /ˈrəʊzi/ *adj* (**rosier**, **rosiest**) **1** sonrosado **2** (*fig*) prometedor

rot /rɒt/ *vt, vi* (**-tt-**) pudrir(se)

rota /ˈrəʊtə/ *n* (*pl* ~**s**) (*GB*) lista (*de turnos*)

rotate /rəʊˈteɪt; *USA* ˈrəʊteɪt/ **1** *vt, vi* (hacer) girar **2** *vt, vi* alternar(se) **rotation** *n* **1** rotación **2** alternancia LOC **in rotation** por turno

rotten /ˈrɒtn/ *adj* **1** podrido **2** (*fig*) asqueroso

rough /rʌf/ ◆ *adj* (**-er**, **-est**) **1** (*superficie*) áspero **2** (*mar*) encrespado **3** (*comportamiento*) violento **4** (*tratamiento*) inconsiderado **5** (*cálculo*) aproximado **6** (*coloq*) malo: *I feel a bit rough.* No me encuentro bien. LOC **to be rough** (**on sb**) (*coloq*) ser duro (con algn) ◆ *adv* (**-er**, **-est**) duro ◆ *n* LOC **in rough** en sucio ◆ *vt* LOC **to rough it** (*coloq*) pasar apuros **roughly** *adv* **1** violentamente **2** aproximadamente

roulette /ruːˈlet/ *n* ruleta

round[1] /raʊnd/ *adj* redondo

round[2] /raʊnd/ *adv* **1** *Ver* AROUND[2] **2** *all year round* durante todo el año ◊ *a shorter way round* un camino más corto ◊ *round the clock* las 24 horas ◊ *round at María's* en casa de María LOC **round about** de alrededor: *the houses round about* las casas de alrededor

round[3] (*tb* **around**) /raʊnd/ *prep* **1** por: *to show sb round the house* enseñarle a algn la casa **2** alrededor de: *She wrapped the towel round her waist.* Se enrolló la toalla alrededor de la cintura. **3** a la vuelta de: *just round the corner* a la vuelta de la esquina

round[4] /raʊnd/ *n* **1** ronda: *a round of talks* una ronda de conversaciones **2** recorrido (*del cartero*), visitas (*del médico*) **3** ronda (*de bebidas*): *It's my round.* Esta ronda la pago yo. **4** (*Dep*) asalto, vuelta **5** *a round of applause* una salva de aplausos **6** tiro, ráfaga

round[5] /raʊnd/ *vt* (*una esquina*) doblar PHR V **to round sth off** terminar algo **to round sth/sb up 1** (*personas*) juntar **2** (*ganado*) acorralar **to round sth up/down** redondear algo por lo alto/bajo (*cifra, precio, etc*)

roundabout /ˈraʊndəbaʊt/ ◆ *adj* indirecto: *in a roundabout way* de forma indirecta/dando un rodeo ◆ *n* **1** (*tb* **carousel**, **merry-go-round**) tiovivo **2** rotonda, glorieta

rouse /raʊz/ *vt* **1** ~ **sb** (**from/out of sth**) (*fml*) despertar a algn (de algo) **2** provocar **rousing** *adj* **1** (*discurso*) enardecedor **2** (*aplauso*) caluroso

rout /raʊt/ ◆ *n* derrota ◆ *vt* derrotar

route /ruːt; *USA* raʊt/ *n* ruta

routine /ruːˈtiːn/ ◆ *n* rutina ◆ *adj* de rutina, rutinario **routinely** *adv* rutinariamente

row[1] /rəʊ/ *n* fila, hilera LOC **in a row** uno tras otro: *the third week in a row* la tercera semana seguida ◊ *four days in a row* cuatro días seguidos

row[2] /rəʊ/ ◆ *vt, vi* remar, navegar a remo: *She rowed the boat to the bank.* Remó hacia la orilla. ◊ *Will you row me across the river?* ¿Me llevas al otro lado del río (en bote)? ◊ *to row across the lake* cruzar el lago a remo ◆ *n*: *to go for a row* salir a remar

row[3] /raʊ/ ◆ *n* (*coloq*) **1** pelea: *to have a row* pelearse ☛ También se dice **argument**. **2** jaleo **3** ruido ◆ *vi* pelear

rowdy /ˈraʊdi/ *adj* (**-ier**, **-iest**) (*pey*) **1** (*persona*) ruidoso, pendenciero **2** (*reunión*) alborotado

royal /ˈrɔɪəl/ *adj* real

Royal Highness *n*: *your/his/her Royal Highness* Su Alteza Real

royalty /ˈrɔɪəlti/ *n* **1** [*sing*] realeza **2** (*pl* **-ties**) derechos de autor

rub /rʌb/ ◆ (**-bb-**) **1** *vt* restregar, frotar: *to rub your hands together* frotarse las manos **2** *vt* friccionar **3** *vi* **to rub** (**on/against sth**) rozar (contra algo) PHR V **to rub off** (**on/onto sb**) pegarse (a algn) **to rub sth out** borrar algo ◆ *n* frote: *to give sth a rub* frotar algo

rubber /ˈrʌbə(r)/ *n* **1** goma, caucho: *rubber/elastic band* goma (elástica) ◊ *rubber stamp* sello de goma **2** (*tb esp USA* **eraser**) goma (*de borrar*)

rubbish /ˈrʌbɪʃ/ *n* [*incontable*] **1** basura: *rubbish dump/tip* vertedero **2** (*pey, fig*) tonterías

rubble /ˈrʌbl/ *n* [*incontable*] escombros

ruby /ˈruːbi/ *n* (*pl* **-ies**) rubí

rucksack /ˈrʌksæk/ (*USA tb* **backpack**) *n* mochila

rudder /ˈrʌdə(r)/ *n* timón

rude /ruːd/ *adj* (**ruder**, **rudest**) **1** grosero, maleducado: *to be rude to do sth* ser de mala educación hacer algo **2** indecente **3** (*chiste, etc*) verde **4** tosco

rudimentary /ˌruːdɪˈmentri/ *adj* rudimentario

ruffle /ˈrʌfl/ *vt* **1** (*superficie*) agitar **2** (*pelo*) alborotar **3** (*plumas*) encrespar **4** (*tela*) arrugar **5** perturbar, desconcertar

rug /rʌg/ *n* **1** alfombra **2** manta de viaje

rugby /ˈrʌgbi/ *n* rugby

rugged /ˈrʌgɪd/ *adj* **1** (*terreno*) escabroso, accidentado **2** (*montaña*) escarpado **3** (*facciones*) duro

ruin /ˈruːɪn/ ◆ *n* (*lit y fig*) ruina ◆ *vt* **1** arruinar, destrozar **2** estropear, malograr

rule /ruːl/ ◆ *n* **1** regla, norma **2** costumbre **3** imperio, dominio, gobierno **4** (*gobierno*) mandato **5** (*de monarca*) reinado LOC **as a (general) rule** en general, por regla general ◆ **1** *vt, vi* ~ (**over sth/sb**) (*Pol*) gobernar (algo/a algn) **2** *vt* dominar, regir **3** *vt, vi* (*Jur*) fallar, decidir **4** *vt* (*línea*) trazar PHR V **to rule sth/sb out (as sth)** descartar algo/a algn (por algo)

ruler /ˈruːlə(r)/ *n* **1** gobernante **2** (*instrumento*) regla

ruling /ˈruːlɪŋ/ ◆ *adj* **1** imperante **2** (*Pol*) en el poder ◆ *n* fallo

rum /rʌm/ *n* ron

rumble /ˈrʌmbl/ ◆ *vi* **1** retumbar, hacer un ruido sordo **2** (*estómago*) sonar ◆ *n* estruendo, ruido sordo

rummage /ˈrʌmɪdʒ/ *vi* **1** ~ **about/around** revolver, rebuscar **2** ~ **among/in/through sth (for sth)** revolver, hurgar (en) algo (en busca de algo)

rumour (*USA* **rumor**) /ˈruːmə(r)/ *n* rumor: *Rumour has it that...* Hay rumores de que...

rump /rʌmp/ *n* **1** grupa, ancas **2** (*tb* **rump steak**) (filete de) cadera

run /rʌn/ ◆ (**-nn-**) (*pret* **ran** /ræn/ *pp* **run**) **1** *vt, vi* correr: *I had to run to catch the bus.* Tuve que correr para coger el autobús. ◊ *I ran nearly ten kilometres.* He corrido casi diez kilómetros. **2** *vt, vi* recorrer: *to run your fingers through sb's hair* pasar los dedos por el pelo de algn ◊ *to run your eyes over sth* echar un vistazo a algo ◊ *She ran her eye around the room.* Recorrió la habitación con la mirada. ◊ *A shiver ran down her spine.* Un escalofrío le recorrió la espalda. ◊ *The tears ran down her cheeks.* Las lágrimas le corrían por las mejillas. **3** *vt, vi* (*máquina, sistema, organización*) (hacer) funcionar: *Everything is running smoothly.* Todo marcha sobre ruedas. ◊ *Run the engine for a few minutes before you start.* Ten el motor en marcha unos minutos antes de arrancar. **4** *vi* extenderse: *The cable runs the length of the wall.* El cable recorre todo el largo de la pared. ◊ *A fence runs round the field.* Una valla circunda el prado. **5** *vi* (*autobús, tren, etc*): *The buses run every hour.* Hay un autobús cada hora. ◊ *The train is running an hour late.* El tren lleva una hora de retraso. **6** *vt* llevar (*en coche*): *Can I run you to the station?* ¿Te puedo llevar a la estación? **7 to run (for...)** (*Teat*) representarse (durante...) **8** *vt*: *to run a bath* preparar un baño **9** *vi*: *to leave the tap running* dejar el grifo abierto **10** *vi* (*nariz*) gotear **11** *vi* (*tinte*) desteñir **12** *vt* (*negocio, etc*) administrar, dirigir **13** *vt* (*servicio, curso, etc*) organizar, ofrecer **14** *vt* (*Informát*) ejecutar **15** *vt* (*vehículo*) mantener: *I can't afford to run a car.* No me puedo permitir mantener un coche. **16** *vi* **to run (for sth)** (*Pol*) presentarse como candidato (a algo) **17** *vt* (*Period*) publicar LOC **to run dry** secarse **to run for it** echar a correr **to run in the family** ser de familia **to run out of steam** (*coloq*) perder el ímpetu **to run riot** desmandarse **to run the risk (of doing sth)** correr el riesgo/peligro (de hacer algo) *Ver tb* DEEP, TEMPERATURE, WASTE PHR V **to run about/around** corretear

to run across sth/sb toparse con algo/algn

to run after sb perseguir a algn

to run at sth: *Inflation is running at 25%.* La inflación alcanza el 25%.

to run away (from sth/sb) huir (de algo/algn)

to run into sth/sb 1 tropezar con algo/algn **2** chocarse con/contra algo, atropellar a algn **to run sth into sth**: *He ran the car into a tree.* Se chocó contra un árbol.

to run off (with sth) huir, escaparse (con algo)

to run out 1 caducar **2** acabarse

agotarse **to run out of sth** quedarse sin algo
to run sb over atropellar a algn
◆ *n* **1** carrera: *to go for a run* salir a correr ◊ *to break into a run* echar a correr **2** paseo (*en coche, etc*) **3** periodo: *a run of bad luck* una temporada de mala suerte **4** (*Teat*) temporada LOC **to be on the run** haberse fugado/estar huido de la justicia *Ver tb* BOLT[2], LONG[1]

runaway /ˈrʌnəweɪ/ ◆ *adj* **1** fugitivo **2** fuera de control **3** fácil ◆ *n* fugitivo, -a

run-down /ˌrʌn ˈdaʊn/ *adj* **1** (*edificio*) en un estado de abandono **2** (*persona*) desmejorado

rung[1] *pp de* RING[2]

rung[2] /rʌŋ/ *n* peldaño

runner /ˈrʌnə(r)/ *n* corredor, -ora

runner-up /ˌrʌnər ˈʌp/ *n* (*pl* **-s-up** /ˌrʌnəz ˈʌp/) subcampeón, -ona

running /ˈrʌnɪŋ/ ◆ *n* **1** atletismo **2** funcionamiento **3** organización LOC **to be in/out of the running (for sth)** (*coloq*) tener/no tener posibilidades (de conseguir algo) ◆ *adj* **1** continuo **2** consecutivo: *four days running* cuatro días seguidos **3** (*agua*) corriente LOC *Ver* ORDER

runny /ˈrʌni/ *adj* (**-ier**, **-iest**) (*coloq*) **1** líquido **2** *to have a runny nose* tener moquita

run-up /ˈrʌn ʌp/ *n* ~ (**to sth**) periodo previo (a algo)

runway /ˈrʌnweɪ/ *n* pista (*de aterrizaje*)

rupture /ˈrʌptʃə(r)/ ◆ *n* (*fml*) ruptura ◆ *vt, vi* desgarrarse

rush /rʌʃ/ ◆ **1** *vi* ir con prisa, apresurarse: *They rushed out of school.* Salieron corriendo del colegio. ◊ *They rushed to help her.* Se apresuraron a ayudarle. **2** *vi* actuar precipitadamente **3** *vt* meterle prisa a: *Don't rush me!* ¡No me metas prisa! **4** *vt* llevar de prisa: *He was rushed to hospital.* Le llevaron al hospital con la mayor urgencia. ◆ *n* **1** [*sing*] precipitación: *There was a rush to the exit.* La gente se precipitó hacia la salida. **2** (*coloq*) prisa: *I'm in a terrible rush.* Tengo una prisa loca. ◊ *There's no rush.* No corre prisa. ◊ *the rush hour* la hora punta

rust /rʌst/ ◆ *n* óxido ◆ *vt, vi* oxidar(se)

rustic /ˈrʌstɪk/ *adj* rústico

rustle /ˈrʌsl/ ◆ *vt, vi* (hacer) crujir, (hacer) susurrar PHR V **to rustle sth up** (*coloq*) preparar algo: *I'll rustle up some coffee for you.* En seguida te preparo un café. ◆ *n* crujido, susurro, frufrú

rusty /ˈrʌsti/ *adj* (**-ier**, **-iest**) **1** oxidado **2** (*fig*) falto de práctica

rut /rʌt/ *n* rodada LOC **to be (stuck) in a rut** estar estancado

ruthless /ˈruːθləs/ *adj* despiadado, implacable **ruthlessly** *adv* despiadadamente **ruthlessness** crueldad, implacabilidad

rye /raɪ/ *n* centeno

Ss

S, s /es/ *n* (*pl* **S's, s's** /ˈesɪz/) S, s: *S for sugar* S de Susana ☛ *Ver ejemplos en* A, a

the Sabbath /ˈsæbəθ/ *n* **1** (*de los cristianos*) domingo **2** (*de los judíos*) sábado

sabotage /ˈsæbətɑːʒ/ ◆ *n* sabotaje ◆ *vt* sabotear

saccharin /ˈsækərɪn/ *n* sacarina

sachet /ˈsæʃeɪ; *USA* sæˈʃeɪ/ *n* bolsita, sobrecito

sack[1] /sæk/ *n* costal, saco

sack[2] /sæk/ *vt* (*coloq, esp GB*) despedir

the sack *n* despido: *to give sb the sack* despedir a algn ◊ *to get the sack* ser despedido

sacred /ˈseɪkrɪd/ *adj* sagrado, sacro

sacrifice /ˈsækrɪfaɪs/ ◆ *n* sacrificio: *to make sacrifices* hacer sacrificios/sacrificarse ◆ *vt* ~ **sth (to/for sth/sb)** sacrificar algo (por algo/algn)

sacrilege /ˈsækrəlɪdʒ/ *n* sacrilegio

sad /sæd/ *adj* (**sadder**, **saddest**) **1** triste **2** (*situación*) lamentable **sadden** *vt* entristecer

saddle /ˈsædl/ ◆ *n* **1** (*para caballo*) silla **2** (*para bicicleta o moto*) sillín ◆ *vt* **1** ~ **sth** ensillar algo **2** ~ **sb with sth** hacer cargar a algn con algo

sadism /ˈseɪdɪzəm/ *n* sadismo

sadly /ˈsædli/ *adv* **1** tristemente, con tristeza **2** lamentablemente, desafortunadamente

sadness /ˈsædnəs/ *n* tristeza, melancolía

safari /səˈfɑːri/ *n* (*pl* ~**s**) safari

safe[1] /seɪf/ *adj* (**safer**, **safest**) **1** ~ (**from sth/sb**) a salvo (de algo/algn) **2** seguro: *Your secret is safe with me.* Tu secreto está seguro conmigo. **3** ileso **4** (*conductor*) prudente LOC **safe and sound** sano y salvo **to be on the safe side** por si acaso: *It's best to be on the safe side.* Es mejor no correr riesgos. *Ver tb* BETTER **safely** *adv* **1** sin novedad, sin ningún percance **2** tranquilamente, sin peligro: *safely locked away* guardado bajo llave en un lugar seguro

safe[2] /seɪf/ *n* caja fuerte

safeguard /ˈseɪfgɑːd/ ◆ *n* ~ (**against sth**) salvaguarda, protección (contra algo) ◆ *vt* ~ **sth/sb** (**against sth/sb**) proteger algo/a algn (de algo/algn)

safety /ˈseɪfti/ *n* seguridad

safety belt *n* cinturón de seguridad

safety net *n* **1** red de seguridad **2** red de protección

safety pin /ˈseɪfti pɪn/ *n* imperdible

safety valve *n* válvula de seguridad

sag /sæg/ *vi* (**-gg-**) **1** (*cama, sofá*) hundirse **2** (*madera*) combarse

Sagittarius /ˌsædʒɪˈteəriəs/ *n* sagitario ☛ *Ver ejemplos en* AQUARIUS

said *pret, pp de* SAY

sail /seɪl/ ◆ *n* vela LOC *Ver* SET[2] ◆ **1** *vt, vi* navegar: *to sail around the world* dar la vuelta al mundo en barco **2** *vi* ~ (**from...**) (**for/to...**) salir (desde...) (para...): *The ship sails at noon.* El barco zarpa a las doce del mediodía. **3** *vi* (*objeto*) volar PHR V **to sail through** (**sth**) hacer (algo) sin dificultad: *She sailed through her exams.* Aprobó los exámenes como quien lava.

sailing /ˈseɪlɪŋ/ *n* **1** navegar: *to go sailing* ir a hacer vela **2** *There are three sailings a day.* Hay tres salidas diarias.

sailing boat *n* velero

sailor /ˈseɪlə(r)/ *n* marinero, marino

saint /seɪnt, snt/ *n* (*abrev* **St**) s… santo, -a: *Saint Bernard/Teresa* S… Bernardo/Santa Teresa

sake /seɪk/ *n* LOC **for God's, go… ness', Heaven's, etc sake** por (el am… de) Dios **for sth's/sb's sake**; **for … sake of sth/sb** por algo/algn, por … bien de algo/algn

salad /ˈsæləd/ *n* ensalada

salary /ˈsæləri/ *n* (*pl* **-ies**) sala… sueldo (*mensual*) ☛ *Comparar* … WAGE

sale /seɪl/ *n* **1** venta: *sales departm…* servicio de ventas **2** rebajas: *to ho… have a sale* tener rebajas **3** subasta L… **for sale** en venta: *For sale.* … vende. **on sale** a la venta

salesman /ˈseɪlzmən/ *n* (*pl* **-m…** /-mən/) vendedor, dependiente

salesperson /ˈseɪlzpɜːsn/ *n* … **-people**) vendedor, -ora, dependien… -a

saleswoman /ˈseɪlzwʊmən/ *n* … **-women**) vendedora, dependienta

saliva /səˈlaɪvə/ *n* saliva

salmon /ˈsæmən/ *n* (*pl* **salm…** salmón

salon /ˈsælɒn; *USA* səˈlɒn/ *n* salón … *belleza*)

saloon /səˈluːn/ *n* **1** salón (*de bar… etc*) **2** (*USA*) bar **3** (*tb* **saloon car**) (… automóvil de dos o cuatro puertas

salt /sɔːlt/ *n* sal **salted** *adj* salado **sa…** (**-ier**, **-iest**) (*tb* **salt**) *adj* salado

salt-water /ˈsɔːlt wɔːtə(r)/ *adj* de a… salada

salutary /ˈsæljətri; *USA* -teri/ *adj* sa… dable

salute /səˈluːt/ ◆ *vt, vi* (*fml*) saludar… *un militar*) ☛ *Comparar con* GREET ◆ **1** saludo **2** salva

salvage /ˈsælvɪdʒ/ ◆ *n* salvamento… *vt* recuperar

salvation /sælˈveɪʃn/ *n* salvación

same /seɪm/ ◆ *adj* mismo, igual (*id… tico*): *the same thing* lo mismo ◊ *I … that same day.* Salí ese mismo día. ☛ … veces se usa para dar énfasis a … oración: *the very same man* el mis… simo hombre. LOC **at the same time** … la vez **2** no obstante, sin embargo … **be in the same boat** estar en el mis… barco ◆ **the same** *adv* de la mis… manera, igual: *to treat everyone* *same* tratar a todos de la misma manera ◆ *pron* **the same (as sth/sb)** el mismo, la misma, etc (que algo/algn): *I think the same as you.* Pienso igual que tú. LOC **all/just the same 1** de todos modos **2** *It's all the same to me.* Me da igual. **same here** (*coloq*) lo mismo digo **(the) same to you** igualmente

sample /ˈsɑːmpl; *USA* ˈsæmpl/ ◆ *n* muestra ◆ *vt* probar

sanatorium /ˌsænəˈtɔːrɪəm/ (*USA tb* **sanitarium** /ˌsænəˈteərɪəm/) *n* (*pl* ~**s** *o* **-ria** /-rɪə/) sanatorio

sanction /ˈsæŋkʃn/ ◆ *n* **1** aprobación **2** sanción: *to lift sanctions* levantar sanciones ◆ *vt* dar el permiso para

sanctuary /ˈsæŋktʃuəri; *USA* -ueri/ *n* (*pl* **-ies**) santuario: *The rebels took sanctuary in the church.* Los rebeldes se refugiaron en la iglesia.

sand /sænd/ *n* **1** arena **2 the sands** [*pl*] la playa

sandal /ˈsændl/ *n* sandalia

sandcastle /ˈsændkɑːsl; *USA* -kæsl/ *n* castillo de arena

sand dune (*tb* **dune**) *n* duna

sandpaper /ˈsændpeɪpə(r)/ *n* papel de lija

sandwich /ˈsænwɪdʒ; *USA* -wɪtʃ/ ◆ *n* bocadillo, sandwich ◆ *vt* apretujar (*entre dos personas o cosas*)

sandy /ˈsændi/ *adj* (**-ier**, **-iest**) arenoso

sane /seɪn/ *adj* (**saner**, **sanest**) **1** cuerdo **2** juicioso

sang *pret de* SING

sanitarium (*USA*) *Ver* SANATORIUM

sanitary /ˈsænətri; *USA* -teri/ *adj* higiénico

sanitary towel *n* compresa

sanitation /ˌsænɪˈteɪʃn/ *n* saneamiento

sanity /ˈsænəti/ *n* **1** cordura **2** sensatez

sank *pret de* SINK

sap /sæp/ ◆ *n* savia ◆ *vt* (**-pp-**) socavar, minar

sapphire /ˈsæfaɪə(r)/ *adj, n* (color) zafiro

sarcasm /ˈsɑːkæzəm/ *n* sarcasmo

sarcastic /sɑːˈkæstɪk/ *adj* sarcástico

sardine /ˌsɑːˈdiːn/ *n* sardina

sash /sæʃ/ *n* fajín

sat *pret, pp de* SIT

satchel /ˈsætʃəl/ *n* cartera (*de colegio*)

satellite /ˈsætəlaɪt/ *n* satélite

satin /ˈsætɪn; *USA* ˈsætn/ *n* raso

satire /ˈsætaɪə(r)/ *n* sátira **satirical** /səˈtɪrɪkl/ *adj* satírico

satisfaction /ˌsætɪsˈfækʃn/ *n* satisfacción

satisfactory /ˌsætɪsˈfæktəri/ *adj* satisfactorio

satisfy /ˈsætɪsfaɪ/ *vt* (*pret, pp* **-fied**) **1** (*curiosidad*) satisfacer **2** (*condiciones, etc*) cumplir con **3** ~ **sb (as to sth)** convencer a algn (de algo) **satisfied** *adj* ~ **(with sth)** satisfecho (con algo) **satisfying** *adj* satisfactorio: *a satisfying meal* una comida que te deja satisfecho

satsuma /sætˈsuːmə/ *n* mandarina

saturate /ˈsætʃəreɪt/ *vt* ~ **sth (with sth)** empapar algo (de algo): *The market is saturated.* El mercado está saturado. **saturation** *n* saturación

Saturday /ˈsætədeɪ, ˈsætədi/ *n* (*abrev* **Sat**) sábado ☛ *Ver ejemplos en* MONDAY

Saturn /ˈsætən/ *n* Saturno

sauce /sɔːs/ *n* salsa

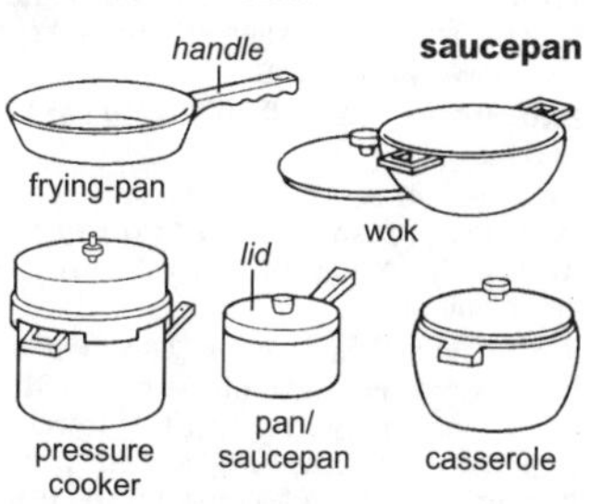

saucepan /ˈsɔːspən; *USA* -pæn/ *n* cazo, cacerola

saucer /ˈsɔːsə(r)/ *n* (*coloq*) platillo ☛ *Ver dibujo en* MUG

sauna /ˈsɔːnə, ˈsaʊnə/ *n* sauna

saunter /ˈsɔːntə(r)/ *vi* pasearse: *He sauntered over to the bar.* Fue hacia la barra con mucha tranquilidad.

sausage /ˈsɒsɪdʒ; *USA* ˈsɔːs-/ *n* salchicha, embutido

sausage roll *n* hojaldre relleno de carne de embutido

savage /ˈsævɪdʒ/ ◆ *adj* **1** salvaje **2** (*perro, etc*) enfurecido **3** (*ataque, régimen*) brutal: *savage cuts in the budget* cortes terribles en el presupuesto ◆ *n* salvaje ◆ *vt* atacar con ferocidad **savagery** *n* salvajismo

save /seɪv/ ◆ *vt* **1** ~ **sb** (**from sth**) salvar a algn (de algo) **2** ~ (**up**) (**for sth**) (*dinero*) ahorrar (para algo) **3** (*Informát*) guardar **4** ~ (**sb**) **sth** evitar (a algn) algo: *That will save us a lot of trouble.* Eso nos evitará muchos problemas. **5** (*Dep*) parar LOC **to save face** guardar las apariencias ◆ *n* parada (*de balón*)

saving /ˈseɪvɪŋ/ *n* **1** ahorro: *a saving of £5* un ahorro de cinco libras **2 savings** [*pl*] ahorros

saviour (*USA* **savior**) /ˈseɪvɪə(r)/ *n* salvador, -ora

savoury (*USA* **savory**) /ˈseɪvəri/ *adj* **1** (*GB*) salado **2** sabroso

saw[1] *pret de* SEE

saw[2] /sɔː/ ◆ *n* sierra ◆ *vt* (*pret* **sawed** *pp* **sawn** /sɔːn/ (*USA* **sawed**)) serrar *Ver tb* CUT PHR V **to saw sth down** talar algo con una sierra **to saw sth off** (**sth**) cortar algo (de algo) con una sierra: *a sawn-off shotgun* una escopeta de cañones recortados **to saw sth up** serrar algo **sawdust** *n* serrín

saxophone /ˈsæksəfəʊn/ (*coloq* **sax**) *n* saxofón

say /seɪ/ ◆ *vt* (*3ª persona sing* **says** /sez/ *pret, pp* **said** /sed/) **1 to say sth** (**to sb**) decir algo (a algn): *to say yes* decir que sí

> **Say** suele utilizarse cuando se mencionan las palabras textuales o para introducir una oración en estilo indirecto precedida por **that**: *'I'll leave at nine', he said.* —Me marcho a las nueve, dijo. ◊ *He said that he would leave at nine.* Dijo que se marcharía a las nueve. **Tell** se utiliza para introducir una oración en estilo indirecto y tiene que ir seguido de un sustantivo, un pronombre o un nombre propio: *He told me that he would leave at nine.* Me dijo que se marcharía a las nueve. Con órdenes o consejos se suele usar **tell**: *I told them to hurry up.* Les dije que se dieran prisa. ◊ *She's always telling me what I ought to do.* Siempre me está diciendo lo que tengo que hacer.

2 digamos, pongamos (que): *Let's take any writer, say Dickens…* Pongamos por caso cualquier escritor, digamos Dickens… ◊ *Say there are 30 in a class…* Pongamos que hay 30 en una clase… **3** *What time does it say on that clock?* ¿Qué hora tiene ese reloj? ◊ *The map says the hotel is on the right.* El plano dice que el hotel está a la derecha. LOC **it goes without saying that…** ni que decir tiene que… **that is to say** es decir *Ver tb* DARE[1], FAREWELL, LET[1], NEEDLESS, SORRY, WORD ◆ *n* LOC **to have a/some say** (**in sth**) tener voz y voto (en algo) **to have your say** expresar su opinión

saying /ˈseɪɪŋ/ *n* dicho, refrán *Ver tb* PROVERB

scab /skæb/ *n* postilla

scaffold /ˈskæfəʊld/ *n* patíbulo

scaffolding /ˈskæfəldɪŋ/ *n* [*incontable*] andamiaje, andamio

scald /skɔːld/ ◆ *vt* escaldar ◆ *n* escaldadura **scalding** *adj* hirviendo

scale[1] /skeɪl/ *n* **1** (*gen, Mús*) escala: *a large-scale map* un mapa a gran escala ◊ *a scale model* una maqueta **2** alcance magnitud, envergadura: *the scale of the problem* la magnitud del problema LOC **to scale** a escala

scale[2] /skeɪl/ *n* escama

scale[3] /skeɪl/ *vt* escalar, trepar

scales /skeɪlz/ *n* [*pl*] balanza, báscula

scalp /skælp/ *n* cuero cabelludo

scalpel /ˈskælpəl/ *n* bisturí

scamper /ˈskæmpə(r)/ *vi* corretear

scampi /ˈskæmpi/ *n* [*pl*] gambas frita rebozadas

scan /skæn/ ◆ *vt* (**-nn-**) **1** escudriñar examinar **2** explorar con un scanner echar un vistazo a ◆ *n* exploració ultrasónica, ecografía

scandal /ˈskændl/ *n* **1** escándalo chisme **scandalize, -ise** *vt* escandaliza **scandalous** *adj* escandaloso

scant /skænt/ *adj* (*fml*) escaso **scant** *adj* (**-ier**, **-iest**) escaso **scantily** *ad* escasamente: *scantily dressed* ligero d ropa

scapegoat /ˈskeɪpgəʊt/ *n* chivo expi torio: *She has been made a scapego for what happened.* Ha cargado con la culpas por lo que pasó.

scar /skɑː(r)/ ◆ *n* cicatriz ◆ *vt* (**-rr** dejar una cicatriz en

scarce /skeəs/ *adj* (**-er**, **-est**) escas *Food was scarce.* Los alimentos escase ban.

scarcely /ˈskeəsli/ *adv* **1** apena

There were scarcely a hundred people present. Apenas había un centenar de personas. **2** *You can scarcely expect me to believe that.* ¿Y esperas que me crea eso? *Ver tb* HARDLY

scarcity /ˈskeəsəti/ *n* (*pl* **-ies**) escasez

scare /ˈskeə(r)/ ◆ *vt* asustar PHR V **to scare sb away/off** ahuyentar a algn ◆ *n* susto: *bomb scare* amenaza de bomba **scared** *adj*: *to be scared* estar asustado/tener miedo ◊ *She's scared of the dark.* Le da miedo la oscuridad. LOC **to be scared stiff** (*coloq*) estar muerto de miedo *Ver tb* WIT

scarecrow /ˈskeəkrəʊ/ *n* espantapájaros

scarf /skɑːf/ *n* (*pl* **scarfs** *o* **scarves** /skɑːvz/) **1** bufanda **2** pañuelo

scarlet /ˈskɑːlət/ *adj, n* escarlata

scary /ˈskeəri/ *adj* (**-ier**, **-iest**) (*coloq*) espeluznante

scathing /ˈskeɪðɪŋ/ *adj* **1** mordaz **2** feroz: *a scathing attack on...* un feroz ataque contra...

scatter /ˈskætə(r)/ **1** *vt, vi* dispersar(se) **2** *vt* esparcir **scattered** *adj* esparcido, disperso: *scattered showers* chubascos aislados

scavenge /ˈskævɪndʒ/ *vi* **1** (*animal, ave*) buscar carroña **2** (*persona*) rebuscar (*en la basura*) **scavenger** *n* **1** animal/ave de carroña **2** persona que rebusca en las basuras

scenario /səˈnɑːriəʊ; *USA* -ˈnær-/ *n* (*pl* ~**s**) **1** (*Teat*) argumento **2** (*fig*) marco hipotético

scene /siːn/ *n* **1** (*gen, Teat*) escena: *a change of scene* un cambio de aires **2** escenario: *the scene of the crime* el lugar del crimen **3** escándalo: *to make a scene* montar un escándalo **4 the scene** [*sing*] (*coloq*) el mundillo: *the music scene* la movida musical LOC *Ver* SET²

scenery /ˈsiːnəri/ *n* [*incontable*] **1** paisaje

La palabra **scenery** tiene un fuerte matiz positivo, tiende a usarse con adjetivos como *beautiful, spectacular, stunning*, etc y se utiliza fundamentalmente para describir paisajes naturales. Por otro lado, **landscape** suele referirse a paisajes construidos por el hombre: *an urban/industrial landscape* un paisaje urbano/industrial ◊ *Trees and hedges are typical features of the British landscape.* Los árboles y los setos son rasgos típicos del paisaje británico.

2 (*Teat*) decorado

scenic /ˈsiːnɪk/ *adj* pintoresco, panorámico

scent /sent/ *n* **1** olor (*agradable*) **2** perfume **3** rastro, pista **scented** *adj* perfumado

sceptic (*USA* **skeptic**) /ˈskeptɪk/ *n* escéptico, -a **sceptical** (*USA* **skep-**) *adj* ~ (**of/about sth**) escéptico (acerca de algo) **scepticism** (*USA* **skep-**) *n* escepticismo

schedule /ˈʃedjuːl; *USA* ˈskedʒʊl/ ◆ *n* **1** programa: *to be two months ahead of/behind schedule* llevar dos meses de adelanto/retraso con respecto al calendario previsto ◊ *to arrive on schedule* llegar a la hora prevista **2** (*USA*) horario ◆ *vt* programar: *scheduled flight* vuelo regular

scheme /skiːm/ ◆ *n* **1** plan, proyecto: *training scheme* programa de formación ◊ *savings/pension scheme* plan de ahorro/de pensiones **2** conspiración **3** *colour scheme* combinación de colores ◆ *vi* conspirar

schizophrenia /ˌskɪtsəˈfriːniə/ *n* esquizofrenia **schizophrenic** /ˌskɪtsəˈfrenɪk/ *adj, n* esquizofrénico, -a

scholar /ˈskɒlə(r)/ *n* **1** becario, -a **2** erudito, -a **scholarship** *n* **1** beca **2** erudición

school /skuːl/ *n* **1** colegio, escuela: *school age/uniform* edad/uniforme escolar *Ver tb* COMPREHENSIVE SCHOOL

Utilizamos las palabras **school**, **church** y **hospital** sin artículo cuando alguien va al colegio como alumno o profesor, a la iglesia para rezar, o al hospital como paciente: *She's gone into hospital.* La han ingresado en el hospital. ◊ *I enjoyed being at school.* Me gustaba ir al colegio. ◊ *We go to church every Sunday.* Vamos a misa todos los domingos. Usamos el artículo cuando nos referimos a estos sitios por algún otro motivo: *I have to go to the school to talk to John's teacher.* Tengo que ir a la escuela a hablar con el profesor de John. ◊ *She works at the hospital.* Trabaja en el hospital.

2 (*USA*) universidad **3** clases: *School begins at nine o'clock.* Las clases empiezan a las nueve. **4** facultad: *law school* facultad de derecho **5** (*Arte, Liter*) escuela LOC **school of thought** escuela de pensamiento

schoolboy /ˈskuːlbɔɪ/ *n* colegial

schoolchild /ˈskuːltʃaɪld/ *n* colegial, -ala

schoolgirl /ˈskuːlgɜːl/ *n* colegiala

schooling /ˈskuːlɪŋ/ *n* educación, estudios

school leaver *n* chico, -a que acaba de terminar la escuela

schoolmaster /ˈskuːlmɑːstə(r)/ *n* maestro

schoolmistress /ˈskuːlmɪstrəs/ *n* maestra

schoolteacher /ˈskuːltiːtʃə(r)/ *n* profesor, -ora

science /ˈsaɪəns/ *n* ciencia: *science fiction* ciencia-ficción **scientific** *adj* científico **scientifically** *adv* científicamente **scientist** *n* científico, -a

sci-fi /ˌsaɪ ˈfaɪ/ *n* (*coloq*) **science fiction** ciencia ficción

scissors /ˈsɪzəz/ *n* [*pl*] tijeras: *a pair of scissors* unas tijeras ☛ *Ver nota en* TIJERA

scoff /skɒf; *USA* skɔːf/ *vi* ~ (**at sth/sb**) mofarse (de algo/algn)

scold /skəʊld/ *vt* ~ **sb** (**for sth**) regañar a algn (por algo)

scoop /skuːp/ ◆ *n* **1** pala: *ice cream scoop* cuchara para servir el helado **2** cucharada: *a scoop of ice-cream* una bola de helado **3** (*Period*) primicia ◆ *vt* cavar, sacar (*con pala*) PHR V **to scoop sth out** sacar algo (*con la mano, una cuchara, etc*)

scooter /ˈskuːtə(r)/ *n* **1** Vespa®, Vespino® **2** patinete

scope /skəʊp/ *n* **1** ~ (**for sth/to do sth**) potencial (para algo/para hacer algo) **2** ámbito, alcance: *within/beyond the scope of this dictionary* dentro/más allá del ámbito de este diccionario

scorch /skɔːtʃ/ *vt, vi* chamuscar(se), quemar(se) **scorching** *adj* abrasador

score /skɔː(r)/ ◆ *n* **1** tanteo: *to keep the score* llevar la cuenta de los tantos ◇ *The final score was 4-3.* El resultado final fue de 4-3. **2** (*Educ*) puntuación **3** **scores** [*pl*] montones **4** (*Mús*) partitura **5** veintena LOC **on that score** en ese sentido ◆ **1** *vt, vi* (*Dep*) marcar **2** *vt* (*Educ*) sacar **scoreboard** *n* marcador

scorn /skɔːn/ ◆ *n* ~ (**for sth/sb**) desdén (hacia algo/algn) ◆ *vt* desdeñar **scornful** *adj* desdeñoso

Scorpio /ˈskɔːpiəʊ/ *n* (*pl* ~**s**) escorpio ☛ *Ver ejemplos en* AQUARIUS

scorpion /ˈskɔːpiən/ *n* escorpión

Scotch /skɒtʃ/ *n* whisky escocés

scour /ˈskaʊə(r)/ *vt* **1** fregar **2** ~ **sth** (**for sth/sb**) registrar, recorrer algo (en busca de algo/algn)

scourge /skɜːdʒ/ *n* azote

scout /ˈskaʊt/ *n* **1** (*Mil*) explorador **2** (*tb* **Boy Scout**, **Scout**) scout

scowl /skaʊl/ ◆ *n* ceño fruncido ◆ *vi* mirar con el ceño fruncido

scrabble /ˈskræbl/ PHR V **to scrabble about** (**for sth**) escarbar (en busca de algo)

scramble /ˈskræmbl/ ◆ **1** *vi* trepar **2** *vi* ~ (**for sth**) pelearse (por algo) ◆ *n* [*sing*] ~ (**for sth**) barullo (por algo)

scrambled eggs *n* huevos revueltos

scrap /skræp/ ◆ *n* **1** pedazo: *a scrap o*[f] *paper* un pedazo de papel ◇ *scraps (o*[f] *food)* sobras **2** [*incontable*] chatarra *scrap paper* papel para apuntes **3** [*sing*] (*fig*) pizca **4** pelea ◆ (**-pp-**) **1** *vt* descar[tar], tar, desechar **2** *vi* pelearse

scrapbook /ˈskræpbʊk/ *n* álbum d[e] recortes

scrape /skreɪp/ ◆ **1** *vt* raspar **2** *vt* **sth away/off** quitar algo raspando **3** ~ **sth off sth** quitar algo de alg[o] raspando **4** *vi* ~ (**against sth**) rozar alg[o] PHR V **to scrape in/into sth** tener éxit[o] conseguir algo por los pelos: *She ju*[st] *scraped into university.* Entró en [la] universidad por los pelos. **to scrap**[e] **sth together/up** reunir algo a dur[as] penas **to scrape through** (**sth**) aproba[r] (algo) por los pelos ◆ *n* raspadura

scratch /skrætʃ/ ◆ **1** *vt, vi* arañar(s[e]) **2** *vt, vi* rascarse **3** *vt* rayar PHR V [**to**] **scratch sth away, off, etc** quitar al[go] de algo raspándolo ◆ *n* **1** rasguñ[o], arañazo **2** [*sing*]: *The dog gave itself* [*a*] *good scratch.* El perro se rascó de lindo. LOC (**to be/come**) **up to scrat**[**ch**] (estar/llegar) a la altura (**to start st**[**h**]) **from scratch** (empezar algo) de cero

scrawl /skrɔːl/ ◆ **1** *vt* garabatear **2** hacer garabatos ◆ *n* [*sing*] garabato

scream /skriːm/ ◆ **1** *vt* gritar **2** *vi* chillar: *to scream with excitement* gritar de emoción ◆ *n* **1** chillido, grito: *a scream of pain* un grito de dolor **2** [*sing*] (*coloq*) algo/algn divertidísimo

screech /skriːtʃ/ ◆ *vi* chillar, chirriar ◆ *n* [*sing*] chillido, chirrido

screen /skriːn/ *n* **1** pantalla ☛ *Ver dibujo en* ORDENADOR **2** biombo

screw /skruː/ ◆ *n* tornillo ◆ *vt* **1** atornillar, fijar con tornillos **2** enroscar PHR V **to screw sth up 1** (*papel*) hacer una pelota con algo **2** (*cara*) torcer algo **3** (*coloq*) (*planes, situación, etc*) jorobar algo

screwdriver /ˈskruːdraɪvə(r)/ *n* destornillador

scribble /ˈskrɪbl/ ◆ **1** *vt* garabatear **2** *vi* hacer garabatos ◆ *n* garabatos

script /skrɪpt/ ◆ *n* **1** guión **2** letra **3** escritura ◆ *vt* escribir el guión para

scripture /ˈskrɪptʃə(r)/ (*tb* **Scripture/ the Scriptures**) *n* las Sagradas Escrituras

scroll /skrəʊl/ *n* **1** pergamino **2** rollo de papel

scrounge /ˈskraʊndʒ/ **1** *vt* gorronear: *Can I scrounge a cigarette off you?* ¿Te puedo gorronear un cigarrillo? **2** *vi* vivir de gorra **3** *vi* ~ **off sb** vivir de algn

scrub[1] /skrʌb/ *n* [*incontable*] matorrales

scrub[2] /skrʌb/ ◆ *vt* (**-bb-**) fregar ◆ *n*: *Give your nails a good scrub.* Cepíllate bien las uñas.

scruff /skrʌf/ *n* LOC **by the scruff of the neck** por el cogote

scruffy /ˈskrʌfi/ *adj* (**-ier**, **-iest**) (*coloq*) desaliñado

scrum /skrʌm/ *n* melé

scruples /ˈskruːplz/ *n* escrúpulos

scrupulous /ˈskruːpjələs/ *adj* escrupuloso **scrupulously** *adv* escrupulosamente: *scrupulously clean* impecable

scrutinize, -ise /ˈskruːtənaɪz/ *vt* **1** examinar **2** inspeccionar

scrutiny /ˈskruːtəni/ *n* **1** examen **2** (*tb Pol*) escrutinio

scuba-diving /ˈskuːbə daɪvɪŋ/ *n* buceo con escafandra

scuff /skʌf/ *vt* hacer rayones en

scuffle /ˈskʌfl/ *n* **1** enfrentamiento **2** forcejeo

sculptor /ˈskʌlptə(r)/ *n* escultor, -ora

sculpture /ˈskʌlptʃə(r)/ *n* escultura

scum /skʌm/ *n* **1** espuma **2** escoria

scurry /ˈskʌri/ *vi* (*pret, pp* **scurried**) ir apresuradamente PHR V **to scurry about/around 1** trajinar **2** corretear

scuttle /ˈskʌtl/ *vi*: *She scuttled back to her car.* Volvió a su coche a toda prisa. ◊ *to scuttle away/off* escabullirse

scythe /saɪð/ *n* guadaña

sea /siː/ *n* **1** mar: *sea creatures* animales marinos ◊ *the sea air/breeze* la brisa marina ◊ *sea port* puerto marítimo ☛ *Ver nota en* MAR **2 seas** [*pl*] mar: *heavy/rough seas* mar gruesa **3** mar: *a sea of people* un mar de gente LOC **at sea** en el mar **to be all at sea** estar en medio de un mar de dudas

seabed /ˈsiːbed/ *n* lecho marino

seafood /ˈsiːfuːd/ *n* marisco

seagull /ˈsiːgʌl/ *n* gaviota

seal[1] /siːl/ *n* foca

seal[2] /siːl/ ◆ *n* sello ◆ *vt* **1** sellar **2** (*documento*) lacrar **3** (*sobre*) cerrar PHR V **to seal sth off** precintar

sea level *n* nivel del mar

seam /siːm/ *n* **1** costura **2** filón

search /sɜːtʃ/ ◆ **1** *vi* ~ **for sth** buscar algo **2** *vt* ~ **sth/sb** (**for sth**) registrar algo/a algn (en busca de algo): *They searched the house for drugs.* Registraron la casa en busca de drogas. ◆ *n* **1** ~ (**for sth/sb**) búsqueda (de algo/algn) **2** (*policial*) registro **searching** *adj* penetrante

searchlight /ˈsɜːtʃlaɪt/ *n* (*foco*) reflector

seashell /ˈsiːʃel/ *n* concha marina

seasick /ˈsiːsɪk/ *adj* mareado

seaside /ˈsiːsaɪd/ *n* **1** playa **2** costa

season[1] /ˈsiːzn/ *n* **1** estación **2** temporada: *season ticket* abono de temporada LOC **in season** que está en temporada *Ver tb* MATING **seasonal** *adj* **1** propio de la estación **2** (*trabajo*) de temporada

season[2] /ˈsiːzn/ *vt* condimentar, sazonar **seasoned** *adj* **1** condimentado **2** (*persona*) con mucha experiencia **seasoning** *n* condimento

seat /siːt/ ◆ *n* **1** (*coche*) asiento **2** (*parque*) banco **3** (*teatro*) butaca **4** (*avión*) plaza **5** (*Pol*) escaño **6** (*Pol*) circunscripción electoral LOC *Ver* DRIVER ◆ *vt* tener cabida para: *The* *stadium can seat 5000 people.* El estadio tiene cabida para 5.000 personas.

seat belt (*tb* **safety belt**) *n* cinturón de seguridad

seating /ˈsiːtɪŋ/ *n* [*incontable*] asientos

seaweed /ˈsiːwiːd/ *n* [*incontable*] alga

secluded /sɪˈkluːdɪd/ *adj* **1** (*lugar*) apartado **2** (*vida*) retirado **seclusion** *n* **1** aislamiento **2** soledad

second (*abrev* **2nd**) /ˈsekənd/ ◆ *adj* segundo LOC **second thoughts**: *We had second thoughts.* Lo reconsideramos. ◊ *On second thoughts...* Pensándolo bien... ◆ *pron, adv* el segundo, la segunda, los segundos, las segundas ◆ *n* **1 the second** el (día) dos **2** (*tb* **second gear**) segunda **3** (*tiempo*) segundo: *the second hand* el segundero ☛ *Ver ejemplos en* FIFTH ◆ *vt* secundar

secondary /ˈsekəndri/ *adj* secundario

second-best /ˌsekənd ˈbest/ *adj* segundo mejor

second-class /ˌsekənd ˈklaːs/ *adj* **1** de segunda clase: *a second-class ticket* un billete de segunda (clase) **2** (*correo*) de franqueo normal

second-hand /ˌsekənd ˈhænd/ *adj, adv* de segunda mano

secondly /ˈsekəndli/ *adv* en segundo lugar

second-rate /ˌsekənd ˈreit/ *adj* de segunda fila

secret /ˈsiːkrət/ *adj, n* secreto **secrecy** *n* **1** secretismo **2** confidencialidad

secretarial /ˌsekrəˈteəriəl/ *adj* **1** (*personal*) administrativo **2** (*trabajo*) de secretario, -a

secretary /ˈsekrətri; *USA* -rəteri/ *n* (*pl* **-ies**) secretario, -a

Secretary of State *n* **1** (*GB*) ministro, -a ☛ *Ver nota en* MINISTRO **2** (*USA*) secretario, -a de Estado

secrete /sɪˈkriːt/ *vt* (*fml*) **1** segregar **2** ocultar **secretion** *n* secreción

secretive /ˈsiːkrətɪv/ *adj* reservado

secretly /ˈsiːkrətli/ *adv* en secreto

sect /sekt/ *n* secta

sectarian /sekˈteəriən/ *adj* sectario

section /ˈsekʃn/ *n* **1** sección, parte **2** (*carretera*) tramo **3** (*sociedad*) sector **4** (*ley, código*) artículo

sector /ˈsektə(r)/ *n* sector

secular /ˈsekjələ(r)/ *adj* laico

secure /sɪˈkjʊə(r)/ ◆ *adj* **1** seguro **2** (*prisión*) de alta seguridad ◆ *vt* **1** fijar **2** (*acuerdo, contrato*) conseguir **securely** *adv* firmemente **security** *n* (*pl* **-ies**) **1** seguridad **2** (*préstamo*) fianza

security guard *n* guardia jurado

sedate /sɪˈdeɪt/ ◆ *adj* serio ◆ *vt* sedar **sedation** *n* sedación LOC **to be under sedation** estar bajo los efectos de calmantes **sedative** *adj, n* /ˈsedətɪv/ sedante

sedentary /ˈsedntri; *USA* -teri/ *adj* sedentario

sediment /ˈsedɪmənt/ *n* sedimento

sedition /sɪˈdɪʃn/ *n* sedición

seduce /sɪˈdjuːs; *USA* -ˈduːs/ *vt* seducir **seduction** *n* seducción **seductive** *adj* seductor

see /siː/ *vt, vi* (*pret* **saw** /sɔː/ *pp* **seen** /siːn/) **1** ver: *I saw a programme on TV about that.* Vi un programa en la tele sobre eso. ◊ *to go and see a film* ir a ver una película ◊ *She'll never see again.* No volverá a ver nunca. ◊ *See page 158.* Véase la página 158. ◊ *Go and see if the postman's been.* Ve a ver si ha llegado el correo. ◊ *Let's see.* Vamos a ver. ◊ *I'm seeing Sue tonight.* He quedado con Sue esta noche. **2** acompañar: *He saw her to the door.* La acompañó hasta la puerta. **3** encargarse: *I'll see that it's done.* Ya me encargaré de que se lleve a cabo. **4** comprender LOC **see you (around)**; **(I'll be seeing you** (*coloq*) hasta luego **seeing that...** en vista de que... ☛ Para otras expresiones con **see** véanse las entradas del sustantivo, adjetivo, etc, p.ej. **to make sb see reason** en REASON. PHR V **to see about sth/doing sth** encargarse de algo/hacer algo **to see sb off 1** ir a despedir a algn **2** echar a algn **to see through sth/sb** calar algo/a algn **to see to sth** ocuparse de algo

seed /siːd/ *n* semilla, simiente

seedy /ˈsiːdi/ *adj* (**-ier**, **-iest**) sórdido

seek /siːk/ *vt, vi* (*pret, pp* **sought** /sɔːt/) (*fml*) **1** ~ **(after/for sth)** buscar (algo) **2** ~ **(to do sth)** intentar (hacer algo) PHR V **to seek sth/sb out** buscar y encontrar algo/a algn

seem /siːm/ *vi* parecer: *It seems that...* Parece que... ☛ No se usa en tiempos continuos. *Ver tb* APPEAR 2 **seemingly** *adv* aparentemente

seen *pp de* SEE

seep /siːp/ *vi* filtrarse

seething /ˈsiːðɪŋ/ *adj* ~ **with sth** abarrotado (de algo)

see-through /ˈsiː θruː/ *adj* transparente

segment /ˈsegmənt/ *n* **1** (*Geom*) segmento **2** (*de naranja, etc*) gajo

segregate /ˈsegrɪgeɪt/ *vt* ~ **sth/sb** (**from sth/sb**) segregar algo/a algn (de algo/algn)

seize /siːz/ *vt* **1** coger: *to seize hold of sth* agarrar algo ◊ *We were seized by panic.* El pánico se apoderó de nosotros. **2** (*armas, drogas, etc*) incautarse de **3** (*personas, edificios*) capturar **4** (*bienes*) embargar **5** (*control*) hacerse con **6** (*oportunidad, etc*) aprovechar: *to seize the initiative* tomar la iniciativa PHR V **to seize on/upon sth** aprovecharse de algo **to seize up** agarrotarse, atascarse **seizure** /ˈsiːʒə(r)/ *n* **1** (*de contrabando, etc*) incautación **2** captura **3** (*Med*) ataque

seldom /ˈseldəm/ *adv* rara vez: *We seldom go out.* Rara vez salimos. ☛ *Ver nota en* ALWAYS

select /sɪˈlekt/ ◆ *vt* ~ **sth/sb** (**as sth**) elegir algo/a algn (como algo) ☛ *Ver nota en* CHOOSE ◆ *adj* selecto **selection** *n* selección **selective** *adj* ~ (**about sth/sb**) selectivo (en cuanto a algo/a algn)

self /self/ *n* (*pl* **selves** /selvz/) ser: *She's her old self again.* Es la misma de siempre otra vez.

self-centred (*USA* **-centered**) /ˌself ˈsentəd/ *adj* egocéntrico

self-confident /ˌself ˈkɒnfɪdənt/ *adj* seguro de sí mismo

self-conscious /ˌself ˈkɒnʃəs/ *adj* inseguro

self-contained /ˌself kənˈteɪnd/ *adj* (*piso*) completo

self-control /ˌself kənˈtrəʊl/ *n* autocontrol

self-defence /ˌself dɪˈfens/ *n* defensa propia

self-determination /ˌself dɪˌtɜːmɪˈneɪʃn/ *n* autodeterminación

self-employed /ˌself ɪmˈplɔɪd/ *adj* (*trabajador*) autónomo

self-interest /ˌself ˈɪntrəst/ *n* interés propio

selfish /ˈselfɪʃ/ *adj* egoísta

self-pity /ˌself ˈpɪti/ *n* autocompasión

self-portrait /ˌself ˈpɔːtreɪt, -trɪt/ *n* autorretrato

self-respect /ˌself rɪˈspekt/ *n* dignidad

self-satisfied /ˌself ˈsætɪsfaɪd/ *adj* excesivamente satisfecho de sí mismo

self-service /ˌself ˈsɜːvɪs/ *adj* autoservicio

sell /sel/ *vt, vi* (*pp, pret* **sold** /səʊld/) ~ (**at/for sth**) vender(se) (a algo) LOC **to be sold out** (**of sth**) haber agotado existencias PHR V **to sell sth off** vender algo a bajo precio **to sell out** (*entradas*) agotarse

sell-by date /ˈsel baɪ deɪt/ *n* fecha de caducidad

seller /ˈselə(r)/ *n* vendedor, -ora

selling /ˈselɪŋ/ *n* venta

Sellotape® /ˈselәteɪp/ ◆ *n* (*GB*) (*tb* **sticky tape**) cinta adhesiva ◆ *vt* pegar con cinta adhesiva

selves *plural de* SELF

semi /ˈsemi/ *n* (*pl* **semis** /ˈsemiz/) (*GB, coloq*) casa o chalé con una pared medianera ☛ *Ver pág 321.*

semicircle /ˈsemisɜːkl/ *n* **1** semicírculo **2** semicircunferencia

semicolon /ˌsemiˈkəʊlən; *USA* ˈsemik-/ *n* punto y coma ☛ *Ver págs 318–19.*

semi-detached /ˌsemi dɪˈtætʃt/ *adj* con una pared medianera: *a semi-detached house* una casa con una pared medianera ☛ *Ver pág 321.*

seminar /ˈsemɪnɑː(r)/ *n* seminario (*clase*)

senate /ˈsenət/ (*tb* **Senate**) *n* [*v sing o pl*] **1** (*Pol*) Senado **2** (*Univ*) junta de gobierno **senator** /ˈsenətə(r)/ (*tb* **Senator**) *n* (*abrev* **Sen**) senador, -ora

send /send/ *vt* (*pret, pp* **sent** /sent/) **1** enviar, mandar: *She was sent to bed without any supper.* La mandaron a la cama sin cenar. **2** hacer (que): *to send sb to sleep* dormir a alguien: *The story sent shivers down my spine.* La historia me dio escalofríos. ◊ *to send sb mad* volver loco a uno LOC *Ver* LOVE
PHR V **to send for sb** llamar a algn, mandar buscar a algn **to send** (**off**) **for sth** pedir/encargar algo
to send sb in enviar a algn (*esp tropas, policía, etc*) **to send sth in** enviar algo: *I sent my application in last week.* Envié mi solicitud la semana pasada.
to send sth off 1 echar algo al correo **2**

despachar algo
to send sth out 1 (*rayos, etc*) emitir algo **2** (*invitaciones, etc*) enviar algo
to send sth/sb up (*GB, coloq*) parodiar algo/a algn
sender *n* remitente

senile /ˈsiːnaɪl/ *adj* senil **senility** /səˈnɪləti/ *n* senilidad

senior /ˈsiːnɪə(r)/ ◆ *adj* **1** superior: *senior partner* socio mayoritario **2** padre: *John Brown, Senior* John Brown, padre ◆ *n* mayor: *She is two years my senior.* Me lleva dos años. **seniority** /ˌsiːniˈɒrəti; *USA* -ˈɔːr-/ *n* antigüedad (*rango, años, etc*)

senior citizen *n* ciudadano de la tercera edad

sensation /senˈseɪʃn/ *n* sensación **sensational** *adj* **1** sensacional **2** (*pey*) sensacionalista

sense /sens/ ◆ *n* **1** sentido: *sense of smell/touch/taste* olfato/tacto/gusto ◊ *a sense of humour* sentido del humor ◊ *It gives him a sense of security.* Le hace sentirse seguro. **2** juicio, sensatez: *to come to your senses* recobrar el juicio ◊ *to make sb see sense* hacer que algn entre en razón LOC **in a sense** en cierto sentido **to make sense** tener sentido **to make sense of sth** descifrar algo **to see sense** entrar en razón ◆ *vt* **1** sentir, ser consciente de **2** (*máquina*) detectar

senseless /ˈsensləs/ *adj* **1** insensato **2** sin sentido (*inconsciente*)

sensibility /ˌsensəˈbɪləti/ *n* sensibilidad

sensible /ˈsensəbl/ *adj* ☛ *Comparar con* SENSITIVE **1** sensato **2** (*decisión*) acertado **sensibly** *adv* **1** (*comportarse*) con prudencia **2** (*vestirse*) adecuadamente

sensitive /ˈsensətɪv/ *adj* ☛ *Comparar con* SENSIBLE **1** sensible: *She's very sensitive to criticism.* Es muy susceptible a la crítica. **2** (*asunto, piel*) delicado: *sensitive documents* documentos confidenciales **sensitivity** /ˌsensəˈtɪvəti/ *n* **1** sensibilidad **2** susceptibilidad **3** (*asunto, piel*) delicadeza

sensual /ˈsenʃuəl/ *adj* sensual **sensuality** /ˌsenʃuˈæləti/ *n* sensualidad

sensuous /ˈsenʃuəs/ *adj* sensual

sent *pret, pp de* SEND

sentence /ˈsentəns/ ◆ *n* **1** (*Gram*) frase, oración **2** sentencia: *a life sentence* cadena perpetua ◆ *vt* sentenciar, condenar

sentiment /ˈsentɪmənt/ *n* **1** sentimentalismo **2** sentimiento **sentimental** /ˌsentɪˈmentl/ *adj* **1** sentimental **2** sensiblero **sentimentality** /ˌsentɪmenˈtæləti/ *n* sentimentalismo, sensiblería

sentry /ˈsentri/ *n* (*pl* **-ies**) centinela

separate /ˈseprət/ ◆ *adj* **1** separado **2** distinto: *It happened on three separate occasions.* Ocurrió en tres ocasiones distintas. ◆ /ˈsepəreɪt/ **1** *vt, vi* separar(se) **2** *vt* dividir: *We separated the children into three groups.* Dividimos a los niños en tres grupos. **separately** *adv* por separado **separation** *n* separación

September /sepˈtembə(r)/ *n* (*abrev* **Sept**) se(p)tiembre ☛ *Ver nota y ejemplos en* JANUARY

sequel /ˈsiːkwəl/ *n* **1** secuela **2** (*película, libro, etc*) continuación

sequence /ˈsiːkwəns/ *n* sucesión, serie

serene /səˈriːn/ *adj* sereno

sergeant /ˈsɑːdʒənt/ *n* sargento

serial /ˈsɪəriəl/ *n* serial, serie: *a radio serial* un serial radiofónico ☛ *Ver nota en* SERIES

series /ˈsɪəriːz/ *n* (*pl* **series**) **1** serie **2** sucesión **3** (*Radio, TV*) serie: *a television series* una serie de televisión

En inglés utilizamos la palabra **series** para referirnos a las series que tratan una historia diferente en cada episodio, y **serial** para referirnos a una sola historia dividida en capítulos.

serious /ˈsɪəriəs/ *adj* **1** serio: *Is he serious (about it)?* ¿Lo dice en serio? ◊ *to be serious about sb* ir en serio con algn **2** (*enfermedad, error, crimen*) grave **seriously** *adv* **1** en serio **2** gravemente **seriousness** *n* **1** seriedad **2** gravedad

sermon /ˈsɜːmən/ *n* sermón

servant /ˈsɜːvənt/ *n* **1** criado, -a **2** *Ver* CIVIL

serve /sɜːv/ ◆ **1** *vt* ~ **sth (up) (to sb)** servir algo (a algn) **2** *vi* ~ **(with sth)** servir (en algo): *He served with the eighth squadron.* Sirvió en el octavo escuadrón. **3** *vt* (*cliente*) atender **4** *vt* (*condena*) cumplir **5** *vt, vi* ~ **(sth) (to**

sb) (*deporte de raqueta*) sacar (algo) (a algn) LOC **to serve sb right**: *It serves them right!* Les está bien empleado. *Ver tb* FIRST PHR V **to serve sth out 1** servir algo **2** distribuir ◆ *n* saque: *Whose serve is it?* ¿A quién le toca sacar?

service /ˈsɜːvɪs/ ◆ *n* **1** servicio: *on active service* en servicio activo ◊ *10% extra for service* un 10% de recargo por servicio ◊ *morning service* los oficios de la mañana **2** (*de coche*) revisión **3** (*deporte de raqueta*) saque ◆ *vt* hacer la revisión

serviceman /ˈsɜːvɪsmən/ *n* (*pl* **-men** /-mən/) militar

service station *n* estación de servicio

servicewoman /ˈsɜːvɪswʊmən/ *n* (*pl* **-women**) militar

session /ˈseʃn/ *n* sesión

set[1] /set/ *n* **1** juego: *a set of saucepans* una batería de cocina **2** (*de personas*) círculo **3** (*Electrón*) aparato **4** (*tenis*) set **5** (*Teat*) decorado **6** (*Cine*) plató **7** *a shampoo and set* lavar y marcar

set[2] /set/ (**-tt-**) (*pret, pp* **set**) **1** *vt* (*localizar*): *The film is set in Austria.* La película se desarrolla en Austria. **2** *vt* (*preparar*) poner: *I've set the alarm clock for seven.* He puesto el despertador para las siete. ◊ *Did you set the video to record that film?* ¿Has programado el vídeo para grabar esa película? **3** *vt* (*fijar*) establecer: *She's set a new world record.* Ha establecido un nuevo récord del mundo. ◊ *They haven't set a date for their wedding yet.* No han fijado la fecha de la boda todavía. ◊ *Can we set a limit to the cost of the trip?* ¿Podemos fijar un límite al coste del viaje? **4** *vt* (*cambio de estado*): *They set the prisoners free.* Pusieron en libertad a los prisioneros. ◊ *It set me thinking.* Me dio que pensar. **5** *vt* (*mandar*) poner: *We've been set a lot of homework today.* Hoy nos han puesto un montón de deberes. **6** *vi* (*el sol*) ponerse **7** *vi* cuajar, fraguar, endurecerse: *Put the jelly in the fridge to set.* Mete la gelatina en la nevera para que cuaje. **8** *vt* (*fml*) poner, colocar: *He set a bowl of soup in front of me.* Me puso un plato de sopa delante. **9** *vt* (*hueso roto*) escayolar **10** *vt* (*pelo*) marcar **11** *vt* engastar LOC **to set a good/bad example** (**to sb**) dar buen/mal ejemplo (a algn) **to set a/the trend** marcar la tónica **to set fire to sth/to set sth on fire** prender fuego a algo **to set light to sth** prender fuego a algo **to set sail** (**to/for**) zarpar (rumbo a) **to set sth alight** pegar fuego a algo **to set the scene** (**for sth**) **1** describir el escenario (para algo) **2** preparar el terreno (para algo) **to set your heart on** (**having/doing**) **sth** poner el corazón en (tener/hacer) algo *Ver tb* BALL, MIND, MOTION, RECORD, RIGHT, WORK[1]

PHR V **to set about** (**doing**) **sth** ponerse a hacer algo

to set off salir: *to set off on a journey* salir de viaje **to set sth off 1** hacer explotar algo **2** ocasionar algo

to set out 1 emprender un viaje **2** salir: *to set out from London* salir de Londres ◊ *They set out for Australia.* Salieron para Australia. **to set out to do sth** proponerse hacer algo

to set sth up 1 levantar algo **2** montar algo

set[3] /set/ *adj* **1** situado **2** determinado LOC **to be all set** (**for sth/to do sth**) estar preparado (para algo/para hacer algo) *Ver tb* MARK[2]

settee /seˈtiː/ *n* sofá

setting /ˈsetɪŋ/ *n* **1** montura **2** ambientación **3** [*sing*] (*del sol*) puesta

settle /ˈsetl/ **1** *vi* establecerse, quedarse a vivir **2** *vi* ~ (**on sth**) posarse (en algo) **3** *vt* (*estómago*) asentar **4** *vt* ~ **sth** (**with sb**) (*disputa*) resolver algo (con algn) **5** *vt* (*cuenta*) pagar **6** *vi* (*sedimento*) depositarse PHR V **to settle down** acostumbrarse: *to marry and settle down* casarse y sentar la cabeza **to settle for sth** aceptar algo **to settle in/into sth** adaptar(se) a algo **to settle on sth** decidirse por algo **to settle up** (**with sb**) liquidar las cuentas (con algn) **settled** *adj* estable

settlement /ˈsetlmənt/ *n* **1** acuerdo **2** colonización, poblado

settler /ˈsetlə(r)/ *n* poblador, -ora

seven /ˈsevn/ *adj, pron, n* siete ☛ *Ver ejemplos en* FIVE **seventh 1** *adj* séptimo **2** *pron, adv* el séptimo, la séptima, los séptimos, las séptimas **3** *n* séptima parte, séptimo ☛ *Ver ejemplos en* FIFTH

seventeen /ˌsevnˈtiːn/ *adj, pron, n* diecisiete ☛ *Ver ejemplos en* FIVE **seventeenth 1** *adj* decimoséptimo **2** *pron, adv* el decimoséptimo, la decimoséptima, los decimoséptimos, las decimoséptimas **3** *n* diecisieteava parte, diecisieteavo ☛ *Ver ejemplos en* FIFTH

seventy /ˈsevnti/ *adj, pron, n* setenta ☛ *Ver ejemplos en* FIFTY, FIVE **seventieth 1** *adj, pron* septuagésimo **2** *n* setentava parte, setentavo ☛ *Ver ejemplos en* FIFTH

sever /ˈsevə(r)/ *vt* (*fml*) **1** ~ **sth (from sth)** cortar algo (de algo) **2** (*relaciones*) romper

several /ˈsevrəl/ *adj, pron* varios, -as

severe /sɪˈvɪə(r)/ *adj* (**-er**, **-est**) **1** (*semblante, castigo*) severo **2** (*tormenta, helada*) fuerte **3** (*dolor*) intenso

sew /səʊ/ *vt, vi* (*pret* **sewed** *pp* **sewn** /səʊn/ *o* **sewed**) coser PHR V **to sew sth up** coser algo: *to sew up a hole* zurcir un agujero

sewage /ˈsuːɪdʒ, ˈsjuː-/ *n* [*incontable*] aguas residuales

sewer /ˈsuːə(r), ˈsjuː-/ *n* alcantarilla, cloaca

sewing /ˈsəʊɪŋ/ *n* costura

sewn *pp de* SEW

sex /seks/ *n* **1** sexo **2** trato sexual: *to have sex (with sb)* tener relaciones sexuales (con algn)

sexism /ˈseksɪzəm/ *n* sexismo

sexual /ˈsekʃuəl/ *adj* sexual: *sexual intercourse* relaciones sexuales, coito **sexuality** /ˌsekʃuˈæləti/ *n* sexualidad

shabby /ˈʃæbi/ *adj* (**-ier**, **-iest**) **1** (*ropa*) raído **2** (*cosas*) en mal estado **3** (*gente*) desharrapado **4** (*comportamiento*) mezquino

shack /ʃæk/ *n* choza

shade /ʃeɪd/ ◆ *n* **1** sombra ☛ *Ver dibujo en* SOMBRA **2** pantalla (*de lámpara*) **3** persiana **4** (*color*) tono **5** (*significado*) matiz ◆ *vt* dar sombra a **shady** *adj* (**-ier**, **-iest**) sombreado

shadow /ˈʃædəʊ/ ◆ *n* **1** sombra ☛ *Ver dibujo en* SOMBRA **2 shadows** [*pl*] tinieblas ◆ *vt* seguir y vigilar secretamente ◆ *adj* de la oposición (*política*) **shadowy** *adj* **1** (*lugar*) oscuro **2** (*fig*) indefinido

shaft /ʃɑːft; *USA* ʃæft/ *n* **1** dardo **2** mango largo **3** fuste **4** eje **5** pozo: *the lift-shaft* el hueco del ascensor **6** ~ **(of sth)** rayo (de algo)

shaggy /ˈʃægi/ *adj* (**-ier**, **-iest**) peludo: *shaggy eyebrows* cejas peludas ◇ *shaggy hair* pelo desgreñado

shake /ʃeɪk/ ◆ (*pret* **shook** /ʃʊk/ *pp* **shaken** /ˈʃeɪkən/) **1** *vt* ~ **sth/sb (about/around)** sacudir, agitar algo/a algn **2** *vi* temblar **3** *vt* ~ **sb (up)** perturbar a algn LOC **to shake sb's hand/shake hands (with sb)/shake sb by the hand** dar la mano a algn **to shake your head** negar con la cabeza PHR V **to shake sb off** quitarse a algn de encima **to shake sb up** dar una sacudida a algn **to shake sth up** agitar algo ◆ *n* [*gen sing*] sacudida: *a shake of the head* una negación con la cabeza **shaky** *adj* (**-ier**, **-iest**) **1** tembloroso **2** poco firme

shall /ʃəl, ʃæl/ ◆ (*contracción* **'ll** *neg* **shall not** *o* **shan't** /ʃɑːnt/) *v aux* (*esp GB*) para formar el futuro: *As we shall see*... Como veremos... ◇ *I shall tell her tomorrow.* Se lo diré mañana.

Shall y **will** se usan para formar el futuro en inglés. **Shall** se utiliza con la primera persona del singular y del plural, **I** y **we**, y **will** con las demás personas. Sin embargo, en inglés hablado **will** (o **'ll**) tiende a utilizarse con todos los pronombres.

◆ *v modal*

Shall es un verbo modal al que sigue un infinitivo sin TO, y las oraciones interrogativas y negativas se construyen sin el auxiliar *do*.

1 (*fml*) (*voluntad, determinación*): *He shall be given a fair trial.* Tendrá un juicio justo. ◇ *I shan't go.* No iré. ☛ En este sentido, **shall** es más formal que **will**, especialmente cuando se usa con pronombres que no sean *I* y *we*. **2** (*oferta, petición*): *Shall we pick you up?* ¿Te vamos a buscar?

shallow /ˈʃæləʊ/ *adj* (**-er**, **-est**) **1** (*agua*) poco profundo **2** (*pey*) (*persona*) superficial

shambles /ˈʃæmblz/ *n* (*coloq*) desastre: *to be (in) a shambles* estar hecho un desastre

shame /ʃeɪm/ ◆ *n* **1** vergüenza **2** deshonra **3 a shame** (*coloq*) lástima: *What a shame!* ¡Qué lástima! LOC **to put sth/sb to shame** dejar a algn a la altura del betún *Ver tb* CRY ◆ *vt* **1** avergonzar **2** deshonrar

shameful /ˈʃeɪmfl/ *adj* vergonzoso

shameless /ˈʃeɪmləs/ *adj* descarado, sinvergüenza

shampoo /ʃæmˈpuː/ ◆ *n* (*pl* **-oos**) champú ◆ *vt* (*pret, pp* **-ooed** *pt pres* **-ooing**) lavar (con champú)

shan't /ʃɑːnt/ = SHALL NOT *Ver* SHALL

shanty town /ˈʃænti taʊn/ *n* barrio de chabolas

shape /ʃeɪp/ ◆ *n* **1** forma **2** figura LOC **in any shape (or form)** (*coloq*) de cualquier tipo **in shape** en forma **out of shape 1** deformado **2** en baja forma **to give shape to sth** (*fig*) plasmar algo **to take shape** ir cobrando forma ◆ *vt* **1** ~ **sth (into sth)** dar forma (de algo) a algo **2** forjar **shapeless** *adj* amorfo

share /ʃeə(r)/ ◆ *n* **1** ~ **(in/of sth)** parte (en/de algo) **2** (*Fin*) acción LOC *Ver* FAIR ◆ **1** *vt* ~ **sth (out) (among/between sb)** repartir algo (entre algn) **2** *vt, vi* ~ **(sth) (with sb)** compartir (algo) (con algn)

shareholder /ˈʃeəhəʊldə(r)/ *n* accionista

shark /ʃɑːk/ *n* tiburón

sharp /ʃɑːp/ ◆ *adj* (**-er**, **-est**) **1** (*cuchillo*) afilado **2** (*curva*) cerrado **3** (*subida*) pronunciado **4** nítido **5** (*sonido*) agudo **6** (*sabor*) ácido **7** (*olor*) acre **8** (*viento*) cortante **9** (*dolor*) agudo **10** poco escrupuloso **11** (*Mús*) sostenido ◆ *n* sostenido ☛ *Comparar con* FLAT ◆ *adv* (*coloq*) en punto **sharpen** *vt, vi* afilar

shatter /ˈʃætə(r)/ *vt, vi* **1** hacer(se) añicos **2** destruir **shattering** *adj* demoledor

shave /ʃeɪv/ *vt, vi* afeitar(se) *Ver tb* CLOSE

she /ʃiː/ ◆ *pron pers* ella (*se usa también para referirse a coches, barcos o naciones*): *She didn't come.* No vino. ☛ El *pron pers* no puede omitirse en inglés. *Comparar con* HER 3 ◆ *n* hembra: *Is it a he or a she?* ¿Es macho o hembra?

shear /ʃɪə(r)/ *vt* (*pret* **sheared** *pp* **shorn** /ʃɔːn/ *o* **sheared**) **1** (*oveja*) esquilar **2** cortar **shears** /ʃɪəz/ *n* [*pl*] podadera

sheath /ʃiːθ/ *n* (*pl* **~s** /ʃiːðz/) vaina, estuche

shed¹ /ʃed/ *n* cobertizo

shed² /ʃed/ *vt* (**-dd-**) (*pret, pp* **shed**) **1** (*hojas*) perder **2** (*la piel*) mudar **3** (*fml*) (*sangre o lágrimas*) derramar **4** ~ (**on sth/sb**) (*luz*) arrojar, difundir algo (sobre algo/algn)

she'd /ʃiːd/ **1** = SHE HAD *Ver* HAVE **2** = SHE WOULD *Ver* WOULD

sheep /ʃiːp/ *n* (*pl* **sheep**) oveja *Ver tb* EWE, RAM ☛ *Ver nota en* CARNE **sheepish** *adj* tímido, avergonzado

sheer /ʃɪə(r)/ *adj* **1** (*absoluto*) puro **2** (*de la tela*) diáfano **3** (*casi vertical*) escarpado

sheet /ʃiːt/ *n* **1** (*para una cama*) sábana **2** (*de papel*) hoja **3** (*de vidrio, metal*) lámina

sheikh /ʃeɪk/ *n* jeque

shelf /ʃelf/ *n* (*pl* **shelves** /ʃelvz/) estante, anaquel

shell¹ /ʃel/ *n* **1** (*de un molusco*) concha **2** (*huevo, nuez*) cáscara ☛ *Ver nota en* PEEL **3** (*tortuga, crustáceo, insecto*) caparazón **4** (*barco*) casco **5** (*edificio*) armazón

shell² /ʃel/ ◆ *n* obús ◆ *vt* bombardear

she'll /ʃiːl/ = SHE WILL *Ver* WILL

shellfish /ˈʃelfɪʃ/ *n* (*pl* **shellfish**) **1** (*Zool*) crustáceo **2** (*como alimento*) marisco

shelter /ˈʃeltə(r)/ ◆ *n* **1** ~ **(from sth)** (*protección*) abrigo, resguardo (contra algo): *to take shelter* refugiarse **2** (*lugar*) refugio ◆ **1** *vt* ~ **sth/sb (from sth/sb)** resguardar, abrigar algo/a algn (de algo/algn) **2** *vi* ~ **(from sth)** refugiarse, ponerse al abrigo (de algo) **sheltered** *adj* **1** (*lugar*) abrigado **2** (*vida*) protegido

shelve /ʃelv/ *vt* archivar

shelves *plural de* SHELF

shelving /ˈʃelvɪŋ/ *n* estantería

shepherd /ˈʃepəd/ *n* pastor

sherry /ˈʃeri/ *n* (*pl* **-ies**) jerez

she's /ʃiːz/ **1** = SHE IS *Ver* BE **2** = SHE HAS *Ver* HAVE

shield /ʃiːld/ ◆ *n* escudo ◆ *vt* ~ **sth/sb (from sth/sb)** proteger algo/a algn (contra algo/algn)

shift /ʃɪft/ ◆ **1** *vi* moverse, cambiar de sitio: *She shifted uneasily in her seat.* Se movió inquietamente en su asiento. **2** *vt* mover, cambiar de sitio: *Help me shift the sofa.* Ayúdame a cambiar el sofá de sitio. ◆ *n* **1** cambio: *a shift in public opinion* un cambio en la opinión pública **2** (*trabajo*) turno

shifty /ˈʃɪfti/ *adj* (**-ier**, **-iest**) sospechoso

shilling /ˈʃɪlɪŋ/ *n* chelín

shimmer /ˈʃɪmə(r)/ *vi* **1** (*agua, seda*) brillar **2** (*luz*) titilar **3** (*luz en agua*) rielar

shin /ʃɪn/ *n* **1** espinilla **2** (*tb* **shin-bone**) tibia

shine /ʃaɪn/ ◆ (*pret, pp* **shone** /ʃɒn; *USA* ʃəʊn/) **1** *vi* brillar: *His face shone with excitement.* Su cara irradiaba excitación. **2** *vt* (*linterna, etc*) dirigir **3** *vi* ~ **at/in sth** brillar: *She's always shone at languages.* Siempre se le han dado muy bien los idiomas. ◆ *n* brillo

shingle /ˈʃɪŋgl/ *n* guijarros

shiny /ˈʃaɪni/ *adj* (**-ier**, **-iest**) brillante, reluciente

ship /ʃɪp/ ◆ *n* barco, buque: *The captain went on board ship.* El capitán subió al barco. ◊ *to launch a ship* botar un barco ◊ *a merchant ship* un buque mercante ☛ *Ver nota en* BOAT ◆ *vt* (**-pp-**) enviar (por vía marítima)

shipbuilding /ˈʃɪpbɪldɪŋ/ *n* construcción naval

shipment /ˈʃɪpmənt/ *n* cargamento

shipping /ˈʃɪpɪŋ/ *n* embarcaciones, buques: *shipping lane/route* vía/ruta de navegación

shipwreck /ˈʃɪprek/ ◆ *n* naufragio ◆ *vt*: *to be shipwrecked* naufragar

shirt /ʃɜːt/ *n* camisa

shiver /ˈʃɪvə(r)/ ◆ *vi* **1** ~ (**with sth**) temblar (de algo) **2** estremecerse ◆ *n* escalofrío

shoal /ʃəʊl/ *n* banco (*de peces*)

shock /ʃɒk/ ◆ *n* **1** conmoción **2** (*tb* **electric shock**) descarga eléctrica **3** (*Med*) shock ◆ **1** *vt* conmover, trastornar **2** *vt, vi* escandalizarse **shocking** *adj* **1** (*comportamiento*) escandaloso **2** (*noticia, crimen, etc*) espantoso **3** (*coloq*) horrible, malísimo

shod *pret, pp de* SHOE

shoddy /ˈʃɒdi/ *adj* (**-ier**, **-iest**) **1** (*producto*) de baja calidad **2** (*trabajo*) chapucero

shoe /ʃuː/ ◆ *n* **1** zapato: *shoe shop* zapatería ◊ *shoe polish* betún ◊ *What shoe size do you take?* ¿Qué número de zapato usas? ☛ *Ver nota en* PAIR **2** *Ver* HORSESHOE ◆ *vt* (*pret, pp* **shod** /ʃɒd/) herrar

shoelace /ˈʃuːleɪs/ *n* cordón de zapato

shoestring /ˈʃuːstrɪŋ/ *n* (*USA*) *Ver* SHOELACE LOC **on a shoestring** con escasos medios

shone *pret, pp de* SHINE

shook *pret de* SHAKE

shoot /ʃuːt/ ◆ (*pret, pp* **shot** /ʃɒt/) **1** *vt* pegar un tiro a: *to shoot rabbits* cazar conejos ◊ *She was shot in the leg.* Recibió un disparo en la pierna. ◊ *to shoot sb dead* matar (a tiros) a algn **2** *vi* ~ **at sth/sb** disparar a algo/contra algn **3** *vt* fusilar **4** *vt* (*mirada*) lanzar **5** *vt* (*película*) rodar **6** *vi* ~ **along, past, out, etc** ir, pasar, salir, etc, volando **7** *vi* (*Dep*) chutar PHR V **to shoot sb down** matar a algn (a tiros) **to shoot sth down** derribar algo (a tiros) **to shoot up 1** (*precios*) dispararse **2** (*planta*) crecer rápidamente **3** (*niño*) espigar ◆ *n* brote

shop /ʃɒp/ ◆ *n* **1** (*USA* **store**) tienda: *a clothes shop* una tienda de ropa ◊ *I'm going to the shops.* Voy a hacer la compra. **2** *Ver* WORKSHOP LOC *Ver* TALK ◆ *vi* (**-pp-**) ir de compras, hacer compras: *to shop for sth* buscar algo (en las tiendas) PHR V **to shop around** (*coloq*) comparar precios

shop assistant *n* dependiente, -a

shopkeeper /ˈʃɒpkiːpə(r)/ (*USA* **storekeeper**) *n* comerciante, tendero, -a

shoplifting /ˈʃɒplɪftɪŋ/ *n* hurto (*en una tienda*): *She was charged with shoplifting.* La acusaron de haberse llevado cosas sin pagar en una tienda. **shoplifter** *n* ladrón, -ona ☛ *Ver nota en* THIEF

shopper /ˈʃɒpə(r)/ *n* comprador, -ora

shopping /ˈʃɒpɪŋ/ *n* compra(s): *to do the shopping* hacer la compra ◊ *She's gone shopping.* Ha salido de compras. ◊ *shopping bag/trolley* bolsa/carrito de la compra

shopping centre (*tb* **shopping mall**) *n* centro comercial

shore /ʃɔː(r)/ *n* **1** costa: *to go on shore* desembarcar **2** orilla (*de mar, lago*): *on the shore(s) of Loch Ness* a orillas del Lago Ness ☛ *Comparar con* BANK[1]

shorn *pp de* SHEAR

short[1] /ʃɔːt/ *adj* (**-er**, **-est**) **1** (*pelo, vestido*) corto: *I was only there for a short while.* Sólo estuve allí un rato. ◊ *a short time ago* hace poco **2** (*persona*) bajo **3** ~ (**of sth**) escaso de algo: *Water is short.* Hay escasez de agua. ◊ *I'm a bit short of time just now.* Ando un poco justo de tiempo en estos momentos.

I'm £5 short. Me faltan cinco libras. **4** ~ **for sth**: *Ben is short for Benjamin.* Ben es el diminutivo de Benjamin. LOC **for short** para abreviar: *He's called Ben for short.* Lo llamamos Ben para abreviar. **in short** resumiendo **to get/ receive short shrift** ser despachado sin contemplaciones **to have a short temper** tener un genio muy vivo *Ver tb* BREATH, TERM

short² /ʃɔːt/ ◆ *adv Ver* CUT, FALL, STOP ◆ *n* **1** *Ver* SHORT-CIRCUIT **2** (*Cine*) corto

shortage /ˈʃɔːtɪdʒ/ *n* escasez

short-circuit /ˌʃɔːt ˈsɜːkɪt/ ◆ **1** *vi* tener un cortocircuito **2** *vt* causar un cortocircuito en ◆ *n* (*tb coloq* **short**) cortocircuito

shortcoming /ˈʃɔːtkʌmɪŋ/ *n* deficiencia: *severe shortcomings in police tactics* graves deficiencias en las tácticas policiales

short cut *n* atajo: *He took a short cut through the park.* Tomó un atajo por el parque.

shorten /ˈʃɔːtn/ *vt, vi* acortar(se)

shorthand /ˈʃɔːthænd/ *n* taquigrafía

short list *n* lista final de candidatos

short-lived /ˌʃɔːt ˈlɪvd; *USA* ˈlaɪvd/ *adj* efímero

shortly /ˈʃɔːtli/ *adv* **1** dentro de poco **2** poco: *shortly afterwards* poco después

shorts /ʃɔːts/ *n* [*pl*] **1** pantalón corto **2** (*USA*) calzoncillos ☛ *Ver nota en* PAIR

short-sighted /ˌʃɔːt ˈsaɪtɪd/ *adj* **1** miope **2** (*fig*) imprudente

short-term /ˈʃɔːt tɜːm/ *adj* a corto plazo: *short-term plans* planes a corto plazo

shot¹ /ʃɒt/ *n* **1** disparo **2** intento: *to have a shot at (doing) sth* intentarlo con algo/intentar hacer algo **3** (*Dep*) golpe **4 the shot** [*sing*] (*Dep*): *to put the shot* lanzar el peso **5** (*Fot*) foto **6** (*coloq*) pico LOC *Ver* BIG

shot² *pret, pp de* SHOOT

shotgun /ˈʃɒtgʌn/ *n* escopeta

should /ʃəd, ʃʊd/ *v modal* (*neg* **should not** *o* **shouldn't** /ˈʃʊdnt/)

> **Should** es un verbo modal al que sigue un infinitivo sin TO, y las oraciones interrogativas y negativas se construyen sin el auxiliar *do*.

1 (*sugerencias y consejos*) deber: *You shouldn't drink and drive.* No deberías conducir si has bebido. ☛ *Comparar con* MUST **2** (*probabilidad*) deber de: *They should be there by now.* Ya deben de haber llegado. **3** *How should I know?* ¿Y yo qué sé?

shoulder /ˈʃəʊldə(r)/ ◆ *n* hombro LOC *Ver* CHIP ◆ *vt* cargar con

shoulder blade *n* omóplato

shout /ʃaʊt/ ◆ *n* grito ◆ *vt, vi* ~ (**sth**) (**out**) (**at/to sb**) gritar (algo) (a algn) PHR V **to shout sb down** callar a algn con abucheos

> Cuando utilizamos **to shout** con **at sb** tiene el sentido de *reñir*, pero cuando lo utilizamos con **to sb** tiene el sentido de *decir a gritos*: *Don't shout at him, he's only little.* No le grites, que es muy pequeño. ◊ *She shouted the number out to me from the car.* Me gritó el número desde el coche.

shove /ʃʌv/ ◆ **1** *vt, vi* empujar **2** *vt* (*coloq*) meter ◆ *n* [*gen sing*] empujón

shovel /ˈʃʌvl/ ◆ *n* pala ◆ *vt* (-**ll**-, *USA* -**l**-) (re)mover con una pala

show /ʃəʊ/ ◆ *n* **1** demostración, función **2** exposición, feria **3** demostración, alarde: *a show of force* una demostración de fuerza ◊ *to make a show of sth* hacer alarde de algo LOC **for show** para impresionar **on show** expuesto ◆ (*pret* **showed** *pp* **shown** /ʃəʊn/ *o* **showed**) **1** *vt* mostrar, enseñar **2** *vi* verse, notarse **3** *vt* demostrar **4** *vt* (*película*) proyectar **5** *vt* (*Arte*) exponer LOC *Ver* ROPE PHR V **to show off** (**to sb**) (*coloq, pey*) fardar (delante de algn) **to show sth/sb off 1** (*aprob*) hacer resaltar algo/a algn **2** (*pey*) presumir de algo/algn **to show up** (*coloq*) presentarse **to show sb up** (*coloq*) avergonzar a algn

show business *n* mundo del espectáculo

showdown /ˈʃəʊdaʊn/ *n* enfrentamiento decisivo

shower /ˈʃaʊə(r)/ ◆ *n* **1** chubasco, chaparrón **2** ~ (**of sth**) lluvia (de algo) **3** ducha: *to take/have a shower* ducharse ◆ *vt* ~ **sb with sth** (*fig*) colmar a algn de algo

showing /ˈʃəʊɪŋ/ *n* **1** (*Cine*) función **2** actuación

shown *pp de* SHOW

showroom /ˈʃəʊruːm/ *n* sala de exposición

shrank *pret de* SHRINK

shrapnel /ˈʃræpnəl/ *n* metralla

shred /ʃred/ ◆ *n* **1** (*de verduras*) tira **2** (*de tabaco*) brizna **3** (*de tela*) jirón **4** ~ **of sth** (*fig*) pizca de algo ◆ *vt* (**-dd-**) hacer tiras

shrewd /ʃruːd/ *adj* (**-er**, **-est**) **1** astuto, perspicaz **2** (*decisión*) inteligente, acertado

shriek /ʃriːk/ ◆ ~ (**with sth**) *vt, vi* gritar, chillar (de algo): *to shriek with laughter* reírse a carcajadas ◆ *n* chillido

shrift /ʃrɪft/ *n Ver* SHORT[1]

shrill /ʃrɪl/ *adj* (**-er**, **-est**) **1** agudo, chillón **2** (*protesta, etc*) estridente

shrimp /ʃrɪmp/ *n* camarón

shrine /ʃraɪn/ *n* **1** santuario **2** sepulcro

shrink /ʃrɪŋk/ *vt, vi* (*pret* **shrank** /ʃræŋk/ *o* **shrunk** /ʃrʌŋk/ *pp* **shrunk**) encoger(se), reducir(se) PHR V **to shrink from sth/doing sth** vacilar ante algo/en hacer algo

shrivel /ˈʃrɪvl/ *vt, vi* (**-ll-**, *USA* **-l-**) ~ (**sth**) (**up**) **1** secar algo/secarse **2** arrugar algo/arrugarse

shroud /ʃraʊd/ ◆ *n* **1** sudario **2** ~ (**of sth**) (*fig*) manto, velo (de algo) ◆ *vt* ~ **sth in sth** envolver algo de algo: *shrouded in secrecy* rodeado del mayor secreto

shrub /ʃrʌb/ *n* arbusto pequeño (*de ornato*) ☛ *Comparar con* BUSH

shrug /ʃrʌg/ ◆ *vt, vi* (**-gg-**) ~ (**your shoulders**) encogerse de hombros PHR V **to shrug sth off** no dar importancia a algo ◆ *n* encogimiento de hombros

shrunk *pret, pp de* SHRINK

shudder /ˈʃʌdə(r)/ ◆ *vi* **1** ~ (**with sth**) estremecerse (de algo) **2** dar sacudidas ◆ *n* **1** estremecimiento, escalofrío **2** sacudida

shuffle /ˈʃʌfl/ **1** *vt, vi* (*baraja*) barajar **2** *vt* ~ **your feet** arrastrar los pies **3** *vi* ~ (**along**) caminar arrastrando los pies

shun /ʃʌn/ *vt* (**-nn-**) evitar, rehuir

shut /ʃʌt/ ◆ *vt, vi* (**-tt-**) (*pret, pp* **shut**) cerrar(se) LOC *Ver* CLICK

PHR V **to shut sth/sb away** encerrar algo/a algn

to shut (sth) down cerrar (algo)

to shut sth in sth pillar(se) algo con algo

to shut sth off cortar algo (*suministro*)

to shut sth/sb off (from sth) aislar algo/a algn (de algo)

to shut sth/sb out (of sth) excluir algo/a algn (de algo)

to shut up (*coloq*) callarse **to shut sb up** (*coloq*) hacer callar a algn **to shut sth up** cerrar algo **to shut sth/sb up (in sth)** encerrar algo/a algn (en algo)

◆ *adj* [*siempre se usa después del verbo*] cerrado: *The door was shut.* La puerta estaba cerrada. ☛ *Comparar con* CLOSED *en* CLOSE[2]

shutter /ˈʃʌtə(r)/ *n* **1** contraventana **2** (*Fot*) obturador

shuttle /ˈʃʌtl/ *n* **1** lanzadera **2** puente (aéreo): *shuttle service* servicio de enlace **3** (*tb* **space shuttle**) lanzadera espacial

shy /ʃaɪ/ ◆ *adj* (**shyer**, **shyest**) tímido: *to be shy of sth/sb* asustarle a uno algo/algn ◆ *vi* (*pret, pp* **shied** /ʃaɪd/) **to shy (at sth)** (*caballo*) espantarse (de algo) PHR V **to shy away from sth/doing sth** asustarse de (hacer) algo **shyness** *n* timidez

sick /sɪk/ ◆ *adj* (**-er**, **-est**) **1** enfermo: *to be off sick* estar de baja ☛ *Ver nota en* ENFERMO **2** mareado **3** ~ **of sth/sb/doing sth** (*coloq*) harto de algo/algn/hacer algo **4** (*coloq*) morboso LOC **to be sick** vomitar **to be sick to death of/sick and tired of sth/sb** (*coloq*) estar hasta las narices de algo/algn **to make sb sick** poner a algn enfermo ◆ *n* (*coloq*) vómito **sicken** *vt* dar asco a algn **sickening** *adj* **1** repugnante **2** irritante

sickly /ˈsɪkli/ *adj* (**-ier**, **-iest**) **1** enfermizo **2** (*gusto, olor*) empalagoso

sickness /ˈsɪknəs/ *n* **1** enfermedad **2** náuseas

side /saɪd/ ◆ *n* **1** cara: *on the other side* al revés **2** lado: *to sit at/by sb's side* sentarse al lado de algn **3** (*de una casa*) costado: *a side door* una puerta lateral **4** (*de una montaña*) ladera **5** (*de un lago*) orilla **6** (*Anat, de una persona*) costado **7** (*de un animal*) flanco **8** parte: *to change sides* pasarse al otro bando ◊ *to be on our side* ser de los nuestros ◊ *Whose side are you on?* ¿De qué lado estás tú? **9** (*GB, Dep*) equipo **10** aspecto: *the different sides of a question* los distintos aspectos de un tema LOC **on/from all sides; on/from every side**

por/de todos lados, por/de todas partes **side by side** uno al lado del otro **to get on the right/wrong side of sb** caer bien/mal a algn **to put sth on/to one side** dejar algo a un lado **to take sides (with sb)** tomar partido (con algn) *Ver tb* LOOK[1], SAFE[1] ◆ **PHR V to side with/against sb** ponerse del lado de/en contra de algn

sideboard /ˈsaɪdbɔːd/ *n* aparador

side effect *n* efecto secundario

side street *n* bocacalle

sidetrack /ˈsaɪdtræk/ *vt* desviar

sidewalk /ˈsaɪdwɔːk/ *n* (*USA*) *Ver* PAVEMENT

sideways /ˈsaɪdweɪz/ *adv, adj* **1** de/hacia un lado **2** (*mirada*) de reojo

siege /siːdʒ/ *n* **1** sitio **2** cerco policial

sieve /sɪv/ ◆ *n* tamiz ◆ *vt* tamizar

sift /sɪft/ *vt* **1** tamizar **2** ~ **(through) sth** (*fig*) examinar algo cuidadosamente

sigh /saɪ/ ◆ *vi* suspirar ◆ *n* suspiro

sight /saɪt/ *n* **1** vista: *to have poor sight* tener mala vista **2 the sights** [*pl*] lugares de interés **LOC at/on sight** en el acto **in sight** a la vista **out of sight, out of mind** ojos que no ven, corazón que no siente *Ver tb* CATCH, LOSE, PRETTY

sightseeing /ˈsaɪtsiːɪŋ/ *n* turismo

sign[1] /saɪn/ *n* **1** signo: *the signs of the Zodiac* los signos del Zodiaco **2** (*tráfico*) señal, letrero **3** señal: *to make a sign at sb* hacerle una señal a algn **4** ~ **(of sth)** señal, indicio (de algo): *a good/bad sign* una buena/mala señal ◊ *there are signs that...* hay indicios de que... **5** ~ **(of sth)** (*Med*) síntoma (de algo)

sign[2] /saɪn/ *vt, vi* firmar **PHR V to sign sb up 1** contratar a algn **2** (*Dep*) fichar a algn **to sign up (for sth) 1** matricularse (en algo) **2** hacerse socio (de algo)

signal /ˈsɪgnəl/ ◆ *n* señal ◆ *vt, vi* **(-ll-,** *USA* **-l-) 1** hacer señas: *to signal (to) sb to do sth* hacer señas a algn para que haga algo **2** mostrar: *to signal your discontent* dar muestras de descontento

signature /ˈsɪgnətʃə(r)/ *n* firma

significant /sɪgˈnɪfɪkənt/ *adj* significativo **significance** *n* **1** significación **2** significado **3** trascendencia

signify /ˈsɪgnɪfaɪ/ *vt* (*pret, pp* **-fied**) **1** significar **2** indicar

sign language *n* lenguaje por señas

signpost /ˈsaɪnpəʊst/ *n* poste indicador

silence /ˈsaɪləns/ ◆ *n, interj* silencio ◆ *vt* acallar

silent /ˈsaɪlənt/ *adj* **1** silencioso **2** callado **3** (*letra, película*) mudo

silhouette /ˌsɪluˈet/ ◆ *n* silueta ◆ *vt* **LOC to be silhouetted (against sth)** dibujarse (sobre algo)

silk /sɪlk/ *n* seda **silky** *adj* **(-ier, -iest)** sedoso

sill /sɪl/ *n* alféizar

silly /ˈsɪli/ *adj* **(-ier, -iest) 1** tonto: *That was a very silly thing to say.* Vaya tontería que has dicho. ☛ *Ver nota en* TONTO **2** ridículo: *to feel/look silly* sentirse/parecer ridículo

silver /ˈsɪlvə(r)/ ◆ *n* **1** plata: *silver paper* papel de plata ◊ *silver-plated* con baño de plata **2** calderilla **3** (vajilla de) plata **LOC** *Ver* WEDDING ◆ *adj* **1** de plata **2** (*color*) plateado **silvery** *adj* plateado

similar /ˈsɪmɪlə(r)/ *adj* ~ **(to sth/sb)** parecido (a algo/algn) **similarity** /ˌsɪməˈlærəti/ *n* (*pl* **-ies**) similitud, semejanza **similarly** *adv* **1** de forma parecida **2** (*también*) del mismo modo, igualmente

simile /ˈsɪməli/ *n* símil

simmer /ˈsɪmə(r)/ *vt, vi* hervir a fuego lento

simple /ˈsɪmpl/ *adj* **(-er, -est) 1** sencillo, simple **2** fácil **3** (*persona*) tonto, lento

simplicity /sɪmˈplɪsəti/ *n* sencillez

simplify /ˈsɪmplɪfaɪ/ *vt* (*pret, pp* **-fied**) simplificar

simplistic /sɪmˈplɪstɪk/ *adj* simplista

simply /ˈsɪmpli/ *adv* **1** sencillamente, simplemente **2** de manera sencilla, modestamente **3** tan sólo

simulate /ˈsɪmjuleɪt/ *vt* simular

simultaneous /ˌsɪmlˈteɪniəs; *USA* ˌsaɪm-/ *adj* ~ **(with sth)** simultáneo (a algo) **simultaneously** *adv* simultáneamente

sin /sɪn/ ◆ *n* pecado ◆ *vi* **(-nn-) to sin (against sth)** pecar (contra algo)

since /sɪns/ ◆ *conj* **1** desde (que): *How long is it since we visited your mother?* ¿Cuánto hace desde que visitamos a tu madre? **2** puesto que ◆ *prep* desde (que): *It was the first time they'd won since 1974.* Era la primera vez que ganaban desde 1974.

tʃ	dʒ	v	θ	ð	s	z	ʃ
chin	June	van	thin	then	so	zoo	she

Tanto **since** como **from** se traducen por "desde" y se usan para especificar el punto de partida de la acción del verbo. **Since** se usa cuando la acción se extiende en el tiempo hasta el momento presente: *She has been here since three.* Ha estado aquí desde las tres. **From** se usa cuando la acción ya ha terminado o no ha empezado todavía: *I was there from three until four.* Estuve allí desde las tres hasta las cuatro. ◊ *I'll be there from three.* Estaré allí a partir de las tres. ☛ *Ver nota en* FOR 3

◆ *adv* desde entonces: *We haven't heard from him since.* No hemos sabido nada desde entonces.

sincere /sɪnˈsɪə(r)/ *adj* sincero **sincerely** *adv* sinceramente LOC *Ver* YOURS **sincerity** /sɪnˈserəti/ *n* sinceridad

sinful /ˈsɪnfl/ *adj* **1** pecador **2** pecaminoso

sing /sɪŋ/ *vt, vi* (*pret* **sang** /sæŋ/ *pp* **sung** /sʌŋ/) ~ (**sth**) (**for/to sb**) cantar (algo) (a algn) **singer** *n* cantante **singing** *n* canto, cantar

single /ˈsɪŋgl/ ◆ *adj* **1** solo, único: *every single day* cada día **2** (*cama*) individual **3** (*USA* **one-way**) (*billete*) de ida ☛ *Comparar con* RETURN **4** soltero: *single parent* madre soltera/padre soltero LOC **in single file** en fila india *Ver tb* BLOW ◆ *n* **1** billete de ida **2** (*disco*) single ☛ *Comparar con* ALBUM **3 singles** [*pl*] (*Dep*) individuales ◆ PHR V **to single sth/sb out** (**for sth**) elegir algo/a algn (para algo)

single-handedly /ˌsɪŋgl ˈhændɪdli/ (*tb* **single-handed**) *adv* sin ayuda

single-minded /ˌsɪŋgl ˈmaɪndɪd/ *adj* decidido, resuelto

singular /ˈsɪŋgjələ(r)/ ◆ *adj* **1** (*Gram*) singular **2** extraordinario, singular ◆ *n*: *in the singular* en singular

sinister /ˈsɪnɪstə(r)/ *adj* amenazador

sink /sɪŋk/ ◆ (*pret* **sank** /sæŋk/ *pp* **sunk** /sʌŋk/) **1** *vt, vi* hundir(se) **2** *vi* bajar **3** *vi* (*sol*) ocultarse **4** *vt* (*coloq*) (*planes*) echar a perder LOC **to be sunk in sth** estar sumido en algo *Ver tb* HEART PHR V **to sink in 1** (*líquido*) absorberse **2** *It hasn't sunk in yet that…* Todavía no me he hecho a la idea de que… **to sink into sth 1** (*líquido*) penetrar en algo **2** (*fig*) sumirse en algo **to sink sth into sth** clavar algo en algo (*dientes, puñal*) ◆ *n* **1** fregadero **2** (*USA*) lavabo ☛ *Comparar con* WASHBASIN

sinus /ˈsaɪnəs/ *n* seno (*de hueso*)

sip /sɪp/ ◆ *vt, vi* (**-pp-**) beber a sorbos ◆ *n* sorbo

sir /sɜː(r)/ *n* **1** *Yes, sir* Sí, señor **2 Sir**: *Dear Sir* Muy señor mío **3 Sir** /sə(r)/: *Sir Laurence Olivier*

siren /ˈsaɪrən/ *n* sirena (*de policía, ambulancia*)

sister /ˈsɪstə(r)/ *n* **1** hermana **2** (*GB, Med*) enfermera jefe **3 Sister** (*Relig*) hermana **4** *sister ship* barco gemelo ◊ *sister organization* organización hermana

sister-in-law /ˈsɪstər ɪn lɔː/ *n* (*pl* **-ers-in-law**) cuñada

sit /sɪt/ (**-tt-**) (*pret, pp* **sat** /sæt/) **1** *vi* sentarse, tomar asiento, estar sentado **2** *vt* **to sit sb** (**down**) (hacer) sentar a algn **3** *vi* **to sit** (**for sb**) (*Arte*) posar (para algn) **4** *vi* (*parlamento*) permanecer en sesión **5** *vi* (*comité, etc*) reunirse **6** *vi* (*objeto*) estar **7** *vt* (*examen*) presentarse a

PHR V **to sit around** esperar sentado: *to sit around doing nothing* pasarse el día sin hacer nada

to sit back ponerse cómodo

to sit (**yourself**) **down** sentarse, tomar asiento

to sit up 1 incorporarse **2** quedarse levantado

site /saɪt/ *n* **1** emplazamiento: *building site* solar de construcción **2** (*de suceso*) lugar

sitting /ˈsɪtɪŋ/ *n* **1** sesión **2** (*para comer*) tanda

sitting room (*esp GB*) *Ver* LIVING ROOM

situated /ˈsɪtʃueɪtɪd/ *adj* situado, ubicado

situation /ˌsɪtʃuˈeɪʃn/ *n* **1** situación **2** (*fml*): *situations vacant* ofertas de trabajo

six /sɪks/ *adj, pron, n* seis ☛ *Ver ejemplos en* FIVE **sixth 1** *adj* sexto **2** *pron, adv* el sexto, la sexta, los sextos, las sextas **3** *n* sexta parte, sexto ☛ *Ver ejemplos en* FIFTH

sixteen /ˌsɪksˈtiːn/ *adj, pron, n* dieciséis ☛ *Ver ejemplos en* FIVE **sixteenth 1** *adj* decimosexto **2** *pron, adv* el decimosexto, la decimosexta, los decimosextos, las decimosextas **3** *n* dieciseisava parte, dieciseisavo ☛ *Ver ejemplos en* FIFTH

sixth form *n* (*GB*) los dos últimos años de la enseñanza secundaria

sixty /ˈsɪksti/ *adj, pron, n* sesenta ☛ *Ver ejemplos en* FIFTY, FIVE **sixtieth 1** *adj, pron* sexagésimo **2** *n* sesentava parte, sesentavo ☛ *Ver ejemplos en* FIFTH

size /saɪz/ ◆ *n* **1** tamaño **2** (*ropa, calzado*) talla: *I take size seven.* Calzo la talla 41. ◆ PHR V **to size sth/sb up** (*coloq*) calibrar algo/a algn: *She sized him up immediately.* Lo caló en seguida. **sizeable** (*tb* **sizable**) *adj* considerable

skate /skeɪt/ ◆ *n* **1** (*tb* **ice-skate**) patín **2** *Ver* ROLLER SKATE ◆ *vi* patinar **skater** *n* patinador, -ora **skating** *n* patinaje

skateboard /ˈskeɪtbɔːd/ *n* monopatín

skeleton /ˈskelɪtn/ ◆ *n* esqueleto ◆ *adj* mínimo: *skeleton staff/service* personal/servicio mínimo

skeptic (*USA*) *Ver* SCEPTIC

sketch /sketʃ/ ◆ *n* **1** bosquejo **2** (*Teat*) sketch ◆ *vt, vi* bosquejar **sketchy** *adj* (**-ier**, **-iest**) (*frec pey*) superficial, vago

ski /skiː/ ◆ *vi* (*pret, pp* **skied** *pt pres* **skiing**) esquiar ◆ *n* esquí **skiing** *n* esquí: *to go skiing* ir a esquiar

skid /skɪd/ ◆ *vi* (**-dd-**) **1** (*coche*) derrapar **2** (*persona*) resbalar ◆ *n* derrape

skies *plural de* SKY

skill /skɪl/ *n* **1** ~ (**at/in sth/doing sth**) habilidad (para algo/hacer algo) **2** destreza **skilful** (*USA* **skillful**) *adj* **1** ~ (**at/in sth/doing sth**) hábil (para algo/hacer algo) **2** (*pintor, jugador*) diestro **skilled** *adj* ~ (**at/in sth/doing sth**) hábil (para algo/hacer algo); experto (en algo/hacer algo): *skilled work/worker* trabajo/trabajador cualificado

skim /skɪm/ *vt* (**-mm-**) **1** descremar, espumar **2** pasar (algo) casi rozando **3** ~ (**through/over**) **sth** leer algo por encima

skin /skɪn/ ◆ *n* **1** (*de animal, persona*) piel **2** (*de fruta, embutidos*) piel, cáscara ☛ *Ver nota en* PEEL **3** (*de leche*) costra LOC **by the skin of your teeth** (*coloq*) por un pelo ◆ *vt* (**-nn-**) despellejar

skinhead /ˈskɪnhed/ *n* (*GB*) cabeza rapada

skinny /ˈskɪni/ *adj* (**-ier**, **-iest**) (*coloq, pey*) flaco ☛ *Ver nota en* DELGADO

skip /skɪp/ ◆ (**-pp-**) **1** *vi* brincar **2** *vi* saltar a la comba: *skipping rope* comba **3** *vt* saltarse ◆ *n* **1** brinco **2** contenedor (*para escombros*)

skipper /ˈskɪpə(r)/ *n* (*coloq*) capitán, -ana (*de barco*)

skirmish /ˈskɜːmɪʃ/ *n* escaramuza

skirt /skɜːt/ ◆ *n* falda ◆ *vt* bordear: *skirting board* rodapié PHR V **to skirt (a)round sth** soslayar algo

skull /skʌl/ *n* calavera, cráneo

sky /skaɪ/ *n* (*pl* **skies**) cielo: *sky-high* por las nubes ◊ *skylight* claraboya ◊ *skyline* línea del horizonte (en una ciudad) ◊ *skyscraper* rascacielos

slab /slæb/ *n* **1** (*mármol*) losa **2** (*hormigón*) bloque **3** (*chocolate*) tableta

slack /slæk/ *adj* (**-er**, **-est**) **1** flojo **2** (*persona*) descuidado

slacken /ˈslækən/ *vt, vi* ~ (**sth**) (**off/up**) aflojar (algo)

slain *pp de* SLAY

slam /slæm/ (**-mm-**) **1** *vt, vi* ~ (**sth**) (**to/shut**) cerrar algo/cerrarse (de golpe) **2** *vt* arrojar, tirar: *to slam your brakes on* frenar de golpe **3** (*coloq*) *vt* (*criticar*) poner verde a

slander /ˈslɑːndə(r); *USA* ˈslæn-/ ◆ *n* calumnia ◆ *vt* calumniar

slang /slæŋ/ *n* argot

slant /slɑːnt; *USA* slænt/ ◆ **1** *vt, vi* inclinar(se), ladear(se) **2** *vt* (*frec pey*) presentar de forma subjetiva ◆ *n* **1** inclinación **2** ~ (**on/to sth**) (*fig*) sesgo (en algo)

slap /slæp/ ◆ *vt* (**-pp-**) **1** (*cara*) abofetear **2** (*espalda*) dar palmadas en **3** arrojar/tirar/dejar caer (con un golpe) ◆ *n* **1** (*espalda*) palmada **2** (*castigo*) palo **3** (*cara*) bofetada ◆ *adv* (*coloq*) de lleno: *slap in the middle* justo en medio

slash /slæʃ/ ◆ *vt* **1** cortar **2** destrozar a navajazos (*ruedas, pinturas, etc*) **3** (*precios, etc*) aplastar ◆ *n* **1** navajazo, cuchillada **2** tajo, corte

slate /sleɪt/ *n* **1** pizarra **2** teja (de pizarra)

slaughter /ˈslɔːtə(r)/ ◆ *n* **1** (*animales*) matanza **2** (*personas*) masacre ◆ *vt* **1** sacrificar (*en matadero*) **2** masacrar **3** (*coloq, esp Dep*) dar una paliza a

slave /sleɪv/ ◆ *n* ~ (**of/to sth/sb**)

esclavo, -a (de algo/algn) ◆ *vi* ~ (**away**) (**at sth**) matarse a trabajar (en algo)

slavery /ˈsleɪvəri/ *n* esclavitud

slay /sleɪ/ *vt* (*pret* **slew** /sluː/ *pp* **slain** /sleɪn/) (*fml o USA*) matar (*violentamente*)

sleazy /ˈsliːzi/ *adj* (**-ier**, **-iest**) (*coloq*) sórdido

sledge /sledʒ/ (*tb* **sled**) *n* trineo (*de nieve*) ☛ *Comparar con* SLEIGH

sleek /sliːk/ *adj* (**-er**, **-est**) lustroso

sleep /sliːp/ ◆ *n* [*sing*] sueñoLOC **to go to sleep** dormirse ◆ (*pret, pp* **slept** /slept/) **1** *vi* dormir: *sleeping bag* saco de dormir ◊ *sleeping pill* pastilla para dormir **2** *vt* albergar, tener camas para PHR V **to sleep in** (*USA*) *Ver* TO LIE IN *en* LIE² **to sleep on sth** consultar algo con la almohada **to sleep sth off** dormir para recuperarse de algo: *to sleep it off* dormirla **to sleep through sth** no ser despertado por algo **to sleep with sb** acostarse con algn

sleeper /ˈsliːpə(r)/ *n* **1** durmiente: *to be a heavy/light sleeper* tener el sueño pesado/ligero **2** (*en las vías del tren*) traviesa **3** (*en el tren*) litera **4** (*en el tren*) coche cama

sleepless /ˈsliːpləs/ *adj* en vela

sleepwalker /ˈsliːpwɔːkə(r)/ *n* sonámbulo, -a

sleepy /ˈsliːpi/ *adj* (**-ier**, **-iest**) **1** somnoliento **2** (*lugar*) tranquilo LOC **to be sleepy** tener sueño

sleet /sliːt/ *n* aguanieve

sleeve /sliːv/ *n* **1** manga **2** (*tb* **album sleeve**) (*de disco*) cubierta LOC **(to have sth) up your sleeve** (tener algo) guardado en la manga **sleeveless** *adj* sin mangas

sleigh /sleɪ/ *n* trineo (*de caballos*) ☛ *Comparar con* SLEDGE

slender /ˈslendə(r)/ *adj* (**-er**, **-est**) **1** delgado **2** (*persona*) esbelto *Ver tb* THIN **3** escaso

slept *pret, pp de* SLEEP

slew *pret de* SLAY

slice /slaɪs/ ◆ *n* **1** (*pan*) rebanada ☛ *Ver dibujo en* PAN **2** (*fruta*) rodaja **3** (*jamón*) loncha **4** (*carne*) tajada **5** (*coloq*) porción ◆ *vt* **1** cortar (*en lonchas, rebanadas, etc*) **2** ~ **through/into sth** cortar algo limpiamente PHR V **to slice sth up** cortar algo en lonchas, rebanadas, etc

slick /slɪk/ ◆ *adj* (**-er**, **-est**) **1** (*representación*) logrado **2** (*vendedor*) astuto ◆ *n* *Ver* OIL SLICK

slide /slaɪd/ ◆ *n* **1** tobogán **2** diapositiva: *slide projector* proyector de diapositivas **3** (*microscopio*) portaobjetos **4** (*fig*) deslizamiento ◆ (*pret, pp* **slid** /slɪd/) **1** *vi* resbalar, deslizarse **2** *vt* deslizar, correr

sliding door *n* puerta corredera

slight /slaɪt/ *adj* (**-er**, **-est**) **1** imperceptible **2** mínimo, ligero: *without the slightest difficulty* sin la menor dificultad **3** (*persona*) delgado, frágil LOC **not in the slightest** ni lo más mínimo **slightly** *adv* ligeramente: *He's slightly better.* Está un poco mejor.

slim /slɪm/ ◆ *adj* (**slimmer**, **slimmest**) **1** (*aprob*) (*persona*) delgado ☛ *Ver nota en* DELGADO **2** (*oportunidad*) escaso **3** (*esperanza*) ligero ◆ *vt, vi* (**-mm-**) ~ (**down**) adelgazar

slime /slaɪm/ *n* **1** cieno **2** baba **slimy** baboso, viscoso

sling¹ /slɪŋ/ *n* cabestrillo

sling² *vt* (*pret, pp* **slung** /slʌŋ/) **1** (*coloq*) lanzar (*con fuerza*) **2** colgar

slink /slɪŋk/ *vi* (*pret, pp* **slunk** /slʌŋk/) deslizarse (*sigilosamente*): *to slink away* largarse furtivamente

slip /slɪp/ ◆ *n* **1** resbalón **2** error, desliz **3** (*ropa*) combinación **4** (*de papel*) resguardo LOC **to give sb the slip** (*coloq*) darle a algn el esquinazo ◆ (**-pp-**) **1** *vt, vi* resbalar, deslizar(se) **2** *vi* ~ **from/out of/through sth** escurrirse de/entre algo **3** *vt* ~ **sth (from/off sth)** soltar algo (de algo) LOC **to slip your mind**: *It slipped my mind.* Se me fue de la cabeza. *Ver tb* LET¹ PHR V **to slip away** escabullirse **to slip sth off** quitarse algo **to slip sth on** ponerse algo **to slip out 1** salir un momento **2** escabullirse **3** *It just slipped out.* Se me escapó. **to slip up (on sth)** (*coloq*) equivocarse (en algo)

slipper /ˈslɪpə(r)/ *n* zapatilla

slippery /ˈslɪpəri/ *adj* **1** (*suelo*) resbaladizo **2** (*pez, persona*) escurridizo

slit /slɪt/ ◆ *n* **1** ranura **2** (*en una falda*) raja **3** corte **4** rendija, abertura ◆ *vt* (**-tt-**) (*pret, pp* **slit**) cortar: *to slit sb's throat* degollar a algn LOC **to slit sth open** abrir algo con un cuchillo

slither /ˈslɪðə(r)/ *vi* **1** deslizarse **2** resbalar, patinar

sliver /ˈslɪvə(r)/ *n* **1** astilla **2** esquirla **3** rodaja fina

slob /slɒb/ *n* (*coloq, GB*) **1** vago **2** guarro

slog /slɒg/ *vi* (**-gg-**) caminar trabajosamente PHR V **to slog (away) at sth** (*coloq*) sudar tinta

slogan /ˈsləʊgən/ *n* eslogan

slop /slɒp/ (**-pp-**) **1** *vt* echar **2** *vt, vi* derramar(se)

slope /sləʊp/ ◆ *n* **1** pendiente **2** (*de esquí*) pista ◆ *vi* tener una pendiente

sloppy /ˈslɒpi/ *adj* (**-ier**, **-iest**) **1** descuidado, chapucero **2** desaliñado **3** (*coloq*) sensiblero

slot /slɒt/ ◆ *n* **1** ranura **2** puesto: *a ten-minute slot on TV* un espacio de diez minutos en la tele ◆ *v* (**-tt-**) PHR V **to slot in** encajar **to slot sth in** introducir/meter algo

slot machine *n* máquina tragaperras

slow /sləʊ/ ◆ *adj* (**-er**, **-est**) **1** lento: *We're making slow progress.* Estamos avanzando lentamente. **2** torpe: *He's a bit slow.* Le cuesta entender las cosas. **3** (*negocio*) flojo: *Business is rather slow today.* El negocio anda bastante flojo hoy. **4** (*reloj*) atrasado: *That clock is five minutes slow.* Ese reloj va cinco minutos atrasado. LOC **in slow motion** a/en cámara lenta **to be slow to do sth/in doing sth** tardar en hacer algo ◆ *adv* (**-er**, **-est**) despacio ◆ **1** *vt* ~ **sth (up/down)** reducir la velocidad de algo: *to slow up the development of research* frenar el desarrollo de la investigación **2** *vi* ~ **(up/down)** reducir la velocidad, ir más despacio: *production has slowed (up/down)* el ritmo de la producción ha disminuido **slowly** *adv* **1** despacio **2** poco a poco

sludge /slʌdʒ/ *n* **1** fango **2** sedimento

slug /slʌg/ *n* babosa **sluggish** *adj* **1** lento **2** aletargado **3** (*Econ*) flojo

slum /slʌm/ *n* **1** (*tb* **slum area**) barrio bajo **2** chabola

slump /slʌmp/ ◆ *vi* **1** (*tb* **to slump down**) desplomarse **2** (*Com*) sufrir un bajón ◆ *n* depresión, bajón

slung *pret, pp de* SLING[2]

slunk *pret, pp de* SLINK

slur[1] /slɜː(r)/ *vt* (**-rr-**) articular mal

slur[2] /slɜː(r)/ *n* calumnia

slush /slʌʃ/ *n* nieve derretida y sucia

sly /slaɪ/ *adj* (**slyer**, **slyest**) **1** astuto **2** (*mirada*) furtivo

smack /smæk/ ◆ *n* cachete ◆ *vt* dar un cachete a PHR V **to smack of sth** oler a algo (*fig*)

small /smɔːl/ *adj* (**-er**, **-est**) **1** pequeño: *a small number of people* unas pocas personas ◊ *small change* calderilla ◊ *in the small hours* de madrugada ◊ *small ads* anuncios por palabras ◊ *to make small talk* hablar de cosas sin importancia **2** (*letra*) minúscula LOC **a small fortune** un dineral **it's a small world** (*refrán*) el mundo es un pañuelo **the small print** la letra pequeña (*en un contrato*)

Small suele utilizarse como el opuesto de **big** o **large** y puede ser modificado por adverbios: *Our house is smaller than yours.* Nuestra casa es más pequeña que la vuestra. ◊ *I have a fairly small income.* Tengo unos ingresos bastante modestos. **Little** no suele ir acompañado por adverbios y a menudo va detrás de otro adjetivo: *He's a horrid little man.* Es un hombre horrible. ◊ *What a lovely little house!* ¡Qué casita tan encantadora!

smallpox /ˈsmɔːlpɒks/ *n* viruela

small-scale /ˈsmɔl skeɪl/ *adj* a pequeña escala

smart /smɑːt/ ◆ *adj* (**-er**, **-est**) **1** elegante **2** listo, astuto ◆ *vi* escocer

smarten PHR V **to smarten (yourself) up** arreglar(se) **to smarten sth up** lavarle la cara a algo

smash /smæʃ/ ◆ **1** *vt* romper, destrozar **2** *vi* hacerse trizas PHR V **to smash against, into, through, etc sth** estrellarse contra algo **to smash sth against, into, through, etc sth** estrellar algo contra algo **to smash sth up** destrozar algo ◆ *n* **1** estrépito **2** (*tb* **smash-up**) accidente de tráfico **3** (*tb* **smash hit**) (*coloq*) exitazo

smashing /ˈsmæʃɪŋ/ *adj* (*GB*) estupendo

smear /smɪə(r)/ *vt* **1** ~ **sth on/over sth** untar algo en algo **2** ~ **sth with sth** untar algo de algo **3** ~ **sth with sth** manchar algo de algo

smell /smel/ ◆ *n* **1** olor: *a smell of gas* un olor a gas ☛ *Ver nota en* ODOUR **2** (*tb* **sense of smell**) olfato: *My sense of smell isn't very good.* No tengo muy buen (sentido del) olfato. ◆ (*pret, pp* **smelt** /smelt/ *o* **smelled**) **1** *vi* ~ (**of sth**) oler (a algo): *It smells of fish.* Huele a pescado. ◊ *What does it smell like?* ¿A qué huele? **2** *vt* oler: *Smell this rose!* ¡Huele esta rosa!

Es muy normal el uso del verbo **smell** con **can** o **could**: *I can smell something burning.* Huele a quemado. ◊ *I could smell gas.* Olía a gas.

3 *vt, vi* olfatear ☛ *Ver nota en* DREAM **smelly** *adj* (**-ier**, **-iest**) (*coloq*) apestoso: *It's smelly in here.* Huele mal aquí.

smile /smaɪl/ ◆ *n* sonrisa: *to give sb a smile* sonreírle a algn LOC *Ver* BRING ◆ *vi* sonreír

smirk /smɜːk/ ◆ *n* sonrisa socarrona o de satisfacción ◆ *vi* sonreír con sorna

smock /smɒk/ *n* guardapolvos (*de pintor*), blusón (*de mujer*)

smog /smɒg/ *n* neblina producida por la contaminación

smoke /sməʊk/ ◆ **1** *vt, vi* fumar: *to smoke a pipe* fumar en pipa **2** *vi* echar humo **3** *vt* (*pescado, etc*) ahumar ◆ *n* **1** humo **2** (*coloq*): *to have a smoke* echar un pitillo **smoker** *n* fumador, -ora **smoking** *n* fumar: *'No Smoking'* 'prohibido fumar' **smoky** (*tb* **smokey**) *adj* (**-ier**, **-iest**) **1** (*habitación*) lleno de humo **2** (*fuego*) humeante **3** (*sabor, color, etc*) ahumado

smooth /smuːð/ ◆ *adj* (**-er**, **-est**) **1** liso **2** (*piel, whisky, etc*) suave **3** (*carretera*) llano **4** (*viaje, periodo*) sin problemas: *The smooth reformist period has ended.* El periodo de reformas sin obstáculos ha acabado. **5** (*salsa, etc*) sin grumos **6** (*pey*) (*persona*) zalamero ◆ *vt* alisar PHR V **to smooth sth over** allanar algo (*dificultades*) **smoothly** *adv*: *to go smoothly* ir sobre ruedas

smother /ˈsmʌðə(r)/ *vt* **1** (*persona*) asfixiar **2** ~ **sth/sb with/in sth** cubrir algo/a algn de algo **3** (*llamas*) sofocar

smoulder (*USA* **smolder**) /ˈsməʊldə(r)/ *vi* consumirse, arder (*sin llama*)

smudge /smʌdʒ/ ◆ *n* borrón, manchón ◆ *vt, vi* emborronar(se)

smug /smʌg/ *adj* (**smugger**, **smuggest**) (*frec pey*) engreído, hueco

smuggle /ˈsmʌgl/ *vt* pasar de contrabando PHR V **to smuggle sth/sb in/out** meter/sacar en secreto algo/a algn **smuggler** *n* contrabandista **smuggling** *n* contrabando

snack /snæk/ ◆ *n* tentempié, refrigerio: *snack bar* cafetería ◊ *to have a snack* tomarse un tentempié ◆ *vi* (*coloq*) picar

snag /snæg/ *n* pega

snail /sneɪl/ *n* caracol

snake /sneɪk/ ◆ *n* serpiente, culebra ◆ *vi* serpentear (*carretera, etc*)

snap /snæp/ ◆ (**-pp-**) **1** *vt, vi* chasquear **2** *vt, vi* romper(se) en dos PHR V **to snap at sb** hablar/contestar bruscamente ◆ *n* **1** (*ruido seco*) chasquido **2** (*tb* **snapshot**) foto ◆ *adj* (*coloq*) repentino (*decisión*)

snapshot /ˈsnæpʃɒt/ *n* foto

snare /sneə(r)/ ◆ *n* cepo ◆ *vt* atrapar

snarl /snɑːl/ ◆ *n* gruñido ◆ *vi* gruñir

snatch /snætʃ/ ◆ *vt* **1** arrebatar, arrancar **2** (*coloq*) robar de un tirón **3** raptar **4** (*oportunidad*) aprovechar, agarrarse a PHR V **to snatch at sth 1** (*objeto*) tirar de algo, coger algo bruscamente **2** (*oportunidad*) agarrarse a algo, aprovechar algo ◆ *n* **1** (*conversación, canción*) fragmento **2** secuestro **3** (*coloq*) robo

sneak /sniːk/ ◆ *vt*: *to sneak a look at sth/sb* mirar algo/a algn a hurtadillas PHR V **to sneak in, out, away, etc** entrar, salir, marcharse a hurtadillas **to sneak into, out of, past, etc sth** entrar en, salir de, pasar por delante de algo a hurtadillas ◆ *n* (*coloq*) soplón, -ona

sneakers /ˈsniːkəz/ *n* [*pl*] (*USA*) zapatillas de deporte

sneer /snɪə(r)/ ◆ *n* **1** sonrisa sarcástica **2** comentario desdeñoso ◆ *vi* ~ (**at sth/sb**) reírse con desprecio (de algo/algn)

sneeze /sniːz/ ◆ *n* estornudo ◆ *vi* estornudar

sniff /snɪf/ ◆ **1** *vi* sorber **2** *vi* husmear **3** *vt* oler **4** *vt* inhalar **5** *vi* gimotear ◆ *n* inhalación

snigger /ˈsnɪgə(r)/ ◆ *n* risita sofocada ◆ *vi* ~ (**at sth/sb**) reírse (con sarcasmo) (de algo/algn)

snip /snɪp/ *vt* (**-pp-**) cortar con tijeras: *to snip sth off* recortar algo

sniper /ˈsnaɪpə(r)/ *n* francotirador, -ora

snob /snɒb/ *n* esnob **snobbery** *n* esnobismo **snobbish** *adj* esnob

snoop /snuːp/ ◆ *vi* (*coloq*) (*tb* **to snoop about/around**) fisgonear ◆ *n* LOC **to have a snoop about/around** reconocer el terreno **to have a snoop about/around sth** fisgonear algo

snore /snɔː(r)/ *vi* roncar

snorkel /ˈsnɔːkl/ *n* tubo de bucear

snort /snɔːt/ ◆ *vi* **1** (*animal*) bufar **2** (*persona*) bufar, gruñir ◆ *n* bufido

snout /snaʊt/ *n* hocico

snow /snəʊ/ ◆ *n* nieve ◆ *vi* nevar LOC **to be snowed in/up** estar aislado por la nieve **to be snowed under (with sth)**: *I was snowed under with work.* Estaba inundado de trabajo.

snowball /ˈsnəʊbɔːl/ ◆ *n* bola de nieve ◆ *vi* multiplicarse (rápidamente)

snowdrop /ˈsnəʊdrɒp/ *n* campanilla blanca (*flor*)

snowfall /ˈsnəʊfɔːl/ *n* nevada

snowflake /ˈsnəʊfleɪk/ *n* copo de nieve

snowman /ˈsnəʊmæn/ *n* (*pl* **-men** /-men/) muñeco de nieve

snowy /ˈsnəʊi/ *adj* (**-ier, -iest**) **1** cubierto de nieve **2** (*día, etc*) de nieve

snub /snʌb/ *vt* (**-bb-**) hacer un desaire a

snug /snʌg/ *adj* (**-gg-**) cómodo y agradable

snuggle /ˈsnʌgl/ *vi* **1** ~ **down** hacerse un ovillo **2** ~ **up to sb** hacerse un ovillo junto a algn

so /səʊ/ *adv, conj* **1** tan: *Don't be so silly!* ¡No seas tan bobo! ◊ *It's so cold!* ¡Qué frío hace! ◊ *I'm so sorry!* ¡Cuánto lo siento! **2** así: *So it seems.* Así parece. ◊ *Hold out your hand, (like) so.* Extiende la mano, así. ◊ *The table is about so big.* La mesa es más o menos así de grande. ◊ *If so,...* Si es así,... **3** *I believe/think so.* Creo que sí. ◊ *I expect/hope so.* Espero que sí. **4** (*para expresar acuerdo*): *'I'm hungry.' 'So am I.'* —Tengo hambre. —Yo también. ☛ En este caso el pronombre o sustantivo va detrás del verbo. **5** (*expresando sorpresa*): *'Philip's gone home.' 'So he has.'* —Philip se ha ido a casa. —Anda, es cierto. **6** [*uso enfático*]: *He's as clever as his brother, maybe more so.* Es tan listo como su hermano, puede que incluso más. ◊ *She has complained, and rightly so.* Se ha quejado, y con mucha razón. **7** así que: *The shops were closed so I didn't get any milk.* Las tiendas estaban cerradas, así que no he comprado leche. **8** entonces: *So why did you do it?* ¿Y entonces, por qué lo hiciste? LOC **and so on (and so forth)** etcétera, etcétera **is that so?** no me digas **so as to do sth** para hacer algo **so many** tantos **so much** tanto **so?; so what?** (*coloq*) ¿y qué? **so that** para que

soak /səʊk/ **1** *vt* remojar, empapar **2** *vi* estar en/a remojo LOC **to get soaked (through)** empaparse PHR V **to soak into sth** ser absorbido por algo **to soak through** calar (*líquido*) **to soak sth up 1** (*líquido*) absorber algo **2** (*fig*) empaparse de algo **soaked** *adj* empapado

soap /səʊp/ *n* [*incontable*] jabón

soap opera *n* culebrón (*televisión*)

soapy /ˈsəʊpi/ *adj* (**-ier, -iest**) jabonoso

soar /sɔː(r)/ *vi* **1** (*avión*) remontarse **2** (*precios*) dispararse **3** (*ave*) planear

sob /sɒb/ ◆ *vi* (**-bb-**) sollozar ◆ *n* sollozo **sobbing** *n* sollozos

sober /ˈsəʊbə(r)/ *adj* **1** sobrio **2** serio

so-called /ˌsəʊ ˈkɔːld/ *adj* (*pey*) (mal) llamado

soccer /ˈsɒkə(r)/ *n* (*coloq*) fútbol ☛ *Ver nota en* FÚTBOL

sociable /ˈsəʊʃəbl/ *adj* (*aprob*) sociable

social /ˈsəʊʃəl/ *adj* social

socialism /ˈsəʊʃəlɪzəm/ *n* socialismo **socialist** *n* socialista

socialize, -ise /ˈsəʊʃəlaɪz/ *vi* ~ **(with sb)** relacionarse (con algn): *He doesn't socialize much.* No sale mucho.

social security (*USA* **welfare**) *n* seguridad social

social services *n* [*pl*] servicios sociales

social work *n* trabajo social **social worker** *n* asistente, -a social

society /səˈsaɪəti/ *n* (*pl* **-ies**) **1** sociedad **2** (*fml*) compañía: *polite society* buena sociedad **3** asociación

sociological /ˌsəʊsiəˈlɒdʒɪkl/ *adj* sociológico

sociologist /ˌsəʊsiˈɒlədʒɪst/ *n* sociólogo, -a **sociology** *n* sociología

sock /sɒk/ *n* calcetín LOC *Ver* PULL ☛ *Ver nota en* PAIR

socket /ˈsɒkɪt/ *n* **1** (*ojo*) cuenca **2** enchufe (*en la pared*) ☛ *Ver dibujo en*

ENCHUFE **3** (*tb* **light socket**) portalámparas

soda /ˈsəʊdə/ *n* **1** soda **2** (*tb* **soda pop**) (*USA, coloq*) gaseosa

sodden /ˈsɒdn/ *adj* empapado

sodium /ˈsəʊdiəm/ *n* sodio

sofa /ˈsəʊfə/ *n* sofá

soft /sɒft; *USA* sɔːft/ *adj* (**-er**, **-est**) **1** blando: *soft option* opción fácil **2** (*piel, color, luz, sonido*) suave **3** (*brisa*) ligero **4** (*voz*) bajo LOC **to have a soft spot for sth/sb** (*coloq*) tener debilidad por algo/algn **softly** *adv* suavemente

soft drink *n* bebida no alcohólica

soften /ˈsɒfn; *USA* ˈsɔːfn/ **1** *vt, vi* ablandar(se) **2** *vt, vi* suavizar(se)

soft-spoken /ˌsɒft ˈspəʊkən/ *adj* de voz suave

software /ˈsɒftweə(r)/ *n* software

soggy /ˈsɒgi/ *adj* (**-ier**, **-iest**) **1** empapado **2** (*pastel, pan, etc*) correoso

soil /sɔɪl/ ◆ *n* tierra ◆ (*fml*) *vt* **1** ensuciar **2** (*reputación*) manchar

solace /ˈsɒləs/ *n* (*fml*) solaz, consuelo

solar /ˈsəʊlə(r)/ *adj* solar: *solar energy* energía solar

sold *pret, pp de* SELL

soldier /ˈsəʊldʒə(r)/ *n* soldado

sole[1] /səʊl/ *n* **1** (*pie*) planta **2** suela

sole[2] /səʊl/ *adj* **1** único: *her sole interest* su único interés **2** exclusivo

solemn /ˈsɒləm/ *adj* **1** (*aspecto, manera*) serio **2** (*acontecimiento, promesa*) solemne **solemnity** /səˈlemnəti/ *n* (*fml*) solemnidad

solicitor /səˈlɪsɪtə(r)/ *n* (*GB*) **1** abogado, -a **2** notario, -a ☛ *Ver nota en* ABOGADO

solid /ˈsɒlɪd/ ◆ *adj* **1** sólido **2** compacto **3** seguido: *I slept for ten hours solid.* Dormí diez horas seguidas. ◆ *n* **1** **solids** [*pl*] alimentos sólidos **2** (*Geom*) figura de tres dimensiones **solidly** *adv* **1** sólidamente **2** sin interrupción

solidarity /ˌsɒlɪˈdærəti/ *n* solidaridad

solidify /səˈlɪdɪfaɪ/ *vi* (*pret, pp* **-fied**) solidificarse

solidity /səˈlɪdəti/ (*tb* **solidness**) *n* solidez

solitary /ˈsɒlətri; *USA* -teri/ *adj* **1** solitario: *to lead a solitary life* llevar una vida retirada **2** (*lugar*) apartado **3** solo LOC **solitary confinement** (*tb coloq* **solitary**) incomunicación

solitude /ˈsɒlɪtjuːd; *USA* -tuːd/ *n* soledad

solo /ˈsəʊləʊ/ ◆ *n* (*pl* ~**s**) solo ◆ *adj, adv* en solitario **soloist** *n* solista

soluble /ˈsɒljəbl/ *adj* soluble

solution /səˈluːʃn/ *n* solución

solve /sɒlv/ *vt* resolver

solvent /ˈsɒlvənt/ *n* disolvente

sombre (*USA* **somber**) /ˈsɒmbə(r)/ *adj* **1** sombrío **2** (*color*) oscuro **3** (*manera, humor*) melancólico

some /səm/ *adj, pron* **1** algo de: *There's some ice in the fridge.* Hay hielo en la nevera. ◇ *Would you like some?* ¿Quieres un poco? **2** unos (cuantos), algunos: *Do you want some crisps?* ¿Quieres patatas fritas?

> ¿**Some** o **any**? Ambos se utilizan con sustantivos incontables o en plural, y aunque muchas veces no se traducen en español, en inglés no se pueden omitir. Normalmente, **some** se usa en las oraciones afirmativas y **any** en las interrogativas y negativas: *I've got some money.* Tengo (algo de) dinero. ◇ *Have you got any children?* ¿Tienes hijos? ◇ *I don't want any sweets.* No quiero caramelos. Sin embargo, **some** se puede usar en oraciones interrogativas cuando se espera una respuesta afirmativa, por ejemplo, para ofrecer o pedir algo: *Would you like some coffee?* ¿Quieres café? ◇ *Can I have some bread, please?* ¿Puedo coger un poco de pan? Cuando **any** se usa en oraciones afirmativas significa "cualquiera": *Any parent would have worried.* Cualquier padre se habría preocupado. *Ver tb ejemplos en* ANY

somebody /ˈsʌmbədi/ (*tb* **someone** /ˈsʌmwʌn/) *pron* alguien: *somebody else* otra persona ☛ La diferencia entre **somebody** y **anybody**, o entre **someone** y **anyone**, es la misma que hay entre **some** y **any**. *Ver nota en* SOME

somehow /ˈsʌmhaʊ/ (*USA tb* **someway** /ˈsʌmweɪ/) *adv* **1** de alguna manera: *Somehow we had got completely lost.* De alguna manera nos hallamos completamente perdidos. **2** por alguna razón: *I somehow get the feeling that I've been here before.* No sé por qué, me da la impresión de que ya he estado aquí.

someone /ˈsʌmwʌn/ *pron Ver* SOMEBODY

somersault /ˈsʌməsɔːlt/ *n* **1** voltereta: *to do a forward/backward somersault* dar una voltereta hacia delante/hacia atrás **2** (*de acróbata*) salto mortal **3** (*de coche*) vuelta de campana

something /ˈsʌmθɪŋ/ *pron* algo: *something else* otra cosa ◊ *something to eat* algo de comer ☛ La diferencia entre **something** y **anything** es la misma que hay entre **some** y **any**. *Ver nota en* SOME

sometime /ˈsʌmtaɪm/ *adv* **1** algún/un día: *sometime or other* un día de estos **2** en algún momento: *Can I see you sometime today?* ¿Podemos hablar hoy en algún momento?

sometimes /ˈsʌmtaɪmz/ *adv* **1** a veces **2** de vez en cuando ☛ *Ver nota en* ALWAYS

somewhat /ˈsʌmwɒt/ *adv* [*con adj o adv*] **1** algo, un tanto: *I have a somewhat different question.* Tengo una pregunta un tanto diferente. **2** bastante: *We missed the bus, which was somewhat unfortunate.* Perdimos el autobús, lo cual fue bastante mala suerte.

somewhere /ˈsʌmweə(r)/ (*USA tb* **someplace**) ◆ *adv* a/en/por algún sitio/lugar: *I've seen your glasses somewhere downstairs.* He visto tus gafas en algún sitio abajo. ◊ *somewhere else* en algún otro lugar ◆ *pron*: *to have somewhere to go* tener algún lugar adonde ir ☛ La diferencia entre **somewhere** y **anywhere** es la misma que hay entre **some** y **any**. *Ver nota en* SOME

son /sʌn/ *n* hijo **LOC** *Ver* FATHER

song /sɒŋ; *USA* sɔːŋ/ *n* **1** canción **2** canto

son-in-law /ˈsʌn ɪn lɔː/ *n* (*pl* **sons-in-law**) yerno

soon /suːn/ *adv* (**-er**, **-est**) pronto, dentro de poco **LOC as soon as** en cuanto, tan pronto como: *as soon as possible* en cuanto sea posible **(just) as soon do sth (as do sth)**: *I'd (just) as soon stay at home as go for a walk.* Lo mismo me da quedarme en casa que ir a dar un paseo. **sooner or later** tarde o temprano **the sooner the better** cuanto antes mejor

soot /sʊt/ *n* hollín

soothe /suːð/ *vt* **1** (*persona, etc*) calmar **2** (*dolor, etc*) aliviar

sophisticated /səˈfɪstɪkeɪtɪd/ *adj* sofisticado **sophistication** *n* sofisticación

soppy /ˈsɒpi/ *adj* (*GB, coloq*) sensiblero

sordid /ˈsɔːdɪd/ *adj* **1** sórdido **2** (*comportamiento*) vil

sore /sɔː(r)/ ◆ *n* llaga ◆ *adj* dolorido: *to have a sore throat* tener dolor de garganta ◊ *I've got sore eyes.* Me duelen los ojos. **LOC a sore point** un asunto delicado **sorely** *adv* (*fml*): *She will be sorely missed.* Se la echará de menos enormemente. ◊ *I was sorely tempted to do it.* Tuve grandes tentaciones de hacerlo.

sorrow /ˈsɒrəʊ/ *n* pesar: *to my great sorrow* con gran pesar mío

sorry /ˈsɒri/ ◆ *interj* **1** (*para disculparse*) ¡perdón! ☛ *Ver nota en* EXCUSE **2 sorry?** ¿cómo dice?, ¿qué has dicho? ◆ *adj* **1** *I'm sorry I'm late.* Siento llegar tarde. ◊ *I'm so sorry!* ¡Lo siento mucho! **2** *He's very sorry for what he's done.* Está muy arrepentido por lo que ha hecho. ◊ *You'll be sorry!* ¡Te arrepentirás! **3** (**-ier**, **-iest**) (*estado*) lastimoso **LOC to say you are sorry** disculparse *Ver tb* BETTER, FEEL

sort /sɔːt/ ◆ *n* **1** tipo: *They sell all sorts of gifts.* Venden toda clase de regalos. **2** (*antic, coloq*) persona: *He's not a bad sort really.* No es mala persona. **LOC a sort of**: *It's a sort of autobiography.* Es una especie de autobiografía. **sort of** (*coloq*): *I feel sort of uneasy.* Me siento como inquieto. *Ver tb* NOTHING ◆ *vt* clasificar **PHR V to sort sth out** arreglar, solucionar algo **to sort through sth** clasificar, ordenar algo

so-so /ˌsəʊ ˈsəʊ, ˈsəʊ səʊ/ *adj, adv* (*coloq*) así así

sought *pret, pp de* SEEK

sought-after /ˈsɔːt ɑːftə(r); *USA* -æf-/ *adj* codiciado

soul /səʊl/ *n* alma: *There wasn't a soul to be seen.* No se veía un alma. ◊ *Poor soul!* ¡El pobre! **LOC** *Ver* BODY

sound[1] /saʊnd/ ◆ *n* **1** sonido: *sound waves* ondas acústicas **2** ruido: *I could hear the sound of voices.* Oía ruido de voces. ◊ *She opened the door without a sound.* Abrió la puerta sin hacer ruido. **3 the sound** volumen: *Can you turn the* *sound up/down?* ¿Puedes subir/bajar el volumen? ◆ **1** *vi* sonar: *Your voice sounds a bit odd.* Tu voz suena un poco rara. **2** *vt* (*trompeta, etc*) tocar **3** *vt* (*alarma*) dar **4** *vt* pronunciar: *You don't sound the 'h'.* No se pronuncia la "h". **5** *vi* parecer: *She sounded very surprised.* Parecía muy sorprendida. ◊ *He sounds a very nice person from his letter.* A juzgar por su carta, parece una persona muy agradable.

sound² /saʊnd/ ◆ *adj* (**-er**, **-est**) **1** sano **2** (*estructura*) sólido **3** (*creencia*) firme **4** (*consejo, paliza*) bueno LOC **being of sound mind** hallándose en plenitud de sus facultades mentales *Ver tb* SAFE¹ ◆ *adv* LOC **to be sound asleep** estar profundamente dormido

sound³ /saʊnd/ *vt* (*mar*) sondar PHR V **to sound sb out** (**about/on sth**) tantear a algn (sobre algo)

soundproof /ˈsaʊndpruːf/ ◆ *adj* insonorizado ◆ *vt* insonorizar

soundtrack /ˈsaʊndtræk/ *n* banda sonora

soup /suːp/ *n* sopa, caldo: *soup spoon* cuchara sopera ◊ *chicken soup* sopa de pollo

sour /ˈsaʊə(r)/ *adj* **1** (*sabor, cara*) agrio **2** (*leche*) cortado LOC **to go/turn sour** agriarse/echarse a perder

source /sɔːs/ *n* **1** (*información*) fuente: *They didn't reveal their sources.* No revelaron sus fuentes. **2** (*río*) nacimiento: *a source of income* una fuente de ingresos

south /saʊθ/ ◆ *n* (*tb* **the south**, **the South**) (*abrev* **S**) (el) sur: *Brighton is in the South of England.* Brighton está al sur de Inglaterra. ◊ *southbound* en/con dirección sur ◆ *adj* (del) sur: *south winds* vientos del sur ◆ *adv* al sur: *The house faces south.* La casa mira hacia el sur. *Ver tb* SOUTHWARD(S)

south-east /ˌsaʊθ ˈiːst/ ◆ *n* (*abrev* **SE**) sureste ◆ *adj* (del) sureste ◆ *adv* hacia el sureste **south-eastern** *adj* (del) sureste

southern /ˈsʌðən/ (*tb* **Southern**) *adj* del sur, meridional: *southern Italy* el sur de Italia ◊ *the southern hemisphere* el hemisferio sur **southerner** *n* sureño, -a

southward(s) /ˈsaʊθwədz/ *adv* hacia el sur *Ver tb* SOUTH *adv*

south-west /ˌsaʊθ ˈwest/ ◆ *n* (*abrev* **SW**) suroeste ◆ *adj* (del) suroeste ◆ *adv* hacia el suroeste **south-western** *adj* (del) suroeste

souvenir /ˌsuːvəˈnɪə(r); *USA* ˈsuːvənɪər/ *n* recuerdo (*objeto*)

sovereign /ˈsɒvrɪn/ *adj, n* soberano, -a **sovereignty** *n* soberanía

sow¹ /saʊ/ *n* cerda ☛ *Ver nota en* CERDO

sow² /səʊ/ *vt* (*pret* **sowed** *pp* **sown** /səʊn/ *o* **sowed**) sembrar

soya /sɔɪə/ (*USA* **soy** /sɔɪ/) *n* soja: *soya bean* semilla de soja

spa /spɑː/ *n* balneario

space /speɪs/ ◆ *n* **1** [*incontable*] (*cabida*) sitio, espacio: *Leave some space for the dogs.* Deja sitio para los perros. ◊ *There's no space for my suitcase.* No queda espacio para mi maleta. **2** (*Aeronáut*) espacio: *a space flight* un vuelo espacial ◊ *to stare into space* mirar al vacío **3** (*periodo*) espacio: *in a short space of time* en un breve espacio de tiempo ◆ *vt* ~ **sth** (**out**) espaciar algo

spacecraft /ˈspeɪskrɑːft; *USA* -kræft/ *n* (*pl* **spacecraft**) (*tb* **spaceship**) nave espacial

spacious /ˈspeɪʃəs/ *adj* espacioso, amplio

spade /speɪd/ *n* **1** pala **2 spades** [*pl*] picas (*cartas*) ☛ *Ver nota en* BARAJA

spaghetti /spəˈgeti/ *n* [*incontable*] espagueti(s)

span /spæn/ ◆ *n* **1** (*de un puente*) luz **2** (*de tiempo*) lapso, duración: *time span/span of time* lapso de tiempo ◆ *vt* (**-nn-**) **1** (*puente*) cruzar **2** abarcar

spank /spæŋk/ *vt* dar una zurra a, dar un(os) azote(s) a

spanner /ˈspænə(r)/ (*esp USA* **wrench**) *n* llave inglesa (*no graduable*)

spare /speə(r)/ ◆ *adj* **1** sobrante, de sobra: *There are no spare seats.* No quedan asientos. ◊ *the spare room* la habitación de invitados **2** de repuesto, de reserva: *a spare tyre/part* una rueda/pieza de repuesto **3** (*tiempo*) libre, de ocio ◆ *n* (pieza de) repuesto ◆ *vt* **1** ~ **sth** (**for sth/sb**) (*tiempo, dinero, etc*) tener algo (para algo/algn) **2** (*la vida de algn*) perdonar **3** escatimar: *No expense was spared.* No repararon en gastos. **4** ahorrar: *Spare me the gory* *details.* Ahórrame los detalles desagradables. LOC **to spare** de sobra: *with two minutes to spare* faltando dos minutos **sparing** *adj* ~ **with/of/in sth** parco en algo; mesurado con algo

spark /spɑːk/ ◆ *n* chispa ◆ PHR V **to spark sth (off)** (*coloq*) provocar algo, ocasionar algo

sparkle /ˈspɑːkl/ ◆ *vi* centellear, destellar ◆ *n* centelleo **sparkling** *adj* **1** (*tb* **sparkly**) centelleante **2** (*vino, etc*) espumoso

sparrow /ˈspærəʊ/ *n* gorrión

sparse /spɑːs/ *adj* **1** escaso, esparcido **2** (*población*) disperso **3** (*pelo*) ralo

spartan /ˈspɑːtn/ *adj* espartano

spasm /ˈspæzəm/ *n* espasmo

spat *pret, pp de* SPIT

spate /speɪt/ *n* racha, ola

spatial /ˈspeɪʃl/ *adj* (*fml*) del espacio (*de una habitación, etc*) ☛ *Comparar con* SPACE

spatter /ˈspætə(r)/ *vt* ~ **sb with sth**; ~ **sth on sb** rociar, salpicar a algn de algo

speak /spiːk/ (*pret* **spoke** /spəʊk/ *pp* **spoken** /spəʊkən/) **1** *vi* hablar: *Can I speak to you a minute, please?* ¿Puedo hablar contigo un minuto, por favor? ☛ *Ver nota en* HABLAR **2** *vt* decir, hablar: *to speak the truth* decir la verdad ◊ *Do you speak French?* ¿Hablas francés? **3** *vi* ~ (**on/about sth**) pronunciar un discurso (sobre algo) **4** (*coloq*) *vi* ~ (**to sb**) hablarse (con algn) LOC **generally, etc speaking** en términos generales **so to speak** por así decirlo **to speak for itself**: *The statistics speak for themselves.* Las estadísticas hablan solas. **to speak for sb** hablar en favor de algn **to speak up** hablar más alto **to speak your mind** hablar sin rodeos *Ver tb* STRICTLY *en* STRICT

speaker /ˈspiːkə(r)/ *n* **1** el/la que habla: *Spanish speaker* hispanohablante **2** (*en público*) orador, -ora, conferenciante **3** (*coloq*) altavoz *Ver* LOUDSPEAKER

spear /spɪə(r)/ **1** *n* lanza **2** (*para pesca*) arpón

special /ˈspeʃl/ ◆ *adj* **1** especial **2** particular: *nothing special* nada en particular **3** (*reunión, edición, pago*) extraordinario ◆ *n* **1** (*tren, programa, etc*) especial **2** (*USA, coloq*) oferta especial **specialist** *n* especialista

speciality /ˌspeʃɪˈæləti/ (*esp USA* **specialty** /ˈspeʃəlti/) *n* (*pl* **-ies**) especialidad

specialize, -ise /ˈspeʃəlaɪz/ *vi* ~ (**in sth**) especializarse (en algo) **specialization, -isation** *n* especialización **specialized, -ised** *adj* especializado

specially /ˈspeʃli/ *adv* **1** especialmente, expresamente

> Aunque **specially** y **especially** tienen significados similares, se usan de forma distinta. **Specially** se usa fundamentalmente con participios y **especially** como conector entre frases: *specially designed for schools* diseñado especialmente para los colegios ◊ *He likes dogs, especially poodles.* Le encantan los perros, sobre todo los caniches.

2 (*tb* **especially**) particularmente, sobre todo

species /ˈspiːʃiːz/ *n* (*pl* **species**) especie

specific /spəˈsɪfɪk/ *adj* específico, preciso, concreto **specifically** *adv* concretamente, específicamente, especialmente

specification /ˌspesɪfɪˈkeɪʃn/ *n* **1** especificación **2** [*gen pl*] especificaciones, plan detallado

specify /ˈspesɪfaɪ/ *vt* (*pret, pp* **-fied**) especificar, precisar

specimen /ˈspesɪmən/ *n* espécimen, ejemplar, muestra

speck /spek/ *n* **1** (*de suciedad*) manchita **2** (*de polvo*) mota **3** *a speck on the horizon* un punto en el horizonte **4** (*pequeño pedazo*) pizca

spectacle /ˈspektəkl/ *n* espectáculo

spectacles /ˈspektəklz/ *n* (*abrev* **specs**) [*pl*] (*fml*) gafas, anteojos ☛ La palabra más normal es **glasses**. *Ver nota en* PAIR

spectacular /spekˈtækjələ(r)/ *adj* espectacular

spectator /spekˈteɪtə(r); *USA* ˈspekteɪtər/ *n* espectador, -ora

spectre (*USA* **specter**) /ˈspektə(r)/ *n* (*fml, lit y fig*) espectro, fantasma: *the spectre of another war* el fantasma de una nueva guerra

spectrum /ˈspektrəm/ *n* (*pl* **-tra**

/ˈspektrə/) **1** espectro **2** espectro, abanico

speculate /ˈspekjuleɪt/ *vi* ~ **(about sth)** especular (sobre/acerca de algo) **speculation** *n* ~ **(on/about sth)** especulación (sobre algo)

speculative /ˈspekjələtɪv; *USA* ˈspekjəleɪtɪv/ *adj* especulativo

speculator /ˈspekjuleɪtə(r)/ *n* especulador, -ora

sped *pret, pp de* SPEED

speech /spiːtʃ/ *n* **1** habla: *freedom of speech* libertad de expresión ◊ *to lose the power of speech* perder el habla ◊ *speech therapy* terapia lingüística **2** discurso: *to make/deliver/give a speech* pronunciar un discurso **3** lenguaje: *children's speech* el lenguaje de los niños **4** (*Teat*) parlamento

speechless /ˈspiːtʃləs/ *adj* sin habla, mudo: *The boy was almost speechless.* El niño apenas podía articular palabra.

speed /spiːd/ ◆ *n* velocidad, rapidez LOC **at speed** a toda velocidad *Ver tb* FULL, PICK ◆ *vt* (*pret, pp* **speeded**) acelerar PHR V **to speed up** apresurarse **to speed sth up** acelerar algo ◆ *vi* (*pret, pp* **sped** /sped/) ir a toda velocidad: *I was fined for speeding.* Me pusieron una multa por exceso de velocidad.

speedily /ˈspiːdɪli/ *adv* rápidamente

speedometer /spiːˈdɒmɪtə(r)/ *n* velocímetro

speedy /ˈspiːdi/ *adj* (**-ier, -iest**) (*frec coloq*) pronto, rápido: *a speedy recovery* una pronta recuperación

spell /spel/ ◆ *n* **1** conjuro, hechizo **2** temporada, racha **3** ~ **(at/on sth)** tanda, turno (en algo) LOC *Ver* CAST ◆ *vt, vi* (*pret, pp* **spelt** /spelt/ *o* **spelled**) ☛ *Ver nota en* DREAM **1** deletrear, escribir **2** suponer, significar PHR V **to spell sth out** explicar algo claramente

spelling /ˈspelɪŋ/ *n* ortografía

spelt *pret, pp de* SPELL

spend /spend/ *vt* (*pret, pp* **spent** /spent/) **1** ~ **sth (on/sth)** gastar algo (en algo) **2** (*tiempo libre, etc*) pasar **3** ~ **sth on sth** dedicar algo a algo **spending** *n* gasto: *public spending* el gasto público

sperm /spɜːm/ *n* (*pl* **sperm**) esperma

sphere /sfɪə(r)/ *n* esfera

sphinx /sfɪŋks/ (*tb* **the Sphinx**) *n* esfinge

spice /spaɪs/ ◆ *n* **1** (*lit*) especia(s) **2** (*fig*) interés: *to add spice to a situation* añadir interés a una situación ◆ *vt* sazonar **spicy** *adj* (**-ier, -iest**) condimentado, picante *Ver tb* HOT

spider /ˈspaɪdə(r)/ *n* araña: *spider's web* telaraña *Ver tb* COBWEB

spied *pret, pp de* SPY

spike /spaɪk/ *n* **1** púa, pincho **2** punta **spiky** *adj* (**-ier, -iest**) erizado de púas, puntiagudo

spill /spɪl/ ◆ *vt, vi* (*pret, pp* **spilt** /spɪlt/ *o* **spilled**) ☛ *Ver nota en* DREAM derramar(se), verter(se) LOC *Ver* CRY PHR V **to spill over** rebosar, desbordarse ◆ *n* (*tb* **spillage**) **1** derramamiento **2** derrame

spin /spɪn/ ◆ (**-nn-**) (*pret, pp* **spun** /spʌn/) **1** *vi* ~ **(round)** dar vueltas, girar **2** *vt* ~ **sth (round)** (hacer) girar algo; dar vueltas a algo **3** *vt, vi* (*lavadora*) centrifugar **4** *vt* hilar PHR V **to spin sth out** alargar algo, prolongar algo ◆ *n* **1** vuelta, giro **2** (*coloq*) (*paseo en coche/moto*) vuelta: *to go for a spin* dar una vuelta

spinach /ˈspɪnɪdʒ; *USA* -ɪtʃ/ *n* [*incontable*] espinaca(s)

spinal /ˈspaɪnl/ *adj* espinal: *spinal column* columna vertebral

spine /spaɪn/ *n* **1** (*Anat*) columna vertebral **2** (*Bot*) espina **3** (*Zool*) púa **4** (*de un libro*) lomo

spinster /ˈspɪnstə(r)/ *n* **1** soltera **2** (*frec ofen*) solterona

spiral /ˈspaɪrəl/ ◆ *n* espiral ◆ *adj* (en espiral, helicoidal: *a spiral staircase* una escalera de caracol

spire /ˈspaɪə(r)/ *n* chapitel, aguja

spirit /ˈspɪrɪt/ *n* **1** espíritu, alma **2** fantasma **3** brío, ánimo **4** temple **5** **spirits** [*pl*] (*bebida alcohólica*) licor **6** **spirits** [*pl*] estado de ánimo, humor: *in high spirits* de muy buen humor **spirited** *adj* animoso, brioso

spiritual /ˈspɪrɪtʃuəl/ *adj* espiritual

spit /spɪt/ ◆ (**-tt-**) (*pret, pp* **spat** /spæt/ *tb esp USA* **spit**) **1** *vt, vi* escupir **2** *vt* (*insulto, etc*) soltar **3** *vi* (*fuego, etc*) chisporrotear PHR V **to spit sth out** escupir algo ◆ *n* **1** saliva, esputo **2** punta (*de tierra*) **3** (*un pincho*) espetón, asador

spite /spaɪt/ ◆ *n* despecho, resent

miento: *out of/from spite* por despecho LOC **in spite of** a pesar de ◆ *vt* molestar, fastidiar **spiteful** *adj* malévolo, rencoroso

splash /splæʃ/ ◆ *n* **1** chapoteo **2** (*mancha*) salpicadura **3** (*de color*) mancha LOC **to make a splash** (*coloq*) causar sensación ◆ **1** *vi* chapotear **2** *vt* ~ **sth/sb (with sth)** salpicar algo/a algn (de algo) PHR V **to splash out (on sth)** (*coloq*) derrochar dinero (en algo), permitirse el lujo de comprar (algo)

splatter /ˈsplætə(r)/ (*tb* **spatter**) *vt* salpicar

splendid /ˈsplendɪd/ *adj* espléndido, magnífico

splendour (*USA* **splendor**) /ˈsplendə(r)/ *n* esplendor

splint /splɪnt/ *n* tablilla (*para entablillar un hueso roto*)

splinter /ˈsplɪntə(r)/ ◆ *n* astilla, esquirla ◆ *vt, vi* **1** astillar(se) **2** dividir(se)

split /splɪt/ ◆ (**-tt-**) (*pret, pp* **split**) **1** *vt, vi* partir(se): *to split sth in two* partir algo en dos **2** *vt, vi* dividir(se) **3** *vt, vi* repartir(se) **4** *vi* henderse, rajarse PHR V **to split up (with sb)** separarse (de algn) ◆ *n* **1** división, ruptura **2** abertura, hendidura **3 the splits** [*pl*]: *to do the splits* hacer el spagat ◆ *adj* partido, dividido

splutter /ˈsplʌtə(r)/ ◆ **1** *vt, vi* farfullar, balbucear **2** *vi* (*tb* **sputter**) (*del fuego, etc*) chisporrotear ◆ *n* chisporroteo

spoil /spɔɪl/ (*pret, pp* **spoilt** /spɔɪlt/ *o* **spoiled**) ☛ *Ver nota en* DREAM **1** *vt, vi* estropear(se), arruinar(se), echar(se) a perder **2** *vt* (*niño*) mimar

spoils /spɔɪlz/ *n* [*pl*] botín (*de robo, guerra, etc*)

spoilt ◆ *pret, pp de* SPOIL ◆ *adj* mimado

spoke /spəʊk/ ◆ *pret de* SPEAK ◆ *n* radio (*de una rueda*)

spoken *pp de* SPEAK

spokesman /ˈspəʊksmən/ *n* (*pl* **-men** /-mən/) portavoz ☛ Se prefiere utilizar la forma **spokesperson**, que se refiere tanto a un hombre como a una mujer.

spokesperson /ˈspəʊkspɜːsn/ *n* portavoz ☛ Se refiere tanto a un hombre como a una mujer. *Comparar con* SPOKESMAN y SPOKESWOMAN

spokeswoman /ˈspəʊkswʊmən/ *n* (*pl* **-women**) portavoz ☛ Se prefiere utilizar la forma **spokesperson**, que se refiere tanto a un hombre como a una mujer.

sponge /spʌndʒ/ ◆ *n* **1** esponja **2** (*tb* **sponge cake**) bizcocho ◆ PHR V **to sponge on/off sb** (*coloq*) vivir a costa de algn

sponsor /ˈspɒnsə(r)/ ◆ *n* patrocinador, -ora ◆ *vt* patrocinar **sponsorship** *n* patrocinio

spontaneous /spɒnˈteɪniəs/ *adj* espontáneo **spontaneity** /ˌspɒntəˈneɪəti/ *n* espontaneidad

spooky /spuːki/ *adj* (*coloq*) (**-ier**, **-iest**) **1** de aspecto embrujado **2** misterioso

spoon /spuːn/ ◆ *n* **1** cuchara: *a serving spoon* un cucharón **2** (*tb* **spoonful**) cucharada ◆ *vt*: *She spooned the mixture out of the bowl.* Sacó la mezcla del tazón con una cuchara.

sporadic /spəˈrædɪk/ *adj* esporádico

sport /spɔːt/ *n* **1** deporte: *sports centre* polideportivo ◊ *sports facilities* instalaciones deportivas ◊ *sports field* campo de deportes **2** (*coloq*) buen chico, buena chica: *a good/bad sport* un buen/mal perdedor **sporting** *adj* deportivo

sports car *n* coche deportivo

sportsman /ˈspɔːtsmən/ *n* (*pl* **-men** /-mən/) deportista **sportsmanlike** *adj* deportivo (*justo*) **sportsmanship** *n* deportividad

sportswoman /ˈspɔːtswʊmən/ *n* (*pl* **-women**) deportista

spot[1] /spɒt/ *vt* (**-tt-**) divisar: *He finally spotted a shirt he liked.* Por fin encontró una camisa que le gustó. ◊ *Nobody spotted the mistake.* Nadie notó el error.

spot[2] /spɒt/ *n* **1** (*diseño*) lunar: *a blue skirt with red spots on it* una falda azul con lunares rojos **2** (*en animales, etc*) mancha **3** (*Med*) grano **4** lugar **5** ~ **of sth** (*coloq, GB*): *Would you like a spot of lunch?* ¿Quieres comer un poco? ◊ *You seem to be having a spot of bother.* Parece que estás pasando por un momento un poco difícil. **6** *Ver* SPOTLIGHT LOC *Ver* SOFT

spotless /ˈspɒtləs/ *adj* **1** (*casa*) inmaculado **2** (*reputación*) intachable

spotlight /ˈspɒtlaɪt/ *n* **1** (*tb* **spot**) foco **2** (*fig*): *to be in the spotlight* ser el centro de la atención

spotted /ˈspɒtɪd/ *adj* **1** (*animal*) con manchas **2** (*ropa*) con lunares

spotty /ˈspɒti/ *adj* (**-ier**, **-iest**) **1** con muchos granos **2** (*tela*) de lunares

spouse /spaʊz; *USA* spaʊs/ *n* (*Jur*) cónyuge

spout /spaʊt/ ◆ *n* **1** (*de tetera*) pitorro **2** (*de canalón*) caño ◆ **1** *vi* ~ (**out/up**) salir a chorros **2** *vi* ~ (**out of/from sth**) salir a chorros, brotar (de algo) **3** *vt* ~ **sth** (**out/up**) echar algo a chorros **4** *vt* (*coloq, frec pey*) recitar **5** *vi* (*coloq, frec pey*) disertar, declamar

sprain /spreɪn/ ◆ *vt*: *to sprain your ankle* torcerse el tobillo ◆ *n* torcedura

sprang *pret de* SPRING

sprawl /sprɔːl/ *vi* **1** ~ (**out**) (**across/in/on sth**) tumbarse, repantigarse (por/en algo) **2** (*ciudad, etc*) extenderse (*desordenadamente*)

spray /spreɪ/ ◆ *n* **1** rociada **2** (*del mar*) espuma **3** (*para el pelo, etc*) spray **4** (*bote*) pulverizador, spray ◆ **1** *vt* ~ **sth on/over sth/sb**; ~ **sth/sb with sth** rociar algo/a algn de algo **2** *vi* ~ (**out**) (**over, across, etc sth/sb**) salpicar (algo/a algn)

spread /spred/ ◆ (*pret, pp* **spread**) **1** *vt* ~ **sth** (**out**) (**on/over sth**) extender, desplegar algo (en/sobre/por algo) **2** *vt* ~ **sth with sth** cubrir algo de/con algo **3** *vt, vi* untar(se) **4** *vt, vi* extender(se), propagar(se) **5** *vt, vi* (*noticia*) divulgar(se) **6** *vt* distribuir ◆ *n* **1** extensión **2** (*alas*) envergadura **3** propagación, difusión **4** paté, queso, etc para untar

spree /spriː/ *n* excursión: *to go on a shopping/spending spree* salir a gastar dinero

spring /sprɪŋ/ ◆ *n* **1** primavera: *spring clean(ing)* limpieza general **2** salto **3** manantial **4** resorte **5** (*colchón, sillón*) muelle **6** elasticidad ◆ *vi* (*pret* **sprang** /spræŋ/ *pp* **sprung** /sprʌŋ/) **1** saltar: *to spring into action* ponerse en acción *Ver tb* JUMP **2** (*líquido*) brotar LOC *Ver* MIND PHR V **to spring back** rebotar **to spring from sth** provenir de algo **to spring sth on sb** (*coloq*) coger a algn de improviso con algo

springboard /ˈsprɪŋbɔːd/ *n* (*lit y fig*) trampolín

springtime /ˈsprɪŋtaɪm/ *n* primavera

sprinkle /ˈsprɪŋkl/ *vt* **1** ~ **sth** (**with sth**) rociar, salpicar algo (de algo) **2** ~ **sth** (**on/onto/over sth**) rociar algo (sobre algo) **sprinkling** *n* ~ (**of sth/sb**) un poquito (de algo); unos, -as cuantos, -as

sprint /sprɪnt/ ◆ *vi* **1** correr a toda velocidad **2** (*Dep*) esprintar ◆ *n* **1** carrera de velocidad **2** sprint

sprout /spraʊt/ ◆ **1** *vi* ~ (**out/up**) (**from sth**) brotar, aparecer (de algo) **2** *vt* (*Bot*) echar (*flores, brotes, etc*) ◆ *n* **1** brote **2** *Ver* BRUSSELS SPROUT

sprung *pp de* SPRING

spun *pret, pp de* SPIN

spur /spɜː(r)/ ◆ *n* **1** espuela **2** a ~ (**to sth**) (*fig*) un acicate (para algo) LOC **on the spur of the moment** impulsivamente ◆ *vt* (**-rr-**) ~ **sth/sb** (**on**) incitar a algn

spurn /spɜːn/ *vt* (*fml*) rechazar

spurt /spɜːt/ ◆ *vi* ~ (**out**) (**from sth**) salir a chorros (de algo) ◆ *n* **1** chorro **2** arranque

spy /spaɪ/ ◆ *n* (*pl* **spies**) espía: *spy thrillers* novelas de espionaje ◆ *vi* (*pret, pp* **spied**) **to spy** (**on sth/sb**) espiar (algo/a algn)

squabble /ˈskwɒbl/ ◆ *vi* ~ (**with sb**) (**about/over sth**) reñir (con algn) (por algo) ◆ *n* riña

squad /skwɒd/ *n* [*v sing o pl*] **1** (*Mil*) escuadrón **2** (*policía*) brigada: *the drug squad* la brigada antidroga **3** (*Dep*) equipo

squadron /ˈskwɒdrən/ *n* [*v sing o pl*] escuadrón

squalid /ˈskwɒlɪd/ *adj* sórdido

squalor /ˈskwɒlə(r)/ *n* miseria

squander /ˈskwɒndə(r)/ *vt* ~ **sth** (**on sth**) **1** (*dinero*) despilfarrar algo (en algo) **2** (*tiempo*) malgastar algo (en algo) **3** (*energía, oportunidad*) desperdiciar algo (en algo)

square /skweə(r)/ ◆ *adj* cuadrado: *one square metre* un metro cuadrado LOC **a square meal** una comida en condiciones **to be** (**all**) **square** (**with sb**) quedar en paz (con algn) *Ver tb* FAIR ◆ *n* **1** (*Mat*) cuadrado **2** cuadro **3** (*en un tablero*) casilla **4** (*abrev* **Sq**) plaza (=Pza.) ◆ PHR V **to square up** (**with sb**) pagar una deuda (a algn)

squarely /ˈskweəli/ *adv* directamente

square root *n* raíz cuadrada

squash /skwɒʃ/ ◆ *vt, vi* aplastar(se): *It was squashed flat.* Estaba aplastado.

n **1** *What a squash!* ¡Qué apretujones! **2** (*GB*) refresco (de frutas edulcorado para diluir) **3** (*fml* **squash rackets**) (*Dep*) squash

squat /skwɒt/ ◆ *vi* (-**tt**-) ~ (**down**) **1** (*persona*) ponerse en cuclillas **2** (*animal*) agazaparse ◆ *adj* (-**tter**, -**ttest**) achatado, rechoncho

squawk /skwɔːk/ ◆ *vi* graznar, chillar ◆ *n* graznido, chillido

squeak /skwiːk/ ◆ *n* **1** (*animal, etc*) chillido **2** (*gozne, etc*) chirrido ◆ *vi* **1** (*animal, etc*) chillar **2** (*gozne*) chirriar **squeaky** *adj* (-**ier**, -**iest**) **1** (*voz*) chillón **2** (*gozne, etc*) que chirría

squeal /skwiːl/ ◆ *n* alarido, chillido ◆ *vt, vi* chillar

squeamish /ˈskwiːmɪʃ/ *adj* delicado, remilgado

squeeze /skwiːz/ ◆ **1** *vt* apretar **2** *vt* exprimir, estrujar **3** *vt, vi* ~ (**sth/sb**) **into, past, through, etc** (**sth**): *to squeeze through a gap in the hedge* pasar con dificultad por un hueco en el seto ◊ *Can you squeeze past/by?* ¿Puedes pasar? ◊ *Can you squeeze anything else into that case?* ¿Puedes meter algo más en esa maleta? ◆ *n* **1** apretón: *a squeeze of lemon* un chorrito de limón **2** apretura **3** (*coloq, Fin*) recortes

squint /ˈskwɪnt/ ◆ *vi* **1** ~ (**at/through sth**) mirar (algo, a través de algo) con los ojos entreabiertos **2** bizquear ◆ *n* estrabismo

squirm /skwɜːm/ *vi* **1** retorcerse **2** abochornarse

squirrel /ˈskwɪrəl; *USA* ˈskwɜːrəl/ *n* ardilla

squirt /skwɜːt/ ◆ **1** *vt*: *to squirt soda-water into a glass* echar un chorro de soda en un vaso **2** *vt* ~ **sth/sb** (**with sth**) cubrir algo/a algn con un chorro (de algo) **3** *vi* ~ (**out of/from sth**) salir a chorros (de algo) ◆ *n* chorro

stab /stæb/ ◆ *vt* (-**bb**-) **1** apuñalar **2** pinchar ◆ *n* puñalada LOC **to have a stab at** (**doing**) **sth** (*coloq*) intentar (hacer) algo **stabbing** *adj* punzante **stabbing** *n* apuñalamiento

stability /stəˈbɪləti/ *n* estabilidad

stabilize, -ise /ˈsteɪbəlaɪz/ *vt, vi* estabilizar(se)

stable[1] /ˈsteɪbl/ *adj* **1** estable **2** equilibrado

stable[2] /ˈsteɪbl/ *n* **1** establo **2** cuadra

stack /stæk/ ◆ *n* **1** pila (*de libros, leña, etc*) **2** ~ **of sth** [*gen pl*] (*coloq*) montón de algo ◆ *vt* ~ **sth** (**up**) apilar algo, amontonar algo

stadium /ˈsteɪdiəm/ *n* (*pl* ~**s** *o* -**dia** /-diə/) estadio

staff /stɑːf; *USA* stæf/ ◆ *n* [*v sing o pl*] personal, plantilla: *teaching staff* cuerpo docente ◊ *The staff are all working long hours.* Todo el personal está trabajando hasta tarde. ◆ *vt* equipar de personal

stag /stæg/ ◆ *n* ciervo ☛ *Ver nota en* CIERVO ◆ *adj*: *stag night/party* despedida de soltero

stage /steɪdʒ/ ◆ *n* **1** escenario **2 the stage** [*sing*] el teatro (*profesión*) **3** etapa: *at this stage* en este momento/a estas alturas LOC **in stages** por etapas **stage by stage** paso por paso **to be/go on the stage** ser/hacerse actor/actriz ◆ *vt* **1** poner en escena **2** (*huelga*) organizar

stagger /ˈstægə(r)/ ◆ **1** *vi* andar tambaleándose: *He staggered back home/to his feet.* Volvió a su casa/Se puso en pie tambaleándose. **2** *vt* dejar atónito **3** *vt* (*viaje, vacaciones*) escalonar ◆ *n* tambaleo **staggering** *adj* asombroso

stagnant /ˈstægnənt/ *adj* estancado

stagnate /stægˈneɪt; *USA* ˈstægneɪt/ *vi* estancarse **stagnation** *n* estancamiento

stain /steɪn/ ◆ *n* **1** mancha **2** tinte (*para la madera*) ☛ *Comparar con* DYE ◆ **1** *vt, vi* manchar(se) **2** *vt* teñir: *stained glass* vidriera **stainless** *adj*: *stainless steel* acero inoxidable

stair /steə(r)/ *n* **1 stairs** [*pl*] escalera: *to go up/down the stairs* subir/bajar las escaleras **2** peldaño

staircase /ˈsteəkeɪs/ (*tb* **stairway**) *n* escalera (*parte de un edificio*) *Ver tb* LADDER

stake /steɪk/ ◆ *n* **1** estaca **2 the stake** la hoguera **3** [*gen pl*] apuesta **4** (*inversión*) participación LOC **at stake** en juego: *His reputation is at stake.* Está en juego su reputación. ◆ *vt* **1** apuntalar **2** ~ **sth** (**on sth**) apostar algo (a algo) LOC **to stake** (**out**) **a/your claim** (**to sth/sb**) mostrar interés (por algo/algn)

stale /steɪl/ *adj* **1** (*pan*) duro **2** (*comida*) pasado **3** (*aire*) rancio **4** (*persona*) anquilosado

stalemate /ˈsteɪlmeɪt/ *n* **1** (*ajedrez*) tablas **2** (*fig*) punto muerto

stalk /stɔːk/ ◆ *n* **1** tallo **2** (*de fruta*) rabo ◆ **1** *vt* (*a un animal*) acechar **2** *vi* ~ (**along**) andar majestuosamente

stall /stɔːl/ ◆ *n* **1** (*en mercado*) puesto **2** (*en establo*) casilla **3 stalls** [*pl*] (*GB*) (*en teatro*) platea ◆ **1** *vt, vi* (*coche, motor*) calar(se) **2** *vi* buscar evasivas

stallion /ˈstæliən/ *n* semental (*caballo*)

stalwart /ˈstɔːlwət/ ◆ *n* incondicional ◆ *adj* (*antic, fml*) recio, fornido

stamina /ˈstæmɪnə/ *n* resistencia

stammer /ˈstæmə(r)/ (*tb* **stutter**) ◆ **1** *vi* tartamudear **2** *vt* ~ **sth** (**out**) decir algo tartamudeando ◆ *n* tartamudeo

stamp /stæmp/ ◆ *n* **1** (*de correos*) sello: *stamp-collecting* filatelia

> En el Reino Unido existen dos tipos de sellos: *first class* y *second class*. Los sellos de primera clase valen un poco más, pero las cartas llegan antes.

2 (*fiscal*) timbre **3** (*de goma*) sello **4** (*para metal*) cuño **5** (*con el pie*) patada ◆ **1** *vt, vi* patear, dar patadas **2** *vi* (*baile*) zapatear **3** *vt* (*carta*) poner sello a, franquear **4** *vt* imprimir, estampar, sellar PHR V **to stamp sth out** (*fig*) erradicar, acabar con algo

stampede /stæmˈpiːd/ ◆ *n* estampida, desbandada ◆ *vi* desbandarse

stance /stɑːns; (*USA*) stæns/ *n* **1** postura **2** ~ (**on sth**) postura, actitud (hacia algo)

stand /stænd/ ◆ *n* **1** ~ (**on sth**) (*fig*) postura, actitud (hacia algo) **2** (*a menudo en compuestos*) pie, soporte: *music stand* atril **3** puesto, quiosco **4** (*Dep*) [*a menudo pl*] tribuna **5** (*USA, Jur*) estrado LOC **to make a stand** (**against sth/sb**) oponer resistencia (a algo/algn) **to take a stand** (**on sth**) posicionarse (sobre algo) ◆ (*pret, pp* **stood** /stʊd/) **1** *vi* estar de pie, mantenerse de pie: *Stand still.* Estáte quieto. **2** *vi* ~ (**up**) ponerse de pie, levantarse **3** *vt* poner, colocar **4** *vi* medir **5** *vi* encontrarse: *A house once stood here.* Antes había una casa aquí. **6** *vi* (*oferta, etc*) seguir en pie **7** *vi* permanecer, estar: *as things stand* tal como están las cosas **8** *vt* aguantar, soportar: *I can't stand him.* No lo aguanto. **9** *vi* ~ (**for sth**) (*Pol*) presentarse (a algo) LOC **it/that stands to reason** es lógico **to stand a chance** (**of sth**) tener posibilidades (de algo) **to stand fast** mantenerse firme *Ver tb* BAIL, LEG, TRIAL PHR V **to stand in** (**for sb**) suplir (a algn) **to stand by sb** apoyar a algn **to stand for sth 1** significar, representar algo **2** apoyar algo **3** (*coloq*) tolerar algo **to stand out** (**from sth/sb**) (*ser mejor*) destacarse (de algo/algn) **to stand sb up** (*coloq*) dejar plantado a algn **to stand up for sth/sb/yourself** defender algo/a algn/defenderse **to stand up to sb** hacer frente a algn

standard /ˈstændəd/ ◆ *n* estándar LOC **to be up to/below standard** (no) ser del nivel requerido ◆ *adj* **1** estándar **2** oficial

standardize, -ise /ˈstændədaɪz/ *vt* estandarizar

standard of living *n* nivel de vida

standby /ˈstændbaɪ/ *n* (*pl* **-bys**) **1** (*cosa*) recurso **2** (*persona*) reserva **3** lista de espera LOC **on standby 1** preparado para partir, ayudar, etc **2** en lista de espera

stand-in /ˈstænd ɪn/ *n* sustituto, -a, suplente

standing /ˈstændɪŋ/ ◆ *n* **1** prestigio **2** *of long standing* duradero ◆ *adj* permanente

standing order *n* domiciliación bancaria

standpoint /ˈstændpɔɪnt/ *n* punto de vista

standstill /ˈstændstɪl/ *n* parado: *to be at/come to/bring sth to a standstill* estar parado/pararse/parar algo LOC *Ver* GRIND

stank *pret de* STINK

staple¹ /ˈsteɪpl/ *adj* principal

staple² /ˈsteɪpl/ ◆ *n* grapa ◆ *vt* grapar **stapler** *n* grapadora

star /stɑː(r)/ ◆ *n* estrella ◆ *vi* (**-rr-**) ~ (**in sth**) protagonizar algo

starboard /ˈstɑːbəd/ *n* estribor

starch /stɑːtʃ/ *n* **1** almidón **2** fécula **starched** *adj* almidonado

stardom /ˈstɑːdəm/ *n* estrellato

stare /steə(r)/ *vi* ~ (**at sth/sb**) mirar fijamente (algo/a algn)

stark /stɑːk/ *adj* (**-er**, **-est**) **1** desolado **2** crudo **3** (*contraste*) manifiesto

starry /ˈstɑːri/ *n* (**-ier**, **-iest**) estrellado

start /stɑːt/ ◆ *n* **1** principio **2 the st**

[*sing*] la salida LOC **for a start** para empezar **to get off to a good, bad, etc start** tener un buen/mal comienzo ◆ **1** *vt, vi* empezar: *It started to rain.* Empezó a llover. **2** *vi* (*coche, motor*) arrancar **3** *vt* (*rumor*) iniciar LOC **to start with** para empezar *Ver tb* BALL, FALSE, SCRATCH PHR V **to start off** salir **to start out (on sth/to do sth)** empezar (con algo/a hacer algo) **to start (sth) up 1** (*motor*) arrancar, poner en marcha **2** (*negocio*) aparecer, montar

tarter /ˈstɑːtə(r)/ *n* (*coloq, esp GB*) primer plato

tarting point *n* punto de partida

tartle /ˈstɑːtl/ *vt* sobresaltar **startling** *adj* asombroso

tarve /stɑːv/ **1** *vi* pasar hambre: *to starve (to death)* morir de hambre **2** *vt* matar de hambre, hacer pasar hambre **3** *vt* ~ **sth/sb of sth** (*fig*) privar algo/a algn de algo LOC **to be starving** (*coloq*) morirse de hambre **starvation** *n* hambre ☛ *Ver nota en* HAMBRE

tate[1] /steɪt/ ◆ *n* **1** estado: *to be in a fit state to drive* estar en condiciones para conducir ◊ *the State* el Estado **2 the States** [*sing*] *coloq*) los Estados Unidos LOC **state of affairs** circunstancias **state of mind** estado mental *Ver tb* REPAIR ◆ *adj* (*tb* **State**) estatal: *a state visit* una visita oficial

tate[2] /steɪt/ *vt* **1** manifestar, afirmar: *State your name.* Haga constar su nombre. **2** establecer: *within the stated limits* en los límites establecidos

tately /ˈsteɪtli/ *adj* (**-ier**, **-iest**) majestuoso

tatement /ˈsteɪtmənt/ *n* declaración: *to issue a statement* dar un informe

tatesman /ˈsteɪtsmən/ *n* (*pl* **-men** /-mən/) estadista

atic[1] /ˈstætɪk/ *adj* estático

atic[2] /ˈstætɪk/ *n* **1** (*Radio*) interferencias **2** (*tb* **static electricity**) electricidad estática

ation[1] /ˈsteɪʃn/ *n* **1** estación: *railway station* estación (de ferrocarril) **2** *nuclear power station* central nuclear ◊ *police station* comisaría ◊ *fire station* parque de bomberos ◊ *petrol station* gasolinera **3** (*Radio*) emisora

ation[2] /ˈsteɪʃn/ *vt* destinar

ationary /ˈsteɪʃənri; *USA* -neri/ *adj* parado

stationer /ˈsteɪʃnə(r)/ *n* dueño, -a de una papelería: *stationer's (shop)* papelería **stationery** /ˈsteɪʃənri; *USA* -neri/ *n* material de escritorio

statistic /stəˈtɪstɪk/ *n* estadística **statistics** *n* [*sing*] estadística (*Mat*)

statue /ˈstætʃuː/ *n* estatua

stature /ˈstætʃə(r)/ *n* **1** (*lit*) estatura **2** (*fig*) talla

status /ˈsteɪtəs/ *n* categoría: *social status* posición social ◊ *marital status* estado civil ◊ *status symbol* símbolo de condición social

statute /ˈstætʃuːt/ *n* estatuto: *statute book* código **statutory** /ˈstætʃətri; *USA* -tɔːri/ *adj* estatutario

staunch /stɔːntʃ/ *adj* (**-er**, **-est**) incondicional

stave /steɪv/ PHR V **to stave sth off 1** (*crisis*) evitar **2** (*ataque*) rechazar

stay /steɪ/ ◆ *vi* quedarse: *to stay (at) home* quedarse en casa ◊ *What hotel are you staying at?* ¿En qué hotel te alojas? ◊ *to stay sober* permanecer sobrio LOC *Ver* CLEAR, COOL PHR V **to stay away (from sth/sb)** permanecer alejado (de algo/algn) **to stay behind** quedarse **to stay in** quedarse en casa **to stay on (at...)** quedarse (en...) **to stay up** no acostarse: *to stay up late* acostarse tarde ◆ *n* estancia

steady /ˈstedi/ ◆ *adj* (**-ier**, **-iest**) **1** firme: *to hold sth steady* sujetar algo con firmeza **2** constante, regular: *a steady boyfriend* un novio formal ◊ *a steady job/income* un empleo/sueldo fijo ◆ (*pret, pp* **steadied**) **1** *vi* estabilizarse **2** *v refl* ~ **yourself** recuperar el equilibrio

steak /steɪk/ *n* filete

steal /stiːl/ (*pret* **stole** /stəʊl/ *pp* **stolen** /ˈstəʊlən/) **1** *vt, vi* ~ **(sth) (from sth/sb)** robar (algo) (a algo/algn) ☛ *Ver nota en* ROB **2** *vi* ~ **in, out, away, etc**: *He stole into the room.* Entró en la habitación a hurtadillas. ◊ *They stole away.* Salieron furtivamente. ◊ *to steal up on sb* acercarse a algn sin ruido

stealth /stelθ/ *n* sigilo: *by stealth* a hurtadillas **stealthy** *adj* (**-ier**, **-iest**) sigiloso

steam /stiːm/ ◆ *n* vapor: *steam engine* máquina/motor de vapor LOC *Ver* LET[1], RUN ◆ **1** *vi* echar vapor: *steaming hot coffee* café caliente humeante **2** *vt* cocinar al vapor LOC **to get (all) steamed up (about/over sth)** (*coloq*) sulfurarse (por algo) PHR V **to steam up** empañarse

steamer /ˈstiːmə(r)/ *n* buque de vapor

steamroller /ˈstiːmˌrəʊlə(r)/ *n* apisonadora

steel /stiːl/ ◆ *n* acero ◆ *v refl* ~ **yourself (against sth)** armarse de valor (para algo)

steep /stiːp/ *adj* (**-er**, **-est**) **1** empinado: *a steep mountain* una montaña escarpada **2** (*coloq*) excesivo

steeply /ˈstiːpli/ *adv* con mucha pendiente: *The plane was climbing steeply.* El avión ascendía vertiginosamente. ◊ *Share prices fell steeply.* Las acciones bajaron en picado.

steer /stɪə(r)/ *vt, vi* **1** conducir, gobernar: *to steer north* seguir rumbo norte ◊ *to steer by the stars* guiarse por las estrellas ◊ *He steered the discussion away from the subject.* Llevó la conversación hacia otro tema. **2** navegar LOC *Ver* CLEAR **steering** *n* dirección

steering wheel *n* volante

stem¹ /stem/ ◆ *n* tallo ◆ *v* (**-mm-**) PHR V **to stem from sth** tener el origen en algo

stem² /stem/ *vt* (**-mm-**) contener

stench /stentʃ/ *n* hedor

step /step/ ◆ *vi* (**-pp-**) dar un paso, andar: *to step on sth* pisar algo ◊ *to step over sth* pasar por encima de algo PHR V **to step down** retirarse **to step in** intervenir **to step up** incrementar ◆ *n* **1** paso **2** escalón, peldaño **3 steps** [*pl*] escaleras LOC **step by step** paso a paso **to be in/out of step (with sth/sb) 1** (*lit*) (no) llevar el paso (de algo/algn) **2** (*fig*) estar de acuerdo/en desacuerdo (con algo/algn) **to take steps to do sth** tomar medidas para hacer algo *Ver tb* WATCH

stepbrother /ˈstepˌbrʌðə(r)/ *n* hermanastro ☛ *Ver nota en* HERMANASTRO

stepchild /ˈsteptʃaɪld/ *n* (*pl* **-children**) hijastro, -a

stepdaughter /ˈstepˌdɔːtə(r)/ *n* hijastra

stepfather /ˈstepˌfɑːðə(r)/ *n* padrastro

stepladder /ˈstepˌlædə(r)/ *n* escalera de tijera

stepmother /ˈstepˌmʌðə(r)/ *n* madrastra

step-parent /ˈstep peərənt/ *n* padrastro, madrastra

stepsister /ˈstepˌsɪstə(r)/ *n* hermanastra ☛ *Ver nota en* HERMANASTRO

stepson /ˈstepsʌn/ *n* hijastro

stereo /ˈsteriəʊ/ *n* (*pl* **~s**) estéreo

stereotype /ˈsteriətaɪp/ *n* estereotipo

sterile /ˈsteraɪl; *USA* ˈsterəl/ *adj* estéril **sterility** /stəˈrɪləti/ *n* esterilidad **sterilize, -ise** /ˈsterəlaɪz/ *vt* esterilizar

sterling /ˈstɜːlɪŋ/ ◆ *adj* **1** (*plata*) de ley **2** (*fig*) excelente ◆ (*tb* **pound sterling**) *n* libra esterlina

stern¹ /stɜːn/ *adj* (**-er**, **-est**) severo, duro

stern² /stɜːn/ *n* popa

stew /stjuː; *USA* stuː/ ◆ *vt, vi* cocer, guisar ◆ *n* guiso, estofado

steward /stjuːəd; *USA* ˈstuːərd/ *n* (*fem* **stewardess**) (*en un avión*) auxiliar de vuelo: *(air) stewardess* azafata **2** (*en un barco*) camarero, -a

stick¹ /stɪk/ *n* **1** palo, vara **2** bastón barra: *a stick of celery* un tallo de apio *a stick of dynamite* un cartucho de dinamita

stick² /stɪk/ (*pret, pp* **stuck** /stʌk/) **1** hincar, clavar: *to stick a needle in your finger* clavarse una aguja en el dedo *to stick your fork into a potato* pinchar una patata con el tenedor **2** *vt,* pegar(se): *Jam sticks to your fingers.* La mermelada se te pega a los dedos. **3** (*coloq*) poner: *He stuck the pen behind his ear.* Se puso el boli detrás de la oreja. **4** *vt* atascarse: *The bus got stuck in the mud.* El autobús se atascó en el barro. ◊ *The lift got stuck between floors six and seven.* El ascensor se atascó entre los pisos seis y siete. **5** *vt* (*coloq*) aguantar: *I can't stick it any longer.* No aguanto más. **6** *vi* ~ **at sth** seguir trabajando, persistir en algo **7** ~ **by** apoyar a algn **8** ~ **to sth** atenerse a algo PHR V **to stick around** (*coloq*) quedarse cerca

to stick out salir: *His ears stick out.* Tiene las orejas muy salidas. **to stick sth out** (*coloq*) aguantar algo **to stick sth out 1** (*lengua, mano*) sacar (*cabeza*) asomar

to stick together mantenerse unidos **to stick up** sobresalir **to stick up f**

yourself/sth/sb defenderse/defender algo/a algn

sticker /ˈstɪkə(r)/ *n* pegatina

sticky /ˈstɪki/ *adj* **1** pegajoso **2** (*coloq*) (*situación*) difícil

stiff /stɪf/ ◆ *adj* (**-er**, **-est**) **1** rígido, duro **2** (*articulación*) agarrotado **3** (*sólido*) espeso **4** difícil, duro **5** (*formal*) tieso **6** (*brisa, bebida alcohólica*) fuerte ◆ *adv* (*coloq*) extremadamente: *bored/ scared stiff* muerto de aburrimiento/ miedo

stiffen /ˈstɪfn/ **1** *vi* ponerse rígido/tieso **2** *vi* (*articulación*) agarrotarse **3** *vt* (*cuello*) almidonar

stifle /ˈstaɪfl/ **1** *vt, vi* ahogar(se) **2** *vt* (*rebelión*) contener **3** *vt* (*bostezo*) ahogar **4** *vt* (*ideas*) ahogar, suprimir **stifling** *adj* sofocante

stigma /ˈstɪgmə/ *n* estigma

still[1] /stɪl/ *adv* **1** todavía, aún

¿**Still** o **yet**? **Still** se usa en frases afirmativas e interrogativas y siempre va detrás de los verbos auxiliares o modales y delante de los demás verbos: *He still talks about her.* Todavía habla de ella. ◊ *Are you still here?* ¿Todavía estás aquí? **Yet** se usa en frases negativas y siempre va al final de la oración: *Aren't they here yet?* ¿Aún no han llegado? ◊ *He hasn't done it yet.* No lo ha hecho todavía. Sin embargo, **still** se puede usar con frases negativas cuando queremos darle énfasis a la oración. En este caso siempre se coloca delante del verbo, aunque sea auxiliar o modal: *He still hasn't done it.* Aún no lo ha hecho. ◊ *He still can't do it.* Todavía no sabe hacerlo.

2 aún así, sin embargo, no obstante: *Still, it didn't turn out badly.* De todos modos, no salió del todo mal.

still[2] /stɪl/ *adj* **1** quieto: *still life* bodegón ◊ *Stand still!* ¡No te muevas! ☞ *Comparar con* QUIET **2** (*agua, viento*) tranquilo **3** (*bebida*) sin gas

stillness /ˈstɪlnəs/ *n* calma, quietud

stilt /stɪlt/ *n* **1** zanco **2** pilote

stilted /ˈstɪltɪd/ *adj* torpe

stimulant /ˈstɪmjələnt/ *n* estimulante

stimulate /ˈstɪmjuleɪt/ *vt* estimular **stimulating** *adj* **1** estimulante **2** interesante

stimulus /ˈstɪmjələs/ *n* (*pl* **-muli** /-laɪ/) estímulo, incentivo

sting /stɪŋ/ ◆ *n* **1** aguijón **2** (*herida*) picadura **3** (*dolor*) picazón ◆ (*pret, pp* **stung** /stʌŋ/) **1** *vt, vi* picar **2** *vi* escocer **3** *vt* (*fig*) herir

stink /stɪŋk/ ◆ *vi* (*pret* **stank** /stæŋk/ *o* **stunk** /stʌŋk/ *pp* **stunk**) (*coloq*) **1** ~ (**of sth**) apestar (a algo) **2** ~ (**of sth**) (*fig*) oler (a algo) PHR V **to stink sth out** apestar algo ◆ *n* (*coloq*) peste, hedor **stinking** *adj* (*coloq*) maldito

stint /stɪnt/ *n* periodo: *a training stint in Lanzarote* un periodo de aprendizaje en Lanzarote

stipulate /ˈstɪpjuleɪt/ *vt* (*fml*) estipular

stir /stɜː(r)/ ◆ (**-rr-**) **1** *vt* remover **2** *vt, vi* mover(se) **3** *vt* (*imaginación, etc*) despertar PHR V **to stir sth up** provocar algo ◆ *n* **1** *to give sth a stir* remover algo **2** alboroto **stirring** *adj* emocionante

stirrup /ˈstɪrəp/ *n* estribo

stitch /stɪtʃ/ ◆ *n* **1** (*costura*) puntada **2** (*tejido*) punto **3** flato: *I got a stitch.* Me dio flato. LOC **in stitches** (*coloq*) muerto de risa ◆ *vt, vi* coser **stitching** *n* costura

stock /stɒk/ ◆ *n* **1** existencias **2** ~ (**of sth**) surtido, reserva (de algo) **3** (*tb* **livestock**) ganado **4** (*Fin*) [*gen pl*] valor **5** (*de empresa*) capital social **6** (*Cocina*) caldo LOC **out of/in stock** agotado/en existencia **to take stock** (**of sth**) pasar revista a algo ◆ *adj* gastado, manido (*frase, etc*) ◆ *vt* tener (existencias de) PHR V **to stock up** (**on/with sth**) abastecerse (de algo)

stockbroker /ˈstɒkˌbrəʊkə(r)/ (*tb* **broker**) *n* corredor, -ora de bolsa

stock exchange (*tb* **stock market**) *n* bolsa

stocking /ˈstɒkɪŋ/ *n* media

stocktaking /ˈstɒkteɪkɪŋ/ *n* inventario (*acción*)

stocky /ˈstɒki/ *adj* (**-ier**, **-iest**) rechoncho

stodgy /ˈstɒdʒi/ *adj* (**-ier**, **-iest**) (*coloq, pey*) pesado (*comida, literatura*)

stoke /stəʊk/ *vt* ~ **sth** (**up**) (**with sth**) cargar algo (de algo)

stole *pret de* STEAL

stolen *pp de* STEAL

stolid /ˈstɒlɪd/ *adj* (*pey*) impasible

stomach /ˈstʌmək/ ◆ *n* **1** estómago: *stomach-ache* dolor de estómago **2** vientre **3** ~ **for sth** (*fig*) ganas de algo ◆ *vt* aguantar: *I can't stomach too much violence in films.* No soporto las películas con demasiada violencia.

stone /stəʊn/ ◆ *n* **1** piedra: *the Stone Age* la Edad de Piedra **2** (*esp USA* **pit**) (*de fruta*) hueso **3** (*GB*) (*pl* **stone**) unidad de peso equivalente a 14 libras o 6,348 kg ◆ *vt* apedrear **stoned** *adj* (*coloq*) **1** como una cuba **2** colocado (*con hachís, etc*)

stony /ˈstəʊni/ *adj* (**-ier**, **-iest**) **1** pedregoso, cubierto de piedras **2** (*mirada*) frío **3** (*silencio*) sepulcral

stood *pret, pp de* STAND

stool /stuːl/ *n* banqueta, taburete

stoop /stuːp/ ◆ *vi* ~ (**down**) agacharse, inclinarse LOC **to stoop so low (as to do sth)** llegar tan bajo (como para hacer algo) ◆ *n*: *to walk with/have a stoop* andar encorvado

stop /stɒp/ ◆ (**-pp-**) **1** *vt, vi* parar(se), detener(se) **2** *vt* (*proceso*) interrumpir **3** *vt* (*injusticia, etc*) acabar con, poner fin a **4** *vt* ~ **doing sth** dejar de hacer algo: *Stop it!* ¡Basta ya! **5** *vt* ~ **sth/sb (from) doing sth** impedir que algo/algn haga algo: *to stop yourself doing sth* hacer un esfuerzo por no hacer algo **6** *vt* cancelar **7** *vt* (*pago*) suspender **8** *vt* (*cheque*) anular **9** *vi* (*GB, coloq*) quedarse LOC **to stop dead/short** pararse en seco **to stop short of (doing) sth** no llegar a (hacer) algo *Ver tb* BUCK[3] PHR V **to stop off (at/in ...)** pasar (por ...) ◆ *n* **1** parada, alto: *to come to a stop* detenerse/parar(se) **2** (*autobús, tren, etc*) parada **3** (*ortografía*) punto **stoppage** *n* **1** paro **2 stoppages** [*pl*] deducciones

stopgap /ˈstɒpgæp/ *n* **1** sustituto, -a **2** recurso provisional

stopover /ˈstɒpəʊvə(r)/ *n* escala (*en un viaje*)

stopper /ˈstɒpə(r)/ (*USA* **plug**) *n* tapón

stopwatch /ˈstɒpwɒtʃ/ *n* cronómetro

storage /ˈstɔːrɪdʒ/ *n* **1** almacenamiento, almacenaje: *storage space* sitio para guardar cosas **2** depósito, almacén

store /stɔː(r)/ ◆ *n* **1** provisión, reserva **2 stores** [*pl*] provisiones, víveres **3** (*esp USA*) tienda, almacén LOC **to be in store for sb** aguardarle a algn (*sorpresa, etc*) **to have in store for sb** tener reservado a algn (*sorpresa, etc*) ◆ *vt* ~ **sth (up/away)** almacenar, guardar, acumular algo

storeroom /ˈstɔːruːm/ *n* despensa, almacén

storey /ˈstɔːri/ *n* (*pl* **storeys**) (*USA* **story**) piso

stork /stɔːk/ *n* cigüeña

storm /stɔːm/ ◆ *n* tormenta, temporal: *a storm of criticism* fuertes críticas ◆ **1** *vi* ~ **in/off/out** entrar/irse/salir furios[o] **2** *vt* (*edificio*) asaltar **stormy** *adj* (**-ier**, **-iest**) **1** tormentoso **2** (*debate*) acalorado **3** (*relación*) turbulento

story[1] /ˈstɔːri/ *n* (*pl* **-ies**) **1** historia **2** cuento **3** (*Period*) noticia

story[2] (*USA*) *Ver* STOREY

stout /staʊt/ *adj* **1** fuerte **2** (*frec eufe*[*mismo*]) gordo *Ver tb* FAT

stove /stəʊv/ *n* **1** cocina **2** estufa

stow /stəʊ/ *vt* ~ **sth (away)** guarda[r] algo

straddle /ˈstrædl/ *vt* poner una pierna a cada lado de

straggle /ˈstrægl/ *vi* **1** (*planta*) desparramarse **2** (*persona*) rezagarse **straggler** *n* rezagado, -a **straggly** *adj* (**-ie**[**r**], **-iest**) desordenado, desaliñado

straight /streɪt/ ◆ *adj* (**-er**, **-est**) recto: *straight hair* pelo liso **2** en orde[n] **3** derecho LOC **to be straight (with s**[**b**]**)** ser franco (con algn) **to keep** [**a**] **straight face** no reírse *Ver tb* RECORD ◆ *adv* (**-er**, **-est**) **1** en línea recta: *Lo*[*ok*] *straight ahead.* Mira recto. **2** (*sentars*[*e*]) derecho **3** (*pensar*) claramente **4** (*irs*[*e*]) directamente LOC **straight away** inmediatamente **straight out** sin vacilar

straighten /ˈstreɪtn/ **1** *vi* volver recto **2** *vt, vi* (*la espalda*) poner(s[e]) derecho **3** *vt* (*corbata, falda*) arregl[ar] PHR V **to straighten sth out** desenmarañar algo **to straighten up** ponerse derecho

straightforward /ˌstreɪtˈfɔːwəd/ *adj* [**1**] (*persona*) honrado **2** franco **3** (*esti*[*lo*]) sencillo

strain /streɪn/ ◆ **1** *vi* esforzarse **2** [*vt*] (*cuerda*) tensar **3** *vt* (*el oído, la vis*[*ta*]) aguzar **4** *vt* (*músculo, espalda*) torce[r] [**5**] *vt* (*vista, voz, corazón*) forzar **6** *vt* ~ **s**[**th**] (**off**) colar algo ◆ *n* **1** tensión: *Th*[*eir*] *relationship is showing signs of stra*[*in*]. Su relación da muestras de tensi[ón]

2 torcedura: *eye strain* vista cansada **strained** *adj* **1** (*risa, tono de voz*) forzado **2** preocupado

strainer /ˈstreɪnə(r)/ *n* colador

straitjacket /ˈstreɪtdʒækɪt/ *n* camisa de fuerza

straits /streɪts/ *n* **1** estrecho: *the Straits of Gibraltar* el Estrecho de Gibraltar **2** *in desperate straits* en una situación desesperada

strand /strænd/ *n* **1** hebra, hilo **2** mechón

stranded /ˈstrændɪd/ *adj* abandonado: *to be left stranded* quedarse colgado

strange /streɪndʒ/ *adj* (**-er**, **-est**) **1** desconocido **2** raro, extraño: *I find it strange that...* Me extraña que... **stranger** *n* **1** desconocido, -a **2** forastero, -a

strangle /ˈstræŋgl/ *vt* estrangular, ahogar

strap /stræp/ ◆ *n* **1** correa, tira ☛ *Ver dibujo en* RELOJ **2** (*de un vestido*) tirante ◆ *vt* ~ **sth (up)** (*Med*) vendar algo PHR V **to strap sth on** amarrar, sujetar algo (*con correas*) **to strap sb in** ponerle cinturón de seguridad a algn

strategy /ˈstrætədʒi/ *n* (*pl* **-ies**) estrategia **strategic** /strəˈtiːdʒɪk/ *adj* estratégico

straw /strɔː/ *n* paja: *a straw hat* un sombrero de paja LOC **the last/final straw** la gota que colma el vaso

strawberry /ˈstrɔːbəri; *USA* -beri/ *n* (*pl* **-ies**) fresa: *strawberries and cream* fresas con nata

stray /streɪ/ ◆ *vi* **1** extraviarse **2** apartarse ◆ *adj* **1** extraviado: *a stray dog* un perro callejero **2** aislado: *a stray bullet* una bala perdida

streak /striːk/ ◆ *n* **1** veta **2** rasgo, vena **3** (*de suerte*) racha: *to be on a winning/losing streak* tener una racha de suerte/mala suerte ◆ **1** *vt* ~ **sth (with sth)** rayar, vetear algo (de algo) **2** *vi* correr como un rayo

stream /striːm/ ◆ *n* **1** arroyo, riachuelo **2** (*de líquido, palabras*) torrente **3** (*de gente*) oleada **4** (*de coches*) caravana ◆ *vt, vi* **1** (*agua, sangre*) manar **2** (*lágrimas*) correr **3** (*luz*) entrar/salir a raudales **4** derramar

streamer /ˈstriːmə(r)/ *n* serpentina

streamline /ˈstriːmlaɪn/ *vt* **1** aerodinamizar **2** (*fig*) racionalizar

street /striːt/ *n* (*abrev* **St**) calle: *the High Street* la calle Mayor ☛ Nótese que cuando **street** va precedido por el nombre de la calle, se escribe con mayúscula. *Ver tb* ROAD *y nota en* CALLE LOC **(right) up your street**: *This job seems right up your street.* Este trabajo te va que ni pintado. **to be streets ahead (of sth/sb)** llevar mucha ventaja (a algo/algn) *Ver tb* MAN[1]

streetcar /ˈstriːtkɑː(r)/ *n* (*USA*) *Ver* TRAM

strength /streŋθ/ *n* **1** [*incontable*] fuerza **2** (*material*) resistencia **3** (*luz, emoción*) intensidad **4** punto fuerte LOC **on the strength of sth** fundándose en algo, confiando en algo **strengthen** *vt, vi* fortalecer(se), reforzar(se)

strenuous /ˈstrenjuəs/ *adj* **1** agotador **2** vigoroso

stress /stres/ ◆ *n* **1** tensión (nerviosa) **2** ~ **(on sth)** énfasis (en algo) **3** (*Ling, Mús*) acento **4** (*Mec*) tensión ◆ *vt* subrayar, recalcar **stressful** *adj* estresante

stretch /stretʃ/ ◆ **1** *vt, vi* estirar(se), alargar(se) **2** *vi* desperezarse **3** *vi* (*terreno, etc*) extenderse **4** *vt* (*persona*) exigir el máximo esfuerzo a LOC **to stretch your legs** estirar las piernas PHR V **to stretch (yourself) out** tenderse ◆ *n* **1** *to have a stretch* estirarse **2** elasticidad **3** ~ **(of sth)** (*terreno*) trecho (de algo) **4** ~ **(of sth)** (*tiempo*) intervalo, periodo (de algo) LOC **at a stretch** sin interrupción, seguidos, -as

stretcher /ˈstretʃə(r)/ *n* camilla

strewn /struːn/ *adj* **1** ~ **(all) over sth** desparramado por algo **2** ~ **with sth** cubierto de algo

stricken /ˈstrɪkən/ *adj* ~ **(by/with sth)** afligido (por algo): *drought-stricken area* zona afectada por la sequía

strict /strɪkt/ *adj* (**-er**, **-est**) **1** severo **2** estricto, preciso LOC **in strictest confidence** con la más absoluta reserva **strictly** *adv* **1** severamente **2** estrictamente: *strictly prohibited* terminantemente prohibido LOC **strictly speaking** en rigor

stride /straɪd/ ◆ *vi* (*pret* **strode** /strəʊd/) **1** andar a pasos largos **2** ~ **up to sth/sb** acercarse resueltamente a algo/algn ◆ *n* **1** zancada **2** (*modo de* *andar*) paso LOC **to take sth in your stride** tomárselo con calma

strident /ˈstraɪdnt/ *adj* estridente

strife /straɪf/ *n* lucha, conflicto

strike /straɪk/ ◆ *n* **1** huelga: *to go on strike* declararse en huelga **2** (*Mil*) ataque ◆ (*pret, pp* **struck** /strʌk/) **1** *vt* golpear, pegar **2** *vt* (*coche, etc*) atropellar **3** *vt* chocar contra **4** *vi* atacar **5** *vt, vi* (*reloj*) dar (la hora) **6** *vt* (*oro, etc*) hallar **7** *vt* (*cerilla*) encender **8** *vt*: *It strikes me that…* Se me ocurre que… **9** *vt* impresionar a, llamar la atención a: *I was struck by the similarity between them.* Me impresionó lo parecidos que eran. LOC *Ver* HOME PHR V **to strike back (at sth/sb)** devolver el golpe (a algo/algn) **to strike (sth) up** empezar a tocar (algo) **to strike up sth (with sb) 1** (*conversación*) entablar algo (con algn) **2** (*amistad*) trabar algo (con algn)

striker /ˈstraɪkə(r)/ *n* **1** huelguista **2** (*Dep*) delantero

striking /ˈstraɪkɪŋ/ *adj* llamativo

string /strɪŋ/ ◆ *n* **1** cuerda: *I need some string to tie up this parcel.* Necesito una cuerda para atar este paquete. **2** (*de perlas, etc*) sarta LOC **(with) no strings attached/without strings** (*coloq*) sin condiciones *Ver tb* PULL ◆ *vt* (*pret, pp* **strung** /strʌŋ/) ~ **sth (up)** colgar algo (*con cuerda, etc*) PHR V **to string (sth) out** extenderse/extender algo **to string sth together** hilar algo

stringent /ˈstrɪndʒənt/ *adj* riguroso

strip¹ /strɪp/ (**-pp-**) **1** *vt* (*una máquina*) desmantelar **2** *vt* (*papel, pintura, etc*) quitar **3** *vt* ~ **sth of sth** despojar a algo de algo **4** *vt* ~ **sb of sth** quitarle algo a algn **5** *vt, vi* ~ **(off)** desnudar(se)

strip² /strɪp/ *n* **1** (*de papel, metal, etc*) tira **2** (*de tierra, agua, etc*) franja

stripe /straɪp/ *n* raya **striped** *adj* de rayas

strive /straɪv/ *vi* (*pret* **strove** /strəʊv/ *pp* **striven** /ˈstrɪvn/) (*fml*) ~ **(for/after sth)** esforzarse (por alcanzar algo)

strode *pret de* STRIDE

stroke¹ /strəʊk/ *n* **1** golpe: *a stroke of luck* un golpe de suerte **2** (*Dep*) brazada **3** trazo (*de lapicero, etc*) **4** campanada **5** (*Med*) apoplejía LOC **at a stroke** de un golpe **not to do a stroke (of work)** no dar ni golpe

stroke² /strəʊk/ *vt* acariciar

stroll /strəʊl/ ◆ *n* paseo: *to go for/take a stroll* dar un paseo ◆ *vi* caminar

strong /strɒŋ; *USA* strɔːŋ/ *adj* (**-er, -est**) fuerte LOC **to be going strong** (*coloq*) estar muy fuerte **to be your/sb's strong point/suit** ser el fuerte de uno/algn

strong-minded /ˌstrɒŋ ˈmaɪndɪd/ *adj* decidido

strove *pret de* STRIVE

struck *pret, pp de* STRIKE

structure /ˈstrʌktʃə(r)/ ◆ *n* **1** estructura **2** construcción ◆ *vt* estructurar

struggle /ˈstrʌgl/ ◆ *vi* **1** luchar **2** ~ **(against/with sth/sb)** forcejear (con algo/algn) ◆ *n* **1** lucha **2** esfuerzo

strung *pret, pp de* STRING

strut /strʌt/ ◆ *n* puntal, riostra ◆ *vi* (**-tt-**) ~ **(about/along)** pavonearse

stub /stʌb/ *n* **1** cabo **2** (*de cigarrillo*) colilla **3** (*de cheque*) resguardo

stubble /ˈstʌbl/ *n* **1** rastrojo **2** barba (incipiente)

stubborn /ˈstʌbən/ *adj* **1** terco, tenaz (*mancha, tos*) rebelde

stuck /stʌk/ ◆ *pret, pp de* STICK² ◆ *adj* **1** atascado: *to get stuck* atascarse (*coloq*): *to be/get stuck with sth/sb* tener que cargar con algo/tener que aguantar a algn

stuck-up /ˌstʌk ˈʌp/ *adj* (*coloq*) engreído

stud /stʌd/ *n* **1** tachuela **2** (*en zapato*) taco **3** caballo semental **4** (*tb* **stud farm**) caballeriza

student /ˈstjuːdnt; *USA* ˈstuː-/ *n* **1** estudiante (*de universidad*) **2** alumno, -a

studied /ˈstʌdid/ *adj* deliberado

studio /ˈstjuːdiəʊ; *USA* ˈstuː-/ *n* (*pl* ~ **1** taller **2** (*Cine, TV*) estudio

studious /ˈstjuːdiəs; *USA* ˈstuː-/ *adj* estudioso **2** (*fml*) deliberado

study /ˈstʌdi/ ◆ *n* (*pl* **-ies**) **1** estudio despacho ◆ *vt, vi* (*pret, pp* **studie**… estudiar

stuff /stʌf/ ◆ *n* **1** material, sustancia (*coloq*) cosas *Ver* FOODSTUFFS ◆ **1** *vt* **sth (with sth)** rellenar algo (con algo) *vt* ~ **sth in**; ~ **sth into sth** meter algo la fuerza (en algo) **3** *v refl* ~ **yours… (with sth)** atiborrarse (de algo) **4** (*animal*) disecar LOC **get stuffed!** (*G… coloq*) ¡véte a hacer puñetas! **stuffing** relleno

stuffy /ˈstʌfi/ *adj* (**-ier**, **-iest**) **1** cargado **2** (*coloq*) (*persona*) estirado

stumble /ˈstʌmbl/ *vi* **1** ~ (**over sth**) dar un traspié (con algo): *stumbling block* obstáculo (fig) **2** ~ (**over sth**) equivocarse (en algo) PHR V **to stumble across/on sth/sb** tropezar con algo/algn

stump /stʌmp/ *n* **1** (*de árbol*) tocón **2** (*de miembro*) muñón

stun /stʌn/ *vt* **1** (**-nn-**) (*fig*) asombrar **2** (*lit*) aturdir **stunning** *adj* (*coloq, aprob*) alucinante, impresionante

stung *pret, pp de* STING

stunk *pret, pp de* STINK

stunt[1] /stʌnt/ *n* (*coloq*) **1** truco **2** acrobacia

stunt[2] /stʌnt/ *vt* frenar el crecimiento de

stupendous /stjuːˈpendəs; *USA* stuː-/ *adj* formidable

stupid /ˈstjuːpɪd; *USA* ˈstuː-/ *adj* (**-er**, **-est**) tonto, estúpido ☛ *Ver nota en* TONTO **stupidity** /stjuːˈpɪdəti; *USA* stuː-/ *n* estupidez

stupor /ˈstjuːpə(r); *USA* ˈstuː-/ *n* [*gen sing*]: *in a drunken stupor* atontado por la bebida

sturdy /ˈstɜːdi/ *adj* (**-ier**, **-iest**) **1** (*zapatos, constitución*) fuerte **2** (*mesa*) sólido **3** (*persona, planta*) robusto

stutter /ˈstʌtə(r)/ (*tb* **stammer**) ◆ *vi* tartamudear ◆ *n* tartamudeo

sty[1] /staɪ/ *n* (*pl* **sties**) pocilga

sty[2] /staɪ/ *n* (*pl* **sties**) (*tb* **stye**) orzuelo

style /staɪl/ *n* **1** estilo **2** modo **3** distinción **4** modelo: *the latest style* la última moda **stylish** *adj* elegante

suave /swɑːv/ *adj* con muy buenas maneras (*a veces excesivamente atento*)

subconscious /ˌsʌbˈkɒnʃəs/ *adj, n* subconsciente

subdivide /ˌsʌbdɪˈvaɪd/ **1** *vt* ~ **sth** (**into sth**) subdividir algo (en algo) **2** *vi* ~ (**into sth**) subdividirse (en algo)

subdue /səbˈdjuː; *USA* -ˈduː/ *vt* someter **subdued** *adj* **1** (*voz*) bajo **2** (*luz, colores*) suave **3** (*persona*) abatido

sub-heading /ˈsʌb hedɪŋ/ *n* subtítulo

subject[1] /ˈsʌbdʒɪkt/ *n* **1** tema **2** asignatura **3** (*Gram*) sujeto **4** súbdito

subject[2] /ˈsʌbdʒɪkt/ *adj* ~ **to sth/sb** sujeto a algo/a algn

subject[3] /səbˈdʒekt/ *vt* ~ **sth/sb** (**to sth**) someter, exponer algo/a algn (a algo) **subjection** *n* sometimiento

subjective /səbˈdʒektɪv/ *adj* subjetivo

subject-matter /ˈsʌbdʒekt mætə(r)/ *n* tema

subjunctive /səbˈdʒʌŋktɪv/ *n* subjuntivo

sublime /səˈblaɪm/ *adj* sublime

submarine /ˌsʌbməˈriːn; *USA* ˈsʌbməriːn/ *adj, n* submarino

submerge /səbˈmɜːdʒ/ **1** *vi* sumergirse **2** *vt* sumergir, inundar

submission /səbˈmɪʃn/ *n* ~ (**to sth/sb**) **1** sumisión (a algo/algn) **2** (*documento, decisión*) presentación

submissive /səbˈmɪsɪv/ *adj* sumiso

submit /səbˈmɪt/ (**-tt-**) **1** *vi* ~ (**to sth/sb**) someterse, rendirse (a algo/algn) **2** *vt* ~ **sth** (**to sth/sb**) presentar algo (a algo/algn): *Applications must be submitted by 31 March.* El plazo de entrega de solicitudes termina el 31 de marzo.

subordinate /səˈbɔːdɪnət; *USA* -dənət/ ◆ *adj, n* subordinado, -a ◆ /səˈbɔːdɪneɪt; *USA* -dəneɪt/ *vt* ~ **sth** (**to sth**) subordinar algo (a algo)

subscribe /səbˈskraɪb/ *vi* ~ (**to sth**) suscribirse (a algo) PHR V **to subscribe to sth** (*fml*) suscribir algo (*opinión*) **subscriber** *n* **1** suscriptor, -ora **2** abonado, -a **subscription** *n* **1** suscripción **2** cuota

subsequent /ˈsʌbsɪkwənt/ *adj* [*sólo antes de sustantivo*] posterior **subsequently** *adv* posteriormente, más tarde **subsequent to** *prep* (*fml*) posterior a, después de

subside /səbˈsaɪd/ *vi* **1** hundirse **2** (*agua*) bajar **3** (*viento*) amainar **4** (*emoción*) calmarse **subsidence** /səbˈsaɪdns, ˈsʌbsɪdns/ *n* hundimiento

subsidiary /səbˈsɪdiəri; *USA* -dieri/ ◆ *adj* secundario, subsidiario ◆ *n* (*pl* **-ies**) filial

subsidize, -ise /ˈsʌbsɪdaɪz/ *vt* subvencionar

subsidy /ˈsʌbsədi/ *n* (*pl* **-ies**) subvención

subsist /səbˈsɪst/ *vi* ~ (**on sth**) (*fml*) subsistir (a base de algo) **subsistence** *n* subsistencia

substance /ˈsʌbstəns/ *n* **1** sustancia **2** esencia

substantial /səbˈstænʃl/ *adj* **1** considerable, importante **2** (*construcción*) sólido **substantially** *adv* **1** considerablemente **2** esencialmente

substitute /ˈsʌbstɪtjuːt; *USA* -tuːt/ ◆ *n* **1** ~ (**for sb**) sustituto (de algn) **2** ~ (**for sth**) sustitutivo (de algo) **3** (*Dep*) reserva ◆ *vt, vi* ~ **A** (**for B**)/(**B with A**) sustituir B (por A): *Substitute honey for sugar/sugar with honey.* Sustituya el azúcar por miel.

subtle /ˈsʌtl/ *adj* (**-er**, **-est**) **1** sutil **2** (*sabor*) delicado **3** (*persona*) agudo, perspicaz **4** (*olor, color*) suave **subtlety** *n* (*pl* **-ies**) sutileza

subtract /səbˈtrækt/ *vt, vi* ~ (**sth**) (**from sth**) restar (algo) (de algo) **subtraction** *n* sustracción

suburb /ˈsʌbɜːb/ *n* barrio residencial de las afueras: *the suburbs* las afueras **suburban** *adj* /səˈbɜːbən/ suburbano: *suburban trains* trenes de cercanías

subversive /səbˈvɜːsɪv/ *adj* subversivo

subway /ˈsʌbweɪ/ *n* **1** paso subterráneo **2** (*USA*) metro *Ver* TUBE

succeed /səkˈsiːd/ **1** *vi* tener éxito, triunfar: *to succeed in doing sth* conseguir/lograr hacer algo **2** *vt, vi* ~ (**sb**) suceder (a algn) **3** *vi* ~ (**to sth**) heredar (algo): *to succeed to the throne* subir al trono

success /səkˈses/ *n* éxito: *to be a success* tener éxito ◊ *hard work is the key to success* el trabajo es la clave del éxito **successful** *adj* exitoso: *a successful writer* un escritor de éxito ◊ *the successful candidate* el candidato elegido ◊ *to be successful in doing sth* lograr hacer algo con éxito

succession /səkˈseʃn/ *n* **1** sucesión **2** serie LOC **in succession**: *three times in quick succession* tres veces seguidas

successor /səkˈsesə(r)/ *n* ~ (**to sth/sb**) sucesor, -ora (a/para algo/de algn): *successor to the former world title holder* sucesor del último campeón del mundo

succumb /səˈkʌm/ *vi* ~ (**to sth**) sucumbir (a algo)

such /sʌtʃ/ *adj, pron* **1** semejante, tal: *Whatever gave you such an idea?* ¿Cómo se te ocurre semejante idea? ◊ *I did no such thing!* ¡Yo no hice tal cosa! ◊ *There's no such thing as ghosts.* Los fantasmas no existen. **2** [*uso enfático*] tan, tanto: *I'm in such a hurry.* Tengo muchísima prisa. ◊ *We had such a wonderful time.* Lo pasamos de maravilla. ☛ **Such** se usa con adjetivos que acompañan a un sustantivo y **so** con adjetivos solos. Compárense los siguientes ejemplos: *The food was so good.* ◊ *We had such good food.* ◊ *You are so intelligent.* ◊ *You are such an intelligent person.* LOC **as such** como tal: *It's not a promotion as such.* No es un ascenso estrictamente dicho. **in such a way that...** de tal manera que... **such as** por ejemplo

suck /sʌk/ *vt, vi* **1** chupar **2** (*bomba*) succionar **sucker** *n* **1** ventosa **2** (*coloq*) primo, -a, bobo, -a

sudden /ˈsʌdn/ *adj* súbito, repentino LOC **all of a sudden** de pronto **suddenly** *adv* de pronto

suds /sʌdz/ *n* [*pl*] espuma

sue /suː, sjuː/ *vt, vi* **to sue** (**sb**) (**for sth**) demandar (a algn) (por algo)

suede /sweɪd/ *n* ante, gamuza

suffer /ˈsʌfə(r)/ **1** *vi* ~ (**from/with sth**) padecer (de algo) **2** *vt, vi* (*dolor, derrota*) sufrir **3** *vi* ser perjudicado **suffering** *n* sufrimiento

sufficient /səˈfɪʃnt/ *adj* ~ (**for sth/sb**) suficiente (para algo/algn)

suffix /ˈsʌfɪks/ *n* sufijo ☛ *Compara con* PREFIX

suffocate /ˈsʌfəkeɪt/ **1** *vt, vi* asfixiar(se) **2** *vi* ahogarse **suffocating** *adj* sofocante **suffocation** *n* asfixia

sugar /ˈʃʊgə(r)/ *n* azúcar: *sugar bowl* azucarero ◊ *sugar lump* terrón de azúcar

suggest /səˈdʒest; *USA* səgˈdʒ-/ *vt* proponer: *I suggest you go to the doctor.* Te aconsejo que vayas al médico. indicar **3** insinuar **suggestion** *n* sugerencia **2** indicio **3** insinuación **suggestive** *adj* **1** ~ (**of sth**) indicativo (de algo) **2** insinuante

suicidal /ˌsuːɪˈsaɪdl/ *adj* **1** suicida **2** punto de suicidarse

suicide /ˈsuːɪsaɪd/ *n* **1** suicidio: *commit suicide* suicidarse **2** suicida

suit /suːt/ ◆ *n* **1** traje: *a two/three-piece suit* un traje de dos/tres piezas (*cartas*) palo ☛ *Ver nota en* BARAJA LOC *Ver* STRONG ◆ *vt* **1** quedar bien convenir **3** sentar bien

suitability /ˌsuːtəˈbɪləti/ (*tb* **suitableness**) *n* aptitud

suitable /ˈsuːtəbl/ *adj* ~ (**for sth/sb**)

adecuado (para algo/algn) **2** conveniente (para algo/algn) **suitably** *adv* debidamente

suitcase /ˈsuːtkeɪs/ *n* maleta

suite /swiːt/ *n* **1** juego: *a three-piece suite* un tresillo **2** (*hotel*) suite

suited /ˈsuːtɪd/ *adj* ~ **(for/to sth/sb)** adecuado (para algo/algn): *He and his wife are well suited (to each other).* Él y su esposa están hechos el uno para el otro.

sulk /sʌlk/ *vi* (*pey*) enfurruñarse, tener la cara larga **sulky** *adj* **(-ier, -iest)** enfurruñado

sullen /ˈsʌlən/ *adj* (*pey*) hosco

sulphur (*USA* **sulfur**) /ˈsʌlfə(r)/ *n* azufre

sultan /ˈsʌltən/ *n* sultán

sultana /sʌlˈtɑːnə; *USA* -ænə/ *n* pasa (*de Esmirna*)

sultry /ˈsʌltri/ *adj* **(-ier, -iest) 1** bochornoso **2** sensual

sum /sʌm/ ◆ *n* suma: *to be good at sums* ser bueno en cálculo ◊ *the sum of £200* la suma de 200 libras ◆ *v* **(-mm-)** PHR V **to sum (sth) up** resumir (*algo*): *to sum up…* en resumen… **to sum sth/sb up** hacerse una idea de algo/algn

summarize, -ise /ˈsʌməraɪz/ *vt, vi* resumir **summary** *n* (*pl* **-ies**) resumen

summer /ˈsʌmə(r)/ *n* verano: *a summer's day* un día de verano ◊ *summer weather* tiempo veraniego **summery** *adj* veraniego

summit /ˈsʌmɪt/ *n* cumbre: *summit conference/meeting* cumbre

summon /ˈsʌmən/ *vt* **1** convocar, llamar: *to summon help* pedir ayuda **2** ~ **sth (up)** (*valor, etc*) hacer acopio de algo, armarse de algo: *I couldn't summon (up) the energy.* No encontré la energía. PHR V **to summon sth up** evocar algo

summons /ˈsʌmənz/ *n* (*pl* **-onses**) citación

sun /sʌn/ ◆ *n* sol: *The sun was shining.* Hacía sol. ◆ *v refl* **(-nn-) to sun yourself** sentarse o tumbarse al sol

sunbathe /ˈsʌnbeɪð/ *vi* tomar el sol

sunbeam /ˈsʌnbiːm/ *n* rayo de sol

sunburn /ˈsʌnbɜːn/ *n* [*incontable*] quemadura de sol: *to get sunburn* quemarse ☛ *Comparar con* SUNTAN **sunburnt** *adj* quemado por el sol

sundae /ˈsʌndeɪ; *USA* -diː/ *n* copa de helado

Sunday /ˈsʌndeɪ, ˈsʌndi/ *n* (*abrev* **Sun**) domingo ☛ *Ver ejemplos en* MONDAY

sundry /ˈsʌndri/ *adj* varios, diversos: *on sundry occasions* en diversas ocasiones LOC **all and sundry** (*coloq*) todos y cada uno

sunflower /ˈsʌnˌflaʊə(r)/ *n* girasol

sung *pp de* SING

sunglasses /ˈsʌnglɑːsɪz/ *n* [*pl*] gafas de sol: *a pair of sunglasses* unas gafas de sol ☛ *Ver nota en* PAIR

sunk *pp de* SINK

sunken /ˈsʌŋkən/ *adj* hundido

sunlight /ˈsʌnlaɪt/ *n* luz solar, luz del sol

sunlit /ˈsʌnlɪt/ *adj* iluminado por el sol

sunny /ˈsʌni/ *adj* **(-ier, -iest) 1** soleado: *It's sunny today.* Hoy hace sol. **2** (*personalidad*) alegre

sunrise /ˈsʌnraɪz/ *n* salida del sol

sunset /ˈsʌnset/ *n* puesta del sol

sunshine /ˈsʌnʃaɪn/ *n* sol: *Let's sit in the sunshine.* Sentémonos al sol.

sunstroke /ˈsʌnstrəʊk/ *n* insolación: *to get sunstroke* coger una insolación

suntan /ˈsʌntæn/ *n* bronceado: *to get a suntan* broncearse ☛ *Comparar con* SUNBURN **suntanned** *adj* bronceado

super /ˈsuːpə(r)/ *adj* estupendo

superb /suːˈpɜːb/ *adj* magnífico **superbly** *adv* de maravilla: *a superbly situated house* una casa en un sitio magnífico

superficial /ˌsuːpəˈfɪʃl/ *adj* superficial **superficiality** /ˌsuːpəˌfɪʃɪˈæləti/ *n* superficialidad **superficially** *adv* superficialmente, aparentemente

superfluous /suːˈpɜːflʊəs/ *adj* superfluo, innecesario: *to be superfluous* estar de más

superhuman /ˌsuːpəˈhjuːmən/ *adj* sobrehumano

superimpose /ˌsuːpərɪmˈpəʊz/ *vt* ~ **sth (on sth)** superponer algo (en algo)

superintendent /ˌsuːpərɪnˈtendənt/ *n* **1** comisario (*de policía*) **2** encargado, -a, superintendente

superior /suːˈpɪəriə(r)/ ◆ *adj* **1** ~ **(to sth/sb)** superior (a algo/algn **2** (*persona, actitud*) soberbio ◆ *n* superior: *Mother Superior* la Madre Superiora **superiority** /suːˌpɪəriˈɒrəti/ *n* ~

(**in sth**); ~ (**over/to sth/sb**) superioridad (en algo); superioridad (sobre algo/ algn)

superlative /suːˈpɜːlətɪv/ *adj*, *n* superlativo

supermarket /ˈsuːpəmɑːkɪt/ *n* supermercado

supernatural /ˌsuːpəˈnætʃrəl/ *adj* **1** sobrenatural **2 the supernatural** *n* el mundo sobrenatural

superpower /ˈsuːpəpaʊə(r)/ *n* superpotencia

supersede /ˌsuːpəˈsiːd/ *vt* reemplazar, sustituir

supersonic /ˌsuːpəˈsɒnɪk/ *adj* supersónico

superstition /ˌsuːpəˈstɪʃn/ *n* superstición **superstitious** *adj* supersticioso

superstore /ˈsuːpəstɔː(r)/ *n* hipermercado

supervise /ˈsuːpəvaɪz/ *vt* supervisar **supervision** /ˌsuːpəˈvɪʒn/ *n* supervisión **supervisor** *n* supervisor, -ora

supper /ˈsʌpə(r)/ *n* cena: *to have supper* cenar ☛ *Ver* pág 320.

supple /ˈsʌpl/ *adj* (**-er**, **-est**) flexible

supplement /ˈsʌplɪmənt/ ◆ *n* **1** suplemento, complemento **2** (*de libro*) apéndice ◆ *vt* complementar, completar: *supplemented by* complementado por

supplementary /ˌsʌplɪˈmentri; *USA* -teri/ *adj* adicional, suplementario

supplier /səˈplaɪə(r)/ *n* proveedor, -ora, suministrador, -ora

supply /səˈplaɪ/ ◆ *vt* (*pret*, *pp* **supplied**) **1** ~ **sb** (**with sth**) proveer, abastecer a algn (de algo) **2** ~ **sth** (**to sb**) suministrar, proporcionar, facilitar algo (a algn) ◆ *n* (*pl* **-ies**) **1** suministro, provisión **2 supplies** [*pl*] víveres **3 supplies** [*pl*] (*Mil*) pertrechos LOC **supply and demand** la oferta y la demanda *Ver tb* PLENTIFUL

support /səˈpɔːt/ ◆ *vt* **1** (*peso*) sostener, soportar **2** (*causa*) apoyar, respaldar: *a supporting role* un papel secundario **3** (*Dep*) seguir: *Which team do you support?* ¿De qué equipo eres? **4** (*persona*) mantener ◆ *n* **1** apoyo **2** soporte **supporter** *n* **1** (*Pol*) partidario, -a **2** (*Dep*) hincha **3** (*de teoría*) seguidor, -ora **supportive** *adj* que ayuda: *to be supportive* apoyar

suppose /səˈpəʊz/ *vt* **1** suponer, imaginarse **2** (*sugerencia*): *Suppose we change the subject?* ¿Qué te parece si cambiamos de tema? LOC **to be supposed to do sth** deber hacer algo **supposed** *adj* supuesto **supposedly** *adv* supuestamente **supposing** (*tb* **supposing that**) *conj* si, en el caso de que

suppress /səˈpres/ *vt* **1** (*rebelión*) reprimir **2** (*información*) ocultar **3** (*sentimiento*) contener, reprimir **4** (*bostezo*) ahogar

supremacy /suːˈpreməsi, sjuː-/ *n* ~ (**over sth/sb**) supremacía (sobre algo/ algn)

supreme /suːˈpriːm, sjuː-/ *adj* supremo, sumo

surcharge /ˈsɜːtʃɑːdʒ/ *n* ~ (**on sth**) recargo (sobre algo)

sure /ʃʊə(r)/ ◆ *adj* (**surer**, **surest**) **1** seguro, cierto: *He's sure to be elected.* Es seguro que será elegido. **2** estable, firme LOC **to be sure of sth** estar seguro de algo **to be sure to do sth**; **to be sure and do sth** no dejar de hacer algo **for sure** (*coloq*) con seguridad **to make sure (of sth/that...** asegurarse (de algo/de que...): *Make sure you are home by nine.* No te olvides de que tienes que estar en casa a las nueve. **sure!** (*coloq*, *esp USA*) ¡claro! ◆ *adv* LOC **sure enough** efectivamente

surely /ˈʃɔːli; *USA* ˈʃʊərli/ *adv* **1** ciertamente, seguramente, por supuesto **2** (*sorpresa*): *Surely you can't agree?* ¿No estarás de acuerdo?

surf /sɜːf/ ◆ *n* **1** oleaje, olas **2** espum (*de las olas*) ◆ *vi* hacer surf

surface /ˈsɜːfɪs/ ◆ *n* **1** superficie: *b surface mail* por correo terrestre marítimo ◊ *the earth's surface* la super ficie de la tierra ◊ *a surface wound* un herida superficial **2** cara ◆ **1** *vt* ~ **st** (**with sth**) recubrir algo (con algo) **2** salir a la superficie

surge /sɜːdʒ/ ◆ *vi*: *They surged into th stadium.* Entraron en tropel en el esta dio. ◆ *n* ~ (**of sth**) oleada (de algo)

surgeon /ˈsɜːdʒən/ *n* cirujano, **surgery** *n* (*pl* **-ies**) **1** cirugía: *bra surgery* neurocirugía ◊ *to underg surgery* someterse a una operació quirúrgica **2** (*GB*) consultorio (*de u médico*): *surgery hours* horas consulta **surgical** *adj* quirúrgico

surly /ˈsɜːli/ *adj* (**-ier**, **-iest**) arisco

surmount /səˈmaʊnt/ *vt* superar

surname /ˈsɜːneɪm/ *n* apellido ☛ *Comparar con* NAME

surpass /səˈpɑːs; *USA* -ˈpæs/ (*fml*) **1** *vt* superar **2** *v refl* ~ **yourself** superarse

surplus /ˈsɜːpləs/ ◆ *n* excedente: *the food surplus in Western Europe* el excedente de alimentos en Europa Occidental ◆ *adj* sobrante

surprise /səˈpraɪz/ ◆ *n* sorpresa LOC **to take sth/sb by surprise** coger algo/a algn por sorpresa ◆ *vt* **1** sorprender: *I wouldn't be surprised if it rained.* No me extrañaría que lloviera. **2** ~ **sb** coger por sorpresa a algn **surprised** *adj* ~ (**at sth/sb**) sorprendido (por algo/con algn): *I'm not surprised!* ¡No me extraña!

surrender /səˈrendə(r)/ ◆ **1** *vi* ~ (**to sb**) rendirse (a algn) **2** *vt* ~ **sth** (**to sb**) (*fml*) entregar algo (a algn) ◆ *n* rendición, entrega

surreptitious /ˌsʌrəpˈtɪʃəs/ *adj* subrepticio, furtivo

surrogate /ˈsʌrəgət/ *n* (*fml*) sustituto, -a: *surrogate mother* madre de alquiler

surround /səˈraʊnd/ *vt* rodear **surrounding** *adj* circundante: *the surrounding countryside* el campo de los alrededores **surroundings** *n* [*pl*] alrededores

surveillance /sɜːˈveɪləns/ *n* vigilancia: *to keep sb under surveillance* mantener a algn bajo vigilancia

survey /səˈveɪ/ ◆ *vt* **1** contemplar **2** (*Geog*) ~ **sth** medir algo; levantar un plano de algo **3** (*GB*) hacer un reconocimiento (*de un edificio*) **4** encuestar ◆ /ˈsɜːveɪ/ *n* **1** panorama **2** (*GB*) inspección (*de una casa, etc*) **3** encuesta **surveying** /sɜːˈveɪɪŋ/ *n* agrimensura, topografía **surveyor** /səˈveɪə(r)/ *n* **1** persona que lleva a cabo la inspección y tasación de edificios **2** agrimensor, -ora, topógrafo, -a

survive /səˈvaɪv/ **1** *vi* sobrevivir **2** *vi* ~ (**on sth**) subsistir (a base de algo) **3** *vt* ~ **sth** (*un naufragio, fuego, etc*) sobrevivir a algo **survival** *n* supervivencia **survivor** *n* superviviente

susceptible /səˈseptəbl/ *adj* **1** ~ **to sth**: *He's very susceptible to flattery.* Se le convence fácilmente con halagos. **2** ~ **to sth** (*Med*) propenso a algo **3** sensible, susceptible

suspect /səˈspekt/ ◆ *vt* **1** sospechar **2** (*motivo, etc*) recelar de **3** ~ **sb** (**of sth/of doing sth**) sospechar de algn; sospechar que algn ha hecho algo ◆ /ˈsʌspekt/ *adj*, *n* sospechoso, -a

suspend /səˈspend/ *vt* **1** ~ **sth** (**from sth**) colgar algo (de algo): *to suspend sth from the ceiling* colgar algo del techo ☛ La palabra más normal es **hang**. **2** suspender: *suspended sentence* pena que no se cumple a menos que se cometa otro crimen

suspender /səˈspendə(r)/ *n* **1** (*GB*) liga **2 suspenders** [*pl*] (*USA*) *Ver* BRACE 2

suspense /səˈspens/ *n* suspense, tensión

suspension /səˈspenʃn/ *n* suspensión: *suspension bridge* puente colgante

suspicion /səˈspɪʃn/ *n* sospecha, recelo: *on suspicion of…* bajo sospecha de…

suspicious /səˈspɪʃəs/ *adj* **1** ~ (**about/of sth/sb**) receloso (de algo/algn): *They're suspicious of foreigners.* Recelan de los extranjeros. **2** sospechoso: *He died in suspicious circumstances.* Murió en circunstancias sospechosas.

sustain /səˈsteɪn/ *vt* **1** (*vida, interés*) mantener: *People have a limited capacity to sustain interest in politics.* La gente tiene una capacidad limitada para mantenerse interesada en la política. **2** sostener: *It is difficult to sustain this argument.* Es difícil sostener este argumento. ◊ *sustained economic growth* crecimiento económico sostenido **3** (*fml*) (*lesión, pérdida, etc*) sufrir

swagger /ˈswægə(r)/ *vi* pavonearse, contonearse

swallow[1] /ˈswɒləʊ/ *n* golondrina

swallow[2] /ˈswɒləʊ/ ◆ **1** *vt*, *vi* tragar **2** *vt* (*coloq*) (*tolerar, creer*) tragarse **3** *vt* ~ **sth/sb** (**up**) (*fig*) tragarse algo/a algn; consumir algo ◆ *n* trago

swam *pret de* SWIM

swamp /swɒmp/ ◆ *n* pantano ◆ *vt* **1** (*lit*) inundar **2** ~ **sth/sb** (**with sth**) (*fig*) inundar algo/a algn (de algo)

swan /swɒn/ *n* cisne

swap (*th* **swop**) /swɒp/ *vt*, *vi* (**-pp-**) (*coloq*) (inter)cambiar: *to swap sth round* cambiar algo de lugar

swarm /swɔːm/ ◆ *n* **1** (*abejas*)

enjambre **2** (*moscas*) nube **3** (*gente*) multitud: *swarms of people* un mar de gente ◆ *v* PHR V **to swarm in/out** entrar/salir en manadas **to swarm with sth/sb** ser un hervidero de algo/algn

swat /swɒt/ *vt* (**-tt-**) aplastar (*un insecto*)

sway /sweɪ/ ◆ **1** *vt, vi* balancear(se), mecer(se) **2** *vi* tambalearse **3** *vt* influir en ◆ *n* **1** balanceo **2** (*fig*) dominio

swear /sweə(r)/ (*pret* **swore** /swɔː(r)/ *pp* **sworn** /swɔːn/) **1** *vi* decir tacos: *swear word* taco ◊ *Your sister swears a lot.* Tu hermana dice muchos tacos. **2** *vt, vi* jurar: *to swear to tell the truth* jurar decir la verdad PHR V **to swear by sth/sb** (*coloq*) confiar plenamente en algo/algn **to swear sb in** tomar juramento a algn

sweat /swet/ ◆ *n* sudor ◆ *vi* sudar LOC **to sweat it out** (*coloq*) aguantar **sweaty** *adj* (**-ier**, **-iest**) sudoroso, que hace sudar

sweater /ˈswetə(r)/ *n* jersey

> Las palabras **sweater**, **jumper**, **pullover** significan "jersey". *Comparar con* CARDIGAN

sweatshirt /ˈswetʃɜːt/ *n* sudadera

swede /swiːd/ *n* colinabo

sweep /swiːp/ ◆ (*pret, pp* **swept** /swept/) **1** *vt, vi* barrer **2** *vt* (*chimenea*) deshollinar **3** *vt* arrastrar **4** *vi* extenderse **5** *vi*: *She swept out of the room.* Salió de la habitación con paso majestuoso. **6** *vt, vi* ~ (**through, over, across, etc**) **sth** recorrer algo; extenderse por algo LOC **to sweep sb off their feet** arrebatarle el corazón a algn PHR V **to sweep (sth) away/up** barrer/limpiar (algo) ◆ *n* **1** barrido **2** movimiento, gesto (amplio) **3** extensión, alcance **4** (*de policía*) redada

sweeping /ˈswiːpɪŋ/ *adj* **1** (*cambio*) radical **2** (*pey*) (*afirmación*) tajante

sweet /swiːt/ ◆ *adj* (**-er**, **-est**) **1** dulce **2** (*olor*) fragante **3** (*sonido*) melodioso **4** (*coloq*) lindo, mono **5** (*carácter*) encantador LOC **to have a sweet tooth** (*coloq*) ser goloso ◆ *n* **1** (*USA* **candy**) caramelo **2** (*GB*) *Ver* DESSERT **sweetness** *n* dulzura

sweetcorn /ˈswiːtkɔːn/ *n* maíz tierno ☛ *Comparar con* MAIZE

sweeten /ˈswiːtn/ *vt* **1** endulzar, poner azúcar a **2** ~ **sb (up)** (*coloq*) ablandar a algn **sweetener** *n* edulcorante

sweetheart /ˈswiːthɑːt/ *n* **1** (*antic*) novio, -a **2** (*tratamiento*) cariño

sweet pea *n* guisante de olor

swell /swel/ *vt, vi* (*pret* **swelled** *pp* **swollen** /ˈswəʊlən/ *o* **swelled**) hinchar(se) **swelling** *n* hinchazón

swept *pret, pp de* SWEEP

swerve /swɜːv/ *vt, vi* dar un viraje brusco, dar un volantazo: *The car swerved to avoid the child.* El coche viró bruscamente para esquivar al niño.

swift /swɪft/ *adj* (**-er**, **-est**) rápido, pronto: *a swift reaction* una pronta reacción

swill /swɪl/ *vt* ~ **sth (out/down)** (*esp GB*) enjuagar algo

swim /swɪm/ ◆ (**-mm-**) (*pret* **swam** /swæm/ *pp* **swum** /swʌm/) **1** *vt, vi* nadar: *to swim the Channel* atravesar el Canal a nado ◊ *to swim breast-stroke* nadar a braza ◊ *to go swimming* ir a bañarse **2** *vi* (*cabeza*) dar vueltas (*cuando uno se marea*) ◆ *n* baño: *to go for a swim* ir a bañarse **swimmer** *n* nadador, -ora **swimming** *n* natación

swimming /ˈswɪmɪŋ/ *n* la natación

swimming costume *Ver* SWIMSUIT

swimming pool *n* piscina

swimming trunks (*USA* **swimming shorts**) *n* [*pl*] bañador (de caballero): *a pair of swimming trunks* un bañador ☛ *Ver nota en* PAIR

swimsuit /ˈswɪmsuːt/ *n* bañador (*de mujer*)

swindle /ˈswɪndl/ ◆ *vt* (*coloq*) estafar, timar ◆ *n* **1** estafa **2** engaño **swindler** *n* estafador, -ora

swing /swɪŋ/ ◆ (*pret, pp* **swung** /swʌŋ/) **1** *vt, vi* balancear(se) **2** *vt, vi* columpiar(se) **3** *vi* [*seguido de adverbio*]: *The door swung open/shut.* La puerta se abrió/cerró. PHR V **to swing (a)round** dar(se) media vuelta ◆ *n* **1** balanceo **2** columpio **3** cambio: *mood swings* cambios bruscos de humor LOC *Ver* FULL

swirl /swɜːl/ *vt, vi* arremolinar(se): *Flakes of snow swirled in the cold wind.* Los copos de nieve se arremolinaban en el frío viento.

switch /swɪtʃ/ ◆ *n* **1** interruptor **2** (*t.* **switch-over**) (*coloq*) cambio: *a switc*

aɪ	aʊ	ɔɪ	ɪə	eə	ʊə	ʒ	h	ŋ
five	now	join	near	hair	pure	vision	how	sing

to Labour un cambio hacia los laboristas ◆ **1** *vi* ~ **(from sth) to sth** cambiar (de algo) a algo **2** *vt* ~ **sth (with sth/sb)** intercambiar algo (con algo/algn) PHR V **to switch (sth) off** desenchufar (algo), apagar (algo) **to switch (sth) on** encender (algo)

switchboard /ˈswɪtʃbɔːd/ *n* centralita

swivel /ˈswɪvl/ *v* (**-ll-**, *USA* **-l-**) PHR V **to swivel round** girar(se)

swollen *pp de* SWELL

swoop /swuːp/ ◆ *vi* ~ **(down) (on sth/sb)** descender en picado (sobre algo/algn) ◆ *n* redada: *Police made a dawn swoop.* La policía hizo una redada al amanecer.

swop *Ver* SWAP

sword /sɔːd/ *n* espada

swore *pret de* SWEAR

sworn *pp de* SWEAR

swum *pp de* SWIM

swung *pret, pp de* SWING

syllable /ˈsɪləbl/ *n* sílaba

syllabus /ˈsɪləbəs/ *n* (*pl* **-buses**) programa (de estudios): *Does the syllabus cover modern literature?* ¿Cubre el programa la literatura moderna?

symbol /ˈsɪmbl/ *n* ~ **(of/for sth)** símbolo (de algo) **symbolic** /sɪmˈbɒlɪk/ *adj* ~ **(of sth)** simbólico (de algo) **symbolism** /ˈsɪmbəlɪzəm/ *n* simbolismo **symbolize, -ise** /ˈsɪmbəlaɪz/ *vt* simbolizar

symmetry /ˈsɪmətri/ *n* simetría **symmetrical** /sɪˈmetrɪkl/ (*tb* **symmetric**) *adj* simétrico

sympathetic /ˌsɪmpəˈθetɪk/ *adj* **1** ~ **(to/towards/with sb)** comprensivo, compasivo (con algn): *They were very sympathetic when I told them I could not sit the exam.* Fueron muy comprensivos cuando les dije que no podía presentarme al examen. ☛ Nótese que “simpático” se dice **nice** o **friendly**. **2** ~ **(to sth/sb)** con buena disposición (hacia algo/algn): *lawyers sympathetic to the peace movement* abogados que apoyan el movimiento pacifista

sympathize, -ise /ˈsɪmpəθaɪz/ *vi* ~ **(with sth/sb)** **1** compadecerse (de algo/algn) **2** estar de acuerdo (con algo/algn) **sympathy** *n* (*pl* **-ies**) **1** ~ **(for/towards sb)** compasión (por/hacia algn) **2** condolencia

symphony /ˈsɪmfəni/ *n* (*pl* **-ies**) sinfonía

symptom /ˈsɪmptəm/ *n* síntoma: *The riots are a symptom of a deeper problem.* Los disturbios son un síntoma de problemas más profundos.

synagogue /ˈsɪnəgɒg/ *n* sinagoga

synchronize, -ise /ˈsɪŋkrənaɪz/ *vt, vi* ~ **(sth) (with sth)** sincronizar (algo) (con algo)

syndicate /ˈsɪndɪkət/ *n* sindicato

syndrome /ˈsɪndrəʊm/ *n* (*Med, fig*) síndrome

synonym /ˈsɪnənɪm/ *n* sinónimo **synonymous** /sɪˈnɒnɪməs/ *adj* ~ **(with sth)** sinónimo (de algo)

syntax /ˈsɪntæks/ *n* sintaxis

synthetic /sɪnˈθetɪk/ *adj* **1** sintético **2** (*coloq, pey*) artificial

syringe /sɪˈrɪndʒ/ *n* jeringa

syrup /ˈsɪrəp/ *n* **1** almíbar **2** jarabe (*para la tos*)

system /ˈsɪstəm/ *n* **1** sistema: *the metric/solar system* el sistema métrico/solar **2** método: *different systems of government* diferentes métodos de gobierno LOC **to get sth out of your system** (*coloq*) desahogarse de algo **systematic** /ˌsɪstəˈmætɪk/ *adj* **1** sistemático **2** metódico

Tt

T, t /tiː/ *n* (*pl* **T's, t's** /tiːz/) T, t: *T for Tommy* T de Tarragona ☛ *Ver ejemplos en* A, a

tab /tæb/ *n* **1** (*de lata de bebida*) anilla **2** etiqueta **3** (*USA*) cuenta

table /ˈteɪbl/ *n* **1** mesa: *bedside/coffee table* mesilla de noche/mesita de café **2** tabla: *table of contents* índice de materias LOC **to lay/set the table** poner la mesa *Ver tb* LAY[1], CLEAR

tablecloth /ˈteɪblklɒθ/ *n* mantel

tablespoon /ˈteɪblspuːn/ *n* **1** cuchara (grande) **2** (*tb* **tablespoonful**) cucharada

tablet /ˈtæblət/ *n* tableta, pastilla

table tennis *n* tenis de mesa

tabloid /ˈtæblɔɪd/ *n* tabloide: *the tabloid press* la prensa sensacionalista

taboo /təˈbuː; *USA* tæˈbuː/ *adj*, *n* (*pl* ~**s**) tabú: *a taboo subject* un tema tabú

tacit /ˈtæsɪt/ *adj* tácito

tack /tæk/ ◆ *vt* clavar (con tachuelas) PHR V **to tack sth on** (**to sth**) (*coloq*) añadir algo (a algo) ◆ *n* tachuela

tackle /ˈtækl/ ◆ *n* **1** [*incontable*] equipo, avíos: *fishing tackle* equipo de pescar **2** (*en fútbol*) entrada **3** (*en rugby*) placaje ◆ *vt* **1** ~ **sth** hacer frente a algo: *to tackle a problem* abordar un problema **2** ~ **sb about/on/over sth** abordar a algn sobre algo **3** (*en fútbol*) hacer una entrada **4** (*en rugby*) placar

tacky /ˈtæki/ *adj* (**-ier**, **-iest**) **1** pegajoso **2** (*coloq*) hortera

tact /tækt/ *n* tacto **tactful** *adj* diplomático, discreto

tactic /ˈtæktɪk/ *n* táctica **tactical** *adj* **1** táctico **2** estratégico: *a tactical decision* una decisión estratégica

tactless /ˈtæktləs/ *adj* indiscreto, poco diplomático: *It was tactless of you to ask him his age.* Fue una indiscreción por tu parte preguntarle su edad.

tadpole /ˈtædpəʊl/ *n* renacuajo

tag /tæg/ ◆ *n* etiqueta ◆ *vt* (**-gg-**) etiquetar PHR V **to tag along** (**behind/with sb**) acompañar a algn, pegarse a algn

tail[1] /teɪl/ *n* **1** rabo, cola **2 tails** [*pl*] frac **3 tails** [*pl*] cruz: *Heads or tails?* ¿Cara o cruz? LOC *Ver* HEAD[1]

tail[2] /teɪl/ *vt* perseguir PHR V **to tail away/off 1** disminuir, desvanecerse **2** (*ruido, etc*) apagarse

tailor /ˈteɪlə(r)/ ◆ *n* sastre, -a ◆ *vt* (*fig*) ~ **sth for/to sth/sb** adaptar algo para/a algo/algn

tailor-made /ˌteɪlə ˈmeɪd/ *adj* **1** a medida **2** (*fig*) a la medida de sus necesidades

taint /teɪnt/ *vt* **1** contaminar **2** (*reputación*) manchar

take

Bring the newspaper.

Fetch the newspaper.

Take the newspaper.

take /teɪk/ *vt* (*pret* **took** /tʊk/ *pp* **taken** /ˈteɪkən/) **1** tomar: *She took it as a compliment.* Se lo tomó como un cumplido. **2** ~ **sth/sb** (**with you**) llevarse algo/a algn: *Take the dog with you.* Llévate el perro. **3** ~ **sth** (**to sb**) llevar algo (a algn) **4** coger: *to take sb's hand/take sb by the hand* coger a algn de la mano ◊ *to take the bus* coger e

iː	i	ɪ	e	æ	ɑː	ʌ	ʊ	uː
see	happy	sit	ten	hat	arm	cup	put	too

autobús **5** ~ **sth from/out of sth** sacar algo de algo **6** (*sin permiso*) llevarse **7** ~ **sth** (**from sb**) quitar algo (a algn) **8** aceptar: *Do you take cheques?* ¿Aceptan cheques? **9** (*tolerar*) soportar **10** (*comprar*) llevarse **11** (*tiempo*) tardar: *It takes an hour to get there.* Se tarda una hora en llegar. ◊ *It won't take long.* No lleva mucho tiempo. **12** (*cualidad*) necesitarse, hacer falta: *It takes courage to speak out.* Se necesita coraje para decir lo que uno piensa. **13** (*talla*) usar: *What size shoes do you take?* ¿Qué número calzas? **14** (*foto*) hacer LOC **to take it (that...)** suponer (que...) **to take some/a lot of doing** (*coloq*) no ser fácil ☛ Para otras expresiones con **take**, véanse las entradas del sustantivo, adjetivo, etc, p.ej. **to take place** en PLACE.

PHR V **to take sb aback** [*gen pasiva*] dejar a algn sorprendido: *It really took me aback.* Me pilló de sorpresa.

to take after sb salir, parecerse a algn

to take sth apart desmontar algo

to take sth/sb away (**from sth/sb**) quitar algo/a algn (de algo/algn)

to take sth back 1 (*tienda*) devolver algo **2** retractarse de algo

to take sth down 1 bajar algo **2** desmontar algo **3** anotar algo

to take sb in 1 dar cobijo a algn **2** engañar a algn **to take sth in** entender, asimilar algo

to take off despegar **to take sth off 1** (*prenda*) quitarse algo **2** *to take the day off* tomarse el día libre

to take sb on contratar a algn **to take sth on** aceptar algo (*trabajo*)

to take it/sth out on sb pagar algo con algn, tomarla con algn **to take sb out** invitar a algn a salir: *I'm taking him out tonight.* Voy a salir con él esta noche. **to take sth out** sacar, extraer algo

to take over from sb sustituir a algn (en algo) **to take sth over 1** adquirir algo (*empresa*) **2** hacerse cargo de algo

to take to sth/sb: *I took to his parents immediately.* Sus padres me cayeron bien inmediatamente.

to take up sth ocupar algo (*espacio, tiempo*) **to take sb up on sth** (*coloq*) aceptar algo de algn (*oferta*) **to take sth up** empezar algo (*como hobby*) **to take sth up with sb** plantear algo a algn

takeaway /ˈteɪkəweɪ/ (*USA* **take-out**) *n* **1** restaurante que vende comida para llevar ☛ *Ver* pág 320. **2** comida para llevar: *We ordered a takeaway.* Encargamos una comida para llevar.

taken *pp de* TAKE

take-off /ˈteɪk ɒf/ *n* despegue

takeover /ˈteɪkəʊvə(r)/ *n* **1** (*empresa*) adquisición: *takeover bid* oferta pública de adquisición **2** (*Mil*) toma del poder

takings /ˈteɪkɪŋz/ *n* [*pl*] recaudación

talc /tælk/ (*tb* **talcum** /ˈtælkəm/) (*tb* **talcum powder**) *n* polvos de talco

tale /teɪl/ *n* **1** cuento, historia **2** chisme

talent /ˈtælənt/ *n* ~ (**for sth**) talento (para algo) **talented** *adj* talentoso, de talento

talk /tɔːk/ ◆ *n* **1** conversación, charla: *to have a talk with sb* tener una conversacion con algn **2 talks** [*pl*] negociaciones ◆ **1** *vi* ~ (**to/with sb**) (**about/of sth/sb**) hablar (con algn) (sobre/de algo/algn) ☛ *Ver nota en* HABLAR **2** *vt* hablar de: *to talk business* hablar de negocios ◊ *to talk sense* hablar con sentido **3** *vi* cotillear LOC **to talk shop** (*pey*) hablar del trabajo **to talk your way out of (doing) sth** librarse de (hacer) algo con labia PHR V **to talk down to sb** hablar a algn como si fuera tonto **to talk sb into/out of doing sth** persuadir a algn para que haga/no haga algo **talkative** *adj* hablador

tall /tɔːl/ *adj* (**-er**, **-est**) alto: *How tall are you?* ¿Cuánto mides? ◊ *Tom is six feet tall.* Tom mide 1.80. ◊ *a tall tree* un árbol alto ◊ *a tall tower* una torre alta ☛ *Ver nota en* ALTO

tambourine /ˌtæmbəˈriːn/ *n* pandereta

tame /teɪm/ ◆ *adj* (**tamer**, **tamest**) **1** domesticado **2** manso **3** (*fiesta, libro*) insulso ◆ *vt* domar

tamper /ˈtæmpə(r)/ PHR V **to tamper with sth** alterar algo

tampon /ˈtæmpɒn/ *n* tampón

tan /tæn/ ◆ *vt, vi* (**-nn-**) broncear(se) ◆ *n* (*tb* **suntan**) bronceado (*del cutis*): *to get a tan* broncearse ◆ *adj* de color canela

tangent /ˈtændʒənt/ *n* tangente LOC **to go/fly off at a tangent** salirse por la tangente

tangerine /ˌtændʒəˈriːn; *USA* ˈtændʒəriːn/ ◆ *n* mandarina ◆ *adj, n* (de) color naranja oscuro

tangle /ˈtæŋgl/ ◆ *n* **1** enredo **2** lío: *to get into a tangle* hacerse un lío ◆ *vt, vi* ~ **(sth) (up)** enredar algo/enredarse **tangled** *adj* enredado

tank /tæŋk/ *n* **1** depósito: *petrol tank* depósito de gasolina **2** pecera **3** (*Mil*) tanque

tanker /ˈtæŋkə(r)/ *n* **1** petrolero **2** camión cisterna

tantalize, -ise /ˈtæntəlaɪz/ *vt* atormentar **tantalizing, -ising** *adj* tentador

tantrum /ˈtæntrəm/ *n* rabieta: *Peter threw/had a tantrum.* A Peter le dio una rabieta.

tap[1] /tæp/ ◆ *n* grifo: *to turn the tap on/off* abrir/cerrar el grifo ◆ **(-pp-) 1** *vt, vi* ~ **(into) sth** explotar algo **2** *vt* (*teléfono*) intervenir

tap[2] /tæp/ ◆ *n* golpecito ◆ *vt* **(-pp-) 1 to tap sth (against/on sth)** dar golpecitos con algo (en algo) **2 to tap sth/sb (on sth) (with sth)** dar golpecitos a algo/algn (en algo) (con algo): *to tap sb on the shoulder* dar una palmadita a alguien en la espalda

tape /teɪp/ ◆ *n* **1** cinta: *sticky tape* cinta adhesiva **2** cinta (*de grabación*): *to have sth on tape* tener algo grabado **3** *Ver* TAPE-MEASURE ◆ **1** *vt* ~ **sth (up)** atar algo con cinta **2** *vt, vi* grabar

tape deck *n* pletina

tape-measure /ˈteɪp meʒə(r)/ (*tb* **tape, measuring tape**) *n* cinta métrica

tape recorder *n* grabadora, casete

tapestry /ˈtæpəstri/ *n* (*pl* **-ies**) tapiz

tar /tɑː(r)/ *n* alquitrán

target /ˈtɑːgɪt/ ◆ *n* **1** blanco, objetivo: *military targets* objetivos militares **2** objetivo: *I'm not going to meet my weekly target* No voy a cumplir mi objetivo semanal. ◆ *vt* **1** ~ **sth/sb** dirigirse a algo/algn: *We're targeting young drivers.* Nos estamos dirigiendo a los conductores jóvenes. **2** ~ **sth at/on sth/sb** dirigir algo a algo/algn

tariff /ˈtærɪf/ *n* **1** tarifa **2** arancel

Tarmac® /ˈtɑːmæk/ *n* **1** (*tb* **tarmacadam**) asfalto **2 tarmac** pista (*de aeropuerto*)

tarnish /ˈtɑːnɪʃ/ **1** *vt, vi* deslucir(se) **2** *vt* (*fig*) desacreditar

tart /tɑːt/ *adj* tarta ☛ *Ver nota en* PIE

tartan /ˈtɑːtn/ *n* tartán

task /tɑːsk; *USA* tæsk/ *n* tarea: *Your first task will be to type these letters.* Su primera tarea será pasar estas cartas a máquina.

taste /teɪst/ ◆ *n* **1** sabor **2** ~ **(for sth)** gusto (por algo) **3** (*tb* **sense of taste**) gusto **4** ~ **(of sth)** (*comida, bebida*) poquito (de algo) **5** ~ **(of sth)** muestra (de algo): *her first taste of life in the city* su primera experiencia de la vida en la ciudad ◆ **1** *vt, vi* notar el sabor (de): *I can't taste anything.* No sabe a nada. **2** *vi* ~ **(of sth)** saber (a algo) **3** *vt* probar **4** *vt* (*fig*) experimentar, conocer

tasteful /ˈteɪstfl/ *adj* de buen gusto

tasteless /ˈteɪstləs/ *adj* **1** insípido, soso **2** de mal gusto

tasty /ˈteɪsti/ *adj* **(-ier, -iest)** sabroso

tattered /ˈtætəd/ *adj* hecho jirones

tatters /ˈtætəz/ *n* [*pl*] harapos LOC **in tatters** hecho jirones

tattoo /təˈtuː; *USA* tæˈtuː/ ◆ *n* (*pl* **~s**) tatuaje ◆ *vt* tatuar

tatty /ˈtæti/ *adj* **(-ier, -iest)** (*GB, coloq*) en mal estado

taught *pret, pp de* TEACH

taunt /tɔːnt/ ◆ *vt* mofarse de ◆ *n* burl

Taurus /ˈtɔːrəs/ *n* tauro ☛ *Ver ejemplos en* AQUARIUS

taut /tɔːt/ *adj* tirante, tenso

tavern /ˈtævən/ *n* (*antic*) taberna

tax /tæks/ ◆ *n* impuesto: *tax return* declaración de (la) renta ◆ *vt* **1** (*artículos*) gravar con un impuesto **2** (*personas*) imponer contribuciones a **3** (*recursos*) exigir demasiado a **4** (*paciencia, etc*) poner a prueba, abusar de **taxable** *adj* imponible **taxation** (recaudación/pago de) impuestos **taxing** *adj* agotador, extenuante

tax-free /ˌtæks ˈfriː/ *adj* libre de impuestos

taxi /ˈtæksi/ ◆ *n* (*tb* **taxicab**, *esp USA* **cab**) taxi: *taxi driver* taxista ◆ *vi* rodar (*avión*)

taxpayer /ˈtæksˌpeɪə(r)/ *n* contribuyente

tea /tiː/ *n* **1** té **2** merienda **3** cena ☛ *Ver* pág 320. LOC *Ver* CUP

teach /tiːtʃ/ (*pret, pp* **taught** /tɔːt/) **1** *vt* enseñar: *Jeremy is teaching us how to use the computer.* Jeremy nos está enseñando a usar el ordenador. **2** *vt, vi* dar clases (de) *Ver tb* COACH LOC **to teach sb a lesson** darle a algn una lección

teacher /ˈtiːtʃə(r)/ *n* profesor, -ora: *English teacher* profesor, -ora de inglés

teaching /ˈtiːtʃɪŋ/ *n* enseñanza: *teaching materials* materiales didácticos ◊ *a teaching career* una carrera docente

team /tiːm/ ◆ *n* [*v sing o pl*] equipo ◆ PHR V **to team up (with sb)** formar equipo (con algn)

teamwork /ˈtiːmwɜːk/ *n* trabajo en equipo

teapot /ˈtiːpɒt/ *n* tetera

tear[1] /tɪə(r)/ *n* lágrima: *He was in tears.* Estaba llorando. LOC *Ver* BRING **tearful** *adj* lloroso

tear[2] /teə(r)/ ◆ (*pret* **tore** /tɔː(r)/ *pp* **torn** /tɔːn/) **1** *vt, vi* rasgar(se) **2** *vt* ~ **sth out** arrancar algo **3** *vi* ~ **along/past** ir/pasar a toda velocidad PHR V **to be torn between A and B** no poder decidirse entre A y B **to tear sth down** derribar algo **to tear sth up** hacer pedazos algo ◆ *n* desgarrón LOC *Ver* WEAR

tearoom /ˈtiːruːm, -rʊm/ (*tb* **tea shop**) *n* salón de té ☛ *Ver* pág 320.

tease /tiːz/ *vt* tomarle el pelo, atormentar

teaspoon /ˈtiːspuːn/ *n* **1** cucharilla **2** (*tb* **teaspoonful**) cucharadita

teatime /ˈtiːtaɪm/ *n* hora del té

technical /ˈteknɪkl/ *adj* **1** técnico **2** según la ley: *a technical point* una cuestión de forma **technicality** /ˌteknɪˈkæləti/ *n* (*pl* **-ies**) **1** detalle técnico, tecnicismo **2** formalismo **technically** *adv* **1** técnicamente, en términos técnicos **2** estrictamente

technical college *n* (*GB*) instituto superior de formación profesional

technician /tekˈnɪʃn/ *n* técnico, -a

technique /tekˈniːk/ *n* técnica

technology /tekˈnɒlədʒi/ *n* (*pl* **-ies**) tecnología **technological** /ˌteknəˈlɒdʒɪkl/ *adj* tecnológico

teddy bear /ˈtedɪ beə(r)/ *n* osito de peluche

tedious /ˈtiːdiəs/ *adj* tedioso

tedium /ˈtiːdiəm/ *n* tedio

teem /tiːm/ *vi* ~ **with sth** estar a rebosar de algo

teenage /ˈtiːneɪdʒ/ *adj* de adolescentes

teenager *n* adolescente

teens /tiːnz/ *n* [*pl*] edad entre los 13 y los 19 años

tee shirt *Ver* T-SHIRT

teeth *plural de* TOOTH

teethe /tiːð/ *vi* echar los dientes LOC **teething problems/troubles** dificultades menores en los inicios de un negocio

telecommunications /ˌtelɪkəˌmjuːnɪˈkeɪʃnz/ *n* [*pl*] telecomunicaciones

telegraph /ˈtelɪgrɑːf; *USA* -græf/ *n* telégrafo

telephone /ˈtelɪfəʊn/ ◆ *n* (*tb* **phone**) teléfono: *telephone call* llamada telefónica ◊ *telephone book/directory* guía telefónica LOC **on the telephone 1** *We're not on the telephone.* No tenemos teléfono. **2** *She's on the telephone.* Está hablando por teléfono. ◆ *vt, vi* llamar por teléfono, telefonear (a algo/algn)

telephone box (*tb* **phone box**, **telephone booth**, **phone booth**) *n* cabina telefónica

telescope /ˈtelɪskəʊp/ *n* telescopio

televise /ˈtelɪvaɪz/ *vt* televisar

television /ˈtelɪvɪʒn/ (*GB, coloq* **telly**) *n* (*abrev* **TV**) **1** televisión: *to watch television* ver la televisión **2** (*tb* **television set**) televisor

> En Gran Bretaña hay cuatro cadenas de televisión nacionales: BBC1, BBC2, ITV y Channel 4. En ITV y Channel 4 hay publicidad (son **commercial channels**). La BBC1 y BBC2 no tienen publicidad y se financian a través del pago de licencias (**TV licence**).

telex /ˈteleks/ *n* télex

tell /tel/ (*pret, pp* **told** /təʊld/) **1** *vt* decir: *to tell the truth* decir la verdad

> En estilo indirecto **tell** va generalmente seguido por un objeto directo de persona: *Tell him to wait.* Dile que espere. ◊ *She told him to hurry up.* Le dijo que se diera prisa. *Ver nota en* SAY

2 *vt* contar: *Tell me all about it.* Cuéntamelo todo. ◊ *Promise you won't tell.* Promete que no lo contarás. **3** *vt, vi* saber: *You can tell she's French.* Salta a la vista que es francesa. **4** *vt* ~ **A from B** distinguir A de B LOC **I told you (so)** (*coloq*) ya te lo dije **there's no telling** es imposible saberlo **to tell the time** (*USA* **to tell time**) decir la hora **you never can tell** nunca se sabe **you're telling me!** (*coloq*) ¡Me lo vas a decir a mí! PHR V **to tell sb off (for sth/doing sth)** (*coloq*) reñir a algn (por algo/hacer algo) **to tell on sb** (*coloq*) chivarse de algn

telling /ˈtelɪŋ/ *adj* revelador, significativo

telling-off /ˌtelɪŋ ˈɒf/ *n* bronca

telly /ˈteli/ *n* (*pl* **-ies**) (*GB, coloq*) tele

temp /temp/ *n* (*coloq*) empleado, -a temporal

temper[1] /ˈtempə(r)/ *n* humor, genio: *to get into a temper* ponerse de mal genio LOC **in a (bad, foul, rotten, etc) temper** de mal genio **to keep/lose your temper** dominarse/perder los estribos *Ver tb* QUICK, SHORT[1]

temper[2] /ˈtempə(r)/ *vt* ~ **sth (with sth)** templar algo (con algo)

temperament /ˈtemprəmənt/ *n* temperamento

temperamental /ˌtemprəˈmentl/ *adj* temperamental

temperate /ˈtempərət/ *adj* **1** (*comportamiento, carácter*) moderado **2** (*clima, región*) templado

temperature /ˈtemprətʃə(r); *USA* -tʃʊər/ *n* temperatura LOC **to have/run a temperature** tener fiebre

template /ˈtempleɪt/ *n* plantilla

temple /ˈtempl/ *n* **1** (*Relig*) templo **2** (*Anat*) sien

tempo /ˈtempəʊ/ *n* (*pl* **~s** *Mús* **tempi** /ˈtempiː/) **1** (*Mús*) tiempo **2** (*fig*) ritmo

temporary /ˈtemprəri; *USA* -pəreri/ *adj* temporal, provisional **temporarily** *adv* temporalmente

tempt /tempt/ *vt* tentar **temptation** *n* tentación **tempting** *adj* tentador

ten /ten/ *adj, pron, n* diez ☛ *Ver ejemplos en* FIVE **tenth 1** *adj* décimo **2** *pron, adv* el décimo, la décima, los décimos, las décimas **3** *n* décima parte, décimo ☛ *Ver ejemplos en* FIFTH

tenacious /təˈneɪʃəs/ *adj* tenaz

tenacity /təˈnæsəti/ *n* tenacidad

tenant /ˈtenənt/ *n* inquilino, -a, arrendatario, -a **tenancy** *n* (*pl* **-ies**) inquilinato, arrendamiento

tend /tend/ **1** *vt* cuidar, atender **2** *vi* ~ **to (do sth)** tender, tener tendencia a (hacer algo) **tendency** *n* (*pl* **-ies**) tendencia, propensión

tender /ˈtendə(r)/ *adj* **1** (*planta/carne*) tierno **2** (*herida*) dolorido **3** (*mirada*) cariñoso **tenderly** *adv* tiernamente, con ternura **tenderness** *n* ternura

tendon /ˈtendən/ *n* tendón

tenement /ˈtenəmənt/ *n*: *a tenement block/tenement house* bloque de pisos

tenner /ˈtenə(r)/ *n* (*GB, coloq*) (billete de) diez libras

tennis /ˈtenɪs/ *n* tenis

tenor /ˈtenə(r)/ *n* tenor

tense[1] /tens/ *adj* (**-er**, **-est**) tenso

tense[2] /tens/ *n* (*Gram*) tiempo: *in the past tense* en tiempo pasado

tension /ˈtenʃn/ *n* tensión, tirantez

tent /tent/ *n* **1** tienda (de campaña) **2** (*de circo*) carpa

tentacle /ˈtentəkl/ *n* tentáculo

tentative /ˈtentətɪv/ *adj* **1** provisional **2** cauteloso

tenth *Ver* TEN

tenuous /ˈtenjuəs/ *adj* tenue

tenure /ˈtenjʊə(r); *USA* -jər/ *n* **1** (*de un puesto*) estancia: *security of tenure* derecho de permanencia **2** (*de tierra, propiedad*) tenencia

tepid /ˈtepɪd/ *adj* tibio

term /tɜːm/ ◆ *n* **1** periodo, plazo: *term of office* mandato (de un gobierno) ◊ *the long-term risks* los riesgos a largo plaz[o] **2** trimestre: *the autumn/spring[/] summer term* el primer/segundo/terce[r] trimestre **3** expresión, término *Ver t[b]* TERMS LOC **in the long/short term** [a] largo/corto plazo ◆ *vt* (*fml*) calificar d[e]

terminal /ˈtɜːmɪnl/ *adj, n* terminal

terminate /ˈtɜːmɪneɪt/ **1** *vt, vi* term[i]nar: *This train terminates at Eusto[n].* Este tren tiene su término en Euston. [2] *vt* (*contrato, etc*) rescindir

terminology /ˌtɜːmɪˈnɒlədʒi/ *n* ([*pl*] **-ies**) terminología

terminus /ˈtɜːmɪnəs/ *n* (*pl* **termi[ni]** /ˈtɜːmɪnaɪ/ *o* **~es** /-nəsɪz/) (estació[n]) terminal

terms /tɜːmz/ *n* [*pl*] **1** condiciones [2] términos LOC **to be on good, bad, e[tc] terms (with sb)** tener buenas, mal[as], etc relaciones con algn **to come [to] terms with sth/sb** aceptar algo/a al[gn] *Ver tb* EQUAL

terrace /ˈterəs/ *n* **1** terraza **2 the te[r]races** [*pl*] (*Dep*) las gradas **3** hilera [de] casas adosadas **4** (*tb* **terraced hous[e]**) casa adosada ☛ *Ver* pág 321. **5** (*Ag[ri]cultura*) bancal, terraza

terrain /təˈreɪn/ *n* terreno

terrible /ˈterəbl/ *adj* **1** (*acciden[te]*

heridas) terrible **2** (*coloq*) fatal, terrible **terribly** *adv* terriblemente: *I'm terribly sorry.* Lo siento muchísimo

terrific /təˈrɪfɪk/ *adj* (*coloq*) **1** tremendo **2** fabuloso: *The food was terrific value.* La comida era baratísima.

terrify /ˈterɪfaɪ/ *vt* (*pret, pp* **-fied**) aterrorizar **terrified** *adj* aterrorizado: *She's terrified of flying.* Le aterra volar. LOC *Ver* WIT **terrifying** *adj* aterrador, espantoso

territorial /ˌterəˈtɔːriəl/ *adj* territorial

territory /ˈterətri; *USA* -tɔːri/ *n* (*pl* **-ies**) territorio **territorial** *adj* territorial

terror /ˈterə(r)/ *n* terror: *to scream with terror* gritar de terror

terrorism /ˈterərɪzəm/ *n* terrorismo **terrorist** *n* terrorista

terrorize, -ise /ˈterəraɪz/ *vt* aterrorizar

terse /tɜːs/ *adj* lacónico: *a terse reply* una respuesta seca

test /test/ ◆ *n* **1** prueba: *blood test* análisis de sangre **2** (*Educ*) test, examen: *I'll give you a test on Thursday.* Os pondré una prueba el jueves. ◆ *vt* **1** probar, poner a prueba **2** ~ **sth for sth** someter algo a pruebas de algo **3** ~ **sb** (**on sth**) (*Educ*) examinar a algn (de algo)

testament /ˈtestəmənt/ *n* (*fml*) ~ (**to sth**) testimonio (de algo)

testicle /ˈtestɪkl/ *n* testículo

testify /ˈtestɪfaɪ/ *vt, vi* (*pret, pp* **-fied**) declarar

testimony /ˈtestɪməni; *USA* -məʊni/ *n* (*pl* **-ies**) testimonio

test tube *n* tubo de ensayo: *test-tube baby* niño probeta

tether /ˈteðə(r)/ ◆ *vt* (*animal*) atar ◆ *n* LOC *Ver* END

text /tekst/ *n* texto: *set text* lectura obligatoria

textbook /ˈtekstbʊk/ *n* libro de texto

textile /ˈtekstaɪl/ *n* [*gen pl*] textil

texture /ˈtekstʃə(r)/ *n* textura

than /ðən, ðæn/ *conj, prep* **1** [*después de comparativo*] que: *faster than ever* más rápido que nunca ◇ *better than he thought* mejor de lo que había pensado **2** (*con tiempo y distancia*) de: *more than an hour/a kilometre* más de una hora/un kilómetro

thank /θæŋk/ *vt* ~ **sb** (**for sth/doing sth**) dar las gracias a algn (por algo/hacer algo); agradecer algo a algn LOC **thank you** gracias

thankful /ˈθæŋkfl/ *adj* agradecido

thanks /θæŋks/ ◆ *interj* (*coloq*) ¡gracias!: *Thanks for coming!* ¡Gracias por venir! ◆ *n* LOC *Ver* VOTE

thanksgiving /ˌθæŋksˈɡɪvɪŋ/ *n* acción de gracias: *Thanksgiving (Day)* Día de Acción de Gracias

that[1] /ðət, ðæt/ *conj* que: *I told him that he should wait.* Le dije que esperase.

that[2] /ðət, ðæt/ *pron rel* **1** [*sujeto*] que: *The letter that came is from him.* La carta que ha llegado es de él. **2** [*complemento*] que: *These are the books (that) I bought.* Estos son los libros que compré. ◇ *the job (that) I applied for* el trabajo que solicité **3** [*con expresiones temporales*] en que: *the year that he died* el año en que murió

that[3] /ðæt/ ◆ *adj* (*pl* **those** /ðəʊz/) ese, aquel ◆ *pron* (*pl* **those** /ðəʊz/) eso, ése, -a, ésos, -as, aquello, aquél, -lla, aquéllos, -llas ☛ *Comparar con* THIS LOC **that is** (**to say**) es decir **that's right/it** eso es ◆ *adv*: *that low* así de bajo ◇ *that near* tan cerca

that[4] /ðæt/ *adv* tan: *It's that long.* Es así de largo. ◇ *that much worse* tanto peor

thatch /θætʃ/ *vt* poner un tejado de paja **thatched** *adj* con tejado de paja

thaw /θɔː/ ◆ *vt, vi* deshelar(se) ◆ *n* deshielo

the /ðə/ ☛ Antes de vocal se pronuncia /ði/ o, si se quiere dar énfasis, /ðiː/. *art def* el/la/lo, los/las LOC **the more/less ... the more/less ...** cuanto más/menos ... más/menos ...

El artículo definido en inglés:

1 No se utiliza con sustantivos contables en plural cuando hablamos en general: *Books are expensive.* Los libros son caros. ◇ *Children learn very fast.* Los niños aprenden muy rápido.

2 Se omite con sustantivos incontables cuando se refieren a una sustancia o a una idea en general: *I like cheese/pop music.* Me gusta el queso/la música pop.

3 Normalmente se omite con nombres propios y con nombres que indican relaciones familiares: *Mrs Smith* la Sra

Smith ◊ *Ana's mother* la madre de Ana ◊ *Granny came yesterday.* Ayer vino la abuela.
4 Con las partes del cuerpo y los objetos personales se suele usar el posesivo en vez del artículo: *Give me **your hand**.* Dame la mano. ◊ *He put **his tie** on.* Se puso la corbata.
5 Hospital, **school** y **church** pueden utilizarse con artículo o sin él, pero el significado es distinto. *Ver nota en* SCHOOL

theatre (*USA* **theater**) /ˈθɪətə(r); *USA* ˈθiːətər/ *n* teatro LOC *Ver* LECTURE

theatrical /θiˈætrɪkl/ *adj* teatral, de teatro

theft /θeft/ *n* robo

Theft es el término que se utiliza para los robos que se realizan sin que nadie los vea y sin recurrir a la violencia: *car/cattle thefts* robos de coches/ganado, **robbery** se refiere a los robos llevados a cabo por medio de la violencia o con amenazas: *armed/bank robbery* robo a mano armada/de un banco y **burglary** se usa para los robos en casas o tiendas cuando los dueños están ausentes. *Ver tb notas en* THIEF *y* ROB

their /ðeə(r)/ *adj pos* su(s) (*de ellos*): *What colour is their cat?* ¿De qué color es su gato? ☛ *Ver nota en* MY

theirs /ðeəz/ *pron pos* suyo, -a, -os, -as (*de ellos*): *a friend of theirs* un amigo suyo ◊ *Our flat is not as big as theirs.* Nuestro piso no es tan grande como el suyo.

them /ðəm, ðem/ *pron pers* **1** [*como objeto directo*] los, las: *I saw them yesterday.* Los vi ayer. **2** [*como objeto indirecto*] les: *Tell them to wait.* Diles que esperen. **3** [*después de preposición o del verbo* **to be**] ellos/ellas: *Go with them.* Ve con ellos. ◊ *They took it with them.* Lo llevaron consigo. ◊ *Was it them at the door?* ¿Eran ellos los que han llamado? ☛ *Comparar con* THEY

theme /θiːm/ *n* tema

themselves /ðəmˈselvz/ *pron* **1** [*uso reflexivo*] se: *They enjoyed themselves a lot.* Se lo pasaron muy bien. **2** [*con preposición*] sí mismos, as: *They were talking about themselves.* Hablaban de sí mismos. **3** [*uso enfático*] ellos, -as mismos, -as: *Did they paint the house themselves?* ¿Pintaron la casa ellos mismos?

then /ðen/ *adv* **1** entonces: *until then* hasta entonces ◊ *from then on* desde entonces **2** en aquella época: *Life was harder then.* La vida era más dura en aquella época. **3** luego, después: *the soup and then the chicken* la sopa y luego el pollo **4** (*así que*) en ese caso, pues: *You're not coming, then?* ¿Así que no vienes?

theology /θiˈɒlədʒi/ *n* teología **theological** /ˌθiːəˈlɒdʒɪkl/ *adj* teológico

theoretical /ˌθɪəˈretɪkl/ *adj* teórico

theory /ˈθɪəri/ *n* (*pl* **-ies**) teoría: *in theory* en teoría

therapeutic /ˌθerəˈpjuːtɪk/ *adj* terapéutico

therapist /ˈθerəpɪst/ *n* terapeuta

therapy /ˈθerəpi/ *n* terapia

there /ðeə(r)/ ◆ *adv* ahí, allí, allá: *My car is there, in front of the pub.* Mi coche está allí, delante del bar. LOC **there and then** en el acto, allí mismo *Ver tb* HERE ◆ *pron* LOC **there + to be**: *There's someone at the door.* Hay alguien en la puerta. ◊ *How many are there?* ¿Cuántos hay? ◊ *There'll be twelve guests at the party.* Habrá doce invitados en la fiesta. ◊ *There was a terrible accident yesterday.* Hubo un accidente horrible ayer. ◊ *There has been very little rain recently.* Ha llovido muy poco últimamente. ☛ *Ver nota en* HABER **there + v modal + be**: *There must be no mistakes.* No debe haber ningún error. ◊ *There might be rain later.* Podría haber chubascos más tarde. ◊ *There shouldn't be any problems.* No creo que haya ningún problema. ◊ *How can there be that many?* ¿Cómo es posible que haya tantos?

There se usa también con **seem** y **appear**: *There seem/appear to be two ways of looking at this problem.* Parece que hay dos formas de ver este problema.

thereafter /ˌðeərˈɑːftə(r); *USA* -ˈæf-/ *adv* (*fml*) a partir de entonces

thereby /ˌðeəˈbaɪ/ *adv* (*fml*) **1** por eso/ello **2** de este modo

therefore /ˈðeəfɔː(r)/ *adv* por (lo) tanto, por consiguiente

thermal /ˈθɜːml/ *adj* **1** térmico **2** (*fuente*) termal

thermometer /θəˈmɒmɪtə(r)/ *n* termómetro

thermostat /ˈθɜːməstæt/ *n* termostato

these /ðiːz/ ◆ *adj* [*pl*] estos, -as ◆ *pron* [*pl*] éstos, -as *Ver tb* THIS

thesis /ˈθiːsɪs/ *n* (*pl* **theses** /ˈθiːsiːz/) tesis

they /ðeɪ/ *pron pers* ellos/ellas: *They didn't like it.* No les gustó. ☛ El *pron pers* no se puede omitir en inglés. *Comparar con* THEM

they'd /ðeɪd/ **1** = THEY HAD *Ver* HAVE **2** = THEY WOULD *Ver* WOULD

they'll /ðeɪl/ = THEY WILL *Ver* WILL

they're /ðeə(r)/ = THEY ARE *Ver* BE

they've /ðeɪv/ = THEY HAVE *Ver* HAVE

thick /θɪk/ ◆ *adj* (**-er**, **-est**) **1** grueso: *The ice was six inches thick.* El hielo tenía quince centímetros de grosor. **2** espeso: *This sauce is too thick.* Esta salsa está demasiado espesa. **3** (*barba*) poblado **4** (*acento*) marcado **5** (*coloq*) (*persona*) negado ◆ *adv* (**-er**, **-est**) (*tb* **thickly**) grueso: *Don't spread the butter too thick.* No te pongas demasiada mantequilla. ◆ *n* LOC **in the thick of sth** en medio de algo **through thick and thin** contra viento y marea **thicken** *vt, vi* espesar(se) **thickly** *adv* **1** gruesamente, espesamente **2** (*poblado*) densamente **thickness** *n* espesor, grosor

thief /θiːf/ *n* (*pl* **thieves** /θiːvz/) ladrón, -ona

Thief es el término general que se utiliza para designar a un ladrón que roba cosas, generalmente sin que nadie lo vea y sin recurrir a la violencia, **robber** se aplica a la persona que roba bancos, tiendas, etc, a menudo mediante la violencia o con amenazas, **burglar** se utiliza para los ladrones que roban en una casa o una tienda cuando no hay nadie y **shoplifter** es la persona que se lleva cosas de una tienda sin pagarlas. *Ver tb notas en* ROB *y* THEFT

thigh /θaɪ/ *n* muslo

thimble /ˈθɪmbl/ *n* dedal

thin /θɪn/ ◆ *adj* (**thinner**, **thinnest**) **1** (*persona*) delgado ☛ *Ver nota en* DELGADO **2** fino, delgado **3** (*sopa*) aguado LOC (**to be**) **thin on the ground** (ser) escaso **to vanish, etc into thin air** desaparecer como por arte de magia *Ver tb* THICK ◆ *adv* (**thinner**, **thinnest**) (*tb* **thinly**) fino ◆ *vt, vi* (**-nn-**) ~ (**sth**) (**out**) hacer algo/hacerse menos denso

thing /θɪŋ/ *n* **1** cosa: *What's that thing on the table?* ¿Qué es eso que hay en la mesa? ◊ *I can't see a thing.* No veo nada. ◊ *the main thing* lo más importante ◊ *the first thing* lo primero ◊ *Forget the whole thing.* Olvídate del asunto. ◊ *to take things seriously* tomárselo todo en serio ◊ *The way things are going...* Tal como está la situación... **2 things** cosas: *You can put your things in that drawer.* Puedes poner tus cosas en ese cajón. **3** *Poor (little) thing!* ¡Pobrecito! **4 the thing**: *Just the thing for tired business people.* Justo lo que necesitan los hombres de negocios cansados. LOC **first/last thing** a primera/última hora **for one thing** para empezar **to be a good thing (that)...** menos mal (que)...: *It was a good thing that...* Menos mal que... **to get/keep things in proportion** ver el asunto en su justa medida **the thing is...** la cosa es que...

think /θɪŋk/ (*pret, pp* **thought** /θɔːt/) **1** *vt, vi* pensar: *What are you thinking (about)?* ¿En qué estás pensando? ◊ *Just think!* ¡Imagínate! ◊ *Who'd have thought it?* ¿Quién lo hubiera pensado? ◊ *The job took longer than we thought.* El trabajo nos llevó más de lo que habíamos pensado. **2** *vi* reflexionar **3** *vt* creer: *I (don't) think so.* Creo que sí/no. ◊ *What do you think (of her)?* ¿Qué opinas (de ella)? ◊ *It would be nice, don't you think?* Sería estupendo, ¿no te parece? ◊ *I think this is the house.* Me parece que ésta es la casa. LOC **I should think so!** ¡faltaría más! **to think the world of sb** tener a algn en alta estima *Ver tb* GREAT

PHR V **to think about sth/sb 1** reflexionar sobre algo/algn **2** recordar algo/a algn **3** tener algo/a algn en cuenta **to think about (doing) sth** pensar en (hacer) algo: *I'll think about it.* Lo pensaré.

to think of sth 1 pensar en algo **2** imaginar algo **3** recordar algo

to think sth out: *a well thought out plan* un plan bien pensado

to think sth over reflexionar sobre algo

to think sth up (*coloq*) inventar/pensar algo

thinker /ˈθɪŋkə(r)/ *n* pensador, -ora

thinking /ˈθɪŋkɪŋ/ ◆ *n* [*incontable*] forma de pensar: *What's your thinking on this?* ¿Qué piensas de esto? ◊ *Quick thinking* ¡Bien pensado! LOC *Ver* WISHFUL *en* WISH ◆ *adj* [*sólo antes de sustantivo*] racional, inteligente: *thinking people* gente inteligente

third (*abrev* **3rd**) /θɜːd/ ◆ *adj* tercero ◆ *pron, adv* el tercero, la tercera, los terceros, las terceras ◆ *n* **1** tercio, tercera parte **2 the third** el (día) tres **3** (*tb* **third gear**) tercera ☛ *Ver ejemplos en* FIFTH **thirdly** *adv* en tercer lugar (*en una enumeración*)

third party *n* tercera persona

the Third World *n* el Tercer Mundo

thirst /θɜːst/ *n* ~ (**for sth**) sed (de algo) **thirsty** *adj* (**-ier**, **-iest**) sediento: *to be thirsty* tener sed

thirteen /ˌθɜːˈtiːn/ *adj, pron, n* trece ☛ *Ver ejemplos en* FIVE **thirteenth 1** *adj* decimotercero **2** *pron, adv* el decimotercero, la decimotercera, los decimoterceros, las decimoterceras **3** *n* treceava parte, treceavo ☛ *Ver ejemplos en* FIFTH

thirty /ˈθɜːti/ *adj, pron, n* treinta ☛ *Ver ejemplos en* FIFTY, FIVE **thirtieth 1** *adj, pron* trigésimo **2** *n* treintava parte, treintavo ☛ *Ver ejemplos en* FIFTH

this /ðɪs/ ◆ *adj* (*pl* **these** /ðiːz/) este, -a, estos, -as: *I don't like this colour.* No me gusta este color. ◊ *This one suits me.* Éste me favorece. ◊ *These shoes are more comfortable than those.* Estos zapatos son más cómodos que ésos. ☛ *Comparar con* THAT[3], TONIGHT ◆ *pron* (*pl* **these** /ðiːz/) **1** éste, -a, éstos, -as: *This is John's father.* Éste es el padre de John. ◊ *I prefer these.* Prefiero éstos. **2** esto: *Listen to this*... Escucha esto... ◆ *adv*: *this high* así de alto ◊ *this far* tan lejos

thistle /ˈθɪsl/ *n* cardo

thorn /θɔːn/ *n* espina (*de rosal, etc*) **thorny** *adj* (**-ier**, **-iest**) espinoso

thorough /ˈθʌrə; *USA* ˈθʌrəʊ/ *adj* **1** (*investigación, conocimiento*) a fondo **2** (*persona*) meticuloso **thoroughly** *adv* **1** a conciencia **2** enormemente

those /ðəʊz/ ◆ *adj* [*pl*] aquellos, -as, esos, -as ◆ *pron* [*pl*] aquéllos, -as, ésos, -as *Ver tb* THAT[3]

though /ðəʊ/ ◆ *conj* aunque, pero ◆ *adv* (*coloq*) de todas formas

thought[1] *pret, pp de* THINK

thought[2] /θɔːt/ *n* **1** pensamiento: *deep/lost in thought* perdido en sus propios pensamientos **2** ~ (**of doing sth**) idea (de hacer algo) LOC *Ver* FOOD, SCHOOL, SECOND, TRAIN[1] **thoughtful** *adj* **1** pensativo **2** atento: *It was very thoughtful of you.* Fue todo un detalle por tu parte. **thoughtless** *adj* desconsiderado

thousand /ˈθaʊznd/ *adj, pron, n* mil ☛ *Ver ejemplos en* FIVE **thousandth 1** *adj, pron* milésimo **2** *n* milésima parte ☛ *Ver ejemplos en* FIFTH

thrash /θræʃ/ *vt* dar una paliza a **thrashing** *n* paliza

thread /θred/ ◆ *n* ~ (**of sth**) hilo (de algo): *a needle and thread* aguja e hilo ◆ *vt* **1** enhebrar **2** (*perlas, cuentas, etc*) ensartar **3** (*cuerda, cable, etc*) pasar

threat /θret/ *n* ~ (**to sth/sb**) (**of sth**) amenaza (para algo/algn) (de algo): *a threat to national security* una amenaza para la seguridad nacional **threaten** *vt* **1** ~ **sth/sb** (**with sth**) amenazar algo/a algn (con algo) **2** ~ **to do sth** amenazar con hacer algo **threatening** *adj* amenazador

three /θriː/ *adj, pron, n* tres ☛ *Ver ejemplos en* FIVE

three-dimensional /ˌθriː daɪˈmenʃənl/ (*tb* **3-D** /ˌθriː ˈdiː/) *adj* tridimensional

threshold /ˈθreʃhəʊld/ *n* umbral

threw *pret de* THROW[1]

thrill /θrɪl/ *n* **1** escalofrío **2** emoción: *What a thrill!* ¡Que emoción! **thrilled** *adj* entusiasmado, emocionado **thriller** *n* obra de suspense (*película, novela, etc*) **thrilling** *adj* emocionante

thrive /θraɪv/ *vi* ~ (**on sth**) prosperar, crecerse (con algo): *a thriving industry* una industria floreciente

throat /θrəʊt/ *n* garganta: *a sore throat* dolor de garganta

throb /θrɒb/ ◆ *vi* (**-bb-**) ~ (**with sth**) vibrar, palpitar (de algo) ◆ *n* vibración, palpitación

throne /θrəʊn/ *n* trono

through (*USA tb* **thru**) /θruː/ ◆ *prep* a través de, por: *She made her way* *through the traffic.* Se hizo paso a través del tráfico. ◊ *to breathe through your nose* respirar por la nariz **2** durante, a lo largo de: *I'm halfway through the book.* Ya voy por la mitad del libro. **3** por (culpa de): *through carelessness* por descuido **4** (*USA*) hasta ... inclusive: *Tuesday through Friday* de martes a viernes ◆ *part adv* **1** de un lado a otro: *Can you get through?* ¿Puedes pasar al otro lado? **2** de principio a fin: *I've read the poem through once.* Me he leído el poema entero una vez. ◊ *all night through* toda la noche ☛ Para los usos de **through** en PHRASAL VERBS ver las entradas de los verbos correspondientes, p.ej. **to break through** en BREAK. ◆ *adj* directo: *a through train* un tren directo ◊ *No through road* Callejón sin salida

throughout /θruːˈaʊt/ ◆ *prep* por todo, durante todo: *throughout his life* toda su vida ◆ *adv* **1** por todas partes **2** todo el tiempo

throw¹ /θrəʊ/ *vt* (*pret* **threw** /θruː/ *pp* **thrown** /θrəʊn/) **1** ~ **sth** (**to sth/sb**) tirar, echar algo (a algo/algn): *Throw the ball to Mary.* Tírale la pelota a Mary. **2** ~ **sth** (**at sth/sb**) tirar, lanzar algo (a algo/algn) ☛ **To throw sth at sth/sb** indica que la intención es de darle a un objeto o de hacerle daño a una persona: *Don't throw stones at the cat.* No le tires piedras al gato. **3** [+ *loc adv*] echar: *He threw back his head.* Echó la cabeza atrás. ◊ *She threw up her hands in horror.* Levantó los brazos horrorizada. **4** (*caballo, etc*) derribar **5** (*coloq*) desconcertar **6** dejar (*de cierta forma*): *to be thrown out of work* quedarse sin trabajo ◊ *We were thrown into confusion by the news.* La noticia nos dejó confusos. **7** (*luz, sombra*) proyectar LOC *Ver* CAUTION, FIT³ PHR V **to throw sth about/around** desparramar algo **to throw sth away** tirar algo (*a la basura*) **to throw sb out** expulsar a algn **to throw sth out 1** (*propuesta, etc*) rechazar algo **2** tirar algo (*a la basura*) **to throw** (**sth**) **up** vomitar (algo)

throw² /θrəʊ/ *n* **1** lanzamiento **2** (*dados, baloncesto, etc*) tiro: *It's your throw.* Te toca a ti (jugar).

thrown *pp de* THROW¹

thru (*USA*) *Ver* THROUGH

thrust /θrʌst/ ◆ (*pret, pp* **thrust**) **1** *vt, vi* meter, clavar, hundir **2** *vt* ~ **sth at sb** tenderle algo a algn (*de malas maneras*) PHR V **to thrust sth/sb on/upon sb** obligar a algn a aceptar algo/a algn, imponer algo a algn ◆ *n* **1** empujón **2** (*de espada*) estocada **3** ~ (**of sth**) idea fundamental (sobre algo)

thud /θʌd/ ◆ *n* ruido (sordo), golpe (sordo) ◆ *vi* (**-dd-**) **1** hacer un ruido sordo, caer con un ruido sordo: *to thud against/into sth* golpear/chocar contra algo con un ruido sordo **2** (*corazón*) latir fuertemente

thug /θʌg/ *n* gamberro, matón

thumb /θʌm/ ◆ *n* pulgar (*de la mano*) LOC *Ver* TWIDDLE ◆ *vi* ~ **through sth** hojear algo LOC **to thumb a lift** hacer dedo *Ver tb* FINGER

thump /θʌmp/ ◆ **1** *vt* golpear, dar un golpe a **2** *vi* (*corazón*) latir fuertemente ◆ *n* **1** puñetazo, porrazo **2** ruido sordo

thunder /ˈθʌndə(r)/ ◆ *n* [*incontable*] trueno: *a clap of thunder* un trueno ◆ *vi* **1** tronar **2** retumbar

thunderstorm /ˈθʌndəstɔːm/ *n* tormenta

Thursday /ˈθɜːzdi, -deɪ/ *n* (*abrev* **Thur**, **Thurs**) jueves ☛ *Ver ejemplos en* MONDAY

thus /ðʌs/ *adv* (*fml*) **1** así, de esta manera **2** (*por esta razón*) por (lo) tanto, así que

thwart /θwɔːt/ *vt* frustrar, impedir

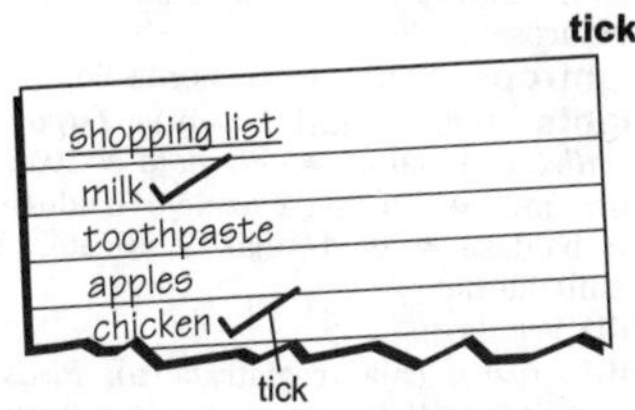

tick /tɪk/ ◆ *n* **1** (*de reloj, etc*) tictac **2** (*marca*) señal ◆ **1** *vi* (*reloj, etc*) hacer tictac **2** *vt*: *to tick sth (off)* marcar algo con una señal PHR V **to tick away/by** pasar **to tick over** ir tirando

ticket /ˈtɪkɪt/ *n* **1** (*tren, etc*) billete **2** (*Teat, Cine*) entrada **3** (*biblioteca*) ficha, tarjeta **4** etiqueta

tickle /ˈtɪkl/ ◆ *vt, vi* hacer cosquillas (a) ◆ *n* cosquilleo, picor

ticklish /ˈtɪklɪʃ/ *adj* que tiene cosquillas: *to be ticklish* tener cosquillas

tidal /ˈtaɪdl/ *adj* de (la) marea

tidal wave *n* maremoto

tide /taɪd/ *n* **1** marea: *The tide is coming in/going out.* La marea está subiendo/bajando. **2** (*fig*) corriente

tidy /ˈtaɪdi/ ◆ *adj* (**tidier**, **tidiest**) **1** ordenado **2** (*apariencia*) pulcro, aseado ◆ *vt* (*pret*, *pp* **tidied**) ~ (**up**) arreglar, ordenar PHR V **to tidy sth away** poner algo en su sitio

tie /taɪ/ ◆ *n* **1** (*tb* **necktie**) corbata **2** [*gen pl*] lazo: *family ties* lazos familiares **3** (*Dep*) empate ◆ *vt, vi* (*pret, pp* **tied** *pt pres* **tying**) **1** atar(se) **2** (*corbata, etc*) anudar(se) **3** (*Dep*) empatar PHR V **to tie sb/yourself down** comprometer(se): *Having young children really ties you down.* Tener niños pequeños ata muchísimo. **to tie sth/sb up** atar algo/a algn

tier /tɪə(r)/ *n* grada, fila, piso

tiger /ˈtaɪgə(r)/ *n* tigre **tigress** *n* tigresa

tight /taɪt/ ◆ *adj* (**-er**, **-est**) **1** apretado, ajustado: *These shoes are too tight.* Estos zapatos me están demasiado justos. **2** tirante **3** (*control*) riguroso ◆ *adv* (**-er**, **-est**) bien, fuertemente: *Hold tight!* ¡Agárrense bien! **tighten** *vt, vi* ~ (**sth**) (**up**) apretar algo/apretarse: *The government wants to tighten immigration controls.* El gobierno quiere hacer más riguroso el control de la inmigración. **tightly** *adv* bien, fuertemente, rigurosamente

tightrope /ˈtaɪtrəʊp/ *n* cuerda floja

tights /taɪts/ *n* [*pl*] **1** pantis **2** (*para ballet, etc*) mallas ☛ *Ver nota en* PAIR

tile /taɪl/ ◆ *n* **1** teja **2** azulejo, baldosín **3** baldosa ◆ *vt* **1** tejar **2** alicatar **3** embaldosar

till[1] *Ver* UNTIL

till[2] /tɪl/ *n* caja (registradora): *Please pay at the till.* Pague en caja, por favor.

tilt /tɪlt/ ◆ *vt, vi* inclinar(se), ladear(se) ◆ *n* inclinación, ladeo

timber /ˈtɪmbə(r)/ *n* **1** madera **2** árboles (madereros) **3** madero, viga

time /taɪm/ ◆ *n* **1** tiempo: *You've been a long time!* ¡Has tardado mucho! **2** hora: *What time is it?/What's the time?* ¿Qué hora es? ◊ *It's time we were going/time for us to go.* Es hora de que nos vayamos. ◊ *by the time we reached home* para cuando llegamos a casa ◊ *(by) this time next year* para estas fechas el año que viene ◊ *at the present time* actualmente **3** vez, ocasión: *last time* la última vez ◊ *every time* cada vez ◊ *for the first time* por primera vez **4** tiempo, época LOC **ahead of time** adelantado **all the time** todo el tiempo (**and**) **about time** (**too**) (*coloq*) ya era hora **at all times** en todo momento **at a time** a la vez: *one at a time* de uno en uno **at one time** en cierta época **at the time** en aquel momento **at times** a veces **for a time** (por) un momento, durante algún tiempo **for the time being** por el momento, de momento **from time to time** de vez en cuando **in good time** temprano, con tiempo **in time** con el tiempo **in time** (**for sth/to do sth**) a tiempo (para algo/para hacer algo) **on time** a la hora, puntual ☛ *Ver nota en* PUNTUAL **time after time**; **time and** (**time**) **again** una y otra vez **to have a good time** pasarlo en grande **to have the time of your life** pasarlo bomba **to take your time** (**over sth/to do sth/doing sth**) tomarse uno el tiempo necesario (para algo/hacer algo) *Ver tb* BIDE, BIG, HARD, KILL, MARK[2], NICK, ONCE, PRESS, SAME, TELL ◆ *vt* **1** programar, prever **2** *to time sth well/badly* escoger un momento oportuno/inoportuno para (hacer) algo **3** medir el tiempo, cronometrar **timer** *n* reloj automático **timing** *n* **1** coordinación: *the timing of the election* la fecha escogida para las elecciones **2** cronometraje

timely /ˈtaɪmli/ *adj* (**-ier**, **-iest**) oportuno

times /taɪmz/ *prep* multiplicado por: *Three times four is twelve.* Cuatro por tres son doce.

timetable /ˈtaɪmteɪbl/ (*esp USA* **schedule**) *n* horario

timid /ˈtɪmɪd/ *adj* apocado, temeroso: *the first timid steps towards...* los primeros tímidos pasos hacia ... ◊ *Don't be timid, and...* No tengáis miedo, y...

tin /tɪn/ *n* **1** estaño: *tin foil* papel de estaño **2** (*tb esp USA* **can**) lata: *tin-opener* abrelatas ☛ *Ver dibujo en* CONTAINER *y nota en* LATA

tinge /tɪndʒ/ ◆ *vt* ~ **sth** (**with sth**) (*lit y fig*) teñir algo (de algo) ◆ *n* tinte, matiz

tingle /ˈtɪŋgl/ *vi* **1** hormiguear **2** ~ **with sth** (*fig*) estremecerse de algo

tinker /ˈtɪŋkə(r)/ *vi* ~ (**with sth**) enredar (con algo)

tinned /tɪnd/ *adj* en lata, de lata

tinsel /ˈtɪnsl/ *n* espumillón

tint /tɪnt/ *n* **1** matiz **2** (*peluquería*) tinte **tinted** *adj* **1** (*pelo*) teñido **2** (*gafas*) ahumado

tiny /ˈtaɪni/ *adj* (**tinier**, **tiniest**) diminuto, minúsculo

tip /tɪp/ ◆ *n* **1** punta **2** vertedero, basurero *Ver tb* DUMP **3** propina **4** consejo ◆ (**-pp-**) **1** *vt, vi* **to tip** (**sth**) (**up**) inclinar algo/inclinarse **2** *vt* tirar, verter **3** *vt, vi* dar (una) propina (a) PHR V **to tip sb off** (*coloq*) dar el soplo a algn **to tip** (**sth**) **over** volcarse, volcar algo

tiptoe /ˈtɪptəʊ/ ◆ *n* LOC **on tiptoe** de puntillas ◆ *vi*: *to tiptoe in/out* entrar/ salir de puntillas

tire[1] /ˈtaɪə(r)/ *vt, vi* cansar(se) *vi* ~ **of sth/sb/of doing sth** cansarse, hartarse de algo/algn/de hacer algo PHR V **to tire sb/yourself out** agotar a algn/agotarse **tired** *adj* cansado LOC **tired out** agotado **to be** (**sick and**) **tired of sth/ sb/doing sth** estar harto de algo/algn/ de hacer algo

tire[2] /ˈtaɪə(r)/ *n* (*USA*) *Ver* TYRE

tireless /ˈtaɪələs/ *adj* incansable

tiresome /ˈtaɪsəm/ *adj* **1** (*tarea*) fastidioso **2** (*persona*) pesado

tiring /ˈtaɪrɪŋ/ *adj* cansado: *a long and tiring journey* un viaje largo y cansado

tissue /ˈtɪʃuː/ *n* **1** (*Biol, Bot*) tejido **2** pañuelo de papel **3** (*tb* **tissue-paper**) papel de seda

tit /tɪt/ *n* **1** (*Ornitología*) herrerillo **2** (*coloq*) teta LOC **tit for tat** ojo por ojo, diente por diente

title /ˈtaɪtl/ *n* **1** título: *title page* portada ◊ *title role* papel principal **2** título nobiliario **3** tratamiento **4** ~ (**to sth**) (*Jur*) derecho (a algo): *title deed* título de propiedad

titter /ˈtɪtə(r)/ ◆ *n* risita ◆ *vi* reírse disimuladamente

to /tə, tuː/ *prep* **1** (*dirección*) a: *to go to the beach* ir a la playa ◊ *the road to Edinburgh* la carretera de Edimburgo **2** [*con objeto indirecto*] a: *He gave it to Bob.* Se lo dio a Bob. **3** hacia: *Move to the left.* Muévete hacia la izquierda. **4** hasta: *faithful to the end/last* leal hasta el final **5** (*duración*): *It lasts two to three hours.* Dura entre dos y tres horas. **6** (*tiempo*): *ten to one* la una menos diez **7** de: *the key to the door* la llave de la puerta **8** (*comparación*) a: *I prefer walking to climbing.* Prefiero andar a escalar. **9** (*proporción*) por: *How many miles to the gallon?* ¿Cuantos kilómetros hace por litro? **10** (*propósito*): *to go to sb's aid* ir en ayuda de algn **11** para: *to my surprise* para mi sorpresa **12** (*opinión*) a, para: *It looks red to me.* A mí me parece rojo. LOC **to and fro** de un lado a otro

> La partícula **to** se utiliza para formar el infinitivo en inglés y tiene varios usos: *to go* ir ◊ *to eat* comer ◊ *I came to see you.* Vine para/a verte. ◊ *He didn't know what to do.* No sabía qué hacer. ◊ *It's for you to decide.* Tienes que decidirlo tú.

toad /təʊd/ *n* sapo

toast /təʊst/ ◆ *n* [*incontable*] **1** tostada: *a slice/piece of toast* una tostada ◊ *toast and jam* tostadas con mermelada ◊ *Would you like some toast?* ¿Quieres tostadas? **2** brindis ◆ *vt* **1** tostar **2** brindar por **toaster** *n* tostadora

tobacco /təˈbækəʊ/ *n* (*pl* ~**s**) tabaco **tobacconist's** *n* estanco ☛ *Ver nota en* ESTANCO

today /təˈdeɪ/ *adv, n* **1** hoy **2** hoy (en) día: *Today's computers are very small.* Los ordenadores de hoy en día son muy pequeños.

toddler /ˈtɒdlə(r)/ *n* niño, -a (*que acaba de aprender a andar*)

toe /təʊ/ ◆ *n* **1** dedo (*del pie*): *big toe* dedo gordo (del pie) ☛ *Comparar con* FINGER **2** punta (*de calcetín*), puntera (*de zapato*) LOC **on your toes** alerta ◆ *vt* (*pret, pp* **toed** *pt pres* **toeing**) LOC **to toe the line** conformarse

toenail /ˈtəʊneɪl/ *n* uña del pie

toffee /ˈtɒfi; *USA* ˈtɔːfi/ *n* caramelo

together /təˈgeðə(r)/ *part adv* **1** juntos: *Can we have lunch together?* ¿Podemos comer juntos? **2** a la vez: *Don't all talk together.* No habléis todos a la vez. LOC **together with** junto con, además de *Ver tb* ACT ☛ Para los usos de **together** en PHRASAL VERBS ver las entradas de los verbos correspondientes, p.ej. **to pull**

yourself together en PULL. **togetherness** *n* unidad, armonía

toil /tɔɪl/ ◆ *vi* (*fml*) trabajar duramente ◆ *n* (*fml*) trabajo, esfuerzo *Ver tb* WORK[1]

toilet /ˈtɔɪlət/ *n* **1** wáter, retrete: *toilet paper* papel higiénico **2** (*en casa*) aseo **3** (*público*) aseos, servicios

En inglés británico se dice **toilet** o **loo** (*coloq*) para referirnos al aseo de las casas particulares (**lavatory** y **WC** han caído en desuso). **The Gents**, **the Ladies**, **the toilets**, **the cloakroom** o **public conveniences** se usan si hablamos de los servicios en lugares públicos.

En inglés norteamericano se dice **lavatory**, **toilet** o **bathroom** si es en una casa particular, y **washroom** o **restroom** en edificios públicos.

toiletries *n* [*pl*] productos de tocador

token /ˈtəʊkən/ ◆ *n* **1** señal, muestra **2** ficha **3** vale ◆ *adj* simbólico (*pago, muestra, etc*)

told *pret, pp de* TELL

tolerate /ˈtɒləreɪt/ *vt* tolerar **tolerance** *n* tolerancia **tolerant** *adj* ~ (**of/towards sth/sb**) tolerante (con algo/algn)

toll /təʊl/ *n* **1** peaje **2** número de víctimas LOC **to take its toll (of sth)** cobrarse su saldo (de algo)

tomato /təˈmɑːtəʊ; *USA* təˈmeɪtəʊ *n*/ (*pl* **-oes**) tomate

tomb /tuːm/ *n* tumba **tombstone** *n* lápida

tom-cat /ˈtɒm kæt/ (*tb* **tom**) *n* gato (macho) ☛ *Ver nota en* GATO

tomorrow /təˈmɒrəʊ/ *n, adv* mañana: *tomorrow morning* mañana por la mañana ◊ *a week tomorrow* dentro de ocho días ◊ *See you tomorrow.* Hasta mañana. LOC *Ver* DAY

ton /tʌn/ *n* **1** 2.240 libras o 1.016 Kg ☛ *Comparar con* TONNE **2 tons** [*pl*] (**of sth**) (*coloq*) montones (de algo)

tone /təʊn/ ◆ *n* **1** tono: *Don't speak to me in that tone of voice.* No me hables en ese tono. **2** tonalidad ◆ PHR V **to tone sth down** suavizar (el tono de) algo

tongs /tɒŋz/ *n* [*pl*] tenazas: *a pair of tongs* unas tenazas ☛ *Ver nota en* PAIR

tongue /tʌŋ/ *n* **1** lengua **2** (*fml*) idioma, lengua *Ver tb* MOTHER TONGUE *en* MOTHER LOC **to put/stick your tongue out** sacar la lengua **(with) tongue in cheek** irónicamente

tonic /ˈtɒnɪk/ *n* **1** tónico **2** (*tb* **tonic water**) (agua) tónica

tonight /təˈnaɪt/ *n, adv* esta noche: *What's on TV tonight?* ¿Qué pasan en la tele esta noche?

tonne /tʌn/ *n* tonelada (métrica) ☛ *Comparar con* TON

tonsil /ˈtɒnsl/ *n* amígdala **tonsillitis** /ˌtɒnsəˈlaɪtɪs/ *n* [*incontable*] amigdalitis

too /tuː/ *adv* **1** también: *I've been to Paris too.* Yo también he estado en París. ☛ *Ver nota en* TAMBIÉN **2** demasiado: *It's too cold outside.* Hace demasiado frío en la calle. **3** para colmo, encima: *Her purse was stolen. And on her birthday too.* Le robaron el monedero, y encima en su cumpleaños. **4** muy: *I'm not too sure.* No estoy muy segura.

took *pret de* TAKE

tool /tuːl/ *n* herramienta: *tool box/kit* caja/juego de herramientas

tooth /tuːθ/ *n* (*pl* **teeth** /tiːθ/) diente: *to have a tooth out* sacarse una muela ◊ *false teeth* dentadura postiza LOC *Ver* FIGHT, GRIT, SKIN, SWEET

toothache /ˈtuːθeɪk/ *n* dolor de muelas

toothbrush /ˈtuːθbrʌʃ/ *n* cepillo de dientes ☛ *Ver dibujo en* BRUSH

toothpaste /ˈtuːθpeɪst/ *n* pasta de dientes

toothpick /ˈtuːθpɪk/ *n* mondadientes

top[1] /tɒp/ ◆ *n* **1** lo más alto, la parte de arriba: *the top of the page* la cabecera de la página **2** (*de colina, fig*) cumbre **3** (*de una lista*) cabeza **4** tapón **5** prenda de vestir que se lleva en la parte superior del cuerpo LOC **at the top of your voice** a voz en grito **to be on top (of sth)** dominar (algo) **off the top of your head** (*coloq*) sin pensarlo **on top** encima **on top of sth/sb 1** sobre algo/algn **2** además de algo/algn: *And on top of all that…* Y para colmo… ◆ *adj* **1** superior: *a top floor flat* un piso en la última planta ◊ *top quality* calidad suprema ◊ *the top jobs* los mejores empleos ◊ *a top British scientist* un científico británico de primera fila **2** máximo ◆ *vt* (**-pp-**) rematar: *ice cream topped with chocolate sauce* helado con crema de chocolate por encima ◊ *and to top it all…* y para acabarlo de rematar... PHR V **to top sth up** rellenar algo: *We topped up our glasses.* Llenamos los vasos otra vez.

top[2] /tɒp/ *n* peonza

top hat (*tb* **topper**) *n* chistera

topic /ˈtɒpɪk/ *n* tema **topical** *adj* actual

topple /ˈtɒpl/ ~ **(over) 1** *vt* hacer caer **2** *vi* caerse

top secret *adj* de alto secreto

torch /tɔːtʃ/ *n* **1** linterna **2** antorcha

tore *pret de* TEAR[2]

torment /ˈtɔːment/ ◆ *n* tormento ◆ /tɔːˈment/ *vt* **1** atormentar **2** fastidiar

torn *pp de* TEAR[2]

tortoise /ˈtɔːtəs/ *n* tortuga (*de tierra*) ☛ *Comparar con* TURTLE

torture /ˈtɔːtʃə(r)/ ◆ *n* **1** tortura **2** (*fig*) tormento ◆ *vt* **1** torturar **2** (*fig*) atormentar **torturer** *n* torturador, -ora

Tory /ˈtɔːri/ *n* (*pl* **-ies**) *adj* conservador, -ora: *the Tory Party* el Partido Conservador *Ver tb* CONSERVATIVE ☛ *Comparar con* LABOUR 4, LIBERAL 3

toss /tɒs; *USA* tɔːs/ ◆ **1** *vt* tirar, echar (*descuidadamente o sin fuerza*) **2** *vt* (*la cabeza*) sacudir **3** *vi* agitarse: *to toss and turn* dar vueltas (en la cama) **4** *vt* (*una moneda*) echar a cara o cruz: *to toss sb for sth* jugarle algo a algn a cara o cruz **5** *vi*: *to toss (up) for sth* jugarse algo a cara o cruz ◆ *n* **1** (*de la cabeza*) sacudida **2** (*de una moneda*) echada LOC **to win/lose the toss** ganar/perder al echar la moneda (*fútbol, etc*)

total /ˈtəʊtl/ ◆ *adj, n* total ◆ *vt* (**-ll-**, *USA tb* **-l-**) **1** sumar **2** ascender a **totally** *adv* totalmente

totter /ˈtɒtə(r)/ *vi* **1** titubear **2** tambalearse

touch[1] /tʌtʃ/ **1** *vt, vi* tocar(se) **2** *vt* rozar **3** *vt* [*en frases negativas*] probar: *You've hardly touched your steak.* Apenas si has probado el filete. **4** *vt* conmover **5** *vt* igualar LOC **touch wood** toca madera PHR V **to touch down** aterrizar **to touch on/upon sth** hablar de pasada de algo

touch[2] /tʌtʃ/ *n* **1** toque: *to put the finishing touches to sth* dar el toque final a algo **2** (*tb* **sense of touch**) tacto: *soft to the touch* suave al tacto **3 a** ~ **(of sth)** una pizca, un poco (de algo): *I've got a touch of flu.* Tengo un poco de gripe. ◊ *a touch more garlic* una pizca más de ajo ◊ *It's a touch colder today.* Hoy hace algo más de fresco. **4** maña: *He hasn't lost his touch.* No ha perdido la maña. LOC **at a touch** al menor roce **in/out of touch (with sb)** en/fuera de contacto (con algn) **to be in/out of touch with sth** estar/no estar al corriente de algo **to get/keep in touch with sb** ponerse/mantenerse en contacto con algn *Ver tb* LOSE

touched /tʌtʃt/ *adj* conmovido **touching** *adj* conmovedor

touchy /ˈtʌtʃi/ *adj* (**-ier**, **-iest**) **1** (*persona*) susceptible **2** (*situación, tema, etc*) delicado

tough /tʌf/ *adj* (**-er**, **-est**) **1** duro **2** fuerte, sólido **3** tenaz **4** (*medida*) severo **5** (*carne*) duro **6** (*una decisión, etc*) difícil: *to have a tough time* pasarlo muy mal **7** (*coloq*): *Tough luck!* ¡Mala pata! LOC **(as) tough as old boots** (*coloq*) duro como una suela **to be/get tough (with sb)** ponerse duro (con algn) **toughen** ~ **(up)** *vt, vi* endurecer(se) **toughness** *n* **1** dureza, resistencia **2** firmeza

tour /tʊə(r)/ ◆ *n* **1** excursión **2** visita: *guided tour* visita con guía **3** gira: *to be on tour/go on tour in Spain* estar de gira/hacer una gira por España ☛ *Ver nota en* VIAJE ◆ **1** *vt* recorrer **2** *vi* viajar **3** *vt, vi* (*cantantes, etc*) efectuar una gira (en)

tourism /ˈtʊərɪzəm, ˈtɔːr-/ *n* turismo

tourist /ˈtʊerɪst, tɔːr-/ *n* turista: *tourist attraction* lugar de interés turístico

tournament /ˈtɔːnəmənt; *USA* ˈtɜːrn-/ *n* torneo

tow /təʊ/ ◆ *vt* remolcar PHR V **to tow sth away** llevarse algo a remolque ◆ *n* [*gen sing*] remolque LOC **in tow** (*coloq*): *He had his family in tow.* Llevaba a la familia a remolque.

towards /təˈwɔːdz; *USA* tɔːrdz/ (*tb* **toward** /təˈwɔːd; *USA* tɔːrd/) *prep* **1** (*dirección, tiempo*) hacia: *towards the end of the film* casi al terminar la película **2** con, respecto a: *to be friendly towards sb* ser amable con algn **3** (*propósito*) para: *to put money towards sth* poner dinero para algo

towel /ˈtaʊəl/ *n* toalla

tower /ˈtaʊə(r)/ ◆ *n* torre: *tower block* bloque de pisos alto ◆ PHR V **to tower**

above/over sth/sb alzarse por encima de algo/algn

town /taʊn/ *n* **1** ciudad **2** centro: *to go into town* ir al centro LOC **(out) on the town** de juerga **to go to town (on sth)** (*coloq*) tirar la casa por la ventana (en algo)

town hall *n* ayuntamiento (*edificio*)

toy /tɔɪ/ ◆ *n* juguete ◆ PHR V **to toy with sth 1** juguetear con algo **2** *to toy with the idea of doing sth* considerar la idea de hacer algo

trace /treɪs/ ◆ *n* rastro, huella: *to disappear without trace* desaparecer sin dejar rastro ◊ *She speaks without a trace of an Irish accent.* Habla sin ningún deje irlandés. ◆ *vt* **1** seguir la pista de **2** ~ **sth/sb (to sth)** dar con algo/algn (en algo) **3** remontar(se): *It can be traced back to the Middle Ages.* Se remonta hasta la Edad Media. **4** ~ **sth (out)** delinear, trazar algo **5** calcar

track /træk/ ◆ *n* **1** [*gen pl*] huella (*de animal, rueda, etc*) **2** camino, senda *Ver tb* PATH **3** (*Dep*) pista, circuito **4** (*Ferrocarril*) vía **5** canción (*de disco o casete*) *Ver tb* SOUNDTRACK LOC **off track** fuera de rumbo **on the right/wrong track** por buen/mal camino **to be on sb's track** seguir la pista a algn **to keep/lose track of sth/sb** seguir/perder la pista de algo/algn: *to lose track of time* perder la noción del tiempo **to make tracks (for...)** (*coloq*) marcharse (a...) *Ver tb* BEAT ◆ *vt* ~ **sb (to sth)** seguir la pista/las huellas de algn (hasta algo) PHR V **to track sth/sb down** localizar algo/a algn

tracksuit /ˈtræksuːt/ *n* chándal

trade /treɪd/ ◆ *n* **1** comercio **2** industria: *the tourist trade* la industria turística **3** oficio: *He's a carpenter by trade.* Es carpintero de oficio. ☛ *Ver nota en* WORK[1] LOC *Ver* ROARING *en* ROAR, TRICK ◆ **1** *vi* comerciar, negociar **2** *vt* ~ **(sb) sth for sth** cambiar (a algn) algo por algo PHR V **to trade sth in (for sth)** dar algo como parte del pago (de algo)

trademark /ˈtreɪdmɑːk/ *n* marca registrada

trader /treɪdə(r)/ *n* comerciante

tradesman /ˈtreɪdzmən/ *n* (*pl* **-men** /-mən/) **1** proveedor: *tradesmen's entrance* entrada de servicio **2** comerciante

trade union *n* sindicato

trading /treɪdɪŋ/ *n* comercio

traffic /ˈtræfɪk/ ◆ *n* tráfico: *traffic jam* atasco ◊ *traffic warden* guardia de tráfico ◆ *vi* (*pret, pp* **trafficked** *pt pres* **trafficking**) ~ **(in sth)** traficar (con algo) **trafficker** *n* traficante

traffic light *n* semáforo

tragedy /ˈtrædʒədi/ *n* (*pl* **-ies**) tragedia

trail /treɪl/ ◆ *n* **1** estela (*de humo*) **2** reguero (*de sangre*) **3** senda **4** rastro (*de un animal*): *to be on sb's trail* seguir la pista a algn ◆ **1** *vi* ~ **along behind (sth/sb)** caminar despacio detrás (de algo/algn) **2** *vi* perder: *trailing by two goals to three* perdiendo por dos goles a tres

trailer /ˈtreɪlə(r)/ *n* **1** remolque **2** (*USA*) *Ver* CARAVAN **3** (*Cine*) trailer

train[1] /treɪn/ *n* **1** tren: *by train* en tren **2** sucesión, serie LOC **train of thought** hilo de pensamiento

train[2] /treɪn/ **1** *vi* estudiar, formarse: *She trained to be a lawyer.* Estudió para abogada. ◊ *to train as a nurse* estudiar enfermería **2** *vt* adiestrar **3** *vt, vi* (*Dep*) entrenar(se), preparar(se) **4** ~ **sth on sth/sb** (*cámara, etc*) apuntarle a algo/algn con algo **trainee** /treɪˈniː/ *n* aprendiz, -iza **trainer** *n* **1** entrenador, -ora (*de atletas*), preparador, -ora (*de animales*) **2** [*gen pl*] zapatilla de deporte **training** *n* **1** (*Dep*) entrenamiento **2** formación, preparación

trait /treɪt/ *n* rasgo (*de personalidad*)

traitor /ˈtreɪtə(r)/ *n* traidor, -ora *Ver tb* BETRAY

tram /træm/ (*USA* **streetcar**) *n* tranvía

tramp /træmp/ ◆ **1** *vi* andar pesadamente **2** *vt* patear ◆ *n* vagabundo, -a

trample /ˈtræmpl/ *vt* ~ **sth/sb (down)**; ~ **on sth/sb** pisotear algo/a algn

tranquillize, -ise /ˈtræŋkwəlaɪz/ *vt* tranquilizar (*sobre todo por medio de sedantes*) **tranquillizer, -iser** *n* tranquilizante: *She's on tranquillizers.* Toma tranquilizantes.

transfer /trænsˈfɜː(r)/ ◆ **(-rr-) 1** *vt, vi* trasladar(se) **2** *vt* transferir **3** *vi* ~ **(from...) (to...)** hacer transbordo (de...) (a...) ◆ /ˈtrænsfɜː(r)/ *n* **1** transferencia, traspaso, traslado **2** (*Dep*) traspaso **3** transbordo **4** (*GB*) calcomanía

transform /trænsˈfɔːm/ *vt* transformar **transformation** *n* transformación

transformer /trænsˈfɔːmə(r)/ (*Electrón*) transformador

translate /trænsˈleɪt/ *vt, vi* traducir(se): *to translate sth from French (in)to Dutch* traducir algo del francés al neerlandés ◊ *It translates as 'fatherland'.* Se traduce como "fatherland". ☛ *Comparar con* INTERPRET **translation** *n* traducción: *translation into/from Spanish* traducción al/del español ◊ *to do a translation* hacer una traducción LOC **in translation**: *Cervantes in translation* Cervantes traducido **translator** *n* traductor, -ora

transmit /trænsˈmɪt/ *vt* (**-tt-**) transmitir **transmitter** *n* (*Electrón*) transmisor, emisora

transparent /trænsˈpærənt/ *adj* **1** (*lit*) transparente **2** (*mentira, etc*) evidente

transplant /trænsˈplɑːnt; *USA* -ˈplænt/ ◆ *vt* (*Bot, Med*) trasplantar ◆ /ˈtrænsplɑːnt/ *n* trasplante: *a heart transplant* un trasplante de corazón

transport /trænˈspɔːt/ ◆ *vt* transportar, llevar ◆ /ˈtrænspɔːt/ *n* (*USA* **transportation**) transporte

transvestite /trænzˈvestaɪt/ *n* travesti

trap /træp/ ◆ *n* trampa: *to lay/set a trap* poner una trampa ◆ *vt* (**-pp-**) **1** atrapar, aprisionar **2** engañar

trapdoor /ˈtræpdɔː(r)/ (*tb* **trap**) *n* escotillón

trapeze /trəˈpiːz; *USA* træ-/ *n* trapecio (*circo*)

trash /træʃ/ *n* (*USA*) **1** (*lit y fig*) basura: *trash can* cubo de la basura ◊ *It's trash.* No vale para nada.

En inglés británico se usa **rubbish** para *basura*, **dustbin** para *cubo de la basura* y **trash** sólo se usa en sentido figurado.

2 (*coloq, pey*) gentuza **trashy** *adj* malo, de mala calidad

travel /ˈtrævl/ ◆ *n* **1** [*incontable*] los viajes, viajar: *travel bag* bolsa de viaje **2 travels** [*pl*]: *to be on your travels* estar de viaje ◊ *Did you see John on your travels?* ¿Viste a John en tus viajes? ☛ *Ver nota en* VIAJE ◆ (**-ll-**, *USA* **-l-**) **1** *vi* viajar: *to travel by car, bus, etc* viajar/ir en coche, autobús, etc **2** *vt* recorrer

travel agency *n* (*pl* **-ies**) agencia de viajes

travel agent *n* empleado de una agencia de viajes

traveller's cheque (*USA* **traveler's check**) *n* cheque de viaje

tray /treɪ/ *n* bandeja

treacherous /ˈtretʃərəs/ *adj* traicionero, pérfido **treachery** *n* **1** traición, perfidia ☛ *Comparar con* TREASON **2** falsedad

tread /tred/ ◆ (*pret* **trod** /trɒd/ *pp* **trodden** /ˈtrɒdn/ *o* **trod**) **1** *vi* ~ (**on/in sth**) pisar (algo) **2** *vt* ~ **sth** (**in/down/out**) aplastar algo **3** *vt* (*camino*) hollar LOC **to tread carefully** andar con pies de plomo ◆ *n* [*sing*] paso

treason /ˈtriːzn/ *n* alta traición ☛ **Treason** se usa específicamente para referirse a un acto de traición hacia el propio país. *Comparar con* TREACHERY *en* TREACHEROUS

treasure /ˈtreʒə(r)/ ◆ *n* tesoro: *art treasures* joyas de arte ◆ *vt* apreciar muchísimo, guardar como un tesoro: *her most treasured possession* su posesión más preciada

treasurer /ˈtreʒərə(r)/ *n* tesorero, -a

the Treasury /ˈtreʒəri/ *n* [*v sing o pl*] Ministerio de Economía y Hacienda

treat /triːt/ ◆ **1** *vt* tratar: *to treat sth as a joke* tomar algo en broma **2** *vt* ~ **sb** (**to sth**) invitar a algn (a algo): *Let me treat you.* Déjame invitarte. **3** *v refl* ~ **yourself** (**to sth**) darse el lujo (de algo) LOC **to treat sb like dirt/a dog** (*coloq*) tratar a algn como a un perro ◆ *n* **1** placer, gusto: *as a special treat* como recompensa especial ◊ *to give yourself a treat* permitirse un lujo **2** *This is my treat.* Invito yo. LOC **a treat** (*coloq*) a las mil maravillas

treatment /ˈtriːtmənt/ *n* **1** tratamiento **2** trato

treaty /ˈtriːti/ *n* (*pl* **-ies**) tratado

treble[1] /ˈtrebl/ ◆ *adj, n* triple ◆ *vt, vi* triplicar(se)

treble[2] /ˈtrebl/ ◆ *n* (*Mús*) **1** tiple **2** [*incontable*] agudos ◆ *adj* atiplado: *treble clef* clave de sol ☛ *Comparar con* BASS

tree /triː/ *n* árbol

trek /trek/ ◆ *n* caminata ◆ *vi* (**-kk-**) caminar (*penosamente*)

tremble /ˈtrembl/ *vi* ~ (**with/at sth**) temblar (de/por algo)

trembling /ˈtremblɪŋ/ ◆ *adj* tembloroso ◆ *n* temblor

tremendous /trəˈmendəs/ *adj* **1** enorme: *a tremendous number* una gran cantidad **2** estupendo **tremendously** *adv* enormemente

tremor /ˈtremə(r)/ *n* temblor, estremecimiento

trench /trentʃ/ *n* **1** (*Mil*) trinchera **2** zanja

trend /trend/ *n* tendencia LOC *Ver* SET[2], BUCK[2]

trendy /ˈtrendi/ *adj* (*coloq*) muy al día

trespass /ˈtrespəs/ *vi* ~ (**on sth**) entrar sin derecho (en algo): *no trespassing* prohibido el paso **trespasser** *n* intruso, -a

trial /ˈtraɪəl/ *n* **1** juicio, proceso **2** prueba: *a trial period* un periodo de prueba ◊ *to take sth on trial* llevarse algo a prueba **3** (*deporte*) preselección LOC **to be/go on trial/stand trial (for sth)** ser procesado (por algo) **trial and error**: *She learnt to type by trial and error.* Aprendió a escribir a máquina a base de cometer errores. **trials and tribulations** tribulaciones

triangle /ˈtraɪæŋgl/ *n* triángulo **triangular** /traɪˈæŋgjələ(r)/ *adj* triangular

tribe /traɪb/ *n* tribu

tribulation /ˌtrɪbjuˈleɪʃn/ *n Ver* TRIAL

tribute /ˈtrɪbjuːt/ *n* **1** homenaje **2 a** ~ (**to sth**): *That is a tribute to his skill.* Eso acredita su habilidad.

trick /trɪk/ ◆ *n* **1** engaño, broma, trampa: *to play a trick on sb* gastarle una broma a algn ◊ *His memory played tricks on him.* La memoria le jugaba malas pasadas. ◊ *a dirty trick* una mala pasada ◊ *a trick question* una pregunta capciosa **2** truco: *The trick is to wait.* El truco está en esperar. ◊ *a trick of the light* un efecto de la luz **3** (*magia*): *conjuring tricks* juegos de manos ◊ *card tricks* trucos con cartas LOC **every/any trick in the book** todos los trucos: *I tried every trick in the book.* Lo intenté todo. **the tricks of the trade** los trucos del oficio *Ver tb* MISS ◆ *vt* engañar: *to trick sb into (doing) sth* embaucar a algn para que haga algo ◊ *to trick sb out of sth* quitarle algo a algn mediante engaño **trickery** *n* engaños, astucia

trickle /ˈtrɪkl/ ◆ *vi* salir en un chorro fino, gotear ◆ *n* **1** hilo: *a trickle of blood* un hilo de sangre **2** ~ (**of sth**) (*fig*) goteo (de algo)

tricky /ˈtrɪki/ *adj* (**-ier**, **-iest**) complicado, difícil

tried *pret, pp de* TRY

trifle /ˈtraɪfl/ ◆ *n* **1** postre hecho a base de capas de bizcocho, fruta, crema y nata **2** nadería, bagatela LOC **a trifle** algo: *a trifle short* un poquito corto ◆ *vi* ~ **with sth/sb** jugar con algo/algn

trigger /ˈtrɪgə(r)/ ◆ *n* gatillo, disparador ◆ *vt* ~ **sth (off) 1** (*fig*) provocar, desencadenar algo **2** (*alarma, etc*) accionar algo

trillion /ˈtrɪljən/ *adj, n* billón ☛ *Ver nota en* BILLION

trim[1] /trɪm/ *adj* (**trimmer**, **trimmest**) (*aprob*) **1** bien cuidado, aseado **2** esbelto, elegante

trim[2] /trɪm/ ◆ *vt* (**-mm-**) **1** recortar **2** ~ **sth off (sth)** quitarle algo (a algo) **3** ~ **sth (with sth)** (*vestido, etc*) adornar algo (con algo) ◆ *n* **1** corte: *to have a trim* hacerse cortar el pelo un poco **2** adorno **trimming** *n* **1** adorno **2 trimmings** [*pl*] (*comida*) guarnición

trip[1] /trɪp/ (**-pp-**) **1** *vi* ~ (**over/up**) tropezar: *She tripped (up) on a stone.* Tropezó con una piedra. **2** *vt* ~ **sb (up)** poner la zancadilla a algn PHR V **to trip (sb) up** confundirse/confundir a algn

trip[2] /trɪp/ *n* viaje, excursión: *to go on a trip* hacer un viaje ◊ *a business trip* un viaje de negocios ◊ *a coach trip* una excursión en autobús ☛ *Ver nota en* VIAJE

triple /ˈtrɪpl/ ◆ *adj, n* triple: *at triple the speed* al triple de velocidad ◆ *vt, vi* triplicar(se)

triplet /ˈtrɪplət/ *n* trillizo, -a

triumph /ˈtraɪʌmf/ ◆ *n* triunfo, éxito: *to return home in triumph* regresar a casa triunfalmente ◊ *a shout of triumph* un grito de júbilo ◆ *vi* ~ (**over sth/sb**) triunfar (sobre algo/algn) **triumphal** /traɪˈʌmfl/ *adj* triunfal (*arco, procesión*) **triumphant** *adj* **1** triunfante **2** jubiloso **triumphantly** *adv* triunfalmente, jubilosamente

trivial /ˈtrɪviəl/ *adj* trivial, insignificante **triviality** /ˌtrɪviˈæləti/ *n* (*pl* **-ies**) trivialidad

trod *pret de* TREAD

trodden *pp de* TREAD

trolley /ˈtrɒli/ *n* (*pl* ~**s**) carrito: *shopping trolley* carrito de la compra

troop /truːp/ ◆ *n* **1** tropel, manada **2 troops** [*pl*] tropas, soldados ◆ PHR V **to troop in(to), out (of), etc** entrar, salir, etc en tropel

trophy /ˈtrəʊfi/ *n* (*pl* **-ies**) trofeo

tropic /ˈtrɒpɪk/ *n* **1** trópico **2 the tropics** [*pl*] el trópico **tropical** *adj* tropical

trot /trɒt/ ◆ *vi* (**-tt-**) trotar, ir al trote ◆ *n* trote LOC **on the trot** (*coloq*) seguidos

trouble /ˈtrʌbl/ ◆ *n* **1** [*incontable*] problemas: *The trouble is (that)...* Lo malo es que... ◊ *What's the trouble?* ¿Qué pasa? **2** problema: *money troubles* dificultades económicas **3** [*incontable*] molestia, esfuerzo: *It's no trouble.* No es molestia. ◊ *It's not worth the trouble.* No vale la pena. **4** disturbios, conflicto **5** (*Med*) dolencia: *back trouble* problemas de espalda LOC **to be in trouble** tener problemas, estar en un apuro: *If I don't get home by ten I'll be in trouble.* Si no llego a casa a las diez me la cargo. **to get into trouble** meterse en un lío: *He got into trouble with the police.* Tuvo problemas con la policía. **to go to a lot of trouble (to do sth)** tomarse muchas molestias (por hacer algo) *Ver tb* ASK, TEETHE ◆ *vt* **1** molestar: *Don't trouble yourself.* No te molestes. **2** preocupar: *What's troubling you?* ¿Qué es lo que te preocupa? **troubled** *adj* **1** (*expresión, voz*) preocupado, afligido **2** (*periodo*) agitado **3** (*vida*) accidentado **troublesome** *adj* molesto

trouble-free /ˌtrʌbl ˈfriː/ *adj* **1** sin problemas **2** (*viaje*) sin ninguna avería

troublemaker /ˈtrʌblˌmeɪkə(r)/ *n* agitador, -ora, alborotador, -ora

trough /trɒf; *USA* trɔːf/ *n* **1** abrevadero **2** comedero **3** canal **4** (*Meteor*) depresión

trousers /ˈtraʊzəz/ *n* [*pl*] pantalones: *a pair of trousers* un pantalón ☛ *Ver nota en* PANTALÓN **trouser** *adj*: *trouser leg/pocket* pierna/bolsillo del pantalón

trout /traʊt/ *n* (*pl* **trout**) trucha

truant /ˈtruːənt/ *n* (*Educ*) novillero, -a LOC *Ver* PLAY

truce /truːs/ *n* tregua

truck /trʌk/ *n* **1** (*GB*) (*ferrocarriles*) vagón **2** (*USA*) camión

true /truː/ *adj* (**truer**, **truest**) **1** cierto, verdad: *It's too good to be true.* Es demasiado bueno para ser verdad. **2** (*historia*) verídico **3** verdadero, auténtico: *the true value of the house* el valor real de la casa **4** fiel: *to be true to your word/principles* cumplir lo prometido/ser fiel a sus principios LOC **to come true** hacerse realidad **true to life** realista

truly /ˈtruːli/ *adv* sinceramente, verdaderamente, realmente LOC *Ver* WELL[2]

trump /trʌmp/ *n* triunfo: *Hearts are trumps.* Pintan corazones.

trumpet /ˈtrʌmpɪt/ *n* trompeta

trundle /ˈtrʌndl/ **1** *vi* rodar lentamente **2** *vt* arrastrar **3** *vt* empujar

trunk /trʌŋk/ *n* **1** (*Anat*, *Bot*) tronco **2** baúl **3** (*elefante*) trompa **4 trunks** [*pl*] bañador (de caballero) **5** (*USA*) maletero

trust /trʌst/ ◆ *n* **1** ~ **(in sth/sb)** confianza (en algo/algn) **2** responsabilidad: *As a teacher you are in a position of trust.* Los profesores están en una posición de responsabilidad. **3** fideicomiso **4** fundación LOC *Ver* BREACH ◆ **1** *vt* fiarse de **2** *vt* ~ **sb with sth** confiar algo a algn PHR V **to trust to sth** confiar en algo **trusted** *adj* de confianza **trusting** *adj* confiado

trustee /trʌˈstiː/ *n* **1** fideicomisario, -a **2** administrador, -ora

trustworthy /ˈtrʌstwɜːði/ *adj* digno de confianza

truth /truːθ/ *n* (*pl* ~**s** /truːðz/) verdad LOC *Ver* ECONOMICAL, MOMENT **truthful** *adj* sincero: *to be truthful* decir la verdad

try /traɪ/ ◆ (*pret*, *pp* **tried**) **1** *vi* intentar ☛ En uso coloquial, **try to + infinitivo** se puede sustituir por **try and + infinitivo**: *I'll try to/and finish it.* Trataré de terminarlo. **2** *vt* probar: *Can I try the soup?* ¿Puedo probar la sopa? **3** *vt* (*Jur*, *caso*) ver **4** *vt* **to try sb (for sth)** (*Jur*) procesar a algn (por algo); juzgar a algn LOC **to try and do sth** intentar hacer algo **to try sb's patience** hacer perder la paciencia a algn *Ver tb* BEST PHR V **to try sth on** probarse algo (*ropa*, *zapatos*, *gafas*, *etc*) ◆ *n* (*pl* **tries**) **1** *I'll give it a try.* Lo intentaré. **2** (*rugby*) ensayo **trying** *adj* difícil

T-shirt /ˈtiː ʃɜːt/ *n* camiseta

tub /tʌb/ *n* **1** tina, barreño **2** tarrina ☛ *Ver dibujo en* CONTAINER **3** bañera

tube /tjuːb; *USA* tuːb/ *n* **1** ~ **(of sth)** tubo (de algo) ☛ *Ver dibujo en* CONTAINER **2 the tube** (*coloq*) (*tb* **the underground**) (*GB*) (el) metro: *by tube* en metro

tuck /tʌk/ *vt* **1** ~ **sth into sth** meter algo en algo **2** ~ **sth round sth/sb** arropar algo/a algn con algo: *to tuck sth round you* arroparse con algo PHR V **to be tucked away** (*coloq*) **1** (*dinero*) estar guardado **2** (*pueblo, edificio*) estar escondido **to tuck sth in** meter algo (*camisa*) **to tuck sb up** meter a algn (*en la cama*)

Tuesday /ˈtjuːzdeɪ, ˈtjuːzdi; *USA* ˈtuː-/ *n* (*abrev* **Tue, Tues**) martes ☛ *Ver ejemplos en* MONDAY

tuft /tʌft/ *n* **1** (*pelo*) mechón **2** (*plumas*) penacho **3** (*hierba*) manojo

tug /tʌg/ ◆ (**-gg-**) **1** *vi* **to tug (at sth)** tirar (con fuerza) de algo: *He tugged at his mother's coat.* Le dio un fuerte tirón al abrigo de su madre. **2** *vt* arrastrar ◆ *n* **1 tug (at/on sth)** tirón (a/de algo) **2** (*tb* **tugboat**) remolcador

tuition /tjuˈɪʃn; *USA* tu-/ *n* (*fml*) instrucción, clases: *private tuition* clases particulares ◊ *tuition fees* matrícula

tulip /ˈtjuːlɪp; *USA* ˈtuː-/ *n* tulipán

tumble /ˈtʌmbl/ ◆ *vi* caer(se), desplomarse PHR V **to tumble down** venirse abajo ◆ *n* caída

tumble-drier (*tb* **tumble-dryer**) /ˌtʌmbl draɪə(r)/ *n* secadora

tumbler /ˈtʌmblə(r)/ *n* vaso

tummy /ˈtʌmi/ *n* (*pl* **-ies**) (*coloq*) barriga: *tummy ache* dolor de tripas

tumour (*USA* **tumor**) /ˈtjuːmə(r); *USA* ˈtuː-/ *n* tumor

tuna /ˈtjuːnə; *USA* ˈtuːnə/ (*pl* **tuna** *o* **~s**) (*tb* **tuna-fish**) *n* atún

tune /tjuːn; *USA* tuːn/ ◆ *n* **1** melodía **2** aire LOC **in/out of tune** afinado/desafinado **in/out of tune with sth/sb** de acuerdo/en desacuerdo (con algo/algn) *Ver tb* CHANGE ◆ *vt* **1** (*piano*) afinar **2** (*motor*) poner a punto PHR V **to tune in (to sth)** sintonizar (algo): *Tune in to us again tomorrow.* Vuelva a sintonizarnos mañana. **to tune up** acordar (instrumentos) **tuneful** *adj* melodioso

tunic /ˈtjuːnɪk; *USA* ˈtuː-/ *n* túnica

tunnel /ˈtʌnl/ ◆ *n* **1** túnel **2** galería ◆ (**-ll-**, *USA* **-l-**) **1** *vi* ~ **(into/through/under sth)** abrir un túnel (en/a través de/debajo de algo) **2** *vt, vi* excavar

turban /ˈtɜːbən/ *n* turbante

turbulence /ˈtɜːbjələns/ *n* turbulencia **turbulent** *adj* **1** turbulento **2** alborotado

turf /tɜːf/ ◆ *n* [*incontable*] césped ◆ *vt* encespedar PHR V **to turf sth/sb out (of sth)** (*GB, coloq*) echar algo/a algn (de algo)

turkey /ˈtɜːki/ *n* (*pl* **~s**) pavo

turmoil /ˈtɜːmɔɪl/ *n* alboroto

turn /tɜːn/ ◆ **1** *vi* girar, dar vueltas **2** *vt* hacer girar, dar (la) vuelta a **3** *vt, vi* volver(se): *She turned her back on Simon and walked off.* Le dio la espalda a Simon y se marchó. **4** *vt* (*página*) pasar **5** *vi*: *to turn left* torcer a la izquierda **6** *vt* (*esquina*) doblar **7** *vi* ponerse, volverse: *to turn white/red* ponerse blanco/colorado ☛ *Ver nota en* BECOME **8** *vt, vi* ~ **(sth/sb) (from A) into B** convertirse, convertir (algo/a algn) (de A) en B **9** *vt*: *to turn 40* cumplir los 40 LOC **to turn a blind eye (to sth)** hacer la vista gorda (ante algo) **to turn back the clock** volver al pasado **to turn over a new leaf** empezar una nueva vida **to turn your back on sth/sb** volverle la espalda a algo/algn *Ver tb* MIND, PALE, SOUR

PHR V **to turn around** girar

to turn away (from sth/sb) apartar la vista (de algo/algn) **to turn sb away** negarse a ayudar a algn **to turn sb away from sth** echar a algn de algo

to turn back volverse hacia atrás **to turn sb back** hacer volverse a algn

to turn sth down bajar algo (*la radio, etc*) **to turn sth/sb down** rechazar algo/a algn

to turn off desviarse (*de un camino*) **to turn sb off** (*coloq*) desanimar/quitarle las ganas a algn **to turn sth off 1** apagar algo **2** (*grifo*) cerrar algo **3** (*fig*) desconectar algo

to turn sb on (*coloq*) excitar a algn **to turn sth on 1** encender algo **2** (*grifo*) abrir algo

to turn out 1 asistir, presentarse **2** resultar, salir **to turn sb out (of/from sth)** echar a algn (de algo) **to turn sth out** apagar algo (*luz*)

to turn (sth/sb) over dar la vuelta (a algo/algn)
to turn (sth/sb) round (*tb* **to turn around**) girar (algo/a algn)
to turn to sb acudir a algn
to turn up presentarse, aparecer
to turn sth up subir algo (*volumen*) ◆ *n* **1** vuelta **2** (*cabeza*) movimiento **3** giro, vuelta: *to take a wrong turn* coger un camino equivocado **4** curva **5** (*circunstancias*) cambio: *to take a turn for the better/worse* empezar a mejorar/empeorar **6** turno, vez: *It's your turn.* Te toca a ti. **7** (*coloq*) susto **8** (*coloq*) ataque, desmayo LOC **a turn of phrase** un giro **in turn** sucesivamente, uno tras otro **to do sb a good/bad turn** hacer un favor/una mala pasada a algn **to take turns (at sth)** turnarse (para/en algo)

turning /ˈtɜːnɪŋ/ *n* bocacalle

turning point *n* momento crítico, punto decisivo

turnip /ˈtɜːnɪp/ *n* nabo

turnout /ˈtɜːnaʊt/ *n* asistencia, concurrencia

turnover /ˈtɜːnˌəʊvə(r)/ *n* **1** (*negocio*) facturación **2** (*personal/mercancías*) movimiento

turntable /ˈtɜːnteɪbl/ *n* (*tocadiscos*) plato

turpentine /ˈtɜːpəntaɪn/ (*tb coloq* **turps** /tɜːps/) *n* aguarrás

turquoise /ˈtɜːkwɔɪz/ ◆ *n* turquesa ◆ *adj* (de) color turquesa

turret /ˈtʌrət/ *n* torreón, torre

turtle /ˈtɜːtl/ *n* tortuga (*marina*) ☛ *Comparar con* TORTOISE

tusk /tʌsk/ *n* colmillo

tutor /ˈtjuːtə(r); *USA* ˈtuː-/ *n* **1** profesor, -ora particular **2** (*GB*) (*universidad*) profesor, -ora

tutorial /tjuːˈtɔːriəl; *USA* tuː-/ ◆ *adj* de tutor ◆ *n* seminario (*clase*)

twang /twæŋ/ *n* **1** (*esp Mús*) punteado (vibrante) **2** (*voz*) gangueo

twelve /twelv/ *adj, pron, n* doce ☛ *Ver ejemplos en* FIVE **twelfth 1** *adj* duodécimo **2** *pron, adv* el duodécimo, la duodécima, los duodécimos, las duodécimas **3** *n* doceava parte, doceavo ☛ *Ver ejemplos en* FIFTH

twenty /ˈtwenti/ *adj, pron, n* veinte ☛ *Ver ejemplos en* FIFTY, FIVE **twentieth 1** *adj, pron* vigésimo **2** *n* veinteava parte, veinteavo ☛ *Ver ejemplos en* FIFTH

twice /twaɪs/ *adv* dos veces: *twice as much/many* el doble LOC *Ver* ONCE

twiddle /ˈtwɪdl/ *vt, vi* ~ **(with) sth** jugar con algo; (hacer) girar algo LOC **to twiddle your thumbs** tocarse las narices

twig /twɪg/ *n* ramita

twilight /ˈtwaɪlaɪt/ *n* crepúsculo

twin /twɪn/ *n* **1** gemelo, -a, mellizo, -a **2** (*de un par*) gemelo, pareja, doble: *twin(-bedded) room* habitación de dos camas

twinge /twɪndʒ/ *n* punzada

twinkle /ˈtwɪŋkl/ *vi* **1** centellear, destellar **2** ~ **(with sth)** (*ojos*) brillar (de algo)

twirl /twɜːl/ *vt, vi* **1** (hacer) girar, dar vueltas (a) **2** retorcer(se)

twist /twɪst/ ◆ **1** *vt, vi* torcer(se), retorcer(se) **2** *vt, vi* enrollar(se), enroscar(se) **3** *vi* (*camino, río*) serpentear **4** *vt* (*palabras, etc*) tergiversar ◆ *n* **1** torsión, torcedura **2** (*camino, río*) recodo, curva **3** (*limón, papel*) pedacito **4** (*cambio*) giro

twit /twɪt/ *n* (*GB, coloq*) tonto, -a

twitch /twɪtʃ/ ◆ *n* **1** movimiento repentino **2** tic **3** tirón ◆ *vt, vi* **1** crispar(se), moverse (nerviosamente) **2** ~ **(at) sth** dar un tirón a algo

twitter /ˈtwɪtə(r)/ *vi* gorjear

two /tuː/ *adj, pron, n* dos ☛ *Ver ejemplos en* FIVE LOC **to put two and two together** atar cabos

two-faced /ˌtuː ˈfeɪst/ *adj* falso

two-way /ˌtuː ˈweɪ/ *adj* **1** (*proceso*) doble **2** (*comunicación*) recíproco

tycoon /taɪˈkuːn/ *n* magnate

tying *Ver* TIE

type /taɪp/ ◆ *n* **1** tipo, clase: *all types of jobs* todo tipo de trabajos ◊ *He's not my type (of person).* No es mi tipo. **2** (*modelo*) tipo: *She's not the artistic type.* No tiene mucha afición por el arte. ◆ *vt, vi* escribir (a máquina), mecanografiar ☛ Se usa a menudo con **out** o **up** : *to type sth up* pasar algo a máquina

typescript /ˈtaɪpskrɪpt/ *n* texto mecanografiado

typewriter /ˈtaɪpˌraɪtə(r)/ *n* máquina de escribir

typhoid (fever) /ˈtaɪfɔɪd/ *n* [*incontable*] (fiebre) tifoidea

typical /ˈtɪpɪkl/ *adj* típico, característico

typically *adv* **1** típicamente **2** por regla general

typify /ˈtɪpɪfaɪ/ *vt* (*pret, pp* **-fied**) tipificar, ser ejemplo de

typing /ˈtaɪpɪŋ/ *n* mecanografía

typist /ˈtaɪpɪst/ *n* mecanógrafo, -a

tyranny /ˈtɪrəni/ *n* tiranía

tyrant /ˈtaɪrənt/ *n* tirano, -a

tyre (*USA* **tire**) /ˈtaɪə(r)/ *n* neumático

Uu

U, u /juː/ *n* (*pl* **U's, u's** /juːz/) U, u: *U for uncle* U de uno ☛ *Ver ejemplos en* A, a

ubiquitous /juːˈbɪkwɪtəs/ *adj* (*fml*) ubicuo

UFO (*tb* **ufo**) /ˌjuː ef ˈəʊ, ˈjuːfəʊ/ *abrev* (*pl* ~s) OVNI (=objeto volador no identificado)

ugh! /ɜː, ʊx/ *interj* ¡uf!, ¡puf!

ugly /ˈʌgli/ *adj* (**uglier, ugliest**) **1** feo **2** siniestro, peligroso

ulcer /ˈʌlsə(r)/ *n* úlcera

ultimate /ˈʌltɪmət/ *adj* **1** último, final **2** mayor **3** principal **ultimately** *adv* **1** al final, finalmente **2** fundamentalmente

umbrella /ʌmˈbrelə/ *n* (*lit y fig*) paraguas

umpire /ˈʌmpaɪə(r)/ *n* árbitro, -a (*tenis, cricket*)

unable /ʌnˈeɪbl/ *adj* (*frec fml*) incapaz, imposibilitado

unacceptable /ˌʌnəkˈseptəbl/ *adj* inaceptable

unaccustomed /ˌʌnəˈkʌstəmd/ *adj* **1** *to be unaccustomed to (doing) sth* no estar acostumbrado a (hacer) algo **2** desacostumbrado, insólito

unambiguous /ˌʌnæmˈbɪgjuəs/ *adj* inequívoco

unanimous /juˈnænɪməs/ *adj* ~ (**in sth**) unánime (en algo)

unarmed /ˌʌnˈɑːmd/ *adj* **1** desarmado, sin armas **2** (*indefenso*) inerme

unattractive /ˌʌnəˈtræktɪv/ *adj* poco atractivo

unavailable /ˌʌnəˈveɪləbl/ *adj* no disponible

unavoidable /ˌʌnəˈvɔɪdəbl/ *adj* inevitable

unaware /ˌʌnəˈweə(r)/ *adj* no consciente: *He was unaware that...* Ignoraba que...

unbearable /ʌnˈbeərəbl/ *adj* insoportable

unbeatable /ʌnˈbiːtəbl/ *adj* invencible, inigualable

unbeaten /ʌnˈbiːtn/ *adj* (*Dep*) nunca superado, imbatido

unbelievable /ˌʌnbɪˈliːvəbl/ *adj* increíble *Ver tb* INCREDIBLE

unbroken /ʌnˈbrəʊkən/ *adj* **1** intacto **2** ininterrumpido **3** (*récord*) imbatido **4** (*espíritu*) indómito

uncanny /ʌnˈkæni/ *adj* (**-ier, -iest**) **1** misterioso **2** asombroso

uncertain /ʌnˈsɜːtn/ *adj* **1** inseguro, dudoso, indeciso **2** incierto: *It is uncertain whether...* No se sabe si... **3** variable **uncertainty** *n* (*pl* **-ies**) incertidumbre, duda

unchanged /ʌnˈtʃeɪndʒd/ *adj* igual, sin alteración

uncle /ˈʌŋkl/ *n* tío

unclear /ˌʌnˈklɪə(r)/ *adj* poco claro, nada claro

uncomfortable /ʌnˈkʌmftəbl; *USA* -fərt-/ *adj* incómodo **uncomfortably** *adv* incómodamente: *The exams are getting uncomfortably close.* Los exámenes se están acercando de manera preocupante.

uncommon /ʌnˈkɒmən/ *adj* poco común, insólito

uncompromising /ʌnˈkɒmprəmaɪzɪŋ/ *adj* inflexible, firme

unconcerned /ˌʌnkənˈsɜːnd/ *adj* **1** ~ (**about/by sth**) indiferente (a algo) **2** despreocupado

unconditional /ˌʌnkənˈdɪʃənl/ *adj* incondicional

unconscious /ʌnˈkɒnʃəs/ ◆ *adj* **1**

inconsciente **2** *to be unconscious of sth* no darse cuenta de algo ◆ **the unconscious** *n* el subconsciente ☛ *Comparar con* SUBCONSCIOUS

unconventional /ˌʌnkənˈvenʃənl/ *adj* poco convencional

unconvincing /ˌʌnkənˈvɪnsɪŋ/ *adj* poco convincente

uncouth /ʌnˈkuːθ/ *adj* grosero

uncover /ʌnˈkʌvə(r)/ *vt* **1** destapar, descubrir **2** (*fig*) descubrir

undecided /ˌʌndɪˈsaɪdɪd/ *adj* **1** pendiente, sin resolver **2** ~ (**about sth/sb**) indeciso (sobre algo/algn)

undeniable /ˌʌndɪˈnaɪəbl/ *adj* innegable, indiscutible **undeniably** *adv* indudablemente

under /ˈʌndə(r)/ *prep* **1** debajo de: *It was under the bed.* Estaba debajo de la cama. **2** (*edad*) menor de **3** (*cantidad*) menos de **4** (*gobierno, mando, etc*) bajo **5** (*Jur*) según (*una ley, etc*) **6** *under construction* en construcción

under- /ˈʌndə(r)/ *pref* **1** insuficientemente: *Women are under-represented in the group.* Las mujeres tienen una representación demasiado pequeña en el grupo. ◊ *under-used* infrautilizado **2** (*edad*) menor de: *the under-fives* los menores de cinco años ◊ *the under-21s* los menores de veintiún años ◊ *the under-21 team* el equipo sub-veintiuno ◊ *under-age drinking* el consumo de bebidas alcohólicas por menores de edad

undercover /ˌʌndəˈkʌvə(r)/ *adj* **1** (*policía*) de paisano, secreto **2** (*operación*) secreto, clandestino

underestimate /ˌʌndərˈestɪmeɪt/ *vt* subestimar, infravalorar

undergo /ˌʌndəˈgəʊ/ *vt* (*pret* **underwent** /-ˈwent/ *pp* **undergone** /-ˈgɒn; *USA* -ˈgɔːn/) **1** experimentar, sufrir **2** (*prueba*) pasar **3** (*curso*) seguir **4** (*tratamiento, cirugía*) someterse a

undergraduate /ˌʌndəˈgrædʒuət/ *n* estudiante no licenciado

underground /ˌʌndəˈgraʊnd/ ◆ *adv* **1** bajo tierra **2** (*fig*) en la clandestinidad ◆ *adj* **1** subterráneo **2** (*fig*) clandestino ◆ *n* **1** (*GB coloq* **the tube**, *USA* **subway**) metro **2** movimiento clandestino

undergrowth /ˈʌndəgrəʊθ/ *n* maleza

underlie /ˌʌndəˈlaɪ/ *vt* (*pret* **underlay** /ˌʌndəˈleɪ/ *pp* **underlain** /-ˈleɪn/) (*fig*) estar detrás de

underline /ˌʌndəˈlaɪn/ (*tb* **underscore**) *vt* subrayar

undermine /ˌʌndəˈmaɪn/ *vt* socavar, debilitar

underneath /ˌʌndəˈniːθ/ ◆ *prep* debajo de ◆ *adv* (por) debajo ◆ **the underneath** *n* [*incontable*] la parte inferior

underpants /ˈʌndəpænts/ (*tb coloq* **pants**) *n* [*pl*] calzoncillos: *a pair of underpants* unos calzoncillos ☛ *Ver nota en* PAIR

underprivileged /ˌʌndəˈprɪvəlɪdʒd/ *adj* desheredado, marginado

underside /ˈʌndəsaɪd/ *n* parte de abajo, costado inferior

understand /ˌʌndəˈstænd/ (*pret, pp* **understood** /-ˈstʊd/) **1** *vt, vi* entender **2** *vt* explicarse **3** *vt* (*saber manejar*) entender de **4** *vt* (*frec fml*) tener entendido **understandable** *adj* comprensible **understandably** *adv* naturalmente

understanding /ˌʌndəˈstændɪŋ/ ◆ *adj* comprensivo ◆ *n* **1** entendimiento, comprensión **2** conocimiento **3** acuerdo (informal) **4** ~ (**of sth**) (*frec fml*) interpretación (de algo)

understate /ˌʌndəˈsteɪt/ *vt* decir que algo es más pequeño o menos importante de lo que es

understatement /ˈʌndəsteɪtmənt/ *n*: *To say they are disappointed would be an understatement.* Decir que están desilusionados sería quedarse corto.

understood *pret, pp de* UNDERSTAND

undertake /ˌʌndəˈteɪk/ *vt* (*pret* **undertook** /-ˈtʊk/ *pp* **undertaken** /-ˈteɪkən/) (*fml*) **1** emprender **2** ~ **to do sth** comprometerse a hacer algo **undertaking** *n* **1** (*fml*) compromiso, obligación **2** [*incontable*] (*Com*) empresa

undertaker /ˈʌndəteɪkə(r)/ *n* director, -ora, de pompas fúnebres **the undertaker's** *n* la funeraria

undertook *pret de* UNDERTAKE

underwater /ˌʌndəˈwɔːtə(r)/ ◆ *adj* submarino ◆ *adv* bajo el agua

underwear /ˈʌndəweə(r)/ *n* ropa interior

underwent *pret de* UNDERGO

the underworld /ˈʌndəwɜːld/ *n* **1** el averno **2** el hampa

undesirable /ˌʌndɪˈzaɪərəbl/ *adj, n* indeseable

undid *pret de* UNDO

undisputed /ˌʌndɪˈspjuːtɪd/ *adj* incuestionable, indiscutible

undisturbed /ˌʌndɪˈstɜːbd/ *adj* **1** (*persona*) tranquilo, sin ser molestado **2** (*cosa*) sin tocar

undo /ʌnˈduː/ *vt* (*pret* **undid** /ʌnˈdɪd/ *pp* **undone** /ʌnˈdʌn/) **1** deshacer **2** desabrochar **3** desatar **4** (*envoltura*) quitar **5** anular: *to undo the damage* reparar el daño **undone** *adj* **1** desabrochado, desatado: *to come undone* desabrocharse/desatarse **2** sin acabar

undoubtedly /ʌnˈdaʊtɪdli/ *adv* indudablemente

undress /ʌnˈdres/ *vt, vi* desnudar(se) ☛ Es más normal decir **to get undressed**. **undressed** *adj* desnudo

undue /ˌʌnˈdjuː; *USA* -ˈduː/ *adj* (*fml*) [*sólo antes de sustantivo*] excesivo **unduly** *adv* (*fml*) excesivamente, en demasía

unearth /ʌnˈɜːθ/ *vt* desenterrar, sacar a la luz

unease /ʌnˈiːz/ *n* malestar

uneasy /ʌnˈiːzi/ *adj* (**-ier**, **-iest**) **1** ~ (**about/at sth**) inquieto (por algo) **2** (*silencio*) incómodo

uneducated /ʌnˈedʒukeɪtɪd/ *adj* inculto

unemployed /ˌʌnɪmˈplɔɪd/ *adj* desempleado, en paro **the unemployed** *n* [*pl*] los parados

unemployment /ˌʌnɪmˈplɔɪmənt/ *n* desempleo, paro

unequal /ʌnˈiːkwəl/ *adj* **1** desigual **2** (*fml*): *to feel unequal to sth* no sentirse a la altura de algo

uneven /ʌnˈiːvn/ *adj* **1** desigual **2** (*pulso*) irregular **3** (*suelo*) desnivelado

uneventful /ˌʌnɪˈventfl/ *adj* sin incidentes, tranquilo

unexpected /ˌʌnɪkˈspektɪd/ *adj* inesperado, imprevisto

unfair /ˌʌnˈfeə(r)/ *adj* **1** ~ (**to/on sb**) injusto (con algn) **2** (*competencia*) desleal **3** (*despido*) improcedente

unfaithful /ʌnˈfeɪθfl/ *adj* **1** infiel **2** (*antic*) desleal

unfamiliar /ˌʌnfəˈmɪliə(r)/ *adj* **1** poco familiar **2** (*persona, cara*) desconocido **3** ~ **with sth** poco familiarizado con algo

unfashionable /ʌnˈfæʃnəbl/ *adj* pasado de moda

unfasten /ʌnˈfɑːsn/ *vt* **1** desabrochar, desatar **2** abrir **3** soltar

unfavourable /ʌnˈfeɪvərəbl/ *adj* **1** adverso, desfavorable **2** poco propicio

unfinished /ʌnˈfɪnɪʃt/ *adj* sin terminar: *unfinished business* asuntos pendientes

unfit /ʌnˈfɪt/ *adj* **1** ~ (**for sth/to do sth**) inadecuado, no apto (para algo/para hacer algo); incapaz (de hacer algo) **2** poco en forma

unfold /ʌnˈfəʊld/ **1** *vt* extender, desplegar **2** *vt, vi* (*fig*) revelar(se)

unforeseen /ˌʌnfɔːˈsiːn/ *adj* imprevisto

unforgettable /ˌʌnfəˈgetəbl/ *adj* inolvidable

unforgivable (*tb* **unforgiveable**) /ˌʌnfəˈgɪvəbl/ *adj* imperdonable

unfortunate /ʌnˈfɔːtʃənət/ *adj* **1** desafortunado: *It is unfortunate (that)*... Es de lamentar que... **2** (*accidente*) desgraciado **3** (*comentario*) inoportuno **unfortunately** *adv* por desgracia, desgraciadamente

unfriendly /ʌnˈfrendli/ *adj* (**-ier**, **-iest**) ~ (**to/towards sb**) antipático (con/hacia algn)

ungrateful /ʌnˈgreɪtfl/ *adj* **1** desagradecido **2** ~ (**to sb**) ingrato (con algn)

unhappy /ʌnˈhæpi/ *adj* (**-ier**, **-iest**) **1** desgraciado, triste **2** ~ (**about/at sth**) preocupado, disgustado (por algo) **unhappiness** *n* infelicidad

unharmed /ʌnˈhɑːmd/ *adj* ileso

unhealthy /ʌnˈhelθi/ *adj* (**-ier**, **-iest**) **1** enfermizo **2** insalubre **3** (*interés*) morboso

unhelpful /ʌnˈhelpfl/ *adj* poco servicial

uniform /ˈjuːnɪfɔːm/ ◆ *adj* uniforme ◆ *n* uniforme LOC **in uniform** de uniforme

unify /ˈjuːnɪfaɪ/ *vt* (*pret, pp* **-fied**) unificar

unimportant /ˌʌnɪmˈpɔːt(ə)nt/ *adj* sin importancia, insignificante

uninhabited /ˌʌnɪnˈhæbɪtɪd/ *adj* deshabitado, despoblado

unintentionally /ˌʌnɪnˈtenʃənəli/ *adv* sin querer

uninterested /ʌnˈɪntrəstɪd/ *adj* ~ (**in sth/sb**) indiferente (a algo/algn); no interesado (en algo/algn)

union /ˈjuːniən/ *n* **1** unión: *the Union Jack* la bandera del Reino Unido **2** *Ver* TRADE UNION

unique /juˈniːk/ *adj* **1** único **2** ~ **to sth/sb** exclusivo de algo/algn **3** (*poco común*) excepcional, extraordinario

unison /ˈjuːnɪsn, ˈjuːnɪzn/ *n* LOC **in unison (with sth/sb)** al unísono (con algo/algn)

unit /ˈjuːnɪt/ *n* **1** unidad **2** (*de mobiliario*) módulo: *kitchen unit* mueble de cocina

unite /juˈnaɪt/ **1** *vt, vi* unir(se) **2** *vi* ~ (**in sth/in doing sth/to do sth**) unirse, juntarse (en algo/para hacer algo)

unity /ˈjuːnəti/ *n* **1** unidad **2** (*concordia*) unidad, armonía

universal /ˌjuːnɪˈvɜːsl/ *adj* universal, general **universally** *adv* universalmente, mundialmente

universe /ˈjuːnɪvɜːs/ *n* (*lit y fig*) universo

university /ˌjuːnɪˈvɜːsəti/ *n* (*pl* **-ies**) universidad: *to go to university* ir a la universidad ☛ *Ver nota en* SCHOOL

unjust /ˌʌnˈdʒʌst/ *adj* injusto

unkempt /ˌʌnˈkempt/ *adj* **1** desaliñado, descuidado **2** (*pelo*) despeinado

unkind /ˌʌnˈkaɪnd/ *adj* **1** (*persona*) poco amable, cruel **2** (*comentario*) cruel

unknown /ˌʌnˈnəʊn/ *adj* ~ (**to sb**) desconocido (para algn)

unlawful /ʌnˈlɔːfl/ *adj* ilegal, ilícito

unleash /ʌnˈliːʃ/ *vt* ~ **sth (against/on sth/sb) 1** (*animal*) soltar algo (contra algo/algn) **2** (*fig*) desatar, desencadenar algo (contra algo/algn)

unless /ənˈles/ *conj* a menos que, a no ser que, si no

unlike /ˌʌnˈlaɪk/ ◆ *adj* **1** distinto **2** (*no típico de*): *It's unlike him to be late.* Es muy raro que llegue tarde. ◆ *prep* a diferencia de

unlikely /ʌnˈlaɪkli/ *adj* (**-ier**, **-iest**) **1** poco probable, improbable **2** (*cuento, excusa, etc*) inverosímil

unlimited /ʌnˈlɪmɪtɪd/ *adj* ilimitado, sin límite

unload /ˌʌnˈləʊd/ *vt, vi* descargar

unlock /ˌʌnˈlɒk/ *vt, vi* abrir(se) (*con llave*)

unlucky /ʌnˈlʌki/ *adj* **1** desgraciado, desafortunado: *to be unlucky* tener mala suerte **2** aciago

unmarried /ˌʌnˈmærid/ *adj* soltero

unmistakable /ˌʌnmɪˈsteɪkəbl/ *adj* inconfundible, inequívoco

unmoved /ˌʌnˈmuːvd/ *adj* impasible

unnatural /ʌnˈnætʃrəl/ *adj* **1** antinatural, anormal **2** contra natura **3** afectado, poco natural

unnecessary /ʌnˈnesəsri; *USA* -seri/ *adj* **1** innecesario **2** (*comentario*) gratuito

unnoticed /ˌʌnˈnəʊtɪst/ *adj* desapercibido, inadvertido

unobtrusive /ˌʌnəbˈtruːsɪv/ *adj* discreto

unofficial /ˌʌnəˈfɪʃl/ *adj* **1** no oficial, extraoficial **2** (*fuente*) oficioso

unorthodox /ʌnˈɔːθədɒks/ *adj* **1** poco ortodoxo **2** (*Relig*) heterodoxo

unpack /ˌʌnˈpæk/ **1** *vi* deshacer las maletas **2** *vt* desempaquetar, desembalar **3** *vt* (*maleta*) deshacer

unpaid /ˌʌnˈpeɪd/ *adj* **1** no pagado **2** (*persona, trabajo*) no retribuido

unpleasant /ʌnˈpleznt/ *adj* **1** desagradable **2** (*persona*) antipático

unpopular /ˌʌnˈpɒpjələ(r)/ *adj* impopular

unprecedented /ʌnˈpresɪdentɪd/ *adj* sin precedentes

unpredictable /ˌʌnprɪˈdɪktəbl/ *adj* imprevisible

unqualified /ʌnˈkwɒlɪfaɪd/ *adj* **1** sin título, no cualificado **2** ~ **to do sth** no competente, inhabilitado para hacer algo

unravel /ʌnˈrævl/ *vt, vi* (**-ll-**, *USA* **-l-**) (*lit y fig*) desenmarañar(se), desenredar(se)

unreal /ˌʌnˈrɪəl/ *adj* irreal, ilusorio

unrealistic /ˌʌnrɪəˈlɪstɪk/ *adj* poco realista

unreasonable /ʌnˈriːznəbl/ *adj* **1** irrazonable, poco razonable **2** excesivo

unreliable /ˌʌnrɪˈlaɪəbl/ *adj* **1** poco fiable **2** (*persona*) poco serio

unrest /ʌnˈrest/ *n* **1** malestar, intranquilidad **2** (*Pol*) disturbios

unruly /ʌnˈruːli/ *adj* indisciplinado, revoltoso

unsafe /ʌnˈseɪf/ *adj* peligroso

unsatisfactory /ˌʌnˌsætɪsˈfæktəri/ *adj* insatisfactorio, inaceptable

unsavoury (*USA* **unsavory**) /ʌnˈseɪvəri/ *adj* **1** desagradable **2** (*persona*) indeseable

unscathed /ʌnˈskeɪðd/ *adj* **1** ileso **2** (*fig*) incólume

unscrew /ˌʌnˈskruː/ *vt, vi* **1** (*tornillo, etc*) desatornillar(se) **2** (*tapa, etc*) desenroscar(se)

unscrupulous /ʌnˈskruːpjələs/ *adj* sin escrúpulos, poco escrupuloso

unseen /ˌʌnˈsiːn/ *adj* invisible, inadvertido, no visto

unsettle /ˌʌnˈsetl/ *vt* perturbar, inquietar **unsettled** *adj* **1** (*persona*) incómodo **2** (*situación*) inestable **3** (*cambiable*) variable, incierto **4** (*asunto*) pendiente **unsettling** *adj* perturbador, inquietante

unshaven /ˌʌnˈʃeɪvn/ *adj* sin afeitar

unsightly /ʌnˈsaɪtli/ *adj* antiestético, feo

unskilled /ˌʌnˈskɪld/ *adj* **1** (*trabajador*) no cualificado **2** (*trabajo*) no especializado

unspoilt /ˌʌnˈspɒɪlt/ (*tb* **unspoiled**) *adj* intacto, sin estropear

unspoken /ˌʌnˈspəʊkən/ *adj* tácito, no expresado

unstable /ʌnˈsteɪbl/ *adj* inestable

unsteady /ʌnˈstedi/ *adj* (**-ier**, **-iest**) **1** inseguro, vacilante **2** (*mano, voz*) tembloroso

unstuck /ˌʌnˈstʌk/ *adj* despegado LOC **to come unstuck 1** despegarse **2** (*coloq, fig*) fracasar

unsuccessful /ˌʌnsəkˈsesfl/ *adj* infructuoso, fracasado: *to be unsuccessful in doing sth* no lograr hacer algo **unsuccessfully** *adv* sin éxito

unsuitable /ˌʌnˈsuːtəbl/ *adj* **1** no apto, inapropiado **2** (*momento*) inoportuno

unsure /ˌʌnˈʃɔː(r); *USA* -ˈʃʊər/ *adj* **1** ~ (**of yourself**) inseguro (de sí mismo) **2 to be ~** (**about/of sth**) no estar seguro (de algo)

unsuspecting /ˌʌnsəˈspektɪŋ/ *adj* confiado

unsympathetic /ˌʌnˌsɪmpəˈθetɪk/ *adj* **1** poco comprensivo **2** (*poco amistoso*) antipático

unthinkable /ʌnˈθɪŋkəbl/ *adj* impensable, inconcebible

untidy /ʌnˈtaɪdi/ *adj* (**-ier**, **-iest**) **1** desordenado **2** (*apariencia*) desaliñado, descuidado **3** (*pelo*) despeinado

untie /ʌnˈtaɪ/ *vt* (*pret, pp* **untied** *pt pres* **untying**) desatar

until /ənˈtɪl/ ◆ (*tb* **till**) *conj* hasta que ◆ *prep* hasta: *until recently* hasta hace poco ☛ *Ver nota en* HASTA

untouched /ʌnˈtʌtʃt/ *adj* ~ (**by sth**) **1** intacto, sin tocar **2** (*comida*) sin probar **3** insensible (a algo) **4** no afectado (por algo) **5** incólume

untrue /ʌnˈtruː/ *adj* **1** falso **2** ~ (**to sth/sb**) infiel (a algo/algn)

unused *adj* **1** /ˌʌnˈjuːzd/ sin usar **2** /ˌʌnˈjuːst/ ~ **to sth/sb** no acostumbrado a algo/algn

unusual /ʌnˈjuːʒuəl/ *adj* **1** inusual, inusitado **2** (*extraño*) raro **3** distintivo **unusually** *adv* inusitadamente, extraordinariamente: *unusually talented* de un talento poco común

unveil /ˌʌnˈveɪl/ *vt* **1** ~ **sth/sb** quitar el velo a algo/algn **2** (*monumento, etc*) descubrir **3** (*fig*) revelar

unwanted /ˌʌnˈwɒntɪd/ *adj* **1** no deseado: *to feel unwanted* sentirse rechazado ◊ *an unwanted pregnancy* un embarazo no deseado **2** superfluo, sobrante

unwarranted /ʌnˈwɒrəntɪd; *USA* -ˈwɔːr-/ *adj* injustificado

unwelcome /ʌnˈwelkəm/ *adj* inoportuno, molesto: *to make you feel unwelcome* hacer a algn sentirse incómodo

unwell /ʌnˈwel/ *adj* indispuesto

unwilling /ʌnˈwɪlɪŋ/ *adj* no dispuesto **unwillingness** *n* falta de voluntad

unwind /ˌʌnˈwaɪnd/ (*pret, pp* **unwound** /-ˈwaʊnd/) **1** *vt, vi* desenrollar(se) **2** (*coloq*) *vi* relajarse

unwise /ˌʌnˈwaɪz/ *adj* imprudente

unwittingly /ʌnˈwɪtɪŋli/ *adv* inconscientemente

unwound *pret, pp de* UNWIND

up /ʌp/ ◆ *part adv* **1** levantado: *Is he up yet?* ¿Está levantado ya? **2** más alto, más arriba: *Pull your socks up.* Súbete los calcetines. **3** ~ (**to sth/sb**): *He came up (to me).* Se (me) acercó. **4** en trozos: *to tear sth up* romper algo en pedazos **5** (*firmemente*): *to lock sth up* guardar/encerrar algo bajo llave **6** (*terminado*): *Your time is up.* Se te acabó el tiempo. **7**

en su sitio, colocado: *Are the curtains up yet?* ¿Están colocadas ya las cortinas? LOC **not to be up to much** no valer mucho **to be up to sb** depender de algn, ser decisión de algn: *It's up to you.* Tú decides. **to be up (with sb)**: *What's up with you?* ¿Qué te pasa? **up and down 1** de arriba a abajo **2** *to jump up and down* dar saltos **up to sth 1** (*tb* **up until sth**) hasta algo: *up to now* hasta ahora **2** capaz de algo, a la altura de algo: *I don't feel up to it.* No me siento capaz de hacerlo. **3** (*coloq*): *What are you up to?* ¿Qué estás haciendo? ◊ *He's up to no good.* Está tramando algo. ☛ Para los usos de **up** en PHRASAL VERBS ver las entradas de los verbos correspondientes, p.ej. **to go up** en GO[1]. ◆ *prep* arriba: *further up the road* calle arriba LOC **up and down sth** de un lado a otro de algo ◆ *n* LOC **ups and downs** altibajos

upbringing /ˈʌpbrɪŋɪŋ/ *n* crianza, educación (*en casa*)

update /ˌʌpˈdeɪt/ ◆ *vt* **1** actualizar **2** ~ **sb (on sth)** poner al día a algn (de algo) ◆ *n* **1** (*tb* **updating**) actualización **2** ~ **(on sth/sb)** información actualizada (sobre algo/algn)

upgrade /ˌʌpˈgreɪd/ *vt* **1** mejorar **2** (*persona*) ascender

upheaval /ʌpˈhiːvl/ *n* agitación

upheld *pret, pp de* UPHOLD

uphill /ˌʌpˈhɪl/ *adj, adv* cuesta arriba: *an uphill struggle* una lucha difícil

uphold /ʌpˈhəʊld/ *vt* (*pret, pp* **upheld** /-ˈheld/) **1** sostener (*decisión, etc*) **2** mantener (*tradición, etc*)

upholstered /ˌʌpˈhəʊlstəd/ *adj* tapizado **upholstery** *n* [*incontable*] tapicería

upkeep /ˈʌpkiːp/ *n* mantenimiento

uplifting /ʌpˈlɪftɪŋ/ *adj* edificante

upon /əˈpɒn/ *prep* (*fml*) = ON LOC *Ver* ONCE

upper /ˈʌpə(r)/ *adj* **1** superior, de arriba: *upper case* mayúsculas ◊ *upper limit* tope **2** alto: *the upper class* la clase alta ☛ *Ver ejemplos en* LOW LOC **to gain, get, etc the upper hand** conseguir, etc ventaja

uppermost /ˈʌpəməʊst/ *adj* más alto (*posición*) LOC **to be uppermost in your mind** ser lo que más preocupa a algn

upright /ˈʌpraɪt/ ◆ *adj* **1** (*posición*) vertical **2** (*persona*) recto, honrado ◆ *adv* derecho, en posición vertical

uprising /ˈʌpraɪzɪŋ/ *n* rebelión

uproar /ˈʌprɔː(r)/ *n* [*incontable*] tumulto, alboroto

uproot /ˌʌpˈruːt/ *vt* **1** arrancar (*con las raíces*) **2** ~ **sb/yourself (from sth)** (*fig*) desarraigarse, desarraigar a algn (de algo)

upset /ˌʌpˈset/ ◆ *vt* (*pret, pp* **upset**) **1** disgustar, afectar **2** (*plan, etc*) desbaratar **3** (*recipiente*) volcar, derramar ◆ *adj* ☛ Se pronuncia /ˈʌpset/ antes de sustantivo. **1** molesto, disgustado **2** (*estómago*) revuelto ◆ /ˈʌpset/ *n* **1** trastorno, disgusto **2** (*Med*) trastorno

upshot /ˈʌpʃɒt/ *n* **the** ~ **(of sth)** el resultado final (de algo)

upside down /ˌʌpsaɪd ˈdaʊn/ *adj, adv* **1** al revés, cabeza abajo ☛ *Ver dibujo en* REVÉS **2** (*coloq, fig*) patas arriba

upstairs /ˌʌpˈsteəz/ ◆ *adv* (en el piso de) arriba ◆ *adj* del piso de arriba ◆ *n* (*coloq*) piso de arriba

upstream /ˌʌpˈstriːm/ *adv* contra corriente (*de un río, etc*)

upsurge /ˈʌpsɜːdʒ/ *n* **1** ~ **(in sth)** aumento (de algo) **2** ~ **(of sth)** oleada (de algo) (*enfado, interés, etc*)

up-to-date /ˌʌp tə ˈdeɪt/ *adj* **1** a la última **2** al día

upturn /ˈʌptɜːn/ *n* ~ **(in sth)** mejora, aumento (en algo)

upturned /ˌʌpˈtɜːnd/ *adj* **1** (*cajón, etc*) dado la vuelta **2** (*nariz*) respingón

upward /ˈʌpwəd/ ◆ *adj* ascendente: *an upward trend* una tendencia al alza ◆ *adv* (*tb* **upwards**) hacia arriba **upwards of** *prep* más de (*cierto número*)

uranium /juˈreɪniəm/ *n* uranio

Uranus /ˈjʊərənəs, jʊˈreɪnəs/ *n* Urano

urban /ˈɜːbən/ *adj* urbano

urge /ɜːdʒ/ ◆ *vt* ~ **sb (to do sth)** animar, instar a algn (a hacer algo) PHR V **to urge sb on** animar a algn ◆ *n* deseo, impulso

urgency /ˈɜːdʒənsi/ *n* apremio, urgencia

urgent /ˈɜːdʒənt/ *adj* **1** urgente: *to be in urgent need of sth* necesitar algo urgentemente **2** apremiante

urine /ˈjʊərɪn/ *n* orina

us /əs, ʌs/ *pron pers* **1** [*como objeto*] nos: *She gave us the job.* Nos dio el trabajo. ◊

He ignored us. No nos hizo caso. ☛ *Ver nota en* LET[1] **2** [*después de preposición y del verbo* **to be**] nosotros, -as: *behind us* detrás de nosotros ◊ *both of us* nosotros dos ◊ *It's us.* Somos nosotros. ☛ *Comparar con* WE

usage /ˈjuːsɪdʒ, ˈjuːzɪdʒ/ *n* uso

use[1] /juːz/ *vt* (*pret, pp* **used** /juːzd/) **1** utilizar, usar, hacer uso de **2** (*esp persona*) utilizar, aprovecharse de **3** consumir, gastar PHR V **to use sth up** agotar algo, acabar algo

use[2] /juːs/ *n* **1** uso: *for your own use* para uso propio ◊ *a machine with many uses* una máquina con múltiples usos ◊ *to find a use for sth* encontrarle alguna utilidad a algo **2** *What's the use of crying?* ¿De qué sirve llorar? ◊ *What's the use?* ¿Para qué? LOC **in use** en uso **to be of use** servir **to be no use 1** no servir de nada **2** ser (un) inútil **to have the use of sth** poder usar algo **to make use of sth** aprovechar algo

used[1] /juːzd/ *adj* usado, de segunda mano

used[2] /juːst/ *adj* acostumbrado: *to get used to sth/doing sth* acostumbrarse a algo/hacer algo ◊ *I am used to being alone.* Estoy acostumbrado a estar solo.

used to /ˈjuːst tə, ˈjuːst tu/ *v modal*

Used to + infinitivo se utiliza para describir hábitos y situaciones que ocurrían en el pasado y que no ocurren en la actualidad: *I used to live in London.* Antes vivía en Londres. Las oraciones interrogativas o negativas se forman generalmente con **did**: *He didn't use to be fat.* Antes no estaba gordo. ◊ *You used to smoke, didn't you?* Antes fumabas, ¿no?

useful /ˈjuːsfl/ *adj* útil, provechoso *Ver tb* HANDY **usefulness** *n* utilidad

useless /ˈjuːsləs/ *adj* **1** inútil, inservible **2** (*coloq*) inepto

user /ˈjuːzə(r)/ *n* usuario, -a: *user-friendly* fácil de manejar

usual /ˈjuːʒuəl/ *adj* acostumbrado, habitual, normal: *later/more than usual* más tarde de lo normal/más que de costumbre ◊ *the usual* lo de siempre LOC **as usual** como siempre

usually /ˈjuːʒuəli/ *adv* normalmente ☛ *Ver nota en* ALWAYS

utensil /juːˈtensl/ *n* [*gen pl*] utensilio

utility /juːˈtɪləti/ *n* (*pl* **-ies**) **1** utilidad **2** [*gen pl*]: *public/privatized utilities* compañía pública/privatizada de suministro

utmost /ˈʌtməʊst/ ◆ *adj* mayor: *with the utmost care* con sumo cuidado ◆ *n* LOC **to do your utmost (to do sth)** hacer todo lo posible (por hacer algo)

utter[1] /ˈʌtə(r)/ *vt* pronunciar, proferir

utter[2] /ˈʌtə(r)/ *adj* total, absoluto **utterly** *adv* totalmente, absolutamente

Vv

V, v /viː/ *n* (*pl* **V's, v's** /viːz/) **1** V, v: *V for Victor* V de Valencia ☛ *Ver ejemplos en* A, a **2** *V-neck* (con) cuello de pico ◊ *v-shaped* en forma de v

vacant /ˈveɪkənt/ *adj* **1** vacante *Ver tb* SITUATION **2** (*mirada*) perdido **3** (*expresión*) distraído **vacancy** *n* (*pl* **-ies**) **1** vacante **2** habitación libre **vacantly** *adv* distraídamente

vacate /vəˈkeɪt; *USA* ˈveɪkeɪt/ *vt* (*fml*) **1** (*casa*) desocupar **2** (*asiento, puesto*) dejar vacío

vacation /vəˈkeɪʃn; *USA* veɪ-/ (*GB tb* **recess**) *n* vacaciones

En Gran Bretaña **vacation** se usa sobre todo para las vacaciones de las universidades y los tribunales de justicia. En el resto de los casos, **holiday** es la palabra más normal. En Estados Unidos **vacation** tiene un uso más generalizado.

vaccination /ˌvæksɪˈneɪʃn/ *n* **1** vacunación **2** vacuna: *polio vaccinations* vacunas contra la polio

vaccine /ˈvæksiːn; *USA* vækˈsiːn/ *n* vacuna
vacuum /ˈvækjuəm/ *n* (*pl* ~**s**) **1** vacío: *vacuum-packed* envasado al vacío **2 vacuum cleaner** aspiradora LOC **in a vacuum** aislado (*de otras personas, acontecimientos*)
vagina /vəˈdʒaɪnə/ *n* (*pl* ~**s**) vagina
vague /veɪg/ *adj* (**-er**, **-est**) **1** vago **2** (*persona*) indeciso **3** (*gesto, expresión*) distraído **vaguely** *adv* **1** vagamente **2** aproximadamente: *It looks vaguely familiar.* Me resulta vagamente familiar. **3** distraídamente
vain /veɪn/ *adj* (**-er**, **-est**) **1** vanidoso **2** (*inútil*) vano LOC **in vain** en vano
valiant /ˈvæliənt/ *adj* valeroso
valid /ˈvælɪd/ *adj* válido **validity** /vəˈlɪdəti/ *n* validez
valley /ˈvæli/ *n* (*pl* **-eys**) valle
valuable /ˈvæljuəbl/ *adj* valioso ☛ *Comparar con* INVALUABLE **valuables** *n* [*pl*] objetos de valor
valuation /ˌvæljuˈeɪʃn/ *n* tasación
value /ˈvæljuː/ ◆ *n* **1** valor **2 values** [*pl*] (*moral*) valores LOC **to be good value** estar muy bien de precio ◆ *vt* **1** ~ **sth** (**at sth**) valorar algo (en algo) **2** ~ **sth/sb** (**as sth**) valorar, apreciar algo/a algn (como algo)
valve /vælv/ *n* válvula
vampire /ˈvæmpaɪə(r)/ *n* vampiro
van /væn/ *n* furgoneta
vandal /ˈvændl/ *n* vándalo, -a **vandalism** *n* vandalismo **vandalize, -ise** *vt* destrozar (*intencionadamente*)
the vanguard /ˈvæŋgɑːd/ *n* la vanguardia
vanilla /vəˈnɪlə/ *n* vainilla
vanish /ˈvænɪʃ/ *vi* desaparecer
vanity /ˈvænəti/ *n* vanidad
vantage point /ˈvɑːntɪdʒ pɔɪnt/ *n* posición estratégica
vapour (*USA* **vapor**) /ˈveɪpə(r)/ *n* vapor
variable /ˈveəriəbl/ *adj, n* variable
variance /ˈveəriəns/ *n* discrepancia LOC **to be at variance** (**with sth/sb**) (*fml*) estar en desacuerdo (con algo/ algn), discrepar de algo
variant /ˈveəriənt/ *n* variante
variation /ˌveəriˈeɪʃn/ *n* ~ (**in/of sth**) variación, variante (en/de algo)
varied /ˈveərid/ *adj* variado
variety /vəˈraɪəti/ *n* (*pl* **-ies**) variedad: *a variety of subjects* varios temas ◇ *variety show* espectáculo de variedades
various /ˈveəriəs/ *adj* varios, diversos
varnish /ˈvɑːnɪʃ/ ◆ *n* barniz ◆ *vt* barnizar
vary /ˈveəri/ *vt, vi* (*pret, pp* **varied**) variar **varying** *adj* variable: *in varying amounts* en diversas cantidades
vase /vɑːz; *USA* veɪs, veɪz/ *n* jarrón, florero
vast /vɑːst; *USA* væst/ *adj* **1** vasto: *the vast majority* la gran mayoría **2** (*coloq*) (*suma, cantidad*) considerable **vastly** *adv* considerablemente
VAT /ˌviː eɪ ˈtiː/ *abrev* **value added tax** IVA
vat /væt/ *n* tinaja
vault /vɔːlt/ ◆ *n* **1** bóveda **2** cripta **3** (*tb* **bank vault**) cámara acorazada **4** salto ◆ *vt, vi* ~ (**over**) **sth** saltar (algo) (*apoyándose en las manos o con pértiga*)
veal /viːl/ *n* ternera ☛ *Ver nota en* CARNE
veer /vɪə(r)/ *vi* **1** virar, desviarse: *to veer off course* salirse del rumbo **2** (*viento*) cambiar (de dirección)
vegetable /ˈvedʒtəbl/ *n* **1** verdura, hortaliza **2** (*persona*) vegetal
vegetarian /ˌvedʒəˈteəriən/ *adj, n* vegetariano, -a
vegetation /ˌvedʒəˈteɪʃn/ *n* vegetación
vehement /ˈviːəmənt/ *adj* vehemente, apasionado
vehicle /ˈviːəkl; *USA* ˈviːhɪkl/ *n* **1** vehículo **2** ~ (**for sth**) (*fig*) vehículo (de/para algo); medio (de algo)
veil /veɪl/ ◆ *n* **1** (*lit y fig*) velo **2** (*de monja*) toca ◆ *vt* (*fig*) velar, disimular, encubrir: *veiled in secrecy* rodeado de secreto **veiled** *adj* (*amenaza*) velado
vein /veɪn/ *n* **1** vena **2** (*Geol*) veta **3** ~ (**of sth**) (*fig*) vena, rasgo (de algo) **4** tono, estilo
velocity /vəˈlɒsəti/ *n* velocidad

> **Velocity** se emplea especialmente en contextos científicos o formales mientras que **speed** es de uso más general.

velvet /ˈvelvɪt/ *n* terciopelo
vending machine /ˈvendɪŋ məʃiːn/ *n* máquina expendedora
vendor /ˈvendə(r)/ *n* (*fml*) vendedor, -ora
veneer /vəˈnɪə(r)/ *n* **1** (*madera,*

plástico) chapa **2** ~ **(of sth)** (*frec pey, fig*) barniz (de algo)

vengeance /ˈvendʒəns/ *n* venganza: *to take vengeance on sb* vengarse de algn LOC **with a vengeance** de veras

venison /ˈvenɪzn, ˈvenɪsn/ *n* (carne de) venado

venom /ˈvenəm/ *n* **1** veneno **2** (*fig*) veneno, odio **venomous** *adj* (*lit y fig*) venenoso

vent /vent/ ◆ *n* **1** respiradero: *air vent* rejilla de ventilación **2** (*chaqueta, etc*) abertura LOC **to give (full) vent to sth** dar rienda suelta a algo ◆ *vt* ~ **sth (on sth/sb)** descargar algo (en algo/algn)

ventilator /ˈventɪleɪtə(r)/ *n* ventilador

venture /ˈventʃə(r)/ ◆ *n* proyecto, empresa *Ver tb* ENTERPRISE ◆ **1** *vi* aventurarse: *They rarely ventured into the city.* Rara vez se aventuraban a ir a la ciudad. **2** *vt* (*fml*) (*opinión, etc*) aventurar

venue /ˈvenjuː/ *n* **1** lugar (*de reunión*) **2** local (*para música*) **3** campo (*para un partido*)

Venus /ˈviːnəs/ *n* Venus

verb /vɜːb/ *n* verbo

verbal /ˈvɜːbl/ *adj* verbal

verdict /ˈvɜːdɪkt/ *n* veredicto

verge /vɜːdʒ/ ◆ *n* borde de hierba (*en camino, jardín, etc*) LOC **on the verge of (doing) sth** al borde de algo, a punto de hacer algo ◆ PHR V **to verge on sth** rayar en algo

verification /ˌverɪfɪˈkeɪʃn/ *n* **1** verificación, comprobación **2** ratificación

verify /ˈverɪfaɪ/ *vt* (*pret, pp* **-fied**) **1** verificar, comprobar **2** (*miedo, etc*) ratificar

veritable /ˈverɪtəbl/ *adj* (*fml, joc*) verdadero

versatile /ˈvɜːsətaɪl; *USA* -tl/ *adj* versátil

verse /vɜːs/ *n* **1** poesía **2** estrofa **3** versículo LOC *Ver* CHAPTER

versed /vɜːst/ *adj* ~ **in sth** versado en algo

version /ˈvɜːʃn; *USA* -ʒn/ *n* versión

vertebra /ˈvɜːtɪbrə/ *n* (*pl* **-brae** /-riː/) vértebra

vertical /ˈvɜːtɪkl/ *adj, n* vertical

verve /vɜːv/ *n* brío, entusiasmo

very /ˈveri/ ◆ *adv* **1** muy: *I'm very sorry.* Lo siento mucho. ◊ *not very much* no mucho **2** *the very best* lo mejor posible ◊ *at the very latest* como muy tarde ◊ *your very own pony* un pony sólo para ti **3** mismo: *the very next day* justo al día siguiente ◆ *adj* **1** *at that very moment* en ese mismísimo momento ◊ *You're the very man I need.* Eres precisamente el hombre que necesito. **2** *at the very end/beginning* justo al final/principio **3** *the very idea/thought of…* la simple idea de…/sólo pensar en… LOC *Ver* EYE, FIRST

vessel /ˈvesl/ *n* **1** (*fml*) buque, barco **2** (*fml*) vasija **3** conducto

vest[1] /vest/ *n* **1** camiseta **2** chaleco **3** (*USA*) *Ver* WAISTCOAT

vest[2] /vest/ *vt* LOC **to have a vested interest in sth** tener intereses creados en algo

vestige /ˈvestɪdʒ/ *n* vestigio

vet[1] /vet/ *vt* (**-tt-**) (*GB*) investigar

vet[2] *Ver* VETERINARY SURGEON

veteran /ˈvetərən/ ◆ *adj, n* veterano, -a ◆ *n* (*USA coloq* **vet**) ex-combatiente

veterinary surgeon *n* veterinario, -a

veto /ˈviːtəʊ/ ◆ *n* (*pl* ~**es**) veto ◆ *vt* (*pt pres* ~**ing**) vetar

via /ˈvaɪə/ *prep* por, vía: *via Paris* vía París

viable /ˈvaɪəbl/ *adj* viable

vibrate /vaɪˈbreɪt; *USA* ˈvaɪbreɪt/ *vt, vi* (hacer) vibrar **vibration** *n* vibración

vicar /ˈvɪkə(r)/ *n* párroco anglicano ☛ *Ver nota en* PRIEST **vicarage** *n* casa del párroco

vice[1] /vaɪs/ *n* vicio

vice[2] (*USA* **vise**) /vaɪs/ *n* tornillo de sujeción de banco (*de carpintero*)

vice- /vaɪs/ *pref* vice-

vice versa /ˌvaɪs ˈvɜːsə/ *adv* viceversa

vicinity /vəˈsɪnəti/ *n* LOC **in the vicinity (of sth)** (*fml*) en el área alrededor (de algo)

vicious /ˈvɪʃəs/ *adj* **1** malicioso, cruel **2** (*ataque, golpe*) con saña **3** (*perro*) fiero LOC **a vicious circle** un círculo vicioso

victim /ˈvɪktɪm/ *n* víctima LOC *Ver* FALL **victimize, -ise** *vt* **1** escoger como víctima **2** tiranizar

victor /ˈvɪktə(r)/ *n* (*fml*) vencedor, -ora

victorious /vɪkˈtɔːriəs/ *adj* **1** ~ **(in sth)** victorioso (en algo) **2** (*equipo*) vencedor

3 to be ~ (over sth/sb) triunfar (sobre algo/algn)

victory /ˈvɪktəri/ *n* (*pl* **-ies**) victoria, triunfo

video /ˈvɪdiəʊ/ *n* (*pl* ~**s**) **1** vídeo **2** (*tb* **video (cassette) recorder**) (aparato de) vídeo **videotape** *n* cinta de vídeo

view /vjuː/ ◆ *n* **1** vista **2 viewing** sesión: *We had a private viewing of the film.* Vimos la película en una sesión privada. **3** [*gen pl*] ~ **(about/on sth)** opinión, parecer (sobre algo) **4** (*modo de entender*) criterio, concepto **5** (*imagen*) visión LOC **in my, etc view** (*fml*) en mi, etc opinión **in view of sth** en vista de algo **with a view to doing sth** (*fml*) con miras a hacer algo *Ver tb* POINT ◆ *vt* **1** mirar, ver **2** ~ **sth (as sth)** ver, considerar algo (como algo) **viewer** *n* **1** telespectador, -ora **2** espectador, -ora **3** (*aparato*) visor **viewpoint** *n* punto de vista

vigil /ˈvɪdʒɪl/ *n* vela, vigilia

vigilant /ˈvɪdʒɪlənt/ *adj* vigilante, alerta

vigorous /ˈvɪgərəs/ *adj* vigoroso, enérgico

vile /vaɪl/ *adj* (**viler**, **vilest**) repugnante, asqueroso

village /ˈvɪlɪdʒ/ *n* **1** pueblo **2** (*pequeño*) aldea **villager** *n* habitante de un pueblo

villain /ˈvɪlən/ *n* **1** (*esp Teat*) malo, -a **2** (*GB, coloq*) delincuente

vindicate /ˈvɪndɪkeɪt/ *vt* **1** rehabilitar **2** justificar

vine /vaɪn/ *n* **1** vid, parra **2** enredadera

vinegar /ˈvɪnɪgə(r)/ *n* vinagre

vineyard /ˈvɪnjəd/ *n* viña, viñedo

vintage /ˈvɪntɪdʒ/ ◆ *n* **1** cosecha **2** vendimia ◆ *adj* **1** (*vino*) añejo **2** (*fig*) clásico **3** (*GB*) (*coche*) antiguo (*fabricado entre 1917 y 1930*)

vinyl /ˈvaɪnl/ *n* vinilo

violate /ˈvaɪəleɪt/ *vt* **1** violar (*ley, normas*)

> **Violate** casi nunca se usa en sentido sexual. En este sentido, utilizamos **rape**.

2 (*confianza*) quebrantar **3** (*intimidad*) invadir

violence /ˈvaɪələns/ *n* **1** violencia **2** (*emociones*) intensidad, violencia

violent /ˈvaɪələnt/ *adj* **1** violento **2** (*emociones*) intenso, violento

violet /ˈvaɪələt/ *adj, n* violeta

violin /ˌvaɪəˈlɪn/ *n* violín

virgin /ˈvɜːdʒɪn/ *adj, n* virgen

Virgo /ˈvɜːgəʊ/ *n* (*pl* **Virgos**) virgo ☛ *Ver ejemplos en* AQUARIUS

virile /ˈvɪraɪl; *USA* ˈvɪrəl/ *adj* viril

virtual /ˈvɜːtʃuəl/ *adj* virtual **virtually** *adv* virtualmente, prácticamente

virtue /ˈvɜːtʃuː/ *n* **1** virtud **2** ventaja LOC **by virtue of sth** (*fml*) en virtud de algo **virtuous** *adj* virtuoso

virus /ˈvaɪrəs/ *n* (*pl* **viruses**) virus

visa /ˈviːzə/ *n* visado

vis-à-vis /ˌviːz ɑː ˈviː/ *prep* (*Fr*) **1** con relación a **2** en comparación con

vise *n* (*USA*) *Ver* VICE[2]

visible /ˈvɪzəbl/ *adj* **1** visible **2** (*fig*) patente **visibly** *adv* visiblemente, notablemente

vision /ˈvɪʒn/ *n* **1** vista **2** (*previsión, sueño*) visión

visit /ˈvɪzɪt/ ◆ **1** *vt, vi* visitar **2** *vt* (*país*) ir a **3** *vt* (*persona*) ir a ver a ◆ *n* visita LOC *Ver* PAY **visiting** *adj* visitante (*equipo, profesor*): *visiting hours* horas de visita **visitor** *n* **1** visitante, visita **2** turista

vista /ˈvɪstə/ *n* (*fml*) **1** vista, panorámica **2** (*fig*) perspectiva

visual /ˈvɪʒuəl/ *adj* visual: *visual display unit* unidad de visualización **visualize, -ise** *vt* **1** ~ **(yourself)** ver(se) **2** prever

vital /ˈvaɪtl/ *adj* **1** ~ **(for/to sth/sb)** vital, imprescindible (para algo/algn): *vital statistics* medidas femeninas **2** (*órgano, carácter*) vital **vitally** *adv*: *vitally important* de vital importancia

vitamin /ˈvɪtəmɪn; *USA* ˈvaɪt-/ *n* vitamina

vivacious /vɪˈveɪʃəs/ *adj* animado

vivid /ˈvɪvɪd/ *adj* vivo (*colores, imaginación, etc*) **vividly** *adv* vivamente

vocabulary /vəˈkæbjələri; *USA* -leri/ *n* (*pl* **-ies**) (*tb coloq* **vocab** /ˈvəʊkæb/) vocabulario

vocal /ˈvəʊkl/ ◆ *adj* **1** vocal: *vocal chords* cuerdas vocales **2** (*que habla mucho*) ruidoso: *a group of very vocal supporters* un grupo de seguidores muy ruidosos ◆ *n* [*gen pl*]: *to do the/be on vocals* ser el cantante/cantar

vocation /vəʊˈkeɪʃn/ *n* ~ (**for/to sth**) vocación (de algo) **vocational** *adj* técnico: *vocational training* formación profesional

vociferous /vəˈsɪfərəs; *USA* vəʊ-/ *adj* vociferante

vogue /vəʊg/ *n* ~ (**for sth**) moda (de algo) LOC **in vogue** en boga

voice /vɔɪs/ ◆ *n* voz: *to raise/lower your voice* levantar/bajar la voz ◊ *to have no voice in the matter* no tener voz en el asunto LOC **to make your voice heard** expresar uno su opinión *Ver tb* TOP[1] ◆ *vt* expresar

void /vɔɪd/ ◆ *n* (*fml*) vacío ◆ *adj* (*fml*) anulado: *to make sth void* anular algo *Ver* NULL

volatile /ˈvɒlətaɪl; *USA* -tl/ *adj* **1** (*frec pey*) (*persona*) voluble **2** (*situación*) inestable

volcano /vɒlˈkeɪnəʊ/ *n* (*pl* **-oes**) volcán

volition /vəˈlɪʃn; *USA* vəʊ-/ *n* (*fml*) LOC **of your own volition** por voluntad propia

volley /ˈvɒli/ *n* (*pl* **-eys**) **1** (*Dep*) volea **2** (*piedras, balas*) lluvia **3** (*fig*) retahíla

volleyball /ˈvɒlibɔːl/ *n* voleibol

volt /vəʊlt/ *n* voltio **voltage** *n* voltaje: *high voltage* tensión alta

volume /ˈvɒljuːm; *USA* -jəm/ *n* **1** volumen **2** (*libro*) volumen, tomo

voluminous /vəˈluːmɪnəs/ *adj* (*fml*) **1** amplio **2** (*escrito*) copioso

voluntary /ˈvɒləntri; *USA* -teri/ *adj* voluntario

volunteer /ˌvɒlənˈtɪə(r)/ ◆ *n* voluntario, -a ◆ **1** *vi* ~ (**for sth/to do sth**) ofrecerse (voluntario) (para algo); ofrecerse (a hacer algo) **2** *vt* ofrecer (*información, sugerencia*)

vomit /ˈvɒmɪt/ ◆ *vt, vi* vomitar ☛ Es más normal decir **to be sick**. ◆ *n* vómito **vomiting** *n* vómitos

voracious /vəˈreɪʃəs/ *adj* voraz, insaciable

vote /vəʊt/ ◆ *n* **1** voto **2** votación: *to take a vote on sth/put sth to the vote* someter algo a votación **3 the vote** derecho al voto LOC **vote of no confidence** voto de censura **vote of thanks** palabras de agradecimiento ◆ **1** *vt, vi* votar: *to vote for/against sth/sb* votar a favor/en contra de algo/a algn **2** *vt* (*dinero*) asignar **3** *vt* ~ (**that...**) (*coloq*) proponer que... **voter** *n* votante **voting** *n* votación

vouch /vaʊtʃ/ *vi* **1** ~ **for sth/sb** responder de algo/algn **2** ~ **for sth/that...** confirmar algo/que...

voucher /ˈvaʊtʃə(r)/ *n* (*GB*) vale, cupón

vow /vaʊ/ ◆ *n* voto, promesa solemne ◆ *vt* **to vow (that).../to do sth** jurar que.../hacer algo

vowel /ˈvaʊəl/ *n* vocal

voyage /ˈvɔɪɪdʒ/ *n* viaje

> **Voyage** se usa generalmente para viajes por mar, por el espacio y en sentido figurado. *Ver nota en* VIAJE

vulgar /ˈvʌlgə(r)/ *adj* **1** vulgar **2** (*chiste, etc*) grosero

vulnerable /ˈvʌlnərəbl/ *adj* vulnerable

vulture /ˈvʌltʃə(r)/ *n* buitre

Ww

W, w /ˈdʌbljuː/ *n* (*pl* **W's, w's** /ˈdʌbljuːz/) W, w: *W for William* W de Wenceslao ☛ *Ver ejemplos en* A, a

wade /weɪd/ **1** *vi* caminar con dificultad por agua, barro, etc **2** *vt, vi* (*riachuelo*) vadear

wafer /ˈweɪfə(r)/ *n* barquillo

wag /wæg/ *vt, vi* (**-gg-**) **1** mover(se) (de un lado a otro) **2** (*cola*) menear(se)

wage /weɪdʒ/ ◆ *n* [*gen pl*] sueldo (*semanal*) ☛ *Comparar con* SALARY ◆ *vt* LOC **to wage (a) war/a battle (against/on sth/sb)** librar una batalla (contra algo/algn)

wagon (*GB tb* **waggon**) /ˈwægən/ *n* carromato **2** (*Ferrocarril*) vagón

wail /weɪl/ ◆ *vi* **1** gemir **2** (*sirena*) aullar ◆ *n* gemido, aullido

waist /weɪst/ *n* cintura: *waistband* cinturilla ◊ *waistline* cintura/talle

waistcoat /ˈweɪskəʊt; *USA* ˈweskət/ (*USA tb* **vest**) *n* chaleco

wait /weɪt/ ◆ **1** *vi* ~ (**for sth/sb**) esperar (algo/a algn): *Wait a minute...* Un momento... ◊ *I can't wait to...* Tengo muchas ganas de... ☛ *Ver nota en* ESPERAR **2** *vt* (*turno*) esperar LOC **to keep sb waiting** hacer esperar a algn PHR V **to wait on sb** servir a algn **to wait up** (**for sb**) esperar levantado (a algn) ◆ *n* espera: *We had a three-hour wait for the bus.* Nos tocó esperar el autobús tres horas. ☛ *Comparar con* AWAIT **waiter** *n* camarero **waitress** *n* camarera

waive /weɪv/ *vt* (*fml*) **1** (*pago*) renunciar a **2** (*norma*) pasar por alto

wake /weɪk/ ◆ *vt, vi* (*pret* **woke** /wəʊk/ *pp* **woken** /ˈwəʊkən/) ~ (**sb**) (**up**) despertarse, despertar a algn ☛ *Ver nota en* AWAKE *y comparar con* AWAKEN PHR V **to wake** (**sb**) **up** despabilarse, despabilar a algn **to wake up to sth** darse cuenta de algo ◆ *n* **1** velatorio **2** (*Náut*) estela LOC **in the wake of sth** después de algo

walk /wɔːk/ ◆ **1** *vi* andar **2** *vt* pasear: *I'll walk you home.* Te acompañaré a casa. **3** *vt* recorrer (a pie) PHR V **to walk away/off** irse **to walk into sth/sb** chocar(se) contra algo/con algn **to walk out** (*coloq*) declararse en huelga **to walk out of sth** largarse de algo ◆ *n* **1** paseo, caminata: *to go for a walk* (ir a) dar un paseo ◊ *It's a ten-minute walk.* Está a diez minutos andando. **2** andar LOC **a walk of life**: *people of all walks of life* gente de todos los tipos o profesiones **walker** *n* paseante **walking** *n* andar: *walking shoes* zapatos para caminar ◊ *walking stick* bastón **walkout** *n* huelga

Walkman® /ˈwɔːkmən/ (*pl* **-mans**) walkman®

wall /wɔːl/ *n* **1** muro, pared **2** (*ciudad, fig*) muralla LOC *Ver* BACK[1] **walled** *adj* **1** amurallado **2** tapiado

wallet /ˈwɒlɪt/ *n* cartera (*para dinero*) ☛ *Comparar con* PURSE, SATCHEL

wallpaper /ˈwɔːlˌpeɪpə(r)/ *n* papel pintado

walnut /ˈwɔːlnʌt/ *n* **1** nuez **2** nogal (*árbol y madera*)

waltz /wɔːls; *USA* wɔːlts/ ◆ *n* vals ◆ *vi* bailar el vals

wand /wɒnd/ *n* vara: *magic wand* varita mágica

wander /ˈwɒndə(r)/ **1** *vi* deambular

> A menudo **wander** va seguido de **around**, **about** u otras preposiciones o adverbios. En estos casos, hay que traducirlo por distintos verbos en español, y tiene el significado de distraídamente, sin propósito: *to wander in* entrar distraídamente ◊ *She wandered across the road.* Cruzó la calle distraídamente.

2 *vi* (*pensamientos*) vagar **3** *vi* (*mirada*) pasear **4** *vt* (*calles, etc*) vagar por PHR V **to wander away/off** extraviarse (*animal*), alejarse

wane /weɪn/ (*tb* **to be on the wane**) *vi* menguar, disminuir (*poder, entusiasmo*)

want /wɒnt; *USA* wɔːnt/ ◆ **1** *vt, vi* querer: *I want some cheese.* Quiero queso. ◊ *Do you want to go?* ¿Quieres ir?

> Nótese que **like** también significa "querer", pero sólo se utiliza para ofrecer algo o para invitar a alguien: *Would you like to come to dinner?* ¿Quieres venir a cenar? ◊ *Would you like something to eat?* ¿Quieres comer algo?

2 *vt* necesitar: *It wants fixing.* Hay que arreglarlo. **3** *vt* buscar, necesitar: *You're wanted upstairs/on the phone.* Te buscan arriba./Te llaman al teléfono. ◆ *n* **1** [*gen pl*] necesidad, deseo **2** ~ **of sth** falta de algo: *for want of* por falta de ◊ *not for want of trying* no por no intentarlo **3** miseria, pobreza **wanting** *adj* ~ (**in sth**) (*fml*) falto (de algo)

war /wɔː(r)/ *n* **1** guerra **2** conflicto **3** ~ (**against sth/sb**) lucha (contra algo/algn) LOC **at war** en guerra **to make/wage war on sth/sb** hacerle la guerra a algo/algn *Ver tb* WAGE

ward /wɔːd/ ◆ *n* sala (*de hospital*) ◆ PHR V **to ward sth off 1** (*ataque*) rechazar algo **2** (*el mal*) ahuyentar algo **3** (*peligro*) prevenir algo

warden /ˈwɔːdn/ *n* guardia, guarda *Ver tb* TRAFFIC

wardrobe /ˈwɔːdrəʊb/ *n* **1** armario (*para colgar ropa*) **2** vestuario

warehouse /ˈweəhaʊs/ *n* almacén

wares /weəz/ *n* [*pl*] (*antic*) mercancías

warfare /ˈwɔːfeə(r)/ *n* guerra

warlike /ˈwɔːlaɪk/ *adj* belicoso

warm /wɔːm/ ◆ *adj* (**-er**, **-est**) **1** (*clima*) templado: *to be warm* hacer calor ☛ *Ver nota en* FRÍO **2** (*cosa*) caliente **3** (*persona*): *to be/get warm* tener calor/calentarse **4** (*ropa*) de abrigo, abrigado **5** (*fig*) caluroso, cordial ◆ *vt, vi* ~ (**sth/yourself**) (**up**) calentar algo; calentarse PHR V **to warm up 1** (*Dep*) calentar **2** (*motor*) calentarse **to warm sth up** recalentar algo (*comida*) **warming** *n*: *global warming* el calentamiento de la tierra **warmly** *adv* **1** calurosamente **2** *warmly dressed* vestido con ropa de abrigo **3** (*dar las gracias*) efusivamente **warmth** *n* **1** calor **2** (*fig*) simpatía, afabilidad, entusiasmo

warn /wɔːn/ *vt* **1** ~ **sb** (**about/of sth**) advertir a algn (de algo); prevenir a algn (contra algo): *They warned us about/of the strike.* Nos advirtieron de la huelga. ◊ *They warned us about the neighbours.* Nos previnieron contra los vecinos. **2** ~ **sb that...** advertir a algn que...: *I warned them that it would be expensive.* Les advertí que sería caro. **3** ~ **sb against doing sth** advertir a algn que no haga algo: *They warned us against going into the forest.* Nos advirtieron que no fuéramos al bosque. **4** ~ **sb** (**not**) **to do sth** ordenar a algn que (no) haga algo (bajo amenaza) **warning** *n* aviso, advertencia

warp /wɔːp/ *vt, vi* combar(se) **warped** *adj* retorcido (*mente*)

warrant /ˈwɒrənt; *USA* ˈwɔːr-/ ◆ *n* (*Jur*) orden: *search-warrant* orden de registro ◆ *vt* (*fml*) justificar

warranty /ˈwɒrənti; *USA* ˈwɔːr-/ *n* (*pl* **-ies**) garantía *Ver tb* GUARANTEE

warren /ˈwɒrən; *USA* ˈwɔːrən/ *n* **1** conejera **2** laberinto

warrior /ˈwɒrɪə(r); *USA* ˈwɔːr-/ *n* guerrero, -a

warship /ˈwɔːʃɪp/ *n* buque de guerra

wart /wɔːt/ *n* verruga

wartime /ˈwɔːtaɪm/ *n* (tiempo de) guerra

wary /ˈweəri/ *adj* (**warier**, **wariest**) cauto: *to be wary of sth/sb* desconfiar de algo/algn

was /wəz, wɒz; *USA* wʌz/ *pret de* BE

wash /wɒʃ/ ◆ *n* **1** lavado: *to have a wash* lavarse **2 the wash** [*sing*]: *All my shirts are in the wash.* Todas mis camisas se están lavando. **3** [*sing*] (*Náut*) estela ◆ **1** *vt, vi* lavar(se): *to wash yourself* lavarse **2** *vi* ~ **over sth** cubrir algo **3** *vi* ~ **over sb** (*fig*) invadir a algn **4** *vt* llevar, arrastrar: *to be washed overboard* ser arrastrado por la borda por las olas PHR V **to wash sth/sb away** arrastrar algo/a algn, llevarse algo/a algn **to wash off** quitarse (lavando) **to wash sth off** quitar algo (lavando) **to wash sth out** lavar algo **to wash up 1** (*GB*) fregar los platos **2** (*USA*) lavarse (*las manos y la cara*) **to wash sth up 1** (*GB*) (*platos*) fregar algo **2** (*mar*) llevar algo a la playa **washable** *adj* lavable

washbasin /ˈwɒʃ beɪsn/ (*USA* **washbowl**) *n* lavabo

washing /ˈwɒʃɪŋ; *USA* ˈwɔː-/ *n* **1** lavado: *washing powder* detergente (de lavadora) **2** ropa sucia **3** colada

washing machine *n* lavadora

washing-up /ˌwɒʃɪŋ ˈʌp/ *n* platos (para fregar): *to do the washing-up* fregar los platos ◊ *washing-up liquid* (detergente) lavavajillas

washroom /ˈwɒʃruːm/ *n* (*USA*, *eufemismo*) aseos ☛ *Ver nota en* TOILET

wasn't /ˈwɒz(ə)nt/ = WAS NOT *Ver* BE

wasp /wɒsp/ *n* avispa

waste /weɪst/ ◆ *adj* **1** *waste material/products* desechos **2** baldío (*terreno*) ◆ *vt* **1** malgastar **2** (*tiempo, ocasión*) perder **3** (*no usar*) desperdiciar LOC **to waste your breath** perder el tiempo PHR V **to waste away** consumirse ◆ *n* **1** pérdida, desperdicio **2** (*acción*) derroche, despilfarro **3** [*incontable*] desperdicios, desechos, basura: *waste disposal* recogida de basura/desechos LOC **to go/run to waste** echarse a perder, desperdiciarse **wasted** *adj* inútil (*viaje, esfuerzo*) **wasteful** *adj* **1** derrochador **2** (*método, proceso*) antieconómico

wasteland /ˈweɪstlænd/ *n* tierra baldía

waste-paper basket *n* papelera

watch /wɒtʃ/ ◆ *n* **1** reloj (*de pulsera*) ☛ *Ver dibujo en* RELOJ **2** (turno de) guardia **3** (*personas*) guardia, vigía LOC **to keep watch** (**over sth/sb**) vigilar (algo/a algn) *Ver tb* CLOSE[1] ◆ **1** *vt, vi* observar, mirar **2** *vt, vi* (*espiar*) vigilar, observar **3** *vt* (*TV, Dep*) ver **4** *vt,*

~ **(over) sth/sb** cuidar (algo/a algn) **5** *vi* ~ **for sth** estar atento a algo; esperar algo **6** *vt* tener cuidado con, fijarse en: *Watch your language.* No digas palabrotas. LOC **to watch your step** tener cuidado PHR V **to watch out** tener cuidado: *Watch out!* ¡Cuidado! **to watch out for sth/sb** estar atento a algo/algn: *Watch out for that hole.* Cuidado con ese hueco. **watchful** *adj* vigilante, alerta

watchdog /ˈwɒtʃdɒg/ *n* organismo de control

water /ˈwɔːtə(r)/ ◆ *n* agua LOC **under water 1** bajo el agua, debajo del agua **2** inundado *Ver tb* FISH ◆ **1** *vt* (*planta*) regar **2** *vi* (*ojos*) llorar **3** *vi* (*boca*) hacerse agua PHR V **to water sth down 1** diluir algo con agua **2** (*fig*) suavizar algo

watercolour (*USA* **-color**) /ˈwɔːtəkʌlə(r)/ *n* acuarela

watercress /ˈwɔːtəkres/ *n* [*incontable*] berro

waterfall /ˈwɔːtəfɔːl/ *n* cascada, catarata

watermelon /ˈwɔːtəmelən/ *n* sandía

waterproof /ˈwɔːtəpruːf/ *adj*, *n* impermeable

watershed /ˈwɔːtəʃed/ *n* momento decisivo/crítico

water-skiing /ˈwɔːtə skiːɪŋ/ *n* esquí acuático

watertight /ˈwɔːtətaɪt/ *adj* **1** estanco, hermético **2** (*argumento*) irrebatible

waterway /ˈwɔːtəweɪ/ *n* vía fluvial, canal

watery /ˈwɔːtəri/ *adj* **1** (*pey*) aguado **2** (*color*) pálido **3** (*ojos*) lloroso

watt /wɒt/ *n* vatio

wave /weɪv/ ◆ **1** *vt*, *vi* agitar(se) **2** *vi* (*bandera*) ondear **3** *vi* ~ **(at/to sb)** hacer señas con la mano (a algn) **4** *vt*, *vi* (*pelo, etc*) ondular(se) PHR V **to wave sth aside** rechazar algo (*protesta*) ◆ *n* **1** ola **2** (*fig*) oleada **3** seña (con la mano) **4** (*Fís, pelo*) onda **wavelength** *n* longitud de onda

waver /ˈweɪvə(r)/ *vi* **1** flaquear **2** (*voz*) temblar **3** vacilar

wavy /ˈweɪvi/ *adj* (**wavier**, **waviest**) **1** ondulado **2** ondulante

wax /wæks/ *n* cera

way /weɪ/ ◆ *n* **1** way **(from ... to ...)** camino (de ... a ...): *to ask/tell sb the way* preguntarle/indicarle a algn por dónde se va ◊ *across/over the way* enfrente/al otro lado de la calle ◊ *a long way (away)* lejos ◊ *way out* salida **2 Way** (*en nombres*) vía **3** paso: *Get out of my way!* ¡Quítate de en medio! **4** dirección: *'Which way?' 'That way.'* —¿Por dónde? —Por ahí. **5** forma, manera: *Do it your own way!* ¡Hazlo como quieras! **6** [*gen pl*] costumbre LOC **by the way** a propósito **in a/one way; in some ways** en cierto modo **no way!** (*coloq*) ¡ni hablar! **one way or another** como sea **on the way** en (el) camino: *to be on your way* irse **the other way (a)round 1** al revés **2** por el otro camino **to divide, split, etc sth two, three, etc ways** dividir algo entre dos, tres, etc **to get/have your own way** salirse con la suya **to give way (to sth/sb) 1** ceder (ante algo/algn) **2** ceder el paso (a algo/algn) **to give way to sth** entregarse (a algo), dejarse dominar por algo **to go out of your way (to do sth)** tomarse la molestia (de hacer algo) **to make way (for sth/sb)** dejar paso (a algo/algn) **to make your way (to/towards sth)** irse (a/hacia algo) **under way** en marcha **way of life** estilo de vida **ways and means** medios *Ver tb* BAR, FEEL, FIGHT, FIND, HARD, HARM, LEAD², LOSE, MEND, PAVE ◆ *adv* (*coloq*) muy: *way ahead* muy por delante LOC **way back** hace mucho tiempo: *way back in the fifties* allá por los años cincuenta

we /wiː/ *pron pers* nosotros: *Why don't we go?* ¿Por qué no vamos? ☛ El *pron pers* no se puede omitir en inglés. *Comparar con* US

weak /wiːk/ *adj* (**-er**, **-est**) **1** débil **2** (*Med*) delicado **3** (*bebida*) flojo **4** ~ **(at/in/on sth)** flojo (en algo) **weaken 1** *vt*, *vi* debilitar(se) **2** *vi* ceder **weakness** *n* **1** debilidad **2** flaqueza

wealth /welθ/ *n* **1** [*incontable*] riqueza **2** ~ **of sth** abundancia de algo **wealthy** *adj* (**-ier**, **-iest**) rico

weapon /ˈwepən/ *n* arma

wear /weə(r)/ ◆ (*pret* **wore** /wɔː(r)/ *pp* **worn** /wɔːn/) **1** *vt* (*ropa, gafas, etc*) llevar **2** *vt* (*expresión*) tener **3** *vt*, *vi* desgastar(se) **4** *vt* (*agujero, etc*) hacer **5** *vi* durar PHR V **to wear (sth) away** desgastar algo/desgastarse por completo **to wear sb down** agotar a algn **to wear sth down** minar algo **to wear (sth) down/out** desgastar algo/ desgastarse **to wear off** desaparecer (*novedad, etc*) **to wear sb out** agotar a algn

¿**Wear** o **carry**? **Wear** se utiliza para referirse a ropa, calzado y complementos, y también a perfumes y gafas: *Do you have to wear a suit at work?* ¿Tienes que llevar traje para ir a trabajar? ◊ *What perfume are you wearing?* ¿Qué perfume llevas? ◊ *He doesn't wear glasses.* No lleva gafas. Utilizamos **carry** cuando nos referimos a objetos que llevamos con nosotros, especialmente en las manos o en los brazos: *She wasn't wearing her raincoat, she was carrying it over her arm.* No llevaba puesta la gabardina, la tenía en el brazo.

◆ *n* **1** desgaste **2** uso **3** ropa: *ladies' wear* ropa de señora LOC **wear and tear** desgaste por el uso

weary /ˈwɪəri/ *adj* (-**ier**, -**iest**) **1** agotado **2** ~ **of sth** hastiado de algo

weather /ˈweðə(r)/ ◆ *n* tiempo: *weather forecast* parte meteorológico LOC **under the weather** (*coloq*) pachucho ◆ *vt* superar (*crisis*)

weave /wiːv/ (*pret* **wove** /wəʊv/ *pp* **woven** /ˈwəʊvn/) **1** *vt* tejer algo (con algo) **2** *vt* ~ **sth into sth** (*fig*) incluir algo (en algo) **3** *vi* (*pret, pp* **weaved**) serpentear

web /web/ *n* **1** telaraña **2** (*fig*) red **3** (*engaños*) sarta

we'd /wiːd/ **1** = WE HAD *Ver* HAVE **2** = WE WOULD *Ver* WOULD

wedding /ˈwedɪŋ/ *n* boda: *wedding ring/cake* alianza/pastel de bodas LOC **golden/silver wedding** bodas de oro/ plata ☛ *Ver nota en* BODA

wedge /wedʒ/ ◆ *n* **1** cuña **2** (*queso, pastel*) pedazo (grande) **3** (*limón*) trozo (*en forma de gajo*) ◆ *vt* **1** *to wedge sth open/shut* mantener algo abierto/ cerrado con calza **2** *to wedge itself/get wedged* atascarse **3** (*esp personas*) apretujar

Wednesday /ˈwenzdeɪ, ˈwenzdi/ *n* (*abrev* **Wed**) miércoles ☛ *Ver ejemplos en* MONDAY

wee /wiː/ *adj* **1** (*Escocia*) pequeñito **2** (*coloq*) poquito: *a wee bit* un poquitín

weed /wiːd/ ◆ *n* **1** mala hierba: *weedkiller* herbicida **2** [*incontable*] (*en agua*) algas **3** (*coloq, pey*) enclenque **4** persona sin carácter: *He's a weed.* No tiene carácter. ◆ *vt* escardar PHR V **to weed sth/sb out** eliminar algo/a algn

week /wiːk/ *n* semana: *35-hour week* semana laboral de 35 horas LOC **a week on Monday/Monday week** el lunes que viene no, el siguiente, del lunes en ocho días **a week today/tomorrow** de hoy/ mañana en ocho días **weekday** *n* día laborable **weekend** /ˌwiːkˈend/ *n* fin de semana

weekly /ˈwiːkli/ ◆ *adj* semanal ◆ *adv* semanalmente ◆ *n* (*pl* -**ies**) semanario

weep /wiːp/ *vi* (*pret, pp* **wept** /wept/) (*fml*) ~ (**for/over sth/sb**) llorar (por algo/algn): *weeping willow* sauce llorón **weeping** *n* llanto

weigh /weɪ/ **1** *vt, vi* pesar **2** *vt* ~ **sth** (**up**) sopesar algo **3** *vi* ~ (**against sth/ sb**) influir (en contra de algo/algn) LOC **to weigh anchor** levar anclas PHR V **to weigh sb down** abrumar a algn **to weigh sth/sb down**: *weighed down with luggage* muy cargado de equipaje

weight /weɪt/ ◆ *n* **1** (*lit y fig*) peso: *by weight* a peso **2** pesa, peso LOC **to lose/ put on weight** (*persona*) adelgazar/ engordar *Ver tb* CARRY, PULL ◆ *vt* **1** poner peso o pesas en **2** ~ **sth (down) (with sth)** sujetar algo (con algo) **weighting** *n* **1** (*GB*): *London weighting* complemento salarial por trabajar en Londres **2** importancia **weightless** *adj* ingrávido **weighty** *adj* (-**ier**, -**iest**) **1** pesado **2** (*fig*) de peso, importante

weir /wɪə(r)/ *n* presa (*colocada en la corriente de un río*)

weird /wɪəd/ *adj* (-**er**, -**est**) **1** sobrenatural, misterioso **2** (*coloq*) raro

welcome /ˈwelkəm/ ◆ *adj* **1** bienvenido **2** agradable LOC **to be welcome to sth/to do sth**: *You're welcome to use my car/to stay.* Mi coche está a tu disposición./Estás invitado a quedarte. **you're welcome** de nada ◆ *n* bienvenida, acogida ◆ *vt* **1** dar la bienvenida a, recibir **2** agradecer **3** acoger, recibir **welcoming** *adj* acogedor

weld /weld/ *vt, vi* soldar(se)

welfare /ˈwelfeə(r)/ *n* **1** bienestar **2** asistencia: *the Welfare State* el Estad del bienestar **3** (*USA*) *Ver* SOCIAL SECURITY

well[1] /wel/ ◆ *n* pozo ◆ *vi* ~ **(out/up)** brotar

well[2] /wel/ ◆ *adj* (*comp* **better** /ˈbetə(r)/ *superl* **best** /best/) bien: *to be well* estar bien ◊ *to get well* reponerse ◆ *adv* (*comp* **better** /ˈbetə(r)/ *superl* **best** /best/) **1** bien **2** [*después de* **can, could, may, might**]: *I can well believe it.* Lo creo totalmente. ◊ *I can't very well leave.* No puedo irme sin más. LOC **as well** también ☛ *Ver nota en* TAMBIÉN **as well as** además de **may/might (just) as well do sth**: *We may/might as well go home.* Bien podríamos irnos a casa. **to do well 1** progresar **2** [*sólo en tiempo continuo*] (*paciente*) recuperarse **well and truly** (*coloq*) completamente *Ver tb* DISPOSED, JUST, MEAN[1], PRETTY

well[3] /wel/ *interj* **1** (*asombro*) ¡vaya!: *Well, look who's here!* ¡Vaya, vaya! Mira quién está aquí. **2** (*resignación*) bueno: *Oh well, that's that then.* Bueno, qué le vamos a hacer. **3** (*interrogación*) ¿y entonces? **4** (*duda*) pues: *Well, I don't know…* Pues, no sé…

we'll /wiːl/ **1** = WE SHALL *Ver* SHALL **2** = WE WILL *Ver* WILL

well behaved *adj* bien educado: *to be well behaved* portarse bien

well-being /ˈwel biːɪŋ/ *n* bienestar

well-earned /ˈwel ɜːnd/ *adj* merecido

wellington /ˈwelɪŋtən/ (*tb* **wellington boot**) *n* [*gen pl*] (*esp GB*) katiusca

well-kept /ˈwel kept/ *adj* **1** cuidado, bien conservado **2** (*secreto*) bien guardado

well known *adj* muy conocido, famoso: *It's a well-known fact that…* Es sabido que…

well meaning *adj* bienintencionado

well off *adj* acomodado, rico

well-to-do /ˌwel tə ˈduː/ *adj* acomodado

went *pret de* GO[1]

wept *pret, pp de* WEEP

were /wə(r), wɜː(r)/ *pret de* BE

we're /wɪə(r)/ = WE ARE *Ver* BE

weren't /wɜːnt/ = WERE NOT *Ver* BE

west /west/ ◆ *n* **1** (*tb* **the west, the West**) (*abrev* **W**) (el) oeste: *I live in the west of Scotland.* Vivo en el oeste de Escocia. ◊ *westbound* en/con dirección oeste **2 the West** (el) Occidente, los países occidentales ◆ *adj* (del) oeste, occidental: *west winds* vientos del oeste ◆ *adv* al oeste: *to travel west* viajar hacia el oeste *Ver tb* WESTWARD(S)

western /ˈwestən/ ◆ *adj* (*tb* **Western**) (del) oeste, occidental ◆ *n* novela o película del oeste **westerner** *n* occidental

westward(s) /ˈwestwəd(z)/ *adv* hacia el oeste *Ver tb* WEST *adv*

wet /wet/ ◆ *adj* (**wetter, wettest**) **1** mojado: *to get wet* mojarse **2** húmedo: *in wet places* en lugares húmedos **3** (*tiempo*) lluvioso **4** (*pintura, etc*) fresco **5** (*GB, coloq, pey*) (*persona*) parado ◆ *n* **1 the wet** lluvia: *Come in out of the wet.* Entra y resguárdate de la lluvia. **2** humedad ◆ (*pret, pp* **wet** *o* **wetted**) **1** *vt* mojar, humedecer: *to wet the/your bed* hacerse pis en la cama **2** *v refl* **to wet yourself** orinarse

we've /wiːv/ = WE HAVE *Ver* HAVE

whack /wæk/ ◆ *vt* (*coloq*) dar un buen golpe a ◆ *n* porrazo

whale /weɪl/ *n* ballena

wharf /wɔːf/ *n* (*pl* **~s** *o* **-ves** /wɔːvz/) muelle

what /wɒt/ ◆ *adj interr* qué: *What time is it?* ¿Qué hora es? ◊ *What colour is it?* ¿De qué color es? ◆ *pron interr* qué: *What did you say?* ¿Qué has dicho? ◊ *What's her phone number?* ¿Cuál es su número de teléfono? ◊ *What's your name?* ¿Cómo te llamas? LOC **what about…? 1** ¿qué te parece si…? **2** ¿y qué es de…?

> **¿Which o what? Which** se refiere a uno o más miembros de un grupo limitado: *Which is your car, this one or that one?* ¿Cuál es tu coche, éste o aquél? **What** se usa cuando el grupo no es tan limitado: *What are your favourite books?* ¿Cuáles son tus libros preferidos?

what if…? ¿y (qué pasa) si…?: *What if it rains?* ¿Y si llueve? ◆ *adj rel, pron rel* el/la/lo que: *what money I have* (todo) el dinero que tenga ◊ *I know what you're thinking.* Sé lo que piensas. ◆ *adj* qué: *What a pity!* ¡Qué pena! ◆ *interj* **1 what!** ¡cómo! **2 what?** (*coloq*) ¿qué?, ¿cómo?

whatever /wɒtˈevə(r)/ ◆ *pron* **1** (todo) lo que: *Give whatever you can.* Dé lo que pueda. **2** *whatever happens* pase lo que pase LOC **or whatever** (*coloq*) o el/la/lo que sea: *…basketball, swimming or whatever.* …baloncesto, natación o el que sea. ◆ *adj* cualquier: *I'll be in whatever time you come.* Estaré a cualquier hora que vengas. ◆ *pron interr* qué (demonios): *Whatever can it be?* ¿Qué demonios puede ser? ◆ *adv* (*tb* **whatsoever**) en absoluto: *nothing whatsoever* nada en absoluto

wheat /wiːt/ *n* trigo

wheel /wiːl/ ◆ *n* **1** rueda **2** volante ◆ **1** *vt* (*bicicleta, etc*) empujar **2** *vt* (*persona*) llevar **3** *vi* (*pájaro*) revolotear **4** *vi* ~ **(a)round** darse la vuelta

wheelbarrow /ˈwiːlbærəʊ/ (*tb* **barrow**) *n* carretilla (*de mano*)

wheelchair /ˈwiːltʃeə(r)/ *n* silla de ruedas

wheeze /wiːz/ *vi* respirar con dificultad, resollar

when /wen/ ◆ *adv interr* cuándo: *When did he die?* ¿Cuándo murió? ◊ *I don't know when she arrived.* No sé cuándo llegó. ◆ *adv rel* en (el/la/los/las) que: *There are times when…* Hay veces en que… ◆ *conj* cuando: *It was raining when I arrived.* Llovía cuando llegué. ◊ *I'll call you when I'm ready.* Te llamaré cuando esté lista.

whenever /wenˈevə(r)/ *conj* **1** cuando: *Come whenever you like.* Ven cuando quieras. **2** (*todas las veces que*) siempre que: *You can borrow my car whenever you want.* Puedes usar mi coche siempre que quieras.

where /weə(r)/ ◆ *adv interr* dónde: *Where are you going?* ¿Adónde vas? ◊ *I don't know where it is.* No sé dónde está. ◆ *adv rel* donde: *the town where I was born* el pueblo en que nací ◆ *conj* donde: *Stay where you are.* Quédate donde estás.

whereabouts /ˈweərəˈbaʊts/ ◆ *adv interr* dónde ◆ *n* [*v sing o pl*] paradero

whereas /ˌweərˈæz/ *conj* (*fml*) mientras que

whereby /weəˈbaɪ/ *adv rel* (*fml*) según/por el/la/lo cual

whereupon /ˌweərəˈpɒn/ *conj* tras lo cual

wherever /ˌweərˈevə(r)/ ◆ *conj* dondequiera que: *wherever you like* donde quieras ◆ *adv interr* dónde (demonios)

whet /wet/ *vt* (-tt-) LOC **to whet sb's appetite** abrir el apetito a algn

whether /ˈweðə(r)/ *conj* si: *I'm not sure whether to resign or stay on.* No sé si dimitir o continuar. ◊ *It depends on whether the letter arrives on time.* Depende de si la carta llega a tiempo. LOC **whether or not**: *whether or not it rains/whether it rains or not* tanto si llueve como si no

which /wɪtʃ/ ◆ *adj interr* qué: *Which book did you take?* ¿Qué libro te has llevado? ◊ *Do you know which one is yours?* ¿Sabes cuál es el tuyo? ☛ *Ver nota en* WHAT ◆ *pron interr* cuál: *Which is your favourite?* ¿Cuál es tu preferido? ☛ *Ver nota en* WHAT ◆ *adj rel, pron rel* **1** [*sujeto*] que: *the book which is on the table* el libro que está sobre la mesa **2** [*complemento*] que: *the article (which) I read yesterday* el artículo que leí ayer **3** (*fml*) [*después de preposición*] el/la/lo cual: *her work, about which I know nothing…* su trabajo, del cual no sé nada… ◊ *in which case* en cuyo caso ◊ *the bag in which I put it* la bolsa en la que lo puse ☛ Este uso es muy formal. Lo más normal es poner la preposición al final: *the bag which I put it in*

whichever /wɪtʃˈevə(r)/ **1** *pron* el/la que: *whichever you like* el que quieras **2** *adj* cualquiera: *It's the same, whichever route you take.* No importa la ruta que elijas.

whiff /wɪf/ *n* ~ (**of sth**) aroma/tufo (a algo); soplo (de algo)

while /waɪl/ ◆ *n* [*sing*] tiempo, rato: *for a while* durante un rato LOC *Ver* ONCE, WORTH ◆ *conj* (*tb* **whilst** /waɪlst/) **1** (*tiempo*) mientras **2** (*contraste*) mientras (que): *I drink coffee while she prefers tea.* Yo tomo café, mientras que ella prefiere el té. **3** (*fml*) aunque: *While I admit that…* Aunque admito que… LOC **while you're at it** ya que estás, va etc ◆ PHR V **to while sth away** pasar algo: *to while the morning away* pasar la mañana

whim /wɪm/ *n* capricho, antojo

whimper /ˈwɪmpə(r)/ ◆ *vi* lloriquear ◆ *n* lloriqueo

whip /wɪp/ ◆ *n* **1** azote, látigo **2** (*Pol*) diputado, -a encargado, -a de la disciplina de su grupo parlamentario ◆ *vt* **1** azotar **2** ~ **sth** (**up**) (**into sth**) (*Cocina*) batir algo (hasta obtener algo): *whipped cream* nata montada PHR V **to whip sth up 1** preparar algo rápidamente **2** causar algo

whirl /wɜːl/ ◆ **1** *vt, vi* (hacer) girar **2** *vi* (*hojas*) arremolinarse **3** *vi* (*cabeza*) dar vueltas ◆ *n* [*sing*] **1** giro **2** remolino: *a whirl of dust* un remolino de polvo **3** (*fig*) torbellino: *My head is in a whirl.* La cabeza me da vueltas.

whirlpool /ˈwɜːlpuːl/ *n* remolino

whirlwind /ˈwɜːlwɪnd/ ◆ *n* torbellino ◆ *adj* (*fig*) relámpago

whirr (*esp USA* **whir**) /wɜː(r)/ ◆ *n* zumbido ◆ *vi* zumbar

whisk /wɪsk/ ◆ *n* batidor, batidora (eléctrica) ◆ *vt* (*Cocina*) batir PHR V **to whisk sth/sb away/off** llevarse algo/a algn volando

whiskers /ˈwɪskəz/ *n* [*pl*] **1** (*de animal*) bigotes **2** (*de hombre*) patillas

whisky /ˈwɪski/ *n* (*pl* **-ies**) (*USA o Irl* **whiskey**) whisky, güisqui

whisper /ˈwɪspə(r)/ ◆ **1** *vi* susurrar **2** *vi* cuchichear **3** *vt* decir en voz baja ◆ *n* **1** cuchicheo **2** susurro

whistle /ˈwɪsl/ ◆ *n* **1** silbido, pitido **2** silbato, pito ◆ *vt, vi* silbar, pitar

white /waɪt/ ◆ *adj* (**-er**, **-est**) **1** blanco: *white coffee* café con leche **2** ~ (**with sth**) pálido (de algo) ◆ *n* **1** blanco **2** clara (*de huevo*) ☛ *Comparar con* YOLK

white-collar /ˌwaɪt ˈkɒlə(r)/ *adj* de oficina: *white-collar workers* oficinistas

whiteness /ˈwaɪtnəs/ *n* blancura

White Paper *n* (*GB*) libro blanco (*de gobierno*)

whitewash /ˈwaɪtwɒʃ/ ◆ *n* lechada de cal, jalbegue ◆ *vt* **1** enjalbegar **2** (*fig*) encubrir

who /huː/ ◆ *pron interr* quién, quiénes: *Who are they?* ¿Quiénes son? ◊ *Who did you meet?* ¿A quién te encontraste? ◊ *Who is it?* ¿Quién es? ◊ *They wanted to know who had rung.* Preguntaron quién había llamado. ◆ *pron rel* **1** [*sujeto*] que: *people who eat garlic* gente que come ajo ◊ *the man who wanted to meet you* el hombre que quería conocerte ◊ *all those who want to go* todos los que quieran ir **2** [*complemento*] que: *I bumped into a woman (who) I knew.* Me topé con una mujer a la que conocía. ◊ *the man (who) I had spoken to* el hombre con el que había hablado ☛ *Ver nota en* WHOM

whoever /huːˈevə(r)/ *pron* **1** quien: *Whoever gets the job...* Quien consiga el puesto de trabajo... **2** quienquiera que

whole /həʊl/ ◆ *adj* **1** entero: *a whole bottle* una botella entera **2** (*coloq*) todo: *to forget the whole thing* olvidar todo el asunto ◆ *n* todo: *the whole of August* todo agosto LOC **on the whole** en general

wholehearted /ˌhəʊlˈhɑːtɪd/ *adj* incondicional **wholeheartedly** sin reservas

wholemeal /ˈhəʊlmiːl/ *adj* integral: *wholemeal bread* pan integral

wholesale /ˈhəʊlseɪl/ *adj, adv* **1** al por mayor **2** total: *wholesale destruction* destrucción total

wholesome /ˈhəʊlsəm/ *adj* sano, saludable

wholly /ˈhəʊlli/ *adv* totalmente

whom /huːm/ ◆ *pron interr* (*fml*) a quién: *Whom did you meet there?* ¿Con quién te encontraste allí? ◊ *To whom did you give the money?* ¿A quién diste el dinero? ☛ Este uso es muy formal. Lo más normal es decir: *Who did you meet there?* ◊ *Who did you give the money to?* ◆ *pron rel* (*fml*): *the investors, some of whom bought shares* los inversores, algunos de los cuales compraron acciones ◊ *the person to whom this letter was addressed* la persona a quien iba dirigida esta carta ☛ Este uso es muy formal. Sería mucho más corriente decir: *the person this letter was addressed to.*

whose /huːz/ ◆ *pron interr, adj interr* de quién: *Whose house is that?* ¿De quién es esa casa? ◊ *I wonder whose it is.* Me pregunto de quién es. ◆ *adj rel* cuyo, -a, -os, -as: *the people whose house* *we stayed in* las personas en cuya casa estuvimos

why /waɪ/ *adv interr, adv rel* por qué: *Why was she so late?* ¿Por qué llegó tan tarde? ◊ *Can you tell me the reason why you are so unhappy?* ¿Me puedes decir por qué eres tan desgraciado? LOC **why not** por qué no: *Why not go to the cinema?* ¿Por qué no vamos al cine?

wicked /ˈwɪkɪd/ *adj* (**-er**, **-est**) **1** malvado **2** malicioso **wickedness** *n* maldad

wicker /ˈwɪkə(r)/ *n* mimbre

wicket /ˈwɪkɪt/ *n* **1** meta, palos **2** terreno

wide /waɪd/ ◆ *adj* (**wider**, **widest**) **1** (*fig*) amplio: *a wide range of possibilities* una amplia gama de posibilidades **2** ancho: *How wide is it?* ¿Cuánto tiene de ancho? ◊ *It's two feet wide.* Tiene dos pies de ancho. ☛ *Ver nota en* BROAD **3** extenso ◆ *adv* muy: *wide awake* completamente despierto LOC **wide open** abierto de par en par *Ver tb* FAR **widely** *adv* extensamente, mucho: *widely used* muy utilizado **widen** *vt, vi* ensanchar(se), ampliar(se)

wide-ranging /ˌwaɪd ˈreɪndʒɪŋ/ *adj* de gran alcance (*investigación, etc*), muy diverso

widespread /ˈwaɪdspred/ *adj* general, difundido

widow /ˈwɪdəʊ/ *n* viuda **widowed** *adj* viudo **widower** *n* viudo

width /wɪdθ, wɪtθ/ *n* anchura, ancho

wield /wiːld/ *vt* **1** (*arma, etc*) empuñar, blandir **2** (*poder*) ejercer

wife /waɪf/ *n* (*pl* **wives** /waɪvz/) mujer, esposa

wig /wɪg/ *n* peluca

wiggle /ˈwɪgl/ *vt, vi* (*coloq*) menear(se)

wild /waɪld/ ◆ *adj* (**-er**, **-est**) **1** salvaje **2** (*planta*) silvestre **3** (*paisaje*) agreste **4** (*tiempo*) tempestuoso **5** desenfrenado **6** (*enojado*) furioso **7** (*coloq*) (*entusiasmado*) loco ◆ *n* **1 the wild** la selva: *in the wild* en estado salvaje **2 the wilds** [*pl*] (las) tierras remotas

wilderness /ˈwɪldənəs/ *n* **1** tierra no cultivada, desierto **2** (*fig*) selva

wildlife /ˈwaɪldlaɪf/ *n* flora y fauna

wildly /ˈwaɪldli/ *adv* **1** locamente, como loco **2** violentamente, furiosamente

wilful (*USA tb* **willful**) /ˈwɪlfl/ *adj* (*pey*) **1** (*acto*) voluntario, intencionado **2** (*delito*) premeditado **3** (*persona*) testarudo **wilfully** *adv* deliberadamente

will /wɪl/ ◆ (*contracción* **'ll** *neg* **will not** *o* **won't** /wəʊnt/) *v aux* para formar el futuro: *He'll come, won't he?* Vendrá, ¿verdad? ◊ *I hope it won't rain.* Espero que no llueva. ◊ *That'll be the postman.* Será el cartero. ◊ *You'll do as you're told.* Harás lo que te manden. ☛ *Ver nota en* SHALL ◆ *v modal*

> **Will** es un verbo modal al que sigue un infinitivo sin TO, y las oraciones interrogativas y negativas se construyen sin el auxiliar *do*.

1 (*voluntad, determinación*): *She won't go.* No quiere ir. ◊ *Will the car start?* ¿El coche arranca o no arranca? ☛ *Ver nota en* SHALL **2** (*oferta, petición*): *Will you help me?* ¿Puedes ayudarme? ◊ *Will you stay for tea?* ¿Quieres quedarte a tomar té? ◊ *Won't you sit down?* ¿No quieres sentarte? **3** (*regla general*): *Oil will float on water.* El aceite flota en el agua. ◆ *n* **1** voluntad **2** deseo **3** (*tb* **testament**) testamento LOC **at will** libremente *Ver tb* FREE

willing /ˈwɪlɪŋ/ *adj* **1** complaciente, bien dispuesto **2** ~ (**to do sth**) dispuesto (a hacer algo) **3** (*apoyo, etc*) espontáneo **willingly** *adv* voluntariamente, de buena gana **willingness** *n* **1** buena voluntad **2** ~ (**to do sth**) voluntad (de hacer algo)

willow /ˈwɪləʊ/ (*tb* **willow tree**) *n* sauce

will-power /ˈwɪl paʊə(r)/ *n* fuerza de voluntad

wilt /wɪlt/ *vi* **1** marchitarse **2** (*fig*) decaer

win /wɪn/ ◆ (**-nn-**) (*pret, pp* **won** /wʌn/) **1** *vi* ganar **2** *vt* ganar, llevarse **3** *vt* (*victoria*) conseguir, lograr **4** *vt* (*apoyo, amigos*) ganarse, granjearse LOC *Ver* TOSS PHR V **to win sth/sb back** recuperar algo/a algn **to win sb over/round (to sth)** convencer a algn (de que haga algo) ◆ *n* victoria

wince /wɪns/ *vi* **1** hacer una mueca de dolor **2** hacer un gesto de disgusto

wind[1] /wɪnd/ *n* **1** viento **2** aliento, resuello **3** [*incontable*] gases LOC **to get wind of sth** enterarse de algo *Ver* CAUTION

wind[2] /waɪnd/ (*pret, pp* **wound**

/waʊnd/) **1** *vi* serpentear **2** *vt* ~ **sth round/onto sth** enrollar algo alrededor de algo **3** *vt* ~ **sth** (**up**) dar cuerda a algo PHR V **to wind down 1** (*persona*) relajarse **2** (*actividad*) llegar a su fin **to wind sb up** (*coloq*) **1** poner nervioso a algn **2** (*fastidiar*) provocar a algn **to wind** (**sth**) **up** terminar (algo), concluir (algo) **to wind sth up** liquidar algo (*negocio*) **winding** *adj* **1** tortuoso, serpenteante **2** (*escalera*) de caracol

windfall /ˈwɪndfɔːl/ *n* **1** fruta caída (del árbol) **2** (*fig*) sorpresa caída del cielo

windmill /ˈwɪndmɪl/ *n* molino de viento

window /ˈwɪndəʊ/ *n* **1** ventana: *windowsill/window ledge* alféizar **2** (*coche, taquilla*) ventanilla **3** (*tb* **window-pane**) cristal, luna **4** escaparate, vitrina: *to go window-shopping* ir de escaparates

windscreen /ˈwɪndskriːn/ (*USA* **windshield**) *n* parabrisas: *(windscreen) wiper* limpiaparabrisas

windsurfing /ˈwɪndsɜːfɪŋ/ *n* windsurf

windy /ˈwɪndi/ *adj* (**-ier**, **-iest**) **1** ventoso **2** (*lugar*) expuesto al viento

wine /waɪn/ *n* vino: *wine glass* copa (para vino)

wing /wɪŋ/ *n* **1** (*gen, Arquit, Pol*) ala: *the right/left wing of the party* el ala derecha/izquierda del partido **2** (*vehículo*) aleta **3 the wings** [*pl*] bastidores

wink /wɪŋk/ ◆ **1** *vi* ~ (**at sb**) guiñar el ojo (a algn) **2** *vi* (*luz*) parpadear, titilar **3** *vt* (*ojo*) guiñar ◆ *n* guiño

winner /ˈwɪnə(r)/ *n* ganador, -ora

winning /ˈwɪnɪŋ/ *adj* **1** ganador **2** premiado **3** cautivador, encantador **winnings** *n* [*pl*] ganancias

winter /ˈwɪntə(r)/ ◆ *n* invierno ◆ *vi* invernar, pasar el invierno

wipe /waɪp/ *vt* **1** ~ **sth** (**from/off sth**) (**on/with sth**) limpiar(se), secar(se) algo (de algo) (con algo) **2** ~ **sth** (**from/off sth**) (*eliminar*) borrar algo (de algo) **3** ~ **sth across, onto, over, etc sth** pasar algo por algo PHR V **to wipe sth away/off/up** limpiar algo, secar algo **to wipe sth out 1** destruir algo **2** (*enfermedad, crimen*) erradicar algo

wire /ˈwaɪə(r)/ ◆ *n* **1** alambre **2** (*Electrón*) cable **3** [*sing*] alambrada **4** (*USA*) telegrama ◆ *vt* **1** ~ **sth** (**up**) hacer la instalación eléctrica de algo **2** ~ **sth** (**up**) **to sth** conectar algo a algo **3** (*USA*) poner un telegrama **wiring** *n* [*incontable*] **1** instalación eléctrica **2** cables

wireless /ˈwaɪələs/ *n* (*antic*) **1** radio (*electrodoméstico*) **2** radiotransmisor

wisdom /ˈwɪzdəm/ *n* **1** sabiduría: *wisdom tooth* muela del juicio **2** prudencia, cordura LOC *Ver* CONVENTIONAL

wise /waɪz/ *adj* (**wiser**, **wisest**) **1** acertado, prudente **2** sabio LOC **to be no wiser/none the wiser**; **not to be any the wiser** seguir sin entender nada

wish /wɪʃ/ ◆ **1** *vi* ~ **for sth** desear algo **2** *vt* ~ **sb sth** desear algo a algn **3** *vt* (*fml*) querer **4** *vt* (*que no se puede realizar*): *I wish he'd go away.* ¡Ojalá se fuera! ◇ *She wished she had gone.* Se arrepintió de no haber ido. ☛ El uso de **were**, y no **was**, con **I, he** o **she** después de **wish** se considera más correcto: *I wish I were rich!* ¡Ojalá fuera rico! **5** *vi* pedir un deseo ◆ *n* **1** ~ (**for sth/to do sth**) deseo (de algo/de hacer algo): *against my wishes* contra mi voluntad **2 wishes** [*pl*]: *(with) best wishes, Mary* un abrazo de Mary LOC *Ver* BEST **wishful** *adj* LOC **wishful thinking**: *It's wishful thinking on my part.* Me estoy haciendo ilusiones.

wistful /ˈwɪstfl/ *adj* triste, melancólico

wit /wɪt/ *n* **1** ingenio **2** (*persona*) persona ingeniosa **3 wits** [*pl*] inteligencia, juicio LOC **to be at your wits' end** estar para volverse loco **to be frightened/terrified/scared out of your wits** estar muerto de miedo

witch /wɪtʃ/ *n* bruja

witchcraft /ˈwɪtʃkrɑːft; *USA* -kræft/ *n* [*incontable*] brujería

witch-hunt /ˈwɪtʃ hʌnt/ *n* (*lit y fig*) caza de brujas

with /wɪð, wɪθ/ *prep* **1** con: *I'll be with you in a minute.* Un minuto y estoy contigo. ◇ *He's with ICI.* Está trabajando en ICI. **2** (*descripciones*) de, con: *the man with the scar* el hombre de la cicatriz ◇ *a house with a garden* una casa con jardín **3** de: *Fill the glass with water.* Llena el vaso de agua. **4** (*apoyo y conformidad*) (de acuerdo) con **5** (*a causa de*) de: *to tremble with fear* temblar de miedo LOC **to be with sb**

(*coloq*) seguir lo que algn dice: *I'm not with you.* No te entiendo. **with it** (*coloq*) **1** al día **2** de moda **3** *He's not with it today.* Hoy no está muy centrado. ☛ Para los usos de **with** en PHRASAL VERBS ver las entradas de los verbos correspondientes, p.ej. **to bear with** en BEAR.

withdraw /wɪð'drɔː, wɪθ'd-/ (*pret* **withdrew** /-'druː/ *pp* **withdrawn** /-'drɔːn/) **1** *vt, vi* retirar(se) **2** *vt* (*dinero*) sacar **3** *vt* (*fml*) (*palabras*) retractar **withdrawal** /-'drɔːəl/ *n* **1** retirada, retractación **2** (*Med*): *withdrawal symptoms* síndrome de abstinencia **withdrawn** *adj* introvertido

wither /'wɪðə(r)/ *vt, vi* ~ (**sth**) (**away/up**) marchitar algo/marchitarse, secar algo/secarse

withhold /wɪð'həʊld, wɪθ'h-/ *vt* (*pret, pp* **withheld** /-'held/) (*fml*) **1** retener **2** (*información*) ocultar **3** (*consentimiento*) negar

within /wɪ'ðɪn/ ◆ *prep* **1** (*tiempo*) en el plazo de: *within a month of having left* al mes de haberse marchado **2** (*distancia*) a menos de **3** al alcance de: *It's within walking distance.* Se puede ir andando. **4** (*fml*) dentro de ◆ *adv* (*fml*) dentro

without /wɪ'ðaʊt/ *prep* sin: *without saying goodbye* sin despedirse ◊ *without him/his knowing* sin que él supiera nada

withstand /wɪð'stænd, wɪθ'stænd/ *vt* (*pret, pp* **withstood** /-'stʊd/) (*fml*) resistir

witness /'wɪtnəs/ ◆ *n* ~ (**to sth**) testigo (de algo) ◆ *vt* **1** presenciar **2** ser testigo de

witness box (*USA* **witness-stand**) *n* estrado

witty /'wɪti/ *adj* (**-ier**, **-iest**) chistoso, ingenioso

wives *plural de* WIFE

wizard /'wɪzəd/ *n* mago, hechicero

wobble /'wɒbl/ **1** *vi* (*persona*) tambalearse **2** *vi* (*silla*) cojear **3** *vi* (*gelatina*) moverse **4** *vt* mover **wobbly** *adj* (*coloq*) **1** que se tambalea **2** cojo **3** *a wobbly tooth* un diente que se mueve

woe /wəʊ/ *n* desgracia LOC **woe betide** (**sb**) pobre de (algn): *Woe betide me if I forget!* ¡Pobre de mí si se me olvida!

wok /wɒk/ *n* sartén china para freír verduras, etc ☛ *Ver dibujo en* SAUCEPAN

woke *pret de* WAKE

woken *pp de* WAKE

wolf /wʊlf/ *n* (*pl* **wolves** /wʊlvz/) lobo *Ver tb* PACK

woman /'wʊmən/ *n* (*pl* **women** /'wɪmɪn/) mujer

womb /wuːm/ *n* matriz (*Anat*)

won *pret, pp de* WIN

wonder /'wʌndə(r)/ ◆ **1** (*fml*) *vi* ~ (**at sth**) admirarse (de algo) **2** *vt, vi* preguntarse: *It makes you wonder.* Te da que pensar. ◊ *I wonder if/whether he's coming.* Me pregunto si va a venir. ◆ *n* **1** asombro **2** maravilla LOC **it's a wonder** (**that**)... es un milagro (que)... **no wonder** (**that...**) no es de extrañar (que)... *Ver tb* MIRACLE

wonderful /'wʌndəfl/ *adj* maravilloso, estupendo

won't /wəʊnt/ = WILL NOT *Ver* WILL

wood /wʊd/ *n* **1** madera **2** leña **3** [*a menudo pl*] bosque: *We went to the woods.* Fuimos al bosque. LOC *Ver* TOUCH[1] **wooded** *adj* arbolado **wooden** *adj* **1** de madera **2** (*pierna*) de palo

woodland /'wʊdlənd/ *n* bosque

woodwind /'wʊdwɪnd/ *n* [*v sing o pl*] instrumentos de viento (*de madera*)

woodwork /'wʊdwɜːk/ *n* **1** maderamen **2** carpintería

wool /wʊl/ *n* lana **woollen** (*tb* **woolly**) *adj* de lana

word /wɜːd/ ◆ *n* palabra LOC **in other words** en otras palabras, es decir **to give sb your word** (**that...**) dar su palabra a algn (de que...) **to have a word** (**with sb**) (**about sth**) hablar (con algn) (de algo) **to keep/break your word** cumplir/faltar a su palabra **to put in/say a** (**good**) **word for sb** recomendar a algn, interceder por algn **to take sb's word for it** (**that...**) creer a algn (cuando dice que...) **without a word** sin decir palabra **words to that effect** *He told me to get out, or words to that effect.* Me dijo que me fuera, o algo parecido. *Ver tb* BREATHE, EAT, LAST, MARK[2], MINCE, PLAY ◆ *vt* expresar, redactar **wording** *n* términos, texto

word processor *n* procesador de textos **word processing** tratamiento de textos

wore *pret de* WEAR

work[1] /wɜːk/ *n* **1** [*incontable*] trabajo: *to leave work* salir del trabajo ◊ *work experience* experiencia laboral/ profesional **2** obra: *Is this your own work?* ¿Lo has hecho tú sola? ◊ *a piece of work* una obra/un trabajo **3** obra: *the complete works of Shakespeare* las obras completas de Shakespeare **4 works** [*pl*] obras: *Danger! Works ahead.* ¡Peligro! Obras. ☛ La palabra más normal es **roadworks**. LOC **at work** en el trabajo **to get (down)/go/set to work (on sth/to do sth)** ponerse a trabajar (en algo/para hacer algo) *Ver tb* STROKE[1]

Las palabras **work** y **job** se diferencian en que **work** es incontable y **job** es contable: *I've found work/a new job at the hospital.* He encontrado un trabajo en el hospital. **Employment** es más formal que **work** y **job**, y se utiliza para referirse a la condición de los que tienen empleo: *Many women are in part-time employment.* Muchas mujeres tienen trabajos a tiempo parcial. **Occupation** es el término que se utiliza en los impresos oficiales: *Occupation: student* Profesión: estudiante. **Profession** se utiliza para referirse a los trabajos que requieren una carrera universitaria: *the medical profession* la profesión médica. **Trade** se usa para designar los oficios que requieren una formación especial: *He's a carpenter by trade.* Es carpintero de profesión.

work[2] /wɜːk/ (*pret, pp* **worked**) **1** *vi* ~ (**away**) (**at/on sth**) trabajar (en algo): *to work as a lawyer* trabajar de abogado ◊ *to work on the assumption that...* basarse en la suposición de que... **2** *vi* ~ **for sth** esforzarse por algo/por hacer algo **3** *vi* (*Mec*) funcionar **4** *vi* surtir efecto: *It will never work.* No será factible. **5** *vt* (*máquina, etc*) manejar **6** *vt* (*persona*) hacer trabajar **7** *vt* (*mina, etc*) explotar **8** *vt* (*tierra*) cultivar LOC **to work free/loose, etc** soltar(se), aflojar (se) **to work like a charm** (*coloq*) tener un efecto mágico **to work your fingers to the bone** matarse trabajando *Ver tb* MIRACLE PHR V **to work out 1** resultar, salir **2** resolverse **3** hacer ejercicio **to work sth out 1** calcular algo **2** solucionar algo **3** planear algo, elaborar algo **to work sth up 1** desarrollar algo **2** *to work up an appetite* abrir el apetito **to work sb up (into sth)** excitar a algn (hasta algo): *to get worked up* exaltarse **workable** *adj* práctico, factible

worker /ˈwɜːkə(r)/ *n* **1** trabajador, -ora **2** obrero, -a

workforce /ˈwɜːkfɔːs/ *n* [*v sing o pl*] mano de obra

working /ˈwɜːkɪŋ/ ◆ *adj* **1** activo **2** de trabajo **3** laboral, laborable **4** que funciona **5** (*conocimiento*) básico LOC *Ver* ORDER ◆ *n* **workings** [*pl*] ~ **(of sth)** funcionamiento (de algo)

working class ◆ *n* (*tb* **working classes**) clase obrera ◆ *adj* (*tb* **working-class**) de clase obrera

workload /ˈwɜːkləʊd/ *n* cantidad de trabajo

workman /ˈwɜːkmən/ *n* (*pl* **-men** /-mən/) obrero **workmanship** *n* **1** (*de persona*) arte **2** (*de producto*) fabricación

workmate /ˈwɜːkmeɪt/ *n* compañero, -a de trabajo

workplace /ˈwɜːkpleɪs/ *n* lugar de trabajo

workshop /ˈwɜːkʃɒp/ *n* taller

worktop /ˈwɜːktɒp/ *n* encimera

world /wɜːld/ *n* **1** mundo: *all over the world/the world over* por el mundo entero ◊ *world-famous* famoso en el mundo entero **2** mundial, universal: *the world population* la población mundial LOC *Ver* SMALL, THINK **worldly** *adj* (**-ier**, **-iest**) **1** mundano **2** (*bienes*) terrenal **3** de mundo

worldwide /ˈwɜːldwaɪd/ ◆ *adj* mundial, universal ◆ *adv* por todo el mundo

worm /wɜːm/ *n* **1** gusano **2** (*tb* **earthworm**) lombriz LOC *Ver* EARLY

worn *pp de* WEAR

worn out *adj* **1** gastado **2** (*persona*) agotado

worry /ˈwʌri/ ◆ (*pret, pp* **worried**) **1** *vi* ~ (**yourself**) (**about sth/sb**) preocuparse (por algo/algn) **2** *vt* preocupar, inquietar: *to be worried by sth* preocuparse por algo ◆ *n* (*pl* **-ies**) **1** [*incontable*] intranquilidad **2** problema: *financial worries* problemas económicos **worried** *adj* **1** ~ (**about sth/sb**) preocupado (por algo/algn) **2 to be ~ that...** preocupar a algn que...: *I'm worried that he might get lost.* Me preocupa que se pueda perder. **worrying** *adj* inquietante, preocupante

worse /wɜːs/ ◆ *adj* (*comp de* **bad**) ~ **(than sth/than doing sth)** peor (que algo/que hacer algo): *to get worse* empeorar *Ver tb* BAD, WORST LOC **to make matters/things worse** para colmo (de desgracias) ◆ *adv* (*comp de* **badly**) peor: *She speaks German even worse than I do.* Habla alemán incluso peor que yo. ◆ *n* lo peor: *to take a turn for the worse* empeorar **worsen** *vt, vi* empeorar, agravar(se)

worship /ˈwɜːʃɪp/ ◆ *n* **1** ~ **(of sth/sb)** veneración (de algo/algn) **2** ~ **(of sth/sb)** (*Relig*) culto (a algo/algn) ◆ (**-pp-**, *USA* **-p-**) **1** *vt, vi* adorar **2** *vt* rendir culto a **worshipper** *n* devoto, -a

worst /wɜːst/ ◆ *adj* (*superl de* **bad**) peor: *My worst fears were confirmed.* Pasó lo que más me temía. *Ver tb* BAD, WORSE ◆ *adv* (*superl de* **badly**) peor: *the worst hit areas* las áreas más afectadas ◆ **the worst** *n* lo peor LOC **at (the) worst**; **if the worst comes to the worst** en el peor de los casos

worth /wɜːθ/ ◆ *adj* **1** con un valor de, que vale: *to be worth £5* valer cinco libras **2** *It's worth reading.* Vale la pena leerlo. LOC **to be worth it** merecer la pena **to be worth sb's while** valer/merecer la pena ◆ *n* **1** valor **2** (*en dinero*): *£10 worth of petrol* diez libras de gasolina **3** (*en tiempo*): *two weeks' worth of supplies* suministros para dos semanas LOC *Ver* MONEY **worthless** *adj* **1** sin valor **2** (*persona*) despreciable

worthwhile /ˌwɜːθˈwaɪl/ *adj* que vale la pena: *to be worthwhile doing/to do sth* valer la pena hacer algo

worthy /ˈwɜːði/ *adj* (**-ier**, **-iest**) **1** meritorio: *to be worthy of sth* ser digno de algo **2** (*causa*) noble **3** (*persona*) respetable

would /wəd, wʊd/ ◆ (*contracción* **'d** *neg* **would not** *o* **wouldn't** /ˈwʊdnt/) *v aux* (*condicional*): *Would you do it if I paid you?* ¿Lo harías si te pagara? ◊ *He said he would come at five.* Dijo que vendría a las cinco. ◆ *v modal*

> **Would** es un verbo modal al que sigue un infinitivo sin TO, y las oraciones interrogativas y negativas se construyen sin el auxiliar *do*.

1 (*oferta, petición*): *Would you like a drink?* ¿Quieres tomar algo? ◊ *Would you come this way?* ¿Quiere venir por aquí? **2** (*propósito*): *I left a note so (that) they'd call us.* Dejé una nota para que nos llamaran. **3** (*voluntad*): *He wouldn't shake my hand.* No quería darme la mano.

wouldn't = WOULD NOT *Ver* WOULD

wound[1] /wuːnd/ ◆ *n* herida ◆ *vt* herir: *He was wounded in the back during the war.* Recibó una herida en la espalda durante la guerra. **the wounded** *n* [*pl*] los heridos ☛ *Ver nota en* HERIDA

wound[2] *pret, pp de* WIND[2]

wove *pret de* WEAVE

woven *pp de* WEAVE

wow! /waʊ/ *interj* (*coloq*) ¡uau!

wrangle /ˈræŋgl/ ◆ *n* ~ **(about/over sth)** disputa (sobre algo) ◆ *vi* discutir

wrap /ræp/ ◆ *vt* (**-pp-**) **1** ~ **sth/sb (up)** envolver algo/a algn **2** ~ **sth (a)round sth/sb** liar algo alrededor de algo/algn LOC **to be wrapped up in sth/sb** estar entregado/dedicado a algo/algn, estar absorto en algo PHR V **to wrap (sb/yourself) up** abrigar a algn/abrigarse **to wrap sth up** (*coloq*) concluir algo ◆ *n* chal **wrapper** *n* envoltura **wrapping** *n* envoltura: *wrapping paper* papel de envolver

wrath /rɒθ; *USA* ræθ/ *n* (*fml*) ira

wreath /riːθ/ *n* (*pl* **~s** /riːðz/) corona (*funeraria*)

wreck /rek/ ◆ *n* **1** naufragio **2** (*coloq, fig*) ruina **3** cacharro ◆ *vt* destrozar, echar abajo **wreckage** *n* restos (*accidente, etc*)

wrench /rentʃ/ ◆ *vt* **1** ~ **sth off (sth)** arrancar algo (de algo) (*de un tirón*) **2** ~ **sth out of sth** sacar algo (de algo) (*de un tirón*) ◆ *n* **1** tirón **2** (*fig*) golpe **3** (*esp USA*) llave inglesa

wrestle /ˈresl/ *vi* (*Dep, fig*) luchar **wrestler** *n* luchador, -ora **wrestling** *n* lucha libre

wretch /retʃ/ *n* desgraciado, -a

wretched /ˈretʃɪd/ *adj* **1** desgraciado, desconsolado **2** (*coloq*) maldito

wriggle /ˈrɪgl/ *vt, vi* **1** ~ **(about)** menear(se), mover(se) **2** retorcer(se): *to wriggle free* conseguir soltarse

wring /rɪŋ/ *vt* (*pret, pp* **wrung** /rʌŋ/) **1** ~ **sth (out)** retorcer, exprimir algo **2** ~ **sth (out)** (*trapo*) escurrir algo **3** ~ **sth**

out of/from sb sacarle algo a algn LOC **to wring sb's neck** (*coloq*) retorcerle el pescuezo a algn

wrinkle /ˈrɪŋkl/ ◆ *n* arruga ◆ **1** *vt, vi* arrugar(se) **2** *vt* (*ceño*) fruncir **3** *vt* (*nariz*) arrugar

wrist /rɪst/ *n* muñeca

write /raɪt/ *vt, vi* (*pret* **wrote** /rəʊt/ *pp* **written** /ˈrɪtn/) escribir

PHR V **to write back (to sb)** contestar (a algn)

to write sth down anotar algo

to write off/away (to sth/sb) for sth escribir (a algo/algn) pidiendo algo **to write sth off 1** anular algo, borrar algo como incobrable **2** dar algo de baja **3** destrozar algo **to write sth/sb off (as sth)** desechar algo/a algn (por algo) **to write sth out 1** escribir algo (en limpio) **2** copiar algo

to write sth up redactar algo

write-off /ˈraɪt ɒf/ *n* desastre: *The car was a write-off.* Al coche lo declararon siniestro total.

writer /ˈraɪtə(r)/ *n* escritor, -ora

writhe /raɪð/ *vi* retorcerse: *to writhe in agony* retorcerse de dolor

writing /ˈraɪtɪŋ/ *n* **1** escribir, escritura **2** escrito **3** estilo de redacción **4** letra **5** **writings** [*pl*] obras LOC **in writing** por escrito

written /ˈrɪtn/ ◆ *adj* por escrito ◆ *pp de* WRITE

wrong /rɒŋ; *USA* rɔːŋ/ ◆ *adj* **1** malo, injusto: *It is wrong to...* No está bien... ◊ *He was wrong to say that.* Hizo mal en decir aquello. **2** equivocado, incorrecto, falso: *to be wrong* estar equivocado/equivocarse **3** inoportuno, equivocado: *the wrong way up/round* cabeza abajo/al revés **4** *What's wrong?* ¿Qué pasa? LOC *Ver* SIDE ◆ *adv* mal, equivocadamente, incorrectamente *Ver tb* WRONGLY LOC **to get sb wrong** (*coloq*) malinterpretar a algn **to get sth wrong** equivocarse en algo **to go wrong 1** equivocarse **2** (*máquina*) estropearse **3** salir/ir mal ◆ *n* **1** mal **2** (*fml*) injusticia LOC **to be in the wrong** estar equivocado **wrongful** *adj* injusto, ilegal **wrongly** *adv* equivocadamente, incorrectamente

wrote *pret de* WRITE

wrought iron /ˌrɔːt ˈaɪən/ *n* hierro forjado

wrung *pret, pp de* WRING

Xx

X, x /eks/ *n* (*pl* **X's**, **x's** /ˈeksɪz/) X, x: *X for Xmas* X de xilófono ☛ *Ver ejemplos en* A, a

Xmas /ˈeksməs, ˈkrɪsməs/ *n* (*coloq*) Navidad

X-ray /ˈeks reɪ/ *n* radiografía: *X-rays* rayos X

xylophone /ˈzaɪləfəʊn/ *n* xilófono

Y, y /waɪ/ *n* (*pl* **Y's**, **y's** /waɪz/) Y, y: *Y for Yellow* Y de yedra ☛ *Ver ejemplos en* A, a

yacht /jɒt/ *n* yate **yachting** *n* navegación a vela

yank /jæŋk/ *vt, vi* (*coloq*) dar un tirón brusco (a) PHR V **to yank sth off/out** quitar/sacar algo de un tirón

Yankee /ˈjæŋki/ (*tb* **Yank**) *n* (*coloq*) yanqui

yard /jɑːd/ *n* **1** patio **2** (*USA*) jardín **3** (*abrev* **yd**) yarda (*0,9144 m*)

yardstick /ˈjɑːdstɪk/ *n* criterio

yarn /jɑːn/ *n* **1** hilo **2** cuento

yawn /jɔːn/ ◆ *vi* bostezar ◆ *n* bostezo **yawning** *adj* **1** (*brecha*) grande **2** (*abismo*) profundo

yeah! /jeə/ *interj* (*coloq*) ¡sí!

year /jɪə(r), jɜː(r)/ *n* **1** año: *for years* durante/desde hace muchos años **2** (*Educ*) curso **3** *a two-year-old (child)* un niño de dos años ◇ *I am ten (years old).* Tengo diez años. ☛ Nótese que cuando expresamos la edad en años, podemos omitir **years old**. *Ver nota en* OLD

yearly /ˈjɪəli/ ◆ *adj* anual ◆ *adv* anualmente, cada año

yearn /jɜːn/ *vi* **1** ~ (**for sth/sb**) suspirar (por algo/algn) **2** ~ (**to do sth**) anhelar (hacer algo) **yearning** *n* **1** ~ (**for sth/sb**) anhelo (de algo); añoranza (de algn) **2** ~ (**to do sth**) ansia (por/de hacer algo)

yeast /jiːst/ *n* levadura

yell /jel/ ◆ *vi* **1** ~ (**out**) (**at sth/sb**) gritar (a algo/algn) **2** ~ (**in/with sth**) gritar (de algo) ◆ *n* grito, alarido

yellow /ˈjeləʊ/ *adj, n* amarillo

yelp /jelp/ *vi* **1** (*animal*) gemir **2** (*persona*) gritar

yes /jes/ ◆ *interj* ¡sí! ◆ *n* (*pl* **yeses** /ˈjesɪz/) sí

yesterday /ˈjestədi, -deɪ/ *adv, n* ayer: *yesterday morning* ayer por la mañana *Ver tb* DAY

yet /jet/ ◆ *adv* **1** [*en frases negativas*] todavía, aún: *not yet* todavía no ◇ *They haven't phoned yet.* Todavía no han llamado. ☛ *Ver nota en* STILL[1] **2** [*en frases interrogativas*] ya

¿**Yet** o **already**? **Yet** sólo se usa en frases interrogativas y siempre va al final de la oración: *Have you finished it yet?* ¿Lo has terminado ya? **Already** se usa en frases afirmativas e interrogativas y normalmente va detrás de los verbos auxiliares o modales y delante de los demás verbos: *Have you finished already?* ¿Has terminado ya? ◇ *He already knew her.* Ya la conocía. Cuando **already** indica sorpresa de que una acción se haya realizado antes de lo esperado se puede poner al final de la frase: *He has found a job already!* ¡Ya ha encontrado trabajo! ◇ *Is it there already? That was quick!* ¿Ya está allí? ¡Qué rapidez! *Ver tb ejemplos en* ALREADY

3 [*después de superlativo*]: *her best novel yet* su mejor novela hasta la fecha **4** [*antes de comparativo*] incluso: *yet more work* aún más trabajo LOC **yet again** otra vez más ◆ *conj* aún así: *It's incredible yet true.* Es increíble pero cierto.

yew /juː/ (*tb* **yew tree**) *n* tejo (*Bot*)

yield /jiːld/ ◆ **1** *vt* producir, dar **2** *vt* (*Fin*) rendir **3** *vi* ~ (**to sth/sb**) (*fml*) rendirse (a algo/algn); ceder (ante algo/algn) ☛ La palabra más normal es **give in**. ◆ *n* **1** producción **2** (*Agricultura*) cosecha **3** (*Fin*) rendimiento **yielding** *adj* **1** flexible **2** sumiso

yoghurt (*tb* **yogurt**, **yoghourt**) /ˈjɒgət; *USA* ˈjəʊgərt/ *n* yogur

yoke /jəʊk/ *n* yugo

yolk /jəʊk/ *n* yema ☛ *Comparar con* WHITE 2

you /juː/ *pron pers* **1** [*como sujeto*] tú, usted, -es, vosotros, -as: *You said that…* Dijiste que… **2** [*en frases impersonales*]: *You can't smoke in here.* No se puede fumar aquí. ☛ En las frases impersonales se puede usar **one** con el mismo significado que **you**, pero es mucho más formal. **3** [*como objeto directo*] te, lo, la, os, los, las **4** [*como objeto indirecto*] te, le, os, les: *I told you to wait.* Te dije que esperaras. **5** [*después de preposición*] ti, usted, -es, vosotros, -as: *Can I go with you?* ¿Puedo ir contigo? ☛ El *pron pers* no se puede omitir en inglés.

you'd /juːd/ **1** = YOU HAD *Ver* HAVE **2** = YOU WOULD *Ver* WOULD

you'll /juːl/ = YOU WILL *Ver* WILL

young /jʌŋ/ ◆ *adj* (**younger** /jʌŋgə(r)/ **youngest** /jʌŋgɪst/) joven: *young people* jóvenes ◇ *He's two years younger than me.* Tiene dos años menos que yo. ◆ *n* [*pl*] **1** (*de animales*) crías **2 the young** los jóvenes

youngster /ˈjʌŋstə(r)/ *n* joven

your /jɔː(r); *USA* jʊər/ *adj pos* tu(s), vuestro(s), -a(s), su(s): *to break your arm* romperse el brazo ◇ *Your room is ready.* Su habitación está lista. ☛ *Ver nota en* MY

you're /jʊə(r), jɔː(r)/ = YOU ARE *Ver* BE

yours /jɔːz; *USA* jʊərz/ *pron pos* tuyo, -a, -os, -as, vuestro, -a, -os, -as, suyo, -a, -os, -as: *Is she a friend of yours?* ¿Es amiga tuya/vuestra/suya? ◇ *Where is yours?* ¿Dónde está el tuyo/vuestro/

suyo? LOC **Yours faithfully/sincerely** Le saluda atentamente ☛ *Ver* págs 314–15.

yourself /jɔːˈself; *USA* jʊərˈself/ *pron* (*pl* **-selves** /-ˈselvz/) **1** [*uso reflexivo*] te, se, os: *Enjoy yourselves!* ¡Pasadlo bien! **2** [*después de prep*] ti (mismo): *proud of yourself* orgulloso de ti mismo **3** [*uso enfático*] tú mismo, -a, vosotros mismos, vosotras mismas LOC **(all) by yourself/yourselves** (completamente) solo(s) **to be yourself/yourselves** ser natural: *Just be yourself.* Simplemente sé tú mismo.

youth /juːθ/ *n* **1** juventud: *In my youth...* Cuando yo era joven... ◊ *youth club/hostel* club para jóvenes/albergue juvenil **2** (*pl* ~**s** /juːðz/) (*frec pey*) joven **youthful** *adj* jovial, juvenil

you've /juːv/ = YOU HAVE *Ver* HAVE

Zz

Z, z /zed; *USA* ziː/ *n* (*pl* **Z's, z's** /zedz; *USA* ziːz/) Z, z: *Z for zebra* Z de Zamora ☛ *Ver ejemplos en* A, a

zeal /ziːl/ *n* entusiasmo, fervor **zealous** /ˈzeləs/ *adj* entusiasta

zebra /ˈzebrə, ˈziːbrə/ *n* (*pl* **zebra** *o* ~s) cebra

zebra crossing *n* (*GB*) paso de cebra

zenith /ˈzenɪθ/ *n* cenit

zero /ˈzɪərəʊ/ *n* (*pl* ~s) *adj, pron* cero

zest /zest/ *n* ~ (**for sth**) entusiasmo, pasión (por algo)

zigzag /ˈzɪgzæg/ ◆ *adj* en zigzag ◆ *n* zigzag

zinc /zɪŋk/ *n* cinc, zinc

zip /zɪp/ ◆ *n* (*USA* **zipper**) cremallera ◆ (**-pp-**) **1** *vt* **to zip sth** (**up**) cerrar la cremallera de algo **2** *vi* **to zip** (**up**) cerrarse con cremallera

zodiac /ˈzəʊdiæk/ *n* zodiaco

zone /zəʊn/ *n* zona

zoo /zuː/ (*pl* **zoos**) (*fml* **zoological gardens**) *n* zoo, parque zoológico

zoology /zuːˈɒlədʒi/ *n* zoología **zoologist** /zuːˈɒlədʒɪst/ *n* zoólogo, -a

zoom /zuːm/ *vi* ir muy deprisa: *to zoom past* pasar zumbando PHR V **to zoom in** (**on sth/sb**) enfocar (algo/a algn) (*con un zoom*)

zoom lens *n* zoom

Apéndices

En esta sección final encontrarás los apéndices a los que hacemos referencia a lo largo del diccionario:

Apéndice 1

Expresiones numéricas

Números

Cardinales		Ordinales	
1	one	**1st**	first
2	two	**2nd**	second
3	three	**3rd**	third
4	four	**4th**	fourth
5	five	**5th**	fifth
6	six	**6th**	sixth
7	seven	**7th**	seventh
8	eight	**8th**	eighth
9	nine	**9th**	ninth
10	ten	**10th**	tenth
11	eleven	**11th**	eleventh
12	twelve	**12th**	twelfth
13	thirteen	**13th**	thirteenth
14	fourteen	**14th**	fourteenth
15	fifteen	**15th**	fifteenth
16	sixteen	**16th**	sixteenth
17	seventeen	**17th**	seventeenth
18	eighteen	**18th**	eighteenth
19	nineteen	**19th**	nineteenth
20	twenty	**20th**	twentieth
21	twenty-one	**21st**	twenty-first
22	twenty-two	**22nd**	twenty-second
30	thirty	**30th**	thirtieth
40	forty	**40th**	fortieth
50	fifty	**50th**	fiftieth
60	sixty	**60th**	sixtieth
70	seventy	**70th**	seventieth
80	eighty	**80th**	eightieth
90	ninety	**90th**	ninetieth
100	a/one hundred	**100th**	hundredth
101	a/one hundred and one	**101st**	hundred and first
200	two hundred	**200th**	two hundredth
1 000	a/one thousand	**1 000th**	thousandth
10 000	ten thousand	**10 000th**	ten thousandth
100 000	a/one hundred thousand	**100 000th**	hundred thousandth
1 000 000	a/one million	**1 000 000th**	millionth

Ejemplos

528	*five hundred and twenty-eight*
2,976	*two thousand, nine hundred and seventy-six*
50 439	*fifty thousand, four hundred and thirty-nine*
2 250 321	*two million, two hundred and fifty thousand, three hundred and twenty-one*

☛ *¡Ojo!* En inglés se utiliza una coma o un espacio (y NO un punto) para marcar el millar, por ejemplo *25 000* o *25,000*.

En cuanto a números como 100, 1 000, 1 000 000, etc, se pueden decir de dos maneras, ***one hundred*** o ***a hundred***, ***one thousand*** o ***a thousand***.

0 (cero) se pronuncia ***nought***, ***zero***, ***nothing***, ***o*** /əʊ/ dependiendo de las expresiones.

Quebrados

½	a half
⅓	a/one third
¼	a quarter
⅖	two fifths
⅛	an/one eighth
⅒	a/one tenth
1/16	a/one sixteenth
1½	one and a half
2⅜	two and three eighths

Hay dos maneras de expresar los quebrados en inglés: lo normal es decir *one eighth of the cake, two thirds of the population, etc;* pero tu profesor de matemáticas te puede pedir que resuelvas el siguiente ejercicio:

Multiply two over five by three over eight (⅖ × ⅜).

Expresiones matemáticas

+	plus
−	minus
×	times o multiplied by
÷	divided by
=	equals
%	per cent
3^2	three squared
5^3	five cubed
6^{10}	six to the power of ten

Ejemplos

6 + 9 = 15 *Six* ***plus*** *nine equals/is fifteen.*

5 × 6 = 30 *Five* ***times*** *six equals thirty./ Five* ***multiplied by*** *six is thirty.*

75% *Seventy-five* ***per cent*** *of the class passed the test.*

Decimales

0.1	(nought) point one
0.25	(nought) point two five
1.75	one point seven five

☛ *¡Ojo!* En inglés se utiliza un punto (y NO una coma) para marcar los decimales.

Peso

		Sistema Imperial (Reino Unido)		Sistema Métrico Decimal	
		1 ounce	(oz)	= 28.35 grams	(g)
16 ounces	=	**1 pound**	(lb)	= 0.454 kilogram	(kg)
14 pounds	=	**1 stone**	(st)	= 6.356 kilograms	

Ejemplos

The baby weighed 7 lb 4 oz (seven pounds four ounces).
For this recipe you need 500g (five hundred grams) of flour.

Longitud

		Sistema Imperial (Reino Unido)		Sistema Métrico Decimal	
		1 inch	(in)	= 25.4 millimetres	(mm)
12 inches	=	**1 foot**	(ft)	= 30.48 centimetres	(cm)
3 feet	=	**1 yard**	(yd)	= 0.914 metre	(m)
1 760 yards	=	**1 mile**		= 1.609 kilometres	(km)

Ejemplos

Height: 5 ft 9 in (five foot nine/five feet nine).
The hotel is 30 yds (thirty yards) from the beach.
The car was doing 50 mph (fifty miles per hour).
The room is 11' × 9'6" (eleven foot by nine foot six/eleven feet by nine feet six).

Superficie

	Sistema Imperial (Reino Unido)	Sistema Métrico Decimal
	1 square inch (sq in)	= 6.452 square centimetres
144 square inches	= **1 square foot** (sq ft)	= 929.03 square centimetres
9 square feet	= **1 square yard** (sq yd)	= 0.836 square metre
4 840 square yards	= **1 acre**	= 0.405 hectare
640 acres	= **1 square mile**	= 2.59 square kilometres/259 hectares

Ejemplos

They have a 200-acre farm.
The fire destroyed 40 square miles of woodland.

Capacidad

	Sistema Imperial (Reino Unido)	Sistema Métrico Decimal
½ (0.5) pint		= 0.284 litre (ℓ)
	1 pint (pt)	= 0.568 litre (ℓ)
2 pints		= 1.136 litres
8 pints	= **1 gallon** (gall)	= 4.546 litres

Ejemplos

I asked the milkman to leave three pints of milk.
The petrol tank holds 40 litres.

Moneda

Reino Unido	Valor de la moneda/billete	Nombre de la moneda/billete
1p	a penny (one p*)	a penny
2p	two pence (two p*)	a two-pence piece
5p	five pence (five p*)	a five-pence piece
10p	ten pence (ten p*)	a ten-pence piece
20p	twenty pence (twenty p*)	a twenty-pence piece
50p	fifty pence (fifty p*)	a fifty-pence piece
£1	a pound	a pound (coin)
£5	five pounds	a five-pound note
£10	ten pounds	a ten-pound note
£20	twenty pounds	a twenty-pound note
£50	fifty pounds	a fifty-pound note

Ejemplos

£5.75: five pounds seventy-five
25p: twenty-five pence
The apples are 65p a pound.
We pay £250 a month in rent.

* Las expresiones que aparecen entre paréntesis son más coloquiales. Nótese que *one p*, *two p*, etc se pronuncian /wʌn piː/, /tuː piː/, etc.

Fechas

Cómo escribirlas:

15/4/95 (EEUU *4/15/95*)

15 April 1995

April 15th, 1995 (es la forma más normal en EEUU)

Cómo decirlas:

April the fifteenth, nineteen ninety-five

The fifteenth of April, nineteen ninety-five (EEUU *April fifteenth*)

Ejemplos

Her birthday is on April 9th (April the ninth/the ninth of April).

The restaurant will be closed May 3–June 1 (from May the third to June the first).

Apéndice 2
Verbos irregulares

Infinitivo	Pasado	Participio
arise	arose	arisen
awake	awoke	awoken
be	was/were	been
bear[2]	bore	borne
beat	beat	beaten
become	became	become
begin	began	begun
bend	bent	bent
bet	bet, betted	bet, betted
bid	bid	bid
bind	bound	bound
bite	bit	bitten
bleed	bled	bled
bless	blessed	blessed
blow	blew	blown
break[1]	broke	broken
breed	bred	bred
bring	brought	brought
broadcast	broadcast	broadcast
build	built	built
burn	burnt, burned	burnt, burned
burst	burst	burst
bust[2]	bust, busted	bust, busted
buy	bought	bought
cast	cast	cast
catch	caught	caught
choose	chose	chosen
cling	clung	clung
come	came	come
cost	cost, costed	cost, costed
creep	crept	crept
cut	cut	cut
deal[3]	dealt	dealt
dig	dug	dug
dive	dived; (*USA*) dove	dived
do[2]	did	done
draw[2]	drew	drawn
dream	dreamt, dreamed	dreamt, dreamed
drink	drank	drunk
drive	drove	driven
eat	ate	eaten
fall	fell	fallen

Infinitivo	Pasado	Participio
feed	fed	fed
feel	felt	felt
fight	fought	fought
find	found	found
flee	fled	fled
fling	flung	flung
fly	flew	flown
forbid	forbade; (*USA*) forbad	forbidden
forecast	forecast, forecasted	forecast, forecasted
forget	forgot	forgotten
forgive	forgave	forgiven
freeze	froze	frozen
get	got	got; (*USA*) gotten
give	gave	given
go[1]	went	gone
grind	ground	ground
grow	grew	grown
hang	hung, hanged	hung, hanged
have	had	had
hear	heard	heard
hide[1]	hid	hidden
hit	hit	hit
hold	held	held
hurt	hurt	hurt
keep	kept	kept
kneel	knelt; (*esp USA*) kneeled	knelt; (*esp USA*) kneeled
knit	knitted	knitted
know	knew	known
lay[1]	laid	laid
lead[2]	led	led
lean[2]	leant, leaned	leant, leaned
leap	leapt, leaped	leapt, leaped
learn	learnt, learned	learnt, learned
leave	left	left
lend	lent	lent
let	let	let
lie[2]	lay	lain
light	lit, lighted	lit, lighted
lose	lost	lost
make[1]	made	made

Infinitivo	Pasado	Participio
mean[1]	meant	meant
meet[1]	met	met
mistake	mistook	mistaken
misunder -stand	misunder -stood	misunder -stood
mow	mowed	mown, mowed
overcome	overcame	overcome
pay	paid	paid
plead	pleaded; (*USA*) pled	pleaded; (*USA*) pled
prove	proved	proved; (*USA*) proven
put	put	put
quit	quit, quitted	quit, quitted
read	read	read
ride	rode	ridden
ring[2]	rang	rung
rise[2]	rose	risen
run[1]	ran	run
saw[2]	sawed	sawn; (*USA*) sawed
say	said	said
see	saw	seen
seek	sought	sought
sell	sold	sold
send	sent	sent
set[2]	set	set
sew	sewed	sewn, sewed
shake	shook	shaken
shed[2]	shed	shed
shine	shone	shone
shoe	shod	shod
shoot	shot	shot
show	showed	shown, showed
shrink	shrank, shrunk	shrunk
shut	shut	shut
sing	sang	sung
sink	sank	sunk
sit	sat	sat
sleep	slept	slept
slide	slid	slid
sling[2]	slung	slung
slit	slit	slit
smell	smelt, smelled	smelt, smelled
sow[2]	sowed	sown, sowed

Infinitivo	Pasado	Participio
speak	spoke	spoken
speed	sped, speeded	sped, speeded
spell	spelt, spelled	spelt, spelled
spend	spent	spent
spill	spilt, spilled	spilt, spilled
spin	spun	spun
spit	spat; (*esp USA*) spit	spat; (*esp USA*) spit
split	split	split
spoil	spoilt, spoiled	spoilt, spoiled
spread	spread	spread
spring	sprang	sprung
stand	stood	stood
steal	stole	stolen
stick[2]	stuck	stuck
sting	stung	stung
stink	stank, stunk	stunk
stride	strode	strode
strike	struck	struck
string	strung	strung
strive	strove	striven
swear	swore	sworn
sweep	swept	swept
swell	swelled	swollen, swelled
swim	swam	swum
swing	swung	swung
take	took	taken
teach	taught	taught
tear[2]	tore	torn
tell	told	told
think	thought	thought
throw[1]	threw	thrown
thrust	thrust	thrust
tread	trod	trodden, trod
wake	woke	woken
wear	wore	worn
weave	wove, weaved	woven, weaved
weep	wept	wept
win	won	won
wind[2]	wound	wound
wring	wrung	wrung
write	wrote	written

Apéndice 3

Nombres de persona

de mujer

Alice /ˈælɪs/
Alison /ˈælɪsn/
Amanda /əˈmændə/; Mandy /ˈmændi/
Angela /ˈændʒələ/
Ann, Anne /æn/
Barbara /ˈbɑːbrə/
Carol, Carole /ˈkærəl/
Caroline /ˈkærəlaɪn/
Catherine /ˈkæθrɪn/; Cathy /ˈkæθi/
Christine /ˈkrɪstiːn/; Chris /krɪs/
Clare, Claire /kleə(r)/
Deborah /ˈdebərə/; Debbie /ˈdebi/
Diana /daɪˈænə/
Elizabeth, Elisabeth /ɪˈlɪzəbəθ/; Liz /lɪz/
Emma /ˈemə/
Frances /ˈfrɑːnsɪs/; Fran /fræn/
Gillian /ˈdʒɪliən/; Gill /dʒɪl/
Fiona /fiˈəʊnə/
Helen /ˈhelən/
Jacqueline /ˈdʒækəlɪn/; Jackie /ˈdʒæki/
Jane /dʒeɪn/
Jennifer /ˈdʒenɪfə(r)/; Jenny /ˈdʒeni/
Joanna /dʒəʊˈænə/; Joanne /dʒəʊˈæn/; Jo /dʒəʊ/
Judith /ˈdʒuːdɪθ/
Julia /ˈdʒuːliə/; Julie /ˈdʒuːli/
Karen /ˈkærən/
Linda /ˈlɪndə/
Margaret /ˈmɑːgrət/; Maggie /ˈmægi/
Mary /ˈmeəri/
Michelle /mɪˈʃel/
Nicola /ˈnɪkələ/; Nicky /ˈnɪki/
Patricia /pəˈtrɪʃə/; Pat /pæt/
Penny /ˈpeni/
Rachel /ˈreɪtʃl/
Rebecca /rɪˈbekə/; Becky /ˈbeki/
Rose /rəʊz/; Rosie /ˈrəʊzi/
Sally /ˈsæli/
Sarah, Sara /ˈseərə/
Sharon /ˈʃærən/
Susan /ˈsuːzn/; Sue /suː/
Tracy, Tracey /ˈtreɪsi/
Victoria /vɪkˈtɔːriə/; Vicki /ˈvɪki/

de hombre

Alan, Allan, Allen /ˈælən/
Andrew /ˈændruː/; Andy /ˈændi/
Anthony /ˈæntəni/; Tony /ˈtəʊni/
Benjamin /ˈbendʒəmɪn/; Ben /ben/
Brian /ˈbraɪən/
Charles /tʃɑːlz/
Christopher /ˈkrɪstəfə(r)/; Chris /krɪs/
David /ˈdeɪvɪd/; Dave /deɪv/
Edward /ˈedwəd/; Ted /ted/
Francis /ˈfrɑːnsɪs/; Frank /fræŋk/
Geoffrey, Jeffrey /ˈdʒefri/; Geoff, Jeff /dʒef/
George /dʒɔːdʒ/
Graham, Grahame, Graeme /ˈgreɪəm/
Henry /ˈhenri/; Harry /ˈhæri/
Ian /ˈiːən/
James /dʒeɪmz/; Jim /dʒɪm/
Jeremy /ˈdʒerəmi/
John /dʒɒn/; Jack /dʒæk/
Jonathan /ˈdʒɒnəθən/; Jon /dʒɒn/
Joseph /ˈdʒəʊzɪf/; Joe /dʒəʊ/
Keith /kiːθ/
Kevin /ˈkevɪn/
Malcolm /ˈmælkəm/
Mark /mɑːk/
Martin /ˈmɑːtɪn/
Matthew /ˈmæθjuː/; Matt /mæt/
Michael /ˈmaɪkl/; Mike /maɪk/
Neil, Neal /niːl/
Nicholas /ˈnɪkələs/; Nick /nɪk/
Nigel /ˈnaɪdʒl/
Patrick /ˈpætrɪk/
Paul /pɔːl/
Peter /ˈpiːtə(r)/; Pete /piːt/
Philip /ˈfɪlɪp/; Phil /fɪl/
Richard /ˈrɪtʃəd/; Rick /rɪk/
Robert /ˈrɒbət/; Bob /bɒb/
Sean /ʃɔːn/
Simon /ˈsaɪmən/
Stephen, Steven /ˈstiːvn/; Steve /stiːv/
Thomas /ˈtɒməs/; Tom /tɒm/
Timothy /ˈtɪməθi/; Tim /tɪm/
William /ˈwɪljəm/; Bill /bɪl/

Apéndice 4

Nombres de lugar

Afghanistan /æfˈɡænɪstɑːn; *USA* -stæn/; Afghan /ˈæfɡæn/, Afghani /æfˈɡɑːni/, Afghanistani /æfˌɡænɪˈstɑːni; *USA* -ˈstæni/
Africa /ˈæfrɪkə/; African /ˈæfrɪkən/
Albania /ælˈbeɪniə/; Albanian /ælˈbeɪniən/
Algeria /ælˈdʒɪəriə/; Algerian /ælˈdʒɪəriən/
America ☛ (the) United States (of America)
America /əˈmerɪkə/; American /əˈmerɪkən/
Andorra /ænˈdɔːrə/; Andorran /ænˈdɔːrən/
Angola /æŋˈɡəʊlə/; Angolan /æŋˈɡəʊlən/
Antarctica /ænˈtɑːktɪkə/; Antarctic
Antigua and Barbuda /ænˌtiːɡə ən bɑːˈbjuːdə/; Antiguan /ænˈtiːɡən/, Barbudan /bɑːˈbjuːdən/
(the) **Arctic Ocean** /ˌɑːktɪk ˈəʊʃn/; Arctic
Argentina /ˌɑːdʒənˈtiːnə/, the Argentine /ˈɑːdʒəntaɪn/; Argentinian /ˌɑːdʒənˈtɪniən/, Argentine
Armenia /ɑːˈmiːniə/; Armenian /ɑːˈmiːniən/
Asia /ˈeɪʃə, ˈeɪʒə/; Asian /ˈeɪʃn, ˈeɪʒn/
Australia /ɒˈstreɪliə, ɔːˈs-/; Australian /ɒˈstreɪliən, ɔːˈs-/
Austria /ˈɒstriə, ˈɔːs-/; Austrian /ˈɒstriən, ˈɔːs-/
(the) **Bahamas** /bəˈhɑːməz/; Bahamian /bəˈheɪmiən/
Bangladesh /ˌbæŋɡləˈdeʃ/; Bangladeshi /ˌbæŋɡləˈdeʃi/
Barbados /bɑːˈbeɪdɒs/; Barbadian /bɑːˈbeɪdiən/
Belgium /ˈbeldʒəm/; Belgian /ˈbeldʒən/
Belize /bəˈliːz/; Belizean /bəˈliːziən/
Bolivia /bəˈlɪviə/; Bolivian /bəˈlɪviən/
Bosnia-Herzegovina /ˌbɒzniə ˌhɜːtsəɡəˈviːnə/; Bosnian /ˈbɒzniən/
Botswana /bɒtˈswɑːnə/; Botswanan /bɒtˈswɑːnən/, *también* the Tswanan /ˈtswɑːnən/
Brazil /brəˈzɪl/; Brazilian /brəˈzɪliən/
Bulgaria /bʌlˈɡeəriə/; Bulgarian /bʌlˈɡeəriən/
Burundi /bʊˈrʊndi /; Burundian /bʊˈrʊndiən/
Cambodia /kæmˈbəʊdiə/; Cambodian /kæmˈbəʊdiən/
Cameroon /ˌkæməˈruːn/; Cameroonian /ˌkæməˈruːniən/
Canada /ˈkænədə/; Canadian /kəˈneɪdiən/
Cape Verde Islands /ˌkeɪp ˈvɜːd aɪləndz/; Cape Verdean /ˌkeɪp ˈvɜːdiən/
(the) **Caribbean Sea** /ˌkærəˌbiːən ˈsiː/; Caribbean
Central African Republic /ˌsentrəl ˌæfrɪkən rɪˈpʌblɪk/
Chad /tʃæd/; Chadian /ˈtʃædiən/
Chile /ˈtʃɪli/; Chilean /ˈtʃɪliən/
China /ˈtʃaɪnə/; Chinese /ˌtʃaɪˈniːz/
Colombia /kəˈlɒmbiə/; Colombian /kəˈlɒmbiən/
Congo /ˈkɒŋɡəʊ/ Congolese /ˌkɒŋɡəˈliːz/
Costa Rica /ˌkɒstə ˈriːkə/; Costa Rican /ˌkɒstə ˈriːkən/
Côte d'Ivoire /ˌkəʊt diːˈvwɑː/
Croatia /krəʊˈeɪʃə/; Croatian /krəʊˈeɪʃən/
Cuba /ˈkjuːbə/; Cuban /ˈkjuːbən/
Cyprus /ˈsaɪprəs/; Cypriot /ˈsɪpriət/
(the) **Czech Republic** /ˌtʃek rɪˈpʌblɪk/; Czech /tʃek/
Denmark /ˈdenmɑːk/; Danish /ˈdeɪnɪʃ/, Dane /deɪn/
(the) **Dominican Republic** /dəˌmɪnɪkən rɪˈpʌblɪk/; Dominican /dəˈmɪnɪkən/
Ecuador /ˈekwədɔː(r)/; Ecuadorian /ˌekwəˈdɔːriən/
Egypt /ˈiːdʒɪpt/; Egyptian /iˈdʒɪpʃn/
El Salvador /el ˈsælvədɔː(r)/; Salvadorean /ˌsælvəˈdɔːriən/
Equatorial Guinea /ˌekwəˌtɔːriəl ˈɡɪni/; Equatorial Guinean /ˌekwəˌtɔːriəl ˈɡɪniən/
Ethiopia /ˌiːθiˈəʊpiə/; Ethiopian /ˌiːθiˈəʊpiən/
Europe /ˈjʊərəp/; European /ˌjʊərəˈpiːən/
Fiji /ˌfiːˈdʒiː; *USA* ˈfiːdʒiː/; Fijian /ˌfiːˈdʒiːən; *USA* ˈfiːdʒiən/
Finland /ˈfɪnlənd/; Finnish /ˈfɪnɪʃ/, Finn /fɪn/
France /frɑːns; *USA* fræns/; French /frentʃ/, Frenchman /ˈfrentʃmən/, Frenchwoman /ˈfrentʃwʊmən/

Gabon /gæˈbɒn; *USA* -ˈbəʊn/; Gabonese /ˌgæbəˈniːz/

The Gambia /ˈgæmbiə/; Gambian /ˈgæmbiən/

Germany /ˈdʒɜːməni/; German /ˈdʒɜːmən/

Ghana /ˈgɑːnə/; Ghanaian /gɑːˈneɪən/

Gibraltar /dʒɪˈbrɔːltə(r)/; Gibraltarian /ˌdʒɪbrɔːlˈteəriən/

Greece /griːs/; Greek /griːk/

Guatemala /ˌgwɑːtəˈmɑːlə/; Guatemalan /ˌgwɑːtəˈmɑːlən/

Guinea /ˈgɪni/; Guinean /ˈgɪniən/

Guinea-Bissau /ˌgɪni bɪˈsaʊ/

Guyana /gaɪˈænə/; Guyanese /ˌgaɪəˈniːz/

Haiti /ˈheɪti/; Haitian /ˈheɪʃn/

Holland /ˈhɒlənd/ ☛ (the) Netherlands

Honduras /hɒnˈdjʊərəs; *USA* -ˈdʊə-/; Honduran /hɒnˈdjʊərən; *USA* -ˈdʊə-/

Hong Kong /ˌhɒŋ ˈkɒŋ/

Hungary /ˈhʌŋgəri/; Hungarian /hʌŋˈgeəriən/

Iceland /ˈaɪslənd/; Icelandic /aɪsˈlændɪk/

India /ˈɪndiə/; Indian /ˈɪndiən/

Indonesia /ˌɪndəˈniːziə; *USA* -ˈniːʒə/; Indonesian /ˌɪndəˈniːzɪən; *USA* -ʒn/

Iran /ɪˈrɑːn/; Iranian /ɪˈreɪniən/

Iraq /ɪˈrɑːk/; Iraqi /ɪˈrɑːki/

(the) **Irish Republic** /ˈaɪərɪʃ rɪˈpʌblɪk/

Israel /ˈɪzreɪl/; Israeli /ɪzˈreɪli/

Italy /ˈɪtəli/; Italian /ɪˈtæliən/

Jamaica /dʒəˈmeɪkə/; Jamaican /dʒəˈmeɪkən/

Japan /dʒəˈpæn/; Japanese /ˌdʒæpəˈniːz/

Jordan /ˈdʒɔːdn/; Jordanian /dʒɔːˈdeɪnˈiən/

Kenya /ˈkenjə/; Kenyan /ˈkenjən/

Korea /kəˈrɪə; *USA* kəˈriːə/; North Korea, North Korean /ˌnɔːθ kəˈrɪən; *USA* kəˈriːən/; South Korea, South Korean /ˌsaʊθ kəˈrɪən; *USA* kəˈriːən/

Kuwait /kuˈweɪt/; Kuwaiti /kuˈweɪti/

Laos /laʊs/; Laotian /ˈlaʊʃn; *USA* leɪˈəʊʃn/

Lebanon /ˈlebənən; *USA* -nɒn/; Lebanese /ˌlebəˈniːz/

Libya /ˈlɪbiə/; Libyan /ˈlɪbiən/

Liechtenstein /ˈlɪktənstaɪn, lɪxt-/; Liechtenstein, Liechtensteiner /ˈlɪktənstaɪnə(r), ˈlɪxt-/

Luxembourg /ˈlʌksəmbɜːg/; Luxembourg, Luxembourger /ˈlʌksəmbɜːgə(r)/

Madagascar /ˌmædəˈgæskə(r)/; Madagascan /ˌmædəˈgæskən/, Malagasy /ˌmæləˈgæsi/

Malawi /məˈlɑːwi/; Malawian /məˈlɑːwiən/

Malaysia /məˈleɪziə; *USA* -ˈleɪʒə/; Malaysian /məˈleɪziən; *USA* -ˈleɪʒn/

Maldives /ˈmɔːldiːvz/; Maldivian /mɔːlˈdɪviən/

Mali /ˈmɑːli/; Malian /ˈmɑːliən/

Malta /ˈmɔːltə/; Maltese /ˌmɔːlˈtiːz/

Mauritania /ˌmɒrɪˈteɪniə; *USA* ˌmɔːr-/; Mauritanian /ˌmɒrɪˈteɪniən; *USA* ˌmɔːr-/

Mauritius /məˈrɪʃəs; *USA* mɔː-/; Mauritian /məˈrɪʃn; *USA* mɔː-/

Mexico /ˈmeksɪkəʊ/; Mexican /ˈmeksɪkən/

Monaco /ˈmɒnəkəʊ/; Monegasque /ˌmɒniˈgæsk/

Mongolia /mɒŋˈgəʊliə/; Mongolian /mɒŋˈgəʊliən/, Mongol /ˈmɒŋgl/

Montserrat /ˌmɒntsəˈræt/; Montserratian /ˌmɒntsəˈreɪʃn/

Morocco /məˈrɒkəʊ/; Moroccan /məˈrɒkən/

Mozambique /ˌməʊzæmˈbiːk/; Mozambiquean /ˌməʊzæmˈbiːkən/

Namibia /nəˈmɪbiə/; Namibian /nəˈmɪbiən/

Nepal /nɪˈpɔːl/; Nepalese /ˌnepəˈliːz/

(the) **Netherlands** /ˈneðələndz/; Dutch /dʌtʃ/, Dutchman /ˈdʌtʃmən/, Dutchwoman /ˈdʌtʃwʊmən/

New Zealand /ˌnjuː ˈziːlənd; *USA* ˌnuː-/; New Zealand, New Zealander /ˌnjuː ˈziːləndə(r); *USA* ˌnuː-/

Nicaragua /ˌnɪkəˈrægjuə; *USA* -ˈrɑːgwə/; Nicaraguan /ˌnɪkəˈrægjuən; *USA* -ˈrɑːgwən/

Niger /niːˈʒeə(r); *USA* ˈnaɪdʒər/; Nigerien /niːˈʒeəriən/

Nigeria /naɪˈdʒɪəriə/ Nigerian /naɪˈdʒɪəriən/

Norway /ˈnɔːweɪ/; Norwegian /nɔːˈwiːdʒən/

Oman /əʊˈmɑːn/; Omani /əʊˈmɑːni/

Pakistan /ˌpɑːkɪˈstɑːn; *USA* ˈpækɪstæn/; Pakistani /ˌpɑːkɪˈstɑːni; *USA* ˌpækɪˈstæni/

Panama /ˈpænəmɑː/; Panamanian /ˌpænəˈmeɪniən/

Papua New Guinea /ˌpæpuə ˌnjuː ˈgɪni; *USA* -ˌnuː-/; Papuan /ˈpæpuən/

Paraguay /ˈpærəgwaɪ; *USA* -gweɪ/; Paraguayan /ˌpærəˈgwaɪən; *USA* -ˈgweɪən/
Peru /pəˈruː/; Peruvian /pəˈruːviən/
(the) **Philippines** /ˈfɪlɪpiːnz/; Philippine /ˈfɪlɪpiːn/, Filipino /ˌfɪlɪˈpiːnəʊ/
Poland /ˈpəʊlənd/; Polish /ˈpəʊlɪʃ/, Pole /pəʊl/
Portugal /ˈpɔːtʃʊgl/; Portuguese /ˌpɔːtʃuˈgiːz/
Romania /ruˈmeɪniə/; Romanian /ruˈmeɪniən/
Russia /ˈrʌʃə/; Russian /ˈrʌʃn/
Rwanda /ruˈændə/; Rwandan /ruˈændən/
San Marino /ˌsæn məˈriːnəʊ/; San Marinese /ˌsæn ˌmærɪˈniːz/
Sao Tomé and Principe /ˌsaʊ təˌmeɪ ən ˈprɪnsɪpeɪ/
Saudi Arabia /ˌsaʊdi əˈreɪbiə/; Saudi /ˈsaʊdi/, Saudi Arabian /ˌsaʊdi əˈreɪbiən/
Senegal /ˌsenɪˈgɔːl/; Senegalese /ˌsenɪgəˈliːz/
(the) **Seychelles** /seɪˈʃelz/; Seychellois /ˌseɪʃelˈwa/
Sierra Leone /siˌerə liˈəʊn/; Sierra Leonean /siˌerə liˈəʊniən/
Singapore /ˌsɪŋəˈpɔː(r), ˌsɪŋgə-; *USA* ˈsɪŋgəpɔːr/; Singaporean /ˌsɪŋəˈpɔːriən, ˌsɪŋgə-/
Slovakia /sləʊˈvɑːkiə, -ˈvæk-/; Slovak /ˈsləʊvæk/
(the) **Solomon Islands** /ˈsɒləmən aɪləndz/
Somalia /səˈmɑːliə/; Somali /səˈmɑːli/
(the Republic of) South Africa /ˌsaʊθ ˈæfrɪkə/; South African /ˌsaʊθ ˈæfrɪkən/
Spain /speɪn/; Spanish /ˈspænɪʃ/, Spaniard /ˈspænɪəd/
Sri Lanka /sri ˈlæŋkə; *USA* -ˈlɑːŋ-/; Sri Lankan /sri ˈlæŋkən; *USA* -ˈlɑːŋ-/
St Lucia /snt ˈluːʃə; *USA* seɪnt-/
Sudan /suˈdɑːn; *USA* -ˈdæn/; Sudanese /ˌsuːdəˈniːz/
Surinam /ˌsʊərɪˈnæm/; Surinamese /ˌsʊərɪnæˈmiːz/
Swaziland /ˈswɑːzilænd/; Swazi /ˈswɑːzi/
Sweden /ˈswiːdn/; Swedish /ˈswiːdiʃ/, Swede /swiːd/
Switzerland /ˈswɪtsələnd/; Swiss /swɪs/
Syria /ˈsɪriə/; Syrian /ˈsɪriən/
Taiwan /taɪˈwɑːn/; Taiwanese /ˌtaɪwəˈniːz/
Tanzania /ˌtænzəˈniːə/; Tanzanian /ˌtænzəˈniːən/
Thailand /ˈtaɪlænd/; Thai /taɪ/
Tibet /tɪˈbet/; Tibetan /tɪˈbetn/
Togo /ˈtəʊgəʊ/; Togolese /ˌtəʊgəˈliːz/
Trinidad and Tobago /ˌtrɪnɪdæd ən təˈbeɪgəʊ/; Trinidadian /ˌtrɪnɪˈdædiən/, Tobagan /təˈbeɪgən/, Tobagonian /ˌtəʊbəˈgəʊniən/
Tunisia /tjuˈnɪziə; *USA* tuˈniːʒə/; Tunisian /tjuˈnɪziən; *USA* tuˈniːʒn/
Turkey /ˈtɜːki/; Turkish /ˈtɜːkɪʃ/, Turk /tɜːk/
Uganda /juːˈgændə/; Ugandan /juːˈgændən/
United Arab Emirates /juˌnaɪtɪd ˌærəb ˈemɪrəts/
(the) **United States of America** /juˌnaɪtɪd ˌsteɪts əv əˈmerɪkə/; American /əˈmerɪkən/
Uruguay /ˈjʊərəgwaɪ/; Uruguayan /ˌjʊərəˈgwaɪən/
Vatican City /ˌvætɪkən ˈsɪti/
Venezuela /ˌvenəˈzweɪlə/; Venezuelan /ˌvenəˈzweɪlən/
Vietnam /viˌetˈnæm; *USA* -ˈnɑːm/; Vietnamese /viˌetnəˈmiːz/
(the) **West Indies** /ˌwest ˈɪndiz/; West Indian /ˌwest ˈɪndiən/
Yemen Republic /ˌjemən rɪˈpʌblɪk/; Yemeni /ˈjeməni/
Yugoslavia /ˌjuːgəʊˈslɑːviə/; Yugoslavian /ˌjuːgəʊˈslɑːviən/, Yugoslav /ˈjuːgəʊslɑːv/
Zaïre /zɑːˈɪə(r)/; Zairean /zɑːˈɪəriən/
Zambia /ˈzæmbiə/; Zambian /ˈzæmbiən/
Zimbabwe /zɪmˈbɑːbwi/; Zimbabwean /zɪmˈbɑːbwiən/

Cómo construir el plural

Para construir el plural debes añadir una ***-s*** al final (p. ej. a *Haitian*, two *Haitians*), excepto en el caso de ***Swiss*** y de palabras acabadas en ***-ese*** (tales como *Japanese*), que son invariables. Las nacionalidades que acaban en ***-man*** o ***-woman*** hacen el plural en ***-men*** y ***-women***, p. ej. three *Frenchmen*.

Apéndice 5

División territorial del Reino Unido

Los condados ingleses

Avon /ˈeɪvən/
Bedfordshire /ˈbedfədʃə(r)/
Berkshire /ˈbɑːkʃə(r)/
Buckinghamshire /ˈbʌkɪŋəmʃə(r)/
Cambridgeshire /ˈkeɪmbrɪdʒʃə(r)/
Cheshire /ˈtʃeʃə(r)/
Cleveland /ˈkliːvlənd/
Cornwall /ˈkɔːnwəl/
Cumbria /ˈkʌmbriə/
Derbyshire /ˈdɑːbɪʃə(r)/
Devon /ˈdevən/
Dorset /ˈdɔːsɪt/
Durham /ˈdʌrəm/
East Sussex /ˌiːst ˈsʌsɪks/
Essex /ˈesɪks/
Gloucestershire /ˈglɒstəʃə(r)/
Greater London /ˌgreɪtə ˈlʌndən/
Greater Manchester /ˌgreɪtə mæntʃəstə(r)/
Hampshire /ˈhæmpʃə(r)/
Hereford and Worcester /ˌherɪfəd ənd wʊstə(r)/
Hertfordshire /ˈhɑːtfədʃə(r)/
Humberside /ˈhʌmbəsaɪd/
Isle of Wight /ˌaɪl əv ˈwaɪt/
Kent /kent/
Lancashire /ˈlæŋkəʃə(r)/
Leicestershire /ˈlestəʃə(r)/
Lincolnshire /ˈlɪŋkənʃə(r)/
Merseyside /ˈmɜːzɪsaɪd/
Norfolk /ˈnɔːfək/
North Yorkshire /ˌnɔːθ ˈjɔːkʃə(r)/
Northamptonshire /nɔːθˈæmptənʃə(r)/
Northumberland /nɔːθˈʌmbələnd/
Nottinghamshire /ˈnɒtɪŋəmʃə(r)/
Oxfordshire /ˈɒksfədʃə(r)/
Shropshire /ˈʃrɒpʃə(r)/
Somerset /ˈsʌməset/
South Yorkshire /ˌsaʊθ ˈjɔːkʃə(r)/
Staffordshire /ˈstæfədʃə(r)/
Suffolk /ˈsʌfək/
Surrey /ˈsʌri/
Tyne and Wear /ˌtaɪn ənd ˈwɪə(r)/
Warwickshire /ˈwɒrɪkʃə(r)/
West Midlands /ˌwest ˈmɪdləndz/
West Sussex /ˌwest ˈsʌsɪks/
West Yorkshire /ˌwest ˈjɔːkʃə(r)/
Wiltshire /ˈwɪltʃə(r)/

Las regiones escocesas

Borders /ˈbɔːdəz/
Central /ˈsentrəl/
Dumfries and Galloway /dʌmˌfriːs ənd gæləweɪ/
Fife /faɪf/
Grampian /ˈgræmpiən/
Highland /ˈhaɪlənd/
Lothian /ˈləʊðiən/
Orkney Islands /ˈɔːkni aɪləndz/
Shetland Islands /ˈʃetlənd aɪləndz/
Strathclyde /ˌstræθˈklaɪd/
Tayside /ˈteɪsaɪd/
Western Isles /ˌwestən ˈaɪlz/

Los condados galeses

Clwyd /ˈkluːɪd/
Dyfed /ˈdʌvɪd/
Gwent /gwent/
Gwynedd /ˈgwɪneð/
Mid Glamorgan /ˌmɪd gləˈmɔːgən/
Powys /ˈpəʊɪs/
South Glamorgan /ˌsaʊθ gləˈmɔːgən/
West Glamorgan /ˌwest gləˈmɔːgən/

Los distritos de Irlanda del Norte

Antrim /ˈæntrɪm/
Ards /ɑːdz/
Armagh /ɑːˈmɑː/
Ballymena /ˌbælɪˈmiːnə/
Ballymoney /ˌbælɪˈmʌni/
Banbridge /ˈbænbrɪdʒ/
Belfast /ˈbelfɑːst/
Carrickfergus /ˌkærɪkˈfɜːgəs/
Castlereagh /ˈkɑːslreɪ/
Coleraine /ˈkəʊləˌreɪn/
Cookstown /ˈkʊkstaʊn/
Craigavon /kreɪgˈævən/
Derry /ˈderi/
Down /daʊn/
Dungannon /dʌŋˈgænən/
Fermanagh /fəˈmænə/
Larne /lɑːn/
Limavady /ˌlɪməˈvædi/
Lisburn /ˈlɪzbən/
Magherafelt /ˈmækerəfelt/
Moyle /mɔɪl/
Newry and Mourne /ˌnjʊəri ənd ˈmɔːn/
Newtownabbey /ˌnjuːtnˈæbi/
North Down /ˌnɔːθ ˈdaʊn/
Omagh /əʊˈmɑː/
Strabane /strəˈbæn/

Reino Unido

1 Belfast
2 Newtownabbey
3 Carrickfergus
4 Castlereagh
5 North Down
6 Ards
7 Down
8 Newry and Mourne
9 Bainbridge
10 Lisburn
11 Craigavon
12 Armagh
13 Dungannon
14 Fermanagh
15 Omagh
16 Cookstown
17 Magherafelt
18 Strabane
19 Derry
20 Limavady
21 Coleraine
22 Ballymoney
23 Moyle
24 Ballymena
25 Larne
26 Antrim
Shetland Islands
Orkney Islands
Western Isles
Highland
Grampian
SCOTLAND
Tayside
Fife
Central
Lothian
Atlantic Ocean
NORTHERN IRELAND
Strathclyde
Borders
Dumfries and Galloway
Northumberland
Tyne and Wear
North Sea
Donegal
Cumbria
Durham
Cleveland
Sligo
Mayo
Leitrim
Cavan
Monaghan
Roscommon
Longford
Louth
Isle of man
North Yorkshire
Galway
West Meath
Meath
Irish Sea
Lancashire
West Yorkshire
Humberside
Offaly
Dublin
Greater Manchester
Merseyside
South Yorkshire
Kildare
Clare
Laois
Wicklow
Cheshire
Derbyshire
Nottinghamshire
Lincolnshire
ENGLAND
Gwynedd
Clwyd
Limerick
Tipperary
Kilkenny
Carlow
Staffordshire
Kerry
Wexford
Shropshire
Leicestershire
Norfolk
WALES
West Midlands
Waterford
Cork
Powys
Hereford and Worcester
Warwickshire
Northamptonshire
Cambridgeshire
Suffolk
IRISH REPUBLIC
Dyfed
Bedfordshire
Buckinghamshire
Hertfordshire
Essex
Mid Glamorgan
Gwent
Gloucestershire
Oxfordshire
West Glamorgan
Greater London
South Glamorgan
Avon
Wiltshire
Berkshire
Surrey
Kent
Somerset
Hampshire
West Sussex
East Sussex
Devon
Dorset
Cornwall
Isle of Wight
Isles of Scilly
English Channel
0 50 100 150 200 km

Apéndice 6

División territorial de los EEUU

Los estados que configuran EEUU

Alabama /ˌæləˈbæmə/
Alaska /əˈlæskə/
Arizona /ˌærɪˈzəʊnə/
Arkansas /ˈɑːkənsɔː/
California /ˌkælɪˈfɔːniə/
Colorado /ˌkɒləˈrɑːdəʊ/
Connecticut /kəˈnetɪkət/
Delaware /ˈdeləweə(r)/
Florida /ˈflɒrɪdə/
Georgia /ˈdʒɔːdʒə/
Hawaii /həˈwaɪi/
Idaho /ˈaɪdəhəʊ/
Illinois /ˌɪlɪˈnɔɪ/
Indiana /ˌɪndɪˈænə/
Iowa /ˈaɪəwə/
Kansas /ˈkænzəs, kænsəs/
Kentucky /kenˈtʌki/
Louisiana /luːˌiːzɪˈænə/
Maine /meɪn/
Maryland /ˈmeərilænd/
Massachusetts /ˌmæsəˈtʃuːsɪts/
Michigan /ˈmɪʃɪgən/
Minnesota /ˌmɪnɪˈsəʊtə/
Mississippi /ˌmɪsɪˈsɪpi/
Missouri /mɪˈzʊri/
Montana /mɒnˈtænə/
Nebraska /nəˈbræskə/
Nevada /nəˈvɑːdə/
New Hampshire /ˌnjuː ˈhæmpʃə(r)/
New Jersey /ˌnjuː ˈdʒɜːzi/
New Mexico /ˌnjuː ˈmeksɪˌkəʊ/
New York /ˌnjuː ˈjɔːk/
North Carolina /ˌnɔːθ kærəˈlaɪnə/
North Dakota /ˌnɔːθ dəˈkəʊtə/
Ohio /əʊˈhaɪəʊ/
Oklahoma /ˌəʊkləˈhəʊmə/
Oregon /ˈɒrɪgən/
Pennsylvania /ˌpensəlˈveɪniə/
Rhode Island /ˌrəʊd ˈaɪlənd/
South Carolina /ˌsaʊθ kærəˈlaɪnə/
South Dakota /ˌsaʊθ dəˈkəʊtə/
Tennessee /ˌtenəˈsiː/
Texas /ˈteksəs/
Utah /ˈjuːtɑː/
Vermont /vɜːrˈmɒnt/
Virginia /vəˈdʒɪniə/
Washington /ˈwɑʃɪŋtən/
West Virginia /ˌwest vəˈdʒɪniə/
Wisconsin /wɪsˈkɒnsɪn/
Wyoming /waɪˈəʊmɪŋ/

Estados Unidos

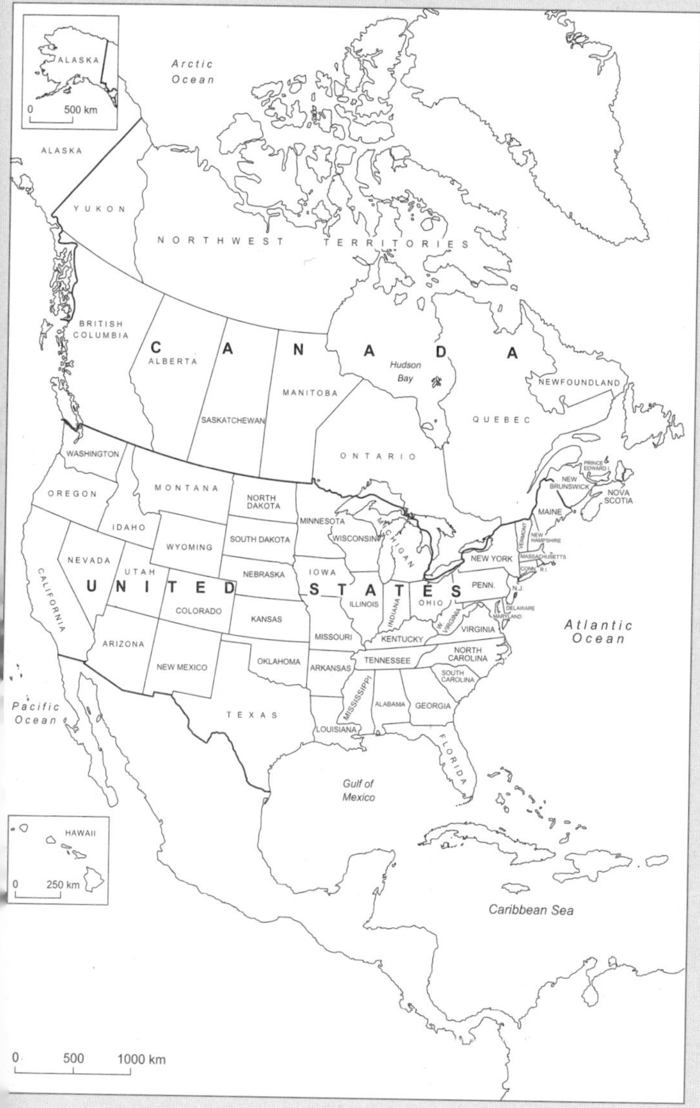

La pronunciación

Hay palabras que tienen más de una pronunciación posible. En el ***Oxford Pocket*** encontrarás las más comunes, ordenadas por su frecuencia de uso.

either /ˈaɪðə(r), ˈiːðə(r)/

Si la pronunciación de la palabra cambia mucho en inglés americano, te lo indicamos mediante la abreviatura *USA*.

address /əˈdres; *USA* ˈædres/

/ˈ/ indica el acento principal de la palabra.
money /ˈmʌni/ lleva el acento en la primera sílaba
lagoon /ləˈguːn/ se acentúa en la segunda sílaba

/ˌ/ muestra el acento secundario de la palabra.
pronunciation /prəˌnʌnsɪˈeɪʃn/ lleva el acento secundario en la sílaba /ˌnʌn/ y el acento principal en la sílaba /ˈeɪʃn/.

(r) En el inglés oral no se pronuncia la **r** final, salvo que la palabra siguiente empiece por vocal.
La **r** no se pronuncia en la frase *His car broke down*, pero sí en *His car is brand new.*

¿Cómo aclaramos esta dificultad? Añadiendo una **r** entre paréntesis en la transcripción fonética.

car /kɑː(r)/

En inglés americano siempre se pronuncia la **r**.

Formas tónicas y átonas

Algunas palabras de uso frecuente (**an**, **as**, **from**, **that**, **of**, etc) tienen dos pronunciaciones posibles, una tónica y otra átona. De las dos, la forma átona es la más frecuente.

Tomemos por ejemplo el caso de la preposición **from** /frəm, frɒm/, que normalmente se pronuncia /frəm/, como en la frase

He comes from Spain.

Ahora bien, si aparece al final de la oración, o le queremos dar un énfasis especial, utilizaremos la pronunciación tónica /frɒm/, como en el caso de

The ˌpresent's not ˈfrom John, it's ˈfor him.

Palabras derivadas

En muchas ocasiones, la pronunciación de una palabra derivada es la suma de la pronunciación de sus elementos. En estos casos no damos la transcipción fonética, ya que es predecible.

slowly = **slow** + **-ly**
/sləʊli/ /sləʊ + li/

astonishingly = **astonish** + **ing** + **ly**
/əˈstɒnɪʃɪŋli/ /əˈstɒnɪʃ + ɪŋ + li/

Pero a veces el acento de la palabra cambia al añadirle las desinencias, y en estos casos sí te mostramos la pronunciación.

photograph /ˈfəʊtəgrɑːf/
photographer /fəˈtɒgrəfə(r)/
photographic /ˌfəʊtəˈgræfɪk/
photography /fəˈtɒgrəfi/

En el caso de las derivadas acabadas en **-tion,** la norma de que el acento recaiga sobre la penúltima sílaba se cumple con regularidad, y por lo tanto no indicamos la pronunciación.

alter /ˈɔːlte(r)/
alteration /ˌɔːltəˈreɪʃn/
confirm /kənˈfɜːm/
confirmation /ˌkɒnfəˈmeɪʃn/